PHILIP'S

ATLAS
OF THE
WORLD

COMPREHENSIVE EDITION

PHILIP'S

ATLAS
OF THE
WORLD

COMPREHENSIVE EDITION

IN ASSOCIATION WITH
THE ROYAL GEOGRAPHICAL SOCIETY
WITH THE INSTITUTE OF BRITISH GEOGRAPHERS

Specialist Geography Consultants

Philip's are grateful to the following people for acting as specialist geography consultants on the 'Introduction to World Geography' front section:

Professor D. Brunsden, Kings College, University of London, UK

Dr C. Clarke, Oxford University, UK

Professor P. Haggett, University of Bristol, UK

Professor M-L. Hsu, University of Minnesota, Minnesota, USA

Professor K. McLachlan, Geopolitical and International Boundaries Research Centre, School of Oriental and African Studies, University of London, UK

Professor M. Monmonier, Syracuse University, New York, USA

Professor M. J. Tooley, University of St Andrews, UK

Dr T. Unwin, Royal Holloway, University of London, UK

Philip's would also like to thank:

Keith Lye

Robin Scagell

Dr I. S. Evans, Durham University, UK

Introduction to World Geography

Picture Acknowledgements
Science Photo Library /BP/NRSC 9, /Earth Satellite Corporation 20, /NOAA 22 bottom left and bottom right

Cartography by Philip's

Illustrations
Stefan Chabluk
William Donohoe
Bernard Thornton Artists /Steve Seymour

Star charts
John Cox and Richard Monkhouse

Published in Great Britain in 1998
by George Philip Limited,
a division of Octopus Publishing Group Limited,
2–4 Heron Quays, London E14 4JP

Copyright © 1998 George Philip Limited

Reprinted 1998, 1999 (twice)

Cartography by Philip's

ISBN 0–540–07538–8

A CIP catalogue record for this book is available from the British Library.

Foreword

Philip's have been mapping the world since 1834. The *Atlas of the World* is the flagship of the Philip's range, an authoritative and serious reference work and one of the finest atlases available anywhere in the world. The atlas incorporates computer-derived maps which have been produced using the very latest in digital cartographic techniques.

Philip's Atlas of the World has been revised and updated with the help of a panel of specialist geography consultants from the United Kingdom and the United States, whose specialities range from the history of cartography, urban and social geography, epidemiology and the European Union to biogeography and applied geomorphology. The result of their valuable input can be seen in the wealth of up-to-date maps and data contained in the '*Introduction to World Geography*' section of this atlas.

How to use the Atlas
The atlas is divided into a number of sections which are explained below.

World Statistics
Six pages of world statistics on topics such as area and population for every country in the world, city populations for the largest cities, climate statistics and physical dimensions – including the largest islands, lakes and seas, the highest mountains and the longest rivers, by continent. Also included in this section is a selection of detailed, up-to-date maps highlighting regions around the world that are currently in the news, such as the former Yugoslavia, Central East Africa, the Caucasus region of the CIS, and Israel.

Introduction to World Geography
A richly informative section comprising 48 pages of up-to-date maps, charts, graphs and clear diagrams which explain key themes about the world in which we live. The topics covered include the Solar System, oceans, climate, the environment, cities, energy and trade. Introductory text on each spread describes and explains the patterns shown by the data.

City Maps
A detailed selection of maps for 66 urban areas around the world. These are useful for planning trips abroad as well as for comparative studies of cities worldwide. Also included is a 16-page index to the city maps.

World Maps
An outstanding collection of 176 pages of distinctive Philip's cartography. The highly acclaimed physical world maps combine relief shading with layer-coloured contours to give a striking visual picture of the Earth's surface. Roads, railways, canals and airports are accurately depicted on the maps, and towns and cities are clearly marked. The maps show the recent place name changes in the countries of the former USSR.

Index
The 75,000-name index to the world maps includes geographical features as well as towns and cities, with both latitude/longitude and letter/figure grid references.

Philip's World Maps

The reference maps which form the main body of this atlas have been prepared in accordance with the highest standards of international cartography to provide an accurate and detailed representation of the Earth. The scales and projections used have been carefully chosen to give balanced coverage of the world, while emphasizing the most densely populated and economically significant regions. A hallmark of Philip's mapping is the use of hill shading and relief colouring to create a graphic impression of landforms: this makes the maps exceptionally easy to read. However, knowledge of the key features employed in the construction and presentation of the maps will enable the reader to derive the fullest benefit from the atlas.

Map Sequence

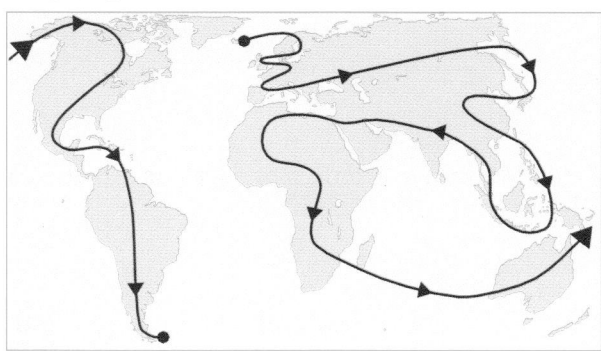

The atlas covers the Earth continent by continent: first Europe; then its land neighbour Asia (mapped north before south, in a clockwise sequence), then Africa, Australia and Oceania, North America and South America. This is the classic arrangement adopted by most cartographers since the 16th century. For each continent, there are maps at a variety of scales. First, physical relief and political maps of the whole continent; then a series of larger-scale maps of the regions within the continent, each followed, where required, by still larger-scale maps of the most important or densely populated areas. The governing principle is that by turning the pages of the atlas, the reader moves steadily from north to south through each continent, with each map overlapping its neighbours. A key map showing this sequence, and the area covered by each map, can be found on the endpapers of the atlas.

Map Presentation

With very few exceptions (e.g. for the Arctic and Antarctic), the maps are drawn with north at the top, regardless of whether they are presented upright or sideways on the page. In the borders will be found the map title; a locator diagram showing the area covered and the page numbers for maps of adjacent areas; the scale; the projection used; the degrees of latitude and longitude; and the letters and figures used in the index for locating place names and geographical features. Physical relief maps also have a height reference panel identifying the colours used for each layer of contouring.

Map Symbols

Each map contains a vast amount of detail which can only be conveyed clearly and accurately by the use of symbols. Points and circles of varying sizes locate and identify the relative importance of towns and cities; different styles of type are employed for administrative, geographical and regional place names to aid identification. A variety of pictorial symbols denote landforms such as glaciers, marshes and coral reefs, and man-made structures including roads, railways, airports and canals. International borders are shown by red lines. Where neighbouring countries are in dispute, for example in parts of the Middle East, the maps show the *de facto* boundary between nations, regardless of the legal or historical situation. The symbols are explained on the first page of the World Maps section of the atlas.

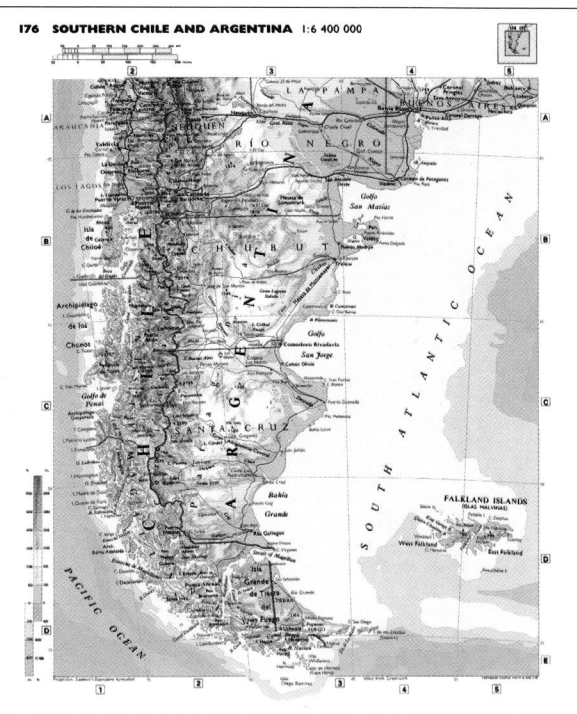

Map Scales

1:16 000 000
1 inch = 252 statute miles

The scale of each map is given in the numerical form known as the 'representative fraction'. The first figure is always one, signifying one unit of distance on the map; the second figure, usually in millions, is the number by which the map unit must be multiplied to give the equivalent distance on the Earth's surface. Calculations can easily be made in centimetres and kilometres, by dividing the Earth units figure by 100 000 (i.e. deleting the last five 0s). Thus 1:1 000 000 means 1 cm = 10 km. The calculation for inches and miles is more laborious, but 1 000 000 divided by 63 360 (the number of inches in a mile) shows that 1:1 000 000 means approximately 1 inch = 16 miles. The table below provides distance equivalents for scales down to 1:50 000 000.

LARGE SCALE		
1:1 000 000	1 cm = 10 km	1 inch = 16 miles
1:2 500 000	1 cm = 25 km	1 inch = 39.5 miles
1:5 000 000	1 cm = 50 km	1 inch = 79 miles
1:6 000 000	1 cm = 60 km	1 inch = 95 miles
1:8 000 000	1 cm = 80 km	1 inch = 126 miles
1:10 000 000	1 cm = 100 km	1 inch = 158 miles
1:15 000 000	1 cm = 150 km	1 inch = 237 miles
1:20 000 000	1 cm = 200 km	1 inch = 316 miles
1:50 000 000	1 cm = 500 km	1 inch = 790 miles
SMALL SCALE		

Measuring Distances

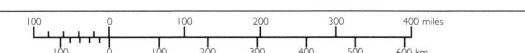

Although each map is accompanied by a scale bar, distances cannot always be measured with confidence because of the distortions involved in portraying the curved surface of the Earth on a flat page. As a general rule, the larger the map scale, the more accurate and reliable will be the distance measured. On small-scale maps such as those of the world and of entire continents, measurement may only be accurate along the 'standard parallels', or central axes, and should not be attempted without considering the map projection.

Map Projections

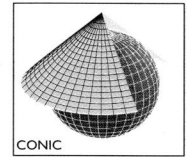 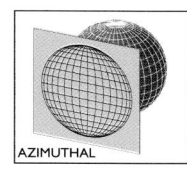 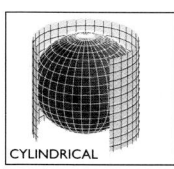

Unlike a globe, no flat map can give a true scale representation of the world in terms of area, shape and position of every region. Each of the numerous systems that have been devised for projecting the curved surface of the Earth on to a flat page involves the sacrifice of accuracy in one or more of these elements. The variations in shape and position of landmasses such as Alaska, Greenland and Australia, for example, can be quite dramatic when different projections are compared.

For this atlas, the guiding principle has been to select projections that involve the least distortion of size and distance. The projection used for each map is noted in the border. Most fall into one of three categories – conic, cylindrical or azimuthal – whose basic concepts are shown above. Each involves plotting the forms of the Earth's surface on a grid of latitude and longitude lines, which may be shown as parallels, curves or radiating spokes.

Latitude and Longitude

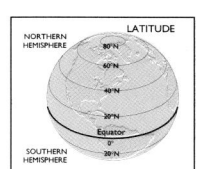 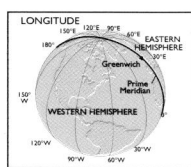 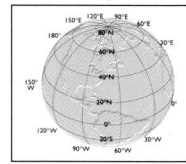

Accurate positioning of individual points on the Earth's surface is made possible by reference to the geometrical system of latitude and longitude. Latitude parallels are drawn west–east around the Earth and numbered by degrees north and south of the Equator, which is designated 0° of latitude. Longitude meridians are drawn north–south and numbered by degrees east and west of the prime meridian, 0° of longitude, which passes through Greenwich in England. By referring to these co-ordinates and their subdivisions of minutes (1/60th of a degree) and seconds (1/60th of a minute), any place on Earth can be located to within a few hundred metres. Latitude and longitude are indicated by blue lines on the maps; they are straight or curved according to the projection employed. Reference to these lines is the easiest way of determining the relative positions of places on different maps, and for plotting compass directions.

Name Forms

For ease of reference, both English and local name forms appear in the atlas. Oceans, seas and countries are shown in English throughout the atlas; country names may be abbreviated to their commonly accepted form (e.g. Germany, not The Federal Republic of Germany). Conventional English forms are also used for place names on the smaller-scale maps of the continents. However, local name forms are used on all large-scale and regional maps, with the English form given in brackets only for important cities – the large-scale map of Russia and Central Asia thus shows Moskva (Moscow). For countries which do not use a Roman script, place names have been transcribed according to the systems adopted by the British and US Geographic Names Authorities. For China, the Pin Yin system has been used, with some more widely known forms appearing in brackets, as with Beijing (Peking). Both English and local names appear in the index, the English form being cross-referenced to the local form.

Contents

World Statistics

Introduction to World Geography

City Maps
1–32

(Scale 1:200 000)

Index to City Maps
33–48

World Maps
1–176

The World

Europe

Scandinavia
1:4 000 000
Norway, Sweden, *Finland*

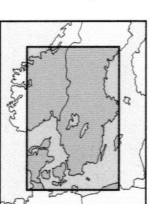

14–15

Denmark and Southern Sweden
1:2 000 000
Denmark, *Norway, Sweden*

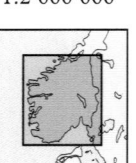

16–17

South Norway
1:2 000 000

18

British Isles and North Sea
1:4 000 000

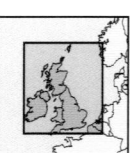

19

England and Wales
1:1 600 000
Isle of Man, Channel Islands

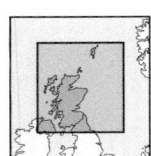

Scotland
1:1 600 000

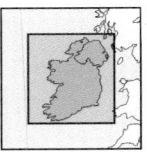

Ireland
1:1 600 000
Irish Republic, Northern Ireland

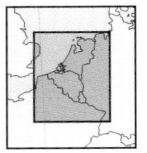

Netherlands, Belgium and Luxembourg
1:2 000 000

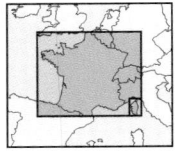

France
1:4 000 000

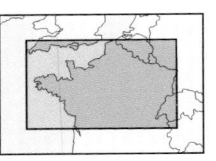

Northern France
1:2 000 000

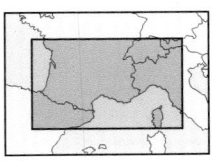

Southern France
1:2 000 000
Monaco

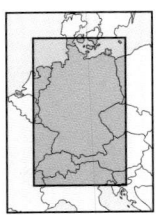

Germany
1:2 000 000

Switzerland
1:800 000
Liechtenstein

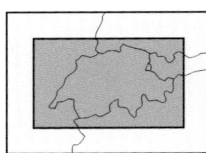

Austria, Czech Republic and Slovak Republic
1:2 000 000

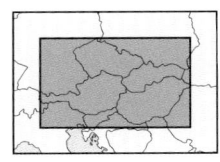

Central Europe
1:4 000 000

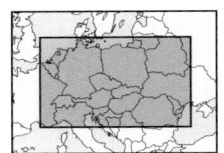

Malta, Crete, Corfu, Rhodes and Cyprus
1:800 000 / 1:1 040 000

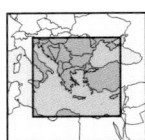

Balearics, Canaries and Madeira
1:800 000 / 1:1 600 000
Mallorca, Menorca, Ibiza

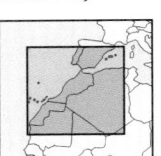

Eastern Spain
1:2 000 000
Andorra

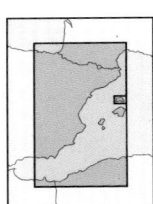

Western Spain and Portugal
1:2 000 000

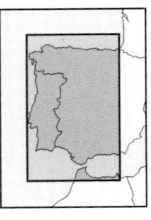

Northern Italy, Slovenia and Croatia
1:2 000 000

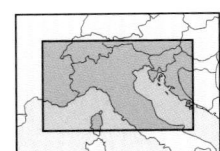

Southern Italy
1:2 000 000

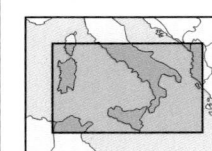

Southern Greece
1:2 000 000
Turkey

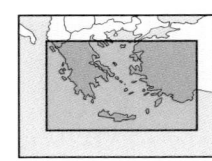

Northern Greece, Bulgaria and Yugoslavia
1:2 000 000
Macedonia

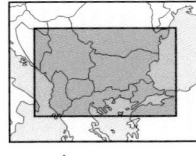

Hungary, Romania and the Lower Danube
1:2 000 000
Moldova

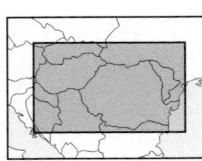

Poland and the Southern Baltic
1:2 000 000
Latvia, Lithuania

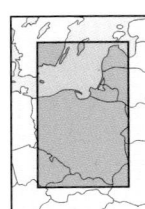

Eastern Europe and Turkey
1:8 000 000

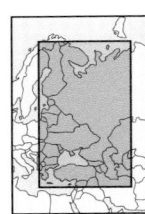

Baltic States, Belarus and Ukraine
1:4 000 000
Russia, Estonia, Latvia, Lithuania, Belarus, Ukraine

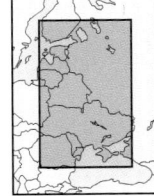

Volga Basin and the Caucasus
1:4 000 000
Russia, Georgia, Armenia, Azerbaijan

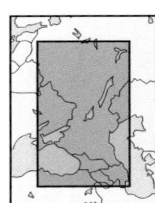

Asia

Southern Urals
1:4 000 000
Russia

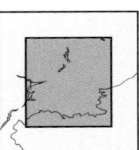

Central Asia
1:4 000 000
Kazakstan, Kyrgyzstan, Tajikistan, Uzbekistan

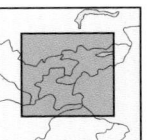

Russia and Central Asia
1:16 000 000
Russia, Kazakstan, Turkmenistan, Uzbekistan

Asia: Physical
1:40 000 000

Asia: Political
1:40 000 000

Japan
1:4 000 000
Ryukyu Islands

Southern Japan
1:2 000 000

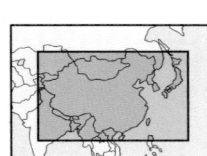
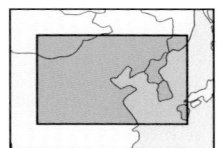
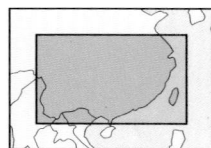
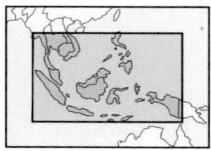
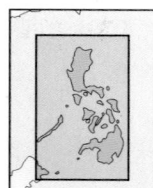
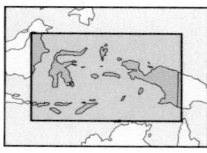
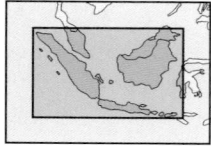
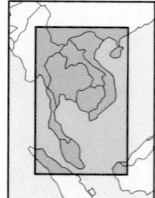
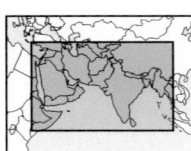
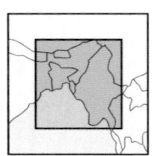
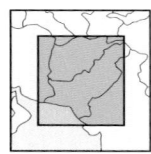
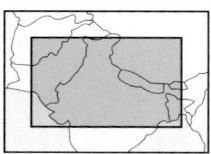
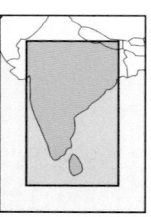
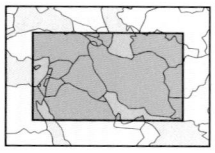
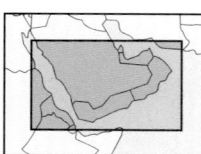
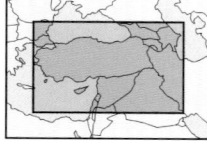
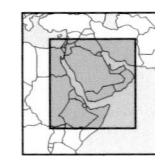
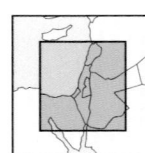
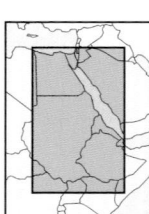
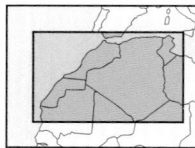
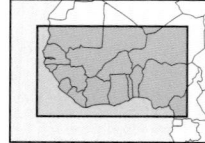
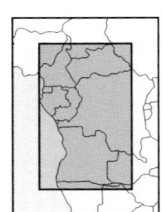
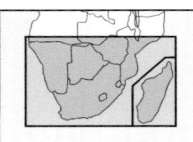
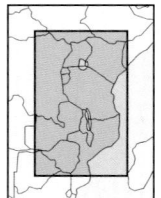
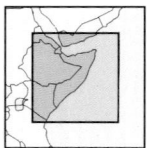
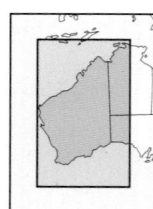

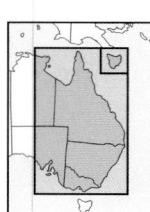
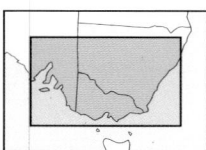
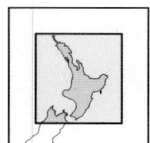
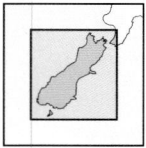
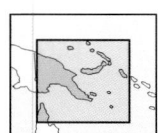
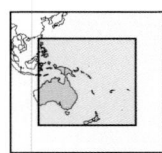
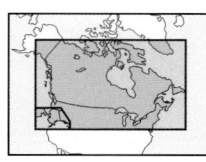
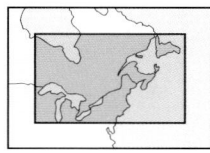
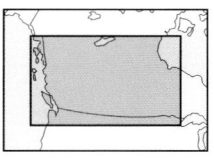
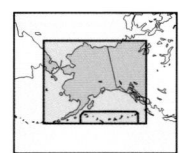
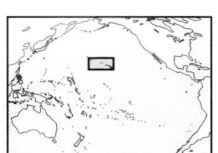
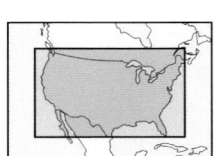
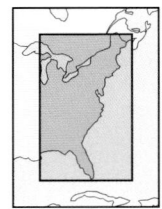
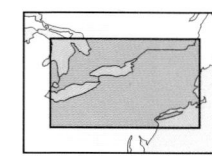
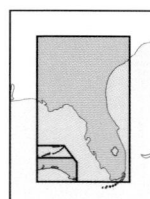
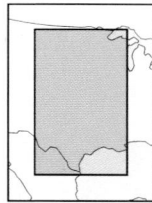
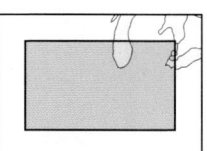
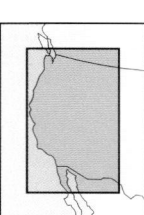
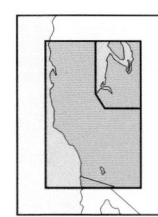
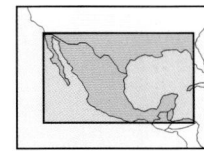
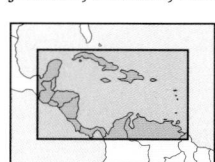
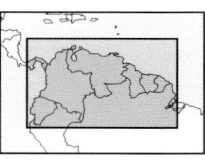

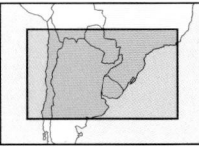
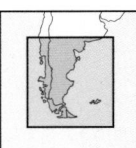

World Statistics: Countries

This alphabetical list includes all the countries and territories of the world. If a territory is not completely independent, then the country it is associated with is named. The area figures give the total area of land, inland water and ice. Units for areas and populations are thousands. The population figures are 1997 estimates. The annual income is the Gross National Product per capita in US dollars. The figures are the latest available, usually 1995.

Country/Territory	Area km² Thousands	Area miles² Thousands	Population Thousands	Capital	Annual Income US $
Adélie Land (France)	432	167	0.03	–	–
Afghanistan	652	252	23,000	Kabul	300
Albania	28.8	11.1	3,600	Tirana	670
Algeria	2,382	920	29,300	Algiers	1,600
American Samoa (US)	0.20	0.08	62	Pago Pago	2,600
Amsterdam Is. (France)	0.05	0.02	0.03	–	–
Andorra	0.45	0.17	75	Andorra-la-Vella	14,000
Angola	1,247	481	11,200	Luanda	410
Anguilla (UK)	0.1	0.04	10	The Valley	6,800
Antigua & Barbuda	0.44	0.17	66	St John's	6,390
Argentina	2,767	1,068	35,400	Buenos Aires	8,030
Armenia	29.8	11.5	3,800	Yerevan	730
Aruba (Netherlands)	0.19	0.07	70	Oranjestad	17,500
Ascension Is. (UK)	0.09	0.03	1.5	Georgetown	–
Australia	7,687	2,968	18,400	Canberra	18,720
Australian Antarctic Terr. (Aus.)	6,120	2,363	0	–	–
Austria	83.9	32.4	8,200	Vienna	26,890
Azerbaijan	86.6	33.4	7,700	Baku	480
Azores (Portugal)	2.2	0.87	238	Ponta Delgada	–
Bahamas	13.9	5.4	280	Nassau	11,940
Bahrain	0.68	0.26	605	Manama	7,840
Bangladesh	144	56	124,000	Dhaka	240
Barbados	0.43	0.17	265	Bridgetown	6,560
Belarus	207.6	80.1	10,500	Minsk	2,070
Belgium	30.5	11.8	10,200	Brussels	24,710
Belize	23	8.9	228	Belmopan	2,630
Benin	113	43	5,800	Porto-Novo	370
Bermuda (UK)	0.05	0.02	65	Hamilton	27,000
Bhutan	47	18.1	1,790	Thimphu	420
Bolivia	1,099	424	7,700	La Paz/Sucre	800
Bosnia-Herzegovina	51	20	3,600	Sarajevo	2,600
Botswana	582	225	1,500	Gaborone	3,020
Bouvet Is. (Norway)	0.05	0.02	0.02	–	–
Brazil	8,512	3,286	159,500	Brasília	3,640
British Antarctic Terr. (UK)	1,709	660	0.3	–	–
British Indian Ocean Terr. (UK)	0.08	0.03	0	–	–
Brunei	5.8	2.2	300	Bandar Seri Begawan	14,500
Bulgaria	111	43	8,600	Sofia	1,330
Burkina Faso	274	106	10,900	Ouagadougou	230
Burma (= Myanmar)	677	261	47,500	Rangoon	1,000
Burundi	27.8	10.7	6,300	Bujumbura	160
Cambodia	181	70	10,500	Phnom Penh	270
Cameroon	475	184	13,800	Yaoundé	650
Canada	9,976	3,852	30,200	Ottawa	19,380
Canary Is. (Spain)	7.3	2.8	1,494	Las Palmas/Santa Cruz	–
Cape Verde Is.	4	1.6	410	Praia	960
Cayman Is. (UK)	0.26	0.10	35	George Town	20,000
Central African Republic	623	241	3,400	Bangui	340
Chad	1,284	496	6,800	Ndjaména	180
Chatham Is. (NZ)	0.96	0.37	0.05	Waitangi	–
Chile	757	292	14,700	Santiago	4,160
China	9,597	3,705	1,210,000	Beijing	620
Christmas Is. (Australia)	0.14	0.05	2	The Settlement	–
Cocos (Keeling) Is. (Australia)	0.01	0.005	1	West Island	–
Colombia	1,139	440	35,900	Bogotá	1,910
Comoros	2.2	0.86	630	Moroni	470
Congo	342	132	2,700	Brazzaville	680
Congo (= Zaïre)	2,345	905	47,200	Kinshasa	120
Cook Is. (NZ)	0.24	0.09	20	Avarua	900
Costa Rica	51.1	19.7	3,500	San José	2,610
Croatia	56.5	21.8	4,900	Zagreb	3,250
Crozet Is. (France)	0.51	0.19	35	–	–
Cuba	111	43	11,300	Havana	1,250
Cyprus	9.3	3.6	800	Nicosia	11,500
Czech Republic	78.9	30.4	10,500	Prague	3,870
Denmark	43.1	16.6	5,400	Copenhagen	29,890
Djibouti	23.2	9	650	Djibouti	1,000
Dominica	0.75	0.29	78	Roseau	2,990
Dominican Republic	48.7	18.8	8,200	Santo Domingo	1,460
Ecuador	284	109	11,800	Quito	1,390
Egypt	1,001	387	63,000	Cairo	790
El Salvador	21	8.1	6,000	San Salvador	1,610
Equatorial Guinea	28.1	10.8	420	Malabo	380
Eritrea	94	36	3,500	Asmara	500
Estonia	44.7	17.3	1,500	Tallinn	2,860
Ethiopia	1,128	436	58,500	Addis Ababa	100
Falkland Is. (UK)	12.2	4.7	2	Stanley	–
Faroe Is. (Denmark)	1.4	0.54	45	Tórshavn	23,660
Fiji	18.3	7.1	800	Suva	2,440
Finland	338	131	5,200	Helsinki	20,580
France	552	213	58,800	Paris	24,990
French Guiana (France)	90	34.7	155	Cayenne	6,500
French Polynesia (France)	4	1.5	226	Papeete	7,500
Gabon	268	103	1,200	Libreville	3,490
Gambia, The	11.3	4.4	1,200	Banjul	320
Georgia	69.7	26.9	5,500	Tbilisi	440
Germany	357	138	82,300	Berlin/Bonn	27,510
Ghana	239	92	18,100	Accra	390
Gibraltar (UK)	0.007	0.003	28	Gibraltar Town	5,000
Greece	132	51	10,600	Athens	8,210
Greenland (Denmark)	2,176	840	57	Nuuk (Godthåb)	9,000
Grenada	0.34	0.13	99	St George's	2,980
Guadeloupe (France)	1.7	0.66	440	Basse-Terre	9,500
Guam (US)	0.55	0.21	161	Agana	6,000
Guatemala	109	42	11,300	Guatemala City	1,340
Guinea	246	95	7,500	Conakry	550
Guinea-Bissau	36.1	13.9	1,200	Bissau	250
Guyana	215	83	820	Georgetown	590
Haiti	27.8	10.7	7,400	Port-au-Prince	250
Honduras	112	43	6,300	Tegucigalpa	600
Hong Kong (China)	1.1	0.40	6,500	–	22,990
Hungary	93	35.9	10,200	Budapest	4,120
Iceland	103	40	275	Reykjavik	24,950
India	3,288	1,269	980,000	New Delhi	340
Indonesia	1,905	735	203,500	Jakarta	980
Iran	1,648	636	69,500	Tehran	4,800
Iraq	438	169	22,500	Baghdad	1,800
Ireland	70.3	27.1	3,600	Dublin	14,710
Israel	27	10.3	5,900	Jerusalem	15,920
Italy	301	116	57,800	Rome	19,020
Ivory Coast	322	125	15,100	Yamoussoukro	660
Jamaica	11	4.2	2,600	Kingston	1,510
Jan Mayen Is. (Norway)	0.38	0.15	0.06	–	–
Japan	378	146	125,900	Tokyo	39,640
Johnston Is. (US)	0.002	0.0009	1	–	–
Jordan	89.2	34.4	5,600	Amman	1,510
Kazakstan	2,717	1,049	17,000	Aqmola	1,330
Kenya	580	224	31,900	Nairobi	280
Kerguelen Is. (France)	7.2	2.8	0.7	–	–
Kermadec Is. (NZ)	0.03	0.01	0.1	–	–
Kiribati	0.72	0.28	85	Tarawa	710
Korea, North	121	47	24,500	Pyŏngyang	1,000
Korea, South	99	38.2	46,100	Seoul	9,700
Kuwait	17.8	6.9	2,050	Kuwait City	17,390
Kyrgyzstan	198.5	76.6	4,700	Bishkek	700
Laos	237	91	5,200	Vientiane	350
Latvia	65	25	2,500	Riga	2,270
Lebanon	10.4	4	3,200	Beirut	2,660
Lesotho	30.4	11.7	2,100	Maseru	770
Liberia	111	43	3,000	Monrovia	850
Libya	1,760	679	5,500	Tripoli	7,000
Liechtenstein	0.16	0.06	32	Vaduz	33,500
Lithuania	65.2	25.2	3,700	Vilnius	1,900
Luxembourg	2.6	1	400	Luxembourg	41,210
Macau (Portugal)	0.02	0.006	450	Macau	7,500
Macedonia	25.7	9.9	2,200	Skopje	860
Madagascar	587	227	15,500	Antananarivo	230
Madeira (Portugal)	0.81	0.31	253	Funchal	–
Malawi	118	46	10,300	Lilongwe	170
Malaysia	330	127	20,900	Kuala Lumpur	3,890
Maldives	0.30	0.12	275	Malé	990
Mali	1,240	479	11,000	Bamako	250
Malta	0.32	0.12	400	Valletta	11,000
Marshall Is.	0.18	0.07	60	Dalap-Uliga-Darrit	1,500
Martinique (France)	1.1	0.42	405	Fort-de-France	10,000
Mauritania	1,030	412	2,400	Nouakchott	460
Mauritius	2.0	0.72	1,200	Port Louis	3,380
Mayotte (France)	0.37	0.14	105	Mamoundzou	1,430
Mexico	1,958	756	97,400	Mexico City	3,320
Micronesia, Fed. States of	0.70	0.27	127	Palikir	1,560
Midway Is. (US)	0.005	0.002	2	–	–
Moldova	33.7	13	4,500	Chişinău	920
Monaco	0.002	0.0001	33	Monaco	16,000
Mongolia	1,567	605	2,500	Ulan Bator	310
Montserrat (UK)	0.10	0.04	12	Plymouth	4,500
Morocco	447	172	28,100	Rabat	1,110
Mozambique	802	309	19,100	Maputo	80
Namibia	825	318	1,700	Windhoek	2,000
Nauru	0.02	0.008	12	Yaren District	10,000
Nepal	141	54	22,100	Katmandu	200
Netherlands	41.5	16	15,900	Amsterdam/The Hague	24,000
Netherlands Antilles (Neths)	0.99	0.38	210	Willemstad	10,500
New Caledonia (France)	18.6	7.2	192	Nouméa	16,000
New Zealand	269	104	3,700	Wellington	14,340
Nicaragua	130	50	4,600	Managua	380
Niger	1,267	489	9,700	Niamey	220
Nigeria	924	357	118,000	Abuja	260
Niue (NZ)	0.26	0.10	2	Alofi	–
Norfolk Is. (Australia)	0.03	0.01	2	Kingston	–
Northern Mariana Is. (US)	0.48	0.18	50	Saipan	11,500
Norway	324	125	4,400	Oslo	31,250
Oman	212	82	2,400	Muscat	4,820
Pakistan	796	307	136,000	Islamabad	460
Palau	0.46	0.18	17	Koror	2,260
Panama	77.1	29.8	2,700	Panama City	2,750
Papua New Guinea	463	179	4,400	Port Moresby	1,160
Paraguay	407	157	5,200	Asunción	1,690
Peru	1,285	496	24,500	Lima	2,310
Peter 1st Is. (Norway)	0.18	0.07	0	–	–
Philippines	300	116	73,500	Manila	1,050
Pitcairn Is. (UK)	0.03	0.01	0.05	Adamstown	–
Poland	313	121	38,800	Warsaw	2,790
Portugal	92.4	35.7	10,100	Lisbon	9,740
Puerto Rico (US)	9	3.5	3,800	San Juan	7,500
Qatar	11	4.2	620	Doha	11,600
Queen Maud Land (Norway)	2,800	1,081	0	–	–
Réunion (France)	2.5	0.97	680	Saint-Denis	4,500
Romania	238	92	22,600	Bucharest	1,480
Ross Dependency (NZ)	435	168	0	–	–
Russia	17,075	6,592	147,800	Moscow	2,240
Rwanda	26.3	10.2	7,000	Kigali	180
St Helena (UK)	0.12	0.05	6	Jamestown	–
St Kitts & Nevis	0.36	0.14	42	Basseterre	4,470
St Lucia	0.62	0.24	150	Castries	3,370
St Paul Is. (France)	0.007	0.003	0	–	–
St Pierre & Miquelon (France)	0.24	0.09	7	Saint Pierre	–
St Vincent & Grenadines	0.39	0.15	114	Kingstown	2,280
San Marino	0.06	0.02	26	San Marino	20,000
São Tomé & Príncipe	0.96	0.37	135	São Tomé	350
Saudi Arabia	2,150	830	19,100	Riyadh	7,040
Senegal	197	76	8,900	Dakar	600
Seychelles	0.46	0.18	78	Victoria	6,370
Sierra Leone	71.7	27.7	4,600	Freetown	180
Singapore	0.62	0.24	3,200	Singapore	26,730
Slovak Republic	49	18.9	5,400	Bratislava	2,950
Slovenia	20.3	7.8	2,000	Ljubljana	8,200
Solomon Is.	28.9	11.2	410	Honiara	910
Somalia	638	246	9,900	Mogadishu	500
South Africa	1,220	471	42,300	C. Town/Pretoria/Bloemfontein	3,160
South Georgia (UK)	3.8	1.4	0.05	–	–
South Sandwich Is. (UK)	0.38	0.15	0	–	–
Spain	505	195	39,300	Madrid	13,580
Sri Lanka	65.6	25.3	18,700	Colombo	700
Sudan	2,506	967	31,000	Khartoum	750
Surinam	163	63	500	Paramaribo	880
Svalbard (Norway)	62.9	24.3	4	Longyearbyen	–
Swaziland	17.4	6.7	1,000	Mbabane	1,170
Sweden	450	174	8,900	Stockholm	23,750
Switzerland	41.3	15.9	7,100	Bern	40,630
Syria	185	71	15,300	Damascus	1,120
Taiwan	36	13.9	21,700	Taipei	12,000
Tajikistan	143.1	55.2	6,000	Dushanbe	340
Tanzania	945	365	31,200	Dodoma	120
Thailand	513	198	60,800	Bangkok	2,740
Togo	56.8	21.9	4,500	Lomé	310
Tokelau (NZ)	0.01	0.005	2	Nukunonu	–
Tonga	0.75	0.29	107	Nuku'alofa	1,610
Trinidad & Tobago	5.1	2	1,300	Port of Spain	3,770
Tristan da Cunha (UK)	0.11	0.04	0.33	Edinburgh	–
Tunisia	164	63	9,200	Tunis	1,820
Turkey	779	301	63,500	Ankara	2,780
Turkmenistan	488.1	188.5	4,800	Ashkhabad	920
Turks & Caicos Is. (UK)	0.43	0.17	15	Cockburn Town	5,000
Tuvalu	0.03	0.01	10	Fongafale	600
Uganda	236	91	20,800	Kampala	240
Ukraine	603.7	233.1	51,500	Kiev	1,630
United Arab Emirates	83.6	32.3	2,400	Abu Dhabi	17,400
United Kingdom	243.3	94	58,600	London	18,700
United States of America	9,373	3,619	268,000	Washington, DC	26,980
Uruguay	177	68	3,300	Montevideo	5,170
Uzbekistan	447.4	172.7	23,800	Tashkent	970
Vanuatu	12.2	4.7	175	Port-Vila	1,200
Vatican City	0.0004	0.0002	1	–	–
Venezuela	912	352	22,500	Caracas	3,020
Vietnam	332	127	77,100	Hanoi	240
Virgin Is. (UK)	0.15	0.06	13	Road Town	–
Virgin Is. (US)	0.34	0.13	105	Charlotte Amalie	12,000
Wake Is.	0.008	0.003	0.30	–	–
Wallis & Futuna Is. (France)	0.20	0.08	15	Mata-Utu	–
Western Sahara	266	103	280	El Aaiún	980
Western Samoa	2.8	1.1	175	Apia	1,120
Yemen	528	204	16,500	Sana	260
Yugoslavia	102.3	39.5	10,500	Belgrade	1,400
Zambia	753	291	9,500	Lusaka	400
Zimbabwe	391	151	12,100	Harare	540

At the time of going to press, the government of Kazakstan planned to rename the capital Aqmola to Astana.

World Statistics: Cities

This list shows the principal cities with more than 500,000 inhabitants (only cities with more than 700,000 inhabitants are included for China and India). The figures are taken from the most recent census or estimate available, and as far as possible are the population of the metropolitan area, e.g. greater New York, Mexico or Paris. All the figures are in thousands. Local name forms have been used for the smaller cities (e.g. Kraków).

Afghanistan
Kabul 1,565
Algeria
Algiers 1,722
Oran 664
Angola
Luanda 2,250
Argentina
Buenos Aires 10,990
Córdoba 1,198
Rosario 1,096
Mendoza 775
La Plata 640
San Miguel de Tucumán 622
Mar del Plata 520
Armenia
Yerevan 1,226
Australia
Sydney 3,713
Melbourne 3,189
Brisbane 1,422
Perth 1,221
Adelaide 1,071
Austria
Vienna 1,560
Azerbaijan
Baku 1,081
Bangladesh
Dhaka 7,832
Chittagong 2,041
Khulna 877
Rajshahi 517
Belarus
Minsk 1,700
Homyel 512
Belgium
Brussels 952
Benin
Cotonou 537
Bolivia
La Paz 1,126
Santa Cruz 767
Bosnia-Herzegovina
Sarajevo 526
Brazil
São Paulo 16,417
Rio de Janeiro 9,888
Salvador 2,056
Belo Horizonte 2,049
Fortaleza 1,758
Brasília 1,596
Curitiba 1,290
Recife 1,290
Nova Iguaçu 1,286
Pôrto Alegre 1,263
Belém 1,246
Manaus 1,011
Goiânia 921
Campinas 846
Guarulhos 781
São Gonçalo 748
São Luís 696
Duque de Caxias 665
Maceió 628
Santo André 614
Natal 607
Teresina 598
São Bernado de Campo 565
Osasco 563
Campo Grande 526
Bulgaria
Sofia 1,117
Burkina Faso
Ouagadougou 690
Burma (Myanmar)
Rangoon 2,513
Mandalay 533
Cambodia
Phnom Penh 920
Cameroon
Douala 884
Yaoundé 750
Canada
Toronto 4,264
Montréal 3,327
Vancouver 1,832
Ottawa-Hull 1,010
Edmonton 863
Calgary 822
Québec 672
Winnipeg 667
Hamilton 624
Central African Rep.
Bangui 706

Chad
Ndjaména 530
Chile
Santiago 5,077
China
Shanghai 15,082
Beijing 12,362
Tianjin 10,687
Hong Kong (SAR)¹ 6,205
Chongqing 3,870
Shenyang 3,762
Wuhan 3,520
Guangzhou 3,114
Harbin 2,505
Nanjing 2,211
Xi'an 2,115
Chengdu 1,933
Dalian 1,855
Changchun 1,810
Jinan 1,660
Taiyuan 1,642
Qingdao 1,584
Fuzhou, Fujian 1,380
Zibo 1,346
Zhengzhou 1,324
Lanzhou 1,296
Anshan 1,252
Fushun 1,246
Kunming 1,242
Changsha 1,198
Hangzhou 1,185
Nanchang 1,169
Shijiazhuang 1,159
Guiyang 1,131
Ürümqi 1,130
Jilin 1,118
Hefei 1,110
Tangshan 1,110
Baotou 1,033
Xuzhou, Jiangsu 937
Handan 894
Wuxi 863
Luoyang 863
Datong 845
Nanning 829
Benxi 805
Yichun, Heilongjiang 800
Huainan 769
Suzhou, Jiangsu 766
Colombia
Bogotá 5,026
Cali 1,719
Medellin 1,621
Barranquilla 1,064
Cartagena 746
Congo
Brazzaville 938
Pointe-Noire 576
Congo (Zaïre)
Kinshasa 3,804
Lubumbashi 739
Mbuji-Mayi 613
Kolwezi 544
Costa Rica
San José 1,186
Croatia
Zagreb 931
Cuba
Havana 2,143
Czech Republic
Prague 1,217
Denmark
Copenhagen 1,353
Dominican Republic
Santo Domingo 2,135
Santiago 691
Ecuador
Guayaquil 1,925
Quito 1,444
Egypt
Cairo 9,656
Alexandria 3,380
El Gîza 2,144
Shubra el Kheima 834
El Salvador
San Salvador 1,522
Ethiopia
Addis Ababa 2,316
Finland
Helsinki 525
France
Paris 9,469
Lyon 1,262
Marseille 1,087
Lille 959

Bordeaux 696
Toulouse 650
Nice 516
Georgia
Tbilisi 1,279
Germany
Berlin 3,472
Hamburg 1,706
Munich 1,245
Cologne 964
Frankfurt 652
Essen 618
Dortmund 601
Stuttgart 588
Düsseldorf 573
Bremen 549
Duisburg 536
Hanover 526
Ghana
Accra 1,781
Kumasi 540
Greece
Athens 3,097
Guatemala
Guatemala 1,814
Guinea
Conakry 1,508
Haiti
Port-au-Prince 1,402
Honduras
Tegucigalpa 739
Hungary
Budapest 1,909
India
Bombay (Mumbai) 15,093
Calcutta 11,673
Delhi 9,882
Madras (Chennai) 5,361
Hyderabad 4,280
Bangalore 4,087
Ahmadabad 3,298
Pune 2,485
Kanpur 2,111
Nagpur 1,661
Lucknow 1,642
Surat 1,517
Jaipur 1,514
Coimbatore 1,136
Vadodara 1,115
Indore 1,104
Patna 1,099
Madurai 1,094
Bhopal 1,064
Vishakhapatnam 1,052
Varanasi 1,026
Ludhiana 1,012
Agra 956
Jabalpur 887
Allahabad 858
Meerut 847
Vijayawada 845
Jamshedpur 834
Trivandrum 826
Dhanbad 818
Thane 797
Asansol 764
Nasik 722
Gwalior 720
Tiruchchirappalli 711
Amritsar 709
Indonesia
Jakarta 11,500
Surabaya 2,701
Bandung 2,368
Medan 1,910
Semarang 1,366
Palembang 1,352
Ujung Pandang 1,092
Bandar Lampung 832
Malang 763
Iran
Tehran 6,750
Mashhad 1,964
Esfahan 1,221
Tabriz 1,166
Shiraz 1,043
Ahvaz 828
Qom 780
Bakhtaran 666
Karaj 588
Iraq
Baghdad 3,841
Diyala 961
As Sulaymaniyah 952
Arbil 770

Al Mawsil 644
Kadhimain 521
Ireland
Dublin 1,024
Israel
Tel Aviv 1,880
Jerusalem 562
Italy
Rome 2,688
Milan 1,334
Naples 1,062
Turin 946
Palermo 695
Genoa 660
Ivory Coast
Abidjan 2,500
Jamaica
Kingston 644
Japan
Tokyo-Yokohama 26,836
Osaka 10,601
Nagoya 2,159
Sapporo 1,732
Kobe 1,509
Kyoto 1,452
Fukuoka 1,269
Kawasaki 1,200
Hiroshima 1,102
Kitakyushu 1,020
Sendai 951
Chiba 851
Sakai 806
Kumamoto 640
Okayama 605
Hamamatsu 561
Sagamihara 560
Funabashi 540
Kagoshima 540
Higashiosaka 515
Jordan
Amman 1,300
Az-Zarqā 609
Kazakstan
Almaty 1,151
Qaraghandy 613
Kenya
Nairobi 2,000
Mombasa 600
Korea, North
Pyŏngyang 2,639
Hamhung 775
Chŏngjin 754
Chinnampo 691
Sinŭiju 500
Korea, South
Seoul 11,641
Pusan 3,814
Taegu 2,449
Inchon 2,308
Taejŏn 1,272
Kwangju 1,258
Ulsan 967
Sŏngnam 869
Puch'on 779
Suwŏn 756
Chŏnju 563
Kyrgyzstan
Bishkek 584
Latvia
Riga 840
Lebanon
Beirut 1,500
Tripoli 500
Libya
Tripoli 960
Lithuania
Vilnius 576
Macedonia
Skopje 541
Madagascar
Antananarivo 1,053
Malaysia
Kuala Lumpur 1,145
Mali
Bamako 746
Mauritania
Nouakchott 600
Mexico
Mexico City 15,643
Guadalajara 2,847
Monterrey 2,522
Puebla 1,055
León 872
Ciudad Juárez 798
Tijuana 743

Culiacán Rosales 602
Mexicali 602
Acapulco de Juárez 592
Mérida 557
Chihuahua 530
San Luis Potosí 526
Aguascalientés 506
Moldova
Chişinău 700
Mongolia
Ulan Bator 619
Morocco
Casablanca 2,943
Rabat-Salé 1,220
Marrakesh 602
Fès 564
Mozambique
Maputo 2,000
Nepal
Katmandu 535
Netherlands
Amsterdam 1,100
Rotterdam 1,074
The Hague 695
Utrecht 546
New Zealand
Auckland 929
Nicaragua
Managua 974
Nigeria
Lagos 10,287
Ibadan 1,365
Ogbomosho 712
Kano 657
Norway
Oslo 714
Pakistan
Karachi 9,863
Lahore 5,085
Faisalabad 1,875
Peshawar 1,676
Gujranwala 1,663
Rawalpindi 1,290
Multan 1,257
Hyderabad 1,107
Paraguay
Asunción 945
Peru
Lima-Callao 6,601
Callao 638
Arequipa 620
Trujillo 509
Philippines
Manila 9,280
Quezon City 1,677
Davao 961
Cebu 688
Caloocan 643
Poland
Warsaw 1,638
Lódz 826
Kraków 745
Wroclaw 643
Poznań 582
Portugal
Lisbon 2,561
Oporto 1,174
Romania
Bucharest 2,061
Russia
Moscow 9,233
St Petersburg 4,883
Nizhniy Novgorod 1,425
Novosibirsk 1,418
Yekaterinburg 1,347
Samara 1,223
Omsk 1,161
Chelyabinsk 1,125
Kazan 1,092
Ufa 1,092
Perm 1,086
Rostov 1,023
Volgograd 1,000
Krasnoyarsk 914
Voronezh 905
Saratov 899
Togliatti 689
Simbirsk 670
Izhevsk 653
Krasnodar 638
Vladivostok 637
Irkutsk 632
Yaroslavl 631
Khabarovsk 609
Barnaul 596

Novokuznetsk 593
Orenburg 558
Penza 551
Tyumen 550
Tula 535
Ryazan 526
Naberezhnyye-Chelny 524
Kemerovo 513
Astrakhan 512
Saudi Arabia
Riyadh 2,000
Jedda 1,400
Mecca 618
Medina 500
Senegal
Dakar 1,729
Sierra Leone
Freetown 505
Singapore
Singapore 2,874
Somalia
Mogadishu 1,000
South Africa
Cape Town 2,350
East Rand 1,379
Johannesburg 1,196
Durban 1,137
Pretoria 1,080
West Rand 870
Port Elizabeth 853
Vanderbijlpark-Vereeniging 774
Soweto 597
Sasolburg 540
Spain
Madrid 3,041
Barcelona 1,631
Valencia 764
Sevilla 714
Zaragoza 607
Málaga 531
Sri Lanka
Colombo 1,863
Sudan
Khartoum 561
Omdurman 526
Sweden
Stockholm 1,553
Göteburg 788
Switzerland
Zürich 915
Syria
Damascus 2,230
Aleppo 1,640
Homs 644
Taiwan
Taipei 2,653
Kaohsiung 1,405
Taichung 817
Tainan 700
Panchiao 544
Tajikistan
Dushanbe 602
Tanzania
Dar-es-Salaam 1,361
Thailand
Bangkok 5,876
Togo
Lomé 590
Tunisia
Tunis 1,827
Turkey
Istanbul 7,490
Ankara 3,028
Izmir 2,333
Adana 1,472
Bursa 1,317
Konya 1,040
Gaziantep 930
Icel 908
Antalya 734
Diyarbakir 677
Kocaeli 661
Urfa 649
Kayseri 648
Manisa 641
Hatay 561
Samsun 557
Eskisehir 508
Balikesir 501
Uganda
Kampala 773
Ukraine
Kiev 2,630
Kharkiv 1,555

Dnipropetrovsk 1,147
Donetsk 1,088
Odesa 1,046
Zaporizhzhya 887
Lviv 802
Kryvyy Rih 720
Mariupol 510
Mykolayiv 508
United Kingdom
London 8,089
Birmingham 2,373
Manchester 2,353
Liverpool 852
Glasgow 832
Leeds 529
Newcastle 525
United States
New York 16,329
Los Angeles 12,410
Chicago 7,668
Philadelphia 4,949
Washington, DC 4,466
Detroit 4,307
Houston 3,653
Atlanta 3,331
Boston 3,240
Dallas 2,898
Minneapolis-St Paul 2,688
San Diego 2,632
St Louis 2,536
Phoenix 2,473
Baltimore 2,458
Pittsburgh 2,402
Cleveland 2,222
San Francisco 2,182
Seattle 2,180
Tampa 2,157
Miami 2,025
Denver 1,796
Portland (Or.) 1,676
Kansas City (Mo.) 1,647
Cincinnati 1,581
San Jose 1,557
Norfolk 1,529
Indianapolis 1,462
Milwaukee 1,456
Sacramento 1,441
San Antonio 1,437
Columbus (Oh.) 1,423
New Orleans 1,309
Charlotte 1,260
Buffalo 1,189
Salt Lake City 1,178
Hartford 1,151
Oklahoma 1,007
Jacksonville 665
Omaha 663
Memphis 614
El Paso 579
Austin 514
Nashville 505
Uruguay
Montevideo 1,326
Uzbekistan
Tashkent 2,106
Venezuela
Caracas 2,784
Maracaibo 1,364
Valencia 1,032
Maracay 800
Barquisimeto 745
Ciudad Guayana 524
Vietnam
Ho Chi Minh City 4,322
Hanoi 3,056
Haiphong 783
Yemen
Sana 972
Yugoslavia
Belgrade 1,137
Zambia
Lusaka 982
Zimbabwe
Harare 1,189
Bulawayo 622

¹ SAR = Special Administrative Region of China

World Statistics: Distances

The table shows air distances in miles and kilometres between 30 major cities. Known as 'Great Circle' distances, these measure the shortest routes between the cities, which aircraft use wherever possible. The maps show the world centred on six cities, and illustrate, for example, why direct flights from Japan to northern America and Europe are across the Arctic regions. The maps have been constructed on an Azimuthal Equidistant projection, on which all distances measured through the centre point are true to scale. The red lines are drawn at 5,000, 10,000 and 15,000 km from the central city.

Upper-right triangle values are in Miles; lower-left triangle values are in Kms.

	Beijing	Bombay	Buenos Aires	Cairo	Calcutta	Caracas	Chicago	Hong Kong	Honolulu	Johannesburg	Lagos	London	Los Angeles	Mexico City	Moscow	Nairobi	New York	Paris	Rio de Janeiro	Rome	Singapore	Sydney	Tokyo	Wellington
Beijing	—	2956	11972	4688	2031	8947	6588	1220	5070	7276	7119	5057	6251	7742	3600	5727	6828	5106	10773	5049	2783	5561	1304	6700
Bombay	4757	—	9275	2706	1034	9024	8048	2683	8024	4334	4730	4467	8700	9728	3126	2816	7793	4356	8332	3837	2432	6313	4189	7686
Buenos Aires	19268	14925	—	7341	10268	3167	5599	11481	7558	5025	4919	6917	6122	4591	8374	6463	5298	6867	1214	6929	9867	7332	11410	6202
Cairo	7544	4355	11814	—	3541	6340	6127	5064	8838	3894	2432	2180	7580	7687	1803	2197	5605	1994	6149	1325	5137	8959	5947	10268
Calcutta	3269	1664	16524	5699	—	9609	7978	1653	7048	5256	5727	4946	8152	9494	3438	3839	7921	4883	9366	4486	1800	5678	3195	7055
Caracas	14399	14522	5096	10203	15464	—	2502	10166	6009	6847	4810	4664	3612	2228	6175	7173	2131	4738	2825	5196	11407	9534	8801	8154
Chicago	10603	12953	9011	3206	12839	4027	—	7783	4247	8689	5973	3949	1742	1694	4971	8005	711	4132	5311	4809	9369	9243	6299	8358
Hong Kong	1963	4317	18478	8150	2659	16360	12526	—	5543	6669	7360	5980	7232	8775	4439	5453	8047	5984	11001	5769	1615	4582	1786	5857
Honolulu	8160	12914	12164	14223	11343	9670	6836	8921	—	11934	10133	7228	2558	3781	7036	10739	4958	7437	8290	8026	6721	5075	3854	4669
Johannesburg	11710	6974	8088	6267	8459	11019	13984	10732	19206	—	2799	5637	10362	9063	5692	1818	7979	5426	4420	4811	5381	6860	8418	7308
Lagos	11457	7612	7916	3915	9216	7741	9612	11845	16308	4505	—	3118	7713	6879	3886	2366	5268	2929	3750	2510	6925	9643	8376	9973
London	8138	7190	11131	3508	7961	7507	6356	9623	11632	9071	5017	—	5442	5552	1552	4237	3463	212	5778	889	6743	10558	5942	11691
Los Angeles	10060	14000	9852	12200	13120	5812	2804	11639	4117	16676	12414	8758	—	1549	6070	9659	2446	5645	6310	6331	8776	7502	5475	6719
Mexico City	12460	15656	7389	12372	15280	3586	2726	14122	6085	14585	11071	8936	2493	—	6664	9207	2090	5717	4780	6365	10321	8058	7024	6897
Moscow	5794	5031	13477	2902	5534	9938	8000	7144	11323	9161	6254	2498	9769	10724	—	3942	4666	1545	7184	1477	5237	9008	4651	10283
Nairobi	9216	4532	10402	3536	6179	11544	12883	8776	17282	2927	3807	6819	15544	14818	6344	—	7358	4029	5548	3350	4635	7552	6996	8490
New York	10988	12541	8526	9020	12747	3430	1145	12950	7980	12841	8477	5572	3936	3264	7510	11842	—	3626	4832	4280	9531	9935	6741	8951
Paris	8217	7010	11051	3210	7858	7625	6650	9630	11968	8732	4714	342	9085	9200	2486	6485	5836	—	5708	687	6671	10539	6038	11798
Rio de Janeiro	17338	13409	1953	9896	15073	4546	8547	17704	13342	7113	6035	9299	10155	7693	11562	8928	7777	9187	—	5725	9763	8389	11551	7367
Rome	8126	6175	11151	2133	7219	8363	7739	9284	12916	7743	4039	1431	10188	10243	2376	5391	6888	1105	9214	—	6229	10143	6127	11523
Singapore	4478	3914	15879	8267	2897	18359	15078	2599	10816	8660	11145	10852	14123	16610	8428	7460	15339	10737	15712	10025	—	3915	3306	5298
Sydney	8949	10160	11800	14418	9138	15343	14875	7374	8168	11040	15519	16992	12073	12969	14497	12153	15989	16962	13501	16324	6300	—	4861	1383
Tokyo	2099	6742	18362	9571	5141	14164	10137	2874	6202	13547	13480	9562	8811	11304	7485	11260	10849	9718	18589	9861	5321	7823	—	5762
Wellington	10782	12370	9981	16524	11354	13122	13451	9427	7513	11761	16050	18814	10814	11100	16549	13664	14405	18987	11855	18545	8526	2226	9273	—

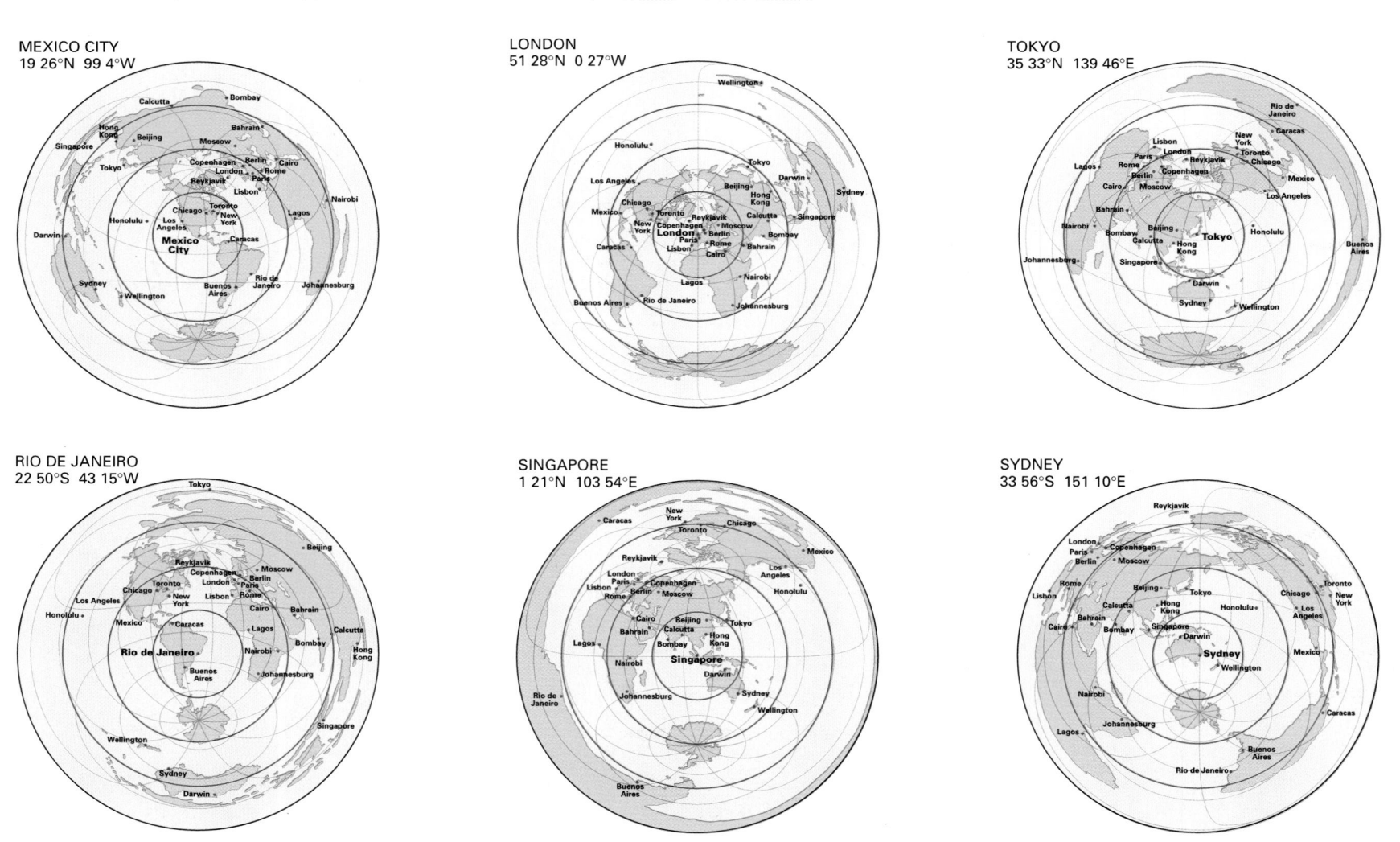

MEXICO CITY 19 26°N 99 4°W

LONDON 51 28°N 0 27°W

TOKYO 35 33°N 139 46°E

RIO DE JANEIRO 22 50°S 43 15°W

SINGAPORE 1 21°N 103 54°E

SYDNEY 33 56°S 151 10°E

World Statistics: Climate

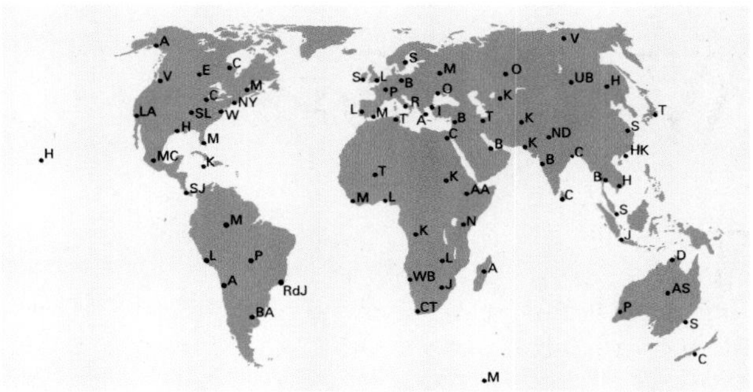

Rainfall and temperature figures are provided for more than 70 cities around the world. As climate is affected by altitude, the height of each city is shown in metres beneath its name. For each month, the figures in blue show the total rainfall or snow in millimetres, and in red the average temperature in degrees Celsius; the total annual rainfall and average annual temperature are at the end of the rows.

	Jan.	Feb.	Mar.	Apr.	May	June	July	Aug.	Sept.	Oct.	Nov.	Dec.	Year
EUROPE													
Athens, Greece	62	37	37	23	23	14	6	7	15	51	56	71	402
107 m	10	10	12	16	20	25	28	28	24	20	15	11	18
Berlin, Germany	46	40	33	42	49	65	73	69	48	49	46	43	603
55 m	−1	0	4	9	14	17	19	18	15	9	5	1	9
Istanbul, Turkey	109	92	72	46	38	34	34	30	58	81	103	119	816
14 m	5	6	7	11	16	20	23	23	20	16	12	8	14
Lisbon, Portugal	111	76	109	54	44	16	3	4	33	62	93	103	708
77 m	11	12	14	16	17	20	22	23	21	18	14	12	17
London, UK	54	40	37	37	46	45	57	59	49	57	64	48	593
5 m	4	5	7	9	12	16	18	17	15	11	8	5	11
Málaga, Spain	61	51	62	46	26	5	1	3	29	64	64	62	474
33 m	12	13	16	17	19	29	25	26	23	20	16	13	18
Moscow, Russia	39	38	36	37	53	58	88	71	58	45	47	54	624
156 m	−13	−10	−4	6	13	16	18	17	12	6	−1	−7	4
Odesa, Ukraine	57	62	30	21	34	34	42	37	37	13	35	71	473
64 m	−3	−1	2	9	15	20	22	22	18	12	9	1	10
Paris, France	56	46	35	42	57	54	59	64	55	50	51	50	619
75 m	3	4	8	11	15	18	20	19	17	12	7	4	12
Rome, Italy	71	62	57	51	46	37	15	21	63	99	129	93	744
17 m	8	9	11	14	18	22	25	25	22	17	13	10	16
Shannon, Irish Republic	94	67	56	53	61	57	77	79	86	86	96	117	929
2 m	5	5	7	9	12	14	16	16	14	11	8	6	10
Stockholm, Sweden	43	30	25	31	34	45	61	76	60	48	53	48	554
44 m	−3	−3	−1	5	10	15	18	17	12	7	3	0	7
ASIA													
Bahrain	8	18	13	8	<3	0	0	0	0	0	18	18	81
5 m	17	18	21	25	29	32	33	34	31	28	24	19	26
Bangkok, Thailand	8	20	36	58	198	160	160	175	305	206	66	5	1,397
2 m	26	28	29	30	29	29	28	28	28	28	26	25	28
Beirut, Lebanon	191	158	94	53	18	3	<3	<3	5	51	132	185	892
34 m	14	14	16	18	22	24	27	28	26	24	19	16	21
Bombay, India	3	3	3	<3	18	485	617	340	264	64	13	3	1,809
11 m	24	24	26	28	30	29	27	27	27	28	27	26	27
Calcutta, India	10	31	36	43	140	297	325	328	252	114	20	5	1,600
6 m	20	22	27	30	30	30	29	29	29	28	23	19	26
Colombo, Sri Lanka	89	69	147	231	371	224	135	109	160	348	315	147	2,365
7 m	26	26	27	28	28	27	27	27	27	27	26	26	27
Harbin, China	6	5	10	23	43	94	112	104	46	33	8	5	488
160 m	−18	−15	−5	6	13	19	22	21	14	4	−6	−16	3
Ho Chi Minh, Vietnam	15	3	13	43	221	330	315	269	335	269	114	56	1,984
9 m	26	27	29	30	29	28	28	28	27	27	27	26	28
Hong Kong, China	33	46	74	137	292	394	381	361	257	114	43	31	2,162
33 m	16	15	18	22	26	28	28	28	27	25	21	18	23
Jakarta, Indonesia	300	300	211	147	114	97	64	43	66	112	142	203	1,798
8 m	26	26	27	27	27	27	27	27	27	27	27	26	27
Kabul, Afghanistan	31	36	94	102	20	5	3	3	<3	15	20	10	338
1,815 m	−3	−1	6	13	18	22	25	24	20	14	7	3	12
Karachi, Pakistan	13	10	8	3	3	18	81	41	13	<3	3	5	196
4 m	19	20	24	28	30	31	30	29	28	28	24	20	26
Kazalinsk, Kazakstan	10	10	13	13	15	5	5	8	8	10	13	15	125
63 m	−12	−11	−3	6	18	23	25	23	16	8	−1	−7	7
New Delhi, India	23	18	13	8	13	74	180	172	117	10	3	10	640
218 m	14	17	23	28	33	34	31	30	29	26	20	15	25
Omsk, Russia	15	8	8	13	31	51	51	51	28	25	18	20	318
85 m	−22	−19	−12	−1	10	16	18	16	10	1	−11	−18	−1
Shanghai, China	48	58	84	94	94	180	147	142	130	71	51	36	1,135
7 m	4	5	9	14	20	24	28	28	23	19	12	7	16
Singapore	252	173	193	188	173	173	170	196	178	208	254	257	2,413
10 m	26	27	28	28	28	28	28	27	27	27	27	27	27
Tehran, Iran	46	38	46	36	13	3	3	3	3	8	20	31	246
1,220 m	2	5	9	16	21	26	30	29	25	18	12	6	17
Tokyo, Japan	48	74	107	135	147	165	142	152	234	208	97	56	1,565
6 m	3	4	7	13	17	21	25	26	23	17	11	6	14
Ulan Bator, Mongolia	<3	<3	3	5	10	28	76	51	23	5	5	3	208
1,325 m	−26	−21	−13	−1	6	14	16	14	8	−1	−13	−22	−3
Verkhoyansk, Russia	5	5	3	5	8	23	28	25	13	8	8	5	134
100 m	−50	−45	−32	−15	0	12	14	9	2	−15	−38	−48	−17
AFRICA													
Addis Ababa, Ethiopia	<3	3	25	135	213	201	206	239	102	28	<3	0	1,151
2,450 m	19	20	20	20	19	18	18	19	21	22	21	20	20
Antananarivo, Madagas.	300	279	178	53	18	8	8	10	18	61	135	287	1,356
1,372 m	21	21	21	19	18	15	14	15	17	19	21	21	19
Cairo, Egypt	5	5	5	3	3	<3	0	0	<3	<3	3	5	28
116 m	13	15	18	21	25	28	28	28	26	24	20	15	22
Cape Town, South Africa	15	8	18	48	79	84	89	66	43	31	18	10	508
17 m	21	21	20	17	14	13	12	13	14	16	18	19	17
Johannesburg, S. Africa	114	109	89	38	25	8	8	8	23	56	107	125	709
1,665 m	20	20	18	16	13	10	11	13	16	18	19	20	16
Khartoum, Sudan	<3	<3	<3	<3	3	8	53	71	18	5	<3	0	158
390 m	24	25	28	31	33	34	32	31	32	32	28	25	29
Kinshasa, Congo (Zaïre)	135	145	196	196	158	8	3	3	31	119	221	142	1,354
325 m	26	26	27	27	26	24	23	24	25	26	26	26	25
Lagos, Nigeria	28	46	102	150	269	460	279	64	140	206	69	25	1,836
3 m	27	28	29	28	28	26	26	25	26	26	28	28	27
Lusaka, Zambia	231	191	142	18	3	<3	<3	0	<3	10	91	150	836
1,277 m	21	22	21	21	19	16	16	18	22	24	23	22	21
Monrovia, Liberia	31	56	97	216	516	973	996	373	744	772	236	130	5,138
23 m	26	26	27	27	26	25	24	25	25	25	26	26	26
Nairobi, Kenya	38	64	125	211	158	46	15	23	31	53	109	86	958
1,820 m	19	19	19	19	18	16	16	16	18	19	18	18	18
Timbuktu, Mali	<3	<3	3	<3	5	23	79	81	38	3	<3	<3	231
301 m	22	24	28	32	34	35	32	30	32	31	28	23	29
Tunis, Tunisia	64	51	41	36	18	8	3	8	33	51	48	61	419
66 m	10	11	13	16	19	23	26	27	25	20	16	11	18
Walvis Bay, Namibia	<3	5	8	3	3	<3	<3	3	<3	<3	<3	<3	23
7 m	19	19	19	18	17	16	15	14	14	15	17	18	18
AUSTRALIA, NEW ZEALAND AND ANTARCTICA													
Alice Springs, Australia	43	33	28	10	15	13	8	8	8	18	31	38	252
579 m	29	28	25	20	15	12	12	14	18	23	26	28	21
Christchurch, N. Zealand	56	43	48	48	66	66	69	48	46	43	48	56	638
10 m	16	16	14	12	9	6	6	7	9	12	14	16	11
Darwin, Australia	386	312	254	97	15	3	<3	3	13	51	119	239	1,491
30 m	29	29	29	29	28	26	25	26	28	29	30	29	28
Mawson, Antarctica	11	30	20	10	44	180	4	40	3	20	0	0	362
14 m	0	−5	−10	−14	−15	−16	−18	−18	−19	−13	−5	−1	−11
Perth, Australia	8	10	20	43	130	180	170	149	86	56	20	13	881
60 m	23	23	22	19	16	14	13	13	15	16	19	22	18
Sydney, Australia	89	102	127	135	127	117	117	76	73	71	73	73	1,181
42 m	22	22	21	18	15	13	12	13	15	18	19	21	17
NORTH AMERICA													
Anchorage, Alaska, USA	20	18	15	10	13	18	41	66	66	56	25	23	371
40 m	−11	−8	−5	2	7	12	14	13	9	2	−5	−11	2
Chicago, Illinois, USA	51	51	66	71	86	89	84	81	79	66	61	51	836
251 m	−4	−3	2	9	14	20	23	22	19	12	5	−1	10
Churchill, Man., Canada	15	13	18	23	32	44	46	58	51	43	39	21	402
13 m	−28	−26	−20	−10	−2	6	12	11	5	−2	−12	−22	−7
Edmonton, Alta., Canada	25	19	19	22	43	77	89	78	39	17	16	25	466
676 m	−15	−10	−5	4	11	15	17	16	11	6	−4	−10	3
Honolulu, Hawaii, USA	104	66	79	48	25	18	23	28	36	48	64	104	643
12 m	23	18	19	20	22	24	25	26	26	24	22	19	22
Houston, Texas, USA	89	76	84	91	119	117	99	99	104	94	89	109	1,171
12 m	12	13	17	21	24	27	28	29	26	22	16	12	21
Kingston, Jamaica	23	15	23	31	102	89	38	91	99	180	74	36	800
34 m	25	25	25	26	26	28	28	28	27	27	26	26	26
Los Angeles, Calif., USA	79	76	71	25	10	3	<3	<3	5	15	31	66	381
95 m	13	14	14	16	17	19	21	22	21	18	16	14	17
Mexico City, Mexico	13	5	10	20	53	119	170	152	130	51	18	8	747
2,309 m	12	13	16	18	19	19	17	18	18	16	14	13	16
Miami, Florida, USA	71	53	64	81	173	178	155	160	203	234	71	51	1,516
8 m	20	20	22	23	25	27	28	28	27	25	22	21	24
Montréal, Que., Canada	72	65	74	74	66	82	90	92	88	76	81	87	946
57 m	−10	−9	−3	−6	13	18	21	20	15	9	2	−7	6
New York City, N.Y., USA	94	97	91	81	81	84	107	109	86	89	76	91	1,092
96 m	−1	−1	3	10	16	20	23	23	21	15	7	2	11
St Louis, Mo., USA	58	64	89	97	114	114	89	86	81	74	71	64	1,001
173 m	0	1	7	13	19	24	26	26	22	15	8	2	14
San José, Costa Rica	15	5	20	46	229	241	211	241	305	300	145	41	1,798
1,146 m	19	19	21	21	22	21	21	21	21	20	20	19	20
Vancouver, B.C., Canada	154	115	101	60	52	45	32	41	67	114	150	182	1,113
14 m	3	5	6	9	12	15	17	17	14	10	6	4	10
Washington, D.C., USA	86	76	91	84	94	99	112	109	94	74	66	79	1,064
22 m	1	2	7	12	18	23	25	24	20	14	8	3	13
SOUTH AMERICA													
Antofagasta, Chile	0	0	0	<3	<3	3	5	3	<3	3	<3	0	13
94 m	21	21	20	18	16	15	14	14	15	16	18	19	17
Buenos Aires, Argentina	79	71	109	89	76	61	56	61	79	86	84	99	950
27 m	23	23	21	17	13	9	10	11	13	15	19	22	16
Lima, Peru	3	<3	<3	<3	5	5	8	8	8	3	3	<3	41
120 m	23	24	24	22	19	17	17	16	17	18	19	21	20
Manaus, Brazil	249	231	262	221	170	84	58	38	46	107	142	203	1,811
44 m	28	28	28	27	28	28	28	28	29	29	29	28	28
Paraná, Brazil	287	236	239	102	13	<3	3	5	28	127	231	310	1,582
260 m	23	23	23	23	23	21	21	22	24	24	24	23	23
Rio de Janeiro, Brazil	125	122	130	107	79	53	41	43	66	79	104	137	1,082
61 m	26	26	25	24	22	21	21	21	21	22	23	25	23

World Statistics: Physical Dimensions

Each topic list is divided into continents and within a continent the items are listed in order of size. The order of the continents is as in the atlas, Europe through to South America. Certain lists down to this mark > are complete; below they are selective. The world top ten are shown in square brackets; in the case of mountains this has not been done because the world top 30 are all in Asia. The figures are rounded as appropriate.

World, Continents, Oceans

	km²	miles²	%
The World	509,450,000	196,672,000	–
Land	149,450,000	57,688,000	29.3
Water	360,000,000	138,984,000	70.7
Asia	44,500,000	17,177,000	29.8
Africa	30,302,000	11,697,000	20.3
North America	24,241,000	9,357,000	16.2
South America	17,793,000	6,868,000	11.9
Antarctica	14,100,000	5,443,000	9.4
Europe	9,957,000	3,843,000	6.7
Australia & Oceania	8,557,000	3,303,000	5.7
Pacific Ocean	179,679,000	69,356,000	49.9
Atlantic Ocean	92,373,000	35,657,000	25.7
Indian Ocean	73,917,000	28,532,000	20.5
Arctic Ocean	14,090,000	5,439,000	3.9

Seas

Pacific

	km²	miles²
South China Sea	2,974,600	1,148,500
Bering Sea	2,268,000	875,000
Sea of Okhotsk	1,528,000	590,000
East China & Yellow	1,249,000	482,000
Sea of Japan	1,008,000	389,000
Gulf of California	162,000	62,500
Bass Strait	75,000	29,000

Atlantic

	km²	miles²
Caribbean Sea	2,766,000	1,068,000
Mediterranean Sea	2,516,000	971,000
Gulf of Mexico	1,543,000	596,000
Hudson Bay	1,232,000	476,000
North Sea	575,000	223,000
Black Sea	462,000	178,000
Baltic Sea	422,170	163,000
Gulf of St Lawrence	238,000	92,000

Indian

	km²	miles²
Red Sea	438,000	169,000
The Gulf	239,000	92,000

Mountains

Europe

		m	ft
Mont Blanc	France/Italy	4,807	15,771
Monte Rosa	Italy/Switzerland	4,634	15,203
Dom	Switzerland	4,545	14,911
Liskamm	Switzerland	4,527	14,852
Weisshorn	Switzerland	4,505	14,780
Taschorn	Switzerland	4,490	14,730
Matterhorn/Cervino	Italy/Switzerland	4,478	14,691
Mont Maudit	France/Italy	4,465	14,649
Dent Blanche	Switzerland	4,356	14,291
> Nadelhorn	Switzerland	4,327	14,196
Grandes Jorasses	France/Italy	4,208	13,806
Jungfrau	Switzerland	4,158	13,642
Barre des Ecrins	France	4,103	13,461
Gran Paradiso	Italy	4,061	13,323
Piz Bernina	Italy/Switzerland	4,049	13,284
Eiger	Switzerland	3,970	13,025
Monte Viso	Italy	3,841	12,602
Grossglockner	Austria	3,797	12,457
Wildspitze	Austria	3,772	12,382
Monte Disgrazia	Italy	3,678	12,066
Mulhacén	Spain	3,478	11,411
Pico de Aneto	Spain	3,404	11,168
Marmolada	Italy	3,342	10,964
Etna	Italy	3,340	10,958
Punta del'Argentera	Italy	3,297	10,817
Zugspitze	Germany	2,962	9,718
Musala	Bulgaria	2,925	9,596
Olympus	Greece	2,917	9,570
Triglav	Slovenia	2,863	9,393
Monte Cinto	France (Corsica)	2,710	8,891
Gerlachovka	Slovak Republic	2,655	8,711
Torre de Cerredo	Spain	2,648	8,688
Galdhöpiggen	Norway	2,468	8,100
Hvannadalshnúkur	Iceland	2,119	6,952
Kebnekaise	Sweden	2,117	6,946
Ben Nevis	UK	1,343	4,406

Asia

		m	ft
Everest	China/Nepal	8,848	29,029
K2 (Godwin Austen)	China/Kashmir	8,611	28,251
Kanchenjunga	India/Nepal	8,598	28,208
Lhotse	China/Nepal	8,516	27,939
Makalu	China/Nepal	8,481	27,824
Cho Oyu	China/Nepal	8,201	26,906
Dhaulagiri	Nepal	8,172	26,811
Manaslu	Nepal	8,156	26,758
Nanga Parbat	Kashmir	8,126	26,660
Annapurna	Nepal	8,078	26,502
Gasherbrum	China/Kashmir	8,068	26,469
Broad Peak	China/Kashmir	8,051	26,414
Xixabangma	China	8,012	26,286
Kangbachen	India/Nepal	7,902	25,925
Jamu	India/Nepal	7,902	25,925
Gayachung Kang	Nepal	7,897	25,909
Himalchuli	Nepal	7,893	25,896
Disteghil Sar	Kashmir	7,885	25,869
Nuptse	Nepal	7,879	25,849
Khunyang Chhish	Kashmir	7,852	25,761
Masherbrum	Kashmir	7,821	25,659
Nanda Devi	India	7,817	25,646
Rakaposhi	Kashmir	7,788	25,551
Batura	Kashmir	7,785	25,541
Namche Barwa	China	7,756	25,446
Kamet	India	7,756	25,446
Soltoro Kangri	Kashmir	7,742	25,400
Gurla Mandhata	China	7,728	25,354
Trivor	Pakistan	7,720	25,328
> Kongur Shan	China	7,719	25,324
Tirich Mir	Pakistan	7,690	25,229
K'ula Shan	Bhutan/China	7,543	24,747
Pik Kommunizma	Tajikistan	7,495	24,590
Elbrus	Russia	5,642	18,510
Demavend	Iran	5,604	18,386
Ararat	Turkey	5,165	16,945
Gunong Kinabalu	Malaysia (Borneo)	4,101	13,455
Yu Shan	Taiwan	3,997	13,113
Fuji-San	Japan	3,776	12,388

Africa

		m	ft
Kilimanjaro	Tanzania	5,895	19,340
Mt Kenya	Kenya	5,199	17,057
Ruwenzori (Margherita)	Uganda/Congo (Z.)	5,109	16,762
Ras Dashan	Ethiopia	4,620	15,157
Meru	Tanzania	4,565	14,977
Karisimbi	Rwanda/Congo (Z.)	4,507	14,787
Mt Elgon	Kenya/Uganda	4,321	14,176
Batu	Ethiopia	4,307	14,130
Guna	Ethiopia	4,231	13,882
Toubkal	Morocco	4,165	13,665
Irhil Mgoun	Morocco	4,071	13,356
Mt Cameroon	Cameroon	4,070	13,353
Amba Ferit	Ethiopia	3,875	13,042
Pico del Teide	Spain (Tenerife)	3,718	12,198
Thabana Ntlenyana	Lesotho	3,482	11,424
> Emi Koussi	Chad	3,415	11,204
Mt aux Sources	Lesotho/S. Africa	3,282	10,768
Mt Piton	Réunion	3,069	10,069

Oceania

		m	ft
Puncak Jaya	Indonesia	5,029	16,499
Puncak Trikora	Indonesia	4,750	15,584
Puncak Mandala	Indonesia	4,702	15,427
> Mt Wilhelm	Papua New Guinea	4,508	14,790
Mauna Kea	USA (Hawaii)	4,205	13,796
Mauna Loa	USA (Hawaii)	4,170	13,681
Mt Cook (Aoraki)	New Zealand	3,753	12,313
Mt Balbi	Solomon Is.	2,439	8,002
Orohena	Tahiti	2,241	7,352
Mt Kosciuszko	Australia	2,237	7,339

North America

		m	ft
Mt McKinley (Denali)	USA (Alaska)	6,194	20,321
Mt Logan	Canada	5,959	19,551
Citlaltepetl	Mexico	5,700	18,701
Mt St Elias	USA/Canada	5,489	18,008
Popocatepetl	Mexico	5,452	17,887
Mt Foraker	USA (Alaska)	5,304	17,401
Ixtaccihuatl	Mexico	5,286	17,342
Lucania	Canada	5,227	17,149
Mt Steele	Canada	5,073	16,644
Mt Bona	USA (Alaska)	5,005	16,420
Mt Blackburn	USA (Alaska)	4,996	16,391
Mt Sanford	USA (Alaska)	4,940	16,207
Mt Wood	Canada	4,848	15,905
Nevado de Toluca	Mexico	4,670	15,321
Mt Fairweather	USA (Alaska)	4,663	15,298
Mt Hunter	USA (Alaska)	4,442	15,573
Mt Whitney	USA	4,418	14,495
Mt Elbert	USA	4,399	14,432
Mt Harvard	USA	4,395	14,419
Mt Rainier	USA	4,392	14,409
Blanca Peak	USA	4,372	14,344
> Longs Peak	USA	4,345	14,255
Tajumulco	Guatemala	4,220	13,845
Grand Teton	USA	4,197	13,770
Mt Waddington	Canada	3,994	13,104
Mt Robson	Canada	3,954	12,972
Chirripó Grande	Costa Rica	3,837	12,589
Mt Assiniboine	Canada	3,619	11,873
Pico Duarte	Dominican Rep.	3,175	10,417

South America

		m	ft
Aconcagua	Argentina	6,960	22,834
Bonete	Argentina	6,872	22,546
Ojos del Salado	Argentina/Chile	6,863	22,516
Pissis	Argentina	6,779	22,241
Mercedario	Argentina/Chile	6,770	22,211
Huascaran	Peru	6,768	22,204
Llullaillaco	Argentina/Chile	6,723	22,057
Nudo de Cachi	Argentina	6,720	22,047
Yerupaja	Peru	6,632	21,758
N. de Tres Cruces	Argentina/Chile	6,620	21,719
Incahuasi	Argentina/Chile	6,601	21,654
Cerro Galan	Argentina	6,600	21,654
Tupungato	Argentina/Chile	6,570	21,555
> Sajama	Bolivia	6,542	21,463
Illimani	Bolivia	6,485	21,276
Coropuna	Peru	6,425	21,079
Ausangate	Peru	6,384	20,945
Cerro del Toro	Argentina	6,380	20,932
Siula Grande	Peru	6,356	20,853
Chimborazo	Ecuador	6,267	20,561
Alpamayo	Peru	5,947	19,511
Cotapaxi	Ecuador	5,896	19,344
Pico Colon	Colombia	5,800	19,029
Pico Bolivar	Venezuela	5,007	16,427

Antarctica

	m	ft
Vinson Massif	4,897	16,066
Mt Kirkpatrick	4,528	14,855
Mt Markham	4,349	14,268

Ocean Depths

Atlantic Ocean

	m	ft	
Puerto Rico (Milwaukee) Deep	9,220	30,249	[7]
Cayman Trench	7,680	25,197	
Gulf of Mexico	5,203	17,070	
Mediterranean Sea	5,121	16,801	
Black Sea	2,211	7,254	
North Sea	660	2,165	
Baltic Sea	463	1,519	

Indian Ocean

	m	ft
Java Trench	7,450	24,442
Red Sea	2,635	8,454
Persian Gulf	73	239

Pacific Ocean

	m	ft	
Mariana Trench	11,022	36,161	[1]
Tonga Trench	10,882	35,702	[2]
Japan Trench	10,554	34,626	[3]
Kuril Trench	10,542	34,587	[4]
Mindanao Trench	10,497	34,439	[5]
Kermadec Trench	10,047	32,962	[6]
New Guinea Trench	9,140	29,987	[8]
Peru–Chile Trench	8,050	26,410	[9]
Aleutian Trench	7,822	25,662	[10]
Middle American Trench	6,662	21,857	

Arctic Ocean

	m	ft
Molloy Deep	5,608	18,399

Land Lows

		m	ft
Caspian Sea	Europe	−28	−92
Dead Sea	Asia	−403	−1,322
Lake Asale	Africa	−116	−381
Lake Eyre North	Oceania	−16	−52
Death Valley	N. America	−86	−282
Valdés Peninsula	S. America	−40	−131

Rivers

Europe

		km	miles	
Volga	Caspian Sea	3,700	2,300	
Danube	Black Sea	2,850	1,770	
Ural	Caspian Sea	2,535	1,575	
Dnepr (Dnipro)	Black Sea	2,285	1,420	
Kama	Volga	2,030	1,260	
Don	Black Sea	1,990	1,240	
Petchora	Arctic Ocean	1,790	1,110	
Oka	Volga	1,480	920	
Belaya	Kama	1,420	880	
Dnister (Dniester)	Black Sea	1,400	870	
Vyatka	Kama	1,370	850	
Rhine	North Sea	1,320	820	
N. Dvina	Arctic Ocean	1,290	800	
Desna	Dnepr (Dnipro)	1,190	740	
Elbe	North Sea	1,145	710	
Wisła	Baltic Sea	1,090	675	
Loire	Atlantic Ocean	1,020	635	
W. Dvina	Baltic Sea	1,019	633	

Asia

		km	miles	
Yangtze	Pacific Ocean	6,380	3,960	[3]
Yenisey–Angara	Arctic Ocean	5,550	3,445	[5]
Huang He	Pacific Ocean	5,464	3,395	[6]
Ob–Irtysh	Arctic Ocean	5,410	3,360	[7]
Mekong	Pacific Ocean	4,500	2,795	[9]
Amur	Pacific Ocean	4,400	2,730	[10]
Lena	Arctic Ocean	4,400	2,730	
Irtysh	Ob	4,250	2,640	
Yenisey	Arctic Ocean	4,090	2,540	
Ob	Arctic Ocean	3,680	2,285	
Indus	Indian Ocean	3,100	1,925	
Brahmaputra	Indian Ocean	2,900	1,800	
Syrdarya	Aral Sea	2,860	1,775	
Salween	Indian Ocean	2,800	1,740	
Euphrates	Indian Ocean	2,700	1,675	
Vilyuy	Lena	2,650	1,645	
Kolyma	Arctic Ocean	2,600	1,615	
Amudarya	Aral Sea	2,540	1,575	
Ural	Caspian Sea	2,535	1,575	
Ganges	Indian Ocean	2,510	1,560	
Si Kiang	Pacific Ocean	2,100	1,305	
Irrawaddy	Indian Ocean	2,010	1,250	
Tarim–Yarkand	Lop Nor	2,000	1,240	
Tigris	Indian Ocean	1,900	1,180	
Angara	Yenisey	1,830	1,135	
Godavari	Indian Ocean	1,470	915	
Sutlej	Indian Ocean	1,450	900	
Yamuna	Indian Ocean	1,400	870	

Africa

		km	miles	
Nile	Mediterranean	6,670	4,140	[1]
Congo	Atlantic Ocean	4,670	2,900	[8]
Niger	Atlantic Ocean	4,180	2,595	
Zambezi	Indian Ocean	3,540	2,200	
Oubangi/Uele	Congo (Zaïre)	2,250	1,400	
Kasai	Congo (Zaïre)	1,950	1,210	
Shaballe	Indian Ocean	1,930	1,200	
Orange	Atlantic Ocean	1,860	1,155	
Cubango	Okavango Swamps	1,800	1,120	
Limpopo	Indian Ocean	1,600	995	
Senegal	Atlantic Ocean	1,600	995	
Volta	Atlantic Ocean	1,500	930	
Benue	Niger	1,350	840	

Australia

		km	miles	
Murray–Darling	Indian Ocean	3,750	2,330	
Darling	Murray	3,070	1,905	
Murray	Indian Ocean	2,575	1,600	
Murrumbidgee	Murray	1,690	1,050	

North America

		km	miles	
Mississippi–Missouri	Gulf of Mexico	6,020	3,740	[4]
Mackenzie	Arctic Ocean	4,240	2,630	
Mississippi	Gulf of Mexico	3,780	2,350	
Missouri	Mississippi	3,780	2,350	
Yukon	Pacific Ocean	3,185	1,980	
Rio Grande	Gulf of Mexico	3,030	1,880	
Arkansas	Mississippi	2,340	1,450	
Colorado	Pacific Ocean	2,330	1,445	
Red	Mississippi	2,040	1,270	
Columbia	Pacific Ocean	1,950	1,210	
Saskatchewan	Lake Winnipeg	1,940	1,205	
Snake	Columbia	1,670	1,040	
Churchill	Hudson Bay	1,600	990	
Ohio	Mississippi	1,580	980	
Brazos	Gulf of Mexico	1,400	870	
St Lawrence	Atlantic Ocean	1,170	730	

South America

		km	miles	
Amazon	Atlantic Ocean	6,450	4,010	[2]
Paraná–Plate	Atlantic Ocean	4,500	2,800	
Purus	Amazon	3,350	2,080	
Madeira	Amazon	3,200	1,990	
São Francisco	Atlantic Ocean	2,900	1,800	
Paraná	Plate	2,800	1,740	
Tocantins	Atlantic Ocean	2,750	1,710	
Paraguay	Paraná	2,550	1,580	
Orinoco	Atlantic Ocean	2,500	1,550	
Pilcomayo	Paraná	2,500	1,550	
Araguaia	Tocantins	2,250	1,400	
Juruá	Amazon	2,000	1,240	
Xingu	Amazon	1,980	1,230	
Ucayali	Amazon	1,900	1,180	
Maranón	Amazon	1,600	990	
Uruguay	Plate	1,600	990	
Magdalena	Caribbean Sea	1,540	960	

Lakes

Europe

		km²	miles²	
Lake Ladoga	Russia	17,700	6,800	
Lake Onega	Russia	9,700	3,700	
Saimaa system	Finland	8,000	3,100	
Vänern	Sweden	5,500	2,100	
Rybinskoye Res.	Russia	4,700	1,800	

Asia

		km²	miles²	
Caspian Sea	Asia	371,800	143,550	[1]
Aral Sea	Kazak./Uzbek.	33,640	13,000	[6]
Lake Baykal	Russia	30,500	11,780	[9]
Tonlé Sap	Cambodia	20,000	7,700	
Lake Balqash	Kazakhstan	18,500	7,100	
Lake Dongting	China	12,000	4,600	
Lake Ysyk	Kyrgyzstan	6,200	2,400	
Lake Orumiyeh	Iran	5,900	2,300	
Lake Koko	China	5,700	2,200	
Lake Poyang	China	5,000	1,900	
Lake Khanka	China/Russia	4,400	1,700	
Lake Van	Turkey	3,500	1,400	
Lake Ubsa	China	3,400	1,300	

Africa

		km²	miles²	
Lake Victoria	E. Africa	68,000	26,000	[3]
Lake Tanganyika	C. Africa	33,000	13,000	[7]
Lake Malawi/Nyasa	E. Africa	29,600	11,430	[10]
Lake Chad	C. Africa	25,000	9,700	
Lake Turkana	Ethiopia/Kenya	8,500	3,300	
Lake Volta	Ghana	8,500	3,300	
Lake Bangweulu	Zambia	8,000	3,100	
Lake Rukwa	Tanzania	7,000	2,700	
Lake Mai-Ndombe	Congo (Zaïre)	6,500	2,500	
Lake Kariba	Zambia/Zimbabwe	5,300	2,000	
Lake Albert	Uganda/Congo (Z.)	5,300	2,000	
Lake Nasser	Egypt/Sudan	5,200	2,000	
Lake Mweru	Zambia/Congo (Z.)	4,900	1,900	
Lake Cabora Bassa	Mozambique	4,500	1,700	
Lake Kyoga	Uganda	4,400	1,700	
Lake Tana	Ethiopia	3,630	1,400	
Lake Kivu	Rwanda/Congo (Z.)	2,650	1,000	
Lake Edward	Uganda/Congo (Z.)	2,200	850	

Australia

		km²	miles²	
Lake Eyre	Australia	8,900	3,400	
Lake Torrens	Australia	5,800	2,200	
Lake Gairdner	Australia	4,800	1,900	

North America

		km²	miles²	
Lake Superior	Canada/USA	82,350	31,800	[2]
Lake Huron	Canada/USA	59,600	23,010	[4]
Lake Michigan	USA	58,000	22,400	[5]
Great Bear Lake	Canada	31,800	12,280	[8]
Great Slave Lake	Canada	28,500	11,000	
Lake Erie	Canada/USA	25,700	9,900	
Lake Winnipeg	Canada	24,400	9,400	
Lake Ontario	Canada/USA	19,500	7,500	
Lake Nicaragua	Nicaragua	8,200	3,200	
Lake Athabasca	Canada	8,100	3,100	
Smallwood Res.	Canada	6,530	2,520	
Reindeer Lake	Canada	6,400	2,500	
Lake Winnipegosis	Canada	5,400	2,100	
Nettilling Lake	Canada	5,500	2,100	
Lake Nipigon	Canada	4,850	1,900	
Lake Manitoba	Canada	4,700	1,800	

South America

		km²	miles²	
Lake Titicaca	Bolivia/Peru	8,300	3,200	
Lake Poopo	Peru	2,800	1,100	

Islands

Europe

		km²	miles²	
Great Britain	UK	229,880	88,700	[8]
Iceland	Atlantic Ocean	103,000	39,800	
Ireland	Ireland/UK	84,400	32,600	
Novaya Zemlya (N.)	Russia	48,200	18,600	
W. Spitzbergen	Norway	39,000	15,100	
Novaya Zemlya (S.)	Russia	33,200	12,800	
Sicily	Italy	25,500	9,800	
Sardinia	Italy	24,000	9,300	
N.E. Spitzbergen	Norway	15,000	5,600	
Corsica	France	8,700	3,400	
Crete	Greece	8,350	3,200	
Zealand	Denmark	6,850	2,600	

Asia

		km²	miles²	
Borneo	S. E. Asia	744,360	287,400	[3]
Sumatra	Indonesia	473,600	182,860	[6]
Honshu	Japan	230,500	88,980	[7]
Sulawesi (Celebes)	Indonesia	189,000	73,000	
Java	Indonesia	126,700	48,900	
Luzon	Philippines	104,700	40,400	
Mindanao	Philippines	101,500	39,200	
Hokkaido	Japan	78,400	30,300	
Sakhalin	Russia	74,060	28,600	
Sri Lanka	Indian Ocean	65,600	25,300	
Taiwan	Pacific Ocean	36,000	13,900	
Kyushu	Japan	35,700	13,800	
Hainan	China	34,000	13,100	
Timor	Indonesia	33,600	13,000	
Shikoku	Japan	18,800	7,300	
Halmahera	Indonesia	18,000	6,900	
Ceram	Indonesia	17,150	6,600	
Sumbawa	Indonesia	15,450	6,000	
Flores	Indonesia	15,200	5,900	
Samar	Philippines	13,100	5,100	
Negros	Philippines	12,700	4,900	
Bangka	Indonesia	12,000	4,600	
Palawan	Philippines	12,000	4,600	
Panay	Philippines	11,500	4,400	
Sumba	Indonesia	11,100	4,300	
Mindoro	Philippines	9,750	3,800	
Buru	Indonesia	9,500	3,700	
Bali	Indonesia	5,600	2,200	
Cyprus	Mediterranean	3,570	1,400	

Africa

		km²	miles²	
Madagascar	Indian Ocean	587,040	226,660	[4]
Socotra	Indian Ocean	3,600	1,400	
Réunion	Indian Ocean	2,500	965	
Tenerife	Atlantic Ocean	2,350	900	
Mauritius	Indian Ocean	1,865	720	

Oceania

		km²	miles²	
New Guinea	Indon./Pap. NG	821,030	317,000	[2]
New Zealand (S.)	Pacific Ocean	150,500	58,100	
New Zealand (N.)	Pacific Ocean	114,700	44,300	
Tasmania	Australia	67,800	26,200	
New Britain	Papua NG	37,800	14,600	
New Caledonia	Pacific Ocean	19,100	7,400	
Viti Levu	Fiji	10,500	4,100	
Hawaii	Pacific Ocean	10,450	4,000	
Bougainville	Papua NG	9,600	3,700	
Guadalcanal	Solomon Is.	6,500	2,500	
Vanua Levu	Fiji	5,550	2,100	
New Ireland	Papua NG	3,200	1,200	

North America

		km²	miles²	
Greenland	Atlantic Ocean	2,175,600	839,800	[1]
Baffin Is.	Canada	508,000	196,100	[5]
Victoria Is.	Canada	212,200	81,900	[9]
Ellesmere Is.	Canada	212,000	81,800	[10]
Cuba	Caribbean Sea	110,860	42,800	
Newfoundland	Canada	110,680	42,700	
Hispaniola	Dom. Rep./Haiti	76,200	29,400	
Banks Is.	Canada	67,000	25,900	
Devon Is.	Canada	54,500	21,000	
Melville Is.	Canada	42,400	16,400	
Vancouver Is.	Canada	32,150	12,400	
Somerset Is.	Canada	24,300	9,400	
Jamaica	Caribbean Sea	11,400	4,400	
Puerto Rico	Atlantic Ocean	8,900	3,400	
Cape Breton Is.	Canada	4,000	1,500	

South America

		km²	miles²	
Tierra del Fuego	Argentina/Chile	47,000	18,100	
Falkland Is. (E.)	Atlantic Ocean	6,800	2,600	
South Georgia	Atlantic Ocean	4,200	1,600	
Galapagos (Isabela)	Pacific Ocean	2,250	870	

World: Regions in the News

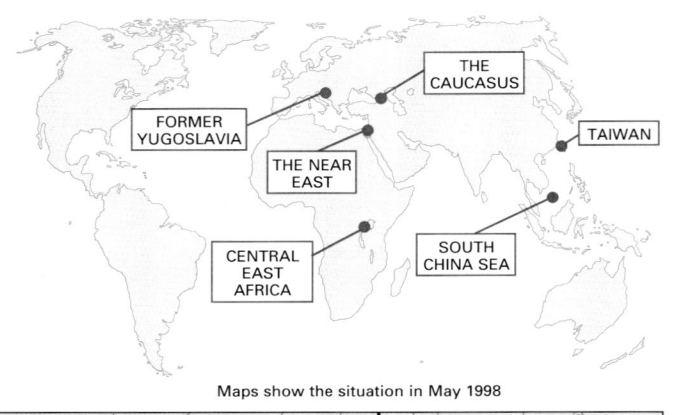

Maps show the situation in May 1998

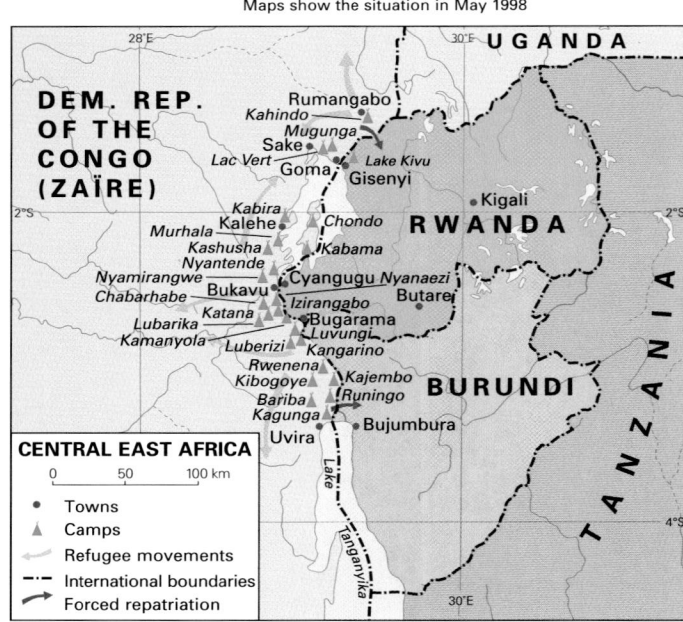

DEM. REP. OF THE CONGO (ZAÏRE)

CENTRAL EAST AFRICA

0   50   100 km

- • Towns
- ▲ Camps
- ← Refugee movements
- ·—·—· International boundaries
- → Forced repatriation

THE NEAR EAST

0   25   50 km

- — — 1949 Armistice Line
- ······· 1974 Cease-fire Lines
- *Efrata* ● Main Jewish settlements in the West Bank and Gaza Strip
- *Halhul* ■ Main Palestinian Arab towns in the West Bank and Gaza Strip
- *'Amman* ■ Capital cities

ISRAEL
Population: 5,696,000 (inc. East Jerusalem and Jewish settlers in the areas under Israeli administration. Jewish 82%, Arab Muslim 13.8%, Arab Christian 2.5%, Druze 1.7%)

West Bank
Population: 1,122,900 (Palestinian Arabs 97% [of whom Arab Muslim 85%, Jewish 7%, Christian 8%])

Gaza Strip
Population: 748,400 (Arab 98%)

JORDAN
Population: 5,547,000 (Arab 99% [of whom about 50% are Palestinian Arab])

LEBANON
Population: 2,971,000 (Arab 93% [of whom 83% are Lebanese Arab and 10% Palestinian Arab])

FORMER YUGOSLAVIA

0   50   100   150   200 km

- ·—··— International boundaries
- ·—·— Republic boundaries
- — — Province boundaries
- ■ Capital cities
- —— Dayton Peace Agreement Boundary
- ▨ Muslim–Croat Federation
- ▨ Bosnian Serb Republic

THE BREAK-UP OF YUGOSLAVIA
The former country of Yugoslavia comprised six republics. In 1991 Slovenia and Croatia declared independence. Bosnia-Herzegovina followed in 1992 and Macedonia in 1993. Yugoslavia now comprises the remaining two republics, Serbia and Montenegro.

YUGOSLAVIA
Population: 10,881,000 (Serb 62.6%, Albanian 16.5%, Montenegrin 5%, Hungarian 3.3%, Muslim 3.2%)

Serbia Population: 6,060,000 (Serb 87.7%, excluding the former autonomous provinces of Kosovo and Vojvodina)
Kosovo Population: 1,989,050
Vojvodina Population: 2,131,900

Montenegro Population: 700,050 (Montenegrin 61.9%, Muslim 14.6%, Albanian 7%)

CROATIA
Population: 4,900,000 (Croat 78.1%, Serb 12.2%)

SLOVENIA
Population: 2,000,000 (Slovene 88%, Croat 3%, Serb 2%)

MACEDONIA (F. Y. R. O. M.)
Population: 2,173,000 (Macedonian 64%, Albanian 21.7%, Turkish 5%, Romanian 3%, Serb 2%)

BOSNIA-HERZEGOVINA
Population: 4,400,000 (Muslim 49%, Serb 31.2%, Croat 17.2%)

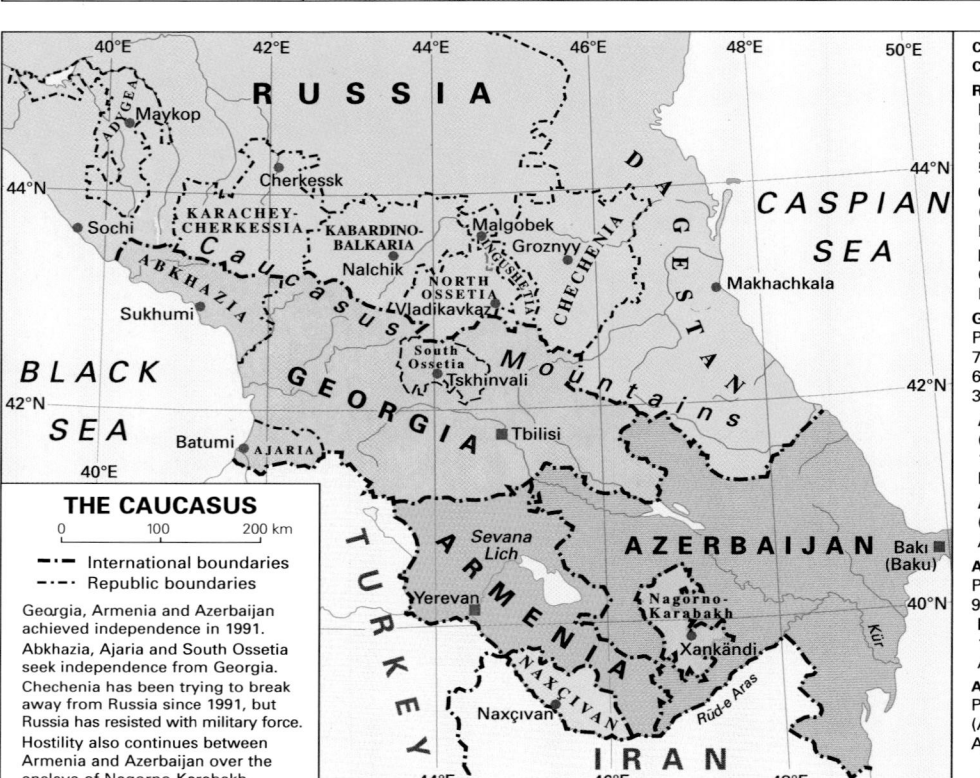

THE CAUCASUS

0   100   200 km

- ·—··— International boundaries
- ·—·— Republic boundaries

Georgia, Armenia and Azerbaijan achieved independence in 1991. Abkhazia, Ajaria and South Ossetia seek independence from Georgia. Chechenia has been trying to break away from Russia since 1991, but Russia has resisted with military force. Hostility also continues between Armenia and Azerbaijan over the enclave of Nagorno-Karabakh.

COUNTRIES AND REPUBLICS OF THE CAUCASUS REGION
RUSSIA
North Ossetia (Alania) Population: 695,000 (Ossetian 53%, Russian 29%, Chechen 5.2%, Armenian 1.9%)

Chechenia Population: 1,308,000 (Chechen and Ingush 70.7%, Russian 23.1%, Armenian 1.2%)

Ingushetia (Split from Chechenia in June 1993) Population: 250,000

GEORGIA
Population: 5,448,000 (Georgian 70.1%, Armenian 8.1%, Russian 6.3%, Azerbaijani 5.7%, Ossetian 3%, Greek 2%, Abkhazian 2%)

Abkhazia Population: 537,500 (Georgian 45.7%, Abkhazian 17.8%, Armenian 14.6%, Russian 14.3%)

Ajaria Population: 382,000 (Georgian 82.8%, Russian 7.7%, Armenian 4%)

ARMENIA
Population: 3,603,000 (Armenian 93%, Azerbaijani 3%)
Nagorno-Karabakh Population: 192,400 (Armenian 76.9%, Azerbaijani 21.5%)

AZERBAIJAN
Population: 7,559,000 (Azerbaijani 83%, Russian 6%, Armenian 6%, Lezgin 2%)
Naxçivan Population: 300,400 (Azerbaijani 95.9%)

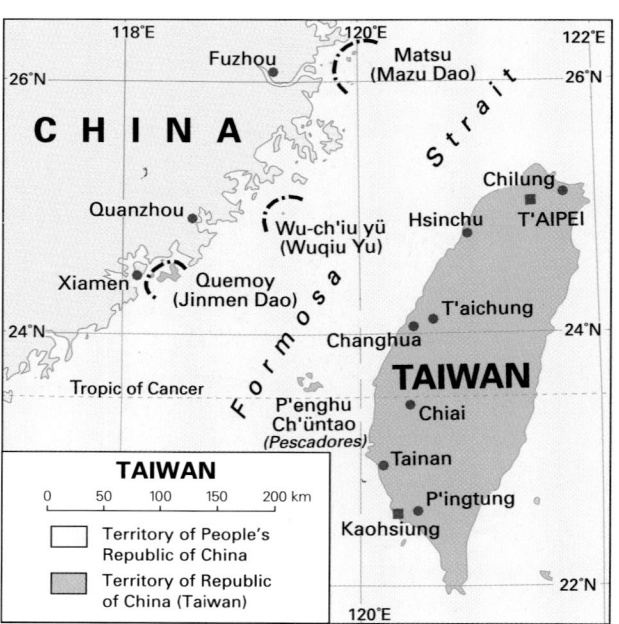

TAIWAN

0   50   100   150   200 km

- ☐ Territory of People's Republic of China
- ▨ Territory of Republic of China (Taiwan)

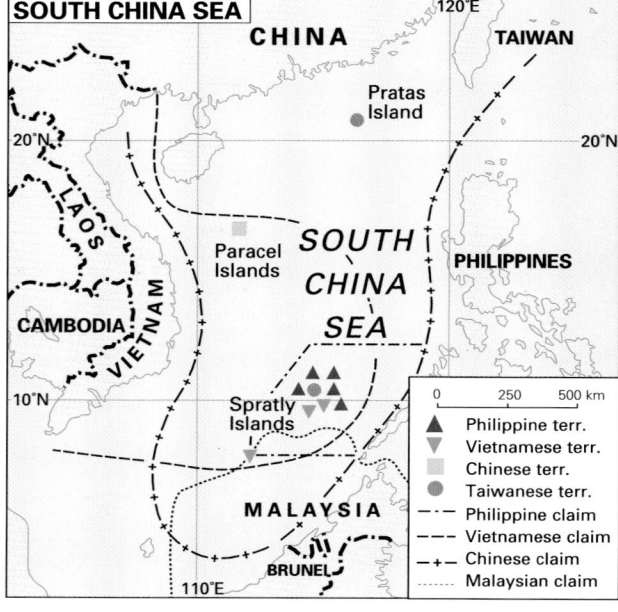

SOUTH CHINA SEA

0   250   500 km

- ▲ Philippine terr.
- ▼ Vietnamese terr.
- ▪ Chinese terr.
- ● Taiwanese terr.
- —— Philippine claim
- — — Vietnamese claim
- —+— Chinese claim
- ······ Malaysian claim

INTRODUCTION TO WORLD GEOGRAPHY

The Universe

About 15 billion years ago, time and space began with the most colossal explosion in cosmic history: the so-called 'Big Bang' that is believed to have initiated the universe. According to current theory, in the first millionth of a second of its existence it expanded from a dimensionless point of infinite mass and density into a fireball about 30 billion kilometres across; and it has been expanding ever since.

It took almost a million years for the primal fireball to cool enough for atoms to form. They were mostly hydrogen, still the most abundant material in the universe. But the new matter was not evenly distributed around the young universe, and a few billion years later atoms in relatively dense regions began to cling together under the influence of gravity, forming distinct masses of gas separated by vast expanses of empty space. To begin with, these first proto-galaxies were dark places: the universe had cooled. But gravitational attraction continued, condensing matter into coherent lumps inside the galactic gas clouds. About three billion years later, some of these masses had contracted so much that internal pressure produced the high temperatures necessary to bring about nuclear fusion: the first stars were born.

There were several generations of stars, each feeding on the wreckage of its extinct predecessors as well as the original galactic gas swirls. With each new generation, progressively larger atoms were forged in stellar furnaces and the galaxy's range of elements, once restricted to hydrogen, grew larger. About 10 billion years after the Big Bang, a star formed on the outskirts of our galaxy with enough matter left over to create a retinue of planets. Nearly five billion years after that human beings evolved.

The Sun is one of more than 100 billion stars in the home galaxy alone. Our galaxy, in turn, forms part of a local group of approximately 30 similar structures, some much larger than our own; there are at least 100 billion other galaxies in the universe as a whole. The most distant ever observed, a highly energetic galactic core known only as quasar PC 1247 +3406, lies about 12 billion light-years away.

Life of a Star

For most of its existence, a star produces energy by the nuclear fusion of hydrogen into helium at its core. The duration of this hydrogen-burning period – known as the main sequence – depends on the star's mass; the greater the mass, the higher the core temperatures and the sooner the star's supply of hydrogen is exhausted. Dim, dwarf stars consume their hydrogen slowly, eking it out over 1,000 billion years or more. The Sun, like other stars of its mass, should spend about 10 billion years on the main sequence; since it was formed less than five billion years ago, it still has half its life left.

Once all a star's core hydrogen has been fused into helium, nuclear activity moves outwards into layers of unconsumed hydrogen. For a time, energy production sharply increases: the star grows hotter and expands enormously, turning into a so-called red giant. Its energy output will increase a thousandfold, and it will swell to a hundred times its present diameter.

After a few hundred million years, helium in the core will become sufficiently compressed to initiate a new cycle of nuclear fusion: from helium to carbon. The star will contract somewhat, before beginning its last expansion, in the Sun's case engulfing the Earth and perhaps Mars. In this bloated condition, the Sun's outer layers will break off into space, leaving a tiny inner core, mainly of carbon, that shrinks progressively under the force of its own gravity: dwarf stars can attain a density more than 10,000 times that of normal matter, with crushing surface gravities to match. Gradually, the nuclear fires will die down, and the Sun will reach its terminal stage: a black dwarf, emitting insignificant amounts of energy.

However, stars more massive than the Sun may undergo another transformation. The additional mass allows gravitational collapse to continue indefinitely: eventually, all the star's remaining matter shrinks to a point, and its density approaches infinity – a state that will not permit even subatomic structures to survive.

The star has become a black hole: an anomalous 'singularity' in the fabric of space and time. Although vast coruscations of radiation will be emitted by any matter falling into its grasp, the singularity itself has an escape velocity that exceeds the speed of light, and nothing can ever be released from it. Within the boundaries of the black hole, the laws of physics are suspended, but no physicist can ever observe the extraordinary events that may occur.

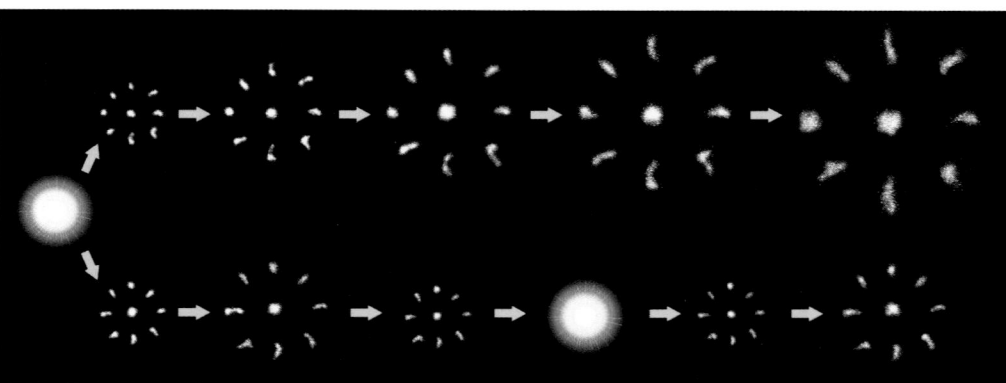

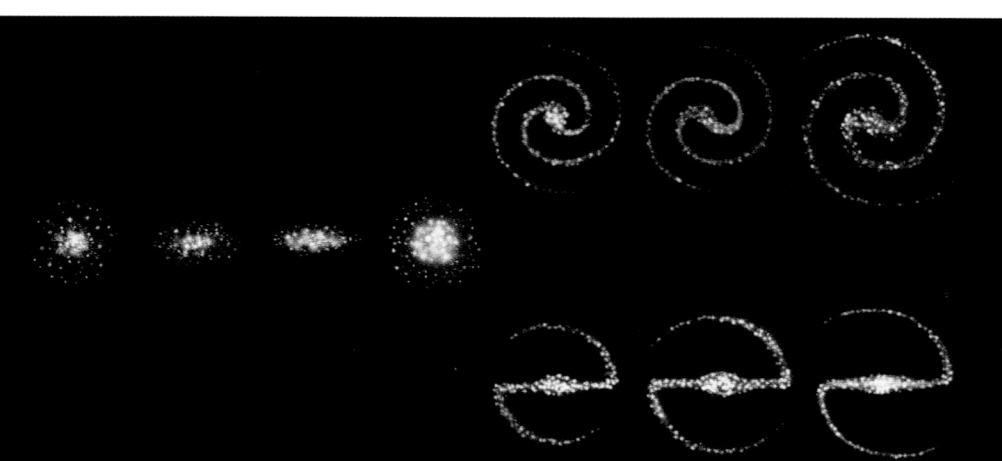

The End of the Universe

The likely fate of the universe is disputed. One theory (top left) dictates that the expansion begun at the time of the Big Bang will continue 'indefinitely', with ageing galaxies moving further and further apart in an immense, dark graveyard. Alternatively, gravity may overcome the expansion (bottom left). Galaxies will fall back together until everything is again concentrated at a single point, followed by a new Big Bang and a new expansion, in an endlessly repeated cycle.

The first theory is supported by the amount of visible matter in the universe; the second assumes there is enough dark material to bring about the gravitational collapse.

Galactic Structures

Many of the universe's 100 billion galaxies show clear structural patterns, originally classified by the American astronomer Edwin Hubble in 1925. Spiral galaxies like our own (top row) have a central, almost spherical bulge and a surrounding disk composed of spiral arms. Barred spirals (bottom row) have a central bar of stars across the nucleus, with spiral arms trailing from the ends of the bar. Elliptical galaxies (far left) have a uniform appearance, ranging from a flattened disk to a near sphere. So-called SO galaxies (left row, right) have a central bulge, but no spiral arms. Most galaxies, however, have no obvious structure at all.

Galaxies also vary enormously in size, from dwarfs only 2,000 light-years across to great assemblies of stars 80 or more times larger.

The Home Galaxy

The Sun and its planets are located in one of the spiral arms, a little less than 28,000 light-years from the galactic centre and orbiting around it in a period of 200 million years. The centre is invisible from the Earth, masked by vast, light-absorbing clouds of interstellar dust. The galaxy is probably around 12 billion years old and, like other spiral galaxies, has three distinct regions. The central bulge is about 30,000 light-years in diameter. The disk in which the Sun is located is not much more than 1,000 light-years thick but 100,000 light-years from end to end. Around the galaxy is the halo, a spherical zone 300,000 light-years across, studded with globular star-clusters and sprinkled with individual suns.

Globular clusters

Bulge

Disk

Solar System

Star charts are drawn as projections of a vast, hollow sphere with the observer in the middle. Each circle below represents slightly more than one hemisphere, centred on the north and south celestial poles respectively – projections of the Earth's poles in the heavens. At the present era, the north pole is marked by the star Polaris; the south pole has no such convenient reference point.

Astronomical co-ordinates are normally given in terms of 'Right Ascension' for longitude and 'Declination' for latitude or altitude. Since the stars appear to rotate around the Earth once every 24 hours, Right Ascension is measured eastwards – anticlockwise – in hours and minutes and is marked around the edge of the map. One hour is equivalent to 15 angular degrees; zero on the scale is the point at which the Sun

crosses the celestial equator at the spring equinox, known to astronomers as the First Point in Aries. Unlike the Sun, stars always rise and set at the same point on the horizon. Declination measures (in degrees) a star's angular distance above or below the celestial equator and is marked on the vertical line.

To use the maps, first choose the one for your hemisphere and hold it with the month at the bottom. The stars in the lower part of the map are then due south (or north, in the southern hemisphere) at about 1 AM local time, not allowing for summer or daylight saving time. Their exact position above the horizon depends on your latitude. The closer to the Equator you live, the higher in the sky these stars will appear. Some additional stars from the map for the other hemisphere will be visible in the lower sky.

Stars near the top of the map will be below the opposite horizon at this date and time but will be visible at other times of the night and year. The sky appears to move anticlockwise around the celestial pole during the course of the day (clockwise in the southern hemisphere), so the same stars will be visible at 11 PM a month earlier.

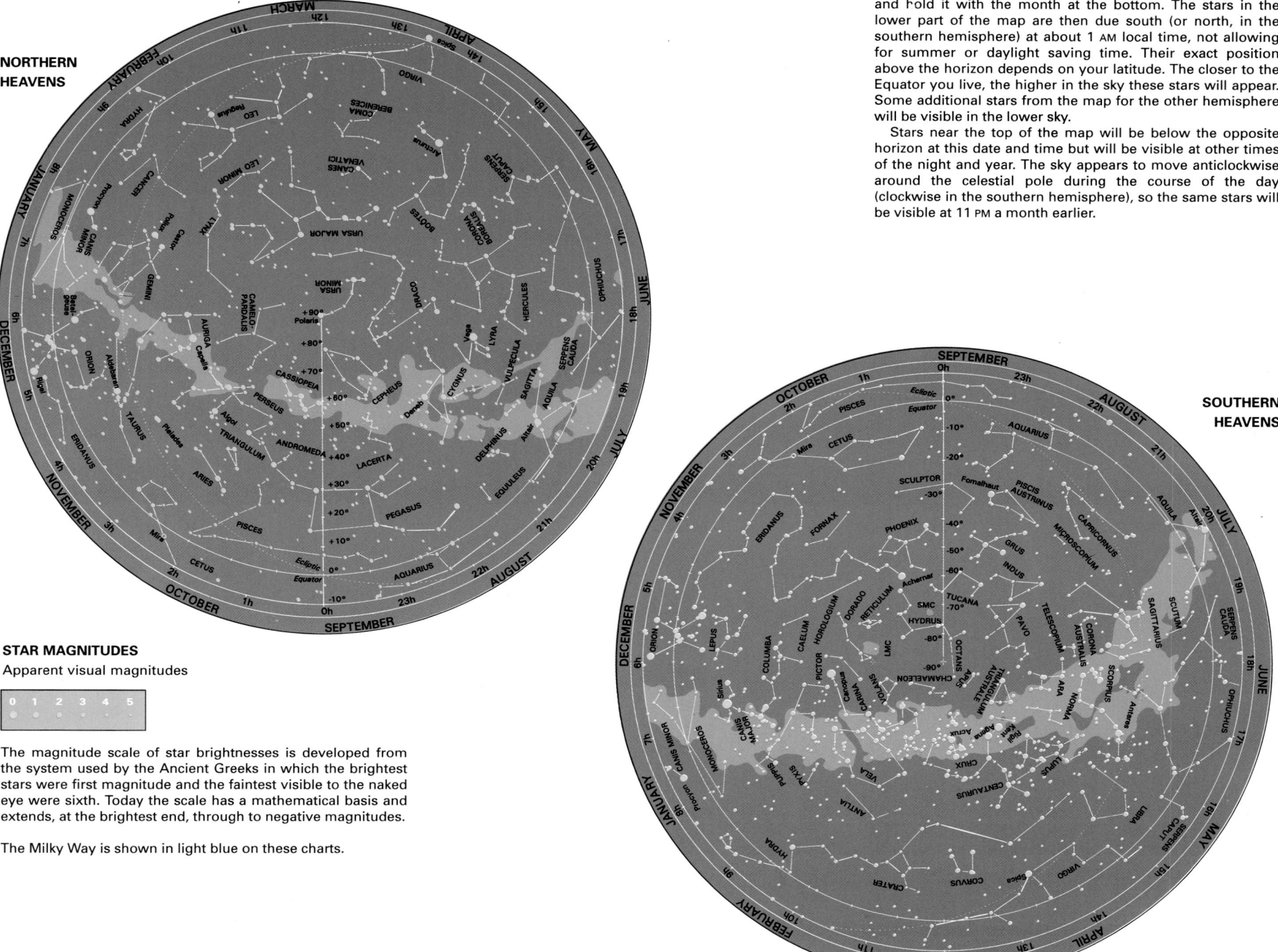

NORTHERN HEAVENS

SOUTHERN HEAVENS

STAR MAGNITUDES

Apparent visual magnitudes

| 0 | 1 | 2 | 3 | 4 | 5 |

The magnitude scale of star brightnesses is developed from the system used by the Ancient Greeks in which the brightest stars were first magnitude and the faintest visible to the naked eye were sixth. Today the scale has a mathematical basis and extends, at the brightest end, through to negative magnitudes.

The Milky Way is shown in light blue on these charts.

THE NEAREST STARS

The 20 nearest stars, excluding the Sun, with their distance from Earth in light-years*

Proxima Centauri	4.25	Many of the nearest stars, like
Alpha Centauri A	4.3	Alpha Centauri A and B, are
Alpha Centauri B	4.3	doubles, orbiting about the
Barnard's Star	6.0	common centre of gravity
Wolf 359	7.8	and to all intents and
Lalande 21185	8.3	purposes equidistant from
Sirius A	8.7	Earth. Many of them are dim
Sirius B	8.7	objects, with no name other
UV Ceti A	8.7	than the designation given
UV Ceti B	8.7	by the astronomers who
Ross 154	9.4	investigated them. However,
Ross 248	10.3	they include Sirius, the
Epsilon Eridani	10.7	brightest star in the sky,
Ross 128	10.9	and Procyon, the seventh
61 Cygni A	11.1	brightest. Both are far larger
61 Cygni B	11.1	than the Sun; of the nearest
Epsilon Indi	11.2	stars, only Epsilon Eridani is
Groombridge 34A	11.2	similar in size and luminosity.
Groombridge 34B	11.2	
L789-6	11.2	* A light-year equals approx.
Procyon A	11.4	9,500,000,000,000 kilometres
Procyon B	11.4	

THE CONSTELLATIONS

The constellations and their English names

Andromeda	Andromeda	Circinus	Compasses	Lacerta	Lizard	Piscis Austrinus	Southern Fish
Antlia	Air Pump	Columba	Dove	Leo	Lion	Puppis	Ship's Stern
Apus	Bird of Paradise	Coma Berenices	Berenice's Hair	Leo Minor	Little Lion	Pyxis	Mariner's Compass
Aquarius	Water Carrier	Corona Australis	Southern Crown	Lepus	Hare	Reticulum	Net
Aquila	Eagle	Corona Borealis	Northern Crown	Libra	Scales	Sagitta	Arrow
Ara	Altar	Corvus	Crow	Lupus	Wolf	Sagittarius	Archer
Aries	Ram	Crater	Cup	Lynx	Lynx	Scorpius	Scorpion
Auriga	Charioteer	Crux	Southern Cross	Lyra	Lyre	Sculptor	Sculptor
Boötes	Herdsman	Cygnus	Swan	Mensa	Table	Scutum	Shield
Caelum	Chisel	Delphinus	Dolphin	Microscopium	Microscope	Serpens	Serpent
Camelopardalis	Giraffe	Dorado	Swordfish	Monoceros	Unicorn	Sextans	Sextant
Cancer	Crab	Draco	Dragon	Musca	Fly	Taurus	Bull
Canes Venatici	Hunting Dogs	Equuleus	Little Horse	Norma	Level	Telescopium	Telescope
Canis Major	Great Dog	Eridanus	Eridanus	Octans	Octant	Triangulum	Triangle
Canis Minor	Little Dog	Fornax	Furnace	Ophiuchus	Serpent Bearer	Triangulum Australe	Southern Triangle
Capricornus	Goat	Gemini	Twins	Orion	Orion	Tucana	Toucan
Carina	Keel	Grus	Crane	Pavo	Peacock	Ursa Major	Great Bear
Cassiopeia	Cassiopeia	Hercules	Hercules	Pegasus	Winged Horse	Ursa Minor	Little Bear
Centaurus	Centaur	Horologium	Clock	Perseus	Perseus	Vela	Sails
Cepheus	Cepheus	Hydra	Water Snake	Phoenix	Phoenix	Virgo	Virgin
Cetus	Whale	Hydrus	Sea Serpent	Pictor	Easel	Volans	Flying Fish
Chamaeleon	Chameleon	Indus	Indian	Pisces	Fishes	Vulpecula	Fox

The Solar System

Lying 28,000 light-years from the centre of one of billions of galaxies that comprise the observable universe, our Solar System contains nine planets and their moons, innumerable asteroids and comets, and a miscellany of dust and gas, all tethered by the immense gravitational field of the Sun, the middling-sized star whose thermonuclear furnaces provide them all with heat and light. The Solar System was formed about 4,600 million years ago, when a spinning cloud of gas, mostly hydrogen but seeded with other, heavier elements, condensed enough to ignite a nuclear reaction and create a star. The Sun still accounts for almost 99.9% of the system's total mass; one planet, Jupiter, contains most of the remainder.

By composition as well as distance, the planetary array divides quite neatly in two: an inner system of four small, solid planets, including the Earth, and an outer system, from Jupiter to Neptune, of four much larger planets composed of lighter materials, such as gas, liquid and ice. Between the two groups lies a scattering of rocky asteroids, perhaps as many as 400,000. They may be debris left over from the inner solar system's formation. The outermost planet, Pluto, may simply be the largest of a number of bodies composed of rock and ice orbiting beyond Neptune, similarly left over from the formation of the outer solar system.

By the 1990s, however, the Solar System also included some newer anomalies: several thousand spacecraft. Most were in orbit around the Earth, but some had probed far and wide around the system. The valuable information beamed back by these robotic investigators has transformed our knowledge of our celestial environment.

Much of the early history of science is the story of people trying to make sense of the errant points of light that were all they knew of the planets. Now, men have themselves stood on the Earth's Moon; probes have landed on Mars and Venus, and orbiting radars have mapped far distant landscapes with astonishing accuracy. In the 1980s, the US *Voyagers* skimmed all four major planets of the outer system, bringing new revelations with each close approach. Only Pluto, inscrutably distant in an orbit that takes it 50 times the Earth's distance from the Sun, remains unvisited by our messengers.

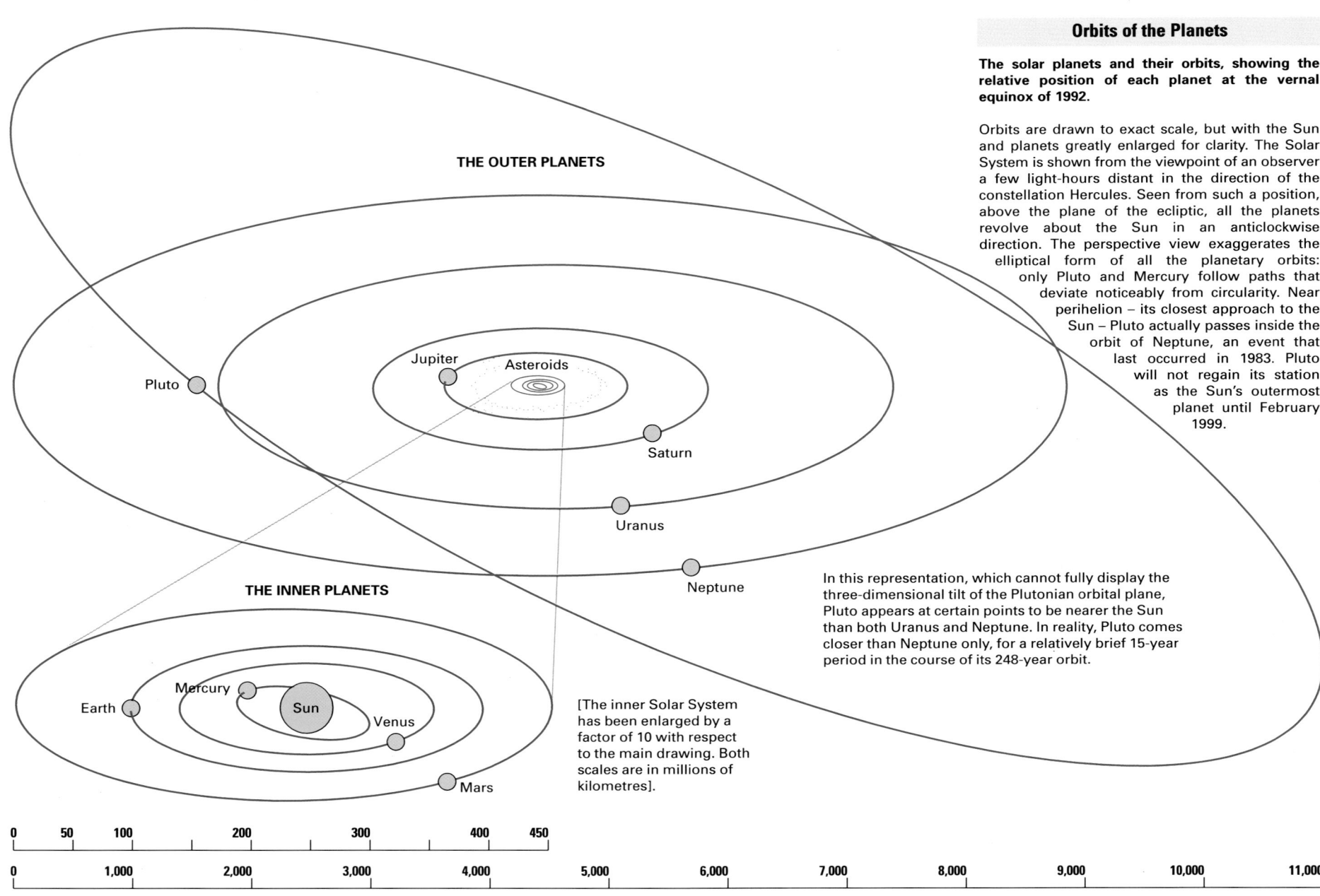

THE OUTER PLANETS

THE INNER PLANETS

Jupiter Asteroids

Pluto

Saturn

Uranus

Neptune

Mercury

Earth Sun Venus

Mars

[The inner Solar System has been enlarged by a factor of 10 with respect to the main drawing. Both scales are in millions of kilometres].

Orbits of the Planets

The solar planets and their orbits, showing the relative position of each planet at the vernal equinox of 1992.

Orbits are drawn to exact scale, but with the Sun and planets greatly enlarged for clarity. The Solar System is shown from the viewpoint of an observer a few light-hours distant in the direction of the constellation Hercules. Seen from such a position, above the plane of the ecliptic, all the planets revolve about the Sun in an anticlockwise direction. The perspective view exaggerates the elliptical form of all the planetary orbits: only Pluto and Mercury follow paths that deviate noticeably from circularity. Near perihelion – its closest approach to the Sun – Pluto actually passes inside the orbit of Neptune, an event that last occurred in 1983. Pluto will not regain its station as the Sun's outermost planet until February 1999.

In this representation, which cannot fully display the three-dimensional tilt of the Plutonian orbital plane, Pluto appears at certain points to be nearer the Sun than both Uranus and Neptune. In reality, Pluto comes closer than Neptune only, for a relatively brief 15-year period in the course of its 248-year orbit.

```
0   50   100      200      300      400  450

0      1,000   2,000    3,000    4,000    5,000    6,000    7,000    8,000    9,000    10,000   11,000
```

Planetary Data

	Mean distance from Sun (million km)	Mass (Earth = 1)	Period of orbit (Earth years)	Period of rotation (Earth days)	Equatorial diameter (km)	Average density (water = 1)	Surface gravity (Earth = 1)	Escape velocity (km/sec)	Number of known satellites
Sun	–	332,946	–	25.38	1,392,000	1.41	27.9	617.5	–
Mercury	57.9	0.06	0.241	58.67	4,878	5.43	0.38	4.25	0
Venus	108.2	0.8	0.615	243.00	12,100	5.24	0.90	10.36	0
Earth	149.6	1.0	1.00	1.00	12,756	5.52	1.00	11.18	1
Mars	227.9	0.1	1.88	1.02	6,794	3.93	0.38	5.03	2
Jupiter	778.3	317.8	11.86	0.41	142,800	1.33	2.69	59.60	16
Saturn	1,426.8	95.2	29.46	0.42	120,000	0.706	1.16	35.60	18
Uranus	2,869.4	14.5	84.01	0.45	52,400	1.25	0.93	21.10	15
Neptune	4,496.3	17.1	164.79	0.71	48,400	1.77	1.21	24.60	8
Pluto	5,900.1	0.002	247.7	6.39	2,445	1.40	0.05	1.20	1

Planetary days are given in sidereal time – that is, with respect to the stars rather than the Sun. Most of the information in the table was confirmed by spacecraft and often obtained from photographs and other data transmitted back to the Earth. In the case of Pluto, however, only earthbound observations have been made, and no spacecraft will encounter it until well into the next century. Given the planet's small size and great distance, figures for its diameter and rotation period have only recently been confirmed.

Pluto is not massive enough to account for the perturbations in the orbits of Uranus and Neptune that led to its 1930 discovery, but it is now widely believed that these perturbations can be explained away as observational errors made by the earlier observers.

The Planets

Mercury is the closest planet to the Sun and hence the fastest-moving. It is very hot with a cratered, wrinkled surface very similar to that of Earth's Moon. It is small and has no gravity, hence there is no significant atmosphere.

Venus has much the same physical dimensions as Earth. Its dense atmosphere is composed of 97% CO_2 resulting in a runaway greenhouse effect that makes the Venusian surface, at 475°C, the hottest of all the planets in the Solar System. Radar mapping shows relatively level land with volcanic regions whose sulphurous discharges explain the sulphuric acid rains reported by soft-landing space probes before they succumbed to Venus' fierce climate.

Earth seen from space is easily the most beautiful of the inner planets; it is also, and more objectively, the largest, as well as the only home of known life. Living things are the main reason why the Earth is able to retain a substantial proportion of corrosive and highly reactive oxygen in its atmosphere, a state of affairs that contradicts the laws of chemical equilibrium; the oxygen in turn supports the life that constantly regenerates it.

Mars, smaller and cooler than the Earth, is nevertheless the most likely planet other than Earth where life may have formed. Vast water channels show that it was once warmer and wetter; there may still be traces of former simple life forms, though whether life could thrive in its current cold, dry and thin atmosphere is doubtful. The ice caps are mainly frozen carbon dioxide, and whatever oxygen the planet once possessed is now locked up in the iron-bearing rock that covers its cratered surface and gives it its characteristic red hue. Mars is a dustbowl with occasional storms whirling the dust high into the air.

Jupiter masses almost three times as much as all the other planets combined; had it scooped up rather more matter during its formation, it might have evolved into a small companion star for the Sun. The planet is mostly gas, under intense pressure in the lower atmosphere above a core of fiercely compressed hydrogen and helium. The upper layers form strikingly-coloured rotating belts, the outward sign of the intense storms created by Jupiter's rapid diurnal rotation. Close approaches by spacecraft have shown an orbiting ring system and discovered several previously unknown moons: Jupiter has at least 16 moons.

Saturn is structurally similar to Jupiter, rotating fast enough to produce an obvious bulge at its equator. It is composed of 89% hydrogen and 11% helium, and has wind velocities in the outer atmosphere of 500 metres per second. Ever since the invention of the telescope, however, Saturn's rings have been the feature that has attracted most observers. *Voyager* probes in 1980 and 1981 sent back detailed pictures that showed them to be composed of thousands of separate ringlets, each in turn made up of tiny icy particles.

Uranus was unknown to the ancients. Although it is faintly visible to the naked eye, it was not discovered until 1781. Its interior is largely water, with an atmosphere of hydrogen, helium and some methane, which gives the planet its blue-green colour. Observations in 1977 suggested the presence of a faint ring system, amply confirmed when *Voyager 2* swung past the planet in 1986.

Neptune is always more than 4,000 million km from Earth, and despite its diameter of almost 50,000 km, it can only be seen by telescope. Its 1846 discovery was the result of mathematical predictions by astronomers seeking to explain irregularities in the orbit of Uranus, but until *Voyager 2* closed with the planet in 1989, little was known of it. Like Uranus, it has a ring system; *Voyager*'s photographs revealed a total of eight moons.

Pluto is the most mysterious of the solar planets, if only because even the most powerful telescopes can scarcely resolve it from a point of light to a disk. It was discovered as recently as 1930, like Neptune as the result of perturbations in the orbits of the two then outermost planets. Its small size, as well as its eccentric and highly tilted orbit, has led to suggestions that it is a former satellite of Neptune, somehow liberated from its primary. In 1978 Pluto was found to have a moon of its own, Charon, apparently half the size of Pluto itself.

Mean distance from the Sun in million kilometres (not to scale)

Mercury	57.9
Venus	108.2
Earth	149.6
Mars	227.9
Jupiter	778.3
Saturn	1,426.8
Uranus	2,869.4
Neptune	4,496.3
Pluto	5,900.1

Diagram not drawn to scale

Time and Motion

The basic unit of time measurement is the day, that is, one rotation of the Earth on its axis. Our present calendar is based on the solar year of 365.24 days, the time taken by the Earth to orbit the Sun.

Calendars based on the movements of the Sun and Moon have been used since ancient times. The average length of the year, according to the Julian Calendar introduced by Julius Caesar, was about 11 minutes too long. The cumulative error was rectified in 1582 by the Gregorian Calendar, when Pope Gregory XIII decreed that the day following 4 October was 15 October, and in that century years did not count as leap years unless they were divisible by 400. England finally adopted the reformed calendar in 1752, when it was 11 days behind the European mainland.

The rotation of the Earth on its axis causes day and night. Because the Earth rotates through 360° every 24 hours, the world is divided into 24 time zones centred on lines of longitude at 15° longitude.

The tilt of the Earth's axis, also called the obliquity of the ecliptic, accounts for the seasons which are so familiar in the middle latitudes. But geological evidence shows that, over long periods of time, climates change and the advances and retreats of the ice during the Pleistocene Ice Age may have been caused by regular variations in the Earth's tilt, its orbit around the Sun, and changes in the season when it is closest to the Sun (perihelion).

Earth Data

Aphelion (maximum distance from Sun):
152,007,016 km

Perihelion (minimum distance from Sun):
147,000,830 km

Angle of tilt (obliquity of the ecliptic): 23° 27' 08"

Length of year – solar tropical (equinox to equinox): 365.24 days

Length of year: 365 days, 5 hours, 48 minutes, 46 seconds of mean solar time

Superficial area:
510,000,000 sq km

Land surface:
149,000,000 sq km (29.2%)

Water surface:
361,000,000 sq km (70.8%)

Equatorial circumference:
40,077 km

Polar circumference:
40,009 km

Equatorial diameter:
12,756.8 km

Polar diameter: 12,713.8 km

Equatorial radius: 6,378.4 km

Polar radius: 6,356.9 km

Volume of the Earth:
1,083,230 x 10⁶ cu km

Mass of the Earth:
5.9 x 10²¹ tonnes

The Seasons

Seasons occur because the Earth's axis is tilted at a constant angle of 23½°. When the northern hemisphere is tilted to a maximum extent towards the Sun, on 21 June, the Sun is overhead at the Tropic of Cancer (latitude 23½° North). This is midsummer, or the summer solstice, in the northern hemisphere.

On 22 or 23 September, the Sun is overhead at the Equator, and day and night are of equal length throughout the world. This is the autumn equinox in the northern hemisphere. On 21 or 22 December, the Sun is overhead at the Tropic of Capricorn (23½° South), the winter solstice in the northern hemisphere. The overhead Sun then tracks north until, on 21 March, it is overhead at the Equator. This is the spring (vernal) equinox in the northern hemisphere.

In the southern hemisphere, the seasons are the reverse of those in the north.

Day and Night

The Sun appears to rise in the east, reach its highest point at noon, and then set in the west, to be followed by night. In reality, it is not the Sun that is moving but the Earth rotating from west to east. The moment when the Sun's upper limb first appears above the horizon is termed sunrise; the moment when the Sun's upper limb disappears below the horizon is sunset.

At the summer solstice in the northern hemisphere (21 June), the Arctic has total daylight and the Antarctic total darkness. The opposite occurs at the winter solstice (21 or 22 December). At the Equator, the length of day and night are almost equal all year.

The Sun's Path

The diagrams on the right illustrate the apparent path of the Sun at (A) the Equator, (B) in mid-latitude (45°), (C) at the Arctic Circle (66½°), and (D) at the North Pole, where there are six months of continuous daylight and six months of continuous night.

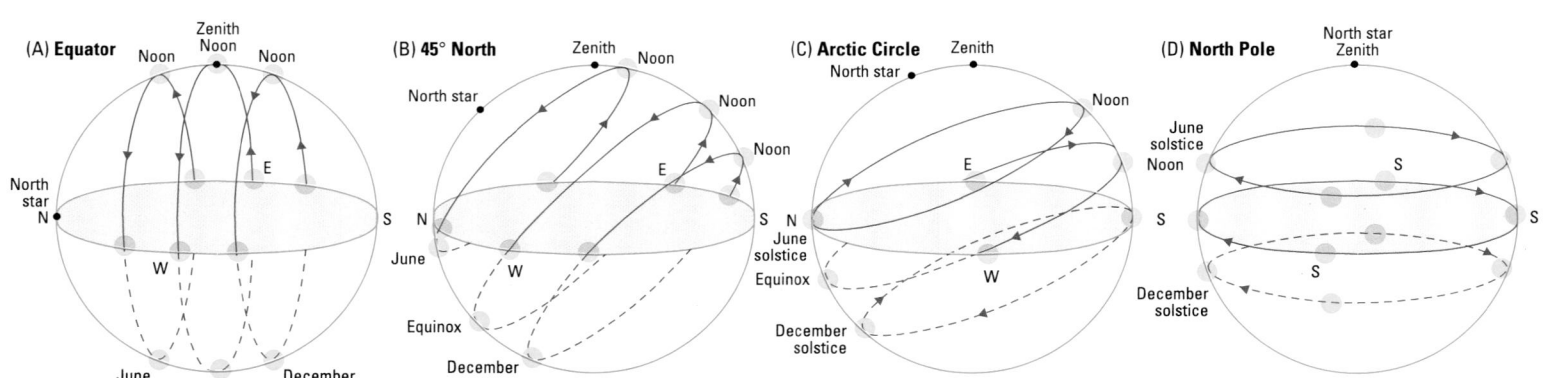

Sunrise and Sunset

The term equinox comes from two Latin words meaning 'equal night'. At the spring and autumn equinoxes, the Sun is vertically overhead at the Equator and all places on Earth have 12 hours of darkness and 12 of daylight. The graphs showing sunrise and sunset show that these occasions occur on 21 March and on 22 or 23 September. The graphs also show that, because the Sun remains high in the sky throughout the year, the length of the day and night at the Equator remain roughly the same throughout the year, with sunrise occurring around 6 AM and sunset at around 6 PM. The further north or south one travels, the greater the difference between the number of hours of daylight and darkness. For example, the graph, right, shows that at latitude 60°N, sunrise varies from just after 9 AM in midwinter (on 22 or 23 December) to about 2.30 AM in midsummer (around the summer solstice on 21 June). By contrast, the second graph, far right, shows that sunset at latitude 60°N occurs at about 2.45 PM in midwinter and 9.20 PM in midsummer.

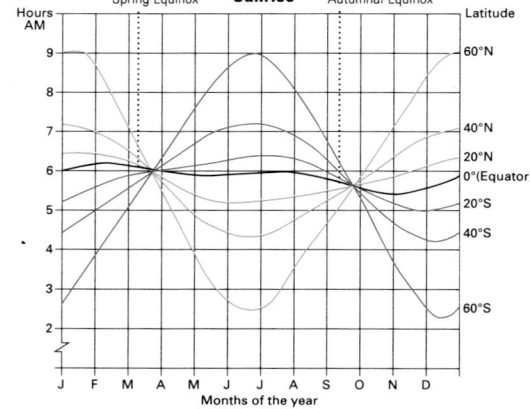

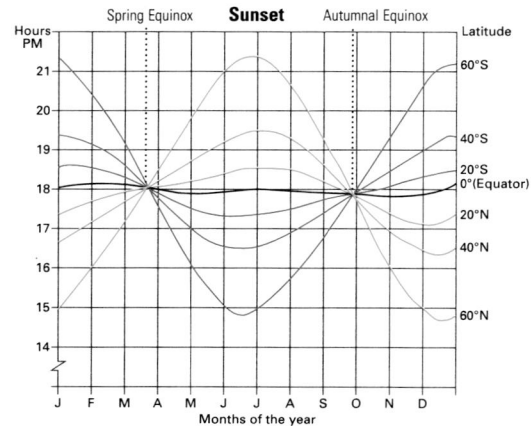

The Moon

The Moon rotates more slowly than the Earth, making one complete turn on its axis in just over 27 days. Since this corresponds to its period of revolution around the Earth, the Moon always presents the same hemisphere or face to us, and we never see 'the dark side'. The interval between one full Moon and the next (and between new Moons) is about 29½ days – a lunar month. The apparent changes in the shape of the Moon are caused by its changing position in relation to the Earth; like the planets, it produces no light of its own and shines only by reflecting the rays of the Sun.

Phases of the Moon

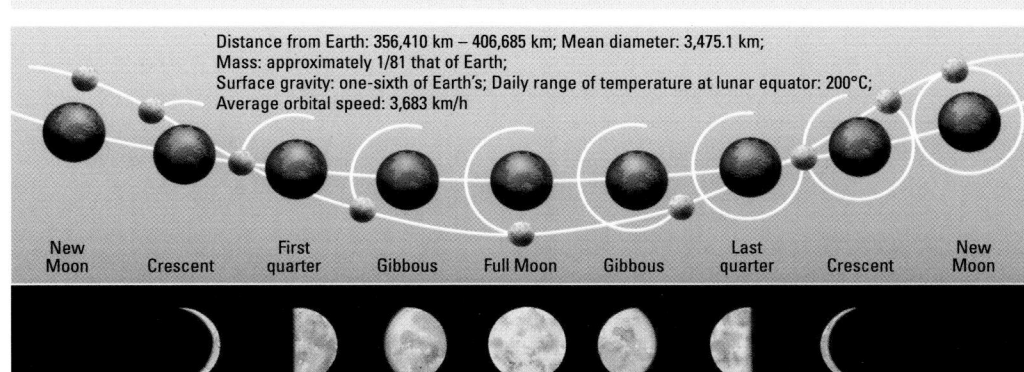

Distance from Earth: 356,410 km – 406,685 km; Mean diameter: 3,475.1 km;
Mass: approximately 1/81 that of Earth;
Surface gravity: one-sixth of Earth's; Daily range of temperature at lunar equator: 200°C;
Average orbital speed: 3,683 km/h

| New Moon | Crescent | First quarter | Gibbous | Full Moon | Gibbous | Last quarter | Crescent | New Moon |

Moon Data

Distance from Earth
The Moon orbits at a mean distance of 384,199.1 km, at an average speed of 3,683 km/h in relation to the Earth.

Size and mass
The average diameter of the Moon is 3,475.1 km. It is 400 times smaller than the Sun but is about 400 times closer to the Earth, so we see them as the same size. The Moon has a mass of $7,348 \times 10^{19}$ tonnes, with a density 3.344 times that of water.

Visibility
Only 59% of the Moon's surface is directly visible from Earth. Reflected light takes 1.25 seconds to reach Earth – compared to 8 minutes 27.3 seconds for light to reach us from the Sun.

Temperature
With the Sun overhead, the temperature on the lunar equator can reach 117.2°C [243°F]. At night it can sink to –162.7°C [–261°F].

Eclipses

When the Moon passes between the Sun and the Earth it causes a partial eclipse of the Sun (1) if the Earth passes through the Moon's outer shadow (P), or a total eclipse (2) if the inner cone shadow crosses the Earth's surface. In a lunar eclipse, the Earth's shadow crosses the Moon and, again, provides either a partial or total eclipse.

Eclipses of the Sun and the Moon do not occur every month because of the 5° difference between the plane of the Moon's orbit and the plane in which the Earth moves. In the 1990s only 14 lunar eclipses are possible, for example, seven partial and seven total; each is visible only from certain, and variable, parts of the world. The same period witnesses 13 solar eclipses – six partial (or annular) and seven total.

Partial eclipse (1)

P P P

Solar eclipse

Total eclipse (2)

Lunar eclipse

Tides

The daily rise and fall of the ocean's tides are the result of the gravitational pull of the Moon and that of the Sun, though the effect of the latter is only 46.6% as strong as that of the Moon. This effect is greatest on the hemisphere facing the Moon and causes a tidal 'bulge'. When the Sun, Earth and Moon are in line, tide-raising forces are at a maximum and Spring tides occur: high tide reaches the highest values, and low tide falls to low levels. When lunar and solar forces are least coincidental with the Sun and Moon at an angle (near the Moon's first and third quarters), Neap tides occur, which have a small tidal range.

Spring tide
Neap tide
Spring tide
Last quarter
Full Moon
New Moon
Gravitational pull by the Sun
Neap tide
First quarter

Time Zones

The Earth rotates through 360° in 24 hours, and so moves 15° every hour. The world is divided into 24 standard time zones, each centred on lines of longitude at 15° intervals. At the centre of the first zone is the Prime meridian or Greenwich meridian. All places to the west of Greenwich are one hour behind for every 15° of longitude; places to the east are ahead by one hour for every 15°. When it is 12 noon at the Greenwich meridian, 180° east it is midnight of the same day – while 180° west the day is just beginning. To overcome this, the International Date Line was established, approximately following the 180° meridian. Thus, if you travelled eastwards from Japan (140° East) to Samoa (170° West), you would pass from Sunday night into Sunday morning.

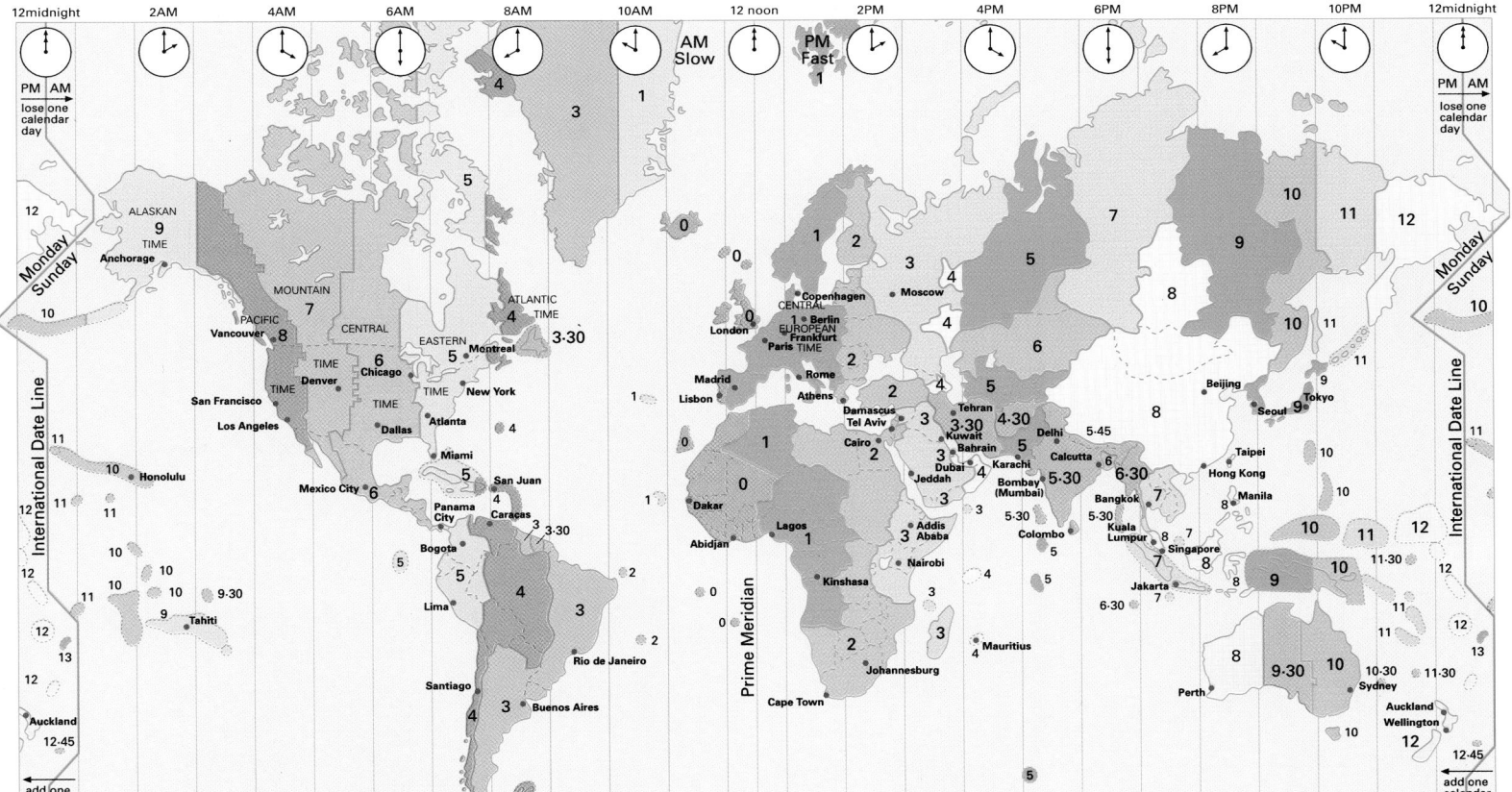

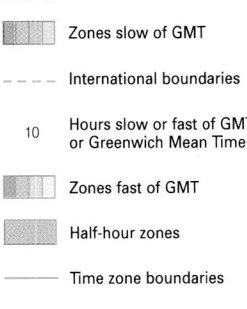

	Zones using GMT
	Zones slow of GMT
– – –	International boundaries
10	Hours slow or fast of GMT or Greenwich Mean Time
	Zones fast of GMT
	Half-hour zones
	Time zone boundaries
	International Date Line

Projection: Mercator

Oceans

The last 40 years have been described as the 'Space Age', but another exciting and perhaps even more important area of discovery, proceeding at the same time, has been the exploration of 'inner space', namely the oceans which cover more than 70% of our planet. The study of the ocean floor and oceanic islands has revealed features that help to explain how continents move, and how the movements are related to earthquakes and volcanic activity.

Manned submersibles have established that life exists even in the deepest trenches, where the pressure reaches 1,000 atmospheres, the equivalent of the force of one tonne bearing down on every square centimetre. Further exploration in the pitch-black environment of the ocean ridges has revealed strange forms of marine life around scalding hot vents. The creatures include giant tubeworms, blind shrimps, and bacteria, some of which are genetically very different from any other known life forms. In 1996, an analysis of one microorganism revealed that at least half of its 1,700 or so genes were hitherto unknown. This environment, which is based on chemicals, not sunlight, may resemble the places where life on Earth first began.

Another vital area of contemporary research concerns the interactions between the oceans and the atmosphere, as exemplified in the El Niño–Southern Oscillation (ENSO), and the bearing that these have on climatic change.

Most geographers divide the world's ocean waters into four areas: the Pacific, Atlantic, Indian and Arctic oceans. The most active zone in the oceans is the sunlit upper layer, where the water is moved around by wind-blown currents. It is the home of most sea life and acts as a membrane through which the ocean breathes,

Seawater

The chemical composition of the sea, by percentage, excluding the elements of water itself

Chloride (Cl)	55.04%
Sodium (Na)	30.61%
Sulphate (SO₄)	7.69%
Magnesium (Mg)	3.69%
Calcium (Ca)	1.16%
Potassium (K)	1.10%
Bicarbonate (HCO₃)	0.41%
Bromide (Br)	0.19%
Boric Acid (H₃BO₃)	0.07%
Strontium (Sr)	0.04%
Fluoride (Fl)	0.003%
Lithium (Li)	trace
Rubidium (Rb)	trace
Phosphorus (P)	trace
Iodine (I)	trace
Barium (Ba)	trace
Arsenic (As)	trace
Cesium (Cs)	trace

Eleven constituents account for over 99% of the salt content of seawater, but seawater also contains virtually every other element. In natural conditions, its composition is broadly consistent across the world's seas and oceans; but in coastal areas especially variations are sometimes substantial. The oceans are about 35 parts water to one part salt.

Life in the Oceans

An imaginary profile of the typical coastal and oceanic zones is shown, with a selection of the life forms that might occur in the water off the Pacific Coast of Central America. The animals illustrated are not drawn to scale as the range of sizes is too great. Most marine life is confined to the first 200 metres, the upper sunlit (photic) zone, where sunlight can still penetrate. Plant and animal plankton, the basis of life in the ocean, occur in great quantities in all zones.

In the pelagic environment (open sea), vertical gradients, including those of light, temperature and salinity, determine the distribution of organisms. From the tidal zone at the coastline, the continental shelf, geologically still part of the continental landmass, drops gently to about 200 metres – the sunlit zone. At the end of the shelf, the seabed falls away in the steeper angle of the continental slope. The subsequent descent to the deep ocean floor, known as the continental rise, is more gentle, with gradients between 1 in 100 and 1 in 700 until the abyssal plains and hills between 2,500 and 6,000 metres below the surface.

The deep sea floor contains seamounts, some of which are capped by coral reefs, ocean ridges, the longest mountain chains on Earth, and deep ocean trenches, especially in the Pacific Ocean where six trenches reach depths of more than 10,000 metres, including the 11,022-metre deep Mariana Trench.

Each of these zones contains a distinctive community of species adapted to the different conditions of salinity, temperature and light intensity. Indeed, a few organisms have been found even in the abyssal darkness of the great ocean trenches.

absorbing great quantities of carbon dioxide and partly exchanging it for oxygen.

As the depth increases, so light fades and temperatures fall until just before 1,000 metres where there is a marked temperature change at the thermocline, the boundary between the warm surface zone and the cold deep zone. Below the thermocline, slow currents are caused by density differences between bodies of water with varying temperatures and salinity.

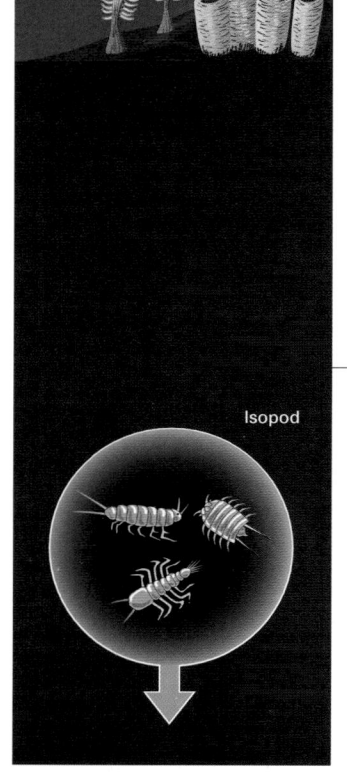

SEA LEVEL

SUNLIT ZONE
200 metres
[650 feet]

TWILIGHT ZONE
1,000 metres
[3,000 feet]

DARK ZONE
6,000 metres
[19,500 feet]

TRENCH ZONE
10,000 metres
[33,000 feet]

Atoll Building

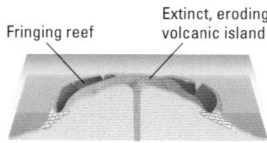

Volcano rises from ocean floor

Fringing reef — Extinct, eroding volcanic island

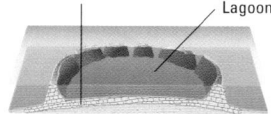

After subsidence, reef covers buried volcanic island — Lagoon

A coral atoll usually begins existence as a bare volcanic peak, thrusting above the surface of the ocean. A colony of coral – organisms with calcium carbonate skeletons – forms itself in the shallow water around the peak. The volcano is eroded and slowly sinks, leaving the coral forming a ring of hard limestone around its remnant. In time, the barrier reef of an atoll is all that remains.

The El Niño Phenomenon

The importance of the ocean–atmosphere interaction is nowhere more dramatically demonstrated than by the El Niño phenomenon in the southern Pacific Ocean.

Under normal conditions, shown in the diagram, top right, surface water flows eastwards from South America under the influence of trade winds while, near the coast, cold, nutrient-rich water (dark blue) rises to the surface and spreads westwards. In the western Pacific, sea surface temperatures reach 28°C or more and warm air rises, creating a low pressure air system and causing heavy rains. The rising warm air spreads out and some of it descends over South America and the eastern Pacific creating a high pressure air system from which winds blow westwards. This rotating system is called a Walker Circulation Cell.

An El Niño event, also called an El Niño–Southern Oscillation cycle, or ENSO cycle, is characterized by a reversal of currents whereby the eastward-moving South Equatorial Current extends much further eastwards and the trade winds weaken. The upwelling of cold water off South America is greatly reduced and surface water temperatures rise, causing a drastic reduction in fish life. The heaviest rainfall is over the eastern Pacific, while South-east Asia is much drier than usual. Warm air rises in the east and spreads out, descending in the western Pacific, which then becomes a high pressure area, as shown on the second diagram, below right.

During an intense El Niño, such as in 1982–83 when sea temperatures in the eastern Pacific rose by 6°C, the effects of the current and wind reversals affect the weather around the world. In Australia and South-east Asia, the monsoon rainfall is reduced, while, in 1983–84, a severe drought occurred in the Sahel, south of the Sahara, and also in southern Africa. The southeast coast of the United States also suffered storms and heavy rainfall, and even Europe experienced changes in weather patterns, possibly as a result of consequent changes in the course of the jet stream.

Scientists have found evidence that the frequency of the El Niño event, which normally occurs every two to seven years, may have increased in recent years with warm conditions persisting in the eastern Pacific from 1990 until mid-1995, an unprecedented length of time during the 114 years for which data exist. Another intense El Niño occurred in 1997–98, with resultant freak weather conditions across the entire Pacific region. Scientists do not know the causes of the El Niño event, though some researchers are investigating possible connections between major volcanic eruptions in the tropical Pacific region, the ENSO cycle and atmospheric circulation.

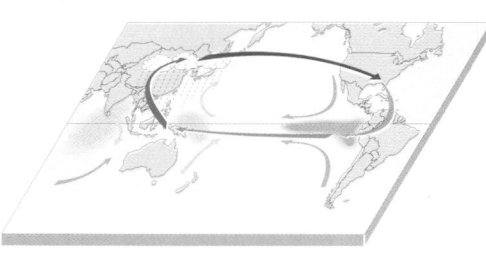

Normal year – Walker Circulation Cell

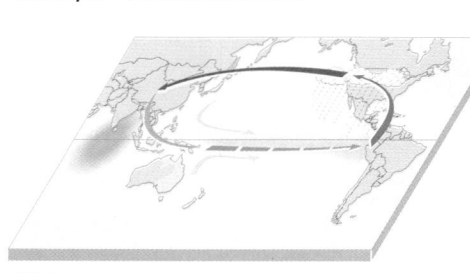

El Niño event

Ocean Currents

JANUARY CURRENTS AND TEMPERATURES
(Northern Hemisphere: winter)

ACTUAL SURFACE
TEMPERATURE

°C
30
20
10
0
−10
−20
−30
−40

OCEAN CURRENTS

Cold	Warm	Speed (knots)
←- -	←—	Less than 0.5
←—	←—	0.5 – 1.0
←—	←—	Over 1.0

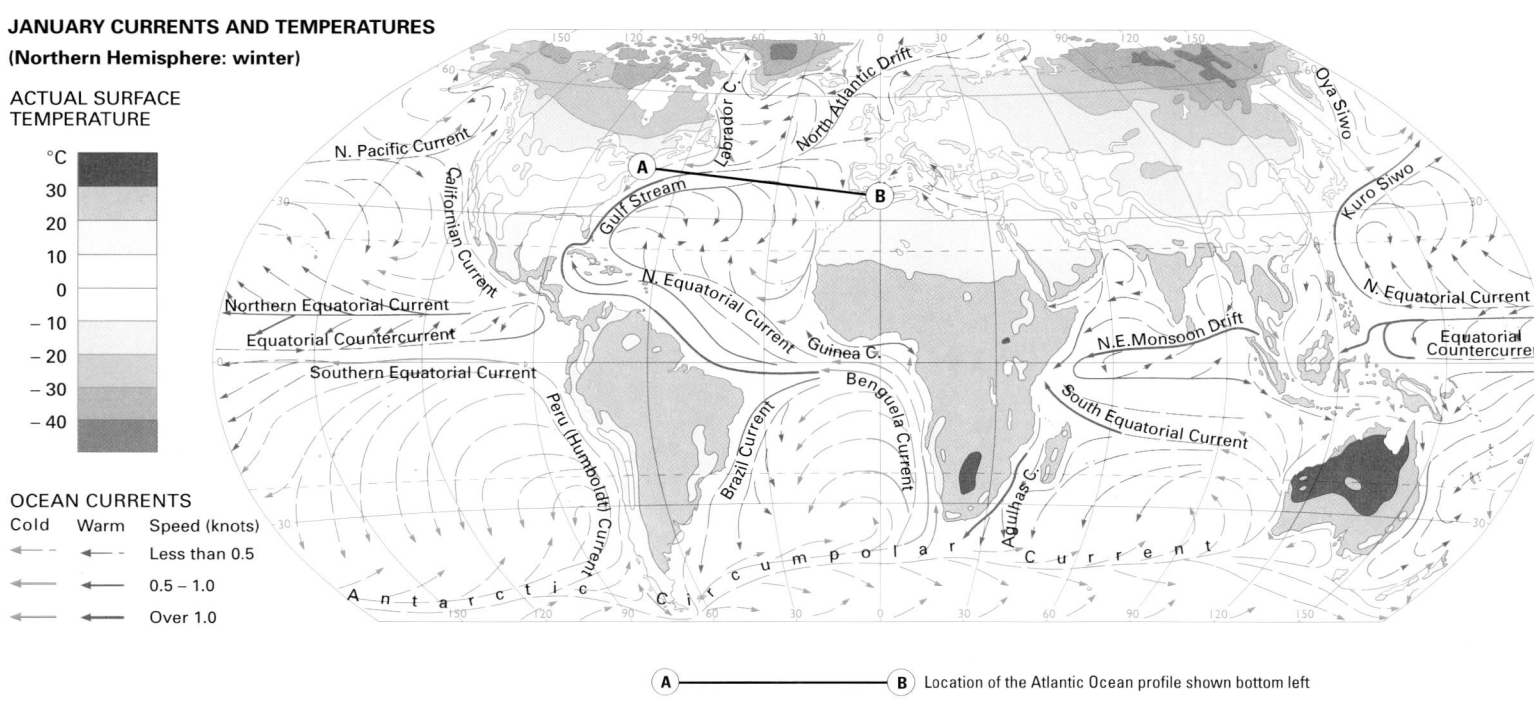

(A)————————**(B)** Location of the Atlantic Ocean profile shown bottom left

JULY CURRENTS AND TEMPERATURES
(Northern Hemisphere: summer)

ACTUAL SURFACE
TEMPERATURE

°C
30
20
10
0
−10

OCEAN CURRENTS

Cold	Warm	Speed (knots)
←- -	←—	Less than 0.5
←—	←—	0.5 – 1.0
←—	←—	Over 1.0

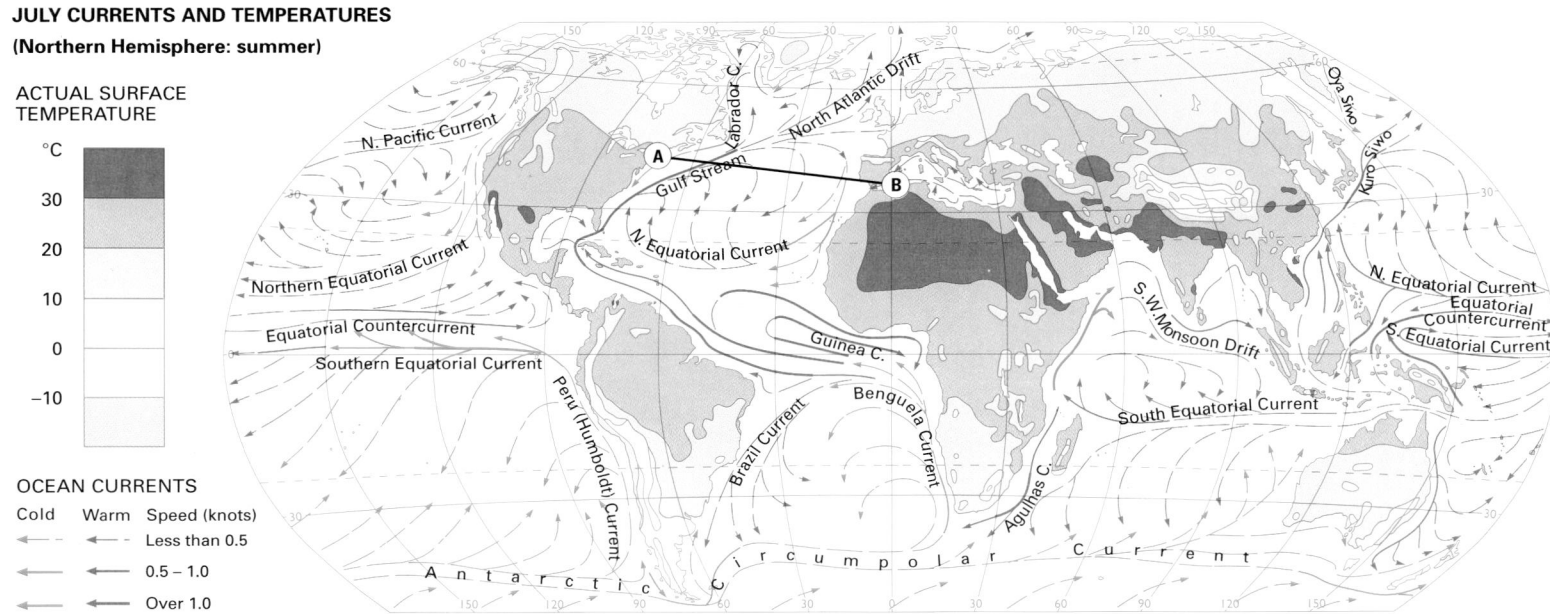

Moving immense quantities of energy as well as billions of tonnes of water every hour, the ocean currents are a vital part of the great heat engine that drives the Earth's climate. They themselves are produced by a twofold mechanism. At the surface, winds push huge masses of water before them; in the deep ocean, below an abrupt temperature gradient that separates the churning surface waters from the still depths, density variations cause slow vertical movements.

The pattern of circulation of the great surface currents is determined by the displacement known as the Coriolis effect. As the Earth turns beneath a moving object – whether it is a tennis ball or a vast mass of water – it appears to be deflected to one side. The deflection is most obvious near the Equator, where the Earth's surface is spinning eastwards at 1,700 km/h; currents moving polewards are curved clockwise in the northern hemisphere and anti-clockwise in the southern.

The result is a system of spinning circles known as gyres. Warm currents move constantly from the Equator towards the poles, while cold water moves in the reverse direction. In this way, ocean currents act like a thermostat, helping to regulate temperatures around the world.

Depending on the annual movements of the prevailing wind belts, some currents on or near the Equator may reverse their direction in the course of the year, a variation on which Asia's monsoon rains depend and whose occasional failure has brought disaster to millions of people.

Topography of the Ocean Floor

Profile of the Atlantic Ocean

The deep ocean floor was once believed to be flat, but maps compiled from readings made by sonar equipment show that it is no more uniform than the surface of the continents. The profile, below, shows some of the features on the Atlantic Ocean floor between Massachusetts in North America and Gibraltar (for location of profile, see maps above). Around the continents are shallow continental shelves composed of rocks which are less dense than the underlying oceanic crust. The continents end at the top of the steep continental slope, which descends to the abyss via the continental rise, made up of sediments washed down from the continental shelves. The abyss contains large plains overlain by oozes but the plains are broken by volcanic seamounts and guyots (flat-topped seamounts), a few of which reach the surface as islands. The other main feature is the Mid-Atlantic Ridge, through which runs a rift valley where new crustal rock is being formed as the plates on either side move apart.

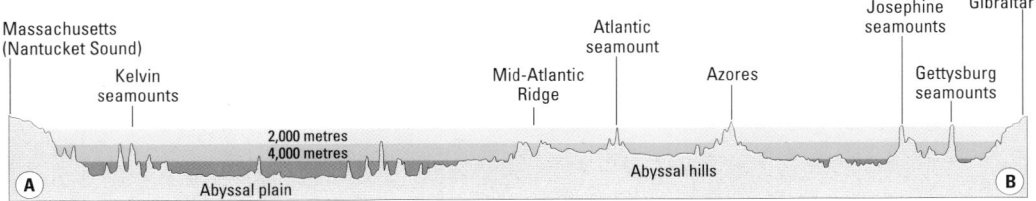

Topography of the ocean floor around Australia

In the image on the right, land areas are shown in grey, with shaded relief. The colours represent sea depth, with red representing the shallowest areas, through yellow and green to dark blue (the deepest). The data for the sea topography are from the Seasat radar satellite. The deep blue area in the upper left is the Java Trench which forms the boundary between the Indo-Australian plate and the Eurasian plate. In the top right, the New Guinea trench, which has a maximum depth of 9,103 metres, forms the border of the Indo-Australian and Pacific plates. Alongside the trenches are volcanic islands formed from magma, created as the edge of the Indo-Australian plate is subducted and melted.

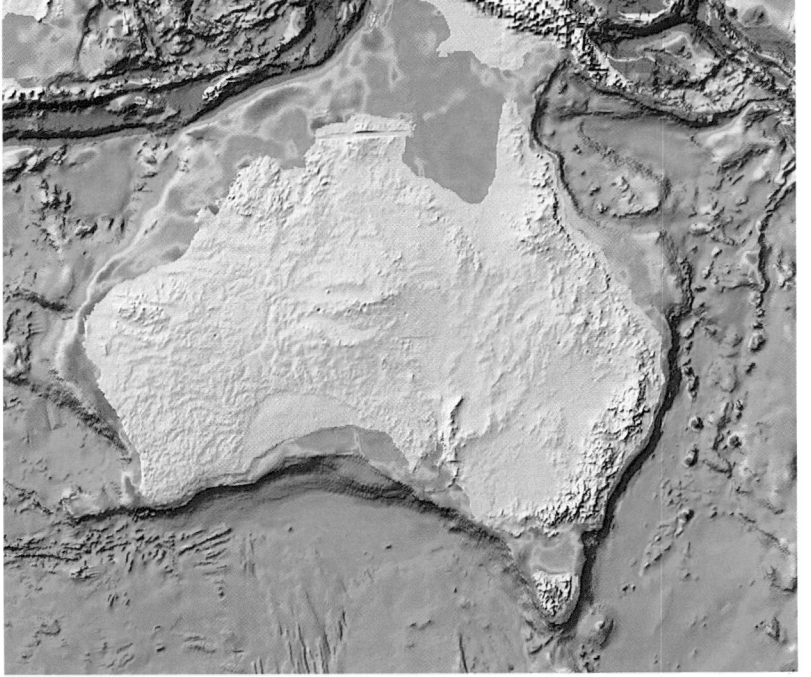

Geology of the Earth

Every year, earthquakes and volcanic eruptions cause much destruction throughout the world. Such phenomena were once thought to be unconnected but since the late 1960s, scientists have understood that these events are surface manifestations of the tremendous forces operating in the Earth's interior that are slowly but constantly changing the face of our planet.

The Earth is divided into three zones. The crust, a brittle, low-density zone, overlies the dense mantle. Separating the crust from the mantle is a distinct boundary called the Mohorovičić (or Moho) discontinuity. Enclosed by the mantle is the Earth's core, which consists mainly of iron and nickel.

Temperatures inside the Earth range from about 870°C in the upper mantle to perhaps 5,000°C in the core. Heat creates convection currents in a semi-molten part of the mantle called the asthenosphere. Above the asthenosphere is the lithosphere, a solid layer about 70 km thick, consisting of the crust and part of the mantle. The lithosphere is divided into rigid plates, moved around by the currents in the asthenosphere, a process named plate tectonics.

The Earth was formed around 4.6 billion years ago. Lighter elements floated towards the surface, where they formed crustal rocks. The oldest rocks so far discovered are nearly 4 billion years old, while the oldest fossils occur in rocks formed around 3.5 billion years ago. An explosion of life occurred at the start of the Cambrian period, 570 million years ago. The fossil record since the start of the Cambrian has enabled scientists to piece together the story of life on Earth.

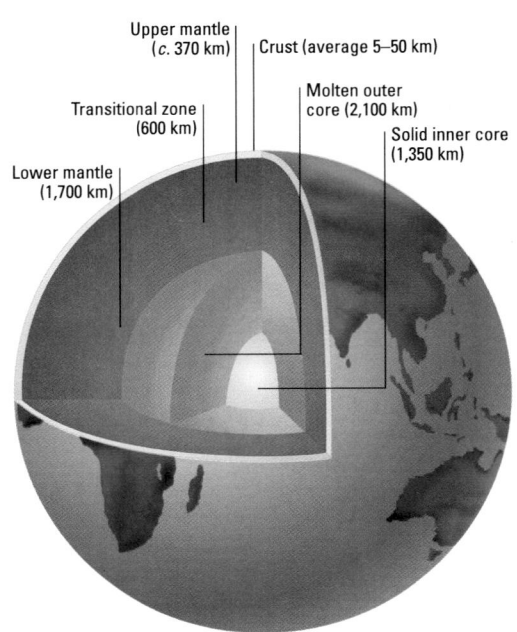

Upper mantle (c. 370 km) | Crust (average 5–50 km)
Molten outer core (2,100 km)
Transitional zone (600 km)
Solid inner core (1,350 km)
Lower mantle (1,700 km)

Plate Tectonics

In the early 20th century, the German scientist Alfred Wegener and others noticed similarities between the shapes of the continents. From a study of rocks and fossils in widely separated continents, they suggested that the continents had once been joined together and that somehow they had drifted apart. But no one knew of a mechanism that might cause continents to drift. However, in the 1950s and 1960s, evidence from studies of the ocean floor suggested that the low-density continents rest on huge slow-moving plates.

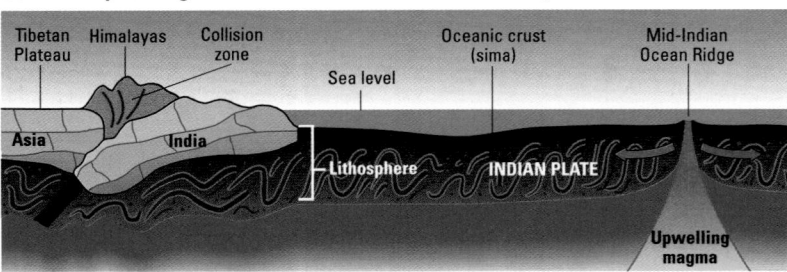

Sea-floor spreading in the Indian Ocean and continental plate collision

Tibetan Plateau | Himalayas | Collision zone | Oceanic crust (sima) | Mid-Indian Ocean Ridge
Sea level
Asia | India | Lithosphere | INDIAN PLATE | Upwelling magma

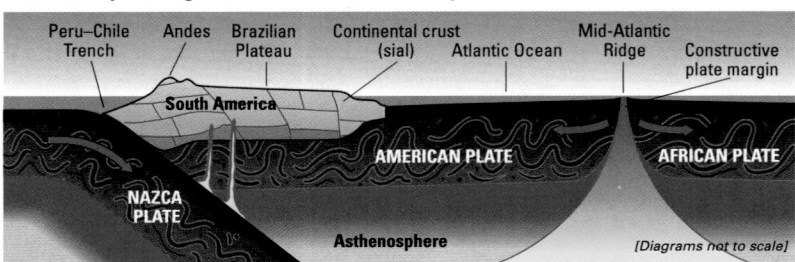

Sea-floor spreading in the Atlantic Ocean and plate collision

Peru–Chile Trench | Andes | Brazilian Plateau | Continental crust (sial) | Atlantic Ocean | Mid-Atlantic Ridge | Constructive plate margin
South America
AMERICAN PLATE | AFRICAN PLATE
NAZCA PLATE
Asthenosphere | [Diagrams not to scale]

The huge ridges that run through the oceans represent boundaries between plates. Here plates are diverging at rates of 20–41 mm a year. Molten magma from the mantle rises along a central rift valley to form new crustal rock. These ocean ridges, which are active zones where earthquakes and volcanic eruptions are common, are called constructive plate margins. Destructive plate margins, which occur when two plates converge, are marked by deep ocean trenches as one plate is forced under the other. The descending plate is melted to produce the magma that fuels volcanoes alongside the trenches. Movements of descending plates are often sudden and violent, triggering earthquakes in overlying continental areas. Where two continents collide, their margins are buckled up to form fold mountain ranges. A third type of plate margin, the transform fault, is not illustrated here. Along these plate margins, such as California's San Andreas fault, plates are moving parallel to each other.

The debate about plate tectonics is not over. Questions still arise as to why some active volcanoes lie far from plate margins, and why major earthquakes occur in mid-plate areas.

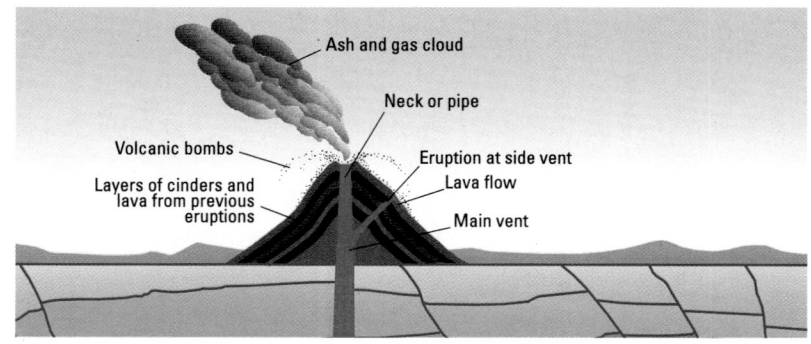

Ash and gas cloud
Neck or pipe
Volcanic bombs
Eruption at side vent
Layers of cinders and lava from previous eruptions
Lava flow
Main vent

Continental Drift

In 1915, Alfred Wegener produced a series of world maps proposing that, around 200 million years ago, the continents had been joined together in a supercontinent which he called Pangaea. This landmass started to break up about 180 million years ago and the parts drifted to their present positions. The arrows on the present day world map shows that the continents are still on the move.

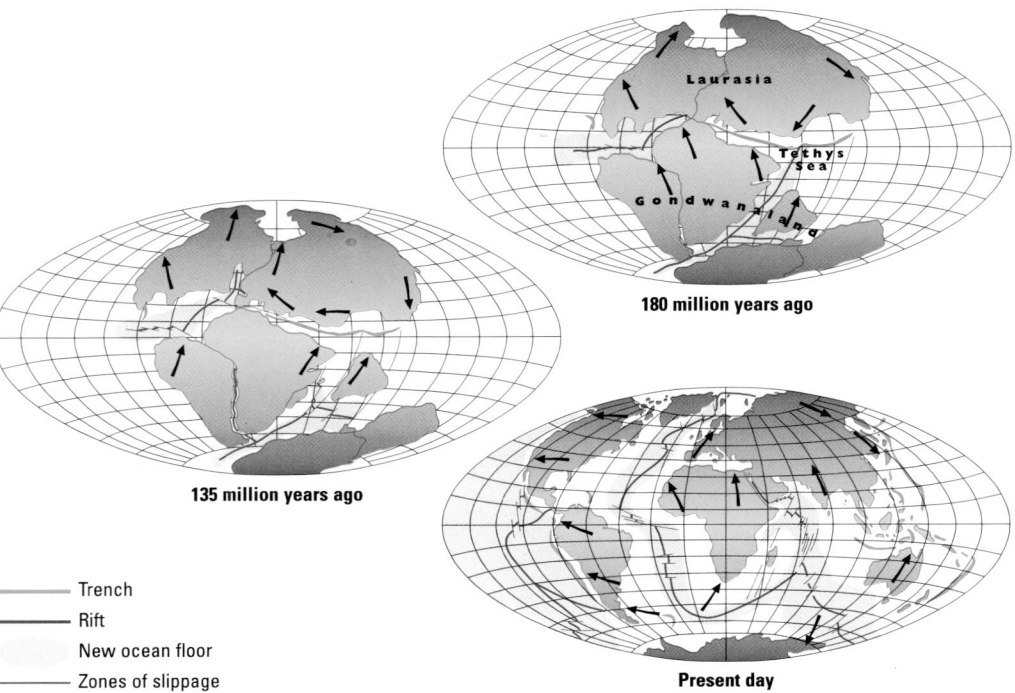

Laurasia | Tethys Sea | Gondwanaland
180 million years ago

135 million years ago

Trench
Rift
New ocean floor
Zones of slippage

Present day

Distribution of Volcanoes

Volcanoes occur when hot liquefied rock beneath the Earth's crust is pushed up by pressure to the surface as molten lava. There are some 550 known active volcanoes, around 20 of which are erupting at any one time.

▲ Land volcanoes active since 1700
5.5 ↗ Direction of movement (cm/year)
⁓ Boundaries of tectonic plates
• Submarine volcanoes
♦ Geysers

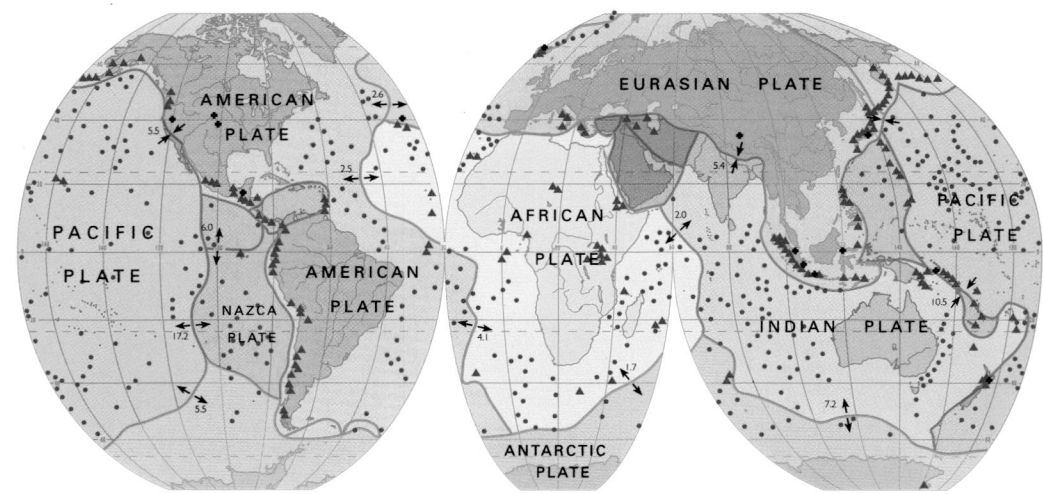

AMERICAN PLATE | EURASIAN PLATE
PACIFIC PLATE | AFRICAN PLATE | PACIFIC PLATE
AMERICAN PLATE
NAZCA PLATE
INDIAN PLATE
ANTARCTIC PLATE

Geological Time

Time, in millions of years before the present, is shown on a sliding scale, greatly compressed in the distant past.

ERA	PERIOD	EPOCH
PRE-CAMBRIAN		
PALEOZOIC	Cambrian	
	Ordovician	
	Silurian	
	Devonian	
	Carboniferous	
	Permian	
MESOZOIC	Triassic	
	Jurassic	
	Cretaceous	
CENOZOIC	Tertiary	Paleocene
		Eocene
		Oligocene
		Miocene
		Pliocene
	Quaternary	Pleistocene
		Holocene 10,000 BP to present

4600, 2000, 1000, 500, 400, 300, 200, 100, 0 (left scale in millions of years)

570, 500, 430, 395, 345, 280, 225, 190, 135, 65, 53, 37, 26, 12, 2

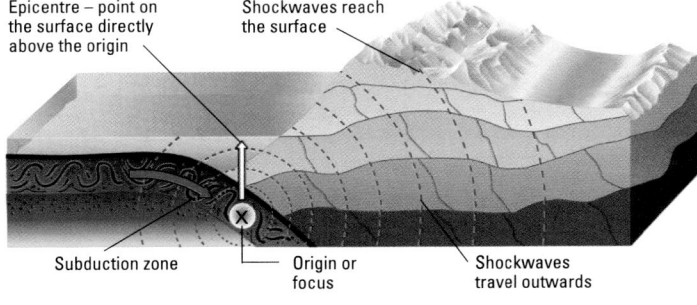

Geologists devised their timescale on the basis of relative, not calendar, ages. Accurate dating was impossible and estimates were often bitterly disputed, but the order in which the rocks were formed could be deduced from careful observation. The advent of radioactive dating – culminating in the 1950s with the development of a mass spectrometer capable of accurately measuring tiny quantities of isotopes – appears to have settled the arguments. The Earth is far older than geologists first imagined, but their painstakingly-created structure of geological time has withstood the advent of high technology.

The 4.6 billion (4,600 million) years since the formation of the Earth are divided into four great eras, further split into periods and, in the case of the most recent era, epochs. The present era is the Cenozoic ('new life'), extending backwards through 'middle life' and 'ancient life' to the Pre-Cambrian, named after the Latin word for Wales, the location of some of the earliest known fossils. Most of the Earth's geological history is encompassed by the Pre-Cambrian: though traces of ancient life have since been found, it was largely the proliferation of fossils from the beginning of the Paleozoic era onwards, some 570 million years ago, which first allowed precise subdivisions to be made.

Like the Cambrian, most are named after regions exemplifying a period's geology. Others – such as the Carboniferous ('coal-bearing') or the Cretaceous ('chalk-bearing') – are more directly descriptive.

- Pre-Cambrian shields
- Sedimentary cover on Pre-Cambrian shields
- Paleozoic (Caledonian and Hercynian) folding
- Sedimentary cover on Paleozoic folding
- Mesozoic folding
- Sedimentary cover on Mesozoic folding
- Cenozoic (Alpine) folding
- Sedimentary cover on Cenozoic folding
- Intensive Mesozoic and Cenozoic vulcanism
- Principal faults
- Oceanic marginal troughs
- Mid-oceanic ridges
- Overthrust faults

Earthquakes

Earthquake magnitude is usually rated according to either the Richter or the Modified Mercalli scale, both devised by seismologists in the 1930s. The Richter scale measures absolute earthquake power with mathematical precision: each step upwards represents a ten-fold increase in the amplitude of the shockwave. Theoretically, there is no upper limit, but the largest earthquakes measured have been rated at between 8.8 and 8.9. The 12-point Mercalli scale, based on observed effects, is often more meaningful, ranging from I (earthquakes noticed only by seismographs) to XII (total destruction); intermediate points include V (people awakened at night; unstable objects overturned), VII (collapse of ordinary buildings; chimneys and monuments fall) and IX (conspicuous cracks in ground; serious damage to reservoirs).

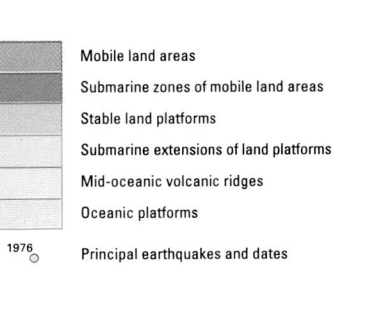

- Mobile land areas
- Submarine zones of mobile land areas
- Stable land platforms
- Submarine extensions of land platforms
- Mid-oceanic volcanic ridges
- Oceanic platforms

1976 ○ Principal earthquakes and dates

Earthquakes are a series of rapid vibrations originating from the slipping or faulting of parts of the Earth's crust when stresses within build up to breaking point. They usually happen at depths varying from 8 km to 30 km. Severe earthquakes cause extensive damage when they take place in populated areas, destroying structures and severing communications. Most initial loss of life occurs due to secondary causes such as falling masonry, fires and flooding.

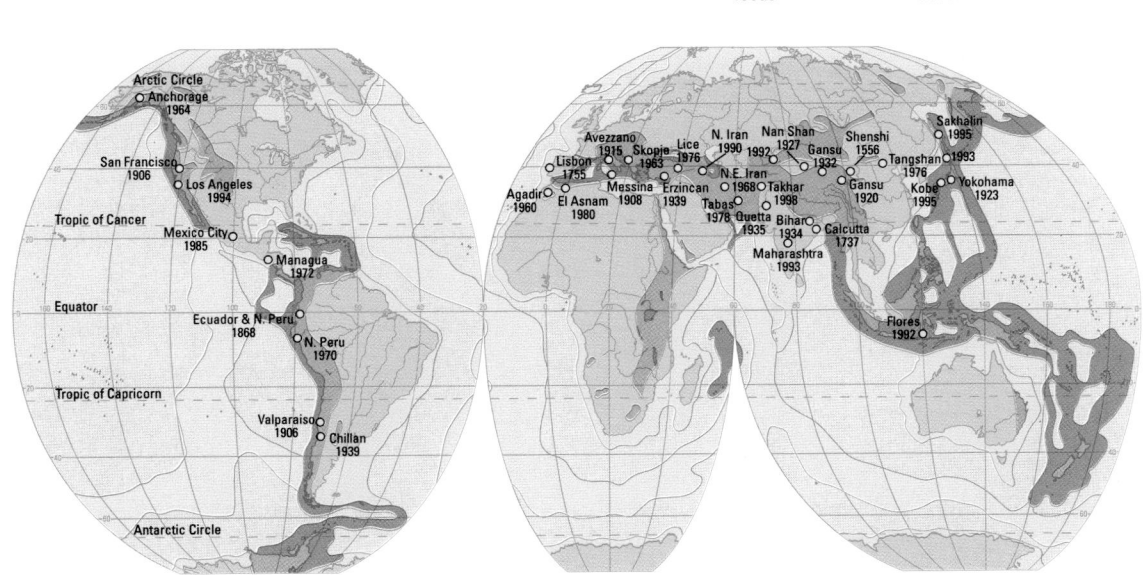

Epicentre – point on the surface directly above the origin

Shockwaves reach the surface

Subduction zone

Origin or focus

Shockwaves travel outwards

Notable Earthquakes Since 1900

Year	Location	Mag.	Deaths
1906	San Francisco, USA	8.3	503
1906	Valparaiso, Chile	8.6	22,000
1908	Messina, Italy	7.5	83,000
1915	Avezzano, Italy	7.5	30,000
1920	Gansu (Kansu), China	8.6	180,000
1923	Yokohama, Japan	8.3	143,000
1927	Nan Shan, China	8.3	200,000
1932	Gansu (Kansu), China	7.6	70,000
1933	Sanriku, Japan	8.9	2,990
1934	Bihar, India/Nepal	8.4	10,700
1935	Quetta, India*	7.5	60,000
1939	Chillan, Chile	8.3	28,000
1939	Erzincan, Turkey	7.9	30,000
1960	Agadir, Morocco	5.8	12,000
1962	Khorasan, Iran	7.1	12,230
1968	N.E. Iran	7.4	12,000
1970	N. Peru	7.7	66,794
1972	Managua, Nicaragua	6.2	5,000
1974	N. Pakistan	6.3	5,200
1976	Guatemala	7.5	22,778
1976	Tangshan, China	8.2	255,000
1978	Tabas, Iran	7.7	25,000
1980	El Asnam, Algeria	7.3	20,000
1980	S. Italy	7.2	4,800
1985	Mexico City, Mexico	8.1	4,200
1988	N.W. Armenia	6.8	55,000
1990	N. Iran	7.7	36,000
1992	Flores, Indonesia	6.8	1,895
1993	Maharashtra, India	6.4	30,000
1994	Los Angeles, USA	6.6	57
1995	Kobe, Japan	7.2	5,000
1995	Sakhalin Is., Russia	7.5	2,000
1996	Yunnan, China	7.0	240
1997	N.E. Iran	7.1	2,400
1998	Takhar, Afghanistan	6.1	4,200

The highest magnitude recorded on the Richter scale is 8.9, in Japan on 2 March 1933 (2,990 deaths). The most devastating quake ever was at Shaanxi (Shenshi) province, central China, on 3 January 1556, when an estimated 830,000 people were killed.

* now Pakistan

Landforms

The theory of plate tectonics has offered new insights as to how the Earth works, elucidating mysteries concerning continental drift, volcanic eruptions and earthquakes. It has also contributed to our understanding of how plate collisions can squeeze up layers of sediments on seabeds into fold mountain ranges, such as the Himalayas.

Yet even as mountains rise, natural forces are wearing them away. In hot, dry climates, mechanical weathering, a result of rapid temperature changes, causes the outer layers of rocks to peel away, while, in cold mountain regions, boulders are prised apart when water freezes in cracks in rocks. Chemical weathering is responsible for hollowing out limestone caves and decomposing granites.

Climatic conditions have a great bearing on the principle agent of erosion in any particular area. Running water is most important in moist temperate regions. In cold regions, ice is the major agent of erosion, and in many mountain ranges, U-shaped valleys are evidence of the erosive power of valley glaciers. Ice sheets moulded much of the Earth's surface during the Ice Ages, the most recent of which, in the northern hemisphere, ended only 10,000 years ago. Polar climates also shape the scenery of the periglacial areas that border bodies of ice. Such areas are subject to constant freeze-thaw action, which creates such features as pingos (domed mounds).

Climatic change has also affected many of the landforms in hot deserts, which were shaped by running water at a time when the deserts enjoyed much wetter climates. However, the major agent of erosion in deserts today is wind-blown sand which erodes rock strata to form mushroom-shaped rocks and caves.

The surface of the Earth is under constant assault from tectonic processes and the agents of erosion. The products of erosion, fragments of rock such as sand, are deposited to form sedimentary rocks. Metamorphic rocks are created when igneous or sedimentary rocks are buried and metamorphosed by heat and pressure. Eventually the rocks are recycled to form magma, which rises upwards to start the rock cycle all over again.

The Rock Cycle

James Hutton first proposed the rock cycle in the late 1700s after he observed the slow but steady effects of erosion.

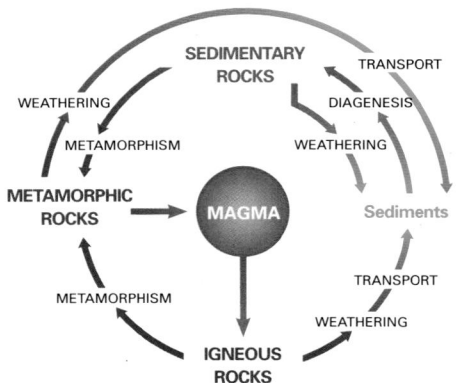

Rocks are divided into three types, according to the way in which they are formed:

Igneous rocks, including granite and basalt, are formed by the cooling of magma from within the Earth's crust.

Metamorphic rocks, such as slate, marble and quartzite, are formed below the Earth's surface by the compression or baking of existing rocks.

Sedimentary rocks, like sandstone and limestone, are formed on the surface of the Earth from the remains of living organisms and eroded fragments of older rocks.

Mountain Building

Mountains are formed when pressures on the Earth's crust caused by continental drift become so intense that the surface buckles or cracks. This happens where oceanic crust is subducted by continental crust or, more dramatically, where two tectonic plates collide: the Rockies, Andes, Alps, Urals and Himalayas resulted from such impacts. These are all known as fold mountains because they were formed by the compression of the rocks, forcing the surface to bend and fold like a crumpled rug. The Himalayas are formed from the folded former sediments of the Tethys Sea which was trapped in the collision zone between the Indian and Eurasian plates.

The other main mountain-building process occurs when the crust fractures to create faults, allowing rock to be forced upwards in large blocks; or when the pressure of magma within the crust forces the surface to bulge into a dome, or erupts to form a volcano. Large mountain ranges may reveal a combination of those features; the Alps, for example, have been compressed so violently that the folds are fragmented by numerous faults and intrusions of molten igneous rock.

Over millions of years, even the greatest mountain ranges can be reduced by the agents of erosion (especially rivers) to a low rugged landscape known as a peneplain.

Types of faults: Faults occur where the crust is being stretched or compressed so violently that the rock strata break in a horizontal or vertical movement. They are classified by the direction in which the blocks of rock have moved. A normal fault results when a vertical movement causes the surface to break apart; compression causes a reverse fault. Horizontal movement causes shearing, known as a strike-slip fault. When the rock breaks in two places, the central block may be pushed up in a horst fault, or sink (creating a rift valley) in a graben fault.

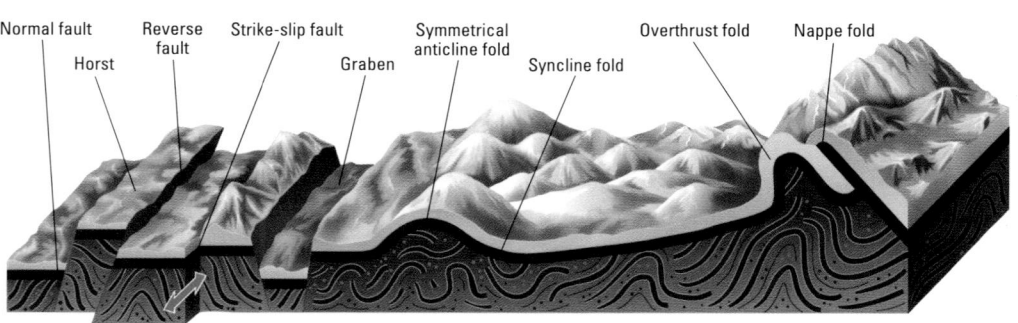

Types of fold: Folds occur when rock strata are squeezed and compressed. They are common, therefore, at destructive plate margins and where plates have collided, forcing the rocks to buckle into mountain ranges. Geographers give different names to the degrees of fold that result from continuing pressure on the rock. A simple fold may be symmetric, with even slopes on either side, but as the pressure builds up, one slope becomes steeper and the fold becomes asymmetric. Later, the ridge or 'anticline' at the top of the fold may slide over the lower ground or 'syncline' to form a recumbent fold. Eventually, the rock strata may break under the pressure to form an overthrust and finally a nappe fold.

Annual Fluctuations for Selected Glaciers

Glacier name and location	Change in mass balance 1970–90
Wolverine, USA	+2,320
Storglaciaren, Sweden	−120
Djankuat, Russia	−1,890
Grasubreen, Norway	−2,530
Ürümqi, China	−3,828
Golubin, Kyrgyzstan	−7,105
Gries, Switzerland	−10,600
Careser, Italy	−11,610
Abramov, Tajikistan	−13,700
Sarennes, France	−15,020
Place, Canada	−15,175

The mass balance is defined as the difference between glacier accumulation and ablation (melting), and is expressed as water equivalent in millimetres. A minus indicates a reduction in the depth or length of a glacier. As can be seen from this geographically diverse selection, glaciers are retreating in many areas worldwide. The most dramatic and serious example of this phenomenon is the continuing distintegration of several large Antarctic ice-shelves.

The extent to which glacial retreat is due to global warming, or to longer term climatic fluctuations remains a matter for debate.

Continental Glaciation

Many landforms in the northern hemisphere were shaped by ice sheets and meltwater during the Pleistocene Ice Age, which began about two million years ago. During the Ice Age, the ice sheets periodically advanced and retreated. The first map shows the ice cover at its greatest extent about 200,000 years BP (before the present), when it covered about 30% of the land surface, as compared with 10% today. About 18,000 years BP, the ice covered most of Canada and as far south as the Bristol Channel in England. Around the ice sheets, land areas experienced periglacial conditions.

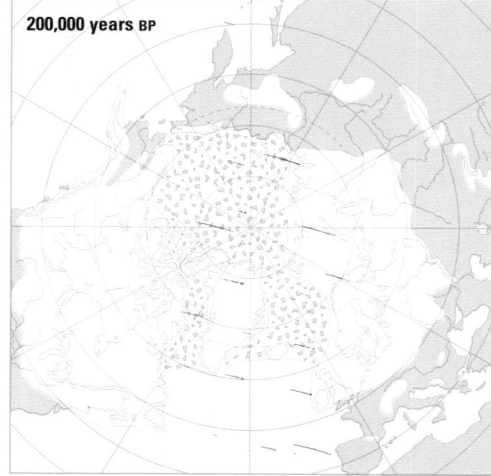

200,000 years BP

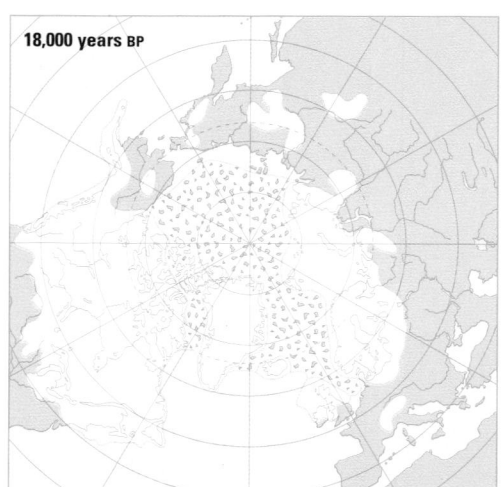

18,000 years BP

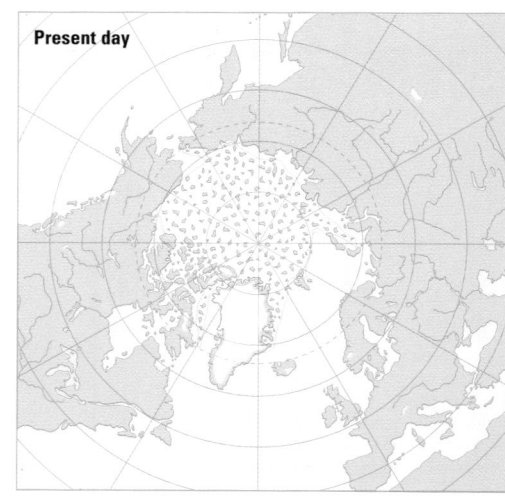

Present day

Natural Landforms

Natural landforms reflect the influence of plate tectonics through mountain-building and the generation of new rocks from the interior, together with the agents of erosion: running water, ice, winds and coastal waves. Over millions of years, mountains are gradually eroded, producing landforms that reflect the major forces that have been at work, as well as the underlying geology, the climatic conditions, which often vary over time, and the vegetation cover. The stylized diagram, below, shows some major natural landforms found in the mid-latitudes.

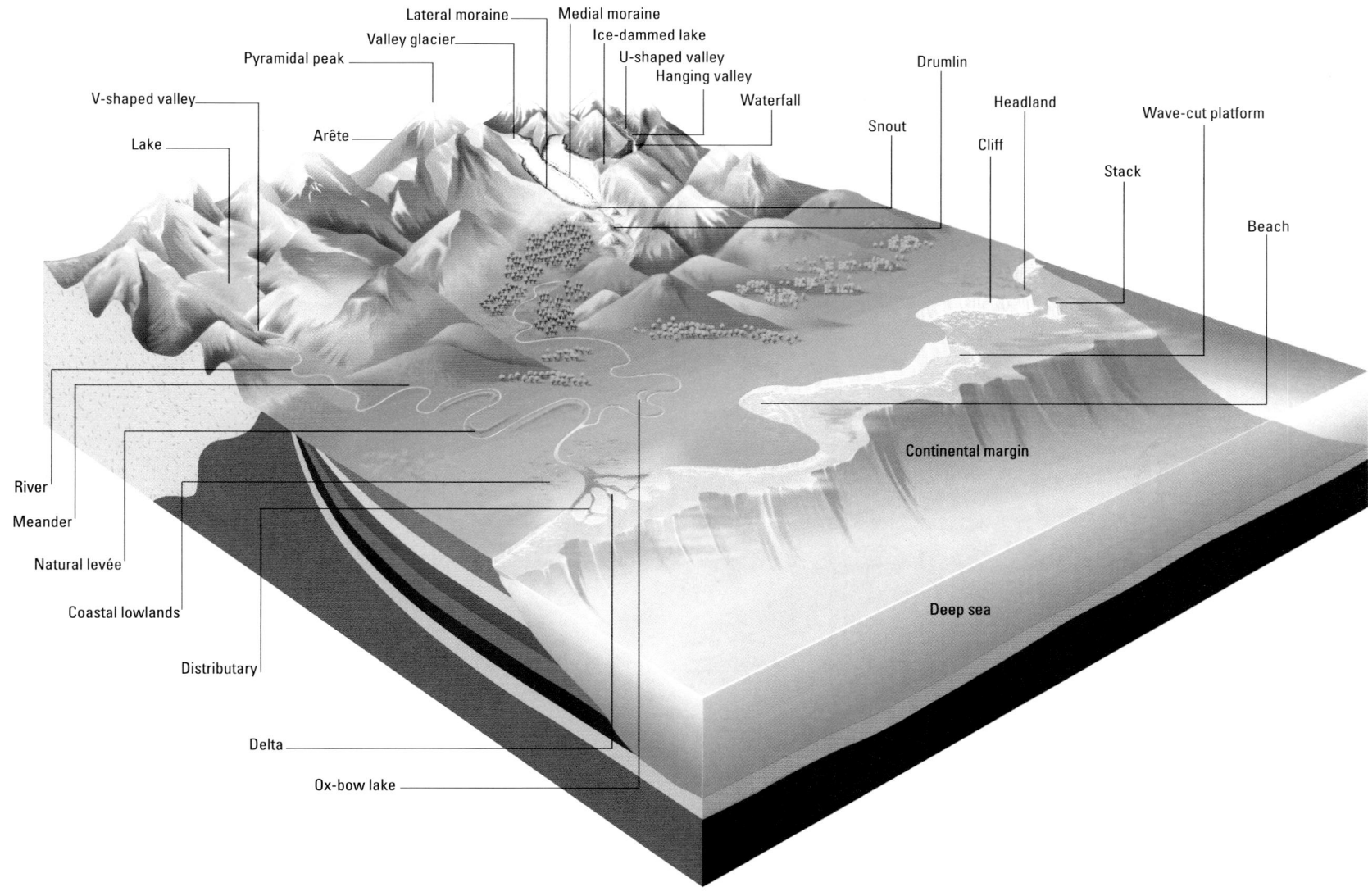

Desert Landforms

Deserts are defined as places with an average annual precipitation of 250 mm per year, though places with a higher rainfall and a high evaporation rate may also qualify as deserts. The three types of desert landforms are known by their Arabic names, a reflection of the fact that the Sahara in North Africa is the world's largest desert. Sand desert, called erg, covers about one-fifth of the world's deserts. The rest is divided between hammada (areas of bare rock) and reg (broad plains covered by loose gravel or pebbles).

The shapes of dunes in sand deserts reflect the character of local winds. Where winds are constant in direction, the sand often piles up in crescent-shaped dunes, called barchans. Barchans are constantly on the move and their forward march, unless halted by vegetation, may overwhelm settlements at oases. Seif dunes, named after the Arabic word for sword, are long ridges of sand which lie parallel to the direction of the wind, but where winds are variable, the sand sheets are often featureless.

Wind-blown sand is an effective agent of erosion but because of the weight of sand grains, this type of erosion is confined to within two metres of the land surface, creating caves and mushroom-shaped rocks.

In assessing desert landforms, it is important to remember that other processes were at work in the past when the climate was very different from today. For example, cave paintings suggest that the Sahara had a much wetter climate after the end of the Ice Age and only began to dry up after about 5000 BC. However, human action, including overgrazing and the cutting down of trees for firewood, can turn a grassland region into desert – a process known as desertification.

Erg

Hammada

Reg

Surface Processes

Catastrophic changes to landforms are periodically caused by such phenomena as avalanches, landslides and volcanic eruptions, but most of the processes that shape the Earth's surface operate extremely slowly in human terms. One estimate, based on a study of landforms in the United States, suggests that, on average, one metre of land is removed from the entire surface of the country every 29,500 years. However, the terrain and the climate have a great effect on the erosion rate. For example, on cold plains, such as the Hudson Bay lowlands, the rate drops to around one metre for every 154,200 years, while in wet, tropical mountain areas, the rate may reach one metre for every 1,300 years.

Chemical weathering is at its greatest in warm, humid regions, while mechanical weathering, or the physical break-up of rocks, predominates in cold mountain or hot desert regions. The most familiar type of chemical weathering is caused by the reaction of rainwater containing dissolved carbon dioxide on limestone. This leads to the creation of labyrinthine cave networks dissolved by groundwater. Mechanical weathering includes frost action, while in hot deserts, rapid temperature changes cause the outer layers of rocks to expand and contract until they crack and peel away, a process called exfoliation.

The most important product of weathering is soil, which consists of rock fragments and humus, the decayed remains of plants and animals, together with living organisms, including vast numbers of micro-organisms. Soils vary in character according to the climate, ranging from the heavily leached, red laterite soils of wet tropical areas to the fertile, brown soils of dry grasslands. Soils are important because they support plants, which in turn anchor the soil and act as a protection against erosion. Soil erosion is greatest on sloping land because the steeper the slope, the greater the tendency for the soil to creep or flow downhill. The degree of movement of soil and rock downhill under the influence of gravity, called mass wasting, depends on a slope's stability. The stability may be disturbed by earthquakes or by heavy rain (water acts as a lubricant and increases the weight of the overlying material) which may trigger flows, slides or large falls of rock.

Running water is probably the world's leading agent of erosion and transportation. The energy of a river depends on several factors, including its velocity and volume, and its erosive power is at its peak when it is in full flood, sweeping soil, pebbles and even boulders along its course, cutting downwards into the bedrock or widening its valley. Sea waves also exert tremendous erosive power during storms when they hurl pebbles and large rocks against the shore, undercutting cliffs and hollowing out caves. Headlands are often attacked on both sides, forming caves, then a natural arch and eventually an isolated stack.

Glacier ice forms in mountain hollows, called cirques, and spills out to form valley glaciers, which transport rocks shattered by frost action. As a glacier moves, rocks embedded in the base and sides scrape away bedrock, eroding steep-sided, flat-bottomed, U-shaped valleys. Evidence of past glaciation in mountain regions includes cirques, knife-edged ridges, or arêtes, and pyramidal peaks, or horns.

Geologists once considered that landforms evolved from 'young', newly uplifted mountainous areas, through a 'mature' hilly stage, to an 'old age' stage when the land was reduced to an almost flat plain, or peneplain. This theory, called the 'cycle of erosion', fell into disuse when it became evident that so many factors, including the effects of plate tectonics and climatic change, constantly interrupt the cycle, which takes no account of the highly complex interactions that shape the surface of our planet.

The Atmosphere

The atmosphere is a meteor shield, a radiation deflector, a thermal blanket and a source of chemical energy for the Earth's diverse life forms. Five-sixths of its mass is in the lowest layer, the troposphere which ranges in thickness from 18 to 10 km between the Equator and the poles. Powered by the Sun, the air is always on the move, flowing generally from high- to low-pressure areas. The troposphere is the layer where virtually all weather phenomena, including clouds, precipitation and winds, occur. Above the troposphere is the stratosphere, which contains the important ozone layer and extends to about 50 km above the Earth's surface. Beyond 100 km, atmospheric density is lower than most laboratory vacuums.

Circulation of the Air

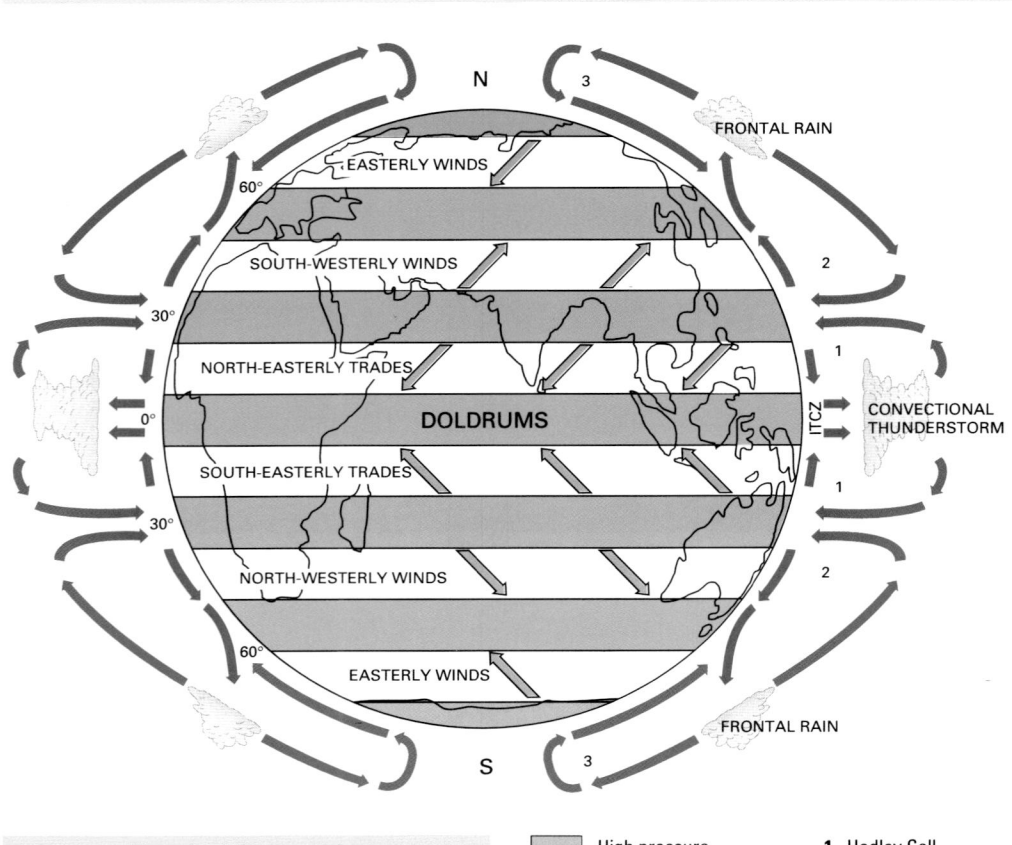

High pressure
Low pressure
Warm air
Cold air
Surface winds
Clouds

1 Hadley Cell
2 Ferrel Cell
3 Polar Cell

ITCZ Intertropical convergence zone

Structure of the Atmosphere

HUBBLE SPACE TELESCOPE
600 km [370 miles] — 600 KM
Pressure 10^{-35} mb

EXOSPHERE
10^{-22} mb

350 KM

MIR SPACE STATION
325 km [200 miles]

300 KM
10^{-16} mb

SPACE SHUTTLE
275 km [170 miles]

250 KM

THERMOSPHERE
200 KM
10^{-10} mb

VOSTOCK MANNED CAPSULE
(first manned space flight, 1961)
175 km [110 miles]

150 KM

AURORAE

METEOR trails 100 KM
10^{-3} mb

MESOSPHERE

50 KM

OZONE LAYER

STRATOSPHERE

CONCORDE
MOUNT EVEREST
8,848 m [29,029 ft]
10 KM
TROPOSPHERE
10^{3} mb

Chemical Composition

Gaseous composition of the principal atmospheric layers

50–100% hydrogen | 25–50% helium
Exosphere
Helium vanishes with increasing altitude. Above 2,400 km the exosphere is almost entirely composed of hydrogen.

70% nitrogen | 15% oxygen | 15% helium
Mesosphere
The high energy of mesospheric gas gives it a notional temperature of more than 2,000°C, although its density is negligible.

80% nitrogen | 18% oxygen | 1% argon | 1% ozone
Stratosphere
Stratospheric air contains enough ozone to make it poisonous, although it is in any case too rarified to breathe.

78% nitrogen | 21% oxygen | 1% argon
Troposphere
The narrowest of all the layers, this thin region contains about 85% of the atmosphere's total mass and almost all of its water vapour. It is also the realm of the Earth's weather.

Frontal Systems

Depressions, or cyclones, form along the polar front where dense polar easterlies meet warm subtropical westerlies. Depressions occur when warm air flows into waves in the polar front, while cold air flows in behind it, creating rotating air systems that bring changeable weather. Along the warm front (the boundary on the ground between the warm and cold air), the warm air flows upwards over the cold air, producing a sequence of clouds which help forecasters to predict a depression's advance. Along the cold front, the advancing cold air forces warm air to rise steeply. Towering cumulonimbus clouds form in the rising air. When the cold front overtakes the warm front, the warm air is pushed above ground level to form an occluded front. Cloud and rain persist along occlusions until temperatures equalize, the air mixes, and the depression dies out.

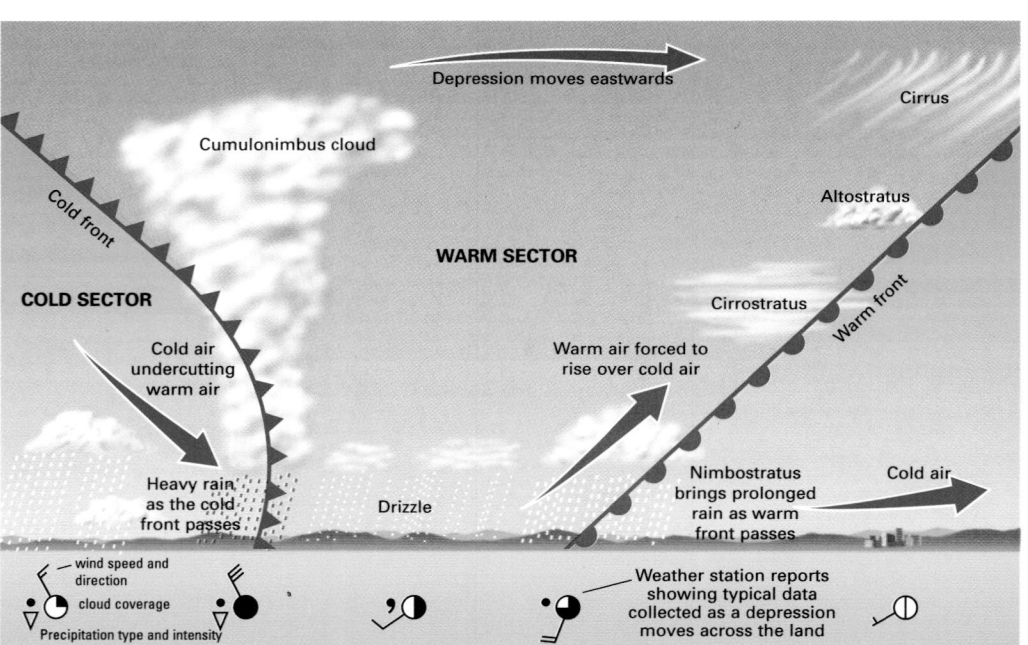

Air Masses

Air masses are bodies of air whose characteristics are broadly the same over a large area. Around the Equator, where the Sun's heat creates relatively high surface temperatures, warm air rises to create a zone of low pressure called the doldrums. The air cools and finally spreads out towards the poles. Around latitudes 30° north and south, the air sinks back to the surface, becoming warmer as it descends and creating zones of high pressure called the horse latitudes.

The high- and low-pressure zones are both areas of comparative calm, but between them lie the prevailing trade wind belts. Air also flows north and south from the high-pressure horse latitudes and these air flows meet up with cold, dense air flowing from the poles along the polar front. This basic circulatory system is complicated by the Coriolis effect, brought about by the spinning Earth. Because of the Coriolis effect, the prevailing winds do not flow directly north–south but are deflected to the right in the northern hemisphere and to the left in the southern. Along the polar front, depressions form where the polar easterlies meet the westerlies.

The first classification of clouds was developed by a London chemist, Luke Howard, in 1803, and it was later modified by the World Meteorological Organization. The main types are divided into three groups according to their altitude, and into subgroups according to their shape, which vary from hairlike filaments (cirrus), heaps or piles (cumulus), and layers (stratus). Each cloud carries some kind of message, though not always a clear one, to weather forecasters.

Classification of Clouds

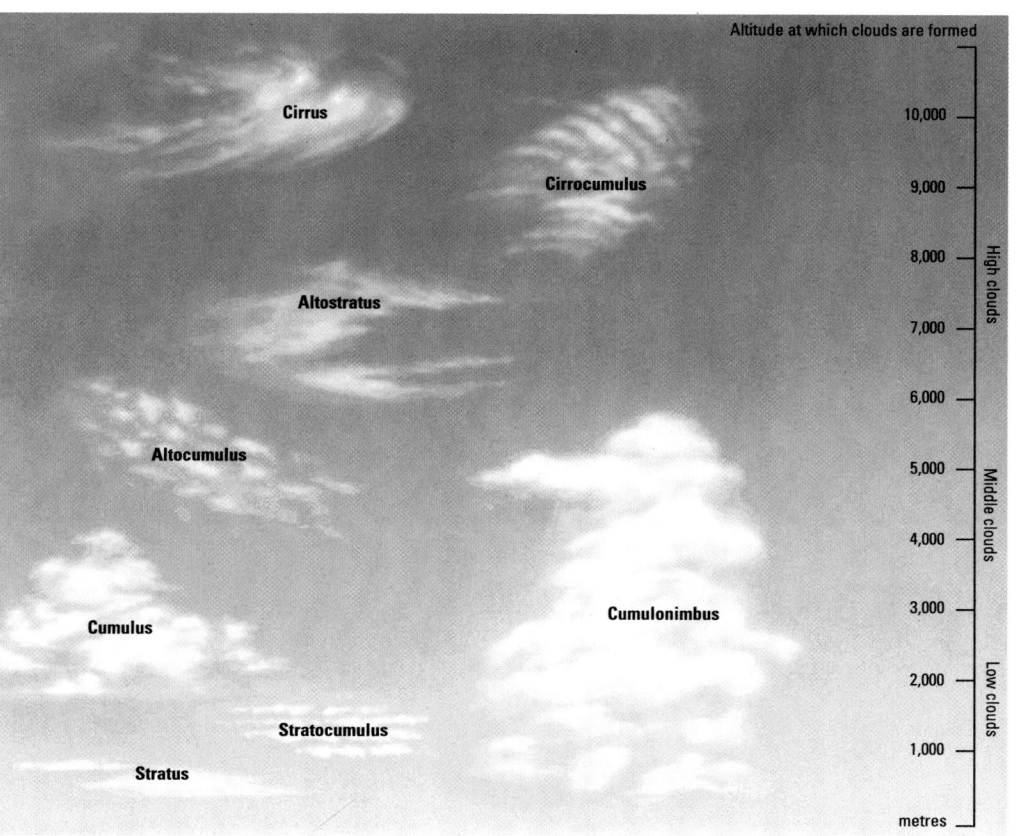

Clouds form when damp, usually rising, air is cooled. Thus they form when a wind rises to cross hills or mountains; when a mass of air rises over, or is pushed up by, another mass of denser air; or when local heating of the ground causes convection currents.

The types of clouds are classified according to altitude as high, middle or low. The high ones, composed of ice crystals, are cirrus, cirrostratus and cirrocumulus. The middle clouds are altostratus, a grey or bluish striated, fibrous or uniform sheet producing light drizzle, and altocumulus, a thicker and fluffier version of cirrocumulus.

Low clouds include nimbostratus, a dark grey layer that brings rain or snow; cumulus, a detached heap, dark at the base; stratus, which forms dull, overcast skies at low levels; and stratocumulus, which consists of fluffy greyish-white layers.

Cumulonimbus, associated with storms and rains, heavy and dense with a flat base and a high, fluffy outline, can be tall enough to occupy middle as well as low altitudes.

Pressure and Surface Winds

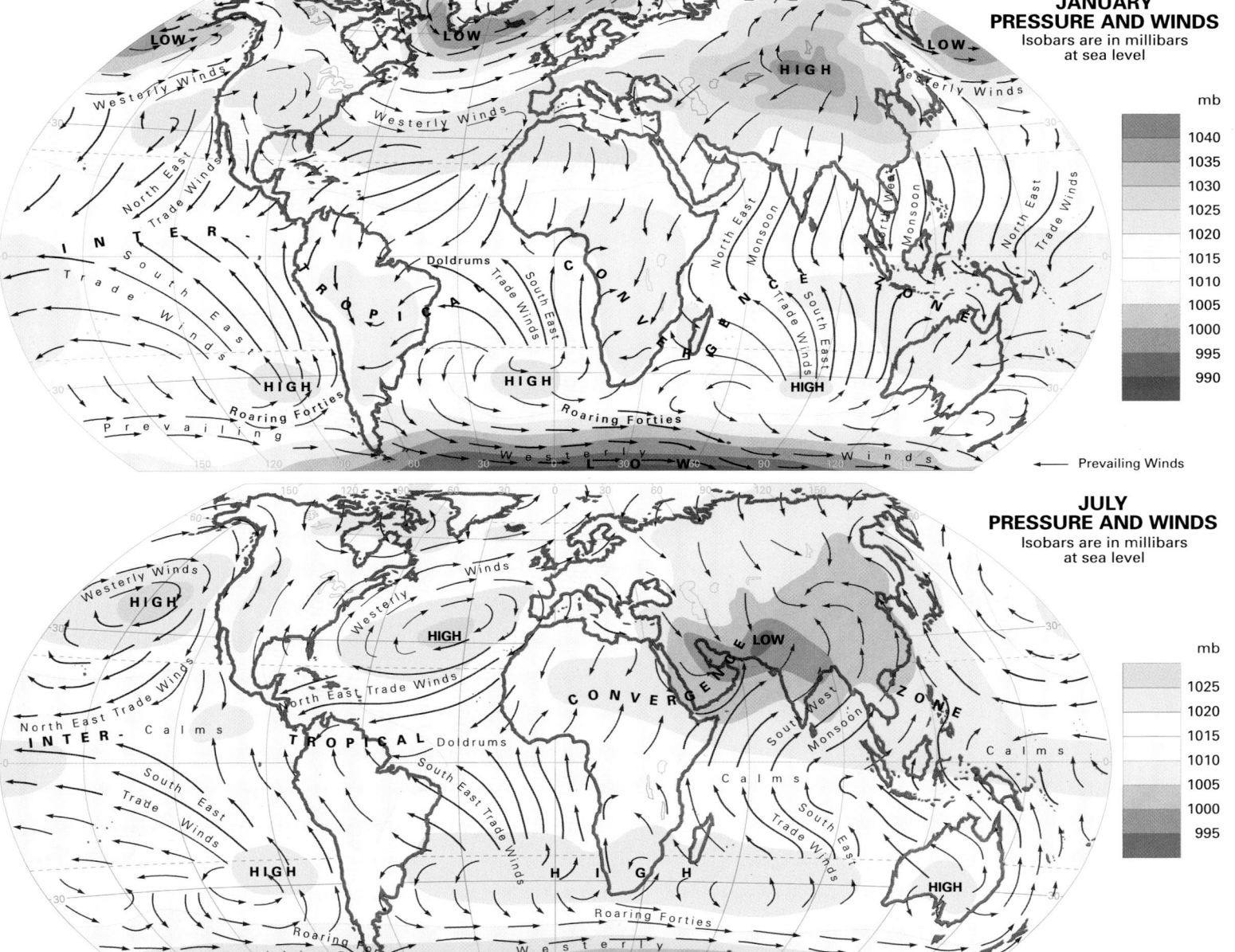

Climate Records

Pressure and winds

Highest barometric pressure: Agata, Siberia, 1,083.8 mb at altitude 262 m [862 ft], 31 December 1968.

Lowest barometric pressure: Typhoon Tip, 480 km [300 mls] west of Guam, Pacific Ocean, 870 mb, 12 October 1979.

Highest recorded wind speed: Mt Washington, New Hampshire, USA, 371 km/h [231 mph], 12 April 1934. This is three times as strong as hurricane force on the Beaufort Scale.

Windiest place: Commonwealth Bay, George V Coast, Antarctica, where gales frequently reach over 320 km/h [200 mph].

Worst recorded storm: Bangladesh (then East Pakistan) cyclone*, 13 November 1970 – over 300,000 dead or missing. The 1991 cyclone, Bangladesh's and the world's second worst in terms of loss of life, killed an estimated 138,000 people.

Worst recorded tornado: Missouri/Illinois/Indiana, USA, 18 March 1925 – 792 deaths. The tornado was only 275 m [300 yds] wide.

Tropical cyclones are known as hurricanes in Central and North America, as typhoons in the Far East, and as willy-willies in northern Australia.

Climate

For more information:

9 Ocean currents
14 Circulation of the air
15 Classification of clouds
Pressure and winds
18 Hydrological cycle
19 Natural vegetation
21 Greenhouse effect
22 Global warming

Weather is the day-to-day or hour-to-hour condition of the air, while climate is weather in the long term, the seasonal pattern of hot and cold, wet and dry, averaged over a long period. Most classifications of climate are based on a system developed by a Russian meteorologist, Vladimir Köppen, in the early 19th century. Using a code based on letters and a classification centred on two main features, temperature and precipitation, he identified five main climatic types: tropical (A), dry (B), warm temperate (C), cold temperate (D), and polar (E). A highland mountain climate (H), was added later to account for the variety of altitudinal climatic zones on high mountains. Each of these main regions was then further subdivided.

Latitude is a major factor in determining climate, but other factors add to the complexity. They include the differential heating of land and sea, the distance from the sea, the effect of mountains on winds, and the influence of ocean currents. For example, New York City, Naples and the Gobi Desert share almost the same latitude, but their climates are very different.

Climates are not indefinitely stable. During the last Ice Age, the Earth underwent alternating cold periods, called glacials, separated by warm interglacials. The Milankovich theory suggests such cycles may be caused by variations in the Earth's path around the Sun, changing from almost circular to elliptical every 95,000 years, and variations in the Earth's tilt from 21.5° to 24.5° every 42,000 years. Another factor is that the Earth is now closest to the Sun in the middle of winter in the northern hemisphere and furthest away in summer. But 12,000 years ago, at the height of the last glacial period, the northern winter fell with the Sun at its most distant.

Studies of these cycles suggest that we are now in an interglacial with a new glacial period on the way. However, many scientists believe that global warming, largely a result of burning fossil fuels and deforestation, may be occurring much faster than the great, slow cycles of the Solar System.

Tropical rainy climates
All mean monthly temperatures above 18°C.

- Af Rainforest climate
- Am Monsoon climate
- Aw Savanna climate

Dry climates
Low rainfall combined with a wide range of temperatures

- BS Steppe climate
- BW Desert climate

Warm temperate rainy climates
The mean temperature is below 18°C but above −3°C and that of the warmest month is over 10°C.

- Cw Dry winter climate
- Cs Dry summer climate
- Cf Climate with no dry season

Cold temperate rainy climates
The mean temperature of the coldest month is below −3°C but that of the warmest month is still over 10°C.

- Dw Dry winter climate
- Df Climate with no dry season

Polar climates
The mean temperature of the warmest month is below 10°C, giving permanently frozen subsoil.

- ET Tundra climate

The mean temperature of the warmest month is below 0°C, giving permanent ice and snow.

- EF Polar climate

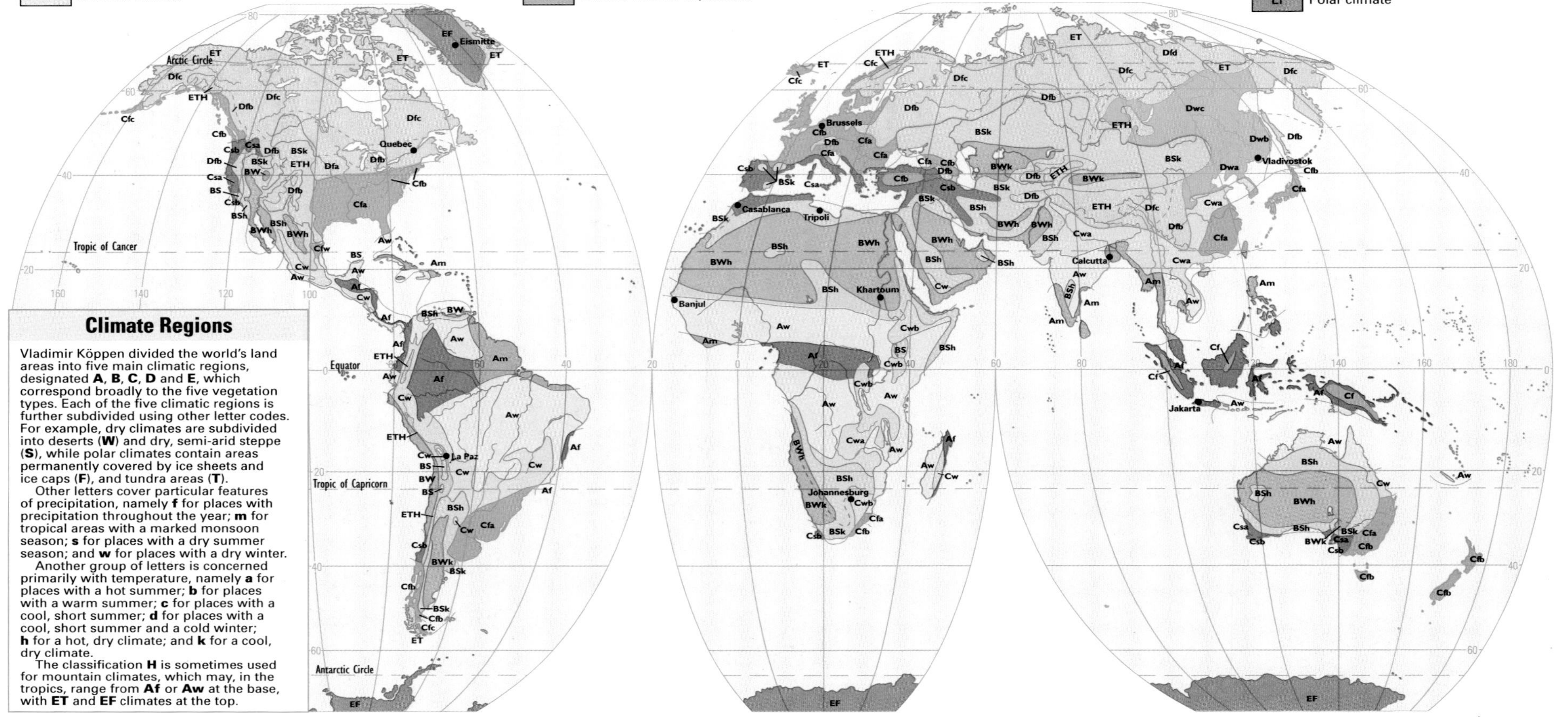

Climate Regions

Vladimir Köppen divided the world's land areas into five main climatic regions, designated **A**, **B**, **C**, **D** and **E**, which correspond broadly to the five vegetation types. Each of the five climatic regions is further subdivided using other letter codes. For example, dry climates are subdivided into deserts (**W**) and dry, semi-arid steppe (**S**), while polar climates contain areas permanently covered by ice sheets and ice caps (**F**), and tundra areas (**T**).

Other letters cover particular features of precipitation, namely **f** for places with precipitation throughout the year; **m** for tropical areas with a marked monsoon season; **s** for places with a dry summer season; and **w** for places with a dry winter.

Another group of letters is concerned primarily with temperature, namely **a** for places with a hot summer; **b** for places with a warm summer; **c** for places with a cool, short summer; **d** for places with a cool, short summer and a cold winter; **h** for a hot, dry climate; and **k** for a cool, dry climate.

The classification **H** is sometimes used for mountain climates, which may, in the tropics, range from **Af** or **Aw** at the base, with **ET** and **EF** climates at the top.

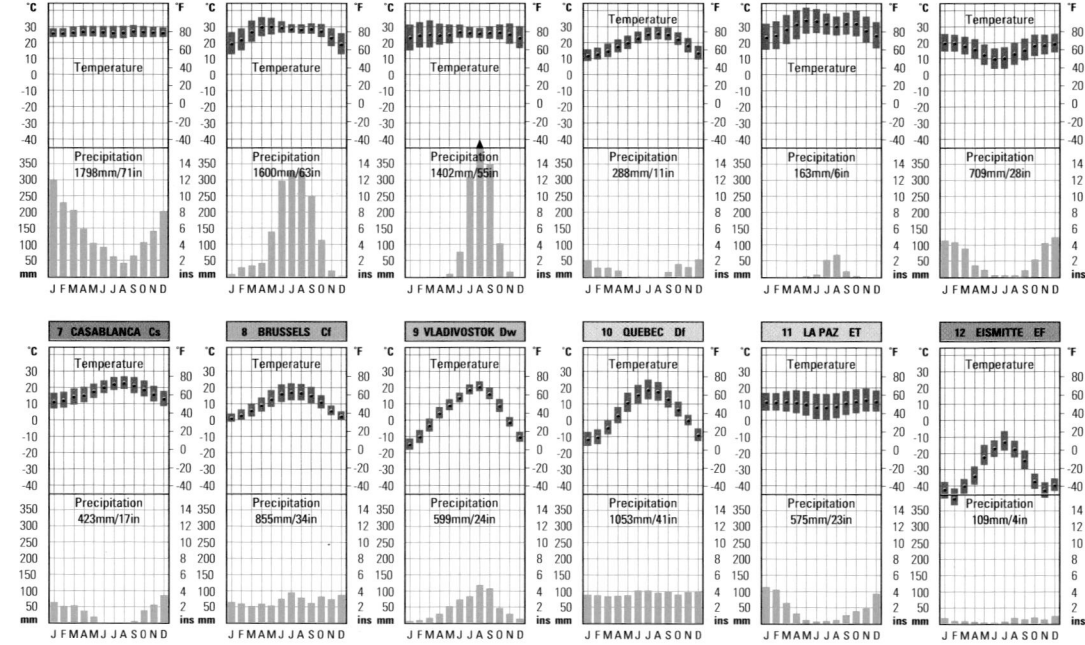

Climate and Weather Terms

Anticyclone: area of high pressure with light winds and generally quiet weather.
Absolute humidity: amount of water vapour contained in a given volume of air.
Cloud cover: amount of cloud in the sky; measured in oktas (from 1 – 8), with 0 clear, and 8 total cover.
Condensation: the conversion of water vapour, or moisture in the air, into liquid.
Cyclone: violent storm resulting from anticlockwise rotation of winds in the northern hemisphere and clockwise in the southern: called hurricane in N. America, typhoon in the Far East.
Depression: area of low pressure. The pressure gradient is towards the centre.
Dew: water droplets condensed out of the air after the ground has cooled at night.
Dew point: temperature at which air becomes saturated (reaches a relative humidity of 100%) at a constant pressure.
Drizzle: precipitation where drops are less than 0.5 mm [0.02 in] in diameter.
Evaporation: conversion of water from liquid into vapour, or moisture in the air.
Front: the dividing line between two air masses.
Frost: dew that has frozen when the air temperature falls below freezing point.
Hail: frozen rain; small balls of ice, often falling during thunderstorms.
Hoar frost: formed on objects when the dew point is below freezing point.
Humidity: amount of moisture in the air.
Isobar: cartographic line connecting places of equal atmospheric pressure.
Isotherm: cartographic line connecting places of equal temperature.
Lightning: massive electrical discharge released in thunderstorm from cloud to cloud or cloud to ground, the result of the tip becoming positively charged and the bottom negatively charged.
Precipitation: measurable rain, snow, sleet or hail.
Prevailing wind: most common direction of wind at a given location.
Rain: precipitation of liquid particles with diameter larger than 0.5 mm [0.02 in].
Relative humidity: amount of water vapour contained in a given volume of air at a given temperature.
Snow: formed when water vapour condenses below freezing point.
Thunder: sound produced by the rapid expansion of air heated by lightning.
Tornado: severe funnel-shaped storm that twists as hot air spins vertically (waterspout at sea).
Whirlwind: rapidly rotating column of air, only a few metres across, made visible by dust.

Climate Change

Human factors, such as the emission of greenhouse gases through the burning of fossil fuels and deforestation, have contributed to global warming. The histogram, below, shows in blue the average global temperatures from 1860 (when sufficient observations became available for global averages to be calculated) to 1996. The red line is a 10-year running average. Overall, there is an upward trend, particularly so since the 1970s, when global warming became a matter of concern in scientific circles. The large year-to-year changes indicate the Earth's natural climatic variability and the influence of such factors as major volcanic eruptions.

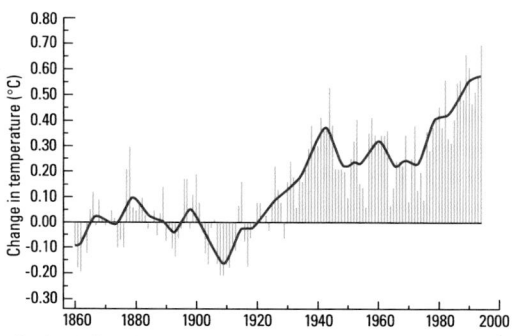

Data from the Hadley Centre for Climate Research and Prediction

Beaufort Wind Scale

Named after the 19th-century British naval officer who devised it, Admiral Beaufort, the Beaufort Scale assesses wind speed according to its effects. It was originally designed as an aid for sailors, but has since been adapted for use on the land. It is used internationally.

Scale	Wind speed km/h	mph	Effect
0	0–1	0–1	**Calm** Smoke rises vertically
1	1–5	1–3	**Light air** Wind direction shown only by smoke drift
2	6–11	4–7	**Light breeze** Wind felt on face; leaves rustle; vanes moved by wind
3	12–19	8–12	**Gentle breeze** Leaves and small twigs in constant motion; wind extends small flag
4	20–28	13–18	**Moderate** Raises dust and loose paper; small branches move
5	29–38	19–24	**Fresh** Small trees in leaf sway; crested wavelets on inland waters
6	39–49	25–31	**Strong** Large branches move; difficult to use umbrellas; overhead wires whistle
7	50–61	32–38	**Near gale** Whole trees in motion; difficult to walk against wind
8	62–74	39–46	**Gale** Twigs break from trees; walking very difficult
9	75–88	47–54	**Strong gale** Slight structural damage
10	89–102	55–63	**Storm** Trees uprooted; serious structural damage
11	103–117	64–72	**Violent storm** Widespread damage
12	118+	73+	**Hurricane**

The Monsoon

Monsoon is the term given to the seasonal reversal of wind direction, most noticeably in South-east Asia. It results from a combination of factors: the extreme heating and cooling of large landmasses in relation to the less marked changes in temperature of the adjacent seas; the northwards movement of the Intertropical Convergence Zone (ITCZ); and the effect of the Himalayas on the circulation of the air.

In early March, which normally marks the end of the sub-continent's cool season and the start of the hot season, winds blow outwards from the mainland. But as the overhead Sun and the ITCZ move northwards, the land is intensely heated, and a low-pressure system develops. The south-east trade winds, which are drawn across the Equator, change direction and are sucked into the interior to become south-westerly winds, bringing heavy rain. By November, the overhead Sun and the ITCZ have again moved southwards, and the wind directions are again reversed. Cool winds blow from the Asian interior to the sea, losing any moisture on the Himalayas before descending to the coast.

Temperature

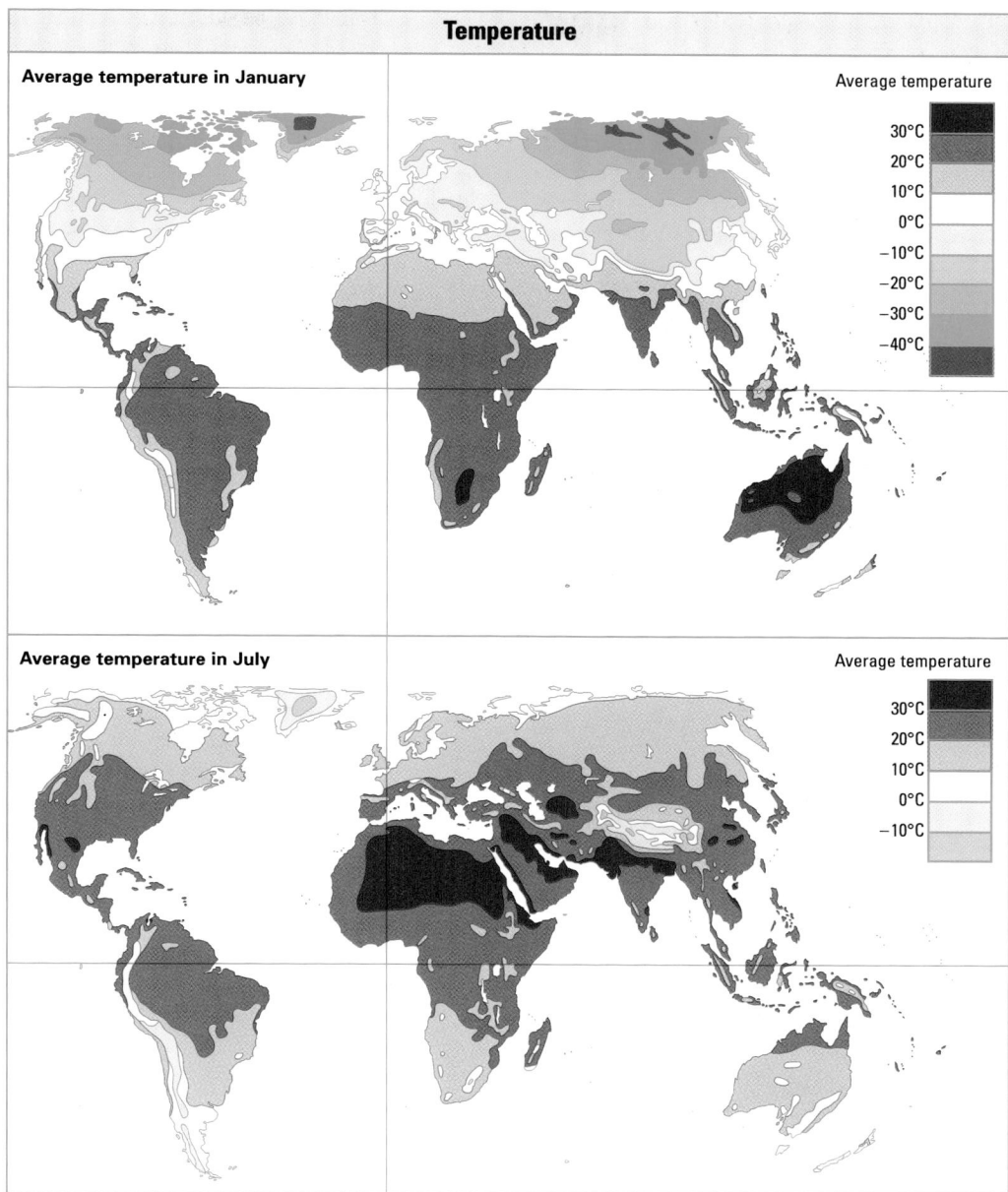

Average temperature in January

Average temperature

30°C / 20°C / 10°C / 0°C / −10°C / −20°C / −30°C / −40°C

Average temperature in July

Average temperature

30°C / 20°C / 10°C / 0°C / −10°C

Precipitation

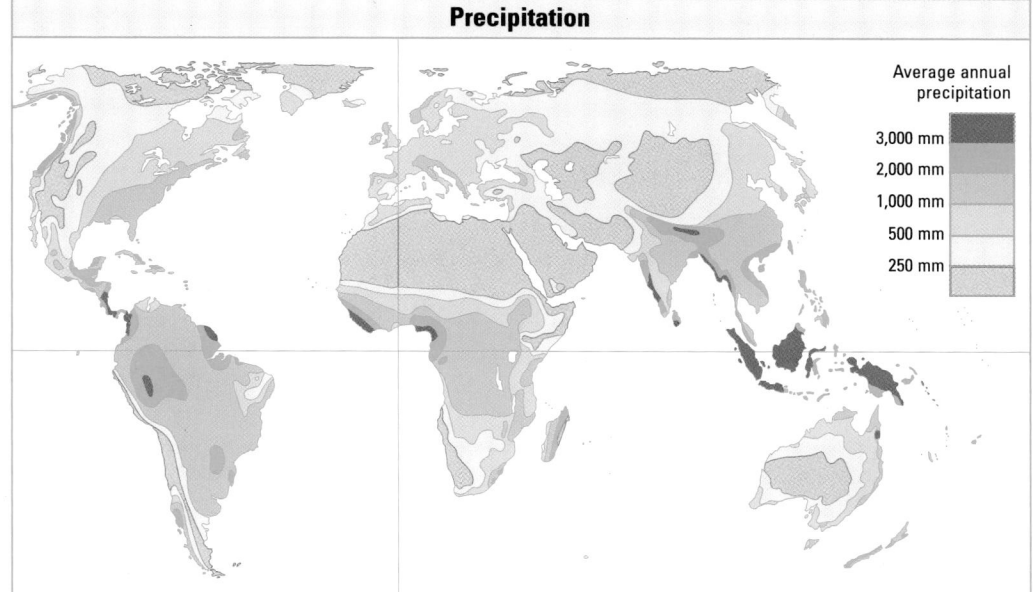

Average annual precipitation

3,000 mm / 2,000 mm / 1,000 mm / 500 mm / 250 mm

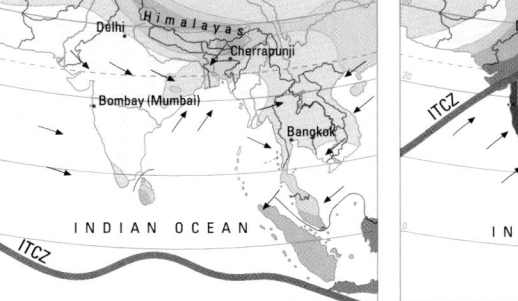

March – Start of the hot, dry season. The ITCZ is over the southern Indian Ocean.

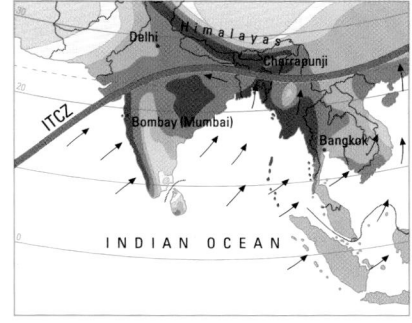

July – The rainy season. The ITCZ has migrated northwards; winds blow onshore.

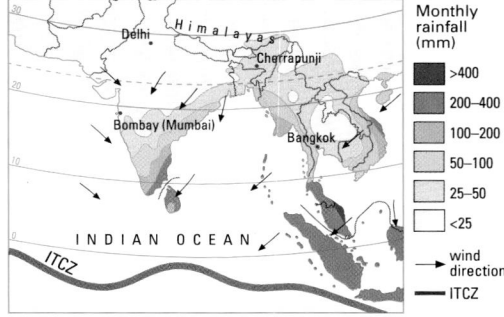

November – The ITCZ has returned south. The offshore winds are cool and dry.

Monthly rainfall (mm)

>400 / 200–400 / 100–200 / 50–100 / 25–50 / <25

→ wind direction
— ITCZ

Climate Records

Temperature

Highest recorded temperature: Al Aziziyah, Libya, 58°C [136.4°F], 13 September 1922.

Highest mean annual temperature: Dallol, Ethiopia, 34.4°C [94°F], 1960–66.

Longest heatwave: Marble Bar, W. Australia, 162 days over 38°C [100°F], 23 October 1923 to 7 April 1924.

Lowest recorded temperature (outside poles): Verkhoyansk, Siberia, −68°C [−90°F], 6 February 1933. Verkhoyansk also registered the greatest annual range of temperature: −70°C to 37°C [−94°F to 98°F].

Lowest mean annual temperature: Polus Nedostupnosti, Pole of Cold, Antarctica, −57.8°C [−72°F].

Precipitation

Driest place: Calama, N. Chile: no recorded rainfall in 400 years to 1971.

Wettest place (average): Tututendo, Colombia: mean annual rainfall 11,770 mm [463.4 in].

Wettest place (12 months): Cherrapunji, Meghalaya, N.E. India, 26,470 mm [1,040 in], August 1860 to August 1861. Cherrapunji also holds the record for rainfall in one month: 2,930 mm [115 in], July 1861. (See maps below.)

Wettest place (24 hours): Cilaos, Réunion, Indian Ocean, 1,870 mm [73.6 in], 15–16 March 1952.

Heaviest hailstones: Gopalganj, Bangladesh, up to 1.02 kg [2.25 lb], 14 April 1986 (killed 92 people).

Heaviest snowfall (continuous): Bessans, Savoie, France, 1,730 mm [68 in] in 19 hours, 5–6 April 1969.

Heaviest snowfall (season/year): Paradise Ranger Station, Mt Rainier, Washington, USA, 31,102 mm [1,224.5 in], 19 February 1971 to 18 February 1972.

CARTOGRAPHY BY PHILIP'S. COPYRIGHT GEORGE PHILIP LTD

Water and Vegetation

Without the hydrological cycle, whereby water is constantly recycled between the oceans, the atmosphere and the land, the continents would be barren. Precipitation enables plants to grow and soils to form, creating the world's natural vegetation regions and the ecosystems that support animal life. Running water also plays a major role in shaping landforms. Yet in many parts of the world, people do not have safe water to drink and suffer from diseases caused by water-borne organisms or pollution. In addition, the limited water supplies have to be shared with agriculture and industry.

In 1996, UN experts argued that the demand for water is increasing at about twice the rate of population growth. They predict that, by 2025, two-thirds of the world's population will face water shortages. This could lead to conflict and even boundary wars, especially because 300 major rivers cross national frontiers and access to their water is likely to be disputed.

The Hydrological Cycle

The world's water balance is regulated by the constant recycling of water between the oceans, atmosphere and land. The movement of water between these three reservoirs is known as the hydrological cycle. The oceans play a vital role in the hydrological cycle: 74% of the total precipitation falls over the oceans and 84% of the total evaporation comes from the oceans. Water vapour in the atmosphere circulates around the planet, transporting energy as well as the water itself. When the vapour cools, it falls as rain or snow. The whole cycle is driven by the Sun.

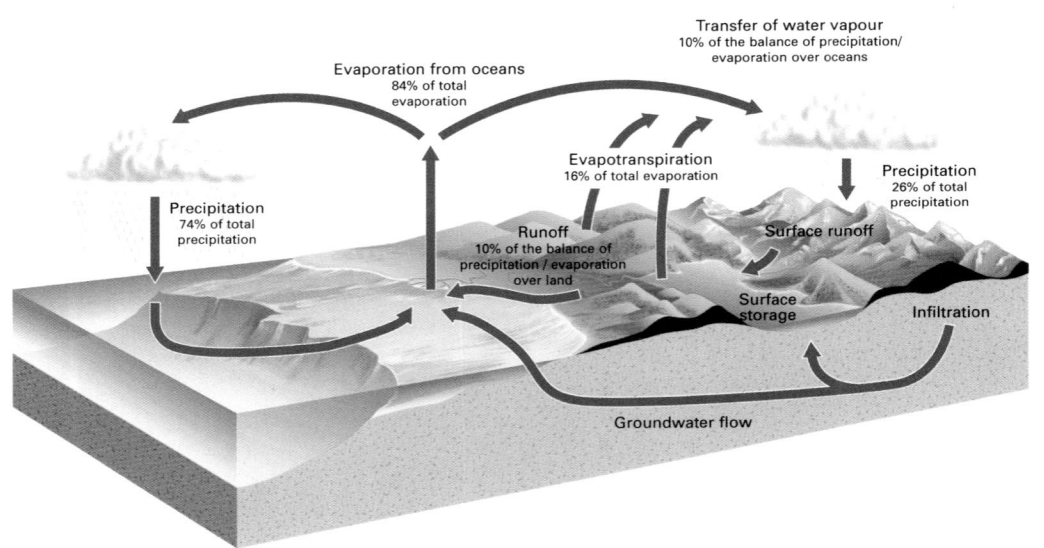

Water Distribution

The distribution of planetary water, by percentage. Oceans and ice caps together account for more than 99% of the total; the breakdown of the remainder is estimated.

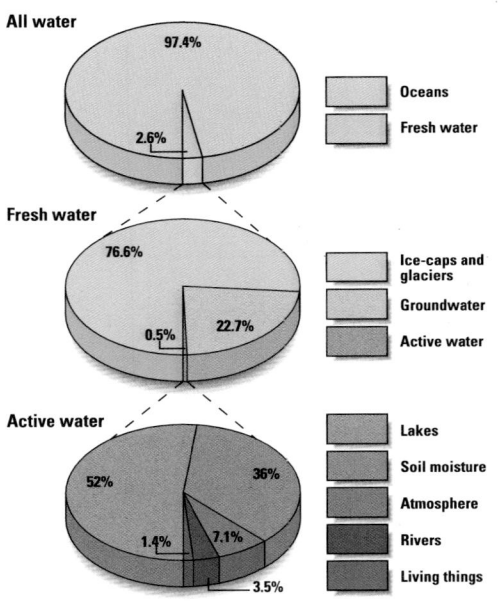

Almost all the world's water is 3,000 million years old, and all of it cycles endlessly through the hydrosphere, though at different rates. Water vapour circulates over days, even hours; deep ocean water circulates over millennia; and ice-cap water remains solid for millions of years.

Water Utilization

The percentage breakdown of water usage by sector, selected countries (latest available year)

Domestic
Industrial
Agriculture

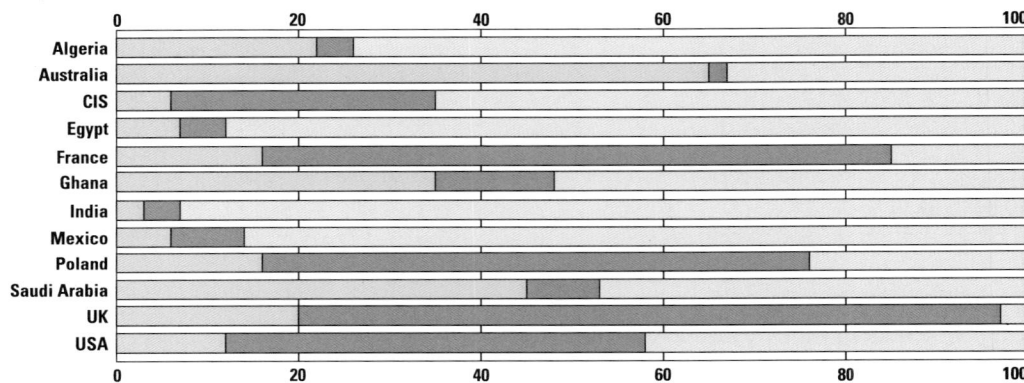

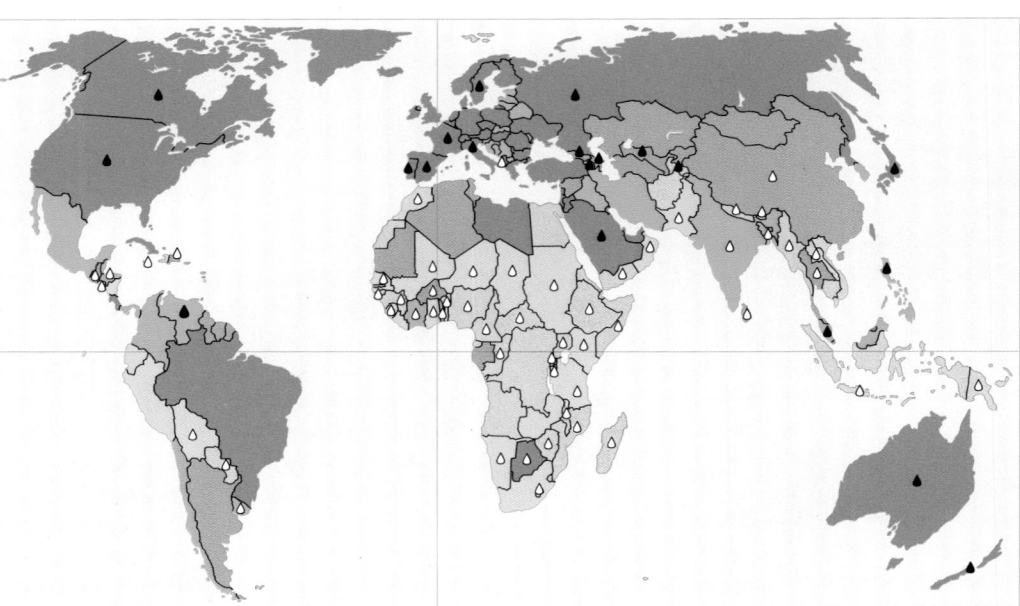

Water Runoff

Annual freshwater runoff by continent in cubic kilometres

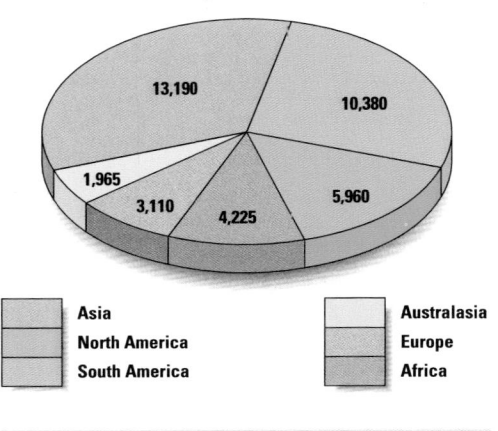

Asia	Australasia
North America	Europe
South America	Africa

Water Supply

Percentage of total population with access to safe drinking water (latest available year)

- Over 90% with safe water
- 75 – 90% with safe water
- 60 – 75% with safe water
- 45 – 60% with safe water
- 30 – 45% with safe water
- Under 30% with safe water

△ Under 80 litres average per capita daily water consumption

▲ Over 320 litres average per capita daily water consumption

Least well-provided countries

Central African Rep	12%	Afghanistan	23%
Uganda	15%	Madagascar	23%
Ethiopia	18%	Guinea-Bissau	25%
Mozambique	22%	Laos	28%

Watersheds

The world's major rivers; the rank of the world's 20 longest is shown in square brackets, led by the Nile and the Amazon.

Where the rivers run

- Pacific Ocean
- Indian Ocean
- Arctic Ocean
- Atlantic Ocean
- Caribbean Sea–Gulf of Mexico
- Mediterranean Sea
- Inland basins, ice caps and deserts

The map shows the direction of freshwater flow on a continental scale; the water runoff chart on the facing page indicates the quantities involved. The rate of runoff varies seasonally and is affected by the surface vegetation. Most of the world's major rivers discharge into the Atlantic Ocean.

Annual Sediment Yield

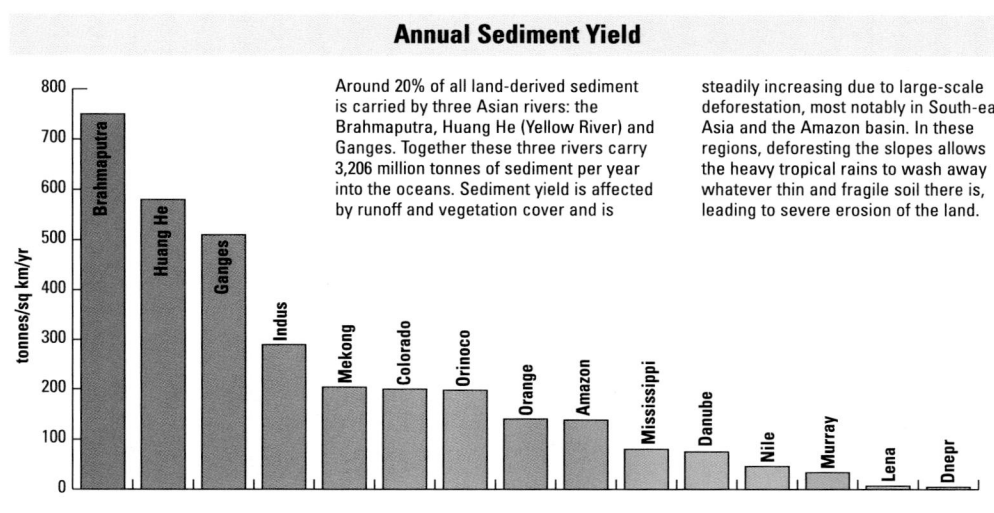

Around 20% of all land-derived sediment is carried by three Asian rivers: the Brahmaputra, Huang He (Yellow River) and Ganges. Together these three rivers carry 3,206 million tonnes of sediment per year into the oceans. Sediment yield is affected by runoff and vegetation cover and is steadily increasing due to large-scale deforestation, most notably in South-east Asia and the Amazon basin. In these regions, deforesting the slopes allows the heavy tropical rains to wash away whatever thin and fragile soil there is, leading to severe erosion of the land.

Land Use by Continent

The proportion of productive land has reached its upper limit in Europe, and in Asia more than 80% of potential cropland is already under cultivation.

- Forest
- Permanent pasture and rough grazing
- Permanent crops and plantations
- Arable
- Non-productive

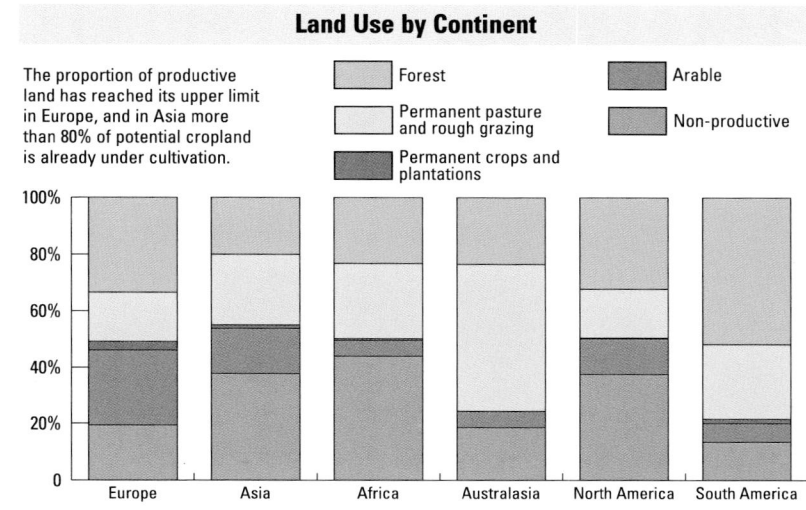

Natural Vegetation

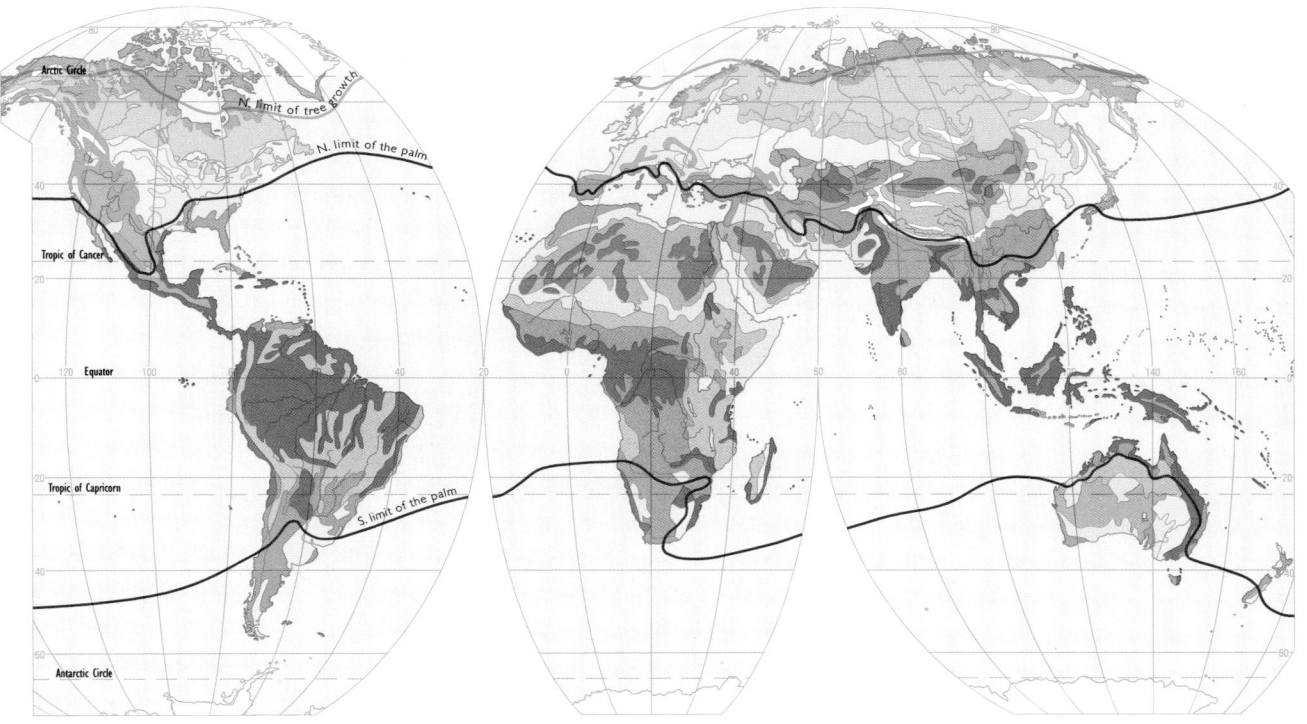

- Tropical rainforest
- Subtropical and temperate rainforest
- Monsoon woodland and open jungle
- Subtropical and temperate woodland, scrub and bush
- Tropical savanna, with low trees and bush
- Tropical savanna and grasslands
- Dry semi-desert, with shrub and grass
- Desert shrub
- Desert
- Dry steppe and shrub
- Temperate grasslands, prairie and steppe
- Mediterranean hardwood forest and scrub
- Temperate deciduous forest and meadow
- Temperate deciduous and coniferous forest
- Northern coniferous forest (taiga)
- Mountainous forest, mainly coniferous
- High plateau steppe and tundra
- Arctic tundra
- Polar and mountainous ice desert

The map illustrates the natural 'climax vegetation' of a region, as dictated by its climate and topography. In most cases, human agricultural activity has drastically altered the vegetation pattern. Western Europe, for example, lost most of its broadleaf forest many centuries ago, while elsewhere irrigation has turned some natural semi-desert into productive land. The various vegetation regions support different kinds of animals and, in an undisturbed state, they are highly developed biological communities, or biomes.

The blue line on the map represents the northern limit of tree growth, and the red lines indicate the northern and southern limits of palm growth.

The Natural Environment

Recent discoveries of life forms in some of the world's most hostile environments, such as around the black smokers along the ocean ridges, prepared the way for the announcement by NASA scientists in 1996 that they had found microfossils in a Martian meteorite. But other scientists were sceptical, believing them to be natural mineral structures and not evidence of extraterrestrial life.

Until further evidence is available, the Earth remains the only planet where we know for sure that life exists. According to the fossil record, life on Earth appeared at least 3,500 million years ago. Since then, it has evolved from its primitive beginnings to its modern biodiversity, including millions of plants, animals and micro-organisms. Living organisms have not only adapted to the environ-ment but they have also changed their environment to suit themselves. For example, the Earth's early atmosphere contained little oxygen but the emergence of multi-celled, oxygen-producing algae, around 2,000 million years ago, led to the creation of an oxygen-rich atmosphere. This enabled land animals to populate the ancient continents.

The amount of the greenhouse gas carbon dioxide in the atmosphere would steadily increase from its present 0.03% were it not for plants. Without them, the Earth's atmos-phere would, in a few million years, be similar to that of Venus, where surface temperatures reach 475°C. The Earth has evolved into a complex control system, sensing and reacting to changes and tending always to maintain the balance it has achieved.

Much discussion has centred on how that balance changes. Only recently, scientists were suggesting that we may be living in an interglacial stage of the Pleistocene Ice Age. From the 1980s, however, predictions of future climates have concentrated more on global warming, caused by pollution which has led to an increase in greenhouse gases in the atmosphere. Interference in the natural cycles that control the environment may have consequences that are hard to predict.

Furthermore, we are currently experien-cing a period of mass extinction of species, causing a rapid reduction in our planet's biodiversity. A report by the World Conser-vation Union in 1996 stated that, of the 4,327 known mammal species, 1,096 were at risk and 169 'critically endangered'.

Biodiversity in California

The photograph, left, is a false-colour satellite image of central California in the south-western United States. The large inlet of the Pacific Ocean is San Francisco Bay. San Francisco lies just below the entrance to the bay, with Oakland on the far side and San Jose to the south-east. California, nicknamed the Golden State, is the third largest state in the United States and the most populous.

Because of its varied terrain and climate, California has a wide range of diverse habitats within a relatively small area. East of the forested Coast Ranges (the grey and red areas just inland from the bay) lies the fertile Central Valley, which appears as a red and blue chequerboard. The Sierra Nevada is the red area in the top right corner. In the north-west and south-west of the state, not shown here, lie parts of the Basin and Range region, much of which is desert. It includes Death Valley, which contains the country's lowest point on land at 86 m below sea level.

Forests cover about 40% of California and they include bristlecone pines, thought to be the oldest living things on Earth, together with coastal red-woods, the world's tallest trees. Wildlife is still abundant, though some species, such as the rare California condor, are on the endangered list.

The state has achieved much to protect its biodiversity. It contains eight of the 54 national parks in the United States. Two of them, Death Valley and Joshua Tree, were designated national parks as recently as 1994, as part of a conservation measure, including the protection of large areas of wilderness in the deserts.

California has vast resources and, were it a separate nation, it would rank among the world's ten most productive in terms of the total value of its goods and services. This means that, like the United States as a whole, it has resources, which many developing countries lack, to finance conservation measures. For example, the World Conservation Union reported in 1996 that 8% of mammals were threatened in the United States, as compared with 32% in the Philippines and 44% in Madagascar, two countries where habitat destruction has been on a large scale.

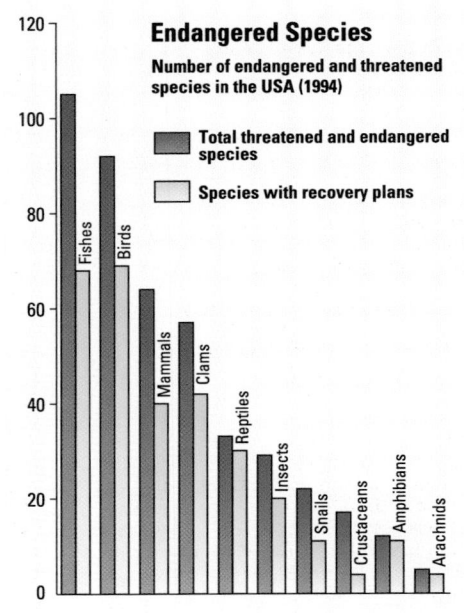

Endangered Species

Number of endangered and threatened species in the USA (1994)

- Total threatened and endangered species
- Species with recovery plans

(Categories shown: Fishes, Birds, Mammals, Clams, Reptiles, Insects, Snails, Crustaceans, Amphibians, Arachnids)

Threatened Mammals

Percentage of mammal species classified as threatened (1996). Many scientists believe we are currently experiencing a period of mass extinction of species rivalling five other periods in the past half a billion years. Among the most threatened mammals are elephants, primates and rhinoceroses.

- Over 20%
- 15 – 19.9%
- 10 – 14.9%
- Less than 10%
- No data available

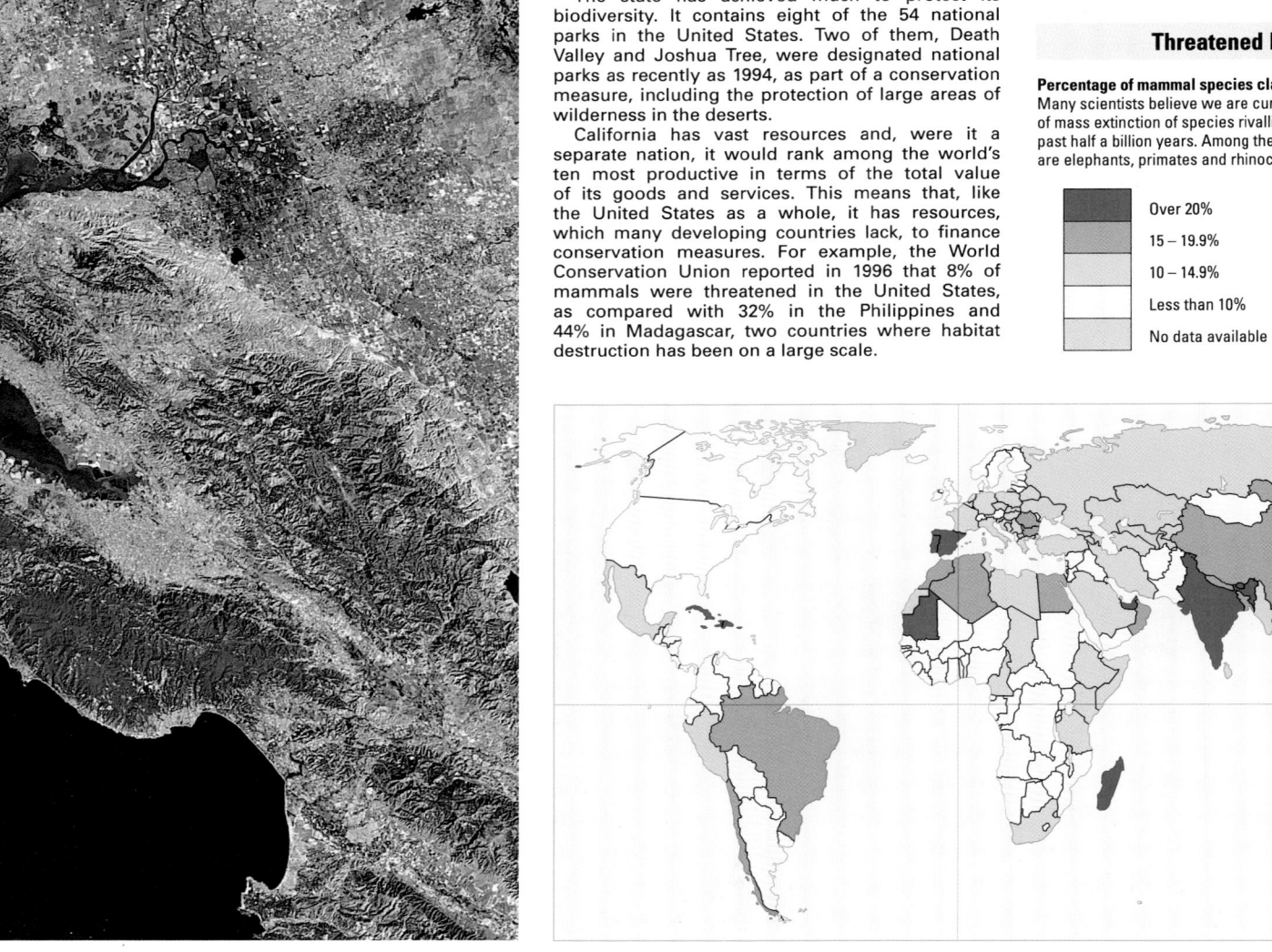

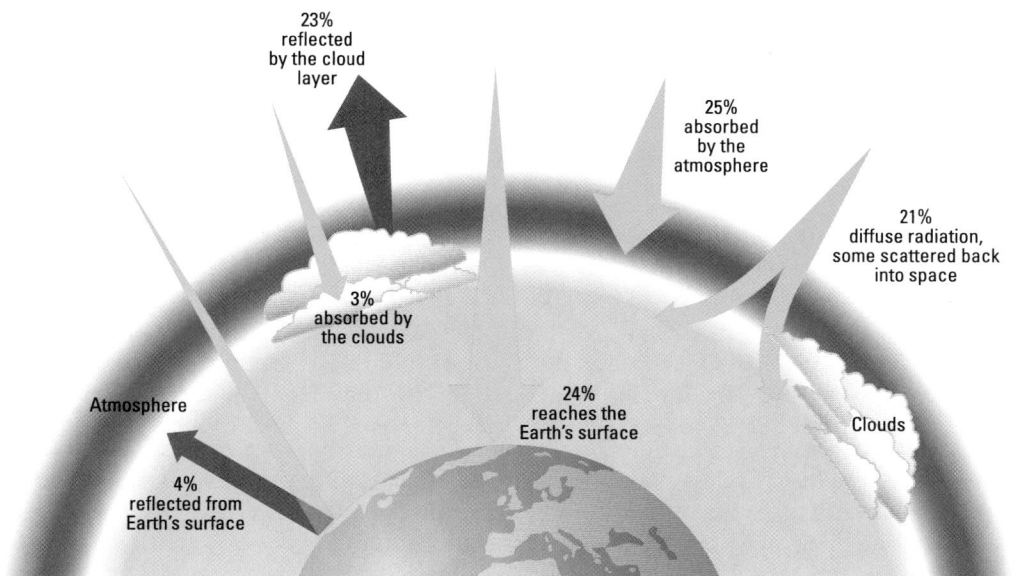

23% reflected by the cloud layer

25% absorbed by the atmosphere

3% absorbed by the clouds

21% diffuse radiation, some scattered back into space

Atmosphere

24% reaches the Earth's surface

Clouds

4% reflected from Earth's surface

The Earth's Energy Balance

Apart from a modest quantity of internal heat from its molten core, the Earth receives all of its energy from the Sun. If the planet is to remain at a constant temperature, it must reradiate exactly as much energy as it receives. Even a minute surplus would lead to a warmer Earth, a deficit to a cooler one. The temperature at which thermal equilibrium is reached depends on a multitude of interconnected factors. Two of the most important are the relative brightness of the Earth – its index of reflectivity, called the 'albedo' – and the heat-trapping capacity of the atmosphere – the celebrated 'greenhouse effect' (see below).

Because the Sun is very hot, most of its energy arrives in the form of relatively short-wave radiation: the shorter the waves, the more energy they carry. Some of the incoming energy is reflected straight back into space, exactly as it arrived; some is absorbed by the atmosphere on its way towards the surface; some is absorbed by the Earth itself. Absorbed energy heats the Earth and its atmosphere alike. But since its temperature is very much lower than that of the Sun, the outgoing energy is emitted at much longer infra-red wavelengths. Some of the outgoing radiation escapes directly into outer space; some of it is reabsorbed by the atmosphere. Atmospheric energy eventually finds its way back into space, too, after a complex series of interactions. These include the air movements we call the weather and, almost incidentally, the maintenance of life on Earth.

This diagram does not attempt to illustrate the actual mechanisms of heat exchange, but gives a reasonable account (in percentages) of what happens to 100 energy 'units'. Short-wave radiation is shown in yellow, long-wave in orange.

The Carbon Cycle

Most of the constituents of the atmosphere are kept in constant balance by complex cycles in which life plays an essential and indeed a dominant part. The control of carbon dioxide, which if left to its own devices would be the dominant atmospheric gas, is possibly the most important, although since all the Earth's biological and geophysical cycles interact and interlock, it is hard to separate them even in theory and quite impossible in practice.

The Earth has a huge supply of carbon, only a small quantity of which is in the form of carbon dioxide. Of that, around 98% is dissolved in the sea; the fraction circulating in the air amounts to only 340 parts per million of the atmosphere, where its capacity as a greenhouse gas is the key regulator of the planetary temperature. In turn, life regulates the regulator, keeping carbon dioxide concentrations below danger level.

If all life were to vanish from the Earth tomorrow, the atmosphere would begin the process of change immediately, although it might take several million years to achieve a new, inorganic stability. First, the oxygen content would begin to fall away; with no more assistance than a little solar radiation, a few electrical storms and its own high chemical potential, oxygen would steadily combine with atmospheric nitrogen and volcanic outgassing. In doing so, it would yield sufficient acid to react with carbonaceous rocks such as limestone, releasing carbon dioxide. Once carbon dioxide levels exceeded about 1%, its greenhouse power would increase disproportionately. Rising temperatures – well above the boiling point of water – would speed chemical reactions; in time, the Earth's atmosphere would consist of little more than carbon dioxide and superheated water vapour.

Living things, however, circulate carbon. They do so first by simply existing: after all, the carbon atom is the basic building block of living matter.

During life, plants absorb carbon dioxide from the atmosphere and, along with various chemicals, as soluble salts from the soil, incorporating the carbon into their structure – leaves and trunks in the case of land plants, shells in the case of plankton and the tiny creatures that feed on it. The oxygen thereby freed is added to the atmosphere, at least for a time. The carbon is returned to circulation when the plants die or is passed up the food chain to the herbivores and then the carnivores that feed on them. As organisms at each of these trophic levels die, they decay, releasing the carbon which then combines once more with the oxygen released during life. However, a small proportion of carbon, about one part in 1,000, is removed almost permanently, buried beneath mud on land or at sea, sinking as dead matter to the ocean floor. In time, it is slowly compressed into sedimentary rocks such as limestone and chalk.

But in the evolution of the Earth, nothing is quite permanent. On an even longer timescale, the planet's crustal movements force new rock upwards in mid-ocean ridges. Limestone deposits are moved, and sea levels change; ancient carbon-iferous rocks are exposed to weathering, and a little of their carbon is released to be fixed in turn by the current generation of plants.

The carbon cycle has continued quietly for an immensely long time, and without gross disturbance there is no reason why it would not continue almost indefinitely in the future. However, human beings have found a way to release fixed carbon at a rate far faster than existing global systems can recirculate it. The fossil fuels, coal, oil, gas and peat deposits, represent the work of millions of years of carbon accumulation; but it has taken only a few human generations of high-energy scavenging to endanger the entire complex regulatory cycle.

pool of CO_2 in atmosphere

combustion   photosynthesis

respiration   respiration   respiration

CO_2

CO_2

decay organisms

respiration

death

carbonification, gradual production of fossil fuels

death

decay organisms

peat

coal

oil and gas

The Greenhouse Effect

Constituting less than 1% of the atmosphere, the natural greenhouse gases (water vapour, carbon dioxide, methane, nitrous oxide and ozone) have a hugely disproportionate effect on the Earth's climate and even its habitability. Like the glass panes in a greenhouse, the gases are transparent to most incoming short-wave radiation, which passes freely to heat the planet beneath. But when the warmed Earth retransmits that energy, in the form of longer-wave infra-red radiation, the gases function as an opaque shield preventing some of it from escaping, so that the planetary surface (like the interior of a greenhouse) stays relatively hot.

Over the last 150 years, there has been a gradual increase in the levels of greenhouse gases (with the exception of water vapour which remains a constant in the system). These increases are causing alarm – global warming associated with a runaway greenhouse effect could bring disaster – and what is more, predictions suggest that there could be a further rise of 1.5–4.5°C by the year 2100. A serious reduction in the greenhouse gases would be just as damaging; a total absence of CO_2, for example, would leave the planet with a temperature roughly 33°C colder than at present.

N.B. The thickness of the Earth's atmosphere is proportionately much thinner than the peel of an apple.

Sun

Less heat escapes into space

Outgoing long-wave radiation (infra-red) is radiated back into space

Increased greenhouse gases means that more long-wave radiation is reflected back to Earth

Atmosphere

The atmosphere of the Earth gets hotter as more heat is trapped

Increased greenhouse gases act as a shield to long-wave radiation

Incoming short-wave radiation (ultraviolet) reaches the surface of the Earth

People and the Environment

In 1996, the Intergovernmental Panel on Climate Change issued a report stating that 'The balance of evidence suggests a discernible human influence on global climate through emissions of carbon dioxide and other greenhouse gases.' The report acknowledged that average global temperatures have risen by about 0.5°C since the mid-19th century, but there were still reasons for caution, such as discrepancies between measurements of temperatures around the world. Furthermore, our knowledge about how climates change of their own accord is incomplete, as is our understanding of human interference, how this varies in different parts of the world and how it differs from natural climatic variability.

Human interference with nature is nothing new, at least since people turned from hunting and gathering to agriculture more than 10,000 years ago. At first, human actions seemed to have no ill effects because the systems that regulate the global environment were able to absorb damage. But from the late 18th century, the Industrial Revolution and the population explosion have caused pollution on a scale that threatens to overwhelm the Earth's ability to cope.

The 20th century has seen many disasters, including the dumping of industrial wastes in rivers and seas, accidents at nuclear power stations, and the creation of acid rain through the release of sulphur dioxides and nitrous oxides by the burning of fossil fuels. The release of greenhouse gases are held to be the main reason for global warming, while CFCs (chlorofluorocarbons) have damaged the ozone layer in the stratosphere, the planet's screen against ultraviolet radiation.

Global warming will lead to melting ice sheets and the flooding of fertile coastal plains. Computer models suggest that it might affect ocean currents so that northwestern Europe, which owes its mild climate to the Gulf Stream, could expect bitterly cold winters. Some models have suggested that cloud cover could increase, reflecting more solar energy back into space and so start a new Ice Age.

In many tropical areas, deforestation is making productive land barren, while in the dry grasslands bordering deserts, the removal of plant cover is causing desertification. But human ingenuity can respond to this crisis in planet management.

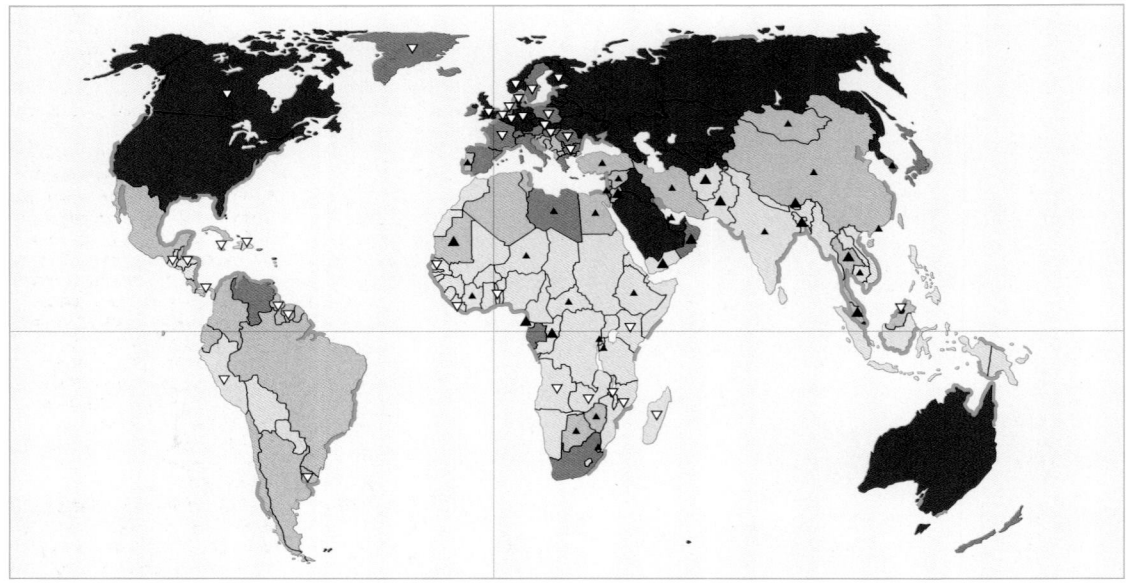

Global Warming

Carbon dioxide emissions in tonnes per person per year (latest available year)

- Over 10 tonnes of CO_2
- 5 – 10 tonnes of CO_2
- 1 – 5 tonnes of CO_2
- Under 1 tonne of CO_2

Changes in CO_2 emissions 1980–90

- ▲ Over 100% increase
- ▲ 50–100% increase
- ▽ Reduction
- ─ Coasts in danger of flooding from rising sea levels

Records of global mean surface temperatures from 1860 to the present show that 1995 was the warmest year and that nine of the ten warmest years have occurred since 1983. This evidence of global warming is attributed mainly to the Greenhouse Effect, caused by the emission of certain gases, notably carbon dioxide (CO_2), into the atmosphere since the start of the Industrial Revolution. At first, much of the CO_2 was absorbed by the oceans. However, the vast increase in fuel combustion since 1950 has led CO_2 content in the atmosphere to increase gradually from 280 parts per million to more than 350 parts per million. Despite international action to control the emissions of some greenhouse gases, CO_2 levels are still rising.

Greenhouse Power

Relative contributions to the Greenhouse Effect by the major heat-absorbing gases in the atmosphere

The chart combines greenhouse potency and volume. Carbon dioxide has a greenhouse potential of only 1, but its concentration of 350 parts per million makes it predominate. CFC 12, with 25,000 times the absorption capacity of CO_2, is present only as 0.00044 ppm.

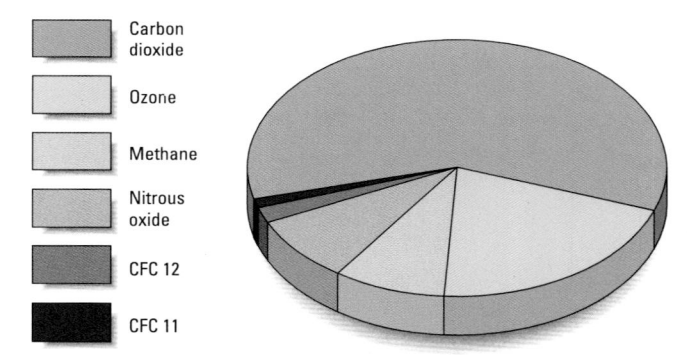

- Carbon dioxide
- Ozone
- Methane
- Nitrous oxide
- CFC 12
- CFC 11

Carbon Dioxide

Carbon dioxide released in millions of tonnes (latest available year)

USA 4,932
Former USSR 3,581
China 2,543
Japan
Germany
India
UK
Iraq
Canada
Italy
France
Mexico

Temperature Rise

The rise in average temperatures caused by carbon dioxide and other greenhouse gases (1960–2020)

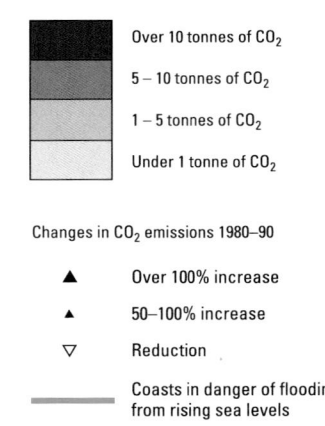

- assumes present trends continue
- assumes drastic emissions cuts in the 1990s

Recorded change | Projected changes

1960 1970 1980 1990 2000 2010 2020

°C +1.5 +1.0 +0.5 0 -0.5

The Thinning Ozone Layer

Total atmospheric ozone concentration in the southern and northern hemispheres (Dobson units, 1995)

In 1985, scientists working in Antarctica discovered a thinning of the ozone layer, commonly known as an 'ozone hole'. This caused immediate alarm because the ozone layer absorbs most of the Sun's dangerous ultraviolet radiation, which is believed to cause an increase in skin cancer, cataracts and damage to the immune system. Since 1985, ozone depletion has increased and, by 1996, the ozone hole over the South Pole was estimated to be as large as North America. The false colour images, right, show the total atmospheric ozone concentration in the southern hemisphere (in October 1995) and the northern hemisphere (in March 1995) with the ozone hole clearly identifiable at the centre. The data are from the Tiros Ozone Vertical Sounder, an instrument on the American TIROS weather satellite. The colours represent the ozone concentration in Dobson Units (DU). Normal healthy values are around 280 DU but the lowest value in the northern hemisphere reached 98 DU. Scientists agree that ozone depletion is caused by CFCs, a group of manufactured chemicals used in air conditioning systems and refrigerators. In a 1987 treaty most industrial nations agreed to phase out CFCs and a complete ban on most CFCs was agreed after the end of 1995. However, scientists believe that the chemicals will remain in the atmosphere for 50 to 100 years. As a result, ozone depletion will continue for many years.

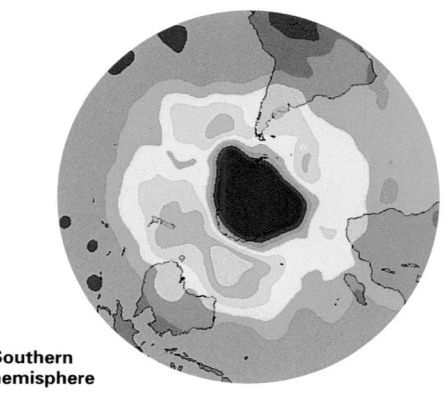

Southern hemisphere

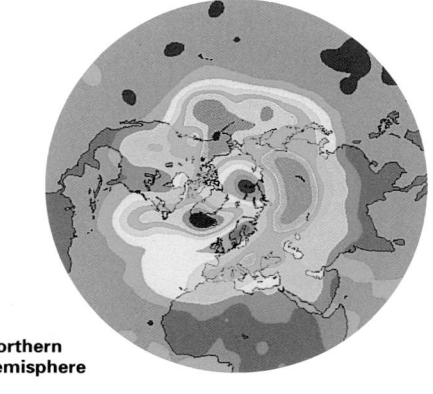

Northern hemisphere

World Pollution

Acid rain and sources of acidic emissions (latest available year)

Acid rain is caused by high levels of sulphur and nitrogen in the atmosphere. They combine with water vapour and oxygen to form acids (H_2SO_4 and HNO_3) which fall as precipitation.

 Regions where sulphur and nitrogen oxides are released in high concentrations, mainly from fossil fuel combustion

• Major cities with high levels of air pollution (including nitrogen and sulphur emissions)

Areas of heavy acid deposition

pH numbers indicate acidity, decreasing from a neutral 7. Normal rain, slightly acid from dissolved carbon dioxide, never exceeds a pH of 5.6.

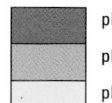
pH less than 4.0 (most acidic)
pH 4.0 to 4.5
pH 4.5 to 5.0

Areas where acid rain is a potential problem

Desertification

 Existing deserts

Areas with a high risk of desertification

Areas with a moderate risk of desertification

Former areas of rainforest

Existing rainforest

Deforestation

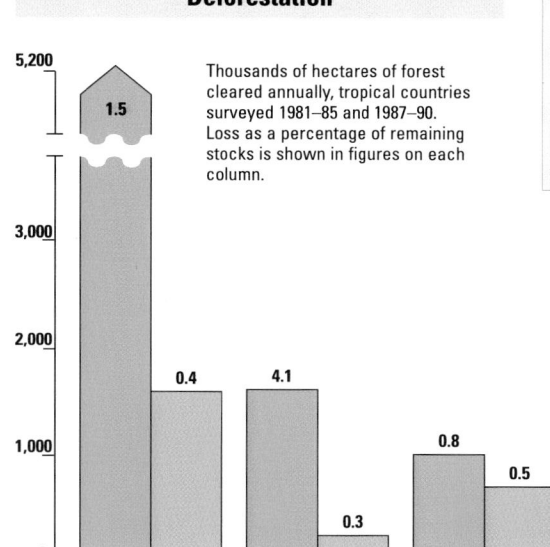

Thousands of hectares of forest cleared annually, tropical countries surveyed 1981–85 and 1987–90. Loss as a percentage of remaining stocks is shown in figures on each column.

1987–90   1981–85

Water Pollution

 Severely polluted sea areas and lakes

Polluted sea areas and lakes

Areas of frequent oil pollution by shipping

 Major oil tanker spills

▲ Major oil rig blow-outs

▼ Offshore dumpsites for industrial and municipal waste

—— Severely polluted rivers and estuaries

The most notorious tanker spillage of the 1980s occurred when the *Exxon Valdez* ran aground in Prince William Sound, Alaska, in 1989, spilling 267,000 barrels of crude oil close to shore in a sensitive ecological area. This rates as the world's 28th worst spill in terms of volume.

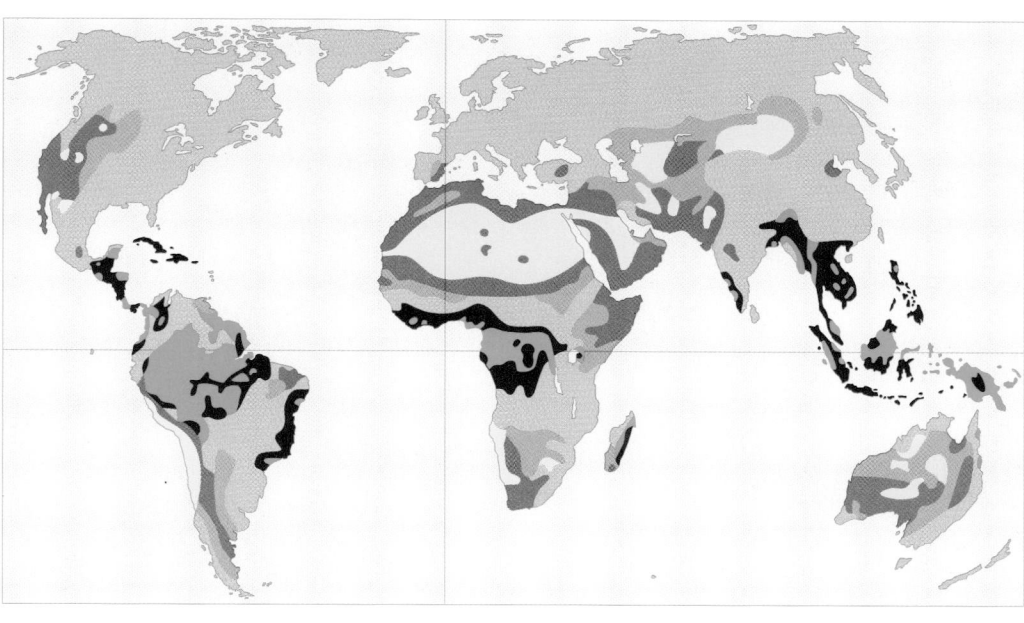

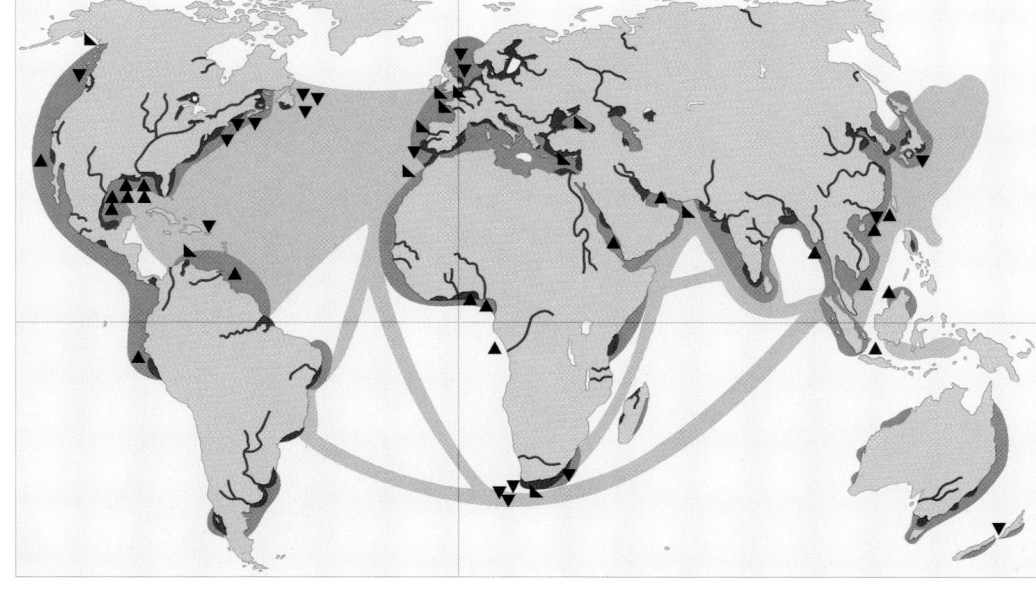

Antarctica

The vast Antarctic ice sheet, containing some 70% of the Earth's fresh water, plays a crucial role in the circulation of the atmosphere and oceans, and hence in determining the planetary climate. The frozen southern continent is also the last remaining wilderness – the largest area to remain free from human colonization.

Ever since Amundsen and Scott raced for the South Pole in 1911, various countries have pressed territorial claims over sections of Antarctica, spurred in recent years by its known and suspected mineral wealth: enough iron ore to supply the world at present levels for 200 years, large oil reserves and, probably, the biggest coal deposits on Earth.

However, the 1961 Antarctic Treaty set aside the area for peaceful uses only, guaranteeing freedom of scientific investigation, banning waste disposal and nuclear testing, and suspending the issue of territorial rights. By 1990, the original 12 signatories had grown to 25, with a further 15 nations granted observer status in subsequent deliberations. However, the Treaty itself was threatened by wrangles between different countries, government agencies and international pressure groups.

Finally, in July 1991, the belated agreement of the UK and the USA assured unanimity on a new accord to ban all mineral exploration for a further 50 years. The ban can only be rescinded if all the present signatories, plus a majority of any future adherents, agree. While the treaty has always lacked a formal mechanism for enforcement, it is firmly underwritten by public concern generated by the efforts of environmental pressure groups such as Greenpeace, which has been foremost in the campaign to have Antarctica declared a 'World Park'.

However, from the mid-1990s, the continent appeared to be under threat from global warming, which some scientists believe was the cause of the break-up of ice shelves along the Antarctic peninsula. Rising temperatures have also disturbed the breeding patterns of Adelie penguins.

Poisoned rivers, domestic sewage and oil spillage have combined in recent years to reduce the world's oceans to a sorry state of contamination, notably near the crowded coasts of industrialized nations. Shipping routes, too, are constantly affected by tanker discharges. Oil spills of all kinds, however, declined significantly during the 1980s, from a peak of 750,000 tonnes in 1979 to under 50,000 tonnes in 1990. The most notorious tanker spill of that period – when the *Exxon Valdez* (94,999 grt) ran aground in Prince William Sound, Alaska, in March 1989 – released only 267,000 barrels, a relatively small amount compared to the results of blow-outs and war damage. Over 2,500,000 barrels were spilled during the Gulf War of 1991. The worst tanker accident in history occurred in July 1979, when the *Atlantic Empress* and the Aegean Captain collided off Trinidad, polluting the Caribbean with 1,890,000 barrels of crude oil.

Population

In 8000 BC, following the development of agriculture, the world had an estimated population of 8 million and by AD 1000 it was about 300 million. The onset of the Industrial Revolution in the late 18th century led to a population explosion. The 1,000 million mark was passed by 1850, it doubled by the 1920s and doubled again to 4,000 million by 1975.

As the 20th century draws to a close, the world's population is increasing by nearly 10,000 every hour. Estimates in 1996 suggested that the population of 5,800 million will continue to increase, peaking at 10,600 million in 2080. It will then fall, reaching 10,350 million by 2100. Rapid population growth is concentrated in the developing world; the populations of some developed countries, such as Belgium and Germany, are static or have even begun to decline.

The developing world includes what the World Bank describes as low-income economies, with an average per capita GNP of US $380, and middle-income economies, with a per capita GNP of $2,520. Most developing countries are in Africa, Asia and Latin America. The developed world, made up of high-income, industrialized economies with an average per capita GNP of $23,420, contains Australasia, most of Europe and North America, and Japan in Asia.

In the poorer developing countries, a high proportion of the population is young, and they face high levels of expenditure on education and health until population growth rates start to decline. In developed countries, where the population pyramids are becoming increasingly top-heavy, expenditure on pensions and healthcare for the elderly is becoming a major social problem.

Largest Nations

The world's most populous nations, in millions (1997)

1.	China	1,210
2.	India	980
3.	USA	268
4.	Indonesia	204
5.	Brazil	160
6.	Russia	148
7.	Pakistan	136
8.	Japan	126
9.	Bangladesh	124
10.	Nigeria	118
11.	Mexico	97
12.	Germany	82
13.	Vietnam	77
14.	Philippines	74
15.	Iran	70
16.	Turkey	64
17.	Egypt	63
18.	Thailand	61
19.	France	59
20.	UK	59
21.	Ethiopia	59
22.	Italy	58
23.	Ukraine	52
24.	Burma (Myanmar)	48

Crowded Nations

Population per square kilometre (1997), excluding nations of less than 1 million

1.	Singapore	5,246
2.	Bangladesh	953
3.	Taiwan	603
4.	Mauritius	569
5.	Netherlands	469
6.	South Korea	466
7.	Puerto Rico	432
8.	Belgium	335
9.	Japan	334
10.	India	330
11.	Lebanon	313
12.	Sri Lanka	289
13.	El Salvador	287
14.	Israel	286
15.	Rwanda	284
16.	Haiti	269
17.	Trinidad & Tobago	253
18.	Philippines	247
19.	UK	243
20.	Jamaica	240

Population Density

Inhabitants per square kilometre

- Over 200
- 100 – 200
- 50 – 100
- 25 – 50
- 6 – 25
- 3 – 6
- 1 – 3
- Under 1

Urban population

- ■ Over 10,000,000
- ● 5,000,000 – 10,000,000
- • 1,000,000 – 5,000,000

Places marked are conurbations, not city limits; San Francisco itself, for example, has an official population of less than a million.

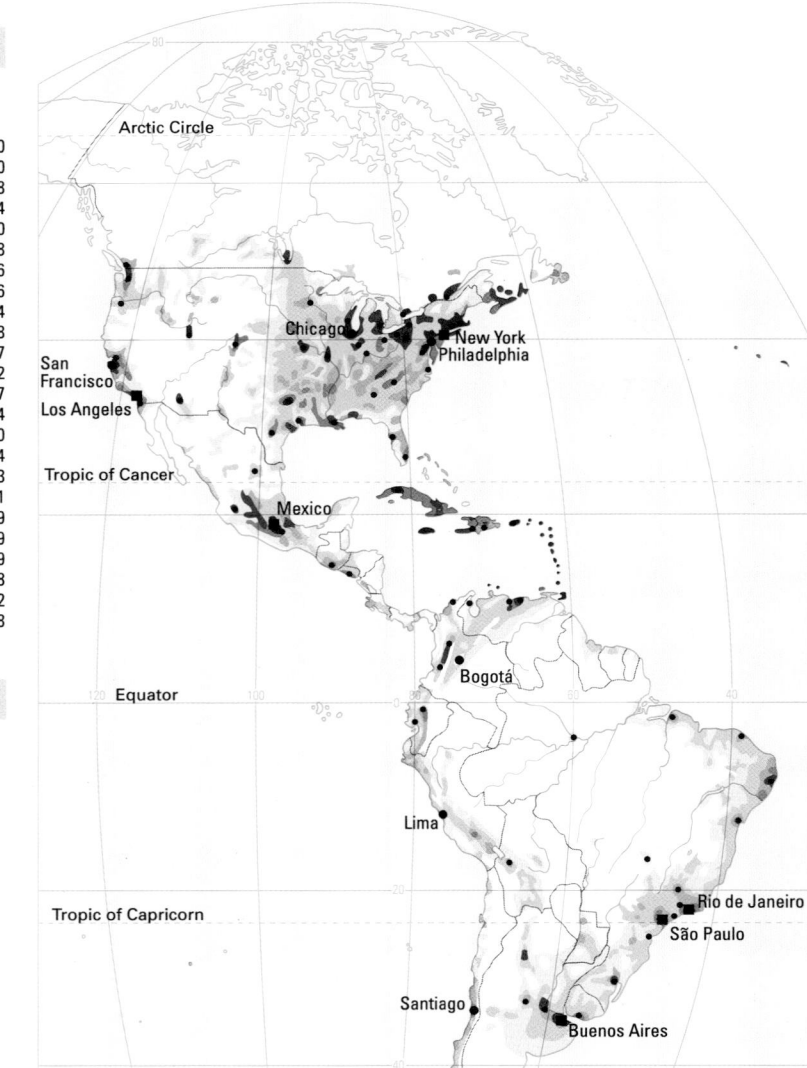

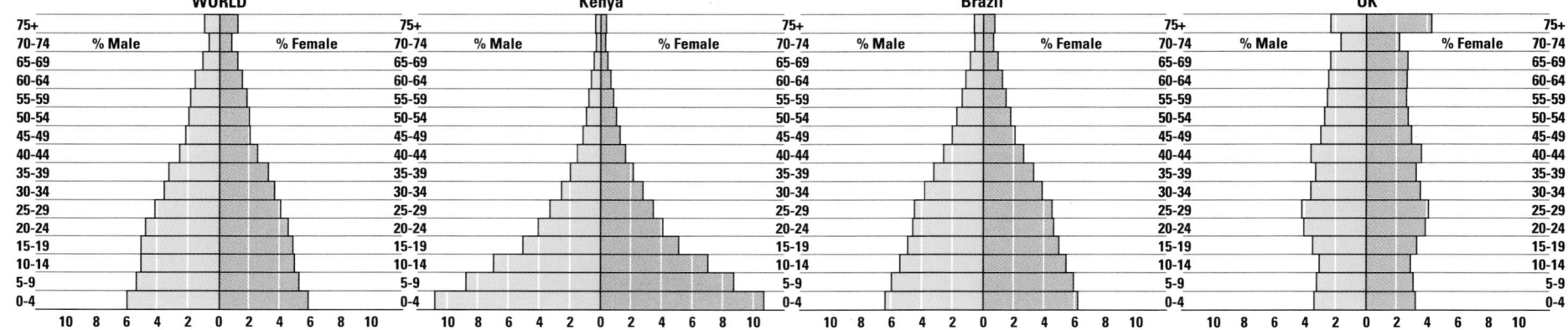

WORLD	Kenya	Brazil	UK

Age groups: 75+, 70-74, 65-69, 60-64, 55-59, 50-54, 45-49, 40-44, 35-39, 30-34, 25-29, 20-24, 15-19, 10-14, 5-9, 0-4 (% Male / % Female)

Rates of Growth

The world population doubled between 1950 and 1990. Small rates of population growth lead to dramatic increases over two or three generations. The table below translates annual percentage growth into the number of years required to double a population.

% change	Doubling time
0.5	139.0
1.0	69.7
1.5	46.6
2.0	35.0
2.5	28.1
3.0	23.4
3.5	20.1
4.0	17.7

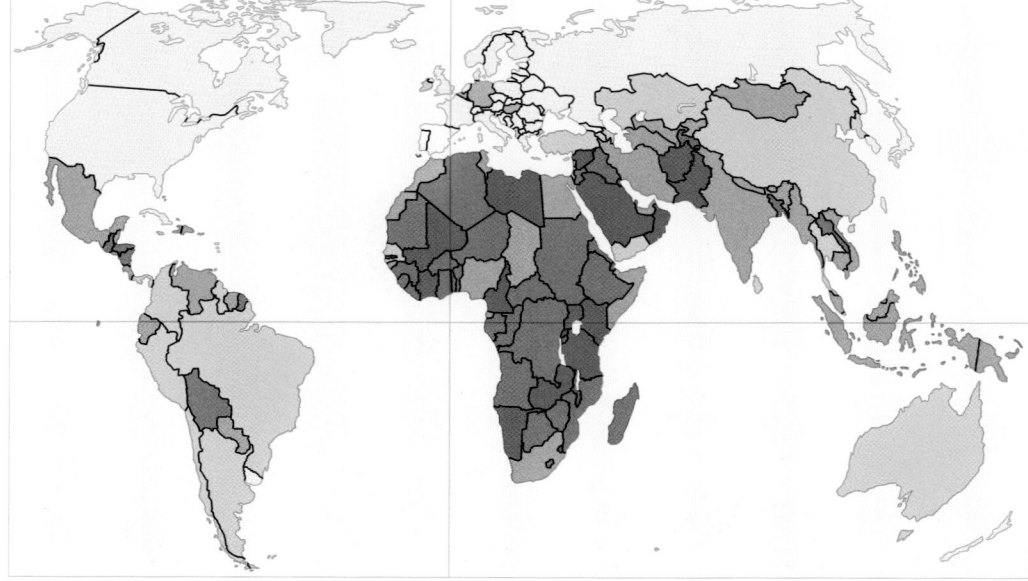

Population Change 1990–2000

The predicted population change for the years 1990–2000

- Over 40% population gain
- 30 – 40% population gain
- 20 – 30% population gain
- 10 – 20% population gain
- 0 – 10% population gain
- No change or population loss

Top 5 countries		Bottom 5 countries	
Kuwait	+75.9%	Belgium	−0.1%
Namibia	+62.5%	Hungary	−0.2%
Afghanistan	+60.1%	Grenada	−2.4%
Mali	+55.5%	Germany	−3.2%
Tanzania	+54.6%	Tonga	−3.2%

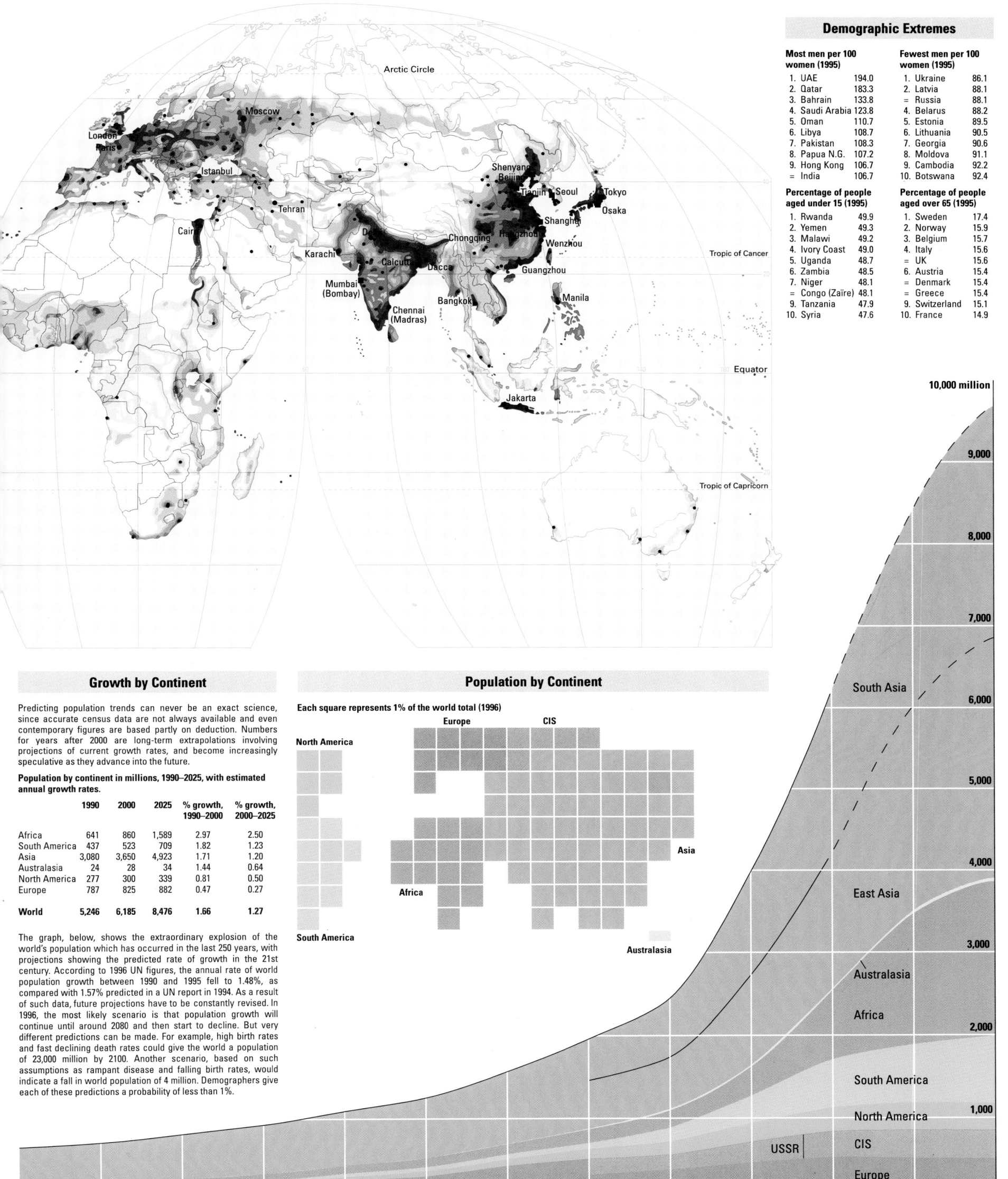

Arctic Circle

Moscow

London
Paris

Istanbul

Tehran

Cairo

Shenyang
Beijing
Tianjin Seoul Tokyo
Osaka
Shanghai
Chongqing Hangzhou
Wenzhou
Guangzhou

Karachi

Mumbai
(Bombay)
Calcutta Dacca

Chennai
(Madras)
Bangkok Manila

Tropic of Cancer

Equator

Jakarta

Tropic of Capricorn

Demographic Extremes

Most men per 100 women (1995)		Fewest men per 100 women (1995)	
1. UAE	194.0	1. Ukraine	86.1
2. Qatar	183.3	2. Latvia	88.1
3. Bahrain	133.8	= Russia	88.1
4. Saudi Arabia	123.8	4. Belarus	88.2
5. Oman	110.7	5. Estonia	89.5
6. Libya	108.7	6. Lithuania	90.5
7. Pakistan	108.3	7. Georgia	90.6
8. Papua N.G.	107.2	8. Moldova	91.1
9. Hong Kong	106.7	9. Cambodia	92.2
= India	106.7	10. Botswana	92.4

Percentage of people aged under 15 (1995)		Percentage of people aged over 65 (1995)	
1. Rwanda	49.9	1. Sweden	17.4
2. Yemen	49.3	2. Norway	15.9
3. Malawi	49.2	3. Belgium	15.7
4. Ivory Coast	49.0	4. Italy	15.6
5. Uganda	48.7	= UK	15.6
6. Zambia	48.5	6. Austria	15.4
7. Niger	48.1	= Denmark	15.4
= Congo (Zaïre)	48.1	= Greece	15.4
9. Tanzania	47.9	9. Switzerland	15.1
10. Syria	47.6	10. France	14.9

Growth by Continent

Predicting population trends can never be an exact science, since accurate census data are not always available and even contemporary figures are based partly on deduction. Numbers for years after 2000 are long-term extrapolations involving projections of current growth rates, and become increasingly speculative as they advance into the future.

Population by continent in millions, 1990–2025, with estimated annual growth rates.

	1990	2000	2025	% growth, 1990–2000	% growth, 2000–2025
Africa	641	860	1,589	2.97	2.50
South America	437	523	709	1.82	1.23
Asia	3,080	3,650	4,923	1.71	1.20
Australasia	24	28	34	1.44	0.64
North America	277	300	339	0.81	0.50
Europe	787	825	882	0.47	0.27
World	**5,246**	**6,185**	**8,476**	**1.66**	**1.27**

The graph, below, shows the extraordinary explosion of the world's population which has occurred in the last 250 years, with projections showing the predicted rate of growth in the 21st century. According to 1996 UN figures, the annual rate of world population growth between 1990 and 1995 fell to 1.48%, as compared with 1.57% predicted in a UN report in 1994. As a result of such data, future projections have to be constantly revised. In 1996, the most likely scenario is that population growth will continue until around 2080 and then start to decline. But very different predictions can be made. For example, high birth rates and fast declining death rates could give the world a population of 23,000 million by 2100. Another scenario, based on such assumptions as rampant disease and falling birth rates, would indicate a fall in world population of 4 million. Demographers give each of these predictions a probability of less than 1%.

Population by Continent

Each square represents 1% of the world total (1996)

North America
Europe
CIS
Asia
Africa
South America
Australasia

10,000 million
9,000
8,000
7,000

South Asia

6,000

5,000

East Asia

4,000

Australasia

Africa

3,000

South America

North America

2,000

1,000

USSR
CIS

Europe

1750   1775   1800   1825   1850   1875   1900   1925   1950   1975   2000   2025   2050

Cities

Following the development of agriculture more than 10,000 years ago, people began to live in farming villages. Around 5,500 years ago, the world's first cities appeared in the lower Tigris and Euphrates valleys in Mesopotamia. Cities were founded in Ancient Egypt around 5,000 years ago and in China around 3,600 years ago. By contrast with the villages, most people in the early cities were not engaged in farming. Instead, they worked in craft industries, in government services, in religion and in trade. The cities became centres of early civilizations and, through trade, their influence spread far and wide. However, they were dependent on the surrounding farming communities for their food and other materials.

In 1750, prior to the start of the Industrial Revolution, barely 3% of the world's population lived in urban areas. By 1850, London and Paris had more than a million people, and, by 1900, 14% of the world's population lived in cities. By 1950, the world had 83 cities with more than a million people, and by 1996, there were 280. By 2015, experts predict that there will be more than 500. New York City was the only city with a population in excess of 10 million in 1950; by 2015 the experts predict 27 such cities worldwide, the majority located in the developing world.

By the end of the 20th century, more than half of the world's population was living in urban areas. Despite the rapid growth of cities in developing countries, urbanization is highest in industrialized countries. For example, 78% of the people in the United States live in urban areas, with the European Union not far behind with 77%. But in countries with low-income economies, which contained nearly 60% of the world's total population in 1996, only 28% lived in urban areas.

The rapid rate of urbanization has created problems, especially in cities which have not been able to provide enough jobs and services for the expanding population. Most new city dwellers are people from rural areas and because many of them are young there is a consequent acceleration in the rate of city population growth. In developed countries, with highly mechanized agriculture, it is population pressure that drives many people into urban areas. In developing countries, the grinding poverty of rural life and the lack of services leads to migration to urban areas.

A typical city in a developing country contains millions of people living, often illegally, in shanty towns (or 'informal settlements' in politically correct parlance), while thousands live on the streets. Yet many of these shanty towns are healthier than the industrial cities of 19th-century Europe and North America. Indeed, surveys have shown that the migrants to the cities in developing countries are less likely to face poverty than they are in rural areas, while benefiting from greater access to healthcare services and education.

Modern cities face many problems, including pollution, crime and unemployment. Yet, given competent central and local government, they are capable of generating the wealth they need to solve them, as well as making a major contribution to the economy.

The Urbanization of the Earth

City-building, 1850–2000; each white spot represents a city of at least 1 million inhabitants.

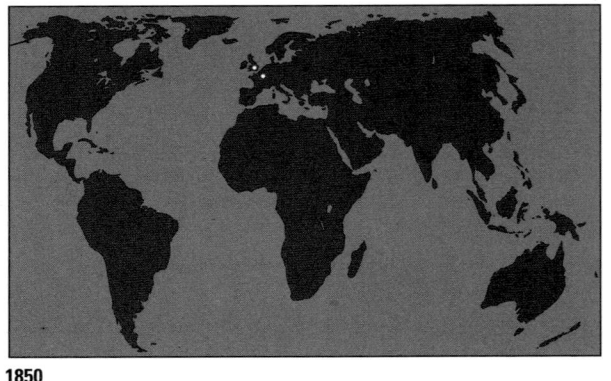
1850

1900

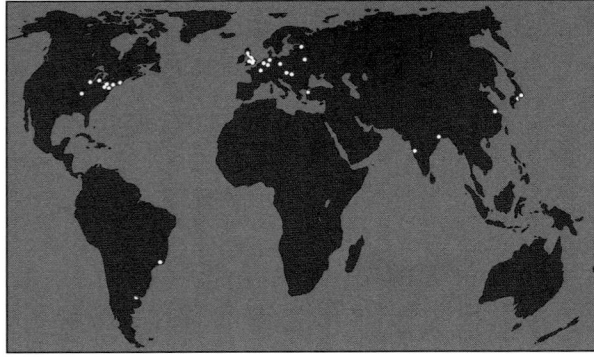
1925

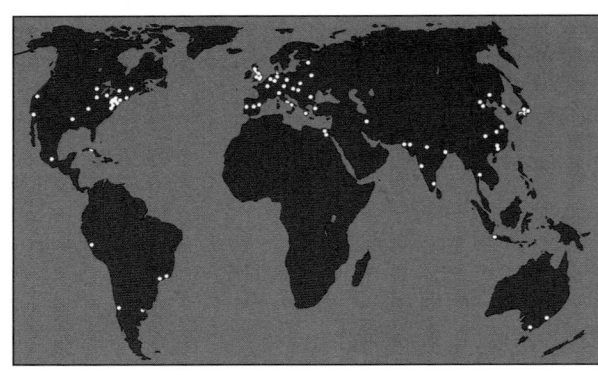
1950

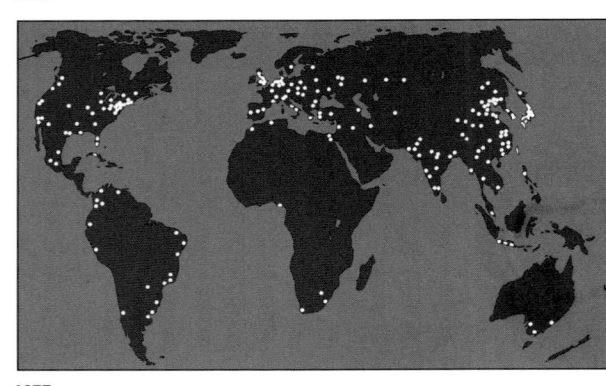
1975

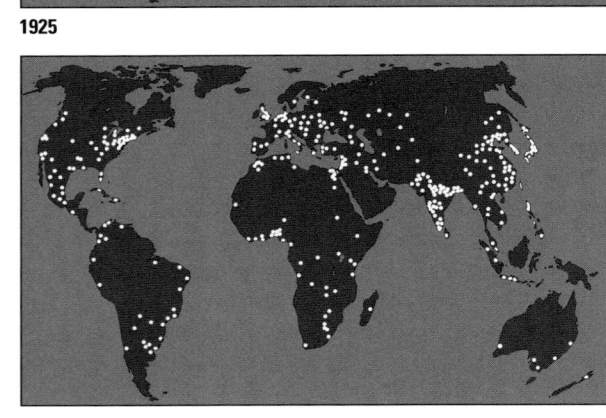
2000

Urban Population

Percentage of total population living in towns and cities (1995)

Most urbanized

Singapore	100%	Over 75%
Belgium	97%	50 – 75%
Kuwait	95%	25 – 50%
Iceland	93%	10 – 25%
Venezuela	91%	Under 10%

[UK 89%] [USA 78%]

Least urbanized

Rwanda	6%
Bhutan	8%
Burundi	9%
Nepal	12%
Malawi	12%

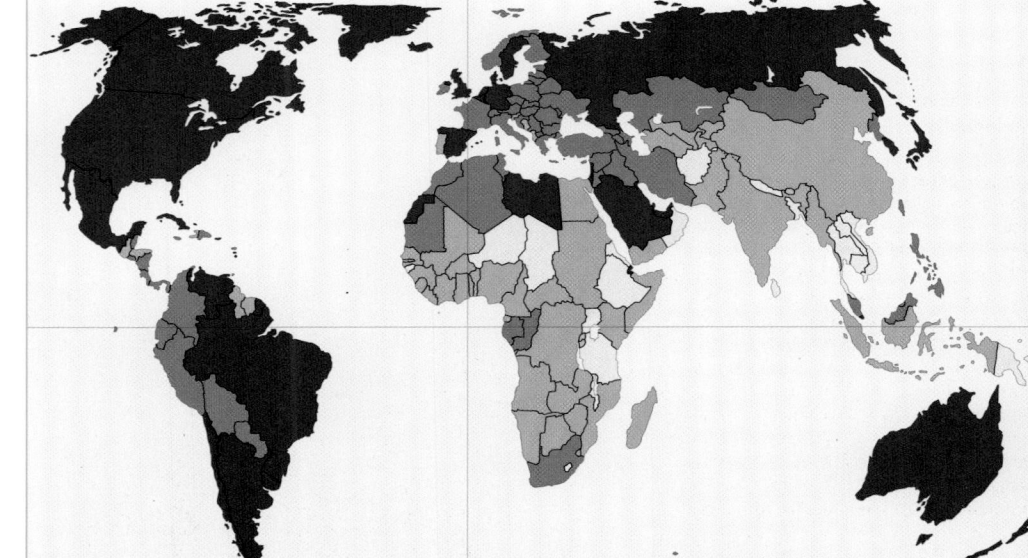

Expanding Cities

The growth of some of the world's largest cities in millions, 1950–2015.
Comparisons of city populations over time are problematic due to changes in the definition of the city limits.
These figures attempt to take such changes into consideration. The figure for London is the metropolitan region.

■ 1950   ■ 2015

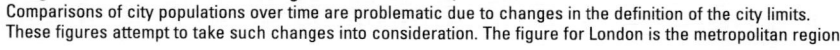
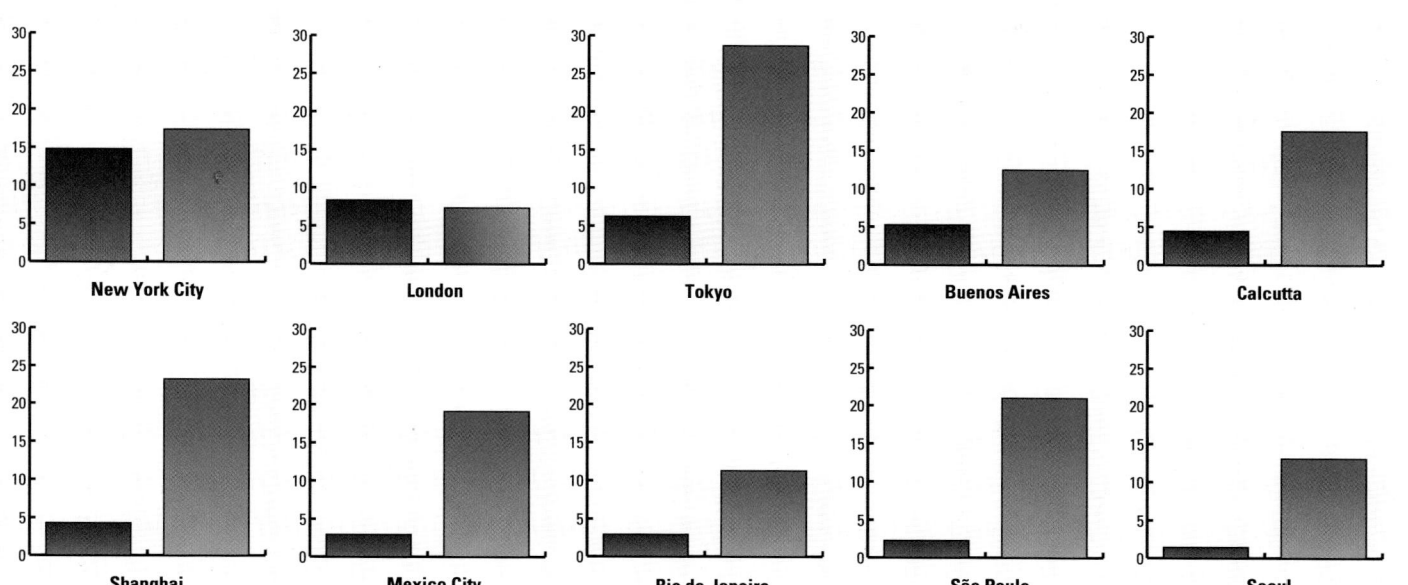

New York City   London   Tokyo   Buenos Aires   Calcutta

Shanghai   Mexico City   Rio de Janeiro   São Paulo   Seoul

The graphs show the projected growth of megacities between 1950 and 2015. New York City, the world's largest city in 1950, reached a peak in 1970, but it has experienced periods of negative growth. London's population also declined between 1970 and 1985, before resuming a modest rate of increase. In both cases, the divergence from world trends is explained in part by counting methods. Each lies at the centre of a great agglomeration, and definitions of the 'city limits' may vary over time. Also, in developing countries, many areas around the megacities which are counted as urban, are rural in character. The rates of city population growth in developing countries have also often been over-estimated. For example, it was once predicted that Calcutta would have a population of 40 million by the late 1990s. The reason why many estimates have proven incorrect is partly explained by a new trend, namely that rapid urban growth is now greatest, in some regions, in the smaller cities. For example, the main expansion in West Bengal is no longer in Calcutta, but in a rash of small cities across the state.

Cities in Danger

As the decade of the 1980s advanced, most industrial countries, alarmed by acid rain and urban smog, took significant steps to limit air pollution. Well into the 1990s, however, these controls have proved expensive to install and difficult to enforce, and clean air remains a luxury most developed as well as developing cities must live without.

Those taking part in the United Nations' Global Environment Monitoring System (see right) frequently show dangerous levels of pollutants ranging from soot to sulphur dioxide and photo-chemical smog; air in the majority of cities without such sampling equipment is likely to be at least as bad. Traffic, a major source of air pollution worldwide, loses Thailand's workforce 44 working days each year.

Urban Air Pollution

The world's most polluted cities: number of days each year when sulphur dioxide levels exceeded the WHO threshold of 150 micrograms per cubic metre (averaged over 4 to 15 years, 1970s – 1980s)

Sulphur dioxide is the main pollutant associated with industrial cities. According to the World Health Organization, more than seven days in a year above 150 μg per cubic metre bring a serious risk of respiratory disease: at least 600 million people live in urban areas where SO_2 concentrations regularly reach damaging levels.

Manila, Philippines
Calcutta, India
Milan, Italy
Zagreb, Croatia
Guangzhou, China
Madrid, Spain
Beijing, China
Xian, China
Seoul, South Korea
Tehran, Iran
Shenyang, China

120   90   60   30

Urban Housing Needs

Proportion of the population living in squatter settlements and the number of homeless per thousand, for selected cities (1993)

Urbanization in most developing countries has been proceeding so rapidly that local governments have been unable to provide the necessary services and housing. In some cities, many people find their homes in squatter settlements, frequently without power, water and sanitation. Yet these communities are often a dynamic part of the city's economy, while their inhabitants sometimes take all kinds of initiatives, including the setting up of their own local government and self-help associations. Some of the world's richest cities also have a homeless underclass, although calculating the numbers of people involved is problematic. Yet it is the case that homelessness and unemployment are currently affecting an increasing number of people in the developed world.

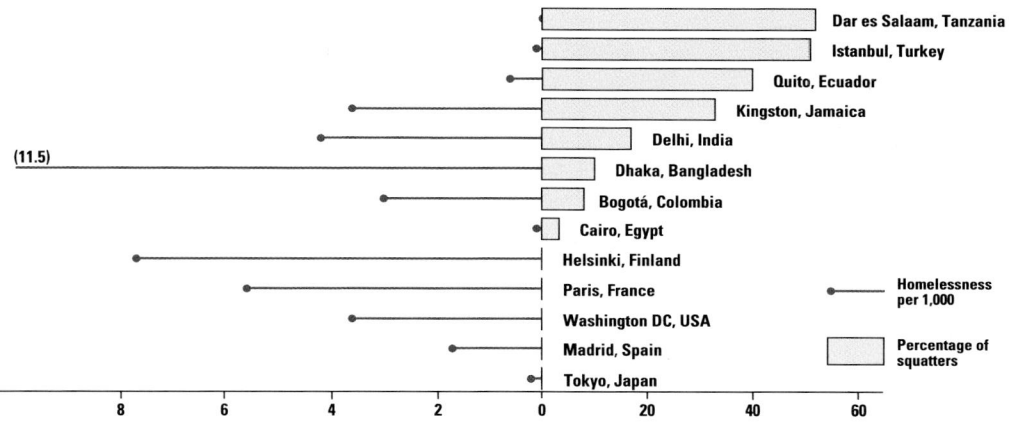

Dar es Salaam, Tanzania
Istanbul, Turkey
Quito, Ecuador
Kingston, Jamaica
Delhi, India
Dhaka, Bangladesh
Bogotá, Colombia
Cairo, Egypt
Helsinki, Finland
Paris, France
Washington DC, USA
Madrid, Spain
Tokyo, Japan

(11.5)

Homelessness per 1,000
Percentage of squatters

8   6   4   2   0   20   40   60

Largest Cities

By early next century for the first time in history, the majority of the world's population will live in cities. Below is a list of all the cities with more than 10 million inhabitants, based on estimates for the year 2015.*

1.	Tokyo–Yokohama	28.7
2.	Bombay	27.4
3.	Lagos	24.1
4.	Shanghai	23.2
5.	Jakarta	21.5
6.	São Paulo	21.0
7.	Karachi	20.6
8.	Beijing	19.6
9.	Dhaka	19.2
10.	Mexico City	19.1
11.	Calcutta	17.6
12.	Delhi	17.5
13.	New York City	17.4
14.	Tianjin	17.1
15.	Manila	14.9
16.	Cairo	14.7
17.	Los Angeles	14.5
18.	Seoul	13.1
19.	Buenos Aires	12.5
20.	Istanbul	12.1
21.	Rio de Janeiro	11.3
22.	Lahore	10.9
23.	Hyderabad	10.6
24.	Bangkok	10.4
25.	Osaka	10.2
26.	Lima	10.1
27.	Tehran	10.0

City populations are based on urban agglomerations rather than legal city limits. In some cases where two adjacent cities have merged into one concentration, such as Tokyo–Yokohama, they have been regarded as a single unit.

* For a list of current city estimates, see page XI.

Urban Advantages

Despite overcrowding and poor housing, living standards in the developing world's cities are almost invariably better than in the surrounding countryside. Resources – financial, material and administrative – are concentrated in the towns, which are usually also the centres of political activity and pressure. Governments – frequently unstable, and rarely established on a solid democratic base – are usually more responsive to urban discontent than rural misery.

In many countries, especially in Africa, food prices are kept artificially low, appeasing underemployed urban masses at the expense of agricultural development. The imbalance encourages further cityward migration, helping to account for the astonishing rate of post-1950 urbanization and putting great strain on the ability of many nations to provide even modest improvements for their people.

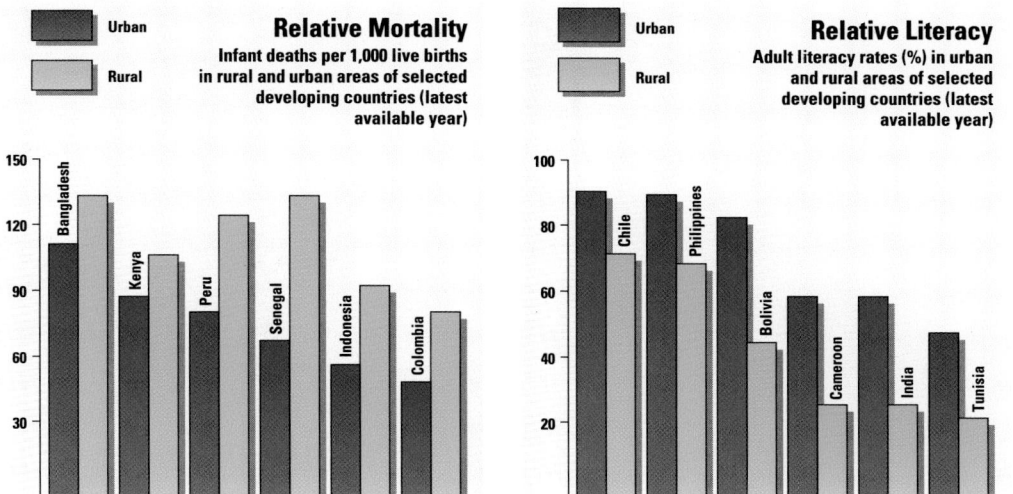

■ Urban   ■ Rural

Relative Mortality
Infant deaths per 1,000 live births in rural and urban areas of selected developing countries (latest available year)

Bangladesh   Kenya   Peru   Senegal   Indonesia   Colombia

150   120   90   60   30

■ Urban   ■ Rural

Relative Literacy
Adult literacy rates (%) in urban and rural areas of selected developing countries (latest available year)

Chile   Philippines   Bolivia   Cameroon   India   Tunisia

100   80   60   40   20

The Human Family

Racial, language and religious differences have led to appalling acts of inhumanity throughout history. Yet strictly speaking, all human beings belong to one species, *Homo sapiens*, which has no subspecies. The differences between the three racial types which most people identify – namely Caucasoid, Mongoloid and Negroid – reflect not so much evolutionary differences as long periods of separation.

Migration has recently mingled the various groups to an unprecedented extent, and most nations now have some degree of racial mixing. For example, the United States has often been called a melting pot, because of the large numbers of people from various geographical locations which make up the population. The country has

no official language but, until recently, English was spoken by the vast majority of the people. But in recent years, some of the immigrants from Mexico, Cuba and other parts of Latin America have not learned English and speak only Spanish. This development disturbs those Americans who believe that the use of English binds the nation together, and several states have passed laws stating that English is their only official language.

Language is fundamental to human culture and any particular language is almost the definition of that particular culture. Because definitions of languages vary, estimates of the total number range from 3,000 to 6,000, although most are spoken by only a few people. The world's languages

are grouped into families, the largest of which are the Indo-European and Sino-Tibetan. Chinese, a Sino-Tibetan language, is spoken by more people as a first language than any other. English, an Indo-European tongue, ranks second, but it is the leading international language, because so many people speak it as their second tongue.

Like language, religion encourages cohesion in single human groups and it satisfies a deep human need by assigning people a place in a divinely ordered world. Religion is a way in which a culture can express its individuality. For example, the rise of Islamic fundamentalism in the late 20th century is partly an expression of resentment that secular Western values are being imposed on Muslims.

World Migration

The greatest voluntary migration was the colonization of North America by 30–35 million European settlers during the 19th century. The greatest forced migration involved 9–11 million Africans taken as slaves to America between 1550 and 1860. The migrations shown on the map below are mostly international, as population movements within borders are not usually recorded. Many of the statistics are necessarily estimates as so many refugees and migrant workers enter countries illegally and unrecorded. Emigrants may have a variety of motives for leaving, thus making it difficult to distinguish between voluntary and involuntary migrations.

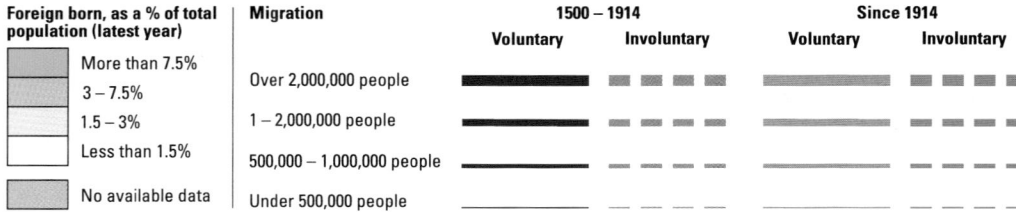

Foreign born, as a % of total population (latest year)
- More than 7.5%
- 3 – 7.5%
- 1.5 – 3%
- Less than 1.5%
- No available data

Migration
- Over 2,000,000 people
- 1 – 2,000,000 people
- 500,000 – 1,000,000 people
- Under 500,000 people

	1500 – 1914		Since 1914	
	Voluntary	Involuntary	Voluntary	Involuntary

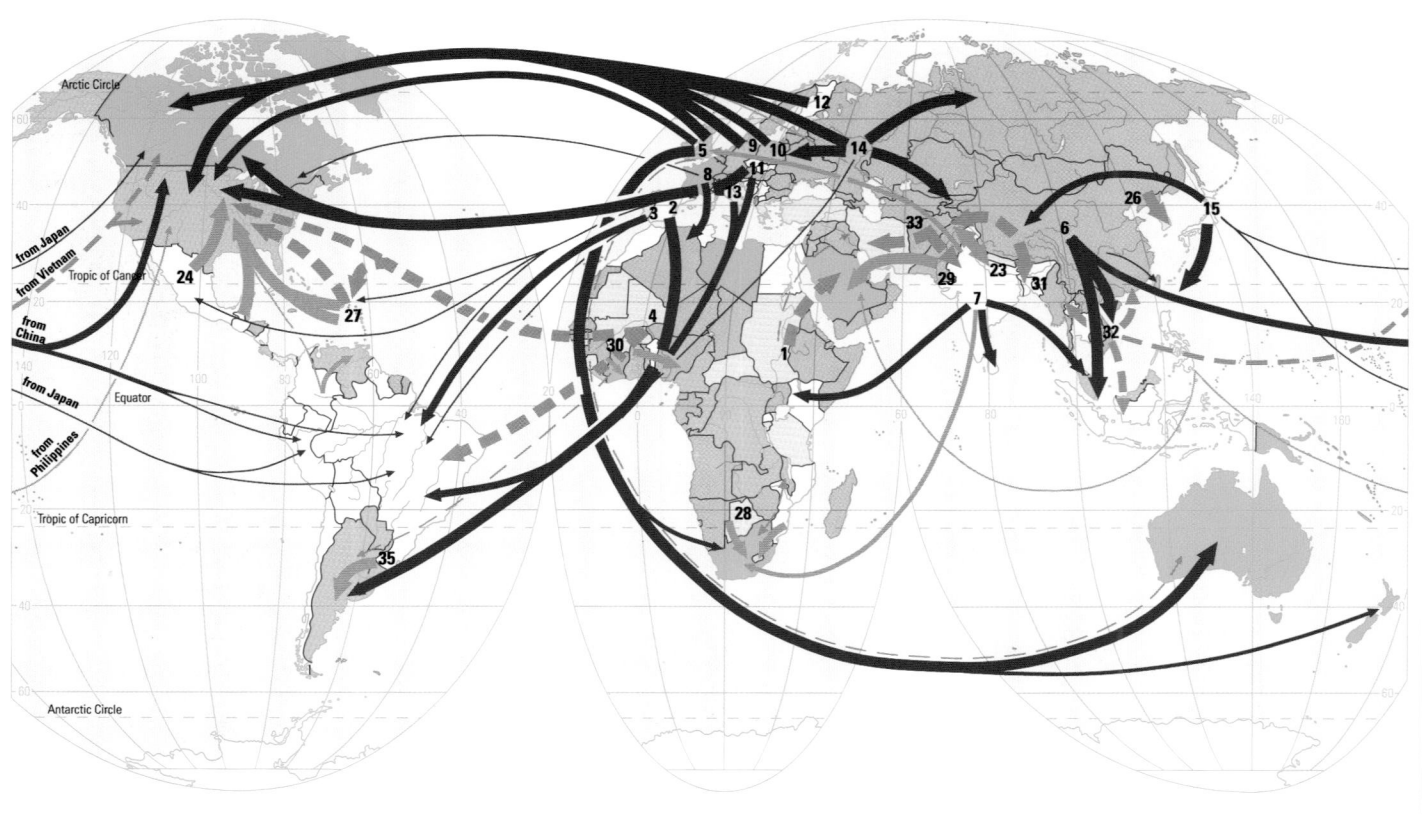

Europe Migrations since 1918

Middle East Migrations since 1945

Building the USA

So starts Emma Lazarus's poem 'The New Colossus', inscribed on the Statue of Liberty. For decades the USA was the magnet that attracted millions of immigrants, notably from Central and Eastern Europe, the flow peaking in the early years of this century. By the mid-1990s the proportion of immigrants had increased again to pre-World War II rates. In 1993/4, net immigration accounted for 30% of US population growth. Of the 904,000 immigrants, 40% were from Asia and 31% from Central America and the Caribbean.

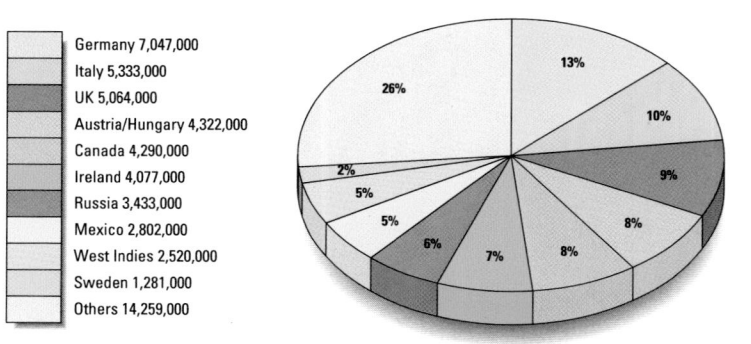

Germany 7,047,000
Italy 5,333,000
UK 5,064,000
Austria/Hungary 4,322,000
Canada 4,290,000
Ireland 4,077,000
Russia 3,433,000
Mexico 2,802,000
West Indies 2,520,000
Sweden 1,281,000
Others 14,259,000

Major world migrations since 1500 (over 1,000,000 people)
1. North and East African slaves to Arabia (4.3m)..........1500–1900
2. Spanish to South and Central America (2.3m)............1530–1914
3. Portuguese to Brazil (1.4m) 1530–1914
4. West African slaves to South America (4.6m)............1550–1860
   to Caribbean (4m) 1580–1860
   to North/Central America (1m)...1650–1820
5. British and Irish to North America (13.5m) 1620–1914
   to Australasia and
   South Africa (3m)...............1790–1914
6. Chinese to South-east Asia (22m) 1820–1914
   to North America (1m) 1880–1914
7. Indian migrant workers (3m) 1850–1914
8. French to North Africa (1.5m) 1850–1914
9. Germans to North America (5m) 1850–1914
10. Poles to North America (3.6m) 1850–1914
11. Austro-Hungarians to North America (3.2m) 1850–1914
    to Western Europe (3.4m).......1850–1914
    to South America (1.8m)..........1850–1914
12. Scandinavians to North America (2.7m) 1850–1914
13. Italians to North America (5m) 1860–1914
    to South America (3.7m) 1860–1914
14. Russians to North America (2.2m) 1850–1914
    to Western Europe (2.2m)................1880–1914
    to Siberia (6m) 1880–1914
    to Central Asia (4m)........................1880–1914

15. Japanese to Eastern Asia, South-east Asia
    and America (8m)...1900–1914
16. Poles to Western Europe (1m) 1920–1940
17. Greeks and Armenians from Turkey (1.6m) 1922–1923
18. European Jews to extermination camps (5m).............1940–1944
19. Turks to Western Europe (1.9m) 1940–
20. Yugoslavs to Western Europe (2m) 1940–
21. Germans to Western Europe (9.8m) 1945–1947
22. Palestinian refugees (2m) 1947–
23. Indian and Pakistani refugees (15m) 1947
24. Mexicans to North America (9m) 1950–
25. North Africans to Western Europe (1.1m) 1950–
26. Korean refugees (5m)..1950–1954
27. Latin Americans and West Indians to
    North America (4.7m)......................................1960–
28. Migrant workers to South Africa (1.5m) 1960–
29. Indians and Pakistanis to The Gulf (2.4m).................1970–
30. Migrant workers to Nigeria and Ivory Coast (3m) 1970–
31. Bangladeshi and Pakistani refugees (2m) 1972
32. Vietnamese and Cambodian refugees (1.5m) 1975–
33. Afghan refugees (6.1m) 1979–
34. Egyptians to The Gulf and Libya (2.9m) 1980–
35. Migrant workers to Argentina (2m) 1980–
36. Mozambique refugees (1.7m) 1985–
37. Yugoslav/Balkan refugees (1.7m) 1992–
38. Rwanda/Burundi refugees (2.6m) 1994–

Predominant Languages

	INDO-EUROPEAN FAMILY		AFRO-ASIATIC FAMILY		ALTAIC FAMILY		AUSTRO-ASIATIC FAMILY
1	Balto-Slavic group (incl. Russian, Ukrainian)	11	Semitic group (incl. Arabic)	18	Turkic group	25	Mon-Khmer group
2	Germanic group (incl. English, German)	12	Kushitic group	19	Mongolian group	26	Munda group
3	Celtic group	13	Berber group	20	Tungus-Manchu group	27	Vietnamese
4	Greek			21	Japanese and Korean		
5	Albanian	14	KHOISAN FAMILY			28	DRAVIDIAN FAMILY (incl. Telugu, Tamil)
6	Iranian group				SINO-TIBETAN FAMILY		
7	Armenian	15	NIGER-CONGO FAMILY	22	Sinitic (Chinese) languages	29	AUSTRONESIAN FAMILY (incl. Malay-Indonesian)
8	Romance group (incl. Spanish, Portuguese, French, Italian)	16	NILO-SAHARAN FAMILY	23	Tibetic-Burmic languages		
9	Indo-Aryan group (incl. Hindi, Bengali, Urdu, Punjabi, Marathi)						
10	CAUCASIAN FAMILY	17	URALIC FAMILY	24	TAI FAMILY	30	OTHER LANGUAGES

Official Languages

Language	Total population	World %
English	1,400m	27.0%
Chinese	1,070m	19.1%
Hindi	700m	13.5%
Spanish	280m	5.4%
Russian	270m	5.2%
French	220m	4.2%
Arabic	170m	3.3%
Portuguese	160m	3.0%
Malay	160m	3.0%
Bengali	150m	2.9%
Japanese	120m	2.3%

Languages form a kind of tree of development, splitting from a few ancient proto-tongues into branches that have grown apart and further divided with the passage of time. English and Hindi, for example, both belong to the great Indo-European family, although the relationship is only apparent after much analysis and comparison with non-Indo-European languages such as Chinese or Arabic; Hindi is part of the Indo-Aryan subgroup, whereas English is a member of Indo-European's Germanic branch; French, another Indo-European tongue, traces its descent through the Latin, or Romance, branch. A few languages – Basque is one example – have no apparent links with any other, living or dead. Most modern languages, of course, have acquired enormous quantities of vocabulary from each other.

Distribution of Living Languages

The figures refer to the number of languages currently in use in the regions shown.

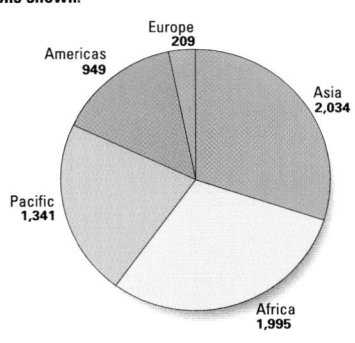

Europe 209
Americas 949
Asia 2,034
Pacific 1,341
Africa 1,995

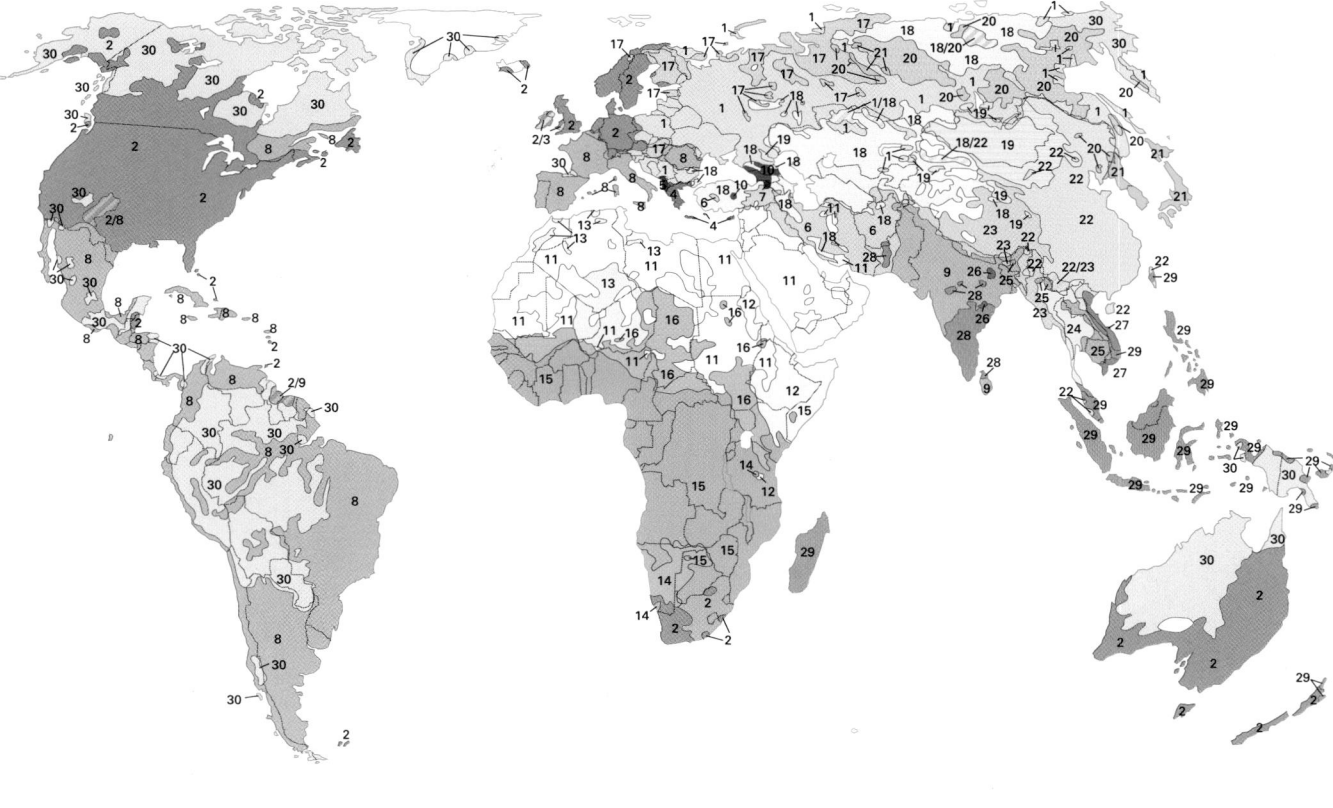

Predominant Religions

- ▲ Roman Catholicism
- Orthodox and other Eastern Churches
- • Protestantism
- Sunni Islam
- Shia Islam
- Buddhism
- Hinduism
- Confucianism
- ✻ Judaism
- Shintoism
- Tribal Religions

Religions are not as easily mapped as the physical contours of the land. Divisions are often blurred and frequently overlapping: most nations include people of many different faiths – or no faith at all. Some religions, like Islam and Christianity, have proselytes worldwide; others, like Hinduism and Confucianism, are restricted to a particular area, though modern migrations have taken some Indians and Chinese very far from their cultural origins. It is also difficult to show the degree to which religion controls daily life: Christian Western Europe, for example, is now far less dominated by its religion than are the Islamic nations of the Middle East. Similarly, figures for the major faiths' adherents make no distinction between nominal believers enrolled at birth and those for whom religion is a vital part of existence.

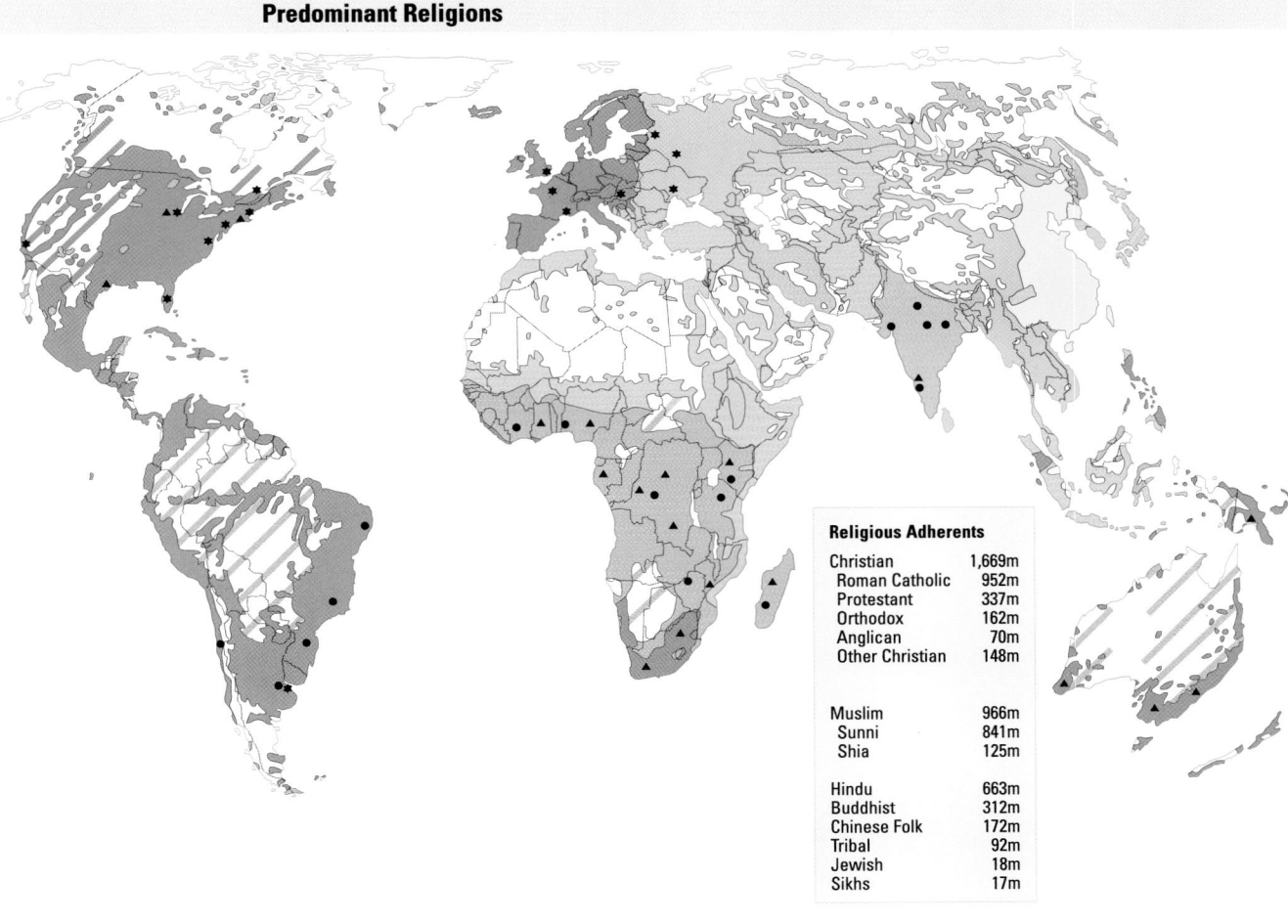

Religious Adherents

Christian	1,669m
Roman Catholic	952m
Protestant	337m
Orthodox	162m
Anglican	70m
Other Christian	148m
Muslim	966m
Sunni	841m
Shia	125m
Hindu	663m
Buddhist	312m
Chinese Folk	172m
Tribal	92m
Jewish	18m
Sikhs	17m

Conflict and Co-operation

For more information:
28 Migration
29 Religion

The 20th century has witnessed two world wars, followed by a Cold War which several times threatened to erupt into a third world war, fought with nuclear weapons. The Cold War was marked by a great number of conflicts. Some were colonial wars, as the empires of the first half of the century fell apart, some were border wars, and some were civil wars. All the wars have caused great suffering among civilians, many of whom were forced to join the ranks of the world's refugees.

In the late 1980s, many people hoped that the end of the Cold War, following the collapse of Communist regimes in the former Soviet Union and Eastern Europe, would herald a new era of international stability. Instead, old ethnic and religious antagonisms surfaced in many areas, leading to civil war in such places as Chechenia, in Russia, and the former Yugoslavia. Nationalist rivalries, suppressed under Communist rule, replaced ideological factors as the major cause of conflict.

War is a very human activity, with no real equivalent in any other species. Yet humans also function well when they co-operate. Evolution has made this so. Hunter-gatherers in co-operative bands were far more effective than animals that prowled. Agriculture, urbanization and industrialization all depend on the ability of humans to co-operate.

The creation of the United Nations in 1945 held out hope that the world's nations, tired of war, would have the means to control humanity's aggressive instincts. Although the UN lacks the power to halt conflicts, it has often helped to achieve negotiation. Economic pressures have led to another kind of co-operation, the creation of common markets and economic unions, such as ASEAN in South-east Asia, the European Union and NAFTA in North America.

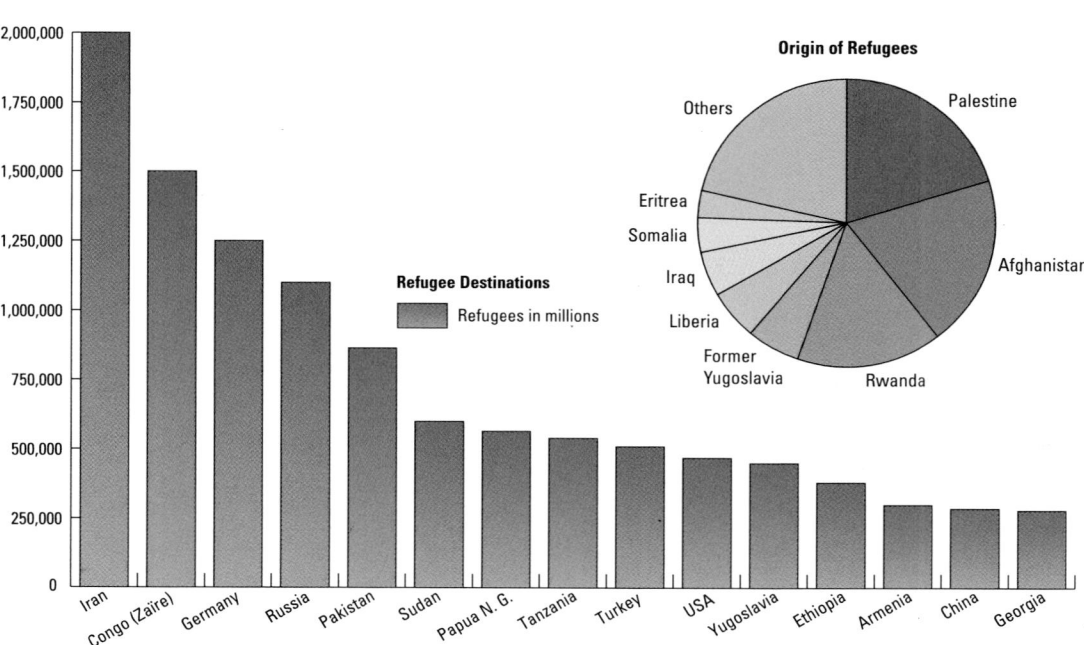

The World's Refugees

Refugees by host nation (bar-chart, left) and by nation of origin (pie-chart, left) (1995). The source is the United Nations High Commission for Refugees (UNHCR). The 3.2 million Palestinian refugees living in Jordan, Syria, Lebanon, Gaza and the West Bank fall under the mandate of United Nations Relief and Works Agency (UNRWA) and are not included on the bar-chart.

The pie-chart shows the origins of the world's refugees, while the bar-chart below shows their destinations. According to the United Nations High Commission for Refugees (UNHCR) in 1995 there were 14.5 million refugees. However, the UNHCR definition of a refugee, 'a person who has left or remains outside their own country because they have a well-founded fear of persecution, or because their safety is threatened by events seriously disturbing public order', does not include people who are in a refugee-like situation but who have not been formally recognized. In 1995, there were a further 3.5 million of these people worldwide and a further 4.5 million people who were internally displaced.

All but a few who cross international boundaries seek asylum in neighbouring countries, which are often the least equipped to deal with them. Lacking any rights or power, they frequently become an unwelcome burden to their hosts. Usually, the best any refugee can hope for is rudimentary food and shelter in temporary camps. Many Palestinians have been forced to live in camps since 1948.

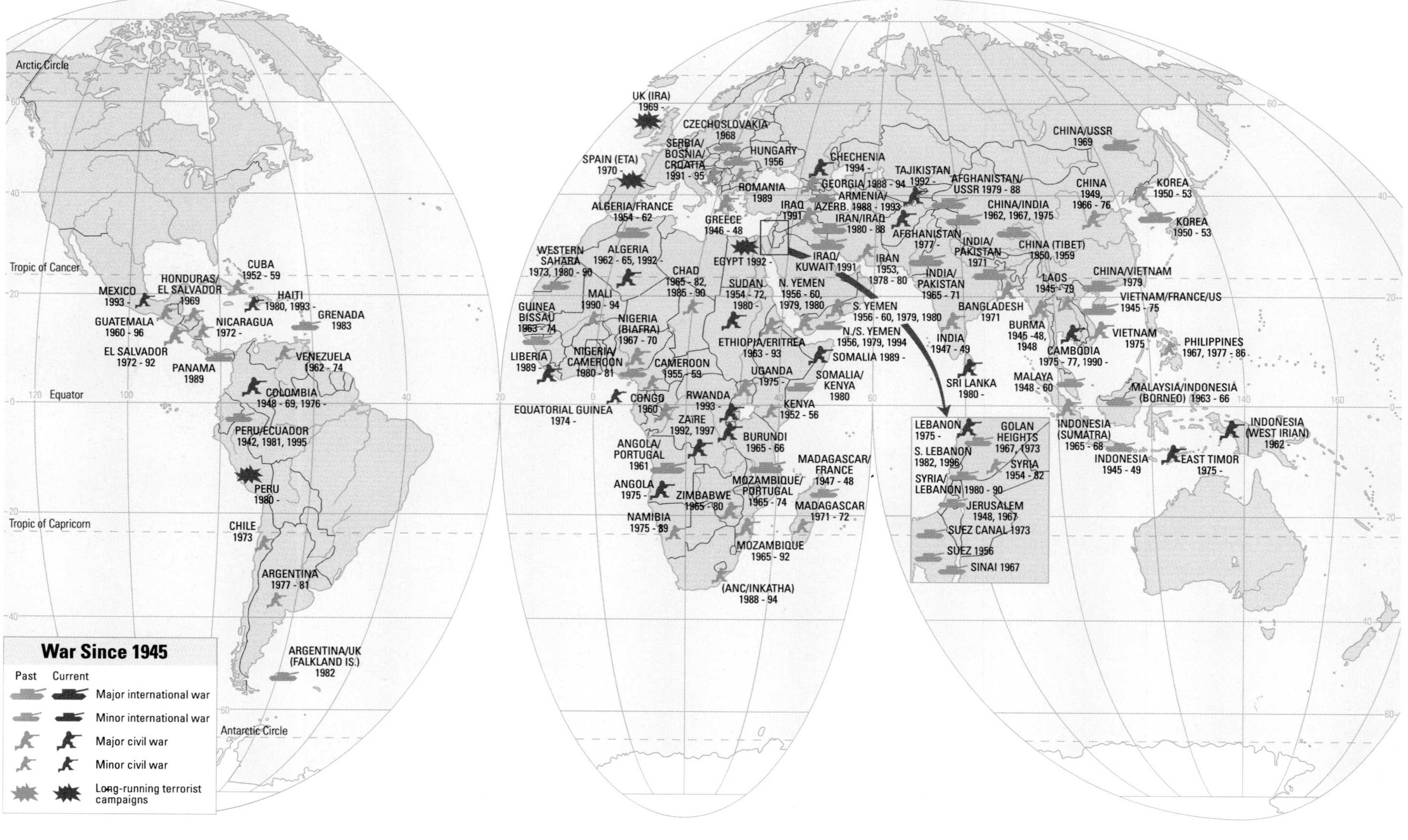

CARTOGRAPHY BY PHILIP'S. COPYRIGHT GEORGE PHILIP LTD

United Nations

The United Nations Organization was born as World War II drew to its conclusion. Six years of strife had strengthened the world's desire for peace, but an effective international organization was needed to help achieve it. That body would replace the League of Nations which, since its inception in 1920, had failed to curb the aggression of at least some of its member nations. At the United Nations Conference on International Organization held in San Francisco, the United Nations Charter was drawn up. Ratified by the Security Council and signed by the 51 original members, it came into effect on 24 October 1945.

The Charter set out the aims of the organization: to maintain peace and security, and develop friendly relations between nations; to achieve international co-operation in solving economic, social, cultural and humanitarian problems; to promote respect for human rights and fundamental freedoms; and to harmonize the activities of nations in order to achieve these common goals.

The United Nations has five principal organs :
The General Assembly
The forum at which member nations discuss moral and political issues affecting world development, peace and security meets annually in September, under a newly-elected President whose tenure lasts one year. Any member can bring business to the agenda, and each member nation has one vote.
The Security Council
A legislative and executive body, the Security Council is the primary instrument for establishing and maintaining international peace by attempting to settle disputes between nations. It has the power to dispatch UN forces and member nations undertake to provide armed forces, assistance and facilities. The Security Council has ten temporary members elected by the General Assembly for two-year terms, and five permanent members – China, France, Russia, UK and USA.
The Economic and Social Council
By far the largest United Nations executive, the Council operates as a conduit between the General Assembly and the many United Nations agencies it instructs to implement Assembly decisions, and whose work it co-ordinates. The Council also commissions studies on economic conditions, collects data and makes recommendations to the Assembly.
The Secretariat
This is the staff of the United Nations, and its task is to administer the policies and programmes of the UN and its organs, and assist and advise the Head of the Secretariat, the Secretary-General – a full-time, non-political appointment made by the General Assembly.
The Trusteeship Council
This no longer administers any of the original 11 trust territories as they are all now independent.
The International Court of Justice (the World Court)
The World Court is the judicial organ of the United Nations. It deals only with United Nations disputes and all members are subject to its jurisdiction. There are 15 judges, elected for nine-year terms by the General Assembly and the Security Council.

The social and humanitarian operations of the UN include:
United Nations Development Programme (UNDP) Plans and funds projects to help developing countries make better use of their resources.
United Nations International Childrens' Fund (UNICEF) Created at the General Assembly's first session in 1945 to help children in the aftermath of World War II, it now provides basic health care and aid worldwide.
Food and Agriculture Organization (FAO) Aims to raise living standards and nutrition levels in rural areas by improving food production and distribution.
United Nations Educational, Scientific and Cultural Organization (UNESCO) Promotes international co-operation through broader and better education.
World Health Organization (WHO) Promotes and provides for better health care, public and environmental health and medical research.

United Nations agencies are involved in many aspects of international trade, safety and security:
International Maritime Organization (IMO) Promotes unity amongst merchant shipping, especially in regard to safety, marine pollution and standardization.
International Labour Organization (ILO) Seeks to improve labour conditions and promote productive employment to raise living standards.
World Meteorological Organization (WMO) Promotes co-operation in weather observation, reporting and forecasting.
World Trade Organization (WTO) On 1 January 1995 the WTO replaced GATT. It advocates a common code of conduct and its aim is the liberalization of world trade.
Disarmament Commission Considers and makes recommendations to the General Assembly on disarmament issues.
International Atomic Energy Agency (IAEA) Fosters development of peaceful uses for nuclear energy and establishes safety standards.

The World Bank comprises three United Nations agencies:
International Monetary Fund (IMF) Cultivates international monetary co-operation and expansion of trade.
International Bank for Reconstruction and Development (IBRD) Provides funds and technical assistance to developing countries.
International Finance Corporation (IFC) Encourages the growth of productive private enterprise in less developed countries.

Membership There are seven independent states which are not members of the UN – Kiribati, Nauru, Switzerland, Taiwan, Tonga, Tuvalu and Vatican City. Official languages are Chinese, English, French, Russian, Spanish and Arabic.
Funding The UN budget for 1996–97 was US $2.6 billion. Contributions are assessed by the members' ability to pay, with the maximum 25% of the total, the minimum 0.01%.
Peacekeeping The UN has been involved in 43 peacekeeping operations worldwide since 1948. At the end of 1996 there were 16 areas of UN patrol and 25,649 'blue berets'.

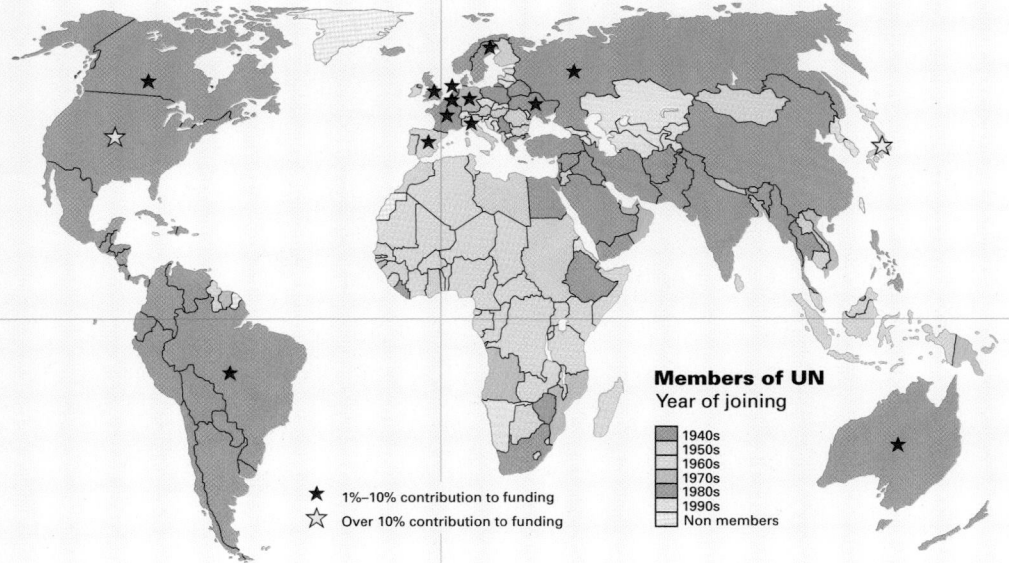

Members of UN
Year of joining

- 1940s
- 1950s
- 1960s
- 1970s
- 1980s
- 1990s
- Non members

★ 1%–10% contribution to funding
☆ Over 10% contribution to funding

Military Spending

Military expenditure as a % of GNP or GDP, ranked selection of countries (1994)

1. Iraq	74.9%	14. Jordan	7.5%
2. North Korea	26.3%	15. Laos	7.4%
3. Angola	23.9%	16. Pakistan	6.0%
4. Oman	18.1%	17. UAE	5.7%
5. Syria	17.9%	18. Seychelles	5.6%
6. Sudan	17.1%	19. Sierra Leone	4.9%
7. Saudi Arabia	14.2%	20. Taiwan	4.8%
8. Yemen	14.1%	21. Liberia	4.8%
9. Russia	12.4%	22. Singapore	4.5%
10. Kuwait	11.1%	23. Sri Lanka	4.5%
11. Mozambique	8.7%	24. USA	4.3%
12. Israel	8.6%	25. Malaysia	4.2%
13. Rwanda	7.6%		

It is worth noting that the total amount of expenditure varies considerably depending on the size of the economy, so that although the percentages show the importance given to military spending within each country, they give no idea as to the total expenditure. In 1997, for example, the USA spent a total of US $271 billion, Russia US $70 billion, and the UK US $36 billion. In 1993, the USA also provided the most military assistance worldwide, providing US $3.4 billion, compared to a total of US $0.9 billion from Western Europe.

The period 1987–94 saw a decline in global military spending which generated what the United Nations Development Programme term a 'peace dividend' of US $935 billion. Unfortunately, there is no clear link between reduced military spending and enhanced expenditure on human development. Moreover, the poorest regions of the world (notably sub-Saharan Africa) failed to contain their military spending and, in some cases, it increased.

International Organizations

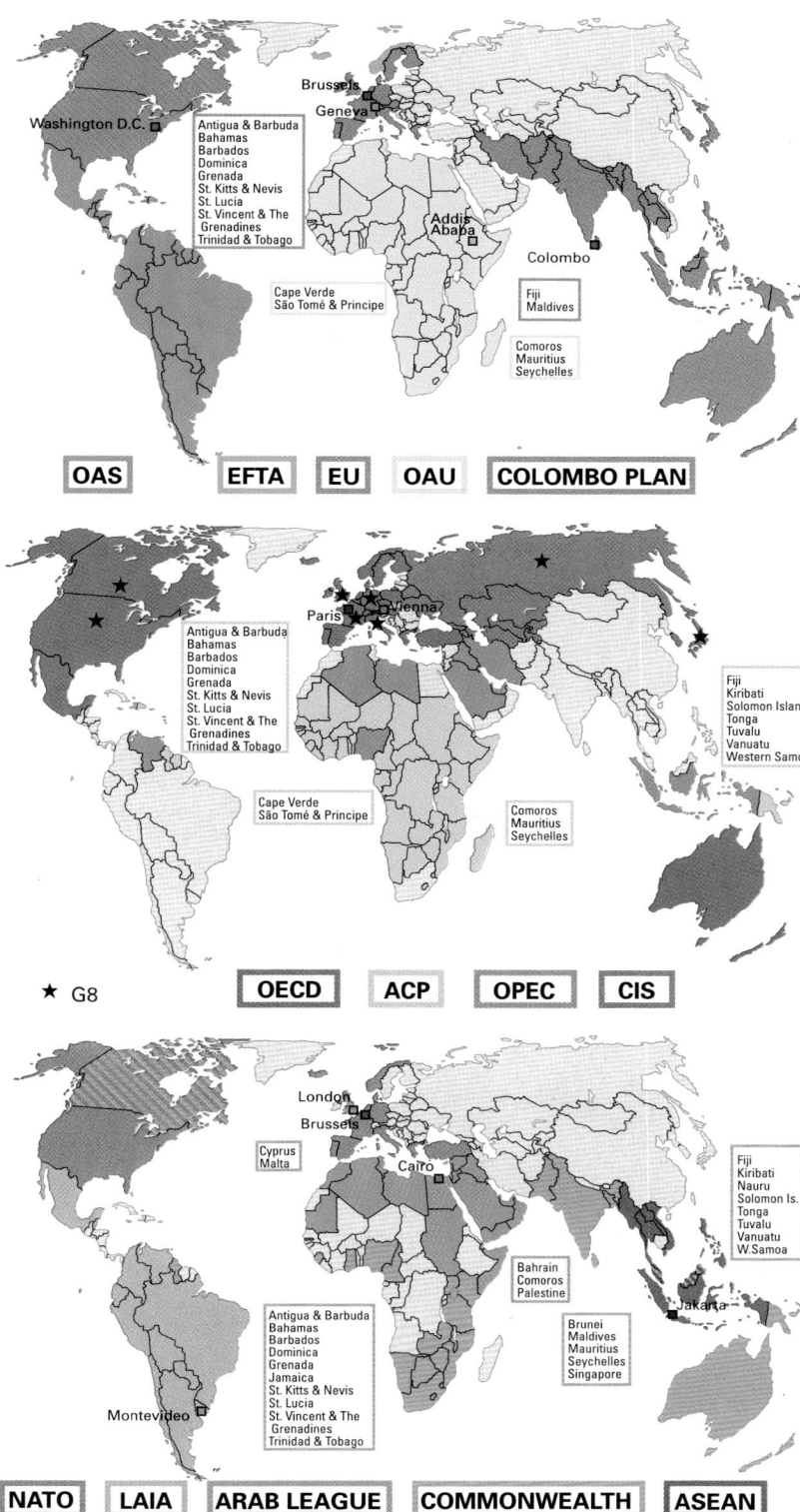

OAS   **EFTA**   **EU**   **OAU**   **COLOMBO PLAN**

★ G8   **OECD**   **ACP**   **OPEC**   **CIS**

NATO   **LAIA**   **ARAB LEAGUE**   **COMMONWEALTH**   **ASEAN**

EU The European Union evolved from the European Community (EC) in 1993. The original body, the European Coal and Steel Community (ECSC), was created in 1951 following the signing of the Treaty of Paris. The 15 members of the EU – Austria, Belgium, Denmark, Finland, France, Germany, Greece, Ireland, Italy, Luxembourg, Netherlands, Portugal, Spain, Sweden and the UK – aim to integrate economies, co-ordinate social developments and bring about political union. These members, of what is now the world's biggest market, share agricultural and industrial policies and tariffs on trade.
EFTA European Free Trade Association (formed in 1960). Portugal left the original 'Seven' in 1989 to join what was then the EC, followed by Austria, Finland and Sweden in 1995. There are now only four members: Norway, Iceland, Liechtenstein and Switzerland.
ACP African-Caribbean-Pacific (formed in 1963). Members enjoy economic ties with the EU.
NATO North Atlantic Treaty Organization (formed in 1949). It continues despite the winding up of the Warsaw Pact in 1991. There are 16 member countries.
OAS Organization of American States (formed in 1948). It aims to promote social and economic co-operation between countries in the developed North America and developing Latin America.
ASEAN Association of South-east Asian Nations (formed in 1967). Burma and Laos joined in 1997.
OAU Organization of African Unity (1963). Its 53 members represent over 94% of Africa's population. Arabic, French, Portuguese and English are recognized as working languages.
LAIA The Latin American Integration Association (formed in 1980) superceded the Latin American Free Trade Association formed in 1961. Its aim is to promote freer regional trade.
OECD Organization for Economic Co-operation and Development (formed in 1961). It comprises 29 major free-market economies. The 'G8' is its 'inner group' of leading industrial nations, comprising Canada, France, Germany, Italy, Japan, Russia, UK and the USA.
COMMONWEALTH The Commonwealth of Nations evolved from the British Empire; it comprises 16 nations recognizing the British monarch as head of state, 32 republics and 5 indigenous monarchies, giving a total of 53. Nigeria was suspended in 1995.
CIS The Commonwealth of Independent States (formed in 1991) comprises the countries of the former Soviet Union except for Estonia, Latvia and Lithuania.
OPEC Organization of Petroleum Exporting Countries (formed in 1960). It controls about three-quarters of the world's oil supply. Gabon formally withdrew from OPEC in August 1996.
ARAB LEAGUE (1945) Aims to promote economic, social, political and military co-operation.
COLOMBO PLAN (formed in 1951) Its 26 members aim to promote economic and social development in Asia and the Pacific.

Agriculture

Bad harvests in 1995 caused a drop in world grain reserves to a 20-year low. This revived the ongoing debate as to whether the population explosion will cause major food crises in the 21st century.

Experts estimate that 3 billion tonnes of cereals will be needed to feed the world's population in 25 years' time, as compared with 1.9 billion tonnes at present. To expand food production to this extent, some argue, will place great strain on the environment. One suggestion to alleviate the situation is that people in developed countries should eat less meat. This would release more grain, which is used as cattle fodder, to feed people.

Other experts argue that there should be no food crises. World grain production tripled between 1950 and 1990, largely as a result of the Green Revolution, during which genetically improved, high-yield varieties of maize, rice and wheat, the world's three leading staple crops, were developed. These new varieties have helped many developing countries to achieve food surpluses and prevent widespread starvation.

The only region of the world which seems likely to suffer food shortages in the 21st century is sub-Saharan Africa, where in the late 1990s the average daily calorie intake was 6% less than what was needed and where the population is expected to double in 20 years. Improved land management and a huge increase in global trade, especially in food distribution, is necessary if sub-Saharan Africans are not to go hungry.

The development of agriculture more than 10,000 years ago transformed human existence more than any other major advance. By supporting larger populations, it led to the growth of early civilizations and later it sustained people in the industrial cities which sprang up in the 19th century.

Today, agricultural production varies a great deal between the developed world, where it is highly mechanized and employs few people, such as 3% of the workforce in the United States, and the developing world, such as sub-Saharan Africa, where it employs 66% of the workforce. Many Africans are engaged in subsistence farming, providing the basic needs of their families but not contributing to the national economy. Much of Africa also suffers from economic mismanagement, as well as civil war and banditry.

Political problems have also affected food production in other parts of the world. The former USSR had much excellent farmland, but the failure of the collectives and state farms to maintain sufficiently high levels of production helped to bring about the collapse of Communism.

Farmers are under great pressure not only to maintain high levels of production but to increase them. However, the cultivation of marginal areas is one of the prime causes of soil erosion and desertification.

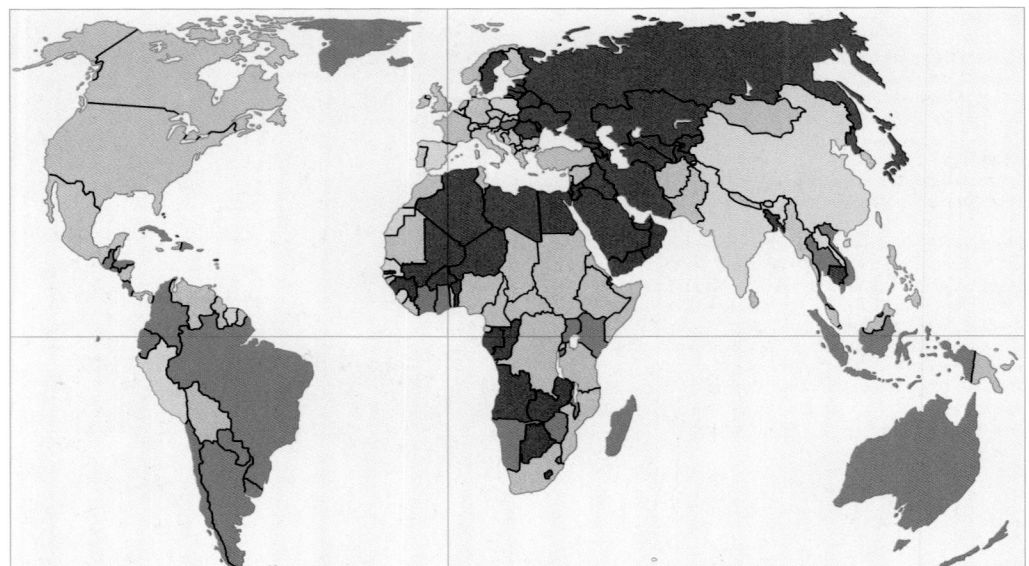

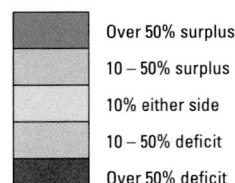

Self-sufficiency in Food

Balance of trade in food products as a percentage of total trade in food products – S.I.T.C. Classes 0, 1 and 4 (latest available year)

- Over 50% surplus
- 10 – 50% surplus
- 10% either side
- 10 – 50% deficit
- Over 50% deficit

Most self-sufficient		Least self-sufficient	
Argentina	95%	Algeria	−98%
Zimbabwe	87%	Djibouti	−97%
Honduras	81%	Yemen	−95%
Malawi	81%	Zambia	−95%
Costa Rica	79%	Japan	−91%
Iceland	78%	Gabon	−90%
Chile	75%	Kuwait	−90%
Uruguay	75%	Brunei	−89%
Ecuador	74%	Burkina Faso	−82%

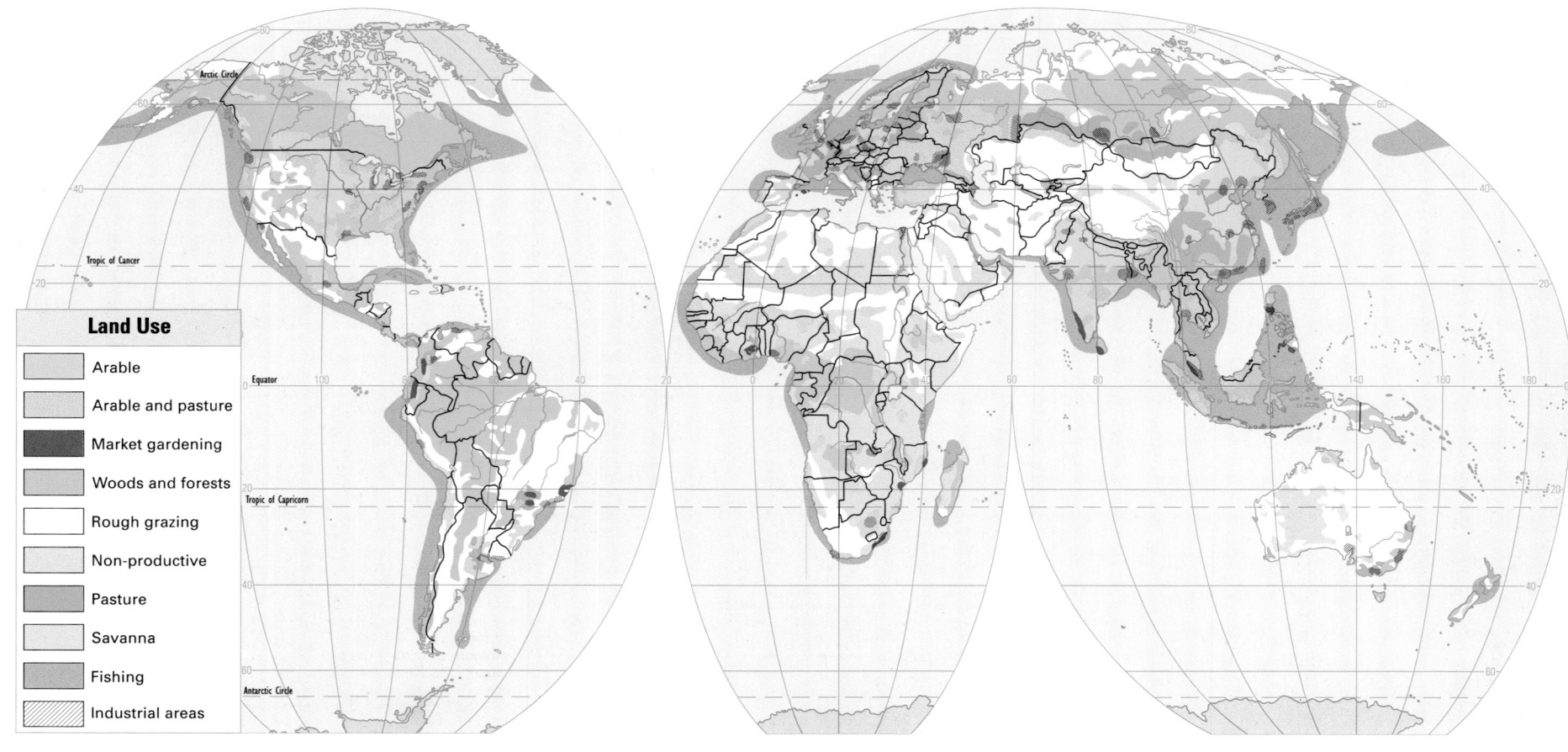

Land Use

- Arable
- Arable and pasture
- Market gardening
- Woods and forests
- Rough grazing
- Non-productive
- Pasture
- Savanna
- Fishing
- Industrial areas

Staple Crops

Wheat: Grown in a range of climates, with most varieties – including the highest-quality bread wheats – requiring temperate conditions. Mainly used in baking, it is also used for pasta and breakfast cereals.

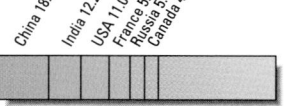

World total (1996): 584,874,000 tonnes

Maize: Originating in the New World and still an important human food in Africa and Latin America, in the developed world it is processed into breakfast cereals, oil, starches and adhesives. It is also used for animal feed.

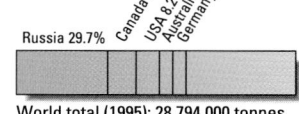

World total (1996): 576,821,000 tonnes

Oats: Most widely used to feed livestock, but eaten by humans as oatmeal or porridge. Oats have a beneficial effect on the cardiovascular system, and human consumption is likely to increase.

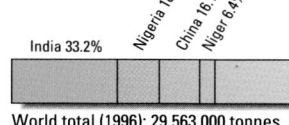

World total (1995): 28,794,000 tonnes

Millet: The name covers a number of small-grained cereals, members of the grass family with a short growing season. Used to produce flour, meal and animal feed, and fermented to make beer, especially in Africa.

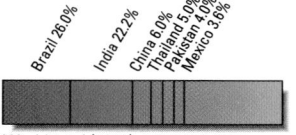

World total (1996): 29,563,000 tonnes

Sugars

Sugar cane: Confined to tropical regions, cane sugar accounts for the bulk of international trade in sugar. Most is produced as a foodstuff, but some countries, notably Brazil and South Africa, distill sugar cane to make motor fuels.

World total (1996): 1,192,555,000 tonnes

Cereals are grasses with starchy, edible seeds; every important civilization has depended on them as a source of food. The major cereal grains contain about 10% protein and 75% carbohydrate. Grain contributes more than any other group of foods to the energy and protein content of human diet. Starchy tuber crops or root crops are second in importance after cereals as staple foods; easily cultivated, they provide high yields for little effort.

Rice: Thrives on the high humidity and temperatures of the Far East, where it is the traditional staple food of half the human race. Usually grown standing in water, rice responds well to continuous cultivation, with three or four crops annually.

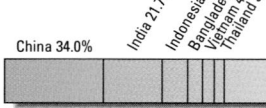

World total (1996): 562,259,000 tonnes

Potatoes: The most important of the edible tubers, potatoes grow in well-watered, temperate areas. Weight for weight less nutritious than grain, they are a human staple as well as an important animal feed.

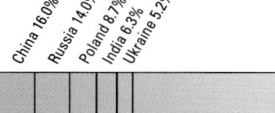

World total (1996): 294,834,000 tonnes

Soya: Beans from soya bushes are very high (30–40%) in protein. Most are processed into oil and proprietary protein foods. Consumption since 1950 has tripled, mainly due to the health-conscious developed world.

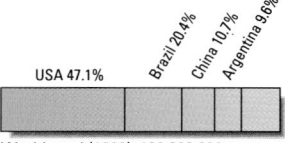

World total (1996): 130,302,000 tonnes

Cassava: A tropical shrub that needs high rainfall (over 1,000 mm annually) and a 10–30 month growing season to produce its large, edible tubers. Used as flour by humans, as cattle feed and in industrial starches.

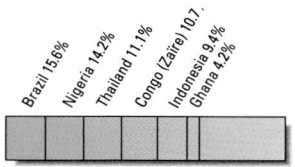

World total (1996): 167,942,000 tonnes

Sugar beet: Closely related to the beetroot, sugar beet's yield after processing is indistinguishable from cane sugar. It is replacing sugar-cane imports in Europe, to the detriment of the developing countries that rely on it as a major cash crop.

World total (1996): 255,500,000 tonnes

Food and Population

Comparison of food production and population by continent.

The left column indicates the % of world food production and the right shows population in proportion.

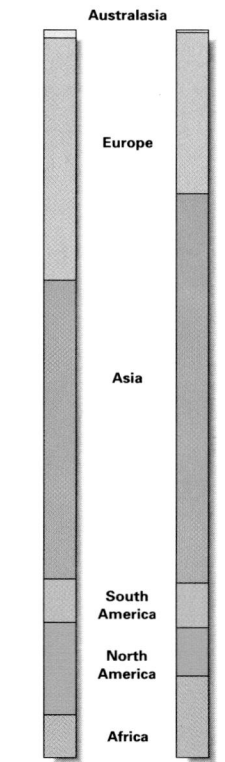

Agricultural Population

Percentage of the total population dependent on agriculture for their livelihood (1994)

- Over 75% dependent
- 50 – 75% dependent
- 25 – 50% dependent
- 10 – 25% dependent
- Under 10% dependent

▲ Over 75% of the total workforce employed in agriculture, forestry and fishing in 1995

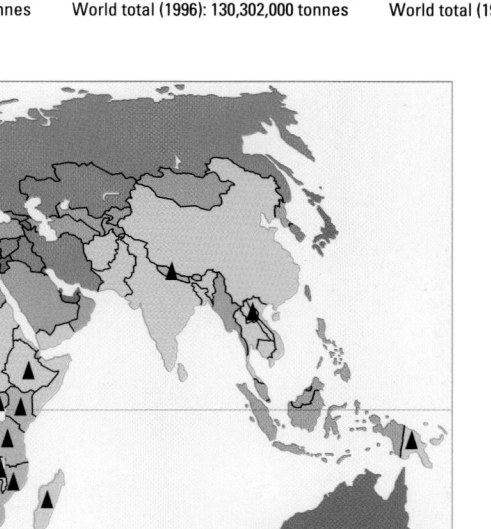

Top 5 countries (1995)		Bottom 5 countries (1995)	
Bhutan	94%	Macau	0.2%
Nepal	93%	Singapore	1.0%
Burkina Faso	92%	Hong Kong	1.0%
Rwanda	91%	Kuwait	1.0%
Burundi	91%	Guam	1.0%

Animal Products

Traditionally, food animals subsisted on land unsuitable for cultivation, supporting agricultural production with their fertilizing dung. But free-ranging animals grow slowly and yield less meat than those more intensively reared; the demands of urban markets in the developed world have encouraged the growth of factory-like production methods. A large proportion of staple crops, especially cereals, are fed to animals, an inefficient way to produce protein but one likely to continue as long as people value meat and dairy products in their diet.

Cheese: Least perishable of all dairy products, cheese is milk fermented with selected bacterial strains to produce a foodstuff with a potentially immense range of flavours and textures. The vast majority of cheeses are made from cow's milk, although sheep and goat cheeses are highly prized.

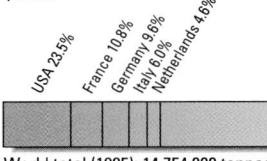

World total (1995): 14,754,000 tonnes

Beef and Veal: Most beef and veal is reared for home markets, and the top five producers are also the biggest consumers. The USA produces nearly a quarter of the world's beef and eats even more.

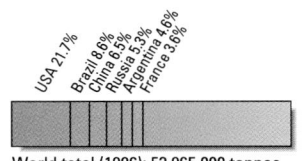

World total (1996): 53,965,000 tonnes

Milk: Many human groups, including most Asians, find raw milk indigestible after infancy, and it is often only the starting point for other dairy products such as butter, cheese and yoghurt. Most world milk production comes from cows, but sheep's milk and goats' milk are also important.

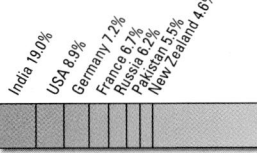

World total (1996): 466,317,000 tonnes

Butter: A traditional source of vitamin A as well as calories, butter has lost much popularity in the developed world for health reasons, although it remains a valuable food. Most butter from India, the world's largest producer, is clarified into ghee, which has religious as well as nutritional importance.

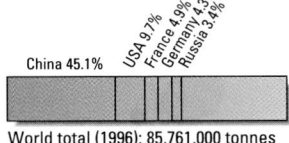

World total (1996): 6,565,000 tonnes

Pork: Although pork is forbidden to many millions, notably Muslims, on religious grounds, more is produced than any other meat in the world, mainly because it is the cheapest. It accounts for about 90% of China's meat output, although per capita meat consumption is relatively low.

China 45.1%

World total (1996): 85,761,000 tonnes

Crisis in Africa

Each year 40 million people, almost half of whom are children, die from starvation and related diseases. By the year 2000, an estimated 600 million people worldwide will be suffering from malnutrition. Africa suffers from more natural disasters than any other continent; pests such as locusts destroy crops, and tropical storms and flooding ruin harvests. Famines periodically affect parts of Africa causing widespread hardship, even though enough food is produced worldwide to feed everyone.

- Areas liable to invasions by locusts
- Areas liable to flood
- ⇒ Paths of tropical storms
- ■ Major famines since 1900 (with dates)

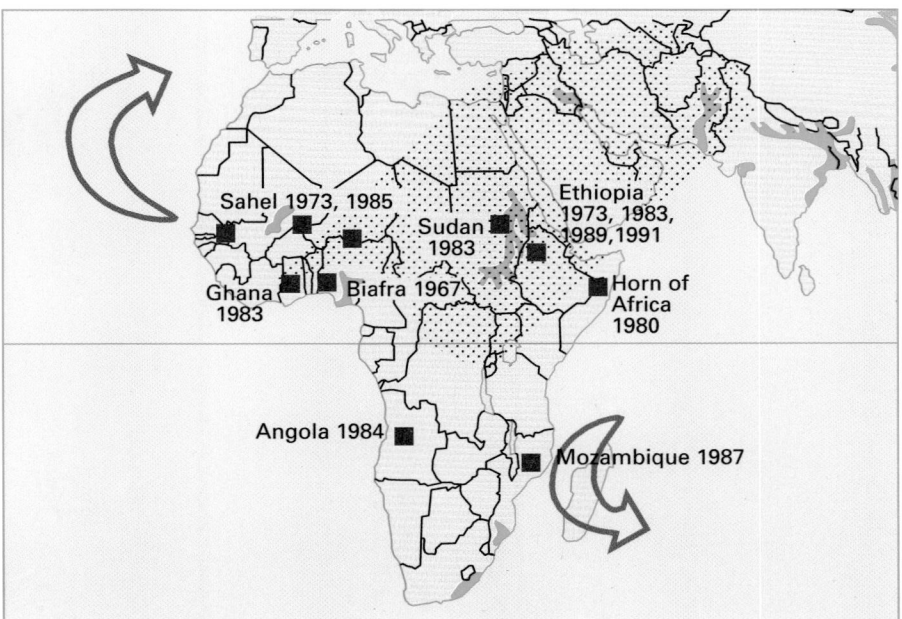

Sahel 1973, 1985
Ethiopia 1973, 1983, 1989, 1991
Sudan 1983
Ghana 1983
Biafra 1967
Horn of Africa 1980
Angola 1984
Mozambique 1987

CARTOGRAPHY BY PHILIP'S. COPYRIGHT GEORGE PHILIP LTD

Energy

Every year, the world's energy consumption is about the equivalent of what would come from burning 8,000 million tonnes of oil (8,000 MtOe) – a twenty-fold increase since 1850. Two-fifths of this total actually comes from burning oil and most of the rest comes from coal and natural gas.

The oil crises in the 1970s precipitated concern over dependence on finite fossil fuels as the primary source of energy and growing environmental awareness has added impetus to the search for alternative energy resources.

Fossil fuel combustion damages the environment through the release of gases and particulate matter but two other major sources of energy, hydroelectricity and nuclear power, are also controversial. For example, hydroelectricity production involves flooding large areas to create reservoirs, while nuclear power stations, which are costly to build, generate dangerous radioactive wastes, and can lead to disasters on an international scale.

Alternative energy resources may soon provide a much larger proportion of the world's energy consumption, especially in developing countries where millions of people currently have no access to electricity. Experts have predicted that solar and wind energy may have an important future in such countries as China and India, while other areas under development, such as tidal, wave and geothermal power, all have potential in appropriate areas. World Bank experts have calculated that solar power could, in theory, supply between five and ten times the present electricity supply of developing countries.

Conversions

For historical reasons, oil is still traded in barrels. The weight and volume equivalents shown below are all based on average density 'Arabian light' crude oil, and should be considered approximate.

The energy equivalents given for a tonne of oil are also somewhat imprecise: oil and coal of different qualities will have varying energy contents, a fact usually reflected in their price on world markets.

1 barrel:
   0.136 tonnes
   159 litres
   35 Imperial gallons
   42 US gallons

1 tonne:
   7.33 barrels
   1185 litres
   256 Imperial gallons
   261 US gallons

1 tonne oil:
   1.5 tonnes hard coal
   3.0 tonnes lignite
   12,000 kWh

1 gallon (Imperial):
   227,42 inches
   1.201 US gallons
   4,546 litres

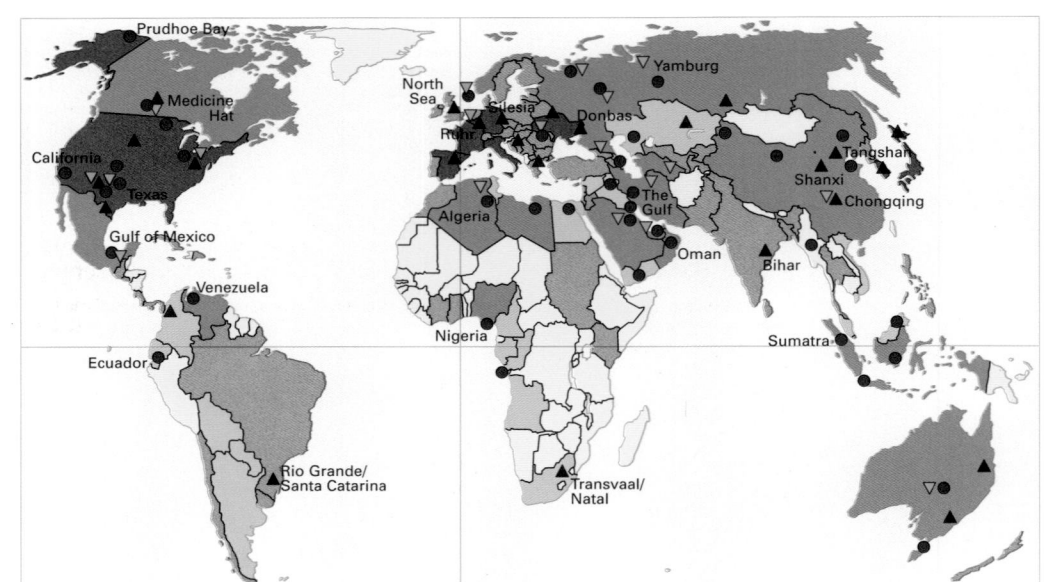

Energy Balance

Difference between energy production and consumption in millions of tonnes of oil equivalent (MtOe) (latest available year)

Energy deficit ↑

- Over 35 MtOe
- 1 – 35 MtOe
- Approx. balance
- 1 – 35 MtOe
- Over 35 MtOe

Energy surplus ↓

- ● Major oilfields
- ▽ Major gasfields
- ▲ Major coalfields

World Energy Consumption

Energy consumed by world regions, measured in million tonnes of oil equivalent in 1993. Total world consumption was 7,804 MtOe. Only energy from oil, gas, coal, nuclear and hydroelectric sources are included. Excluded are fuels such as wood, peat, animal waste, wind, solar and geothermal which, though important in some countries, are unreliably documented in terms of consumption statistics.

- Oil
- Gas
- Coal
- Nuclear
- Hydro

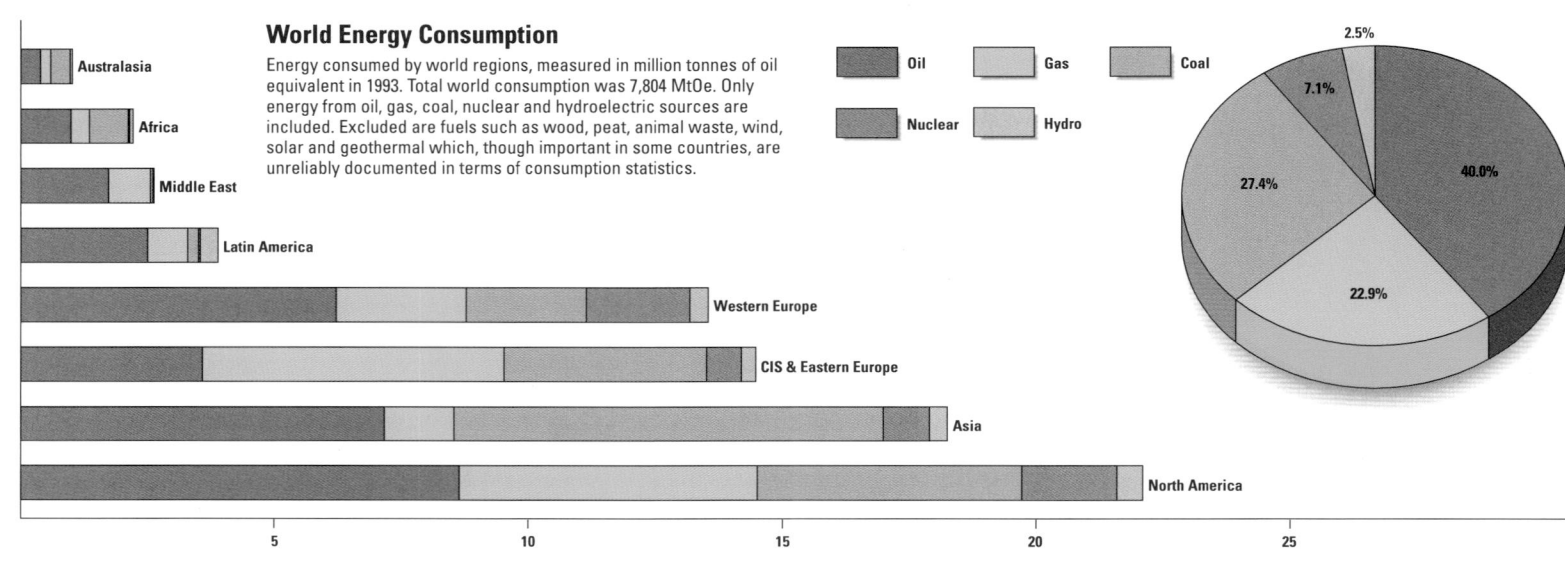

Energy Production

Primary energy production expressed in kilograms of coal equivalent per person (1994)

In developing countries traditional fuels are still very important. These so-called biomass fuels include wood, charcoal and dried dung. The pie-chart highlights the importance of biomass in terms of energy consumption in Nigeria. Collecting fuelwood can be a time-consuming task, sometimes taking all day.

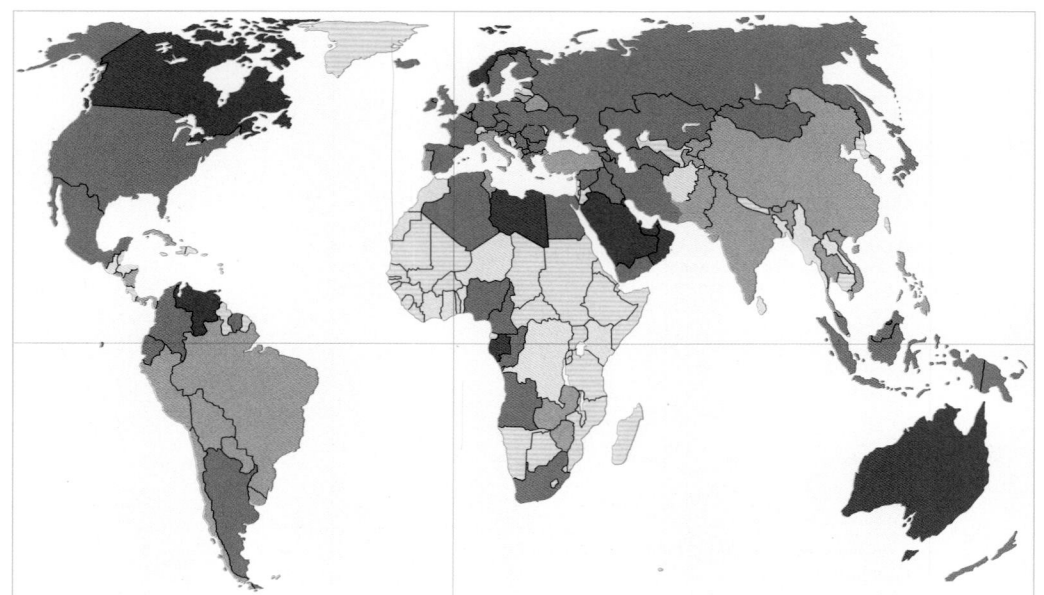

- Over 10,000 kg per person
- 1,000 – 10,000 kg per person
- 100 – 1,000 kg per person
- 10 – 100 kg per person
- Under 10 kg per person

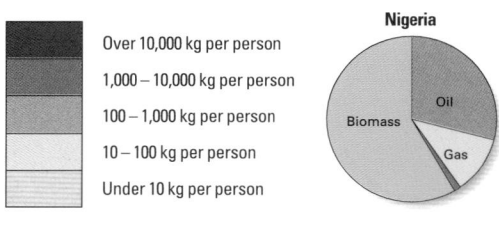

Nigeria

34

Major world movements of oil in millions of tonnes (1995)

Middle East to Asia (not Japan)	253.8
Middle East to Japan	206.8
Middle East to Western Europe	178.1
South and Central America to USA	112.9
North Africa to Western Europe	99.7
CIS to Western Europe	80.2
Middle East to USA	79.8
Canada to USA	65.7
West Africa to USA	62.9
Mexico to USA	53.1
West Africa to Western Europe	42.3
Western Europe to USA	36.7
Middle East to Africa	33.6
Middle East to South and Central America	33.1
CIS to Central Europe	25.6
Western Europe to Canada	16.6

Total world imports ....1,815,400,000 million tonnes

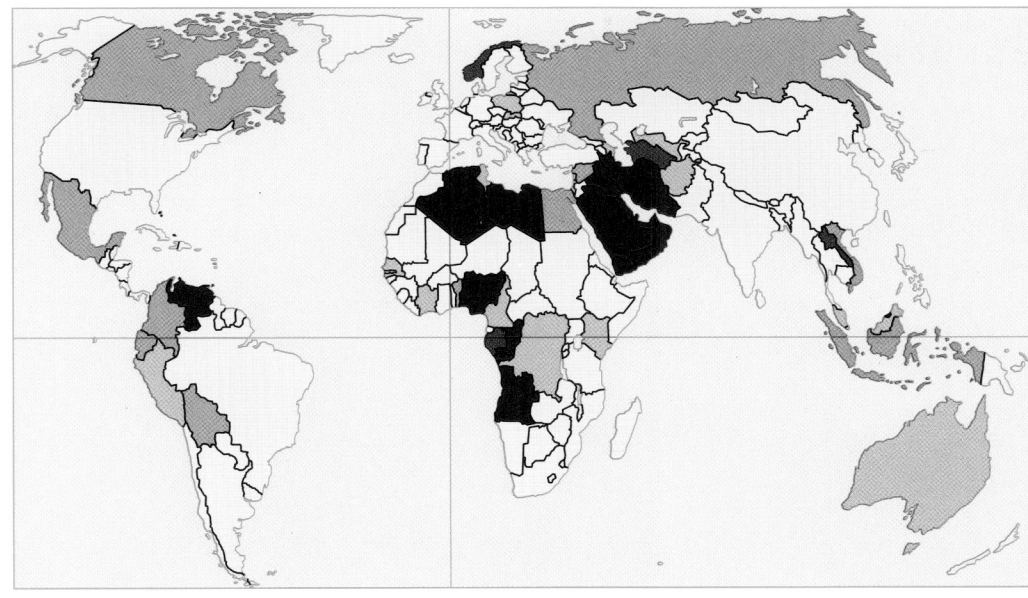

Fuel Exports

Fuels as a percentage of total value of exports (latest available year)

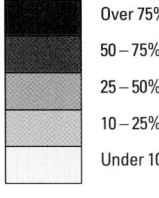

- Over 75%
- 50 – 75%
- 25 – 50%
- 10 – 25%
- Under 10%

Oil exports became a major political issue when OPEC (Organization of Oil Exporting Countries) sought, in the 1970s, to increase the influence of developing countries in world affairs by raising oil prices and restricting production. But its power was short-lived, following a fall in the demand for oil in the 1980s, due to increased energy efficiency and the development of alternative energy resources, such as natural gas and nuclear power.

Coal Reserves

Proved coal reserves in place by region and country, thousand million tonnes (1993)

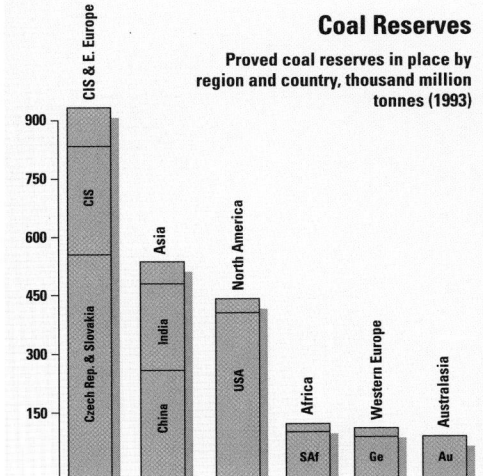

Gas Reserves

Proved recoverable natural gas reserves by region and country, thousand million tonnes (1993)

Oil Reserves

Crude oil reserves by region and country, thousand million tonnes (1993)

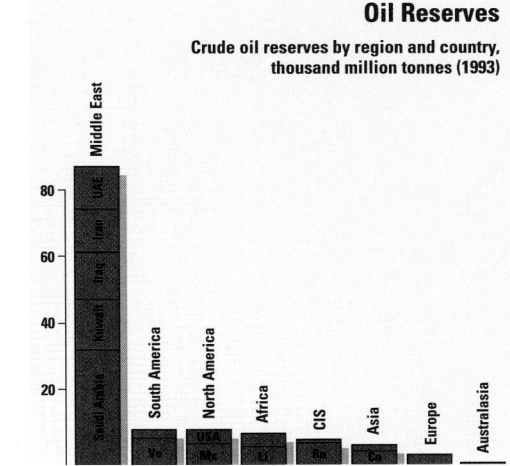

Al: Algeria
Au: Australia
Ca: Canada
Cn: China
Ge: Germany
Iq: Iraq
Ka: Kazakstan
Li: Libya
Ma: Malaysia
Mx: Mexico
Ni: Nigeria
No: Norway
Qa: Qatar
Ru: Russia
SA: Saudi Arabia
SAf: South Africa
Tm: Turkmenistan
Uk: Ukraine
Ve: Venezuela

Nuclear Power

Percentage of electricity generated by nuclear power stations, leading nations (1995)

1.	Lithuania	85%	11.	Spain	33%
2.	France	77%	12.	Finland	30%
3.	Belgium	56%	13.	Germany	29%
4.	Slovak Rep.	49%	14.	Japan	29%
5.	Sweden	48%	15.	UK	27%
6.	Bulgaria	41%	16.	Ukraine	27%
7.	Hungary	41%	17.	Czech Rep.	22%
8.	Switzerland	39%	18.	Canada	19%
9.	Slovenia	38%	19.	USA	18%
10.	South Korea	33%	20.	Russia	12%

Although the 1980s were a bad time for the nuclear power industry (major projects ran over budget and fears of long-term environmental damage were heavily reinforced by the 1986 disaster at Chernobyl), the industry picked up in the early 1990s. Whilst the number of reactors is still increasing, however, orders for new plants have shrunk. In 1997, the Swedish government began to decommission the country's 12 nuclear power plants; a bold environmental decision that could cost US $50 billion.

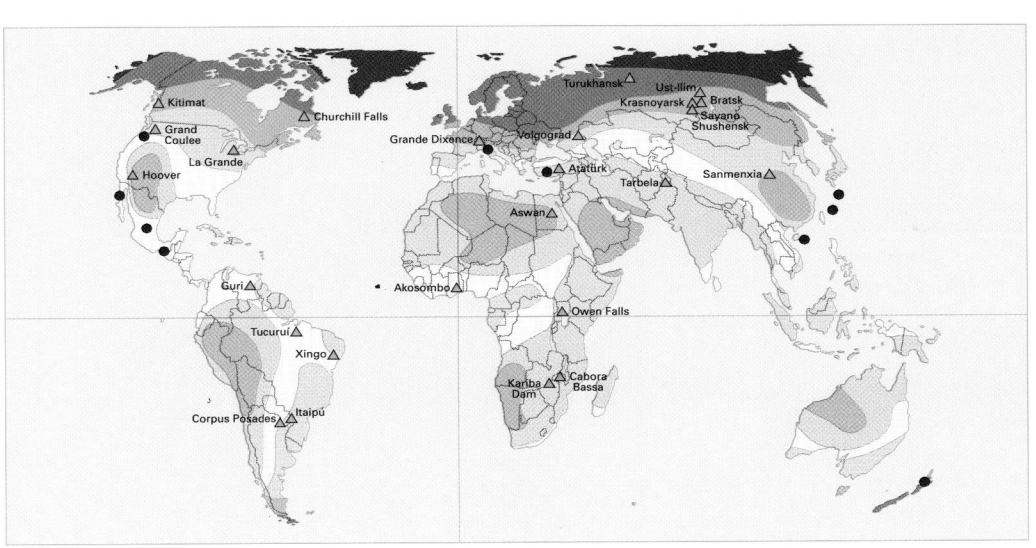

Renewable Energy

Average annual solar irradiance in kWh/m², with selected major hydroelectric and geothermal power stations

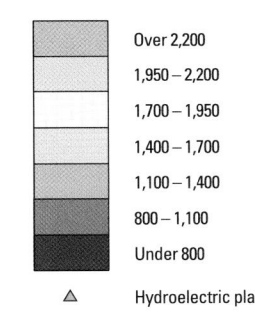

- Over 2,200
- 1,950 – 2,200
- 1,700 – 1,950
- 1,400 – 1,700
- 1,100 – 1,400
- 800 – 1,100
- Under 800

△ Hydroelectric plants
● Geothermal plants

Hydroelectricity

Percentage of electricity generated by hydroelectric power stations, leading nations (1995)

1.	Paraguay	99.9%	11.	Rwanda	97.6%
2.	Congo (Zaïre)	99.7%	12.	Malawi	97.6%
3.	Bhutan	99.6%	13.	Cameroon	96.9%
4.	Zambia	99.5%	14.	Nepal	96.7%
5.	Norway	99.4%	15.	Laos	95.3%
6.	Ghana	99.3%	16.	Albania	95.2%
7.	Congo	99.3%	17.	Iceland	94.0%
8.	Uganda	99.1%	18.	Brazil	92.2%
9.	Burundi	98.3%	19.	Honduras	87.6%
10.	Uruguay	98.0%	20.	Tanzania	87.1%

Countries heavily reliant on hydroelectricity are usually small and non-industrial: a high proportion of hydroelectric power more often reflects a modest energy budget than vast hydroelectric resources. The USA, for instance, produces only 9% of power requirements from hydroelectricity; yet that 9% amounts to more than three times the hydropower generated by the whole of Africa.

Alternative Energy Resources

Solar: Each year the Sun bestows upon the Earth almost a million times as much energy as is locked up in all the planet's oil reserves, but only an insignificant fraction is trapped and used commercially. In a few installations around the world, mirrors focus the Sun's rays on to boilers, whose steam generates electricity by spinning turbines.

Wind: Caused by uneven heating of the Earth, winds are themselves a form of solar energy. Windmills have been used for centuries to turn wind power into mechanical work; recent models, often arranged in banks on wind-swept high ground, usually generate electricity. Figures for wind power worldwide are given in the table, right.

Tidal: The energy from tides is potentially enormous, although only a few installations have so far been built to exploit it. In theory at least, waves and currents could also provide almost unimaginable power, and the thermal differences in the ocean depths are another huge well of potential energy. But work on extracting it is still in the experimental stage.

Geothermal: The Earth's temperature rises by 1°C for every 30 metres descent, with much steeper temperature gradients in geologically active areas. El Salvador, for example, produces 39% of its electricity from geothermal power stations, whilst the USA, the world leader, produced 3,331 megawatts in 1993. Some of the oldest and most successful applications are in Iceland, where 86% of all households are heated by geothermal energy.

Biomass: The oldest of human fuels ranges from animal dung, still burned in cooking fires in much of North Africa and elsewhere, to sugar cane plantations feeding high-technology distilleries to produce ethanol for motor vehicle engines. In Brazil and South Africa, plant ethanol provides up to 25% of motor fuel. Throughout the developing world, most biomass energy comes from firewood: although accurate figures are impossible to obtain, it may yield as much as 10% of the world's total energy consumption.

Wind Power

World wind energy generating capacity, in megawatts

1980	10
1981	25
1982	90
1983	210
1984	600
1985	1,020
1986	1,270
1987	1,580
1988	1,580
1989	1,730
1990	1,930
1991	2,170
1992	2,510
1993	3,050
1994	3,710

Wind power is the fastest growing source of energy worldwide but still provides only 1% of the world's energy. Output grew by 33% in 1995.

Minerals

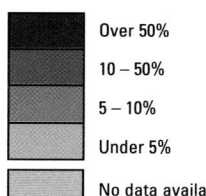

For more information:
10 Geology
39 Patterns of production
41 World shipping

The use of metals played a vital part in the evolving technologies of early peoples. Copper first came into use around 10,000 years ago, bronze about 5,000 years ago, and iron 3,300 years ago. In the early stages of the Industrial Revolution, the location of coal, iron ore and water power usually determined the location of new industries. But due to continuing improvements in transport, in-cluding oil pipelines, industries can now be located almost anywhere.

Minerals are distributed unevenly and some industrial countries, lacking their own mineral resources, import most of the raw materials they need. Some imports come from mineral-rich countries, such as Australia but others come from developing countries, especially in Africa and South America. Most of the developing countries export unpro-cessed ores, losing out on the much higher revenues gained from exporting metals.

Most minerals come from land deposits, because undersea deposits, with the exception of oil reserves under the continental shelves, have been regarded as inaccessible. But short-ages of terrestrial minerals may one day encourage exploitation of the ocean floor.

Mineral Exports

Minerals and metals as a percentage of total exports (latest available year)

- Over 50%
- 10 – 50%
- 5 – 10%
- Under 5%
- No data available

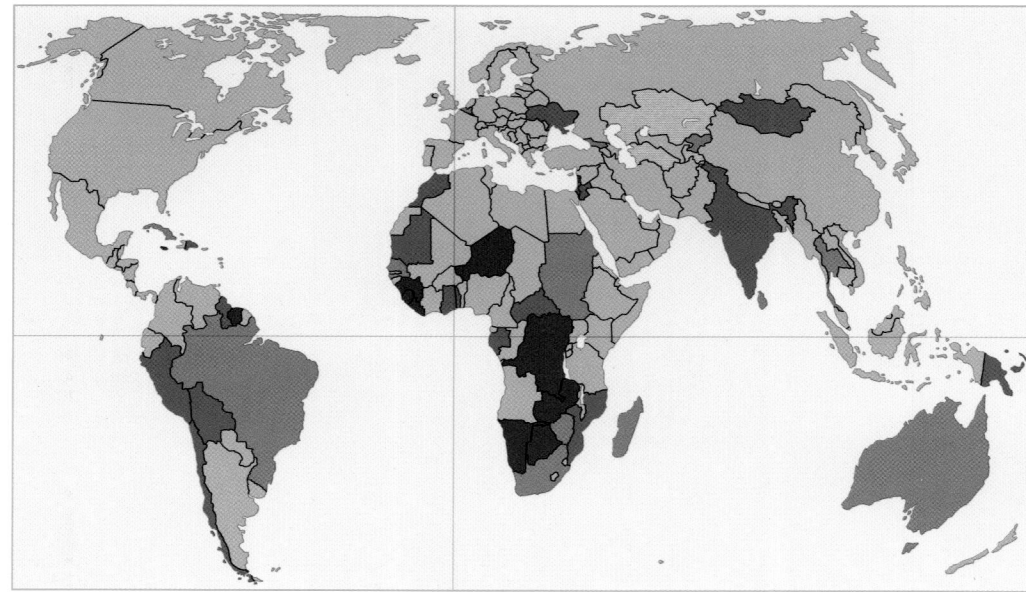

Uranium

In its pure state, uranium is an immensely heavy, white metal; but although spent uranium is employed as projectiles in anti-missile cannons, where its mass ensures a lethal punch, its main use is as a fuel in nuclear reactors, and in nuclear weaponry. Uranium is very scarce: the main source is the rare ore pitchblende, which itself contains only 0.2% uranium oxide. Only a minute fraction of that is the radioactive U^{235} isotope, though so-called breeder reactors can transmute the more common U^{238} into highly radioactive plutonium.

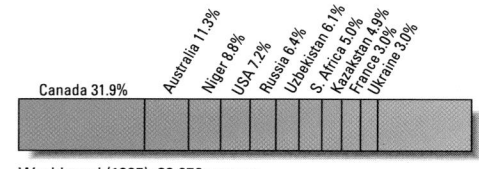

Canada 31.9% | Australia 11.3% | Niger 8.8% | USA 7.2% | Russia 6.4% | Uzbekistan 6.1% | S. Africa 5.0% | Kazakstan 4.9% | France 3.0% | Ukraine 3.0%

World total (1995): 32,976 tonnes

Metals

* Figures for aluminium are for refined metal; all other figures refer to ore production.

The world's leading producers of aluminium ore (bauxite) in 1995 were as follows:

1. Australia 41.9%
2. Papua New Guinea 14.3%
3. Jamaica 10.8%
4. Brazil 10.1%
5. Russia 6.7%
6. China 5.7%
7. India 5.0%
8. Surinam 2.8%
9. Venezuela 2.6%
10. Greece 1.9%

The figures shown above are in stark contrast to the figures showing aluminium production on the right. Australia, for example, produces 41.9% of the world's bauxite but only 5.9% of the aluminium metal. Papua New Guinea and Jamaica account for 25% of the bauxite mined but have no smelters and export virtually all of it to countries like the USA and Canada.

Diamond

Most of the world's diamond is found in kimberlite, or 'blue ground', a basic peridotite rock; erosion may wash the diamond from its kimberlite matrix and deposit it with sand or gravel on river beds. Only a small proportion of the world's diamond, the most flawless, is cut into gemstones – 'diamonds'; most is used in industry, where the material's remarkable hardness and abrasion resistance finds a use in cutting tools, drills and dies, as well as in styluses. Australia, not among the top 12 producers at the beginning of the 1980s, had by 1986 become world leader and by 1993 was the source of 40.6% of world production. The other main producers were Congo (Zaïre) (16.3%), Botswana (14.6%), Russia (11.4%) and South Africa (9.7%). Between them, these five nations accounted for over 82% of the world total of 100,850,000 carats.

Aluminium: Produced mainly from its oxide, bauxite, which yields 25% of its weight in aluminium. The cost of refining and production is often too high for producer-countries to bear, so bauxite is largely exported. Lightweight and corrosion resistant, aluminium alloys are widely used in aircraft, vehicles, cans and packaging.

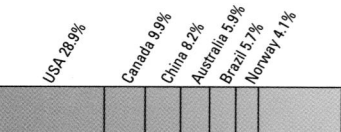

USA 28.9% | Canada 9.9% | China 8.2% | Australia 5.9% | Brazil 5.7% | Norway 4.1%

World total (1995): 22,706,000 tonnes *

Lead: A soft metal, obtained mainly from galena (lead sulphide), which occurs in veins associated with iron, zinc and silver sulphides. Its use in vehicle batteries accounts for the USA's prime consumer status; lead is also made into sheeting and piping. Its use as an additive to paints and petrol is decreasing.

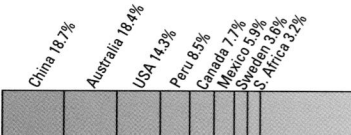

China 18.7% | Australia 18.4% | USA 14.3% | Peru 8.5% | Canada 7.7% | Mexico 5.9% | Sweden 3.6% | S. Africa 3.2%

World total (1995): 2,751,000 tonnes *

Tin: Soft, pliable and non-toxic, used to coat 'tin' (tin-plated steel) cans, in the manufacture of foils and in alloys. The principal tin-bearing mineral is cassiterite (SnO_2), found in ore formed from molten rock. Producers and refiners were hit by a price collapse in 1991.

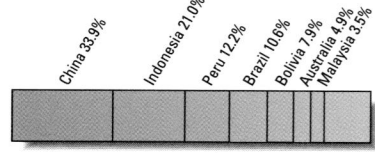

China 33.9% | Indonesia 21.0% | Peru 12.2% | Brazil 10.6% | Bolivia 7.9% | Australia 4.9% | Malaysia 3.5%

World total (1995): 182,518 tonnes *

Gold: Regarded for centuries as the most valuable metal in the world and used to make coins, gold is still recognized as the monetary standard. A soft metal, it is alloyed to make jewellery; the electronics industry values its corrosion resistance and conductivity.

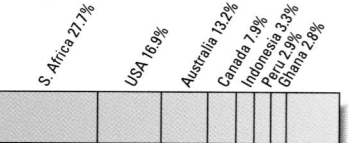

S. Africa 27.7% | USA 16.9% | Australia 13.2% | Canada 7.9% | Indonesia 3.3% | Peru 2.9% | Ghana 2.8%

World total (1995): 1,889 tonnes *

Copper: Derived from low-yielding sulphide ores, copper is an important export for several developing countries. An excellent conductor of heat and electricity, it forms part of most electrical items, and is used in the manufacture of brass and bronze. Major importers include Japan and Germany.

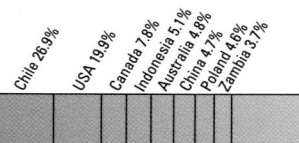

Chile 26.5% | USA 19.9% | Canada 7.8% | Indonesia 5.1% | Australia 4.8% | China 4.7% | Poland 4.6% | Zambia 3.7%

World total (1995): 9,311,000 tonnes *

Mercury: The only metal that is liquid at normal temperatures, most is derived from its sulphide, cinnabar, found only in small quantities in volcanic areas. Apart from its value in thermometers and other instruments, most mercury production is used in anti-fungal and anti-fouling preparations, and to make detonators.

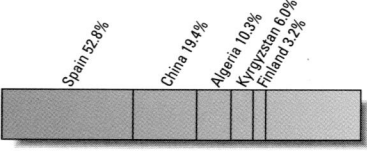

Spain 52.9% | China 18.4% | Algeria 10.3% | Kyrgyzstan 6.0% | Finland 3.2%

World total (1995): 2,837 tonnes *

Zinc: Often found in association with lead ores, zinc is highly resistant to corrosion, and about 40% of the refined metal is used to plate sheet steel, particularly vehicle bodies – a process known as galvanizing. Zinc is also used in dry batteries, paints and dyes.

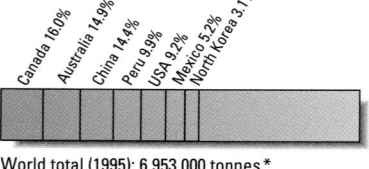

Canada 16.0% | Australia 14.9% | China 14.4% | Peru 9.9% | USA 9.2% | Mexico 5.2% | North Korea 3.1%

World total (1995): 6,953,000 tonnes *

Silver: Most silver comes from ores mined and processed for other metals (including lead and copper). Pure or alloyed with harder metals, it is used for jewellery and ornaments. Industrial use includes dentistry, electronics, photography and as a chemical catalyst.

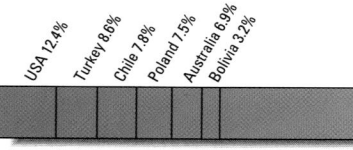

USA 12.4% | Turkey 8.6% | Chile 7.8% | Poland 7.5% | Australia 6.9% | Bolivia 3.2%

World total (1995): 13,266 tonnes *

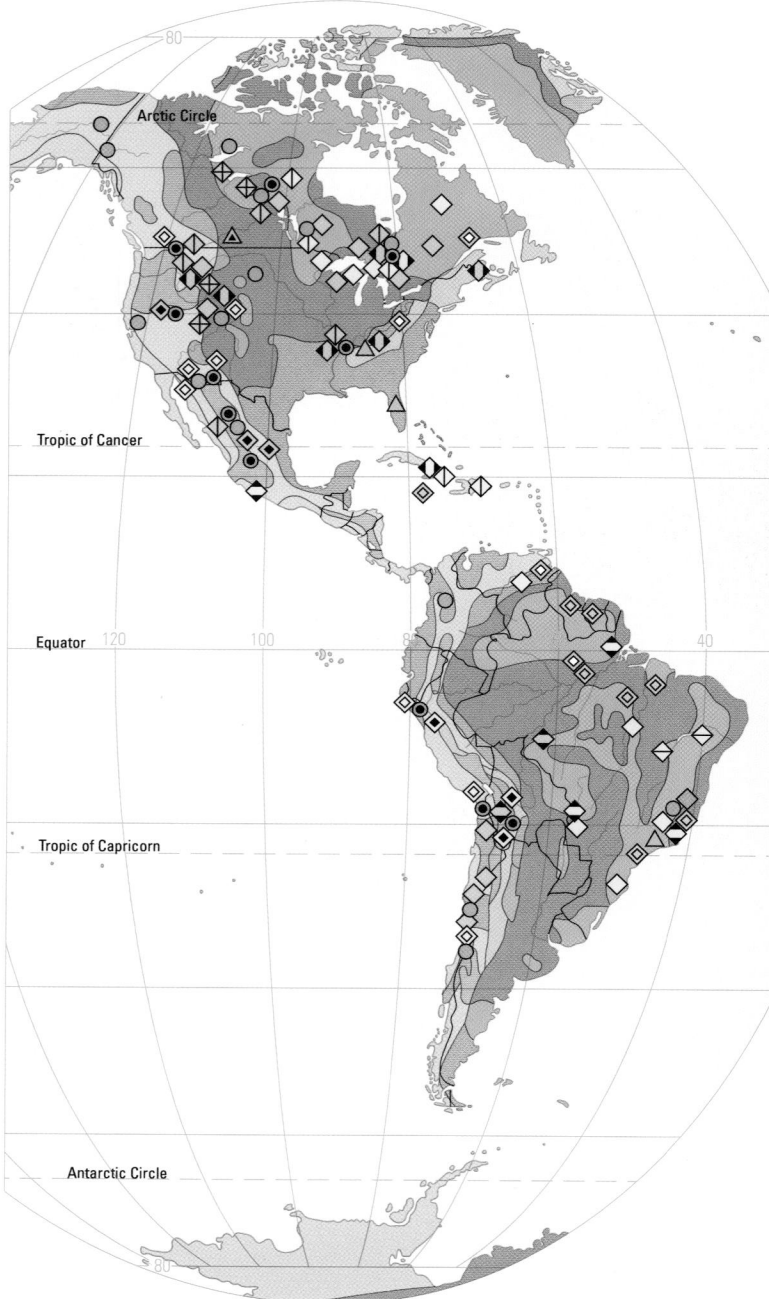

Strategic Minerals

Ever since the art of high-temperature smelting was discovered, some time in the second millennium BC, iron has been by far the most important metal known to man. The earliest iron ploughs transformed primitive agriculture and led to the first human population explosion, while iron weapons – or the lack of them – ensured the rise or fall of entire cultures.

Widely distributed around the world, iron ores usually contain 25–60% iron; blast furnaces process the raw product into pig-iron, which is then alloyed with carbon and other minerals to produce steels of various qualities. From the time of the Industrial Revolution, steel has been almost literally the backbone of modern civilization, the prime structural material on which all else is built.

Iron smelting usually developed close to the sources of ore and, later, to the coalfields that fuelled the furnaces. Today, most ore comes from a few richly-endowed locations where large-scale mining is possible. Iron and steel plants are generally built at coastal sites so that giant ore carriers, which account for a sizeable proportion of the world's merchant fleet, can easily discharge their cargoes.

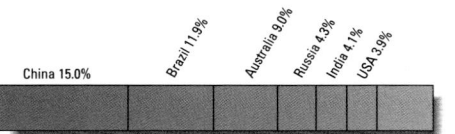
World total production of iron ore (1995): 1,020,000,000 tonnes

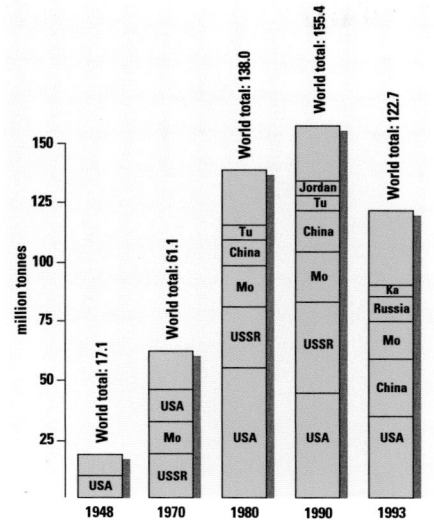

World production of phosphates in millions of tonnes (1993). Phosphate production is vital to the economies of several small countries. Nauru, for example, is heavily dependent on phosphate exports – the island has one of the world's richest deposits. In 1994, 613,000 tonnes were mined, employing 1,000 people. In Togo, earnings from phosphate exports have superseded all agricultural exports.

Percentage of total world phosphate production (1994)

1. USA	32.4%	7. Israel	3.1%
2. China	20.2%	8. Brazil	2.6%
3. Morocco	15.4%	9. South Africa	2.0%
4. Russia	6.2%	10. Togo	1.7%
5. Tunisia	4.4%	11. Kazakstan	1.6%
6. Jordan	3.3%	12. Senegal	1.4%

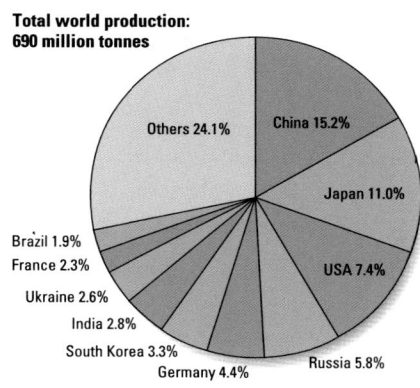

World production of pig-iron and ferro-alloys (1995). All countries with an annual output of more than 1 million tonnes are shown

Total world production: 690 million tonnes

China 15.2%, Japan 11.0%, USA 7.4%, Russia 5.8%, Germany 4.4%, South Korea 3.3%, India 2.8%, Ukraine 2.6%, France 2.3%, Brazil 1.9%, Others 24.1%

Manganese: In its pure state, manganese is a hard, brittle metal. Alloyed with chrome, iron and nickel, it produces abrasion-resistant steels; manganese-aluminium alloys are light but tough. Found in batteries and inks, manganese is also used in glass production. Manganese ores are frequently found in the same location as sedimentary iron ores. Pyrolusite (MnO_2) and psilomelane are the main economically-exploitable sources.

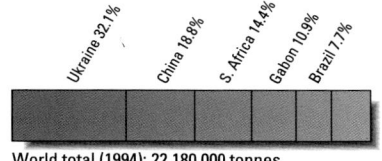
World total (1994): 22,180,000 tonnes

Chromium: Most of the world's chromium production is alloyed with iron and other metals to produce steels with various different properties. Combined with iron, nickel, cobalt and tungsten, chromium produces an exceptionally hard steel, resistant to heat; chrome steels are used for many household items where utility must be matched with appearance – cutlery, for example. Chromium is also used in production of refractory bricks, and its salts for tanning and dyeing leather and cloth.

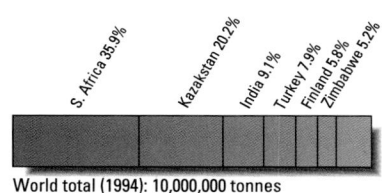
World total (1994): 10,000,000 tonnes

Nickel: Combined with chrome and iron, nickel produces stainless and high-strength steels; similar alloys go to make magnets and electrical heating elements. Nickel combined with copper is widely used to make coins; cupro-nickel alloy is very resistant to corrosion. Its ores yield only modest quantities of nickel – 0.5% to 3.0% – but also contain copper, iron and small amounts of precious metals. Japan, USA, UK, Germany and France are the principal importers.

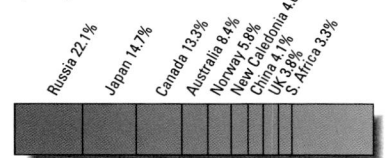
World total (1995): 920,000 tonnes

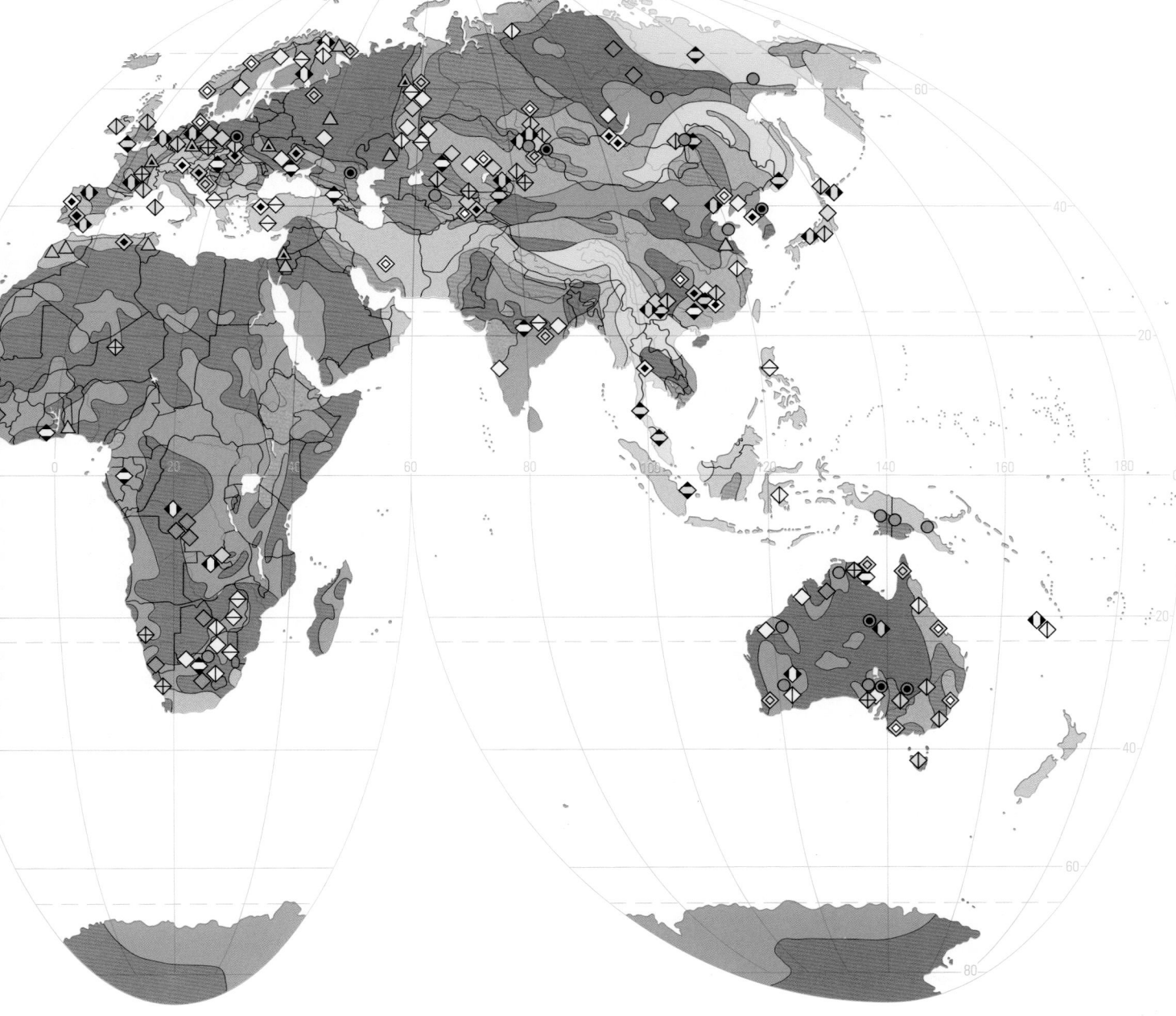

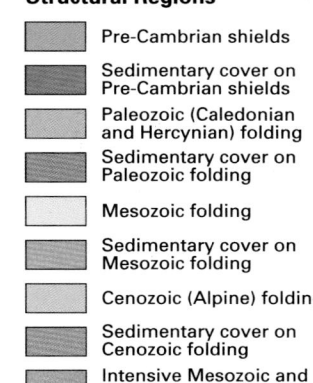

Distribution of Minerals

Structural Regions

- Pre-Cambrian shields
- Sedimentary cover on Pre-Cambrian shields
- Paleozoic (Caledonian and Hercynian) folding
- Sedimentary cover on Paleozoic folding
- Mesozoic folding
- Sedimentary cover on Mesozoic folding
- Cenozoic (Alpine) folding
- Sedimentary cover on Cenozoic folding
- Intensive Mesozoic and Cenozoic vulcanism

Distribution
Iron and ferro-alloys

- Chrome
- Cobalt
- Iron Ore
- Manganese
- Molybdenum
- Nickel Ore
- Tungsten

Non-ferrous metals

- Bauxite (Aluminium)
- Copper
- Lead
- Mercury
- Tin
- Zinc
- Uranium

Precious metals and stones

- Diamonds
- Gold
- Silver

Fertilizers

- Phosphates
- Potash

Manufacturing

The Industrial Revolution which began in Britain in the late 18th century, represented a major technological advance in the evolution of human society. It enabled a group of countries to become prosperous by replacing expensive human labour with increasingly sophisticated machinery. In economic terms, manufacturing is the transformation of raw materials, energy, labour and machines into finished goods, which have a higher value than the various elements used in production.

The economies of countries can be compared by reference to their per capita Gross National Products (or per capita GNPs), namely, the total value of goods and services produced in a country in a year, divided by the population.

The industrialized, or developed, countries accounted for 15% of the world's population in 1994 with an average per capita GNP of US $23,420. On the other hand, developing countries, with comparatively small industrial sectors and low-income economies, accounted for 57% of the world's population, with an average per capita GNP of just $380.

Kenya, with its low-income economy, had a per capita GNP in 1995 of $280. Agriculture employs 80% of the people, industry 7% and services 13%. The major industries are the processing of agricultural products and import substitution (the manufacture of such necessities as cement, footwear and textiles). Heavy industry plays a comparatively small part in the economy. By contrast, Germany, a major industrialized nation, had a per capita GNP in 1995

of $27,510. Agriculture employs only 4% of the population, with 38% in industry, and 58% in services. Germany's industrial sector differs greatly from Kenya's, with an emphasis on the manufacture of vehicles, machinery and chemicals.

Since the 1970s, some former developing countries in Asia have been tranformed by rapid industrialization. These 'economic tigers', including China, Malaysia, South Korea, Singapore, Taiwan and Thailand, owe their success partly to low labour costs, but also to substantial investment in education, together with advances in transport, telecommunications and computers, which have made technology more readily transferable around the world than ever before. They have also benefited from economic freedom and trade liberalization.

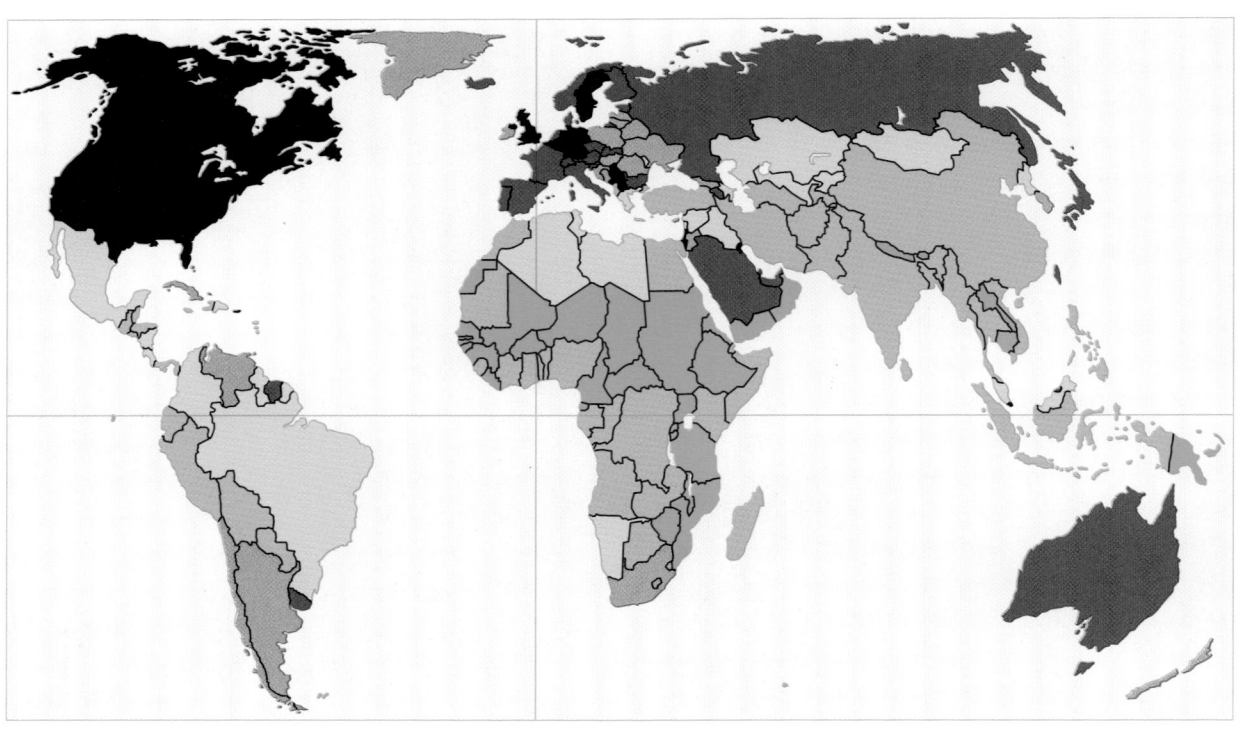

Employment

The number of workers employed in manufacturing for every 100 workers engaged in agriculture (latest available year)

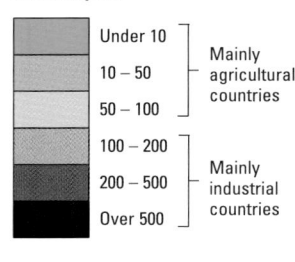

Under 10 — Mainly agricultural countries
10 – 50
50 – 100
100 – 200
200 – 500 — Mainly industrial countries
Over 500

Selected countries (latest available year)

Singapore	8,860
UK	1,270
Belgium	820
Germany	800
Kuwait	767
Bahrain	660
USA	657
Israel	633

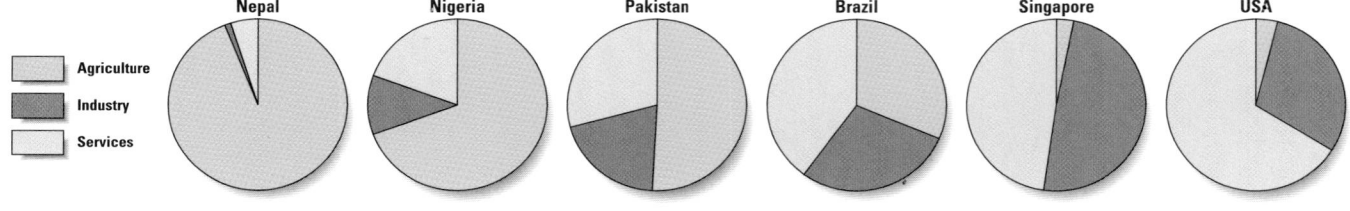

Nepal   Nigeria   Pakistan   Brazil   Singapore   USA

Agriculture
Industry
Services

Division of Employment

Distribution of workers between agriculture, industry and services, selected countries (latest available year)

The six countries selected illustrate the usual stages of economic development, from dependence on agriculture through industrial growth to the expansion of the service sector.

The Workforce

Percentages of men and women between 15 and 64 in employment, selected countries (latest available year)

The figures include employees and the self-employed, who in developing countries are often subsistence farmers. People in full-time education are excluded. Because of the population age structure in developing countries, the employed population has to support a far larger number of non-workers than its industrial equivalent. For example, more than 52% of Kenya's people are under 15, an age group that makes up less than a tenth of the UK population.

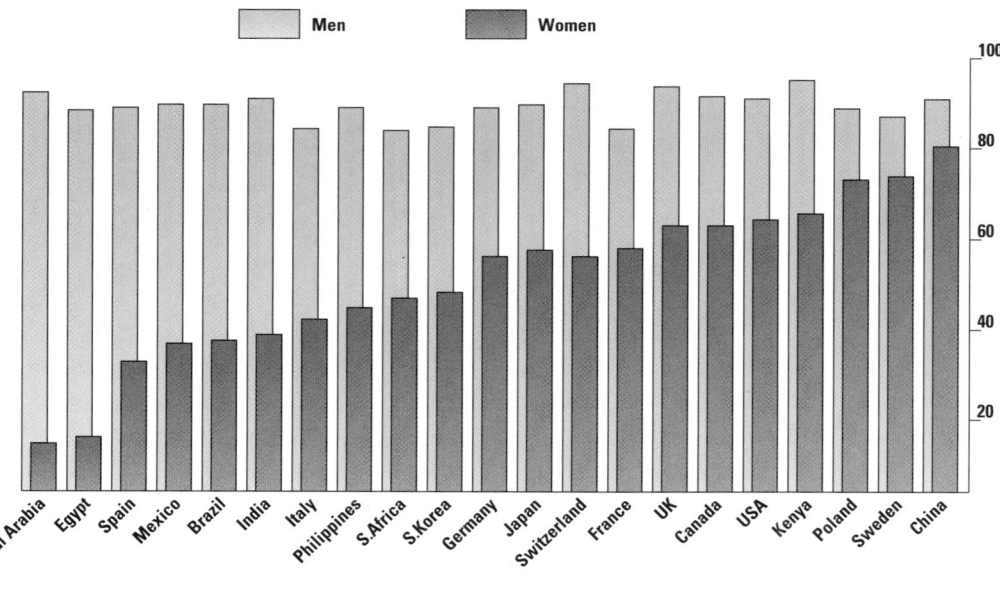

Men   Women

Saudi Arabia Egypt Spain Mexico Brazil India Italy Philippines S.Africa S.Korea Germany Japan Switzerland France UK Canada USA Kenya Poland Sweden China

Wealth Creation

The Gross National Product (GNP) of the world's largest economies, US $ million (1995)

1.	USA	7,100,007	21.	Austria	216,547
2.	Japan	4,963,587	22.	Sweden	209,720
3.	Germany	2,252,343	23.	Indonesia	190,105
4.	France	1,451,051	24.	Turkey	169,452
5.	UK	1,094,734	25.	Thailand	159,630
6.	Italy	1,088,085	26.	Denmark	156,027
7.	China	744,890	27.	Hong Kong	142,332
8.	Brazil	579,787	28.	Norway	136,077
9.	Canada	573,695	29.	Saudi Arabia	133,540
10.	Spain	532,347	30.	South Africa	130,918
11.	South Korea	435,137	31.	Poland	107,829
12.	Netherlands	371,039	32.	Finland	105,174
13.	Australia	337,909	33.	Portugal	96,689
14.	Russia	331,948	34.	Israel	87,875
15.	India	319,660	35.	Greece	85,885
16.	Mexico	304,596	36.	Ukraine	84,084
17.	Switzerland	286,014	37.	Singapore	79,831
18.	Argentina	278,431	38.	Malaysia	78,321
19.	Taiwan	256,300	39.	Philippines	71,865
20.	Belgium	250,710	40.	Colombia	70,263

Patterns of Production

Breakdown of industrial output by value, selected countries (latest available year)

	Food & agric. products	Textiles & clothing	Machinery & transport	Chemicals	Other
Algeria	26%	20%	11%	1%	41%
Argentina	24%	10%	16%	12%	37%
Australia	18%	7%	21%	8%	45%
Austria	17%	8%	25%	6%	43%
Belgium	19%	8%	23%	13%	36%
Brazil	15%	12%	24%	9%	40%
Burkina Faso	62%	18%	2%	1%	17%
Canada	15%	7%	25%	9%	44%
Denmark	22%	6%	23%	10%	39%
Egypt	20%	27%	13%	10%	31%
Finland	13%	6%	24%	7%	50%
France	18%	7%	33%	9%	33%
Germany	12%	5%	38%	10%	36%
Greece	20%	22%	14%	7%	38%
Hungary	6%	11%	37%	11%	35%
India	11%	16%	26%	15%	32%
Indonesia	23%	11%	10%	10%	47%
Iran	13%	22%	22%	7%	36%
Israel	13%	10%	28%	8%	42%
Ireland	28%	7%	20%	15%	28%
Italy	7%	13%	32%	10%	38%
Japan	10%	6%	38%	10%	37%
Kenya	35%	12%	14%	9%	29%
Malaysia	21%	5%	23%	14%	37%
Mexico	24%	12%	14%	12%	39%
Netherlands	19%	4%	28%	11%	38%
New Zealand	26%	10%	16%	6%	43%
Norway	21%	3%	26%	7%	44%
Pakistan	34%	21%	8%	12%	25%
Philippines	40%	7%	7%	10%	35%
Poland	15%	16%	30%	6%	33%
Portugal	17%	22%	16%	8%	38%
Singapore	6%	5%	46%	8%	36%
South Africa	14%	8%	17%	11%	49%
South Korea	15%	17%	24%	9%	35%
Spain	17%	9%	22%	9%	43%
Sweden	10%	2%	35%	8%	44%
Thailand	30%	17%	14%	6%	33%
Turkey	20%	14%	15%	8%	43%
UK	14%	6%	32%	11%	36%
USA	12%	5%	35%	10%	38%
Venezuela	23%	8%	9%	11%	49%

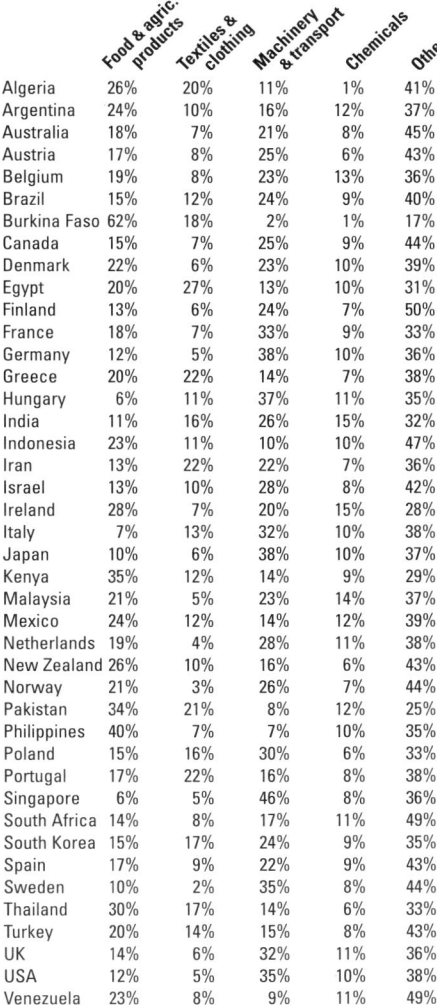

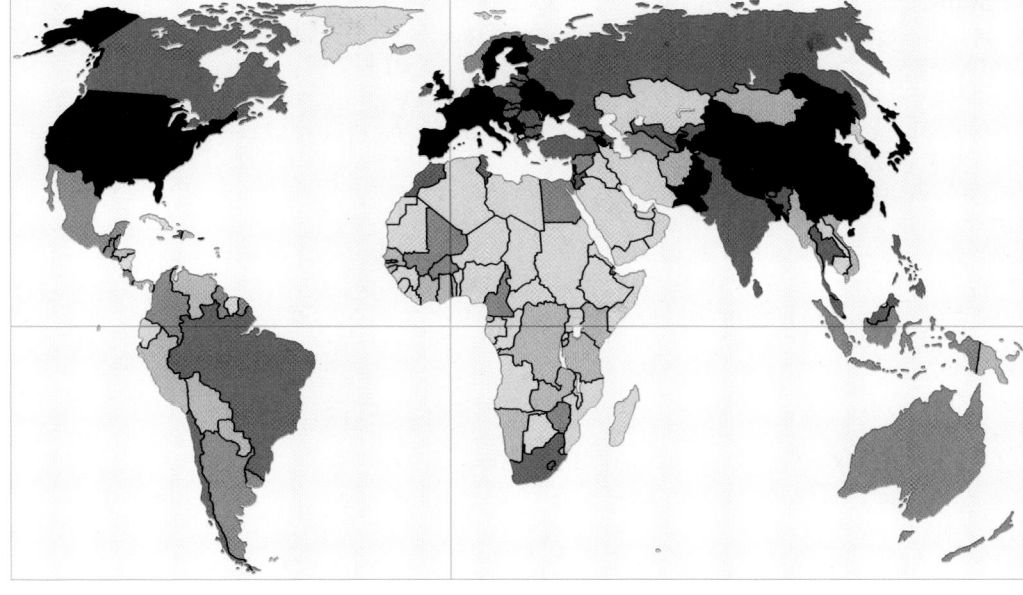

Manufactured goods (including machinery and transport) as a percentage of total exports (latest available year)

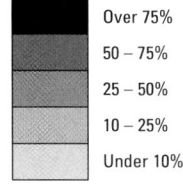

	Over 75%
	50 – 75%
	25 – 50%
	10 – 25%
	Under 10%

The Far East and South-east Asia (Japan 98.3%, Macau 97.8%, Taiwan 92.7%, Hong Kong [now part of China] 93.0%, South Korea 93.4%) are most dominant, but many countries in Europe (e.g. Slovenia 92.4%) are also heavily dependent on manufactured goods.

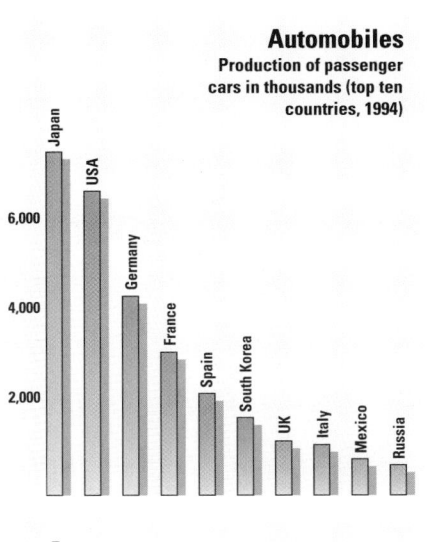

Automobiles
Production of passenger cars in thousands (top ten countries, 1994)

(Japan, USA, Germany, France, Spain, South Korea, UK, Italy, Mexico, Russia)

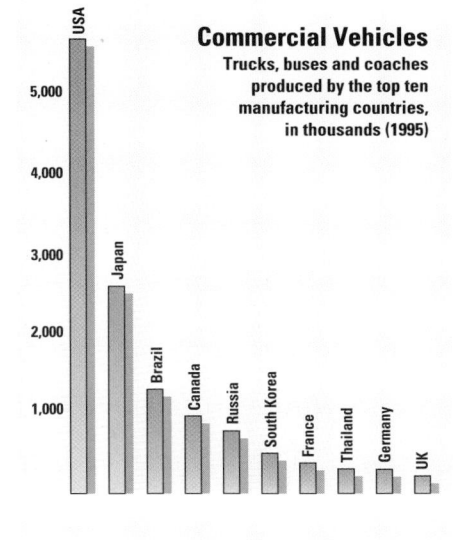

Commercial Vehicles
Trucks, buses and coaches produced by the top ten manufacturing countries, in thousands (1995)

(USA, Japan, Brazil, Canada, Russia, South Korea, France, Thailand, Germany, UK)

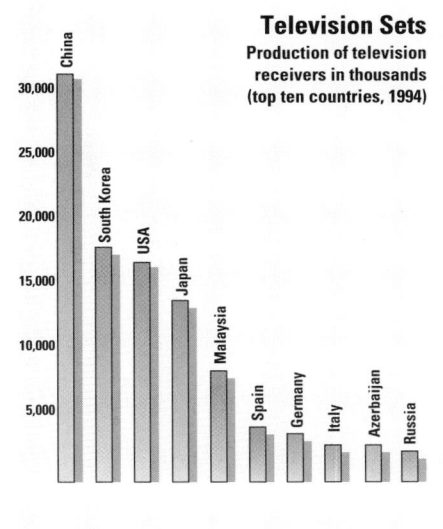

Television Sets
Production of television receivers in thousands (top ten countries, 1994)

(China, South Korea, USA, Japan, Malaysia, Spain, Germany, Italy, Azerbaijan, Russia)

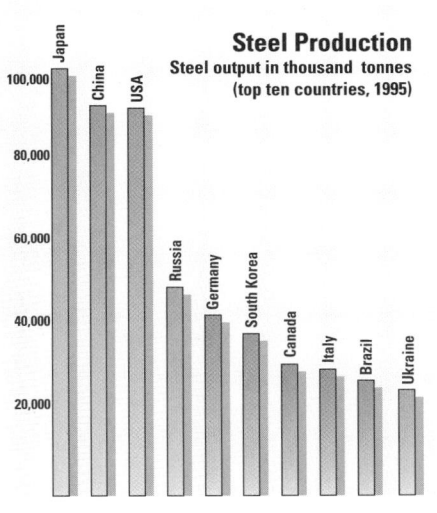

Steel Production
Steel output in thousand tonnes (top ten countries, 1995)

(Japan, China, USA, Russia, Germany, South Korea, Canada, Italy, Brazil, Ukraine)

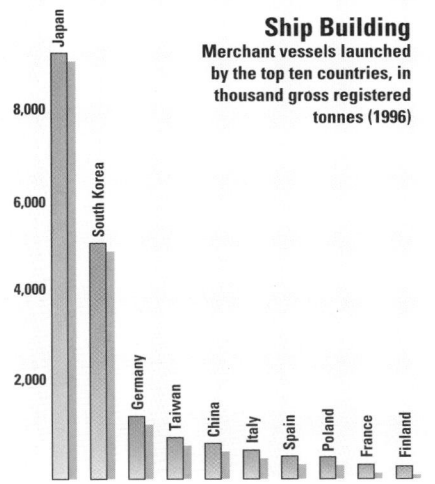

Ship Building
Merchant vessels launched by the top ten countries, in thousand gross registered tonnes (1996)

(Japan, South Korea, Germany, Taiwan, China, Italy, Spain, Poland, France, Finland)

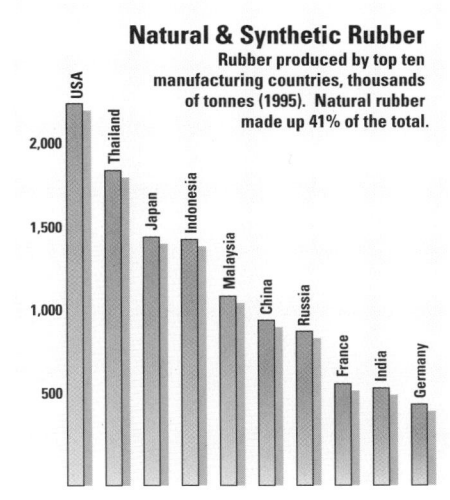

Natural & Synthetic Rubber
Rubber produced by top ten manufacturing countries, thousands of tonnes (1995). Natural rubber made up 41% of the total.

(USA, Thailand, Japan, Indonesia, Malaysia, China, Russia, France, India, Germany)

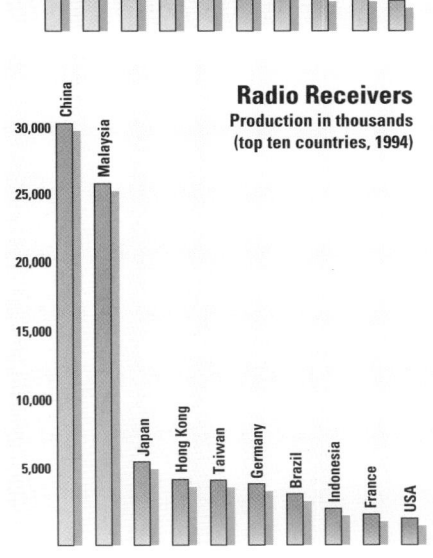

Radio Receivers
Production in thousands (top ten countries, 1994)

(China, Malaysia, Japan, Hong Kong, Taiwan, Germany, Brazil, Indonesia, France, USA)

Industrial Output

Industrial output (mining, manufacturing, construction, energy and water production), US $ billion (1994)

1.	Japan	1,836	21.	Saudi Arabia	59
2.	USA	1,496	=	Sweden	59
3.	Germany	777	23.	Thailand	56
4.	France	373	24.	Ukraine	46
5.	UK	326	25.	Turkey	41
6.	Italy	318	26.	Denmark	39
7.	China	245	27.	Norway	38
8.	Brazil	216	=	South Africa	38
9.	South Korea	162	29.	Poland	37
10.	Canada	154	30.	Finland	31
11.	Russia	143	31.	Malaysia	30
12.	Mexico	106	32.	Philippines	26
13.	Australia	100	33.	Singapore	25
14.	Netherlands	92	34.	Venezuela	24
15.	Argentina	85	=	Greece	24
16.	India	82	=	Hong Kong	24
17.	Indonesia	72	=	Israel	24
18.	Switzerland	68	=	Iran	24
19.	Austria	67	39.	Colombia	22
=	Belgium	67	40.	UAE	20

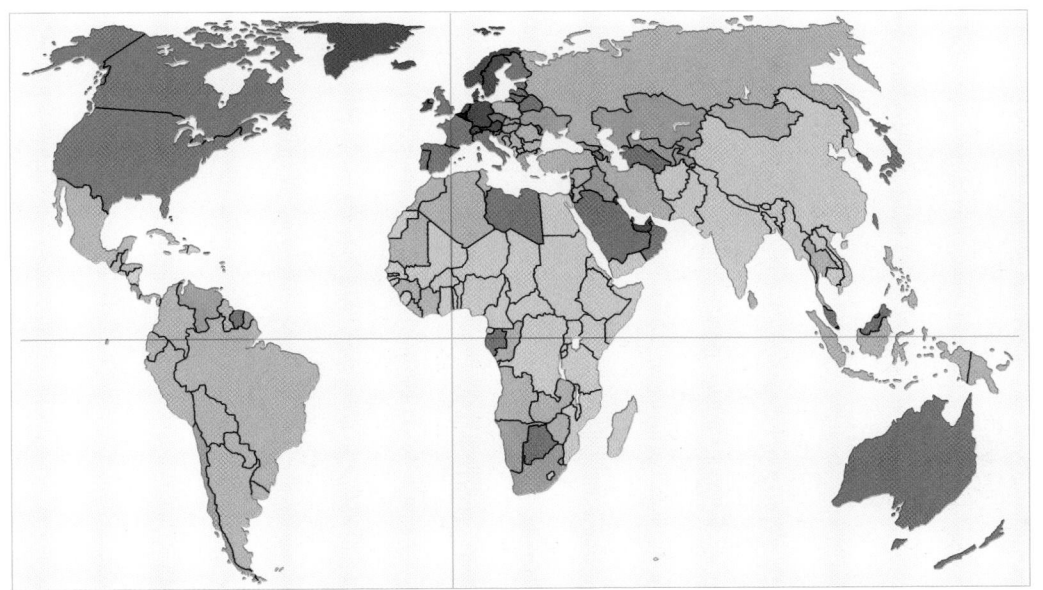

Exports Per Capita

Value of exports in US $, divided by total population (latest available year)

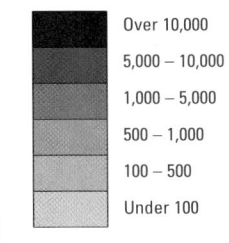

	Over 10,000
	5,000 – 10,000
	1,000 – 5,000
	500 – 1,000
	100 – 500
	Under 100

[UK 3,135]   [USA 1,967]

Highest per capita exports (1993)
Singapore	25,787
Hong Kong	22,339
Benelux	12,295
Brunei	8,778
Netherlands	8,578
Switzerland	8,457

Trade

Trade played a vital role in the growth of early civilizations and it was later a spur to European exploration and colonization. The colonial powers grew rich by exporting cheap manufactures, such as clothing and footwear, while obtaining primary products from their colonies.

From the late 19th century to the early 1950s, as transport technology improved, primary products, especially oil in the later stages of this period, dominated world trade. However, since that time, manufactures have become the chief commodities in world trade, which is dominated by the industrialized countries. Nearly half of all world trade flows between the developed market economies of the European Union, the United States and Japan, although the Asian 'tiger economies', notably Singapore, South Korea, Taiwan, Malaysia and Thailand, have increased their share in recent years. Recent predictions suggest that the next 'tigers' might include Argentina and Chile in South America, Indonesia, the Philippines and Vietnam in Asia, and the Czech Republic and Poland in Europe.

There is little trade between developing countries, although some mineral- and oil-rich nations obtain a high proportion of their GNP from export sales. Growth in world trade is regarded as a sign of economic health, as is a favourable balance of trade (or trade surplus) in any country.

World Trade

Percentage share of total world exports by value (1995)

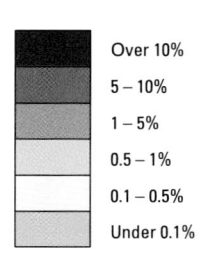

- Over 10%
- 5 – 10%
- 1 – 5%
- 0.5 – 1%
- 0.1 – 0.5%
- Under 0.1%

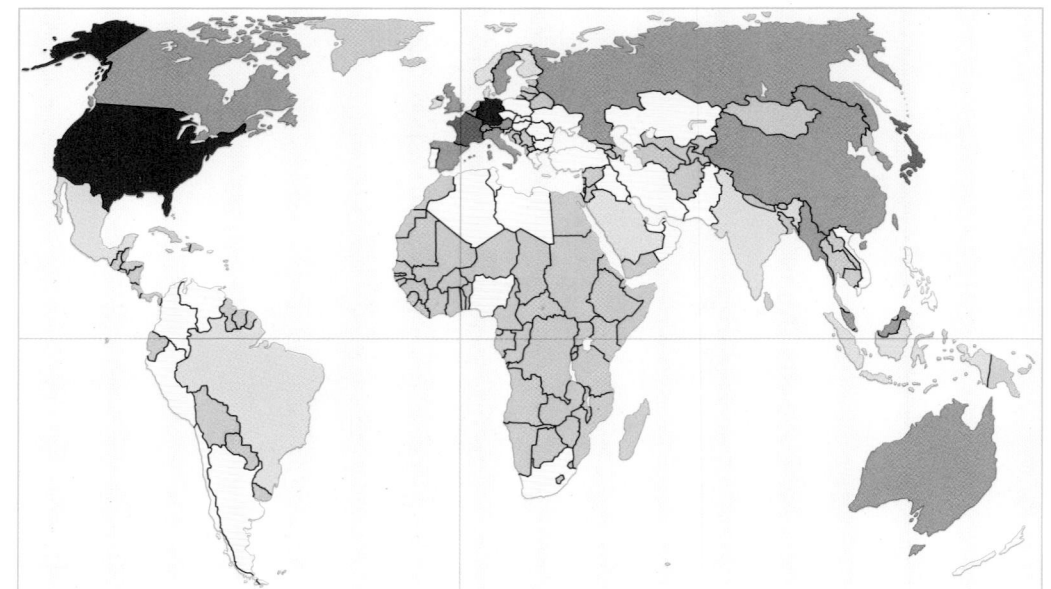

The Main Trading Nations

The imports and exports of the top ten trading nations as a percentage of world trade (1994). Each country's trade in manufactured goods is shown in dark blue. The graph shows that, in 1994, virtually all of Japan's imports and exports were manufactured goods.

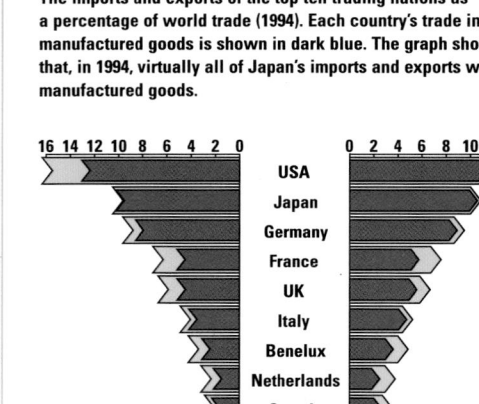

Imports   Exports

USA
Japan
Germany
France
UK
Italy
Benelux
Netherlands
Canada
Switzerland
Taiwan
South Korea

Dependence on Trade

Value of exports as a percentage of Gross National Product (1995)

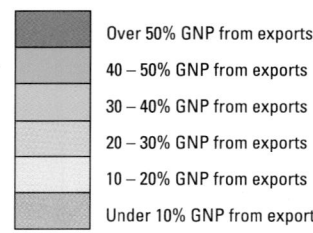

- Over 50% GNP from exports
- 40 – 50% GNP from exports
- 30 – 40% GNP from exports
- 20 – 30% GNP from exports
- 10 – 20% GNP from exports
- Under 10% GNP from exports

- ● Most dependent on industrial exports (over 75% of total exports)
- ○ Most dependent on fuel exports (over 75% of total exports)
- ● Most dependent on metal and mineral exports (over 75% of total exports)

Major Exports

Leading manufactured items and their exporters, by percentage of world total in US $ (latest available year)

Leading manufactured items and their exporters, by percentage of world total in US $ (latest available year)

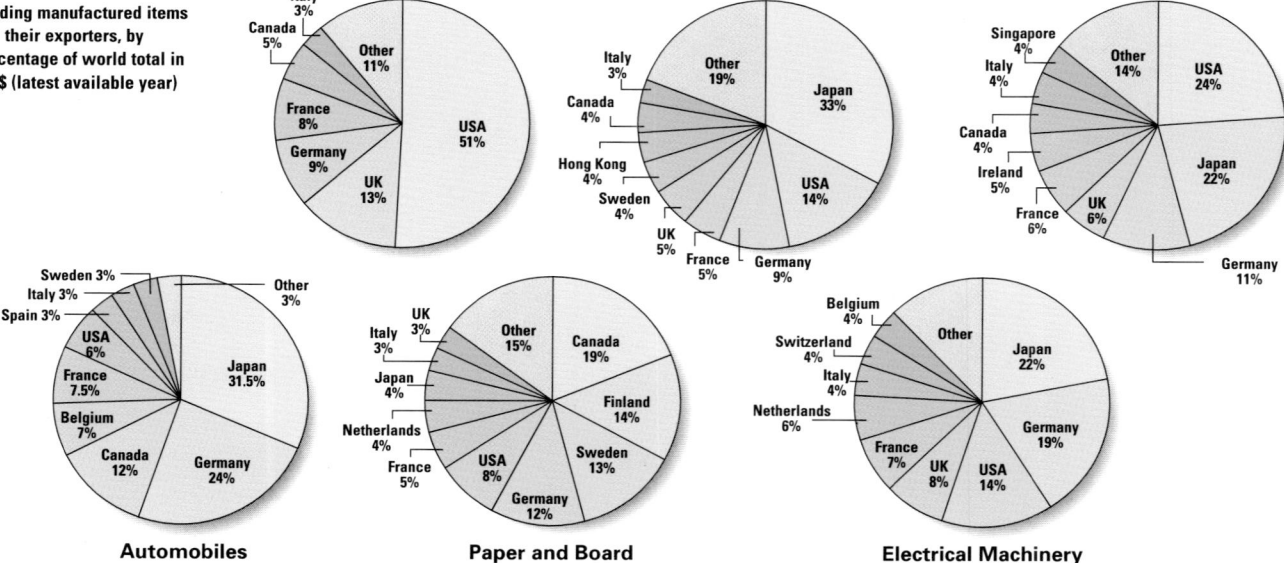

Aircraft
Italy 3%, Canada 5%, Other 11%, France 8%, Germany 9%, UK 13%, USA 51%

Telecommunications Gear
Italy 3%, Canada 4%, Hong Kong 4%, Sweden 4%, UK 5%, France 5%, Germany 5%, Other 19%, Japan 33%, USA 14%

Data Processing Equipment
Singapore 4%, Italy 4%, Canada 4%, Ireland 5%, France 6%, UK 6%, Other 14%, USA 24%, Japan 22%, Germany 11%

Automobiles
Sweden 3%, Italy 3%, Spain 3%, USA 6%, France 7.5%, Belgium 7%, Canada 12%, Germany 24%, Japan 31.5%, Other 3%

Paper and Board
UK 3%, Italy 3%, Japan 4%, Netherlands 4%, France 5%, USA 8%, Germany 12%, Other 15%, Canada 19%, Finland 14%, Sweden 13%

Electrical Machinery
Belgium 4%, Switzerland 4%, Italy 4%, Netherlands 6%, France 7%, UK 8%, USA 14%, Other, Japan 22%, Germany 19%

Traded Products

Top ten manufactures traded, by value in billions of US $ (latest available year)

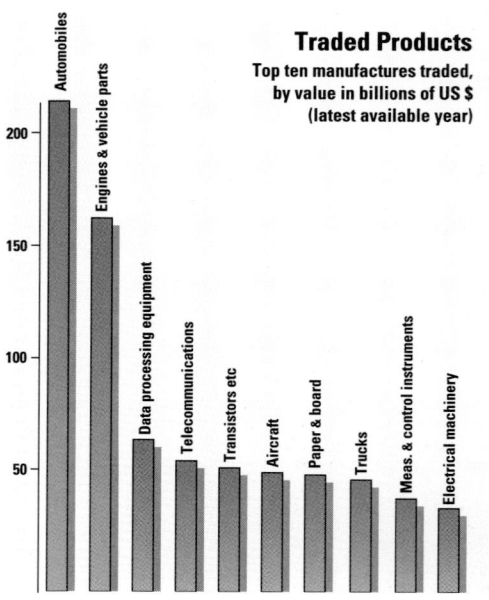

- Automobiles
- Engines & vehicle parts
- Data processing equipment
- Telecommunications
- Transistors etc
- Aircraft
- Paper & board
- Trucks
- Meas. & control instruments
- Electrical machinery

World Shipping

While ocean passenger traffic is nowadays relatively modest, sea transport still carries most of the world's trade. Oil and bulk carriers make up the majority of the world fleet, although the general cargo category is the fastest growing. Two innovations have revolutionized sea transport. The first is the development of the roll-on/roll-off (Ro-Ro) method where lorries or even trains loaded with freight are driven straight on to the ship, thus saving time. The second is containerization in which goods are packed into containers (the dimensions of which are fixed) at the factory, driven to the port and loaded on board by specialist machinery.

Almost 30% of world shipping sails under a 'flag of convenience', whereby owners take advantage of low taxes by registering their vessels in a foreign country the ships will never see, notably Panama and Liberia.

Merchant Fleets

Merchant fleets in thousand gross tonnage (1994). A large number of vessels are registered in Liberia and Panama but they are not part of the national fleet.

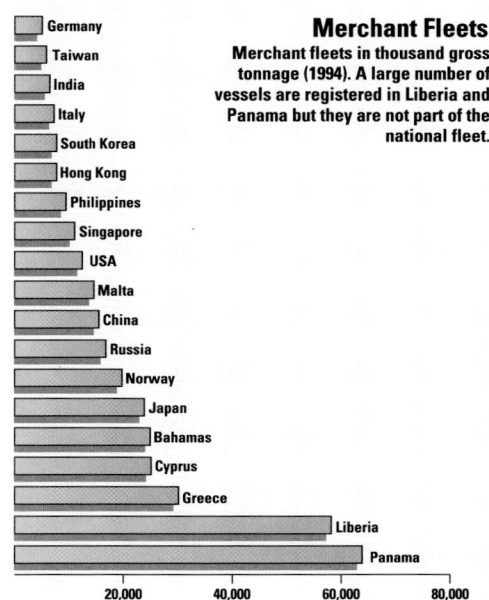

Germany
Taiwan
India
Italy
South Korea
Hong Kong
Philippines
Singapore
USA
Malta
China
Russia
Norway
Japan
Bahamas
Cyprus
Greece
Liberia
Panama

20,000 40,000 60,000 80,000

Types of Vessels

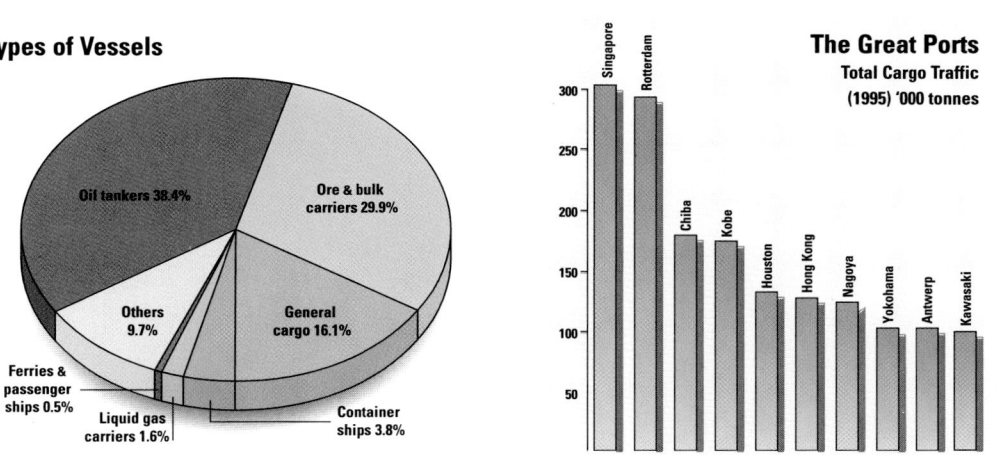

Oil tankers 38.4%
Ore & bulk carriers 29.9%
General cargo 16.1%
Others 9.7%
Container ships 3.8%
Liquid gas carriers 1.6%
Ferries & passenger ships 0.5%

The Great Ports

Total Cargo Traffic (1995) '000 tonnes

Singapore
Rotterdam
Chiba
Kobe
Houston
Hong Kong
Nagoya
Yokohama
Antwerp
Kawasaki

50 100 150 200 250 300

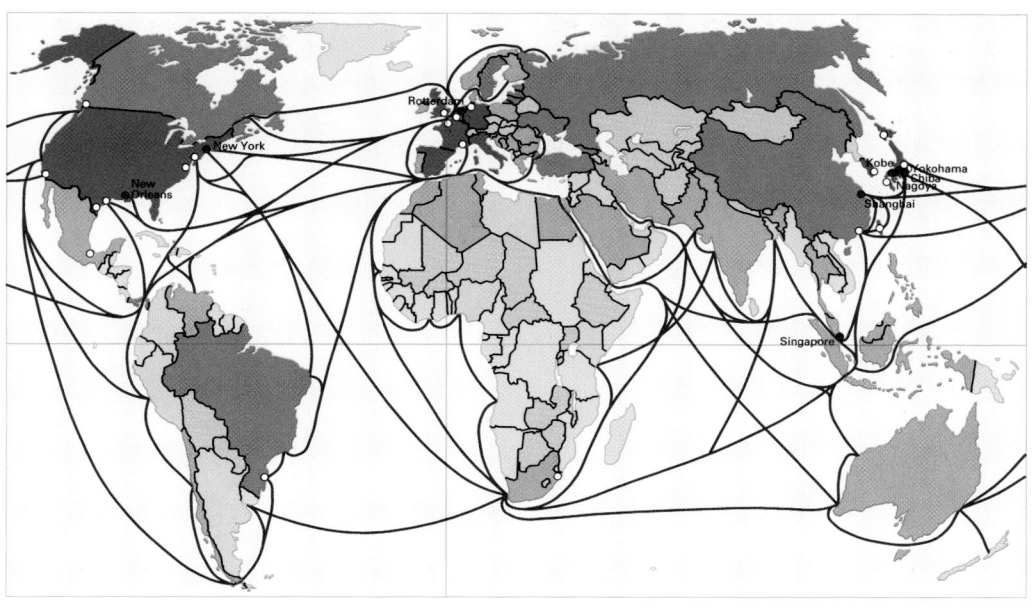

New Orleans
New York
Rotterdam
Kobe Yokohama
Nagoya Chiba
Shanghai
Singapore

Freight

Freight unloaded in millions of tonnes (latest available year)

- Over 100
- 50 – 100
- 10 – 50
- 5 – 10
- Under 5
- Landlocked countries

Major seaports

- ● Over 100 million tonnes per year
- ○ 50 – 100 million tonnes per year
- ── major shipping routes

Trade in Primary Products

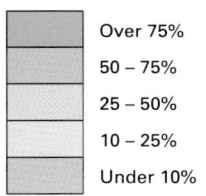

Primary products (excluding fuels, minerals and metals) as a percentage of total export value (latest available year)

- Over 75%
- 50 – 75%
- 25 – 50%
- 10 – 25%
- Under 10%

Primary products are raw materials or partly processed products which form the basis for manufacturing. They are the necessary requirements of industries and include agricultural products, minerals and timber, as well as many semi-manufactured goods such as cotton, which has been spun but not woven, wood pulp or flour. Many developed countries have few natural resources and rely on imports for the majority of their primary products. The countries of South-east Asia export hardwoods to the rest of the world, whilst many South American countries are heavily dependent on coffee exports.

Balance of Trade

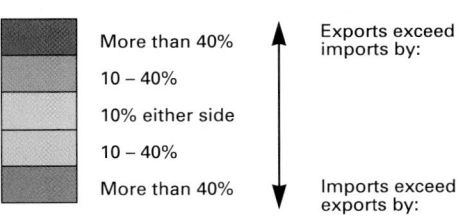

Value of exports in proportion to the value of imports (1995)

Exports exceed imports by:
- More than 40%
- 10 – 40%
- 10% either side
- 10 – 40%
- More than 40%
Imports exceed exports by:

The total world trade balance should amount to zero, since exports must equal imports on a global scale. In practice, at least $100 billion in exports go unrecorded, leaving the world with an apparent deficit and many countries in a better position than public accounting reveals. However, a favourable trade balance is not necessarily a sign of prosperity: many poorer countries must maintain a high surplus in order to service debts, and do so by restricting imports below the levels needed to sustain successful economies.

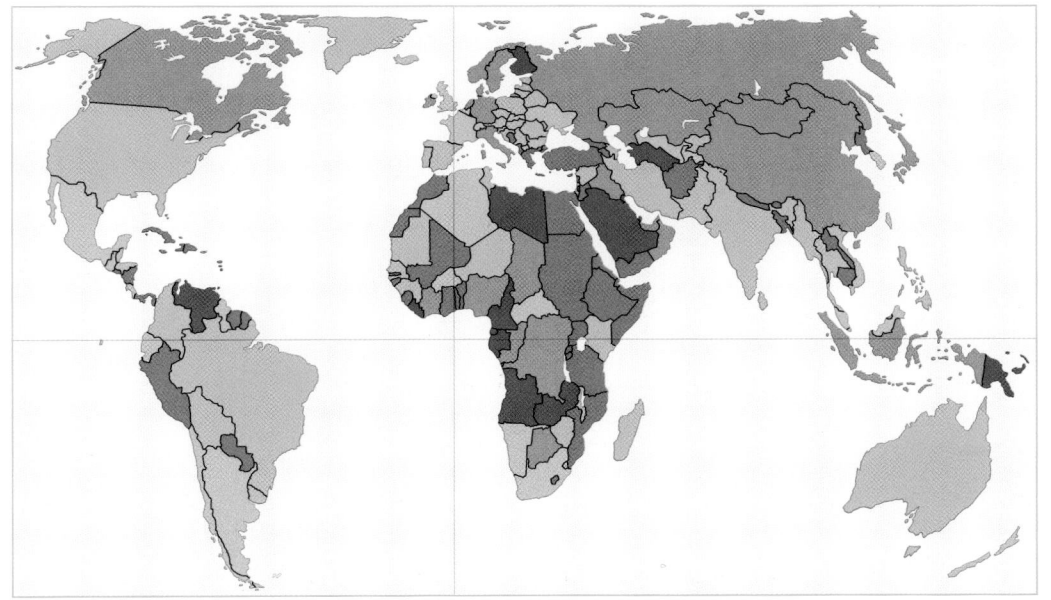

Air Freight

Trends in air freight in million tonne-km*, selected countries (1988–92)

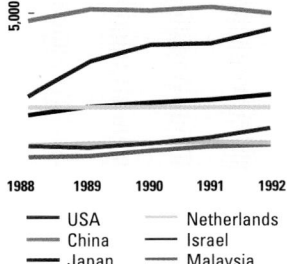

20,000
15,000
10,000
5,000

1988 1989 1990 1991 1992

- USA
- China
- Japan
- UK
- Netherlands
- Israel
- Malaysia

* Equivalent to million tonnes of air freight flown over 1 million kilometres per year.

Air transport is important to countries of considerable size; where ground terrain is difficult; when crossing short stretches of sea; and where goods are of high value, light in weight or perishable. Recent deregulation of airlines (in the USA since 1978 and the EU in 1993) has led to increased competition and lower fares.

Health

Average life expectancies all over the world have never been higher. They range from an average of 77 years in high-income economies, to 67 years in middle-income economies and 63 in low-income economies. Even in poverty-stricken and strife-torn Burundi and Ethiopia, average life expectancies are around 50 years, as compared with less than 30 years for a citizen of Berlin in 1880.

In global terms, the radical improvements in health have much to do with improvements in agriculture and, hence, nutrition, as well as health education, an increase in sanitation and the quality of drinking water, together with advances in medicine. These radical changes have been responsible for falling death rates and rapid population growth, together with the expectation by most people that improvements in health will continue.

Health standards, life expectancies and causes of death vary considerably between the developed and developing world. The map on this page shows that in most of Africa, Asia and Latin America, the average daily calorie supply per person is so low as to cause malnutrition. (The daily requirement rated adequate by the World Health Organization is between 2,300 and 2,500 calories per person per day.) Malnutrition is a serious condition.

For example, among pregnant women it causes high rates of child mortality.

Deficiency diseases occur when people do not have a balanced diet. Protein deficiency causes stunting and kwashiorkor, which can be fatal, especially among young children, while vitamin deficiencies cause such illnesses as beri beri, pellagra, scurvy and rickets. Iron deficiency causes anaemia, while a lack of iodine causes mental retardation. A UN report in the early 1990s reported that iodine deficiency affected 458 million women world-wide, as compared with 238 million men. Women's nutritional problems are especially acute in southern Asia. For example, the UN report stated that 88% of pregnant women in India were anaemic, as compared with 15% in developed countries.

Infectious diseases in association, directly or indirectly, with deficient diets, continue to affect people in developing countries, especially the 48 countries in the low human development category, where, in 1990–95, only 32% of the people had access to sanitation and 68% to safe water supplies.

A World Health report in 1996 stated that infectious diseases cause 17 million deaths per year. Most of the victims are young and otherwise fit people in developing countries. The major killers in 1995 were respiratory infections, including pneumonia (which caused

4.4 million deaths), cholera, typhoid, dysentery (3.1 million together), tuberculosis (almost 3 million), malaria (2.1 million), hepatitis B (1.1 million), AIDS and measles (more than 1 million each). Many of these diseases are preventable and, according to the United Nations Children's Fund, an investment of US $25,000 million per year, about half the money spent annually on cigarettes in Europe alone, would save the lives of all the children who currently die from avoidable diseases.

Infectious diseases are much less important as causes of death in developed countries, where cancer and circulatory diseases, such as atherosclerosis and hypertension, which cause strokes and heart attacks, are the most common causes of fatality. Because these diseases tend to kill older people, they are relatively less important in developing countries where people have shorter lifespans.

Harmful habits are also generally practised more by the rich than the poor. For example, smoking is an important cause of death in developed countries, though, curiously, the Japanese, with an average life expectancy of 79 years in 1996, are among the highest tobacco consumers. Similarly, high alcohol consumption, although it has bad effects on health, does not seem to affect longevity. The leading consumers, the French, had a life expectancy of 78 in 1996.

Food Consumption

Average daily food intake in calories per person (latest available year)

- Over 3,500 calories
- 3,000 – 3,500 calories
- 2,500 – 3,000 calories
- 2,000 – 2,500 calories
- Under 2,000 calories
- No available data

Top 5 countries

Ireland	3,847 calories
Greece	3,815 calories
Cyprus	3,779 calories
USA	3,732 calories
Spain	3,708 calories

Bottom 5 countries

Somalia	1,499 calories
Afghanistan	1,523 calories
Ethiopia	1,610 calories
Liberia	1,640 calories
Mozambique	1,680 calories

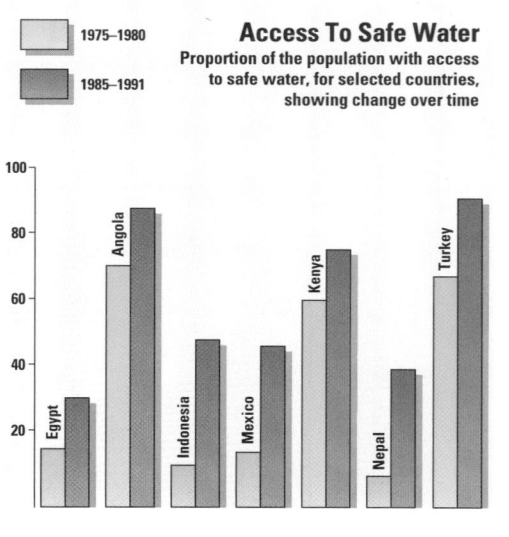

Access To Safe Water
Proportion of the population with access to safe water, for selected countries, showing change over time

1975–1980
1985–1991

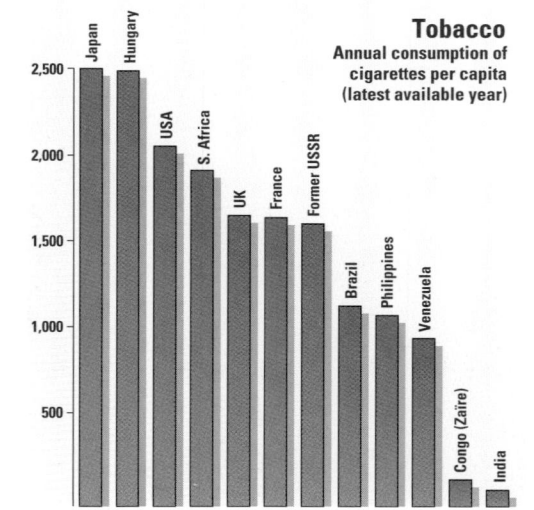

Tobacco
Annual consumption of cigarettes per capita (latest available year)

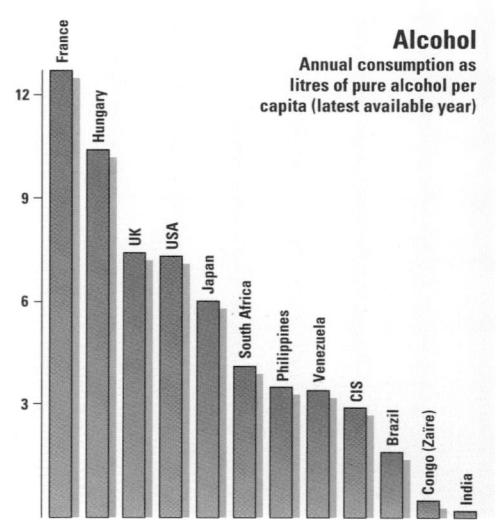

Alcohol
Annual consumption as litres of pure alcohol per capita (latest available year)

Life Expectancy

Years of life expectancy at birth, selected countries (1997)

The chart shows combined data for both sexes. On average, women live longer than men worldwide, even in developing countries with high maternal mortality rates. Overall, life expectancy is steadily rising, though the difference between rich and poor nations remains dramatic.

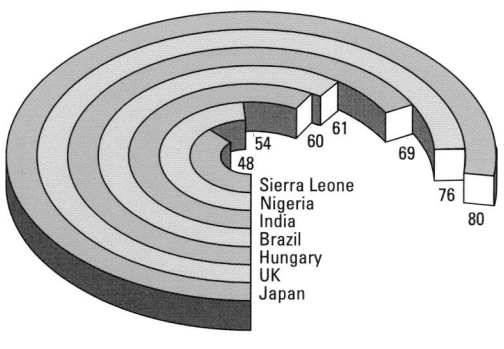

Sierra Leone	48
Nigeria	54
India	60
Brazil	61
Hungary	69
UK	76
Japan	80

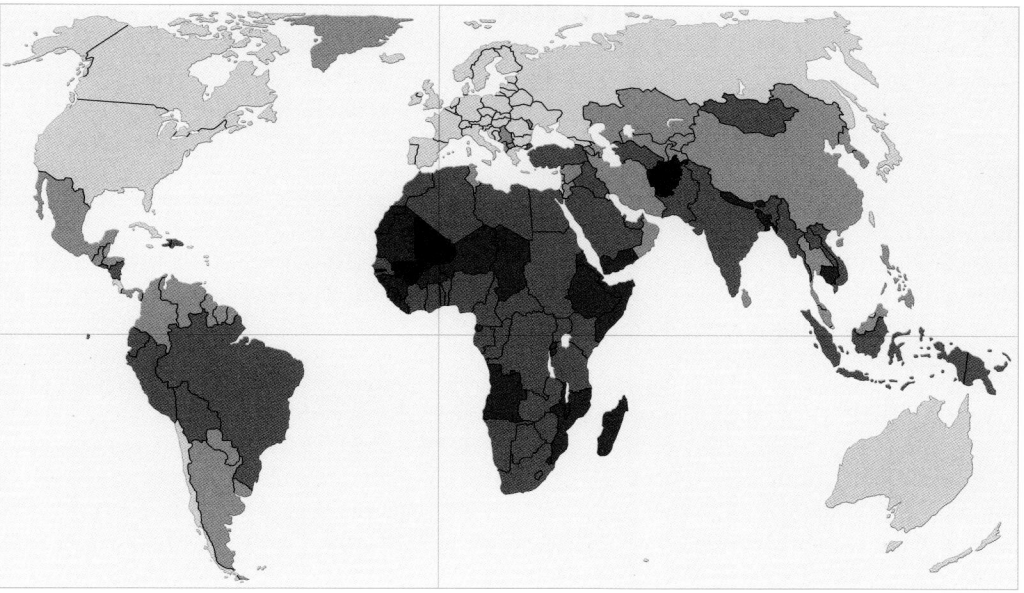

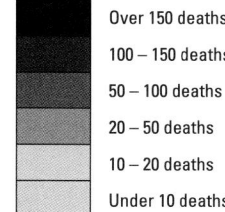

	Over 150 deaths
	100 – 150 deaths
	50 – 100 deaths
	20 – 50 deaths
	10 – 20 deaths
	Under 10 deaths

Highest child mortality
Afghanistan .... 162 deaths
Mali .... 159 deaths

Lowest child mortality
Iceland .... 5 deaths
Finland .... 5 deaths

[UK 8 deaths] [USA 8 deaths]

Expenditure on Health

Public expenditure on health as a percentage of GNP (latest available year)

Countries with the highest spending		Countries with the lowest spending	
Costa Rica	30.0	Syria	0.4
Panama	21.8	Sudan	0.5
Grenada	15.6	Indonesia	0.7
St Vincent & G.	15.1	Qatar	0.8
Bahamas	14.5	Congo (Zaïre)	0.8
Bermuda	14.5	Morocco	0.9
USA	13.3	Somalia	0.9
Barbados	12.0	Cameroon	1.0
Lesotho	11.5	Laos	1.0

[UK 6.6 – in 1995 this amounted to US $1,300 per head]

The allocation of limited funds for health care in developing countries is rarely evenly spread – the quality of treatment can vary enormously from place to place within the same country. Urban dwellers tend to have much better access to health provisions than those living in rural areas.

Medical Provision

Doctors per 100,000 population, selected countries (latest available year, 1988–92)

Although the ratio of people to doctors gives a good approximation of a country's health provision, it is not an absolute indicator. Raw numbers may mask inefficiency and other weaknesses: the high proportion of physicians in Hungary, for example, has not prevented infant mortality rates more than twice as high as in the United Kingdom.

The definition of a doctor also varies from nation to nation. As well as registered medical practitioners, it may include trained medical assistants – an especially important category in developing countries, where they provide many of the same services as fully qualified physicians, including simple operations.

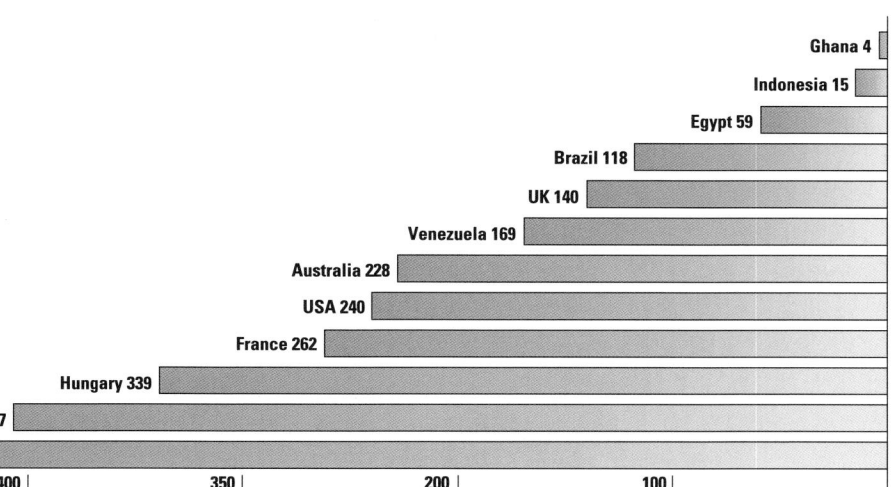

Ghana 4
Indonesia 15
Egypt 59
Brazil 118
UK 140
Venezuela 169
Australia 228
USA 240
France 262
Hungary 339
Latvia 407
Italy 439

400   350   200   100

The Aids Crisis

The Acquired Immune Deficiency Syndrome (AIDS) was first identified in 1981 when American doctors found otherwise healthy young men succumbing to rare infections. By 1984 the cause had been traced to the Human Immunodeficiency Virus (HIV) which can remain dormant for many years and perhaps indefinitely: only half of those known to carry the virus in 1981 had developed AIDS ten years later.

In Western countries in the mid-1990s, most AIDS deaths were among male homosexuals or needle-sharing drug-users. However, the disease is spreading fastest among heterosexual men and women, which is its usual vector in the developing world where most of its victims live.

The World Health Organization estimated that 1.3 million people died of AIDS in 1995 and that by the end of the same year 22 million people were HIV-positive. India has the largest number of HIV infections totalling more than 3 million, but two-thirds of all infections are in sub-Saharan Africa (where, unlike the rest of the world, more women are infected than men). It is estimated that two million African children will die of AIDS before the year 2000 and some 10 million will be orphaned.

Causes of Death

▪ Accidents, poisoning & violence	▪ Metabolic disorders
▪ Respiratory & digestive diseases	▪ Cancers
▪ Nervous & circulatory diseases	▪ Infectious & parasitic diseases

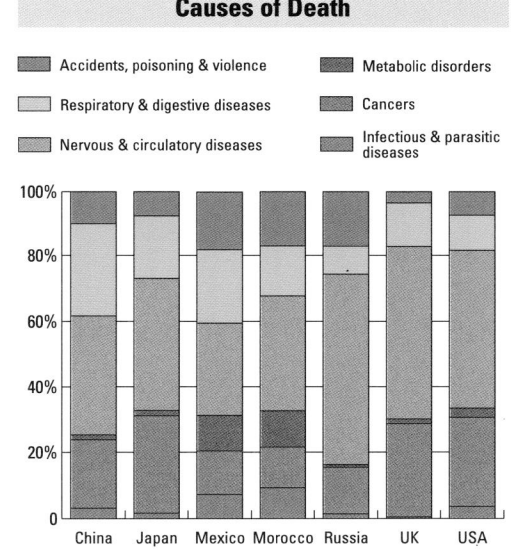

China   Japan   Mexico   Morocco   Russia   UK   USA

Circulatory Disease in Europe

Diseases of the circulatory system per 100,000 people (latest available year 1992–95)

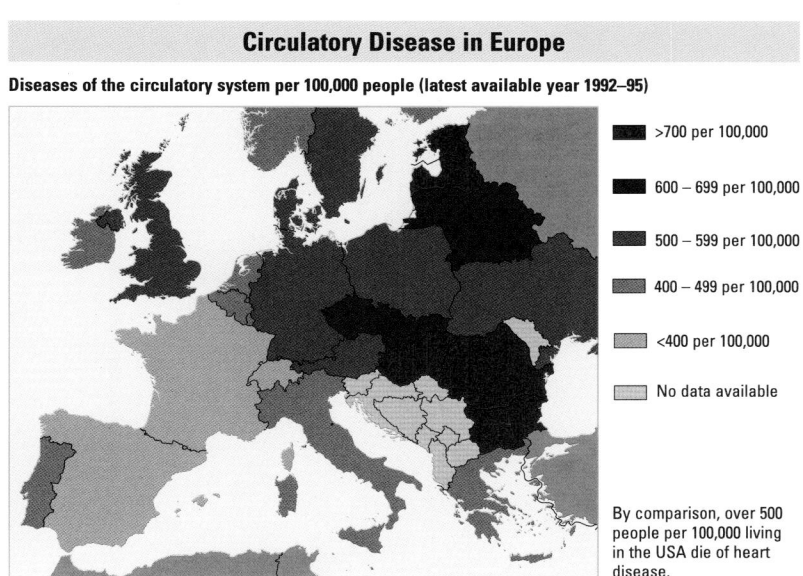

▪	>700 per 100,000
▪	600 – 699 per 100,000
▪	500 – 599 per 100,000
▪	400 – 499 per 100,000
▪	<400 per 100,000
▪	No data available

By comparison, over 500 people per 100,000 living in the USA die of heart disease.

Aids

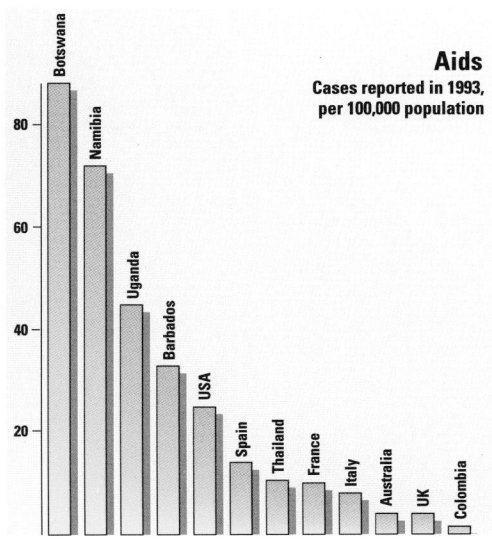

Cases reported in 1993, per 100,000 population

Botswana, Namibia, Uganda, Barbados, USA, Spain, Thailand, France, Italy, Australia, UK, Colombia

Sanitation

▪ Urban	
▪ Rural	

Percentage of the population with access to sanitation services, selected countries (latest available year)

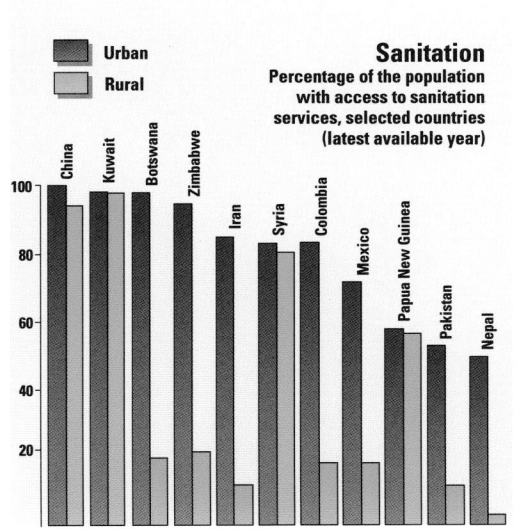

China, Kuwait, Botswana, Zimbabwe, Iran, Syria, Colombia, Mexico, Papua New Guinea, Pakistan, Nepal

Malaria

Cases of malaria per 100,000 people exposed to malaria-infected environments, selected countries* (latest available year)

* data are not available for Africa where 80% of malaria cases occur

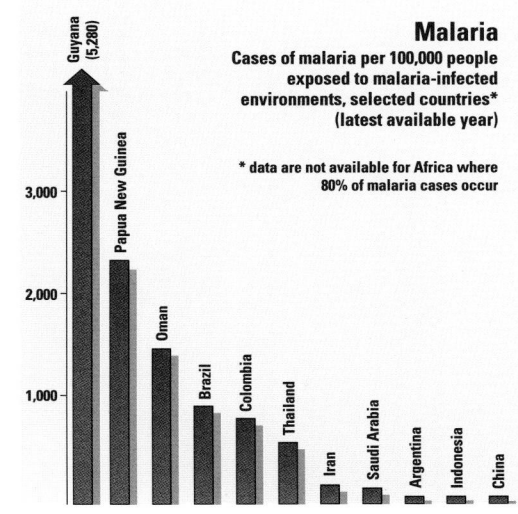

Guyana (5,280)
Papua New Guinea
Oman
Brazil
Colombia
Thailand
Iran
Saudi Arabia
Argentina
Indonesia
China

Infectious and parasitic diseases, such as malaria, which claimed 2.1 million lives in 1995, remain a scourge in the developing countries. Respiratory infections and injury also claim more lives in developing countries, which lack the drugs and the medical personnel to deal with them. Developing countries lack the basic services taken for granted in developed nations. For example, in sub-Saharan Africa in 1990–95, only 31% of the population had access to sanitation and 45% to safe water, with the situation being worse in rural areas. By contrast, circulatory diseases and cancer are the main causes of death in the rich, industrialized countries. For example, in the UK in the mid-1990s, circulatory diseases, which cause heart attacks and strokes, accounted for nearly half the deaths, with cancer accounting for nearly a quarter.

Wealth

For more information:
38 Wealth creation
39 Industrial power
   Exports per capita
40 World trade
   Major exports
41 Balance of trade
47 Distribution of
   spending
   Distribution of
   income

Currencies

Currency units of the world's most powerful economies

1. USA: US dollar ($, US $) = 100 cents
2. Japan: Yen (Y, ¥) = 100 sen
3. Germany: Deutsche Mark (DM) = 100 Pfennig
4. France: French franc (Fr) = 100 centimes
5. Italy: Italian lira (L, £, Lit) = 100 centesimi
6. UK: Pound sterling (£) = 100 pence
7. Canada: Canadian dollar (C$, Can$) = 100 cents
8. China: Renminbi yuan (RMBY, $, Y) = 10 jiao = 100 fen
9. Brazil: Cruzeiro real (BRC) = 100 centavos
10. Spain: Peseta (Pta, Pa) = 100 céntimos
11. India: Indian rupee (Re, Rs) = 100 paisa
12. Australia: Australian dollar ($A) = 100 cents
13. Netherlands: Guilder, florin (Gld, f) = 100 centimes
14. Switzerland: Swiss franc (SFr, SwF) = 100 centimes
15. South Korea: Won (W) = 100 chon
16. Sweden: Swedish krona (SKr) = 100 öre
17. Mexico: Mexican peso (Mex$) = 100 centavos
18. Belgium: Belgian franc (BFr) = 100 centimes
19. Austria: Schilling (S, Sch) = 100 Groschen
20. Finland: Markka (FMk) = 100 penniä
21. Denmark: Danish krone (DKr) = 100 øre
22. Norway: Norwegian krone (NKr) = 100 øre
23. Saudi Arabia: Riyal (SAR, SRI$) = 100 halalah
24. Indonesia: Rupiah (Rp) = 100 sen
25. South Africa: Rand (R) = 100 cents

Indicators

The gap between the world's rich and poor is now so great that it is difficult to illustrate on a single graph. Within each income group (as defined by the World Bank), however, comparisons have some meaning; the Chinese, perhaps because of propaganda value, have many more TV sets than Indians, whereas Nigerians prefer to spend their money on vehicles. However, the wealth gap in many developing countries is wide, with a small, rich class and a large, impoverished majority, while many high-income countries contain an underclass of unemployed and homeless people.

Perhaps the most glaring differences in the world today are those between the rich and the poor. The World Bank divides countries into three main groups based on average economic production expressed in terms of per capita GNP (Gross National Product). They are the low-income economies, including most African countries and much of Asia; the middle-income economies, including most of Latin America and most of the former USSR; and the high-income economies of Canada, the United States, Western Europe, Japan and Australia.

Per capita GNPs are a measure of the total goods and services produced by a country divided by the population, and then converted into US dollars at official exchange rates. They are useful indicators of a country's prosperity, though, like all statistics, they must be treated with care. For example, the prices for goods and services in China are far cheaper than they are in the United States. China's per capita GNP in 1995 was $620 (as compared with $26,980 in the USA) but the PPP (Purchasing-Power Parity) estimate of China's per capita GNP was considerably higher at $2,920. Another problem with per capita GNPs is that they are averages, which often conceal wide internal variations.

The pattern of poverty varies from region to region. In Latin America, much progress has been made through industrialization, though startling inequalities still exist between rich and poor. In Asia, the 'tiger economies' have followed Japan's example in pursuing export-led industrial policies, while the success of China's Special Economic Zones, where foreign investment is encouraged, has led to a huge rise in China's per capita GNP, as shown on the map on page 45, bottom right.

Solutions to poverty in Africa are much harder to find because of its high population growth, civil wars, natural disasters and high inflation rates. Although Africa receives more aid than any other continent, aid is only a partial solution. Much aid has been wasted on overambitious projects, in the servicing of huge national debts, or lost by inexperienced or corrupt governments. One initiative in some African countries has been to improve the infrastructure and develop tourism, creating employment and providing much-needed foreign currency. But tourism alone cannot solve the problems of under-development.

The International Monetary Fund and the World Bank argue that real economic progress in Africa will be achieved only when African countries create market-friendly economies that encourage trade through export-led manufacturing, while at the same time strictly controlling public spending on welfare, the civil service and other areas.

Continental Shares

Shares of population and of wealth (GNP) by continent

These generalized continental figures show the startling difference between rich and poor but mask the successes or failures of individual countries. Japan, for example, with less than 4% of Asia's population, produces almost 70% of the continent's output. Within countries, the difference between rich and poor can also be startling. In Brazil, for example, the richest 20% of the population own 60% of the wealth.

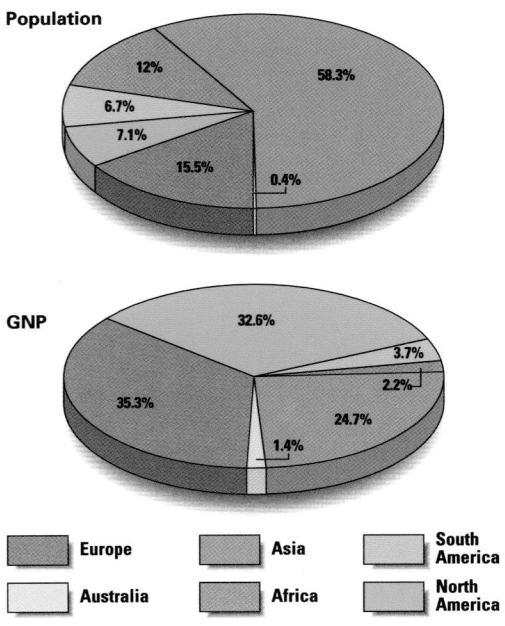

	Europe		Asia		South America
	Australia		Africa		North America

Levels of Income

Gross National Product per capita: the value of total production divided by the population (1995)

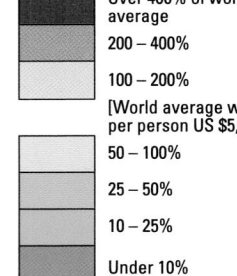

- Over 400% of world average
- 200 – 400%
- 100 – 200%

[World average wealth per person US $5,714]

- 50 – 100%
- 25 – 50%
- 10 – 25%
- Under 10%

Top 5 countries
Luxembourg $41,210
Switzerland $40,630
Japan $39,640
Norway $31,250
Denmark $29,890

Bottom 5 countries
Mozambique $80
Ethiopia $100
Congo (Zaïre) $120
Tanzania $120
Burundi $160

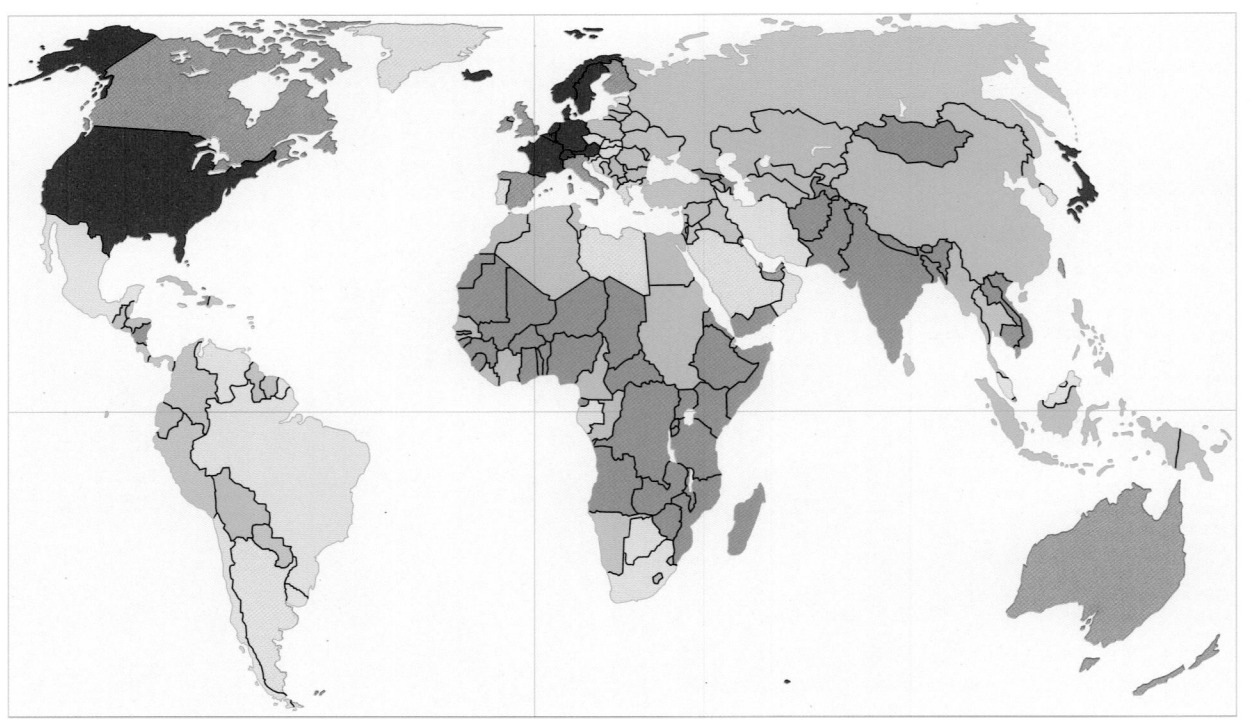

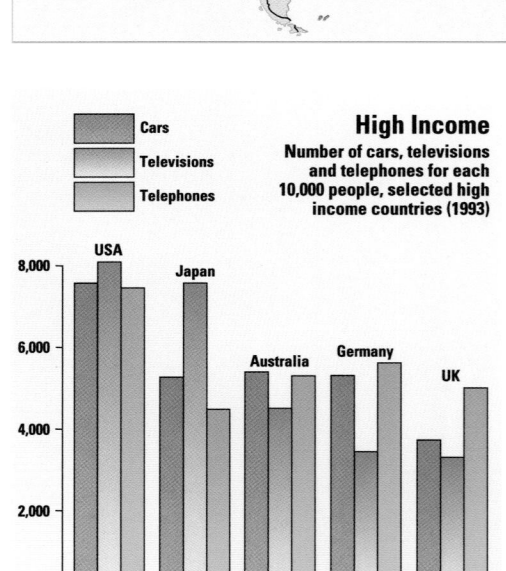

High Income
Number of cars, televisions and telephones for each 10,000 people, selected high income countries (1993)

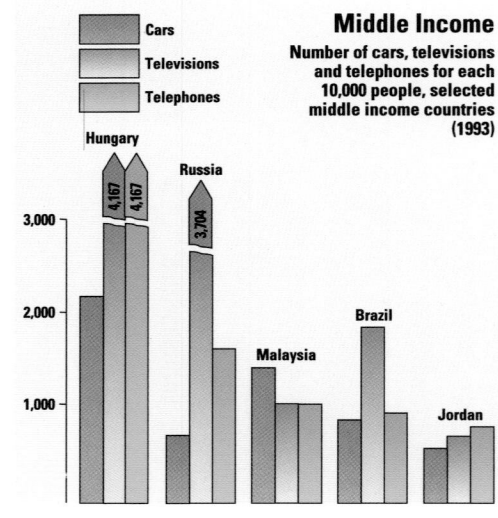

Middle Income
Number of cars, televisions and telephones for each 10,000 people, selected middle income countries (1993)

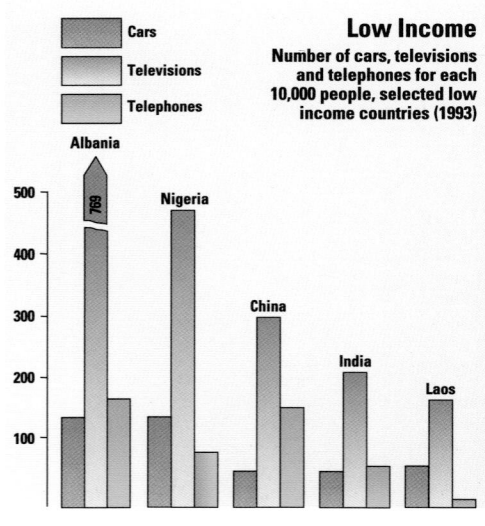

Low Income
Number of cars, televisions and telephones for each 10,000 people, selected low income countries (1993)

World Tourism

Passenger km (the number of passengers carried, multiplied by distance flown from airport of origin) (1994)

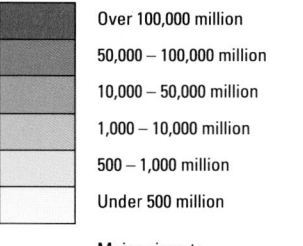

- Over 100,000 million
- 50,000 – 100,000 million
- 10,000 – 50,000 million
- 1,000 – 10,000 million
- 500 – 1,000 million
- Under 500 million

○ Major airports (handling over 25 million passengers in 1995)

Leisure and tourism is the world's second largest industry in terms of revenue generated. Small economies in attractive areas are often completely dominated by tourism: in some Caribbean islands, tourist spending provides over 90% of the total income and is the biggest foreign exchange earner. In cash terms the USA is the world leader: its 1996 earnings exceeded US $64 billion, though that sum amounted to only 0.9% of its total GDP. Of the 44.7 million visitors to the USA, 34% came from Canada and 25% from Mexico. The USA also spends the most on overseas tourism; in 1993 the USA spent over US $40,000 million abroad. The next biggest spenders were Germany, Japan and the UK.

The world's busiest airport in terms of total number of passengers is Chicago's O'Hare Airport (67.3 million passengers in 1996); the busiest international airport is Heathrow, the largest of London's airports.

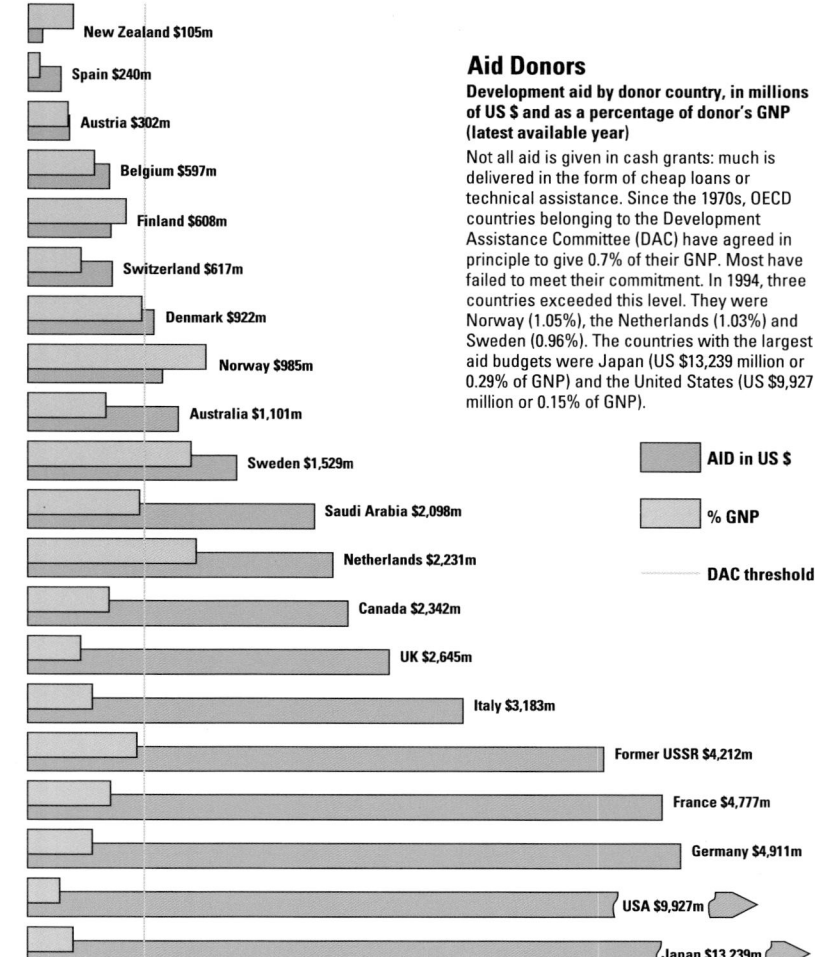

Aid Donors

Development aid by donor country, in millions of US $ and as a percentage of donor's GNP (latest available year)

Not all aid is given in cash grants: much is delivered in the form of cheap loans or technical assistance. Since the 1970s, OECD countries belonging to the Development Assistance Committee (DAC) have agreed in principle to give 0.7% of their GNP. Most have failed to meet their commitment. In 1994, three countries exceeded this level. They were Norway (1.05%), the Netherlands (1.03%) and Sweden (0.96%). The countries with the largest aid budgets were Japan (US $13,239 million or 0.29% of GNP) and the United States (US $9,927 million or 0.15% of GNP).

- AID in US $
- % GNP
- DAC threshold

New Zealand $105m
Spain $240m
Austria $302m
Belgium $597m
Finland $608m
Switzerland $617m
Denmark $922m
Norway $985m
Australia $1,101m
Sweden $1,529m
Saudi Arabia $2,098m
Netherlands $2,231m
Canada $2,342m
UK $2,645m
Italy $3,183m
Former USSR $4,212m
France $4,777m
Germany $4,911m
USA $9,927m
Japan $13,239m

0.5% 1% 1.5% 2% 2.5%

State Finance

Inflation rates, shown on the map, right, are an index of a country's financial stability and usually of its prosperity. Annual inflation rates above 20% are usually marked by slow or even negative growth of the GNP. Above 50%, it becomes hyperinflation and an economy is reeling. In the late 1980s and early 1990s, many high-income countries had to contend with annual inflation rates of 10% or more, while Japan, the growth leader, had an average inflation rate of 1.3% between 1985 and 1994.

The per capita GNP figures listed below are useful indicators of economic success or failure, but they do not account for living costs. Nor do they reveal the gaps between the rich and poor within countries.

Market-friendly policies, including low taxes and state spending, liberal trade policies and a welcome for foreign investors, are major factors in countries which have enjoyed rapid economic growth since 1980. For example, the setting up of Special Economic Zones in eastern China has led to a spectacular rise in the per capita GNP. Other successful countries include the 'tiger economies' of South Korea, Thailand and Singapore, although an Asian market crash in 1997 temporarily halted the dramatic economic expansion in these countries.

Inflation

Average annual rate of inflation (1980–93)

- Over 50%
- 20 – 50%
- 7.5 – 20%
- 1 – 7.5%
- Negative inflation
- No data available

Highest average inflation
Nicaragua	665%
Brazil	423%
Argentina	374%

Lowest average inflation
Brunei	–5.1%
Oman	–2.3%
Saudi Arabia	–2.1%

The Wealth Gap

The world's richest and poorest countries, by Gross National Product per capita in US $ (1995)

1. Luxembourg	41,210		1. Mozambique	80
2. Switzerland	40,630		2. Ethiopia	100
3. Japan	39,640		3. Congo (Zaïre)	120
4. Liechtenstein	38,520		4. Tanzania	120
5. Norway	31,250		5. Burundi	160
6. Denmark	29,890		6. Malawi	170
7. Germany	27,510		7. Sierra Leone	180
8. USA	26,980		8. Rwanda	180
9. Austria	26,890		9. Chad	180
10. Singapore	26,730		10. Nepal	200
11. France	24,990		11. Niger	220
12. Iceland	24,950		12. Madagascar	230
13. Belgium	24,710		13. Burkina Faso	230
14. Sweden	23,750		14. Vietnam	240
15. Hong Kong	22,990		15. Uganda	240
16. Finland	20,580		16. Bangladesh	240
17. Canada	19,380		17. Haiti	250
18. Italy	19,020		18. Guinea-Bissau	250
19. Australia	18,720		19. Yemen	250
20. UK	18,700		20. Nigeria	260

GNP per capita is calculated by dividing a country's Gross National Product by its total population.

Growth in GNP

GNP per capita annual growth rate (1980–93)

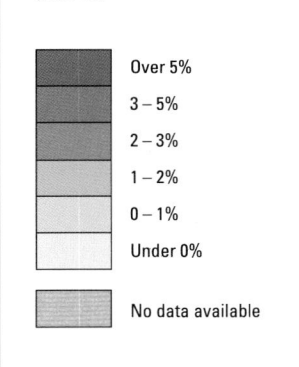

- Over 5%
- 3 – 5%
- 2 – 3%
- 1 – 2%
- 0 – 1%
- Under 0%
- No data available

Countries with highest growth rates
China	8.2%
South Korea	8.2%
Thailand	6.4%
Botswana	6.2%
Singapore	6.1%

Standards of Living

Wealth is a basic factor in determining standards of living. Everywhere, the rich have more of everything, including higher average life expectancies, while the poor have to spend most of their income on basic human needs, such as food and clothing. Yet poverty and wealth are relative terms. Slum dwellers living on social security in an industrial society feel their poverty acutely, but they have far more resources than an average African living in a rural area.

In 1990 the United Nations Development Programme published its first Human Development Index (HDI), an attempt to construct a comparative scale by which a simplified form of well-being might be measured. The HDI, expressed as a value between 0 and 0.999, combines figures for life expectancy and literacy with a wealth scale, based on Purchasing-Power Parity. The world's countries are divided into three groups, those with a high HDI (0.800 and above); those with a medium HDI (0.500 to 0.799); and those with a low HDI (below 0.500).

National scores for 1993 ranged from 0.951 for Canada to a low of 0.204 in Niger. In fact, of the 48 countries with a low HDI, 37 were from Africa, 10 from Asia, plus Haiti from the Caribbean.

Besides having low per capita GNPs, the average life expectancy in these countries was 56 years, while the adult literacy rate was 49%. By comparison, the average life expectancy at birth in countries in the high HDI group was 74 years, while the literacy rate was 97%.

Comparisons between countries with similar per capita GNPs reveal the effects of government actions. For example, the World Bank classifies both India and China as low-income economies, but India's HDI at 0.436 is much lower than that of China, at 0.609. This reflects not only China's economic progress in the 1980s and 1990s, but also differences in average life expectancies (61 years in India and 69 years in China), and adult literacy rates (51% in India and 80% in China).

Disparities in standards of living exist not only between countries but also between individuals, groups and regions within countries. For example, income distribution figures for 1995 show that, in the United States, the poorest 20% of households received less than 4% of the income.

Other contrasts exist in developing countries between rural communities, where incomes are low and basic services are often in short supply, and urban areas, where even those living in slums are generally better off than their rural neighbours. Other striking differences exist between men and women. For example, while adult literacy rates for men and women living in developed countries are more or less the same, large differences exist in many developing countries. In 1995, in countries in the lowest HDI category, only 37% of women were literate, as compared with 62% of men.

Female education is a factor in population control, especially as women's fertility rates appear to fall in direct proportion to the amount of secondary education they receive. This point was acknowledged in 1994 by the UN Population Fund, which defined four main objectives relating to women and population control. They were: the reduction of maternal, infant and child mortality; better education, especially for girls; universal access to reproductive health services; and gender equality.

Statistical analysis presents many problems of interpretation, especially when trying to define such intangible factors as a sense of well-being. For example, education helps create wealth; but are rich countries wealthy because their people are well-educated, or are they well-educated because they are rich?

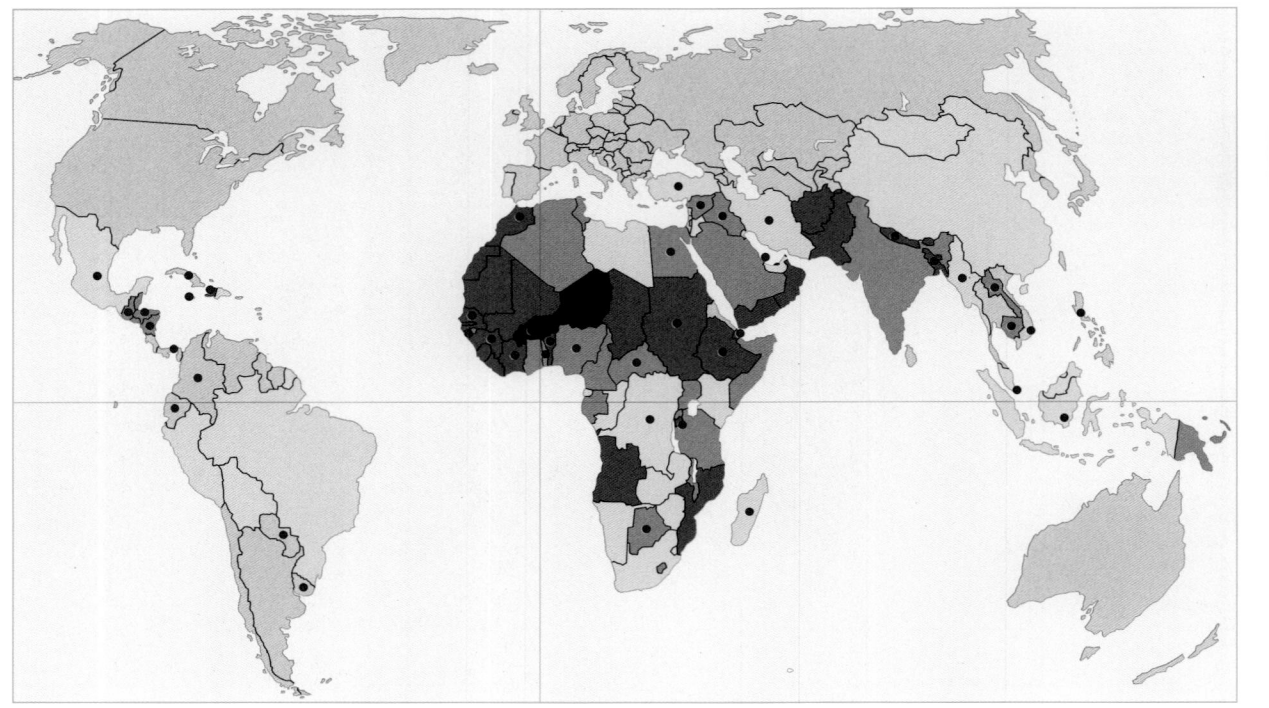

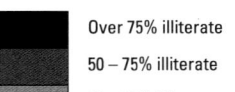

Illiteracy

% of the total population unable to read or write (latest available year)

- Over 75% illiterate
- 50 – 75% illiterate
- 25 – 50% illiterate
- 10 – 15% illiterate
- Under 10% illiterate

• Less than 6 years compulsory education per child

Educational expenditure per person (latest available year)

Top 5 countries

Norway	$2,820
Denmark	$2,450
Switzerland	$2,256
Japan	$1,853
Finland	$1,706

Bottom 5 countries

Congo (Zaïre)	$1
Somalia	$2
Sierra Leone	$2
Nigeria	$3
Haiti	$3

Education

The developing countries made great efforts in the 1970s and 1980s to bring at least a basic education to their people. Primary school enrolments rose above 60% in all but the poorest nations. Figures often include teenagers or young adults, however, and there are still an estimated 300 million children worldwide who receive no schooling at all. A lack of resources has restricted the development of secondary and higher education. Most primary education is free in the poorer countries, but fees are often paid for secondary and higher education, thus heightening the differences between rich and poor.

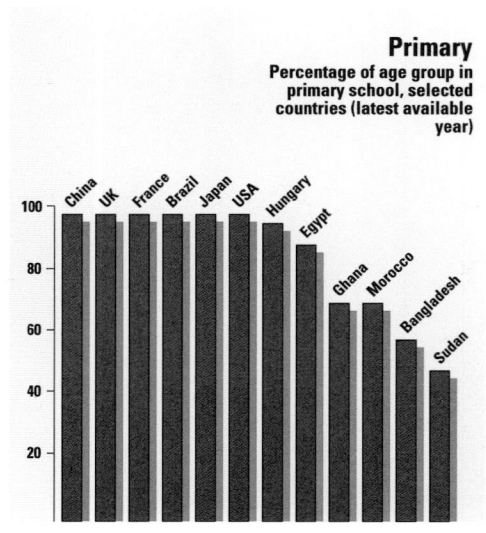

Primary
Percentage of age group in primary school, selected countries (latest available year)

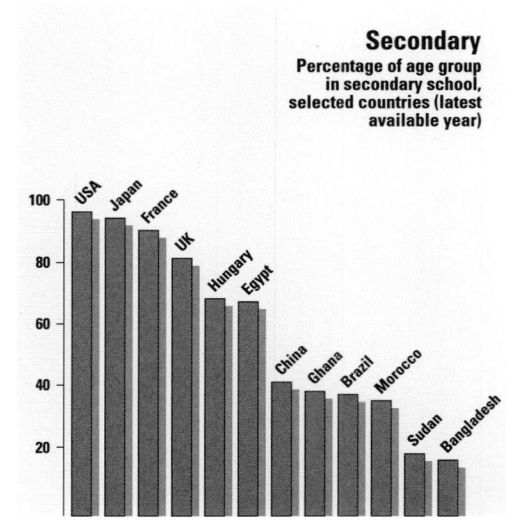

Secondary
Percentage of age group in secondary school, selected countries (latest available year)

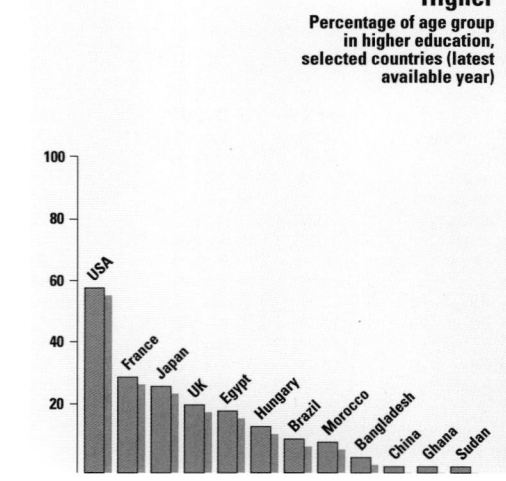

Higher
Percentage of age group in higher education, selected countries (latest available year)

Distribution of Spending

Percentage share of household spending (latest available year)

A high proportion of the average income of households in developing nations is spent on basic needs such as food and clothing. In most Western countries food and clothing account for less than 25% of expenditure.

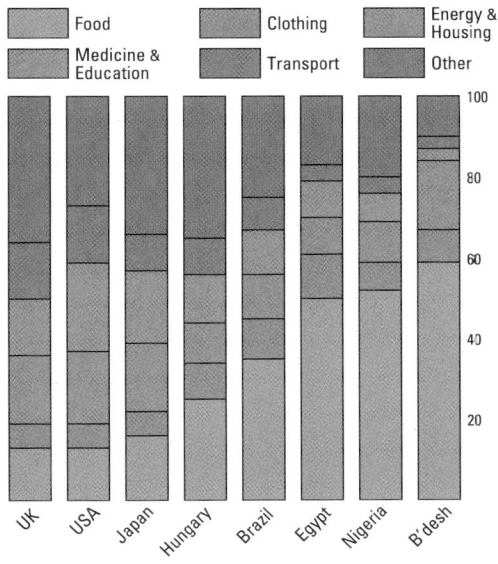

- Food
- Medicine & Education
- Clothing
- Transport
- Energy & Housing
- Other

UK, USA, Japan, Hungary, Brazil, Egypt, Nigeria, B'desh

Distribution of Income

Percentage share of household income from poorest fifth to richest fifth, selected countries (latest available year)

The graph below shows that wealth is not distributed evenly throughout the population of the six countries. In every country worldwide the richest 20% of the population have a disproportionately high percentage of the income. This disparity between rich and poor is nowhere more pronounced than in Brazil, where the richest 20% of the population have over 60% of the income. The poorest 20%, on the other hand, have less than 5%.

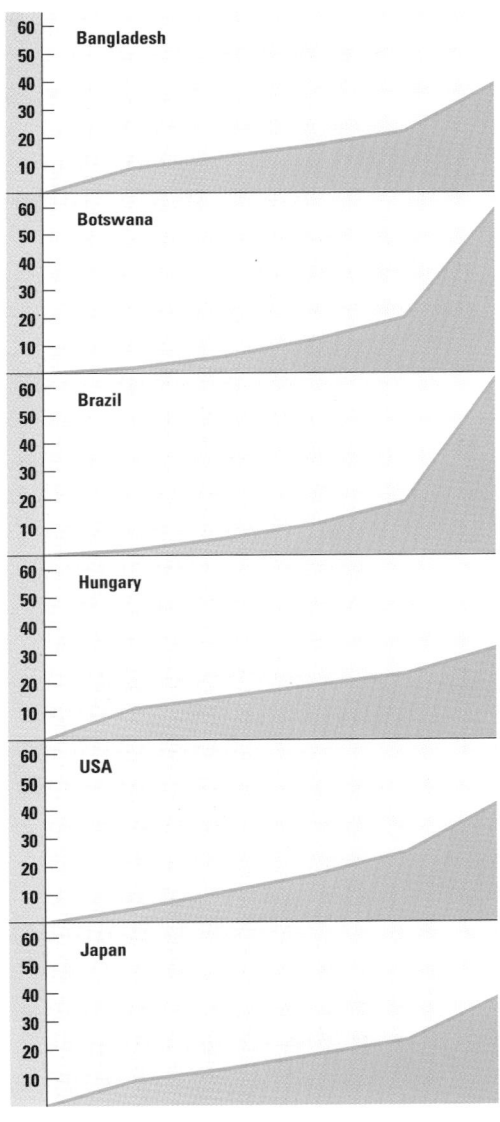

Bangladesh, Botswana, Brazil, Hungary, USA, Japan

Fertility and Education

Fertility rates compared with female education, selected countries (1992–95)

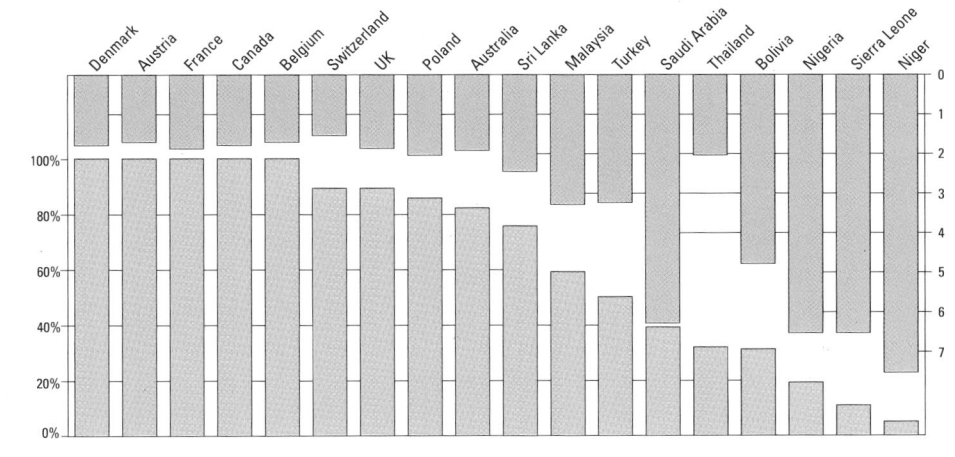

Denmark, Austria, France, Canada, Belgium, Switzerland, UK, Poland, Australia, Sri Lanka, Malaysia, Turkey, Saudi Arabia, Thailand, Bolivia, Nigeria, Sierra Leone, Niger

- Percentage of females aged 12–17 in secondary education
- Fertility rate: average number of children borne per woman

Access to secondary education is closely linked to low fertility rates in developed countries. By contrast, in many developing countries, women's lives are dominated by agriculture, or they lack access to secondary and higher education for cultural reasons, as in Muslim countries. Such disparities are reflected in women's parliamentary representation which is only one-seventh that of men, despite the emergence of such figures as Mrs Indira Gandhi, India's former prime minister. Female wages are also, on average, only two-thirds of those of men.

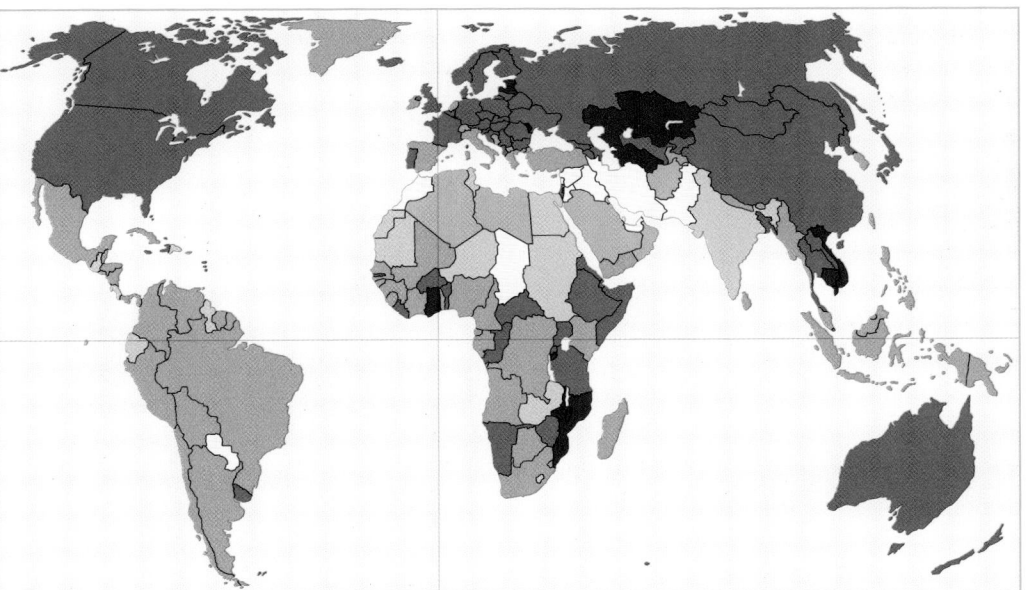

Women at Work

Women in paid employment as a percentage of the total workforce (latest available year)

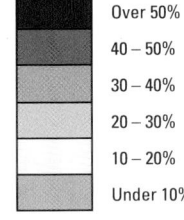

- Over 50%
- 40 – 50%
- 30 – 40%
- 20 – 30%
- 10 – 20%
- Under 10%

Most women in work
Cambodia	56%
Kazakstan	54%
Burundi	53%

Fewest women in work
Saudi Arabia	4%
Oman	6%
Afghanistan	8%

Car Ownership

Proportion of the world's vehicles, by region (1994)

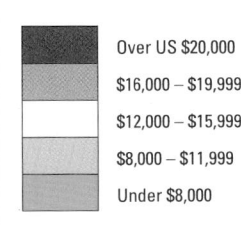

North America, Western Europe, Asia, E.Europe & CIS, Others

TOTAL = 270 million vehicles

Motor cars per 100 people (1994)
USA	75
Italy	52
Israel	19
Bulgaria	16
Chile	8
Zimbabwe	4
Philippines	2

Standards of Living in the USA by Race, Age and Region

A comparison of measures of income and education, by selected characteristics (1995)

Median income per household (US $), by age and region
15–24 years	20,979
25–34 years	34,701
35–44 years	43,465
45–54 years	48,058
55–64 years	38.077
65 years and over	19,096
North-east	36,111
Mid-west	35,839
South	30,942
West	35,979

Per capita income (US $), by race and Hispanic origin of householder
ALL RACES	17,227
White	18,304
Black	10,982
Asian & Pacific Is.	16,567
Hispanic (any race)	9,300

The poorest 20% of households received just 3.6% of the income, whereas the richest 20% received 48.2%.

Percentage of persons aged 25 and over who have completed High School, by race or origin
ALL RACES	1975	62.5
	1995	81.7
White	1975	64.5
	1995	83.0
Black	1975	42.5
	1995	73.8
Hispanic	1975	37.9
	1995	53.4

Regional Inequality in Italy

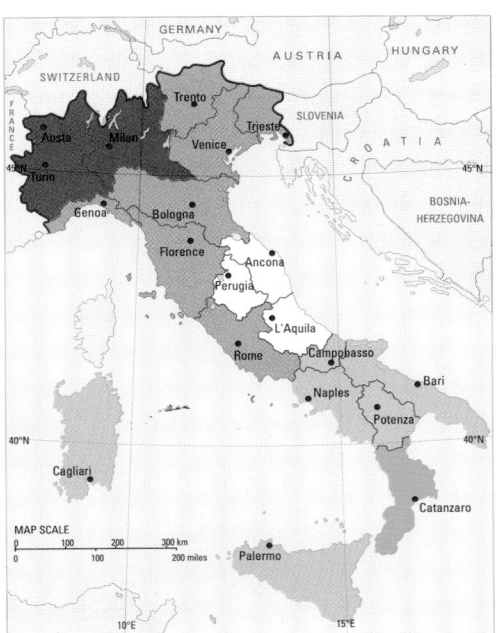

Gross Domestic Product (GDP) per capita in Italy, by region (1993)

- Over US $20,000
- $16,000 – $19,999
- $12,000 – $15,999
- $8,000 – $11,999
- Under $8,000

Average GDP per capita for Italy was $18,878. The per capita GDP, by comparison, for the UK was $17,920; for the USA $25,650; and for the EU $25,900.

The number of inhabitants per doctor, another social indicator, varies from less than 500 in the north-west of Italy to over 800 in the far south, with a national average of 607.

The southern part of Italy, known as the *Mezzogiorno* (or 'Land of the midday sun'), has been described as the poorest part of the European Union. It is identifiable on the map, left, as all the regions with a GDP per capita of less than $12,000 (including the two islands of Sicily and Sardinia), plus Abruzzi whose capital is L'Aquila.

The *Mezzogiorno* region suffers from a lack of mineral and energy resources, industry, commerce, services and skilled labour. As a result, standards of living in the region are well below the rest of Italy and Europe. Employment is predominantly agricultural and small-scale.

The north of Italy accounts for 60% of the population but 80% of the GDP, whereas the *Mezzogiorno* accounts for 40% of the population and only 20% of the GDP. Manpower surpluses in the south led to emigration to other parts of Europe and the Americas. It has also led, especially in the last 50 years, to inter-regional migration from the islands and the southern mainland to the north. The main regions attracting migrants were the north-west – the prosperous Liguria–Piedmont–Lombardy triangle with its great industrial cities of Genoa, Milan and Turin – and the Venetia region in the north-east. As a result, the north has experienced much higher population growth rates than the rest of Italy.

In 1996 the Northern League, one of Italy's political parties, exploited the regional differences by declaring the north to be the independent 'Republic of Padania'. However, only a small minority of northerners supports secession.

CITY
MAPS

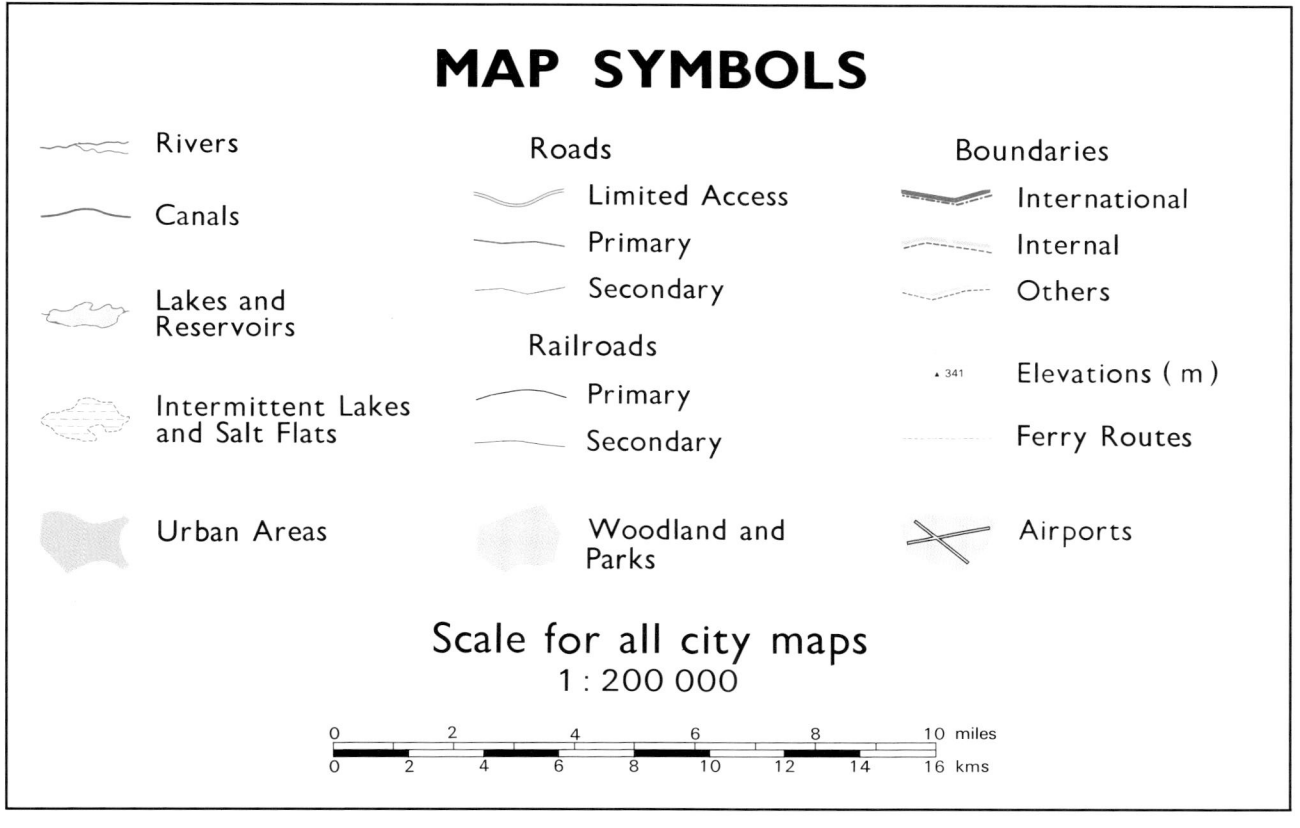

MAP SYMBOLS

Rivers

Canals

Lakes and
Reservoirs

Intermittent Lakes
and Salt Flats

Urban Areas

Roads
   Limited Access
   Primary
   Secondary

Railroads
   Primary
   Secondary

Woodland and
Parks

Boundaries
   International
   Internal
   Others

• 341   Elevations (m)

Ferry Routes

Airports

Scale for all city maps
1 : 200 000

0   2   4   6   8   10 miles
0 2 4 6 8 10 12 14 16 kms

1: 200 000

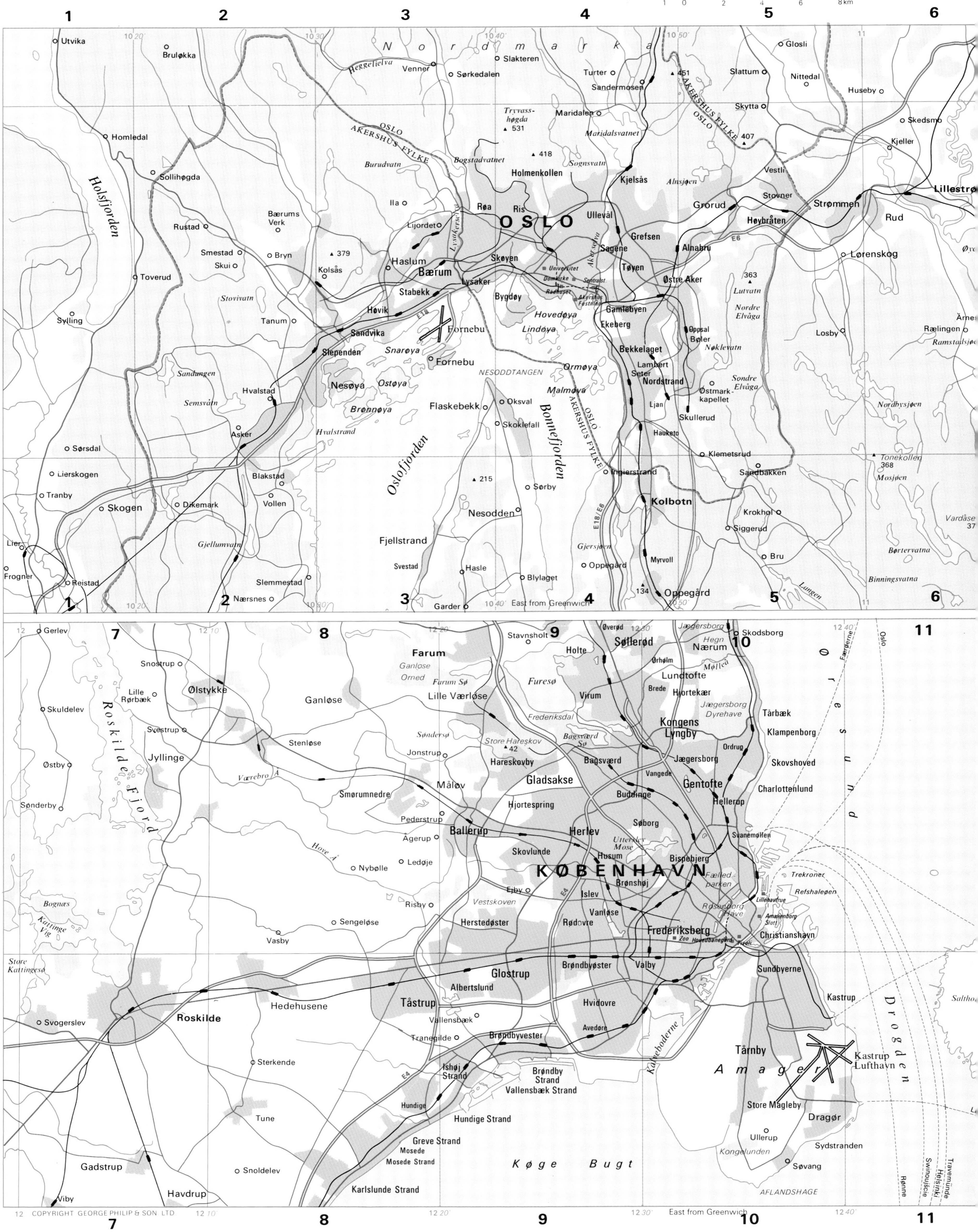

5 miles
8 km

Grid references (top): 1 2 3 4 5 6

A

Utvika
Bruløkka
Glosli
Nordmarka
Slakteren
Venner
Sørkedalen
Turter
Slattum
Nittedal
451
Huseby
Sandermosen
Heggelielva
Homledal
60
Skedsmo
Tryvass-høgda
531
Maridalen
Skytta
Kjeller
OSLO
AKERSHUS FYLKE
Maridalsvatnet
407
Vestli
Sollihøgda
418
Sognsvatn
Holmenkollen
Kjelsås
Alnsjøen
Stovner
Strømmen
Lillestrø
Burudvatn
Bogstadvatnet
Grorud
Ila
Røa Ris
OSLO
Ulleval
Grefsen
Høybråten
Rud
Bærums Verk
Smestad
Skui
379
Bryn
Lijordet
Skøyen
Sagene
Alnabru
E6
Rustad
Haslum
Universitet
Tøyen
Østre Aker
363
Lørenskog
Øve

B

Toverud
Kolsås
Bærum
Lysaker
Domkirke
Sentralst
Lutvatn
Stovivatn
Stabekk
Bygdøy
Akershus Festning
Gamlebyen
Oppsal
Nordre Elvåga
Sylling
Tanum
Høvik
Hovedøya
Ekeberg
Bøler
Losby
Rælingen
Sandvika
Fornebu
Lindøya
Bekkelaget
Nøklevatn
Ramstalsjø
Slependen
Snarøya
Fornebu
Ormøya
Lambert Seter
Nesøya
Ostøya
NESODDTANGEN
Malmøya
Nordstrand
Østmark kapellet
Hvalstad
Brønnøya
Flaskebekk
Oksval
Ljan
Sondre Elvåga
Nordbysjøen
Asker
Semsvatn
Hvalstrand
Skøttefall
Skullerud
Hauketo

C

Sørsdal
Oslofjorden
Skoklefall
AKERSHUS FYLKE
OSLO
Klemetsrud
Tonekollen 368
Lierskogen
215
Ingierstrand
Sandbakken
Mosjøen
Tranby
Blakstad
Sørby
Kolbotn
Skogen
Dikemark
Vollen
Krokhol
Siggerud
Bru
Børtervatna
Lier
Gjellumvatn
Nesodden
Fjellstrand
Gjersjøen
Myrvoll
Vardåse 37
Frogner
Reistad
Slemmestad
Svestad
Hasle
Oppegård
134
Oppegård
Binningsvatna
59 50
Næsnes
Garder
East from Greenwich
Langen

Grid references (bottom left): 1 2 3 4 5 6

Grid references (lower map): 7 8 9 10 11

D

Gerlev
Øverød
Jægersborg
Skodsborg
Oslo
Stavnsholt
Holte
Søllerød
Hegn
Nærum
Færgerne
Snostrup
Farum
Ganløse Orned
Furum Sø
Ørholm
Lundtofte
Lille Rørbæk
Ølstykke
Ganløse
Lille Værløse
Brede
Hjortekær
Tårbæk
Skuldelev
Svestrup
Furesø
Virum
Jægersborg Dyrehave
Roskilde Fjord
Stenløse
Frederiksdal
Kongens Lyngby
Klampenborg
Østby
Jyllinge
Værebro Å
Søndersø
Store Hareskov
Bagsværd Sø
Ordrup
Skovshoved
42
Jonstrup
Bagsværd
Jægersborg
Charlottenlund
Sønderby
Måløv
Hareskovby
Vangede
Gentofte
Smørumnedre
Gladsakse
Buddinge
Hellerup
Hove Å
Hjortespring
Pederstrup
Søborg
Svanemøllen
Ågerup
Ballerup
Herlev
Utterslev Mose
Øresund
Ledøje
Skovlunde
Husum
Bispebjerg
Nybølle
KØBENHAVN
Fælled parken
Trekroner
Risby
Ejby
Brønshøj
Refshaleøen
Bognæs
Islev
Rosenborg Have
Lillehavrue
Vestskoven
Vanløse
Sengeløse
Herstedøster
Rødovre
Frederiksberg
Christianshavn
Zoo Hovedbanegård
Kattinge Vig
Vasby
55 40
Glostrup
Brøndbyøster
Valby
Sundbyerne
Store Kattingesø
Albertslund
Svogerslev
Hedehusene
Tåstrup
Hvidovre
Kastrup
Drogden
Roskilde
Vallensbæk
Brøndbyvester
Avedøre
Tårnby
Kastrup Lufthavn
Sterkende
Tranegilde
Amager
Kalvebodeme
Ishøj Strand
Brøndby Strand
Store Magleby
Vallensbæk Strand
Dragør
Hundige
Gadstrup
Tune
Hundige Strand
Ullerup
Sydstranden
Greve Strand
Mosede
Mosede Strand
Kongelunden
Søvang
Viby
Havdrup
Snoldelev
Karlslunde Strand
Køge Bugt
AFLANDSHAGE
Travemünde Helsingfors
Swinoujscie
Rønne

E

Grid references (bottom): 7 8 9 10 11

1: 200 000

0 5 miles
0 8 km

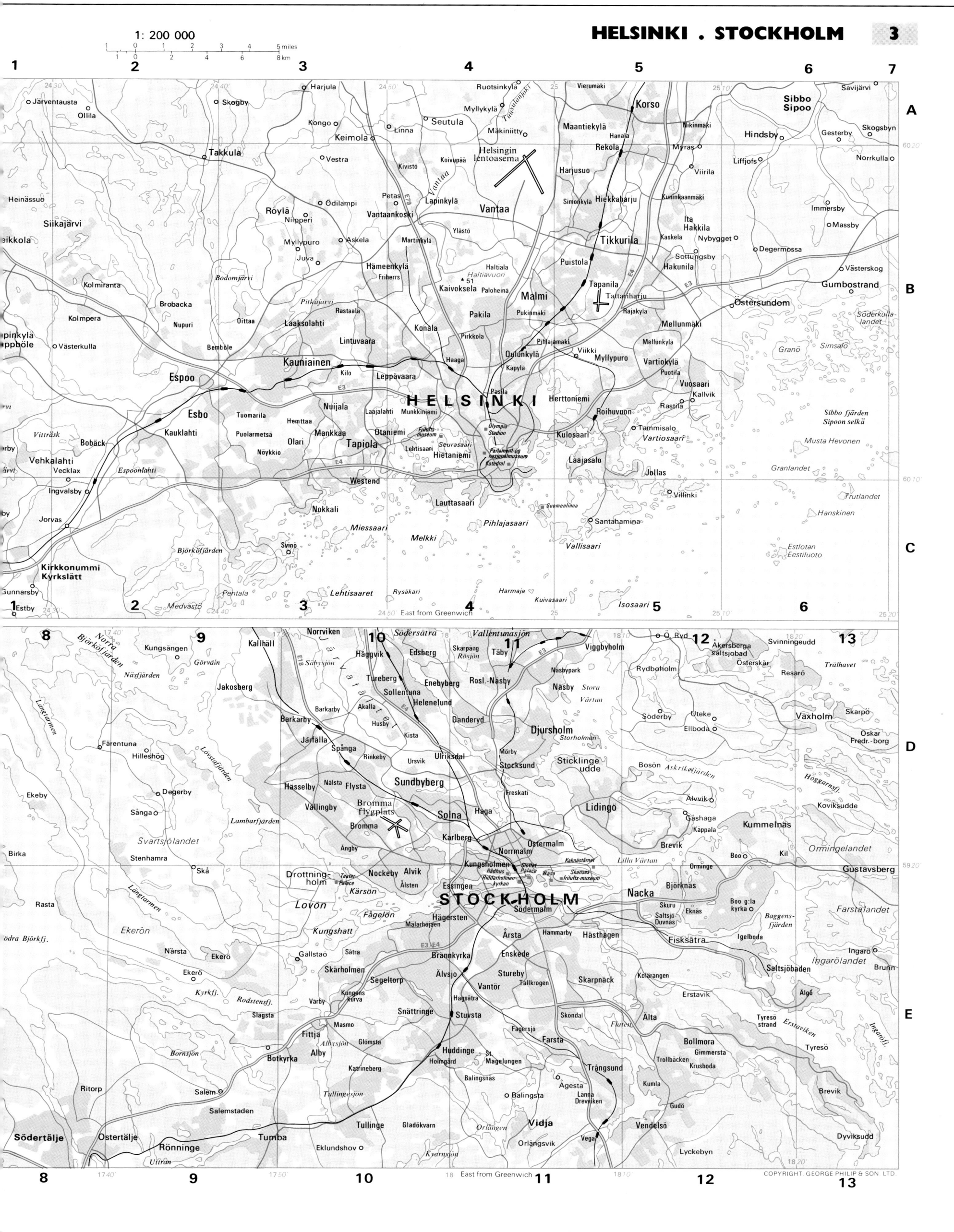

1   2   3   4   5   6   7

Järventausta
Ollila
Skogby
Harjula
Ruotsinkylä
Vierumäki
Savijärvi
Sibbo
Sipoo

Kongo
Myllykylä
Tuusulanjkt
Korso
Skogsbyn

Seutula
Makiniitty
Maantiekylä
Hanala
Nikinmäki
Hindsby
Gesterby

Heinässuo
Keimola
Linna
Rekola
Myräs
Lifjofs

Takkula
Vestra
Koivupaa
Harjusuo
Kuninkaanmäki
Viirila
Norrkulla

Siikajärvi
Ödilampi
Helsingin
lentoasema
Simonkylä
Hiekkaharju
Immersby
Massby

Röylä
Petas
Lapinkylä
Vantaa
Tikkurila
Kaskela
Nybygget
Degermossa

Nipperi
Vantaankoski
Ylasto
Puistola
Sottungsby
Hakunila
Västerskog

Myllypuro
Askela
Martinkyla
Haltiala
Tapanila
Gumbostrand

Kolmiranta
Juva
Hämeenkylä
Friherrs
Haltiavuori
Paloheinä
Tautiharju
Rajakyla
Östersundom

Brobacka
Kaivoksela
Malmi
Pukinmäki
Mellunmäki

Kolmpera
Nupuri
Oittaa
Rastaala
Pakila
Pihlajamäki
Viikki
Mellunkyla

Västerkulla
Bemböle
Laaksolahti
Konala
Pirkkola
Haaga
Oulunkylä
Kapyla
Myllypuro
Vartiokylä
Puotila

Kauniainen
Kilo
Leppävaara
Pasila
Herttoniemi
Vuosaari
Kallvik

Espoo
HELSINKI
Roihuvuori
Rastila

Esbo
Nuijala
Laajalahti
Munkkiniemi
Kulosaari

Tuomarila
Hemttaa
Otaniemi
Tammisalo
Vartiosaari

Kauklahti
Puolarmetsä
Mankkaa
Tapiola
Lehtisaari
Seurasaari
Laajasalo

Vehkalahti
Olari
Nöykkio
Hietaniemi
Katedral
Jollas

Vecklax
Westend
Lauttasaari
Villinki

Ingvalsby
Nokkali
Santahamina
Estlotan
Eestiluoto

Jorvas
Miessaari
Melkki
Pihlajasaari
Suomenlinna

Kirkkonummi
Kyrkslätt
Svinö
Vallisaari

Gunnarsby
Estby
Medvästö
Pentala
Lehtisaaret
Rysäkari
Harmaja
Kuivasaari
Isosaari

East from Greenwich

1   2   3   4   5   6

8   9   10   11   12   13

Kallhäll
Norrviken
Södersätra
Vallentunasjön
Ö. Ryd
Åkersberga
saltsjobad
Svinningeudd

Kungsängen
Häggvik
Edsberg
Skarpang
Rösjön
Täby
Viggbyholm
Österskär

Görväln
Tureberg
Näsbypark
Rydboholm
Trälhavet

Jakosberg
Sollentuna
Enebyberg
Rosl.-Näsby
Näsby
Söderby
Uteke
Resarö

Barkarby
Akalla
Helenelund
Storavärtan
Ellbödä
Växholm

Barkarby
Husby
Danderyd
Djursholm
Skarpö

Färentuna
Järfälla
Kista
Storholmen
Oskar
Fredr.-borg

Hilleshög
Spånga
Rinkeby
Ursvik
Ulriksdal
Mörby
Sticklinge
udde
Boson
Askrikefjärden
Höggarnsfj.

Degerby
Hässelby
Nalsta
Flysta
Sundbyberg
Stocksund
Älvvik
Koviksudde

Sånga
Vällingby
Bromma
flygplats
Haga
Freskati
Lidingö
Gashaga
Kappala
Kummelnäs

Ekeby
Bromma
Solna
Karlberg
Östermalm
Brevik
Kil

Birka
Angby
Norrmalm
Kaknästornet
Boo
Ormingelandet

Skå
Nockeby
Alvik
Kungsholmen
Slottet
Palace
Orminge
Gustavsberg

Drottning-
holm
Teater
Palace
Ålsten
Riddarholmen
kyrkan
Skansens
frilufts-museum
Björknäs
Nacka

Lovön
Kärsön
Essingen
STOCKHOLM
Södermalm
Skuru
Saltsjo-
Duvnäs
Boo g:la
kyrka
Baggens-
fjärden
Farstalandet

Fågelön
Hägersten
Mälarhöjden
Årsta
Hammarby
Hästhägen
Fisksätra
Igelboda
Ingarö
Ingarölandet

Kungshatt
Satra
Brännkyrka
Enskede
Kolarängen
Saltsjöbaden
Algö
Brunn

Rasta
Ekerön
Gallsta
Skärholmen
Stureby
Skarpnäck

Närsta
Ekerö
Segeltorp
Älvsjö
Vantör
Tallkrogen
Erstavik
Alta
Tyresö
strand

Ekerö
Varby
Kungens
kurva
Hagsätra
Erstaviken

Slagsta
Snättringe
Stuvsta
Skondal
Farsta
Bollmora
Gimmersta
Tyresö

Fittja
Masmo
Fagersjo
Trollbäcken
Krusboda

Rönninge
Alby
Glomsta
Huddinge
St
Magelungen
Trångsund
Kumla
Brevik

Ritorp
Salem
Katrineberg
Holmgård
Balingsnas
Ågesta
Lanna
Dvärviken
Gudö

Söderälje
Östertälje
Rönninge
Tumba
Tullinge
Gladökvarn
Orlången
Vidja
Vendelsö
Dyviksudd

Eklundshov
Kvarnsjön
Orlångsvik
Balingsta
Vega
Lyckebyn

Södra Björkfj.
Bornsjön
Tullingesjön
Salemstaden

East from Greenwich

COPYRIGHT. GEORGE PHILIP & SON. LTD.

8   9   10   11   12   13

1: 200 000

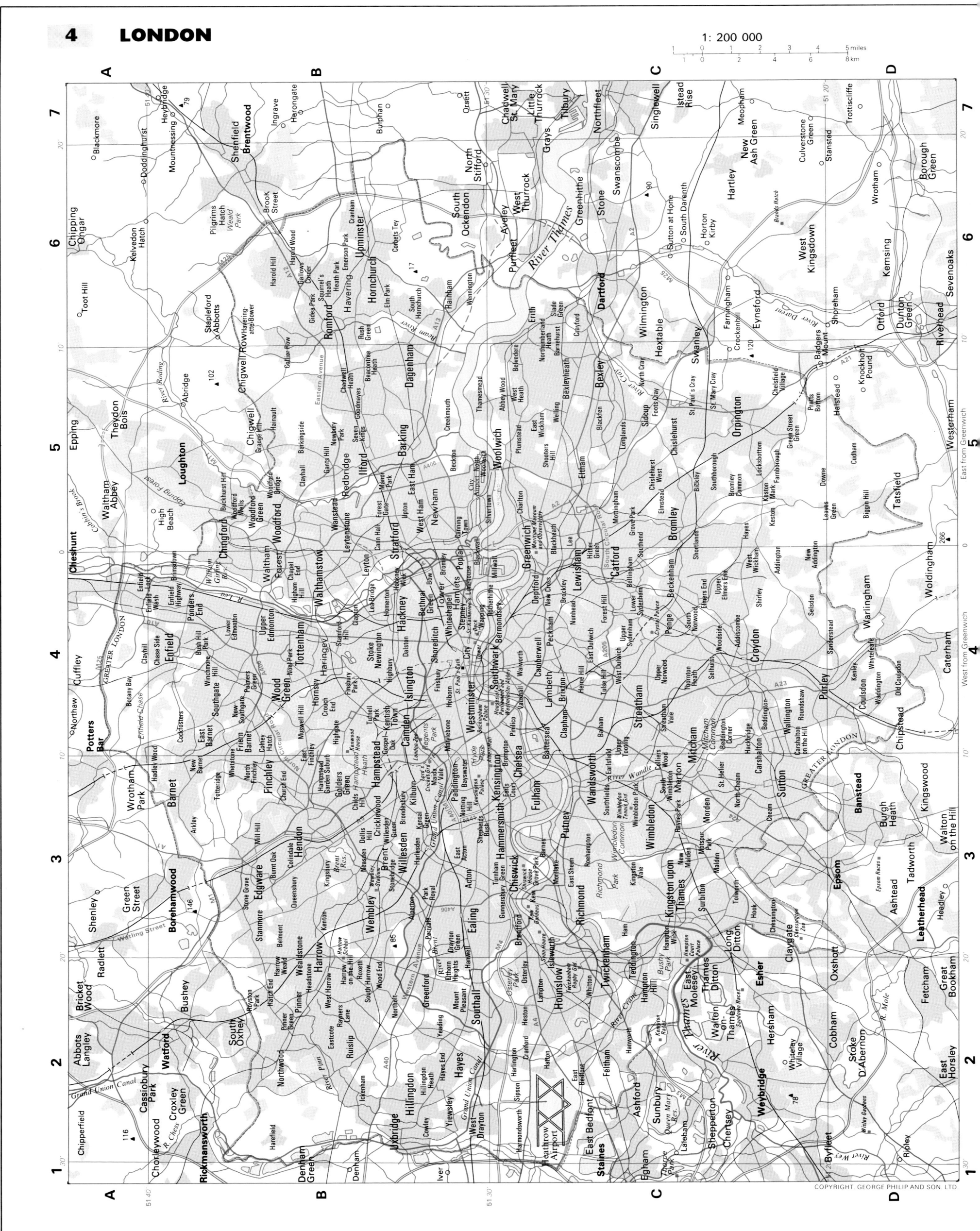

1 : 200 000

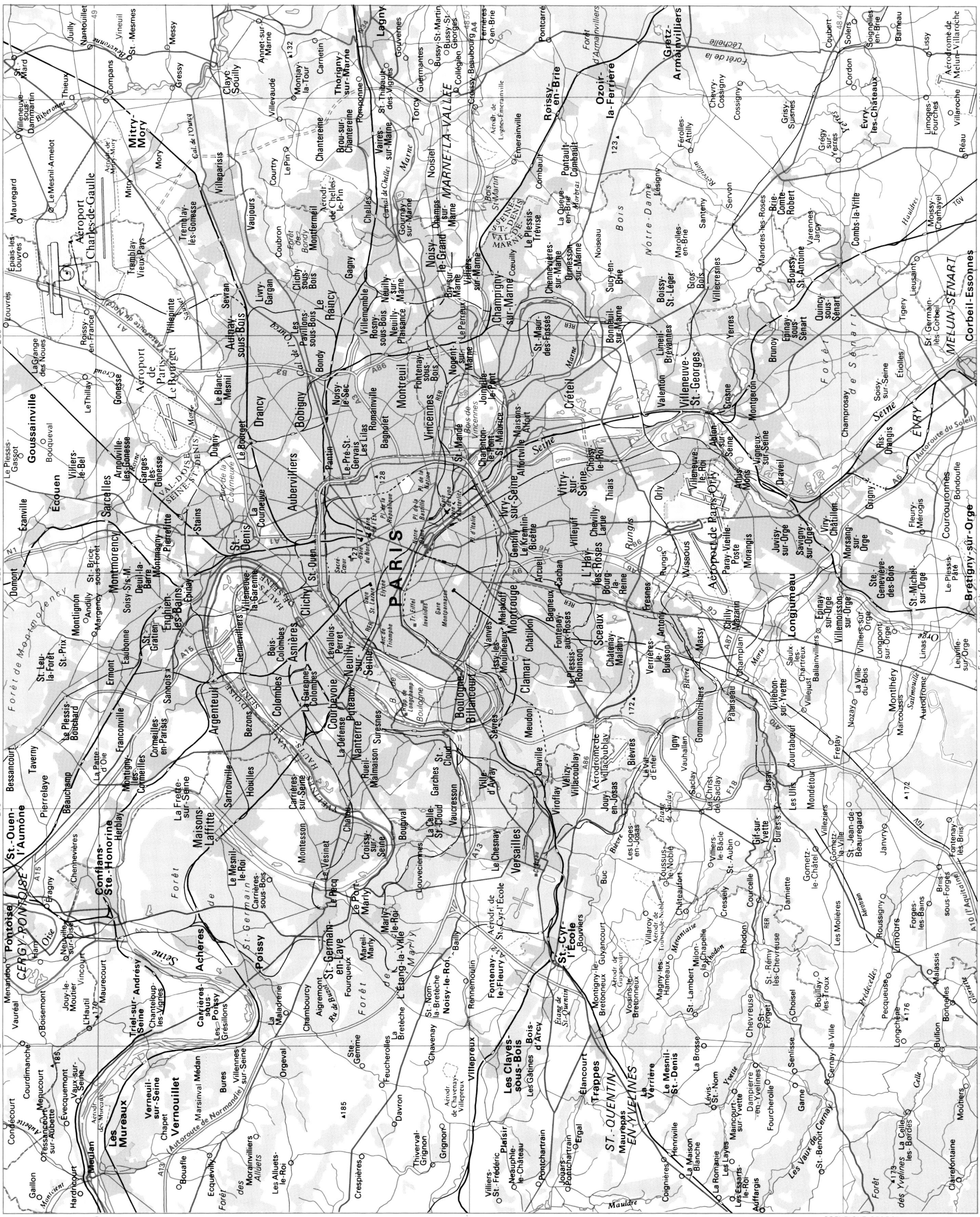

5 miles
8 km

PARIS

MARNE-LA-VALLÉE

ST-QUENTIN EN-YVELINES

MELUN-SÉNART

EVRY

Aéroport Charles-de-Gaulle

Aéroport de Paris-Orly

Aéroport de Paris-Le Bourget

Forêt de Notre-Dame

Forêt de Sénart

Bois de Vincennes

Bois de Boulogne

East from Greenwich

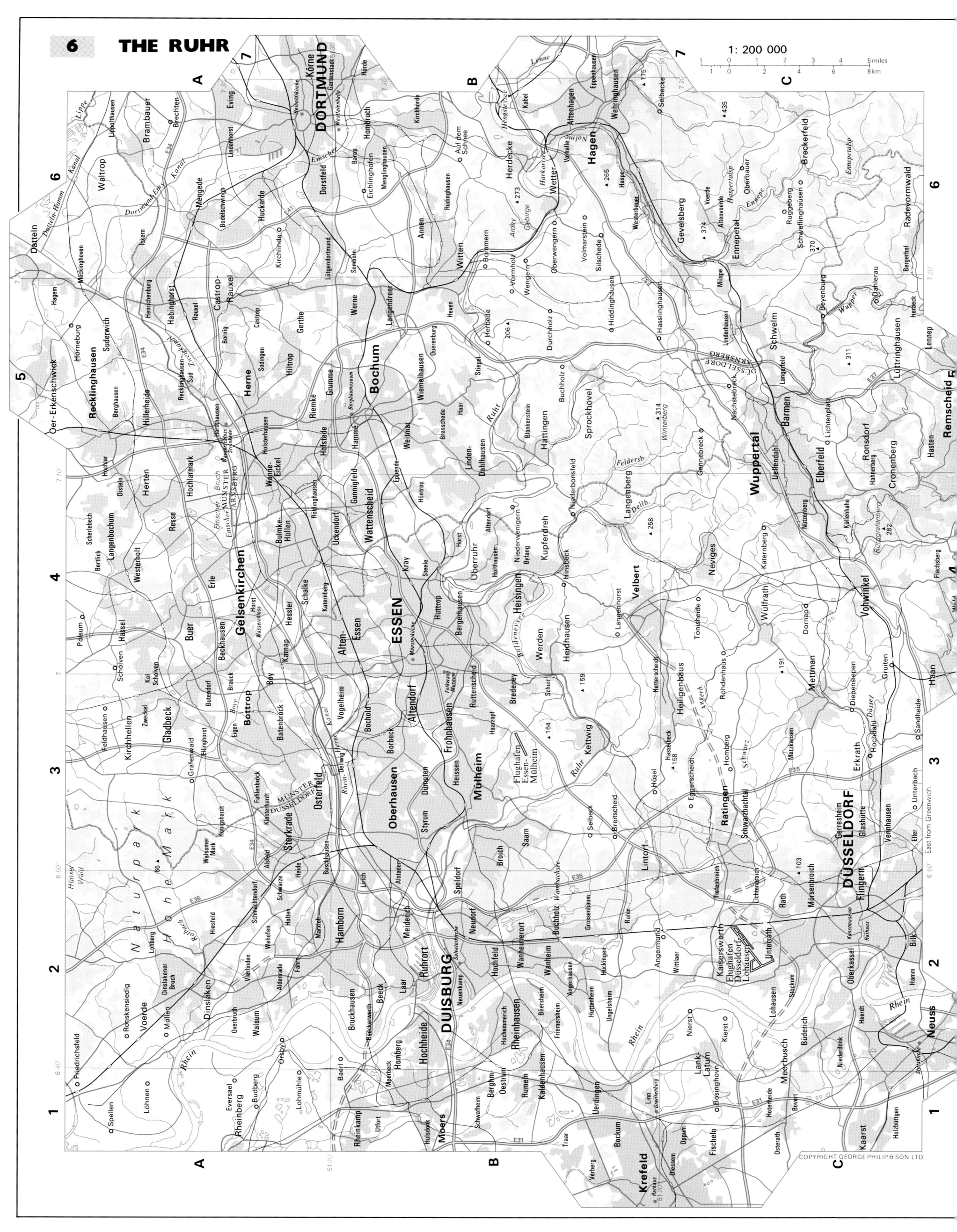

1 : 200 000

1: 200 000

1 2 3 4 5

Berlin map (top section):

Pausin · Wansdorf · Bötzow · Frohnau · Glienicke · Schildow · Rontgental · Zepernick · Birkenhöhe · Elisenau · Stienitzsee · Amselhain · Werneuchen

Schönwalde · Hennigsdorf · Stolpe-Süd · Hermsdorf · Lübars · Blankenfelde · Buch · Schwanebeck · Birkholzaue · Birkholz · Löhme · Seefeld · Rudolfshöhe

Havelkanal · Nieder Neuendorf · Schulzendorf · Heiligensee · Waidmannslust · Buchholz · Neu Buch · Karow · Neu Lindenberg · Lindenberg · 89 · Wegendorf · Krummensee

Alter Finkenkrug · Siedlung Schönwalde · Konradshöhe · Tegel · Wittenau · Rosenthal · Niederschönhausen · Blankenburg · BRANDENBURG BERLIN · Ahrensfelde · Trappenfelde · Paulshof · Altlandsberg Nord · Neuhonow

A Waldheim · Falkensee · Johannesstift · Tegeler See · Scharfenberg · Flughafen Tegel · Reinickendorf · Pankow · Heinersdorf · Malchow · Wartenberg · 67 · Eiche · Mehrow · Seeberg · Friedrichslust · Altlandsberg **A**

Finkenkrug · Falkenhagen · Seegefeld · Haselhorst · Volkspark Jungfernheide · Wedding · Weissensee · Hohenschönhausen · Eiche Süd · Honow · Fredersdorf Nord

Spandau · Siemensstadt · Schlossgarten · Tiergarten · Mitte · Volkspark Friedrichshain · Lichtenburg · Marzahn · Neuenhagen · Fredersdorf

Döberitz · Dallgow · Staaken · Spree · Charlottenburg · Schloss Charlottenburg · University · Cathedral · Friedrichshain · Wuhlgarten · Birkenstein · Mühlenfliess · Bollensdorf

Seeburg · Zitadelle · Olympic Stadium · Deutsche Oper · Zoo Station · Humboldt University · Braudenburg Gate · Biesdorf · Dahlwitz-Hoppegarten

B Gross Glienicke · Gatow · 74 · Grunewald · 120 · Teufelsberg · BERLIN · Kreuzberg · Landwehr kanal · Treptow · Friedrichsfelde · Kaulsdorf · Mahlsdorf · Münchehofe · Vogelsdorf **B**

Krampnitz · Grosser · Schmargendorf · Schöneberg · Neukölln · Flughafen Tempelhof · Karlshorst · Kleinschönebeck · Schöneiche

Neu Fahrland · Sacrower See · Kladow · Schwanenwerder · Krumme Lanke · Dahlem · Friedenau · Tempelhof · Niederschöneweide · Oberschöneweide · Heidemühle · Waldesruh · Gratzwalde

Nedlitz · Sacrow · Schlachtensee · Steglitz · Teltow kanal · Johannisthal · Aldershof · Köpenick · Fichtenau · Schönblick

Pfaueninsel · Wannsee · Nikolassee · Lichterfelde · Mariendorf · Niederschöneweide · Grünau · Grosse Müggelsee · Rahnsdorf · Wilmshagen · Springeberg · Erkner

Cecilienhof · 103 · Zehlendorf · Lankwitz · Buckow · Müggelberge · Müggelheim · Dämeritzsee

Potsdam · Klein Glienicke · Dreilinden · Kleinmachnow · Seehof · Marienfelde · Rudow · Grossziethen · Altglienicke · Bohnsdorf · Wendenschloss · 115 · Langer See · Gr. Krumpe · Neu Buchhorst

Babelsberg · Kienwerder · Stahnsdorf · Teltow · Heinersdorf · Osdorf · Lichtenrade · Schönefeld · Flughafen Schönefeld · Eichwalde · Karolinenhof · Seddinsee · Gosen · Neu Zittau

Steinstücken · Ruhlsdorf · Friederikenhof · Kleinziethen · Schmöckwitz

East from Greenwich

6 7 8 9 10 11

Hamburg map (bottom left):

Quickborn · Harksheide · Tangstedter Forst · Duvenstedter Brook

Rantzau · Renzel · Norderstedt · Glasmoor · Wulksfelde · Duvenstedt · Ammersbek

C Hohenraden · Wulfsmühle · Hasloh · Haslohfeld · Ochsenzoll · Glashütte · Wohldorf-Ohlstedt **C**

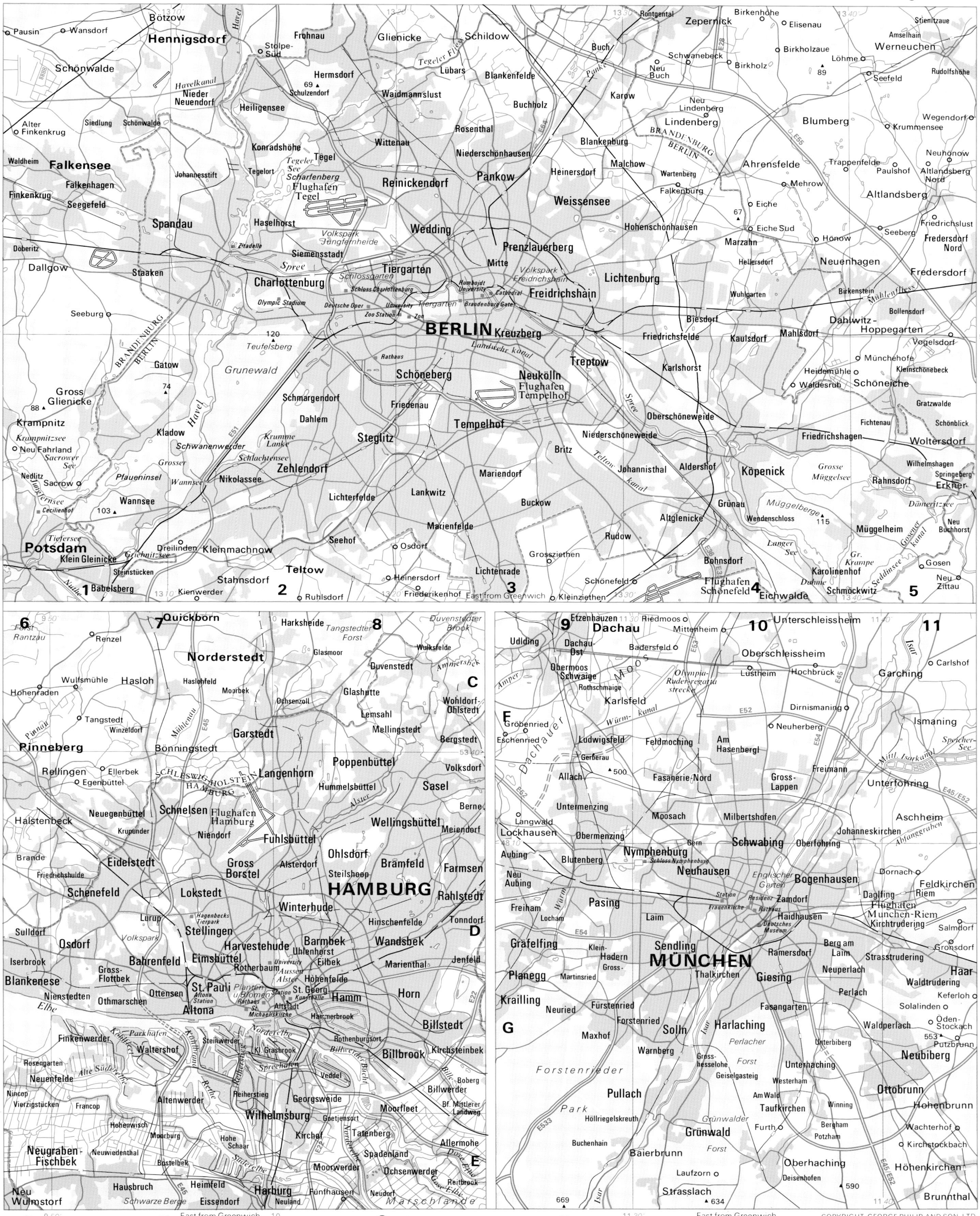

Tangstedt · Winzeldorf · Bönningstedt · Garstedt · Lemsahl · Mellingstedt · Bergstedt

Pinneberg · Langenhorn · Hummelsbüttel · Poppenbüttel · Volksdorf

Rellingen · Ellerbek · Neuegenbüttel · Schnelsen · Flughafen Hamburg · Niendorf · Sasel · Berne · Meiendorf

Egenbüttel · Krupunder · Fuhlsbüttel · Ohlsdorf · Wellingsbüttel

D Halstenbek · Brande · Eidelstedt · Gross Borstel · Alsterdorf · Bramfeld · Steilshoop · Farmsen · Rahlstedt **D**

Friedrichshulde · Schenefeld · Lokstedt · Winterhude · Hinschenfelde · Tonndorf · Jenfeld

Sülldorf · Lürup · Hagenbecks Tierpark · Stellingen · HAMBURG · Wandsbek · Marienthal

Iserbrook · Osdorf · Bahrenfeld · Harvestehude · Barmbek · Uhlenhorst · Hoheluft · Hamm · Horn · Billstedt

Blankenese · Gross-Flottbek · Eimsbüttel · Rotherbaum · University · Aussen Alster · St. Georg · Kunsthalle · Kirchsteinbek

Nienstedten · Othmarschen · Ottensen · St. Pauli · Altona · St. Michaelis · Altstadt · Hammerbrook · Billbrook

Finkenwerder · Waltershof · Steinwerder · Kl. Grasbrook · Rothenburgsort · Bf. Mittlerer Landweg · Boberg

Rosengarten · Parkhafen · Veddel · Billwerder

Neuenfelde · Köhlbrand · Kl. Grasbrook · Georgswerder · Moorfleet

Nincop · Vierzigstücken · Francop · Hohenwisch · Moorburg · Wilhelmsburg · Goetjensort · Tatenberg · Allermohe

Hohe Schaar · Kirchof · Spadenland · Ochsenwerder

E Neugraben-Fischbek · Neuwiedenthal · Bostelbek · Süderelbe · Moorwerder **E**

Neu Wulmstorf · Hausbruch · Schwarze Berge · Heimfeld · Harburg · Eissendorf · Neuland · Fünfhausen · Neudorf · Reitbrook · Marschlande

East from Greenwich

Munich map (bottom right):

Etzenhausen · Riedmoos · Dachau · Mittenheim · Unterschleissheim · Isar

Udling · Dachau-Ost · Badersfeld · Oberschleissheim · Carlshof

C Obermoos Schwaige · Olympia-Ruder-regatta-strecke · Lustheim · Hochbrück · Garching **C**

Amper · Moos · Rothschwaige · Karlsfeld · Dirnismaning · Ismaning

F Gröbenried · Würm-kanal · E52 · Neuherberg · Speicher See **F**

Eschenried · Ludwigsfeld · Feldmoching · Am Hasenbergl

Gerberau · 500 · Fasanerie-Nord · Freimann · Unterföhring

Dachauer · Allach · Untermenzing · Moosach · Milbertshofen · Gross-Lappen · Aschheim

Langwied · Obermenzing · Lochhausen · Schwabing · Oberföhring · Johanneskirchen

Aubing · Bern · Nymphenburg · Schloss Nymphenburg · Englischer Garten · Bogenhausen · Feldkirchen · Riem

Neu Aubing · Blutenberg · Neuhausen · Dornach

Freiham · Pasing · Station · Residenz · Zamdorf · Daglfing · Flughafen München-Riem

Würm · Locham · Frauenkirche · Rathaus · Haidhausen · Deutsches Museum · Kirchtrudering · Salmdorf

Laim · Berg am Laim · Strasstrudering · Gronsdorf

D Gräfelfing · Klein-Hadern · Giesing · Ramersdorf · Neuperlach · Haar · Waldtrudering **D**

Planegg · Martinsried · Gross-Hadern · MÜNCHEN · Thalkirchen · Perlach · Keferloh

Krailling · Neuried · Fürstenried · Fasangarten · Oden-Stockach · Solalinden

G Forstenried · Solln · Harlaching · Unterbiberg · Waldperlach · 553 · Putzbrunn **G**

Maxhof · Warnberg · Perlacher · Forst · Neubiberg

Grosshesselohe · Unterhaching · Bergham · Ottobrunn

Forstenrieder Park · Pullach · Geiselgasteig · Westerham · Winning · Höhenbrunn

Höllriegelskreuth · Grünwalder · Furth · Wachterhof

E Buchenhain · Taufkirchen · Potzham · Grünwald · Kirchstockbach · Höhenkirchen **E**

Baierbrunn · Am Wald · Grünwald · Forst · Oberhaching · Deisenhofen

669 · Laufzorn · 634 · Strasslach · Isar · 590 · Brunnthal

East from Greenwich

9 10 11

1: 200 000

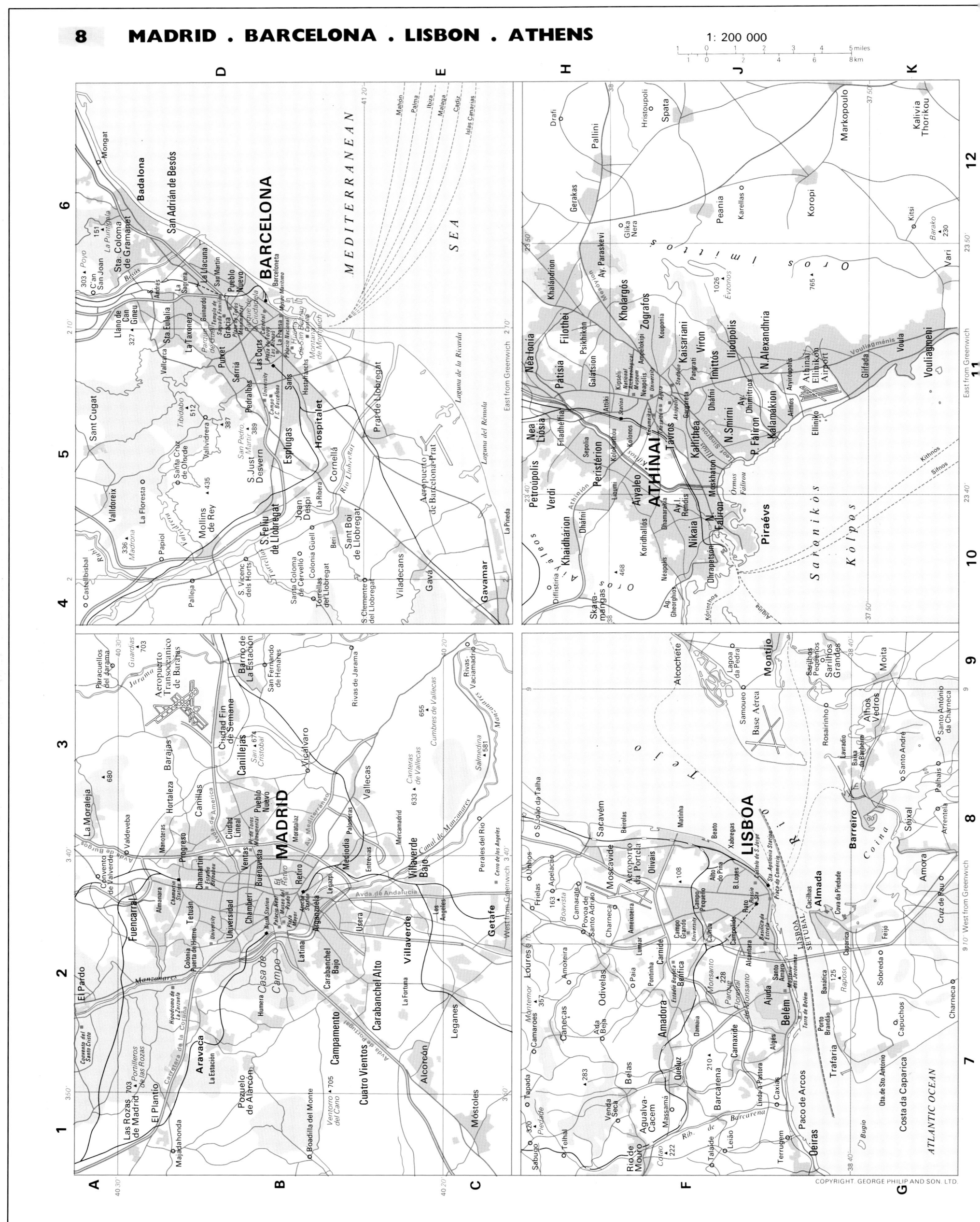

1 : 200 000

0 1 2 3 4 5 miles
0 1 2 3 4 5 6 8 km

MILANO

Monza, Lissone, Desio, Cinisello Balsamo, Sesto S. Giovanni, Brughério, Cologno Monz., Cernusco s. Nav., Concorezzo, Vedano, Villasanta, Carugate, Caponago, Muggiò, Nova Mil., Bresso, Cusano Mil., Paderno, Cormano, Novate Mil., Bollate, Garbagnate Mil., Senago, Limbiate Varedo, Cesate, Solaro, Caronno Pert., Saronno, Ceriano, Uboldo, Origgio, Lainate, Arese, Rho, Pero, Cornaredo, Vighignolo, Settimo Mil., Trenno, Baggio, Córsico, Buccinasco, Trezzano s. Nav., Assago, Rozzano, Opera, S. Giuliano Mil., S. Donato Mil., Segrate, Peschiera Borromeo, Pioltello, Vimodrone, Cassina de' Pecchi, Gorgonzola, Melzo, Aeroporto Internaz. di Linate, Triulzo, Metanópoli, Chiaravalle, Vigentino, Morivione, Lambrate, Ortica, Città degli Studi, Crescenzago, Greco, Affori, Bovisa, Bovisio, Mombello, Masciago, Bruzzano, Buzzago, Palazzolo, Incirano, Dugnano, Mu) Robbiano, Turbigo

Pregnana Mil., Vanzago, Pogliano, Nerviano, Parabiago, Villastanza, Cerro Magg., Cantalupo, Rescaldina, S. Ilario, S. Lorenzo, Canegrate, Barbaiana, Passirana, Terrazzano, Ospiate, Valera, Vittuone, Sedriano, S. Pietro all'Olmo, Bareggio, Cisliano, Cusago, Cesano Bosc., Romano Banco, Quinto Rom., Cesano Bosc., Quartiere Zingone, Rosio, Fagnano, Bestazzo, S. Pietro Best., Mantegazza, S. Vito, Seguro, Monzoro, Settimo Mil., Vighignolo, Pero, Figino

TORINO

Settimo Tor., Volpiano, Léini, Brandizzo, Castiglione Torinese, Gassino Torinese, S. Mauro Tor., Superga, Pino Torinese, Pecetto Tor., Chieri, Baldissero Tor., Pavarolo, Córdova, Cipresso, Andezeno, Castelvecchio, Mongreno, S. Margherita, S. Pietro, Mad. di Scala, Madonna della Scala, Castelletto di Cervere, Reáglie, Bertolla, Barca, Rivodora, Basilica di Superga, Colle di Maddalena, Abbadia di Stura, Venaria, Borgaro Torinese, Cast. S. Cristina, Villaretto, Lucento, Parco M. Carrara, Palazzo Reale, Stupinigi, Mirafiori, Lingotto, Moncalieri, Nichelino, Cavoretto, Testona, S. Vito, Borgaretto, Beinasco, Doirone, Tetti Neirotti, Grugliasco, Collegno, Pianezza, Regina Margherita, Druento, Mándria, Rubianetta, Savonera, Robassomero, Fornacino, Caselle Tor., Aeroporto di Caselle, Malanghero, Banna, S. Maurizio, S. Gillio, La Cassa, Brione, Val della Torre, Givoletto, Montelera, Rivasacco, Moncolombone, Truc di Miola, Mte. Lera 1371, Caselette, Alpignano, Pianezza, Rivoli, Rivalta di Torino, Orbassano, Rosta, Corbiglia, Villarbasse, Sangano, Bruno, Roncáglia, Pancrázio, Regina Margherita, Venaria Reale, Mte. Musinè 1150, Cast. di Camp.

NÁPOLI

Napoli, Portici, S. Giovanni a Ted., Barra, Ponticelli, Torre del Greco, Ercolano, Résina, Torre Annunziata, Boscotrecase, Boscoreale, Trecase, Pompei, Terzigno, S. Giuseppe Vesuviano, Ottaviano, S. Anastasia, Somma Ves., Pollena, S. Sebastiano al Ves., Troochia, S. Giorgio a Crem., Cércola, Volla, Casalnuovo di Náp., Pomigliano d'Arco, Brusciano, Mariglianella, Marigliano, Castello, Cisterna, Acerra, Afragola, Frattamaggiore, Caivano, Cardito, Crispano, Frattaminore, Casoria, Arzano, Grumo Nevano, S. Pietro a Pat., Secondigliano, Capodichino, Aeroporto di Capodichino, Miano, Bosco di Capodimonte, Capodimonte, Vomero, Posillipo, Mergellina, Sta. Lucia, Marechiaro, C. di Posillipo, Bagnoli, Agnano Terme, Camp. Flegrei, Campi Flegrei, Pozzuoli, Quarto, Pianura, Soccavo, Pianura, Marano di Náp., Mugnano di Náp., Chiaiano, Marianella, Villaricca, Calvizzano, S. Antimo, S. Pietro, Melito di Náp., Casandrino, Casavatore, Casoria, Giugliano in Camp., Qualiano, Lauro, Aiperti, Scisciano, Saviano, Faibano, Palazzuolo, Mte. Somma 1132, Vesuvio 1277, Coroglio, I. di Nisida, Pròcida, Íschia, Capri

Golfo di Nápoli

ROMA

Roma, Città del Vaticano, Trastevere, Monteverde Nuovo, Magliana, Valcannuta, Montespaccato, Primavalle, Torrevecchia, Ottavia, La Giustiniana, Prima Porta, Tomba di Nerone, Foro Itálico, Mte. Mario 139, Trionfale, Aurelio, S. Pietro, Villa Borghese, Parioli, Villa Ada, Villa Trieste, Nomentano, Pietralata, Mte. Sacro, Tufello, S. Basilio, Tre Cervara, Tor Sapienza, Torre Nova, Centocelle, Cinecittà, Quadraro, Tuscolano, Prenestino, Labicano, Tor Pignattara, Gabatella, EUR, Ostiense, Cecchignola, Spinaceto, Vallerano, Vitínia, Acilia, Casalotti, La Monachina, La Pisana, Corviale, Aeroporto d. Urbe, Casal Bruciato, Stazione Termini, Università, Foro Romano, Via Nomentana, Via Tiburtina, Via Prenestina, Via Casilina, Via Tuscolana, Via Appia, Via Anagnina, Via Latina, Via Ardeatina, G.R.A., Acrop. d. Ciampino, Aeroporto Ciampino, Moreno, Torricola, Sto. Ricola, Ponte Galéria, Cast. Malnome, Boccea, Centrone, La Bottáccia, Cast. di Guido, Le Selce, La Selce, S. Nicola, Galéria, Tregháta, Malagrotta, Via Aurelia, Via Cassia, Via Flaminia, Via del Mare, Via Portuense, Via Ostiense, Via Laurentina, Ag

ro Romano, Tévere, Arrone, Bottácia, Via del Porto, Aeroporto Intercontinentale Leonardo da Vinci, A12

East from Greenwich

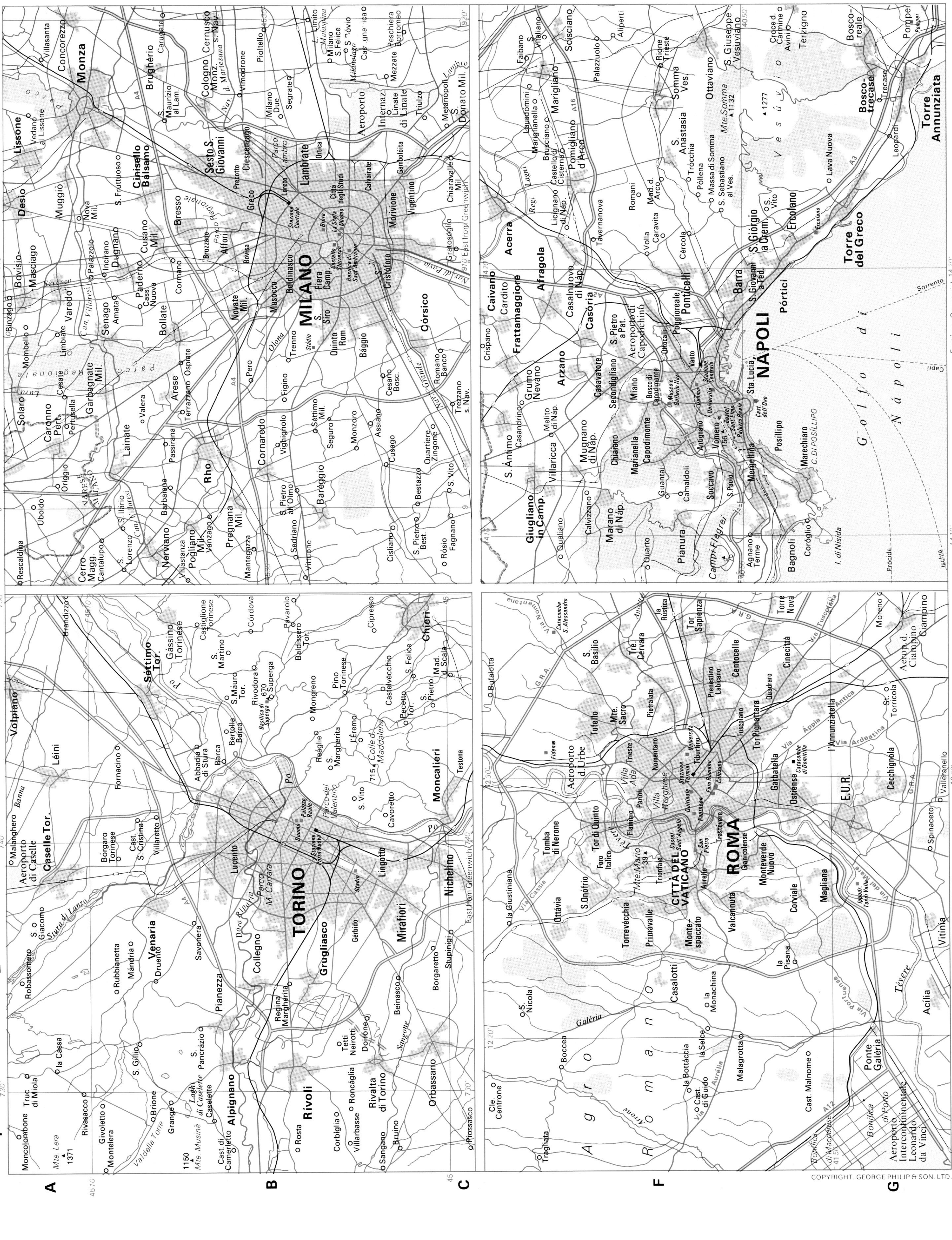

COPYRIGHT. GEORGE PHILIP & SON. LTD

1: 200 000

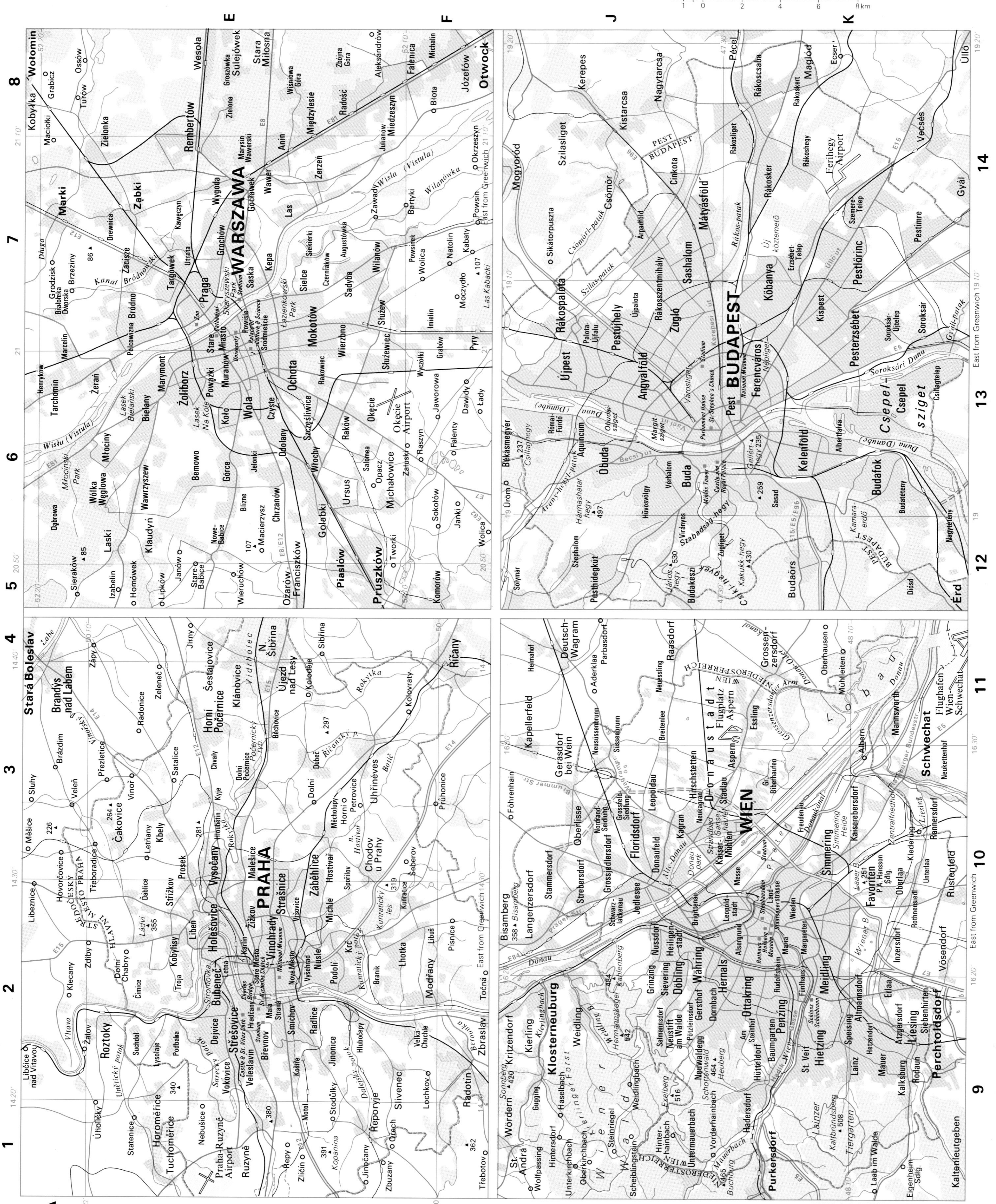

1 0 1 2 3 4 5 miles
1 0 2 4 6 8 km

WARSZAWA

PRAHA

WIEN

BUDAPEST

Praga

Pest

Buda

Óbuda

Újpest

Klosterneuburg

Perchtoldsdorf

Schwechat

Stará Boleslav

Brandýs nad Labem

Říčany

Otwock

Wołomin

Pruszków

Piaslów

COPYRIGHT GEORGE PHILIP AND SON LTD

East from Greenwich

1: 200 000

1 0 1 2 3 4 5 miles
1 0 2 4 6 8 km

1   2   3   4   5   6

A

30   10'   Lisiy Nos   Olgino   Kolomyagi Novaya Derevnya   Udelnaya   Ruchyi   30 20   Gorely   Berngardovka   Lubya   30 40'   **Vsevolozhsk**   A
60   O. Verperluda   Oz. Lakhtinskiy Razliv   Lesnoy   Grazhdanka   Rybatskaya   Rzhevka   Noyoye Kovalyova   Kalytino   60
Lakhtinskiy   Bobylyskaya   Polyustrovo   Krasnaya Gorka
Staraya Derevnya   Bolshaya Nevka   O. Trudyashchikhsya   Vyborgskaya Storona   Finland Station   Selytsy
Kirov Stadium   Ostrova Kirovskiye   Apterkarskiy Ostrov   Khirvosti   Koltushi
Petrogradskaya Storona   Bolshaya-Okhta   Zanevka   Yanino   Pavlovo
O. Volynyy   Malaya Neva   Dekabristov   Staraya
B   Ostrov Vasilyevskiy   Hermitage & Winter Palace   Admiralteyskaya Storona   Oz. Korkinskoye   B
Old Admiralty   Neva   Moskva Station   Malaya-Okhta   Kudrovo   Tavry
St. Isaac's Cathedral   Alexander Nevsky Abbey   Novosergiyevka   Razmitelevo
SANKT-PETERBURG   Vitebsk Station   Volodarskoye   Cornaya   Myaglovo   Ozerki
Fontanka   Baltic Station   Vesolyy Posolok   Khaboye
Obvodnyy kanal   Warszawa Station
Ostrov Kanonerskiy   Ostrov Gutuyevskiy   Volynkina-Derevnya   Obukhovo   Volkovka   Farforovskaya
Avtovo   Aleksandrovskoye   Lesnozavodskaya   Neva   Novosaratovka
59 50   Strelyna   Kikenka   Posolok Lenina   Uritsk   Ulyanka   Dakhnoye   Kupchino   Novoaleksandrovskoye   Novosaratovka   59 50
C   30   Sosnovaya   Ligovo   30 10'   Airport   30 20'   Srednaya Rogatka   Rybatskoye   Ust-Slavyanka   30 30   East from Greenwich   C
1   2   3   4   5   6

7   8   9   10   11   12

D   Sheremetyevo Airport   37 20'   **Khimki**   Moskovskaya   Kolytsevaya   Automobilynaya Doroga   37 40'   Chelobityevo   **Mytishchi**   37 50   Zhegalovo   **12**   D
Kurkino   Lianozovo   Vatutino   Yauza   Tayninka   Tsentralynyy   Oboldino   Medvezhiy Ozyora
Saburovo   Novokhovrino   **Beskudnikovo**   **Medvedkovo**   Druzhba
Maryino   Sinicka   Putilkovo   Bratsevo   Degunino   Vladykino   Shosse   Meavezhiy Ozyora   Almazovo
Mitino   Khimki-Khovrino   Likhoborka   Babushkin   Pekhra-Pokrovskoye
55 50   Novonikolyskoye   Penyagino   Nikolskiy   157   55 50
Chernovo   Tushino   Petrovsko-Razumovskoye   Dzerzhinskiy Park   Abramtsevo   Vostochnyy
Krasnogorsk   Timiryazev Park   Ostankino   Yauza   Galyanovo   140   **Balashikha**
Pavshino   Pokrovsko-Sresnevo   Sokolniki Park   Bogorodskoye   Novaya
Golyevo   Myakinino   Strogino   Leningradskiy Prospekt   Petrovsky Park   Sokolniki   **Izmaylovo**   Gorenki   Pekhra-Yakovievskaya
Arkhangelyskoye   Troitse-Lykovo   Frunze   Riga Station   Serebryanka   Vishnyaki   Nikolyskoye
Zakharkovo   Rublovo   Khorosovo   Dzerzhinskiy   Izmayloskiy Park   Saltykovka
E   Razdory   Tatarovo   Mnevniki   **MOSKVA**   Sverdlov   Leningrad Station   Kazan Station   Leportovo   150   Enturiastou Shosse   **Reutov**   Kutsino   E
Barvikha   Cachenka   Cherepkovo   Krasno-Presnenskaya   Bolshoi Theatre   Bauman   Novogireyevo   Serebryanka   **Zheleznodorozhnyy**
Romashkovo   Krylatskoye   Moskva   Red Square, St. Basil's Cathedral, Lenin Mausoleum   **Perovo**   Fenino
Poduskino   Kuntsevo   **Fili-Mazilovo**   Kremlin   Kuskovo   Plyushchevo   Veshnyaki   Rudnevka   Temnikovo
Nemchinovka   Kiyev Sta.   Tretiakov Art Gallery   Zhdanov   Vykhino   Kosino   Kozhukhovo
Novoivanovskoye   Davidkovo   Luzhniki Sports Centre, Lenin Stadium   Gorkiy Park   Lenin   Paveletz Station   Vykhino   94   Mikhelysona   Marusino
Lochino   Aminyevo   Moskvoretskiy   Volgoaradskyy Prospekt   Zhulebino
Mamonovo   Ochakovo   Lomonosov University   Leninskiye Gory   150   Oktyabrskiy   Kuzyminki   Nekrasovka
55 40   Bakovka   Zarechye   Ramenki   Leninsky Prospekt   Nogatino   **Lyublino**   **Lyubertsy**   Koreno vo   55 40
Odintsovo   Meshcherskiy   Nikulino   Yugo-Zarad   Cheryomushki   Kolomenskoye   Kotelynik i   Tomilino
Choboty   Solntsevo   Zyuzino   Dyakovo   Maryino   Kapotnya   Kraskovo   **Malakhovka**
Peredelkino   Orlovo   Rumyantsevo   Volkhonka Zil   Kuryanovo   Chkalova   Dzerzhinskiy   Udelnaya
Rasskazovka   Setunka   Sosenka   **Belyayevo Bogorodskoye**   Certanovka   Lenino   Borisovo   Besedy   Tokarevo
Vnukovo   Nikolo-Khovanskoye   250   **Certanovo**   Uzkoye   Brateyevo   Petrovskoye   Oktyabrskiy   Vereya
F   Vnukovo Airport   Teplyy Star   Pokrovskoye   Yasenevo   Ashcherino   Lytkarino   Pechorka   F
Serednevo   Peredelytsy   Likova   Sosenka   Kr. Stroitel   Mamonovo   Ostrovtsy
Valuyevo   Letovo   Baturino   Yasenevo   **Biryulyovo**   Molokovo   38   Zaozerye
Kommunarka   Mikhaylovskoye   Bitsa   East from Greenwich   COPYRIGHT. GEORGE PHILIP & SON. LTD.

7   8   9   37 40'   10   37 50   11   12

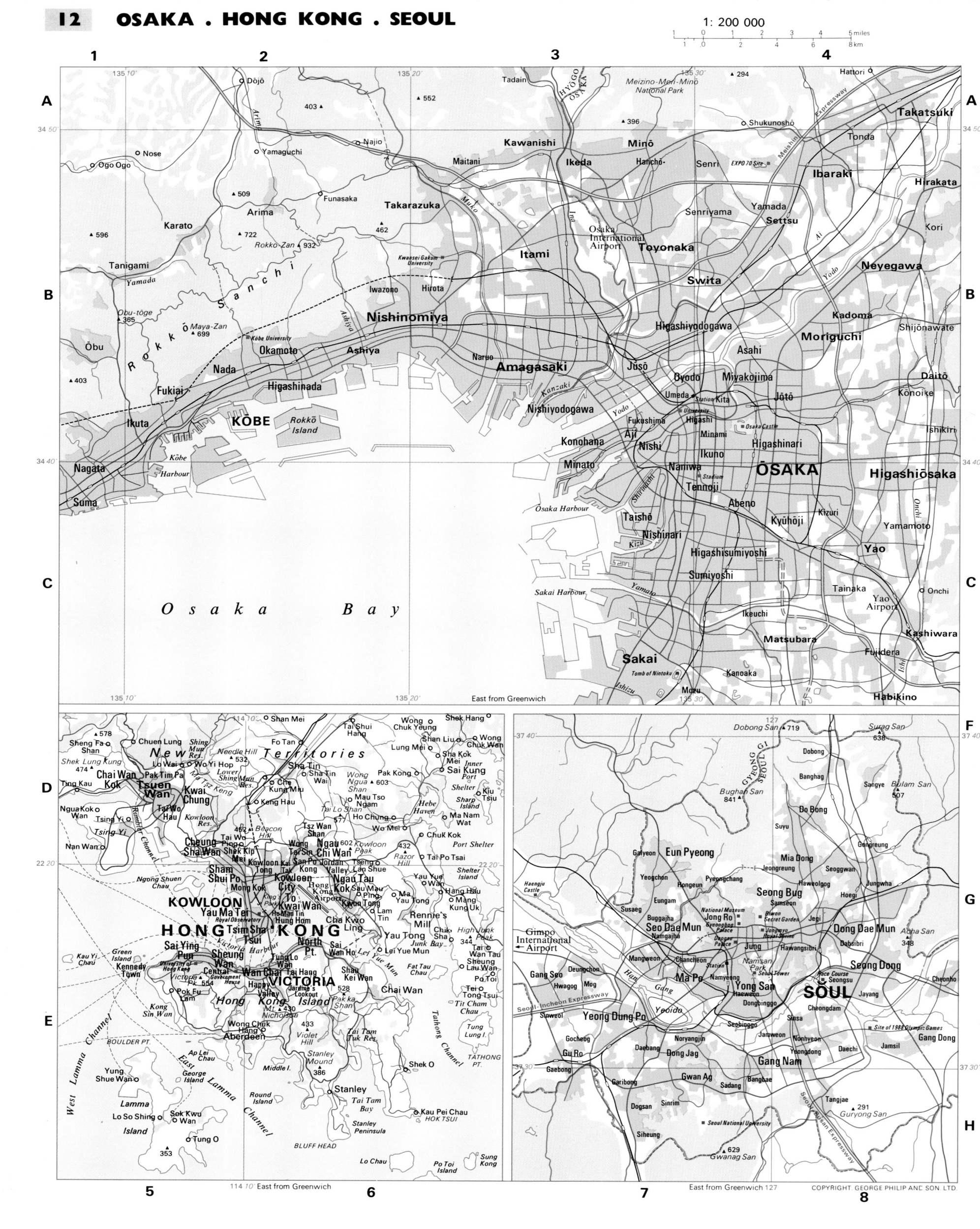

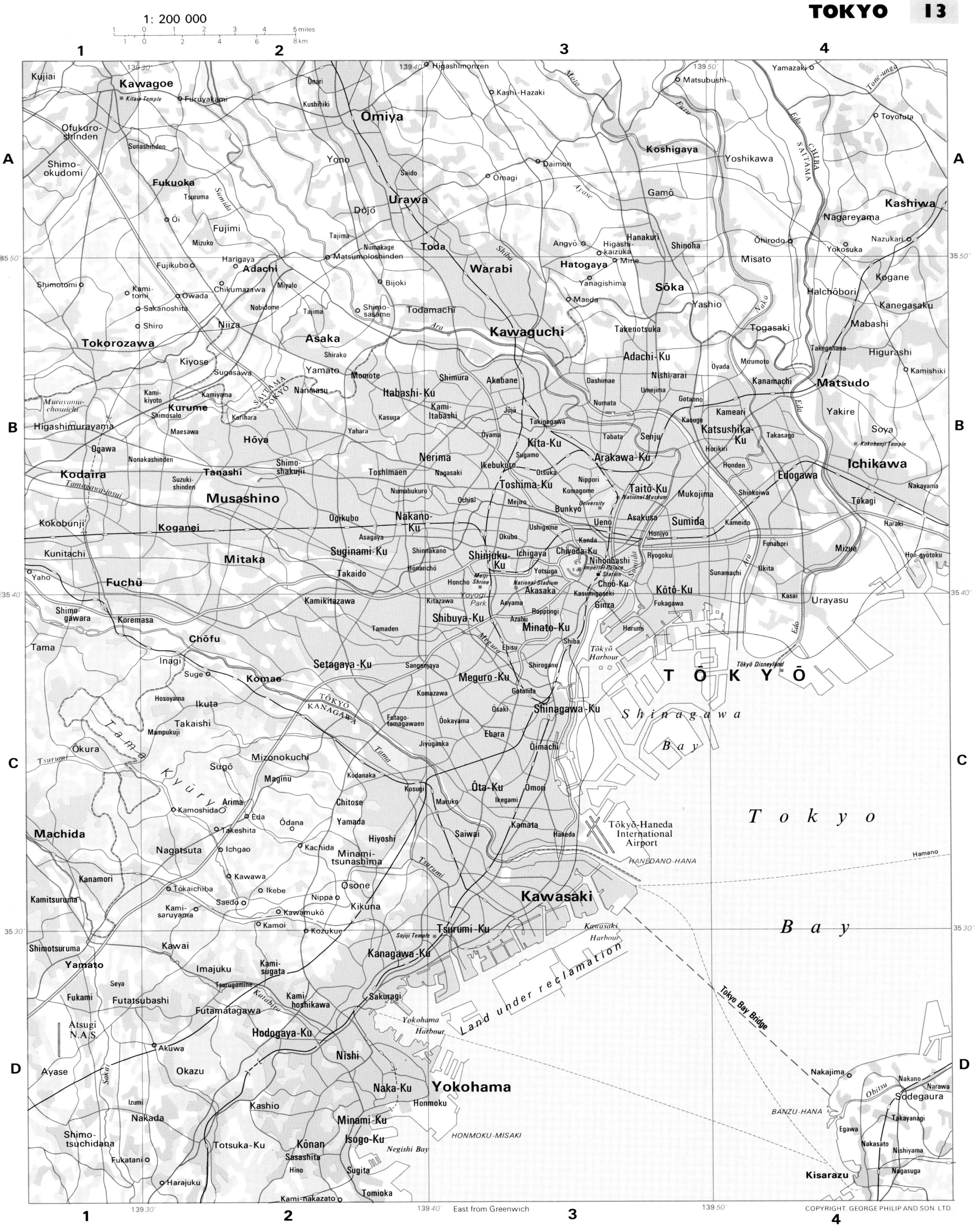

1 : 200 000

1 2 0 3 4 5 miles
1 0 2 4 6 8 km

1 **2** **3** **4**

139 30' 139 40' Higashimonzen 139 50' Yamazaki Tone-unga

Kujiai
Kawagoe Ōnari Kushihiki Kashi-Hazaki Matsubushi Toyofuta
Ōmiya Yono Saido Ōmagi Koshigaya Yoshikawa Nagareyama Nazukari
A Ofukuro-shinden Suriashinden Daimon Gamō Kashiwa
Shimo-okudomi Urawa Angyō Higashi-kaizuka Mine Shinoha Ōhirodo Yokosuka Kogane **A**
Fukuoka Tsuruma Dōjō Higashi Misato Kanegasaku
Ōi Fujimi Tajima Numakage Warabi Hatogaya Yanagishima Sōka Yashio Haichōbori Mabashi
Mizuko Toda Maeda Takenotsuka Togasaki Takegahana Higurashi
Shimotomi Harigaya Matsumotoshinden Kawaguchi Takenotsuka Kamishiki
Kami-tomi Fujikubo Adachi Bijoki Shimo-sasame Todamachi Adachi-Ku Ōyada Kanamachi **B**
Sakanoshita Ōwada Chikumazawa Miyalo Nobidome Shirako Shimura Dashimae Nishi-arai Mizumoto Matsudo
Shiro Niiza Asaka Yamato Momote Akabane Numata Umejima Gotanno Kameari Katsushika-Ku
Tokorozawa Kiyose Sugesawa Narimasu Yahara Kasuga Jūjō Takinegawa Tabata Senju Kasuge Horikiri Takasago Soya
B Higashimurayama Ogawa Kurume Shimosalo Kurihara Kita-Ku Ōyama Arakawa-Ku Honden Takasago Kokobunji Temple Ichikawa
Murayama-chosuichi Nonakashinden Kami-kiyoto Kamiyama Maesawa Itabashi-Ku Kami-Itabashi Sugamo Otsuka Nippori Komagome Nakayama
Kodaira Suzuki-shinden Tanashi Hōya Shimo-shakujii Nerima Ikebukuro Toshimaen Nagasaki Toshima-Ku Mejiro University Ueno Taitō-Ku Mukojima Shinkoiwa Edogawa Tōkagi
Tamagawa-josui Numabukuro National Museum Asakusa Sumida Haraki
Kokobunji Musashino Ōgikubo Nakano-Ku Ochiai Ushigome Kanda Honjyo Kameido Mizue
C Koganei Asagaya Shinnakano Mejiro Bunkyō Nihonbashi Ryogoku Funabori Hon-gyotoku
Kunitachi Mitaka Suginami-Ku Honanchō Shinjuku-Ku Ichigaya Chiyoda-Ku Imperial Palace Sunamachi Ukita Urayasu
Yaho Fuchū Takaido Kitazawa Meiji Shrine Yotsuya Station Chūō-Ku Kasai
Shimo-gawara Kamikitazawa Yoyogi Park National Stadium Akasaka Kasumigaseki Kōtō-Ku Fukagawa
Koremasa Tamaden Shibuya-Ku Aoyama Roppongi Ginza Harumi
Tama Chōfu Azabu Minato-Ku Shiba Tōkyō Disneyland
Inagi Suge Komae Setagaya-Ku Sangenjaya Meguro-Ku Shirogane Tōkyō Harbour **TŌKYŌ**
Hosoyama Ikuta Komazawa Gotanda Shinagawa Bay
Takaishi Mampukuji F Futago-tamagawaen Jiyugaoka Ōsaki Shinagawa-Ku
C Okura Sugō Mizonokuchi Kodanaka Ebara Ōimachi **C**
Tsurumi Maginu Kosugi Ōta-Ku Ōmori Tokyo Bay Hamano
Machida Arima Chitose Yamada Maruko Ikegami Tōkyō-Haneda International Airport
Kamoshida Ēda Ōdana Hiyoshi Saiwai Kamata Haneda HANEDANO-HANA
Nagatsuta Takeshita Ichgao Minami-tsunashima Nippa Osone Tsurumi
Kanamori Kawawa Ikebe Kikuna Kawasaki
Kamitsuruma Tōkaichiba Saedō Kawamukō Kawasaki Harbour
Kami-saruyama Kamoi Kozukue Tsurumi-Ku Shōji Temple
D Shimotsuruma Kawai Kanagawa-Ku Land under reclamation Tokyo Bay Bridge Nakajima Nakano Narawa **D**
Yamato Seya Imajuku Kami-sugata Tsurugamine Sakuragi Yokohama Harbour Sodegaura
Fukami Futatsubashi Futamatagawa Kami-hoshikawa Obitsu
Atsugi N.A.S. Hodogaya-Ku Egawa Takayanagi
Ayase Akuwa Nishi BANZU-HANA Nakasato Nishiyama
Okazu Naka-Ku Yokohama Nagasuga
Izumi Kashio Honmoku Minami-Ku Kisarazu
Nakada Kōnan Isogo-Ku Negishi Bay
Shimo-tsuchidana Totsuka-Ku Sasashita HONMOKU-MISAKI
Fukatani Hino Sugita
Harajuku Kami-nakazato Tomioka

1 139 30' **2** 139 40' East from Greenwich **3** 139 50' **4**

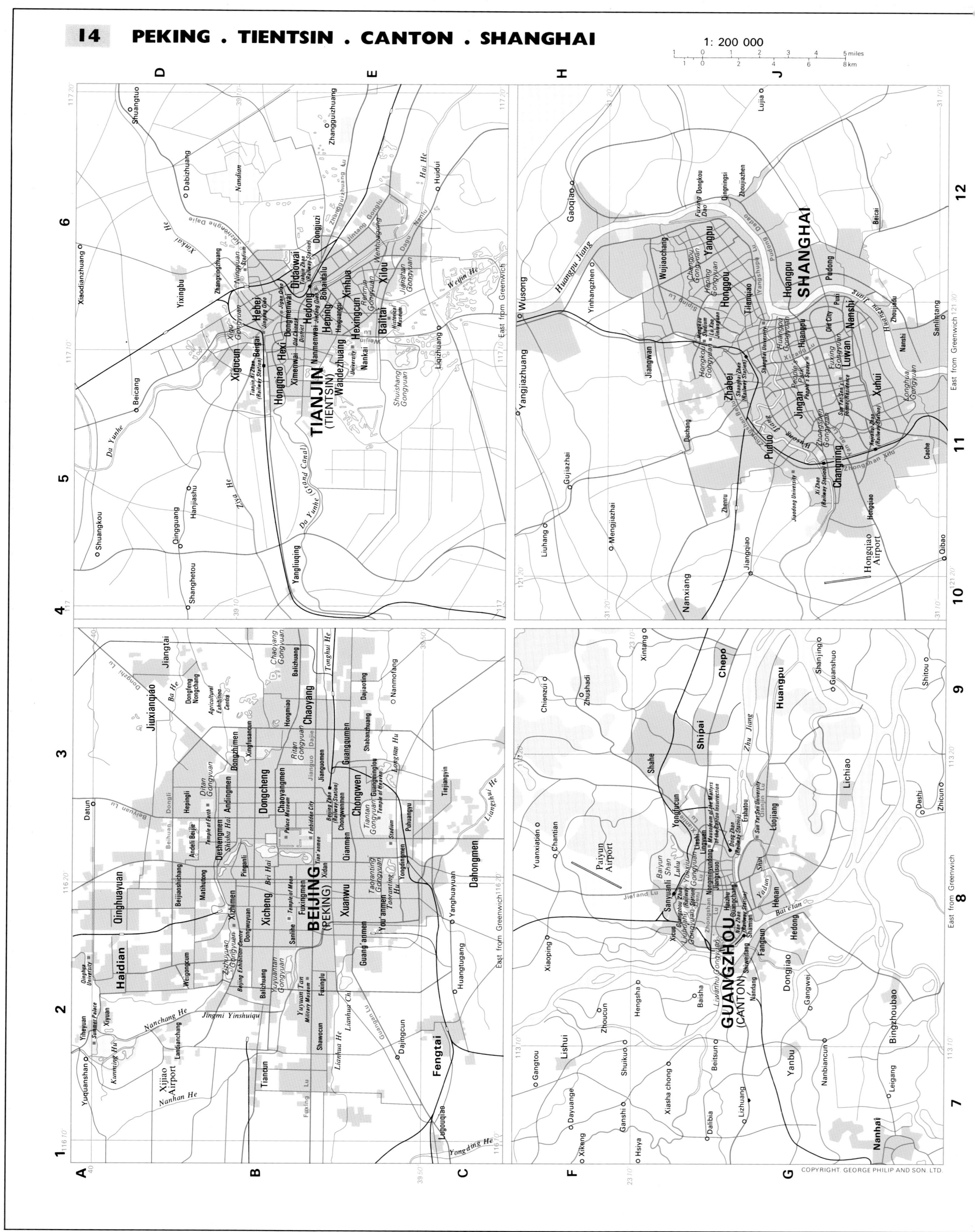

1 : 200 000

1 0 1 2 3 4 5 miles
1 0 2 4 6 8 km

COPYRIGHT. GEORGE PHILIP AND SON. LTD.

1 : 200 000

1 0 1 2 3 4 5 miles
1 0 1 2 3 4 6 8 km

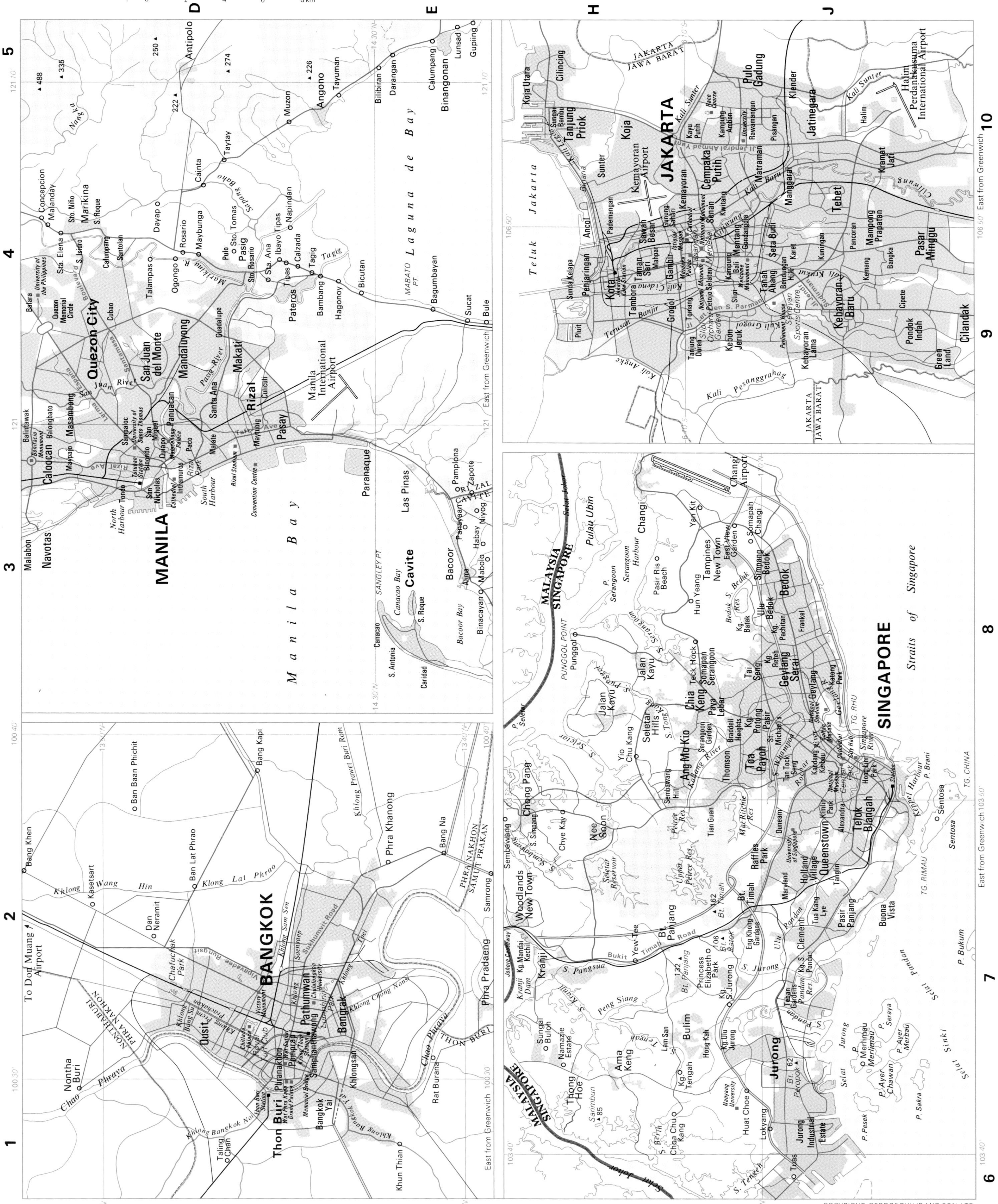

MANILA

Quezon City
San Juan del Monte
Mandaluyong
Makati
Rizal
Pasay
Santa Ana
Paco
Manila International Airport
Paranaque
Las Pinas
Pamplona
Zapote
CAVITE
Cavite
Bacoor
Caridad
S. Antonia
Canacao
Sangley Pt.
Bacoor Bay
Canacao Bay

Manila Bay

University of the Philippines
Quezon Memorial Circle
Bonifacio Monument
Caloocan
Navotas
Malabon
North Harbour
South Harbour
Convention Centre
Rizal Park
Rizal Stadium
Balintawak
Balonghato
Masambong
Maypajo
San Juan
Mariblana
Mandaluyong

Antipolo
250
274
226
Angono
Binangonan
Lunsad
Guping
Calumpang
Darangan
Bilibiran
Tayuman
Muzon
Cainta
Taytay
488
335
222
Nangka
Concepcion
Malanday
Sto. Niño
Marikina
S. Roque
Sta. Elena
Cubao
Davap
Rosario
Maybunga
Ogongo
Talampas
Santolan
Pasig
Sto. Tomas
Napindan
Ibayo Tipas
Calzada
Tagig
Bambang
Bagumbayan
Bicutan
Hagonoy
Pateros
Sucat
Bule

Laguna de Bay
MABATO PT.

BANGKOK

Thon Buri
Dusit
Pathumwan
Pinklao
Phranakhon
Bangkak
Phra Pradaeng
Bangkok Yai
Khlongsan
Rat Burana
Taling Chan
Khun Thian
Nontha Buri
Bang Khen
Bang Kapi
Ban Baan Phichit
Kasetsart
Dan Neramit
Ban Lat Phrao
Bang Na
Phra Khanong
Samrong
To Don Muang Airport
Chatuchak Park
Vibhavadee Rangsit
Sukhumvit Road

PHRA NAKHON SAMUT PRAKAN
THON BURI
NONTHABURI
PHRA NAKHON

Chao Phraya
Khlong Bangkok Noi
Khlong Bangkok Yai
Khlong Chong Nonsi
Khlong Prawet Buri Rum
Klong Lat Phrao

JAKARTA

Koja Utara
Clincing
Tanjung Priok
Koja
Pulo Gadung
Klender
Halim Perdanakusuma International Airport
Jatinegara
Kramat Jati
Kenayoran Airport
Kemayoran
Cempaka Putih
Sunter
Antol
Pademangan
Penjaringan
Sunda Kelapa
Pluit
Kota
Taman Sari
Tambora
Banjir
Grogol
Gambir
Senen
Matraman
Manggarai
Tebet
Seta Buti
Mampong Prapatan
Kebayoran Baru
Pasar Minggu
Cilandak
Pondok Indah
Green Land
Kebayoran Lama
Mentang
Gondangdia
Tanah Abang
Karet
Setiabudi
Duren Sawit
Kebon Jeruk
Kampung
Pancoran
Cipete
Kemang
Bangka
Kuningan

Teluk Jakarta
Kali Jakarta
JAKARTA JAWA BARAT

SINGAPORE

Changi Airport
Changi
Yan Kit
East View Garden
Somapah Changi
Tampines New Town
Pasir Ris Beach
Bedok
Hun Yeang
Geylang Serai
Kg. Batak
Kg. Pachitan
Frankel
Paya Lebar
Teck Hock
Chia Keng
Jalan Kayu
Seletar Hills
Ang Mo Kio
Yio Chu Kang
Bradell Heights
Toa Payoh
Thomson
Serangoon
Potong Pasir
Tai Seng
Geylang
Telok Blangah
Queenstown
Holland Village
Raffles Park
Buona Vista
Pasir Panjang
Clementi
Jurong
Jurong Industrial Estate
Woodlands New Town
Sembawang
Nee Soon
Chong Pang
Chye Kay
Bt. Timah
Bt. Panjang
Kranji
Sungai Kadut
Peng Siang
Bulim
Hong Kah
Ama Keng
Thong Hoe
Choa Chu Kang
Lokyang
Huat Choe
Sarimbun
Namazie Estate
Princess Elizabeth Park
Sembawang Hill
Bukit Timah
Nanyang University

Straits of Singapore
Johor Strait
Selat Johor
MALAYSIA
SINGAPORE
Pulau Ubin
Serangoon Harbour
Sentosa
P. Brani
Keppel Harbour
TG CHINA
TG RIMAU
TG RHU

Peirce Reservoir
MacRitchie Res.
Seletar Reservoir
Upper Peirce Res.
University of Singapore

1: 200 000

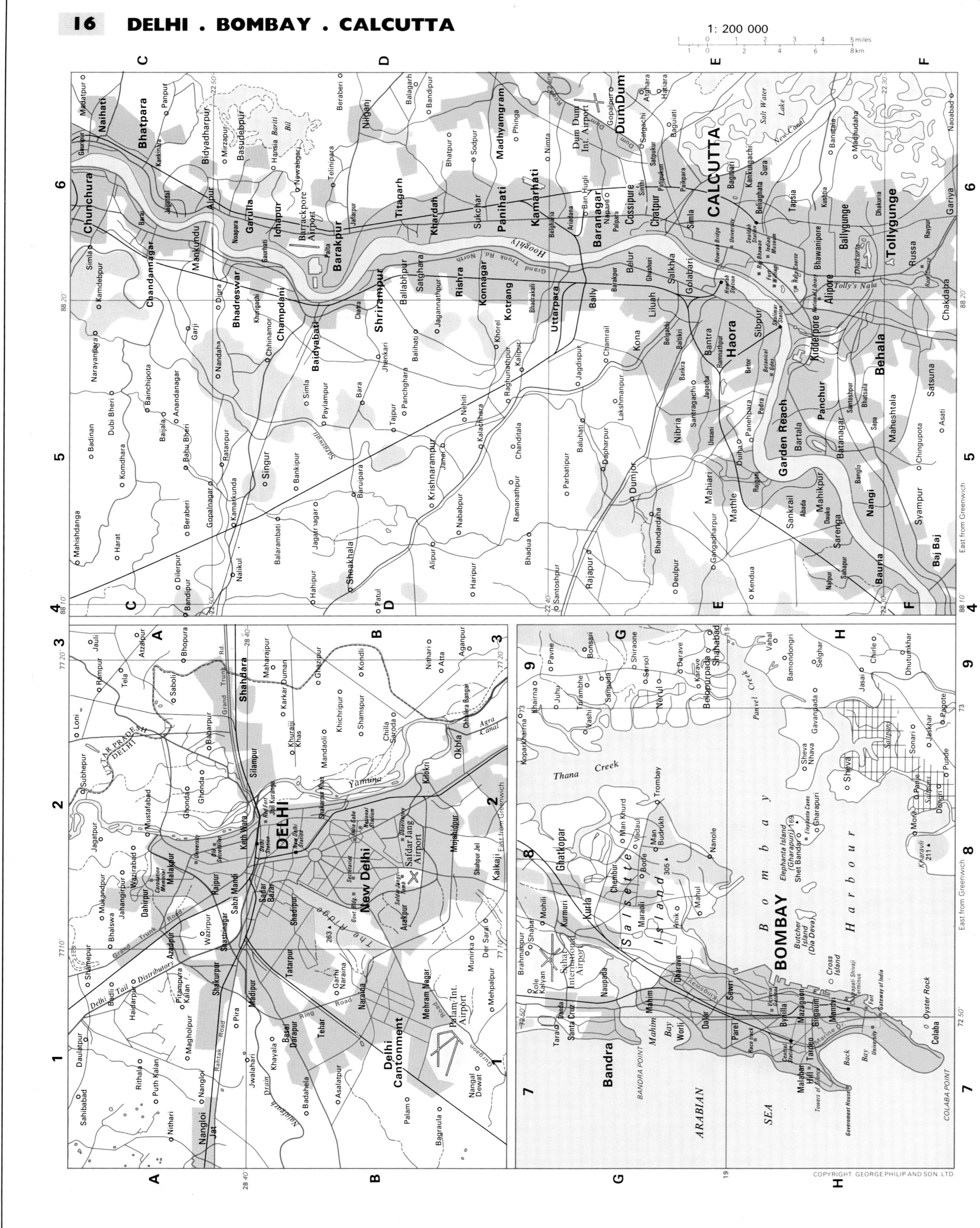

COPYRIGHT GEORGE PHILIP AND SON LTD.

1: 200 000

TEHRAN

Niávarán · Ekhtiyárieh · Shemirānāt · Qolhak · Bâvudiyeh · Vanak · Ewin · Pârk-e-Shâhanshâhi · Kuy-e-Mekânir · Bâgh-e-Feiz · Kuy-e-Gishâ · Yusofâ'id · Amirâbâd · University · Imperial Palace · Jamshidiâbâd · Baer Course · Kan · Hasanâbâd · Mehrābād Airport · 1214 · Firuz Bahram · Guldasteh · Magidiyeh · Nâmak · Eshratâbâd · Nira-ye Havâ'i · Majlis · Sepah Sahir Mosque · Golistan Palace · Bazâr · Shah Mosque · Aktaabâd · Westanâd · Nemahâbâd · Qasr-e-Firózéh · Farahâbâd · Doshan Tappeh Airfield · Qasemâbâd · Tehrān Pars · Dulâb · Dowlatâbâd · Jawâdiyeh · Qual'eh Muraghi Airfield · Shâhr-e-Rey · Yaftâbâd · Tepe Saif · Mesagarâbâd

Teheran Highway

ISTANBUL

Beykoz · Paşabahce · Çubuklu · Kanlica · Yeniköy · Istinye · Anadoluhisari · Kandilli · Vanıköy · Umraniye · İçerenköy · Bostancı · Erenköy · Feherbahçe · Kısıklı · Bebek · Rumelihisari · Çengelköy · Beylerbeyi · Üsküdar · Kadiköy · Boyacıköy · Balmumcu · Ortaköy · Kuruçeşme · Arnavutköy · Mecidiyeköy · Şişli · Beşiktaş · Taksim · Galata · Dolmabahçe Saray · Maslak · Kuçukkoy · Küçükköy · Kâğıthane · Eyüp · Hasköy · Beyoğlu · Eminönü · Fatih · Laleli · Aksaray · Topkapi · Yenikapi · Samatya · Zeytinburnu · Bakırköy · Yeşilköy · İstanbul Hava Alanı · Ayvazaga · Kâğıthane · Alibeyköy · Topçular · Karagümrük · Fatih · Sultanahmet Cami · Kızkulesi · Zeytinburnu

Golden Horn (Haliç)

Boğaziçi (Bosphorus) · İstanbul Boğazı

285 · 438 · 128

Avcılar · Cebeciköy · Küçükçekmece · Ayişalen · Esenler · Mahmutbey · Güngören · Esenler · Mahmutbey · Kocasinan · Safraköy · Şenlikköy · Havalimanı

MARMARA DENIZI

KARACHI

Malir Cantonment · Karachi Intl. Airport · Drigh Road · Phihái · Bhambo Khân · Qarmati · Korangi · Punjápur · Mahmodâbâd · Sharea Fuisal · Nazimabad · Gothi Goti Mâr · Lülükhei · Sadr · Ghizri · Clifton · Chhota Andai · Barra Andai · Oyster Rocks · Gandhi Zoo · Race Course · University · Zoological Garden · Goth Sher Shâh · Layâri · City · Sind · Bulbai · Qadri-i-Azam · Kiamari · Manora · West Wharf · Bâba I. · Bunker · Masroor · Chauki · Mauripur · Ghizri Creek · Tower of Silence

ARABIAN SEA

BAGHDAD

Saddam City · Khansâ · Amin · Huwaydi · Ishlijîa · Idrîs · New Baghdad · Muthana · Riyad · Khalij · Quds · Nazlal Hikmat Beg · Mustansiriya · Nil · Shebab Stadium · Shebâb · Wahda · Al 'Azamiyah · Waziriya · Shaikh Aâmir · Saadun · Nidâl · Jizira · Tunis · Maghreb · Al Mansur · Rusâfa · Karkh · Shaikh · Aâlam · Tishriyaa · Karâdah · Dôra · Atfiya · Karama · Sûqs · Bâb al Moâaham · Baghdad Univ. · Salam · Ramadan · Mutaalab · Madinat Al Mansur · Tâjiblus · Reşaf · Um Al Khanâzir Island · Jizî er · Huriya · Zafra · Mutanabi · Kindi · Adel · Zâhra · Khudiâ · Andalus · Hamrâ · Firdows · Apal Qadisiya · Ta'imm · Maarifa · Jihad · Shaala · Abu Ghraib Expressway · Site of Ancient Road · City of Baghdad · Saddam Intl. Airport · Dôra Expressway · AMANAT AL-ASIMA

East from Greenwich

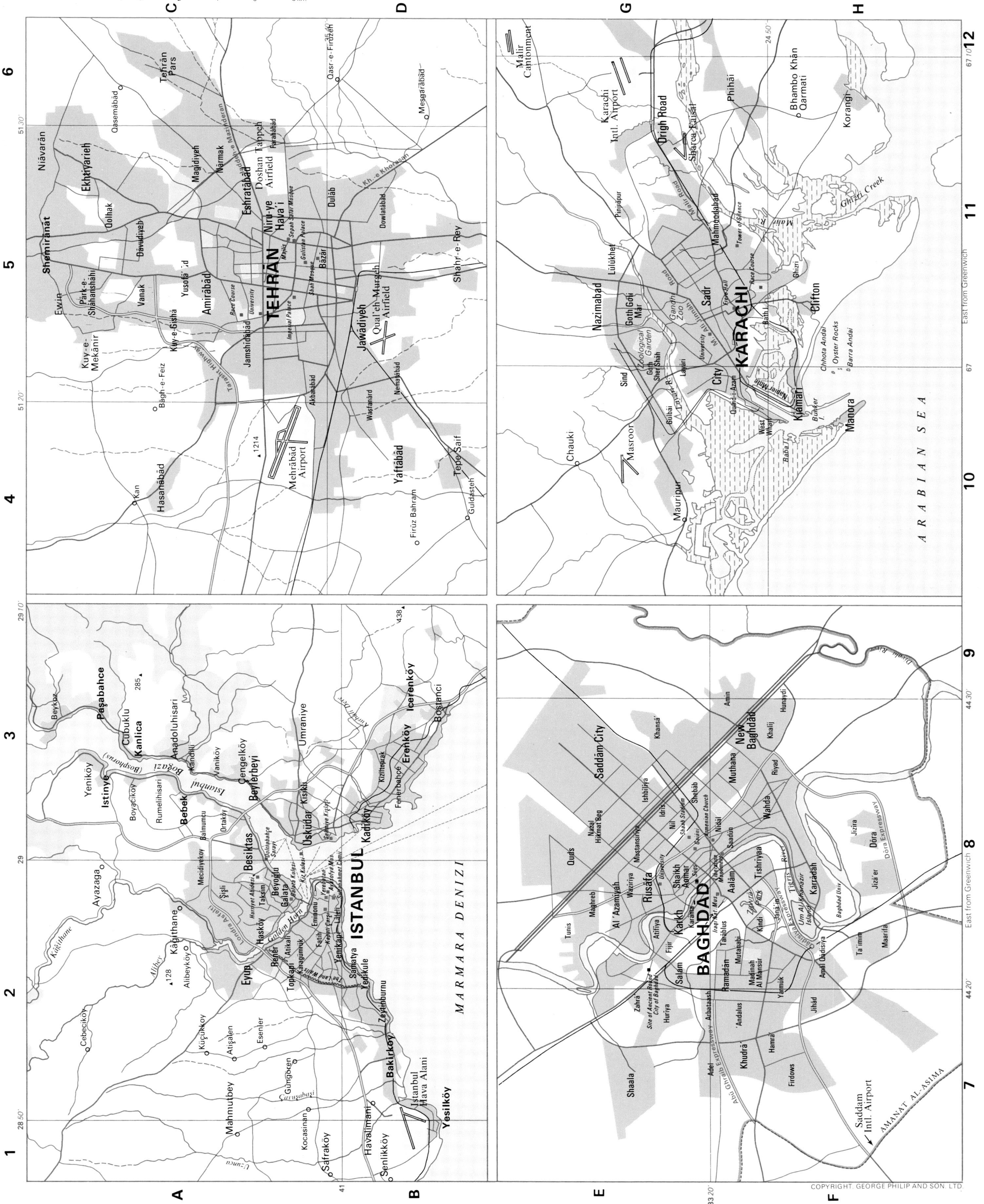

COPYRIGHT. GEORGE PHILIP AND SON. LTD

1: 200 000

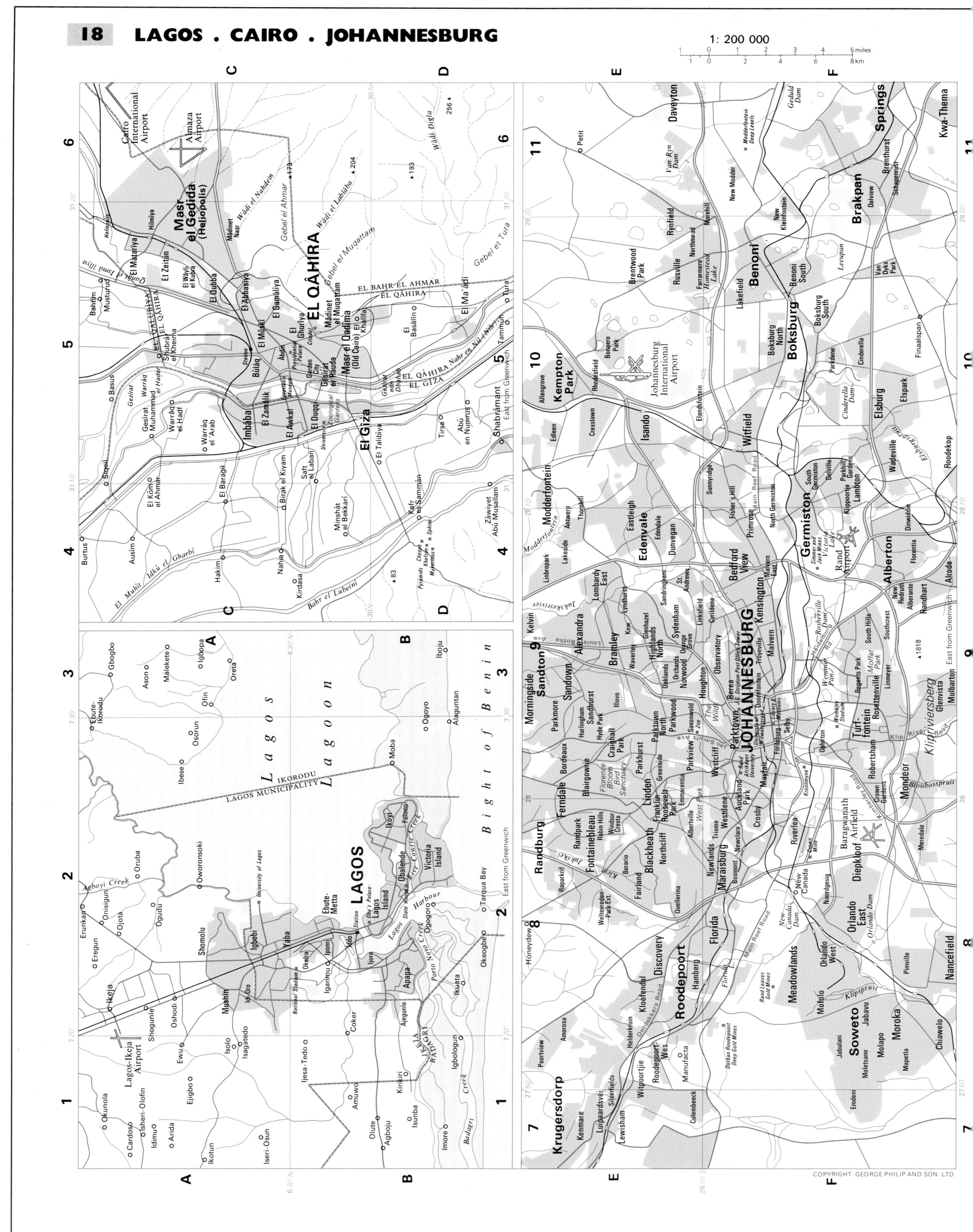

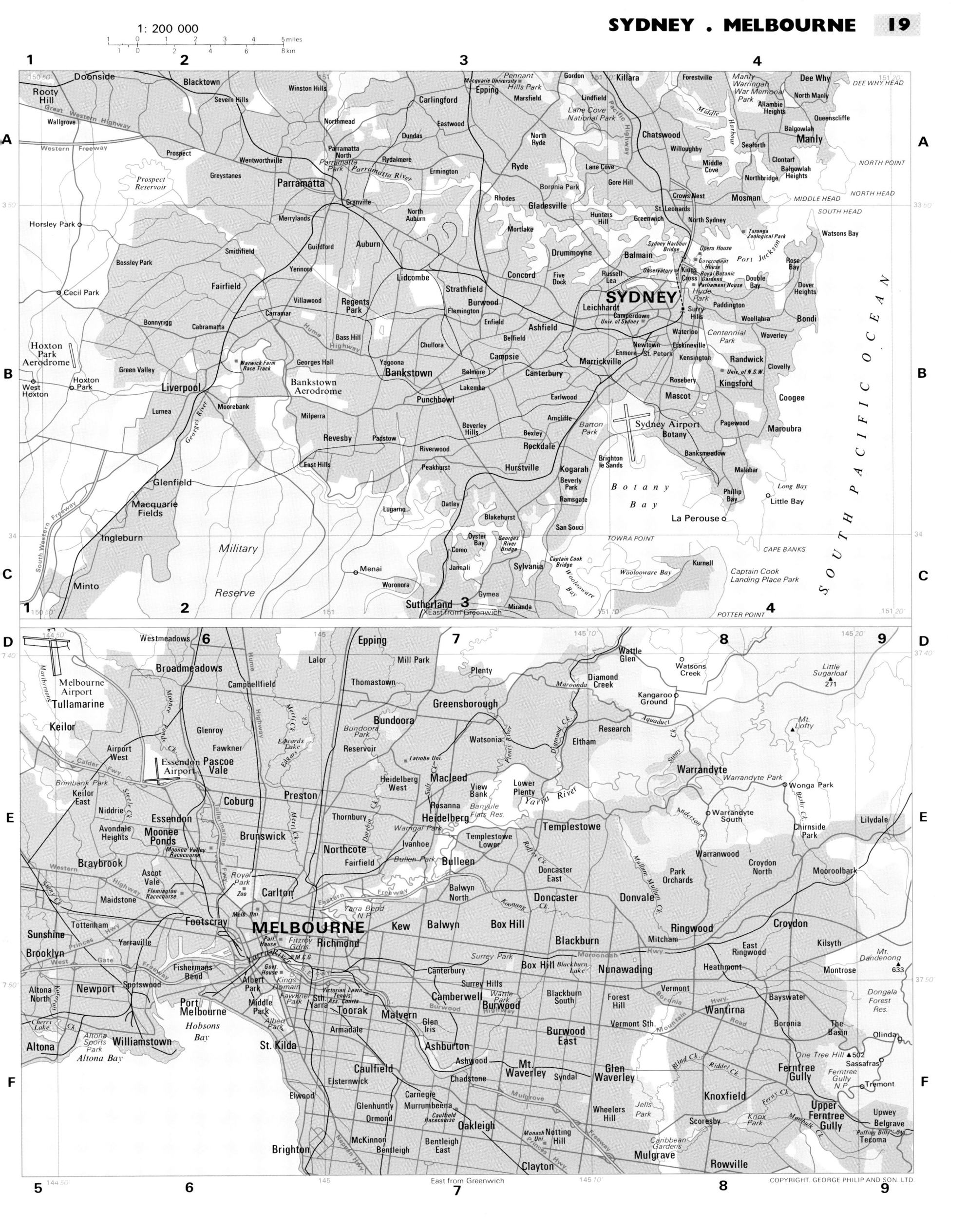

1: 200 000

1 : 200 000

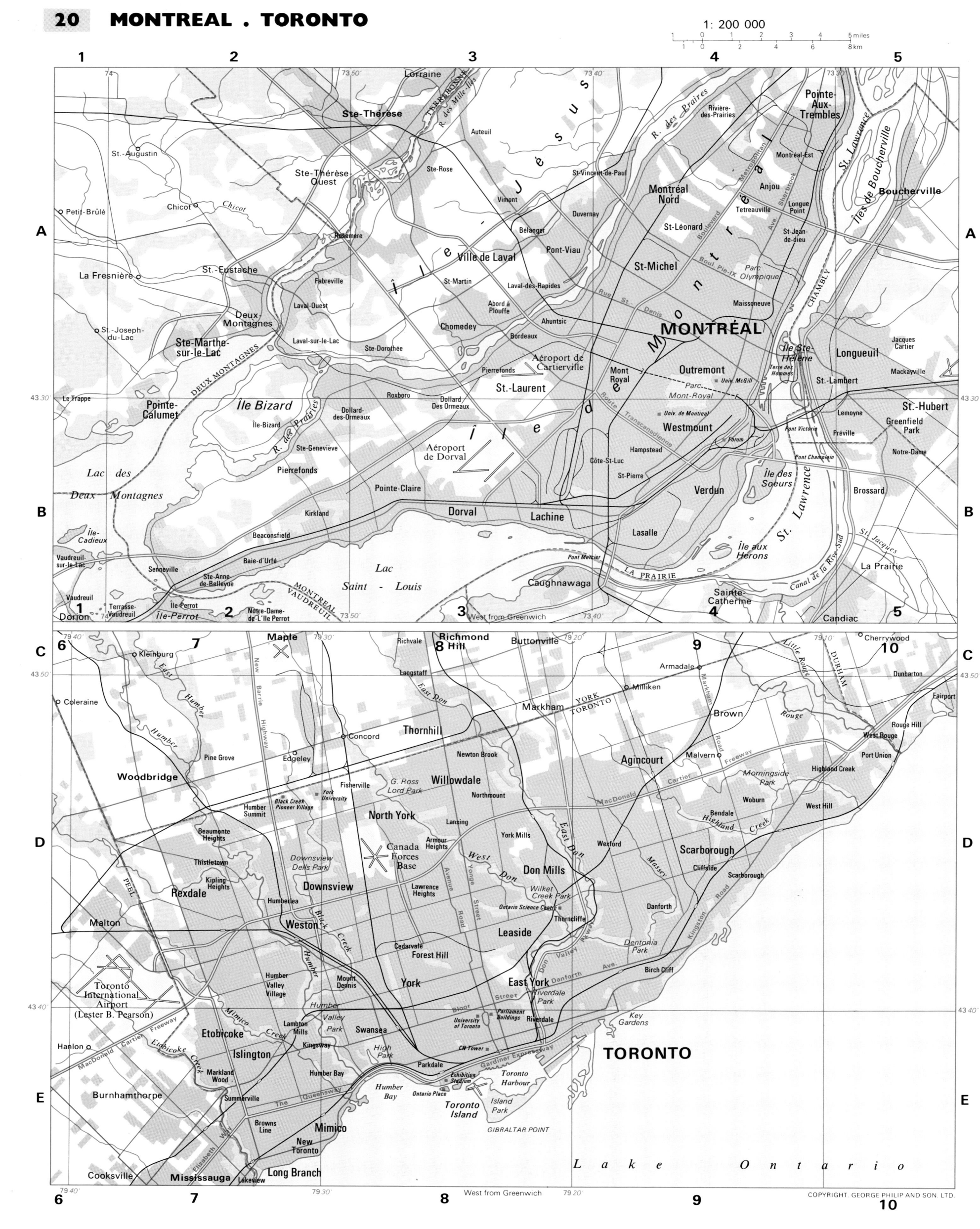

1: 200 000

5 miles
8 km

1   2   3   4

New Hampshire
Massachusetts

Seavey Hill   Peters Pond   **Methuen**   **Lawrence**   ▲65   Rowley
West Boxford   ▲108   Chaplinville
Long Pond   Lake Cochichewick   Baldpate Hill   Georgetown   Ipswich
Muscuppic Lake   Collinsville   Dracut   North Andover   Baldpate Pond   Rowley
Lowell Dracut State Forest   Kenwood   South Lawrence   Town Farm Hill ▲87   State Forest   Hood Pond   Willowdale   Turner Hill ▲81   State
North Chelmsford   West Andover   Shawsheen Village   Woodchuck Hill   Boxford   Fish Brook   Boxford   Topsfield   Ipswich Forest
West Chelmsford   Wood Hill   Andover   Boston Hill   State Forest   Harold   Bald Hill ▲75   Wenham   South Hamilton
Haggetts Pond   Ballardvale   Parker   Salem Turnpike   Putnamville Res.   Wenham Lake
Lowell   North Tewksbury   State Forest   ESSEX MIDDLESEX   Middleton   Danvers   Beverly Municipal Airport   North Beverly
Ames Hill ▲111   Tewksbury   Fosters Pond   Middleton Pond   Beverly
Chelmsford   North Billerica   Martins Pond   N. Reading   Uptons Hill ▲73   Davensport
▲124 Warren Hill   East Billerica   North Wilmington   Lynnfield   Peabody   Witch House   Salem Maritime Nat. Hist. Site
Manning State Park   South Chelmsford   Silver Lake   Reading   Suntaug Lake   South Lynnfield   South Peabody   Salem   Salem Harbor
Heart Pond   River Pines   Billerica   Wilmington   Reading Highlands   L. Quannapowitt   Salem
Rail Tree Hill   Nutting Lake   Pinehurst   Wakefield   Saugus R.   North Saugus   Marblehead
North Acton   Riverside   Burlington   North Woburn (Route 128)   Mishawum Lake   Greenwood   Spring Pond   Clifton   Beverley Harbor
Carlisle   Bedford   Wynmere Lake   Saugus   Lynn   Swampscott
North Acton   West Bedford   Woburn   Stoneham   Breakheart Reservation   West Lynn   Nahant Bay
East Acton   Old Manse   Laurence G. Hanscom Field   Harn Pond   North Res.   Middlesex Fells Reservation   Spot Pond   Melrose   Lynn Harbor   Nahant
West Concord   Concord   North Lexington   North Res.   Mt. Hood Mem. Park   Malden   East Point
Minute Man National Historic Park   ▲114   Winchester   South Res.   Revere   Nahant Harbor
Fairhaven Hill   Lexington   Arlington Heights   Mystic Lakes   West Medford   Everett   Chelsea   Beachmont   Broad Sound   Essex Suffolk
Fairhaven Bay   Sandy Pond   East Lexington   Concord   Medford   Orient Hts.   Winthrop
Farrar Pond   Lincoln   Arlington   Belmont   Somerville   Charlestown   East Boston   Boston Bay
North Sudbury   Cambridge Reservoir   ▲146 Prospect Hill   Waverley   N. Cambridge   Harvard University   Bunker Hill Mon.
Sudbury   South Lincoln   Waltham Park   Fresh Pond   Cambridge   Old North Church   Logan International Airport   Deer Island
Cat Rock Hill   Kendall Green   Watertown   North Brighton   Mass. Inst. of Tech.   New State House   BOSTON   Boston Harbor   Outer Brewster Island
Goodman Hill   Weston   Allston   John F. Kennedy Nat. Hist. Site   Northeastern Univ.   South Boston   Calf Island   Middle Brewster Island
South Sudbury   Heard Pond   Weston Reservoir   Auburndale   Museum of Fine Arts   Dorchester Hts. Nat. Hist. Site   Spectacle Island   Great Brewster Island
Wayland   Reeves Hill ▲124   Newtonville   Old Harbor   Thompson Island   Long Island   Georges Island
Hultman Aqueduct   Cochituate   Norumbega Reservoir   Newton   Chestnut Hill   Roxbury   Blake House   Grove Hall   Fields Corner   Point Allerton
Saxonville   Newton Highlands   Brookline   Jamaica Plain   Franklin Park   Dorchester Bay   Hull   Peddocks Island
Framingham   Wellesley Fells   Boylston St.   Arnold Arboretum   Squantum   Hingham Bay   Grape Island   Nantasket Beach
Morses Pond   Wellesley Hills   Oak Hill Park   Roslindale   Dorchester   Quincy Bay   Houghs Neck   Hingham Harbor   North Cohasset
Wellesley   Needham Heights   W. Roxbury   Mattapan   Wollaston   Grape Island
Natick   Needham   Middlesex   Stony Brook Res.   Milton Village   Woolaston   North Weymouth
Lake Cochituate   Suffolk Norfolk   Hyde Park   Milton   South Quincy   East Braintree   East Weymouth
Brush Hill ▲121   ▲125 Dover   Strawberry Hill ▲118   Quincy   Hingham
Sherborn   Farm Pond   Islington   Fowl Meadow Res.   Blue Hills Reservation   Southeast Expy.   North Weymouth   Whitmans Pond
East Holliston   Westwood   Gt. Blue Hill ▲194   Adams Nat. Hist. Site   South Quincy   Weymouth   South Hingham
Harding   ▲158   Braintree   East Braintree   Liberty Plain
Middlesex Norfolk   Norwood   Medfield   North Randolph   South Braintree   South Weymouth   Accord
Millis   Ponkapog   Ponkapog Pond   Great Pond   Pilgrims Hy.   Accord Pond
Norwood Memorial Airport   Reservoir Pond   Randolph   Norfolk Plymouth
Willett Pond   Canton   Nepon.   Yankee Division Hy.

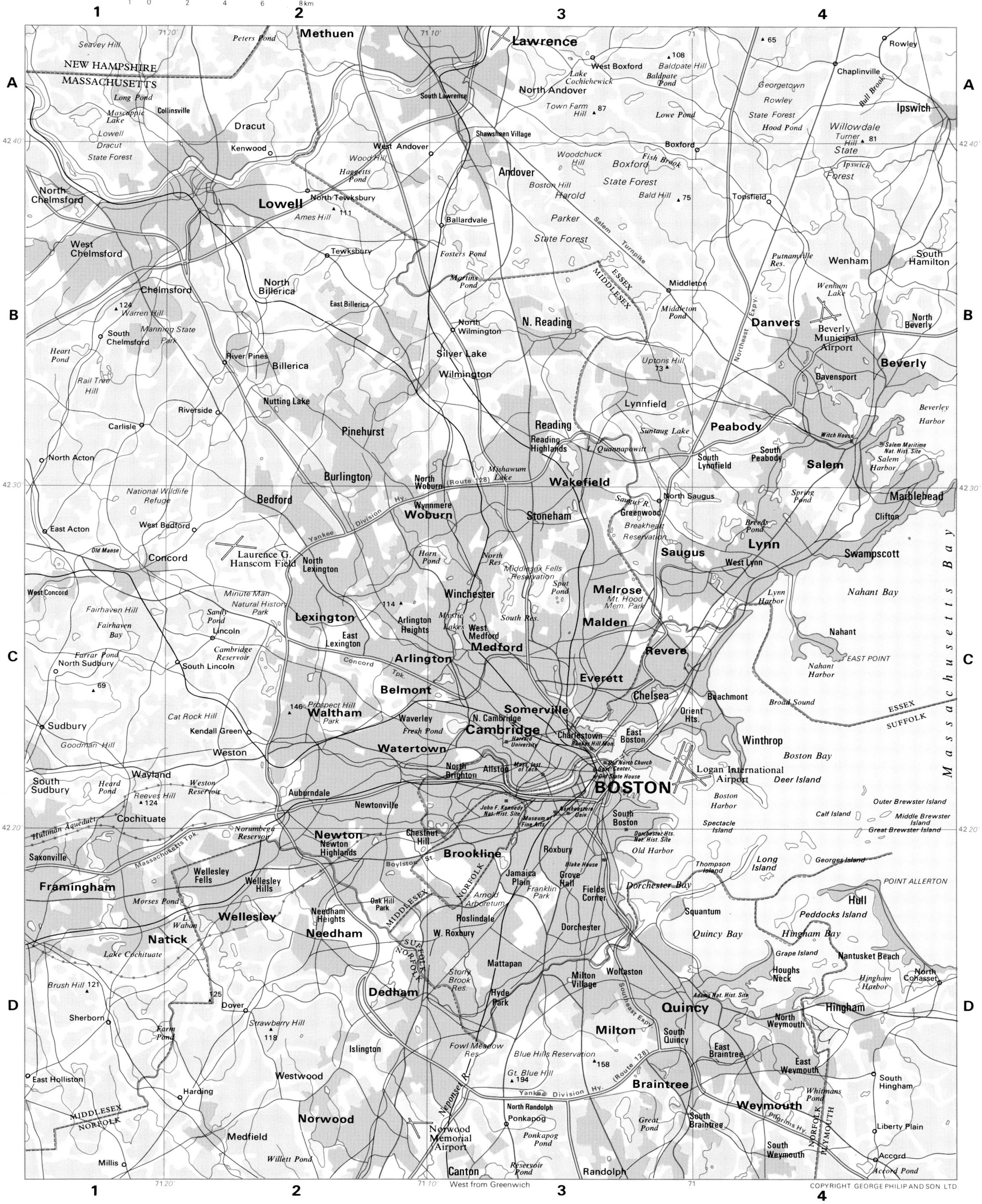

West from Greenwich

Massachusetts Bay

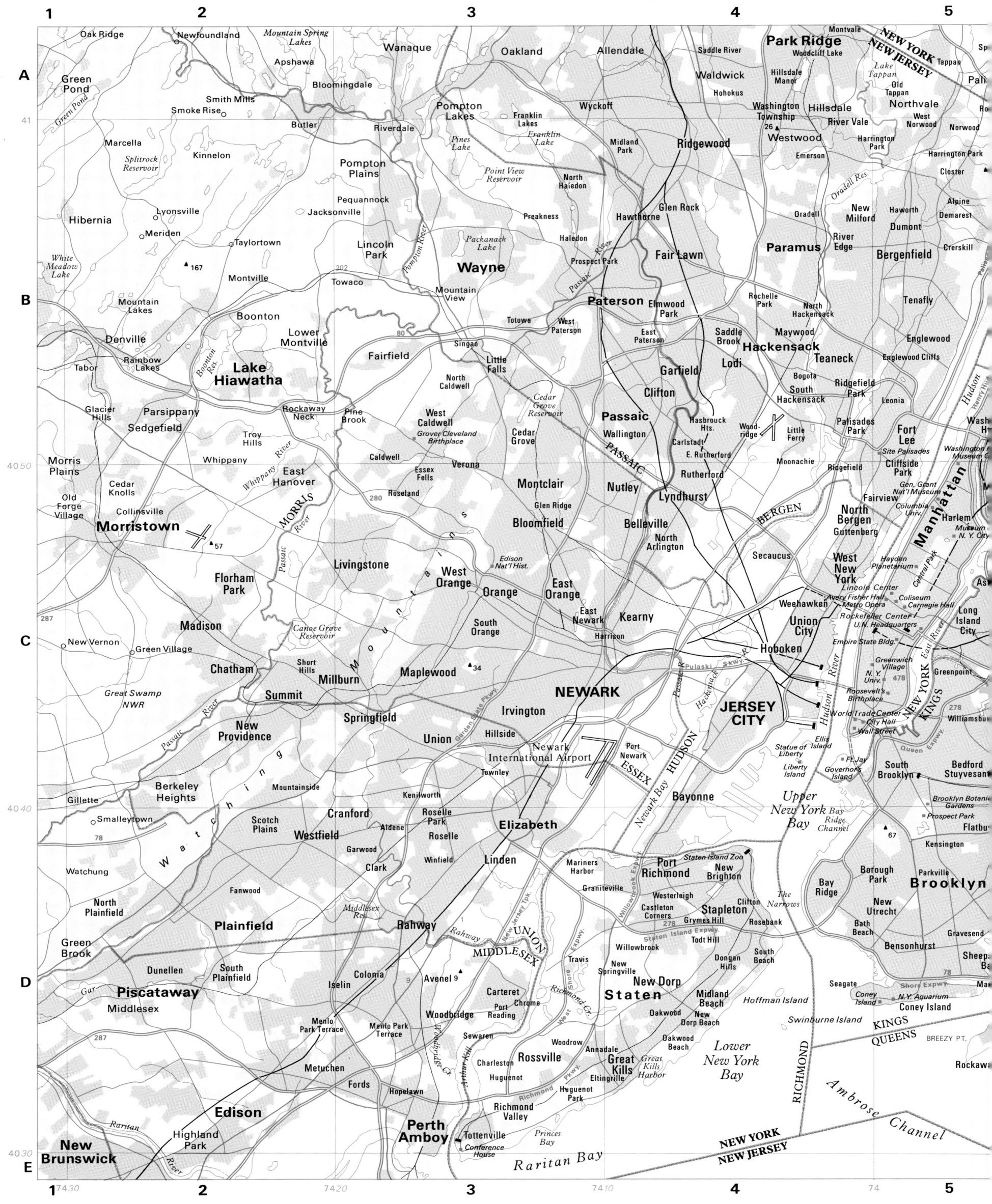

1   2   3   4   5

Oak Ridge   Newfoundland   Mountain Spring Lakes   Wanaque   Oakland   Allendale   Saddle River   Park Ridge   Montvale   Tappan   Sp

A   Green Pond   Apshawa   Bloomingdale   Pompton Lakes   Franklin Lakes   Wyckoff   Woodcliff Lake   Hillsdale Manor   Old Tappan   Pali

Smith Mills   Smoke Rise   Butler   Riverdale   Pines Lake   Franklin Lake   Midland Park   Ridgewood   Washington Township   Hillsdale   River Vale   Northvale   West Norwood   Norwood

41   Marcella   Kinnelon   Pompton Plains   Point View Reservoir   North Haledon   Glen Rock   Hawthorne   Oradell   New Milford   Harrington Park   Harrington Park   Closter

Splitrock Reservoir   Preakness   Prospect Park   Fair Lawn   Rochelle Park   North Hackensack   River Edge   Bergenfield   Alpine   Demarest

Hibernia   Lyonsville   Jacksonville   Lincoln Park   202   Packanack Lake   Haledon   Paterson   Elmwood Park   Saddle Brook   Maywood   Hackensack   Teaneck   Englewood

Meriden   Taylortown   167   Montville   Towaco   Wayne   Totowa   West Paterson   East Paterson   Garfield   Lodi   Bogota   South Hackensack   Ridgefield Park   Leonia   Englewood Cliffs

B   White Meadow Lake   Mountain Lakes   Boonton   Lower Montville   Fairfield   Singac   Little Falls   Clifton   Hasbrouck Hts.   Carlstadt   E. Rutherford   Wood-ridge   Little Ferry   Palisades Park   Fort Lee

Denville   Rainbow Lakes   80   North Caldwell   Cedar Grove Reservoir   Passaic   Wallington   Moonachie   Ridgefield   Cliffside Park

Tabor   West Caldwell   Grover Cleveland Birthplace   Cedar Grove   Rutherford   Fairview   Columbia Univ.

Glacier Hills   Parsippany   Rockaway Neck   Pine Brook   Caldwell   Essex Fells   Verona   Montclair   Nutley   Lyndhurst   BERGEN   North Bergen   Guttenberg   Harlem   N.Y. City

40 50   Morris Plains   Sedgefield   Troy Hills   Whippany   East Hanover   280   Roseland   Glen Ridge   Bloomfield   Belleville   North Arlington   Secaucus   West New York   Hayden Planetarium   Lincoln Center

Old Forge Village   Cedar Knolls   MORRIS   Livingstone   West Orange   Orange   East Orange   Kearny   Weehawken   Avery Fisher Hall–Metro Opera   Rockefeller Center   U.N. Headquarters

Collinsville   Morristown   57   East Newark   Harrison   Union City   Empire State Bldg.   Long Island City

C   New Vernon   Green Village   Madison   Canoe Grove Reservoir   Chatham   34   South Orange   Maplewood   NEWARK   Hoboken   Greenwich Village   N.Y. Univ.   478   Greenpoint

287   Short Hills   Millburn   Irvington   JERSEY CITY   Hudson River   Roosevelt's Birthplace   World Trade Center   KINGS   278   Williamsburg

Great Swamp NWR   Summit   Springfield   Hillside   Ellis Island   City Hall   Wall Street

New Providence   Union   Newark International Airport   Port Newark   Statue of Liberty   Ft. Jay   Governors Island   South Brooklyn   Bedford Stuyvesant

Gillette   Berkeley Heights   Mountainside   Kenilworth   Townley   Liberty Island   Upper New York Bay   Brooklyn Botanic Gardens   Prospect Park   Flatbu

40 40   Smalleytown   Scotch Plains   Cranford   Roselle Park   Bayonne   67   Kensington

Watchung   Westfield   Garwood   Roselle   Elizabeth   Mariners Harbor   Port Richmond   Staten Island Zoo   New Brighton   Bay Ridge   Borough Park   Brooklyn

North Plainfield   Fanwood   Clark   Winfield   Linden   Graniteville   Westerleigh   Clifton   The Narrows   New Utrecht   Bath Beach   Gravesend

Plainfield   Middlesex Res.   Rahway   Castleton Corners   278   Stapleton   Rosebank   Bay Ridge Channel   Bensonhurst   Sheepsh   Bay

Green Brook   Rahway River   UNION   Travis   Willowbrook   Grymes Hill   Todt Hill   Dongan Hills   South Beach   Seagate   Shore Expwy.   78

D   Dunellen   South Plainfield   Colonia   Avenel   9   MIDDLESEX   New Springville   New Dorp   Midland Beach   Coney Island   N.Y. Aquarium   Coney Island

Piscataway   Iselin   Carteret   Chrome   Travis   Dongan Hills   Hoffman Island

Middlesex   Menlo Park Terrace   Woodbridge   Port Reading   Oakwood   New Dorp Beach   Swinburne Island   KINGS   QUEENS   BREEZY PT.

287   Menlo Park Terrace   9   Sewaren   Woodrow   Annadale   Oakwood Beach   Lower New York Bay   Rockaw

Metuchen   Fords   Charleston   Rossville   Great Kills   Great Kills Harbor   RICHMOND

E   New Brunswick   Edison   Highland Park   Perth Amboy   Tottenville   Conference House   Huguenot   Eltingville   Richmond Valley   Huguenot Park   Princes Bay   Lower New York Bay   NEW YORK NEW JERSEY   Ambrose Channel

Raritan River   Raritan Bay

1   74 30   2   74 20   3   74 10   4   74   5

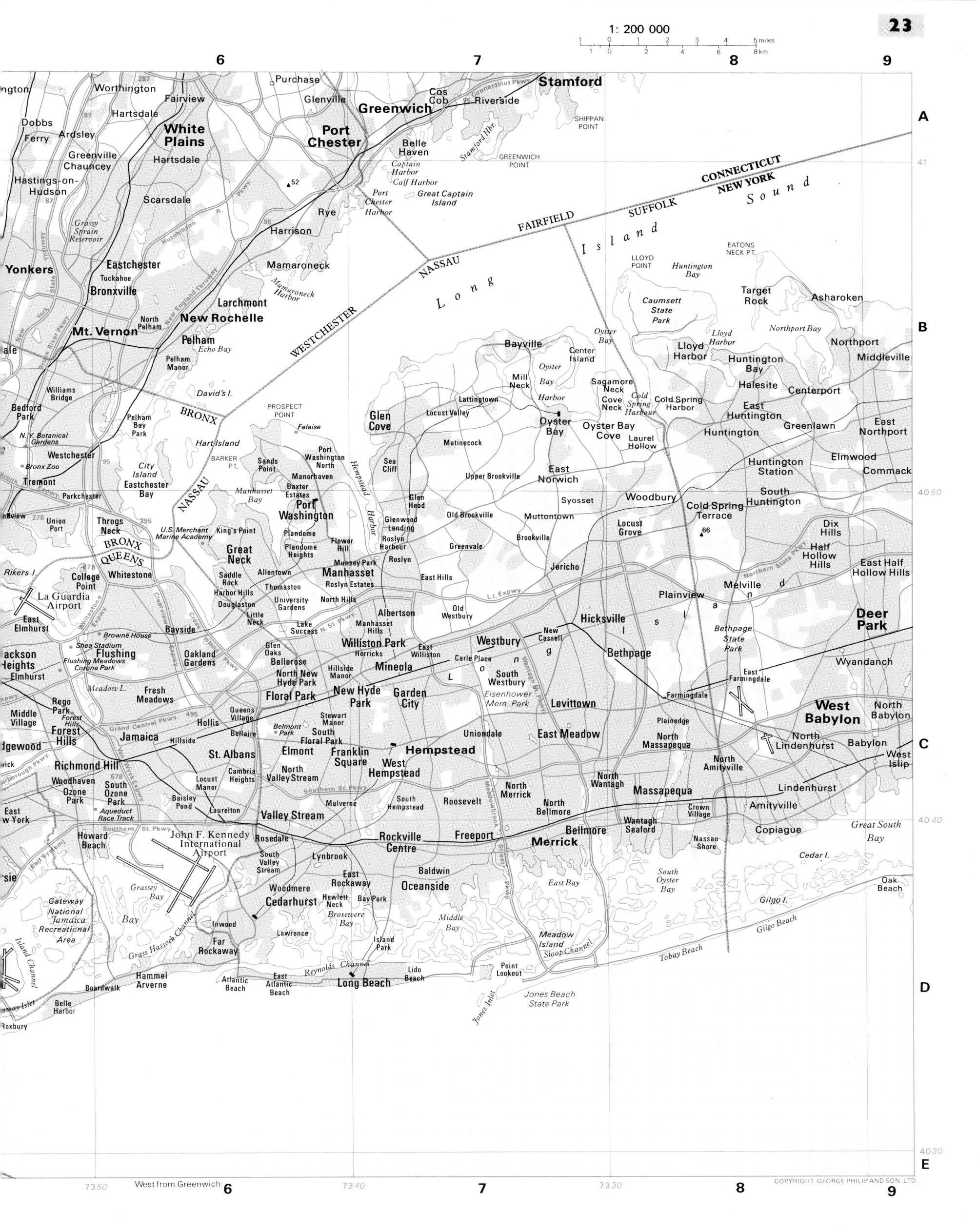

1: 200 000

5 miles
8 km

Worthington
Purchase
Glenville
Cos Cob
Stamford
Fairview
Greenwich
Riverside
Hartsdale
SHIPPAN POINT
Dobbs Ferry
Ardsley
White Plains
Port Chester
Belle Haven
Captain Harbor
Calf Harbor
GREENWICH POINT
Greenville Chauncey
Hartsdale
Port Chester Harbor
Great Captain Island
Hastings-on-Hudson
Scarsdale
52
Rye
Harrison
CONNECTICUT
NEW YORK
Grassy Sprain Reservoir
Mamaroneck
FAIRFIELD
SUFFOLK
Sound
A
41
Yonkers
Eastchester
Tuckahoe
Bronxville
Mamaroneck Harbor
NASSAU
Long
Island
EATONS NECK PT.
LLOYD POINT
Huntington Bay
Target Rock
Asharoken
Mt. Vernon
North Pelham
Larchmont
New Rochelle
WESTCHESTER
Caumsett State Park
Lloyd Harbor
Northport Bay
B
Pelham
Echo Bay
Bayville
Center Island
Oyster Bay
Lloyd Harbor
Northport
Pelham Manor
David's I.
Mill Neck
Oyster Bay Harbor
Sagamore Neck
Cold Spring Harbour
Huntington Bay
Halesite
Centerport
Middleville
Bedford Park
PROSPECT POINT
Falaise
Glen Cove
Locust Valley
Lattingtown
Matinecock
Cold Spring Harbor
East Huntington
N.Y. Botanical Gardens
BRONX
Hart Island
Sea Cliff
Oyster Bay Cove
Laurel Hollow
Greenlawn
East Northport
Westchester
Bronx Zoo
City Island
Eastchester Bay
BARKER PT.
Sands Point
Port Washington North
Manorhaven
Baxter Estates
Glen Head
Upper Brookville
East Norwich
Huntington
Huntington Station
Elmwood
Commack
Tremont
Parkchester
NASSAU
Manhasset Bay
Port Washington
Plandome
Flower Hill
Glenwood Landing
Old Brookville
Muttontown
Woodbury
Cold Spring Terrace
South Huntington
40 50
Union Port
Throgs Neck
U.S. Merchant Marine Academy
King's Point
Plandome Heights
Munsey Park
Roslyn
Syosset
Locust Grove
66
Dix Hills
Rikers I.
BRONX
QUEENS
Saddle Rock
Harbor Hills
Thomaston
Roslyn Estates
East Hills
Greenvale
Brookville
Jericho
Melville
Half Hollow Hills
Great Neck
Allentown
Manhasset
East Half Hollow Hills
College Point
Whitestone
University Gardens
Douglaston
North Hills
Old Westbury
Plainview
La Guardia Airport
Little Neck
Lake Success
Manhasset Hills
Albertson
New Cassell
Hicksville
Bethpage State Park
Deer Park
East Elmhurst
Bayside
Oakland Gardens
Williston Park
Herricks
East Williston
Westbury
Bethpage
Browne House
Glen Oaks
Bellerose
Carle Place
Mineola
Wyandanch
Jackson Heights
Flushing
Flushing Meadows Corona Park
North New Hyde Park
Hillside Manor
South Westbury
Eisenhower Mem. Park
East Farmingdale
Elmhurst
Meadow L.
Fresh Meadows
Floral Park
New Hyde Park
Garden City
Levittown
Farmingdale
West Babylon
North Babylon
Rego Park
Forest Hills
Queens Village
Stewart Manor
Bellaire
South Floral Park
Uniondale
East Meadow
Plainedge
North Massapequa
North Lindenhurst
Middle Village
Hollis
Belmont Park
Hempstead
North Amityville
West Islip
dgewood
Forest Hills
Jamaica
Hillside
St. Albans
Elmont
Franklin Square
West Hempstead
North Merrick
North Wantagh
Massapequa
Lindenhurst
Amityville
C
40 40
Richmond Hill
Woodhaven
Ozone Park
South Ozone Park
Locust Manor
Cambria Heights
North Valley Stream
South Hempstead
Roosevelt
North Bellmore
Wantagh Seaford
Crown Village
Copiague
East w York
Aqueduct Race Track
Baisley Pond
Laurelton
Malverne
Valley Stream
Freeport
Bellmore
Nassau Shore
Howard Beach
Rosedale
South Valley Stream
Lynbrook
Rockville Centre
Merrick
Great South Bay
Cedar I.
Grassey Bay
East Rockaway
Baldwin
East Bay
South Oyster Bay
Gilgo I.
Oak Beach
Gateway National Jamaica Recreational Area
Woodmere
Cedarhurst
Hewlett Neck
Bay Park
Oceanside
Gilgo Beach
sie
Lawrence
Brosevere Bay
Middle Bay
Meadow Island
Sloop Channel
Island Channel
Inwood
Far Rockaway
Island Park
Meadow Island
Tobay Beach
Boardwalk
Hammel Arverne
Belle Harbor
Atlantic Beach
East Atlantic Beach
Reynolds Channel
Long Beach
Lido Beach
Point Lookout
Jones Inlet
Jones Beach State Park
D
Roxbury
Grass Hassock Channel
E
40 30

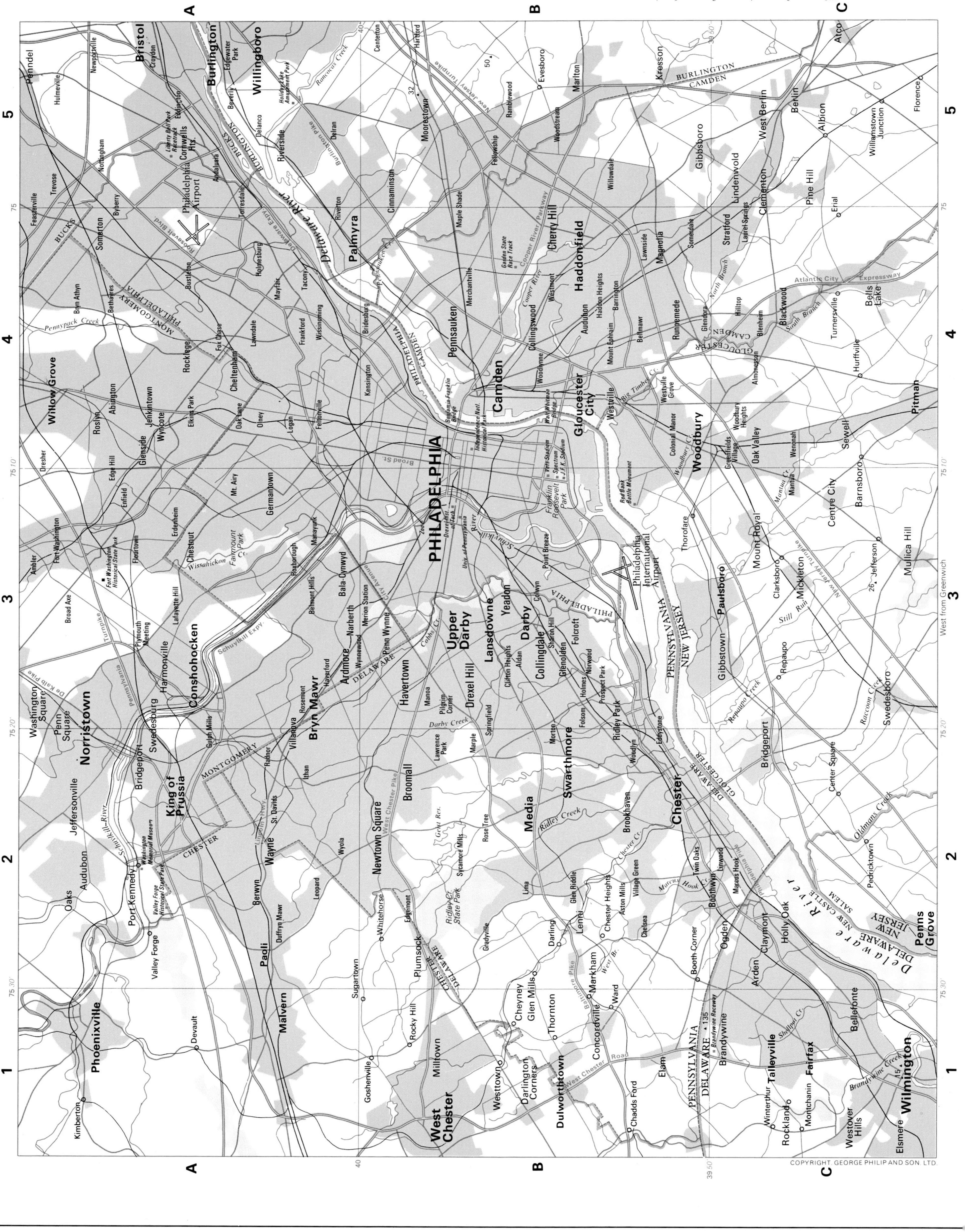

1 : 200 000

5 miles
8 km

PHILADELPHIA

Camden

Norristown

King of Prussia

Conshohocken

Bryn Mawr

Wayne

Paoli

Malvern

Phoenixville

Valley Forge

West Chester

Newtown Square

Broomall

Media

Swarthmore

Chester

Upper Darby

Lansdowne

Darby

Havertown

Drexel Hill

Collingdale

Brookhaven

Woodbury

Gloucester City

Pennsauken

Haddonfield

Cherry Hill

Palmyra

Bristol

Burlington

Willingboro

Wilmington

Penns Grove

Pitman

Paulsboro

West Berlin

Berlin

PENNSYLVANIA
NEW JERSEY

DELAWARE
NEW JERSEY

Delaware River

Schuylkill River

Philadelphia International Airport

Philadelphia Airport

COPYRIGHT GEORGE PHILIP AND SON LTD.

1 : 200 000

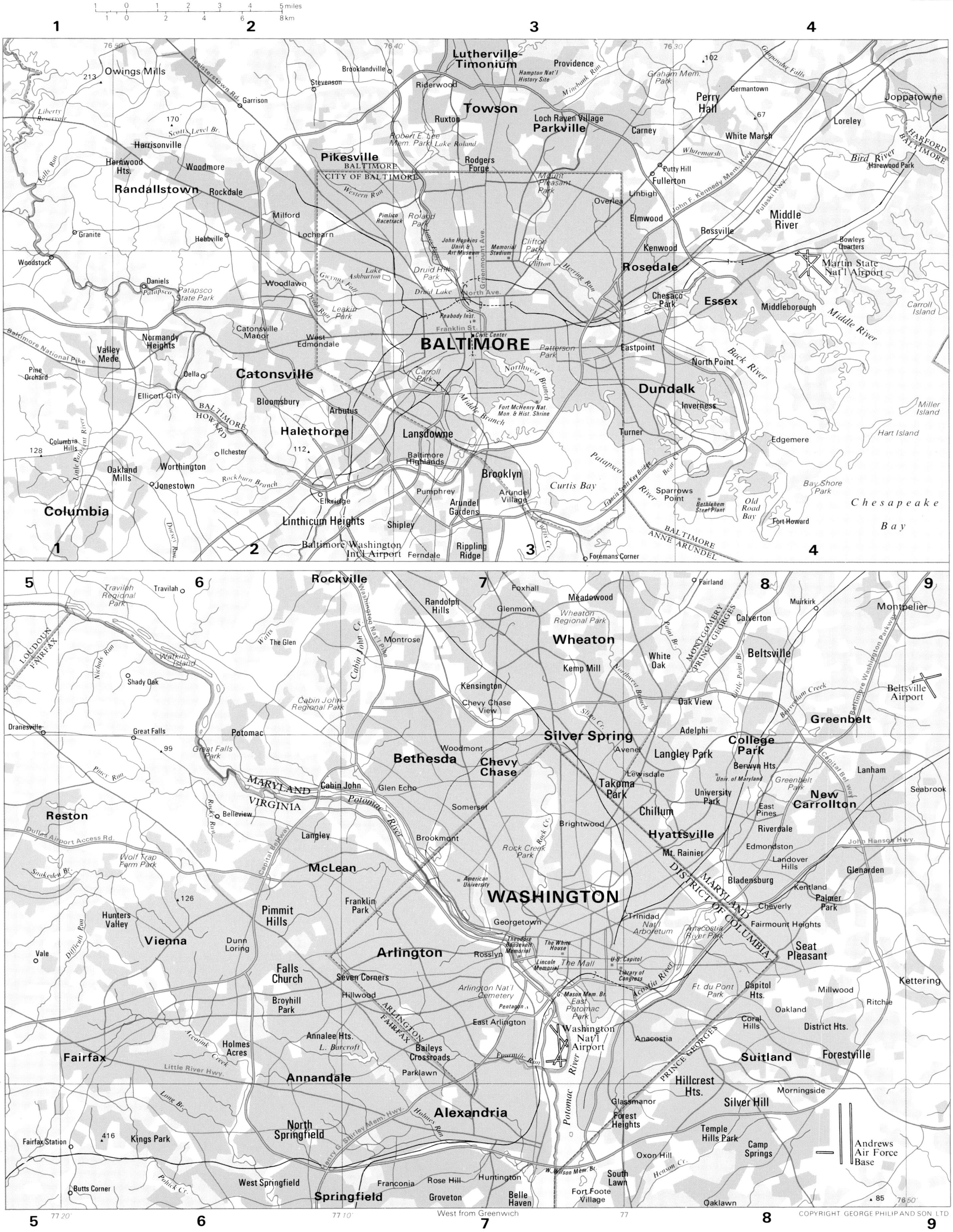

5 miles
8 km

1 **2** **3** **4**

76 50 76 40 76 30

213 · Owings Mills
Liberty Reservoir
Falls Run
Harrisonville
Woodmore
170
Scott Level Br.
Garrison
Riderwood
Brooklandville
Stevenson
Lutherville Timonium
Providence
Hampton Nat'l History Site
Graham Mem. Park
102
Germantown
Glenmonkn Falls
A
Perry Hall
67
Joppatowne
Loreley
HARFORD BALTIMORE
Bird River
Harewood Park

Hernwood Hts.
Randallstown
Rockdale
Granite
Woodstock
Hebbville
Pikesville
BALTIMORE
CITY OF BALTIMORE
Milford
Lochearn
Robert E. Lee Mem. Park
Lake Roland
Towson
Ruxton
Rodgers Forge
Loch Raven Village
Parkville
Carney
Putty Hill
Fullerton
Linbigh
White Marsh
Whitemarsh
John F. Kennedy Mem. Hwy.
Pulaski Hwy.
Middle River
Bowleys Quarters
Carroll Island

39 20
Woodstock
Daniels
Patapsco
Patapsco State Park
Woodlawn
Pimlico Racetrack
Roland Park
John Hopkins Univ. & Art Museum
Druid Hill Park
Lake Ashburton
Druid Lake
North Ave.
Peabody Inst.
Memorial Stadium
Clifton Park
Clifton
Herring Run
Mount Pleasant Park
Overlea
Elmwood
Kenwood
Rosedale
Chesaco Park
Essex
Middleborough
Martin State Nat'l Airport
39 20

B
Normandy Heights
Valley Mede
Pine Orchard
Catonsville Manor
Oella
Catonsville
West Edmondale
Franklin St.
Civic Center
BALTIMORE
Patterson Park
Eastpoint
North Point
Back River
Miller Island

Ellicott City
Columbia Hills
128
Oakland Mills
Worthington
Jonestown
Bloomsbury
Halethorpe
Arbutus
112
Lansdowne
Carroll Park
Baltimore Highlands
Northwest Branch
Middle Branch
Fort McHenry Nat. Mon & Hist. Shrine
Dundalk
Inverness
Turner
Edgemere
Hart Island

Columbia
Little Patuxent River
Elkridge
Linthicum Heights
Pumphrey
Shipley
Arundel Gardens
Arundel Village
Brooklyn
Curtis Bay
Patapsco
River
Sparrows Point
Bethlehem Steel Plant
Old Road Bay
Bay Shore Park
Chesapeake Bay

Baltimore Washington Int'l Airport
Ferndale
Rippling Ridge
BALTIMORE
ANNE ARUNDEL
Foremans Corner
Francis Scott Key Bridge
Fort Howard

1 **2** **3** **4**

5 **6** **7** **8** **9**

Travilah Regional Park
Travilah
Rockville
Foxhall
Randolph Hills
Glenmont
Meadowood
Fairland
Muirkirk
Montpelier

LOUDOUN FAIRFAX
Watkins Island
Nichols Run
Shady Oak
The Glen
Montrose
Wheaton Regional Park
Calverton
C
Wheaton
White Oak
Beltsville
Beltsville Airport

Dranesville
Great Falls
99
Potomac
Cabin John Regional Park
Kensington
Chevy Chase View
Kemp Mill
Northwest Branch
Oak View
Adelphi
Greenbelt
39
Great Falls Park
Great Falls
Silver Spring
Avenel
Lewisdale
Berwyn Hts.
College Park
Lanham
Seabrook

Reston
Pinec Run
Bethesda
Woodmont
Chevy Chase
Somerset
Langley Park
Univ. of Maryland
University Park
Greenbelt Park
New Carrollton
MARYLAND
VIRGINIA
Cabin John
Glen Echo
Brookmont
Brightwood
Takoma Park
Chillum
East Pines
Riverdale
Edmondston

Dulles Airport Access Rd.
Bellaview
Langley
Rock Creek Park
Hyattsville
Mt. Rainier
Landover Hills
Glenarden

Wolf Trap Farm Park
McLean
Franklin Park
American University
Georgetown
Trinidad Nat'l Arboretum
Bladensburg
Kentland
Cheverly
Fairmount Heights
D
126
Pimmit Hills
Rosslyn
The White House
Lincoln Memorial
The Mall
U.S. Capitol
Anacostia River Park
Seat Pleasant

Hunters Valley
Vale
Vienna
Dunn Loring
Arlington
Theodore Roosevelt Memorial
WASHINGTON
Library of Congress
Ft. du Pont Park
Capitol Hts.
Oakland
Millwood
Ritchie
Kettering

Falls Church
Seven Corners
Hillwood
Arlington Nat'l Cemetery
Pentagon
East Potomac Park
Coral Hills
District Hts.

Broyhill Park
Annalee Hts.
L. Barcroft
Baileys Crossroads
East Arlington
Washington Nat'l Airport
Anacostia
Suitland
Forestville
416
Holmes Acres
Little River Hwy.
Parklawn
E
Fairfax
Acotink Creek
Annandale
Potomac River
Glassmanor
Forest Heights
Hillcrest Hts.
Morningside
38 50

Fairfax Station
Kings Park
Long Br.
North Springfield
Alexandria
Oxon Hill
Temple Hills Park
Silver Hill
Camp Springs
Andrews Air Force Base

Butts Corner
Patrick Cr.
West Springfield
Franconia
Rose Hill
Huntington
Springfield
Groveton
Belle Haven Village
Fort Foote Village
South Lawn
Henson Cr.
Oxlawn
85
76 50

5 **6** **7** **8** **9**

77 20 77 10 West from Greenwich 77

COPYRIGHT GEORGE PHILIP AND SON LTD

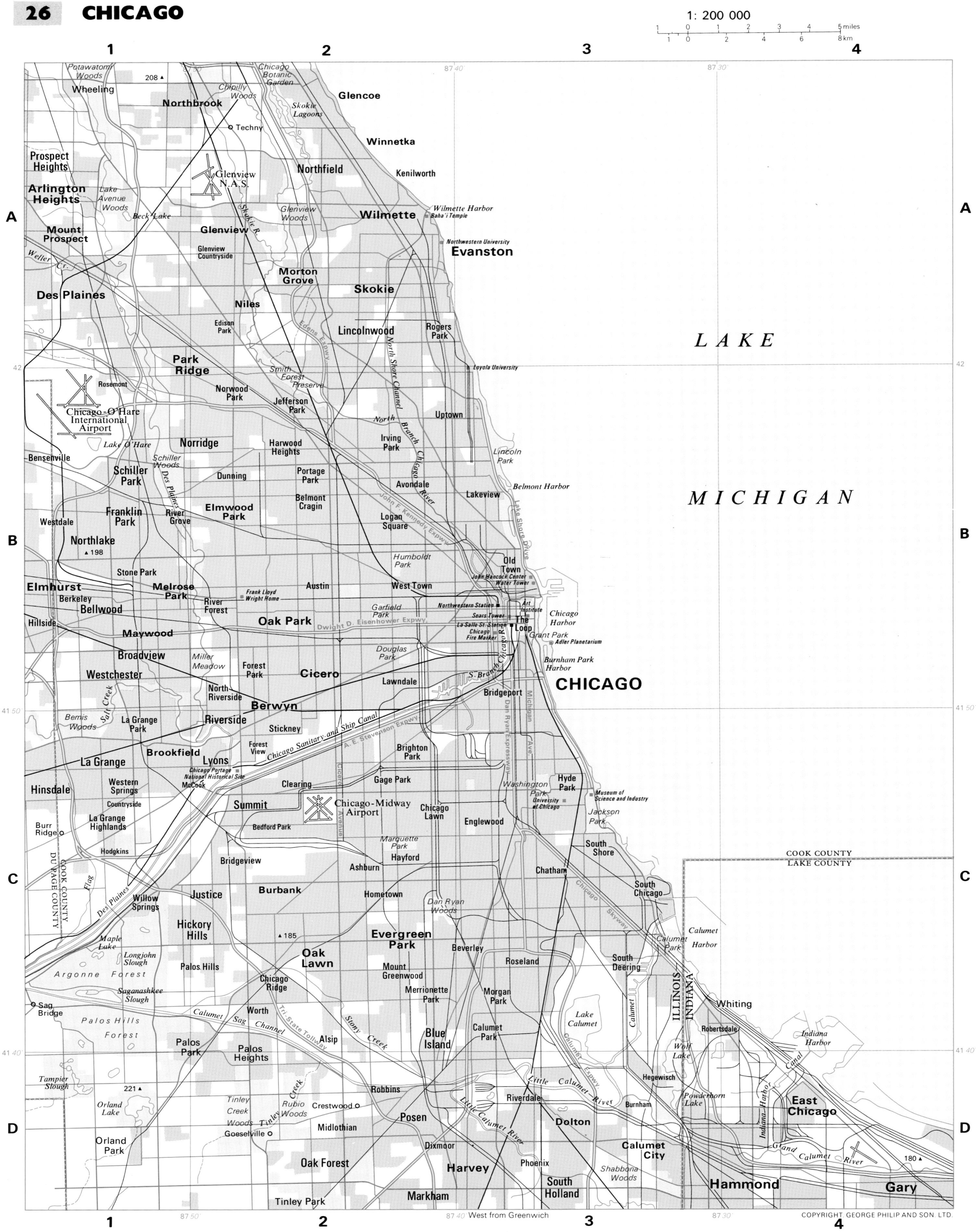

1: 200 000

5 miles
8 km

1   2   3   4

A

LAKE

MICHIGAN

B

C

COOK COUNTY
LAKE COUNTY

D

Potawatomi Woods
208 ▲
Wheeling
Northbrook
Chicago Botanic Garden
Glencoe
Chipilly Woods
Skokie Lagoons
Techny
Winnetka
Prospect Heights
Glenview N.A.S.
Northfield
Kenilworth
Arlington Heights
Lake Avenue Woods
Beck Lake
Glenview Woods
Wilmette Harbor
Baha'i Temple
Wilmette
Mount Prospect
Glenview
Glenview Countryside
Northwestern University
Evanston
Des Plaines
Weller Cr.
Morton Grove
Niles
Skokie
Edison Park
Lincolnwood
Rogers Park
Park Ridge
Smith Forest Preserve
Jefferson Park
Loyola University
Rosemont
Chicago-O'Hare International Airport
Norwood Park
North Shore Channel
Uptown
Chicago River
Bensenville
Lake O'Hare
Norridge
Schiller Woods
Harwood Heights
Irving Park
Lincoln Park
Belmont Harbor
Schiller Park
Dunning
Portage Park
Avondale
Lakeview
Westdale
Franklin Park
Elmwood Park
River Grove
Belmont Cragin
Logan Square
John F. Kennedy Expwy
Lake Shore Drive
Northlake
▲ 198
Humboldt Park
Old Town
John Hancock Center
Water Tower
Stone Park
Austin
West Town
Elmhurst
Melrose Park
Frank Lloyd Wright Home
Northwestern Station
Art Institute
Berkeley
River Forest
Garfield Park
Sears Tower
The Loop
Chicago Harbor
Bellwood
La Salle St. Station
Chicago Fire Marker
Grant Park
Hillside
Oak Park
Dwight D. Eisenhower Expwy
Adler Planetarium
Maywood
Douglas Park
Burnham Park Harbor
Broadview
Miller Meadow
Forest Park
S. Branch Chicago R.
CHICAGO
Westchester
Cicero
Lawndale
Bridgeport
North Riverside
Berwyn
Dan Ryan Expressway
Bernis Woods
La Grange Park
Riverside
Stickney
Chicago Sanitary and Ship Canal
Brighton Park
Salt Creek
Brookfield
Lyons
Forest View
A. E. Stevenson Expwy
Michigan Ave.
La Grange
Chicago Portage National Historical Site
McCook
Clearing
Gage Park
Washington Park
Hyde Park
Museum of Science and Industry
Hinsdale
Western Springs
University of Chicago
Countryside
Chicago-Midway Airport
Chicago Lawn
Englewood
Jackson Park
Burr Ridge
La Grange Highlands
Summit
Bedford Park
Hodgkins
Bridgeview
Marquette Park
Hayford
South Shore
Justice
Ashburn
Chatham
Flag
Des Plaines
Willow Springs
Burbank
Hometown
Dan Ryan Woods
South Chicago
Maple Lake
Hickory Hills
▲ 185
Evergreen Park
Beverley
Chicago Skyway
Calumet Park
Calumet Harbor
Longjohn Slough
Oak Lawn
Roseland
South Deering
Argonne Forest
Palos Hills
Chicago Ridge
Mount Greenwood
Merrionette Park
Morgan Park
ILLINOIS
INDIANA
Whiting
Saganashkee Slough
Worth
Lake Calumet
Calumet R.
Robertsdale
Sag Bridge
Calumet
Sag Channel
Alsip
Stony Creek
Blue Island
Calumet Park
Calumet Expwy
Wolf Lake
Indiana Harbor
Palos Hills Forest
Palos Park
Palos Heights
Tri-State Tollway
Robbins
Riverdale
Little Calumet River
Hegewisch
Powderhorn Lake
Indiana Harbor Canal
Tampier Slough
221 ▲
Tinley Creek Woods
Rubio Woods
Crestwood
Posen
Dolton
Burnham
East Chicago
Orland Lake
Little Calumet River
Shabbona Woods
Grand Calumet River
Orland Park
Goeselville
Midlothian
Dixmoor
Calumet City
180 ▲
Oak Forest
Harvey
Phoenix
South Holland
Hammond
Gary
Tinley Park
Markham

1: 200 000

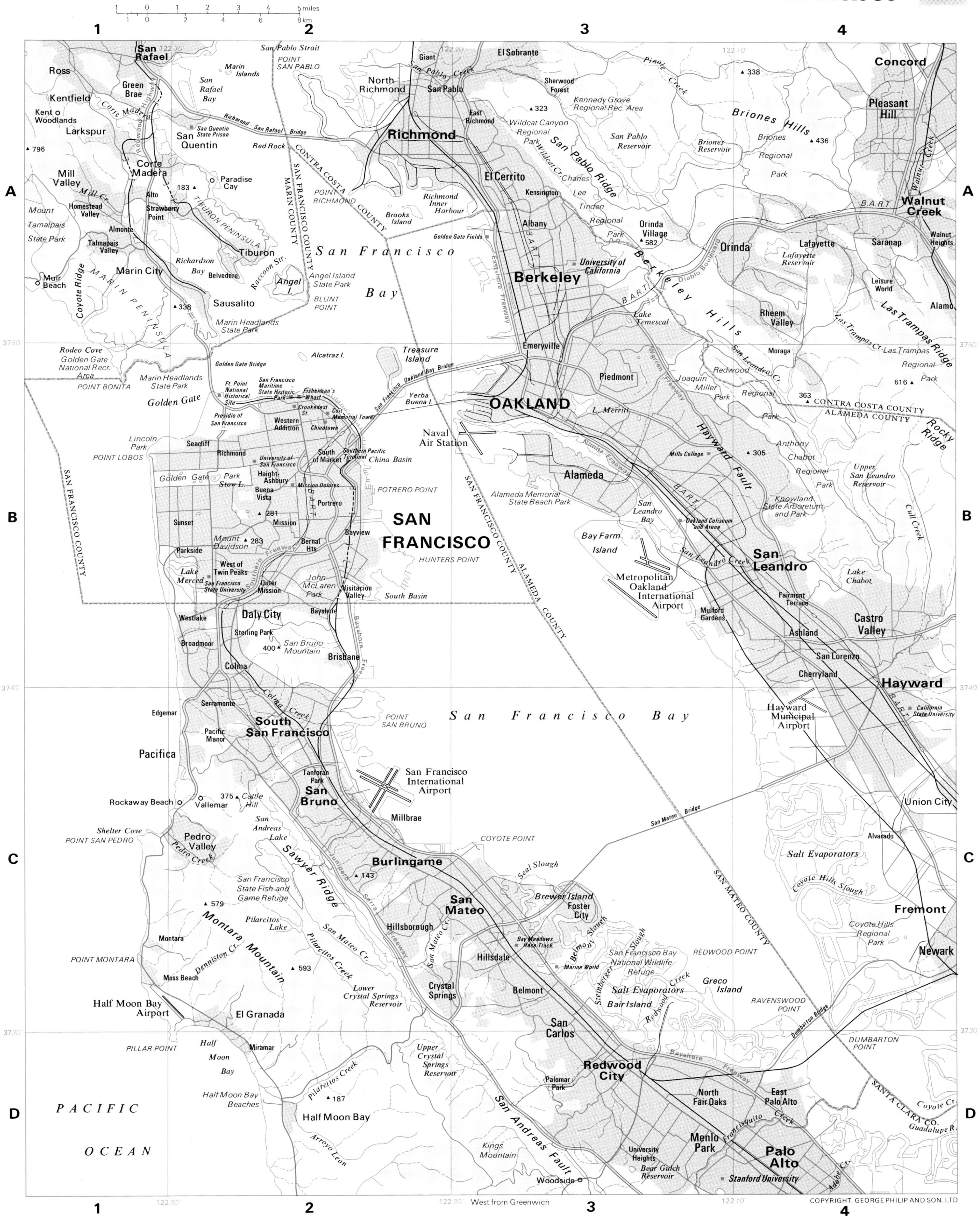

0 1 2 3 4 5 miles
0 2 4 6 8 km

1 **2** **3** **4**

Ross
San Rafael
Marin Islands
San Pablo Strait
POINT SAN PABLO
El Sobrante
Giant
San Pablo Creek
Concord
Green Brae
Kentfield
Kent Woodlands
Larkspur
San Rafael Bay
San Rafael
North Richmond
San Pablo
East Richmond
Sherwood Forest
Kennedy Grove Regional Rec. Area
▲ 338
Pleasant Hill
▲ 796
Corte Madera
Redwood Highway
San Quentin State Prison
Richmond San Rafael Bridge
Red Rock
▲ 323
Wildcat Canyon Regional Park
San Pablo Reservoir
Briones Hills
Briones
▲ 436
Briones Regional Park

A
Mount Tamalpais State Park
Homestead Valley
Almonte
Alto
183 ▲
Paradise Cay
Strawberry Point
Richmond
El Cerrito
Kensington
Wildcat Cr.
Charles
Lee
Tilden
San Pablo Ridge
Berkeley
Orinda Village
▲ 582
Orinda
Lafayette
Saranap
Walnut Heights
B.A.R.T
Walnut Creek
Alamo
A

Mill Valley
Talmapais Valley
Tiburon Peninsula
▲ 338
Richardson Bay
Belvedere
Tiburon
Angel I.
Raccoon Str.
San Francisco Bay
Brooks Island
Richmond Inner Harbour
Golden Gate Fields
Albany
University of California
Berkeley
B.A.R.T
Lake Temescal
Berkeley Hills
Lafayette Reservoir
Leisure World
Las Trampas Ridge
Marin City
Coyote Ridge
Marin Peninsula
Sausalito
Angel Island State Park
BLUNT POINT
Emeryville
Piedmont
Moraga
Redwood Regional Park
Rheem Valley
616 ▲
Las Trampas Cr.-Las Trampas Regional Park

Mount Tamalpais State Park
Muir Beach
Marin Headlands State Park
Treasure Island
Alcatraz I.
San Francisco Oakland Bay Bridge
Yerba Buena I.
OAKLAND
L. Merritt
Joaquin Miller Park
363 ▲
CONTRA COSTA COUNTY
ALAMEDA COUNTY

B
Rodeo Cove
Golden Gate National Recr. Area
POINT BONITA
Marin Headlands State Park
Golden Gate Bridge
Golden Gate
Ft. Point National Historical Site
San Francisco Maritime State Historic Park
Fisherman's Wharf
Crookedest St.
Coit Memorial Tower
Chinatown
Naval Air Station
Mills College
▲ 305
Anthony Chabot Regional Park
Upper San Leandro Reservoir
Rocky Ridge
B

Lincoln Park
POINT LOBOS
Presidio of San Francisco
Western Addition
Seacliff
Richmond
University of San Francisco
South of Market
Southern Pacific Terminal
China Basin
Hayward Fault
Knowland State Arboretum and Park
Cull Creek

SAN FRANCISCO COUNTY
Golden Gate Park
Stow L.
Haight-Ashbury
Buena Vista
Mission Dolores
POTRERO POINT
Alameda
B.A.R.T

Sunset
▲ 281
Mission
Portrero
SAN FRANCISCO
Alameda Memorial State Beach Park
San Leandro Bay
Oakland Coliseum and Arena
San Leandro
Lake Chabot

Parkside
Mount Davidson
▲ 283
Bernal Hts.
Bayview
HUNTERS POINT
Bay Farm Island
San Leandro Creek
Fairmont Terrace
Castro Valley

West of Twin Peaks
San Francisco State University
Outer Mission
John McLaren Park
Visitacion Valley
South Basin
Metropolitan Oakland International Airport
Mulford Gardens
Ashland

Lake Merced
Westlake
Daly City
Bayshore
Broadmoor
Sterling Park
400 ▲ San Bruno Mountain
Brisbane
Baylands Fwy.
San Lorenzo
Cherryland
Hayward
California State University

C
Colma
Edgemar
Serramonte
Colma Creek
POINT SAN BRUNO
San Francisco Bay
Hayward Municipal Airport
C

Pacific Manor
South San Francisco
Pacifica
San Francisco International Airport
Tanforan Park
San Bruno
Millbrae
Union City

Rockaway Beach
Vallemar
375 ▲ Cattle Hill
San Andreas Lake
Coyote Point
San Mateo Bridge
Alvarado

Shelter Cove
POINT SAN PEDRO
Pedro Valley
Pedro Creek
Sawyer Ridge
San Francisco State Fish and Game Refuge
Burlingame
▲ 143
Seal Slough
Brewer Island
Foster City
Belmont Slough
Salt Evaporators
Fremont
Coyote Hills Regional Park

▲ 579
Pilarcitos Lake
Pilarcitos Creek
San Mateo Cr.
San Mateo
Hillsborough
Bay Meadows Race Track
Marine World
San Francisco Bay National Wildlife Refuge
REDWOOD POINT
Newark

Montara Mountain
Montara
▲ 593
Hillsdale
Crystal Springs
Belmont
Marine World
Salt Evaporators
Bair Island
Greco Island
RAVENSWOOD POINT
Dumbarton Bridge

POINT MONTARA
Moss Beach
Lower Crystal Springs Reservoir
San Carlos
Redwood City
Steinberger Slough
DUMBARTON POINT

D
Half Moon Bay Airport
El Granada
PILLAR POINT
Miramar
▲ 187
Half Moon Bay Beaches
Half Moon Bay
Upper Crystal Springs Reservoir
Palomar Park
North Fair Oaks
East Palo Alto
SANTA CLARA CO.
Coyote Cr.
Guadalupe R.
D

PACIFIC OCEAN
Half Moon Bay
Kings Mountain
San Andreas Fault
University Heights
Bear Gulch Reservoir
Woodside
Menlo Park
Stanford University
Palo Alto
Adobe Cr.

Arroyo Leon

1 **2** West from Greenwich **3** **4**

COPYRIGHT. GEORGE PHILIP AND SON. LTD.

1 : 200 000

5 miles
8 km

A   B   C

Waterman Mountain
Silver Mountain
San Gabriel River
Strawberry Peak
Josephine Pk.
Mount Disappointment
San Gabriel Peak 1877
Mount Markham
Mount Lowe
Echo Mountain
Mount Harvard
Mt. Wilson
Mt. Wilson Observatory

Angeles National Forest

Big Tujunga Canyon
Mount Lukens
Tujunga
Highway Highlands
Foothill Fwy.
La Crescenta
Montrose
La Cañada
Altadena
San Rafael Hills
Flint Peak 575
Rose Bowl
Pasadena
California Inst. of Tech.
South Pasadena
El Sereno

Azusa
Irwindale
Santa Fe Flood Control Basin
San Gabriel River
Duarte
Las Lomas
Monrovia
Sierra Madre
Colorado Fwy.
Arcadia
Temple City
San Marino
Rosemead
San Gabriel

West Covina
La Puente
Rowland
Fallon
Baldwin Park
Bassett
Hacienda Hts.
Hillgrove District
Puente Hills
El Monte
South San Gabriel
Monterey Park

Los Angeles / Orange
La Habra Heights
Sunshine Acres
La Habra
Fuller Park
Buena Park
Whittier
Santa Fe Springs
Los Nietos
Pico Rivera
Rio Hondo
Montebello
Commerce
Bell Gardens
Downey
Norwalk
Artesia
Bellflower
Clearwater
Hynes
North Long Beach

Sunland
Stonehurst
Verdugo Mountains
617
Glendale
Los Angeles River
Golden State Fwy.
Burbank
Hollywood-Burbank Airport
San Valley
243
N.B.C.
Universal City
Cahuenga Pass
Cahuenga Peak 555
Griffith Park
Hollywood Fwy.
Hollywood Bowl

Eagle Rock
Highland Park
Garvanza
Lincoln Heights
Dodger Stadium
California State University
Civic Center
Boyle Heights
East Los Angeles
Alhambra

LOS ANGELES

Maywood
Huntington Park
Florence
South Gate
Lynwood
Willowbrook
Compton
Gardena
Paramount
Holydale
Lawndale
Artesia Fwy.

San Fernando Airport
San Fernando
Pacoima
Panorama City
Sepulveda
Hansen Flood Control Basin
North Hollywood
Studio City
Tujunga Wash
Ventura Fwy.
Van Nuys Airport
Van Nuys
Reseda
Northridge
Granada Hills
Lower Van Norman Lake
Aliso Canyon Wash
San Fernando Valley
Winnetka
Tarzana
216
Encino
Encino Reservoir
Sherman Oaks
459
Glen Aire Golf Club
Sepulveda Flood Control Basin
Stone Canyon Mts.
Stone Canyon Reservoir
Santa Monica Mts.
Bel Air
Beverly Glen
Westwood Village
Franklin Reservoir
Beverly Hills
West Hollywood
Twentieth Century Fox
648
Brentwood Park
Will Rogers State Historical Park
J. Paul Getty Museum
Santa Ynez Canyon
Pacific Palisades
Santa Monica
Santa Monica Municipal Airport
Venice
San Diego Fwy.
Santa Monica Fwy.
Culver City
Baldwin Hills Reservoir
Baldwin Hills
The Forum
Inglewood
The Coliseum
Harbour Fwy.
Lennox
Los Angeles Intl. Airport
El Segundo
Hawthorne
Manhattan Beach
Hermosa Beach

Santa Monica Bay

West from Greenwich

COPYRIGHT GEORGE PHILIP AND SON LTD.

1: 200 000

0 1 2 3 4 5 miles
0 2 4 6 8 km

1
2
3
4
A
B
C
D
99 20'
99 10'
99
19 30'
19 20'
19 10'
West from Greenwich
CIUDAD DE MÉXICO
Hila
La Colmena
San Mateo Tecoloapan
Barrientos
Cerro el Picacho
2968
Ecatepec de Morelos
Santa Isabel Ixtapan
Planta de Evaporación
Río Nexipayac
Gran Canal
Vía Morelos
Santa María Tulpetlac
Cuautepec El Alto
Ciudad López Mateos
Santa Clara
San Andrés Atenco
Santa Cecilia
Cuautepec de Madero
Ciudad Azteca
Tlalnepantla
Pirámide de Tenayuca
La Loma
Río Tlalnepantla
San Nicolás Viejo
Ticomán
San Juan Ixtacala
Progreso Nacional
San Pedro Zacatenco
Juan González Romero
Ciudad Satélite
Reynosa Tamaulipas
Lago de Texcoco
Presa de Rancho Colorado
Indios Verdes
Nueva Atzacoalco
Villa Gustavo A. Madero
Río Los Remedios
Azcapotzalco
Villa de Guadalupe
Basílica de Guadalupe
Santiago Tepatlaxco
Naucalpan de Juárez
San Juan Toltotepec
Presa Tenanitongo
Parque Nacional de los Remedios
Zoológico
San Juan de Aragón
Parque San Juan de Aragón
Río Sn. Lorenzo
Cuajimalpa
Gustavo Madero
Azcapotzalco
Nueva Tenochtitlán
San Rafael Chamapa
El Toreo
Central Station
Tlatelolco
Av. Río Consulado
Venustiano Carranza
Tacuba
San José Río Hondo
San Francisco Chimalpa
Hipódromo de las Americas
Catedral
Tenochtitlán
Palacio Nacional
Bellas Artes
Ciudadela
Lomas Chapultepec
Paseo de la Reforma
Bosque de Chapultepec
Castillo de Chapultepec
Tlaxcoaque
Aeropuerto Internacional
Chimalhuacán
San Pablo
San Pedro
Xochitenco
Xochiaca
La Magdalena Chichicaspa
Tecamachaleo
Presa Los Jazmines
Miguel Hidalgo
Av. General Ignacio
Pantitlán
Netzahualcóyotl
Lomas Reforma
Viaducto Presidente Miguel Alemán
Palacio de los Deportes
Ciudad Deportiva
Los Pirules
San Lorenzo Chimalco
Tacubaya
Juan Escutia
Agricola Oriental
Río Colorado
San Bartolomé Coatepec
Av. Constituyentes
Estado de México
Distrito Federal
Iztacalco
Tepalcates
San Agustín Atlapulco
Santa Cruz Ayotusco
Unidad Santa Fe
Olivar del Conde
Av. Insurgentes Sur
Calzada de Tlalpan
Benito Juárez
Iztacalco
Iztapalapa
Dos Ríos
Río Huixquilucan
Molino de Rosas
Mixcoac
Héroes de Churubusco
Iztapalapa
Santa Martha Acatitla
La Magdalena Atlipac
Huixquilucan
Chimalpa
Presa de Mixcoac
Presa Tarango
Río Cañada de los Helechos
Av. Río Churubusco
Universidad Ibero-Americana
Santa María Aztahuacán
Los Reyes
Tecamachalco
Cuajimalpa
Olivar de los Padres
Villa Obregon
Coyoacan
Prado Churubusco
Los Reyes
Santiago Acahualtepec
General Ignacio Allende
Contadero
Lomas de San Angel Inn
San Angel
Rosedal
La Candelaria
Parque Nacional
2460
Cerro de la Estrella
Santa Cruz Meyehualco
Tlaltenango
San Bartolo Ameyalco
Tizapán
Estadio Olimpico
Ciudad Universitaria
San Francisco Culhuacán
Santa Rosa Xochiac
San Lorenzo Acopilco
Parque Nacional Desierto de los Leones
San Jerónimo Lidice
Jardines del Pedregal de San Angel
El Reloj
San Lorenzo Tezonco
Iztapalapa
Tlahuac
Tlapitzáhuac
El Vergel
La Marquesa
Cuajimalpa
Alvaro Obregon
La Magdalena Contreras
Coyoacan
Tlalpan
Pirámide de Cuicuilco
Tlalpan
Estadio Azteca
La Nopalera
Zapotitlán
Parque Nacional del Insurgente Miguel Hidalgo
San Nicolás Totolapan
Las Fuentes Brotantes
Viaducto Tlalpan
Tepepan
Lago de Xochimilco
Jardines Flotantes
Tlaltenco
Santa Ursula Xitla
San Pedro Martir
Tlahuac
Xitle
Xochitepec
San Lucas Xochimanca
Xochimilco
San Gregorio Atlapulco
San Luis Tlaxialtemalco
Gran Canal
Cerro Xico
2346
Tulyehualco
Contreras
Tlalpan
Cerro Xitle
3128
San Andrés Totoltepec
Santiago Tepalcatlalpan
Nativitas
Santa Cruz Alcapixca
Xochimilco
Tlahuac
San Juan Ixtayopan
La Magdalena Petlalco
San Miguel Xicalco
San Mateo Xalpa
San Andrés Ahuayucan
Mixquic
San Miguel Ajusco
Santa Cecilia Tepetlapa
San Antonio Tecómitl
Tetelco
Parque Nacional de Ajusco
Cerro Ajusco
3937
San Francisco Tecoxpa
San Jerónimo Miacatlán
San Juan y San Pedro Tezompa
Topilejo
San Pedro Actopan
San Augustín Ohtenco
San Francisco Tlalnepantla
San Salvador Cuauhtenco
Milpa Alta
San Pablo Ostotepec
Santa Ana Tlacotenco
San Lorenzo Tlacoyucan
Aserradero
Cerro Pelado
3620
Cerro Cuautzin
3497
El Guarda Parres
Tlalpan
Milpa Alta
Distrito Federal
Estado de Morelos
Cerro Tláloc
3690
Cerro Chichinautzin
3476
Distrito Federal
Estado de Morelos
Parque Nacional de las Lagunas de Zempoala
Parque Nacional del Tepozteco
Tres Marias
57
85
95
130
15
190

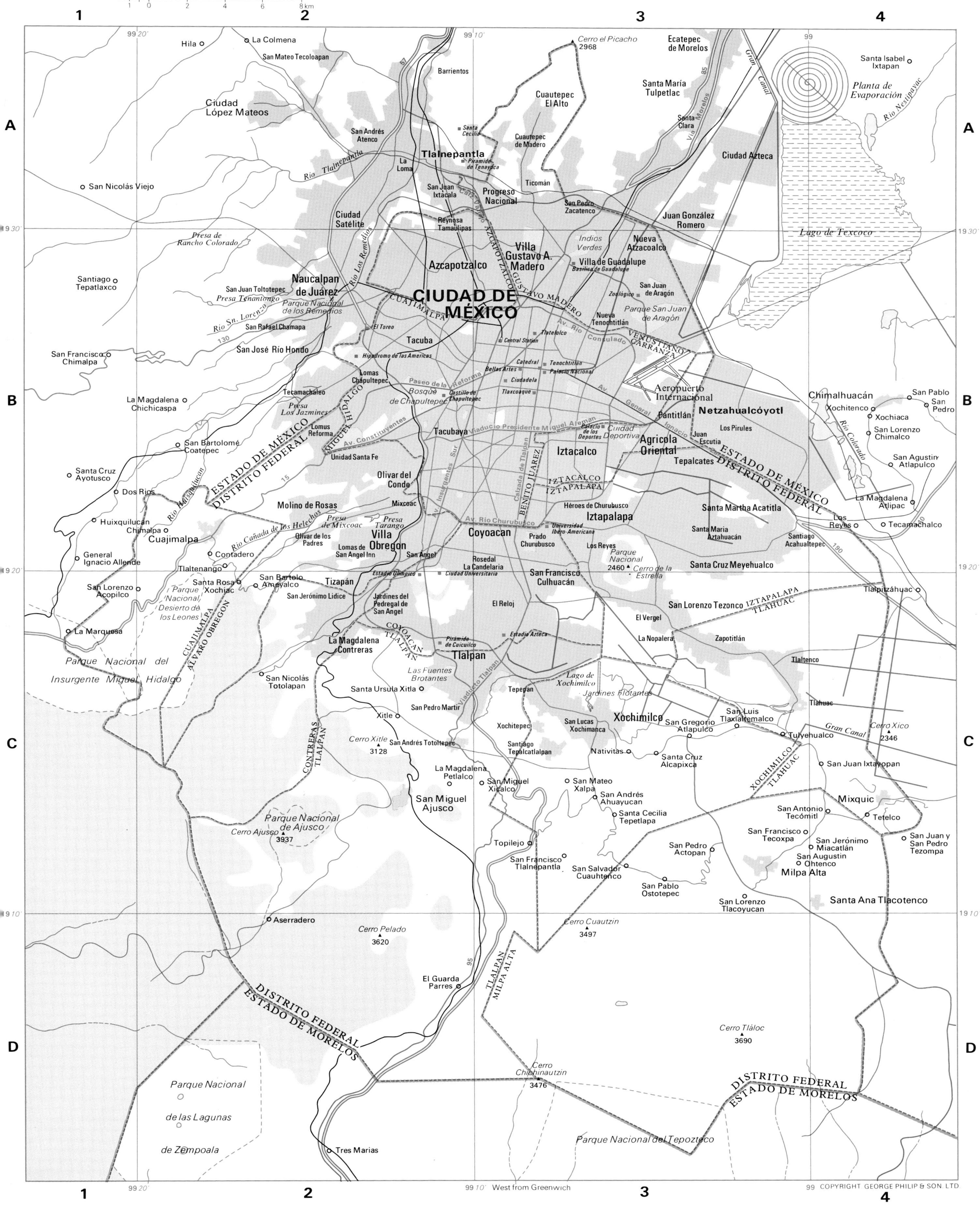

1 : 200 000

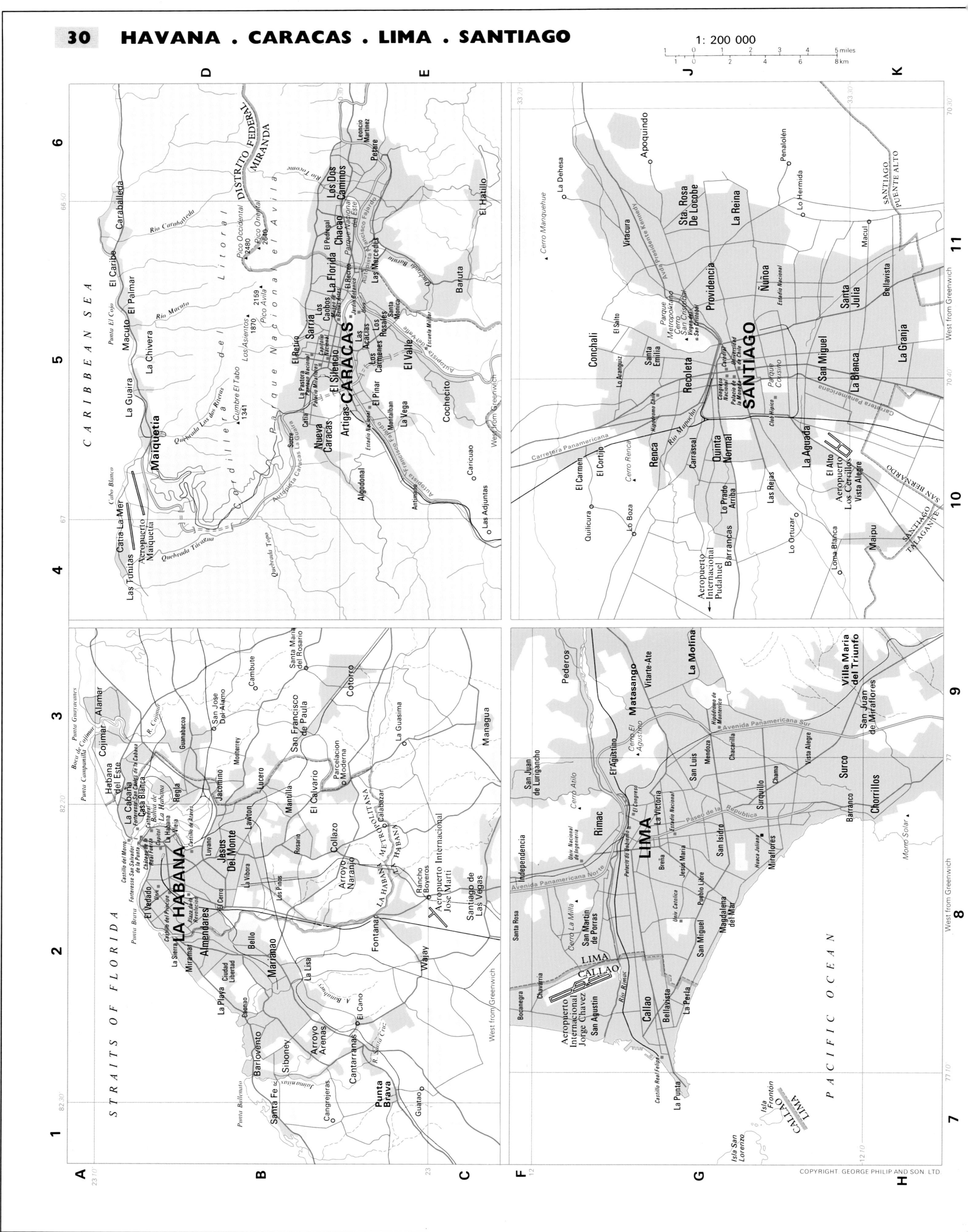

1: 200 000

0 1 2 3 4 5 miles
0 2 4 6 8 km

1   **2**   **3**

Rio de Janeiro (top map)

Mesquita, Eden, Coelho da Rocha, Duque de Caxias, São João de Meriti, Nilópolis, São Mateus, Vigário Geral, Anchieta, Cordovil, Olinda, Guadalupe, Penha, Aéroporto de Gateão, Cocota, Ilha do Governador, Jardim Guanabara, Zumbi, Galeão, Irajá, Olaria, Ilha dos Tavares, São Gonçalo

NITERÓI, RIO DE JANEIRO, Avenida Brasil, Deodoro, Ramos, Ilha da Cidade Universitária, Cidade Universitária, Ilha do Engenho, Barreto, Sete Pontes, Tribobo, Magalhães, Rocha Miranda, Bonsucesso, Baía de, Ilha de Santa Cruz, Neves, Baldeador, Maria Páula

Bangu, Realengo, Bástos, Madureira, Inhaúme, Méier, Benéfica, Caju, Guanabara, Ilha da Conceição, Armação, Centro, S. Domingos, Vila Progresso, Padre Miguel, Cascadura, Piedade, Encantado, Engenho Novo, São Cristóvão, Aéroporto de Manguinho, Ilha das Cobras, Aéroport Santos Dumont, Canto do Rio, Niterói, Icaraí, Badu

Serra do Bangu, Praça Seca, Vila Isabel, Isabel, Maracana, Palacio das Exposições, Zoological Gardens, Estádio Maracanã, National Museum, Lapa, Catete, Monroe Palace, Naval Academy, Enseada de Jurujuba, Pedra Branca 1025, Taquara, Pechincha, Serra do Engenho Velho, Rio Comprido, RIO DE JANEIRO, Museum of the Republic, Morro Boa Vista, Morro de Sta Bárbara 851, Jacarepaguá, Andarai, Larangeiras, Pico da Tijuca 1022, Tijuca, Botofogo, Flamengo, 268 Morro do Macaco, Piratininga

Serra da Carioca, Monumento de Cristo Redebro, 740 Corcovado, Urca 404 Sugar Loaf Mt., L.o de Piratininga, Canto do Pontes, Engenho do Mato, Alto do Bôa-Vista, Botanical Gardens, Jardim Botânico, Hipodromo da Gávea, Gávea, Lagoa Rodrigo de Freitas, Ilha de Cotunduba

Vargem Grande, Guanabara, Ipanema, Copacabana, Ilha do Pai, Itaocaia, Itaipu, Leblon, Niemeyer 535, Forte de Copacabana, Pedra da Gávea 845, Gruta da Imprensa

Rio do Cortado, Lagoa de Marapéndi, Tijucamar, Praia dos Bandeirantes, Lagoa de Tijuca

Ilhas Tijucas, Ilhas Cagarras

A T L A N T I C   O C E A N

West from Greenwich

São Paulo (bottom map)

4   **5**   **6**   **7**

Pico de Jaraguá 1133, Jaraguá, Bananal, Cantareira, Horto Florestal, Tremembé, Piqueri, Vila Galvão, Baquirivu, Pimenta, Congo, Itaberaba, Tucuruvi, Parque Edú Chaves, Guarulhos, Baquirivu-Guaçú, Rio Tietê, Tamboré, Jardim Munhoz, Mutinga, Pirituba, Piqueri, Imirim, Mandaqui, Santana, Ermelino Matarazzo, Itaquaquecetuba, Jaguara, N. Senhora do O., Jardim Munhoz, São Miguel Paulista, Itaim, Carapicuiba, Quitaúna, Jardim Rochidale, Base Aérea de Marte, Vila Maria, Cangaiba, Bairro do Limoeiro, Vila Nova Curuçá

Osasco, Jaguaré, Lapa, Agua Branca, Bom Retiro, Rio Tietê, Penha, Vila Ré, Tatuapé, Vila Matilde, Ferraz de Vasconcelos, Vila Dirce, Sumaré, Barra Funda, Estação Julio Prestes, Pari, Brás, Belenzinho, Itaquera, Jardim Osasco, Cidade de Deus, Perdizes, Sta. Elígena, Estação da Luz, Água Rasa, Arthur Alvim, Bussocaba, Vila Dalva, Rio Pequeno, Cidade Universitária, Consolação, Bela Vista, Liberdade, Cambuci, Moóca, Cidade Líder, Guianazes, Aldeia de Carapicuiba, Jockey Club, Butantã, Jardim América, Aclimação, Vila Formosa, Roseiras

Granja Viana, Jardim Arpoador, Jardim Ouro Preto, Caxingui, Cidade Universitária, Cerqueira Cesar, SÃO PAULO, Vila Mariana, Museu Ipiranga, Alto da Moóca, Vila Prudente, Cidade S. Matheus, Colônia, Cunhas, Vila Sonia, Jardim Paulista, Parque Ibirapuera, Ipiranga, Vila Ema, Canguera, Vila Vista Alegre, Vila Indiana, Taboão da Serra, Estádio do Morumbi, Indianópolis, Cor. do Sapateiro, Parque S. Lucas, Iguassú, Jardim Sapopemba, Jardim Vera Cruz, Mombaça

Jardim Vista Alegre, Campo Belo, Ibirapuera, Brooklin, Bosque da Saúde, Sacoma, São Caetano do Sul, Rio do Oratorio, Capuava, Morro Pelado, Embu, Valo Velho, Vila Andrade, Campo Limpo, Alto da Boa Vista, Aéroporto Congonhas, S. João Climaco, Utinga, Parque das Nações, Jardim S. Francisco, Jardim Vista Alegre, Pirajussara, Parque Zoologico, Santo André, Jardim Zaira, Parque do Estado, Capão Redondo, Vila Remo, Itupu, Jurubatuba, Cupecé, Santo Amaro, Capelinha, Santa Tereza, Vila Pires, Mauá, Jardim Santista, Pilar Velho

Itapecerica da Serra, Jardim S. Bento, Interagos, Pedreira, Zuvuvús, Diadema, Jardim do Mar, Nova Pet., Vila Gonçalves, Jardim Anchieta, Jardim Petrópolis, Ribeirão Pires, Embú-Mirim, M'Boi Mirim, Cidade Ipava, Reservatorio de Guarapiranga, Vila Eldorado, Represa Billings, São Bernardo do Campo, Bairro da Matriz, Vila Bocaina

West from Greenwich

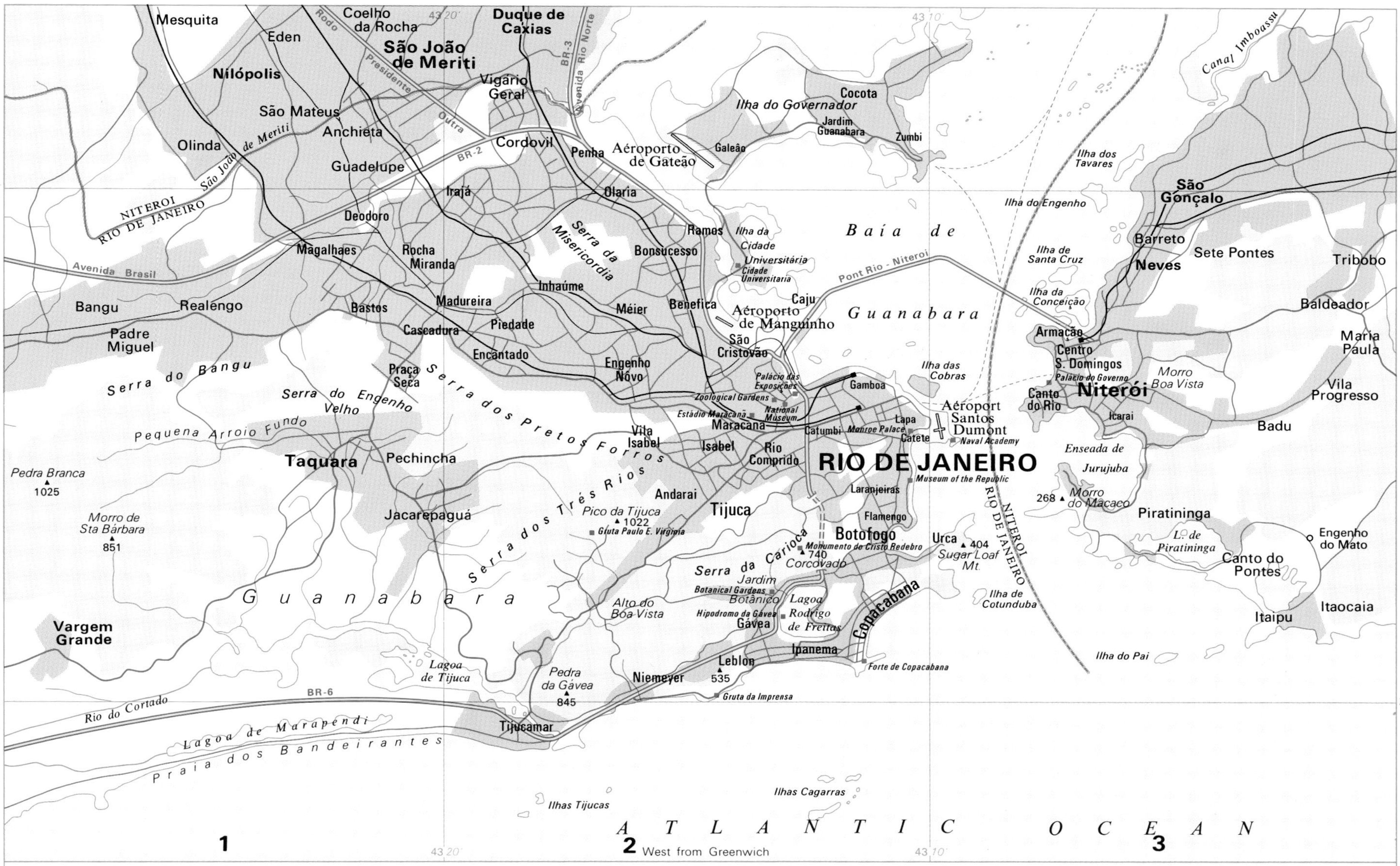

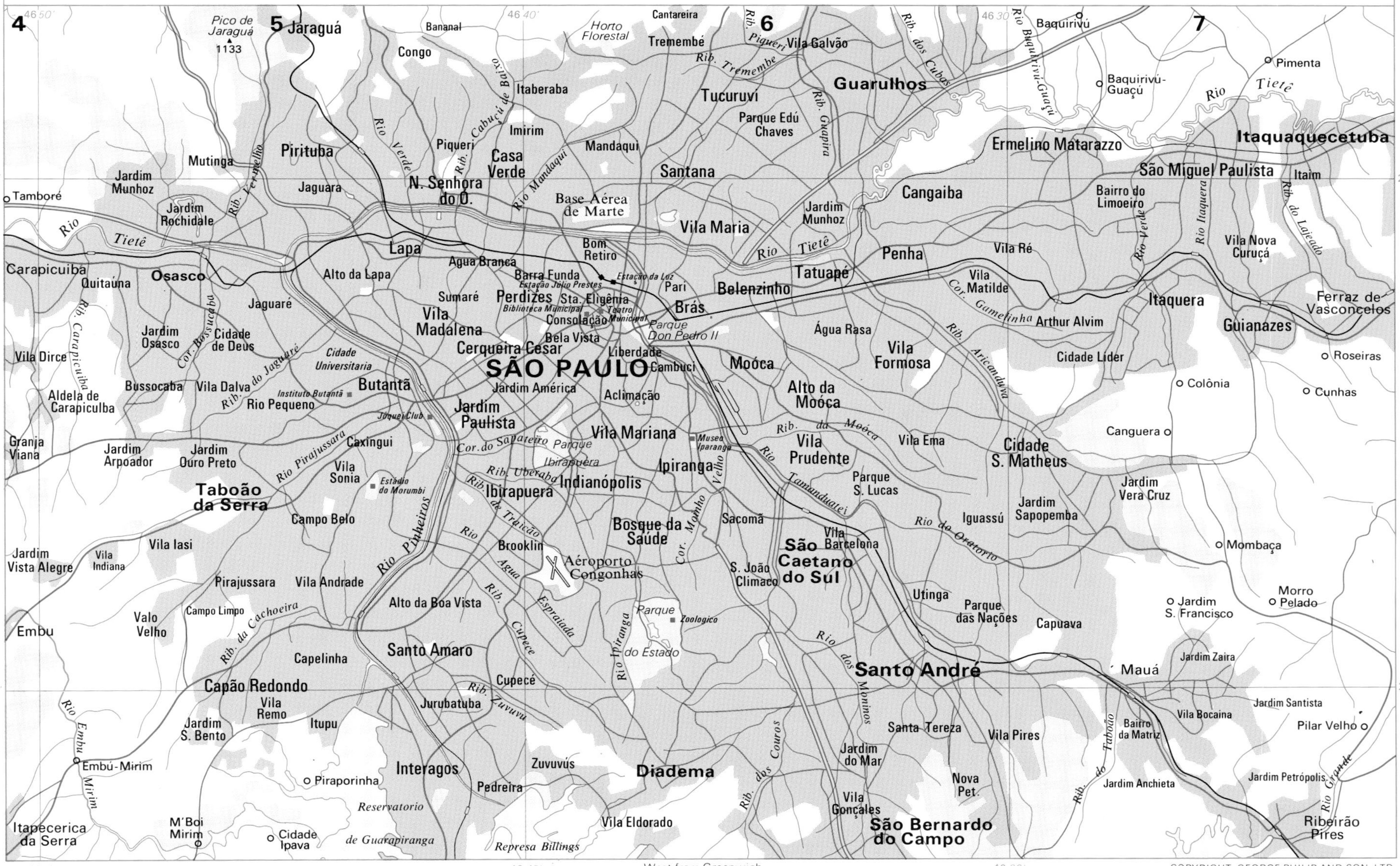

COPYRIGHT GEORGE PHILIP AND SON LTD.

4   **5**   **6**   **7**

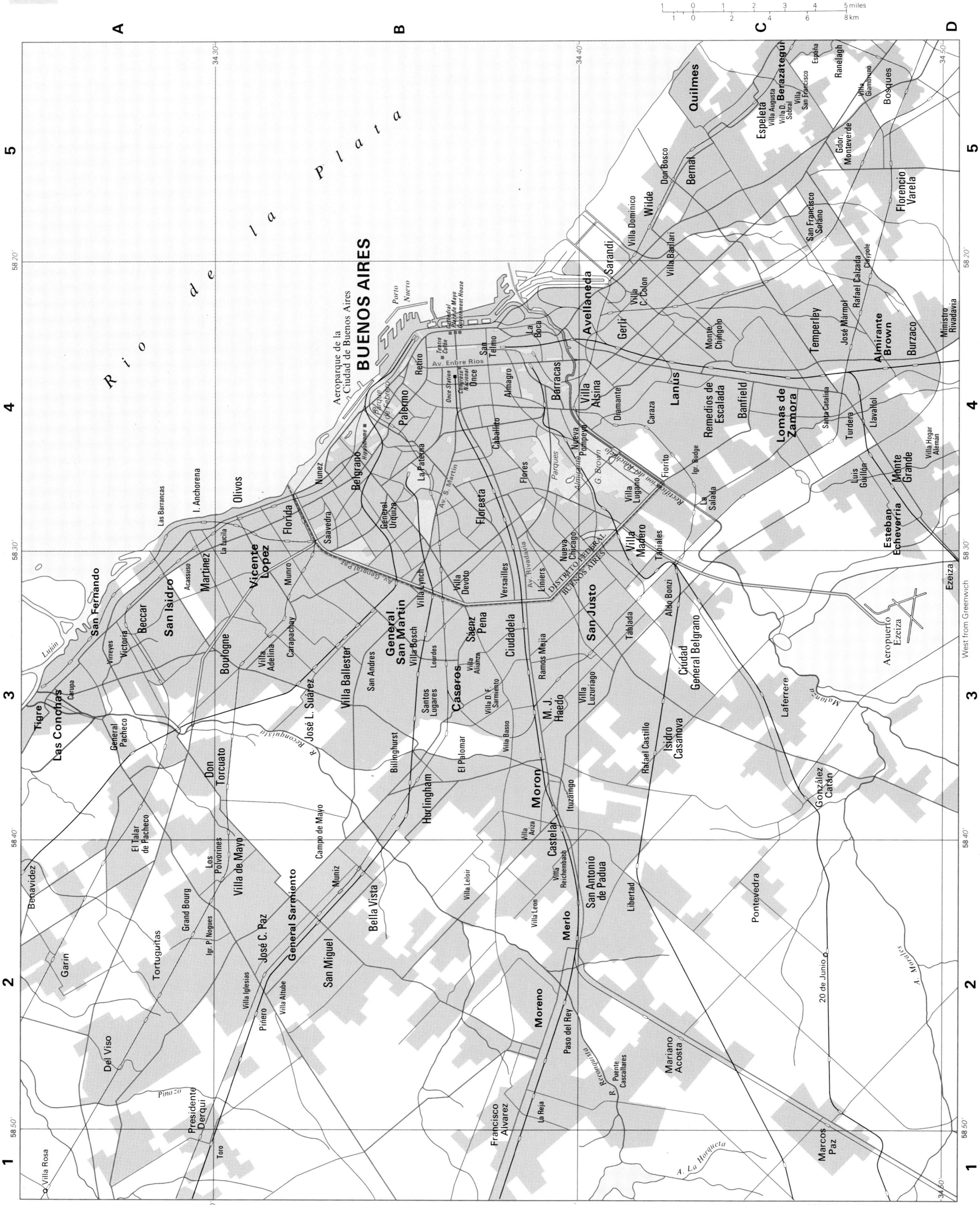

1: 200 000

5 miles
8 km

A B C D

Rio de la Plata

BUENOS AIRES

5
4
3
2
1

Aeroparque de la Ciudad de Buenos Aires

Porto Nuevo

Retiro
Once Station
Teatro Colón
San Telmo
La Boca
Palermo
Belgrano
Núñez
Olivos
Av. Enbre Rios
Almagro
Barracas
Flores
Floresta
Caballito
La Paterna
Av. S. Martín
General Urquiza
Saavedra
Florida
Martínez
Vicente López
Munro
La Lucila
Acassuso
Beccar
Victoria
San Isidro
San Fernando
Tigre
Las Conchas
Carupá
Virreyes
General Pacheco
Boulogne
Villa Adelina
Carapachay
Villa Ballester
San Andrés
José L. Suárez
Santos Lugares
Caseres
General San Martín
Villa Bosch
Lourdes
Villa D.F. Sarmiento
El Palomar
Hurlingham
Billinghurst
Don Torcuato
El Talar de Pacheco
Los Polvorines
Villa de Mayo
Muniz
General Sarmiento
Bella Vista
San Miguel
José C. Paz
Grand Bourg
Tortuguitas
Garín
Benavidez
Villa Rosa
Del Viso
Presidente Derqui
Toro
Pinazo
 Reconquista
Francisco Alvarez
La Reja
Moreno
Paso del Rey
Merlo
San Antonio de Padua
Libertad
Mariano Acosta
Marcos Paz
20 de Junio
Pontevedra
González Catán
Laferrere
Isidro Casanova
Rafael Castillo
Ciudad General Belgrano
Villa Luzuriaga
San Justo
La Tablada
Aldo Bonzi
Villa Madero
Tapiales
Villa Lugano
Mataderos
Liniers
Nueva Chicago
Ciudadela
Ramos Mejía
M. J. Haedo
Morón
Castelar
Ituzaingó
Villa Ariza
Villa Leon
Villa Reichenbach
Villa Leloir
Villa Basso
Versailles
Saenz Peña
Villa Alianza
Villa Devoto
Villa Lynch
Av. Rivadavia
DISTRITO FEDERAL BUENOS AIRES
Av. General Paz
Nueva Pompeya
Villa Alsina
Diamante
Caraza
Fiorito
La Salada
Almirante Brown
Remedios de Escalada
Lanús
Banfield
Gerli
Avellaneda
Sarandí
Wilde
Don Bosco
Bernal
Quilmes
Espeleta
Villa Dominico
Villa Bailari
Villa C. Colón
Monte Chingolo
José Marmol
Temperley
Rafael Calzada
Claypole
San Francisco Solano
Berazategui
Florencio Varela
Bosques
Ranelagh
Espiña
Gdor. Monteverde
Burzaco
Lomas de Zamora
Turdera
Llavallol
Luis Guillón
Monte Grande
Esteban Echeverría
Villa Hogar Alemán
Ministro Rivadavia
Aeropuerto Ezeiza
Ezeiza
West from Greenwich

COPYRIGHT GEORGE PHILIP AND SON. LTD.

INDEX TO CITY MAPS

Place names in this index are given a letter-figure reference to a map square made from the lines of latitude and longitude that appear on the city maps. The full geographic reference is provided in the border of each map.
The letter-figure reference will take the reader directly to the square, and by using the geographical coordinates the place sought can be pinpointed within that square.

The location given is the city or suburban center, and not necessarily the name. Lakes, airports and other features having a large area are given coordinates for their centers. Rivers that enter the sea, lake or main stream within the map area have the coordinates of that entrance.

If the river flows through the map, then the coordinates are given to the name. The same rule applies to canals. A river carries the symbol → after its name.

As an aid to identification, every place name is followed by the city map name or its abbreviation; for example, Oakland in California will be followed by S.F. Some of the place names so described will be completely independent of the main city.

An explanation of the alphabetical order rules is to be found at the beginning of the World Map Index.

ABBREVIATIONS USED IN THE INDEX

Ath. – Athinai (Athens)
B. – Baie, Bahía, Bay, Bucht
B.A. – Buenos Aires
Bagd. – Baghdad
Balt. – Baltimore
Bangk. – Bangkok
Barc. – Barcelona
Beij. – Beijing (Peking)
Berl. – Berlin
Bomb. – Bombay
Bost. – Boston
Bud. – Budapest
C. – Cabo, Cap, Cape
Calc. – Calcutta
Car. – Caracas
Chan. – Channel
Chic. – Chicago
Cr. – Creek
E. – East
El Qâ. – El Qâhira (Cairo)
G. – Golfe, Golfo, Gulf, Guba
Gzh. – Guangzhou (Canton)
H.K. – Hong Kong
Hbg. – Hamburg
Hd. – Head
Hels. – Helsinki
Hts. – Heights
I.(s) – Île, Ilha, Insel, Isla, Island, Isle
Ist. – Istanbul
J. – Jabal, Jebel
Jak. – Jakarta
Jobg. – Johannesburg
K. – Kap, Kapp
Kar. – Karachi
Kep. – Kepulauan
Købn. – København (Copenhagen)
L. – Lac, Lacul, Lago, Lagoa, Lake
L.A. – Los Angeles
La Hab. – La Habana (Havana)
Lisb. – Lisboa (Lisbon)
Lon. – London
Mdrd. – Madrid
Melb. – Melbourne
Méx. – México
Mil. – Milano
Mos. – Moskva (Moscow)
Mt. (e) – Mont, Monte, Monti, Montaña, Mountain
Mtrl. – Montréal
Mün. – München (Munich)
N. – Nord, Norte, North, Northern, Nouveau
Nápl. – Nápoli (Naples)
N.Y. – New York City
Os. – Ostrov
Oz. – Ozero
Pen. – Peninsula, Peninsule
Phil. – Philadelphia
Pk. – Park, Peak
Pra. – Praha (Prague)
Pt. – Point
Pta. – Ponta, Punta
Pte. – Pointe
R. – Rio, River
Ra. (s) – Range(s)
Res. – Reserve, Reservoir
Rio J. – Rio de Janeiro
S. – San, South
S.F. – San Francisco
S. Pau. – São Paulo
Sa. – Serra, Sierra
Sd. – Sound
Shang. – Shanghai
Sing. – Singapore
St. – Saint, Sankt, Sint
St-Pet. – St-Peterburg
Sta. – Santa, Station
Ste. – Sainte
Stgo. – Santiago
Sto. – Santo
Stock. – Stockholm
Str. – Strait, Stretto
Syd. – Sydney
Tehr. – Tehran
Tianj. – Tianjin (Tientsin)
Tori. – Torino (Turin)
Trto. – Toronto
W. – West
Wash. – Washington
Wsaw. – Warszawa (Warsaw)

A

Aalām, *Bagd.* 17 F8 33 19N 44 23 E
Abada, *Calc.* 16 E5 22 32N 88 13 E
Abbadia di Stura, *Tori.* 9 B3 45 7N 7 44 E
Abbey Wood, *Lon.* 4 C5 51 29N 0 7 E
Abbots Langley, *Lon.* 4 A2 51 42N 0 25W
Abeno, *Ōsaka* 12 C4 34 38N 135 31 E
Aberdeen, *H.K.* 12 E6 22 14N 114 8 E
Abfanggraben, *Mün.* 7 F11 48 10N 11 41 E
Abington, *Phil.* 24 A4 40 7N 75 7W
Ablon-sur-Seine, *Paris* 5 C4 48 43N 2 25 E
Abord à Plouffe, *Mtrl.* 20 A3 43 32N 73 43W
Abramtsevo, *Mos.* 11 E10 55 49N 37 49 E
Abridge, *Lon.* 4 B5 51 38N 0 7 E
Abû en Numrus, *El Qâ.* 18 D5 29 57N 31 12 E
Acassuso, *B.A.* 32 A3 34 29 S 58 30W
Accord, *Bost.* 21 D4 42 10N 70 52W
Accord Pond, *Bost.* 21 D4 42 10N 70 53W
Accotink Cr. →, *Wash.* 25 D6 38 51N 77 15W
Acerra, *Nápl.* 9 H13 40 56N 14 22 E
Acha San, *Sŏul* 12 G8 37 33N 127 5 E
Acheres, *Paris* 5 B2 48 57N 2 3 E
Acília, *Rome* 9 G9 41 47N 12 21 E
Aclimação, *S. Pau.* 31 E6 23 34 S 46 37W
Acostia →, *Wash.* 25 D8 38 51N 77 1W
Acton, *Lon.* 4 B3 51 30N 0 16W
Açúcar, Pão de, *Rio J.* 31 B3 22 56 S 43 9W
Ada Beja, *Lisb.* 8 F7 38 47N 9 13W
Adabe Cr. →, *S.F.* 27 D4 37 26N 122 6W
Adachi, *Tōkyō* 13 B2 35 49N 139 34 E
Adachi-Ku, *Tōkyō* 13 B3 35 47N 139 47 E
Adams Nat. Hist. Site, *Bost.* 21 D4 42 15N 71 0W
Addington, *Lon.* 4 C4 51 21N 0 1W
Addiscombe, *Lon.* 4 C4 51 22N 0 4W
Adel, *Bagd.* 17 E7 33 20N 44 17 E
Adelphi, *Wash.* 25 C8 39 0N 76 58W
Aderklaa, *Wien* 10 G11 48 17N 16 32 E
Admiralteyskaya Storona, *St-Pet.* 11 B4 59 56N 30 20 E
Áffori, *Mil.* 9 D6 45 31N 9 10 E
Aflandshage, *Købn.* 2 E10 55 33N 12 35 E
Afragola, *Nápl.* 9 H12 40 55N 14 18 E
Aganpur, *Delhi* 16 B3 28 33N 77 20 E
Agboju, *Lagos* 18 B1 6 27N 7 16 E
Agboyi Cr. →, *Lagos* 18 A2 6 33N 7 24 E
Ågerup, *Købn.* 2 D8 55 43N 12 19 E
Ågesta, *Stock.* 3 E11 59 12N 18 6 E
Agincourt, *Trto.* 20 D9 43 47N 79 16W
Agnano Terme, *Nápl.* 9 J12 40 49N 14 10 E
Agora, *Ath.* 8 J11 37 57N 23 43 E
Agra Canal, *Delhi* 16 B2 28 33N 77 17 E
Agricola Oriental, *Méx.* 29 B3 19 23N 99 4W
Agro Romano, *Rome* 9 F8 41 56N 12 17 E
Agua Branca, *S. Pau.* 31 E5 23 31 S 46 40W
Agua Espraiada →, *S. Pau.* 31 E6 23 36 S 46 41W
Água Rasa, *S. Pau.* 31 E6 23 32 S 46 33W
Agualva-Cacem, *Lisb.* 8 F7 38 46N 9 15W
Agustino, Cerro El, *Lima* 30 G8 12 3 S 76 59W
Ahrensfelde, *Berl.* 7 A4 52 34N 13 34 E
Ahuntsic, *Mtrl.* 20 A3 43 32N 73 41W
Ai →, *Ōsaka* 12 B4 34 46N 135 35 E
Aigremont, *Paris* 5 B2 48 54N 2 1 E
Airport West, *Melb.* 19 E6 37 42 S 144 52 E
Aiyaleo, *Ath.* 8 J11 37 59N 23 40 E
Ajegunle, *Lagos* 18 B2 6 26N 7 20 E
Aji, *Ōsaka* 12 B3 34 40N 135 27 E
Ajuda, *Lisb.* 8 F7 38 42N 9 12W
Ajusco, Parque Nacional de, *Méx.* 29 C2 19 12N 99 15W
Akabane, *Tōkyō* 13 B3 35 46N 139 42 E
Akalla, *Stock.* 3 D10 59 24N 17 55 E
Akasaka, *Tōkyō* 13 B3 35 40N 139 43 E
Akbarābād, *Tehr.* 17 C5 35 40N 51 20 E
Åkersberga Saltsjobad, *Stock.* 3 D12 59 26N 18 15 E
Akerselva →, *Oslo* 2 B4 59 54N 10 45 E
Akrópolis, *Ath.* 8 J11 37 57N 23 43 E
Akuwa, *Tōkyō* 13 D2 35 26N 139 30 E
Al 'Azamiyah, *Bagd.* 17 E8 33 22N 44 22 E
Alaguntan, *Lagos* 18 B2 6 25N 7 29 E
Alamar, *La Hab.* 30 B3 23 9N 82 16W
Alameda, *S.F.* 27 B3 37 46N 122 15W
Alameda Memorial State Beach Park, *S.F.* 27 B3 37 45N 122 16W
Alamo, *S.F.* 27 A4 37 51N 122 2W
Albany, *S.F.* 27 A3 37 53N 122 17W
Alberante, *Jobg.* 18 F9 26 16 S 28 7 E
Albern, *Wien* 10 H10 48 9N 16 29 E
Albert Hall, *Lon.* 4 C3 51 29N 0 10W
Albert Park, *Melb.* 19 F6 37 51 S 144 58 E
Albertfalva, *Bud.* 10 K13 47 26N 19 3 E
Alberton, *Jobg.* 18 F9 26 15 S 28 7 E
Albertslund, *Købn.* 2 E9 55 39N 12 21 E
Albertson, *N.Y.* 23 C7 40 46N 73 38W
Albertville, *Jobg.* 18 E8 26 9 S 27 58 E
Albion, *Phil.* 24 C5 39 46N 74 57W
Alby, *Stock.* 3 E10 59 14N 17 51 E
Albysjön, *Stock.* 3 E10 59 14N 17 52 E
Alcantara, *Lisb.* 8 F7 38 43N 9 10W
Alcatraz I., *S.F.* 27 B2 37 49N 122 25W
Alcochete, *Lisb.* 8 F9 38 45N 8 58W
Alcorcón, *Mdrd.* 8 B2 40 20N 3 48W
Aldan, *Phil.* 24 B3 39 55N 75 17W
Aldela de Carapiculba, *S. Pau.* 31 E5 23 34 S 46 49W
Aldene, *N.Y.* 22 D3 40 39N 74 17W
Aldenrade, *Ruhr* 6 A2 51 31N 6 44 E
Alder Planetarium, *Chic.* 26 B3 41 5N 87 36W
Aldershof, *Berl.* 7 B4 52 26N 13 33 E
Aldo Bonzi, *B.A.* 32 C3 34 42 S 58 31W
Aleksandrovskoye, *St-Pet.* 11 B4 59 51N 30 20 E
Aleksandrów, *Wsaw.* 10 E8 52 10N 21 14 E
Alexander Nevsky Abbey, *St-Pet.* 11 B4 59 54N 30 23 E
Alexandra, *Jobg.* 18 E9 26 6 S 28 5 E
Alexandra, *Sing.* 15 G7 1 17N 103 49 E
Alexandria, *Wash.* 25 E7 38 49N 77 5W
Alfortville, *Paris* 5 C4 48 48N 2 24 E
Algés, *Lisb.* 8 F7 38 42N 9 13W
Älgo, *Stock.* 3 E13 59 16N 18 20 E
Algodonal, *Car.* 30 E5 10 29N 66 58W
Alhambra, *L.A.* 28 B4 34 5N 118 7W
Alhos Vedros, *Lisb.* 8 G8 38 39N 9 1W
Alibey →, *Ist.* 17 A2 41 3N 28 56 E
Alibeyköy, *Ist.* 17 A2 41 4N 28 56 E
Alima, *Manila* 15 E3 14 27N 120 55 E
Alimos, *Ath.* 8 J11 37 52N 23 43 E
Aliperti, *Nápl.* 9 H13 40 53N 14 28 E
Alipore, *Calc.* 16 E6 22 31N 88 20 E
Alipur, *Calc.* 16 D5 22 43N 88 12 E
Aliso Canyon Wash →, *L.A.* 28 A1 34 15N 118 31W
Allach, *Mün.* 7 F9 48 11N 11 27 E
Allambie Heights, *Syd.* 19 A4 33 46 S 151 15 E
Allendale, *N.Y.* 22 A4 41 1N 74 9W
Allengrove, *Jobg.* 18 E10 26 5 S 28 14 E
Allentown, *N.Y.* 23 C6 40 47N 73 43W
Allermohe, *Hbg.* 7 E8 53 29N 10 7 E
Allerton, Pt., *Bost.* 21 D4 42 18N 70 52W
Allston, *Bost.* 21 C3 42 21N 71 7W
Alluets, Forêt des, *Paris* 5 B1 48 56N 1 55 E
Almada, *Lisb.* 8 F8 38 41N 9 8W
Almagro, *B.A.* 32 B4 34 38 S 58 24W
Almanara, *Mdrd.* 8 B2 40 28N 3 41W
Almaza Airport, *El Qâ.* 18 C6 30 5N 31 21 E
Almazovo, *Mos.* 11 D12 55 50N 38 3 E
Almendares, *La Hab.* 30 B2 23 6N 82 23W
Almendares →, *La Hab.* 30 B2 23 7N 82 24W
Almirante Brown, *B.A.* 32 C4 34 48 S 58 23W
Almirante G. Brown, Parques, *B.A.* 32 C4 34 40 S 58 28W
Almonesson, *Phil.* 24 C4 39 48N 75 5W
Almonte, *S.F.* 27 A1 37 53N 122 31W
Alnabru, *Oslo* 2 B5 59 55N 10 50 E
Alnsjøen, *Oslo* 2 B5 59 57N 10 51 E
Alperton, *Lon.* 4 B3 51 32N 0 17W
Alpignano, *Tori.* 9 B1 45 6N 7 31 E
Alpine, *N.Y.* 22 B5 40 57N 73 57W
Alpur, *Calc.* 16 C6 22 50N 88 23 E
Alrode, *Jobg.* 18 F9 26 17 S 28 7 E
Alsergrund, *Wien* 10 G10 48 13N 16 21 E
Alsfeld, *Ruhr* 6 A3 51 31N 6 50 E
Alsip, *Chic.* 26 C2 41 40N 87 44W
Alstaden, *Ruhr* 6 B2 51 28N 6 49 E
Ålsten, *Stock.* 3 E10 59 19N 17 57 E
Alster →, *Hbg.* 7 D8 53 38N 10 4 E
Alsterdorf, *Hbg.* 7 D8 53 36N 10 0 E
Älta, *Stock.* 3 E12 59 15N 18 11 E
Altadena, *L.A.* 28 A4 34 11N 118 8W
Alte-Donau →, *Wien* 10 G10 48 14N 16 25 E
Alte Süderelbe, *Hbg.* 7 D7 53 31N 9 52 E
Alten-Essen, *Ruhr* 6 B4 51 29N 7 1 E
Altendorf, *Ruhr* 6 B3 51 27N 6 58 E
Altenhagen, *Ruhr* 6 B6 51 22N 7 27 E
Altenvoerde, *Ruhr* 6 C6 51 18N 7 22 E
Altenwerder, *Hbg.* 7 D7 53 30N 9 55 E
Alter Finkenkrug, *Berl.* 7 A1 52 35N 13 3 E
Altglenicke, *Berl.* 7 B4 52 25N 13 32 E
Altlandsberg Nord, *Berl.* 7 A5 52 34N 13 43 E
Altmannsdorf, *Wien* 10 H9 48 9N 16 18 E
Alto, *S.F.* 27 A1 37 54N 122 30W
Alto da Boa Vista, *S. Pau.* 31 E5 23 38 S 46 42W
Alto da Lapa, *S. Pau.* 31 E5 23 31 S 46 43W
Alto da Moóca, *S. Pau.* 31 E6 23 34 S 46 33W
Alto do Pina, *Lisb.* 8 F8 38 44N 9 7W
Altona, *Hbg.* 7 D7 53 32N 9 56 E
Altona, *Melb.* 19 F5 37 51 S 144 49 E
Altona B., *Melb.* 19 F6 37 52 S 144 51 E
Altona North, *Melb.* 19 F5 37 50 S 144 49 E
Altona Sports Park, *Melb.* 19 F6 37 51 S 144 51 E
Altstadt, *Hbg.* 7 D8 53 32N 10 0 E
Alvarado, *S.F.* 27 C4 37 35N 122 4W
Alvik, *Stock.* 3 E10 59 19N 17 58 E
Älvsjo, *Stock.* 3 E11 59 16N 18 0 E
Älvvik, *Stock.* 3 D12 59 21N 18 15 E
Am Hasenbergl, *Mün.* 7 F10 48 12N 11 33 E
Am Steinhof, *Wien* 10 G9 48 12N 16 17 E
Am Wald, *Mün.* 7 G10 48 3N 11 36 E
Ama Keng, *Sing.* 15 F7 1 23N 103 41 E
Amadora, *Lisb.* 8 F7 38 45N 9 13W
Amagasaki, *Ōsaka* 12 B3 34 42N 135 23 E
Amager, *Købn.* 2 E10 55 36N 12 35 E
Amāl Qādisiya, *Bagd.* 17 F8 33 16N 44 20 E
Amalienborg Slott, *Købn.* 2 D10 55 41N 12 35 E
Amata, *Mil.* 9 D5 45 34N 9 8 E
Ambler, *Phil.* 24 A3 40 9N 75 13W
Ambrose Channel, *N.Y.* 22 D5 40 31N 73 50W
Ameixoeira, *Lisb.* 8 F8 38 46N 9 8W
Ames Hill, *Bost.* 21 B2 42 38N 71 13W
Amin, *Bagd.* 17 F8 33 19N 44 29 E
Aminyevo, *Mos.* 11 E8 55 41N 37 25 E
Amirābād, *Tehr.* 17 C5 35 43N 51 24 E
Amityville, *N.Y.* 23 C8 40 40N 73 23W
Ammersbek →, *Hbg.* 7 C8 53 42N 10 7 E
Amora, *Lisb.* 8 G8 38 37N 9 6W
Amoreira, *Lisb.* 8 F7 38 48N 9 11W
Amorosa, *Jobg.* 18 E8 26 5 S 27 52 E
Ampelokipi, *Ath.* 8 J11 37 58N 23 47 E
Amper →, *Mün.* 7 F9 48 14N 11 25 E
Amselhain, *Berl.* 7 A5 52 38N 13 43 E
Amuwo, *Lagos* 18 B1 6 28N 7 18 E
Anacostia, *Wash.* 25 D8 38 51N 76 59W
Anacostia River Park, *Wash.* 25 D8 38 54N 76 57W
Anadoluhisari, *Ist.* 17 A3 41 4N 29 3 E
Anandanagar, *Calc.* 16 C5 22 51N 88 16 E
Anchieta, *Rio J.* 31 A1 22 48 S 43 21W
Ancol, *Jak.* 15 H9 6 7 S 106 49 E
Andalus, *Bagd.* 17 F7 33 19N 44 18 E
Andalusia, *Phil.* 24 A5 40 4N 74 58W
Andarai, *Rio J.* 31 B2 22 56 S 43 14W
Andeli Beijie, *Beij.* 14 B3 39 57N 116 21 E
Anderson Cr. →, *Melb.* 19 E8 37 44 S 145 12 E
Andilly, *Paris* 5 A3 49 0N 2 17 E
Andingmen, *Beij.* 14 B3 39 55N 116 23 E
Andover, *Bost.* 21 B3 42 39N 71 7W
Andrésy, *Paris* 5 B2 48 58N 2 3 E
Andrews Air Force Base, *Wash.* 25 E8 38 48N 76 52W
Ang Mo Kio, *Sing.* 15 F8 1 22N 103 50 E
Ängby, *Stock.* 3 D10 59 20N 17 53 E
Angel I., *S.F.* 27 A2 37 52N 122 25W
Angel Island State Park, *S.F.* 27 A2 37 52N 122 25W
Angerbruch →, *Ruhr* 6 C3 51 18N 6 59 E
Angerhausen, *Ruhr* 6 B2 51 22N 6 43 E
Angermund, *Ruhr* 6 C2 51 19N 6 46 E
Angke, Kali →, *Jak.* 15 H9 6 6 S 106 46 E
Angono, *Manila* 15 D4 14 31N 121 8 E
Angyalföld, *Bud.* 10 J13 47 32N 19 5 E
Angyō, *Tōkyō* 13 A3 35 50N 139 45 E
Aniene →, *Rome* 9 F10 41 56N 12 35 E
Anik, *Bomb.* 16 G8 19 1N 72 53 E
Anin, *Wsaw.* 10 E7 52 13N 21 9 E
Anjou, *Mtrl.* 20 A4 43 36N 73 33W
Annadale, *N.Y.* 22 D3 40 32N 74 10W
Annalee Heights, *Wash.* 25 D6 38 51N 77 10W
Annandale, *Wash.* 25 D6 38 50N 77 11W
Annen, *Ruhr* 6 B6 51 27N 7 22 E
Annet-sur-Marne, *Paris* 5 B6 48 55N 2 43 E
Anthony Chabot Regional Park, *S.F.* 27 B4 37 46N 122 7W
Antignano, *Nápl.* 9 H12 40 51N 14 13 E
Antimano, *Car.* 30 E5 10 27N 66 59W
Antipolo, *Manila* 15 D5 14 35N 121 10 E
Antony, *Paris* 5 C3 48 44N 2 17 E
Antwerp, *Jobg.* 18 E9 26 5 S 28 9 E
Aoyama, *Tōkyō* 13 C3 35 39N 139 42 E
Ap Lei Chau, *H.K.* 12 E5 22 14N 114 9 E
Apapa, *Lagos* 18 B2 6 26N 7 21 E
Apelacão, *Lisb.* 8 F8 38 48N 9 7W
Apoquindo, *Stgo* 30 J11 33 23 S 70 30W
Apshawa, *N.Y.* 22 A2 41 1N 74 22W
Apterkarskiy Os., *St-Pet.* 11 B4 59 57N 30 20 E
Aquincum, *Bud.* 10 J13 47 33N 19 3 E
Ara →, *Tōkyō* 13 B4 35 41N 139 50 E
Arakawa-Ku, *Tōkyō* 13 B3 35 44N 139 48 E
Arakpur, *Delhi* 16 B2 28 35N 77 11 E
Arany-hegyi-patak →, *Bud.* 10 J13 47 34N 19 4 E
Aravaca, *Mdrd.* 8 B2 40 27N 3 47W
Arbataash, *Bagd.* 17 E7 33 20N 44 19 E
Arbutus, *Balt.* 25 B2 39 15N 76 41W
Arc de Triomphe, *Paris* 5 B3 48 52N 2 17 E
Arcadia, *L.A.* 28 B4 34 7N 118 1W
Arceuil, *Paris* 5 C3 48 48N 2 19 E
Arden, *Phil.* 24 C2 39 48N 75 29W
Ardey Gebirge, *Ruhr* 6 B6 51 24N 7 23 E
Ardmore, *Phil.* 24 A3 40 0N 75 17W
Ardsley, *N.Y.* 23 A5 41 0N 73 50W
Arese, *Mil.* 9 D5 45 32N 9 4 E
Arganzuela, *Mdrd.* 8 B2 40 23N 3 42W
Argenteuil, *Paris* 5 B3 48 56N 2 15 E
Argonne Forest, *Chic.* 26 C1 41 42N 87 53W
Ariadana, *Calc.* 16 E6 22 39N 88 22 E
Aricanduva →, *S. Pau.* 31 E6 23 31 S 46 33W
Arida, *Lagos* 18 A1 6 33N 7 16 E
Arima, *Ōsaka* 12 B2 34 47N 135 15 E
Arima, *Tōkyō* 13 C2 35 33N 139 33 E
Arima →, *Ōsaka* 12 A2 34 50N 135 14 E
Arkhangelyskoye, *Mos.* 11 E7 55 47N 37 17 E
Arkley, *Lon.* 4 B3 51 38N 0 13W
Arlington, *Bost.* 21 C2 42 24N 71 10W
Arlington, *Wash.* 25 D7 38 53N 77 7W
Arlington Heights, *Bost.* 21 C2 42 25N 71 10W
Arlington Heights, *Chic.* 26 A1 42 5N 87 55W
Arlington Nat. Cemetery, *Wash.* 25 D7 38 52N 77 4W
Armação, *Rio J.* 31 B3 22 52 S 43 6W
Armadale, *Melb.* 19 F7 37 51 S 145 0 E
Armadale, *Trto.* 20 C9 43 50N 79 14W
Armainvilliers, Forêt d', *Paris* 5 C6 48 46N 2 42 E
Armour Heights, *Trto.* 20 D8 43 45N 79 25W
Arncliffe, *Syd.* 19 B3 33 56 S 151 8 E
Arnold Arboretum, *Bost.* 21 D3 42 18N 71 8W
Arnouville-les-Gonesse, *Paris* 5 B4 48 59N 2 24 E
Arrentela, *Lisb.* 8 G8 38 37N 9 6W
Arrone →, *Rome* 9 F8 41 55N 12 16 E
Arroyo Arenas, *La Hab.* 30 B2 23 3N 82 27W
Arroyo Cr. →, *S.F.* 26 D2 37 27N 122 25W
Arroyo Naranjo, *La Hab.* 30 B2 23 2N 82 21W
Årsta, *Stock.* 3 E11 59 17N 18 3 E
Artesia, *L.A.* 28 C4 33 51N 118 4W
Arthur Alvim, *S. Pau.* 31 E7 23 32 S 46 28W
Arthur Kill →, *N.Y.* 22 D3 40 32N 74 15W
Artigas, *Car.* 30 E5 10 29N 66 56W
Arundel Gardens, *Balt.* 25 B3 39 12N 76 37W
Arundel Village, *Balt.* 25 B3 39 13N 76 35W
Aryiróupolis, *Ath.* 8 J11 37 52N 23 44 E
Arzano, *Nápl.* 9 H12 40 54N 14 16 E
Asagaya, *Tōkyō* 13 B2 35 41N 139 38 E
Asahi, *Ōsaka* 12 B4 34 43N 135 31 E
Asaka, *Tōkyō* 13 B2 35 47N 139 35 E
Asakusa, *Tōkyō* 13 B3 35 42N 139 47 E
Asalatpur, *Delhi* 16 B1 28 37N 77 4 E
Asati, *Calc.* 16 F5 22 28N 88 15 E
Aschheim, *Mün.* 7 F11 48 10N 11 42 E
Ascot Vale, *Melb.* 19 E6 37 46 S 144 53 E
Aserradero, *Méx.* 29 D2 19 10N 99 16W
Asharoken, *N.Y.* 23 B8 40 55N 73 21W
Ashburn, *Chic.* 26 C2 41 45N 87 43W
Ashburton, *Melb.* 19 F7 37 51 S 145 4 E

34 Ashburton, L.

Ashburton, L., *Balt.* 25 B2 39 19N 76 40W
Ashchherino, *Mos.* 11 F10 55 36N 37 46 E
Ashfield, *Syd.* 19 B3 33 53 S 151 7 E
Ashford, *Lon.* 4 C2 51 25N 0 26W
Ashiya, *Ōsaka* 12 B2 34 43N 135 18 E
Ashiya →, *Ōsaka* 12 B2 34 42N 135 18 E
Ashland, *S.F.* 27 B4 37 41N 122 7W
Ashstead, *Lon.* 4 D3 51 18N 0 17W
Ashwood, *Melb.* 19 F7 37 52 S 145 5 E
Asker, *Oslo* 2 B2 59 50N 10 25 E
Askisto, *Hels.* 3 B3 60 16N 24 47 E
Askrikefjärden, *Stock.* 3 D12 59 22N 18 13 E
Asnieres, *Paris* 5 B3 48 54N 2 16 E
Ason, *Lagos* 18 A3 6 34N 7 31 E
Aspern, *Wien* 10 G10 48 13N 16 29 E
Aspern, Flugplatz, *Wien* 10 G11 48 13N 16 30 E
Assiano, *Mil.* 9 E5 45 27N 9 3 E
Aston Mills, *Phil.* 24 B2 39 52N 75 26W
Astoria, *N.Y.* 22 C5 40 46N 73 55W
Atares, Castillo de, *La Hab.* 30 B2 23 7N 82 21W
Atco, *Phil.* 24 C5 39 46N 74 53W
Atghara, *Calc.* 16 E6 22 37N 88 26 E
Athens = Athínai, *Ath.* 8 J11 37 58N 23 43 E
Athínai, *Ath.* 8 J11 37 58N 23 43 E
Athinai-Ellinikón Airport, *Ath.* 8 J2 37 51N 23 44 E
Athis-Mons, *Paris* 5 C4 48 42N 2 23 E
Atīfīya, *Bagd.* 17 E8 33 21N 44 21 E
Atikali, *Ist.* 17 A2 41 1N 28 56 E
Atilo, Cerro, *Lima* 30 G8 12 2 S 77 2W
Atişalen, *Ist.* 17 A2 41 3N 28 52 E
Atlandsberg, *Berl.* 7 A5 52 33N 13 43 E
Atlantic Beach, *N.Y.* 23 D6 40 35N 73 44W
Atta, *Delhi* 16 B2 28 34N 77 19 E
Attiki, *Ath.* 8 H11 38 0N 23 43 E
Atzalpur, *Delhi* 16 A3 28 43N 77 20 E
Atzgersdorf, *Wien* 10 H9 48 8N 16 18 E
Aubervilliers, *Paris* 5 B4 48 54N 2 22 E
Aubing, *Mün.* 7 G9 48 9N 11 25 E
Auburn, *Syd.* 19 B3 33 51 S 151 1 E
Auburndale, *Bost.* 21 C2 42 20N 71 14W
Auckland Park, *Jobg.* 18 F9 26 11 S 28 0 E
Audubon, *Phil.* 24 A2 40 7N 75 25W
Auf-dem-Schnee, *Ruhr* 6 B6 51 26N 7 25 E
Auffargis, *Paris* 5 C1 48 42N 1 53 E
Augustówka, *Wsaw.* 10 E7 52 11N 21 5 E
Aulnay-sous-Bois, *Paris* 5 B4 48 56N 2 29 E
Aurelio, *Rome* 9 F9 51 54N 12 26 E
Ausîm, *El Qâ.* 18 C4 30 7N 31 8 E
Aussen Alster, *Hbg.* 7 D8 53 33N 10 0 E
Austerlitz, Gare d', *Paris* 5 B4 48 50N 2 22 E
Austin, *Chic.* 26 B2 41 53N 87 45W
Auteuil, *Mtrl.* 20 A3 43 37N 73 44W
Avedøre, *Købn.* 2 E9 55 37N 12 27 E
Aveley, *Lon.* 4 C6 51 29N 0 15 E
Avellaneda, *B.A.* 32 C4 34 40 S 58 22W
Avenel, *N.Y.* 22 D3 40 34N 74 16W
Avenel, *Wash.* 25 D8 38 59N 76 59W
Avila, Parque National el, *Car.* 30 D5 10 31N 66 52W
Avila, Pico, *Car.* 30 D5 10 32N 66 52W
Avini, *Nápl.* 9 J13 40 48N 14 28 E
Avondale, *Chic.* 26 B2 41 56N 87 41W
Avondale Heights, *Melb.* 19 E6 37 45 S 144 52 E
Avtovo, *St-Pet.* 11 B3 59 51N 30 16 E
Ayase, *Tōkyō* 13 D1 35 25N 139 26 E
Ayase →, *Tōkyō* 13 A3 35 52N 139 45 E
Ayazaga, *Ist.* 17 A2 41 6N 28 59 E
Ayer Chawan, P., *Sing.* 15 G7 1 16N 103 41 E
Ayer Merbau, P., *Sing.* 15 G7 1 16N 103 42 E
Ayía Paraskevi, *Ath.* 8 H11 38 1N 23 49 E
Áyios Dhimitrios, *Ath.* 8 J11 37 53N 23 44 E
Áyios Ioánnis Rendis, *Ath.* 8 J10 37 57N 23 39 E
Azabu, *Tōkyō* 13 C3 35 39N 139 43 E
Azadpur, *Delhi* 16 A2 28 42N 77 10 E
Azcapotzalco, *Méx.* 29 B2 19 28N 99 10W
Azteca, Estadia, *Méx.* 29 C3 19 8N 99 9W
Azusa, *L.A.* 28 B5 34 7N 117 54W

B

Ba He →, *Beij.* 14 B3 39 57N 116 27 E
Baba I., *Kar.* 17 H10 24 49N 66 57 E
Babarpur, *Delhi* 16 A2 28 41N 77 16 E
Babelsberg, *Berl.* 7 B1 52 22N 13 7 E
Babushkin, *Mos.* 11 D10 55 51N 37 42 E
Babylon, *N.Y.* 23 C9 40 42N 73 19W
Back →, *Balt.* 25 B4 39 17N 76 27W
Back B., *Bomb.* 16 H7 18 56N 72 48 E
Bacoor, *Manila* 15 E3 14 27N 120 56 E
Bacoor B., *Manila* 15 E3 14 27N 120 54 E
Badagri Cr. →, *Lagos* 18 B1 6 24N 7 17 E
Badahela, *Delhi* 16 B1 28 38N 77 4 E
Badalona, *Barc.* 8 D6 41 26N 2 14 E
Badersfeld, *Mün.* 7 F10 48 15N 11 31 E
Badgers Mt., *Lon.* 4 C5 51 20N 0 8 E
Badi, *Delhi* 16 A1 28 44N 77 8 E
Badinan, *Calc.* 16 C5 22 53N 88 14 E
Badu, *Rio J.* 31 B3 22 54 S 43 3W
Baerl, *Ruhr* 6 B2 51 29N 6 40 E
Bærum, *Oslo* 2 B3 59 54N 10 36 E
Bærums Verk, *Oslo* 2 B2 59 56N 10 28 E
Baggensfjärden, *Stock.* 3 E12 59 18N 18 19 E
Bággio, *Mil.* 9 E5 45 27N 9 6 E
Bāgh-e-Feiz, *Tehr.* 17 C4 35 44N 51 19 E
Baghdād, *Bagd.* 17 E8 33 20N 44 23 E
Bagmari, *Calc.* 16 E6 22 34N 88 23 E
Bagneux, *Paris* 5 C3 48 47N 2 18 E
Bagnolet, *Paris* 5 B4 48 52N 2 25 E
Bagnoli, *Nápl.* 9 J11 40 48N 14 9 E
Bagraula, *Delhi* 16 B1 28 34N 77 4 E
Bagsværd, *Købn.* 2 D9 55 45N 12 27 E
Bagsværd Sø, *Købn.* 2 D9 55 46N 12 28 E
Baguiati, *Calc.* 16 E6 22 36N 88 25 E
Bagumbayan, *Manila* 15 E4 14 28N 121 3 E
Baha'i Temple, *Chic.* 26 A2 42 4N 87 41W
Bahrenfeld, *Hbg.* 7 D7 53 34N 9 55 E
Bahtîm, *El Qâ.* 18 C5 30 8N 31 16 E
Bahu Bheri, *Calc.* 16 C5 22 50N 88 14 E
Baidyabati, *Calc.* 16 D5 22 46N 88 19 E
Baie-d'Urfé, *Mtrl.* 20 B2 43 25N 73 53W
Baierbrunn, *Mün.* 7 G10 48 1N 11 29 E
Baijala, *Calc.* 16 C5 22 51N 88 16 E
Baileys Crossroads, *Wash.* 25 D7 38 50N 77 6W
Bailly, *Paris* 5 B2 48 50N 2 4 E
Bainchipota, *Calc.* 16 C5 22 51N 88 16 E
Bair I., *S.F.* 27 C3 37 30N 122 13W
Bairro da Matriz, *S. Pau.* 31 F7 23 40 S 46 27W
Bairro do Limoeiro, *S. Pau.* 31 E7 23 30 S 46 27W
Baisha, *Gzh.* 14 G8 23 8N 113 11 E
Baisley Pond, *N.Y.* 23 C6 40 40N 73 47W
Baixa da Banheira, *Lisb.* 8 G8 38 39N 9 2W
Baiyun Shan, *Gzh.* 14 G8 23 8N 113 15 E
Baj Baj, *Calc.* 16 F5 22 28N 88 11 E
Bakirkoy, *Ist.* 17 B2 40 58N 28 52 E
Bakovka, *Mos.* 11 E8 55 40N 37 19 E
Bala-Cynwyd, *Phil.* 24 A3 40 0N 75 15W
Balagarh, *Calc.* 16 D6 22 44N 88 27 E
Balara, *Manila* 15 D4 14 39N 121 3 E
Balarambati, *Calc.* 16 D5 22 48N 88 12 E
Balashikha, *Mos.* 11 E11 55 48N 37 58 E
Bald Hill, *Bost.* 21 B3 42 38N 71 0W
Baldeador, *Rio J.* 31 B3 22 51 S 43 1W
Baldeneysee, *Ruhr* 6 B4 51 24N 7 1 E
Baldissero Torinese, *Tori.* 9 B3 45 4N 7 48 E
Baldpate Hill, *Bost.* 21 A3 42 42N 71 0W
Baldpate Pond, *Bost.* 21 A3 42 41N 71 0W
Baldwin, *N.Y.* 23 D7 40 38N 73 37W
Baldwin Hills, *L.A.* 28 B2 34 0N 118 21W
Baldwin Hills Res., *L.A.* 28 B2 34 0N 118 21W
Baldwin Park, *L.A.* 28 B5 34 5N 117 57W
Bal'etan →, *Gzh.* 14 G8 23 5N 113 14 E
Balgowlah, *Syd.* 19 A4 33 47 S 151 16 E
Balgowlah Heights, *Syd.* 19 A4 33 48 S 151 16 E
Balham, *Lon.* 4 C4 51 26N 0 8W
Balihati, *Calc.* 16 D5 22 44N 88 18 E
Balingsnäs, *Stock.* 3 E11 59 13N 18 0 E
Balingsta, *Stock.* 3 E11 59 12N 18 3 E
Balintawak, *Manila* 15 D3 14 39N 120 59 E
Balitai, *Tianj.* 14 E6 39 5N 117 11 E
Balizhuang, *Beij.* 14 B3 39 53N 116 28 E
Ballabhpur, *Calc.* 16 D6 22 44N 88 20 E
Ballainvilliers, *Paris* 5 C3 48 40N 2 17 E
Ballardvale, *Bost.* 21 B3 42 37N 71 9W
Ballenato, Pta., *La Hab.* 30 B2 23 55N 82 28W
Ballerup, *Købn.* 2 D9 55 43N 12 21 E
Bally, *Calc.* 16 E6 22 38N 88 20 E
Ballygunge, *Calc.* 16 E6 22 31N 88 21 E
Balmain, *Syd.* 19 B4 33 51 S 151 11 E
Balmumcu, *Ist.* 17 A3 41 3N 29 2 E
Balongbato, *Manila* 15 D3 14 39N 120 59 E
Baltikri, *Calc.* 16 E5 22 36N 88 18 E
Baltimore, *Balt.* 25 B3 39 17N 76 37W
Baltimore Highlands, *Balt.* 25 B3 39 14N 76 38W
Baltimore-Washington Int. Airport, *Balt.* 25 B3 39 11N 76 39W
Baluhati, *Calc.* 16 E5 22 39N 88 15 E
Balwyn, *Melb.* 19 E7 37 48 S 145 4 E
Balwyn North, *Melb.* 19 E7 37 47 S 145 4 E
Bambang, *Manila* 15 D4 14 31N 121 4 E
Bamondongri, *Bomb.* 16 H9 18 58N 73 1 E
Ban Baan Phichit, *Bangk.* 15 B2 13 49N 100 37 E
Ban Hugli, *Calc.* 16 E6 22 38N 88 22 E
Ban Lat Phrao, *Bangk.* 15 B2 13 47N 100 35 E
Banabuey →, *La Hab.* 30 B2 23 5N 82 27W
Bananal, *S. Pau.* 31 D5 23 27 S 46 41W
Banática, *Lisb.* 8 F7 38 40N 9 11W
Bandeirantes, Praia dos, *Rio J.* 31 C1 23 0 S 43 23W
Bandipur, *Calc.* 16 D6 22 43N 88 26 E
Bandipur, *Calc.* 16 C4 22 50N 88 9 E
Bandra, *Bomb.* 16 G7 19 3N 72 49 E
Bandra Pt., *Bomb.* 16 G7 19 2N 72 49 E
Banfield, *B.A.* 32 C4 34 44 S 58 24W
Bang Kapi, *Bangk.* 15 B2 13 45N 100 38 E
Bang Khen, *Bangk.* 15 A2 13 52N 100 35 E
Bang Na, *Bangk.* 15 B2 13 40N 100 36 E
Bang Su, Khlong →, *Bangk.* 15 B2 13 47N 100 31 E
Bangbae, *Sŏul* 12 H7 37 29N 126 59 E
Banghag, *Sŏul* 12 G8 37 38N 127 1 E
Bangka, *Jak.* 15 J9 6 15 S 106 48 E
Bangkok, *Bangk.* 15 B2 13 44N 100 30 E
Bangkok Noi, Khlong →, *Bangk.* 15 B1 13 45N 100 29 E
Bangkok Yai, *Bangk.* 15 B1 13 43N 100 29 E
Bangkok Yai, Khlong →, *Bangk.* 15 B1 13 44N 100 29 E
Banglo, *Calc.* 16 E5 22 31N 88 14 E
Bangrak, *Bangk.* 15 B2 13 43N 100 31 E
Bangu, *Rio J.* 31 B1 22 52 S 43 26W
Bangu, Sa. do, *Rio J.* 31 B1 22 53 S 43 24W
Bankipur, *Calc.* 16 D5 22 47N 88 13 E
Bankra, *Calc.* 16 E5 22 36N 88 17 E
Banks, C., *Syd.* 19 C4 34 0 S 151 16 E
Bankstown, *Syd.* 19 B3 33 55 S 151 2 E
Bankstown Aerodrome, *Syd.* 19 B2 33 55 S 150 59 E
Banna →, *Tori.* 9 A3 45 12N 7 42 E
Banstala, *Calc.* 16 E6 22 31N 88 24 E
Banstead, *Lon.* 4 D3 51 18N 0 12W
Bantra, *Calc.* 16 E5 22 35N 88 18 E
Banyule Flats Res., *Melb.* 19 E7 37 44 S 145 5 E
Baquirivú, *S. Pau.* 31 D7 23 26 S 46 28W
Baquirivú-Guaçu, *S. Pau.* 31 D7 23 28 S 46 28W
Bara, *Calc.* 16 D5 22 45N 88 16 E
Baragwanath Airfield, *Jobg.* 18 F8 26 14 S 27 58 E
Barai, *Calc.* 16 C6 22 52N 88 22 E
Barajas, *Mdrd.* 8 B3 40 28N 3 34W
Barajas, Aeropuerto Transoceanico de, *Mdrd.* 8 B3 40 28N 3 33W
Barakpur, *Calc.* 16 D6 22 47N 88 21 E
Baranagar, *Calc.* 16 E6 22 38N 88 22 E
Barbaiana, *Mil.* 9 D5 45 32N 9 1 E
Barca, *Tori.* 9 B3 45 6N 7 43 E
Barcarena, *Lisb.* 8 F7 38 43N 9 16W
Barcarena →, *Lisb.* 8 F7 38 41N 9 16W
Barcelona, *Barc.* 8 D6 41 22N 2 10 E
Barcelona-Prat, Aeropuerta de, *Barc.* 8 E5 41 17N 2 5 E
Barceloneta, *Barc.* 8 D6 41 22N 2 11 E
Barcroft, L., *Wash.* 25 D6 38 50N 77 9W
Baréggio, *Mil.* 9 E5 45 28N 9 0 E
Bariti Bil, *Calc.* 16 D6 22 48N 88 25 E
Barkarby, *Stock.* 3 D10 59 24N 17 52 E
Barker Pt., *N.Y.* 23 B6 40 50N 73 44W
Barking, *Lon.* 4 B5 51 32N 0 5 E
Barkingside, *Lon.* 4 B5 51 35N 0 4 E
Barlovento, *La Hab.* 30 B2 23 5N 82 28W
Barmbek, *Hbg.* 7 D8 53 34N 10 1 E
Barmen, *Ruhr* 6 C5 51 16N 7 12 E
Barneau, *Paris* 5 D6 48 38N 2 43 E
Barnes, *Lon.* 4 C3 51 28N 0 14W
Barnet, *Lon.* 4 B3 51 39N 0 11W
Barnsboro, *Phil.* 24 C4 39 45N 75 9W
Baronia Park, *Syd.* 19 A3 33 49 S 151 8 E
Barop, *Ruhr* 6 B6 51 29N 7 25 E
Barra, *Nápl.* 9 H12 40 50N 14 19 E
Barra Andai, *Kar.* 17 H11 24 47N 66 59 E
Barra Funda, *S. Pau.* 31 E6 23 31 S 46 39W
Barracas, *B.A.* 32 B4 34 39 S 58 24W
Barrackpore Airport, *Calc.* 16 D6 22 46N 88 21 E
Barrancas, *Stgo* 30 J10 33 26 S 70 44W
Barranco, *Lima* 30 G8 12 9 S 77 2W
Barreiro, *Lisb.* 8 G8 38 39N 9 5W
Barreto, *Rio J.* 31 B3 22 50 S 43 5W
Barrientos, *Méx.* 29 A2 19 34N 99 11W
Barrington, *Phil.* 24 B4 39 52N 75 3W
Barrio de La Estación, *Mdrd.* 8 B3 40 26N 3 32W
Bartala, *Calc.* 16 E5 22 32N 88 15 E
Barton Park, *Syd.* 19 B3 33 56 S 151 9 E
Bartyki, *Wsaw.* 10 F7 52 10N 21 6 E
Baru, Kali →, *Jak.* 15 J10 6 12 S 106 51 E
Baruipara, *Calc.* 16 D5 22 45N 88 13 E
Baruta, *Car.* 30 E5 10 26N 66 52W
Barvikha, *Mos.* 11 E7 55 44N 37 16 E
Basai Darapur, *Delhi* 16 B1 28 38N 77 6 E
Bass Hill, *Syd.* 19 B3 33 54 S 151 0 E
Bassett, *L.A.* 28 B5 34 3N 117 59W
Bastille, Place de la, *Paris* 5 B4 48 51N 2 22 E
Bastos, *Rio J.* 31 B1 22 52 S 43 21W
Basudebpur, *Calc.* 16 D6 22 49N 88 24 E
Basus, *El Qâ.* 18 C5 30 7N 31 12 E
Batanagar, *Calc.* 16 E5 22 31N 88 15 E
Batenbrock, *Ruhr* 6 A3 51 31N 6 57 E
Bath Beach, *N.Y.* 22 D4 40 36N 74 0W
Bath I., *Kar.* 17 H11 24 49N 67 1 E
Batok, Bukit, *Sing.* 15 F7 1 21N 103 46 E
Battersea, *Lon.* 4 C4 51 28N 0 9W
Baturino, *Mos.* 11 F9 55 35N 37 30 E
Bauman, *Mos.* 11 E10 55 45N 37 40 E
Baumgarten, *Wien* 10 G9 48 12N 16 17 E
Bauria, *Calc.* 16 E5 22 30N 88 10 E
Baxter Estates, *N.Y.* 23 B6 40 50N 73 42W
Bay Farm I., *S.F.* 27 B3 37 44N 122 14W
Bay Meadows Race Track, *S.F.* 27 C3 37 32N 122 17W
Bay Park, *N.Y.* 23 D7 40 37N 73 39W
Bay Ridge, *N.Y.* 22 D4 40 37N 74 1W
Bay Ridge Channel, *N.Y.* 22 D4 40 39N 74 1W
Bay Shore Park, *Balt.* 25 B4 39 13N 76 25W
Baykoz, *Ist.* 17 A3 41 7N 29 7 E
Bayonne, *N.Y.* 22 C4 40 40N 74 6W
Bayshore, *S.F.* 27 B3 37 42N 122 24W
Bayside, *N.Y.* 23 C6 40 45N 73 46W
Bayswater, *Lon.* 4 B3 51 30N 0 10W
Bayswater, *Melb.* 19 F8 37 50 S 145 17 E
Bayview, *S.F.* 27 B2 37 44N 122 23W
Bayville, *N.Y.* 23 B7 40 54N 73 33W
Bāzār, *Tehr.* 17 C5 35 40N 51 25 E
Beachmont, *Bost.* 21 C4 42 23N 70 59W
Beacon Hill, *H.K.* 12 D6 22 21N 114 10 E
Beaconsfield, *Mtrl.* 20 B2 43 25N 73 53W
Beacontree Heath, *Lon.* 4 B5 51 33N 0 9 E
Beam →, *Lon.* 4 B6 51 30N 0 10 E
Bear Cr. →, *Balt.* 25 B3 39 13N 76 30W
Bear Gulch Res., *S.F.* 27 D3 37 26N 122 13W
Beato, *Lisb.* 8 F8 38 44N 9 5W
Beauchamp, *Paris* 5 A3 49 0N 2 11 E
Beaumonte Heights, *Trto.* 20 D7 43 45N 79 34W
Beaverdam Cr. →, *Wash.* 25 C8 39 0N 76 5W
Bebek, *Ist.* 17 A3 41 4N 29 2 E
Beccar, *B.A.* 32 A3 34 27 S 58 32W
Běchovice, *Pra.* 10 B3 50 4N 14 36 E
Beck L., *Chic.* 26 A1 42 4N 87 52W
Beckenham, *Lon.* 4 C4 51 24N 0 1W
Beckhausen, *Ruhr* 6 A4 51 33N 7 1 E
Beckton, *Lon.* 4 B5 51 30N 0 4 E
Beddington, *Lon.* 4 C4 51 21N 0 8W
Beddington Corner, *Lon.* 4 C4 51 23N 0 9W
Bedford, *Bost.* 21 C2 42 27N 71 15W
Bedford Park, *Chic.* 26 C2 41 46N 87 46W
Bedford Park, *N.Y.* 23 B5 40 52N 73 52W
Bedford Stuyvesant, *N.Y.* 22 C5 40 41N 73 56W
Bedford View, *Jobg.* 18 F9 26 10 S 28 7 E
Bedok, *Sing.* 15 G8 1 19N 103 56 E
Beeck, *Ruhr* 6 B2 51 28N 6 44 E
Beeckerwerth, *Ruhr* 6 B2 51 28N 6 42 E
Behala, *Calc.* 16 E5 22 30N 88 18 E
Bei Hai, *Beij.* 14 B3 39 54N 116 21 E
Beicai, *Shang.* 14 J12 31 11N 121 32 E
Beicang, *Tianj.* 14 D5 39 13N 117 7 E
Beigai, *Tianj.* 14 E6 39 9N 117 10 E
Beijiaoshichang, *Beij.* 14 B2 39 57N 116 19 E
Beijing, *Beij.* 14 B2 39 53N 116 21 E
Beinasco, *Tori.* 9 B2 45 1N 7 34 E
Beirolas, *Lisb.* 8 F8 38 46N 9 5W
Beitsun, *Gzh.* 14 G8 23 7N 113 10 E
Békásmegyer, *Bud.* 10 J13 47 35N 19 3 E
Bekkelaget, *Oslo* 2 B4 59 53N 10 47 E
Bel Air, *L.A.* 28 B2 34 4N 118 27W
Bela Vista, *S. Pau.* 31 E6 23 33 S 46 38W
Bélanger, *Mtrl.* 20 A3 43 35N 73 42W
Belas, *Lisb.* 8 F7 38 46N 9 17W
Belém, *Lisb.* 8 F7 38 41N 9 12W
Belém, Torre de, *Lisb.* 8 F7 38 41N 9 12W
Belenzinho, *S. Pau.* 31 E6 23 32 S 46 34W
Belfield, *Syd.* 19 B3 33 53 S 151 6 E
Belgachi, *Calc.* 16 E5 22 36N 88 18 E
Belgharia, *Calc.* 16 E6 22 39N 88 22 E
Belgrano, *B.A.* 32 B4 34 33 S 58 27W
Belgrave, *Melb.* 19 F9 37 54 S 145 21 E
Bell Gardens, *L.A.* 28 C4 33 58N 118 9W
Bella Vista, *B.A.* 32 B2 34 34 S 58 41W
Bellaire, *N.Y.* 23 C6 40 42N 73 44W
Bellavista, *Lima* 30 G8 12 4 S 77 8W
Bellavista, *Stgo* 30 K11 33 31 S 70 35W
Belle Harbour, *N.Y.* 23 D5 40 34N 73 51W
Belle Haven, *N.Y.* 23 A7 41 0N 73 37W
Belle Haven, *Wash.* 25 E7 38 46N 77 3W
Bellefonte, *Phil.* 24 C1 39 45N 75 30W
Bellerose, *N.Y.* 23 C6 40 44N 73 42W
Belleview, *Wash.* 25 D6 38 57N 77 14W
Belleville, *N.Y.* 22 C4 40 48N 74 8W
Bellflower, *L.A.* 28 C4 33 53N 118 7W
Bellingham, *Lon.* 4 C4 51 25N 0 1W
Bellmawr, *Phil.* 24 B4 39 52N 75 5W
Bellmore, *N.Y.* 23 D7 40 39N 73 31W
Bello, *La Hab.* 30 B2 23 5N 82 24W
Bells Lake, *Phil.* 24 C4 39 45N 75 3W
Bellwood, *Chic.* 26 B1 41 52N 87 53W
Belmont, *Bost.* 21 C2 42 23N 71 10W
Belmont, *Lon.* 4 B3 51 36N 0 18W
Belmont, *S.F.* 27 C3 37 31N 122 17W
Belmont Cragin, *Chic.* 26 B2 41 56N 87 45W
Belmont Harbor, *Chic.* 26 B3 41 56N 87 38W
Belmont Hills, *Phil.* 24 A3 40 1N 75 15W
Belmont Slough, *S.F.* 27 C3 37 32N 122 15W
Belmore, *Syd.* 19 B3 33 55 S 151 5 E
Belopurpada, *Bomb.* 16 G9 19 0N 73 1 E
Beltsville, *Wash.* 25 C8 39 2N 76 54W
Beltsville Airport, *Wash.* 25 C9 39 1N 76 49W
Belur, *Calc.* 16 E6 22 37N 88 21 E
Belvedere, *Lon.* 4 C5 51 29N 0 9 E
Belvedere, *S.F.* 27 A2 37 52N 122 27W
Belyayevo Bogorodskoye, *Mos.* 11 F9 55 39N 37 31 E
Bemböle, *Hels.* 3 B2 60 13N 24 39 E
Bemis Woods, *Chic.* 26 C1 41 49N 87 54W
Bemowo, *Wsaw.* 10 E6 52 15N 20 53 E
Benavidez, *B.A.* 32 A2 34 24 S 58 41W
Bendale, *Trto.* 20 D9 43 45N 79 13W
Bendungan Hilir, *Jak.* 15 J9 6 12 S 106 48 E
Benefica, *Rio J.* 31 B2 22 52 S 43 14W
Benfica, *Lisb.* 8 F7 38 45N 9 11W
Benin B., *Lagos* 18 B2 6 24N 7 28 E
Benjamin Franklin Br., *Phil.* 24 B4 39 57N 75 8W
Benoni, *Jobg.* 18 F10 26 11 S 28 18 E
Benoni South, *Jobg.* 18 F10 26 12 S 28 17 E
Bensenville, *Chic.* 26 B1 41 57N 87 56W
Bensonhurst, *N.Y.* 22 D5 40 35N 73 59W
Bentleigh, *Melb.* 19 F7 37 54 S 145 2 E
Bentleigh East, *Melb.* 19 F7 37 54 S 145 4 E
Beraberi, *Calc.* 16 D6 22 46N 88 27 E
Berario, *Jobg.* 18 E8 26 7 S 27 57 E
Berazategui, *B.A.* 32 C5 34 45 S 58 15W
Berea, *Jobg.* 18 F9 26 10 S 28 3 E
Berg am Laim, *Mün.* 7 G10 48 7N 11 38 E
Bergbaumuseum, *Ruhr* 6 B5 51 29N 7 13 E
Bergenfield, *N.Y.* 22 B5 40 55N 73 59W
Berger, *Oslo* 2 B6 59 56N 11 7 E
Bergerhausen, *Ruhr* 6 B4 51 26N 7 2 E
Bergerhof, *Ruhr* 6 C6 51 12N 7 21 E
Bergham, *Mün.* 7 G10 48 2N 11 37 E
Berghausen, *Ruhr* 6 A5 51 36N 7 12 E
Berghm-Oestrum, *Ruhr* 6 B1 51 25N 6 39 E
Bergstedt, *Hbg.* 7 C8 53 40N 10 7 E
Beri, *Barc.* 8 D5 41 20N 2 1 E
Berih, Sungei →, *Sing.* 15 F7 1 22N 103 40 E
Berkeley, *Chic.* 26 B1 41 53N 87 54W
Berkeley, *S.F.* 27 A3 37 51N 122 16W
Berkeley Heights, *N.Y.* 22 C2 40 40N 74 26W
Berkeley Hills, *S.F.* 27 A3 37 51N 122 11W
Berlin, *Berl.* 7 A3 52 31N 13 23 E
Berlin, *Phil.* 24 C5 39 47N 74 55W
Bermondsey, *Lon.* 4 C4 51 29N 0 3W
Bernabeu, Estadio, *Mdrd.* 8 B2 40 27N 3 41W
Bernal, *B.A.* 32 C5 34 43 S 58 17W
Bernal Heights, *S.F.* 27 B2 37 44N 122 24W
Berne, *Hbg.* 7 D8 53 38N 10 8 E
Berngardovka, *St-Pet.* 11 A5 60 0N 30 34 E
Berthpage, *N.Y.* 23 C8 40 45N 73 29W
Bertlich, *Ruhr* 6 A4 51 36N 7 4 E
Bertolla Barca, *Tori.* 9 B3 45 6N 7 44 E
Berwyn, *Chic.* 26 B2 41 50N 87 47W
Berwyn, *Phil.* 24 A2 40 2N 75 26W
Berwyn Heights, *Wash.* 25 D8 38 59N 76 55W
Besedy, *Mos.* 11 F10 55 38N 37 47 E
Besiktas, *Ist.* 17 A3 41 2N 29 0 E
Beskudnikovo, *Mos.* 11 D9 55 52N 37 34 E
Besós →, *Barc.* 8 D6 41 24N 2 13 E
Bessancourt, *Paris* 5 A3 49 2N 2 12 E
Bestazzo, *Mil.* 9 E5 45 25N 9 0 E
Bethayres, *Phil.* 24 A4 40 7N 75 3W
Bethesda, *Wash.* 25 D7 38 59N 77 6W
Bethlehem Steel Plant, *Balt.* 25 B4 39 13N 76 29W
Bethnal Green, *Lon.* 4 B4 51 31N 0 2W
Bethpage State Park, *N.Y.* 23 C8 40 45N 73 25W
Betor, *Calc.* 16 E5 22 34N 88 17 E
Beuvronne →, *Paris* 5 B6 48 59N 2 40 E
Beverley, *Chic.* 26 C3 41 42N 87 39W
Beverley Hills, *Syd.* 19 B3 33 56 S 151 5 E
Beverley Park, *Syd.* 19 B3 33 58 S 151 8 E
Beverly, *Bost.* 21 B4 42 34N 70 53W
Beverly, *Phil.* 24 A5 40 3N 74 55W
Beverly Glen, *L.A.* 28 B2 34 6N 118 26W
Beverly Harbor, *Bost.* 21 B4 42 32N 70 51W
Beverly Hills, *L.A.* 28 B2 34 5N 118 24W
Beverly Municipal Airport, *Bost.* 21 B4 42 36N 70 55W
Bexley, *Lon.* 4 C5 51 26N 0 8 E
Bexley, *Syd.* 19 B3 33 56 S 151 7 E
Bexleyheath, *Lon.* 4 C5 51 27N 0 8 E
Beyenburg, *Ruhr* 6 C5 51 15N 7 19 E
Beylerbeyi, *Ist.* 17 A3 41 2N 29 2 E
Beyoğlu, *Ist.* 17 A2 41 1N 28 58 E
Bezons, *Paris* 5 B3 48 56N 2 13 E
Bhadrakali, *Calc.* 16 D6 22 40N 88 20 E
Bhadreswar, *Calc.* 16 D5 22 49N 88 22 E
Bhadua, *Calc.* 16 D5 22 40N 88 12 E
Bhalswa, *Delhi* 16 A2 28 44N 77 10 E
Bhambo Khān Qarmati, *Kar.* 17 H11 24 49N 67 7 E
Bhandardaha, *Calc.* 16 E5 22 37N 88 12 E
Bhatpara, *Calc.* 16 C6 22 52N 88 25 E
Bhatpur, *Calc.* 16 D6 22 43N 88 25 E
Bhatsala, *Calc.* 16 E5 22 30N 88 16 E
Bhawanipore, *Calc.* 16 E6 22 32N 88 21 E
Bhopura, *Delhi* 16 A2 28 41N 77 19 E
Białołeka Dworska, *Wsaw.* 10 E7 52 19N 21 1 E
Bickley, *Lon.* 4 C5 51 23N 0 3 E
Bicutan, *Manila* 15 D4 14 30N 121 3 E
Bidyadharpur, *Calc.* 16 C6 22 50N 88 24 E
Bielany, *Wsaw.* 10 E6 52 17N 20 57 E
Biesdorf, *Berl.* 7 A4 52 30N 13 33 E
Bièvre →, *Paris* 5 C2 48 44N 2 9 E
Bièvres, *Paris* 5 C3 48 45N 2 13 E
Big Timber Cr. →, *Phil.* 24 B4 39 52N 75 7W
Big Tujunga Canyon →, *L.A.* 28 A3 34 16N 118 12W
Biggin Hill, *Lon.* 4 D5 51 18N 0 1 E
Bijoki, *Tōkyō* 13 B2 35 49N 139 38 E
Bilibiran, *Manila* 15 E5 14 29N 121 10 E
Bilk, *Ruhr* 6 C2 51 12N 6 46 E
Billbrook, *Hbg.* 7 D8 53 31N 10 4 E
Bille →, *Hbg.* 7 D8 53 32N 10 4 E
Billerica, *Bost.* 21 B2 42 33N 71 16W
Billinghurst, *B.A.* 32 B3 34 34 S 58 37W
Billings, Represa, *S. Pau.* 31 F6 23 42 S 46 39W
Billstedt, *Hbg.* 7 D8 53 32N 10 6 E
Billwerder, *Hbg.* 7 D8 53 30N 10 7 E
Billwerder B., *Hbg.* 7 D8 53 31N 10 3 E
Binacayan, *Manila* 15 E3 14 27N 120 55 E
Binangonan, *Manila* 15 E5 14 28N 121 10 E
Binaria, *Jak.* 15 H10 6 7 S 106 51 E
Bingzhoubao, *Gzh.* 14 G8 23 2N 113 11 E
Binningsvatna, *Oslo* 2 C6 50 46N 11 3 E
Binondo, *Manila* 15 D3 14 36N 120 58 E
Binzago, *Mil.* 9 D5 45 37N 9 8 E
Birak el Kiyam, *El Qâ.* 18 C4 30 2N 31 9 E
Birch Cliff, *Trto.* 20 D9 43 41N 79 16W
Bird →, *Balt.* 25 A4 39 22N 76 22W
Birka, *Stock.* 3 D8 59 20N 17 33 E
Birkenhöhe, *Berl.* 7 A4 52 38N 13 36 E
Birkenstein, *Berl.* 7 A5 52 31N 13 40 E
Birkholz, *Berl.* 7 A4 52 37N 13 34 E
Birkholzaue, *Berl.* 7 A4 52 38N 13 36 E
Biryulyovo, *Mos.* 11 F10 55 35N 37 40 E
Bisamberg, *Wien* 10 G10 48 19N 16 21 E
Bispebjerg, *Købn.* 2 D10 55 42N 12 31 E
Bitsa, *Mos.* 11 F9 55 35N 37 36 E
Biwon Secret Garden, *Sŏul* 12 G7 37 34N 126 59 E
Bizard, Î., *Mtrl.* 20 B2 43 29N 73 53W
Björknas, *Stock.* 3 E12 59 19N 18 12 E
Björköfjärden, *Hels.* 3 C2 60 7N 24 38 E
Black Cr. →, *Trto.* 20 D8 43 40N 79 30W
Blackburn, *Melb.* 19 E7 37 48 S 145 9 E
Blackburn L., *Melb.* 19 E7 37 49 S 145 9 E
Blackburn South, *Melb.* 19 F7 37 50 S 145 9 E
Blackfen, *Lon.* 4 C5 51 26N 0 6 E
Blackheath, *Jobg.* 18 E8 26 8 S 27 57 E
Blackheath, *Lon.* 4 C5 51 28N 0 0 E
Blackmore, *Lon.* 4 A6 51 41N 0 19 E
Blacktown, *Syd.* 19 A2 33 46 S 150 56 E
Blackwall, *Lon.* 4 B4 51 30N 0 0 E
Blackwood, *Phil.* 24 C4 39 47N 75 4W
Bladensburg, *Wash.* 25 D8 38 55N 76 55W
Blairgowrie, *Jobg.* 18 E9 26 6 S 28 0 E
Blakehurst, *Syd.* 19 B3 33 59 S 151 6 E
Blakstad, *Oslo* 2 C2 50 49N 10 28 E
Blanco, C., *Car.* 30 D5 10 36N 66 59W
Blankenburg, *Berl.* 7 A3 52 35N 13 27 E
Blankenese, *Hbg.* 7 D6 53 33N 9 48 E
Blankenfelde, *Berl.* 7 A3 52 37N 13 23 E
Blankenstein, *Ruhr* 6 B5 51 24N 7 11 E
Blenheim, *Phil.* 24 C4 39 48N 75 4W
Bliersheim, *Ruhr* 6 B2 51 23N 6 42 E
Blind Cr. →, *Melb.* 19 F8 37 53 S 145 12 E
Blizne, *Wsaw.* 10 E6 52 14N 20 52 E
Bloomfield, *N.Y.* 22 C3 40 48N 74 12W
Bloomingdale, *N.Y.* 22 A3 41 0N 74 19W
Bloomsbury, *Balt.* 25 B2 39 15N 76 44W
Błota, *Wsaw.* 10 F8 52 9N 21 11 E
Bloubosspruit →, *Jobg.* 18 F9 26 16 S 28 0 E
Blue Hills Reservation, *Bost.* 21 D3 42 13N 71 5W
Blue Island, *Chic.* 26 C2 41 40N 87 40W
Bluff Hd., *H.K.* 12 E6 22 11N 114 12 E
Blumberg, *Berl.* 7 A4 52 36N 13 39 E
Blunt Pt., *S.F.* 27 A2 37 51N 122 25W
Blutenberg, *Mün.* 7 G9 48 9N 11 27 E
Blylaget, *Oslo* 2 C4 59 46N 10 41 E
Boa Vista, Alto do, *Rio J.* 31 B2 22 58 S 43 16W
Boa Vista, Morro, *Rio J.* 31 B3 22 53 S 43 5W
Boadilla del Monte, *Mdrd.* 8 B1 40 24N 3 52W
Boardwalk, *N.Y.* 23 D6 40 34N 73 49W
Boavista, *Lisb.* 8 F8 38 48N 9 8W
Bobäck, *Hels.* 3 B2 60 10N 24 31 E
Boberg, *Hbg.* 7 D8 53 30N 10 9 E
Bobigny, *Paris* 5 B4 48 54N 2 26 E
Bobylyskaya, *St-Pet.* 11 B3 59 59N 30 10 E
Bocanegra, *Lima* 30 F8 11 59 S 77 7W
Boccea, *Rome* 9 F8 41 57N 12 19 E
Bochold, *Ruhr* 6 B3 51 28N 6 57 E
Bochum, *Ruhr* 6 B5 51 28N 7 13 E
Bockum, *Ruhr* 6 B1 51 21N 6 37 E
Bodelschwingh, *Ruhr* 6 A6 51 33N 7 22 E
Bodomjärvi, *Hels.* 3 B3 60 15N 24 40 E
Bogenhausen, *Mün.* 7 G10 48 8N 11 36 E
Bognæs, *Købn.* 2 D7 55 41N 12 1 E
Bogorodskoye, *Mos.* 11 E10 55 48N 37 42 E
Bogota, *N.Y.* 22 B4 40 52N 74 2W
Bogstadvatnet, *Oslo* 2 B3 59 58N 10 37 E
Bohaidalu, *Tianj.* 14 E6 39 7N 117 12 E
Bohnsdorf, *Berl.* 7 B4 52 23N 13 34 E
Bois-Colombes, *Paris* 5 B3 48 55N 2 16 E
Bois-d'Arcy, *Paris* 5 C2 48 48N 2 1 E
Boisement, *Paris* 5 A2 49 1N 2 0 E
Boissy-St.-Léger, *Paris* 5 C5 48 44N 2 31 E
Boksburg, *Jobg.* 18 F10 26 12 S 28 15 E
Boksburg North, *Jobg.* 18 F10 26 12 S 28 15 E
Boksburg South, *Jobg.* 18 F10 26 13 S 28 16 E
Boldinasco, *Mil.* 9 E5 45 29N 9 8 E
Bøler, *Oslo* 2 B5 59 53N 10 50 E
Bollate, *Mil.* 9 D5 45 32N 9 7 E
Bollensdorf, *Berl.* 7 A5 52 30N 13 42 E
Bollmora, *Stock.* 3 E12 59 14N 18 14 E
Bolshaya Nevka, *St-Pet.* 11 B3 59 58N 30 18 E
Bolshaya-Okhta, *St-Pet.* 11 B4 59 56N 30 26 E
Bolshoi Theatre, *Mos.* 11 E9 55 45N 37 37 E
Bom Retiro, *S. Pau.* 31 E6 23 31 S 46 38W
Bombay, *Bomb.* 16 H8 18 56N 72 50 E
Bombay Harbour, *Bomb.* 16 H8 18 58N 72 55 E
Bombay Univ., *Bomb.* 16 H7 18 55N 72 49 E
Bommern, *Ruhr* 6 B6 51 25N 7 20 E
Bonaero Park, *Jobg.* 18 E10 26 7 S 28 15 E
Bondi, *Syd.* 19 B4 33 53 S 151 16 E
Bondoufle, *Paris* 5 D4 48 36N 2 22 E
Bondy, *Paris* 5 B4 48 54N 2 28 E
Bondy, Forêt de, *Paris* 5 B5 48 54N 2 33 E
Bonifacio Monument, *Manila* 15 D3 14 38N 120 58 E
Bonifica di Maccarese, *Rome* 9 F8 41 50N 12 15 E
Bonifica di Porto, *Rome* 9 G8 41 48N 12 16 E
Bonita, Pt., *S.F.* 27 B1 37 48N 122 31W
Bonnelles, *Paris* 5 D2 48 37N 2 1 E
Bonneuil-sur-Marne, *Paris* 5 C5 48 46N 2 30 E
Bönningstedt, *Hbg.* 7 C7 53 40N 9 54 E
Bonnyrigg, *Syd.* 19 B2 33 53 S 150 54 E
Bonsari, *Bomb.* 16 G9 19 4N 73 1 E
Bonsucesso, *Rio J.* 31 B2 22 51 S 43 15W
Boo, *Stock.* 3 D12 59 20N 18 16 E
Boonton, *N.Y.* 22 B2 40 54N 74 24W
Boonton Res., *N.Y.* 22 B2 40 53N 74 24W
Booth Corner, *Phil.* 24 B2 39 50N 75 29W
Boothwyn, *Phil.* 24 C2 39 49N 75 26W
Borbeck, *Ruhr* 6 B3 51 28N 6 56 E
Bordeaux, *Jobg.* 18 E9 26 5 S 28 1 E
Bordeaux, *Mtrl.* 20 A3 43 31N 73 43W
Borehamwood, *Lon.* 4 B3 51 39N 0 15W
Borgaretto, *Tori.* 9 B2 45 0N 7 35 E
Bórgaro Torinese, *Tori.* 9 B2 45 9N 7 39 E
Borghese, Villa, *Rome* 9 F9 41 54N 12 29 E
Borisovo, *Mos.* 11 F10 55 38N 37 44 E
Borle, *Bomb.* 16 G8 19 2N 72 54 E
Bornig, *Ruhr* 6 A5 51 33N 7 16 E
Bornsjön, *Stock.* 3 E9 59 14N 17 44 E
Boronia, *Melb.* 19 F8 37 51 S 145 17 E
Borough Green, *Lon.* 4 D6 51 17N 0 18 E
Borough Park, *N.Y.* 22 D5 40 38N 73 59W
Børtervatna, *Oslo* 2 C6 50 46N 11 3 E
Boscoreale, *Nápl.* 9 J13 40 46N 14 28 E
Boscotrecase, *Nápl.* 9 J13 40 46N 14 27 E
Bösinghovn, *Ruhr* 6 C1 51 18N 6 38 E
Bosmont, *Jobg.* 18 F8 26 10 S 27 57 E
Bosön, *Stock.* 3 D12 59 22N 18 11 E
Bosporus = Istanbul Boğazi, *Ist.* 17 A3 41 5N 29 3 E
Bosque da Saúde, *S. Pau.* 31 E6 23 36 S 46 37W
Bosques, *B.A.* 32 C5 34 48 S 58 15W
Bossley Park, *Syd.* 19 B2 33 51 S 150 53 E
Bossucaba →, *S. Pau.* 31 E5 23 31 S 46 46W
Bostanci, *Ist.* 17 B3 40 57N 29 5 E
Bostelbek, *Hbg.* 7 E7 53 28N 9 55 E
Boston, *Bost.* 21 C3 42 21N 71 3W
Boston B., *Bost.* 21 C4 42 22N 70 55W
Boston Harbor, *Bost.* 21 C4 42 20N 70 58W
Boston Hill, *Bost.* 21 B3 42 38N 71 5W
Botany, *Syd.* 19 B4 33 56 S 151 12 E
Botany B., *Lon.* 4 A4 51 40N 0 7W
Botany B., *Syd.* 19 B4 33 58 S 151 11 E
Botič →, *Pra.* 10 B3 50 4N 14 26 E
Botkyrka, *Stock.* 3 E9 59 15N 17 49 E
Botofogo, *Rio J.* 31 B2 22 56 S 43 10W
Bottrop, *Ruhr* 6 A3 51 32N 6 57 E
Bötzow, *Berl.* 7 A1 52 39N 13 8 E
Bouafle, *Paris* 5 B1 48 57N 1 54 E
Boucherville, *Mtrl.* 20 A5 43 36N 73 28W
Boucherville, Îs. de, *Mtrl.* 20 A5 43 36N 73 28W
Bougival, *Paris* 5 B2 48 51N 2 8 E
Boulder Pt., *H.K.* 12 E5 22 14N 114 6 E

Choisy-le-Roi 35

Boullay-les-Troux, Paris 5 C2 48 40N 2 2 E
Boulogne, B.A. 32 B3 34 30 S 58 33W
Boulogne, Bois de, Paris 5 B3 48 51N 2 14 E
Boulogne-Billancourt, Paris 5 B3 48 50N 2 14 E
Bouqueval, Paris 5 A4 49 1N 2 25 E
Bourg-la-Reine, Paris 5 C3 48 46N 2 19 E
Boussy-St.-Antoine, Paris 5 C5 48 41N 2 33 E
Bouviers, Paris 5 C2 48 46N 2 4 E
Bovert, Ruhr 6 C1 51 16N 6 37 E
Bovisa, Mil. 9 D6 45 30N 9 10 E
Bovísio-Masciago, Mil. 9 D5 45 36N 9 8 E
Bow, Lon. 4 B4 51 31N 0 1W
Bowleys Quarters, Balt. 25 A4 39 20N 76 24W
Box Hill, Melb. 19 E7 37 48 S 145 6 E
Boxford State Forest, Bost. 21 B3 42 39N 71 2W
Boy, Ruhr 6 A3 51 31N 7 0 E
Boyaciköy, Ist. 17 A3 41 5N 29 2 E
Boye →, Ruhr 6 A3 51 30N 6 59 E
Boyle Heights, L.A. 28 B3 34 1N 118 12 E
Braddell Heights, Sing. 15 F8 1 20N 103 51 E
Brahmanpur, Bomb. 16 G8 19 5N 72 52 E
Braintree, Bost. 21 D3 42 12N 71 0W
Brakpan, Jobg. 18 F11 26 14 S 28 20 E
Brambauer, Ruhr 6 A6 51 35N 7 26 E
Bramfeld, Hbg. 7 D8 53 36N 10 5 E
Bramley, Jobg. 18 E9 26 7 S 28 4 E
Brande, Hbg. 7 D6 53 37N 9 49 E
Brandenburg Gate, Berl. 7 A3 52 30N 13 21 E
Brandizzo, Tori. 9 A3 45 10N 7 49 E
Brands Hatch, Lon. 4 C6 51 21N 0 15 E
Brandýs nad Labem, Pra. 10 A3 50 10N 14 39 E
Brandywine, Phil. 24 C1 39 49N 75 32W
Brandywine Cr. →, Phil. 24 C1 39 43N 75 31W
Brani, P., Sing. 15 G8 1 15N 103 50 E
Branik, Pra. 10 B2 50 1N 14 25 E
Brännkyrka, Stock. 3 E11 59 17N 18 0 E
Brás, S. Pau. 31 E6 23 32 S 46 36W
Brateyevo, Mos. 11 F10 55 39N 37 45 E
Bratsevo, Mos. 11 D8 55 51N 37 24 E
Brauck, Ruhr 6 A3 51 32N 7 0 E
Brava, Pta., La Hab. 30 B2 23 8N 82 23W
Braybrook, Melb. 19 E6 37 46 S 144 51 E
Brázdim, Pra. 10 A3 50 10N 14 35 E
Breakheart Reservation, Bost. 21 C3 42 28N 71 1W
Brechten, Ruhr 6 A6 51 34N 7 27 E
Breckerfeld, Ruhr 6 C6 51 15N 7 28 E
Brede, Købn. 2 D10 55 47N 12 30 E
Bredeney, Ruhr 6 B3 51 24N 6 59 E
Breeds Pond, Bost. 21 C4 42 28N 70 58W
Breezy Pt., N.Y. 22 D5 40 33N 73 56W
Breitenlee, Wien 10 G11 48 15N 16 30 E
Breitscheid, Ruhr 6 B3 51 21N 6 51 E
Breña, Lima 30 G8 12 3 S 77 3W
Brenschede, Ruhr 6 B5 51 26N 7 12 E
Brent, Lon. 4 B3 51 33N 0 15W
Brent →, Lon. 4 B2 51 30N 0 20W
Brent Res., Lon. 4 B3 51 34N 0 14W
Brentford, Lon. 4 C3 51 28N 0 18W
Brenthurst, Jobg. 18 F11 26 15 S 28 21 E
Brentwood, Lon. 4 B6 51 36N 0 18 E
Brentwood Park, Jobg. 18 E10 26 7 S 28 17 E
Brentwood Park, L.A. 28 B2 34 3N 118 29W
Brera, Mil. 9 E6 45 28N 9 11 E
Bresso, Mil. 9 D6 45 32N 9 11 E
Brétigny-sur-Orge, Paris 5 D3 48 36N 2 18 E
Brevik, Stock. 3 D12 59 20N 18 12 E
Břevnov, Pra. 10 B2 50 4N 14 22 E
Brewer I., S.F. 27 C3 37 33N 122 16W
Bricket Wood, Lon. 4 A2 51 42N 0 21W
Bridesburg, Phil. 24 B4 39 59N 75 4W
Bridgeport, Chic. 26 B3 41 50N 87 38W
Bridgeport, Phil. 24 A2 40 6N 75 21W
Bridgeview, Chic. 26 C2 41 45N 87 48W
Brie-Comte-Robert, Paris 5 C5 48 41N 2 36 E
Brighton, Melb. 19 F6 37 55 S 144 59 E
Brighton le Sands, Syd. 19 B3 33 57 S 151 9 E
Brighton Park, Chic. 26 C2 41 48N 87 41W
Brightwood, Wash. 25 D7 38 57N 77 1W
Brigittenau, Wien 10 G10 48 14N 16 22 E
Briis-sous-Forges, Paris 5 D2 48 37N 2 7 E
Brimbank Park, Melb. 19 E6 37 43 S 144 50 E
Brimsdown, Lon. 4 B4 51 39N 0 0 E
Brione, Tori. 9 B1 45 8N 7 28 E
Briones Hills, S.F. 27 A4 37 56N 122 8W
Briones Regional Park, S.F. 27 A4 37 55N 122 8W
Briones Res., S.F. 27 A3 37 55N 122 11W
Brisbane, S.F. 27 B2 37 40N 122 23W
Bristol, Phil. 24 A5 40 6N 74 53W
Britz, Berl. 7 B3 52 26N 13 27 E
Brixton, Lon. 4 C4 51 27N 0 8W
Broad Axe, Phil. 24 A3 40 8N 75 14W
Broad Sd., Bost. 21 C4 42 23N 70 56W
Broadmeadows, Melb. 19 E6 37 40 S 144 55 E
Broadmoor, S.F. 27 B2 37 41N 122 29W
Broadview, Chic. 26 B1 41 51N 87 52W
Brobacka, Hels. 3 B2 60 15N 24 36 E
Brockley, Lon. 4 C4 51 27N 0 2W
Bródno, Wsaw. 10 E7 52 17N 21 1 E
Bródnowski, Kanal, Wsaw. 10 E7 52 17N 21 3 E
Broich, Ruhr 6 B3 51 25N 6 50 E
Bromley, Lon. 4 C5 51 24N 0 0 E
Bromley-by-Bow, Lon. 4 B4 51 31N 0 0 E
Bromley Common, Lon. 4 C5 51 22N 0 2 E
Bromma, Stock. 3 D10 59 21N 17 55 E
Bromma flygplats, Stock. 3 D10 59 21N 17 56 E
Brompton, Lon. 4 C3 51 29N 0 10W
Brøndby Strand, Købn. 2 E9 55 36N 12 25 E
Brøndbyøster, Købn. 2 E9 55 39N 12 26 E
Brøndbyvester, Købn. 2 E9 55 37N 12 23 E
Brondesbury, Lon. 4 B3 51 32N 0 12W
Brønnøya, Oslo 2 B3 59 51N 10 32 E
Brønshøj, Købn. 2 D9 55 41N 12 29 E
Bronx Zoo, N.Y. 23 B5 40 50N 73 51W
Bronxville, N.Y. 23 B6 40 56N 73 49W
Brook Street, Lon. 4 B6 51 36N 0 17 E
Brookfield, Chic. 26 C1 41 48N 87 50W
Brookhaven, Phil. 24 B2 39 52N 75 23W
Brooklandville, Balt. 25 A2 39 25N 76 40W
Brooklin, S. Pau. 31 E6 23 37 S 46 39W
Brookline, Bost. 21 D3 42 19N 71 8W
Brooklyn, Balt. 25 B3 39 13N 76 36W
Brooklyn, Melb. 19 E5 37 49 S 144 49 E
Brooklyn, N.Y. 22 D5 40 37N 73 57W
Brookmont, Wash. 25 D7 38 57N 77 7W
Brooks I., S.F. 27 A2 37 53N 122 21W
Brookville, N.Y. 23 C7 40 48N 73 33W
Broomall, Phil. 24 B2 39 58N 75 22W
Brosewere B., N.Y. 23 D6 40 37N 73 40W
Brossard, Mtrl. 20 B5 43 27N 73 28W
Brou-sur-Chantereine, Paris 5 B5 48 53N 2 37 E
Brown, Trto. 20 D9 43 48N 79 14W
Browns Line, Trto. 20 E7 43 36N 79 32W
Broyhill Park, Wash. 25 D6 38 52N 77 12W
Bru, Oslo 2 C5 59 47N 10 54 E
Bruckhausen, Ruhr 6 B2 51 29N 6 43 E
Brughério, Mil. 9 D6 45 33N 9 17 E
Bruino, Tori. 9 B1 45 1N 7 27 E
Bruløkka, Oslo 2 A2 60 1N 10 22 E
Brunn, Stock. 3 E13 59 17N 18 25 E
Brunnthal, Mün. 7 G11 48 0N 11 41 E
Brunoy, Paris 5 C4 48 41N 2 29 E
Brunswick, Melb. 19 E6 37 45 S 144 57 E
Brusciano, Nápl. 9 H13 40 55N 14 25 E
Brush Hill, Bost. 21 D1 42 15N 71 22W
Bruzzano, Mil. 9 D6 45 31N 9 10 E
Bry-sur-Marne, Paris 5 B5 48 50N 2 32 E
Bryn, Oslo 2 B2 59 55N 10 27 E
Bryn Athyn, Phil. 24 A4 40 8N 75 3W
Bryn Mawr, Phil. 24 A3 40 1N 75 19W
Brzeziny, Wsaw. 10 E7 52 19N 21 2 E
Bubeneč, Pra. 10 B2 50 6N 14 24 E
Buc, Paris 5 C2 48 46N 2 7 E
Buch, Berl. 7 A3 52 38N 13 29 E
Buchburg, Wien 10 G9 48 13N 16 11 E
Buchenhain, Mün. 7 G9 48 1N 11 29 E
Buchholz, Berl. 7 A3 52 36N 13 25 E
Buchholz, Ruhr 6 B2 51 23N 6 46 E
Buckhurst Hill, Lon. 4 B5 51 37N 0 2 E
Buckingham Palace, Lon. 4 B4 51 30N 0 8W
Buckow, Berl. 7 B3 52 25N 13 26 E
Buda, Bud. 10 J13 47 30N 19 2 E
Budafok, Bud. 10 K13 47 25N 19 2 E
Budakeszi, Bud. 10 J12 47 30N 18 56 E
Budaörs, Bud. 10 K12 47 27N 18 57 E
Budapest, Bud. 10 K13 47 29N 19 3 E
Budatétény, Bud. 10 K13 47 25N 19 1 E
Budberg, Ruhr 6 A1 51 32N 6 38 E
Buddinge, Købn. 2 D10 55 44N 12 30 E
Büderich, Ruhr 6 C2 51 15N 6 41 E
Buena Park, L.A. 28 C4 33 51N 118 1W
Buena Vista, S.F. 27 B2 37 45N 122 26W
Buenavista, Mdrd. 8 B2 40 25N 3 40W
Buenos Aires, B.A. 32 B4 34 36 S 58 22W
Buenos Aires, Aeroparque de la Ciudad de, B.A. 32 B4 34 34 S 58 25W
Buer, Ruhr 6 A4 51 34N 7 2 E
Bufalotta, Rome 9 F10 41 59N 12 33 E
Buggajha, Sŏul 12 G7 37 34N 126 55 E
Bughan San, Sŏul 12 G7 37 38N 126 58 E
Bugio, Lisb. 8 G7 38 39N 9 18W
Bukit Panjang, Sing. 15 F7 1 22N 103 45 E
Bukit Timah, Sing. 15 F7 1 20N 103 47 E
Bulam San, Sŏul 12 G8 37 38N 127 4 E
Bûlâq, El Qâ. 18 C5 30 3N 31 14 E
Bule, Manila 15 E4 14 26N 121 2 E
Bulim, Sing. 15 F7 1 22N 103 43 E
Bull Brook →, Bost. 21 A4 42 41N 70 52W
Bulleen, Melb. 19 E7 37 46 S 145 4 E
Bullen Park, Melb. 19 E7 37 46 S 145 4 E
Bullion, Paris 5 D1 48 37N 1 59 E
Bulmke-Hüllen, Ruhr 6 A4 51 31N 7 7 E
Bulphan, Lon. 4 B7 51 32N 0 21 E
Bundoora, Melb. 19 E7 37 41 S 145 2 E
Bundoora Park, Melb. 19 E7 37 42 S 145 2 E
Bunker I., Kar. 17 H10 24 48N 66 57 E
Bunkyo, Tōkyō 13 B3 35 42N 139 45 E
Bunnefjorden, Oslo 2 B4 59 50N 10 44 E
Buona Vista, Sing. 15 G7 1 16N 103 47 E
Buquirivú-Guaçu →, S. Pau. 31 D7 23 28 S 46 28W
Burbank, Chic. 26 C2 41 44N 87 46W
Burbank, L.A. 28 A3 34 12N 118 18W
Bures, Paris 5 B1 48 56N 1 57 E
Bures-sur-Yvette, Paris 5 C2 48 41N 2 9 E
Burggrafenberg, Ruhr 6 C4 51 13N 7 7 E
Burgh Heath, Lon. 4 D3 51 18N 0 13W
Burlingame, S.F. 27 C2 37 34N 122 20W
Burlington, Bost. 21 B2 42 30N 71 13W
Burlington, Phil. 24 A5 40 4N 74 53W
Burnham, Chic. 26 D3 41 38N 87 33W
Burnham Park Harbor, Chic. 26 B3 41 51N 87 36W
Burnhamthorpe, Trto. 20 E7 43 37N 79 35W
Burnt Oak, Lon. 4 B3 51 36N 0 15W
Burr Ridge, Chic. 26 C1 41 46N 87 54W
Burtus, El Qâ. 18 C4 30 8N 31 8 E
Burudvatn, Oslo 2 B3 59 58N 10 35 E
Burwood, Melb. 19 F7 37 50 S 145 6 E
Burwood, Syd. 19 B3 33 52 S 151 5 E
Burwood East, Melb. 19 F7 37 51 S 145 8 E
Burzaco, B.A. 32 C4 34 49 S 58 23W
Buschhausen, Ruhr 6 A3 51 30N 6 50 E
Bush Hill Park, Lon. 4 B4 51 38N 0 4W
Bushey, Lon. 4 B2 51 38N 0 22W
Bushwick, N.Y. 23 C5 40 41N 73 54W
Bushy Cr. →, Melb. 19 E8 37 42 S 145 17 E
Bushy Park, Lon. 4 C2 51 24N 0 20W
Bussocaba, S. Pau. 31 E5 23 34 S 46 47W
Bussy-St.-Georges, Paris 5 B6 48 50N 2 41 E
Bussy-St.-Martin, Paris 5 B6 48 50N 2 41 E
Bustleton, Phil. 24 A4 40 4N 75 2W
Butantã, S. Pau. 31 E5 23 34 S 46 42W
Butcher I., Bomb. 16 H8 18 57N 72 53 E
Butendorf, Ruhr 6 A3 51 33N 6 59 E
Butler, N.Y. 22 B2 40 59N 74 20W
Buttonville, Trto. 20 C8 43 51N 79 20W
Butts Corner, Wash. 25 E6 38 46N 77 19W
Byailla, Bomb. 16 H8 18 58N 72 50 E
Byberry, Phil. 24 A5 40 6N 74 59W
Byfang, Ruhr 6 B4 51 24N 7 5 E
Byfleet, Lon. 4 D2 51 19N 0 28W
Bygdøy, Oslo 2 B4 59 54N 10 40 E

C

C.N. Tower, Trto. 20 E8 43 38N 79 23W
Caballito, B.A. 32 B4 34 37 S 58 25W
Cabin John, Wash. 25 D6 38 58N 77 10W
Cabin John Cr. →, Wash. 25 C7 39 2N 77 8W
Cabin John Regional Park, Wash. 25 C6 39 0N 77 10W
Cabramatta, Syd. 19 B2 33 53 S 150 56 E
Cabuçú de Baixo →, S. Pau. 31 D5 23 30 S 46 40W
Cachan, Paris 5 C3 48 47N 2 19 E
Cachenka →, Mos. 11 E7 55 46N 37 17 E
Cachoeira →, S. Pau. 31 E5 23 38 S 46 43W
Cacilhas, Lisb. 8 F8 38 41N 9 8W
Cadieux, Î., Mtrl. 20 B1 43 25N 74 1W
Cagarras, Is., Rio J. 31 C2 23 1 S 43 12W
Cahuenga Pk., L.A. 28 B3 34 8N 118 19 E
Cainta, Manila 15 D4 14 34N 121 6 E
Cairo = El Qâhira, El Qâ. 18 C5 30 2N 31 13 E
Cairo Int. Airport, El Qâ. 18 C6 30 7N 31 23 E
Caivano, Nápl. 9 H12 40 57N 14 18 E
Caju, Rio J. 31 B2 22 52 S 43 12W
Čakovice, Pra. 10 B3 50 9N 14 31 E
Calabazar, La Hab. 30 B2 23 1N 82 20W
Calcutta, Calc. 16 E6 22 34N 88 21 E
Caldwell, N.Y. 22 B3 40 50N 74 19W
Calf Harbour, N.Y. 23 B7 40 59N 73 37W
Calf I., Bost. 21 C4 42 20N 70 53W
Calhua, Lisb. 8 F8 38 44N 9 9W
California, Univ. of, S.F. 27 A3 37 52N 122 16W
California Inst. of Tech., L.A. 28 B4 34 8N 118 8W
California State Univ., L.A. 28 B3 34 4N 118 10W
California State Univ., S.F. 27 C4 37 39N 122 6W
Callao, Lima 30 G8 12 3 S 77 8W
Caloocan, Manila 15 D3 14 39N 120 58 E
Calumet →, Chic. 26 C3 41 43N 87 31W
Calumet, L., Chic. 26 C3 41 40N 87 35W
Calumet City, Chic. 26 D3 41 36N 87 32W
Calumet Harbor, Chic. 26 C3 41 43N 87 30W
Calumet Park, Chic. 26 C3 41 40N 87 39W
Calumet Sag Channel →, Chic. 26 C2 41 40N 87 47W
Calumpang, Manila 15 D4 14 37N 121 5 E
Calvairate, Mil. 9 E6 45 27N 9 13 E
Calverton, Wash. 25 C8 39 3N 76 56W
Calvizzano, Nápl. 9 H12 40 54N 14 11 E
Calzada, Manila 15 D4 14 32N 121 4 E
Camarate, Lisb. 8 F8 38 48N 9 7W
Camaroes, Lisb. 8 F7 38 49N 9 14W
Camberwell, Lon. 4 C4 51 28N 0 5W
Camberwell, Melb. 19 F7 37 50 S 145 5 E
Cambria Heights, N.Y. 23 C6 40 41N 73 44W
Cambridge, Bost. 21 C3 42 23N 71 7W
Cambridge Res., Bost. 21 C2 42 24N 71 16W
Cambuci, S. Pau. 31 E6 23 33 S 46 47W
Cambute, La Hab. 30 B3 23 5N 82 16W
Camden, Lon. 4 B4 51 32N 0 8W
Camden, Phil. 24 B4 39 56N 75 7W
Camp Springs, Wash. 25 E8 38 48N 76 55W
Campamento, Mdrd. 8 B2 40 23N 3 46W
Campanilla, Pta., La Hab. 30 A3 23 10N 82 18W
Campbellfield, Melb. 19 E6 37 40 S 144 57 E
Camperdown, Syd. 19 B4 33 53 S 151 11 E
Campi Flegrei, Nápl. 9 H11 40 50N 14 9 E
Campo, Casa de, Mdrd. 8 B2 40 25N 3 45W
Campo Belo, S. Pau. 31 E5 23 36 S 46 44W
Campo de Mayo, B.A. 32 B2 34 32 S 58 40W
Campo Grando, Lisb. 8 F8 38 45N 9 9W
Campo Limpo, S. Pau. 31 E5 23 38 S 46 46W
Campo Pequeño, Lisb. 8 F8 38 44N 9 8W
Campolide, Lisb. 8 F8 38 43N 9 9W
Campsie, Syd. 19 B3 33 54 S 151 6 E
C'an San Joan, Barc. 8 D6 41 28N 2 11 E
Canacao, Manila 15 E3 14 29N 120 54 E
Canacao B., Manila 15 E3 14 29N 120 54 E
Cañada de los Helechos →, Méx. 29 B2 19 21N 99 15W
Canarsie, N.Y. 23 D5 40 38N 73 53W
Candiac, Mtrl. 20 B5 43 23N 73 29W
Caneças, Lisb. 8 F7 38 48N 9 13W
Cangaiba, S. Pau. 31 E6 23 30 S 46 31W
Cangrejeras, La Hab. 30 B1 23 3N 82 30W
Canguera, S. Pau. 31 E7 23 34 S 46 26W
Canillas, Mdrd. 8 B3 40 27N 3 38W
Canillejas, Mdrd. 8 B3 40 26N 3 36W
Cann Hall, Lon. 4 B5 51 33N 0 0 E
Canning Town, Lon. 4 B5 51 30N 0 1 E
Canoe Grove Res., N.Y. 22 C2 40 45N 74 21W
Cantalupo, Mil. 9 D4 45 34N 8 58 E
Cantareira, S. Pau. 31 D6 23 26 S 46 36W
Cantarranas, La Hab. 30 B2 23 2N 82 28W
Canteras de Vallecas, Mdrd. 8 B3 40 20N 3 37W
Canterbury, Melb. 19 E7 37 49 S 145 4 E
Canterbury, Syd. 19 B3 33 55 S 151 7 E
Canto do Rio, Rio J. 31 B3 22 54 S 43 7W
Canton, Bost. 21 D3 42 10N 71 8W
Caohe, Shang. 14 J11 31 10N 121 24 E
Caonao, La Hab. 30 B2 23 5N 82 24W
Capão Redondo, S. Pau. 31 E5 23 39 S 46 45W
Caparica, Lisb. 8 F8 38 40N 9 9W
Caparica, Costa da, Lisb. 8 G7 38 38N 9 15W
Capelinha, S. Pau. 31 E5 23 39 S 46 44W
Capitol Heights, Wash. 25 D8 38 52N 76 55W
Capodichino, Aeroporto di, Nápl. 9 H12 40 52N 14 17 E
Capodimonte, Nápl. 9 H12 40 52N 14 14 E
Capodimonte, Bosco di, Nápl. 9 H12 40 52N 14 15 E
Captain Cook Bridge, Syd. 19 C3 34 0 S 151 7 E
Captain Cook Landing Place Park, Syd. 19 C4 34 1 S 151 14 E
Captain Harbour, N.Y. 23 B7 40 59N 73 37W
Capuava, S. Pau. 31 E7 23 38 S 46 28W
Capuchos, Lisb. 8 G7 38 38N 9 16W
Caraballeda, Car. 30 D5 10 36N 66 50W
Carabanchel Alto, Mdrd. 8 B2 40 22N 3 44W
Carabanchel Bajo, Mdrd. 8 B2 40 23N 3 44W
Carabatteda →, Car. 30 D5 10 37N 66 51W
Caracas, Car. 30 E5 10 30N 66 54W
Carapachay, B.A. 32 B3 34 31 S 58 32W
Carapicuiba, S. Pau. 31 E5 23 31 S 46 49W
Carapicuiba →, S. Pau. 31 E5 23 31 S 46 49W
Caravita, Nápl. 9 H13 40 52N 14 21 E
Caraza, B.A. 32 C4 34 41 S 58 25W
Cardito, Nápl. 9 H12 40 56N 14 17 E
Cardoso, Lagos 18 A1 6 34N 7 16 E
Caribbean Gardens, Melb. 19 F8 37 54 S 145 12 E
Caricuao, Car. 30 E5 10 25N 66 58W
Caridad, Manila 15 E3 14 28N 120 53 E
Carioca, Sa. da, Rio J. 31 B2 22 57 S 43 13W
Carle Place, N.Y. 23 C7 40 44N 73 35W
Carlingford, Syd. 19 A3 33 46 S 151 3 E
Carlisle, Bost. 21 B1 42 31N 71 20W
Carlshof, Mün. 7 F11 48 15N 11 41 E
Carlstadt, N.Y. 22 B4 40 50N 74 6W
Carlton, Melb. 19 E6 37 47 S 144 57 E
Carnaxide, Lisb. 8 F7 38 43N 9 14W
Carnegie, Melb. 19 F7 37 53 S 145 3 E
Carnegie Hall, N.Y. 22 C5 40 45N 73 59W
Carnetin, Paris 5 B6 48 54N 2 42 E
Carney, Balt. 25 A3 39 23N 76 31W
Carnide, Lisb. 8 F7 38 45N 9 10W
Caronno Pert, Mil. 9 D5 45 35N 9 2 E
Carramar, Syd. 19 B2 33 51 S 150 58 E
Carrascal, Stgo 30 J10 33 25 S 70 42W
Carrières-sous-Bois, Paris 5 B2 48 55N 2 6 E
Carrières-sous-Poissy, Paris 5 B2 48 56N 2 2 E
Carrières-sur-Seine, Paris 5 B3 48 55N 2 11 E
Carroll I., Balt. 25 B4 39 19N 76 20W
Carroll Park, Balt. 25 B3 39 16N 76 38W
Carshalton, Lon. 4 C3 51 22N 0 10W
Carshalton on the Hill, Lon. 4 C4 51 20N 0 9W
Carteret, N.Y. 22 D3 40 34N 74 13W
Cartierville, Aéroport de, Mtrl. 20 A3 43 31N 73 42 E
Carugate, Mil. 9 D6 45 32N 9 20 E
Carupa, B.A. 32 A3 34 25 S 58 33W
Casa Blanca, La Hab. 30 B3 23 8N 82 19W
Casa Verde, S. Pau. 31 D5 23 29 S 46 40W
Casalnuovo di Nápoli, Nápl. 9 H12 40 54N 14 20 E
Casalotti, Rome 9 F9 41 54N 12 22 E
Casandrino, Nápl. 9 H12 40 56N 14 15 E
Casavatore, Nápl. 9 H12 40 53N 14 15 E
Cascadura, Rio J. 31 B2 22 52 S 43 19W
Caselette, Tori. 9 B1 45 6N 7 28 E
Caselette, Laghi di, Tori. 9 B1 45 7N 7 29 E
Caselle Torinese, Tori. 9 A3 45 10N 7 38 E
Caseros, B.A. 32 B3 34 36 S 58 34W
Casória, Nápl. 9 H12 40 54N 14 17 E
Cassignanica, Mil. 9 E7 45 27N 9 20 E
Cassiobury Park, Lon. 4 B2 51 39N 0 25W
Castel di Camerletto, Tori. 9 B1 45 6N 7 27 E
Castel di Guido, Rome 9 F8 41 53N 12 17 E
Castel Malnome, Rome 9 F8 41 50N 12 19 E
Castel San Cristina, Tori. 9 B3 45 8N 7 40 E
Castel Sant'Angelo, Rome 9 F9 41 54N 12 27 E
Castelar, B.A. 32 B3 34 39 S 58 39W
Castellbisbal, Barc. 8 D4 41 28N 1 58 E
Castello di Cisterna, Nápl. 9 H13 40 54N 14 24 E
Castelvécchio, Tori. 9 B3 45 1N 7 46 E
Castiglione Torinese, Tori. 9 B3 45 6N 7 48 E
Castleton Corners, N.Y. 22 D4 40 36N 74 8W
Castro Valley, S.F. 27 B4 37 41N 122 5W
Castrop, Ruhr 6 A5 51 32N 7 18 E
Castrop-Rauxel, Ruhr 6 A5 51 33N 7 18 E
Cat Rock Hill, Bost. 21 C2 42 23N 71 18W
Caterham, Lon. 4 D4 51 16N 0 5W
Catete, Rio J. 31 B2 22 54 S 43 10W
Catford, Lon. 4 C4 51 26N 0 1W
Catia, Car. 30 D5 10 31N 66 56W
Catia La Mer, Car. 30 D4 10 36N 67 0W
Catonsville, Balt. 25 B2 39 16N 76 43W
Catonsville Manor, Balt. 25 B2 39 17N 76 44W
Cattle Hill, S.F. 27 C2 37 36N 122 27W
Catumbi, Rio J. 31 B2 22 54 S 43 12W
Caughnawaga, Mtrl. 20 B3 43 24N 73 40W
Caulfield, Melb. 19 F7 37 52 S 145 1 E
Caulfield Racecourse, Melb. 19 F7 37 53 S 145 4 E
Caumsett State Park, N.Y. 23 B8 40 55N 73 27W
Cavite, Manila 15 E3 14 29N 120 54 E
Cavoretto, Tori. 9 B3 45 1N 7 41 E
Caxias, Lisb. 8 F7 38 42N 9 16W
Caxingui, S. Pau. 31 E5 23 35 S 46 43W
Cebeciköy, Ist. 17 A2 41 7N 28 53 E
Cecchignola, Rome 9 G10 41 48N 12 29 E
Cecil Park, Syd. 19 B2 33 52 S 150 51 E
Cecilienhof, Berl. 7 B1 52 35N 13 5 E
Cedar Grove, N.Y. 22 B3 40 50N 74 13W
Cedar Grove Res., N.Y. 22 B3 40 51N 74 12W
Cedar I., N.Y. 23 D8 40 38N 73 22W
Cedar Knolls, N.Y. 22 C2 40 49N 74 27W
Cedarhurst, N.Y. 23 D6 40 37N 73 43W
Cedarvale, Trto. 20 D8 43 41N 79 26W
Celle →, Paris 5 D1 48 36N 1 59 E
Cempaka Putih, Jak. 15 J10 6 10 S 106 51 E
Çengelköy, Ist. 17 A3 41 2N 29 3 E
Centennial Park, Syd. 19 B4 33 53 S 151 14 E
Center Square, Phil. 24 C2 39 46N 75 22W
Centerport, N.Y. 23 B8 40 53N 73 22W
Centerton, Phil. 24 B5 39 59N 74 53W
Centocelle, Rome 9 F10 41 52N 12 34 E
Central Park, N.Y. 22 C5 40 47N 73 58W
Central Park, Sing. 15 G8 1 17N 103 50 E
Centre City, Phil. 24 C3 39 46N 75 11W
Centre I., N.Y. 23 B7 40 54N 73 31W
Cércola, Nápl. 9 H13 40 51N 14 21 E
Cergy-Pontoise, Paris 5 A2 49 1N 2 4 E
Cernay-la-Ville, Paris 5 C1 48 40N 1 58 E
Cernusco sul Navíglio, Mil. 9 D6 45 31N 9 19 E
Cerqueira Cesar, S. Pau. 31 E5 23 33 S 46 40W
Cerro Ajusco, Méx. 29 C2 19 12N 99 15W
Cerro de la Estrella, Méx. 29 B3 19 20N 99 5W
Cerro de los Angeles, Mdrd. 8 C2 40 18N 3 41W
Cerro el Picacho, Méx. 29 A3 19 35N 99 6W
Cerro Maggiore, Mil. 9 D4 45 35N 8 57 E
Certanovka →, Mos. 11 F9 55 38N 37 48 E
Certanovo, Mos. 11 F9 55 38N 37 36 E
Cesano Boscone, Mil. 9 E5 45 26N 9 5 E
Cesate, Mil. 9 D5 45 35N 9 4 E
Cha Kwo Ling, H.K. 12 E6 22 18N 114 13 E
Chabot, L., S.F. 27 B4 37 43N 122 6W
Chacao, Car. 30 D5 10 30N 66 50W
Chacarilla, Lima 30 G9 12 6 S 76 59W
Chadds Ford, Phil. 24 B1 39 52N 75 35W
Chadstone, Melb. 19 F7 37 52 S 145 5 E
Chadwell Heath, Lon. 4 B5 51 34N 0 8 E
Chadwell St. Mary, Lon. 4 C7 51 29N 0 20 E
Chai Wan, H.K. 12 E6 22 16N 114 14 E
Chai Wan Kok, H.K. 12 D5 22 22N 114 6 E
Chakdaha, Calc. 16 F5 22 28N 88 19 E
Chama, Lima 30 G8 12 7 S 77 0W
Chamartin, Mdrd. 8 B2 40 27N 3 40W
Chamberi, Mdrd. 8 B2 40 26N 3 42W
Chambourcy, Paris 5 B2 48 54N 2 2 E
Champdani, Calc. 16 D5 22 48N 88 19 E
Champigny-sur-Marne, Paris 5 C5 48 49N 2 30 E
Champlain, Pont, Mtrl. 20 B4 43 28N 73 31W
Champlan, Paris 5 C3 48 42N 2 16 E
Champrosay, Paris 5 D4 48 39N 2 25 E
Champs-sur-Marne, Paris 5 B5 48 50N 2 34 E
Chamrail, Calc. 16 E5 22 38N 88 17 E
Chancheon, Sŏul 12 G7 37 33N 126 56 E
Chandernagore, Calc. 16 C6 22 51N 88 21 E
Chanditala, Calc. 16 D5 22 41N 88 15 E
Changi, Sing. 15 F8 1 23N 103 59 E
Changi Airport, Sing. 15 F8 1 21N 103 59 E
Changning, Shang. 14 J11 31 13N 121 24 E
Changpu Gongyuan, Shang. 14 J12 31 17N 121 31 E
Chanteloup-les-Vignes, Paris 5 B2 48 58N 2 1 E
Chantereine, Paris 5 B5 48 53N 2 37 E
Chantian, Gzh. 14 F8 23 12N 113 16 E
Chao Phraya →, Bangk. 15 B2 13 40N 100 31 E
Chaoyang, Beij. 14 B3 39 53N 116 26 E
Chaoyang Gongyuan, Beij. 14 B3 39 54N 116 28 E
Chaoyangmen, Beij. 14 B3 39 54N 116 23 E
Chapel End, Lon. 4 B4 51 35N 0 1W
Chapet, Paris 5 B1 48 58N 1 55 E
Chaplinville, Bost. 21 A4 42 42N 70 54W
Chapultepec, Bosque de, Méx. 29 B2 19 25N 99 11W
Chapultepec, Castillo de, Méx. 29 B2 19 25N 99 10W
Charenton-le-Pont, Paris 5 C4 48 49N 2 25 E
Charles-de-Gaulle, Aéroport, Paris 5 A5 49 0N 2 33 E
Charles Lee Tinden Regional Park, S.F. 27 A3 37 53N 122 14W
Charleston, N.Y. 22 D3 40 32N 74 14W
Charlestown, Bost. 21 C3 42 22N 71 4W
Charlottenburg, Berl. 7 A2 52 31N 13 14 E
Charlottenburg, Schloss, Berl. 7 A2 52 31N 13 18 E
Charlottenlund, Købn. 2 D10 55 44N 12 35 E
Charlton, Lon. 4 C5 51 29N 0 1 E
Charneca, Lisb. 8 F8 38 47N 9 8W
Charneca, Lisb. 8 G7 38 37N 9 12W
Chase Side, Lon. 4 B4 51 39N 0 4W
Châteaufort, Paris 5 C2 48 44N 2 5 E
Châtenay-Malabry, Paris 5 C3 48 46N 2 16 E
Chatham, Chic. 26 C3 41 45N 87 36W
Chatham, N.Y. 22 C2 40 44N 74 23W
Châtillon, Paris 5 C3 48 48N 2 17 E
Chatou, Paris 5 B2 48 53N 2 9 E
Chatpur, Calc. 16 E6 22 36N 88 22 E
Chatra, Calc. 16 D5 22 45N 88 19 E
Chatswood, Syd. 19 A4 33 47 S 151 11 E
Chauki, Kar. 17 G10 24 55N 66 56 E
Chavarria, Lima 30 G8 12 0 S 77 7W
Chavenay, Paris 5 B1 48 51N 1 59 E
Chavenay-Villepreux, Aérodrôme de, Paris 5 B1 48 50N 1 58 E
Chaville, Paris 5 C3 48 48N 2 11 E
Che Kung Miu, H.K. 12 D6 22 22N 114 10 E
Cheam, Lon. 4 C3 51 21N 0 12W
Chelles, Paris 5 B5 48 53N 2 35 E
Chelles, Canal de, Paris 5 B5 48 51N 2 35 E
Chells-le-Pin, Aérodrome, Paris 5 B5 48 53N 2 36 E
Chelmsford, Bost. 21 B1 42 35N 71 20W
Chelobityevo, Mos. 11 D10 55 54N 37 40 E
Chelsea, Bost. 21 C3 42 23N 71 1W
Chelsea, Lon. 4 C3 51 29N 0 10W
Chelsea, Phil. 24 B2 39 51N 75 27W
Chelsfield Village, Lon. 4 C5 51 21N 0 8 E
Cheltenham, Phil. 24 A4 40 3N 75 6W
Chembur, Bomb. 16 G8 19 3N 72 53 E
Chennevières, Paris 5 A2 49 0N 2 6 E
Chennevières-sur-Marne, Paris 5 C5 48 47N 2 31 E
Cheongdam, Sŏul 12 G8 37 31N 127 2 E
Cheonho, Sŏul 12 G8 37 32N 127 6 E
Cheops, El Qâ. 18 D4 29 58N 31 8 E
Chepo, Gzh. 14 G9 23 7N 113 23 E
Cherepkovo, Mos. 11 E8 55 45N 37 21 E
Chernyovo, Mos. 11 D7 55 50N 37 17 E
Cherry Hill, Phil. 24 B4 39 54N 75 1W
Cherry L., Melb. 19 F5 37 51 S 144 49 E
Cherryland, S.F. 27 B4 37 40N 122 7W
Cherrywood, Trto. 20 C10 43 51N 79 8W
Chertsey, Lon. 4 C2 51 23N 0 29W
Cheryomushki, Mos. 11 E9 55 40N 37 35 E
Chesaco Park, Balt. 25 B3 39 18N 76 30W
Chesapeake B., Balt. 25 B4 39 12N 76 22W
Cheshunt, Lon. 4 A4 51 42N 0 0 E
Chess →, Lon. 4 B2 51 38N 0 27W
Chessington, Lon. 4 C3 51 21N 0 18W
Chessington Zoo, Lon. 4 C3 51 20N 0 19W
Chester, Phil. 24 B2 39 50N 75 23W
Chester Cr. →, Phil. 24 B2 39 50N 75 21W
Chester Heights, Phil. 24 B2 39 53N 75 27W
Chestnut, Phil. 24 A3 40 4N 75 13W
Chestnut Hill, Bost. 21 D2 42 19N 71 10W
Cheung Sha Wan, H.K. 12 D5 22 20N 114 8 E
Cheverly, Wash. 25 D8 38 55N 76 54W
Chevilly-Larue, Paris 5 C4 48 46N 2 21 E
Chevreuse, Paris 5 C2 48 42N 2 2 E
Chevry-Cossigny, Paris 5 C5 48 43N 2 39 E
Chevy Chase, Wash. 25 D7 38 59N 77 4W
Chevy Chase View, Wash. 25 C7 39 0N 77 4W
Cheyney, Phil. 24 B1 39 55N 75 31W
Chhalera Bangar, Delhi 16 B2 28 33N 77 17 E
Chhinamor, Calc. 16 D5 22 48N 88 17 E
Chhota Andai, Kar. 17 H11 24 48N 66 59 E
Chia Keng, Sing. 15 F8 1 21N 103 52 E
Chiaíano, Nápl. 9 H12 40 53N 14 13 E
Chiaravalle Milanese, Mil. 9 E6 45 24N 9 16 E
Chiawelo, Jobg. 18 F8 26 17 S 27 51 E
Chicago, Chic. 26 B3 41 52N 87 38W
Chicago, Univ. of, Chic. 26 C3 41 47N 87 35W
Chicago Harbor, Chic. 26 B3 41 52N 87 36W
Chicago Lawn, Chic. 26 C2 41 47N 87 40W
Chicago-Midway Airport, Chic. 26 C2 41 47N 87 45W
Chicago-O'Hare Int. Airport, Chic. 26 B1 41 58N 87 53W
Chicago Ridge, Chic. 26 C2 41 41N 87 46W
Chicago Sanitary and Ship Canal, Chic. 26 C2 41 49N 87 45W
Chichinautzin, Cerro, Méx. 29 D3 19 6N 99 8W
Chicot, Mtrl. 20 A2 43 35N 73 56W
Chicot →, Mtrl. 20 A2 43 34N 73 51W
Chienzui, Gzh. 14 F9 23 12N 113 22 E
Chieri, Tori. 9 B3 45 0N 7 49 E
Chigwell, Lon. 4 B5 51 36N 0 6 E
Chigwell Row, Lon. 4 B5 51 37N 0 7 E
Chik Sha, H.K. 12 E6 22 17N 114 16 E
Chikumazawa, Tōkyō 13 B2 35 49N 139 32 E
Childs Hill, Lon. 4 B3 51 33N 0 12W
Chilla Saroda, Delhi 16 B2 28 35N 77 18 E
Chillum, Wash. 25 D8 38 57N 76 58W
Chilly-Mazarin, Paris 5 C3 48 42N 2 17 E
Chimalhuacán, Méx. 29 B4 19 25N 89 57 E
Chimalpa, Méx. 29 B2 19 21N 99 19W
China, Tg., Sing. 15 G8 1 14N 103 50 E
China Basin, S.F. 27 B2 37 46N 122 22W
Chingford, Lon. 4 B5 51 37N 0 0 E
Chingupota, Calc. 16 F5 22 29N 88 14 E
Chipilly Woods, Chic. 26 A2 42 8N 87 48W
Chipperfield, Lon. 4 A2 51 42N 0 29W
Chipping Ongar, Lon. 4 A6 51 41N 0 15 E
Chipstead, Lon. 4 D4 51 17N 0 8W
Chirle, Bomb. 16 H9 18 55N 73 2 E
Chirnside Park, Melb. 19 E8 37 45 S 145 18 E
Chislehurst, Lon. 4 C5 51 24N 0 6 E
Chislehurst West, Lon. 4 C5 51 25N 0 3 E
Chiswick, Lon. 4 C3 51 29N 0 16W
Chiswick House, Lon. 4 C3 51 28N 0 15W
Chitlade Palace, Bangk. 15 B2 13 45N 100 31 E
Chitose, Tōkyō 13 C2 35 33N 139 37 E
Chiyoda-Ku, Tōkyō 13 B3 35 41N 139 44 E
Chkalova, Mos. 11 F11 55 39N 37 56 E
Choa Chu Kang, Sing. 15 F7 1 22N 103 40 E
Choboty, Mos. 11 F8 55 39N 37 21 E
Chodov u Prahy, Pra. 10 B3 50 1N 14 30 E
Chōfu, Tōkyō 13 C2 35 38N 139 32 E
Choisel, Paris 5 C2 48 41N 2 1 E
Choisy-le-Roi, Paris 5 C4 48 46N 2 24 E

Gerthe **37**

Ebute-Metta, *Lagos* **18 B2** 6 28N 7 23 E
Ecatepec de Morelos, *Méx.* **29 A3** 19 35N 99 2W
Echo B., *N.Y.* **23 B6** 40 54N 73 45W
Echo Mt., *L.A.* **28 A4** 34 12N 118 8W
Écouen, *Paris* **5 A4** 49 1N 2 22 E
Ecquevilly, *Paris* **5 B1** 48 57N 1 55 E
Ecser, *Bud.* **10 K14** 47 26N 19 19 E
Eda, *Tōkyō* **13 C2** 35 33N 139 33 E
Eddington, *Phil.* **24 A5** 40 5N 74 55W
Eddystone, *Phil.* **24 B2** 39 51N 75 20W
Eden, *Rio J.* **31 A1** 22 47 S 43 23W
Edendale, *Jobg.* **18 E9** 26 8 S 28 9 E
Edenvale, *Jobg.* **18 E9** 26 8 S 28 9 E
Edgars Cr. →, *Melb.* **19 E6** 37 43 S 144 58 E
Edge Hill, *Phil.* **24 A4** 40 7N 75 9W
Edgeley, *Trto.* **20 D7** 43 47N 79 31W
Edgemar, *S.F.* **27 C2** 37 39N 122 29W
Edgemere, *Balt.* **25 B4** 39 14N 76 26W
Edgemont, *Phil.* **24 B2** 39 58N 75 26W
Edgewater Park, *Phil.* **24 A5** 40 3N 74 54W
Edgware, *Lon.* **4 B3** 51 36N 0 15W
Edison, *N.Y.* **22 D2** 40 31N 74 23W
Edison Park, *Chic.* **26 A2** 42 1N 87 48W
Edleen, *Jobg.* **18 E10** 26 5 S 28 12 E
Edmondston, *Wash.* **25 D8** 38 56N 76 54W
Edo →, *Tōkyō* **13 C4** 35 38N 139 52 E
Edogawa, *Tōkyō* **13 B4** 35 43N 139 52 E
Edsberg, *Stock.* **3 D10** 59 26N 17 57 E
Edwards L., *Melb.* **19 E6** 37 42 S 144 59 E
Eestiluoto, *Hels.* **3 C6** 60 7N 25 13 E
Egawa, *Tōkyō* **13 D4** 35 22N 139 54 E
Egenbüttel, *Hbg.* **7 D7** 53 39N 9 51 E
Eggerscheidt, *Ruhr* **6 C3** 51 19N 6 53 E
Egham, *Lon.* **4 C1** 51 25N 0 30W
Eiche, *Berl.* **7 A4** 52 33N 13 35 E
Eiche Sud, *Berl.* **7 A4** 52 33N 13 35 E
Eichlinghofen, *Ruhr* **6 B6** 51 29N 7 24 E
Eichwalde, *Berl.* **7 B4** 52 22N 13 37 E
Eidelstedt, *Hbg.* **7 D7** 53 36N 9 54 E
Eiffel, Tour, *Paris* **5 B3** 48 51N 2 17 E
Eigen, *Ruhr* **6 A3** 51 32N 6 56 E
Eilbek, *Hbg.* **7 D8** 53 34N 10 2 E
Eimsbüttel, *Hbg.* **7 D7** 53 34N 9 57 E
Eissendorf, *Hbg.* **7 E7** 53 27N 9 57 E
Ejby, *Købn.* **2 D9** 55 41N 12 24 E
Ejigbo, *Lagos* **18 A1** 6 33N 7 18 E
Ekeberg, *Oslo* **2 B4** 59 53N 10 46 E
Ekeby, *Stock.* **3 D8** 59 21N 17 35 E
Ekerö, *Stock.* **3 E9** 59 17N 17 46 E
Ekerön, *Stock.* **3 E9** 59 18N 17 41 E
Ekhtiyarieh, *Tehr.* **17 C5** 35 46N 51 28 E
Eklundshov, *Stock.* **3 E10** 59 11N 17 54 E
Eknäs, *Stock.* **3 E12** 59 18N 18 13 E
El 'Abbasiya, *El Qâ.* **18 C5** 30 3N 31 16 E
El Agustino, *Lima* **30 G8** 12 2 S 77 0W
El Alto, *Stgo* **30 J10** 33 29 S 70 42W
El Awkal, *El Qâ.* **18 C5** 30 2N 31 12 E
El Baragil, *El Qâ.* **18 C4** 30 4N 31 9 E
El Basâlîn, *El Qâ.* **18 D5** 29 58N 31 16 E
El Calvario, *La Hab.* **30 B3** 23 3N 82 19W
El Cano, *La Hab.* **30 B2** 23 2N 82 27W
El Caribe, *Car.* **30 D5** 10 36N 66 52W
El Carmen, *Stgo* **30 J10** 33 22 S 70 43W
El Cerrito, *S.F.* **27 A3** 37 54N 122 18W
El Cerro, *La Hab.* **30 B2** 23 6N 82 23W
El Cojo, Pta., *Car.* **30 D5** 10 36N 66 53W
El Cortijo, *Stgo* **30 J10** 33 22 S 70 42W
El Duqqi, *El Qâ.* **18 C5** 30 1N 31 12 E
El Gamâlîya, *El Qâ.* **18 C5** 30 2N 31 15 E
El Ghurîya, *El Qâ.* **18 C5** 30 2N 31 15 E
El Gîza, *El Qâ.* **18 C5** 30 0N 31 12 E
El Granada, *S.F.* **27 C2** 37 30N 122 27W
El Guarda Parres, *Méx.* **29 D2** 19 9N 99 11W
El Hatillo, *Car.* **30 E6** 10 25N 66 49W
El Khalîfa, *El Qâ.* **18 C5** 30 0N 31 15 E
El Kôm el Ahmar, *El Qâ.* **18 C5** 30 6N 31 10 E
El Ma'âdi, *El Qâ.* **18 D5** 29 57N 31 15 E
El Matarîya, *El Qâ.* **18 C5** 30 7N 31 18 E
El Monte, *L.A.* **28 B4** 34 3N 118 1W
El Muhît Idkû el Gharbî →, *El Qâ.* **18 C4** 30 6N 31 6 E
El Mûskî, *El Qâ.* **18 C5** 30 3N 31 15 E
El Palmar, *Car.* **30 D5** 10 36N 66 53W
El Palomar, *B.A.* **32 B3** 34 36 S 58 37W
El Pardo, *Mdrd.* **8 A2** 40 30N 3 46W
El Pedregal, *Car.* **30 D5** 10 30N 66 51W
El Pinar, *Car.* **30 E5** 10 28N 66 56W
El Plantio, *Mdrd.* **8 B1** 40 28N 3 51W
El Qâhira, *El Qâ.* **18 C5** 30 2N 31 13 E
El Qubba, *El Qâ.* **18 C5** 30 4N 31 16 E
El Recreo, *Car.* **30 E5** 10 29N 66 52W
El Reloj, *Méx.* **29 C3** 19 19N 99 9W
El Retiro, *Car.* **30 D5** 10 31N 66 54W
El Salto, *Stgo* **30 J11** 33 22 S 70 38W
El Segundo, *L.A.* **28 C2** 33 55N 118 24W
El Sereno, *L.A.* **28 B3** 34 6N 118 10 E
El Silencio, *Car.* **30 D5** 10 30N 66 55W
El Sobrante, *S.F.* **27 A3** 37 58N 122 17W
El Talar de Pacheco, *B.A.* **32 A3** 34 27 S 58 38W
El Talibîya, *El Qâ.* **18 D5** 29 59N 31 10 E
El Valle, *Car.* **30 E5** 10 29N 66 54W
El Vedado, *La Hab.* **30 B2** 23 8N 82 23W
El Vergel, *Méx.* **29 C3** 19 18N 99 5W
El Wâyli el Kubra, *El Qâ.* **18 C5** 30 5N 31 17 E
El Zamalik, *El Qâ.* **18 C5** 30 3N 31 12 E
Elam, *Phil.* **24 B1** 39 51N 75 32W
Élancourt, *Paris* **5 C1** 48 47N 1 57 E
Elandsfortein, *Jobg.* **18 E10** 26 9 S 28 13 E
Elbe →, *Hbg.* **7 D6** 53 32N 9 49 E
Elberfeld, *Ruhr* **6 C4** 51 15N 7 9 E
Elephanta Caves, *Bomb.* **16 H8** 18 57N 72 57 E
Elephanta I., *Bomb.* **16 H8** 18 57N 72 56 E
Elisenau, *Berl.* **7 A4** 52 38N 13 37 E
Elizabeth, *N.Y.* **22 D3** 40 39N 74 13W
Elkins Park, *Phil.* **24 A4** 40 4N 75 8W
Elkridge, *Balt.* **25 B2** 39 13N 76 42W
Ellboda, *Stock.* **3 D12** 59 24N 18 15 E
Eller, *Ruhr* **6 C3** 51 12N 6 51 E
Ellerbek, *Hbg.* **7 D7** 53 39N 9 52 E
Ellicott City, *Balt.* **25 B2** 39 15N 76 49W
Ellinghorst, *Ruhr* **6 A3** 51 33N 6 57 E
Ellinikón, *Ath.* **8 J11** 37 50N 23 45 E
Ellis I., *N.Y.* **22 C4** 40 41N 74 2W
Elm Park, *Lon.* **4 B6** 51 32N 0 12 E
Elmers End, *Lon.* **4 C4** 51 23N 0 2W
Elmhurst, *Chic.* **26 B1** 41 53N 87 55W
Elmhurst, *N.Y.* **23 C5** 40 44N 73 53W
Elmont, *N.Y.* **23 C6** 40 42N 73 42W
Elmstead, *Lon.* **4 C5** 51 24N 0 2 E
Elmwood, *Balt.* **25 A3** 39 20N 76 31W
Elmwood, *N.Y.* **23 B8** 40 51N 73 20W
Elmwood Park, *Chic.* **26 B2** 41 55N 87 48W
Elmwood Park, *N.Y.* **22 B4** 40 54N 74 7W
Elsburg, *Jobg.* **18 F10** 26 15 S 28 13 E
Elsburgspruit →, *Jobg.* **18 F10** 26 16 S 28 12 E
Elsmere, *Phil.* **24 C1** 39 44N 75 35W
Elspark, *Jobg.* **18 F10** 26 15 S 28 13 E
Elsternwick, *Melb.* **19 F7** 37 52 S 145 0 E
Eltham, *Lon.* **4 C5** 51 27N 0 3 E
Eltham, *Melb.* **19 E7** 37 42 S 145 9 E
Elthorn Heights, *Lon.* **4 B2** 51 31N 0 20W
Eltingrille, *N.Y.* **22 D4** 40 32N 74 9W
Elwood, *Melb.* **19 F6** 37 53 S 144 59 E
Élysée, *Paris* **5 B3** 48 52N 2 19 E
Embu, *S. Pau.* **31 E4** 23 38 S 46 50W
Embu-Mirim, *S. Pau.* **31 F5** 23 41 S 46 49W
Embu Mirim →, *S. Pau.* **31 F5** 23 43 S 46 47W
Emdeni, *Jobg.* **18 F7** 26 14 S 27 49 E
Émerainville, *Paris* **5 C5** 48 48N 2 37 E
Emerson, *N.Y.* **22 B4** 40 57N 74 2W
Emerson Park, *Lon.* **4 B6** 51 34N 0 13 E
Emeryville, *S.F.* **27 B3** 37 49N 122 17W
Eminonu, *Ist.* **17 A2** 41 0N 28 57 E
Emmarentia, *Jobg.* **18 E9** 26 9 S 28 0 E
Emperor's Palace, *Tōkyō* **13 B3** 35 40N 139 45 E
Empire State Building, *N.Y.* **22 C5** 40 44N 73 59W
Emscher →, *Ruhr* **6 A6** 51 30N 7 26 E
Emscher Bruch, *Ruhr* **6 A4** 51 33N 7 8 E
Emscher Zweigkanal, *Ruhr* **6 A4** 51 33N 7 9 E
Encantado, *Rio J.* **31 B2** 22 53 S 43 19W
Encino, *L.A.* **28 B2** 34 9N 118 28W
Encino Res., *L.A.* **28 B1** 34 8N 118 30W
Enebyberg, *Stock.* **3 D10** 59 25N 17 59 E
Enfield, *Lon.* **4 B4** 51 39N 0 4W
Enfield, *Phil.* **24 A3** 40 6N 75 11W
Enfield, *Syd.* **19 B3** 33 53 S 151 6 E
Enfield Chase, *Lon.* **4 A4** 51 40N 0 8W
Enfield Highway, *Lon.* **4 B4** 51 39N 0 2W
Enfield Lock, *Lon.* **4 A4** 51 40N 0 1W
Enfield Wash, *Lon.* **4 B4** 51 39N 0 2W
Eng Khong Gardens, *Sing.* **15 F7** 1 20N 103 46 E
Engenho, I. do, *Rio J.* **31 B3** 22 50 S 43 6W
Engenho Nôvo, *Rio J.* **31 B2** 22 53 S 43 17W
Engenho Velho, Sa. do, *Rio J.* **31 B1** 22 54 S 43 21W
Engenno do Mato, *Rio J.* **31 B3** 22 56 S 43 2W
Enghein-les-Bains, *Paris* **5 B3** 48 58N 2 18 E
Englewood, *Chic.* **26 C3** 41 46N 87 38W
Englewood, *N.Y.* **22 B5** 40 53N 73 58W
Englewood Cliffs, *N.Y.* **22 B5** 40 53N 73 59W
Englischer Garten, *Mün.* **7 G10** 48 9N 11 35 E
Enmore, *Syd.* **19 B4** 33 54 S 151 10 E
Ennepe →, *Ruhr* **6 C6** 51 17N 7 23 E
Ennepetal, *Ruhr* **6 C6** 51 17N 7 21 E
Ennepetalsp →, *Ruhr* **6 C6** 51 14N 7 24 E
Enskede, *Stock.* **3 E11** 59 17N 18 4 E
Entrevias, *Mdrd.* **8 B2** 40 22N 3 40W
Épiais-les-Louvres, *Paris* **5 A5** 49 1N 2 33 E
Epinay, *Paris* **5 B3** 48 57N 2 19 E
Epinay-sous-Sénart, *Paris* **5 C5** 48 41N 2 30 E
Epinay-sur-Orge, *Paris* **5 C3** 48 40N 2 19 E
Eppende, *Ruhr* **6 B4** 51 28N 7 9 E
Eppenhausen, *Ruhr* **6 B6** 51 22N 7 29 E
Epping, *Lon.* **4 A5** 51 41N 0 6 E
Epping, *Melb.* **19 D7** 37 39 S 145 1 E
Epping, *Syd.* **19 A3** 33 46 S 151 5 E
Epping Forest, *Lon.* **4 B5** 51 39N 0 2 E
Epsom, *Lon.* **4 D3** 51 19N 0 15W
Epsom Racecourse, *Lon.* **4 D3** 51 18N 0 15W
Éragny, *Paris* **5 A2** 49 1N 2 5 E
Ercolano, *Nápl.* **9 J13** 40 48N 14 21 E
Érd, *Bud.* **10 K12** 47 23N 18 56 E
Erdenheim, *Phil.* **24 A3** 40 5N 75 12W
Eregun, *Lagos* **18 A2** 6 35N 7 22 E
Erenköy, *Ist.* **17 B3** 40 58N 29 3 E
Ergal, *Paris* **5 C1** 48 47N 1 55 E
Erial, *Phil.* **24 C4** 39 46N 75 0W
Erith, *Lon.* **4 C6** 51 28N 0 11 E
Erkner, *Berl.* **7 B5** 52 25N 13 44 E
Erkrath, *Ruhr* **6 C3** 51 13N 6 54 E
Erlaa, *Wien* **10 H9** 48 9N 16 19 E
Erle, *Ruhr* **6 A4** 51 33N 7 4 E
Ermelino Matarazzo, *S. Pau.* **31 D7** 23 29 S 46 28W
Ermington, *Syd.* **19 A3** 33 48 S 151 4 E
Ermont, *Paris* **5 B3** 48 59N 2 15 E
Ersébet-Telep, *Bud.* **10 K14** 47 27N 19 10 E
Ershatou, *Gzh.* **14 G8** 23 6N 113 18 E
Erskineville, *Syd.* **19 B4** 33 54 S 151 12 E
Erstavik, *Stock.* **3 E12** 59 16N 18 14 E
Erstaviken, *Stock.* **3 E12** 59 16N 18 20 E
Erunkan, *Lagos* **18 A2** 6 36N 7 23 E
Eschenried, *Mün.* **7 F9** 48 13N 11 24 E
Esenler, *Ist.* **17 A2** 41 1N 28 52 E
Esher, *Lon.* **4 C2** 51 22N 0 20W
Eshratābād, *Tehr.* **17 C5** 35 42N 51 27 E
España, *B.A.* **32 C5** 34 46 S 58 14W
Espeleta, *B.A.* **32 C5** 34 45 S 58 15W
Esplugas, *Barc.* **8 D5** 41 22N 2 5 E
Espoo, *Hels.* **3 B2** 60 13N 24 38 E
Espoonlahti, *Hels.* **3 B2** 60 9N 24 31 E
Esposizione Univ. di Roma (E.U.R.), *Rome* **9 G9** 41 49N 12 28 E
Essen, *Ruhr* **6 B4** 51 27N 7 0 E
Essen-Mülheim, Flughafen, *Ruhr* **6 B3** 51 24N 6 56 E
Essendon, *Melb.* **19 E6** 37 44 S 144 55 E
Essendon Airport, *Melb.* **19 E6** 37 43 S 144 54 E
Essex, *Balt.* **25 B4** 39 18N 76 28W
Essex Falls, *N.Y.* **22 C3** 40 49N 74 16W
Essingen, *Stock.* **3 E10** 59 19N 17 59 E
Essling, *Wien* **10 G11** 48 12N 16 30 E
Est, Gare de l', *Paris* **5 B4** 48 52N 2 21 E
Estado, Parque do, *S. Pau.* **31 E6** 23 38 S 46 38W
Estby, *Hels.* **3 C1** 60 5N 24 27W
Este, Parque Nacional del, *Car.* **30 E5** 10 29N 66 50W
Esteban Echeverria, *B.A.* **32 C4** 34 48 S 58 29W
Estlotan, *Hels.* **3 C6** 60 7N 25 13 E
Estrela, Basilica da, *Lisb.* **8 F8** 38 42N 9 9W
Étiolles, *Paris* **5 D4** 48 38N 2 28 E
Etobicoke, *Trto.* **20 E7** 43 39N 79 34W
Etobicoke Cr. →, *Trto.* **20 E7** 43 35N 79 32W
Etzenhauzen, *Mün.* **7 F9** 48 16N 11 27 E
Eun Pyeong, *Sŏul* **12 G7** 37 36N 126 56 E
Eungam, *Sŏul* **12 G7** 37 34N 126 55 E
Evanston, *Chic.* **26 A2** 42 3N 87 40W
Évecquemont, *Paris* **5 A1** 49 0N 1 56 E
Everett, *Bost.* **21 C3** 42 24N 71 3W
Evergreen Park, *Chic.* **26 C2** 41 43N 87 42W
Eversael, *Ruhr* **6 A1** 51 32N 6 39 E
Evesboro, *Phil.* **24 B5** 39 54N 74 55W
Eving, *Ruhr* **6 A6** 51 33N 7 28 E
Evry, *Paris* **5 D4** 48 38N 2 26 E
Évry-les-Châteaux, *Paris* **5 D5** 48 39N 2 38 E
Évzonos, *Ath.* **8 J11** 37 55N 23 49 E
Ewin, *Tehr.* **17 C5** 35 47N 51 23 E
Ewu, *Lagos* **18 A1** 6 33N 7 19 E
Exelberg, *Wien* **10 G9** 48 14N 16 15 E
Eynsford, *Lon.* **4 C6** 51 21N 0 12 E
Eyup, *Ist.* **17 A2** 41 2N 28 55 E
Ez Zeitûn, *El Qâ.* **18 C5** 30 6N 31 18 E
Ézanville, *Paris* **5 A4** 49 1N 2 21 E
Ezeiza, *B.A.* **32 D3** 34 50 S 58 31W
Ezeiza, Aeropuerto, *B.A.* **32 C3** 34 48 S 58 32W

F

Fabreville, *Mtrl.* **20 A2** 43 33N 73 51W
Fælledparken, *Købn.* **2 D10** 55 42N 12 34 E
Fågelön, *Stock.* **3 E10** 59 18N 17 55 E
Fagersjo, *Stock.* **3 E11** 59 14N 18 4 E
Fagnano, *Mil.* **9 E4** 45 24N 8 59 E
Fahrn, *Ruhr* **6 A2** 51 30N 6 45 E
Faibano, *Nápl.* **9 H13** 40 55N 14 27 E
Fair Lawn, *N.Y.* **22 B4** 40 55N 74 7W
Fairfax, *Phil.* **24 C1** 39 47N 75 33W
Fairfax, *Wash.* **25 D6** 38 50N 77 19W
Fairfax Station, *Wash.* **25 E6** 38 48N 77 19W
Fairfield, *Melb.* **19 E7** 37 46 S 145 2 E
Fairfield, *N.Y.* **22 B3** 40 53N 74 17W
Fairfield, *Syd.* **19 B2** 33 52 S 150 56 E
Fairhaven B., *Bost.* **21 C1** 42 25N 71 21W
Fairhaven Hill, *Bost.* **21 C1** 42 26N 71 21W
Fairland, *Jobg.* **18 E8** 26 8 S 27 57 E
Fairland, *Wash.* **25 C8** 39 4N 76 57W
Fairmont Terrace, *S.F.* **27 B4** 37 42N 122 7W
Fairmount Heights, *Wash.* **25 D8** 38 54N 76 54W
Fairmount Park, *Phil.* **24 A3** 40 3N 75 13W
Fairport, *Trto.* **20 D10** 43 49N 79 4W
Fairview, *N.Y.* **22 C5** 40 48N 73 59W
Fairview, *N.Y.* **23 A6** 41 1N 73 46W
Falenica, *Wsaw.* **10 F8** 52 9N 21 12 E
Falenty, *Wsaw.* **10 F6** 52 8N 20 55 E
Falkenburg, *Berl.* **7 A4** 52 34N 13 32 E
Falkenhagen, *Berl.* **7 A1** 52 34N 13 5 E
Falkensee, *Berl.* **7 A1** 52 34N 13 4 E
Fallon, *L.A.* **28 C5** 33 59N 117 54W
Falls Church, *Wash.* **25 D6** 38 53N 77 12W
Falls Run →, *Balt.* **25 A1** 39 21N 76 52W
Falomo, *Lagos* **18 B2** 6 26N 7 26 E
Fangcun, *Gzh.* **14 G8** 23 6N 113 13 E
Fanwood, *N.Y.* **22 D2** 40 37N 74 23W
Far Rockaway, *N.Y.* **23 D6** 40 36N 73 45W
Farahābād, *Tehr.* **17 C5** 35 41N 51 29 E
Färentuna, *Stock.* **3 D8** 59 23N 17 39 E
Farforovskaya, *St-Pet.* **11 B4** 59 52N 30 27 E
Farm Pond, *Bost.* **21 D2** 42 13N 71 20W
Farmingdale, *N.Y.* **23 C8** 40 43N 73 27W
Farmsen, *Hbg.* **7 D8** 53 36N 10 8 E
Farnborough, *Lon.* **4 C5** 51 21N 0 3 E
Farningham, *Lon.* **4 C6** 51 23N 0 12 E
Farrar Pond, *Bost.* **21 C1** 42 24N 71 21W
Farrarmere, *Jobg.* **18 E10** 26 9 S 28 18 E
Farsta, *Stock.* **3 E11** 59 14N 18 5 E
Farstalandet, *Stock.* **3 E13** 59 18N 18 23 E
Farum, *Købn.* **2 D8** 55 48N 12 21 E
Farum Sø, *Købn.* **2 D9** 55 48N 12 21 E
Fasanerie-Nord, *Mün.* **7 F10** 48 11N 11 32 E
Fasangarten, *Mün.* **7 G10** 48 5N 11 36 E
Fat Tau Chau, *H.K.* **12 E6** 22 16N 114 16 E
Fatih, *Ist.* **17 A2** 41 0N 28 56 E
Favoriten, *Wien* **10 H10** 48 9N 16 23 E
Fawkner, *Melb.* **19 E6** 37 42 S 144 56 E
Fawkner Park, *Melb.* **19 F6** 37 50 S 144 58 E
Feasterville, *Phil.* **24 A4** 40 9N 75 0W
Febrero, Parque de, *B.A.* **32 B4** 34 36 S 58 25W
Feijó, *Lisb.* **8 G8** 38 39N 9 9W
Feldersbruch →, *Ruhr* **6 B5** 51 23N 7 4 E
Feldhausen, *Ruhr* **6 A3** 51 36N 6 58 E
Feldkirchen, *Mün.* **7 G11** 48 8N 11 43 E
Feldmoching, *Mün.* **7 F10** 48 14N 11 32 E
Fellowship, *Phil.* **24 B5** 39 56N 74 57W
Feltham, *Lon.* **4 C2** 51 26N 0 24W
Feltonville, *Phil.* **24 A4** 40 1N 75 8W
Fenerbahce, *Ist.* **17 B3** 40 58N 29 2 E
Fengtai, *Beij.* **14 C2** 39 49N 116 14 E
Fenino, *Mos.* **11 E11** 55 43N 37 56 E
Ferencváros, *Bud.* **10 K13** 47 29N 19 5 E
Ferihegyi Airport, *Bud.* **10 K14** 47 26N 19 14 E
Ferndale, *Balt.* **25 B3** 39 11N 76 38W
Ferndale, *Jobg.* **18 E9** 26 5 S 28 0 E
Ferntree Gully, *Melb.* **19 F8** 37 52 S 145 17 E
Ferntree Gully Nat. Park, *Melb.* **19 F8** 37 52 S 145 19 E
Ferny Cr. →, *Melb.* **19 F8** 37 54 S 145 16 E
Férolles-Attilly, *Paris* **5 C5** 48 44N 2 37 E
Ferraz de Vasconcelos, *S. Pau.* **31 E7** 23 32 S 46 22W
Ferrières-en-Brie, *Paris* **5 C6** 48 49N 2 42 E
Ferry, *N.Y.* **23 A5** 41 0N 73 52W
Fetcham, *Lon.* **4 D2** 51 17N 0 21W
Feucherolles, *Paris* **5 B1** 48 52N 1 58 E
Fichtenau, *Berl.* **7 B5** 52 27N 13 42 E
Fields Corner, *Bost.* **21 D3** 42 18N 71 3W
Fiera Camp, *Mil.* **9 E5** 45 28N 9 9 E
Figino, *Mil.* **9 E5** 45 29N 9 4 E
Fijir, *Bagd.* **17 E8** 33 21N 44 21 E
Filadhélfia, *Ath.* **8 H11** 38 2N 23 43 E
Fili-Masilovo, *Mos.* **11 E8** 55 44N 37 29 E
Filothei, *Ath.* **8 H11** 38 2N 23 46 E
Finaalspan, *Jobg.* **18 F10** 26 16 S 28 16 E
Finchley, *Lon.* **4 B3** 51 36N 0 11W
Finkenkrug, *Berl.* **7 A1** 52 33N 13 3 E
Finkenwerder, *Hbg.* **7 D7** 53 32N 9 51 E
Finsbury, *Lon.* **4 B4** 51 31N 0 6W
Finsbury Park, *Lon.* **4 B4** 51 34N 0 6W
Fiorito, *B.A.* **32 C4** 34 42 S 58 26W
Firdows, *Bagd.* **17 F7** 33 17N 44 17 E
Firōz Bahram, *Tehr.* **17 D4** 35 37N 51 14 E
Fischeln, *Ruhr* **6 C1** 51 18N 6 35 E
Fish Brook →, *Bost.* **21 B3** 42 39N 71 1W
Fishermans Bend, *Melb.* **19 E6** 37 49 S 144 55 E
Fisher's Hill, *Jobg.* **18 F10** 26 10 S 28 10 E
Fisherville, *Trto.* **20 D8** 43 46N 79 28W
Fisksätra, *Stock.* **3 E12** 59 17N 18 13 E
Fittja, *Stock.* **3 E10** 59 14N 17 51 E
Fitzroy Gardens, *Melb.* **19 E6** 37 48 S 144 58 E
Five Cowrie Cr. →, *Lagos* **18 B2** 6 26N 7 25 E
Five Dock, *Syd.* **19 B3** 33 52 S 151 8 E
Fjellstrand, *Oslo* **2 C3** 59 47N 10 36 E
Flachsberg, *Ruhr* **6 C4** 51 11N 7 4 E
Flag →, *Chic.* **26 C1** 41 43N 87 55W
Flamengo, *Rio J.* **31 B2** 22 56 S 43 11W
Flaminio, *Rome* **9 F9** 41 55N 12 28 E
Flaskebekk, *Oslo* **2 B3** 59 51N 10 39 E
Flatbush, *N.Y.* **22 D5** 40 39N 73 56W
Flaten, *Stock.* **3 E11** 59 15N 18 9 E
Flemington, *Syd.* **19 B3** 33 53 S 151 4 E
Flemington Racecourse, *Melb.* **19 E6** 37 47 S 144 54 E
Fleury-Mérogis, *Paris* **5 D4** 48 37N 2 21 E
Flingern, *Ruhr* **6 C2** 51 13N 6 48 E
Flint Pk., *L.A.* **28 B3** 34 9N 118 11 E
Floral Park, *N.Y.* **23 C6** 40 43N 73 42W
Florence, *L.A.* **28 C3** 33 57N 118 13W
Florence, *Phil.* **24 C5** 39 44N 74 55W
Florence Bloom Bird Sanctuary, *Jobg.* **18 E9** 26 7 S 28 0 E
Florencio Varela, *B.A.* **32 C5** 34 49 S 58 18W
Florentia, *Jobg.* **18 F9** 26 16 S 28 8 E
Flores, *B.A.* **32 B4** 34 38 S 58 27W
Floresta, *B.A.* **32 B4** 34 37 S 58 27W
Florham Park, *N.Y.* **22 C2** 40 46N 74 23W
Florida, *B.A.* **32 B4** 34 31 S 58 28W
Florida, *Jobg.* **18 F8** 26 10 S 27 55 E
Florida L., *Jobg.* **18 F8** 26 10 S 27 54 E
Floridsdorf, *Wien* **10 G10** 48 15N 16 26 E
Flourtown, *Phil.* **24 A3** 40 6N 75 13W
Flower Hill, *N.Y.* **23 C6** 40 48N 73 40W
Flushing, *N.Y.* **23 C6** 40 45N 73 49W
Flushing Meadows Corona Park, *N.Y.* **23 C5** 40 44N 73 50W
Flysta, *Stock.* **3 D10** 59 22N 17 54 E
Fo Tan, *H.K.* **12 D6** 22 23N 114 11 E
Föhrenhain, *Wien* **10 G10** 48 19N 16 26 E
Folcroft, *Phil.* **24 B3** 39 53N 75 16W
Folsom, *Phil.* **24 B3** 39 53N 75 19W
Fontainebleau, *Jobg.* **18 E8** 26 6 S 27 57 E
Fontana, *La Hab.* **30 B2** 23 1N 82 24W
Fontanka, *St-Pet.* **11 B3** 59 54N 30 16 E
Fontenay-aux-Roses, *Paris* **5 C3** 48 47N 2 17 E
Fontenay-le-Fleury, *Paris* **5 C2** 48 48N 2 2 E
Fontenay-lès-Briis, *Paris* **5 D2** 48 37N 2 9 E
Fontenay-sous-Bois, *Paris* **5 B4** 48 51N 2 28 E
Foots Cray, *Lon.* **4 C5** 51 24N 0 7 E
Footscray, *Melb.* **19 E6** 37 48 S 144 56 E
Forbidden City, *Beij.* **14 B3** 39 53N 116 21 E
Fordham Univ., *N.Y.* **23 B5** 40 51N 73 51W
Fords, *N.Y.* **22 D3** 40 31N 74 19W
Fordsburg, *Jobg.* **18 F9** 26 12 S 28 2 E
Foremans Corner, *Balt.* **25 B3** 39 11N 76 33W
Forest Gate, *Lon.* **4 B5** 51 32N 0 1 E
Forest Heights, *Wash.* **25 E7** 38 48N 77 0W
Forest Hill, *Lon.* **4 C4** 51 26N 0 2W
Forest Hill, *Melb.* **19 F8** 37 50 S 145 10 E
Forest Hill, *Trto.* **20 D8** 43 41N 79 25W
Forest Hills, *N.Y.* **23 C5** 40 42N 73 51W
Forest Park, *Chic.* **26 B2** 41 51N 87 47W
Forest View, *Chic.* **26 C2** 41 48N 87 47W
Forestville, *Syd.* **19 A4** 33 46 S 151 12 E
Forestville, *Wash.* **25 D8** 38 50N 76 52W
Forges-les-Bains, *Paris* **5 D2** 48 37N 2 5 E
Fornacino, *Tori.* **9 B3** 45 9N 7 44 E
Fornebu, *Oslo* **2 B3** 59 53N 10 36 E
Fornebu Airport, *Oslo* **2 B3** 59 56N 10 37 E
Foro Italico, *Rome* **9 F9** 41 56N 12 26 E
Foro Romano, *Rome* **9 F9** 41 53N 12 29 E
Forst Rantzau, *Hbg.* **7 C6** 53 43N 9 49 E
Forstenried, *Mün.* **7 G9** 48 5N 11 29 E
Forstenrieder Park, *Mün.* **7 G9** 48 3N 11 27 E
Fort du Pont Park, *Wash.* **25 D8** 38 52N 76 56W
Fort Foote Village, *Wash.* **25 E7** 38 46N 77 1W
Fort Howard, *Balt.* **25 B4** 39 12N 76 26W
Fort Lee, *N.Y.* **22 B5** 40 50N 73 58W
Fort McHenry Nat. Mon., *Balt.* **25 B3** 35 15N 76 35W
Fort Washington, *Phil.* **24 A3** 40 8N 75 13W
Fort William, *Calc.* **16 E6** 22 33N 88 20 E
Foster City, *S.F.* **27 C3** 37 33N 122 15W
Fosters Pond, *Bost.* **21 B3** 42 36N 71 8W
Fourcherolle, *Paris* **5 C1** 48 42N 1 58 E
Fourmile Run →, *Wash.* **25 D7** 38 50N 77 2W
Fourqueux, *Paris* **5 B2** 48 53N 2 3 E
Fowl Meadow Res., *Bost.* **21 D3** 42 13N 71 8W
Fox Chase, *Phil.* **24 A4** 40 4N 75 5W
Foxhall, *Wash.* **25 C7** 39 4N 77 3W
Framingham, *Bost.* **21 D1** 42 18N 71 24W
Francisco Alvarez, *B.A.* **32 B1** 34 38 S 58 50W
Francisquito Cr. →, *S.F.* **27 D4** 37 27N 122 9W
Franconia, *Wash.* **25 E7** 38 47N 77 7W
Franconville, *Paris* **5 B3** 48 59N 2 13 E
Francop, *Hbg.* **7 D7** 53 30N 9 51 E
Frankel, *Sing.* **15 G8** 1 18N 103 55 E
Frankford, *Phil.* **24 A4** 40 1N 75 5W
Franklin L., *N.Y.* **22 B3** 40 59N 74 13W
Franklin Lakes, *N.Y.* **22 B3** 40 59N 74 13W
Franklin Park, *Bost.* **21 D3** 42 18N 71 5W
Franklin Park, *Chic.* **26 B1** 41 55N 87 52W
Franklin Park, *Wash.* **25 D7** 38 55N 77 9W
Franklin Res., *L.A.* **28 B2** 34 5N 118 24W
Franklin Roosevelt Park, *Jobg.* **18 E8** 26 8 S 27 59 E
Franklin Roosevelt Park, *Phil.* **24 B3** 39 54N 75 10W
Franklin Square, *N.Y.* **23 C6** 40 42N 73 40W
Frattamaggiore, *Nápl.* **9 H12** 40 56N 14 16 E
Frauenkirche, *Mün.* **7 G10** 48 8N 11 34 E
Frederiksberg, *Købn.* **2 D10** 55 40N 12 33 E
Frederiksdal, *Købn.* **2 D9** 55 46N 12 25 E
Fredersdorf, *Berl.* **7 A5** 52 31N 13 45 E
Fredersdorf Nord, *Berl.* **7 A5** 52 32N 13 45 E
Freeport, *N.Y.* **23 D7** 40 39N 73 35W
Freidrichshain, Volkspark, *Berl.* **7 A3** 52 31N 13 25 E
Freiham, *Mün.* **7 G9** 48 8N 11 25 E
Freimann, *Mün.* **7 F10** 48 11N 11 37 E
Fremont, *S.F.* **27 C4** 37 33N 122 2W
Fresh Meadows, *N.Y.* **23 C6** 40 43N 73 47W
Fresh Pond, *Bost.* **21 C3** 42 22N 71 8W
Freskati, *Stock.* **3 D11** 59 22N 18 3 E
Fresnes, *Paris* **5 C3** 48 45N 2 18 E
Fretay, *Paris* **5 C3** 48 40N 2 12 E
Freudenau, *Wien* **10 G10** 48 11N 16 25 E
Friedenau, *Berl.* **7 B3** 52 28N 31 20 E
Friederikenhof, *Berl.* **7 B3** 52 23N 13 21 E
Friedrichsfeld, *Ruhr* **6 A1** 51 37N 6 39 E
Friedrichsfelde, *Berl.* **7 B4** 52 29N 13 33 E
Friedrichshagen, *Berl.* **7 B4** 52 27N 13 37 E
Friedrichshain, *Berl.* **7 A3** 52 31N 13 25 E
Friedrichshulde, *Hbg.* **7 D7** 53 36N 9 51 E
Friedrichslust, *Berl.* **7 A5** 52 33N 13 43 E
Frielas, *Lisb.* **8 F8** 38 49N 9 6W
Friemersheim, *Ruhr* **6 B2** 51 23N 6 42 E
Friern Barnet, *Lon.* **4 B4** 51 37N 0 9W
Friherrs, *Hels.* **3 B3** 60 16N 24 49 E
Frogner, *Oslo* **2 A6** 60 1N 11 6 E
Frohnau, *Berl.* **7 A2** 52 38N 13 16 E
Frohnhausen, *Ruhr* **6 B3** 51 26N 6 56 E
Frontón, I., *Lima* **30 G7** 12 7 S 77 11W
Frunze, *Mos.* **11 E9** 55 47N 37 33 E
Fuchź, *Tōkyō* **13 B1** 35 40N 139 29 E
Fuencarral, *Mdrd.* **8 B2** 40 29N 3 42W
Fuhlenbrock, *Ruhr* **6 A3** 51 32N 6 54 E
Fuhlsbüttel, *Hbg.* **7 D8** 53 37N 10 1 E
Fujidera, *Ōsaka* **12 C4** 34 34N 135 36 E
Fujikubo, *Tōkyō* **13 B2** 35 49N 139 31 E
Fujimi, *Tōkyō* **13 A2** 35 50N 139 33 E
Fukagawa, *Tōkyō* **13 C3** 35 39N 139 48 E
Fukami, *Tōkyō* **13 D1** 35 28N 139 27 E
Fukiai, *Ōsaka* **12 B2** 34 42N 135 12 E
Fukuoka, *Tōkyō* **13 A2** 35 52N 139 31 E
Fukushima, *Ōsaka* **12 B3** 34 41N 135 28 E
Fulatani, *Tōkyō* **13 D1** 35 22N 139 30 E
Fulham, *Lon.* **4 C3** 51 28N 0 12W
Fuller Park, *L.A.* **28 C5** 33 51N 117 56W
Fullerton, *Balt.* **25 A3** 39 22N 76 30W
Funabori, *Tōkyō* **13 B4** 35 41N 139 52 E
Funasaka, *Ōsaka* **12 B2** 34 48N 135 16 E
Fünfhaus, *Wien* **10 G10** 48 11N 16 20 E
Fünfhausen, *Hbg.* **7 E8** 53 27N 10 2 E
Furesø, *Købn.* **2 D9** 55 47N 12 25 E
Fürstenried, *Mün.* **7 G9** 48 5N 11 28 E
Furth, *Mün.* **7 G10** 48 2N 11 35 E
Furu →, *Tōkyō* **13 A3** 35 54N 139 49 E
Furuyakami, *Tōkyō* **13 A2** 35 54N 139 31 E
Futago-tamagawaen, *Tōkyō* **13 C2** 35 36N 139 39 E
Futamatagawa, *Tōkyō* **13 D2** 35 27N 139 31 E
Futatsubashi, *Tōkyō* **13 D1** 35 28N 139 29 E
Fuxing Dao, *Shang.* **14 J12** 31 16N 121 33 E
Fuxing Gongyuan, *Shang.* **14 J11** 31 13N 121 27 E
Fuxinglu, *Beij.* **14 B2** 39 52N 116 16 E
Fuxingmen, *Beij.* **14 B2** 39 53N 116 19 E

G

Gadstrup, *Købn.* **2 E7** 55 34N 12 5 E
Gaebong, *Sŏul* **12 H7** 37 29N 126 52 E
Gage Park, *Chic.* **26 C2** 41 47N 87 42W
Gagny, *Paris* **5 B5** 48 53N 2 32 E
Gaillon, *Paris* **5 A1** 49 1N 1 53 E
Galata, *Ist.* **17 A2** 41 1N 28 58 E
Galátsion, *Ath.* **8 H11** 38 1N 23 45 E
Galeâo, *Rio J.* **31 A2** 22 49 S 43 14W
Galéria →, *Rome* **9 F9** 41 57N 12 20 E
Gallows Corner, *Lon.* **4 B6** 51 35N 0 13 E
Gällstaö, *Stock.* **3 E10** 59 17N 17 51 E
Galyanovo, *Mos.* **11 E10** 55 48N 37 47 E
Galyeon, *Sŏul* **12 G7** 37 36N 126 55 E
Gambir, *Jak.* **15 H9** 6 9 S 106 48 E
Gamboa, *Rio J.* **31 B2** 22 53 S 43 11W
Gambolóita, *Mil.* **9 E6** 45 26N 9 13 E
Gamelinha →, *S. Pau.* **31 E6** 23 31 S 46 31W
Gamlebyen, *Oslo* **2 B4** 59 54N 10 46 E
Gamlebyen, *Shang.* **14 J11** 31 13N 121 29 E
Gamō, *Tōkyō* **13 A3** 35 52N 139 48 E
Gang Dong, *Sŏul* **12 G8** 37 30N 127 5 E
Gang Nam, *Sŏul* **12 G7** 37 30N 126 59 E
Gang Sea, *Sŏul* **12 G7** 37 32N 126 51 E
Gangadharpur, *Calc.* **16 E5** 22 35N 88 11 E
Gangtou, *Gzh.* **14 F7** 23 12N 113 8 E
Gangwei, *Gzh.* **14 G8** 23 4N 113 11 E
Ganløse, *Købn.* **2 D8** 55 47N 12 15 E
Ganløse Orned, *Købn.* **2 D8** 55 48N 12 18 E
Ganshi, *Gzh.* **14 F7** 23 10N 113 8 E
Gants Hill, *Lon.* **4 B5** 51 34N 0 4 E
Gaoqiao, *Shang.* **14 H12** 31 21N 121 34 E
Garbagnate Milanese, *Mil.* **9 D5** 45 34N 9 4 E
Garbatella, *Rome* **9 F10** 41 51N 12 30 E
Garches, *Paris* **5 B3** 48 50N 2 11 E
Garching, *Mün.* **7 F11** 48 14N 11 39 E
Garden City, *El Qâ.* **18 C5** 30 2N 31 14 E
Garden City, *N.Y.* **23 C7** 40 43N 73 37W
Garden Reach, *Calc.* **16 E5** 22 33N 88 15 E
Gardena, *L.A.* **28 C3** 33 53N 118 18W
Garder, *Oslo* **2 C3** 59 45N 10 38 E
Garfield, *N.Y.* **22 B4** 40 52N 74 7W
Garfield Park, *Chic.* **26 B2** 41 52N 87 42W
Gargareta, *Ath.* **8 J11** 37 57N 23 43 E
Garges-lès-Gonesse, *Paris* **5 B4** 48 58N 2 25 E
Garhi Naraina, *Delhi* **16 B1** 28 37N 77 8 E
Garibong, *Sŏul* **12 H7** 37 29N 126 54 E
Garin, *B.A.* **32 A2** 34 25 S 58 44W
Gariya, *Calc.* **16 F6** 22 28N 88 23 E
Garji, *Calc.* **16 C5** 22 50N 88 19 E
Garne, *Paris* **5 C1** 48 41N 1 58 E
Garrison, *Balt.* **25 A2** 39 24N 76 45W
Garstedt, *Hbg.* **7 C7** 53 40N 9 59 E
Gartenstadt, *Ruhr* **6 B6** 51 30N 7 30 E
Garulia, *Calc.* **16 D6** 22 48N 88 22 E
Garvanza, *L.A.* **28 B3** 34 6N 118 11 E
Garwood, *N.Y.* **22 D3** 40 38N 74 18W
Gary, *Chic.* **26 D4** 41 35N 87 23W
Gåshaga, *Stock.* **3 D12** 59 21N 18 13 E
Gássino Torinese, *Tori.* **9 B3** 45 7N 7 49 E
Gästerby, *Hels.* **3 C1** 60 8N 24 27 E
Gateão, Aéroporto de, *Rio J.* **31 A2** 22 49 S 43 15W
Gateway of India, *Bomb.* **16 H8** 18 55N 72 50 E
Gatow, *Berl.* **7 B1** 52 29N 13 11 E
Gaurhati, *Calc.* **16 D6** 22 48N 88 21 E
Gauripur, *Calc.* **16 C6** 22 53N 88 25 E
Gavá, *Barc.* **8 E5** 41 18N 2 0 E
Gavamar, *Barc.* **8 E4** 41 16N 1 58 E
Gavanpada, *Bomb.* **16 H9** 18 57N 73 0 E
Gávea, *Rio J.* **31 B2** 22 58 S 43 13W
Gávea, Pedra da, *Rio J.* **31 B2** 22 59 S 43 18W
Gbogbo, *Lagos* **18 A3** 6 35N 7 31 E
Gebel el Ahmar, *El Qâ.* **18 C5** 30 2N 31 19 E
Gebel el Muqattam, *El Qâ.* **18 C5** 30 1N 31 17 E
Gebel et Tura, *El Qâ.* **18 D5** 29 56N 31 15 E
Geduld Dam, *Jobg.* **18 F11** 26 12 S 28 24 E
Geiselgasteig, *Mün.* **7 G10** 48 3N 11 33 E
Geist Res., *Phil.* **24 B2** 39 57N 75 24W
Gellért hegy, *Bud.* **10 K13** 47 29N 19 3 E
Gelsenkirchen, *Ruhr* **6 A4** 51 32N 7 2 E
General Ignacio Allende, *Méx.* **29 B1** 19 20N 99 21W
General Pacheco, *B.A.* **32 A3** 34 27 S 58 36W
General San Martin, *B.A.* **32 B3** 34 35 S 58 32W
General Sarmiento, *B.A.* **32 B2** 34 32 S 58 43W
General Urquiza, *B.A.* **32 B4** 34 34 S 58 28W
Gennebreck, *Ruhr* **6 C5** 51 18N 7 12 E
Gennevilliers, *Paris* **5 B3** 48 56N 2 17 E
Gentilly, *Paris* **5 C4** 48 48N 2 21 E
Gentofte, *Købn.* **2 D10** 55 44N 12 32 E
Georges →, *Syd.* **19 B2** 33 56 S 150 55 E
Georges Hall, *Syd.* **19 B2** 33 54 S 150 59 E
Georges I., *Bost.* **21 D4** 42 19N 70 55W
Georges River Bridge, *Syd.* **19 C3** 34 0 S 151 6 E
Georgetown, *Wash.* **25 D7** 38 54N 77 3W
Georgetown Rowley State Forest, *Bost.* **21 A4** 42 41N 70 56W
Georgsweide, *Hbg.* **7 D8** 53 30N 10 1 E
Gerasdorf bei Wein, *Wien* **10 G10** 48 17N 16 28 E
Gerberau, *Mün.* **7 F9** 48 12N 11 27 E
Gérbido, *Tori.* **9 B2** 45 2N 7 36 E
Gerlev, *Købn.* **2 D7** 55 49N 12 0 E
Gerli, *B.A.* **32 C4** 34 41 S 58 22W
Germantown, *Balt.* **25 A4** 39 24N 76 28W
Germantown, *Phil.* **24 A3** 40 2N 75 11W
Germiston, *Jobg.* **18 F9** 26 13 S 28 10 E
Gerresheim, *Ruhr* **6 C3** 51 14N 6 51 E
Gersthof, *Wien* **10 G9** 48 14N 16 18 E
Gerthe, *Ruhr* **6 A5** 51 31N 7 16 E

38 Gesîrat el Rauda

Gesîrat el Rauda, *El Qâ.* 18 C5 30 1N 31 13 E
Gesîrat Muhammad, *El Qâ.* 18 C5 30 6N 31 11 E
Gesterby, *Hels.* 3 A6 60 20N 25 17 E
Getafe, *Mdrd.* 8 C2 40 18N 3 43W
Gevelsberg, *Ruhr* 6 C6 51 19N 7 21 E
Geylang, *Sing.* 15 G8 1 18N 103 53 E
Geylang →, *Sing.* 15 G8 1 18N 103 52 E
Geylang Serai, *Sing.* 15 G8 1 19N 103 53 E
Gezîrat edn Dhahab, *El Qâ.* 18 D5 29 59N 31 13 E
Gezîrat Warrâq el Hadar, *El Qâ.* 18 C5 30 6N 31 13 E
Gharapuri, *Bomb.* 16 H8 18 57N 72 57 E
Ghatkopar, *Bomb.* 16 G8 19 4N 72 54 E
Ghazipur, *Delhi* 16 B2 28 37N 77 19 E
Ghizri, *Kar.* 17 H11 24 49N 67 2 E
Ghizri Cr. →, *Kar.* 17 H11 24 47N 67 5 E
Ghonda, *Delhi* 16 A2 28 41N 77 16 E
Ghushuri, *Calc.* 16 E6 22 37N 88 21 E
Gianicolense, *Rome* 9 F9 51 53N 12 28 E
Giant, *S.F.* 27 A2 37 58N 122 20W
Gibbsboro, *Phil.* 24 B5 39 50N 74 57W
Gibbstown, *Phil.* 24 C3 39 49N 75 17W
Gibraltar Pt., *Trto.* 20 E8 43 36N 79 23W
Gidea Park, *Lon.* 4 B6 51 35N 0 11 E
Giesing, *Mün.* 7 G10 48 6N 11 35 E
Gif-sur-Yvette, *Paris* 5 C2 48 42N 2 8 E
Gilgo Beach, *N.Y.* 23 D8 40 36N 73 24W
Gilgo I., *N.Y.* 23 D8 40 37N 73 23W
Gillette, *N.Y.* 22 C2 40 40N 74 29W
Gimmersta, *Stock.* 3 E12 59 14N 18 14 E
Ginza, *Tōkyō* 13 C3 35 39N 139 46 E
Girgaum, *Bomb.* 16 H8 18 57N 72 50 E
Giugliano in Campània, *Nápl.* 9 H12 40 55N 14 12 E
Givoletto, *Tori.* 9 B1 45 9N 7 29 E
Gjellumvatn, *Oslo* 2 C2 59 47N 10 26 E
Gjersjøen, *Oslo* 2 C4 59 47N 10 47 E
Glacier Hills, *N.Y.* 22 B2 40 51N 74 28W
Gladbeck, *Ruhr* 6 A3 51 34N 6 58 E
Gladesville, *Syd.* 19 B3 33 50 S 151 8 E
Gladökvarn, *Stock.* 3 E10 59 11N 17 59 E
Gladsakse, *Købn.* 2 D9 55 45N 12 25 E
Glashutte, *Hbg.* 7 C8 53 41N 10 2 E
Glashütte, *Ruhr* 6 C3 51 13N 6 51 E
Glasmoor, *Hbg.* 7 C8 53 42N 10 1 E
Glassmanor, *Wash.* 25 E7 38 49N 77 0W
Glen Cove, *N.Y.* 23 B7 40 52N 73 38W
Glen Echo, *Wash.* 25 D7 38 58N 77 8W
Glen Hd., *N.Y.* 23 C7 40 49N 73 37W
Glen Iris, *Melb.* 19 F7 37 51 S 145 3 E
Glen Mills, *Phil.* 24 B2 39 55N 75 29W
Glen Oaks, *N.Y.* 23 C6 40 45N 73 43W
Glen Riddle, *Phil.* 24 B2 39 53N 75 26W
Glen Ridge, *N.Y.* 22 C3 40 48N 74 12W
Glen Rock, *N.Y.* 22 B4 40 57N 74 7W
Glen Waverley, *Melb.* 19 F8 37 52 S 145 10 E
Glenardon, *Wash.* 25 D8 38 56N 76 51W
Glencoe, *Chic.* 26 A2 42 7N 87 44W
Glendale, *L.A.* 28 B3 34 9N 118 15 E
Glendora, *Phil.* 24 B4 39 50N 75 4W
Glenfield, *Syd.* 19 B2 33 58 S 150 53 E
Glenhazel, *Jobg.* 18 E9 26 8 S 28 6 E
Glenhuntly, *Melb.* 19 F7 37 52 S 145 1 E
Glenmont, *Wash.* 25 C7 39 3N 77 4W
Glenolden, *Phil.* 24 B3 39 54N 75 17W
Glenroy, *Melb.* 19 E6 37 42 S 144 55 E
Glenside, *Phil.* 24 A4 40 6N 75 9W
Glenview, *Chic.* 26 A2 42 3N 87 48W
Glenview Countryside, *Chic.* 26 A2 42 3N 87 49W
Glenview Woods, *Chic.* 26 A2 42 4N 87 46W
Glenville, *N.Y.* 23 A6 41 1N 73 41W
Glenvista, *Jobg.* 18 F9 26 17 S 28 3 E
Glenwood Landing, *N.Y.* 23 C7 40 48N 73 38W
Glienicke, *Berl.* 7 A2 52 38N 13 18 E
Glömsta, *Stock.* 3 E10 59 14N 17 55 E
Glosli, *Oslo* 2 A5 60 1N 10 55 E
Glostrup, *Købn.* 2 E9 55 39N 12 23 E
Gloucester City, *Phil.* 24 B4 39 53N 75 7W
Gocheog, *Sŏul* 12 G7 37 30N 126 52 E
Gocławek, *Wsaw.* 10 E7 52 14N 21 7 E
Goeselville, *Chic.* 26 D2 41 37N 87 46W
Goetjensort, *Hbg.* 7 E8 53 29N 10 2 E
Golabari, *Calc.* 16 E6 22 35N 88 20 E
Golabki, *Wsaw.* 10 E6 52 12N 20 52 E
Golden Gate, *S.F.* 27 B2 37 48N 122 29W
Golden Gate Bridge, *S.F.* 27 B2 37 49N 122 28W
Golden Gate National Recreation Area, *S.F.* 27 B1 37 49N 122 31W
Golden Gate Park, *S.F.* 27 B2 37 46N 122 28W
Golden Horn, *Ist.* 17 A2 41 1N 28 57 E
Golders Green, *Lon.* 4 B3 51 34N 0 11W
Golyevo, *Mos.* 11 E7 55 48N 37 18 E
Gometz-la-Ville, *Paris* 5 C2 48 40N 2 7 E
Gometz-le-Châtel, *Paris* 5 C2 48 40N 2 8 E
Gondangdra, *Jak.* 15 J9 6 11 S 106 49 E
Gonesse, *Paris* 5 B4 48 59N 2 26 E
Gongreung, *Sŏul* 12 G8 37 36N 127 3 E
González Catán, *B.A.* 32 C3 34 46 S 58 38W
Goodman Hill, *Bost.* 21 C1 42 22N 71 23W
Goodmayes, *Lon.* 4 B5 51 33N 0 6 E
Gopalnagar, *Calc.* 16 E5 22 50N 88 13 E
Gopalpur, *Calc.* 16 E6 22 38N 88 26 E
Górce, *Wsaw.* 10 E6 52 15N 20 55 E
Gordon, *Syd.* 19 A3 33 46 S 151 8 E
Gore Hill, *Syd.* 19 A4 33 49 S 151 10 E
Gorelyy →, *St-Pet.* 11 A5 60 1N 30 30 E
Gorenki, *Mos.* 11 E11 55 47N 37 53 E
Gorkiy Park, *Mos.* 11 E9 55 43N 37 36 E
Görväln, *Stock.* 3 D9 59 26N 17 45 E
Gose Elbe →, *Hbg.* 7 E8 53 28N 10 6 E
Gosen, *Berl.* 7 B5 52 23N 13 43 E
Gosener kanal, *Berl.* 7 B5 52 24N 13 42 E
Goshenville, *Phil.* 24 B1 39 59N 75 32W
Gospel Oak, *Lon.* 4 B4 51 32N 0 9W
Gotanda, *Tōkyō* 13 C3 35 37N 139 43 E
Gotanno, *Tōkyō* 13 B3 35 45N 139 49 E
Goth Goli Mār, *Kar.* 17 G11 24 53N 67 1 E
Goth Sher Shāh, *Kar.* 17 G10 24 53N 66 59 E
Gournay-sur-Marne, *Paris* 5 B5 48 51N 2 34 E
Goussainville, *Paris* 5 A4 49 1N 2 27 E
Gouvernes, *Paris* 5 B6 48 51N 2 41 E
Governador, I. do, *Rio J.* 31 A2 22 48 S 43 13W
Governor's I., *N.Y.* 22 C4 40 41N 74 1W
Grabicz, *Wsaw.* 10 E8 52 19N 21 12 E
Grabów, *Wsaw.* 10 E6 52 8N 20 59 E
Gracia, *Barc.* 8 D6 41 24N 2 10 E
Gradyville, *Phil.* 24 B2 39 56N 75 27W
Gräfelfing, *Mün.* 7 G9 48 7N 11 25 E
Grafenwald, *Ruhr* 6 A3 51 34N 6 54 E
Graham Memorial Park, *Balt.* 25 A4 39 25N 76 29W
Gran Canal, *Méx.* 29 A3 19 34N 99 1W
Granada Hills, *L.A.* 28 A2 34 16N 118 30W
Grand Bourg, *B.A.* 32 A2 34 29 S 58 42W
Grand Calumet →, *Chic.* 26 D4 41 37N 87 28W
Grand Union Canal, *Lon.* 4 A2 51 42N 0 26W
Grande →, *S. Pau.* 31 F7 23 43 S 46 24W
Grange, *Tori.* 9 B1 45 7N 7 29 E
Grange Hill, *Lon.* 4 B5 51 36N 0 5 E
Granite, *Balt.* 25 A1 39 20N 76 51W
Graniteville, *N.Y.* 22 D3 40 37N 74 10W
Granja Viana, *S. Pau.* 31 E4 23 35 S 46 50W
Granlandet, *Hels.* 3 B6 60 10N 25 15 E
Granö, *Hels.* 3 B6 60 13N 25 14 E
Grant Park, *Chic.* 26 B3 41 52N 87 37W
Granville, *Syd.* 19 A3 33 49 S 151 1 E
Grape I., *Bost.* 21 D4 42 16N 70 55W
Grass Hassock Channel, *N.Y.* 23 D6 40 36N 73 47W
Grassey B., *N.Y.* 23 D6 40 37N 73 47W
Grassy Sprain Res., *N.Y.* 23 B5 40 58N 73 50W
Gratosóglio, *Mil.* 9 E6 45 24N 9 1 E
Gratzwalde, *Berl.* 7 B5 52 28N 13 42 E
Gravesend, *N.Y.* 22 D5 40 36N 73 56W
Grays, *Lon.* 4 C6 51 28N 0 19 E
Grazhdanka, *St-Pet.* 11 B4 59 59N 30 24 E
Great Blue Hill, *Bost.* 21 D3 42 12N 71 4W
Great Bookham, *Lon.* 4 D2 51 16N 0 21W
Great Brewster I., *Bost.* 21 C4 42 19N 70 53W
Great Captain I., *N.Y.* 23 B7 40 59N 73 37W
Great Falls, *Wash.* 25 D6 38 59N 77 17W
Great Falls Park, *Wash.* 25 D6 38 59N 77 14W
Great Kills, *N.Y.* 22 D4 40 32N 74 9W
Great Kills Harbour, *N.Y.* 22 D4 40 32N 74 8W
Great Neck, *N.Y.* 23 C6 40 48N 73 44W
Great Pond, *Bost.* 21 D3 42 11N 71 2W
Great South B., *N.Y.* 23 D9 40 39N 73 19W
Greco, *Mil.* 9 D6 45 30N 9 12 E
Greco I., *S.F.* 27 C3 37 30N 122 10W
Green Brae, *S.F.* 27 A1 37 57N 122 31W
Green Brook, *N.Y.* 22 D2 40 35N 74 26W
Green Is., *H.K.* 12 E5 22 17N 114 6 E
Green Land, *Jak.* 15 J9 6 17 S 106 46 E
Green Pond, *N.Y.* 22 A2 41 1N 74 29W
Green Street, *Lon.* 4 A3 51 40N 0 16W
Green Street Green, *Lon.* 4 C5 51 21N 0 5 E
Green Valley, *Syd.* 19 B2 33 54 S 150 53 E
Green Village, *N.Y.* 22 C2 40 44N 74 27W
Greenbelt, *Wash.* 25 C8 39 0N 76 52W
Greenbelt Park, *Wash.* 25 D8 38 58N 76 53W
Greenfield Park, *Mtrl.* 20 B5 43 29N 73 28W
Greenfields Village, *Phil.* 24 C4 39 49N 75 9W
Greenford, *Lon.* 4 B2 51 31N 0 21W
Greenhithe, *Lon.* 4 C6 51 27N 0 17 E
Greenlawn, *N.Y.* 23 B8 40 52N 73 22W
Greenpoint, *N.Y.* 22 C5 40 43N 73 57W
Greensborough, *Melb.* 19 E7 37 41 S 145 5 E
Greenside, *Jobg.* 18 E9 26 8 S 28 1 E
Greenvale, *N.Y.* 23 C7 40 48N 73 35W
Greenville Chauncey, *N.Y.* 23 B5 40 59N 73 50W
Greenwich, *Lon.* 4 C4 51 28N 0 0 E
Greenwich, *N.Y.* 23 A7 41 1N 73 37W
Greenwich, *Syd.* 19 B4 33 50 S 151 11 E
Greenwich Observatory, *Lon.* 4 C4 51 28N 0 0 E
Greenwich Pt., *N.Y.* 23 A7 41 0N 73 34W
Greenwich Village, *N.Y.* 22 C5 40 44N 73 59W
Greenwood, *Bost.* 21 C3 42 29N 71 2W
Grefsen, *Oslo* 2 B4 59 56N 10 47 E
Grégy-sur-Yerres, *Paris* 5 C5 48 40N 2 37 E
Greiffenburg, *Ruhr* 6 B1 51 20N 6 37 E
Gressy, *Paris* 5 B6 48 58N 2 40 E
Greve Strand, *Købn.* 2 E8 55 34N 12 18 E
Greystanes, *Syd.* 19 A2 33 49 S 150 58 E
Griebnitzsee, *Berl.* 7 B1 52 23N 13 8 E
Griffith Park, *L.A.* 28 B3 34 7N 118 18 E
Grignon, *Paris* 5 B1 48 50N 1 56 E
Grigny, *Paris* 5 D4 48 39N 2 23 E
Grinzing, *Wien* 10 G10 48 15N 16 20 E
Grisy-Suisnes, *Paris* 5 C6 48 41N 2 40 E
Gröbenried, *Mün.* 7 F9 48 13N 11 25 E
Grochów, *Wsaw.* 10 E7 52 15N 21 5 E
Grodzisk, *Wsaw.* 10 E7 52 19N 21 4 E
Grogol, *Jak.* 15 H9 6 9 S 106 47 E
Grogol, Kali →, *Jak.* 15 J9 6 11 S 106 47 E
Gronsdorf, *Mün.* 7 G11 48 7N 11 42 E
Grorud, *Oslo* 2 B5 59 57N 10 52 E
Gross Borstel, *Hbg.* 7 D7 53 36N 9 59 E
Gross Flottbek, *Hbg.* 7 D7 53 33N 9 53 E
Gross Glienicke, *Berl.* 7 B1 52 28N 13 6 E
Gross-Hadern, *Mün.* 7 G9 48 6N 11 29 E
Gross-Lappen, *Mün.* 7 F10 48 11N 11 35 E
Grosse Krampe, *Berl.* 7 B5 52 23N 13 40 E
Grosse Müggelsee, *Berl.* 7 B4 52 26N 13 38 E
Grossenbaum, *Ruhr* 6 B2 51 22N 6 46 E
Grossenzersdorf, *Wien* 10 G11 48 12N 16 33 E
Grossenzersdorfer Arm →, *Wien* 10 G11 48 12N 16 31 E
Grosser Biberhaufen, *Wien* 10 G10 48 12N 16 28 E
Grosser Wannsee, *Berl.* 7 B2 52 25N 13 10 E
Grossfeld-Siedlung, *Wien* 10 G10 48 16N 16 26 E
Grosshesselohe, *Mün.* 7 G10 48 3N 11 32 E
Grossjedlersdorf, *Wien* 10 G10 48 16N 16 23 E
Grossziethen, *Berl.* 7 B3 52 23N 13 26 E
Grozsówka, *Wsaw.* 10 E8 52 14N 21 13 E
Grove Hall, *Bost.* 21 D3 42 18N 71 4W
Grove Park, *Lon.* 4 C5 51 25N 0 1 E
Grove Park, *Lon.* 4 C3 51 28N 0 15W
Groveton, *Wash.* 25 E7 38 46N 77 6W
Grugliasco, *Tori.* 9 B2 45 5N 7 34 E
Gruiten, *Ruhr* 6 C4 51 12N 7 0 E
Grumme, *Ruhr* 6 B5 51 30N 7 15 E
Grumo Nevano, *Nápl.* 9 H12 40 56N 14 15 E
Grünau, *Berl.* 7 B4 52 24N 13 34 E
Grunewald, *Berl.* 7 B2 52 28N 13 15 E
Grünwald, *Mün.* 7 G10 48 2N 11 31 E
Grünwalder Forst, *Mün.* 7 G10 48 2N 11 33 E
Grymes Hill, *N.Y.* 22 D4 40 36N 74 6W
Gu Ro, *Sŏul* 12 G7 37 30N 126 51 E
Guadalupe, *Manila* 15 D4 14 34N 121 2 E
Guadalupe →, *S.F.* 27 D4 37 28N 122 4W
Guadalupe, Basilica de, *Méx.* 29 B3 19 29N 99 7W
Guadelupe, *Rio J.* 31 A1 22 49 S 43 20W
Guanabacoa, *La Hab.* 30 B3 23 7N 82 17W
Guanabara, *Rio J.* 31 B1 22 57 S 43 18W
Guanabara, B. de, *Rio J.* 31 B2 22 52 S 43 10W
Guanabara, Jardim, *Rio J.* 31 A2 22 48 S 43 11W
Guang'anmen, *Beij.* 14 B2 39 51N 116 18 E
Guangminglou, *Beij.* 14 B2 39 51N 116 23 E
Guangqumen, *Beij.* 14 B3 39 52N 116 25 E
Guangzhou, *Gzh.* 14 G8 23 6N 113 13 E
Guanshuo, *Gzh.* 14 G9 23 4N 113 22 E
Guantai, *Nápl.* 9 H12 40 52N 14 11 E
Guapira →, *S. Pau.* 31 D6 23 30 S 46 33W
Guarapiranga, Res. de, *S. Pau.* 31 F5 23 42 S 46 43W
Guardias, *Mdrd.* 8 B3 40 29N 3 31W
Guarulhos, *S. Pau.* 31 D6 23 28 S 46 32W
Guatao, *La Hab.* 30 B2 23 0N 82 29W
Guayacanes, Pta., *La Hab.* 30 A3 23 10N 82 16W
Gubernador Monteverde, *B.A.* 32 C5 34 47 S 58 16W
Gudö, *Stock.* 3 E12 59 12N 18 12 E
Güell, Parque de, *Barc.* 8 D6 41 24N 2 10 E
Guermantes, *Paris* 5 B6 48 51N 2 42 E
Gugging, *Wien* 10 G9 48 18N 16 15 E
Guianazes, *S. Pau.* 31 E7 23 32 S 46 24W
Guildford, *Syd.* 19 B2 33 51 S 150 59 E
Guinardó, *Barc.* 8 D6 41 24N 2 10 E
Gujiazhai, *Shang.* 14 H11 31 21N 121 23 E
Gulbāi, *Kar.* 17 G10 24 52N 66 58 E
Guldasteh, *Tehr.* 17 D4 35 36N 51 15 E
Gulistan Palace, *Tehr.* 17 C5 35 40N 51 24 E
Gulph Mills, *Phil.* 24 A2 40 4N 75 20W
Gumbostrand, *Hels.* 3 B6 60 15N 25 17 E
Güngören, *Ist.* 17 A2 41 1N 28 52 E
Gunnarsby, *Hels.* 3 C1 60 6N 24 28W
Gunnersbury, *Lon.* 4 C3 51 29N 0 17W
Gunnigfeld, *Ruhr* 6 B4 51 29N 7 8 E
Gunpowder Falls →, *Balt.* 25 A4 39 23N 76 36W
Gunung Sahari, *Jak.* 15 H9 6 9 S 106 49 E
Gupiing, *Manila* 15 E5 14 27N 121 11 E
Guryong San, *Sŏul* 12 H8 37 28N 127 3 E
Gustavsberg, *Stock.* 3 E13 59 19N 18 23 E
Guttenberg, *N.Y.* 22 C4 40 48N 74 0W
Gutuyevskiy, Os., *St-Pet.* 11 B3 59 53N 30 15 E
Guyancourt, *Paris* 5 C2 48 46N 2 4 E
Guyancourt, Aérodrome de, *Paris* 5 C2 48 45N 2 3 E
Gvali-patak →, *Bud.* 10 K13 47 23N 19 7 E
Gwan Ag, *Sŏul* 12 H7 37 29N 126 57 E
Gwanag San, *Sŏul* 12 H7 37 27N 126 58 E
Gwynns Falls →, *Balt.* 25 B2 39 19N 76 42W
Gyál, *Bud.* 10 K14 47 23N 19 13 E
Gyeongbong Palace, *Sŏul* 12 G7 37 34N 126 58 E
Gynea, *Syd.* 19 C3 34 1 S 151 5 E

H

Haaga, *Hels.* 3 B4 60 13N 24 53 E
Haan, *Ruhr* 6 C3 51 11N 6 59 E
Haar, *Mün.* 7 G11 48 6N 11 43 E
Haar, *Ruhr* 6 B5 51 26N 7 13 E
Haarzopf, *Ruhr* 6 B3 51 25N 6 57 E
Habana del Este, *La Hab.* 30 B3 23 9N 82 19W
Habay, *Manila* 15 E3 14 27N 120 56 E
Habikino, *Ōsaka* 12 C4 34 33N 135 36 E
Habinghorst, *Ruhr* 6 A5 51 34N 7 18 E
Hacienda Heights, *L.A.* 28 C5 33 59N 117 59W
Hackbridge, *Lon.* 4 C4 51 23N 0 9W
Hackensack, *N.Y.* 22 B4 40 52N 74 4W
Hackney, *Lon.* 4 B4 51 32N 0 3W
Hackney Wick, *Lon.* 4 B4 51 32N 0 1W
Haddon Heights, *Phil.* 24 B4 39 53N 75 3W
Haddonfield, *Phil.* 24 B4 39 53N 75 3W
Hadersdorf, *Wien* 10 G9 48 12N 16 14 E
Hadley Wood, *Lon.* 4 B3 51 39N 0 10W
Haga, *Stock.* 3 D11 59 21N 18 1 E
Hagem, *Ruhr* 6 A5 51 33N 7 19 E
Hagen, *Ruhr* 6 B6 51 21N 7 27 E
Hägersten, *Stock.* 3 E10 59 18N 17 59 E
Haggetts Pond, *Bost.* 21 B2 42 39N 71 11W
Häggvik, *Stock.* 3 D10 59 26N 17 56 E
Hagonoy, *Manila* 15 D4 14 30N 121 4 E
Hagsätra, *Stock.* 3 E11 59 15N 18 0 E
Hahipur, *Calc.* 16 D5 22 47N 88 10 E
Hahnenberg, *Ruhr* 6 C4 51 12N 7 9 E
Hai He →, *Tianj.* 14 E6 39 4N 117 17 E
Haidarpur, *Delhi* 16 A1 28 43N 77 8 E
Haidhausen, *Mün.* 7 G10 48 7N 11 36 E
Haidian, *Beij.* 14 B2 39 59N 116 16 E
Haight-Ashbury, *S.F.* 27 B2 37 46N 122 26W
Haiguangsi, *Tianj.* 14 E6 39 7N 117 11 E
Hainault, *Lon.* 4 B5 51 36N 0 6 E
Haizhu Guangchang, *Gzh.* 14 G8 23 6N 113 14 E
Hakim, *El Qâ.* 18 C4 30 4N 31 7 E
Hakunila, *Hels.* 3 B5 60 16N 25 6 E
Halchōbori, *Tōkyō* 13 B4 35 48N 139 55 E
Haledon, *N.Y.* 22 B3 40 56N 74 11W
Halesite, *N.Y.* 23 B8 40 53N 73 24W
Halethorpe, *Balt.* 25 B2 39 14N 76 41W
Half Hollow Hills, *N.Y.* 23 C8 40 48N 73 21W
Half Moon B., *S.F.* 26 D2 37 27N 122 25W
Half Moon Bay Airport, *S.F.* 27 C1 37 31N 122 30W
Half Moon Bay Beaches, *S.F.* 26 D2 37 28N 122 28W
Halim, *Jak.* 15 J10 6 15 S 106 53 E
Halim Perdanakusuma Airport, *Jak.* 15 J10 6 16 S 106 53 E
Halstead, *Lon.* 4 C5 51 19N 0 8 E
Halstenbeck, *Hbg.* 7 D7 53 38N 9 50 E
Haltiala, *Hels.* 3 B4 60 16N 24 57 E
Haltiavuori, *Hels.* 3 B4 60 16N 24 56 E
Ham, *Lon.* 4 C3 51 25N 0 18W
Ham, *Paris* 5 A2 49 1N 2 3 E
Hamberg, *Jobg.* 18 E8 26 9 S 27 54 E
Hamborn, *Ruhr* 6 B2 51 29N 6 46 E
Hamburg, *Hbg.* 7 D8 53 33N 10 0 E
Hamburg Flughafen, *Hbg.* 7 D7 53 38N 9 59 E
Hämeenkylä, *Hels.* 3 B3 60 16N 24 48 E
Hamm, *Hbg.* 7 D8 53 33N 10 2 E
Hamm, *Ruhr* 6 C2 51 12N 6 44 E
Hammarby, *Stock.* 3 E11 59 17N 18 5 E
Hamme, *Ruhr* 6 B5 51 29N 7 12 E
Hammel Arverne, *N.Y.* 23 D6 40 35N 73 48W
Hammerbrook, *Hbg.* 7 D8 53 32N 10 1 E
Hammersmith, *Lon.* 4 C3 51 29N 0 13W
Hammond, *Chic.* 26 D4 41 36N 87 29W
Hampstead, *Lon.* 4 B3 51 33N 0 10W
Hampstead, *Mtrl.* 20 B4 43 28N 73 37W
Hampstead Garden Suburb, *Lon.* 4 B3 51 34N 0 11W
Hampstead Heath, *Lon.* 4 B3 51 33N 0 10W
Hampton Court Palace, *Lon.* 4 C2 51 24N 0 20W
Hampton Hill, *Lon.* 4 C2 51 25N 0 21W
Hampton Wick, *Lon.* 4 C3 51 24N 0 18W
Hamrā, *Bagd.* 17 F7 33 18N 44 18 E
Han Gang →, *Sŏul* 12 G7 37 32N 126 55 E
Hanakuri, *Tōkyō* 13 A3 35 50N 139 47 E
Hanala, *Hels.* 3 A5 60 20N 25 4 E
Hancho, *Ōsaka* 12 B3 34 48N 135 28 E
Haneda, *Tōkyō* 13 C3 35 32N 139 44 E
Hang Hau, *H.K.* 12 E6 22 19N 114 16 E
Hanjiashu, *Tianj.* 14 D5 39 11N 117 4 E
Hanlon, *Trto.* 20 E7 43 38N 79 39W
Hansen Flood Control Basin, *L.A.* 28 A2 34 15N 118 23W
Hansia, *Calc.* 16 E6 22 48N 88 24 E
Hanskinen, *Hels.* 3 C6 60 8N 25 15 E
Hanwell, *Lon.* 4 B2 51 30N 0 20W
Hanworth, *Lon.* 4 C2 51 26N 0 23W
Haora, *Calc.* 16 E5 22 34N 88 18 E
Happy Valley, *H.K.* 12 E6 22 16N 114 11 E
Harajuku, *Tōkyō* 13 D2 35 22N 139 30 E
Haraki, *Tōkyō* 13 B4 35 42N 139 56 E
Harat, *Calc.* 16 C5 22 52N 88 11 E
Harbor Hills, *N.Y.* 23 C6 40 46N 73 44W
Harburg, *Hbg.* 7 E7 53 27N 9 59 E
Harding, *Bost.* 21 D2 42 12N 71 19W
Hardricourt, *Paris* 5 A1 49 0N 1 53 E
Harefield, *Lon.* 4 B2 51 36N 0 28W
Hareskovby, *Købn.* 2 D9 55 45N 12 23 E
Harewood Park, *Balt.* 25 A4 39 22N 76 21W
Harigaya, *Tōkyō* 13 B2 35 49N 139 33 E
Haringey, *Lon.* 4 B4 51 34N 0 4W
Haripur, *Calc.* 16 D5 22 42N 88 10 E
Harjula, *Hels.* 3 C5 60 6N 25 3 E
Harjusuo, *Hels.* 3 B5 60 19N 25 0 E
Harkortsee, *Ruhr* 6 B6 51 23N 7 24 E
Harksheide, *Hbg.* 7 C8 53 43N 10 0 E
Harlaching, *Mün.* 7 G10 48 5N 11 33 E
Harlem, *N.Y.* 22 C5 40 48N 73 56W
Harlesden, *Lon.* 4 B3 51 32N 0 14W
Harlington, *Lon.* 4 C2 51 29N 0 25W
Harmaja, *Hels.* 3 C4 60 6N 24 58 E
Harmashatar hegy, *Bud.* 10 J13 47 33N 19 0 E
Harmondsworth, *Lon.* 4 C2 51 29N 0 29W
Harmonville, *Phil.* 24 A3 40 5N 75 18W
Harold Hill, *Lon.* 4 B6 51 36N 0 14 E
Harold Parker State Forest, *Bost.* 21 B3 42 37N 71 4W
Harold Wood, *Lon.* 4 B6 51 35N 0 14 E
Harrington Park, *N.Y.* 22 B5 40 59N 73 59W
Harrison, *N.Y.* 22 C4 40 44N 74 9W
Harrison, *N.Y.* 23 B6 40 57N 73 42W
Harrisonville, *Balt.* 25 A2 39 22N 76 49W
Harrow, *Lon.* 4 B2 51 34N 0 20W
Harrow on the Hill, *Lon.* 4 B2 51 34N 0 21W
Harrow School, *Lon.* 4 B2 51 34N 0 20W
Harrow Weald, *Lon.* 4 B2 51 36N 0 20W
Hart I., *Balt.* 25 B4 39 14N 76 23W
Hart I., *N.Y.* 23 B6 40 51N 73 46W
Hartford, *Phil.* 24 B5 39 58N 74 53W
Hartley, *Lon.* 4 C6 51 22N 0 18 E
Hartsdale, *N.Y.* 23 A6 41 1N 73 48W
Harumi, *Tōkyō* 13 C3 35 38N 139 47 E
Harvard, Mt., *L.A.* 28 A4 34 12N 118 4W
Harvard Univ., *Bost.* 21 C3 42 23N 71 7W
Harvestehude, *Hbg.* 7 D7 53 34N 9 58 E
Harvey, *Chic.* 26 D3 41 36N 87 39W
Harwood Heights, *Chic.* 26 B2 41 57N 87 46W
Hasanābād, *Tehr.* 17 C4 35 44N 51 16 E
Hasbrouck Heights, *N.Y.* 22 B4 40 51N 74 6W
Haselbach, *Wien* 10 G9 48 18N 16 14 E
Haselhorst, *Berl.* 7 A2 52 33N 13 14 E
Hasköy, *Ist.* 17 A2 41 2N 28 57 E
Hasle, *Oslo* 2 C3 59 46N 10 38 E
Hasloh, *Hbg.* 7 C7 53 41N 9 54 E
Haslohfeld, *Hbg.* 7 C7 53 41N 9 56 E
Haslum, *Oslo* 2 B3 59 55N 10 34 E
Haspe, *Ruhr* 6 B6 51 21N 7 25 E
Haspertalsp, *Ruhr* 6 C6 51 17N 7 24 E
Hasselbeck, *Ruhr* 6 C3 51 19N 6 56 E
Hässelby, *Stock.* 3 D10 59 22N 17 50 E
Hasslinghausen, *Ruhr* 6 C5 51 20N 7 16 E
Hasten, *Ruhr* 6 C5 51 11N 7 11 E
Hästhagen, *Stock.* 3 E11 59 18N 18 9 E
Hastings-on-Hudson, *N.Y.* 23 B5 40 59N 73 51W
Hatch End, *Lon.* 4 B2 51 36N 0 22W
Hatiara, *Calc.* 16 E6 22 36N 88 26 E
Hatogaya, *Tōkyō* 13 B3 35 49N 139 44 E
Hattingen, *Ruhr* 6 B5 51 23N 7 11 E
Hatton, *Lon.* 4 C2 51 28N 0 25W
Hattori, *Ōsaka* 12 A4 34 51N 135 36 E
Haukoto, *Oslo* 2 B4 59 50N 10 48 E
Hauldres →, *Paris* 5 D5 48 37N 2 37 E
Hausbruch, *Hbg.* 7 E7 53 28N 9 53 E
Havalimani, *Ist.* 17 B2 40 59N 28 50 E
Havana = La Habana, *La Hab.* 30 B2 23 7N 82 21W
Havdrup, *Købn.* 2 E7 55 33N 12 7 E
Havel →, *Berl.* 7 A2 52 37N 13 11 E
Havelkanal, *Berl.* 7 A2 52 36N 13 10 E
Haverford, *Phil.* 24 A3 40 0N 75 18W
Havering, *Lon.* 4 B6 51 33N 0 12 E
Havering-atte-Bower, *Lon.* 4 B6 51 37N 0 11 E
Havertown, *Phil.* 24 B3 39 58N 75 18W
Hawangsibri, *Sŏul* 12 G8 37 33N 127 1 E
Haweolgog, *Sŏul* 12 G8 37 35N 127 1 E
Haworth, *N.Y.* 22 B5 40 57N 73 59W
Hawthorne, *L.A.* 28 C2 33 54N 118 21W
Hawthorne, *N.Y.* 22 B4 40 57N 74 8W
Hayes, *Lon.* 4 C5 51 22N 0 0 E
Hayes, *Lon.* 4 B2 51 30N 0 25W
Hayes End, *Lon.* 4 B2 51 31N 0 26W
Hayford, *Chic.* 26 C2 41 45N 87 42W
Hayward, *S.F.* 27 B4 37 40N 122 4W
Hayward Fault, *S.F.* 27 B3 37 46N 122 10W
Haywood Municipal Airport, *S.F.* 27 C4 32 39N 122 9W
Headley, *Lon.* 4 D3 51 16N 0 16W
Headstone, *Lon.* 4 B2 51 35N 0 21W
Heard Pond, *Bost.* 21 C1 42 20N 71 23W
Heart Pond, *Bost.* 21 B1 42 33N 71 23W
Heath Park, *Lon.* 4 B6 51 34N 0 12 E
Heathmont, *Melb.* 19 E8 37 49 S 145 14 E
Heathrow Airport, *Lon.* 4 C2 51 28N 0 27W
Hebbville, *Balt.* 25 A2 39 20N 76 45W
Hebe Haven, *H.K.* 12 D6 22 21N 114 15 E
Hebei, *Tianj.* 14 E6 39 9N 117 11 E
Hedehusene, *Købn.* 2 E8 55 39N 12 11 E
Hedong, *Gzh.* 14 G8 23 5N 113 14 E
Hedong, *Tianj.* 14 E6 39 7N 117 11 E
Heerdt, *Ruhr* 6 C2 51 13N 6 42 E
Hegewisch, *Chic.* 26 D3 41 39N 87 32W
Heggelielva →, *Oslo* 2 A3 60 1N 10 36 E
Heide, *Ruhr* 6 A3 51 31N 6 50 E
Heidelberg, *Melb.* 19 E7 37 45 S 145 4 E
Heidelberg West, *Melb.* 19 E7 37 43 S 145 2 E
Heidemühle, *Berl.* 7 B5 52 29N 13 40 E
Heidhausen, *Ruhr* 6 B4 51 22N 7 1 E
Heiligenhaus, *Ruhr* 6 B3 51 19N 6 57 E
Heiligensee, *Berl.* 7 A2 52 36N 13 13 E
Heiligenstadt, *Wien* 10 G10 48 14N 16 21 E
Heimfeld, *Hbg.* 7 E7 53 28N 9 57 E
Heinässuo, *Hels.* 3 B1 60 18N 24 27 E
Heinersdorf, *Berl.* 7 A3 52 34N 13 26 E
Heisingen, *Ruhr* 6 B4 51 24N 7 3 E
Heissen, *Ruhr* 6 B3 51 26N 6 54 E
Heiskerkruin, *Jobg.* 18 E8 26 7 S 27 51 E
Helenelund, *Stock.* 3 D10 59 24N 17 58 E
Heliopolis, *El Qâ.* 18 C5 30 5N 31 19 E
Hellersdorf, *Berl.* 7 A4 52 32N 13 35 E
Hellerup, *Købn.* 2 D10 55 44N 12 33 E
Helmahof, *Wien* 10 G11 48 18N 16 34 E
Helsingfors = Helsinki, *Hels.* 3 B4 60 10N 24 55 E
Helsinki, *Hels.* 3 B4 60 10N 24 55 E
Helsinki Airport, *Hels.* 3 B4 60 18N 24 58 E
Hempstead, *N.Y.* 23 C7 40 42N 73 37W
Hempstead Harbor, *N.Y.* 23 B7 40 50N 73 39W
Henan, *Gzh.* 14 G8 23 5N 113 14 E
Hendon, *Lon.* 4 B3 51 35N 0 14W
Hengsha, *Gzh.* 14 G8 23 9N 113 12 E
Hengsteysee, *Ruhr* 6 B6 51 24N 7 27 E
Hennigsdorf, *Berl.* 7 A2 52 38N 13 12 E
Henrichenburg, *Ruhr* 6 A5 51 35N 7 19 E
Henriville, *Paris* 5 C1 48 44N 1 56 E
Henrykow, *Wsaw.* 10 E6 52 19N 20 58 E
Henson Cr. →, *Wash.* 25 E8 38 47N 76 58W
Henttaa, *Hels.* 3 B3 60 11N 24 45 E
Heping, *Tianj.* 14 E6 39 7N 117 11 E
Heping Gongyuan, *Shang.* 14 J12 31 16N 121 30 E
Hepingli, *Beij.* 14 B3 39 57N 116 23 E
Herbeck, *Ruhr* 6 C5 51 12N 7 18 E
Herbede, *Ruhr* 6 B5 51 25N 7 16 E
Herblay, *Paris* 5 A2 48 59N 2 9 E
Herdecke, *Ruhr* 6 B6 51 24N 7 26 E
Herlev, *Købn.* 2 D9 55 43N 12 27 E
Hermannskogel, *Wien* 10 G9 48 16N 16 17 E
Hermitage and Winter Palace, *St-Pet.* 11 B3 59 55N 30 19 E
Hermosa Beach, *L.A.* 28 C2 33 51N 118 23W
Hermsdorf, *Berl.* 7 A2 52 37N 13 18 E
Hernals, *Wien* 10 G10 48 13N 16 20 E
Herne, *Ruhr* 6 A5 51 32N 7 13 E
Herne Hill, *Lon.* 4 C4 51 27N 0 6W
Hernwood Heights, *Balt.* 25 A2 39 22N 76 49W
Héroes de Churubusco, *Méx.* 29 B3 19 21N 99 6W
Herongate, *Lon.* 4 B7 51 35N 0 21 E
Herons, Î. aux, *Mtrl.* 20 B4 43 25N 73 34W
Herricks, *N.Y.* 23 C7 40 45N 73 39W
Herring Run →, *Balt.* 25 B3 39 18N 76 30W
Hersham, *Lon.* 4 C2 51 21N 0 22W
Herstedøster, *Købn.* 2 D9 55 40N 12 22 E
Herten, *Ruhr* 6 A4 51 35N 7 8 E
Hertoniemi, *Hels.* 3 B5 60 12N 25 2 E
Hessler, *Ruhr* 6 A4 51 31N 7 3 E
Heston, *Lon.* 4 C2 51 28N 0 22W
Hetterscheidt, *Ruhr* 6 A3 51 20N 6 59 E
Hetzendorf, *Wien* 10 H9 48 9N 16 17 E
Heuberg, *Wien* 10 G9 48 13N 16 16 E
Heven, *Ruhr* 6 B5 51 26N 7 18 E
Hewlett Neck, *N.Y.* 23 D6 40 37N 73 41W
Hexi, *Tianj.* 14 E5 39 8N 117 9 E
Hexingcun, *Tianj.* 14 E6 39 6N 117 10 E
Hextable, *Lon.* 4 C6 51 24N 0 10 E
Heybridge, *Lon.* 4 B7 51 39N 0 22 E
Hibernia, *N.Y.* 22 B2 40 57N 74 29W
Hickory Hills, *Chic.* 26 C2 41 43N 87 49W
Hicksville, *N.Y.* 23 C7 40 46N 73 30W
Hiddinghausen, *Ruhr* 6 B5 51 21N 7 17 E
Hiekkaharju, *Hels.* 3 B5 60 18N 25 2 E
Hiesfeld, *Ruhr* 6 A2 51 33N 6 46 E
Hietaniemi, *Hels.* 3 B4 60 10N 24 54 E
Hietzing, *Wien* 10 G9 48 10N 16 17 E
Higashi, *Ōsaka* 12 B4 34 41N 135 30 E
Higashi-kaizuka, *Tōkyō* 13 A3 35 50N 139 46 E
Higashimonzen, *Tōkyō* 13 A3 35 55N 139 40 E
Higashimurayama, *Tōkyō* 13 B1 35 45N 139 26 E
Higashinada, *Ōsaka* 12 B2 34 42N 135 15 E
Higashinari, *Ōsaka* 12 B4 34 40N 135 32 E
Higashiōsaka, *Ōsaka* 12 C4 34 39N 135 37 E
Higashisumiyoshi, *Ōsaka* 12 C4 34 37N 135 31 E
Higashiyodogawa, *Ōsaka* 12 B3 34 44N 135 28 E
High Beach, *Lon.* 4 B5 51 39N 0 1 E
High Junk Pk., *H.K.* 12 E6 22 17N 114 17 E
High Park, *Trto.* 20 E8 43 38N 79 27W
Higham Hill, *Lon.* 4 B4 51 35N 0 2W
Highbury, *Lon.* 4 B4 51 33N 0 6W
Highgate, *Lon.* 4 B4 51 34N 0 8W
Highland Cr. →, *Trto.* 20 D9 43 45N 79 13W
Highland Creek, *Trto.* 20 D9 43 46N 79 8W
Highland Park, *L.A.* 28 B3 34 7N 118 13 E
Highland Park, *N.Y.* 22 D2 40 30N 74 25W
Highlands North, *Jobg.* 18 E9 26 8 S 28 5 E
Highway Highlands, *L.A.* 28 A3 34 14N 118 16W
Higurashi, *Tōkyō* 13 B4 35 47N 139 55 E
Hila, *Méx.* 29 A2 19 35N 99 17W
Hillcrest Heights, *Wash.* 25 E8 38 49N 76 57W
Hillerheide, *Ruhr* 6 A5 51 35N 7 12 E
Hilleshög, *Stock.* 3 D9 59 23N 17 42 E
Hillgrove District, *L.A.* 28 B5 34 1N 117 58W
Hillingdon, *Lon.* 4 B2 51 32N 0 27W
Hillingdon Heath, *Lon.* 4 B2 51 31N 0 26W
Hillsborough, *S.F.* 27 C2 37 32N 122 21W
Hillsdale, *N.Y.* 22 A4 41 0N 74 1W
Hillsdale, *S.F.* 27 C3 37 32N 122 18W
Hillsdale Manor, *N.Y.* 22 A4 41 1N 74 3W
Hillside, *Chic.* 26 B1 41 52N 87 55W
Hillside, *N.Y.* 23 C6 40 42N 73 46W
Hillside Manor, *N.Y.* 23 C6 40 44N 73 40W
Hilltop, *Phil.* 24 C4 39 49N 75 4W
Hillwood, *Wash.* 25 D7 38 52N 77 9W
Hilmīya, *El Qâ.* 18 C5 30 6N 31 19 E
Hiltrop, *Ruhr* 6 A5 51 31N 7 15 E
Hindsby, *Hels.* 3 A6 60 20N 25 13 E
Hingham, *Bost.* 21 D4 42 14N 70 54W
Hingham B., *Bost.* 21 D4 42 17N 70 56W
Hingham Harbor, *Bost.* 21 D4 42 15N 70 53W
Hino, *Tōkyō* 13 C1 35 23N 139 35 E
Hinsbeck, *Ruhr* 6 B4 51 22N 7 4 E
Hinschenfelde, *Hbg.* 7 D8 53 35N 10 0 E
Hinsdale, *Chic.* 26 C1 41 47N 87 55W
Hinterhainbach, *Wien* 10 G9 48 14N 16 13 E
Hintersdorf, *Wien* 10 G9 48 18N 16 13 E
Hirakata, *Ōsaka* 12 B4 34 48N 135 38 E
Hirota, *Ōsaka* 12 B3 34 44N 135 20 E
Hirschstetten, *Wien* 10 G10 48 14N 16 27 E
Hither Green, *Lon.* 4 C4 51 26N 0 0 E
Hiyoshi, *Tōkyō* 13 C2 35 32N 139 38 E
Hjortekær, *Købn.* 2 D10 55 47N 12 32 E
Hjortespring, *Købn.* 2 D9 55 44N 12 25 E
Hlubočepy, *Pra.* 10 C2 50 2N 14 23 E
Ho Chung, *H.K.* 12 D6 22 21N 114 14 E
Ho Man Tin, *H.K.* 12 E6 22 18N 114 11 E
Hoboken, *N.Y.* 22 C4 40 44N 74 3W
Hobsons B., *Melb.* 19 F6 37 51 S 144 55 E
Hochbrück, *Mün.* 7 F10 48 14N 11 37 E
Hochdahl, *Ruhr* 6 C3 51 13N 6 55 E
Hochemmerich, *Ruhr* 6 B2 51 24N 6 41 E
Hochfeld, *Ruhr* 6 B2 51 25N 6 45 E
Hochheide, *Ruhr* 6 B2 51 27N 6 40 E
Hochlar, *Ruhr* 6 A5 51 36N 7 11 E
Hochlarmark, *Ruhr* 6 A4 51 34N 7 11 E
Hodgkins, *Chic.* 26 C1 41 46N 87 53W
Hodogaya-Ku, *Tōkyō* 13 D2 35 26N 139 35 E
Hoegi, *Sŏul* 12 G8 37 35N 127 3 E
Hofberg, *Wien* 10 G10 48 12N 16 21 E
Hoffman I., *N.Y.* 22 D4 40 34N 74 3W
Hofstede, *Ruhr* 6 A5 51 30N 7 11 E
Höggarnsfjärden, *Stock.* 3 D13 59 22N 18 22 E
Hohe Mark, Naturpark, *Ruhr* 6 A2 51 35N 6 49 E
Hohe Schaar, *Hbg.* 7 E7 53 29N 9 58 E
Hohenbrunn, *Mün.* 7 G11 48 2N 11 42 E
Hohenfelde, *Hbg.* 7 D8 53 33N 10 1 E
Hohenkirchen, *Mün.* 7 G11 48 1N 11 42 E
Hohenraden, *Hbg.* 7 C6 53 41N 9 49 E
Hohenschönhausen, *Berl.* 7 A4 52 33N 13 30 E
Hohenwisch, *Hbg.* 7 E7 53 29N 9 53 E

Kennedy Grove Regional Rec. Area 39

Hohokus, *N.Y.* 22 A4 41 0N 74 5W
Hok Tsui, *H.K.* 12 E6 22 12N 114 15 E
Holborn, *Lon.* 4 B4 51 31N 0 7W
Holečovice, *Pra.* 10 B2 50 6N 14 28 E
Holland Village, *Sing.* 15 G7 1 18N 103 47 E
Hollis, *N.Y.* 23 C6 40 42N 73 45W
Höllriegelskreuth, *Mün.* 7 G9 48 2N 11 30 E
Holly Oak, *Phil.* 24 C2 39 47N 75 27W
Hollydale, *L.A.* 28 C4 33 55N 118 10W
Hollywood Bowl, *L.A.* 28 B2 34 6N 118 21W
Hollywood-Burbank Airport, *L.A.* 28 A2 34 11N 118 21W
Holmenkollen, *Oslo* 2 B4 59 57N 10 41 E
Holmes, *Phil.* 24 B3 39 53N 75 18W
Holmes Acres, *Wash.* 25 D6 38 51N 77 13W
Holmes Run →, *Wash.* 25 E7 38 48N 77 6W
Holmesburg, *Phil.* 24 A4 40 2N 75 2W
Holmgård, *Stock.* 3 E10 59 14N 18 0 E
Holsfjorden, *Oslo* 2 B1 59 58N 10 17 E
Holsterhausen, *Ruhr* 6 A5 51 32N 7 11 E
Holte, *Købn.* 2 D9 55 48N 12 27 E
Holten, *Ruhr* 6 A2 51 31N 6 47 E
Holthausen, *Ruhr* 6 B4 51 25N 7 5 E
Holzbüttgen, *Ruhr* 6 C1 51 13N 6 37 E
Homberg, *Ruhr* 6 B2 51 27N 6 41 E
Hombruch, *Ruhr* 6 B6 51 28N 7 27 E
Homerton, *Lon.* 4 B4 51 32N 0 2W
Homestead Lake, *Jobg.* 18 F10 26 10 S 28 17 E
Homestead Valley, *S.F.* 27 A1 37 53N 122 32W
Hometown, *Chic.* 26 C2 41 44N 87 42W
Homledal, *Oslo* 2 B1 59 59N 10 18 E
Homówek, *Wsaw.* 10 E5 52 17N 20 48 E
Hon-gyōtoku, *Tōkyō* 13 B4 35 41N 139 57 E
Hōnanchō, *Tōkyō* 13 B2 35 40N 139 39 E
Honcho, *Tōkyō* 13 B3 35 40N 139 41 E
Honden, *Tōkyō* 13 B4 35 43N 139 50 E
Honeydew, *Jobg.* 18 E8 26 4 S 27 55 E
Hong Kah, *Sing.* 15 F7 1 21N 103 43 E
Hong Kong, *H.K.* 12 E5 22 17N 114 11 E
Hong Kong, Univ. of, *H.K.* 12 E5 22 16N 114 8 E
Hong Kong Airport, *H.K.* 12 E6 22 19N 114 11 E
Hong Kong I., *H.K.* 12 E6 22 16N 114 11 E
Hong Lim Park, *Sing.* 15 G8 1 17N 103 50 E
Hongeun, *Sŏul* 12 G7 37 35N 126 56 E
Honggiao, *Shang.* 14 J11 31 12N 121 22 E
Honggou, *Shang.* 14 J11 31 16N 121 29 E
Hongkou Gongyuan, *Shang.* 14 J11 31 17N 121 28 E
Hongmiao, *Beij.* 14 B3 39 54N 116 26 E
Hongqiao, *Tianj.* 14 E5 39 8N 117 9 E
Hongqiao Airport, *Shang.* 14 J10 31 12N 121 19 E
Honjyo, *Tōkyō* 13 B3 35 41N 139 48 E
Honmoku, *Tōkyō* 13 D2 35 24N 139 39 E
Hönow, *Berl.* 7 A4 52 32N 13 38 E
Höntrop, *Ruhr* 6 B4 51 27N 7 9 E
Hood Pond, *Bost.* 21 A4 42 40N 70 57W
Hooghly →, *Calc.* 16 D6 22 41N 88 21 E
Hook, *Lon.* 4 C3 51 22N 0 17W
Hopelawn, *N.Y.* 22 D3 40 31N 74 17W
Hörde, *Ruhr* 6 B7 51 29N 7 30 E
Horikiri, *Tōkyō* 13 B4 35 44N 139 50 E
Horn, *Hbg.* 7 D8 53 33N 10 5 E
Horn Pond, *Bost.* 21 C2 42 28N 71 9W
Hornchurch, *Lon.* 4 B6 51 33N 0 14 E
Horneburg, *Ruhr* 6 A5 51 37N 7 17 E
Horni, *Pra.* 10 B3 50 2N 14 33 E
Horni Počernice, *Pra.* 10 B3 50 6N 14 36 E
Hornsey, *Lon.* 4 B4 51 35N 0 7W
Horoměřice, *Pra.* 10 B1 50 8N 14 20 E
Horsley Park, *Syd.* 19 B2 33 50 S 150 51 E
Horst, *Ruhr* 6 B4 51 26N 7 6 E
Horsthausen, *Ruhr* 6 A5 51 33N 7 12 E
Hortaleza, *Mdrd.* 8 B3 40 28N 3 38W
Horto Florestal, *S. Pau.* 31 D6 23 27 S 46 38W
Horton Kirby, *Lon.* 4 C6 51 23N 0 14 E
Hösel, *Ruhr* 6 B3 51 20N 6 53 E
Hosoyama, *Tōkyō* 13 C2 35 36N 139 31 E
Hospitalet, *Barc.* 8 D5 41 21N 2 6 E
Hostafranchs, *Barc.* 8 D5 41 21N 2 8 E
Hoterheide, *Ruhr* 6 C1 51 16N 6 37 E
Houbetin, *Pra.* 10 B3 50 6N 14 33 E
Houghs Neck, *Bost.* 21 D4 42 15N 70 57W
Houghton, *Jobg.* 18 F9 26 10 S 28 3 E
Houilles, *Paris* 5 B3 48 56N 2 11 E
Hounslow, *Lon.* 4 C2 51 28N 0 21W
Houses of Parliament, *Lon.* 4 C4 51 29N 0 7W
Hove Å →, *Købn.* 2 D8 55 43N 12 7 E
Hovedøya, *Oslo* 2 B4 59 53N 10 43 E
Høvik, *Oslo* 2 B3 59 54N 10 34 E
Hovorčovice, *Pra.* 10 A3 50 10N 14 31 E
Howard Beach, *N.Y.* 23 D5 40 39N 73 50W
Hoxton Park, *Syd.* 19 B2 33 55 S 150 51 E
Hoxton Park Aerodrome, *Syd.* 19 B2 33 54 S 150 50 E
Hōya, *Tōkyō* 13 B2 35 44N 139 34 E
Høybråten, *Oslo* 2 B5 59 56N 10 55 E
Hradčany, *Pra.* 10 B2 50 5N 14 24 E
Hsiya, *Gzh.* 14 G7 23 9N 113 6 E
Huangpu, *Gzh.* 14 G9 23 5N 113 23 E
Huangpu, *Shang.* 14 J12 31 14N 121 30 E
Huangpu Gongyuan, *Shang.* 14 J11 31 14N 121 29 E
Huangpu Jiang →, *Shang.* 14 J11 31 11N 121 29 E
Huangtugang, *Beij.* 14 C2 39 49N 116 15 E
Huat Choe, *Sing.* 15 F7 1 20N 103 41 E
Huckarde, *Ruhr* 6 A6 51 32N 7 24 E
Huckingen, *Ruhr* 6 B2 51 21N 6 44 E
Huddinge, *Stock.* 3 E11 59 14N 18 0 E
Hudson →, *N.Y.* 22 B5 40 43N 73 6W
Huertas de San Beltran, *Barc.* 8 D5 41 22N 2 9 E
Huguenot, *N.Y.* 22 D3 40 32N 74 13W
Huguenot Park, *N.Y.* 22 D3 40 31N 74 12W
Huidui, *Tianj.* 14 E6 39 4N 117 16 E
Huisquilucan →, *Méx.* 29 B2 19 24N 99 17W
Huixquilucan, *Méx.* 29 B1 19 21N 99 21W
Hull, *Bost.* 21 D4 42 18N 70 54W
Hulman Aqueduct, *Bost.* 21 C1 42 20N 71 23W
Hulmeville, *Phil.* 24 A5 40 8N 74 55W
Hulsdonk, *Ruhr* 6 B1 51 27N 6 36 E
Humaljärvi, *Hels.* 3 B1 60 10N 24 26 E
Humber →, *Trto.* 20 D7 43 47N 79 38W
Humber B., *Trto.* 20 E8 43 37N 79 27W
Humber Bay, *Trto.* 20 E8 43 38N 79 29W
Humber Summit, *Trto.* 20 D7 43 45N 79 32W
Humber Valley Park, *Trto.* 20 E8 43 39N 79 29W
Humber Valley Village, *Trto.* 20 D7 43 40N 79 31W
Humberlea, *Trto.* 20 D7 43 43N 79 31W
Humboldt Park, *Chic.* 26 B2 41 54N 87 42W
Humera, *Mdrd.* 8 B2 40 25N 3 46W
Hummelsbüttel, *Hbg.* 7 D8 53 39N 10 4 E
Hun Yeang, *Sing.* 15 F8 1 21N 103 55 E
Hunaydī, *Bagd.* 17 F8 33 18N 44 29 E
Hundige, *Købn.* 2 E8 55 35N 12 18 E
Hundige Strand, *Købn.* 2 E9 55 35N 12 20 E
Hung Hom, *H.K.* 12 E6 22 18N 114 11 E
Hunters Hill, *Syd.* 19 B3 33 50 S 151 9 E
Hunters Pt., *S.F.* 27 B2 37 43N 122 21W
Hunters Valley, *Wash.* 25 D6 38 54N 77 17W
Huntington, *N.Y.* 23 B8 40 51N 73 25W
Huntington, *Wash.* 25 E7 38 47N 77 4W
Huntington B., *N.Y.* 23 B8 40 54N 73 24W
Huntington Bay, *N.Y.* 23 B8 40 56N 73 26W
Huntington Park, *L.A.* 28 C3 33 58N 118 13W
Huntington Station, *N.Y.* 23 B8 40 50N 73 23W
Hünxer Wald, *Ruhr* 6 A2 51 37N 6 49 E
Hurffville, *Phil.* 24 C4 39 45N 75 6W
Hurīya, *Bagd.* 17 E7 33 21N 44 19 E
Hurlingham, *B.A.* 32 B3 34 35 S 58 37W
Hurlingham, *Jobg.* 18 E9 26 6 S 28 2 E
Hurstville, *Syd.* 19 B3 33 57 S 151 6 E
Husby, *Stock.* 3 D10 59 24N 17 56 E
Huseby, *Oslo* 2 A6 60 0N 11 1 E
Hustivař, *Pra.* 10 B3 50 3N 14 31 E
Husum, *Købn.* 2 D9 55 42N 12 27 E
Hütteldorf, *Wien* 10 G9 48 12N 16 15 E
Hüttenheim, *Ruhr* 6 B2 51 21N 6 43 E
Huttrop, *Ruhr* 6 B4 51 26N 7 3 E
Hüvösvölgy, *Bud.* 10 J13 47 32N 19 0 E
Hvalstad, *Oslo* 2 B2 59 51N 10 27 E
Hvalstrand, *Oslo* 2 B3 59 50N 10 30 E
Hvidovre, *Købn.* 2 E9 55 38N 12 27 E
Hwagog, *Sŏul* 12 G7 37 32N 126 51 E
Hyattsville, *Wash.* 25 D8 38 57N 76 57W
Hyde Park, *Bost.* 21 D3 42 15N 71 7W
Hyde Park, *Chic.* 26 C3 41 47N 87 35W
Hyde Park, *Jobg.* 18 E9 26 6 S 28 2 E
Hyde Park, *Lon.* 4 B3 51 30N 0 10W
Hyde Park, *Syd.* 19 B4 33 52 S 151 12 E
Hynes, *L.A.* 28 C3 33 52N 118 10W

I

Ibaraki, *Ōsaka* 12 B4 34 48N 135 34 E
Ibayo Tipas, *Manila* 15 D4 14 32N 121 4 E
Ibese, *Lagos* 18 A2 6 33N 7 28 E
Ibirapuera, *S. Pau.* 31 E5 23 36 S 46 40W
Ibirapuera, Parque, *S. Pau.* 31 E6 23 35 S 46 38W
Iboju, *Lagos* 18 B3 6 25N 7 31 E
Icarai, *Rio J.* 31 B3 22 54 S 43 6W
Icerenköy, *Ist.* 17 B3 40 58N 29 6 E
Ichapur, *Calc.* 16 D6 22 48N 88 22 E
Ichgao, *Tōkyō* 13 C2 35 32N 139 32 E
Ichigaya, *Tōkyō* 13 B3 35 41N 139 43 E
Ichikawa, *Tōkyō* 13 B4 35 43N 139 54 E
Ickenham, *Lon.* 4 B2 51 33N 0 26W
Ickern, *Ruhr* 6 A6 51 35N 7 21 E
Iddo, *Lagos* 18 B2 6 28N 7 22 E
Idi-Oro, *Lagos* 18 A2 6 31N 7 21 E
Idimu, *Lagos* 18 A1 6 34N 7 17 E
Idrīs, *Bagd.* 17 E8 33 22N 44 27 E
Iganmu, *Lagos* 18 B2 6 28N 7 22 E
Igbobi, *Lagos* 18 A2 6 31N 7 22 E
Igbologun, *Lagos* 18 B1 6 24N 7 19 E
Igbopa, *Lagos* 18 A3 6 32N 7 31 E
Igelboda, *Stock.* 3 E12 59 17N 18 17 E
Igny, *Paris* 5 C3 48 44N 2 13 E
Iguassú, *S. Pau.* 31 E6 23 36 S 46 30W
Ijesa-Tedo, *Lagos* 18 B1 6 29N 7 19 E
Ijora, *Lagos* 18 B2 6 27N 7 22 E
Ikebe, *Tōkyō* 13 C2 35 31N 139 34 E
Ikebukuro, *Tōkyō* 13 B3 35 43N 139 42 E
Ikeda, *Ōsaka* 12 B3 34 48N 135 25 E
Ikegami, *Tōkyō* 13 C3 35 33N 139 42 E
Ikeja, *Lagos* 18 A2 6 35N 7 20 E
Ikeuchi, *Ōsaka* 12 C4 34 35N 135 32 E
Ikotun, *Lagos* 18 A1 6 32N 7 16 E
Ikoyi, *Lagos* 18 B2 6 27N 7 26 E
Ikuata, *Lagos* 18 B2 6 24N 7 21 E
Ikuno, *Ōsaka* 12 B4 34 40N 135 30 E
Ikuta, *Ōsaka* 12 B2 34 41N 135 10 E
Ikuta, *Tōkyō* 13 C2 35 36N 139 32 E
Ila, *Oslo* 2 B3 59 57N 10 35 E
Ilchester, *Balt.* 25 B2 39 14N 76 46W
Ilford, *Lon.* 4 B5 51 33N 0 4 E
Ilioúpolis, *Ath.* 8 J11 37 54N 23 47 E
Illovo, *Jobg.* 18 E9 26 7 S 28 3 E
Ilsós →, *Ath.* 8 J11 37 55N 23 41 E
Imajuku, *Tōkyō* 13 D2 35 28N 139 32 E
Imbâba, *El Qâ.* 18 C5 30 3N 31 12 E
Imielin, *Wsaw.* 10 F7 52 9N 21 0 E
Imirim, *S. Pau.* 31 D6 23 29 S 46 39W
Imittós, *Ath.* 8 J11 37 55N 23 45 E
Immersby, *Hels.* 3 B6 60 18N 25 16 E
Imore, *Lagos* 18 B1 6 25N 7 17 E
Imperial Palace, *Tōkyō* 13 B3 35 41N 139 45 E
Ina →, *Ōsaka* 12 B3 34 48N 135 27 E
Inagi, *Tōkyō* 13 C2 35 38N 139 31 E
Incirano, *Mil.* 9 D5 45 34N 9 9 E
Independencia, *Lima* 30 F8 11 59 S 77 3W
Indian Gabe, *Delhi* 16 B2 28 36N 77 13 E
Indian Museum, *Calc.* 16 E6 22 33N 88 21 E
Indiana Harbor, *Chic.* 26 C4 41 40N 87 26W
Indiana Harbor Canal, *Chic.* 26 D4 41 39N 87 26W
Indianópolis, *S. Pau.* 31 E6 23 35 S 46 38W
Indios Verdes, *Méx.* 29 B3 19 29N 99 6W
Ingarö, *Stock.* 3 E13 59 17N 18 24 E
Ingaröfjärden, *Stock.* 3 E13 59 14N 18 25 E
Ingarölandet, *Stock.* 3 E13 59 17N 18 22 E
Ingenieur Budge, *B.A.* 32 C4 34 43 S 58 27W
Ingierstrand, *Oslo* 2 C4 59 49N 10 46 E
Ingleburn, *Syd.* 19 C2 34 0 S 150 52 E
Inglewood, *L.A.* 28 C3 33 57N 118 19W
Ingrave, *Lon.* 4 B7 51 35N 0 20 E
Ingvalsby, *Hels.* 3 C2 60 9N 24 32 E
Inhaúme, *Rio J.* 31 B2 22 51 S 43 17W
Inner Port Shelter, *H.K.* 12 D6 22 22N 114 17 E
Interagos, *S. Pau.* 31 F5 23 41 S 46 42W
Intramuros, *Manila* 15 D3 14 35N 120 57 E
Invalides, *Paris* 5 B3 48 51N 2 18 E
Inverness, *Balt.* 25 B4 39 15N 76 29W
Inwood, *N.Y.* 23 D6 40 36N 73 45W
Inzersdorf, *Wien* 10 H10 48 8N 16 21 E
Ipanema, *Rio J.* 31 B2 22 59 S 43 12W
Ipiranga, *S. Pau.* 31 E6 23 35 S 46 36W
Ipiranga →, *S. Pau.* 31 E6 23 37 S 46 37W
Iponri, *Lagos* 18 B2 6 28N 7 22 E
Ipswich, *Bost.* 21 A4 42 41N 70 50W
Ipswich →, *Bost.* 21 B4 42 39N 70 53W
Irajá, *Rio J.* 31 B2 22 50 S 43 19W
Irving Park, *Chic.* 26 B2 41 57N 87 42W
Irvington, *N.Y.* 23 A5 41 2N 73 52W
Irwindale, *L.A.* 28 B5 34 6N 117 54W
Isabel, *Rio J.* 31 B2 22 55 S 43 14W
Isagatedo, *Lagos* 18 A1 6 31N 7 19 E
Isando, *Jobg.* 18 E10 26 8 S 28 12 E
Isar →, *Mün.* 7 F11 48 15N 11 41 E
Iselin, *N.Y.* 22 D3 40 34N 74 19W
Iserbrook, *Hbg.* 7 D6 53 34N 9 49 E
Iseri-Osun, *Lagos* 18 A1 6 30N 7 16 E
Ishbīlīya, *Bagd.* 17 E8 33 21N 44 26 E
Isheri-Olofin, *Lagos* 18 A1 6 34N 7 16 E
Ishi →, *Ōsaka* 12 C4 34 34N 135 37 E
Ishikiri, *Ōsaka* 12 B4 34 40N 135 39 E
Ishizu →, *Ōsaka* 12 C3 34 33N 135 26 E
Ishøj Strand, *Købn.* 2 E9 55 36N 12 20 E
Isidro Casanova, *B.A.* 32 C3 34 42 S 58 36W
Island Channel, *N.Y.* 23 D5 40 35N 73 52W
Island Park, *N.Y.* 23 D7 40 36N 73 38W
Island Park, *Trto.* 20 E8 43 37N 79 22W
Islev, *Købn.* 2 D9 55 41N 12 27 E
Isleworth, *Lon.* 4 C3 51 28N 0 19W
Islington, *Bost.* 21 D2 42 13N 71 13W
Islington, *Lon.* 4 B4 51 32N 0 6W
Islington, *Trto.* 20 E7 43 38N 79 30W
Ismaning, *Mün.* 7 F11 48 13N 11 40 E
Ismayloskiypark, *Mos.* 11 E10 55 46N 37 46 E
Isogo-Ku, *Tōkyō* 13 D2 35 23N 139 37 E
Isolo, *Lagos* 18 A1 6 31N 7 19 E
Isosaari, *Hels.* 3 C5 60 6N 25 3 E
Issy-les-Moulineaux, *Paris* 5 C3 48 49N 2 15 E
Istanbul, *Ist.* 17 B2 41 0N 28 58 E
Istanbul Boğazi, *Ist.* 17 A3 41 5N 29 3 E
Istanbul Hava Alani, *Ist.* 17 B2 40 58N 28 50 E
Istead Rise, *Lon.* 4 C7 51 24N 0 21 E
Istinye, *Ist.* 17 A3 41 6N 29 3 E
Isunba, *Lagos* 18 B1 6 25N 7 17 E
Itä Hakkila, *Hels.* 3 B5 60 17N 25 7 E
Itabashi-Ku, *Tōkyō* 13 B2 35 46N 139 38 E
Itaberaba, *S. Pau.* 31 D6 23 28 S 46 39W
Itaeweon, *Sŏul* 12 G7 37 32N 126 58 E
Itaim, *S. Pau.* 31 D7 23 29 S 46 23W
Itaipu, *Rio J.* 31 B3 22 58 S 43 2W
Italie, Place d', *Paris* 5 C4 48 49N 2 22 E
Itami, *Ōsaka* 12 B3 34 46N 135 24 E
Itaocaia, *Rio J.* 31 B3 22 58 S 43 2W
Itapecerica da Serra, *S. Pau.* 31 F5 23 42 S 46 50W
Itaquaquecetuba, *S. Pau.* 31 D7 23 29 S 46 23W
Itaquera, *S. Pau.* 31 E7 23 32 S 46 27W
Itaquera →, *S. Pau.* 31 E7 23 28 S 46 26W
Ithan, *Phil.* 24 A2 40 1N 75 21W
Itupu, *S. Pau.* 31 F5 23 40 S 46 43W
Ituzaingo, *B.A.* 32 B3 34 39 S 58 38W
Ivanhoe, *Melb.* 19 E7 37 45 S 145 3 E
Iver, *Lon.* 4 B1 51 32N 0 30W
Ivry-sur-Seine, *Paris* 5 C4 48 49N 2 22 E
Iwazono, *Ōsaka* 12 B2 34 45N 135 18 E
Izabelin, *Wsaw.* 10 E5 52 17N 20 48 E
Izmaylovo, *Mos.* 11 E10 55 47N 37 47 E
Iztacalco, *Méx.* 29 B3 19 23N 99 6W
Iztapalapa, *Méx.* 29 B3 19 21N 99 6W
Izumi, *Tōkyō* 13 D1 35 25N 139 29 E

J

J. G. Strijdom Post Office Tower, *Jobg.* 18 F9 26 11 S 28 2 E
J. Paul Getty Museum, *L.A.* 28 B1 34 2N 118 33W
Jabavu, *Jobg.* 18 F8 26 14 S 27 52 E
Jabulani, *Jobg.* 18 F8 26 14 S 27 51 E
Jacarepaguá, *Rio J.* 31 B1 22 56 S 43 20W
Jackson Heights, *N.Y.* 23 C5 40 44N 73 53W
Jackson Park, *Chic.* 26 C3 41 46N 87 34W
Jacksonville, *N.Y.* 22 B3 40 57N 74 18W
Jacomino, *La Hab.* 30 B3 23 6N 82 19W
Jacques Cartier, *Mtrl.* 20 A5 43 31N 73 27W
Jægersborg, *Købn.* 2 D10 55 45N 12 31 E
Jægersborg Dyrehave, *Købn.* 2 D10 55 46N 12 33 E
Jægersborg Hegn, *Købn.* 2 D10 55 49N 12 33 E
Jafarpur, *Calc.* 16 D6 22 45N 88 22 E
Jagacha, *Calc.* 16 E5 22 35N 88 17 E
Jagannathpur, *Calc.* 16 D5 22 43N 88 18 E
Jagatdal, *Calc.* 16 C6 22 51N 88 23 E
Jagatmagar, *Calc.* 16 D5 22 46N 88 13 E
Jagatpur, *Delhi* 16 A2 28 44N 77 13 E
Jagdispur, *Calc.* 16 E5 22 39N 88 17 E
Jaguara, *S. Pau.* 31 E5 23 30 S 46 45W
Jaguaré, *S. Pau.* 31 E5 23 32 S 46 45W
Jaguaré →, *S. Pau.* 31 E5 23 32 S 46 45W
Jahangirpur, *Delhi* 16 A2 28 43N 77 12 E
Jaimanitas →, *La Hab.* 30 B2 23 5N 82 29W
Jakarta, *Jak.* 15 H10 6 9 S 106 52 E
Jakarta, Teluk, *Jak.* 15 H9 6 5 S 106 50 E
Jakosberg, *Stock.* 3 D9 59 25N 17 47 E
Jalan Kayu, *Sing.* 15 F8 1 24N 103 52 E
Jamaica, *N.Y.* 23 C6 40 42N 73 48W
Jamaica B., *N.Y.* 23 D6 40 36N 73 49W
Jamaica Plain, *Bost.* 21 D3 42 18N 71 6W
Jamshīdābād, *Tehr.* 17 C5 35 42N 51 22 E
Jamsil, *Sŏul* 12 G8 37 30N 127 4 E
Jamweon, *Sŏul* 12 G8 37 30N 127 0 E
Jan Smuts Airport, *Jobg.* 18 E10 26 7 S 28 14 E
Janai, *Calc.* 16 D5 22 43N 88 15 E
Janā'in, *Bagd.* 17 F8 33 18N 44 22 E
Janki, *Wsaw.* 10 F6 52 8N 20 52 E
Jannali, *Syd.* 19 C3 34 0 S 151 4 E
Jánoshegy, *Bud.* 10 J12 47 31N 18 57 E
Janów, *Wsaw.* 10 E6 52 16N 20 50 E
Janvry, *Paris* 5 D2 48 38N 2 9 E
Jaraguá, *S. Pau.* 31 D5 23 27 S 46 44W
Jaraguá, Pico de, *S. Pau.* 31 D5 23 27 S 46 46W
Jarama →, *Mdrd.* 8 B3 40 29N 3 32W
Jardim América, *S. Pau.* 31 E6 23 34 S 46 39W
Jardim Anchieta, *S. Pau.* 31 F7 23 41 S 46 27W
Jardim Arpoador, *S. Pau.* 31 E5 23 35 S 46 48W
Jardim do Mar, *S. Pau.* 31 F6 23 41 S 46 33W
Jardim Munhoz, *S. Pau.* 31 E6 23 30 S 46 33W
Jardim Osasco, *S. Pau.* 31 E5 23 33 S 46 47W
Jardim Ouro Preto, *S. Pau.* 31 E5 23 35 S 46 46W
Jardim Paulista, *S. Pau.* 31 E5 23 34 S 46 41W
Jardim Petrópolis, *S. Pau.* 31 F7 23 41 S 46 23W
Jardim Rochidale, *S. Pau.* 31 E5 23 30 S 46 46W
Jardim Santista, *S. Pau.* 31 F7 23 40 S 46 24W
Jardim São Bento, *S. Pau.* 31 F5 23 40 S 46 46W
Jardim São Francisco, *S. Pau.* 31 E7 23 38 S 46 26W
Jardim Sapopemba, *S. Pau.* 31 E7 23 36 S 46 29W
Jardim Vera Cruz, *S. Pau.* 31 E7 23 35 S 46 27W
Jardim Vista Alegre, *S. Pau.* 31 E5 23 37 S 46 49W
Jardim Zaira, *S. Pau.* 31 E7 23 39 S 46 25W
Jardines Flotantes, *Méx.* 29 C3 19 16N 99 6W
Jardine's Lookout, *H.K.* 12 E6 22 16N 114 11 E
Järfälla, *Stock.* 3 D10 59 23N 17 51 E
Järvafältet, *Stock.* 3 D10 59 25N 17 54 E
Järventausta, *Hels.* 3 A1 60 21N 24 28 E
Jasai, *Bomb.* 16 H9 18 56N 73 1 E
Jaskhar, *Bomb.* 16 H8 18 54N 72 58 E
Jatinegara, *Jak.* 15 J10 6 13 S 106 52 E
Jauli, *Delhi* 16 A3 28 44N 77 20 E
Jawādiyeh, *Tehr.* 17 D5 35 39N 51 22 E
Jaworowa, *Wsaw.* 10 F6 52 9N 20 56 E
Jayang, *Sŏul* 12 G8 37 32N 127 3 E
Jedlesee, *Wien* 10 G10 48 15N 16 23 E
Jefferson, *Phil.* 24 C3 39 45N 75 12W
Jefferson Park, *Chic.* 26 B2 41 58N 87 46W
Jeffersonville, *Phil.* 24 A2 40 8N 75 23W
Jegi, *Sŏul* 12 G8 37 34N 127 1 E
Jells Park, *Melb.* 19 F8 37 53 S 145 11 E
Jelonki, *Wsaw.* 10 E6 52 14N 20 54 E
Jenfeld, *Hbg.* 7 D8 53 34N 10 8 E
Jenkintown, *Phil.* 24 A4 40 6N 75 8W
Jeongreung, *Sŏul* 12 G8 37 35N 127 0 E
Jericho, *N.Y.* 23 C7 40 47N 73 32W
Jerónimes, Mosteiro dos, *Lisb.* 8 F7 38 41N 9 11W
Jersey City, *N.Y.* 22 C4 40 42N 74 4W
Jésus, Î., *Mtrl.* 20 A3 43 36N 73 44W
Jesus Del Monte, *La Hab.* 30 B2 23 6N 82 21W
Jesús Maria, *Lima* 30 G8 12 4 S 77 3W
Jhenkari, *Calc.* 16 D5 22 45N 88 18 E
Jhil Kuranga, *Delhi* 16 B2 28 39N 77 14 E
Jiangqiao, *Shang.* 14 J11 31 15N 121 20 E
Jiangtai, *Beij.* 14 B3 39 57N 116 28 E
Jianguomen, *Beij.* 14 B3 39 53N 116 24 E
Jiangwan, *Shang.* 14 J11 31 18N 121 28 E
Jianshan Gongyuan, *Tianj.* 14 E6 39 5N 117 12 E
Jihād, *Bagd.* 17 F7 33 17N 44 19 E
Jingan, *Shang.* 14 J11 31 14N 121 25 E
Jinočany, *Pra.* 10 B1 50 2N 14 16 E
Jinonice, *Pra.* 10 B2 50 3N 14 22 E
Jirny, *Pra.* 10 B4 50 7N 14 41 E
Jiuxianqiao, *Beij.* 14 B3 39 58N 116 28 E
Jiyźgaoka, *Tōkyō* 13 C3 35 35N 139 40 E
Jizā'er, *Bagd.* 17 F8 33 15N 44 23 E
Jizīra, *Bagd.* 17 F8 33 15N 44 25 E
Joan Despi, *Barc.* 8 D5 41 22N 2 2 E
Joaquin Miller Park, *S.F.* 27 B3 37 48N 122 11W
Johannesburg, *Jobg.* 18 F9 26 11 S 28 2 E
Johanneskirchen, *Mün.* 7 F10 48 10N 11 38 E
Johannesstift, *Berl.* 7 A2 52 34N 13 12 E
Johannisthal, *Berl.* 7 B4 52 26N 13 30 E
John F. Kennedy Int. Airport, *N.Y.* 23 D6 40 39N 73 45W
John F. Kennedy Nat. Hist. Site, *Bost.* 21 C3 42 20N 71 7W
John Hancock Center, *Chic.* 26 B3 41 53N 87 37W
John Hopkins Univ., *Balt.* 25 B3 39 19N 76 37W
John McLaren Park, *S.F.* 27 B2 37 43N 122 24W
Joinville-le-Pont, *Paris* 5 C4 48 49N 2 27 E
Jollas, *Hels.* 3 B5 60 10N 25 5 E
Jones Beach State Park, *N.Y.* 23 D7 40 35N 73 32W
Jones Falls →, *Balt.* 25 B3 39 20N 76 36W
Jones Inlet, *N.Y.* 23 D7 40 34N 73 34W
Jonestown, *Balt.* 25 B2 39 13N 76 48W
Jong Ro, *Sŏul* 12 G7 37 34N 126 58 E
Jongmyo Royal Shrine, *Sŏul* 12 G7 37 34N 126 59 E
Jonstrup, *Købn.* 2 D9 55 45N 12 20 E
Joppatowne, *Balt.* 25 A4 39 24N 76 20W
Jordan Valley, *H.K.* 12 D6 22 20N 114 12 E
Jorge Chavez, Aeropuerto Int., *Lima* 30 G8 12 2 S 77 8W
Jorvas, *Hels.* 3 C2 60 8N 24 30 E
José C. Paz, *B.A.* 32 B2 34 31 S 58 44W
José L. Suárez, *B.A.* 32 B3 34 32 S 58 34W
José Mármol, *B.A.* 32 C4 34 47 S 58 22W
Jose Marti, Aeropuerto Int., *La Hab.* 30 C2 22 59N 82 22W
Josephine Pk., *L.A.* 28 A4 34 17N 118 7W
Jōsō, *Ōsaka* 12 B3 34 42N 135 27 E
Jōtō, *Ōsaka* 12 B4 34 42N 135 33 E
Jouars-Pontchartrain, *Paris* 5 C1 48 47N 1 53 E
Jouy-en-Josas, *Paris* 5 C3 48 46N 2 10 E
Jouy-le-Moutier, *Paris* 5 A2 49 0N 2 2 E
Józefów, *Wsaw.* 10 F8 52 8N 21 13 E
Juan Escutia, *Méx.* 29 B3 19 23N 99 3W
Juan González Romero, *Méx.* 29 A3 19 30N 99 3W
Juhu, *Bomb.* 16 G9 19 5N 73 0 E
Juilly, *Paris* 5 A6 49 0N 2 42 E
Jūjā, *Tōkyō* 13 B3 35 45N 139 43 E
Jukskeirivier →, *Jobg.* 18 E9 26 5 S 28 6 E
Julianów, *Wsaw.* 10 E7 52 10N 21 9 E
Jung, *Sŏul* 12 G7 37 33N 126 59 E
Jungfernheide, Volkspark, *Berl.* 7 A2 52 32N 13 18 E
Jungfernsee, *Berl.* 7 B1 52 25N 13 6 E
Jungwha, *Sŏul* 12 G8 37 35N 127 3 E
Junk B., *H.K.* 12 E6 22 17N 114 15 E
Jurong, *Sing.* 15 G7 1 19N 103 40 E
Jurong, Selat, *Sing.* 15 G7 1 17N 103 42 E
Jurong, Sungei →, *Sing.* 15 G7 1 17N 103 45 E
Jurubatuba, *S. Pau.* 31 F5 23 40 S 46 41W
Jurujuba, Enseada de, *Rio J.* 31 B3 22 54 S 43 6W
Justice, *Chic.* 26 C2 41 44N 87 49W
Juusjärvi, *Hels.* 3 B1 60 12N 24 26 E
Juva, *Hels.* 3 B3 60 16N 24 45 E
Juvisy-sur-Orge, *Paris* 5 C4 48 41N 2 21 E
Jwalahari, *Delhi* 16 B1 28 40N 77 6 E
Jyllinge, *Købn.* 2 D7 55 45N 12 6 E

K

Kaarst, *Ruhr* 6 C1 51 13N 6 36 E
Kabaty, *Wsaw.* 10 F7 52 8N 21 4 E
Kabel, *Ruhr* 6 B6 51 24N 7 28 E
Kadiköy, *Ist.* 17 B3 40 59N 29 1 E
Kadoma, *Ōsaka* 12 B4 34 44N 135 35 E
Kafr es Sammân, *El Qâ.* 18 D4 29 58N 31 8 E
Kâğithane, *Ist.* 17 A2 41 4N 28 58 E
Kâğithane →, *Ist.* 17 A2 41 9N 28 56 E
Kagran, *Wien* 10 G10 48 14N 16 26 E
Kahlenberg, *Wien* 10 G9 48 16N 16 19 E
Kai Tak, *H.K.* 12 D6 22 20N 114 11 E
Kaisariani, *Ath.* 8 J11 37 57N 23 46 E
Kaiser-Mühlen, *Wien* 10 G10 48 13N 16 25 E
Kaiserebersdorf, *Wien* 10 H10 48 9N 16 26 E
Kaiserswerth, *Ruhr* 6 C2 51 18N 6 44 E
Kaivoksela, *Hels.* 3 B4 60 15N 24 53 E
Kakukk-hegy, *Bud.* 10 K12 47 29N 18 57 E
Kalachhara, *Calc.* 16 D5 22 42N 88 15 E
Kalamákion, *Ath.* 8 J11 37 52N 23 43 E
Kaldenhausen, *Ruhr* 6 B1 51 23N 6 39 E
Kalipur, *Calc.* 16 D5 22 40N 88 17 E
Kalkaji, *Delhi* 16 B2 28 32N 77 12 E
Kalksburg, *Wien* 10 H9 48 8N 16 15 E
Kallang →, *Sing.* 15 F8 1 21N 103 51 E
Kallhäll, *Stock.* 3 D9 59 26N 17 48 E
Kallithéa, *Ath.* 8 J11 37 56N 23 43 E
Kallvik, *Hels.* 3 B5 60 12N 25 8 E
Kaltbründsberg, *Wien* 10 G9 48 10N 16 13 E
Kaltenleutgeben, *Wien* 10 H9 48 7N 16 11 E
Kalveboderne, *Købn.* 2 E10 55 37N 12 31 E
Kalytino, *St-Pet.* 11 B5 59 59N 30 39 E
Kamaraerdö, *Bud.* 10 K12 47 26N 18 59 E
Kamarhati, *Calc.* 16 D6 22 40N 88 23 E
Kamarkunda, *Calc.* 16 D5 22 49N 88 12 E
Kamata, *Tōkyō* 13 C3 35 33N 139 43 E
Kamdebpur, *Calc.* 16 C5 22 53N 88 19 E
Kameari, *Tōkyō* 13 B4 35 45N 139 50 E
Kameido, *Tōkyō* 13 B4 35 42N 139 50 E
Kami-hoshikawa, *Tōkyō* 13 D2 35 27N 139 35 E
Kami-Itabashi, *Tōkyō* 13 B3 35 45N 139 40 E
Kami-nakazato, *Tōkyō* 13 D2 35 22N 139 36 E
Kami-saruyama, *Tōkyō* 13 C2 35 30N 139 31 E
Kami-sugata, *Tōkyō* 13 D2 35 28N 139 34 E
Kami-tomi, *Tōkyō* 13 B1 35 48N 139 29 E
Kamikitazawa, *Tōkyō* 13 C2 35 39N 139 36 E
Kamikiyoto, *Tōkyō* 13 B2 35 45N 139 30 E
Kamishiki, *Tōkyō* 13 B4 35 46N 139 57 E
Kamitsuruma, *Tōkyō* 13 C1 35 30N 139 26 E
Kamiyama, *Tōkyō* 13 B2 35 46N 139 32 E
Kamoi, *Tōkyō* 13 C2 35 30N 139 34 E
Kamoshida, *Tōkyō* 13 C2 35 33N 139 31 E
Kampong Batak, *Sing.* 15 F8 1 20N 103 54 E
Kampong Mandai Kechil, *Sing.* 15 F7 1 26N 103 46 E
Kampong Pachitan, *Sing.* 15 G8 1 19N 103 54 E
Kampong Potong Pasir, *Sing.* 15 F8 1 20N 103 52 E
Kampong Reteh, *Sing.* 15 G8 1 19N 103 53 E
Kampong Tengah, *Sing.* 15 F7 1 22N 103 42 E
Kampong Ulu Jurong, *Sing.* 15 F7 1 20N 103 42 E
Kampung Ambon, *Jak.* 15 J10 6 11 S 106 53 E
Kampung Bali, *Jak.* 15 J9 6 11 S 106 48 E
Kan, *Tehr.* 17 C4 35 45N 51 16 E
Kanagawa-Ku, *Tōkyō* 13 D2 35 29N 139 38 E
Kanamachi, *Tōkyō* 13 B4 35 46N 139 52 E
Kanamori, *Tōkyō* 13 C1 35 31N 139 27 E
Kanda, *Tōkyō* 13 B3 35 41N 139 45 E
Kandang Kerbau, *Sing.* 15 G8 1 18N 103 51 E
Kandilli, *Ist.* 17 A3 41 4N 29 3 E
Kanegasaku, *Tōkyō* 13 B4 35 48N 139 56 E
Kangaroo Ground, *Melb.* 19 E8 37 41 S 145 13 E
Kankinara, *Calc.* 16 C6 22 51N 88 24 E
Kankurgachi, *Calc.* 16 E6 22 34N 88 23 E
Kanlica, *Ist.* 17 A3 41 5N 29 3 E
Kanoaka, *Ōsaka* 12 C4 34 33N 135 31 E
Kanonerskiy, Os., *St-Pet.* 11 B3 59 53N 30 13 E
Kanzaki →, *Ōsaka* 12 B3 34 41N 135 24 E
Kapellerfeld, *Wien* 10 G10 48 18N 16 29 E
Kapotnya, *Mos.* 11 F10 55 39N 37 48 E
Käppala, *Stock.* 3 D12 59 21N 18 13 E
Käpylä, *Hels.* 3 B4 60 13N 24 57 E
Karachi, *Kar.* 17 G11 24 50N 67 0 E
Karachi Int. Airport, *Kar.* 17 G11 24 5N 67 9 E
Karachi Univ., *Kar.* 17 G11 24 51N 67 0 E
Karagümrük, *Ist.* 17 A2 41 1N 28 56 E
Karāma, *Bagd.* 17 E8 33 20N 44 22 E
Karato, *Ōsaka* 12 B2 34 46N 135 12 E
Karave, *Bomb.* 16 G9 19 0N 73 0 E
Karet, *Jak.* 15 J9 6 12 S 106 49 E
Karkar Duman, *Delhi* 16 B2 28 39N 77 18 E
Karkh, *Bagd.* 17 E8 33 20N 44 22 E
Karlberg, *Stock.* 3 D11 59 20N 18 1 E
Karlin, *Pra.* 10 B2 50 5N 14 26 E
Karlsfeld, *Mün.* 7 F9 48 13N 11 28 E
Karlshorst, *Berl.* 7 B4 52 29N 13 31 E
Karlslunde Strand, *Købn.* 2 E8 55 33N 12 15 E
Karnap, *Ruhr* 6 A4 51 31N 7 0 E
Karolinenhof, *Berl.* 7 B4 52 23N 13 38 E
Karow, *Berl.* 7 A3 52 36N 13 29 E
Karrādah, *Bagd.* 17 F8 33 17N 44 23 E
Kärsön, *Stock.* 3 E10 59 19N 17 54 E
Kasai, *Tōkyō* 13 C4 35 39N 139 52 E
Kasetsart, *Bangk.* 15 A2 13 50N 100 34 E
Kashi-Hazaki, *Tōkyō* 13 A3 35 54N 139 42 E
Kashio, *Tōkyō* 13 D2 35 24N 139 34 E
Kashiwa, *Tōkyō* 13 A4 35 51N 139 57 E
Kashiwara, *Ōsaka* 12 C4 34 34N 135 37 E
Kaskela, *Hels.* 3 B5 60 17N 25 6 E
Kastrup, *Købn.* 2 E10 55 38N 12 39 E
Kastrup Lufthavn, *Købn.* 2 E11 55 37N 12 14 E
Kasuga, *Tōkyō* 13 B2 35 45N 139 38 E
Kasuge, *Tōkyō* 13 B3 35 45N 139 49 E
Kasumigasek, *Tōkyō* 13 C3 35 40N 139 46 E
Katabira →, *Tōkyō* 13 D2 35 27N 139 38 E
Katernberg, *Ruhr* 6 A4 51 30N 7 4 E
Katong Park, *Sing.* 15 G8 1 18N 103 53 E
Katrineberg, *Stock.* 3 E10 59 13N 17 54 E
Katsushika-Ku, *Tōkyō* 13 B4 35 44N 139 51 E
Kattinge Vig, *Købn.* 2 D7 55 40N 12 1 E
Kau Pei Chau, *H.K.* 12 E6 22 12N 114 15 E
Kau Yi Chau, *H.K.* 12 E5 22 17N 114 4 E
Kauklahti, *Hels.* 3 B2 60 11N 24 36 E
Kaulsdorf, *Berl.* 7 B4 52 29N 13 34 E
Kauniainen, *Hels.* 3 B3 60 13N 24 44 E
Kawagoe, *Tōkyō* 13 A1 35 54N 139 29 E
Kawaguchi, *Tōkyō* 13 B3 35 47N 139 43 E
Kawai, *Tōkyō* 13 D2 35 29N 139 31 E
Kawamukō, *Tōkyō* 13 C2 35 30N 139 34 E
Kawanishi, *Ōsaka* 12 B3 34 49N 135 24 E
Kawasaki, *Tōkyō* 13 C3 35 31N 139 43 E
Kawasaki Harbour, *Tōkyō* 13 D3 35 30N 139 47 E
Kawawa, *Tōkyō* 13 C2 35 31N 139 33 E
Kawęczyn, *Wsaw.* 10 E7 52 16N 21 5 E
Kayu Putih, *Jak.* 15 J10 6 10 S 106 53 E
Kbely, *Pra.* 10 B3 50 8N 14 32 E
Kearny, *N.Y.* 22 C4 40 45N 74 8W
Kebayoran Baru, *Jak.* 15 J9 6 14 S 106 47 E
Kebayoran Lama, *Jak.* 15 J9 6 13 S 106 46 E
Kebon Jeruk, *Jak.* 15 J9 6 11 S 106 46 E
Keferloh, *Mün.* 7 G11 48 5N 11 43 E
Keilor, *Melb.* 19 E6 37 42 S 144 50 E
Keilor East, *Melb.* 19 E6 37 44 S 144 51 E
Keimola, *Hels.* 3 A3 60 20N 24 49 E
Kelenföld, *Bud.* 10 K13 47 27N 19 2 E
Kelvedon Hatch, *Lon.* 4 A6 51 40N 0 16 E
Kelvin, *Jobg.* 18 E9 26 4 S 28 5 E
Kemang, *Jak.* 15 J9 6 15 S 106 48 E
Kemayoran, *Jak.* 15 J10 6 10 S 106 51 E
Kemayoran Airport, *Jak.* 15 H10 6 8 S 106 50 E
Kemp Mill, *Wash.* 25 C7 39 0N 77 1W
Kempton Park, *Jobg.* 18 E10 26 5 S 28 14 E
Kempton Racecourse, *Lon.* 4 C2 51 24N 0 23W
Kemsing, *Lon.* 4 D6 51 18N 0 12 E
Kendall Green, *Bost.* 21 C2 42 22N 71 16W
Kendua, *Calc.* 16 E5 22 34N 88 10 E
Keng Hau, *H.K.* 12 D6 22 22N 114 10 E
Kenilworth, *Chic.* 26 A2 42 5N 87 42W
Kenilworth, *N.Y.* 22 C3 40 40N 74 16W
Kenley, *Lon.* 4 D4 51 19N 0 6W
Kenmare, *Jobg.* 18 E7 26 6 S 27 48 E
Kennedy Grove Regional Rec. Area, *S.F.* 27 A3 37 56N 122 14W

40 Kennedy Town

Kennedy Town, *H.K.* 12 E5 22 16N 114 6 E
Kensal Green, *Lon.* 4 B3 51 32N 0 13W
Kensington, *Jobg.* 18 F9 26 11 S 28 6 E
Kensington, *Lon.* 4 C3 51 29N 0 10W
Kensington, *N.Y.* 22 D5 40 38N 73 57W
Kensington, *Phil.* 24 B4 39 59N 75 6W
Kensington, *S.F.* 27 A3 37 54N 122 17W
Kensington, *Syd.* 19 B4 33 54 S 151 13 E
Kensington, *Wash.* 25 C7 39 1N 77 4W
Kensington Palace, *Lon.* 4 B3 51 30N 0 11W
Kent Woodlands, *S.F.* 27 A1 37 56N 122 34W
Kentfield, *S.F.* 27 A1 37 57N 122 33W
Kentish Town, *Lon.* 4 B4 51 32N 0 8W
Kentland, *Wash.* 25 D8 38 55N 76 53W
Kenton, *Lon.* 4 B3 51 34N 0 17W
Kenwood, *Balt.* 25 A4 39 20N 76 30W
Kenwood, *Bost.* 21 B2 42 40N 71 14W
Kenwood House, *Lon.* 4 B4 51 34N 0 9W
Kepa, *Wsaw.* 10 E7 52 13N 21 3 E
Keppel Harbour, *Sing.* 15 G7 1 15N 103 49 E
Kerameikos, *Ath.* 8 J11 37 58N 23 42 E
Kerepes, *Bud.* 10 J14 47 33N 19 17 E
Keston, *Lon.* 4 C5 51 21N 0 1 E
Keston Mark, *Lon.* 4 C5 51 21N 0 2 E
Keth Wara, *Delhi* 16 A2 28 40N 77 13 E
Kettering, *Wash.* 25 D9 38 53N 76 49W
Kettwig, *Ruhr* 6 B3 51 22N 6 56 E
Kew, *Jobg.* 18 E9 26 7 S 28 5 E
Kew, *Lon.* 4 C3 51 28N 0 17W
Kew, *Melb.* 19 E7 37 48 S 145 2 E
Kew Gardens, *Lon.* 4 C3 51 28N 0 17W
Key Gardens, *Trto.* 20 E9 43 39N 79 18W
Khaboye, *St-Pet.* 11 B6 59 53N 30 44 E
Khaidhárion, *Ath.* 8 H10 38 2N 23 38 E
Khairna, *Bomb.* 16 G9 19 5N 73 0 E
Khalándrion, *Ath.* 8 H11 38 3N 23 48 E
Khalīj, *Bagd.* 17 F8 33 18N 44 28 E
Khansā, *Bagd.* 17 E8 33 21N 44 28 E
Kharavli, *Bomb.* 16 H8 18 54N 72 55 E
Khardah, *Calc.* 16 D6 22 43N 88 22 E
Khayala, *Delhi* 16 B1 28 39N 77 6 E
Khefren, *El Qâ.* 18 D4 29 58N 31 8 E
Khichripur, *Delhi* 16 B2 28 37N 77 18 E
Khimki, *Mos.* 11 D8 55 53N 37 24 E
Khimki-Khovrino, *Mos.* 11 D9 55 51N 37 31 E
Khimkinskoye Vdkr., *Mos.* 11 D8 55 51N 37 27 E
Khirvosti, *St-Pet.* 11 B5 59 56N 30 37 E
Khlongsan, *Bangk.* 15 B1 13 43N 100 29 E
Kholargós, *Ath.* 8 J11 37 59N 23 48 E
Khorel, *Calc.* 16 D5 22 41N 88 18 E
Khorosovo, *Mos.* 11 E8 55 46N 37 27 E
Khudrā, *Bagd.* 17 F7 33 19N 44 17 E
Khun Thian, *Bangk.* 15 B1 13 41N 100 27 E
Khuraiji Khas, *Delhi* 16 B2 28 38N 77 16 E
Khurigachi, *Calc.* 16 D5 22 48N 88 21 E
Kiamari, *Kar.* 17 H10 24 49N 66 58 E
Kidderpore, *Calc.* 16 E5 22 32N 88 19 E
Kienwerder, *Berl.* 7 B2 52 22N 13 11 E
Kierling, *Wien* 10 G9 48 18N 16 16 E
Kierlingbach →, *Wien* 10 G9 48 18N 16 19 E
Kierlinger Forst, *Wien* 10 G9 48 17N 16 14 E
Kierst, *Ruhr* 6 C2 51 18N 6 42 E
Kifisós →, *Ath.* 8 J11 37 58N 23 42 E
Kikenka →, *St-Pet.* 11 B2 59 50N 30 3 E
Kikuna, *Tōkyō* 13 C2 35 30N 139 37 E
Kil, *Stock.* 3 D12 59 20N 18 19 E
Kilburn, *Lon.* 4 B3 51 32N 0 11W
Killara, *Syd.* 19 A4 33 46 S 151 10 E
Kilo, *Hels.* 3 B3 60 13N 24 47 E
Kilokri, *Delhi* 16 B2 28 34N 77 15 E
Kilsyth, *Melb.* 19 E8 37 48 S 145 18 E
Kimberton, *Phil.* 24 A1 40 7N 75 34W
Kimlin Park, *Sing.* 15 G7 1 18N 103 49 E
Kindi, *Bagd.* 17 F8 33 18N 44 22 E
King of Prussia, *Phil.* 24 A2 40 5N 75 22W
Kings Cross, *Syd.* 19 B4 33 52 S 151 12 E
Kings Domain, *Melb.* 19 E6 37 49 S 144 58 E
Kings Mt., *S.F.* 27 D3 37 27N 122 19W
King's Park, *H.K.* 12 E6 22 18N 114 10 E
Kings Park, *Wash.* 25 E6 38 48N 77 17W
King's Point, *N.Y.* 23 C6 40 48N 73 45W
Kingsbury, *Lon.* 4 B3 51 34N 0 15W
Kingsford, *Syd.* 19 B4 33 55 S 151 14 E
Kingston upon Thames, *Lon.* 4 C3 51 24N 0 17W
Kingston Vale, *Lon.* 4 C3 51 25N 0 25W
Kingsway, *Trto.* 20 E7 43 38N 79 32W
Kingswood, *Lon.* 4 D3 51 17N 0 12W
Kinnelon, *N.Y.* 22 B2 40 59N 74 23W
Kipling Heights, *Trto.* 20 D7 43 43N 79 34W
Kipséli, *Ath.* 8 J11 37 59N 23 45 E
Kirchhellen, *Ruhr* 6 A3 51 36N 6 56 E
Kirchhörde, *Ruhr* 6 B6 51 27N 7 27 E
Kirchlinde, *Ruhr* 6 A6 51 31N 7 22 E
Kirchof, *Hbg.* 7 E8 53 29N 10 1 E
Kirchsteinbek, *Hbg.* 7 D8 53 31N 10 7 E
Kirchstockbach, *Mün.* 7 G11 48 1N 11 40 E
Kirchtrudering, *Mün.* 7 G11 48 7N 11 40 E
Kirdasa, *El Qâ.* 18 C4 30 2N 31 6 E
Kirikiri, *Lagos* 18 B1 6 26N 7 18 E
Kirkkonummi, *Hels.* 3 C1 60 6N 24 28W
Kirkland, *Mtrl.* 20 B2 43 26N 73 51W
Kirovskiye, Os., *St-Pet.* 11 B3 59 57N 30 14 E
Kisarazu, *Tōkyō* 13 D4 35 21N 139 54 E
Kisikli, *Ist.* 17 A3 41 1N 29 2 E
Kispest, *Bud.* 10 K13 47 27N 19 8 E
Kista, *Stock.* 3 D10 59 24N 17 57 E
Kistarcsa, *Bud.* 10 J14 47 32N 19 16 E
Kita, *Ōsaka* 12 B4 34 41N 135 30 E
Kita-Ku, *Tōkyō* 13 B3 35 44N 139 44 E
Kitain-Temple, *Tōkyō* 13 A1 35 54N 139 29 E
Kitazawa, *Tōkyō* 13 C3 35 39N 139 40 E
Kiu Tsiu, *H.K.* 12 D6 22 22N 114 17 E
Kivistö, *Hels.* 3 B4 60 18N 24 50 E
Kiyose, *Tōkyō* 13 B2 35 46N 139 31 E
Kiziltoprak, *Ist.* 17 B3 40 58N 29 3 E
Kizu →, *Ōsaka* 12 C3 34 37N 135 27 E
Kizuri, *Ōsaka* 12 C4 34 38N 135 34 E
Kjeller, *Oslo* 2 B6 59 58N 11 1 E
Kjelsås, *Oslo* 2 B4 59 57N 10 47 E
Kladow, *Berl.* 7 B1 52 27N 13 9 E
Klampenborg, *Købn.* 2 D10 55 46N 12 35 E
Klánovice, *Pra.* 10 B3 50 5N 14 40 E
Klaudyń, *Wsaw.* 10 E6 52 17N 20 50 E
Klecany, *Pra.* 10 A2 50 10N 14 24 E
Kledering, *Wien* 10 H10 48 8N 16 26 E
Klein Gleinicke, *Berl.* 7 B1 52 23N 13 5 E
Klein-Hadern, *Mün.* 7 G9 48 7N 11 28 E
Klein Jukskei →, *Jobg.* 18 E8 26 6 S 27 57 E
Kleinburg, *Trto.* 20 C7 43 51N 79 37W
Kleine Grasbrook, *Hbg.* 7 D7 53 31N 9 59 E
Kleinmachnow, *Berl.* 7 B2 52 24N 13 14 E
Kleinschönebeck, *Berl.* 7 B5 52 29N 13 42 E
Kleinziethen, *Berl.* 7 B3 52 22N 13 26 E
Klemetsrud, *Oslo* 2 B5 59 50N 10 51 E
Klender, *Jak.* 15 J10 6 12 S 106 53 E
Klippoortje, *Jobg.* 18 F10 26 14 S 28 10 E
Klipriviersberg, *Jobg.* 18 F9 26 16 S 28 2 E
Klipspruit →, *Jobg.* 18 F8 26 14 S 27 53 E
Kloofendal, *Jobg.* 18 E8 26 8 S 27 52 E
Klosterhardt, *Ruhr* 6 A3 51 32N 6 52 E
Klosterneuburg, *Wien* 10 G9 48 18N 16 19 E
Knockholt Pound, *Lon.* 4 D5 51 18N 0 7 E
Knowland State Arboretum and Park, *S.F.* 27 B4 37 45N 122 7W
Knox Park, *Melb.* 19 F8 37 54 S 145 15 E
Knoxville, *Melb.* 19 F8 37 53 S 145 14 E
Kőbánya, *Bud.* 10 K13 47 28N 19 9 E
Kobe, *Ōsaka* 12 B2 34 41N 135 13 E
Kōbe Harbour, *Ōsaka* 12 C2 34 39N 135 11 E
København, *Købn.* 2 D9 55 40N 12 26 E
Kobylisy, *Pra.* 10 B2 50 7N 14 26 E
Kobyłka, *Wsaw.* 10 D8 52 20N 21 10 E
Kocasinan, *Ist.* 17 A2 41 1N 28 50 E
Kočife, *Pra.* 10 B2 50 3N 14 21 E
Kodaira, *Tōkyō* 13 B1 35 43N 139 28 E
Kodanaka, *Tōkyō* 13 C2 35 34N 139 37 E
Kogane, *Tōkyō* 13 B4 35 49N 139 55 E
Koganei, *Tōkyō* 13 B2 35 42N 139 31 E
Kogarah, *Syd.* 19 B3 33 57 S 151 8 E
Køge Bugt, *Købn.* 2 E9 55 34N 12 24 E
Köhlbrand Rethe, *Hbg.* 7 D7 53 31N 9 56 E
Köhlfleet, *Hbg.* 7 D7 53 32N 9 53 E
Koivupää, *Hels.* 3 B4 60 18N 24 53 E
Koja, *Jak.* 15 H10 6 8 S 106 52 E
Koja Utara, *Jak.* 15 H10 6 5 S 106 53 E
Kokobunji, *Tōkyō* 13 B1 35 42N 139 27 E
Kokobunji-Temple, *Tōkyō* 13 B4 35 44N 139 55 E
Kol Scholven, *Ruhr* 6 A3 51 35N 6 59 E
Kolarängen, *Stock.* 3 E12 59 16N 18 10 E
Kolbotn, *Oslo* 2 C4 59 48N 10 48 E
Kole Kalyan, *Bomb.* 16 G8 19 5N 72 50 E
Kolmiranta, *Hels.* 3 B2 60 15N 24 31 E
Kolmperä, *Hels.* 3 B2 60 15N 24 32 E
Koło, *Wsaw.* 10 E6 52 14N 20 56 E
Kolodeje, *Pra.* 10 B3 50 3N 14 38 E
Kolokinthou, *Ath.* 8 J11 38 0N 23 42 E
Kolomenskoye, *Mos.* 11 E10 55 40N 37 40 E
Kolomyagi, *St-Pet.* 11 A3 60 0N 30 19 E
Kolónos, *Ath.* 8 J11 37 59N 23 43 E
Kolovraty, *Pra.* 10 B3 50 0N 14 37 E
Kolsås, *Oslo* 2 B3 59 55N 10 30 E
Koltushi, *St-Pet.* 11 B5 59 55N 30 38 E
Komae, *Tōkyō* 13 C2 35 37N 139 34 E
Komagome, *Tōkyō* 13 B3 35 43N 139 45 E
Komazawa, *Tōkyō* 13 C3 35 37N 139 40 E
Komdhara, *Calc.* 16 C5 22 52N 88 14 E
Kommunarka, *Mos.* 11 F8 55 35N 37 29 E
Komorów, *Wsaw.* 10 F5 52 9N 20 48 E
Kona, *Calc.* 16 E5 22 37N 88 18 E
Konala, *Hels.* 3 B4 60 14N 24 52 E
Kōnan, *Tōkyō* 13 D2 35 23N 139 35 E
Kondli, *Delhi* 16 B2 28 36N 77 19 E
Kong Sin Wan, *H.K.* 12 E5 22 15N 114 7 E
Kongelunden, *Købn.* 2 E10 55 34N 12 34 E
Kongens Lyngby, *Købn.* 2 D10 55 46N 12 30 E
Kongo, *Hels.* 3 A3 60 20N 24 47 E
Königshardt, *Ruhr* 6 A3 51 33N 6 51 E
Konnagar, *Calc.* 16 D6 22 42N 88 21 E
Konohana, *Ōsaka* 12 B3 34 40N 135 26 E
Kōnoike, *Ōsaka* 12 B4 34 42N 135 37 E
Konradshöhe, *Berl.* 7 A2 52 35N 13 13 E
Koonung Cr. →, *Melb.* 19 E7 37 46 S 145 4 E
Kopanina, *Pra.* 10 B1 50 3N 14 17 E
Koparkhairna, *Bomb.* 16 G8 19 6N 72 59 E
Köpenick, *Berl.* 7 B4 52 26N 13 35 E
Korangi, *Kar.* 17 H11 24 47N 67 8 E
Koremasa, *Tōkyō* 13 C1 35 39N 139 29 E
Korenevo, *Mos.* 11 E12 55 40N 38 0 E
Kori, *Ōsaka* 12 B4 34 47N 135 38 E
Koridhallós, *Ath.* 8 J10 37 59N 23 39 E
Korkinskoye, Oz., *St-Pet.* 11 B6 59 55N 30 42 E
Korne, *Ruhr* 6 A7 51 30N 7 30 E
Korso, *Hels.* 3 A5 60 21N 25 5 E
Koshigaya, *Tōkyō* 13 A3 35 53N 139 47 E
Kosino, *Mos.* 11 E11 55 43N 37 50 E
Kosugi, *Tōkyō* 13 C2 35 34N 139 39 E
Kota, *Jak.* 15 H9 6 7 S 106 48 E
Kotelyniki, *Mos.* 11 F11 55 39N 37 52 E
Kōtō-Ku, *Tōkyō* 13 B3 35 40N 139 48 E
Kotrang, *Calc.* 16 D6 22 41N 88 20 E
Koupónia, *Ath.* 8 J11 37 57N 23 47 E
Koviksudde, *Stock.* 3 D13 59 21N 18 21 E
Kowloon, *H.K.* 12 E5 22 18N 114 10 E
Kowloon City, *H.K.* 12 E6 22 19N 114 11 E
Kowloon Pk., *H.K.* 12 D6 22 20N 114 10 E
Kowloon Res., *H.K.* 12 E6 22 21N 114 9 E
Kowloon Tong, *H.K.* 12 D6 22 20N 114 10 E
Kozhukhovo, *Mos.* 11 E11 55 43N 37 53 E
Kozukue, *Tōkyō* 13 C2 35 30N 139 35 E
Krailling, *Mün.* 7 G9 48 5N 11 25 E
Kramat Jati, *Jak.* 15 J10 6 15 S 106 51 E
Krampnitz, *Berl.* 7 B1 52 27N 13 3 E
Krampnitzsee, *Berl.* 7 B1 52 28N 13 4 E
Kranji, *Sing.* 15 F7 1 26N 103 45 E
Kranji, Sungei →, *Sing.* 15 F7 1 26N 103 44 E
Kranji Dam, *Sing.* 15 F7 1 26N 103 44 E
Kraskovo, *Mos.* 11 F11 55 39N 37 58 E
Krasnaya Gorka, *St-Pet.* 11 B5 59 58N 30 38 E
Krasno-Presnenskaya, *Mos.* 11 E9 55 45N 37 32 E
Krasnogorsk, *Mos.* 11 E7 55 49N 37 18 E
Krasnyj Stroitel, *Mos.* 11 F9 55 36N 37 35 E
Krč, *Pra.* 10 B2 50 2N 14 26 E
Krefeld, *Ruhr* 6 B1 51 20N 6 33 E
Kremlin, *Mos.* 11 E9 55 45N 37 38 E
Kresson, *Phil.* 24 B5 39 51N 74 54W
Kreuzberg, *Berl.* 7 A3 52 30N 13 24 E
Krishnarampur, *Calc.* 16 D5 22 43N 88 13 E
Kritzendorf, *Wien* 10 G9 48 19N 16 18 E
Krokhol, *Oslo* 2 C5 59 48N 10 55 E
Krugersdorp, *Jobg.* 18 E7 26 6 S 27 48 E
Krukut, Kali →, *Jak.* 15 J9 6 13 S 106 48 E
Krumme Lanke, *Berl.* 7 B2 52 27N 13 14 E
Krummensee, *Berl.* 7 A5 52 35N 13 42 E
Krupunder, *Hbg.* 7 D7 53 37N 9 53 E
Krusboda, *Stock.* 3 E12 59 13N 18 14 E
Krylatskoye, *Mos.* 11 E8 55 44N 37 23 E
Küçükkoy, *Ist.* 17 A2 41 3N 28 52 E
Kuivasaari, *Hels.* 3 C5 60 8N 25 0 E
Kujiai, *Tōkyō* 13 A1 35 57N 139 26 E
Küllenhahn, *Ruhr* 6 C4 51 14N 7 8 E
Kulosaari, *Hels.* 3 B5 60 11N 25 0 E
Kulturpalasset, *Wsaw.* 10 E7 52 14N 21 0 E
Kumla, *Stock.* 3 E12 59 13N 18 11 E
Kummelnäs, *Stock.* 3 D12 59 21N 18 16 E
Kungens kurva, *Stock.* 3 E10 59 15N 17 53 E
Kungsängen, *Stock.* 3 D9 59 26N 17 43 E
Kungshatt, *Stock.* 3 E10 59 17N 17 53 E
Kungsholmen, *Stock.* 3 D11 59 20N 18 2 E
Kuningan, *Jak.* 15 J9 6 13 S 106 49 E
Kunninkaanmäki, *Hels.* 3 B5 60 18N 25 7 E
Kunitachi, *Tōkyō* 13 B1 35 41N 139 27 E
Kunming Hu, *Beij.* 14 B2 39 59N 116 13 E
Kunratice, *Pra.* 10 B2 50 0N 14 28 E
Kunratický →, *Pra.* 10 B2 50 2N 14 24 E
Kunsthalle, *Hbg.* 7 D8 53 33N 10 0 E
Kuntsevo, *Mos.* 11 E8 55 43N 37 24 E
Kupchino, *St-Pet.* 11 B4 59 50N 30 22 E
Kupferdreh, *Ruhr* 6 B4 51 23N 7 5 E
Kurbali Dere →, *Ist.* 17 B3 40 58N 29 1 E
Kurihara, *Tōkyō* 13 B2 35 45N 139 34 E
Kurkino, *Mos.* 11 D8 55 53N 37 22 E
Kurla, *Bomb.* 16 G8 19 4N 72 52 E
Kurmuri, *Bomb.* 16 G8 19 4N 72 53 E
Kurnell, *Syd.* 19 C4 34 0 S 151 10 E
Kurume, *Tōkyō* 13 B2 35 45N 139 31 E
Kuryanovo, *Mos.* 11 F10 55 39N 37 42 E
Kushihiki, *Tōkyō* 13 A2 35 54N 139 36 E
Kushtia, *Calc.* 16 E6 22 31N 88 23 E
Kuskovo, *Mos.* 11 E10 55 44N 37 48 E
Kutsino, *Mos.* 11 E11 55 44N 37 55 E
Kuy-e-Gishā, *Tehr.* 17 C5 35 44N 51 23 E
Kuy-e-Mekānir, *Tehr.* 17 C5 35 46N 51 22 E
Kuzyminki, *Mos.* 11 E10 55 42N 37 46 E
Kvarnsjön, *Stock.* 3 E10 59 11N 17 58 E
Kwa-Thema, *Jobg.* 18 F11 26 17 S 28 23 E
Kwai Chung, *H.K.* 12 D5 22 22N 114 7 E
Kwitang, *Jak.* 15 J10 6 11 S 106 50 E
Kwun Tong, *H.K.* 12 E6 22 18N 114 13 E
Kyje, *Pra.* 10 B3 50 6N 14 33 E
Kyōhōji, *Ōsaka* 12 C4 34 38N 135 33 E
Kyrkfjärden, *Stock.* 3 E9 59 16N 17 45 E
Kyrkslätt, *Hels.* 3 C1 60 6N 24 28W

L

La Aguada, *Stgo* 30 J10 33 28 S 70 40W
La Blanca, *Stgo* 30 K11 33 30 S 70 40W
La Boca, *B.A.* 32 B4 34 38 S 58 22W
La Bottáccia, *Rome* 9 F8 41 54N 12 18 E
La Bretèche, *Paris* 5 B2 48 51N 2 1 E
La Brosse, *Paris* 5 C1 48 43N 1 20 E
La Cabana, *La Hab.* 30 B3 23 8N 82 20W
La Canada, *L.A.* 28 A3 34 12N 118 12W
La Cassa, *Tori.* 9 A2 45 11N 7 30 E
La Celle-les-Bordes, *Paris* 5 D1 48 38N 1 57 E
La Celle-St.-Cloud, *Paris* 5 B2 48 50N 2 9 E
La Chivera, *Car.* 30 D5 10 35N 66 54W
La Colmena, *Méx.* 29 A2 19 35N 99 16W
La Courneuve, *Paris* 5 B4 48 55N 2 22 E
La Crescenta, *L.A.* 28 A3 34 13N 118 14W
La Défense, *Paris* 5 B3 48 53N 2 13 E
La Dehesa, *Stgo* 30 J11 33 21 S 70 33W
La Estación, *Mdrd.* 8 B2 40 27N 3 48W
La Floresta, *Barc.* 8 D5 41 26N 2 3 E
La Florida, *Car.* 30 D5 10 30N 66 52W
La Fortuna, *Mdrd.* 8 B2 40 21N 3 46W
La Fransa, *Barc.* 8 D5 41 22N 2 9 E
La Fresnière, *Mtrl.* 20 A2 43 33N 73 58W
La Frette-sur-Seine, *Paris* 5 B3 48 58N 2 11 E
La Garenne-Colombes, *Paris* 5 B3 48 54N 2 15 E
La Giustiniana, *Rome* 9 F9 41 59N 12 24 E
La Grange, *Chic.* 26 C1 41 48N 87 53W
La Grange des Noues, *Paris* 5 A4 49 1N 2 28 E
La Grange Highlands, *Chic.* 26 C1 41 46N 87 53W
La Grange Park, *Chic.* 26 C1 41 49N 87 51W
La Granja, *Stgo* 30 K11 33 31 S 70 38W
La Guaira, *Car.* 30 D5 10 36N 66 55W
La Guardia Airport, *N.Y.* 23 C5 40 46N 73 52W
La Guasima, *La Hab.* 30 B3 23 0N 82 17W
La Habana, *La Hab.* 30 B2 23 7N 82 21W
La habana, B. de, *La Hab.* 30 B3 23 7N 82 20W
La Habana Vieia, *La Hab.* 30 B2 23 7N 82 20W
La Habra, *L.A.* 28 C5 33 56N 117 57W
La Habre Heights, *L.A.* 28 B5 33 59N 117 56W
La Horqueta →, *B.A.* 32 C1 34 43 S 58 51W
La Lisa, *La Hab.* 30 B2 23 3N 82 25W
La Llacuna, *Barc.* 8 D6 41 24N 2 12 E
La Loma, *Méx.* 29 A2 19 31N 99 11W
La Lucila, *B.A.* 32 B4 34 30 S 58 29W
La Magdalena Atlipac, *Méx.* 29 B4 19 22N 89 56 E
La Magdalena Chichicaspa, *Méx.* 29 B2 19 24N 99 18W
La Magdalena Contreras, *Méx.* 29 C2 19 17N 99 13W
La Magdalena Petlalco, *Méx.* 29 C2 19 13N 99 10W
La Maison Blanche, *Paris* 5 C1 48 44N 1 54 E
La Maladrerie, *Paris* 5 B2 48 54N 2 1 E
La Marquesa, *Méx.* 29 C1 19 18N 99 22W
La Milla, Cerro, *Lima* 30 G8 12 2 S 77 5W
La Molina, *Lima* 30 G9 12 4 S 76 56W
La Monachina, *Rome* 9 F9 41 53N 12 21 E
La Moraleja, *Mdrd.* 8 A3 40 30N 30 38W
La Nopalera, *Méx.* 29 C3 19 18N 99 5W
La Pastora, *Car.* 30 D5 10 31N 66 55W
La Paterna, *B.A.* 32 B4 34 35 S 58 26W
La Patte-d'Oie, *Paris* 5 A3 49 0N 2 10 E
La Perla, *Lima* 30 G8 12 4 S 77 7W
La Perouse, *Syd.* 19 B4 33 59 S 151 14 E
La Pineda, *Barc.* 8 E5 41 15N 2 1 E
La Pisana, *Rome* 9 F8 41 51N 12 23 E
La Playa, *La Hab.* 30 B2 23 5N 82 26W
La Prairie, *Mtrl.* 20 B5 43 25N 73 29W
La Puente, *L.A.* 28 B5 34 1N 117 54W
La Punta, *Lima* 30 G7 12 4 S 77 10W
La Puntigala, *Barc.* 8 D6 41 27N 2 13 E
La Queue-en-Brie, *Paris* 5 C5 48 47N 2 34 E
La Reina, *Stgo* 30 J11 33 26 S 70 33W
La Reja, *B.A.* 32 B2 34 38 S 58 48W
La Ribera, *Barc.* 8 D5 41 21N 2 4 E
La Romanie, *Paris* 5 C1 48 43N 1 53 E
La Rústica, *Rome* 9 F10 41 54N 12 36 E
La Sagrera, *Barc.* 8 D6 41 25N 2 11 E
La Salada, *B.A.* 32 C4 34 43 S 58 28W
La Scala, *Mil.* 9 E6 45 28N 9 11 E
La Selce, *Rome* 9 G10 41 53N 12 20 E
La Sierra, *La Hab.* 30 B2 23 7N 82 24W
La Taxonera, *Barc.* 8 D6 41 25N 2 10 E
La Vega, *Car.* 30 E5 10 28N 66 56W
La Verrière, *Paris* 5 C1 48 45N 1 57 E
La Víbora, *La Hab.* 30 B2 23 4N 82 21W
La Victoria, *Lima* 30 G8 12 3 S 77 2W
La Ville-du-Bois, *Paris* 5 C3 48 39N 2 16 E
Laab im Walde, *Wien* 10 H9 48 9N 16 10 E
Laaer Berg, *Wien* 10 H10 48 9N 16 24 E
Laajalahti, *Hels.* 3 B3 60 11N 24 48 E
Laajasalo, *Hels.* 3 B5 60 10N 25 3 E
Laaksolahti, *Hels.* 3 B3 60 14N 24 45 E
Laar, *Ruhr* 6 B2 51 27N 6 44 E
Lablāba, W. el →, *El Qâ.* 18 C5 30 1N 31 19 E
Lachine, *Mtrl.* 20 B3 43 26N 73 42W
Ládví, *Pra.* 10 B2 50 8N 14 27 E
Łady, *Wsaw.* 10 F6 52 8N 20 57 E
Lafayette, *S.F.* 27 A4 37 52N 122 6W
Lafayette Hill, *Phil.* 24 A3 40 5N 75 15W
Lafayette Res., *S.F.* 27 A4 37 52N 122 8W
Laferrere, *B.A.* 32 C3 34 44 S 58 35W
Lagny, *Paris* 5 B6 48 52N 2 42 E
Lagoa da Pedra, *Lisb.* 8 F9 38 43N 8 58W
Lagos, *Lagos* 18 B2 6 27N 7 23 E
Lagos Harbour, *Lagos* 18 B2 6 26N 7 23 E
Lagos-Ikeja Airport, *Lagos* 18 A1 6 34N 7 19 E
Lagos Island, *Lagos* 18 B2 6 26N 7 23 E
Lagos Lagoon, *Lagos* 18 B2 6 30N 7 28 E
Laguna de B., *Manila* 15 E4 14 29N 121 6 E
Laim, *Mün.* 7 G10 48 7N 11 30 E
Lainate, *Mil.* 9 D5 45 34N 9 1 E
Lainz, *Wien* 10 H9 48 10N 16 16 E
Lainzer Tiergarten, *Wien* 10 G9 48 10N 16 13 E
Lajeado →, *S. Pau.* 31 E7 23 28 S 46 24W
Lake Avenue Woods, *Chic.* 26 A1 42 4N 87 53W
Lake Hiawatha, *N.Y.* 22 B2 40 52N 74 23W
Lakefield, *Jobg.* 18 F10 26 11 S 28 17 E
Lakemba, *Syd.* 19 B3 33 55 S 151 5 E
Lakeside, *Jobg.* 18 E9 26 5 S 28 8 E
Lakeview, *Chic.* 26 B3 41 56N 87 38W
Lakeview, *Trto.* 20 E7 43 35N 79 32W
Lakhtinskiy, *St-Pet.* 11 B2 59 59N 30 9 E
Lakhtinskiy Razliv, Oz., *St-Pet.* 11 B2 59 59N 30 12 E
Lakshmanpur, *Calc.* 16 E5 22 38N 88 16 E
Laleham, *Lon.* 4 C2 51 24N 0 29W
Lâleli, *Ist.* 17 A2 41 0N 28 57 E
Lalor, *Melb.* 19 E6 37 40 S 144 59 E
Lam San, *Sing.* 15 F7 1 22N 103 43 E
Lam Tin, *H.K.* 12 E6 22 18N 114 14 E
Lambarfjärden, *Stock.* 3 D9 59 21N 17 48 E
Lambert, *Oslo* 2 B4 59 52N 10 48 E
Lambeth, *Lon.* 4 C4 51 28N 0 6W
Lambrate, *Mil.* 9 E6 45 28N 9 16 E
Lambro →, *Mil.* 9 E6 45 24N 9 17 E
Lambro, Parco, *Mil.* 9 E6 45 29N 9 14 E
Lambton, *Jobg.* 18 F10 26 14 S 28 10 E
Lambton Hills, *Trto.* 20 E7 43 39N 79 30W
Lamma I., *H.K.* 12 E5 22 12N 114 7 E
Lampton, *Lon.* 4 C2 51 28N 0 21W
Landianchang, *Beij.* 14 B2 39 57N 116 13 E
Landover Hills, *Wash.* 25 D8 38 56N 76 54W
Landstrasse, *Wien* 10 G10 48 12N 16 23 E
Landwehr kanal, *Berl.* 7 B3 52 29N 13 24 E
Lane Cove, *Syd.* 19 A3 33 48 S 151 9 E
Lane Cove National Park, *Syd.* 19 A3 33 47 S 151 8 E
Langen, *Oslo* 2 C5 59 44N 10 57 E
Langenberg, *Ruhr* 6 B4 51 20N 7 7 E
Langenbochum, *Ruhr* 6 A4 51 36N 7 7 E
Langendreer, *Ruhr* 6 B5 51 27N 7 18 E
Langenhorn, *Hbg.* 7 D7 53 39N 9 59 E
Langenhorst, *Ruhr* 6 B4 51 21N 7 1 E
Langenzersdorf, *Wien* 10 G10 48 18N 16 21 E
Langer See, *Berl.* 7 B4 52 24N 13 37 E
Langerfeld, *Ruhr* 6 C5 51 16N 7 14 E
Langley, *Wash.* 25 D6 38 57N 77 11W
Langley Park, *Wash.* 25 D8 38 59N 76 58W
Langstaff, *Trto.* 20 C8 43 50N 79 26W
Längtarmen, *Stock.* 3 D8 59 24N 17 36 E
Langwald, *Mün.* 7 F9 48 10N 11 25 E
Lanham, *Wash.* 25 D8 38 59N 76 51W
Lank-Latum, *Ruhr* 6 C2 51 18N 6 40 E
Lankwitz, *Berl.* 7 B3 52 25N 13 21 E
Länna Drevviken, *Stock.* 3 E11 59 12N 18 8 E
L'Annunziatella, *Rome* 9 G10 41 49N 12 33 E
Lansdowne, *Balt.* 25 B3 39 14N 76 38W
Lansdowne, *Phil.* 24 B3 39 56N 75 16W
Lansing, *Trto.* 20 D8 43 45N 79 24W
Lanús, *B.A.* 32 C4 34 42 S 58 23W
Lapa, *Rio J.* 31 B2 22 54 S 43 10W
Lapa, *S. Pau.* 31 E5 23 31 S 46 42W
Lapangan Merdeka, *Jak.* 15 J9 6 10 S 106 49 E
Lapinkylä, *Hels.* 3 B4 60 18N 24 51 E
Lapinkylä, *Hels.* 3 B1 60 13N 24 27 E
Lappböle, *Hels.* 3 B1 60 13N 24 27 E
Laranjeiras, *Rio J.* 31 B2 22 55 S 43 10W
Larchmont, *N.Y.* 23 B6 40 55N 73 44W
Larkspur, *S.F.* 27 A1 37 55N 122 31W
Las, *Wsaw.* 10 E7 52 13N 21 6 E
Las Acacias, *Car.* 30 E5 10 29N 66 54W
Las Adjuntas, *Car.* 30 E4 10 25N 67 0W
Las Barrancas, *B.A.* 32 A4 34 28 S 58 29W
Las Conchas, *B.A.* 32 A3 34 25 S 58 34W
Las Corts, *Barc.* 8 D5 41 23N 2 9 E
Las Fuentes Brotantes, *Méx.* 29 C2 19 16N 99 11W
Las Kabacki, *Wsaw.* 10 F7 52 7N 21 2 E
Las Lomas, *L.A.* 28 B5 34 8N 117 59W
Las Mercedes, *Car.* 30 E5 10 28N 66 51W
Las Pinas, *Manila* 15 E3 14 29N 120 58 E
Las Rejas, *Stgo* 30 J10 33 27 S 70 42W
Las Rozas de Madrid, *Mdrd.* 8 B1 40 29N 3 52W
Las Trampas Cr. →, *S.F.* 27 A4 37 53N 122 6W
Las Trampas Regional Park, *S.F.* 27 B4 37 49N 122 3W
Las Trampas Ridge, *S.F.* 27 A4 37 50N 122 3W
Las Tunitas, *Car.* 30 D4 10 36N 67 1W
Lasalle, *Mtrl.* 20 B4 43 26N 73 37W
Lasek Bielański, *Wsaw.* 10 E6 52 17N 20 57 E
Lasek Na Kole, *Wsaw.* 10 E6 52 15N 20 56 E
Laski, *Wsaw.* 10 E6 52 18N 20 50 E
Latina, *Mdrd.* 8 B2 40 24N 3 44W
Latrobe Univ., *Melb.* 19 E7 37 43 S 145 3 E
Lattingtown, *N.Y.* 23 B7 40 52N 73 34W
Laufzorn, *Mün.* 7 G10 48 0N 11 33 E
Laurel Hollow, *N.Y.* 23 B8 40 51N 73 28W
Laurel Springs, *Phil.* 24 C4 39 49N 75 0W
Laurelton, *N.Y.* 23 C6 40 40N 73 45W
Laurence Hanscom Field, *Bost.* 21 C2 42 28N 71 16W
Lausdomini, *Nápl.* 9 H13 40 55N 14 26 E
Lauttasaari, *Hels.* 3 C4 60 9N 24 53 E
Lava Nuova, *Nápl.* 9 J13 40 47N 14 23 E
Laval-des-Rapides, *Mtrl.* 20 A3 43 33N 73 41W
Laval-Ouest, *Mtrl.* 20 A2 43 32N 73 52W
Laval-sur-le-Lac, *Mtrl.* 20 A2 43 31N 73 52W
Lavradio, *Lisb.* 8 F8 38 40N 9 2W
Lawndale, *Chic.* 26 B2 41 50N 87 42W
Lawndale, *L.A.* 28 C3 33 52N 118 22W
Lawndale, *Phil.* 24 A4 40 3N 75 5W
Lawnside, *Phil.* 24 B4 39 52N 75 2W
Lawrence, *Bost.* 21 A3 42 43N 71 7W
Lawrence, *N.Y.* 23 D6 40 36N 73 43W
Lawrence Heights, *Trto.* 20 D8 43 43N 79 25W
Lawrence Park, *Phil.* 24 B2 39 57N 75 20W
Lawton, *La Hab.* 30 B2 23 5N 82 21W
Layāri, *Kar.* 17 G11 24 52N 67 0 E
Layāri →, *Kar.* 17 G10 24 52N 66 58 E
Lazienkowski Park, *Wsaw.* 10 E7 52 13N 21 1 E
Le Blanc-Mesnil, *Paris* 5 B4 48 56N 2 27 E
Le Bourget, *Paris* 5 B4 48 56N 2 25 E
Le Chesnay, *Paris* 5 C2 48 49N 2 8 E
Le Christ de Saclay, *Paris* 5 C3 48 43N 1 59 E
Le Kremlin-Bicêtre, *Paris* 5 C4 48 48N 2 21 E
Le Mesnil-Amelot, *Paris* 5 A5 49 1N 2 35 E
Le Mesnil-le-Roi, *Paris* 5 B2 48 56N 2 7 E
Le Mesnil-St.-Denis, *Paris* 5 C1 48 44N 1 57 E
Le Pecq, *Paris* 5 B2 48 53N 2 6 E
Le Perreux, *Paris* 5 B4 48 50N 2 29 E
Le Pin, *Paris* 5 B5 48 54N 2 37 E
Le Plessis-Bouchard, *Paris* 5 A3 49 0N 2 14 E
Le Plessis-Gassot, *Paris* 5 A4 49 2N 2 24 E
Le Plessis-Pâté, *Paris* 5 D3 48 36N 2 19 E
Le Plessis-Robinson, *Paris* 5 C3 48 47N 2 15 E
Le Plessis-Trévise, *Paris* 5 C5 48 48N 2 34 E
Le Port-Marly, *Paris* 5 B2 48 52N 2 6 E
Le Pré-St.-Gervais, *Paris* 5 B4 48 53N 2 23 E
Le Raincy, *Paris* 5 B4 48 53N 2 31 E
Le Thillay, *Paris* 5 A4 49 0N 2 28 E
Le Trappe, *Mtrl.* 20 B1 43 30N 74 1W
Le Val d'Enfer, *Paris* 5 C3 48 45N 2 11 E
Le Vésinet, *Paris* 5 B2 48 54N 2 8 E
Lea →, *Lon.* 4 B4 51 30N 0 2W
Lea Bridge, *Lon.* 4 B4 51 33N 0 2W
Leakin Park, *Balt.* 25 B2 39 18N 76 41W
Leaside, *Trto.* 20 D8 43 42N 79 22W
Leatherhead, *Lon.* 4 D3 51 17N 0 19W
Leaves Green, *Lon.* 4 D5 51 19N 0 1 E
Leblon, *Rio J.* 31 B2 22 59 S 43 14W
Léchelle, Forêt de la, *Paris* 5 C6 48 43N 2 41 E
Ledøje, *Købn.* 2 D8 55 42N 12 18 E
Lee, *Lon.* 4 C5 51 27N 0 0 E
Leeupan, *Jobg.* 18 F10 26 13 S 28 18 E
Leganes, *Mdrd.* 8 C2 40 19N 3 45W
Legazpi, *Mdrd.* 8 B2 40 23N 3 41W
Legoa, Kali →, *Jak.* 15 H10 6 6 S 106 52 E
Lehtisaaret, *Hels.* 3 C3 60 6N 24 46 E
Lehtisaari, *Hels.* 3 B4 60 10N 24 51 E
Lei Yue Mun, *H.K.* 12 E6 22 17N 114 14 E
Leião, *Lisb.* 8 F7 38 43N 9 17W
Leichhardt, *Syd.* 19 B3 33 53 S 151 9 E
Leigang, *Gzh.* 14 G7 23 2N 113 6 E
Léini, *Tori.* 9 A3 45 11N 7 42 E
Leisure World, *S.F.* 27 A4 37 51N 122 4W
Lemoyne, *Mtrl.* 20 B5 43 29N 73 29W
Lemsahl, *Hbg.* 7 C8 53 41N 10 5 E
Lenin, *Mos.* 11 E9 55 43N 37 34 E
Leningrad = St. Petersburg, *St-Pet.* 11 B3 59 55N 30 15 E
Lenino, *Mos.* 11 F9 55 38N 37 39 E
Leninskiye Gory, *Mos.* 11 E9 55 41N 37 32 E
Lenne →, *Ruhr* 6 B7 51 25N 7 30 E
Lennep, *Ruhr* 6 C5 51 11N 7 15 E
Lenni, *Phil.* 24 B2 39 53N 75 27W
Lennox, *L.A.* 28 C2 33 56N 118 20W
Leonardo da Vinci, Aeroporto Int., *Rome* 9 G8 41 47N 12 15 E
Leoncio Martinez, *Car.* 30 E6 10 29N 66 48W
Leonia, *N.Y.* 22 B5 40 51N 73 59W
Leopard, *Phil.* 24 A2 40 1N 75 26W
Leopardi, *Nápl.* 9 J13 40 45N 14 24 E
Leopoldau, *Wien* 10 G10 48 15N 16 26 E
Leopoldstadt, *Wien* 10 G10 48 13N 16 22 E
Leportovo, *Mos.* 11 E10 55 46N 37 43 E
Leppävaara, *Hels.* 3 B3 60 13N 24 49 E
Lera, Mte., *Tori.* 9 A1 45 10N 7 27 E
L'Éremo, *Tori.* 9 B3 45 2N 7 44 E
Les Alluets-le-Roi, *Paris* 5 B1 48 54N 1 55 E
Les Clayes-sous-Bois, *Paris* 5 C1 48 49N 1 59 E
Les Essarts-le-Roi, *Paris* 5 C1 48 42N 1 53 E
Les Gâtines, *Paris* 5 C1 48 48N 1 58 E
Les Grésillons, *Paris* 5 B2 48 56N 2 1 E
Les Layes, *Paris* 5 C1 48 43N 1 55 E
Les Lilas, *Paris* 5 B4 48 52N 2 25 E
Les Loges-en-Josas, *Paris* 5 C2 48 45N 2 8 E
Les Molières, *Paris* 5 C2 48 40N 2 4 E
Les Mureaux, *Paris* 5 B1 48 59N 1 54 E
Les Pavillons-sous-Bois, *Paris* 5 B5 48 54N 2 30 E
Les Vaux de Cernay →, *Paris* 5 C1 48 41N 1 59 E
Lésigny, *Paris* 5 C5 48 44N 2 37 E
Lesnosavodskaya, *St-Pet.* 11 B4 59 51N 30 29 E
Lesnoy, *St-Pet.* 11 B4 59 59N 30 22 E
Lester B. Pearson Int. Airport, *Trto.* 20 D7 43 40N 79 38 E
L'Étang-la-Ville, *Paris* 5 B2 48 52N 2 4 E
Letná, *Pra.* 10 B2 50 0 S 14 26 E
Lethany, *Pra.* 10 B3 50 8N 14 30 E
Letovo, *Mos.* 11 F8 55 34N 37 24 E
Leuville-sur-Orge, *Paris* 5 D3 48 36N 2 16 E
Levallois-Perret, *Paris* 5 B3 48 53N 2 16 E
Lévis St.-Nom, *Paris* 5 C1 48 43N 1 57 E
Levittown, *N.Y.* 23 C7 40 43N 73 31W
Lewisdale, *Wash.* 25 D8 38 58N 76 59W
Lewisham, *Jobg.* 18 E7 26 7 S 27 49 E
Lewisham, *Lon.* 4 C4 51 27N 0 1W
Lexington, *Bost.* 21 C2 42 25N 71 12W
Leyton, *Lon.* 4 B4 51 33N 0 1W
Leytonstone, *Lon.* 4 B5 51 34N 0 0 E
L'Hautil, *Paris* 5 A2 49 0N 2 0 E
L'Hay-les-Roses, *Paris* 5 C4 48 46N 2 20 E
Lhotka, *Pra.* 10 B2 50 1N 14 26 E
Liangshui He →, *Beij.* 14 C3 39 48N 116 23 E
Lianhua Chi, *Beij.* 14 B2 39 52N 116 21 E
Lianhua He →, *Beij.* 14 B2 39 52N 116 15 E
Lianozovo, *Mos.* 11 D9 55 53N 37 34 E
Libčice nad Vitavou, *Pra.* 10 A2 50 11N 14 22 E
Liben, *Pra.* 10 B2 50 6N 14 27 E
Liberdade, *S. Pau.* 31 E6 23 33 S 46 37W
Libertad, *B.A.* 32 C2 34 41 S 58 41W
Liberty I., *N.Y.* 22 C4 40 41N 74 2W
Liberty Plain, *Bost.* 21 D4 42 11N 70 52W
Liberty Res., *Balt.* 25 A1 39 23N 76 52W
Libeznice, *Pra.* 10 A2 50 11N 14 29 E
Library of Congress, *Wash.* 25 D7 38 53N 77 0W
Libuč, *Pra.* 10 B2 50 0N 14 27 E
Lichiao, *Gzh.* 14 G8 23 3N 113 18 E
Lichtenbroich, *Ruhr* 6 C2 51 17N 6 49 E
Lichtenburg, *Berl.* 7 A4 52 31N 13 30 E
Lichtenplatz, *Ruhr* 6 C5 51 14N 7 11 E
Lichtenrade, *Berl.* 7 B3 52 23N 13 24 E
Lichterfelde, *Berl.* 7 B3 52 26N 13 19 E
Licignano di Nápoli, *Nápl.* 9 H13 40 54N 14 21 E
Lidcombe, *Syd.* 19 B3 33 52 S 151 3 E
Lidingö, *Stock.* 3 D11 59 21N 18 8 E
Lido Beach, *N.Y.* 23 D7 40 35N 73 37W
Lier, *Oslo* 2 C1 59 47N 10 13 E
Lierskogen, *Oslo* 2 C1 59 49N 10 15 E
Lieshi Lingyuan, *Gzh.* 14 G8 23 7N 113 16 E
Liesing, *Wien* 10 H9 48 8N 16 17 E
Liesing →, *Wien* 10 H10 48 8N 16 21 E
Lieusant, *Paris* 5 D5 48 38N 2 33 E
Liffjofs, *Hels.* 3 B6 60 19N 25 12 E
Ligovo, *St-Pet.* 11 C3 59 50N 30 12 E
Lijordet, *Oslo* 2 B3 59 56N 10 36 E
Likhoborka →, *Mos.* 11 D9 55 50N 37 37 E
Likova →, *Mos.* 11 F8 55 36N 37 20 E
Lilla Värtan, *Stock.* 3 D12 59 20N 18 7 E
Lille Rørbæk, *Købn.* 2 D7 55 47N 12 6 E

Midland Park 41

Lille Værløse, *Købn.* .. 2 D9 55 47N 12 22 E
Lillehavfrue, *Købn.* .. 2 D10 55 42N 12 35 E
Lillestrøm, *Oslo* .... 2 B6 59 57N 11 3 E
Liluah, *Calc.* .... 16 E5 22 37N 88 19 E
Lilydale, *Melb.* ..... 19 E9 37 45 S 145 21 E
Lima, *Lima* .... 30 G8 12 3 S 77 2W
Lima, *Phil.* 24 B2 39 55N 75 26W
Limbiate, *Mil.* ...... 9 D5 45 35N 9 7 E
Limehouse, *Lon.* 4 B4 51 30N 0 1W
Limeil-Brévannes, *Paris* 5 C4 48 44N 2 29 E
Limito, *Mil.* .... 9 E6 45 28N 9 19 E
Limoges-Fourches, *Paris* 5 D5 48 37N 2 39 E
Limours, *Paris* ...... 5 D2 48 38N 2 4 E
Linas, *Paris* .... 5 D3 48 37N 2 16 E
Linate, *Mil.* .... 9 E6 45 26N 9 16 E
Linate, Aeroporto Internazionale di, *Mil.* 9 E6 45 26N 9 16 E
Linbigh, *Balt.* 25 A3 39 21N 76 31W
Linbropark, *Jobg.* .... 18 E9 26 5 S 28 7 E
Lincoln, *Bost.* 21 C2 42 25N 71 18W
Lincoln Center, *N.Y.* .. 22 C5 40 46N 73 59W
Lincoln Heights, *L.A.* . 28 B3 34 4N 118 12 E
Lincoln Memorial, *Wash.* 25 D7 38 53N 77 2W
Lincoln Park, *Chic.* ... 26 B3 41 57N 87 38W
Lincoln Park, *N.Y.* ... 22 B3 40 56N 74 18W
Lincoln Park, *S.F.* ... 27 B1 37 47N 122 30W
Lincolnwood, *Chic.* ... 26 A2 42 1N 87 43W
Linda-a-Pastora, *Lisb.* . 8 F7 38 42N 9 15W
Linden, *Jobg.* .... 18 E9 26 8 S 28 0 E
Linden, *N.Y.* 22 D3 40 38N 74 14W
Linden-Dahlhausen, *Ruhr* .... 6 B5 51 25N 7 10 E
Lindenberg, *Berl.* .... 7 A4 52 36N 13 31 E
Lindenhorst, *Ruhr* .... 6 A6 51 33N 7 27 E
Lindenhurst, *N.Y.* 23 C8 40 40N 73 22W
Lindenwold, *Phil.* 24 C5 39 49N 74 59W
Linderhausen, *Ruhr* ... 6 C5 51 17N 7 17 E
Lindfield, *Syd.* ...... 19 A3 33 46 S 151 9 E
Lindøya, *Oslo* .... 2 B4 59 53N 10 42 E
Lingotto, *Tori.* ...... 9 B2 45 1N 7 39 E
Liniers, *B.A.* .... 32 B3 34 39 S 58 30W
Linksfield, *Jobg.* .... 18 E9 26 9 S 28 6 E
Linmeyer, *Jobg.* ..... 18 F9 26 15 S 28 4 E
Linn, *Ruhr* .... 6 B1 51 20N 6 38 E
Linna, *Hels.* .... 3 A4 60 20N 24 50 E
Linthicum Heights, *Balt.* 25 B2 39 12N 76 47W
Lintorf, *Ruhr* .... 6 B3 51 20N 6 50 E
Lintuvaara, *Hels.* .... 3 B3 60 14N 24 49 E
Linwood, *Phil.* 24 C2 39 49N 75 25W
Lioúmi, *Ath.* .... 8 J11 38 0N 23 40 E
Lipków, *Wsaw.* ...... 10 E5 52 16N 20 48 E
Lippalthausen, *Ruhr* .. 6 A6 51 36N 7 26 E
Liqizhuang, *Tianj.* ... 14 E6 39 4N 117 10 E
Lirich, *Ruhr* .... 6 B2 51 29N 6 49 E
Lisboa, *Lisb.* 8 F8 38 42N 9 8W
Lisbon = Lisboa, *Lisb.* 8 F8 38 42N 9 8W
Lishui, *Gzh.* .... 14 F7 23 12N 113 9 E
Lisiy Nos, *St-Pet.* ... 11 A2 60 1N 30 0 E
Lissone, *Mil.* .... 9 D6 45 36N 9 14 E
Lissy, *Paris* .... 5 D6 48 38N 2 42 E
Litoral, Cord. del, *Car.* 30 D5 10 33N 66 54W
Little B., *Syd.* ...... 19 B4 33 58 S 151 15 E
Little Calumet →, *Chic.* 26 D3 41 39N 87 34W
Little Falls, *N.Y.* ... 22 B3 40 52N 74 14W
Little Ferry, *N.Y.* ... 22 B4 40 50N 74 2W
Little Neck, *N.Y.* 23 C6 40 46N 73 43W
Little Paint Br. →, *Wash.* 25 C8 39 0N 76 55W
Little Patuxent →, *Balt.* 25 B1 39 13N 76 51W
Little Rouge →, *Trto.* 20 C9 43 45N 79 11W
Little Sugarloaf, *Melb.* 19 E8 37 40 S 145 18 E
Little Thurrock, *Lon.* . 4 C7 51 29N 0 20 E
Liuhang, *Shang.* ..... 14 H11 31 21N 121 21 E
Liuhuahu Gongyuan, *Gzh.* .... 14 G8 23 8N 113 14 E
Liverpool, *Syd.* ...... 19 B2 33 55 S 150 55 E
Livingstone, *N.Y.* 22 C3 40 47N 74 19W
Livry-Gargan, *Paris* .. 5 B5 48 55N 2 31 E
Liwanhu Gongyuan, *Gzh.* .... 14 G8 23 7N 113 13 E
Lizhuang, *Gzh.* ..... 14 G7 23 6N 113 7 E
Ljan, *Oslo* .... 2 B4 59 51N 10 48 E
Llano de Can Gineu, *Barc.* .... 8 D6 41 27N 2 10 E
Llavallol, *B.A.* ...... 32 C4 34 48 S 58 25W
Llobregat →, *Barc.* .. 8 D5 41 19N 2 5 E
Lloyd Harbor, *N.Y.* .. 23 B8 40 54N 73 26W
Lloyd Pt., *N.Y.* 23 B8 40 56N 73 29W
Lo Aranguiz, *Stgo* ... 30 J11 33 23 S 70 40W
Lo Boza, *Stgo* ...... 30 J10 33 23 S 70 43W
Lo Chau, *H.K.* ...... 12 E6 22 11N 114 15 E
Lo Hermida, *Stgo* ... 30 J11 33 28 S 70 33W
Lo Ortuzar, *Stgo* .... 30 J10 33 28 S 70 43W
Lo Prado Arriba, *Stgo* 30 J10 33 26 S 70 42W
Lo So Shing, *H.K.* ... 12 E5 22 12N 114 7 E
Lo Wai, *H.K.* .... 12 D5 22 22N 114 8 E
Lobau, *Wien* .... 10 G11 48 10N 16 31 E
Lobos, Pt., *S.F.* 27 B1 37 46N 122 30W
Loch Raven Village, *Balt.* 25 A3 39 23N 76 34W
Locham, *Mün.* ...... 7 G9 48 7N 11 26 E
Lochearn, *Balt.* 25 A2 39 20N 76 43W
Lochino, *Mos.* ...... 11 E7 55 41N 37 17 E
Lochkov, *Pra.* ...... 10 B2 50 0N 14 21 E
Lockhausen, *Mün.* ... 7 F9 48 10N 11 24 E
Locksbottom, *Lon.* ... 4 C5 51 21N 0 3 E
Locust Grove, *N.Y.* .. 23 C8 40 48N 73 29W
Locust Manor, *N.Y.* .. 23 C6 40 41N 73 45W
Locust Valley, *N.Y.* .. 23 B7 40 52N 73 36W
Lodi, *N.Y.* 22 B4 40 52N 74 5W
Lofty, Mt., *Melb.* ... 19 E8 37 42 S 145 17 E
Logan, *Phil.* 24 A4 40 2N 75 8W
Logan Int. Airport, *Bost.* 21 C4 42 22N 71 0W
Logan Square, *Chic.* .. 26 B2 41 55N 87 42W
Lognes-Emerainville, Aérodrome de, *Paris* 5 C5 48 49N 2 37 E
Lohausen, *Ruhr* ..... 6 C2 51 16N 6 44 E
Lohberg, *Ruhr* ...... 6 A2 51 34N 6 45 E
Löhme, *Berl.* .... 7 A5 52 37N 13 40 E
Lohmühle, *Ruhr* ..... 6 A4 51 31N 6 59 E
Löhnen, *Ruhr* ...... 6 A1 51 35N 6 39 E
Lokstedt, *Hbg.* ..... 7 D7 53 36N 9 56 E
Lokyang, *Sing.* ...... 15 G7 1 19N 103 40 E
Lōlōkhet, *Kar.* ..... 17 G11 24 54N 67 2 E
Loma Blanca, *Stgo* ... 30 J10 33 29 S 70 43W
Lomas Chapultepec, *Méx.* 29 B2 19 25N 99 12W
Lomas de San Angel Inn, *Méx.* 29 B2 19 20N 99 13W
Lomas de Zamora, *B.A.* 32 C4 34 45 S 58 24W
Lombardy East, *Jobg.* . 18 E9 26 6 S 28 7 E
Lomonosov Univ., *Mos.* .... 11 E9 55 42N 37 31 E
Lomus Reforma, *Méx.* . 29 B2 19 24N 99 14W
London, *Lon.* 4 B4 51 30N 0 6W
London, City of, *Lon.* . 4 B4 51 30N 0 5W
London, Tower of, *Lon.* 4 B4 51 30N 0 4W
London Zoo, *Lon.* ... 4 B4 51 31N 0 9W
Long B., *Syd.* .... 19 B4 33 59 S 151 15 E
Long Beach, *N.Y.* 23 D7 40 35N 73 39W
Long Branch, *Trto.* ... 20 E7 43 35N 79 31W
Long Brook →, *Wash.* 25 E6 38 49N 77 15W
Long Ditton, *Lon.* 4 C3 51 22N 0 19W
Long I., *Bost.* 21 D4 42 19N 70 59W
Long I., *N.Y.* 23 C7 40 45N 73 30W
Long Island City, *N.Y.* 22 C5 40 45N 73 56W
Long Island Sd., *N.Y.* . 23 B7 40 57N 73 30W
Long Pond, *Bost.* 21 A1 42 41N 71 22W
Longchamp, Hippodrôme de, *Paris* 5 B3 48 51N 2 13 E
Longchêne, *Paris* .... 5 D2 48 38N 2 0 E
Longhua Gongyuan, *Shang.* .... 14 J11 31 10N 121 26 E
Longjohn Slough, *Chic.* 26 C1 41 42N 87 52W
Longjumeau, *Paris* ... 5 C3 48 41N 2 17 E
Longlands, *Lon.* ..... 4 C5 51 25N 0 5 E
Longpont-sur-Orge, *Paris* .... 5 D3 48 38N 2 17 E
Longtan Hu →, *Beij.* 14 B3 39 51N 116 24 E
Longue Point, *Mtrl.* .. 20 A4 43 31N 73 31W
Longueuil, *Mtrl.* 20 A5 43 31N 73 29W
Loni, *Delhi* .... 16 A2 28 45N 77 17 E
Lord's Cricket Ground, *Lon.* 4 B3 51 31N 0 10W
Loreley, *Balt.* 25 A4 39 23N 76 24W
Lørenskog, *Oslo* .... 2 B5 59 55N 10 59 E
Loreto, *Mil.* .... 9 E6 45 29N 9 12 E
Lorraine, *Mtrl.* 20 A3 43 39N 73 46W
Los Angeles, *L.A.* ... 28 B3 34 3N 118 14 E
Los Angeles, *Mdrd.* .. 8 B2 40 20N 3 41W
Los Angeles →, *L.A.* 28 C3 33 55N 118 10W
Los Angeles Int. Airport, *L.A.* 28 C2 33 56N 118 23W
Los Asientos, *Car.* ... 30 D5 10 32N 66 53W
Los Caobos, *Car.* 30 D5 10 30N 66 53W
Los Carmenes, *Car.* .. 30 E5 10 28N 66 54W
Los Cerrillas, Aeroporto, *Stgo* .... 30 J10 33 29 S 70 42W
Los Dos Caminos, *Car.* 30 D6 10 30N 66 49W
Los dos Riteras →, *Car.* 30 D5 10 35N 66 57W
Los Jazmines, Presa, *Méx.* 29 B2 19 25N 99 15W
Los Nietos, *L.A.* 28 C4 33 57N 118 4W
Los Pinos, *La Hab.* .. 30 B2 23 4N 82 22W
Los Pirules, *Méx.* ... 29 B3 19 24N 99 2W
Los Polvorines, *B.A.* . 32 B2 34 30 S 58 41W
Los Remedios →, *Méx.* 29 B2 19 28N 99 13W
Los Remedios, Parque Nacional de, *Méx.* .. 29 B2 19 27N 99 15W
Los Reyes, *Méx.* 29 B4 19 21N 99 6W
Los Rosales, *Car.* ... 30 E5 10 28N 66 53W
Losby, *Oslo* .... 2 B5 59 53N 10 59 E
Loughton, *Lon.* ..... 4 B5 51 38N 0 4 E
Loures, *Lisb.* 8 F7 38 49N 9 10W
Louveciennes, *Paris* .. 5 B2 48 51N 2 8 E
Louvres, *Paris* ...... 5 A5 49 2N 2 30 E
Lövholmen, *Stock.* ... 3 E10 59 18N 17 51 E
Lövön, *Stock.* .... 3 E9 59 19N 17 51 E
Lövstafjärden, *Stock.* . 3 D9 59 23N 17 46 E
Lowe, Mt., *L.A.* 28 A4 34 13N 118 5W
Lowe Pond, *Bost.* ... 21 A3 42 41N 71 0W
Lowell, *Bost.* 21 B2 42 38N 71 16W
Lowell Dracut State Forest, *Bost.* 21 B1 42 39N 71 22W
Lower Crystal Springs Res., *S.F.* 27 C2 37 31N 122 21W
Lower Edmonton, *Lon.* 4 B4 51 37N 0 3W
Lower Montville, *N.Y.* 22 B2 40 53N 74 21W
Lower New York B., *N.Y.* 22 D4 40 32N 74 5W
Lower Plenty, *Melb.* . 19 E7 37 44 S 145 7 E
Lower Shing Mun Res., *H.K.* .... 12 D5 22 22N 114 9 E
Lower Sydenham, *Lon.* 4 C4 51 25N 0 2W
Lower Van Norman L., *L.A.* 28 A2 34 17N 118 28W
Lübars, *Berl.* ...... 7 A3 52 37N 13 21 E
Lubeinī, Bahr el →, *El Qâ.* .... 18 C4 30 1N 31 5 E
Lubya →, *St-Pet.* ... 11 A5 60 1N 30 39 E
Lucento, *Tori.* ...... 9 B2 45 5N 7 39 E
Lucero, *La Hab.* 30 B3 23 5N 82 19W
Ludwigsfeld, *Mün.* .. 7 F9 48 12N 11 27 E
Lugarno, *Syd.* ...... 19 B3 33 59 S 151 2 E
Lugouqiao, *Beij.* .... 14 C2 39 49N 116 10 E
Luhu, *Gzh.* .... 14 G8 23 9N 113 16 E
Luipaardsvei, *Jobg.* .. 18 E7 26 6 S 27 49 E
Luis Guillón, *B.A.* .. 32 C4 34 48 S 58 26W
Lujia, *Shang.* ...... 14 J12 31 15N 121 37 E
Lukens, Mt., *L.A.* ... 28 A3 34 16N 118 12W
Lumiar, *Lisb.* 8 F8 38 4N 9 10W
Lundtofte, *Købn.* ... 2 D10 55 47N 12 32 E
Lung Mei, *H.K.* ..... 12 D6 22 23N 114 15 E
Lunsad, *Manila* ..... 15 E5 14 27N 121 11 E
Luojiang, *Gzh.* ..... 14 G8 23 5N 113 17 E
Lura →, *Mil.* ...... 9 D5 45 34N 9 5 E
Lurnea, *Syd.* .... 19 B2 33 56 S 150 54 E
Lurup, *Hbg.* .... 7 D7 53 35N 9 54 E
Lustheim, *Mün.* .... 7 F10 48 14N 11 34 E
Lütgendortmund, *Ruhr* 6 A6 51 30N 7 20 E
Lutherville-Timonium, *Balt.* 25 A3 39 25N 76 36W
Lüttringhausen, *Ruhr* . 6 C5 51 12N 7 14 E
Lutvann, *Oslo* ...... 2 B5 59 54N 10 52 E
Luwan, *Shang.* ..... 14 J11 31 12N 121 27 E
Luyano, *La Hab.* 30 B2 23 6N 82 21W
Luzhniki Sports Centre, *Mos.* .... 11 E9 55 43N 37 31 E
Lyckebyn, *Stock.* .... 3 E12 59 11N 18 13 E
Lynbrook, *N.Y.* 23 D6 40 38N 73 41W
Lyndhurst, *Jobg.* .... 18 E9 26 7 S 28 6 E
Lyndhurst, *N.Y.* 22 C4 40 49N 74 7W
Lynn, *Bost.* 21 C4 42 28N 70 57W
Lynn Harbor, *Bost.* .. 21 C4 42 26N 70 56W
Lynnfield, *Bost.* 21 B3 42 32N 71 2W
Lynwood, *L.A.* 28 C3 33 55N 118 11W
Lyon, Gare de, *Paris* . 5 B4 48 50N 2 22 E
Lyons, *Chic.* 26 C2 41 48N 87 49W
Lyonsville, *N.Y.* 22 B2 40 57N 74 26W
Lysaker, *Oslo* ...... 2 B3 59 54N 10 38 E
Lysakerselva →, *Oslo* 2 B3 59 54N 10 38 E
Lysolaje, *Pra.* ...... 10 B2 50 8N 14 22 E
Lytkarino, *Mos.* .... 11 F11 55 35N 37 55 E
Lyubertsy, *Mos.* .... 11 E11 55 40N 37 51 E
Lyublino, *Mos.* ..... 11 E10 55 40N 37 44 E

M

Ma Nam Wat, *H.K.* ... 12 D6 22 21N 114 16 E
Ma Po, *Sŏul* .... 12 G7 37 32N 126 56 E
Ma Tsz Keng, *H.K.* .. 12 D5 22 25N 114 7 E
Ma Yau Tong, *H.K.* .. 12 E6 22 19N 114 14 E
Maantiekylä, *Hels.* .. 3 A5 60 20N 25 0 E
Maarifa, *Bagd.* ..... 17 F8 33 15N 44 21 E
Mabashi, *Tōkyō* .... 13 B4 35 48N 139 54 E
Mabato Pt., *Manila* .. 15 E4 14 29N 121 3 E
Mabolo, *Manila* .... 15 E3 14 26N 120 56 E
Macaco, Morro do, *Rio J.* .... 31 B3 22 56 S 43 6W
McCook, *Chic.* 26 C2 41 47N 87 49W
McGill Univ., *Mtrl.* . 20 A4 43 30N 73 35W
Machida, *Tōkyō* .... 13 C1 35 32N 139 26 E
Macierzysz, *Wsaw.* .... 10 E6 52 13N 20 50 E
Maciołki, *Wsaw.* ..... 10 E7 52 19N 21 9 E
Mackayville, *Mtrl.* ... 20 A5 43 30N 73 26W
McKinnon, *Melb.* .... 19 F7 37 54 S 145 1 E
Mclean, *Wash.* 25 D6 38 56N 77 10W
Macleod, *Melb.* ..... 19 E7 37 43 S 145 4 E
Macopocho →, *Stgo* . 30 J10 33 24 S 70 40W
Macquarie Fields, *Syd.* 19 B2 33 59 S 150 53 E
Macquarie Univ., *Syd.* 19 A3 33 46 S 151 7 E
MacRitchie Res., *Sing.* 15 F7 1 20N 103 49 E
Macul, *Stgo* .... 30 K11 33 30 S 70 35W
Macuto, *Car.* 30 D5 10 36N 66 53W
Macuto →, *Car.* 30 D5 10 36N 66 53W
Madatpur, *Calc.* ..... 16 C6 22 53N 88 27 E
Maddalena, Colle della, *Tori.* .... 9 B3 45 2N 7 43 E
Madhudaha, *Calc.* ... 16 E6 22 30N 88 24 E
Madhyamgram, *Calc.* . 16 D6 22 41N 88 26 E
Madīnah Al Mansōr, *Bagd.* .... 17 F8 33 18N 44 20 E
Mâdinet el Muqattam, *El Qâ.* .... 18 C5 30 1N 31 15 E
Mâdinet Nasr, *El Qâ.* . 18 C5 30 4N 31 18 E
Madipur, *Delhi* ..... 16 B1 28 40N 77 8 E
Madison, *N.Y.* 22 C2 40 45N 74 24W
Madonna della Scala, *Tori.* .... 9 B3 44 59N 7 46 E
Madonna dell'Arco, *Nápl.* .... 9 H13 40 52N 14 23 E
Madrid, *Mdrd.* 8 B2 40 24N 3 42W
Madrona, *Barc.* ..... 8 D5 41 27N 2 1 E
Madureira, *Rio J.* ... 31 B2 22 52 S 43 19W
Maeda, *Tōkyō* ...... 13 B3 35 48N 139 45 E
Maesawa, *Tōkyō* .... 13 B2 35 44N 139 31 E
Magalhaes, *Rio J.* ... 31 B1 22 51 S 43 22W
Magdalena del Mar, *Lima* .... 30 G8 12 5 S 77 5W
Magholpur, *Delhi* .... 16 A1 28 41N 77 6 E
Maghreb, *Bagd.* .... 17 E8 33 23N 44 22 E
Magidiyeh, *Tehr.* ... 17 C5 35 43N 51 28 E
Maginu, *Tōkyō* ..... 13 C2 35 35N 139 34 E
Magliana, *Rome* ..... 9 F9 41 50N 12 26 E
Maglód, *Bud.* ...... 10 K14 47 27N 19 18 E
Magnolia, *Phil.* 24 B4 39 51N 75 1W
Magny-les-Hameaux, *Paris* .... 5 C2 48 44N 2 3 E
Maharajpur, *Delhi* ... 16 B2 28 39N 77 19 E
Maheshtala, *Calc.* ... 16 E5 22 29N 88 15 E
Mahiari, *Calc.* ...... 16 E5 22 35N 88 14 E
Mahikpur, *Calc.* .... 16 E5 22 32N 88 13 E
Mahim, *Bomb.* ..... 16 G8 19 2N 72 50 E
Mahim B., *Bomb.* ... 16 G7 19 2N 72 49 E
Mahishdanga, *Calc.* .. 16 C6 22 53N 88 11 E
Mahlsdorf, *Berl.* .... 7 A4 52 30N 13 37 E
Mahmoodabad, *Kar.* . 17 G11 24 51N 67 4 E
Mahmutbey, *Ist.* .... 17 A1 41 2N 28 49 E
Mahpar, *Jak.* ...... 15 H9 6 9 S 106 49 E
Mahul, *Bomb.* ..... 16 G8 19 1N 72 53 E
Maida Vale, *Lon.* ... 4 B3 51 31N 0 10W
Maidstone, *Melb.* ... 19 E6 37 47 S 144 52 E
Maincourt-sur-Yvette, *Paris* .... 5 C1 48 42N 1 58 E
Maipu, *Stgo* .... 30 K10 33 30 S 70 45W
Maiquetia, *Car.* 30 D5 10 35N 66 57W
Maiquetia Aeropuerto, *Car.* 30 D4 10 36N 67 0W
Maisons-Alfort, *Paris* . 5 C4 48 48N 2 26 E
Maisons-Laffitte, *Paris* 5 B2 48 57N 2 8 E
Maissoneuve, *Mtrl.* .. 20 A4 43 32N 73 33W
Maitani, *Ōsaka* ..... 12 B3 34 48N 135 22 E
Majadahonda, *Mdrd.* . 8 B1 40 28N 3 52W
Majlis, *Tehr.* ...... 17 C5 35 41N 51 25 E
Makati, *Manila* .... 15 D4 14 33N 121 7 E
Mäkiniittty, *Hels.* .. 3 A4 60 20N 24 58 E
Mala Straná, *Pra.* ... 10 B2 50 4N 14 24 E
Malabar, *Syd.* ..... 19 B4 33 58 S 151 14 E
Malabar Hill, *Bomb.* . 16 H7 18 57N 72 48 E
Malabon, *Manila* ... 15 D3 14 39N 120 56 E
Malacanang Palace, *Manila* .... 15 D3 14 35N 120 59 E
Malagrotta, *Rome* ... 9 F9 41 52N 12 20 E
Malakhovka, *Mos.* ... 11 F12 55 39N 38 0 E
Malakoff, *Paris* .... 5 C3 48 49N 2 18 E
Malakpur, *Delhi* ... 16 A2 28 42N 77 12 E
Malanday, *Manila* ... 15 D4 14 38N 121 5 E
Malanghero, *Tori.* ... 9 A2 45 12N 7 39 E
Mälarhöjaen, *Stock.* . 3 E10 59 18N 17 58 E
Malaspina, L., *Mil.* . 9 E6 45 28N 9 18 E
Malassis, *Paris* .... 5 D2 48 37N 2 3 E
Malate, *Manila* .... 15 D3 14 34N 120 59 E
Malaya Neva, *St-Pet.* . 11 B3 59 56N 30 15 E
Malaya-Okhta, *St-Pet.* 11 B4 59 55N 30 25 E
Malchow, *Berl.* ..... 7 A3 52 34N 13 29 E
Malden, *Bost.* 21 C3 42 26N 71 3W
Malden, *Lon.* 4 C3 51 23N 0 15W
Malečice, *Pra.* ..... 10 B3 50 5N 14 30 E
Malekete, *Lagos* .... 18 A3 6 33N 7 32 E
Malir →, *Kar.* ..... 17 H11 24 49N 67 4 E
Malir Cantonment, *Kar.* 17 G12 24 58N 67 10 E
Malmi, *Hels.* ...... 3 B4 60 15N 24 59 E
Malmøya, *Oslo* ..... 2 B4 59 52N 10 45 E
Måløv, *Købn.* ..... 2 D9 55 44N 12 20 E
Malton, *Trto.* 20 D7 43 42N 79 38W
Malvern, *Jobg.* ..... 18 F9 26 11 S 28 5 E
Malvern, *Melb.* .... 19 F7 37 50 S 145 2 E
Malvern, *Phil.* 24 A1 40 2N 75 31W
Malvern, *Trto.* 20 D9 43 47N 79 13W
Malvern East, *Jobg.* . 18 F9 26 11 S 28 7 E
Malverne, *N.Y.* 23 C6 40 40N 73 40W
Mamaroneck, *N.Y.* .. 23 B6 40 56N 73 43W
Mamaroneck Harbour, *N.Y.* 23 B6 40 56N 73 41W
Mamonovo, *Mos.* ... 11 F10 55 36N 37 49 E
Mamonovo, *Mos.* ... 11 E8 55 41N 37 18 E
Mampong Prapatan, *Jak.* .... 15 J9 6 15 S 106 49 E
Mampukuji, *Tōkyō* .. 13 C2 35 36N 139 31 E
Man Budrukh, *Bomb.* . 16 G8 19 2N 72 55 E
Man Khurd, *Bomb.* .. 16 G8 19 3N 72 55 E
Managua, *La Hab.* .. 30 C3 22 58N 82 17W
Manayunk, *Phil.* 24 A3 40 1N 75 12W
Mandaluyong, *Manila* . 15 D4 14 35N 121 1 E
Mandaoli, *Delhi* .... 16 B2 28 37N 77 17 E
Mandaqui, *S. Pau.* .. 31 D6 23 29 S 46 37W
Mandaqui →, *S. Pau.* 31 D6 23 30 S 46 40W
Mandres-les-Roses, *Paris* .... 5 C5 48 42N 2 32 E
Mandvi, *Bomb.* .... 16 H8 18 56N 72 50 E
Mang Kung Uk, *H.K.* . 12 E6 22 18N 114 16 E
Manggarai, *Jak.* .... 15 J10 6 12 S 106 50 E
Manguinho, Aéroporto de, *Rio J.* .... 31 B2 22 52 S 43 14W
Mangweon, *Sŏul* ... 12 G7 37 33N 126 55 E
Manhasset, *N.Y.* ... 23 C6 40 47N 73 40W
Manhasset B., *N.Y.* . 23 C6 40 49N 73 43W
Manhasset Hills, *N.Y.* 23 C7 40 45N 73 39W
Manhattan, *N.Y.* ... 22 C5 40 48N 73 57W
Manhattan Beach, *L.A.* 28 C2 33 53N 118 24W
Manhatten, *N.Y.* ... 22 D5 40 34N 73 56W
Manila, *Manila* .... 15 D3 14 35N 120 58 E
Manila B., *Manila* .. 15 D3 14 32N 120 56 E
Manila Int. Airport, *Manila* .... 15 D4 14 31N 121 0 E
Mankkaa, *Hels.* ..... 3 B3 60 11N 24 47 E
Mankunda, *Calc.* ... 16 C6 22 50N 88 22 E
Manly, *Syd.* .... 19 A4 33 47 S 151 17 E
Manly Warringah War Memorial Park, *Syd.* 19 A4 33 46 S 151 15 E
Manning State Park, *Bost.* 21 B1 42 34N 71 20W
Mannsworth, *Wien* ... 10 H11 48 8N 16 30 E
Manoa, *Phil.* 24 B3 39 58N 75 18W
Manor Park, *Lon.* .. 4 B5 51 32N 0 1 E
Manora, *Kar.* ...... 17 H10 24 47N 66 58 E
Manorhaven, *N.Y.* .. 23 B6 40 50N 73 41W
Manoteras, *Mdrd.* .. 8 B3 40 28N 3 39W
Manquehue, Cerro, *Stgo* 30 J11 33 21 S 70 35W
Mantegazza, *Mil.* .. 9 D4 45 30N 8 58 E
Mantilla, *La Hab.* .. 30 B3 23 4N 82 20W
Mantua, *Phil.* 24 C3 39 47N 75 10W
Mantua Cr. →, *Phil.* . 24 C3 39 47N 75 13W
Manufacta, *Jobg.* .. 18 E8 26 9 S 27 51 E
Manzanares, Canal de, *Mdrd.* 8 C3 40 19N 3 38W
Mapetla, *Jobg.* .... 18 F8 26 16 S 27 51 E
Maple, *Trto.* 20 C7 43 51N 79 30W
Maple L., *Chic.* ... 26 C1 41 43N 87 53W
Maple Shade, *Phil.* . 24 B4 39 57N 75 0W
Maplewood, *N.Y.* .. 22 C3 40 43N 74 16W
Maracana, *Rio J.* ... 31 B2 22 54 S 43 13W
Maraisburg, *Jobg.* .. 18 F8 26 10 S 27 57 E
Marano di Nápoli, *Nápl.* 9 H12 40 53N 14 11 E
Maraoli, *Bomb.* ... 16 G8 19 2N 72 53 E
Marapendi, L. de, *Rio J.* .... 31 C1 23 0 S 43 23W
Marblehead, *Bost.* .. 21 C4 42 29N 70 51W
Marcelin, *Wsaw.* .. 10 E6 52 19N 20 59 E
Marcella, *N.Y.* 22 B2 40 59N 74 29W
Marcos Paz, *B.A.* .. 32 C2 34 46 S 58 49W
Marcoussis, *Paris* .. 5 D3 48 38N 2 13 E
Marcus Hook, *Phil.* . 24 C2 39 49N 75 25W
Marcus Hook Cr. →, *Phil.* 24 B2 39 49N 75 24W
Marechiaro, *Nápl.* .. 9 J12 40 48N 14 12 E
Mareil-Marly, *Paris* .. 5 B2 48 52N 2 4 E
Margareten, *Wien* ... 10 G10 48 11N 16 20 E
Margency, *Paris* ... 5 A3 49 0N 2 17 E
Margitsziget, *Bud.* .. 10 J13 47 31N 19 2 E
Maria, *Wien* .... 10 G10 48 11N 16 21 E
Maria Paula, *Rio J.* . 31 B3 22 53 S 43 1W
Marianao, *La Hab.* . 30 B2 23 4N 82 25W
Marianella, *Nápl.* .. 9 H12 40 53N 14 13 E
Mariano Acosta, *B.A.* . 32 C2 34 42 S 58 47W
Mariano J. Haedo, *B.A.* 32 B3 34 39 S 58 35W
Maridalen, *Oslo* ... 2 B4 59 59N 10 45 E
Maridalsvatnet, *Oslo* . 2 B4 59 59N 10 46 E
Mariendorf, *Berl.* .. 7 B3 52 26N 13 23 E
Marienfelde, *Berl.* . 7 B3 52 24N 13 23 E
Marienthal, *Hbg.* .. 7 D8 53 34N 10 4 E
Mariglanella, *Nápl.* . 9 H13 40 55N 14 26 E
Mariglano, *Nápl.* .. 9 H13 40 55N 14 27 E
Marikina, *Manila* ... 15 D4 14 38N 121 5 E
Marikina →, *Manila* . 15 D4 14 33N 121 3 E
Marin City, *S.F.* ... 27 A1 37 52N 122 30W
Marin Headlands State Park, *S.F.* 27 A2 37 50N 122 28W
Marin Is., *S.F.* 27 A2 37 57N 122 27W
Marin Pen., *S.F.* ... 27 A1 37 50N 122 30W
Marine World, *S.F.* . 27 C3 37 32N 122 16W
Mariners Harbour, *N.Y.* 22 D3 40 38N 74 10W
Mario, Mt., *Rome* .. 9 F9 41 55N 12 27 E
Markham, *Chic.* 26 D2 41 35N 87 40W
Markham, *Phil.* 24 B1 39 53N 75 30W
Markham, *Trto.* 20 D8 43 49N 79 22W
Markham, Mt., *L.A.* . 28 A4 34 14N 118 6W
Marki, *Wsaw.* ..... 10 E7 52 19N 21 6 E
Markland Wood, *Trto.* 20 E7 43 38N 79 34W
Marlton, *Phil.* 24 B5 39 53N 74 55W
Marly, Forêt de, *Paris* 5 B2 48 52N 2 2 E
Marly-le-Roi, *Paris* . 5 B2 48 52N 2 5 E
Marne →, *Paris* .... 5 C4 48 47N 2 29 E
Marne-la-Vallée, *Paris* 5 B5 48 50N 2 37 E
Marolles-en-Brie, *Paris* 5 C5 48 44N 2 33 E
Maroonda Aquaduct, *Melb.* .... 19 E7 37 40 S 145 9 E
Maroubra, *Syd.* .... 19 B4 33 56 S 151 16 E
Marple, *Phil.* 24 B2 39 56N 75 20W
Marquette Park, *Chic.* 26 C2 41 46N 87 42W
Marrickville, *Syd.* .. 19 B3 33 54 S 151 9 E
Marschlande, *Hbg.* . 7 E8 53 27N 10 6 E
Marsfield, *Syd.* .... 19 A3 33 46 S 151 7 E
Marte, Base Aérea de, *S. Pau.* .... 31 E6 23 30 S 46 38W
Martesana, Navíglio della, *Mil.* .... 9 D6 45 31N 9 17 E
Martin State Nat. Airport, *Balt.* 25 B4 39 19N 76 24W
Martinez, *B.A.* .... 32 A3 34 29 S 58 31W
Martinkylä, *Hels.* .. 3 B4 60 17N 24 51 E
Martins Pond, *Bost.* . 21 B3 42 35N 71 7W
Martinsried, *Mün.* . 7 G9 48 6N 11 27 E
Maruko, *Tōkyō* .... 13 C3 35 33N 139 40 E
Marusino, *Mos.* ... 11 E11 55 41N 37 58 E
Marxloh, *Ruhr* .... 6 A2 51 30N 6 47 E
Maryino, *Mos.* ... 11 E10 55 40N 37 45 E
Maryland, *Sing.* ... 15 G7 1 19N 103 47 E
Maryland, Univ. of, *Wash.* 25 D8 39 58N 76 56W
Marylebone, *Lon.* .. 4 B4 51 31N 0 9W
Marymont, *Wsaw.* .. 10 E6 52 16N 20 58 E
Marysin Wawerski, *Wsaw.* .... 10 E7 52 14N 21 9 E
Marzahn, *Berl.* .... 7 A4 52 32N 13 34 E
Masambong, *Manila* . 15 D4 14 38N 121 0 E
Mascot, *Syd.* ...... 19 B4 33 55 S 151 12 E
Mascuppic L., *Bost.* . 21 A1 42 40N 71 23W
Masmo, *Stock.* .... 3 E10 59 15N 17 53 E
Maspeth, *N.Y.* 22 C5 40 43N 73 55W
Masr el Gedida, *El Qâ.* 18 C5 30 5N 31 19 E
Masr el Qadîma, *El Qâ.* 18 C5 30 0N 31 14 E
Masroor Airport, *Kar.* 17 G10 24 53N 66 56 E
Massa di Somma, *Nápl.* 9 H13 40 50N 14 22 E
Massachusetts B., *Bost.* 21 C4 42 25N 70 50W
Massachusetts Inst. of Tech., *Bost.* 21 C3 42 22N 71 6W
Massamá, *Lisb.* 8 F7 38 45N 9 16W
Massapequa, *N.Y.* .. 23 C8 40 40N 73 28W
Massby, *Hels.* ..... 3 B6 60 17N 25 16 E
Massey →, *Trto.* .. 20 D9 43 42N 79 19W
Massy, *Paris* ..... 5 C3 48 43N 2 16 E
Matarza →, *B.A.* .. 32 C3 34 47 S 58 35W
Matasango, *Lima* ... 30 G9 12 8 S 76 58W
Mathile, *Calc.* .... 16 E5 22 34N 88 13 E
Mathitong, *Beij.* ... 14 B2 39 56N 116 19 E
Matinecock, *N.Y.* . 23 B7 40 51N 73 36W
Matinha, *Lisb.* 8 F8 38 45N 9 5W
Matramam, *Jak.* ... 15 J10 6 12 S 106 51 E
Matsubara, *Ōsaka* .. 12 C4 34 34N 135 33 E
Matsubushi, *Tōkyō* . 13 A3 35 55N 139 49 E
Matsudo, *Tōkyō* ... 13 B4 35 46N 139 54 E
Matsumoloshinden, *Tōkyō* .... 13 B2 35 50N 139 36 E
Mattapan, *Bost.* ... 21 D3 42 15N 71 6W
Mátyásföld, *Bud.* .. 10 J14 47 30N 19 12 E
Mau Tso Ngam, *H.K.* 12 D6 22 22N 114 13 E
Mauá, *S. Pau.* .... 31 E7 23 39 S 46 27W
Mauer, *Wien* ...... 10 H9 48 9N 16 16 E
Mauerbach →, *Wien* . 10 G9 48 12N 16 13 E
Mauldre, *Paris* ... 5 C1 48 56N 1 53 E
Maurecourt, *Paris* .. 5 B2 48 59N 2 3 E
Mauregard, *Paris* .... 5 A5 49 2N 2 34 E
Maurepas, *Paris* .... 5 C1 48 46N 1 55 E
Mauripur, *Kar.* ..... 17 G10 24 52N 66 55 E
Maxhof, *Mün.* ...... 7 G9 48 4N 11 29 E
Maya-Zan, *Ōsaka* ... 12 B2 34 43N 135 12 E
Maybunga, *Manila* ... 15 D4 14 34N 121 4 E
Mayfair, *Jobg.* ..... 18 F9 26 11 S 28 0 E
Mayfair, *Phil.* 24 A4 40 2N 75 3W
Maypajo, *Manila* ... 15 D3 14 38N 120 58 E
Maytubig, *Manila* ... 15 D3 14 33N 120 59 E
Maywood, *Chic.* ... 26 B1 41 52N 87 51W
Maywood, *L.A.* 28 C3 33 59N 118 12W
Maywood, *N.Y.* 22 B4 40 53N 74 3W
Mazagaon, *Bomb.* .. 16 H8 18 57N 72 50 E
M'Boi Mirim, *S. Pau.* 31 F5 23 42 S 46 46W
Meadow I., *N.Y.* ... 23 D7 40 36N 73 32W
Meadow L., *N.Y.* ... 23 C6 40 44N 73 50W
Meadowlands, *Jobg.* . 18 F8 26 12 S 27 53 E
Meadowood, *Wash.* . 25 C7 39 4N 77 0W
Měcholupy, *Pra.* ... 10 B3 50 3N 14 32 E
Měčice, *Pra.* ...... 10 A3 50 11N 14 31 E
Mecidiyekoy, *Ist.* .. 17 A3 41 4N 29 0 E
Meckinghoven, *Ruhr* . 6 A5 51 37N 7 19 E
Médan, *Paris* ..... 5 B1 48 57N 1 59 E
Medfield, *Bost.* ... 21 D2 42 11N 71 18W
Medford, *Bost.* 21 C3 42 25N 71 7W
Media, *Phil.* 24 B3 39 55N 75 23W
Mediodia, *Mdrd.* .. 8 F5 40 22N 3 39W
Medvastö, *Hels.* .. 3 C2 60 5N 24 38 E
Medvedkovo, *Mos.* . 11 D9 55 52N 37 37 E
Medvezhiy Ozyora, *Mos.* .... 11 D11 55 52N 37 59 E
Meerbeck, *Ruhr* ... 6 B1 51 28N 6 38 E
Meerbusch, *Ruhr* .. 6 C2 51 16N 6 40 E
Meguro →, *Tōkyō* . 13 C3 35 37N 139 45 E
Meguro-Ku, *Tōkyō* . 13 C3 35 37N 139 42 E
Mehpalpur, *Delhi* .. 16 B1 28 32N 77 7 E
Mehrābād Airport, *Tehr.* .... 17 C4 35 41N 51 18 E
Mehram Nagar, *Delhi* 16 B1 28 34N 77 8 E
Mehrow, *Berl.* .... 7 A4 52 34N 13 37 E
Meiderich, *Ruhr* .. 6 B2 51 27N 6 47 E
Meidling, *Wien* ... 10 G10 48 10N 16 20 E
Meiendorf, *Hbg.* .. 7 D8 53 37N 10 8 E
Méier, *Rio J.* .... 31 B2 22 52 S 43 15W
Meiji Shrine, *Tōkyō* 13 B3 35 41N 139 41 E
Meizino-Mori-Minō National Park, *Ōsaka* 12 A3 34 51N 135 28 E
Mejiro, *Tōkyō* .... 13 B3 35 43N 139 43 E
Melbourne, *Melb.* . 19 E6 37 48 S 144 58 E
Melbourne Airport, *Melb.* .... 19 E6 37 40 S 144 50 E
Melbourne Univ., *Melb.* 19 E6 37 47 S 144 57 E
Melito di Nápoli, *Nápl.* 9 H12 40 55N 14 13 E
Melkki, *Hels.* .... 3 C4 60 8N 24 53 E
Mellingstedt, *Hbg.* . 7 C8 53 40N 10 6 E
Mellunkylä, *Hels.* . 3 B5 60 14N 25 5 E
Mellunmäki, *Hels.* . 3 B5 60 14N 25 6 E
Melrose, *Bost.* ... 21 C3 42 27N 71 2W
Melrose, *N.Y.* 22 C5 40 49N 73 55W
Melrose Park, *Chic.* 26 B1 41 53N 87 50W
Melun-Sénart, *Paris* . 5 D5 48 3N 2 31 E
Melun-Villaroche, Aérodrome de, *Paris* 5 D6 48 37N 2 41 E
Melville, *N.Y.* ... 23 C8 40 47N 73 24W
Menai, *Syd.* ...... 19 C3 34 1 S 151 1 E
Menandon, *Paris* .. 5 A2 49 2N 2 3 E
Mendoza, *Lima* ... 30 G9 12 5 S 76 59W
Mengede, *Ruhr* ... 6 A6 51 34N 7 23 E
Mengjiazhai, *Shang.* 14 J11 31 19N 121 21 E
Menglinghausen, *Ruhr* 6 B6 51 28N 7 26 E
Menlo Park, *S.F.* . 27 D3 37 27N 122 11W
Menlo Park Terrace, *N.Y.* 22 D3 40 34N 74 18W
Mentang, *Jak.* ... 15 J9 6 11 S 106 49 E
Menucourt, *Paris* . 5 A1 49 1N 1 59 E
Meopham, *Lon.* .. 4 C7 51 22N 0 21 E
Mérantaise →, *Paris* . 5 C2 48 42N 2 8 E
Mercamadrid, *Mdrd.* 8 B3 40 21N 3 39W
Merced, L., *S.F.* . 27 B2 37 43N 122 29W
Merchantville, *Phil.* 24 B4 39 56N 75 3W
Mercier, Pont, *Mtrl.* 20 B4 43 24N 73 39W
Merdeka Palace, *Jak.* 15 J9 6 10 S 106 49 E
Meredale, *Jobg.* .. 18 F8 26 16 S 27 58 E
Mergellina, *Nápl.* . 9 J12 40 49N 14 13 E
Meriden, *N.Y.* ... 22 B2 40 56N 74 27W
Merion Station, *Phil.* 24 B3 39 59N 75 15W
Merlimau, *Sing.* .. 15 G7 1 17N 103 42 E
Merlimau, P., *Sing.* 15 G7 1 17N 103 42 E
Merlo, *B.A.* ..... 32 B2 34 39 S 58 43W
Merri Cr. →, *Melb.* 19 E6 37 47 S 144 59 E
Merrick, *N.Y.* ... 23 D7 40 39N 73 32W
Merrionette Park, *Chic.* 26 C2 41 41N 87 42W
Merritt, L., *S.F.* . 27 B3 37 48N 122 15W
Merrylands, *Syd.* . 19 B3 33 50 S 150 59 E
Merton, *Lon.* 4 C3 51 25N 0 11W
Mesgarābād, *Tehr.* . 17 D6 35 27N 51 30 E
Meshcherskiy, *Mos.* 11 E8 55 40N 37 23 E
Mesquita, *Rio J.* .. 31 A1 22 46 S 43 25W
Messe, *Wien* .... 10 G10 48 13N 16 24 E
Messy, *Paris* .... 5 B6 48 58N 2 42 E
Metanópoli, *Mil.* . 9 E6 45 24N 9 15 E
Methuen, *Bost.* .. 21 A2 42 42N 71 12W
Metropolitan Opera, *N.Y.* 22 C5 40 46N 74 59W
Mettman, *Ruhr* .. 6 C3 51 15N 6 58 E
Metuchen, *N.Y.* . 22 D2 40 32N 74 21W
Metzkausen, *Ruhr* 6 C3 51 16N 6 57 E
Meudon, *Paris* .. 5 C3 48 48N 2 14 E
Meulan, *Paris* .. 5 A1 49 0N 1 54 E
México, Aeropuerto Int. de, *Méx.* 29 B3 19 25N 99 4W
México, Ciudad de, *Méx.* 29 B2 19 25N 99 7W
Mezzate, *Mil.* .... 9 E6 45 26N 9 17 E
Mia Dong, *Sŏul* .. 12 G8 37 36N 127 0 E
Miano, *Nápl.* .... 9 H12 40 53N 14 15 E
Miasto, *Wsaw.* ... 10 E7 52 15N 21 0 E
Michalin, *Wsaw.* . 10 F8 52 9N 21 13 E
Michałowice, *Wsaw.* 10 E6 52 10N 20 52 E
Michle, *Pra.* .... 10 B2 50 3N 14 28 E
Mickleton, *Phil.* . 24 C3 39 47N 75 14W
Middle →, *Balt.* . 25 B4 39 18N 76 24W
Middle B., *N.Y.* . 23 D7 40 36N 73 36W
Middle Branch →, *Balt.* 25 B3 39 15N 76 37W
Middle Brewster I., *Bost.* 21 C4 42 20N 70 51W
Middle Cove, *Syd.* 19 A4 33 48 S 151 13 E
Middle Harbour, *Syd.* 19 A4 33 48 S 151 14 E
Middle Hd., *Syd.* . 19 A4 33 49 S 151 16 E
Middle I., *H.K.* .. 12 E6 22 16N 114 10 E
Middle Park, *Melb.* 19 F6 37 50 S 144 57 E
Middle River, *Balt.* 25 A4 39 20N 76 26W
Middle Village, *N.Y.* 23 C5 40 43N 73 52W
Middleborough, *Balt.* 25 B4 39 18N 76 25W
Middlesex, *N.Y.* . 22 D2 40 34N 74 27W
Middlesex Fells Reservation, *Bost.* . 21 C3 42 27N 71 6W
Middlesex Res., *N.Y.* 22 C3 40 37N 74 26W
Middleton, *Bost.* . 21 B3 42 35N 71 0W
Middleton Pond, *Bost.* 21 B3 42 35N 71 1W
Middleville, *N.Y.* . 23 B9 40 54N 73 19W
Midland Beach, *N.Y.* 22 D4 40 33N 74 5W
Midland Park, *N.Y.* . 22 B4 40 59N 74 9W

42 Midlothian

Midlothian, *Chic.* **26 D2** 41 37N 87 43W
Miedzeszyn, *Wsaw.* **10 E8** 52 10N 21 11 E
Międzylesie, *Wsaw.* **10 E8** 52 12N 21 10 E
Miessaari, *Hels.* **3 C3** 60 8N 24 47 E
Mikhaylovskoye, *Mos.* **11 F9** 55 35N 37 35 E
Mikhelysona, *Mos.* **11 E11** 55 42N 37 52 E
Milano, *Mil.* **9 E5** 45 28N 9 10 E
Milano Due, *Mil.* **9 E6** 45 29N 9 16 E
Milano San Felice, *Mil.* **9 E6** 45 28N 9 18 E
Milanolago, *Mil.* **9 E6** 45 27N 9 17 E
Milbertshofen, *Mün.* **7 F10** 48 10N 11 34 E
Milburn, *N.Y.* **22 C3** 40 43N 74 19W
Milford, *Balt.* **25 A2** 39 21N 76 43W
Mill Cr. →, *S.F.* **27 A1** 37 53N 122 31W
Mill Hill, *Lon.* **4 B3** 51 37N 0 14W
Mill Neck, *N.Y.* **23 B7** 40 53N 73 33W
Mill Park, *Melb.* **19 E7** 37 40 S 145 3 E
Mill Valley, *S.F.* **27 A1** 37 54N 122 33W
Millbrae, *S.F.* **27 C2** 37 35N 122 22W
Mille-Iles, R. des →, *Mtrl.* **20 A3** 43 39N 73 46W
Miller I., *Balt.* **25 B4** 39 15N 76 21W
Miller Meadow, *Chic.* **26 B2** 41 51N 87 49W
Milliken, *Trto.* **20 D9** 43 49N 79 17W
Millis, *Bost.* **21 D1** 42 10N 71 21W
Mills College, *S.F.* **27 B3** 37 46N 122 10W
Milltown, *Phil.* **24 B1** 39 57N 75 32W
Millwall, *Lon.* **4 C4** 51 29N 0 0 E
Millwood, *Wash.* **25 D8** 38 52N 76 52W
Milon-la-Chapelle, *Paris* **5 C2** 48 43N 2 3 E
Milpa Alta, *Méx.* **29 C3** 19 11N 99 0W
Milperra, *Syd.* **19 B2** 33 56 S 150 59 E
Milspe, *Ruhr* **6 C5** 51 18N 7 19 E
Milton, *Bost.* **21 D3** 42 14N 71 2W
Milton Village, *Bost.* **21 D3** 42 15N 71 4W
Mimico, *Trto.* **20 E8** 43 36N 79 29W
Mimico Cr. →, *Trto.* **20 E7** 43 37N 79 33W
Minami, *Ōsaka* **12 B4** 34 40N 135 30 E
Minami-Ku, *Tōkyō* **13 D2** 35 24N 139 37 E
Minami-tsunashima, *Tōkyō* **13 C2** 35 32N 139 37 E
Minato, *Ōsaka* **12 C3** 34 39N 135 25 E
Minato-Ku, *Tōkyō* **13 C3** 35 39N 139 44 E
Mine, *Tōkyō* **13 B3** 35 49N 139 46 E
Minebank Run →, *Balt.* **25 A3** 39 24N 76 33W
Mineola, *N.Y.* **23 C7** 40 44N 73 38W
Ministro Rivadavia, *B.A.* **32 D4** 34 50 S 58 22W
Minō, *Ōsaka* **12 B3** 34 49N 135 28 E
Minshât el Bekkarî, *El Qâ.* **18 C4** 30 0N 31 8 E
Minto, *Syd.* **19 C2** 34 1 S 150 51 E
Minute Man Nat. Hist. Park, *Bost.* **21 C2** 42 25N 71 16W
Mirafiori, *Tori.* **9 B2** 45 1N 7 36 E
Miraflores, *Lima* **30 G8** 12 7 S 77 2W
Miramar, *La Hab.* **30 B2** 23 7N 82 25W
Miramar, *S.F.* **27 D2** 37 29N 122 27W
Miranda, *Syd.* **19 C3** 34 2 S 151 6 E
Mirzapur, *Calc.* **16 D6** 22 49N 88 24 E
Misato, *Tōkyō* **13 B4** 35 49N 139 51 E
Misericordia, Sa. da, *Rio J.* **31 B2** 22 51 S 43 17W
Mishawum L., *Bost.* **21 B3** 42 30N 71 8W
Mission, *S.F.* **27 B2** 37 44N 122 25W
Mississauga, *Trto.* **20 E7** 43 35N 79 34W
Mitaka, *Tōkyō* **13 B2** 35 41N 139 34 E
Mitcham, *Lon.* **4 C3** 51 23N 0 10W
Mitcham, *Melb.* **19 E8** 37 48 S 145 12 E
Mitcham Common, *Lon.* **4 C4** 51 23N 0 8W
Mitino, *Mos.* **11 D8** 55 51N 37 20 E
Mitry, *Paris* **5 B5** 48 59N 2 36 E
Mitry-Mory, *Paris* **5 B5** 48 59N 2 38 E
Mitry-Mory, Aérodrome de, *Paris* **5 B5** 48 59N 2 37 E
Mitte, *Berl.* **7 A3** 52 32N 13 24 E
Mittel Isarkanal, *Mün.* **7 F11** 48 12N 11 40 E
Mittenheim, *Mün.* **7 F10** 48 15N 11 33 E
Mixcoac, Presa de, *Méx.* **29 B2** 19 21N 99 14W
Mixquic, *Méx.* **29 C4** 19 13N 98 58W
Miyakojima, *Ōsaka* **12 B4** 34 42N 135 31 E
Miyalo, *Tōkyō* **13 B2** 35 49N 139 35 E
Mizonokuchi, *Tōkyō* **13 C2** 35 35N 139 34 E
Mizue, *Tōkyō* **13 B4** 35 41N 139 54 E
Mizuko, *Tōkyō* **13 A2** 35 50N 139 32 E
Mizumoto, *Tōkyō* **13 B4** 35 46N 139 52 E
Młocinski Park, *Wsaw.* **10 E6** 52 19N 20 57 E
Młociny, *Wsaw.* **10 E6** 52 18N 20 55 E
Mnevniki, *Mos.* **11 E8** 55 45N 37 28 E
Moba, *Lagos* **18 B2** 6 26N 7 28 E
Moczydło, *Wsaw.* **10 F7** 52 8N 21 2 E
Modderfontein, *Jobg.* **18 E10** 26 5 S 28 10 E
Modderfontein →, *Jobg.* **18 E9** 26 5 S 28 10 E
Modřany, *Pra.* **10 B2** 50 0N 14 24 E
Moers, *Ruhr* **6 B1** 51 26N 6 37 E
Moffat Park, *Jobg.* **18 F9** 26 15 S 28 4 E
Mofolo, *Jobg.* **18 F8** 26 13 S 27 53 E
Mog, *Sŏul* **12 G7** 37 32N 126 52 E
Mogyorod, *Bud.* **10 J14** 47 35N 19 14 E
Mohili, *Bomb.* **16 G8** 19 5N 72 52 E
Moinho Velho →, *S. Pau.* **31 E6** 23 35 S 46 35W
Moissy-Cramayel, *Paris* **5 D5** 48 37N 2 35 E
Moita, *Lisb.* **8 G9** 38 39N 8 59W
Mokotów, *Wsaw.* **10 E7** 52 12N 21 0 E
Molapo, *Jobg.* **18 F8** 26 15 S 27 51 E
Mole →, *Lon.* **4 D2** 51 14N 0 20W
Moletsane, *Jobg.* **18 F8** 26 14 S 27 50 E
Molino de Rosas, *Méx.* **29 B2** 19 21N 99 14W
Mølleå →, *Købn.* **2 D10** 55 48N 12 35 E
Möllen, *Ruhr* **6 A2** 51 35N 6 41 E
Mollins de Rey, *Barc.* **8 D5** 41 24N 2 1 E
Molokovo, *Mos.* **11 F11** 55 35N 37 53 E
Mombaça, *S. Pau.* **31 E7** 23 37 S 46 25W
Mombello, *Mil.* **9 D5** 45 36N 9 7 E
Momote, *Tōkyō* **13 B2** 35 46N 139 37 E
Monash Univ., *Melb.* **19 F7** 37 54 S 145 8 E
Monbulk Cr. →, *Melb.* **19 F8** 37 55 S 145 12 E
Moncalieri, *Tori.* **9 B3** 45 0N 7 41 E
Moncolombone, *Tori.* **9 A1** 45 12N 7 28 E
Mondeor, *Jobg.* **18 F9** 26 16 S 28 0 E
Moneda, Palacio de la, *Stgo* **30 J11** 33 26 S 70 39W
Mong Kok, *H.K.* **12 E6** 22 19N 114 10 E
Mongat, *Barc.* **8 D6** 41 27N 2 16 E
Mongreno, *Tori.* **9 B3** 45 3N 7 45 E
Moninos →, *S. Pau.* **31 F6** 23 40 S 46 33W
Monrovia, *L.A.* **28 B4** 34 9N 118 1W
Monsanto, *Lisb.* **8 F7** 38 44N 9 12W
Monsanto, Parque Florestal de, *Lisb.* **8 F7** 38 43N 9 11W
Mont Royal, *Mtrl.* **20 A4** 43 30N 73 38W
Mont-Royal, Parc, *Mtrl.* **20 A4** 43 30N 73 36W
Montalban, *Car.* **30 E5** 10 28N 66 56W
Montana de Montjuich, *Barc.* **8 D5** 41 21N 2 9 E
Montara, *S.F.* **27 C2** 37 32N 122 30W
Montara, Pt., *S.F.* **27 C1** 37 32N 122 31W
Montara Mt., *S.F.* **27 C2** 37 32N 122 27W
Montchanin, *Phil.* **24 C1** 39 47N 75 35W
Montclair, *N.Y.* **22 C3** 40 49N 74 12W
Monte Chingolo, *B.A.* **32 C4** 34 43 S 58 22W
Monte Grande, *B.A.* **32 C4** 34 48 S 58 27W
Monte Sacro, *Rome* **9 F10** 41 56N 12 32 E
Montebello, *L.A.* **28 B4** 34 1N 118 8W
Montelera, *Tori.* **9 B1** 45 9N 7 26 E
Montemor, *Lisb.* **8 F7** 38 49N 9 12W
Monterey Park, *L.A.* **28 B4** 34 3N 118 7W
Monterrey, *La Hab.* **30 B3** 23 5N 82 18W
Montespaccato, *Rome* **9 F9** 41 54N 12 23 E
Montesson, *Paris* **5 B2** 48 54N 2 8 E
Monteverde Nuovo, *Rome* **9 F9** 41 52N 12 26 E
Montfermeil, *Paris* **5 B5** 48 54N 2 33 E
Montgeron, *Paris* **5 C4** 48 42N 2 27 E
Montigny-le-Bretonneux, *Paris* **5 C2** 48 46N 2 1 E
Montigny-les-Cormeilles, *Paris* **5 B3** 48 59N 2 11 E
Montijo, *Lisb.* **8 F9** 38 42N 8 58W
Montjay-la-Tour, *Paris* **5 B6** 48 54N 2 40 E
Montlhéry, *Paris* **5 D3** 48 38N 2 16 E
Montlignon, *Paris* **5 A3** 49 0N 2 16 E
Montmagny, *Paris* **5 B4** 48 58N 2 21 E
Montmorency, *Paris* **5 B3** 48 59N 2 19 E
Montmorency, Forêt de, *Paris* **5 A3** 49 2N 2 16 E
Montparnasse, Gare, *Paris* **5 B3** 48 50N 2 19 E
Montpelier, *Wash.* **25 C8** 39 3N 76 50W
Montréal, *Mtrl.* **20 A4** 43 30N 73 33W
Montréal, Î. de, *Mtrl.* **20 A4** 43 30N 73 40W
Montréal, Univ. de, *Mtrl.* **20 B4** 43 29N 73 37W
Montréal-Est, *Mtrl.* **20 A4** 43 37N 73 31W
Montréal Nord, *Mtrl.* **20 A4** 43 36N 73 36W
Montreuil, *Paris* **5 B4** 48 51N 2 27 E
Montrose, *L.A.* **28 A3** 34 12N 118 12W
Montrose, *Melb.* **19 E8** 37 49 S 145 19 E
Montrose, *Wash.* **25 C7** 39 2N 77 7W
Montrouge, *Paris* **5 C3** 48 48N 2 18 E
Montvale, *N.Y.* **22 A4** 41 2N 74 1W
Montville, *N.Y.* **22 B2** 40 55N 74 23W
Monza, *Mil.* **9 D6** 45 35N 9 16 E
Monzoro, *Mil.* **9 E5** 45 27N 9 2 E
Moóca, *S. Pau.* **31 E6** 23 33 S 46 35W
Moóca →, *S. Pau.* **31 E6** 23 35 S 46 35W
Moonachie, *N.Y.* **22 C4** 40 50N 74 2W
Moonee Ponds, *Melb.* **19 E6** 37 45 S 144 53 E
Moonee Valley Racecourse, *Melb.* **19 E6** 37 45 S 144 55 E
Moorbek, *Hbg.* **7 C7** 53 41N 9 58 E
Moorburg, *Hbg.* **7 E7** 53 29N 9 55 E
Moorebank, *Syd.* **19 B2** 33 56 S 150 56 E
Moorestown, *Phil.* **24 B5** 39 58N 74 56W
Moorfleet, *Hbg.* **7 D8** 53 30N 10 4 E
Mooroolbark, *Melb.* **19 E8** 37 46 S 145 19 E
Moorwerder, *Hbg.* **7 E8** 53 28N 10 3 E
Moosach, *Mün.* **7 F10** 48 10N 11 30 E
Mora, *Bomb.* **16 H8** 18 54N 72 55 E
Moraga, *S.F.* **27 B4** 37 49N 122 7W
Morainvilliers, *Paris* **5 B1** 48 55N 1 56 E
Morales →, *B.A.* **32 C2** 34 47 S 58 35W
Morangis, *Paris* **5 C4** 48 42N 2 20 E
Moratalaz, *Mdrd.* **8 B3** 40 24N 3 39W
Morbras →, *Paris* **5 C5** 48 46N 2 30 E
Mörby, *Stock.* **3 D11** 59 23N 18 3 E
Morce →, *Paris* **5 B4** 48 57N 2 25 E
Morden, *Lon.* **4 C3** 51 24N 0 13W
Morehill, *Jobg.* **18 F11** 26 10 S 28 20 E
Moreno, *B.A.* **32 B2** 34 38 S 58 45W
Moreno, *Rome* **9 G10** 41 48N 12 37 E
Morgan Park, *Chic.* **26 C3** 41 41N 87 38W
Moriguchi, *Ōsaka* **12 B4** 34 43N 135 34 E
Morivione, *Mil.* **9 E6** 45 26N 9 12 E
Morningside, *Jobg.* **18 E9** 26 4 S 28 3 E
Morningside, *Wash.* **25 E8** 38 49N 76 53W
Morningside Park, *Trto.* **20 D9** 43 46N 79 12W
Moroka, *Jobg.* **18 F8** 26 15 S 27 52 E
Moron, *B.A.* **32 B3** 34 39 S 58 37W
Morris Plains, *N.Y.* **22 C2** 40 49N 74 29W
Morristown, *N.Y.* **22 C2** 40 47N 74 28W
Morro, Castillo del, *La Hab.* **30 B2** 23 8N 82 21W
Morro Pelado, *S. Pau.* **31 E7** 23 38 S 46 24W
Morro Solar, *Lima* **30 H8** 12 11 S 77 1W
Morsang-sur-Orge, *Paris* **5 D4** 48 39N 2 21 E
Mörsenbroich, *Ruhr* **6 C2** 51 15N 6 48 E
Morses Pond, *Bost.* **21 D2** 42 17N 71 19W
Morte →, *Paris* **5 C3** 48 40N 2 16 E
Mortlake, *Lon.* **4 C3** 51 27N 0 15W
Mortlake, *Syd.* **19 B3** 33 50 S 151 6 E
Morton, *Phil.* **24 B2** 39 54N 75 20W
Morton Grove, *Chic.* **26 A2** 42 2N 87 46W
Mory, *Paris* **5 B5** 48 58N 2 37 E
Moscavide, *Lisb.* **8 F8** 38 47N 9 6W
Moscow = Moskva, *Mos.* **11 E9** 55 45N 37 37 E
Mosede, *Købn.* **2 E8** 55 34N 12 17 E
Mosede Strand, *Købn.* **2 E8** 55 34N 12 17 E
Mosjøen, *Oslo* **2 C6** 50 49N 11 0 E
Moskhaton, *Ath.* **8 J11** 37 55N 23 40 E
Moskva, *Mos.* **11 E9** 55 45N 37 37 E
Moskvoretskiy, *Mos.* **11 E9** 55 42N 37 37 E
Mosman, *Syd.* **19 A4** 33 49 S 151 15 E
Moss Beach, *S.F.* **27 C2** 37 31N 122 30W
Móstoles, *Mdrd.* **8 C1** 40 18N 3 51W
Moto →, *Tōkyō* **13 A3** 35 53N 139 45 E
Motol, *Pra.* **10 B1** 50 3N 14 19 E
Motspur Park, *Lon.* **4 C3** 51 23N 0 14W
Mottingham, *Lon.* **4 C5** 51 26N 0 1 E
Mount Airy, *Phil.* **24 A3** 40 3N 75 10W
Mount Dennis, *Trto.* **20 D8** 43 40N 79 28W
Mount Ephraim, *Phil.* **24 B4** 39 52N 75 5W
Mount Greenwood, *Chic.* **26 C2** 41 42N 87 42W
Mount Hood Memorial Park, *Bost.* **21 C3** 42 26N 71 1W
Mount Pleasant, *Lon.* **4 B2** 51 30N 0 22W
Mount Pleasant Park, *Balt.* **25 A3** 39 22N 76 34W
Mount Prospect, *Chic.* **26 A1** 42 3N 87 54W
Mount Royal, *Phil.* **24 C3** 39 48N 75 12W
Mount Tamalpais State Park, *S.F.* **27 A1** 37 53N 122 34W
Mount Vernon, *N.Y.* **23 B6** 40 54N 73 49W
Mount Waverley, *Melb.* **19 F7** 37 52 S 145 7 E
Mount Wilson Observatory, *L.A.* **28 A4** 34 13N 118 4W
Mountain Lakes, *N.Y.* **22 B2** 40 54N 74 27W
Mountain Spring Ls., *N.Y.* **22 A2** 41 2N 74 21W
Mountain View, *N.Y.* **22 B3** 40 55N 74 15W
Mountainside, *N.Y.* **22 C2** 40 40N 74 21W
Mountnessing, *Lon.* **4 B7** 51 39N 0 21 E
Moûtiers, *Paris* **5 D1** 48 36N 1 58 E
Mozu, *Ōsaka* **12 C3** 34 33N 135 29 E
Müggelberge, *Berl.* **7 B4** 52 25N 13 37 E
Müggelheim, *Berl.* **7 B5** 52 24N 13 40 E
Muggiò, *Mil.* **9 D6** 45 35N 9 13 E
Mugnano di Nápoli, *Nápl.* **9 H12** 40 54N 14 12 E
Mühleiten, *Wien* **10 G11** 48 10N 16 33 E
Mühlenau →, *Hbg.* **7 C7** 53 41N 9 56 E
Mühlenfliess →, *Berl.* **7 A5** 52 32N 13 42 E
Muir Beach, *S.F.* **27 A1** 37 51N 122 34W
Muirkirk, *Wash.* **25 C8** 39 3N 76 53W
Mujahidpur, *Delhi* **16 B2** 28 33N 77 14 E
Mukandpur, *Delhi* **16 A2** 28 44N 77 10 E
Muko →, *Ōsaka* **12 B3** 34 48N 135 22 E
Mukojima, *Tōkyō* **13 B3** 35 43N 139 49 E
Mulbarton, *Jobg.* **18 F9** 26 17 S 28 3 E
Mulford Gardens, *S.F.* **27 B3** 37 42N 122 10W
Mulgrave, *Melb.* **19 F8** 37 55 S 145 12 E
Mülheim, *Ruhr* **6 B3** 51 25N 6 53 E
Mullica Hill, *Phil.* **24 C3** 39 44N 75 13W
Mullum Mullum Cr. →, *Melb.* **19 E8** 37 44 S 145 10 E
Münchehofe, *Berl.* **7 B5** 52 29N 13 40 E
München, *Mün.* **7 G10** 48 8N 11 34 E
Munchen-Riem, Flughafen, *Mün.* **7 G11** 48 7N 11 42 E
Munich = München, *Mün.* **7 G10** 48 8N 11 34 E
Munirka, *Delhi* **16 B2** 28 33N 77 10 E
Muniz, *B.A.* **32 B2** 34 33 S 58 41W
Munkkiniemi, *Hels.* **3 B4** 60 11N 24 52 E
Munro, *B.A.* **32 B3** 34 31 S 58 31W
Munsey Park, *N.Y.* **23 C6** 40 47N 73 40W
Münsterkirche, *Ruhr* **6 B4** 51 27N 7 0 E
Muranów, *Wsaw.* **10 E6** 52 14N 20 58 E
Murayama-chosuichi, *Tōkyō* **13 B1** 35 45N 139 26 E
Murrumbeena, *Melb.* **19 F7** 37 53 S 145 4 E
Musashino, *Tōkyō* **13 B2** 35 42N 139 33 E
Mushin, *Lagos* **18 A2** 6 31N 7 21 E
Musinè, Mte., *Tori.* **9 B1** 45 7N 7 27 E
Musocco, *Mil.* **9 E5** 45 29N 9 8 E
Musta Hevonen, *Hels.* **3 B6** 60 11N 25 14 E
Mustafabad, *Delhi* **16 A2** 28 43N 77 13 E
Mustansiriya, *Bagd.* **17 E8** 33 22N 44 24 E
Musturud, *El Qâ.* **18 C5** 30 8N 31 17 E
Muswell Hill, *Lon.* **4 B4** 51 35N 0 8W
Mutanabi, *Bagd.* **17 F8** 33 19N 44 21 E
Muthana, *Bagd.* **17 F8** 33 19N 44 27 E
Mutinga, *S. Pau.* **31 D5** 23 29 S 46 46W
Muttontown, *N.Y.* **23 C7** 40 49N 73 32W
Muzon, *Manila* **15 D4** 14 32N 121 8 E
Myaglovo, *St-Pet.* **11 B5** 59 53N 30 39 E
Myakinino, *Mos.* **11 E8** 55 48N 37 22 E
Mykerinos, *El Qâ.* **18 D4** 29 28N 31 8 E
Myllykylä, *Hels.* **3 A4** 60 21N 24 57 E
Myllypuro, *Hels.* **3 B5** 60 13N 25 3 E
Myras, *Hels.* **3 B5** 60 19N 25 6 E
Myrvoll, *Oslo* **2 C4** 59 47N 10 48 E
Mystic Lakes, *Bost.* **21 C3** 42 26N 71 8W
Mytishchi, *Mos.* **11 D10** 55 53N 37 44 E

N

Nababpur, *Calc.* **16 D5** 22 42N 88 12 E
Nações, Parque das, *S. Pau.* **31 E6** 23 38 S 46 30W
Nachstebreck, *Ruhr* **6 C5** 51 17N 7 14 E
Nacka, *Stock.* **3 E12** 59 19N 18 10 E
Nada, *Ōsaka* **12 B2** 34 42N 135 13 E
Nærsnes, *Oslo* **2 C2** 59 45N 10 27 E
Nærum, *Købn.* **2 D10** 55 48N 12 33 E
Nagareyama, *Tōkyō* **13 A4** 35 51N 139 54 E
Nagasaki, *Tōkyō* **13 B3** 35 43N 139 40 E
Nagasuga, *Tōkyō* **13 D4** 35 21N 139 57 E
Nagata, *Ōsaka* **12 C1** 34 39N 135 8 E
Nagatsuta, *Tōkyō* **13 C2** 35 32N 139 31 E
Nagytarcsa, *Bud.* **10 J14** 47 31N 19 17 E
Nagytétény, *Bud.* **10 K12** 47 23N 18 59 E
Nahant, *Bost.* **21 C4** 42 25N 70 54W
Nahant B., *Bost.* **21 C4** 42 26N 70 54W
Nahant Harbor, *Bost.* **21 C4** 42 25N 70 55W
Nahdein, W. el →, *El Qâ.* **18 C5** 30 3N 31 19 E
Nahia, *El Qâ.* **18 C4** 30 2N 31 7 E
Naihati, *Calc.* **16 C6** 22 53N 88 25 E
Najafgarh Drain →, *Delhi* **16 B1** 28 39N 77 4 E
Najio, *Ōsaka* **12 B2** 34 49N 135 18 E
Naka →, *Tōkyō* **13 B4** 35 49N 139 52 E
Naka-Ku, *Tōkyō* **13 D2** 35 25N 139 38 E
Nakada, *Tōkyō* **13 D2** 35 24N 139 30 E
Nakajima, *Tōkyō* **13 D4** 35 25N 139 54 E
Nakano, *Tōkyō* **13 D4** 35 25N 139 56 E
Nakano-Ku, *Tōkyō* **13 B2** 35 42N 139 39 E
Nakasato, *Tōkyō* **13 D4** 35 22N 139 55 E
Nakayama, *Tōkyō* **13 B4** 35 43N 139 57 E
Nalikul, *Calc.* **16 D5** 22 49N 88 10 E
Nalpur, *Calc.* **16 E5** 22 31N 88 10 E
Namazie Estate, *Sing.* **15 F7** 1 25N 103 42 E
Namgajha, *Sŏul* **12 G7** 37 33N 126 55 E
Namsan Park, *Sŏul* **12 G7** 37 32N 126 59 E
Namyeong, *Sŏul* **12 G7** 37 32N 126 57 E
Nan Wan, *H.K.* **12 D5** 22 20N 114 5 E
Nanbiancun, *Gzh.* **14 G7** 23 4N 113 10 E
Nancefield, *Jobg.* **18 F8** 26 17 S 27 54 E
Nanchang He →, *Beij.* **14 B2** 39 58N 116 14 E
Nandaha, *Calc.* **16 D5** 22 49N 88 18 E
Nandang, *Gzh.* **14 G8** 23 6N 113 12 E
Nandian, *Tianj.* **14 D6** 39 10N 117 16 E
Nangal Dewat, *Delhi* **16 B1** 28 33N 77 5 E
Nangi, *Calc.* **16 E5** 22 30N 88 13 E
Nangka →, *Manila* **15 D4** 14 38N 121 8 E
Nangloi, *Delhi* **16 A1** 28 41N 77 4 E
Nangloi Jat, *Delhi* **16 A1** 28 41N 77 3 E
Nanhai, *Gzh.* **14 G7** 23 2N 113 6 E
Nanhan He →, *Beij.* **14 B2** 39 57N 116 11 E
Naniwa, *Ōsaka* **12 C3** 34 39N 135 29 E
Nankai, *Tianj.* **14 E5** 39 7N 117 10 E
Nanmenwai, *Tianj.* **14 E6** 39 8N 117 10 E
Nanole, *Bomb.* **16 G8** 19 0N 72 55 E
Nanshi, *Shang.* **14 J11** 31 12N 121 29 E
Nanterre, *Paris* **5 B3** 48 53N 2 12 E
Nantouillet, *Paris* **5 A6** 49 0N 2 42 E
Nantusket Beach, *Bost.* **21 D4** 42 16N 70 52W
Nanxiang, *Shang.* **14 J10** 31 17N 121 18 E
Naoabad, *Calc.* **16 F6** 22 28N 88 26 E
Napara, *Calc.* **16 E6** 22 38N 88 23 E
Napier Mole, *Kar.* **17 H10** 24 49N 66 58 E
Napindan, *Manila* **15 D4** 14 32N 121 5 E
Naples = Nápoli, *Nápl.* **9 J12** 40 50N 14 14 E
Nápoli, *Nápl.* **9 J12** 40 50N 14 14 E
Nápoli, G. di, *Nápl.* **9 J12** 40 46N 14 15 E
Naraina, *Delhi* **16 B1** 28 36N 77 8 E
Narawa, *Tōkyō* **13 D4** 35 25N 139 58 E
Narayanpara, *Calc.* **16 C5** 22 53N 88 18 E
Narberth, *Phil.* **24 A3** 40 0N 75 16W
Narimasu, *Tōkyō* **13 B2** 35 46N 139 35 E
Nārmak, *Tehr.* **17 C5** 35 42N 51 28 E
Närsta, *Stock.* **3 E9** 59 17N 17 43 E
Naruo, *Ōsaka* **12 B3** 34 43N 135 22 E
Näsby, *Stock.* **3 D11** 59 25N 18 5 E
Näsbypark, *Stock.* **3 D11** 59 25N 18 5 E
Näsfjärden, *Stock.* **3 D9** 59 25N 17 41 E
Nassau Shore, *N.Y.* **23 D8** 40 39N 73 26W
Natick, *Bost.* **21 D2** 42 16N 71 19W
Nation, Place de la, *Paris* **5 B4** 48 51N 2 23 E
National Arboretum, *Wash.* **25 D8** 39 54N 76 59W
Nativitas, *Méx.* **29 C3** 19 15N 99 5W
Natolin, *Wsaw.* **10 F7** 52 8N 21 4 E
Naucalpan de Juárez, *Méx.* **29 B2** 19 28N 99 14W
Naupada, *Bomb.* **16 G8** 19 3N 72 50 E
Navíglio di Pavia, *Mil.* **9 E5** 45 24N 9 9 E
Navíglio Grande, *Mil.* **9 E5** 45 25N 9 5 E
Navotas, *Manila* **15 D3** 14 39N 120 56 E
Nazal Hikmat Beg, *Bagd.* **17 E8** 33 23N 44 25 E
Nazimabad, *Kar.* **17 G11** 24 54N 67 1 E
Nazukari, *Tōkyō* **13 A4** 35 50N 139 57 E
Néa Alexandhria, *Ath.* **8 J11** 37 52N 23 46 E
Néa Faliron, *Ath.* **8 J10** 37 55N 23 39 E
Néa Ionía, *Ath.* **8 H11** 38 3N 23 45 E
Néa Liósia, *Ath.* **8 H11** 38 3N 23 43 E
Néa Smirni, *Ath.* **8 J11** 37 54N 23 43 E
Neapolis, *Ath.* **8 J11** 37 58N 23 45 E
Neasden, *Lon.* **4 B3** 51 35N 0 16W
Neauphle-le-Château, *Paris* **5 C1** 48 48N 1 53 E
Nebučice, *Pra.* **10 B1** 50 6N 14 19 E
Nedlitz, *Berl.* **7 B1** 52 25N 13 3 E
Nee Soon, *Sing.* **15 F7** 1 24N 103 49 E
Needham, *Bost.* **21 D2** 42 16N 71 13W
Needham Heights, *Bost.* **21 D2** 42 17N 71 14W
Needle Hill, *H.K.* **12 D5** 22 23N 114 9 E
Negishi B., *Tōkyō* **13 D2** 35 23N 139 38 E
Nehiti, *Calc.* **16 D5** 22 42N 88 16 E
Nekrasovka, *Mos.* **11 E11** 55 41N 37 55 E
Nematābād, *Tehr.* **17 D5** 35 38N 51 21 E
Nemchinovka, *Mos.* **11 E7** 55 42N 37 19 E
Népliget, *Bud.* **10 K13** 47 29N 19 7 E
Neponset →, *Bost.* **21 D3** 42 12N 71 9W
Nerima, *Tōkyō* **13 B3** 35 44N 139 40 E
Nerul, *Bomb.* **16 G9** 19 2N 73 0 E
Nerviano, *Mil.* **9 D4** 45 32N 8 58 E
Nesodden, *Oslo* **2 C4** 59 48N 10 41 E
Nesoddtangen, *Oslo* **2 B4** 59 52N 10 41 E
Nesøya, *Oslo* **2 B3** 59 52N 10 31 E
Nestipayac →, *Méx.* **29 A4** 19 33N 89 57W
Netzahualcóyotl, *Méx.* **29 B3** 19 24N 99 2W
Neu Aubing, *Mün.* **7 G9** 48 8N 11 25 E
Neu Buch, *Berl.* **7 A4** 52 37N 13 31 E
Neu Buchhorst, *Berl.* **7 B5** 52 24N 13 44 E
Neu Fahrland, *Berl.* **7 B1** 52 26N 13 3 E
Neu Lindenberg, *Berl.* **7 A4** 52 36N 13 33 E
Neu Wulmstorf, *Hbg.* **7 E6** 53 27N 9 48 E
Neu Zittau, *Berl.* **7 B5** 52 23N 13 44 E
Neubiberg, *Mün.* **7 G11** 48 4N 11 40 E
Neudorf, *Hbg.* **7 E8** 53 27N 10 4 E
Neudorf, *Ruhr* **6 B2** 51 25N 6 47 E
Neuegenbüttel, *Hbg.* **7 D7** 53 38N 9 54 E
Neuenfelde, *Hbg.* **7 D6** 53 31N 9 48 E
Neuenhagen, *Berl.* **7 A4** 52 32N 13 38 E
Neuenkamp, *Ruhr* **6 B2** 51 26N 6 43 E
Neuessling, *Wien* **10 G11** 48 15N 16 32 E
Neugraben-Fischbek, *Hbg.* **7 E6** 53 28N 9 49 E
Neuhausen, *Mün.* **7 G10** 48 9N 11 32 E
Neuherberg, *Mün.* **7 F10** 48 13N 11 35 E
Neuhönow, *Berl.* **7 A5** 52 34N 13 44 E
Neuilly-Plaisance, *Paris* **5 B5** 48 51N 2 30 E
Neuilly-sur-Marne, *Paris* **5 B5** 48 51N 2 31 E
Neuilly-sur-Seine, *Paris* **5 B3** 48 53N 2 15 E
Neukagran, *Wien* **10 G10** 48 14N 16 27 E
Neukettenhof, *Wien* **10 H10** 48 7N 16 28 E
Neukölln, *Berl.* **7 B3** 52 28N 13 25 E
Neuland, *Hbg.* **7 E8** 53 27N 10 0 E
Neuperlach, *Mün.* **7 G10** 48 6N 11 37 E
Neuried, *Mün.* **7 G9** 48 5N 11 27 E
Neuss, *Ruhr* **6 C2** 51 12N 6 42 E
Neustift am Walde, *Wien* **10 G9** 48 14N 16 17 E
Neusüssenbrunn, *Wien* **10 G10** 48 16N 16 29 E
Neuville-sur-Oise, *Paris* **5 A2** 49 0N 2 3 E
Neuwaldegg, *Wien* **10 G9** 48 14N 16 17 E
Neuwiedenthal, *Hbg.* **7 E7** 53 28N 9 52 E
Neva →, *St-Pet.* **11 B4** 59 56N 30 20 E
Neves, *Rio J.* **31 B3** 22 51 S 43 5W
Neviges, *Ruhr* **6 C4** 51 18N 7 6 E
New Addington, *Lon.* **4 C4** 51 20N 0 0 E
New Ash Green, *Lon.* **4 C6** 51 22N 0 18 E
New Baghdād, *Bagd.* **17 F8** 33 18N 44 28 E
New Barnet, *Lon.* **4 B3** 51 38N 0 10W
New Brighton, *N.Y.* **22 D4** 40 38N 74 5W
New Brunswick, *N.Y.* **22 D2** 40 30N 74 29W
New Canada, *Jobg.* **18 F8** 26 12 S 27 56 E
New Canada Dam, *Jobg.* **18 F8** 26 12 S 27 56 E
New Canal →, *Calc.* **16 E6** 22 33N 88 25 E
New Carrollton, *Wash.* **25 D8** 38 58N 76 52W
New Cassell, *N.Y.* **23 C7** 40 45N 73 32W
New Cross, *Lon.* **4 C4** 51 28N 0 1W
New Delhi, *Delhi* **16 B2** 28 36N 77 11 E
New Dorp, *N.Y.* **22 D4** 40 34N 74 7W
New Dorp Beach, *N.Y.* **22 D4** 40 33N 74 6W
New Hyde Park, *N.Y.* **23 C7** 40 43N 73 39W
New Kleinfontein, *Jobg.* **18 F11** 26 11 S 20 20 E
New Malden, *Lon.* **4 C3** 51 24N 0 15W
New Milford, *N.Y.* **22 B4** 40 56N 74 0W
New Modder, *Jobg.* **18 F11** 26 10 S 28 21 E
New Providence, *N.Y.* **22 C2** 40 42N 74 23W
New Redruth, *Jobg.* **18 F9** 26 15 S 28 7 E
New Rochelle, *N.Y.* **23 B6** 40 55N 73 45W
New South Wales, Univ. of, *Syd.* **19 B4** 33 55 S 151 14 E
New Southgate, *Lon.* **4 B4** 51 37N 0 7W
New Springville, *N.Y.* **22 D4** 40 35N 74 9W
New Territories, *H.K.* **12 D5** 22 23N 114 10 E
New Toronto, *Trto.* **20 E7** 43 35N 79 30W
New Utrecht, *N.Y.* **22 D5** 40 36N 73 59W
New Vernon, *N.Y.* **22 C2** 40 44N 74 30W
New York Aquarium, *N.Y.* **22 D5** 40 33N 73 59W
New York Botanical Gdns., *N.Y.* **23 B5** 40 51N 73 51W
New York Univ., *N.Y.* **22 C5** 40 43N 74 59W
Newabgarj, *Calc.* **16 D6** 22 47N 88 23 E
Newark, *N.Y.* **22 C3** 40 43N 74 10W
Newark, *S.F.* **27 C4** 37 32N 122 2W
Newark B., *N.Y.* **22 C4** 40 40N 74 8W
Newark Int. Airport, *N.Y.* **22 C3** 40 41N 74 10W
Newbury Park, *Lon.* **4 B5** 51 34N 0 5 E
Newclare, *Jobg.* **18 F8** 26 11 S 27 58 E
Newfoundland, *N.Y.* **22 A2** 41 2N 74 25W
Newham, *Lon.* **4 B5** 51 31N 0 1 E
Newlands, *Jobg.* **18 F8** 26 10 S 27 57 E
Newport, *Melb.* **19 F6** 37 50 S 144 51 E
Newportville, *Phil.* **24 A5** 40 7N 74 53W
Newton, *Bost.* **21 D2** 42 19N 71 13W
Newton Brook, *Trto.* **20 D8** 43 47N 79 24W
Newton Highlands, *Bost.* **21 D2** 42 19N 71 13W
Newtonville, *Bost.* **21 C2** 42 20N 71 11W
Newtown, *Syd.* **19 B4** 33 54 S 151 11 E
Newtown Square, *Phil.* **24 B2** 39 59N 75 24W
Neyegawa, *Ōsaka* **12 B4** 34 45N 135 36 E
Ngau Chi Wan, *H.K.* **12 D6** 22 20N 114 12 E
Ngau Tau Kok, *H.K.* **12 E6** 22 19N 114 12 E
Ngong Shuen Chau, *H.K.* **12 E5** 22 19N 114 8 E
Ngua Kok Wan, *H.K.* **12 D5** 22 21N 114 5 E
Niāvarān, *Tehr.* **17 C5** 35 47N 51 29 E
Nibria, *Calc.* **16 E5** 22 36N 88 15 E
Nichelino, *Tori.* **9 C2** 44 59N 7 38 E
Nichols Run →, *Wash.* **25 C6** 39 2N 77 17W
Nicholson, Mt., *H.K.* **12 E6** 22 15N 114 11 E
Nidāl, *Bagd.* **17 F8** 33 19N 44 25 E
Niddrie, *Melb.* **19 E6** 37 44 S 144 51 E
Nieder Neuendorf, *Berl.* **7 A2** 52 36N 13 12 E
Niederbonsfeld, *Ruhr* **6 B4** 51 22N 7 8 E
Niederdonk, *Ruhr* **6 C2** 51 14N 6 41 E
Niederschöneweide, *Berl.* **7 B3** 52 27N 13 30 E
Niederschönhausen, *Berl.* **7 A3** 52 35N 13 25 E
Niederwenigern, *Ruhr* **6 B4** 51 24N 7 8 E
Niemeyer, *Rio J.* **31 B2** 22 59 S 43 16W
Niendorf, *Hbg.* **7 D7** 53 37N 9 57 E
Nienstedten, *Hbg.* **7 D7** 53 33N 9 51 E
Nierst, *Ruhr* **6 C2** 51 19N 6 43 E
Nihonbashi, *Tōkyō* **13 B3** 35 41N 139 46 E
Niipperi, *Hels.* **3 B3** 60 18N 24 45 E
Niiza, *Tōkyō* **13 B2** 35 48N 139 33 E
Nikaia, *Ath.* **8 J10** 37 57N 23 38 E
Nikinmäki, *Hels.* **3 A5** 60 20N 25 8 E
Nikolassee, *Berl.* **7 B2** 52 25N 13 12 E
Nikolo-Khovanskoye, *Mos.* **11 F8** 55 36N 37 27 E
Nikolskiy, *Mos.* **11 E8** 55 49N 37 29 E
Nikolyskoye, *Mos.* **11 E11** 55 46N 37 53 E
Nikulino, *Mos.* **11 E8** 55 40N 37 25 E
Nil, *Bagd.* **17 E8** 33 21N 44 25 E
Nil, Nahr en →, *El Qâ.* **18 D5** 29 57N 31 14 E
Nile = Nil, Nahr en →, *El Qâ.* **18 D5** 29 57N 31 14 E
Niles, *Chic.* **26 A2** 42 1N 87 48W
Nilganj, *Calc.* **16 D6** 22 45N 88 25 E
Nilópolis, *Rio J.* **31 A1** 22 47 S 43 23W
Nimta, *Calc.* **16 D6** 22 40N 88 24 E
Nincop, *Hbg.* **7 D6** 53 30N 9 48 E
Ningyuan, *Tianj.* **14 E6** 39 9N 117 12 E
Nippa, *Tōkyō* **13 C2** 35 31N 139 36 E
Nippori, *Tōkyō* **13 B3** 35 43N 139 45 E
Niru-ye-Hava'i, *Tehr.* **17 C5** 35 41N 51 26 E
Nishi, *Ōsaka* **12 B3** 34 40N 135 28 E
Nishi, *Tōkyō* **13 D2** 35 26N 139 37 E
Nishi-arai, *Tōkyō* **13 B3** 35 46N 139 48 E
Nishinari, *Ōsaka* **12 C3** 34 37N 135 28 E
Nishinomiya, *Ōsaka* **12 B2** 34 44N 135 18 E
Nishiyama, *Tōkyō* **13 D4** 35 22N 139 57 E
Nishiyodogawa, *Ōsaka* **12 B3** 34 41N 135 24 E
Nisida, I. di, *Nápl.* **9 J11** 40 47N 14 10 E
Niterói, *Rio J.* **31 B3** 22 53 S 43 7W
Nithari, *Delhi* **16 B3** 28 34N 77 20 E
Nittedal, *Oslo* **2 A5** 60 0N 10 57 E
Niyog, *Manila* **15 E3** 14 27N 120 57 E
Noapara, *Calc.* **16 D6** 22 49N 88 22 E
Nobidome, *Tōkyō* **13 B2** 35 48N 139 34 E
Nockeby, *Stock.* **3 E10** 59 19N 17 56 E
Noel Park, *Lon.* **4 B4** 51 35N 0 5W
Nogatino, *Mos.* **11 E10** 55 41N 37 41 E
Nogent-sur-Marne, *Paris* **5 B4** 48 50N 2 28 E
Noiseau, *Paris* **5 C5** 48 46N 2 32 E
Noisiel, *Paris* **5 B5** 48 51N 2 37 E
Noisy-le-Grand, *Paris* **5 B5** 48 50N 2 33 E
Noisy-le-Roi, *Paris* **5 B2** 48 50N 2 3 E
Noisy-le-Sec, *Paris* **5 B4** 48 53N 2 27 E
Nokkala, *Hels.* **3 C3** 60 8N 24 45 E
Nøklevatn, *Oslo* **2 B5** 59 52N 10 52 E
Nolme →, *Ruhr* **6 B6** 51 23N 7 26 E
Nomentano, *Rome* **9 F10** 41 55N 12 30 E
Nonakashinden, *Tōkyō* **13 B2** 35 44N 139 30 E
Nongminyundong Jiangxisuo, *Gzh.* **14 G8** 23 7N 113 15 E
Nonhyeon, *Sŏul* **12 G8** 37 30N 127 1 E
Nontha Buri, *Bangk.* **15 A1** 13 50N 100 29 E
Noordgesig, *Jobg.* **18 F8** 26 13 S 27 56 E
Nord, Gare du, *Paris* **5 B4** 48 52N 2 21 E
Nordbysjøen, *Oslo* **2 B6** 59 51N 11 1 E
Nordereble, *Hbg.* **7 D7** 53 32N 9 59 E
Norderelbe →, *Hbg.* **7 E8** 53 29N 10 3 E
Norderstedt, *Hbg.* **7 C7** 53 42N 9 59 E
Nordmarka, *Oslo* **2 A4** 60 1N 10 38 E
Nordrand-Seidlung, *Wien* **10 G10** 48 16N 16 26 E
Nordre Elvåga, *Oslo* **2 B5** 59 53N 10 54 E
Nordstrand, *Oslo* **2 B4** 59 52N 10 48 E
Normandy Heights, *Balt.* **25 B2** 39 17N 76 48W
Norra Björköfjärden, *Stock.* **3 D8** 59 26N 17 39 E
Norridge, *Chic.* **26 B2** 41 57N 87 49W
Norristown, *Phil.* **24 A2** 40 7N 75 20W
Norrkula, *Hels.* **3 B6** 60 19N 25 20 E
Norrmalm, *Stock.* **3 D11** 59 20N 18 3 E
Norrviken, *Stock.* **3 D10** 59 27N 17 52 E
North Acton, *Bost.* **21 B1** 42 30N 71 23W
North Amityville, *N.Y.* **23 C8** 40 41N 73 25W
North Andover, *Bost.* **21 A3** 42 41N 71 7W
North Arlington, *N.Y.* **22 C4** 40 47N 74 7W
North Auburn, *Syd.* **19 B3** 33 50 S 151 3 E
North Babylon, *N.Y.* **23 C9** 40 43N 73 19W
North Bellmore, *N.Y.* **23 C7** 40 40N 73 32W
North Bergen, *N.Y.* **22 C4** 40 48N 74 0W
North Beverly, *Bost.* **21 B4** 42 34N 70 51W
North Billerica, *Bost.* **21 B2** 42 35N 71 16W
North Branch →, *Phil.* **24 C4** 39 50N 75 5W
North Branch Chicago River →, *Chic.* **26 B2** 41 53N 87 42W
North Brighton, *Bost.* **21 C3** 42 21N 71 8W
North Caldwell, *N.Y.* **22 B3** 40 52N 74 15W
North Cambridge, *Bost.* **21 C3** 42 23N 71 7W
North Cheam, *Lon.* **4 C3** 51 22N 0 11W
North Chelmsford, *Bost.* **21 B1** 42 38N 71 23W
North Cohasset, *Bost.* **21 D4** 42 15N 70 50W
North Cray, *Lon.* **4 C5** 51 25N 0 8 E
North Fair Oaks, *S.F.* **27 D3** 37 28N 122 11W
North Finchley, *Lon.* **4 B3** 51 36N 0 10W
North Germiston, *Jobg.* **18 F9** 26 12 S 28 9 E
North Hackensack, *N.Y.* **22 B4** 40 54N 74 2W
North Haledon, *N.Y.* **22 B3** 40 58N 74 11W
North Harbour, *Manila* **15 D3** 14 37N 120 57 E
North Hd., *Syd.* **19 A4** 33 49 S 151 18 E
North Hills, *N.Y.* **23 C6** 40 46N 73 40W
North Hollywood, *L.A.* **28 B2** 34 9N 118 22W
North Lexington, *Bost.* **21 C2** 42 27N 71 14W
North Lindenhurst, *N.Y.* **23 C8** 40 42N 73 22W
North Long Beach, *L.A.* **28 C3** 33 53N 118 10W
North Manly, *Syd.* **19 A4** 33 46 S 151 17 E
North Massapequa, *N.Y.* **23 C8** 40 42N 73 27W
North Merrick, *N.Y.* **23 C7** 40 41N 73 33W
North New Hyde Park, *N.Y.* **23 C6** 40 44N 73 42W
North Pelham, *N.Y.* **23 B6** 40 54N 73 46W
North Plainfield, *N.Y.* **22 D2** 40 37N 74 27W
North Point, *Balt.* **25 B4** 39 16N 76 29W
North Pt., *H.K.* **12 E6** 22 17N 114 12 E
North Pt., *Syd.* **19 A4** 33 48 S 151 18 E
North Randolph, *Bost.* **21 D3** 42 11N 71 5W
North Reading, *Bost.* **21 B3** 42 34N 71 5W
North Res., *Bost.* **21 C3** 42 27N 71 6W
North Richmond, *S.F.* **27 A2** 37 57N 122 22W
North Riverside, *Chic.* **26 B2** 41 50N 87 48W
North Ryde, *Syd.* **19 A3** 33 47 S 151 7 E
North Saugus, *Bost.* **21 C3** 42 29N 71 0W
North Shore Channel →, *Chic.* **26 B2** 41 58N 87 42W

Pitampura Kalan 43

North Springfield, *Wash.* 25 E6 38 48N 77 11W
North Stifford, *Lon.* 4 B6 51 30N 0 18 E
North Sudbury, *Bost.* 21 C1 42 24N 71 24W
North Sydney, *Syd.* 19 B4 33 50 S 151 13 E
North Tewksbury, *Bost.* 21 B2 42 38N 71 14W
North Valley Stream, *N.Y.* 23 C6 40 41N 73 42W
North Wantagh, *N.Y.* 23 C7 40 41N 73 30W
North Weymouth, *Bost.* 21 D4 42 14N 70 56W
North Wilmington, *Bost.* 21 B3 42 34N 71 9W
North Woburn, *Bost.* 21 B2 42 30N 71 10W
North Woolwich, *Lon.* 4 B5 51 30N 0 3 E
North York, *Trto.* 20 D8 43 45N 79 27W
Northaw, *Lon.* 4 A4 51 42N 0 8W
Northbridge, *Syd.* 19 A4 33 49 S 151 15 E
Northbrook, *Chic.* 26 A1 42 7N 87 50W
Northcliff, *Jobg.* 18 E8 26 8 S 27 58 E
Northcote, *Melb.* 19 E7 37 46 S 145 0 E
Northeastern Univ., *Bost.* 21 C3 42 20N 71 4W
Northfield, *Chic.* 26 A2 42 6N 87 45W
Northfleet, *Lon.* 4 C7 51 26N 0 21 E
Northlake, *Chic.* 26 B1 41 54N 87 53W
Northmead, *Jobg.* 18 E10 26 9 S 28 19 E
Northmead, *Syd.* 19 A3 33 47 S 151 0 E
Northmount, *Trto.* 20 D8 43 46N 79 23W
Northolt, *Lon.* 4 B2 51 32N 0 22W
Northport, *N.Y.* 23 B8 40 54N 73 20W
Northport B., *N.Y.* 23 B8 40 54N 73 22W
Northridge, *L.A.* 28 A1 34 14N 118 30W
Northumberland Heath, *Lon.* 4 C6 51 28N 0 10 E
Northvale, *N.Y.* 22 A5 41 0N 73 59W
Northwest Branch →, *Balt.* 25 B3 39 16N 76 35W
Northwest Branch →, *Wash.* 25 C8 39 2N 76 56W
Northwestern Univ., *Chic.* 26 A2 42 3N 87 40W
Northwood, *Lon.* 4 B2 51 36N 0 25W
Norumbega Res., *Bost.* 21 D2 42 19N 71 17W
Norwalk, *L.A.* 28 C4 33 53N 118 4W
Norwood, *Bost.* 21 D2 42 11N 71 13W
Norwood, *Jobg.* 18 E9 26 9 S 28 4 E
Norwood, *N.Y.* 22 B5 40 59N 73 57W
Norwood, *Phil.* 24 B3 39 53N 75 17W
Norwood Memorial Airport, *Bost.* 21 D3 42 11N 71 9W
Norwood Park, *Chic.* 26 B2 41 59N 87 48W
Noryangjin, *Sŏul* 12 G7 37 30N 126 56 E
Nose, *Ōsaka* 12 B2 34 49N 135 10 E
Nossa Senhora do Ó, *S. Pau.* 31 E5 23 30 S 46 41W
Notre-Dame, *Mtrl.* 20 B5 43 28N 73 28W
Notre-Dame, *Paris* 5 B4 48 51N 2 21 E
Notre-Dame, Bois, *Paris* 5 C5 48 45N 2 34 E
Notre Dame de L'Île Perrot, *Mtrl.* 20 B2 43 23N 73 53W
Notting Hill, *Lon.* 4 B3 51 30N 0 12W
Notting Hill, *Melb.* 19 F7 37 54 S 145 9 E
Nottingham, *Phil.* 24 A5 40 7N 74 58W
Nova Milanese, *Mil.* 9 D6 45 35N 9 12 E
Novate Milanese, *Mil.* 9 D5 45 30N 9 8 E
Novaya Derevnya, *St-Pet.* 11 A3 60 0N 30 19 E
Nové Mesto, *Pra.* 10 B2 50 4N 14 25 E
Novoaleksandrovskoye, *St-Pet.* 11 B4 59 50N 30 31 E
Novogireyevo, *Mos.* 11 E10 55 45N 37 46 E
Novoivanovskoye, *Mos.* 11 E7 55 42N 37 21 E
Novokhovrino, *Mos.* 11 D8 55 53N 37 27 E
Novonikolyskoye, *Mos.* 11 D7 55 50N 37 14 E
Novosaratovka, *St-Pet.* 11 B5 59 50N 30 32 E
Novosergiyevka, *St-Pet.* 11 B5 59 54N 30 34 E
Nowe-Babice, *Wsaw.* 10 E6 52 15N 20 51 E
Nöykkiö, *Hels.* 3 B3 60 10N 24 42 E
Noyoye Kovalyova, *St-Pet.* 11 B5 59 58N 30 34 E
Nozay, *Paris* 5 D3 48 39N 2 14 E
Nueva Atzacoalco, *Méx.* 29 B3 19 29N 99 4W
Nueva Caracas, *Car.* 30 D5 10 30N 66 57W
Nueva Chicago, *B.A.* 32 B4 34 39 S 58 29W
Nueva Pompeya, *B.A.* 32 C4 34 40 S 58 25W
Nueva Tenochtitlán, *Méx.* 29 B3 19 27N 99 5W
Nuijala, *Hels.* 3 B3 60 12N 24 46 E
Numabukuro, *Tōkyō* 13 B2 35 43N 139 39 E
Numakage, *Tōkyō* 13 A2 35 50N 139 37 E
Numata, *Tōkyō* 13 B3 35 45N 139 46 E
Nunawading, *Melb.* 19 E8 37 49 S 145 10 E
Nunez, *B.A.* 32 B4 34 32 S 58 27W
Nunhead, *Lon.* 4 C4 51 27N 0 3W
Ñuñoa, *Stgo* 30 J11 33 27 S 70 35W
Nupuri, *Hels.* 3 B2 60 14N 24 36 E
Nusle, *Pra.* 10 B2 50 3N 14 26 E
Nussdorf, *Wien* 10 G10 48 15N 16 21 E
Nuthe →, *Berl.* 7 B1 52 22N 13 5 E
Nutley, *N.Y.* 22 C4 40 49N 74 9W
Nutting L., *Bost.* 21 B2 42 32N 71 16W
Nützenberg, *Ruhr* 6 C4 51 15N 7 8 E
Nybølle, *Købn.* 2 D8 55 42N 12 15 E
Nybygget, *Hels.* 3 B6 60 17N 25 11 E
Nymphenburg, *Mün.* 7 G10 48 9N 11 30 E
Nymphenburg, Schloss, *Mün.* 7 G10 48 9N 11 30 E

O

Oak Beach, *N.Y.* 23 D9 40 38N 73 19W
Oak Forest, *Chic.* 26 D2 41 36N 87 44W
Oak Hill Park, *Bost.* 21 D2 42 17N 71 11W
Oak Lane, *Phil.* 24 A4 40 3N 75 8W
Oak Lawn, *Chic.* 26 C2 41 42N 87 45W
Oak Park, *Chic.* 26 B2 41 52N 87 47W
Oak Ridge, *N.Y.* 22 A2 41 2N 74 28W
Oak Valley, *Phil.* 24 C4 39 48N 75 9W
Oak View, *Wash.* 25 C8 39 1N 76 58W
Oakland, *N.Y.* 22 A3 41 1N 74 13W
Oakland, *S.F.* 27 B3 37 48N 122 18W
Oakland, *Wash.* 25 D8 38 52N 76 54W
Oakland Coliseum, *S.F.* 27 B3 37 44N 122 11W
Oakland Gardens, *N.Y.* 23 C6 40 45N 73 46W
Oakland Int. Airport, *S.F.* 27 B3 37 43N 122 12W
Oakland Mills, *Balt.* 25 B2 39 13N 76 49W
Oakland Naval Air Station, *S.F.* 27 B3 37 47N 122 19W
Oaklands, *Jobg.* 18 E9 26 8 S 28 4 E
Oaklawn, *Wash.* 25 E8 38 46N 76 56W
Oakleigh, *Melb.* 19 F7 37 54 S 145 5 E
Oaks, *Phil.* 24 A2 40 8N 75 26W
Oakwood, *N.Y.* 22 D4 40 34N 74 7W
Oakwood Beach, *N.Y.* 22 D4 40 33N 74 7W
Oatley, *Syd.* 19 B3 33 59 S 151 4 E
Obalende, *Lagos* 18 B2 6 26N 7 25 E
Oba's Palace, *Lagos* 18 B2 6 26N 7 22 E
Oberbauer, *Ruhr* 6 C6 51 17N 7 25 E
Oberföhring, *Mün.* 7 G10 48 10N 11 37 E
Oberhaching, *Mün.* 7 G10 48 1N 11 35 E
Oberhausen, *Ruhr* 6 B3 51 28N 6 54 E
Oberhausen, *Wien* 10 G11 48 10N 16 34 E
Oberkassel, *Ruhr* 6 C2 51 14N 6 45 E
Oberkirchbach, *Wien* 10 G9 48 17N 16 12 E
Oberlaa, *Wien* 10 H10 48 8N 16 24 E
Oberlisse, *Wien* 10 G10 48 17N 16 26 E
Obermenzing, *Mün.* 7 F9 48 10N 11 28 E
Obermoos Schwaige, *Mün.* 7 F9 48 14N 11 27 E
Oberschleissheim, *Mün.* 7 F10 48 15N 11 33 E
Oberschöneweide, *Berl.* 7 B4 52 27N 13 31 E
Oberwengern, *Ruhr* 6 B6 51 23N 7 22 E
Obitsu →, *Tōkyō* 13 D4 35 25N 139 56 E
Oboldino, *Mos.* 11 D11 55 53N 37 56 E
Observatory, *Jobg.* 18 F9 26 10 S 28 4 E
Ōbu, *Ōsaka* 12 B1 34 43N 135 8 E
Obu-tōge, *Ōsaka* 12 B1 34 44N 135 9 E
Óbuda, *Bud.* 10 J13 47 33N 19 2 E
Obudaisziget, *Bud.* 10 J13 47 33N 19 3 E
Obukhovo, *St-Pet.* 11 B4 59 53N 30 22 E
Occidental, Pico, *Car.* 30 D5 10 32N 66 51W
Oceanside, *N.Y.* 23 D7 40 38N 73 37W
Ochakovo, *Mos.* 11 E8 55 41N 37 26 E
Ochiai, *Tōkyō* 13 B3 35 43N 139 42 E
Ochota, *Wsaw.* 10 E6 52 13N 20 58 E
Ochsenwerder, *Hbg.* 7 E8 53 28N 10 4 E
Ochsenzoll, *Hbg.* 7 C8 53 41N 10 0 E
Ōdana, *Tōkyō* 13 C2 35 33N 139 35 E
Oden-Stockach, *Mün.* 7 G11 48 5N 11 41 E
Odilampi, *Hels.* 3 B3 60 18N 24 45 E
Odintsovo, *Mos.* 11 E7 55 40N 37 16 E
Odivelas, *Lisb.* 8 F7 38 47N 9 10W
Odolany, *Wsaw.* 10 E6 52 13N 20 55 E
Oeiras, *Lisb.* 8 F7 38 41N 9 18W
Oella, *Balt.* 25 B2 39 16N 76 46W
Oer-Erkenschwick, *Ruhr* 6 A5 51 38N 7 15 E
Oern, *Mün.* 7 G10 48 10N 11 32 E
Ofin, *Lagos* 18 A3 6 32N 7 30 E
Ofukuro-shinden, *Tōkyō* 13 A1 35 53N 139 28 E
Ogawa, *Tōkyō* 13 B1 35 44N 139 28 E
Ogden, *Phil.* 24 C2 39 49N 75 27W
Ogikubo, *Tōkyō* 13 B2 35 42N 139 37 E
Ogo Ogo, *Ōsaka* 12 B1 34 49N 135 8 E
Ogogoro, *Lagos* 18 B2 6 25N 7 24 E
Ogongo, *Manila* 15 D4 14 35N 121 4 E
Ogoyo, *Lagos* 18 B2 6 25N 7 29 E
Ogudu, *Lagos* 18 A2 6 34N 7 24 E
O'Hare, L., *Chic.* 26 B1 41 57N 87 53W
Ōhirodo, *Tōkyō* 13 A4 35 50N 139 53 E
Ohlsdorf, *Hbg.* 7 D8 53 37N 10 3 E
Ōi, *Tōkyō* 13 A2 35 51N 139 31 E
Ōimachi, *Tōkyō* 13 C3 35 35N 139 43 E
Oise →, *Paris* 5 A2 49 2N 2 5 E
Oittaa, *Hels.* 3 B3 60 15N 24 42 E
Ojota, *Lagos* 18 A2 6 35N 7 23 E
Okamoto, *Ōsaka* 12 B2 34 43N 135 15 E
Okazu, *Tōkyō* 13 D2 35 25N 139 31 E
Okęcie, *Wsaw.* 10 E6 52 11N 20 56 E
Okęcie Airport, *Wsaw.* 10 E6 52 10N 20 57 E
Okelra, *Lagos* 18 B2 6 29N 7 22 E
Okeogbe, *Lagos* 18 B2 6 24N 7 23 E
Okhla, *Delhi* 16 B2 28 33N 77 16 E
Okhta →, *St-Pet.* 11 B4 59 56N 30 25 E
Okkervil →, *St-Pet.* 11 B4 59 56N 30 30 E
Okrzeszyn, *Wsaw.* 10 F7 52 8N 21 8 E
Oksval, *Oslo* 2 B4 59 51N 10 40 E
Oktyabrskiy, *Mos.* 11 F11 55 37N 37 58 E
Oktyabrskiy, *Mos.* 11 E9 55 41N 37 35 E
Okubo, *Tōkyō* 13 B3 35 41N 139 42 E
Okunola, *Lagos* 18 A1 6 35N 7 17 E
Ōkura, *Tōkyō* 13 C1 35 35N 139 27 E
Olari, *Hels.* 3 B3 60 10N 24 44 E
Olaria, *Rio J.* 31 B2 22 50 S 43 16W
Old Brookville, *N.Y.* 23 C7 40 49N 73 35W
Old Cairo, *El Qâ.* 18 C5 30 0N 31 14 E
Old Coulsdon, *Lon.* 4 D4 51 17N 0 6W
Old Forge Village, *N.Y.* 22 C2 40 48N 74 29W
Old Harbor, *Bost.* 21 D3 42 19N 71 1W
Old Road B., *Balt.* 25 B4 39 12N 76 27W
Old Tappan, *N.Y.* 22 A5 41 0N 73 59W
Old Town, *Chic.* 26 B3 41 54N 87 37W
Old Westbury, *N.Y.* 23 C7 40 46N 73 35W
Oldmans Cr. →, *Phil.* 24 C2 39 47N 75 26W
Olgino, *St-Pet.* 11 A3 60 0N 30 10 E
Olimpico, Estadio, *Méx.* 29 C2 19 19N 99 11W
Olinda, *Melb.* 19 F9 37 51 S 145 21 E
Olinda, *Rio J.* 31 A1 22 49 S 43 25W
Olivais, *Lisb.* 8 F8 38 45N 9 7W
Olivar de los Padres, *Méx.* 29 B2 19 21N 99 14W
Olivar del Conde, *Méx.* 29 B2 19 22N 99 12W
Olivos, *B.A.* 32 B4 34 30 S 58 28W
Ollila, *Hels.* 3 A2 60 20N 24 32 E
Olney, *Phil.* 24 A4 40 2N 75 8W
Olona →, *Mil.* 9 E5 45 29N 9 6 E
Ølstykke, *Købn.* 2 D7 55 47N 12 8 E
Olute, *Lagos* 18 B1 6 27N 7 17 E
Olympia-Stadion, *Hels.* 3 B4 60 11N 24 55 E
Olympique Parc, *Mtrl.* 20 A4 43 33N 73 33W
Ōmagi, *Tōkyō* 13 A3 35 52N 139 43 E
Ōmiya, *Tōkyō* 13 A3 35 54N 139 37 E
Ōmori, *Tōkyō* 13 B3 35 34N 139 43 E
Ōnari, *Tōkyō* 13 A2 35 56N 139 38 E
Once, *B.A.* 32 B4 34 37 S 58 24W
Onchi, *Ōsaka* 12 C4 34 34N 135 37 E
Onchi →, *Ōsaka* 12 C4 34 38N 135 37 E
One Tree Hill, *Melb.* 19 F8 37 52 S 145 19 E
Onigbongbo, *Lagos* 18 A2 6 34N 7 23 E
Onisigun, *Lagos* 18 B2 6 25N 7 24 E
Ōokayama, *Tōkyō* 13 C3 35 36N 139 40 E
Opacz, *Wsaw.* 10 E6 52 10N 20 53 E
Ophirton, *Jobg.* 18 F9 26 13 S 28 1 E
Oppegård, *Oslo* 2 C4 59 45N 10 49 E
Oppsal, *Oslo* 2 B5 59 53N 10 51 E
Oppum, *Ruhr* 6 C1 51 19N 6 36 E
Oradell, *N.Y.* 22 B4 40 57N 74 2W
Oradell Res., *N.Y.* 22 B4 40 58N 74 0W
Orange, *N.Y.* 22 C3 40 46N 74 13W
Orange Grove, *Jobg.* 18 F9 26 9 S 28 5 E
Oratorio →, *S. Pau.* 31 E6 23 36 S 46 32W
Orbassano, *Tori.* 9 B2 45 0N 7 32 E
Orchards, *Jobg.* 18 E9 26 9 S 28 4 E
Ordrup, *Købn.* 2 D10 55 45N 12 35 E
Orech, *Pra.* 10 B1 50 1N 14 17 E
Øresund, *Købn.* 2 D11 55 45N 12 40 E
Oreta, *Lagos* 18 A3 6 31N 7 31 E
Orge →, *Paris* 5 D3 48 42N 2 22 E
Orgeval, *Paris* 5 B1 48 55N 1 58 E
Orhølm, *Købn.* 2 D10 55 48N 12 30 E
Orient Heights, *Bost.* 21 C4 42 23N 70 59W
Oriental, Pico, *Car.* 30 D5 10 30N 66 50W
Origgio, *Mil.* 9 D5 45 35N 9 1 E
Orinda, *S.F.* 27 A3 37 52N 122 10W
Orinda Village, *S.F.* 27 A3 37 53N 122 12W
Orland L., *Chic.* 26 D1 41 38N 87 52W
Orland Park, *Chic.* 26 D1 41 37N 87 50W
Orlando, *Jobg.* 18 F8 26 15 S 27 55 E
Orlando East, *Jobg.* 18 F8 26 14 S 27 55 E
Orlando West, *Jobg.* 18 F8 26 13 S 27 54 E
Orlången, *Stock.* 3 E11 59 11N 18 2 E
Orlångsvik, *Stock.* 3 E11 59 11N 18 2 E
Orlovo, *Mos.* 11 F8 55 38N 37 20 E
Orly, *Paris* 5 C4 48 45N 2 23 E
Ormesson-sur-Marne, *Paris* 5 C5 48 47N 2 32 E
Orminge, *Stock.* 3 E12 59 19N 18 17 E
Ormingelandet, *Stock.* 3 D13 59 20N 18 22 E
Ormond, *Melb.* 19 F7 37 54 S 145 1 E
Órmos Fálirou, *Ath.* 8 J11 37 54N 23 40 E
Ormøya, *Oslo* 2 B4 59 52N 10 45 E
Oros Aiyáleos, *Ath.* 8 J10 38 0N 23 36 E
Oros Imittós, *Ath.* 8 J11 37 53N 23 48 E
Örpadfold, *Bud.* 10 J14 47 32N 19 12 E
Orpington, *Lon.* 4 C5 51 22N 0 6 E
Orsay, *Paris* 5 C3 48 41N 2 11 E
Orsby, *Ruhr* 6 A2 51 31N 6 41 E
Orsett, *Lon.* 4 B7 51 30N 0 22 E
Ortaköy, *Ist.* 17 A3 41 3N 29 1 E
Ortica, *Mil.* 9 E6 45 28N 9 16 E
Oruba, *Lagos* 18 A2 6 34N 7 24 E
Ōsaka, *Ōsaka* 12 C4 34 42N 135 30 E
Ōsaka B., *Ōsaka* 12 C2 34 35N 135 18 E
Ōsaka Castle, *Ōsaka* 12 B4 34 41N 135 30 E
Ōsaka Harbour, *Ōsaka* 12 C3 34 38N 135 25 E
Ōsaka Univ., *Ōsaka* 12 B3 34 41N 135 29 E
Ōsaki, *Tōkyō* 13 C3 35 36N 139 42 E
Osasco, *S. Pau.* 31 E5 23 31 S 46 46W
Osdorf, *Berl.* 7 B3 52 24N 13 20 E
Osdorf, *Hbg.* 7 D7 53 34N 9 50 E
Oshodi, *Lagos* 18 A2 6 33N 7 21 E
Oskar Frederikborg, *Stock.* 3 D13 59 24N 18 24 E
Oslo, *Oslo* 2 B4 59 54N 10 43 E
Oslofjorden, *Oslo* 2 C3 59 40N 10 35 E
Ōsone, *Tōkyō* 13 C2 35 31N 139 37 E
Osorun, *Lagos* 18 A2 6 33N 7 29 E
Ospiate, *Mil.* 9 D5 45 32N 9 6 E
Ossów, *Wsaw.* 10 E8 52 18N 21 12 E
Ostankino, *Mos.* 11 E9 55 49N 37 37 E
Østby, *Købn.* 2 D7 55 45N 12 2 E
Osterath, *Ruhr* 6 C1 51 16N 6 36 E
Österby, *Hels.* 3 B1 60 10N 24 25 E
Osterfeld, *Ruhr* 6 A3 51 30N 6 53 E
Osterley, *Lon.* 4 C2 51 28N 0 21W
Osterley Park, *Lon.* 4 C2 51 29N 0 21W
Östermalm, *Stock.* 3 D11 59 20N 18 4 E
Österskär, *Stock.* 3 D12 59 26N 18 16 E
Östersundom, *Hels.* 3 B6 60 15N 25 10 E
Ostertälje, *Stock.* 3 E8 59 11N 17 39 E
Ostiense, *Rome* 9 F9 41 51N 12 29 E
Østmarkkapellet, *Oslo* 2 B5 59 52N 10 51 E
Østøya, *Oslo* 2 B3 59 52N 10 34 E
Östra Ryd, *Stock.* 3 D12 59 27N 18 11 E
Østre Aker, *Oslo* 2 B4 59 54N 10 49 E
Ostrov, *Mos.* 11 F11 55 36N 37 50 E
Ostrovtsy, *Mos.* 11 F12 55 36N 38 0 E
Ōta-Ku, *Tōkyō* 13 C3 35 34N 139 41 E
Otaniemi, *Hels.* 3 B3 60 11N 24 49 E
Otford, *Lon.* 4 D6 51 18N 0 11 E
Othmarschen, *Hbg.* 7 D7 53 33N 9 53 E
Otsuka, *Tōkyō* 13 B3 35 43N 139 44 E
Ottakring, *Wien* 10 G9 48 12N 16 18 E
Ottávia, *Rome* 9 F9 41 57N 12 24 E
Ottaviano, *Nápl.* 9 H13 40 50N 14 28 E
Ottensen, *Hbg.* 7 D7 53 33N 9 55 E
Ottobrunn, *Mün.* 7 G11 48 3N 11 40 E
Ottocalli, *Nápl.* 9 H12 40 52N 14 17 E
Otwock, *Wsaw.* 10 F8 52 8N 21 13 E
Ouerenburg, *Ruhr* 6 B5 51 27N 7 16 E
Ouiapo, *Manila* 15 D3 14 35N 120 59 E
Oulunkylä, *Hels.* 3 B4 60 13N 24 58 E
Ourcq, Canal de l', *Paris* 5 B4 48 54N 2 28 E
Ousit, *Bangk.* 15 B2 13 47N 100 31 E
Outer Brewster I., *Bost.* 21 C4 42 20N 70 52W
Outer Mission, *S.F.* 27 B2 37 43N 122 26W
Outremont, *Mtrl.* 20 A4 43 31N 73 36W
Overbruch, *Ruhr* 6 A2 51 32N 6 43 E
Overlea, *Balt.* 25 B3 39 21N 76 32W
Øverød, *Købn.* 2 D9 55 48N 12 28 E
Ōwada, *Tōkyō* 13 B2 35 48N 139 31 E
Owings Mills, *Balt.* 25 A2 39 25N 76 47W
Oworonsoki, *Lagos* 18 A2 6 32N 7 24 E
Oxon Hill, *Wash.* 25 E8 38 48N 76 59W
Oxshott, *Lon.* 4 D2 51 19N 0 21W
Oyada, *Tōkyō* 13 B4 35 46N 139 50 E
Ōyama, *Tōkyō* 13 B3 35 44N 139 42 E
Øyeren, *Oslo* 2 B6 59 55N 11 6 E
Oyodo, *Ōsaka* 12 B3 34 42N 135 29 E
Oyster B., *N.Y.* 23 B7 40 53N 73 31W
Oyster B., *Syd.* 19 C3 34 0 S 151 5 E
Oyster Bay Cove, *N.Y.* 23 B8 40 51N 73 29W
Oyster Bay Harbour, *N.Y.* 23 B7 40 53N 73 32W
Oyster Rock, *Bomb.* 16 H7 18 54N 72 49 E
Oyster Rocks, *Kar.* 17 H11 24 48N 66 59 E
Ozarów-Franciszków, *Wsaw.* 10 E5 52 13N 20 48 E
Ozerki, *St-Pet.* 11 B6 59 53N 30 42 E
Ozoir-la-Ferrière, *Paris* 5 C6 48 46N 2 40 E
Ozone Park, *N.Y.* 23 C5 40 40N 73 50W

P

Pacific Manor, *S.F.* 27 C2 37 38N 122 29W
Pacific Palisades, *L.A.* 28 B1 34 2N 118 32W
Pacifica, *S.F.* 27 C2 37 37N 122 29W
Packanack L., *N.Y.* 22 B3 40 56N 74 15W
Paco, *Manila* 15 D3 14 35N 120 59 E
Paco de Arcos, *Lisb.* 8 F7 38 41N 9 17W
Paddington, *Lon.* 4 B3 51 30N 0 10W
Paddington, *Syd.* 19 B4 33 53 S 151 14 E
Pademangan, *Jak.* 15 H9 6 7 S 106 49 E
Padenor, *Mil.* 9 E6 45 33N 9 9 E
Padre Miguel, *Rio J.* 31 B1 22 52 S 43 26W
Padstow, *Syd.* 19 B3 33 57 S 151 2 E
Pagewood, *Syd.* 19 B4 33 56 S 151 14 E
Pagote, *Bomb.* 16 H8 18 53N 72 59 E
Pai, I. do, *Rio J.* 31 B3 22 59 S 43 5W
Paia, *Lisb.* 8 F7 38 46N 9 11W
Paikpara, *Calc.* 16 E6 22 36N 88 23 E
Paint Br. →, *Wash.* 25 C8 38 57N 76 55W
Paiyun Airport, *Gzh.* 14 F8 23 10N 113 15 E
Pak ka Shan, *H.K.* 12 E6 22 16N 114 13 E
Pak Kong, *H.K.* 12 D6 22 22N 114 15 E
Pak Tim Pa, *H.K.* 12 D5 22 23N 114 7 E
Pakila, *Hels.* 3 B4 60 15N 24 55 E
Palace Museum, *Beij.* 14 B3 39 54N 116 21 E
Palaión Fáliron, *Ath.* 8 J11 37 53N 23 42 E
Palaiseau, *Paris* 5 C3 48 42N 2 14 E
Palam, *Delhi* 16 B1 28 35N 77 4 E
Palam Int. Airport, *Delhi* 16 B1 28 32N 77 8 E
Palazzo Reale, *Nápl.* 9 H12 40 50N 14 15 E
Palazzo Reale, *Tori.* 9 B3 45 4N 7 40 E
Palazzolo, *Mil.* 9 D6 45 36N 9 11 E
Palazzuolo, *Nápl.* 9 H13 40 54N 14 28 E
Palermo, *B.A.* 32 B4 34 34 S 58 25W
Palhais, *Lisb.* 8 G8 38 37N 9 2W
Palisades, *N.Y.* 22 A5 41 1N 73 57W
Palisades Park, *N.Y.* 22 B4 40 50N 74 1W
Palleja, *Barc.* 8 D5 41 25N 2 0 E
Palmer Park, *Wash.* 25 D8 38 55N 76 52W
Palmers Green, *Lon.* 4 B4 51 36N 0 6W
Palmira, *Phil.* 24 A4 40 0N 75 1W
Palo Alto, *S.F.* 27 D4 37 27N 122 8W
Paloheinä, *Hels.* 3 B4 60 15N 24 55 E
Palomar Park, *S.F.* 27 D3 37 29N 122 16W
Palomeras, *Mdrd.* 8 B3 40 23N 3 39W
Palos Heights, *Chic.* 26 D2 41 39N 87 47W
Palos Hills, *Chic.* 26 C2 41 42N 87 49W
Palos Hills Forest, *Chic.* 26 C1 41 40N 87 52W
Palos Park, *Chic.* 26 C1 41 40N 87 50W
Palota-Újfalu, *Bud.* 10 J13 47 33N 19 7 E
Palpara, *Calc.* 16 E6 22 38N 88 22 E
Palta, *Calc.* 16 D6 22 46N 88 23 E
Pamplona, *Manila* 15 E3 14 27N 120 58 E
Panayaan, *Manila* 15 E3 14 27N 120 57 E
Panchghara, *Calc.* 16 D5 22 44N 88 16 E
Panchur, *Calc.* 16 E5 22 32N 88 16 E
Pancoran, *Jak.* 15 J9 6 14 S 106 49 E
Pandan, Selat, *Sing.* 15 G7 1 16N 103 45 E
Pandan, Sungei →, *Sing.* 15 G7 1 18N 103 43 E
Pandan Res., *Sing.* 15 G7 1 18N 103 44 E
Panehpara, *Calc.* 16 E5 22 34N 88 15 E
Pangrati, *Ath.* 8 J11 37 56N 23 45 E
Pangsua, Sungei →, *Sing.* 15 F7 1 25N 103 45 E
Panihati, *Calc.* 16 D6 22 41N 88 22 E
Panjang, Bukit, *Sing.* 15 F7 1 22N 103 45 E
Panje, *Bomb.* 16 H8 18 54N 72 57 E
Panke →, *Berl.* 7 A3 52 31N 13 22 E
Pankow, *Berl.* 7 A3 52 34N 13 23 E
Panorama City, *L.A.* 28 A2 34 13N 118 26W
Panpur, *Calc.* 16 C6 22 51N 88 26 E
Pantheon, *Rome* 9 F9 41 53N 12 28 E
Pantin, *Paris* 5 B4 48 53N 2 24 E
Pantitlán, *Méx.* 29 B3 19 24N 99 4W
Panuacan, *Manila* 15 D4 14 35N 121 0 E
Panvel Cr. →, *Bomb.* 16 H9 18 59N 73 0 E
Paoli, *Phil.* 24 A2 40 2N 75 28W
Papiol, *Barc.* 8 D5 41 25N 2 0 E
Paracuellos del Jarama, *Mdrd.* 8 A3 40 30N 3 31W
Paradise Cay, *S.F.* 27 A2 37 54N 122 28W
Paramount, *L.A.* 28 C3 33 53N 118 11W
Paramus, *N.Y.* 22 B4 40 56N 74 2W
Paranaque, *Manila* 15 D3 14 30N 120 59 E
Paray-Vieille-Poste, *Paris* 5 C4 48 42N 2 20 E
Parbasdorf, *Wien* 10 G11 48 16N 16 35 E
Parbatipur, *Calc.* 16 E5 22 39N 88 13 E
Parcelacion Moderna, *La Hab.* 30 B3 23 2N 82 19W
Parco Regionale, *Mil.* 9 D5 45 35N 9 5 E
Parel, *Bomb.* 16 H7 18 59N 72 49 E
Pari, *S. Pau.* 31 E6 23 32 S 46 36W
Parioli, *Rome* 9 F9 41 55N 12 29 E
Paris, *Paris* 5 B4 48 53N 2 20 E
Paris-Le Bourget, Aéroport de, *Paris* 5 B4 48 58N 2 26 E
Paris-Orly, Aéroport de, *Paris* 5 C4 48 43N 2 22 E
Pārk-e-Shahānshāh, *Tehr.* 17 C5 35 46N 51 24 E
Park Orchards, *Melb.* 19 E8 37 46 S 145 13 E
Park Ridge, *Chic.* 26 A1 42 0N 87 50W
Park Ridge, *N.Y.* 22 A4 41 2N 74 2W
Park Royal, *Lon.* 4 B3 51 31N 0 16W
Parkchester, *N.Y.* 23 C5 40 49N 73 50W
Parkdale, *Trto.* 20 E8 43 38N 79 25W
Parkdene, *Jobg.* 18 F10 26 11 S 28 15 E
Parkhafen, *Hbg.* 7 D7 53 32N 9 54 E
Parkhill Gardens, *Jobg.* 18 F10 26 14 S 28 11 E
Parkhurst, *Jobg.* 18 E9 26 8 S 28 1 E
Parklawn, *Wash.* 25 D7 38 50N 77 7W
Parkmore, *Jobg.* 18 E9 26 5 S 28 2 E
Parkside, *S.F.* 27 B2 37 44N 122 29W
Parktown, *Jobg.* 18 F9 26 10 S 28 3 E
Parktown North, *Jobg.* 18 E9 26 8 S 28 2 E
Parkview, *Jobg.* 18 E9 26 9 S 28 1 E
Parkville, *Balt.* 25 A3 39 23N 76 34W
Parkville, *N.Y.* 22 D5 40 38N 73 57W
Parkwood, *Jobg.* 18 E9 26 9 S 28 2 E
Parque Edú Chaves, *S. Pau.* 31 D6 23 29 S 46 34W
Parramatta, *Syd.* 19 A2 33 49 S 150 59 E
Parramatta →, *Syd.* 19 A3 33 49 S 151 1 E
Parramatta North, *Syd.* 19 A3 33 48 S 151 0 E
Parramatta Park, *Syd.* 19 A3 33 48 S 151 0 E
Parsippany, *N.Y.* 22 B2 40 51N 74 26W
Paşabahçe, *Ist.* 17 A3 41 6N 29 5 E
Pasadena, *L.A.* 28 B4 34 9N 118 8W
Pasar Minggu, *Jak.* 15 J9 6 16 S 106 49 E
Pasay, *Manila* 15 D3 14 32N 120 59 E
Pascoe Vale, *Melb.* 19 E6 37 43 S 144 55 E
Pasig, *Manila* 15 D4 14 33N 121 4 E
Pasig →, *Manila* 15 D4 14 31N 121 0 E
Pasila, *Hels.* 3 B4 60 12N 24 56 E
Pasing, *Mün.* 7 G9 48 8N 11 28 E
Pasir Panjang, *Sing.* 15 G7 1 17N 103 46 E
Pasir Ris Beach, *Sing.* 15 F8 1 22N 103 56 E
Paso del Rey, *B.A.* 32 B2 34 39 S 58 45W
Passaic, *N.Y.* 22 B4 40 51N 74 9W
Passaic →, *N.Y.* 22 B3 40 42N 74 10W
Passirana, *Mil.* 9 D5 45 32N 9 2 E
Patapsco →, *Balt.* 25 B2 39 19N 76 49W
Patapsco State Park, *Balt.* 25 B2 39 18N 76 47W
Pateres, *Manila* 15 D4 14 32N 121 3 E
Paterson, *N.Y.* 22 B4 40 54N 74 9W
Pathumwan, *Bangk.* 15 B2 13 44N 100 31 E
Patipukur, *Calc.* 16 E6 22 36N 88 24 E
Patisia, *Ath.* 8 H11 38 2N 23 45 E
Patterson Park, *Balt.* 25 B3 39 17N 76 34W
Patul, *Calc.* 16 D4 22 45N 88 9 E
Paulo E. Virginia, Gruta, *Rio J.* 31 B2 22 56 S 43 16W
Paulsboro, *Phil.* 24 C3 39 49N 75 14W
Paulshof, *Berl.* 7 A5 52 34N 13 40 E
Pausin, *Berl.* 7 A1 52 38N 13 2 E
Pavarolo, *Tori.* 9 B3 45 4N 7 50 E
Pavlovo, *St-Pet.* 11 B5 59 55N 30 38 E
Pavne, *Bomb.* 16 G9 19 5N 73 1 E
Pavshino, *Mos.* 11 E7 55 49N 37 20 E
Paya Lebar, *Sing.* 15 F8 1 21N 103 52 E
Paylampur, *Calc.* 16 D5 22 46N 88 15 E
Peabody, *Bost.* 21 B4 42 31N 70 55W
Peabody Inst., *Balt.* 25 B3 39 17N 76 37W
Peakhurst, *Syd.* 19 B3 33 57 S 151 3 E
Pécel, *Bud.* 10 K14 47 29N 19 20 E
Pecetto Torinese, *Tori.* 9 B3 45 1N 7 44 E
Pechincha, *Rio J.* 31 B1 22 55 S 43 20W
Pechorka →, *Mos.* 11 F12 55 37N 38 2 E
Peckham, *Lon.* 4 C4 51 28N 0 3W
Pecqueuse, *Paris* 5 D2 48 38N 2 3 E
Peddocks I., *Bost.* 21 D4 42 17N 70 56W
Pederstrup, *Købn.* 2 D9 55 44N 12 20 E
Pedra Branca, *Rio J.* 31 B1 22 55 S 43 26W
Pedralbes, *Barc.* 8 D5 41 23N 2 7 E
Pedregal de San Angel, Jardines del, *Méx.* 29 C2 19 19N 99 12W
Pedreira, *S. Pau.* 31 F5 23 41 S 46 40W
Pedreiras, *Lima* 30 G8 12 2 S 76 57W
Pedricktown, *Phil.* 24 C2 39 45N 75 24W
Pedro Cr. →, *S.F.* 27 C2 37 35N 122 30W
Pedro Valley, *S.F.* 27 C2 37 35N 122 29W
Peirce Res., *Sing.* 15 F7 1 22N 103 49 E
Pekhra-Pokrovskoye, *Mos.* 11 D11 55 50N 37 57 E
Pekhra-Yakovievskaya, *Mos.* 11 E11 55 47N 37 57 E
Peking = Beijing, *Beij.* 14 B2 39 53N 116 21 E
Pelado, Cerro, *Méx.* 29 D2 19 9N 99 12W
Pelcowizna, *Wsaw.* 10 E7 52 17N 21 0 E
Pelham, *N.Y.* 23 B6 40 54N 73 46W
Pelham B. Park, *N.Y.* 23 B6 40 51N 73 48W
Pelham Manor, *N.Y.* 23 B6 40 53N 73 46W
Penalolén, *Stgo* 30 J11 33 28 S 70 30W
Peng Siang →, *Sing.* 15 F7 1 24N 103 43 E
Penge, *Lon.* 4 C4 51 24N 0 3W
Penha, *Rio J.* 31 A2 22 49 S 43 17W
Penha, *S. Pau.* 31 E6 23 31 S 46 32W
Penjaringan, *Jak.* 15 H9 6 7 S 106 48 E
Penn Square, *Phil.* 24 A3 40 8N 75 19W
Penn Wynne, *Phil.* 24 B3 39 59N 75 16W
Pennant Hills Park, *Syd.* 19 A3 33 45 S 151 6 E
Penndel, *Phil.* 24 A5 40 9N 74 54W
Penns Grove, *Phil.* 24 C2 39 44N 75 27W
Pennsauken, *Phil.* 24 B4 39 57N 75 5W
Pennsauken Cr. →, *Phil.* 24 B4 39 59N 75 3W
Pennsylvania, Univ. of, *Phil.* 24 B3 39 51N 75 11W
Pennypack Cr. →, *Phil.* 24 A4 40 0N 75 3W
Pentala, *Hels.* 3 C3 60 6N 24 40 E
Penyagino, *Mos.* 11 D8 55 50N 37 20 E
Penzing, *Wien* 10 G9 48 11N 16 18 E
Pequannock, *N.Y.* 22 B3 40 57N 74 17W
Pequena Arroio Fundo →, *Rio J.* 31 B1 22 58 S 43 21W
Perales del Rio, *Mdrd.* 8 C3 40 18N 3 38W
Perchtoldsdorf, *Wien* 10 H9 48 7N 16 17 E
Perdizes, *S. Pau.* 31 E6 23 32 S 46 39W
Peredelkino, *Mos.* 11 F8 55 38N 37 20 E
Peredeltsy, *Mos.* 11 F8 55 36N 37 21 E
Peristérion, *Ath.* 8 H11 38 1N 23 42 E
Perivale, *Lon.* 4 B3 51 31N 0 18W
Perlach, *Mün.* 7 G10 48 5N 11 37 E
Perlacher Forst, *Mün.* 7 G10 48 4N 11 34 E
Pero, *Mil.* 9 D5 45 30N 9 5 E
Peropok, Bukit, *Sing.* 15 G7 1 19N 103 42 E
Perovo, *Mos.* 11 E10 55 44N 37 45 E
Perrot, Î., *Mtrl.* 20 B2 43 23N 73 56W
Perry Hall, *Balt.* 25 A4 39 24N 76 28W
Perth Amboy, *N.Y.* 22 D3 40 30N 74 16W
Pertusella, *Mil.* 9 D5 45 35N 9 3 E
Pesanggrahag, Kali →, *Jak.* 15 J9 6 10 S 106 44 E
Peschiera Borromeo, *Mil.* 9 E6 45 26N 9 19 E
Pesek, P., *Sing.* 15 G7 1 17N 103 41 E
Pest, *Bud.* 10 K13 47 29N 19 4 E
Pesterzsébet, *Bud.* 10 K13 47 26N 19 6 E
Pesthidegkút, *Bud.* 10 J12 47 33N 18 57 E
Pestimre, *Bud.* 10 K14 47 24N 19 11 E
Pestlőrinc, *Bud.* 10 K14 47 26N 19 11 E
Pestujhely, *Bud.* 10 J13 47 32N 19 7 E
Petare, *Car.* 30 E6 10 29N 66 48W
Petas, *Hels.* 3 B4 60 15N 24 50 E
Peters Pond, *Bost.* 21 A2 42 43N 71 15W
Petit, *Jobg.* 18 E11 26 6 S 28 22 E
Petit-Brûlé, *Mtrl.* 20 A1 43 35N 74 2W
Petojo Selatan, *Jak.* 15 J9 6 10 S 106 48 E
Petrograd = St. Petersburg, *St-Pet.* 11 B3 59 55N 30 15 E
Petrogradskaya Storona, *St-Pet.* 11 B4 59 56N 30 20 E
Petroúpolis, *Ath.* 8 H11 38 3N 23 40 E
Petrovice, *Pra.* 10 B3 50 2N 14 33 E
Petrovsko-Rasumovskoye, *Mos.* 11 E9 55 49N 37 34 E
Petrovskoye, *Mos.* 11 F11 55 36N 37 53 E
Petrovsky Park, *Mos.* 11 E9 55 47N 37 34 E
Pfaueninsel, *Berl.* 7 B1 52 26N 13 7 E
Phihāi, *Kar.* 17 G11 24 50N 67 8 E
Philadelphia, *Phil.* 24 B3 39 57N 75 11W
Philadelphia Airport, *Phil.* 24 A5 40 4N 75 0W
Philadelphia Int. Airport, *Phil.* 24 B3 39 52N 75 16W
Phillip B., *Syd.* 19 B4 33 58 S 151 14 E
Phinga, *Calc.* 16 D6 22 41N 88 25 E
Phoenix, *Chic.* 26 D3 41 36N 87 37W
Phoenixville, *Phil.* 24 A1 40 7N 75 31W
Phra Khanong, *Bangk.* 15 B2 13 40N 100 36 E
Phra Pradaeng, *Bangk.* 15 C2 13 39N 100 33 E
Phranakhon, *Bangk.* 15 B1 13 44N 100 29 E
Pianezza, *Tori.* 9 B2 45 6N 7 32 E
Pianura, *Nápl.* 9 H11 40 51N 14 10 E
Piaslów, *Wsaw.* 10 E5 52 11N 20 49 E
Pico Rivera, *L.A.* 28 C4 33 59N 118 5W
Piedade, *Lisb.* 8 F7 38 49N 9 14W
Piedade, *Rio J.* 31 B2 22 52 S 43 18W
Piedade, Cova da, *Lisb.* 8 F8 38 40N 9 8W
Piedmont, *S.F.* 27 B3 37 49N 122 14W
Pierrefitte, *Paris* 5 B4 48 58N 2 21 E
Pierrefonds, *Mtrl.* 20 B2 43 29N 73 51W
Pierrelaye, *Paris* 5 A2 49 1N 2 8 E
Pietralata, *Rome* 9 F10 41 55N 12 33 E
Pihlajamäki, *Hels.* 3 B4 60 14N 24 58 E
Pihlajasaari, *Hels.* 3 C4 60 8N 24 55 E
Pikesville, *Balt.* 25 A2 39 22N 76 42W
Pilar Velho, *S. Pau.* 31 F7 23 40 S 46 22W
Pilarcitos Cr. →, *S.F.* 27 C3 37 33N 122 24W
Pilarcitos L., *S.F.* 27 C2 37 33N 122 25W
Pilgrim Corner, *Phil.* 24 A3 40 6N 75 12W
Pilgrims Hatch, *Lon.* 4 B6 51 37N 0 17 E
Pillar Pt., *S.F.* 26 D2 37 29N 122 30W
Pimenta, *S. Pau.* 31 D7 23 27 S 46 24W
Pimlico, *Lon.* 4 C4 51 29N 0 8W
Pimmit Hills, *Wash.* 25 D6 38 54N 77 12W
Pimville, *Jobg.* 18 F8 26 16 S 27 54 E
Pinazo →, *B.A.* 32 A2 34 29 S 58 49W
Pine Brook, *N.Y.* 22 B3 40 51N 74 20W
Pine Grove, *Trto.* 20 D7 43 47N 79 34W
Pine Hill, *Phil.* 24 C5 39 47N 74 59W
Pine Orchard, *Balt.* 25 B1 39 16N 76 52W
Pinehurst, *Bost.* 21 B2 42 31N 71 12W
Piñero, *B.A.* 32 B2 34 31 S 58 46W
Pines Lake, *N.Y.* 22 B3 40 59N 74 15W
Piney Run →, *Wash.* 25 D6 38 58N 77 14W
Pinganli, *Beij.* 14 B3 39 56N 116 21 E
Pinheiros →, *S. Pau.* 31 E5 23 37 S 46 44W
Pinjrāpur, *Kar.* 17 G11 24 53N 67 4 E
Pinn →, *Lon.* 4 B2 51 30N 0 28W
Pinnau →, *Hbg.* 7 C6 53 40N 9 49 E
Pinneberg, *Hbg.* 7 C6 53 40N 9 48 E
Pinner, *Lon.* 4 B2 51 35N 0 22W
Pinner Green, *Lon.* 4 B2 51 35N 0 23W
Pino Torinese, *Tori.* 9 B3 45 2N 7 46 E
Pinole Cr. →, *S.F.* 27 A3 37 58N 122 12W
Pioltello, *Mil.* 9 D6 45 30N 9 19 E
Piossasco, *Tori.* 9 C1 44 59N 7 27 E
Piqueri, *S. Pau.* 31 D5 23 29 S 46 41W
Piqueri →, *S. Pau.* 31 D5 23 29 S 46 34W
Pira, *Delhi* 16 A1 28 40N 77 7 E
Piraévs, *Ath.* 8 J10 37 57N 23 39 E
Pirajussara, *S. Pau.* 31 E5 23 34 S 46 45W
Pirajussara →, *S. Pau.* 31 E5 23 33 S 46 42W
Piraporinha, *S. Pau.* 31 F5 23 40 S 46 33W
Piratininga, *Rio J.* 31 B3 22 56 S 43 4W
Piratininga, L. de, *Rio J.* 31 B3 22 56 S 43 4W
Pirituba, *S. Pau.* 31 D5 23 29 S 46 44W
Pirkkola, *Hels.* 3 B4 60 14N 24 55 E
Pisangan, *Jak.* 15 J10 6 12 S 106 52 E
Piscataway, *N.Y.* 22 D2 40 34N 74 27W
Pisnice, *Pra.* 10 C2 49 59N 14 28 E
Pitampura Kalan, *Delhi* 16 A1 28 41N 77 8 E

Pitkäjärvi, *Hels.* 3 B3 60 15N 24 45 E
Pitman, *Phil.* 24 C4 39 44N 75 7W
Plainedge, *N.Y.* 23 C8 40 43N 73 27W
Plainfield, *N.Y.* 22 D2 40 36N 74 23W
Plainview, *N.Y.* 23 C8 40 46N 73 27W
Plaisir, *Paris* 5 C1 48 49N 1 56 E
Plandome, *N.Y.* 23 C6 40 48N 73 42W
Plandome Heights, *N.Y.* 23 C6 40 48N 73 42W
Planegg, *Mün.* 7 G9 48 6N 11 25 E
Plazo Mayor, *Mdrd.* 8 B2 40 25N 3 43W
Pleasant Hill, *S.F.* 27 A4 37 56N 122 4W
Plenty, *Melb.* 19 E7 37 40 S 145 5 E
Pluit, *Jak.* 15 H9 6 7 S 106 47 E
Plumsock, *Phil.* 24 B2 39 58N 75 28W
Plumstead, *Lon.* 4 C5 51 29N 0 5 E
Plymouth Meeting, *Phil.* 24 A3 40 6N 75 16W
Plyushchevo, *Mos.* 11 E10 55 44N 37 45 E
Po →, *Tori.* 9 B3 45 7N 7 46 E
Po Toi, *H.K.* 12 E6 22 16N 114 17 E
Po Toi I., *H.K.* 12 E6 22 10N 114 15 E
Podbaba, *Pra.* 10 B2 50 7N 14 22 E
Podoli, *Pra.* 10 B2 50 2N 14 25 E
Podra, *Calc.* 16 E5 22 33N 88 16 E
Poduskino, *Mos.* 11 E7 55 43N 37 15 E
Poggioreale, *Nápl.* 9 H12 40 51N 14 17 E
Pogliano Milanese, *Mil.* 9 D4 45 32N 8 59 E
Pohick Cr. →, *Wash.* 25 E6 38 47N 77 16W
Point Breeze, *Phil.* 24 B3 39 54N 75 13W
Point Lookout, *N.Y.* 23 D7 40 35N 73 34W
Point View Res., *N.Y.* 22 B3 40 58N 74 14W
Pointe-Aux-Trembles, *Mtrl.* 20 A4 43 38N 73 30W
Pointe-Calumet, *Mtrl.* 20 B2 43 29N 73 58W
Pointe-Claire, *Mtrl.* 20 B3 43 27N 73 48W
Poissy, *Paris* 5 B2 48 55N 2 2 E
Pok Fu Lam, *H.K.* 12 E5 22 16N 114 7 E
Pokrovsko-Sresnevo, *Mos.* 11 E8 55 48N 37 27 E
Pokrovskoye, *Mos.* 11 F9 55 37N 37 36 E
Póllena, *Nápl.* 9 H13 40 51N 14 22 E
Polsum, *Ruhr* 6 A4 51 37N 7 2 E
Polyustrovo, *St-Pet.* 11 B4 59 57N 30 25 E
Pomigliano d'Arco, *Nápl.* 9 H13 40 54N 14 23 E
Pompei, *Nápl.* 9 J13 40 45N 14 29 E
Pomponne, *Paris* 5 B6 48 52N 2 40 E
Pomprap, *Bangk.* 15 B2 13 44N 100 30 E
Pompton →, *N.Y.* 22 B3 40 53N 74 16W
Pompton Lakes, *N.Y.* 22 A3 41 0N 74 15W
Pompton Plains, *N.Y.* 22 B3 40 58N 74 18W
Ponders End, *Lon.* 4 B4 51 38N 0 2W
Pondok Indah, *Jak.* 15 J9 6 16 S 106 46 E
Ponkapog, *Bost.* 21 D3 42 11N 71 4W
Ponkapog Pond, *Bost.* 21 D3 42 11N 71 5W
Pont-Viau, *Mtrl.* 20 A3 43 34N 73 41W
Pontault-Combault, *Paris* 5 C5 48 47N 2 36 E
Pontcarré, *Paris* 5 C6 48 47N 2 42 E
Pontchartrain, *Paris* 5 C1 48 48N 1 54 E
Ponte Galéria, *Rome* 9 G8 41 48N 12 19 E
Pontes, Canto do, *Rio J.* 31 B3 22 56 S 43 3W
Pontevedra, *B.A.* 32 C2 34 44 S 58 41W
Ponticelli, *Nápl.* 9 H12 40 51N 14 19 E
Pontinha, *Lisb.* 8 F7 38 45N 9 11W
Pontoise, *Paris* 5 A2 49 2N 2 4 E
Poortview, *Jobg.* 18 E8 26 5 S 27 51 E
Poplar, *Lon.* 4 B4 51 30N 0 0 E
Poppenbüttel, *Hbg.* 7 D8 53 39N 10 4 E
Port Chester, *N.Y.* 23 A6 41 0N 73 40W
Port Chester Harbour, *N.Y.* 23 B7 40 58N 73 38W
Port Jackson, *Syd.* 19 B4 33 51 S 151 14 E
Port Kennedy, *Phil.* 24 A2 40 6N 75 25W
Port Melbourne, *Melb.* 19 F6 37 50 S 144 54 E
Port Newark, *N.Y.* 22 C4 40 41N 74 9W
Port Reading, *N.Y.* 22 D3 40 34N 74 13W
Port Richmond, *N.Y.* 22 D4 40 38N 74 7W
Port Shelter, *H.K.* 12 D6 22 20N 114 17 E
Port Union, *Trto.* 20 D10 43 47N 79 7W
Port Washington, *N.Y.* 23 C6 40 49N 73 42W
Port Washington North, *N.Y.* 23 B6 40 50N 73 41W
Portage Park, *Chic.* 26 B2 41 56N 87 45W
Portela, Aeroporto da, *Lisb.* 8 F8 38 46N 9 7W
Pórtici, *Nápl.* 9 J12 40 48N 14 19 E
Porto Brandão, *Lisb.* 8 F7 38 40N 9 12W
Porto Novo Cr. →, *Lagos* 18 B2 6 25N 7 22 E
Porto Nuevo, *B.A.* 32 B4 34 35 S 58 22W
Portrero, *S.F.* 27 B3 37 46N 122 25W
Posen, *Chic.* 26 D2 41 38N 87 41W
Posíllipo, *Nápl.* 9 J12 40 49N 14 13 E
Posíllipo, C. di, *Nápl.* 9 J12 40 48N 14 12 E
Posolok Lenina, *St-Pet.* 11 C2 59 50N 30 5 E
Potawatomi Woods, *Chic.* 26 A1 42 8N 87 53W
Potomac, *Wash.* 25 D6 38 59N 77 13W
Potomac →, *Wash.* 25 D7 38 58N 77 9W
Potrero Pt., *S.F.* 27 B2 37 45N 122 22W
Potsdam, *Berl.* 7 B1 52 23N 13 3 E
Potter Pt., *Syd.* 19 C4 34 2 S 151 13 E
Potters Bar, *Lon.* 4 A4 51 41N 0 10W
Potzham, *Mün.* 7 G10 48 1N 11 36 E
Pötzleinsdorf, *Wien* 10 G9 48 14N 16 17 E
Povoa de Santo Adriao, *Lisb.* 8 F8 38 47N 9 9W
Powderhorn L., *Chic.* 26 D3 41 38N 87 31W
Powičle, *Wsaw.* 10 E7 52 14N 21 1 E
Powõzki, *Wsaw.* 10 E6 52 15N 20 58 E
Powsin, *Wsaw.* 10 F7 52 8N 21 6 E
Powsinek, *Wsaw.* 10 F7 52 9N 21 6 E
Poyo, *Barc.* 8 D6 41 28N 2 12 E
Pozuelo de Alarcón, *Mdrd.* 8 B2 40 25N 3 48W
Praça Seca, *Rio J.* 31 B1 22 53 S 43 20W
Prado, Museo del, *Mdrd.* 8 B2 40 25N 3 42W
Prado Churubusco, *Méx.* 29 B3 19 20N 99 8W
Praga, *Wsaw.* 10 E7 52 15N 21 2 E
Prague = Praha, *Pra.* 10 B2 50 4N 14 25 E
Praha, *Pra.* 10 B2 50 4N 14 25 E
Praha-Ruzyně Airport, *Pra.* 10 B1 50 6N 14 16 E
Praires, R. des →, *Mtrl.* 20 A4 43 38N 73 36W
Prat de Llobregat, *Barc.* 8 E5 41 19N 2 5 E
Prater, *Wien* 10 G10 48 12N 16 25 E
Pratts Bottom, *Lon.* 4 C5 51 20N 0 7 E
Prawet Buri Rom, Khlong →, *Bangk.* 15 B2 13 43N 100 38 E
Preakness, *N.Y.* 22 B3 40 56N 74 12W
Precotto, *Mil.* 9 D6 45 30N 9 13 E
Prédecelles →, *Paris* 5 D2 48 36N 2 7 E
Pregnana Milanese, *Mil.* 9 D4 45 30N 9 0 E
Prem Prachakan, Khlong →, *Bangk.* 15 B2 13 46N 100 35 E
Prenestino Labicano, *Rome* 9 F10 41 53N 12 33 E
Prenzlauerberg, *Berl.* 7 A3 52 32N 13 24 E
Presidente Derqui, *B.A.* 32 A1 34 29 S 58 50W
Presidente Outra, Rodo, *Rio J.* 31 A1 22 47 S 43 21W
Preston, *Melb.* 19 E6 37 44 S 144 59 E
Pretos Forros, Sa. dos, *Rio J.* 31 B2 22 54 S 43 17W
Préville, *Mtrl.* 20 B5 43 28N 73 29W
Přezletice, *Pra.* 10 B3 50 9N 14 34 E
Primavalle, *Rome* 9 F9 41 55N 12 25 E
Primrose, *Jobg.* 18 F9 26 11 S 28 9 E
Princes B., *N.Y.* 22 D3 40 30N 74 12W
Princess Elizabeth Park, *Sing.* 15 F7 1 21N 103 45 E
Progreso, *Mdrd.* 8 B3 40 27N 3 39W
Progreso Nacional, *Méx.* 29 A3 19 30N 99 9W
Prosek, *Pra.* 10 B3 50 7N 14 30 E
Prospect, *Syd.* 19 A2 33 48 S 150 55 E
Prospect Heights, *Chic.* 26 A1 42 5N 87 55W
Prospect Hill Park, *Bost.* 21 C2 42 23N 71 13W
Prospect Park, *N.Y.* 22 B3 40 55N 74 10W
Prospect Park, *Phil.* 24 B3 39 53N 75 18W
Prospect Pt., *N.Y.* 23 B6 40 52N 73 42W
Prospect Res., *Syd.* 19 A2 33 49 S 150 53 E
Providence, *Balt.* 25 A3 39 25N 76 34W
Providencia, *Stgo* 30 J11 33 25 S 70 36W
Průhonice, *Pra.* 10 C3 50 0N 14 33 E
Pruszków, *Wsaw.* 10 E5 52 10N 20 48 E
Psikhikón, *Ath.* 8 H11 38 1N 23 46 E
Pudong, *Shang.* 14 J12 31 13N 121 30 E
Puduo, *Shang.* 14 J11 31 15N 121 24 E
Pueblo Libre, *Lima* 30 G8 12 5 S 77 4W
Pueblo Nuevo, *Barc.* 8 D6 41 23N 2 11 E
Pueblo Nuevo, *Mdrd.* 8 B3 40 25N 3 37W
Puente Cascallares, *B.A.* 32 C2 34 41 S 58 48W
Puente Hills, *L.A.* 28 C5 33 59N 117 59W
Puffing Billy Station, *Melb.* 19 F9 37 54 S 145 20 E
Puhuangyu, *Beij.* 14 B3 39 50N 116 22 E
Puistola, *Hels.* 3 B5 60 16N 25 2 E
Pukinmäki, *Hels.* 3 B4 60 15N 24 57 E
Pullach, *Mün.* 7 G9 48 3N 11 31 E
Pulo, *Manila* 15 D4 14 34N 121 4 E
Pulo Gadung, *Jak.* 15 J10 6 11 S 106 54 E
Pumphrey, *Balt.* 25 B3 39 13N 76 39W
Punchbowl, *Syd.* 19 B3 33 55 S 151 3 E
Punde, *Bomb.* 16 H8 18 53N 72 57 E
Punggol, *Sing.* 15 F8 1 23N 103 54 E
Punggol, Sungei →, *Sing.* 15 F8 1 24N 103 54 E
Punggol Pt., *Sing.* 15 F8 1 24N 103 54 E
Punta Brava, *La Hab.* 30 B2 23 1N 82 29W
Puolarmetsä, *Hels.* 3 B3 60 11N 24 41 E
Puotila, *Hels.* 3 B5 60 13N 25 6 E
Purchase, *N.Y.* 23 A6 41 2N 73 43W
Purfleet, *Lon.* 4 C6 51 29N 0 14 E
Purkersdorf, *Wien* 10 G9 48 12N 16 11 E
Purley, *Lon.* 4 C4 51 20N 0 6W
Puteaux, *Paris* 5 B3 48 53N 2 14 E
Puth Kalan, *Delhi* 16 A1 28 42N 77 4 E
Putilkovo, *Mos.* 11 D8 55 51N 37 22 E
Putnamville Res., *Bost.* 21 B4 42 36N 70 56W
Putney, *Lon.* 4 C3 51 27N 0 13W
Putty Hill, *Balt.* 25 A3 39 22N 76 30W
Putxet, *Barc.* 8 D5 41 24N 2 8 E
Putzbrunn, *Mün.* 7 G11 48 4N 11 42 E
Pyeongchang, *Sŏul* 12 G7 37 35N 126 57 E
Pyramids, *El Qâ.* 18 D4 29 58N 31 7 E
Pyry, *Wsaw.* 10 F6 52 8N 21 0 E

Q

Qanât el Ismâilîya, *El Qâ.* 18 C5 30 7N 31 17 E
Qasemābād, *Tehr.* 17 C6 35 4N 51 3 E
Qasr-e-Firōzeh, *Tehr.* 17 D6 35 29N 51 31 E
Qianmen, *Beij.* 14 B3 39 51N 116 21 E
Qibao, *Shang.* 14 K11 31 9N 121 20 E
Qingguang, *Tianj.* 14 D5 39 11N 117 2 E
Qinghua Univ., *Beij.* 14 A2 40 0N 116 17 E
Qinghuayuan, *Beij.* 14 B2 39 59N 116 19 E
Qingningsi, *Shang.* 14 J12 31 16N 121 33 E
Qolhak, *Tehr.* 17 C5 35 45N 51 26 E
Quadraro, *Rome* 9 F10 41 51N 12 33 E
Quaid-i-Azam, *Kar.* 17 G10 24 50N 66 59 E
Qual'eh Murgeh Airport, *Tehr.* 17 D5 35 38N 51 22 E
Qualiano, *Nápl.* 9 H11 40 55N 14 9 E
Quannapowitt, L., *Bost.* 21 B3 42 30N 71 4W
Quartiere Zingone, *Mil.* 9 E5 45 25N 9 3 E
Quarto, *Nápl.* 9 H11 40 52N 14 8 E
Quds, *Bagd.* 17 E8 33 23N 44 24 E
Quebrada Baruta →, *Car.* 30 E5 10 29N 66 53W
Quebrada Tácagua →, *Car.* 30 D4 10 36N 67 1W
Quebrada Topo →, *Car.* 30 D4 10 32N 67 0W
Queen Mary Res., *Lon.* 4 C2 51 24N 0 27W
Queens Village, *N.Y.* 23 C6 40 43N 73 44W
Queensbury, *Lon.* 4 B3 51 35N 0 16W
Queenscliffe, *Syd.* 19 A4 33 47 S 151 17 E
Queenstown, *Sing.* 15 G7 1 18N 103 48 E
Quellerina, *Jobg.* 18 E8 26 9 S 27 56 E
Queluz, *Lisb.* 8 F7 38 45N 9 14W
Quezon City, *Manila* 15 D4 14 37N 121 2 E
Quickborn, *Hbg.* 7 C7 53 43N 9 54 E
Quilicura, *Stgo* 30 J10 33 22 S 70 43W
Quilmes, *B.A.* 32 C5 34 43 S 58 15W
Quincy, *Bost.* 21 D3 42 14N 71 0W
Quincy B., *Bost.* 21 D4 42 16N 70 59W
Quincy-sous-Sénart, *Paris* 5 C5 48 40N 2 32 E
Quinta Normal, *Stgo* 30 J10 33 26 S 70 40W
Quinto Romano, *Mil.* 9 E5 45 28N 9 7 E
Quirinale, *Rome* 9 F9 41 53N 12 29 E
Quitaúna, *S. Pau.* 31 E5 23 31 S 46 48W

R

Raasdorf, *Wien* 10 G11 48 14N 16 33 E
Raccoon Cr. →, *Phil.* 24 C3 39 48N 75 21W
Raccoon Str., *S.F.* 27 A2 37 52N 122 26W
Radevormwald, *Ruhr* 6 C6 51 12N 7 22 E
Radlett, *Lon.* 4 A3 51 41N 0 19W
Radlice, *Pra.* 10 B2 50 3N 14 23 E
Radnor, *Phil.* 24 A2 40 2N 75 21W
Radonice, *Pra.* 10 B3 50 8N 14 36 E
Radotin, *Pra.* 10 C2 49 59N 14 21 E
Rælingen, *Oslo* 2 B6 59 53N 11 5 E
Rafael Calzada, *B.A.* 32 C4 34 47 S 58 21W
Rafael Castillo, *B.A.* 32 C3 34 42 S 58 36W
Raffles Park, *Sing.* 15 G7 1 19N 103 48 E
Raghunathpur, *Calc.* 16 D5 22 41N 88 16 E
Rahlstedt, *Hbg.* 7 D8 53 35N 10 7 E
Rahm, *Ruhr* 6 B2 51 21N 6 47 E
Rahnsdorf, *Berl.* 7 B5 52 25N 13 41 E
Rahway, *N.Y.* 22 D3 40 36N 74 17W
Rail Tree Hill, *Bost.* 21 B1 42 32N 71 22W
Rainbow Lakes, *N.Y.* 22 B2 40 53N 74 27W
Rainham, *Lon.* 4 B6 51 31N 0 11 E
Rainier, Mt., *Wash.* 25 D8 38 56N 76 57W
Raj Bhawan, *Calc.* 16 E6 22 33N 88 20 E
Rajakylä, *Hels.* 3 B5 60 15N 25 5 E
Rajapur, *Calc.* 16 E5 22 39N 88 11 E
Rajganj, *Calc.* 16 E5 22 34N 88 14 E
Rajpur, *Delhi* 16 A2 28 41N 77 12 E
Rákos-patak →, *Bud.* 10 K14 47 29N 19 12 E
Rákoscsaba, *Bud.* 10 K14 47 28N 19 17 E
Rákoshegy, *Bud.* 10 K14 47 27N 19 14 E
Rákosker, *Bud.* 10 K14 47 28N 19 14 E
Rákoskert, *Bud.* 10 K14 47 27N 19 18 E
Rákosliget, *Bud.* 10 K14 47 29N 19 16 E
Rákospalota, *Bud.* 10 J13 47 34N 19 7 E
Rákosszentmihály, *Bud.* 10 J13 47 31N 19 8 E
Raków, *Wsaw.* 10 E6 52 11N 20 56 E
Rakowiec, *Wsaw.* 10 E6 52 12N 20 58 E
Ramadān, *Bagd.* 17 F8 33 19N 44 20 E
Ramanathpur, *Calc.* 16 D5 22 41N 88 14 E
Rambler Channel, *H.K.* 12 D5 22 21N 114 6 E
Ramblewood, *Phil.* 24 B5 39 55N 74 56W
Ramenki, *Mos.* 11 E8 55 41N 37 28 E
Ramersdorf, *Mün.* 7 G10 48 6N 11 35 E
Ramnathpur, *Calc.* 16 E5 22 35N 88 18 E
Ramos, *Rio J.* 31 B2 22 50 S 43 14W
Ramos Mejia, *B.A.* 32 B3 34 39 S 58 33W
Rampur, *Delhi* 16 A2 28 44N 77 18 E
Ramsgate, *Syd.* 19 B3 33 58 S 151 8 E
Ramstadjøen, *Oslo* 2 B6 59 53N 11 3 E
Rancho Boyeros, *La Hab.* 30 C2 22 59N 82 22W
Rancho Colorado, Presa de, *Méx.* 29 B2 19 29N 99 16W
Rancocas Cr. →, *Phil.* 24 A5 40 2N 74 58W
Rand Afrikaans Univ., *Jobg.* 18 F9 26 11 S 28 0 E
Rand Airport, *Jobg.* 18 F9 26 14 S 28 8 E
Randallstown, *Balt.* 25 A2 39 21N 76 46W
Randburg, *Jobg.* 18 E8 26 5 S 27 57 E
Randhart, *Jobg.* 18 F9 26 16 S 28 7 E
Randolph, *Bost.* 21 D3 42 10N 71 3W
Randolph Hills, *Wash.* 25 C7 39 3N 77 6W
Randpark, *Jobg.* 18 E8 26 6 S 27 58 E
Randwick, *Syd.* 19 B4 33 54 S 151 14 E
Ranelagh, *B.A.* 32 C5 34 47 S 58 14W
Rannersdorf, *Wien* 10 H10 48 7N 16 27 E
Raparkrif, *Jobg.* 18 E8 26 5 S 27 57 E
Raposo, *Lisb.* 8 F7 38 40N 9 11W
Raritan →, *N.Y.* 22 D2 40 30N 74 27W
Raritan B., *N.Y.* 22 E3 40 29N 74 12W
Rasskazovka, *Mos.* 11 F8 55 38N 37 20 E
Rasta, *Stock.* 3 E8 59 18N 17 37 E
Rastaala, *Hels.* 3 B3 60 15N 24 47 E
Rastila, *Hels.* 3 B5 60 12N 25 7 E
Raszyn, *Wsaw.* 10 F6 52 9N 20 54 E
Rat Burana, *Bangk.* 15 B2 13 40N 100 30 E
Ratanpur, *Calc.* 16 D5 22 49N 88 14 E
Rath, *Ruhr* 6 C2 51 16N 6 49 E
Ratingen, *Ruhr* 6 C3 51 18N 6 52 E
Rato, *Lisb.* 8 F8 38 43N 9 8W
Rauxel, *Ruhr* 6 A5 51 34N 7 18 E
Ravenswood Pt., *S.F.* 27 C4 37 30N 122 8W
Rawamangun, *Jak.* 15 J10 6 11 S 106 52 E
Rayners Lane, *Lon.* 4 B2 51 34N 0 23W
Raynes Park, *Lon.* 4 C3 51 24N 0 12W
Raypur, *Calc.* 16 F6 22 28N 88 22 E
Razdory, *Mos.* 11 E7 55 44N 37 17 E
Razmitelevo, *St-Pet.* 11 B5 59 54N 30 39 E
Razor Hill, *H.K.* 12 D6 22 20N 114 15 E
Reading, *Bost.* 21 B3 42 31N 71 5W
Reading Highlands, *Bost.* 21 B3 42 31N 71 5W
Reáglie, *Tori.* 9 B3 45 3N 7 44 E
Real, Palacio, *Mdrd.* 8 B2 40 25N 3 43W
Real Felipe, Castillo, *Lima* 30 G8 12 4 S 77 9W
Real Fuerta, Château de la, *La Hab.* 30 B2 23 8N 82 20W
Realengo, *Rio J.* 31 B1 22 52 S 43 24W
Réau, *Paris* 5 D5 48 36N 2 37 E
Recklinghausen, *Ruhr* 6 A5 51 37N 7 12 E
Recklinghausen-Süd, *Ruhr* 6 A5 51 34N 7 14 E
Recoleta, *Stgo* 30 J11 33 25 S 70 40W
Reconquista →, *B.A.* 32 B3 34 35 S 58 35W
Red Bank Battle Mon., *Phil.* 24 B3 39 52N 75 11W
Red Fort, *Delhi* 16 B2 28 39N 77 14 E
Red Rock, *S.F.* 27 A2 37 55N 122 25W
Red Square, *Mos.* 11 E9 55 45N 37 37 E
Redbridge, *Lon.* 4 B5 51 34N 0 3 E
Redwood City, *S.F.* 27 D3 37 29N 122 14W
Redwood Cr. →, *S.F.* 27 C3 37 31N 122 11W
Redwood Pt., *S.F.* 27 C3 37 32N 122 11W
Redwood Regional Park, *S.F.* 27 B4 37 48N 122 8W
Reeves Hill, *Bost.* 21 C1 42 20N 71 20W
Refshaleøen, *Købn.* 2 D10 55 41N 12 36 E
Regents Park, *Jobg.* 18 F9 26 14 S 28 3 E
Regents Park, *Lon.* 4 B4 51 31N 0 9W
Regents Park, *Syd.* 19 B3 33 52 S 151 1 E
Regi Lagni →, *Nápl.* 9 H13 40 56N 14 23 E
Regina Margherita, *Tori.* 9 B2 45 4N 7 34 E
Regla, *La Hab.* 30 B3 23 7N 82 19W
Rego Park, *N.Y.* 23 C5 40 43N 73 51W
Reiherstieg, *Hbg.* 7 D7 53 30N 9 58 E
Reinickendorf, *Berl.* 7 A3 52 34N 13 22 E
Reinoldikirche, *Ruhr* 6 A6 51 30N 7 28 E
Reistad, *Oslo* 2 C1 59 46N 10 16 E
Reitbrook, *Hbg.* 7 E8 53 28N 10 8 E
Rekola, *Hels.* 3 B5 60 19N 25 4 E
Rellingen, *Hbg.* 7 D7 53 39N 9 50 E
Rembertów, *Wsaw.* 10 E7 52 15N 21 9 E
Remedios de Escalada, *B.A.* 32 C4 34 43 S 58 24W
Rémola, Laguna del, *Barc.* 8 E5 41 16N 2 4 E
Remscheid, *Ruhr* 6 C5 51 11N 7 11 E
Renca, *Stgo* 30 J10 33 24 S 70 42W
Renca, Cerro, *Stgo* 30 J10 33 23 S 70 40W
Rener, *Ist.* 17 A2 41 1N 28 56 E
Renmin Gongyuan, *Tianj.* 14 E6 39 6N 117 12 E
Rennemoulin, *Paris* 5 B2 48 50N 2 2 E
Rennie's Mill, *H.K.* 12 E6 22 18N 114 15 E
Renzel, *Hbg.* 7 C7 53 43N 9 52 E
Repaupo, *Phil.* 24 C3 39 48N 75 18W
Repaupo Cr. →, *Phil.* 24 C3 39 49N 75 20W
Řeporyje, *Pra.* 10 B1 50 1N 14 18 E
République, Place de la, *Paris* 5 B4 48 52N 2 22 E
Repy, *Pra.* 10 B1 50 4N 14 17 E
Resarö, *Stock.* 3 D13 59 25N 18 20 E
Rescaldna, *Mil.* 9 D4 45 36N 8 57 E
Research, *Melb.* 19 E8 37 42 S 145 10 E
Reseda, *L.A.* 28 A1 34 12N 118 31W
Reservoir, *Melb.* 19 E7 37 42 S 145 1 E
Reservoir Pond, *Bost.* 21 D3 42 10N 71 7W
Residenz, *Mün.* 7 G10 48 8N 11 34 E
Resse, *Ruhr* 6 A4 51 34N 7 6 E
Reston, *Wash.* 25 D6 38 57N 77 20W
Retiro, *B.A.* 32 B4 34 35 S 58 23W
Retiro, *Mdrd.* 8 B2 40 24N 3 40W
Reutov, *Mos.* 11 E11 55 45N 37 50 E
Réveillon →, *Paris* 5 C5 48 42N 2 30 E
Revere, *Bost.* 21 C3 42 25N 71 0W
Revesby, *Syd.* 19 B3 33 57 S 151 0 E
Revolucion, Plaza de la, *La Hab.* 30 B2 23 7N 82 23W
Rexdale, *Trto.* 20 D7 43 43N 79 35W
Reynolds Channel, *N.Y.* 23 D6 40 35N 73 41W
Reynosa Tamaulipas, *Méx.* 29 A2 19 30N 99 10W
Rheem Valley, *S.F.* 27 A4 37 50N 122 8W
Rhein-Herne Kanal, *Ruhr* 6 B3 51 29N 6 59 E
Rheinberg, *Ruhr* 6 A1 51 32N 6 37 E
Rheinhausen, *Ruhr* 6 B2 51 24N 6 43 E
Rheinkamp, *Ruhr* 6 B1 51 29N 6 36 E
Rho, *Mil.* 9 D5 45 31N 9 2 E
Rhodes, *Syd.* 19 A3 33 49 S 151 6 E
Rhodesfield, *Jobg.* 18 E10 26 6 S 28 14 E
Rhodon, *Paris* 5 C2 48 42N 2 3 E
Rhodon →, *Paris* 5 C2 48 42N 2 4 E
Rhu, Tg., *Sing.* 15 G8 1 17N 103 51 E
Ribeirão Pires, *S. Pau.* 31 F7 23 42 S 46 23W
Říčanský →, *Pra.* 10 B3 50 5N 14 36 E
Říčany, *Pra.* 10 C3 49 59N 14 39 E
Ricarda, Laguna de la, *Barc.* 8 E5 41 17N 2 6 E
Richardson B., *S.F.* 27 A2 37 52N 122 29W
Richmond, *Lon.* 4 C3 51 27N 0 17W
Richmond, *Melb.* 19 E7 37 48 S 145 0 E
Richmond, *S.F.* 27 B2 37 46N 122 27W
Richmond, *S.F.* 27 A2 37 56N 122 21W
Richmond →, *N.Y.* 22 D3 40 34N 74 11W
Richmond, Pt., *S.F.* 27 A2 37 54N 122 23W
Richmond Hill, *N.Y.* 23 C5 40 41N 73 51W
Richmond Hill, *Trto.* 20 C8 43 51N 79 24W
Richmond Inner Harbour, *S.F.* 27 A2 37 54N 122 20W
Richmond Park, *Lon.* 4 C3 51 26N 0 16W
Richmond Valley, *N.Y.* 22 D3 40 31N 74 13W
Richvale, *Trto.* 20 C8 43 51N 79 26W
Rickers I., *N.Y.* 23 C5 40 47N 73 53W
Rickmansworth, *Lon.* 4 B2 51 38N 0 28W
Riddel Cr. →, *Melb.* 19 F8 37 52 S 145 13 E
Riderwood, *Balt.* 25 A3 39 24N 76 37W
Ridgefield, *N.Y.* 22 C4 40 49N 74 0W
Ridgefield Park, *N.Y.* 22 B4 40 52N 74 1W
Ridgewood, *N.Y.* 23 C5 40 42N 73 53W
Ridley Cr. →, *Phil.* 24 B2 39 51N 75 20W
Ridley Creek State Park, *Phil.* 24 B2 39 57N 75 26W
Ridley Park, *Phil.* 24 B3 39 52N 75 19W
Riedmoos, *Mün.* 7 F10 48 16N 11 32 E
Riem, *Mün.* 7 G11 48 8N 11 41 E
Riemke, *Ruhr* 6 A5 51 30N 7 12 E
Rimac, *Lima* 30 G8 12 2 S 77 2W
Rimau, Tg., *Sing.* 15 G7 1 15N 103 48 E
Ringwood, *Melb.* 19 E8 37 48 S 145 4 E
Rinkeby, *Stock.* 3 D10 59 23N 17 55 E
Rio Comprido, *Rio J.* 31 B2 22 55 S 43 12W
Rio de Janeiro, *Rio J.* 31 B2 22 54 S 43 12W
Rio de Mouro, *Lisb.* 8 F7 38 46N 9 15W
Rio Hondo →, *L.A.* 28 B4 34 2N 118 15W
Rio Pequeno, *S. Pau.* 31 E5 23 34 S 46 44W
Rione Trieste, *Nápl.* 9 H13 40 52N 14 27 E
Ripley, *Lon.* 4 D2 51 17N 0 29W
Rippling Ridge, *Balt.* 25 B3 39 11N 76 37W
Ris, *Oslo* 2 B4 59 56N 10 41 E
Ris-Orangis, *Paris* 5 D4 48 38N 2 24 E
Risby, *Købn.* 2 D8 55 41N 12 19 E
Rishra, *Calc.* 16 D6 22 42N 88 20 E
Ritan Gongyuan, *Beij.* 14 B3 39 53N 116 24 E
Ritchie, *Wash.* 25 D8 38 52N 76 51W
Rithala, *Delhi* 16 A1 28 43N 77 6 E
Ritorp, *Stock.* 3 E8 59 12N 17 38 E
Rivalta di Torino, *Tori.* 9 B1 45 2N 7 31 E
Rivas de Jarama, *Mdrd.* 8 B3 40 22N 3 31W
Rivas-Vaciamadrio, *Mdrd.* 8 C3 40 19N 3 30W
Rivasacco, *Tori.* 9 A1 45 10N 7 29 E
Rive Sud, Canal de la, *Mtrl.* 20 B4 43 24N 73 31W
River Edge, *N.Y.* 22 B4 40 56N 74 1W
River Forest, *Chic.* 26 B2 41 53N 87 49W
River Grove, *Chic.* 26 B1 41 55N 87 50W
River Pines, *Bost.* 21 B2 42 33N 71 17W
River Vale, *N.Y.* 22 B4 40 59N 74 1W
Riverdale, *Chic.* 26 D3 41 38N 87 37W
Riverdale, *N.Y.* 22 B3 40 59N 74 17W
Riverdale, *Trto.* 20 E8 43 39N 79 21W
Riverdale, *Wash.* 25 D8 38 57N 76 54W
Riverdale Park, *Trto.* 20 D8 43 40N 79 21W
Riverhead, *Lon.* 4 D6 51 16N 0 10 E
Riverlea, *Jobg.* 18 F8 26 12 S 27 58 E
Riverside, *Bost.* 21 B2 42 32N 71 18W
Riverside, *Chic.* 26 C2 41 49N 87 49W
Riverside, *N.Y.* 23 B5 40 54N 73 54W
Riverside, *N.Y.* 23 A7 41 1N 73 34W
Riverside, *Phil.* 24 A5 40 2N 74 57W
Riverton, *Phil.* 24 A4 40 0N 75 0W
Riverwood, *Syd.* 19 B3 33 57 S 151 3 E
Rivière-des-Praires, *Mtrl.* 20 A4 43 38N 73 34W
Rivodora, *Tori.* 9 B3 45 5N 7 47 E
Rivoli, *Tori.* 9 B1 45 4N 7 30 E
Riyad, *Bagd.* 17 F8 33 18N 44 27 E
Rizal, *Manila* 15 D4 14 33N 121 0 E
Rizal Park, *Manila* 15 D3 14 35N 120 58 E
Rizel Stadium, *Manila* 15 D3 14 34N 120 59 E
Røa, *Oslo* 2 B3 59 57N 10 39 E
Robassomero, *Tori.* 9 A2 45 11N 7 34 E
Robbins, *Chic.* 26 D2 41 38N 87 42W
Robert E. Lee Memorial Park, *Balt.* 25 A3 39 23N 76 40 E
Robertsdale, *Chic.* 26 C3 41 40N 87 30W
Robertsham, *Jobg.* 18 F9 26 15 S 28 1 E
Robin Hills, *Jobg.* 18 E8 26 6 S 27 58 E
Rocha Miranda, *Rio J.* 31 B1 22 51 S 43 20W
Rochar →, *Sing.* 15 G8 1 18N 103 52 E
Rochelle Park, *N.Y.* 22 B4 40 54N 74 4W
Rock Cr. →, *Wash.* 25 D7 38 54N 77 3W
Rock Creek Park, *Wash.* 25 D7 38 56N 77 2W
Rockaway, *N.Y.* 22 D5 40 32N 73 56W
Rockaway Beach, *S.F.* 27 C2 37 36N 122 29W
Rockaway Islet, *N.Y.* 23 D5 40 34N 73 53W
Rockaway Neck, *N.Y.* 22 B2 40 51N 74 21W
Rockaway Point, *N.Y.* 23 D5 40 33N 73 54W
Rockburn Branch →, *Balt.* 25 B2 39 13N 76 43W
Rockdale, *Balt.* 25 A2 39 21N 76 46W
Rockdale, *Syd.* 19 B3 33 57 S 151 8 E
Rockland, *Phil.* 24 C1 39 47N 75 34W
Rocklege, *Phil.* 24 A4 40 4N 75 5W
Rockleigh, *N.Y.* 22 A5 41 0N 73 55W
Rockville, *Wash.* 25 C6 39 4N 77 10W
Rockville Centre, *N.Y.* 23 D7 40 39N 73 38W
Rocky Hill, *Phil.* 24 B1 39 58N 75 32W
Rocky Ridge, *S.F.* 27 B4 37 47N 122 2W
Rocky Run →, *Wash.* 25 D6 38 58N 77 14W
Rodaon, *Wien* 10 H9 48 8N 16 16 E
Rodeo Cove, *S.F.* 27 B1 37 49N 122 32W
Rodgers Forge, *Balt.* 25 A3 39 22N 76 37W
Roding →, *Lon.* 4 B5 51 30N 0 5 E
Rodość, *Wsaw.* 10 E8 52 11N 21 11 E
Rødovre, *Købn.* 2 D9 55 40N 12 26 E
Rodrigo de Freitas, L., *Rio J.* 31 B2 22 58 S 43 12W
Rodstensfjärden, *Stock.* 3 E9 59 16N 17 48 E
Roehampton, *Lon.* 4 C3 51 27N 0 15W
Rogers Park, *Chic.* 26 A2 42 0N 87 40W
Rohdenhaus, *Ruhr* 6 C4 51 18N 7 0 E
Röhlinghausen, *Ruhr* 6 A4 51 30N 7 9 E
Roihuvuori, *Hels.* 3 B5 60 11N 25 2 E
Roissy, *Paris* 5 C5 48 47N 2 39 E
Roissy-en-France, *Paris* 5 A5 49 0N 2 30 E
Rokkō Sanchi, *Ōsaka* 12 B2 34 44N 135 13 E
Rokko-Zan, *Ōsaka* 12 B2 34 46N 135 16 E
Rokytka →, *Pra.* 10 B3 50 6N 14 27 E
Roland Lake, *Balt.* 25 A3 39 23N 76 38W
Roland Park, *Balt.* 25 A3 39 20N 76 39W
Roma, *Rome* 9 F9 41 54N 12 28 E
Római-Fürdö, *Bud.* 10 J13 47 34N 19 4 E
Romainville, *Paris* 5 B4 48 52N 2 26 E
Romani, *Nápl.* 9 H13 40 52N 14 22 E
Romano Banco, *Mil.* 9 E5 45 25N 9 6 E
Romashkovo, *Mos.* 11 E7 55 43N 37 19 E
Rome = Roma, *Rome* 9 F9 41 54N 12 28 E
Romford, *Lon.* 4 B6 51 34N 0 11 E
Roncáglia, *Tori.* 9 B1 45 2N 7 29 E
Rönninge, *Stock.* 3 E9 59 12N 17 45 E
Ronsdorf, *Ruhr* 6 C5 51 13N 7 11 E
Ronskensiedig, *Ruhr* 6 A2 51 36N 6 41 E
Rontgental, *Berl.* 7 A4 52 38N 13 31 E
Roodekop, *Jobg.* 18 F10 26 17 S 28 11 E
Roodepoort, *Jobg.* 18 E8 26 9 S 27 53 E
Roodepoort-Wes, *Jobg.* 18 E8 26 8 S 27 51 E
Roosevelt, *N.Y.* 23 C7 40 40N 73 35W
Rooty Hill, *Syd.* 19 A2 33 46 S 150 50 E
Roppongi, *Tōkyō* 13 C3 35 39N 139 44 E
Rosairinho, *Lisb.* 8 F8 38 40N 9 0W
Rosanna, *Melb.* 19 E7 37 44 S 145 4 E
Rosario, *La Hab.* 30 B2 23 3N 82 21W
Rosario, *Manila* 15 D4 14 35N 121 4 E
Rose B., *Syd.* 19 B4 33 51 S 151 16 E
Rose Hill, *Wash.* 25 E7 38 47N 77 6W
Rose Tree, *Phil.* 24 B2 39 56N 75 23W
Rosebank, *N.Y.* 22 D4 40 36N 74 4W
Rosebery, *Syd.* 19 B4 33 55 S 151 12 E
Rosedal La Candelaria, *Méx.* 29 B3 19 20N 99 10W
Rosedale, *Balt.* 25 B3 39 19N 76 31W
Rosedale, *N.Y.* 23 D6 40 39N 73 43W
Roseiras, *S. Pau.* 31 E7 23 33 S 46 23W
Roseland, *Chic.* 26 C3 41 42N 87 37W
Roseland, *N.Y.* 22 C3 40 49N 74 17W
Roselle, *N.Y.* 22 D3 40 39N 74 15W
Roselle Park, *N.Y.* 22 D3 40 39N 74 16W
Rosemead, *L.A.* 28 B4 34 4N 118 4W
Rosemere, *Mtrl.* 20 A2 43 34N 73 50W
Rosemont, *Chic.* 26 B1 41 59N 87 52W
Rosemont, *Phil.* 24 A3 40 1N 75 19W
Rosenborg Have, *Købn.* 2 D10 55 41N 12 33 E
Rosengarten, *Hbg.* 7 D6 53 31N 9 49 E
Rosenthal, *Berl.* 7 A3 52 35N 13 22 E
Rosettenville, *Jobg.* 18 F9 26 15 S 28 3 E
Rosherville Dam, *Jobg.* 18 F9 26 13 S 28 6 E
Rósio, *Mil.* 9 E4 45 25N 8 57 E
Rösjön, *Stock.* 3 D11 59 26N 18 0 E
Roskilde, *Købn.* 2 E7 55 38N 12 5 E
Roskilde Fjord, *Købn.* 2 D7 55 45N 12 4 E
Roslags-Näsby, *Stock.* 3 D11 59 25N 18 2 E
Roslindale, *Bost.* 21 D3 42 17N 71 7W
Roslyn, *N.Y.* 23 C7 40 47N 73 38W
Roslyn, *Phil.* 24 A4 40 7N 75 8W
Roslyn Estates, *N.Y.* 23 C6 40 47N 73 40W
Roslyn Harbour, *N.Y.* 23 C7 40 48N 73 38W
Rosne →, *Paris* 5 B4 48 58N 2 25 E
Rosny-sous-Bois, *Paris* 5 B5 48 52N 2 30 E
Ross, *S.F.* 27 A1 37 57N 122 33W
Rosslyn, *Wash.* 25 D7 38 53N 77 4W
Rossville, *Balt.* 25 A4 39 20N 76 28W
Rossville, *N.Y.* 22 D3 40 32N 74 12W
Rosta, *Tori.* 9 B1 45 4N 7 27 E
Rotbach →, *Ruhr* 6 A2 51 34N 6 41 E
Rothenburgsort, *Hbg.* 7 D8 53 32N 10 2 E
Rotherbaum, *Hbg.* 7 D7 53 33N 9 58 E
Rotherhithe, *Lon.* 4 C4 51 29N 0 2W
Rothneusiedl, *Wien* 10 H10 48 8N 16 23 E
Rothschmaige, *Mün.* 7 F9 48 14N 11 27 E
Rouge →, *Trto.* 20 D9 43 47N 79 12W
Rouge Hill, *Trto.* 20 D10 43 48N 79 6W
Round I., *H.K.* 12 E6 22 13N 114 11 E
Roundshaw, *Lon.* 4 C4 51 20N 0 7W
Roussigny, *Paris* 5 D2 48 38N 2 6 E
Rowland, *L.A.* 28 B5 34 0N 117 55W
Rowley, *Bost.* 21 A4 42 43N 70 52W
Rowville, *Melb.* 19 F8 37 55 S 145 14 E
Roxboro, *Mtrl.* 20 A3 43 30N 73 48W
Roxborough, *Phil.* 24 A3 40 1N 75 13W
Roxbury, *Bost.* 21 D3 42 19N 71 5W
Roxbury, *N.Y.* 23 D5 40 33N 73 53W
Roxeth, *Lon.* 4 B2 51 33N 0 20W
Royal Observatory, *H.K.* 12 E6 22 18N 114 10 E
Royal Park, *Melb.* 19 E6 37 46 S 144 57 E
Röylä, *Hels.* 3 B3 60 18N 24 42 E
Royston Park, *Lon.* 4 B2 51 36N 0 22W
Rozas, Portilleros de las, *Mdrd.* 8 B2 40 29N 3 49W
Roztoky, *Pra.* 10 B2 50 9N 14 23 E
Rubbianetta, *Tori.* 9 B2 45 9N 7 34 E
Rubi →, *Barc.* 8 D5 41 26N 2 0 E
Rubio Woods, *Chic.* 26 D2 41 38N 87 45W
Rublovo, *Mos.* 11 E8 55 47N 37 21 E
Ruchyi, *St-Pet.* 11 A4 60 0N 30 25 E
Rud, *Oslo* 2 B6 59 56N 11 0 E
Rüdinghausen, *Ruhr* 6 B6 51 26N 7 22 E
Rudnevka →, *Mos.* 11 E11 55 43N 37 56 E
Rudolfsheim, *Wien* 10 G10 48 12N 16 20 E
Rudolfshöhe, *Berl.* 7 A5 52 37N 13 44 E
Rudow, *Berl.* 7 B3 52 24N 13 29 E
Rueil-Malmaison, *Paris* 5 B3 48 52N 2 11 E
Ruffys Cr. →, *Melb.* 19 E7 37 45 S 145 7 E
Ruggeberg, *Ruhr* 6 C6 51 16N 7 23 E
Ruhlsdorf, *Berl.* 7 B2 52 22N 13 15 E
Ruhr →, *Ruhr* 6 B3 51 27N 6 56 E
Ruhrort, *Ruhr* 6 B2 51 27N 6 44 E
Ruislip, *Lon.* 4 B2 51 34N 0 24W
Rumelihisari, *Ist.* 17 A3 41 4N 29 2 E
Rumeln, *Ruhr* 6 B1 51 24N 6 39 E
Rumyantsevo, *Mos.* 11 F8 55 38N 37 25 E
Rungis, *Paris* 5 C4 48 44N 2 20 E
Runnemede, *Phil.* 24 B4 39 50N 75 4W
Ruotsinkylä, *Hels.* 3 A4 60 21N 24 57 E
Rusāfa, *Bagd.* 17 E8 33 21N 44 23 E
Rush Green, *Lon.* 4 B6 51 33N 0 10 E
Russa, *Calc.* 16 F6 22 29N 88 21 E
Russell Lea, *Syd.* 19 B4 33 52 S 151 10 E
Rustad, *Oslo* 2 B2 59 56N 10 24 E
Rustenfeld, *Wien* 10 H10 48 7N 16 23 E
Rusville, *Jobg.* 18 E10 26 9 S 28 18 E
Rutherford, *N.Y.* 22 C4 40 49N 74 6W
Rüttenscheid, *Ruhr* 6 B3 51 25N 6 58 E
Ruxton, *Balt.* 25 A3 39 23N 76 38W
Ruzyně, *Pra.* 10 B1 50 5N 14 17 E
Rybatskaya, *St-Pet.* 11 B4 59 59N 30 29 E
Rybatskoye, *St-Pet.* 11 B4 59 50N 30 29 E
Rydalmere, *Syd.* 19 A3 33 48 S 151 2 E
Rydboholm, *Stock.* 3 D12 59 26N 18 12 E
Ryde, *Syd.* 19 A3 33 48 S 151 6 E
Rye, *N.Y.* 23 B6 40 58N 73 40W
Rynfield, *Jobg.* 18 E10 26 9 S 28 19 E
Ryogoku, *Tōkyō* 13 B3 35 40N 139 48 E
Rysäkari, *Hels.* 3 C4 60 6N 24 50 E
Rzhevka, *St-Pet.* 11 B5 59 59N 30 31 E

Serangoon Garden 45

S

Saadōn, *Bagd.* 17 F8 33 19N 44 25 E
Saarn, *Ruhr* 6 B3 51 24N 6 51 E
Saavedra, *B.A.* 32 B4 34 33 S 58 29W
Saboli, *Delhi* 16 A2 28 42N 77 18 E
Sabugo, *Lisb.* 8 F7 38 49N 9 17W
Saburovo, *Mos.* 11 D7 55 53N 37 15 E
Säbysjön, *Stock.* 3 D10 59 26N 17 52 E
Sabzi Mandi, *Delhi* 16 A2 28 40N 77 12 E
Sacavém, *Lisb.* 8 F8 38 47N 9 5W
Saclay, *Paris* 5 C3 48 43N 2 10 E
Saclay, Étang de, *Paris* 5 C2 48 44N 2 9 E
Sacoma, *S. Pau.* 31 E6 23 36 S 46 35W
Sacré-Coeur, *Paris* 5 B4 48 53N 2 20 E
Sacrow, *Berl.* 7 B1 52 25N 13 6 E
Sacrower See, *Berl.* 7 B1 52 26N 13 6 E
Sadang, *Sŏul* 12 H7 37 29N 126 58 E
Sadar Bazar, *Delhi* 16 B2 28 39N 77 11 E
Saddām City, *Bagd.* 17 E8 33 23N 44 27 E
Saddle Brook, *N.Y.* 22 B4 40 53N 74 5W
Saddle River, *N.Y.* 22 A4 41 1N 74 6W
Saddle Rock, *N.Y.* 23 C6 40 47N 73 45W
Sadr, *Kar.* 17 G11 24 51N 67 2 E
Sadyba, *Wsaw.* 10 E7 52 11N 21 3 E
Saedo, *Tōkyō* 13 C2 35 30N 139 33 E
Saensaep, Khlong →, *Bangk.* 15 B2 13 44N 100 32 E
Sáenz Pena, *B.A.* 32 B3 34 37 S 58 32W
Safdar Jang Airport, *Delhi* 16 B2 28 35N 77 12 E
Safdar Jangs Tomb, *Delhi* 16 B2 28 35N 77 12 E
Safraköy, *Ist.* 17 A1 41 0N 28 48 E
Saft el Laban, *El Qâ.* 18 C5 30 1N 31 10 E
Sag Bridge, *Chic.* 26 C1 41 41N 87 55W
Sagamore Neck, *N.Y.* 23 B8 40 53N 73 29W
Saganashkee Slough, *Chic.* 26 C1 41 41N 87 53W
Sagene, *Oslo* 2 B4 59 55N 10 46 E
Sagrada Família, Temple de, *Barc.* 8 D6 41 24N 2 10 E
Sahapur, *Calc.* 16 E5 22 31N 88 11 E
Sahibabad, *Delhi* 16 A1 28 45N 77 4 E
Sai Kung, *H.K.* 12 D6 22 22N 114 16 E
Sai Wan Ho, *H.K.* 12 E6 22 17N 114 12 E
Sai Ying Pun, *H.K.* 12 E5 22 17N 114 8 E
Saido, *Tōkyō* 13 A2 35 52N 139 39 E
Sailmouille →, *Paris* 5 D3 48 37N 2 17 E
St. Albans, *N.Y.* 23 C6 40 42N 73 44W
St. Andrä, *Wien* 10 G9 48 19N 16 12 E
St. Andrews, *Jobg.* 18 E9 26 9 S 28 7 E
St. Aubin, *Paris* 5 C2 48 44N 2 8 E
St. Augustin, *Mtrl.* 20 A2 43 37N 73 58W
St. Basil's Cathedral, *Mos.* 11 E9 55 45N 37 38 E
St.-Benoit, *Paris* 5 C1 48 40N 1 54 E
St.-Brice-sous-Forêt, *Paris* 5 A4 49 0N 2 21 E
St.-Cloud, *Paris* 5 B3 48 50N 2 12 E
St.-Cyr-l'École, *Paris* 5 B2 48 47N 2 4 E
St.-Cyr-l'École, Aérodrome de, *Paris* 5 C2 48 48N 2 4 E
St. Davids, *Phil.* 24 A2 40 2N 75 23W
St.-Denis, *Paris* 5 B4 48 56N 2 20 E
St. Eustache, *Mtrl.* 20 A2 43 33N 73 54W
St.-Forget, *Paris* 5 C2 48 42N 2 0 E
St. Georg, *Hbg.* 7 D8 53 33N 10 1 E
St.-Germain, Forêt de, *Paris* 5 B2 48 57N 2 5 E
St. Germain-en-Laye, *Paris* 5 B2 48 53N 2 4 E
St.-Germain-lès-Corbeil, *Paris* 5 D4 48 37N 2 29 E
St.-Gratien, *Paris* 5 B3 48 58N 2 17 E
St. Helier, *Lon.* 4 C3 51 23N 0 11W
St.-Hubert, *Mtrl.* 20 B5 43 29N 73 25W
St. Isaac's Cathedral, *St-Pet.* 11 B3 59 55N 30 19 E
St. Jacques →, *Mtrl.* 20 B5 43 26N 73 29W
St.-Jean-de-Beauregard, *Paris* 5 D3 48 39N 2 10 E
St.-Jean-de-dieu, *Mtrl.* 20 A4 43 34N 73 31W
St. Joseph-du-Lac, *Mtrl.* 20 A1 43 32N 74 0W
St. Katherine's Dock, *Lon.* 4 B4 51 30N 0 5W
St. Kilda, *Melb.* 19 F6 37 51 S 144 58 E
St. Lambert, *Mtrl.* 20 A5 43 30N 73 29W
St.-Lambert, *Paris* 5 C2 48 43N 2 1 E
St.-Laurent, *Mtrl.* 20 A3 43 30N 73 43W
St. Lawrence, *Mtrl.* 20 A5 43 26N 73 29W
St.-Lazare, Gare, *Paris* 5 B3 48 52N 2 19 E
St.-Léonard, *Mtrl.* 20 A4 43 35N 73 34W
St. Leonards, *Syd.* 19 B4 33 50 S 151 12 E
St. Leu-la-Forêt, *Paris* 5 A3 49 1N 2 14 E
St.-Louis, L., *Mtrl.* 20 B3 43 24N 73 48W
St. Magelungen, *Stock.* 3 E11 59 13N 18 4 E
St.-Mandé, *Paris* 5 B4 48 50N 2 24 E
St.-Mard, *Paris* 5 A6 49 2N 2 41 E
St.-Martin, *Mtrl.* 20 A3 43 33N 73 45W
St.-Martin, Bois, *Paris* 5 C5 48 48N 2 35 E
St. Mary Cray, *Lon.* 4 C5 51 23N 0 7 E
St.-Maur-des-Fossés, *Paris* 5 C4 48 48N 2 29 E
St.-Maurice, *Paris* 5 C4 48 49N 2 24 E
St.-Mesmes, *Paris* 5 B6 48 59N 2 41 E
St. Michaeliskirche, *Hbg.* 7 D7 53 32N 9 59 E
St. Michael's, *Sing.* 15 G8 1 19N 103 51 E
St.-Michel, *Mtrl.* 20 A4 43 34N 73 37W
St.-Michel-sur-Orge, *Paris* 5 D3 48 38N 2 18 E
St. Nikolaus-Kirken, *Pra.* 10 B2 50 5N 14 23 E
St. Nom-la-Bretèche, *Paris* 5 B2 48 51N 2 1 E
St.-Ouen, *Paris* 5 B4 48 56N 2 20 E
St. Ouen-l'Aumône, *Paris* 5 A2 49 2N 2 6 E
St. Pauli, *Hbg.* 7 D7 53 33N 9 57 E
St. Pauls Cathedral, *Lon.* 4 B4 51 30N 0 5W
St. Paul's Cray, *Lon.* 4 C5 51 23N 0 6 E
St. Petersburg, *St-Pet.* 11 B3 59 55N 30 15 E
St.-Pierre, *Mtrl.* 20 B4 43 27N 73 38W
St. Prix, *Paris* 5 A3 49 0N 2 15 E
St.-Quentin, Étang de, *Paris* 5 C2 48 47N 2 0 E
St. Quentin-en-Yvelines, *Paris* 5 C1 48 46N 1 57 E
St.-Rémy-lès-Chevreuse, *Paris* 5 C2 48 42N 2 4 E
St.-Thibault-des-Vignes, *Paris* 5 B6 48 52N 2 41 E
St. Veit, *Wien* 10 G9 48 11N 16 16 E
St.-Vincent-de-Paul, *Mtrl.* 20 A4 43 36N 73 39W
Ste.-Anne-de-Bellevue, *Mtrl.* 20 B2 43 24N 73 55W
Ste.-Catherine, *Mtrl.* 20 B4 43 24N 73 34W
Ste.-Dorothée, *Mtrl.* 20 A3 43 31N 73 48W
Ste.-Gemme, *Paris* 5 B1 48 52N 1 59 E
Ste.-Geneviève, *Mtrl.* 20 B2 43 28N 73 51W
Ste.-Geneviève-des-Bois, *Paris* 5 D3 48 38N 2 19 E
Ste.-Hélène, Î., *Mtrl.* 20 A4 43 31N 73 32W
Ste. Marthe-sur-le-Lac, *Mtrl.* 20 A2 43 31N 73 56W
Ste.-Rose, *Mtrl.* 20 A3 43 37N 73 46W
Ste. Thérèse, *Mtrl.* 20 A3 43 38N 73 49W
Ste. Thérèse-Ouest, *Mtrl.* 20 A2 43 36N 73 50W
Saiwai, *Tōkyō* 13 C3 35 32N 139 41 E
Sakai, *Ōsaka* 12 C3 34 34N 135 27 E
Sakai →, *Tōkyō* 13 D1 35 27N 139 29 E
Sakai Harbour, *Ōsaka* 12 C3 34 36N 135 26 E
Sakanoshita, *Tōkyō* 13 B2 35 48N 139 30 E
Sakra, P., *Sing.* 15 G7 1 15N 103 41 E
Sakuragi, *Tōkyō* 13 D2 35 28N 139 38 E
Salam, *Bagd.* 17 E8 33 20N 44 20 E
Salaryevo, *Mos.* 11 F8 55 37N 37 25 E
Salem, *Bost.* 21 B4 42 30N 70 54W
Salem, *Stock.* 3 E9 59 13N 17 46 E
Salem Harbor, *Bost.* 21 B4 42 30N 70 52W
Salem Maritime Nat. Hist. Site, *Bost.* 21 B4 42 31N 70 52W
Salemstaden, *Stock.* 3 E9 59 13N 17 46 E
Salkhia, *Calc.* 16 E6 22 36N 88 21 E
Salmannsdorf, *Wien* 10 G9 48 14N 16 14 E
Salmdorf, *Mün.* 7 G11 48 7N 11 43 E
Salmedina, *Mdrd.* 8 C3 40 18N 3 35W
Salomea, *Wsaw.* 10 E6 52 11N 20 55 E
Salsette I., *Bomb.* 16 G8 19 2N 72 53 E
Salt Cr. →, *Chic.* 26 C1 41 51N 87 54W
Salt Cr. →, *Melb.* 19 E7 37 45 S 145 4 E
Salt Water L., *Calc.* 16 E6 22 33N 88 26 E
Saltholm, *Købn.* 2 E11 55 38N 12 46 E
Saltsjö-Duvnäs, *Stock.* 3 E12 59 18N 18 12 E
Saltsjöbaden, *Stock.* 3 E12 59 16N 18 18 E
Saltykovka, *Mos.* 11 E11 55 45N 37 54 E
Salvatorkirche, *Ruhr* 6 B2 51 26N 6 45 E
Sam Sen, Khlong →, *Bangk.* 15 B2 13 45N 100 33 E
Samatya, *Ist.* 17 B2 40 59N 28 55 E
Samoueo, *Lisb.* 8 F8 38 43N 8 59W
Sampaloc, *Manila* 15 D3 14 36N 120 59 E
Samphanthawong, *Bangk.* 15 B2 13 44N 100 31 E
Samrong, *Bangk.* 15 C2 13 39N 100 35 E
Samseon, *Sŏul* 12 G8 37 34N 127 0 E
San Agustin, *Lima* 30 G8 12 1 S 77 9W
San Agustin Atlapulco, *Méx.* 29 B4 19 23N 89 57 E
San Andreas Fault, *S.F.* 27 D3 37 27N 122 18W
San Andreas L., *S.F.* 27 C2 37 35N 122 25W
San Andrés, *B.A.* 32 B3 34 34 S 58 33W
San Andrés, *Barc.* 8 D6 41 26N 2 11 E
San Andrés Ahuayucan, *Méx.* 29 C3 19 13N 99 7W
San Andrés Atenco, *Méx.* 29 A2 19 32N 99 13W
San Andrés Totoltepec, *Méx.* 29 C2 19 15N 99 10W
San Andrián de Besós, *Barc.* 8 D6 41 25N 2 13 E
San Angel, *Méx.* 29 B2 19 20N 99 11W
San Antonia, *Manila* 15 E3 14 29N 120 53 E
San Antonio de Padua, *B.A.* 32 C2 34 40 S 58 42W
San Augustin Ohtenco, *Méx.* 29 C3 19 12N 99 0W
San Bartolo Ameyalco, *Méx.* 29 C2 19 19N 99 16W
San Bartolomé Coatepec, *Méx.* 29 B2 19 23N 99 18W
San Basilio, *Rome* 9 F10 41 56N 12 35 E
San Bóvio, *Mil.* 9 E6 45 27N 9 18 E
San Bruno, *S.F.* 27 C2 37 36N 122 24W
San Bruno, Pt., *S.F.* 27 C2 37 39N 122 23W
San Bruno Mt., *S.F.* 27 B2 37 41N 122 26W
San Carlos, *S.F.* 27 C3 37 30N 122 16W
San Carlos de la Cabana, Forteresse, *La Hab.* 30 B2 23 8N 82 20W
San Clemente del Llobregat, *Barc.* 8 E4 41 19N 1 59 E
San Cristobal, *Mdrd.* 8 B3 40 25N 3 35W
San Cristobal, Cerro, *Stgo* 30 J11 33 25 S 70 38W
San Cristoforo, *Mil.* 9 E5 45 26N 9 9 E
San Donato Milanese, *Mil.* 9 E6 45 24N 9 16 E
San Felice, *Tori.* 9 B3 45 1N 7 46 E
San Feliu de Llobregat, *Barc.* 8 D5 41 22N 2 2 E
San Fernando, *B.A.* 32 A3 34 26 S 58 32W
San Fernando, *L.A.* 28 A2 34 17N 118 26W
San Fernando Airport, *L.A.* 28 A2 34 17N 118 25W
San Fernando de Henares, *Mdrd.* 8 B3 40 25N 3 31W
San Fernando Valley, *L.A.* 28 A1 34 12N 118 31W
San Francisco, *S.F.* 27 B2 37 46N 122 23W
San Francisco, Univ. of, *S.F.* 27 B2 37 47N 122 27W
San Francisco B., *S.F.* 27 C3 37 39N 122 14W
San Francisco Chimalpa, *Méx.* 29 B1 19 26N 99 20W
San Francisco Culhuacán, *Méx.* 29 C3 19 19N 99 8W
San Francisco de Paula, *La Hab.* 30 B3 23 3N 82 17W
San Francisco Int. Airport, *S.F.* 27 C2 37 37N 122 22W
San Francisco Solano, *B.A.* 32 C5 34 46 S 58 19W
San Francisco State Univ., *S.F.* 27 B2 37 43N 122 28W
San Francisco Tecoxpa, *Méx.* 29 C3 19 12N 99 0W
San Francisco Tlalnepantla, *Méx.* 29 C3 19 12N 99 8W
San Fruttuoso, *Mil.* 9 D6 45 34N 9 14 E
San Gabriel, *L.A.* 28 B4 34 5N 118 5W
San Gabriel →, *L.A.* 28 C4 33 53N 118 6W
San Gabriel Pk., *L.A.* 28 A4 34 14N 118 5W
San Giacomo, *Tori.* 9 A2 45 11N 7 36 E
San Gillio, *Tori.* 9 B2 45 8N 7 32 E
San Giórgio a Crem, *Nápl.* 9 J13 40 50N 14 20 E
San Giovanni a Teduccio, *Nápl.* 9 J12 40 49N 14 18 E
San Giuseppe Vesuviano, *Nápl.* 9 H13 40 50N 14 29 E
San Gregorio Atlapulco, *Méx.* 29 C3 19 15N 99 4W
San Isidro, *B.A.* 32 A3 34 28 S 58 30W
San Isidro, *Lima* 30 G8 12 5 S 77 2W
San Isidro, *Manila* 15 D4 14 38N 121 5 E
San Jerónimo Lídice, *Méx.* 29 C2 19 19N 99 14W
San Jerónimo Miacatlán, *Méx.* 29 C4 19 12N 98 59W
San Jorge, Castelo de, *Lisb.* 8 F8 38 42N 9 8W
San Jose Del Alamo, *La Hab.* 30 B3 23 6N 82 17W
San José Rio Hondo, *Méx.* 29 B2 19 26N 99 14W
San Juan →, *Manila* 15 D4 14 35N 121 0 E
San Juan de Aragón, *Méx.* 29 B3 19 28N 99 4W
San Juan de Aragón, Parque, *Méx.* 29 B3 19 27N 99 4W
San Juan de Lurigancho, *Lima* 30 F8 11 59 S 77 0W
San Juan de Miraflores, *Lima* 30 H9 12 10 S 76 58W
San Juan del Monte, *Manila* 15 D4 14 36N 121 1 E
San Juan Ixtacala, *Méx.* 29 A2 19 31N 99 10W
San Juan Ixtayopan, *Méx.* 29 C4 19 14N 98 59W
San Juan Toltotepec, *Méx.* 29 B2 19 28N 99 15W
San Juan y San Pedro Tezompa, *Méx.* 29 C4 19 12N 98 57W
San Just Desvern, *Barc.* 8 D5 41 22N 2 4 E
San Justo, *B.A.* 32 C3 34 40 S 58 33W
San Leandro, *S.F.* 27 B4 37 43N 122 9W
San Leandro B., *S.F.* 27 B3 37 45N 122 13W
San Leandro Cr. →, *S.F.* 27 B3 37 44N 122 12W
San Lorenzo, *Mil.* 9 D4 45 34N 8 57 E
San Lorenzo, *S.F.* 27 B4 37 41N 122 6W
San Lorenzo →, *Méx.* 29 B2 19 28N 99 17W
San Lorenzo, I., *Lima* 30 G7 12 6 S 77 12W
San Lorenzo Acopilco, *Méx.* 29 C1 19 19N 99 20 E
San Lorenzo Chimalco, *Méx.* 29 B4 19 24N 89 58 E
San Lorenzo Tezonco, *Méx.* 29 C3 19 19N 99 3W
San Lorenzo Tlacoyucan, *Méx.* 29 C3 19 10N 99 2W
San Lucas Xochimanca, *Méx.* 29 C3 19 15N 99 6W
San Luis, *Lima* 30 G8 12 4 S 77 0W
San Luis Tlaxialtemalco, *Méx.* 29 C3 19 16N 99 2W
San Marino, *L.A.* 28 B4 34 7N 118 5W
San Martin, *Barc.* 8 D6 41 24N 2 11 E
San Martin de Porras, *Lima* 30 G8 12 1 S 77 5W
San Martino, *Tori.* 9 B3 45 6N 7 47 E
San Mateo, *S.F.* 27 C3 37 33N 122 19W
San Mateo Cr. →, *S.F.* 27 C2 37 31N 122 22W
San Mateo Tecoloapan, *Méx.* 29 A2 19 35N 99 14W
San Mateo Xalpa, *Méx.* 29 C3 19 13N 99 8W
San Máuro Torinese, *Tori.* 9 B3 45 6N 7 45 E
San Miguel, *B.A.* 32 B2 34 32 S 58 43W
San Miguel, *Lima* 30 G8 12 5 S 77 6W
San Miguel, *Manila* 15 D3 14 36N 120 59 E
San Miguel, *Stgo* 30 J11 33 29 S 70 39W
San Miguel Ajusco, *Méx.* 29 C2 19 13N 99 12W
San Miguel Xicalco, *Méx.* 29 C3 19 13N 99 9W
San Nicholas, *Manila* 15 D3 14 36N 120 57 E
San Nicola, *Rome* 9 F9 41 58N 12 21 E
San Nicolás Totolapan, *Méx.* 29 C2 19 16N 99 16W
San Nicolás Viejo, *Méx.* 29 A1 19 31N 99 21W
San Onófrio, *Rome* 9 F9 41 57N 12 25 E
San Pablo, *Méx.* 29 B4 19 25N 89 56 E
San Pablo, *S.F.* 27 A2 37 57N 122 20W
San Pablo, Pt., *S.F.* 27 A2 37 57N 122 25W
San Pablo Cr. →, *S.F.* 27 A2 37 58N 122 22W
San Pablo Ostotepec, *Méx.* 29 C3 19 11N 99 5W
San Pablo Res., *S.F.* 27 A3 37 55N 122 14W
San Pablo Ridge, *S.F.* 27 A3 37 55N 122 15W
San Pablo Str., *S.F.* 27 A2 37 58N 122 25W
San Pancrázio, *Tori.* 9 B2 45 6N 7 32 E
San Pedro, *Méx.* 29 B4 19 24N 89 56 E
San Pedro, Pt., *S.F.* 27 C1 37 35N 122 31W
San Pedro Actopan, *Méx.* 29 C3 19 12N 99 4W
San Pedro Martir, *Barc.* 8 D5 41 23N 2 6 E
San Pedro Martir, *Méx.* 29 C2 19 16N 99 10W
San Pedro Zacatenco, *Méx.* 29 A3 19 30N 99 6W
San Pietro, *Rome* 9 F9 41 53N 12 27 E
San Pietro, *Tori.* 9 B3 45 1N 7 45 E
San Pietro a Patierno, *Nápl.* 9 H12 40 53N 14 17 E
San Pietro all'Olmo, *Mil.* 9 E5 45 29N 9 0 E
San Po Kong, *H.K.* 12 D6 22 20N 114 11 E
San Quentin, *S.F.* 27 A2 37 56N 122 27W
San Rafael, *S.F.* 27 A1 37 58N 122 30W
San Rafael B., *S.F.* 27 A2 37 57N 122 28W
San Rafael Chamapa, *Méx.* 29 B2 19 27N 99 15W
San Rafael Hills, *L.A.* 28 A3 34 10N 118 12W
San Roque, *Manila* 15 D4 14 37N 121 5 E
San Salvador Cuauhtenco, *Méx.* 29 C3 19 11N 99 8W
San Salvador de la Punta, Forteresse, *La Hab.* 30 B2 23 8N 82 21W
San Sebastiano al Vesúvio, *Nápl.* 9 H13 40 50N 14 22 E
San Siro, *Mil.* 9 E5 45 28N 9 7 E
San Souci, *Syd.* 19 B3 33 59 S 151 8 E
San Telmo, *B.A.* 32 B4 34 37 S 58 23W
San Vicenc dels Horts, *Barc.* 8 D5 41 23N 2 0 E
San Vitaliano, *Nápl.* 9 H13 40 55N 14 28 E
San Vito, *Mil.* 9 E5 45 24N 9 0 E
San Vito, *Nápl.* 9 J13 40 49N 14 22 E
San Vito, *Tori.* 9 B3 45 2N 7 41 E
Sandbakken, *Oslo* 2 C5 59 49N 10 54 E
Sandermosen, *Oslo* 2 A4 60 0N 10 48 E
Sanderstead, *Lon.* 4 D4 51 19N 0 4W
Sandheide, *Ruhr* 6 C3 51 12N 6 56 E
Sandhurst, *Jobg.* 18 E9 26 6 S 28 3 E
Sandown, *Jobg.* 18 E9 26 5 S 28 4 E
Sandown Racecourse, *Lon.* 4 C2 51 22N 0 21W
Sandringham, *Jobg.* 18 E9 26 8 S 28 6 E
Sands Point, *N.Y.* 23 B6 40 51N 73 43W
Sandton, *Jobg.* 18 E9 26 5 S 28 4 E
Sandungen, *Oslo* 2 B3 59 52N 10 21 E
Sandvika, *Oslo* 2 B3 59 53N 10 32 E
Sandy Pond, *Bost.* 21 C2 42 26N 71 18W
Sånga, *Stock.* 3 D9 59 21N 17 42 E
Sangenjaya, *Tōkyō* 13 C2 35 37N 139 39 E
Sangley Pt., *Manila* 15 E3 14 29N 120 54 E
Sangone →, *Tori.* 9 B2 45 1N 7 32 E
Sangye, *Sŏul* 12 G8 37 38N 127 3 E
Sankrail, *Calc.* 16 E5 22 33N 88 13 E
Sanlihe, *Beij.* 14 B2 39 53N 116 18 E
Sanlintang, *Shang.* 14 K11 31 9N 121 29 E
Sannois, *Paris* 5 B3 48 58N 2 15 E
Sanpada, *Bomb.* 16 G9 19 3N 73 0 E
Sans, *Barc.* 8 D5 41 22N 2 7 E
Sant Ambrogio, Basilica di, *Mil.* 9 E6 45 27N 9 10 E
Sant Boi de Llobregat, *Barc.* 8 D5 41 20N 2 2 E
Sant Cugat, *Barc.* 8 D5 41 28N 2 5 E
Santa Ana, *Manila* 15 D4 14 34N 121 0 E
Santa Ana Tlacotenco, *Méx.* 29 C4 19 11N 98 58W
Santa Bárbara, Morro de, *Rio J.* 31 B1 22 56 S 43 26W
Santa Catalina, *B.A.* 32 C4 34 47 S 58 24W
Santa Cecilia Tepetlapa, *Méx.* 29 C3 19 13N 99 5W
Santa Clara, *Méx.* 29 A3 19 33N 99 3W
Santa Coloma de Cervelló, *Barc.* 8 D5 41 21N 2 0 E
Santa Coloma de Gramanet, *Barc.* 8 D6 41 27N 2 12 E
Santa Cruz, *Bomb.* 16 G7 19 4N 72 51 E
Santa Cruz →, *La Hab.* 30 B2 23 4N 82 29W
Santa Cruz, Ilhe de, *Rio J.* 31 B3 22 51 S 43 7W
Santa Cruz Alcapixca, *Méx.* 29 C3 19 14N 99 4W
Santa Cruz Ayotusco, *Méx.* 29 B1 19 22N 99 21W
Santa Cruz de Olorde, *Barc.* 8 D5 41 25N 2 3 E
Santa Cruz Int. Airport, *Bomb.* 16 G8 19 5N 72 51 E
Santa Cruz Meyehualco, *Méx.* 29 B3 19 20N 99 2W
Santa Elena, *Manila* 15 D4 14 38N 121 5 E
Santa Eligênia Consolação, *S. Pau.* 31 E6 23 32 S 46 38W
Santa Emilia, *Stgo* 30 J11 33 23 S 70 39W
Santa Eulalia, *Barc.* 8 D6 41 25N 2 10 E
Santa Fe, *La Hab.* 30 B2 23 4N 82 30W
Santa Fe Flood Control Basin, *L.A.* 28 B5 34 7N 117 57W
Santa Fe Springs, *L.A.* 28 C4 33 56N 118 3W
Santa Isabel Ixtapan, *Méx.* 29 A4 19 35N 89 57W
Santa Julia, *Stgo* 30 K11 33 30 S 70 35W
Santa Lucia, *Nápl.* 9 J12 40 49N 14 15 E
Santa Margherita, *Tori.* 9 B3 45 3N 7 43 E
Santa Maria Aztahuacán, *Méx.* 29 B3 19 21N 99 2W
Santa Maria del Rosario, *La Hab.* 30 B3 23 3N 82 15W
Santa Maria Tulpetlac, *Méx.* 29 A3 19 34N 99 3W
Santa Martha Acatitla, *Méx.* 29 B3 19 21N 99 2W
Santa Monica, *Car.* 30 E5 10 28N 66 53W
Santa Monica, *L.A.* 28 C2 34 1N 118 29W
Santa Monica B., *L.A.* 28 C1 33 58N 118 30W
Santa Monica Mt., *L.A.* 28 B2 34 6N 118 29W
Santa Rosa, *Lima* 30 F8 11 59 S 77 5W
Santa Rosa De Locobe, *Stgo* 30 J11 33 25 S 70 33W
Santa Rosa Xochiac, *Méx.* 29 C2 19 19N 99 17W
Santa Tereza, *S. Pau.* 31 F6 23 40 S 46 33W
Santa Ursula Xitla, *Méx.* 29 C2 19 16N 99 11W
Santa Ynez Canyon →, *L.A.* 28 B1 34 2N 118 33W
Santahamina, *Hels.* 3 C5 60 8N 25 2 E
Santana, *S. Pau.* 31 D6 23 29 S 46 36W
Sant'Anastasia, *Nápl.* 9 H13 40 51N 14 24 E
Sant'Antimo, *Nápl.* 9 H12 40 56N 14 14 E
Santeny, *Paris* 5 C5 48 43N 2 34 E
Santiago, *Stgo* 30 J11 33 26 S 70 40W
Santiago Acahualtepec, *Méx.* 29 B3 19 20N 99 0W
Santiago de Las Vegas, *La Hab.* 30 C2 22 58N 82 22W
Santiago Tepalcatlalpan, *Méx.* 29 C3 19 14N 99 8W
Santiago Tepatlaxco, *Méx.* 29 B1 19 28N 99 20W
Sant'Ilário, *Mil.* 9 D4 45 34N 8 59 E
Santo Amaro, *Lisb.* 8 F7 38 42N 9 11W
Santo Amaro, *S. Pau.* 31 E5 23 39 S 46 42W
Santo Andre, *Lisb.* 8 G8 38 38N 9 3W
Santo André, *S. Pau.* 31 E6 23 39 S 46 41W
Santo Antonio, Qta. de, *Lisb.* 8 G7 38 39N 9 15W
Santo António da Charneca, *Lisb.* 8 G8 38 37N 9 1W
Santo Niño, *Manila* 15 D4 14 38N 121 5 E
Santo Rosario, *Manila* 15 D4 14 33N 121 4 E
Santo Thomas, Univ. of, *Manila* 15 D3 14 36N 120 59 E
Santo Tomas, *Manila* 15 D4 14 33N 121 4 E
Santolan, *Manila* 15 D4 14 36N 121 4 E
Santos Dumont, Aéroport, *Rio J.* 31 B3 22 54 S 43 9W
Santos Lugares, *B.A.* 32 B3 34 35 S 58 35W
Santoshpur, *Calc.* 16 E5 22 31N 88 16 E
Santragachi, *Calc.* 16 E5 22 35N 88 17 E
Sanyuanli, *Gzh.* 14 G8 23 8N 113 14 E
São Bernardo do Campo, *S. Pau.* 31 F6 23 42 S 46 32W
São Caetano do Sul, *S. Pau.* 31 E6 23 37 S 46 34W
São Cristovão, *Rio J.* 31 B2 22 53 S 43 13W
São Domingos, Centro, *Rio J.* 31 B3 22 53 S 43 6W
São Gonçalo, *Rio J.* 31 A3 22 49 S 43 4W
São João Clímaco, *S. Pau.* 31 E6 23 37 S 46 35W
São João da Talha, *Lisb.* 8 F8 38 49N 9 5W
São João de Meriti, *Rio J.* 31 A1 22 47 S 43 18W
São Lucas, Parque, *S. Pau.* 31 E6 23 35 S 46 32W
São Mateus, *Rio J.* 31 A1 22 48 S 43 22W
São Miguel Paulista, *S. Pau.* 31 D7 23 29 S 46 26W
São Paulo, *S. Pau.* 31 E6 23 32 S 46 38W
Sapa, *Calc.* 16 E5 22 30N 88 15 E
Sapang Baho →, *Manila* 15 D4 14 33N 121 10 E
Sapateiro →, *S. Pau.* 31 E5 23 35 S 46 41W
Saranap, *S.F.* 27 A4 37 52N 122 4W
Sarandi, *B.A.* 32 C4 34 40 S 58 20W
Saraswati →, *Calc.* 16 D5 22 46N 88 15 E
Sarcelles, *Paris* 5 B4 48 59N 2 22 E
Sarecky →, *Pra.* 10 B2 50 7N 14 23 E
Sarenga, *Calc.* 16 E5 22 31N 88 12 E
Sarilhos Grandes, *Lisb.* 8 F9 38 40N 8 58W
Sarilhos Pequenos, *Lisb.* 8 F9 38 40N 8 58W
Sarimbun, *Sing.* 15 F7 1 24N 103 40 E
Saronikòs Kólpos, *Ath.* 8 J10 37 52N 23 38 E
Sarriá, *Barc.* 8 D5 41 22N 2 8 E
Sarria, *Car.* 30 D5 10 30N 66 53W
Sarsol, *Bomb.* 16 G9 19 2N 73 0 E
Sartrouville, *Paris* 5 B3 48 56N 2 10 E
Sasad, *Bud.* 10 K13 47 28N 19 0 E
Sasashita, *Tōkyō* 13 D2 35 23N 139 35 E
Sasel, *Hbg.* 7 D8 53 39N 10 7 E
Sashalom, *Bud.* 10 J14 47 30N 19 10 E
Saska, *Wsaw.* 10 E7 52 13N 21 4 E
Sassafras, *Melb.* 19 F9 37 52 S 145 20 E
Satalice, *Pra.* 10 B3 50 7N 14 34 E
Satgachi, *Calc.* 16 E6 22 37N 88 25 E
Satghara, *Calc.* 16 E6 22 43N 88 21 E
Satpukur, *Calc.* 16 E6 22 37N 88 24 E
Sätra, *Stock.* 3 E10 59 17N 17 54 E
Satsuna, *Calc.* 16 F5 22 28N 88 17 E
Sau Mau Ping, *H.K.* 12 E6 22 19N 114 13 E
Saugus, *Bost.* 21 C3 42 28N 71 0W
Saugus →, *Bost.* 21 C3 42 27N 70 58W
Saulx-les-Chartreux, *Paris* 5 C3 48 41N 2 16 E
Sausalito, *S.F.* 27 A2 37 51N 122 28W
Sausset →, *Paris* 5 B5 48 56N 2 28 E
Savigny-sur-Orge, *Paris* 5 C4 48 40N 2 21 E
Savijärvi, *Hels.* 3 A6 60 21N 25 19 E
Savonera, *Tori.* 9 B2 45 7N 7 36 E
Sawah Besar, *Jak.* 15 H9 6 8 S 106 49 E
Sawyer Ridge, *S.F.* 27 C2 37 34N 122 24W
Saxonville, *Bost.* 21 D1 42 19N 71 24W
Saxonwold, *Jobg.* 18 E9 26 9 S 28 2 E
Scarborough, *Trto.* 20 D9 43 44N 79 14W
Scarsdale, *N.Y.* 23 B6 40 58N 73 47W
Sceaux, *Paris* 5 C3 48 46N 2 17 E
Schalke, *Ruhr* 6 A4 51 33N 7 4 E
Schapenrust, *Jobg.* 18 F11 26 15 S 28 21 E
Scharfenberg, *Berl.* 7 A2 52 35N 13 15 E
Scheiblingstein, *Wien* 10 G9 48 16N 16 13 E
Schenefeld, *Hbg.* 7 D7 53 36N 9 52 E
Scherlebech, *Ruhr* 6 A4 51 37N 7 8 E
Schildow, *Berl.* 7 A3 52 38N 13 22 E
Schiller Park, *Chic.* 26 B1 41 56N 87 52W
Schiller Woods, *Chic.* 26 B1 41 57N 87 51W
Schlachtensee, *Berl.* 7 B2 52 26N 13 13 E
Schlossgarten, *Berl.* 7 A2 52 31N 13 18 E
Schmachtendorf, *Ruhr* 6 A2 51 32N 6 48 E
Schmargendorf, *Berl.* 7 B2 52 28N 13 17 E
Schmöckwitz, *Berl.* 7 B5 52 22N 13 38 E
Schnelsen, *Hbg.* 7 D7 53 38N 9 54 E
Scholven, *Ruhr* 6 A4 51 36N 7 0 E
Schönblick, *Berl.* 7 B5 52 27N 13 43 E
Schönbrunn, Schloss, *Wien* 10 G9 48 10N 16 19 E
Schöneberg, *Berl.* 7 B3 52 28N 13 20 E
Schönefeld, *Berl.* 7 B4 52 23N 13 30 E
Schöneiche, *Berl.* 7 B5 52 28N 13 41 E
Schönwalde, *Berl.* 7 A1 52 37N 13 7 E
Schottenwald, *Wien* 10 G9 48 13N 16 16 E
Schuir, *Ruhr* 6 B3 51 23N 6 59 E
Schulzendorf, *Berl.* 7 A2 52 36N 13 16 E
Schuylkill →, *Phil.* 24 B3 39 53N 75 11W
Schwabing, *Mün.* 7 G10 48 10N 11 35 E
Schwafheim, *Ruhr* 6 B1 51 25N 6 36 E
Schwanebeck, *Berl.* 7 A4 52 37N 13 32 E
Schwanenwerder, *Berl.* 7 B2 52 26N 13 10 E
Schwarz →, *Ruhr* 6 C3 51 19N 6 44 E
Schwarzbachtal, *Ruhr* 6 C3 51 17N 6 51 E
Schwarze, *Ruhr* 6 A2 51 31N 6 48 E
Schwarze Berge, *Hbg.* 7 E7 53 27N 9 54 E
Schwarzlackenau, *Wien* 10 G10 48 16N 16 23 E
Schwechat, *Wien* 10 H10 48 8N 16 28 E
Schweflinghaüsen, *Ruhr* 6 C6 51 15N 7 24 E
Schwelm, *Ruhr* 6 C5 51 16N 7 16 E
Scisciano, *Nápl.* 9 H13 40 54N 14 28 E
Scoresby, *Melb.* 19 F8 37 54 S 145 14 E
Scotch Plains, *N.Y.* 22 D2 40 39N 74 22W
Scotts Level Br. →, *Balt.* 25 A2 39 23N 76 45W
Sea Cliff, *N.Y.* 23 B7 40 50N 73 38W
Seabrook, *Wash.* 25 D9 38 58N 76 49W
Seacliff, *S.F.* 27 B2 37 47N 122 28W
Seaforth, *Syd.* 19 A4 33 48 S 151 15 E
Seagate, *N.Y.* 22 D4 40 34N 74 0W
Seal Slough, *S.F.* 27 C3 37 34N 122 17W
Sears Tower, *Chic.* 26 B3 41 52N 87 38W
Seat Pleasant, *Wash.* 25 D8 38 53N 76 53W
Seavey Hill, *Bost.* 21 A1 42 42N 71 23W
Šeberov, *Pra.* 10 B3 50 0N 14 30 E
Secaucus, *N.Y.* 22 C4 40 47N 74 3W
Secondigliano, *Nápl.* 9 H12 40 53N 14 15 E
Seddinsee, *Berl.* 7 B5 52 23N 13 41 E
Sedgefield, *N.Y.* 22 B4 40 52N 74 26W
Sedriano, *Mil.* 9 E4 45 29N 8 58 E
Seeberg, *Berl.* 7 A5 52 33N 13 41 E
Seeburg, *Berl.* 7 A1 52 30N 13 7 E
Seefeld, *Berl.* 7 A5 52 37N 13 40 E
Seegefeld, *Berl.* 7 A1 52 33N 13 5 E
Seehof, *Berl.* 7 B2 52 24N 13 17 E
Segeltorp, *Stock.* 3 E10 59 16N 17 56 E
Segrate, *Mil.* 9 E6 45 29N 9 17 E
Seguro, *Mil.* 9 E5 45 28N 9 3 E
Seine →, *Paris* 5 C4 48 48N 2 25 E
Seixal, *Lisb.* 8 G8 38 38N 9 5W
Selbeck, *Ruhr* 6 B3 51 22N 6 51 E
Selbecke, *Ruhr* 6 C5 51 20N 7 28 E
Selby, *Jobg.* 18 F9 26 12 S 28 2 E
Seletar, P., *Sing.* 15 F8 1 26N 103 51 E
Seletar, Sungei →, *Sing.* 15 F8 1 23N 103 52 E
Seletar Hills, *Sing.* 15 F8 1 23N 103 52 E
Seletar Res., *Sing.* 15 F7 1 24N 103 48 E
Selghar, *Bomb.* 16 H9 18 57N 73 1 E
Selhurst, *Lon.* 4 C4 51 23N 0 5W
Selsdon, *Lon.* 4 C4 51 20N 0 3W
Selytsy, *St-Pet.* 11 B6 59 56N 30 42 E
Sembawang, *Sing.* 15 F7 1 26N 103 49 E
Sembawang, Sungei →, *Sing.* 15 F7 1 26N 103 48 E
Sembawang Hill, *Sing.* 15 F7 1 22N 103 49 E
Semsvatn, *Oslo* 2 B2 59 51N 10 25 E
Senago, *Mil.* 9 D5 45 34N 9 7 E
Senan, *Jak.* 15 J10 6 10 S 106 50 E
Sénart, Forêt de, *Paris* 5 D4 48 40N 2 28 E
Senayan Sports Centre, *Jak.* 15 J9 6 12 S 106 47 E
Sendling, *Mün.* 7 G10 48 7N 11 31 E
Søngeløse, *Købn.* 2 D8 55 40N 12 14 E
Senju, *Tōkyō* 13 B3 35 44N 139 48 E
Senlikköy, *Ist.* 17 B1 40 58N 28 47 E
Senlisse, *Paris* 5 C1 48 41N 1 59 E
Senneville, *Mtrl.* 20 B2 43 24N 73 57W
Senri, *Ōsaka* 12 B4 34 49N 135 30 E
Senriyama, *Ōsaka* 12 B4 34 47N 135 30 E
Sentosa, *Sing.* 15 G7 1 15N 103 49 E
Sentosa, P., *Sing.* 15 G7 1 15N 103 49 E
Seo Dae Mun, *Sŏul* 12 G7 37 34N 126 55 E
Seobinngo, *Sŏul* 12 G7 37 31N 126 58 E
Seoggwan, *Sŏul* 12 G8 37 35N 127 2 E
Seong Bug, *Sŏul* 12 G8 37 35N 127 0 E
Seong Dong, *Sŏul* 12 G8 37 33N 127 3 E
Seongsu, *Sŏul* 12 G8 37 32N 127 2 E
Seoul = Sŏul, *Sŏul* 12 G7 37 34N 127 0 E
Seoul National Univ., *Sŏul* 12 H7 37 28N 126 57 E
Seoul Tower, *Sŏul* 12 G7 37 32N 126 59 E
Sepah Salar Mosque, *Tehr.* 17 C5 35 40N 51 25 E
Sepolia, *Ath.* 8 H11 38 1N 23 42 E
Sepulveda, *L.A.* 28 A2 34 13N 118 27W
Sepulveda Flood Control Basin, *L.A.* 28 A2 34 10N 118 28W
Serangoon, P., *Sing.* 15 F8 1 23N 103 55 E
Serangoon, Sungei →, *Sing.* 15 F8 1 23N 103 55 E
Serangoon Garden, *Sing.* 15 F8 1 21N 103 51 E

46 Serangoon Harbour

Serangoon Harbour, *Sing.* **15 F8** 1 23N 103 57 E
Seraya, P., *Sing.* **15 G7** 1 16N 103 43 E
Serebryanka, *Mos.* **11 E11** 55 44N 37 53 E
Serebryanka →, *Mos.* **11 E10** 55 47N 37 44 E
Serednevo, *Mos.* **11 F7** 55 35N 37 18 E
Serramonte, *S.F.* **27 C2** 37 39N 122 28W
Servon, *Paris* **5 C5** 48 43N 2 35 E
Šestajovice, *Pra.* **10 B3** 50 6N 14 40 E
Sesto San Giovanni, *Mil.* **9 D6** 45 31N 9 13 E
Seta Budi, *Jak.* **15 J9** 6 12 S 106 49 E
Setagaya-Ku, *Tōkyō* **13 C2** 35 37N 139 36 E
Sete Pontes, *Rio J.* **31 B3** 22 50 S 43 4W
Seter, *Oslo* **2 B4** 59 52N 10 47 E
Séttimo Milanese, *Mil.* **9 E5** 45 28N 9 3 E
Séttimo Torinese, *Tori.* **9 B3** 45 8N 7 46 E
Settsu, *Ōsaka* **12 B4** 34 47N 135 33 E
Setuny →, *Mos.* **11 E8** 55 43N 37 21 E
Seurasaari, *Hels.* **3 B4** 60 11N 24 53 E
Seutula, *Hels.* **3 A4** 60 20N 24 52 E
Seven Corners, *Wash.* **25 D7** 38 53N 77 9W
Seven Kings, *Lon.* **4 B5** 51 33N 0 5 E
Sevenoaks, *Lon.* **4 D6** 51 16N 0 11 E
Severn Hills, *Syd.* **19 A2** 33 46 S 150 57 E
Sévesco →, *Mil.* **9 D5** 45 35N 9 9 E
Sevran, *Paris* **5 B5** 48 56N 2 31 E
Sèvres, *Paris* **5 C3** 48 49N 2 13 E
Sewaren, *N.Y.* **22 D3** 40 33N 74 15W
Sewell, *Phil.* **24 C4** 39 46N 75 8W
Sewri, *Bomb.* **16 H8** 18 59N 72 50 E
Seya, *Tōkyō* **13 D1** 35 28N 139 28 E
Sforzesso, Castello, *Mil.* **9 E6** 45 28N 9 10 E
Sha Kok Mei, *H.K.* **12 D6** 22 23N 114 16 E
Sha Tin, *H.K.* **12 D6** 22 23N 114 11 E
Sha Tin Wai, *H.K.* **12 D6** 22 22N 114 11 E
Shaala, *Bagd.* **17 E7** 33 22N 44 16 E
Shabanzhuang, *Beij.* **14 B3** 39 51N 116 25 E
Shabbona Woods, *Chic.* **26 D3** 41 36N 87 33W
Shabrâmant, *El Qâ.* **18 D5** 29 56N 31 11 E
Shadipur, *Delhi* **16 B2** 28 38N 77 11 E
Shady Oak, *Wash.* **25 C6** 39 1N 77 17W
Shahabad, *Bomb.* **16 G9** 19 0N 73 2 E
Shahar, *Bomb.* **16 G8** 19 5N 72 52 E
Shahdara, *Delhi* **16 A2** 28 40N 77 18 E
Shahe, *Gzh.* **14 G8** 23 9N 113 19 E
Shahpur Jel, *Delhi* **16 B2** 28 33N 77 12 E
Shahr-e-Rey, *Tehr.* **17 D5** 35 36N 51 25 E
Shaikh Aomar, *Bagd.* **17 E8** 33 20N 44 23 E
Shakarpor Khas, *Delhi* **16 B2** 28 37N 77 14 E
Shakurpur, *Delhi* **16 A1** 28 40N 77 8 E
Sham Shui Po, *H.K.* **12 E5** 22 19N 114 9 E
Shamepur, *Delhi* **16 A1** 28 44N 77 8 E
Shamian, *Gzh.* **14 G8** 23 6N 113 13 E
Shamspur, *Delhi* **16 B2** 28 36N 77 17 E
Shan Liu, *H.K.* **12 D6** 22 23N 114 16 E
Shan Mei, *H.K.* **12 D6** 22 24N 114 10 E
Shanghai, *Shang.* **14 J12** 31 14N 121 28 E
Shanghetou, *Tianj.* **14 D5** 39 11N 117 0 E
Shanjing, *Gzh.* **14 G9** 23 4N 113 23 E
Sharea Faisal, *Kar.* **17 G11** 24 52N 67 8 E
Sharon Hill, *Phil.* **24 B3** 39 54N 75 16W
Sharp I., *H.K.* **12 D6** 22 21N 114 17 E
Sharp Park, *S.F.* **27 C2** 37 38N 122 29W
Shau Kei Wan, *H.K.* **12 E6** 22 16N 114 13 E
Shawocun, *Beij.* **14 B2** 39 53N 116 13 E
Shawsheen Village, *Bost.* **21 A3** 42 40N 71 7W
Shea Stadium, *N.Y.* **23 C5** 40 45N 73 50W
Sheakhala, *Calc.* **16 D5** 22 45N 88 10 E
Shebāb, *Bagd.* **17 E8** 33 20N 44 26 E
Sheepshead B., *N.Y.* **22 D5** 40 35N 73 55W
Shek Hang, *H.K.* **12 D6** 22 24N 114 17 E
Shek Kip Mei, *H.K.* **12 D5** 22 20N 114 9 E
Shek Lung Kung, *H.K.* **12 D5** 22 23N 114 5 E
Shek O, *H.K.* **12 E6** 22 13N 114 15 E
Shellpot Cr. →, *Phil.* **24 C1** 39 44N 75 30W
Shelter Cove, *S.F.* **27 C1** 37 35N 122 30W
Shelter I., *H.K.* **12 E6** 22 19N 114 17 E
Shemirānāt, *Tehr.* **17 C5** 35 47N 51 25 E
Shenfield, *Lon.* **4 B6** 51 37N 0 19 E
Sheng Fa Shan, *H.K.* **12 D5** 22 23N 114 5 E
Shenley, *Lon.* **4 A3** 51 41N 0 16W
Shepherds Bush, *Lon.* **4 B3** 51 30N 0 13W
Shepperton, *Lon.* **4 C2** 51 23N 0 26W
Sherborn, *Bost.* **21 D1** 42 14N 71 22W
Sherman Oaks, *L.A.* **28 B2** 34 8N 118 29W
Sherwood Forest, *S.F.* **27 A3** 37 57N 122 16W
Shet Bandar, *Bomb.* **16 H8** 18 57N 72 55 E
Sheung Lau Wan, *H.K.* **12 E6** 22 16N 114 16 E
Sheung Wan, *H.K.* **12 E5** 22 16N 114 9 E
Sheva, *Bomb.* **16 H8** 18 56N 72 57 E
Sheva Nhava, *Bomb.* **16 H8** 18 57N 72 57 E
Shiba, *Tōkyō* **13 C3** 35 38N 139 45 E
Shiba →, *Tōkyō* **13 A3** 35 50N 139 44 E
Shibuya-Ku, *Tōkyō* **13 C3** 35 39N 139 41 E
Shijōnawate, *Ōsaka* **12 B4** 34 44N 135 37 E
Shimo-okudomi, *Tōkyō* **13 A1** 35 52N 139 27 E
Shimo-tsuchidana, *Tōkyō* **13 D1** 35 24N 139 27 E
Shimogawara, *Tōkyō* **13 C1** 35 39N 139 27 E
Shimosalo, *Tōkyō* **13 B2** 35 45N 139 31 E
Shimosasame, *Tōkyō* **13 B2** 35 48N 139 37 E
Shimoshakujii, *Tōkyō* **13 B2** 35 43N 139 35 E
Shimotomi, *Tōkyō* **13 B1** 35 49N 139 27 E
Shimotsuruma, *Tōkyō* **13 D1** 35 29N 139 26 E
Shimura, *Tōkyō* **13 B3** 35 46N 139 41 E
Shinagawa B., *Tōkyō* **13 C3** 35 35N 139 48 E
Shinagawa-Ku, *Tōkyō* **13 C3** 35 36N 139 44 E
Shing Mun Res., *H.K.* **12 D5** 22 23N 114 8 E
Shinjuku-Ku, *Tōkyō* **13 B3** 35 41N 139 42 E
Shinkoiwa, *Tōkyō* **13 B4** 35 43N 139 51 E
Shinnakano, *Tōkyō* **13 B3** 35 41N 139 40 E
Shinoha, *Tōkyō* **13 A3** 35 50N 139 49 E
Shipai, *Gzh.* **14 G9** 23 8N 113 20 E
Shipley, *Balt.* **25 B3** 39 12N 76 39W
Shippan Pt., *N.Y.* **23 A7** 41 1N 73 31W
Shirako, *Tōkyō* **13 B2** 35 47N 139 36 E
Shiraone, *Bomb.* **16 G9** 19 2N 73 1 E
Shirinashi →, *Ōsaka* **12 C3** 34 38N 135 27 E
Shirley, *Lon.* **4 C4** 51 22N 0 2W
Shiro, *Tōkyō* **13 B2** 35 48N 139 30 E
Shirogane, *Tōkyō* **13 C3** 35 37N 139 44 E
Shisha Hai, *Beij.* **14 B3** 39 55N 116 21 E
Shitou, *Gzh.* **14 G9** 23 1N 113 23 E
Shiweitang, *Gzh.* **14 G8** 23 6N 113 12 E
Shogunle, *Lagos* **18 A2** 6 34N 7 20 E
Shomolu, *Lagos* **18 A2** 6 32N 7 22 E
Shooters Hill, *Lon.* **4 C5** 51 28N 0 4 E
Shoreditch, *Lon.* **4 B4** 51 31N 0 4W
Shoreham, *Lon.* **4 D6** 51 19N 0 10 E
Short Hills, *N.Y.* **22 C2** 40 44N 74 21W
Shortlands, *Lon.* **4 C5** 51 23N 0 0 E
Shrirampur, *Calc.* **16 D5** 22 45N 88 21 E
Shuangkou, *Tianj.* **14 D5** 39 14N 117 2 E
Shuangtuo, *Tianj.* **14 D6** 39 13N 117 19 E
Shubrâ el Kheima, *El Qâ.* **18 C5** 30 6N 31 14 E
Shuikuo, *Gzh.* **14 F8** 23 10N 113 10 E
Shuishang Gongyuan, *Tianj.* **14 E5** 39 5N 117 9 E
Shukunoshō, *Ōsaka* **12 A4** 34 50N 135 31 E
Sibbo, *Hels.* **3 A6** 60 21N 25 14 E
Sibbo fjärden, *Hels.* **3 B6** 60 11N 25 17 E
Siboney, *La Hab.* **30 B2** 23 4N 82 28W
Sibpur, *Calc.* **16 E5** 22 34N 88 19 E
Sibřina, *Pra.* **10 B4** 50 3N 14 40 E
Sidcup, *Lon.* **4 C5** 51 25N 0 6 E
Siebenhirten, *Wien* **10 H9** 48 8N 16 17 E
Siedlung, *Berl.* **7 A1** 52 35N 13 7 E
Siekierki, *Wsaw.* **10 E7** 52 12N 21 4 E
Sielce, *Wsaw.* **10 E7** 52 12N 21 2 E
Siemensstadt, *Berl.* **7 A2** 52 32N 13 16 E
Sieraków, *Wsaw.* **10 E5** 52 19N 20 48 E
Sierra Madre, *L.A.* **28 B4** 34 9N 118 3W
Sievering, *Wien* **10 G10** 48 15N 16 20 E
Siggerud, *Oslo* **2 C5** 59 47N 10 52 E
Siheung, *Sŏul* **12 H7** 37 28N 126 54 E
Siikajärvi, *Hels.* **3 B2** 60 17N 24 31 E
Sikátorpuszta, *Bud.* **10 J14** 47 34N 19 10 E
Silampur, *Delhi* **16 B2** 28 39N 77 16 E
Silschede, *Ruhr* **6 B6** 51 21N 7 22 E
Silver Hill, *Wash.* **25 E8** 38 49N 76 55W
Silver L., *Bost.* **21 B3** 42 33N 71 9W
Silver Mt., *L.A.* **28 A5** 34 12N 117 55W
Silver Spring, *Wash.* **25 D7** 38 59N 77 2W
Silverfields, *Jobg.* **18 E7** 26 7 S 27 49 E
Silvertown, *Lon.* **4 C5** 51 29N 0 1 E
Simla, *Calc.* **16 E6** 22 35N 88 22 E
Simmer and Jack Mines, *Jobg.* **18 F9** 26 12 S 28 8 E
Simmering, *Wien* **10 G10** 48 10N 16 24 E
Simmering Heide, *Wien* **10 G10** 48 10N 16 26 E
Simonkylä, *Hels.* **3 B5** 60 18N 25 1 E
Simpang Bedok, *Sing.* **15 G8** 1 19N 103 56 E
Simsalö, *Hels.* **3 B6** 60 14N 25 17 E
Singao, *N.Y.* **22 B3** 40 53N 74 14W
Singapore, *Sing.* **15 G8** 1 17N 103 51 E
Singapore →, *Sing.* **15 G8** 1 17N 103 51 E
Singapore, Univ. of, *Sing.* **15 G7** 1 19N 103 49 E
Singapore Airport, *Sing.* **15 F8** 1 21N 103 54 E
Singlewell, *Lon.* **4 C7** 51 25N 0 21 E
Singur, *Calc.* **16 D5** 22 48N 88 13 E
Sinicka →, *Mos.* **11 D7** 55 52N 37 18 E
Sinki, Selat, *Sing.* **15 G7** 1 15N 103 42 E
Sinrim, *Sŏul* **12 H7** 37 28N 126 56 E
Sinsa, *Sŏul* **12 G8** 37 31N 127 0 E
Sinthi, *Calc.* **16 E6** 22 37N 88 23 E
Sinweol, *Sŏul* **12 G7** 37 31N 126 51 E
Sipoo, *Hels.* **3 A6** 60 21N 25 14 E
Sipoon selkä, *Hels.* **3 B6** 60 11N 25 17 E
Sipson, *Lon.* **4 C2** 51 29N 0 26W
Siqeil, *El Qâ.* **18 C4** 30 7N 31 10 E
Şişli, *Ist.* **17 A2** 41 3N 28 58 E
Skå, *Stock.* **3 E9** 59 19N 17 44 E
Skärholmen, *Stock.* **3 E10** 59 16N 17 53 E
Skarpäng, *Stock.* **3 D11** 59 26N 18 0 E
Skarpnäck, *Stock.* **3 E11** 59 16N 18 7 E
Skarpö, *Stock.* **3 D13** 59 24N 18 22 E
Skedsmo, *Oslo* **2 B6** 59 59N 11 2 E
Skhodnya →, *Mos.* **11 D8** 55 53N 37 23 E
Skodsborg, *Købn.* **2 D10** 55 49N 12 34 E
Skogby, *Hels.* **3 A2** 60 21N 24 40 E
Skogen, *Oslo* **2 C1** 59 48N 10 18 E
Skogsbyn, *Hels.* **3 A6** 60 20N 25 18 E
Skokie, *Chic.* **26 A2** 42 2N 87 43W
Skokie →, *Chic.* **26 A2** 42 3N 87 46W
Skokie Lagoons, *Chic.* **26 A2** 42 7N 87 46W
Skoklefall, *Oslo* **2 B4** 59 50N 10 40 E
Sköndal, *Stock.* **3 E11** 59 15N 18 6 E
Skovlunde, *Købn.* **2 D9** 55 42N 12 25 E
Skovshoved, *Købn.* **2 D10** 55 45N 12 35 E
Skøyen, *Oslo* **2 B4** 59 55N 10 40 E
Skui, *Oslo* **2 B2** 59 55N 10 25 E
Skuldelev, *Købn.* **2 D7** 55 46N 12 1 E
Skullerud, *Oslo* **2 B5** 59 51N 10 50 E
Skuru, *Stock.* **3 E12** 59 18N 18 12 E
Skytta, *Oslo* **2 B5** 59 59N 10 54 E
Slade Green, *Lon.* **4 C6** 51 27N 0 11 E
Slagsta, *Stock.* **3 E9** 59 15N 17 48 E
Slakteren, *Oslo* **2 A4** 60 1N 10 40 E
Slattum, *Oslo* **2 A5** 60 0N 10 55 E
Slemmestad, *Oslo* **2 C2** 59 46N 10 29 E
Slependen, *Oslo* **2 B3** 59 52N 10 30 E
Sligo Cr. →, *Wash.* **25 C7** 39 0N 77 1W
Slipi, *Jak.* **15 J9** 6 11 S 106 47 E
Slipi Orchard Garden, *Jak.* **15 J9** 6 10 S 106 46 E
Slivenec, *Pra.* **10 B2** 50 1N 14 21 E
Slone Canyon Res., *L.A.* **28 B2** 34 6N 118 27W
Sloop Channel, *N.Y.* **23 D7** 40 36N 73 31W
Sluhy, *Pra.* **10 A3** 50 11N 14 33 E
Służew, *Wsaw.* **10 E7** 52 10N 21 1 E
Służewiec, *Wsaw.* **10 E7** 52 10N 21 0 E
Smalleytown, *N.Y.* **22 D2** 40 39N 74 28W
Smestad, *Oslo* **2 B2** 59 55N 10 25 E
Smichov, *Pra.* **10 B2** 50 4N 14 23 E
Smith Forest Preserve, *Chic.* **26 B2** 41 59N 87 45W
Smith Mills, *N.Y.* **22 A2** 41 0N 74 23W
Smithfield, *Syd.* **19 B2** 33 51 S 150 56 E
Smoke Rise, *N.Y.* **22 A2** 41 0N 74 24W
Smørumnedre, *Købn.* **2 D8** 55 44N 12 7 E
Snakeden Br. →, *Wash.* **25 D6** 38 58N 77 17W
Snarøya, *Oslo* **2 B3** 59 52N 10 33 E
Snättringe, *Stock.* **3 E10** 59 15N 17 58 E
Snoldelev, *Købn.* **2 E8** 55 33N 12 10 E
Snostrup, *Købn.* **2 D7** 55 48N 12 7 E
Søborg, *Købn.* **2 D9** 55 43N 12 29 E
Sobreda, *Lisb.* **8 G7** 38 39N 9 11W
Soccavo, *Nápl.* **9 H12** 40 50N 14 11 E
Sodegaura, *Tōkyō* **13 D4** 35 24N 139 57 E
Söderby, *Stock.* **3 D12** 59 24N 18 12 E
Söderkullalandet, *Hels.* **3 B6** 60 14N 25 19 E
Södermalm, *Stock.* **3 E11** 59 18N 18 4 E
Södersätra, *Stock.* **3 D10** 59 27N 17 56 E
Södertälje, *Stock.* **3 E8** 59 11N 17 36 E
Sodingen, *Ruhr* **6 A5** 51 32N 7 15 E
Sodpur, *Calc.* **16 D6** 22 42N 88 24 E
Södra Björkfjärden, *Stock.* **3 E8** 59 17N 17 34 E
Soeurs, Î. des, *Mtrl.* **20 B4** 43 27N 73 32W
Sognsvatn, *Oslo* **2 B4** 59 58N 10 43 E
Soignolles-en-Brie, *Paris* **5 D6** 48 39N 2 43 E
Soisy-sous-Montmorency, *Paris* **5 B3** 48 59N 2 17 E
Soisy-sur-Seine, *Paris* **5 D4** 48 39N 2 27 E
Sojiji Temple, *Tōkyō* **13 D3** 35 29N 139 40 E
Sok Kwu Wan, *H.K.* **12 E5** 22 12N 114 7 E
Sōka, *Tōkyō* **13 B3** 35 49N 139 48 E
Sokolniki, *Mos.* **11 E10** 55 47N 37 40 E
Sokolniki Park, *Mos.* **11 E10** 55 48N 37 40 E
Sokołów, *Wsaw.* **10 F6** 52 9N 20 51 E
Solalinden, *Mün.* **7 G11** 48 5N 11 42 E
Solaro, *Mil.* **9 D5** 45 36N 9 6 E
Solers, *Paris* **5 D6** 48 39N 2 43 E
Solingen, *Ruhr* **6 C4** 51 10N 7 5 E
Sollentuna, *Stock.* **3 D10** 59 25N 17 56 E
Søllerød, *Købn.* **2 D9** 55 48N 12 29 E
Sollihøgda, *Oslo* **2 B2** 59 58N 10 21 E
Solln, *Mün.* **7 G10** 48 4N 11 31 E
Solna, *Stock.* **3 D10** 59 21N 17 59 E
Solntsevo, *Mos.* **11 F8** 55 39N 37 24 E
Solymár, *Bud.* **10 J12** 47 35N 18 56 E
Somapah Changi, *Sing.* **15 F8** 1 20N 103 57 E
Somapan Serangoon, *Sing.* **15 F8** 1 21N 103 53 E
Somborn, *Ruhr* **6 B6** 51 29N 7 20 E
Somerdale, *Phil.* **24 B4** 39 50N 75 1W
Somerset, *Wash.* **25 D7** 38 57N 77 5W
Somerton, *Phil.* **24 A4** 40 7N 75 1W
Somerville, *Bost.* **21 C3** 42 22N 71 5W
Somma, Mte., *Nápl.* **9 H13** 40 50N 14 25 E
Somma Vesuviana, *Nápl.* **9 H13** 40 52N 14 26 E
Sonari, *Bomb.* **16 H8** 18 54N 72 59 E
Sønderby, *Købn.* **2 D7** 55 44N 12 2 E
Søndersø, *Købn.* **2 D9** 55 46N 12 21 E
Sondre Elvåga, *Oslo* **2 B5** 59 51N 10 54 E
Sonnberg, *Wien* **10 G9** 48 19N 16 15 E
Sørby, *Oslo* **2 C4** 59 49N 10 41 E
Sørkedalen, *Oslo* **2 A3** 60 1N 10 37 E
Soroksár, *Bud.* **10 K13** 47 24N 19 7 E
Soroksár-Újtelep, *Bud.* **10 K13** 47 25N 19 7 E
Soroksari Duna →, *Bud.* **10 K13** 47 25N 19 5 E
Sørsdal, *Oslo* **2 B1** 59 50N 10 16 E
Sosenka →, *Mos.* **11 E10** 55 46N 37 42 E
Sosnovaya, *St-Pet.* **11 C2** 59 49N 30 8 E
Sottungsby, *Hels.* **3 B5** 60 16N 25 8 E
Sŏul, *Sŏul* **12 G8** 37 34N 127 51 E
Soundview, *N.Y.* **23 C5** 40 49N 73 53W
South Basin, *S.F.* **27 B2** 37 42N 122 22W
South Beach, *N.Y.* **22 D4** 40 35N 74 4W
South Boston, *Bost.* **21 C3** 42 20N 71 2W
South Braintree, *Bost.* **21 D4** 42 11N 70 59W
South Branch →, *Phil.* **24 C4** 39 50N 75 5W
South Brooklyn, *N.Y.* **22 C5** 40 41N 73 59W
South Chelmsford, *Bost.* **21 B1** 42 34N 71 22W
South Chicago, *Chic.* **26 C3** 41 44N 87 32W
South Darenth, *Lon.* **4 C6** 51 23N 0 15 E
South Deering, *Chic.* **26 C3** 41 42N 87 33W
South Floral Park, *N.Y.* **23 C6** 40 42N 73 41W
South Gate, *L.A.* **28 C3** 33 56N 118 12W
South Germiston, *Jobg.* **18 F10** 26 11 S 28 13 E
South Hackensack, *N.Y.* **22 B4** 40 51N 74 2W
South Hamilton, *Bost.* **21 B4** 42 36N 70 52W
South Harbour, *Manila* **15 D3** 14 34N 120 58 E
South Harrow, *Lon.* **4 B2** 51 33N 0 21W
South Hd., *Syd.* **19 B4** 33 50 S 151 16 E
South Hempstead, *N.Y.* **23 C7** 40 40N 73 37W
South Hills, *Jobg.* **18 F9** 26 14 S 28 5 E
South Hingham, *Bost.* **21 D4** 42 12N 70 53W
South Holland, *Chic.* **26 D3** 41 36N 87 35W
South Hornchurch, *Lon.* **4 B6** 51 32N 0 11 E
South Huntington, *N.Y.* **23 C8** 40 49N 73 23W
South Lawn, *Wash.* **25 E7** 38 47N 77 0W
South Lawrence, *Bost.* **21 A3** 42 41N 71 9W
South Lincoln, *Bost.* **21 C2** 42 24N 71 19W
South Lynnfield, *Bost.* **21 B4** 42 30N 70 59W
South Norwood, *Lon.* **4 C4** 51 23N 0 3W
South Ockendon, *Lon.* **4 B6** 51 30N 0 16 E
South of Market, *S.F.* **27 B2** 37 46N 122 24W
South Orange, *N.Y.* **22 C3** 40 45N 74 14W
South Oxley, *Lon.* **4 B2** 51 37N 0 23W
South Oyster B., *N.Y.* **23 D8** 40 38N 73 27W
South Ozone Park, *N.Y.* **23 C6** 40 41N 73 49W
South Pasadena, *L.A.* **28 B4** 34 7N 118 8W
South Peabody, *Bost.* **21 B4** 42 30N 70 57W
South Peters, *Syd.* **19 B4** 33 54 S 151 11 E
South Plainfield, *N.Y.* **22 D2** 40 35N 74 24W
South Quincy, *Bost.* **21 D3** 42 13N 71 0W
South Res., *Bost.* **21 C3** 42 26N 71 6W
South San Francisco, *S.F.* **27 C2** 37 38N 122 26W
South San Gabriel, *L.A.* **28 B4** 34 3N 118 6W
South Shore, *Chic.* **26 C3** 41 45N 87 34W
South Sudbury, *Bost.* **21 C1** 42 21N 71 24W
South Valley Stream, *N.Y.* **23 D6** 40 38N 73 43W
South Westbury, *N.Y.* **23 C7** 40 44N 73 34W
South Weymouth, *Bost.* **21 D4** 42 10N 70 56W
South Wimbledon, *Lon.* **4 C3** 51 24N 0 11W
South Yarra, *Melb.* **19 F6** 37 50 S 144 59 E
Southall, *Lon.* **4 B2** 51 30N 0 22W
Southborough, *Lon.* **4 C5** 51 23N 0 3 E
Southcrest, *Jobg.* **18 F9** 26 15 S 28 5 E
Southend, *Lon.* **4 C4** 51 25N 0 0 E
Southfields, *Lon.* **4 C3** 51 26N 0 11W
Southgate, *Lon.* **4 B4** 51 38N 0 7W
Southwark, *Lon.* **4 C4** 51 29N 0 5W
Søvang, *Købn.* **2 E10** 55 34N 12 37 E
Soweto, *Jobg.* **18 F8** 26 14 S 27 52 E
Soya, *Tōkyō* **13 B4** 35 44N 139 55 E
Spadenland, *Hbg.* **7 E8** 53 28N 10 3 E
Spandau, *Berl.* **7 A1** 52 33N 13 9 E
Spånga, *Stock.* **3 D10** 59 23N 17 53 E
Sparkhill, *N.Y.* **22 A5** 41 1N 73 55W
Sparrows Point, *Balt.* **25 B4** 39 13N 76 29W
Spectacle I., *Bost.* **21 C4** 42 19N 70 59W
Speicher-See, *Mün.* **7 F11** 48 12N 11 42 E
Speising, *Wien* **10 H9** 48 10N 16 17 E
Speldorf, *Ruhr* **6 B2** 51 26N 6 49 E
Spellen, *Ruhr* **6 A1** 51 36N 6 36 E
Sphinx, *El Qâ.* **18 D4** 29 58N 31 8 E
Spinaceto, *Rome* **9 G9** 41 47N 12 27 E
Splitrock Res., *N.Y.* **22 B2** 40 58N 74 26W
Spořilov, *Pra.* **10 B3** 50 2N 14 29 E
Spot Pond, *Bost.* **21 C3** 42 26N 71 4W
Spotswood, *Melb.* **19 F6** 37 50 S 144 52 E
Spree →, *Berl.* **7 A2** 52 32N 13 12 E
Spreehafen, *Hbg.* **7 D7** 53 31N 9 59 E
Spring Pond, *Bost.* **21 C4** 42 29N 70 56W
Springeberg, *Berl.* **7 B5** 52 26N 13 43 E
Springfield, *N.Y.* **22 C3** 40 42N 74 18W
Springfield, *Phil.* **24 B3** 39 56N 75 19W
Springfield, *Wash.* **25 E6** 38 46N 77 10W
Springs, *Jobg.* **18 F11** 26 15 S 28 23 E
Sprockhövel, *Ruhr* **6 B5** 51 22N 7 14 E
Squantum, *Bost.* **21 D3** 42 17N 71 0W
Squirrel's Heath, *Lon.* **4 B6** 51 34N 0 12 E
Srednaya Rogatka, *St-Pet.* **11 C4** 59 49N 30 22 E
Śródmieście, *Wsaw.* **10 E7** 52 13N 21 0 E
Staaken, *Berl.* **7 A1** 52 31N 13 8 E
Staatsoper, *Wien* **10 G10** 48 12N 16 21 E
Stabekk, *Oslo* **2 B3** 59 54N 10 36 E
Stadlau, *Wien* **10 G10** 48 13N 16 27 E
Stahnsdorf, *Berl.* **7 B2** 52 23N 13 12 E
Staines, *Lon.* **4 C2** 51 26N 0 29W
Stains, *Paris* **5 B4** 48 57N 2 22 E
Stamford, *N.Y.* **23 A7** 41 2N 73 32W
Stamford Harbor, *N.Y.* **23 A7** 41 0N 73 34W
Stamford Hill, *Lon.* **4 B4** 51 34N 0 4W
Stammersdorf, *Wien* **10 G10** 48 18N 16 24 E
Stanford Univ., *S.F.* **27 D4** 37 26N 122 10W
Stanley, *H.K.* **12 E6** 22 13N 114 12 E
Stanley Mound, *H.K.* **12 E6** 22 13N 114 12 E
Stanley Pen., *H.K.* **12 E6** 22 12N 114 12 E
Stanmore, *Lon.* **4 B3** 51 37N 0 18W
Stansted, *Lon.* **4 C6** 51 20N 0 18 E
Stapleford Abbotts, *Lon.* **4 B6** 51 37N 0 10 E
Stapleton, *N.Y.* **22 D4** 40 36N 74 5W
Stará Boleslav, *Pra.* **10 A3** 50 11N 14 39 E
Stara Milosna, *Wsaw.* **10 E8** 52 15N 21 12 E
Staraya, *St-Pet.* **11 B5** 59 55N 30 37 E
Staraya Derevnya, *St-Pet.* **11 B3** 59 58N 30 15 E
Stare, *Wsaw.* **10 E7** 52 15N 21 0 E
Stare Babice, *Wsaw.* **10 E5** 52 15N 20 49 E
Staré Mesto, *Pra.* **10 B2** 50 5N 14 25 E
State House, *Lagos* **18 B2** 6 26N 7 24 E
Staten, *N.Y.* **22 D4** 40 34N 74 7W
Staten Island Zoo, *N.Y.* **22 D4** 40 38N 74 6W
Statenice, *Pra.* **10 B1** 50 9N 14 19 E
Stavnsholt, *Købn.* **2 D9** 55 48N 12 24 E
Steele, *Ruhr* **6 B4** 51 27N 7 4 E
Steele Creek, *Melb.* **19 E6** 37 44 S 144 52 E
Steglitz, *Berl.* **7 B2** 52 27N 13 19 E
Stehstücken, *Berl.* **7 B1** 52 23N 13 7 E
Steilshoop, *Hbg.* **7 D8** 53 36N 10 2 E
Steinberger Slough, *S.F.* **27 C3** 37 32N 122 13W
Steinriegel, *Wien* **10 G9** 48 16N 16 12 E
Steinstücken, *Berl.* **7 B1** 52 21N 13 7 E
Steinwerder, *Hbg.* **7 D7** 53 32N 9 57 E
Stellingen, *Hbg.* **7 D7** 53 35N 9 56 E
Stenhamra, *Stock.* **3 D9** 59 20N 17 40 E
Stenløse, *Købn.* **2 D8** 55 46N 12 11 E
Stephansdom, *Wien* **10 G10** 48 12N 16 21 E
Stepney, *Lon.* **4 B4** 51 30N 0 3W
Sterkende, *Købn.* **2 E8** 55 36N 12 10 E
Sterkrade, *Ruhr* **6 A3** 51 31N 6 52 E
Sterling Park, *S.F.* **27 B2** 37 41N 122 27W
Stevenson, *Balt.* **25 A2** 39 24N 76 42W
Stewart Manor, *N.Y.* **23 C6** 40 43N 73 40W
Sticklinge udde, *Stock.* **3 D11** 59 23N 18 6 E
Stickney, *Chic.* **26 C2** 41 49N 87 46W
Stienitzaue, *Berl.* **7 A5** 52 38N 13 44 E
Stiepel, *Ruhr* **6 B5** 51 25N 7 14 E
Stiftskirche, *Ruhr* **6 C2** 51 12N 6 41 E
Still Run →, *Phil.* **24 C3** 39 47N 75 16W
Stockholm, *Stock.* **3 E11** 59 19N 18 4 E
Stocksund, *Stock.* **3 D11** 59 23N 18 3 E
Stockum, *Ruhr* **6 C2** 51 16N 6 44 E
Stodůlky, *Pra.* **10 B1** 50 3N 14 19 E
Stoke D'Abernon, *Lon.* **4 D2** 51 19N 0 23W
Stoke Newington, *Lon.* **4 B4** 51 33N 0 4W
Stolpe-Süd, *Berl.* **7 A2** 52 37N 13 14 E
Stone, *Lon.* **4 C6** 51 26N 0 16 E
Stone Grove, *Lon.* **4 B3** 51 37N 0 16W
Stone Park, *Chic.* **26 B1** 41 53N 87 52W
Stonebridge, *Lon.* **4 B3** 51 32N 0 16W
Stoneham, *Bost.* **21 C3** 42 29N 71 5W
Stonehurst, *L.A.* **28 A2** 34 15N 118 21W
Stony Brook Res., *Bost.* **21 D3** 42 15N 71 8W
Stony Cr. →, *Chic.* **26 C2** 41 40N 87 45W
Stony Cr. →, *Melb.* **19 E6** 37 49 S 144 53 E
Stora Värtan, *Stock.* **3 D11** 59 25N 18 7 E
Store Hareskov, *Købn.* **2 D9** 55 46N 12 23 E
Store Kattingesø, *Købn.* **2 E7** 55 39N 12 0 E
Store Magleby, *Købn.* **2 E10** 55 35N 12 35 E
Storholmen, *Stock.* **3 D11** 59 23N 18 8 E
Stovivatn, *Oslo* **2 B2** 59 54N 10 26 E
Stovner, *Oslo* **2 B5** 59 57N 10 55 E
Stow L., *S.F.* **27 B2** 37 46N 122 28W
Stračnice, *Pra.* **10 B2** 50 4N 14 28 E
Strandbad Gansehäufe, *Wien* **10 G10** 48 13N 16 26 E
Strasslach, *Mün.* **7 G10** 48 0N 11 30 E
Strasstrudering, *Mün.* **7 G11** 48 6N 11 41 E
Stratford, *Lon.* **4 B5** 51 33N 0 0 E
Stratford, *Phil.* **24 C4** 39 49N 75 0W
Strathfield, *Syd.* **19 B3** 33 52 S 151 5 E
Strawberry Hill, *Bost.* **21 D2** 42 14N 71 15W
Strawberry Pk., *L.A.* **28 A4** 34 16N 118 7W
Strawberry Pt., *S.F.* **27 A1** 37 53N 122 30W
Streatham, *Lon.* **4 C4** 51 25N 0 7W
Streatham Vale, *Lon.* **4 C4** 51 24N 0 8W
Strebersdorf, *Wien* **10 G10** 48 17N 16 23 E
Střešovice, *Pra.* **10 B2** 50 5N 14 23 E
Strelyna, *St-Pet.* **11 C1** 59 49N 30 0 E
Střížkov, *Pra.* **10 B2** 50 7N 14 28 E
Strogino, *Mos.* **11 E8** 55 48N 37 24 E
Strømmen, *Oslo* **2 B5** 59 56N 10 59 E
Stromovka, *Pra.* **10 B2** 50 6N 14 25 E
Strunkede Wasserschloss, *Ruhr* **6 A5** 51 33N 7 12 E
Studio City, *L.A.* **28 B2** 34 8N 118 24W
Stupinigi, *Tori.* **9 C2** 44 59N 7 36 E
Stura di Lanzo →, *Tori.* **9 A2** 45 11N 7 47 E
Stureby, *Stock.* **3 E11** 59 15N 18 4 E
Stuvsta, *Stock.* **3 E11** 59 15N 18 0 E
Styrum, *Ruhr* **6 B3** 51 27N 6 52 E
Subhepur, *Delhi* **16 A2** 28 44N 77 15 E
Sucat, *Manila* **15 E4** 14 27N 121 2 E
Success, L., *N.Y.* **23 C6** 40 45N 73 42W
Suchdol, *Pra.* **10 B2** 50 8N 14 22 E
Sucre, *Car.* **30 D5** 10 31N 66 57W
Sucy-en-Brie, *Paris* **5 C5** 48 46N 2 31 E
Sudberg, *Ruhr* **6 C4** 51 10N 7 6 E
Sudbury, *Bost.* **21 C1** 42 22N 71 24W
Suderelbe →, *Hbg.* **7 E7** 53 28N 9 58 E
Suderwich, *Ruhr* **6 A5** 51 36N 7 16 E
Sugamo, *Tōkyō* **13 B3** 35 44N 139 43 E
Sugar Loaf Mt. = Açúcar, Pão de, *Rio J.* **31 B3** 22 56 S 43 9W
Sugartown, *Phil.* **24 B1** 39 59N 75 30W
Sugasawa, *Tōkyō* **13 B2** 35 46N 139 32 E
Suge, *Tōkyō* **13 C2** 35 37N 139 32 E
Suginami-Ku, *Tōkyō* **13 B2** 35 41N 139 37 E
Sugita, *Tōkyō* **13 D2** 35 22N 139 37 E
Sugō, *Tōkyō* **13 C2** 35 34N 139 33 E
Suitland, *Wash.* **25 D8** 38 50N 76 55W
Sukchar, *Calc.* **16 D6** 22 42N 88 22 E
Sulejówek, *Wsaw.* **10 E8** 52 14N 21 14 E
Sulldorf, *Hbg.* **7 D6** 53 34N 9 49 E
Sultan Mosque, *Sing.* **15 G8** 1 18N 103 51 E
Suma, *Ōsaka* **12 C1** 34 38N 135 8 E
Sumaré, *S. Pau.* **31 E5** 23 32 S 46 41W
Sumida, *Tōkyō* **13 B3** 35 42N 139 49 E
Sumida →, *Tōkyō* **13 B3** 35 39N 139 45 E
Sumiyoshi, *Ōsaka* **12 C4** 34 36N 135 30 E
Summer Palace, *Beij.* **14 B2** 39 59N 116 13 E
Summerville, *Trto.* **20 E7** 43 37N 79 33W
Summit, *Chic.* **26 C2** 41 47N 87 47W
Summit, *N.Y.* **22 C2** 40 43N 74 22W
Sun Valley, *L.A.* **28 A2** 34 13N 118 21W
Sunamachi, *Tōkyō* **13 B4** 35 40N 139 50 E
Sunashinden, *Tōkyō* **13 A2** 35 53N 139 30 E
Sunbury, *Lon.* **4 C2** 51 25N 0 26W
Sunda Kelapa, *Jak.* **15 H9** 6 6 S 106 48 E
Sundbyberg, *Stock.* **3 D10** 59 22N 17 57 E
Sundbyerne, *Købn.* **2 E10** 55 39N 12 36 E
Sung Kong, *H.K.* **12 E6** 22 11N 114 17 E
Sungai Bambu, *Jak.* **15 H10** 6 6 S 106 53 E
Sungai Buloh, *Sing.* **15 F7** 1 25N 103 42 E
Sungei Simpang, *Sing.* **15 F7** 1 26N 103 49 E
Sunland, *L.A.* **28 A3** 34 15N 118 18W
Sunnyridge, *Jobg.* **18 F10** 26 10 S 28 10 E
Sunset, *S.F.* **27 B2** 37 44N 122 29W
Sunshine, *Melb.* **19 E5** 37 48 S 144 49 E
Sunshine Acres, *L.A.* **28 C5** 33 56N 117 59W
Suntaug L., *Bost.* **21 B3** 42 31N 71 0W
Sunter, *Jak.* **15 H10** 6 7 S 106 51 E
Sunter, Kali, *Jak.* **15 J10** 6 10 S 106 53 E
Suomenlinna, *Hels.* **3 C4** 60 9N 24 59 E
Superga, *Tori.* **9 B3** 45 4N 7 46 E
Superga, Basilica di, *Tori.* **9 B3** 45 5N 7 45 E
Sura, *Calc.* **16 E6** 22 33N 88 24 E
Surag San, *Sŏul* **12 F8** 37 40N 127 4 E
Surbiton, *Lon.* **4 C3** 51 23N 0 17W
Surco, *Lima* **30 G8** 12 9 S 77 0W
Suresnes, *Paris* **5 B3** 48 52N 2 13 E
Surquillo, *Lima* **30 G8** 12 6 S 77 1W
Surrey Hills, *Melb.* **19 F7** 37 50 S 145 5 E
Surrey Hills, *Syd.* **19 B4** 33 53 S 151 13 E
Surrey Park, *Melb.* **19 E7** 37 49 S 145 6 E
Susaeg, *Sŏul* **12 G7** 37 34N 126 54 E
Süssenbrunn, *Wien* **10 G10** 48 16N 16 29 E
Sutherland, *Syd.* **19 C3** 34 2 S 151 3 E
Sutton, *Lon.* **4 C3** 51 21N 0 11W
Sutton at Hone, *Lon.* **4 C6** 51 24N 0 14 E
Suyu, *Sŏul* **12 G8** 37 37N 127 0 E
Suzukishinden, *Tōkyō* **13 B2** 35 43N 139 31 E
Svanemøllen, *Købn.* **2 D10** 55 43N 12 34 E
Svartsjölandet, *Stock.* **3 D9** 59 20N 17 43 E
Sverdlov, *Mos.* **11 E9** 55 46N 37 36 E
Svestad, *Oslo* **2 C3** 59 46N 10 36 E
Svestrup, *Købn.* **2 D7** 55 46N 12 8 E
Svinningeudd, *Stock.* **3 D12** 59 26N 18 17 E
Svinö, *Hels.* **3 C3** 60 7N 24 44 E
Svogerslev, *Købn.* **2 E7** 55 38N 12 0 E
Swampscott, *Bost.* **21 C4** 42 28N 70 53W
Swanley, *Lon.* **4 C5** 51 23N 0 9 E
Swanscombe, *Lon.* **4 C6** 51 26N 0 18 E
Swansea, *Trto.* **20 E8** 43 39N 79 27W
Swarthmore, *Phil.* **24 B2** 39 54N 75 22W
Swedesboro, *Phil.* **24 C3** 39 45N 75 17W
Swedesburg, *Phil.* **24 A3** 40 5N 75 19W
Swinburne I., *N.Y.* **22 D4** 40 33N 74 3W
Swita, *Ōsaka* **12 B4** 34 45N 135 30 E
Syampur, *Calc.* **16 F5** 22 28N 88 12 E
Sycamore Mills, *Phil.* **24 B2** 39 57N 75 25W
Sydenham, *Jobg.* **18 E9** 26 9 S 28 5 E
Sydney, *Syd.* **19 B4** 33 52 S 151 12 E
Sydney, Univ. of, *Syd.* **19 B4** 33 54 S 151 11 E
Sydney Airport, *Syd.* **19 B4** 33 56 S 151 10 E
Sydney Harbour Bridge, *Syd.* **19 B4** 33 51 S 151 12 E
Sydstranden, *Købn.* **2 E10** 55 34N 12 38 E
Sylling, *Oslo* **2 B1** 59 54N 10 16 E
Sylvania, *Syd.* **19 C3** 34 0 S 151 7 E
Syndal, *Melb.* **19 F7** 37 52 S 145 9 E
Syon House, *Lon.* **4 C3** 51 28N 0 18W
Syosset, *N.Y.* **23 C7** 40 49N 73 30W
Szabadság-hegy, *Bud.* **10 J12** 47 30N 18 59 E
Szczęśliwice, *Wsaw.* **10 E6** 52 12N 20 57 E
Szemere-Telep, *Bud.* **10 K14** 47 26N 19 13 E
Széphalom, *Bud.* **10 J12** 47 34N 18 57 E
Szilasliget, *Bud.* **10 J14** 47 34N 19 16 E

T

Tabata, *Tōkyō* **13 B3** 35 44N 139 46 E
Tablada, *B.A.* **32 C3** 34 41 S 58 32W
Taboão →, *S. Pau.* **31 F7** 23 40 S 46 27W
Taboão da Serra, *S. Pau.* **31 E5** 23 36 S 46 45W
Tabor, *N.Y.* **22 B2** 40 52N 74 28W
Täby, *Stock.* **3 D11** 59 26N 18 2 E
Tacony, *Phil.* **24 A4** 40 1N 75 2W
Tacuba, *Méx.* **29 B2** 19 26N 99 11W
Tacubaya, *Méx.* **29 B2** 19 24N 99 10W
Tadain, *Ōsaka* **12 A3** 34 51N 135 24 E
Tadworth, *Lon.* **4 D3** 51 17N 0 14W
Tagig, *Manila* **15 D4** 14 31N 121 4 E
Tagig →, *Manila* **15 D4** 14 31N 121 5 E
Tai Hang, *H.K.* **12 E6** 22 16N 114 11 E
Tai Lo Shan, *H.K.* **12 D6** 22 21N 114 13 E
Tai Po Tsai, *H.K.* **12 D6** 22 20N 114 15 E
Tai Seng, *Sing.* **15 F8** 1 20N 103 53 E
Tai Shui Hang, *H.K.* **12 D6** 22 24N 114 13 E
Tai Tam B., *H.K.* **12 E6** 22 12N 114 13 E
Tai Tam Tuk Res., *H.K.* **12 E6** 22 14N 114 13 E
Tai Wan Tau, *H.K.* **12 E6** 22 17N 114 17 E
Tai Wo Hau, *H.K.* **12 D5** 22 21N 114 7 E
Tai Wo Ping, *H.K.* **12 D5** 22 20N 114 9 E
Ta'imim, *Bagd.* **17 F8** 33 15N 44 21 E
Tainaka, *Ōsaka* **12 C4** 34 36N 135 35 E
Taishō, *Ōsaka* **12 C3** 34 38N 135 27 E
Taitō-Ku, *Tōkyō* **13 B3** 35 43N 139 47 E
Tajima, *Tōkyō* **13 B2** 35 48N 139 36 E
Tajpur, *Calc.* **16 D5** 22 44N 88 15 E
Takaido, *Tōkyō* **13 B2** 35 40N 139 37 E
Takaishi, *Tōkyō* **13 C2** 35 36N 139 31 E
Takarazuka, *Ōsaka* **12 B2** 34 47N 135 20 E
Takasago, *Tōkyō* **13 B4** 35 44N 139 52 E
Takatsuki, *Ōsaka* **12 A4** 34 50N 135 37 E
Takayanagi, *Tōkyō* **13 D4** 35 23N 139 57 E
Takegahana, *Tōkyō* **13 B4** 35 47N 139 54 E
Takenotsuka, *Tōkyō* **13 B3** 35 47N 139 47 E
Takeshita, *Tōkyō* **13 C2** 35 33N 139 32 E
Takinegawa, *Tōkyō* **13 B3** 35 45N 139 44 E
Takkula, *Hels.* **3 B2** 60 19N 24 38 E
Takoma Park, *Wash.* **25 D7** 38 58N 77 0W
Taksim, *Ist.* **17 A2** 41 2N 28 58 E
Talaide, *Lisb.* **8 F7** 38 44N 9 18W
Talampas, *Manila* **15 D4** 14 36N 121 4 E
Taling Chan, *Bangk.* **15 B1** 13 46N 100 27 E
Talleyville, *Phil.* **24 C1** 39 48N 75 32W
Tallkrogen, *Stock.* **3 E11** 59 16N 18 4 E
Talmapais Valley, *S.F.* **27 A1** 37 52N 122 32W
Tama, *Tōkyō* **13 C1** 35 38N 139 26 E
Tama →, *Tōkyō* **13 C2** 35 32N 139 39 E
Tama Kyźryō, *Tōkyō* **13 C2** 35 34N 139 30 E
Tamaden, *Tōkyō* **13 C2** 35 39N 139 38 E
Tamagawa-josui →, *Tōkyō* **13 B1** 35 41N 139 47 E
Taman Sari, *Jak.* **15 H9** 6 8 S 106 48 E
Tamanduatei →, *S. Pau.* **31 E6** 23 37 S 46 38W
Tambora, *Jak.* **15 H9** 6 8 S 106 47 E
Tamboré, *S. Pau.* **31 E4** 23 30 S 46 50W
Tammisalo, *Hels.* **3 B5** 60 11N 25 5 E
Tammûh, *El Qâ.* **18 D5** 29 55N 31 15 E
Tampier Slough, *Chic.* **26 D1** 41 39N 87 54W
Tan Tock Seng, *Sing.* **15 G8** 1 19N 103 50 E
Tanah Abang, *Jak.* **15 J9** 6 12 S 106 48 E
Tanashi, *Tōkyō* **13 B2** 35 43N 139 32 E
Tanforan Park, *S.F.* **27 C2** 37 37N 122 24W
Tangjae, *Sŏul* **12 H8** 37 29N 127 2 E
Tanglin, *Sing.* **15 G7** 1 18N 103 47 E
Tangstedt, *Hbg.* **7 C7** 53 40N 9 51 E
Tangstedter Forst, *Hbg.* **7 C8** 53 43N 10 3 E
Tanigami, *Ōsaka* **12 B2** 34 45N 135 10 E
Tanjung Duren, *Jak.* **15 J9** 6 10 S 106 46 E
Tanjung Priok, *Jak.* **15 H10** 6 6 S 106 52 E
Tanum, *Oslo* **2 B2** 59 53N 10 28 E
Taoranting Gongyuan, *Beij.* **14 B3** 39 51N 116 20 E
Taoranting Hu, *Beij.* **14 B3** 39 50N 116 20 E
Tapada, *Lisb.* **8 F7** 38 49N 9 16W
Tapanila, *Hels.* **3 B5** 60 15N 25 2 E
Tapiales, *B.A.* **32 C3** 34 42 S 58 30W
Tapiola, *Hels.* **3 B3** 60 10N 24 48 E
Tappan, *N.Y.* **22 A5** 41 1N 73 57W
Tappan, L., *N.Y.* **22 A5** 41 1N 73 59W
Tappeh, *Tehr.* **17 C5** 35 41N 51 29 E
Tapsia, *Calc.* **16 E6** 22 32N 88 23 E
Taquara, *Rio J.* **31 B1** 22 55 S 43 21W
Tara, *Bomb.* **16 G7** 19 5N 72 49 E
Tarāblus, *Bagd.* **17 F8** 33 19N 44 21 E
Tarango, Presa, *Méx.* **29 B2** 19 21N 99 12W
Tårbæk, *Købn.* **2 D10** 55 46N 12 35 E
Tarchomin, *Wsaw.* **10 E6** 52 19N 20 58 E
Tardeo, *Bomb.* **16 H7** 18 57N 72 48 E
Target Rock, *N.Y.* **23 B8** 40 55N 73 24W
Targówek, *Wsaw.* **10 E7** 52 16N 21 3 E
Tårnby, *Købn.* **2 E10** 55 37N 12 35 E

Villecresnes 47

Taronga Zoo. Park, *Syd.* 19 B4 33 50 S 151 14 E
Tarqua B., *Lagos* 18 B2 6 24N 7 23 E
Tarzana, *L.A.* 28 A1 34 10N 118 32W
Tåstrup, *Købn.* 2 E8 55 39N 12 18 E
Tatarovo, *Mos.* 11 E8 55 45N 37 24 E
Tatarpur, *Delhi* 16 B1 28 38N 77 9 E
Tatenberg, *Hbg.* 7 E8 53 29N 10 3 E
Tathong Channel, *H.K.* 12 E6 22 15N 114 16 E
Tathong Pt., *H.K.* 12 E6 22 14N 114 17 E
Tatsfield, *Lon.* 4 D5 51 17N 0 1 E
Tattariharju, *Hels.* 3 B5 60 15N 25 2 E
Tatuapé, *S. Pau.* 31 E6 23 31 S 46 33W
Taufkirchen, *Mün.* 7 G10 48 2N 11 36 E
Tavares, I. dos, *Rio J.* 31 A3 22 49 S 43 6W
Tavernanova, *Nápl.* 9 H13 40 54N 14 21 E
Taverny, *Paris* 5 A3 49 1N 2 13 E
Távros, *Ath.* 8 J11 37 57N 23 43 E
Tavry, *St-Pet.* 11 B6 59 54N 30 40 E
Taylortown, *N.Y.* 22 B2 40 56N 74 23W
Tayninka, *Mos.* 11 D10 55 53N 37 45 E
Taytay, *Manila* 15 D4 14 34N 121 7 E
Tayuman, *Manila* 15 D4 14 31N 121 9 E
Teaneck, *N.Y.* 22 B4 40 52N 74 1W
Teatro Colón, *B.A.* 32 B4 34 36 S 58 23 E
Teban Gardens, *Sing.* 15 G7 1 19N 103 44 E
Tebet, *Jak.* 15 J10 6 14 S 106 50 E
Tecamachaleo, *Méx.* 29 B2 19 25N 99 14W
Techny, *Chic.* 26 A2 42 6N 87 48W
Teck Hock, *Sing.* 15 F8 1 21N 103 54 E
Tecoma, *Melb.* 19 F9 37 54 S 145 20 E
Teddington, *Lon.* 4 C2 51 25N 0 20W
Tegel, *Berl.* 7 A2 52 34N 13 16 E
Tegel, Flughafen, *Berl.* 7 A2 52 33N 13 15 E
Tegeler Fliess →, *Berl.* 7 A3 52 37N 13 21 E
Tegeler See, *Berl.* 7 A2 52 34N 13 15 E
Tegelort, *Berl.* 7 A2 52 34N 13 13 E
Tehar, *Delhi* 16 B1 28 37N 77 7 E
Tehrān, *Tehr.* 17 C5 35 41N 51 25 E
Tehrān Pars, *Tehr.* 17 C5 35 44N 51 32 E
Tei Tong Tsui, *H.K.* 12 E6 22 16N 114 17 E
Tejo →, *Lisb.* 8 F8 38 45N 9 3W
Tekstilyshchik, *Mos.* 11 E10 55 42N 37 41 E
Tela, *Delhi* 16 A2 28 43N 77 19 E
Telhal, *Lisb.* 8 F7 38 48N 9 18W
Telinipara, *Calc.* 16 D6 22 46N 88 23 E
Telok Blangah, *Sing.* 15 G7 1 17N 103 49 E
Teltow, *Berl.* 7 B2 52 23N 13 17 E
Teltow kanal, *Berl.* 7 B3 52 26N 13 29 E
Temescal, L., *S.F.* 27 A3 37 50N 122 13W
Temnikovo, *Mos.* 11 E12 55 43N 38 1 E
Tempelhof, *Berl.* 7 B3 52 27N 13 23 E
Tempelhof, Flughafen, *Berl.* 7 B3 52 28N 13 27 E
Temperley, *B.A.* 32 C4 34 46 S 58 22W
Temple City, *L.A.* 28 B4 34 6N 118 3W
Temple Hills Park, *Wash.* 25 E8 38 48N 76 56W
Templestowe, *Melb.* 19 E7 37 45 S 145 8 E
Templestowe Lower, *Melb.* 19 E7 37 45 S 145 6 E
Tenafly, *N.Y.* 22 B5 40 54N 73 58W
Tenantongo, Presa, *Méx.* 29 B2 19 28N 99 15W
Tengah →, *Sing.* 15 F7 1 23N 103 43 E
Tengeh, Sungei →, *Sing.* 15 F6 1 20N 103 39 E
Tennoji, *Ōsaka* 12 C4 34 39N 135 30 E
Tenochtitlán, *Méx.* 29 B3 19 26N 99 7W
Tepalcates, *Méx.* 29 B3 19 23N 99 3W
Tepe Saif, *Tehr.* 17 D4 35 36N 51 17 E
Tepepan, *Méx.* 29 C3 19 16N 99 9W
Teplyy Star, *Mos.* 11 F9 55 37N 37 30 E
Tepozteco, Parque Nac. del, *Méx.* 29 D3 19 3N 99 5W
Terrasse Vaudreuil, *Mtrl.* 20 B2 43 23N 73 59W
Terrazzano, *Mil.* 9 D5 45 32N 9 4 E
Terrugem, *Lisb.* 8 F7 38 41N 9 17W
Terusan Banjir, *Jak.* 15 H9 6 7 S 106 46 E
Terzigno, *Nápl.* 9 J13 40 48N 14 29 E
Tessancourt-sur-Aubette, *Paris* 5 A1 49 1N 1 55 E
Testona, *Tori.* 9 C3 44 59N 7 42 E
Tetelco, *Méx.* 29 C4 19 12N 98 57W
Tetreauville, *Mtrl.* 20 A4 43 35N 73 32W
Tetti Neirotti, *Tori.* 9 B2 45 3N 7 32 E
Tetuán, *Mdrd.* 8 B2 40 27N 3 42W
Teufelsberg, *Berl.* 7 B2 52 29N 13 14 E
Tévere →, *Rome* 9 F9 41 56N 12 27 E
Tewksbury, *Bost.* 21 B2 42 37N 71 12W
Texcoco, L. de, *Méx.* 29 B4 19 30N 89 58 E
Thalkirchen, *Mün.* 7 G10 48 6N 11 32 E
Thames Ditton, *Lon.* 4 C2 51 23N 0 20W
Thamesmead, *Lon.* 4 B5 51 30N 0 7 E
Thana Cr. →, *Bomb.* 16 G8 19 2N 72 54 E
The Basin, *Melb.* 19 F8 37 51 S 145 19 E
The Glen, *Wash.* 25 C6 39 2N 77 12W
The Loop, *Chic.* 26 B3 41 52N 87 37W
The Narrows, *N.Y.* 22 D4 40 37N 74 3W
The Ridge, *Delhi* 16 B2 28 37N 77 10 E
The White House, *Wash.* 25 D7 38 53N 77 1W
The Wilds, *Jobg.* 18 F9 26 10 S 28 2 E
Theseión, *Ath.* 8 J11 37 57N 23 43 E
Theydon Bois, *Lon.* 4 A5 51 40N 0 6 E
Thiais, *Paris* 5 C4 48 46N 2 23 E
Thieux, *Paris* 5 A6 49 0N 2 40 E
Thistletown, *Trto.* 20 D7 43 44N 79 34W
Thiverval-Grignon, *Paris* 5 B1 48 51N 1 55 E
Thomaston, *N.Y.* 23 C6 40 47N 73 43W
Thomastown, *Melb.* 19 E7 37 40 S 145 2 E
Thompson I., *Bost.* 21 D4 42 19N 70 59W
Thomson, *Sing.* 15 F8 1 20N 103 50 E
Thon Buri, *Bangk.* 15 B1 13 45N 100 29 E
Thong Hoe, *Sing.* 15 F7 1 25N 103 42 E
Thorigny-sur-Marne, *Paris* 5 B6 48 53N 2 41 E
Thornbury, *Melb.* 19 E7 37 44 S 145 1 E
Thorncliffe, *Trto.* 20 D8 43 42N 79 20W
Thornhill, *Jobg.* 18 E9 26 6 S 28 9 E
Thornhill, *Trto.* 20 D8 43 48N 79 25W
Thornton, *Phil.* 24 B1 39 54N 75 31W
Thornton Heath, *Lon.* 4 C4 51 23N 0 6W
Thorofare, *Phil.* 24 B3 39 50N 75 11W
Throgs Neck, *N.Y.* 23 C6 40 48N 73 49W
Tian Guan, *Sing.* 15 F7 1 21N 103 40 E
Tian'anmen, *Beij.* 14 B3 39 53N 116 21 E
Tiancun, *Beij.* 14 B2 39 54N 116 12 E
Tianjin, *Tianj.* 14 E5 39 7N 117 12 E
Tiantan Gongyuan, *Beij.* 14 B3 39 51N 116 22 E
Tiateloco, *Méx.* 29 B3 19 27N 99 8W
Tibidabo, *Barc.* 8 D5 41 25N 2 6 E
Tiburon, *S.F.* 27 A2 37 52N 122 27W
Tiburon Pen., *S.F.* 27 A2 37 53N 122 28W
Tiburtino, *Rome* 9 F10 41 53N 12 30 E
Ticomán, *Méx.* 29 A3 19 31N 99 8W
Tiefenbroich, *Ruhr* 6 C2 51 18N 6 49 E
Tiefersee, *Berl.* 7 B1 52 24N 13 5 E
Tiejiangyin, *Beij.* 14 C3 39 49N 116 23 E
Tientsin = Tianjin, *Tianj.* 14 E5 39 7N 117 12 E
Tiergarten, *Berl.* 7 A3 52 31N 13 20 E
Tietê →, *S. Pau.* 31 D7 23 28 S 46 24W
Tigery, *Paris* 5 D5 48 38N 2 30 E
Tigre, *B.A.* 32 A3 34 25 S 58 34W
Tigris →, *Bagd.* 17 F8 33 17N 44 23 E
Tijuca, *Rio J.* 31 B2 22 56 S 43 13W
Tijuca, L. de, *Rio J.* 31 B2 22 59 S 43 20W
Tijuca, Pico da, *Rio J.* 31 B2 22 56 S 43 15W
Tijucamar, *Rio J.* 31 C2 23 0 S 43 18W
Tijucas, Is., *Rio J.* 31 C2 23 1 S 43 17W
Tikkurila, *Hels.* 3 B5 60 17N 25 2 E
Tilanqiao, *Shang.* 14 J11 31 15N 121 29 E
Tilbury, *Lon.* 4 C7 51 27N 0 21 E
Timah, Bukit, *Sing.* 15 F7 1 21N 103 46 E
Timiryazev Park, *Mos.* 11 E9 55 49N 37 33 E
Ting Kau, *H.K.* 12 D5 22 22N 114 4 E
Tinley Cr. →, *Chic.* 26 D2 41 39N 87 45W
Tinley Creek Woods, *Chic.* 26 D2 41 38N 87 48W
Tinley Park, *Chic.* 26 D2 41 35N 87 46W
Tipas, *Manila* 15 D4 14 32N 121 4 E
Tirsa, *El Qâ.* 18 D5 29 57N 31 12 E
Tishrīyaa, *Bagd.* 17 F8 33 18N 44 24 E
Tit Cham Chau, *H.K.* 12 E6 22 15N 114 17 E
Titagarh, *Calc.* 16 D6 22 44N 88 22 E
Tivoli, *Købn.* 2 D10 55 40N 12 35 E
Tizapán, *Méx.* 29 C2 19 19N 99 13W
Tlalnepantla, *Méx.* 29 A2 19 32N 99 11W
Tlalnepantla →, *Méx.* 29 A2 19 30N 99 18W
Tlâloc, Cerro, *Méx.* 29 D3 19 7N 99 3W
Tlalpan, *Méx.* 29 C2 19 17N 99 10W
Tlalpitzáhuac, *Méx.* 29 C4 19 19N 98 56W
Tlaltenango, *Méx.* 29 B2 19 20N 99 17W
Tlaltenco, *Méx.* 29 C3 19 19N 99 0W
Tlaxcoaque, *Méx.* 29 B3 19 25N 99 8W
To Kwai Wan, *H.K.* 12 E6 22 18N 114 11 E
Toa Payoh, *Sing.* 15 F8 1 20N 103 50 E
Tobay Beach, *N.Y.* 23 D8 40 36N 73 26W
Točná, *Pra.* 10 C2 49 58N 14 25 E
Tocome →, *Car.* 30 D6 10 28N 66 49W
Toda, *Tōkyō* 13 A2 35 50N 139 40 E
Todamachi, *Tōkyō* 13 B3 35 48N 139 39 E
Todt Hill, *N.Y.* 22 D4 40 36N 74 6W
Toei, Khlong →, *Bangk.* 15 B2 13 43N 100 32 E
Togasaki, *Tōkyō* 13 B4 35 47N 139 51 E
Tōkagi, *Tōkyō* 13 B4 35 42N 139 55 E
Tōkaichiba, *Tōkyō* 13 C2 35 31N 139 30 E
Tokarevo, *Mos.* 11 F11 55 38N 37 54 E
Tokorozawa, *Tōkyō* 13 B1 35 47N 139 28 E
Tōkyō, *Tōkyō* 13 C3 35 43N 139 45 E
Tōkyō B., *Tōkyō* 13 C4 35 33N 139 53 E
Tōkyō-Haneda Int. Airport, *Tōkyō* 13 C3 35 33N 139 45 E
Tōkyō Harbour, *Tōkyō* 13 C3 35 38N 139 46 E
Tokyo Univ., *Tōkyō* 13 B3 35 42N 139 46 E
Tollygunge, *Calc.* 16 F6 22 29N 88 21 E
Tolly's Nala, *Calc.* 16 E6 22 33N 88 19 E
Tolworth, *Lon.* 4 C3 51 22N 0 17W
Tomang, *Jak.* 15 J9 6 10 S 106 47 E
Tomba di Nerone, *Rome* 9 F9 41 58N 12 26 E
Tomilino, *Mos.* 11 F11 55 39N 37 55 E
Tomioka, *Tōkyō* 13 D2 35 22N 139 37 E
Tonda, *Ōsaka* 12 B4 34 49N 135 35 E
Tondo, *Manila* 15 D3 14 36N 120 57 E
Tone-unga →, *Tōkyō* 13 A4 35 55N 139 56 E
Tonekollen, *Oslo* 2 C6 50 49N 11 0 E
Tong Kang, Sungei →, *Sing.* 15 F8 1 23N 103 53 E
Tonghui He →, *Beij.* 14 B3 39 53N 116 28 E
Tönisheide, *Ruhr* 6 C4 51 18N 7 3 E
Tonndorf, *Hbg.* 7 D8 53 35N 10 8 E
Toorak, *Melb.* 19 F7 37 50 S 145 1 E
Toot Hill, *Lon.* 4 A6 51 41N 0 11 E
Topilejo, *Méx.* 29 C3 19 12N 99 9W
Topkapi, *Ist.* 17 A2 41 1N 28 55 E
Topsfield, *Bost.* 21 B4 42 38N 70 57W
Tor di Quinto, *Rome* 9 F9 41 56N 12 27 E
Tor Pignattara, *Rome* 9 F10 41 52N 12 31 E
Tor Sapienza, *Rome* 9 F10 41 53N 12 35 E
Torcy, *Paris* 5 B5 48 51N 2 39 E
Torino, *Tori.* 9 B3 45 5N 7 39 E
Toro, *B.A.* 32 B1 34 30 S 58 50W
Toronto, *Trto.* 20 E9 43 39N 79 23W
Toronto, Univ. of, *Trto.* 20 E8 43 39N 79 23W
Toronto Harbour, *Trto.* 20 E8 43 38N 79 21W
Toronto I., *Trto.* 20 E8 43 37N 79 23W
Toronto Int. Airport, *Trto.* 20 D7 43 40N 79 38 E
Torre Annunziata, *Nápl.* 9 J13 40 45N 14 26 E
Torre Cervara, *Rome* 9 F10 41 55N 12 35 E
Torre del Greco, *Nápl.* 9 J13 40 47N 14 21 E
Torre Nova, *Rome* 9 F10 41 51N 12 36 E
Torrellas →, *Barc.* 8 D5 41 23N 2 1 E
Torrellas del Llobregat, *Barc.* 8 D4 41 20N 1 59 E
Torresdale, *Phil.* 24 A5 40 3N 74 59W
Torrevécchia, *Rome* 9 F9 41 55N 12 25 E
Tortuguitas, *B.A.* 32 A2 34 28 S 58 44W
Toshima-Ku, *Tōkyō* 13 B3 35 43N 139 43 E
Toshimaen, *Tōkyō* 13 B3 35 44N 139 38 E
Totowa, *N.Y.* 22 B3 40 54N 74 13W
Totsuka-Ku, *Tōkyō* 13 D2 35 23N 139 32 E
Tottenham, *Lon.* 4 B4 51 35N 0 4W
Tottenham, *Melb.* 19 E6 37 48 S 144 51 E
Tottenville, *N.Y.* 22 D3 40 30N 74 14W
Totteridge, *Lon.* 4 B3 51 37N 0 11W
Toussus-le-Noble, *Paris* 5 C2 48 44N 2 6 E
Toussus-le-Noble, Aérodrome de, *Paris* 5 C2 48 44N 2 6 E
Toverud, *Oslo* 2 B4 59 55N 10 20 E
Towaco, *N.Y.* 22 B3 40 55N 74 18W
Tower Hamlets, *Lon.* 4 B4 51 31N 0 2W
Town Farm Hill, *Bost.* 21 A3 42 40N 71 3W
Townley, *N.Y.* 22 C3 40 41N 74 14W
Towra Pt., *Syd.* 19 C4 34 0 S 151 10 E
Towson, *Balt.* 25 A3 39 24N 76 36W
Tøyen, *Oslo* 2 B4 59 55N 10 47 E
Toyofuta, *Tōkyō* 13 A3 35 54N 139 55 E
Toyonaka, *Ōsaka* 12 B3 34 46N 135 28 E
Traar, *Ruhr* 6 B1 51 22N 6 36 E
Trafaria, *Lisb.* 8 F7 38 40N 9 13W
Tragliata, *Rome* 9 F8 41 58N 12 14 E
Traicão →, *S. Pau.* 31 E6 23 35 S 46 41W
Trålhavet, *Stock.* 3 D13 59 26N 18 22 E
Tranby, *Oslo* 2 C1 59 49N 10 14 E
Tranegilde, *Købn.* 2 E9 55 37N 12 22 E
Trångsund, *Stock.* 3 E11 59 13N 18 7 E
Trappenfelde, *Berl.* 7 A4 52 34N 13 39 E
Trappes, *Paris* 5 C1 48 46N 2 0 E
Trastévere, *Rome* 9 F9 51 53N 12 28 E
Travilah, *Wash.* 25 C6 39 4N 77 15W
Travilah Regional Park, *Wash.* 25 C6 39 4N 77 17W
Travis, *N.Y.* 22 D3 40 35N 74 11W
Treasure I., *S.F.* 27 B2 37 49N 122 22W
Třeboradice, *Pra.* 10 B3 50 9N 14 31 E
Třebotov, *Pra.* 10 C1 49 58N 14 17 E
Trecase, *Nápl.* 9 J13 40 46N 14 26 E
Trekroner, *Købn.* 2 D10 55 40N 12 37 E
Tremblay-lès-Gonesse, *Paris* 5 B5 48 58N 2 30 E
Tremembé, *S. Pau.* 31 D6 23 27 S 46 36W
Tremembe →, *S. Pau.* 31 D6 23 28 S 46 34W
Tremont, *Melb.* 19 F9 37 53 S 145 20 E
Tremont, *N.Y.* 23 B5 40 50N 73 52W
Trenno, *Mil.* 9 E5 45 29N 9 6 E
Treptow, *Berl.* 7 B3 52 29N 13 27 E
Tres Marias, *Méx.* 29 D2 19 3N 99 15W
Três Rios, Sa. dos, *Rio J.* 31 B2 22 56 S 43 17W
Tretiakov Art Gallery, *Mos.* 11 E9 55 44N 37 38 E
Trevose, *Phil.* 24 A5 40 8N 74 59W
Trezzano sul Naviglio, *Mil.* 9 E5 45 24N 9 4 E
Tribobo, *Rio J.* 31 B3 22 50 S 43 0W
Triel-sur-Seine, *Paris* 5 B2 48 58N 2 0 E
Trieste, *Rome* 9 F10 41 55N 12 30 E
Trinidad, *Wash.* 25 D8 38 54N 76 59W
Triome, *Jobg.* 18 F8 26 10 S 27 58 E
Trionfale, *Rome* 9 F9 41 54N 12 26 E
Triulzo, *Mil.* 9 E6 45 25N 9 16 E
Trócchia, *Nápl.* 9 H13 40 51N 14 23 E
Troitse-Lykovo, *Mos.* 11 E8 55 47N 37 23 E
Troja, *Pra.* 10 B2 50 7N 14 25 E
Trollbäcken, *Stock.* 3 E12 59 14N 18 12 E
Trombay, *Bomb.* 16 G8 19 2N 72 56 E
Troparevo, *Mos.* 11 F8 55 39N 37 29 E
Trottiscliffe, *Lon.* 4 D7 51 18N 0 21 E
Troy Hills, *N.Y.* 22 B2 40 50N 74 23W
Troyeville, *Jobg.* 18 F9 26 11 S 28 4 E
Truc di Miola, *Tori.* 9 A2 45 11N 7 30 E
Trudyashchikhsya, Os., *St-Pet.* 11 B3 59 58N 30 18 E
Trutlandet, *Hels.* 3 C6 60 9N 25 17 E
Tryvasshøgda, *Oslo* 2 B4 59 59N 10 40 E
Tseng Lan Shue, *H.K.* 12 D6 22 20N 114 14 E
Tsentralnyy, *Mos.* 11 D11 55 53N 37 51 E
Tsim Sha Tsui, *H.K.* 12 E6 22 17N 114 10 E
Tsing Yi, *H.K.* 12 D5 22 21N 114 6 E
Tsuen Wan, *H.K.* 12 D5 22 22N 114 7 E
Tsurugamine, *Tōkyō* 13 D2 35 28N 139 33 E
Tsuruma, *Tōkyō* 13 A2 35 52N 139 31 E
Tsurumi →, *Tōkyō* 13 C3 35 32N 139 40 E
Tsurumi-Ku, *Tōkyō* 13 D3 35 30N 139 41 E
Tsz Wan Shan, *H.K.* 12 D6 22 20N 114 11 E
Tua Kang Lye, *Sing.* 15 G7 1 18N 103 46 E
Tuas, *Sing.* 15 G6 1 19N 103 39 E
Tuchoměřice, *Pra.* 10 B1 50 7N 14 16 E
Tuckahoe, *N.Y.* 23 B6 40 56N 73 49W
Tucuruvi, *S. Pau.* 31 D6 23 28 S 46 35W
Tufello, *Rome* 9 F10 41 56N 12 32 E
Tufnell Park, *Lon.* 4 B4 51 33N 0 8W
Tujunga, *L.A.* 28 A3 34 15N 118 16W
Tujunga Wash →, *L.A.* 28 A2 34 12N 118 23W
Tullamarine, *Melb.* 19 E6 37 41 S 144 50 E
Tullinge, *Stock.* 3 E10 59 12N 17 54 E
Tullingesjön, *Stock.* 3 E10 59 12N 17 52 E
Tulse Hill, *Lon.* 4 C4 51 26N 0 6W
Tulyehualco, *Méx.* 29 C3 19 15N 99 0W
Tumba, *Stock.* 3 E9 59 12N 17 49 E
Tune, *Købn.* 2 E8 55 35N 12 10 E
Tung Lo Wan, *H.K.* 12 E6 22 17N 114 11 E
Tung Lung I., *H.K.* 12 E6 22 15N 114 17 E
Tung O, *H.K.* 12 E5 22 11N 114 8 E
Tunis, *Bagd.* 17 E8 33 23N 44 21 E
Tuomarila, *Hels.* 3 B3 60 11N 24 41 E
Tura, *El Qâ.* 18 D5 29 55N 31 16 E
Turambhe, *Bomb.* 16 G9 19 4N 73 0 E
Turdera, *B.A.* 32 C4 34 48 S 58 26W
Tureberg, *Stock.* 3 D10 59 25N 17 55 E
Turffontein, *Jobg.* 18 F9 26 14 S 28 2 E
Turin = Torino, *Tori.* 9 B2 45 5N 7 39 E
Turner, *Balt.* 25 B4 39 14N 76 31W
Turner Hill, *Bost.* 21 A4 42 40N 70 53W
Turnersville, *Phil.* 24 C4 39 46N 75 3W
Turnham Green, *Lon.* 4 C3 51 29N 0 16W
Turów, *Wsaw.* 10 E8 52 19N 21 11 E
Turter, *Oslo* 2 A4 60 0N 10 46 E
Tuscolano, *Rome* 9 F10 41 52N 12 31 E
Tushino, *Mos.* 11 D8 55 50N 37 24 E
Tuusulanjoki →, *Hels.* 3 A4 60 20N 24 54 E
Twickenham, *Lon.* 4 C2 51 26N 0 20W
Twickenham Rugby Ground, *Lon.* 4 C2 51 27N 0 20W
Twin Oaks, *Phil.* 24 B2 39 50N 75 25W
Twórki, *Wsaw.* 10 E5 52 10N 20 49 E
Tyresö, *Stock.* 3 E13 59 14N 18 20 E
Tyresö strand, *Stock.* 3 E12 59 15N 18 17 E

U

Uberaba →, *S. Pau.* 31 E6 23 35 S 46 41W
Uberruhr, *Ruhr* 6 B4 51 25N 7 4 E
Ubin, P., *Sing.* 15 F8 1 24N 103 57 E
Uboldo, *Mil.* 9 D5 45 36N 9 0 E
Uckendorf, *Ruhr* 6 B4 51 29N 7 7 E
Udelnaya, *St-Pet.* 11 A4 60 0N 30 21 E
Udelnyaya, *Mos.* 11 F11 55 38N 37 59 E
Udlding, *Mün.* 7 F9 48 15N 11 25 E
Uellendahl, *Ruhr* 6 C5 51 16N 7 10 E
Ueno, *Tōkyō* 13 B3 35 42N 139 46 E
Uerdingen, *Ruhr* 6 B1 51 20N 6 38 E
Uhlenhorst, *Hbg.* 7 D8 53 34N 10 1 E
Úholičky, *Pra.* 10 B1 50 9N 14 19 E
Uhříněves, *Pra.* 10 B3 50 2N 14 35 E
Újezd nad Lesy, *Pra.* 10 B3 50 4N 14 39 E
Újpalota, *Bud.* 10 J13 47 32N 19 8 E
Újpest, *Bud.* 10 J13 47 33N 19 5 E
Ukita, *Tōkyō* 13 B4 35 38N 139 51 E
Ullerup, *Købn.* 2 E10 55 34N 12 36 E
Ullevål, *Oslo* 2 B4 59 56N 10 46 E
Üllo, *Bud.* 10 K14 47 23N 19 20 E
Ulriksdal, *Stock.* 3 D10 59 23N 17 59 E
Ulu Bedok, *Sing.* 15 G8 1 19N 103 55 E
Ulu Pandan →, *Sing.* 15 G7 1 19N 103 45 E
Ulyanka, *St-Pet.* 11 B3 59 50N 30 14 E
Um Al-Khanazir, *Bagd.* 17 F8 33 17N 44 22 E
Umeda, *Ōsaka* 12 B3 34 41N 135 29 E
Umejima, *Tōkyō* 13 B3 35 46N 139 48 E
Umraniye, *Ist.* 17 A3 41 1N 29 4 E
Uněticky →, *Pra.* 10 B2 50 9N 14 24 E
Ungelsheim, *Ruhr* 6 B2 51 21N 6 43 E
Unhos, *Lisb.* 8 F8 38 49N 9 7W
Unidad Santa Fe, *Méx.* 29 B2 19 23N 99 13W
Union, *N.Y.* 22 C3 40 42N 74 16W
Union City, *N.Y.* 22 C4 40 45N 74 2W
Union City, *S.F.* 27 C4 37 36N 122 2W
Union Port, *N.Y.* 23 C5 40 48N 73 51W
Uniondale, *N.Y.* 23 C7 40 42N 73 35W
United Nations H.Q., *N.Y.* 22 C5 40 45N 73 59W
Universal City, *L.A.* 28 B2 34 8N 118 21W
Universidad de Chila, *Stgo* 30 J11 33 26 S 70 39W
University Gardens, *N.Y.* 23 C6 40 46N 73 42W
University Heights, *S.F.* 27 D3 37 26N 122 13W
University Park, *Wash.* 25 D8 38 58N 76 56W
Unsani, *Calc.* 16 E5 22 35N 88 15 E
Unterbach, *Ruhr* 6 C3 51 12N 6 53 E
Unterbiberg, *Mün.* 7 G10 48 6N 11 38 E
Unterföhring, *Mün.* 7 F11 48 11N 11 38 E
Unterhaching, *Mün.* 7 G10 48 3N 11 37 E
Unterkirchbach, *Wien* 10 G9 48 17N 16 12 E
Unterlaa, *Wien* 10 H10 48 7N 16 25 E
Untermauerbach, *Wien* 10 G9 48 14N 16 11 E
Untermenzing, *Mün.* 7 F9 48 10N 11 28 E
Unterrath, *Ruhr* 6 C2 51 16N 6 45 E
Unterschleissheim, *Mün.* 7 F10 48 16N 11 35 E
Upminster, *Lon.* 4 B6 51 33N 0 14 E
Upper Brookville, *N.Y.* 23 B7 40 50N 73 35W
Upper Crystal Springs Res., *S.F.* 26 D2 37 28N 122 20W
Upper Darby, *Phil.* 24 B3 39 57N 75 16W
Upper Edmonton, *Lon.* 4 B4 51 36N 0 3W
Upper Elmers End, *Lon.* 4 C4 51 23N 0 1W
Upper Fern Tree Gully, *Melb.* 19 F8 37 53 S 145 18 E
Upper New York B., *N.Y.* 22 D4 40 39N 74 3W
Upper Norwood, *Lon.* 4 C4 51 24N 0 6W
Upper Peirce Res., *Sing.* 15 F7 1 22N 103 47 E
Upper San Leandro Res., *S.F.* 27 B4 37 46N 122 6W
Upper Sydenham, *Lon.* 4 C4 51 26N 0 4W
Upper Tooting, *Lon.* 4 C4 51 25N 0 9W
Upton, *Lon.* 4 B5 51 32N 0 1 E
Uptons Hill, *Bost.* 21 B3 42 33N 71 0W
Uptown, *Chic.* 26 B2 41 58N 87 40W
Upwey, *Melb.* 19 F9 37 53 S 145 20 E
Urawa, *Tōkyō* 13 A2 35 51N 139 39 E
Urayasu, *Tōkyō* 13 C4 35 39N 139 53 E
Urbe, Aeroporto d', *Rome* 9 F10 41 57N 12 30 E
Urca, *Rio J.* 31 B3 22 56 S 43 9W
Uritsk, *St-Pet.* 11 C3 59 49N 30 10 E
Üröm, *Bud.* 10 J13 47 35N 19 1 E
Ursus, *Wsaw.* 10 E6 52 11N 20 52 E
Ursvik, *Stock.* 3 D10 59 23N 17 57 E
Usera, *Mdrd.* 8 B2 40 22N 3 42W
Ushigome, *Tōkyō* 13 B3 35 42N 139 44 E
Usküdar, *Ist.* 17 A3 41 1N 29 0 E
Ust-Slavyanka, *St-Pet.* 11 C5 59 51N 30 32 E
Uteke, *Stock.* 3 D12 59 24N 18 15 E
Utfort, *Ruhr* 6 B1 51 28N 6 37 E
Utinga, *S. Pau.* 31 E6 23 38 S 46 31W
Utrata, *Wsaw.* 10 E7 52 15N 21 4 E
Uttarpara, *Calc.* 16 E5 22 39N 88 21 E
Utterslev Mose, *Købn.* 2 D9 55 42N 12 29 E
Uttran, *Stock.* 3 E9 59 12N 17 43 E
Utvika, *Oslo* 2 A1 60 2N 10 15 E
Uxbridge, *Lon.* 4 B2 51 32N 0 28W
Uzkoye, *Mos.* 11 F9 55 37N 37 32 E
Uzunca →, *Ist.* 17 A1 41 54N 28 50 E

V

Vadaul, *Bomb.* 16 G8 19 2N 72 55 E
Værebro Å →, *Købn.* 2 D8 55 47N 12 7 E
Vahal, *Bomb.* 16 H9 18 58N 73 2 E
Vaires-sur-Marne, *Paris* 5 B5 48 52N 2 38 E
Val della Torre, *Tori.* 9 B1 45 8N 7 27 E
Valby, *Købn.* 2 E9 55 39N 12 29 E
Valcannuta, *Rome* 9 F9 41 52N 12 25 E
Valdeveba, *Mdrd.* 8 B3 40 29N 3 39W
Vale, *Wash.* 25 D5 38 55N 77 20W
Valentino, Parco del, *Tori.* 9 B3 45 3N 7 41 E
Valenton, *Paris* 5 C4 48 44N 2 27 E
Valera, *Mil.* 9 D5 45 33N 9 3 E
Vallcarca, *Barc.* 8 D5 41 25N 2 9 E
Valldoreix, *Barc.* 8 D5 41 27N 2 3 E
Vallecas, *Mdrd.* 8 B3 40 22N 3 37W
Vallemar, *S.F.* 27 C2 37 36N 122 28W
Vallensbæk, *Købn.* 2 E9 55 38N 12 21 E
Vallensbæk Strand, *Købn.* 2 E9 55 36N 12 23 E
Vallentunasjön, *Stock.* 3 D11 59 27N 18 1 E
Valleranello, *Rome* 9 G9 41 46N 12 29 E
Valley Forge, *Phil.* 24 A2 40 5N 75 27W
Valley Forge Hist. State Park, *Phil.* 24 A2 40 5N 75 27W
Valley Mede, *Balt.* 25 B1 39 16N 76 50W
Valley Stream, *N.Y.* 23 C6 40 40N 73 43W
Vällingby, *Stock.* 3 D10 59 21N 17 52 E
Vallisaari, *Hels.* 3 C5 60 7N 25 0 E
Vallvidrera, *Barc.* 8 D5 41 24N 2 6 E
Valo Velho, *S. Pau.* 31 E5 23 38 S 46 47W
Valuyevo, *Mos.* 11 F8 55 30N 37 21 E
Valvidrera →, *Barc.* 8 D5 41 25N 2 0 E
Van Dyks Park, *Jobg.* 18 F10 26 15 S 28 18 E
Van Nuys, *L.A.* 28 A2 34 11N 118 27W
Van Nuys Airport, *L.A.* 28 A2 34 12N 118 29W
Van Ryn Dam, *Jobg.* 18 E11 26 8 S 28 21 E
Vanak, *Tehr.* 17 C5 35 45N 51 23 E
Vangede, *Købn.* 2 D10 55 45N 12 31 E
Vaniköy, *Ist.* 17 A3 41 3N 29 3 E
Vanløse, *Købn.* 2 D9 55 41N 12 28 E
Vantaa, *Hels.* 3 B4 60 18N 24 56 E
Vantaa →, *Hels.* 3 B4 60 13N 24 53 E
Vantaankoski, *Hels.* 3 B4 60 18N 24 50 E
Vantör, *Stock.* 3 E11 59 16N 18 2 E
Vanves, *Paris* 5 C3 48 49N 2 17 E
Vanzago, *Mil.* 9 D4 45 31N 8 59 E
Vårby, *Stock.* 3 E10 59 15N 17 52 E
Vardåsen, *Oslo* 2 C6 50 48N 11 6 E
Varedo, *Mil.* 9 D5 45 35N 9 8 E
Varennes-Jarcy, *Paris* 5 C5 48 40N 2 33 E
Vargem Grande, *Rio J.* 31 B1 22 58 S 43 27W
Városliget, *Bud.* 10 J13 47 30N 19 5 E
Vartiokylä, *Hels.* 3 B5 60 13N 25 6 E
Vartiosaari, *Hels.* 3 B5 60 11N 25 5 E
Vasby, *Købn.* 2 D8 55 40N 12 12 E
Vashi, *Bomb.* 16 G8 19 4N 72 59 E
Vasilyevskiy, Os., *St-Pet.* 11 B3 59 55N 30 16 E
Västerkulla, *Hels.* 3 B5 60 16N 24 31 E
Västerskog, *Hels.* 3 B6 60 16N 25 17 E
Vasto, *Nápl.* 9 H12 40 51N 14 16 E
Vatutino, *Mos.* 11 D10 55 52N 37 40 E
Vaucresson, *Paris* 5 B2 48 50N 2 9 E
Vaudreuil, *Mtrl.* 20 B1 43 24N 74 1W
Vaudreuil-sur-le Lac, *Mtrl.* 20 B1 43 25N 74 1W
Vauhallan, *Paris* 5 C3 48 44N 2 12 E
Vaujours, *Paris* 5 B5 48 56N 2 34 E
Vauréal, *Paris* 5 A2 49 2N 2 1 E
Vaux-sur-Seine, *Paris* 5 A1 49 0N 1 57 E
Vauxhall, *Lon.* 4 C4 51 29N 0 7W
Vaxholm, *Stock.* 3 D13 59 24N 18 20 E
Vecklax, *Hels.* 3 B2 60 10N 24 31 E
Vecsés, *Bud.* 10 K14 47 24N 19 16 E
Vedano al Lissone, *Mil.* 9 D6 45 36N 9 16 E
Veddel, *Hbg.* 7 D8 53 31N 10 2 E
Vega, *Stock.* 3 E11 59 11N 18 8 E
Vehkalahti, *Hels.* 3 B2 60 11N 24 30 E
Veikkola, *Hels.* 3 B1 60 16N 24 26 E
Velbert, *Ruhr* 6 B4 51 21N 7 1 E
Veleň, *Pra.* 10 A3 50 10N 14 33 E
Veleslavin, *Pra.* 10 B2 50 5N 14 21 E
Vélizy-Villacoublay, *Paris* 5 C3 48 47N 2 11 E
Velka-Chuchle, *Pra.* 10 B2 50 0N 14 23 E
Venaria, *Tori.* 9 B2 45 8N 7 37 E
Venda Seca, *Lisb.* 8 F7 38 46N 9 15W
Vendelsö, *Stock.* 3 E12 59 12N 18 11 E
Venice, *L.A.* 28 C2 33 59N 118 27W
Venner, *Oslo* 2 A3 60 1N 10 36 E
Vennhausen, *Ruhr* 6 C3 51 13N 6 51 E
Ventas, *Mdrd.* 8 B2 40 26N 3 40W
Ventorro del Cano, *Mdrd.* 8 B2 40 23N 3 49W
Verberg, *Ruhr* 6 B1 51 21N 6 34 E
Verde →, *S. Pau.* 31 E7 23 29 S 46 27W
Verdi, *Ath.* 8 H11 38 2N 23 40 E
Verdugo Mt., *L.A.* 28 A3 34 12N 118 17W
Verdun, *Mtrl.* 20 B4 43 27N 73 35W
Vereya, *Mos.* 11 F12 55 37N 38 2 E
Vérhalom, *Bud.* 10 J13 47 31N 19 1 E
Vermelho →, *S. Pau.* 31 E5 23 30 S 46 46W
Vermont, *Melb.* 19 F8 37 50 S 145 12 E
Vermont South, *Melb.* 19 F8 37 51 S 145 11 E
Verneuil-sur-Seine, *Paris* 5 B1 48 58N 1 59 E
Vernouillet, *Paris* 5 B1 48 58N 1 56 E
Verona, *N.Y.* 22 C3 40 49N 74 15W
Verperluda, Os., *St-Pet.* 11 B2 59 59N 30 0 E
Verrières-le-Buisson, *Paris* 5 C3 48 44N 2 16 E
Versailles, *B.A.* 32 B3 34 38 S 58 31W
Versailles, *Paris* 5 C2 48 48N 2 7 E
Veshnyaki, *Mos.* 11 E10 55 43N 37 48 E
Vesolyy Posolok, *St-Pet.* 11 B4 59 53N 30 28 E
Vestli, *Oslo* 2 B5 59 58N 10 55 E
Vestra, *Hels.* 3 B3 60 19N 24 46 E
Vestskoven, *Købn.* 2 D9 55 41N 12 23 E
Vesuvio, *Nápl.* 9 J13 40 49N 14 25 E
Vets Stadium, *Phil.* 24 B3 39 54N 75 10W
Viby, *Købn.* 2 E7 55 33N 12 1 E
Vicálvaro, *Mdrd.* 8 B3 40 24N 3 36W
Vicente Lopez, *B.A.* 32 B4 34 31 S 58 30W
Victoria, *B.A.* 32 A3 34 27 S 58 32W
Victoria, *H.K.* 12 E6 22 17N 114 11 E
Victoria, Pont, *Mtrl.* 20 B4 43 29N 73 32W
Victoria Gardens, *Bomb.* 16 H8 18 58N 72 50 E
Victoria Harbour, *H.K.* 12 E5 22 17N 114 10 E
Victoria Island, *Lagos* 18 B2 6 25N 7 25 E
Victoria L., *Jobg.* 18 F9 26 13 S 28 9 E
Victoria Lawn Tennis Courts, *Melb.* 19 F7 37 50 S 145 1 E
Victoria Park, *H.K.* 12 E5 22 16N 114 8 E
Vidja, *Stock.* 3 E11 59 12N 18 4 E
Vidrholec, *Pra.* 10 B3 50 5N 14 39 E
Vienna = Wien, *Wien* 10 G10 48 12N 16 22 E
Vienna, *Wash.* 25 D6 38 54N 77 16W
Vieringhausen, *Ruhr* 6 C4 51 10N 7 9 E
Vierlinden, *Ruhr* 6 A2 51 32N 6 45 E
Vierumäki, *Hels.* 3 A5 60 21N 25 2 E
Vierzigstücken, *Hbg.* 7 D6 53 30N 9 49 E
View Bank, *Melb.* 19 E7 37 43 S 145 6 E
Vigário Geral, *Rio J.* 31 A2 22 48 S 43 16W
Vigentino, *Mil.* 9 E6 45 26N 9 13 E
Viggbyholm, *Stock.* 3 D11 59 26N 18 7 E
Vighignolo, *Mil.* 9 E5 45 29N 9 2 E
Vigneux-sur-Seine, *Paris* 5 C4 48 42N 2 24 E
Viikki, *Hels.* 3 B5 60 13N 25 1 E
Viirilä, *Hels.* 3 B5 60 19N 25 8 E
Vila Andrade, *S. Pau.* 31 E5 23 37 S 46 44W
Vila Barcelona, *S. Pau.* 31 E6 23 37 S 46 33W
Vila Bocaina, *S. Pau.* 31 F7 23 40 S 46 26W
Vila Dalva, *S. Pau.* 31 E5 23 34 S 46 46W
Vila Dirce, *S. Pau.* 31 E4 23 33 S 46 50W
Vila Eldorado, *S. Pau.* 31 F6 23 42 S 46 38W
Vila Ema, *S. Pau.* 31 E6 23 35 S 46 31W
Vila Formosa, *S. Pau.* 31 E6 23 34 S 46 32W
Vila Galvão, *S. Pau.* 31 D6 23 27 S 46 34W
Vila Gonçales, *S. Pau.* 31 F6 23 42 S 46 33W
Vila Iasi, *S. Pau.* 31 E5 23 37 S 46 47W
Vila Indiana, *S. Pau.* 31 E5 23 34 S 46 48W
Vila Isabel, *Rio J.* 31 B2 22 54 S 43 15W
Vila Madalena, *S. Pau.* 31 E5 23 32 S 46 41W
Vila Maria, *S. Pau.* 31 E6 23 31 S 46 36W
Vila Mariana, *S. Pau.* 31 E6 23 35 S 46 37W
Vila Matilde, *S. Pau.* 31 E6 23 31 S 46 30W
Vila Nova Curuçá, *S. Pau.* 31 E7 23 31 S 46 25W
Vila Pires, *S. Pau.* 31 F6 23 41 S 46 30W
Vila Progresso, *Rio J.* 31 B3 22 53 S 43 1W
Vila Prudente, *S. Pau.* 31 E6 23 35 S 46 33W
Vila Ré, *S. Pau.* 31 E6 23 31 S 46 29W
Vila Remo, *S. Pau.* 31 F5 23 40 S 46 45W
Vila Sonia, *S. Pau.* 31 E5 23 35 S 46 43W
Viladecans, *Barc.* 8 E5 41 18N 2 1 E
Villa Ada, *Rome* 9 F10 41 55N 12 30 E
Villa Adelina, *B.A.* 32 B3 34 31 S 58 33W
Villa Alianza, *B.A.* 32 B3 34 37 S 58 33W
Villa Alsina, *B.A.* 32 C4 34 40 S 58 24W
Villa Altube, *B.A.* 32 B2 34 31 S 58 45W
Villa Ariza, *B.A.* 32 B3 34 38 S 58 39W
Villa Augusta, *B.A.* 32 C5 34 45 S 58 15W
Villa Ballester, *B.A.* 32 B3 34 33 S 58 33W
Villa Barilari, *B.A.* 32 C4 34 42 S 58 20W
Villa Basso, *B.A.* 32 B3 34 33 S 58 33W
Villa Bosch, *B.A.* 32 B3 34 35 S 58 33W
Villa C. Colon, *B.A.* 32 C4 34 41 S 58 21W
Villa D. F. Sarmiento, *B.A.* 32 B3 34 38 S 58 35W
Villa D. Sobral, *B.A.* 32 C5 34 45 S 58 15W
Villa de Guadalupe, *Méx.* 29 B3 19 29N 99 6W
Villa de Mayo, *B.A.* 32 B2 34 30 S 58 40W
Villa Devoto, *B.A.* 32 B3 34 36 S 58 31W
Villa Dominico, *B.A.* 32 C5 34 41 S 58 19W
Villa Giambruno, *B.A.* 32 C5 34 48 S 58 15W
Villa Gustavo A. Madero, *Méx.* 29 B3 19 29N 99 8W
Villa Hogar Alemán, *B.A.* 32 C4 34 42 S 58 26W
Villa Iglesias, *B.A.* 32 B3 34 30 S 58 45W
Villa Leloir, *B.A.* 32 B2 34 35 S 58 41W
Villa Leon, *B.A.* 32 B3 34 38 S 58 41W
Villa Lugano, *B.A.* 32 C4 34 41 S 58 27W
Villa Luzuriago, *B.A.* 32 C3 34 40 S 58 34W
Villa Lynch, *B.A.* 32 B3 34 35 S 58 31W
Villa Madero, *B.A.* 32 C3 34 41 S 58 30W
Villa Maria del Triunfo, *Lima* 30 G9 12 9 S 76 57W
Villa Obregon, *Méx.* 29 B2 19 20N 99 12W
Villa Reichembach, *B.A.* 32 B2 34 39 S 58 40W
Villa Rosa, *B.A.* 32 A1 34 25 S 58 5W
Villa San Francisco, *B.A.* 32 C5 34 46 S 58 15W
Villacoublay, Aérodrome de, *Paris* 5 C3 48 46N 2 12 E
Village Green, *Phil.* 24 B2 39 52N 75 26W
Villanova, *Phil.* 24 A2 40 1N 75 20W
Villarbasse, *Tori.* 9 B1 45 2N 7 27 E
Villaretto, *Tori.* 9 B3 45 7N 7 42 E
Villaricca, *Nápl.* 9 H12 40 55N 14 11 E
Villaroche, *Paris* 5 D5 48 37N 2 39 E
Villaroy, *Paris* 5 C2 48 46N 2 5 E
Villastanza, *Mil.* 9 D4 45 32N 8 57 E
Villaverde, *Mdrd.* 8 B2 40 21N 3 42W
Villaverde Bajo, *Mdrd.* 8 B2 40 20N 3 40W
Villawood, *Syd.* 19 B2 33 53 S 150 58 E
Ville-d'Avray, *Paris* 5 C3 48 49N 2 11 E
Ville de Laval, *Mtrl.* 20 A3 43 34N 73 43W
Villebon-sur-Yvette, *Paris* 5 C3 48 41N 2 14 E
Villecresnes, *Paris* 5 C5 48 43N 2 31 E

48 Villejuif

Villejuif, Paris 5 C4 48 47N 2 21 E
Villejust, Paris 5 C3 48 41N 2 15 E
Villemoisson-sur-Orge, Paris 5 C3 48 40N 2 19 E
Villemomble, Paris 5 B5 48 52N 2 30 E
Villeneuve-la-Garenne, Paris 5 B3 48 56N 2 19 E
Villeneuve-le-Roi, Paris 5 C4 48 43N 2 24 E
Villeneuve-St.-Georges, Paris 5 C4 48 43N 2 27 E
Villeneuve-sous-Dammartin, Paris 5 A5 49 2N 2 38 E
Villennes-sur-Seine, Paris 5 B1 48 56N 2 0 E
Villeparisis, Paris 5 B5 48 56N 2 36 E
Villepinte, Paris 5 B5 48 57N 2 30 E
Villepreux, Paris 5 C1 48 49N 1 59 E
Villevaudé, Paris 5 B5 48 55N 2 39 E
Villeziers, Paris 5 C3 48 40N 2 10 E
Villiers-le-Bâcle, Paris 5 C2 48 44N 2 8 E
Villiers-le-Bel, Paris 5 A4 49 0N 2 23 E
Villiers-St. Frédéric, Paris 5 C1 48 49N 1 53 E
Villiers-sur-Marne, Paris 5 C5 48 49N 2 32 E
Villiers-sur-Orge, Paris 5 D3 48 39N 2 18 E
Villinki, Hels. 3 C5 60 9N 25 6 E
Villoresi, Canale, Mil. 9 D4 45 33N 8 59 E
Vimodrone, Mil. 9 D6 45 30N 9 16 E
Vimont, Mtrl. 20 A3 43 36N 73 43W
Vincennes, Paris 5 B4 48 51N 2 26 E
Vincennes, Bois de, Paris 5 C4 48 49N 2 26 E
Vinohrady, Pra. 10 B2 50 4N 14 26 E
Vinoř, Pra. 10 B3 50 8N 14 34 E
Vinořský →, Pra. 10 A3 50 11N 14 39 E
Violet Hill, H.K. 12 E6 22 15N 114 11 E
Virányos, Bud. 10 J12 47 31N 18 59 E
Virgeo del San Cristóbal, Stgo 30 J11 33 25 S 70 38W
Viroflay, Paris 5 C3 48 48N 2 10 E
Viron, Ath. 8 J11 37 55N 23 46 E
Virreyes, B.A. 32 A3 34 27 S 58 33W
Virum, Købn. 2 D9 55 47N 12 27 E
Viry-Châtillon, Paris 5 C4 48 40N 2 21 E
Vishnyaki, Mos. 11 E11 55 46N 37 53 E
Visitacion Valley, S.F. 27 B2 37 42N 122 23W
Vista Alegre, Lima 30 G9 12 8 S 76 59W
Vista Alegre, Stgo 30 K10 33 30 S 70 43W
Vitacura, Stgo 30 J11 33 23 S 70 35W
Vitarte-Ate, Lima 30 G9 12 3 S 76 57W
Vitinia, Rome 9 G9 41 47N 12 24 E
Vitry-sur-Seine, Paris 5 C4 48 47N 2 23 E
Vitträsk, Hels. 3 B1 60 11N 24 29 E
Vittuone, Mil. 9 E4 45 28N 8 57 E
Vladykino, Mos. 11 D9 55 51N 37 35 E
Vltava →, Pra. 10 B2 50 10N 14 2 E
Vnukovo, Mos. 11 F7 55 37N 37 17 E
Voerde, Ruhr 6 C6 51 18N 7 23 E
Voerde, Ruhr 6 A2 51 35N 6 42 E
Vogelheim, Ruhr 6 B3 51 29N 6 59 E
Vohwinkel, Ruhr 6 C4 51 13N 7 4 E
Voisins-le-Bretonneux, Paris 5 C2 48 45N 2 3 E
Vokovice, Pra. 10 B2 50 5N 14 21 E
Volgelsdorf, Berl. 7 B5 52 30N 13 44 E
Volkhonka-Zil, Mos. 11 F9 55 39N 37 37 E
Volkovka →, St-Pet. 11 B4 59 54N 30 25 E
Volksdorf, Hbg. 7 D8 53 39N 10 8 E
Volla, Nápl. 9 H13 40 52N 14 20 E
Vollen, Oslo 2 C2 59 48N 10 27 E
Volmarstein, Ruhr 6 B6 51 22N 7 22 E
Volodarskoye, St-Pet. 11 B4 59 54N 30 23 E
Volpiano, Tori. 9 A3 45 12N 7 46 E
Volynkina-Derevnya, St-Pet. 11 B3 59 53N 30 18 E
Volynyy, Os., St-Pet. 11 B3 59 57N 30 14 E
Vomero, Nápl. 9 H12 40 50N 14 13 E
Vorderhainbach, Wien 10 G9 48 13N 16 12 E
Vorhalle, Ruhr 6 B6 51 23N 7 26 E
Vormholz, Ruhr 6 B5 51 24N 7 19 E
Vösendorf, Wien 10 H10 48 7N 16 20 E
Vostochnyy, Mos. 11 E11 55 49N 37 51 E
Vouliagmeni, Ath. 8 K11 37 50N 23 46 E
Vrčovice, Pra. 10 B2 50 4N 14 28 E
Vsevolozhsk, St-Pet. 11 A5 60 0N 30 39 E
Vuosaari, Hels. 3 B5 60 13N 25 8 E
Vyborgskaya Storona, St-Pet. 11 B4 59 57N 30 22 E
Vyčehrad, Pra. 10 B2 50 3N 14 25 E
Vykhino, Mos. 11 E10 55 42N 37 48 E
Vysočany, Pra. 10 B2 50 6N 14 29 E

W

Waban, L., Bost. 21 D2 42 17N 71 18W
Wachterhof, Mün. 7 G11 48 2N 11 42 E
Waddington, Lon. 4 D3 51 18N 0 7W
Wadeville, Jobg. 18 F10 26 15 S 28 11 E
Wahda, Bagd. 17 F8 33 18N 44 26 E
Währing, Wien 10 G10 48 14N 16 20 E
Waidmannslust, Berl. 7 A3 52 36N 13 20 E
Wajay, La Hab. 30 B2 23 0N 82 25W
Wakefield, Bost. 21 B3 42 30N 71 5W
Wald, Ruhr 6 C4 51 11N 7 3 E
Waldesruh, Berl. 7 B4 52 28N 13 37 E
Waldheim, Berl. 7 A1 52 34N 13 3 E
Waldperlach, Mün. 7 G10 48 4N 11 40 E
Waldtrudering, Mün. 7 G11 48 6N 11 42 E
Waldwick, N.Y. 22 A4 41 1N 74 5W
Wall Street, N.Y. 22 C4 40 42N 74 0W
Wallgrove, Syd. 19 A2 33 47 S 150 51 E
Wallington, Lon. 4 C4 51 21N 0 8W
Wallington, N.Y. 22 B4 40 50N 74 8W
Walnut Cr. →, S.F. 27 A4 37 55N 122 3W
Walnut Creek, S.F. 27 A4 37 53N 122 3W
Walnut Heights, S.F. 27 A4 37 52N 122 2W
Walsum, Ruhr 6 A2 51 32N 6 42 E
Walsumer Mark, Ruhr 6 A3 51 33N 6 50 E
Walt Whitman Br., Phil. 24 B4 39 4N 75 9W
Waltershof, Hbg. 7 D7 53 31N 9 54 E
Waltham, Bost. 21 C2 42 23N 71 14W
Waltham Abbey, Lon. 4 A5 51 41N 0 1 E
Waltham Forest, Lon. 4 B4 51 35N 0 1 E
Walthamstow, Lon. 4 B4 51 34N 0 1W
Walton on Thames, Lon. 4 C2 51 22N 0 23W
Walton on the Hill, Lon. 4 D3 51 16N 0 14W
Waltrop, Ruhr 6 A6 51 36N 7 25 E
Walworth, Lon. 4 C4 51 29N 0 5W
Wambachsee, Ruhr 6 C4 51 23N 6 47 E
Wan Chai, H.K. 12 E6 22 16N 114 10 E
Wanaque, N.Y. 22 A3 41 2N 74 17W
Wandezhuang, Tianj. 14 E5 39 6N 117 10 E
Wandle →, Lon. 4 C3 51 27N 0 11W
Wandsbek, Hbg. 7 D8 53 34N 10 4 E
Wandsworth, Lon. 4 C3 51 27N 0 11W
Wang Hin, Khlong →, Bangk. 15 A2 13 50N 100 35 E
Wanheim, Ruhr 6 B2 51 23N 6 45 E
Wanheimerort, Ruhr 6 B2 51 24N 6 45 E
Wanne-Eickel, Ruhr 6 A4 51 31N 7 9 E
Wannsee, Berl. 7 B1 52 25N 13 9 E
Wansdorf, Berl. 7 A1 52 38N 13 5 E
Wanstead, Lon. 4 B5 51 34N 0 1 E
Wantagh Seaford, N.Y. 23 D8 40 39N 73 28W
Wantirna, Melb. 19 F8 37 50 S 145 14 E
Wapping, Lon. 4 B4 51 30N 0 3W
Warabi, Tōkyō 13 B3 35 49N 139 42 E
Ward, Phil. 24 B1 39 52N 75 30W
Warlingham, Lon. 4 D4 51 18N 0 2W
Warnberg, Mün. 7 G10 48 4N 11 31 E
Warngal Park, Melb. 19 E7 37 45 S 145 4 E
Warrandyte, Melb. 19 E8 37 43 S 145 13 E
Warrandyte Park, Melb. 19 E8 37 44 S 145 14 E
Warrandyte South, Melb. 19 E8 37 44 S 145 14 E
Warranwood, Melb. 19 E8 37 46 S 145 14 E
Warrâq el 'Arab, El Qâ. 18 C5 30 4N 31 11 E
Warrâq el Hadf, El Qâ. 18 C5 30 5N 31 12 E
Warren Hill, Bost. 21 B1 42 35N 71 21W
Warsaw = Warszawa, Wsaw. 10 E7 52 14N 21 0 E
Warszawa, Wsaw. 10 E7 52 14N 21 0 E
Wartenberg, Berl. 7 A4 52 34N 13 31 E
Warwick Farm Racetrack, Syd. 19 B2 33 54 S 150 56 E
Wasa, Stock. 3 E11 59 19N 18 5 E
Wasfanârd, Tehr. 17 D5 35 38N 51 20 E
Washington, Wash. 25 D7 38 53N 77 2W
Washington Heights, N.Y. 22 B5 40 51N 73 56W
Washington Memorial Museum, Phil. 24 A2 40 5N 75 26W
Washington Nat. Airport, Wash. 25 D7 38 51N 77 2W
Washington Park, Chic. 26 C3 41 47N 87 36W
Washington Square, Phil. 24 A3 40 9N 75 19W
Washington Township, N.Y. 22 A4 41 0N 74 3W
Wasserschloss, Ruhr 6 A4 51 32N 7 1 E
Watching Mts., N.Y. 22 C2 40 43N 74 20W
Watchung, N.Y. 22 D2 40 38N 74 29W
Waterloo, Syd. 19 B4 33 53 S 151 12 E
Waterman Mt., L.A. 28 A5 34 14N 117 56W
Watertown, Bost. 21 C2 42 22N 71 10W
Watford, Lon. 4 A2 51 40N 0 27W
Watkins Island, Wash. 25 C6 39 2N 77 15W
Watsonia, Melb. 19 E7 37 43 S 145 6 E
Watsons B., Syd. 19 B4 33 50 S 151 18 E
Watsons Creek, Melb. 19 E8 37 40 S 145 13 E
Wattenscheid, Ruhr 6 B4 51 28N 7 8 E
Wattle Glen, Melb. 19 E8 37 39 S 145 11 E
Wattle Park, Melb. 19 F7 37 50 S 145 6 E
Watts →, Wash. 25 C6 39 2N 77 15W
Waverley, Bost. 21 C2 42 23N 71 10W
Waverley, Jobg. 18 E9 26 7 S 28 4 E
Waverley, Syd. 19 B4 33 53 S 151 15 E
Wawer, Wsaw. 10 E8 52 13N 21 8 E
Wawrzyszew, Wsaw. 10 E6 52 17N 20 53 E
Wayland, Bost. 21 C1 42 21N 71 20W
Wayne, N.Y. 22 B3 40 55N 74 15W
Wayne, Phil. 24 A2 40 2N 75 24W
Wazirabad, Delhi 16 A2 28 43N 77 13 E
Wazīrīya, Bagd. 17 E8 33 22N 44 23 E
Wazirpur, Delhi 16 A2 28 41N 77 10 E
Weald Park, Lon. 4 B6 51 37N 0 16 E
Wedding, Berl. 7 A3 52 32N 13 21 E
Weehawken, N.Y. 22 C4 40 45N 74 2W
Wegendorf, Berl. 7 A5 52 36N 13 45 E
Wehofen, Ruhr 6 A2 51 31N 6 46 E
Wehringhausen, Ruhr 6 B6 51 21N 7 28 E
Weidling, Wien 10 G9 48 17N 16 18 E
Weidling →, Wien 10 G9 48 17N 16 19 E
Weidlingbach, Wien 10 G9 48 16N 16 15 E
Weigongcum, Beij. 14 B2 39 57N 116 16 E
Weijin He →, Tianj. 14 E6 39 3N 117 12 E
Weissensee, Berl. 7 A3 52 33N 13 27 E
Weitmar, Ruhr 6 B5 51 27N 7 11 E
Welcome Monument, Jak. 15 J9 6 12N 106 49 E
Weller Creek, Chic. 26 A1 42 2N 87 52W
Wellesley, Bost. 21 D2 42 17N 71 17W
Wellesley Fells, Bost. 21 D2 42 18N 71 18W
Wellesley Hills, Bost. 21 D2 42 18N 71 16W
Welling, Lon. 4 C5 51 27N 0 6 E
Wellingsbüttel, Hbg. 7 D8 53 38N 10 6 E
Weltevreden Park Extension, Jobg. 18 E8 26 7 S 27 56 E
Wembley, Lon. 4 B3 51 33N 0 17W
Wembley Stadium, Jobg. 18 F9 26 13 S 28 1 E
Wembley Stadium, Lon. 4 B3 51 33N 0 16W
Wemmer Pan, Jobg. 18 F9 26 13 S 28 3 E
Wendenschloss, Berl. 7 B4 52 24N 13 35 E
Wengern, Ruhr 6 B6 51 24N 7 20 E
Wenham, Bost. 21 B4 42 36N 70 53W
Wenham L., Bost. 21 B4 42 35N 70 53W
Wenhuagong, Tianj. 14 E6 39 5N 117 14 E
Wennington, Lon. 4 B6 51 30N 0 12 E
Wenonah, Phil. 24 C4 39 47N 75 9W
Wentworthville, Syd. 19 A2 33 48 S 150 58 E
Werden, Ruhr 6 B4 51 23N 7 1 E
Werne, Ruhr 6 B5 51 29N 7 18 E
Werneuchen, Berl. 7 A5 52 38N 13 44 E
Wesoła, Wsaw. 10 E8 52 15N 21 13 E
West Andover, Bost. 21 A2 42 39N 71 10W
West Babylon, N.Y. 23 C8 40 43N 73 20W
West Bedford, Bost. 21 C2 42 28N 71 18W
West Berlin, Phil. 24 C5 39 48N 74 56W
West Boxford, Bost. 21 A3 42 42N 71 3W
West Caldwell, N.Y. 22 B3 40 50N 74 16W
West Chelmsford, Bost. 21 B1 42 36N 71 23W
West Chester, Phil. 24 B1 39 57N 75 35W
West Concord, Bost. 21 C1 42 27N 71 24W
West Covina, L.A. 28 B5 34 4N 117 55W
West Don →, Trto. 20 D8 43 44N 79 24W
West Drayton, Lon. 4 B2 51 30N 0 28W
West Dulwich, Lon. 4 C4 51 26N 0 5W
West Edmondale, Balt. 25 B2 39 17N 76 42W
West Ham, Lon. 4 B5 51 31N 0 1 E
West Harrow, Lon. 4 B2 51 34N 0 21W
West Heath, Lon. 4 C5 51 29N 0 7 E
West Hempstead, N.Y. 23 C7 40 41N 73 38W
West Hill, Trto. 20 D9 43 46N 79 11W
West Hollywood, L.A. 28 B2 34 5N 118 21W
West Hoxton, Syd. 19 B1 33 55 S 150 49 E
West Islip, N.Y. 23 C9 40 42N 73 18W
West Kingsdown, Lon. 4 C6 51 20N 0 15 E
West Lamma Channel, H.K. 12 E5 22 14N 114 4 E
West Lynn, Bost. 21 C4 42 28N 70 58W
West Medford, Bost. 21 C3 42 25N 71 7W
West New York, N.Y. 22 C4 40 46N 74 1W
West Norwood, N.Y. 22 A5 41 0N 73 58W
West of Twin Peaks, S.F. 27 B2 37 43N 122 27W
West Orange, N.Y. 22 C3 40 46N 74 15W
West Park, Jobg. 18 E8 26 9 S 27 59 E
West Paterson, N.Y. 22 B4 40 53N 74 11W
West Rouge, Trto. 20 D10 43 48N 79 7W
West Roxbury, Bost. 21 D3 42 16N 71 9W
West Springfield, Wash. 25 E6 38 47N 77 13W
West Thurrock, Lon. 4 C7 51 28N 0 16 E
West Town, Chic. 26 B2 41 53N 87 42W
West Wharf, Kar. 17 H10 24 49N 66 58 E
West Wickham, Lon. 4 C4 51 22N 0 0 E
Westbury, N.Y. 23 C7 40 45N 73 34W
Westchester, Chic. 26 B1 41 51N 87 53W
Westchester, N.Y. 23 B5 40 51N 73 51W
Westcliff, Jobg. 18 F9 26 10 S 28 1 E
Westdale, Chic. 26 B1 41 55N 87 54W
Westdene, Jobg. 18 F8 26 10 S 27 59 E
Westend, Hels. 3 C3 60 9N 24 48 E
Westerbauer, Ruhr 6 B6 51 20N 7 23 E
Westerham, Lon. 4 D5 51 16N 0 4 E
Westerham, Mün. 7 G10 48 3N 11 36 E
Westerholt, Ruhr 6 A4 51 36N 7 5 E
Westerleigh, N.Y. 22 D4 40 37N 74 7W
Western Addition, S.F. 27 B2 37 47N 122 25W
Western Run →, Balt. 25 A2 39 22N 76 39W
Western Springs, Chic. 26 C1 41 47N 87 52W
Westfalenhalle, Ruhr 6 B6 51 29N 7 27 E
Westfield, N.Y. 22 D2 40 39N 74 21W
Westlake, S.F. 27 B2 37 42N 122 29W
Westmeadows, Melb. 19 D6 37 39 S 144 55 E
Westminster, Lon. 4 B4 51 30N 0 7W
Westminster Abbey, Lon. 4 C4 51 29N 0 7W
Westmont, Phil. 24 B4 39 54N 75 3W
Westmount, Mtrl. 20 B4 43 29N 73 35W
Weston, Bost. 21 C2 42 22N 71 16W
Weston, Trto. 20 D7 43 42N 79 30W
Weston Res., Bost. 21 C2 42 20N 71 11W
Westover Hills, Phil. 24 C1 39 45N 75 35W
Westtown, Phil. 24 B1 39 56N 75 32W
Westville, Phil. 24 B4 39 52N 75 7W
Westville Grove, Phil. 24 B4 39 51N 75 7W
Westwood, Bost. 21 D2 42 12N 71 14W
Westwood, N.Y. 22 B4 40 59N 74 3W
Westwood Village, L.A. 28 B2 34 3N 118 26W
Wetter, Ruhr 6 B6 51 23N 7 23 E
Wexford, Trto. 20 D9 43 45N 79 18W
Wey →, Lon. 4 D2 51 18N 0 27W
Weybridge, Lon. 4 C2 51 22N 0 27W
Weyer, Ruhr 6 C4 51 10N 7 1 E
Weymouth, Bost. 21 D4 42 12N 70 57W
Whampoa, Sungei →, Sing. 15 G8 1 18N 103 52 E
Wheaton, Wash. 25 C7 39 2N 77 2W
Wheaton Regional Park, Wash. 25 C7 39 3N 77 1W
Wheelers Hill, Melb. 19 F8 37 53 S 145 10 E
Wheeling, Chic. 26 A1 42 8N 87 54W
Whetstone, Lon. 4 B3 51 37N 0 10W
Whippany, N.Y. 22 B2 40 49N 74 24W
Whippany →, N.Y. 22 B2 40 50N 74 20W
White Marsh, Balt. 25 A4 39 23N 76 28W
White Meadow L., N.Y. 22 B1 40 55N 74 30W
White Oak, Wash. 25 C8 39 2N 76 59W
White Plains, N.Y. 23 A6 41 0N 73 46W
Whitechapel, Lon. 4 B4 51 31N 0 3W
Whitehorse, Phil. 24 B2 39 59N 75 28W
Whiteley Village, Lon. 4 C2 51 21N 0 25W
Whitemarsh →, Balt. 25 A4 39 22N 76 29W
Whitestone, N.Y. 23 C6 40 47N 73 48W
Whiting, Chic. 26 C4 41 41N 87 30W
Whitmans Pond, Bost. 21 D4 42 12N 70 55W
Whittier, L.A. 28 C4 33 58N 118 2W
Whitton, Lon. 4 C2 51 27N 0 21W
Whyteleafe, Lon. 4 D4 51 18N 0 5W
Wieden, Wien 10 G10 48 11N 16 22 E
Wiemelhausen, Ruhr 6 B5 51 27N 7 13 E
Wien, Wien 10 G10 48 12N 16 22 E
Wien-Schwechat, Flughafen, Wien 10 H11 48 6N 16 34 E
Wiener Berg, Wien 10 H10 48 9N 16 21 E
Wiener Wald, Wien 10 G9 48 13N 16 14 E
Wieruchów, Wsaw. 10 E5 52 14N 20 49 E
Wierzbno, Wsaw. 10 E7 52 11N 21 1 E
Wilanów, Wsaw. 10 E7 52 10N 21 4 E
Wilanówka →, Wsaw. 10 F7 52 10N 21 6 E
Wildcat Canyon Regional Park, S.F. 27 A3 37 56N 122 17W
Wildcat Cr. →, S.F. 27 A3 37 57N 122 15W
Wilde, B.A. 32 C5 34 24 S 58 18W
Wilhelmsburg, Hbg. 7 E7 53 29N 9 59 E
Wilhelmshagen, Berl. 7 B5 52 26N 13 42 E
Wilket Creek Park, Trto. 20 D8 43 43N 79 21W
Willesden, Lon. 4 B3 51 32N 0 15W
Willesden Green, Lon. 4 B3 51 32N 0 13W
Willett Pond, Bost. 21 D2 42 10N 71 14W
William Girling Res., Lon. 4 B4 51 38N 0 1W
Williams Bridge, N.Y. 23 B5 40 52N 73 51W
Williamsburg, N.Y. 22 C5 40 42N 73 56W
Williamstown, Melb. 19 F6 37 51 S 144 52 E
Williamstown Junction, Phil. 24 C5 39 45N 74 56W
Willingboro, Phil. 24 A5 40 2N 74 53W
Williston Park, N.Y. 23 C7 40 45N 73 38W
Willoughby, Syd. 19 A4 33 48 S 151 12 E
Willow Grove, Phil. 24 A4 40 8N 75 7W
Willow Springs, Chic. 26 C1 41 44N 87 51W
Willowbrook, L.A. 28 C3 33 54N 118 13W
Willowbrook, N.Y. 22 D4 40 35N 74 8W
Willowdale, Phil. 24 B5 39 52N 74 58W
Willowdale, Trto. 20 D8 43 46N 79 25W
Willowdale State Forest, Bost. 21 B4 42 39N 70 54W
Wilmette, Chic. 26 A2 42 4N 87 42W
Wilmette Harbor, Chic. 26 A2 42 4N 87 41W
Wilmington, Bost. 21 B3 42 33N 71 9W
Wilmington, Lon. 4 C6 51 25N 0 12 E
Wilmington, Phil. 24 C1 39 44N 75 33W
Wilson, Mt., L.A. 28 A4 34 13N 118 4W
Wimbledon, Lon. 4 C3 51 25N 0 13W
Wimbledon Common, Lon. 4 C3 51 26N 0 14W
Wimbledon Park, Lon. 4 C3 51 25N 0 11W
Wimbledon Tennis Ground, Lon. 4 C3 51 25N 0 12W
Winchester, Bost. 21 C3 42 26N 71 8W
Winchmore Hill, Lon. 4 B4 51 38N 0 5W
Windsor Cresta, Jobg. 18 E8 26 7 S 27 59 E
Winfield, N.Y. 22 D3 40 38N 74 16W
Winnetka, Chic. 26 A2 42 6N 87 43W
Winnetka, L.A. 28 A1 34 10N 118 32W
Winning, Mün. 7 G10 48 2N 11 37 E
Winston Hills, Syd. 19 A2 33 46 S 150 57 E
Winterberg, Ruhr 6 C5 51 19N 7 12 E
Winterhude, Hbg. 7 D8 53 35N 10 0 E
Winterthur, Phil. 24 C1 39 48N 75 35W
Winthrop, Bost. 21 C4 42 22N 70 58W
Winzeldorf, Hbg. 7 C7 53 40N 9 54 E
Wisley Gardens, Lon. 4 D2 51 18N 0 28W
Wiśniowa Góra, Wsaw. 10 E8 52 13N 21 12 E
Wissahickon Cr. →, Phil. 24 A3 40 0N 75 12W
Wissinoming, Phil. 24 A4 40 1N 75 4W
Wissous, Paris 5 C3 48 44N 2 19 E
Witch House, Bost. 21 B4 42 31N 70 54W
Witfield, Jobg. 18 F10 26 11 S 28 12 E
Witpoortjie, Jobg. 18 E8 26 8 S 27 50 E
Witten, Ruhr 6 B6 51 26N 7 20 E
Wittenau, Berl. 7 A2 52 35N 13 19 E
Wittlaer, Ruhr 6 C2 51 19N 6 44 E
Witwatersrand, Univ. of, Jobg. 18 F9 26 11 S 28 1 E
Włochy, Wsaw. 10 E6 52 12N 20 54 E
Wo Mei, H.K. 12 D6 22 21N 114 15 E
Wo Yi Hop, H.K. 12 D5 22 23N 114 8 E
Woburn, Bost. 21 C3 42 29N 71 9W
Woburn, Trto. 20 D9 43 46N 79 12W
Wohldorf-Ohlstedt, Hbg. 7 C8 53 41N 10 7 E
Wola, Wsaw. 10 E6 52 14N 20 57 E
Woldingham, Lon. 4 D4 51 16N 0 1W
Wolf Lake, Chic. 26 D3 41 39N 87 31W
Wolf Trap Farm Park, Wash. 25 D6 38 56N 77 17W
Wolfpassing, Wien 10 G9 48 18N 16 10 E
Wolica, Wsaw. 10 F7 52 9N 21 3 E
Wolica, Wsaw. 10 F6 52 7N 20 51 E
Wólka Węglowa, Wsaw. 10 E6 52 18N 20 52 E
Wollaston, Bost. 21 D3 42 15N 71 2W
Wołomin, Wsaw. 10 D8 52 20N 21 12 E
Woltersdorf, Berl. 7 B5 52 27N 13 44 E
Wong Chuk Hang, H.K. 12 E6 22 15N 114 10 E
Wong Chuk Wan, H.K. 12 D6 22 23N 114 17 E
Wong Chuk Yeung, H.K. 12 D6 22 24N 114 15 E
Wong Ngua Shan, H.K. 12 D6 22 22N 114 14 E
Wong Tai Sin, H.K. 12 D6 22 20N 114 11 E
Wonga Park, Melb. 19 E8 37 44 S 145 17 E
Wood End, Lon. 4 B2 51 33N 0 21W
Wood Green, Lon. 4 B4 51 36N 0 6W
Wood Hill, Bost. 21 B2 42 39N 71 11W
Woodbridge, N.Y. 22 D3 40 33N 74 16W
Woodbridge, Trto. 20 D7 43 47N 79 35W
Woodbridge Cr. →, N.Y. 22 D3 40 32N 74 15W
Woodbury, N.Y. 23 C8 40 49N 73 28W
Woodbury, Phil. 24 B4 39 50N 75 9W
Woodbury Cr. →, Phil. 24 B4 39 51N 75 11W
Woodbury Heights, Phil. 24 C4 39 49N 75 7W
Woodchuck Hill, Bost. 21 B3 42 39N 71 4W
Woodcliff Lake, N.Y. 22 A4 41 1N 74 2W
Woodford, Lon. 4 B5 51 36N 0 1 E
Woodford Bridge, Lon. 4 B5 51 36N 0 3 E
Woodford Green, Lon. 4 B5 51 36N 0 1 E
Woodford Wells, Lon. 4 B5 51 37N 0 1 E
Woodhaven, N.Y. 23 C5 40 41N 73 51W
Woodlands, Sing. 15 F7 1 26N 103 46 E
Woodlawn, Balt. 25 B2 39 19N 76 44W
Woodlyn, Phil. 24 B2 39 52N 75 21W
Woodlynne, Phil. 24 B4 39 54N 75 6W
Woodmere, N.Y. 23 D6 40 38N 73 43W
Woodmont, Wash. 25 D7 38 59N 77 5W
Woodmore, Balt. 25 A2 39 22N 76 47W
Woodridge, N.Y. 22 B4 40 50N 74 4W
Woodrow, N.Y. 22 D3 40 32N 74 11W
Woodside, Lon. 4 C4 51 23N 0 4W
Woodside, N.Y. 23 C5 40 44N 73 54W
Woodside, S.F. 27 D3 37 26N 122 16W
Woodstock, Balt. 25 B1 39 19N 76 52W
Woodstream, Phil. 24 B5 39 54N 74 57W
Woollahra, Syd. 19 B4 33 53 S 151 15 E
Wooloware B., Syd. 19 C3 34 1 S 151 8 E
Woolwich, Lon. 4 C5 51 29N 0 4 E
Wördern, Wien 10 G9 48 19N 16 12 E
World Trade Center, N.Y. 22 C4 40 42N 74 0W
Worli, Bomb. 16 G7 19 1N 72 49 E
Woronora, Syd. 19 C3 34 1 S 151 2 E
Worth, Chic. 26 C2 41 41N 87 47W
Worthington, Balt. 25 B1 39 14N 76 47W
Worthington, N.Y. 23 A6 41 2N 73 49W
Wrotham, Lon. 4 D6 51 18N 0 18 E
Wrotham Park, Lon. 4 A3 51 40N 0 10W
Wuhlgarten, Berl. 7 A4 52 31N 13 34 E
Wujiaochang, Shang. 14 J12 31 18N 121 31 E
Wülfrath, Ruhr 6 C4 51 16N 7 2 E
Wulfsmühle, Hbg. 7 C7 53 41N 9 51 E
Wulksfelde, Hbg. 7 C8 53 42N 10 6 E
Wupper →, Ruhr 6 C5 51 14N 7 18 E
Wuppertal, Ruhr 6 C5 51 17N 7 8 E
Würm →, Mün. 7 G9 48 8N 11 27 E
Würm-kanal, Mün. 7 F9 48 13N 11 29 E
Wusong, Shang. 14 H11 31 22N 121 29 E
Wusong Jiang →, Shang. 14 J11 31 15N 121 29 E
Wyandanch, N.Y. 23 C8 40 44N 73 20W
Wyckoff, N.Y. 22 A3 41 0N 74 10W
Wyczólki, Wsaw. 10 F6 52 9N 20 59 E
Wygoda, Wsaw. 10 E7 52 15N 21 7 E
Wyncote, Phil. 24 A4 40 5N 75 8W
Wynnewood, Phil. 24 A3 40 0N 75 17W
Wynnmere, Bost. 21 C3 42 29N 71 9W
Wyola, Phil. 24 A2 40 0N 75 24W

X

Xabregas, Lisb. 8 F8 38 43N 9 6W
Xiaodianzhuang, Tianj. 14 D6 39 14N 117 14 E
Xiaoping, Gzh. 14 F8 23 12N 113 13 E
Xiasha chong, Gzh. 14 G7 23 8N 113 9 E
Xicheng, Beij. 14 B2 39 54N 116 19 E
Xico, Cerro, Méx. 29 C4 19 15N 98 56W
Xicun, Gzh. 14 G8 23 8N 113 13 E
Xidan, Beij. 14 B3 39 52N 116 20 E
Xigu Gongyuan, Tianj. 14 D6 39 10N 117 10 E
Xigucun, Tianj. 14 D5 39 10N 117 9 E
Xijiao Airport, Beij. 14 B2 39 57N 116 12 E
Xikeng, Gzh. 14 F7 23 11N 113 6 E
Xilou, Tianj. 14 E6 39 5N 117 12 E
Ximenwai, Tianj. 14 E5 39 8N 117 9 E
Xingfusancun, Beij. 14 B3 39 55N 116 25 E
Xinhua, Tianj. 14 E6 39 6N 117 12 E
Xinkai He →, Tianj. 14 D6 39 12N 117 15 E
Xintang, Gzh. 14 G9 23 9N 113 24 E
Xitle, Méx. 29 C2 19 15N 99 12W
Xitle, Cerro, Méx. 29 C2 19 14N 99 12W
Xiyuan, Beij. 14 B2 39 59N 116 14 E
Xizhimen, Beij. 14 B2 39 55N 116 19 E
Xochiaca, Méx. 29 B4 19 24N 89 58 E
Xochimilco, Méx. 29 C3 19 15N 99 5W
Xochimilco, L. de, Méx. 29 C3 19 16N 99 7W
Xochitenco, Méx. 29 B4 19 24N 89 58 E
Xochitepec, Méx. 29 C3 19 15N 99 9W
Xuanwu, Beij. 14 B2 39 52N 116 19 E
Xuhui, Shang. 14 J11 31 11N 121 26 E

Y

Yaba, Lagos 18 A2 6 30N 7 22 E
Yadun Shui, Gzh. 14 G8 23 5N 113 15 E
Yaftābād, Tehr. 17 D4 35 37N 51 17 E
Yagoona, Syd. 19 B3 33 54 S 151 2 E
Yahara, Tōkyō 13 B2 35 44N 139 37 E
Yaho, Tōkyō 13 B1 35 40N 139 26 E
Yakire, Tōkyō 13 B4 35 44N 139 51 E
Yamada, Ōsaka 12 B4 34 47N 135 32 E
Yamada, Tōkyō 13 C2 35 33N 139 37 E
Yamada →, Ōsaka 12 B3 34 45N 135 10 E
Yamaguchi, Ōsaka 12 B4 34 47N 135 35 E
Yamamoto, Ōsaka 12 C4 34 38N 135 37 E
Yamato, Tōkyō 13 B2 35 46N 139 36 E
Yamato, Tōkyō 13 D1 35 29N 139 27 E
Yamato →, Ōsaka 12 C3 34 36N 135 26 E
Yamazaki, Tōkyō 13 A4 35 55N 139 53 E
Yamuna →, Delhi 16 B2 28 37N 77 15 E
Yan Kit, Sing. 15 F8 1 21N 103 58 E
Yanagishima, Tōkyō 13 B3 35 49N 139 45 E
Yanbu, Gzh. 14 G7 23 5N 113 9 E
Yanghuayuan, Beij. 14 C2 39 49N 116 18 E
Yangjiazhuang, Shang. 14 H11 31 22N 121 25 E
Yangliuqing, Tianj. 14 E5 39 8N 117 0 E
Yangpu, Shang. 14 J12 31 16N 121 32 E
Yanino, St-Pet. 11 B5 59 55N 30 36 E
Yao, Ōsaka 12 C4 34 37N 135 36 E
Yao Airport, Ōsaka 12 C4 34 35N 135 36 E
Yarmōk, Bagd. 17 F7 33 18N 44 19 E
Yarra →, Melb. 19 E6 37 51 S 144 53 E
Yarra Bend Nat. Park, Melb. 19 E7 37 47 S 145 0 E
Yarraville, Melb. 19 E6 37 48 S 144 53 E
Yasenevo, Mos. 11 F9 55 36N 37 21 E
Yashio, Tōkyō 13 B3 35 48N 139 49 E
Yau Ma Tei, H.K. 12 E5 22 18N 114 10 E
Yau Tong, H.K. 12 E6 22 17N 114 14 E
Yau Yue Wan, H.K. 12 E6 22 19N 114 15 E
Yauza →, Mos. 11 D10 55 54N 37 43 E
Yeading, Lon. 4 B2 51 31N 0 23W
Yeadon, Phil. 24 B3 39 55N 75 15W
Yedikule, Ist. 17 B2 40 59N 28 55 E
Yenikapi, Ist. 17 A2 41 0N 28 56 E
Yeniköy, Ist. 17 A3 41 6N 29 3 E
Yennora, Syd. 19 B2 33 51 S 150 58 E
Yeogchon, Sŏul 12 G7 37 35N 126 55 E
Yeoido, Sŏul 12 G7 37 31N 126 55 E
Yeong Dung Po, Sŏul 12 G7 37 31N 126 54 E
Yeongdong, Sŏul 12 G8 37 30N 127 1 E
Yerba Buena I., S.F. 27 B2 37 48N 122 21W
Yerres, Paris 5 C5 48 43N 2 30 E
Yerres →, Paris 5 C5 48 43N 2 26 E
Yesilköy, Ist. 17 B2 40 57N 28 50 E
Yew Tee, Sing. 15 F7 1 23N 103 45 E
Yiewsley, Lon. 4 B2 51 31N 0 27W
Yiheyuan, Beij. 14 A2 40 0N 116 14 E
Yinhangzhen, Shang. 14 H12 31 20N 121 31 E
Yio Chu Kang, Sing. 15 F8 1 23N 103 51 E
Yixingbu, Tianj. 14 D6 39 11N 117 12 E
Ylästö, Hels. 3 B4 60 17N 24 35 E
Yodo →, Ōsaka 12 B4 34 45N 135 35 E
Yokohama, Tōkyō 13 D3 35 26N 139 41 E
Yokohama Harbour, Tōkyō 13 D2 35 27N 139 39 E
Yokosuka, Tōkyō 13 A4 35 50N 139 54 E
Yong San, Sŏul 12 G7 37 32N 126 58 E
Yongding He →, Beij. 14 C1 39 49N 116 10 E
Yongdingmen, Beij. 14 B3 39 50N 116 20 E
Yongfucun, Gzh. 14 G8 23 8N 113 17 E
Yonkers, N.Y. 23 B5 40 56N 73 52W
Yono, Tōkyō 13 A2 35 52N 139 37 E
York, Trto. 20 D8 43 40N 79 26W
York Mills, Trto. 20 D8 43 45N 79 22W
Yoshikawa, Tōkyō 13 A4 35 53N 139 50 E
Yotsuga, Tōkyō 13 B3 35 40N 139 44 E
You'anmen, Beij. 14 B2 39 51N 116 19 E
Yoyogi Park, Tōkyō 13 C3 35 40N 139 41 E
Yuanxiatian, Gzh. 14 F8 23 12N 113 17 E
Yuexiu Gongyuan, Gzh. 14 G8 23 8N 113 16 E
Yugo-Zarad, Mos. 11 E9 55 40N 37 30 E
Yung Shue Wan, H.K. 12 E5 22 13N 114 6 E
Yuquanshan, Beij. 14 A2 40 0N 116 13 E
Yusofābād, Tehr. 17 C5 35 43N 51 24 E
Yuyuan Tan, Beij. 14 B2 39 53N 116 16 E
Yuyuantan Gongyuan, Beij. 14 B2 39 54N 116 16 E
Yvelines, Forêt des, Paris 5 D1 48 38N 1 53 E
Yvette →, Paris 5 C1 48 43N 1 57 E

Z

Záběhlice, Pra. 10 B2 50 3N 14 29 E
Żacisze, Wsaw. 10 E7 52 17N 21 4 E
Zahrā, Bagd. 17 E7 33 22N 44 19 E
Zakharkovo, Mos. 11 E7 55 46N 37 18 E
Żalov, Pra. 10 A2 50 10N 14 22 E
Załuski, Wsaw. 10 F6 52 9N 20 55 E
Zamdorf, Mün. 7 G10 48 8N 11 35 E
Zanevka, St-Pet. 11 B5 59 55N 30 31 E
Zaozerye, Mos. 11 F12 55 35N 38 1 E
Zapote, Manila 15 E3 14 27N 120 56 E
Zapotitlán, Méx. 29 C3 19 18N 99 2W
Zápy, Pra. 10 B4 50 9N 14 40 E
Zarechye, Mos. 11 E8 55 41N 37 22 E
Zawady, Wsaw. 10 E7 52 10N 21 6 E
Zâwiyet Abû Musallam, El Qâ. 18 D4 29 56N 31 9 E
Zawrā Park, Bagd. 17 F8 33 18N 44 23 E
Zbójna Góra, Wsaw. 10 E8 52 11N 21 13 E
Zbraslav, Pra. 10 C2 49 58N 14 23 E
Zbuzany, Pra. 10 B1 50 1N 14 17 E
Zdiby, Pra. 10 B2 50 9N 14 27 E
Zehlendorf, Berl. 7 B2 52 26N 13 16 E
Zeleneč, Pra. 10 B3 50 8N 14 39 E
Zempoala, Parque Nac. de las Lagunas de, Méx. 29 D2 19 5N 99 18W
Zepernick, Berl. 7 A4 52 38N 13 33 E
Żerań, Wsaw. 10 E6 52 18N 20 58 E
Zerzeń, Wsaw. 10 E7 52 12N 21 7 E
Zeytinburnu, Ist. 17 B2 40 58N 28 53 E
Zhabei, Shang. 14 J11 31 16N 121 26 E
Zhangguizhuang, Tianj. 14 E6 39 7N 117 19 E
Zhangxingzhuang, Tianj. 14 D6 39 10N 117 12 E
Zhdanov, Mos. 11 E10 55 44N 37 41 E
Zhegalovo, Mos. 11 D11 55 54N 37 59 E
Zheleznodorozhnyy, Mos. 11 E12 55 45N 38 0 E
Zhenru, Shang. 14 J11 31 16N 121 22 E
Zhicun, Gzh. 14 G8 23 0N 113 18 E
Zhongshan Gongyuan, Shang. 14 J11 31 13N 121 24 E
Zhoucun, Gzh. 14 F8 23 11N 113 11 E
Zhoujiadu, Shang. 14 J11 31 11N 121 29 E
Zhoujiazhen, Shang. 14 J12 31 16N 121 33 E
Zhu Jiang →, Gzh. 14 G9 23 6N 113 20 E
Zhulebino, Mos. 11 E11 55 42N 37 50 E
Zhushadi, Gzh. 14 F9 23 11N 113 22 E
Zielona, Wsaw. 10 E8 52 14N 21 11 E
Zielonka, Wsaw. 10 E7 52 18N 21 9 E
Zitadella, Berl. 7 A2 52 31N 13 11 E
Zizhuyuan Gongyuan, Beij. 14 B2 39 55N 116 17 E
Žižkov, Pra. 10 B2 50 5N 14 28 E
Zličin, Pra. 10 B1 50 3N 14 17 E
Zōbki, Wsaw. 10 E7 52 17N 21 6 E
Zografos, Ath. 8 J11 37 58N 23 47 E
Żoliborz, Wsaw. 10 E6 52 16N 20 57 E
Zugliget, Bud. 10 K12 47 30N 18 59 E
Zugló, Bud. 10 J13 47 31N 19 8 E
Zumbi, Rio J. 31 A2 22 49 S 43 10W
Zuvuvu →, S. Pau. 31 F5 23 40 S 46 42W
Zuvuvus, S. Pau. 31 F6 23 41 S 46 39W
Zweckel, Ruhr 6 A3 51 35N 6 57 E
Zyuzino, Mos. 11 F9 55 39N 37 34 E

WORLD MAPS

MAP SYMBOLS

─────── SETTLEMENTS ───────

◻ PARIS   ▣ Berne   ◉ Livorno   ⊚ Brugge   ⊙ Algeciras   ○ Fréjus   ○ Oberammergau   ○ Thira

Settlement symbols and type styles vary according to the scale of each map and indicate the importance
of towns on the map rather than specific population figures

∴ Ruins or Archæological Sites   ᵛ Wells in Desert

─────── ADMINISTRATION ───────

Boundaries	National Parks	Country Names
─────── International		NICARAGUA
▬ ▬ ▬ International (Undefined or Disputed)	International boundaries show the *de facto* situation where there are rival claims to territory.	Administrative Areas
﹏﹏﹏ Internal		KENT
		CALABRIA

─────── COMMUNICATIONS ───────

Roads	Railroads	✈ ☼ Airfields
─────── Primary	⌢ Primary	⋈ Passes
⌢ Secondary	⌢ Secondary	⊣---⊢ Railroad Tunnels
-⌐--⌐- Trails and Seasonal	--⌐-- Under Construction	﹍﹍ Principal Canals

─────── PHYSICAL FEATURES ───────

⌁ Perennial Streams	⌁ Intermittent Lakes	▲ 2259 Elevations (m)
﹍ Intermittent Streams	⌁ Swamps and Marshes	▼ 2604 Sea Depths (m)
⬭ Perennial Lakes	⌁ Permanent Ice and Glaciers	*408* Elevation of Lake Surface Above Sea Level (m)

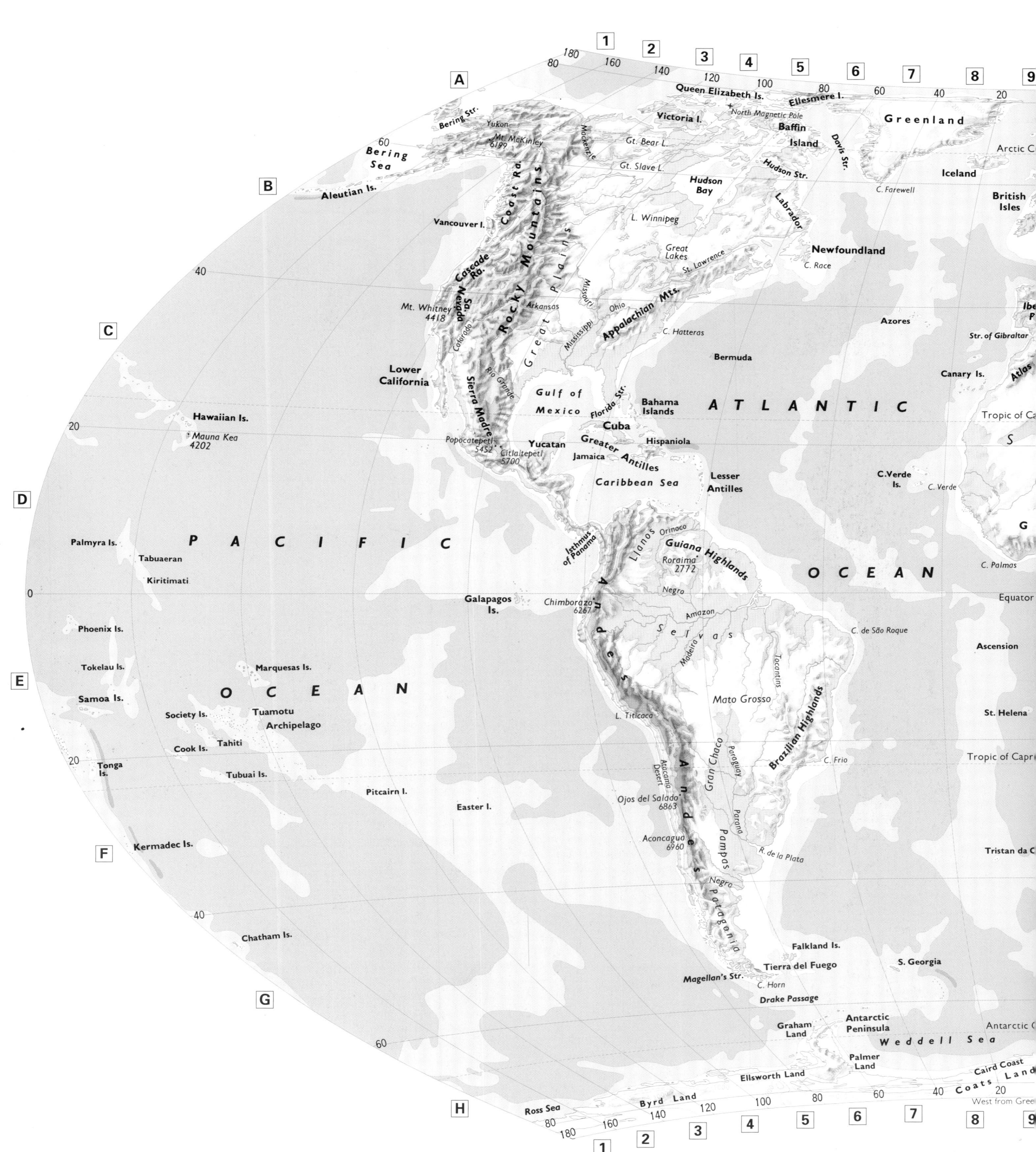

Projection: Hammer Equal Area

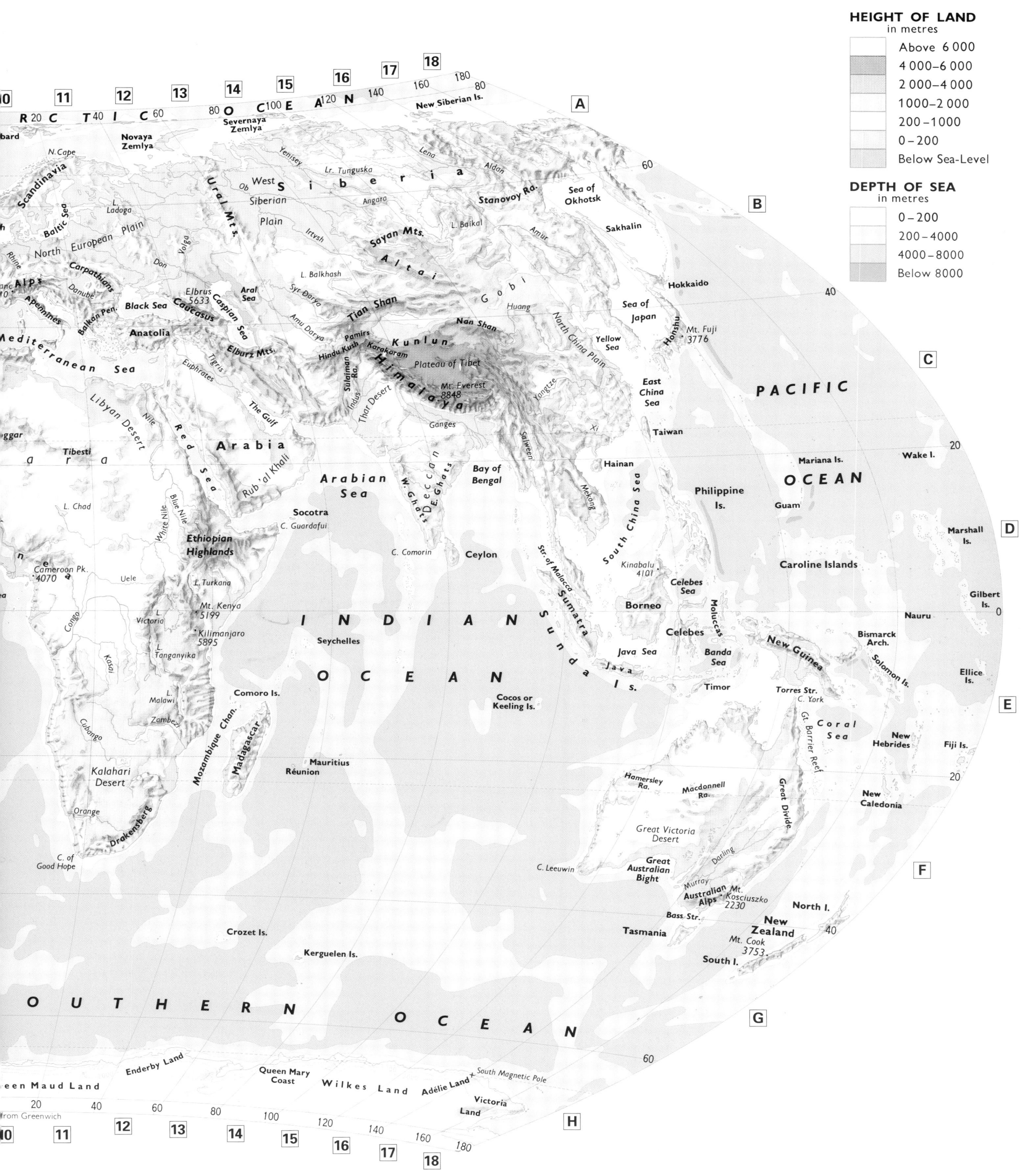

HEIGHT OF LAND
in metres

Above 6 000
4 000 – 6 000
2 000 – 4 000
1000 – 2 000
200 – 1000
0 – 200
Below Sea-Level

DEPTH OF SEA
in metres

0 – 200
200 – 4000
4000 – 8000
Below 8000

R 20 C T 40 I C 60 O C E A N 80 140 160 180 80

10   11   12   13   14   15   16   17   18

New Siberian Is.

A

Svalbard   N. Cape   Novaya Zemlya   Severnaya Zemlya

Scandinavia   West   Yenisey   Lr. Tunguska   Lena   Aldan

Baltic Sea   L. Ladoga   Ob   Siberian Plain   S i b e r i a   Stanovoy Ra.   Sea of Okhotsk

North European Plain   Ural Mts.   Irtysh   Angara   L. Baikal   Amur   Sakhalin   Hokkaido

Rhine   Carpathians   Volga   Don   Sayan Mts.   Altai   Gobi   Sea of Japan

60

40

Alps   Danube   Elbrus 5633   Aral Sea   Syr Darya   L. Balkhash   Tian Shan   Nan Shan   Huang   North China Plain   Honshu   Mt. Fuji 3776

Apennines   Black Sea   Caucasus   Caspian Sea   Amu Darya   Pamirs   Kunlun   Yellow Sea   East China Sea

Mediterranean Sea   Anatolia   Elburz Mts.   Hindu Kush   Karakoram   Plateau of Tibet   Yangtze   Taiwan   PACIFIC

The Gulf   Euphrates   Tigris   Sulaiman Ra.   Himalaya   Mt. Everest 8848   Ganges   Xi   Hainan   OCEAN

Libyan Desert   Nile   Thar Desert   Indus   Mariana Is.   Wake I.

Hoggar   Tibesti   Arabia   Rub'al Khali   Arabian Sea   W.Ghats   Deccan   E.Ghats   Bay of Bengal   Mekong   Philippine Is.   Guam

Sahara   Red Sea   Socotra   C. Guardafui   Salween   South China Sea   Marshall Is.

L. Chad   Blue Nile   White Nile   C. Comorin   Ceylon   Str. of Malacca   Caroline Islands   Gilbert Is.

Cameroon Pk. 4070   Ethiopian Highlands   L. Turkana   Kinabalu 4101   Borneo   Celebes Sea   Nauru

Uele   Mt. Kenya 5199   Sumatra   I N D I A N   Seychelles   Celebes   Moluccas   Bismarck Arch.

Congo   Kasai   L. Victoria   Kilimanjaro 5895   L. Tanganyika   O C E A N   S u n d a   I s.   Java Sea   Banda Sea   New Guinea   Solomon Is.   Ellice Is.

L. Malawi   Zambezi   Comoro Is.   Java   Timor   Torres Str.   New Hebrides   Fiji Is.

Cubango   Mozambique Chan.   Madagascar   Cocos or Keeling Is.   C. York   Coral Sea

Kalahari Desert   Mauritius   Réunion   Hamersley Ra.   Macdonnell Ra.   Gt. Barrier Reef   New Caledonia

Orange   Drakensberg   Great Victoria Desert   Darling   Great Divide   20

C. of Good Hope   C. Leeuwin   Great Australian Bight   Murray   Australian Alps   Mt. Kosciuszko 2230   North I.

Crozet Is.   Bass Str.   Tasmania   New Zealand   Mt. Cook 3753   40

Kerguelen Is.   South I.

S O U T H E R N   O C E A N

Green Maud Land   Enderby Land   Queen Mary Coast   Wilkes Land   Adélie Land   South Magnetic Pole   Victoria Land

from Greenwich   20   40   60   80   100   120   140   160   180   60

10   11   12   13   14   15   16   17   18

A   B   C   D   E   F   G   H

Projection: Hammer Equal Area

10 **11** **12** **13** **14** **15** **16** **17** **18**

A R C T I C   O C E A N

A

B

C

PACIFIC

OCEAN

D

E

F

G

H

10 **11** **12** **13** **14** **15** **16** **17** **18**

S O U T H E R N   O C E A N

Hanoi ● Capital Cities

Maximum extent of sea ice

Summer extent of sea ice

Ice caps and permanent ice shelf

Projection : Zenithal Equidistant

West from Greenwich   East from Greenwich

CARTOGRAPHY BY PHILIP'S. COPYRIGHT REED INTERNATIONAL BOOKS LTD

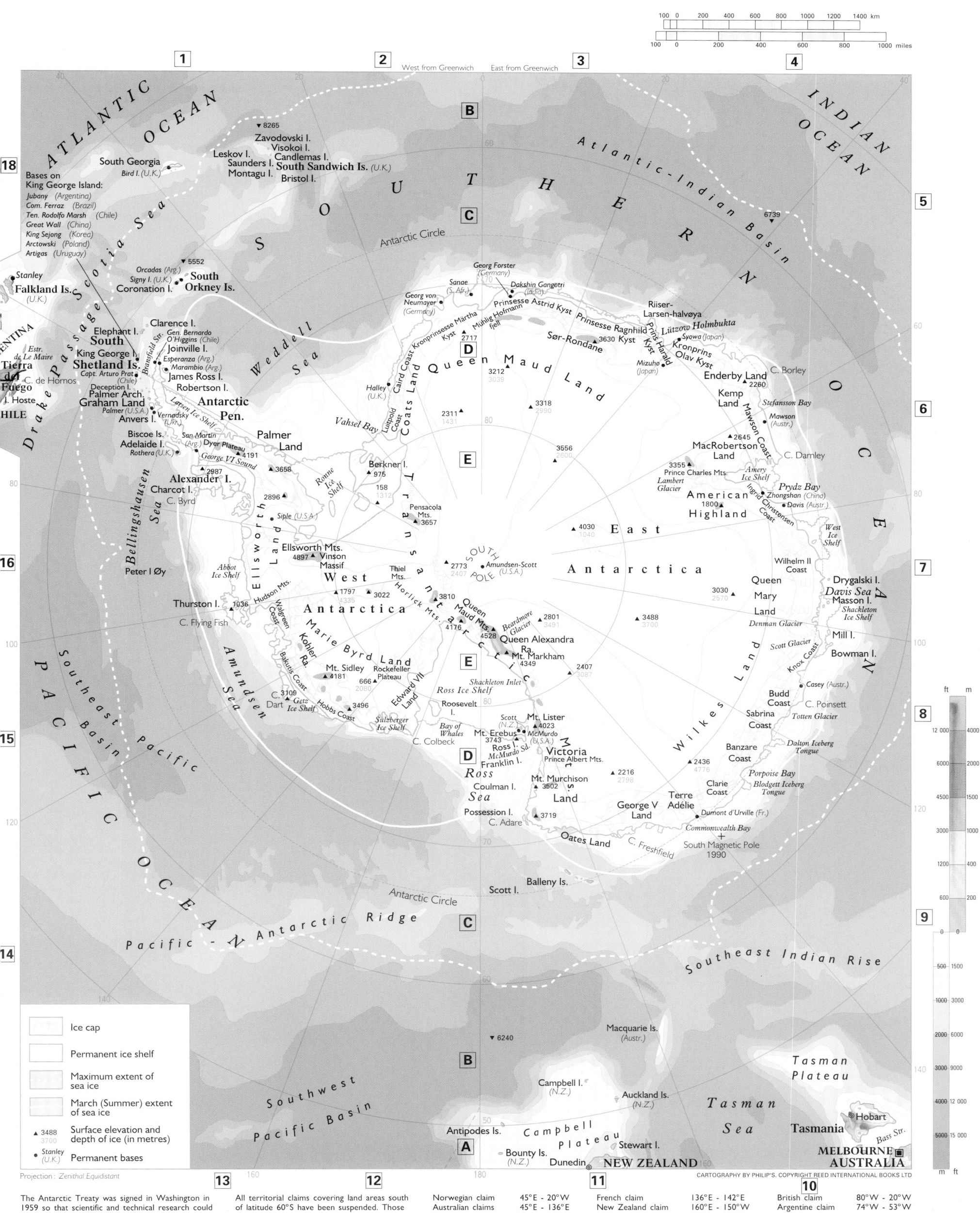

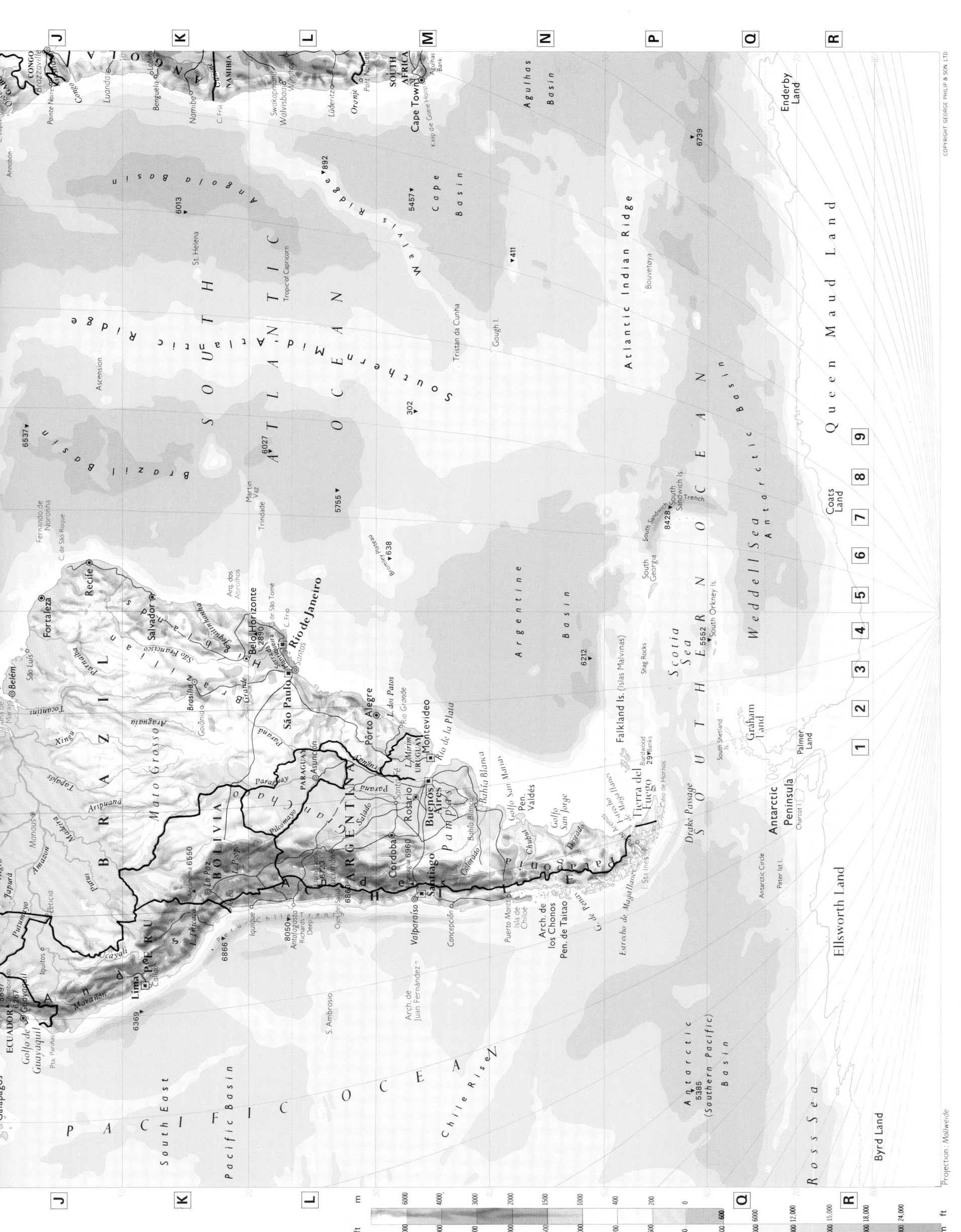

SOUTH ATLANTIC OCEAN

SOUTHERN OCEAN

PACIFIC OCEAN

BRAZIL

PERU

BOLIVIA

PARAGUAY

ARGENTINA

URUGUAY

Chile

Rio de Janeiro
São Paulo
Buenos Aires
Montevideo
Santiago
Valparaíso
Córdoba
Rosario
Pôrto Alegre
Belo Horizonte
Salvador
Recife
Fortaleza
Belém
La Paz
Lima
Iquitos
Guayaquil

ECUADOR

CONGO
Brazzaville
Luanda
Benguela
Namibe
Swakopmund
Walvisbaai
Windhoek
Lüderitz

NAMIBIA

SOUTH AFRICA
Cape Town

Agulhas Basin
Cape Basin
Angola Basin
Brazil Basin
Argentine Basin
Weddell Sea
Scotia Sea
Antarctic Basin
Atlantic Indian Ridge
Mid Atlantic Ridge
Chile Rise
South East Pacific Basin

Queen Maud Land
Enderby Land
Coats Land
Ellsworth Land
Byrd Land
Ross Sea

Antarctic Peninsula
Graham Land
Palmer Land

Falkland Is. (Islas Malvinas)
South Georgia
South Sandwich Is.
South Orkney Is.
South Shetland
Tristan da Cunha
Gough I.
St. Helena
Ascension
Bouvetøya

Tierra del Fuego
Cabo de Hornos
Drake Passage

Tropic of Capricorn

Projection: Mollweide

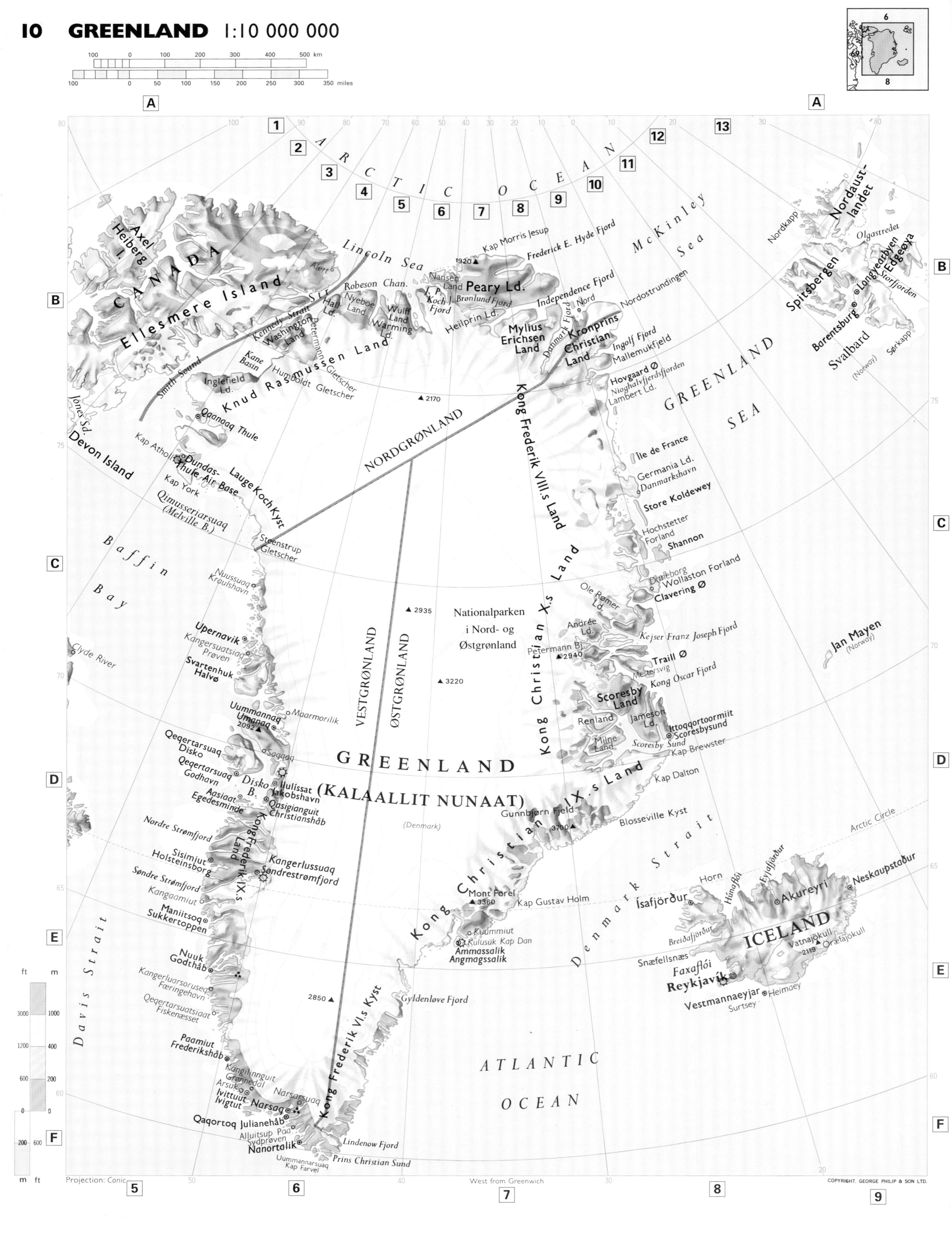

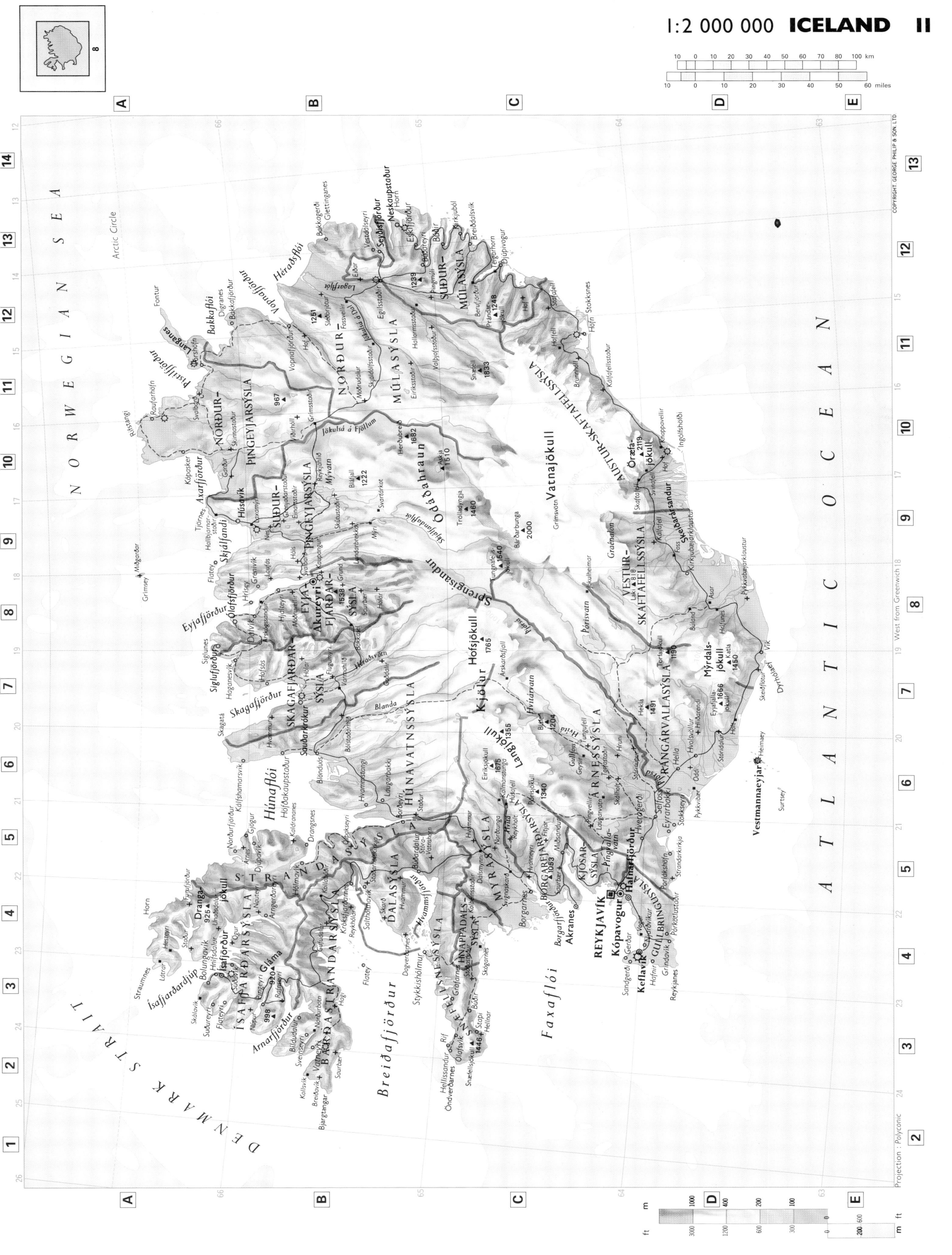

Projection : Polyconic

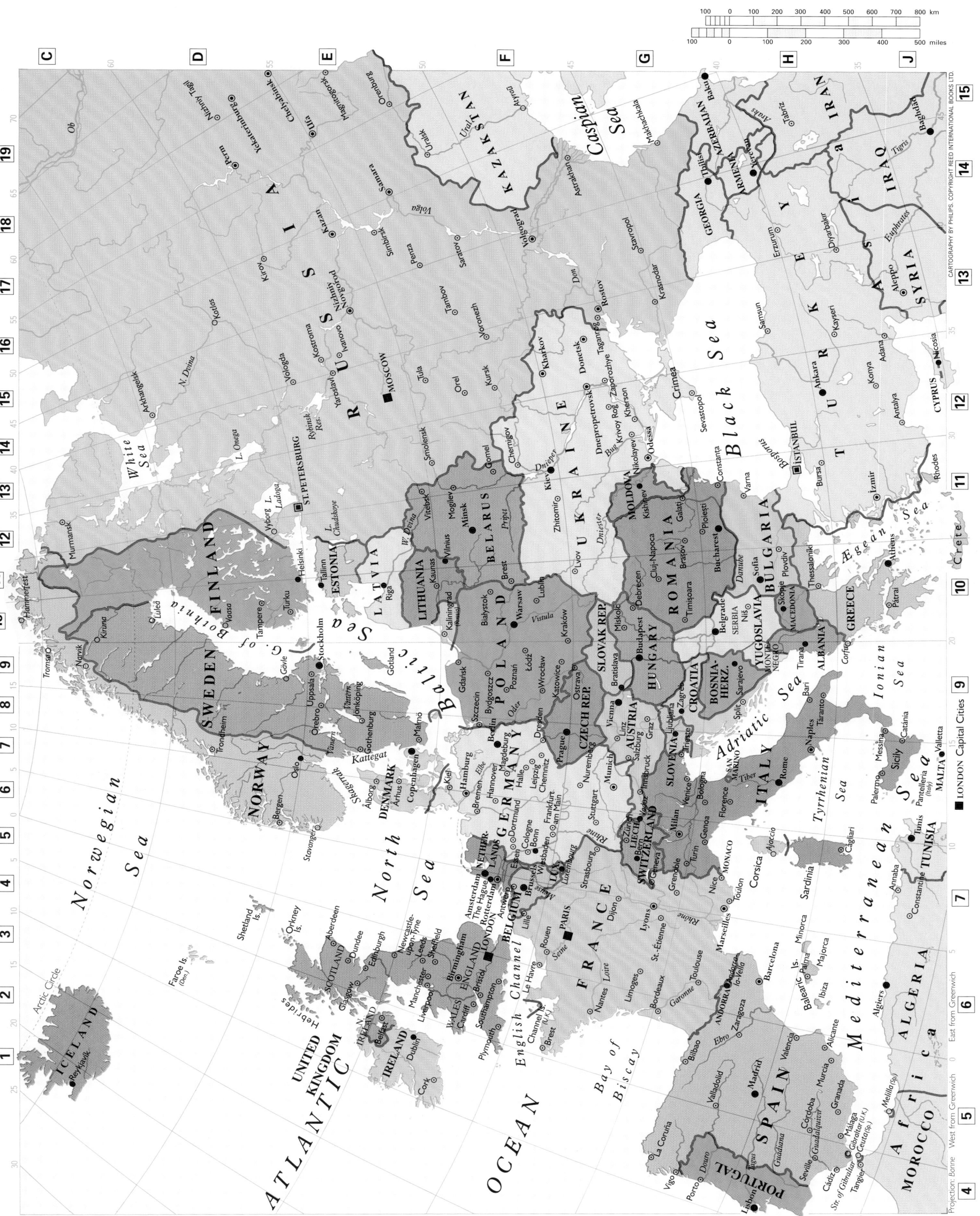

100   0   100   200   300   400   500   600   700   800 km
100   0   100   200   300   400   500 miles

CARTOGRAPHY BY PHILIP'S. COPYRIGHT REED INTERNATIONAL BOOKS LTD.

■ LONDON Capital Cities

Projection: Bonne

East from Greenwich   West from Greenwich

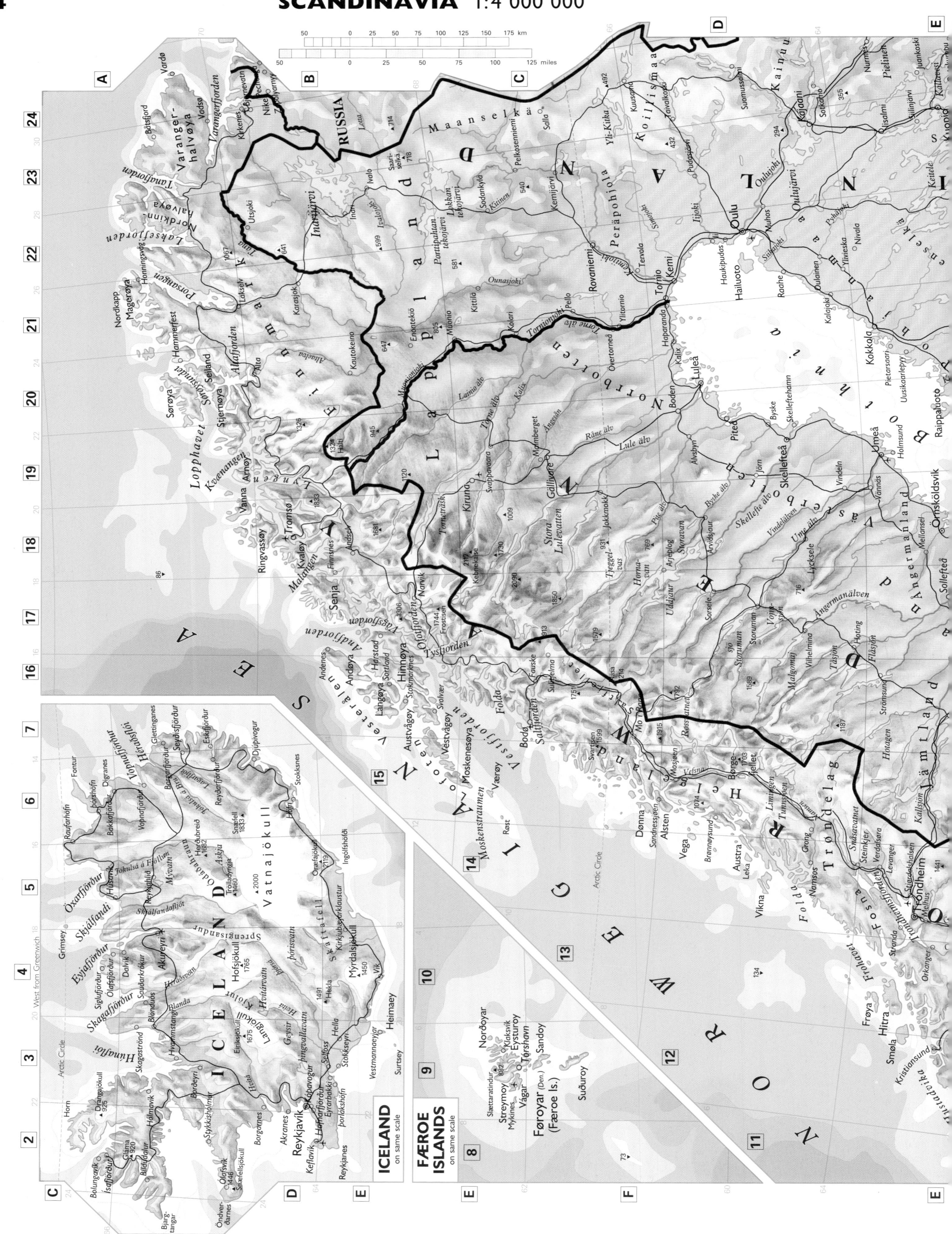

ICELAND
on same scale

FÆROE
ISLANDS
on same scale

Føroyar
(Faroe Is.)

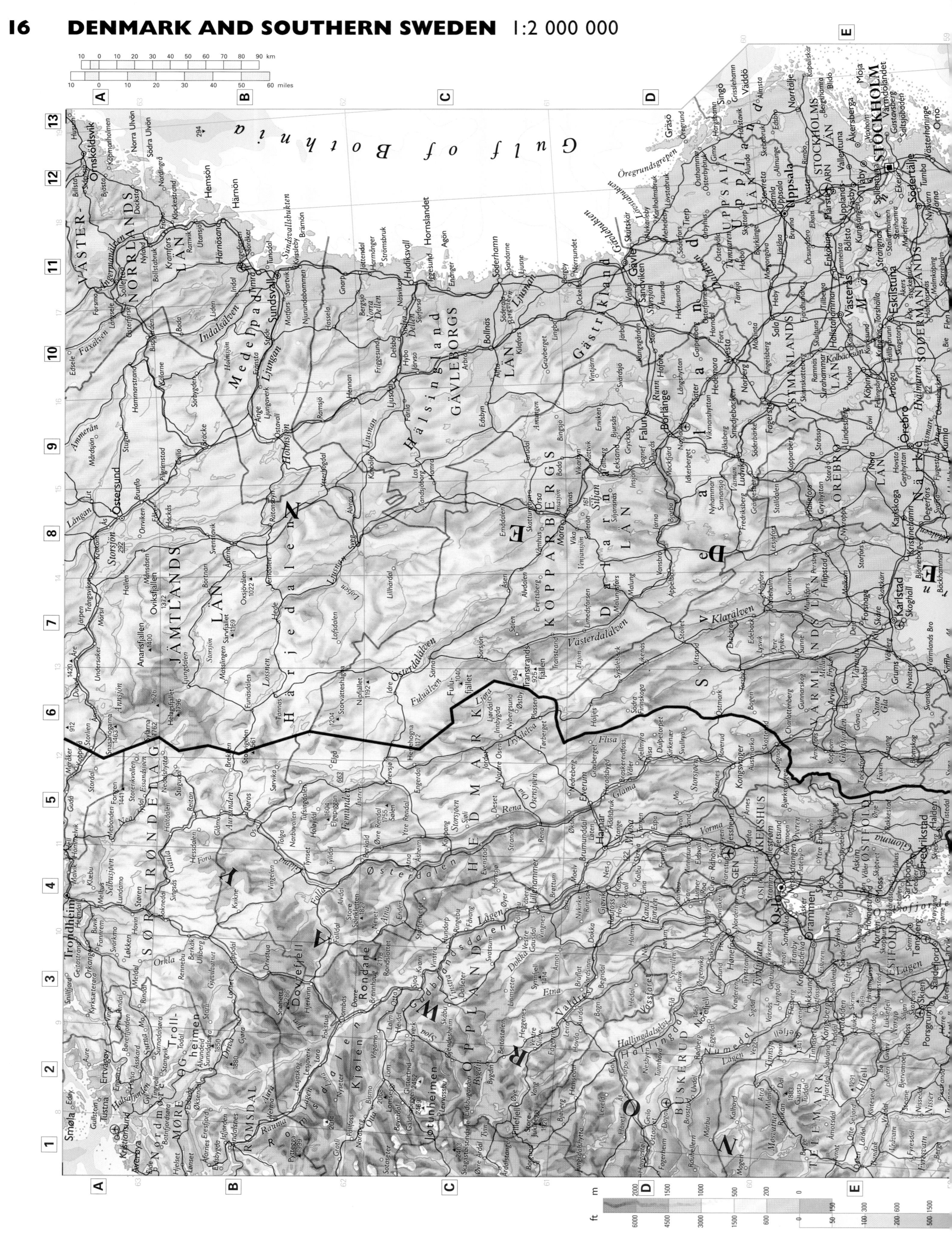

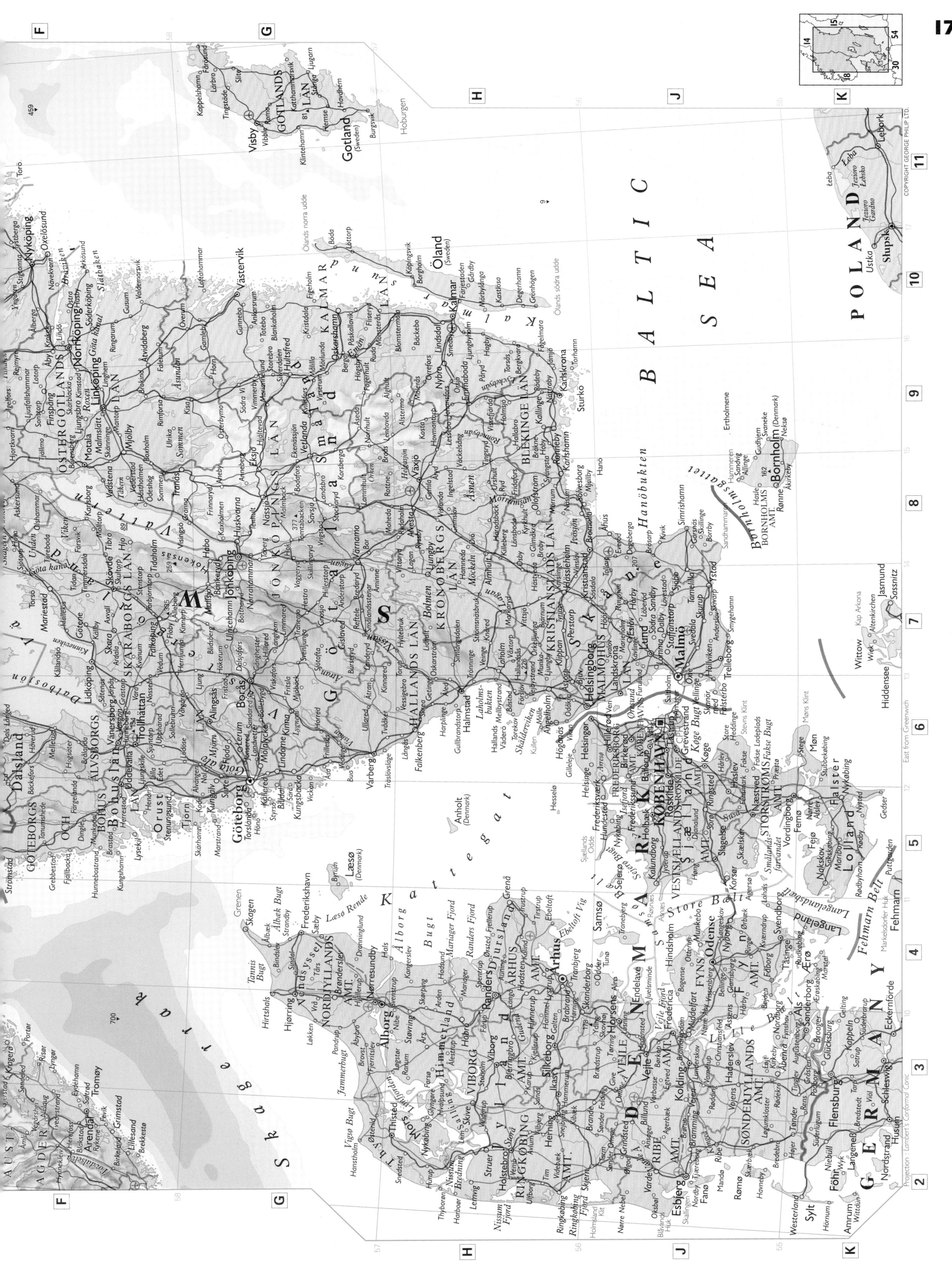

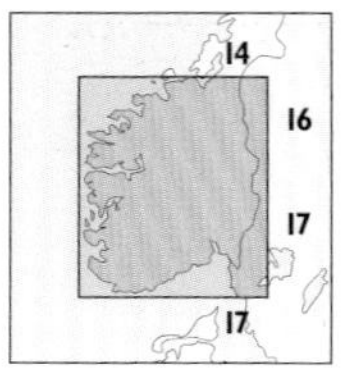

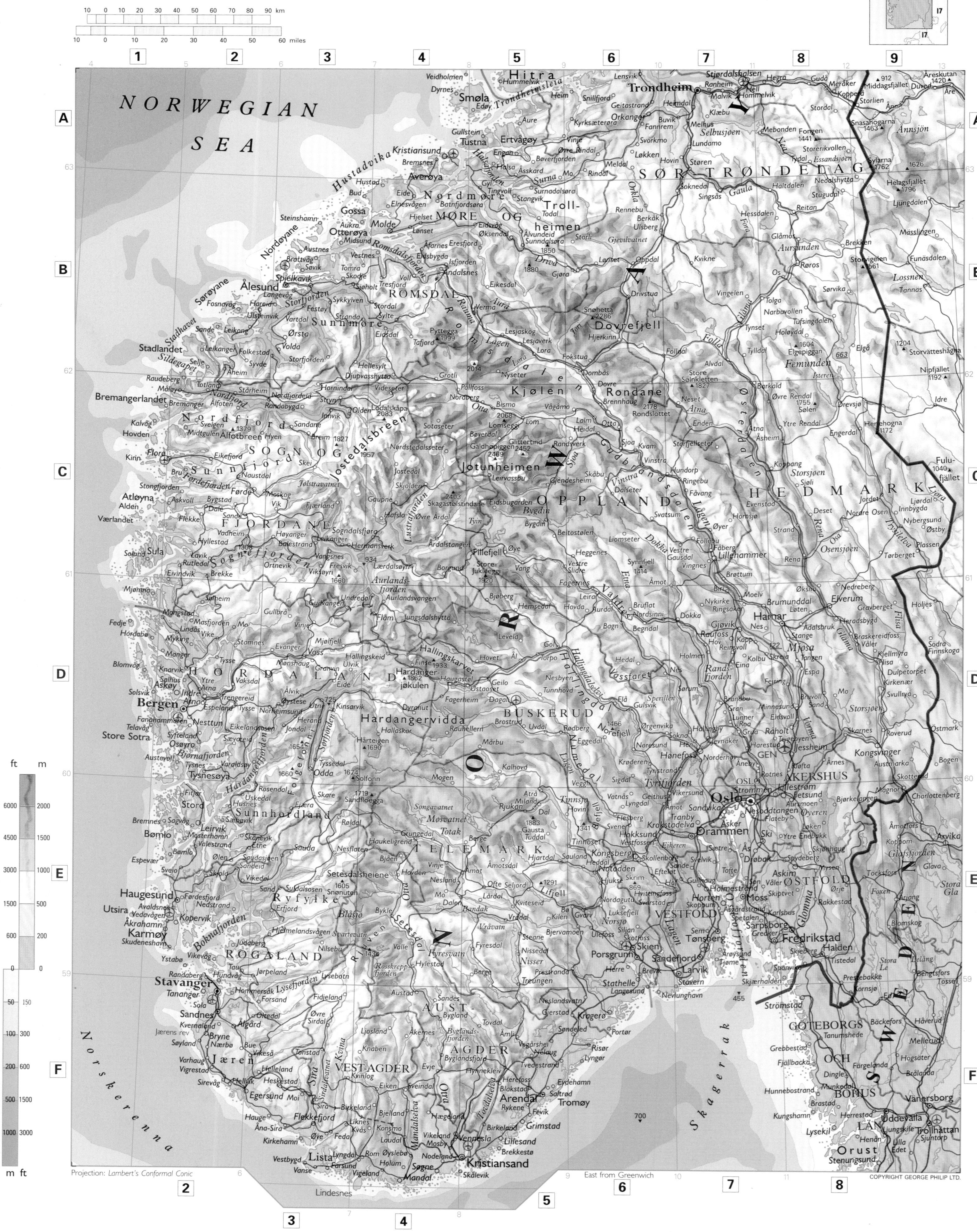

10 0 10 20 30 40 50 60 70 80 90 km
10 0 10 20 30 40 50 60 miles

NORWEGIAN SEA

SØR TRØNDELAG

Trondheim

Hitra

MØRE OG ROMSDAL

Troll-heimen

Dovrefjell

Kristiansund

Molde

Ålesund

ROMSDAL

Sunnmøre

Kjølen

Rondane

HEDMARK

Femunden

Nordfjord

SOGN OG FJORDANE

Jotunheimen

OPPLAND

Lillehammer

Sognefjorden

Hamar

Mjøsa

Bergen

HORDALAND

Hardangervidda

Hardangerjøkulen

BUSKERUD

Elverum

AKERSHUS

Oslo

Drammen

ØSTFOLD

Haugesund

ROGALAND

TELEMARK

VESTFOLD

Tønsberg

Larvik

Fredrikstad

Halden

Stavanger

Sandnes

Jæren

VEST-AGDER

AUST-AGDER

Arendal

Skagerrak

SWEDEN

GÖTEBORGS OCH BOHUS LÄN

Kristiansand

Mandal

Lindesnes

Norskerenna

Projection: Lambert's Conformal Conic

East from Greenwich

COPYRIGHT GEORGE PHILIP LTD.

ft m
6000 2000
4500 1500
3000 1000
1500 500
600 200
0 0
50 150
100 300
200 600
500 1500
1000 3000
m ft

ATLANTIC OCEAN

NORWAY
Bergen
Askøy
Osøyra
Stord
Bømlo
Leirvik
Haugesund
Kopervik
Åkrahamn
Boknafjorden
Stavanger
Sandnes
Bryne
Nærbø

Shetland Is.
Yell
Unst
Fetlar
Foula
Mainland
Lerwick
Fair Isle

Orkney Is.
Westray
Sanday
Stronsay
Mainland
Kirkwall
Hoy
South Ronaldsay

Lewis
Stornoway
C. Wrath
Thurso
Wick

Pentland Firth

North Minch
Ullapool
Lairg
Helmsdale

St. Kilda
Harris
789
North Uist
Benbecula
South Uist
Portree
Skye
Rhum
Eigg
Coll
Tiree
Mull
Oban
Colonsay
Jura
Islay
Tobermory

Outer Hebrides
Inner Hebrides

North West Highlands
Invergordon
Dingwall
L. Ness
1182
Inverness
Aviemore
Ben Nevis
1342
Fort William

Moray Firth
Tain
Nairn
Elgin
Buckie
Banff
Fraserburgh
Peterhead
Huntly
Inverurie
Aberdeen
Spey
Don
Dee
1311
Ballater
Stonehaven

Grampian Mts.
SCOTLAND
1214
Forfar
Arbroath
Perth
Dundee
St. Andrews

L. Lomond
973
Stirling
Glenrothes
Kirkcaldy
Dunfermline

NORTH SEA
238

Greenock
Paisley
Glasgow
Edinburgh
East Kilbride
Hamilton
Clyde
Berwick-upon-Tweed
Campbeltown
Arran
Kilmarnock
Ayr
Irvine
840
Galashiels
Southern Uplands
Jedburgh
Hawick
Cheviot Hills
816
Alnwick

Malin Hd.
Buncrana
Coleraine
Ballymena
Larne
Bangor
North Channel
Dumfries
Annan
Newcastle-upon-Tyne
South Shields
Sunderland
Hexham
Gateshead
Durham
Hartlepool
Redcar

Aran I.
Letterkenny
Lifford
Londonderry
NORTHERN IRELAND
Antrim
Firth of Clyde
Kirkcudbright
Stranraer
Carlisle
Workington
Whitehaven
Cumbrian Mts.
978
Darlington
Middlesbrough
Stockton-on-Tees
893
Scarborough

Donegal
Ulster
Omagh
Lough Neagh
Belfast
Lisburn
Portadown
Lurgan
Mull of Galloway
Pennines
16

Bundoran
Lower L. Erne
Enniskillen
Armagh
Newry
Douglas
I. of Man
Barrow-in-Furness
Lancaster
Harrogate
Bridlington

Ballina
L. Corn
Sligo
Leitrim
Cavan
Castleblaney
Dundalk
UNITED
KINGDOM
Blackpool
Preston
Blackburn
Burnley
Keighley
Bradford
Leeds
York
Beverley
Kingston upon Hull

Achill I.
Castlebar
Westport
Roscommon
Ceanannus Mor
Drogheda
Boyne
IRISH SEA
Southport
Bolton
Halifax
Huddersfield
Barnsley
Doncaster
Scunthorpe
Grimsby
Humber

Lough Mask
Connemara
Lough Conn
Lough Carra
Ballinasloe
Athlone
Longford
Mullingar
Liffey
Manchester
Warrington
Stockport
Oldham
636
Sheffield
Chesterfield
Mansfield
Rotherham
Lincoln
Louth
Skegness

Galway B.
Galway
Aran Is.
Birr
Lough Ree
Tullamore
Dublin
Dun Laoghaire
Bray
Holyhead
Anglesey
Bangor
Colwyn Bay
Chester
Crewe
Liverpool
Stoke-on-Trent
Derby
Nottingham
Grantham
King's Lynn
The Wash
Cromer

Ennis
Lough Derg
DIRELAND
Port Laoise
Athy
Wrexham
Snowdon
1085
Shrewsbury
Stafford
Telford
Nuneaton
Leicester
Corby
Peterborough
Norwich
Great Yarmouth
Lowestoft

953
Dingle
Limerick
Nenagh
Thurles
Kilkenny
Carlow
926
Wicklow Mts.
Arklow
Pwllheli
Cambrian Mts.
ENGLAND
Cardigan Bay
Wolverhampton
BIRMINGHAM
Coventry
Rugby
Northampton
Bedford
Cambridge
Ipswich
Bury St. Edmunds
Thetford

Tralee
Killarney
Macgillycuddy's Reeks
1041
Tipperary
Carrick-on-Suir
Clonmel
Wexford
Aberystwyth
WALES
Redditch
Worcester
Hereford
Leamington Spa
Ely
Stevenage
NETHERLANDS
's-Gravenhage
(Den Haag)
Hoek van Holland
ROTTERDAM
Dordrecht
Texel
Den Helder
Alkmaar
Haarlem

Carrauntoohill
Mallow
Waterford
Dungarvan
Youghal
Fishguard
St. George's Channel
Rosslare
Carmarthen
886
Merthyr Tydfil
Brecon
Cheltenham
Gloucester
Oxford
Hemel Hempstead
High Wycombe
Milton Keynes
Luton
Harlow
Colchester
Chelmsford
Harwich
Felixstowe
Vlissingen

encia I.
Bandon
Cork
Cóbh
Kinsale
Haverfordwest
Milford Haven
Pembroke
Llanelli
Neath
Cwmbran
Swansea
Port Talbot
Rhondda
Newport
Cardiff
Bristol
Bath
Swindon
Newbury
Reading
LONDON
Thames
Southend-on-Sea
Margate
Zeebrugge
Oostende
BELGIUM
Antwerpen
Gent
Mechelen
BRUSSEL
(Bruxelles)
36

C. Clear
Bantry
99
Barry
Bristol Channel
Weston-super-Mare
Barnstaple
Exmoor
Bude
618
Dartmoor
Exeter
Taunton
Yeovil
Salisbury
Winchester
Basingstoke
Guildford
Crawley
Reigate
Maidstone
Ashford
Dover
Canterbury
Chatham
Folkestone
Str. of Dover
Calais
Dunkerque
St. Omer
Boulogne-sur-Mer
Béthune
Lille
Roubaix
Tourcoing
Mechelen
Bruay-la-Buissière
Lens
Armentières
BELGIUM
Tournai
Valenciennes
Cambrai

CELTIC SEA
Newquay
Truro
St. Austell
Plymouth
Torbay
Exmouth
Weymouth
Poole
Bournemouth
Southampton
Fareham
Portsmouth
Isle of Wight
Worthing
Brighton
Eastbourne
Hastings
Havant
Le Touquet-Paris-Plage
33
Le Tréport
Abbeville
FRANCE
Picardie
Amiens
St-Quentin

Land's End
Penzance
Falmouth
Isles of Scilly
English Channel
West from Greenwich
C. de la Hague
Alderney
Pte. de Barfleur
Fécamp
Dieppe
Pays de Caux
Bolbec
Rouen
Seine
Elbeuf
East from Greenwich

Guernsey
St. Peter Port
Sark
Cherbourg
Valognes
Le Havre
Trouville-sur-Mer
Lisieux

Channel Is.
(U.K.)
St. Helier
Jersey
Cotentin
Bayeux
Caen

CARTOGRAPHY BY PHILIP'S
COPYRIGHT REED INTERNATIONAL BOOKS LTD

Projection: Conical with two standard parallels

ft m
3000 1000
1500 500
600 200
0 0
50 150
100 300
200 600
500 1500
1000 3000
2000 6000
m ft

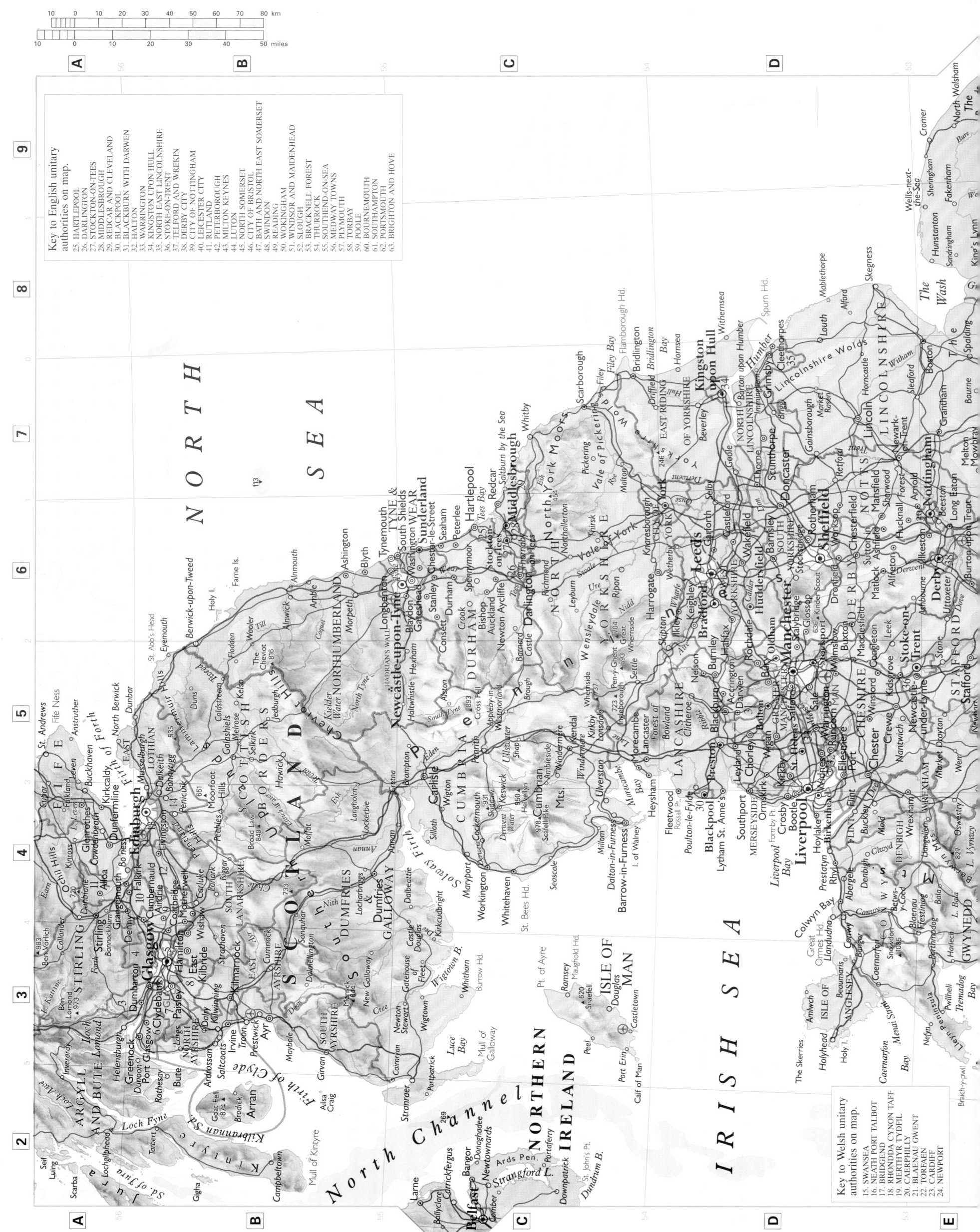

NORTH SEA

IRISH SEA

North Channel

NORTHERN IRELAND

SCOTLAND

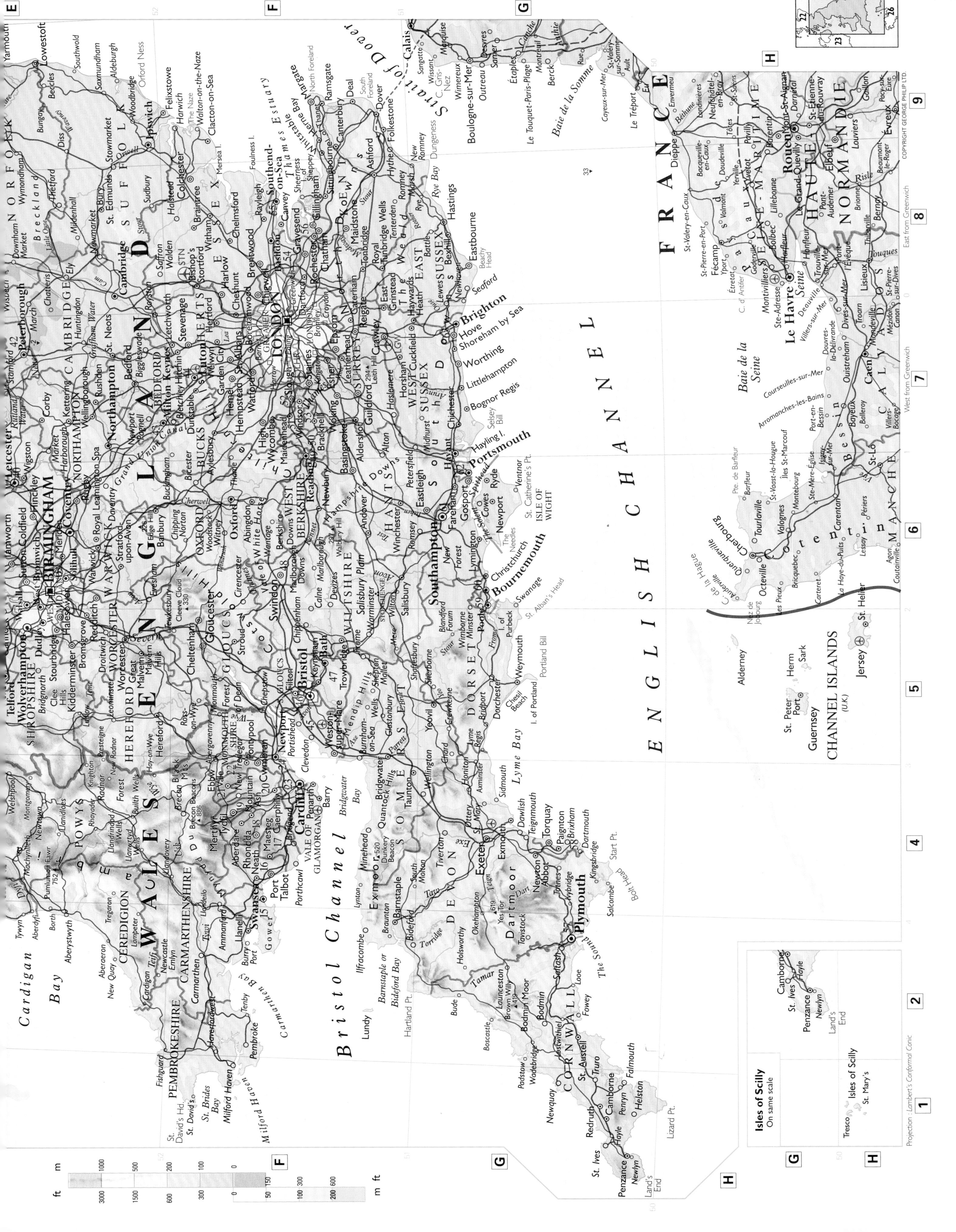

ENGLAND

WALES

FRANCE

HAUTE-NORMANDIE

SEINE-MARITIME

CALVADOS

MANCHE

London

Birmingham

Bristol

Cardiff

Southampton

Portsmouth

Plymouth

Brighton

Bournemouth

Swansea

Le Havre

Rouen

Cherbourg

Strait of Dover

ENGLISH CHANNEL

Bristol Channel

Cardigan Bay

Baie de la Seine

Baie de la Somme

CHANNEL ISLANDS (U.K.)

Jersey • St. Helier

Guernsey • St. Peter Port

Alderney

Sark

Herm

CORNWALL

DEVON

SOMERSET

DORSET

WILTSHIRE

HAMPSHIRE

BERKSHIRE

SURREY

WEST SUSSEX

EAST SUSSEX

KENT

ESSEX

SUFFOLK

NORFOLK

CAMBRIDGE

BEDFORD

NORTHAMPTON

LEICESTER

WARWICK

OXFORD

GLOUCS

HEREFORD

SHROPSHIRE

WEST GLAMORGAN

VALE OF GLAMORGAN

POWYS

CEREDIGION

CARMARTHENSHIRE

PEMBROKESHIRE

COTENTIN

PAYS de CAUX

Isles of Scilly (On same scale)

Tresco • St. Mary's

St. Ives • Camborne • Hayle

Penzance • Newlyn

Land's End

Lowestoft, Yarmouth, Southwold, Beccles, Bungay, Diss, Aldeburgh, Saxmundham, Woodbridge, Orford Ness, Felixstowe, Harwich, Clacton-on-Sea, Walton-on-the-Naze, Ipswich, Stowmarket, Bury St. Edmunds, Sudbury, Colchester, Halstead, Braintree, Witham, Chelmsford, Maldon, Southend-on-Sea, Thetford, Brandon, Mildenhall, Newmarket, Ely, Cambridge, Royston, Saffron Walden, Bishop's Stortford, Harlow, Brentwood, Gravesend, Sheerness, Margate, Ramsgate, Deal, Dover, Folkestone, Canterbury, Whitstable, Herne Bay, Sandwich, Ashford, Hythe, Romney, Rye, Hastings, Bexhill, Eastbourne, Seaford, Newhaven, Lewes, Uckfield, Tunbridge Wells, Tonbridge, Maidstone, Rochester, Chatham, Sevenoaks, Crawley, East Grinstead, Haywards Heath, Horsham, Worthing, Littlehampton, Bognor Regis, Chichester, Petersfield, Haslemere, Guildford, Woking, Reading, Basingstoke, Andover, Winchester, Eastleigh, Fareham, Gosport, Ryde, Newport, Cowes, Ventnor, ISLE OF WIGHT, The Needles, Lymington, New Milton, Christchurch, Ringwood, Wareham, Swanage, Poole, Wimborne Minster, Blandford Forum, Dorchester, Weymouth, Portland Bill, Bridport, Lyme Regis, Axminster, Honiton, Sidmouth, Exmouth, Dawlish, Teignmouth, Torquay, Paignton, Brixham, Dartmouth, Kingsbridge, Salcombe, Start Pt., Bolt Head, Plymouth, Saltash, Looe, Fowey, St. Austell, Newquay, Wadebridge, Padstow, Boscastle, Bude, Bodmin, Liskeard, Launceston, Okehampton, Tavistock, Dartmoor, Exeter, Tiverton, Cullompton, Taunton, Bridgwater, Minehead, Ilfracombe, Barnstaple, Bideford, Lynton, Exmoor, Wellington, Yeovil, Sherborne, Crewkerne, Chard, Ilminster, Glastonbury, Wells, Shepton Mallet, Frome, Warminster, Shaftesbury, Salisbury, Devizes, Calne, Chippenham, Trowbridge, Bath, Keynsham, Bristol, Weston-super-Mare, Burnham-on-Sea, Clevedon, Portishead, Chepstow, Monmouth, Newport, Cwmbran, Pontypool, Abergavenny, Merthyr Tydfil, Aberdare, Pontypridd, Caerphilly, Bridgend, Porthcawl, Port Talbot, Neath, Llanelli, Carmarthen, Tenby, Pembroke, Milford Haven, Haverfordwest, Fishguard, St. David's, Cardigan, Aberystwyth, Aberaeron, New Quay, Newcastle Emlyn, Lampeter, Tregaron, Llandovery, Brecon, Builth Wells, Llandrindod Wells, Rhayader, Newtown, Montgomery, Welshpool, Machynlleth, Knighton, Presteigne, Leominster, Hereford, Ross-on-Wye, Ledbury, Malvern, Worcester, Droitwich, Kidderminster, Stourbridge, Bromsgrove, Redditch, Stratford-upon-Avon, Warwick, Royal Leamington Spa, Rugby, Daventry, Banbury, Chipping Norton, Witney, Woodstock, Oxford, Abingdon, Wantage, Wallingford, Henley, Marlow, High Wycombe, Aylesbury, Buckingham, Bicester, Milton Keynes, Bedford, Biggleswade, Hitchin, Stevenage, Welwyn Garden City, Hatfield, St. Albans, Hemel Hempstead, Watford, Luton, Dunstable, Leighton Buzzard, Northampton, Wellingborough, Kettering, Corby, Market Harborough, Leicester, Loughborough, Wigston, Hinckley, Nuneaton, Coventry, Solihull, Sutton Coldfield, Walsall, Wolverhampton, Telford, Dudley, Halesowen

Dieppe, Le Tréport, Eu, Fécamp, Étretat, St-Valery-en-Caux, Yvetot, Bolbec, Lillebonne, Pont-Audemer, Honfleur, Trouville, Deauville, Cabourg, Ouistreham, Caen, Bayeux, Arromanches-les-Bains, Courseulles-sur-Mer, Carentan, Ste-Mère-Église, Valognes, Cherbourg, Octeville, Tourlaville, Barfleur, Coutances, St-Lô, Lessay, Évreux, Louviers, Elbeuf, Pont-de-l'Arche, Gisors, Les Andelys, Vernon, Gournay-en-Bray, Forges-les-Eaux, Neufchâtel-en-Bray, Blangy-sur-Bresle, Aumale

Calais, Boulogne-sur-Mer, Le Touquet-Paris-Plage, Berck, Étaples, Montreuil, Marquise, Wimereux, Wissant, Cap Gris-Nez, Desvres, Samer, Hucqueliers

Copyright George Philip Ltd.

Projection: Lambert's Conformal Conic

East from Greenwich

West from Greenwich

10 0 10 20 30 40 50 60 70 80 km
10 0 10 20 30 40 50 miles

Key to Scottish unitary authorities on map

1. CITY OF ABERDEEN
2. DUNDEE CITY
3. WEST DUNBARTONSHIRE
4. EAST DUNBARTONSHIRE
5. CITY OF GLASGOW
6. INVERCLYDE
7. RENFREWSHIRE
8. EAST RENFREWSHIRE
9. NORTH LANARKSHIRE
10. FALKIRK
11. CLACKMANNANSHIRE
12. WEST LOTHIAN
13. CITY OF EDINBURGH
14. MIDLOTHIAN

ORKNEY IS.
On same scale

ORKNEY

North Ronaldsay
Papa Westray
Westray
Rousay
Eday
Sanday
Stronsay
Brough Hd.
Mainland
Shapinsay
Stromness
Kirkwall
Hoy
481
Scapa Flow
St. Mary's
Burray
South Ronaldsay
Burwick
Dunnet Hd. Stroma
Duncansby Head
John o' Groats
Sinclair's Bay
Thurso
Pentland Firth

SHETLAND IS.
On same scale

Unst
Haroldswick
Fetlar
Yell
Ulsta
Whalsay
Esha Ness
Yell Sound
St. Magnus Bay
Papa Stour
Voe
Walls
Scalloway
Lerwick
Bressay
Foula
West Burra
Boddam
Sumburgh Hd.
453

ft m
3000 1000
1500 500
600 200
300 100
0 0
50 150
100 300
200 600
500 1500
1000 3000
m ft

ATLANTIC OCEAN

WESTERN ISLES

Flannan Is.
Butt of Lewis
Stornoway
Broad Bay
Eye Peninsula
Gallan Hd.
Lewis
Scarp
Taransay
799 Clisham
Harris
Toe Hd.
Pabbay
Berneray
North Uist
Lochmaddy
Baleshare
Grimsay
Benbecula
Ardivachar Pt.
Wiay
South Uist
Lochboisdale
Eriskay
Barra
Vatersay
Sandray
Barra Hd.
268

Outer Hebrides
Sound of Harris
Sound of Barra

Inner Hebrides

North Minch
Little Minch
Sound of Raasay

C. Wrath
Durness
Strathy Pt.
Dounreay
Dunnet Hd.
Thurso
Stroma
John o' Groats
Scapa Flow
Hoy 481
Burwick
Pentland Firth
Noss Hd.
Sinclair's Bay
Wick
Lybster
Halkirk
Thurso
L. Eriboll
Tongue
Ben Hope 927
Naver
Reay Forest
L. Laxford
Eddrachillis B.
Pt. of Stoer
961
Lochinver
Enard B.
Rubha Coigeach
L. Assynt
Ben More Assynt 998
L. Shin
Laing
Brora
Golspie
Helmsdale
705
Ord of Caithness
Helmsdale
1081 Ben Dearg
1109
L. Broom
Ullapool
Dornoch Firth
Tarbat Ness
Dornoch
Tain
Kinnairds Hd.
Fraserburgh
Rattray Hd.
Peterhead
Buchan Ness
Ellon
Oldmeldrum

Greenstone Pt.
Gruinard B.
L. Ewe
Gairloch
L. Maree 1053
Rubha Hunish
Uig
Rona
Raasay
Scalpay
Portree
L. Monar 1083
Carn Eige 1182
Glen Affric
1068
Kyle of Lochalsh
Stromeferry
Dornie
L. Carron
L. Torridon
L. Fannich 1045
Ben Wyvis
Strathpeffer
Dingwall
Fortrose
Beauly
Inverness
Loch Ness
Fort Augustus
Glen Moriston
Glen Garry
MONADHLIATH MTS.
941
Newtonmore
Kingussie
Carn Ban
Aviemore
Grantown-on-Spey
Strath Spey
CAIRNGORM MTS.
1309 Cairn Gorm 1245
1309 Ben Macdhui
Braemar
Tomintoul
MORAY
Elgin
Lossiemouth
Portknockie Portsoy
Buckie Cullen Banff Macduff
Nairn
Forres
Rothes
Keith
Aberchirder
Turriff
Huntly
Dufftown
Alford
Inverurie
Westhill
ABERDEENSHIRE
Dyce
Aberdeen 1
Girdle Ness
Peterculter
Banchory
Aboyne
Balloter
1154 Lochnagar
Stonehaven
Inverbervie
Laurencekirk
Brechin
Montrose
ANGUS
Forfar
Arbroath
Carnoustie
Monifieth
Dundee 2

Skye
Cuillin Hills 992
Cuillin Sound
Sd. of Sleat
Canna
Rhum
Eigg
Muck
Mallaig
L. Morar
Arisaig
Pt. of Ardnamurchan
Coll
Tiree
Passage of Tiree
Tobermory
Staffa
Ulva
Iona
966 Ben More
Mull
Kerrera
Oban
Lismore
Seil
Luing
Scarba
Colonsay
Oronsay
Jura
Islay
Bowmore
Port Ellen
Rhinns Pt.
Mull of Oa
Rubh' a' Mhail
Ardnave Pt.
Gigha
Kintyre
Campbeltown
Mull of Kintyre

L. Shiel
L. Eil
Ben Nevis 1342
Fort William
Glen Coe 1148
Ballachulish
Morvern
Sound of Mull
Loch Linnhe
L. Sunart
L. Moidart
L. Arkaig 1128
L. Lochy
Glen Spean
Spean 1148
Lochaber
L. Leven
Ben Cruachan 1126
L. Awe
Loch Etive
L. Fyne
Inveraray
Lochgilphead
ARGYLL AND BUTE
Loch Lomond
Ben Lomond 973
Tarbert
Loch Fyne
Sd. of Jura
Kilbrannan Sd.
Arran
Goat Fell 874
Brodick
Firth of Clyde
Bute
Rothesay
Largs
Dunoon
Port Glasgow
Greenock
Helensburgh
Dumbarton
Clydebank
Glasgow
Paisley
Rannoch Moor
L. Rannoch
Forest of Atholl 1121
Blair Atholl
1148
Garry
Ben Lawers 1214
L. Tay
Aberfeldy
Pitlochry
Kirriemuir
Alyth
Blairgowrie
Dunkeld
PERTH
KINROSS
Crieff
Comrie
Callander
983 Ben Vorlich
Ben More 1174
Crianlarich
STIRLING
Dunblane
Stirling
Bannockburn
Alloa
Dollar
Ochil Hills
720
CLACKMANNANSHIRE
Kinross
L. Leven
Falkland
FIFE
Cupar
St. Andrews
Fife Ness
Leven
Anstruther
Buckhaven
Kirkcaldy
Glenrothes
Cowdenbeath
Dunfermline
Firth of Forth
North Berwick
Dunbar
St. Abb's Head
Eyemouth
EAST LOTHIAN
Musselburgh
Edinburgh 13
Livingston
Bo'ness
Grangemouth
Denny
Cumbernauld
Falkirk 10
Airdrie
Coatbridge
Motherwell
Hamilton
East Kilbride
Wishaw
Carluke
Lanark
NORTH AYRSHIRE
Kilwinning
Dalry
Ardrossan
Saltcoats
Irvine
Kilmarnock
Troon
Prestwick
Ayr
EAST AYRSHIRE
Cumnock
Maybole
Girvan
Ailsa Craig
SOUTH AYRSHIRE
Dalmellington
Sanquhar
SOUTH LANARKSHIRE
Strathaven
Biggar
Broad Law 840
Peebles
Moorfoot Hills
Penicuik
Dalkeith
Bonnyrigg
651
Pentland Hills
Tweed
Galashiels
Melrose
Selkirk
535
Lammermuir Hills
Duns
Coldstream
Kelso
SCOTTISH BORDERS
Hawick
Jedburgh
The Cheviot 816
Cheviot Hills
Flodden
Wooler
Holy I.
Farne Is.
Berwick-upon-Tweed
Alnmouth
Amble
NORTHUMBERLAND
Morpeth
Newcastle-upon-Tyne
Blaydon
Gateshead
Stanley
Consett
DURHAM
Bishop Auckland
Crook
Barnard Castle

L. Ryan
Stranraer
Portpatrick
Luce Bay
Wigtown B.
Whithorn
Burrow Hd.
Mull of Galloway
Cairnryan
Newton Stewart
Gatehouse of Fleet
Kirkcudbright
Wigtown
Castle Douglas
Dalbeattie
DUMFRIES & GALLOWAY
Merrick 844
New Galloway
733
Moniaive
Thornhill
Dumfries
Lochmaben
Lockerbie
Langholm
Moffat
Annan
Gretna
Carlisle
Brampton
Silloth
Maryport
Workington
Cockermouth
Whitehaven
St. Bees Hd.
CUMBRIA
Wigton
Penrith
Keswick
Skiddaw 931
Derwent Water
Ullswater
950 Helvellyn
893 Cross Fell
Alston
Haltwhistle
Hexham
Appleby-in-Westmorland
Brough

Galloway
Solway Firth

Firth of Lorn
Firth of Tay
Strathmore
Sidlaw Hills
N. Esk
S. Esk

SCOTLAND

NORTH SEA

ATLANTIC OCEAN

NORTHERN IRELAND
Larne
Carrickfergus
Belfast L.
Belfast
Bangor
Donaghadee
Newtownards
269

North Channel

ENGLAND

West from Greenwich

Projection: Lambert's Conformal Conic

COPYRIGHT GEORGE PHILIP LTD.

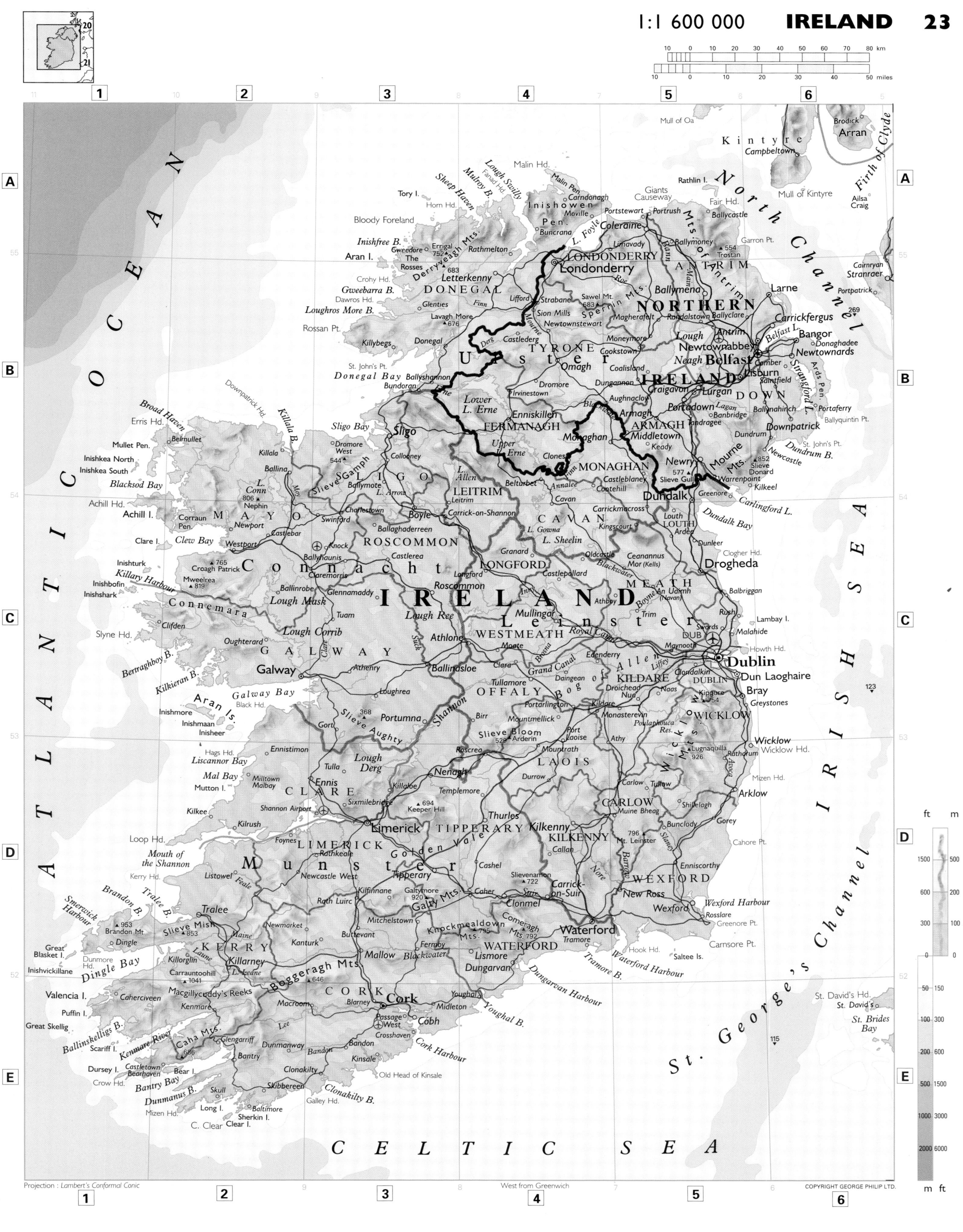

10 0 10 20 30 40 50 60 70 80 km
10 0 10 20 30 40 50 miles

20
21

ft m

ATLANTIC OCEAN

North Channel

Mull of Oa
Kintyre
Campbeltown
Brodick
Arran
Firth of Clyde
Mull of Kintyre
Ailsa Craig

Tory I.
Sheep Haven
Mulroy B.
Lough Swilly
Fanad Hd.
Malin Hd.
Malin Hd.
Malin Pen.
Inishowen Pen.
Carndonagh
Meville
Bunerana
Giants Causeway
Portstewart Portrush
Rathlin I.
Ballycastle
Fair Hd.
Garron Pt.
Cairnryan
Stranraer
Portpatrick

Bloody Foreland
Inishfree B.
Gweedore
Errigal 752
The Rosses
Crohy Hd.
Gweebarra B.
Dawros Hd.
Aran I.
683
Derryveagh Mts.
L. Foyle
Coleraine
Limavady
Rae
Ballymoney
Moneymore
Garron Pt.
554 Trostan
ANTRIM
Larne

Loughros More B.
Rossan Pt.
Killybegs
Donegal
DONEGAL
Letterkenny
Rathmelton
Lifford
Strabane
Sion Mills
Newtownstewart
Sawel Mt. 683
Spelrin Mts.
Magherafelt
Cookstown
Randalstown Ballyclare
NORTHERN
IRELAND
Ballymena
Antrim
Lough Neagh
Carrickfergus 269
Belfast L.
Bangor
Donaghadee
Newtownabbey
Belfast
Comber
Newtownards
Ards Pen.

Ulster
Castlederg
TYRONE
Omagh
Dungannon
Coalisland
Craigavon
Lurgan
Portadown
Lagan
Lisburn
Saintfield
Strangford L.
Ballynahinch
Banbridge
Dromore
DOWN
Dundrum
Downpatrick
Ballyquintin Pt.
Portaferry

St. John's Pt.
Donegal Bay
Ballyshannon
Bundoran
Lower L. Erne
Enniskillen
FERMANAGH
Irvinestown
Dromore
Monaghan
Aughnacloy
ARMAGH
Armagh
Middletown
Keady
Newry
Clogher Hd.
St. John's Pt.
Dundrum B.
852 Slieve Donard
Newcastle
Mourne Mts.
Kilkeel
Warrenpoint
Greenore

Downpatrick Hd.
Killala B.
Broad Haven
Erris Hd.
Mullet Pen.
Belmullet
Inishkea North
Inishkea South
Blacksod Bay
Achill Hd.
Achill I.
Corraun Pen.
Nephin 806
L. Conn
Ballina
Killala
SLIGO
Slieve Gamph
544 Dromore West
Sligo Bay
Sligo
Collooney
Ballymote
L. Arrow
L. Allen
LEITRIM
Leitrim
Carrick-on-Shannon
Upper L. Erne
Clones
Belturbet
MONAGHAN
Monaghan
Castleblaney
Cootehill
Annalee
577 Slieve Gullion
Dundalk
Carlingford L.
Carrickmacross
Louth
LOUTH
Ardee
Dundalk Bay

Connacht
MAYO
Newport
Castlebar
Clew Bay
Westport
Clare I.
Inishturk
Killary Harbour
Inishbofin
Inishshark
Croagh Patrick 765
Mweelrea 819
Connemara
Clifden
Slyne Hd.
Knock
Swinford
Charlestown
Ballyhaunis
Claremorris
Ballinrobe
Ballaghaderreen
Boyle
ROSCOMMON
Castlerea
Roscommon
Longford
LONGFORD
L. Gowna
CAVAN
Cavan
L. Sheelin
Granard
Castlepollard
Oldcastle
Ceanannus Mor (Kells)
Blackwater
Kingscourt
Dunleer
Clogher Hd.
Drogheda
Balbriggan

Bertraghboy B.
Kilkieran B.
Inishmore
Aran Is.
Inishmaan
Inisheer
Oughterard
Lough Corrib
GALWAY
Tuam
Athenry
Galway
Galway Bay
Black Hd.
Lough Mask
Lough Corrib
Glennamaddy
Loughrea
Ballinasloe
Lough Ree
Athlone
Moate
WESTMEATH
Mullingar
Edenderry
An Uaimh (Navan)
Athboy
Trim
Boyne
MEATH
Royal Canal
Maynooth
Swords
DUB
Malahide
Lambay I.
Howth Hd.

IRELAND
Leinster

Hags Hd.
Liscannor Bay
Mal Bay
Mutton I.
Ennistimon
Slieve Aughty
368
Gort
Portumna
Birr
Shannon
Slieve Bloom
Arderin 528
OFFALY
Tullamore
Daingean
Bog of Allen
Grand Canal
Clara
Kildare
KILDARE
Naas
Droichead Nua
Kilcock 254
Clondalkin
Dublin
Dun Laoghaire
Bray
Greystones
123

Loop Hd.
Kilkee
Kilrush
CLARE
Tulla
Ennis
Sixmilebridge
Shannon Airport
Lough Derg
Nenagh
Killaloe
Keeper Hill 694
Templemore
Roscrea
Mountmellick
Port Laoise
Portarlington
Mountrath
Athy
LAOIS
Mt. Leinster 796
Durrow
Carlow
CARLOW
Muine Bheag
Tullow
Shillelagh
Gorey
Bunclody
WICKLOW
Lugnaquilla 926
Wicklow Mts.
Rathdrum
Wicklow
Wicklow Hd.
Arklow
Mizen Hd.

Mouth of the Shannon
Kerry Hd.
Listowel
Rathkeale
LIMERICK
Newcastle West
Limerick
TIPPERARY
Golden Vale
Tipperary
Thurles
Cashel
Munster
Kilkenny
KILKENNY
Callan
Thomastown
Mt. Leinster
Enniscorthy
WEXFORD
New Ross
Cahore Pt.

Smerwick Harbour
Brandon B.
Brandon Mt. 953
Dingle
Slieve Mish 853
Tralee B.
Tralee
Great Blasket I.
Dunmore Hd.
Dingle Bay
Inishvickillane
Maine
KERRY
Killorglin
Newmarket
Kanturk
Buttevant
Mitchelstown
Fermoy
Galty Mts.
Galtymore 920
Kilfinnane
Rath Luirc
Mallow
Blackwater
Lismore
Knockmealdown Mts. 795 792
Comeragh Mts.
Clonmel
Carrick-on-Suir
Slievenamon 722
Caher
Tipperary
WATERFORD
Dungarvan
Dungarvan Harbour
Tramore
Tramore B.
Waterford
Waterford Harbour
Hook Hd.
Saltee Is.
Wexford
Rosslare
Greenore Pt.
Carnsore Pt.

Valencia I.
Puffin I.
Great Skellig
Ballinskelligs B.
Scariff I.
Dursey I.
Crow Hd.
Bear I.
Bantry Bay
Dunmanus B.
Mizen Hd.
Long I.
Skull
Cahersiveen
Kenmare
Macgillycuddy's Reeks
Carrauntoohill 1041
L. Leane
Killarney
Laune
Kenmare River
Caha Mts. 686
Glengarriff
Castletown Bearhaven
Bantry
Dunmanway
Bandon
Clonakilty
Skibbereen
Clonakilty B.
Galley Hd.
Baltimore
Sherkin I.
Clear I.
C. Clear
Boggeragh Mts. 646
CORK
Macroom
Blarney
Cork
Lee
Passage West
Cobh
Crosshaven
Cork Harbour
Midleton
Youghal
Youghal B.
Old Head of Kinsale
Kinsale
Bandon

CELTIC SEA

IRISH SEA

St. George's Channel

St. David's Hd.
St. David's
St. Brides Bay
115

ft m
1500 500
600 200
300 100
0
50 150
100 300
500 600
1000 3000
2000 6000
m ft

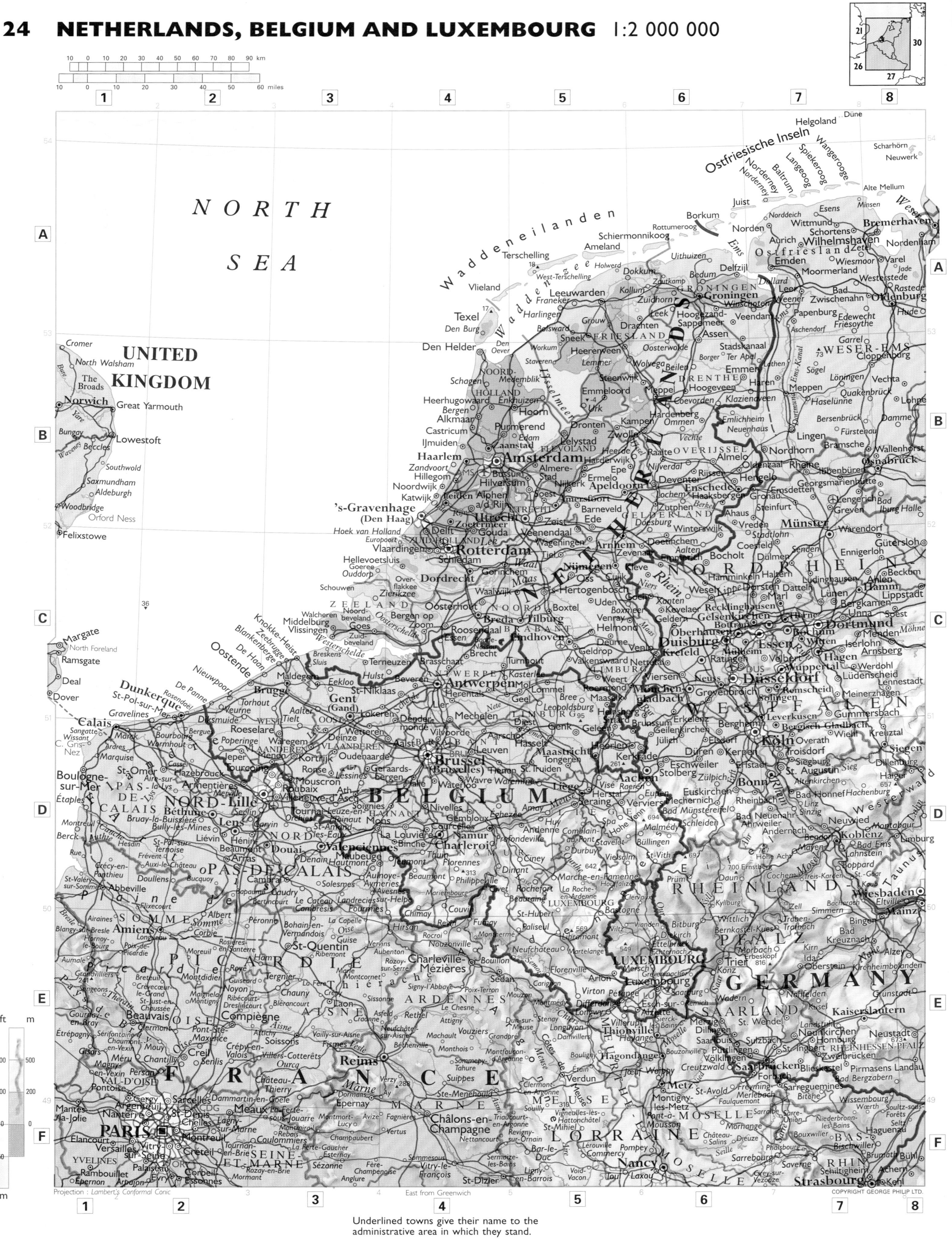

Projection : Lambert's Conformal Conic

East from Greenwich

COPYRIGHT GEORGE PHILIP LTD.

Underlined towns give their name to the
administrative area in which they stand.

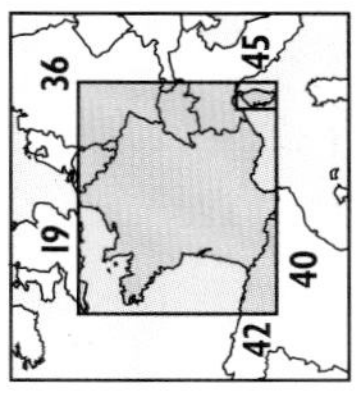

km scale: 50 25 0 25 50 75 100 125 150 175 km
miles scale: 50 25 0 25 50 75 100 125 miles

Corse (Corsica)

C. Corse
Bastia
Calvi
Mte. Cinto 2710
Ajaccio
Porto-Vecchio
Bonifacio

GERMANY

UNITED KINGDOM

BELGIUM

LUXEMBOURG

SWITZERLAND

AUSTRIA

ITALY

FRANCE

SPAIN

ANDORRA

MONACO

MEDITERRANEAN SEA

English Channel

Bay of Biscay

Golfe de Gascogne

Golfe du Lion

Côte d'Azur

PARIS
MARSEILLE
LYON
TORINO (Turin)
MILANO
GENOVA (Genoa)
Bordeaux
Toulouse
Nantes
Strasbourg
Stuttgart
Zürich
Bern
Genève

Projection: Conical with two standard parallels

West from Greenwich

East from Greenwich

m ft elevation scale:
4000 12000
3000 9000
2000 6000
1500 4500
1000 3000
500 1500
200 600
0
ft m

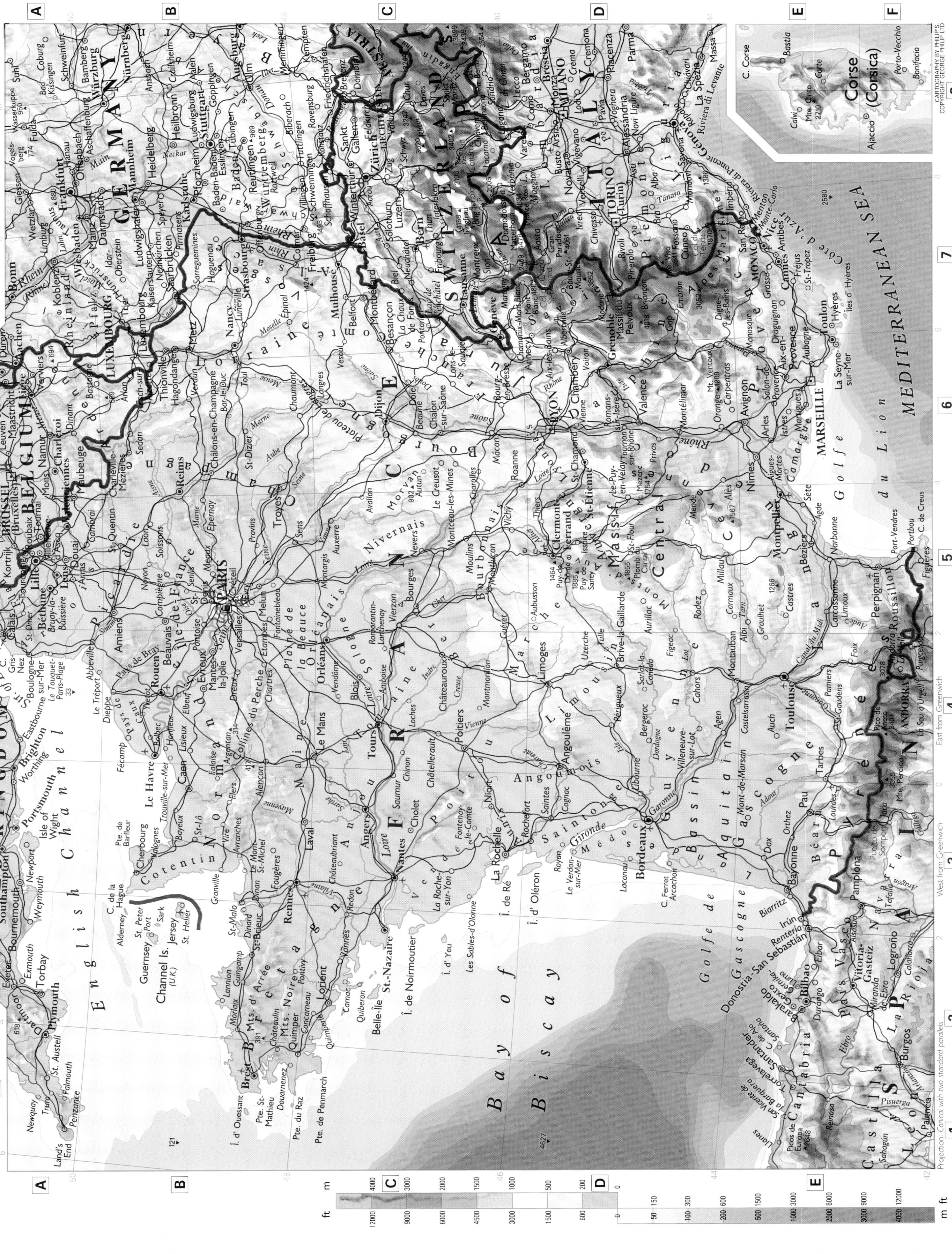

DÉPARTEMENTS IN THE PARIS AREA
1. Ville de Paris   3. Val-de-Marne
2. Seine-St-Denis   4. Hauts-de-Seine

Projection : Lambert's Conformal Conic

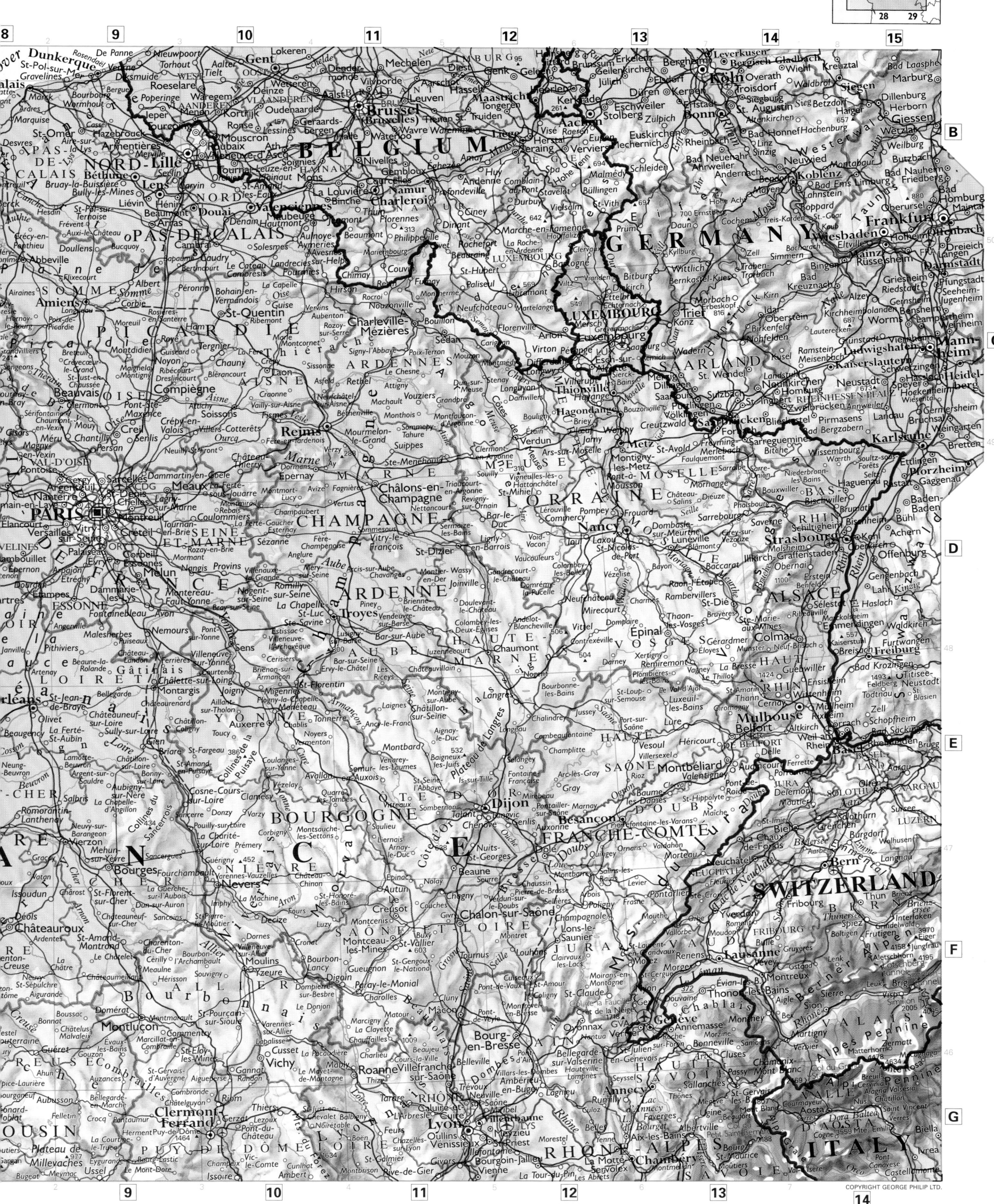

Underlined towns give their name to the
administrative area in which they stand.

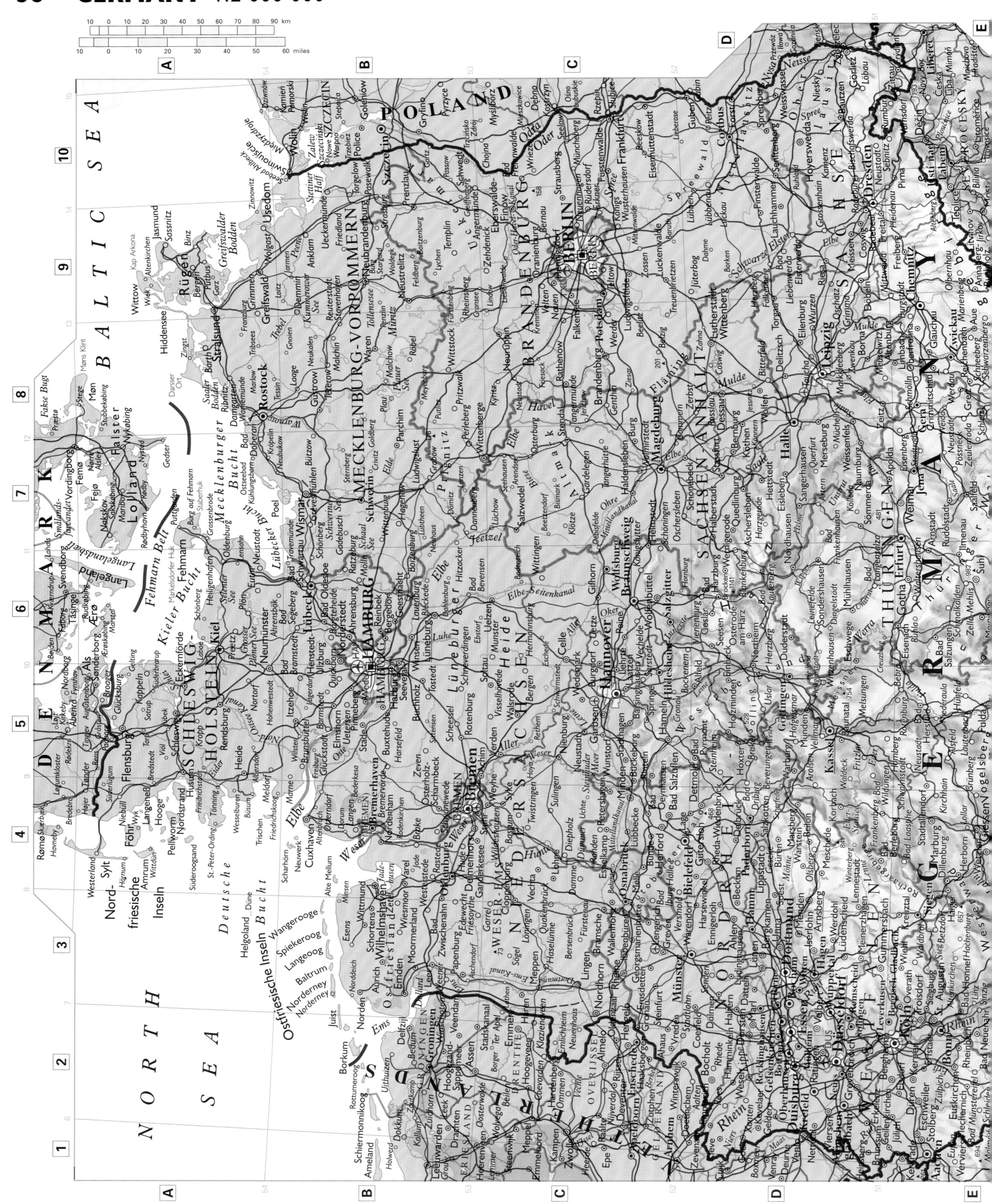

Underlined towns give their name to the
administrative area in which they stand.

Projection : Lambert's Conformal Conic

East from Greenwich

COPYRIGHT GEORGE PHILIP LTD.

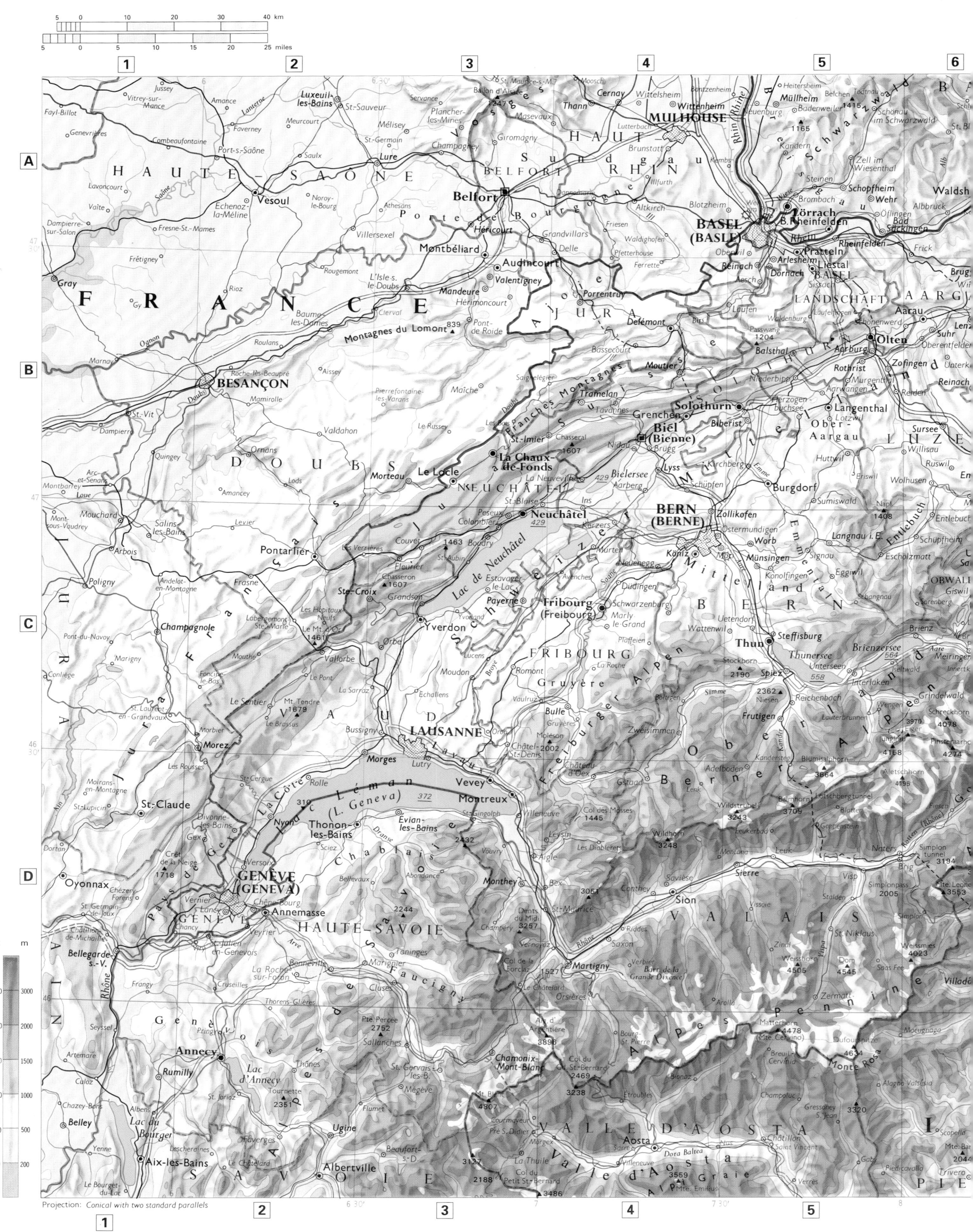

Underlined towns give their name to the
administrative area in which they stand.

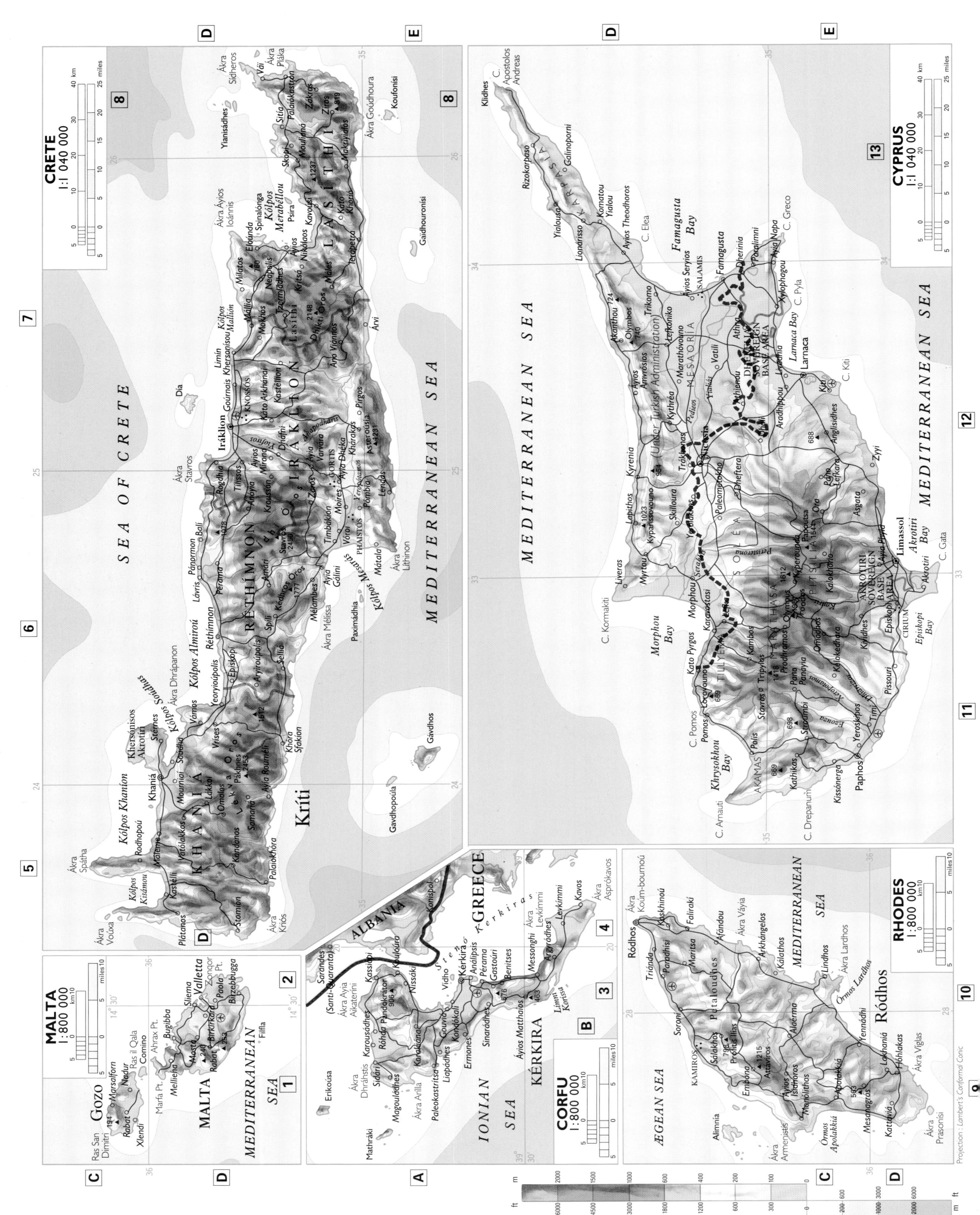

CRETE
1:1 040 000

CYPRUS
1:1 040 000

MALTA
1:800 000

CORFU
1:800 000

RHODES
1:800 000

SEA OF CRETE

MEDITERRANEAN SEA

Kríti

KHANIA

RÉTHIMNON

Óros Ídhi

IRÁKLION

LASÍTHI

Iráklion

Réthimnon

Khaniá

MEDITERRANEAN SEA

Famagusta Bay

MESAORIA

Nicosia

Kyrenia

Limassol

Larnaca

Paphos

ARAKHNÍ OROS

AKAMAS

TÍLLÍRIA

Morphou Bay

SOLÉA

KARPASÍA

MEDITERRANEAN SEA

IONIAN SEA

GREECE

ALBANIA

KÉRKIRA

Kérkira

AEGEAN SEA

Ródhos

Ródhos

MEDITERRANEAN SEA

MALTA

GOZO

Valletta

MEDITERRANEAN SEA

Projection : Lambert's Conformal Conic

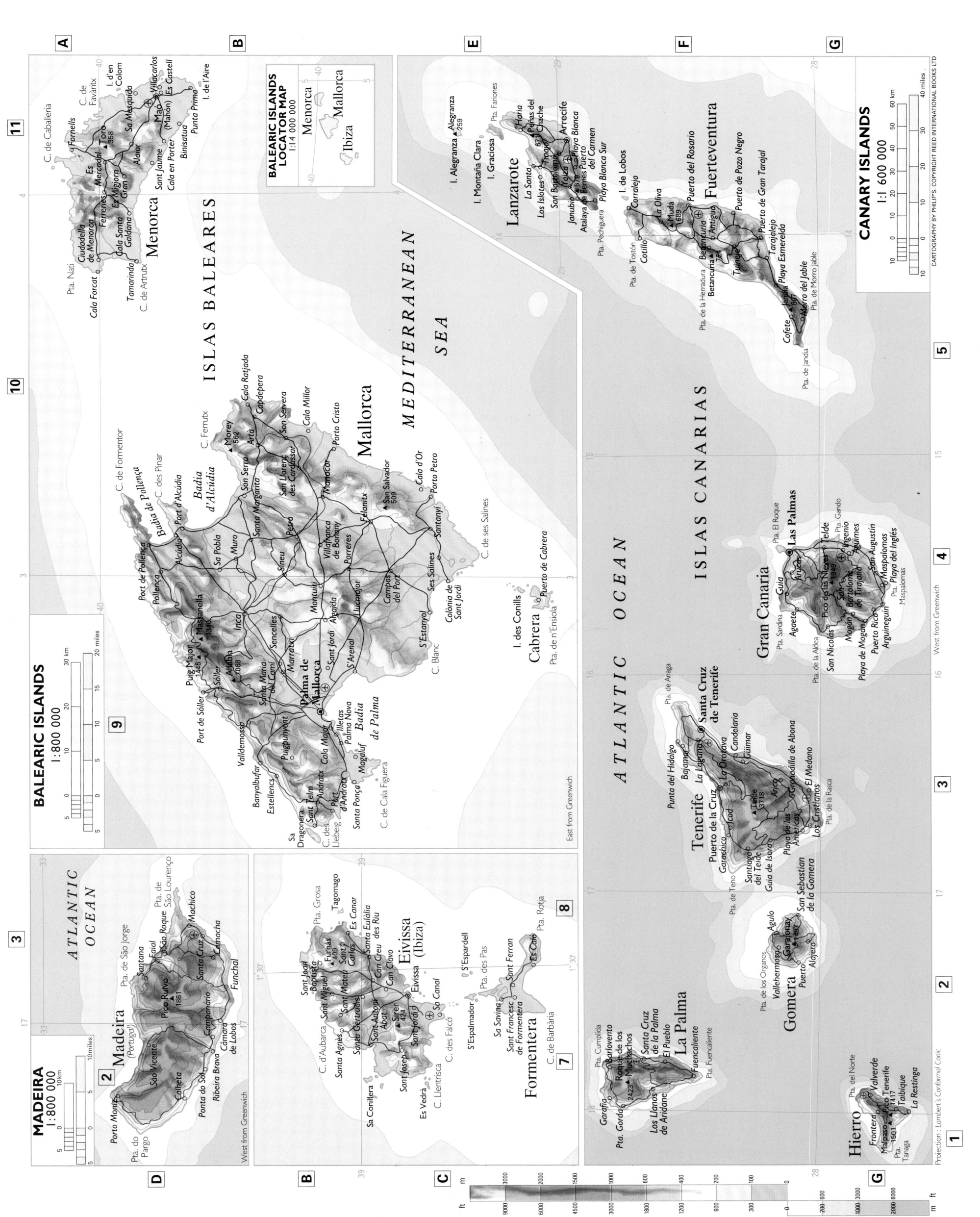

MEDITERRANEAN SEA

ALGERIA

ALGER (Algiers)

Blida
Médéa
DJELFA
Ech Cheliff
Tiaret
MOSTAGANEM
Mostaganem
Relizane
Mascara
Oran
(Ouahran)
Sidi-bel-Abbès
TÉMOUCHENT

ISLA de VALENCIA

Golfo de Valencia

Valencia

EIVISSA (IBIZA)
Formentera

Cabrera

CASTILLA-LA MANCHA

Albacete

CIUDAD REAL

ALBACETE

VALENCIA

ALICANTE

Alicante
Elche
Cartagena

MURCIA

Murcia
Lorca

GRANADA

Granada

ALMERÍA

Almería

Costa del Sol

Melilla (Sp.)
Nador

Alborán (Sp.)

Islas Chafarinas (Sp.)

Copyright George Philip Ltd.

West from Greenwich

East from Greenwich

Projection - Lambert's Conformal Conic

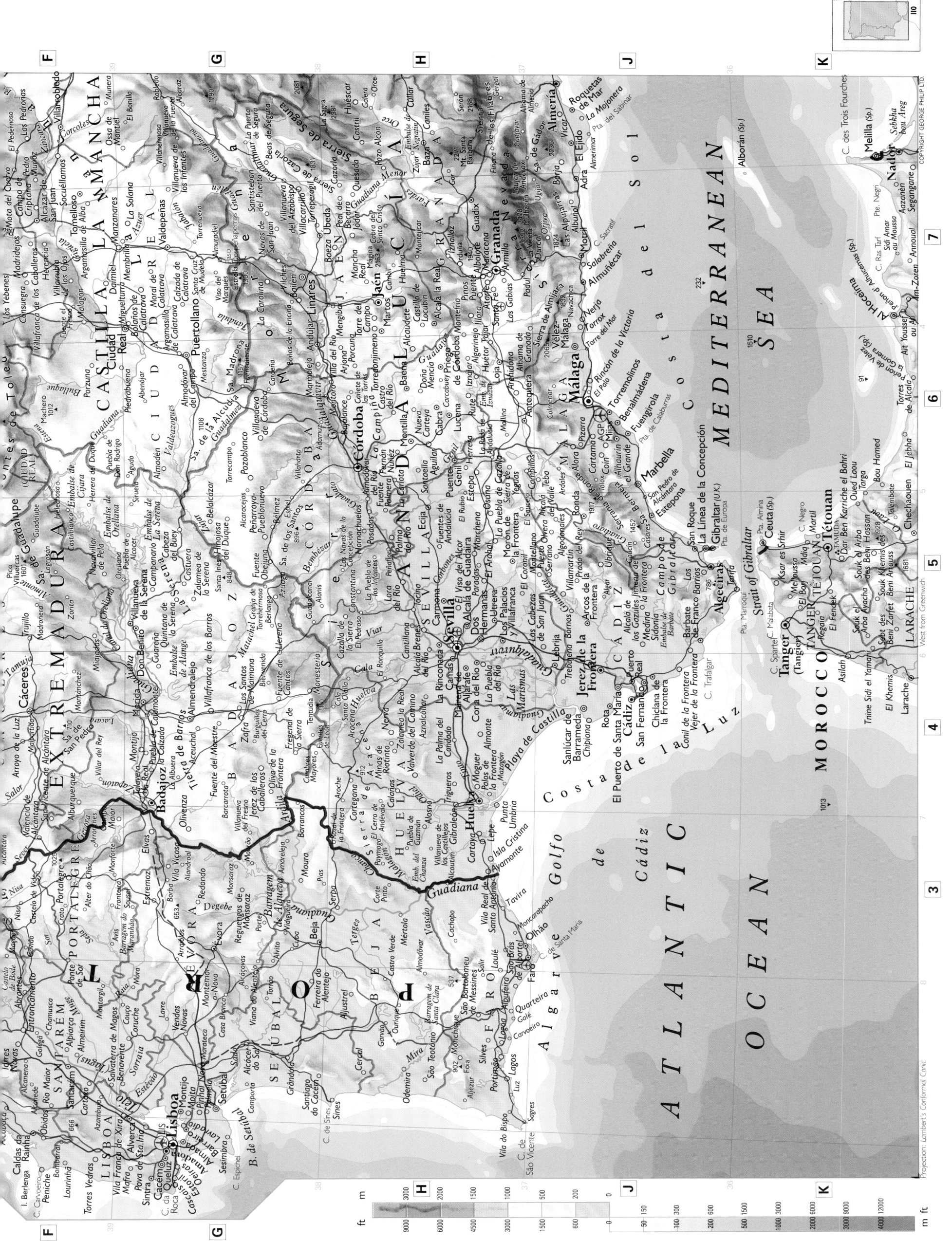

Projection : Lambert's Conformal Conic

East from Greenwich

Underlined towns give their name to
administrative area in which they stan

Administrative divisions in Croatia:
rodsko-Posavska   4. Medimurska   8. Virovitičko-Podravska
oprivničko-Križevačka 6. Požeško-Slavonska 10. Zagrebačka
rapinsko-Zagorska   7. Varaždinska

Inter-entity boundaries as agreed
at the 1995 Dayton Peace Agreement.

COPYRIGHT GEORGE PHILIP LTD.

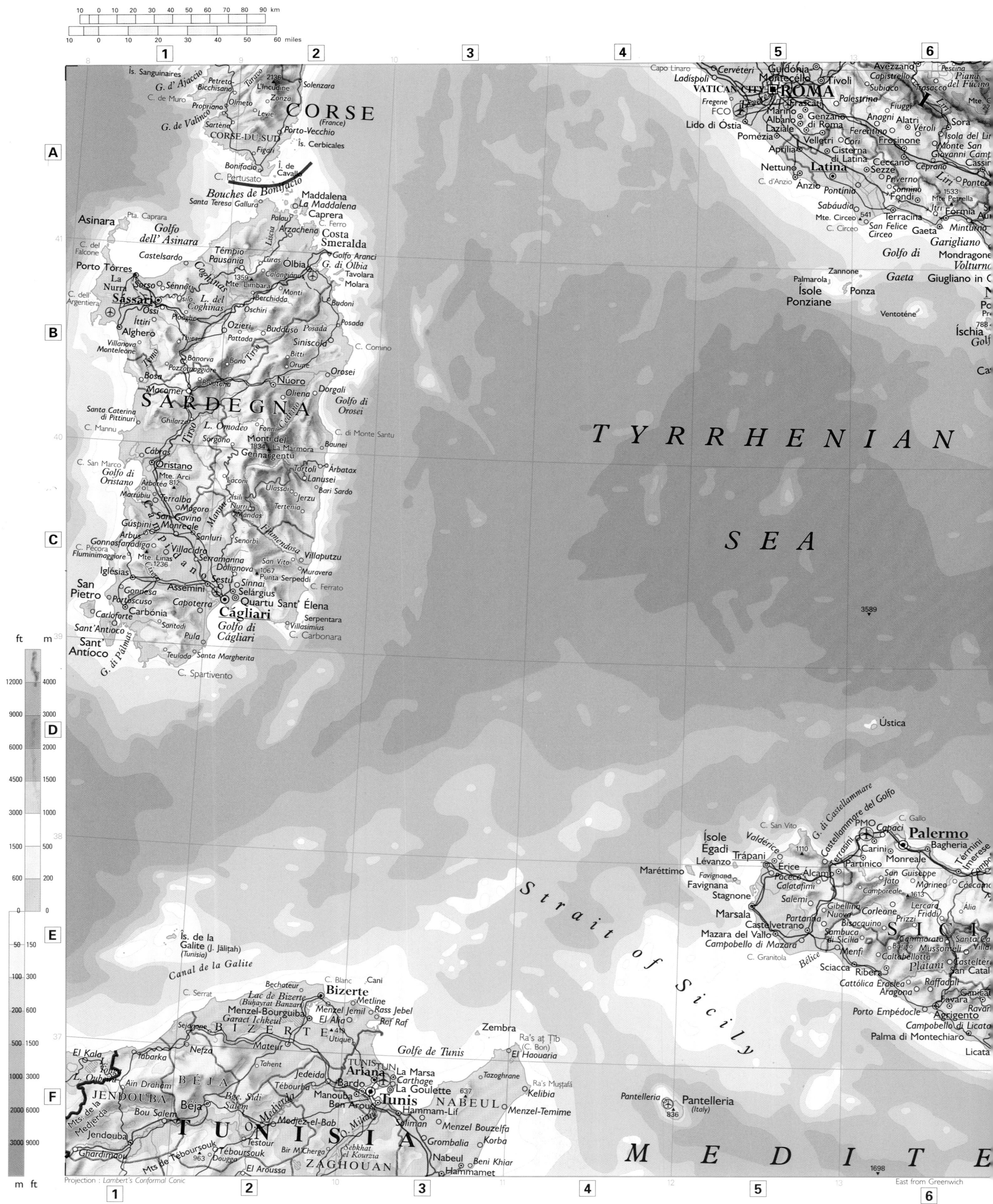

Underlined towns give their name to the
administrative area in which they stand.

COPYRIGHT GEORGE PHILIP LTD.

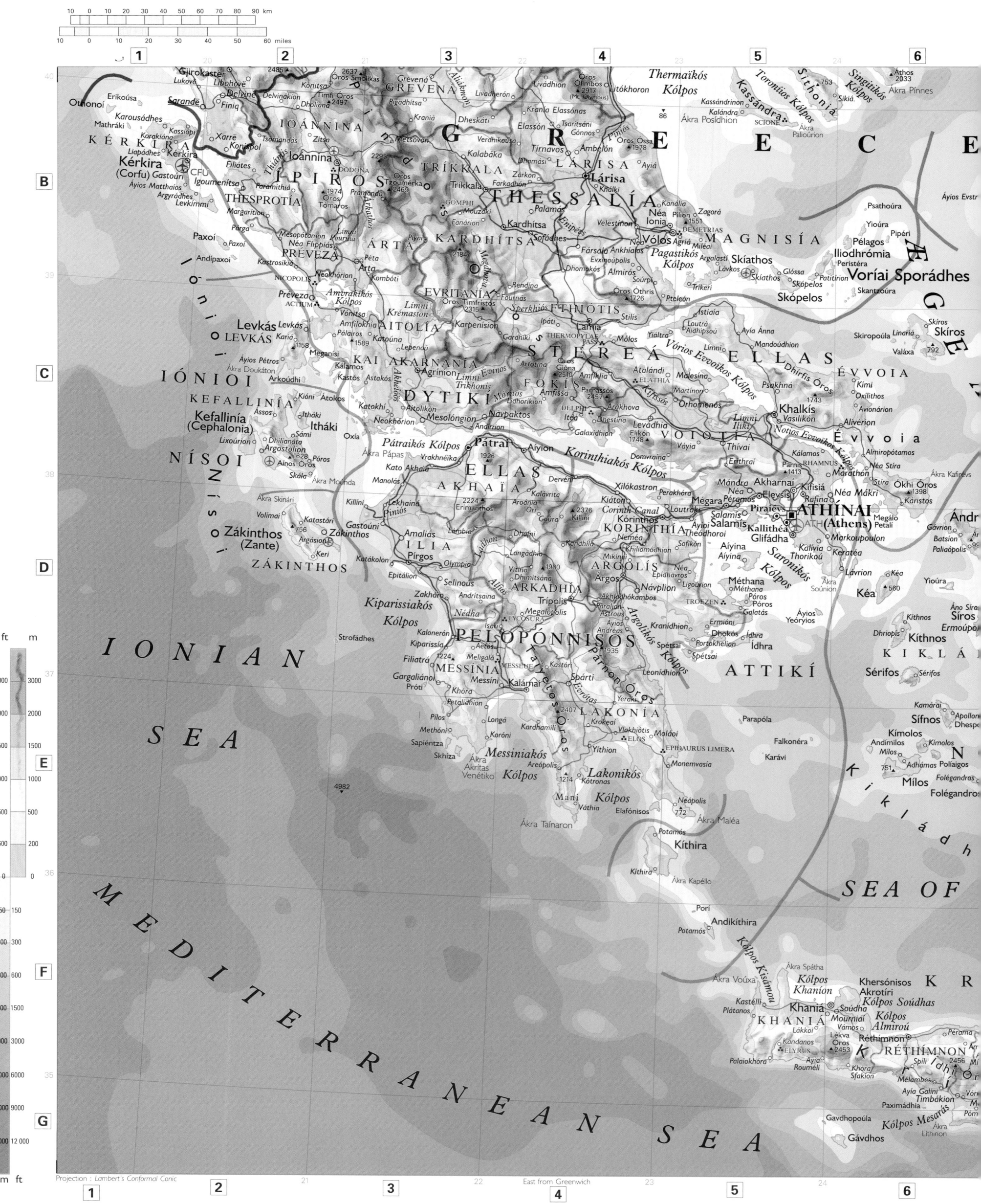

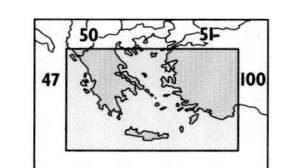

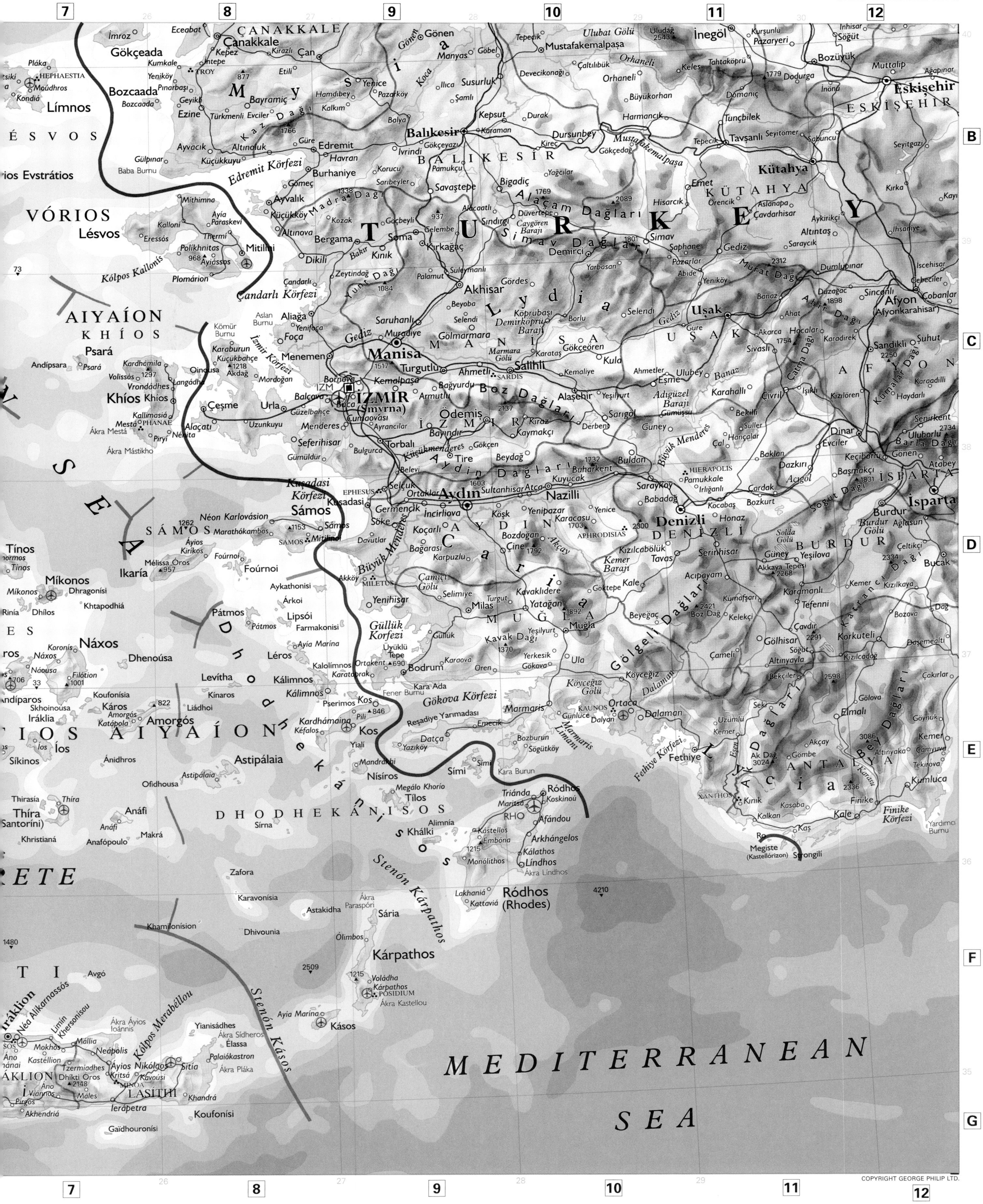

Projection : Lambert's Conformal Conic

East from Greenwich

Inter-entity boundaries as agreed
at the 1995 Dayton Peace Agreement.

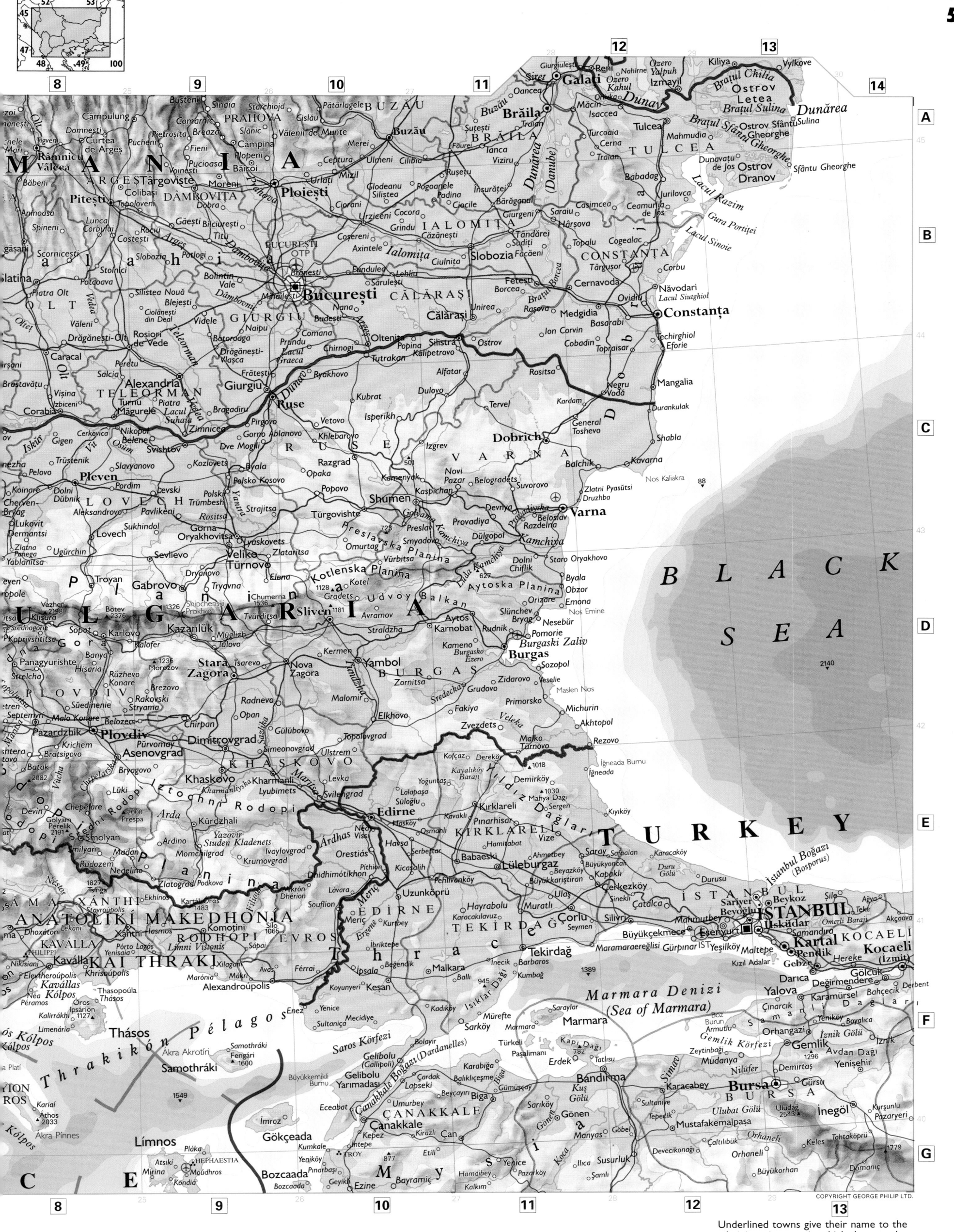

Underlined towns give their name to the
administrative area in which they stand.

COPYRIGHT GEORGE PHILIP LTD.

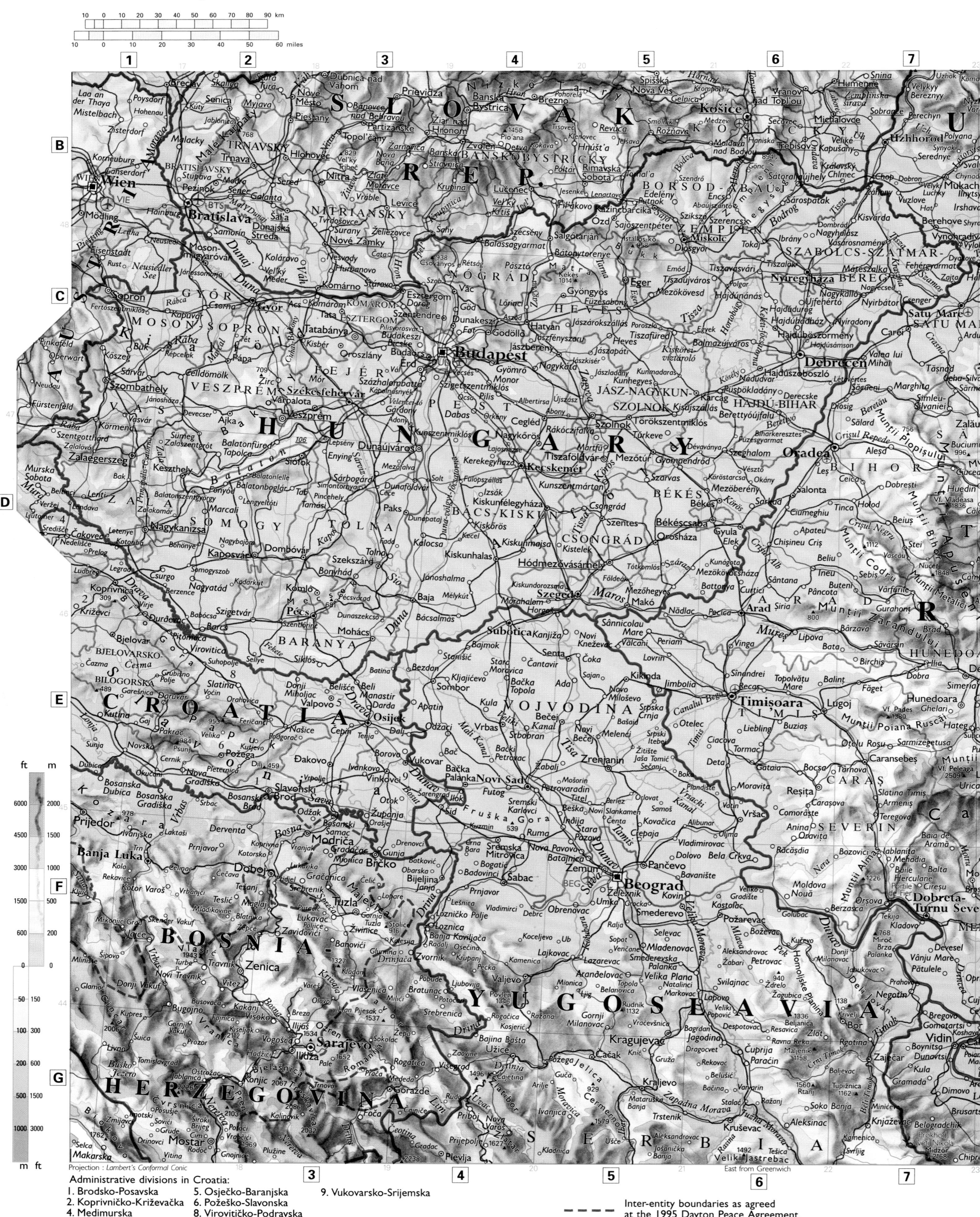

Administrative divisions in Croatia:
1. Brodsko-Posavska
2. Koprivničko-Križevačka
3. (blank)
4. Međimurska
5. Osječko-Baranjska
6. Požeško-Slavonska
7. (blank)
8. Virovitičko-Podravska
9. Vukovarsko-Srijemska

Inter-entity boundaries as agreed at the 1995 Dayton Peace Agreement.

Underlined towns give their name to the
administrative area in which they stand.

Underlined towns give their name to the
administrative area in which they stand.

Projection : Lambert's Conformal Conic

East from Greenwich

Division between Greeks and Turks
in Cyprus: Turks to the North.

Projection: Conical with two standard parallels

East from Greenwich

COPYRIGHT: GEORGE PHILIP & SON LTD.

1. Crimea (Ukr.)
2. Adygea (Russ.)
3. Karachey-Cherkessia (Russ.)
4. Kabardino-Balkaria (Russ.)
5. North Ossetia (Russ.)
6. Ingushetia (Russ.)
7. Chechenia (Russ.)
8. Naxçıvan (Azer.)

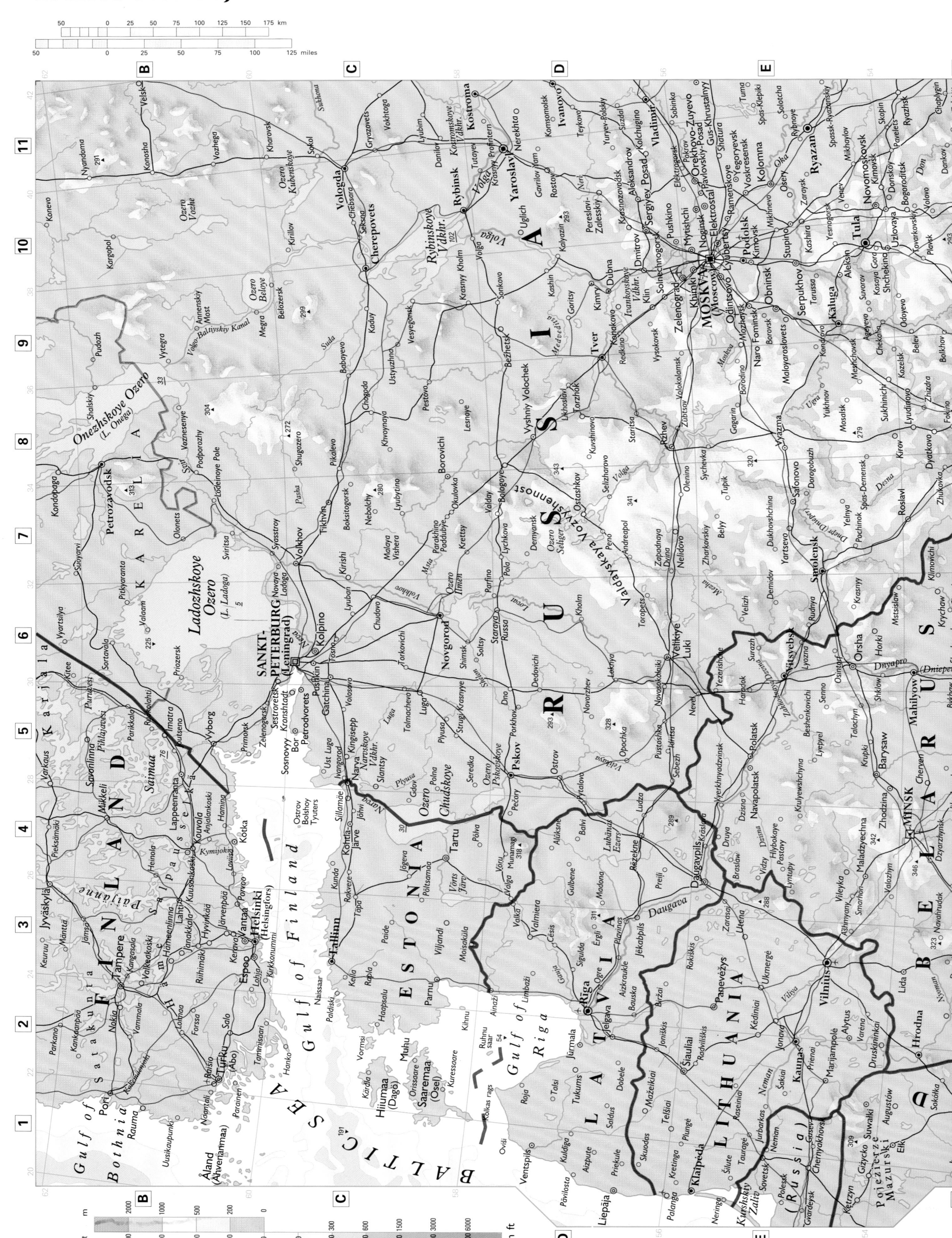

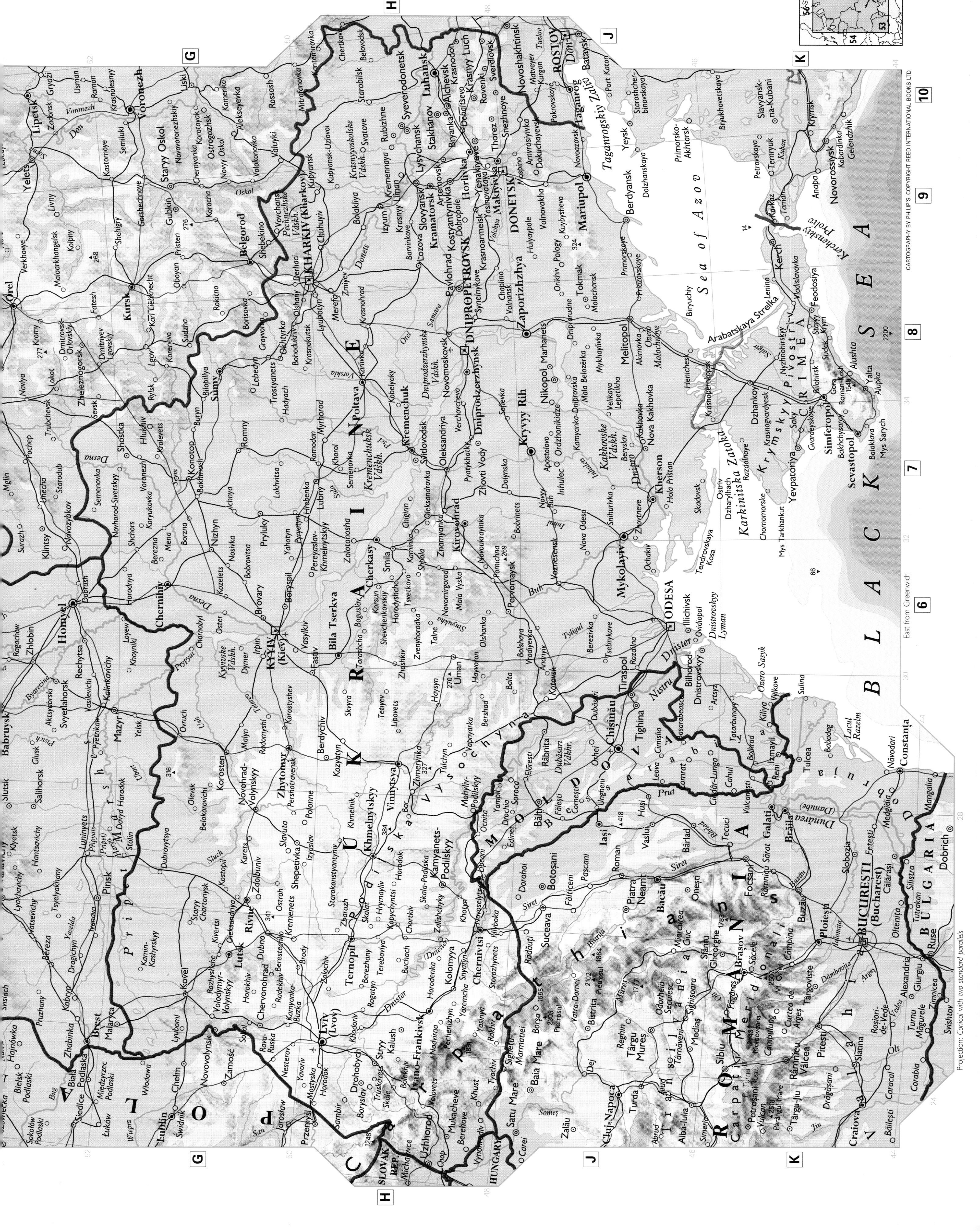

Projection: Conical with two standard parallels

East from Greenwich

Countries / regions

UKRAINE
ROMANIA
BULGARIA
MOLDOVA
SLOVAK REP.
HUNGARY
CRIMEA
BLACK SEA
Sea of Azov
Taganrogskiy Zaliv
Kerchenskiy Proliv
Karkinitska Zatoka
Krymskiy P-ov
Carpathian Mountains
Transylvanian Alps
Prut
Dnister / Nistru
Danube (Dunărea)
Desna
Pripet
Don

Major cities

Orel, Yelets, Lipetsk, Voronezh, Kursk, Belgorod, Rostov, Taganrog, Novoshakhtinsk
KHARKIV (Kharkov), Luhansk, Sumy, Poltava, DONETSK, DNIPROPETROVSK, Zaporizhzhya, Mariupol, Berdyansk
Chernihiv, Homyel, KYIV (Kiev), Cherkasy, Kremenchuk, Kirovohrad, Kryvyy Rih, Kherson, Mykolayiv, ODESA
Babruysk, Pinsk, Zhytomyr, Vinnytsya, Khmelnytskyy, Chernivtsi, Chişinău, Tiraspol, Tighina
Brest, Lutsk, Rivne, Ternopil, Lviv (Lvov), Ivano-Frankivsk, Uzhhorod, Mukacheve, Satu Mare
Iaşi, Botoşani, Suceava, Bacău, Galaţi, Brăila, Buzău, Ploieşti, BUCUREŞTI (Bucharest)
Cluj-Napoca, Sibiu, Braşov, Târgu Mureş, Piteşti, Craiova, Constanţa, Dobrich, Ruse, Silistra

Novorossiysk, Anapa, Kerch, Feodosiya, Yalta, Sevastopol, Simferopol, Yevpatoriya, Dzhankoy

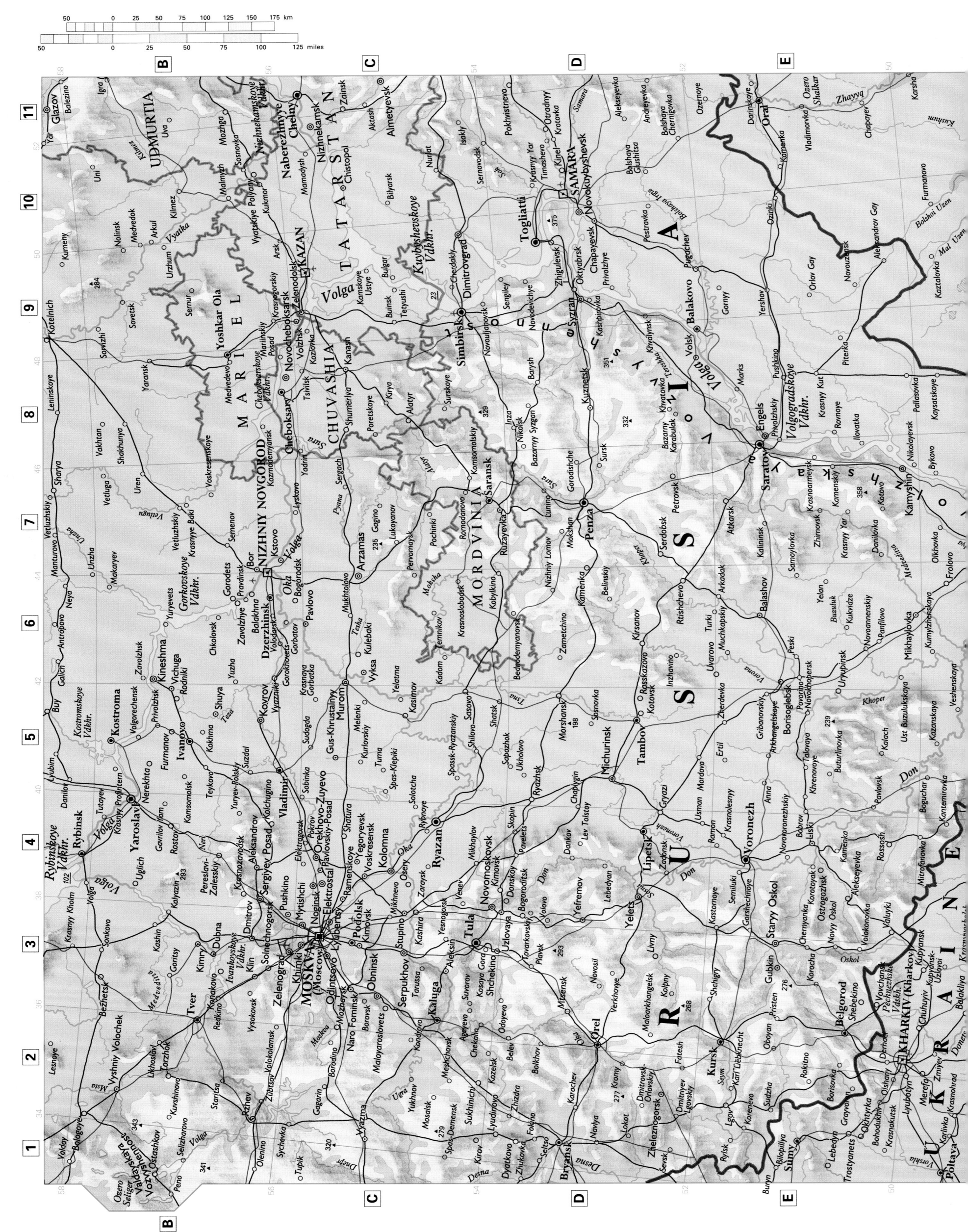

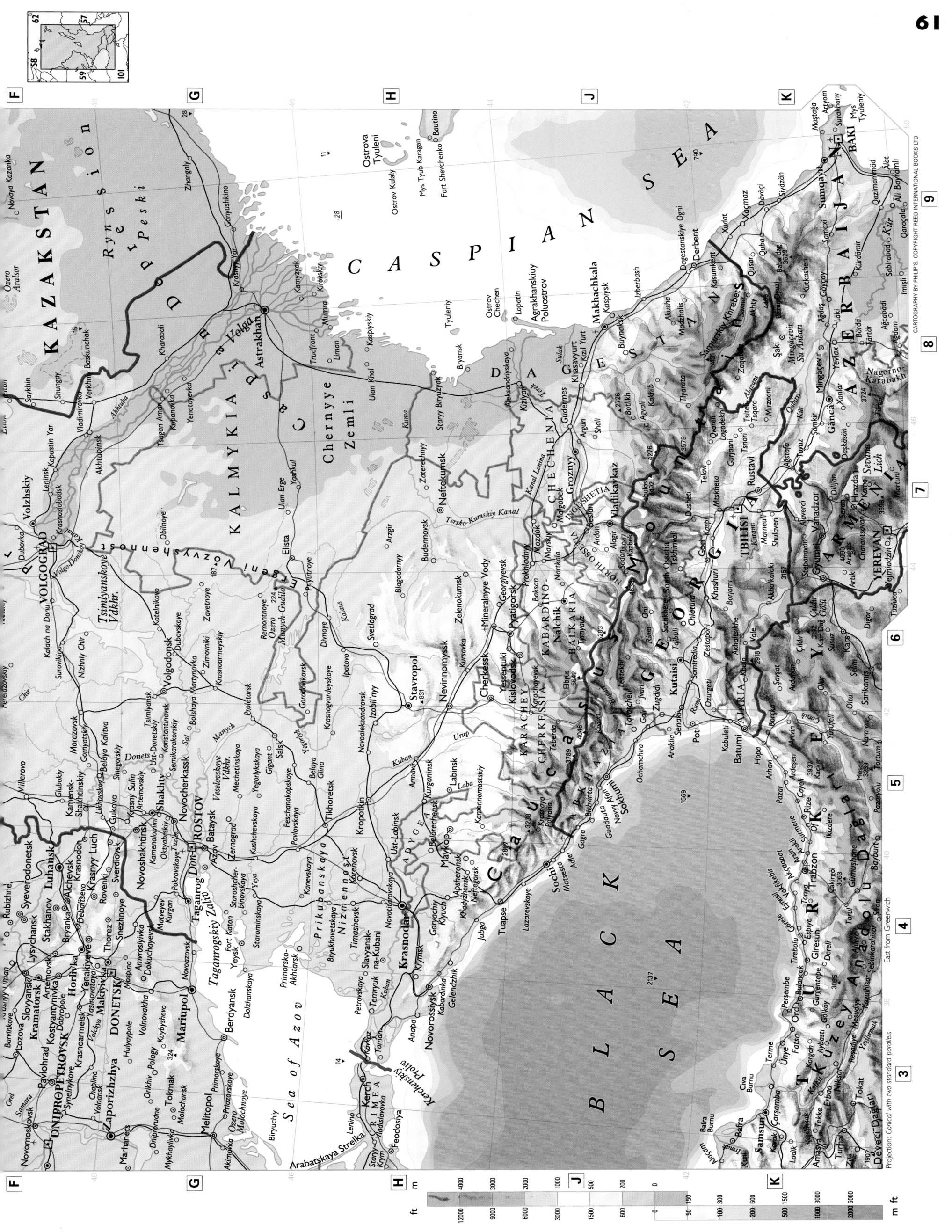

CARTOGRAPHY BY PHILIP'S. COPYRIGHT REED INTERNATIONAL BOOKS LTD.

Projection: Conical with two standard parallels

East from Greenwich

50 0 25 50 75 100 125 150 175 km
50 0 25 50 75 100 125 miles

1 2 3 4 5 6 7 8 9

KOMI

Severnyye Uvaly

RUSSIA

UDMURTIA

MARIEL

TATARSTAN

BASHKORTOSTAN

Ural

KAZAKSTAN

Kirgiziya Steppe

Mugodzhary

Turgayskaya Stolovaya Strana

Cities and towns:
Pinyug, Kazhim, Veslyana, Gayny, Kama, Cherdyn, Krasnovishersk, Gora Denezhkin Kamen 1493, Kalya, Severouralsk

Murashi, Krasnoye, Milonia, Nagorsk, Kirs, Kosa, Yuria, Borovsk, Solikamsk, Usolye, Pozhva, Kudymkar, Kamskoye Vdkhr., 1065, Pokrovsk-Uralskiy, Volchansk, Konzhakovskiy Kamen 1569, Karpinsk, Serov, Pelym

Yurya, Slobodskoy, Khalturin, Kirov, Novovyatsk, Kirovo-Chepetsk, Zuyevka, Belaya Kholunitsa, Chernaya Kholunitsa, Peskovka, Omutninsk, Zalazna, 337, Chermoz, Aleksandrovsk, Kizel, Ugleuralskiy, Gubakha 993, Gremyachinsk, Kachkanar, Novaya Lyalya, Verkhoturye, Lobva, Sosva, Gari, Bolotovskoye

Kotelnich, Chapetsk, Falenki, Glazov, Vereshchagino, Nytva, Ocher, Krasnokamsk, PERM, Sylva, Chusovaya, Chusovoy, Pashiya, Verkhnyaya Tura, Krasnouralsk, Kushva, Nizhnyaya Salda, Tura, Turinsk

Sorvizhi, 284, Nolinsk, Kez, Igra, Zura, Balezino, Dobryanka, Lysva, 482, Nizhniy Tagil, Verkhnyaya Salda, Alapayevsk, Nitsa, Irbit

Yaransk, Sovetsk, Medvedok, Arkul, Kilmez, Uni, Kungur, 452, Verkhniy Tagil, 746, Nevyansk, Rezh, Artemovskiy, Troitskiy, Talitsa

Sernur, Urzhum, Vyatka, Kilmez, Malmyzh, Uva, Yakshur Bodya, Votkinsk, Osa, Achit, Kuzino, Revda, Pervouralsk, YEKATERINBURG, Beloyarskiy, Bogdanovich, Kamensk Uralskiy, Kamyshlov, Psheira

Yoshkar Ola, Medvedevo, Izhevsk, Chaykovskiy, Votkinskoye Vdkhr., Krasnoufimsk, Nizhniye Sergi, Polevskoy, Sysert, Asbest, Sukhoy Log, Kataysk, Dalmatovo

Mariinskiy Posad, Krasnogorskiy, Volzhsk, Zelenodolsk, Arsk, Kukmor, Mozhga, Sosnovka, Sarapul, Kambarka, Yanaul, Chernushka, Oktyabrskiy, Mikhaylovski, 678, Verkhniy Ufaley, Kasli, Shadrinsk

Kozlovka, KAZAN, Vyatskiye Polyany, Nizhnekamskoye Vdkhr., Neftekamsk, Belaya, Ufa, 517, Verkhniye Kigi, Kyshtym, Karabash, Argayash, Miass

Buinsk, Tetyushi, Bulgar, Bilyarsk, Mamadysh, Yelabuga, Menzelinsk, Naberezhnyye Chelny, Nizhnekamsk, Ik, Birsk, Krashyy Klyuch, Kusa, Berdyaush, Zlatoust, CHELYABINSK, Kopeysk, Shchuchye, Shumikha

Kamskoye Ustye, Chistopol, Zainsk, Aktash, Almetyevsk, Kushnarenkovo, Blagoveshchensk, Dyurtyuli, Ay, Minyar, Asha, Katav Ivanovsk, Satka, Bakal, Miass, Chebarkul, Novosineglazovskiy, Korkino, Yemanzhelinsk

Kuybyshevskoye Vdkhr., 23, Leninogorsk, Bugulma, Tuymazy, Chishmy, UFA, Iglino, Yuryuzan, 1406, Gora Iremel 1582, Yuzhnouralsk, Uvelskiy, Oktyabrskoye

Simbirsk, Novoulyanovsk, Sengiley, Cherdakly, Dimitrovgrad, Isakly, Bugulma, 383, Belebey, 420, Rayevskiy, Davlekanovo, Inzer, Gora Yamantau 1638, Tirlyanskiy, Uchaly, Plast, Troitsk, Uy

Novodevichye, Togliatti, Zhigulevsk, Krasnyy Yar, Timashevo, Kinel, Buguruslan, Priyutovo, Beloretsk, Verkhneuralsk, Stepnoye, Buskul, Toguzak, Komsomolets

Oktyabrsk, Syzran, Kashpirovka, 375, SAMARA, Novokuybyshevsk, Otradnyy, Krotovka, Sterlitamak, Petrovskoye, Krasnousolskiy, Verkhniy Avzyan 1118, 452, Varna, Magnitogorsk, Kartaly, Rudnyy

Chapayevsk, Privolzhye, Alekseyevka, Buzuluk, Grachevka, Ishimbay, Salavat, 481, 1039, 659, Sibay, Kizilskoye, Tobol, Lisakovsk

Pestravka, Bolshaya Glushitsa, Totskoye, Sorochinsk, Ponomarevka, Meleuz, Kumertau, Baymak, 758, Bredy, Ordzhonikidze

Pugachev, Bolshaya Chernigovka, Novo-Sergiyevskiy, Bulanovo, 405, Tyulgan, Verkhn Otrag, Iriklinskoye Vdkhr., 414, Zhetiqara, Zhaima

Ozernoye, Perevolotskiy, Ilek, Orenburg, Saraktash, Krasnoyarskiy, Aydyrlinsky, Energetik, Yelizavetinka, Adamovka, Ozërnyy

Ozinki, Darinskoye, Burli, Krasnyy Kholm, Ural, Pervomayskiy, Kuvandyk, Gay, Novoorsk, 418, Kumak, Yasnyy, Svetlyy

Oral, Zhayyq, Kamenka, Aksay, Ilek, Sol Iletsk, Akbulak, Mednogorsk, Novotroitsk, Orsk, Dombarovskiy, Aktasty, Tolybay

Vladimirovka, Ozero Shalkar, Chingirlau, Ueda, Martuk, Leninskoye 509, Novorossiyskoye, Khromtau, Irgiz, Qarabutaq, Zhabasak

Furmanov, Bolshoi Uzen, Shalkar, Chapayev, Dzhambeyty, Aqtöbe, Novoalekseyevka, Alga, Oktyabrsk, Karatobe

Projection: Conical with two standard parallels

East from Greenwich

50 0 25 50 75 100 125 150 175 km

50 0 25 50 75 100 125 miles

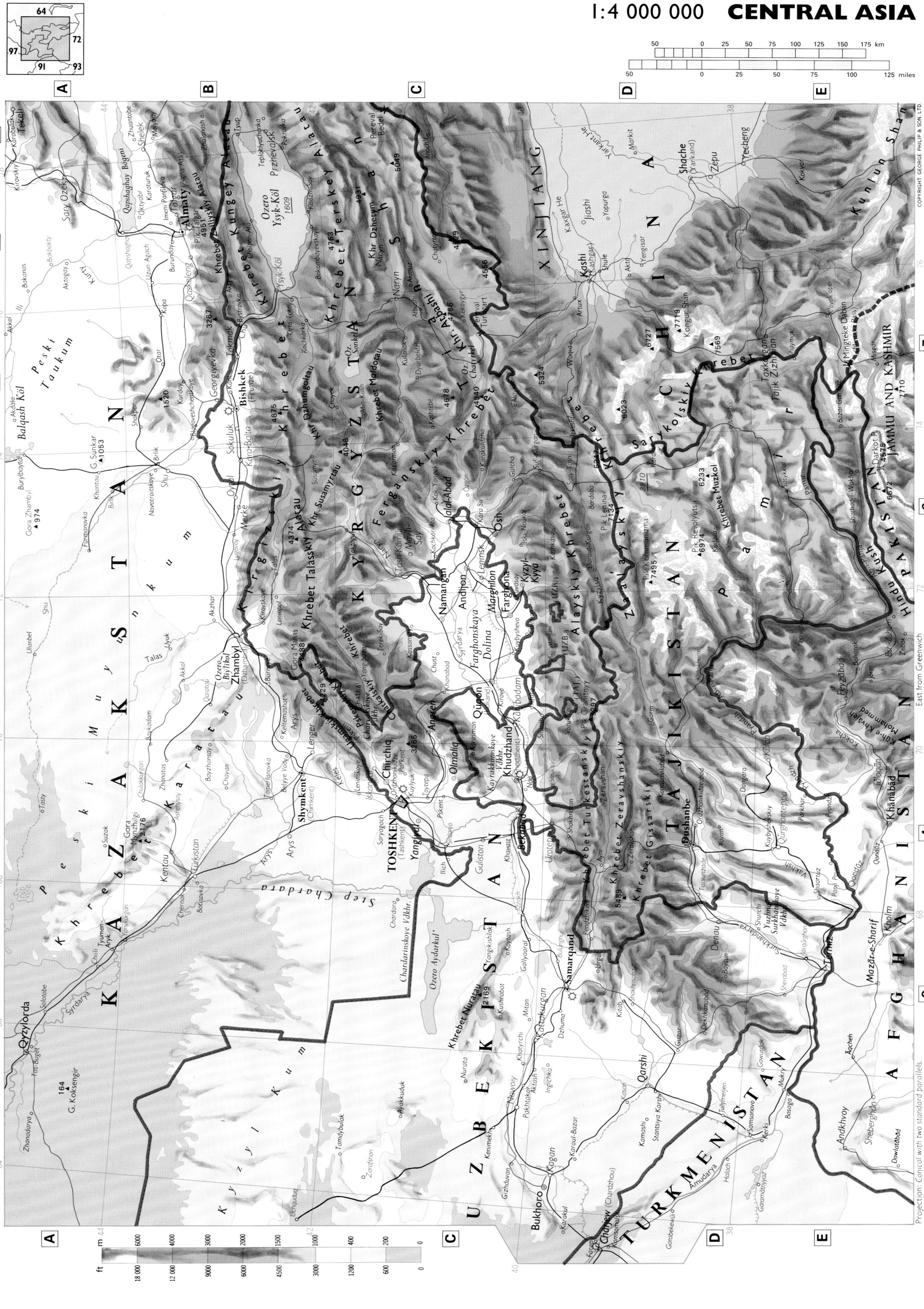

COPYRIGHT GEORGE PHILIP & SON LTD

Projection: Conical with two standard parallels.

East from Greenwich

KAZAKSTAN

KYRGYZSTAN

UZBEKISTAN

TAJIKISTAN

TURKMENISTAN

AFGHANISTAN

XINJIANG

CHINA

JAMMU AND KASHMIR

PAKISTAN

Peski Taukum

Balqash Köl

Peski Ozero

Kyzyl Kum

Step Chardara

Kunlun Shan

Hindu Kush

Pamir

TOSHKENT (Tashkent)

Bishkek (Frunze)

Almaty

Shymkent

Khudzhand

Dushanbe

Samarqand

Bukhoro

Qarshi

Termiz

Mazâr-e-Sharif

Andkhvoy

Chärjew (Chardzhou)

Kashi

Shache (Yarkand)

Yecheng

Namangan

Andijon

Farghona

Margilon

Osh

Jalal-Abad

Ozero Ysyk-Köl 1609

Khrebet Zailiyskiy Alatau

Khrebet Kungey Alatau

Khrebet Terskey Alatau

Kirgizskiy Khrebet

Khrebet Talasskiy Alatau

Ferganskiy Khrebet

Alayskiy Khrebet

Zaalayskiy Khrebet

Khrebet Zeravshanskiy

Khrebet Gissarskiy

Khrebet Turkestanskiy

Sarykolskiy Khrebet

Khrebet Karatau

Oʻyqylay

Qyzylorda

Zhambyl

Talas

Taraz

Qsyl-Kyya

Syrdarya

Amudarya

RUSSIA
1 Adygea
2 Karachey-Cherkessia
3 Kabardino-Balkaria
4 North Ossetia
5 Ingushetia
6 Chechenia
7 Dagestan
8 Mordvinia
9 Chuvashia
10 Mari El
11 Tatarstan
12 Udmurtia
13 Khakassia
AZERBAIJAN
14 Naxçivan
GEORGIA   UKRAINE
15 Ajaria   17 Crimea
16 Abkhazia

Projection: Conical Orthomorphic with two standard parallels

East from Greenwich

CARTOGRAPHY BY PHILIP'S
COPYRIGHT REED INTERNATIONAL BOOKS LTD.

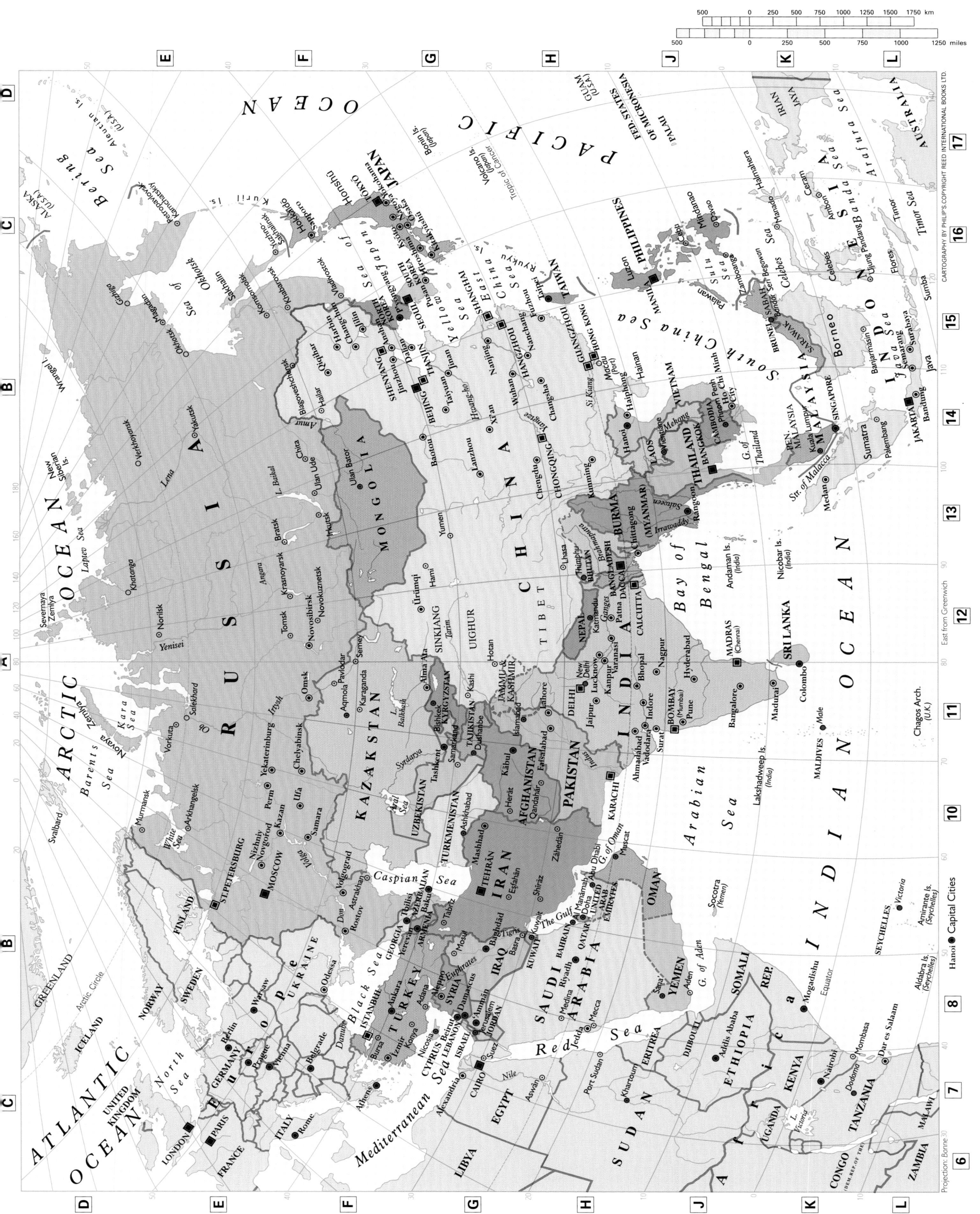

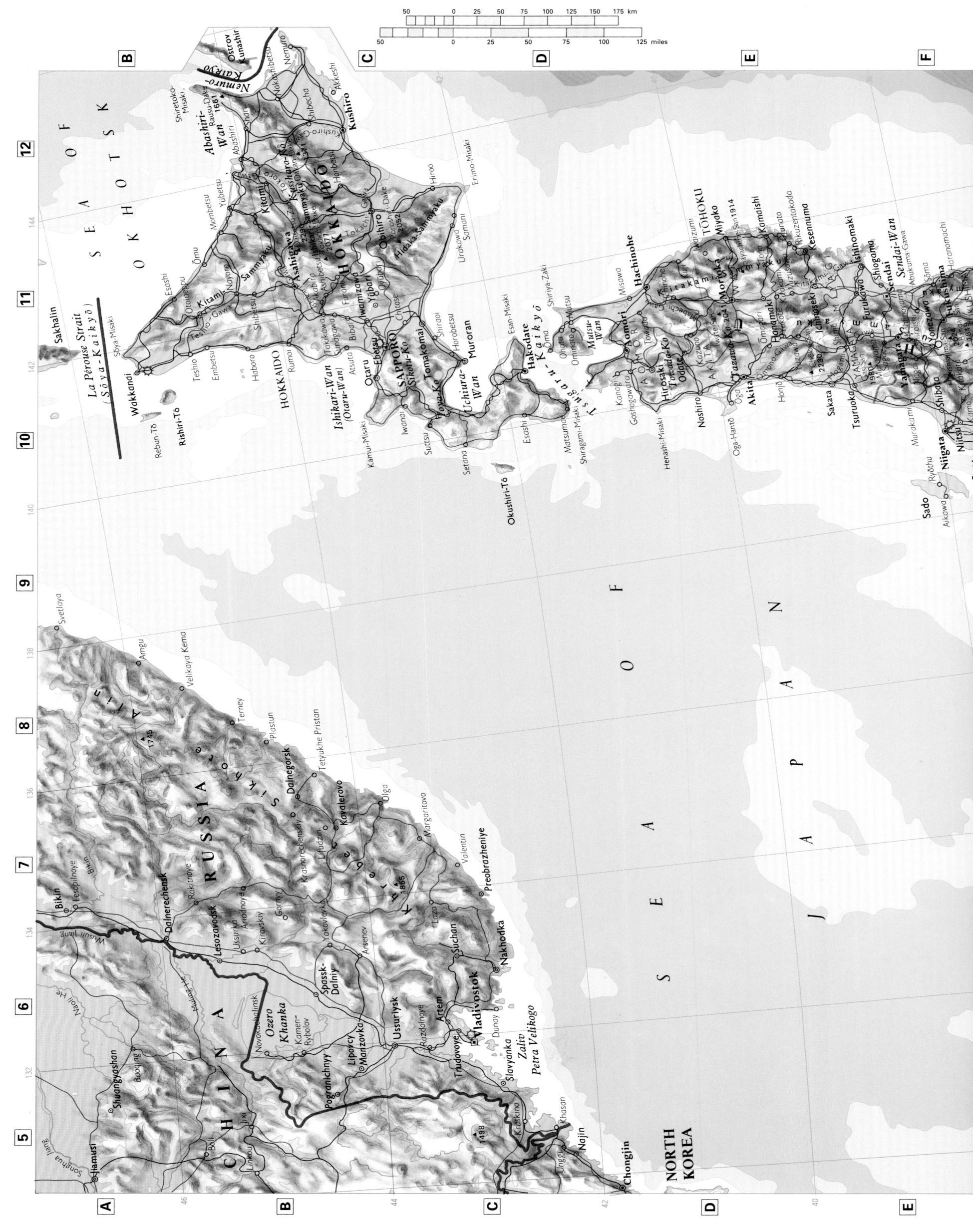

B   C   D   E   F

12

Ostrov Kunashir
Nemuro-Kaikyō
Kaigyō
Nemuro
Nosappu-Misaki
Abashiri-Wan 1661
Shiretoko-Misaki
Rausu-Dake
Abashiri
Akkeshi
Shibecha
Kushiro
Mombetsu
Yūbetsu
Kitami
HOKKAIDO
Hiroo

11
Sakhalin
Esashi
Otoineppu
Kitami
Asahigawa 2290
2077
Obihiro
Hidaka-Sammyaku
Tokachi-Dake
Erimo-Misaki
TŌHOKU
Miyako
San 1914
Kamaishi
Rikuzentakada
Kesennuma
Ishinomaki

10
La Pérouse Strait
(Sōya-Kaikyō)
Sōya-Misaki
Wakkanai
Teshio
Embetsu
Haboro
Rumoi
HOKKAIDO
Ishikari-Wan
(Otaru-Wan)
SAPPORO
Shihoro-Ko
Tomakomai
Muroran
Uchiura-Wan
Noboribetsu
Horobetsu
Hakodate
Esan-Misaki
Tsugaru-Kaikyō
Mutsu-Wan
Aomori
Hachinohe
Misawa
Shirakami
Morioka
Ōfunato
Sendai-Wan
Shiogama
Sendai
Ishinomaki
Soma

Rishiri-Tō
Rebun-Tō
Kamui-Misaki
Suttsu
Iwanai
Setana
Shiraoi
Shiranuka
Okushiri-Tō
Esashi
Matsumae
Shiriya-Zaki
Ōma
Ōminato
Henashi-Misaki
Oga-Hantō
Hirosaki
Odate
Towada
Noshiro
Oga
Akita
AKITA
Honjo
Sakata
YAMAGATA
2230
Tsuruoka
Murakami
Niigata
Ryōtsu
Sado
Aikawa
Shibata

9

Svetlaya
O F

8
Amgu
Velikaya Kema
Terney
1745
Plastun
Tetyukhe Pristan

S E A

7
Dalnegorsk
Olga
Kavalerovo
Margaritovo

O F

6
Bikin
Lesozavodsk
Dalnerechensk
RUSSIA
Sikhote Alin
Rokitnoye
Krasno rechenskiy
Lifudzin
Iman
1855
Gornyy
Yakovlevka
Arsenev
Valentin
Preobrazheniye

J A P A N

5
Hamusi
Shuangyashan
Baoqing
CHINA
Wusuri Jiang
Nmol He
Hulin
Jixi
Songhua Jiang
Dalnerechensk
Novorossiya
Ozero Khanka
Kamen-Rybolov
Spassk-Dalniy
Ussuriysk
Artem
Vladivostok
Nakhodka
Zaliv
Petra Velikogo
Trudovoye
Slavyanka
Khasan
498
Najin
Chongjin
NORTH
KOREA

A   B   C   D   E

RYUKYU ISLANDS
on same scale

SOUTH
KOREA

PACIFIC

OCEAN

CHŪGOKU

SHIKOKU

KINKI

KANTŌ

FUKUOKA

KITAKYŪSHŪ

KYŪSHŪ

Projection: Conical with two standard parallels

140 COPYRIGHT GEORGE PHILIP & SON LTD

East from Greenwich

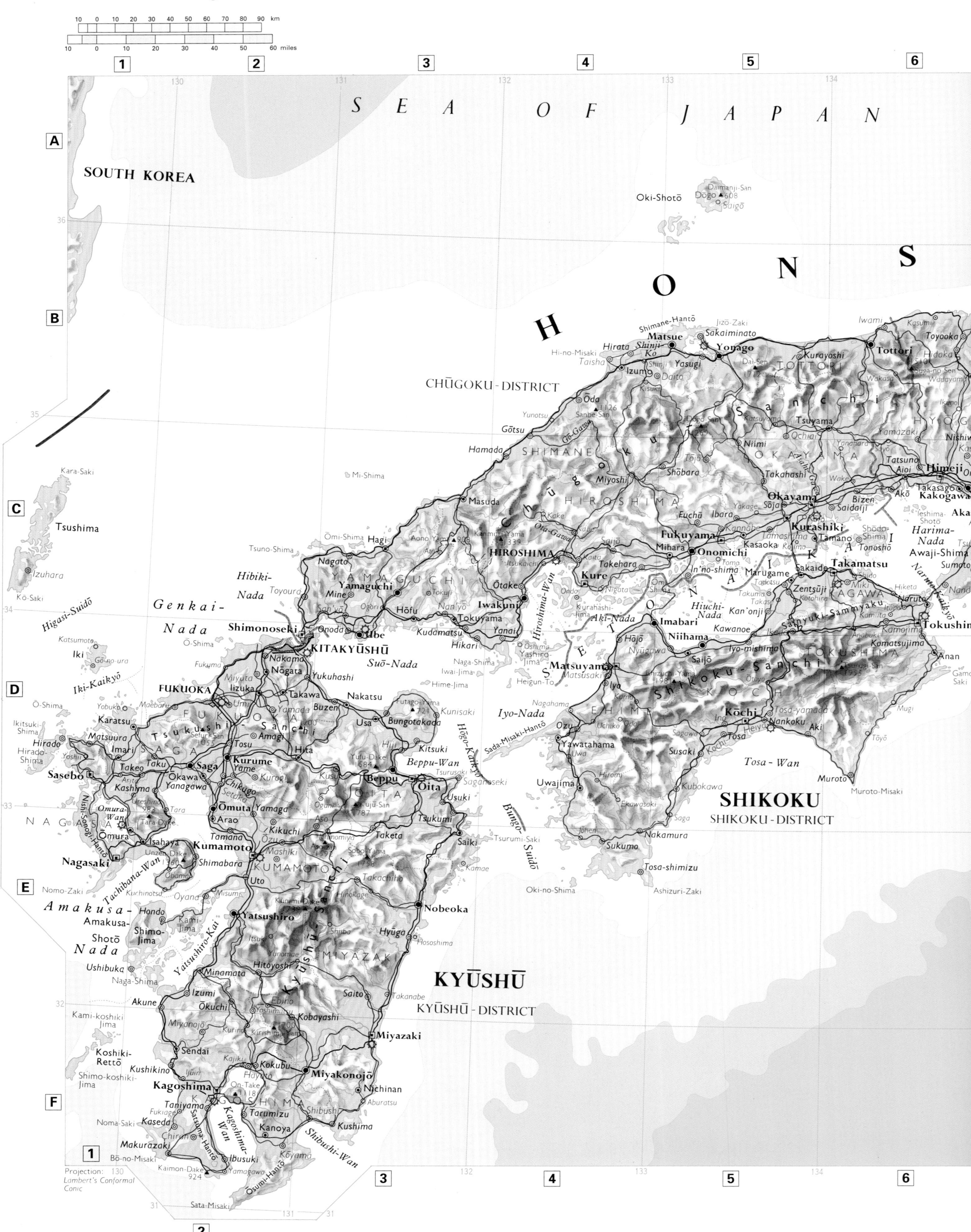

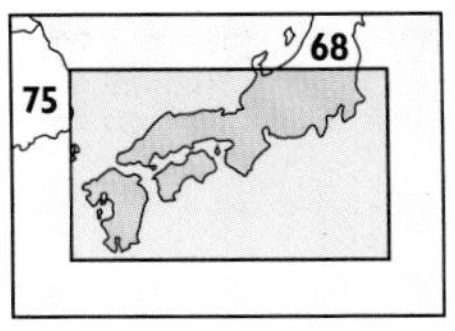

7 8 9 10 11 12

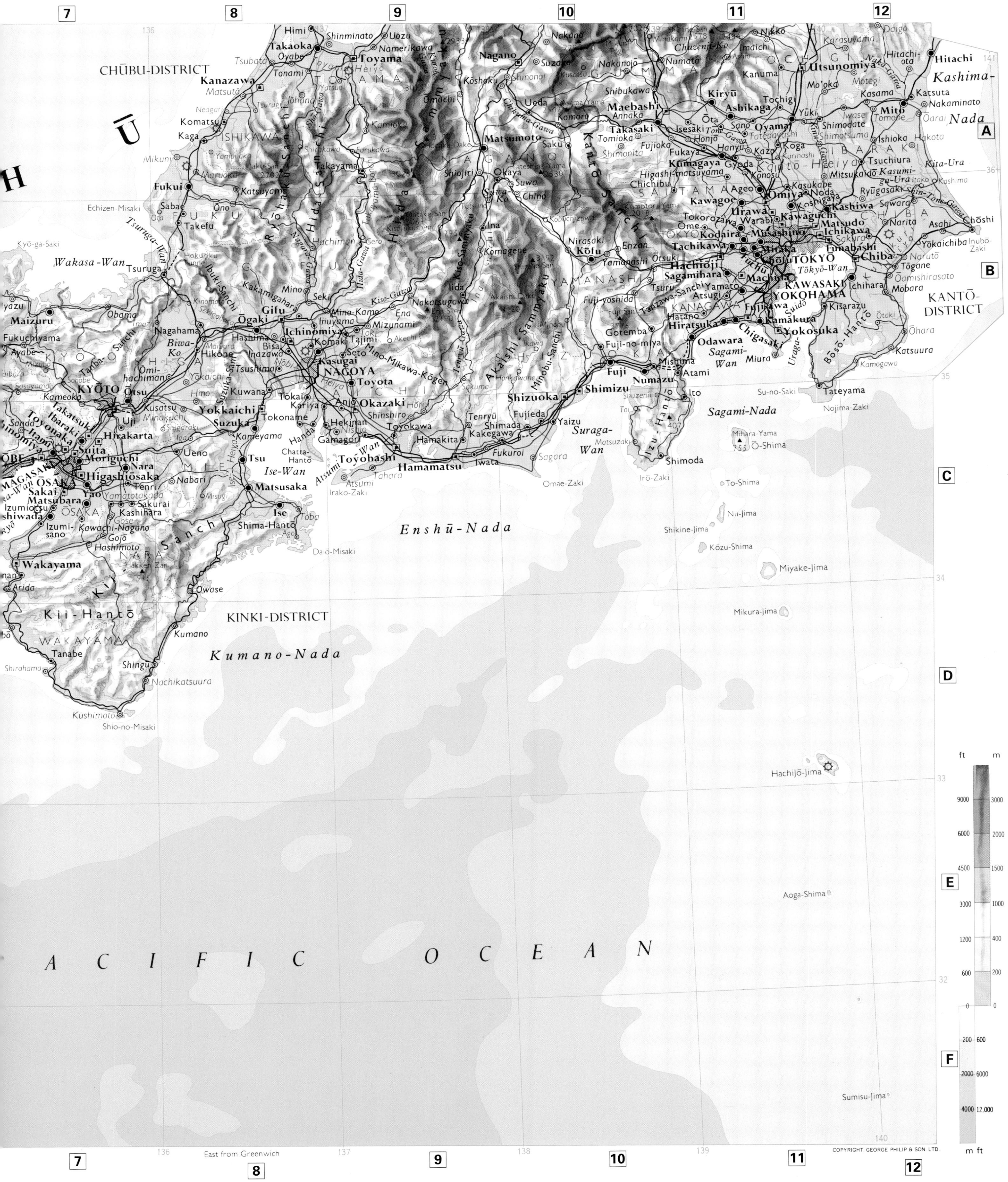

CHŪBU-DISTRICT

H Ū

H

Himi Shinminato Uozu Nakano Nikko Karasuyama Hitachi
Takaoka Namerikawa Nagano Suzaka Nakanojo Numata Imaichi Kashima-
Tsubata Oyabe Toyama Kōshoku Shinonoi Kusatsu Chūzenji-Ko Utsunomiya Katsuta Nada
Kanazawa Tonami Yatsuo Omachi Kamioka Shibukawa Maebashi Kanuma Kasama Nakaminato
Matsutō Neagari Itoigawa Furukawa Ueda Komoro Annaka Kiryū Tochigi Mo-oka Mito Ōarai
Komatsu Takayama Saku Takasaki Ashikaga Yūki Shimodate Tsuchiura Kita-Ura
Kaga Hachiman Matsumoto Shiojiri Tomioka Isesaki Ōta Sano Oyama Koga Mitsukaido Kasumi-ga-Ura Itako
Fukui Maruoka Katsuyama Okaya Suwa Fujioka Honjo Hanyū Kazo Konosu Ageo
Sabae Takayama Chichibu Kumagaya Gyoda Kasukabe Noda Ryūgasaki Sawara Chōshi
Takefu Ōno Higashi-matsuyama Kawagoe Omiya Narita Asahi
Tsuruga Nirasaki Tokorozawa Urawa Kawaguchi Kashiwa Yokaichiba
Biwa-Ko Kōfu Enzan Ōme Kodaira Matsudo Ichikawa
Gifu Ina Komagane Yamanashi Ōtsuki TŌKYŌ Tachikawa Mitaka Funabashi Chiba
Ichinomiya Mino-Kamo Mizunami Akechi Hachioji Tsuru Machida KAWASAKI Chiba
NAGOYA Toyota Seto Okazaki Shinshiro Tenryū Fujieda Atsugi Fujisawa YOKOHAMA Ichihara Mobara
KYŌTO Ōtsu Kariya Hekinan Toyokawa Hamakita Shimada Yaizu Hiratsuka Kamakura Yokosuka Kisarazu
Yokkaichi Suzuka Handa Gamagori Toyohashi Hamamatsu Iwata Kakegawa Odawara Chigasaki Ōtaki
Tsu Matsusaka Fukuroi Sagara Shizuoka Shimizu Numazu Atami Mishima Miura Katsuura Tateyama
OSAKA Nara Ise Toba Omae-Zaki Fuji Fuji-no-miya Gotemba Ito Shimoda
Wakayama Kushimoto Kumano Shingu Nachikatsuura Tanabe Shirahama

Enshū-Nada
Kumano-Nada
Suruga-Wan
Sagami-Nada
Sagami-Wan
Ise-Wan
Wakasa-Wan
Tsuruga-Wan

O-Shima Mihara-Yama 755
To-Shima Nii-Jima Kōzu-Shima Shikine-Jima
Miyake-Jima Mikura-Jima Hachijō-Jima Aoga-Shima Sumisu-Jima

KINKI-DISTRICT
KANTŌ-DISTRICT
Kashima-Nada

PACIFIC OCEAN

East from Greenwich

ft m
9000 3000
6000 2000
4500 1500
3000 1000
1200 400
600 200
0
200 600
2000 6000
4000 12,000
m ft

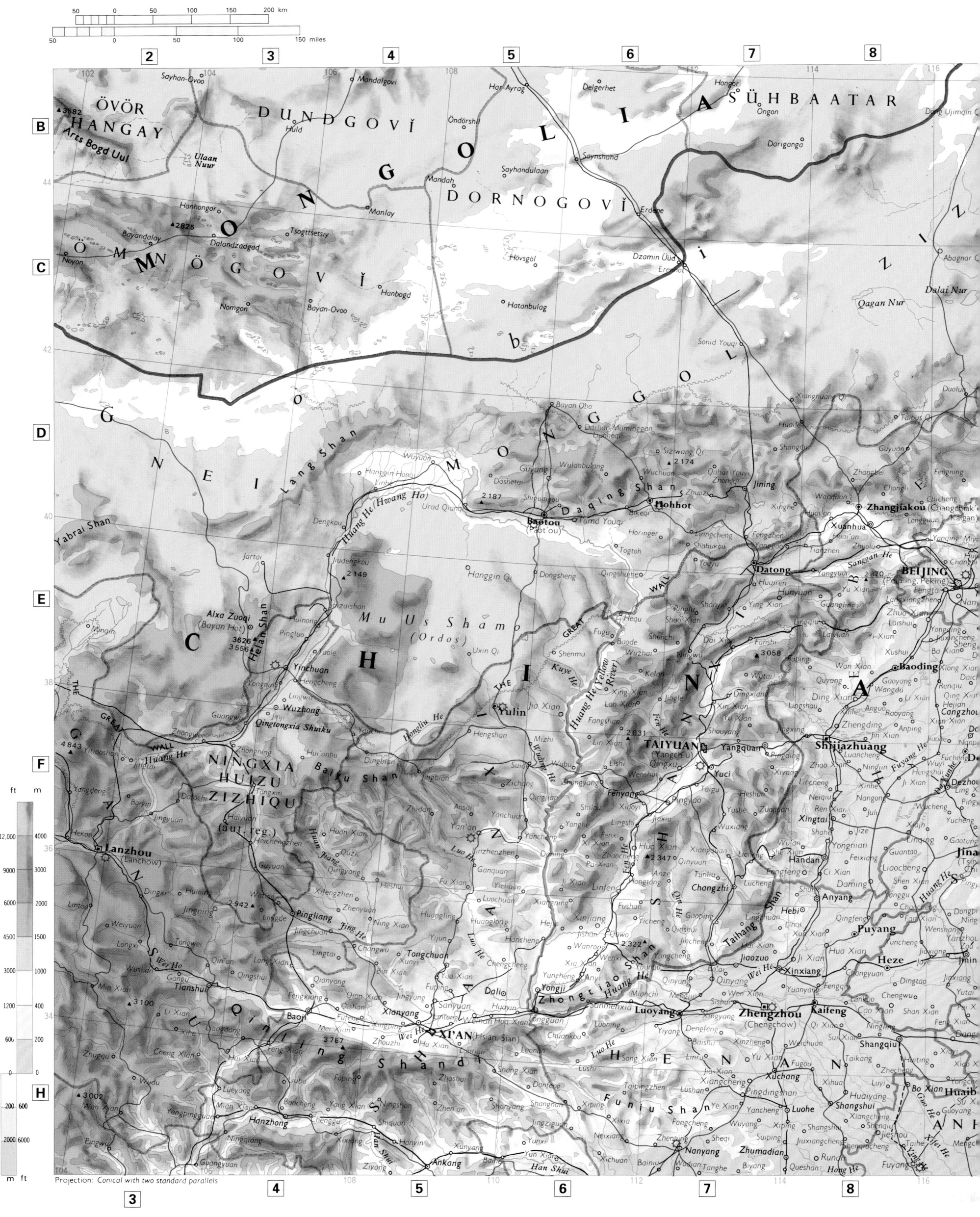

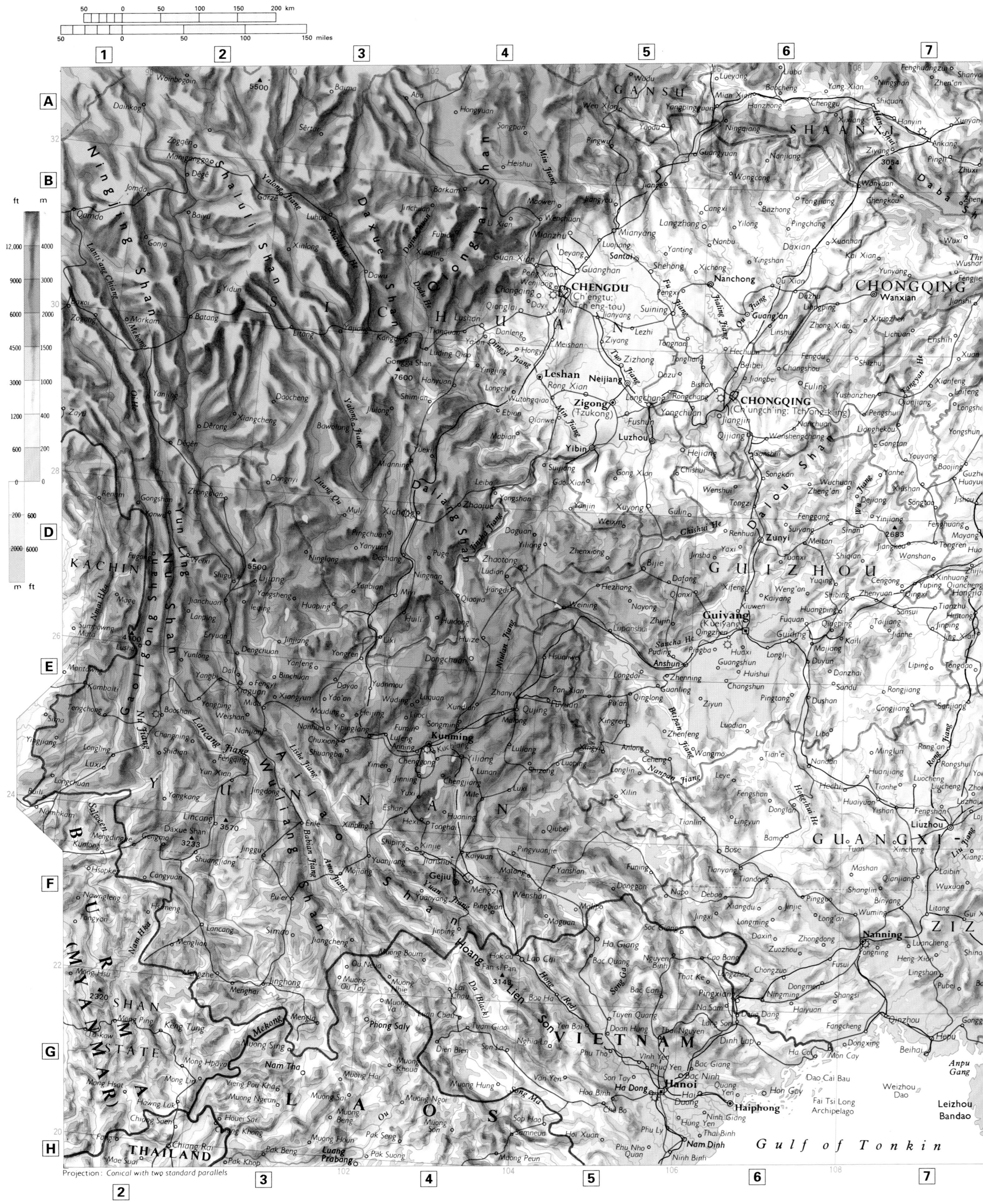

8 9 10 11 12 13 14

A

Shangnan Xiping
Jingziguan Wuyang Xiping Xiangcheng Shangqiu Guzhen Wuhe Hongze Xinghua Dongtai
Neixiang Xixia Fangcheng Suiping Jiuxiangcheng Linquan Yingshang Huaiyuan Guoyang Wuhe Hu Gaoyou Hu Haian
Yunxi Jingshan Zhenping Nanyang Zhumadian Runan Fuyang Madian Fengyang Tianchang Yangzhou Taizhou Tai Xian Rugao
Han Shui Deng Xian Wadian Tanghe Biyang Queshan Xinyang Zhengyangguan Shou Xian Changfeng Dingyuan Luhe Yizheng Guazhou Taixing
Shiyan Xinye Zaoyang Tongbai Xi Xian Huoqiu Chuxian Yangzhou JIANGSU
Xiangfan Baokang Zhengyang Huangchuan Chengdong Hefei Nanjing Chenchiang Jurong Changzhou Jiangyin Haimen Qidong
Nanzhang Hu Nanking Ch'angchou Chongming Dao
Dongjinwan Jingshan Huoshan Wuwei Ma'anshan Wuxi Changshu Jiading Chang Jiang
Wuhan ANHUI Wuhu Danyang Wuhu Suzhou Kunshan SHANGHAI
Macheng Nanling Nanjing Songjiang
WUHAN Hankou

SOUTH CHINA SEA

Projection: Mercator

East from Greenwich

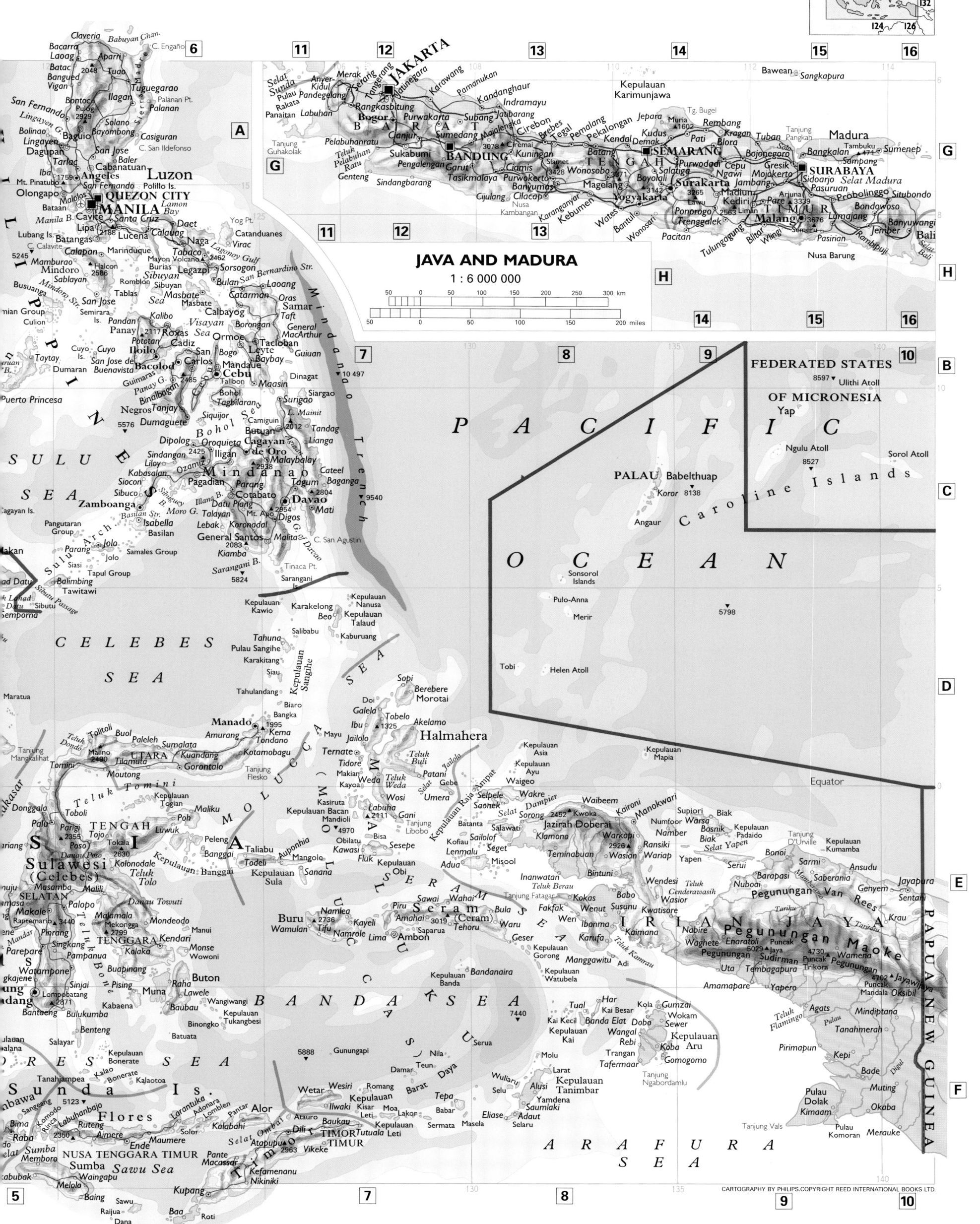

JAVA AND MADURA

1 : 6 000 000

CARTOGRAPHY BY PHILIPS.COPYRIGHT REED INTERNATIONAL BOOKS LTD.

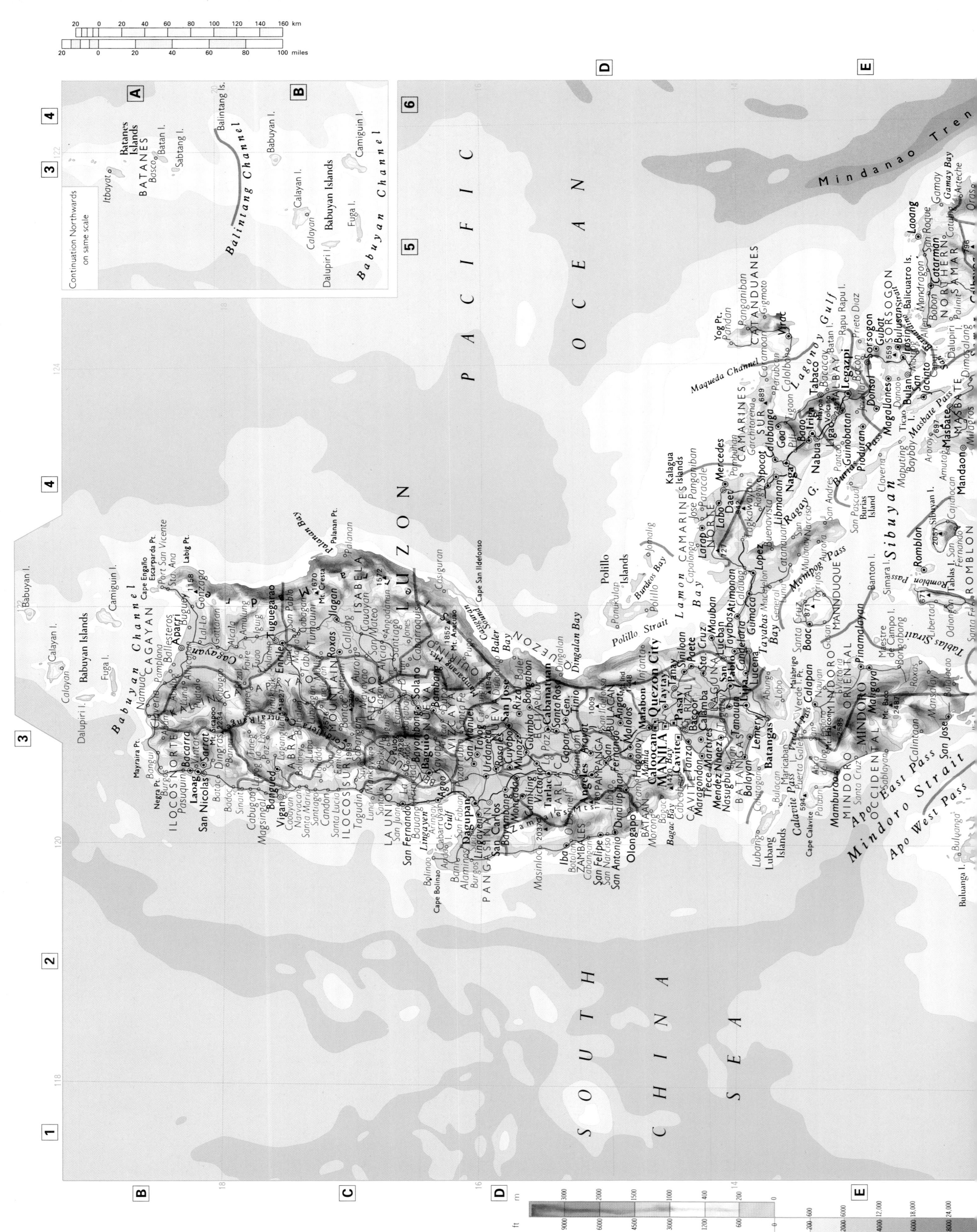

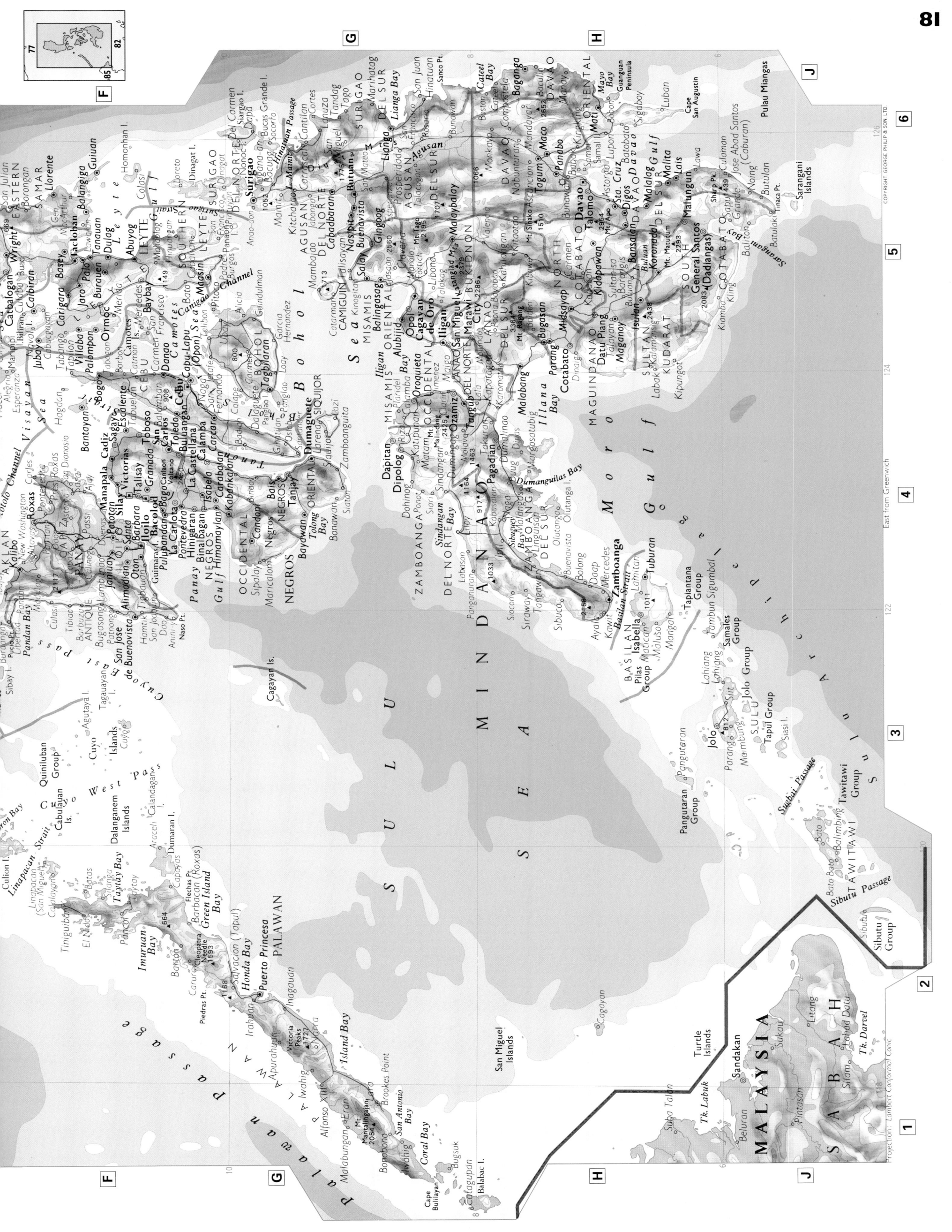

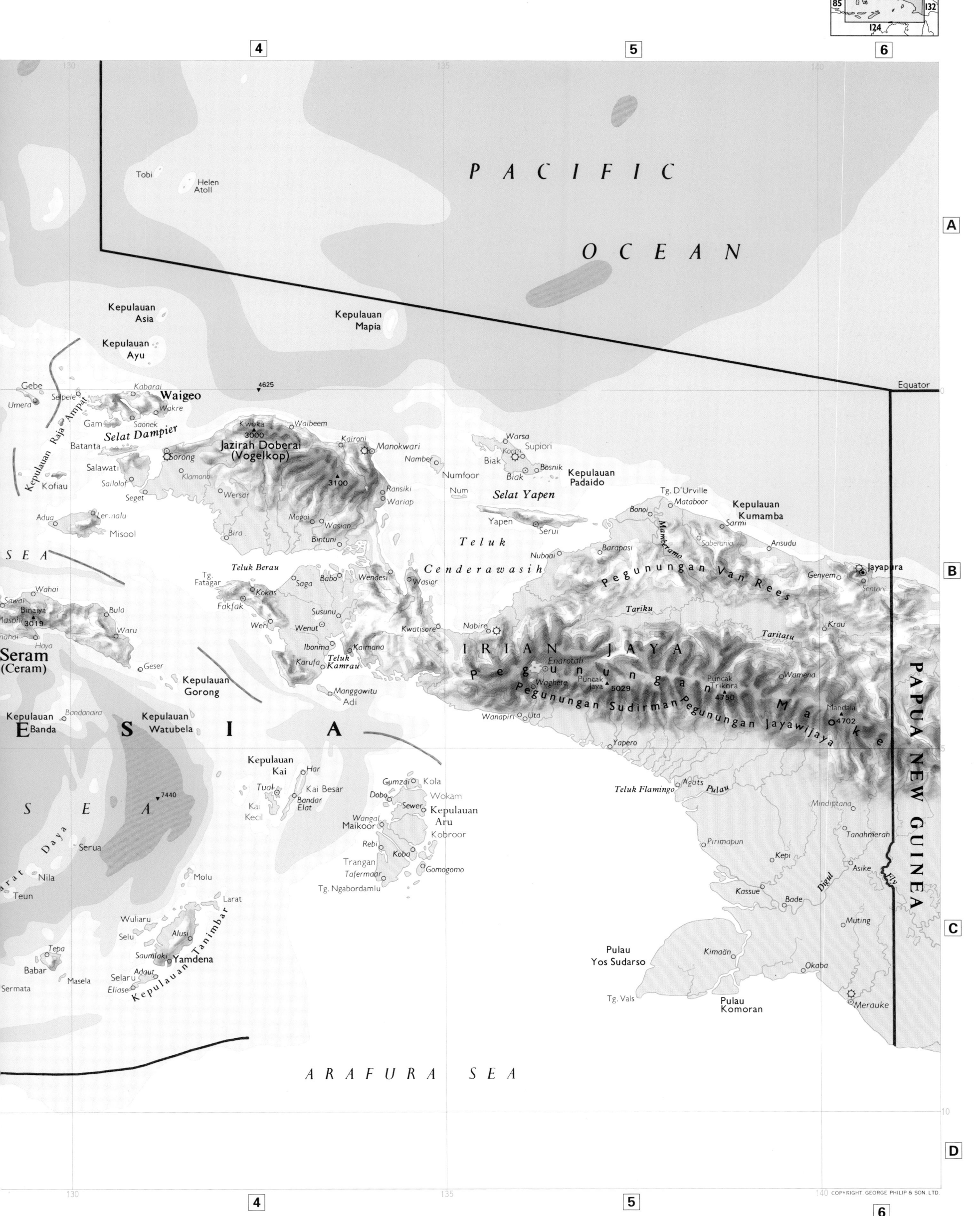

4   5   6

PACIFIC

OCEAN

A

Tobi   Helen
            Atoll

Kepulauan
Asia   Kepulauan
                       Mapia
Kepulauan
Ayu

Gebe   Kabarai   4625   Equator
Umera   Selpele   Waigeo   Waibeem
              Wakre   Warsa
                   Saonek   Kwoka   Kaironi   Korim   Supiori
Batanta   3000   Jazirah Doberai   Manokwari   Biak   Bosnik   Kepulauan
Salawati   Klamono   (Vogelkop)   Namber   Biak   Padaido
        Sorong   Numfoor
Sailolof   Wersar   3100   Ransiki   Num   Selat Yapen   Kepulauan   B
Adua   Lermalu   Mogoi   Wasian   Wariap   Yapen   Serui   Kumamba
       Misool   Bira   Bintuni   Sarmi
                                                          Teluk   Bonoi   Tg. D'Urville   Mataboor
SEA   Teluk Berau   Babo   Wendesi   Cenderawasih   Mamberamo   Saberania   Ansudu
       Wahai   Tg.   Saga   Wasior   Nubaai   Barapasi   Pegunungan Van Rees   Genyem   Jayapura
Sawai   Fatagar   Kokas   Kwatisore   Nabire   Tariku   Krau   Sentani
Binaiya   Susunu   Weri   Nabire   Tariku   Taritatu
3019   Masohi   Wenut   Ibonma   IRIAN   JAYA   Wamena   B
Haya   Karufa   Kaimana   Pegunungan   Enarotali   Puncak   Mandala
Seram   Kepulauan Teluk   Wanapiri   Uta   Waghete   Jaya 5029   Puncak   Mamberamo 4702
(Ceram)   Gorong   Kamrau   Pegunungan Sudirman Trikora   Maoke
       Bandanaira   Manggawitu Adi   Pegunungan Jayawijaya 4750
Kepulauan   Kepulauan   Yapero
E Banda   Watubela   S I   A   Agats   Teluk Flaminggo   Pulau
                                                                  Mindiptana
                   Kepulauan Kai   Har   C
SEA   Tual   Kai Besar   Kola   Gumzai   Pirimapun   Kepi   Asike
                   Kai   Bandar Dobo Sewer   Wokam   Tanahmerah
7440   Kecil   Elat   Kobroor   Kepulauan   Kassue   Bade   Muting
Daya   Serua   Wangal   Maikoor   Rebi   Aru   Digul
Nila   Koba   Okaba
Teun   Molu   Trangan   Gomogomo   Pulau   C
                   Larat   Tafermaar   Yos Sudarso   Kimaän
Wuliaru   Tg. Ngabordamlu   Okaba
Selu   Alusi   Tg. Vals   Pulau
Tepa   Saumlaki Yamdena   Komoran   Merauke
Babar   Adaut Selaru
Sermata Masela Eliase Kepulauan Tanimbar

ARAFURA   SEA   D

COPYRIGHT GEORGE PHILIP & SON LTD

4   5   6

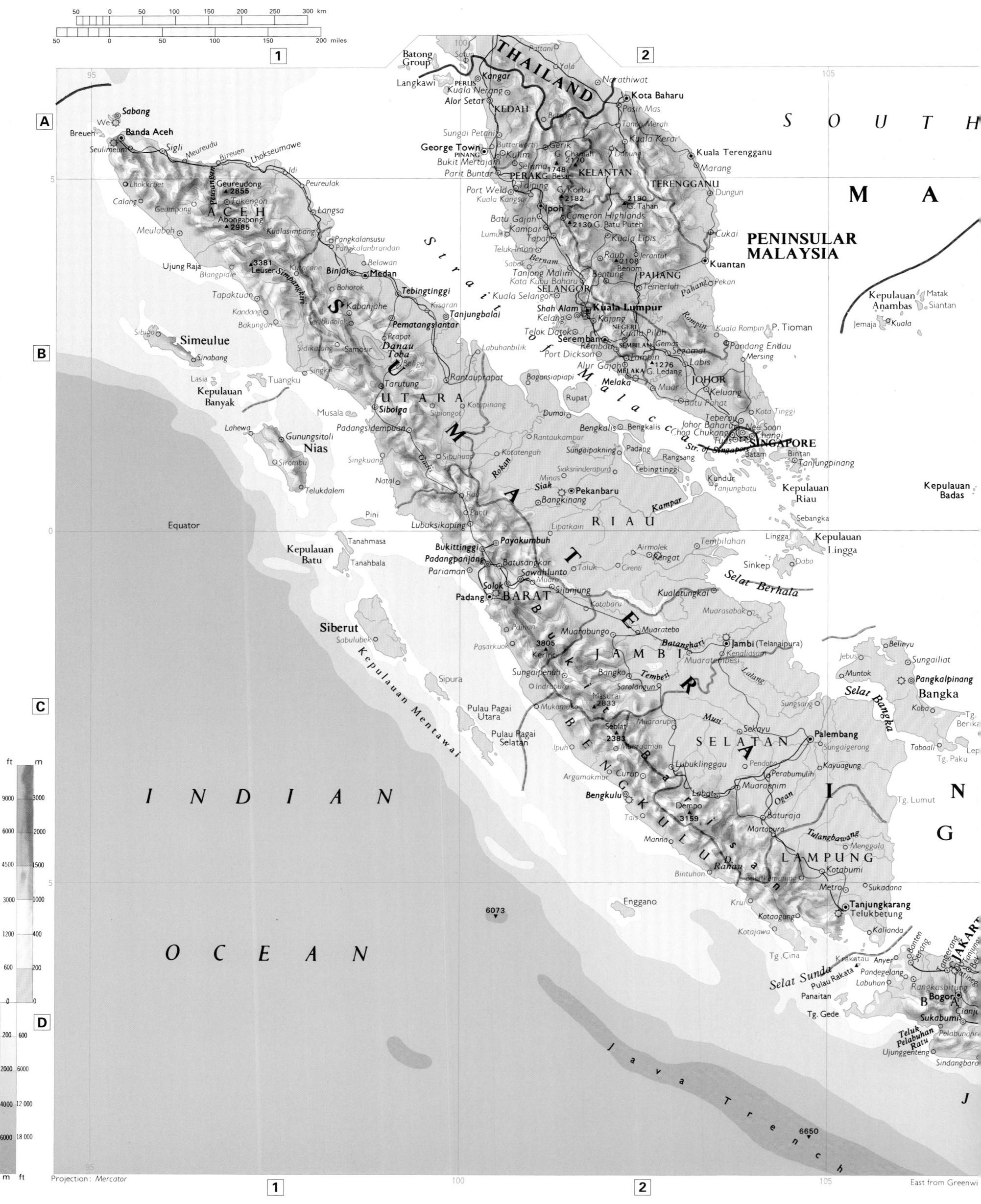

Projection: Mercator

East from Greenwich

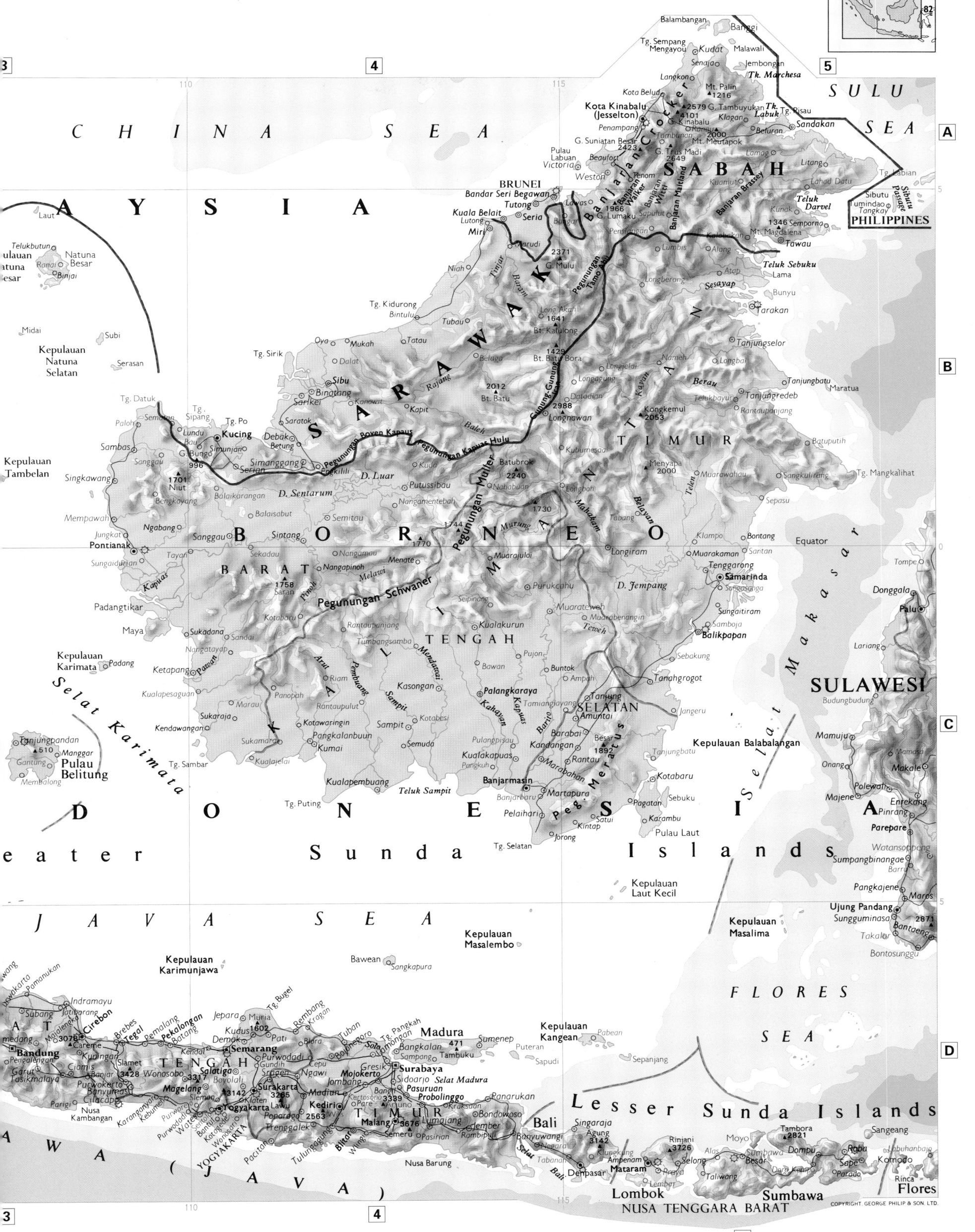

CHINA SEA

SULU SEA

MALAYSIA

AYSIA

Laut

Telukbutun
Pulauan
Natuna
esar

Ranai
Binjai
Natuna
Besar

Midai

Subi

Kepulauan
Natuna
Selatan

Serasan

Tg. Datuk

Kepulauan
Tambelan

Balambangan
Banggi

Tg. Sempang
Mengayou
Kudat
Malawali

Langkon
Senajau
Jembongan

Kota Belud
Mt. Palin
1216

Tk. Marchesa

Kota Kinabalu
(Jesselton)
2579 G. Tambuyukon
4101
Kinabalu
Klagan
Beluran
Sandakan

Penampang
Kumbi
2000

SABAH

G. Suniatan Besar
2423
Kimanis
2649

G. Trus Madi

Mt. Meutapok
Lamag

Litang

Tk.
Labuk
Tg. Risau

Beaufort

BRUNEI
Bandar Seri Begawan
Tutong
Seria
Kuala Belait
Lutong
Miri

Weston
Walker

1966
G. Lumaku

Penom

Banjaran Maitland

Banjaran Brassey

Lahad Datu
Teluk
Darvel

Mt. Magdalena
1346 Semporna
Tawau

PHILIPPINES

Teluk Sebuku

Lumbis
Alang
Atap
Lama

Sibutu
Tangkay
Tumindao

Sibutu
Passage

Labian

Niah
2371
G. Mulu

Marudi
Tiniar

Baram

S
A
R
A
W
A
K

Banjaran Tanaku

Longberang

Sesayap

Bunyu

Tarakan

Tg. Kidurong
Bintulu

Long Akah
1641
Bt. Katulong

Tubau

Tatau

Oya
Mukah
Dalat

Tg. Sirik

Sibu

Binatang
Sarikei
Saratok

Kanowit
Kapit

Rajang

1429
Bt. Batu Bora
Belaga

2012
Bt. Batu

2988
Longnawan

T
I
M
U
R

Longajan

Tanjungselor
Longbai

Longgung

Datadian

Berau

Tanjungredeb

Maratua

Kubumesaai

Kongkemul
2053

Telukbayur

Tanjungbatu

Batuputih

Sepasu

Tg. Mangkalihat

Palohn
Semunjan
Tg.
Sipang

Tg. Po

Kucing

Lundu
Bau
G.
Bungo
996
Simunjan

Debak
Betung

Pejkilili

Serian

Pegunungan Boyen Kapuas

Balaikarangan

Sambas

Singkawang

Sanggau

Tg. Datuk

Kepulauan
Tambelan

1701
Niut

Bengkayang

Balaisabut

Mempawah

Ngabang

1758
Saran

Pegunungan Kapuas Hulu

D. Luar

Kuda

Batubrok
2240

Putussibau

Nangamentebah

Semitau

D. Sentarum

Pegunungan Muller

Nangapinoh

Murung

1730

1744
1770

Mahakam

Longiram

Muarajulai

Muarakaman

Santan

Equator

Tompe

Sintang

B O R N E O

Ngabang

Sungaiduri

Pontianak

Tayan

Jungkat

Kapuas

B A R A T

Sanggau

Sekadau

Nangamau

Menate

Muaratewah

Muarabengangin
Teleh

Sungaisiram

Samboja

Sangasanga

Samarinda

Tenggarong

Donggala

Palu

Padangtikar

Maya

Sukadana

Kepulauan
Karimata

Padang

Kotabaru

Nangatayap

Pembuang

Pegunungan Schwaner

Rantaupanjang

Pinoh

1758
Saran

Arut

Tumbangsamba

Mendawai

Seipinang

Purukcahu

D. Jempang

Balikpapan

Sebakung

Tanahgrogot

SULAWESI

Budungbudung

Lariang

Ketapang

Kualapesaguan

Kendawangan

Sandai

Sukaraja

Marau

Kotabaru

Riam

Kasongan

Sampit

Bawan

Pujon

Buntok

Ampah

Sungaisiram

Mamuju

Onang

Mamasa

Makale

Kepulauan
Karimata

Padang

T E N G A H

Palangkaraya

Kahayan

Barito

Tamianglayang

Tanjung
S E L A T A N

Amuntai

Kepulauan
Balabalangan

Majene

Polewali
Enrekang
Pinrang

Kalapembuang

Kualapembuang

Sukamara

Pangkalanbuun

Kumai

Semuda

Tg. Sambar

Kualajelai

Pangkalpisau

Kualakapuas

Pangkih

Barabai
Kandangan

Rantau

1892

Peg.

Meratus

Tanjungbatu

Kotabaru

Parepare

Watansoppeng

Sumpangbinangae

Tanjungpandan
Gantung

510

Manggar

Membalong

Pulau
Belitung

D O

Teluk Sampit

Tg. Puting

N

Banjarmasin

Banjarbaru

Martapura

Pelaihari

Pagatan

Karambu

Sebuku

Pulau Laut

E

Kintap

Jorong

S

Tg. Selatan

I

A

Pangkajene

Maros

Selat Karimata

G r e a t e r   S u n d a

Tg. Selatan

I s l a n d s

Selat Makasar

Ujung Pandang
Sungguminasa

Bantaeng
2871

Takalar

Bontosunggu

JAVA SEA

Kepulauan
Masalembo

Kepulauan
Laut Kecil

Kepulauan
Masalima

FLORES SEA

Bawean
Sangkapura

Kepulauan
Karimunjawa

J A V A   S E A

Indramayu
Jatibarang

Cirebon

Brebes
Tegal
Pemalang
Batang

Pekalongan

Kudus
1602
Pati

Muria

Jepara

Rembang
Kragan

Tuban

Demak

Tg. Bugel

Tg. Pangkah

Madura

Sumenep

Kepulauan
Kangean

Pabean

Subang

Majalengka

3078
Careme

Kuningan

Pengalengan

Slamet

T E N G A H

3428 Wonosobo

Magelang

3317

Salatiga

Semarang

Gundih

Kendal

Blora

Cepu

Ngawi

Bojonegoro

Solo

Bangkalan

Gresik

Mojokerto

Surabaya

Sidoarjo

Jombang

Sampang

Pamekasan

Tambuku

Selat Madura

Sapudi

Puteran

Sepanjang

Lesser Sunda Islands

Sangeang

Bandung

Garut
Tasikmalaya

Banjar
Ciamis

Purwokerto

Banyumas

Cilacap

Nusa
Kambangan

Karangnyar
Kebumen

3142

Kloten

Slamet

3265

Surakarta

Madiun

Sragen

Kertosono

Pare

Kediri

3339

Pasuruan

Probolinggo

Bondowoso

Panarukan

Bali

Singaraja

YOGYAKARTA

Wonogiri

Wates

Ponorogo

2563

Lawu

Trenggalek

Tulungagung

Blitar

Malang
3676

Lumajang

Semeru

Jember

Rambipuji

Banyuwangi

Agung
3142

Klungkung

Tabanan

Rinjani
3726

Moyo

Tambora
2821

Dompu

Raba

Sape

Parado

Komodo

Yogyakarta

Pacitan

T I M U R

Bantul

Denpasar

Mataram

Selat
Bali

Lombok

Ampenam

Praya

Selong

Alas

Sumbawa
Besar

Taliwang

Dompu

Labuhanbajo

Flores

Nusa Barung

S A W A   (J A V A)

NUSA TENGGARA BARAT

Sumbawa

Rinca

COPYRIGHT GEORGE PHILIP & SON LTD.

50 0 50 100 150 200 km
50 0 50 100 150 miles

A B C D E F

8 7 6 5 4 3 2 1

G. of Tonkin

HAINAN

CHINA

YUNNAN

GUANGXI ZHUANGZU

BURMA (MYANMAR)

SHAN

KAYAH

KAWTHULE

TENASSERIM

THAILAND

Khorat

Chao Phraya Lowlands

LAOS

VIETNAM

Hoang Lien Son

Bac Phan

Trung Phan

Annam

Annam Cordillera

CAMBODIA

Phnom Dangrek

Cao Nguyen

Mekong

Lancang Jiang

Salween

Tanen Dong Dan

Moscos Islands

RANGOON
Mandalay
HANOI
Haiphong
Vientiane
BANGKOK
Thon Buri
Da Nang
Hue
ANGKOR

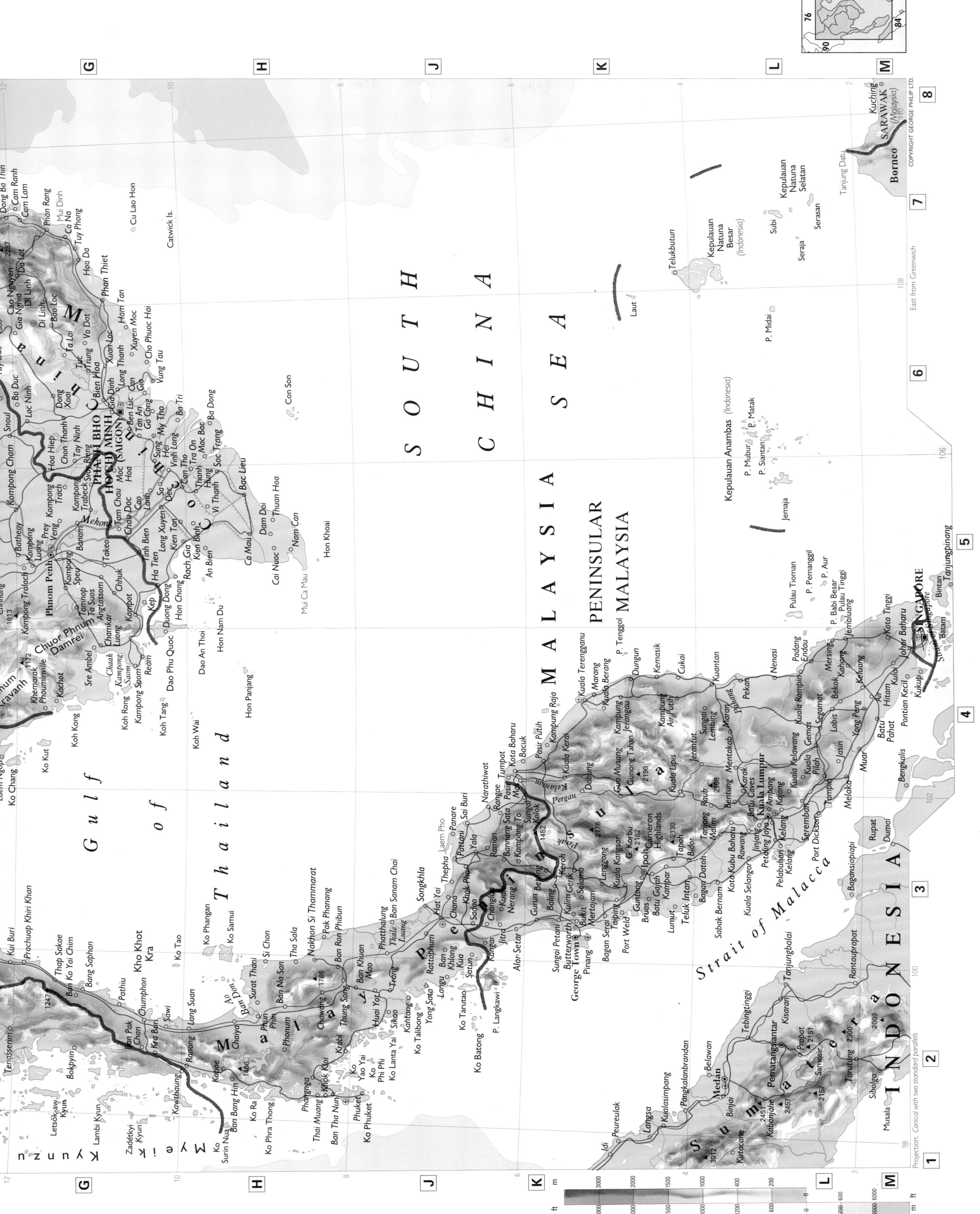

SARAWAK (Malaysia)
Kuching
Tanjung Datu
Borneo

Kepulauan
Natuna
Selatan

Subi
Serasan

S O U T H

C H I N A

S E A

Telukbutun

Kepulauan
Natuna
Besar
(Indonesia)

Seraja

P. Midai

Laut

Kepulauan Anambas (Indonesia)

P. Mubur
P. Matak
P. Siantan

Jemaja

M
A
L
A
Y
S
I
A

PENINSULAR
MALAYSIA

Tanjungpinang

East from Greenwich

Con Son

Hon Khoai

Kuala Terengganu
Marang
Kuala Berang

Dungun

P. Tenggol

Kemasik
Cukai

Kuantan

Pekan

Nenasi

Padang
Endau

Pulau Tioman

P. Pemanggil

P. Aur

P. Babi Besar
Pulau Tinggi

Bintan

Batam

SINGAPORE

Kota Tinggi
Johor Baharu

Jemaluang

Mersing

Kukup

Pontian Kecil

Kluang

Bekok
Kahang

Yong Peng

Batu
Pahat

Labis
Segamat

Muar

Bengkalis

Rupat

Dumai

Bagansiapiapi

Strait of Malacca

Rantauprapat

INDONESIA

Tebingtinggi

Tanjungbalai

Kisaran

Belawan
Medan
Binjai

Kualasimpang
Pangkalanbrandan

Langsa

Idi

Peureulak

Kutacane

Kabanjahe

Pematangsiantar

Prapat
Samosir

Parapat
2151

3007
2457

Tarutung

2300
Sidikalang

Musala
Sibolga

2009

S
u
m
a
t
e
r
a

G u l f

o f

T h a i l a n d

Gulf of Thailand

Ko Chang

Ko Kut

Koh Kong

Koh Rong

Koh Tang

Koh Wai

Koh Tao

Loem Ngop

Kampong Saom

Ream

Hon Nam Du

Dao Phu Quoc

Dao An Thoi

Hon Panjang

Mui Ca Mau

Cai Nuoc

Ca Mau

Dam Doi

Nam Can

Bac Lieu

Soc Trang

Thanh

Vi Thanh

Thuan Hoa

Ba Dong

Tra On

My Tho

Vinh Long

Can Tho

Cao
Lanh

Chau Doc

Long Xuyen

Kien Tan

Rach Gia

Kien Binh

An Bien

Ha Tien

Tinh Bien

Duong Dong

Hon Chong

Kep

Kampot

Angtassom

Takeo

Chhuk

Tani

THAILAND

M y a n m a r

Tenasserim

Letsôk-aw
Kyun

Zadètkyi
Kyun

Lambi Kyun

Bokpyin

Kawthaung

Thap Sakae

Prachuap Khiri Khan

Kui Buri

Bang Saphan

Ban Ko Yai Chim

Ban Pak
Chan

Kra Buri

Ko Phra Thong

Ko Ra

Phangnga

Thai Muang

Phuket

Ko Phuket

Ko Yao Yai

Ko Phi Phi

Krabi

Ko Lanta Yai

Ko Klok Klai

Ko Talibong

Sikao

Trang

Huai Yot

Palian

Yong Sata

Ko Tarutao

Ko Batong

Satun

P. Langkawi

Langu

Ko Lipe

Rattaphum

Hat Yai

Sadao

Changlun

Kangar

Jitra

Alor Setar

Kuala Kangsar

Kulim

Bukit
Mertajam

George Town

Pinang

Butterworth

Sungai Petani

Baling

Gerik

Grik

Keroh

Bagan Serai

Port Weld

Kuala Kurau

Taiping

Bruas

Lumut

Teluk Intan

Bagan Datoh

Sitiawan

Ipoh

Gua Musang

Kuala Lipis

Jerantut

Kampung
Air Putih

Kampung
Jerangau

Dabong

Tanah Merah

Kota Baharu

Pasir Mas

Pasir Putih

Tumpat

Kampung To
Kelok

Rantau
Panjang

Sungai
Kolok

Golok

Tak Bai

Narathiwat

Yala

Betong

Pattani

Thepha

Panare

Saiburi

Laem Pho

Songkhla

Chana

Thale
Luang

Phatthalung

Phunphin

Sai Buri

Ban Khuan

Ron Phibun

Surat Thani

Khao Phloi

Khlong
Thom

Ban Na San

Khuan Niang

Chaiya

Ao Ban Don

Phun
Phin

Ban Nam Som

Chumphon

Lang Suan

Pathiu

Sawi

Ranong

Nakhon Si Thammarat

Pak Phanang

Si Chon

Tha Sala

Chawang
1786

Thung Song

Ko Samui

Ko Phangan

M
a
l
a
y
P
e
n
i
n
s
u
l
a

M
a
l
a
c
c
a

Klang

Melaka

Kelang
Pelabuhan
Kelang

Petaling Jaya
Kuala Lumpur

Ampang
Bentong
Karak

Kajang

Seremban

Port Dickson

Kuala Pilah

Tampin

Rompin

Kuala Rompin

Bidor

Tapah

Raub

Gunong Tahan
2190

Benta

Cameron
Highlands

Batu Gajah

Kampar

Kuala Kubu Bharu

Rawang

Batu
Caves

Kuala Selangor

Sabak Bernam

Kuala Selangor

Banting

Sepang

Kuala Krai

Kuala Lipis

2182

2176

Perak

Kelantan

Pergau

1452

2130

P h n o m C h u o r   P h n u m   D â m r ê i

S a i g o n   PHANH BHO
HO CHI MINH
(SAIGON)

Phnom Penh
1813

Kompong Cham
Kompong Trach

Snoul

Bo Duc

Loc Ninh

Kompong Tralach

Kompong Speu

Kampong

Kompong
Trabeck

Kracheh

Kompong
Trabeck

Prey Veng

Banam

Svay Rieng

Soc Trang

Chhlong

M
e
k
o
n
g

Mekong

Con Son

Vung Tau

Ba Ria

Bien Hoa

Thu Duc

Xuyen Moc

Long Thanh

Cho Phuoc Hai

Phan Thiet

Phan Rang

Phan Rang

Di Linh

Đa Lat

Cam Ranh

Cam Lam

Dong Ba Thin

Ca Na

Tuy Phong

Mui Ne

Cu Lao Hon

Catwick Is.

Ham Tan

Vo Dat

La Lai

Gia Nghia

Cao Nguyen
2287

Kampong
Saom

Chuor Phnum
Kravanh

Chuor Phnum
Damrei
1772

Khemarak
Phoumiville

Sre Ambel

Chaak

Phsar Ream

Kampong Speu

1247

Projection: Conical with two standard parallels

f t   m
9000   3000
6000   2000
4500   1500
3000   1000
1200   400
600   200
0   0
2000   600
4000   1200
6000   2000

f t   m

Projection : Alber's Equal Area with two standard Parallels

East from Greenwich

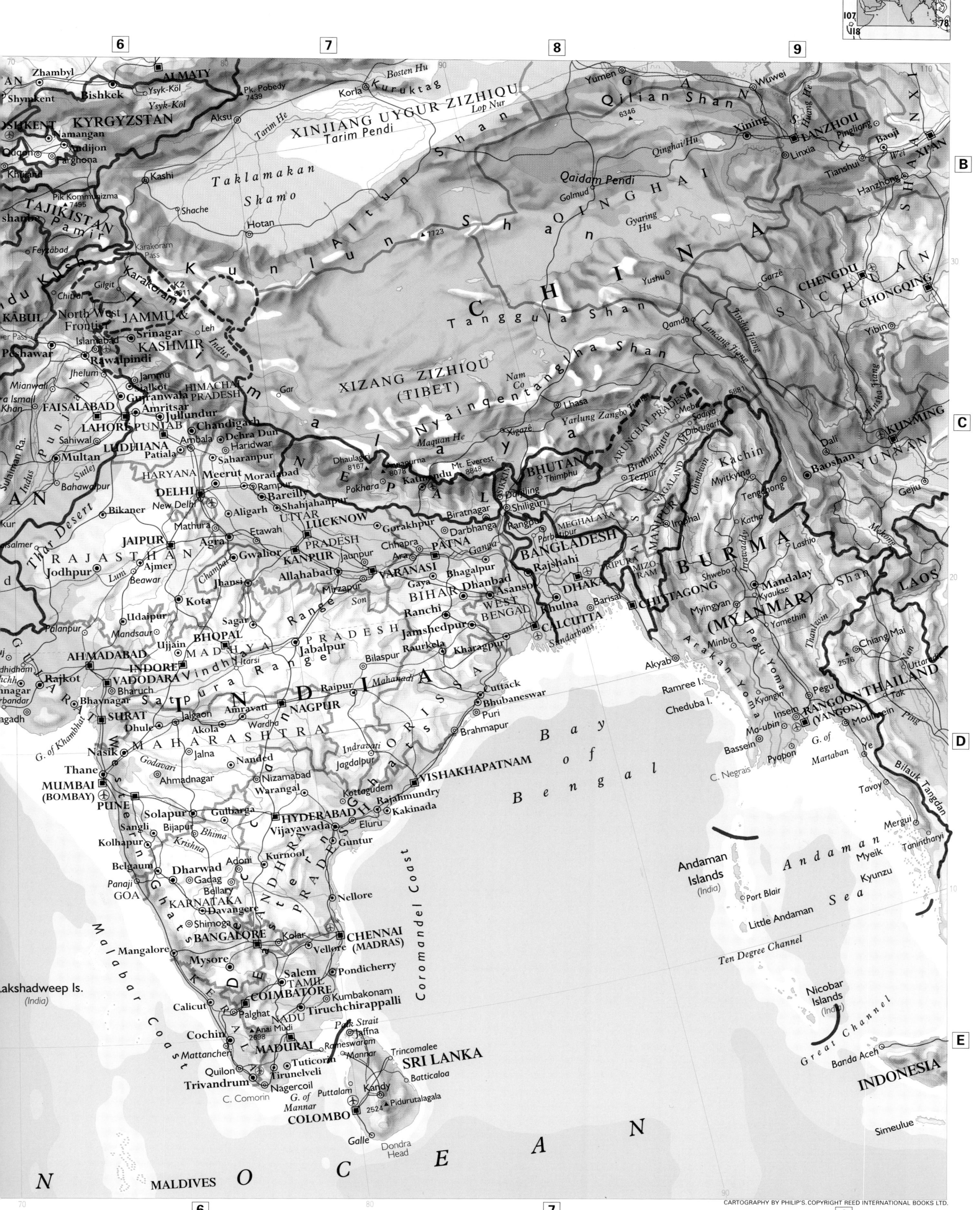

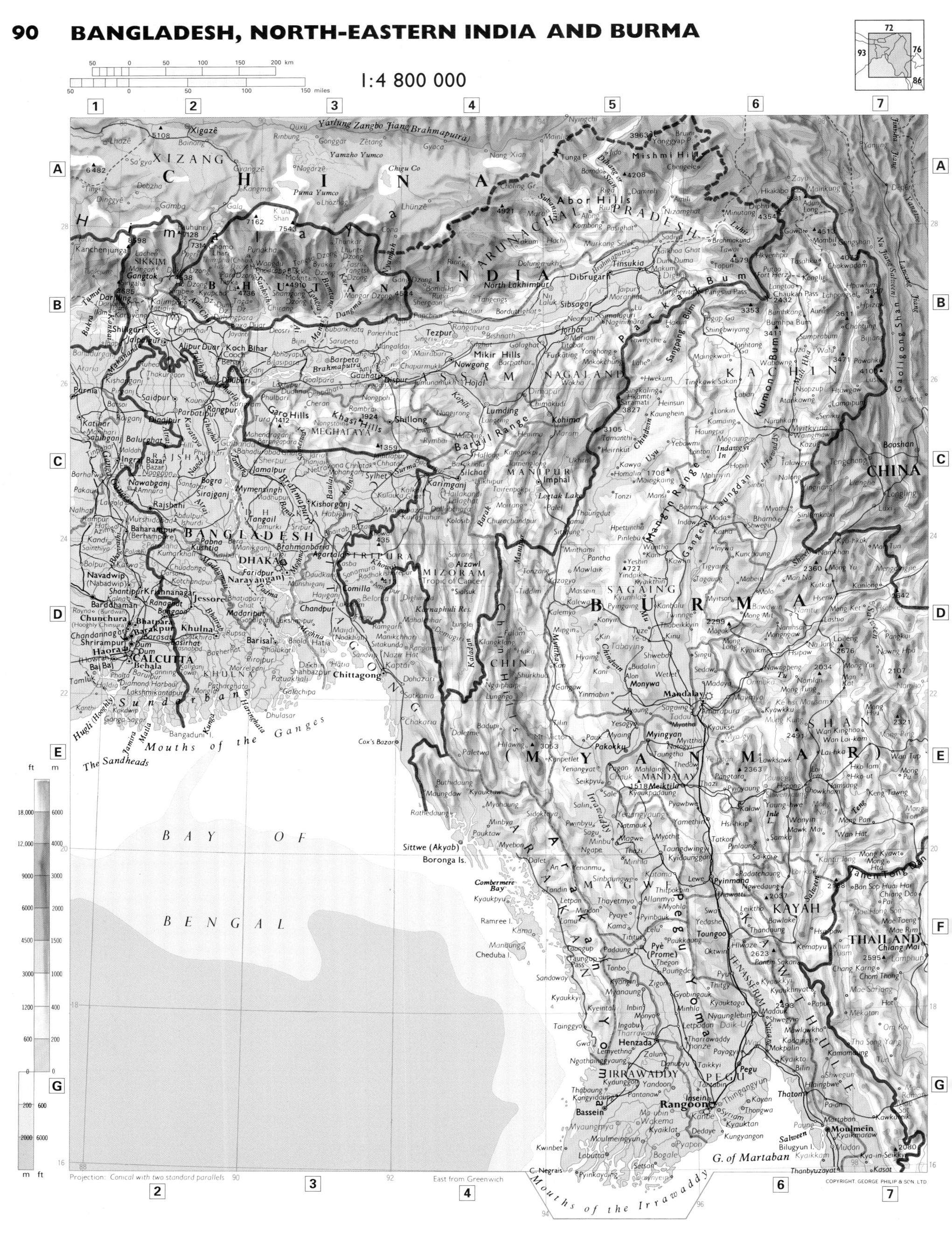

1:4 800 000

50   0   50   100   150   200 km
50   0   50   100   150 miles

Projection: Conical with two standard parallels

East from Greenwich

COPYRIGHT GEORGE PHILIP & SON LTD

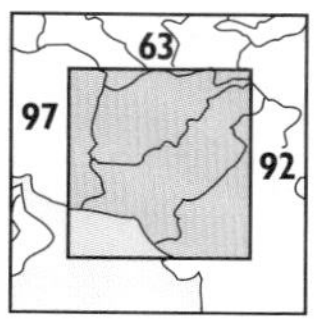

50 0 50 100 150 200 250 300 km
50 0 50 100 150 200 miles

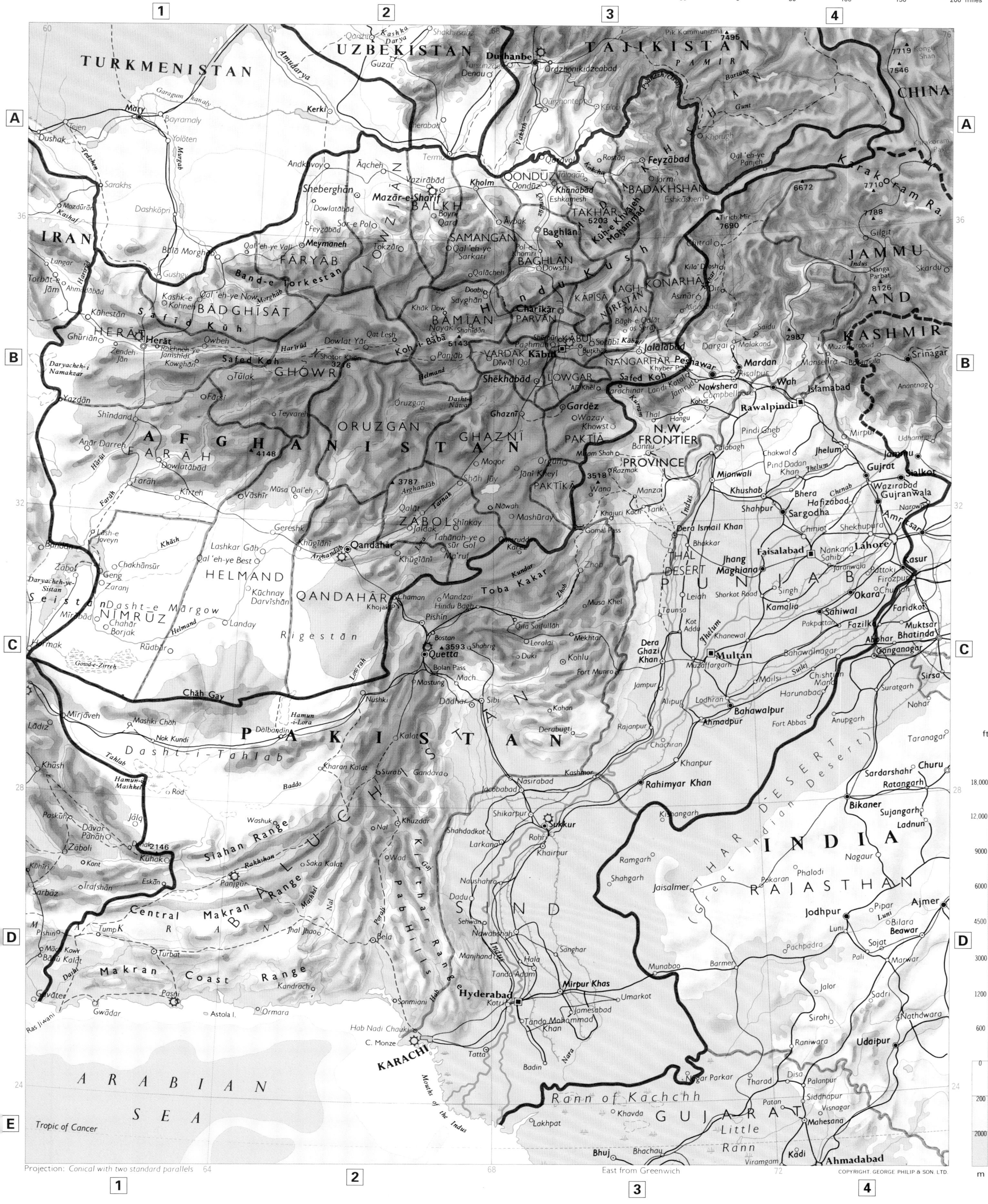

TURKMENISTAN

UZBEKISTAN

TAJIKISTAN

CHINA

IRAN

PAMIR

BADAKHSHAN

JAMMU AND KASHMIR

HINDU KUSH

Dushanbe
Guzar
Denau
Termiz
Qarshi
Kashka Darya
Shakhrisabz

Mary
Bayramaly
Yölöten
Kerki
Garagum kanaly
Amudarya

Tejen
Dushak
Tedzhen

Sarakhs
Mozdūrān
Kashaf

Andkvoy
Sheberghan
Āqcheh
Vazirābad
Kholm
QONDŪZ
Qonduz
Khanabad
Feyzābād
Jorm
Eshkamesh

Mazār-e-Sharīf
BALKH
Dowlatābād
Sor-e Pol
Pol-e
SAMANGAN
Āybak
Baghlān
BAGHLĀN
Dowshi

Meymaneh
Qal'eh-ye Vali
Tokzār
FĀRYĀB
JOWZJĀN
Sheberghan

Bālā Morghāb
Qal'eh-ye Now
Band-e Torkestan
Khāk Dow
BĀMIĀN
Bāmiān
CHARĪKĀR
PARVĀN
KĀPĪSĀ
LAGHMAN
NŪRESTĀN
KONARHĀ
Chitral

HERĀT
Herāt
Owbeh
Safīd Kūh
GHOWR
Koh-i-Bābā
5143
VARDAK
Kābul
KABUL
Jalālābād
NANGARHĀR
Peshawar
Mardan
Risalpur

BĀDGHĪSĀT

Zendeh Jān
Kūhestān
Ghūriān
Daryācheh-ye Namakzar

FARĀH
4148
AFGHANISTAN
ORUZGAN
Oruzgan
GHAZNĪ
Ghaznī
Gardēz
Khowst
PAKTĪĀ
LOWGAR
Shēkhābād

N.W. FRONTIER PROVINCE

HELMAND
Gereshk
ZĀBOL
Qalāt
3787
Arghandāb
Tarnak

QANDAHĀR
Qandahār
Chaman
Pishin
Toba Kakar
Zhob

NIMRŪZ
Dasht-e Mārgow
Rigestān
Rūdbār

Chāh Gay
Dālbandīn
Dasht-i-Tahlab
PAKISTAN
BALUCHISTAN

Quetta
3593
Bolan Pass
Mastung
Mach
Sibi

Siahan Range
Central Makran Range
Kharan Kalat
Surab
Gandava

Makran Coast Range
Panjgur
Turbat
Bela

PUNJAB
THAL DESERT
Dera Ismail Khan
Bannu
Gomal Pass

Mianwali
Khushab
Sargodha
Jhang
Faisalabad
Lahore
Kasur
Okara
Sāhiwal

Dera Ghazi Khan
Multan
Bahawalpur
Ahmadpur

Rawalpindi
Islamabad
Jhelum
Gujrat
Sialkot
Wazirabad
Gujranwala
Amritsar
Firozpur
Faridkot
Muktsar
Bhatinda
Ganganagar

THAR DESERT
(Great Indian Desert)
INDIA
RAJASTHAN

Bikaner
Churu
Ratangarh
Ladnun
Nagaur
Jodhpur
Ajmer
Beawar

SIND
Sukkur
Larkana
Nawabshah
Hyderabad
Mirpur Khas

KARACHI
C. Monze
Mouths of the Indus

ARABIAN SEA

Tropic of Cancer

Rann of Kachchh
GUJARAT
Little Rann
Bhuj
Ahmadabad
Udaipur

ft m
18,000 6000
12,000 4000
9000 3000
6000 2000
4500 1500
3000 1000
1200 400
600 200
0 0
200 600
2000 6000
m ft

Projection: Conical with two standard parallels
East from Greenwich
COPYRIGHT GEORGE PHILIP & SON LTD.

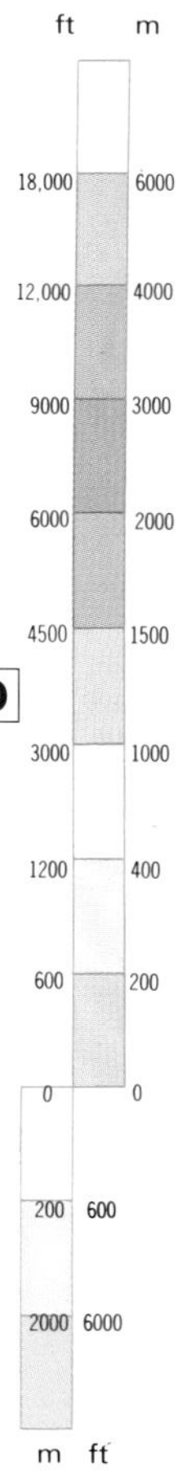

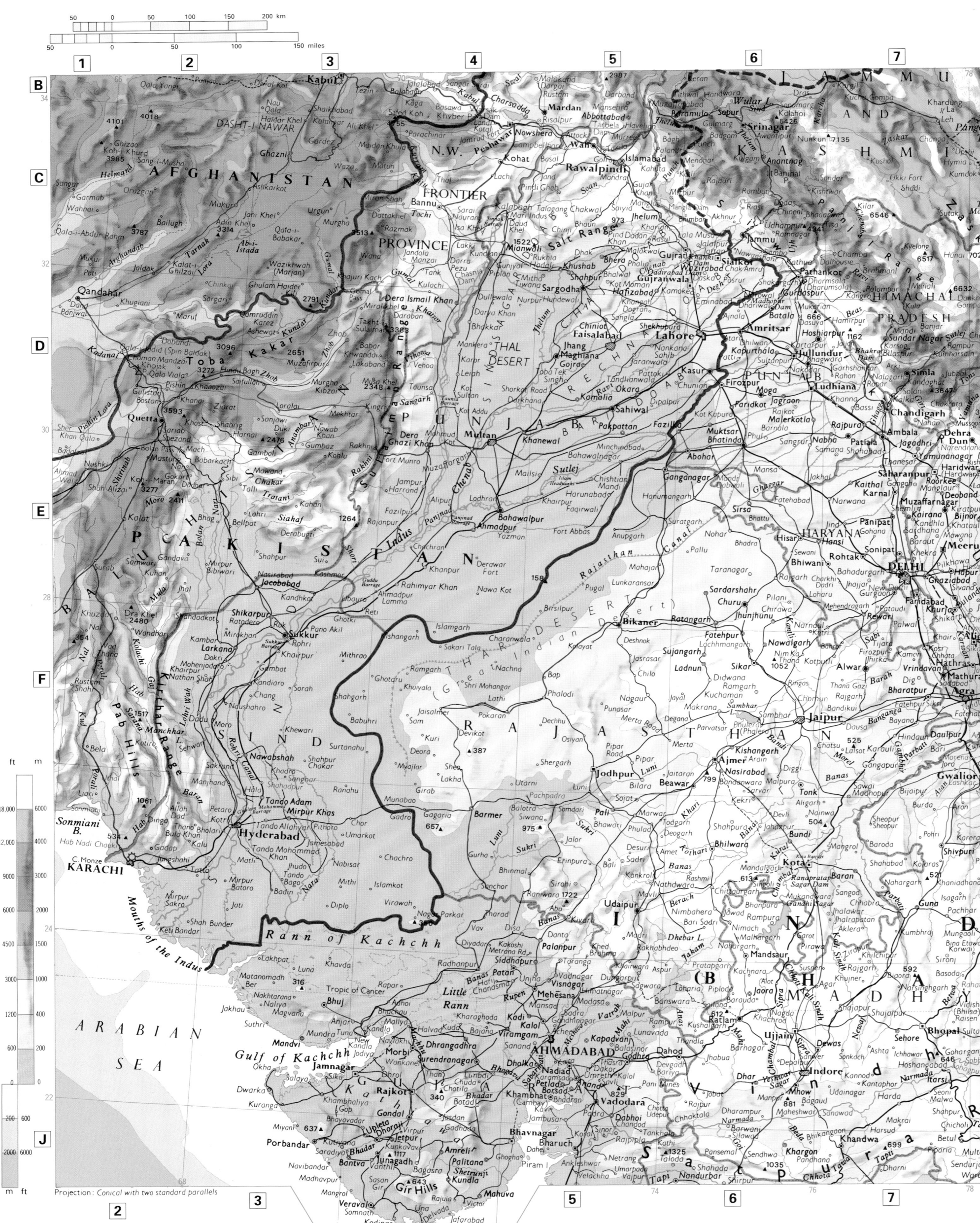

Projection: Conical with two standard parallels

JAMMU AND KASHMIR
On same scale as Main Map

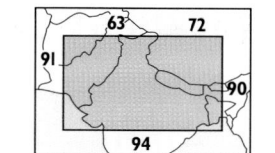

East from Greenwich

COPYRIGHT. GEORGE PHILIP & SON. LTD

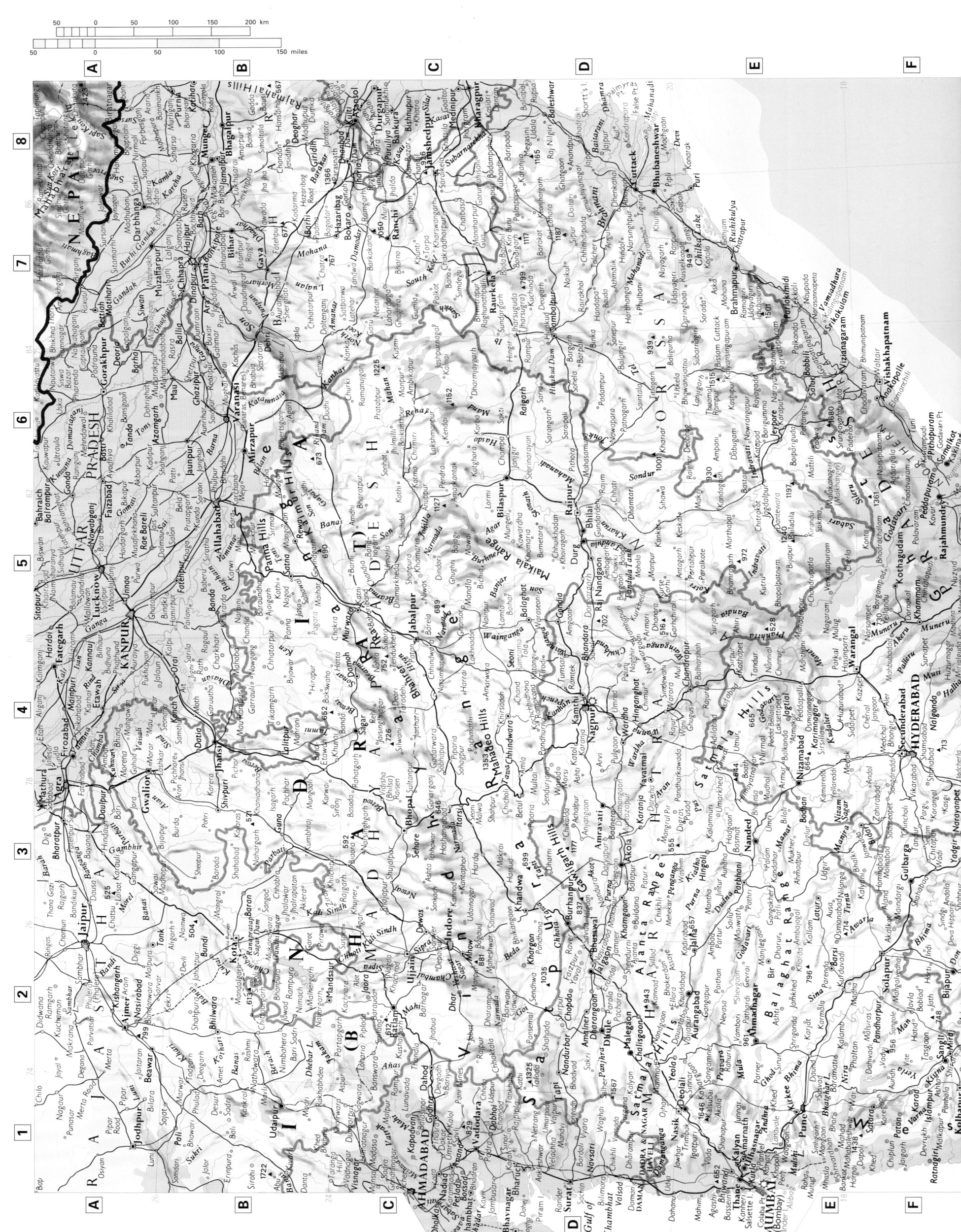

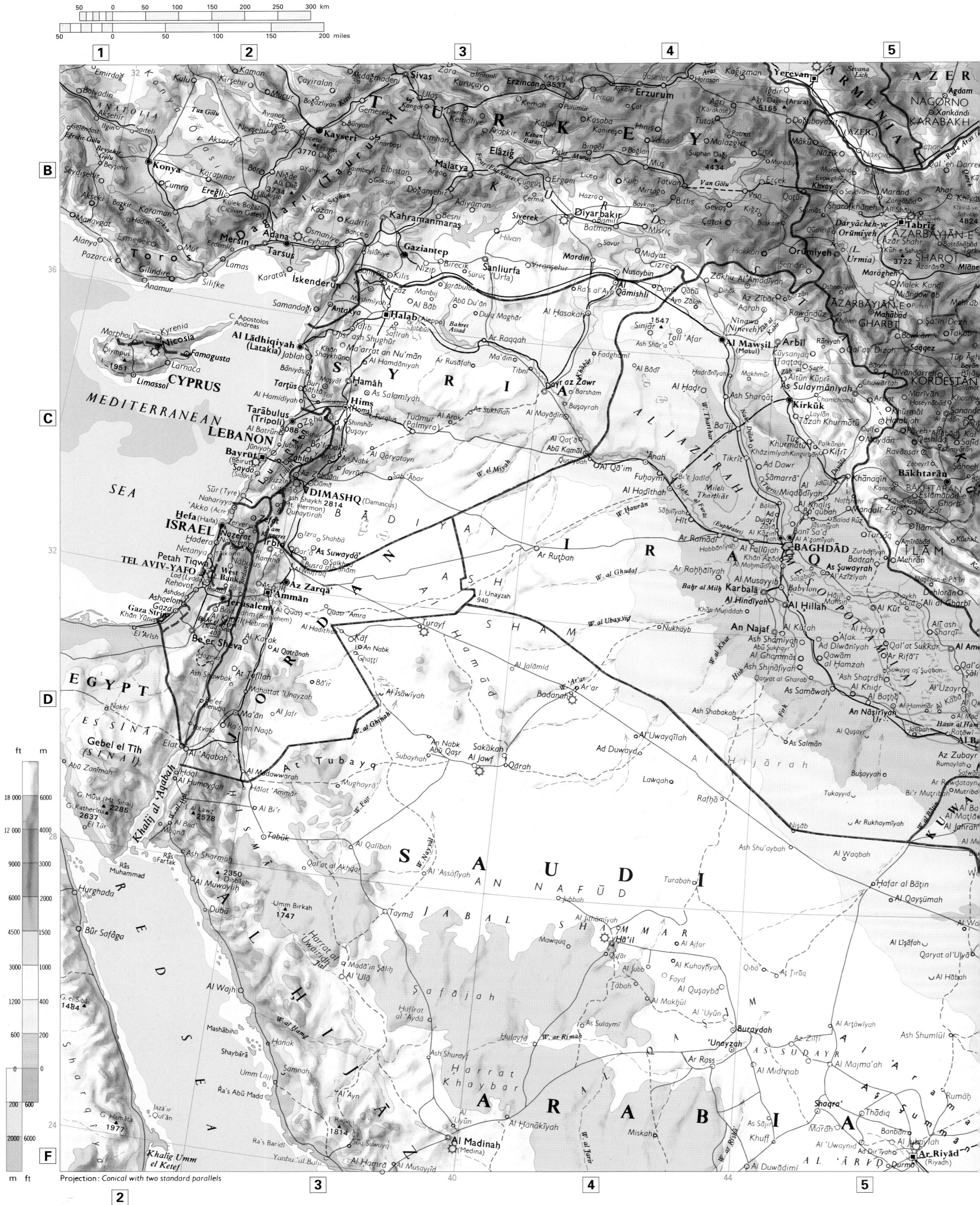

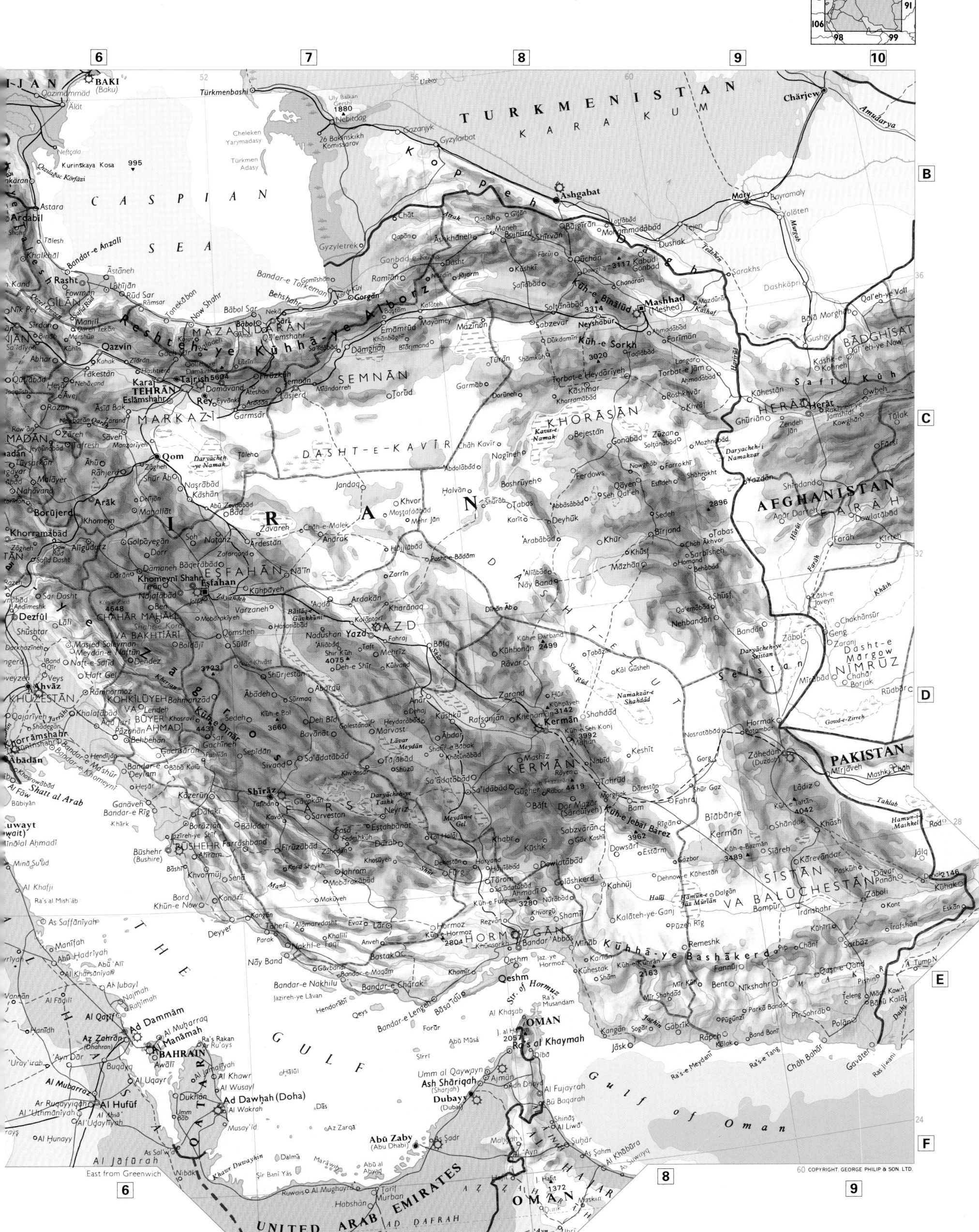

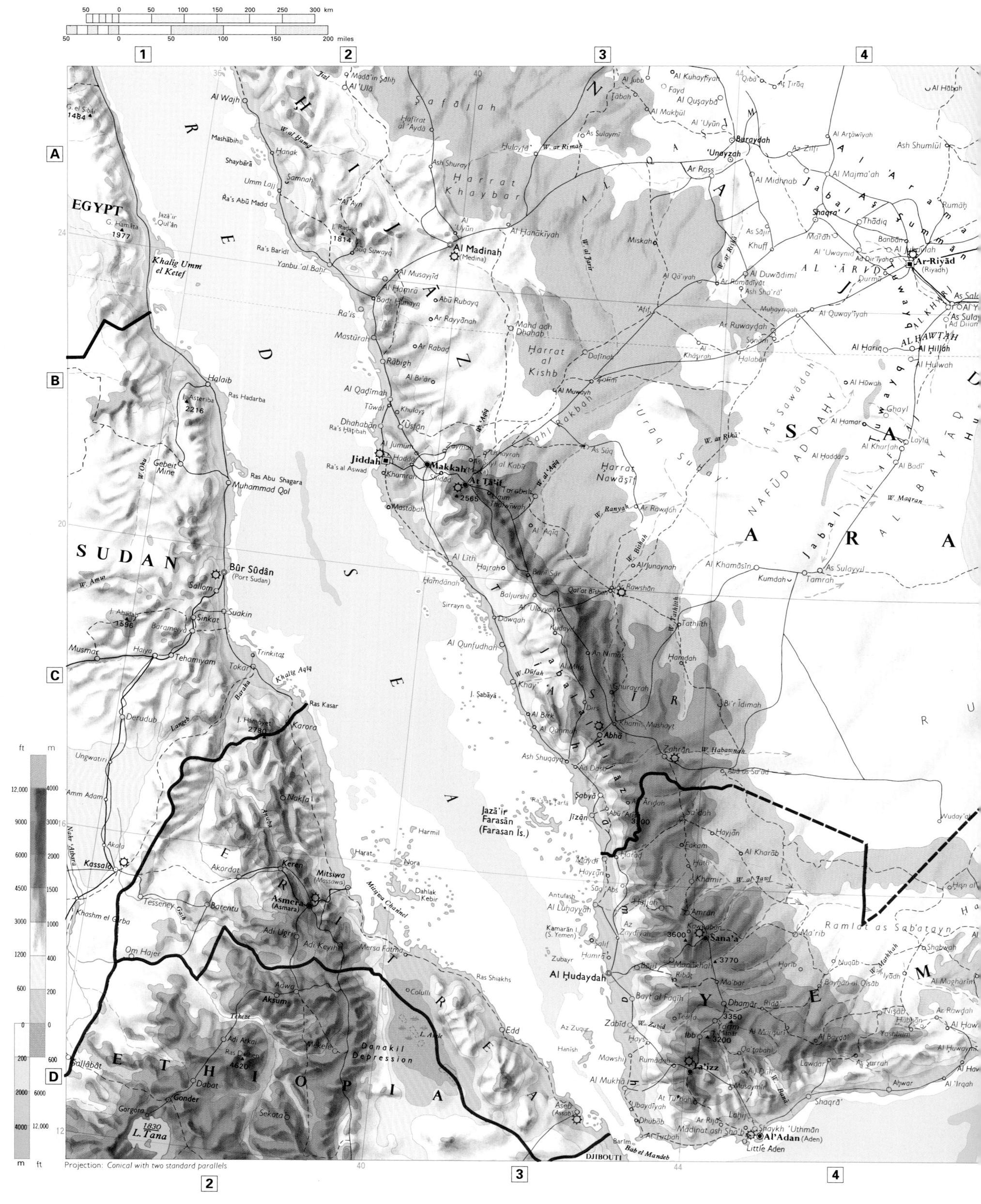

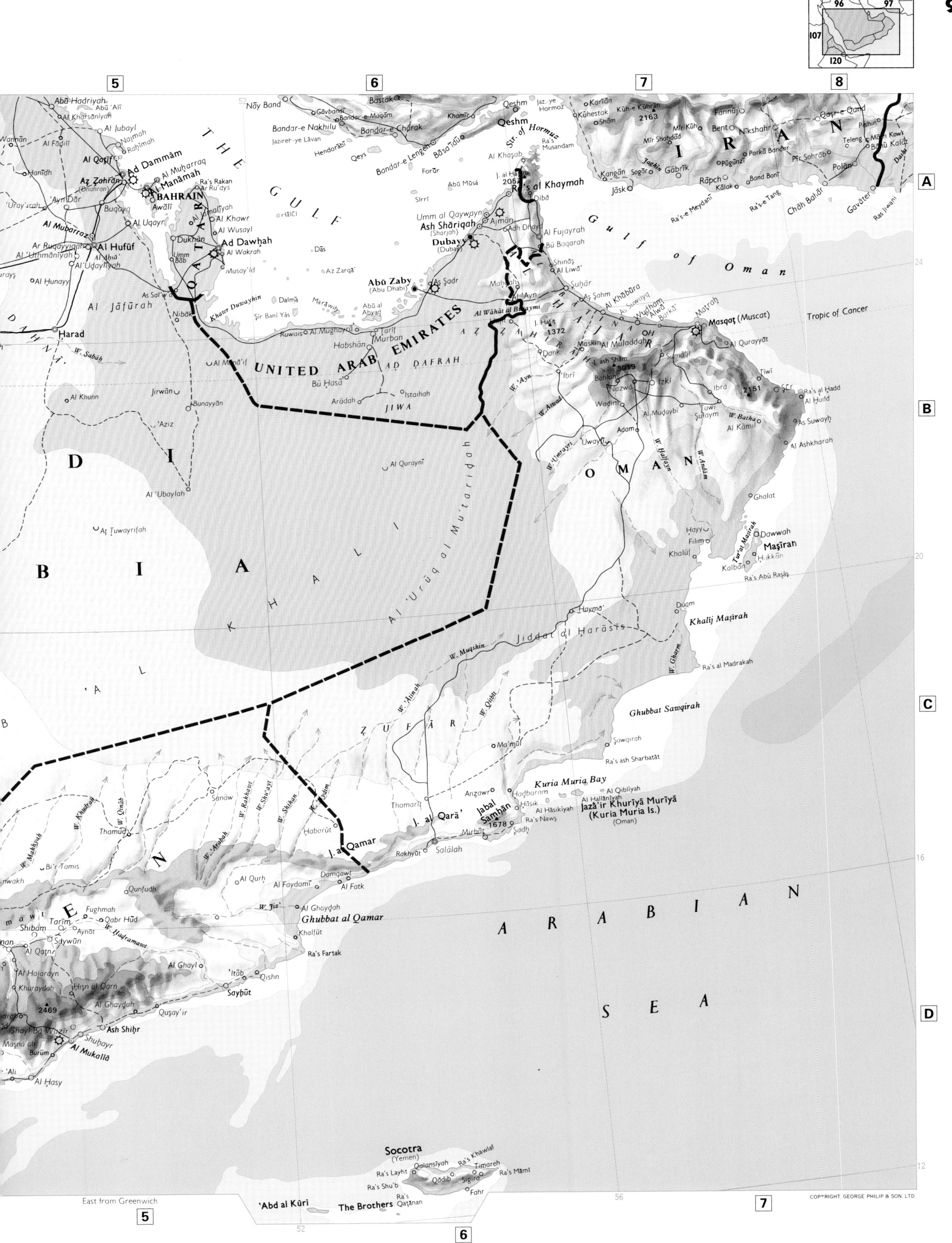

5   6   7   8

Abū Hadriyah
Abū 'Alī
Al Khabsāniyah
Al Jubayl
Warbān
Al Fagili
Najmah
Rahīmah
'Uray'irah
'Aynūn
Az Zahrān (Dhahran)
Al Qatīf
Ad Dammām
Al Muharraq
Manāmah
BAHRAIN
Awālī
Ra's Rakan
Ra's ad'ays
Buqayq
Al Mubarraz
Al 'Uthmānīyah
Ar Ruqayyiqah
Al Hufūf
Al 'Udayliyah
Al Hunayy
'urays
Hanīdh
Harad
Dahnā'
Al Khunn

THE GULF

Nāy Band
Bandar-e Nakhilu
Jazīret-ye Lāvan
Qeys
Hendorābī
Forūr
Bū Mūsā
Sirrī
Az Zarqā'

Gāvbandi
Bandar-e Maqām
Bandar-e Chārak
Bandar-e Lengeh
Bāsa'īdū

Khamīr
Qeshm
Jaz.-ye Hormoz

Str. of Hormuz
Al Khasab
Ra's al Khaymah
Dibā
Umm al Qaywayn
Ajmān
Ash Shāriqah (Sharjah)
Adh Dhayd
Al Fujayrah
Dubayy (Dubai)
Shinās
Al Liwā'
Suhār

Qeshm
Kūhestak
Shām
2163
Mīr Shahdād
Jāchīn
Kangān
Sogar
Jāsk
Ra's-e Meydanī

Kāriān
Kūh-e Kūhrān
Mīr Kūh
Pūgūnzī
Gābrīk
Band Bonī
Ra's-e Tang

Fannūj
Nīkshahr
Parkā Bander
Pīr Sohrāb
Polān
Ra's Tang
Chāh Bahār

IRAN

Qasr-e Qand
Bent
Teleng
Telang
Gāvēter
Gāvāter
Bāhū Kalāt
Ras Jīwānī
Pishīn

A

'Aynūn
As Sal'wā
QATAR
Al Khawr
Al Wusayl
Al Wakrah
Musay'īd
Dukhān
Ad Dawhah
Umm Bāb
Al Uqayr

Dās
Das

Umm al Qaywayn
Aş Şadr
Al 'Ayn
J. al Hafīt
Mahyah
Aş Şahm
Al Khābūra
Aş Şuwayq
Wudham 'Alwā
Burkā
Masqat (Muscat)
Matrah

Tropic of Cancer

24

B

Al Jāfūrah
Nibāk
Khawr Duwayhin
Sīr Banī Yās
Ruwais
Al Mughayra
Tarīf
Murban
Habshān
Bū Hasa
Arādah
Al Ma'nā'if
Abū al Abyad
Dalmā
Marāwih

UNITED ARAB EMIRATES
AD DAFRAH
JIWA

Al Wāhāt al Buraymi
Az Zāhirāh
Dank
Maskin
1372
Al Muladdah
Ibrī
3019
Bahlā
Nazwā
Izkī
Adam
Al Mudaybi
Sulaym

Bidbid
Ibrā
2151
Tiwī
Ra's al Hadd
Al Hadd
Samā'il
Wadi'ra
Tuwī
As Suwayh
Al Kāmil
Ghalat
Al Ashkharah

OMAN

Jirwān
Bunayyān
'Azīz
Al Quraynī
Aţ Ţuwayrifah

R U B   'A L   K H A L I

Al 'Ubaylah

Hayy
Filim
Khalūf
Kalbān

Tuw al Matrah
Dawwah
Hikkān
Masīrah

20

C

B
B I   A

Al Uraug al Mu'tarīqah

W. 'Ayn
W. Amdām
W. Halfayn
W. Aridām

Haymā'
Jiddat al Harāsīs

Duqm
Khalīj Masīrah
Ra's Abū Rasās

Ghalat

Ra's al Madrakah

R U B   'A L   K H A L I

W. Muqshin
W. 'Aimah
W. Qitbī

'A   L
B

ZUFĀR

Ghubbat Sawqirah
Ma'mūl
Sawqirah
Ra's ash Sharbātat

W. Khudrah
W. Qinab
Sānāw
W. Rakhyūt
W. Shu'yt
Thamūd
W. 'Arabah
W. Shihan
W. Aydim

Thamarīt
Anzawr
Haqbaram
Hāsik
Al Hāsikiyah
Al Qibliyah

Kuria Muria Bay
Al Hallānīyah
Jazā'ir Khurīyā Murīyā
(Kuria Muria Is.)
(Oman)

W. Makhūth
Bi'r Tamīs
Thamūd
Habarūt
J. al Qarā'
1678
Mirbāt
Rakhyūt
Salālah
Sādh
Ra's Naws
Jabal Samhān

16

D

mawt
Shibam
Tarīm
Aynāt
Qabr Hūd
W. Hadramawt
Al Qatn
Al Hajarayn
Khuraybah
Hisn al Qarn
2469
Al Ghaydah
Qunfudh
Al Qurh
Al Faydamī
W. Jīz
Al Ghaydah
'Itāb
Qishn
Sayhūt
Ghubbat al Qamar
Khalfūt
Ra's Fartak
Damqawt
Al Fatk

J. al Qamar

Ghubbat al Qamar

A R A B I A N

S E A

Ghayl Bā Wazir
Shuqrah
Al Mukallā
Maşna'ah
Burūm
'Alī
Al Hasy
Qusay'ir
Ash Shihr

East from Greenwich

'Abd al Kūri
The Brothers

Socotra
(Yemen)
Qalansīyah
Ra's Khawlaf
Ra's Layht
Ra's Shu'b
Qādib
Sigiro
Fahr
Timareh
Ra's Mamī

Ra's Qatanan

COPYRIGHT GEORGE PHILIP & SON LTD

5   6   7

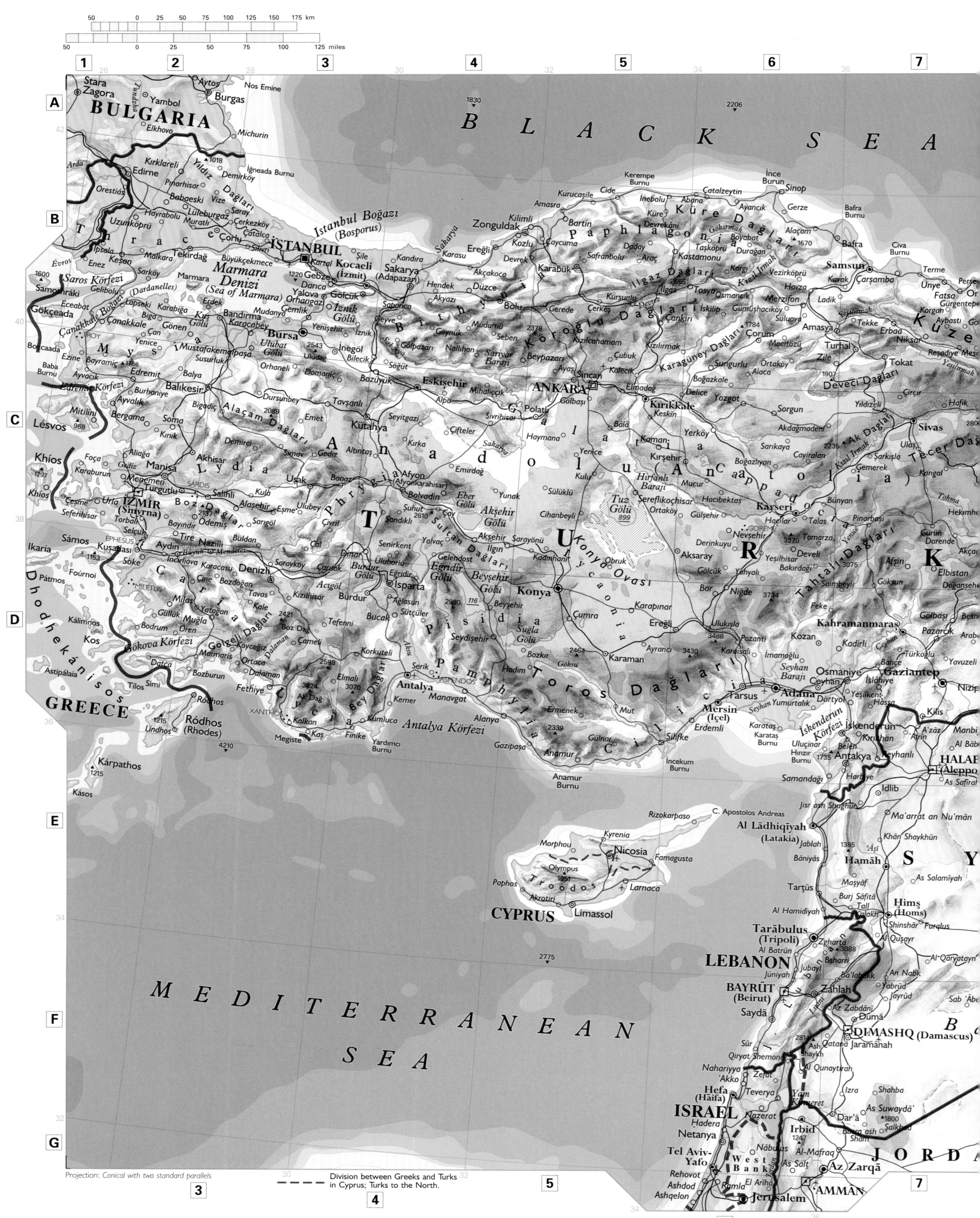

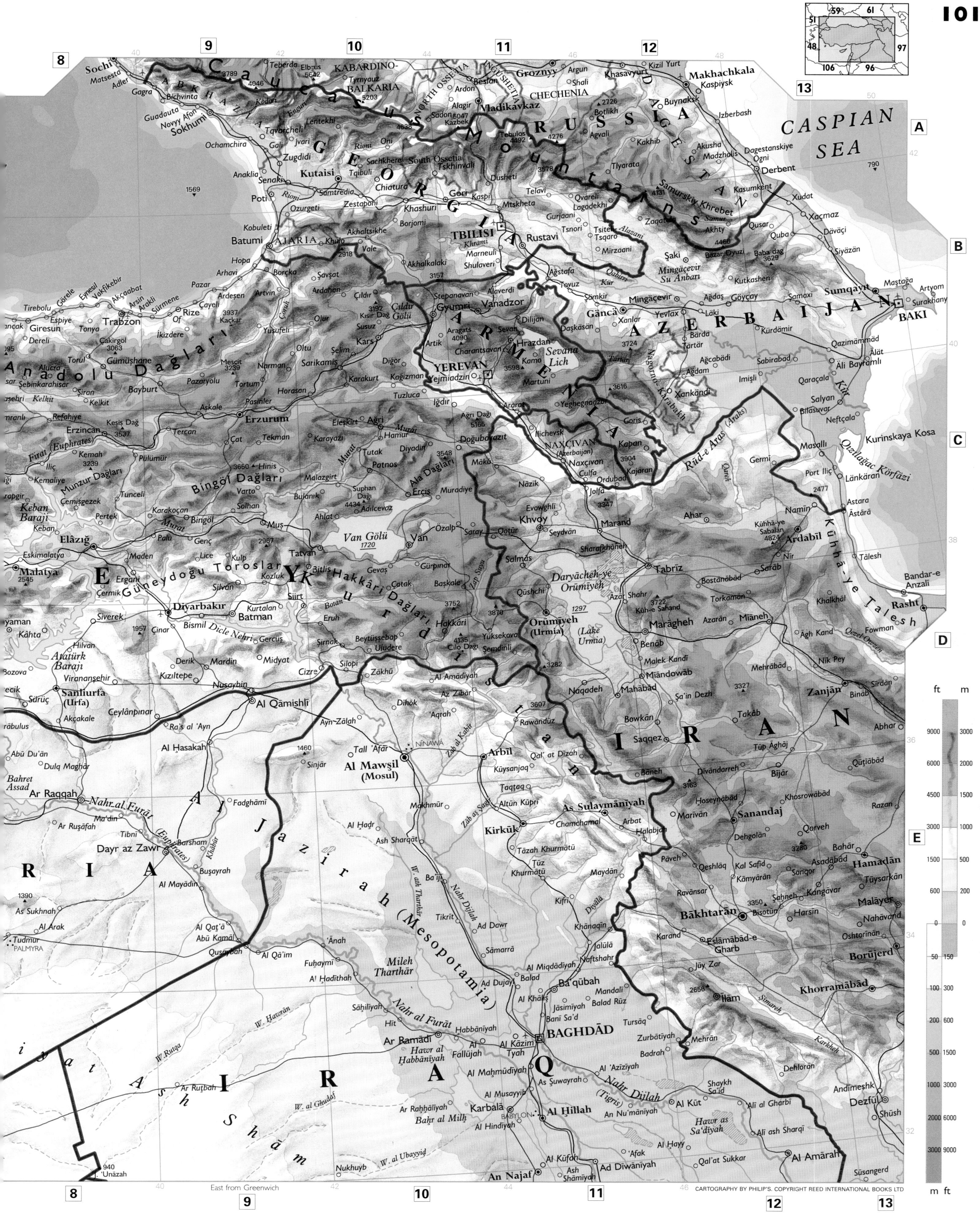

CASPIAN SEA

RUSSIA

GEORGIA

ARMENIA

AZERBAIJAN

TBILISI

YEREVAN

BAKI

Sumqayıt

NAXÇIVAN (Azerbaijan)

Nagorno-Karabakh

IRAN

IRAQ

SYRIA

Al Jazirah (Mesopotamia)

BAGHDAD

Van Gölü 1720

Daryācheh-ye Orūmīyeh (Lake Urmia)

Rūd-e Aras (Araks)

Anadolu Dağları

Güneydoğu Toroslar

Hakkâri Dağları

Bingöl Dağları

Caucasus Mountains

KABARDINO-BALKARIA

NORTH OSSETIA

SOUTH OSSETIA

CHECHENIA

INGUSHETIA

DAGESTAN

ABKHAZIA

AJARIA

KURDISTAN

Kutaisi

Batumi

Poti

Trabzon

Giresun

Erzurum

Erzincan

Elâzığ

Malatya

Diyarbakır

Şanlıurfa (Urfa)

Al Qāmishlī

Al Ḥasakah

Ar Raqqah

Dayr az Zawr

Al Mawşil (Mosul)

Arbīl

Kirkūk

As Sulaymānīyah

Tabrīz

Orūmīyeh (Urmia)

Marāgheh

Sanandaj

Hamadān

Bākhtarān

Rasht

Ardabīl

Zanjān

Khorramābād

Borūjerd

Karbalā

An Najaf

Al Ḥillah

Al Amārah

Makhachkala

Groznyy

Vladikavkaz

Gori

Rustavi

Gyumri

Vanadzor

Gäncä

Mingäçevir

Khvoy

Marand

Kaspiysk

Derbent

East from Greenwich

CARTOGRAPHY BY PHILIP'S. COPYRIGHT REED INTERNATIONAL BOOKS LTD

ft m

m ft

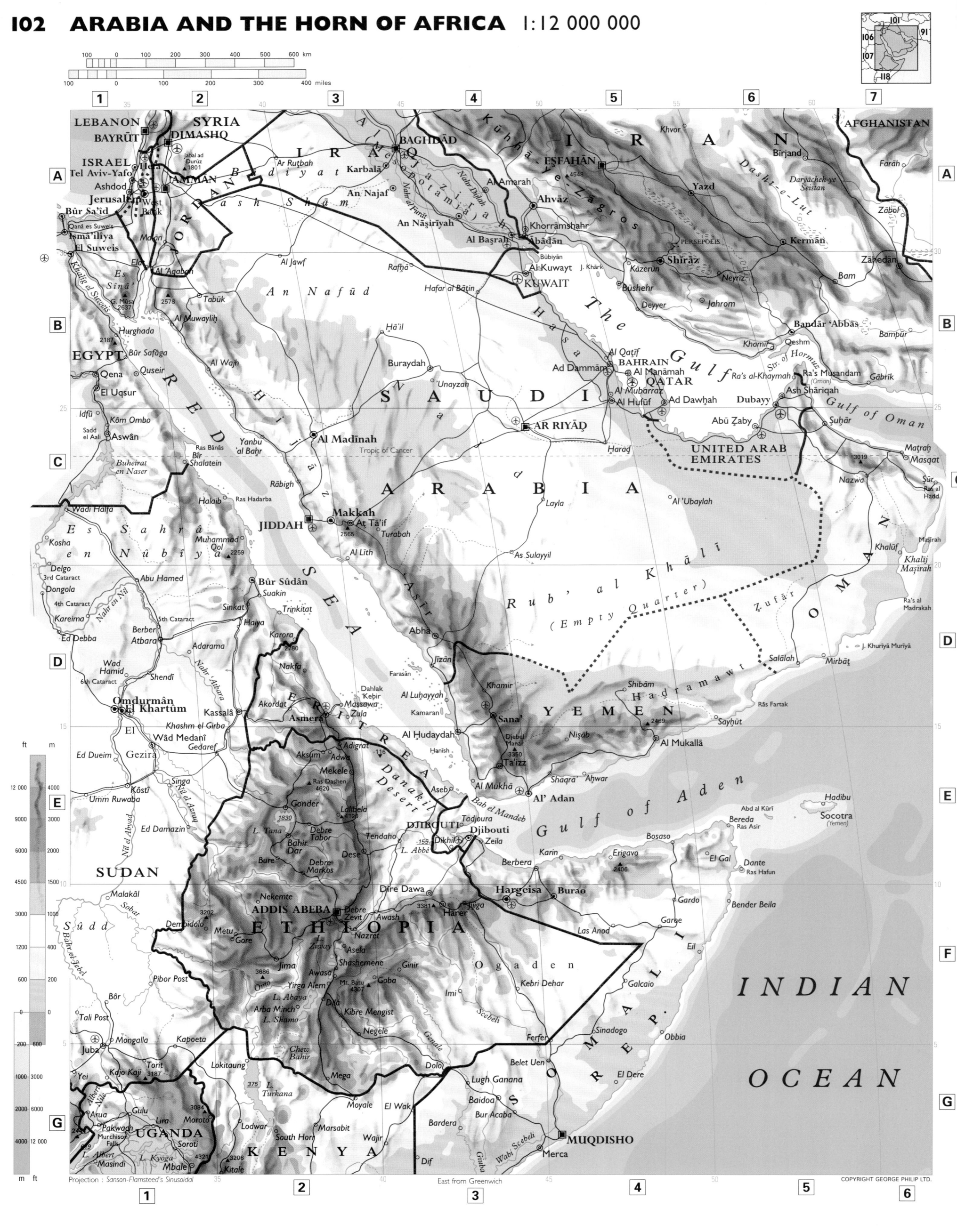

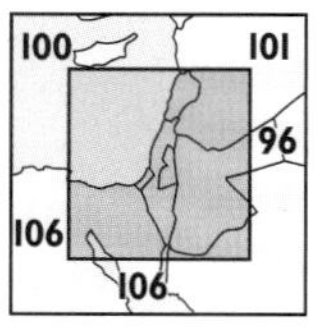

100 101
96
106 106

10 0 10 20 30 40 50 60 70 80 100 km
10 0 10 20 30 40 50 60 miles

1 **2** **3** **4** **5** **6**

Paphos
Episkopi
Episkopi Bay
Limassol
Akrotiri Bay
C. Gata

CYPRUS

M E D I T E R R A N E A N

S E A

Al Ḥamīdiyah
Tall Kalakh
Shinshār
Furqlus
Ḥims (Homs)

ASH SHAMĀL
Ḥalbā
Al Qusayr
Al Qaryatayn

Al Minā'
Ṭarābulus (Tripoli)
Zgharta
Qurnat as Sawdā'
3088
Al Hirmil
Al Buṟayj
2464

Al Batrūn
Jubayl
Qarṭabā
Ibrāhīm
Bsharri
2616
Baʻlabakk
Yabrūd
An Nabk
Biʼr Ghadīr

JABAL LUBNĀN
AL BIQĀ (Bekaa Valley)
2628
Sannīn

BAYRŪT (Beirut)
Bikfayyā
Alayh
Zaḥlah
Khān Abū Shāmat

Ash Shuwayfāt
Ad Dāmūr
1942
J. al Bārūk
Az Zabadānī
Dūmā
Dūmayr

LEBANON

Saydā (Sidon)
Jazzīn
ash Shaykh
DIMASHQ (Damascus)
DIMASHQ

An Nabaṭīyah at Taḥta
Marj ʻUyūn
Dārayyā
Al Kiswah
Al Hājānah

SYRIA

Ṣūr (Tyre)
Qiryat
AL JANŪB
Al ʻArīḍah
Golan Heights
Qoṭanā
Burāq
Aʻwaj

Nahariyya
Me'ona
1197
Al Qunayṭirah
As Sanamayn

ʻAkko (Acre)
Mifraz Hefa
Karmi'el
DARĀ
Ar Rafīd
Shahbā

Hagalil
Zefat
Fiq
Shaykh Miskīn
W. Al Harīr
AS SUWAYDĀ'

Ḥefa (Haifa)
Qiryat Ata
Teverya (Tiberias)
Yam 210
Kinneret
Saham al Jawlān
As Suwaydā'
1800
Sālah

Nazerat (Nazareth)
HAZAFON
Dār'ā
Ad Durūz

Dāliyat el Karmel
Afula
Yarmūk
TEL MEGIDDO
Umm el Fahm
Bet She'an
Irbid
Busrā ash Shām
Salkhad

CAESAREA
Jenin
IRBID
Al Mafraq

Hadera
Shomrōn
Tūbās SAMARIA
Umm ad Darab
Umm al Qittayn

ISRAEL
Netanya
Ṭulkarm
Ailūn
1247
Jarash

HAMERKAZ
Herzliyya
Nāblus
Nahr az Zarqā'
AL BALQĀ'

Benē Beraq
Kefar Sava
SHILO
As Salt

Tel Aviv-Yafo
Petah Tiqwa
Rama Gan
Wādī as Sīr
AMMĀN
Az Zarqā

Bat Yam
Rishon le Ziyyon
Lod
West Bank
Karama
Naʻūr
Azraq ash Shīshān

Yavne
Ramla
Rām Allāh
At Tunayb

Ashdod
Rehovot
El Arīḥā
'AMMĀN

Qiryat Malʼakhi
Bet Shemesh
Jerusalem (Yerushalayim)
(Al Quds)
Maʻdabā

Ashqelon
Qiryat Gat
Bayt Laḥm (Bethlehem)
Yehuda
W. al Haydān
Dhībān

LAKHISH
Al Khalīl (Hebron)
Al Ḥadīthah

Gaza Strip
Gaza
N. Shiqma
Sederot
Az Ẓāhirīyah
403
Arad

Khān Yūnis
Rafah
Be'er Sheva (Beersheba)
Sedom
1305
Al Karak
Al Mazār

Bûr Saʻîd (Port Said)
Bûr Fu'ad
Râs Burûn
El Daheir
Bor Mashash
Dimona
333
W. al Ḥasā
AL KARAK

Khalîg El Tîna
Sabkhet el Bardawîl
HADAROM
Sedom
Bāʼir

Români
Bîr el 'Abd
El 'Arîsh
Bîr Lahfân
Qezi'ot
Sedé Boqér
121
At Ṭafīlah
W. al Māqaʻ

El Qantara
Bîr el Duweidar
Bîr el Garârât
Birein
W. al Ghadaf
Al Qaṭrānah

Wâhid
Bîr Kaseiba
W. el 'Arîsh
Muweilih
Mizpe Ramon
1072
J. ash Shawmarī

Bîr Madkûr
El Quseima
Nijil
Mahattat 'Unayzah

Ismâ'ilîya
SÎNÎ
Bîr Hascna
Sedé Boqér
Ha 'Arava
Rujm Tal'at al Jamālah
1736
W. Abu Safāt

Talâta
G. Yi 'Allaq
1094
Bîr Beida
Hanegev
Bi'r ad Dabbāghāt
PETRA
Qa'el Jafr

Khamsa
El Buheirat el Murrat el Kubra (Great Bitter L.)
Bîr el Thamâda
W. el Brûk
W. Qiraiya
El 'Agrûd
N. Paran
N. Ḥiyyon
Ma'ān
MAʻĀN

Ginefa
Mamarr Mitlâ
Bîr Gebeil Hisn
W. el Sabha
Wâdî el 'Arîsh
El Kuntilla
Ra's an Naqb
Mahattat ash Shīdīyah

EGYPT
Sînâ (Sinai)
948
G. el Kabrît
El Thamad
Bîr Abu Muhammad
'En 'Avrona
Ra's an Māqb
1435
Baṭn al Ghūl

El Suweis (Suez)
Adabiya
Uyûn Mûsa
Nakhl
W. el Agaba
W. el Tamarânî
Bîr al Butayhât
Bi'r al Mārī
Al Mudawwarah

Bîr Bad
Gebel el Tîh
Bîr el Biarât
1592
El Thamad
1435

Ghubbet el Bûs
Râs Matarma
El Wabeira
W. Abu el Gan
Bîr Taba
Al ʻAqabah
SAUDI

Bîr Abu Sanûra
1272
EL SUWEIS
Shibh Jazîrat Sinâ'
Bîr el Heisi
1165
Gulf of Aqaba
Haql
Al Mudawwarah
At Tubayq
ARABIA

JORDAN

ft m
9000 3000
6000 2000
4500 1500
3000 1000
1200 400
600 200
200 600
2000 6000
m ft

Projection: Polyconic
East from Greenwich
CARTOGRAPHY BY PHILIP'S. COPYRIGHT REED INTERNATIONAL BOOKS LTD.

━━━ 1974 Cease Fire Lines

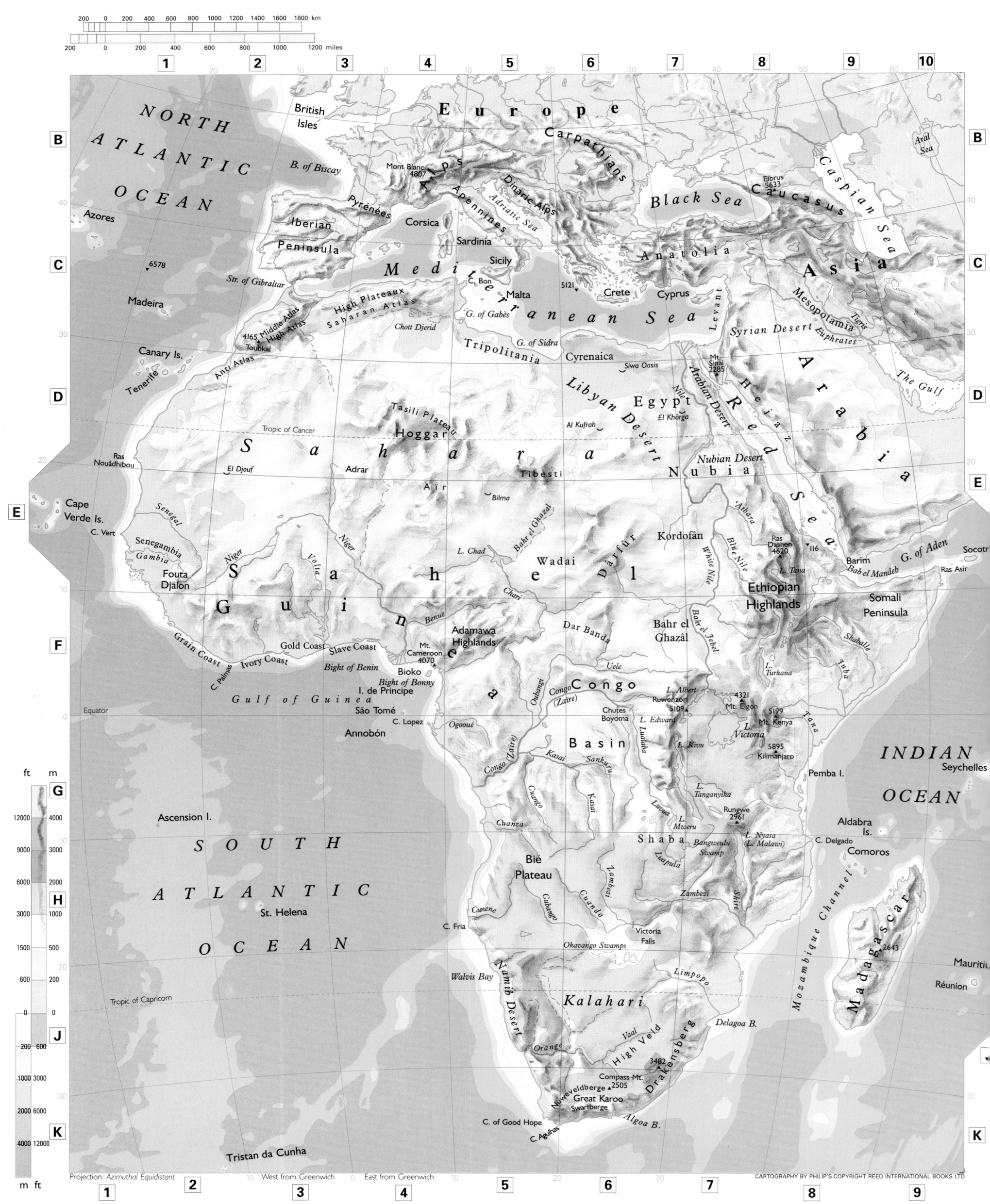

200 0   200 400 600 800 1000 1200 1400 1600 1800 km
200 0   200 400 600 800 1000 1200 miles

1 2 3 4 5 6 7 8 9 10

NORTH
ATLANTIC
OCEAN

UNITED KINGDOM NETH.
LONDON BELG. GERMANY POLAND Warsaw RUSSIA KAZAKSTAN
PARIS Prague CZECH REP. Kiev Volgograd Aral Sea
FRANCE SWITZ. Vienna SLOVAK REP. UKRAINE
B. of Biscay AUSTRIA HUNGARY Odessa
CROATIA ROMANIA Black Sea GEORGIA Caspian Sea
BOS.-HERZ. YUG. BULGARIA ARM. Baku AZER. TURKMEN.
ITALY Ankara TURKEY
PORTUGAL SPAIN Madrid Corsica Rome ALB. MAC. Aleppo TEHRÄN
Lisbon Sardinia GREECE CYPRUS SYRIA Mosul Esfahän
Algiers Annaba Athens Crete Tel Aviv Damascus Baghdäd
Rabat Tétouan Tunis MALTA -Jaffa ISRAEL Jerusalem I R A Q IRAN
Casablanca Fès Constantine Sfax JORDAN Syrian Desert Basra KUWAIT
MOROCCO Tripoli Misrätah Benghazi Alexandria Port Said Suez The Gulf
Marrakesh Chott Djerid CAIRO El Faiyûm SAUDI BAHRAIN
Canary Is. ALGERIA LIBYA Asyût Riyadh QATAR
(Sp.) In Salah EGYPT ARABIA
WESTERN SAHARA Tropic of Cancer Marzûq Aswân Red Medina
Dakhla Al Jawf Wadi Halfa Jedda
Ras Nouâdhibou Fdérik S a h a r a Port Sudan Mecca
MAURITANIA Sea YEMEN
VERDE IS. Nouakchott NIGER CHAD Atbara 'Atbara Mesewa G. of Aden
St-Louis Tombouctou Agadès Omdurmân Khartoum ERITREA Asmera Socotra
Praia Senegal L. Chad Abéché SUDAN Wäd Medani DJIBOUTI (Yemen)
C. Vert Niger Niamey El Fâsher Djibouti Ras Asir
Dakar SENEGAL MALI Kano El Obeid White Nile Berbera
GAMBIA Banjul BURKINA Maiduguri Ndjamena Blue Nile Addis Ababa Harer
GUINEA Bamako FASO Ouagadougou NIGERIA Chari L. Tana ETHIOPIA
BISSAU Bissau Bobo Abuja Wau Bahr el Jebel Shabelle
Conakry GUINEA Dioulasso BENIN Benue CENTRAL L. Turkana SOMALI REP.
Freetown SIERRA IVORY GHANA Ibadan Enugu AFRICAN REP. Mogadishu
LEONE COAST Bouaké Kumasi TOGO Lagos Bangui Kisangani KENYA Juba
Monrovia Yamoussoukro Lomé CAMEROON Ouham L. Albert UGANDA Kampala Kismayu
LIBERIA Abidjan Accra Porto Douala Yaoundé Congo Mbandaka L. Edward Kisumu Nairobi
Sekondi- Novo Port Malabo (Zaïre) RWANDA L. Mombasa
Takoradi Bight of Benin Harcourt EQUATORIAL GABON CONGO Kigali Victoria INDIAN
Gulf of Guinea GUINEA Libreville (DEM. REP. OF THE) L. Kivu BURUNDI SEYCHELLES
Equator SÃO TOMÉ & PRINCIPE C. Lopez Kasai Bujumbura OCEAN
Annobón Pointe-Noire Brazzaville Zaïre TANZANIA Zanzibar
CABINDA Kinshasa Kananga Dodoma Dar es Salaam Aldabra Is.
(Angola) Matadi Cuango L. Tanganyika C. Delgado COMOROS
Ascension I. Luanda L. Mweru L. Malawi Mayotte Antsiranana
(U.K.) Likasi MALAWI (Fr.)
SOUTH ANGOLA Lubumbashi Lilongwe Moçambique Mahajanga
Lobito ZAMBIA Ndola MOZAMBIQUE
ATLANTIC Namibe Huambo Lusaka Blantyre Zambezi Toamasina
St. Helena Cunene ZIMBABWE Livingstone Harare Beira MADAGASCAR Antananarivo
(U.K.) C. Fria Bulawayo Limpopo Fianarantsoa MAURITIUS
OCEAN NAMIBIA BOTSWANA Réunion
Windhoek (Fr.)
Tropic of Capricorn Gaborone Pretoria Maputo
Johannesburg Mbabane SWAZ.
Kimberley Vaal Maseru Durban
SOUTH AFRICA LESOTHO East
Cape Town London
C. of Good Hope Port Elizabeth
C. Agulhas

Tristan da Cunha
(U.K.)

Projection: Azimuthal Equidistant West from Greenwich East from Greenwich ● Dakar Capital Cities

CARTOGRAPHY BY PHILIP'S. COPYRIGHT REED INTERNATIONAL BOOKS LTD

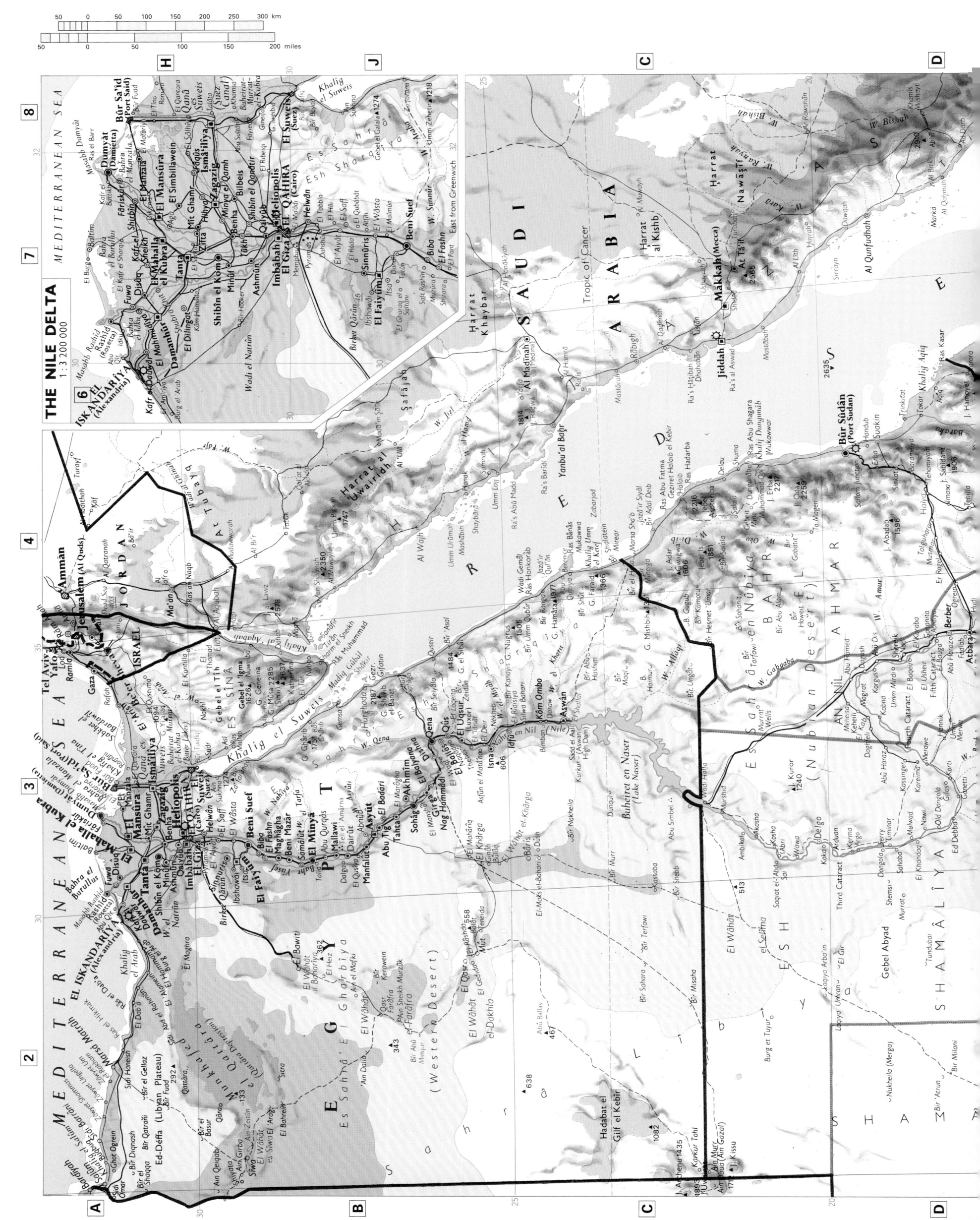

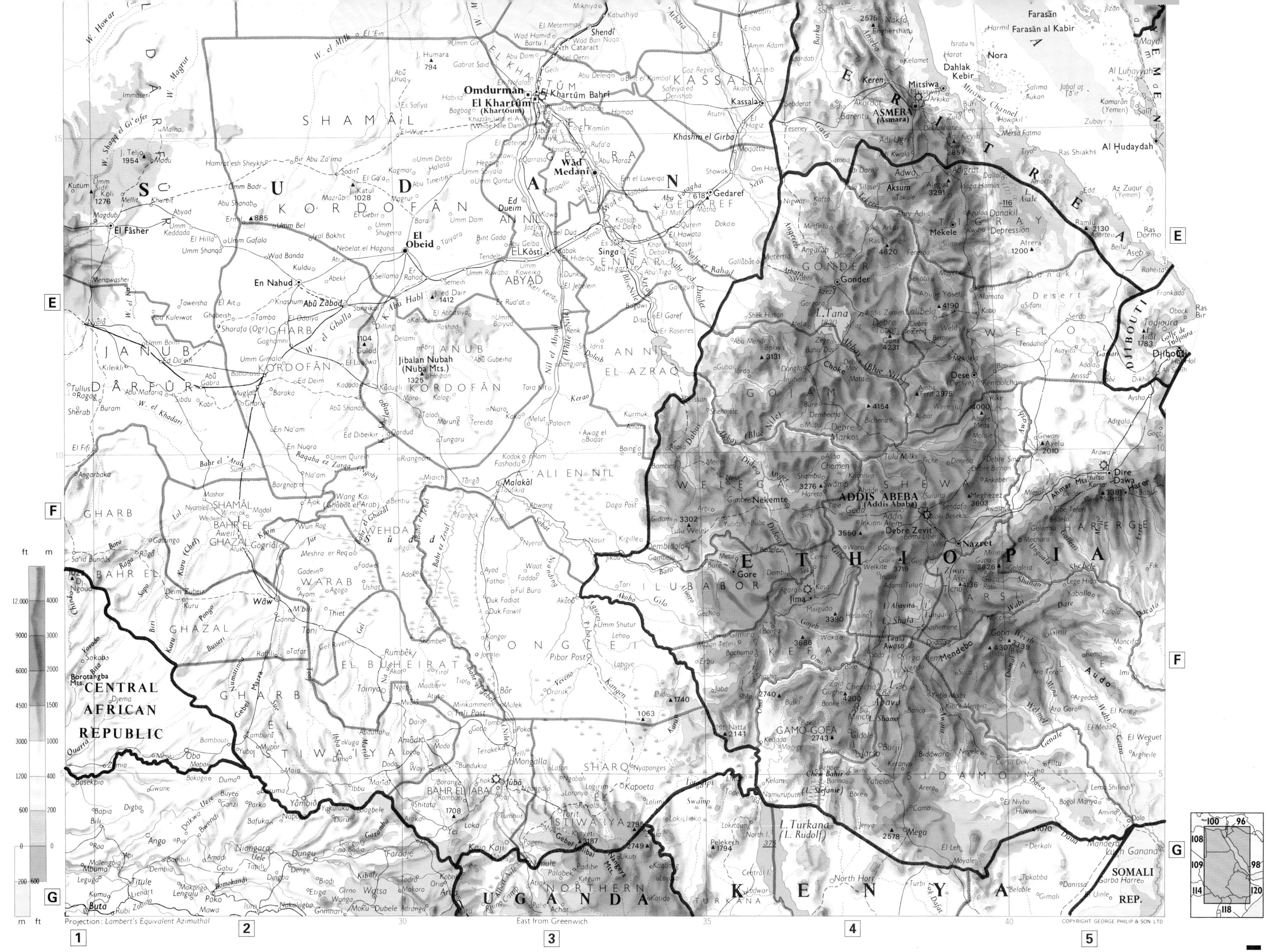

YEMEN

ERITREA

ASMERA (Asmara)
Keren
Mitsiwa

DJIBOUTI
Djibouti

E T H I O P I A

ADDIS ABEBA
(Addis Abäba)
Debre Zeyit
Nazret
Dese
Gonder
Aksum
Makele
L. Tana

Jima
Nekemte
Gore

SUDAN

Omdurman
El Khartûm (Khartoum)
Wad Medani
Kassala
Gedaref
El Obeid
En Nahud
El Fasher
El Kosti
Ed Dueim

KORDOFAN
DARFUR
KASSALA
GEDAREF
BAHR EL GHAZAL

KENYA

L. Turkana
(L. Rudolf)

UGANDA

NORTHERN

SOMALI REP.

CENTRAL AFRICAN REPUBLIC

SOMALI

Juba

East from Greenwich

Projection: Lambert's Equivalent Azimuthal

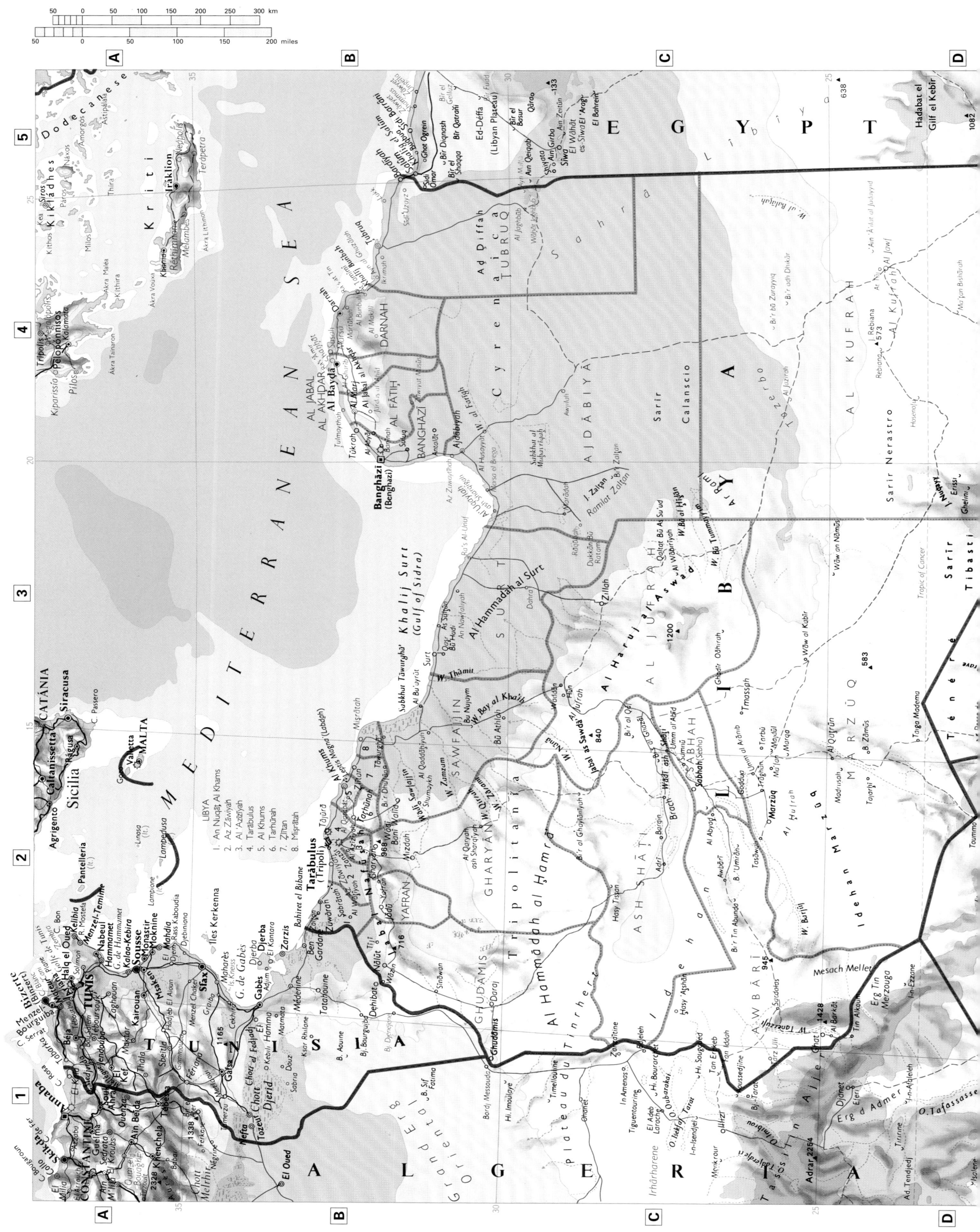

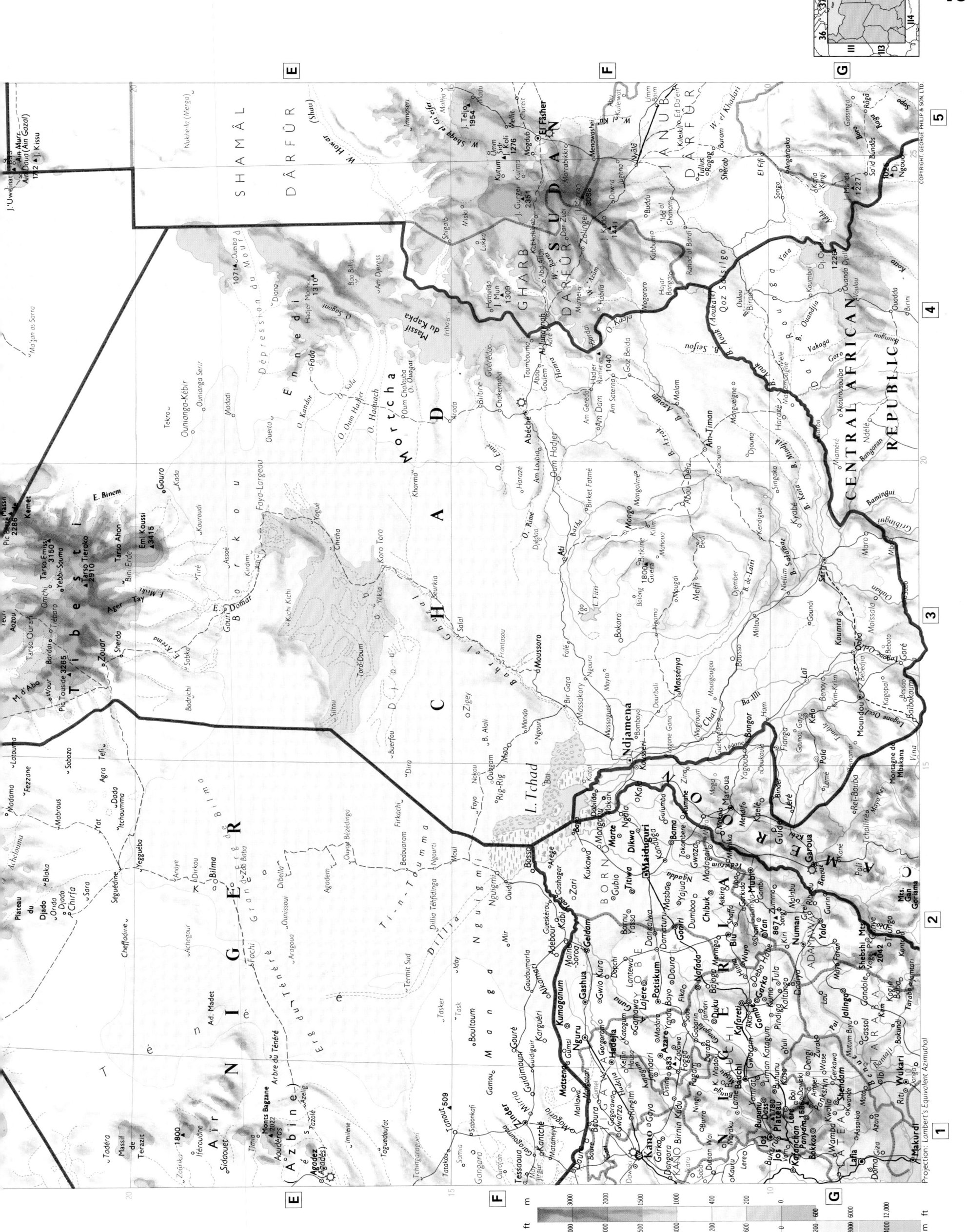

Projection: Lambert's Equivalent Azimuthal

COPYRIGHT GEORGE PHILIP & SON, LTD.

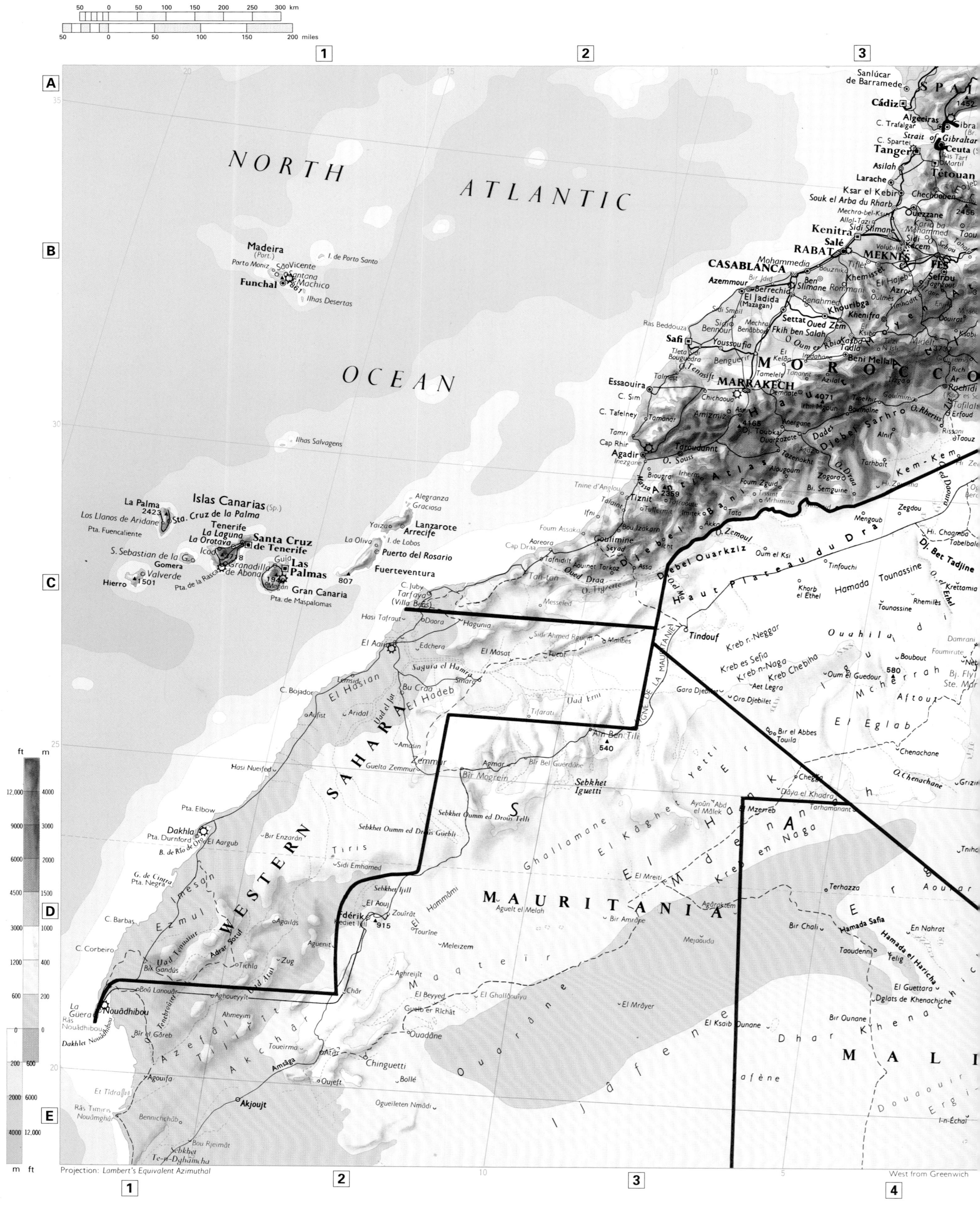

Projection: Lambert's Equivalent Azimuthal

West from Greenwich

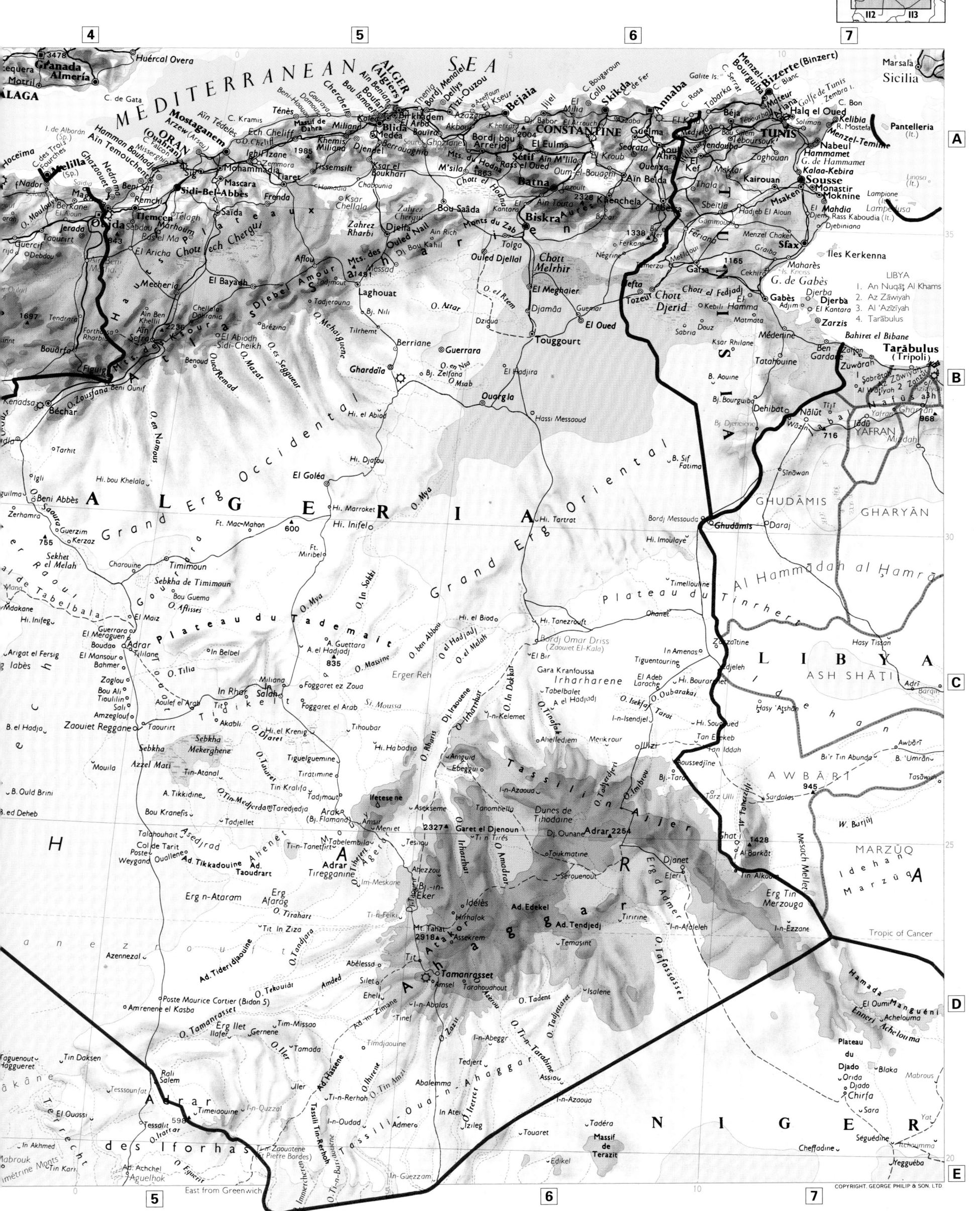

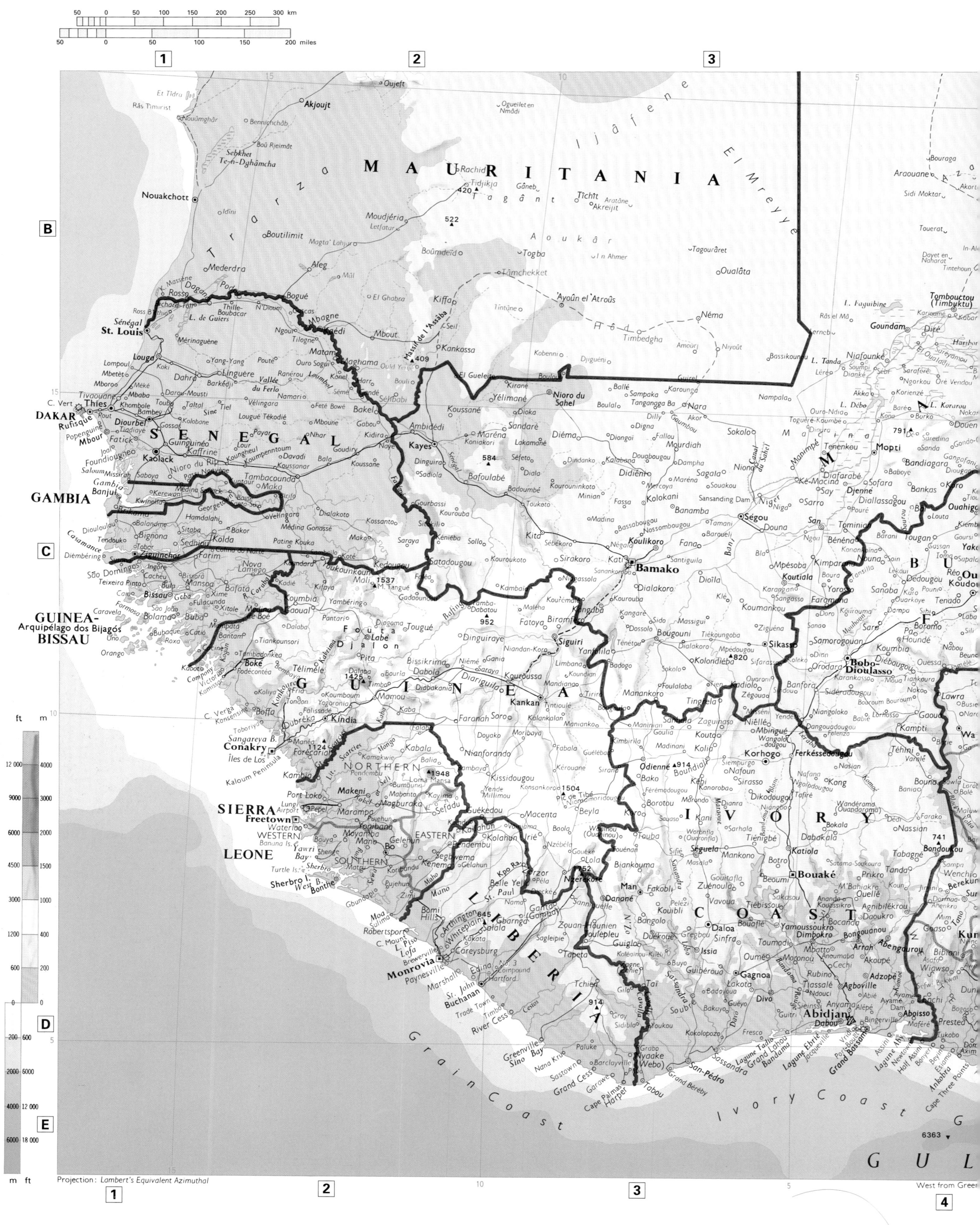

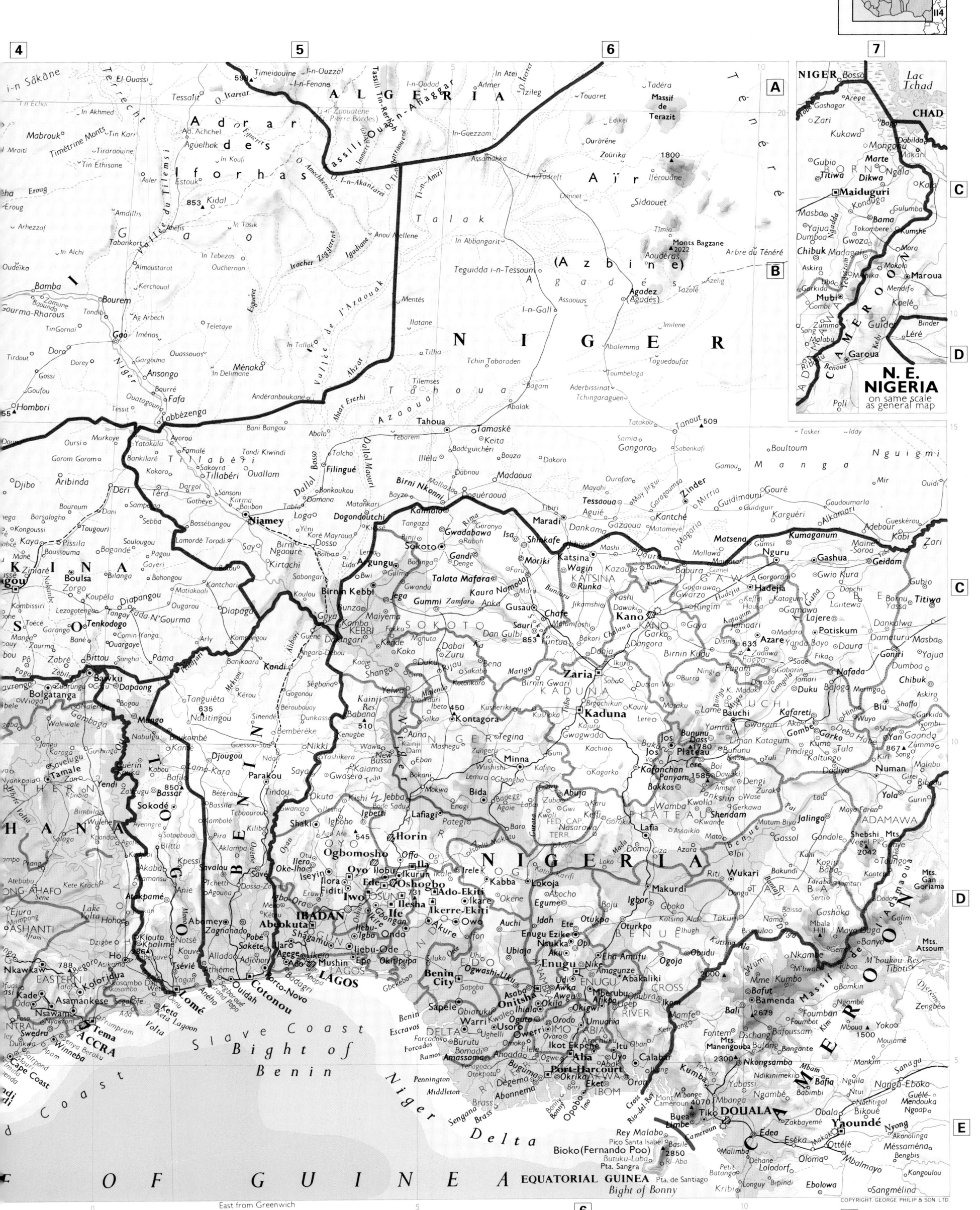

N. E. NIGERIA
on same scale
as general map

COPYRIGHT GEORGE PHILIP & SON, LTD

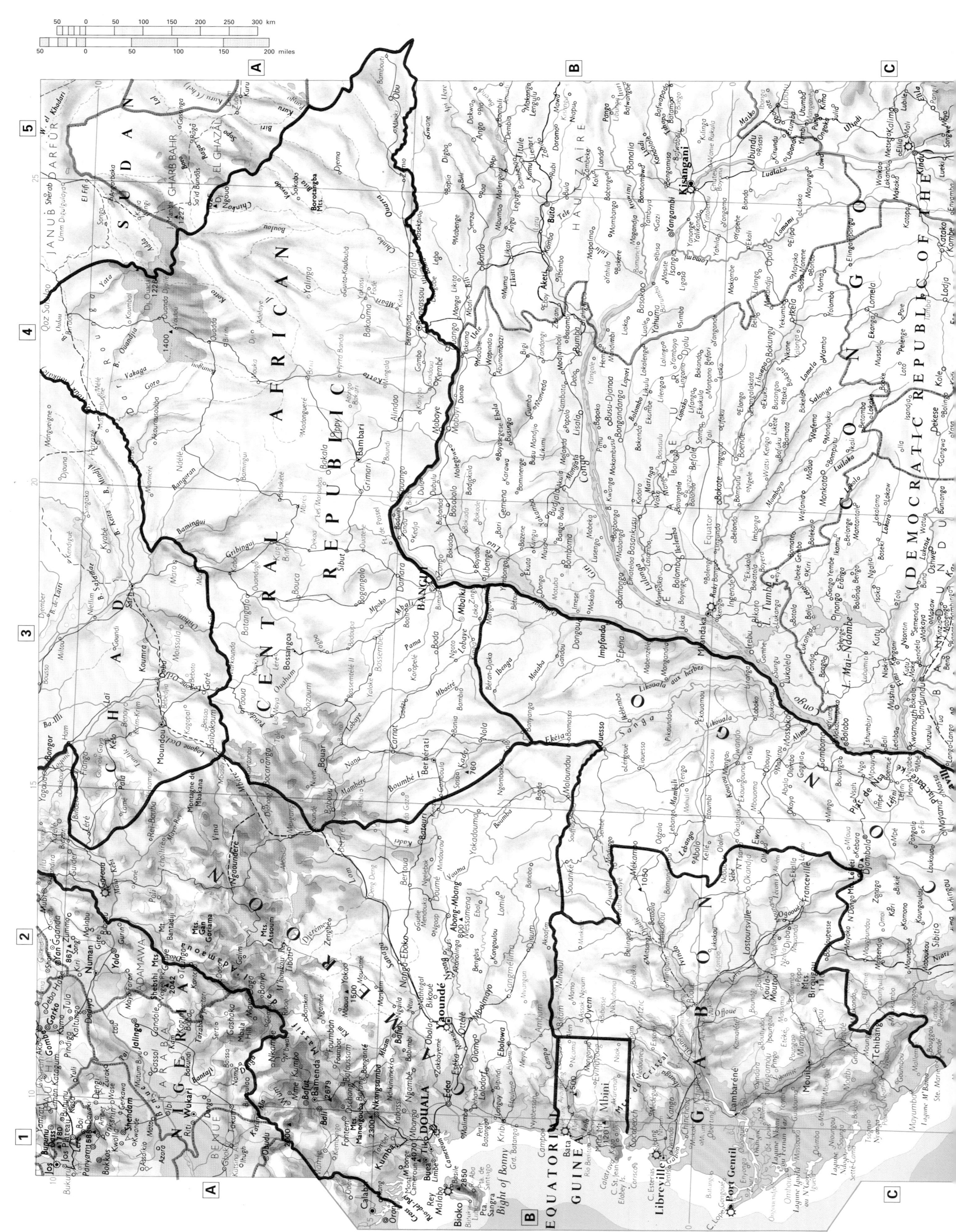

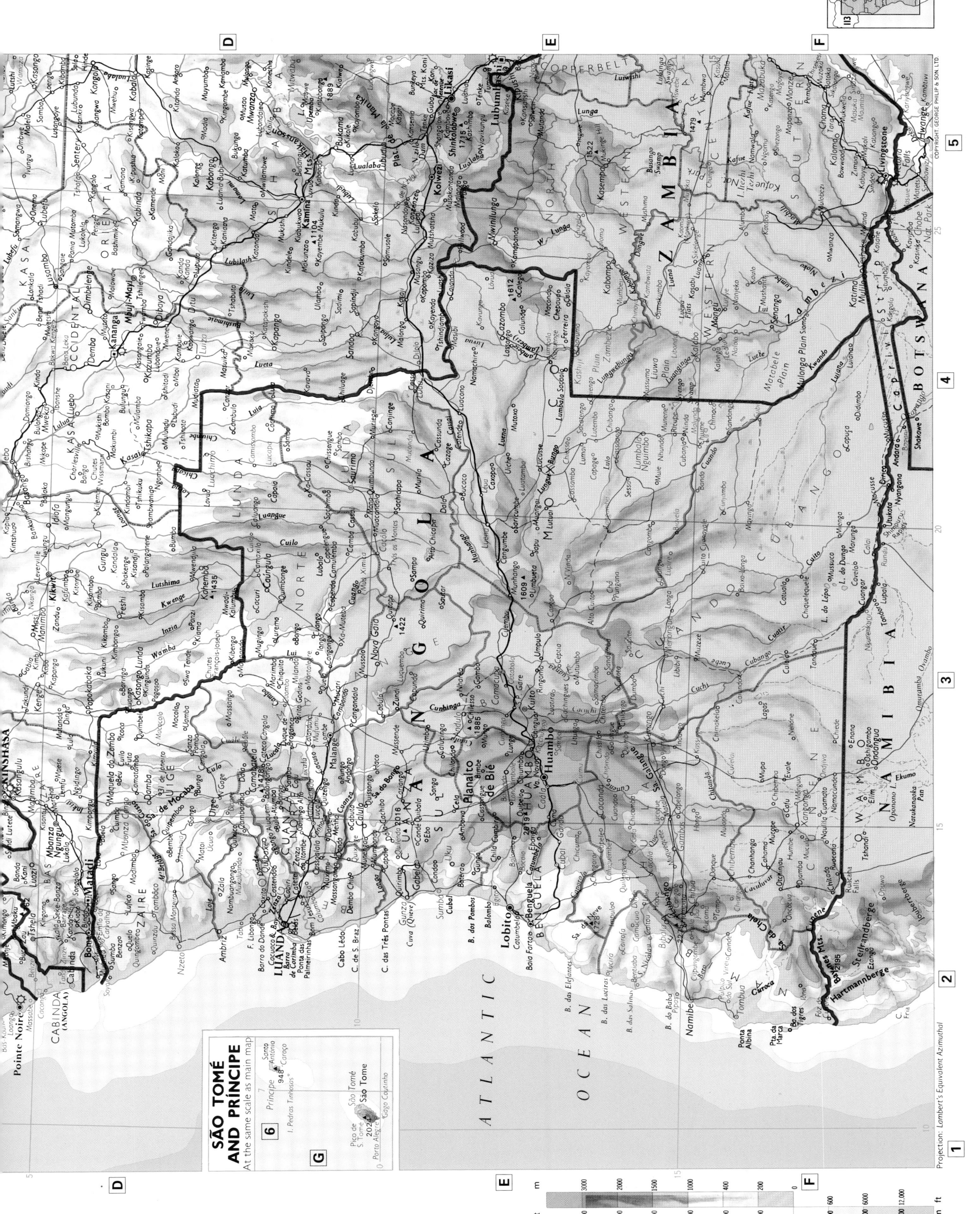

SÃO TOMÉ AND PRÍNCIPE
At the same scale as main map.

Projection: Lambert's Equivalent Azimuthal

COPYRIGHT GEORGE PHILIP & SON, LTD.

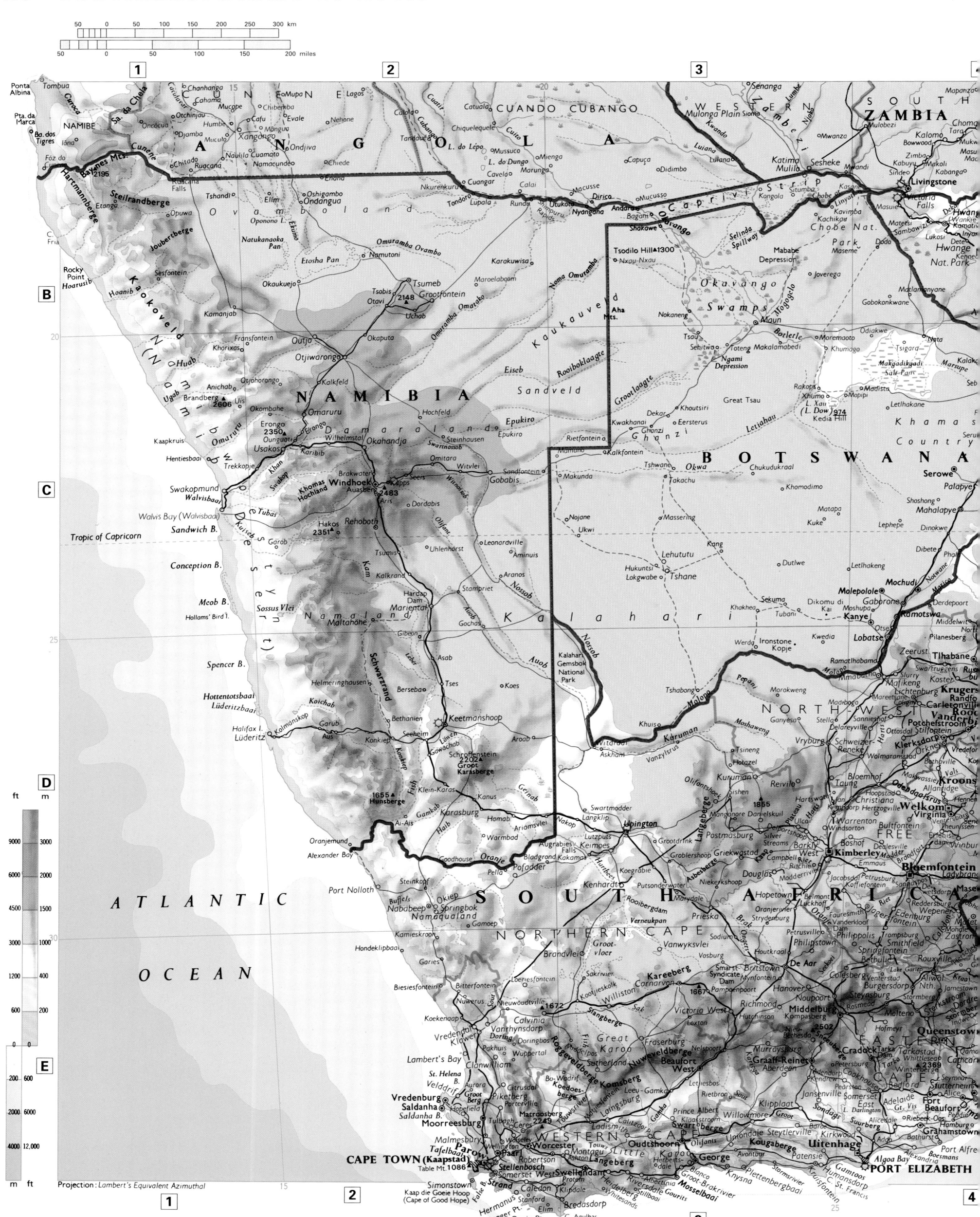

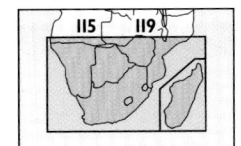

MADAGASCAR

On same scale as General Map

COPYRIGHT. GEORGE PHILIP & SON. LTD.

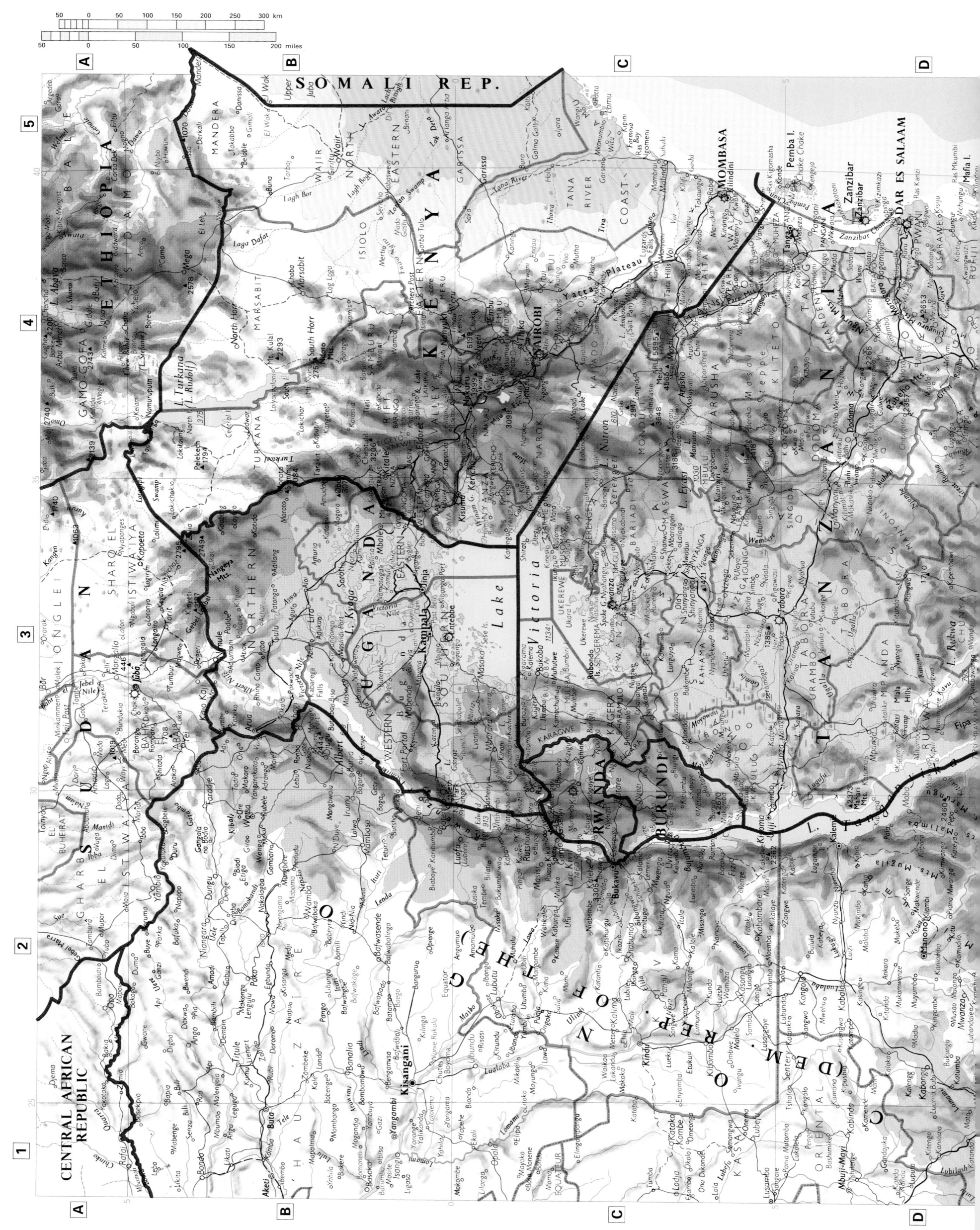

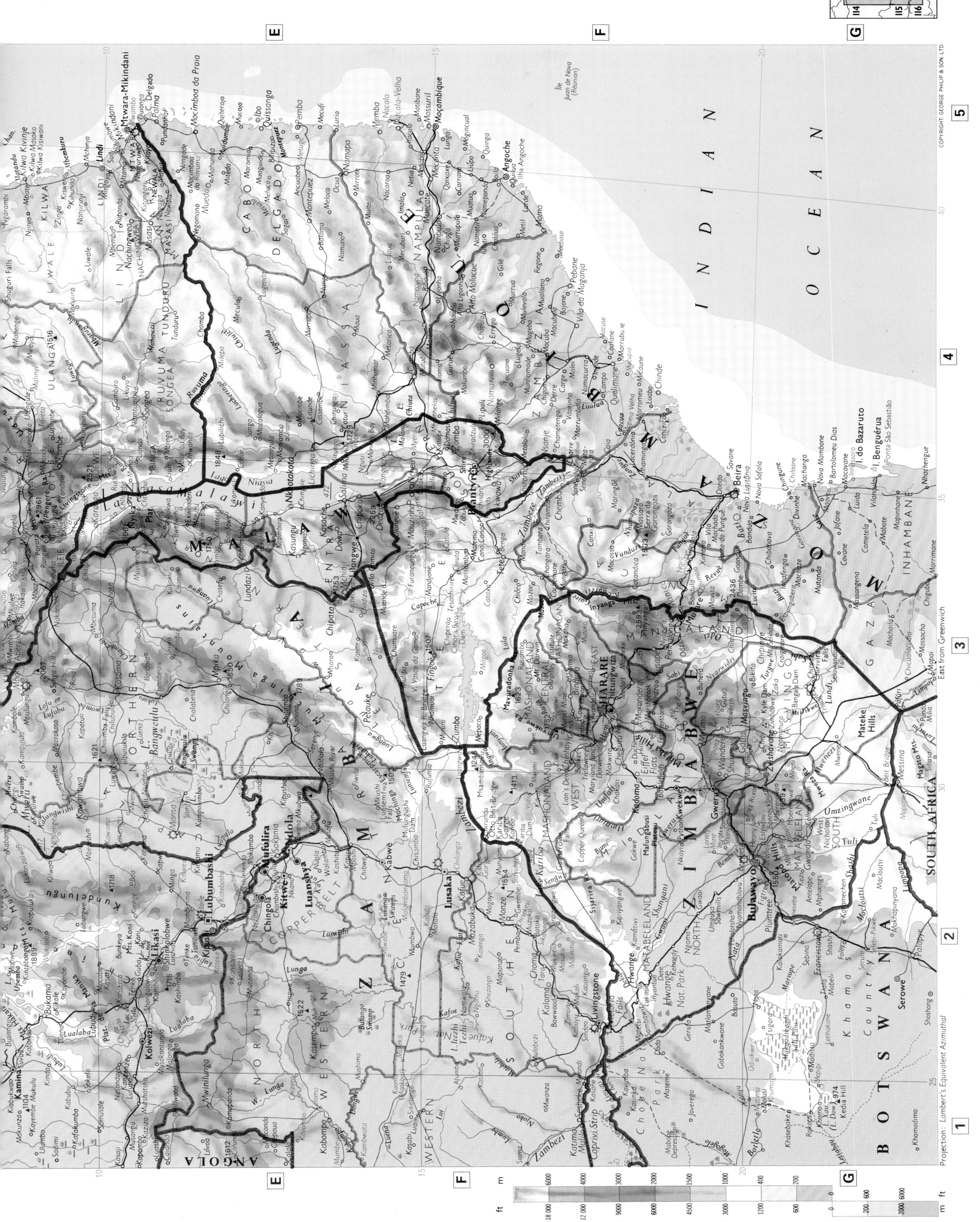

Projection: Lambert's Equivalent Azimuthal

East from Greenwich

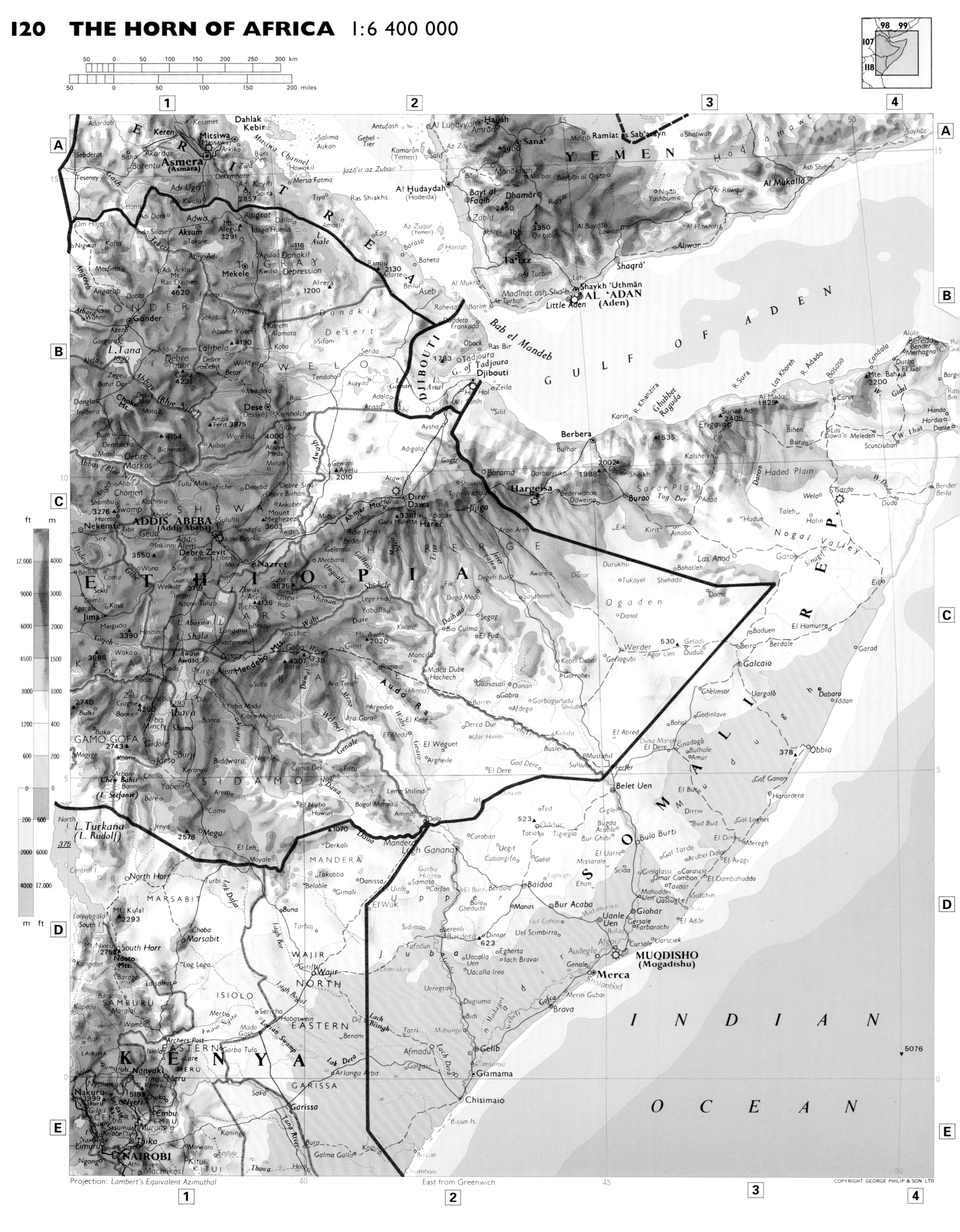

Projection: Lambert's Equivalent Azimuthal   East from Greenwich

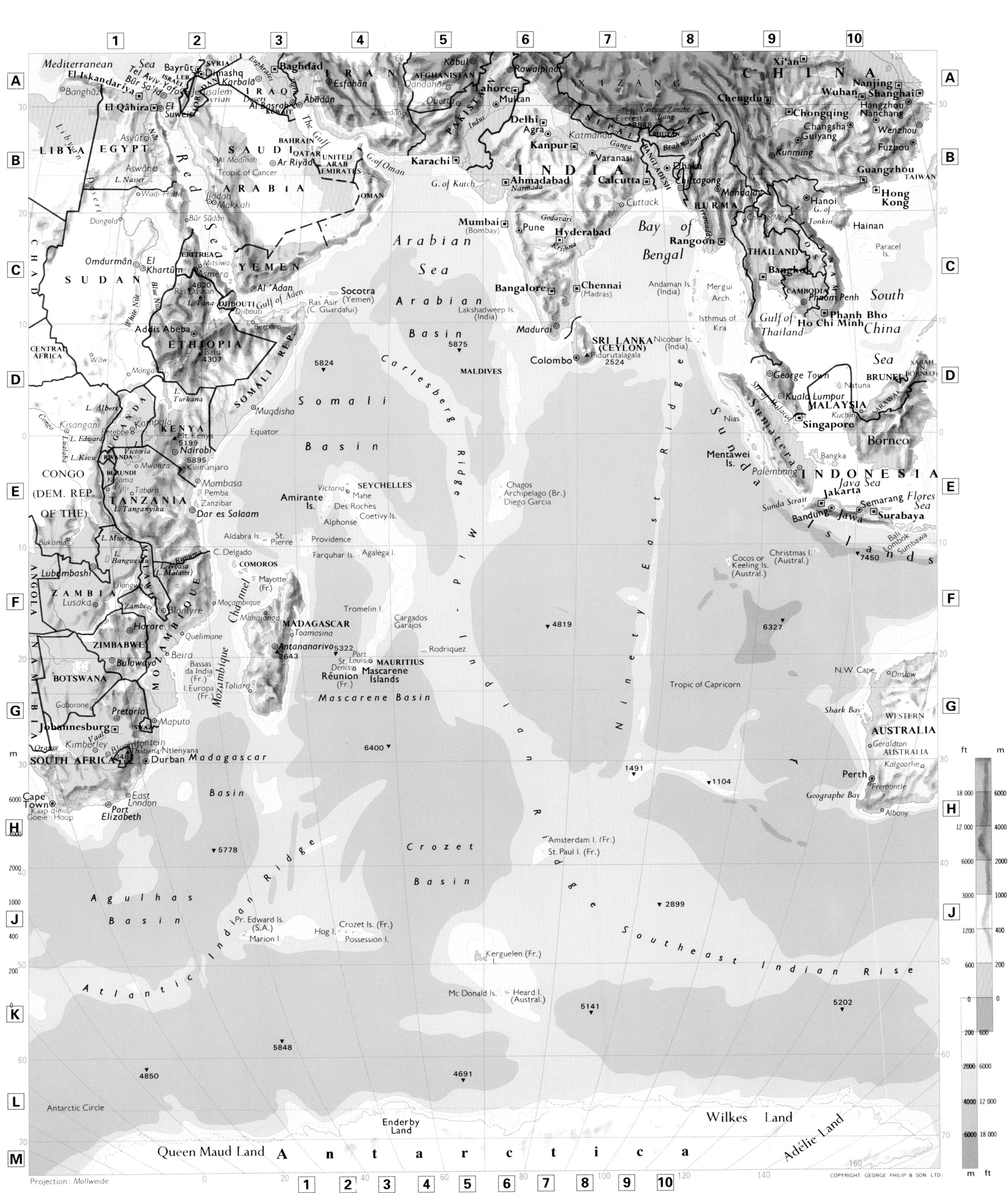

Projection: Mollweide

Projection : Lambert's Equivalent Azimuthal

M e l a n e s i a

³ Bougainville
bi
ch.
New Georgia
Choiseul
Santa Isabel
SOLOMON
ISLANDS
Malaita
Honiara ▲2331
Guadalcanal
San Cristóbal
Rennell
▼ 7223

NAURU

Tamana

K I R I B A T I

Baker
Equator

Namumea

Abariringa
Phoenix Is.

Carondelet

TUVALU
(Ellice Is.) Funafuti ○ Funafuti
Nukulaelae

Tokelau Is.
(N.Z.)

ea

Santa Cruz Is.
Fataka

Rotuma

Banks Is.

Espíritu Santo ▲1880
VANUATU
(New Hebrides)
Malakula
Port-Vila ○ Efate

Mata-Utu ○ Uvea
Wallis & Futuna
Horn (Fr.)

WESTERN
SAMOA
Savai'i ○ ○ Apia
Upolu
Tutuila

American Samoa

Niuafo'ou

Chesterfield Is.

New Caledonia (Fr.)
▲ 1628
Noumea ○

Loyalty Is.
▼ 7569

Vanua Levu
Viti Levu
▲1324 ○ Suva
FIJI
Lau Is.

Vavau Is.
Ha'apai Is.
TONGA

○ Niue (N.Z.)

Matthew
Ceve-i-Ra

Nuku'Alofa ○
Tongatapu Is.

Cook Is. (N.Z.)

P A C I F I C
▼ 5303
O C E A N

Tonga Trench
10 882 ▼

Tropic of Capricorn

Norfolk (Austr.)

Lord Howe (Austr.) ▼ 734

Kermadec Is. (N.Z.)
Raoul

Kermadec Trench
10 047 ▼

asman Sea

North C.
Kaitaia
Whangarei
Auckland ○ North Island
Hamilton
Bay of Plenty
New Plymouth Rotorua
Raupehu 2797
Wanganui
NEW ZEALAND
Gisborne
Napier

International Date Line

▼ 5267

Palmerston North
Wellington
Nelson Cook Strait
Blenheim
Greymouth
South Island
Southern Alps
Mt.Cook 3753
Christchurch
Wakatipu
Timaru
Invercargill Dunedin
Stewart

Chatham (N.Z.)

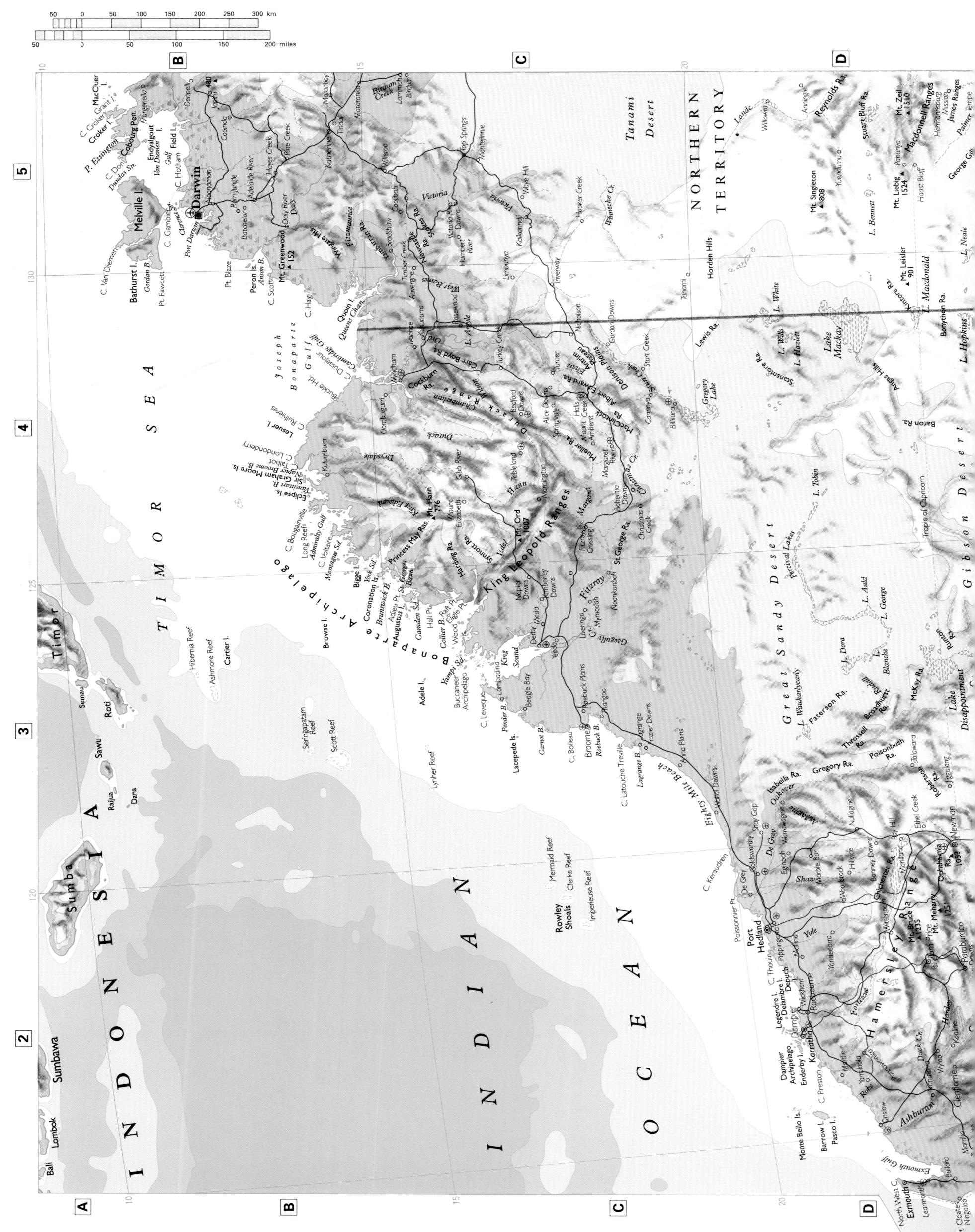

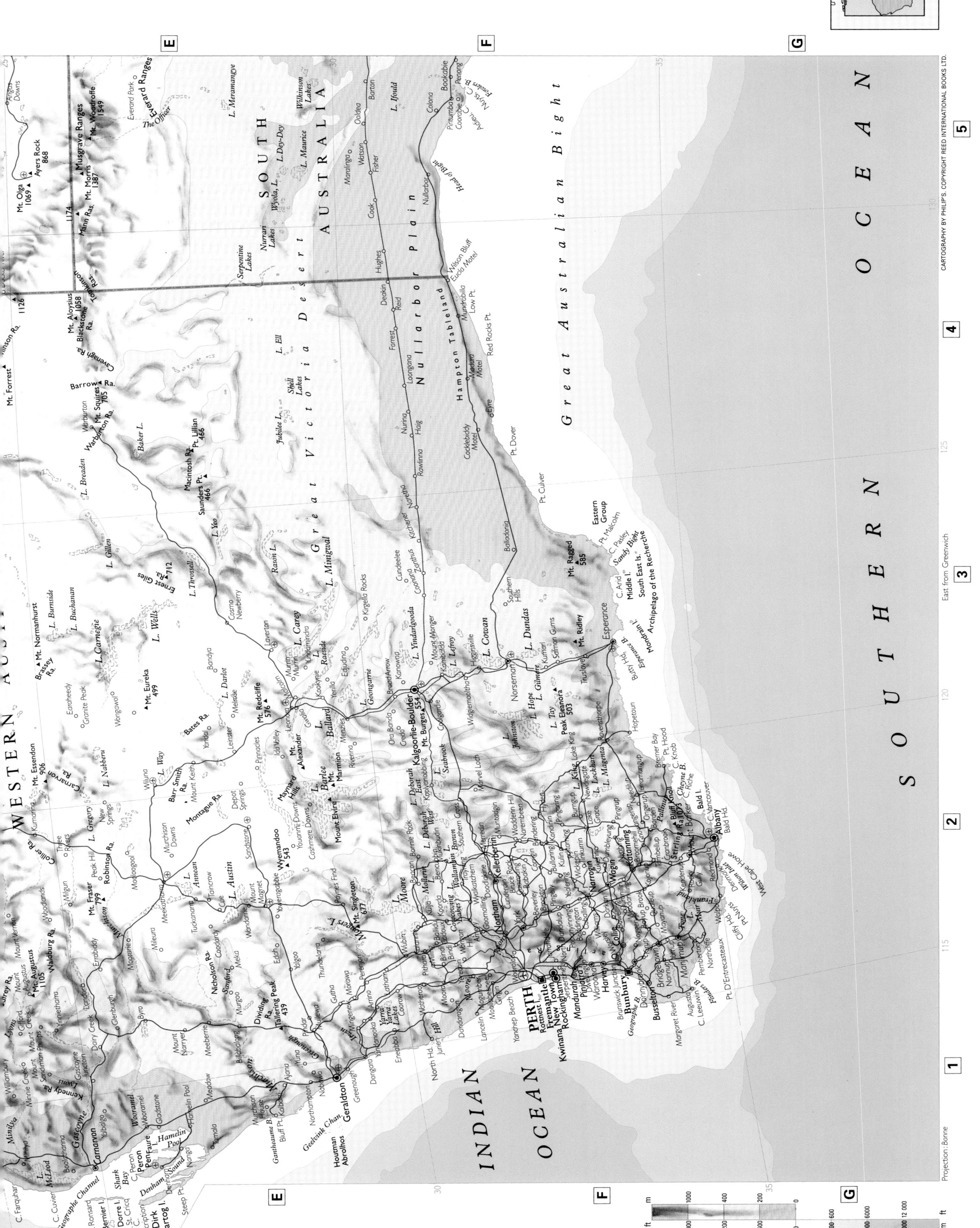

WESTERN AUST

SOUTH AUSTRALIA

INDIAN OCEAN

SOUTHERN OCEAN

Great Victoria Desert

Great Australian Bight

Nullarbor Plain

Hampton Tableland

PERTH
Fremantle
Kalgoorlie-Boulder
Geraldton
Carnarvon
Bunbury
Albany
Esperance
Norseman

Ayers Rock
868

Musgrave Ranges
Mt. Woodroffe
1549

Everard Ranges

East from Greenwich

Projection: Bonne

CARTOGRAPHY BY PHILIP'S. COPYRIGHT REED INTERNATIONAL BOOKS LTD.

m
1000
400
200
0

ft
3000
1200
600
0

ft
12 000
6000
2000
600
200
0
200-600

m
4000
2000
600
200
0

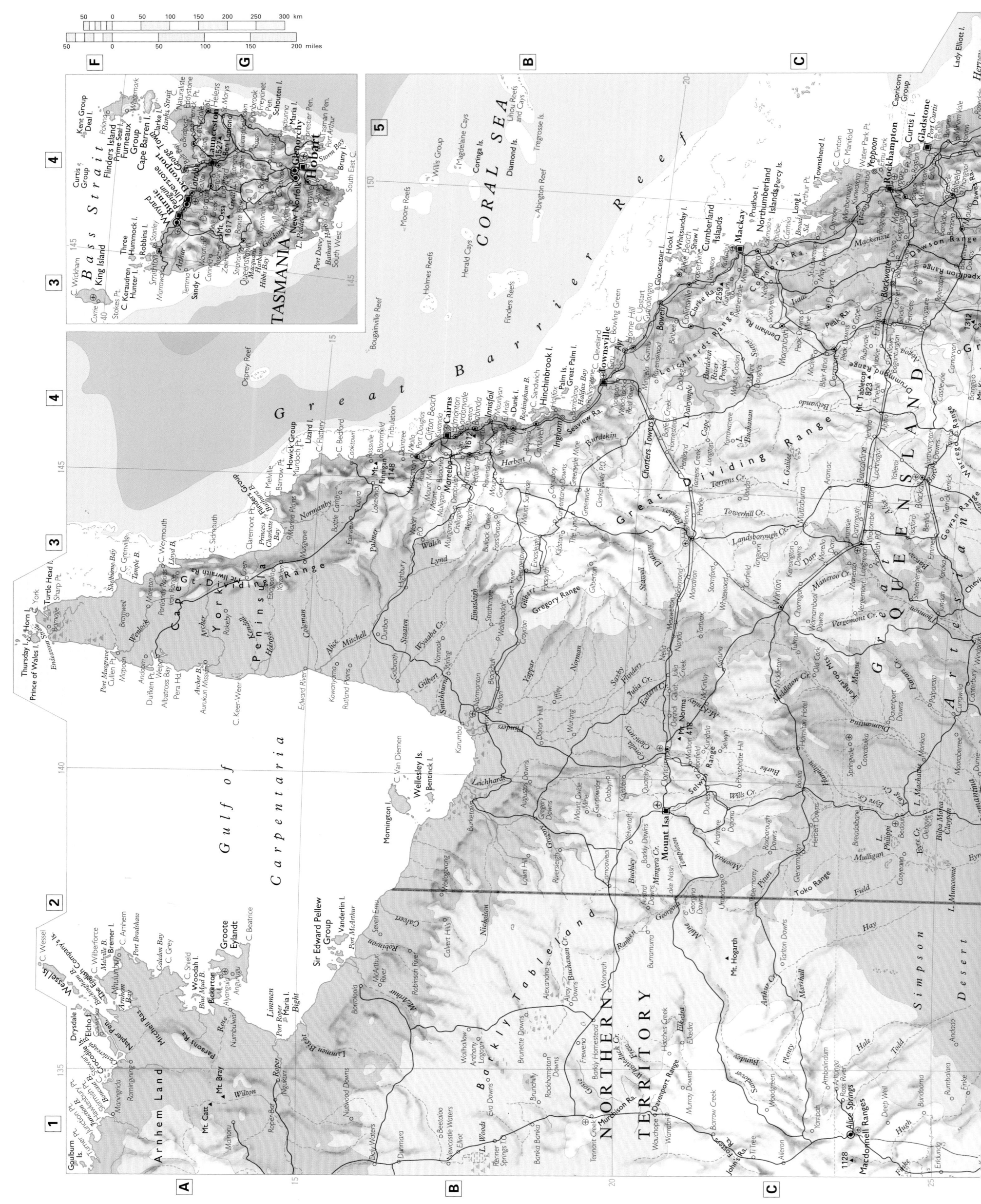

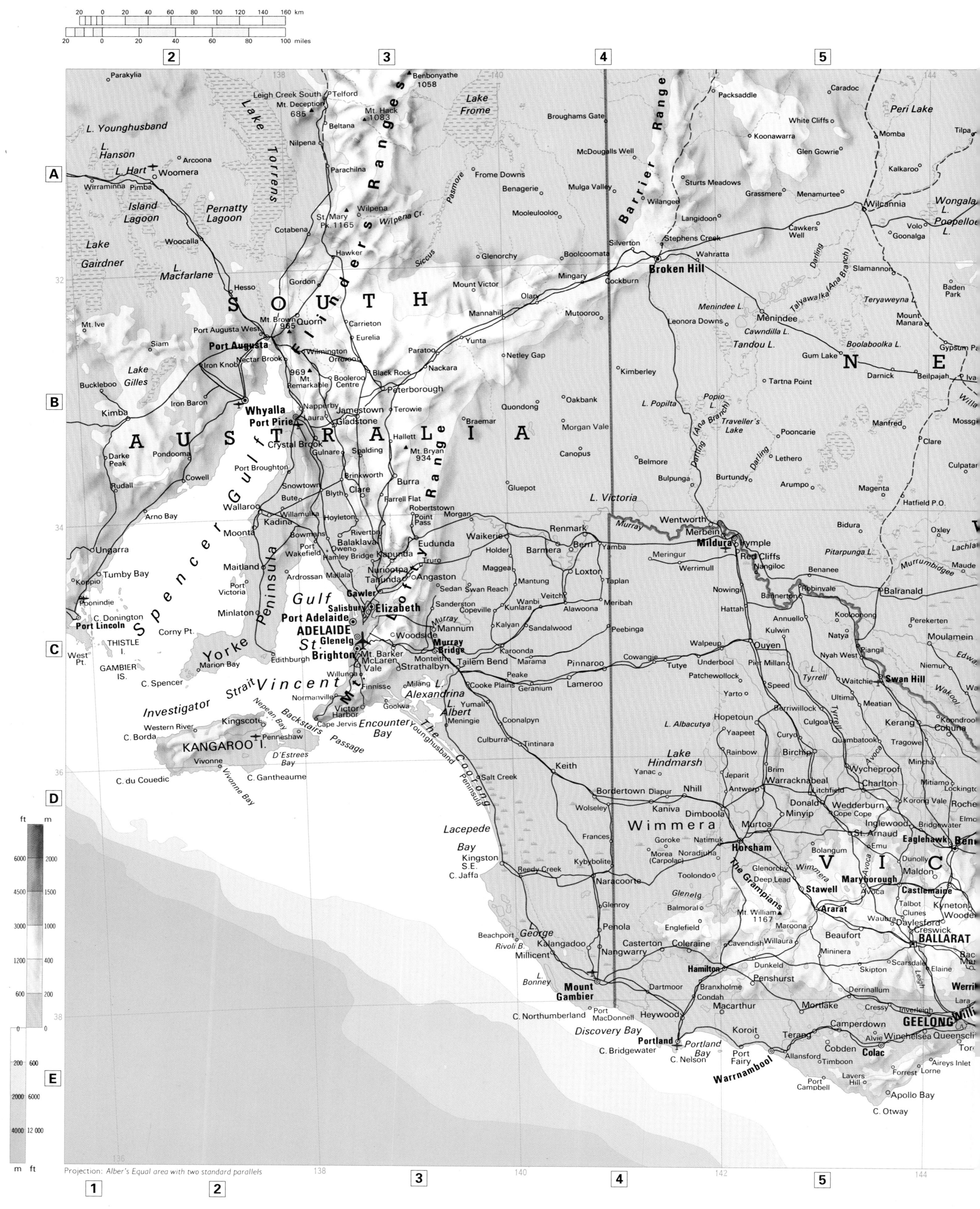

Projection: Alber's Equal area with two standard parallels

6   **7**   **8**   **9**   **10**

Louth
Curraweena
Byrock
Carinda
Gwabegar
Turrawan
Barraba
Black Mountain
1684
Coffs Harbour
Dorrigo

anyalpa
Wilgaroon
Glenariff
Colossal
Coonamble
Baradine
Coonabarabran
Boggabri
Namoi
Manilla
Upper Manilla
Kingstown
Chandlers Pk.
Bellingen

Burnamwood
Coolabah
Pine Ridge
Girilambone
Gombara
Yearinan
Ulamambri
Gunnedah
Peel
Attunga
Manilla
Armidale
Uralla
Kentucky
Nambucca Heads
Macksville

Cobar
Canbelego
Haddon Rig
Armatree
Castlereagh
Liverpool
Plains
Tamworth
Bendemeer
Walcha Road
Walcha
Hastings
Range
Mt. Banda Banda
1263
Kempsey

A

Elsinore
Hermidale
Nyngan
Mullengudgery
Warren
Collie
Gilgandra
Neilrex
Oakley Creek
Coolah
Murrurundi
Willow Tree
Nowendoc
Comboyne
Kendall
Port Macquarie

Rest Downs
Nevertire
Buddabadah
Trangie
Brocklehurst
Dunedoo
Merrygoen
Wingen
Ellerston
Yarras
Wauchope

verdale
Taringo Downs
Nymagee
Bobadah
Tottenham
Narromine
Minore
Albert
Geurie
Talbragar
Craboon
Scone
Barrington Tops
1555
Gloucester
Wingham
Lansdowne

32

Yathong
Gilgunnia
Gunebang
Tullamore
Toongi
Tomingley
Gulgong
Merriwa
Gungal
Aberdeen
Muswellbrook
Denman
Stratford
Wards River
Taree

W S O U T H

Tiarra
Mt. Hope
Melrose
Peak Hill
Yeoval
Wellington
Mudgee
Lue
Baerami
Creek
Ravensworth
Singleton
Paterson
Dungog
Stroud Road
Forster
Tuncurry

noble
Wee Elwah
Trida
Roto
Matakana
Condobolin
Ootha
Bogan
Gate
Parkes
Molong
Store Creek
Eucharena
Rylstone
Kandos
Putty
Branxton
Maitland
Karuah
Bulahdelah
Booral

B

arrowie Cr.
Cowl Cowl
Hillston
Naradhan
Lake Cargelligo
Tullibigeal
Ungarie
Marsden
Caragabal
Goonumbla
Cumnock
Boomey
Orange
Bathurst
Spring Hill
Blayney
Olinda
Coricudgy
1257
Lithgow
Kurrajong
Cessnock
Kurri Kurri
Toronto
Wallsend
NEWCASTLE
Belmont
Swansea

Booligal
Merriwagga
Rankins
Springs
Kikoira
West Wyalong
Pullabooka
Grenfell
Forbes
Eugowra
Carcoar
Oberon
Richmond
Windsor
Penrith
Parramatta
Fairfield
Hornsby
Manly
Morisset
Wyong
Budgewoi
Gosford
The Entrance
Woy Woy

34

Beabula
Goolgowi
Bellarwi
Barmedman
Mirrool
Reefton
Young
Frogmore
Peelwood
Woodstock
Wyangala
Res.
Lake
Burragorang
Katoomba
Liverpool
SYDNEY
Sutherland
Cronulla

Griffith
Hanwood
Yenda
Ardlethan
Temora
Murrumburrah
Boorowa
Crookwell
Roslyn
Camden
The Oaks
Picton
Campbelltown
Helensburgh
Bulli
Woonona

Willbriggie
Leeton
Yanco
Cootamundra
Harden
Galong
Binalong
Yass
Mittagong
Bargo
Port Kembla
WOLLONGONG
Shellharbour

Hay
Narrandera
Ganmain
Bethungra
Muttama
Murrumbateman
Goulburn
Marulan
Moss Vale
Robertson
Berry
Kiama

A L E S

Morundah
Coolamon
Junee
Pettitts
Gundagai
Burrinjuck
Res.
L.
George
Bowral
Gerringong
Bomaderry

C

Yanco Cr.
Wanganella
Borea Creek
Lockhart
Wagga
Wagga
Alfred Town
Nowra

Conargo
Bundure
Urana
Pleasant
Hills
The Rock
Adelong
Tumut
CANBERRA
A.C.T.
Queanbeyan
Braidwood
Ulladulla

Deniliquin
Jerilderie
Oaklands
Rand
Henty
Culcairn
Holbrook
Gilmore
Humula
Kunama
Batlow
Royalla
Captains
Flat
Marlow
St. Georges
Hd.
Jervis Bay (Commonwealth
Territory)

Finley
Berrigan
Balldale
Walla Walla
Gerogery
Tumbarumba
Bimberi Pk.
1910
Colinton
Bredbo
Majors Creek
East Lynne
Batemans Bay
Bateman's Bay

Tocumwal
Mathoura
Cobram
Yarrawonga
Mulwala
Corowa
Rutherglen
Albury
Walwa
Adaminaby
Numbugga
Moruya

arnes
Nathalia
Numurkah
Katamatite
Springhurst
Chiltern
Wodonga
L. Hume
(Res.)
Mt. Jagungal
2060
L. Eucumbene
Tuross Head

36

chuca
Kyabram
North
Wangaratta
Yackandandah
Cudgewa
Corryong
Murray
Yowrie
Narooma
C. Dromedary

ala
Tatura
Shepparton
Mooroopna
Glenrowan
Beechworth
Everton
Mt. Benambra
1476
Jindabyne
Rock Flat
Bega
Goalen Hd.

hope
Rushworth
Benalla
Ovens
Bright
Mt. Bogong
1986
Mt. Kosciuszko
2230
Nimmitabel
Tathra
Candelo

binabbin
Euroa
Violet Town
Whitfield
Mount
Beauty
Snowy Mts.
Cooma
Bombala
Cathcart
Eden

D

eymour
Carisbrook
Mansfield
Mt. Buller
1806
Glen Valley
Mt. Cobberas
1836
Corrowidgie
Rowes
Delegate
Towamba
Twofold Bay

ttlesea
Junc.
L. Eildon
Omeo
Swifts Creek
Bonang
Wonboyn
Green C.
Disaster B.

dford
Kilmore
Heathcote
Glenburn
Eildon
Mt.
Tamboritha
1646
Buchan
Mt. Ellery
1297
Genoa
C. Howe

GREAT DIVIDING RANGE

Sunshine
Healesville
Warburton
Cobbannah
Club Terrace
Orbost
Cann
River
Mallacoota
Mallacoota Inlet

MELBOURNE
Eltham
Aberfeldy
Walhalla
Heyfield
Maffra
Stratford
Bairnsdale
Nowa
Nowa
C.
Conran
Ram Head

Dandenong
Pakenham
Hill End
Yallourn
Sale
L. Wellington
Lakes Entrance

Seaford
Drouin
Moe
Traralgon
Seaspray

chelsea
ton
Frankston
Warragul
Nyora
Trafalgar
Morwell
Churchill

Hastings
FRENCH
Korumburra
San Remo
Mirboo
North
Yarram
Woodside

sebud
PHILLIP
Koonwarra
Meeniyan
The
Ninety
Mile

C. Woolamai
Anderson
Inverloch
Toora
Port Albert

E

Wonthaggi
C. Liptrap
SNAKE I.
Wilsons
Promontory
Waratah B.
Venus
B.

38

COPYRIGHT GEORGE PHILIP & SON LTD

6   **7**   **8**   **9**   **10**

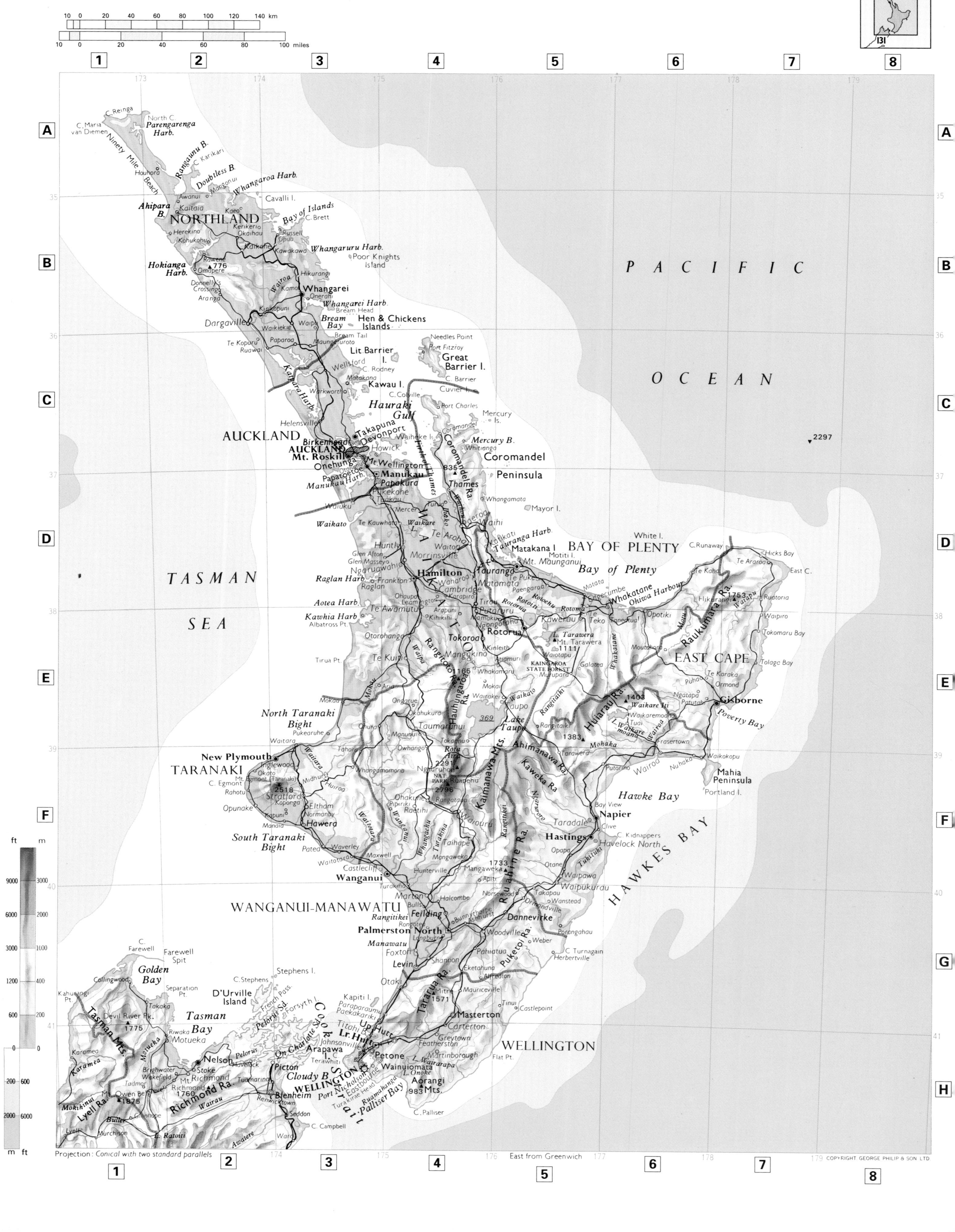

10 0 20 40 60 80 100 120 140 km
10 0 20 40 60 80 100 miles

1 **2** **3** **4** **5** **6** **7** **8**

131

173 174 175 176 177 178 179

A

C. Reinga
C. Maria van Diemen
North C.
Parengarenga Harb.
Houhora
Rangaunu B.
C. Karikari
Doubtless B.
Whangaroa Harb.
Ahipara B.
Awanui
Kaitaia
Keo
Cavalli I.
Kaikohe
Kerikeri
Okaihau
NORTHLAND
Bay of Islands
C. Brett
Herekino
Kohukohu
Russell
Opua
Kawakawa
Whangaruru Harb.
Hokianga Harb.
776
Omapere
Rawene
Donnelly's Crossing
Kamo
Hikurangi
Poor Knights Island
Aranga
Kirikopuni
Whangarei
Dargaville
Whangarei Harb.
Bream Head
Maungaturoto
Te Kopuru
Bream Bay
Hen & Chickens Islands
Ruawai
Bream Tail
Paparoa
Waikiekie
Waipu
Needles Point
Port Fitzroy
Lit. Barrier I.
Wellsford
Great Barrier I.
C. Rodney
Matakana
Warkworth
Kawau I.
C. Barrier
Cuvier I.
Kaipara Harb.
Hauraki Gulf
C. Colville
C. Coromandel
Port Charles
Mercury Is.
Helensville
AUCKLAND
Takapuna
Devonport
Waiheke I.
Mercury B.
Birkenhead
Howick
Whitianga
AUCKLAND
Mt. Roskill
Mt. Wellington
835
Coromandel
Onehunga
Papatoetoe
Manukau
Peninsula
Papakura
Thames
Manukau Harb.
Pukekohe
Whangamata
Waiuku
Mercer
Mayor I.
Te Kauwhata
Waihi
Waikato
Kopuku
Huntly
Tauranga Harb.
White I.
Ngaruawahia
Morrinsville
Matakana I.
Te Aroha
Motiti I.
BAY OF PLENTY
Glen Afton
Waitoa
Tauranga
C. Runaway
Glen Massey
Mt. Maunganui
Hicks Bay
Hamilton
Waharoa
Te Kaha
Te Araroa
Raglan Harb.
Cambridge
Te Puke
Bay of Plenty
Raglan
Matamata
Pyes Pa
Matata
East C.
Aotea Harb.
Karapiro
Paengaroa
Whakatane
Te Awamutu
Arapuni
Rotoehu
Ohiwa Harbour
Kihikihi
Tirau
Rotorua
Kawerau
Opotiki
Kawhia Harb.
Putaruru
Rotorua
Te Teko
Albatross Pt.
Tokoroa
Rotoma
Whakatane
1753
Hikarangi
Waipu
Ruatoria
Tirua Pt.
Mangakino
Ngongotaha
Raukumara Ra.
P. Waipiro
Te Kuiti
Okahukura
Whakamaru
Tokomaru Bay
Mokau
Mangakino
Waikite
Waiotapu
Galatea
1165
Murupara
Kainga
Roa State Forest
Tolaga Bay
EAST CAPE
North Taranaki Bight
Ohura
Pukearuhe
Ongarue
Taumarunui
L. Waikaremoana
1403
Waikare Iti
Gisborne
Waitara
Tahora
Whangamomona
Taupo
Rangitaiki
Ngatapa
Patutahi
Poverty Bay
New Plymouth
Inglewood
Mt. Egmont
Lake Taupo
1383
Mohaka
Ormond
Okato
Mt. Egmont (Taranaki)
TARANAKI
Midhirst
Tarawera
Frasertown
Mahia Peninsula
Rahotu
2518
Stratford
Whangamomona
Ngaruhoe
2291
Ahimanawa Ra.
Waikokopu
Opunake
Kopanga
Eltham
Rangataua
2796
Rangatoto
Portland I.
Manaia
Normanby
Raetihi
Ohakune
Kaweka Ra.
Hawke Bay
Hawera
Pipiriki
Rangataua
Napier
South Taranaki Bight
Waverley
Raetihi
Bay View
Patea
Taihape
Clive
Waitotara
Mangaweka
Ruahine Ra.
C. Kidnappers
Maxwell
Hunterville
1733
Hastings
Castlecliff
Havelock North
Opapa
Wanganui
Turakina
Marton
Otane
WANGANUI-MANAWATU
Bulls
Halcombe
Waipawa
Rangitikei
Feilding
Waipukurau
Ormondville
Palmerston North
Takapau
Manawatu
Rongotea
Dannevirke
Woodville
Weber
Foxton
Shannon
Pahiatua
Porangahau
Levin
Eketahuna
C. Turnagain
Otaki
Alfredton
Herbertville
Waikanae
Tararua Ra.
Masterton
Paraparaumu
1571
Paekakariki
Carterton
Kapiti I.
Mauriceville
Greytown
Tinui
Castlepoint
Flat Pt.
Titahi B.
Lr. Hutt
Up. Hutt
WELLINGTON
Martinborough
Petone
Featherston
Wainuiomata
Wairarapa

TASMAN SEA

PACIFIC OCEAN

2297

D

E

F

G

H

35 36 37 38 39 40 41

ft m
9000 3000
6000 2000
3000 1000
1200 400
600 200
0 0
200 600
2000 6000
m ft

C. Farewell
Farewell Spit
Golden Bay
Collingwood
Stephens I.
Kahurangi Pt.
C. Stephens
Separation Pt.
Takaka
D'Urville Island
French Pass
Tasman Mts.
1775
Tasman Bay
Riwaka
Pelorus Sd.
Motueka
Queen Charlotte Sd.
Kaiteriteri
Brightwater
Nelson
Arapawa I.
Stoke
Pelorus
Havelock
Picton
Cloudy B.
Wakefield
Mt. Richmond
Tuamarina
Richmond Ra.
1760
WELLINGTON
Karamea
Owen
Renwick
Port Nicholson
Tadmor
1875
Blenheim
Wairau
C. Palliser
Palliser Bay
Lyell Ra.
Richmond Ra.
Aorangi 983 Mts.
Mokihinui
Buller
Seddon
Murchison
Ratotii
Lyell
Awatere
Wai—

Projection: Conical with two standard parallels

1 **2** **3** **4** **5** **6** **7** **8**

173 174 175 176 177 178 179

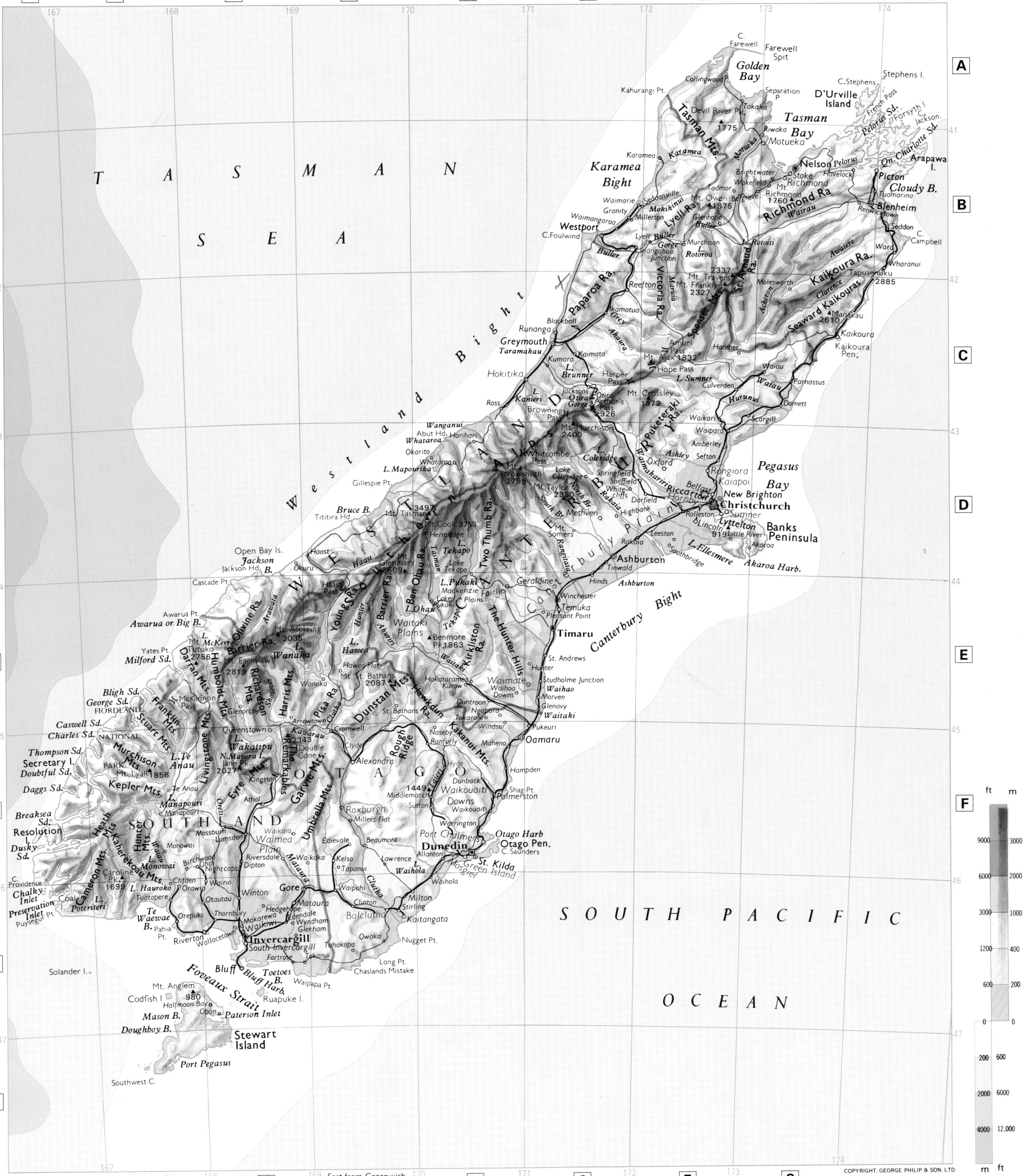

10 0 20 40 60 80 100 120 140 km
10 0 20 40 60 80 100 miles

1 2 3 4 5 6 7 8 9

A B C D E F G H

167 168 169 170 171 172 173 174

T A S M A N   S E A

S O U T H   P A C I F I C

O C E A N

C. Farewell
Farewell Spit
Golden Bay
C. Stephens
Stephens I.
D'Urville Island
Separation P
French Pass
Pelorus Sd.
Q'n Charlotte Sd.
Jackson
Collingwood
Kahurangi Pt.
Devil River Pt.
Takaka
Riwaka
Motueka
Tasman Bay
Arapawa I.
Tasman Mts.
1775
Karamea
Brightwater
Stoke
Nelson
Richmond
Havelock
Picton
Cloudy B.
Renwicktown
Blenheim
Seddon
C. Campbell
Mt. Owen
Mt Richmond 1760
Richmond Ra.
Wairau
Ward
Wharanui
Tapuaenuku 2885
Manakau 2610
Kaikoura Ra.
Seaward Kaikouras
Kaikoura
Kaikoura Pen.
Karamea
Seddonville
Waimarie
Granity
Millerton
Westport
C. Foulwind
Lyell Ra. 1875
Lyell
Buller
Murchison
L. Rotoroa
L. Rotoiti
Mt. Travers 2337
Mt. Franklyn 2327
St. Arnaud
Spenser Mts.
Molesworth
Hanmer
Awatere
Clarence
Waiau
Karamea Bight
Mokihinui
Waimangaroa
Tadmor
Glenhope
Wakefield
Tuamarina
Reefton
Inangahua Junction
Buller Gorge
Grey
Ahaura
Murchison
Inaka
Amuri Pass
Mt. Ajax 1832
Hope Pass
L. Sumner
Hurunui
Waiau
Culverden
Parnassus
Domett
Westland Bight
Runanga
Blackball
Greymouth
Taramakau
Hokitika
Kumara
L. Brunner
Kaimata
Harper Pass
Mt. Crossley 1872
Waiau
Scargill
Ross
L. Kanieri
Otira Gorge
Arthur's Pass
Browning's Pass
Mt. Murchison 2400
Hurunui
Waikari
Waipara
Ashley
Sefton
Oxford
Amberley
Rangiora
Kaiapoi
Pegasus Bay
Wanganui
Abut Hd.
Harihari
Whataroa
Okarito
Whataroa
L. Mapourika
Gillespie Pt.
Whitcombe Pass
Mt. Oslesmith 2795
Lake Coleridge
Coleridge
Springfield
Sheffield
White-cliffs
Belfast
Riccarton
New Brighton
Christchurch
Hornby
Sumner
Lyttelton
Little River 919
Banks Peninsula
Akaroa Harb.
Akaroa
Bruce B.
Tititira Hd.
Mt. Tasman 3497
Mt. Cook 3753
Hermitage
Mt. Taylor 2330
North Br.
Rakaia
Darfield
Rolleston
Lincoln
Leeston
Southbridge
L. Ellesmere
Mt. Somers
Methven
Highbank
Mt. Glenmary 2609
L. Tekapo
Lake Tekapo
Two Thumb Ra.
Tasman
Rangitata
Hinds
Ashburton
Tinwald
Open Bay Is.
Jackson
Jackson Hd.
B.
Okuru
Haast Pass
Ben Ohau Ra.
L. Pukaki
Mackenzie Plains
Fairlie
Geraldine
Winchester
Temuka
Pleasant Point
Cascade Pt.
Haast
Burke
Barrier Ra.
L. Ohau
Lake Ohau
Tekapo
Pukaki
Canterbury Bight
Timaru
Awarua Pt.
Awarua or Big B.
Yates Pt.
Milford Sd.
Mt. McKerrow
Utuko 2756
Olivine Ra.
Darran Mts.
Mt. Aspiring 3035
L. Wanaka
Mt. Earnslaw 2819
Richardson Mts.
Harris Mts.
Pisa Ra.
Hunter
L. Hawea
Hawea
Hawea Flat
Mt. Bathans 2087
Waitaki
Waitaki Plains
Hakataramea
Kurow
Waimate
Waihao
Waihao Downs
Studholme Junction
St. Andrews
Hunter
The Hunter Hills
Benmore Pk. 1863
Kirkliston Ra.
Waitaki
Bligh Sd.
George Sd.
FIORDLAND
McKinnon Pass
Stuart Mts.
Glenorchy
Arrowtown
Queenstown
Kawarau
L. Wakatipu
2343
The Remarkables
N. Matara I.
Jane Pk. 2027
Cromwell
Clyde
St. Bathans
Dunstan Mts.
Hawkdun Ra.
Naseby
Kokanui Mts.
Duntroon
Ngapara
Tokarahi
Windsor
Pukeuri
Oamaru
Moheno
Hampden
Caswell Sd.
Charles Sd.
Thompson Sd.
Secretary I.
Doubtful Sd.
Daggs Sd.
Murchison Mts.
Mt. Lyall 1858
NATIONAL PARK
Te Anau
L. Te Anau
Eyre Mts.
Garvie Mts.
Rough Ridge
Double Cone
Alexandra
Roxburgh
Millers Flat
Waikaia
Middlemarch 1449
Hyde
Dunback
Shag Pt.
Palmerston
Ranfurly
Kepler Mts.
Manapouri
L. Manapouri
Mararoa
Te Anau
Umbrella Mts.
Clutha
Waikaia
Waimea Plain
Waipahi
Clinton
Kaitangata
Lawrence
Tapanui
Beaumont
Port Chalmers
Otago Harb.
Otago Pen.
C. Saunders
Dunedin
Allanton
Mosgiel
Green Island
St. Kilda
Breaksea Sd.
Resolution I.
Dusky Sd.
Heath Mts.
Mahwerekou Mts.
Hunt Mts.
Wairio
Ohai
Nightcaps
Birchwood
Dipton
Riversdale
Mossburn
Lumsden
Athol
Balfour
SOUTHLAND
Monowai
L. Monowai
Caroline 1699
Coals
L. Poteriteri
Clifden
Orawia
Otautau
Thornbury
Winton
Gore
Mataura
Edendale
Wyndham
Glenham
Owaka
Nugget Pt.
Waihola
Milton
Stirling
Balclutha
Kaitangata
Chalky Inlet
Preservation Inlet
Puysegur Pt.
C. Providence
Cameron Mts.
L. Hauroko
Te Waewae
Tuatapere
Pahia
Te Waewae B.
Pahia Pt.
Riverton
Wallacetown
Waikiwi
Invercargill
South Invercargill
Fortrose
Tokanui
Tahakopa
Chaslands Mistake
Long Pt.
Waipapa Pt.
Solander I.
Foveaux Strait
Bluff
Bluff Harb.
Toetoes B.
Ruapuke I.
Mt. Anglem 980
Codfish I.
Halfmoon Bay
Oban
Paterson Inlet
Mason B.
Doughboy B.
Stewart Island
Port Pegasus
Southwest C.

Projection: Conical with two standard parallels

East from Greenwich

COPYRIGHT. GEORGE PHILIP & SON. LTD.

ft m
9000 3000
6000 2000
3000 1000
1500 400
600 200
0 0
200 600
2000 6000
4000 12,000
m ft

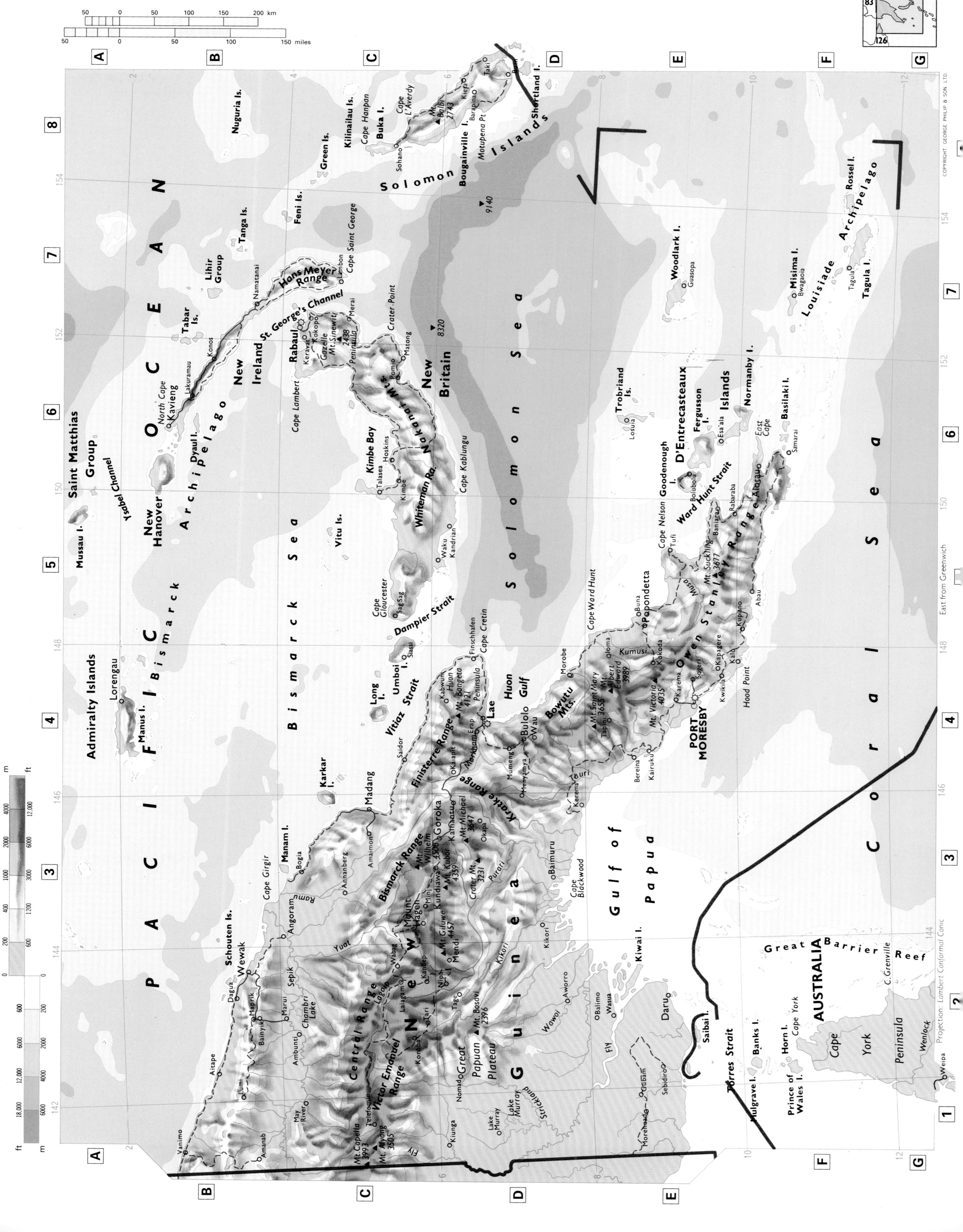

50 0 50 100 150 200 km

50 0 50 100 150 miles

| A | B | C | D | E | F | G |

P A C I F I C   O C E A N

Nuguria Is.

Green Is.
Kilinailau Is.
Cape Hanpan
Buka I.
Cape L'Averdy
Taki
Bulfi
2743
Kunua
Barapino
Kieta
Motupena Pt
Sohano

Solomon Islands
Bougainville I.
Shortland I.

Tanga Is.
Feni Is.
Cape Saint George
9140
8320

Lihir Group
Namatanai

Hans Meyer Range

Saint Matthias Group
Mussau I.

Tabar Is.
Konos
Lakuramau

New Ireland
St. George's Channel
Rabaul
Kavieng
North Cape
Ysabel Channel

New Hanover

Bismarck Archipelago

Gazelle Peninsula
Keravat
Kokopo
Mt. Sinewit
2438
Merai
Matong
Pomio
Crater Point

New Britain

Cape Lambert
Kimbe Bay
Hoskins
Kimbe
Talasea

Nakanai Mts.
Cape Kablungu

Whiteman Ra.
Waku
Kandrian

Solomon Sea

Woodlark I.
Guasopa

Misima I.
Bwagaoia

Louisiade Archipelago
Tagula
Rossell I.
Tagula I.

Bismarck Sea

Vitu Is.

Cape Gloucester
Sag Sag
Dampier Strait

Long I.
Umboi I.
Siassi
Vitiaz Strait
Cape Cretin
Finschhafen

Huon Peninsula
Kabwum
Huon
Mt. Bangeta
4121
Saidor

Admiralty Islands
Lorengau
Manus I.

Karkar I.

Manam I.

Schouten Is.
Bogia
Madang
Cape Girgir

Amaimon
Annanberg

Wewak
Aitape
Vanimo

Dagua
Maprik
Marui
Angoram
Chambri Lake
Sepik

Ramu
Yuat

Finisterre Range
Mt. Kerigomna
3653
Leron
Markham
Lae
Bulolo
Wau

Huon Gulf

Bowutu Mts.
Morobe

Mt. Saint Mary
3655
Mambare
Kumusi
Oloma
Kokoda
Buna
Popondetta

Owen Stanley Range
Mt. Suckling
Mt. Albert Edward
3989
Mt. Victoria
4035
Karema
Kwikila
Okapagere
Abau

Cape Nelson
Tufi

D'Entrecasteaux Islands
Goodenough I.
Fergusson I.
Esa'ala
Normanby I.
Ward Hunt Strait
Basilaki I.
East Cape
Samarai
Alotau
Rabaraba
Baniara

Trobriand Is.
Losuia

Kratke Range
Goroka
Kainantu
Mt. Michael
3647
Okapa
Okari
Crater Mt.
3231

Bismarck Range
Mt. Wilhelm
4508
Mt. Hagen
Minj
Mendi
Mt. Giluwe
4367
Mt. Kubor
4359

Central Range
Wabag
Laiagam
Wapenamanda
Kandep
Tari
Nipa
Koroba

Victor Emanuel Range
Mt. Capella
3992
Mt. Aiyang
3505
Telefomin

N E W   G U I N E A

Great Papuan Plateau
Mt. Bosavi
2396

May River
Amanab

Kiunga
Nomad
Lake Murray
Fly

Kikori
Kukipi
Kerema
Baimuru
Cape Blackwood

Gulf of Papua

Kiwai I.
Daru
Wasua
Balimo
Obalimo
Awaba
Wawoi
Strickland
Morehead
Sebidiro
Wepa

Banks I.
Mulgrave I.

Torres Strait
Saibai I.
Prince of Wales I.
Horn I.
Cape York

C o r a l   S e a

Cape Ward Hunt

Hood Point

PORT MORESBY
Bereina
Kairuku
Iuri

AUSTRALIA
Great Barrier Reef
Cape Grenville
C. Grenville

Cape York Peninsula
Wenlock

East from Greenwich

Projection: Lambert Conformal Conic

m / ft
18,000 / 6000
12,000 / 4000
6000 / 2000
4000 / 1200
3000 / 1000
2000 / 600
1000 / 300
600 / 200
200 / 0
0
ft / m

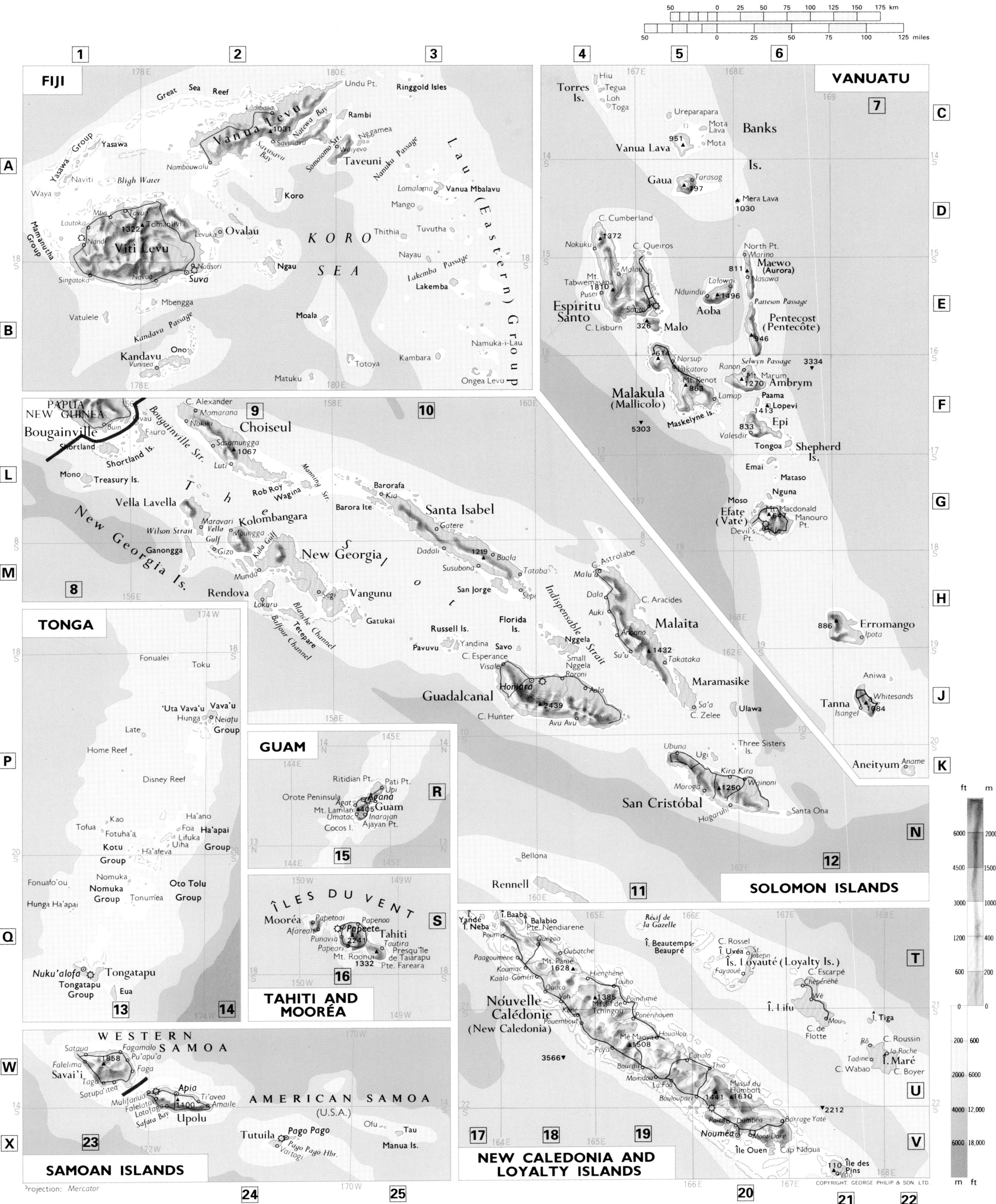

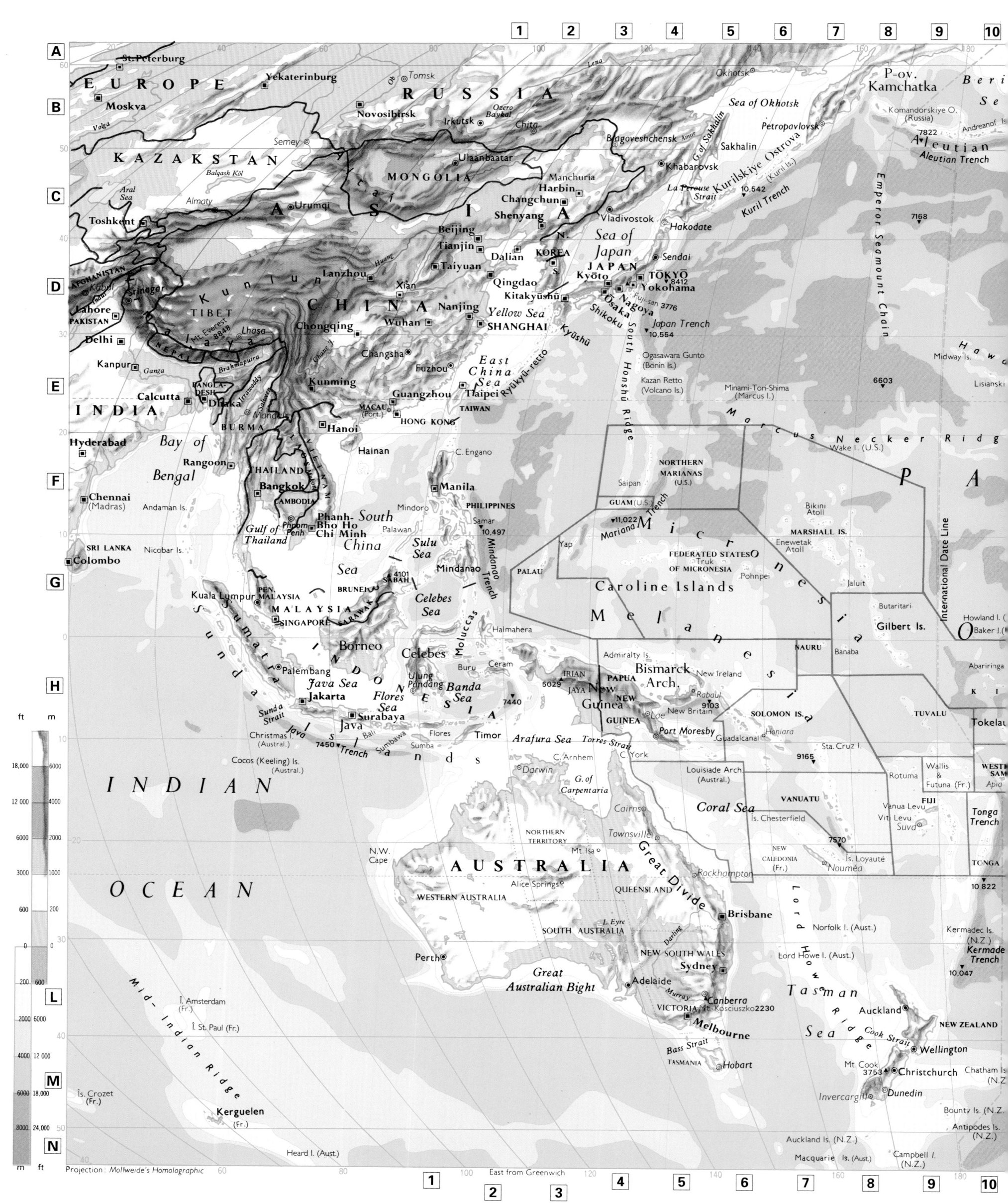

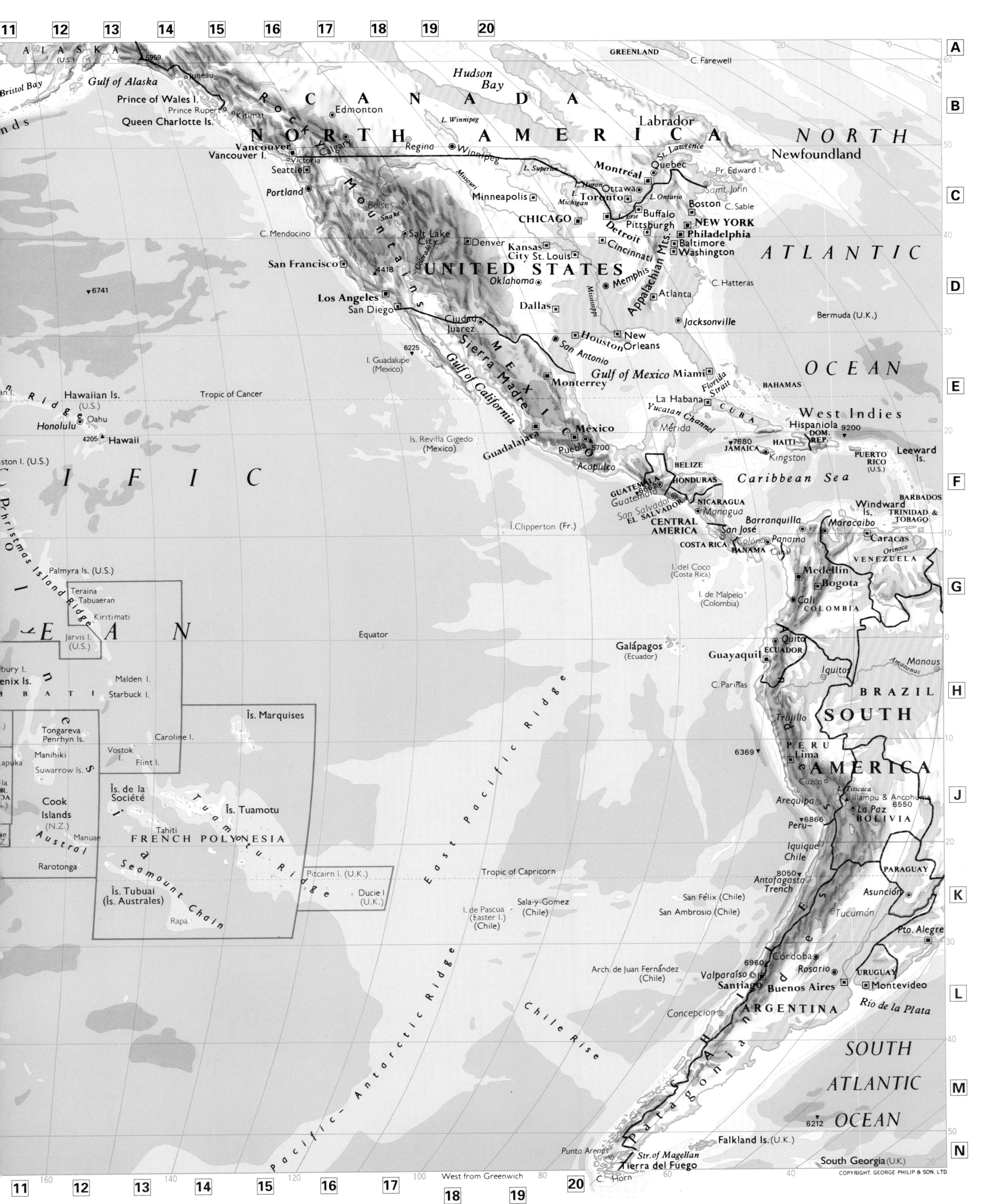

11 **12** **13** **14** **15** **16** **17** **18** **19** **20**

A

GREENLAND

C. Farewell

ALASKA
(U.S.)

60

5959

Bristol Bay

Gulf of Alaska

B

Hudson
Bay

C A N A D A

NORTH AMERICA

NORTH

Juneau

Prince of Wales I.
Prince Rupert
Kitimat
Queen Charlotte Is.

Edmonton

L. Winnipeg

Labrador

Newfoundland

50

Vancouver
Vancouver I.
Victoria
Calgary
Regina
Winnipeg

Montréal
Quebec

St. Lawrence

C

Pr. Edward I.
Saint John

Seattle

L. Superior
Ottawa
Toronto
Michigan
L. Huron

CHICAGO

L. Ontario
Erie
Buffalo
Pittsburgh
Detroit

Boston

NEW YORK

C. Sable

Portland

Boise
Snake

Salt Lake
City

Denver

Kansas
City St. Louis

Cincinnati

Philadelphia
Baltimore
Washington

ATLANTIC

40

C. Mendocino

4418

UNITED STATES

Memphis

Appalachian Mts.

C. Hatteras

D

San Francisco

Oklahoma

Atlanta

6741

Los Angeles
San Diego

Ciudad
Juárez

Dallas

Jacksonville

Bermuda (U.K.)

30

I. Guadalupe
(Mexico)

6225

Houston

San Antonio

New
Orleans

Miami

OCEAN

Hawaiian Is.
(U.S.)

Tropic of Cancer

Sierra Madre

M E X I C O

Gulf of Mexico

Florida
Strait

BAHAMAS

E

Honolulu
Oahu

Gulf of California

Monterrey

La Habana

CUBA

West Indies

20

4205
Hawaii

I. Revilla Gigedo
(Mexico)

México
Guadalajara
Puebla 5700
Acapulco

Yucatan Channel
Mérida

Hispaniola
JAMAICA
7680
HAITI

DOM.
REP.
9200

PUERTO
RICO
(U.S.)

Leeward
Is.

F

P A C I F I C

Kingston

BELIZE
HONDURAS

Caribbean Sea

BARBADOS

GUATEMALA
Guatemala 6862
San Salvador
EL SALVADOR

NICARAGUA
Managua

Windward
Is.

TRINIDAD &
TOBAGO

Î. Clipperton (Fr.)

CENTRAL
AMERICA

Barranquilla
San José
Colón Panama

Maracaibo

Caracas

10

Palmyra Is. (U.S.)

COSTA RICA
PANAMA

Panama
Canal

VENEZUELA

Orinoco

Christmas Island Ridge

Teraina
Tabuaeran
Kiritimati

I. del Coco
(Costa Rica)

Medellín
Bogota

G

Jarvis I.
(U.S.)

I. de Malpelo
(Colombia)

Cali

COLOMBIA

E A N

Equator

Galápagos
(Ecuador)

Quito
ECUADOR

Manaus

0

bury I.
nix Is.

Malden I.

Starbuck I.

Guayaquil

Iquitos

Amazonas

Manihiki
Suwarrow Is.

Vostok
I.
Flint I.

Caroline I.

C. Pariñas

BRAZIL

H

SOUTH

Î. Marquises

Trujillo

PERU

10

Cook
Islands
(N.Z.)

Îs. de la
Société

Îs. Tuamotu

6369

Lima

AMERICA

Manuae

Cuzco

J

Rarotonga

Tahiti
FRENCH POLYNESIA

Austral

Seamount Chain

Tuamotu Ridge

L. Titicaca
Illampu & Ancohuma
6550
La Paz
BOLIVIA

Arequipa

6866
Peru-

20

Îs. Tubuai
(Îs. Australes)

Rapa

Pitcairn I. (U.K.)

Tropic of Capricorn

Iquique
Chile

Ducie I.
(U.K.)

Sala-y-Gomez
(Chile)

8050
Antofagasta
Trench

PARAGUAY

K

East Pacific Ridge

I. de Pascua
(Easter I.)
(Chile)

San Félix (Chile)

San Ambrosio (Chile)

Asunción

Tucumán

Pto. Alegre

30

Arch. de Juan Fernández
(Chile)

6960
Córdoba
Rosario

URUGUAY

Chile Rise

Valparaíso
Santiago
Concepción

Buenos Aires

Montevideo

ARGENTINA

Rio de la Plata

L

Pacific - Antarctic Ridge

Andes

SOUTH

40

Patagonia

ATLANTIC

M

6212

OCEAN

50

Punta Arenas

Falkland Is.(U.K.)

N

Str. of Magellan
Tierra del Fuego
C. Horn

South Georgia (U.K.)

11 **12** **13** **14** **15** **16** **17** **18** **19** **20**

West from Greenwich

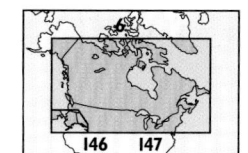

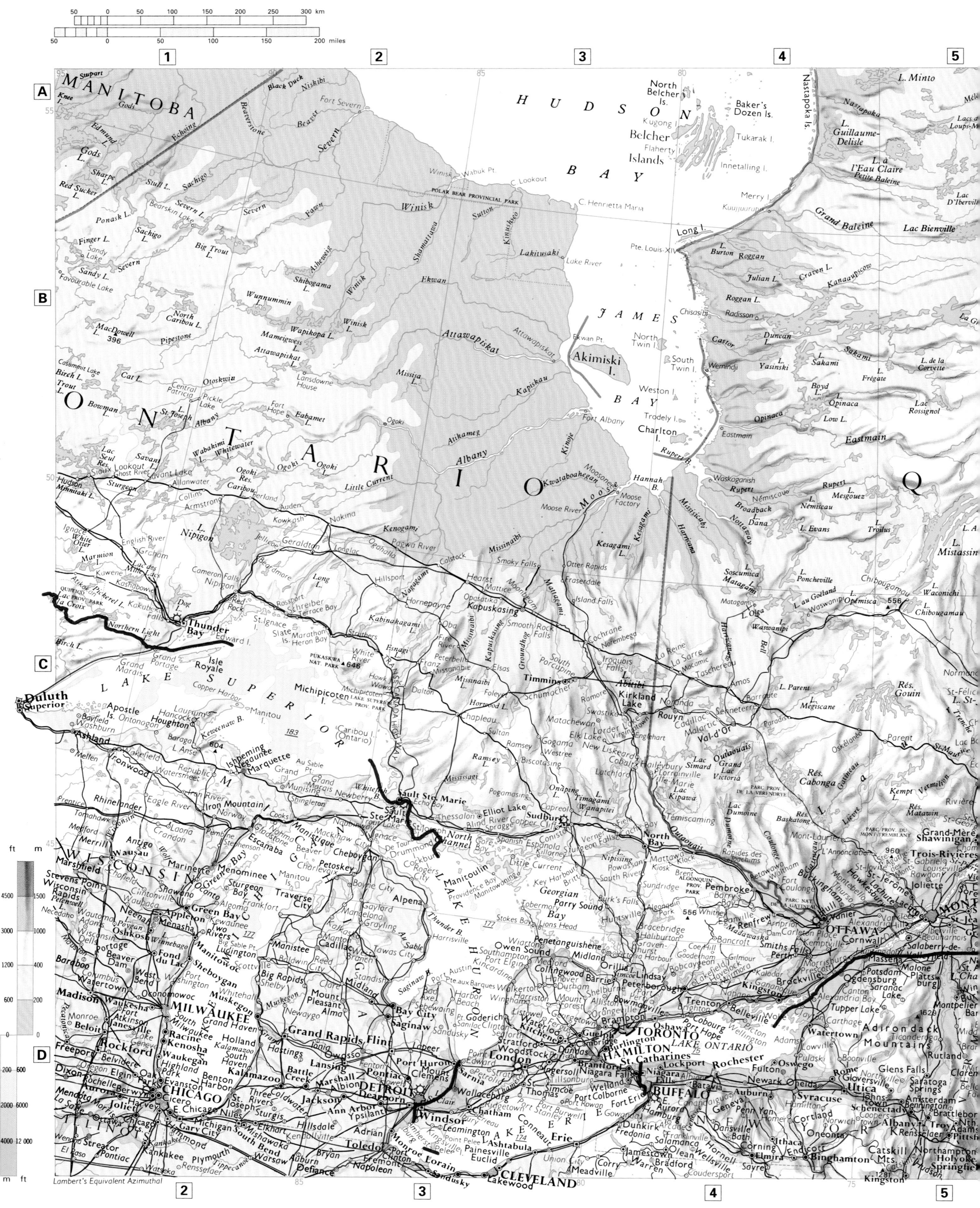

COPYRIGHT GEORGE PHILIP & SON LTD

Projection: Lambert's Equivalent Azimuthal

West from Greenwich

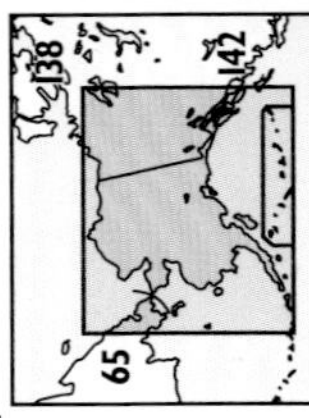

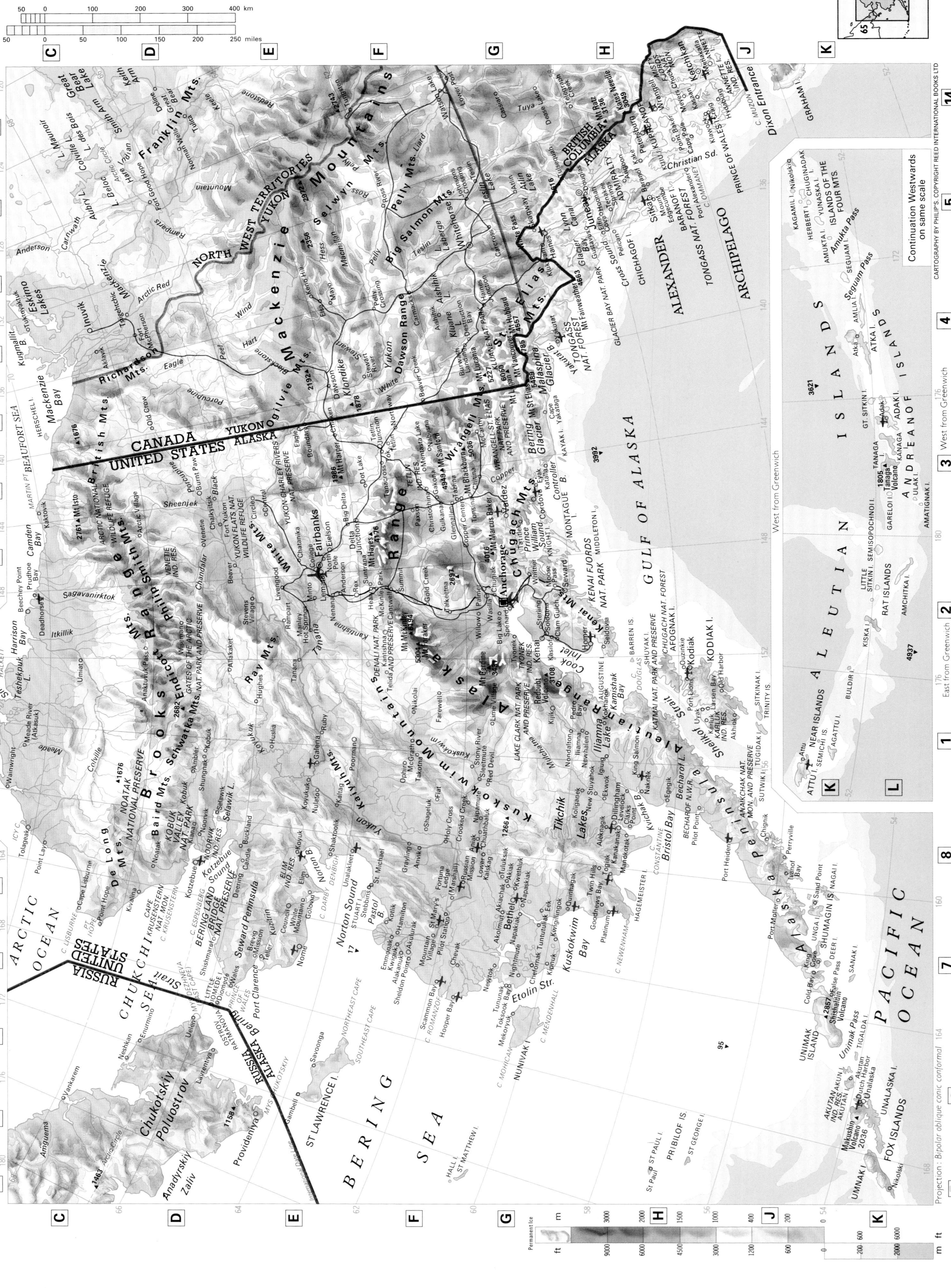

CARTOGRAPHY BY PHILIP'S. COPYRIGHT REED INTERNATIONAL BOOKS LTD

Continuation Westwards on same scale

Projection: Bipolar oblique conic conformal

ARCTIC OCEAN

BEAUFORT SEA

CHUKCHI SEA

BERING SEA

GULF OF ALASKA

PACIFIC OCEAN

CANADA
UNITED STATES
YUKON
ALASKA

NORTH WEST TERRITORIES
YUKON

BRITISH COLUMBIA

RUSSIA
UNITED STATES

Brooks Range

Mackenzie Mountains

Selwyn Mts.

Alaska Range

Chugach Mts.

Wrangell Mts.

St. Elias Mts.

ALEUTIAN ISLANDS

ALEXANDER ARCHIPELAGO

ANDREANOF ISLANDS

RAT ISLANDS

NEAR ISLANDS

FOX ISLANDS

Fairbanks

Anchorage

Nome

Barrow

Kodiak

Ketchikan

Juneau

Alaska Peninsula

Seward Peninsula

Kenai Peninsula

Permanent ice

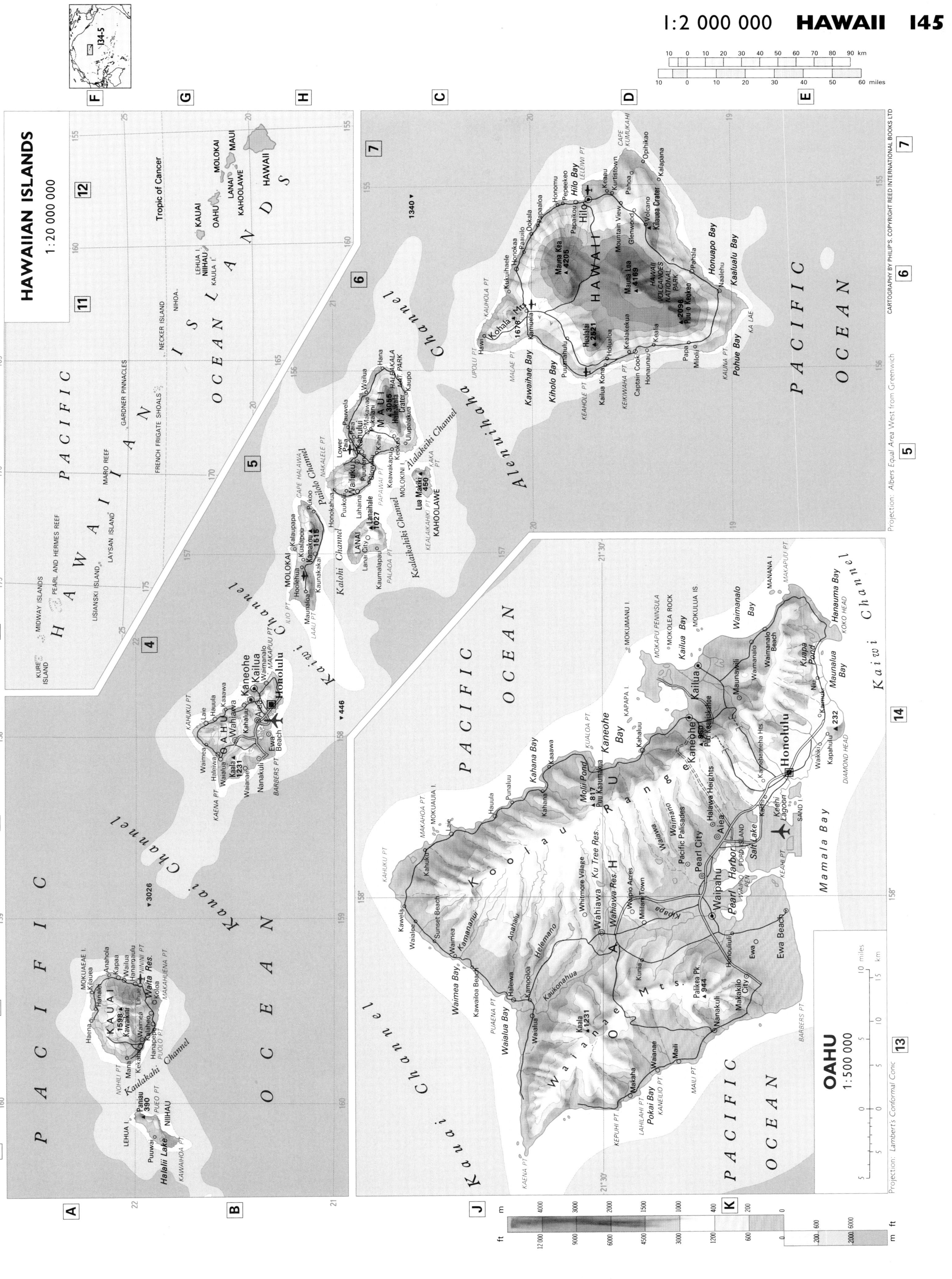

HAWAIIAN ISLANDS
1:20 000 000

km / miles scale

10 0 10 20 30 40 50 60 70 80 90 km
10 0 10 20 30 40 50 60 miles

Tropic of Cancer

KAUAI OAHU MOLOKAI MAUI
LEHUA I. LANAI KAHOOLAWE
NIIHAU HAWAII
KAULA I.
NIHOA

H A W A I I A N   I S L A N D S

PACIFIC   OCEAN

KURE ISLAND
MIDWAY ISLANDS
PEARL AND HERMES REEF
LISIANSKI ISLAND
LAYSAN ISLAND
MARO REEF
GARDNER PINNACLES
FRENCH FRIGATE SHOALS
NECKER ISLAND
NIHOA

CARTOGRAPHY BY PHILIP'S. COPYRIGHT REED INTERNATIONAL BOOKS LTD
Projection: Albers Equal Area West from Greenwich

HAWAII

Upolu Pt
Hawi Kapaau
Kohala Mts 1678
Kukuihaele
Honokaa
Paauilo
Ookala
Laupahoehoe
Honohina
Pepeekeo
Honomu
Papaikou
Hilo Hilo Bay
LELEIWI PT
Keaau
Pahoa
Kurtistown
Mountain View
Glenwood Volcano
Kilauea Crater
Kalapana
Opihikao
CAPE KUMUKAHI
Mauna Kea 4205
Mauna Loa 4169
HAWAII VOLCANOES NATIONAL PARK
Puu o Keokeo 2096
HAWAII
Hualalai 2521
Kailua Kona
Kealakekua
Captain Cook
Honaunau
Keokea
Keei
Kealia
Papa
Miloli
Naalehu
Waiohinu
Pahala
Punaluu
KA LAE
KAUNA PT
Pohue Bay
Kealulua Bay
Honuapo Bay
Prahala
KEAHOLE PT
Kiholo Bay
Kawaihae Bay
MALAE PT
Kamuela
KAUHOLA PT
KEKUAHAHA PT
1340

Alalakeiki Channel
Alenuihaha Channel
Kealaikahiki Channel
Kealakahiki Channel

MAUI
Wailuku Kahului
Paia Lower Paia
Haiku
Hana
Keanae
Wailua
Kipahulu
Kaupo
Ulupalakua
HALEAKALA 3055
Haleakala Crater
HALEAKALA NAT. PARK
Puunene
Kihei
Makena
Lahaina
Kaanapali
Honokohau
Kapalua
Olowalu
PAPAWAI PT
MAKENA PT

MOLOKAI
Kaunakakai 1515
Kualapuu
Kalaupapa
Kalae
Hoolehua
Maunaloa
Mapulehu
Kamalo
CAPE HALAWA
Pailolo Channel
MAKALELE PT
ILIO PT
LAAU PT
Kalohi Channel

LANAI
Lanai City 1027
PALAOA PT
Kaumalapau

KAHOOLAWE
Lua Makika 450
KAKA PT

Kaiwi Channel

OAHU
Honolulu
Kaneohe Kailua
Waialua Haleiwa
Waianae
Wahiawa
Ewa Beach
Kaala 1231
KAENA PT
MAKAPUU PT
BARBERS PT
446

Kaieie Channel
Kauai Channel
Kaulakahi Channel
3026

KAUAI
Lihue
Kapaa
Wailua
Anahola
Kilauea
Hanalei
Haena
Kekaha
Waimea
Kalaheo
Koloa
Hanapepe
Kawaikini 1598
Mana
Waita Res.
MOKUAEAE I.
NOHILI PT
MAKAHUENA PT
NIUMALU PT
PUOLO PT

NIIHAU
Puuwai
LEHUA I.
Halalii Lake
Paniau 390
KAWAIHOA PT
KIKEPA PT

P A C I F I C   O C E A N

OAHU
1:500 000

Projection: Lambert's Conformal Conic

P A C I F I C   O C E A N

Kaena Pt
Waialua Haleiwa
Mokuleia
Kawailoa
Waimea Bay
Sunset Beach
Kahuku
Laie
Hauula
Punaluu
Kahana Kahana Bay
Kaaawa
Kualoa Pt
Kahaluu
Waiahole
Kaneohe Kaneohe Bay
MOKAPU PENINSULA
MOKOLEA ROCK
MOKULUA IS.
MOKUMANU I.
MANANA I.
Kailua Kailua Bay
Waimanalo Waimanalo Bay
Waimanalo Beach
MAKAPUU PT
Kuapa Pond
Hanauma Bay
KOKO HEAD
DIAMOND HEAD
Honolulu
Waikiki
Pearl Harbor
FORD ISLAND
SAND I.
Keehi Lagoon
Pearl City
Aiea
Waipahu
Waipio
Waimalu
Pacific Palisades
Halawa Heights
Pearl City
Kapolei
Ewa Ewa Beach
Iroquois Point
Kapalama
Kalihi
Kaneohe
Pali Highway
Koolau Range
Mount Olympus
Pali
Maunawili
Kaalaea
Heeia
Waipahu
Wahiawa
Mililani Town
Whitmore Village
Wahiawa Res.
Ku Tree Res.
Schofield Barracks
Pupukea
Moii Pond
Puu Kaaumakua 817
Kunia
Makakilo City
Nanakuli
Maili Maili Pt
Waianae
Makaha
Lualualei
Pokai Bay
Kaneilio Pt
LAHILAHI PT
KEPUHI PT
PUAENA PT
KAHUKU PT
Haleiwa
Waialua Bay
Kaukonahua
Paalaa
Helemano
Anahulu
Kaena
Waialua
Kaiaka
Kaukonahua
Kaala 1231
Waianae Range
Koolau Range
Palikea Pk 944
232
Kamehameha Hts
BARBERS PT
KAENA PT
KAHUKU PT
Mamala Bay
KAIWI Channel
KEAHI PT

m / ft elevation scale

4000 3000 2000 1500 1000 400 200 m
12 000 9000 6000 4500 3000 1200 600 ft

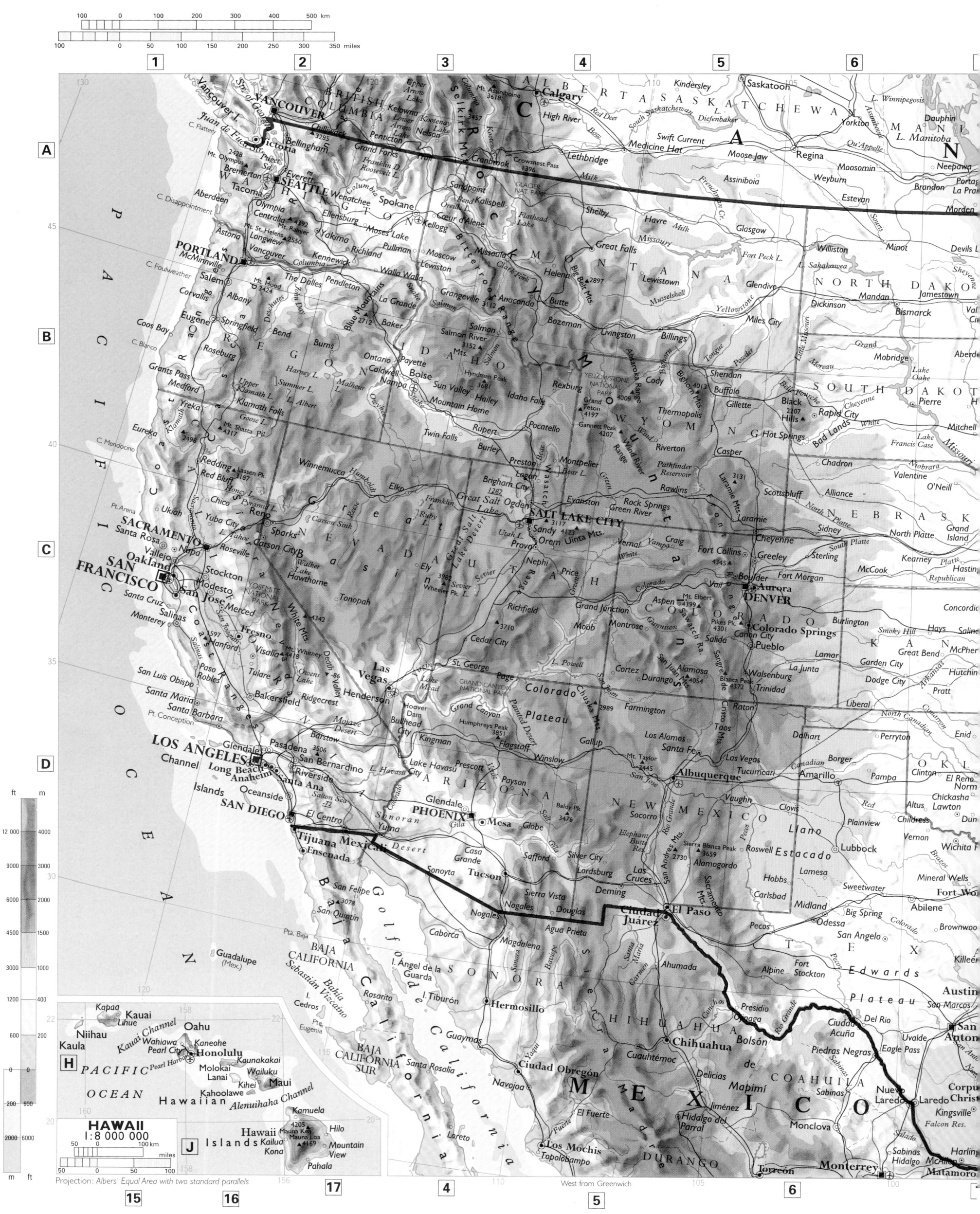

ft   m

12 000   4000

9000   3000

6000   2000

4500   1500

3000   1000

1200   400

600   200

0   0

200   600

2000   6000

m   ft

HAWAII 1:8 000 000

Projection: Albers' Equal Area with two standard parallels

West from Greenwich

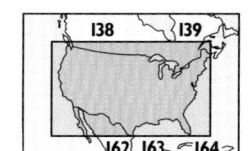

8 9 10 11 12 13

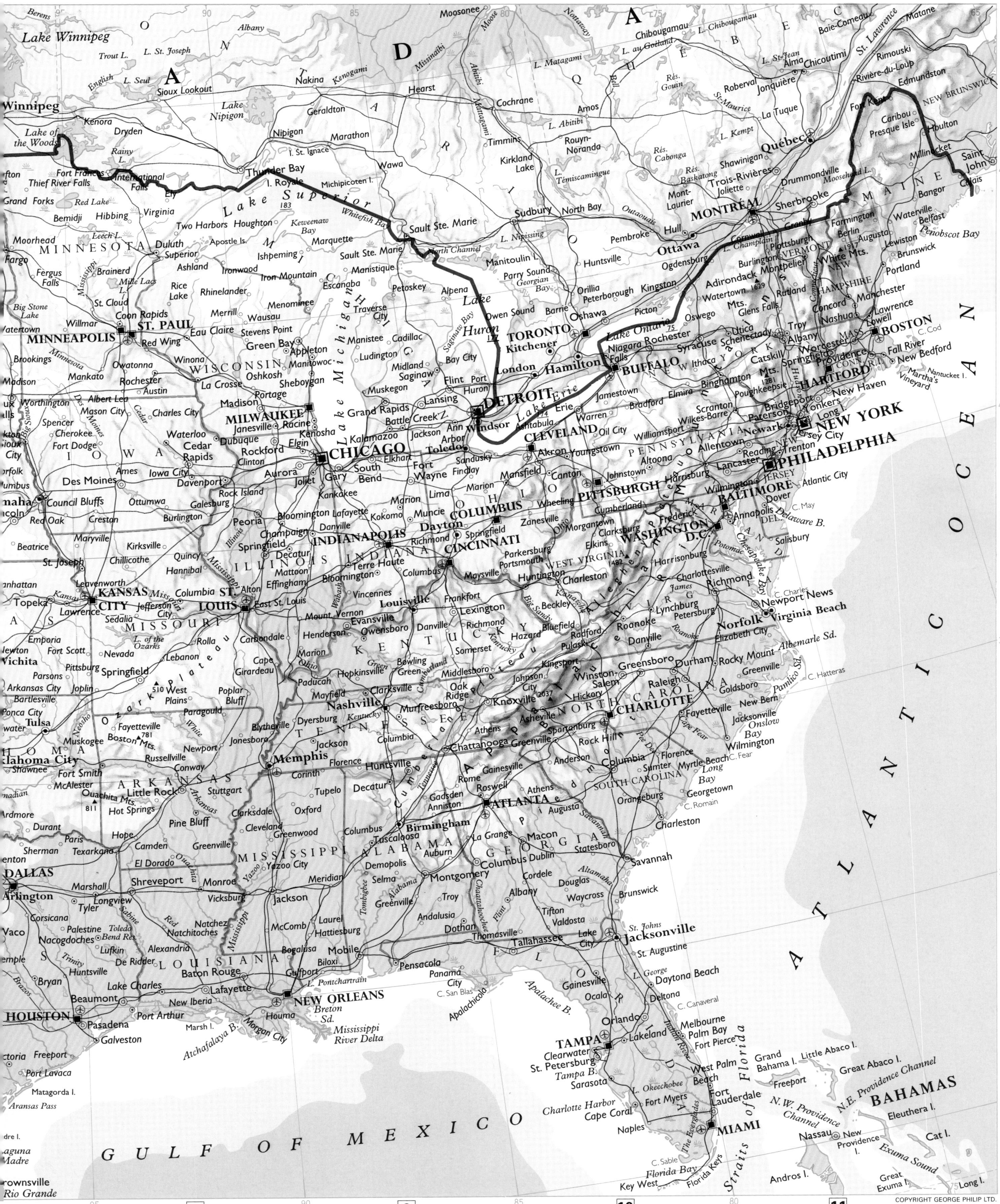

A D A

Lake Winnipeg

Winnipeg
Lake of the Woods

MINNESOTA

Thunder Bay
Lake Superior

MINNEAPOLIS
ST. PAUL

Duluth

WISCONSIN

MILWAUKEE

Madison

Sault Ste. Marie

Lake Michigan
Lake Huron

TORONTO

Lake Ontario
BUFFALO

MONTREAL

Quebec

MAINE
NEW BRUNSWICK

Saint John
Calais
Bangor

Ottawa

NEW HAMPSHIRE
VERMONT

BOSTON
HARTFORD
NEW YORK
Long I.

DETROIT
Windsor
CLEVELAND

CHICAGO
IOWA

Des Moines

ILLINOIS

INDIANAPOLIS

COLUMBUS
CINCINNATI

OHIO

PITTSBURGH

PHILADELPHIA
BALTIMORE
WASHINGTON, D.C.

WEST VIRGINIA

PENNSYLVANIA

Atlantic City
DELAWARE

VIRGINIA

KANSAS CITY
ST. LOUIS

MISSOURI

KENTUCKY

Louisville
Lexington

Norfolk
Virginia Beach
Newport News

C. Hatteras

Nashville
TENNESSEE

NORTH CAROLINA
CHARLOTTE

Raleigh

Memphis

ARKANSAS

Little Rock

ALABAMA
MISSISSIPPI

ATLANTA
GEORGIA

SOUTH CAROLINA

Charleston

DALLAS
Arlington

LOUISIANA

Jackson

Montgomery

Savannah

Jacksonville

NEW ORLEANS

HOUSTON

GULF OF MEXICO

FLORIDA

TAMPA
Orlando

Melbourne

West Palm Beach
Fort Lauderdale

MIAMI

BAHAMAS

Great Abaco I.

ATLANTIC OCEAN

Key West
Florida Keys

GULF OF MEXICO

ATLANTIC OCEAN

BAHAMAS

TENNESSEE

NORTH CAROLINA

SOUTH CAROLINA

GEORGIA

ALABAMA

MISSISSIPPI

FLORIDA

MAINE

NEW HAMPSHIRE

CANADA

Continuation Eastwards On same scale.

Projection: Alber's Equal Area with two standard parallels

West from Greenwich

COPYRIGHT. GEORGE PHILIP & SON LTD.

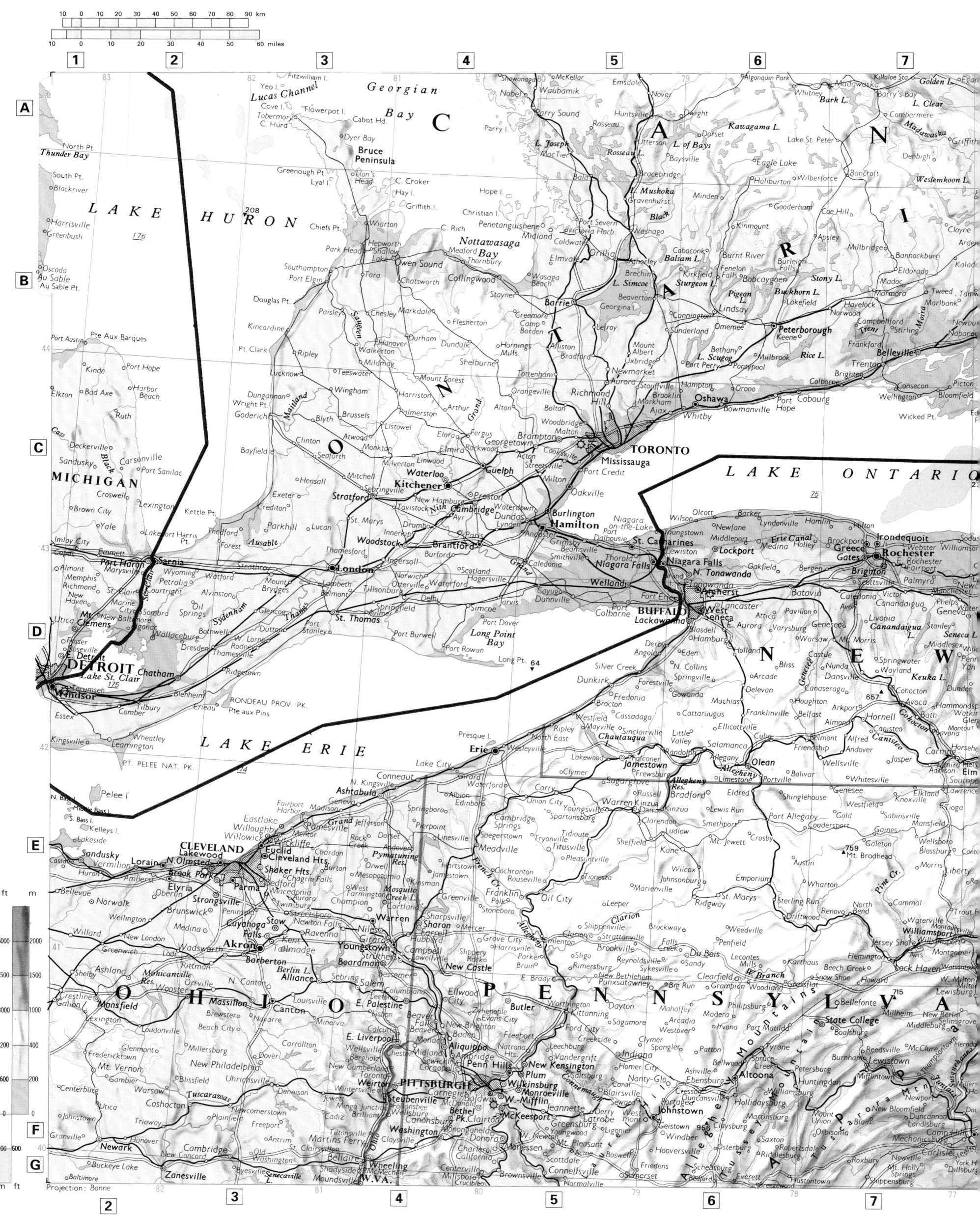

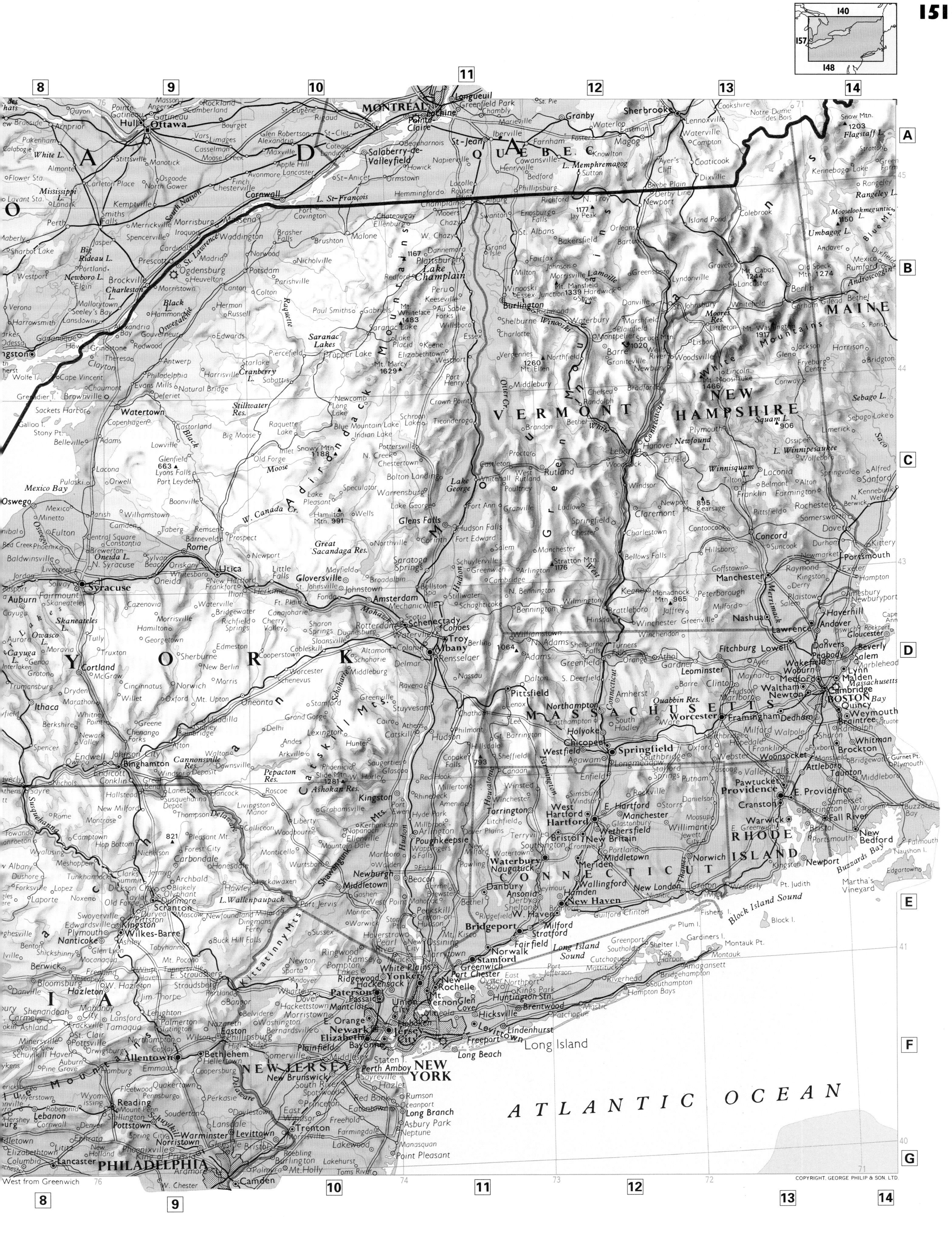
140
157
148
8
9
10
11
12
13
14
A
B
C
D
E
F
G
MONTREAL
Ottawa
Hull
Sherbrooke
Q U É B E C
Granby
Magog
L. Memphremagog
Cornwall
Salaberry-de-Valleyfield
L. St-François
Ogdensburg
Brockville
Lake Champlain
Plattsburgh
Burlington
Montpelier
Barre
VERMONT
Green Mountains
Rutland
Mt. Mansfield 1339
Adirondack Mountains
Mt. Marcy 1629
Saranac Lake
Watertown
Lake George
Glens Falls
Saratoga Springs
Great Sacandaga Res.
Oswego
Syracuse
Utica
Rome
Oneida L.
Mexico Bay
Schenectady
Troy
Albany
Amsterdam
Gloversville
Mohawk
Catskill Mts.
Slide Mtn. 1281
Ashokan Res.
Kingston
Poughkeepsie
Newburgh
Middletown
Binghamton
Ithaca
Cortland
Cayuga L.
Y O R K
NEW HAMPSHIRE
White Mountains
Mt. Washington 1917
Mt. Cabot 1244
Concord
Manchester
Nashua
Portsmouth
L. Winnipesaukee
MAINE
Rangeley L.
Umbagog L.
Berlin
MASSACHUSETTS
BOSTON
Cambridge
Lowell
Lawrence
Worcester
Springfield
Pittsfield
Northampton
Holyoke
Quabbin Res.
Fitchburg
RHODE ISLAND
Providence
Pawtucket
Newport
CONNECTICUT
Hartford
New Haven
New London
Waterbury
Bridgeport
Stamford
Block Island Sound
Long Island Sound
Long Island
Montauk Pt.
Martha's Vineyard
Buzzards Bay
Cape Cod Bay
NEW YORK
Yonkers
Paterson
Newark
Jersey City
Elizabeth
NEW JERSEY
Trenton
New Brunswick
Perth Amboy
Asbury Park
Long Branch
PHILADELPHIA
Camden
Allentown
Bethlehem
Reading
Lancaster
Scranton
Wilkes-Barre
Hazleton
Kittatinny Mts.
Blue Mountain
Delaware
Susquehanna
Hudson
Connecticut
ATLANTIC OCEAN
West from Greenwich
76
74
73
72
71
45
44
43
41
40
COPYRIGHT. GEORGE PHILIP & SON, LTD.

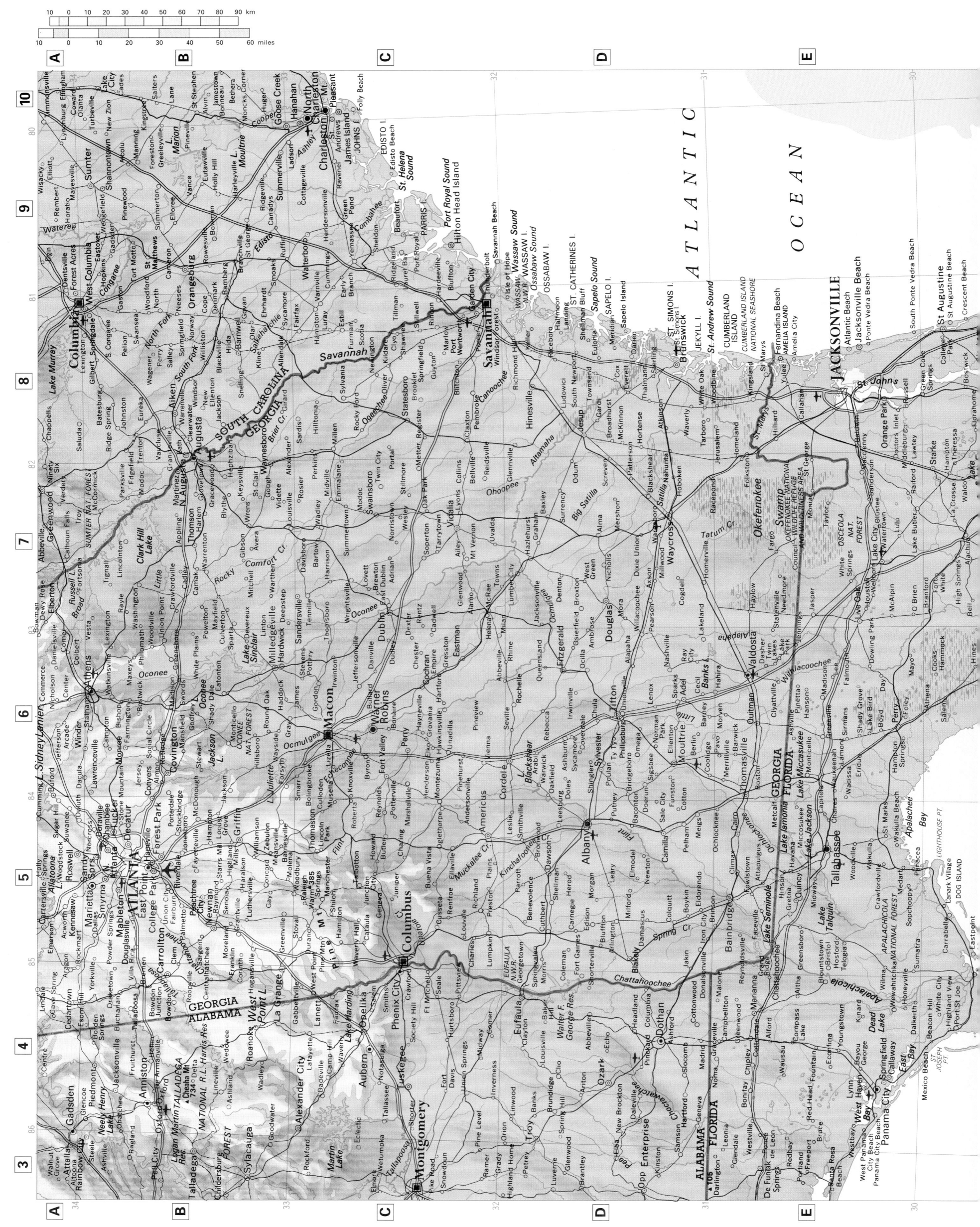

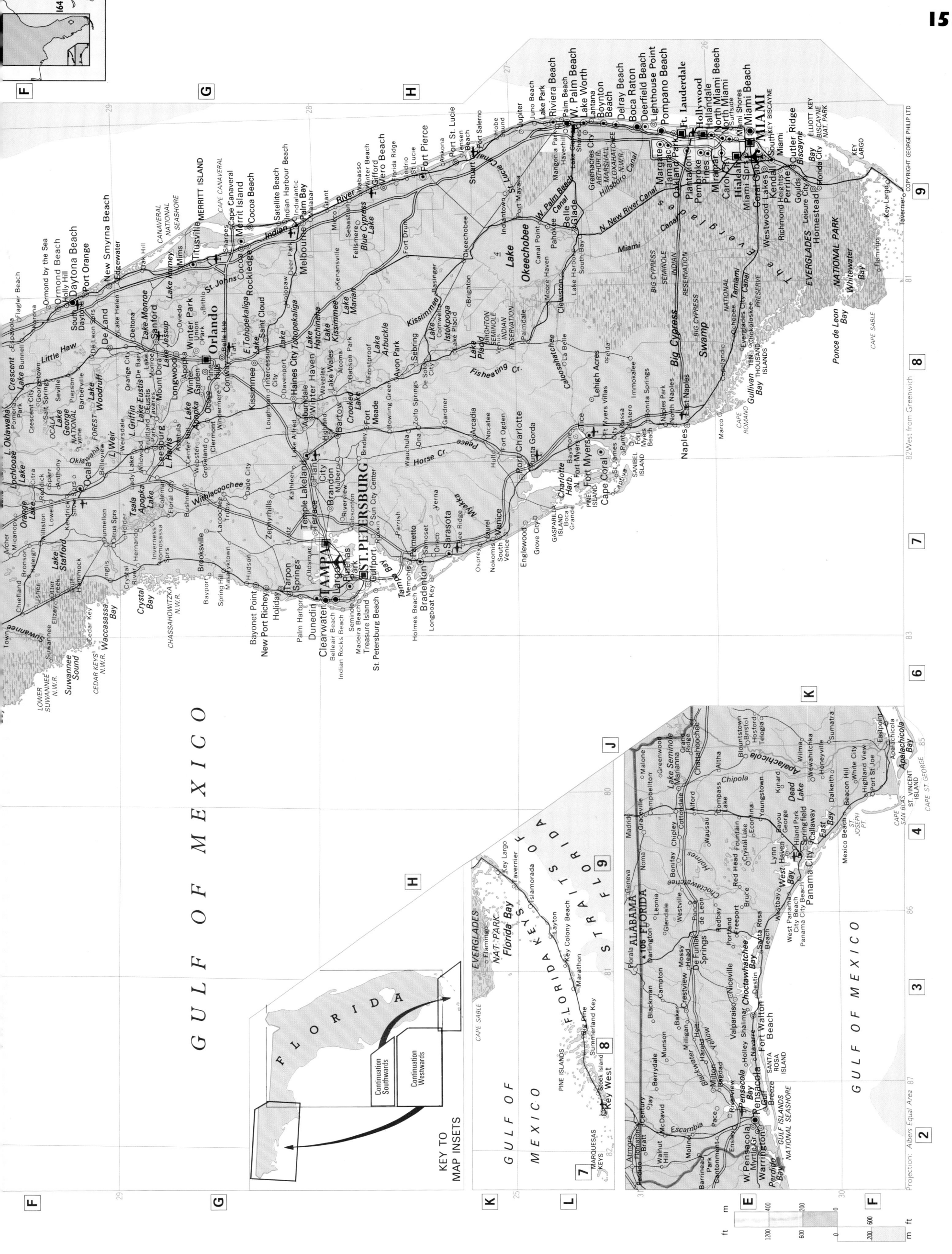

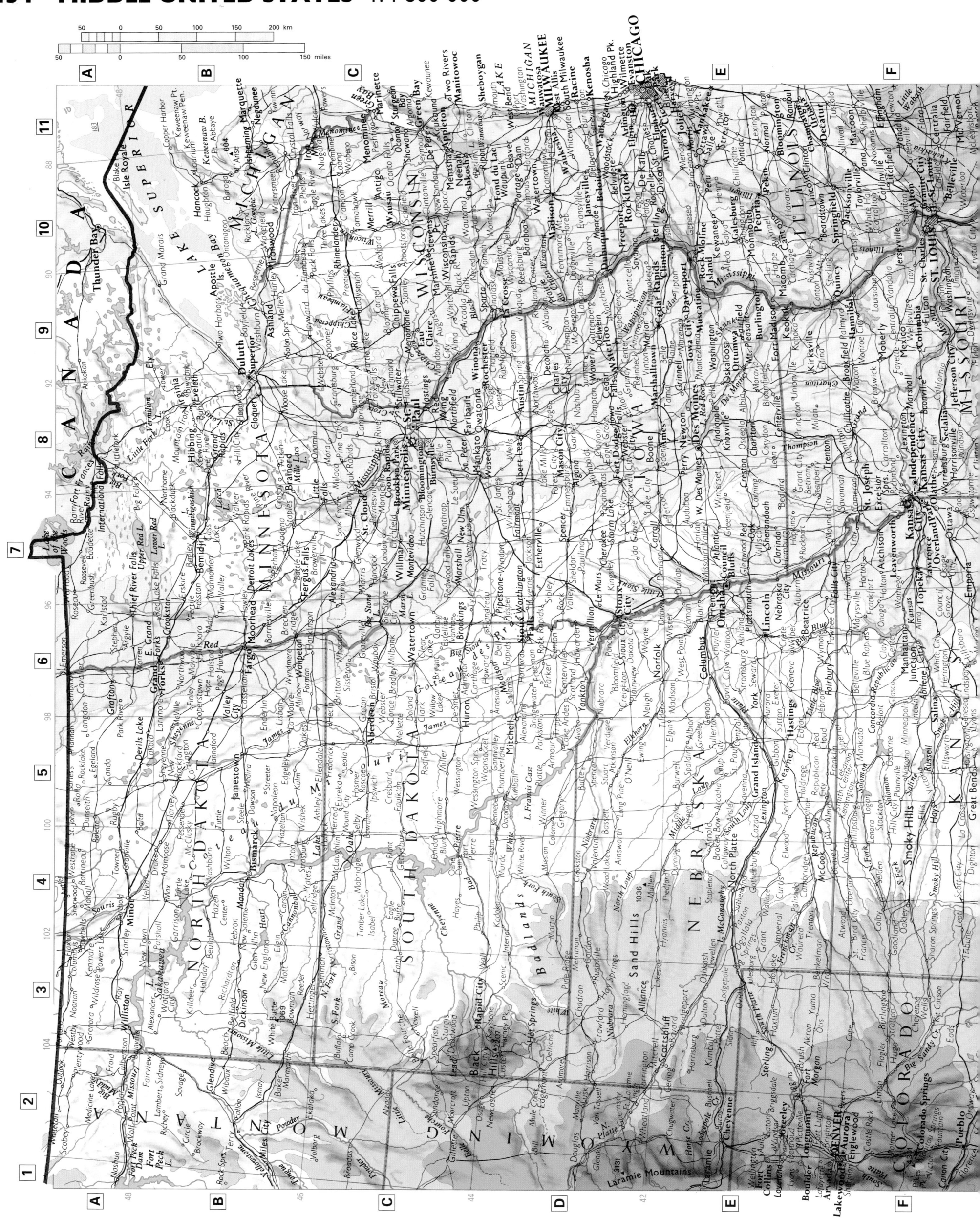

M

Continuation Southwards on same scale

West from Greenwich

GULF OF MEXICO

Projection: Albers' Equal Area with two standard parallels

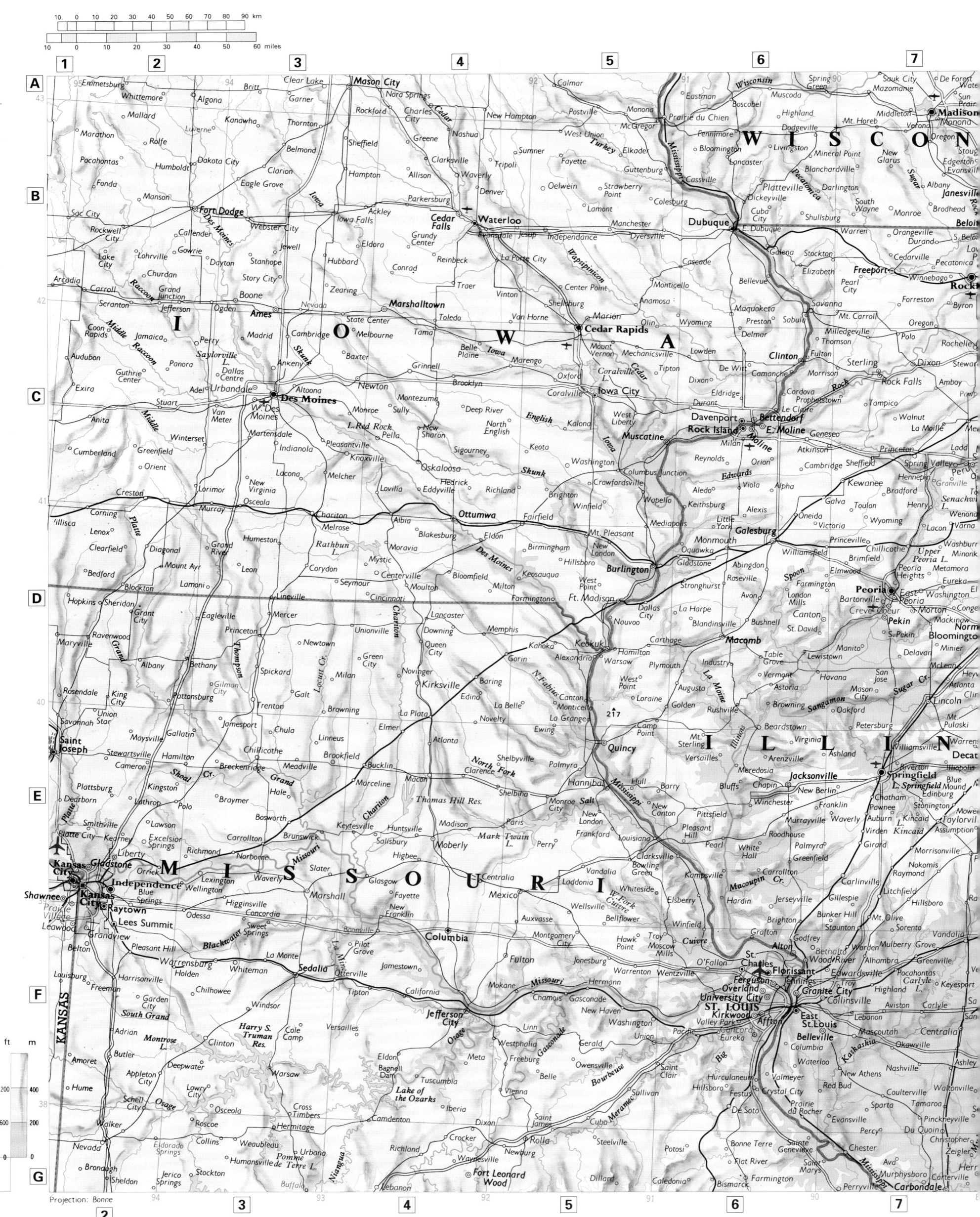

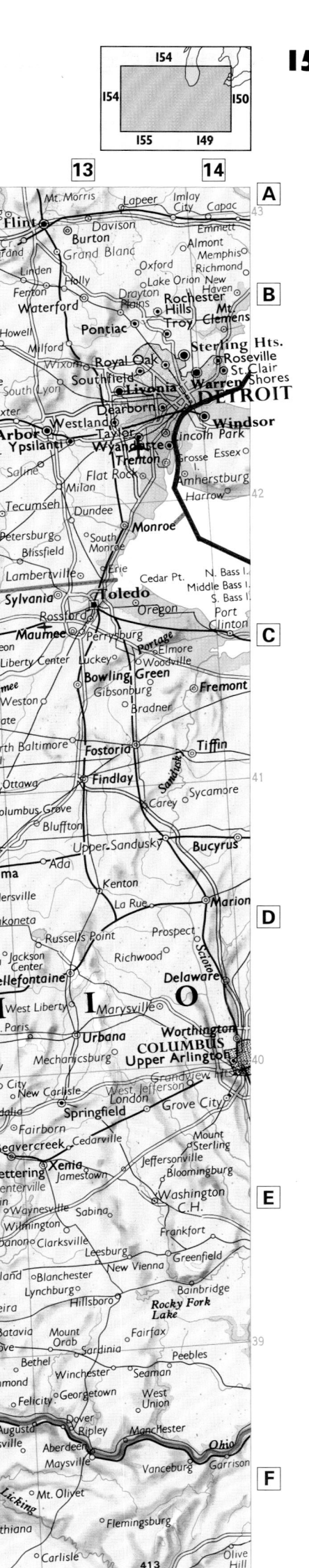

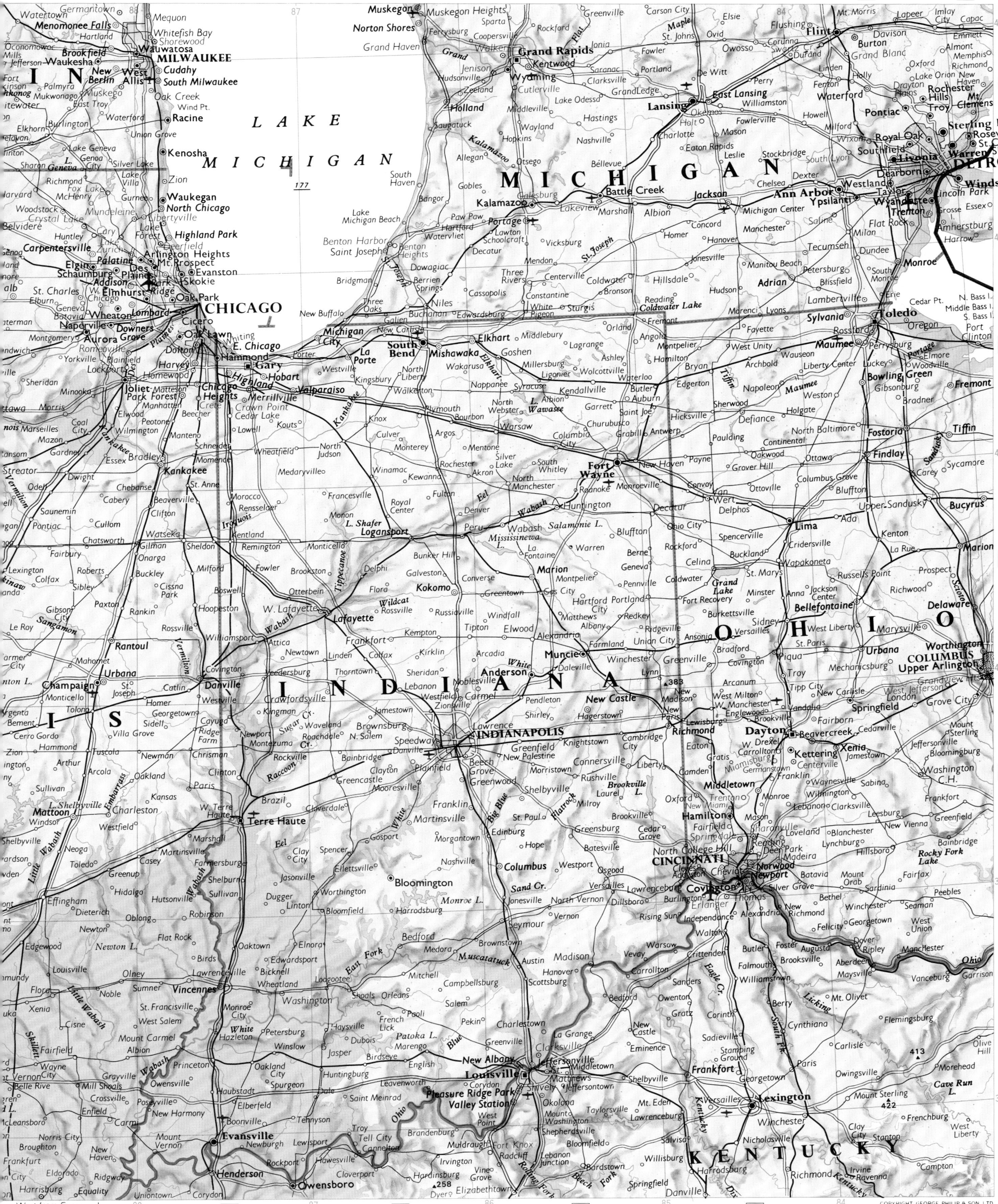

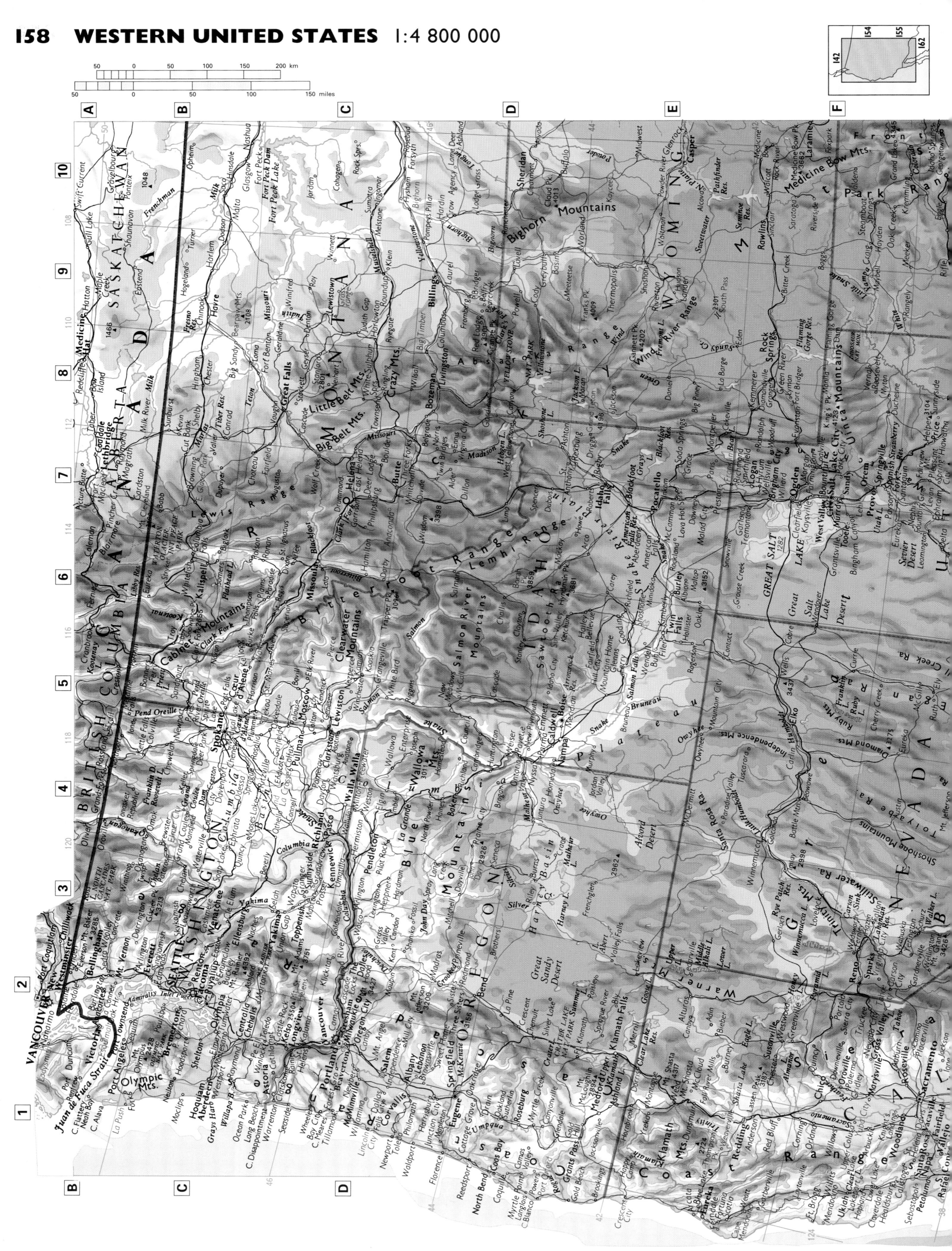

WESTERN WASHINGTON
REGION
On same scale

158 159 162

M

13

12

11

10

9

8

H J K L M

Projection: Bonne

West from Greenwich

L M N

NEVADA

ARIZONA

CALIFORNIA

MEXICO

PACIFIC OCEAN

Meadow Valley Wash

Jumbo Peak 857

Overton

Moapa

Logandale

Lake Mead

LAKE MEAD NATIONAL RECREATION AREA

Mt Tipton 2179

Chloride

Kingman

Hualapai

Yucca

Valentine

Peach Springs

Nelson Reef

Signal

Alamo Crossing

Wenden

Salome

Hope

Bouse

Vicksburg

Wickenburg

Sunrise Manor

North Las Vegas

Las Vegas

Paradise

Henderson

Boulder City

Hoover Dam

Davis Dam

Bullhead City

Oatman

Topock

Needles

Parker Dam

Poston

Parker

Bill Williams R.

Signal Peak 1487

Blythe

Ehrenberg

Quartzsite

Cibola

Palo Verde

Ripley

Winterhaven

Yuma

Imperial Res.

Imperial Dam

Laguna Dam

Ogilby

Glamis

Midway

Holtville

El Centro

Mexicali

Calexico

Heber

Calipatria

Niland

Westmorland

Brawley

Imperial

Indian Springs

Mercury

Charleston Peak 3633

Mountain Pass 1442

Kingston Peak 2252

Pahrump

Johnnie

Sandy

Sloan

Arden

Jean

Goodsprings

Searchlight

Nipton

Cima

McCullough Mtn 2142

Searles L.

Amargosa Range

2043

Death Valley

Telescope Pk 3366

Furnace Creek

Amargosa

Avawatz Mts 1816

Silver Lake L.

Baker

Bigbird

Cadiz

Baghdad

Amboy

Twentynine Palms

Old Dale

JOSHUA TREE NAT. MON.

Joshua Tree

Desert Hot Springs

Indio

Coachella

Mecca

Salton Sea

Oasis

Desert Center

Eagle Mountain

Midland

Sonora Desert

Colorado R. Aqueduct

Chocolate Mts.

Coachella Canal

Imperial Valley

Niland

El Centro

Argus Peak 2600

2487

INYO

Coso Junction

Little Lake

Ridgecrest

China Lake

Inyokern

Randsburg

Johannesburg

Red Mountain

Trona

Westend

Coso Range

MOJAVE

Mojave

Rosamond

Lancaster

Palmdale

Edwards

Boron

Kramer Junction

Hinkley

Barstow

Lenwood

Daggett

Yermo

Newberry Springs

Ludlow

Bagdad

Lavic

Victorville

Adelanto

Hesperia

Apple Valley

Lucerne Valley

Big Bear City

Barstow

Hi Vista

Gorman

Tehachapi Mts

Tehachapi

Keene

Cummings Mtn 2311

Frazier Mtn 2485

Wheeler Ridge

Maricopa

Taft

Bakersfield

Lamont

Arvin

Oildale

Delano

McFarland

Wasco

Shafter

Buttonwillow

Buena Vista L.

Tupman

Ford City

Temblor Range

San Emigdio Mts

Pine Mtn 2692

SAN BERNARDINO

Redlands

L. Arrowhead

San Gorgonio Mtn 3505

Banning

Beaumont

Moreno Valley

Hemet

San Jacinto Peak 3293

Idyllwild

Palm Springs

Cathedral City

Rancho Mirage

Palm Desert

La Quinta

ANZA BORREGO DESERT STATE PARK

2637

Borrego Springs

Santa Rosa Mtn 2637

Coyote Wells

El Centro

Ocotillo

Mount Signal 1717

Calexico

Plaster City

Seeley

Riverside

Corona

Perris

Elsinore

Sun City

Temecula

Murrieta

Fallbrook

Vista

San Marcos

Escondido

Ramona

Julian

Santa Ysabel

Warner Springs

Aguanga

Pala

Valley Center

Poway

Lakeside

El Cajon

Santee

La Mesa

Alpine

Pine Valley

Campo

Tecate

Ontario

Cucamonga

Rancho Cucamonga

Upland

Claremont

Pomona

Chino

Riverside

Pasadena

Glendale

Burbank

Alhambra

Monterey Park

Covina

West Covina

El Monte

Whittier

La Habra

Fullerton

Anaheim

Orange

Santa Ana

Garden Grove

Costa Mesa

Irvine

Mission Viejo

San Juan Capistrano

Dana Point

San Clemente

San Onofre

Oceanside

Carlsbad

Encinitas

Leucadia

Cardiff-by-the-Sea

Del Mar

Laguna Beach

SAN DIEGO

National City

Coronado

Imperial Beach

Chula Vista

Lemon Grove

Spring Valley

TIJUANA

Rosarito

La Puerta

Pta. Descanso

El Descanso

Mt San Antonio 3068

Wrightwood

Palmdale

Santa Clarita

San Fernando

Newhall

Castaic

Piru

Fillmore

Santa Paula

Ojai

Moorpark

Simi Valley

Thousand Oaks

Agoura

Malibu

Santa Monica

LOS ANGELES

Inglewood

Torrance

Redondo Beach

Palos Verdes

Palos Verdes Pt.

San Pedro

Long Beach

Carson

Compton

Downey

Norwalk

Lakewood

Bellflower

Cerritos

Buena Park

Huntington Beach

Newport Beach

Gulf of Santa Catalina

Avalon

Santa Catalina

San Pedro Channel

Channel Islands

Anacapa I.

Santa Cruz I.

Santa Rosa I.

San Miguel I.

Santa Barbara I.

San Nicolas I.

San Clemente I.

Ventura

Oxnard

Port Hueneme

El Rio

Camarillo

San Buenaventura

Santa Barbara

Montecito

Carpinteria

Goleta

Isla Vista

Santa Barbara Channel

Pt. Conception

Pt. Arguello

Lompoc

Vandenberg

Surf

Guadalupe

Santa Maria

Nipomo

Arroyo Grande

Grover City

Pismo Beach

San Luis Obispo

Los Osos

Morro Bay

Cambria

Shandon

Paso Robles

Atascadero

Templeton

Santa Margarita

Creston

Los Alamos

Buellton

Solvang

Santa Ynez

Los Olivos

Santa Ynez Mts

Santa Ynez R.

San Rafael Mts

Sisquoc

New Cuyama

Cuyama

Maricopa

Lake Isabella

Kernville

Wofford Heights

Lake Isabella

Hillcrest Center

Bodfish

Weldon

Onyx

Keysville

Breckenridge Mtn 2303

Woody

Glennville

Piute Mtns

Walker Pass 1578

Kelso Valley

3035

Sierra Nevada

Owens Peak 2468

Freeman Junction

Telescope Pk

San Andreas Fault

L. Havasu

L. Havasu City

Vidal Junction

Vidal

10 0 10 20 30 40 50 60 70 80 90 km

10 0 10 20 30 40 50 60 miles

m

4000

3000

2000

1500

1000

400

200

0

ft

12 000

9000

6000

4500

3000

1200

600

0

m ft

6000

2000

200

0

0

200

600

km
50 0 50 100 150 200 250 300 km
miles
50 0 50 100 150 200 miles

1 2 3 4

A

B

C

D

REFERENCE TO NUMBERS
1 Federal District   5 México
2 Aguascalientes   6 Morelos
3 Guanajuato   7 Querétaro
4 Hidalgo   8 Tlaxcala

Projection: Bi-polar oblique Conical Orthomorphic

West from Greenwich

ft m
12,000 4000
9000 3000
6000 2000
4500 1500
3000 1000
1200 400
600 200
0 0
200 600
2000 6000
4000 12,000
m ft

PACIFIC

OCEAN

5   **6**   **7**   **8**

Wichita
Falls
Possum
Kingdom
Res.
FORT WORTH
Ranger
Abilene
Cleburne
Denton
DALLAS
Denison
Sherman
Greenville
Paris
Texarkana
Red
Hope
Camden
ARKANSAS
El Dorado
Monroe
Greenville
Tuscaloosa
Opelika
Columbus
McRde
Ocmulgee

A

Brownwood
Hillsboro
Waco
Temple
Austin
Corsicana
Palestine
Tyler
Longview
Marshall
Shreveport
Nacogdoches
Toledo
Bend
Res.
Lufkin
Sam
Rayburn Res.
Alexandria
Natchez
Vicksburg
Jackson
Meridian
Laurel
Hattiesburg
McComb
Montgomery
Troy
Selma
Phenix City
Americus
Dothan
Jim Woodruff Res.
Flomaton
Albany
GEORGIA
Tifton
Cordele
Waycross
Valdosta
Chattahoochee
Lake
City
FLORIDA

D
A
L
L
A
S

Brownwood

MISSISSIPPI
ALABAMA
STATES

SAN
ANTONIO
Dilley
Alice
Laredo
Kingsville
Nuevo Laredo
Zapata
Corpus Christi
Victoria
Huntsville
Bryan
HOUSTON
Beaumont
Rosenberg
Port
Arthur
Galveston
Lake Charles
Lafayette
Baton
Rouge
Hammond
NEW
ORLEANS
Biloxi
Gulfport
Pensacola
Panama City
Apalachee
Bay
Apalachicola
C. San Blas
Suwannee
Clearwater

B

GULF   OF

GULF   O F

Laguna Madre
McAllen
Harlingen
Brownsville
Matamoros
Valle Hermoso
Santa Teresa
Laguna Madre

M E X I C O

Tropic of Cancer

C

CUBA
Guane
La Fé
La Esperanza
C. San Antonio
C.
Corrientes
Canal de Yucatán

M E X I C O

GULF
O F

Golfo
de
Campeche

Golfo
de
Campeche

Ciudad del
Carmen
Campeche
QUINTANA
ROO
Chetumal
Ambergris Cay
Turneffe Is.
Belize
City
BELIZE
Islas de
la Bahía

D

Tropic of Cancer

5   95   90

E

GULF OF MEXICO

U.S.A.
West Palm Beach
Fort Myers
Boca Raton
Fort Lauderdale
Naples
C. Romano
The Everglades
Hialeah
MIAMI
Everglades
C. Sable
Florida Bay
Florida City
Key West
Dry Tortugas
Florida Keys
Straits of Florida

Little Abaco I.
Normans Castle
West End
Grand Bahama I.
Freeport
Hope Town
Great Abaco I.
Grand Guana Cay
Bimini Is.
Berry Is.
Northwest Providence Channel
Nassau
New Providence
Eleuthera I.
Andros Town
Andros Island
Great Exuma I.
Exuma Sound
Northeast Providence Channel
Dunmore Town
BA...
GREAT BAHAMA BANK

Isla Desterrada
Isla Pérez
Canal de Yucatán

Pta. Yalkubul
Progreso
Dzilam de Bravo
Dzibichaltún
Motul
MÉRIDA
Temax
Tizimín
El Cuyo
C. Catoche
Izamal
Maxcanú
Ticul
Espita
Cancún
Pto. Juárez
YUCATÁN
Mayapán
Chichén Itzá
Valladolid
El Díaz
Puerto Morelos
Sotuta
Peto
Tenabo
Campeche
Champotón
San José Carpizo
Hopelchén
Bolonchenticul
Felipe Carrillo Puerto
Vigía Chico
Isla Cozumel
Chenkán
Juárez
Pedro Antonio Santos
QUINTANA ROO
B. de la Ascensión
B. del Espíritu Santo
Ciudad del Carmen
Laguna de Términos
Pital
Palizada
Concepción
CAMPECHE
Chetumal
B. de Corozal
Banco Chinchorro
Orange Walk
Matorras
Tenosique
Uaxactún
Maya Mts.
Ambergris Cay

Canal de Yucatán

(Havana) LA HABANA
Guanabacoa
MARIANAO
San Antonio de los Baños
Guanajay
Bahía Honda
La Esperanza
Pinar del Rio
Los Palacios
Guane
La Fé
San Luis
Isla de la Juventud
Nueva Gerona
Corrientes
C. San Antonio
Santo Cruz del Norte
Matanzas
Canal Nicolás
Cárdenas
Colón
Jovellanos
Güines
Batabanó
Jagüey Grande
Playa Larga
Cienfuegos
Sagua la Grande
Santa Clara
Caibarién
Placetas
Morón
Ciego de Ávila
Trinidad
Sancti-Spíritus
Júcaro
Tunas de Zaza
Arch. de los Jardines de la Reina
Archipiélago de los Canarreos
CUBA
GREATER
Nuevitas
Camagüey
Florida
Victoria de las Tunas
Santa Cruz del Sur
Golfo de Guacanayabo
Manzanillo
Bayamo
Holguín
Puerto Padre
Gibara
Palma Soriano
Sierra Maestra
SANTIAGO DE CUBA
2000

Canal Viejo de Bahama
Jumento Cays
Cay Sal Bank
Santaren Channel

Cayman Islands (Br.)
Georgetown
Grand Cayman
Cayman Brac
Little Cayman
C. Cruz
7680

Swan Islands (U.S.A. & Honduras)

Montego Bay
Lucea
Falmouth
St. Ann's Bay
Port Maria
Annotto Bay
Savanna la Mar
JAMAICA
Port Antonio
South Negril Pt.
Cambridge
Black River
Mandeville
May Pen
Spanish Town
KINGSTON
Pedro Cays (Jamaica)

Belize City
Turneffe Is.
BELIZE
Middlesex
Danriga
Benque Viejo
Flores
L. Petén Itzá
La Libertad
Tikal
San Ignacio
San Luis
Usumacinta
Lacantún
L. Independencia
Comitán
GUATEMALA
Cuchumatanes
Huehuetenango
Cobán
Sa. de las Minas
San Marcos
Totonicapán
Sololá
Jalapa
Zacapa
Chiquimula
Quezaltenango
Retalhuleu
Antigua
GUATEMALA
Amatitlán
Escuintla
Mazatenango
Santa Rosa de Copán
Copán
San Pedro Sula
El Progreso
Santa Bárbara
HONDURAS
Sula
Comayagua
Yoro
Juticalpa
Catacamas
Golfo de Honduras
Punta Gorda
Monkey River
Livingston
Puerto Barrios
Puerto Cortés
Tela
La Ceiba
Balfate
Trujillo
Olanchito
Islas de la Bahía
Roatán
Puerto Castilla
Iriona
C. Camarón
Pta. Patuca
Brus laguna
C. Falso
Laguna Caratasca
Mosquitia
C. Gracias á Dios
Puerto Cabo Gracias á Dios
Kisalaya
Cayos Miskitos (Nicaragua)
Pta. Gorda
Puerto Cabezas

Comayagüela
TEGUCIGALPA
Danlí
Jinotega
Cholutega
Segovia
Coco
Patuca
Olancho
Siuna
Bonanza
Rosita

Santa Ana
Suchitoto
Cojutepeque
Zacatecoluca
Ahuachapán
Sonsonate
Nueva San Salvador (Santa Tecla)
SAN SALVADOR
Usulután
EL SALVADOR
San Miguel
San Vicente
La Unión
Golfo de Fonseca
Chinandega
León
La Paz Centro
Corinto
Esteli
Matagalpa
Muy Muy
NICARAGUA
Boaco
Juigalpa
Siquia
Santo Domingo
Rama
Rio Grande
Prinzapolca
I. de San Pedro
Tuma
Tungla
San Carlos
Bluefields
El Bluff
Pta. Mico
Cord. de Yolaina
Bahía de San Juan del Norte
San Juan del Norte
C. Gracias á Dios

I. de Providencia (Colombia)
I. de San Andrés (Colombia)
Cayos de Albuquerque (Colombia)
Bajo Nuevo (Colombia)
Cayos Roncador (U.S.A. & Colombia)

CARIBBEAN

MANAGUA
Masaya
Granada
Diriamba
Jinotepe
L. de Managua
Lago de Nicaragua
Isla de Ometepe
Rivas
San Juan del Sur
B. de Salinas
C. Sta. Elena
Golfo de Papagayo
Liberia
Cord. de Guanacaste
Santa Cruz
Nicoya
C. Velas
Islas del Maíz (Nicaragua, U.S.A.)
San Juan

COSTA RICA
Cord. Central
Guápiles
Siquirres
Alajuela
Puntarenas
Pen. de Nicoya
C. Blanco
Golfo de Nicoya
San José
Cartago
Limón
Pta. Mona
Puerto Quepos
Cord. de Talamanca
3867
Bahía de Coronado
Buenos Aires
Puerto Cortes
Pen. de Osa
Golfo Dulce
Puerto Armuelles
Pta. Burica
Golfo de Chiriquí
David
Boquete
Volcán Barú
3370
Laguna de Chiriquí
Golfo de los Mosquitos
Bocas del Toro
Almirante
Remedios
Rio Hato
Santiago
Serranía de Tabasará
Aguadulce
Penonomé
La Chorrera
Chepo
PANAMÁ
Colón
Nombre de Dios
Portobelo
Archipiélago de San Blas
Sierranía de San Blas
Golfo del Darién
Gatún I.
Balboa
Pta. San Bernardo
Is. de San Bernardo
Chimán
San Miguel
I. del Rey
Arch. de las Perlas
Golfo de Panamá
Chitré
Las Tablas
Pen. de Azuera
Pocri
I. de Coiba
I. de Cebaco
Pta. Mala
Pta. Mariato
CARTAG...
DARIÉN
La Palma
El Real
Turbo
Golfo de Urabá
G. de Morrosquillo

Projection: Bi-polar oblique Conical Orthomorphic

MAS

A T L A N T I C   O C E A N

Tropic of Cancer

ur's Town
The Bight
Cat I.
San Salvador
(Watling I., Guanahani)
Conception I.
Rum Cay
Long I.
Clarence Town
Crooked I. Passage
Richmond
Crooked I.
Plana Cays
Albert Town
Snug Corner
Mayaguana I.
Cay Verde
Acklins I.
Mira por vos Cay
Hogsty Reef
Little Inagua I.
Caicos Passage
Caicos Islands (Br.)
Turks I. Passage
Turks Islands (Br.)
Lake Rose
Great Inagua I.
Matthew Town
Puerto Rico Trench
Milwaukee Deep 9220

Baracoa
Pta. de Maisi
Paso de los Vientos (Windward Passage)
Guantánamo
Cap-à-Foux
Î. de la Tortue
port-de-Paix
Cap-Haïtien
Fort-Liberté
Monte Cristi
La Isabela
Puerto Plata
Santiago de los Cabelleros
Vega
San Francisco de Macorís
Nagua
C. Frances Viejo
Sánchez
Sabana de la Mar
San Juan
Bayamón SAN JUAN
Carolina
Virgin Is. Anegada
Virgin Gorda Tortola (Br.)
Sombrero (Anguilla)
Anguilla (Br.)
St.-Martin (Guad.)
St.-Barthélemy (Fr.)
Barbuda
ANTIGUA & BARBUDA
Antigua
Montserrat
Guadeloupe Passage
Ste-Rose Moule Désirade
GUADELOUPE
Basse-Terre Pointe-à-Pitre
Marie-Galante Grand-Bourg
Dominica Passage
Portsmouth DOMINICA
Roseau
Martinique Passage
Ste-Marie
Mt. Pelée 1397 François
Rivière-Pilote
Fort-de-France MARTINIQUE
St. Lucia Channel (Fr.)
Castries ST. LUCIA
Soufrière
St. Vincent Passage
Speightstown
Soufrière 1234 ST. VINCENT
Kingstown Bridgetown & THE BARBADOS
Hillsborough GRENADINES
The Grenadines
St. George's GRENADA

HAITI
DOMINICAN REP
PORT-AU-PRINCE
San Juan
Jérémie
Dame Marie
Massif de la Hotte
Les Cayes
Aquin
Jacmel
3175
HISPANIOLA
ANTILLES
Golfe de la Gonâve
Gonaïves Hinche
St.-Marc
2280
Barahona
SANTO DOMINGO
San Cristóbal
San Pedro de Macorís
La Romana
Higüey
C. Engano
Hato Mayor
Mayagüez
Isla Mona
PUERTO RICO (U.S.A.)
Ponce
Caguas
Guayama
Charlotte Amalie
Frederiksted St. Croix
Christiansted
St. Kitts & Nevis
Basseterre
St. Eustatius (Neth.)
Saba (Neth.)
St. Maarten (Neth.)
Redonda
LEEWARD ISLANDS
WINDWARD ISLANDS
LESSER ANTILLES
I. de Aves (Bird I.) (Venezuela)

Arecibo
Aguadilla
Fajardo

BEAN SEA

LESSER ANTILLES

Aruba (Neth)
Curaçao
Bonaire
NETH. ANTILLES
Willemstad
Is. de Aves (Ven.)
I. Orchila (Ven.)
I. Los Roques (Ven.)
I. Blanquilla (Ven.)
I. Los Hermanos (Ven.)
I. Los Testigos (Ven.)
Tobago
Scarborough
Galera Pt.
Port of Spain
Arima Trinidad
TRINIDAD & TOBAGO
San Fernando
Serpent's Mouth

Pta. Gallinas
C. San Román
Pen. de Paraguaná
Punto Fijo
Puerto Cumarebo
Coro La Vela de Coro
Tucacas
Puerto Cabello
Maiquetía La Guaira
CARACAS
Distrito Federal
I. La Tortuga (Ven.)
I. Margarita La Asunción
NUEVA ESPARTA
Porlamar
Pen. de Paria
Carúpano
Río Caribe Güira
Golfo de Paria
Cumaná
SUCRE
Carúpano
Caripito

Ríohacha
Uribia
Golfo de Venezuela
Punta Cardón
Pen. de la Guajira
GUAJIRA
San Juan de Guía
Santa Marta
Ciénaga
MARACAIBO
La Concepción
Santa Rita
Cabimas
Ciudad Ojeda
Lago de Maracaibo
La Ceiba
Barquisimeto
San Felipe
YARACUY
Valencia
Villa de Cura
Maracay
S. Juan de los Morros
Higuerote
Puerto La Cruz
Barcelona
ANZOATEGUI
Anaco MONAGAS
Maturín
DELTA AMACURO
Tucupita
Valledupar
Villa del Rosario
CESAR
Machiques
ZULIA
TRUJILLO
Valera
MÉRIDA
Ciudad Bolivia
Barinas
BARINAS
San Fernando de Apure
GUÁRICO
Calabozo
Valle de la Pascua
El Sombrero
El Baúl
PORTUGUESA
Guanare
Acarigua
San Carlos
COJEDES
San Carlos del Zulia
El Tocuyo
Trujillo
LARA
FALCÓN
Altagracia
Mene de Mauroa
Carora
Aragua de Barcelona
Santa María de Ipire
Pariaguán
Cantaura
El Tigre
El Pao
Ciudad Guayana
Upata
Sierra Imataca
Soledad
Ciudad Bolívar
BOLÍVAR
Caicara
Cabruta
Caroní
Guasipati
Tumeremo
El Callao
VENEZUELA
Orinoco
Apure
Meta
Cúcuta
TÁCHIRA
San Cristóbal
Barbacoas

West from Greenwich

COPYRIGHT GEORGE PHILIP & SON LTD.

Projection: Lambert's Azimuthal Equal Area

Projection: *Lambert's Azimuthal Equal Area*

■ LIMA Capital Cities

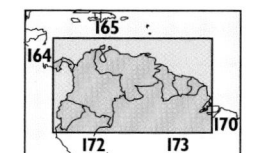

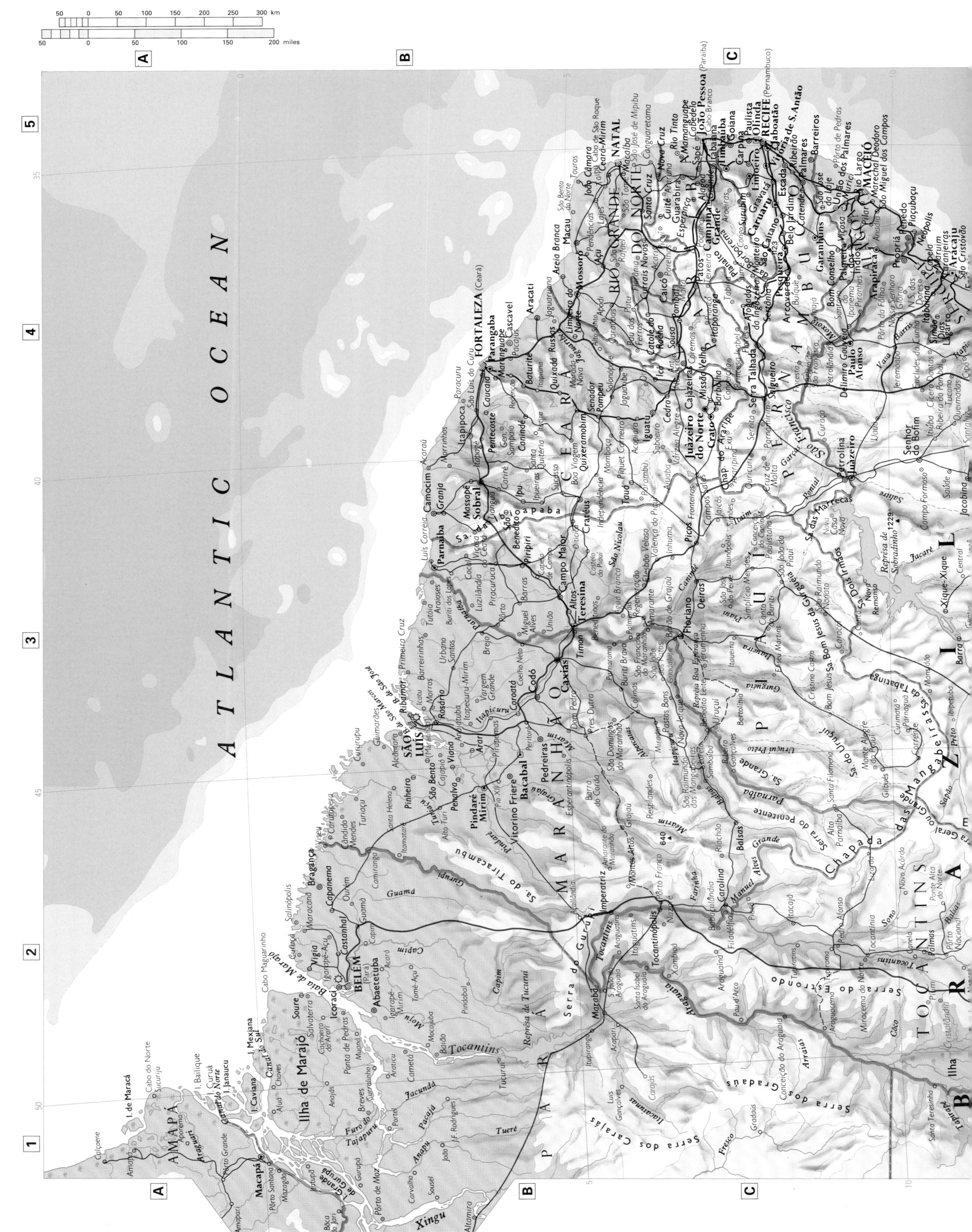

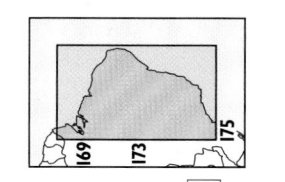

Projection: Lambert's Equivalent Azimuthal

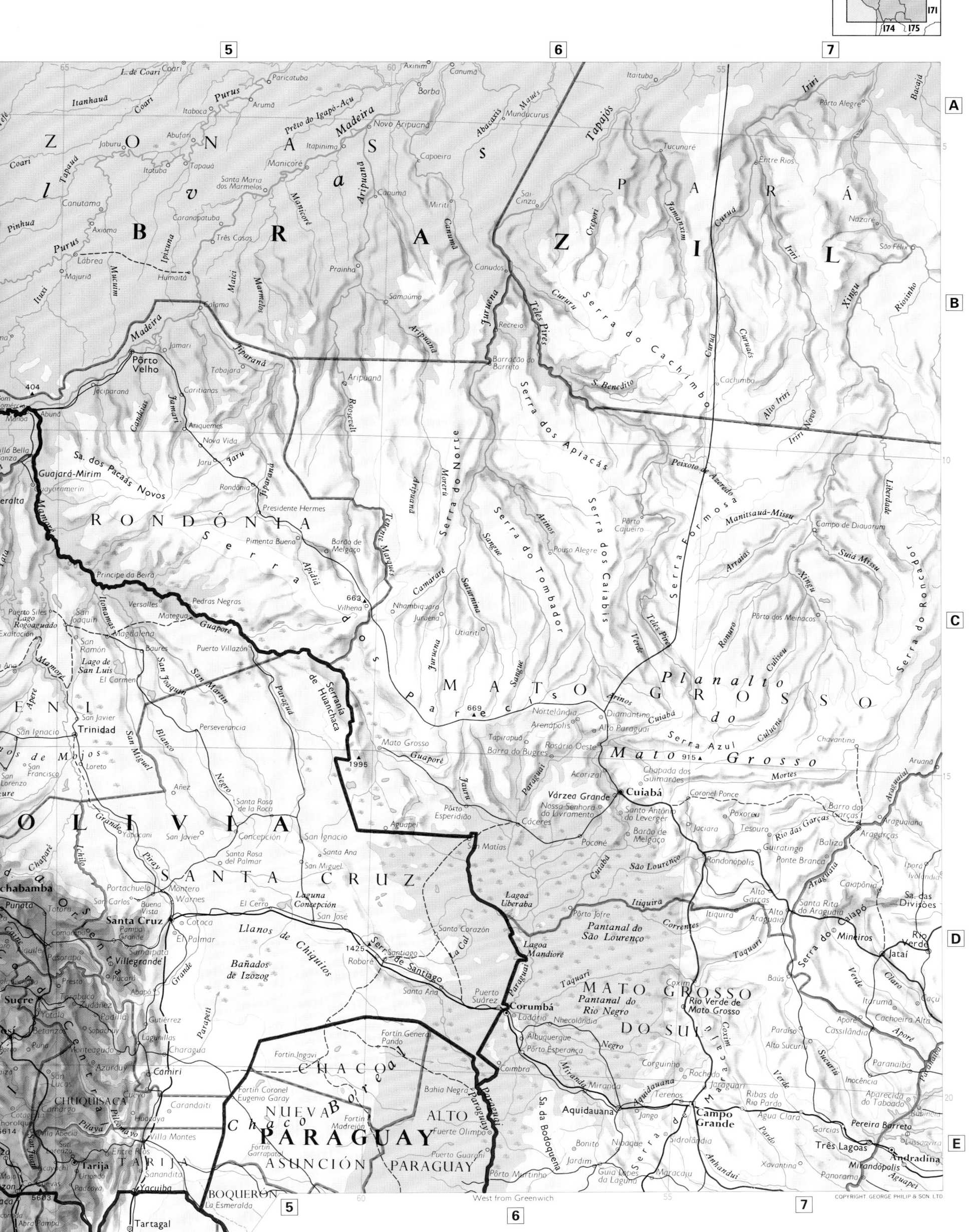

COPYRIGHT GEORGE PHILIP & SON. LTD

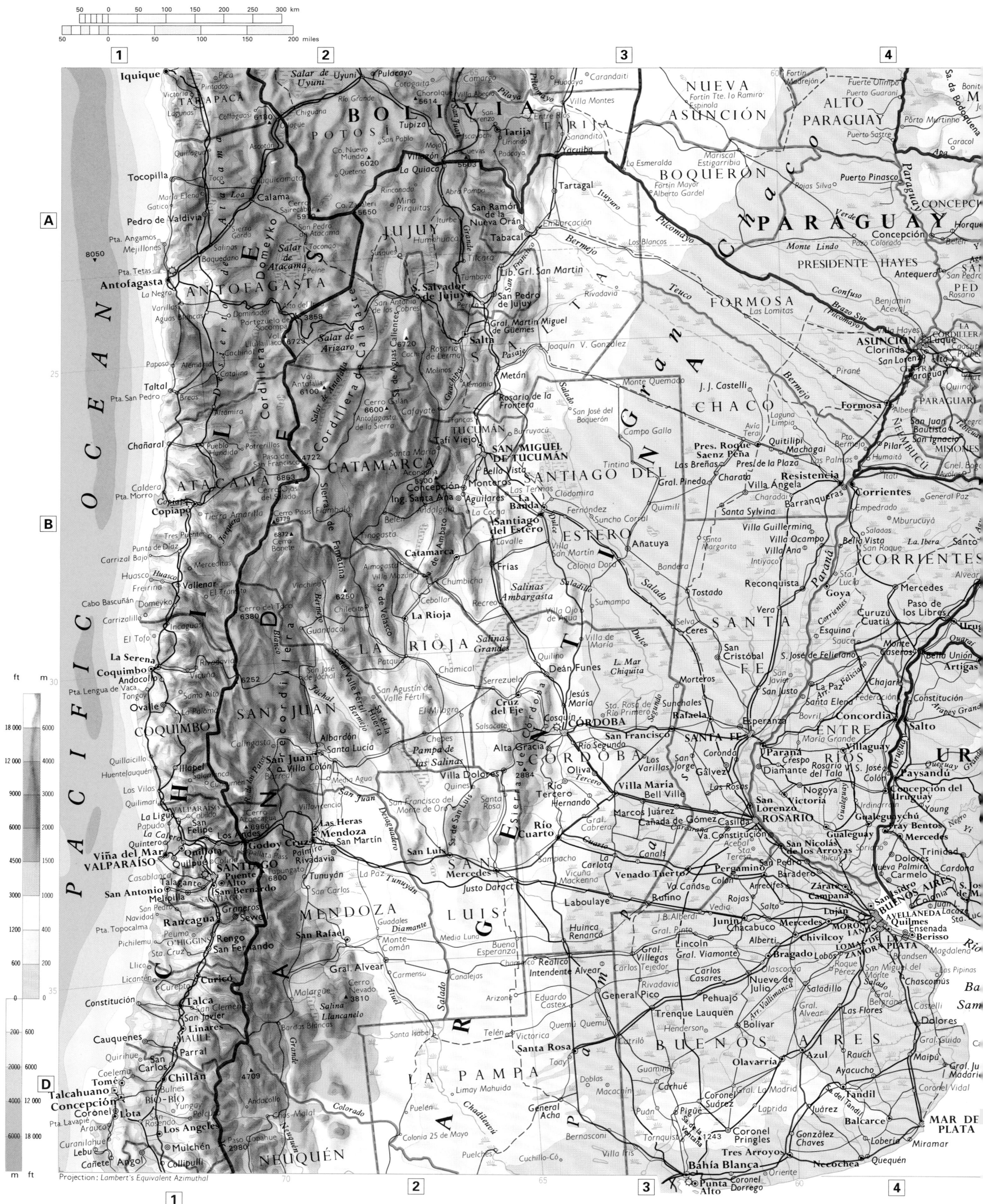

Projection: Lambert's Equivalent Azimuthal

BELO
HORIZONTE
Lima
Itabirito
Congonhas
Cons.
Lafaiete
Ouro
Prêto
Ponte Nova
Carangola
Vitória
Itaquari
Vila
Velha
Guarapari
Picada
Bandeira
2890

Três Lagoas
Andradina
Mirassol
S. Olímpia
Passos
Batatais
Oliveira
Campo Belo
São João
del Rei
Ubá
Muriaé
Itaperuna
Cachoeiro
de Itapemirim

MATO GROSSO
DO SUL
Xavantina
Mirandópolis
Araçatuba
S. José
do Rio Prêto
Caranduva
Ribeirão
Prêto
Bebedouro
São Seb.
do Paraíso
Guaxupé
Três
Pontas
Lavras
Barbacena
Cataguases
Carangola
Alegre
Castelo

Maracaju
Panorama
Birigui
Taquaritinga
Japoticabal
Mococa
Alfenas
Poços de
Caldas
Varginha
Três
Corações
Juiz de Fora
Leopoldina
Guarus

Dourados
Pardo
Rio Brilhante
Santo Anastácio
Adamantina
Tupã
SÃO
Lins
Novo
Horizonte
Araraquara
Casa
Branca
Pinhal
Ouro Fino
Pouso
Alegre
Itajubá
Cruzeiro
Volta
Redonda
Barra do Piraí
Nova Friburgo
CAMPOS

Pôrto São José
Pres.
Epitácio
Presidente
Prudente
Martinópolis
Marília
Garça
Jaú
São
Carlos
Rio Claro
São João
da Boa Vista
Mogi Mirim
Americana
São
Lourenço
Mantiqueira
Três
Rios
Além Paraíba
Cabo de
São Tomé

Pedro Juan Caballero
Rancharia
Paraguaçu
Paulista
Bauru
Bariri
Limeira
Piracicaba
CAMPINAS
Guaratinguetá
Bragança
Paulista
Mansa
Nova Iguaçu
RIO DE
JANEIRO
Macaé

Ponta Porã
Paranavaí
Nova
Esperança
Rolândia
Assis
Santa Cruz
do Rio Pardo
Ourinhos
Botucatu
Avaré
Tietê
Paulista
Angra dos Reis
PARQUE DE
CAXIAS
SÃO GONÇALO
La. de Araruama
Cabo Frio

Maringá
Londrina
Cambará
Cornélio
Procópio
Jacarèzinho
Tatuí
Sorocaba
Itu
Jundiaí
S. J. dos Campos
NITERÓI
RIO DE
JANEIRO
Tropic of Capricorn

Umuarama
Cruzeiro
do Oeste
Goio
Erê
Mandaguari
Apucarana
Arapongas
Joaquim
Távora
Ibaiti
Itapetininga
Itapeva
São Bernardo
do Campo
SÃO PAULO
Mogi das Cruzes
SANTO ANDRÉ
SANTOS
Ilha de São Sebastião
Pta. do Boi

CANINDEYU
Guaíra
PARANÁ
Cândido de Abreu
Castro
Jaguariaíva
São Vicente
Guarujá
Itanhaém

Igatimi
Pto. Mendes
Pitanga
1889
Apiaí
Juquiá
Registro
Iguape

BRAZIL
Cascavel
Sa. das Araras
Prudentópolis
Guarapuava
Ponta Grossa
Palmeira
CURITIBA
Antonina
Ilha Comprida

AZÚ
ALTO
PARANÁ
Foz do Iguaçu
Cat. del
Iguaçu
Laranjeiras
do Sul
Irati
Lapa
Paranaguá
Ilha do Cardoso

Óvido
Ciudad
del Este
Bernardo
de Irigoyen
União da
Vitória
Rio Negro
Guaratuba
25

Represa de Itaipú
Chopim
Pto.
União
Mafra
São Francisco do Sul

APUÁ
MISIONES
Eldorado
San Pedro
Clevelândia
Palmas
Sa. do
Espigão
Joinville

Corpus
Oberá
Montecarlo
Uruguaí
340
Caçador
Itajaí

Encarnación
Leandro N. Alem
Santa Rosa
Chapecó
Joaçaba
SANTA
Campos Novos
Santa Cecília
Blumenau
Brusque

San
Javier
Erechim
CATARINA
Rio do Sul
Ilha de Santa Catarina

Apóstoles
Ijuí
Caràzinho
Passo Fundo
Lajes
1808
Florianópolis

Santo Ângelo
Cruz
Alta
Vacaria
Tubarão
Laguna

São Luís
Gonzaga
Guaporé
Bento Gonçalves
Criciúma
Cabo Santa Marta Grande

Borja
RIO GRANDE
Caxias do Sul
Araranguá

Santiago
Passo
Fundo
Nôvo Hamburgo

DO SUL
Santa Maria
Santa Cruz
do Sul
Montenegro
Taquara

Alegrete
rio do Sul
Cachoeira do Sul
Canoas
São
Leopoldo
Osorio

Santana do
Livramento
São
Gabriel
Viamão
PORTO ALEGRE

Rivera
Dom Pedro
Caçapava
do Sul
Sa. Encantadas
30

Bagé
Camaquã
Lagoa dos Patos
Mostardas

acuarembó
Sa. do Canguçu
Canguçu
Pelotas

UAY
Melo
Jaguarão
Rio Grande

San Gregorio
Blanquillo
Sta. Clara
de Olimar
Mirim
Lagoa Mangueira

A T L A N T I C

Sarandí del Yi
José Batlle
y Ordóñez
Lascano

Minas
Aigua
Castillos
Treinta y Tres
Santa Vitória do Palmar

MONTEVIDEO
Rocha
San Carlos
Maldonado

Plata
35

O C E A N

5304

West from Greenwich
COPYRIGHT. GEORGE PHILIP & SON. LTD

50 0 50 100 150 200 250 300 km
50 0 50 100 150 200 miles

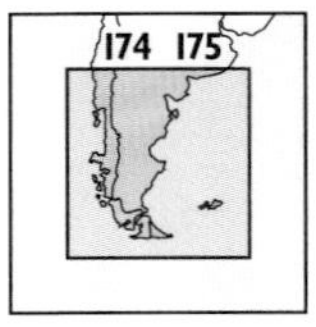

2 **3** **4** **5**

PACIFIC OCEAN

SOUTH ATLANTIC OCEAN

LA PAMPA
BUENOS AIRES
RÍO NEGRO
NEUQUÉN
CHUBUT
SANTA CRUZ
ARAUCANIA
LOS LAGOS

Colonia 25 de Mayo
Bernasconi
Tornquist 1243
Coronel Pringles
González Chaves
Balcarce
Loberia
Tres Arroyos
Necochea
Quequén
Coronel Dorrego
Punta Alta
Bahía Blanca
Medanos
B. Blanca
I. Trinidad
Mayor Buratovich
Cuchillo-Co
Villa Iris
Puelches

Angol
Mulchén
Victoria
Curacautín
Lautaro
Temuco
Zapala
Paso Pino Hachado
Neuquén
Cipolletti
Allen
Gral. Roca
Río Colorado
Colorado
Choele Choel
Río Colorado
Lamarque
Gral. Conesa
Stroede
Viedma
Carmen de Patagones
Pta. Rasa
B. Anegada

Valdivia
Osorno
Río Bueno
La Unión
Ranco
San Martín de los Andes
El Cuy
Salina Gualicho
San Antonio Oeste
Valcheta
Aguada Cecilio
Los Menucos
Comallo
Maquinchao
Ingeniero Jacobacci
El Cain
Quetrequile
Sierra Grande
Puerto Lobos
Golfo San Matías
Pta. Norte
Pen. Valdés
Puerto Pirámides
Punta Delgada
G. Nuevo
Puerto Madryn

Puerto Varas
Puerto Montt
G. de los Coronados
Maullín
Ancud
Isla de Chiloé
Castro
Achao
Chaitén
Esquel
Tecka
Gualjaina
Gan Gan
Gastre
Leleque
Telsen
Gaimán
Rawson
Trelew
San Carlos de Bariloche
El Bolsón
Norquinco
L. Nahuel Huapi
Meseta de Somuncurá
Cona Niyeu
Verde

Archipiélago de los Chonos
C. Taitao
Peninsula de Taitao
C. Tres Montes
Golfo de Penas
Archipiélago Guayaneco
I. Campana
I. Patricio Lynch
I. Esmeralda
I. Javier
Coihaique
Puerto Aisén
Balmaceda
Alto Río Senguer
Mayo
Río Mayo
L. Buenos Aires
Perito Moreno
Los Antiguos
Lago Posadas
Cochrane
Las Horquetas
L. Pueyrredón
Comodoro Rivadavia
Golfo San Jorge
Colonia Las Heras
Caleta Olivia
Pico Truncado
Fitz Roy
Jaramillo
Mazarredo
C. Tres Puntas
C. Blanco
Deseado
Puerto Deseado
Pta. Medanosa
Bahía Laura

SANTA CRUZ
Gob. Gregores
Gran Altiplanicie Central
L. San Martín
L. Cardiel
Mte. Fitzroy
L. Viedma
Tres Lagos
Shehuen
Cmte. Luis Piedrabuena
L. Argentino
Calafate
Puerto Coig
Bahía Grande
Esperanza
Coig
Santa Cruz
San Julián

Puerto Natales
El Turbio
Gallegos
Río Gallegos
Guer Aike
Monte Dinero
C. Virgenes
Strait of Magellan

FALKLAND ISLANDS
(ISLAS MALVINAS)
Jason Is.
King George B.
Queen Charlotte B.
Pebble I.
C. Dolphin
Mt. Adam 700
Mt. Usborne 705
Weddell I.
West Falkland
Port Darwin
Stanley
East Falkland
C. Meredith
Beauchêne I.

Punta Arenas
Pen. Brunswick
Santa Inés
Porvenir
Isla Grande de Tierra del Fuego
Río Grande
San Sebastián
TIERRA DEL FUEGO
Ushuaia
L. Fagnano
Canal Beagle
Navarino
Picton
Nueva
Lennox
Cabo de Hornos (Cape Horn)
Islas Diego Ramírez
Islas Wollaston
Is. Hermite

PACIFIC OCEAN

Projection: Lambert's Equivalent Azimuthal

West from Greenwich

COPYRIGHT: GEORGE PHILIP & SON. LTD.

ft m
9000 3000
6000 2000
4500 1500
3000 1000
1200 400
600 200
0 0
200 600
2000 6000
4000 12,000
m ft

INDEX

The index contains the names of all the principal places and features shown on the World Maps. Each name is followed by an additional entry in italics giving the country or region within which it is located. The alphabetical order of names composed of two or more words is governed primarily by the first word and then by the second. This is an example of the rule:

Mīr Kūh, *Iran*	**97 E8**	26 22N	58 55E
Mīr Shahdād, *Iran*	**97 E8**	26 15N	58 29E
Mira, *Italy*	**45 C9**	45 26N	12 8E
Mira por vos Cay, *Bahamas* .	**165 B5**	22 9N	74 30W
Mīrābād, *Afghan*	**91 C1**	30 25N	61 50E

Physical features composed of a proper name (Erie) and a description (Lake) are positioned alphabetically by the proper name. The description is positioned after the proper name and is usually abbreviated:

Erie, L., *N. Amer.* **150 D4** 42 15N 81 0W

Where a description forms part of a settlement or administrative name however, it is always written in full and put in its true alphabetic position:

Mount Morris, *U.S.A.* **150 D7** 42 44N 77 52W

Names beginning with M' and Mc are indexed as if they were spelled Mac. Names beginning St. are alphabetised under Saint, but Sankt, Sint, Sant', Santa and San are all spelt in full and are alphabetised accordingly. If the same place name occurs two or more times in the index and all are in the same country, each is followed by the name of the administrative subdivision in which it is located. The names are placed in the alphabetical order of the subdivisions. For example:

Jackson, *Ky., U.S.A.*	**148 G4**	37 33N	83 23W
Jackson, *Mich., U.S.A.*	**157D12**	42 15N	84 24W
Jackson, *Minn., U.S.A.*	**154 D7**	43 37N	95 1W

The number in bold type which follows each name in the index refers to the number of the map page where that feature or place will be found. This is usually the largest scale at which the place or feature appears.

The letter and figure which are in bold type immediately after the page number give the grid square on the map page, within which the feature is situated. The letter represents the latitude and the figure the longitude.

In some cases the feature itself may fall within the specified square, while the name is outside. This is usually the case only with features which are larger than a grid square.

For a more precise location the geographical coordinates which follow the letter/figure references give the latitude and the longitude of each place. The first set of figures represent the latitude which is the distance north or south of the Equator measured as an angle at the centre of the earth. The Equator is latitude 0°, the North Pole is 90°N, and the South Pole 90°S.

The second set of figures represent the longitude, which is the distance East or West of the prime meridian, which runs through Greenwich, England. Longitude is also measured as an angle at the centre of the earth and is given East or West of the prime meridian, from 0° to 180° in either direction.

The unit of measurement for latitude and longitude is the degree, which is subdivided into 60 minutes. Each index entry states the position of a place in degrees and minutes, a space being left between the degrees and the minutes.

The latitude is followed by N(orth) or S(outh) and the longitude by E(ast) or W(est).

Rivers are indexed to their mouths or confluences, and carry the symbol ➙ after their names. A solid square ■ follows the name of a country, while an open square □ refers to a first order administrative area.

ABBREVIATIONS USED IN THE INDEX

A.C.T. – Australian Capital Territory
Afghan. – Afghanistan
Ala. – Alabama
Alta. – Alberta
Amer. – America(n)
Arch. – Archipelago
Ariz. – Arizona
Ark. – Arkansas
Atl. Oc. – Atlantic Ocean
B. – Baie, Bahia, Bay, Bucht, Bugt
B.C. – British Columbia
Bangla. – Bangladesh
Barr. – Barrage
Bos.-H. – Bosnia-Herzegovina
C. – Cabo, Cap, Cape, Coast
C.A.R. – Central African Republic
C. Prov. – Cape Province
Calif. – California
Cent. – Central
Chan. – Channel
Colo. – Colorado
Conn. – Connecticut
Cord. – Cordillera
Cr. – Creek
Czech. – Czech Republic
D.C. – District of Columbia
Del. – Delaware
Dep. – Dependency
Des. – Desert
Dist. – District
Dj. – Djebel
Domin. – Dominica
Dom. Rep. – Dominican Republic
E. – East

E. Salv. – El Salvador
Eq. Guin. – Equatorial Guinea
Fla. – Florida
Falk. Is. – Falkland Is.
G. – Golfe, Golfo, Gulf, Guba, Gebel
Ga. – Georgia
Gt. – Great, Greater
Guinea-Biss. – Guinea-Bissau
H.K. – Hong Kong
H.P. – Himachal Pradesh
Hants. – Hampshire
Harb. – Harbor, Harbour
Hd. – Head
Hts. – Heights
I. (s). – Île, Ilha, Insel, Isla, Island, Isle
Ill. – Illinois
Ind. – Indiana
Ind. Oc. – Indian Ocean
Ivory C. – Ivory Coast
J. – Jabal, Jebel, Jazira
Junc. – Junction
K. – Kap, Kapp
Kans. – Kansas
Kep. – Kepulauan
Ky. – Kentucky
L. – Lac, Lacul, Lago, Lagoa, Lake, Limni, Loch, Lough
La. – Louisiana
Liech. – Liechtenstein
Lux. – Luxembourg
Mad. P. – Madhya Pradesh
Madag. – Madagascar
Man. – Manitoba
Mass. – Massachusetts

Md. – Maryland
Me. – Maine
Medit. S. – Mediterranean Sea
Mich. – Michigan
Minn. – Minnesota
Miss. – Mississippi
Mo. – Missouri
Mont. – Montana
Mozam. – Mozambique
Mt.(e) – Mont, Monte, Monti, Montaña, Mountain
N. – Nord, Norte, North, Northern, Nouveau
N.B. – New Brunswick
N.C. – North Carolina
N. Cal. – New Caledonia
N. Dak. – North Dakota
N.H. – New Hampshire
N.I. – North Island
N.J. – New Jersey
N. Mex. – New Mexico
N.S. – Nova Scotia
N.S.W. – New South Wales
N.W.T. – North West Territory
N.Y. – New York
N.Z. – New Zealand
Nebr. – Nebraska
Neths. – Netherlands
Nev. – Nevada
Nfld. – Newfoundland
Nic. – Nicaragua
O. – Oued, Ouadi
Occ. – Occidentale
Okla. – Oklahoma
Ont. – Ontario
Or. – Orientale

Oreg. – Oregon
Os. – Ostrov
Oz. – Ozero
P. – Pass, Passo, Pasul, Pulau
P.E.I. – Prince Edward Island
Pa. – Pennsylvania
Pac. Oc. – Pacific Ocean
Papua N.G. – Papua New Guinea
Pass. – Passage
Pen. – Peninsula, Péninsule
Phil. – Philippines
Pk. – Park, Peak
Plat. – Plateau
Prov. – Province, Provincial
Pt. – Point
Pta. – Ponta, Punta
Pte. – Pointe
Qué. – Québec
Queens. – Queensland
R. – Rio, River
R.I. – Rhode Island
Ra. (s). – Range(s)
Raj. – Rajasthan
Reg. – Region
Rep. – Republic
Res. – Reserve, Reservoir
S. – San, South, Sea
Si. Arabia – Saudi Arabia
S.C. – South Carolina
S. Dak. – South Dakota
S.I. – South Island
S. Leone – Sierra Leone
Sa. – Serra, Sierra
Sask. – Saskatchewan
Scot. – Scotland
Sd. – Sound

Sev. – Severnaya
Sib. – Siberia
Sprs. – Springs
St. – Saint
Sta. – Santa, Station
Ste. – Sainte
Sto. – Santo
Str. – Strait, Stretto
Switz. – Switzerland
Tas. – Tasmania
Tenn. – Tennessee
Tex. – Texas
Tg. – Tanjung
Trin. & Tob. – Trinidad & Tobago
U.A.E. – United Arab Emirates
U.K. – United Kingdom
U.S.A. – United States of America
Ut. P. – Uttar Pradesh
Va. – Virginia
Vdkhr. – Vodokhranilishche
Vf. – Virful
Vic. – Victoria
Vol. – Volcano
Vt. – Vermont
W. – Wadi, West
W. Va. – West Virginia
Wash. – Washington
Wis. – Wisconsin
Wlkp. – Wielkopolski
Wyo. – Wyoming
Yorks. – Yorkshire
Yug. – Yugoslavia

178 A Baña

A

A Baña, *Spain* **42 C2** 42 58N 8 46W
A Cañiza, *Spain* **42 C2** 42 13N 8 16W
A Coruña, *Spain* **42 B2** 43 20N 8 25W
A Estrada, *Spain* **42 C2** 42 43N 8 27W
A Fonsagrada, *Spain* **42 B3** 43 8N 7 4W
A Guarda, *Spain* **42 D2** 41 56N 8 52W
A Gudiña, *Spain* **42 C3** 42 4N 7 8W
A Rúa, *Spain* **42 C3** 42 24N 7 6W
Aachen, *Germany* **30 E2** 50 45N 6 6 E
Aadorf, *Switz.* **33 B7** 47 30N 8 55 E
Aalborg = Ålborg, *Denmark* **17 G3** 57 2N 9 54 E
Aalen, *Germany* **31 G6** 48 51N 10 6 E
A'âli en Nîl □, *Sudan* **107 F3** 9 30N 33 0 E
Aalst, *Belgium* **24 D4** 50 56N 4 2 E
Aalten, *Neths.* **24 C6** 51 56N 6 35 E
Aalter, *Belgium* **24 C3** 51 5N 3 28 E
Äänekoski, *Finland* **15 E21** 62 36N 25 44 E
Aarau, *Switz.* **32 B6** 47 23N 8 4 E
Aarberg, *Switz.* **32 B4** 47 2N 7 16 E
Aare →, *Switz.* **32 A6** 47 33N 8 14 E
Aargau □, *Switz.* **32 B6** 47 26N 8 10 E
Aarhus = Århus, *Denmark* **17 H4** 56 8N 10 11 E
Aarschot, *Belgium* **24 D4** 50 59N 4 49 E
Aarwangen, *Switz.* **32 B5** 47 15N 7 46 E
Aasiaat = Egedesminde,
Greenland **10 D5** 68 43N 52 56W
Aba, *China* **76 A3** 32 59N 101 42 E
Aba,
Dem. Rep. of the Congo **118 B3** 3 58N 30 17 E
Aba, *Nigeria* **113 D6** 5 10N 7 19 E
Âbâ, Jazîrat, *Sudan* **107 E3** 13 30N 32 31 E
Abacaxis →, *Brazil* **169 D6** 3 54 S 58 47W
Ābādān, *Iran* **97 D6** 30 22N 48 20 E
Abade, *Ethiopia* **107 F4** 9 22N 38 3 E
Ābādeh, *Iran* **97 D7** 31 8N 52 40 E
Abadin, *Spain* **42 B3** 43 21N 7 29W
Abadla, *Algeria* **111 B4** 31 2N 2 45W
Abaeté, *Brazil* **171 E2** 19 9 S 45 27W
Abaeté →, *Brazil* **171 E2** 18 2 S 45 12W
Abaetetuba, *Brazil* **170 B2** 1 40 S 48 50W
Abagnar Qi, *China* **74 C9** 43 52N 116 2 E
Abai, *Paraguay* **175 B4** 25 58 S 55 54W
Abak, *Nigeria* **113 E6** 4 58N 7 50 E
Abakaliki, *Nigeria* **113 D6** 6 22N 8 2 E
Abakan, *Russia* **65 D10** 53 40N 91 10 E
Abalemma, *Niger* **113 B6** 16 12N 7 50 E
Abana, *Turkey* **100 B6** 41 59N 34 1 E
Abancay, *Peru* **172 C3** 13 35 S 72 55W
Abano Terme, *Italy* **45 C8** 45 22N 11 46 E
Abapó, *Bolivia* **173 D5** 18 48 S 63 25W
Abarán, *Spain* **41 G3** 38 12N 1 23W
Abariringa, *Kiribati* **134 H10** 2 50 S 171 40W
Abarqū, *Iran* **97 D7** 31 10N 53 20 E
Abashiri, *Japan* **68 C12** 44 0N 144 15 E
Abashiri-Wan, *Japan* **68 C12** 44 0N 144 30 E
Abau, *Papua N. G.* **132 F5** 10 11 S 148 46 E
Abaújszántó, *Hungary* **52 B6** 48 16N 21 12 E
Abava →, *Latvia* **54 A8** 57 6N 21 54 E
Abay, *Kazakstan* **64 E8** 49 38N 72 53 E
Abaya, L., *Ethiopia* **107 F4** 6 30N 37 50 E
Abaza, *Russia* **64 D10** 52 39N 90 6 E
Abbadia San Salvatore, *Italy* **45 F8** 42 53N 11 41 E
'Abbāsābād, *Iran* **97 C8** 33 34N 58 23 E
Abbay = Nîl el Azraq →,
Sudan **107 D3** 15 38N 32 31 E
Abbaye, Pt., *U.S.A.* **148 B1** 46 58N 88 8W
Abbé, L., *Ethiopia* **107 E5** 11 8N 41 47 E
Abbeville, *France* **27 B8** 50 6N 1 49 E
Abbeville, *Ala., U.S.A.* **152 D4** 31 34N 85 15W
Abbeville, *Ga., U.S.A.* **152 D6** 31 59N 83 18W
Abbeville, *La., U.S.A.* **155 L8** 29 58N 92 8W
Abbeville, *S.C., U.S.A.* **152 A7** 34 11N 82 23W
Abbiategrasso, *Italy* **44 C5** 45 24N 8 54 E
Abbieglassie, *Australia* **127 D4** 27 15 S 147 28 E
Abbot Ice Shelf, *Antarctica* **7 D16** 73 0 S 92 0W
Abbotsford, *Canada* **142 D4** 49 5N 122 20W
Abbotsford, *U.S.A.* **154 C9** 44 57N 90 19W
Abbottabad, *Pakistan* **92 B5** 34 10N 73 15 E
Abd al Kūrī, *Ind. Oc.* **99 D6** 12 5N 52 20 E
Ābdar, *Iran* **97 D7** 30 16N 55 19 E
'Abdolābād, *Iran* **97 C8** 34 12N 56 30 E
Abdulino, *Russia* **62 E4** 53 42N 53 40 E
Abéché, *Chad* **109 F4** 13 50N 20 35 E
Abejar, *Spain* **40 D2** 41 48N 2 47W
Abekr, *Sudan* **107 E2** 12 45N 28 50 E
Abêlessa, *Algeria* **111 D5** 22 58N 4 47 E
Abengourou, *Ivory C.* **112 D4** 6 42N 3 27W
Abenójar, *Spain* **43 G6** 38 53N 4 21W
Åbenrå, *Denmark* **17 J3** 55 3N 9 25 E
Abensberg, *Germany* **31 G7** 48 48N 11 51 E
Abeokuta, *Nigeria* **113 D5** 7 3N 3 19 E
Aber, *Uganda* **118 B3** 2 12N 32 25 E
Aberaeron, *U.K.* **21 E3** 52 15N 4 15W
Aberayron = Aberaeron,
U.K. **21 E3** 52 15N 4 15W
Aberchirder, *U.K.* **22 D6** 57 34N 2 37W
Abercorn = Mbala, *Zambia* **119 D3** 8 46 S 31 24 E
Abercorn, *Australia* **127 D5** 25 12 S 151 5 E
Aberdare, *U.K.* **21 F4** 51 43N 3 27W
Aberdare Ra., *Kenya* **118 C4** 0 15 S 36 50 E
Aberdeen, *Australia* **129 B9** 32 9 S 150 56 E
Aberdeen, *Canada* **143 C7** 52 20N 106 8W
Aberdeen, *S. Africa* **116 E3** 32 28 S 24 2 E
Aberdeen, *U.K.* **22 D6** 57 9N 2 5W
Aberdeen, *Ala., U.S.A.* **149 J1** 33 49N 88 33W
Aberdeen, *Idaho, U.S.A.* **158 E7** 42 57N 112 50W
Aberdeen, *Ohio, U.S.A.* **157 F13** 38 39N 83 46W
Aberdeen, *S. Dak., U.S.A.* **154 C5** 45 28N 98 29W
Aberdeen, *Wash., U.S.A.* **160 D3** 46 59N 123 50W
Aberdeen, City of □, *U.K.* **22 D6** 57 10N 2 10W
Aberdeenshire □, *U.K.* **22 D6** 57 17N 2 36W
Aberdovey = Aberdyfi, *U.K.* **21 E3** 52 33N 4 3W
Aberdyfi, *U.K.* **21 E3** 52 33N 4 3W
Aberfeldy, *Australia* **129 D7** 37 42 S 146 22 E
Aberfeldy, *U.K.* **22 E5** 56 37N 3 51W
Abergavenny, *U.K.* **21 F4** 51 49N 3 1W
Abergele, *U.K.* **20 D4** 53 17N 3 35W
Abernathy, *U.S.A.* **155 J4** 33 50N 101 51W
Abert, L., *U.S.A.* **158 E3** 42 38N 120 14W
Aberystwyth, *U.K.* **21 E3** 52 25N 4 5W
Abha, *Si. Arabia* **106 D5** 18 0N 42 34 E
Abhar, *Iran* **97 B6** 36 9N 49 13 E
Abhayapuri, *India* **90 B3** 26 24N 90 38 E
Abia □, *Nigeria* **113 D6** 5 30N 7 35 E
Abide, *Turkey* **49 C11** 38 55N 29 20 E
Abidiya, *Sudan* **106 D3** 18 18N 34 3 E
Abidjan, *Ivory C.* **112 D4** 5 26N 3 58W
Abilene, *Kans., U.S.A.* **154 F6** 38 55N 97 13W
Abilene, *Tex., U.S.A.* **155 J5** 32 28N 99 43W
Abingdon, *U.K.* **21 F6** 51 40N 1 17W
Abingdon, *Ill., U.S.A.* **156 D6** 40 48N 90 24W
Abingdon, *Va., U.S.A.* **149 G5** 36 43N 81 59W
Abington Reef, *Australia* **126 B4** 18 0 S 149 35 E
Abitau →, *Canada* **143 B7** 59 53N 109 3W
Abitau L., *Canada* **143 A7** 60 27N 107 15W
Abitibi L., *Canada* **140 C4** 48 40N 79 40W
Abiy Adi, *Ethiopia* **107 E4** 13 39N 39 3 E
Abkhaz Republic □ =
Abkhazia □, *Georgia* **61 J5** 43 12N 41 5 E
Abkhazia □, *Georgia* **61 J5** 43 12N 41 5 E
Abminga, *Australia* **127 D1** 26 8 S 134 51 E
Abnûb, *Egypt* **106 B3** 27 18N 31 4 E
Åbo = Turku, *Finland* **15 F20** 60 30N 22 19 E
Abo, Massif d', *Chad* **109 D3** 21 41N 16 8 E
Abocho, *Nigeria* **113 D6** 7 35N 6 56 E
Abohar, *India* **92 D6** 30 10N 74 10 E
Aboisso, *Ivory C.* **112 D4** 5 30N 3 5W
Abolo, *Congo* **114 B2** 0 8N 14 16 E
Abomey, *Benin* **113 D5** 7 10N 2 5 E
Abong-Mbang, *Cameroon* **114 B2** 4 0N 13 8 E
Abongabong, *Indonesia* **84 B1** 4 15N 96 48 E
Abonnema, *Nigeria* **113 E6** 4 41N 6 49 E
Abony, *Hungary* **52 C5** 47 12N 20 3 E
Aboso, *Ghana* **112 D4** 5 23N 1 57W
Abou-Deïa, *Chad* **109 F3** 11 20N 19 20 E
Abou Goulem, *Chad* **109 F4** 13 37N 21 38 E
Aboyne, *U.K.* **22 D6** 57 4N 2 47W
Abra □, *Phil.* **80 C3** 17 35N 120 45 E
Abra de Ilog, *Phil.* **80 E3** 13 27N 120 44 E
Abra Pampa, *Argentina* **174 A2** 22 43 S 65 42W
Abrantes, *Portugal* **43 F2** 39 24N 8 7W
Abreojos, Pta., *Mexico* **162 B2** 26 50N 113 40W
Abri, *Esh Shamâliya, Sudan* **106 C3** 20 50N 30 27 E
Abri, *Janub Kordofân,*
Sudan **107 E3** 11 40N 30 21 E
Abrolhos, Banka, *Brazil* **171 E4** 18 0 S 38 0W
Abrud, *Romania* **52 D8** 46 19N 23 5 E
Abruzzo □, *Italy* **45 F10** 42 15N 14 0 E
Absaroka Range, *U.S.A.* **158 D9** 44 45N 109 50W
Abtenau, *Austria* **34 D6** 47 33N 13 21 E
Abū al Khaṣīb, *Iraq* **97 D6** 30 25N 48 0 E
Abū 'Alī, *Si. Arabia* **97 E6** 27 20N 49 27 E
Abū 'Alī →, *Lebanon* **103 A4** 34 25N 35 50 E
Abu 'Arīsh, *Si. Arabia* **106 D5** 16 53N 42 48 E
Abû Ballas, *Egypt* **106 C2** 24 26N 27 36 E
Abu Deleiq, *Sudan* **107 D3** 15 57N 33 48 E
Abu Dhabi = Abū Ẓāby,
U.A.E. **97 E7** 24 28N 54 22 E
Abû Dis, *Sudan* **106 D3** 19 12N 33 38 E
Abû Dom, *Sudan* **107 D3** 16 18N 32 25 E
Abû Du'ân, *Syria* **101 D8** 36 25N 38 15 E
Abu el Gairi, W. →, *Egypt* **103 F2** 29 35N 33 30 E
Abû Gabra, *Sudan* **107 E2** 11 2N 26 50 E
Abu Ga'da, W. →, *Egypt* **103 F1** 29 15N 32 53 E
Abû Gubeiha, *Sudan* **107 E3** 11 30N 31 15 E
Abu Habl, Khawr →,
Sudan **107 E3** 12 37N 31 0 E
Abū Ḩadrīyah, *Si. Arabia* **97 E6** 27 20N 48 58 E
Abu Hamed, *Sudan* **106 D3** 19 32N 33 13 E
Abu Haraz, *An Nîl el Azraq,*
Sudan **107 E3** 14 35N 33 30 E
Abû Haraz, *Esh Shamâliya,*
Sudan **106 D3** 19 8N 32 18 E
Abû Higar, *Sudan* **107 E3** 12 50N 33 59 E
Abū Kamāl, *Syria* **101 E9** 34 30N 41 0 E
Abū Madd, Ra's, *Si. Arabia* **96 E3** 24 50N 37 7 E
Abu Matariq, *Sudan* **107 E2** 10 59N 26 9 E
Abu Qir, *Egypt* **106 H7** 31 18N 30 0 E
Abu Qireiya, *Egypt* **106 C4** 24 5N 35 28 E
Abu Qurqâs, *Egypt* **106 J7** 28 1N 30 44 E
Abū Raṣāş, Ra's, *Oman* **99 B7** 20 10N 58 38 E
Abû Rubayq, *Si. Arabia* **98 B2** 23 44N 39 42 E
Abu Şafāt, W. →, *Jordan* **103 E5** 30 24N 36 7 E
Abû Simbel, *Egypt* **106 C3** 22 18N 31 40 E
Abū Şukhayr, *Iraq* **101 G11** 31 54N 44 30 E
Abu Tig, *Egypt* **106 B3** 27 4N 31 15 E
Abu Tiga, *Sudan* **107 E3** 12 47N 34 12 E
Abû Zabad, *Sudan* **107 E2** 12 25N 29 10 E
Abū Ẓāby, *U.A.E.* **97 E7** 24 28N 54 22 E
Abū Zeydābād, *Iran* **97 C6** 33 54N 51 45 E
Abufari, *Brazil* **173 B5** 5 25 S 62 59W
Abuja, *Nigeria* **113 D6** 9 16N 7 2 E
Abukuma-Gawa →, *Japan* **68 E10** 38 6N 140 52 E
Abukuma-Sammyaku, *Japan* **68 F10** 37 30N 140 45 E
Abulug, *Phil.* **80 B3** 18 27N 121 27 E
Abumombazi,
Dem. Rep. of the Congo **114 B4** 3 42N 22 10 E
Abunã, *Brazil* **173 B4** 9 40 S 65 20W
Abunã →, *Brazil* **173 B4** 9 41 S 65 20W
Abung, *Phil.* **80 E3** 13 46N 121 26 E
Aburatsu, *Japan* **70 F3** 31 34N 131 24 E
Aburo,
Dem. Rep. of the Congo **118 B3** 2 4N 30 53 E
Abut Hd., *N.Z.* **131 D5** 43 7 S 170 15 E
Abwong, *Sudan* **107 F3** 9 2N 32 14 E
Åby, *Sweden* **17 F10** 58 40N 16 10 E
Aby, Lagune, *Ivory C.* **112 D4** 5 15N 3 14W
Åbybro, *Denmark* **17 G3** 57 10N 9 44 E
Acacías, *Colombia* **168 C3** 3 59N 73 46W
Acajutla, *El Salv.* **164 D2** 13 36N 89 50W
Açailândia, *Brazil* **170 C2** 5 0 S 47 30W
Acámbaro, *Mexico* **162 D4** 20 0N 100 40W
Acanthus, *Greece* **50 F7** 40 27N 23 47 E
Acaponeta, *Mexico* **162 C3** 22 30N 105 20W
Acapulco, *Mexico* **163 D5** 16 51N 99 56W
Acarai, Serra, *Brazil* **169 C6** 1 50N 57 50W
Acaraú, *Brazil* **170 B3** 2 53 S 40 7W
Acari, *Brazil* **170 C4** 6 31 S 36 38W
Acarí, *Peru* **172 D3** 15 25 S 74 36W
Acarigua, *Venezuela* **168 B4** 9 33N 69 12W
Acatlán, *Mexico* **163 D5** 18 10N 98 3W
Acayucan, *Mexico* **163 D6** 17 59N 94 58W
Accéglio, *Italy* **44 D3** 44 28N 7 0 E
Accomac, *U.S.A.* **148 G8** 37 43N 75 40W
Accous, *France* **28 E3** 43 0N 0 36W
Accra, *Ghana* **113 D4** 5 35N 0 6W
Accrington, *U.K.* **20 D5** 53 45N 2 22W
Acebal, *Argentina* **174 C3** 33 20 S 60 50W
Aceh □, *Indonesia* **84 B1** 4 15N 97 30 E
Acerra, *Italy* **47 B7** 40 57N 14 22 E
Aceuchal, *Spain* **43 G4** 38 39N 6 30W
Achacachi, *Bolivia* **172 D4** 16 3 S 68 43W
Achaguas, *Venezuela* **168 B4** 7 46N 68 14W
Achalpur, *India* **94 D3** 21 22N 77 32 E
Achao, *Chile* **176 B2** 42 28 S 73 30W
Acheng, *China* **75 B14** 45 30N 126 58 E
Achenkirch, *Austria* **34 D4** 47 32N 11 45 E
Achensee, *Austria* **34 D4** 47 26N 11 45 E
Acher, *India* **92 H5** 23 10N 72 32 E
Achern, *Germany* **31 G4** 48 37N 8 4 E
Acheron →, *N.Z.* **131 C8** 42 16 S 173 4 E
Achill Hd., *Ireland* **23 C1** 53 58N 10 15W
Achill I., *Ireland* **23 C1** 53 58N 10 1W
Achim, *Germany* **30 B5** 53 1N 9 3 E
Achinsk, *Russia* **65 D10** 56 20N 90 20 E
Achisay = Ashchysay,
Kazakstan **63 B4** 43 35N 68 53 E
Achit, *Russia* **62 C6** 56 48N 57 54 E
Achol, *Sudan* **107 F3** 6 35N 31 32 E
Acıgöl, *Turkey* **49 D11** 37 50N 29 50 E
Acıpayam, *Turkey* **49 D11** 37 26N 29 22 E
Acireale, *Italy* **47 E8** 37 37N 15 10 E
Ackerman, *U.S.A.* **155 J10** 33 19N 89 11W
Ackley, *U.S.A.* **156 B3** 42 33N 93 3W
Acklins I., *Bahamas* **165 B5** 22 30N 74 0W
Acme, *Canada* **142 C6** 51 33N 113 30W
Acobamba, *Peru* **172 C3** 12 52 S 74 35W
Acomayo, *Peru* **172 C3** 13 55 S 71 38W
Aconcagua, Cerro, *Argentina* **174 C2** 32 39 S 70 0W
Aconquija, Mt., *Argentina* **174 B2** 27 0 S 66 0W
Acopiara, *Brazil* **170 C4** 6 6 S 39 27W
Açores, Is. dos = Azores,
Atl. Oc. **8 E6** 38 44N 29 0W
Acorizal, *Brazil* **173 D6** 15 12 S 56 22W
Acquapendente, *Italy* **45 F8** 42 44N 11 52 E
Acquasanta Terme, *Italy* **45 F10** 42 46N 13 24 E
Acquasparta, *Italy* **45 F9** 42 41N 12 33 E
Acquaviva delle Fonti, *Italy* **47 B9** 40 54N 16 50 E
Ácqui Terme, *Italy* **44 D5** 44 41N 8 28 E
Acraman, L., *Australia* **127 E2** 32 2 S 135 23 E
Acre = 'Akko, *Israel* **103 C4** 32 55N 35 4 E
Acre □, *Brazil* **172 B3** 9 1 S 71 0W
Acre →, *Brazil* **172 B4** 8 45 S 67 22W
Acri, *Italy* **47 C9** 39 29N 16 23 E
Acs, *Hungary* **52 C3** 47 42N 18 2 E
Actium, *Greece* **48 C2** 38 57N 20 45 E
Acton, *Canada* **150 C4** 43 38N 80 3W
Açu, *Brazil* **170 C4** 5 34 S 36 54W
Acworth, *U.S.A.* **152 A5** 34 4N 84 41W
Ad Dahnā, *Si. Arabia* **99 A5** 24 30N 48 10 E
Ad Ḑālī', *Yemen* **98 D4** 13 42N 44 44 E
Ad Dammām, *Si. Arabia* **97 E6** 26 20N 50 5 E
Ad Darb, *Si. Arabia* **98 C3** 18 2N 43 7 E
Ad Dawhah, *Qatar* **97 E6** 25 15N 51 35 E
Ad Dawr, *Iraq* **101 E10** 34 27N 43 47 E
Ad Ḑiffah, *Libya* **108 B4** 30 30N 24 30 E
Ad Dilam, *Si. Arabia* **98 B4** 23 55N 47 10 E
Ad Dir'īyah, *Si. Arabia* **96 E5** 24 44N 46 35 E
Ad Dīwānīyah, *Iraq* **101 F11** 32 0N 45 0 E
Ad Dujayl, *Iraq* **101 F11** 33 51N 44 14 E
Ada, *Ghana* **113 D5** 5 44N 0 40 E
Ada, *Serbia, Yug.* **52 E5** 45 49N 20 9 E
Ada, *Minn., U.S.A.* **154 B6** 47 18N 96 31W
Ada, *Ohio, U.S.A.* **157 D13** 40 46N 83 49W
Ada, *Okla., U.S.A.* **155 H6** 34 46N 96 41W
Adad, *Somali Rep.* **120 C3** 9 27N 46 49 E
Adaja →, *Spain* **42 D6** 41 32N 4 52W
Adak, *U.S.A.* **144 L3** 51 45N 176 45W
Adak I., *U.S.A.* **144 L3** 51 45N 176 45W
Ådalsbruk, *Norway* **18 D8** 60 43N 11 19 E
Adam, *Oman* **99 B7** 22 15N 57 28 E
Adam, Mt., *Falk. Is.* **176 D4** 51 34 S 60 4W
Adamantina, *Brazil* **171 F1** 21 42 S 51 4W
Adamaoua, Massif de l',
Cameroon **113 D7** 7 20N 12 20 E
Adamawa □, *Nigeria* **113 D7** 9 20N 12 30 E
Adamawa Highlands =
Adamaoua, Massif de l',
Cameroon **113 D7** 7 20N 12 20 E
Adamello, Mte., *Italy* **44 B7** 46 9N 10 30 E
Adami Tulu, *Ethiopia* **107 F4** 7 53N 38 41 E
Adaminaby, *Australia* **129 D8** 36 0 S 148 45 E
Adamovka, *Russia* **62 F7** 51 32N 59 56 E
Adams, *Phil.* **80 B3** 18 28N 120 54 E
Adams, *Mass., U.S.A.* **151 D11** 42 38N 73 7W
Adams, *N.Y., U.S.A.* **151 C8** 43 49N 76 1W
Adams, *Wis., U.S.A.* **154 D10** 43 57N 89 49W
Adam's Bridge, *Sri Lanka* **95 K4** 9 15N 79 40 E
Adams L., *Canada* **142 C5** 51 10N 119 40W
Adams Mt., *U.S.A.* **160 D5** 46 12N 121 30W
Adam's Peak, *Sri Lanka* **95 L5** 6 48N 80 30 E
Adamuz, *Spain* **43 G6** 38 2N 4 32W
Adana, *Turkey* **100 D6** 37 0N 35 16 E
Adanero, *Spain* **42 E6** 40 56N 4 36W
Adapazarı, *Turkey* **100 B4** 40 48N 30 25 E
Adarama, *Sudan* **107 D3** 17 10N 34 52 E
Adare, C., *Antarctica* **7 D11** 71 0 S 171 0 E
Adaut, *Indonesia* **83 C4** 8 8 S 131 7 E
Adavale, *Australia* **127 D3** 25 52 S 144 32 E
Adda →, *Italy* **44 C6** 45 8N 9 53 E
Addis Ababa = Addis
Abeba, *Ethiopia* **107 F4** 9 2N 38 42 E
Addis Abeba, *Ethiopia* **107 F4** 9 2N 38 42 E
Addis Alem, *Ethiopia* **107 F4** 9 0N 38 17 E
Addison, *Ill., U.S.A.* **157 C8** 41 55N 88 0W
Addison, *N.Y., U.S.A.* **150 D7** 42 1N 77 14W
Addo, *S. Africa* **116 E4** 33 32 S 25 45 E
Addyston, *U.S.A.* **157 E12** 39 8N 84 43W
Adebour, *Niger* **109 F2** 13 17N 11 50 E
Ādeh, *Iran* **96 B5** 37 42N 45 11 E
Adel, *Ga., U.S.A.* **152 D6** 31 8N 83 25W
Adel, *Iowa, U.S.A.* **156 C2** 41 37N 94 1W
Adelaide, *Australia* **128 C3** 34 52 S 138 30 E
Adelaide, *Bahamas* **164 A4** 25 4N 77 31W
Adelaide, *S. Africa* **116 E4** 32 42 S 26 20 E
Adelaide I., *Antarctica* **7 C17** 67 15 S 68 30W
Adelaide Pen., *Canada* **138 B10** 68 15N 97 30W
Adelaide River, *Australia* **124 B5** 13 15 S 131 7 E
Adelanto, *U.S.A.* **161 L9** 34 35N 117 22W
Adelboden, *Switz.* **32 D5** 46 29N 7 33 E
Adele I., *Australia* **124 C3** 15 32 S 123 9 E
Adélie, Terre, *Antarctica* **7 C10** 68 0 S 140 0 E
Adélie Land = Adélie,
Terre, *Antarctica* **7 C10** 68 0 S 140 0 E
Ademuz, *Spain* **40 E3** 40 5N 1 13W
Aden = Al 'Adan, *Yemen* **98 D4** 12 45N 45 0 E
Aden, G. of, *Asia* **102 E4** 12 30N 47 30 E
Adendorp, *S. Africa* **116 E3** 32 15 S 24 30 E
Adh Dhayd, *U.A.E.* **97 E7** 25 17N 55 53 E
Adhoi, *India* **92 H4** 23 26N 70 32 E
Adi, *Indonesia* **83 B4** 4 15 S 133 30 E
Adi Daro, *Ethiopia* **107 E4** 14 20N 38 14 E
Adi Keyih, *Eritrea* **107 E4** 14 51N 39 22 E
Adi Kwala, *Eritrea* **107 E4** 14 38N 38 48 E
Adi Ugri, *Eritrea* **107 E4** 14 58N 38 48 E
Adieu, C., *Australia* **125 F5** 32 0 S 132 10 E
Adieu Pt., *Australia* **124 C3** 15 14 S 124 35 E
Adigala, *Ethiopia* **107 E5** 10 24N 42 15 E
Adige →, *Italy* **45 C9** 45 9N 12 20 E
Adigrat, *Ethiopia* **107 E4** 14 20N 39 26 E
Adıgüzel Barajı, *Turkey* **49 C11** 38 13N 29 14 E
Adilabad, *India* **94 E4** 19 33N 78 20 E
Adilcevaz, *Turkey* **101 C10** 38 47N 42 43 E
Adin, *U.S.A.* **158 F3** 41 12N 120 57W
Adirondack Mts., *U.S.A.* **151 C10** 44 0N 74 0W
Adıyaman, *Turkey* **101 D8** 37 45N 38 16 E
Adjim, *Tunisia* **108 B2** 33 47N 10 50 E
Adjohon, *Benin* **113 D5** 6 41N 2 32 E
Adjud, *Romania* **53 D12** 46 7N 27 10 E
Adjumani, *Uganda* **118 B3** 3 20N 31 50 E
Adlavik Is., *Canada* **141 A8** 55 2N 57 45W
Adler, *Russia* **61 J4** 43 28N 39 52 E
Adliswil, *Switz.* **33 B7** 47 19N 8 32 E
Admer, *Algeria* **111 D6** 20 21N 5 27 E
Admer, Erg d', *Algeria* **111 D6** 24 0N 9 5 E
Admiralty G., *Australia* **124 B4** 14 20 S 125 55 E
Admiralty I., *U.S.A.* **138 C6** 57 30N 134 30W
Admiralty Inlet, *U.S.A.* **158 C2** 48 8N 122 58W
Admiralty Is., *Papua N. G.* **132 B4** 2 0 S 147 0 E
Ado, *Nigeria* **113 D5** 6 36N 2 56 E
Ado-Ekiti, *Nigeria* **113 D6** 7 38N 5 12 E
Adok, *Sudan* **107 F3** 8 10N 30 20 E
Adola, *Ethiopia* **107 E5** 11 14N 41 44 E
Adonara, *Indonesia* **82 C2** 8 15 S 123 5 E
Adoni, *India* **95 G3** 15 33N 77 18 E
Adony, *Hungary* **52 C3** 47 6N 18 52 E
Adour →, *France* **28 E2** 43 32N 1 32W
Adra, *India* **93 H12** 23 30N 86 42 E
Adra, *Spain* **43 J7** 36 43N 3 3W
Adrano, *Italy* **47 E7** 37 40N 14 50 E
Adrar, *Algeria* **111 C4** 27 51N 0 11W
Adrasman, *Tajikistan* **63 C4** 40 38N 69 58 E
Adré, *Chad* **109 F4** 13 40N 22 20 E
Adrī, *Libya* **108 C2** 27 32N 13 2 E
Ádria, *Italy* **45 C9** 45 3N 12 3 E
Adrian, *Ga., U.S.A.* **152 C7** 32 33N 82 35W
Adrian, *Mich., U.S.A.* **157 C12** 41 54N 84 2W
Adrian, *Mo., U.S.A.* **156 F2** 38 24N 94 21W
Adrian, *Tex., U.S.A.* **155 H3** 35 16N 102 40W
Adriatic Sea, *Medit. S.* **12 G9** 43 0N 16 0 E
Adua, *Indonesia* **83 B3** 1 45 S 129 50 E
Adula, *Switz.* **33 D8** 46 30N 9 3 E
Adung Long, *Burma* **90 A6** 28 7N 97 42 E
Adur, *India* **95 K3** 9 8N 76 40 E
Adwa, *Ethiopia* **107 E4** 14 15N 38 52 E
Adygea □, *Russia* **61 H5** 45 0N 40 0 E
Adzhar Republic □ =
Ajaria □, *Georgia* **61 K6** 41 30N 42 0 E
Adzopé, *Ivory C.* **112 D4** 6 7N 3 49W
Ægean Sea, *Medit. S.* **49 C7** 38 30N 25 0 E
Aerhtai Shan, *Mongolia* **72 B4** 46 40N 92 45 E
Ærø, *Denmark* **17 K4** 54 52N 10 25 E
Ærøskøbing, *Denmark* **17 K4** 54 53N 10 24 E
Aesch, *Switz.* **32 B5** 47 28N 7 36 E
Aëtós, *Greece* **48 D3** 37 15N 21 50 E
Afafi, Massif d', *Niger* **109 D3** 22 11N 15 10 E
'Afak, *Iraq* **101 F11** 32 4N 45 15 E
Afándou, *Greece* **38 C10** 36 18N 28 12 E
Afarag, Erg, *Algeria* **111 D5** 23 50N 2 47 E
Åfarnes, *Norway* **18 B4** 62 40N 7 32 E
Afdega, *Ethiopia* **120 C2** 6 4N 43 30 E
Affreville = Khemis Miliana,
Algeria **111 A5** 36 11N 2 14 E
Affton, *U.S.A.* **156 F6** 38 33N 90 20W
Afghanistan ■, *Asia* **91 B2** 33 0N 65 0 E
Afgoi, *Somali Rep.* **120 D2** 2 7N 44 59 E
'Afīf, *Si. Arabia* **98 B3** 23 53N 42 56 E
Afikpo, *Nigeria* **113 D6** 5 53N 7 54 E
Aflou, *Algeria* **111 B5** 34 7N 2 3 E
Afmadu, *Somali Rep.* **120 D2** 0 31N 42 4 E
Afogados da Ingàzeira,
Brazil **170 C4** 7 45 S 37 39W
Afragóla, *Italy* **47 B7** 40 55N 14 18 E
Afrera, *Ethiopia* **107 E5** 13 16N 41 5 E
'Afrīn, *Syria* **100 D7** 36 32N 36 50 E
Afşin, *Turkey* **100 C7** 38 14N 36 55 E
Afton, *U.S.A.* **151 D9** 42 14N 75 32W
Aftout, *Algeria* **110 C4** 26 50N 3 45W
Afuá, *Brazil* **169 D7** 0 15 S 50 20W
'Afula, *Israel* **103 C4** 32 37N 35 17 E
Afyon, *Turkey* **57 G5** 38 45N 30 33 E
Afyon □, *Turkey* **49 C12** 38 25N 30 30 E
Afyonkarahisar = Afyon,
Turkey **57 G5** 38 45N 30 33 E
Aga, *Egypt* **106 H7** 30 55N 31 10 E
Agadès = Agadez, *Niger* **109 E1** 16 58N 7 59 E
Agadez, *Niger* **109 E1** 16 58N 7 59 E
Agadir, *Morocco* **110 B3** 30 28N 9 55W
Agaete, *Canary Is.* **39 F4** 28 6N 15 43W
Agaiás, *Mauritania* **110 D2** 22 37N 14 22W
Agana, *Guam* **133 R15** 13 28N 144 45 E
Ağapınar, *Turkey* **49 B12** 39 48N 30 47 E
Agar, *India* **92 H7** 23 40N 76 2 E
Agaro, *Ethiopia* **107 F4** 7 50N 36 38 E
Agartala, *India* **90 D3** 23 50N 91 23 E
Agăş, *Romania* **53 D11** 46 28N 26 15 E
Agassiz, *Canada* **142 D4** 49 14N 121 46W
Agats, *Indonesia* **83 C5** 5 33 S 138 0 E
Agattu I., *U.S.A.* **144 K4** 52 25N 173 35 E
Agbélouvé, *Togo* **113 D5** 6 35N 1 14 E
Agboville, *Ivory C.* **112 D4** 5 55N 4 15W
Ağcabädi, *Azerbaijan* **61 K8** 40 5N 47 27 E
Agcogan, *Phil.* **80 E3** 12 4N 121 57 E
Ağdam, *Azerbaijan* **61 L8** 40 0N 46 58 E
Ağdaş, *Azerbaijan* **61 K8** 40 44N 47 22 E
Agde, *France* **28 E7** 43 19N 3 28 E
Agde, C. d', *France* **28 E7** 43 16N 3 28 E
Agdz, *Morocco* **110 B3** 30 47N 6 30W
Agdzhabedi = Ağcabädi,
Azerbaijan **61 K8** 40 5N 47 27 E
Agen, *France* **28 D4** 44 12N 0 38 E
Ageo, *Japan* **71 B11** 35 58N 139 36 E
Ager Tay, *Chad* **109 E3** 20 0N 17 41 E
Agerbæk, *Denmark* **17 J2** 55 36N 8 48 E
Agersø, *Denmark* **17 J5** 55 13N 11 12 E
Ageyevo, *Russia* **58 E9** 54 10N 36 27 E
Āgh Kand, *Iran* **97 B6** 37 15N 48 4 E
Aghireşu, *Romania* **53 D8** 46 53N 23 15 E
Aghoueyyît, *Mauritania* **110 D1** 21 10N 15 6W
Aginskoye, *Russia* **65 D12** 51 6N 114 32 E
Ağlasun, *Turkey* **49 D12** 37 39N 30 31 E
Agly →, *France* **28 F7** 42 46N 3 3 E
Agnibilékrou, *Ivory C.* **112 D4** 7 10N 3 11W
Agnita, *Romania* **53 E9** 45 59N 24 40 E
Agnone, *Italy* **45 G11** 41 48N 14 22 E
Ago, *Japan* **71 C8** 34 20N 136 51 E
Agofie, *Ghana* **113 D5** 8 27N 0 15 E

Al Khums 179

Agogna →, Italy 44 C5 45 4N 8 54 E
Agogo, Sudan 107 F2 7 50N 28 45 E
Agön, Sweden 16 C11 61 34N 17 23 E
Agon Coutainville, France 26 C5 49 2N 1 34W
Agoo, Phil. 80 C3 16 20N 120 22 E
Ágordo, Italy 45 B9 46 18N 12 2 E
Agout →, France 28 E5 43 47N 1 41 E
Agra, India 92 F7 27 17N 77 58 E
Agrakhanskiy Poluostrov, Russia 61 J8 43 42N 47 36 E
Agramunt, Spain 40 D6 41 48N 1 6 E
Agreda, Spain 40 D3 41 51N 1 55W
Ağri, Turkey 101 C10 39 44N 43 4 E
Agri →, Italy 47 B9 40 13N 16 44 E
Ağrı Dağı, Turkey 101 C11 39 50N 44 15 E
Ağrı Karakose, Turkey 57 G7 39 44N 43 3 E
Agriá, Greece 48 B5 39 20N 23 1 E
Agrigento, Italy 46 E6 37 19N 13 34 E
Agrínion, Greece 48 C3 38 37N 21 27 E
Agrópoli, Italy 47 B7 40 21N 14 59 E
Ağstafa, Azerbaijan 61 K7 41 7N 45 27 E
Água Branca, Brazil 170 C3 5 50 S 42 40W
Agua Caliente, Baja Calif., Mexico 161 N10 32 29N 116 59W
Agua Caliente, Sinaloa, Mexico 162 B3 26 30N 108 20W
Agua Caliente Springs, U.S.A. 161 N10 32 56N 116 19W
Água Clara, Brazil 173 E7 20 25 S 52 45W
Agua Hechicero, Mexico 161 N10 32 26N 116 14W
Agua Preta →, Brazil 169 D5 1 41 S 63 48W
Agua Prieta, Mexico 162 A3 31 20N 109 32W
Aguachica, Colombia 168 B3 8 19N 73 38W
Aguada Cecilio, Argentina 176 B3 40 51 S 65 51W
Aguadas, Colombia 168 B2 5 40N 75 38W
Aguadilla, Puerto Rico 165 C6 18 26N 67 10W
Aguadulce, Panama 164 E3 8 15N 80 32W
Aguanga, U.S.A. 161 M10 33 27N 116 51W
Aguanish, Canada 141 B7 50 14N 62 2W
Aguanus →, Canada 141 B7 50 13N 62 5W
Aguapeí, Brazil 173 D6 16 12 S 59 43W
Aguapeí →, Brazil 171 F1 21 0 S 51 0W
Aguapey →, Argentina 174 B4 29 7 S 56 36W
Aguaray Guazú →, Paraguay 174 A4 24 47 S 57 19W
Aguarico →, Ecuador 168 D2 0 59 S 75 11W
Aguas →, Spain 40 D4 41 20N 0 30W
Aguas Blancas, Chile 174 A2 24 15 S 69 55W
Aguas Calientes, Sierra de, Argentina 174 B2 25 26 S 66 40W
Águas Formosas, Brazil 171 E3 17 5 S 40 57W
Aguascalientes, Mexico 162 C4 21 53N 102 12W
Aguascalientes □, Mexico 162 C4 22 0N 102 20W
Agudo, Spain 43 G6 38 59N 4 52W
Águeda, Portugal 42 E2 40 34N 8 27W
Agueda →, Spain 42 D4 41 2N 6 56W
Aguié, Niger 113 C6 13 31N 7 46 E
Aguilafuente, Spain 42 D6 41 13N 4 7W
Aguilar, Spain 43 H6 37 31N 4 40W
Aguilar de Campóo, Spain 42 C6 42 47N 4 15W
Aguilares, Argentina 174 B2 27 26 S 65 35W
Aguilas, Spain 41 H3 37 23N 1 35W
Agüimes, Canary Is. 39 G4 27 58N 15 27W
Aguja, C. de la, Colombia 168 A3 11 18N 74 12W
Agulaa, Ethiopia 107 E4 13 40N 39 40 E
Agulhas, C., S. Africa 116 E3 34 52 S 20 0 E
Agulo, Canary Is. 39 F2 28 11N 17 12W
Agung, Indonesia 85 D5 8 20 S 115 28 E
Agur, Uganda 118 B3 2 28N 32 55 E
Agusan →, Phil. 81 G5 9 0N 125 30 E
Agusan del Norte □, Phil. 81 G5 9 20N 125 10 E
Agusan del Sur □, Phil. 81 G5 8 30N 125 30 E
Agustín Codazzi, Colombia 168 A3 10 2N 73 14W
Agutaya I., Phil. 81 F3 11 9N 120 58 E
Ağva, Turkey 51 E13 41 8N 29 51 E
Agvali, Russia 61 J8 42 36N 46 8 E
Aha Mts., Botswana 116 B3 19 45 S 21 0 E
Ahaggar, Algeria 111 D6 23 0N 6 30 E
Ahamansu, Ghana 113 D5 7 38N 0 35 E
Ahar, Iran 101 C12 38 35N 47 0 E
Ahat, Turkey 49 C11 38 39N 29 47 E
Ahaura →, N.Z. 131 C6 42 21 S 171 34 E
Ahaus, Germany 30 C2 52 4N 7 0 E
Åheim, Norway 18 B2 62 2N 5 13 E
Ahelledjem, Algeria 111 C6 26 37N 6 58 E
Ahimanawa Ra., N.Z. 130 F5 39 3 S 176 30 E
Ahipara B., N.Z. 130 B2 35 5 S 173 5 E
Ahir Dağı, Turkey 49 C12 38 45N 30 10 E
Ahiri, India 94 E5 19 30N 80 0 E
Ahlat, Turkey 101 C10 38 45N 42 29 E
Ahlen, Germany 30 D3 51 45N 7 53 E
Ahmad Wal, Pakistan 92 E1 29 18N 65 58 E
Ahmadabad, India 92 H5 23 0N 72 40 E
Aḩmadābād, Khorāsān, Iran 97 C9 35 3N 60 50 E
Aḩmadābād, Khorāsān, Iran 97 C8 35 49N 59 42 E
Aḩmadī, Iran 97 E8 27 56N 56 42 E
Ahmadnagar, India 94 E2 19 7N 74 46 E
Ahmadpur, Pakistan 92 E4 29 12N 71 10 E
Ahmar, Ethiopia 107 F5 9 20N 41 15 E
Ahmedabad = Ahmadabad, India 92 H5 23 0N 72 40 E
Ahmednagar = Ahmadnagar, India 94 E2 19 7N 74 46 E
Ahmetbey, Turkey 51 E11 41 26N 27 34 E
Ahmetler, Turkey 49 C11 38 28N 29 5 E
Ahmetli, Turkey 49 C9 38 32N 27 57 E
Ahoada, Nigeria 113 D6 5 8N 6 36 E
Ahome, Mexico 162 B3 25 55N 109 11W
Ahr →, Germany 30 E3 50 32N 7 16 E
Ahram, Iran 97 D6 28 52N 51 16 E
Ahrax Pt., Malta 38 D1 35 59N 14 22 E
Ahrensbök, Germany 30 A6 54 2N 10 35 E
Ahrensburg, Germany 30 B6 53 40N 10 13 E
Āhū, Iran 97 C6 34 33N 50 2 E
Ahuachapán, El Salv. 164 D2 13 54N 89 52W
Ahun, France 27 F9 46 4N 2 5 E
Ahuriri →, N.Z. 131 E5 44 31 S 170 12 E
Åhus, Sweden 17 J8 55 56N 14 18 E
Ahvāz, Iran 97 D6 31 20N 48 40 E
Ahvenanmaa = Åland, Finland 15 F19 60 15N 20 0 E
Aḩwar, Yemen 98 D4 13 30N 46 40 E
Ahzar, Mali 113 B5 15 30N 3 20 E
Aiari →, Brazil 168 C4 1 22N 68 36W
Aichach, Germany 31 G7 48 27N 11 8 E
Aichi □, Japan 71 C9 35 0N 137 15 E
Aiea, U.S.A. 145 K14 21 23N 157 56W
Aigle, Switz. 32 D3 46 18N 6 58 E
Aignay-le-Duc, France 27 E11 47 40N 4 43 E
Aigoual, Mt., France 28 D7 44 8N 3 35 E
Aigre, France 28 C4 45 54N 0 1 E
Aigua, Uruguay 175 C5 34 13 S 54 46W
Aigueperse, France 27 F10 46 3N 3 13 E
Aigues →, France 29 D8 44 7N 4 43 E
Aigues-Mortes, France 29 E8 43 35N 4 12 E
Aigues-Mortes, G. d', France 29 E8 43 31N 4 3 E
Aiguilles, France 29 D10 44 47N 6 51 E
Aiguillon, France 28 D4 44 18N 0 21 E
Aigurande, France 27 F8 46 27N 1 49 E
Aihui, China 73 A7 50 10N 127 30 E
Aija, Peru 172 B2 9 50 S 77 45W
Aikawa, Japan 68 E9 38 2N 138 15 E
Aiken, U.S.A. 152 B9 33 34N 81 43W
Ailao Shan, China 76 F3 24 0N 101 20 E
Ailey, U.S.A. 152 C7 32 11N 82 34W
Aillant-sur-Tholon, France 27 E10 47 52N 3 20 E
Aillik, Canada 141 A8 55 11N 59 18W
Ailsa Craig, U.K. 22 F3 55 15N 5 6W
'Ailūn, Jordan 103 C4 32 18N 35 47 E
Aim, Russia 65 D14 59 0N 133 55 E
Aimere, Indonesia 82 C2 8 45 S 121 3 E
Aimogasta, Argentina 174 B2 28 33 S 66 50W
Aimorés, Brazil 171 E3 19 30 S 41 4W
Ain □, France 27 F12 46 5N 5 20 E
Ain →, France 29 C9 45 45N 5 11 E
Aïn Beïda, Algeria 111 A6 35 50N 7 29 E
Aïn Ben Khellil, Algeria 111 B4 33 15N 0 49W
Aïn Ben Tili, Mauritania 110 C3 25 59N 9 27W
Aïn Beni Mathar, Morocco 111 B4 34 1N 2 0W
Aïn Benian, Algeria 111 A5 36 48N 2 55 E
Ain Dalla, Egypt 106 B2 27 20N 27 23 E
Ain el Mafki, Egypt 106 B2 27 30N 28 15 E
Ain Girba, Egypt 106 B2 29 20N 25 14 E
Aïn M'lila, Algeria 111 A6 36 2N 6 35 E
Ain Qeiqab, Egypt 106 B1 29 42N 24 55 E
Aïn-Sefra, Algeria 111 B4 32 47N 0 37W
Ain Sheikh Murzûk, Egypt 106 B2 26 47N 27 45 E
'Ain Sudr, Egypt 103 F2 29 50N 33 6 E
Ain Sukhna, Egypt 106 J8 29 32N 32 20 E
Aïn Tédelès, Algeria 111 A5 36 0N 0 21 E
Aïn-Témouchent, Algeria 111 A4 35 16N 1 8W
Aïn Touta, Algeria 111 A6 35 26N 5 54 E
Ain Zeitûn, Egypt 106 B2 29 10N 25 48 E
Aïn Zorah, Morocco 111 B4 34 37N 3 32W
Ainabo, Somali Rep. 120 C3 9 0N 46 25 E
Ainaži, Latvia 15 H21 57 50N 24 24 E
Aínos Óros, Greece 48 C2 38 10N 20 35 E
Ainsworth, U.S.A. 154 D5 42 33N 99 52W
Aioi, Japan 70 C6 34 48N 134 28 E
Aipe, Colombia 168 C2 3 13N 75 15W
Aiquile, Bolivia 173 D4 18 10 S 65 10W
Aïr, Niger 109 E1 18 30N 8 0 E
Air Hitam, Malaysia 87 M4 1 55N 103 11 E
Airaines, France 27 C8 49 58N 1 55 E
Airão, Brazil 169 D5 1 56 S 61 22W
Airdrie, U.K. 22 F5 55 52N 3 57W
Aire →, France 27 C11 49 18N 4 49 E
Aire →, U.K. 20 D7 53 43N 0 55W
Aire, I. de l', Spain 39 B11 39 48N 4 16 E
Aire-sur-la-Lys, France 27 B9 50 37N 2 22 E
Aire-sur-l'Adour, France 28 E3 43 42N 0 15W
Aireys Inlet, Australia 128 E6 38 29 S 144 5 E
Airlie Beach, Australia 126 C4 20 16 S 148 43 E
Airolo, Switz. 33 C7 46 32N 8 37 E
Airvault, France 26 F6 46 50N 0 8W
Aisch →, Germany 31 F6 49 49N 10 58 E
Aisen □, Chile 176 C2 46 30 S 73 0W
Aisne □, France 27 C10 49 42N 3 40 E
Aisne →, France 27 C9 49 26N 2 50 E
Aitana, Sierra de, Spain 41 G4 38 35N 0 24W
Aitape, Papua N. G. 132 B2 3 11 S 142 22 E
Aitkin, U.S.A. 154 B8 46 32N 93 42W
Aitolía Kai Akarnanía □, Greece 48 C3 38 45N 21 18 E
Aitolikón, Greece 48 C3 38 26N 21 21 E
Aiuaba, Brazil 170 C3 6 38 S 40 7W
Aiud, Romania 53 D8 46 19N 23 44 E
Aix-en-Provence, France 29 E9 43 32N 5 27 E
Aix-la-Chapelle = Aachen, Germany 30 E2 50 45N 6 6 E
Aix-les-Bains, France 29 C9 45 41N 5 53 E
Aixe-sur-Vienne, France 28 C5 45 47N 1 9 E
Aiyang, Mt., Papua N. G. 132 C1 5 10 S 141 20 E
Aiyansh, Canada 142 B3 55 17N 129 2W
Aíyina, Greece 48 D5 37 45N 23 26 E
Aiyínion, Greece 50 F6 40 28N 22 28 E
Aíyion, Greece 48 C4 38 15N 22 5 E
Aizawl, India 90 D4 23 40N 92 44 E
Aizenay, France 26 F5 46 44N 1 38W
Aizkraukle, Latvia 15 H21 56 36N 25 11 E
Aizpute, Latvia 15 H19 56 43N 21 40 E
Aizuwakamatsu, Japan 68 F9 37 30N 139 56 E
Ajaccio, France 29 G12 41 55N 8 40 E
Ajaccio, G. d', France 29 G12 41 52N 8 40 E
Ajaju →, Colombia 168 C3 0 59N 72 20W
Ajalpan, Mexico 163 D5 18 22N 97 15W
Ajanta Ra., India 94 D2 20 28N 75 50 E
Ajari Rep. = Ajaria □, Georgia 61 K6 41 30N 42 0 E
Ajaria □, Georgia 61 K6 41 30N 42 0 E
Ajax, Canada 150 C5 43 50N 79 1W
Ajax, Mt., N.Z. 131 C7 42 35 S 172 5 E
Ajayan Pt., Guam 133 R15 13 15N 144 43 E
Ajdâbiyah, Libya 108 B4 30 54N 20 4 E
Ajdovščina, Slovenia 45 C10 45 54N 13 54 E
Ajibar, Ethiopia 107 E4 10 35N 38 36 E
Ajka, Hungary 52 C2 47 4N 17 31 E
'Ajmān, U.A.E. 97 E7 25 25N 55 30 E
Ajmer, India 92 F6 26 28N 74 37 E
Ajo, U.S.A. 159 K7 32 22N 112 52W
Ajo, C. de, Spain 42 B7 43 31N 3 35W
Ajoie, Switz. 32 B4 47 22N 7 0 E
Ajok, Sudan 107 F2 9 15N 28 28 E
Ajuy, Phil. 81 F4 11 10N 123 1 E
Ak Dağ, Turkey 49 E11 36 30N 29 32 E
Ak Dağlari, Muğla, Turkey 49 E11 36 30N 29 30 E
Ak Dağları, Sivas, Turkey 100 C7 39 32N 36 12 E
Akaba, Togo 113 D5 8 10N 1 2 E
Akabira, Japan 68 C11 43 33N 142 5 E
Akabli, Algeria 111 C5 26 49N 1 31 E
Akaishi-Dake, Japan 71 B10 35 27N 138 9 E
Akaishi-Sammyaku, Japan 71 B10 35 25N 138 10 E
Akaki Beseka, Ethiopia 107 F4 8 55N 38 45 E
Akala, Sudan 107 D4 15 39N 36 13 E
Akamas □, Cyprus 38 D11 35 3N 32 18 E
Akanthou, Cyprus 38 D12 35 22N 33 45 E
Akarca, Turkey 49 C11 38 20N 29 51 E
Akaroa, N.Z. 131 D7 43 49 S 172 59 E
Akaroa Harbour, N.Z. 131 D7 43 50 S 172 55 E
Akasha, Sudan 106 C3 21 10N 30 32 E
Akashi, Japan 70 C6 34 45N 134 58 E
Akbou, Algeria 111 A5 36 31N 4 31 E
Akbulak, Russia 62 F5 51 1N 55 37 E
Akçaabat, Turkey 101 B8 41 1N 39 34 E
Akçadağ, Turkey 100 C7 38 27N 37 43 E
Akçakale, Turkey 101 D8 36 41N 38 56 E
Akçakoca, Turkey 100 B4 41 5N 31 8 E
Akçaova, Turkey 51 E13 41 3N 29 57 E
Akçay, Turkey 49 E11 36 36N 29 45 E
Akçay →, Turkey 49 D10 37 50N 28 15 E
Akchâr, Mauritania 110 D2 20 20N 14 28W
Akdağ, Turkey 49 C8 38 33N 26 30 E
Akdağmadeni, Turkey 100 C6 39 39N 35 53 E
Akdala, Kazakstan 63 A7 45 2N 74 35 E
Akechi, Japan 71 B9 35 18N 137 23 E
Akelamo, Indonesia 82 A3 1 35N 129 40 E
Åkernes, Norway 18 F4 58 45N 7 30 E
Åkers styckebruk, Sweden 16 E11 59 15N 17 5 E
Åkersberga, Sweden 16 E12 59 29N 18 18 E
Akershus □, Norway 18 D8 60 0N 11 10 E
Akeru →, India 94 F5 17 25N 80 5 E
Aketi, Dem. Rep. of the Congo 114 B4 2 38N 23 47 E
Akhaïa □, Greece 48 C3 38 5N 21 45 E
Akhalkalaki, Georgia 61 K6 41 27N 43 25 E
Akhaltsikhe, Georgia 61 K6 41 40N 43 0 E
Akharnaí, Greece 48 C5 38 5N 23 44 E
Akhelóös →, Greece 48 C3 38 19N 21 7 E
Akhendriá, Greece 49 G7 34 59N 25 13 E
Akhiok, U.S.A. 144 H9 56 57N 154 10W
Akhisar, Turkey 49 C9 38 56N 27 48 E
Akhladhókambos, Greece 48 D4 37 31N 22 35 E
Akhmîm, Egypt 106 B3 26 31N 31 47 E
Akhnur, India 93 C6 32 52N 74 45 E
Akhtopol, Bulgaria 51 D11 42 6N 27 56 E
Akhtuba →, Russia 61 G8 47 41N 46 55 E
Akhtubinsk, Russia 61 F8 48 13N 46 7 E
Akhty, Russia 61 K8 41 30N 47 45 E
Akhtyrka = Okhtyrka, Ukraine 59 G8 50 25N 35 0 E
Aki, Japan 70 D5 33 30N 133 54 E
Aki-Nada, Japan 70 C4 34 5N 132 40 E
Akiachak, U.S.A. 144 F7 60 55N 161 26W
Akiéni, Gabon 114 C2 1 11 S 13 53 E
Akimiski I., Canada 140 B3 52 50N 81 30W
Akimovka, Ukraine 59 J8 46 44N 35 0 E
Åkirkeby, Denmark 17 J8 55 4N 14 55 E
Akita, Japan 68 E10 39 45N 140 7 E
Akita □, Japan 68 E10 39 40N 140 30 E
Akjoujt, Mauritania 112 B2 19 45N 14 15W
Akka, Morocco 110 C3 29 22N 8 9W
Akkaya Tepesi, Turkey 49 D11 37 25N 29 38 E
Akkeshi, Japan 68 C12 43 2N 144 51 E
'Akko, Israel 103 C4 32 55N 35 4 E
Akkol, Kazakstan 63 B5 43 36N 70 45 E
Akköy, Turkey 49 D9 37 29N 27 15 E
Aklampa, Benin 113 D5 8 15N 2 10 E
Aklan □, Phil. 81 F4 11 50N 122 30 E
Aklavik, Canada 138 B6 68 12N 135 0W
Akmenė, Lithuania 54 B9 56 15N 22 45 E
Akmenrags, Latvia 54 B8 56 50N 21 4 E
Akmolinsk = Aqmola, Kazakstan 64 D8 51 10N 71 30 E
Akmonte = Almonte, Spain 43 H4 37 13N 6 38W
Akmuz, Kyrgyzstan 63 C8 41 15N 76 10 E
Aknoul, Morocco 111 B4 34 40N 3 55W
Akō, Japan 70 C6 34 45N 134 24 E
Ako, Nigeria 113 C7 10 19N 10 48 E
Akobo →, Ethiopia 107 F3 7 48N 33 3 E
Akola, India 94 D3 20 42N 77 2 E
Akolmiut, U.S.A. 144 F7 60 55N 162 20W
Akonolinga, Cameroon 113 E7 3 50N 12 18 E
Akordat, Eritrea 107 D4 15 30N 37 40 E
Akosombo Dam, Ghana 113 D5 6 20N 0 5 E
Akot, India 94 D3 21 10N 77 10 E
Akot, Sudan 107 F3 6 31N 30 9 E
Akpatok I., Canada 139 B13 60 25N 68 8W
Åkrahamn, Norway 15 G11 59 15N 5 10 E
Akranes, Iceland 11 C4 64 19N 22 5W
Akreïjit, Mauritania 112 B3 18 19N 9 11W
Akrítas Venétiko, Ákra, Greece 48 E3 36 43N 21 54 E
Akron, Colo., U.S.A. 154 E3 40 10N 103 13W
Akron, Ind., U.S.A. 157 C10 41 2N 86 1W
Akron, Ohio, U.S.A. 150 E3 41 5N 81 31W
Akrotiri, Cyprus 38 E11 34 36N 32 57 E
Akrotíri, Ákra, Greece 51 F9 40 26N 25 27 E
Akrotiri Bay, Cyprus 38 E12 34 35N 33 10 E
Aksai Chin, India 93 B8 35 15N 79 55 E
Aksaray, Turkey 100 C6 38 25N 34 2 E
Aksay, Kazakstan 62 F4 51 11N 53 0 E
Akşehir, Turkey 100 C4 38 18N 31 30 E
Akşehir Gölü, Turkey 100 C4 38 30N 31 25 E
Akstafa = Ağstafa, Azerbaijan 61 K7 41 7N 45 27 E
Aksu, China 72 B3 41 5N 80 10 E
Aksu →, Turkey 100 D4 36 52N 30 57 E
Aksum, Ethiopia 107 E4 14 5N 38 40 E
Aktash, Russia 60 C11 55 2N 52 0 E
Aktash, Uzbekistan 63 D2 39 55N 65 55 E
Aktasty, Kazakstan 62 F8 50 42N 61 42 E
Aktogay, Almaty, Kazakstan 63 A8 44 25N 76 44 E
Aktogay, Semey, Kazakstan 64 E8 46 57N 79 40 E
Aktsyabrski, Belarus 59 F5 52 38N 28 53 E
Aktyubinsk = Aqtöbe, Kazakstan 57 D10 50 17N 57 10 E
Aktyuz, Kyrgyzstan 63 B8 42 54N 76 7 E
Aku, Nigeria 113 D6 6 40N 7 18 E
Akula, Dem. Rep. of the Congo 114 B4 2 22N 20 12 E
Akune, Japan 70 E2 32 1N 130 12 E
Akure, Nigeria 113 D6 7 15N 5 5 E
Akureyri, Iceland 11 B8 65 40N 18 6W
Akuseki-Shima, Japan 69 K4 29 27N 129 37 E
Akusha, Russia 61 J8 42 18N 47 30 E
Akutan, U.S.A. 144 J6 54 8N 165 46W
Akutan Indian Reservation, U.S.A. 144 J6 54 10N 166 0W
Akwa-Ibom □, Nigeria 113 E6 4 30N 7 30 E
Akyab = Sittwe, Burma 90 E4 20 18N 92 45 E
Akyazı, Turkey 100 B4 40 40N 30 38 E
Akzhar, Kazakstan 63 B5 43 8N 71 37 E
Ål, Norway 18 D5 60 38N 8 33 E
Al Abyār, Libya 108 B4 32 9N 20 29 E
Al 'Adan, Yemen 98 D4 12 45N 45 0 E
Al Aḩsā, Si. Arabia 97 E6 25 50N 49 0 E
Al Ajfar, Si. Arabia 96 E4 27 26N 43 0 E
Al Amādīyah, Iraq 101 D10 37 5N 43 30 E
Al Amārah, Iraq 101 G12 31 55N 47 15 E
Al 'Aqabah, Jordan 103 F4 29 31N 35 0 E
Al 'Aqīq, Si. Arabia 98 B3 20 39N 41 25 E
Al Arak, Syria 101 E8 34 38N 38 35 E
Al 'Aramah, Si. Arabia 96 E5 25 30N 46 0 E
Al 'Ariḑah, Si. Arabia 98 C3 17 3N 43 5 E
Al Arţāwīyah, Si. Arabia 96 E5 26 31N 45 20 E
Al Ashkhara, Oman 99 B7 21 50N 59 30 E
Al 'Āşimah = 'Ammān □, Jordan 103 D5 31 40N 36 30 E
Al 'Assāfīyah, Si. Arabia 96 D3 28 17N 38 59 E
Al 'Ayn, Oman 97 E7 24 15N 55 45 E
Al 'Ayn, Si. Arabia 96 E3 25 4N 38 6 E
Al A'ẓamīyah, Iraq 96 C5 33 22N 44 22 E
Al 'Azīzīyah, Iraq 101 F11 32 54N 45 4 E
Al 'Azīzīyah, Libya 108 B2 32 30N 13 1 E
Al Bāb, Syria 100 D7 36 23N 37 29 E
Al Bad', Si. Arabia 96 D2 28 28N 35 1 E
Al Bādī, Iraq 96 C4 35 56N 41 32 E
Al Badī', Si. Arabia 98 B4 22 0N 46 35 E
Al Baḩrah, Kuwait 96 D5 29 40N 47 52 E
Al Baḩral Mayyit = Dead Sea, Asia 103 D4 31 30N 35 30 E
Al Balqā' □, Jordan 103 C4 32 5N 35 45 E
Al Barkāt, Libya 108 D2 24 56N 10 14 E
Al Bārūk, J., Lebanon 103 B4 33 39N 35 40 E
Al Başrah, Iraq 96 D5 30 30N 47 50 E
Al Baţḩā, Iraq 96 D5 31 6N 45 53 E
Al Batrūn, Lebanon 103 A4 34 15N 35 40 E
Al Bayāḑ, Si. Arabia 98 B4 22 0N 47 0 E
Al Bayḑā, Libya 108 B4 32 50N 21 44 E
Al Bayḑā', Yemen 98 D4 14 5N 45 42 E
Al Bayḑā □, Libya 108 B4 32 0N 21 30 E
Al Bi'ār, Si. Arabia 98 B2 22 39N 39 40 E
Al Biqā □, Lebanon 103 A5 34 10N 36 10 E
Al Bi'r, Si. Arabia 96 D3 28 51N 36 16 E
Al Birk, Si. Arabia 98 C3 18 13N 41 33 E
Al Bu'ayrāt al Ḩasūn, Libya 108 B3 31 24N 15 44 E
Al Burayj, Syria 103 A5 34 15N 36 46 E
Al Fallūjah, Iraq 101 F10 33 20N 43 55 E
Al Fatk, Yemen 99 C6 16 31N 52 41 E
Al Fāw, Iraq 97 D6 30 0N 48 30 E
Al Faydamī, Yemen 99 C6 16 25N 52 26 E
Al Fujayrah, U.A.E. 97 E8 25 7N 56 18 E
Al Ghadaf, W. →, Jordan 103 D5 31 26N 36 43 E
Al Ghammās, Iraq 96 D5 31 45N 44 37 E
Al Gharīb, Libya 108 B4 32 35N 21 11 E
Al Ghayḑah, Yemen 99 C6 16 13N 52 11 E
Al Ghayḑah, Yemen 99 D5 14 55N 50 0 E
Al Ghayl, Yemen 99 D5 15 30N 50 54 E
Al Hābah, Si. Arabia 96 E5 27 10N 47 0 E
Al Ḩadd, Oman 99 B7 22 32N 59 48 E
Al Ḩaddār, Si. Arabia 98 B4 21 58N 45 57 E
Al Ḩadīthah, Iraq 101 E10 34 0N 41 13 E
Al Ḩadīthah, Si. Arabia 96 D3 31 28N 37 8 E
Al Ḩaḑr, Iraq 101 E10 35 35N 42 44 E
Al Hājānah, Syria 103 B5 33 20N 36 33 E
Al Hajarayn, Yemen 99 D5 15 29N 48 20 E
Al Hallānīyah, Oman 99 C7 17 30N 56 1 E
Al Hāmad, Si. Arabia 96 D3 31 30N 39 30 E
Al Ḩamar, Si. Arabia 98 B4 22 26N 46 12 E
Al Hamdānīyah, Syria 96 C3 35 25N 36 50 E
Al Ḩamīdīyah, Syria 103 A4 34 42N 35 57 E
Al Ḩammādah al Ḩamrā', Libya 108 C2 29 30N 12 0 E
Al Ḩammār, Iraq 96 D5 30 57N 46 51 E
Al Ḩamrā', Si. Arabia 98 A2 24 2N 38 55 E
Al Ḩarīq, Si. Arabia 98 B4 23 29N 46 27 E
Al Harīr, W. →, Syria 103 C4 32 44N 35 59 E
Al Harūj al Aswad, Libya 108 C3 27 0N 17 10 E
Al Ḩasā, W. →, Jordan 103 D4 31 4N 35 29 E
Al Ḩasakah, Syria 101 D9 36 35N 40 45 E
Al Hāsikīyah, Oman 99 C6 17 28N 55 36 E
Al Ḩasy, Yemen 99 D5 14 3N 48 40 E
Al Ḩawrah, Yemen 98 D4 13 50N 47 35 E
Al Ḩawṯah, Yemen 98 D4 14 23N 47 24 E
Al Ḩawṯah □, Si. Arabia 98 B4 23 30N 47 0 E
Al Haydān, W. →, Jordan 103 D4 31 29N 35 34 E
Al Ḩayy, Iraq 101 F12 32 5N 46 5 E
Al Ḩillah, Iraq 101 F11 32 30N 44 25 E
Al Ḩillah, Si. Arabia 98 B4 23 35N 46 50 E
Al Hindīyah, Iraq 101 F11 32 30N 44 10 E
Al Hirmil, Lebanon 103 A5 34 26N 36 24 E
Al Hoceïma, Morocco 110 A4 35 8N 3 58W
Al Ḩudaydah, Yemen 98 D3 14 50N 43 0 E
Al Ḩufrah, Libya 108 C2 25 32N 14 1 E
Al Hufūf, Si. Arabia 97 E6 25 25N 49 45 E
Al Ḩulwah, Si. Arabia 98 B4 23 24N 46 48 E
Al Ḩumayḑah, Si. Arabia 96 D2 29 14N 34 56 E
Al Ḩunayy, Si. Arabia 97 E6 25 58N 48 45 E
Al Ḩurayḑah, Yemen 99 D5 15 36N 48 12 E
Al Husayyāt, Libya 108 B4 30 24N 20 37 E
Al Hūwah, Si. Arabia 98 B4 23 2N 45 48 E
Al Ḩuwaymī, Yemen 98 D4 13 23N 44 28 E
Al 'Irqah, Yemen 98 D4 13 39N 47 22 E
Al Īsāwīyah, Si. Arabia 96 D3 30 43N 37 59 E
Al Ittihad = Madīnat ash Sha'b, Yemen 98 D4 12 50N 45 0 E
Al Jafr, Jordan 103 E5 30 18N 36 14 E
Al Jaghbūb, Libya 108 C4 29 42N 24 38 E
Al Jahrah, Kuwait 96 D5 29 25N 47 40 E
Al Jalāmīd, Si. Arabia 96 D3 31 20N 39 45 E
Al Jamalīyah, Qatar 97 E6 25 37N 51 5 E
Al Janūb □, Lebanon 103 B4 33 20N 35 20 E
Al Jawf, Libya 108 D4 24 10N 23 24 E
Al Jawf, Si. Arabia 96 D3 29 55N 39 40 E
Al Jazirah, Iraq 101 E10 33 30N 44 0 E
Al Jazirah, Libya 108 C4 26 10N 21 20 E
Al Jithāmīyah, Si. Arabia 96 E4 27 41N 41 43 E
Al Jubayl, Si. Arabia 97 E6 27 0N 49 50 E
Al Jubaylah, Si. Arabia 96 E5 24 55N 46 25 E
Al Jubb, Si. Arabia 96 E4 27 11N 42 17 E
Al Jumūm, Si. Arabia 98 B2 21 37N 39 42 E
Al Junaynah, Sudan 109 F4 13 27N 22 45 E
Al Kabā'ish, Iraq 96 D5 30 58N 47 0 E
Al Kāmil, Oman 99 B7 22 13N 59 12 E
Al Karak, Jordan 103 D4 31 11N 35 42 E
Al Karak □, Jordan 103 E5 31 0N 36 0 E
Al Kāzim Tyah, Iraq 101 F11 33 22N 44 12 E
Al Khābūra, Oman 99 B7 23 57N 57 5 E
Al Khalīl, West Bank 103 D4 31 32N 35 6 E
Al Khāliş, Iraq 101 F11 33 49N 44 32 E
Al Khamāsīn, Si. Arabia 98 C4 20 29N 44 46 E
Al Kharāb, Yemen 98 C4 16 29N 44 18 E
Al Kharfah, Si. Arabia 98 B4 22 0N 46 35 E
Al Kharj, Si. Arabia 98 B4 24 0N 47 0 E
Al Khāşirah, Si. Arabia 98 B3 23 30N 43 47 E
Al Khawr, Qatar 97 E6 25 41N 51 30 E
Al Khiḑr, Iraq 96 D5 31 12N 45 33 E
Al Khiyām, Lebanon 103 B4 33 20N 35 36 E
Al Khums, Libya 108 B2 32 40N 14 17 E
Al Khums □, Libya 108 B2 31 20N 14 10 E

Allanton, *N.Z.* **131 F5** 45 55 S 170 15 E
Allanwater, *Canada* **140 B1** 50 14N 90 10W
Allaqi, Wadi →, *Egypt* **106 C3** 23 7N 32 47 E
Allariz, *Spain* **42 C3** 42 11N 7 50W
Allassac, *France* **28 C5** 45 15N 1 29 E
Allatoona L., *U.S.A.* **152 A5** 34 10N 84 44W
Ålleberg, *Sweden* **17 F7** 58 8N 13 36 E
Allegan, *U.S.A.* **157 B11** 42 32N 85 51W
Allegany, *U.S.A.* **150 D6** 42 6N 78 30W
Allegheny →, *U.S.A.* **150 F5** 40 27N 80 1W
Allegheny Mts., *U.S.A.* **136 F11** 38 15N 80 10W
Allegheny Plateau, *U.S.A.* **148 G6** 38 0N 80 0W
Allegheny Reservoir, *U.S.A.* **150 E6** 41 50N 79 0W
Allègre, *France* **28 C7** 45 12N 3 41 E
Allen, *Argentina* **176 A3** 38 58 S 67 50W
Allen, *Phil.* **80 E5** 12 30N 124 17 E
Allen, Bog of, *Ireland* **23 C5** 53 15N 7 0W
Allen, L., *Ireland* **23 B3** 54 8N 8 4W
Allendale, *U.S.A.* **152 B9** 33 1N 81 18W
Allende, *Mexico* **162 B4** 28 20N 100 50W
Allentown, *U.S.A.* **151 F9** 40 37N 75 29W
Allentsteig, *Austria* **34 C8** 48 41N 15 20 E
Alleppey, *India* **95 K3** 9 30N 76 28 E
Allepuz, *Spain* **40 E4** 40 29N 0 44W
Aller →, *Germany* **30 C5** 52 56N 9 12 E
Alliance, *Surinam* **169 B7** 5 50N 54 50W
Alliance, *Nebr., U.S.A.* **154 D3** 42 6N 102 52W
Alliance, *Ohio, U.S.A.* **150 F3** 40 55N 81 6W
Allier □, *France* **27 F9** 46 25N 2 40 E
Allier →, *France* **27 F10** 46 57N 3 4 E
Allinge, *Denmark* **17 J8** 55 17N 14 50 E
Allison, *U.S.A.* **156 B4** 42 45N 92 48W
Alliston, *Canada* **140 D4** 44 9N 79 52W
Alloa, *U.K.* **22 E5** 56 7N 3 47W
Allones, *France* **26 D8** 48 20N 1 40 E
Allora, *Australia* **127 D5** 28 2 S 152 0 E
Allos, *France* **29 D10** 44 15N 6 38 E
Alluitsup Paa = Sydprøven, *Greenland* **10 E6** 60 30N 45 35W
Alma, *Canada* **141 C5** 48 35N 71 40W
Alma, *Ga., U.S.A.* **152 D7** 31 33N 82 28W
Alma, *Kans., U.S.A.* **154 F6** 39 1N 96 17W
Alma, *Mich., U.S.A.* **148 D3** 43 23N 84 39W
Alma, *Nebr., U.S.A.* **154 E5** 40 6N 99 22W
Alma, *Wis., U.S.A.* **154 C9** 44 20N 91 55W
Alma Ata = Almaty, *Kazakstan* **63 B8** 43 15N 76 57 E
Almacelles, *Spain* **40 D5** 41 43N 0 27 E
Almada, *Portugal* **43 G1** 38 40N 9 9W
Almaden, *Australia* **126 B3** 17 22 S 144 40 E
Almadén, *Spain* **43 G6** 38 49N 4 52W
Almagro I., *Phil.* **81 F5** 11 56N 124 18 E
Almalyk = Olmaliq, *Uzbekistan* **63 C4** 40 50N 69 35 E
Almanor, L., *U.S.A.* **158 F3** 40 14N 121 9W
Almansa, *Spain* **41 G3** 38 51N 1 5W
Almanza, *Spain* **42 C5** 42 39N 5 3W
Almanzor, Pico, *Spain* **42 E5** 40 15N 5 18W
Almanzora →, *Spain* **41 H3** 37 14N 1 46W
Almas, *Brazil* **171 D2** 11 33 S 47 9W
Almaş, Munţii, *Romania* **52 F7** 44 49N 22 12 E
Almassora, *Spain* **40 F4** 39 57N 0 3W
Almaty, *Kazakstan* **63 B8** 43 15N 76 57 E
Almazán, *Spain* **40 D2** 41 30N 2 30W
Almeirim, *Brazil* **169 D7** 1 30 S 52 34W
Almeirim, *Portugal* **43 F2** 39 12N 8 37W
Almelo, *Neths.* **24 B6** 52 22N 6 42 E
Almenar de Soria, *Spain* **40 D2** 41 43N 2 12W
Almenara, *Brazil* **171 E3** 16 11 S 40 42W
Almenara, *Spain* **40 F4** 39 46N 0 14W
Almenara, Sierra de la, *Spain* **41 H3** 37 34N 1 32W
Almendra, Embalse de, *Spain* **42 D4** 41 10N 6 5W
Almendralejo, *Spain* **43 G4** 38 41N 6 26W
Almere-Stad, *Neths.* **24 B5** 52 20N 5 15 E
Almería, *Spain* **43 J8** 36 52N 2 27W
Almería □, *Spain* **41 H2** 37 20N 2 20W
Almería, G. de, *Spain* **41 J2** 36 41N 2 28W
Almetyevsk, *Russia* **60 C11** 54 53N 52 20 E
Älmhult, *Sweden* **17 H8** 56 33N 14 8 E
Almirante, *Panama* **164 E3** 9 10N 82 30W
Almirante Montt, G., *Chile* **176 D2** 51 52 S 72 50W
Almirópótamos, *Greece* **48 C6** 38 16N 24 11 E
Almirós, *Greece* **48 B4** 39 11N 22 45 E
Almiroú, Kólpos, *Greece* **38 D6** 35 23N 24 20 E
Almodôvar, *Portugal* **43 H2** 37 31N 8 2W
Almodóvar del Campo, *Spain* **43 G6** 38 43N 4 10W
Almodóvar del Río, *Spain* **43 H5** 37 48N 5 1W
Almon, *U.S.A.* **152 B6** 33 37N 83 56W
Almont, *U.S.A.* **150 D1** 42 55N 83 3W
Almonte, *Canada* **151 A8** 45 14N 76 12W
Almonte, *Spain* **43 H4** 37 13N 6 38W
Almora, *India* **93 E8** 29 38N 79 40 E
Almoradí, *Spain* **41 G4** 38 7N 0 46W
Almorox, *Spain* **42 E6** 40 14N 4 24W
Almoustarat, *Mali* **113 B5** 17 35N 0 8 E
Älmsta, *Sweden* **16 E12** 59 58N 18 50 E
Almudévar, *Spain* **40 C4** 42 3N 0 35W
Almuñécar, *Spain* **43 J7** 36 43N 3 41W
Almunge, *Sweden* **16 E12** 59 53N 18 3 E
Almuradiel, *Spain* **43 G7** 38 32N 3 28W
Alness, *U.K.* **22 D4** 57 41N 4 16W
Alnif, *Morocco* **110 B3** 31 10N 5 8W
Alnmouth, *U.K.* **20 B6** 55 24N 1 37W
Alnwick, *U.K.* **20 B6** 55 24N 1 42W
Aloi, *Uganda* **118 B3** 2 16N 33 10 E
Alon, *Burma* **90 D5** 22 12N 95 5 E
Alor, *Indonesia* **82 C2** 8 15 S 124 30 E
Alor Setar, *Malaysia* **87 J3** 6 7N 100 22 E
Álora, *Spain* **43 J6** 36 49N 4 46W
Alosno, *Spain* **43 H3** 37 33N 7 7W
Alotau, *Papua N. G.* **132 F6** 10 16 S 150 30 E
Alougoum, *Morocco* **110 B3** 30 17N 6 56W
Aloysius, Mt., *Australia* **125 E4** 26 0 S 128 38 E
Alpaugh, *U.S.A.* **160 K7** 35 53N 119 29W
Alpedrinha, *Portugal* **42 E3** 40 6N 7 27W
Alpena, *U.S.A.* **148 C4** 45 4N 83 27W
Alpercatas →, *Brazil* **170 C3** 6 2 S 44 19W
Alpes-de-Haute-Provence □, *France* **29 D10** 44 8N 6 10 E
Alpes-Maritimes □, *France* **29 E11** 43 55N 7 10 E
Alpha, *Australia* **126 C4** 23 39 S 146 37 E
Alpha, *U.S.A.* **156 C6** 41 12N 90 23W
Alphen aan den Rijn, *Neths.* **24 B4** 52 7N 4 40 E
Alphonse, *Seychelles* **121 E4** 7 0 S 52 45 E
Alpiarça, *Portugal* **43 F2** 39 15N 8 35W
Alpine, *Ariz., U.S.A.* **159 K9** 33 51N 109 9W
Alpine, *Calif., U.S.A.* **161 N10** 32 50N 116 46W
Alpine, *Tex., U.S.A.* **155 K3** 30 22N 103 40W
Alpnach, *Switz.* **33 C6** 46 57N 8 17 E
Alps, *Europe* **12 F7** 46 30N 9 30 E
Alpu, *Turkey* **100 C4** 39 46N 30 58 E
Alqueta, Barragem do, *Portugal* **43 G3** 38 20N 7 25W
Alrø, *Denmark* **17 J4** 55 52N 10 5 E
Alroy Downs, *Australia* **126 B2** 19 20 S 136 5 E
Als, *Denmark* **17 K3** 54 59N 9 55 E
Alsace, *France* **27 D14** 48 15N 7 25 E
Alsask, *Canada* **143 C7** 51 21N 109 59W
Alsasua, *Spain* **40 C2** 42 54N 2 10W
Alsfeld, *Germany* **30 E5** 50 44N 9 16 E
Alsten, *Norway* **14 D15** 65 58N 12 40 E
Alstermo, *Sweden* **17 H9** 56 58N 15 38 E
Alston, *U.K.* **20 C5** 54 49N 2 25W
Alta, *Norway* **14 B20** 69 57N 23 10 E
Alta, Sierra, *Spain* **40 E3** 40 31N 1 30W
Alta Gracia, *Argentina* **174 C3** 31 40 S 64 30W
Alta Lake, *Canada* **142 C4** 50 10N 123 0W
Alta Sierra, *U.S.A.* **161 K8** 35 42N 118 33W
Altaelva →, *Norway* **14 B20** 69 54N 23 17 E
Altafjorden, *Norway* **14 A20** 70 5N 23 5 E
Altagracia, *Venezuela* **168 A3** 10 45N 71 30W
Altagracia de Orituco, *Venezuela* **168 B4** 9 52N 66 23W
Altai = Aerhtai Shan, *Mongolia* **72 B4** 46 40N 92 45 E
Altamachi →, *Bolivia* **172 D4** 16 8 S 66 50W
Altamaha →, *U.S.A.* **152 D8** 31 20N 81 20W
Altamira, *Brazil* **169 D7** 3 12 S 52 10W
Altamira, *Chile* **174 B2** 25 47 S 69 51W
Altamira, *Colombia* **168 C2** 2 3N 75 47W
Altamira, *Mexico* **163 C5** 22 24N 97 55W
Altamira, Cuevas de, *Spain* **42 B6** 43 20N 4 5W
Altamont, *Ill., U.S.A.* **157 E8** 39 4N 88 45W
Altamont, *N.Y., U.S.A.* **151 D10** 42 43N 74 3W
Altamura, *Italy* **47 B9** 40 49N 16 33 E
Altanbulag, *Mongolia* **72 A5** 50 16N 106 30 E
Altar, *Mexico* **162 A2** 30 40N 111 50W
Altata, *Mexico* **162 C3** 24 30N 108 0W
Altavas, *Phil.* **81 F4** 11 32N 122 29 E
Altavista, *U.S.A.* **148 G6** 37 6N 79 17W
Altay, *China* **72 B3** 47 48N 88 10 E
Altdorf, *Switz.* **33 C7** 46 52N 8 36 E
Alte Mellum, *Germany* **30 B4** 53 43N 8 10 E
Altea, *Spain* **41 G4** 38 38N 0 2W
Altenberg, *Germany* **30 E9** 50 45N 13 45 E
Altenbruch, *Germany* **30 B4** 53 49N 8 46 E
Altenburg, *Germany* **30 E8** 50 59N 12 25 E
Altenkirchen, *Mecklenburg-Vorpommern, Germany* **30 A9** 54 38N 13 22 E
Altenkirchen, *Rhld-Pfz., Germany* **30 E3** 50 41N 7 39 E
Altenmarkt, *Austria* **34 D7** 47 43N 14 39 E
Alter do Chão, *Portugal* **43 F3** 39 12N 7 40W
Altha, *U.S.A.* **152 E4** 30 34N 85 8W
Altınoluk, *Turkey* **49 B8** 39 34N 26 45 E
Altınova, *Turkey* **49 B8** 39 12N 26 47 E
Altıntaş, *Turkey* **49 B12** 39 4N 30 7 E
Altınyaka, *Turkey* **49 E12** 36 33N 30 20 E
Altınyayla, *Turkey* **49 D11** 37 0N 29 33 E
Altiplano, *Bolivia* **172 D4** 17 0 S 68 0W
Altkirch, *France* **27 E14** 47 37N 7 15 E
Altmark, *Germany* **30 C7** 52 45N 11 30 E
Altmühl →, *Germany* **31 G7** 48 54N 11 52 E
Altmunster, *Austria* **34 D6** 47 54N 13 45 E
Alto Adige = Trentino-Alto Adige □, *Italy* **45 B8** 46 30N 11 20 E
Alto Araguaia, *Brazil* **173 D7** 17 15 S 53 20W
Alto Cuchumatanes = Cuchumatanes, Sierra de los, *Guatemala* **164 C1** 15 35N 91 25W
Alto Cuito, *Angola* **115 E3** 13 27 S 18 49 E
Alto del Inca, *Chile* **174 A2** 24 10 S 68 10W
Alto Garças, *Brazil* **173 D7** 16 56 S 53 32W
Alto Iriri →, *Brazil* **173 B7** 8 50 S 53 25W
Alto Ligonha, *Mozam.* **119 F4** 15 30 S 38 11 E
Alto Molocue, *Mozam.* **119 F4** 15 50 S 37 35 E
Alto Paraguai, *Brazil* **173 C6** 14 30 S 56 31W
Alto Paraguay □, *Paraguay* **174 A4** 21 0 S 58 30W
Alto Paraná □, *Paraguay* **175 B5** 25 30 S 54 50W
Alto Parnaíba, *Brazil* **170 C2** 9 6 S 45 57W
Alto Purús →, *Peru* **172 B3** 9 12 S 70 28W
Alto Río Senguerr, *Argentina* **176 C2** 45 2 S 70 50W
Alto Santo, *Brazil* **170 C4** 5 31 S 38 15W
Alto Sucuriú, *Brazil* **173 D7** 19 19 S 52 47W
Alto Turi, *Brazil* **170 B2** 2 54 S 45 38W
Alton, *Canada* **150 C4** 43 54N 80 5W
Alton, *U.K.* **21 F7** 51 9N 0 59W
Alton, *U.S.A.* **156 F6** 38 53N 90 11W
Alton Downs, *Australia* **127 D2** 26 7 S 138 57 E
Altoona, *Ala., U.S.A.* **152 A3** 34 2N 86 20W
Altoona, *Iowa, U.S.A.* **156 C3** 41 39N 93 28W
Altoona, *Pa., U.S.A.* **150 F6** 40 31N 78 24W
Altos, *Brazil* **170 C3** 5 3 S 42 28W
Altötting, *Germany* **31 G8** 48 12N 12 39 E
Altstätten, *Switz.* **33 B9** 47 22N 9 33 E
Altūn Kūprī, *Iraq* **101 E11** 35 45N 44 9 E
Altun Shan, *China* **72 C3** 38 30N 88 0 E
Alturas, *U.S.A.* **158 F3** 41 29N 120 32W
Altus, *U.S.A.* **155 H5** 34 38N 99 20W
Alubijid, *Phil.* **81 G5** 8 35N 124 29 E
Alucra, *Turkey* **101 B8** 40 22N 38 47 E
Alūksne, *Latvia* **15 H22** 57 24N 27 3 E
Alùla, *Somali Rep.* **120 B4** 11 50N 50 45 E
Alunda, *Sweden* **16 D12** 60 4N 18 5 E
Alunite, *U.S.A.* **161 K12** 35 59N 114 55W
Alupka, *Ukraine* **59 K8** 44 23N 34 2 E
Alur Gajah, *Malaysia* **84 B2** 2 23N 102 13 E
Alushta, *Ukraine* **59 K8** 44 40N 34 25 E
Alusi, *Indonesia* **83 C4** 7 35 S 131 40 E
Alustante, *Spain* **40 E3** 40 36N 1 40W
Al'Uzayr, *Iraq* **96 D5** 31 19N 47 25 E
Alva, *U.S.A.* **155 G5** 36 48N 98 40W
Alvaiázere, *Portugal* **42 F2** 39 49N 8 23W
Älvängen, *Sweden* **17 G6** 57 58N 12 8 E
Alvarado, *Mexico* **163 D5** 18 40N 95 50W
Alvarado, *U.S.A.* **155 J6** 32 24N 97 13W
Alvarães, *Brazil* **169 D5** 3 12 S 64 50W
Alvaro Obregón, Presa, *Mexico* **162 B3** 27 55N 109 52W
Alvdal, *Norway* **18 B7** 62 6N 10 37 E
Älvdalen, *Sweden* **16 C8** 61 13N 14 4 E
Alvear, *Argentina* **174 B4** 29 5 S 56 30W
Alverca, *Portugal* **43 G1** 38 56N 9 1W
Alvesta, *Sweden* **17 H8** 56 54N 14 35 E
Alvie, *Australia* **128 E5** 38 14 S 143 30 E
Ålvik, *Norway* **18 D3** 60 26N 6 26 E
Alvin, *S.C., U.S.A.* **152 B10** 33 22N 79 48W
Alvin, *Tex., U.S.A.* **155 L7** 29 26N 95 15W
Alvinston, *Canada* **150 D3** 42 49N 81 52W
Alvito, *Portugal* **43 G3** 38 15N 7 58W
Älvkarleby, *Sweden* **16 D11** 60 34N 17 26 E
Älvros, *Sweden* **16 B8** 62 3N 14 38 E
Älvsborgs län □, *Sweden* **17 F6** 58 30N 12 30 E
Älvsbyn, *Sweden* **14 D19** 65 40N 21 0 E
Ålvundeid, *Norway* **18 B5** 62 45N 8 33 E
Alwar, *India* **92 F7** 27 38N 76 34 E
Alwaye, *India* **95 J3** 10 8N 76 24 E
Alxa Zuoqi, *China* **74 E3** 38 50N 105 40 E
Alyata = Älät, *Azerbaijan* **61 L9** 39 58N 49 25 E
Alyth, *U.K.* **22 E5** 56 38N 3 13W
Alytus, *Lithuania* **15 J21** 54 24N 24 3 E
Alzada, *U.S.A.* **154 C2** 45 2N 104 25W
Alzey, *Germany* **31 F4** 49 45N 8 7 E
Alzira, *Spain* **41 F4** 39 9N 0 30W
Am Dam, *Chad* **109 F4** 12 40N 20 35 E
Am Géréda, *Chad* **109 F4** 12 53N 21 14 E
Am-Timan, *Chad* **109 F4** 11 0N 20 10 E
Amacuro □, *Venezuela* **169 B5** 8 50N 61 5W
Amadeus, L., *Australia* **125 D5** 24 54 S 131 0 E
Amadi, *Dem. Rep. of the Congo* **118 B2** 3 40N 26 40 E
Amâdi, *Sudan* **107 F3** 5 29N 30 25 E
Amadjuak L., *Canada* **139 B12** 65 0N 71 8W
Amadora, *Portugal* **43 G1** 38 45N 9 13W
Amagasaki, *Japan* **71 C7** 34 42N 135 20 E
Amager, *Denmark* **17 J6** 55 37N 12 35 E
Amagi, *Japan* **70 D2** 33 25N 130 39 E
Amahai, *Indonesia* **83 B3** 3 20 S 128 55 E
Amaimon, *Papua N. G.* **132 C3** 5 12 S 145 30 E
Amakusa-Nada, *Japan* **70 E2** 32 35N 130 5 E
Amakusa-Shotō, *Japan* **70 E2** 32 15N 130 10 E
Åmål, *Sweden* **16 E6** 59 3N 12 42 E
Amalapuram, *India* **95 F5** 16 35N 81 55 E
Amalfi, *Colombia* **168 B2** 6 55N 75 4W
Amalfi, *Italy* **47 B7** 40 38N 14 36 E
Amaliás, *Greece* **48 D3** 37 47N 21 22 E
Amalner, *India* **94 D2** 21 5N 75 5 E
Amambaí, *Brazil* **175 A4** 23 5 S 55 13W
Amambaí →, *Brazil* **175 A5** 23 22 S 53 56W
Amambay □, *Paraguay* **175 A4** 23 0 S 56 0W
Amambay, Cordillera de, *S. Amer.* **175 A4** 23 0 S 55 45W
Amami-Guntō, *Japan* **69 L4** 27 16N 129 21 E
Amami-Ō-Shima, *Japan* **69 L4** 28 0N 129 0 E
Amana →, *Venezuela* **169 B5** 9 45N 62 39W
Amaná, L., *Brazil* **169 D5** 2 35 S 64 40W
Amanab, *Papua N. G.* **132 B1** 3 40 S 141 14 E
Amanda Park, *U.S.A.* **160 C3** 47 28N 123 55W
Amangeldy, *Kazakstan* **64 D7** 50 10N 65 10 E
Amantea, *Italy* **47 C9** 39 8N 16 4 E
Amapá, *Brazil* **169 C7** 2 5N 50 50W
Amapá □, *Brazil* **169 C7** 1 40N 52 0W
Amapari, *Brazil* **169 C7** 0 37N 51 39W
Amara, *Sudan* **107 E3** 10 25N 34 10 E
Amarante, *Brazil* **170 C3** 6 14 S 42 50W
Amarante, *Portugal* **42 D2** 41 16N 8 5W
Amarante do Maranhão, *Brazil* **170 C2** 5 36 S 46 45W
Amaranth, *Canada* **143 C9** 50 36N 98 43W
Amarapura, *Burma* **90 E6** 21 54N 96 3 E
Amaravati →, *India* **95 J4** 11 0N 78 15 E
Amareleja, *Portugal* **43 G3** 38 12N 7 13W
Amargosa, *Brazil* **171 D4** 13 2 S 39 36W
Amargosa →, *U.S.A.* **161 J10** 36 14N 116 51W
Amargosa Range, *U.S.A.* **161 J10** 36 20N 116 45W
Amári, *Greece* **38 D6** 35 13N 24 40 E
Amarillo, *U.S.A.* **155 H4** 35 13N 101 50W
Amarnath, *India* **94 E1** 19 12N 73 22 E
Amaro, Mte., *Italy* **45 F11** 42 5N 14 5 E
Amaro Leite, *Brazil* **171 D2** 13 58 S 49 9W
Amarpur, *India* **93 G12** 25 5N 87 0 E
Amasra, *Turkey* **100 B5** 41 45N 32 23 E
Amassama, *Nigeria* **113 D6** 5 1N 6 2 E
Amasya, *Turkey* **100 B6** 40 40N 35 50 E
Amataurá, *Brazil* **168 D4** 3 29 S 68 6W
Amatikulu, *S. Africa* **117 D5** 29 3 S 31 33 E
Amatitlán, *Guatemala* **164 D1** 14 29N 90 38W
Amatrice, *Italy* **45 F10** 42 38N 13 17 E
Amay, *Belgium* **24 D5** 50 33N 5 19 E
Amazon = Amazonas →, *S. Amer.* **169 D8** 0 5 S 50 0W
Amazonas □, *Brazil* **173 B5** 5 0 S 65 0W
Amazonas □, *Peru* **172 B2** 5 0 S 78 0W
Amazonas □, *Venezuela* **168 C4** 3 30N 66 0W
Amazonas →, *S. Amer.* **169 D8** 0 5 S 50 0W
Ambad, *India* **94 E2** 19 38N 75 50 E
Ambahakily, *Madag.* **117 C7** 21 36 S 43 41 E
Ambala, *India* **92 D7** 30 23N 76 56 E
Ambalangoda, *Sri Lanka* **95 L5** 6 15N 80 5 E
Ambalapulai, *India* **95 K3** 9 25N 76 25 E
Ambalavao, *Madag.* **117 C8** 21 50 S 46 56 E
Ambalindum, *Australia* **126 C2** 23 23 S 135 0 E
Ambam, *Cameroon* **114 B2** 2 20N 11 15 E
Ambanja, *Madag.* **117 A8** 13 40 S 48 27 E
Ambarchik, *Russia* **65 C17** 69 40N 162 20 E
Ambarijeby, *Madag.* **117 A8** 14 56 S 47 41 E
Ambaro, Helodranon', *Madag.* **117 A8** 13 23 S 48 38 E
Ambasamudram, *India* **95 K3** 8 43N 77 25 E
Ambato, *Ecuador* **168 D2** 1 5 S 78 42W
Ambato, Sierra de, *Argentina* **174 B2** 28 25 S 66 10W
Ambato Boeny, *Madag.* **117 B8** 16 28 S 46 43 E
Ambatofinandrahana, *Madag.* **117 C8** 20 33 S 46 48 E
Ambatolampy, *Madag.* **117 B8** 19 20 S 47 35 E
Ambatondrazaka, *Madag.* **117 B8** 17 55 S 48 28 E
Ambatosoratra, *Madag.* **117 B8** 17 37 S 48 31 E
Ambelón, *Greece* **48 B4** 39 45N 22 22 E
Ambenja, *Madag.* **117 B8** 15 17 S 46 58 E
Amberg, *Germany* **31 F7** 49 26N 11 52 E
Ambergris Cay, *Belize* **163 D7** 18 0N 88 0W
Ambérieu-en-Bugey, *France* **29 C9** 45 57N 5 20 E
Amberley, *N.Z.* **131 D7** 43 9 S 172 44 E
Ambert, *France* **28 C7** 45 33N 3 44 E
Ambidédi, *Mali* **112 C2** 14 35N 11 47W
Ambikapur, *India* **93 H10** 23 15N 83 15 E
Ambikol, *Sudan* **106 C3** 21 20N 30 50 E
Ambilobé, *Madag.* **117 A8** 13 10 S 49 3 E
Ambinanindrano, *Madag.* **117 C8** 20 5 S 48 23 E
Amble, *U.K.* **20 B6** 55 20N 1 36W
Ambler, *U.S.A.* **144 C8** 67 5N 157 52W
Ambleside, *U.K.* **20 C5** 54 26N 2 58W
Ambo, *Ethiopia* **107 E4** 12 20N 37 30 E
Ambo, *Peru* **172 C2** 10 5 S 76 10W
Ambodifototra, *Madag.* **117 B8** 16 59 S 49 52 E
Ambodilazana, *Madag.* **117 B8** 18 6 S 49 10 E
Ambohimahasoa, *Madag.* **117 C8** 21 7 S 47 13 E
Ambohimanga, *Madag.* **117 C8** 20 52 S 47 36 E
Ambohitra, *Madag.* **117 A8** 12 30 S 49 10 E
Amboise, *France* **26 E8** 47 24N 1 2 E
Ambon, *Indonesia* **82 B3** 3 43 S 128 12 E
Amboseli, L., *Kenya* **118 C4** 2 40 S 37 10 E
Ambositra, *Madag.* **117 C8** 20 31 S 47 25 E
Ambovombé, *Madag.* **117 D8** 25 11 S 46 5 E
Amboy, *Calif., U.S.A.* **161 L11** 34 33N 115 45W
Amboy, *Ill., U.S.A.* **156 C7** 41 44N 89 20W
Ambridge, *U.S.A.* **150 F4** 40 36N 80 14W
Ambriz, *Angola* **115 D2** 7 48 S 13 8 E
Ambrose, *U.S.A.* **152 D6** 31 36N 83 1W
Ambrym, *Vanuatu* **133 F6** 16 15 S 168 10 E
Ambunti, *Papua N. G.* **132 C2** 4 13 S 142 52 E
Ambur, *India* **95 H4** 12 48N 78 43 E
Amby, *Australia* **127 D4** 26 30 S 148 11 E
Amchitka I., *U.S.A.* **138 C1** 51 32N 179 0 E
Amderma, *Russia* **64 C7** 69 45N 61 30 E
Ameca, *Mexico* **162 C4** 20 30N 104 0W
Ameca →, *Mexico* **162 C3** 20 40N 105 15W
Amecameca, *Mexico* **163 D5** 19 7N 98 46W
Ameland, *Neths.* **24 A5** 53 27N 5 45 E
Amélia, *Italy* **45 F9** 42 33N 12 25 E
Amelia City, *U.S.A.* **152 E8** 30 35N 81 28W
Amelia I., *U.S.A.* **152 E8** 30 40N 81 25W
Amendolara, *Italy* **47 C9** 39 57N 16 35 E
American Falls, *U.S.A.* **158 E7** 42 47N 112 51W
American Falls Reservoir, *U.S.A.* **158 E7** 42 47N 112 52W
American Highland, *Antarctica* **7 D6** 73 0 S 75 0 E
American Samoa ■, *Pac. Oc.* **133 X24** 14 20 S 170 40W
Americana, *Brazil* **175 A6** 22 45 S 47 20W
Americus, *U.S.A.* **152 C5** 32 4N 84 14W
Amersfoort, *Neths.* **24 B5** 52 9N 5 23 E
Amersfoort, *S. Africa* **117 D4** 26 59 S 29 53 E
Amery, *Australia* **125 F2** 31 9 S 117 5 E
Amery, *Canada* **143 B10** 56 34N 94 3W
Amery Ice Shelf, *Antarctica* **7 C6** 69 30 S 72 0 E
Ames, *Spain* **42 C2** 42 54N 8 38W
Ames, *U.S.A.* **156 C3** 42 2N 93 37W
Amesbury, *U.S.A.* **151 D14** 42 51N 70 56W
Amfíklia, *Greece* **48 C4** 38 38N 22 35 E
Amfilokhía, *Greece* **48 C3** 38 52N 21 9 E
Amfípolis, *Greece* **50 F7** 40 48N 23 52 E
Ámfissa, *Greece* **48 C4** 38 32N 22 22 E
Amga, *Russia* **65 C14** 60 50N 132 0 E
Amga →, *Russia* **65 C14** 62 38N 134 32 E
Amgu, *Russia* **68 B8** 45 45N 137 15 E
Amgun →, *Russia* **65 D14** 52 56N 139 38 E
Amherst, *Canada* **141 C7** 45 48N 64 8W
Amherst, *Mass., U.S.A.* **151 D12** 42 23N 72 31W
Amherst, *N.Y., U.S.A.* **150 D6** 42 59N 78 48W
Amherst, *Ohio, U.S.A.* **150 E2** 41 24N 82 14W
Amherst, *Tex., U.S.A.* **155 J3** 34 1N 102 25W
Amherst I., *Canada* **151 B8** 44 8N 76 43W
Amherstburg, *Canada* **140 D3** 42 6N 83 6W
Amiata, Mte., *Italy* **45 F8** 42 53N 11 37 E
Amiens, *France* **27 C9** 49 54N 2 16 E
Amili, *India* **90 A5** 28 25N 95 52 E
Amindaion, *Greece* **50 F5** 40 42N 21 42 E
Åminne, *Sweden* **17 G7** 57 7N 14 0 E
Amīrābād, *Iran* **96 C5** 33 20N 46 16 E
Amirante Is., *Seychelles* **121 E4** 6 0 S 53 0 E
Amisk L., *Canada* **143 C8** 54 35N 102 15W
Amistad, Presa de la, *Mexico* **162 B4** 29 24N 101 0W
Amite, *U.S.A.* **155 K9** 30 44N 90 30W
Amizmiz, *Morocco* **110 B3** 31 12N 8 15W
Åmli, *Norway* **18 F5** 58 45N 8 32 E
Amlwch, *U.K.* **20 D3** 53 24N 4 20W
Amm Adam, *Sudan* **107 D4** 16 20N 36 1 E
'Ammān, *Jordan* **103 D4** 31 57N 35 52 E
'Ammān □, *Jordan* **103 D5** 31 40N 36 30 E
Ammanford, *U.K.* **21 F4** 51 48N 3 59W
Ammassalik = Angmagssalik, *Greenland* **10 D7** 65 40N 37 20W
Ammerån →, *Sweden* **16 A10** 63 9N 16 13 E
Ammersee, *Germany* **31 G7** 48 0N 11 7 E
Amnat Charoen, *Thailand* **86 E5** 15 51N 104 38 E
Amo Jiang →, *China* **76 F3** 23 0N 101 50 E
Āmol, *Iran* **97 B7** 36 23N 52 20 E
Amoret, *U.S.A.* **156 F2** 38 15N 94 35W
Amorgós, *Greece* **49 E7** 36 50N 25 58 E
Amory, *U.S.A.* **149 J1** 33 59N 88 29W
Amos, *Canada* **140 C4** 48 35N 78 5W
Åmot, *Buskerud, Norway* **15 G13** 59 57N 9 54 E
Åmot, *Oppland, Norway* **18 D7** 61 0N 10 2 E
Åmot, *Telemark, Norway* **18 E5** 59 34N 8 0 E
Åmotfors, *Sweden* **16 E6** 59 47N 12 22 E
Åmotsdal, *Norway* **18 E5** 59 37N 8 26 E
Amour, Djebel, *Algeria* **111 B5** 33 42N 1 37 E
Amoy = Xiamen, *China* **77 E12** 24 25N 118 4 E
Ampang, *Malaysia* **87 L3** 3 8N 101 45 E
Ampanihy, *Madag.* **117 C7** 24 40 S 44 45 E
Ampasindava, Helodranon', *Madag.* **117 A8** 13 40 S 48 15 E
Ampasindava, Saikanosy, *Madag.* **117 A8** 13 42 S 47 55 E
Ampato, Nevado, *Peru* **172 D3** 15 40 S 71 56W
Ampenan, *Indonesia* **85 D5** 8 35 S 116 13 E
Amper, *Nigeria* **113 D6** 9 25N 9 40 E
Amper →, *Germany* **31 G7** 48 29N 11 55 E
Ampezzo, *Italy* **45 B9** 46 25N 12 48 E
Amposta, *Spain* **40 E5** 40 43N 0 34 E
Ampotaka, *Madag.* **117 D7** 25 3 S 44 41 E
Ampoza, *Madag.* **117 C7** 22 20 S 44 44 E
Amqui, *Canada* **141 C6** 48 28N 67 27W
'Amrān, *Yemen* **98 D3** 15 41N 43 55 E
Amravati, *India* **94 D3** 20 55N 77 45 E
Amreli, *India* **92 J4** 21 35N 71 17 E
Amrenene el Kasba, *Algeria* **111 D5** 22 10N 0 30 E
Amriswil, *Switz.* **33 A8** 47 33N 9 18 E
Amritsar, *India* **92 D6** 31 35N 74 57 E
Amroha, *India* **93 E8** 28 53N 78 30 E
Amrum, *Germany* **30 A4** 54 38N 8 22 E
Amsel, *Algeria* **111 D6** 22 47N 5 29 E
Amsterdam, *Neths.* **24 B4** 52 23N 4 54 E
Amsterdam, *U.S.A.* **151 D10** 42 56N 74 11W
Amsterdam, I., *Ind. Oc.* **121 H6** 38 30 S 77 30 E
Amstetten, *Austria* **34 C7** 48 7N 14 51 E
Amudarya →, *Uzbekistan* **64 E6** 43 58N 59 34 E
Amukta Pass, *U.S.A.* **144 L5** 52 0N 171 0W
Amulung, *Phil.* **80 C3** 17 50N 121 43 E
Amundsen Gulf, *Canada* **138 A7** 71 0N 124 0W
Amundsen Sea, *Antarctica* **7 D15** 72 0 S 115 0W
Amungen, *Sweden* **16 C9** 61 10N 15 40 E
Amuntai, *Indonesia* **85 C5** 2 28 S 115 25 E
Amur, *Somali Rep.* **120 C3** 5 16N 46 30 E

Amur →, *Russia* **65 D15** 52 56N 141 10 E
Amurang, *Indonesia* **82 A2** 1 5N 124 40 E
Amuri Pass, *N.Z.* **131 C7** 42 31 S 172 11 E
Amurrio, *Spain* **40 B1** 43 3N 3 0W
Amursk, *Russia* **65 D14** 50 14N 136 54 E
Amusco, *Spain* **42 C6** 42 10N 4 28W
Amutag, *Phil.* **80 E4** 12 23N 123 16 E
Amvrakikós Kólpos, *Greece* **48 C2** 39 0N 20 55 E
Amvrosiyivka, *Ukraine* **59 J10** 47 43N 38 30 E
Amyderya = Amudarya →, *Uzbekistan* **64 E6** 43 58N 59 34 E
Amzeglouf, *Algeria* **111 C5** 26 50N 0 1 E
An, *Burma* **90 F5** 19 48N 94 0 E
An Bien, *Vietnam* **87 H5** 9 45N 105 0 E
An Hoa, *Vietnam* **86 E7** 15 40N 108 5 E
An Nabatīyah at Tahta, *Lebanon* **103 B4** 33 23N 35 27 E
An Nabk, *Si. Arabia* **96 D3** 31 20N 37 20 E
An Nabk, *Syria* **103 A5** 34 2N 36 44 E
An Nabk Abū Qaşr, *Si. Arabia* **96 D3** 30 21N 38 34 E
An Nafūd, *Si. Arabia* **96 D4** 28 15N 41 0 E
An Najaf, *Iraq* **101 G11** 32 3N 44 15 E
An Nāşirīyah, *Iraq* **96 D5** 31 0N 46 15 E
An Nawfalīyah, *Libya* **108 B3** 30 54N 17 58 E
An Nhon, *Vietnam* **86 F7** 13 55N 109 7 E
An Nîl □, *Sudan* **106 D3** 19 30N 33 0 E
An Nîl el Abyad □, *Sudan* **107 E3** 14 0N 32 15 E
An Nîl el Azraq □, *Sudan* **107 E3** 11 30N 34 30 E
An Nimāş, *Si. Arabia* **98 C3** 19 7N 42 8 E
An Nu'ayrīyah, *Si. Arabia* **97 E6** 27 30N 48 30 E
An Nu'mānīyah, *Iraq* **101 F11** 32 32N 45 25 E
An Nuwayb'ī, W. →, *Si. Arabia* **103 F3** 29 18N 34 57 E
An Thoi, Dao, *Vietnam* **87 H5** 9 58N 104 0 E
An Uaimh, *Ireland* **23 C5** 53 39N 6 41W
Åna-Sira, *Norway* **18 F3** 58 17N 6 25 E
Anabar →, *Russia* **65 B12** 73 8N 113 36 E
'Anabtā, *West Bank* **103 C4** 32 19N 35 7 E
Anabuki, *Japan* **70 C6** 34 2N 134 11 E
Anaco, *Venezuela* **169 B5** 9 27N 64 28W
Anaconda, *U.S.A.* **158 C7** 46 8N 112 57W
Anacortes, *U.S.A.* **160 B4** 48 30N 122 37W
Anacuao, Mt., *Phil.* **80 C3** 16 16N 121 53 E
Anadarko, *U.S.A.* **155 H5** 35 4N 98 15W
Anadia, *Brazil* **170 C4** 9 42 S 36 18W
Anadia, *Portugal* **42 E2** 40 26N 8 27W
Anadolu, *Turkey* **100 C5** 39 0N 30 0 E
Anadyr, *Russia* **65 C18** 64 35N 177 20 E
Anadyr →, *Russia* **65 C18** 64 55N 176 5 E
Anadyrskiy Zaliv, *Russia* **65 C19** 64 0N 180 0 E
Anáfi, *Greece* **49 E7** 36 22N 25 48 E
Anafópoulo, *Greece* **49 E7** 36 17N 25 50 E
Anaga, Pta. de, *Canary Is.* **39 F3** 28 34N 16 9W
Anagni, *Italy* **45 G10** 41 44N 13 9 E
'Ānah, *Iraq* **101 E10** 34 25N 42 0 E
Anahalu →, *U.S.A.* **145 J13** 21 37N 158 6W
Anaheim, *U.S.A.* **161 M9** 33 50N 117 55W
Anahim Lake, *Canada* **142 C3** 52 28N 125 18W
Anahola, *U.S.A.* **145 A2** 22 9N 159 19W
Anáhuac, *Mexico* **162 B4** 27 14N 100 9W
Anai Mudi, *India* **95 J3** 10 12N 77 4 E
Anaimalai Hills, *India* **95 J3** 10 20N 76 40 E
Anajás, *Brazil* **170 B2** 0 59 S 49 57W
Anajatuba, *Brazil* **170 B3** 3 16 S 44 37W
Anakapalle, *India* **94 F6** 17 42N 83 6 E
Anakie, *Australia* **126 C4** 23 32 S 147 45 E
Anaklia, *Georgia* **61 J5** 42 22N 41 35 E
Anaktuvuk Pass, *U.S.A.* **144 B10** 68 8N 151 45W
Analalava, *Madag.* **117 A8** 14 35 S 48 0 E
Análipsis, *Greece* **38 A3** 39 36N 19 55 E
Anamã, *Brazil* **169 D5** 3 35 S 61 22W
Anambar →, *Pakistan* **92 D3** 30 15N 68 50 E
Anambas, Kepulauan, *Indonesia* **87 L6** 3 20N 106 30 E
Anambas Is. = Anambas, Kepulauan, *Indonesia* **87 L6** 3 20N 106 30 E
Anambra □, *Nigeria* **113 D6** 6 20N 7 0 E
Aname, *Vanuatu* **133 K7** 20 8 S 169 47 E
Anamoose, *U.S.A.* **154 B4** 47 53N 100 15W
Anamosa, *U.S.A.* **156 B5** 42 7N 91 17W
Anamur, *Turkey* **100 D5** 36 8N 32 58 E
Anamur Burnu, *Turkey* **100 D5** 36 2N 32 47 E
Anan, *Japan* **70 D6** 33 54N 134 40 E
Anand, *India* **92 H5** 22 32N 72 59 E
Anandpur, *India* **94 D8** 21 16N 86 13 E
Anánes, *Greece* **48 E6** 36 33N 24 9 E
Anantapur, *India* **95 G3** 14 39N 77 42 E
Anantnag, *India* **93 C6** 33 45N 75 10 E
Ananyiv, *Ukraine* **59 J5** 47 44N 29 58 E
Anao-aon, *Phil.* **81 G5** 9 47N 125 25 E
Anapa, *Russia* **59 K9** 44 55N 37 25 E
Anapodháris →, *Greece* **38 E7** 34 59N 25 20 E
Anápolis, *Brazil* **171 E2** 16 15 S 48 50W
Anapu →, *Brazil* **169 D7** 1 53 S 50 53W
Anār, *Iran* **97 D7** 30 55N 55 13 E
Anār Darreh, *Afghan.* **91 B1** 32 46N 61 39 E
Anārak, *Iran* **97 C7** 33 25N 53 40 E
Anarisfjällen, *Sweden* **16 A7** 63 6N 13 10 E
Anatolia = Anadolu, *Turkey* **100 C5** 39 0N 30 0 E
Anatone, *U.S.A.* **158 C5** 46 8N 117 8W
Anatsogno, *Madag.* **117 C7** 23 33 S 43 46 E
Añatuya, *Argentina* **174 B3** 28 20 S 62 50W
Anauá →, *Brazil* **169 C5** 0 58N 61 21W
Anaunethad L., *Canada* **143 A8** 60 55N 104 25W
Anavilhanas, Arquipélago das, *Brazil* **169 D5** 2 42 S 60 45W
Anaye, *Niger* **109 E2** 19 15N 12 50 E
Anbyŏn, *N. Korea* **75 E14** 39 1N 127 35 E
Ancares, Sierra de, *Spain* **42 C4** 42 51N 6 52W
Ancash □, *Peru* **172 B2** 9 30 S 77 45W
Ancenis, *France* **26 E5** 47 21N 1 10W
Ancho, Canal, *Chile* **176 D2** 50 0 S 74 20W
Anchor Bay, *U.S.A.* **160 G3** 38 48N 123 34W
Anchorage, *U.S.A.* **138 B5** 61 13N 149 54W
Anci, *China* **74 E9** 39 20N 116 40 E
Ancohuma, Nevada, *Bolivia* **172 D4** 16 0 S 68 50W
Ancón, *Peru* **172 C2** 11 50 S 77 10W
Ancona, *Italy* **45 E10** 43 38N 13 30 E
Ancud, *Chile* **176 B2** 42 0 S 73 50W
Ancud, G. de, *Chile* **176 B2** 42 0 S 73 0W
Ancy-le-Franc, *France* **27 E11** 47 46N 4 10 E
Anda, *China* **73 B7** 46 24N 125 19 E
Anda, *Phil.* **80 C2** 16 17N 119 57 E
Andacollo, *Argentina* **174 D1** 37 10 S 70 42W
Andacollo, *Chile* **174 C1** 30 5 S 71 10W
Andado, *Australia* **126 D2** 25 25 S 135 15 E
Andahuaylas, *Peru* **172 C3** 13 40 S 73 25W
Andalgalá, *Argentina* **174 B2** 27 40 S 66 30W
Åndalsnes, *Norway* **15 E12** 62 35N 7 43 E
Andalucía □, *Spain* **43 H6** 37 35N 5 0W
Andalusia, *U.S.A.* **149 K2** 31 18N 86 29W
Andalusia □ = Andalucía □, *Spain* **43 H6** 37 35N 5 0W
Andaman Is., *Ind. Oc.* **121 C8** 12 30N 92 30 E
Andara, *Namibia* **116 B3** 18 2 S 21 9 E
Andaraí, *Brazil* **171 D3** 12 48 S 41 20W
Andeer, *Switz.* **33 C8** 46 36N 9 26 E
Andelfingen, *Switz.* **33 A7** 47 36N 8 41 E
Andelot-Blancheville, *France* **27 D12** 48 15N 5 18 E
Andenes, *Norway* **14 B17** 69 19N 16 18 E
Andenne, *Belgium* **24 D5** 50 28N 5 5 E
Andéranboukane, *Mali* **113 B5** 15 26N 3 2 E
Andermatt, *Switz.* **33 C7** 46 38N 8 35 E
Andernach, *Germany* **30 E3** 50 26N 7 24 E
Andernos-les-Bains, *France* **28 D2** 44 44N 1 6W
Anderslöv, *Sweden* **17 J7** 55 26N 13 19 E
Anderson, *Alaska, U.S.A.* **144 D10** 64 25N 149 15W
Anderson, *Calif., U.S.A.* **158 F2** 40 27N 122 18W
Anderson, *Ind., U.S.A.* **157 D11** 40 10N 85 41W
Anderson, *Mo., U.S.A.* **155 G7** 36 39N 94 27W
Anderson, *S.C., U.S.A.* **149 H4** 34 31N 82 39W
Anderson →, *Canada* **138 B7** 69 42N 129 0W
Andersonville, *U.S.A.* **152 C5** 32 12N 84 9W
Anderstorp, *Sweden* **17 G7** 57 19N 13 39 E
Andes, Cord. de los, *S. Amer.* **172 E4** 20 0 S 68 0W
Andfjorden, *Norway* **14 B17** 69 10N 16 20 E
Andhra, L., *India* **94 E1** 18 54N 73 32 E
Andhra Pradesh □, *India* **95 F4** 18 0N 79 0 E
Andijon, *Uzbekistan* **63 C6** 41 10N 72 15 E
Andikíthira, *Greece* **48 F5** 35 52N 23 15 E
Andīmeshk, *Iran* **97 C6** 32 27N 48 21 E
Andímilos, *Greece* **48 E6** 36 47N 24 12 E
Andíparos, *Greece* **49 D7** 37 0N 25 3 E
Andípaxoi, *Greece* **48 B2** 39 9N 20 13 E
Andípsara, *Greece* **49 C7** 38 30N 25 29 E
Andírrion, *Greece* **48 C3** 38 20N 21 46 E
Andizhan = Andijon, *Uzbekistan* **63 C6** 41 10N 72 15 E
Andkhvoy, *Afghan.* **91 A2** 36 52N 65 8 E
Andoain, *Spain* **40 B2** 43 13N 2 1W
Andoany, *Madag.* **117 A8** 13 25 S 48 16 E
Andoas, *Peru* **168 D2** 2 55 S 76 25W
Andol, *India* **94 F4** 17 51N 78 4 E
Andong, *S. Korea* **75 F15** 36 40N 128 43 E
Andongwei, *China* **75 G10** 35 6N 119 20 E
Andorra, *Spain* **40 E4** 40 59N 0 28W
Andorra ■, *Europe* **28 F5** 42 30N 1 30 E
Andorra La Vella, *Andorra* **28 F5** 42 31N 1 32 E
Andover, *U.K.* **21 F6** 51 12N 1 29W
Andover, *Mass., U.S.A.* **151 D13** 42 40N 71 8W
Andover, *N.Y., U.S.A.* **150 D7** 42 10N 77 48W
Andover, *Ohio, U.S.A.* **150 E4** 41 36N 80 34W
Andøya, *Norway* **14 B16** 69 10N 15 50 E
Andradina, *Brazil* **171 F1** 20 54 S 51 23W
Andrahary, Mt., *Madag.* **117 A8** 13 37 S 49 17 E
Andramasina, *Madag.* **117 B8** 19 11 S 47 35 E
Andranopasy, *Madag.* **117 C7** 21 17 S 43 44 E
Andratx, *Spain* **39 B9** 39 39N 2 25 E
Andreanof Is., *U.S.A.* **144 L4** 51 30N 176 0W
Andreapol, *Russia* **56 D7** 56 40N 32 17 E
Andrée Land, *Greenland* **10 C8** 73 40N 26 0W
Andrewilla, *Australia* **127 D2** 26 31 S 139 17 E
Andrews, *S.C., U.S.A.* **149 J6** 33 27N 79 34W
Andrews, *Tex., U.S.A.* **155 J3** 32 19N 102 33W
Andreyevka, *Russia* **60 D10** 52 19N 51 55 E
Ándria, *Italy* **47 A9** 41 13N 16 17 E
Andriba, *Madag.* **117 B8** 17 30 S 46 58 E
Andrijevica, *Montenegro, Yug.* **50 D3** 42 45N 19 48 E
Andrítsaina, *Greece* **48 D3** 37 29N 21 52 E
Androka, *Madag.* **117 C7** 24 58 S 44 2 E
Andropov = Rybinsk, *Russia* **58 C10** 58 5N 38 50 E
Ándros, *Greece* **48 D6** 37 50N 24 57 E
Andros I., *Bahamas* **164 B4** 24 30N 78 0W
Andros Town, *Bahamas* **164 B4** 24 43N 77 47W
Andrychów, *Poland* **55 J6** 49 51N 19 18 E
Andselv, *Norway* **14 B18** 69 4N 18 34 E
Andújar, *Spain* **43 G6** 38 3N 4 5W
Andulo, *Angola* **115 E3** 11 25 S 16 45 E
Aneby, *Norway* **16 D4** 60 5N 10 51 E
Aneby, *Sweden* **17 G8** 57 48N 14 49 E
Anegada, B., *Argentina* **176 B4** 40 20 S 62 20W
Anegada I., *Virgin Is.* **165 C7** 18 45N 64 20W
Anegada Passage, *W. Indies* **165 C7** 18 15N 63 45W
Aného, *Togo* **113 D5** 6 12N 1 34 E
Aneityum, *Vanuatu* **133 K7** 20 12 S 169 45 E
Añelo, *Argentina* **176 A3** 38 20 S 68 45W
Anenni-Noi, *Moldova* **53 D14** 46 53N 29 15 E
Anergane, *Morocco* **110 B3** 31 4N 7 14W
Aneto, Pico de, *Spain* **40 C5** 42 37N 0 40 E
Añez, *Bolivia* **173 D5** 15 40 S 63 10W
Anfu, *China* **77 D10** 27 21N 114 40 E
Ang Thong, *Thailand* **86 E3** 14 35N 100 31 E
Angadanan, *Phil.* **80 C3** 16 45N 121 45 E
Angamos, Punta, *Chile* **174 A1** 23 1 S 70 32W
Angara →, *Russia* **65 D10** 58 5N 94 20 E
Angarab, *Ethiopia* **107 E4** 13 11N 37 7 E
Angarsk, *Russia* **65 D11** 52 30N 104 0 E
Angas Downs, *Australia* **125 E5** 25 2 S 132 14 E
Angas Hills, *Australia* **124 D4** 23 0 S 127 50 E
Angaston, *Australia* **128 C3** 34 30 S 139 8 E
Angat, *Phil.* **80 D3** 14 56N 121 2 E
Ånge, *Sweden* **16 B9** 62 31N 15 35 E
Ángel, Salto = Angel Falls, *Venezuela* **169 B5** 5 57N 62 30W
Ángel de la Guarda, I., *Mexico* **162 B2** 29 30N 113 30W
Angel Falls, *Venezuela* **169 B5** 5 57N 62 30W
Angeles, *Phil.* **80 D3** 15 9N 120 33 E
Ängelholm, *Sweden* **17 H6** 56 15N 12 58 E
Angellala, *Australia* **127 D4** 26 24 S 146 54 E
Angels Camp, *U.S.A.* **160 G6** 38 4N 120 32W
Ängelsberg, *Sweden* **16 E10** 59 58N 16 0 E
Anger →, *Ethiopia* **107 F4** 9 37N 36 6 E
Angereb →, *Ethiopia* **107 E4** 13 45N 36 40 E
Ångermanälven →, *Sweden* **16 B11** 62 40N 18 0 E
Ångermanland, *Sweden* **14 E18** 63 36N 17 45 E
Angermünde, *Germany* **30 B9** 53 0N 14 0 E
Angers, *Canada* **151 A9** 45 31N 75 29W
Angers, *France* **26 E6** 47 30N 0 35W
Angerville, *France* **27 D9** 48 19N 2 0 E
Ängesån →, *Sweden* **14 C20** 66 16N 22 47 E
Angical, *Brazil* **171 D3** 12 0 S 44 42W
Angikuni L., *Canada* **143 A9** 62 0N 100 0W
Angkor, *Cambodia* **86 F4** 13 22N 103 50 E
Anglem Mt., *N.Z.* **131 G2** 46 45 S 167 53 E
Anglès, *Spain* **40 D7** 41 57N 2 38 E
Anglesey, *U.K.* **20 D3** 53 17N 4 20W
Anglesey, Isle of □, *U.K.* **20 D3** 53 16N 4 18W
Anglet, *France* **28 E2** 43 29N 1 31W
Angleton, *U.S.A.* **155 L7** 29 10N 95 26W
Anglin →, *France* **28 B4** 46 42N 0 52 E
Anglisidhes, *Cyprus* **38 E12** 34 51N 33 27 E
Anglure, *France* **27 D10** 48 35N 3 50 E
Angmagssalik, *Greenland* **10 D7** 65 40N 37 20W
Ango, *Dem. Rep. of the Congo* **118 B2** 4 10N 26 5 E
Angoche, *Mozam.* **119 F4** 16 8 S 39 55 E
Angoche, I., *Mozam.* **119 F4** 16 20 S 39 50 E
Angol, *Chile* **174 D1** 37 56 S 72 45W
Angola, *Ind., U.S.A.* **157 C12** 41 38N 85 0W
Angola, *N.Y., U.S.A.* **150 D5** 42 38N 79 2W
Angola ■, *Africa* **115 E3** 12 0 S 18 0 E
Angoon, *U.S.A.* **142 B2** 57 30N 134 35W
Angoram, *Papua N. G.* **132 C3** 4 4 S 144 4 E
Angoulême, *France* **28 C4** 45 39N 0 10 E
Angoumois, *France* **28 C4** 45 50N 0 25 E
Angra dos Reis, *Brazil* **175 A7** 23 0 S 44 10W
Angren, *Uzbekistan* **63 C5** 41 1N 70 12 E
Angtassom, *Cambodia* **87 G5** 11 1N 104 41 E
Angu, *Dem. Rep. of the Congo* **118 B1** 3 25N 24 28 E
Anguang, *China* **75 B12** 45 15N 123 45 E
Anguilla ■, *W. Indies* **165 C7** 18 14N 63 5W
Anguo, *China* **74 E8** 38 28N 115 15 E
Angurugu, *Australia* **126 A2** 14 0 S 136 25 E
Angus □, *U.K.* **22 E6** 56 46N 2 56W
Anhanduí →, *Brazil* **175 A5** 21 46 S 52 9W
Anholt, *Denmark* **17 H5** 56 42N 11 33 E
Anhua, *China* **77 C8** 28 23N 111 12 E
Anhui □, *China* **77 B11** 32 0N 117 0 E
Anhwei □ = Anhui □, *China* **77 B11** 32 0N 117 0 E
Anichab, *Namibia* **116 C1** 21 0 S 14 46 E
Anicuns, *Brazil* **171 E2** 16 28 S 49 58W
Ánidhros, *Greece* **49 E7** 36 38N 25 43 E
Anié, *Togo* **113 D5** 7 42N 1 8 E
Animas, *U.S.A.* **159 L9** 31 57N 108 48W
Anina, *Romania* **52 E6** 45 6N 21 51 E
Anini-y, *Phil.* **81 F3** 10 25N 121 55 E
Aninoasa, *Romania* **53 F9** 44 47N 24 10 E
Anita, *U.S.A.* **156 C2** 41 27N 94 46W
Anivorano, *Madag.* **117 B8** 18 44 S 48 58 E
Aniwa, *Vanuatu* **133 J7** 19 17 S 169 35 E
Anjalankoski, *Finland* **15 F22** 60 45N 26 51 E
Anjangaon, *India* **94 D3** 21 10N 77 20 E
Anjar, *India* **92 H4** 23 6N 70 10 E
Anjidiv I., *India* **95 G2** 14 40N 74 10 E
Anjō, *Japan* **71 C9** 34 57N 137 5 E
Anjou, *France* **26 E6** 47 20N 0 15W
Anjozorobe, *Madag.* **117 B8** 18 22 S 47 52 E
Anju, *N. Korea* **75 E13** 39 36N 125 40 E
Anka, *Nigeria* **113 C6** 12 13N 5 58 E
Ankaboa, Tanjona, *Madag.* **117 C7** 21 58 S 43 20 E
Ankang, *China* **74 H5** 32 40N 109 1 E
Ankara, *Turkey* **100 C5** 39 57N 32 54 E
Ankaramena, *Madag.* **117 C8** 21 57 S 46 39 E
Ankarsrum, *Sweden* **17 G10** 57 41N 16 20 E
Ankazoabo, *Madag.* **117 C7** 22 18 S 44 31 E
Ankazobe, *Madag.* **117 B8** 18 20 S 47 10 E
Ankeny, *U.S.A.* **156 C3** 41 44N 93 36W
Ankisabe, *Madag.* **117 B8** 19 17 S 46 29 E
Anklam, *Germany* **30 B9** 53 51N 13 41 E
Ankleshwar, *India* **94 D1** 21 38N 73 3 E
Ankober, *Ethiopia* **107 F4** 9 35N 39 40 E
Ankona, *U.S.A.* **153 H9** 27 21N 80 17W
Ankoro, *Dem. Rep. of the Congo* **118 D2** 6 45 S 26 55 E
Anlong, *China* **76 E5** 25 2N 105 27 E
Anlu, *China* **77 B9** 31 15N 113 45 E
Anmyŏn-do, *S. Korea* **75 F14** 36 25N 126 25 E
Ånn, *Sweden* **16 A6** 63 16N 12 34 E
Ann, C., *U.S.A.* **151 D14** 42 38N 70 35W
Ann Arbor, *U.S.A.* **157 B13** 42 17N 83 45W
Anna, *Russia* **60 E5** 51 28N 40 23 E
Anna, *Ill., U.S.A.* **155 G10** 37 28N 89 15W
Anna, *Ohio, U.S.A.* **157 D12** 40 24N 84 11W
Anna Plains, *Australia* **124 C3** 19 17 S 121 37 E
Anna Regina, *Guyana* **169 B6** 7 10N 58 30W
Annaba, *Algeria* **111 A6** 36 50N 7 46 E
Annaberg-Buchholz, *Germany* **30 E9** 50 34N 13 0 E
Annaka, *Japan* **71 A10** 36 19N 138 54 E
Annalee →, *Ireland* **23 B4** 54 2N 7 24W
Annam, *Vietnam* **86 E7** 16 0N 108 0 E
Annamitique, Chaîne, *Asia* **86 D6** 17 0N 106 0 E
Annan, *U.K.* **22 G5** 54 59N 3 16W
Annan →, *U.K.* **22 G5** 54 58N 3 16W
Annanberg, *Papua N. G.* **132 C3** 4 52 S 144 42 E
Annapolis, *U.S.A.* **148 F7** 38 59N 76 30W
Annapolis Royal, *Canada* **141 D6** 44 44N 65 32W
Annapurna, *Nepal* **93 E10** 28 34N 83 50 E
Annean, L., *Australia* **125 E2** 26 54 S 118 14 E
Anneberg, *Sweden* **17 G8** 57 44N 14 49 E
Annecy, *France* **29 C10** 45 55N 6 8 E
Annecy, L. d', *France* **29 C10** 45 52N 6 10 E
Annemasse, *France* **27 F13** 46 12N 6 16 E
Annenskiy Most, *Russia* **58 B9** 60 45N 37 10 E
Annette I., *U.S.A.* **144 J15** 55 9N 131 28W
Annette Island Indian Reservation, *U.S.A.* **144 J15** 55 5N 131 30W
Anning, *China* **76 E4** 24 55N 102 26 E
Anningie, *Australia* **124 D5** 21 50 S 133 7 E
Anniston, *U.S.A.* **152 B4** 33 39N 85 50W
Annobón, *Atl. Oc.* **105 G4** 1 25 S 5 36 E
Annonay, *France* **29 C8** 45 15N 4 40 E
Annot, *France* **29 E10** 43 58N 6 38 E
Annotto Bay, *Jamaica* **164 C4** 18 17N 76 45W
Annsjön, *Sweden* **16 A6** 63 19N 12 34 E
Annuello, *Australia* **128 C5** 34 53 S 142 55 E
Annville, *U.S.A.* **151 F8** 40 20N 76 31W
Annweiler, *Germany* **31 F3** 49 12N 7 57 E
Áno Arkhánai, *Greece* **49 F7** 35 16N 25 11 E
Áno Porróia, *Greece* **50 E7** 41 17N 23 2 E
Áno Síros, *Greece* **48 D6** 37 29N 24 56 E
Áno Viánnos, *Greece* **38 D7** 35 2N 25 21 E
Anoano, *Solomon Is.* **133 M11** 8 59 S 160 46 E
Anoka, *U.S.A.* **147 A8** 45 12N 93 23W
Anorotsangana, *Madag.* **117 A8** 13 56 S 47 55 E
Anóyia, *Greece* **38 D6** 35 16N 24 52 E
Anping, *Hebei, China* **74 E8** 38 15N 115 30 E
Anping, *Liaoning, China* **75 D12** 41 5N 123 30 E
Anpu Gang, *China* **76 G7** 21 25N 109 50 E
Anqing, *China* **77 B11** 30 30N 117 3 E
Anqiu, *China* **75 F10** 36 25N 119 10 E
Anren, *China* **77 D9** 26 43N 113 18 E
Ansager, *Denmark* **17 J2** 55 42N 8 45 E
Ansai, *China* **74 F5** 36 50N 109 20 E
Ansbach, *Germany* **31 F6** 49 28N 10 34 E
Anseba →, *Eritrea* **107 D4** 16 0N 38 30 E
Anserma, *Colombia* **168 B2** 5 13N 75 48W
Ansfelden, *Austria* **34 C7** 48 12N 14 17 E
Anshan, *China* **75 D12** 41 5N 122 58 E
Anshun, *China* **76 D5** 26 18N 105 57 E
Ansião, *Portugal* **42 F2** 39 56N 8 27W
Ansley, *U.S.A.* **154 E5** 41 18N 99 23W
Ansó, *Spain* **40 C4** 42 51N 0 48W
Ansoain, *Spain* **40 C3** 42 50N 1 38W
Anson, *U.S.A.* **155 J5** 32 45N 99 54W
Anson B., *Australia* **124 B5** 13 20 S 130 6 E
Ansongo, *Mali* **113 B5** 15 25N 0 35 E
Ansonia, *Conn., U.S.A.* **151 E11** 41 21N 73 5W
Ansonia, *Ohio, U.S.A.* **157 D12** 40 13N 84 38W
Anstruther, *U.K.* **22 E6** 56 14N 2 41W
Ansudu, *Indonesia* **83 B5** 2 11 S 139 22 E
Antabamba, *Peru* **172 C3** 14 40 S 73 0W
Antakya, *Turkey* **100 D7** 36 14N 36 10 E
Antalaha, *Madag.* **117 A9** 14 57 S 50 20 E
Antalya, *Turkey* **100 D4** 36 52N 30 45 E
Antalya □, *Turkey* **49 E12** 36 30N 30 0 E
Antalya Körfezi, *Turkey* **100 D4** 36 15N 31 30 E
Antananarivo, *Madag.* **117 B8** 18 55 S 47 31 E
Antananarivo □, *Madag.* **117 B8** 19 0 S 47 0 E
Antanimbaribe, *Madag.* **117 C7** 21 30 S 44 48 E
Antarctic Pen., *Antarctica* **7 C18** 67 0 S 60 0W
Antarctica **7 E3** 90 0 S 0 0 E
Antelope, *Zimbabwe* **119 G2** 21 2 S 28 31 E
Antenor Navarro, *Brazil* **170 C4** 6 44 S 38 27W
Antequera, *Paraguay* **174 A4** 24 8 S 57 7W
Antequera, *Spain* **43 H6** 37 5N 4 33W
Antero, Mt., *U.S.A.* **159 G10** 38 41N 106 15W
Anthemoús, *Greece* **50 F7** 40 31N 23 15 E
Anthony, *Fla., U.S.A.* **153 F7** 29 18N 82 7W
Anthony, *Kans., U.S.A.* **155 G5** 37 9N 98 2W
Anthony, *N. Mex., U.S.A.* **159 K10** 32 0N 106 36W
Anthony Lagoon, *Australia* **126 B2** 18 0 S 135 30 E
Anti Atlas, *Morocco* **110 C3** 30 0N 8 30W
Anti-Lebanon = Ash Sharqi, Al Jabal, *Lebanon* **103 B5** 33 40N 36 10 E
Antibes, *France* **29 E11** 43 34N 7 6 E
Antibes, C. d', *France* **29 E11** 43 31N 7 7 E
Anticosti, Î. d', *Canada* **141 C7** 49 30N 63 0W
Antifer, C. d', *France* **26 C7** 49 41N 0 10 E
Antigo, *U.S.A.* **154 C10** 45 9N 89 9W
Antigonish, *Canada* **141 C7** 45 38N 61 58W
Antigua, *Canary Is.* **39 F5** 28 24N 14 1W
Antigua, *W. Indies* **165 C7** 17 0N 61 50W
Antigua & Barbuda ■, *W. Indies* **165 C7** 17 20N 61 48W
Antigua Guatemala, *Guatemala* **164 D1** 14 34N 90 41W
Antilla, *Cuba* **164 B4** 20 40N 75 50W
Antimony, *U.S.A.* **159 G8** 38 7N 112 0W
Antioch, *U.S.A.* **160 G5** 38 1N 121 48W
Antioche, Pertuis d', *France* **28 B2** 46 6N 1 20W
Antioquia, *Colombia* **168 B2** 6 40N 75 55W
Antioquia □, *Colombia* **168 B2** 7 0N 75 30W
Antipodes Is., *Pac. Oc.* **134 M9** 49 45 S 178 40 E
Antique □, *Phil.* **81 F4** 11 10N 122 5 E
Antler, *U.S.A.* **154 A4** 48 59N 101 17W
Antler →, *Canada* **143 D8** 49 8N 101 0W
Antlers, *U.S.A.* **155 H7** 34 14N 95 37W
Antofagasta, *Chile* **174 A1** 23 50 S 70 30W
Antofagasta □, *Chile* **174 A2** 24 0 S 69 0W
Antofagasta de la Sierra, *Argentina* **174 B2** 26 5 S 67 20W
Antofalla, *Argentina* **174 B2** 25 30 S 68 5W
Antofalla, Salar de, *Argentina* **174 B2** 25 40 S 67 45W
Anton, *U.S.A.* **155 J3** 33 49N 102 10W
Anton Chico, *U.S.A.* **159 J11** 35 12N 105 9W
Antongila, Helodrano, *Madag.* **117 B8** 15 30 S 49 50 E
Antonibé, *Madag.* **117 B8** 15 7 S 47 24 E
Antonibé, Presqu'île d', *Madag.* **117 A8** 14 55 S 47 20 E
Antonina, *Brazil* **175 B6** 25 26 S 48 42W
Antonito, *U.S.A.* **159 H10** 37 5N 106 0W
Antrain, *France* **26 D5** 48 28N 1 30W
Antrim, *U.K.* **23 B5** 54 43N 6 14W
Antrim □, *U.K.* **23 B5** 54 56N 6 25W
Antrim, Mts. of, *U.K.* **23 A5** 55 3N 6 14W
Antrim Plateau, *Australia* **124 C4** 18 8 S 128 20 E
Antrodoco, *Italy* **45 F10** 42 25N 13 5 E
Antropovo, *Russia* **60 A6** 58 24N 43 6 E
Antsalova, *Madag.* **117 B7** 18 40 S 44 37 E
Antsirabe, *Madag.* **117 B8** 19 55 S 47 2 E
Antsiranana, *Madag.* **117 A8** 12 25 S 49 20 E
Antsohihy, *Madag.* **117 A8** 14 50 S 47 59 E
Antsohimbondrona Seranana, *Madag.* **117 A8** 13 7 S 48 48 E
Antu, *China* **75 C15** 42 30N 128 20 E
Antufash, *Yemen* **98 D3** 15 42N 42 25 E
Antwerp = Antwerpen, *Belgium* **24 C4** 51 13N 4 25 E
Antwerp, *Australia* **128 D5** 36 17 S 142 4 E
Antwerp, *N.Y., U.S.A.* **151 B9** 44 12N 75 37W
Antwerp, *Ohio, U.S.A.* **157 C12** 41 11N 84 45W
Antwerpen, *Belgium* **24 C4** 51 13N 4 25 E
Antwerpen □, *Belgium* **24 C4** 51 15N 4 40 E
Anupgarh, *India* **92 E5** 29 10N 73 10 E
Anuradhapura, *Sri Lanka* **95 K5** 8 22N 80 28 E
Anveh, *Iran* **97 E7** 27 23N 54 11 E
Anvers = Antwerpen, *Belgium* **24 C4** 51 13N 4 25 E
Anvers I., *Antarctica* **7 C17** 64 30 S 63 40W
Anxi, *Fujian, China* **77 E12** 25 2N 118 12 E
Anxi, *Gansu, China* **72 B4** 40 30N 95 43 E
Anxiang, *China* **77 C9** 29 27N 112 11 E
Anxious B., *Australia* **127 E1** 33 24 S 134 45 E
Anyama, *Ivory C.* **112 D4** 5 30N 4 3W
Anyang, *China* **74 F8** 36 5N 114 21 E
Anyer, *Indonesia* **84 D3** 6 4 S 105 53 E
Anyi, *Jiangxi, China* **77 C10** 28 49N 115 25 E
Anyi, *Shanxi, China* **74 G6** 35 2N 111 2 E
Anyuan, *China* **77 E10** 25 9N 115 21 E
Anza, *U.S.A.* **161 M10** 33 35N 116 39W
Anzawr, *Oman* **99 C6** 17 28N 52 50 E
Anze, *China* **74 F7** 36 10N 112 12 E
Anzhero-Sudzhensk, *Russia* **64 D9** 56 10N 86 0 E
Ánzio, *Italy* **46 A5** 41 27N 12 37 E
Anzoátegui □, *Venezuela* **169 B5** 9 0N 64 30W
Aoba, *Vanuatu* **133 E5** 15 25 S 167 50 E
Aoga-Shima, *Japan* **71 E11** 32 28N 139 46 E
Aoiz, *Spain* **40 C3** 42 46N 1 22W
Aomori, *Japan* **68 D10** 40 45N 140 45 E
Aomori □, *Japan* **68 D10** 40 45N 140 40 E
Aonla, *India* **93 E8** 28 16N 79 11 E

Azzano Décimo 185

Athabasca, *Canada* **142 C6** 54 45N 113 20W
Athabasca →, *Canada* **143 B6** 58 40N 110 50W
Athabasca, L., *Canada* **143 B7** 59 15N 109 15W
Athboy, *Ireland* **23 C5** 53 37N 6 56W
Athena, *U.S.A.* **152 F6** 29 59N 83 30W
Athenry, *Ireland* **23 C3** 53 18N 8 44W
Athens = Athínai, *Greece* **48 D5** 37 58N 23 46 E
Athens, *Ala., U.S.A.* **149 H2** 34 48N 86 58W
Athens, *Ga., U.S.A.* **152 B6** 33 57N 83 23W
Athens, *N.Y., U.S.A.* **151 D11** 42 16N 73 49W
Athens, *Ohio, U.S.A.* **148 F4** 39 20N 82 6W
Athens, *Pa., U.S.A.* **151 E8** 41 57N 76 31W
Athens, *Tenn., U.S.A.* **149 H3** 35 27N 84 36W
Athens, *Tex., U.S.A.* **155 J7** 32 12N 95 51W
Atherley, *Canada* **150 B5** 44 37N 79 20W
Atherton, *Australia* **126 B4** 17 17 S 145 30 E
Athiéme, *Benin* **113 D5** 6 37N 1 40 E
Athienou, *Cyprus* **38 D12** 35 3N 33 32 E
Athínai, *Greece* **48 D5** 37 58N 23 46 E
Athlone, *Ireland* **23 C4** 53 25N 7 56W
Athna, *Cyprus* **38 D12** 35 3N 33 47 E
Athni, *India* **94 F2** 16 44N 75 6 E
Athol, *N.Z.* **131 F3** 45 30 S 168 35 E
Atholl, Forest of, *U.K.* **22 E5** 56 51N 3 50W
Atholl, Kap, *Greenland* **10 B4** 76 25N 69 30W
Atholville, *Canada* **141 C6** 47 59N 66 43W
Áthos, *Greece* **51 F8** 40 9N 24 22 E
Athy, *Ireland* **23 C5** 53 0N 7 0W
Ati, *Chad* **109 F3** 13 13N 18 20 E
Ati, *Sudan* **107 E2** 13 5N 29 2 E
Atiak, *Uganda* **118 B3** 3 12N 32 2 E
Atiamuri, *N.Z.* **130 E5** 38 24 S 176 5 E
Atico, *Peru* **172 D3** 16 14 S 73 40W
Atienza, *Spain* **40 D2** 41 12N 2 52W
Atikokan, *Canada* **140 C1** 48 45N 91 37W
Atikonak L., *Canada* **141 B7** 52 40N 64 32W
Atimonan, *Phil.* **80 D3** 14 0N 121 55 E
'Ātinah, W. →, *Oman* **99 C6** 18 23N 53 28 E
Atirampattinam, *India* **95 J4** 10 28N 79 20 E
Atka, *Russia* **65 C16** 60 50N 151 48 E
Atka, *U.S.A.* **144 K4** 52 12N 174 12W
Atka I., *U.S.A.* **144 K4** 52 7N 174 30W
Atkarsk, *Russia* **60 E7** 51 55N 45 2 E
Atkasuk = Meade River, *U.S.A.* **144 A8** 70 28N 157 24W
Atkinson, *Ga., U.S.A.* **152 D8** 31 13N 81 47W
Atkinson, *Ill., U.S.A.* **156 C6** 41 25N 90 1W
Atkinson, *Nebr., U.S.A.* **154 D5** 42 32N 98 59W
Atlanta, *Ga., U.S.A.* **152 B5** 33 45N 84 23W
Atlanta, *Ill., U.S.A.* **156 D7** 40 16N 89 14W
Atlanta, *Mo., U.S.A.* **156 E4** 39 54N 92 29W
Atlanta, *Tex., U.S.A.* **155 J7** 33 7N 94 10W
Atlantic, *U.S.A.* **154 E7** 41 24N 95 1W
Atlantic Beach, *U.S.A.* **152 E8** 30 20N 81 24W
Atlantic City, *U.S.A.* **148 F8** 39 21N 74 27W
Atlantic Ocean **8 H7** 0 0 20 0W
Atlántico □, *Colombia* **168 A3** 10 45N 75 0W
Atlas Mts. = Haut Atlas, *Morocco* **110 B4** 32 30N 5 0W
Atlin, *Canada* **142 B2** 59 31N 133 41W
Atlin, L., *Canada* **142 B2** 59 26N 133 45W
Atløyna, *Norway* **18 C1** 61 21N 4 58 E
Atmakur, *India* **95 G4** 14 37N 79 40 E
Atmore, *U.S.A.* **149 K2** 31 2N 87 29W
Atna, *Norway* **18 C7** 61 44N 10 49 E
Atna →, *Norway* **18 C7** 61 44N 10 49 E
Atō, *Japan* **70 C3** 34 25N 131 40 E
Atok, *Phil.* **80 C3** 16 35N 120 41 E
Atoka, *U.S.A.* **155 H6** 34 23N 96 8W
Átokos, *Greece* **48 C2** 38 28N 20 49 E
Atolia, *U.S.A.* **161 K9** 35 19N 117 37W
Atoyac →, *Mexico* **163 D5** 16 30N 97 31W
Atrå, *Norway* **18 E5** 59 59N 8 45 E
Atrak → = Atrek →, *Turkmenistan* **97 B8** 37 35N 53 58 E
Ätran, *Sweden* **17 G6** 57 7N 12 57 E
Ätran →, *Sweden* **17 H6** 56 53N 12 30 E
Atrato →, *Colombia* **168 B2** 8 17N 76 58W
Atrauli, *India* **92 E8** 28 2N 78 20 E
Atrek →, *Turkmenistan* **97 B8** 37 35N 53 58 E
Atri, *Italy* **45 F10** 42 35N 13 58 E
Atsbi, *Ethiopia* **107 E4** 13 52N 39 50 E
Atsikí, *Greece* **49 B7** 39 56N 25 13 E
Atsoum, Mts., *Cameroon* **113 D7** 6 41N 12 57 E
Atsugi, *Japan* **71 B11** 35 25N 139 21 E
Atsumi, *Japan* **71 C9** 34 35N 137 4 E
Atsumi-Wan, *Japan* **71 C9** 34 44N 137 13 E
Atsuta, *Japan* **68 C10** 43 24N 141 26 E
Attalla, *U.S.A.* **152 A3** 34 1N 86 6W
Attapu, *Laos* **86 E6** 14 48N 106 50 E
Attapulgus, *U.S.A.* **152 E5** 30 45N 84 29W
Attáviros, *Greece* **38 C9** 36 12N 27 50 E
Attawapiskat, *Canada* **140 B3** 52 56N 82 24W
Attawapiskat →, *Canada* **140 B3** 52 57N 82 18W
Attawapiskat, L., *Canada* **140 B2** 52 18N 87 54W
Attersee, *Austria* **34 D6** 47 55N 13 32 E
Attica, *U.S.A.* **157 D9** 40 18N 87 15W
Attichy, *France* **27 C10** 49 25N 3 3 E
Attigny, *France* **27 C11** 49 28N 4 35 E
Attikamagen L., *Canada* **141 B6** 55 0N 66 30W
Attikí □, *Greece* **48 D5** 37 10N 23 40 E
Attleboro, *U.S.A.* **151 E13** 41 57N 71 17W
Attock, *Pakistan* **92 C5** 33 52N 72 20 E
Attopeu = Attapu, *Laos* **86 E6** 14 48N 106 50 E
Attu I., *U.S.A.* **144 K1** 52 55N 172 55 E
Attunga, *Australia* **129 A9** 30 55 S 150 50 E
Attur, *India* **95 J4** 11 35N 78 30 E
'Atūd, *Yemen* **99 D5** 14 53N 48 10 E
Atuel →, *Argentina* **174 D2** 36 17 S 66 50W
Åtvidaberg, *Sweden* **17 F10** 58 12N 16 0 E
Atwater, *U.S.A.* **160 H6** 37 21N 120 37W
Atwood, *Canada* **150 C3** 43 40N 81 1W
Atwood, *U.S.A.* **154 F4** 39 48N 101 3W
Atyraū, *Kazakstan* **57 E9** 47 5N 52 0 E
Au Sable →, *U.S.A.* **148 C4** 44 25N 83 20W
Au Sable Pt., *U.S.A.* **140 C2** 46 40N 86 10W
Aubagne, *France* **29 E9** 43 17N 5 37 E
Aubarca, C., *Spain* **39 B7** 39 4N 1 22 E
Aube □, *France* **27 D11** 48 15N 4 10 E
Aube →, *France* **27 D10** 48 34N 3 43 E
Aubenas, *France* **29 D8** 44 37N 4 24 E
Aubenton, *France* **27 C11** 49 50N 4 12 E
Auberry, *U.S.A.* **160 H7** 37 7N 119 29W
Aubigny-sur-Nère, *France* **27 E9** 47 30N 2 24 E
Aubin, *France* **28 D6** 44 33N 2 15 E
Aubrac, Mts. d', *France* **28 D7** 44 40N 3 2 E
Auburn, *Ala., U.S.A.* **152 C4** 32 36N 85 29W
Auburn, *Calif., U.S.A.* **160 G5** 38 54N 121 4W
Auburn, *Ill., U.S.A.* **156 E7** 39 36N 89 45W
Auburn, *Ind., U.S.A.* **157 C11** 41 22N 85 4W
Auburn, *N.Y., U.S.A.* **151 D8** 42 56N 76 34W
Auburn, *Nebr., U.S.A.* **154 E7** 40 23N 95 51W
Auburn, *Wash., U.S.A.* **160 C4** 47 18N 122 14W
Auburn Ra., *Australia* **127 D5** 25 15 S 150 30 E
Auburndale, *U.S.A.* **149 L5** 28 4N 81 48W
Aubusson, *France* **28 C6** 45 57N 2 11 E
Auce, *Latvia* **54 B9** 56 28N 22 53 E
Auch, *France* **28 E4** 43 39N 0 36 E
Auchi, *Nigeria* **113 D6** 7 6N 6 13 E
Aucilla →, *U.S.A.* **152 E6** 30 5N 83 59W
Auckland, *N.Z.* **130 C3** 36 52 S 174 46 E
Auckland □, *N.Z.* **130 E6** 36 50 S 175 0 E
Auckland Is., *Pac. Oc.* **134 N8** 50 40 S 166 5 E
Aude □, *France* **28 E6** 43 8N 2 28 E
Aude →, *France* **28 E7** 43 13N 3 14 E
Audegle, *Somali Rep.* **120 D2** 1 59N 44 50 E
Auden, *Canada* **140 B2** 50 14N 87 53W
Auderville, *France* **26 C5** 49 43N 1 57W
Audierne, *France* **26 D2** 48 1N 4 34W
Audincourt, *France* **27 E13** 47 30N 6 50 E
Audo, *Ethiopia* **107 F5** 6 20N 41 50 E
Audubon, *U.S.A.* **156 C2** 41 43N 94 56W
Aue, *Germany* **30 E8** 50 35N 12 41 E
Auerbach, *Germany* **30 E8** 50 30N 12 24 E
Aueti Paraná →, *Brazil* **168 D4** 1 51 S 65 37W
Aufist, *W. Sahara* **110 C2** 25 44N 14 39W
Augathella, *Australia* **127 D4** 25 48 S 146 35 E
Aughnacloy, *U.K.* **23 B5** 54 25N 6 59W
Augrabies Falls, *S. Africa* **116 D3** 28 35 S 20 20 E
Augsburg, *Germany* **31 G6** 48 25N 10 52 E
Augusta, *Italy* **47 E8** 37 13N 15 13 E
Augusta, *Ark., U.S.A.* **155 H9** 35 17N 91 22W
Augusta, *Ga., U.S.A.* **152 B8** 33 28N 81 58W
Augusta, *Ill., U.S.A.* **156 D6** 40 14N 90 57W
Augusta, *Kans., U.S.A.* **155 G6** 37 41N 96 59W
Augusta, *Ky., U.S.A.* **157 F13** 38 47N 84 0W
Augusta, *Maine, U.S.A.* **141 D6** 44 19N 69 47W
Augusta, *Mont., U.S.A.* **158 C7** 47 30N 112 24W
Augusta, *Wis., U.S.A.* **154 C9** 44 41N 91 7W
Augustenborg, *Denmark* **17 K3** 54 57N 9 53 E
Augustine I., *U.S.A.* **144 G9** 59 22N 153 26W
Augustów, *Poland* **54 E9** 53 51N 23 0 E
Augustus, Mt., *Australia* **124 D2** 24 20 S 116 50 E
Augustus Downs, *Australia* **126 B2** 18 35 S 139 55 E
Augustus I., *Australia* **124 C3** 15 20 S 124 30 E
Aukan, *Eritrea* **107 D5** 15 29N 40 50 E
Auki, *Solomon Is.* **133 M11** 8 45 S 160 42 E
Aukra, *Norway* **18 B3** 62 47N 6 55 E
Aukum, *U.S.A.* **160 G6** 38 34N 120 43W
Auld, L., *Australia* **124 D3** 22 25 S 123 50 E
Aulla, *Italy* **44 D6** 44 12N 9 58 E
Aulnay, *France* **28 B3** 46 2N 0 22W
Aulne →, *France* **26 D2** 48 17N 4 16W
Aulnoye-Aymeries, *France* **27 B10** 50 12N 3 50 E
Ault, *France* **26 B8** 50 8N 1 26 E
Ault, *U.S.A.* **154 E2** 40 35N 104 44W
Aulus-les-Bains, *France* **28 F5** 42 49N 1 19 E
Aumale, *France* **27 C8** 49 46N 1 46 E
Aumont-Aubrac, *France* **28 D7** 44 43N 3 17 E
Auna, *Nigeria* **113 C5** 10 9N 4 42 E
Aundh, *India* **94 F2** 17 33N 74 23 E
Auning, *Denmark* **17 H4** 56 26N 10 22 E
Aunis, *France* **28 B3** 46 5N 0 50W
Auponhia, *Indonesia* **82 B3** 1 58 S 125 27 E
Aups, *France* **29 E10** 43 37N 6 15 E
Aur, Pulau, *Malaysia* **87 L5** 2 35N 104 10 E
Aura, *Burma* **90 B6** 26 59N 97 57 E
Auraiya, *India* **93 F8** 26 28N 79 33 E
Aurangabad, *Bihar, India* **93 G11** 24 45N 84 18 E
Aurangabad, *Maharashtra, India* **94 E2** 19 50N 75 23 E
Auray, *France* **26 E4** 47 40N 2 59W
Aurdal, *Norway* **18 D6** 60 55N 9 26 E
Aure, *Norway* **18 A5** 63 16N 8 33 E
Aurès, *Algeria* **111 A6** 35 8N 6 30 E
Aurich, *Germany* **30 B3** 53 28N 7 28 E
Aurilândia, *Brazil* **171 E1** 16 44 S 50 28W
Aurillac, *France* **28 D6** 44 55N 2 26 E
Aurlandsfjorden, *Norway* **18 C4** 61 3N 7 1 E
Aurlandsvangen, *Norway* **18 D4** 60 55N 7 12 E
Auronzo di Cadore, *Italy* **45 B9** 46 33N 12 26 E
Aurora = Maéwo, *Vanuatu* **133 E6** 15 10 S 168 10 E
Aurora, *Canada* **150 C5** 44 0N 79 28W
Aurora, *Isabela, Phil.* **80 C3** 16 59N 121 38 E
Aurora, *Quezon, Phil.* **80 E4** 13 21N 122 31 E
Aurora, *S. Africa* **116 E2** 32 40 S 18 29 E
Aurora, *Colo., U.S.A.* **154 F2** 39 44N 104 52W
Aurora, *Ill., U.S.A.* **157 C8** 41 45N 88 19W
Aurora, *Mo., U.S.A.* **155 G8** 36 58N 93 43W
Aurora, *Nebr., U.S.A.* **154 E6** 40 52N 98 0W
Aurora, *Ohio, U.S.A.* **150 E3** 41 21N 81 20W
Aursmoen, *Norway* **18 E8** 59 55N 11 26 E
Aursunden, *Norway* **18 B8** 62 40N 11 40 E
Aurukun Mission, *Australia* **126 A3** 13 20 S 141 45 E
Aus, *Namibia* **116 D2** 26 35 S 16 12 E
Auschwitz = Oświęcim, *Poland* **55 H6** 50 2N 19 11 E
Ausiait, *Greenland* **10 D5** 68 43N 52 56W
Aust-Agder □, *Norway* **18 F4** 58 45N 8 0 E
Austad, *Norway* **18 F4** 58 58N 7 37 E
Austerlitz = Slavkov u Brna, *Czech Rep.* **35 B9** 49 10N 16 52 E
Austevoll, *Norway* **18 D2** 60 5N 5 13 E
Austin, *Ind., U.S.A.* **157 F11** 38 45N 85 49W
Austin, *Minn., U.S.A.* **154 D8** 43 40N 92 58W
Austin, *Nev., U.S.A.* **158 G5** 39 30N 117 4W
Austin, *Pa., U.S.A.* **150 E6** 41 38N 78 6W
Austin, *Tex., U.S.A.* **155 K6** 30 17N 97 45W
Austin, L., *Australia* **125 E2** 27 40 S 118 0 E
Austmarka, *Norway* **18 D9** 60 6N 12 20 E
Austnes, *Norway* **18 B3** 62 38N 6 16 E
Austra, *Norway* **14 D14** 65 8N 11 55 E
Austral Downs, *Australia* **126 C2** 20 30 S 137 45 E
Austral Is. = Tubuai Is., *Pac. Oc.* **135 K13** 25 0 S 150 0W
Austral Seamount Chain, *Pac. Oc.* **135 K13** 24 0 S 150 0W
Australia ■, *Oceania* **134 K5** 23 0 S 135 0 E
Australian Alps, *Australia* **129 D8** 36 30 S 148 30 E
Australian Capital Territory □, *Australia* **127 F4** 35 30 S 149 0 E
Austria ■, *Europe* **34 E7** 47 0N 14 0 E
Austur-Skaftafellssýsla □, *Iceland* **11 C10** 64 15N 16 0W
Austvågøy, *Norway* **14 B16** 68 20N 14 40 E
Autazes, *Brazil* **169 D6** 3 35 S 59 8W
Auterive, *France* **28 E5** 43 21N 1 29 E
Authie →, *France* **27 B8** 50 22N 1 38 E
Authon-du-Perche, *France* **26 D7** 48 12N 0 54 E
Autlán, *Mexico* **162 D4** 19 40N 104 30W
Autun, *France* **27 F11** 46 58N 4 17 E
Auvergne, *Australia* **124 C5** 15 39 S 130 1 E
Auvergne, *France* **28 C7** 45 20N 3 15 E
Auvergne, Mts. d', *France* **28 C6** 45 20N 2 55 E
Auvézère →, *France* **28 C4** 45 12N 0 50 E
Auxerre, *France* **27 E10** 47 48N 3 32 E
Auxi-le-Château, *France* **27 B9** 50 15N 2 8 E
Auxonne, *France* **27 E12** 47 10N 5 20 E
Auxvasse, *U.S.A.* **156 E5** 39 1N 91 54W
Auzances, *France* **27 F9** 46 2N 2 30 E
Ava, *U.S.A.* **156 G7** 37 53N 89 30W
Availdsnes, *Norway* **18 E2** 59 21N 5 20 E
Avallon, *France* **27 E10** 47 30N 3 53 E
Avalon, *U.S.A.* **161 M8** 33 21N 118 20W
Avalon Pen., *Canada* **141 C9** 47 30N 53 20W
Avanigadda, *India* **95 G5** 16 0N 80 56 E
Avaré, *Brazil* **175 A6** 23 4 S 48 58W
Ávas, *Greece* **51 F9** 40 57N 25 56 E
Avawatz Mts., *U.S.A.* **161 K10** 35 40N 116 30W
Avdan Dağı, *Turkey* **51 F13** 40 23N 29 46 E
Aveiro, *Brazil* **169 D6** 3 10 S 55 5W
Aveiro, *Portugal* **42 E2** 40 37N 8 38W
Aveiro □, *Portugal* **42 E2** 40 40N 8 35W
Āvej, *Iran* **97 C6** 35 40N 49 15 E
Avellaneda, *Argentina* **174 C4** 34 50 S 58 10W
Avellino, *Italy* **47 B7** 40 54N 14 47 E
Avenal, *U.S.A.* **160 K6** 36 0N 120 8W
Avenches, *Switz.* **32 C4** 46 53N 7 2 E
Avera, *U.S.A.* **152 B7** 33 12N 82 32W
Averøya, *Norway* **18 A4** 63 0N 7 35 E
Aversa, *Italy* **47 B7** 40 58N 14 12 E
Avery, *U.S.A.* **158 C6** 47 15N 115 49W
Aves, I. de, *W. Indies* **165 C7** 15 45N 63 55W
Aves, Is. de, *Venezuela* **165 D6** 12 0N 67 30W
Avesnes-sur-Helpe, *France* **27 B10** 50 8N 3 55 E
Avesta, *Sweden* **16 D10** 60 9N 16 10 E
Aveyron □, *France* **28 D6** 44 22N 2 45 E
Aveyron →, *France* **28 D5** 44 5N 1 16 E
Avezzano, *Italy* **45 F10** 42 2N 13 25 E
Avgó, *Greece* **49 F7** 35 33N 25 37 E
Aviá Terai, *Argentina* **174 B3** 26 45 S 60 50W
Aviano, *Italy* **45 B9** 46 4N 12 36 E
Aviemore, *U.K.* **22 D5** 57 12N 3 50W
Avigliana, *Italy* **44 C4** 45 5N 7 23 E
Avigliano, *Italy* **47 B8** 40 44N 15 43 E
Avignon, *France* **29 E8** 43 57N 4 50 E
Ávila, *Spain* **42 E6** 40 39N 4 43W
Ávila □, *Spain* **42 E6** 40 30N 5 0W
Ávila, Sierra de, *Spain* **42 E5** 40 40N 5 15W
Avila Beach, *U.S.A.* **161 K6** 35 11N 120 44W
Avilés, *Spain* **42 B5** 43 35N 5 57W
Avintes, *Portugal* **42 D2** 41 7N 8 33W
Avionárion, *Greece* **48 C6** 38 31N 24 8 E
Avis, *Portugal* **43 F3** 39 4N 7 53W
Avisio →, *Italy* **44 B8** 46 7N 11 5 E
Aviston, *U.S.A.* **156 F7** 38 36N 89 36W
Aviz = Avis, *Portugal* **43 F3** 39 4N 7 53W
Avize, *France* **27 D11** 48 59N 4 1 E
Avlum, *Denmark* **17 H2** 56 16N 8 47 E
Avoca, *U.S.A.* **150 D7** 42 25N 77 25W
Avoca →, *Australia* **128 C5** 35 40 S 143 43 E
Avoca →, *Ireland* **23 D5** 52 48N 6 10W
Avola, *Canada* **142 C5** 51 45N 119 19W
Avola, *Italy* **47 F8** 36 56N 15 7 E
Avon, *Ill., U.S.A.* **156 D6** 40 40N 90 26W
Avon, *N.Y., U.S.A.* **150 D7** 42 55N 77 45W
Avon, *S. Dak., U.S.A.* **154 D5** 43 0N 98 4W
Avon →, *Australia* **125 F2** 31 40 S 116 7 E
Avon →, *Bristol, U.K.* **21 F5** 51 29N 2 41W
Avon →, *Dorset, U.K.* **21 G6** 50 44N 1 46W
Avon →, *Warks., U.K.* **21 E5** 52 0N 2 8W
Avon Park, *U.S.A.* **153 H8** 27 36N 81 31W
Avondale, *Zimbabwe* **119 F3** 17 43 S 30 58 E
Avonlea, *Canada* **143 D8** 50 0N 105 0W
Avonmore, *Canada* **151 A10** 45 10N 74 58W
Avramov, *Bulgaria* **51 D10** 42 45N 26 38 E
Avranches, *France* **26 D5** 48 40N 1 20W
Avre →, *France* **26 D8** 48 47N 1 22 E
Avrig, *Romania* **53 E9** 45 43N 24 21 E
Avrillé, *France* **26 E6** 47 30N 0 35W
Avtovac, *Bos.-H.* **50 C2** 43 9N 18 35 E
Avu Avu, *Solomon Is.* **133 M11** 9 50 S 160 22 E
Awag el Baqar, *Sudan* **107 E3** 10 10N 33 10 E
A'waj →, *Syria* **103 B5** 33 23N 36 20 E
Awaji, *Japan* **71 C7** 34 32N 135 1 E
Awaji-Shima, *Japan* **70 C6** 34 30N 134 50 E
'Awālī, *Bahrain* **97 E6** 26 0N 50 30 E
Awantipur, *India* **93 C6** 33 55N 75 3 E
Awanui, *N.Z.* **130 B2** 35 4 S 173 17 E
Awarja →, *India* **94 F3** 17 5N 76 15 E
Awarua B., *N.Z.* **131 E3** 44 28 S 168 4 E
Awarua Pt., *N.Z.* **131 E3** 44 15 S 168 5 E
Awasa, L., *Ethiopia* **107 F4** 7 0N 38 30 E
Awash, *Ethiopia* **107 F5** 9 1N 40 10 E
Awash →, *Ethiopia* **107 E5** 11 45N 41 5 E
Awaso, *Ghana* **112 D4** 6 15N 2 22W
Awatere →, *N.Z.* **131 B9** 41 37 S 174 10 E
Awbārī, *Libya* **108 C2** 26 46N 12 57 E
Awbārī □, *Libya* **108 C2** 26 35N 12 46 E
Awe, L., *U.K.* **22 E3** 56 17N 5 16W
Aweil, *Sudan* **107 F2** 8 42N 27 20 E
Awgu, *Nigeria* **113 D6** 6 4N 7 24 E
Awjilah, *Libya* **108 C4** 29 8N 21 7 E
Aworro, *Papua N. G.* **132 D2** 7 43 S 143 11 E
Ax-les-Thermes, *France* **28 F5** 42 44N 1 50 E
Axat, *France* **28 F6** 42 48N 2 13 E
Axe →, *U.K.* **21 F5** 50 42N 3 4W
Axel Heiberg I., *Canada* **6 B3** 80 0N 90 0W
Axim, *Ghana* **112 E4** 4 51N 2 15W
Axinim, *Brazil* **169 D6** 4 2 S 59 22W
Axintele, *Romania* **53 F11** 44 37N 26 47 E
Axioma, *Brazil* **173 B5** 6 45 S 64 31W
Axiós →, *Greece* **50 F6** 40 57N 22 35 E
Axminster, *U.K.* **21 G4** 50 46N 3 0W
Axson, *U.S.A.* **152 D7** 31 17N 82 44W
Axvall, *Sweden* **17 F7** 58 23N 13 34 E
Ay, *France* **27 C11** 49 3N 4 1 E
Ay →, *Russia* **62 C6** 56 8N 57 40 E
Ayaantang, *Eq. Guin.* **114 B2** 1 58N 10 24 E
Ayabaca, *Peru* **172 A2** 4 40 S 79 53W
Ayabe, *Japan* **71 B7** 35 20N 135 20 E
Ayacucho, *Argentina* **174 D4** 37 5 S 58 20W
Ayacucho, *Peru* **172 C3** 13 0 S 74 0W
Ayaguz, *Kazakstan* **64 E9** 48 10N 80 10 E
Ayakkuduk, *Uzbekistan* **63 C2** 41 12N 65 12 E
Ayakudi, *India* **95 J3** 10 28N 77 56 E
Ayala, *Phil.* **81 H3** 6 57N 121 57 E
Ayamonte, *Spain* **43 H3** 37 12N 7 24W
Ayan, *Russia* **65 D14** 56 30N 138 16 E
Ayancık, *Turkey* **100 B6** 41 57N 34 35 E
Ayapel, *Colombia* **168 B2** 8 19N 75 9W
Ayas, *Turkey* **100 B5** 40 2N 32 21 E
Ayaviri, *Peru* **172 C3** 14 50 S 70 35W
Āybak, *Afghan.* **91 A3** 36 15N 68 5 E
Aybastı, *Turkey* **100 B7** 40 41N 37 23 E
Aydim, W. →, *Oman* **99 C6** 18 8N 53 8 E
Aydın, *Turkey* **100 D2** 37 51N 27 51 E
Aydin □, *Turkey* **49 D9** 37 50N 28 0 E
Aydin Dağları, *Turkey* **49 D10** 38 0N 28 0 E
Aydyrlinskiy, *Russia* **62 E7** 52 3N 59 50 E
Ayenngré, *Togo* **113 D5** 8 40N 1 1 E
Ayerbe, *Spain* **40 C4** 42 17N 0 41W
Ayer's Cliff, *Canada* **151 A12** 45 10N 72 3W
Ayers Rock, *Australia* **125 E5** 25 23 S 131 5 E
Ayiá, *Greece* **48 B4** 39 43N 22 45 E
Ayia Aikateríni, Ákra, *Greece* **38 A3** 39 50N 19 50 E
Ayía Ánna, *Greece* **48 C5** 38 52N 23 24 E
Ayia Dhéka, *Greece* **38 D6** 35 3N 24 58 E
Ayia Gálini, *Greece* **38 D6** 35 6N 24 41 E
Ayia Marína, *Kásos, Greece* **49 F8** 35 27N 26 53 E
Ayía Marína, *Léros, Greece* **49 D8** 37 11N 26 48 E
Ayia Napa, *Cyprus* **38 E13** 34 59N 34 0 E
Ayía Paraskeví, *Greece* **49 B8** 39 14N 26 21 E
Ayia Phyla, *Cyprus* **38 E12** 34 43N 33 1 E
Ayía Rouméli, *Greece* **48 F5** 35 14N 23 58 E
Ayia Varvára, *Greece* **38 D7** 35 8N 25 1 E
Ayiássos, *Greece* **49 B8** 39 5N 26 23 E
Áyioi Theódhoroi, *Greece* **48 D5** 37 55N 23 9 E
Áyion Óros □, *Greece* **51 F8** 40 25N 24 6 E
Áyios Amvrósios, *Cyprus* **38 D12** 35 20N 33 35 E
Áyios Andréas, *Greece* **48 D4** 37 21N 22 45 E
Áyios Evstrátios, *Greece* **48 B6** 39 34N 24 58 E
Áyios Ioánnis, Ákra, *Greece* **38 D7** 35 20N 25 40 E
Áyios Isidhoros, *Greece* **38 C9** 36 9N 27 51 E
Áyios Kiríkos, *Greece* **49 D8** 37 34N 26 17 E
Áyios Matthaíos, *Greece* **38 B3** 39 30N 19 47 E
Áyios Mírono, *Greece* **49 F7** 35 15N 25 1 E
Áyios Nikólaos, *Greece* **38 D7** 35 11N 25 41 E
Áyios Pétros, *Greece* **48 C2** 38 38N 20 33 E
Áyios Seryios, *Cyprus* **38 D12** 35 12N 33 53 E
Áyios Theodhoros, *Cyprus* **38 D13** 35 22N 34 1 E
Áyios Yeóryios, *Greece* **48 D5** 37 28N 23 57 E
Aykathonisi, *Greece* **49 D8** 37 28N 27 0 E
Aykino, *Russia* **56 B8** 62 15N 49 56 E
Aykirikçi, *Turkey* **49 B12** 39 8N 30 9 E
Aylesbury, *U.K.* **21 F7** 51 49N 0 49W
Aylmer, *Canada* **150 D4** 42 46N 80 59W
Aylmer, L., *Canada* **138 B8** 64 0N 110 8W
'Ayn al Ghazālah, *Libya* **108 B4** 32 10N 23 20 E
Ayn Zālah, *Iraq* **101 D10** 36 45N 42 35 E
Ayna, *Spain* **41 G2** 38 34N 2 3W
Aynāt, *Yemen* **99 C5** 16 4N 49 9 E
Ayni, *Tajikistan* **63 D4** 39 23N 68 32 E
Ayolas, *Paraguay* **174 B4** 27 10 S 56 59W
Ayom, *Sudan* **107 F2** 7 49N 28 23 E
Ayon, Ostrov, *Russia* **65 C17** 69 50N 169 0 E
Ayora, *Spain* **41 F3** 39 3N 1 3W
Ayr, *Australia* **126 B4** 19 35 S 147 25 E
Ayr, *U.K.* **22 F4** 55 28N 4 38W
Ayr →, *U.K.* **22 F4** 55 28N 4 38W
Ayrancı, *Turkey* **100 D5** 37 21N 33 41 E
Ayrancılar, *Turkey* **49 C9** 38 15N 27 18 E
Ayre, Pt. of, *U.K.* **20 C3** 54 25N 4 21W
Aysha, *Ethiopia* **107 E5** 10 50N 42 23 E
Aytos, *Bulgaria* **51 D11** 42 42N 27 16 E
Aytoska Planina, *Bulgaria* **51 D11** 42 45N 27 30 E
Ayu, Kepulauan, *Indonesia* **83 A4** 0 35N 131 5 E
Ayutla, *Guatemala* **164 D1** 14 40N 92 10W
Ayutla, *Mexico* **163 D5** 16 58N 99 17W
Ayvacık, *Turkey* **100 C2** 39 36N 26 24 E
Ayvalık, *Turkey* **57 G4** 39 20N 26 46 E
Az Zabadānī, *Syria* **103 B5** 33 43N 36 5 E
Az Ẓāhirīyah, *West Bank* **103 D3** 31 25N 34 58 E
Az Ẓahrān, *Si. Arabia* **97 E6** 26 10N 50 7 E
Az Zarqā, *Jordan* **103 C5** 32 5N 36 4 E
Az Zāwiyah, *Libya* **108 B2** 32 52N 12 56 E
Az Zaydīyah, *Yemen* **98 D3** 15 20N 43 1 E
Az Zībār, *Iraq* **101 D11** 36 52N 44 4 E
Az-Zilfī, *Si. Arabia* **96 E5** 26 12N 44 52 E
Az Zubayr, *Iraq* **96 D5** 30 26N 47 40 E
Az Zuqur, *Yemen* **98 D3** 14 0N 42 45 E
Az Zuwaytīnah, *Libya* **108 B4** 30 58N 20 7 E
Azambuja, *Portugal* **43 F2** 39 4N 8 51W
Azamgarh, *India* **93 F10** 26 5N 83 13 E
Azangaro, *Peru* **172 C3** 14 55 S 70 13W
Azaouak, Vallée de l', *Mali* **113 B5** 15 50N 3 20 E
Āzār Shahr, *Iran* **101 D11** 37 45N 45 59 E
Azarān, *Iran* **101 D12** 37 25N 47 16 E
Azärbayjan = Azerbaijan ■, *Asia* **61 K9** 40 20N 48 0 E
Āzarbāyjān-e Gharbī □, *Iran* **96 B5** 37 0N 44 30 E
Āzarbāyjān-e Sharqī □, *Iran* **96 B5** 37 20N 47 0 E
Azare, *Nigeria* **113 C7** 11 55N 10 10 E
Azay-le-Rideau, *France* **26 E7** 47 16N 0 30 E
A'zāz, *Syria* **100 D7** 36 36N 37 4 E
Azazga, *Algeria* **111 A5** 36 48N 4 22 E
Azbine = Aïr, *Niger* **109 E1** 18 30N 8 0 E
Azefal, *Mauritania* **110 D2** 21 0N 14 45W
Azeffoun, *Algeria* **111 A5** 36 51N 4 26 E
Azemmour, *Morocco* **110 B3** 33 20N 9 20W
Azerbaijan ■, *Asia* **61 K9** 40 20N 48 0 E
Azerbaijchan = Azerbaijan ■, *Asia* **61 K9** 40 20N 48 0 E
Azezo, *Ethiopia* **107 E4** 12 28N 37 15 E
Azimganj, *India* **93 G13** 24 14N 88 16 E
Aznalcóllar, *Spain* **43 H4** 37 32N 6 17W
Azogues, *Ecuador* **168 D2** 2 35 S 78 0W
Azores, *Atl. Oc.* **8 E6** 38 44N 29 0W
Azov, *Russia* **59 J10** 47 3N 39 25 E
Azov, Sea of, *Europe* **59 J9** 46 0N 36 30 E
Azovskoye More = Azov, Sea of, *Europe* **59 J9** 46 0N 36 30 E
Azpeitia, *Spain* **40 B2** 43 12N 2 19W
Azrou, *Morocco* **110 B3** 33 28N 5 19W
Aztec, *U.S.A.* **159 H10** 36 49N 107 59W
Azúa, *Dom. Rep.* **165 C5** 18 25N 70 44W
Azuaga, *Spain* **43 G5** 38 16N 5 39W
Azuara, *Spain* **40 D4** 41 15N 0 53W
Azuay □, *Ecuador* **168 D2** 2 55 S 79 0W
Azuer →, *Spain* **43 F7** 39 8N 3 36W
Azuero, Pen. de, *Panama* **164 E3** 7 30N 80 30W
Azuga, *Romania* **53 E10** 45 27N 25 33 E
Azul, *Argentina* **174 D4** 36 42 S 59 43W
Azul, Serra, *Brazil* **173 C7** 14 50 S 54 50W
Azurduy, *Bolivia* **173 D5** 19 59 S 64 29W
Azusa, *U.S.A.* **161 L9** 34 8N 117 52W
Azzaba, *Algeria* **111 A6** 36 48N 7 6 E
Azzano Décimo, *Italy* **45 C9** 45 52N 12 56 E

B

Bardejov 187

Balfour Channel, *Solomon Is.* **133 M9** 8 43 S 157 27 E
Balharshah, *India* **94 E4** 19 50N 79 23 E
Bali, *Cameroon* **113 D7** 5 54N 10 0 E
Balí, *Greece* **38 D6** 35 25N 24 47 E
Bali, *Indonesia* **85 D5** 8 20 S 115 0 E
Bali □, *Indonesia* **85 D4** 8 20 S 115 0 E
Bali, Selat, *Indonesia* **85 D4** 8 18 S 114 25 E
Balicuatro Is., *Phil.* **80 E5** 12 39N 124 24 E
Baligród, *Poland* **55 J9** 49 20N 22 17 E
Balikeşir, *Turkey* **57 G4** 39 39N 27 53 E
Balikeşir □, *Turkey* **49 B9** 39 45N 28 0 E
Balıklıçeşme, *Turkey* **51 F11** 40 18N 27 5 E
Balikpapan, *Indonesia* **85 C5** 1 10 S 116 55 E
Balimbing, *Phil.* **81 J2** 5 5N 119 58 E
Balimo, *Papua N. G.* **132 E2** 8 6 S 142 57 E
Baling, *Malaysia* **87 K3** 5 41N 100 55 E
Balingen, *Germany* **31 G4** 48 16N 8 51 E
Balinţ, *Romania* **52 E6** 45 48N 21 54 E
Balintang Channel, *Phil.* **80 B3** 19 49N 121 40 E
Balintang Is., *Phil.* **80 B4** 19 58N 122 9 E
Baliton, *Phil.* **81 J5** 5 44N 125 14 E
Baliza, *Brazil* **173 D7** 16 0 S 52 20W
Baljurshi, *Si. Arabia* **98 C3** 19 51N 41 33 E
Balkan Mts. = Stara Planina, *Bulgaria* **50 C7** 43 15N 23 0 E
Balkh □, *Afghan.* **91 A2** 36 50N 67 0 E
Balkhash = Balqash, *Kazakstan* **64 E8** 46 50N 74 50 E
Balkhash, Ozero = Balqash Köl, *Kazakstan* **64 E8** 46 0N 74 50 E
Ballachulish, *U.K.* **22 E3** 56 41N 5 8W
Balladonia, *Australia* **125 F3** 32 27 S 123 51 E
Ballaghaderreen, *Ireland* **23 C3** 53 55N 8 34W
Ballara, *Australia* **128 B4** 32 19 S 140 45 E
Ballarat, *Australia* **127 F3** 37 33 S 143 50 E
Ballard, L., *Australia* **125 E3** 29 20 S 120 40 E
Ballater, *U.K.* **22 D5** 57 3N 3 3W
Balldale, *Australia* **129 C7** 35 50 S 146 33 E
Ballenas, Canal de, *Mexico* **162 B2** 29 10N 113 45W
Balleny Is., *Antarctica* **7 C11** 66 30 S 163 0 E
Balleroy, *France* **26 C6** 49 11N 0 50W
Ballerup, *Denmark* **17 J6** 55 44N 12 21 E
Ballesteros, *Phil.* **80 B3** 18 25N 121 31 E
Ballı, *Turkey* **51 F11** 40 50N 27 3 E
Ballia, *India* **93 G11** 25 46N 84 12 E
Ballidu, *Australia* **125 F2** 30 35 S 116 45 E
Ballina, *Australia* **127 D5** 28 50 S 153 31 E
Ballina, *Ireland* **23 B2** 54 7N 9 9W
Ballinasloe, *Ireland* **23 C3** 53 20N 8 13W
Ballinger, *U.S.A.* **155 K5** 31 45N 99 57W
Ballinrobe, *Ireland* **23 C2** 53 38N 9 13W
Ballinskelligs B., *Ireland* **23 E1** 51 48N 10 13W
Ballon, *France* **26 D7** 48 10N 0 14 E
Ballsh, *Albania* **50 F3** 40 36N 19 44 E
Ballycastle, *U.K.* **23 A5** 55 12N 6 15W
Ballyclare, *U.K.* **23 B5** 54 46N 6 0W
Ballyhaunis, *Ireland* **23 C3** 53 46N 8 46W
Ballymena, *U.K.* **23 B5** 54 52N 6 17W
Ballymoney, *U.K.* **23 A5** 55 5N 6 31W
Ballymote, *Ireland* **23 B3** 54 5N 8 31W
Ballynahinch, *U.K.* **23 B6** 54 24N 5 54W
Ballyquintin Pt., *U.K.* **23 B6** 54 20N 5 30W
Ballyshannon, *Ireland* **23 B3** 54 30N 8 11W
Balmaceda, *Chile* **176 C2** 46 0 S 71 50W
Balmaseda, *Spain* **40 B1** 43 11N 3 12W
Balmazújváros, *Hungary* **52 C6** 47 37N 21 21 E
Balmhorn, *Switz.* **32 D5** 46 26N 7 42 E
Balmoral, *Australia* **128 D4** 37 15 S 141 48 E
Balmorhea, *U.S.A.* **155 K3** 30 59N 103 45W
Balombo, *Angola* **115 E2** 12 21 S 14 46 E
Balonne →, *Australia* **127 D4** 28 47 S 147 56 E
Balqash, *Kazakstan* **64 E8** 46 50N 74 50 E
Balqash Köl, *Kazakstan* **64 E8** 46 0N 74 50 E
Balrampur, *India* **93 F10** 27 30N 82 20 E
Balranald, *Australia* **128 C5** 34 38 S 143 33 E
Balş, *Romania* **53 F9** 44 22N 24 5 E
Balsapuerto, *Peru* **172 B2** 5 48 S 76 33W
Balsas, *Mexico* **163 D5** 18 0N 99 40W
Balsas →, *Maranhão, Brazil* **170 C3** 7 15 S 44 35W
Balsas →, *Tocantins, Brazil* **170 C2** 9 58 S 47 52W
Balsas →, *Mexico* **162 D4** 17 55N 102 10W
Bålsta, *Sweden* **16 E11** 59 35N 17 30 E
Balsthal, *Switz.* **32 B5** 47 19N 7 41 E
Balston Spa, *U.S.A.* **151 D11** 43 0N 73 52W
Balta, *Romania* **52 F7** 44 54N 22 38 E
Balta, *Ukraine* **59 H5** 48 2N 29 45 E
Balta, *U.S.A.* **154 A4** 48 10N 100 2W
Baltanás, *Spain* **42 D6** 41 56N 4 15W
Bălţi, *Moldova* **53 C12** 47 48N 27 58 E
Baltic Sea, *Europe* **15 H18** 57 0N 19 0 E
Baltîm, *Egypt* **106 H7** 31 35N 31 10 E
Baltimore, *Ireland* **23 E2** 51 29N 9 22W
Baltimore, *U.S.A.* **148 F7** 39 17N 76 37W
Baltit, *Pakistan* **93 A6** 36 15N 74 40 E
Baltiysk, *Russia* **15 J18** 54 41N 19 58 E
Baltrum, *Germany* **30 B3** 53 43N 7 24 E
Baluchistan □, *Pakistan* **91 D2** 27 30N 65 0 E
Balud, *Phil.* **80 E4** 12 2N 123 12 E
Balurghat, *India* **93 G13** 25 15N 88 44 E
Balvi, *Latvia* **15 H22** 57 8N 27 15 E
Balya, *Turkey* **49 B9** 39 44N 27 35 E
Balzar, *Ecuador* **168 D2** 2 2 S 79 54W
Bam, *Iran* **97 D8** 29 7N 58 14 E
Bama, *China* **76 E6** 24 8N 107 12 E
Bama, *Nigeria* **113 C7** 11 33N 13 41 E
Bamako, *Mali* **112 C3** 12 34N 7 55W
Bamba, *Dem. Rep. of the Congo* **115 D3** 5 45 S 18 23 E
Bamba, *Mali* **113 B4** 17 5N 1 24W
Bambam, *Phil.* **80 D3** 15 40N 120 20 E
Bambamarca, *Peru* **172 B2** 6 36 S 78 32W
Bambang, *Phil.* **80 C3** 16 23N 121 6 E
Bambari, *C.A.R.* **114 A4** 5 40N 20 35 E
Bambaroo, *Australia* **126 B4** 18 50 S 146 10 E
Bamberg, *Germany* **31 F6** 49 54N 10 54 E
Bamberg, *U.S.A.* **152 B9** 33 18N 81 2W
Bambesi, *Ethiopia* **107 F3** 9 45N 34 40 E
Bambey, *Senegal* **112 C1** 14 42N 16 28W
Bambili, *Dem. Rep. of the Congo* **118 B2** 3 40N 26 0 E
Bambuí, *Brazil* **171 F2** 20 1 S 45 58W
Bamenda, *Cameroon* **113 D7** 5 57N 10 11 E
Bamfield, *Canada* **142 D3** 48 45N 125 10W
Bāmīān □, *Afghan.* **91 B2** 35 0N 67 0 E
Bamiancheng, *China* **75 C13** 43 15N 124 2 E
Bamingui, *C.A.R.* **114 A4** 7 34N 20 11 E
Bamkin, *Cameroon* **113 D7** 6 3N 11 27 E
Bampūr, *Iran* **97 E9** 27 15N 60 21 E
Ban Ban, *Laos* **86 C4** 19 31N 103 30 E
Ban Bang Hin, *Thailand* **87 H2** 9 32N 98 35 E
Ban Chiang Klang, *Thailand* **86 C3** 19 25N 100 55 E
Ban Chik, *Laos* **86 D4** 17 15N 102 22 E
Ban Choho, *Thailand* **86 E4** 15 2N 102 9 E
Ban Dan Lan Hoi, *Thailand* **86 D2** 17 0N 99 35 E
Ban Don = Surat Thani, *Thailand* **87 H2** 9 6N 99 20 E
Ban Don, *Vietnam* **86 F6** 12 53N 107 48 E
Ban Don, Ao →, *Thailand* **87 H2** 9 20N 99 25 E
Ban Dong, *Thailand* **86 C3** 19 30N 100 59 E
Ban Hong, *Thailand* **86 C2** 18 18N 98 50 E
Ban Kaeng, *Thailand* **86 D3** 17 29N 100 7 E
Ban Kantang, *Thailand* **87 J2** 7 25N 99 31 E
Ban Keun, *Laos* **86 C4** 18 22N 102 35 E
Ban Khai, *Thailand* **86 F3** 12 46N 101 18 E
Ban Kheun, *Laos* **86 B3** 20 13N 101 7 E
Ban Khlong Kua, *Thailand* **87 J3** 6 57N 100 8 E
Ban Khuan Mao, *Thailand* **87 J2** 7 50N 99 37 E
Ban Ko Yai Chim, *Thailand* **87 G2** 11 17N 99 26 E
Ban Kok, *Thailand* **86 D4** 16 40N 103 40 E
Ban Laem, *Thailand* **86 F2** 13 13N 99 59 E
Ban Lao Ngam, *Laos* **86 E6** 15 28N 106 10 E
Ban Le Kathe, *Thailand* **86 E2** 15 49N 98 53 E
Ban Mae Chedi, *Thailand* **86 C2** 19 11N 99 31 E
Ban Mae Laeng, *Thailand* **86 B2** 20 1N 99 17 E
Ban Mae Sariang, *Thailand* **86 C1** 18 10N 97 56 E
Ban Mê Thuôt = Buon Ma Thuot, *Vietnam* **86 F7** 12 40N 108 3 E
Ban Mi, *Thailand* **86 E3** 15 3N 100 32 E
Ban Muong Mo, *Laos* **86 C4** 19 4N 103 58 E
Ban Na Mo, *Laos* **86 D5** 17 7N 105 40 E
Ban Na San, *Thailand* **87 H2** 8 53N 99 52 E
Ban Na Tong, *Laos* **86 B3** 20 56N 101 47 E
Ban Nam Bac, *Laos* **86 B4** 20 38N 102 20 E
Ban Nam Ma, *Laos* **86 A3** 22 2N 101 37 E
Ban Ngang, *Laos* **86 E6** 15 59N 106 11 E
Ban Nong Bok, *Laos* **86 D5** 17 5N 104 48 E
Ban Nong Boua, *Laos* **86 E6** 15 40N 106 33 E
Ban Nong Pling, *Thailand* **86 E3** 15 40N 100 10 E
Ban Pak Chan, *Thailand* **87 G2** 10 32N 98 51 E
Ban Phai, *Thailand* **86 D4** 16 4N 102 44 E
Ban Pong, *Thailand* **86 F2** 13 50N 99 55 E
Ban Ron Phibun, *Thailand* **87 H2** 8 9N 99 51 E
Ban Sanam Chai, *Thailand* **87 J3** 7 33N 100 25 E
Ban Sangkha, *Thailand* **86 E4** 14 37N 103 52 E
Ban Tak, *Thailand* **86 D2** 17 2N 99 4 E
Ban Tako, *Thailand* **86 E4** 14 5N 102 40 E
Ban Tha Dua, *Thailand* **86 D2** 17 59N 98 39 E
Ban Tha Li, *Thailand* **86 D3** 17 37N 101 25 E
Ban Tha Nun, *Thailand* **87 H2** 8 12N 98 18 E
Ban Thahine, *Laos* **86 E5** 14 12N 105 33 E
Ban Xien Kok, *Laos* **86 B3** 20 54N 100 39 E
Ban Yen Nhan, *Vietnam* **86 B6** 20 57N 106 2 E
Banā, W. →, *Yemen* **98 D4** 13 3N 45 24 E
Banaba, *Kiribati* **134 H8** 0 45 S 169 50 E
Bañalbufar, *Spain* **39 B9** 39 42N 2 31 E
Banalia, *Dem. Rep. of the Congo* **118 B2** 1 32N 25 5 E
Banam, *Cambodia* **87 G5** 11 20N 105 17 E
Banamba, *Mali* **112 C3** 13 29N 7 22W
Banana, *Australia* **126 C5** 24 28 S 150 8 E
Bananal, I. do, *Brazil* **171 D1** 11 30 S 50 30W
Banaras = Varanasi, *India* **93 G10** 25 22N 83 0 E
Banas →, *Gujarat, India* **92 H4** 23 45N 71 25 E
Banas →, *Mad. P., India* **93 G9** 24 15N 81 30 E
Bânâs, Ras, *Egypt* **106 C4** 23 57N 35 59 E
Banaz, *Turkey* **49 C11** 38 46N 29 46 E
Banaz →, *Turkey* **49 C11** 38 12N 29 14 E
Banbān, *Si. Arabia* **96 E5** 25 1N 46 35 E
Banbridge, *U.K.* **23 B5** 54 22N 6 16W
Banbury, *U.K.* **21 E6** 52 4N 1 20W
Banchory, *U.K.* **22 D6** 57 3N 2 29W
Bancroft, *Canada* **140 C4** 45 3N 77 51W
Band, *Romania* **53 D9** 46 30N 24 25 E
Band Bonī, *Iran* **97 E8** 25 30N 59 33 E
Band-e Torkestān, *Afghan.* **91 B2** 35 30N 64 0 E
Band Qīr, *Iran* **97 D6** 31 39N 48 53 E
Banda, *Cameroon* **114 B2** 3 58N 14 32 E
Banda, *India* **93 G9** 25 30N 80 26 E
Banda, Kepulauan, *Indonesia* **83 B3** 4 37 S 129 50 E
Banda Aceh, *Indonesia* **84 A1** 5 35N 95 20 E
Banda Banda, Mt., *Australia* **129 A10** 31 10 S 152 28 E
Banda Elat, *Indonesia* **83 C4** 5 40 S 133 5 E
Banda Is. = Banda, Kepulauan, *Indonesia* **83 B3** 4 37 S 129 50 E
Banda Sea, *Indonesia* **82 C3** 6 0 S 130 0 E
Bandai-San, *Japan* **68 F10** 37 36N 140 4 E
Bandak, *Norway* **18 E5** 59 23N 8 29 E
Bandama →, *Ivory C.* **112 D3** 6 32N 5 30W
Bandān, *Iran* **97 D9** 31 23N 60 44 E
Bandanaira, *Indonesia* **83 B3** 4 32 S 129 54 E
Bandanwara, *India* **92 F6** 26 9N 74 38 E
Bandar = Machilipatnam, *India* **95 F5** 16 12N 81 8 E
Bandār 'Abbās, *Iran* **97 E8** 27 15N 56 15 E
Bandar-e Anzalī, *Iran* **97 B6** 37 30N 49 30 E
Bandar-e Bushehr = Būshehr, *Iran* **97 D6** 28 55N 50 55 E
Bandar-e Chārak, *Iran* **97 E7** 26 45N 54 20 E
Bandar-e Deylam, *Iran* **97 D6** 30 5N 50 10 E
Bandar-e Khomeynı, *Iran* **97 D6** 30 30N 49 5 E
Bandar-e Lengeh, *Iran* **97 E7** 26 35N 54 58 E
Bandar-e Maqām, *Iran* **97 E7** 26 56N 53 29 E
Bandar-e Ma'shur, *Iran* **97 D6** 30 35N 49 10 E
Bandar-e Nakhīlū, *Iran* **97 E7** 26 58N 53 30 E
Bandar-e Rīg, *Iran* **97 D6** 29 29N 50 38 E
Bandar-e Torkeman, *Iran* **97 B7** 37 0N 54 10 E
Bandar Maharani = Muar, *Malaysia* **87 L4** 2 3N 102 34 E
Bandar Penggaram = Batu Pahat, *Malaysia* **87 M4** 1 50N 102 56 E
Bandar Seri Begawan, *Brunei* **85 B4** 4 52N 115 0 E
Bandar Sri Aman, *Malaysia* **85 B4** 1 15N 111 32 E
Bandawe, *Malawi* **119 E3** 11 58 S 34 5 E
Bande, *Spain* **42 C3** 42 3N 7 58W
Bandeira, Pico da, *Brazil* **171 F3** 20 26 S 41 47W
Bandeirante, *Brazil* **171 D1** 13 41 S 50 48W
Bandera, *Argentina* **174 B3** 28 55 S 62 20W
Bandera, *U.S.A.* **155 L5** 29 44N 99 5W
Banderas, B. de, *Mexico* **162 C3** 20 40N 105 30W
Bandia →, *India* **94 E5** 19 2N 80 28 E
Bandiagara, *Mali* **112 C4** 14 12N 3 29W
Bandırma, *Turkey* **51 F11** 40 20N 28 0 E
Bandol, *France* **29 E9** 43 8N 5 46 E
Bandon, *Ireland* **23 E3** 51 44N 8 44W
Bandon →, *Ireland* **23 E3** 51 43N 8 37W
Bandoua, *C.A.R.* **114 B4** 4 39N 21 42 E
Bandula, *Mozam.* **119 F3** 19 0 S 33 7 E
Bandundu, *Dem. Rep. of the Congo* **114 C3** 3 15 S 17 22 E
Bandung, *Indonesia* **85 D3** 6 54 S 107 36 E
Bandya, *Australia* **125 E3** 27 40 S 122 5 E
Băneasa, *Romania* **53 E12** 45 56N 27 55 E
Bāneh, *Iran* **101 E11** 35 59N 45 53 E
Bañeres, *Spain* **41 G4** 38 44N 0 38W
Banes, *Cuba* **165 B4** 21 0N 75 42W
Banff, *Canada* **142 C5** 51 10N 115 34W
Banff, *U.K.* **22 D6** 57 40N 2 33W
Banff Nat. Park, *Canada* **142 C5** 51 30N 116 15W
Banfora, *Burkina Faso* **112 C4** 10 40N 4 40W
Bang Fai →, *Laos* **86 D5** 16 57N 104 45 E
Bang Hieng →, *Laos* **86 D5** 16 10N 105 10 E
Bang Krathum, *Thailand* **86 D3** 16 34N 100 18 E
Bang Lamung, *Thailand* **86 F3** 13 3N 100 56 E
Bang Mun Nak, *Thailand* **86 D3** 16 2N 100 23 E
Bang Pa In, *Thailand* **86 E3** 14 14N 100 35 E
Bang Rakam, *Thailand* **86 D3** 16 45N 100 7 E
Bang Saphan, *Thailand* **87 G2** 11 14N 99 28 E
Bangala Dam, *Zimbabwe* **119 G3** 21 7 S 31 25 E
Bangalore, *India* **95 H3** 12 59N 77 40 E
Bangangté, *Cameroon* **113 D7** 5 8N 10 32 E
Bangaon, *India* **93 H13** 23 0N 88 47 E
Bangassou, *C.A.R.* **114 B4** 4 55N 23 7 E
Bangeta, Mt., *Papua N. G.* **132 D4** 6 21 S 147 3 E
Banggai, Kepulauan, *Indonesia* **82 B2** 1 40 S 123 30 E
Banggai Arch. = Banggai, Kepulauan, *Indonesia* **82 B2** 1 40 S 123 30 E
Banggi, *Malaysia* **85 A5** 7 17N 117 12 E
Banghāzī, *Libya* **108 B4** 32 11N 20 3 E
Banghāzī □, *Libya* **108 B4** 32 7N 20 4 E
Bangil, *Indonesia* **85 D4** 7 36 S 112 50 E
Bangjang, *Sudan* **107 E3** 11 23N 32 41 E
Bangka, *Sulawesi, Indonesia* **82 A3** 1 50N 125 5 E
Bangka, *Sumatera, Indonesia* **84 C3** 2 0 S 105 50 E
Bangka, Selat, *Indonesia* **84 C3** 2 30 S 105 30 E
Bangkalan, *Indonesia* **85 D4** 7 2 S 112 46 E
Bangkinang, *Indonesia* **84 B2** 0 18N 101 5 E
Bangko, *Indonesia* **84 C2** 2 5 S 102 9 E
Bangkok, *Thailand* **86 F3** 13 45N 100 35 E
Bangladesh ■, *Asia* **90 D3** 24 0N 90 0 E
Bangolo, *Ivory C.* **112 D3** 7 1N 7 29W
Bangong Co, *India* **93 B8** 35 50N 79 20 E
Bangor, *Down, U.K.* **23 B6** 54 40N 5 40W
Bangor, *Gwynedd, U.K.* **20 D3** 53 14N 4 8W
Bangor, *Maine, U.S.A.* **141 D6** 44 48N 68 46W
Bangor, *Mich., U.S.A.* **157 B10** 42 18N 86 7W
Bangor, *Pa., U.S.A.* **151 F9** 40 52N 75 13W
Bangu, *Dem. Rep. of the Congo* **114 C3** 0 3 S 19 12 E
Bangued, *Phil.* **80 C3** 17 40N 120 37 E
Bangui, *C.A.R.* **114 B3** 4 23N 18 35 E
Bangui, *Phil.* **80 B3** 18 32N 120 46 E
Banguru, *Dem. Rep. of the Congo* **118 B2** 0 30N 27 10 E
Bangweulu, L., *Zambia* **119 E3** 11 0 S 30 0 E
Bangweulu Swamp, *Zambia* **119 E3** 11 20 S 30 15 E
Bani, *Dom. Rep.* **165 C5** 18 16N 70 22W
Bani, *Phil.* **80 C2** 16 11N 119 52 E
Bani →, *Mali* **112 C4** 14 30N 4 12W
Bani, Djebel, *Morocco* **110 C3** 29 16N 8 0W
Bani Bangou, *Niger* **113 B5** 15 3N 2 42 E
Banī Sa'd, *Iraq* **101 F11** 33 34N 44 32 E
Banī Sār, *Si. Arabia* **98 B3** 20 6N 41 27 E
Banī Walīd, *Libya* **108 B2** 31 36N 13 53 E
Bania, *Ivory C.* **112 D4** 9 4N 3 6W
Baniara, *Papua N. G.* **132 E5** 9 44 S 149 54 E
Banihal Pass, *India* **93 C6** 33 30N 75 12 E
Banīnah, *Libya* **108 B4** 32 0N 20 12 E
Bāniyās, *Syria* **100 E6** 35 10N 36 0 E
Banja Luka, *Bos.-H.* **52 F2** 44 49N 17 11 E
Banjar, *Indonesia* **85 D3** 7 24 S 108 30 E
Banjarmasin, *Indonesia* **85 C4** 3 20 S 114 35 E
Banjarnegara, *Indonesia* **85 D3** 7 24 S 109 42 E
Banjul, *Gambia* **112 C1** 13 28N 16 40W
Banka Banka, *Australia* **126 B1** 18 50 S 134 0 E
Bankeryd, *Sweden* **17 G8** 57 53N 14 6 E
Banket, *Zimbabwe* **119 F3** 17 27 S 30 19 E
Bankilaré, *Niger* **113 C5** 14 35N 0 44 E
Bankipore, *India* **93 G11** 25 35N 85 10 E
Banks, *U.S.A.* **152 D4** 31 49N 85 51W
Banks, Is., *Vanuatu* **133 C5** 13 50 S 167 30 E
Banks I., *B.C., Canada* **142 C3** 53 20N 130 0W
Banks I., *N.W.T., Canada* **138 A7** 73 15N 121 30W
Banks I., *Papua N. G.* **132 F2** 10 10 S 142 15 E
Banks L., *U.S.A.* **152 D6** 31 2N 83 6W
Banks Pen., *N.Z.* **131 D8** 43 45 S 173 15 E
Banks Str., *Australia* **126 G4** 40 40 S 148 10 E
Bankura, *India* **93 H12** 23 11N 87 18 E
Bankya, *Bulgaria* **50 D7** 42 43N 23 8 E
Bann →, *Arm., U.K.* **23 B5** 54 30N 6 31W
Bann →, *L'derry., U.K.* **23 A5** 55 8N 6 41W
Banna, *Phil.* **80 C3** 17 59N 120 39 E
Bannalec, *France* **26 E3** 47 57N 3 42W
Bannang Sata, *Thailand* **87 J3** 6 16N 101 16 E
Bannerton, *Australia* **128 C5** 34 42 S 142 47 E
Banning, *U.S.A.* **161 M10** 33 56N 116 53W
Banningville = Bandundu, *Dem. Rep. of the Congo* **114 C3** 3 15 S 17 22 E
Bannockburn, *Canada* **150 B7** 44 39N 77 33W
Bannockburn, *U.K.* **22 E5** 56 5N 3 55W
Bannockburn, *Zimbabwe* **119 G2** 20 17 S 29 48 E
Bannu, *Pakistan* **91 B3** 33 0N 70 18 E
Bañolas = Banyoles, *Spain* **40 C7** 42 16N 2 44 E
Banon, *France* **29 D9** 44 2N 5 38 E
Baños de la Encina, *Spain* **43 G7** 38 10N 3 46W
Baños de Molgas, *Spain* **42 C3** 42 15N 7 40W
Bánovce nad Bebravou, *Slovak Rep.* **35 C11** 48 44N 18 16 E
Banovići, *Bos.-H.* **52 F3** 44 25N 18 32 E
Bansilan □, *Phil.* **81 H3** 6 40N 121 40 E
Banská Bystrica, *Slovak Rep.* **35 C12** 48 46N 19 14 E
Banská Štiavnica, *Slovak Rep.* **35 C11** 48 25N 18 55 E
Bansko, *Bulgaria* **50 E7** 41 52N 23 28 E
Banskobystrický □, *Slovak Rep.* **35 C12** 48 20N 19 0 E
Banswara, *India* **92 H6** 23 32N 74 24 E
Bantayan, *Phil.* **81 F4** 11 10N 123 43 E
Bantayan I., *Phil.* **81 F4** 11 13N 123 44 E
Banten, *Indonesia* **84 D3** 6 5 S 106 8 E
Banton I., *Phil.* **80 E4** 12 56N 122 4 E
Bantry, *Ireland* **23 E2** 51 41N 9 27W
Bantry B., *Ireland* **23 E2** 51 37N 9 44W
Bantul, *Indonesia* **85 D4** 7 55 S 110 19 E
Bantva, *India* **92 J4** 21 29N 70 12 E
Bantval, *India* **95 H2** 12 55N 75 0 E
Banya, *Bulgaria* **51 D8** 42 33N 24 50 E
Banyak, Kepulauan, *Indonesia* **84 B1** 2 10N 97 10 E
Banyo, *Cameroon* **113 D7** 6 52N 11 45 E
Banyoles, *Spain* **40 C7** 42 16N 2 44 E
Banyuls-sur-Mer, *France* **28 F7** 42 28N 3 8 E
Banyumas, *Indonesia* **85 D3** 7 32 S 109 18 E
Banyuwangi, *Indonesia* **85 D4** 8 13 S 114 21 E
Banzare Coast, *Antarctica* **7 C9** 68 0 S 125 0 E
Banzyville = Mobayi, *Dem. Rep. of the Congo* **114 B4** 4 15N 21 8 E
Bao Ha, *Vietnam* **86 A5** 22 11N 104 21 E
Bao Lac, *Vietnam* **86 A5** 22 57N 105 40 E
Bao Loc, *Vietnam* **87 G6** 11 32N 107 48 E
Bao'an = Shenzhen, *China* **77 F10** 22 27N 114 10 E
Baocheng, *China* **74 H4** 33 12N 106 56 E
Baode, *China* **74 E6** 39 1N 111 5 E
Baodi, *China* **75 E9** 39 38N 117 20 E
Baoding, *China* **74 E8** 38 50N 115 28 E
Baoji, *China* **74 G4** 34 20N 107 5 E
Baojing, *China* **76 C7** 28 45N 109 41 E
Baokang, *China* **77 B8** 31 54N 111 12 E
Baoro, *C.A.R.* **114 A3** 5 40N 15 58 E
Baoshan, *Shanghai, China* **77 B13** 31 27N 121 26 E
Baoshan, *Yunnan, China* **76 E2** 25 10N 99 5 E
Baotou, *China* **74 D6** 40 32N 110 2 E
Baoying, *China* **75 H10** 33 17N 119 20 E
Bap, *India* **92 F5** 27 23N 72 18 E
Bapatla, *India* **95 G5** 15 55N 80 30 E
Bapaume, *France* **27 B9** 50 7N 2 50 E
Bāqerābād, *Iran* **97 C6** 33 2N 51 58 E
Ba'qūbah, *Iraq* **101 F11** 33 45N 44 50 E
Baquedano, *Chile* **174 A2** 23 20 S 69 52W
Bar, *Montenegro, Yug.* **50 D3** 42 8N 19 6 E
Bar, *Ukraine* **59 H4** 49 4N 27 40 E
Bar Bigha, *India* **93 G11** 25 21N 85 47 E
Bar Harbor, *U.S.A.* **141 D6** 44 23N 68 13W
Bar-le-Duc, *France* **27 D12** 48 47N 5 10 E
Bar-sur-Aube, *France* **27 D11** 48 14N 4 40 E
Bar-sur-Seine, *France* **27 D11** 48 7N 4 20 E
Băra, *Romania* **53 C12** 47 2N 27 3 E
Barabai, *Indonesia* **85 C5** 2 32 S 115 34 E
Baraboo, *U.S.A.* **154 D10** 43 28N 89 45W
Baracoa, *Cuba* **165 B5** 20 20N 74 30W
Baradā →, *Syria* **103 B5** 33 33N 36 34 E
Baradero, *Argentina* **174 C4** 33 52 S 59 29W
Baradine, *Australia* **129 A8** 30 56 S 149 4 E
Baraga, *U.S.A.* **154 B10** 46 47N 88 30W
Bărăganul, *Romania* **53 F12** 44 49N 27 31 E
Barahona, *Dom. Rep.* **165 C5** 18 13N 71 7W
Barahona, *Spain* **40 D2** 41 17N 2 39W
Baraka →, *Sudan* **106 D4** 18 13N 37 35 E
Barakaldo, *Spain* **40 B2** 43 18N 2 59W
Barakot, *India* **93 J11** 21 33N 84 59 E
Barakpur, *India* **93 H13** 22 44N 88 30 E
Barakula, *Australia* **127 D5** 26 30 S 150 33 E
Baralaba, *Australia* **126 C4** 24 13 S 149 50 E
Baralla, *Spain* **42 C3** 42 53N 7 15W
Baralzon L., *Canada* **143 B9** 60 0N 98 3W
Baram →, *Malaysia* **85 B4** 4 35N 113 58 E
Baramati, *India* **94 E2** 18 11N 74 33 E
Baramba, *India* **94 D7** 20 25N 85 23 E
Barameiya, *Sudan* **106 D4** 18 32N 36 38 E
Baramula, *India* **93 B6** 34 15N 74 20 E
Baran, *India* **92 G7** 25 9N 76 40 E
Barañain, *Spain* **40 C3** 42 48N 1 40W
Baranavichy, *Belarus* **59 F4** 53 10N 26 0 E
Baranoa, *Colombia* **168 A3** 10 48N 74 55W
Baranof, *U.S.A.* **144 H14** 57 5N 134 50W
Baranof I., *U.S.A.* **142 B1** 57 0N 135 0W
Baranów Sandomierski, *Poland* **55 H8** 50 29N 21 30 E
Baranya □, *Hungary* **52 E3** 46 0N 18 15 E
Barão de Cocais, *Brazil* **171 E3** 19 56 S 43 28W
Barão de Grajaú, *Brazil* **170 C3** 6 45 S 43 1W
Barão de Melgaço, *Mato Grosso, Brazil* **173 D6** 16 14 S 55 52W
Barão de Melgaço, *Rondônia, Brazil* **173 C5** 11 50 S 60 45W
Baraolt, *Romania* **53 D10** 46 5N 25 34 E
Barapasi, *Indonesia* **83 B5** 2 15 S 137 5 E
Barapina, *Papua N. G.* **132 D8** 6 21 S 155 25 E
Barasat, *India* **93 H13** 22 46N 88 31 E
Barat Daya, Kepulauan, *Indonesia* **82 C3** 7 30 S 128 0 E
Barataria B., *U.S.A.* **155 L10** 29 20N 89 55W
Baraut, *India* **92 E7** 29 13N 77 7 E
Baraya, *Colombia* **168 C2** 3 10N 75 4W
Barbacan, *Phil.* **81 F2** 10 20N 119 21 E
Barbacena, *Brazil* **171 F3** 21 15 S 43 56W
Barbacoas, *Colombia* **168 C2** 1 45N 78 0W
Barbacoas, *Venezuela* **168 B4** 9 29N 66 58W
Barbados ■, *W. Indies* **165 D8** 13 10N 59 30W
Barbalha, *Brazil* **170 C4** 7 19 S 39 17W
Barban, *Croatia* **45 C11** 45 5N 14 2 E
Barbària, C. de, *Spain* **39 C7** 38 39N 1 24 E
Barbaros, *Turkey* **51 F11** 40 54N 27 27 E
Barbastro, *Spain* **40 C5** 42 2N 0 5 E
Barbate = Barbate de Franco, *Spain* **43 J5** 36 13N 5 56W
Barbate de Franco, *Spain* **43 J5** 36 13N 5 56W
Barbaza, *Phil.* **81 F4** 11 12N 122 2 E
Barberino di Mugello, *Italy* **45 E8** 44 0N 11 15 E
Barbers Pt., *U.S.A.* **145 K13** 21 18N 158 7W
Barberton, *S. Africa* **117 D5** 25 42 S 31 2 E
Barberton, *U.S.A.* **150 E3** 41 0N 81 39W
Barberville, *U.S.A.* **153 F8** 29 11N 81 26W
Barbezieux-St-Hilaire, *France* **28 C3** 45 28N 0 9W
Barbosa, *Colombia* **168 B3** 5 57N 73 37W
Barbourville, *U.S.A.* **149 G4** 36 52N 83 53W
Barbuda, *W. Indies* **165 C7** 17 30N 61 40W
Bârca, *Romania* **53 G8** 43 59N 23 36 E
Barcaldine, *Australia* **126 C4** 23 43 S 145 6 E
Barcarrota, *Spain* **43 G4** 38 31N 6 51W
Barcellona Pozzo di Gotto, *Italy* **47 D8** 38 9N 15 13 E
Barcelona, *Spain* **40 D7** 41 21N 2 10 E
Barcelona, *Venezuela* **169 A5** 10 10N 64 40W
Barcelona □, *Spain* **40 D7** 41 30N 2 0 E
Barcelonette, *France* **29 D10** 44 23N 6 40 E
Barcelos, *Brazil* **169 D5** 1 0 S 63 0W
Barcin, *Poland* **55 F4** 52 52N 17 55 E
Barcoo →, *Australia* **126 D3** 25 30 S 142 50 E
Barcs, *Hungary* **52 E2** 45 58N 17 28 E
Barczewo, *Poland* **54 E7** 53 50N 20 42 E
Bärdä, *Azerbaijan* **61 K8** 40 25N 47 10 E
Barda del Medio, *Argentina* **176 A3** 38 45 S 68 11W
Bardaï, *Chad* **109 D3** 21 25N 17 0 E
Bardas Blancas, *Argentina* **174 D2** 35 49 S 69 45W
Barddhaman, *India* **93 H12** 23 14N 87 39 E
Bardejov, *Slovak Rep.* **35 B14** 49 18N 21 15 E

Bengal, Bay of 189

Beach City, *U.S.A.* **150 F3** 40 39N 81 35W
Beachport, *Australia* **128 D4** 37 29 S 140 0 E
Beachy Hd., *U.K.* **21 G8** 50 44N 0 15 E
Beacon, *Australia* **125 F2** 30 26 S 117 52 E
Beacon, *U.S.A.* **151 E11** 41 30N 73 58W
Beacon Hill, *U.S.A.* **152 F4** 29 55N 85 23W
Beaconia, *Canada* **143 C9** 50 25N 96 31W
Beagle, Canal, *S. Amer.* **176 E3** 55 0 S 68 30W
Beagle Bay, *Australia* **124 C3** 16 58 S 122 40 E
Bealanana, *Madag.* **117 A8** 14 33 S 48 44 E
Beamsville, *Canada* **150 C5** 43 12N 79 28W
Bear →, *U.S.A.* **160 G5** 38 56N 121 36W
Béar, C., *France* **28 F7** 42 31N 3 8 E
Bear I., *Ireland* **23 E2** 51 38N 9 50W
Bear L., *B.C., Canada* **142 B3** 56 10N 126 52W
Bear L., *Man., Canada* **143 B9** 55 8N 96 0W
Bear L., *U.S.A.* **158 F8** 41 59N 111 21W
Bearcreek, *U.S.A.* **158 D9** 45 11N 109 6W
Beardmore, *Canada* **140 C2** 49 36N 87 57W
Beardmore Glacier, *Antarctica* **7 E11** 84 30 S 170 0 E
Beardstown, *U.S.A.* **156 E6** 40 1N 90 26W
Béarn, *France* **28 E3** 43 20N 0 30W
Bearpaw Mts., *U.S.A.* **158 B9** 48 12N 109 30W
Bearskin Lake, *Canada* **140 B1** 53 58N 91 2W
Beas de Segura, *Spain* **43 G8** 38 15N 2 53W
Beasain, *Spain* **40 B2** 43 3N 2 11W
Beata, C., *Dom. Rep.* **165 C5** 17 40N 71 30W
Beata, I., *Dom. Rep.* **165 C5** 17 34N 71 31W
Beatrice, *U.S.A.* **154 E6** 40 16N 96 45W
Beatrice, *Zimbabwe* **119 F3** 18 15 S 30 55 E
Beatrice, C., *Australia* **126 A2** 14 20 S 136 55 E
Beatton →, *Canada* **142 B4** 56 15N 120 45W
Beatton River, *Canada* **142 B4** 57 26N 121 20W
Beatty, *U.S.A.* **160 J10** 36 54N 116 46W
Beaucaire, *France* **29 E8** 43 48N 4 39 E
Beauce, Plaine de la, *France* **27 D8** 48 10N 1 45 E
Beauceville, *Canada* **141 C5** 46 13N 70 46W
Beauchêne, I., *Falk. Is.* **176 D5** 52 55 S 59 15W
Beaudesert, *Australia* **127 D5** 27 59 S 153 0 E
Beaufort, *Australia* **128 D5** 37 25 S 143 25 E
Beaufort, *France* **29 C10** 45 44N 6 34 E
Beaufort, *Malaysia* **85 A5** 5 30N 115 40 E
Beaufort, *N.C., U.S.A.* **149 H7** 34 43N 76 40W
Beaufort, *S.C., U.S.A.* **152 C9** 32 26N 80 40W
Beaufort Sea, *Arctic* **6 B1** 72 0N 140 0W
Beaufort West, *S. Africa* **116 E3** 32 18 S 22 36 E
Beaugency, *France* **27 E8** 47 47N 1 38 E
Beauharnois, *Canada* **140 C5** 45 20N 73 52W
Beaujeu, *France* **27 F11** 46 10N 4 35 E
Beaujolais, *France* **27 F11** 46 0N 4 22 E
Beaulieu →, *Canada* **142 A6** 62 3N 113 11W
Beaulieu-sur-Dordogne, *France* **28 D5** 44 58N 1 50 E
Beaulieu-sur-Mer, *France* **29 E11** 43 42N 7 20 E
Beauly, *U.K.* **22 D4** 57 30N 4 28W
Beauly →, *U.K.* **22 D4** 57 29N 4 27W
Beaumaris, *U.K.* **20 D3** 53 16N 4 6W
Beaumont, *Belgium* **24 D4** 50 15N 4 14 E
Beaumont, *France* **28 D4** 44 45N 0 46 E
Beaumont, *N.Z.* **131 F4** 45 50 S 169 33 E
Beaumont, *U.S.A.* **155 K7** 30 5N 94 6W
Beaumont-de-Lomagne, *France* **28 E5** 43 53N 1 0 E
Beaumont-le-Roger, *France* **26 C7** 49 4N 0 47 E
Beaumont-sur-Sarthe, *France* **26 D7** 48 13N 0 8 E
Beaune, *France* **27 E11** 47 2N 4 50 E
Beaune-la-Rolande, *France* **27 D9** 48 4N 2 25 E
Beaupréau, *France* **26 E6** 47 12N 1 0W
Beauraing, *Belgium* **24 D4** 50 7N 4 57 E
Beaurepaire, *France* **29 C9** 45 22N 5 1 E
Beauséjour, *Canada* **143 C9** 50 5N 96 35W
Beautemps-Beaupré, I., *N. Cal.* **133 K4** 20 24 S 166 9 E
Beauvais, *France* **27 C9** 49 25N 2 8 E
Beauval, *Canada* **143 B7** 55 9N 107 37W
Beauvoir-sur-Mer, *France* **26 F4** 46 55N 2 2W
Beauvoir-sur-Niort, *France* **28 B3** 46 12N 0 30W
Beaver, *Okla., U.S.A.* **155 G4** 36 49N 100 31W
Beaver, *Pa., U.S.A.* **150 F4** 40 42N 80 19W
Beaver, *Utah, U.S.A.* **159 G7** 38 17N 112 38W
Beaver →, *B.C., Canada* **142 B4** 59 52N 124 20W
Beaver →, *Ont., Canada* **140 A2** 55 55N 87 48W
Beaver →, *Sask., Canada* **143 B7** 55 26N 107 45W
Beaver City, *U.S.A.* **154 E5** 40 8N 99 50W
Beaver Dam, *U.S.A.* **154 D10** 43 28N 88 50W
Beaver Falls, *U.S.A.* **150 F4** 40 46N 80 20W
Beaver Hill L., *Canada* **143 C10** 54 5N 94 50W
Beaver I., *U.S.A.* **148 C3** 45 40N 85 33W
Beavercreek, *U.S.A.* **157 E12** 39 43N 84 11W
Beaverhill L., *Alta., Canada* **142 C6** 53 27N 112 32W
Beaverhill L., *N.W.T., Canada* **143 A8** 63 2N 104 22W
Beaverlodge, *Canada* **142 B5** 55 11N 119 29W
Beavermouth, *Canada* **142 C5** 51 32N 117 23W
Beaverstone →, *Canada* **140 B2** 54 59N 89 25W
Beaverton, *Canada* **150 B5** 44 26N 79 9W
Beaverton, *U.S.A.* **160 E4** 45 29N 122 48W
Beaverville, *U.S.A.* **157 D9** 40 57N 87 39W
Beawar, *India* **92 F6** 26 3N 74 18 E
Bebedouro, *Brazil* **175 A6** 21 0 S 48 25W
Beboa, *Madag.* **117 B7** 17 22 S 44 33 E
Bebra, *Germany* **30 E5** 50 58N 9 48 E
Beccles, *U.K.* **21 E9** 52 27N 1 35 E
Bečej, *Serbia, Yug.* **52 E5** 45 36N 20 3 E
Beceni, *Romania* **53 E11** 45 23N 26 48 E
Becerreá, *Spain* **42 C3** 42 51N 7 10W
Béchar, *Algeria* **111 B4** 31 38N 2 18W
Bechyně, *Czech Rep.* **34 B7** 49 17N 14 29 E
Beckley, *U.S.A.* **148 G5** 37 47N 81 11W
Beckum, *Germany* **30 D4** 51 45N 8 3 E
Beclean, *Romania* **53 C9** 47 11N 24 11 E
Bečov nad Teplou, *Czech Rep.* **34 A5** 50 5N 12 49 E
Bečva →, *Czech Rep.* **35 B10** 49 31N 17 20 E
Bédar, *Spain* **41 H3** 37 11N 1 59W
Bédarieux, *France* **28 E7** 43 37N 3 10 E
Beddouza, Ras, *Morocco* **110 B3** 32 33N 9 9W
Bedel, Pereval, *Kyrgyzstan* **63 C9** 41 26N 78 26 E
Bedele, *Ethiopia* **107 F4** 8 31N 36 23 E
Bederkesa, *Germany* **30 B4** 53 37N 8 50 E
Bederwanak, *Somali Rep.* **120 C2** 9 34N 44 23 E
Bedeso, *Ethiopia* **107 F5** 9 58N 40 52 E
Bedford, *Canada* **140 C5** 45 7N 72 59W
Bedford, *S. Africa* **116 E4** 32 40 S 26 10 E
Bedford, *U.K.* **21 E7** 52 8N 0 28W
Bedford, *Ind., U.S.A.* **157 F10** 38 52N 86 29W
Bedford, *Iowa, U.S.A.* **156 D2** 40 40N 94 44W
Bedford, *Ky., U.S.A.* **157 F11** 38 36N 85 19W
Bedford, *Ohio, U.S.A.* **150 E3** 41 23N 81 32W
Bedford, *Pa., U.S.A.* **150 F6** 40 1N 78 30W
Bedford, *Va., U.S.A.* **148 G6** 37 20N 79 31W
Bedford, C., *Australia* **126 B4** 15 14 S 145 21 E
Bedford Downs, *Australia* **124 C4** 17 19 S 127 20 E
Bedfordshire □, *U.K.* **21 E7** 52 4N 0 28W
Bedi, *Chad* **109 F3** 11 6N 18 33 E
Będków, *Poland* **55 G6** 51 36N 19 44 E
Bednja →, *Croatia* **45 B13** 46 20N 16 52 E
Bednodemyanovsk, *Russia* **60 D6** 53 55N 43 15 E
Bedónia, *Italy* **44 D6** 44 30N 9 38 E
Bedourie, *Australia* **126 C2** 24 30 S 139 30 E
Bedretto, *Switz.* **33 C7** 46 31N 8 31 E
Bedum, *Neths.* **24 A6** 53 18N 6 36 E
Będzin, *Poland* **55 H6** 50 19N 19 7 E
Bee Ridge, *U.S.A.* **153 H7** 27 17N 82 29W
Beech Fork →, *U.S.A.* **157 G11** 37 46N 85 41W
Beech Grove, *U.S.A.* **157 E10** 39 44N 86 3W
Beecher, *U.S.A.* **157 C9** 41 21N 87 38W
Beechworth, *Australia* **129 D7** 36 22 S 146 43 E
Beechy, *Canada* **143 C7** 50 53N 107 24W
Beelitz, *Germany* **30 C8** 52 14N 12 58 E
Beenleigh, *Australia* **127 D5** 27 43 S 153 10 E
Be'er Menuha, *Israel* **96 D2** 30 19N 35 8 E
Be'er Sheva, *Israel* **103 D3** 31 15N 34 48 E
Beersheba = Be'er Sheva, *Israel* **103 D3** 31 15N 34 48 E
Beeskow, *Germany* **30 C10** 52 10N 14 15 E
Beeston, *U.K.* **20 E6** 52 55N 1 14W
Beetaloo, *Australia* **126 B1** 17 15 S 133 50 E
Beetzendorf, *Germany* **30 C7** 52 42N 11 6 E
Beeville, *U.S.A.* **155 L6** 28 24N 97 45W
Befale, *Dem. Rep. of the Congo* **114 B4** 0 25N 20 45 E
Befandriana, *Madag.* **117 C7** 21 55 S 44 0 E
Befotaka, *Madag.* **117 C8** 23 49 S 47 0 E
Bega, *Australia* **129 D8** 36 41 S 149 51 E
Bega, Canalul, *Romania* **52 E5** 45 37N 20 46 E
Bégard, *France* **26 D3** 48 38N 3 18W
Beğendik, *Turkey* **51 F10** 40 55N 26 34 E
Begndal, *Norway* **18 D6** 60 49N 9 46 E
Begusarai, *India* **93 G12** 25 24N 86 9 E
Behābād, *Iran* **97 C8** 32 24N 59 47 E
Behara, *Madag.* **117 C8** 24 55 S 46 20 E
Behbehān, *Iran* **97 D6** 30 30N 50 15 E
Behshahr, *Iran* **97 B7** 36 45N 53 35 E
Bei Jiang →, *China* **77 F9** 23 2N 112 58 E
Bei'an, *China* **73 B7** 48 10N 126 20 E
Beihai, *China* **76 G7** 21 28N 109 6 E
Beijing, *China* **74 E9** 39 55N 116 20 E
Beijing □, *China* **74 E9** 39 55N 116 20 E
Beilen, *Neths.* **24 B6** 52 52N 6 27 E
Beiliu, *China* **77 F8** 22 41N 110 21 E
Beilngries, *Germany* **31 F7** 49 2N 11 28 E
Beilpajah, *Australia* **128 B5** 32 54 S 143 52 E
Beilul, *Eritrea* **107 E5** 13 2N 42 20 E
Beinn na Faoghla = Benbecula, *U.K.* **22 D1** 57 26N 7 21W
Beipiao, *China* **75 D11** 41 52N 120 32 E
Beira, *Mozam.* **119 F3** 19 50 S 34 52 E
Beira, *Somali Rep.* **120 C3** 6 57N 47 19 E
Beirut = Bayrūt, *Lebanon* **103 B4** 33 53N 35 31 E
Beitaolaizhao, *China* **75 B13** 44 58N 125 58 E
Beitbridge, *Zimbabwe* **119 G3** 22 12 S 30 0 E
Beiuş, *Romania* **52 D7** 46 40N 22 21 E
Beizhen, *Liaoning, China* **75 D11** 41 38N 121 54 E
Beizhen, *Shandong, China* **75 F10** 37 20N 118 2 E
Beizhengzhen, *China* **75 B12** 44 31N 123 30 E
Beja, *Portugal* **43 G3** 38 2N 7 53W
Béja, *Tunisia* **108 A1** 36 43N 9 12 E
Beja □, *Portugal* **43 H3** 37 55N 7 55W
Bejaia, *Algeria* **111 A6** 36 42N 5 2 E
Béjar, *Spain* **42 E5** 40 23N 5 46W
Bejestān, *Iran* **97 C8** 34 30N 58 5 E
Bekabad, *Uzbekistan* **63 C4** 40 13N 69 14 E
Bekasi, *Indonesia* **84 D3** 6 14 S 106 59 E
Bekçiler, *Turkey* **49 E11** 36 56N 29 44 E
Békés, *Hungary* **52 D6** 46 47N 21 9 E
Békés □, *Hungary* **52 D6** 46 45N 21 0 E
Békéscsaba, *Hungary* **52 D6** 46 40N 21 5 E
Bekilli, *Turkey* **49 C11** 38 17N 29 27 E
Bekily, *Madag.* **117 C8** 24 13 S 45 19 E
Bekoji, *Ethiopia* **107 F4** 7 40N 39 17 E
Bekok, *Malaysia* **87 L4** 2 20N 103 7 E
Bekwai, *Ghana* **113 D4** 6 30N 1 34W
Bela, *India* **93 G10** 25 50N 82 0 E
Bela, *Pakistan* **91 D2** 26 12N 66 20 E
Bela Crkva, *Serbia, Yug.* **52 F6** 44 55N 21 27 E
Bela Palanka, *Serbia, Yug.* **50 C6** 43 13N 22 17 E
Bela Vista, *Brazil* **174 A4** 22 12 S 56 20W
Bela Vista, *Mozam.* **117 D5** 26 10 S 32 44 E
Bélâbre, *France* **28 B5** 46 34N 1 8 E
Belaga, *Malaysia* **85 B4** 2 42N 113 47 E
Belalcázar, *Spain* **43 G5** 38 35N 5 10W
Belanovica, *Serbia, Yug.* **50 B4** 44 15N 20 23 E
Belarus ■, *Europe* **58 F4** 53 30N 27 0 E
Belas, *Angola* **115 D2** 8 55 S 13 9 E
Belau = Palau ■, *Pac. Oc.* **134 G5** 7 30N 134 30 E
Belavenona, *Madag.* **117 C8** 24 50 S 47 4 E
Belawan, *Indonesia* **84 B1** 3 33N 98 32 E
Belaya, *Ethiopia* **107 E4** 11 25N 36 8 E
Belaya →, *Russia* **62 D6** 54 40N 56 0 E
Belaya Glina, *Russia* **61 G5** 46 5N 40 48 E
Belaya Kalitva, *Russia* **61 F5** 48 13N 40 50 E
Belaya Kholunitsa, *Russia* **62 B5** 58 51N 50 53 E
Belaya Tserkov = Bila Tserkva, *Ukraine* **59 H6** 49 45N 30 10 E
Belayan →, *Indonesia* **85 C5** 0 14 S 116 36 E
Belceşti, *Romania* **53 C12** 47 19N 27 7 E
Bełchatów, *Poland* **55 G6** 51 21N 19 22 E
Belcher Is., *Canada* **139 C12** 56 15N 78 45W
Belchite, *Spain* **40 D4** 41 18N 0 43W
Belden, *U.S.A.* **160 E5** 40 2N 121 17W
Belebey, *Russia* **62 D5** 54 7N 54 7 E
Belém, *Brazil* **170 B2** 1 20 S 48 30W
Belém de São Francisco, *Brazil* **170 C4** 8 46 S 38 58W
Belén, *Argentina* **174 B2** 27 40 S 67 5W
Belén, *Colombia* **168 C2** 1 26N 75 56W
Belén, *Paraguay* **174 A4** 23 30 S 57 6W
Belen, *U.S.A.* **159 J10** 34 40N 106 46W
Belene, *Bulgaria* **51 C9** 43 39N 25 10 E
Beleni, *Turkey* **100 D7** 36 31N 36 10 E
Bélesta, *France* **28 F5** 42 55N 1 56 E
Belet Uen, *Somali Rep.* **120 D3** 4 30N 45 5 E
Belev, *Russia* **58 F9** 53 50N 36 5 E
Belevi, *Turkey* **49 C9** 38 0N 27 28 E
Belfair, *U.S.A.* **160 C4** 47 27N 122 50W
Belfast, *N.Z.* **131 D7** 43 27 S 172 39 E
Belfast, *S. Africa* **117 D5** 25 42 S 30 2 E
Belfast, *U.K.* **23 B6** 54 37N 5 56W
Belfast, *Maine, U.S.A.* **141 D6** 44 26N 69 1W
Belfast, *N.Y., U.S.A.* **150 D6** 42 21N 78 7W
Belfast L., *U.K.* **23 B6** 54 40N 5 50W
Belfield, *U.S.A.* **154 B3** 46 53N 103 12W
Belfort, *France* **27 E13** 47 38N 6 50 E
Belfort, Territoire de □, *France* **27 E13** 47 40N 6 55 E
Belfry, *U.S.A.* **158 D9** 45 9N 109 1W
Belgaum, *India* **95 G2** 15 55N 74 35 E
Belgioioso, *Italy* **44 C6** 45 10N 9 19 E
Belgium ■, *Europe* **24 D4** 50 30N 5 0 E
Belgodère, *France* **29 F13** 42 35N 9 1 E
Belgorod, *Russia* **59 G9** 50 35N 36 35 E
Belgorod-Dnestrovskiy = Bilhorod-Dnistrovskyy, *Ukraine* **59 J6** 46 11N 30 23 E
Belgrade = Beograd, *Serbia, Yug.* **50 B4** 44 50N 20 37 E
Belgrade, *U.S.A.* **158 D8** 45 47N 111 11W
Belgrove, *N.Z.* **131 B7** 41 27 S 172 59 E
Belhaven, *U.S.A.* **149 H7** 35 33N 76 37W
Beli Drim →, *Europe* **50 D4** 42 6N 20 25 E
Beli Manastir, *Croatia* **52 E3** 45 45N 18 36 E
Beli Timok →, *Serbia, Yug.* **50 C6** 43 53N 22 14 E
Bélice →, *Italy* **46 E5** 37 35N 12 55 E
Belinga, *Gabon* **114 B2** 1 10N 13 2 E
Belinskiy, *Russia* **60 D6** 53 0N 43 25 E
Belinyu, *Indonesia* **84 C3** 1 35 S 105 50 E
Beliton Is. = Belitung, *Indonesia* **85 C3** 3 10 S 107 50 E
Belitung, *Indonesia* **85 C3** 3 10 S 107 50 E
Beliu, *Romania* **52 D6** 46 30N 22 0 E
Belize ■, *Cent. Amer.* **163 D7** 17 0N 88 30W
Belize City, *Belize* **163 D7** 17 25N 88 0W
Beljakovci, *Macedonia* **50 D5** 42 6N 21 59 E
Beljanica, *Serbia, Yug.* **50 B5** 44 8N 21 43 E
Belkovskiy, Ostrov, *Russia* **65 B14** 75 32N 135 44 E
Bell, *U.S.A.* **152 F7** 29 45N 82 52W
Bell →, *Canada* **140 C4** 49 48N 77 38W
Bell Bay, *Australia* **126 G4** 41 6 S 146 53 E
Bell I., *Canada* **141 B8** 50 46N 55 35W
Bell-Irving →, *Canada* **142 B3** 56 12N 129 5W
Bell Peninsula, *Canada* **139 B11** 63 50N 82 0W
Bell Ville, *Argentina* **174 C3** 32 40 S 62 40W
Bella, *Italy* **47 B8** 40 45N 15 32 E
Bella Bella, *Canada* **142 C3** 52 10N 128 10W
Bella Coola, *Canada* **142 C3** 52 25N 126 40W
Bella Flor, *Bolivia* **172 C4** 11 9 S 67 49W
Bella Unión, *Uruguay* **174 C4** 30 15 S 57 40W
Bella Vista, *Corrientes, Argentina* **174 B4** 28 33 S 59 0W
Bella Vista, *Tucuman, Argentina* **174 B2** 27 10 S 65 25W
Bellac, *France* **28 B5** 46 7N 1 3 E
Bellágio, *Italy* **44 C6** 45 59N 9 15 E
Bellaire, *U.S.A.* **150 F4** 40 1N 80 45W
Bellária, *Italy* **45 D9** 44 9N 12 28 E
Bellary, *India* **95 G3** 15 10N 76 56 E
Bellata, *Australia* **127 D4** 29 53 S 149 46 E
Belle, *U.S.A.* **156 F5** 38 17N 91 43W
Belle Fourche, *U.S.A.* **154 C3** 44 40N 103 51W
Belle Fourche →, *U.S.A.* **154 C3** 44 26N 102 18W
Belle Glade, *U.S.A.* **149 M5** 26 41N 80 40W
Belle-Île, *France* **26 E3** 47 20N 3 10W
Belle Isle, *Canada* **141 B8** 51 57N 55 25W
Belle Isle, *U.S.A.* **153 G8** 28 27N 81 21W
Belle Isle, Str. of, *Canada* **141 B8** 51 30N 56 30W
Belle Plaine, *Iowa, U.S.A.* **156 C4** 41 54N 92 17W
Belle Plaine, *Minn., U.S.A.* **154 C8** 44 37N 93 46W
Belle Rive, *U.S.A.* **157 F8** 38 14N 88 45W
Belle Yella, *Liberia* **112 D3** 7 24N 10 0W
Belledonne, *France* **29 C10** 45 20N 6 10 E
Belledune, *Canada* **141 C6** 47 55N 65 50W
Bellefontaine, *U.S.A.* **157 D13** 40 22N 83 46W
Bellefonte, *U.S.A.* **150 F7** 40 55N 77 47W
Bellegarde, *France* **27 E9** 47 59N 2 26 E
Bellegarde-en-Marche, *France* **28 C6** 45 59N 2 18 E
Bellegarde-sur-Valserine, *France* **27 F12** 46 4N 5 50 E
Bellême, *France* **26 D7** 48 22N 0 34 E
Belleoram, *Canada* **141 C8** 47 31N 55 25W
Belleview, *U.S.A.* **153 F7** 29 4N 82 3W
Belleville, *Canada* **140 D4** 44 10N 77 23W
Belleville, *France* **27 F11** 46 7N 4 45 E
Belleville, *Ill., U.S.A.* **156 F7** 38 31N 89 59W
Belleville, *Kans., U.S.A.* **154 F6** 39 50N 97 38W
Belleville, *N.Y., U.S.A.* **151 C8** 43 46N 76 10W
Belleville-sur-Vie, *France* **26 F5** 46 46N 1 25W
Bellevue, *Canada* **142 D6** 49 35N 114 22W
Bellevue, *Idaho, U.S.A.* **158 E6** 43 28N 114 16W
Bellevue, *Iowa, U.S.A.* **156 B6** 42 16N 90 26W
Bellevue, *Mich., U.S.A.* **157 B11** 42 27N 85 1W
Bellevue, *Ohio, U.S.A.* **150 E2** 41 17N 82 51W
Bellevue, *Wash., U.S.A.* **160 C4** 47 37N 122 12W
Belley, *France* **29 C9** 45 46N 5 41 E
Bellflower, *U.S.A.* **156 F5** 39 0N 91 21W
Bellin = Kangirsuk, *Canada* **139 C13** 60 0N 70 0W
Bellinge, *Denmark* **17 J4** 55 20N 10 20 E
Bellingen, *Australia* **129 A10** 30 25 S 152 50 E
Bellingham, *U.S.A.* **160 B4** 48 46N 122 29W
Bellingshausen Sea, *Antarctica* **7 C17** 66 0 S 80 0W
Bellinzona, *Switz.* **33 D8** 46 11N 9 1 E
Bello, *Colombia* **168 B2** 6 20N 75 33W
Bellona, *Solomon Is.* **133 N10** 11 17 S 159 47 E
Bellows Falls, *U.S.A.* **151 C12** 43 8N 72 27W
Bellpat, *Pakistan* **92 E3** 29 0N 68 5 E
Bellpuig d'Urgell, *Spain* **40 D6** 41 37N 1 1 E
Belluno, *Italy* **45 B9** 46 9N 12 13 E
Bellville, *Ga., U.S.A.* **152 C8** 32 9N 81 59W
Bellville, *Tex., U.S.A.* **155 L6** 29 57N 96 15W
Bellwood, *U.S.A.* **150 F6** 40 36N 78 20W
Bélmez, *Spain* **43 G5** 38 17N 5 17W
Belmond, *U.S.A.* **156 B3** 42 51N 93 37W
Belmont, *Australia* **129 B9** 33 4 S 151 42 E
Belmont, *Canada* **150 D3** 42 53N 81 5W
Belmont, *S. Africa* **116 D3** 29 28 S 24 22 E
Belmont, *U.S.A.* **150 D6** 42 14N 78 2W
Belmonte, *Brazil* **171 E4** 16 0 S 39 0W
Belmonte, *Portugal* **42 E3** 40 21N 7 20W
Belmonte, *Spain* **41 F2** 39 34N 2 43W
Belmopan, *Belize* **163 D7** 17 18N 88 30W
Belmore, *Australia* **128 B4** 33 34 S 141 13 E
Belmullet, *Ireland* **23 B2** 54 14N 9 58W
Belo Horizonte, *Brazil* **171 E3** 19 55 S 43 56W
Belo Jardim, *Brazil* **170 C4** 8 20 S 36 26W
Belo-sur-Mer, *Madag.* **117 C7** 20 42 S 44 0 E
Belo-Tsiribihina, *Madag.* **117 B7** 19 40 S 44 30 E
Belogorsk = Bilohirsk, *Ukraine* **59 K8** 45 3N 34 35 E
Belogorsk, *Russia* **65 D13** 51 0N 128 20 E
Belogradchik, *Bulgaria* **50 C6** 43 53N 22 42 E
Belogradets, *Bulgaria* **51 C11** 43 22N 27 18 E
Beloha, *Madag.* **117 D8** 25 10 S 45 3 E
Beloit, *Kans., U.S.A.* **154 F5** 39 28N 98 6W
Beloit, *Wis., U.S.A.* **156 B7** 42 31N 89 2W
Belokorovichi, *Ukraine* **59 G5** 51 7N 28 2 E
Belomorsk, *Russia* **56 B5** 64 35N 34 54 E
Belonia, *India* **90 D3** 23 15N 91 30 E
Belopolye = Bilopillya, *Ukraine* **59 G8** 51 14N 34 20 E
Belorechensk, *Russia* **61 H4** 44 46N 39 52 E
Beloretsk, *Russia* **62 E7** 53 58N 58 24 E
Belorussia = Belarus ■, *Europe* **58 F4** 53 30N 27 0 E
Beloslav, *Bulgaria* **51 C11** 43 11N 27 42 E
Belovo, *Bulgaria* **51 D8** 42 13N 24 1 E
Belovo, *Russia* **64 D9** 54 30N 86 0 E
Belovodsk, *Ukraine* **59 H10** 49 13N 39 36 E
Beloyarskiy, *Russia* **62 C8** 56 45N 61 24 E
Beloye, Ozero, *Russia* **58 B9** 60 10N 37 35 E
Beloye More, *Russia* **56 A6** 66 30N 38 0 E
Belozem, *Bulgaria* **51 D9** 42 12N 25 2 E
Belozersk, *Russia* **58 B9** 60 1N 37 45 E
Belpasso, *Italy* **47 E7** 37 35N 14 58 E
Beltana, *Australia* **128 A3** 30 48 S 138 25 E
Belterra, *Brazil* **169 D7** 2 45 S 55 0W
Beltinci, *Slovenia* **45 B13** 46 37N 16 20 E
Belton, *S.C., U.S.A.* **149 H4** 34 31N 82 30W
Belton, *Tex., U.S.A.* **155 K6** 31 3N 97 28W
Belton Res., *U.S.A.* **155 K6** 31 8N 97 32W
Beltsy = Bălţi, *Moldova* **53 C12** 47 48N 27 58 E
Belturbet, *Ireland* **23 B4** 54 6N 7 26W
Belukha, *Russia* **64 E9** 49 50N 86 50 E
Beluša, *Slovak Rep.* **35 B11** 49 5N 18 17 E
Belušić, *Serbia, Yug.* **50 C5** 43 50N 21 10 E
Belvedere Maríttimo, *Italy* **47 C8** 39 37N 15 52 E
Belvès, *France* **28 D5** 44 46N 1 0 E
Belvidere, *Ill., U.S.A.* **154 D10** 42 15N 88 50W
Belvidere, *N.J., U.S.A.* **151 F9** 40 50N 75 5W
Belvis de la Jara, *Spain* **42 F6** 39 45N 4 57W
Belyando →, *Australia* **126 C4** 21 38 S 146 50 E
Belyy, *Russia* **58 E7** 55 49N 33 5 E
Belyy, Ostrov, *Russia* **64 B8** 73 30N 71 0 E
Belyy Yar, *Russia* **64 D9** 58 26N 84 39 E
Belyye Vody, *Kazakstan* **63 B4** 42 25N 69 50 E
Bełżec, *Poland* **55 H10** 50 23N 23 26 E
Belzig, *Germany* **30 C8** 52 8N 12 35 E
Belzoni, *U.S.A.* **155 J9** 33 11N 90 29W
Bełżyce, *Poland* **55 G9** 51 11N 22 17 E
Bemaraha, Lembalemban' i, *Madag.* **117 B7** 18 40 S 44 45 E
Bemarivo, *Madag.* **117 C7** 21 45 S 44 45 E
Bemarivo →, *Madag.* **117 B8** 15 27 S 47 40 E
Bemavo, *Madag.* **117 C8** 21 33 S 45 25 E
Bembéréke, *Benin* **113 C5** 10 11N 2 43 E
Bembesi, *Zimbabwe* **119 G2** 20 0 S 28 58 E
Bembesi →, *Zimbabwe* **119 F2** 18 57 S 27 47 E
Bembézar →, *Spain* **43 H5** 37 45N 5 13W
Bembibre, *Spain* **42 C4** 42 37N 6 25W
Bement, *U.S.A.* **157 E8** 39 55N 88 34W
Bemidji, *U.S.A.* **154 B7** 47 28N 94 53W
Ben, *Iran* **97 C6** 32 32N 50 45 E
Ben Bullen, *Australia* **129 B9** 33 12 S 150 2 E
Ben Cruachan, *U.K.* **22 E3** 56 26N 5 8W
Ben Dearg, *U.K.* **22 D4** 57 47N 4 56W
Ben Gardane, *Tunisia* **108 B2** 33 11N 11 11 E
Ben Hope, *U.K.* **22 C4** 58 25N 4 36W
Ben Lawers, *U.K.* **22 E4** 56 32N 4 14W
Ben Lomond, *N.S.W., Australia* **127 E5** 30 1 S 151 43 E
Ben Lomond, *Tas., Australia* **126 G4** 41 38 S 147 42 E
Ben Lomond, *U.K.* **22 E4** 56 11N 4 38W
Ben Luc, *Vietnam* **87 G6** 10 39N 106 29 E
Ben Macdhui, *U.K.* **22 D5** 57 4N 3 40W
Ben Mhor, *U.K.* **22 D1** 57 15N 7 18W
Ben More, *Arg. & Bute, U.K.* **22 E2** 56 26N 6 1W
Ben More, *Stirl., U.K.* **22 E4** 56 23N 4 32W
Ben More Assynt, *U.K.* **22 C4** 58 8N 4 52W
Ben Nevis, *U.K.* **22 E3** 56 48N 5 1W
Ben Ohau Ra., *N.Z.* **131 E5** 44 1 S 170 4 E
Ben Quang, *Vietnam* **86 D6** 17 3N 106 55 E
Ben Slimane, *Morocco* **110 B3** 33 38N 7 7W
Ben Vorlich, *U.K.* **22 E4** 56 21N 4 14W
Ben Wyvis, *U.K.* **22 D4** 57 40N 4 35W
Bena, *Nigeria* **113 C6** 11 20N 5 50 E
Bena Dibele, *Dem. Rep. of the Congo* **115 C4** 4 4 S 22 50 E
Bena-Leka, *Dem. Rep. of the Congo* **115 D4** 5 8 S 22 10 E
Bena-Tshadi, *Dem. Rep. of the Congo* **115 C4** 4 40 S 22 49 E
Benāb, *Iran* **101 D12** 37 20N 46 4 E
Benadir, *Somali Rep.* **120 D2** 1 30N 44 30 E
Benagerie, *Australia* **128 A4** 31 25 S 140 22 E
Benahmed, *Morocco* **110 B3** 33 4N 7 9W
Benalla, *Australia* **129 D7** 36 30 S 146 0 E
Benalmádena, *Spain* **43 J6** 36 36N 4 34W
Benambra, Mt., *Australia* **129 D7** 36 31 S 147 34 E
Benares = Varanasi, *India* **93 G10** 25 22N 83 0 E
Bénat, C., *France* **29 E10** 43 5N 6 22 E
Benavente, *Portugal* **43 G2** 38 59N 8 49W
Benavente, *Spain* **42 C5** 42 2N 5 43W
Benavides, *U.S.A.* **155 M5** 27 36N 98 25W
Benavides de Órbigo, *Spain* **42 C5** 42 30N 5 54W
Benbecula, *U.K.* **22 D1** 57 26N 7 21W
Benbonyathe, *Australia* **128 A3** 30 25 S 139 11 E
Bencubbin, *Australia* **125 F2** 30 48 S 117 52 E
Bend, *U.S.A.* **158 D3** 44 4N 121 19W
Bendela, *Dem. Rep. of the Congo* **114 C3** 3 18 S 17 36 E
Bender Beila, *Somali Rep.* **120 C4** 9 30N 50 48 E
Bender Merchagno, *Somali Rep.* **120 B4** 11 41N 50 34 E
Bendering, *Australia* **125 F2** 32 23 S 118 18 E
Bendery = Tighina, *Moldova* **53 D14** 46 50N 29 30 E
Bendigo, *Australia* **128 D6** 36 40 S 144 15 E
Bendorf, *Germany* **30 E3** 50 25N 7 35 E
Benē Beraq, *Israel* **103 C3** 32 6N 34 51 E
Beneditinos, *Brazil* **170 C3** 5 27 S 42 22W
Benedito Leite, *Brazil* **170 C3** 7 13 S 44 34W
Bénéna, *Mali* **112 C4** 13 9N 4 17W
Benenitra, *Madag.* **117 C8** 23 27 S 45 5 E
Benešov, *Czech Rep.* **34 B7** 49 46N 14 41 E
Benevento, *Italy* **47 A7** 41 8N 14 45 E
Benevolence, *U.S.A.* **152 D5** 31 53N 84 44W
Benfeld, *France* **27 D14** 48 22N 7 34 E
Benga, *Mozam.* **119 F3** 16 11 S 33 40 E
Bengal, Bay of, *Ind. Oc.* **66 H12** 15 0N 90 0 E

Blairsden 191

Big Lake, *Alaska, U.S.A.* **144 C10** 67 30N 149 27W
Big Lake, *Tex., U.S.A.* **155 K4** 31 12N 101 28W
Big Moose, *U.S.A.* **151 C10** 43 49N 74 58W
Big Muddy →, *U.S.A.* **156 G8** 38 0N 89 0W
Big Muddy Cr. →, *U.S.A.* **154 A2** 48 8N 104 36W
Big Pine, *Calif., U.S.A.* **160 H8** 37 10N 118 17W
Big Pine, *Fla., U.S.A.* **153 L8** 24 40N 81 21W
Big Piney, *U.S.A.* **158 E8** 42 32N 110 7W
Big Quill L., *Canada* **143 C8** 51 55N 104 50W
Big Rapids, *U.S.A.* **148 D3** 43 42N 85 29W
Big River, *Canada* **143 C7** 53 50N 107 0W
Big Run, *U.S.A.* **150 F6** 40 57N 78 55W
Big Sable Pt., *U.S.A.* **148 C2** 44 3N 86 1W
Big Sand L., *Canada* **143 B9** 57 45N 99 45W
Big Sandy, *U.S.A.* **158 B8** 48 11N 110 7W
Big Sandy Cr. →, *U.S.A.* **154 F3** 38 7N 102 29W
Big Satilla →, *U.S.A.* **152 D7** 31 27N 82 3W
Big Sioux →, *U.S.A.* **154 D6** 42 29N 96 27W
Big Spring, *U.S.A.* **155 J4** 32 15N 101 28W
Big Springs, *U.S.A.* **154 E3** 41 4N 102 5W
Big Stone City, *U.S.A.* **154 C6** 45 18N 96 28W
Big Stone Gap, *U.S.A.* **149 G4** 36 52N 82 47W
Big Stone L., *U.S.A.* **154 C6** 45 30N 96 35W
Big Sur, *U.S.A.* **160 J5** 36 15N 121 48W
Big Timber, *U.S.A.* **158 D9** 45 50N 109 57W
Big Trout L., *Canada* **140 B2** 53 40N 90 0W
Biğa, *Turkey* **51 F11** 40 13N 27 14 E
Biga →, *Turkey* **51 F11** 40 20N 27 14 E
Bigadiç, *Turkey* **49 B10** 39 22N 28 7 E
Biganos, *France* **28 D3** 44 39N 0 59W
Bigfork, *U.S.A.* **158 B6** 48 4N 114 4W
Biggar, *Canada* **143 C7** 52 4N 108 0W
Biggar, *U.K.* **22 F5** 55 38N 3 32W
Bigge I., *Australia* **124 B4** 14 35 S 125 10 E
Biggenden, *Australia* **127 D5** 25 31 S 152 4 E
Biggleswade, *U.K.* **21 E7** 52 5N 0 14W
Biggs, *U.S.A.* **160 F5** 39 25N 121 43W
Bighorn, *U.S.A.* **158 C10** 46 10N 107 27W
Bighorn →, *U.S.A.* **158 C10** 46 10N 107 28W
Bighorn Mts., *U.S.A.* **158 D10** 44 30N 107 30W
Bignona, *Senegal* **112 C1** 12 52N 16 14W
Bigorre, *France* **28 E4** 43 10N 0 5 E
Bigstone L., *Canada* **143 C9** 53 42N 95 44W
Biguglia, Étang de, *France* **29 F13** 42 36N 9 29 E
Bigwa, *Tanzania* **118 D4** 7 10 S 39 10 E
Bihać, *Bos.-H.* **45 D12** 44 49N 15 57 E
Bihar, *India* **93 G11** 25 5N 85 40 E
Bihar □, *India* **93 G12** 25 0N 86 0 E
Biharamulo, *Tanzania* **118 C3** 2 25 S 31 25 E
Biharamulo □, *Tanzania* **118 C3** 2 30 S 31 20 E
Biharkeresztes, *Hungary* **52 C6** 47 8N 21 44 E
Bihor □, *Romania* **52 D7** 47 0N 22 10 E
Bihor, Munţii, *Romania* **52 D7** 46 29N 22 47 E
Bijagós, Arquipélago dos, *Guinea-Biss.* **112 C1** 11 15N 16 10W
Bijaipur, *India* **92 F7** 26 2N 77 20 E
Bijapur, *Karnataka, India* **94 F2** 16 50N 75 55 E
Bijapur, *Mad. P., India* **94 E5** 18 50N 80 50 E
Bījār, *Iran* **101 E12** 35 52N 47 35 E
Bijeljina, *Bos.-H.* **52 F4** 44 46N 19 14 E
Bijelo Polje, *Montenegro, Yug.* **50 C3** 43 1N 19 45 E
Bijie, *China* **76 D5** 27 20N 105 16 E
Bijni, *India* **90 B3** 26 30N 90 40 E
Bijnor, *India* **92 E8** 29 27N 78 11 E
Bikaner, *India* **92 E5** 28 2N 73 18 E
Bikapur, *India* **93 F10** 26 30N 82 7 E
Bikeqi, *China* **74 D6** 40 43N 111 20 E
Bikfayyā, *Lebanon* **103 B4** 33 55N 35 41 E
Bikin, *Russia* **65 E14** 46 50N 134 20 E
Bikin →, *Russia* **68 A7** 46 51N 134 2 E
Bikini Atoll, *Pac. Oc.* **134 F8** 12 0N 167 30 E
Bikoro, *Dem. Rep. of the Congo* **114 C3** 0 48 S 18 15 E
Bikoué, *Cameroon* **113 E7** 3 55N 11 50 E
Bila Tserkva, *Ukraine* **59 H6** 49 45N 30 10 E
Bilara, *India* **92 F5** 26 14N 73 53 E
Bilaspara, *India* **90 B3** 26 13N 90 14 E
Bilaspur, *Mad. P., India* **93 H10** 22 2N 82 15 E
Bilaspur, *Punjab, India* **92 D7** 31 19N 76 50 E
Biläsuvar, *Azerbaijan* **101 C13** 39 27N 48 32 E
Bilauk Taungdan, *Thailand* **86 F2** 13 0N 99 0 E
Bilbao, *Spain* **40 B2** 43 16N 2 56W
Bilbeis, *Egypt* **106 H7** 30 25N 31 34 E
Bilbo = Bilbao, *Spain* **40 B2** 43 16N 2 56W
Bilbor, *Romania* **53 C10** 47 6N 25 30 E
Bilciureşti, *Romania* **53 F10** 44 44N 25 48 E
Bíldudalur, *Iceland* **11 B3** 65 41N 23 36W
Bílé Karpaty, *Europe* **35 B11** 49 5N 18 0 E
Bileća, *Bos.-H.* **50 D2** 42 53N 18 27 E
Bilecik, *Turkey* **100 B4** 40 5N 30 5 E
Biłgoraj, *Poland* **55 H9** 50 33N 22 42 E
Bilhorod-Dnistrovskyy, *Ukraine* **59 J6** 46 11N 30 23 E
Bilibino, *Russia* **65 C17** 68 3N 166 20 E
Bilibiza, *Mozam.* **119 E5** 12 30 S 40 20 E
Bilin, *Burma* **90 G6** 17 14N 97 15 E
Biliran I., *Phil.* **81 F5** 11 35N 124 28 E
Bilishti, *Albania* **50 F5** 40 37N 21 2 E
Bill, *U.S.A.* **154 D2** 43 14N 105 16W
Billabalong, *Australia* **125 E2** 27 25 S 115 49 E
Billdal, *Sweden* **17 G5** 57 35N 11 57 E
Billiluna, *Australia* **124 C4** 19 37 S 127 41 E
Billings, *U.S.A.* **158 D9** 45 47N 108 30W
Billiton Is. = Belitung, *Indonesia* **85 C3** 3 10 S 107 50 E
Billsta, *Sweden* **16 A12** 63 20N 18 28 E
Billund, *Denmark* **17 J3** 55 44N 9 6 E
Bilma, *Niger* **109 E2** 18 50N 13 30 E
Bilo Gora, *Croatia* **52 E2** 45 53N 17 15 E
Biloela, *Australia* **126 C5** 24 24 S 150 31 E
Bilohirsk, *Ukraine* **59 K8** 45 3N 34 35 E
Biloku, *Guyana* **169 C6** 1 50N 58 25W
Bilopillya, *Ukraine* **59 G8** 51 14N 34 20 E
Biloxi, *U.S.A.* **155 K10** 30 24N 88 53W
Bilpa Morea Claypan, *Australia* **126 D3** 25 0 S 140 0 E
Biltine, *Chad* **109 F4** 14 40N 20 50 E
Bilugyun, *Burma* **90 G6** 16 24N 97 32 E
Bilyana, *Australia* **126 B4** 18 5 S 145 50 E
Bilyarsk, *Russia* **60 C10** 54 58N 50 22 E
Bima, *Indonesia* **85 D5** 8 22 S 118 49 E
Bimban, *Egypt* **106 C3** 24 24N 32 54 E
Bimberi Pk., *Australia* **129 C8** 35 44 S 148 51 E
Bimbila, *Ghana* **113 D5** 8 54N 0 5 E
Bimbo, *C.A.R.* **114 B3** 4 15N 18 33 E
Bimini Is., *Bahamas* **164 A4** 25 42N 79 25W
Bin Xian, *Heilongjiang, China* **75 B14** 45 42N 127 32 E
Bin Xian, *Shaanxi, China* **74 G5** 35 2N 108 4 E
Bina-Etawah, *India* **92 G8** 24 13N 78 14 E
Bināb, *Iran* **97 B6** 36 35N 48 41 E
Binaiya, *Indonesia* **83 B3** 3 11 S 129 26 E
Binalbagan, *Phil.* **81 F4** 10 12N 122 50 E
Binalong, *Australia* **129 C8** 34 40 S 148 39 E
Bīnālūd, Kūh-e, *Iran* **97 B8** 36 30N 58 30 E
Binatang = Bintangor, *Malaysia* **85 B4** 2 10N 111 40 E
Binbee, *Australia* **126 C4** 20 19 S 147 56 E
Binche, *Belgium* **24 D4** 50 26N 4 10 E
Binchuan, *China* **76 E3** 25 42N 100 38 E
Binda, *Australia* **127 D4** 27 52 S 147 21 E
Binda, *Dem. Rep. of the Congo* **115 D2** 5 52 S 13 14 E
Bindle, *Australia* **127 D4** 27 40 S 148 45 E
Bindoy, *Phil.* **81 G4** 9 48N 123 5 E
Bindslev, *Denmark* **17 G4** 57 33N 10 11 E
Bindura, *Zimbabwe* **119 F3** 17 18 S 31 18 E
Binefar, *Spain* **40 D5** 41 51N 0 18 E
Bingara, *N.S.W., Australia* **127 D5** 29 52 S 150 36 E
Bingara, *Queens., Australia* **127 D3** 28 10 S 144 37 E
Bingen, *Germany* **31 F3** 49 57N 7 55 E
Bingerville, *Ivory C.* **112 D4** 5 18N 3 49W
Bingham, *U.S.A.* **141 C6** 45 3N 69 53W
Bingham Canyon, *U.S.A.* **158 F7** 40 32N 112 9W
Binghamton, *U.S.A.* **151 D9** 42 6N 75 55W
Bingöl, *Turkey* **101 C9** 38 53N 40 29 E
Bingöl Dağları, *Turkey* **101 C9** 39 16N 41 9 E
Bingsjö, *Sweden* **16 C9** 61 1N 15 39 E
Binh Dinh = An Nhon, *Vietnam* **86 F7** 13 55N 109 7 E
Binh Khe, *Vietnam* **86 F7** 13 57N 108 51 E
Binh Son, *Vietnam* **86 E7** 15 20N 108 40 E
Binhai, *China* **75 G10** 34 2N 119 49 E
Binic, *France* **26 D4** 48 46N 2 50W
Binisatua, *Spain* **39 B11** 39 50N 4 11 E
Binjai, *Indonesia* **84 B1** 3 20N 98 30 E
Binnaway, *Australia* **129 A8** 31 28 S 149 24 E
Binongko, *Indonesia* **82 C2** 5 55 S 123 55 E
Binscarth, *Canada* **143 C8** 50 37N 101 17W
Bintan, *Indonesia* **84 B2** 1 0N 104 0 E
Bintangor, *Malaysia* **85 B4** 2 10N 111 40 E
Bintuni, *Indonesia* **83 B4** 2 7 S 133 32 E
Binyang, *China* **76 F7** 23 12N 108 47 E
Binz, *Germany* **30 A9** 54 24N 13 35 E
Binza, *Dem. Rep. of the Congo* **115 C3** 4 21 S 15 14 E
Binzert = Bizerte, *Tunisia* **108 A1** 37 15N 9 50 E
Bío Bío □, *Chile* **174 D1** 37 35 S 72 0W
Biograd na Moru, *Croatia* **45 E12** 43 56N 15 29 E
Bioko, *Eq. Guin.* **113 E6** 3 30N 8 40 E
Biokovo, *Croatia* **45 E14** 43 23N 17 0 E
Biougra, *Morocco* **110 B3** 30 15N 9 14W
Bir, *India* **94 E2** 19 4N 75 46 E
Bir, Ras, *Djibouti* **107 E5** 12 0N 43 20 E
Bîr Abu Hashim, *Egypt* **106 C3** 23 42N 34 6 E
Bîr Abu M'nqar, *Egypt* **106 B2** 26 33N 27 33 E
Bîr Abu Muḥammad, *Egypt* **103 F3** 29 44N 34 14 E
Bi'r ad Dabbāghāt, *Jordan* **103 E4** 30 26N 35 32 E
Bîr Adal Deib, *Sudan* **106 C4** 22 35N 36 10 E
Bi'r al Butayyihāt, *Jordan* **103 F4** 29 47N 35 20 E
Bi'r al Mārī, *Jordan* **103 E4** 30 4N 35 33 E
Bi'r al Qattār, *Jordan* **103 F4** 29 47N 35 32 E
Bir 'Ali, *Yemen* **99 D5** 14 1N 48 20 E
Bir Aouine, *Tunisia* **108 B1** 32 25N 9 18 E
Bîr 'Asal, *Egypt* **106 B3** 25 55N 34 20 E
Bir Autrun, *Sudan* **106 D2** 18 15N 26 40 E
Bîr Beiḍa, *Egypt* **103 E3** 30 25N 34 29 E
Bi'r Dhu'fān, *Libya* **108 B2** 31 59N 14 32 E
Bîr Diqnash, *Egypt* **106 A2** 31 3N 25 23 E
Bir el Abbes, *Algeria* **110 C3** 26 7N 6 9W
Bîr el 'Abd, *Egypt* **103 D2** 31 2N 33 0 E
Bir el Ater, *Algeria* **111 B6** 34 46N 8 3 E
Bîr el Basur, *Egypt* **106 B2** 29 51N 25 49 E
Bîr el Biarât, *Egypt* **103 F3** 29 30N 34 43 E
Bîr el Duweidar, *Egypt* **103 E1** 30 56N 32 32 E
Bîr el Garârât, *Egypt* **103 D2** 31 3N 33 34 E
Bîr el Gellaz, *Egypt* **106 A2** 30 50N 26 40 E
Bîr el Heisi, *Egypt* **103 F3** 29 22N 34 36 E
Bîr el Jafir, *Egypt* **103 E1** 30 50N 32 41 E
Bîr el Mâlḥi, *Egypt* **103 E2** 30 38N 33 19 E
Bîr el Shaqqa, *Egypt* **106 A2** 30 54N 25 1 E
Bîr el Thamâda, *Egypt* **103 E2** 30 12N 33 27 E
Bîr Fuad, *Egypt* **106 A2** 30 35N 26 28 E
Bîr Gara, *Chad* **109 F3** 13 11N 15 58 E
Bîr Gebeil Ḥiṣn, *Egypt* **103 E2** 30 2N 33 18 E
Bi'r Ghadīr, *Syria* **103 A6** 34 6N 37 3 E
Bîr Haimur, *Egypt* **106 C3** 22 45N 33 40 E
Bîr Ḥasana, *Egypt* **103 E2** 30 29N 33 46 E
Bi'r Īdimah, *Si. Arabia* **98 C4** 18 31N 44 12 E
Bi'r Jadīd, *Iraq* **96 C4** 34 1N 42 54 E
Bir Jdid, *Morocco* **110 B3** 33 26N 8 0W
Bîr Kanayis, *Egypt* **106 C3** 24 59N 33 15 E
Bîr Kaseiba, *Egypt* **103 E2** 31 0N 33 17 E
Bîr Kerawein, *Egypt* **106 B2** 27 10N 28 25 E
Bîr Lahfân, *Egypt* **103 E2** 31 0N 33 51 E
Bir Lahrache, *Algeria* **111 B6** 32 1N 8 12 E
Bîr Madkûr, *Egypt* **103 E1** 30 44N 32 33 E
Bîr Maql, *Egypt* **106 C3** 23 7N 33 40 E
Bîr Misaha, *Egypt* **106 C2** 22 13N 27 59 E
Bir Mogreïn, *Mauritania* **110 C2** 25 10N 11 25W
Bîr Murr, *Egypt* **106 C3** 23 28N 30 10 E
Bi'r Muṭribah, *Kuwait* **96 D5** 29 54N 47 17 E
Bîr Nakheila, *Egypt* **106 C3** 24 1N 30 50 E
Bîr Qaṭia, *Egypt* **103 E1** 30 58N 32 45 E
Bîr Qatrani, *Egypt* **106 A2** 30 55N 26 10 E
Bîr Ranga, *Egypt* **106 C4** 24 25N 35 15 E
Bîr Sahara, *Egypt* **106 C2** 22 54N 28 40 E
Bîr Seiyâla, *Egypt* **106 B3** 26 10N 33 50 E
Bir Semguine, *Morocco* **110 B3** 30 1N 5 39W
Bîr Shalatein, *Egypt* **106 C4** 23 5N 35 25 E
Bîr Shebb, *Egypt* **106 C2** 22 25N 29 40 E
Bîr Shût, *Egypt* **106 C4** 23 50N 35 15 E
Bi'r Tamis, *Yemen* **99 C5** 16 45N 48 48 E
Bîr Terfawi, *Egypt* **106 C2** 22 57N 28 55 E
Bîr Umm Qubûr, *Egypt* **106 C3** 24 35N 34 2 E
Bîr Ungât, *Egypt* **106 C3** 22 8N 33 48 E
Bîr Za'farâna, *Egypt* **106 J8** 29 10N 32 40 E
Bîr Zāmūs, *Libya* **108 D3** 24 16N 15 6 E
Bîr Zeidûn, *Egypt* **106 B3** 25 45N 33 40 E
Bira, *Indonesia* **83 B4** 2 3 S 132 2 E
Biramféro, *Guinea* **112 C3** 11 40N 9 10W
Birao, *C.A.R.* **114 A4** 10 20N 22 47 E
Biratnagar, *Nepal* **93 F12** 26 27N 87 17 E
Birawa, *Dem. Rep. of the Congo* **118 C2** 2 20 S 28 48 E
Birch Hills, *Canada* **143 C7** 52 59N 105 25W
Birch I., *Canada* **143 C9** 52 26N 99 54W
Birch L., *N.W.T., Canada* **142 A5** 62 4N 116 33W
Birch L., *Ont., Canada* **140 B1** 51 23N 92 18W
Birch L., *U.S.A.* **140 C1** 47 45N 91 51W
Birch Mts., *Canada* **142 B6** 57 30N 113 10W
Birch River, *Canada* **143 C8** 52 24N 101 6W
Birchip, *Australia* **128 C5** 35 56 S 142 55 E
Birchiş, *Romania* **52 E7** 45 58N 22 9 E
Birchwood, *N.Z.* **131 F2** 45 55 S 167 53 E
Bird, *Canada* **143 B10** 56 30N 94 13W
Bird City, *U.S.A.* **154 F4** 39 45N 101 32W
Bird I. = Aves, I. de, *W. Indies* **165 C7** 15 45N 63 55W
Birds, *U.S.A.* **157 F9** 38 50N 87 40W
Birdseye, *U.S.A.* **157 F10** 38 19N 86 42W
Birdsville, *Australia* **126 D2** 25 51 S 139 20 E
Birdum, *Australia* **124 C5** 15 39 S 133 13 E
Birecik, *Turkey* **101 D8** 37 2N 38 0 E
Birein, *Israel* **103 E3** 30 50N 34 28 E
Bireuen, *Indonesia* **84 A1** 5 14N 96 39 E
Biri, *Norway* **18 D7** 60 58N 10 35 E
Birifo, *Gambia* **112 C2** 13 30N 14 0W
Birigui, *Brazil* **175 A5** 21 18 S 50 16W
Birini, *C.A.R.* **114 A4** 7 51N 22 24 E
Birkenfeld, *Germany* **31 F3** 49 38N 7 9 E
Birkenhead, *N.Z.* **130 C3** 36 49 S 174 46 E
Birkenhead, *U.K.* **20 D4** 53 23N 3 2W
Birkerød, *Denmark* **17 J6** 55 50N 12 25 E
Birket Qârûn, *Egypt* **106 J7** 29 30N 30 40 E
Birkfeld, *Austria* **34 D8** 47 21N 15 45 E
Birkhadem, *Algeria* **111 A5** 36 43N 3 3 E
Bîrlad = Bârlad, *Romania* **53 D12** 46 15N 27 38 E
Birlik, *Kazakstan* **63 A6** 44 5N 73 31 E
Birmingham, *U.K.* **21 E6** 52 29N 1 52W
Birmingham, *Ala., U.S.A.* **149 J2** 33 31N 86 48W
Birmingham, *Iowa, U.S.A.* **156 D5** 40 53N 91 57W
Birmitrapur, *India* **94 C7** 22 24N 84 46 E
Birni Ngaouré, *Niger* **113 C5** 13 5N 2 51 E
Birni Nkonni, *Niger* **113 C6** 13 55N 5 15 E
Birnin Gwari, *Nigeria* **113 C6** 11 0N 6 45 E
Birnin Kebbi, *Nigeria* **113 C5** 12 32N 4 12 E
Birnin Kudu, *Nigeria* **113 C6** 11 30N 9 29 E
Birobidzhan, *Russia* **65 E14** 48 50N 132 50 E
Birougou, Mts., *Gabon* **114 C2** 1 51 S 12 20 E
Birr, *Ireland* **23 C4** 53 6N 7 54W
Birrie →, *Australia* **127 D4** 29 43 S 146 37 E
Birs →, *Switz.* **32 B5** 47 24N 7 32 E
Birsilpur, *India* **92 E5** 28 11N 72 15 E
Birsk, *Russia* **62 D5** 55 25N 55 30 E
Birštonas, *Lithuania* **54 D11** 54 37N 24 2 E
Birtle, *Canada* **143 C8** 50 30N 101 5W
Biryuchiy, *Ukraine* **59 J8** 46 10N 35 0 E
Biržai, *Lithuania* **15 H21** 56 11N 24 45 E
Birżebbugga, *Malta* **38 D2** 35 49N 14 32 E
Bisa, *Indonesia* **82 B3** 1 15 S 127 28 E
Bisáccia, *Italy* **47 A8** 41 1N 15 22 E
Bisacquino, *Italy* **46 E6** 37 42N 13 15 E
Bisai, *Japan* **71 B8** 35 16N 136 44 E
Bisalpur, *India* **93 E8** 28 14N 79 48 E
Bisbee, *U.S.A.* **159 L9** 31 27N 109 55W
Biscarosse, *France* **28 D2** 44 22N 1 20W
Biscarrosse et de Parentis, Étang de, *France* **28 D2** 44 21N 1 10W
Biscay, B. of, *Atl. Oc.* **8 D8** 45 0N 2 0W
Biscayne B., *U.S.A.* **149 N5** 25 40N 80 12W
Biscayne National Park, *U.S.A.* **153 K9** 25 25N 80 12W
Biscéglie, *Italy* **47 A9** 41 14N 16 30 E
Bischheim, *France* **27 D14** 48 37N 7 46 E
Bischofshofen, *Austria* **34 D6** 47 26N 13 14 E
Bischofswerda, *Germany* **30 D10** 51 7N 14 10 E
Bischofszell, *Switz.* **33 B8** 47 29N 9 15 E
Bischwiller, *France* **27 D14** 48 46N 7 50 E
Biscoe Bay, *Antarctica* **7 D13** 77 0 S 152 0W
Biscoe Is., *Antarctica* **7 C17** 66 0 S 67 0W
Biscostasing, *Canada* **140 C3** 47 18N 82 9W
Biscucuy, *Venezuela* **168 B4** 9 22N 69 59W
Biševo, *Croatia* **45 F13** 42 57N 16 3 E
Bisha, *Eritrea* **107 D4** 15 30N 37 31 E
Bishah, W. →, *Si. Arabia* **98 B3** 21 24N 43 26 E
Bishan, *China* **76 C6** 29 33N 106 12 E
Bishkek, *Kyrgyzstan* **63 B7** 42 54N 74 46 E
Bishnupur, *India* **93 H12** 23 8N 87 20 E
Bisho, *S. Africa* **117 E4** 32 50 S 27 23 E
Bishop, *Calif., U.S.A.* **160 H8** 37 22N 118 24W
Bishop, *Ga., U.S.A.* **152 B6** 33 49N 83 26W
Bishop, *Tex., U.S.A.* **155 M6** 27 35N 97 48W
Bishop Auckland, *U.K.* **20 C6** 54 39N 1 40W
Bishop's Falls, *Canada* **141 C8** 49 2N 55 30W
Bishop's Stortford, *U.K.* **21 F8** 51 52N 0 10 E
Bisignano, *Italy* **47 C9** 39 31N 16 17 E
Bisina, L., *Uganda* **118 B3** 1 38N 33 56 E
Biskra, *Algeria* **111 B6** 34 50N 5 44 E
Biskupiec, *Poland* **54 E7** 53 53N 20 58 E
Bismarck, *Mo., U.S.A.* **156 G6** 37 46N 90 38W
Bismarck, *N. Dak., U.S.A.* **154 B4** 46 48N 100 47W
Bismarck Arch., *Papua N. G.* **132 B6** 2 30 S 150 0 E
Bismarck Ra., *Papua N. G.* **132 C3** 5 35 S 145 0 E
Bismarck Sea, *Papua N. G.* **132 C4** 4 10 S 146 50 E
Bismark, *Germany* **30 C7** 52 40N 11 33 E
Bismil, *Turkey* **101 D9** 37 51N 40 40 E
Bismo, *Norway* **18 C5** 61 54N 8 15 E
Biso, *Uganda* **118 B3** 1 44N 31 26 E
Bison, *U.S.A.* **154 C3** 45 31N 102 28W
Bīsotūn, *Iran* **101 E12** 34 23N 47 26 E
Bispgården, *Sweden* **16 A10** 63 2N 16 40 E
Bissagos = Bijagós, Arquipélago dos, *Guinea-Biss.* **112 C1** 11 15N 16 10W
Bissau, *Guinea-Biss.* **112 C1** 11 45N 15 45W
Bissett, *Canada* **143 C9** 51 2N 95 41W
Bissikrima, *Guinea* **112 C2** 10 50N 10 58W
Bistcho L., *Canada* **142 B5** 59 45N 118 50W
Bistreţ, *Romania* **53 G8** 43 54N 23 23 E
Bistrica = Ilirska-Bistrica, *Slovenia* **45 C11** 45 34N 14 14 E
Bistriţa, *Romania* **53 C9** 47 9N 24 35 E
Bistriţa →, *Romania* **53 D11** 46 30N 26 57 E
Bistriţa Năsăud □, *Romania* **53 C9** 47 15N 24 30 E
Bistriţei, Munţii, *Romania* **53 C10** 47 15N 25 40 E
Biswan, *India* **93 F9** 27 29N 81 2 E
Bisztynek, *Poland* **54 D7** 54 8N 20 53 E
Bitam, *Gabon* **114 B2** 2 5N 11 25 E
Bitburg, *Germany* **31 F2** 49 58N 6 31 E
Bitche, *France* **27 C14** 49 2N 7 25 E
Bithlo, *U.S.A.* **153 G8** 28 33N 81 6W
Bithynia, *Turkey* **100 B4** 40 40N 31 0 E
Bitkine, *Chad* **109 F3** 11 59N 18 13 E
Bitlis, *Turkey* **101 C10** 38 20N 42 3 E
Bitola, *Macedonia* **50 E5** 41 1N 21 20 E
Bitolj = Bitola, *Macedonia* **50 E5** 41 1N 21 20 E
Bitonto, *Italy* **47 A9** 41 6N 16 41 E
Bitter Creek, *U.S.A.* **158 F9** 41 33N 108 33W
Bitter L. = Buheirat-Murrat-el-Kubra, *Egypt* **106 H8** 30 18N 32 26 E
Bitterfeld, *Germany* **30 D8** 51 37N 12 20 E
Bitterfontein, *S. Africa* **116 E2** 31 1 S 18 32 E
Bitterroot →, *U.S.A.* **158 C6** 46 52N 114 7W
Bitterroot Range, *U.S.A.* **158 D6** 46 0N 114 20W
Bitterwater, *U.S.A.* **160 J6** 36 23N 121 0W
Bitti, *Italy* **46 B2** 40 29N 9 23 E
Bittou, *Burkina Faso* **113 C4** 11 17N 0 18W
Biu, *Nigeria* **113 C7** 10 40N 12 3 E
Bivolari, *Romania* **53 C12** 47 31N 27 27 E
Bivolu, Vf., *Romania* **53 C10** 47 16N 25 58 E
Biwa-Ko, *Japan* **71 B8** 35 15N 136 10 E
Biwabik, *U.S.A.* **154 B8** 47 32N 92 21W
Bixad, *Romania* **53 C8** 47 56N 23 28 E
Biyang, *China* **74 H7** 32 38N 113 21 E
Biylikol, Ozero, *Kazakstan* **63 B5** 43 5N 70 45 E
Biysk, *Russia* **64 D9** 52 40N 85 0 E
Bizana, *S. Africa* **117 E4** 30 50 S 29 52 E
Bizen, *Japan* **70 C6** 34 43N 134 8 E
Bizerte, *Tunisia* **108 A1** 37 15N 9 50 E
Bjåen, *Norway* **18 E4** 59 37N 7 26 E
Bjargtangar, *Iceland* **11 B2** 65 30N 24 30W
Bjärnum, *Sweden* **17 H7** 56 17N 13 43 E
Bjästa, *Sweden* **16 A12** 63 12N 18 29 E
Bjelasica, *Montenegro, Yug.* **50 D3** 42 50N 19 40 E
Bjelašnica, *Bos.-H.* **52 G3** 43 43N 18 9 E
Bjelland, *Norway* **18 F4** 58 23N 7 32 E
Bjelovar, *Croatia* **45 C13** 45 56N 16 49 E
Bjerringbro, *Denmark* **17 H3** 56 23N 9 39 E
Bjervamoen, *Norway* **18 E6** 59 17N 9 5 E
Bjøberg, *Norway* **18 D5** 60 56N 8 13 E
Björbo, *Sweden* **16 D8** 60 27N 14 44 E
Bjørkelangen, *Norway* **18 E8** 59 53N 11 34 E
Björklinge, *Sweden* **16 D11** 60 2N 17 33 E
Bjørnafjorden, *Norway* **18 D2** 60 7N 5 28 E
Björneborg, *Sweden* **16 E8** 59 14N 14 16 E
Bjørnevatn, *Norway* **14 B23** 69 40N 30 0 E
Bjørnøya, *Arctic* **6 B8** 74 30N 19 0 E
Bjursås, *Sweden* **16 D9** 60 44N 15 25 E
Bjuv, *Sweden* **17 H6** 56 5N 12 55 E
Blace, *Serbia, Yug.* **50 C5** 43 18N 21 17 E
Blachownia, *Poland* **55 H5** 50 49N 18 56 E
Black = Da →, *Vietnam* **86 B5** 21 15N 105 20 E
Black →, *Canada* **150 B5** 44 42N 79 19W
Black →, *Alaska, U.S.A.* **144 C11** 66 42N 144 42W
Black →, *Ark., U.S.A.* **155 H9** 35 38N 91 20W
Black →, *N.Y., U.S.A.* **151 C8** 43 59N 76 4W
Black →, *Wis., U.S.A.* **154 D9** 43 57N 91 22W
Black Diamond, *Canada* **142 C6** 50 45N 114 14W
Black Forest = Schwarzwald, *Germany* **31 G4** 48 30N 8 20 E
Black Hd., *Ireland* **23 C2** 53 9N 9 16W
Black Hills, *U.S.A.* **154 D3** 44 0N 103 45W
Black I., *Canada* **143 C9** 51 12N 96 30W
Black L., *Canada* **143 B7** 59 12N 105 15W
Black L., *U.S.A.* **148 C3** 45 28N 84 16W
Black Mesa, *U.S.A.* **155 G3** 36 58N 102 58W
Black Mountain, *Australia* **129 A9** 30 18 S 151 39 E
Black Mt. = Mynydd Du, *U.K.* **21 F4** 51 52N 3 50W
Black Mts., *U.K.* **21 F4** 51 55N 3 7W
Black Range, *U.S.A.* **159 K10** 33 15N 107 50W
Black River, *Jamaica* **164 C4** 18 0N 77 50W
Black River Falls, *U.S.A.* **154 C9** 44 18N 90 51W
Black Rock, *Australia* **128 B3** 32 50 S 138 44 E
Black Sea, *Eurasia* **57 F6** 43 30N 35 0 E
Black Volta →, *Africa* **112 D4** 8 41N 1 33W
Black Warrior →, *U.S.A.* **149 J2** 32 32N 87 51W
Blackall, *Australia* **126 C4** 24 25 S 145 45 E
Blackball, *N.Z.* **131 C6** 42 22 S 171 26 E
Blackbull, *Australia* **126 B3** 17 55 S 141 45 E
Blackburn, *U.K.* **20 D5** 53 45N 2 29W
Blackburn with Darwen □, *U.K.* **20 D5** 53 45N 2 29W
Blackduck, *U.S.A.* **154 B7** 47 44N 94 33W
Blackfoot, *U.S.A.* **158 E7** 43 11N 112 21W
Blackfoot →, *U.S.A.* **158 C7** 46 52N 113 53W
Blackfoot River Reservoir, *U.S.A.* **158 E8** 43 0N 111 43W
Blackie, *Canada* **142 C6** 50 36N 113 37W
Blackman, *U.S.A.* **153 E3** 30 56N 86 38W
Blackpool, *U.K.* **20 D4** 53 49N 3 3W
Blackpool □, *U.K.* **20 D4** 53 49N 3 3W
Blackriver, *U.S.A.* **150 B1** 44 46N 83 17W
Blacks Harbour, *Canada* **141 C6** 45 3N 66 49W
Blacksburg, *U.S.A.* **148 G5** 37 14N 80 25W
Blackshear, *U.S.A.* **152 D7** 31 18N 82 14W
Blackshear L., *U.S.A.* **152 D6** 31 51N 83 56W
Blacksod B., *Ireland* **23 B1** 54 6N 10 0W
Blackstone, *U.S.A.* **148 G7** 37 4N 78 0W
Blackstone →, *Canada* **142 A4** 61 5N 122 55W
Blackstone Ra., *Australia* **125 E4** 26 0 S 128 30 E
Blackville, *Canada* **141 C6** 46 44N 65 50W
Blackville, *U.S.A.* **152 B9** 33 22N 81 16W
Blackwater, *Australia* **126 C4** 23 35 S 148 53 E
Blackwater →, *Meath, Ireland* **23 C4** 53 39N 6 41W
Blackwater →, *Waterford, Ireland* **23 D4** 52 4N 7 52W
Blackwater →, *U.K.* **23 B5** 54 31N 6 35W
Blackwater →, *Fla., U.S.A.* **153 E2** 30 36N 87 2W
Blackwater →, *Mo., U.S.A.* **156 F4** 38 59N 92 59W
Blackwater Cr. →, *Australia* **127 D3** 25 56 S 144 30 E
Blackwell, *U.S.A.* **155 G6** 36 48N 97 17W
Blackwells Corner, *U.S.A.* **161 K7** 35 37N 119 47W
Blackwood, C., *Papua N. G.* **132 D3** 7 49 S 144 31 E
Blaenau Ffestiniog, *U.K.* **20 E4** 53 0N 3 56W
Blaenau Gwent □, *U.K.* **21 F4** 51 48N 3 12W
Bláfell, *Iceland* **11 C7** 64 30N 19 51W
Bláfjall, *Iceland* **11 B10** 65 26N 16 50W
Blagaj, *Bos.-H.* **50 C1** 43 16N 17 55 E
Blagnac, *France* **28 E5** 43 37N 1 23 E
Blagodarnyy, *Russia* **61 H6** 45 7N 43 37 E
Blagoevgrad, *Bulgaria* **50 D7** 42 2N 23 5 E
Blagoveshchensk, *Amur, Russia* **65 D13** 50 20N 127 30 E
Blagoveshchensk, *Bashkortostan, Russia* **62 D5** 55 1N 55 59 E
Blagoveshchenskoye, *Kazakstan* **63 B7** 43 18N 74 12 E
Blain, *France* **26 E5** 47 29N 1 45W
Blaine, *U.S.A.* **160 B4** 48 59N 122 45W
Blaine Lake, *Canada* **143 C7** 52 51N 106 52W
Blair, *U.S.A.* **154 E6** 41 33N 96 8W
Blair Athol, *Australia* **126 C4** 22 42 S 147 31 E
Blair Atholl, *U.K.* **22 E5** 56 46N 3 50W
Blairgowrie, *U.K.* **22 E5** 56 35N 3 21W
Blairmore, *Canada* **142 D6** 49 40N 114 25W
Blairsden, *U.S.A.* **160 F6** 39 47N 120 37W

Branchville 193

Bonney, L., *Australia* . . . . . . **128 D4** 37 50 S 140 20 E
Bonnie Doon, *Australia* . . . . **129 D6** 37 2 S 145 53 E
Bonnie Downs, *Australia* . . . **126 C3** 22 7 S 143 50 E
Bonnie Rock, *Australia* . . . . **125 F2** 30 29 S 118 22 E
Bonny, *Nigeria* . . . . **113 E6** 4 25N 7 13 E
Bonny →, *Nigeria* . . . . **113 E6** 4 20N 7 10 E
Bonny, Bight of, *Africa* . . . . **113 E6** 3 30N 9 20 E
Bonny-sur-Loire, *France* . . . **27 E9** 47 33N 2 50 E
Bonnyrigg, *U.K.* **22 F5** 55 53N 3 6W
Bonnyville, *Canada* **143 C6** 54 20N 110 45W
Bono, *Italy* . . . . **46 B2** 40 25N 9 2 E
Bonobono, *Phil.* . . . . **81 G1** 8 40N 117 36 E
Bonoi, *Indonesia* . . . . **83 B5** 1 45 S 137 41 E
Bonorva, *Italy* . . . . **46 B1** 40 25N 8 46 E
Bonsall, *U.S.A.* **161 M9** 33 16N 117 14W
Bontang, *Indonesia* . . . . **85 B5** 0 10N 117 30 E
Bonthain, *Indonesia* . . . . **82 C1** 5 34 S 119 56 E
Bonthe, *S. Leone* **112 D2** 7 30N 12 33W
Bontoc, *Phil.* . . . . **80 C3** 17 7N 120 58 E
Bontosunggu, *Indonesia* . . . . **82 C1** 5 41 S 119 42 E
Bonyeri, *Ghana* **112 D4** 5 1N 2 46W
Bonyhád, *Hungary* . . . . **52 D3** 46 18N 18 32 E
Bonython Ra., *Australia* . . . **124 D4** 23 40 S 128 45 E
Bookabie, *Australia* . . . . **125 F5** 31 50 S 132 41 E
Booker, *U.S.A.* **155 G4** 36 27N 100 32W
Boolaboolka L., *Australia* . . **128 B5** 32 38 S 143 10 E
Boolarra, *Australia* . . . . **129 E7** 38 20 S 146 20 E
Boolcoomatta, *Australia* . . . . **128 A4** 31 57 S 140 33 E
Booleroo Centre, *Australia* . **128 B3** 32 53 S 138 21 E
Booligal, *Australia* . . . . **129 B6** 33 58 S 144 53 E
Boonah, *Australia* . . . . **127 D5** 27 58 S 152 41 E
Boone, *Iowa, U.S.A.* **156 B3** 42 4N 93 53W
Boone, *N.C., U.S.A.* **149 G5** 36 13N 81 41W
Booneville, *Ark., U.S.A.* **155 H8** 35 8N 93 55W
Booneville, *Miss., U.S.A.* . . . **149 H1** 34 39N 88 34W
Boonville, *Calif., U.S.A.* **160 F3** 39 1N 123 22W
Boonville, *Ind., U.S.A.* **157 F9** 38 3N 87 16W
Boonville, *Mo., U.S.A.* **156 F4** 38 58N 92 44W
Boonville, *N.Y., U.S.A.* **151 C9** 43 29N 75 20W
Booral, *Australia* . . . . **129 B9** 32 30 S 151 56 E
Boorindal, *Australia* . . . . **127 E4** 30 22 S 146 11 E
Booroomugga, *Australia* . . . . **129 A7** 31 17 S 146 27 E
Boorowa, *Australia* . . . . **129 C8** 34 28 S 148 44 E
Boothia, Gulf of, *Canada* . . . **139 A11** 71 0N 90 0W
Boothia Pen., *Canada* **138 A10** 71 0N 94 0W
Bootle, *U.K.* **20 D4** 53 28N 3 1W
Booué, *Gabon* . . . . **114 C2** 0 5 S 11 55 E
Boppard, *Germany* . . . . **31 E3** 50 13N 7 35 E
Boquerón □, *Paraguay* . . . . . **173 E6** 23 0 S 60 0W
Boquete, *Panama* **164 E3** 8 46N 82 27W
Boquilla, Presa de la, *Mexico* **162 B3** 27 40N 105 30W
Boquillas del Carmen,
Mexico **162 B4** 29 17N 102 53W
Bor, *Czech Rep.* . . . . **34 B5** 49 41N 12 45 E
Bor, *Russia* . . . . **60 B7** 56 28N 43 59 E
Bor, *Serbia, Yug.* . . . . **50 B6** 44 5N 22 7 E
Bôr, *Sudan* . . . . **107 F3** 6 10N 31 40 E
Bor, *Sweden* . . . . **17 G8** 57 9N 14 10 E
Bor, *Turkey* . . . . **100 D6** 37 54N 34 32 E
Bor Mashash, *Israel* . . . . **103 D3** 31 7N 34 50 E
Borah Peak, *U.S.A.* **158 D7** 44 8N 113 47W
Borama, *Somali Rep.* . . . . **120 C2** 9 55N 43 7 E
Borang, *Sudan* . . . . **107 G3** 4 50N 30 59 E
Borangapara, *India* . . . . **90 C3** 25 14N 90 14 E
Borås, *Sweden* . . . . **17 G6** 57 43N 12 56 E
Borāzjān, *Iran* . . . . **97 D6** 29 22N 51 10 E
Borba, *Brazil* . . . . **169 D6** 4 12 S 59 34W
Borba, *Portugal* **43 G3** 38 50N 7 26W
Borbon, *Phil.* . . . . **81 F5** 10 50N 124 2 E
Borborema, Planalto da,
Brazil . . . . **170 C4** 7 0 S 37 0W
Borcea, *Romania* . . . . **53 F12** 44 20N 27 45 E
Borçka, *Turkey* . . . . **101 B9** 41 25N 41 41 E
Bord Khūn-e Now, *Iran* . . . . **97 D6** 28 3N 51 28 E
Borda, C., *Australia* . . . . **128 C2** 35 45 S 136 34 E
Bordeaux, *France* **28 D3** 44 50N 0 36W
Borden, *Australia* . . . . **125 F2** 34 3 S 118 12 E
Borden, *Canada* **141 C7** 46 18N 63 47W
Borden I., *Canada* **6 B2** 78 30N 111 30W
Borden Springs, *U.S.A.* **152 B4** 33 56N 85 28W
Bordertown, *Australia* . . . . . . **128 D4** 36 19 S 140 45 E
Borðeyri, *Iceland* **11 B5** 65 12N 21 6W
Bordighera, *Italy* . . . . **44 E4** 43 46N 7 39 E
Bordj bou Arreridj, *Algeria* . **111 A5** 36 4N 4 45 E
Bordj Bourguiba, *Tunisia* . . **108 B2** 32 12N 10 2 E
Bordj Fly Ste. Marie, *Algeria* **110 C4** 27 19N 2 32W
Bordj-in-Eker, *Algeria* . . . . . **111 D6** 24 9N 5 3 E
Bordj Menaiel, *Algeria* . . . . . **111 A5** 36 46N 3 43 E
Bordj Messouda, *Algeria* . . . **111 B6** 30 12N 9 25 E
Bordj Nili, *Algeria* . . . . **111 B5** 33 28N 3 2 E
Bordj Omar Driss, *Algeria* . . **111 C6** 28 10N 6 40 E
Bordj Sif Fatima, *Algeria* . . . **111 B6** 31 6N 8 41 E
Bordj-Tarat, *Algeria* . . . . **111 C6** 25 55N 9 3 E
Bordj Zelfana, *Algeria* . . . . . **111 B5** 32 27N 4 15 E
Bordoba, *Kyrgyzstan* . . . . . . **63 D6** 39 31N 73 16 E
Borea Creek, *Australia* . . . . . **129 C7** 35 5 S 146 35 E
Borehamwood, *U.K.* **21 F7** 51 40N 0 15W
Borek Wielkopolski, *Poland* . **55 G4** 51 54N 17 11 E
Boremore, *Australia* . . . . **129 B8** 33 15 S 149 0 E
Boren Kapuas, Pegunungan,
Malaysia . . . . **85 B4** 1 25N 113 15 E
Borensberg, *Sweden* . . . . **17 F9** 58 34N 15 17 E
Borgå = Porvoo, *Finland* . . . **15 F21** 60 24N 25 40 E
Borgarfjarðarsýsla □, *Iceland* **11 C5** 64 30N 21 30W
Borgarfjörður, *Iceland* **11 C4** 64 30N 22 0W
Borgarfjörður, *Iceland* **11 B13** 65 31N 13 49W
Borgarnes, *Iceland* **11 C5** 64 32N 21 55W
Børgefjellet, *Norway* . . . . . . **14 D15** 65 20N 13 45 E
Borger, *Neths.* . . . . **24 B6** 52 54N 6 44 E
Borger, *U.S.A.* **155 H4** 35 39N 101 24W
Borgholm, *Sweden* . . . . **17 H10** 56 52N 16 39 E
Bórgia, *Italy* . . . . **47 D9** 38 49N 16 30 E
Borgo San Dalmazzo, *Italy* . . **44 D4** 44 20N 7 30 E
Borgo San Lorenzo, *Italy* . . . **45 E8** 43 57N 11 23 E
Borgo Val di Taro, *Italy* . . . . **44 D6** 44 29N 9 46 E
Borgo Valsugana, *Italy* . . . . . **45 B8** 46 3N 11 27 E
Borgomanero, *Italy* . . . . **44 C5** 45 42N 8 28 E
Borgorose, *Italy* . . . . **45 F10** 42 11N 13 13 E
Borgosésia, *Italy* . . . . **44 C5** 45 43N 8 16 E
Borgund, *Norway* . . . . **18 C4** 61 3N 7 48 E
Borikhane, *Laos* . . . . **86 C4** 18 33N 103 43 E
Borisoglebsk, *Russia* . . . . **60 E6** 51 27N 42 5 E
Borisov = Barysaw, *Belarus* . **58 E5** 54 17N 28 28 E
Borisovka, *Kazakstan* . . . . . . **63 B4** 43 15N 68 10 E
Borisovka, *Russia* . . . . **59 G9** 50 36N 36 1 E
Borja, *Peru* . . . . **168 D2** 4 20 S 77 40W
Borja, *Spain* **40 D3** 41 48N 1 34W
Borjas Blancas = Les Borges
Blanques, *Spain* . . . . **40 D5** 41 31N 0 52 E
Borjomi, *Georgia* . . . . **61 K6** 41 48N 43 28 E
Borken, *Germany* . . . . **30 D9** 51 40N 13 10 E
Børkop, *Denmark* . . . . **17 J3** 55 39N 9 39 E
Borkou, *Chad* . . . . **109 E3** 18 15N 18 50 E
Borkum, *Germany* . . . . **30 B2** 53 34N 6 40 E
Borlänge, *Sweden* . . . . **16 D9** 60 29N 15 26 E
Borley, C., *Antarctica* . . . . . **7 C5** 66 15 S 52 30 E
Borlu, *Turkey* . . . . **49 C10** 38 44N 28 27 E
Bormida →, *Italy* . . . . **44 D5** 44 23N 8 13 E
Bórmio, *Italy* . . . . **44 B7** 46 28N 10 22 E
Borna, *Germany* . . . . **30 D8** 51 7N 12 29 E
Borne Sulinowo, *Poland* . . . . **54 E3** 53 32N 16 36 E
Borneo, *E. Indies* . . . . **85 B4** 1 0N 115 0 E
Bornholm, *Denmark* . . . . **17 J8** 55 10N 15 0 E
Bornholms
Amtskommune □,
Denmark . . . . **17 J8** 55 5N 15 0 E
Bornholmsgattet, *Europe* . . . **17 J8** 55 15N 14 20 E
Borno □, *Nigeria* . . . . **113 C7** 11 30N 13 0 E
Bornos, *Spain* **43 J5** 36 48N 5 42W
Bornova, *Turkey* . . . . **49 C9** 38 27N 27 14 E
Bornu Yassa, *Nigeria* . . . . . . **113 C7** 12 14N 12 25 E
Borobudur, *Indonesia* . . . . . . **85 D4** 7 36 S 110 13 E
Borodino, *Russia* . . . . **58 E8** 55 31N 35 40 E
Borogontsy, *Russia* . . . . **65 C14** 62 42N 131 8 E
Boromo, *Burkina Faso* **112 C4** 11 45N 2 58W
Boron, *U.S.A.* **161 L9** 35 0N 117 39W
Boronga Is., *Burma* . . . . **90 F4** 19 58N 93 6 E
Borongan, *Phil.* . . . . **81 F5** 11 37N 125 26 E
Bororen, *Australia* . . . . **126 C5** 24 13 S 151 33 E
Borotangba Mts., *C.A.R.* . . . **107 F2** 6 30N 25 0 E
Borovan, *Bulgaria* . . . . **50 C7** 43 27N 23 45 E
Borovichi, *Russia* . . . . **58 C7** 58 25N 33 55 E
Borovsk, *Berezniki, Russia* . **62 B6** 59 43N 56 40 E
Borovsk, *Moskva, Russia* . . . **58 E9** 55 12N 36 24 E
Borrby, *Sweden* . . . . **17 J8** 55 27N 14 10 E
Borrego Springs, *U.S.A.* **161 M10** 33 15N 116 23W
Borriol, *Spain* **40 E4** 40 4N 0 4W
Borroloola, *Australia* . . . . **126 B2** 16 4 S 136 17 E
Borşa, *Cluj, Romania* . . . . . . **53 D8** 46 56N 23 40 E
Borşa, *Maramureş, Romania* **53 C9** 47 41N 24 50 E
Borsec, *Romania* . . . . **53 D10** 46 57N 25 34 E
Borsod-Abaúj-Zemplén □,
Hungary . . . . **52 B6** 48 20N 21 0 E
Bort-les-Orgues, *France* . . . . **28 C6** 45 24N 2 29 E
Borth, *U.K.* **21 E3** 52 29N 4 2W
Börtnan, *Sweden* . . . . **16 B7** 62 45N 13 50 E
Borūjerd, *Iran* . . . . **97 C6** 33 55N 48 50 E
Boryslav, *Ukraine* . . . . **59 H2** 49 18N 23 28 E
Boryspil, *Ukraine* . . . . **59 G6** 50 21N 30 59 E
Borzhomi = Borjomi,
Georgia . . . . **61 K6** 41 48N 43 28 E
Borzna, *Ukraine* . . . . **59 G7** 51 18N 32 26 E
Borzya, *Russia* . . . . **65 D12** 50 24N 116 31 E
Bosa, *Italy* . . . . **46 B1** 40 18N 8 30 E
Bosaga, *Turkmenistan* . . . . . **63 E2** 37 33N 65 41 E
Bosanska Dubica, *Bos.-H.* . . **45 C13** 45 10N 16 50 E
Bosanska Gradiška, *Bos.-H.* . **52 E2** 45 10N 17 15 E
Bosanska Kostajnica,
Bos.-H. . . . . **45 C13** 45 11N 16 33 E
Bosanska Krupa, *Bos.-H.* . . . **45 D13** 44 53N 16 10 E
Bosanski Brod, *Bos.-H.* . . . . **52 E2** 45 10N 18 0 E
Bosanski Novi, *Bos.-H.* . . . . **45 C13** 45 2N 16 22 E
Bosanski Petrovac, *Bos.-H.* . **45 D13** 44 35N 16 21 E
Bosanski Šamac, *Bos.-H.* . . . **52 E3** 45 3N 18 29 E
Bosansko Grahovo, *Bos.-H.* . **45 D13** 44 12N 16 26 E
Bosaso, *Somali Rep.* . . . . **120 B3** 11 12N 49 18 E
Bosavi, Mt., *Papua N. G.* . . . **132 D2** 6 30 S 142 49 E
Boscastle, *U.K.* **21 G3** 50 41N 4 42W
Boscobel, *U.S.A.* **156 A6** 43 8N 90 42W
Bose, *China* . . . . **76 F6** 23 53N 106 35 E
Boshan, *China* . . . . **75 F9** 36 28N 117 49 E
Boshof, *S. Africa* . . . . **116 D4** 28 31 S 25 13 E
Boshrūyeh, *Iran* . . . . **97 C8** 33 50N 57 30 E
Bosilegrad, *Serbia, Yug.* . . . **50 D6** 42 30N 22 27 E
Boskovice, *Czech Rep.* . . . . . **35 B9** 49 29N 16 40 E
Bosna →, *Bos.-H.* . . . . **52 E3** 45 4N 18 29 E
Bosna i Hercegovina =
Bosnia-Herzegovina ■,
Europe . . . . **52 G2** 44 0N 18 0 E
Bosnia-Herzegovina ■,
Europe . . . . **52 G2** 44 0N 18 0 E
Bosnik, *Indonesia* . . . . **83 B5** 1 5 S 136 10 E
Bōsō-Hantō, *Japan* . . . . **71 B12** 35 20N 140 20 E
Bosobolo,
Dem. Rep. of the Congo . **114 B3** 4 15N 19 50 E
Bosporus = İstanbul Boğazı,
Turkey . . . . **51 E13** 41 10N 29 10 E
Bossangoa, *C.A.R.* . . . . **114 A3** 6 35N 17 30 E
Bossembélé, *C.A.R.* . . . . **114 A3** 5 25N 17 40 E
Bossembélé II, *C.A.R.* . . . . . . **114 A3** 5 41N 16 38 E
Bossier City, *U.S.A.* **155 J8** 32 31N 93 44W
Bosso, *Niger* . . . . **109 F2** 13 43N 13 19 E
Bostānābād, *Iran* . . . . **101 D12** 37 50N 46 50 E
Bosten Hu, *China* . . . . **72 B3** 41 55N 87 40 E
Boston, *Phil.* . . . . **81 H6** 7 52N 126 22 E
Boston, *U.K.* **20 E7** 52 59N 0 2W
Boston, *Ga., U.S.A.* **152 E6** 30 47N 83 47W
Boston, *Mass., U.S.A.* **151 D13** 42 22N 71 4W
Boston Bar, *Canada* **142 D4** 49 52N 121 30W
Bostwick, *Fla., U.S.A.* **152 F8** 29 46N 81 38W
Bostwick, *Ga., U.S.A.* **152 B6** 33 44N 83 31W
Bosusulu,
Dem. Rep. of the Congo . **114 B4** 0 50N 20 45 E
Bosut →, *Croatia* . . . . **52 E3** 45 20N 18 45 E
Boswell, *Canada* **142 D5** 49 28N 116 45W
Boswell, *Ind., U.S.A.* **157 D9** 40 31N 87 23W
Boswell, *Okla., U.S.A.* **155 H7** 34 2N 95 52W
Boswell, *Pa., U.S.A.* **150 F5** 40 10N 79 2W
Bosworth, *U.S.A.* **156 E3** 39 28N 93 20W
Botad, *India* . . . . **92 H4** 22 15N 71 40 E
Botan →, *Turkey* . . . . **101 D10** 37 57N 42 2 E
Botany B., *Australia* . . . . **127 E5** 34 0 S 151 14 E
Botene, *Laos* . . . . **86 D3** 17 35N 101 12 E
Botev, *Bulgaria* . . . . **51 D8** 42 44N 24 52 E
Botevgrad, *Bulgaria* . . . . **50 D7** 42 55N 23 47 E
Bothaville, *S. Africa* . . . . **116 D4** 27 23 S 26 34 E
Bothnia, G. of, *Europe* . . . . . **14 E19** 63 0N 20 15 E
Bothwell, *Australia* . . . . **126 G4** 42 20 S 147 1 E
Bothwell, *Canada* **150 D3** 42 38N 81 52W
Boticas, *Portugal* **42 D3** 41 41N 7 40W
Botletle →, *Botswana* . . . . . . **116 C3** 20 10 S 23 15 E
Botlikh, *Russia* . . . . **61 J8** 42 39N 46 11 E
Botna →, *Moldova* . . . . **53 D14** 46 45N 29 34 E
Botolan, *Phil.* . . . . **80 D3** 15 17N 120 1 E
Botoroaga, *Romania* . . . . **53 F10** 44 8N 25 32 E
Botoşani, *Romania* . . . . **53 C11** 47 42N 26 41 E
Botoşani □, *Romania* . . . . **53 C11** 47 50N 26 50 E
Botricello, *Italy* . . . . **47 D9** 38 56N 16 51 E
Botro, *Ivory C.* **112 D3** 7 51N 5 19W
Botswana ■, *Africa* . . . . **116 C3** 22 0 S 24 0 E
Bottineau, *U.S.A.* **154 A4** 48 50N 100 27W
Bottnaryd, *Sweden* . . . . **17 G7** 57 47N 13 50 E
Bottrop, *Germany* . . . . **30 D2** 51 31N 6 58 E
Botucatu, *Brazil* . . . . **175 A6** 22 55 S 48 30W
Botwood, *Canada* **141 C8** 49 6N 55 23W
Bou Alam, *Algeria* . . . . **111 B5** 33 50N 1 26 E
Bou Ali, *Algeria* **111 C5** 27 11N 0 4W
Bou Djébéha, *Mali* **112 B4** 18 25N 2 45W
Bou Guema, *Algeria* . . . . **111 C5** 28 49N 0 19 E
Bou Ismael, *Algeria* . . . . **111 A5** 36 38N 2 42 E
Bou Izakarn, *Morocco* **110 C3** 29 12N 9 46W
Boû Lanouâr, *Mauritania* . . . **110 D1** 21 12N 16 34W
Bou Saâda, *Algeria* . . . . **111 A5** 35 11N 4 9 E
Bou Salem, *Tunisia* . . . . **108 A1** 36 45N 9 2 E
Bouaflé, *Ivory C.* **112 D3** 7 1N 5 47W
Bouaké, *Ivory C.* **112 D3** 7 40N 5 2W
Bouanga, *Congo* . . . . **114 C3** 2 7 S 16 8 E
Bouar, *C.A.R.* . . . . **114 A3** 6 0N 15 40 E
Bouârfa, *Morocco* **111 B4** 32 32N 1 58W
Bouca, *C.A.R.* . . . . **114 A3** 6 45N 18 25 E
Boucaut B., *Australia* . . . . . . **126 A1** 12 0 S 134 25 E
Bouches-du-Rhône □, *France* **29 E9** 43 37N 5 2 E
Bouda, *Algeria* **111 C4** 27 50N 0 27W
Boudenib, *Morocco* **110 B4** 31 59N 3 31W
Boudry, *Switz.* . . . . **32 C3** 46 57N 6 50 E
Boufarik, *Algeria* . . . . **111 A5** 36 34N 2 58 E
Bougainville, C., *Australia* . . **124 B4** 13 57 S 126 4 E
Bougainville I., *Solomon Is.* . **133 L8** 6 0 S 155 0 E
Bougainville Reef, *Australia* **126 B4** 15 30 S 147 5 E
Bougainville Str.,
Solomon Is. . . . . **133 L9** 6 40 S 156 10 E
Bougaroun, C., *Algeria* . . . . . **111 A6** 37 6N 6 30 E
Bougie = Bejaia, *Algeria* . . . . **111 A6** 36 42N 5 2 E
Bougouni, *Mali* **112 C3** 11 30N 7 20W
Bouillon, *Belgium* . . . . **24 E5** 49 44N 5 3 E
Bouïra, *Algeria* . . . . **111 A5** 36 20N 3 59 E
Boulazac, *France* . . . . **28 C4** 45 10N 0 47 E
Boulder, *Colo., U.S.A.* **154 E2** 40 1N 105 17W
Boulder, *Mont., U.S.A.* **158 C7** 46 14N 112 7W
Boulder City, *U.S.A.* **161 K12** 35 59N 114 50W
Boulder Creek, *U.S.A.* **160 H4** 37 7N 122 7W
Boulder Dam = Hoover
Dam, *U.S.A.* **161 K12** 36 1N 114 44W
Boulembo, *Gabon* . . . . **114 C2** 1 26 S 12 0 E
Bouli, *Mauritania* **112 B2** 15 17N 12 18W
Boulia, *Australia* . . . . **126 C2** 22 52 S 139 51 E
Bouligny, *France* . . . . **27 C12** 49 17N 5 45 E
Boulogne →, *France* **26 E5** 47 12N 1 47W
Boulogne-sur-Gesse, *France* . **28 E4** 43 18N 0 38 E
Boulogne-sur-Mer, *France* . . **27 B8** 50 42N 1 36 E
Bouloire, *France* . . . . **26 E7** 47 59N 0 45 E
Bouloupari, *N. Cal.* . . . . **133 U20** 21 52 S 166 4 E
Boulsa, *Burkina Faso* **113 C4** 12 39N 0 34W
Boultoum, *Niger* . . . . **109 F2** 14 45N 10 25 E
Boumalne, *Morocco* **110 B3** 31 25N 6 0W
Boun Neua, *Laos* . . . . **86 B3** 21 38N 101 54 E
Boun Tai, *Laos* . . . . **86 B3** 21 23N 101 58 E
Bouna, *Ivory C.* **112 D4** 9 10N 3 0W
Boundary Peak, *U.S.A.* **160 H8** 37 51N 118 21W
Boundiali, *Ivory C.* **112 D3** 9 30N 6 20W
Bountiful, *U.S.A.* **158 F8** 40 53N 111 53W
Bounty Is., *Pac. Oc.* . . . . **134 M9** 48 0 S 178 30 E
Bourail, *N. Cal.* . . . . **133 U19** 21 34 S 165 30 E
Bourbeuse →, *U.S.A.* **156 F6** 38 24N 90 53W
Bourbon, *U.S.A.* **157 C10** 41 18N 86 7W
Bourbon-Lancy, *France* . . . . . **27 F10** 46 37N 3 45 E
Bourbon-l'Archambault,
France . . . . **27 F10** 46 36N 3 4 E
Bourbonnais, *France* . . . . **27 F10** 46 28N 3 0 E
Bourbonne-les-Bains, *France* **27 E12** 47 54N 5 45 E
Bourbourg, *France* . . . . **27 B9** 50 56N 2 12 E
Bourem, *Mali* **113 B4** 17 0N 0 24W
Bourg, *France* **28 C3** 45 3N 0 34W
Bourg-Argental, *France* . . . . . **29 C8** 45 18N 4 32 E
Bourg-de-Péage, *France* . . . . . **29 C9** 45 2N 5 3 E
Bourg-en-Bresse, *France* . . . . **27 F12** 46 13N 5 12 E
Bourg-Lastic, *France* . . . . **28 C6** 45 39N 2 35 E
Bourg-Madame, *France* . . . . . **28 F5** 42 26N 1 55 E
Bourg-St-Andéol, *France* . . . . **29 D8** 44 23N 4 39 E
Bourg-St-Maurice, *France* . . . **29 C10** 45 35N 6 46 E
Bourg-St.-Pierre, *Switz.* . . . . . **32 E4** 45 57N 7 12 E
Bourganeuf, *France* . . . . **28 C5** 45 57N 1 45 E
Bourges, *France* . . . . **27 E9** 47 9N 2 25 E
Bourget, *Canada* **151 A9** 45 26N 75 9W
Bourget, L. du, *France* . . . . . . **29 C9** 45 44N 5 52 E
Bourgneuf, B. de, *France* **26 E4** 47 3N 2 10W
Bourgneuf-en-Retz, *France* . . **26 E5** 47 2N 1 58W
Bourgogne, *France* . . . . **27 F11** 47 0N 4 50 E
Bourgoin-Jallieu, *France* . . . . **29 C9** 45 36N 5 17 E
Bourgueil, *France* . . . . **26 E7** 47 17N 0 10 E
Bourke, *Australia* . . . . **127 E4** 30 8 S 145 55 E
Bourne, *U.K.* **20 E7** 52 47N 0 22W
Bournemouth, *U.K.* **21 G6** 50 43N 1 52W
Bournemouth □, *U.K.* **21 G6** 50 43N 1 52W
Bouse, *U.S.A.* **161 M13** 33 56N 114 0W
Boussac, *France* . . . . **27 F9** 46 22N 2 13 E
Bousso, *Chad* . . . . **109 F3** 10 34N 16 52 E
Boutilimit, *Mauritania* **112 B2** 17 45N 14 40W
Boutonne →, *France* **28 C3** 45 54N 0 50W
Bouvet I. = Bouvetøya,
Antarctica . . . . **9 P9** 54 26 S 3 24 E
Bouvetøya, *Antarctica* . . . . . . **9 P9** 54 26 S 3 24 E
Bouxwiller, *France* . . . . **27 D14** 48 49N 7 27 E
Bouznika, *Morocco* **110 B3** 33 46N 7 6W
Bouzonville, *France* . . . . **27 C13** 49 17N 6 32 E
Bova Marina, *Italy* . . . . **47 E8** 37 56N 15 55 E
Bovalino Marina, *Italy* . . . . . . **47 D9** 38 10N 16 10 E
Bovec, *Slovenia* . . . . **45 B10** 46 20N 13 33 E
Bøverdal, *Norway* . . . . **18 C5** 61 44N 8 20 E
Bøverfjorden, *Norway* . . . . . . **18 A5** 63 1N 8 32 E
Bovill, *U.S.A.* **158 C5** 46 51N 116 24W
Bovino, *Italy* . . . . **47 A8** 41 15N 15 20 E
Bow Island, *Canada* **142 D6** 49 50N 111 23W
Bowbells, *U.S.A.* **154 A3** 48 48N 102 15W
Bowdle, *U.S.A.* **154 C5** 45 27N 99 39W
Bowdon, *U.S.A.* **152 B4** 33 32N 85 15W
Bowdon Junction, *U.S.A.* **152 B4** 33 40N 85 9W
Bowelling, *Australia* . . . . **125 F2** 33 25 S 116 30 E
Bowen, *Australia* . . . . **126 C4** 20 0 S 148 16 E
Bowen Mts., *Australia* . . . . . . **129 D7** 37 0 S 147 50 E
Bowie, *Ariz., U.S.A.* **159 K9** 32 19N 109 29W
Bowie, *Tex., U.S.A.* **155 J6** 33 34N 97 51W
Bowkān, *Iran* . . . . **101 D12** 36 31N 46 12 E
Bowland, Forest of, *U.K.* **20 D5** 54 0N 2 30W
Bowling Green, *Fla., U.S.A.* . **153 H8** 27 38N 81 50W
Bowling Green, *Ky., U.S.A.* . **148 G2** 36 59N 86 27W
Bowling Green, *Mo., U.S.A.* . **156 E5** 39 21N 91 12W
Bowling Green, *Ohio,*
U.S.A. **157 C13** 41 23N 83 39W
Bowling Green, C., *Australia* **126 B4** 19 19 S 147 25 E
Bowman, *N. Dak., U.S.A.* . . . **154 B3** 46 11N 103 24W
Bowman, *S.C., U.S.A.* **152 B9** 33 21N 80 41W
Bowman I., *Antarctica* . . . . . . **7 C8** 65 0 S 104 0 E
Bowmans, *Australia* . . . . **128 C3** 34 10 S 138 17 E
Bowmanville, *Canada* **140 D4** 43 55N 78 41W
Bowmore, *U.K.* **22 F2** 55 45N 6 17W
Bowral, *Australia* . . . . **129 C9** 34 26 S 150 27 E
Bowraville, *Australia* . . . . **127 E5** 30 37 S 152 52 E
Bowron →, *Canada* **142 C4** 54 3N 121 50W
Bowser L., *Canada* **142 B3** 56 30N 129 30W
Bowsman, *Canada* **143 C8** 52 14N 101 12W
Bowutu Mts., *Papua N. G.* . . **132 D4** 7 45 S 147 10 E
Bowwood, *Zambia* . . . . **119 F2** 17 5 S 26 20 E
Boxholm, *Sweden* . . . . **17 F9** 58 12N 15 3 E
Boxmeer, *Neths.* . . . . **24 C5** 51 38N 5 56 E
Boxtel, *Neths.* . . . . **24 C5** 51 36N 5 20 E
Boyabat, *Turkey* . . . . **100 B6** 41 28N 34 47 E
Boyabo,
Dem. Rep. of the Congo . **114 B3** 3 43N 18 46 E
Boyaca = Casanare □,
Colombia **168 B3** 5 30N 72 0W
Boyalıca, *Turkey* . . . . **51 F13** 40 29N 29 33 E
Boyce, *U.S.A.* **155 K8** 31 23N 92 40W
Boyd, *U.S.A.* **152 E6** 30 11N 83 37W
Boyer →, *Canada* **142 B5** 58 27N 115 57W
Boyer, C., *N. Cal.* . . . . **133 U22** 21 37 S 168 6 E
Boykin, *U.S.A.* **152 D5** 31 6N 84 41W
Boyle, *Ireland* **23 C3** 53 59N 8 18W
Boyne →, *Ireland* **23 C5** 53 43N 6 15W
Boyne City, *U.S.A.* **148 C3** 45 13N 85 1W
Boyni Qara, *Afghan.* . . . . **91 A2** 36 20N 67 0 E
Boynitsa, *Bulgaria* . . . . **50 C6** 43 58N 22 32 E
Boynton Beach, *U.S.A.* **149 M5** 26 32N 80 4W
Boyolali, *Indonesia* . . . . **85 D4** 7 32 S 110 35 E
Boyoma, Chutes,
Dem. Rep. of the Congo . **114 B5** 0 35N 25 23 E
Boyup Brook, *Australia* . . . . . **125 F2** 33 50 S 116 23 E
Boz Burun, *Turkey* . . . . **51 F12** 40 32N 28 46 E
Boz Dağ, *Turkey* . . . . **49 D11** 37 18N 29 11 E
Boz Dağları, *Turkey* . . . . **49 C10** 38 20N 28 0 E
Bozburun, *Turkey* . . . . **49 E10** 36 43N 28 4 E
Bozcaada, *Turkey* . . . . **49 B8** 39 50N 26 4 E
Bozdoğan, *Turkey* . . . . **49 D10** 37 40N 28 17 E
Bozeman, *U.S.A.* **158 D8** 45 41N 111 2W
Bozen = Bolzano, *Italy* . . . . . **45 B8** 46 31N 11 22 E
Bozene,
Dem. Rep. of the Congo . **114 B3** 2 56N 19 12 E
Boževac, *Serbia, Yug.* . . . . . . **50 B5** 44 32N 21 24 E
Bozkır, *Turkey* . . . . **100 D5** 37 11N 32 14 E
Bozkurt, *Turkey* . . . . **49 D11** 37 50N 29 37 E
Bozouls, *France* . . . . **28 D6** 44 28N 2 43 E
Bozoum, *C.A.R.* . . . . **114 A3** 6 25N 16 35 E
Bozova, *Antalya, Turkey* . . . . **49 D12** 37 13N 30 18 E
Bozova, *Sanliurfa, Turkey* . . . **101 D8** 37 21N 38 32 E
Bozovici, *Romania* . . . . **52 F7** 44 56N 22 0 E
Bozüyük, *Turkey* . . . . **49 B12** 39 54N 30 3 E
Bra, *Italy* . . . . **44 D4** 44 42N 7 51 E
Braås, *Sweden* . . . . **17 G9** 57 4N 15 3 E
Brabant □, *Belgium* . . . . **24 D4** 50 46N 4 30 E
Brabant L., *Canada* **143 B8** 55 58N 103 43W
Brabrand, *Denmark* . . . . **17 H4** 56 9N 10 7 E
Brač, *Croatia* . . . . **45 E13** 43 20N 16 40 E
Bracadale, L., *U.K.* **22 D2** 57 20N 6 30W
Bracciano, *Italy* . . . . **45 F9** 42 6N 12 10 E
Bracciano, L. di, *Italy* . . . . . . **45 F9** 42 7N 12 14 E
Bracebridge, *Canada* **140 C4** 45 2N 79 19W
Brach, *Libya* . . . . **108 C2** 27 31N 14 20 E
Bracieux, *France* . . . . **26 E8** 47 30N 1 30 E
Bräcke, *Sweden* . . . . **16 B9** 62 45N 15 26 E
Brackettville, *U.S.A.* **155 L4** 29 19N 100 25W
Bracki Kanal, *Croatia* . . . . **45 E13** 43 24N 16 40 E
Bracknell, *U.K.* **21 F7** 51 25N 0 43W
Bracknell Forest □, *U.K.* . . . **21 F7** 51 25N 0 44W
Brad, *Romania* . . . . **52 D7** 46 10N 22 50 E
Brádano →, *Italy* . . . . **47 B9** 40 23N 16 51 E
Bradenton, *U.S.A.* **149 M4** 27 30N 82 34W
Bradford, *Canada* **150 B5** 44 7N 79 34W
Bradford, *U.K.* **20 D6** 53 47N 1 45W
Bradford, *Ill., U.S.A.* **156 C7** 41 11N 89 39W
Bradford, *Ohio, U.S.A.* **157 D12** 40 8N 84 27W
Bradford, *Pa., U.S.A.* **150 E6** 41 58N 78 38W
Bradford, *Vt., U.S.A.* **151 C12** 43 59N 72 9W
Bradley, *Ark., U.S.A.* **155 J8** 33 6N 93 39W
Bradley, *Calif., U.S.A.* **160 K6** 35 52N 120 48W
Bradley, *Fla., U.S.A.* **153 H8** 27 48N 81 59W
Bradley, *Ill., U.S.A.* **157 C9** 41 9N 87 52W
Bradley, *S. Dak., U.S.A.* **154 C6** 45 5N 97 39W
Bradley Institute, *Zimbabwe* **119 F3** 17 7 S 31 25 E
Bradore Bay, *Canada* **141 B8** 51 27N 57 18W
Bradshaw, *Australia* . . . . **124 C5** 15 21 S 130 16 E
Brady, *U.S.A.* **155 K5** 31 9N 99 20W
Brædstrup, *Denmark* . . . . **17 J3** 55 58N 9 37 E
Braemar, *Australia* . . . . **128 B3** 33 12 S 139 35 E
Braemar, *U.K.* **22 D5** 57 0N 3 23W
Braeside, *Canada* **151 A8** 45 28N 76 24W
Braga, *Portugal* **42 D2** 41 35N 8 25W
Braga □, *Portugal* **42 D2** 41 30N 8 30W
Bragadiru, *Romania* . . . . **53 G10** 43 46N 25 31 E
Bragado, *Argentina* . . . . **174 D3** 35 2 S 60 27W
Bragança, *Brazil* . . . . **170 B2** 1 0 S 47 2W
Bragança, *Portugal* **42 D4** 41 48N 6 50W
Bragança □, *Portugal* **42 D4** 41 30N 6 45W
Bragança Paulista, *Brazil* . . . **175 A6** 22 55 S 46 32W
Brahmanbaria, *Bangla.* . . . . . **90 D3** 23 58N 91 15 E
Brahmani →, *India* . . . . **94 D8** 20 39N 86 46 E
Brahmapur, *India* . . . . **94 E7** 19 15N 84 54 E
Brahmaputra →, *India* . . . . . **90 D2** 23 58N 89 50 E
Braich-y-pwll, *U.K.* **20 E3** 52 47N 4 46W
Braidwood, *Australia* . . . . **129 C8** 35 27 S 149 49 E
Brăila, *Romania* . . . . **53 E12** 45 19N 27 59 E
Brăila □, *Romania* . . . . **53 E12** 45 5N 27 30 E
Brainerd, *U.S.A.* **154 B7** 46 22N 94 12W
Braintree, *U.K.* . . . . **21 F8** 51 53N 0 34 E
Braintree, *U.S.A.* **151 D14** 42 13N 71 0W
Brak →, *S. Africa* . . . . **116 D3** 29 35 S 22 55 E
Brake, *Germany* . . . . **30 B4** 53 20N 8 28 E
Brakel, *Germany* . . . . **30 D5** 51 42N 9 11 E
Bräkne-Hoby, *Sweden* . . . . . . **17 H9** 56 14N 15 6 E
Brakwater, *Namibia* . . . . **116 C2** 22 28 S 17 3 E
Brålanda, *Sweden* . . . . **17 F6** 58 34N 12 21 E
Bralorne, *Canada* **142 C4** 50 50N 122 50W
Bramberg, *Germany* . . . . **31 E6** 50 6N 10 40 E
Bramdrupdam, *Denmark* . . . . **17 J3** 55 31N 9 28 E
Bramming, *Denmark* . . . . **17 J2** 55 28N 8 42 E
Brämön, *Sweden* . . . . **16 B11** 62 14N 17 40 E
Brampton, *Canada* **140 D4** 43 45N 79 45W
Brampton, *U.K.* **20 C5** 54 57N 2 44W
Bramsche, *Germany* . . . . **30 C3** 52 24N 7 59 E
Bramwell, *Australia* . . . . **126 A3** 12 8 S 142 37 E
Branchville, *U.S.A.* **152 B9** 33 15N 80 49W

194 Branco

Branco →, *Brazil* 169 D5 1 20 S 61 50W
Branco, C., *Brazil* 170 C5 7 9 S 34 47W
Brandbu, *Norway* 18 D7 60 26N 10 28 E
Brande, *Denmark* 17 J3 55 57N 9 8 E
Brandenburg =
Neubrandenburg, *Germany* 30 B9 53 33N 13 15 E
Brandenburg, *Germany* 30 C8 52 25N 12 33 E
Brandenburg, *U.S.A.* 157 G10 38 0N 86 10W
Brandenburg □, *Germany* 30 C9 52 50N 13 0 E
Brandfort, *S. Africa* 116 D4 28 40 S 26 30 E
Brando, *France* 29 F13 42 47N 9 27 E
Brandon, *Canada* 143 D9 49 50N 99 57W
Brandon, *Fla., U.S.A.* 153 H7 27 56N 82 17W
Brandon, *Vt., U.S.A.* 151 C11 43 48N 73 4W
Brandon B., *Ireland* 23 D1 52 17N 10 8W
Brandon Mt., *Ireland* 23 D1 52 15N 10 15W
Brandsen, *Argentina* 174 D4 35 10 S 58 15W
Brandvlei, *S. Africa* 116 E3 30 25 S 20 30 E
Brandýs nad Labem,
Czech Rep. 34 A7 50 10N 14 40 E
Brănești, *Romania* 53 F11 44 27N 26 20 E
Branford, *Conn., U.S.A.* 151 E12 41 17N 72 49W
Branford, *Fla., U.S.A.* 152 F7 29 58N 82 56W
Braniewo, *Poland* 54 D6 54 25N 19 50 E
Bransfield Str., *Antarctica* 7 C18 63 0 S 59 0W
Brańsk, *Poland* 55 F9 52 45N 22 50 E
Branson, *Colo., U.S.A.* 155 G3 37 1N 103 53W
Branson, *Mo., U.S.A.* 155 G8 36 39N 93 13W
Brantford, *Canada* 140 D3 43 10N 80 15W
Brantley, *U.S.A.* 152 D3 31 35N 86 16W
Brantôme, *France* 28 C4 45 22N 0 39 E
Branxholme, *Australia* 128 D4 37 52 S 141 49 E
Branxton, *Australia* 129 B9 32 38 S 151 21 E
Branzi, *Italy* 44 B6 46 1N 9 46 E
Bras d'Or, L., *Canada* 141 C7 45 50N 60 50W
Brasil, Planalto, *Brazil* 166 E6 18 0 S 46 30W
Brasiléia, *Brazil* 172 C4 11 0 S 68 45W
Brasília, *Brazil* 171 E2 15 47 S 47 55W
Brasília Legal, *Brazil* 169 D6 3 49 S 55 36W
Braskereidfoss, *Norway* 18 D8 60 44N 11 46 E
Braslaw, *Belarus* 15 J22 55 38N 27 0 E
Braslovče, *Slovenia* 45 B12 46 21N 15 3 E
Brașov, *Romania* 53 E10 45 38N 25 35 E
Brașov □, *Romania* 53 E10 45 45N 25 15 E
Brass, *Nigeria* 113 E6 4 35N 6 14 E
Brass →, *Nigeria* 113 E6 4 15N 6 13 E
Brassac-les-Mines, *France* 28 C7 45 24N 3 20 E
Brasschaat, *Belgium* 24 C4 51 19N 4 27 E
Brassey, Banjaran, *Malaysia* 85 B5 5 0N 117 15 E
Brassey Ra., *Australia* 125 E3 25 8 S 122 15 E
Brasstown Bald, *U.S.A.* 149 H4 34 53N 83 49W
Brastad, *Sweden* 17 F5 58 23N 11 30 E
Brastavățu, *Romania* 53 G9 43 55N 24 24 E
Bratan = Morozov, *Bulgaria* 51 D9 42 30N 25 10 E
Brateș, *Romania* 53 E11 45 50N 26 4 E
Bratislava, *Slovak Rep.* 35 C10 48 10N 17 7 E
Bratislavský □, *Slovak Rep.* 35 C10 48 15N 17 20 E
Bratsigovo, *Bulgaria* 51 D8 42 1N 24 22 E
Bratsk, *Russia* 65 D11 56 10N 101 30 E
Bratt, *U.S.A.* 153 E2 30 58N 87 26W
Brattleboro, *U.S.A.* 151 D12 42 51N 72 34W
Brattvåg, *Norway* 18 B3 62 37N 6 25 E
Bratunac, *Bos.-H.* 52 F4 44 13N 19 21 E
Braunau, *Austria* 34 C6 48 15N 13 3 E
Braunschweig, *Germany* 30 C6 52 15N 10 31 E
Braunton, *U.K.* 21 F3 51 7N 4 10W
Brava, *Somali Rep.* 120 D2 1 20N 44 8 E
Bravicea, *Moldova* 53 C13 47 22N 28 27 E
Bråviken, *Sweden* 17 F10 58 38N 16 32 E
Bravo del Norte →, *Mexico* 162 B5 25 57N 97 9W
Bravo del Norte, Rio → =
Grande, Rio →, *U.S.A.* 155 N6 25 58N 97 9W
Brawley, *U.S.A.* 161 N11 32 59N 115 31W
Bray, *Ireland* 23 C5 53 13N 6 7W
Bray, Mt., *Australia* 126 A1 14 0 S 134 30 E
Bray-sur-Seine, *France* 27 D10 48 25N 3 14 E
Braymer, *U.S.A.* 156 E3 39 35N 93 48W
Brazeau →, *Canada* 142 C5 52 55N 115 14W
Brazil, *U.S.A.* 157 E9 39 32N 87 8W
Brazil ■, *S. Amer.* 171 D2 12 0 S 50 0W
Brazilian Highlands = Brasil,
Planalto, *Brazil* 166 E6 18 0 S 46 30W
Brazo Sur →, *S. Amer.* 174 B4 25 21 S 57 42W
Brazos →, *U.S.A.* 155 L7 28 53N 95 23W
Brazzaville, *Congo* 115 C3 4 9 S 15 12 E
Brčko, *Bos.-H.* 52 F3 44 54N 18 46 E
Brda →, *Poland* 55 E5 53 8N 18 8 E
Brdy, *Czech Rep.* 34 B6 49 43N 13 55 E
Brea, *Peru* 172 A1 4 40 S 81 7W
Breadalbane, *Australia* 126 C2 23 50 S 139 35 E
Breaden, L., *Australia* 125 E4 25 51 S 125 28 E
Breaksea Sd., *N.Z.* 131 F1 45 35 S 166 35 E
Bream B., *N.Z.* 130 B3 35 56 S 174 28 E
Bream Hd., *N.Z.* 130 B3 35 51 S 174 36 E
Bream Tail, *N.Z.* 130 C3 36 3 S 174 36 E
Breas, *Chile* 174 B1 25 29 S 70 24W
Breaza, *Romania* 53 E10 45 11N 25 40 E
Brebes, *Indonesia* 85 D3 6 52 S 109 3 E
Brechin, *Canada* 150 B5 44 32N 79 10W
Brechin, *U.K.* 22 E6 56 44N 2 39W
Brecht, *Belgium* 24 C4 51 21N 4 38 E
Breckenridge, *Colo., U.S.A.* 158 G10 39 29N 106 3W
Breckenridge, *Minn., U.S.A.* 154 B6 46 16N 96 35W
Breckenridge, *Mo., U.S.A.* 156 E3 39 46N 93 48W
Breckenridge, *Tex., U.S.A.* 155 J5 32 45N 98 54W
Breckland, *U.K.* 21 E8 52 30N 0 40 E
Brecknock, Pen., *Chile* 176 D2 54 35 S 71 30W
Břeclav, *Czech Rep.* 35 C9 48 46N 16 53 E
Brecon, *U.K.* 21 F4 51 57N 3 23W
Brecon Beacons, *U.K.* 21 F4 51 53N 3 26W
Breda, *Neths.* 24 C4 51 35N 4 45 E
Bredaryd, *Sweden* 17 G7 57 10N 13 45 E
Bredasdorp, *S. Africa* 116 E3 34 33 S 20 2 E
Bredbo, *Australia* 129 C8 35 58 S 149 10 E
Bredebro, *Denmark* 17 J2 55 4N 8 50 E
Bredstedt, *Germany* 30 A4 54 37N 8 55 E
Bredy, *Russia* 62 E8 52 26N 60 21 E
Bree, *Belgium* 24 C5 51 8N 5 35 E
Bregalnica →, *Macedonia* 50 E6 41 43N 22 9 E
Bregenz, *Austria* 34 D2 47 30N 9 45 E
Bregovo, *Bulgaria* 50 B6 44 9N 22 39 E
Bréhal, *France* 26 D5 48 53N 1 30W
Bréhat, Î. de, *France* 26 D4 48 51N 3 0W
Breiðafjörður, *Iceland* 11 B3 65 15N 23 15W
Breiðavík, *Iceland* 11 B2 65 33N 24 21W
Breiðdalsvík, *Iceland* 11 C13 64 44N 14 0W
Breil-sur-Roya, *France* 29 E11 43 56N 7 31 E
Breim, *Norway* 18 C3 61 44N 6 25 E
Breisach, *Germany* 31 G3 48 1N 7 36 E
Brejinho de Nazaré, *Brazil* 170 D2 11 1 S 48 34W
Brejo, *Brazil* 170 B3 3 41 S 42 47W
Brekke, *Norway* 18 C2 61 1N 5 26 E
Brekken, *Norway* 18 B8 62 40N 11 51 E
Brekkestø, *Norway* 18 F5 58 11N 8 22 E
Bremanger, *Norway* 18 C1 61 51N 4 58 E
Bremangerlandet, *Norway* 18 C1 61 51N 5 0 E
Bremen, *Germany* 30 B4 53 4N 8 47 E
Bremen, *U.S.A.* 152 B4 33 43N 85 9W
Bremen □, *Germany* 30 B4 53 4N 8 50 E
Bremer I., *Australia* 126 A2 12 5 S 136 45 E
Bremerhaven, *Germany* 30 B4 53 33N 8 36 E
Bremerton, *U.S.A.* 160 C4 47 34N 122 38W
Bremervörde, *Germany* 30 B5 53 29N 9 8 E
Bremnes, *Norway* 18 E2 59 47N 5 8 E
Bremsnes, *Norway* 18 A4 63 6N 7 40 E
Brenes, *Spain* 43 H5 37 32N 5 54W
Brenham, *U.S.A.* 155 K6 30 10N 96 24W
Brenne, *France* 28 B5 46 44N 1 14 E
Brennerpass, *Austria* 34 D4 47 2N 11 30 E
Brennhaug, *Norway* 18 C6 61 54N 9 21 E
Breno, *Italy* 44 C7 45 57N 10 18 E
Brent, *Canada* 140 C4 46 2N 78 29W
Brenta →, *Italy* 45 C9 45 11N 12 18 E
Brentwood, *U.K.* 21 F8 51 37N 0 19 E
Brentwood, *U.S.A.* 151 F11 40 47N 73 15W
Bréscia, *Italy* 44 C7 45 33N 10 15 E
Breskens, *Neths.* 24 C3 51 23N 3 33 E
Breslau = Wrocław, *Poland* 55 G4 51 5N 17 5 E
Bresle →, *France* 26 B8 50 4N 1 22 E
Bressanone, *Italy* 45 B8 46 43N 11 39 E
Bressay, *U.K.* 22 A7 60 9N 1 6W
Bresse, *France* 27 F12 46 50N 5 10 E
Bressuire, *France* 26 F6 46 51N 0 30W
Brest, *Belarus* 59 F2 52 10N 23 40 E
Brest, *France* 26 D2 48 24N 4 31W
Brest-Litovsk = Brest,
Belarus 59 F2 52 10N 23 40 E
Bretagne, *France* 26 D3 48 10N 3 0W
Bretçu, *Romania* 53 D11 46 7N 26 18 E
Bretenoux, *France* 28 D5 44 54N 1 51 E
Breteuil, *Eure, France* 26 D7 48 50N 0 57 E
Breteuil, *Oise, France* 27 C9 49 38N 2 18 E
Breton, *Canada* 142 C6 53 7N 114 28W
Breton, Pertuis, *France* 28 B2 46 17N 1 25W
Breton Sd., *U.S.A.* 155 L10 29 35N 89 15W
Brett, C., *N.Z.* 130 B3 35 10 S 174 20 E
Bretten, *Germany* 31 F4 49 2N 8 42 E
Breuil-Cervínia, *Italy* 44 C4 45 56N 7 38 E
Brevard, *U.S.A.* 149 H4 35 14N 82 44W
Breves, *Brazil* 170 B1 1 40 S 50 29W
Brevig Mission, *U.S.A.* 144 D6 65 20N 166 29W
Brevik, *Norway* 18 E6 59 4N 9 42 E
Brewarrina, *Australia* 127 E4 30 0 S 146 51 E
Brewer, *U.S.A.* 141 D6 44 48N 68 46W
Brewer, Mt., *U.S.A.* 160 J8 36 44N 118 28W
Brewster, *N.Y., U.S.A.* 151 E11 41 23N 73 37W
Brewster, *Wash., U.S.A.* 158 B4 48 6N 119 47W
Brewster, Kap, *Greenland* 10 C8 70 7N 22 0W
Brewton, *Ala., U.S.A.* 149 K2 31 7N 87 4W
Brewton, *Ga., U.S.A.* 152 C7 32 36N 82 48W
Breyten, *S. Africa* 117 D5 26 16 S 30 0 E
Breza, *Bos.-H.* 52 F3 44 2N 18 16 E
Brezhnev = Naberezhnyye
Chelny, *Russia* 60 C11 55 42N 52 19 E
Brežice, *Slovenia* 45 C12 45 54N 15 35 E
Brézina, *Algeria* 111 B5 33 4N 1 14 E
Březnice, *Czech Rep.* 34 B6 49 32N 13 57 E
Breznik, *Bulgaria* 50 D6 42 44N 22 55 E
Brezno, *Slovak Rep.* 35 C12 48 50N 19 40 E
Brezoi, *Romania* 53 E9 45 21N 24 15 E
Brezovo, *Bulgaria* 51 D9 42 21N 25 5 E
Bria, *C.A.R.* 114 A4 6 30N 21 58 E
Briançon, *France* 29 D10 44 54N 6 39 E
Briare, *France* 27 E9 47 38N 2 45 E
Briático, *Italy* 47 D9 38 43N 16 2 E
Bribbaree, *Australia* 129 C7 34 10 S 147 51 E
Bribie I., *Australia* 127 D5 27 0 S 153 10 E
Briceni, *Moldova* 53 B12 48 22N 27 6 E
Bricquebec, *France* 26 C5 49 28N 1 38W
Bridgeboro, *U.S.A.* 152 D6 31 24N 83 59W
Bridgehampton, *U.S.A.* 151 F12 40 56N 72 19W
Bridgend, *U.K.* 21 F4 51 30N 3 34W
Bridgend □, *U.K.* 21 F4 51 36N 3 36W
Bridgeport, *Calif., U.S.A.* 160 G7 38 15N 119 14W
Bridgeport, *Conn., U.S.A.* 151 E11 41 11N 73 12W
Bridgeport, *Nebr., U.S.A.* 154 E3 41 40N 103 6W
Bridgeport, *Tex., U.S.A.* 155 J6 33 13N 97 45W
Bridger, *U.S.A.* 158 D9 45 18N 108 55W
Bridgeton, *U.S.A.* 148 F8 39 26N 75 14W
Bridgetown, *Australia* 125 F2 33 58 S 116 7 E
Bridgetown, *Barbados* 165 D8 13 5N 59 30W
Bridgetown, *Canada* 141 D6 44 55N 65 18W
Bridgewater, *Australia* 128 D5 36 36 S 143 59 E
Bridgewater, *Canada* 141 D7 44 25N 64 31W
Bridgewater, *Mass., U.S.A.* 151 E14 41 59N 70 58W
Bridgewater, *S. Dak.,
U.S.A.* 154 D6 43 33N 97 30W
Bridgewater, C., *Australia* 128 E4 38 23 S 141 23 E
Bridgman, *U.S.A.* 157 C10 41 57N 86 33W
Bridgnorth, *U.K.* 21 E5 52 32N 2 25W
Bridgton, *U.S.A.* 151 B14 44 3N 70 42W
Bridgwater, *U.K.* 21 F5 51 8N 2 59W
Bridgwater B., *U.K.* 21 F4 51 15N 3 15W
Bridlington, *U.K.* 20 C7 54 5N 0 12W
Bridlington B., *U.K.* 20 C7 54 4N 0 10W
Bridport, *Australia* 126 G4 40 59 S 147 23 E
Bridport, *U.K.* 21 G5 50 44N 2 45W
Briec, *France* 26 D2 48 6N 4 0W
Brienne-le-Château, *France* 27 D11 48 24N 4 30 E
Brienon-sur-Armançon,
France 27 E10 47 59N 3 38 E
Brienz, *Switz.* 32 C6 46 46N 8 2 E
Brienzersee, *Switz.* 32 C5 46 44N 7 53 E
Brier Cr. →, *U.S.A.* 152 C8 32 44N 81 26W
Brig, *Switz.* 32 D5 46 18N 7 59 E
Brigg, *U.K.* 20 D7 53 34N 0 28W
Briggsdale, *U.S.A.* 154 E2 40 38N 104 20W
Brigham City, *U.S.A.* 158 F7 41 31N 112 1W
Bright, *Australia* 129 D7 36 42 S 146 56 E
Brighton, *Australia* 128 C3 35 5 S 138 30 E
Brighton, *Canada* 140 D4 44 2N 77 44W
Brighton, *U.K.* 21 G7 50 49N 0 7W
Brighton, *Colo., U.S.A.* 154 F2 39 59N 104 49W
Brighton, *Fla., U.S.A.* 153 H8 27 14N 81 6W
Brighton, *Ill., U.S.A.* 156 E6 39 2N 90 8W
Brighton, *Iowa, U.S.A.* 156 C5 41 10N 91 49W
Brighton Seminole Indian
Reservation, *U.S.A.* 153 H8 27 0N 81 15W
Brightwater, *N.Z.* 131 B8 41 22 S 173 9 E
Brignogan-Plage, *France* 26 D2 48 40N 4 20W
Brignoles, *France* 29 E10 43 25N 6 5 E
Brihuega, *Spain* 40 E2 40 45N 2 52W
Brikama, *Gambia* 112 C1 13 15N 16 45W
Brilliant, *Canada* 142 D5 49 19N 117 38W
Brilliant, *U.S.A.* 150 F4 40 15N 80 39W
Brilon, *Germany* 30 D4 51 23N 8 35 E
Brim, *Australia* 128 D5 36 3 S 142 27 E
Brimfield, *U.S.A.* 156 D7 40 50N 89 53W
Bríndisi, *Italy* 47 B10 40 39N 17 55 E
Brinje, *Croatia* 45 D12 44 59N 15 9 E
Brinkley, *U.S.A.* 155 H9 34 53N 91 12W
Brinkworth, *Australia* 128 B3 33 42 S 138 26 E
Brinnon, *U.S.A.* 160 C4 47 41N 122 54W
Brinson, *U.S.A.* 152 E5 30 59N 84 44W
Brion, I., *Canada* 141 C7 47 46N 61 26W
Brionne, *France* 26 C7 49 11N 0 43 E
Brionski, *Croatia* 45 D10 44 55N 13 45 E
Brioude, *France* 28 C7 45 18N 3 24 E
Briouze, *France* 26 D6 48 42N 0 23W
Brisbane, *Australia* 127 D5 27 25 S 153 2 E
Brisbane →, *Australia* 127 D5 27 24 S 153 9 E
Brisighella, *Italy* 45 D8 44 13N 11 46 E
Bristol, *U.K.* 21 F5 51 26N 2 35W
Bristol, *Conn., U.S.A.* 151 E12 41 40N 72 57W
Bristol, *Fla., U.S.A.* 152 E5 30 26N 84 59W
Bristol, *Pa., U.S.A.* 151 F10 40 6N 74 51W
Bristol, *R.I., U.S.A.* 151 E13 41 40N 71 16W
Bristol, *S. Dak., U.S.A.* 154 C6 45 21N 97 45W
Bristol, *Tenn., U.S.A.* 149 G4 36 36N 82 11W
Bristol, City of □, *U.K.* 21 F5 51 27N 2 36W
Bristol B., *U.S.A.* 138 C4 58 0N 160 0W
Bristol Channel, *U.K.* 21 F3 51 18N 4 30W
Bristol I., *Antarctica* 7 B1 58 45 S 28 0W
Bristol L., *U.S.A.* 159 J5 34 23N 116 50W
Bristow, *U.S.A.* 155 H6 35 50N 96 23W
British Columbia □, *Canada* 142 C3 55 0N 125 15W
British Isles, *Europe* 12 E5 54 0N 4 0W
Brits, *S. Africa* 117 D4 25 37 S 27 48 E
Britstown, *S. Africa* 116 E3 30 37 S 23 30 E
Britt, *Canada* 140 C3 45 46N 80 34W
Britt, *U.S.A.* 156 A3 43 6N 93 48W
Brittany = Bretagne, *France* 26 D3 48 10N 3 0W
Britton, *U.S.A.* 154 C6 45 48N 97 45W
Brive-la-Gaillarde, *France* 28 C5 45 10N 1 32 E
Briviesca, *Spain* 42 C7 42 32N 3 19W
Brixen = Bressanone, *Italy* 45 B8 46 43N 11 39 E
Brixham, *U.K.* 21 G4 50 23N 3 31W
Brixton, *Australia* 126 C3 23 32 S 144 57 E
Brlik = Birlik, *Kazakstan* 63 A6 44 5N 73 31 E
Brlik, *Kazakstan* 63 B6 43 40N 73 49 E
Brnaze, *Croatia* 45 E13 43 41N 16 40 E
Brno, *Czech Rep.* 35 B9 49 10N 16 35 E
Broach = Bharuch, *India* 94 D1 21 47N 73 0 E
Broad →, *Ga., U.S.A.* 152 B7 33 59N 82 39W
Broad →, *S.C., U.S.A.* 149 J5 34 1N 81 4W
Broad Arrow, *Australia* 125 F3 30 23 S 121 15 E
Broad B., *U.K.* 22 C2 58 14N 6 18W
Broad Haven, *Ireland* 23 B2 54 20N 9 55W
Broad Law, *U.K.* 22 F5 55 30N 3 21W
Broad Sd., *Australia* 126 C4 22 0 S 149 45 E
Broadford, *Australia* 129 D6 37 14 S 145 4 E
Broadhurst, *U.S.A.* 152 D8 31 28N 81 55W
Broadhurst Ra., *Australia* 124 D3 22 30 S 122 30 E
Broads, The, *U.K.* 20 E9 52 45N 1 30 E
Broadus, *U.S.A.* 154 C2 45 27N 105 25W
Broadview, *Canada* 143 C8 50 22N 102 35W
Broager, *Denmark* 17 K3 54 53N 9 40 E
Broby, *Sweden* 17 H8 56 15N 14 4 E
Broceni, *Latvia* 54 B9 56 42N 22 32 E
Brochet, *Canada* 143 B8 57 53N 101 40W
Brochet, L., *Canada* 143 B8 58 36N 101 35W
Brock, *Canada* 143 C7 51 26N 108 43W
Brocken, *Germany* 30 D6 51 47N 10 37 E
Brocklehurst, *Australia* 129 B8 32 9 S 148 38 E
Brockport, *U.S.A.* 150 C7 43 13N 77 56W
Brockton, *U.S.A.* 151 D13 42 5N 71 1W
Brockville, *Canada* 140 D4 44 35N 75 41W
Brockway, *Mont., U.S.A.* 154 B2 47 18N 105 45W
Brockway, *Pa., U.S.A.* 150 E6 41 15N 78 47W
Brocton, *U.S.A.* 150 D5 42 23N 79 26W
Brod, *Macedonia* 50 E5 41 32N 21 17 E
Brodarevo, *Serbia, Yug.* 50 C3 43 14N 19 44 E
Brodeur Pen., *Canada* 139 A11 72 30N 88 10W
Brodhead, *U.S.A.* 156 B7 42 37N 89 22W
Brodick, *U.K.* 22 F3 55 35N 5 9W
Brodnica, *Poland* 55 E6 53 15N 19 25 E
Brody, *Ukraine* 59 G3 50 5N 25 10 E
Brogan, *U.S.A.* 158 D5 44 15N 117 31W
Broglie, *France* 26 C7 49 2N 0 30 E
Brok, *Poland* 55 F8 52 43N 21 52 E
Broken Arrow, *U.S.A.* 155 G7 36 3N 95 48W
Broken Bow, *Nebr., U.S.A.* 154 E5 41 24N 99 38W
Broken Bow, *Okla., U.S.A.* 155 H7 34 2N 94 44W
Broken Hill = Kabwe,
Zambia 119 E2 14 30 S 28 29 E
Broken Hill, *Australia* 128 A4 31 58 S 141 29 E
Brokind, *Sweden* 17 F9 58 13N 15 42 E
Brokopondo, *Surinam* 169 B7 5 3N 54 59W
Brokopondo □, *Surinam* 169 C6 4 30N 55 30W
Bromley, *U.K.* 21 F8 51 24N 0 2 E
Bromölla, *Sweden* 17 H8 56 5N 14 28 E
Bromsgrove, *U.K.* 21 E5 52 21N 2 2W
Bronaugh, *U.S.A.* 156 G2 37 41N 94 28W
Brønderslev, *Denmark* 17 G3 57 16N 9 57 E
Brong-Ahafo □, *Ghana* 112 D4 7 50N 2 0W
Broni, *Italy* 44 C6 45 4N 9 16 E
Bronkhorstspruit, *S. Africa* 117 D4 25 46 S 28 45 E
Brønnøysund, *Norway* 14 D15 65 28N 12 14 E
Bronson, *Fla., U.S.A.* 153 F7 29 27N 82 39W
Bronson, *Mich., U.S.A.* 157 C11 41 52N 85 12W
Bronte, *Italy* 47 E7 37 47N 14 50 E
Bronte, *U.S.A.* 155 K4 31 53N 100 18W
Bronte Park, *Australia* 126 G4 42 8 S 146 30 E
Bronwood, *U.S.A.* 152 D5 31 50N 84 22W
Brook Park, *U.S.A.* 150 E4 41 24N 80 51W
Brookes Point, *Phil.* 81 G1 8 47N 117 50 E
Brookfield, *U.S.A.* 156 E3 39 47N 93 4W
Brookhaven, *U.S.A.* 155 K9 31 35N 90 26W
Brookings, *Oreg., U.S.A.* 158 E1 42 3N 124 17W
Brookings, *S. Dak., U.S.A.* 154 C6 44 19N 96 48W
Brooklet, *U.S.A.* 152 C8 32 23N 81 40W
Brooklin, *Canada* 150 C6 43 55N 78 55W
Brooklyn, *U.S.A.* 156 C4 41 44N 92 27W
Brooklyn Park, *U.S.A.* 154 C8 45 6N 93 23W
Brookmere, *Canada* 142 D4 49 52N 120 53W
Brooks, *Canada* 142 C6 50 35N 111 55W
Brooks B., *Canada* 142 C3 50 15N 127 55W
Brooks L., *Canada* 143 A7 61 55N 106 35W
Brooks Range, *U.S.A.* 144 C10 68 0N 152 0W
Brookston, *U.S.A.* 157 D10 40 36N 86 52W
Brooksville, *Fla., U.S.A.* 149 L4 28 33N 82 23W
Brooksville, *Ky., U.S.A.* 157 F12 38 41N 84 4W
Brookville, *U.S.A.* 157 E12 39 25N 85 1W
Brooloo, *Australia* 127 D5 26 30 S 152 43 E
Broom, L., *U.K.* 22 D3 57 55N 5 15W
Broome, *Australia* 124 C3 18 0 S 122 15 E
Broomehill, *Australia* 125 F2 33 51 S 117 39 E
Broons, *France* 26 D4 48 20N 2 16W
Brora, *U.K.* 22 C5 58 0N 3 52W
Brora →, *U.K.* 22 C5 58 0N 3 51W
Brørup, *Denmark* 17 J2 55 29N 9 1 E
Brösarp, *Sweden* 17 J8 55 43N 14 6 E
Brosna →, *Ireland* 23 C4 53 14N 7 58W
Broșteni, *Mehedinți,
Romania* 52 F7 44 45N 22 59 E
Broșteni, *Suceava, Romania* 53 C10 47 14N 25 43 E
Brostrud, *Norway* 18 D5 60 18N 8 34 E
Brotas de Macaúbas, *Brazil* 171 D3 12 0 S 42 38W
Brothers, *U.S.A.* 158 E3 43 49N 120 36W
Brøttum, *Norway* 18 C7 61 2N 10 34 E
Brou, *France* 26 D8 48 13N 1 11 E
Brouage, *France* 28 C2 45 52N 1 4W
Brough, *U.K.* 20 C5 54 32N 2 18W
Brough Hd., *U.K.* 22 B5 59 8N 3 20W
Broughams Gate, *Australia* 128 A4 30 51 S 140 59 E
Broughton, *U.S.A.* 157 G8 37 56N 88 27W
Broughton Island, *Canada* 139 B13 67 33N 63 0W
Broumov, *Czech Rep.* 35 A9 50 35N 16 20 E
Brovary, *Ukraine* 59 G6 50 34N 30 48 E
Brovst, *Denmark* 17 G3 57 6N 9 31 E
Browerville, *U.S.A.* 154 B7 46 5N 94 52W
Brown, Mt., *Australia* 128 B3 32 30 S 138 0 E
Brown, Pt., *Australia* 127 E1 32 32 S 133 50 E
Brown Willy, *U.K.* 21 G3 50 35N 4 37W
Brownfield, *U.S.A.* 155 J3 33 11N 102 17W
Browning, *Ill., U.S.A.* 156 D6 40 8N 90 22W
Browning, *Mo., U.S.A.* 156 D3 40 3N 93 12W
Browning, *Mont., U.S.A.* 158 B7 48 34N 113 1W
Browning Pass, *N.Z.* 131 C6 42 55 S 171 22 E
Brownlee, *Canada* 143 C7 50 43N 106 1W
Brownsburg, *U.S.A.* 157 E10 39 51N 86 24W
Brownstown, *U.S.A.* 157 F10 38 53N 86 3W
Brownsville, *Oreg., U.S.A.* 158 D2 44 24N 122 59W
Brownsville, *Tenn., U.S.A.* 155 H10 35 36N 89 16W
Brownsville, *Tex., U.S.A.* 155 N6 25 54N 97 30W
Brownsweg, *Surinam* 169 B6 5 5N 55 15W
Brownwood, *U.S.A.* 155 K5 31 43N 98 59W
Brownwood, L., *U.S.A.* 155 K5 31 51N 98 35W
Browse I., *Australia* 124 B3 14 7 S 123 33 E
Broxton, *U.S.A.* 152 D7 31 38N 82 53W
Broye →, *Switz.* 32 C3 46 52N 6 58 E
Bru, *Norway* 18 C2 61 32N 5 11 E
Bruas, *Malaysia* 87 K3 4 30N 100 47 E
Bruay-la-Buissière, *France* 27 B9 50 29N 2 33 E
Bruce, *U.S.A.* 152 E4 30 28N 85 58W
Bruce, Mt., *Australia* 124 D2 22 37 S 118 8 E
Bruce B., *N.Z.* 131 D4 43 35 S 169 42 E
Bruce Pen., *Canada* 150 B3 45 0N 81 30W
Bruce Rock, *Australia* 125 F2 31 52 S 118 8 E
Bruche →, *France* 27 D14 48 34N 7 43 E
Bruchsal, *Germany* 31 F4 49 7N 8 35 E
Bruck an der Leitha, *Austria* 35 C9 48 1N 16 47 E
Bruck an der Mur, *Austria* 34 D8 47 24N 15 16 E
Brue →, *U.K.* 21 F5 51 13N 2 59W
Bruflat, *Norway* 18 D6 60 53N 9 37 E
Bruges = Brugge, *Belgium* 24 C3 51 13N 3 13 E
Brugg, *Switz.* 32 B6 47 29N 8 11 E
Brugge, *Belgium* 24 C3 51 13N 3 13 E
Brûlé, *Canada* 142 C5 53 15N 117 58W
Brûlon, *France* 26 E6 47 58N 0 15W
Brumado, *Brazil* 171 D3 14 14 S 41 40W
Brumado →, *Brazil* 171 D3 14 13 S 41 40W
Brumath, *France* 27 D14 48 43N 7 40 E
Brumunddal, *Norway* 15 F14 60 53N 10 56 E
Brunchilly, *Australia* 126 B1 18 50 S 134 30 E
Brundidge, *U.S.A.* 152 D4 31 43N 85 49W
Bruneau, *U.S.A.* 158 E6 42 53N 115 48W
Bruneau →, *U.S.A.* 158 E6 42 56N 115 57W
Bruneck = Brunico, *Italy* 45 B8 46 48N 11 56 E
Brunei = Bandar Seri
Begawan, *Brunei* 85 B4 4 52N 115 0 E
Brunei ■, *Asia* 85 B4 4 50N 115 0 E
Brunette Downs, *Australia* 126 B2 18 40 S 135 55 E
Brunflo, *Sweden* 16 A8 63 5N 14 50 E
Brunico, *Italy* 45 B8 46 48N 11 56 E
Brünig, P., *Switz.* 32 C6 46 46N 8 8 E
Brunna, *Sweden* 16 E11 59 52N 17 25 E
Brunnen, *Switz.* 33 C7 46 59N 8 37 E
Brunner, L., *N.Z.* 131 C6 42 37 S 171 27 E
Brunnhóll, *Iceland* 11 C11 64 17N 15 26W
Bruno, *Canada* 143 C7 52 20N 105 30W
Brunsbüttel, *Germany* 30 B5 53 53N 9 6 E
Brunssum, *Neths.* 24 D5 50 57N 5 59 E
Brunswick = Braunschweig,
Germany 30 C6 52 15N 10 31 E
Brunswick, *Ga., U.S.A.* 152 D8 31 10N 81 30W
Brunswick, *Maine, U.S.A.* 141 D6 43 55N 69 58W
Brunswick, *Md., U.S.A.* 148 F7 39 19N 77 38W
Brunswick, *Mo., U.S.A.* 156 E3 39 26N 93 8W
Brunswick, *Ohio, U.S.A.* 150 E3 41 14N 81 51W
Brunswick, Pen. de, *Chile* 176 D2 53 30 S 71 30W
Brunswick B., *Australia* 124 C3 15 15 S 124 50 E
Brunswick Junction,
Australia 125 F2 33 15 S 115 50 E
Bruntál, *Czech Rep.* 35 B10 49 59N 17 27 E
Bruny I., *Australia* 126 G4 43 20 S 147 15 E
Brus Laguna, *Honduras* 164 C3 15 47N 84 35W
Brusartsi, *Bulgaria* 50 C7 43 40N 23 5 E
Brush, *U.S.A.* 154 E3 40 15N 103 37W
Brushton, *U.S.A.* 151 B10 44 50N 74 31W
Brusio, *Switz.* 33 D10 46 14N 10 8 E
Brusque, *Brazil* 175 B6 27 5 S 49 0W
Brussel, *Belgium* 24 D4 50 51N 4 21 E
Brussels = Brussel, *Belgium* 24 D4 50 51N 4 21 E
Brussels, *Canada* 150 C3 43 44N 81 15W
Brusy, *Poland* 54 E4 53 53N 17 43 E
Bruthen, *Australia* 129 D7 37 42 S 147 50 E
Bruvoll, *Norway* 18 D8 60 27N 11 29 E
Bruxelles = Brussel, *Belgium* 24 D4 50 51N 4 21 E
Bruyères, *France* 27 D13 48 10N 6 40 E
Bruz, *France* 26 D5 48 1N 1 46W
Brwinów, *Poland* 55 F7 52 9N 20 40 E
Bryagovo, *Bulgaria* 51 E9 41 58N 25 8 E
Bryan, *Ohio, U.S.A.* 157 C12 41 28N 84 33W
Bryan, *Tex., U.S.A.* 155 K6 30 40N 96 22W
Bryan, Mt., *Australia* 128 B3 33 30 S 139 0 E
Bryanka, *Ukraine* 59 H10 48 32N 38 45 E
Bryansk, *Bryansk, Russia* 59 F8 53 13N 34 25 E
Bryansk, *Dagestan, Russia* 61 H8 44 20N 47 10 E
Bryanskoye = Bryansk,
Russia 61 H8 44 20N 47 10 E

Bussolengo 195

Bryant, U.S.A. 154 C6 44 35N 97 28W
Bryne, Norway 15 G11 58 44N 5 38 E
Bryson City, U.S.A. 149 H4 35 26N 83 27W
Bryukhovetskaya, Russia 59 K10 45 48N 39 0 E
Brza Palanka, Serbia, Yug. 50 B6 44 28N 22 27 E
Brzeg, Poland 55 H4 50 52N 17 30 E
Brzeg Dolny, Poland 55 G3 51 16N 16 41 E
Brześć Kujawski, Poland 55 F5 52 36N 18 55 E
Brzesko, Poland 55 J7 49 59N 20 34 E
Brzeziny, Poland 55 G6 51 49N 19 42 E
Brzozów, Poland 55 J9 49 41N 22 3 E
Bsharri, Lebanon 103 A5 34 15N 36 0 E
Bū Athlah, Libya 108 B3 30 9N 15 39 E
Bū Baqarah, U.A.E. 97 E8 25 35N 56 25 E
Bu Craa, W. Sahara 110 C2 26 45N 12 50W
Bū Ḩasā, U.A.E. 97 F7 23 30N 53 20 E
Bua, Sweden 17 G6 57 14N 12 7 E
Bua Yai, Thailand 86 E4 15 33N 102 26 E
Buad I., Phil. 81 F5 11 40N 124 51 E
Buala, Solomon Is. 133 M10 8 10 S 159 35 E
Buapinang, Indonesia 82 B2 4 40 S 121 30 E
Buba, Guinea-Biss. 112 C2 11 40N 14 59W
Bubanda, Dem. Rep. of the Congo 114 B3 4 14N 19 38 E
Bubanza, Burundi 118 C2 3 6 S 29 23 E
Būbiyān, Kuwait 97 D6 29 45N 48 15 E
Buca, Turkey 49 C9 38 22N 27 11 E
Bucak, Turkey 49 D12 37 28N 30 36 E
Bucaramanga, Colombia 168 B3 7 0N 73 0W
Bucas Grande I., Phil. 81 G5 9 40N 125 57 E
Buccaneer Arch., Australia 124 C3 16 7 S 123 20 E
Buccino, Italy 47 B8 40 38N 15 22 E
Bucecea, Romania 53 C11 47 47N 26 28 E
Buchach, Ukraine 59 H3 49 5N 25 25 E
Buchan, Australia 129 D8 37 30 S 148 12 E
Buchan, U.K. 22 D6 57 32N 2 21W
Buchan Ness, U.K. 22 D7 57 29N 1 46W
Buchanan, Canada 143 C8 51 40N 102 45W
Buchanan, Liberia 112 D2 5 57N 10 2W
Buchanan, Ga., U.S.A. 152 B4 33 48N 85 11W
Buchanan, Mich., U.S.A. 157 C10 41 50N 86 22W
Buchanan, L., Queens., Australia 126 C4 21 35 S 145 52 E
Buchanan, L., W. Austral., Australia 125 E3 25 33 S 123 2 E
Buchanan, L., U.S.A. 155 K5 30 45N 98 25W
Buchanan Cr. →, Australia 126 B2 19 13 S 136 33 E
Buchans, Canada 141 C8 48 50N 56 52W
Bucharest = Bucureşti, Romania 53 F11 44 27N 26 10 E
Buchen, Germany 31 F5 49 32N 9 20 E
Buchholz, Germany 30 B5 53 19N 9 52 E
Buchloe, Germany 31 G6 48 1N 10 44 E
Buchon, Pt., U.S.A. 160 K6 35 15N 120 54W
Buchs, Switz. 33 B8 47 10N 9 28 E
Buciumi, Romania 52 C8 47 3N 23 1 E
Bückeburg, Germany 30 C5 52 16N 9 7 E
Buckeye, U.S.A. 159 K7 33 22N 112 35W
Buckhannon, U.S.A. 148 F5 39 0N 80 8W
Buckhaven, U.K. 22 E5 56 11N 3 3W
Buckie, U.K. 22 D6 57 41N 2 58W
Buckingham, Canada 140 C4 45 37N 75 24W
Buckingham, U.K. 21 F7 51 59N 0 57W
Buckingham B., Australia 126 A2 12 10 S 135 40 E
Buckingham Canal, India 95 H5 14 0N 80 5 E
Buckinghamshire ☐, U.K. 21 F7 51 53N 0 55W
Buckland, U.S.A. 157 D12 40 37N 84 16W
Buckle Hd., Australia 124 B4 14 26 S 127 52 E
Buckleboo, Australia 128 B2 32 54 S 136 12 E
Buckley, U.K. 20 D4 53 10N 3 5W
Buckley, Ill., U.S.A. 157 D8 40 36N 88 2W
Buckley, Wash., U.S.A. 158 C2 47 10N 122 2W
Buckley →, Australia 126 C2 20 10 S 138 49 E
Bucklin, Kans., U.S.A. 155 G5 37 33N 99 38W
Bucklin, Mo., U.S.A. 156 E4 39 47N 92 53W
Bucks L., U.S.A. 160 F5 39 54N 121 12W
Buco Zau, Angola 115 C2 4 46 S 12 33 E
Bucquoy, France 27 B9 50 9N 2 43 E
Buctouche, Canada 141 C7 46 30N 64 45W
Bucureşti, Romania 53 F11 44 27N 26 10 E
Bucyrus, U.S.A. 157 D14 40 48N 82 59W
Bud, Norway 18 B3 62 55N 6 55 E
Budacu, Vf., Romania 53 C10 47 7N 25 41 E
Budalin, Burma 90 D5 22 20N 95 10 E
Budaörs, Hungary 52 C3 47 27N 18 58 E
Budapest, Hungary 52 C4 47 29N 19 5 E
Budapest ☐, Hungary 52 C4 47 29N 19 5 E
Budaun, India 93 E8 28 5N 79 10 E
Budd Coast, Antarctica 7 C8 68 0 S 112 0 E
Buddabadah, Australia 129 A7 31 56 S 147 14 E
Buddusò, Italy 46 B2 40 35N 9 15 E
Bude, U.K. 21 G3 50 49N 4 34W
Budennovsk, Russia 61 H7 44 50N 44 10 E
Budeşti, Romania 53 F11 44 13N 26 30 E
Budge Budge = Baj Baj, India 93 H13 22 30N 88 5 E
Budgewoi, Australia 129 B9 33 13 S 151 34 E
Búðardalur, Iceland 11 B5 65 7N 21 46W
Búðir, Snæfellsnessýsla, Iceland 11 C3 64 49N 23 23W
Búðir, Suður-Múlasýsla, Iceland 11 C12 64 56N 14 1W
Budia, Spain 40 E2 40 38N 2 46W
Büdingen, Germany 31 E5 50 16N 9 7 E
Budjala, Dem. Rep. of the Congo 114 B3 2 50N 19 40 E
Budoni, Italy 46 B2 40 40N 9 45 E
Búdrio, Italy 45 D8 44 32N 11 32 E
Budva, Montenegro, Yug. 50 D2 42 17N 18 50 E
Budzyń, Poland 55 F3 52 54N 16 59 E
Bue, Norway 18 F2 58 40N 5 58 E
Buea, Cameroon 113 E6 4 10N 9 9 E
Buellton, U.S.A. 161 L6 34 37N 120 12W
Buena Park, U.S.A. 161 M9 33 52N 117 59W
Buena Vista, Bolivia 173 D5 17 27 S 63 40W
Buena Vista, Colo., U.S.A. 159 G10 38 51N 106 8W
Buena Vista, Ga., U.S.A. 152 C5 32 19N 84 31W
Buena Vista, Va., U.S.A. 148 G6 37 44N 79 21W
Buena Vista L., U.S.A. 161 K7 35 12N 119 18W
Buenaventura, Colombia 168 C2 3 53N 77 4W
Buenaventura, Mexico 162 B3 29 50N 107 30W
Buenaventura, B. de, Colombia 168 C2 3 48N 77 17W
Buenavista, Luzon, Phil. 80 E4 13 35N 122 34 E
Buenavista, Mindanao, Phil. 81 G5 8 59N 125 24 E
Buenavista, Zamboanga del S., Phil. 81 H4 7 15N 122 16 E
Buendía, Embalse de, Spain 40 E2 40 25N 2 43W
Buenópolis, Brazil 171 E3 17 54 S 44 11W
Buenos Aires, Argentina 174 C4 34 30 S 58 20W
Buenos Aires, Colombia 168 C3 1 36N 73 18W
Buenos Aires, Costa Rica 164 E3 9 10N 83 20W
Buenos Aires ☐, Argentina 174 D4 36 30 S 60 0W
Buenos Aires, L., Chile 176 C2 46 35 S 72 30W
Buesaco, Colombia 168 C2 1 23N 77 9W
Buffalo, Mo., U.S.A. 155 G8 37 39N 93 6W
Buffalo, N.Y., U.S.A. 150 D6 42 53N 78 53W
Buffalo, Okla., U.S.A. 155 G5 36 50N 99 38W
Buffalo, S. Dak., U.S.A. 154 C3 45 35N 103 33W
Buffalo, Wyo., U.S.A. 158 D10 44 21N 106 42W
Buffalo →, Canada 142 A5 60 5N 115 5W
Buffalo Head Hills, Canada 142 B5 57 25N 115 55W
Buffalo L., Canada 142 C6 52 27N 112 54W
Buffalo Narrows, Canada 143 B7 55 51N 108 29W
Buffels →, S. Africa 116 D2 29 36 S 17 3 E
Buford, U.S.A. 149 H4 34 10N 84 0W
Bug → = Buh →, Ukraine 59 J6 46 59N 31 58 E
Bug →, Poland 55 F8 52 31N 21 5 E
Buga, Colombia 168 C2 4 0N 76 15W
Buganda, Uganda 118 C3 0 0 31 30 E
Buganga, Uganda 118 C3 0 3 S 32 0 E
Bugasan, Phil. 81 H5 7 27N 124 14 E
Bugasong, Phil. 81 F4 11 3N 122 4 E
Bugeat, France 28 C5 45 36N 1 55 E
Bugel, Tanjung, Indonesia 85 D4 6 26 S 111 3 E
Bugibba, Malta 38 D1 35 57N 14 25 E
Bugojno, Bos.-H. 52 F2 44 2N 17 25 E
Bugsuk, Phil. 81 G1 8 15N 117 15 E
Buguey, Phil. 80 B3 18 17N 121 50 E
Bugulma, Russia 62 D4 54 33N 52 48 E
Buguma, Nigeria 113 E6 4 42N 6 55 E
Bugun Shara, Mongolia 72 B5 49 0N 104 0 E
Buguruslan, Russia 62 E4 53 39N 52 26 E
Buh →, Ukraine 59 J6 46 59N 31 58 E
Buharkent, Turkey 49 D10 37 58N 28 44 E
Buheirat-Murrat-el-Kubra, Egypt 106 H8 30 18N 32 26 E
Bühl, Germany 31 G4 48 40N 8 8 E
Buhl, Idaho, U.S.A. 158 E6 42 36N 114 46W
Buhl, Minn., U.S.A. 154 B8 47 30N 92 46W
Buhuşi, Romania 53 D11 46 41N 26 45 E
Buick, U.S.A. 155 G9 37 38N 91 2W
Builth Wells, U.K. 21 E4 52 9N 3 25W
Buin, Papua N. G. 133 L8 6 48 S 155 42 E
Buinsk, Russia 60 C9 55 0N 48 18 E
Buíque, Brazil 170 C4 8 37 S 37 9W
Buir Nur, Mongolia 73 B6 47 50N 117 42 E
Buis-les-Baronnies, France 29 D9 44 17N 5 16 E
Buitrago = Buitrago del Lozoya, Spain 42 E7 40 58N 3 38W
Buitrago del Lozoya, Spain 42 E7 40 58N 3 38W
Bujalance, Spain 43 H6 37 54N 4 23W
Bujanovac, Serbia, Yug. 50 D5 42 28N 21 44 E
Bujaraloz, Spain 40 D4 41 29N 0 10W
Buje, Croatia 45 C10 45 24N 13 39 E
Bujumbura, Burundi 118 C2 3 16 S 29 18 E
Bük, Hungary 52 C1 47 22N 16 45 E
Buk, Poland 55 F3 52 21N 16 30 E
Buka I., Papua N. G. 132 C8 5 10 S 154 35 E
Bukachacha, Russia 65 D12 52 55N 116 50 E
Bukama, Dem. Rep. of the Congo 119 D2 9 10 S 25 50 E
Bukavu, Dem. Rep. of the Congo 118 C2 2 20 S 28 52 E
Bukene, Tanzania 118 C3 4 15 S 32 48 E
Bukhara = Bukhoro, Uzbekistan 63 D2 39 48N 64 25 E
Bukhoro, Uzbekistan 63 D2 39 48N 64 25 E
Bukidnon ☐, Phil. 81 H5 8 0N 125 0 E
Bukima, Tanzania 118 C3 1 50 S 33 25 E
Bukit Mertajam, Malaysia 87 K3 5 22N 100 28 E
Bukittinggi, Indonesia 84 C2 0 20 S 100 20 E
Bükk, Hungary 52 B5 48 0N 20 30 E
Bukkapatnam, India 95 G3 14 14N 77 46 E
Bukoba, Tanzania 118 C3 1 20 S 31 49 E
Bukoba ☐, Tanzania 118 C3 1 30 S 32 0 E
Bukuru, Nigeria 113 D6 9 42N 8 48 E
Bukuya, Uganda 118 B3 0 40N 31 52 E
Bula, Guinea-Biss. 112 C1 12 7N 15 43W
Bula, Indonesia 83 B4 3 6 S 130 30 E
Bulacan, Phil. 80 E3 13 40N 120 21 E
Bulacan ☐, Phil. 80 D3 15 0N 121 5 E
Bülach, Switz. 33 A7 47 31N 8 32 E
Bulahdelah, Australia 129 B10 32 23 S 152 13 E
Bulalacao, Phil. 80 E3 12 31N 121 26 E
Bulan, Phil. 80 E4 12 40N 123 52 E
Bulanash, Russia 62 C9 57 16N 62 0 E
Bulancak, Turkey 101 B8 40 56N 38 14 E
Búland, Iceland 11 D8 63 46N 18 30W
Bulandshahr, India 92 E7 28 28N 77 51 E
Bulanık, Turkey 101 C10 39 4N 42 14 E
Bulanovo, Russia 62 E5 52 27N 55 10 E
Bûlâq, Egypt 106 B3 25 10N 30 38 E
Bulawayo, Zimbabwe 119 G2 20 7 S 28 32 E
Buldan, Turkey 49 C10 38 2N 28 50 E
Buldana, India 94 D3 20 30N 76 18 E
Buldon, Phil. 81 H5 7 33N 124 25 E
Bulgar, Russia 60 C9 54 57N 49 4 E
Bulgaria ■, Europe 51 D9 42 35N 25 30 E
Bulgheria, Monte, Italy 47 B8 40 4N 15 26 E
Bulgroo, Australia 127 D3 25 47 S 143 58 E
Bulgunnia, Australia 127 E1 30 10 S 134 53 E
Bulgurca, Turkey 49 C9 38 9N 27 9 E
Bulhale, Somali Rep. 120 C3 5 20N 46 29 E
Bulhar, Somali Rep. 120 B2 10 25N 44 30 E
Buli, Teluk, Indonesia 82 A3 1 5N 128 25 E
Buliluyan, C., Phil. 81 G1 8 20N 117 15 E
Bulki, Ethiopia 107 F4 6 11N 36 31 E
Bulkley →, Canada 142 B3 55 15N 127 40W
Bull Shoals L., U.S.A. 155 G8 36 22N 92 35W
Bullaque →, Spain 43 G6 38 59N 4 17W
Bullara, Australia 124 D1 22 40 S 114 3 E
Bullard, U.S.A. 152 C6 32 38N 83 30W
Bullaring, Australia 125 F2 32 30 S 117 45 E
Bullas, Spain 41 G3 38 2N 1 40W
Bulle, Switz. 32 C4 46 37N 7 3 E
Buller →, N.Z. 131 B6 41 44 S 171 36 E
Buller, Mt., Australia 129 D7 37 10 S 146 28 E
Buller Gorge, N.Z. 131 B7 41 40 S 172 10 E
Bulli, Australia 129 C9 34 15 S 150 57 E
Büllingen, Belgium 24 D6 50 25N 6 16 E
Bullock Creek, Australia 126 B3 17 43 S 144 31 E
Bulloo →, Australia 127 D3 28 43 S 142 30 E
Bulloo Downs, Queens., Australia 127 D3 28 31 S 142 57 E
Bulloo Downs, W. Austral., Australia 124 D2 24 0 S 119 32 E
Bulloo L., Australia 127 D3 28 43 S 142 25 E
Bulls, N.Z. 130 G4 40 10 S 175 24 E
Bully-les-Mines, France 27 B9 50 27N 2 44 E
Bulnes, Chile 174 D1 36 42 S 72 19W
Bulo Burti, Somali Rep. 120 D3 3 50N 45 33 E
Bulo Ghedudo, Somali Rep. 120 D2 2 52N 43 1 E
Bulolo, Papua N. G. 132 D4 7 10 S 146 40 E
Bulongo, Dem. Rep. of the Congo 115 C4 4 45 S 21 30 E
Bulpunga, Australia 128 B4 33 47 S 141 45 E
Bulqiza, Albania 50 E4 41 30N 20 21 E
Bulsar = Valsad, India 94 D1 20 40N 72 58 E
Bultfontein, S. Africa 116 D4 28 18 S 26 10 E
Buluan, L., Phil. 81 H5 6 40N 124 49 E
Buluangan, Phil. 81 F4 10 24N 123 20 E
Bulukumba, Indonesia 82 C2 5 33 S 120 11 E
Bulun, Russia 65 B13 70 37N 127 30 E
Bulunghur, Uzbekistan 63 D3 39 46N 67 16 E
Bulungu, Dem. Rep. of the Congo 115 D4 6 4 S 21 54 E
Bulusan, Phil. 80 E5 12 45N 124 8 E
Bumba, Dem. Rep. of the Congo 114 B4 2 13N 22 30 E
Bumbeşti-Jiu, Romania 53 E8 45 10N 23 24 E
Bumbiri I., Tanzania 118 C3 1 40 S 31 55 E
Bumhkang, Burma 90 B6 26 51N 97 40 E
Bumhpa Bum, Burma 90 B6 26 51N 97 14 E
Bumi →, Zimbabwe 119 F2 17 0 S 28 20 E
Bumtang →, Bhutan 90 B3 26 56N 90 53 E
Buna, Kenya 118 B4 2 58N 39 30 E
Buna, Papua N. G. 132 E5 8 42 S 148 27 E
Bunawan, Agusan del S., Phil. 81 G5 8 12N 125 57 E
Bunawan, Davao del S., Phil. 81 H5 7 14N 125 38 E
Bunazi, Tanzania 118 C3 1 3 S 31 23 E
Bunbah, Khalīj, Libya 108 B4 32 20N 23 15 E
Bunbury, Australia 125 F2 33 20 S 115 35 E
Bunclody, Ireland 23 D5 52 39N 6 40W
Buncrana, Ireland 23 A4 55 8N 7 27W
Bundaberg, Australia 127 C5 24 54 S 152 22 E
Bünde, Germany 30 C4 52 11N 8 35 E
Bundey →, Australia 126 C2 21 46 S 135 37 E
Bundi, India 92 G6 25 30N 75 35 E
Bundooma, Australia 126 C1 24 54 S 134 16 E
Bundoran, Ireland 23 B3 54 28N 8 16W
Bundukia, Sudan 107 F3 5 14N 30 55 E
Bundure, Australia 129 C7 35 10 S 146 1 E
Bung Kan, Thailand 86 C4 18 23N 103 37 E
Bungatakada, Japan 70 D3 33 35N 131 25 E
Bungay, U.K. 21 E9 52 27N 1 28 E
Bungendore, Australia 129 C8 35 14 S 149 30 E
Bungil Cr. →, Australia 126 D4 27 5 S 149 5 E
Bungo, Gunong, Malaysia 85 B4 1 16N 110 9 E
Bungo-Suidō, Japan 70 E4 33 0N 132 15 E
Bungoma, Kenya 118 B3 0 34N 34 34 E
Bungu, Tanzania 118 D4 7 35 S 39 0 E
Bunia, Dem. Rep. of the Congo 118 B3 1 35N 30 20 E
Bunji, Pakistan 93 B6 35 45N 74 40 E
Bunker Hill, Ill., U.S.A. 156 E7 39 3N 89 57W
Bunker Hill, Ind., U.S.A. 157 D10 40 40N 86 6W
Bunkie, U.S.A. 155 K8 30 57N 92 11W
Bunnell, U.S.A. 149 L5 29 28N 81 16W
Bunnythorpe, N.Z. 130 G4 40 16 S 175 39 E
Buñol, Spain 41 F4 39 25N 0 47W
Buntok, Indonesia 85 C4 1 40 S 114 58 E
Bununu, Nigeria 113 D6 9 51N 9 32 E
Bununu Dass, Nigeria 113 C6 10 5N 9 31 E
Bünyan, Turkey 100 C6 38 51N 35 51 E
Bunyu, Indonesia 85 B5 3 35N 117 50 E
Bunza, Nigeria 113 C5 12 8N 4 0 E
Buol, Indonesia 82 A2 1 15N 121 32 E
Buon Brieng, Vietnam 86 F7 13 9N 108 12 E
Buon Ma Thuot, Vietnam 86 F7 12 40N 108 3 E
Buong Long, Cambodia 86 F6 13 44N 106 59 E
Buorkhaya, Mys, Russia 65 B14 71 50N 132 40 E
Buqayq, Si. Arabia 97 E6 26 0N 49 45 E
Buqbuq, Egypt 106 A2 31 29N 25 29 E
Bur Acaba, Somali Rep. 120 D2 3 12N 44 20 E
Bûr Fuad, Egypt 106 H8 31 15N 32 20 E
Bur Ghibi, Somali Rep. 120 D3 3 56N 45 7 E
Bûr Safâga, Egypt 106 B3 26 43N 33 57 E
Bûr Sa'îd, Egypt 106 H8 31 16N 32 18 E
Bûr Sûdân, Sudan 106 D4 19 32N 37 9 E
Bûr Taufiq, Egypt 106 J8 29 54N 32 32 E
Bura, Kenya 118 C4 1 4 S 39 58 E
Buran, Somali Rep. 120 B3 10 14N 48 44 E
Burao, Somali Rep. 120 C3 9 32N 45 32 E
Burāq, Syria 103 B5 33 11N 36 29 E
Buras, U.S.A. 155 L10 29 22N 89 32W
Burauen, Phil. 81 F5 10 58N 124 53 E
Buraydah, Si. Arabia 96 E5 26 20N 44 8 E
Burbank, U.S.A. 161 L8 34 11N 118 19W
Burcher, Australia 129 B7 33 30 S 147 16 E
Burdekin →, Australia 126 B4 19 38 S 147 25 E
Burdeos Bay, Phil. 80 D4 14 44N 122 6 E
Burdett, Canada 142 D6 49 50N 111 32W
Burdur, Turkey 57 G5 37 45N 30 17 E
Burdur ☐, Turkey 49 D12 37 45N 30 0 E
Burdur Gölü, Turkey 49 D12 37 44N 30 10 E
Burdwan = Barddhaman, India 93 H12 23 14N 87 39 E
Bure, Ethiopia 107 E4 10 40N 37 4 E
Bure →, U.K. 20 E9 52 38N 1 43 E
Büren, Germany 30 D4 51 33N 8 35 E
Bureya →, Russia 65 E13 49 27N 129 30 E
Burford, Canada 150 C4 43 7N 80 27W
Burg, Germany 30 C7 52 16N 11 51 E
Burg auf Fehmarn, Germany 30 A7 54 28N 11 9 E
Burg el Arab, Egypt 106 H6 30 54N 29 32 E
Burg et Tuyur, Sudan 106 C2 20 55N 27 56 E
Burg Stargard, Germany 30 B9 53 29N 13 18 E
Burgas, Bulgaria 51 D11 42 33N 27 29 E
Burgas ☐, Bulgaria 51 D10 42 30N 26 50 E
Burgaski Zaliv, Bulgaria 51 D11 42 30N 27 39 E
Burgdorf, Germany 30 C6 52 27N 10 1 E
Burgdorf, Switz. 32 B5 47 3N 7 37 E
Burgenland ☐, Austria 35 D9 47 20N 16 20 E
Burgeo, Canada 141 C8 47 37N 57 38W
Burgersdorp, S. Africa 116 E4 31 0 S 26 20 E
Burges, Mt., Australia 125 F3 30 50 S 121 5 E
Burghausen, Germany 31 G8 48 9N 12 49 E
Búrgio, Italy 46 E6 37 36N 13 17 E
Bürglen, Switz. 33 C7 46 53N 8 40 E
Burglengenfeld, Germany 31 F8 49 12N 12 2 E
Burgohondo, Spain 42 E6 40 26N 4 47W
Burgos, Ilocos N., Phil. 80 B3 18 31N 120 39 E
Burgos, Pangasinan, Phil. 80 C2 16 4N 119 52 E
Burgos, Spain 42 C7 42 21N 3 41W
Burgos ☐, Spain 42 C7 42 21N 3 42W
Burgstädt, Germany 30 E8 50 54N 12 49 E
Burgsvik, Sweden 17 G12 57 3N 18 19 E
Burguillos del Cerro, Spain 43 G4 38 23N 6 35W
Burgundy = Bourgogne, France 27 F11 47 0N 4 50 E
Burhaniye, Turkey 49 B8 39 30N 26 58 E
Burhanpur, India 94 D3 21 18N 76 14 E
Buri Pen., Eritrea 107 D4 15 25N 39 55 E
Burias, Phil. 80 E4 12 55N 123 5 E
Burias Pass, Phil. 80 E4 13 0N 123 15 E
Burica, Pta., Costa Rica 164 E3 8 3N 82 51W
Burigi, L., Tanzania 118 C3 2 2 S 31 22 E
Burin, Canada 141 C8 47 1N 55 14W
Buriram, Thailand 86 E4 15 0N 103 0 E
Buriti Alegre, Brazil 171 E2 18 9 S 49 3W
Buriti Bravo, Brazil 170 C3 5 50 S 43 50W
Buriti dos Lopes, Brazil 170 B3 3 10 S 41 52W
Burj Sāfitā, Syria 100 E7 34 48N 36 7 E
Burji, Ethiopia 107 F4 5 29N 37 51 E
Burkburnett, U.S.A. 155 H5 34 6N 98 34W
Burke, U.S.A. 158 C6 47 31N 115 49W
Burke →, Australia 126 C2 23 12 S 139 33 E
Burketown, Australia 126 B2 17 45 S 139 33 E
Burkettsville, U.S.A. 157 D12 40 21N 84 39W
Burkina Faso ■, Africa 112 C4 12 0N 1 0W
Burk's Falls, Canada 140 C4 45 37N 79 24W
Burlada, Spain 40 C3 42 49N 1 36W
Burley, U.S.A. 158 E7 42 32N 113 48W
Burli, Kazakstan 62 F4 51 25N 52 40 E
Burlingame, U.S.A. 160 H4 37 35N 122 21W
Burlington, Canada 150 C5 43 18N 79 45W
Burlington, Colo., U.S.A. 154 F3 39 18N 102 16W
Burlington, Ill., U.S.A. 157 B8 42 3N 88 33W
Burlington, Iowa, U.S.A. 156 D5 40 49N 91 14W
Burlington, Kans., U.S.A. 154 F7 38 12N 95 45W
Burlington, Ky., U.S.A. 157 E12 39 2N 84 43W
Burlington, N.C., U.S.A. 149 G6 36 6N 79 26W
Burlington, N.J., U.S.A. 151 F10 40 4N 74 51W
Burlington, Vt., U.S.A. 151 B11 44 29N 73 12W
Burlington, Wash., U.S.A. 160 B4 48 28N 122 20W
Burlington, Wis., U.S.A. 148 D1 42 41N 88 17W
Burlyu-Tyube, Kazakstan 64 E8 46 30N 79 10 E
Burma ■, Asia 90 E6 21 0N 96 30 E
Burnaby I., Canada 142 C2 52 25N 131 19W
Burnamwood, Australia 129 A6 31 7 S 144 53 E
Burnet, U.S.A. 155 K5 30 45N 98 14W
Burney, U.S.A. 158 F3 40 53N 121 40W
Burngup, Australia 125 F2 33 2 S 118 42 E
Burnham, U.S.A. 150 F7 40 38N 77 34W
Burnham-on-Sea, U.K. 21 F5 51 14N 3 0W
Burnie, Australia 126 G4 41 4 S 145 56 E
Burnley, U.K. 20 D5 53 47N 2 14W
Burnoye, Kazakstan 63 B5 42 36N 70 47 E
Burns, Oreg., U.S.A. 158 E4 43 35N 119 3W
Burns, Wyo., U.S.A. 154 E2 41 12N 104 21W
Burns Lake, Canada 142 C3 54 20N 125 45W
Burnside →, Canada 138 B9 66 51N 108 4W
Burnside, L., Australia 125 E3 25 22 S 123 0 E
Burnsville, U.S.A. 154 C8 44 47N 93 17W
Burnt River, Canada 150 B6 44 41N 78 42W
Burntwood →, Canada 143 B9 56 8N 96 34W
Burntwood L., Canada 143 B8 55 22N 100 26W
Burqān, Kuwait 96 D5 29 0N 47 57 E
Burra, Australia 128 B3 33 40 S 138 55 E
Burragorang, L., Australia 129 B9 33 52 S 150 37 E
Burramurra, Australia 126 C2 20 25 S 137 15 E
Burray, U.K. 22 C6 58 51N 2 54W
Burreli, Albania 50 E4 41 36N 20 1 E
Burren Junction, Australia 127 E4 30 7 S 148 59 E
Burrendong, L., Australia 129 B8 32 45 S 149 10 E
Burrendong Dam, Australia 127 E4 32 39 S 149 6 E
Burriana, Spain 40 F4 39 50N 0 4W
Burrinjuck Res., Australia 129 C8 35 0 S 148 36 E
Burro, Serranías del, Mexico 162 B4 29 0N 102 0W
Burrow Hd., U.K. 22 G4 54 41N 4 24W
Burruyacú, Argentina 174 B3 26 30 S 64 40W
Burry Port, U.K. 21 F3 51 41N 4 15W
Bursa, Turkey 51 F13 40 15N 29 5 E
Burserud, Sweden 17 G7 57 12N 13 17 E
Burstall, Canada 143 C7 50 39N 109 54W
Burton, U.S.A. 157 B13 43 0N 83 40W
Burton L., Canada 140 B4 54 45N 78 20W
Burton upon Trent, U.K. 20 E6 52 48N 1 38W
Burtundy, Australia 128 B5 33 45 S 142 15 E
Buru, Indonesia 82 B3 3 30 S 126 30 E
Buruanga, Phil. 81 F3 11 51N 121 53 E
Burullus, Bahra el, Egypt 106 H7 31 25N 31 0 E
Burûm, Yemen 99 D5 14 22N 48 59 E
Burûn, Râs, Egypt 103 D2 31 14N 33 7 E
Burunday, Kazakstan 63 B8 43 20N 76 51 E
Burundi ■, Africa 118 C3 3 15 S 30 0 E
Bururi, Burundi 118 C2 3 57 S 29 37 E
Burutu, Nigeria 113 D6 5 20N 5 29 E
Burwell, U.S.A. 154 E5 41 47N 99 8W
Burwick, U.K. 22 C5 58 45N 2 58W
Bury, U.K. 20 D5 53 35N 2 17W
Bury St. Edmunds, U.K. 21 E8 52 15N 0 43 E
Buryatia ☐, Russia 65 D12 53 0N 110 0 E
Buryn, Ukraine 59 G7 51 13N 33 50 E
Burzenin, Poland 55 G5 51 28N 18 47 E
Busalla, Italy 44 D5 44 34N 8 57 E
Busango Swamp, Zambia 119 E2 14 15 S 25 45 E
Buşayrah, Syria 101 E9 35 9N 40 26 E
Buşayyah, Iraq 96 D5 30 0N 46 10 E
Busca, Italy 44 D4 44 31N 7 29 E
Bushati, Albania 50 E3 41 58N 19 34 E
Būshehr, Iran 97 D6 28 55N 50 55 E
Būshehr ☐, Iran 97 D6 28 20N 51 45 E
Bushell, Canada 143 B7 59 31N 108 45W
Bushenyi, Uganda 118 C3 0 35 S 30 10 E
Bushire = Būshehr, Iran 97 D6 28 55N 50 55 E
Bushnell, Fla., U.S.A. 153 G7 28 40N 82 7W
Bushnell, Ill., U.S.A. 154 E9 40 33N 90 31W
Bushnell, Nebr., U.S.A. 154 E3 41 14N 103 54W
Busia ☐, Kenya 118 B3 0 25N 34 6 E
Busie, Ghana 112 C4 10 29N 2 22W
Businga, Dem. Rep. of the Congo 114 B4 3 16N 20 59 E
Buskerud ☐, Norway 18 D5 60 20N 9 0 E
Busko-Zdrój, Poland 55 H7 50 28N 20 42 E
Buskul, Kazakstan 62 E8 53 45N 61 12 E
Buslei, Ethiopia 120 C2 5 28N 44 25 E
Busovača, Bos.-H. 52 F2 44 6N 17 53 E
Buşra ash Shām, Syria 103 C5 32 30N 36 25 E
Busselton, Australia 125 F2 33 42 S 115 15 E
Busseto, Italy 44 D7 44 59N 10 2 E
Bussière-Badil, France 28 C4 45 39N 0 36 E
Bussigny, Switz. 32 C3 46 33N 6 33 E
Bussolengo, Italy 44 C7 45 28N 10 51 E

204 Coronel Pringles

Coronel Pringles, *Argentina* **174 D3** 38 0 S 61 30W
Coronel Suárez, *Argentina* **174 D3** 37 30 S 61 52W
Coronel Vidal, *Argentina* **174 D4** 37 28 S 57 45W
Corongo, *Peru* **172 B2** 8 30 S 77 53W
Coronie □, *Surinam* **169 B6** 5 55N 56 20W
Coropuna, Nevado, *Peru* **172 D3** 15 30 S 72 41W
Çorovoda, *Albania* **50 F4** 40 31N 20 14 E
Corowa, *Australia* **129 C7** 35 58 S 146 21 E
Corozal, *Belize* **163 D7** 18 23N 88 23W
Corozal, *Colombia* **168 B2** 9 19N 75 18W
Corps, *France* **29 D9** 44 50N 5 56 E
Corpus, *Argentina* **175 B4** 27 10 S 55 30W
Corpus Christi, *U.S.A.* **155 M6** 27 47N 97 24W
Corpus Christi, L., *U.S.A.* **155 L6** 28 2N 97 52W
Corque, *Bolivia* **172 D4** 18 20 S 67 41W
Corral, *Chile* **176 A2** 39 52 S 73 26W
Corral de Almaguer, *Spain* **42 F7** 39 45N 3 10W
Corralejo, *Canary Is.* **39 F6** 28 43N 13 53W
Corraun Pen., *Ireland* **23 C2** 53 54N 9 54W
Corréggio, *Italy* **44 D7** 44 46N 10 47 E
Corrente, *Brazil* **170 D2** 10 27 S 45 10W
Corrente →, *Brazil* **171 D3** 13 8 S 43 28W
Correntes →, *Brazil* **173 D6** 17 38 S 55 8W
Correntes, C. das, *Mozam.* **117 C6** 24 6 S 35 34 E
Correntina, *Brazil* **171 D3** 13 20 S 44 39W
Corrèze □, *France* **28 C5** 45 20N 1 45 E
Corrèze →, *France* **28 C5** 45 10N 1 28 E
Corrib, L., *Ireland* **23 C2** 53 27N 9 16W
Corridónia, *Italy* **45 E10** 43 15N 13 30 E
Corrientes, *Argentina* **174 B4** 27 30 S 58 45W
Corrientes □, *Argentina* **174 B4** 28 0 S 57 0W
Corrientes →, *Argentina* **174 C4** 30 42 S 59 38W
Corrientes →, *Peru* **168 D3** 3 43 S 74 35W
Corrientes, C., *Colombia* **168 B2** 5 30N 77 34W
Corrientes, C., *Cuba* **164 B3** 21 43N 84 30W
Corrientes, C., *Mexico* **162 C3** 20 25N 105 42W
Corrigan, *U.S.A.* **155 K7** 31 0N 94 52W
Corrigin, *Australia* **125 F2** 32 20 S 117 53 E
Corrowidgie, *Australia* **129 D8** 36 56 S 148 50 E
Corry, *U.S.A.* **150 E5** 41 55N 79 39W
Corryong, *Australia* **129 D7** 36 12 S 147 53 E
Corse, *France* **29 G13** 42 0N 9 0 E
Corse, C., *France* **29 E13** 43 1N 9 25 E
Corse-du-Sud □, *France* **29 G13** 41 45N 9 0 E
Corsica = Corse, *France* **29 G13** 42 0N 9 0 E
Corsicana, *U.S.A.* **155 J6** 32 6N 96 28W
Corte, *France* **29 F13** 42 19N 9 11 E
Corte Pinto, *Portugal* **43 H3** 37 42N 7 29W
Cortegana, *Spain* **43 H4** 37 52N 6 49W
Cortes, *Phil.* **81 G6** 9 17N 126 11 E
Cortez, *U.S.A.* **159 H9** 37 21N 108 35W
Cortina d'Ampezzo, *Italy* **45 B9** 46 32N 12 8 E
Cortland, *U.S.A.* **151 D8** 42 36N 76 11W
Cortona, *Italy* **45 E8** 43 16N 11 59 E
Coruche, *Portugal* **43 G2** 38 57N 8 30W
Çoruh →, *Turkey* **61 K5** 41 38N 41 38 E
Çorum, *Turkey* **100 B6** 40 30N 34 57 E
Corumbá, *Brazil* **173 D6** 19 0 S 57 30W
Corumbá →, *Brazil* **171 E2** 18 19 S 48 55W
Corumbá de Goiás, *Brazil* **171 E2** 16 0 S 48 50W
Corumbaíba, *Brazil* **171 E2** 18 9 S 48 34W
Corund, *Romania* **53 D10** 46 30N 25 13 E
Corunna = A Coruña, *Spain* **42 B2** 43 20N 8 25W
Corunna, *U.S.A.* **157 B12** 42 59N 84 7W
Corvallis, *U.S.A.* **158 D2** 44 34N 123 16W
Corvette, L. de la, *Canada* **140 B5** 53 25N 74 3W
Corydon, *Ind., U.S.A.* **157 F10** 38 13N 86 7W
Corydon, *Iowa, U.S.A.* **156 D3** 40 46N 93 19W
Corydon, *Ky., U.S.A.* **157 G9** 37 44N 87 43W
Cosalá, *Mexico* **162 C3** 24 28N 106 40W
Cosamaloapan, *Mexico* **163 D5** 18 23N 95 50W
Cosenza, *Italy* **47 C9** 39 18N 16 15 E
Coşereni, *Romania* **53 F11** 44 38N 26 35 E
Coshocton, *U.S.A.* **150 F3** 40 16N 81 51W
Cosmo Newberry, *Australia* **125 E3** 28 0 S 122 54 E
Cosne-Cours-sur-Loire, *France* **27 E9** 47 24N 2 54 E
Coso Junction, *U.S.A.* **161 J9** 36 3N 117 57W
Coso Pk., *U.S.A.* **161 J9** 36 13N 117 44W
Cospeito, *Spain* **42 B3** 43 12N 7 34W
Cosquín, *Argentina* **174 C3** 31 15 S 64 30W
Cossato, *Italy* **44 C5** 45 34N 8 10 E
Cossé-le-Vivien, *France* **26 E6** 47 57N 0 54W
Cosson →, *France* **26 E8** 47 30N 1 15 E
Costa Blanca, *Spain* **41 G4** 38 25N 0 10W
Costa Brava, *Spain* **40 D8** 41 30N 3 0 E
Costa del Sol, *Spain* **43 J6** 36 30N 4 30W
Costa Dorada, *Spain* **40 D6** 41 12N 1 15 E
Costa Mesa, *U.S.A.* **161 M9** 33 38N 117 55W
Costa Rica ■, *Cent. Amer.* **164 E3** 10 0N 84 0W
Costa Smeralda, *Italy* **46 A2** 41 5N 9 35 E
Costeşti, *Romania* **53 F9** 44 40N 24 53 E
Costigliole d'Asti, *Italy* **44 D5** 44 47N 8 11 E
Costilla, *U.S.A.* **159 H11** 36 59N 105 32W
Cosumnes →, *U.S.A.* **160 G5** 38 16N 121 26W
Coswig, *Sachsen, Germany* **30 D9** 51 7N 13 34 E
Coswig, *Sachsen-Anhalt, Germany* **30 D8** 51 53N 12 27 E
Cotabato, *Phil.* **81 H5** 7 14N 124 15 E
Cotabena, *Australia* **128 A3** 31 42 S 138 11 E
Cotacajes →, *Bolivia* **172 D4** 16 0 S 67 1W
Cotagaita, *Bolivia* **174 A2** 20 45 S 65 40W
Cotahuasi, *Peru* **172 D3** 15 12 S 72 50W
Côte d'Azur, *France* **29 E11** 43 25N 7 10 E
Côte-d'Ivoire = Ivory Coast ■, *Africa* **112 D4** 7 30N 5 0W
Côte d'Or, *France* **27 E11** 47 10N 4 50 E
Côte-d'Or □, *France* **27 E11** 47 30N 4 50 E
Coteau des Prairies, *U.S.A.* **154 C6** 45 20N 97 50W
Coteau du Missouri, *U.S.A.* **154 B4** 47 0N 100 0W
Coteau Landing, *Canada* **151 A10** 45 15N 74 13W
Cotegipe, *Brazil* **171 D3** 12 2 S 44 15W
Cotentin, *France* **26 C5** 49 15N 1 30W
Côtes-d'Armor □, *France* **26 D4** 48 25N 2 40W
Côtes de Meuse, *France* **27 C12** 49 15N 5 22 E
Côtes-du-Nord = Côtes-d'Armor □, *France* **26 D4** 48 25N 2 40W
Cotiella, *Spain* **40 C5** 42 31N 0 19 E
Cotillo, *Canary Is.* **39 F5** 28 41N 14 1W
Cotiujeni, *Moldova* **53 C13** 47 51N 28 33 E
Cotoca, *Bolivia* **173 D5** 17 49 S 63 3W
Cotonou, *Benin* **113 D5** 6 20N 2 25 E
Cotopaxi, *Ecuador* **168 D2** 0 40 S 78 30W
Cotopaxi □, *Ecuador* **168 D2** 0 5 S 78 55W
Cotronei, *Italy* **47 C9** 39 9N 16 47 E
Cotswold Hills, *U.K.* **21 F5** 51 42N 2 10W
Cottage Grove, *U.S.A.* **158 E2** 43 48N 123 3W
Cottageville, *U.S.A.* **152 C9** 32 56N 80 29W
Cottbus, *Germany* **30 D10** 51 45N 14 20 E
Cotton, *U.S.A.* **152 D5** 31 10N 84 4W
Cottondale, *U.S.A.* **152 E4** 30 48N 85 23W
Cottonwood, *Ala., U.S.A.* **152 D4** 31 3N 85 18W
Cottonwood, *Ariz., U.S.A.* **159 J7** 34 45N 112 1W
Cotulla, *U.S.A.* **155 L5** 28 26N 99 14W
Coubre, Pte. de la, *France* **28 C2** 45 42N 1 15W
Couches, *France* **27 F11** 46 53N 4 30 E
Couço, *Portugal* **43 G2** 38 59N 8 17W
Coudersport, *U.S.A.* **150 E6** 41 46N 78 1W
Couedic, C. du, *Australia* **128 D2** 36 5 S 136 40 E
Couëron, *France* **26 E5** 47 13N 1 44W
Couesnon →, *France* **26 D5** 48 38N 1 32W
Couhé, *France* **28 B4** 46 17N 0 11 E
Coulanges-sur-Yonne, *France* **27 E10** 47 31N 3 33 E
Coulee City, *U.S.A.* **158 C4** 47 37N 119 17W
Coulman I., *Antarctica* **7 D11** 73 35 S 170 0 E
Coulommiers, *France* **27 D10** 48 50N 3 3 E
Coulon →, *France* **29 E9** 43 51N 5 6 E
Coulonge →, *Canada* **140 C4** 45 52N 76 46W
Coulonges-sur-l'Autize, *France* **28 B3** 46 29N 0 36W
Coulounieix-Chamiers, *France* **28 C4** 45 11N 0 42 E
Coulterville, *Calif., U.S.A.* **160 H6** 37 43N 120 12W
Coulterville, *Ill., U.S.A.* **156 F7** 38 11N 89 36W
Council, *Ga., U.S.A.* **152 E7** 30 37N 82 31W
Council, *Idaho, U.S.A.* **158 D5** 44 44N 116 26W
Council Bluffs, *U.S.A.* **154 E7** 41 16N 95 52W
Council Grove, *U.S.A.* **154 F6** 38 40N 96 29W
Coupeville, *U.S.A.* **160 B4** 48 13N 122 41W
Courantyne →, *S. Amer.* **169 B6** 5 55N 57 5W
Courcelles, *Belgium* **24 D4** 50 28N 4 22 E
Courçon, *France* **28 B3** 46 15N 0 50W
Courmayeur, *Italy* **44 C3** 45 47N 6 58 E
Couronne, C., *France* **29 E9** 43 19N 5 3 E
Cours-la-Ville, *France* **27 F11** 46 7N 4 19 E
Coursan, *France* **28 E7** 43 14N 3 4 E
Courseulles-sur-Mer, *France* **26 C6** 49 20N 0 29W
Courtenay, *Canada* **142 D4** 49 45N 125 0W
Courtenay, *France* **27 D10** 48 2N 3 3 E
Courtland, *U.S.A.* **160 G5** 38 20N 121 34W
Courtrai = Kortrijk, *Belgium* **24 D3** 50 50N 3 17 E
Courtright, *Canada* **150 D2** 42 49N 82 28W
Coushatta, *U.S.A.* **155 J8** 32 1N 93 21W
Coutances, *France* **26 C5** 49 3N 1 28W
Coutras, *France* **28 C3** 45 3N 0 8W
Coutts, *Canada* **142 D6** 49 0N 111 57W
Couvet, *Switz.* **32 C3** 46 57N 6 38 E
Couvin, *Belgium* **24 D4** 50 3N 4 29 E
Covarrubias, *Spain* **42 C7** 42 4N 3 31W
Covasna, *Romania* **53 E11** 45 50N 26 10 E
Covasna □, *Romania* **53 E10** 45 50N 26 0 E
Coveñas, *Colombia* **168 B2** 9 24N 75 44W
Coventry, *U.K.* **21 E6** 52 25N 1 28W
Coventry L., *Canada* **143 A7** 61 15N 106 15W
Coverdale, *U.S.A.* **152 D6** 31 38N 83 58W
Covilhã, *Portugal* **42 E3** 40 17N 7 31W
Covington, *Ga., U.S.A.* **152 B6** 33 36N 83 51W
Covington, *Ind., U.S.A.* **157 D9** 40 9N 87 24W
Covington, *Ky., U.S.A.* **157 E12** 39 5N 84 31W
Covington, *Ohio, U.S.A.* **157 D12** 40 7N 84 21W
Covington, *Okla., U.S.A.* **155 G6** 36 18N 97 35W
Covington, *Tenn., U.S.A.* **155 H10** 35 34N 89 39W
Cowal, L., *Australia* **129 B7** 33 40 S 147 25 E
Cowan, *Canada* **143 C8** 52 5N 100 45W
Cowan, L., *Australia* **125 F3** 31 45 S 121 45 E
Cowan L., *Canada* **143 C7** 54 0N 107 15W
Cowangie, *Australia* **128 C4** 35 12 S 141 26 E
Cowansville, *Canada* **151 A12** 45 14N 72 46W
Coward, *U.S.A.* **152 B10** 33 58N 79 45W
Cowarie, *Australia* **127 D2** 27 45 S 138 15 E
Cowcowing Lakes, *Australia* **125 F2** 30 55 S 117 20 E
Cowden, *U.S.A.* **157 E8** 39 15N 88 52W
Cowdenbeath, *U.K.* **22 E5** 56 7N 3 21W
Cowell, *Australia* **128 B2** 33 39 S 136 56 E
Cowes, *U.K.* **21 G6** 50 45N 1 18W
Cowl Cowl, *Australia* **129 B6** 33 36 S 145 18 E
Cowlitz →, *U.S.A.* **160 D4** 46 6N 122 55W
Cowra, *Australia* **129 B8** 33 49 S 148 42 E
Cox, *Spain* **41 G4** 38 8N 0 53W
Cox, *U.S.A.* **152 D8** 31 27N 81 34W
Coxilha Grande, *Brazil* **175 B5** 28 18 S 51 30W
Coxim, *Brazil* **173 D7** 18 30 S 54 55W
Coxim →, *Brazil* **173 D7** 18 34 S 54 46W
Cox's Bazar, *Bangla.* **90 E3** 21 26N 91 59 E
Cox's Cove, *Canada* **141 C8** 49 7N 58 5W
Coyame, *Mexico* **162 B3** 29 28N 105 6W
Coyote Wells, *U.S.A.* **161 N11** 32 44N 115 58W
Coyuca de Benítez, *Mexico* **163 D4** 17 1N 100 8W
Coyuca de Catalan, *Mexico* **162 D4** 18 18N 100 41W
Cozad, *U.S.A.* **154 E5** 40 52N 99 59W
Cozes, *France* **28 C3** 45 34N 0 49W
Cozumel, *Mexico* **163 C7** 20 31N 86 55W
Cozumel, I. de, *Mexico* **163 C7** 20 30N 86 40W
Craboon, *Australia* **129 B8** 32 3 S 149 30 E
Cracow = Kraków, *Poland* **55 H6** 50 4N 19 57 E
Cracow, *Australia* **127 D5** 25 17 S 150 17 E
Cradock, *S. Africa* **116 E4** 32 8 S 25 36 E
Craig, *Alaska, U.S.A.* **142 B2** 55 29N 133 9W
Craig, *Colo., U.S.A.* **158 F10** 40 31N 107 33W
Craigavon, *U.K.* **23 B5** 54 27N 6 23W
Craigmore, *Zimbabwe* **119 G3** 20 28 S 32 50 E
Crailsheim, *Germany* **31 F6** 49 8N 10 5 E
Craiova, *Romania* **53 F8** 44 21N 23 48 E
Cramsie, *Australia* **126 C3** 23 20 S 144 15 E
Cranberry Portage, *Canada* **143 C8** 54 35N 101 23W
Cranbrook, *Tas., Australia* **126 G4** 42 0 S 148 5 E
Cranbrook, *W. Austral., Australia* **125 F2** 34 18 S 117 33 E
Cranbrook, *Canada* **142 D5** 49 30N 115 46W
Crandon, *U.S.A.* **154 C10** 45 34N 88 54W
Crane, *Oreg., U.S.A.* **158 E4** 43 25N 118 35W
Crane, *Tex., U.S.A.* **155 K3** 31 24N 102 21W
Cranston, *U.S.A.* **151 E13** 41 47N 71 26W
Craon, *France* **26 E6** 47 50N 0 58W
Craonne, *France* **27 C10** 49 27N 3 46 E
Craponne-sur-Arzon, *France* **28 C7** 45 19N 3 51 E
Crasna, *Romania* **53 D12** 46 32N 27 51 E
Crasna →, *Romania* **52 C7** 47 44N 22 35 E
Crasnei, Munţii, *Romania* **53 C8** 47 0N 23 20 E
Crater L., *U.S.A.* **158 E2** 42 56N 122 6W
Crater Mt., *Papua N. G.* **132 D3** 6 37 S 145 7 E
Crater Pt., *Papua N. G.* **132 C7** 5 25 S 152 9 E
Crateús, *Brazil* **170 C3** 5 10 S 40 39W
Crati →, *Italy* **47 C9** 39 43N 16 31 E
Crato, *Brazil* **170 C4** 7 10 S 39 25W
Crato, *Portugal* **43 F3** 39 16N 7 39W
Cravo Norte, *Colombia* **168 B3** 6 18N 70 12W
Cravo Norte →, *Colombia* **168 B3** 6 18N 70 12W
Crawford, *Ala., U.S.A.* **152 C4** 32 27N 85 11W
Crawford, *Nebr., U.S.A.* **154 D3** 42 41N 103 25W
Crawfordsville, *U.S.A.* **157 D10** 40 2N 86 54W
Crawfordville, *Fla., U.S.A.* **152 E5** 30 11N 84 23W
Crawfordville, *Ga., U.S.A.* **152 B7** 33 33N 82 54W
Crawley, *U.K.* **21 F7** 51 7N 0 11W
Crazy Mts., *U.S.A.* **158 C8** 46 12N 110 20W
Crean L., *Canada* **143 C7** 54 5N 106 9W
Crécy-en-Ponthieu, *France* **27 B8** 50 15N 1 53 E
Crediton, *Canada* **150 C3** 43 17N 81 33W
Credo, *Australia* **125 F3** 30 28 S 120 45 E
Cree →, *Canada* **143 B7** 58 57N 105 47W
Cree →, *U.K.* **22 G4** 54 55N 4 25W
Cree L., *Canada* **143 B7** 57 30N 106 30W
Creede, *U.S.A.* **159 H10** 37 51N 106 56W
Creel, *Mexico* **162 B3** 27 45N 107 38W
Creighton, *U.S.A.* **154 D6** 42 28N 97 54W
Creil, *France* **27 C9** 49 15N 2 29 E
Crema, *Italy* **44 C6** 45 22N 9 41 E
Cremona, *Italy* **44 C7** 45 7N 10 2 E
Crepaja, *Serbia, Yug.* **50 B4** 45 1N 20 38 E
Crepori →, *Brazil* **173 B6** 5 42 S 57 8W
Crépy, *France* **27 C10** 49 35N 3 32 E
Crépy-en-Valois, *France* **27 C9** 49 14N 2 54 E
Cres, *Croatia* **45 D11** 44 58N 14 25 E
Cresbard, *U.S.A.* **154 C5** 45 10N 98 57W
Crescent, *Okla., U.S.A.* **155 H6** 35 57N 97 36W
Crescent, *Oreg., U.S.A.* **158 E3** 43 28N 121 42W
Crescent Beach, *U.S.A.* **152 F8** 29 46N 81 15W
Crescent City, *Calif., U.S.A.* **158 F1** 41 45N 124 12W
Crescent City, *Fla., U.S.A.* **153 F8** 29 26N 81 31W
Crescent L., *U.S.A.* **153 F8** 29 28N 81 30W
Crescentino, *Italy* **44 C5** 45 11N 8 6 E
Crespo, *Argentina* **174 C3** 32 2 S 60 19W
Cressy, *Australia* **128 E5** 38 2 S 143 40 E
Crest, *France* **29 D9** 44 44N 5 2 E
Cresta, Mt., *Phil.* **80 C4** 17 17N 122 6 E
Crested Butte, *U.S.A.* **159 G10** 38 52N 106 59W
Crestline, *Calif., U.S.A.* **161 L9** 34 14N 117 18W
Crestline, *Ohio, U.S.A.* **150 F2** 40 47N 82 44W
Creston, *Canada* **142 D5** 49 10N 116 31W
Creston, *Calif., U.S.A.* **160 K6** 35 32N 120 33W
Creston, *Iowa, U.S.A.* **156 C2** 41 4N 94 22W
Creston, *Wash., U.S.A.* **158 C4** 47 46N 118 31W
Crestview, *Calif., U.S.A.* **160 H8** 37 46N 118 58W
Crestview, *Fla., U.S.A.* **149 K2** 30 46N 86 34W
Creswick, *Australia* **128 D5** 37 25 S 143 58 E
Crêt de la Neige, *France* **27 F12** 46 16N 5 58 E
Crete = Kríti, *Greece* **38 D7** 35 15N 25 0 E
Crete, *U.S.A.* **154 E6** 40 38N 96 58W
Crete, Sea of, *Greece* **49 E7** 36 0N 25 0 E
Créteil, *France* **27 D9** 48 47N 2 28 E
Cretin, C., *Papua N. G.* **132 D4** 6 40 S 147 53 E
Creus, C. de, *Spain* **40 C8** 42 20N 3 19 E
Creuse □, *France* **27 F9** 46 10N 2 0 E
Creuse →, *France* **28 B4** 47 0N 0 34 E
Creutzwald, *France* **27 C13** 49 12N 6 42 E
Creuzburg, *Germany* **30 D6** 51 3N 10 14 E
Crèvecœur-le-Grand, *France* **27 C9** 49 37N 2 5 E
Crevillente, *Spain* **41 G4** 38 12N 0 48W
Crewe, *U.K.* **20 D5** 53 6N 2 26W
Crewkerne, *U.K.* **21 G5** 50 53N 2 48W
Criciúma, *Brazil* **175 B6** 28 40 S 49 23W
Cricova, *Moldova* **53 C13** 47 8N 28 52 E
Cridersville, *U.S.A.* **157 D12** 40 39N 84 9W
Crieff, *U.K.* **22 E5** 56 22N 3 50W
Crikvenica, *Croatia* **45 C11** 45 11N 14 40 E
Crimea □, *Ukraine* **59 K8** 45 30N 33 10 E
Crimean Pen. = Krymskyy Pivostriv, *Ukraine* **59 K8** 45 0N 34 0 E
Crimmitschau, *Germany* **30 E8** 50 48N 12 24 E
Cristal, Mts. de, *Gabon* **114 B2** 0 30N 10 30 E
Cristalândia, *Brazil* **170 D2** 10 36 S 49 11W
Cristino Castro, *Brazil* **170 C3** 8 49 S 44 13W
Cristuru Secuiesc, *Romania* **53 D10** 46 17N 25 2 E
Crişul Alb →, *Romania* **52 D6** 46 42N 21 17 E
Crişul Negru →, *Romania* **52 D6** 46 42N 21 16 E
Crişul Repede →, *Romania* **52 D5** 46 55N 20 59 E
Crittenden, *U.S.A.* **157 F12** 38 47N 84 36W
Criuleni, *Moldova* **53 C14** 47 13N 29 10 E
Crivitz, *Germany* **30 B7** 53 34N 11 39 E
Crixás, *Brazil* **171 D2** 14 27 S 49 58W
Crna →, *Macedonia* **50 E5** 41 33N 21 59 E
Crna Gora = Montenegro □, *Yugoslavia* **50 D3** 42 40N 19 20 E
Crna Gora, *Macedonia* **50 D5** 42 10N 21 30 E
Crna Reka = Crna →, *Macedonia* **50 E5** 41 33N 21 59 E
Crna Trava, *Serbia, Yug.* **50 D6** 42 49N 22 19 E
Crni Drim →, *Macedonia* **50 E4** 41 17N 20 40 E
Crni Timok →, *Serbia, Yug.* **50 C6** 43 53N 22 15 E
Crnoljeva Planina, *Serbia, Yug.* **50 D5** 42 20N 21 0 E
Črnomelj, *Slovenia* **45 C12** 45 33N 15 10 E
Croagh Patrick, *Ireland* **23 C2** 53 46N 9 40W
Croatia ■, *Europe* **45 C13** 45 20N 16 0 E
Crocker, *U.S.A.* **156 G4** 37 57N 92 16W
Crocker, Banjaran, *Malaysia* **85 A5** 5 40N 116 30 E
Crockett, *U.S.A.* **155 K7** 31 19N 95 27W
Crocodile = Krokodil →, *Mozam.* **117 D5** 25 14 S 32 18 E
Crocodile Is., *Australia* **126 A1** 12 3 S 134 58 E
Crocq, *France* **28 C6** 45 52N 2 21 E
Crodo, *Italy* **44 B5** 46 13N 8 19 E
Crohy Hd., *Ireland* **23 B3** 54 55N 8 26W
Croisette, C., *France* **29 E9** 43 14N 5 22 E
Croisic, Pte. du, *France* **26 E4** 47 19N 2 31W
Croix, L. La, *Canada* **140 C1** 48 20N 92 15W
Croker, C., *Australia* **124 B5** 10 58 S 132 35 E
Croker I., *Australia* **124 B5** 11 12 S 132 32 E
Cromarty, *Canada* **143 B10** 58 3N 94 9W
Cromarty, *U.K.* **22 D4** 57 40N 4 2W
Cromer, *U.K.* **20 E9** 52 56N 1 17 E
Cromwell, *N.Z.* **131 F4** 45 3 S 169 14 E
Cronat, *France* **27 F10** 46 43N 3 40 E
Cronulla, *Australia* **129 C9** 34 3 S 151 8 E
Crook, *U.K.* **20 C6** 54 43N 1 45W
Crooked →, *Canada* **142 C4** 54 50N 122 54W
Crooked →, *U.S.A.* **158 D3** 44 32N 121 16W
Crooked Creek, *U.S.A.* **144 F8** 61 52N 158 7W
Crooked I., *Bahamas* **165 B5** 22 50N 74 10W
Crooked Island Passage, *Bahamas* **165 B5** 23 0N 74 30W
Crooked L., *U.S.A.* **153 H8** 27 48N 81 35W
Crookston, *Minn., U.S.A.* **154 B6** 47 47N 96 37W
Crookston, *Nebr., U.S.A.* **154 D4** 42 56N 100 45W
Crooksville, *U.S.A.* **148 F4** 39 46N 82 6W
Crookwell, *Australia* **129 C8** 34 28 S 149 24 E
Crosby, *U.K.* **20 D4** 53 30N 3 3W
Crosby, *Minn., U.S.A.* **154 B8** 46 29N 93 58W
Crosby, *N. Dak., U.S.A.* **143 D8** 48 55N 103 18W
Crosby, *Pa., U.S.A.* **150 E6** 41 45N 78 23W
Crosbyton, *U.S.A.* **155 J4** 33 40N 101 14W
Crosía, *Italy* **47 C9** 39 35N 16 45 E
Cross →, *Nigeria* **113 E6** 4 42N 8 21 E
Cross City, *U.S.A.* **153 F6** 29 38N 83 7W
Cross Fell, *U.K.* **20 C5** 54 43N 2 28W
Cross L., *Canada* **143 C9** 54 45N 97 30W
Cross Plains, *U.S.A.* **155 J5** 32 8N 99 11W
Cross River □, *Nigeria* **113 D6** 6 0N 8 0 E
Cross Sound, *U.S.A.* **138 C6** 58 0N 135 0W
Cross Timbers, *U.S.A.* **156 F3** 38 1N 93 14W
Crossett, *U.S.A.* **155 J9** 33 8N 91 58W
Crossfield, *Canada* **142 C6** 51 25N 114 0W
Crosshaven, *Ireland* **23 E3** 51 47N 8 17W
Crossley, Mt., *N.Z.* **131 C7** 42 50 S 172 5 E
Crossville, *U.S.A.* **157 F8** 38 10N 88 4W
Croton-on-Hudson, *U.S.A.* **151 E11** 41 12N 73 55W
Crotone, *Italy* **47 C10** 39 5N 17 8 E
Crow →, *Canada* **142 B4** 59 41N 124 20W
Crow Agency, *U.S.A.* **158 D10** 45 36N 107 28W
Crow Hd., *Ireland* **23 E1** 51 35N 10 9W
Crowell, *U.S.A.* **155 J5** 33 59N 99 43W
Crowl Creek, *Australia* **129 B6** 32 0 S 145 30 E
Crowley, *U.S.A.* **155 K8** 30 13N 92 22W
Crowley, L., *U.S.A.* **160 H8** 37 35N 118 42W
Crown Point, *U.S.A.* **157 C9** 41 25N 87 22W
Crows Landing, *U.S.A.* **160 H5** 37 23N 121 6W
Crows Nest, *Australia* **127 D5** 27 16 S 152 4 E
Crowsnest Pass, *Canada* **142 D6** 49 40N 114 40W
Croydon, *Australia* **126 B3** 18 13 S 142 14 E
Croydon, *U.K.* **21 F7** 51 22N 0 5W
Crozet Is., *Ind. Oc.* **121 J4** 46 27 S 52 0 E
Crozon, *France* **26 D2** 48 15N 4 30W
Cruz, C., *Cuba* **164 C4** 19 50N 77 50W
Cruz Alta, *Brazil* **175 B5** 28 45 S 53 40W
Cruz das Almas, *Brazil* **171 D4** 12 0 S 39 6W
Cruz de Incio, *Spain* **42 C3** 42 39N 7 21W
Cruz de Malta, *Brazil* **170 C3** 8 15 S 40 20W
Cruz del Eje, *Argentina* **174 C3** 30 45 S 64 50W
Cruzeiro, *Brazil* **171 F3** 22 33 S 45 0W
Cruzeiro do Oeste, *Brazil* **175 A5** 23 46 S 53 4W
Cruzeiro do Sul, *Brazil* **172 B3** 7 35 S 72 35W
Cry L., *Canada* **142 B3** 58 45N 129 0W
Crystal B., *U.S.A.* **153 G7** 28 50N 82 45W
Crystal Bay, *U.S.A.* **160 F7** 39 15N 120 0W
Crystal Brook, *Australia* **128 B3** 33 21 S 138 12 E
Crystal City, *Mo., U.S.A.* **156 F6** 38 13N 90 23W
Crystal City, *Tex., U.S.A.* **155 L5** 28 41N 99 50W
Crystal Falls, *U.S.A.* **148 B1** 46 5N 88 20W
Crystal Lake, *Fla., U.S.A.* **152 E4** 30 26N 85 42W
Crystal Lake, *Ill., U.S.A.* **157 B8** 42 14N 88 19W
Crystal River, *U.S.A.* **149 L4** 28 54N 82 35W
Crystal Springs, *U.S.A.* **155 K9** 31 59N 90 21W
Csenger, *Hungary* **52 C7** 47 50N 22 41 E
Csongrád, *Hungary* **52 D5** 46 43N 20 12 E
Csongrád □, *Hungary* **52 D5** 46 32N 20 15 E
Csorna, *Hungary* **52 C2** 47 38N 17 18 E
Csurgo, *Hungary* **52 D2** 46 16N 17 9 E
Cu Lao Hon, *Vietnam* **87 G7** 10 54N 108 18 E
Cua Rao, *Vietnam* **86 C5** 19 16N 104 27 E
Cuácua →, *Mozam.* **119 F4** 17 54 S 37 0 E
Cuamato, *Angola* **115 F3** 17 2 S 15 7 E
Cuamba, *Mozam.* **119 E4** 14 45 S 36 22 E
Cuando →, *Angola* **115 F4** 17 30 S 23 15 E
Cuando Cubango □, *Angola* **115 F4** 16 25 S 20 0 E
Cuangar, *Angola* **115 F3** 17 36 S 18 39 E
Cuango, *Angola* **115 D3** 6 15 S 16 42 E
Cuanza →, *Angola* **115 D2** 9 2 S 13 30 E
Cuanza Norte □, *Angola* **115 D2** 8 50 S 14 30 E
Cuanza Sul □, *Angola* **115 E2** 10 50 S 14 50 E
Cuarto →, *Argentina* **174 C3** 33 25 S 63 2W
Cuatrociénegas, *Mexico* **162 B4** 26 59N 102 5W
Cuauhtémoc, *Mexico* **162 B3** 28 25N 106 52W
Cuba, *Portugal* **43 G3** 38 10N 7 54W
Cuba, *Mo., U.S.A.* **156 F5** 38 4N 91 24W
Cuba, *N. Mex., U.S.A.* **159 J10** 36 1N 107 4W
Cuba, *N.Y., U.S.A.* **150 D6** 42 13N 78 17W
Cuba ■, *W. Indies* **164 B4** 22 0N 79 0W
Cuba City, *U.S.A.* **156 B6** 42 36N 90 26W
Cubal, *Angola* **115 E2** 12 26 S 14 3 E
Cuballing, *Australia* **125 F2** 32 50 S 117 10 E
Cubango →, *Africa* **115 F4** 18 50 S 22 25 E
Cubanja, *Angola* **115 E4** 14 49 S 21 20 E
Cubia, *Angola* **115 F4** 15 58 S 21 42 E
Çubuk, *Turkey* **100 B5** 40 14N 33 3 E
Cuchi, *Angola* **115 E3** 14 37 S 16 58 E
Cuchillo-Có, *Argentina* **176 A4** 38 20 S 64 37W
Cuchivero →, *Venezuela* **168 B4** 7 40N 65 57W
Cuchumatanes, Sierra de los, *Guatemala* **164 C1** 15 35N 91 25W
Cuckfield, *U.K.* **21 F7** 51 1N 0 8W
Cucuí, *Brazil* **168 C4** 1 12N 66 50W
Cucurpe, *Mexico* **162 A2** 30 20N 110 43W
Cucurrupí, *Colombia* **168 C2** 4 23N 76 56W
Cúcuta, *Colombia* **168 B3** 7 54N 72 31W
Cudahy, *U.S.A.* **157 B9** 42 58N 87 52W
Cudalbi, *Romania* **53 E12** 45 46N 27 41 E
Cuddalore, *India* **95 J4** 11 46N 79 45 E
Cuddapah, *India* **95 G4** 14 30N 78 47 E
Cuddapan, L., *Australia* **126 D3** 25 45 S 141 26 E
Cudgewa, *Australia* **129 D7** 36 10 S 147 42 E
Cudillero, *Spain* **42 B4** 43 33N 6 9W
Cue, *Australia* **125 E2** 27 25 S 117 54 E
Cuéllar, *Spain* **42 D6** 41 23N 4 21W
Cuemba, *Angola* **115 E3** 11 50 S 17 42 E
Cuenca, *Ecuador* **168 D2** 2 50 S 79 9W
Cuenca, *Spain* **40 E2** 40 5N 2 10W
Cuenca □, *Spain* **40 F3** 40 0N 2 0W
Cuenca, Serranía de, *Spain* **40 F3** 39 55N 1 50W
Cuerdo del Pozo, Embalse de la, *Spain* **40 D2** 41 51N 2 44W
Cuernavaca, *Mexico* **163 D5** 18 55N 99 15W
Cuero, *U.S.A.* **155 L6** 29 6N 97 17W
Cuers, *France* **29 E10** 43 14N 6 5 E
Cuervo, *U.S.A.* **155 H2** 35 2N 104 25W
Cuevas, Cerro, *Bolivia* **173 E4** 22 0 S 65 12W
Cuevas del Almanzora, *Spain* **41 H3** 37 18N 1 58W
Cuevo, *Bolivia* **173 E5** 20 15 S 63 30W
Cugir, *Romania* **53 E8** 45 48N 23 25 E
Cugnaux, *France* **28 E5** 43 32N 1 20 E
Cuhai-Bakony →, *Hungary* **52 C2** 47 35N 17 54 E
Cuiabá, *Brazil* **173 D6** 15 30 S 56 0W
Cuiabá →, *Brazil* **173 D6** 17 5 S 56 36W
Cuijk, *Neths.* **24 C5** 51 44N 5 50 E
Cuilco, *Guatemala* **164 C1** 15 24N 91 58W
Cuillin Hills, *U.K.* **22 D2** 57 23N 6 15W
Cuillin Sd., *U.K.* **22 D2** 57 4N 6 20W
Cuima, *Angola* **115 E3** 13 25 S 15 45 E
Cuiseaux, *France* **27 F12** 46 30N 5 22 E
Cuité, *Brazil* **170 C4** 6 29 S 36 9W
Cuito →, *Angola* **115 F4** 18 1 S 20 48 E

Dantan 205

Cuito Cuanavale, *Angola* . . . **115 F3** 15 10 S 19 10 E
Cuitzeo, L. de, *Mexico* **162 D4** 19 55N 101 5W
Cuiuni →, *Brazil* . . . . **169 D5** 0 45 S 63 7W
Cuivre →, *U.S.A.* **156 F6** 38 55N 90 44W
Cuivre, West Fork →, *U.S.A.* **156 E6** 39 2N 90 58W
Cujmir, *Romania* . . . . **52 F7** 44 13N 22 57 E
Cukai, *Malaysia* . . . . **87 K4** 4 13N 103 25 E
Culaba, *Phil.* . . . . **81 F5** 11 40N 124 32 E
Culasi, *Phil.* . . . . **81 F4** 11 26N 122 3 E
Culauan, *Phil.* . . . . **81 J5** 5 58N 125 40 E
Culbertson, *U.S.A.* **154 A2** 48 9N 104 31W
Culburra, *Australia* . . . . **128 C3** 35 50 S 139 58 E
Culcairn, *Australia* . . . . **127 F4** 35 41 S 147 3 E
Culebra, Sierra de la, *Spain* **42 D4** 41 55N 6 20W
Culfa, *Azerbaijan* . . . . **101 C11** 38 57N 45 38 E
Culgoa, *Australia* . . . . **128 C5** 35 44 S 143 6 E
Culgoa →, *Australia* . . . . . . **127 D4** 29 56 S 146 20 E
Culiacán, *Mexico* **162 C3** 24 50N 107 23W
Culiacán →, *Mexico* **162 C3** 24 30N 107 42W
Culion, *Phil.* . . . . **81 F3** 11 54N 119 58 E
Culiseu →, *Brazil* . . . . **173 C7** 12 14 S 53 17W
Cúllar, *Spain* **43 H8** 37 35N 2 34W
Cullarin Ra., *Australia* . . . . . **129 C8** 34 30 S 149 30 E
Cullen, *U.K.* **22 D6** 57 42N 2 49W
Cullen Pt., *Australia* . . . . . . **126 A3** 11 57 S 141 54 E
Cullera, *Spain* **41 F4** 39 9N 0 17W
Cullman, *U.S.A.* **149 H2** 34 11N 86 51W
Culloden, *U.S.A.* **152 C5** 32 52N 84 6W
Cullom, *U.S.A.* **157 D8** 40 53N 88 16W
Culoz, *France* . . . . **29 C9** 45 47N 5 46 E
Culpataro, *Australia* . . . . . . **128 B6** 33 40 S 144 22 E
Culpeper, *U.S.A.* **148 F7** 38 30N 78 0W
Culuene →, *Brazil* . . . . **173 C7** 12 56 S 52 51W
Culver, *U.S.A.* **157 C10** 41 13N 86 25W
Culver, Pt., *Australia* . . . . . . **125 F3** 32 54 S 124 43 E
Culverden, *N.Z.* . . . . **131 C7** 42 47 S 172 49 E
Culverton, *U.S.A.* **152 B7** 33 19N 82 54W
Cuma, *Angola* . . . . **115 E3** 12 52 S 15 5 E
Cumaná, *Venezuela* **169 A5** 10 30N 64 5W
Cumaovası, *Turkey* . . . . **49 C9** 38 15N 27 9 E
Cumare, *Colombia* **168 C3** 0 49N 72 32W
Cumari, *Brazil* . . . . **171 E2** 18 16 S 48 11W
Cumberland, *Canada* **142 D4** 49 40N 125 0W
Cumberland, *Iowa, U.S.A.* . . **156 C2** 41 16N 94 52W
Cumberland, *Md., U.S.A.* . . **148 F6** 39 39N 78 46W
Cumberland, *Wis., U.S.A.* . . **154 C8** 45 32N 92 1W
Cumberland →, *U.S.A.* . . . **149 G2** 36 15N 87 0W
Cumberland, C., *Vanuatu* . . **133 D4** 14 39 S 166 37 E
Cumberland I., *U.S.A.* **152 E8** 30 50N 81 25W
Cumberland I. Nat. Seashore, *U.S.A.* **152 E8** 30 12N 81 24W
Cumberland Is., *Australia* . . **126 C4** 20 35 S 149 10 E
Cumberland L., *Canada* **143 C8** 54 3N 102 18W
Cumberland Pen., *Canada* . **139 B13** 67 0N 64 0W
Cumberland Plateau, *U.S.A.* **149 H3** 36 0N 85 0W
Cumberland Sd., *Canada* . . . **139 B13** 65 30N 66 0W
Cumbernauld, *U.K.* **22 F5** 55 57N 3 58W
Cumborah, *Australia* . . . . . . **127 D4** 29 40 S 147 45 E
Cumbres Mayores, *Spain* . . . **43 G4** 38 4N 6 39W
Cumbria □, *U.K.* **20 C5** 54 42N 2 52W
Cumbrian Mts., *U.K.* **20 C5** 54 30N 3 0W
Cumbum, *India* . . . . **95 G4** 15 40N 79 10 E
Cuminá →, *Brazil* . . . . **169 D6** 1 30 S 56 0W
Cuminapanema →, *Brazil* . **169 D7** 1 9 S 54 54W
Cummings, *U.S.A.* **152 C9** 32 47N 80 59W
Cummings Mt., *U.S.A.* **161 K8** 35 2N 118 34W
Cummins, *Australia* . . . . **127 E2** 34 16 S 135 43 E
Cumnock, *Australia* . . . . **129 B8** 32 59 S 148 46 E
Cumnock, *U.K.* **22 F4** 55 28N 4 17W
Cumpas, *Mexico* **162 B3** 30 0N 109 48W
Cumplida, Pta., *Canary Is.* . **39 F2** 28 50N 17 48W
Çumra, *Turkey* . . . . **100 D5** 37 34N 32 45 E
Cuncumén, *Chile* . . . . **174 C1** 31 53 S 70 38W
Cundeelee, *Australia* . . . . . . **125 F3** 30 43 S 123 26 E
Cunderdin, *Australia* . . . . . . **125 F2** 31 37 S 117 12 E
Cundinamarca □, *Colombia* **168 C3** 5 0N 74 0W
Cunene □, *Angola* . . . . **115 F3** 16 30 S 15 0 E
Cunene →, *Angola* . . . . **115 F2** 17 20 S 11 50 E
Cúneo, *Italy* . . . . **44 D4** 44 23N 7 32 E
Cunhinga, *Angola* . . . . **115 E3** 12 11 S 16 47 E
Cunillera, I. = Sa Conillera, *Spain* . . . . **39 C7** 38 59N 1 13 E
Cunjamba, *Angola* . . . . **115 F4** 15 27 S 20 10 E
Cunlhat, *France* . . . . **28 C7** 45 38N 3 32 E
Cunnamulla, *Australia* . . . . **127 D4** 28 2 S 145 38 E
Cuorgnè, *Italy* . . . . **44 C4** 45 23N 7 39 E
Cupar, *Canada* **143 C8** 50 57N 104 10W
Cupar, *U.K.* **22 E5** 56 19N 3 1W
Cupcini, *Moldova* . . . . **53 B12** 48 6N 27 23 E
Cupica, G. de, *Colombia* . . . **168 B2** 6 25N 77 30W
Ćuprija, *Serbia, Yug.* . . . . . . **50 C5** 43 57N 21 26 E
Curaçá, *Brazil* . . . . **170 C4** 8 59 S 39 54W
Curaçao, *Neth. Ant.* **165 D6** 12 10N 69 0W
Curacautín, *Chile* . . . . **176 A2** 38 26 S 71 53W
Curahuara de Carangas, *Bolivia* . . . . **172 D4** 17 52 S 68 26W
Curanilahue, *Chile* . . . . **174 D1** 37 29 S 73 28W
Curaray →, *Peru* . . . . **168 D3** 2 20 S 74 5W
Curatabaca, *Venezuela* **169 B5** 6 19N 62 51W
Cure →, *France* . . . . **27 E10** 47 40N 3 41 E
Curepto, *Chile* . . . . **174 D1** 35 8 S 72 1W
Curiapo, *Venezuela* **169 B5** 8 33N 61 5W
Curicó, *Chile* . . . . **174 C1** 34 55 S 71 20W
Curicó □, *Chile* . . . . **174 C1** 34 50 S 71 15W
Curicuriari →, *Brazil* . . . . . **168 D4** 0 14 S 66 48W
Curimatá, *Brazil* . . . . **170 D3** 10 2 S 44 17W
Curinga, *Italy* . . . . **47 D9** 38 49N 16 19 E
Curiplaya, *Colombia* **168 C3** 0 16N 74 52W
Curitiba, *Brazil* . . . . **175 B6** 25 20 S 49 10W
Currabubula, *Australia* . . . . **129 A9** 31 16 S 150 44 E
Currais Novos, *Brazil* . . . . . **170 C4** 6 13 S 36 30W
Curralinho, *Brazil* . . . . **170 B2** 1 45 S 49 46W
Currant, *U.S.A.* **158 G6** 38 51N 115 32W
Curranyalpa, *Australia* . . . . **129 A6** 30 53 S 144 39 E
Curraweena, *Australia* . . . . **129 A6** 30 47 S 145 54 E
Currawilla, *Australia* . . . . . **126 D3** 25 10 S 141 20 E
Current →, *U.S.A.* **155 G9** 36 15N 90 55W
Currie, *Australia* . . . . **126 F3** 39 56 S 143 53 E
Currie, *U.S.A.* **158 F6** 40 16N 114 45W
Currituck Sd., *U.S.A.* **149 G8** 36 20N 75 52W
Cursole, *Somali Rep.* . . . . . . **120 D3** 2 14N 45 25 E
Curtea de Argeş, *Romania* . **53 E9** 45 12N 24 42 E
Curtici, *Romania* . . . . **52 D6** 46 21N 21 18 E
Curtis, *U.S.A.* **154 E4** 40 38N 100 31W
Curtis Group, *Australia* . . . . **126 F4** 39 30 S 146 37 E
Curtis I., *Australia* . . . . **126 C5** 23 35 S 151 10 E
Curuá →, *Pará, Brazil* . . . . **169 D7** 2 24 S 54 5W
Curuá →, *Pará, Brazil* . . . . **173 B7** 5 23 S 54 22W
Curuá, I., *Brazil* **170 A1** 0 48N 50 10W
Curuaés →, *Brazil* . . . . **173 B7** 7 30 S 54 45W
Curuápanema →, *Brazil* . . **169 D6** 2 25 S 55 2W
Curuçá, *Brazil* . . . . **170 B2** 0 43 S 47 50W
Curuguaty, *Paraguay* . . . . . . **175 A4** 24 31 S 55 42W
Çürüksu Çayi →, *Turkey* . . **57 G4** 37 27N 27 11 E
Curup, *Indonesia* . . . . **84 C2** 4 26 S 102 13 E
Curupira, Serra, *S. Amer.* . . **169 C5** 1 25N 64 30W
Cururu →, *Brazil* . . . . **173 B6** 7 12 S 58 3W
Cururupu, *Brazil* . . . . **170 B3** 1 50 S 44 50W
Curuzú Cuatiá, *Argentina* . . **174 B4** 29 50 S 58 5W
Curvelo, *Brazil* . . . . **171 E3** 18 45 S 44 27W
Curyo, *Australia* . . . . **128 C5** 35 50 S 142 47 E
Cushing, *U.S.A.* **155 H6** 35 59N 96 46W
Cushing, Mt., *Canada* **142 B3** 57 35N 126 57W
Cusihuiriáchic, *Mexico* **162 B3** 28 10N 106 50W
Cusna, Mte., *Italy* . . . . **44 D7** 44 17N 10 23 E
Cusset, *France* . . . . **27 F10** 46 8N 3 28 E
Cusseta, *U.S.A.* **152 C5** 32 18N 84 47W
Custer, *U.S.A.* **154 D3** 43 46N 103 36W
Cut Bank, *U.S.A.* **158 B7** 48 38N 112 20W
Cutervo, *Peru* . . . . **172 B2** 6 25 S 78 55W
Cuthbert, *U.S.A.* **152 D5** 31 46N 84 48W
Cutler, *U.S.A.* **160 J7** 36 31N 119 17W
Cutler Ridge, *U.S.A.* **153 K9** 25 35N 80 20W
Cutral-Có, *Argentina* . . . . . . **176 A3** 38 58 S 69 15W
Cutro, *Italy* . . . . **47 C9** 39 2N 16 59 E
Cuttaburra →, *Australia* . . **127 D3** 29 43 S 144 22 E
Cuttack, *India* . . . . **94 D7** 20 25N 85 57 E
Cuvelai, *Angola* . . . . **115 F3** 15 44 S 15 50 E
Cuvier, C., *Australia* . . . . . . **125 D1** 23 14 S 113 22 E
Cuvier I., *N.Z.* . . . . **130 C4** 36 27 S 175 50 E
Cuxhaven, *Germany* . . . . **30 B4** 53 51N 8 41 E
Cuyabeno, *Ecuador* . . . . **168 D2** 0 16 S 75 53W
Cuyahoga Falls, *U.S.A.* **150 E3** 41 8N 81 29W
Cuyapo, *Phil.* . . . . **80 D3** 15 46N 120 40 E
Cuyo, *Phil.* . . . . **81 F3** 10 50N 121 5 E
Cuyo East Pass, *Phil.* . . . . . . **81 F3** 11 0N 121 28 E
Cuyo I., *Phil.* . . . . **81 F3** 10 51N 121 2 E
Cuyo West Pass, *Phil.* . . . . . **81 F3** 11 0N 120 30 E
Cuyuni →, *Guyana* **169 B6** 6 23N 58 41W
Cuzco, *Bolivia* . . . . **172 E4** 20 0 S 66 50W
Cuzco, *Peru* . . . . **172 C3** 13 32 S 72 0W
Cuzco □, *Peru* . . . . **172 C3** 13 31 S 71 59W
Čvrsnica, *Bos.-H.* . . . . **52 G2** 43 36N 17 35 E
Cwmbran, *U.K.* **21 F4** 51 39N 3 2W
Cyangugu, *Rwanda* . . . . **118 C2** 2 29 S 28 54 E
Cybinka, *Poland* . . . . **55 F1** 52 12N 14 46 E
Cyclades = Kikládhes, *Greece* . . . . **48 E6** 37 0N 24 30 E
Cygnet, *Australia* . . . . **126 G4** 43 8 S 147 1 E
Cynthiana, *U.S.A.* **157 F12** 38 23N 84 18W
Cypress Hills, *Canada* **143 D7** 49 40N 109 30W
Cyprus ■, *Asia* . . . . **38 E12** 35 0N 33 0 E
Cyrenaica, *Libya* . . . . **108 B4** 27 0N 23 0 E
Cyrene = Shaḥḥāt, *Libya* . . **108 B4** 32 48N 21 54 E
Czaplinek, *Poland* . . . . **54 E3** 53 34N 16 14 E
Czar, *Canada* **143 C6** 52 27N 110 50W
Czarna →, Piotrkow Trybunalski, *Poland* . . . . **55 G6** 51 18N 19 55 E
Czarna →, *Tarnobrzeg, Poland* . . . . **55 H8** 50 28N 21 21 E
Czarna Białostocka, *Poland* **55 E10** 53 18N 23 17 E
Czarna Woda, *Poland* . . . . . . **54 E5** 53 51N 18 6 E
Czarne, *Poland* . . . . **54 E3** 53 42N 16 58 E
Czarnków, *Poland* . . . . **55 F3** 52 55N 16 38 E
Czech Rep. ■, *Europe* . . . . . **34 B8** 50 0N 15 0 E
Czechowice-Dziedzice, *Poland* . . . . **55 J5** 49 54N 18 59 E
Czempiń, *Poland* . . . . **55 F3** 52 9N 16 43 E
Czeremcha, *Poland* . . . . **55 F10** 52 31N 23 21 E
Czerniejewo, *Poland* . . . . **55 F4** 52 26N 17 30 E
Czersk, *Poland* . . . . **54 E4** 53 46N 17 58 E
Czerwieńsk, *Poland* . . . . **55 F2** 52 1N 15 23 E
Czerwionka-Leszczyny, *Poland* . . . . **55 H5** 50 7N 18 37 E
Częstochowa, *Poland* . . . . . . **55 H6** 50 49N 19 7 E
Częstochowa □, *Poland* . . . . **55 H6** 50 45N 19 0 E
Człopa, *Poland* . . . . **55 E3** 53 6N 16 6 E
Człuchów, *Poland* . . . . **54 E4** 53 41N 17 22 E
Czyżew-Osada, *Poland* . . . . . **55 F9** 52 48N 22 19 E

D

Da →, *Vietnam* . . . . **86 B5** 21 15N 105 20 E
Da Hinggan Ling, *China* . . . **73 B7** 48 0N 121 0 E
Da Lat, *Vietnam* . . . . **87 G7** 11 56N 108 25 E
Da Nang, *Vietnam* . . . . **86 D7** 16 4N 108 13 E
Da Qaidam, *China* . . . . **72 C4** 37 50N 95 15 E
Da Yunhe →, *China* . . . . **75 G11** 34 25N 120 5 E
Da'an, *China* . . . . **75 B13** 45 30N 124 7 E
Daap, *Phil.* . . . . **81 H4** 7 4N 122 12 E
Dab'a, Râs el, *Egypt* . . . . . . **106 H6** 31 3N 28 31 E
Daba Shan, *China* . . . . **76 B7** 32 0N 109 0 E
Dabai, *Nigeria* . . . . **113 C6** 11 25N 5 15 E
Dabajuro, *Venezuela* **168 A3** 11 2N 70 40W
Dabakala, *Ivory C.* **112 D4** 8 15N 4 20W
Dabaro, *Somali Rep.* . . . . **120 C3** 6 21N 48 43 E
Dabas, *Hungary* . . . . **52 C4** 47 11N 19 19 E
Dabeiba, *Colombia* **168 B2** 7 1N 76 16W
Dabhoi, *India* . . . . **92 H5** 22 10N 73 20 E
Dąbie, *Poland* . . . . **55 F5** 52 5N 18 50 E
Dabie Shan, *China* . . . . **77 B10** 31 20N 115 20 E
Dabo = Pasirkuning, *Indonesia* . . . . **84 C2** 0 30 S 104 33 E
Dabola, *Guinea* **112 C2** 10 50N 11 5W
Dabou, *Ivory C.* **112 D4** 5 20N 4 23W
Daboya, *Ghana* **113 D4** 9 30N 1 20W
Dąbrowa Białostocka, *Poland* . . . . **54 E10** 53 40N 23 21 E
Dąbrowa Górnicza, *Poland* . **55 H6** 50 15N 19 10 E
Dąbrowa Tarnowska, *Poland* **55 H7** 50 10N 20 59 E
Dabu, *China* . . . . **77 E11** 24 22N 116 41 E
Dabung, *Malaysia* . . . . **87 K4** 5 23N 102 1 E
Dabus →, *Ethiopia* . . . . **107 E4** 10 48N 35 10 E
Dacato →, *Ethiopia* . . . . **107 F5** 7 25N 42 40 E
Dacca = Dhaka, *Bangla.* . . . **90 D3** 23 43N 90 26 E
Dacca = Dhaka □, *Bangla.* . **90 C3** 24 25N 90 25 E
Dachau, *Germany* . . . . **31 G7** 48 15N 11 26 E
Dachstein, Hoher, *Austria* . . **34 D6** 47 28N 13 35 E
Dačice, *Czech Rep.* . . . . **34 B8** 49 5N 15 26 E
Dacula, *U.S.A.* **152 B6** 33 59N 83 54W
Dadali, *Solomon Is.* . . . . **133 M10** 8 7 S 159 6 E
Dadanawa, *Guyana* **169 C6** 2 50N 59 30W
Daday, *Turkey* . . . . **100 B5** 41 28N 33 27 E
Dade City, *U.S.A.* **149 L4** 28 22N 82 11W
Dades, Oued →, *Morocco* . . **110 B3** 30 58N 6 44W
Dadeville, *U.S.A.* **152 C4** 32 50N 85 46W
Dadiya, *Nigeria* . . . . **113 D7** 9 35N 11 24 E
Dadra & Nagar Haveli □, *India* . . . . **94 D1** 20 5N 73 0 E
Dadri = Charkhi Dadri, *India* . . . . **92 E7** 28 37N 76 17 E
Dadu, *Pakistan* . . . . **91 D2** 26 45N 67 45 E
Dadu He →, *China* . . . . **76 C4** 29 31N 103 46 E
Daet, *Phil.* . . . . **80 D4** 14 2N 122 55 E
Dafang, *China* . . . . **76 D5** 27 9N 105 39 E
Dağ, *Turkey* . . . . **49 D12** 37 12N 30 31 E
Dagali, *Norway* . . . . **18 D5** 60 25N 8 28 E
Dagana, *Senegal* **112 B1** 16 30N 15 35W
Dagash, *Sudan* . . . . **106 D3** 19 19N 33 25 E
Dagestan □, *Russia* . . . . **61 J8** 42 30N 47 0 E
Dagestanskiye Ogni, *Russia* **61 J9** 42 6N 48 12 E
Dagg Sd., *N.Z.* . . . . **131 F1** 45 23 S 166 45 E
Daggett, *U.S.A.* **161 L10** 34 52N 116 52W
Daghestan Republic = Dagestan □, *Russia* . . . . . **61 J8** 42 30N 47 0 E
Daghfeli, *Sudan* . . . . **106 D3** 19 18N 32 40 E
Dağlıq Qarabağ = Nagorno-Karabakh, *Azerbaijan* . . . **101 C12** 39 55N 46 45 E
Dagö = Hiiumaa, *Estonia* . . **15 G20** 58 50N 22 45 E
Dagu, *China* . . . . **75 E9** 38 59N 117 40 E
Dagua, *Papua N. G.* . . . . **132 B2** 3 27 S 143 20 E
Daguan, *China* . . . . **76 D4** 27 43N 103 56 E
Dagupan, *Phil.* . . . . **80 C3** 16 3N 120 20 E
Dagverðarnes, *Iceland* **11 B4** 65 10N 22 32W
Dahab, *Egypt* . . . . **106 B3** 28 31N 34 31 E
Dahlak Kebir, *Eritrea* . . . . . . **107 D5** 15 50N 40 10 E
Dahlenburg, *Germany* . . . . . . **30 B6** 53 11N 10 44 E
Dahlgren, *U.S.A.* **157 F8** 38 12N 88 41W
Dahlonega, *U.S.A.* **149 H4** 34 32N 83 59W
Dahme, *Germany* . . . . **30 D9** 51 52N 13 25 E
Dahod, *India* . . . . **92 H6** 22 50N 74 15 E
Dahomey = Benin ■, *Africa* **113 D5** 10 0N 2 0 E
Dahong Shan, *China* . . . . **77 B9** 31 25N 113 0 E
Dahra, *Senegal* **112 B1** 15 22N 15 30W
Dahra, Massif de, *Algeria* . . **111 A5** 36 7N 1 21 E
Daḥy, Nafūd ad, *Si. Arabia* **98 B4** 22 0N 45 25 E
Dai Hao, *Vietnam* . . . . **86 C6** 18 1N 106 25 E
Dai-Sen, *Japan* . . . . **70 B5** 35 22N 133 32 E
Dai Shan, *China* . . . . **77 B14** 30 25N 122 10 E
Dai Xian, *China* . . . . **74 E7** 39 4N 112 58 E
Daicheng, *China* . . . . **74 E9** 38 42N 116 38 E
Daigo, *Japan* . . . . **71 A12** 36 46N 140 21 E
Daimanji-San, *Japan* . . . . **70 A5** 36 14N 133 20 E
Daimiel, *Spain* **43 F7** 39 5N 3 35W
Daingean, *Ireland* **23 C4** 53 18N 7 17W
Dainkog, *China* . . . . **76 A1** 32 30N 97 58 E
Daintree, *Australia* . . . . **126 B4** 16 20 S 145 20 E
Daiō-Misaki, *Japan* . . . . **71 C8** 34 15N 136 45 E
Dairût, *Egypt* . . . . **106 B3** 27 34N 30 43 E
Daisetsu-Zan, *Japan* . . . . **68 C11** 43 30N 142 57 E
Daitari, *India* . . . . **94 D7** 21 10N 85 46 E
Daito, *Japan* . . . . **70 B4** 35 19N 132 58 E
Dajarra, *Australia* . . . . **126 C2** 21 42 S 139 30 E
Dajin Chuan →, *China* . . . . . **76 B3** 31 16N 101 59 E
Dak Dam, *Cambodia* . . . . **86 F6** 12 20N 107 21 E
Dak Nhe, *Vietnam* . . . . **86 E6** 15 28N 107 48 E
Dak Pek, *Vietnam* . . . . **86 E6** 15 4N 107 44 E
Dak Song, *Vietnam* . . . . **87 F6** 12 19N 107 35 E
Dak Sui, *Vietnam* . . . . **86 E6** 14 55N 107 43 E
Dakar, *Senegal* **112 C1** 14 34N 17 29W
Dakhla, *W. Sahara* **110 D1** 23 50N 15 53W
Dakhla, El Wâhât el-, *Egypt* **106 B2** 25 30N 28 50 E
Dakhovskaya, *Russia* . . . . **57 F7** 44 13N 40 13 E
Dakingari, *Nigeria* . . . . **113 C5** 11 37N 4 1 E
Dakor, *India* . . . . **92 H5** 22 45N 73 11 E
Dakoro, *Niger* . . . . **113 C6** 14 31N 6 46 E
Dakota City, *Iowa, U.S.A.* . . **156 B2** 42 43N 94 12W
Dakota City, *Nebr., U.S.A.* . **154 D6** 42 25N 96 25W
Đakovica, *Serbia, Yug.* . . . . . **50 D4** 42 22N 20 26 E
Đakovo, *Croatia* . . . . **52 E3** 45 19N 18 24 E
Dal, *Norway* . . . . **18 E5** 59 53N 8 40 E
Dala, *Angola* . . . . **115 E4** 11 3 S 20 17 E
Dala, *Solomon Is.* . . . . **133 M11** 8 30 S 160 41 E
Dalaba, *Guinea* **112 C2** 10 42N 12 15W
Dalachi, *China* . . . . **74 F3** 36 48N 105 0 E
Dalaguete, *Phil.* . . . . **81 G4** 9 46N 123 32 E
Dalai Nur, *China* . . . . **74 C9** 43 20N 116 45 E
Dālakī, *Iran* . . . . **97 D6** 29 26N 51 17 E
Dalälven, *Sweden* . . . . **16 D10** 60 12N 16 43 E
Dalaman, *Turkey* . . . . **49 E10** 36 48N 28 47 E
Dalaman →, *Turkey* . . . . **49 E10** 36 41N 28 43 E
Dalandzadgad, *Mongolia* . . . **74 C3** 43 27N 104 30 E
Dalanganem Is., *Phil.* . . . . . . **81 F3** 10 40N 120 17 E
Dalarna, *Sweden* . . . . **16 D8** 61 0N 14 0 E
Dalasýsla □, *Iceland* **11 B4** 65 15N 22 0W
Dalat, *Malaysia* . . . . **85 B4** 2 44N 111 56 E
Dālbandīn, *Pakistan* . . . . **91 C2** 29 0N 64 23 E
Dalbeattie, *U.K.* **22 G5** 54 56N 3 50W
Dalbosjön, *Sweden* . . . . **17 F6** 58 40N 12 45 E
Dalby, *Australia* . . . . **127 D5** 27 10 S 151 17 E
Dalby, *Sweden* . . . . **17 J7** 55 40N 13 22 E
Dale, *Norway* . . . . **18 C2** 61 22N 5 23 E
Dale, *U.S.A.* **157 F10** 38 10N 86 59W
Dalen, *Norway* . . . . **18 E4** 59 26N 8 0 E
Dalet, *Burma* . . . . **90 F4** 19 59N 93 51 E
Daletme, *Burma* . . . . **90 E4** 21 36N 92 46 E
Daleville, *Ala., U.S.A.* **152 D4** 31 19N 85 43W
Daleville, *Ind., U.S.A.* **157 D11** 40 7N 85 33W
Dalga, *Egypt* . . . . **106 B3** 27 39N 30 41 E
Dalgān, *Iran* . . . . **97 E8** 27 31N 59 19 E
Dalhart, *U.S.A.* **155 G3** 36 4N 102 31W
Dalhousie, *Canada* **141 C6** 48 5N 66 26W
Dalhousie, *India* . . . . **92 C6** 32 38N 75 58 E
Dali, *Shaanxi, China* . . . . **74 G5** 34 48N 109 58 E
Dali, *Yunnan, China* . . . . **76 E3** 25 40N 100 10 E
Dalian, *China* . . . . **75 E11** 38 50N 121 40 E
Daliang Shan, *China* . . . . **76 D4** 28 0N 102 45 E
Daling He →, *China* . . . . **75 D11** 40 55N 121 40 E
Dāliyat el Karmel, *Israel* . . **103 C4** 32 43N 35 2 E
Dalj, *Croatia* . . . . **52 E3** 45 29N 18 59 E
Dalkeith, *U.K.* **22 F5** 55 54N 3 4W
Dalkeith, *U.S.A.* **152 E4** 30 0N 85 9W
Dall I., *U.S.A.* **142 C2** 54 59N 133 25W
Dallarnil, *Australia* . . . . **127 D5** 25 19 S 152 2 E
Dallas, *Ga., U.S.A.* **152 B5** 33 55N 84 51W
Dallas, *Oreg., U.S.A.* **158 D2** 44 55N 123 19W
Dallas, *Tex., U.S.A.* **155 J6** 32 47N 96 49W
Dallas Center, *U.S.A.* **156 C3** 41 41N 93 58W
Dallas City, *U.S.A.* **156 D5** 40 38N 91 10W
Dallol, *Ethiopia* . . . . **107 E5** 14 14N 40 17 E
Dalmacija, *Croatia* . . . . **45 E13** 43 20N 17 0 E
Dalmatia = Dalmacija, *Croatia* . . . . **45 E13** 43 20N 17 0 E
Dalmatovo, *Russia* . . . . **62 C9** 56 16N 62 56 E
Dalmellington, *U.K.* **22 F4** 55 19N 4 23W
Dalnegorsk, *Russia* . . . . **68 B7** 44 32N 135 33 E
Dalnerechensk, *Russia* . . . . . **68 B6** 45 50N 133 40 E
Daloa, *Ivory C.* **112 D3** 7 0N 6 30W
Dalou Shan, *China* . . . . **76 C6** 28 15N 107 0 E
Dalry, *U.K.* **22 F4** 55 42N 4 43W
Dals Långed, *Sweden* . . . . . . **17 F6** 58 56N 12 18 E
Dalseter, *Norway* . . . . **18 C6** 61 28N 9 26 E
Dalsjöfors, *Sweden* . . . . **17 G7** 57 46N 13 5 E
Dalsland, *Sweden* . . . . **17 F6** 58 50N 12 15 E
Dalsmynni, *Iceland* **11 C5** 64 48N 21 29W
Daltenganj, *India* . . . . **93 H11** 24 0N 84 4 E
Dalton, *Canada* **140 C3** 48 11N 84 1W
Dalton, *Ga., U.S.A.* **149 H3** 34 46N 84 58W
Dalton, *Mass., U.S.A.* **151 D11** 42 28N 73 11W
Dalton, *Nebr., U.S.A.* **154 E3** 41 25N 102 58W
Dalton, Kap, *Greenland* **10 D8** 69 25N 24 3W
Dalton Iceberg Tongue, *Antarctica* . . . . **7 C9** 66 15 S 121 30 E
Dalton-in-Furness, *U.K.* **20 C4** 54 10N 3 11W
Dalupiri I., *Cagayan, Phil.* . . **80 B3** 19 5N 121 12 E
Dalupiri I., *N. Samar, Phil.* . . **80 E5** 12 25N 124 16 E
Dalvík, *Iceland* **11 B8** 65 58N 18 32W
Daly →, *Australia* . . . . **124 B5** 13 35 S 130 19 E
Daly City, *U.S.A.* **160 H4** 37 42N 122 28W
Daly L., *Canada* **143 B7** 56 32N 105 39W
Daly Waters, *Australia* . . . . . **126 B1** 16 15 S 133 24 E
Dalyan, *Turkey* . . . . **49 E10** 36 50N 28 39 E
Dam Doi, *Vietnam* . . . . **87 H5** 8 50N 105 12 E
Dam Ha, *Vietnam* . . . . **86 B6** 21 21N 107 36 E
Daman, *India* . . . . **94 D1** 20 25N 72 57 E
Daman & Diu □, *India* . . . . . **94 D1** 20 25N 72 58 E
Dāmaneh, *Iran* . . . . **97 C6** 33 1N 50 29 E
Damanhûr, *Egypt* . . . . **106 H7** 31 0N 30 30 E
Damanzhuang, *China* . . . . **74 E9** 38 5N 116 35 E
Damar, *Indonesia* . . . . **82 C3** 7 7 S 128 40 E
Damara, *C.A.R.* . . . . **114 B3** 4 58N 18 42 E
Damaraland, *Namibia* . . . . . . **116 C2** 20 0 S 15 0 E
Damascus = Dimashq, *Syria* **103 B5** 33 30N 36 18 E
Damascus, *U.S.A.* **152 D5** 31 18N 84 43W
Damaturu, *Nigeria* . . . . **113 C7** 11 45N 11 55 E
Damāvand, *Iran* . . . . **97 C7** 35 47N 52 0 E
Damāvand, Qolleh-ye, *Iran* **97 C7** 35 56N 52 10 E
Damba, *Angola* . . . . **115 D3** 6 44 S 15 20 E
Dâmboviţa □, *Romania* . . . . **53 F10** 45 0N 25 30 E
Dâmboviţa →, *Romania* . . . . **53 F11** 44 12N 26 26 E
Dâmbovnic →, *Romania* . . . **53 F10** 44 28N 25 18 E
Dame Marie, *Haiti* **165 C5** 18 36N 74 26W
Dāmghān, *Iran* . . . . **97 B7** 36 10N 54 17 E
Dămienesti, *Romania* . . . . . . **53 D11** 46 44N 26 59 E
Damietta = Dumyât, *Egypt* **106 H7** 31 24N 31 48 E
Daming, *China* . . . . **74 F8** 36 15N 115 6 E
Damīr Qābū, *Syria* . . . . **96 B4** 36 58N 41 51 E
Dammam = Ad Dammām, *Si. Arabia* . . . . **97 E6** 26 20N 50 5 E
Dammarie-les-Lys, *France* . . **27 D9** 48 31N 2 39 E
Dammartin-en-Goële, *France* **27 C9** 49 3N 2 41 E
Dammastock, *Switz.* . . . . **33 C6** 46 38N 8 24 E
Damme, *Germany* . . . . **30 C4** 52 32N 8 11 E
Damodar →, *India* . . . . **93 H12** 23 17N 87 35 E
Damoh, *India* . . . . **93 H8** 23 50N 79 28 E
Damous, *Algeria* . . . . **111 A5** 36 31N 1 42 E
Dampier, *Australia* . . . . **124 D2** 20 41 S 116 42 E
Dampier, Selat, *Indonesia* . . **83 B4** 0 40 S 131 0 E
Dampier Arch., *Australia* . . **124 D2** 20 38 S 116 32 E
Dampier Str., *Papua N. G.* . . **132 C5** 5 50 S 148 0 E
Damqawt, *Yemen* . . . . **99 C6** 16 34N 52 50 E
Damrei, Chuor Phnum, *Cambodia* . . . . **87 G4** 11 30N 103 0 E
Damvillers, *France* . . . . **27 C12** 49 20N 5 21 E
Dan-Gulbi, *Nigeria* . . . . **113 C6** 11 40N 6 15 E
Dan Xian, *China* . . . . **86 C7** 19 31N 109 33 E
Dana, *Indonesia* . . . . **82 D2** 11 0 S 122 52 E
Dana, L., *Canada* **140 B4** 50 53N 77 20W
Dana, Mt., *U.S.A.* **160 H7** 37 54N 119 12W
Danakil Depression, *Ethiopia* **107 E5** 12 45N 41 0 E
Danao, *Cebu, Phil.* . . . . **81 F5** 10 31N 124 1 E
Danao, *Sorsogon, Phil.* . . . . . **80 E4** 12 44N 123 51 E
Danbury, *U.S.A.* **151 E11** 41 24N 73 28W
Danby L., *U.S.A.* **159 J6** 34 13N 115 5W
Dand, *Afghan.* . . . . **92 D1** 31 28N 65 32 E
Dandaragan, *Australia* . . . . . . **125 F2** 30 40 S 115 40 E
Dandeldhura, *Nepal* . . . . **93 E9** 29 20N 80 35 E
Dandenong, *Australia* . . . . . . **129 E6** 38 0 S 145 15 E
Dandong, *China* . . . . **75 D13** 40 10N 124 20 E
Danfeng, *China* . . . . **74 H6** 33 45N 110 25 E
Danforth, *U.S.A.* **141 C6** 45 40N 67 52W
Dangan Liedao, *China* . . . . . . **77 F10** 22 2N 114 8 E
Dangara, *Tajikistan* . . . . **63 D4** 38 6N 69 22 E
Dangé-St.-Romain, *France* . . **28 B4** 46 56N 0 36 E
Dângeni, *Romania* . . . . **53 C11** 47 51N 26 58 E
Danger Is. = Pukapuka, *Cook Is.* . . . . **135 J11** 10 53 S 165 49W
Danger Pt., *S. Africa* . . . . **116 E2** 34 40 S 19 17 E
Dangla, *Ethiopia* . . . . **107 E4** 11 18N 36 56 E
Dangla Shan = Tanggula Shan, *China* . . . . **72 C4** 32 40N 92 10 E
Dangora, *Nigeria* . . . . **113 C6** 11 30N 8 7 E
Dangrek, Phnom, *Thailand* . **86 E5** 14 15N 105 0 E
Dangriga, *Belize* **163 D7** 17 0N 88 13W
Dangshan, *China* . . . . **74 G9** 34 27N 116 22 E
Dangtu, *China* . . . . **77 B12** 31 32N 118 25 E
Dangyang, *China* . . . . **77 B8** 30 52N 111 44 E
Daniel, *U.S.A.* **158 E8** 42 52N 110 4W
Daniel's Harbour, *Canada* . . **141 B8** 50 13N 57 35W
Danielskuil, *S. Africa* . . . . . . **116 D3** 28 11 S 23 33 E
Danielson, *U.S.A.* **151 E13** 41 48N 71 53W
Danielsville, *U.S.A.* **152 A6** 34 8N 83 13W
Danilov, *Russia* . . . . **58 C11** 58 16N 40 13 E
Danilovgrad, *Montenegro, Yug.* . . . . **50 D3** 42 38N 19 4 E
Danilovka, *Russia* . . . . **60 E7** 50 25N 44 12 E
Daning, *China* . . . . **74 F6** 36 28N 110 45 E
Danissa, *Kenya* . . . . **118 B5** 3 15N 40 58 E
Danja, *Nigeria* . . . . **113 C6** 11 21N 7 30 E
Danje-ia-Menha, *Angola* . . . . **115 D2** 9 32 S 14 39 E
Ḑank, *Oman* . . . . **99 B7** 23 33N 56 16 E
Dankalwa, *Nigeria* . . . . **113 C7** 11 52N 12 12 E
Dankama, *Nigeria* . . . . **113 C6** 13 20N 7 44 E
Dankov, *Russia* . . . . **58 F10** 53 20N 39 5 E
Danleng, *China* . . . . **76 B4** 30 1N 103 31 E
Danlí, *Honduras* **164 D2** 14 4N 86 35W
Danmark Fjord, *Greenland* . **10 A8** 81 30N 22 0W
Danmarkshavn, *Greenland* . **10 B9** 76 45N 18 50W
Dannemora, *U.S.A.* **151 B11** 44 43N 73 44W
Dannenberg, *Germany* . . . . . . **30 B7** 53 7N 11 4 E
Dannevirke, *N.Z.* . . . . **130 G5** 40 12 S 176 8 E
Dannhauser, *S. Africa* . . . . . . **117 D5** 28 0 S 30 3 E
Danot, *Ethiopia* . . . . **120 C3** 7 33N 45 17 E
Dansville, *U.S.A.* **150 D7** 42 34N 77 42W
Dantan, *India* . . . . **93 J12** 21 57N 87 20 E

Eppingen 211

El Metemma, Sudan 107 D3 16 50N 33 10 E
El Miamo, Venezuela 169 B5 7 39N 61 46W
El Milagro, Argentina 174 C2 30 59 S 65 59W
El Milia, Algeria 111 A6 36 51N 6 13 E
El Minyâ, Egypt 106 J7 28 7N 30 33 E
El Monte, U.S.A. 161 L8 34 4N 118 1W
El Montseny, Spain 40 D7 41 55N 2 25 E
El Mreyye, Mauritania 112 B3 18 0N 6 0W
El Nido, Phil. 81 F2 11 10N 119 25 E
El Obeid, Sudan 107 E3 13 8N 30 10 E
El Odaiya, Sudan 107 E2 12 8N 28 12 E
El Oro, Mexico 163 D4 19 48N 100 8W
El Oro □, Ecuador 168 D2 3 30 S 79 50W
El Oued, Algeria 111 B6 33 20N 6 58 E
El Palmar, Bolivia 173 D5 17 50 S 63 9W
El Palmar, Venezuela 169 B5 7 58N 61 53W
El Palmito, Presa, Mexico 162 B3 25 40N 105 30W
El Paso, Ill., U.S.A. 156 D7 40 44N 89 1W
El Paso, Tex., U.S.A. 159 L10 31 45N 106 29W
El Paso Robles, U.S.A. 160 K6 35 38N 120 41W
El Pedernoso, Spain 41 F2 39 29N 2 45W
El Pedroso, Spain 43 H5 37 51N 5 45W
El Pobo de Dueñas, Spain 40 E3 40 46N 1 39W
El Portal, U.S.A. 160 H7 37 41N 119 47W
El Porvenir, Mexico 162 A3 31 15N 105 51W
El Prat de Llobregat, Spain 40 D7 41 18N 2 3 E
El Progreso, Honduras 164 C2 15 26N 87 51W
El Pueblito, Mexico 162 B3 29 3N 105 4W
El Pueblo, Canary Is. 39 F2 28 36N 17 47W
El Puente del Arzobispo, Spain 42 F5 39 48N 5 10W
El Puerto de Santa María, Spain 43 J4 36 36N 6 13W
El Qâhira, Egypt 106 H7 30 1N 31 14 E
El Qantara, Egypt 103 E1 30 51N 32 20 E
El Qasr, Egypt 106 B2 25 44N 28 42 E
El Quseima, Egypt 103 E3 30 40N 34 15 E
El Qusîya, Egypt 106 B3 27 29N 30 44 E
El Râshda, Egypt 106 B2 25 36N 28 57 E
El Reno, U.S.A. 155 H6 35 32N 97 57W
El Rîdisiya, Egypt 106 C3 24 56N 32 51 E
El Rio, U.S.A. 161 L7 34 14N 119 10W
El Ronquillo, Spain 43 H4 37 44N 6 10W
El Roque, Pta., Canary Is. 39 F4 28 10N 15 25W
El Rosarito, Mexico 162 B2 28 38N 114 4W
El Rubio, Spain 43 H5 37 22N 5 0W
El Saff, Egypt 106 J7 29 34N 31 16 E
El Saheira, W. →, Egypt 103 E2 30 5N 33 25 E
El Salto, Mexico 162 C3 23 47N 105 22W
El Salvador ■, Cent. Amer. 164 D2 13 50N 89 0W
El Sauce, Nic. 164 D2 13 0N 86 40W
El Saucejo, Spain 43 H5 37 4N 5 6W
El Shallal, Egypt 106 C3 24 0N 32 53 E
El Simbillawein, Egypt 106 H7 30 48N 31 13 E
El Sombrero, Venezuela 168 B4 9 23N 67 3W
El Suweis, Egypt 106 J8 29 58N 32 31 E
El Tamarâni, W. →, Egypt 103 E3 30 7N 34 43 E
El Thamad, Egypt 103 F3 29 40N 34 28 E
El Tigre, Venezuela 169 B5 8 44N 64 15W
El Tîh, G., Egypt 103 F2 29 40N 33 50 E
El Tîna, Khalîg, Egypt 103 D1 31 10N 32 40 E
El Tocuyo, Venezuela 168 B4 9 47N 69 48W
El Tofo, Chile 174 B1 29 22 S 71 18W
El Tránsito, Chile 174 B1 28 52 S 70 17W
El Tûr, Egypt 106 J8 28 14N 33 36 E
El Turbio, Argentina 176 D2 51 45 S 72 5W
El Uinle, Somali Rep. 120 D2 3 4N 41 42 E
El Uqsur, Egypt 106 B3 25 41N 32 38 E
El Venado, Mexico 162 C4 22 56N 101 10W
El Vendrell, Spain 40 D6 41 10N 1 30 E
El Vigía, Venezuela 168 B3 8 38N 71 39W
El Viso del Alcor, Spain 43 H5 37 23N 5 43W
El Wabeira, Egypt 103 F2 29 34N 33 6 E
El Wak, Kenya 118 B5 2 49N 40 56 E
El Wak, Somali Rep. 120 D2 2 44N 41 1 E
El Waqf, Egypt 106 B3 25 45N 32 15 E
El Wâsta, Egypt 106 J7 29 19N 31 12 E
El Weguet, Ethiopia 107 F5 5 28N 42 17 E
El Wuz, Sudan 107 D3 15 5N 30 7 E
Elafónisos, Greece 48 E4 36 29N 22 56 E
Elaine, Australia 128 D6 37 44 S 144 2 E
Elamanchili, India 94 F6 17 33N 82 50 E
Élancourt, France 27 D8 48 47N 1 58 E
Elands, Australia 129 A10 31 37 S 152 20 E
Élassa, Greece 49 F8 35 18N 26 21 E
Elassón, Greece 48 B4 39 53N 22 12 E
Elat, Israel 103 F3 29 30N 34 56 E
Eláthia, Greece 48 C4 38 37N 22 46 E
Elâzığ, Turkey 101 C8 38 37N 39 14 E
Elba, Italy 44 F7 42 46N 10 17 E
Elba, U.S.A. 152 D3 31 25N 86 4W
Elbasani, Albania 50 E4 41 9N 20 9 E
Elbe, U.S.A. 160 D4 46 45N 122 10W
Elbe →, Europe 30 B4 53 50N 9 0 E
Elbe-Seitenkanal, Germany 30 C6 52 45N 10 32 E
Elberfeld, U.S.A. 157 F9 38 10N 87 27W
Elbert, Mt., U.S.A. 159 G10 39 7N 106 27W
Elberta, U.S.A. 148 C2 44 37N 86 14W
Elberton, U.S.A. 152 A7 34 7N 82 52W
Elbeuf, France 26 C8 49 17N 1 2 E
Elbing = Elbląg, Poland 54 D6 54 10N 19 25 E
Elbistan, Turkey 100 C7 38 13N 37 15 E
Elbląg, Poland 54 D6 54 10N 19 25 E
Elbląg □, Poland 54 D6 54 15N 19 30 E
Elbow, Canada 143 C7 51 7N 106 35W
Elbrus, Asia 61 J6 43 21N 42 30 E
Elburn, U.S.A. 157 C8 41 54N 88 28W
Elburz Mts. = Alborz, Reshteh-ye Kūhhā-ye, Iran 97 C7 36 0N 52 0 E
Elche, Spain 41 G4 38 15N 0 42W
Elche de la Sierra, Spain 41 G2 38 27N 2 3W
Elcho I., Australia 126 A2 11 55 S 135 45 E
Elda, Spain 41 G4 38 29N 0 47W
Elde →, Germany 30 B7 53 7N 11 15 E
Eldon, Mo., U.S.A. 156 F4 38 21N 92 35W
Eldon, Wash., U.S.A. 160 C3 47 33N 123 3W
Eldora, U.S.A. 156 B3 42 22N 93 5W
Eldorado, Argentina 175 B5 26 28 S 54 43W
Eldorado, Canada 143 B7 59 35N 108 30W
Eldorado, Mexico 162 C3 24 20N 107 22W
Eldorado, Ill., U.S.A. 157 G8 37 49N 88 26W
Eldorado, Tex., U.S.A. 155 K4 30 52N 100 36W
Eldorado Springs, U.S.A. 155 G8 37 52N 94 1W
Eldorendo, U.S.A. 152 D5 31 3N 84 39W
Eldoret, Kenya 118 B4 0 30N 35 17 E
Eldred, U.S.A. 150 E6 41 58N 78 23W
Eldridge, U.S.A. 156 C6 41 39N 90 35W
Elea, C., Cyprus 38 D13 35 19N 34 4 E
Electra, U.S.A. 155 H5 34 2N 98 55W
Elefantes →, Mozam. 117 C5 24 10 S 32 40 E
Elefantes, G., Chile 176 C2 46 28 S 73 49W
Elektrogorsk, Russia 58 E10 55 56N 38 50 E
Elektrostal, Russia 58 E10 55 41N 38 32 E
Elele, Nigeria 113 D6 5 5N 6 50 E
Elena, Bulgaria 51 D9 42 55N 25 53 E
Elephant Butte Reservoir, U.S.A. 159 K10 33 9N 107 11W
Elephant I., Antarctica 7 C18 61 0 S 55 0W
Elephant Pass, Sri Lanka 95 K5 9 35N 80 25 E
Elesbão Veloso, Brazil 170 C3 6 13 S 42 8W
Eleshnitsa, Bulgaria 50 E7 41 52N 23 36 E
Eleşkirt, Turkey 101 C10 39 50N 42 50 E
Eleuthera, Bahamas 164 B4 25 0N 76 20W
Elevsís, Greece 48 C5 38 4N 23 26 E
Elevtheroúpolis, Greece 51 F8 40 52N 24 20 E
Elgå, Norway 18 B8 62 10N 11 56 E
Elgepiggen, Norway 18 B8 62 10N 11 21 E
Elgeyo-Marakwet □, Kenya 118 B4 0 45N 35 30 E
Elgg, Switz. 33 B7 47 29N 8 52 E
Elgin, N.B., Canada 141 C6 45 48N 65 10W
Elgin, Ont., Canada 151 B8 44 36N 76 13W
Elgin, U.K. 22 D5 57 39N 3 19W
Elgin, Ill., U.S.A. 157 B8 42 2N 88 17W
Elgin, N. Dak., U.S.A. 154 B4 46 24N 101 51W
Elgin, Nebr., U.S.A. 154 E5 41 59N 98 5W
Elgin, Nev., U.S.A. 159 H6 37 21N 114 32W
Elgin, Oreg., U.S.A. 158 D5 45 34N 117 55W
Elgin, S.C., U.S.A. 152 A9 34 10N 80 48W
Elgin, Tex., U.S.A. 155 K6 30 21N 97 22W
Elgoibar, Spain 40 B2 43 13N 2 24W
Elgon, Mt., Africa 118 B3 1 10N 34 30 E
Eliase, Indonesia 83 C4 8 21 S 130 48 E
Elida, U.S.A. 155 J3 33 57N 103 39W
Elikón, Greece 48 C4 38 18N 22 45 E
Elim, S. Africa 116 E2 34 35 S 19 45 E
Elim Indian Reservation, U.S.A. 144 D7 64 40N 162 0W
Elin Pelin, Bulgaria 50 D7 42 40N 23 36 E
Elisabethville = Lubumbashi, Dem. Rep. of the Congo 119 E2 11 40 S 27 28 E
Eliseu Martins, Brazil 170 C3 8 13 S 43 42W
Elista, Russia 61 G7 46 16N 44 14 E
Elizabeth, Australia 128 C3 34 42 S 138 41 E
Elizabeth, Ill., U.S.A. 156 B6 42 19N 90 13W
Elizabeth, N.J., U.S.A. 151 F10 40 40N 74 13W
Elizabeth City, U.S.A. 149 G7 36 18N 76 14W
Elizabethton, U.S.A. 149 G4 36 21N 82 13W
Elizabethtown, Ky., U.S.A. 148 G3 37 42N 85 52W
Elizabethtown, N.Y., U.S.A. 151 B11 44 13N 73 36W
Elizabethtown, Pa., U.S.A. 151 F8 40 9N 76 36W
Elizondo, Spain 40 B3 43 12N 1 30W
Elk, Poland 54 E9 53 50N 22 21 E
Elk →, Poland 54 E9 53 41N 22 28 E
Elk City, U.S.A. 155 H5 35 25N 99 25W
Elk Creek, U.S.A. 160 F4 39 36N 122 32W
Elk Grove, U.S.A. 160 G5 38 25N 121 22W
Elk Island Nat. Park, Canada 142 C6 53 35N 112 59W
Elk Lake, Canada 140 C3 47 40N 80 25W
Elk Point, Canada 143 C6 53 54N 110 55W
Elk River, Idaho, U.S.A. 158 C5 46 47N 116 11W
Elk River, Minn., U.S.A. 154 C8 45 18N 93 35W
Elkader, U.S.A. 156 B5 42 51N 91 24W
Elkedra, Australia 126 C2 21 9 S 135 33 E
Elkedra →, Australia 126 C2 21 8 S 136 22 E
Elkhart, Ind., U.S.A. 157 C11 41 41N 85 58W
Elkhart, Kans., U.S.A. 155 G4 37 0N 101 54W
Elkhart →, U.S.A. 157 C11 41 41N 85 58W
Elkhorn, Canada 143 D8 49 59N 101 14W
Elkhorn, U.S.A. 157 B8 42 40N 88 33W
Elkhorn →, U.S.A. 154 E6 41 8N 96 19W
Elkhovo, Bulgaria 51 D10 42 10N 26 35 E
Elkin, U.S.A. 149 G5 36 15N 80 51W
Elkins, U.S.A. 148 F6 38 55N 79 51W
Elko, Canada 142 D5 49 20N 115 10W
Elko, Ga., U.S.A. 152 C6 32 20N 83 42W
Elko, Nev., U.S.A. 158 F6 40 50N 115 46W
Ell, L., Australia 125 E4 29 13 S 127 46 E
Ellaville, U.S.A. 152 C5 32 14N 84 19W
Ellef Ringnes I., Canada 6 B2 78 30N 102 2W
Ellendale, Australia 124 C3 17 56 S 124 48 E
Ellendale, U.S.A. 154 B5 46 0N 98 32W
Ellensburg, U.S.A. 158 C3 46 59N 120 34W
Ellenton, U.S.A. 152 D6 31 11N 83 35W
Ellenville, U.S.A. 151 E10 41 43N 74 24W
Ellerston, Australia 129 A9 31 49 S 151 20 E
Ellery, Mt., Australia 129 D8 37 28 S 148 47 E
Ellesmere, L., N.Z. 131 H7 47 47 S 172 28 E
Ellesmere I., Canada 6 B4 79 30N 80 0W
Ellesmere Port, U.K. 20 D5 53 17N 2 54W
Ellettsville, U.S.A. 157 E10 39 14N 86 38W
Ellice Is. = Tuvalu ■, Pac. Oc. 134 H9 8 0 S 178 0 E
Ellinwood, U.S.A. 154 F5 38 21N 98 35W
Elliot, Australia 126 B1 17 33 S 133 32 E
Elliot, S. Africa 117 E4 31 22 S 27 48 E
Elliot Lake, Canada 140 C3 46 25N 82 35W
Elliotdale = Xhora, S. Africa 117 E4 31 55 S 28 38 E
Elliott, U.S.A. 152 A9 34 6N 80 10W
Elliott Key, U.S.A. 153 K9 25 27N 80 12W
Ellis, U.S.A. 154 F5 38 56N 99 34W
Elliston, Australia 127 E1 33 39 S 134 53 E
Ellisville, U.S.A. 155 K10 31 36N 89 12W
Ellon, U.K. 22 D6 57 22N 2 4W
Ellore = Eluru, India 94 F5 16 48N 81 8 E
Elloree, U.S.A. 152 B9 33 32N 80 34W
Ells →, Canada 142 B6 57 18N 111 40W
Ellsworth, U.S.A. 154 F5 38 44N 98 14W
Ellsworth Land, Antarctica 7 D16 76 0 S 89 0W
Ellsworth Mts., Antarctica 7 D16 78 30 S 85 0W
Ellwangen, Germany 31 G6 48 57N 10 8 E
Ellwood City, U.S.A. 150 F4 40 52N 80 17W
Ellzey, U.S.A. 153 F7 29 19N 82 48W
Elm, Switz. 33 C8 46 54N 9 10 E
Elma, Canada 143 D9 49 52N 95 55W
Elma, U.S.A. 160 D3 47 0N 123 25W
Elmadağ, Turkey 100 C5 39 55N 33 14 E
Elmalı, Turkey 57 G4 36 44N 29 56 E
Elmer, U.S.A. 156 E4 39 57N 92 39W
Elmhurst, U.S.A. 157 C9 41 53N 87 56W
Elmina, Ghana 113 D4 5 5N 1 21W
Elmira, Canada 150 C4 43 36N 80 33W
Elmira, U.S.A. 150 D8 42 6N 76 48W
Elmodel, U.S.A. 152 D5 31 21N 84 29W
Elmore, Australia 128 D6 36 30 S 144 37 E
Elmore, Ala., U.S.A. 152 C3 32 32N 86 19W
Elmore, Calif., U.S.A. 161 M11 33 7N 115 49W
Elmore, Minn., U.S.A. 157 C13 41 29N 83 18W
Elmshorn, Germany 30 B5 53 43N 9 40 E
Elmvale, Canada 150 B5 44 35N 79 52W
Elmwood, U.S.A. 156 D7 40 47N 89 58W
Elne, France 28 F6 42 36N 2 58 E
Elnesvågen, Norway 18 B4 62 52N 7 10 E
Elnora, U.S.A. 157 F9 38 53N 87 5W
Elora, Canada 150 C4 43 41N 80 26W
Elorza, Venezuela 168 B4 7 3N 69 31W
Elos, Greece 48 E4 36 46N 22 43 E
Eloúnda, Greece 38 D7 35 16N 25 42 E
Eloy, U.S.A. 159 K8 32 45N 111 33W
Éloyes, France 27 D13 48 6N 6 36 E
Elrose, Canada 143 C7 51 12N 108 0W
Elsas, Canada 140 C3 48 32N 82 55W
Elsdorf, Germany 30 E2 50 55N 6 34 E
Elsie, U.S.A. 160 E3 45 52N 123 36W
Elsinore = Helsingør, Denmark 17 H6 56 2N 12 35 E
Elsinore, Australia 129 A6 31 35 S 145 11 E
Elsinore, U.S.A. 159 G7 38 41N 112 9W
Elster →, Germany 30 D7 51 25N 11 57 E
Elsterwerda, Germany 30 D9 51 27N 13 31 E
Eltham, Australia 129 D6 37 43 S 145 12 E
Eltham, N.Z. 130 F3 39 26 S 174 19 E
Elton, Russia 61 F8 49 5N 46 52 E
Elton, Ozero, Russia 61 F8 49 5N 46 42 E
Eltville, Germany 31 E4 50 2N 8 7 E
Eluru, India 94 F5 16 48N 81 8 E
Elvas, Portugal 43 G3 38 50N 7 10W
Elven, France 26 E4 47 44N 2 36W
Elverum, Norway 15 F14 60 53N 11 34 E
Elvire →, Australia 124 C4 17 51 S 128 11 E
Elvo →, Italy 44 C5 45 23N 8 21 E
Elwood, Ill., U.S.A. 157 C8 41 24N 88 7W
Elwood, Ind., U.S.A. 157 D11 40 17N 85 50W
Elwood, Nebr., U.S.A. 154 E5 40 36N 99 52W
Elx = Elche, Spain 41 G4 38 15N 0 42W
Ely, U.K. 21 E8 52 24N 0 16 E
Ely, Minn., U.S.A. 154 B9 47 55N 91 51W
Ely, Nev., U.S.A. 158 G6 39 15N 114 54W
Elyria, U.S.A. 150 E2 41 22N 82 7W
Elyrus, Greece 48 F5 35 15N 23 45 E
Elz →, Germany 31 G3 48 18N 7 44 E
Emådalen, Sweden 16 C8 61 20N 14 44 E
Emai, Vanuatu 133 G6 17 4 S 168 24 E
Emāmrūd, Iran 97 B7 36 30N 55 0 E
Emån →, Sweden 17 G10 57 8N 16 30 E
Emba, Kazakstan 64 E6 48 50N 58 8 E
Emba →, Kazakstan 57 E9 46 55N 53 28 E
Embarcación, Argentina 174 A3 23 10 S 64 0W
Embarras →, U.S.A. 157 F9 38 39N 87 37W
Embarras Portage, Canada 143 B6 58 27N 111 28W
Embetsu, Japan 68 B10 44 44N 141 47 E
Embi = Emba, Kazakstan 64 E6 48 50N 58 8 E
Embi → = Emba →, Kazakstan 57 E9 46 55N 53 28 E
Embira →, Brazil 172 B3 7 19 S 70 15W
Embóna, Greece 38 C9 36 13N 27 51 E
Embrach, Switz. 33 B7 47 30N 8 36 E
Embrun, France 29 D10 44 34N 6 30 E
Embu, Kenya 118 C4 0 32 S 37 38 E
Embu □, Kenya 118 C4 0 30 S 37 35 E
Emden, Germany 30 B3 53 21N 7 12 E
Emecik, Turkey 49 E9 36 46N 27 49 E
Emerald, Australia 126 C4 23 32 S 148 10 E
Emerson, Canada 143 D9 49 0N 97 10W
Emerson, U.S.A. 152 A5 34 8N 84 45W
Emery, U.S.A. 159 G8 38 55N 111 15W
Emet, Turkey 49 B11 39 20N 29 15 E
Emi Koussi, Chad 109 E3 19 45N 18 55 E
Emília-Romagna □, Italy 44 D8 44 45N 11 0 E
Emilius, Mte., Italy 44 C4 45 45N 7 20 E
Eminabad, Pakistan 92 C6 32 2N 74 8 E
Emine, Nos, Bulgaria 51 D11 42 40N 27 56 E
Eminence, U.S.A. 157 F11 38 22N 85 11W
Emirdağ, Turkey 100 C4 39 2N 31 8 E
Emlenton, U.S.A. 150 E5 41 11N 79 43W
Emlichheim, Germany 30 C2 52 37N 6 51 E
Emmaboda, Sweden 17 H9 56 37N 15 32 E
Emmalane, U.S.A. 152 C7 32 46N 82 0W
Emme →, Switz. 32 B5 47 14N 7 32 E
Emmeloord, Neths. 24 B5 52 44N 5 46 E
Emmen, Neths. 24 B6 52 48N 6 57 E
Emmen, Switz. 31 H4 47 5N 8 18 E
Emmendingen, Germany 31 G3 48 6N 7 51 E
Emmental, Switz. 32 C4 46 55N 7 40 E
Emmerich, Germany 30 D2 51 50N 6 14 E
Emmet, Australia 126 C3 24 45 S 144 30 E
Emmetsburg, U.S.A. 156 A2 43 7N 94 41W
Emmett, U.S.A. 158 E5 43 52N 116 30W
Emmonak, U.S.A. 144 E6 62 46N 164 30W
Emőd, Hungary 52 C5 47 57N 20 47 E
Emona, Bulgaria 51 D11 42 43N 27 53 E
Empalme, Mexico 162 B2 28 1N 110 49W
Empangeni, S. Africa 117 D5 28 50 S 31 52 E
Empedrado, Argentina 174 B4 28 0 S 58 46W
Emperor Seamount Chain, Pac. Oc. 134 D9 40 0N 170 0 E
Empire, U.S.A. 152 C6 32 21N 83 18W
Empoli, Italy 44 E7 43 43N 10 57 E
Emporia, Kans., U.S.A. 154 F6 38 25N 96 11W
Emporia, Va., U.S.A. 149 G7 36 42N 77 32W
Emporium, U.S.A. 150 E6 41 31N 78 14W
Empress, Canada 143 C7 50 57N 110 0W
Empty Quarter = Rub' al Khālī, Si. Arabia 99 C5 18 0N 48 0 E
Ems →, Germany 30 B3 53 20N 7 12 E
Emsdale, Canada 150 A5 45 32N 79 19W
Emsdetten, Germany 30 C3 52 10N 7 32 E
Emu, Australia 128 D5 36 44 S 143 26 E
Emu, China 75 C15 43 40N 128 6 E
Emu Park, Australia 126 C5 23 13 S 150 50 E
'En 'Avrona, Israel 103 F4 29 43N 35 0 E
En Nahud, Sudan 107 E2 12 45N 28 25 E
Ena, Japan 71 B9 35 25N 137 25 E
Ena-San, Japan 71 B9 35 26N 137 36 E
Enambú, Colombia 168 C3 1 1N 70 17W
Enana, Namibia 116 B2 17 30 S 16 23 E
Enånger, Sweden 16 C11 61 30N 17 9 E
Enaratoli, Indonesia 83 B5 3 55 S 136 21 E
Enard B., U.K. 22 C3 58 5N 5 20W
Enare = Inarijärvi, Finland 14 B22 69 0N 28 0 E
Encantadas, Serra, Brazil 175 C5 30 40 S 53 0W
Encarnación, Paraguay 175 B4 27 15 S 55 50W
Encarnación de Diaz, Mexico 162 C4 21 30N 102 13W
Enchi, Ghana 112 D4 5 53N 2 48W
Encinal, U.S.A. 155 L5 28 2N 99 21W
Encinitas, U.S.A. 161 M9 33 3N 117 17W
Encino, U.S.A. 159 J11 34 39N 105 28W
Encontrados, Venezuela 168 B3 9 3N 72 14W
Encounter B., Australia 128 C3 35 45 S 138 45 E
Encruzilhada, Brazil 171 E3 15 31 S 40 54W
Encs, Hungary 52 B6 48 20N 21 8 E
Ende, Indonesia 82 C2 8 45 S 121 40 E
Endeavour, Canada 143 C8 52 10N 102 39W
Endeavour Str., Australia 126 A3 10 45 S 142 0 E
Endelave, Denmark 17 J4 55 46N 10 18 E
Enden, Norway 18 C7 61 47N 10 15 E
Enderbury I., Kiribati 134 H10 3 8 S 171 5W
Enderby, Canada 142 C5 50 35N 119 10W
Enderby I., Australia 124 D2 20 35 S 116 30 E
Enderby Land, Antarctica 7 C5 66 0 S 53 0 E
Enderlin, U.S.A. 154 B6 46 38N 97 36W
Endicott, N.Y., U.S.A. 151 D8 42 6N 76 4W
Endicott, Wash., U.S.A. 158 C5 46 56N 117 41W
Endimari →, Brazil 172 B4 8 46 S 66 7W
Endyalgout I., Australia 124 B5 11 40 S 132 35 E
Ene →, Peru 172 C3 11 10 S 74 18W
Energetik, Russia 62 F7 51 45N 58 45 E
Enewetak Atoll, Pac. Oc. 134 F8 11 30N 162 15 E
Enez, Turkey 51 F10 40 45N 26 5 E
Enfield, U.S.A. 157 F8 38 6N 88 20W
Engadin, Switz. 31 J6 46 45N 10 10 E
Engan, Norway 18 A5 63 8N 8 31 E
Engaño, C., Dom. Rep. 165 C6 18 30N 68 20W
Engaño, C., Phil. 80 B4 18 35N 122 23 E
Engcobo, S. Africa 117 E4 31 37 S 28 0 E
Engelberg, Switz. 33 C6 46 48N 8 26 E
Engels, Russia 60 E8 51 28N 46 6 E
Engemann L., Canada 143 B7 58 0N 106 55W
Engerdal, Norway 18 C8 61 45N 11 58 E
Enggano, Indonesia 84 D2 5 20 S 102 40 E
Engil, Morocco 110 B4 33 12N 4 32W
Engkilili, Malaysia 85 B4 1 3N 111 42 E
England, U.S.A. 155 H9 34 33N 91 58W
England □, U.K. 20 D7 53 0N 2 0W
Englee, Canada 141 B8 50 45N 56 5W
Englefield, Australia 128 D4 37 21 S 141 48 E
Englehart, Canada 140 C4 47 49N 79 52W
Engler L., Canada 143 B7 59 8N 106 52W
Englewood, Colo., U.S.A. 154 F2 39 39N 104 59W
Englewood, Fla., U.S.A. 153 J7 26 58N 82 21W
Englewood, Kans., U.S.A. 155 G5 37 2N 99 59W
Englewood, Ohio, U.S.A. 157 E12 39 53N 84 18W
English, U.S.A. 157 F10 38 20N 86 28W
English →, Canada 143 C10 50 35N 93 30W
English →, U.S.A. 156 C5 41 29N 91 32W
English Bazar = Ingraj Bazar, India 93 G13 24 58N 88 10 E
English Channel, Europe 21 G6 50 0N 2 0W
English River, Canada 140 C1 49 14N 91 0W
Engures ezers, Latvia 54 A10 57 16N 23 6 E
Enguri →, Georgia 61 J5 42 27N 41 38 E
Enid, U.S.A. 155 G6 36 24N 97 53W
Enipévs →, Greece 48 B4 39 22N 22 17 E
Enkhuizen, Neths. 24 B5 52 42N 5 17 E
Enköping, Sweden 16 E11 59 37N 17 4 E
Enle, China 76 F3 24 0N 101 9 E
Enna, Italy 47 E7 37 34N 14 16 E
Ennadai, Canada 143 A8 61 8N 100 53W
Ennadai L., Canada 143 A8 61 0N 101 0W
Ennedi, Chad 109 E4 17 15N 22 0 E
Enngonia, Australia 127 D4 29 21 S 145 50 E
Ennigerloh, Germany 30 D4 51 50N 8 2 E
Ennis, Ireland 23 D3 52 51N 8 59W
Ennis, Mont., U.S.A. 158 D8 45 21N 111 44W
Ennis, Tex., U.S.A. 155 J6 32 20N 96 38W
Enniscorthy, Ireland 23 D5 52 30N 6 34W
Enniskillen, U.K. 23 B4 54 21N 7 39W
Ennistimon, Ireland 23 D2 52 57N 9 17W
Enns, Austria 34 C7 48 12N 14 28 E
Enns →, Austria 34 C7 48 14N 14 32 E
Enontekiö, Finland 14 B20 68 23N 23 37 E
Enping, China 77 F9 22 16N 112 21 E
Enrekang, Indonesia 82 B1 3 34 S 119 47 E
Enrile, Phil. 80 C3 17 34N 121 42 E
Enriquillo, L., Dom. Rep. 165 C5 18 20N 72 5W
Enschede, Neths. 24 B6 52 13N 6 53 E
Ensenada, Argentina 174 C4 34 55 S 57 55W
Ensenada, Mexico 162 A1 31 50N 116 50W
Enshi, China 76 B7 30 18N 109 29 E
Enshū-Nada, Japan 71 C9 34 27N 137 38 E
Ensiola, Pta., Spain 39 B9 39 7N 2 55 E
Ensisheim, France 27 E14 47 50N 7 20 E
Ensley, U.S.A. 153 E2 30 31N 87 16W
Entebbe, Uganda 118 B3 0 4N 32 28 E
Enterprise, Canada 142 A5 60 47N 115 45W
Enterprise, Ala., U.S.A. 152 D4 31 19N 85 51W
Enterprise, Oreg., U.S.A. 158 D5 45 25N 117 17W
Enterprise, Utah, U.S.A. 159 H7 37 34N 113 43W
Entlebuch, Switz. 32 C6 46 59N 8 4 E
Entraygues-sur-Truyère, France 28 D6 44 38N 2 35 E
Entre Ríos, Bolivia 174 A3 21 30 S 64 25W
Entre Rios, Bahia, Brazil 171 D4 11 56 S 38 5W
Entre Rios, Pará, Brazil 173 B7 5 24 S 54 21W
Entre Ríos □, Argentina 174 C4 30 30 S 58 30W
Entrepeñas, Embalse de, Spain 40 E2 40 34N 2 42W
Entroncamento, Portugal 43 F2 39 28N 8 28W
Enugu, Nigeria 113 D6 6 20N 7 30 E
Enugu □, Nigeria 113 D6 6 30N 7 45 E
Enugu Ezike, Nigeria 113 D6 7 0N 7 29 E
Enumclaw, U.S.A. 160 C5 47 12N 121 59W
Envermeu, France 26 C8 49 53N 1 15 E
Envigado, Colombia 168 B2 6 10N 75 35W
Enviken, Sweden 16 D9 60 49N 15 46 E
Envira, Brazil 172 B3 7 18 S 70 13W
Enying, Hungary 52 D3 46 56N 18 15 E
Enza →, Italy 44 D7 44 54N 10 31 E
Enzan, Japan 71 B10 35 42N 138 44 E
Eólie, Ís., Italy 47 D7 38 30N 14 57 E
Epanomí, Greece 50 F6 40 25N 22 59 E
Epe, Neths. 24 B5 52 21N 5 59 E
Epe, Nigeria 113 D5 6 36N 3 59 E
Epéna, Congo 114 B3 1 22N 17 29 E
Épernay, France 27 C10 49 3N 3 56 E
Épernon, France 27 D8 48 35N 1 40 E
Ephesus, Turkey 49 D9 37 55N 27 22 E
Ephraim, U.S.A. 158 G8 39 22N 111 35W
Ephrata, U.S.A. 158 C4 47 19N 119 33W
Epi, Vanuatu 133 F6 16 43 S 168 15 E
Epidaurus Limera, Greece 48 E5 36 46N 23 0 E
Épila, Spain 40 D3 41 36N 1 17W
Épinac, France 27 F11 46 59N 4 31 E
Épinal, France 27 D13 48 10N 6 27 E
Epira, Guyana 169 B6 5 5N 57 20W
Episkopi, Cyprus 38 E11 34 40N 32 54 E
Episkopí, Greece 38 D6 35 20N 24 20 E
Episkopi Bay, Cyprus 38 E11 34 35N 32 50 E
Epitálion, Greece 48 D3 37 37N 21 30 E
Eppan = Appiano, Italy 45 B8 46 28N 11 15 E
Eppingen, Germany 31 F4 49 8N 8 53 E

212 Epsom

Epsom, *U.K.* **21 F7** 51 19N 0 16W
Epukiro, *Namibia* **116 C2** 21 40 S 19 9 E
Equality, *U.S.A.* **157 G8** 37 44N 88 20W
Equatorial Guinea ■, *Africa* **114 B1** 2 0N 8 0 E
Equeipa, *Venezuela* **169 B5** 5 22N 62 43W
Er Rahad, *Sudan* **107 E3** 12 45N 30 32 E
Er Rif, *Morocco* **111 A4** 35 1N 4 1W
Er Roseires, *Sudan* **107 E3** 11 55N 34 30 E
Er Yébigué, *Chad* **109 D3** 22 30N 17 30 E
Eraclea, *Italy* **45 C9** 45 35N 12 40 E
Eran, *Phil.* **81 G1** 9 4N 117 42 E
Erandol, *India* **94 D2** 20 56N 75 20 E
Erap, *Papua N. G.* **132 D4** 6 37 S 146 51 E
Erāwadī Myit = Irrawaddy →, *Burma* **90 G5** 15 50N 95 6 E
Erba, *Italy* **44 C6** 45 48N 9 15 E
Erba, *Sudan* **106 D4** 19 5N 36 51 E
Erbaa, *Turkey* **100 B7** 40 42N 36 36 E
Erbeskopf, *Germany* **31 F3** 49 44N 7 2 E
Erbil = Arbīl, *Iraq* **101 D11** 36 15N 44 5 E
Erçis, *Turkey* **101 C10** 39 2N 43 21 E
Erciyaş Dağı, *Turkey* **57 G6** 38 30N 35 30 E
Érd, *Hungary* **52 C3** 47 22N 18 56 E
Erdao Jiang →, *China* **75 C14** 43 0N 127 0 E
Erdek, *Turkey* **51 F11** 40 23N 27 47 E
Erdemli, *Turkey* **100 D6** 36 36N 34 19 E
Erdene, *Mongolia* **74 B6** 44 13N 111 10 E
Erding, *Germany* **31 G7** 48 18N 11 54 E
Erdre →, *France* **26 E5** 47 13N 1 32W
Erebato →, *Venezuela* **169 B5** 5 54N 64 16W
Erebus, Mt., *Antarctica* **7 D11** 77 35 S 167 0 E
Erechim, *Brazil* **175 B5** 27 35 S 52 15W
Ereğli, *Konya, Turkey* **100 D6** 37 31N 34 4 E
Ereğli, *Zonguldak, Turkey* **100 B4** 41 15N 31 24 E
Erei, Monti, *Italy* **47 E7** 37 20N 14 20 E
Erenhot, *China* **74 C7** 43 48N 112 2 E
Eresfjord, *Norway* **18 B5** 62 40N 8 8 E
Eresma →, *Spain* **42 D6** 41 26N 4 45W
Eressós, *Greece* **49 B7** 39 11N 25 57 E
Erfenisdam, *S. Africa* **116 D4** 28 30 S 26 50 E
Erfjord, *Norway* **18 E3** 59 20N 6 14 E
Erfoud, *Morocco* **110 B4** 31 30N 4 15W
Erfstadt, *Germany* **30 E2** 50 50N 6 50 E
Erft →, *Germany* **30 D2** 51 11N 6 44 E
Erfurt, *Germany* **30 E7** 50 58N 11 2 E
Ergani, *Turkey* **101 C8** 38 17N 39 49 E
Ergene →, *Turkey* **51 E10** 41 1N 26 22 E
Ergeni Vozvyshennost, *Russia* **61 G7** 47 0N 44 0 E
Ērgli, *Latvia* **15 H21** 56 54N 25 38 E
Erhlin, *Taiwan* **77 F13** 23 54N 120 22 E
Eria →, *Spain* **42 C5** 42 3N 5 44W
Eriba, *Sudan* **107 D4** 16 40N 36 10 E
Eriboll, L., *U.K.* **22 C4** 58 30N 4 42W
Érice, *Italy* **46 D5** 38 2N 12 35 E
Eridu, *U.S.A.* **152 E6** 30 18N 83 45W
Erie, *Mich., U.S.A.* **157 C13** 41 47N 83 31W
Erie, *Pa., U.S.A.* **150 D4** 42 8N 80 5W
Erie, L., *N. Amer.* **150 D4** 42 15N 81 0W
Erie Canal, *U.S.A.* **150 C7** 43 5N 78 43W
Erieau, *Canada* **150 D3** 42 16N 81 57W
Erigavo, *Somali Rep.* **120 B3** 10 35N 47 20 E
Erikoúsa, *Greece* **38 A3** 39 53N 19 34 E
Eriksdale, *Canada* **143 C9** 50 52N 98 7W
Erímanthos, *Greece* **48 D3** 37 57N 21 50 E
Erimo-misaki, *Japan* **68 D11** 41 50N 143 15 E
Eriskay, *U.K.* **22 D1** 57 4N 7 18W
Eriswil, *Switz.* **32 B5** 47 5N 7 46 E
Erithraí, *Greece* **48 C5** 38 13N 23 20 E
Eritrea ■, *Africa* **107 E4** 14 0N 38 30 E
Erjas →, *Portugal* **42 F3** 39 40N 7 1W
Erkelenz, *Germany* **30 D2** 51 4N 6 19 E
Erkner, *Germany* **30 C9** 52 25N 13 44 E
Erlangen, *Germany* **31 F6** 49 36N 11 0 E
Erldunda, *Australia* **126 D1** 25 14 S 133 12 E
Ermelo, *Neths.* **24 B5** 52 18N 5 35 E
Ermelo, *S. Africa* **117 D4** 26 31 S 29 59 E
Ermenek, *Turkey* **100 D5** 36 38N 33 0 E
Ermióni, *Greece* **48 D5** 37 23N 23 15 E
Ermones, *Greece* **38 A3** 39 37N 19 46 E
Ernakulam = Cochin, *India* **95 K3** 9 59N 76 22 E
Erne →, *Ireland* **23 B3** 54 30N 8 16W
Erne, Lower L., *U.K.* **23 B4** 54 28N 7 47W
Erne, Upper L., *U.K.* **23 B4** 54 14N 7 32W
Ernée, *France* **26 D6** 48 18N 0 56W
Ernest Giles Ra., *Australia* **125 E3** 27 0 S 123 45 E
Ernstberg, *Germany* **31 E2** 50 13N 6 47 E
Erode, *India* **95 J3** 11 24N 77 45 E
Eromanga, *Australia* **127 D3** 26 40 S 143 11 E
Erongo, *Namibia* **116 C2** 21 39 S 15 58 E
Erquy, *France* **26 D4** 48 38N 2 29W
Err, Piz d', *Switz.* **33 C9** 46 34N 9 43 E
Errabiddy, *Australia* **125 E2** 25 25 S 117 5 E
Erramala Hills, *India* **95 G4** 15 30N 78 15 E
Errer →, *Ethiopia* **107 F5** 7 32N 42 35 E
Errigal, *Ireland* **23 A3** 55 2N 8 6W
Erris Hd., *Ireland* **23 B1** 54 19N 10 0W
Erromango, *Vanuatu* **133 H7** 18 45 S 169 5 E
Erseka, *Albania* **50 F4** 40 22N 20 40 E
Erskine, *U.S.A.* **154 B7** 47 40N 96 0W
Erstein, *France* **27 D14** 48 25N 7 38 E
Erstfeld, *Switz.* **33 C7** 46 50N 8 38 E
Ertholmene, *Denmark* **17 J9** 55 19N 15 11 E
Ertil, *Russia* **60 E5** 51 55N 40 50 E
Ertis → = Irtysh →, *Russia* **64 C7** 61 4N 68 52 E
Ertvågøy, *Norway* **18 A5** 63 13N 8 26 E
Eruh, *Turkey* **101 D10** 37 46N 42 13 E
Eruwa, *Nigeria* **113 D5** 7 33N 3 26 E
Ervy-le-Châtel, *France* **27 D10** 48 2N 3 55 E
Erwin, *U.S.A.* **149 G4** 36 9N 82 25W
Eryuan, *China* **76 D2** 26 7N 99 57 E
Erzgebirge, *Germany* **30 E8** 50 27N 12 55 E
Erzin, *Russia* **65 D10** 50 15N 95 10 E
Erzincan, *Turkey* **101 C8** 39 46N 39 30 E
Erzurum, *Turkey* **101 C9** 39 57N 41 15 E
Es Caló, *Spain* **39 C8** 38 40N 1 30 E
Es Caná, *Spain* **39 B8** 39 2N 1 36 E
Es Mercadal, *Spain* **39 B11** 39 59N 4 5 E
Es Sahrâ' Esh Sharqîya, *Egypt* **106 B3** 27 30N 32 30 E
Es Sînâ', *Egypt* **106 J8** 29 0N 34 0 E
Es Sûkî, *Sudan* **107 E3** 13 20N 33 58 E
Es Vedrà, *Spain* **39 C7** 38 52N 1 12 E
Esa'ala, *Papua N. G.* **132 E6** 9 45 S 150 49 E
Esambo, *Dem. Rep. of the Congo* **114 C4** 3 48 S 23 30 E
Esan-Misaki, *Japan* **68 D10** 41 40N 141 10 E
Esashi, *Hokkaidō, Japan* **68 B11** 44 56N 142 35 E
Esashi, *Hokkaidō, Japan* **68 D10** 41 52N 140 7 E
Esbjerg, *Denmark* **17 J2** 55 29N 8 29 E
Escada, *Brazil* **170 C4** 8 22 S 35 8W
Escalante, *U.S.A.* **159 H8** 37 47N 111 36W
Escalante →, *U.S.A.* **159 H8** 37 24N 110 57W
Escalente, *Phil.* **81 F4** 10 50N 123 33 E
Escalón, *Mexico* **162 B4** 26 46N 104 20W
Escambia →, *U.S.A.* **149 K2** 30 32N 87 11W
Escanaba, *U.S.A.* **148 C2** 45 45N 87 4W
Escarparda Pt., *Phil.* **80 B4** 18 31N 122 13 E
Escarpé, C., *Vanuatu* **133 K5** 20 41 S 167 13 E
Esch-sur-Alzette, *Lux.* **24 E6** 49 32N 6 0 E
Eschede, *Germany* **30 C6** 52 44N 10 14 E
Escholzmatt, *Switz.* **32 C5** 46 55N 7 56 E
Eschwege, *Germany* **30 D6** 51 11N 10 2 E
Eschweiler, *Germany* **30 E2** 50 49N 6 15 E
Escoma, *Bolivia* **172 D4** 15 40 S 69 8W
Escondido, *U.S.A.* **161 M9** 33 7N 117 5W
Escuinapa, *Mexico* **162 C3** 22 50N 105 50W
Escuintla, *Guatemala* **164 D1** 14 20N 90 48W
Eséka, *Cameroon* **113 E7** 3 41N 10 44 E
Eşen →, *Turkey* **49 E11** 36 27N 29 16 E
Esenguly, *Turkmenistan* **64 F6** 37 37N 53 59 E
Esens, *Germany* **30 B3** 53 38N 7 36 E
Esenyurt, *Turkey* **51 E12** 41 3N 28 48 E
Esera →, *Spain* **40 C5** 42 6N 0 15 E
Eşfahān, *Iran* **97 C6** 32 39N 51 43 E
Esfīdeh, *Iran* **97 C8** 33 39N 59 46 E
Esgueva →, *Spain* **42 D6** 41 40N 4 43W
Esh Sham = Dimashq, *Syria* **103 B5** 33 30N 36 18 E
Esh Shamâlîya □, *Sudan* **106 D2** 19 0N 29 0 E
Esha Ness, *U.K.* **22 A7** 60 29N 1 38W
Eshan, *China* **76 E4** 24 11N 102 24 E
Esher, *U.K.* **21 F7** 51 21N 0 20W
Eshkāshem, *Tajikistan* **63 E5** 36 44N 71 37 E
Eshowe, *S. Africa* **117 D5** 28 50 S 31 30 E
Esiama, *Ghana* **112 E4** 4 56N 2 25W
Esil → = Ishim →, *Russia* **64 D8** 57 45N 71 10 E
Esino →, *Italy* **45 E10** 43 39N 13 22 E
Esk →, *Cumb., U.K.* **22 G5** 54 58N 3 2W
Esk →, *N. Yorks., U.K.* **20 C7** 54 30N 0 37W
Eskān, *Iran* **91 D1** 26 48N 63 9 E
Eskifjörður, *Iceland* **11 B13** 65 3N 13 55W
Eskilsäter, *Sweden* **17 F7** 58 57N 13 10 E
Eskilstuna, *Sweden* **16 E10** 59 22N 16 32 E
Eskimalatya, *Turkey* **101 C8** 38 24N 38 22 E
Eskimo Pt., *Canada* **143 A10** 61 10N 94 15W
Eskişehir, *Turkey* **57 G5** 39 50N 30 30 E
Eskişehir □, *Turkey* **49 B12** 39 40N 31 0 E
Esla →, *Spain* **42 D4** 41 29N 6 3W
Eslāmābād-e Gharb, *Iran* **101 E12** 34 10N 46 30 E
Eslöv, *Sweden* **17 J7** 55 50N 13 20 E
Eşme, *Turkey* **49 C10** 38 23N 28 58 E
Esmeralda, I., *Chile* **176 C1** 48 55 S 75 25W
Esmeraldas, *Ecuador* **168 C2** 1 0N 79 40W
Esmeraldas □, *Ecuador* **168 C2** 0 40N 79 30W
Esmeraldas →, *Ecuador* **168 C2** 0 58N 79 38W
Esom Hill, *U.S.A.* **152 B4** 33 57N 85 23W
Espa, *Norway* **18 D8** 60 34N 11 16 E
Espada, Pta., *Colombia* **168 A3** 12 5N 71 7W
Espalion, *France* **28 D6** 44 32N 2 47 E
Espanola, *Canada* **140 C3** 46 15N 81 46W
Espanola, *U.S.A.* **153 F8** 29 31N 81 19W
Esparreguera, *Spain* **40 D6** 41 33N 1 52 E
Esparta, *Costa Rica* **164 E3** 9 59N 84 40W
Espeland, *Norway* **18 D2** 60 23N 5 28 E
Espelkamp, *Germany* **30 C4** 52 24N 8 36 E
Esperança, *Brazil* **170 C4** 7 1 S 35 51W
Esperance, *Australia* **125 F3** 33 45 S 121 55 E
Esperance B., *Australia* **125 F3** 33 48 S 121 55 E
Esperantinópolis, *Brazil* **170 B3** 4 53 S 44 53W
Esperanza, *Santa Cruz, Argentina* **176 D2** 51 1 S 70 49W
Esperanza, *Santa Fe, Argentina* **174 C3** 31 29 S 61 3W
Esperanza, *Masbate, Phil.* **81 F5** 11 45N 124 3 E
Esperanza, *Mindanao, Phil.* **81 G5** 8 43N 125 36 E
Espéraza, *France* **28 F6** 42 56N 2 14 E
Espevær, *Norway* **18 E2** 59 35N 5 7 E
Espichel, C., *Portugal* **43 G1** 38 22N 9 16W
Espiel, *Spain* **43 G5** 38 11N 5 1W
Espigão, Serra do, *Brazil* **175 B5** 26 35 S 50 30W
Espinal, *Colombia* **168 C3** 4 9N 74 53W
Espinar, *Peru* **172 C3** 14 51 S 71 24W
Espinazo, Sierra del = Espinhaço, Serra do, *Brazil* **171 E3** 17 30 S 43 30W
Espinhaço, Serra do, *Brazil* **171 E3** 17 30 S 43 30W
Espinho, *Portugal* **42 D2** 41 1N 8 38W
Espinilho, Serra do, *Brazil* **175 B5** 28 30 S 55 0W
Espino, *Venezuela* **168 B4** 8 34N 66 1W
Espinosa de los Monteros, *Spain* **42 B7** 43 5N 3 34W
Espírito Santo □, *Brazil* **171 F3** 20 0 S 40 45W
Espíritu Santo, *Vanuatu* **133 E4** 15 15 S 166 50 E
Espíritu Santo, B. del, *Mexico* **163 D7** 19 15N 87 0W
Espíritu Santo, I., *Mexico* **162 C2** 24 30N 110 23W
Espita, *Mexico* **163 C7** 21 1N 88 19W
Espiye, *Turkey* **101 B8** 40 56N 38 43 E
Esplanada, *Brazil* **171 D4** 11 47 S 37 57W
Espluga de Francolí, *Spain* **40 D6** 41 24N 1 7 E
Espoo, *Finland* **15 F21** 60 12N 24 40 E
Espuña, Sierra de, *Spain* **41 H3** 37 51N 1 35W
Espungabera, *Mozam.* **117 C5** 20 29 S 32 45 E
Esquel, *Argentina* **176 B2** 42 55 S 71 20W
Esquina, *Argentina* **174 C4** 30 0 S 59 30W
Essandsjøen, *Norway* **18 A8** 63 0N 12 0 E
Essaouira, *Morocco* **110 B3** 31 32N 9 42W
Essebie, *Dem. Rep. of the Congo* **118 B3** 2 58N 30 40 E
Essen, *Belgium* **24 C4** 51 28N 4 28 E
Essen, *Germany* **30 D3** 51 28N 7 2 E
Essendon, Mt., *Australia* **125 E3** 25 0 S 120 29 E
Essequibo →, *Guyana* **169 B6** 6 50N 58 30W
Essex, *Canada* **150 D2** 42 10N 82 49W
Essex, *Calif., U.S.A.* **161 L11** 34 44N 115 15W
Essex, *Ill., U.S.A.* **157 C8** 41 11N 88 11W
Essex, *N.Y., U.S.A.* **151 B11** 44 19N 73 21W
Essex □, *U.K.* **21 F8** 51 54N 0 27 E
Esslingen, *Germany* **31 G5** 48 44N 9 18 E
Essonne □, *France* **27 D9** 48 30N 2 20 E
Estaca de Bares, C. de, *Spain* **42 B3** 43 46N 7 42W
Estadilla, *Spain* **40 C5** 42 4N 0 16 E
Estados, I. de Los, *Argentina* **176 D4** 54 40 S 64 30W
Estagel, *France* **28 F6** 42 47N 2 40 E
Eşţahbānāt, *Iran* **97 D7** 29 8N 54 4 E
Estallenchs, *Spain* **39 B9** 39 39N 2 29 E
Estância, *Brazil* **170 D4** 11 16 S 37 26W
Estancia, *U.S.A.* **159 J10** 34 46N 106 4W
Estārm, *Iran* **97 D8** 28 21N 58 21 E
Estarreja, *Portugal* **42 E2** 40 45N 8 35W
Estats, Pic d', *Spain* **40 C6** 42 40N 1 24 E
Estavayer-le-Lac, *Switz.* **32 C3** 46 51N 6 51 E
Estcourt, *S. Africa* **117 D4** 29 0 S 29 53 E
Este, *Italy* **45 C8** 45 14N 11 39 E
Estelí, *Nic.* **164 D2** 13 9N 86 22W
Estella, *Spain* **40 C2** 42 40N 2 2W
Estelline, *S. Dak., U.S.A.* **154 C6** 44 35N 96 54W
Estelline, *Tex., U.S.A.* **155 H4** 34 33N 100 26W
Estena →, *Spain* **43 F6** 39 23N 4 44W
Estepa, *Spain* **43 H6** 37 17N 4 52W
Estepona, *Spain* **43 J5** 36 24N 5 7W
Esterhazy, *Canada* **143 C8** 50 37N 102 5W
Esternay, *France* **27 D10** 48 44N 3 33 E
Estero, *U.S.A.* **153 J8** 26 26N 81 49W
Esterri d'Aneu, *Spain* **40 C6** 42 38N 1 5 E
Estevan, *Canada* **143 D8** 49 10N 102 59W
Estevan Group, *Canada* **142 C3** 53 3N 129 38W
Estherville, *U.S.A.* **154 D7** 43 24N 94 50W
Estill, *U.S.A.* **152 C8** 32 45N 81 15W
Estissac, *France* **27 D10** 48 16N 3 48 E
Eston, *Canada* **143 C7** 51 8N 108 40W
Estonia ■, *Europe* **15 G21** 58 30N 25 30 E
Estoril, *Portugal* **43 G1** 38 42N 9 23W
Estouk, *Mali* **113 B5** 18 14N 1 2 E
Estrela, Serra da, *Portugal* **42 E3** 40 10N 7 45W
Estrella, *Spain* **43 G7** 38 25N 3 35W
Estremoz, *Portugal* **43 G3** 38 51N 7 39W
Estrondo, Serra do, *Brazil* **170 C2** 7 20 S 48 0W
Esztergom, *Hungary* **52 C3** 47 47N 18 44 E
Et Tîdra, *Mauritania* **112 B1** 19 45N 16 20W
Etadunna, *Australia* **127 D2** 28 43 S 138 38 E
Etah, *India* **93 F8** 27 35N 78 40 E
Étain, *France* **27 C12** 49 13N 5 38 E
Etamamu, *Canada* **141 B8** 50 18N 59 59W
Étampes, *France* **27 D9** 48 26N 2 10 E
Etanga, *Namibia* **116 B1** 17 55 S 13 0 E
Étaples, *France* **27 B8** 50 30N 1 39 E
Etawah, *India* **93 F8** 26 48N 79 6 E
Etawah →, *U.S.A.* **149 H3** 34 20N 84 15W
Etawney L., *Canada* **143 B9** 57 50N 96 50W
Ete, *Nigeria* **113 D6** 7 2N 7 28 E
Ethel, *U.S.A.* **160 D4** 46 32N 122 46W
Ethel, Oued el →, *Algeria* **110 C4** 28 31N 3 37W
Ethel Creek, *Australia* **124 D3** 22 55 S 120 11 E
Ethelbert, *Canada* **143 C8** 51 32N 100 25W
Ethiopia ■, *Africa* **102 F3** 8 0N 40 0 E
Ethiopian Highlands, *Ethiopia* **66 J7** 10 0N 37 0 E
Etili, *Turkey* **51 G10** 39 59N 26 54 E
Etive, L., *U.K.* **22 E3** 56 29N 5 10W
Etna, *Italy* **47 E7** 37 50N 14 55 E
Etna →, *Norway* **18 C6** 60 49N 10 7 E
Etne, *Norway* **18 E2** 59 40N 5 58 E
Etoile, *Dem. Rep. of the Congo* **119 E2** 11 33 S 27 30 E
Etolin I., *U.S.A.* **142 B2** 56 5N 132 20W
Etolin Strait, *U.S.A.* **144 F6** 60 20N 165 15W
Etosha Pan, *Namibia* **116 B2** 18 40 S 16 30 E
Etoumbi, *Congo* **114 C2** 0 1 S 14 57 E
Etowah, *U.S.A.* **149 H3** 35 20N 84 32W
Étréchy, *France* **27 D9** 48 30N 2 12 E
Étrépagny, *France* **27 C8** 49 18N 1 36 E
Étretat, *France* **26 C7** 49 42N 0 12 E
Etropole, *Bulgaria* **51 D8** 42 50N 24 0 E
Ettelbruck, *Lux.* **24 E6** 49 51N 6 5 E
Ettlingen, *Germany* **31 G4** 48 56N 8 25 E
Ettrick Water →, *U.K.* **22 F6** 55 31N 2 55W
Etuku, *Dem. Rep. of the Congo* **114 C5** 3 42 S 25 45 E
Etulia, *Moldova* **53 E13** 45 32N 28 27 E
Etzatlán, *Mexico* **162 C4** 20 48N 104 5W
Eu, *France* **26 B8** 50 3N 1 26 E
Eua, *Tonga* **133 Q13** 21 22 S 174 56W
Euboea = Évvoia, *Greece* **48 C6** 38 30N 24 0 E
Euchareena, *Australia* **129 B8** 32 57 S 149 6 E
Eucla Motel, *Australia* **125 F4** 31 41 S 128 52 E
Euclid, *U.S.A.* **150 E3** 41 34N 81 32W
Euclides da Cunha, *Brazil* **170 D4** 10 31 S 39 1W
Eucumbene, L., *Australia* **129 D8** 36 2 S 148 40 E
Eudora, *U.S.A.* **155 J9** 33 7N 91 16W
Eudunda, *Australia* **128 C3** 34 12 S 139 7 E
Eufaula, *Ala., U.S.A.* **152 D4** 31 54N 85 9W
Eufaula, *Okla., U.S.A.* **155 H7** 35 17N 95 35W
Eufaula L., *U.S.A.* **155 H7** 35 18N 95 21W
Eugene, *U.S.A.* **158 E2** 44 5N 123 4W
Eugowra, *Australia* **129 B8** 33 22 S 148 24 E
Eulo, *Australia* **127 D4** 28 10 S 145 3 E
Eulonia, *U.S.A.* **152 D8** 31 32N 81 26W
Eumungerie, *Australia* **129 A8** 31 56 S 148 36 E
Eunice, *La., U.S.A.* **155 K8** 30 30N 92 25W
Eunice, *N. Mex., U.S.A.* **155 J3** 32 26N 103 10W
Eupen, *Belgium* **24 D6** 50 37N 6 3 E
Euphrates = Furāt, Nahr al →, *Asia* **96 D5** 31 0N 47 25 E
Eure □, *France* **26 C8** 49 10N 1 0 E
Eure →, *France* **26 C8** 49 18N 1 12 E
Eure-et-Loir □, *France* **26 D8** 48 22N 1 30 E
Eureka, *Canada* **6 B3** 80 0N 85 56W
Eureka, *Calif., U.S.A.* **158 F1** 40 47N 124 9W
Eureka, *Ill., U.S.A.* **156 D7** 40 43N 89 16W
Eureka, *Kans., U.S.A.* **155 G6** 37 49N 96 17W
Eureka, *Mo., U.S.A.* **156 F6** 38 30N 90 38W
Eureka, *Mont., U.S.A.* **158 B6** 48 53N 115 3W
Eureka, *Nev., U.S.A.* **158 G5** 39 31N 115 58W
Eureka, *S.C., U.S.A.* **152 B9** 33 42N 81 46W
Eureka, *S. Dak., U.S.A.* **154 C5** 45 46N 99 38W
Eureka, *Utah, U.S.A.* **158 G7** 39 58N 112 7W
Eureka, Mt., *Australia* **125 E3** 26 35 S 121 35 E
Eurelia, *Australia* **128 B3** 32 33 S 138 35 E
Euroa, *Australia* **129 D6** 36 44 S 145 35 E
Europa, Picos de, *Spain* **42 B6** 43 10N 4 49W
Europa, Pta. de, *Gib.* **43 J5** 36 3N 5 21W
Europoort, *Neths.* **24 C4** 51 57N 4 10 E
Euskirchen, *Germany* **30 E2** 50 39N 6 48 E
Eustis, *U.S.A.* **149 L5** 28 51N 81 41W
Eustis, L., *U.S.A.* **153 G8** 28 50N 81 44W
Eutawville, *U.S.A.* **152 B9** 33 24N 80 21W
Eutin, *Germany* **30 A6** 54 8N 10 36 E
Eutsuk L., *Canada* **142 C3** 53 20N 126 45W
Eva, *Brazil* **169 D6** 3 9 S 59 56W
Eva Downs, *Australia* **126 B1** 18 1 S 134 52 E
Evale, *Angola* **115 F3** 16 33 S 15 44 E
Evanger, *Norway* **18 D3** 60 39N 6 7 E
Evans, *U.S.A.* **154 E2** 40 23N 104 41W
Evans Head, *Australia* **127 D5** 29 7 S 153 27 E
Evans L., *Canada* **140 B4** 50 50N 77 0W
Evans Mills, *U.S.A.* **151 B9** 44 6N 75 48W
Evansdale, *U.S.A.* **156 B4** 42 30N 92 17W
Evanston, *Ill., U.S.A.* **157 C9** 42 3N 87 41W
Evanston, *Wyo., U.S.A.* **158 F8** 41 16N 110 58W
Evansville, *Ill., U.S.A.* **156 F7** 38 5N 89 56W
Evansville, *Ind., U.S.A.* **157 G9** 37 58N 87 35W
Evansville, *Wis., U.S.A.* **156 D7** 42 47N 89 18W
Évaux-les-Bains, *France* **27 F9** 46 12N 2 29 E
Evaz, *Iran* **97 E7** 27 46N 53 59 E
Evciler, *Afyon, Turkey* **49 C11** 38 4N 29 54 E
Evciler, *Çanakkale, Turkey* **49 B8** 39 47N 26 44 E
Eveleth, *U.S.A.* **154 B8** 47 28N 92 32W
Evensk, *Russia* **65 C16** 62 12N 159 30 E
Evenstad, *Norway* **18 C8** 61 25N 11 7 E
Everard, L., *Australia* **127 E2** 31 30 S 135 0 E
Everard Park, *Australia* **125 E5** 27 1 S 132 43 E
Everard Ranges, *Australia* **125 E5** 27 5 S 132 28 E
Everdale, *Australia* **129 A6** 31 52 S 144 46 E
Everest, Mt., *Nepal* **93 E12** 28 5N 86 58 E
Everett, *Ga., U.S.A.* **152 D8** 31 24N 81 38W
Everett, *Pa., U.S.A.* **150 F6** 40 1N 78 23W
Everett, *Wash., U.S.A.* **160 C4** 47 59N 122 12W
Everglades, The, *U.S.A.* **149 N5** 25 50N 81 0W
Everglades City, *U.S.A.* **149 N5** 25 52N 81 23W
Everglades National Park, *U.S.A.* **149 N5** 25 30N 81 0W
Evergreen, *U.S.A.* **149 K2** 31 26N 86 57W
Everöd, *Sweden* **17 J8** 55 53N 14 5 E
Everson, *U.S.A.* **158 B2** 48 57N 122 22W
Everton, *Australia* **129 D7** 36 25 S 146 33 E
Evertsberg, *Sweden* **16 C7** 61 8N 13 58 E
Evesham, *U.K.* **21 E6** 52 6N 1 56W
Évian-les-Bains, *France* **27 F13** 46 24N 6 35 E
Evinayong, *Eq. Guin.* **114 B2** 1 26N 10 35 E
Évinos →, *Greece* **48 C3** 38 27N 21 40 E
Évisa, *France* **29 F12** 42 15N 8 48 E
Evje, *Norway* **15 G12** 58 36N 7 51 E
Évora, *Portugal* **43 G3** 38 33N 7 57W
Évora □, *Portugal* **43 G3** 38 33N 7 50W
Evowghlī, *Iran* **101 C11** 38 43N 45 13 E
Évreux, *France* **26 C8** 49 3N 1 8 E
Evritanía □, *Greece* **48 B3** 39 5N 21 30 E
Évron, *France* **26 D6** 48 10N 0 24W
Évros □, *Greece* **51 E10** 41 10N 26 0 E
Évros →, *Bulgaria* **100 B2** 41 40N 26 34 E
Evrótas →, *Greece* **48 E4** 36 50N 22 40 E
Évry, *France* **27 D9** 48 38N 2 27 E
Évvoia, *Greece* **48 C6** 38 30N 24 0 E
Évvoia □, *Greece* **48 C5** 38 40N 23 40 E
Evxinoúpolis, *Greece* **48 B4** 39 12N 22 42 E
Ewa, *U.S.A.* **145 K13** 21 20N 158 3W
Ewa Beach, *U.S.A.* **145 K13** 21 19N 158 1W
Ewe, L., *U.K.* **22 D3** 57 49N 5 38W
Ewing, *Mo., U.S.A.* **156 E5** 40 6N 91 43W
Ewing, *Nebr., U.S.A.* **154 D5** 42 16N 98 21W
Ewo, *Congo* **114 C2** 0 48 S 14 45 E
Exaltación, *Bolivia* **173 C4** 13 10 S 65 20W
Excelsior Springs, *U.S.A.* **156 E2** 39 20N 94 13W
Excideuil, *France* **28 C5** 45 20N 1 4 E
Exe →, *U.K.* **21 G4** 50 41N 3 29W
Exeter, *Canada* **150 C3** 43 21N 81 29W
Exeter, *U.K.* **21 G4** 50 43N 3 31W
Exeter, *Calif., U.S.A.* **160 J7** 36 18N 119 9W
Exeter, *N.H., U.S.A.* **151 D14** 42 59N 70 57W
Exeter, *Nebr., U.S.A.* **154 E6** 40 39N 97 27W
Exira, *U.S.A.* **156 C2** 41 35N 94 52W
Exmoor, *U.K.* **21 F4** 51 12N 3 45W
Exmouth, *Australia* **124 D1** 21 54 S 114 10 E
Exmouth, *U.K.* **21 G4** 50 37N 3 25W
Exmouth G., *Australia* **124 D1** 22 15 S 114 15 E
Expedition Ra., *Australia* **126 C4** 24 30 S 149 12 E
Extremadura □, *Spain* **43 F4** 39 30N 6 5W
Exuma Sound, *Bahamas* **164 B4** 24 30N 76 20W
Eyak, *U.S.A.* **144 F11** 60 32N 145 36W
Eyasi, L., *Tanzania* **118 C4** 3 30 S 35 0 E
Eydehamn, *Norway* **18 F5** 58 30N 8 53 E
Eye Pen., *U.K.* **22 C2** 58 13N 6 10W
Eyeberry L., *Canada* **143 A8** 63 8N 104 43W
Eyemouth, *U.K.* **22 F6** 55 52N 2 5W
Eygurande, *France* **27 G9** 45 40N 2 26 E
Eyjafjallajökull, *Iceland* **11 D7** 63 38N 19 36W
Eyjafjarðarsýsla □, *Iceland* **11 B8** 65 30N 18 30W
Eyjafjörður, *Iceland* **11 A8** 66 15N 18 30W
Eymet, *France* **28 D4** 44 40N 0 25 E
Eymoutiers, *France* **28 C5** 45 40N 1 45 E
Eynesil, *Turkey* **101 B8** 41 4N 39 9 E
Eyrarbakki, *Iceland* **11 D5** 63 52N 21 9W
Eyre, *Australia* **125 F4** 32 15 S 126 18 E
Eyre (North), L., *Australia* **127 D2** 28 30 S 137 20 E
Eyre (South), L., *Australia* **127 D2** 29 18 S 137 25 E
Eyre, L., *Australia* **122 F6** 29 30 S 137 26 E
Eyre Cr. →, *Australia* **127 D2** 26 40 S 139 0 E
Eyre Mts., *N.Z.* **131 F3** 45 25 S 168 25 E
Eyre Pen., *Australia* **127 E2** 33 30 S 136 17 E
Eysturoy, *Færoe Is.* **14 E9** 62 13N 6 54W
Eyvānkī, *Iran* **97 C6** 35 24N 51 56 E
Ez Zeidab, *Sudan* **106 D3** 17 25N 33 55 E
Ezcaray, *Spain* **40 C1** 42 19N 3 0W
Ežerėlis, *Lithuania* **54 D10** 54 53N 23 37 E
Ezine, *Turkey* **49 B8** 39 48N 26 20 E
Ezmul, *Mauritania* **110 D1** 22 15N 15 40W
Ezouza →, *Cyprus* **38 E11** 34 44N 32 27 E

F

F.Y.R.O.M. = Macedonia ■, *Europe* **50 E5** 41 53N 21 40 E
Fabens, *U.S.A.* **159 L10** 31 30N 106 10W
Fåberg, *Norway* **18 C7** 61 10N 10 25 E
Fabero, *Spain* **42 C4** 42 46N 6 37W
Fåborg, *Denmark* **17 J4** 55 6N 10 15 E
Fabriano, *Italy* **45 E9** 43 20N 12 54 E
Făcăeni, *Romania* **53 F12** 44 32N 27 53 E
Facatativá, *Colombia* **168 C3** 4 49N 74 22W
Faceville, *U.S.A.* **152 E5** 30 45N 84 38W
Fachi, *Niger* **109 E2** 18 6N 11 34 E
Fada, *Chad* **109 E4** 17 13N 21 34 E
Fada-n-Gourma, *Burkina Faso* **113 C5** 12 10N 0 30 E
Fadd, *Hungary* **52 D3** 46 28N 18 49 E
Faddeyevskiy, Ostrov, *Russia* **65 B15** 76 0N 144 0 E
Fadghāmī, *Syria* **101 E9** 35 53N 40 52 E
Fadlab, *Sudan* **106 D3** 17 42N 34 2 E
Faenza, *Italy* **45 D8** 44 17N 11 53 E
Færingehavn, *Greenland* **10 E5** 63 45N 51 27W
Færoe Is. = Føroyar, *Atl. Oc.* **8 B8** 62 0N 7 0W
Fafa, *Mali* **113 B5** 15 22N 0 48 E
Fafe, *Portugal* **42 D2** 41 27N 8 11W

Fusui 215

Fort William, U.K. 22 E3 56 49N 5 7W
Fort Worth, U.S.A. 155 J6 32 45N 97 18W
Fort Yates, U.S.A. 154 B4 46 5N 100 38W
Fort Yukon, U.S.A. 138 B5 66 34N 145 16W
Fortaleza, Bolivia 172 C4 12 6 S 66 49W
Fortaleza, Brazil 170 B4 3 45 S 38 35W
Forteau, Canada 141 B8 51 28N 56 58W
Forth →, U.K. 22 E5 56 9N 3 50W
Forth, Firth of, U.K. 22 E6 56 5N 2 55W
Forthassa Rharbia, Algeria 111 B4 32 52N 1 18W
Fortín Garrapatal, Paraguay 173 E5 21 27 S 61 30W
Fortín General Pando, Paraguay 173 D6 19 45 S 59 47W
Fortín Madrejón, Paraguay 173 E6 20 45 S 59 52W
Fortín Uno, Argentina 176 A3 38 50 S 65 18W
Fortore →, Italy 45 G12 41 55N 15 17 E
Fortrose, N.Z. 131 G3 46 38 S 168 45 E
Fortrose, U.K. 22 D4 57 35N 4 9W
Fortsonia, U.S.A. 152 A7 34 1N 82 47W
Fortuna, Spain 41 G3 38 11N 1 7W
Fortuna, Calif., U.S.A. 158 F1 40 36N 124 9W
Fortuna, N. Dak., U.S.A. 154 A3 48 55N 103 47W
Fortune B., Canada 141 C8 47 30N 55 22W
Fos-sur-Mer, France 29 E8 43 26N 4 56 E
Foshan, China 77 F9 23 4N 113 5 E
Fosna, Norway 14 E14 63 50N 10 20 E
Fosnavåg, Norway 15 E11 62 22N 5 38 E
Foss, Iceland 11 D9 63 51N 17 52W
Fossano, Italy 44 D4 44 33N 7 43 E
Fossil, U.S.A. 158 D3 45 0N 120 9W
Fossilbrook, Australia 126 B3 17 47 S 144 29 E
Fossombrone, Italy 45 E9 43 41N 12 48 E
Fosston, U.S.A. 154 B7 47 35N 95 45W
Fossvellir, Iceland 11 B12 65 27N 14 37W
Foster, Canada 151 A12 45 17N 72 30W
Foster, U.S.A. 157 F12 38 48N 84 13W
Foster →, Canada 143 B7 55 47N 105 49W
Fosters Ra., Australia 126 C1 21 35 S 133 48 E
Fostoria, U.S.A. 157 C13 41 10N 83 25W
Fotuha'a, Tonga 133 P13 19 49 S 174 44W
Fouesnant, France 26 E2 47 53N 4 1W
Fougamou, Gabon 114 C2 1 16 S 10 30 E
Fougères, France 26 D5 48 21N 1 14W
Foul Pt., Sri Lanka 95 K5 8 35N 81 18 E
Foula, U.K. 22 A6 60 10N 2 5W
Foulness I., U.K. 21 F8 51 36N 0 55 E
Foulpointe, Madag. 117 B8 17 41 S 49 31 E
Foulwind, C., N.Z. 131 B6 41 45 S 171 28 E
Foum Assaka, Morocco 110 C2 29 8N 10 24W
Foum Zguid, Morocco 110 B3 30 2N 6 59W
Foumban, Cameroon 113 D7 5 45N 10 50 E
Foundiougne, Senegal 112 C1 14 5N 16 32W
Fountain, Colo., U.S.A. 154 F2 38 41N 104 42W
Fountain, Fla., U.S.A. 152 E4 30 29N 85 25W
Fountain, Utah, U.S.A. 158 G8 39 41N 111 37W
Fountain Springs, U.S.A. 161 K8 35 54N 118 51W
Fourchambault, France 27 E10 47 2N 3 3 E
Fourchu, Canada 141 C7 45 43N 60 17W
Fouriesburg, S. Africa 116 D4 28 38 S 28 14 E
Fourmies, France 27 B11 50 1N 4 2 E
Fournás, Greece 48 B3 39 3N 21 52 E
Foúrnoi, Greece 49 D8 37 36N 26 32 E
Fours, France 27 F10 46 50N 3 42 E
Fouta Djalon, Guinea 112 C2 11 20N 12 10W
Foux, Cap-à-, Haiti 165 C5 19 43N 73 27W
Foveaux Str., N.Z. 131 G3 46 42 S 168 10 E
Fowey, U.K. 21 G3 50 20N 4 39W
Fowler, Calif., U.S.A. 160 J7 36 38N 119 41W
Fowler, Colo., U.S.A. 154 F3 38 8N 104 2W
Fowler, Ind., U.S.A. 157 D9 40 37N 87 19W
Fowler, Kans., U.S.A. 155 G4 37 23N 100 12W
Fowler, Mich., U.S.A. 157 B12 43 0N 84 45W
Fowlers B., Australia 125 F5 31 59 S 132 34 E
Fowlerton, U.S.A. 155 L5 28 28N 98 48W
Fowlerville, U.S.A. 157 B12 42 40N 84 4W
Fowlstown, U.S.A. 152 E5 30 48N 84 33W
Fowman, Iran 101 D13 37 13N 49 19 E
Fox →, Canada 143 B10 56 3N 93 18W
Fox Is., U.S.A. 144 K6 53 0N 168 0W
Fox Valley, Canada 143 C7 50 30N 109 25W
Foxe Basin, Canada 139 B12 66 0N 77 0W
Foxe Chan., Canada 139 B12 65 0N 80 0W
Foxe Pen., Canada 139 B12 65 0N 76 0W
Foxen, Sweden 16 E5 59 25N 11 55 E
Foxpark, U.S.A. 158 F10 41 5N 106 9W
Foxton, N.Z. 130 G4 40 29 S 175 18 E
Foyle, Lough, U.K. 23 A4 55 7N 7 4W
Foynes, Ireland 23 D2 52 37N 9 7W
Foz, Spain 42 B3 43 33N 7 20W
Foz do Cunene, Angola 115 F2 17 15 S 11 48 E
Foz do Gregório, Brazil 172 B3 6 47 S 70 44W
Foz do Iguaçu, Brazil 175 B5 25 30 S 54 30W
Foz do Riosinho, Brazil 172 B3 7 11 S 71 50W
Frackville, U.S.A. 151 F8 40 47N 76 14W
Fraga, Spain 40 D5 41 32N 0 21 E
Framingham, U.S.A. 151 D13 42 17N 71 25W
Frampol, Poland 55 H9 50 41N 22 40 E
Franca, Brazil 171 F2 20 33 S 47 30W
Francavilla al Mare, Italy 45 F11 42 25N 14 17 E
Francavilla Fontana, Italy 47 B10 40 32N 17 35 E
France ■, Europe 13 F6 47 0N 3 0 E
Frances, Australia 128 D4 36 41 S 140 55 E
Frances →, Canada 142 A3 60 16N 129 10W
Frances L., Canada 142 A3 61 23N 129 30W
Francés Viejo, C., Dom. Rep. 165 C6 19 40N 69 55W
Francesville, U.S.A. 157 D10 40 59N 86 53W
Franceville, Gabon 114 C2 1 40 S 13 32 E
Franche-Comté, France 27 F12 46 50N 5 55 E
Franches Montagnes, Switz. 32 B4 47 10N 7 0 E
Francisco de Orellana, Ecuador 168 D2 0 28 S 76 58W
Francisco I. Madero, Coahuila, Mexico 162 B4 25 48N 103 18W
Francisco I. Madero, Durango, Mexico 162 C4 24 32N 104 22W
Francisco Sá, Brazil 171 E3 16 28 S 43 30W
Francistown, Botswana 117 C4 21 7 S 27 33 E
Francofonte, Italy 47 E7 37 14N 14 53 E
François, Canada 141 C8 47 35N 56 45W
François L., Canada 142 C3 54 0N 125 30W
Franeker, Neths. 24 A5 53 12N 5 33 E
Frankado, Djibouti 107 E5 12 30N 43 12 E
Frankenberg, Germany 30 D4 51 3N 8 48 E
Frankenwald, Germany 31 E7 50 20N 11 30 E
Frankford, U.S.A. 156 E5 39 29N 91 19W
Frankfort, S. Africa 117 D4 27 17 S 28 30 E
Frankfort, Ind., U.S.A. 157 D10 40 17N 86 31W
Frankfort, Kans., U.S.A. 154 F6 39 42N 96 25W
Frankfort, Ky., U.S.A. 157 F12 38 12N 84 52W
Frankfort, Mich., U.S.A. 148 C2 44 38N 86 14W
Frankfort, Ohio, U.S.A. 157 E13 39 24N 83 11W
Frankfurt, Brandenburg, Germany 30 C10 52 20N 14 32 E
Frankfurt, Hessen, Germany 31 E4 50 7N 8 41 E
Fränkische Alb, Germany 31 F7 49 10N 11 23 E
Fränkische Rezat →, Germany 31 F7 49 11N 11 1 E
Fränkische Saale →, Germany 31 E5 50 3N 9 42 E
Fränkische Schweiz, Germany 31 F7 49 50N 11 16 E
Frankland →, Australia 125 G2 35 0 S 116 48 E
Franklin, Ga., U.S.A. 152 B4 33 17N 85 6W
Franklin, Ill., U.S.A. 156 E6 39 37N 90 3W
Franklin, Ind., U.S.A. 157 E10 39 29N 86 3W
Franklin, Ky., U.S.A. 149 G2 36 43N 86 35W
Franklin, La., U.S.A. 155 L9 29 48N 91 30W
Franklin, Mass., U.S.A. 151 D13 42 5N 71 24W
Franklin, N.H., U.S.A. 151 C13 43 27N 71 39W
Franklin, Nebr., U.S.A. 154 E5 40 6N 98 57W
Franklin, Ohio, U.S.A. 157 E12 39 34N 84 18W
Franklin, Pa., U.S.A. 150 E5 41 24N 79 50W
Franklin, Tenn., U.S.A. 149 H2 35 55N 86 52W
Franklin, Va., U.S.A. 149 G7 36 41N 76 56W
Franklin, W. Va., U.S.A. 148 F6 38 39N 79 20W
Franklin, Pt., U.S.A. 144 A8 70 55N 158 48W
Franklin B., Canada 138 B7 69 45N 126 0W
Franklin D. Roosevelt L., U.S.A. 158 B4 48 18N 118 9W
Franklin I., Antarctica 7 D11 76 10 S 168 30 E
Franklin L., U.S.A. 158 F6 40 25N 115 22W
Franklin Mts., Canada 138 B7 65 0N 125 0W
Franklin Mts., N.Z. 131 E2 44 55 S 167 45 E
Franklin Str., Canada 138 A10 72 0N 96 0W
Franklinton, U.S.A. 155 K9 30 51N 90 9W
Franklinville, U.S.A. 150 D6 42 20N 78 27W
Franklyn Mt., N.Z. 131 C7 42 4 S 172 42 E
Franks Pk., U.S.A. 158 E9 43 58N 109 18W
Frankston, Australia 129 E6 38 8 S 145 8 E
Frankton Junc., N.Z. 130 D4 37 47 S 175 16 E
Frånö, Sweden 16 B11 62 55N 17 50 E
Fränsta, Sweden 16 B10 62 30N 16 11 E
Frantsa Iosifa, Zemlya, Russia 64 A6 82 0N 55 0 E
Franz, Canada 140 C3 48 25N 84 30W
Franz Josef Land = Frantsa Iosifa, Zemlya, Russia 64 A6 82 0N 55 0 E
Franzburg, Germany 30 A8 54 11N 12 51 E
Frascati, Italy 45 G9 41 48N 12 41 E
Fraser →, B.C., Canada 142 D4 49 7N 123 11W
Fraser →, Nfld., Canada 141 A7 56 39N 62 10W
Fraser, Mt., Australia 125 E2 25 35 S 118 20 E
Fraser I., Australia 127 D5 25 15 S 153 10 E
Fraser Lake, Canada 142 C4 54 0N 124 50W
Fraserburg, S. Africa 116 E3 31 55 S 21 30 E
Fraserburgh, U.K. 22 D6 57 42N 2 1W
Fraserdale, Canada 140 C3 49 55N 81 37W
Frasertown, N.Z. 130 E6 38 58 S 177 28 E
Frashëri, Albania 50 F4 40 23N 20 30 E
Frasne, France 27 F13 46 50N 6 10 E
Frăteşti, Romania 53 G10 43 58N 25 58 E
Frauenfeld, Switz. 33 A7 47 34N 8 54 E
Fray Bentos, Uruguay 174 C4 33 10 S 58 15W
Frazier Downs, Australia 124 C3 18 48 S 121 42 E
Frechilla, Spain 42 C6 42 8N 4 50W
Fredericia, Denmark 17 J3 55 34N 9 45 E
Frederick, Md., U.S.A. 148 F7 39 25N 77 25W
Frederick, Okla., U.S.A. 155 H5 34 23N 99 1W
Frederick, S. Dak., U.S.A. 154 C5 45 50N 98 31W
Frederick E. Hyde Fjord, Greenland 10 A8 83 25N 29 0W
Frederick Sd., U.S.A. 142 B2 57 10N 134 0W
Fredericksburg, Tex., U.S.A. 155 K5 30 16N 98 52W
Fredericksburg, Va., U.S.A. 148 F7 38 18N 77 28W
Fredericktown, U.S.A. 155 G9 37 34N 90 18W
Frederico I. Madero, Presa, Mexico 162 B3 28 7N 105 40W
Fredericton, Canada 141 C6 45 57N 66 40W
Fredericton Junc., Canada 141 C6 45 41N 66 40W
Frederiksborg Amtskommune □, Denmark 17 J6 55 50N 12 10 E
Frederikshåb, Greenland 10 E6 62 0N 49 43W
Frederikshavn, Denmark 17 G4 57 28N 10 31 E
Frederikssund, Denmark 17 J6 55 50N 12 3 E
Frederiksted, Virgin Is. 165 C7 17 43N 64 53W
Frederiksværk, Denmark 17 J6 55 58N 12 4 E
Fredonia, Ariz., U.S.A. 159 H7 36 57N 112 32W
Fredonia, Kans., U.S.A. 155 G7 37 32N 95 49W
Fredonia, N.Y., U.S.A. 150 D5 42 26N 79 20W
Fredriksberg, Sweden 16 D8 60 8N 14 23 E
Fredrikstad, Norway 15 G14 59 13N 10 57 E
Free State □, S. Africa 116 D4 28 30 S 27 0 E
Freeburg, U.S.A. 156 F5 38 19N 91 56W
Freehold, U.S.A. 151 F10 40 16N 74 17W
Freel Peak, U.S.A. 160 G7 38 52N 119 54W
Freeland, U.S.A. 151 E9 41 1N 75 54W
Freels, C., Canada 141 C9 49 15N 53 30W
Freeman, Calif., U.S.A. 161 K9 35 35N 117 53W
Freeman, Mo., U.S.A. 156 F2 38 37N 94 30W
Freeman, S. Dak., U.S.A. 154 D6 43 21N 97 26W
Freeport, Bahamas 164 A4 26 30N 78 47W
Freeport, Canada 141 D6 44 15N 66 20W
Freeport, Fla., U.S.A. 152 E3 30 30N 86 8W
Freeport, Ill., U.S.A. 156 B7 42 17N 89 36W
Freeport, N.Y., U.S.A. 151 F11 40 39N 73 35W
Freeport, Tex., U.S.A. 155 L7 28 57N 95 21W
Freetown, S. Leone 112 D2 8 30N 13 17W
Frégate, L., Canada 140 B5 53 15N 74 45W
Fregenal de la Sierra, Spain 43 G4 38 10N 6 39W
Fregene, Italy 45 G9 41 51N 12 12 E
Fréhel, C., France 26 D4 48 40N 2 20W
Freiberg, Germany 30 E9 50 55N 13 20 E
Freibourg = Fribourg, Switz. 32 C4 46 49N 7 9 E
Freiburg, Baden-W., Germany 31 H3 47 59N 7 51 E
Freiburg, Niedersachsen, Germany 30 B5 53 49N 9 16 E
Freiburger Alpen, Switz. 32 C4 46 37N 7 10 E
Freilassing, Germany 31 H8 47 50N 12 58 E
Freire, Chile 176 A2 38 54 S 72 38W
Freirina, Chile 174 B1 28 30 S 71 10W
Freising, Germany 31 G7 48 24N 11 45 E
Freistadt, Austria 34 C7 48 30N 14 30 E
Freital, Germany 30 D9 51 1N 13 39 E
Fréjus, France 29 E10 43 25N 6 44 E
Fremantle, Australia 125 F2 32 7 S 115 47 E
Fremont, Calif., U.S.A. 160 H4 37 32N 121 57W
Fremont, Ind., U.S.A. 157 C12 41 44N 84 56W
Fremont, Mich., U.S.A. 148 D3 43 28N 85 57W
Fremont, Nebr., U.S.A. 154 E6 41 26N 96 30W
Fremont, Ohio, U.S.A. 157 C13 41 21N 83 7W
Fremont →, U.S.A. 159 G8 38 24N 110 42W
Fremont L., U.S.A. 158 E9 42 57N 109 48W
French Camp, U.S.A. 160 H5 37 53N 121 16W
French Creek →, U.S.A. 150 E5 41 24N 79 50W
French Frigate Shoals, U.S.A. 145 G10 23 45N 166 10W
French Guiana ■, S. Amer. 169 C7 4 0N 53 0W
French I., Australia 129 E6 38 20 S 145 22 E
French Lick, U.S.A. 157 F10 38 33N 86 37W
French Pass, N.Z. 131 A8 40 55 S 173 55 E
French Polynesia ■, Pac. Oc. 135 K13 20 0 S 145 0W
Frenchburg, U.S.A. 157 G13 37 57N 83 38W
Frenchglen, U.S.A. 158 E4 42 50N 118 55W
Frenchman Butte, Canada 143 C7 53 35N 109 38W
Frenchman Cr. →, Mont., U.S.A. 158 B10 48 31N 107 10W
Frenchman Cr. →, Nebr., U.S.A. 154 E4 40 14N 100 50W
Frenda, Algeria 111 A5 35 2N 1 1 E
Frenštát pod Radhoštěm, Czech Rep. 35 B11 49 33N 18 13 E
Fresco →, Brazil 173 B7 7 15 S 51 30W
Freshfield, C., Antarctica 7 C10 68 25 S 151 10 E
Fresnay-sur-Sarthe, France 26 D7 48 17N 0 1 E
Fresnillo, Mexico 162 C4 23 10N 103 0W
Fresno, U.S.A. 160 J7 36 44N 119 47W
Fresno Alhandiga, Spain 42 E5 40 42N 5 37W
Fresno Reservoir, U.S.A. 158 B9 48 36N 109 57W
Fresvik, Norway 18 C3 61 4N 6 55 E
Freudenstadt, Germany 31 G4 48 27N 8 24 E
Frévent, France 27 B9 50 15N 2 17 E
Frew →, Australia 126 C2 20 0 S 135 38 E
Frewena, Australia 126 B2 19 25 S 135 25 E
Freycinet Pen., Australia 126 G4 42 10 S 148 25 E
Freyming-Merlebach, France 27 C13 49 8N 6 48 E
Freyung, Germany 31 G9 48 48N 13 31 E
Fria, Guinea 112 C2 10 27N 13 38W
Fria, C., Namibia 116 B1 18 0 S 12 0 E
Friant, U.S.A. 160 J7 36 59N 119 43W
Frías, Argentina 174 B2 28 40 S 65 5W
Fribourg, Switz. 32 C4 46 49N 7 9 E
Fribourg □, Switz. 32 C4 46 40N 7 0 E
Frick, Switz. 32 A6 47 31N 8 1 E
Fridafors, Sweden 17 H8 56 25N 14 39 E
Friday Harbor, U.S.A. 160 B3 48 32N 123 1W
Friedberg, Bayern, Germany 31 G6 48 21N 10 59 E
Friedberg, Hessen, Germany 31 E4 50 19N 8 45 E
Friedland, Germany 30 B9 53 40N 13 33 E
Friedrichshafen, Germany 31 H5 47 39N 9 30 E
Friedrichskoog, Germany 30 A4 54 1N 8 53 E
Friedrichstadt, Germany 30 A5 54 23N 9 6 E
Friendly Is. = Tonga ■, Pac. Oc. 133 P13 19 50 S 174 30W
Friesach, Austria 34 E7 46 57N 14 24 E
Friesack, Germany 30 C8 52 44N 12 34 E
Friesland □, Neths. 24 A5 53 5N 5 50 E
Friesoythe, Germany 30 B3 53 1N 7 51 E
Friggesund, Sweden 16 C10 61 54N 16 33 E
Frillesås, Sweden 17 G6 57 20N 12 12 E
Frinnaryd, Sweden 17 G8 57 55N 14 50 E
Frio →, U.S.A. 155 L5 28 26N 98 11W
Frio, C., Brazil 166 F6 22 50 S 41 50W
Friol, Spain 42 B3 43 2N 7 47W
Friona, U.S.A. 155 H3 34 38N 102 43W
Fristad, Sweden 17 G6 57 50N 13 0 E
Fritch, U.S.A. 155 H4 35 38N 101 36W
Fritsla, Sweden 17 G6 57 33N 12 47 E
Fritzlar, Germany 30 D5 51 7N 9 16 E
Friuli-Venézia Giulia □, Italy 45 B9 46 0N 13 0 E
Frobisher B., Canada 139 B13 62 30N 66 0W
Frobisher Bay = Iqaluit, Canada 139 B13 63 44N 68 31W
Frobisher L., Canada 143 B7 56 20N 108 15W
Frogmore, Australia 129 C8 34 15 S 148 52 E
Frohavet, Norway 14 E13 64 0N 9 30 E
Frohnleiten, Austria 34 D8 47 16N 15 19 E
Froid, U.S.A. 154 A2 48 20N 104 30W
Frolovo, Russia 60 F6 49 45N 43 40 E
Fromberg, U.S.A. 158 D9 45 24N 108 54W
Frombork, Poland 54 D6 54 21N 19 41 E
Frome, U.K. 21 F5 51 14N 2 19W
Frome →, U.K. 21 G5 50 41N 2 6W
Frome, L., Australia 128 A3 30 45 S 139 45 E
Frome Downs, Australia 128 A3 31 13 S 139 45 E
Frómista, Spain 42 C6 42 16N 4 25W
Front Range, U.S.A. 158 G11 40 25N 105 45W
Front Royal, U.S.A. 148 F6 38 55N 78 12W
Fronteira, Portugal 43 F3 39 3N 7 39W
Fronteiras, Brazil 170 C3 7 5 S 40 37W
Frontera, Canary Is. 39 G2 27 47N 17 59W
Frontera, Mexico 163 D6 18 30N 92 40W
Frontignan, France 28 E7 43 27N 3 45 E
Frosinone, Italy 46 A6 41 38N 13 19 E
Frostburg, U.S.A. 148 F6 39 39N 78 56W
Frostisen, Norway 14 B17 68 14N 17 10 E
Frostproof, U.S.A. 153 H8 27 45N 81 32W
Frouard, France 27 D13 48 47N 6 8 E
Frövi, Sweden 16 E9 59 28N 15 24 E
Frøya, Norway 14 E13 63 43N 8 40 E
Fruithurst, U.S.A. 152 B4 33 44N 85 26W
Fruitland Park, U.S.A. 153 G8 28 51N 81 54W
Frumoasa, Romania 53 D10 46 28N 25 48 E
Frunze = Bishkek, Kyrgyzstan 63 B7 42 54N 74 46 E
Fruška Gora, Serbia, Yug. 52 E4 45 7N 19 30 E
Frutal, Brazil 171 F2 20 0 S 49 0W
Frutigen, Switz. 32 C5 46 35N 7 38 E
Frýdek-Místek, Czech Rep. 35 B11 49 40N 18 20 E
Frýdlant, Czech Rep. 34 A8 50 56N 15 9 E
Fryvaldov = Jeseník, Czech Rep. 35 A10 50 14N 17 8 E
Fthiótis □, Greece 48 C4 38 50N 22 25 E
Fu Jiang →, China 76 C6 30 0N 106 16 E
Fu Xian, Liaoning, China 75 E11 39 38N 121 58 E
Fu Xian, Shaanxi, China 74 G5 36 0N 109 20 E
Fu'an, China 77 D12 27 11N 119 36 E
Fubian, China 76 B4 31 17N 102 22 E
Fucécchio, Italy 44 E7 43 44N 10 48 E
Fucheng, China 74 F9 37 50N 116 10 E
Fuchou = Fuzhou, China 77 D12 26 5N 119 16 E
Fuchū, Hiroshima, Japan 70 C5 34 34N 133 14 E
Fuchū, Tōkyō, Japan 71 B11 35 40N 139 29 E
Fuchuan, China 77 E8 24 50N 111 5 E
Fuchun Jiang →, China 77 B13 30 5N 120 5 E
Fúcino, Piana del, Italy 45 F10 42 1N 13 31 E
Fuding, China 77 D13 27 20N 120 12 E
Fuencaliente, Canary Is. 39 F2 28 28N 17 50W
Fuencaliente, Spain 43 G6 38 25N 4 18W
Fuencaliente, Pta., Canary Is. 39 F2 28 27N 17 51W
Fuengirola, Spain 43 J6 36 32N 4 41W
Fuenlabrada, Spain 42 E7 40 17N 3 48W
Fuensalida, Spain 42 E6 40 3N 4 12W
Fuente-Álamo, Spain 41 G3 38 44N 1 24W
Fuente-Álamo de Murcia, Spain 41 H3 37 42N 1 6W
Fuente de Cantos, Spain 43 G4 38 15N 6 18W
Fuente del Maestre, Spain 43 G4 38 31N 6 28W
Fuente el Fresno, Spain 43 F7 39 14N 3 46W
Fuente Obejuna, Spain 43 G5 38 15N 5 25W
Fuente Ovejuna = Fuente Obejuna, Spain 43 G5 38 15N 5 25W
Fuente Palmera, Spain 43 H5 37 42N 5 6W
Fuentes de Andalucía, Spain 43 H5 37 28N 5 20W
Fuentes de Ebro, Spain 40 D4 41 31N 0 38W
Fuentes de León, Spain 43 G4 38 5N 6 32W
Fuentes de Oñoro, Spain 42 E4 40 33N 6 52W
Fuentesaúco, Spain 42 D5 41 15N 5 30W
Fuerte →, Mexico 162 B3 25 50N 109 25W
Fuerte Olimpo, Paraguay 174 A4 21 0 S 57 51W
Fuerteventura, Canary Is. 39 F6 28 30N 14 0W
Fufeng, China 74 G5 34 22N 108 0 E
Fuga I., Phil. 80 B3 18 52N 121 20 E
Fughmah, Yemen 99 C5 16 9N 49 26 E
Fugong, China 76 D2 27 5N 98 47 E
Fugou, China 74 G8 34 3N 114 25 E
Fugu, China 74 E6 39 2N 111 3 E
Fuhai, China 72 B3 47 2N 87 25 E
Fuḩaymī, Iraq 101 E10 34 16N 42 10 E
Fuji, Japan 71 B10 35 9N 138 39 E
Fuji-San, Japan 71 B10 35 22N 138 44 E
Fuji-yoshida, Japan 71 B10 35 30N 138 46 E
Fujian □, China 77 E12 26 0N 118 0 E
Fujieda, Japan 71 C10 34 52N 138 16 E
Fujinomiya, Japan 71 B10 35 10N 138 40 E
Fujioka, Japan 71 A11 36 15N 139 5 E
Fujisawa, Japan 71 B11 35 22N 139 29 E
Fukaya, Japan 71 A11 36 12N 139 12 E
Fukien = Fujian □, China 77 E12 26 0N 118 0 E
Fukuchiyama, Japan 71 B7 35 19N 135 9 E
Fukue-Shima, Japan 69 H4 32 40N 128 45 E
Fukui, Japan 71 A8 36 5N 136 10 E
Fukui □, Japan 71 B8 36 0N 136 12 E
Fukuma, Japan 70 D2 33 46N 130 28 E
Fukuoka, Japan 70 D2 33 39N 130 21 E
Fukuoka □, Japan 70 D3 33 30N 131 0 E
Fukuroi, Japan 71 C9 34 45N 137 55 E
Fukushima, Japan 68 F10 37 44N 140 28 E
Fukushima □, Japan 68 F10 37 30N 140 15 E
Fukuyama, Japan 70 C5 34 35N 133 20 E
Fulda, Germany 30 E5 50 32N 9 40 E
Fulda →, Germany 30 D5 51 25N 9 39 E
Fuling, China 76 C6 29 40N 107 20 E
Fullerton, Calif., U.S.A. 161 M9 33 53N 117 56W
Fullerton, Nebr., U.S.A. 154 E6 41 22N 97 58W
Fulongquan, China 75 B13 44 20N 124 42 E
Fülöpszállás, Hungary 52 D4 46 49N 19 15 E
Fulton, Ill., U.S.A. 156 C6 41 52N 90 11W
Fulton, Ind., U.S.A. 157 D10 40 57N 86 16W
Fulton, Mo., U.S.A. 156 F5 38 52N 91 57W
Fulton, N.Y., U.S.A. 151 C8 43 19N 76 25W
Fulton, Tenn., U.S.A. 149 G1 36 31N 88 53W
Fuluälven →, Sweden 16 C7 61 18N 13 4 E
Fulufjället, Sweden 16 C6 61 32N 12 41 E
Fumay, France 27 C11 49 58N 4 40 E
Fumel, France 28 D4 44 30N 0 58 E
Fumin, China 76 E4 25 10N 102 20 E
Funabashi, Japan 71 B12 35 45N 140 0 E
Funafuti, Pac. Oc. 123 B14 8 30 S 179 0 E
Funäsdalen, Sweden 16 B6 62 33N 12 32 E
Funchal, Madeira 39 D3 32 38N 16 54W
Fundación, Colombia 168 A3 10 31N 74 11W
Fundão, Brazil 171 E3 19 55 S 40 24W
Fundão, Portugal 42 E3 40 8N 7 30W
Fundu Moldovei, Romania 53 C10 47 32N 25 24 E
Fundulea, Romania 53 F11 44 28N 26 31 E
Fundy, B. of, Canada 141 D6 45 0N 66 0W
Funing, Hebei, China 75 E10 39 53N 119 12 E
Funing, Jiangsu, China 75 H10 33 45N 119 50 E
Funing, Yunnan, China 76 F5 23 35N 105 45 E
Funiu Shan, China 74 H7 33 30N 112 20 E
Funsi, Ghana 112 C4 10 21N 1 54W
Funston, U.S.A. 152 D6 31 12N 83 52W
Funtua, Nigeria 113 C6 11 30N 7 18 E
Fuping, Hebei, China 74 E8 38 48N 114 12 E
Fuping, Shaanxi, China 74 G5 34 42N 109 10 E
Fuqing, China 77 E12 25 41N 119 21 E
Fuquan, China 76 D6 26 40N 107 27 E
Furano, Japan 68 C11 43 21N 142 23 E
Furāt, Nahr al →, Asia 96 D5 31 0N 47 25 E
Fürg, Iran 97 D7 28 18N 55 13 E
Furkapass, Switz. 33 C7 46 34N 8 35 E
Furman, U.S.A. 152 C8 32 41N 81 11W
Furmanov, Russia 60 B5 57 10N 41 9 E
Furmanovka, Kazakstan 63 A6 44 17N 72 57 E
Furmanovo, Kazakstan 60 F9 49 42N 49 25 E
Furnás, Spain 39 B8 39 3N 1 32 E
Furnas, Reprêsa de, Brazil 171 F2 20 50 S 45 30W
Furneaux Group, Australia 126 G4 40 10 S 147 50 E
Furqlus, Syria 103 A6 34 36N 37 8 E
Fürstenau, Germany 30 C3 52 31N 7 40 E
Fürstenberg, Germany 30 B9 53 10N 13 8 E
Fürstenfeld, Austria 34 D9 47 3N 16 3 E
Fürstenfeldbruck, Germany 31 G7 48 11N 11 15 E
Fürstenwalde, Germany 30 C10 52 22N 14 3 E
Fürth, Germany 31 F6 49 28N 10 59 E
Furth im Wald, Germany 31 F8 49 18N 12 50 E
Furtwangen, Germany 31 G4 48 2N 8 12 E
Furudal, Sweden 16 C9 61 10N 15 11 E
Furufjörður, Iceland 11 A4 66 16N 22 15W
Furukawa, Japan 68 E10 38 34N 140 58 E
Furulund, Sweden 17 J7 55 46N 13 6 E
Fury and Hecla Str., Canada 139 B11 69 56N 84 0W
Fusagasuga, Colombia 168 C3 4 21N 74 22W
Fuscaldo, Italy 47 C9 39 25N 16 2 E
Fushan, Shandong, China 75 F11 37 30N 121 15 E
Fushan, Shanxi, China 74 G6 35 58N 111 51 E
Fushë Arrëzi, Albania 50 D4 42 4N 20 2 E
Fushë-Krujë, Albania 50 E3 41 29N 19 43 E
Fushun, Liaoning, China 75 D12 41 50N 123 56 E
Fushun, Sichuan, China 76 C5 29 13N 104 52 E
Fusio, Switz. 33 D7 46 27N 8 40 E
Fusong, China 75 C14 42 20N 127 15 E
Füssen, Germany 31 H6 47 35N 10 42 E
Fusui, China 76 F6 22 40N 107 56 E

216 Futago-Yama

Futago-Yama, Japan 70 D3 33 35N 131 36 E
Futog, Yugoslavia 52 E4 45 15N 19 42 E
Futrono, Chile 176 B2 40 8 S 72 24W
Futuna, Wall. & F. Is. 134 J9 14 25 S 178 20 E
Fuwa, Egypt 106 H7 31 12N 30 33 E
Fuxin, China 75 C11 42 5N 121 48 E
Fuyang, Anhui, China 74 H8 33 0N 115 48 E
Fuyang, Zhejiang, China 77 B12 30 5N 119 57 E
Fuyang He →, China 74 E9 38 12N 117 0 E
Fuying Dao, China 77 D13 26 34N 120 9 E
Fuyu, China 75 B13 45 12N 124 43 E
Fuyuan, China 76 E5 25 40N 104 16 E
Füzesgyarmat, Hungary 52 C6 47 6N 21 14 E
Fuzhou, China 77 D12 26 5N 119 16 E
Fylde, U.K. 20 D5 53 50N 2 58W
Fyn, Denmark 17 J4 55 20N 10 30 E
Fyne, L., U.K. 22 F3 55 59N 5 23W
Fyns Amtskommune □, Denmark 17 J4 55 15N 10 30 E
Fynshav, Denmark 17 K3 54 59N 9 59 E
Fyresdal, Norway 18 E5 59 11N 8 5 E
Fyresvatn, Norway 18 E5 59 6N 8 10 E

G

Gaanda, Nigeria 113 C7 10 10N 12 27 E
Gabarin, Nigeria 113 C7 11 8N 10 27 E
Gabas →, France 28 E3 43 46N 0 42W
Gabbettville, U.S.A. 152 C4 32 57N 85 8W
Gabela, Angola 115 E2 11 0 S 14 24 E
Gabès, Tunisia 108 B2 33 53N 10 2 E
Gabès, G. de, Tunisia 108 B2 34 0N 10 30 E
Gabgaba, W. →, Egypt 106 C3 22 10N 33 5 E
Gąbin, Poland 55 F6 52 23N 19 41 E
Gabon ■, Africa 114 C2 0 10 S 10 0 E
Gaborone, Botswana 116 C4 24 45 S 25 57 E
Gabriels, U.S.A. 151 B10 44 26N 74 12W
Gābrīk, Iran 97 E8 25 44N 58 28 E
Gabro, Ethiopia 120 C2 6 18N 43 16 E
Gabrovo, Bulgaria 51 D9 42 52N 25 19 E
Gacé, France 26 D7 48 49N 0 20 E
Gāch Sār, Iran 97 B6 36 7N 51 19 E
Gachsārān, Iran 97 D6 30 15N 50 45 E
Gacko, Bos.-H. 50 C2 43 10N 18 33 E
Gadag, India 95 G2 15 30N 75 45 E
Gadamai, Sudan 107 D4 17 11N 36 10 E
Gadap, Pakistan 92 G2 25 5N 67 28 E
Gadarwara, India 93 H8 22 50N 78 50 E
Gadebusch, Germany 30 B7 53 42N 11 7 E
Gadein, Sudan 107 F2 8 10N 28 45 E
Gadhada, India 92 J4 22 0N 71 35 E
Gadmen, Switz. 33 C6 46 45N 8 16 E
Gádor, Sierra de, Spain 43 J8 36 57N 2 45W
Gadsden, Ala., U.S.A. 152 A3 34 1N 86 1W
Gadsden, Ariz., U.S.A. 159 K6 32 33N 114 47W
Gadsden, S.C., U.S.A. 152 B9 33 51N 80 46W
Gadwal, India 95 F3 16 10N 77 50 E
Gadyach = Hadyach, Ukraine 59 G8 50 21N 34 0 E
Gadzi, C.A.R. 114 B3 4 47N 16 42 E
Găeşti, Romania 53 F10 44 48N 25 19 E
Gaeta, Italy 46 A6 41 12N 13 35 E
Gaeta, G. di, Italy 46 A6 41 6N 13 30 E
Gaffney, U.S.A. 149 H5 35 5N 81 39W
Gafsa, Tunisia 108 B1 34 24N 8 43 E
Gagarin, Russia 58 E8 55 38N 35 0 E
Gagetown, Canada 141 C6 45 46N 66 10W
Gaggenau, Germany 31 G4 48 48N 8 18 E
Gagino, Russia 60 C7 55 15N 45 1 E
Gagliano del Capo, Italy 47 C11 39 50N 18 22 E
Gagnef, Sweden 16 D9 60 36N 15 5 E
Gagnoa, Ivory C. 112 D3 6 56N 5 16W
Gagnon, Canada 141 B6 51 50N 68 5W
Gagnon, L., Canada 143 A6 62 3N 110 27W
Gagra, Georgia 61 J5 43 20N 40 10 E
Gahini, Rwanda 118 C3 1 50 S 30 30 E
Gahmar, India 93 G10 25 27N 83 49 E
Gai Xian, China 75 D12 40 22N 122 20 E
Gaibanda, Bangla. 90 C2 25 20N 89 36 E
Gaïdhouronísi, Greece 38 E7 34 53N 25 41 E
Gail, U.S.A. 155 J4 32 46N 101 27W
Gail →, Austria 34 E6 46 36N 13 53 E
Gaillac, France 28 E5 43 54N 1 54 E
Gaillimh = Galway, Ireland 23 C2 53 17N 9 3W
Gaillon, France 26 C8 49 10N 1 20 E
Gaimán, Argentina 176 B3 43 10 S 65 25W
Gaines, U.S.A. 150 E7 41 46N 77 35W
Gainesville, Fla., U.S.A. 153 F7 29 40N 82 20W
Gainesville, Ga., U.S.A. 149 H4 34 18N 83 50W
Gainesville, Mo., U.S.A. 155 G8 36 36N 92 26W
Gainesville, Tex., U.S.A. 155 J6 33 38N 97 8W
Gainsborough, U.K. 20 D7 53 24N 0 46W
Gairdner, L., Australia 128 A2 31 30 S 136 0 E
Gairloch, L., U.K. 22 D3 57 43N 5 45W
Gais, Switz. 33 B8 47 22N 9 27 E
Gaj, Croatia 52 E2 45 28N 17 3 E
Gakona, U.S.A. 144 E11 62 18N 145 18W
Gakuch, Pakistan 93 A5 36 7N 73 45 E
Gal Laghet, Somali Rep. 120 D3 4 9N 47 10 E
Gal Oya Res., Sri Lanka 95 L5 7 5N 81 30 E
Gal Tardo, Somali Rep. 120 D3 3 34N 45 58 E
Galachipa, Bangla. 90 D3 22 8N 90 26 E
Galán, Cerro, Argentina 174 B2 25 55 S 66 52W
Galana →, Kenya 118 C5 3 9 S 40 8 E
Galangue, Angola 115 E3 13 42 S 16 9 E
Galangue, Serra, Angola 115 E3 14 18 S 15 52 E
Galanta, Slovak Rep. 35 C10 48 11N 17 45 E
Galapagar, Spain 42 E7 40 36N 3 58W
Galápagos, Pac. Oc. 135 H18 0 0 91 0W
Galashiels, U.K. 22 F6 55 37N 2 49W
Galatás, Greece 48 D5 37 30N 23 26 E
Galatea, N.Z. 130 E5 38 24 S 176 45 E
Galaţi, Romania 53 E13 45 27N 28 2 E
Galaţi □, Romania 53 E12 45 45N 27 30 E
Galatia, Turkey 100 C5 39 30N 33 0 E
Galatina, Italy 47 B11 40 10N 18 10 E
Galátone, Italy 47 B11 40 9N 18 4 E
Galax, U.S.A. 149 G5 36 40N 80 56W
Galaxídhion, Greece 48 C4 38 22N 22 23 E
Galbraith, Australia 126 B3 16 25 S 141 30 E
Galcaio, Somali Rep. 102 F4 6 30N 47 30 E
Galdhøpiggen, Norway 15 F12 61 38N 8 18 E
Galeana, Mexico 162 C4 24 50N 100 4W
Galela, Indonesia 82 A3 1 50N 127 49 E
Galena, U.S.A. 156 B6 42 25N 90 26W
Galera, Spain 41 H2 37 45N 2 33W
Galera, Pta., Chile 176 A2 39 59 S 73 43W
Galera Point, Trin. & Tob. 165 D7 10 8N 61 0W
Galesburg, Ill., U.S.A. 156 D6 40 57N 90 22W
Galesburg, Mich., U.S.A. 157 B11 42 17N 85 26W
Galeton, U.S.A. 150 E7 41 44N 77 39W
Galgasc, Somali Rep. 120 D2 0 11N 41 38 E
Galheirão →, Brazil 171 D2 12 23 S 45 5W
Galheiros, Brazil 171 D2 13 18 S 46 25W
Gali, Georgia 61 J5 42 37N 41 46 E
Galicea Mare, Romania 53 F8 44 4N 23 19 E
Galich, Russia 60 A6 58 22N 42 24 E
Galiche, Bulgaria 50 C7 43 34N 23 53 E
Galicia □, Spain 42 C3 42 43N 7 45W
Galien, U.S.A. 157 C10 41 48N 86 30W
Galilee = Hagalil, Israel 103 C4 32 53N 35 18 E
Galilee, L., Australia 126 C4 22 20 S 145 50 E
Galilee, Sea of = Yam Kinneret, Israel 103 C4 32 45N 35 35 E
Galinoporni, Cyprus 38 D13 35 31N 34 18 E
Galion, U.S.A. 150 F2 40 44N 82 47W
Galite, Îs. de la, Tunisia 111 A6 37 30N 8 59 E
Galiuro Mts., U.S.A. 159 K8 32 30N 110 20W
Gallabat, Sudan 107 E4 12 58N 36 11 E
Gallan Hd., U.K. 22 C1 58 15N 7 2W
Gallarate, Italy 44 C5 45 40N 8 48 E
Gallatin, Mo., U.S.A. 156 E3 39 55N 93 58W
Gallatin, Tenn., U.S.A. 149 G2 36 24N 86 27W
Galle, Sri Lanka 95 L5 6 5N 80 10 E
Gállego →, Spain 40 D4 41 39N 0 51W
Gallegos →, Argentina 176 D3 51 35 S 69 0W
Galley Hd., Ireland 23 E3 51 32N 8 55W
Galliate, Italy 44 C5 45 29N 8 42 E
Gallinas, Pta., Colombia 168 A3 12 28N 71 40W
Gallipoli = Gelibolu, Turkey 51 F10 40 28N 26 43 E
Gallípoli, Italy 47 B10 40 3N 17 58 E
Gallipolis, U.S.A. 148 F4 38 49N 82 12W
Gällivare, Sweden 14 C19 67 9N 20 40 E
Gallneukirchen, Austria 34 C7 48 21N 14 25 E
Gällö, Sweden 16 B9 62 55N 15 13 E
Gallo, C., Italy 46 D6 38 13N 13 19 E
Gallocanta, L. de, Spain 40 E3 40 58N 1 30W
Galloway, U.K. 22 F4 55 1N 4 29W
Galloway, Mull of, U.K. 22 G4 54 39N 4 52W
Gallup, U.S.A. 159 J9 35 32N 108 45W
Gallur, Spain 40 D3 41 52N 1 19W
Gallyaaral, Uzbekistan 63 C3 40 2N 67 35 E
Galong, Australia 129 C8 34 37 S 148 34 E
Galt, Calif., U.S.A. 160 G5 38 15N 121 18W
Galt, Mo., U.S.A. 156 D3 40 8N 93 23W
Galten, Denmark 17 H3 56 9N 9 54 E
Galtür, Austria 34 E3 46 58N 10 11 E
Galty Mts., Ireland 23 D3 52 22N 8 10W
Galtymore, Ireland 23 D3 52 21N 8 11W
Galva, U.S.A. 156 C6 41 10N 90 3W
Galvarino, Chile 176 A2 38 24 S 72 47W
Galve de Sorbe, Spain 40 D1 41 13N 3 10W
Galveston, Ind., U.S.A. 157 D10 40 35N 86 11W
Galveston, Tex., U.S.A. 155 L7 29 18N 94 48W
Galveston B., U.S.A. 155 L7 29 36N 94 50W
Gálvez, Argentina 174 C3 32 0 S 61 14W
Galway, Ireland 23 C2 53 17N 9 3W
Galway □, Ireland 23 C2 53 22N 9 1W
Galway B., Ireland 23 C2 53 13N 9 10W
Gam, Indonesia 83 B4 0 27 S 130 36 E
Gam →, Vietnam 86 B5 21 55N 105 12 E
Gamagori, Japan 71 C9 34 50N 137 14 E
Gamari, L., Ethiopia 107 E5 11 32N 41 40 E
Gamawa, Nigeria 113 C7 12 10N 10 31 E
Gamay, Phil. 80 E5 12 23N 125 18 E
Gamay Bay, Phil. 80 E5 12 21N 125 21 E
Gamba, Angola 115 E3 11 42 S 17 14 E
Gambaga, Ghana 113 C4 10 30N 0 28W
Gambat, Pakistan 92 F3 27 17N 68 26 E
Gambela, Ethiopia 107 F3 8 14N 34 38 E
Gambia ■, W. Afr. 112 C1 13 25N 16 0W
Gambia →, W. Afr. 112 C1 13 28N 16 34W
Gambier, C., Australia 124 B5 11 56 S 130 57 E
Gambier Is., Australia 128 C2 35 3 S 136 30 E
Gambo, C.A.R. 114 B4 4 39N 22 16 E
Gamboli, Pakistan 92 E3 29 53N 68 24 E
Gamboma, Congo 114 C3 1 55 S 15 52 E
Gamboula, C.A.R. 114 B3 4 8N 15 9 E
Gambuta, Indonesia 82 A2 0 30N 123 20 E
Gamerco, U.S.A. 159 J9 35 34N 108 46W
Gamla Uppsala, Sweden 16 E11 59 54N 17 40 E
Gamlakarleby = Kokkola, Finland 14 E20 63 50N 23 8 E
Gamleby, Sweden 17 G10 57 54N 16 24 E
Gammon →, Canada 143 C9 51 24N 95 44W
Gammouda, Tunisia 108 A1 35 3N 9 39 E
Gamoda-Saki, Japan 70 D6 33 50N 134 45 E
Gamu-Gofa □, Ethiopia 107 F4 5 40N 36 40 E
Gan, France 28 E3 43 12N 0 27W
Gan Gan, Argentina 176 B3 42 30 S 68 10W
Gan Goriama, Mts., Cameroon 113 D7 7 44N 12 45 E
Gan Jiang →, China 77 C11 29 15N 116 0 E
Ganado, Ariz., U.S.A. 159 J9 35 43N 109 33W
Ganado, Tex., U.S.A. 155 L6 29 2N 96 31W
Gananoque, Canada 140 D4 44 20N 76 10W
Ganāveh, Iran 97 D6 29 35N 50 35 E
Gäncä, Azerbaijan 61 K8 40 45N 46 20 E
Gancheng, China 86 C7 18 51N 108 37 E
Gand = Gent, Belgium 24 C3 51 2N 3 42 E
Ganda, Angola 115 E2 13 3 S 14 35 E
Gandak →, India 93 G11 25 39N 85 13 E
Gandara, Phil. 80 E5 12 1N 124 49 E
Gandava, Pakistan 91 C2 28 32N 67 32 E
Gander, Canada 141 C9 48 58N 54 35W
Gander L., Canada 141 C9 48 58N 54 35W
Ganderkesee, Germany 30 B4 53 2N 8 32 E
Ganderowe Falls, Zimbabwe 119 F2 17 20 S 29 10 E
Gandesa, Spain 40 D5 41 3N 0 26 E
Gandhi Sagar, India 92 G6 24 40N 75 40 E
Gandi, Nigeria 113 C6 12 55N 5 49 E
Gandía, Spain 41 G4 38 58N 0 9W
Gandino, Italy 44 C6 45 49N 9 54 E
Gando, Pta., Canary Is. 39 G4 27 55N 15 22W
Gandole, Nigeria 113 D7 8 28N 11 35 E
Gandu, Brazil 171 D4 13 45 S 39 30W
Ganedidalem = Gani, Indonesia 82 B3 0 48 S 128 14 E
Ganetti, Sudan 106 D3 18 0N 31 10 E
Ganga →, India 93 H14 23 20N 90 30 E
Ganganagar, India 92 E5 29 56N 73 56 E
Gangapur, India 92 F7 26 32N 76 49 E
Gangara, Niger 109 F1 14 35N 8 29 E
Gangaw, Burma 90 D5 22 5N 94 5 E
Gangawati, India 95 G3 15 30N 76 36 E
Ganges = Ganga →, India 93 H14 23 20N 90 30 E
Ganges, France 28 E7 43 56N 3 42 E
Ganges, Mouths of the, India 93 J14 21 30N 90 0 E
Gånghester, Sweden 17 G7 57 42N 13 1 E
Gangi, Italy 47 E7 37 48N 14 12 E
Gângiova, Romania 53 G8 43 54N 23 50 E
Gangoh, India 92 E7 29 46N 77 18 E
Gangtok, India 90 B2 27 20N 88 37 E
Gangu, China 74 G3 34 40N 105 15 E
Gangyao, China 75 B14 44 12N 126 37 E
Gani, Indonesia 82 B3 0 48 S 128 14 E
Ganj, India 93 F8 27 45N 78 57 E
Gannat, France 27 F10 46 7N 3 11 E
Gannett Peak, U.S.A. 158 E9 43 11N 109 39W
Gannvalley, U.S.A. 154 C5 44 2N 98 59W
Ganongga, Solomon Is. 133 M9 8 5 S 156 35 E
Ganquan, China 74 F5 36 20N 109 20 E
Gänserdorf, Austria 35 C9 48 20N 16 43 E
Ganshui, China 76 C6 28 40N 106 40 E
Gansu □, China 74 G3 36 0N 104 0 E
Ganta, Liberia 112 D3 7 15N 8 59W
Gantheaume, C., Australia 128 D2 36 4 S 137 32 E
Gantheaume B., Australia 125 E1 27 40 S 114 10 E
Gantsevichi = Hantsavichy, Belarus 59 F4 52 49N 26 30 E
Ganyem = Genyem, Indonesia 83 B6 2 46 S 140 12 E
Ganyu, China 75 G10 34 50N 119 8 E
Ganyushkino, Kazakstan 61 G9 46 35N 49 20 E
Ganzhou, China 77 E10 25 51N 114 56 E
Gao, Mali 113 B5 18 0N 1 0 E
Gao Xian, China 76 C5 28 21N 104 32 E
Gao'an, China 77 C10 28 26N 115 17 E
Gaohe, China 77 F9 22 46N 112 57 E
Gaohebu, China 77 B11 30 43N 116 49 E
Gaokeng, China 77 D9 27 40N 113 58 E
Gaolan Dao, China 77 G9 21 55N 113 10 E
Gaoligong Shan, China 76 E2 24 45N 98 45 E
Gaomi, China 75 F10 36 20N 119 42 E
Gaoping, China 74 G7 35 45N 112 55 E
Gaotang, China 74 F9 36 50N 116 15 E
Gaoua, Burkina Faso 112 C4 10 20N 3 8W
Gaoual, Guinea 112 C2 11 45N 13 25W
Gaoxiong = Kaohsiung, Taiwan 77 F13 22 35N 120 16 E
Gaoyang, China 74 E8 38 40N 115 45 E
Gaoyou, China 77 A12 32 47N 119 26 E
Gaoyou Hu, China 75 H10 32 45N 119 20 E
Gaoyuan, China 75 F9 37 8N 117 58 E
Gaozhou, China 77 G8 21 58N 110 50 E
Gap, France 29 D10 44 33N 6 5 E
Gapan, Phil. 80 D3 15 19N 120 57 E
Gar, China 72 C2 32 10N 79 58 E
Garabekewüi, Turkmenistan 63 D2 38 30N 64 8 E
Garabogazköl Aylagy, Turkmenistan 57 F9 41 0N 53 30 E
Garachico, Canary Is. 39 F3 28 22N 16 46W
Garachiné, Panama 164 E4 8 0N 78 12W
Garad, Somali Rep. 120 C3 6 57N 49 24 E
Garafia, Canary Is. 39 F2 28 48N 17 57W
Garajonay, Canary Is. 39 F2 28 7N 17 14W
Garamätnyyaz, Turkmenistan 63 E2 37 45N 64 34 E
Garanhuns, Brazil 170 C4 8 50 S 36 30W
Garawe, Liberia 112 E3 4 35N 8 0W
Garba Harre, Somali Rep. 120 D2 3 19N 42 13 E
Garba Tula, Kenya 118 B4 0 30N 38 32 E
Garbagududu, Ethiopia 120 C2 6 12N 43 50 E
Garber, U.S.A. 155 G6 36 26N 97 35W
Garberville, U.S.A. 158 F2 40 6N 123 48W
Garbsen, Germany 30 C5 52 26N 9 31 E
Garça, Brazil 171 F2 22 14 S 49 37W
Garças →, Mato Grosso, Brazil 173 D7 15 54 S 52 16W
Garças →, Pernambuco, Brazil 170 C4 8 43 S 39 41W
Garchitorena, Phil. 80 E4 13 52N 123 40 E
Garcia Hernandez, Phil. 81 G5 9 37N 124 18 E
Garcias, Brazil 173 E7 20 34 S 52 13W
Gard □, France 29 D8 44 2N 4 10 E
Gard →, France 29 E8 43 51N 4 37 E
Garda, L. di, Italy 44 C7 45 40N 10 41 E
Gardanne, France 29 E9 43 27N 5 27 E
Gårdby, Sweden 17 H10 56 36N 16 38 E
Garde L., Canada 143 A7 62 50N 106 13W
Gardelegen, Germany 30 C7 52 32N 11 24 E
Garden City, Ga., U.S.A. 152 C8 32 6N 81 9W
Garden City, Kans., U.S.A. 155 G4 37 58N 100 53W
Garden City, Mo., U.S.A. 156 F2 38 34N 94 12W
Garden City, Tex., U.S.A. 155 K4 31 52N 101 29W
Garden Grove, U.S.A. 161 M9 33 47N 117 55W
Gardēz, Afghan. 91 B3 33 37N 69 9 E
Gardhíki, Greece 48 C3 38 50N 21 55 E
Garður, Iceland 11 A10 66 4N 16 46W
Gardi, U.S.A. 152 D8 31 32N 81 48W
Gardiner, U.S.A. 158 D8 45 2N 110 22W
Gardiners I., U.S.A. 151 E12 41 6N 72 6W
Gardner, Fla., U.S.A. 153 H8 27 21N 81 48W
Gardner, Ill., U.S.A. 157 C8 41 12N 88 17W
Gardner, Mass., U.S.A. 151 D13 42 34N 71 59W
Gardner Canal, Canada 142 C3 53 27N 128 8W
Gardner Pinnacles, U.S.A. 145 G10 25 0N 167 55W
Gardnerville, U.S.A. 160 G7 38 56N 119 45W
Gardno, Jezioro, Poland 54 D4 54 40N 17 7 E
Gardo, Somali Rep. 120 C3 9 30N 49 6 E
Gardone Val Trómpia, Italy 44 C7 45 41N 10 11 E
Gárdony, Hungary 52 C3 47 12N 18 39 E
Gare Tigre, Fr. Guiana 169 C7 4 58N 53 9W
Garešnica, Croatia 45 C13 45 36N 16 56 E
Garéssio, Italy 44 D5 44 12N 8 2 E
Garey, U.S.A. 161 L6 34 53N 120 19W
Garfield, U.S.A. 158 C5 47 1N 117 9W
Garforth, U.K. 20 D6 53 47N 1 24W
Gargaliánoi, Greece 48 D3 37 4N 21 38 E
Gargan, Mt., France 28 C5 45 37N 1 39 E
Gargouna, Mali 113 B5 15 56N 0 13 E
Gargždai, Lithuania 54 C8 55 43N 21 24 E
Garhshankar, India 92 D7 31 13N 76 11 E
Gari, Russia 62 B9 59 26N 62 21 E
Garibaldi Prov. Park, Canada 142 D4 49 50N 122 40W
Garies, S. Africa 116 E2 30 32 S 17 59 E
Garigliano →, Italy 46 A6 41 13N 13 45 E
Garissa, Kenya 118 C4 0 25 S 39 40 E
Garissa □, Kenya 118 C5 0 20 S 40 0 E
Garkida, Nigeria 113 C7 10 27N 12 36 E
Garko, Nigeria 113 C6 11 45N 8 53 E
Garland, Tex., U.S.A. 155 J6 32 55N 96 38W
Garland, Utah, U.S.A. 158 F7 41 47N 112 10W
Garlasco, Italy 44 C5 45 12N 8 55 E
Garliava, Lithuania 54 D10 54 49N 23 52 E
Garlin, France 28 E3 43 33N 0 16W
Garm, Tajikistan 63 D5 39 0N 70 20 E
Garmāb, Iran 97 C8 35 25N 56 45 E
Garmisch-Partenkirchen, Germany 31 H7 47 30N 11 6 E
Garmsār, Iran 97 C7 35 20N 52 25 E
Garner, U.S.A. 156 A3 43 6N 93 36W
Garnett, U.S.A. 154 F7 38 17N 95 14W
Garo Hills, India 93 G14 25 30N 90 30 E
Garoe, Somali Rep. 120 C3 8 25N 48 33 E
Garonne →, France 28 C3 45 2N 0 36W
Garonne, Canal Latéral à la →, France 28 D4 44 15N 0 18 E
Garoua, Cameroon 113 D7 9 19N 13 21 E
Garpenberg, Sweden 16 D10 60 19N 16 12 E
Garphyttan, Sweden 16 E8 59 18N 14 56 E
Garrel, Germany 30 C4 52 57N 8 1 E
Garrett, U.S.A. 157 C11 41 21N 85 8W
Garrigue = Garrigues, France 28 E7 43 40N 3 55 E
Garrigues, France 28 E7 43 40N 3 55 E
Garrison, Ky., U.S.A. 157 F13 38 36N 83 10W
Garrison, Mont., U.S.A. 158 C7 46 31N 112 49W
Garrison, N. Dak., U.S.A. 154 B4 47 40N 101 25W
Garrison, Tex., U.S.A. 155 K7 31 49N 94 30W
Garrison Res. = Sakakawea, L., U.S.A. 154 B4 47 30N 101 25W
Garron Pt., U.K. 23 A6 55 3N 5 59W
Garrovillas, Spain 43 F4 39 40N 6 33W
Garrucha, Spain 41 H3 37 11N 1 49W
Garry →, U.K. 22 E5 56 44N 3 47W
Garry, L., Canada 138 B9 65 58N 100 18W
Garsen, Kenya 118 C5 2 20 S 40 5 E
Gärsnäs, Sweden 17 J8 55 32N 14 10 E
Garson L., Canada 143 B6 56 19N 110 2W
Gartempe →, France 28 B4 46 47N 0 49 E
Gartz, Germany 30 B10 53 13N 14 22 E
Garu, Ghana 113 C4 10 55N 0 11W
Garub, Namibia 116 D2 26 37 S 16 0 E
Garut, Indonesia 85 D3 7 14 S 107 53 E
Garvão, Portugal 43 H2 37 42N 8 21W
Garvie Mts., N.Z. 131 F3 45 30 S 168 50 E
Garwa = Garoua, Cameroon 113 D7 9 19N 13 21 E
Garwa, India 93 G10 24 11N 83 47 E
Garwolin, Poland 55 G8 51 55N 21 38 E
Gary, U.S.A. 157 C9 41 36N 87 20W
Garz, Germany 30 A9 54 19N 13 20 E
Garzê, China 76 B3 31 38N 100 1 E
Garzón, Colombia 168 C2 2 10N 75 40W
Gas City, U.S.A. 157 D11 40 29N 85 37W
Gas-San, Japan 68 E10 38 32N 140 1 E
Gasan, Phil. 80 E3 13 19N 121 51 E
Gasan Kuli = Esenguly, Turkmenistan 64 F6 37 37N 53 59 E
Gascogne, France 28 E4 43 45N 0 20 E
Gascogne, G. de, Europe 28 E2 44 0N 2 0W
Gasconade, U.S.A. 156 F5 38 40N 91 34W
Gasconade →, U.S.A. 156 F5 38 41N 91 33W
Gascony = Gascogne, France 28 E4 43 45N 0 20 E
Gascoyne →, Australia 125 D1 24 52 S 113 37 E
Gascoyne Junc. T.O., Australia 125 E2 25 2 S 115 17 E
Gascueña, Spain 40 E2 40 18N 2 31W
Gash, Wadi →, Ethiopia 107 D4 16 48N 35 51 E
Gashaka, Nigeria 113 D7 7 20N 11 29 E
Gasherbrum, Pakistan 93 B7 35 40N 76 40 E
Gashua, Nigeria 113 C7 12 54N 11 0 E
Gasparilla I., U.S.A. 153 J7 26 46N 82 16W
Gaspé, Canada 141 C7 48 52N 64 30W
Gaspé, C. de, Canada 141 C7 48 48N 64 7W
Gaspé, Pén. de, Canada 141 C6 48 45N 65 40W
Gaspésie, Parc Prov. de la, Canada 141 C6 48 55N 65 50W
Gassaway, U.S.A. 148 F5 38 41N 80 47W
Gassol, Nigeria 113 D7 8 34N 10 25 E
Gasteiz = Vitoria-Gasteiz, Spain 40 C2 42 50N 2 41W
Gaston, U.S.A. 152 B9 33 49N 81 5W
Gastonia, U.S.A. 149 H5 35 16N 81 11W
Gastoúni, Greece 48 D3 37 51N 21 15 E
Gastoúri, Greece 48 B1 39 34N 19 54 E
Gastre, Argentina 176 B3 42 20 S 69 15W
Gästrikland, Sweden 16 D10 60 45N 16 40 E
Gata, C., Cyprus 38 E12 34 34N 33 2 E
Gata, C. de, Spain 41 J2 36 41N 2 13W
Gata, Sierra de, Spain 42 E4 40 20N 6 45W
Gataga →, Canada 142 B3 58 35N 126 59W
Gătaia, Romania 52 E6 45 26N 21 30 E
Gatchina, Russia 58 C6 59 35N 30 9 E
Gatehouse of Fleet, U.K. 22 G4 54 53N 4 12W
Gates, U.S.A. 150 C7 43 9N 77 42W
Gateshead, U.K. 20 C6 54 57N 1 35W
Gatesville, U.S.A. 155 K6 31 26N 97 45W
Gaths, Zimbabwe 119 G3 20 2 S 30 32 E
Gatico, Chile 174 A1 22 29 S 70 20W
Gâtinais, France 27 D9 48 5N 2 40 E
Gâtine, Hauteurs de, France 28 B3 46 35N 0 45W
Gatineau →, Canada 140 C4 45 27N 75 42W
Gatineau, Parc de la, Canada 140 C4 45 40N 76 0W
Gattaran, Phil. 80 B3 18 4N 121 38 E
Gattinara, Italy 44 C5 45 37N 8 22 E
Gatukai, Solomon Is. 133 M10 8 45 S 158 15 E
Gatun, L., Panama 164 E4 9 7N 79 56W
Gatyana, S. Africa 117 E4 32 16 S 28 31 E
Gau, Fiji 133 B2 18 2 S 179 18 E
Gaua, Vanuatu 133 D5 14 15 S 167 30 E
Gaucín, Spain 43 J5 36 31N 5 19W
Gauer L., Canada 143 B9 57 0N 97 50W
Gauhati, India 93 F14 26 10N 91 45 E
Gauja →, Latvia 15 H21 57 10N 24 16 E
Gaula →, Norway 14 E14 63 21N 10 14 E
Gaupne, Norway 18 C4 61 25N 7 18 E
Gaurdak = Gowurdak, Turkmenistan 63 E3 37 50N 66 4 E
Gausta, Norway 15 G13 59 48N 8 40 E
Gauteng □, S. Africa 117 D4 26 0 S 28 0 E
Gāv Koshī, Iran 97 D8 28 38N 57 12 E
Gāvakān, Iran 97 D7 29 37N 53 10 E
Gavarnie, France 28 F3 42 44N 0 1W
Gavāter, Iran 97 E9 25 10N 61 31 E
Gāvbandī, Iran 97 E7 27 12N 53 4 E
Gavdhopoúla, Greece 38 E6 34 56N 24 0 E
Gávdhos, Greece 38 E6 34 50N 24 5 E
Gavi, Italy 44 D5 44 41N 8 49 E
Gavião, Portugal 43 F3 39 28N 7 56W
Gaviota, U.S.A. 161 L6 34 29N 120 13W
Gävle, Sweden 16 D11 60 40N 17 9 E
Gävleborgs län □, Sweden 16 C10 61 30N 16 15 E
Gävlebukten, Sweden 16 D11 60 40N 17 20 E
Gavorrano, Italy 44 F7 42 55N 10 54 E
Gavray, France 26 D5 48 55N 1 20W
Gavrilov Yam, Russia 58 D10 57 18N 39 49 E

220 Greenacres City

Greenacres City, *U.S.A.* ... **153 J9** 26 38N 80 7W
Greenbank, *U.S.A.* ... **160 B4** 48 6N 122 34W
Greenbush, *Mich., U.S.A.* . **150 B1** 44 35N 83 19W
Greenbush, *Minn., U.S.A.* . **154 A6** 48 42N 96 11W
Greencastle, *U.S.A.* ... **157 E10** 39 38N 86 52W
Greene, *Iowa, U.S.A.* ... **156 B4** 42 54N 92 48W
Greene, *N.Y., U.S.A.* ... **151 D9** 42 20N 75 46W
Greenfield, *Calif., U.S.A.* .. **160 J5** 36 19N 121 15W
Greenfield, *Calif., U.S.A.* .. **161 K8** 35 15N 119 0W
Greenfield, *Ill., U.S.A.* ... **156 E6** 39 21N 90 12W
Greenfield, *Ind., U.S.A.* ... **157 E11** 39 47N 85 46W
Greenfield, *Iowa, U.S.A.* .. **156 C2** 41 18N 94 28W
Greenfield, *Mass., U.S.A.* .. **151 D12** 42 35N 72 36W
Greenfield, *Mo., U.S.A.* ... **155 G8** 37 25N 93 51W
Greenfield, *Ohio, U.S.A.* .. **157 E13** 39 21N 83 23W
Greenfield Park, *Canada* .. **151 A11** 45 29N 73 29W
Greenland ■, *N. Amer.* ... **10 D6** 66 0N 45 0W
Greenland Sea, *Arctic* ... **10 B10** 73 0N 10 0W
Greenock, *U.K.* ... **22 F4** 55 57N 4 46W
Greenore, *Ireland* ... **23 B5** 54 2N 6 8W
Greenore Pt., *Ireland* ... **23 D5** 52 14N 6 19W
Greenough →, *Australia* .. **125 E1** 28 51 S 114 38 E
Greenport, *U.S.A.* ... **151 E12** 41 6N 72 22W
Greensboro, *Fla., U.S.A.* .. **152 E5** 30 34N 84 45W
Greensboro, *Ga., U.S.A.* .. **152 B6** 33 35N 83 11W
Greensboro, *N.C., U.S.A.* . **149 G6** 36 4N 79 48W
Greensburg, *Ind., U.S.A.* .. **157 E11** 39 20N 85 29W
Greensburg, *Kans., U.S.A.* . **155 G5** 37 36N 99 18W
Greensburg, *Pa., U.S.A.* ... **150 F5** 40 18N 79 33W
Greenstone Pt., *U.K.* ... **22 D3** 57 55N 5 37W
Greentown, *U.S.A.* ... **157 D11** 40 29N 85 58W
Greenup, *U.S.A.* ... **157 E8** 39 15N 88 10W
Greenville, *Liberia* ... **112 D3** 5 1N 9 6W
Greenville, *Ala., U.S.A.* ... **149 K2** 31 50N 86 38W
Greenville, *Calif., U.S.A.* .. **160 E6** 40 8N 120 57W
Greenville, *Fla., U.S.A.* ... **152 E6** 30 28N 83 38W
Greenville, *Ga., U.S.A.* ... **152 B5** 33 2N 84 43W
Greenville, *Ill., U.S.A.* ... **156 F7** 38 53N 89 25W
Greenville, *Ind., U.S.A.* ... **157 F11** 38 22N 85 59W
Greenville, *Maine, U.S.A.* .. **141 C6** 45 28N 69 35W
Greenville, *Mich., U.S.A.* .. **157 A11** 43 11N 85 15W
Greenville, *Miss., U.S.A.* .. **155 J9** 33 24N 91 4W
Greenville, *N.C., U.S.A.* .. **149 H7** 35 37N 77 23W
Greenville, *Ohio, U.S.A.* .. **157 D12** 40 6N 84 38W
Greenville, *Pa., U.S.A.* ... **150 E4** 41 24N 80 23W
Greenville, *S.C., U.S.A.* ... **149 H4** 34 51N 82 24W
Greenville, *Tenn., U.S.A.* .. **149 G4** 36 13N 82 51W
Greenville, *Tex., U.S.A.* ... **155 J6** 33 8N 96 7W
Greenwater Lake Prov. Park, *Canada* ... **143 C8** 52 32N 103 30W
Greenwich, *U.K.* ... **21 F8** 51 29N 0 1 E
Greenwich, *Conn., U.S.A.* . **151 E11** 41 2N 73 38W
Greenwich, *N.Y., U.S.A.* .. **151 C11** 43 5N 73 30W
Greenwich, *Ohio, U.S.A.* .. **150 E2** 41 2N 82 31W
Greenwood, *Canada* ... **142 D5** 49 10N 118 40W
Greenwood, *Fla., U.S.A.* .. **152 E4** 30 52N 85 10W
Greenwood, *Ind., U.S.A.* .. **157 E10** 39 37N 86 7W
Greenwood, *Miss., U.S.A.* . **155 J9** 33 31N 90 11W
Greenwood, *S.C., U.S.A.* .. **149 H4** 34 12N 82 10W
Greenwood, Mt., *Australia* . **124 B5** 13 48 S 130 4 E
Greenwood L., *U.S.A.* ... **151 E10** 41 8N 74 21W
Gregório →, *Brazil* ... **172 B3** 6 50 S 70 46W
Gregory, *U.S.A.* ... **154 D5** 43 14N 99 20W
Gregory →, *Australia* ... **126 B2** 17 53 S 139 17 E
Gregory, L., *S. Austral., Australia* ... **127 D2** 28 55 S 139 0 E
Gregory, L., *W. Austral., Australia* ... **125 E2** 25 38 S 119 58 E
Gregory Downs, *Australia* .. **126 B2** 18 35 S 138 45 E
Gregory L., *Australia* ... **124 D4** 20 0 S 127 40 E
Gregory Ra., *Queens., Australia* ... **126 B3** 19 30 S 143 40 E
Gregory Ra., *W. Austral., Australia* ... **124 D3** 21 20 S 121 12 E
Greiffenberg, *Germany* ... **30 B9** 53 5N 13 57 E
Greifswald, *Germany* ... **30 A9** 54 5N 13 23 E
Greifswalder Bodden, *Germany* ... **30 A9** 54 12N 13 35 E
Grein, *Austria* ... **34 C7** 48 14N 14 51 E
Greiz, *Germany* ... **30 E8** 50 39N 12 10 E
Gremikha, *Russia* ... **56 A6** 67 59N 39 47 E
Gremyachinsk, *Russia* ... **62 B6** 58 34N 57 51 E
Grenå, *Denmark* ... **17 H4** 56 25N 10 53 E
Grenada, *U.S.A.* ... **155 J10** 33 47N 89 49W
Grenada ■, *W. Indies* ... **165 D7** 12 10N 61 40W
Grenade, *France* ... **28 E5** 43 47N 1 17 E
Grenadines, *W. Indies* ... **165 D7** 12 40N 61 20W
Grenchen, *Switz.* ... **32 B4** 47 12N 7 24 E
Grenen, *Denmark* ... **17 G4** 57 44N 10 40 E
Grenfell, *Australia* ... **129 B8** 33 52 S 148 8 E
Grenfell, *Canada* ... **143 C8** 50 30N 102 56W
Grenivík, *Iceland* ... **11 B8** 65 57N 18 11W
Grenjaðarstaður, *Iceland* ... **11 B9** 65 49N 17 21W
Grenoble, *France* ... **29 C9** 45 12N 5 42 E
Grenora, *U.S.A.* ... **154 A3** 48 37N 103 56W
Grenville, C., *Australia* ... **126 A3** 12 0 S 143 13 E
Grenville Chan., *Canada* ... **142 C3** 53 40N 129 46W
Gréoux-les-Bains, *France* ... **29 E9** 43 45N 5 52 E
Gresham, *U.S.A.* ... **160 E4** 45 30N 122 26W
Gresik, *Indonesia* ... **85 D4** 7 13 S 112 38 E
Gresston, *U.S.A.* ... **152 C6** 32 17N 83 15W
Gretna, *U.K.* ... **22 F5** 55 0N 3 3W
Gretna, *U.S.A.* ... **152 E5** 30 37N 84 40W
Greven, *Germany* ... **30 C3** 52 6N 7 37 E
Grevená, *Greece* ... **50 F5** 40 4N 21 25 E
Grevená □, *Greece* ... **50 F5** 40 2N 21 25 E
Grevenbroich, *Germany* ... **30 D2** 51 5N 6 35 E
Grevenmacher, *Lux.* ... **24 E6** 49 41N 6 26 E
Grevesmühlen, *Germany* ... **30 B7** 53 52N 11 12 E
Grevestrand, *Denmark* ... **17 J6** 55 36N 12 19 E
Grey →, *N.Z.* ... **131 C6** 42 27 S 171 12 E
Grey, C., *Australia* ... **126 A2** 13 0 S 136 35 E
Grey Ra., *Australia* ... **127 D3** 27 0 S 143 30 E
Grey Res., *Canada* ... **141 C8** 48 20N 56 30W
Greybull, *U.S.A.* ... **158 D9** 44 30N 108 3W
Greymouth, *N.Z.* ... **131 C6** 42 29 S 171 13 E
Greystones, *Ireland* ... **23 C5** 53 9N 6 5W
Greytown, *N.Z.* ... **130 H4** 41 5 S 175 29 E
Greytown, *S. Africa* ... **117 D5** 29 1 S 30 36 E
Gribanovskiy, *Russia* ... **60 E5** 51 28N 41 50 E
Gribbell I., *Canada* ... **142 C3** 53 23N 129 0W
Gridley, *U.S.A.* ... **160 F5** 39 22N 121 42W
Griekwastad, *S. Africa* ... **116 D3** 28 49 S 23 15 E
Griesheim, *Germany* ... **31 F4** 49 51N 8 34 E
Grieskirchen, *Austria* ... **34 C6** 48 16N 13 48 E
Griffin, *U.S.A.* ... **152 B5** 33 15N 84 16W
Griffin, L., *U.S.A.* ... **153 G8** 28 52N 81 51W
Griffith, *Australia* ... **129 C7** 34 18 S 146 2 E
Grignols, *France* ... **28 D3** 44 23N 0 2W
Grigoriopol, *Moldova* ... **53 C14** 47 9N 29 18 E
Grimari, *C.A.R.* ... **114 A4** 5 43N 20 6 E
Grimaylov = Hrymayliv, *Ukraine* ... **59 H4** 49 20N 26 5 E
Grimes, *U.S.A.* ... **160 F5** 39 4N 121 54W
Grimma, *Germany* ... **30 D8** 51 14N 12 43 E
Grimmen, *Germany* ... **30 A9** 54 7N 13 3 E
Grimsay, *U.K.* ... **22 D1** 57 29N 7 14W
Grimsby, *Canada* ... **150 C5** 43 12N 79 34W
Grimsby, *U.K.* ... **20 D7** 53 34N 0 5W
Grimselpass, *Switz.* ... **33 C6** 46 34N 8 23 E
Grímsey, *Iceland* ... **11 A9** 66 33N 17 58W
Grimshaw, *Canada* ... **142 B5** 56 10N 117 40W
Grimslöv, *Sweden* ... **17 H8** 56 44N 14 34 E
Grímsstaðir, *Iceland* ... **11 B10** 65 39N 16 7W
Grimstad, *Norway* ... **15 G13** 58 20N 8 35 E
Grímsvötn, *Iceland* ... **11 C9** 64 26N 17 22W
Grindavík, *Iceland* ... **11 D4** 63 50N 22 26W
Grindelwald, *Switz.* ... **32 C6** 46 38N 8 2 E
Grindsted, *Denmark* ... **17 J2** 55 46N 8 55 E
Grindu, *Romania* ... **53 F11** 44 44N 26 50 E
Grinnell, *U.S.A.* ... **156 C4** 41 45N 92 43W
Grintavec, *Slovenia* ... **45 B11** 46 22N 14 32 E
Gris-Nez, C., *France* ... **27 B8** 50 52N 1 35 E
Grisolles, *France* ... **28 E5** 43 49N 1 19 E
Grisons = Graubünden □, *Switz.* ... **33 C9** 46 45N 9 30 E
Grisslehamn, *Sweden* ... **16 D12** 60 5N 18 49 E
Grmeč Planina, *Bos.-H.* ... **45 D13** 44 43N 16 16 E
Groais I., *Canada* ... **141 B8** 50 55N 55 35W
Grobiņa, *Latvia* ... **54 B8** 56 33N 21 10 E
Groblersdal, *S. Africa* ... **117 D4** 25 15 S 29 25 E
Grobming, *Austria* ... **34 D6** 47 27N 13 54 E
Grocka, *Serbia, Yug.* ... **50 B4** 44 40N 20 42 E
Gródek, *Poland* ... **55 E10** 53 6N 23 40 E
Grodków, *Poland* ... **55 H4** 50 43N 17 21 E
Grodno = Hrodna, *Belarus* . **58 F2** 53 42N 23 52 E
Grodzisk Mazowiecki, *Poland* ... **55 F7** 52 7N 20 37 E
Grodzisk Wielkopolski, *Poland* ... **55 F3** 52 15N 16 22 E
Grodzyanka = Hrodzyanka, *Belarus* ... **58 F5** 53 31N 28 42 E
Groesbeck, *U.S.A.* ... **155 K6** 31 31N 96 31W
Groix, *France* ... **26 E3** 47 38N 3 29W
Groix, Î. de, *France* ... **26 E3** 47 38N 3 28W
Grójec, *Poland* ... **55 G7** 51 50N 20 58 E
Gronau, *Niedersachsen, Germany* ... **30 C5** 52 5N 9 47 E
Gronau, *Nordrhein-Westfalen, Germany* ... **30 C3** 52 12N 7 2 E
Grong, *Norway* ... **14 D15** 64 25N 12 8 E
Grönhögen, *Sweden* ... **17 H10** 56 16N 16 24 E
Groningen, *Neths.* ... **24 A6** 53 15N 6 35 E
Groningen, *Surinam* ... **169 B6** 5 48N 55 28W
Groningen □, *Neths.* ... **24 A6** 53 16N 6 40 E
Grønnedal, *Greenland* ... **10 E6** 61 20N 47 57W
Groom, *U.S.A.* ... **155 H4** 35 12N 101 6W
Groot →, *S. Africa* ... **116 E3** 33 45 S 24 36 E
Groot Berg →, *S. Africa* .. **116 E2** 32 47 S 18 8 E
Groot-Brakrivier, *S. Africa* . **116 E3** 34 2 S 22 18 E
Groot-Kei →, *S. Africa* ... **117 E4** 32 41 S 28 22 E
Groot Vis →, *S. Africa* ... **116 E4** 33 28 S 27 5 E
Groote Eylandt, *Australia* .. **126 A2** 14 0 S 136 40 E
Grootfontein, *Namibia* ... **116 B2** 19 31 S 18 6 E
Grootlaagte →, *Africa* ... **116 C3** 20 55 S 21 27 E
Grootvloer, *S. Africa* ... **116 E3** 30 0 S 20 40 E
Gros C., *Canada* ... **142 A6** 61 59N 113 32W
Grósio, *Italy* ... **44 B7** 46 18N 10 16 E
Grosne →, *France* ... **27 F11** 46 42N 4 56 E
Grossa, Pta., *Spain* ... **39 B8** 39 6N 1 36 E
Grossenbrode, *Germany* ... **30 A7** 54 21N 11 4 E
Grossenhain, *Germany* ... **30 D9** 51 17N 13 32 E
Grosser Arber, *Germany* ... **31 F9** 49 6N 13 8 E
Grosser Plöner See, *Germany* ... **30 A6** 54 10N 10 22 E
Grosseto, *Italy* ... **45 F8** 42 46N 11 8 E
Grossgerungs, *Austria* ... **34 C7** 48 34N 14 57 E
Grossglockner, *Austria* ... **34 D5** 47 5N 12 40 E
Groswater B., *Canada* ... **141 B8** 54 20N 57 40W
Grotli, *Norway* ... **18 B4** 62 2N 7 42 E
Groton, *Conn., U.S.A.* ... **151 E12** 41 21N 72 5W
Groton, *S. Dak., U.S.A.* ... **154 C5** 45 27N 98 6W
Grottáglie, *Italy* ... **47 B10** 40 32N 17 26 E
Grottaminarda, *Italy* ... **47 A8** 41 4N 15 2 E
Grottammare, *Italy* ... **45 F10** 42 59N 13 52 E
Grouard Mission, *Canada* .. **142 B5** 55 33N 116 9W
Grouin, Pte. du, *France* ... **26 D5** 48 43N 1 51W
Groundhog →, *Canada* ... **140 C3** 48 45N 82 58W
Grouse Creek, *U.S.A.* ... **158 F7** 41 42N 113 53W
Grouw, *Neths.* ... **24 A5** 53 5N 5 51 E
Grovania, *U.S.A.* ... **152 C6** 32 22N 83 40W
Grove City, *Ohio, U.S.A.* .. **157 E13** 39 53N 83 6W
Grove City, *Pa., U.S.A.* ... **150 E4** 41 10N 80 5W
Groveland, *Calif., U.S.A.* .. **160 H6** 37 50N 120 14W
Groveland, *Fla., U.S.A.* ... **153 G8** 28 34N 81 51W
Grover City, *U.S.A.* ... **161 K6** 35 7N 120 37W
Grover Hill, *U.S.A.* ... **157 C12** 41 1N 84 29W
Groveton, *N.H., U.S.A.* ... **151 B13** 44 36N 71 31W
Groveton, *Tex., U.S.A.* ... **155 K7** 31 4N 95 8W
Grovetown, *U.S.A.* ... **152 B7** 33 27N 82 12W
Grožnjan, *Croatia* ... **45 C10** 45 22N 13 43 E
Groznyy, *Russia* ... **61 J7** 43 20N 45 45 E
Grua, *Norway* ... **18 D7** 60 16N 10 40 E
Grubišno Polje, *Croatia* ... **52 E2** 45 44N 17 12 E
Grudovo, *Bulgaria* ... **51 D11** 42 21N 27 10 E
Grudusk, *Poland* ... **55 E7** 53 3N 20 38 E
Grudziądz, *Poland* ... **54 E5** 53 30N 18 47 E
Gruinard B., *U.K.* ... **22 D3** 57 56N 5 35W
Gruissan, *France* ... **28 E7** 43 8N 3 7 E
Grumo Áppula, *Italy* ... **47 A9** 41 1N 16 42 E
Grums, *Sweden* ... **16 E7** 59 22N 13 5 E
Grünberg, *Germany* ... **30 E4** 50 35N 8 58 E
Grund, *Iceland* ... **11 B8** 65 31N 18 9W
Gründau, *Germany* ... **31 E5** 50 10N 9 9 E
Grundy Center, *U.S.A.* ... **156 B4** 42 22N 92 47W
Grungedal, *Norway* ... **18 E4** 59 44N 7 43 E
Grünstadt, *Germany* ... **31 F4** 49 34N 8 9 E
Gruvberget, *Sweden* ... **16 C10** 61 6N 16 10 E
Gruver, *U.S.A.* ... **155 G4** 36 16N 101 24W
Gruyères, *Switz.* ... **32 C4** 46 35N 7 4 E
Gruža, *Serbia, Yug.* ... **50 C4** 43 54N 20 46 E
Gryazi, *Russia* ... **59 F10** 52 30N 39 58 E
Gryazovets, *Russia* ... **58 C11** 58 50N 40 10 E
Grybów, *Poland* ... **55 J7** 49 36N 20 55 E
Gryckbo, *Sweden* ... **16 D9** 60 40N 15 29 E
Gryfice, *Poland* ... **54 E2** 53 55N 15 13 E
Gryfino, *Poland* ... **55 E1** 53 16N 14 29 E
Gryfów Śląski, *Poland* ... **55 G2** 51 2N 15 24 E
Grythyttan, *Sweden* ... **16 E8** 59 41N 14 32 E
Gstaad, *Switz.* ... **32 D4** 46 28N 7 18 E
Gua Musang, *Malaysia* ... **87 K3** 4 53N 101 58 E
Guacanayabo, G. de, *Cuba* . **164 B4** 20 40N 77 20W
Guacara, *Venezuela* ... **168 A4** 10 14N 67 53W
Guachípas →, *Argentina* .. **174 B2** 25 40 S 65 30W
Guachiría →, *Colombia* ... **168 B3** 5 27N 70 36W
Guadajoz →, *Spain* ... **43 H6** 37 50N 4 51W
Guadalajara, *Mexico* ... **162 C4** 20 40N 103 20W
Guadalajara, *Spain* ... **40 E1** 40 37N 3 12W
Guadalajara □, *Spain* ... **40 E2** 40 47N 2 30W
Guadalcanal, *Solomon Is.* .. **133 M11** 9 32 S 160 12 E
Guadalcanal, *Spain* ... **43 G5** 38 5N 5 52W
Guadalén →, *Spain* ... **43 G7** 38 5N 3 32W
Guadales, *Argentina* ... **174 C2** 34 30 S 67 55W
Guadalete →, *Spain* ... **43 J4** 36 35N 6 13W
Guadalimar →, *Spain* ... **43 G7** 38 5N 3 28W
Guadalmena →, *Spain* ... **43 G8** 38 19N 2 56W
Guadalmez →, *Spain* ... **43 G5** 38 46N 5 4W
Guadalope →, *Spain* ... **40 D4** 41 15N 0 3W
Guadalquivir →, *Spain* ... **43 J4** 36 47N 6 22W
Guadalupe = Guadeloupe ■, *W. Indies* ... **165 C7** 16 20N 61 40W
Guadalupe, *Brazil* ... **170 C3** 6 44 S 43 47W
Guadalupe, *Mexico* ... **161 N10** 32 4N 116 32W
Guadalupe, *Spain* ... **43 F5** 39 27N 5 17W
Guadalupe, *U.S.A.* ... **161 L6** 34 59N 120 33W
Guadalupe →, *Mexico* ... **161 N10** 32 6N 116 51W
Guadalupe →, *U.S.A.* ... **155 L6** 28 27N 96 47W
Guadalupe, Sierra de, *Spain* **43 F5** 39 28N 5 30W
Guadalupe Bravos, *Mexico* . **162 A3** 31 20N 106 10W
Guadalupe I., *Pac. Oc.* ... **136 G8** 29 0N 118 50W
Guadalupe Peak, *U.S.A.* ... **159 L11** 31 50N 104 52W
Guadalupe y Calvo, *Mexico* **162 B3** 26 6N 106 58W
Guadarrama, Sierra de, *Spain* ... **42 E7** 41 0N 4 0W
Guadauta, *Georgia* ... **61 J5** 43 7N 40 32 E
Guadeloupe ■, *W. Indies* ... **165 C7** 16 20N 61 40W
Guadeloupe Passage, *W. Indies* ... **165 C7** 16 50N 62 15W
Guadiamar →, *Spain* ... **43 J4** 36 55N 6 24W
Guadiana →, *Portugal* ... **43 H3** 37 14N 7 22W
Guadiana Menor →, *Spain* . **43 H7** 37 56N 3 15W
Guadiaro →, *Spain* ... **43 J5** 36 17N 5 17W
Guadiato →, *Spain* ... **43 H5** 37 48N 5 5W
Guadiela →, *Spain* ... **40 E2** 40 22N 2 49W
Guadix, *Spain* ... **43 H7** 37 18N 3 11W
Guafo, Boca del, *Chile* ... **176 B2** 43 35 S 74 0W
Guafo, I., *Chile* ... **176 B2** 43 35 S 74 50W
Guainía □, *Colombia* ... **168 C4** 2 30N 69 0W
Guainía →, *Colombia* ... **168 C4** 2 1N 67 7W
Guaíra, *Brazil* ... **175 A5** 24 5 S 54 10W
Guaitecas, Is., *Chile* ... **176 B2** 44 0 S 74 30W
Guajará-Mirim, *Brazil* ... **173 C4** 10 50 S 65 20W
Guajira □, *Colombia* ... **168 A3** 11 30N 72 30W
Guajira, Pen. de la, *Colombia* ... **168 A3** 12 0N 72 0W
Gualaceo, *Ecuador* ... **168 D2** 2 54 S 78 47W
Gualán, *Guatemala* ... **164 C2** 15 8N 89 22W
Gualdo Tadino, *Italy* ... **45 E9** 43 14N 12 47 E
Gualeguay, *Argentina* ... **174 C4** 33 10 S 59 14W
Gualeguaychú, *Argentina* ... **174 C4** 33 3 S 59 31W
Gualicho, Salina, *Argentina* **176 B3** 40 25 S 65 20W
Gualjaina, *Argentina* ... **176 B2** 42 45 S 70 30W
Guam ■, *Pac. Oc.* ... **133 R15** 13 27N 144 45 E
Guamá, *Brazil* ... **170 B2** 1 37 S 47 29W
Guamá →, *Brazil* ... **170 B2** 1 29 S 48 30W
Guamblin, I., *Chile* ... **176 B1** 44 50 S 75 0W
Guaminí, *Argentina* ... **174 D3** 37 1 S 62 28W
Guamote, *Ecuador* ... **168 D2** 1 56 S 78 43W
Guampí, Sierra de, *Venezuela* ... **169 B4** 6 0N 65 35W
Guamúchil, *Mexico* ... **162 B3** 25 25N 108 3W
Guan Xian, *China* ... **76 B4** 31 2N 103 38 E
Guanabacoa, *Cuba* ... **164 B3** 23 8N 82 18W
Guanacaste, Cordillera del, *Costa Rica* ... **164 D2** 10 40N 85 4W
Guanaceví, *Mexico* ... **162 B3** 25 40N 106 0W
Guanahani = San Salvador, *Bahamas* ... **165 B5** 24 0N 74 40W
Guanajay, *Cuba* ... **164 B3** 22 56N 82 42W
Guanajuato, *Mexico* ... **162 C4** 21 0N 101 20W
Guanajuato □, *Mexico* ... **162 C4** 20 40N 101 20W
Guanambi, *Brazil* ... **171 D3** 14 13 S 42 47W
Guanare, *Venezuela* ... **168 B4** 8 42N 69 12W
Guanare →, *Venezuela* ... **168 B4** 8 13N 67 46W
Guandacol, *Argentina* ... **174 B2** 29 30 S 68 40W
Guane, *Cuba* ... **164 B3** 22 10N 84 7W
Guang'an, *China* ... **76 B6** 30 28N 106 35 E
Guangchang, *China* ... **77 D11** 26 50N 116 21 E
Guangde, *China* ... **77 B12** 30 54N 119 25 E
Guangdong □, *China* ... **77 F9** 23 0N 113 0 E
Guangfeng, *China* ... **77 C12** 28 20N 118 15 E
Guanghan, *China* ... **76 B5** 30 58N 104 17 E
Guanghua, *China* ... **77 A8** 32 22N 111 38 E
Guangji, *China* ... **77 C10** 29 52N 115 30 E
Guangling, *China* ... **74 E8** 39 47N 114 22 E
Guangning, *China* ... **77 F9** 23 40N 112 22 E
Guangrao, *China* ... **75 F10** 37 5N 118 25 E
Guangshun, *China* ... **76 D6** 26 8N 106 21 E
Guanguan Peninsula, *Phil.* . **81 H6** 6 50N 126 19 E
Guangwu, *China* ... **74 F3** 37 48N 105 57 E
Guangxi Zhuangzu Zizhiqu □, *China* ... **76 F7** 24 0N 109 0 E
Guangyuan, *China* ... **76 A5** 32 26N 105 51 E
Guangze, *China* ... **77 D11** 27 30N 117 12 E
Guangzhou, *China* ... **77 F9** 23 5N 113 10 E
Guanhães, *Brazil* ... **171 E3** 18 47 S 42 57W
Guanipa →, *Venezuela* ... **169 B5** 9 56N 62 26W
Guanling, *China* ... **76 E5** 25 56N 105 35 E
Guannan, *China* ... **75 G10** 34 8N 119 21 E
Guanta, *Venezuela* ... **169 A5** 10 14N 64 36W
Guantánamo, *Cuba* ... **165 B4** 20 10N 75 14W
Guantao, *China* ... **74 F8** 36 42N 115 25 E
Guanyang, *China* ... **77 E8** 25 30N 111 8 E
Guanyun, *China* ... **75 G10** 34 20N 119 18 E
Guapí, *Colombia* ... **168 C2** 2 36N 77 54W
Guápiles, *Costa Rica* ... **164 D3** 10 10N 83 46W
Guaporé →, *Brazil* ... **173 C4** 11 55 S 65 4W
Guaqui, *Bolivia* ... **172 D4** 16 41 S 68 54W
Guara, Sierra de, *Spain* ... **40 C4** 42 19N 0 15W
Guarabira, *Brazil* ... **170 C4** 6 51 S 35 29W
Guaranda, *Ecuador* ... **168 D2** 1 36 S 79 0W
Guarapari, *Brazil* ... **171 F3** 20 40 S 40 30W
Guarapuava, *Brazil* ... **171 G1** 25 20 S 51 30W
Guaratinguetá, *Brazil* ... **175 A6** 22 49 S 45 9W
Guaratuba, *Brazil* ... **175 B6** 25 53 S 48 38W
Guarda, *Portugal* ... **42 E3** 40 32N 7 20W
Guarda □, *Portugal* ... **42 E3** 40 40N 7 20W
Guardafui, C. = Asir, Ras, *Somali Rep.* ... **120 B4** 11 55N 51 10 E
Guardamar del Segura, *Spain* **41 G4** 38 5N 0 39W
Guardavalle, *Italy* ... **47 D9** 38 30N 16 30 E
Guárdia Sanframondi, *Italy* . **47 A7** 41 15N 14 36 E
Guardiagrele, *Italy* ... **45 F11** 42 11N 14 13 E
Guardo, *Spain* ... **42 C6** 42 47N 4 50W
Guareña, *Spain* ... **43 G4** 38 51N 6 6W
Guareña →, *Spain* ... **42 D5** 41 29N 5 23W
Guaria □, *Paraguay* ... **174 B4** 25 45 S 56 30W
Guárico □, *Venezuela* ... **168 B4** 8 40N 66 35W
Guarrojo →, *Colombia* ... **168 C3** 4 6N 70 42W
Guarujá, *Brazil* ... **175 A6** 24 2 S 46 25W
Guarus, *Brazil* ... **171 F3** 21 44 S 41 20W
Guasave, *Mexico* ... **162 B3** 25 34N 108 27W
Guascama, Pta., *Colombia* . **168 C2** 2 32N 78 24W
Guasdualito, *Venezuela* ... **168 B3** 7 15N 70 44W
Guasipati, *Venezuela* ... **169 B5** 7 28N 61 54W
Guasopa, *Papua N. G.* ... **132 E7** 9 12 S 152 56 E
Guastalla, *Italy* ... **44 D7** 44 55N 10 39 E
Guatemala, *Guatemala* ... **164 D1** 14 40N 90 22W
Guatemala ■, *Cent. Amer.* . **164 C1** 15 40N 90 30W
Guatire, *Venezuela* ... **168 A4** 10 28N 66 32W
Guaviare □, *Colombia* ... **168 C3** 2 0N 72 30W
Guaviare →, *Colombia* ... **168 C4** 4 3N 67 44W
Guaxupé, *Brazil* ... **175 A6** 21 10 S 47 5W
Guayabero →, *Colombia* .. **168 C3** 2 36N 72 47W
Guayama, *Puerto Rico* ... **165 C6** 17 59N 66 7W
Guayaneco, Arch., *Chile* ... **176 C1** 47 45 S 75 10W
Guayaquil, *Ecuador* ... **168 D2** 2 15 S 79 52W
Guayaquil, G. de, *Ecuador* . **168 D1** 3 10 S 81 0W
Guayaramerín, *Bolivia* ... **173 C4** 10 48 S 65 23W
Guayas →, *Ecuador* ... **168 D2** 2 36 S 79 52W
Guaymas, *Mexico* ... **162 B2** 27 59N 110 54W
Guazhou, *China* ... **77 A12** 32 17N 119 21 E
Guba, *Dem. Rep. of the Congo* . **119 E2** 10 38 S 26 27 E
Gubakha, *Russia* ... **62 B6** 58 52N 57 36 E
Gûbâl, Madîq, *Egypt* ... **106 B3** 27 30N 34 0 E
Gubam, *Papua N. G.* ... **132 E1** 8 39 S 141 53 E
Gubat, *Phil.* ... **80 E5** 12 55N 124 7 E
Gúbbio, *Italy* ... **45 E9** 43 21N 12 35 E
Guben, *Germany* ... **30 D10** 51 57N 14 42 E
Gubin, *Poland* ... **55 G1** 51 57N 14 43 E
Gubio, *Nigeria* ... **113 C7** 12 30N 12 42 E
Gubkin, *Russia* ... **59 G9** 51 17N 37 32 E
Guča, *Serbia, Yug.* ... **50 C4** 43 46N 20 15 E
Gudå, *Norway* ... **18 A8** 63 27N 11 26 E
Gudalur, *India* ... **95 J3** 11 30N 76 29 E
Gudata = Guadauta, *Georgia* ... **61 J5** 43 7N 40 32 E
Gudbrandsdalen, *Norway* .. **15 F14** 61 33N 10 10 E
Gudenå →, *Denmark* ... **17 H4** 56 29N 10 13 E
Gudermes, *Russia* ... **61 J8** 43 24N 46 5 E
Gudhjem, *Denmark* ... **17 J8** 55 12N 14 58 E
Gudivada, *India* ... **95 F5** 16 30N 81 3 E
Gudiyattam, *India* ... **95 H4** 12 57N 78 55 E
Gudur, *India* ... **95 G4** 14 12N 79 55 E
Gudvangen, *Norway* ... **18 D3** 60 52N 6 49 E
Guebwiller, *France* ... **27 E14** 47 55N 7 12 E
Guecho = Getxo, *Spain* ... **40 B2** 43 21N 2 59W
Guékédou, *Guinea* ... **112 D2** 8 40N 10 5W
Guelma, *Algeria* ... **111 A6** 36 25N 7 29 E
Guelph, *Canada* ... **140 D3** 43 35N 80 20W
Guemar, *Algeria* ... **111 B6** 33 30N 6 49 E
Guéméné-Penfao, *France* ... **26 E5** 47 38N 1 50W
Guéméné-sur-Scorff, *France* **26 D3** 48 4N 3 13W
Guéné, *Benin* ... **113 C5** 11 44N 3 16 E
Güepi, *Peru* ... **168 D2** 0 9 S 75 10W
Guer, *France* ... **26 E4** 47 54N 2 8W
Güer Aike, *Argentina* ... **176 D3** 51 39 S 69 35W
Guera Pk., *Chad* ... **109 F3** 11 55N 18 12 E
Guérande, *France* ... **26 E4** 47 20N 2 26W
Guercif, *Morocco* ... **111 B4** 34 14N 3 21W
Guéréda, *Chad* ... **109 F4** 14 31N 22 5 E
Guéret, *France* ... **27 F8** 46 11N 1 51 E
Guérigny, *France* ... **27 E10** 47 6N 3 10 E
Guerneville, *U.S.A.* ... **160 G4** 38 30N 123 0W
Guernica = Gernika-Lumo, *Spain* ... **40 B2** 43 19N 2 40W
Guernsey, *U.K.* ... **21 H5** 49 26N 2 35W
Guernsey, *U.S.A.* ... **154 D2** 42 19N 104 45W
Guerrara, *Oasis, Algeria* ... **111 B5** 32 51N 4 22 E
Guerrara, *Saoura, Algeria* .. **111 C4** 28 5N 0 8W
Guerrero □, *Mexico* ... **163 D5** 17 30N 100 0W
Guerzim, *Algeria* ... **111 C4** 29 39N 1 40W
Gueugnon, *France* ... **27 F11** 46 36N 4 4 E
Gueydan, *U.S.A.* ... **155 K8** 30 2N 92 31W
Gufuðalur, *Iceland* ... **11 B4** 65 34N 22 25W
Gügher, *Iran* ... **99 D8** 29 28N 56 27 E
Guglionesi, *Italy* ... **45 G11** 41 55N 14 55 E
Gui Jiang →, *China* ... **77 F8** 23 30N 111 15 E
Gui Xian, *China* ... **76 F7** 23 8N 109 35 E
Guia, *Canary Is.* ... **39 F4** 28 8N 15 38W
Guia de Isora, *Canary Is.* .. **39 F3** 28 12N 16 46W
Guia Lopes da Laguna, *Brazil* ... **175 A4** 21 26 S 56 7W
Guiana, *S. Amer.* ... **166 C4** 5 10N 60 40W
Guichi, *China* ... **77 B11** 30 39N 117 27 E
Guider, *Cameroon* ... **113 D7** 9 56N 13 57 E
Guidimouni, *Niger* ... **109 F1** 13 42N 9 31 E
Guiding, *China* ... **76 D6** 26 34N 107 11 E
Guidong, *China* ... **77 D9** 26 7N 113 57 E
Guidónia-Montecélio, *Italy* . **45 F9** 42 1N 12 45 E
Guiglo, *Ivory C.* ... **112 D3** 6 45N 7 30W
Guijá, *Mozam.* ... **117 C5** 24 27 S 33 0 E
Guijuelo, *Spain* ... **42 E5** 40 33N 5 40W
Guildford, *U.K.* ... **21 F7** 51 14N 0 34W
Guilford, *U.S.A.* ... **141 C6** 45 10N 69 23W
Guilin, *China* ... **77 E8** 25 18N 110 15 E
Guillaumes, *France* ... **29 D10** 44 5N 6 52 E
Guillestre, *France* ... **29 D10** 44 39N 6 40 E
Guilvinec, *France* ... **26 E2** 47 48N 4 17W
Güimar, *Canary Is.* ... **39 F3** 28 18N 16 24W
Guimarães, *Brazil* ... **170 B3** 2 9 S 44 42W
Guimarães, *Portugal* ... **42 D2** 41 28N 8 24W
Guimaras, *Phil.* ... **81 F4** 10 35N 122 37 E
Guimba, *Phil.* ... **80 D3** 15 40N 120 46 E
Guinda, *U.S.A.* ... **160 G4** 38 50N 122 12W
Guindulman, *Phil.* ... **81 G5** 9 46N 124 29 E
Guinea, *Africa* ... **104 F4** 8 0N 8 0 E
Guinea ■, *W. Afr.* ... **112 C2** 10 20N 11 30W
Guinea, Gulf of, *Atl. Oc.* .. **113 E5** 3 0N 2 30 E
Guinea-Bissau ■, *Africa* ... **112 C2** 12 0N 15 0W
Güines, *Cuba* ... **164 B3** 22 50N 82 0W
Guingamp, *France* ... **26 D3** 48 34N 3 10W
Guinobatan, *Phil.* ... **80 E4** 13 11N 123 36 E
Guiom, *Phil.* ... **81 F4** 11 59N 123 44 E
Guipavas, *France* ... **26 D2** 48 26N 4 29W
Guiping, *China* ... **77 F8** 23 21N 110 2 E
Guipúzcoa □, *Spain* ... **40 B2** 43 12N 2 15W
Guir, O. →, *Algeria* ... **111 B4** 31 29N 2 17W

Hymia 225

Horodok, Khmelnytskyy, Ukraine 59 H4 49 10N 26 34 E
Horodok, Lviv, Ukraine 59 H2 49 46N 23 32 E
Horodyshche, Ukraine 59 H6 49 17N 31 27 E
Horokhiv, Ukraine 59 G3 50 30N 24 45 E
Horovice, Czech Rep. 34 B6 49 48N 13 53 E
Horqin Youyi Qianqi, China 75 A12 46 5N 122 3 E
Horqueta, Paraguay 174 A4 23 15 S 56 55W
Horred, Sweden 17 G6 57 22N 12 28 E
Horse Cr. →, U.S.A. 153 H8 27 6N 81 58W
Horse Creek, U.S.A. 154 E3 41 57N 105 10W
Horse Is., Canada 141 B8 50 15N 55 50W
Horsefly L., Canada 142 C4 52 25N 121 0W
Horsens, Denmark 17 J3 55 52N 9 51 E
Horsham, Australia 128 D5 36 44 S 142 13 E
Horsham, U.K. 21 F7 51 4N 0 20W
Horšovský Týn, Czech Rep. 34 B5 49 31N 12 58 E
Horten, Norway 15 G14 59 25N 10 32 E
Hortense, U.S.A. 152 D8 31 20N 81 57W
Hortobágy →, Hungary 52 C6 47 30N 21 6 E
Horton, U.S.A. 154 F7 39 40N 95 32W
Horton →, Canada 138 B7 69 56N 126 52W
Horw, Switz. 33 B6 47 1N 8 19 E
Horwood, L., Canada 140 C3 48 5N 82 20W
Hosaina, Ethiopia 107 F4 7 30N 37 47 E
Hosdurga, India 95 H3 13 49N 76 17 E
Ḩoseynābād, Khuzestān, Iran 97 C6 32 45N 48 20 E
Ḩoseynābād, Kordestān, Iran 101 E12 35 33N 47 8 E
Hosford, U.S.A. 152 E5 30 23N 84 48W
Hoshangabad, India 92 H7 22 45N 77 45 E
Hoshiarpur, India 92 D6 31 30N 75 58 E
Hoskins, Papua N. G. 132 C6 5 29 S 150 27 E
Hosmer, U.S.A. 154 C5 45 34N 99 28W
Hososhima, Japan 70 E3 32 26N 131 40 E
Hospental, Switz. 33 C7 46 37N 8 34 E
Hospet, India 95 G3 15 15N 76 20 E
Hoste, I., Chile 176 E3 55 0 S 69 0W
Hostens, France 28 D3 44 30N 0 40W
Hot, Thailand 86 C2 18 8N 98 29 E
Hot Creek Range, U.S.A. 158 G6 38 40N 116 20W
Hot Springs, Ark., U.S.A. 155 H8 34 31N 93 3W
Hot Springs, S. Dak., U.S.A. 154 D3 43 26N 103 29W
Hotagen, Sweden 14 E16 63 50N 14 30 E
Hotan, China 72 C2 37 25N 79 55 E
Hotazel, S. Africa 116 D3 27 17 S 22 58 E
Hotchkiss, U.S.A. 159 G10 38 48N 107 43W
Hotham, C., Australia 124 B5 12 2 S 131 18 E
Hoting, Sweden 14 D17 64 8N 16 15 E
Hotolishti, Albania 50 E4 41 10N 20 25 E
Hotte, Massif de la, Haiti 165 C5 18 30N 73 45W
Hottentotsbaai, Namibia 116 D1 26 8 S 14 59 E
Houailou, N. Cal. 133 U19 21 17 S 165 38 E
Houat, Î. de, France 26 E4 47 24N 2 58W
Houck, U.S.A. 159 J9 35 20N 109 10W
Houdan, France 27 D8 48 48N 1 35 E
Houei Sai, Laos 86 B3 20 18N 100 26 E
Houeillès, France 28 D4 44 12N 0 2 E
Houffalize, Belgium 24 D5 50 8N 5 48 E
Houghton, U.S.A. 154 B10 47 7N 88 34W
Houghton L., U.S.A. 148 C3 44 21N 84 44W
Houhora Heads, N.Z. 130 A2 34 49 S 173 9 E
Houlton, U.S.A. 141 C6 46 8N 67 51W
Houma, U.S.A. 155 L9 29 36N 90 43W
Houndé, Burkina Faso 112 C4 11 34N 3 31W
Hourtin, France 28 C2 45 11N 1 4W
Hourtin-Carcans, Étang d', France 28 C2 45 10N 1 6W
Houston, Canada 142 C3 54 25N 126 39W
Houston, Fla., U.S.A. 152 E7 30 15N 82 54W
Houston, Mo., U.S.A. 155 G9 37 22N 91 58W
Houston, Tex., U.S.A. 155 L7 29 46N 95 22W
Houtman Abrolhos, Australia 125 E1 28 43 S 113 48 E
Hov, Norway 18 D7 60 42N 10 20 E
Hovd, Mongolia 72 B4 48 2N 91 37 E
Hovda, Norway 18 D6 60 53N 9 11 E
Hovden, Aust-Agder, Norway 18 E4 59 33N 7 22 E
Hovden, Sogn og Fjordane, Norway 18 C1 61 41N 4 52 E
Hove, U.K. 21 G7 50 50N 0 10W
Hovet, Norway 18 D5 60 38N 8 8 E
Hoveyzeh, Iran 97 D6 31 27N 48 4 E
Hovgaard Ø, Greenland 10 B9 79 55N 18 50W
Hovin, Norway 18 E6 59 51N 9 0 E
Hovmantorp, Sweden 17 H9 56 47N 15 7 E
Hövsgöl, Mongolia 74 C5 43 37N 109 39 E
Hövsgöl Nuur, Mongolia 72 A5 51 0N 100 30 E
Hovsta, Sweden 16 E9 59 22N 15 15 E
Howakil, Eritrea 107 D5 15 10N 40 16 E
Howar, Wadi →, Sudan 107 D2 17 30N 27 8 E
Howard, Australia 127 D5 25 16 S 152 32 E
Howard, Ga., U.S.A. 152 C5 32 36N 84 23W
Howard, Kans., U.S.A. 155 G6 37 28N 96 16W
Howard, Pa., U.S.A. 150 F7 41 1N 77 40W
Howard, S. Dak., U.S.A. 154 C6 44 1N 97 32W
Howard I., Australia 126 A2 12 10 S 135 24 E
Howard L., Canada 143 A7 62 15N 105 57W
Howe, U.S.A. 158 E7 43 48N 113 0W
Howe, C., Australia 129 D9 37 30 S 150 0 E
Howell, U.S.A. 157 B13 42 36N 83 56W
Howick, Canada 151 A11 45 11N 73 51W
Howick, N.Z. 130 C3 36 54 S 174 56 E
Howick, S. Africa 117 D5 29 28 S 30 14 E
Howick Group, Australia 126 A4 14 20 S 145 30 E
Howitt, L., Australia 127 D2 27 40 S 138 40 E
Howland I., Pac. Oc. 134 G10 0 48N 176 38W
Howley, Canada 141 C8 49 12N 57 2W
Howrah = Haora, India 93 H13 22 37N 88 20 E
Howth Hd., Ireland 23 C5 53 22N 6 3W
Höxter, Germany 30 D5 51 46N 9 22 E
Hoy, U.K. 22 C5 58 50N 3 15W
Hoya, Germany 30 C5 52 49N 9 8 E
Høyanger, Norway 15 F12 61 13N 6 4 E
Hoyerswerda, Germany 30 D10 51 26N 14 14 E
Hoylake, U.K. 20 D4 53 24N 3 10W
Hoyleton, Australia 128 C3 34 2 S 138 34 E
Hoyos, Spain 42 E4 40 9N 6 45W
Hpawlum, Burma 90 B7 27 12N 98 12 E
Hpettintha, Burma 90 C5 24 14N 95 23 E
Hpizow, Burma 90 B7 26 57N 98 24 E
Hradec Králové, Czech Rep. 34 A8 50 15N 15 50 E
Hrádek, Czech Rep. 35 C9 48 46N 16 16 E
Hrafnseyri, Iceland 11 B3 65 46N 23 28W
Hranice, Czech Rep. 35 B10 49 34N 17 45 E
Hrazdan, Armenia 61 K7 40 30N 44 46 E
Hrebenka, Ukraine 59 G7 50 9N 32 22 E
Hrífunes, Iceland 11 D8 63 38N 18 30W
Hrísey, Iceland 11 B8 66 0N 18 23W
Hrodna, Belarus 58 F2 53 42N 23 52 E
Hrodzyanka, Belarus 58 F5 53 31N 28 42 E
Hron →, Slovak Rep. 35 D11 47 49N 18 45 E
Hrubieszów, Poland 55 H10 50 49N 23 51 E
Hrubý Jeseník, Czech Rep. 35 A10 50 5N 17 10 E
Hruni, Iceland 11 C6 64 8N 20 16W
Hrvatska = Croatia ■, Europe 45 C13 45 20N 16 0 E
Hrymayliv, Ukraine 59 H4 49 20N 26 5 E
Hsenwi, Burma 90 D6 23 22N 97 55 E
Hsiamen = Xiamen, China 77 E12 24 25N 118 4 E
Hsian = Xi'an, China 74 G5 34 15N 109 0 E
Hsinchu, Taiwan 77 E13 24 48N 120 58 E
Hsinhailien = Lianyungang, China 75 G10 34 40N 119 11 E
Hsipaw, Burma 90 D6 22 37N 97 18 E
Hsüchou = Xuzhou, China 75 G9 34 18N 117 10 E
Htawgaw, Burma 90 C7 25 57N 98 23 E
Hu Xian, China 74 G5 34 8N 108 42 E
Hua Hin, Thailand 86 F2 12 34N 99 58 E
Hua Xian, Henan, China 74 G8 35 30N 114 30 E
Hua Xian, Shaanxi, China 74 G5 34 30N 109 48 E
Hua'an, China 77 E11 25 1N 117 32 E
Huacaya, Bolivia 173 E5 20 45 S 63 43W
Huacheng, China 77 E10 24 4N 115 37 E
Huachinera, Mexico 162 A3 30 9N 108 55W
Huacho, Peru 172 C2 11 10 S 77 35W
Huachón, Peru 172 C2 10 35 S 76 0W
Huade, China 74 D7 41 55N 113 59 E
Huadian, China 75 C14 43 0N 126 40 E
Huai He →, China 77 A12 33 0N 118 30 E
Huai Yot, Thailand 87 J2 7 45N 99 37 E
Huai'an, Hebei, China 74 D8 40 30N 114 20 E
Huai'an, Jiangsu, China 75 H10 33 30N 119 10 E
Huaibei, China 74 G9 34 0N 116 48 E
Huaide, China 75 C13 43 30N 124 40 E
Huaidezhen, China 75 C13 43 48N 124 50 E
Huaihua, China 76 D7 27 32N 109 57 E
Huaiji, China 77 F9 23 55N 112 12 E
Huainan, China 77 A11 32 38N 116 58 E
Huaining, China 77 B11 30 24N 116 40 E
Huairen, China 74 E7 39 48N 113 20 E
Huairou, China 74 D9 40 20N 116 35 E
Huaiyang, China 74 H8 33 40N 114 52 E
Huaiyuan, Anhui, China 75 H9 32 55N 117 10 E
Huaiyuan, Guangxi Zhuangzu, China 76 E7 24 31N 108 22 E
Huajianzi, China 75 D13 41 23N 125 20 E
Huajuapan de Leon, Mexico 163 D5 17 50N 97 48W
Hualalai, U.S.A. 145 D6 19 42N 155 52W
Hualapai Peak, U.S.A. 159 J7 35 5N 113 54W
Hualien, Taiwan 77 E13 24 0N 121 30 E
Huallaga →, Peru 172 B2 5 15 S 75 30W
Huallanca, Peru 172 B2 8 50 S 77 56W
Huamachuco, Peru 172 B2 7 50 S 78 5W
Huambo, Angola 115 E3 12 42 S 15 54 E
Huambo □, Angola 115 E3 13 0 S 16 0 E
Huan Jiang →, China 74 G5 34 28N 109 0 E
Huan Xian, China 74 F4 36 33N 107 7 E
Huancabamba, Peru 172 B2 5 10 S 79 15W
Huancane, Peru 172 D4 15 10 S 69 44W
Huancapi, Peru 172 C3 13 40 S 74 0W
Huancavelica, Peru 172 C2 12 50 S 75 5W
Huancavelica □, Peru 172 C3 13 0 S 75 0W
Huancayo, Peru 172 C2 12 5 S 75 12W
Huanchaca, Bolivia 172 E4 20 15 S 66 40W
Huanchaca, Serranía de, Bolivia 173 C5 14 30 S 60 39W
Huang Hai = Yellow Sea, China 75 G12 35 0N 123 0 E
Huang He →, China 75 F10 37 55N 118 50 E
Huang Xian, China 75 F11 37 38N 120 30 E
Huangchuan, China 77 A10 32 15N 115 10 E
Huanggang, China 77 B10 30 29N 114 52 E
Huangling, China 74 G5 35 34N 109 15 E
Huanglong, China 74 G5 35 30N 109 59 E
Huanglongtan, China 77 A8 32 40N 110 33 E
Huangmei, China 77 B10 30 5N 115 56 E
Huangpi, China 77 B10 30 50N 114 22 E
Huangping, China 76 D6 26 52N 107 54 E
Huangshi, China 77 B10 30 10N 115 3 E
Huangsongdian, China 75 C14 43 45N 127 25 E
Huangyan, China 77 C13 28 38N 121 19 E
Huangyangsi, China 77 D8 26 33N 111 39 E
Huaning, China 76 E4 24 17N 102 56 E
Huanjiang, China 76 E7 24 50N 108 18 E
Huanta, Peru 172 C3 12 55 S 74 20W
Huantai, China 75 F9 36 58N 117 56 E
Huánuco, Peru 172 B2 9 55 S 76 15W
Huánuco □, Peru 172 B2 9 55 S 76 14W
Huanuni, Bolivia 172 D4 18 16 S 66 51W
Huanzo, Cordillera de, Peru 172 C3 14 35 S 73 20W
Huaping, China 76 D3 26 46N 101 25 E
Huaral, Peru 172 C2 11 32 S 77 13W
Huaraz, Peru 172 B2 9 30 S 77 32W
Huari, Peru 172 B2 9 14 S 77 14W
Huarmey, Peru 172 C2 10 5 S 78 5W
Huarochirí, Peru 172 C2 12 9 S 76 15W
Huarocondo, Peru 172 C3 13 26 S 72 14W
Huarong, China 77 C9 29 29N 112 30 E
Huascarán, Peru 172 B2 9 8 S 77 36W
Huascarán, Nevado, Peru 172 B2 9 7 S 77 37W
Huasco, Chile 174 B1 28 30 S 71 15W
Huasco →, Chile 174 B1 28 27 S 71 13W
Huasna, U.S.A. 161 K6 35 6N 120 24W
Huatabampo, Mexico 162 B3 26 50N 109 50W
Huauchinango, Mexico 163 C5 20 11N 98 3W
Huautla de Jiménez, Mexico 163 D5 18 8N 96 51W
Huaxi, China 76 D6 26 25N 106 40 E
Huay Namota, Mexico 162 C4 21 56N 104 30W
Huayin, China 74 G6 34 35N 110 5 E
Huayllay, Peru 172 C2 11 3 S 76 21W
Huayuan, China 76 C7 28 37N 109 29 E
Huazhou, China 77 G8 21 33N 110 33 E
Hubbard, Iowa, U.S.A. 156 B3 42 18N 93 18W
Hubbard, Tex., U.S.A. 155 K6 31 51N 96 48W
Hubbart Pt., Canada 143 B10 59 21N 94 41W
Hubei □, China 77 B9 31 0N 112 0 E
Hubli-Dharwad = Dharwad, India 95 G2 15 22N 75 15 E
Huchang, N. Korea 75 D14 41 25N 127 2 E
Hucknall, U.K. 20 D6 53 3N 1 13W
Huddersfield, U.K. 20 D6 53 39N 1 47W
Hude, Germany 30 B4 53 7N 8 26 E
Hudi, Sudan 106 D3 17 43N 34 18 E
Hudiksvall, Sweden 16 C11 61 43N 17 10 E
Hudson, Canada 143 C10 50 6N 92 9W
Hudson, Fla., U.S.A. 153 G7 28 22N 82 42W
Hudson, Mass., U.S.A. 151 D13 42 23N 71 34W
Hudson, Mich., U.S.A. 157 C12 41 51N 84 21W
Hudson, N.Y., U.S.A. 151 D11 42 15N 73 46W
Hudson, Wis., U.S.A. 154 C8 44 58N 92 45W
Hudson, Wyo., U.S.A. 158 E9 42 54N 108 35W
Hudson →, U.S.A. 151 F10 40 42N 74 2W
Hudson Bay, N.W.T., Canada 139 C11 60 0N 86 0W
Hudson Bay, Sask., Canada 143 C8 52 51N 102 23W
Hudson Falls, U.S.A. 151 C11 43 18N 73 35W
Hudson Mts., Antarctica 7 D16 74 32 S 99 20W
Hudson Str., Canada 139 B13 62 0N 70 0W
Hudson's Hope, Canada 142 B4 56 0N 121 54W
Hudsonville, U.S.A. 157 B11 42 52N 85 52W
Hue, Vietnam 86 D6 16 30N 107 35 E
Huebra →, Spain 42 D4 41 2N 6 48W
Huechucuicui, Pta., Chile 176 B2 41 48 S 74 2W
Huedin, Romania 52 D8 46 52N 23 2 E
Huehuetenango, Guatemala 164 C1 15 20N 91 28W
Huejúcar, Mexico 162 C4 22 21N 103 13W
Huélamo, Spain 40 E3 40 17N 1 48W
Huelgoat, France 26 D3 48 22N 3 46W
Huelma, Spain 43 H7 37 39N 3 28W
Huelva, Spain 43 H4 37 18N 6 57W
Huelva □, Spain 43 H4 37 40N 7 0W
Huelva →, Spain 43 H5 37 27N 6 0W
Huentelauquén, Chile 174 C1 31 38 S 71 33W
Huércal-Overa, Spain 41 H3 37 23N 1 57W
Huerta, Sa. de la, Argentina 174 C2 31 10 S 67 30W
Huertas, C. de las, Spain 41 G4 38 21N 0 24W
Huerva →, Spain 40 D4 41 39N 0 52W
Huesca, Spain 40 C4 42 8N 0 25W
Huesca □, Spain 40 C5 42 20N 0 1 E
Huéscar, Spain 41 H2 37 44N 2 35W
Huetamo, Mexico 162 D4 18 36N 100 54W
Huete, Spain 40 E2 40 10N 2 43W
Huger, U.S.A. 152 B10 33 6N 79 48W
Hugh →, Australia 126 D1 25 1 S 134 1 E
Hughenden, Australia 126 C3 20 52 S 144 10 E
Hughes, Australia 125 F4 30 42 S 129 31 E
Hugli →, India 93 J13 21 56N 88 4 E
Hugo, U.S.A. 154 F3 39 8N 103 28W
Hugoton, U.S.A. 155 G4 37 11N 101 21W
Hui Xian, Gansu, China 74 H4 33 50N 106 4 E
Hui Xian, Henan, China 74 G7 35 27N 113 12 E
Hui'an, China 77 E12 25 1N 118 43 E
Hui'anbu, China 74 F4 37 28N 106 38 E
Huiarau Ra., N.Z. 130 E5 38 45 S 176 55 E
Huichang, China 77 E10 25 32N 115 45 E
Huichapán, Mexico 163 C5 20 24N 99 40W
Huidong, China 76 D4 26 34N 102 35 E
Huifa He →, China 75 C14 43 0N 127 50 E
Huíla, Angola 115 F2 15 4 S 13 32 E
Huila □, Colombia 168 C2 2 30N 75 45W
Huila, Nevado del, Colombia 168 C2 3 0N 76 0W
Huilai, China 77 F11 23 0N 116 18 E
Huili, China 76 D4 26 35N 102 17 E
Huimin, China 75 F9 37 27N 117 28 E
Huinan, China 75 C14 42 40N 126 2 E
Huinca Renancó, Argentina 174 C3 34 51 S 64 22W
Huining, China 74 G3 35 38N 105 0 E
Huinong, China 74 E4 39 5N 106 35 E
Huiroa, N.Z. 130 F3 39 15 S 174 30 E
Huishui, China 76 D6 26 7N 106 38 E
Huisne →, France 26 E7 47 59N 0 11 E
Huiting, China 74 G9 34 5N 116 5 E
Huitong, China 76 D7 26 51N 109 45 E
Huixtla, Mexico 163 D6 15 9N 92 28W
Huize, China 76 D4 26 24N 103 15 E
Huizhou, China 77 F10 23 0N 114 23 E
Hukou, China 77 C11 29 45N 116 21 E
Hukuntsi, Botswana 116 C3 23 58 S 21 45 E
Hula, Ethiopia 107 F4 6 33N 38 30 E
Ḩulayfā', Si. Arabia 96 E4 25 58N 40 45 E
Huld, Mongolia 74 B3 45 5N 105 30 E
Hulin He →, China 75 B12 45 0N 122 10 E
Hull = Kingston upon Hull, U.K. 20 D7 53 45N 0 21W
Hull, Canada 140 C4 45 25N 75 44W
Hull, Fla., U.S.A. 153 H8 27 7N 81 56W
Hull, Ill., U.S.A. 156 E5 39 43N 91 13W
Hull →, U.K. 20 D7 53 44N 0 20W
Hulst, Neths. 24 C4 51 17N 4 2 E
Hultsfred, Sweden 17 G9 57 30N 15 52 E
Hulun Nur, China 73 B6 49 0N 117 30 E
Hulyaypole, Ukraine 59 J9 47 45N 36 21 E
Humahuaca, Argentina 174 A2 23 10 S 65 25W
Humaitá, Brazil 173 B5 7 35 S 63 1W
Humaitá, Paraguay 174 B4 27 2 S 58 31W
Humansdorp, S. Africa 116 E3 34 2 S 24 46 E
Humansville, U.S.A. 156 G3 37 48N 93 35W
Humbe, Angola 115 F2 16 40 S 14 55 E
Humber →, U.K. 20 D7 53 42N 0 27W
Humbert River, Australia 124 C5 16 30 S 130 45 E
Humble, U.S.A. 155 L8 29 59N 93 18W
Humboldt, Canada 143 C7 52 15N 105 9W
Humboldt, Iowa, U.S.A. 156 B2 42 44N 94 13W
Humboldt, Tenn., U.S.A. 155 H10 35 50N 88 55W
Humboldt →, U.S.A. 158 F4 39 59N 118 36W
Humboldt Gletscher, Greenland 10 B4 79 30N 62 0W
Humboldt Mts., N.Z. 131 E3 44 30 S 168 15 E
Humbolt, Massif du, N. Cal. 133 U20 21 53 S 166 25 E
Hume, Calif., U.S.A. 160 J8 36 48N 118 54W
Hume, Mo., U.S.A. 156 F2 38 6N 94 34W
Hume, L., Australia 129 D7 36 0 S 147 5 E
Humenné, Slovak Rep. 35 C14 48 55N 21 50 E
Humeston, U.S.A. 156 D3 40 52N 93 30W
Hummelsta, Sweden 16 E10 59 34N 16 58 E
Hummelvik, Norway 18 A5 63 29N 8 19 E
Humpata, Angola 115 F2 15 2 S 13 24 E
Humphreys, Mt., U.S.A. 160 H8 37 17N 118 40W
Humphreys Peak, U.S.A. 159 J8 35 21N 111 41W
Humpolec, Czech Rep. 34 B8 49 31N 15 20 E
Humptulips, U.S.A. 160 C3 47 14N 123 57W
Humula, Australia 129 C7 35 30 S 147 46 E
Hūn, Libya 108 C3 29 2N 16 0 E
Hun Jiang →, China 75 D13 40 50N 125 38 E
Húnaflói, Iceland 11 B6 65 50N 20 50W
Hunan □, China 77 D9 27 30N 112 0 E
Húnavatnssýsla □, Iceland 11 B6 65 30N 20 25W
Hunchun, China 75 C16 42 52N 130 28 E
Hundested, Denmark 17 J5 55 58N 11 52 E
Hundorp, Norway 18 C7 61 33N 9 59 E
Hundred Mile House, Canada 142 C4 51 38N 121 18W
Hundvåg, Norway 18 E2 59 0N 5 43 E
Hunedoara, Romania 52 E7 45 40N 22 50 E
Hunedoara □, Romania 52 E7 45 50N 22 54 E
Hünfeld, Germany 30 E5 50 39N 9 46 E
Hung Yen, Vietnam 86 B6 20 39N 106 4 E
Hunga, Tonga 133 P13 18 41 S 174 7W
Hunga Ha'api, Tonga 133 Q13 20 41 S 175 7W
Hungary ■, Europe 35 D12 47 20N 19 20 E
Hungary, Plain of, Europe 12 F10 47 0N 20 0 E
Hungerford, Australia 127 D3 28 58 S 144 24 E
Hŭngnam, N. Korea 75 E14 39 49N 127 45 E
Huni Valley, Ghana 112 D4 5 33N 1 56W
Hunneberg, Sweden 17 F6 58 18N 12 30 E
Hunnebostrand, Sweden 17 F5 58 27N 11 18 E
Hunsberge, Namibia 116 D2 27 45 S 17 12 E
Hunsrück, Germany 31 F3 49 56N 7 27 E
Hunstanton, U.K. 20 E8 52 56N 0 29 E
Hunsur, India 95 H3 12 16N 76 16 E
Hunte →, Germany 30 B4 53 14N 8 28 E
Hunter, N.Z. 131 E6 44 36 S 171 2 E
Hunter, N. Dak., U.S.A. 154 B6 47 12N 97 13W
Hunter, N.Y., U.S.A. 151 D10 42 13N 74 13W
Hunter →, N.Z. 131 E4 44 21 S 169 27 E
Hunter, C., Solomon Is. 133 M10 9 48 S 159 50 E
Hunter I., Australia 126 G3 40 30 S 144 45 E
Hunter I., Canada 142 C3 51 55N 128 0W
Hunter Mts., N.Z. 131 F2 45 43 S 167 25 E
Hunter Ra., Australia 129 B9 32 45 S 150 15 E
Hunters Road, Zimbabwe 119 F2 19 9 S 29 49 E
Hunterville, N.Z. 130 F4 39 56 S 175 35 E
Huntingburg, U.S.A. 157 F10 38 18N 86 57W
Huntingdon, Canada 140 C5 45 6N 74 10W
Huntingdon, U.K. 21 E7 52 20N 0 11W
Huntingdon, U.S.A. 150 F6 40 30N 78 1W
Huntington, Ind., U.S.A. 157 D11 40 53N 85 30W
Huntington, N.Y., U.S.A. 151 F11 40 52N 73 26W
Huntington, Oreg., U.S.A. 158 D5 44 21N 117 16W
Huntington, Utah, U.S.A. 158 G8 39 20N 110 58W
Huntington, W. Va., U.S.A. 148 F4 38 25N 82 27W
Huntington Beach, U.S.A. 161 M9 33 40N 118 5W
Huntington Park, U.S.A. 159 K4 33 58N 118 15W
Huntley, U.S.A. 157 B8 42 10N 88 26W
Huntly, N.Z. 130 D4 37 34 S 175 11 E
Huntly, U.K. 22 D6 57 27N 2 47W
Huntsville, Canada 140 C4 45 20N 79 14W
Huntsville, Ala., U.S.A. 149 H2 34 44N 86 35W
Huntsville, Mo., U.S.A. 156 E4 39 26N 92 33W
Huntsville, Tex., U.S.A. 155 K7 30 43N 95 33W
Hunyani →, Zimbabwe 119 F3 15 57 S 30 39 E
Hunyuan, China 74 E7 39 42N 113 42 E
Hunza →, India 93 B6 35 54N 74 20 E
Huo Xian, China 74 F6 36 36N 111 42 E
Huon G., Papua N. G. 132 D4 7 0 S 147 30 E
Huon Pen., Papua N. G. 132 D4 6 20 S 147 30 E
Huong Hoa, Vietnam 86 D6 16 37N 106 45 E
Huong Khe, Vietnam 86 C5 18 13N 105 41 E
Huonville, Australia 126 G4 43 0 S 147 5 E
Huoqiu, China 77 A11 32 20N 116 12 E
Huoshan, Anhui, China 77 A12 32 28N 118 30 E
Huoshan, Anhui, China 77 B11 31 25N 116 20 E
Hupeh = Hubei □, China 77 B9 31 0N 112 0 E
Ḩūr, Iran 97 D8 30 50N 57 7 E
Hurbanovo, Slovak Rep. 35 D11 47 51N 18 11 E
Hure Qi, China 75 C11 42 45N 121 45 E
Hurezani, Romania 53 F8 44 49N 23 40 E
Hurghada, Egypt 106 B3 27 15N 33 50 E
Hurley, N. Mex., U.S.A. 159 K9 32 42N 108 8W
Hurley, Wis., U.S.A. 154 B9 46 27N 90 11W
Huron, Calif., U.S.A. 160 J6 36 12N 120 6W
Huron, Ohio, U.S.A. 150 E2 41 24N 82 33W
Huron, S. Dak., U.S.A. 154 C5 44 22N 98 13W
Huron, L., U.S.A. 150 B2 44 30N 82 40W
Hurricane, U.S.A. 159 H7 37 11N 113 17W
Hurso, Ethiopia 107 F5 9 35N 41 33 E
Hurstboro, U.S.A. 152 C4 32 15N 85 25W
Hurunui →, N.Z. 131 C8 42 54 S 173 18 E
Hurup, Denmark 17 H2 56 46N 8 25 E
Húsafell, Iceland 11 C6 64 42N 20 53W
Húsavík, Iceland 11 A9 66 3N 17 21W
Huşi, Romania 53 D13 46 41N 28 7 E
Huskvarna, Sweden 17 G8 57 47N 14 15 E
Husnes, Norway 18 E2 59 52N 5 45 E
Hussar, Canada 142 C6 51 3N 112 41W
Hustad, Norway 18 B4 62 57N 7 6 E
Hustadvika, Norway 14 E12 63 0N 7 0 E
Hustopeče, Czech Rep. 35 C9 48 57N 16 43 E
Husum, Germany 30 A5 54 28N 9 4 E
Husum, Sweden 16 A13 63 21N 19 12 E
Hutchinson, Kans., U.S.A. 155 F6 38 5N 97 56W
Hutchinson, Minn., U.S.A. 154 C7 44 54N 94 22W
Ḩūth, Yemen 98 C3 16 14N 43 58 E
Hutsonville, U.S.A. 157 E9 39 7N 87 40W
Hüttenberg, Austria 34 E7 46 56N 14 33 E
Huttig, U.S.A. 155 J8 33 2N 92 11W
Hutton, Mt., Australia 127 D4 25 51 S 148 20 E
Huttwil, Switz. 32 B5 47 7N 7 50 E
Huwun, Ethiopia 107 G5 4 23N 40 6 E
Huy, Belgium 24 D5 50 31N 5 15 E
Hvalpsund, Denmark 17 H3 56 42N 9 11 E
Hvammsfjörður, Iceland 11 B4 65 4N 22 5W
Hvammstangi, Iceland 11 B6 65 24N 20 57W
Hvammur, Dalasýsla, Iceland 11 B5 65 13N 21 49W
Hvammur, Mýrasýsla, Iceland 11 C5 64 50N 21 21W
Hvammur, Skagafjarðarsýsla, Iceland 11 B7 65 53N 19 51W
Hvanneyri, Iceland 11 C5 64 34N 21 36W
Hvar, Croatia 45 E13 43 11N 16 28 E
Hvarski Kanal, Croatia 45 E13 43 15N 16 35 E
Hveragerði, Iceland 11 C5 64 0N 21 12W
Hvítá →, Iceland 11 C5 64 30N 21 58W
Hvítárvatn, Iceland 11 C7 64 37N 19 50W
Hvittingfoss, Norway 18 E7 59 29N 10 0 E
Hvolsvöllur, Iceland 11 D6 63 45N 20 14W
Hwachon-chosuji, S. Korea 75 E14 38 5N 127 50 E
Hwang Ho = Huang He →, China 75 F10 37 55N 118 50 E
Hwange, Zimbabwe 119 F2 18 18 S 26 30 E
Hwange Nat. Park, Zimbabwe 116 B4 19 0 S 26 30 E
Hwekum, Burma 90 B5 26 7N 95 22 E
Hyannis, U.S.A. 154 E4 42 0N 101 46W
Hyargas Nuur, Mongolia 72 B4 49 0N 93 0 E
Hybo, Sweden 16 C10 61 49N 16 15 E
Hyde, N.Z. 131 F5 45 18 S 170 16 E
Hyde Park, Guyana 169 B6 6 30N 58 16W
Hyden, Australia 125 F2 32 24 S 118 53 E
Hyderabad, India 94 F4 17 22N 78 29 E
Hyderabad, Pakistan 91 D3 25 23N 68 24 E
Hyen, Norway 18 C2 61 44N 5 56 E
Hyères, France 29 E10 43 8N 6 9 E
Hyères, Îs. d', France 29 F10 43 0N 6 20 E
Hyesan, N. Korea 75 D15 41 20N 128 10 E
Hyland →, Canada 142 B3 59 52N 128 12W
Hylestad, Norway 18 E4 59 6N 7 29 E
Hyllestad, Norway 18 C2 61 10N 5 17 E
Hyltebruk, Sweden 17 H7 56 59N 13 15 E
Hymia, India 93 C8 33 40N 78 2 E

Ituiutaba 227

Ingul → = Inhul →, Ukraine 59 J7 46 50N 32 0 E
Ingulec = Inhulec, Ukraine 59 J7 47 42N 33 14 E
Ingulets → = Inhulets →, Ukraine 59 J7 46 46N 32 47 E
Inguri → = Enguri →, Georgia 61 J5 42 27N 41 38 E
Ingushetia □, Russia 61 J7 43 20N 44 50 E
Ingwavuma, S. Africa 117 D5 27 9 S 31 59 E
Inhaca, I., Mozam. 117 D5 26 1 S 32 57 E
Inhafenga, Mozam. 117 C5 20 36 S 33 53 E
Inhambane, Mozam. 117 C6 23 54 S 35 30 E
Inhambane □, Mozam. 117 C5 22 30 S 34 20 E
Inhambupe, Brazil 171 D4 11 47 S 38 21W
Inhaminga, Mozam. 119 F4 18 26 S 35 0 E
Inharrime, Mozam. 117 C6 24 30 S 35 0 E
Inharrime →, Mozam. 117 C6 24 30 S 35 0 E
Inhisar, Turkey 49 A12 40 3N 30 23 E
Inhul →, Ukraine 59 J7 46 50N 32 0 E
Inhulec, Ukraine 59 J7 47 42N 33 14 E
Inhulets →, Ukraine 59 J7 46 46N 32 47 E
Inhuma, Brazil 170 C3 6 40 S 41 42W
Inhumas, Brazil 171 E2 16 22 S 49 30W
Iniesta, Spain 41 F3 39 27N 1 45W
Ining = Yining, China 64 E9 43 58N 81 10 E
Inini □, Fr. Guiana 169 C7 4 0N 53 0W
Inírida →, Colombia 168 C4 3 55N 67 52W
Inishbofin, Ireland 23 C1 53 37N 10 13W
Inisheer, Ireland 23 C2 53 3N 9 32W
Inishfree B., Ireland 23 A3 55 4N 8 23W
Inishkea North, Ireland 23 B1 54 9N 10 11W
Inishkea South, Ireland 23 B1 54 7N 10 12W
Inishmaan, Ireland 23 C2 53 5N 9 35W
Inishmore, Ireland 23 C2 53 8N 9 45W
Inishowen Pen., Ireland 23 A4 55 14N 7 15W
Inishshark, Ireland 23 C1 53 37N 10 16W
Inishturk, Ireland 23 C1 53 42N 10 7W
Inishvickillane, Ireland 23 D1 52 3N 10 37W
Injune, Australia 127 D4 25 53 S 148 32 E
Inklin, Canada 142 B2 58 56N 133 5W
Inklin →, Canada 142 B2 58 50N 133 10W
Inkom, U.S.A. 158 E7 42 48N 112 15W
Inle L., Burma 90 E6 20 30N 96 58 E
Inn →, Austria 34 C6 48 35N 13 28 E
Innamincka, Australia 127 D3 27 44 S 140 46 E
Innbygda, Norway 18 C9 61 19N 12 17 E
Inner Hebrides, U.K. 22 E2 57 0N 6 30W
Inner Mongolia = Nei Monggol Zizhiqu □, China 74 D7 42 0N 112 0 E
Inner Sound, U.K. 22 D3 57 30N 5 55W
Innerkip, Canada 150 C4 43 13N 80 42W
Innerkirchen, Switz. 32 C6 46 43N 8 14 E
Innetalling I., Canada 140 A4 56 0N 79 0W
Innisfail, Australia 126 B4 17 33 S 146 5 E
Innisfail, Canada 142 C6 52 0N 113 57W
In'no-shima, Japan 70 C5 34 19N 133 10 E
Innsbruck, Austria 34 D4 47 16N 11 23 E
Innviertel, Austria 34 C6 48 15N 13 15 E
Innvik, Norway 18 C3 61 51N 6 37 E
Inny →, Ireland 23 C4 53 30N 7 50W
Ino, Japan 70 D5 33 33N 133 26 E
Inocência, Brazil 171 E1 19 47 S 51 48W
Inongo, Dem. Rep. of the Congo 114 C3 1 55 S 18 30 E
Inoni, Congo 114 C3 3 4 S 15 39 E
Inönü, Turkey 49 B12 39 48N 30 9 E
Inoucdjouac = Inukjuak, Canada 139 C12 58 25N 78 15W
Inowrocław, Poland 55 F5 52 50N 18 12 E
Inpundong, N. Korea 75 D14 41 25N 126 34 E
Inquisivi, Bolivia 172 D4 16 50 S 67 10W
Ins, Switz. 32 B4 47 1N 7 7 E
Inscription, C., Australia 125 E1 25 29 S 112 59 E
Insein, Burma 90 G6 16 50N 96 5 E
Insjön, Sweden 16 D9 60 41N 15 6 E
Ińsko, Poland 54 E2 53 25N 15 32 E
Însurăţei, Romania 53 F12 44 50N 27 40 E
Inta, Russia 56 A11 66 5N 60 8 E
Intendente Alvear, Argentina 174 D3 35 12 S 63 32W
Intepe, Turkey 49 A8 40 1N 26 20 E
Intercession City, U.S.A. 153 G8 28 16N 81 31W
Interior, U.S.A. 154 D4 43 44N 101 59W
Interlachen, U.S.A. 153 F8 29 37N 81 53W
Interlaken, Switz. 32 C5 46 41N 7 50 E
International Falls, U.S.A. 154 A8 48 36N 93 25W
Intiyaco, Argentina 174 B3 28 43 S 60 5W
Întorsura Buzăului, Romania 53 E11 45 41N 26 2 E
Intragna, Switz. 33 D7 46 11N 8 42 E
Intutu, Peru 168 D3 3 32 S 74 48W
Inubō-Zaki, Japan 71 B12 35 42N 140 52 E
Inukjuak, Canada 139 C12 58 25N 78 15W
Inútil, B., Chile 176 D2 53 30 S 70 15W
Inuvik, Canada 138 B6 68 16N 133 40W
Inuyama, Japan 71 B8 35 23N 136 56 E
Inveraray, U.K. 22 E3 56 14N 5 5W
Inverbervie, U.K. 22 E6 56 51N 2 17W
Invercargill, N.Z. 131 G3 46 24 S 168 24 E
Inverclyde □, U.K. 22 F4 55 55N 4 49W
Inverell, Australia 127 D5 29 45 S 151 8 E
Invergordon, U.K. 22 D4 57 41N 4 10W
Inverleigh, Australia 128 E6 38 6 S 144 3 E
Invermere, Canada 142 C5 50 30N 116 2W
Inverness, Canada 141 C7 46 15N 61 19W
Inverness, U.K. 22 D4 57 29N 4 13W
Inverness, Ala., U.S.A. 152 C4 32 1N 85 45W
Inverness, Fla., U.S.A. 149 L4 28 50N 82 20W
Inverurie, U.K. 22 D6 57 17N 2 23W
Inverway, Australia 124 C4 17 50 S 129 38 E
Investigator Group, Australia 127 E1 34 45 S 134 20 E
Investigator Str., Australia 128 C2 35 30 S 137 0 E
Inya, Russia 64 D9 50 28N 86 37 E
Inyanga, Zimbabwe 119 F3 18 12 S 32 40 E
Inyangani, Zimbabwe 119 F3 18 5 S 32 50 E
Inyantue, Zimbabwe 119 F2 18 30 S 26 40 E
Inyo Mts., U.S.A. 159 H5 36 40N 118 0W
Inyokern, U.S.A. 161 K9 35 39N 117 49W
Inywa, Burma 90 D6 23 56N 96 17 E
Inza, Russia 60 D8 53 55N 46 25 E
Inzer, Russia 62 D6 54 14N 57 34 E
Inzhavino, Russia 60 D6 52 22N 42 30 E
Iō-Jima, Japan 69 J5 30 48N 130 18 E
Ioánnina, Greece 48 B2 39 42N 20 47 E
Ioánnina □, Greece 48 B2 39 39N 20 57 E
Iola, U.S.A. 155 G7 37 55N 95 24W
Ioma, Papua N. G. 132 E4 8 19 S 147 52 E
Ion Corvin, Romania 53 F12 44 7N 27 50 E
Iona, U.K. 22 E2 56 20N 6 25W
Ione, Calif., U.S.A. 160 G6 38 21N 120 56W
Ione, Wash., U.S.A. 158 B5 48 45N 117 25W
Ionia, U.S.A. 157 B11 42 59N 85 4W
Ionian Sea, Medit. S. 12 H9 37 30N 17 30 E
Iónioi Nísoi □, Greece 48 C2 38 40N 20 0 E
Íos, Greece 49 E7 36 41N 25 20 E
Iowa □, U.S.A. 154 D8 42 18N 93 30W
Iowa →, U.S.A. 156 C5 41 10N 91 1W
Iowa City, U.S.A. 156 C5 41 40N 91 32W
Iowa Falls, U.S.A. 156 B3 42 31N 93 16W
Ipala, Tanzania 118 C3 4 30 S 32 52 E
Ipameri, Brazil 171 E2 17 44 S 48 9W
Iparía, Peru 172 B3 9 17 S 74 29W
Ipáti, Greece 48 C4 38 52N 22 14 E
Ipatinga, Brazil 171 E3 19 32 S 42 30W
Ipatovo, Russia 61 H6 45 45N 42 50 E
Ipel' →, Europe 35 D11 47 48N 18 53 E
Ipiales, Colombia 168 C2 0 50N 77 37W
Ipiaú, Brazil 171 D4 14 8 S 39 44W
Ipil, Phil. 81 H4 7 47N 122 35 E
Ipin = Yibin, China 76 C5 28 45N 104 32 E
Ipirá, Brazil 171 D4 12 10 S 39 44W
Ipiranga, Brazil 168 D4 3 13 S 65 57W
Ípiros □, Greece 48 B2 39 30N 20 30 E
Ipixuna, Brazil 172 B3 7 0 S 71 40W
Ipixuna →, Amazonas, Brazil 172 B3 7 11 S 71 51W
Ipixuna →, Amazonas, Brazil 173 B5 5 45 S 63 2W
Ipoh, Malaysia 87 K3 4 35N 101 5 E
Iporá, Brazil 171 D1 11 23 S 50 40W
Ippy, C.A.R. 114 A4 6 5N 21 7 E
Ipsala, Turkey 51 F10 40 55N 26 23 E
Ipsárion, Óros, Greece 51 F8 40 40N 24 40 E
Ipswich, Australia 127 D5 27 35 S 152 40 E
Ipswich, U.K. 21 E9 52 4N 1 10 E
Ipswich, Mass., U.S.A. 151 D14 42 41N 70 50W
Ipswich, S. Dak., U.S.A. 154 C5 45 27N 99 2W
Ipu, Brazil 170 B3 4 23 S 40 44W
Ipueiras, Brazil 170 B3 4 33 S 40 43W
Ipupiara, Brazil 171 D3 11 49 S 42 37W
Iqaluit, Canada 139 B13 63 44N 68 31W
Iquique, Chile 172 E3 20 19 S 70 5W
Iquitos, Peru 168 D3 3 45 S 73 10W
Irabu-Jima, Japan 69 M2 24 50N 125 10 E
Iracoubo, Fr. Guiana 169 B7 5 30N 53 10W
Īrafshān, Iran 97 E9 26 42N 61 56 E
Irahuan, Phil. 81 G2 9 48N 118 41 E
Iráklia, Kikládhes, Greece 49 E7 36 50N 25 28 E
Iráklia, Sérrai, Greece 50 E7 41 10N 23 16 E
Iráklion, Greece 38 D7 35 20N 25 12 E
Iráklion □, Greece 38 D7 35 10N 25 10 E
Irako-Zaki, Japan 71 C9 34 35N 137 1 E
Irala, Paraguay 175 B5 25 55 S 54 35W
Iramba □, Tanzania 118 C3 4 30 S 34 30 E
Iran ■, Asia 97 C7 33 0N 53 0 E
Iran, Gunung-Gunung, Malaysia 85 B4 2 20N 114 50 E
Iran, Plateau of, Asia 66 F9 32 0N 55 0 E
Iran Ra. = Iran, Gunung-Gunung, Malaysia 85 B4 2 20N 114 50 E
Iranamadu Tank, Sri Lanka 95 K5 9 23N 80 29 E
Īrānshahr, Iran 97 E9 27 15N 60 40 E
Irapa, Venezuela 169 A5 10 34N 62 35W
Irapuato, Mexico 162 C4 20 40N 101 30W
Iraq ■, Asia 101 F10 33 0N 44 0 E
Irarrar, O. →, Mali 111 E5 20 0N 1 30 E
Irati, Brazil 175 B5 25 25 S 50 38W
Irbes saurums, Latvia 54 A9 57 45N 22 5 E
Irbid, Jordan 103 C4 32 35N 35 48 E
Irbid □, Jordan 103 C5 32 15N 36 35 E
Irbit, Russia 62 C9 57 41N 63 3 E
Irebu, Dem. Rep. of the Congo 114 C3 0 40 S 17 46 E
Irecê, Brazil 170 D3 11 18 S 41 52W
Iregua →, Spain 40 C7 42 27N 2 24 E
Ireland ■, Europe 23 C4 53 50N 7 52W
Irele, Nigeria 113 D6 7 40N 5 40 E
Iremel, Gora, Russia 62 D7 54 33N 58 50 E
Ireng →, Brazil 169 C6 3 33N 59 51W
Irgiz, Bolshaya →, Russia 60 D9 52 10N 49 10 E
Irhârharene, Algeria 111 C6 27 37N 7 30 E
Irharrhar, O. →, Algeria 111 C6 28 3N 6 15 E
Irherm, Morocco 110 B3 30 7N 8 18W
Irhil Mgoun, Morocco 110 B3 31 30N 6 28W
Irhyangdong, N. Korea 75 D15 41 15N 129 30 E
Iri, S. Korea 75 G14 35 59N 127 0 E
Irian Jaya □, Indonesia 83 B5 4 0 S 137 0 E
Iriba, Chad 109 E4 15 7N 22 15 E
Irid, Mt., Phil. 80 D3 14 47N 121 19 E
Irié, Guinea 112 D3 8 15N 9 10W
Iriga, Phil. 80 E4 13 25N 123 25 E
Iriklinskiy, Russia 62 F7 51 39N 58 38 E
Iriklinskoye Vdkhr., Russia 62 F7 52 0N 59 0 E
Iringa, Tanzania 118 D4 7 48 S 35 43 E
Iringa □, Tanzania 118 D4 7 48 S 35 43 E
Irinjalakuda, India 95 J3 10 21N 76 14 E
Iriomote-Jima, Japan 69 M1 24 19N 123 48 E
Iriona, Honduras 164 C2 15 57N 85 11W
Iriri →, Brazil 169 D7 3 52 S 52 37W
Iriri Novo →, Brazil 173 B7 8 46 S 53 22W
Irish Republic ■, Europe 23 C3 53 0N 8 0W
Irish Sea, U.K. 20 D3 53 38N 4 48W
Irkeshtam, Kyrgyzstan 63 D6 39 41N 73 55 E
Irkutsk, Russia 65 D11 52 18N 104 20 E
Irlığanlı, Turkey 49 D11 37 53N 29 12 E
Irma, Canada 143 C6 52 55N 111 14W
Irō-Zaki, Japan 71 C10 34 36N 138 51 E
Iroise, Mer d', France 26 D2 48 15N 4 45W
Iron Baron, Australia 128 B2 32 58 S 137 11 E
Iron City, U.S.A. 152 D5 31 1N 84 49W
Iron Gate = Portile de Fier, Europe 52 F7 44 44N 22 30 E
Iron Knob, Australia 128 B2 32 46 S 137 8 E
Iron Mountain, U.S.A. 148 C1 45 49N 88 4W
Iron Ra., Australia 126 A3 12 46 S 143 16 E
Iron River, U.S.A. 154 B10 46 6N 88 39W
Irondequoit, U.S.A. 150 C7 43 13N 77 35W
Ironstone Kopje, Botswana 116 D3 25 17 S 24 5 E
Ironton, Mo., U.S.A. 155 G9 37 36N 90 38W
Ironton, Ohio, U.S.A. 148 F4 38 32N 82 41W
Ironwood, U.S.A. 154 B9 46 27N 90 9W
Iroquois →, U.S.A. 157 C9 41 5N 87 49W
Iroquois Falls, Canada 140 C3 48 46N 80 41W
Irosin, Phil. 80 E5 12 42N 124 2 E
Irpin, Ukraine 59 G6 50 30N 30 15 E
Irrara Cr. →, Australia 127 D4 29 35 S 145 31 E
Irrawaddy □, Burma 90 G5 17 0N 95 0 E
Irrawaddy →, Burma 90 G5 15 50N 95 6 E
Irsina, Italy 47 B9 40 45N 16 14 E
Irtysh →, Russia 64 C7 61 4N 68 52 E
Irumu, Dem. Rep. of the Congo 118 B2 1 32N 29 53 E
Irún, Spain 40 B3 43 20N 1 52W
Irunea = Pamplona, Spain 40 C3 42 48N 1 38W
Irurzun, Spain 40 C3 42 55N 1 50W
Irvine, Canada 143 D6 49 57N 110 16W
Irvine, U.K. 22 F4 55 37N 4 41W
Irvine, Calif., U.S.A. 161 M9 33 41N 117 46W
Irvine, Ky., U.S.A. 157 G13 37 42N 83 58W
Irvinestown, U.K. 23 B4 54 28N 7 39W
Irving, U.S.A. 155 J6 32 49N 96 56W
Irvington, U.S.A. 157 G10 37 53N 86 17W
Irvona, U.S.A. 150 F6 40 46N 78 33W
Irwin →, Australia 125 E1 29 15 S 114 54 E
Irwinton, U.S.A. 152 C6 32 49N 83 10W
Irwinville, U.S.A. 152 D6 31 39N 83 23W
Irymple, Australia 128 C5 34 14 S 142 8 E
Is-sur-Tille, France 27 E12 47 30N 5 8 E
Isa, Nigeria 113 C6 13 14N 6 24 E
Isaac →, Australia 126 C4 22 55 S 149 20 E
Isabel, U.S.A. 154 C4 45 24N 101 26W
Isabela, Phil. 81 F4 10 12N 122 59 E
Isabela □, Phil. 80 C4 17 0N 122 0 E
Isabela, I., Mexico 162 C3 21 51N 105 55W
Isabelia, Cord., Nic. 164 D2 13 30N 85 25W
Isabella, Phil. 81 H4 6 40N 122 10 E
Isabella Ra., Australia 124 D3 21 0 S 121 4 E
Isaccea, Romania 53 E13 45 16N 28 28 E
Ísafjarðardjúp, Iceland 11 A3 66 10N 23 0W
Ísafjarðarsýsla □, Iceland 11 B3 66 0N 23 0W
Ísafjörður, Iceland 11 A3 66 5N 23 9W
Isagarh, India 92 G7 24 48N 77 51 E
Isahaya, Japan 70 E2 32 52N 130 2 E
Isaka, Tanzania 118 C3 3 56 S 32 59 E
Isakly, Russia 60 C10 54 8N 51 32 E
Işalniţa, Romania 53 F8 44 24N 23 44 E
Isana = Içana →, Brazil 168 C4 0 26N 67 19W
Isangi, Dem. Rep. of the Congo 114 B4 0 52N 24 10 E
Isar →, Germany 31 G8 48 48N 12 57 E
Isarco →, Italy 45 B8 46 27N 11 18 E
Ísari, Greece 48 D3 37 22N 22 0 E
Íscar, Spain 42 D6 41 22N 4 32W
Iscayachi, Bolivia 173 E4 21 31 S 65 3W
İscehisar, Turkey 49 C12 38 51N 30 45 E
Íschia, Italy 46 B6 40 44N 13 57 E
Iscuandé, Colombia 168 C2 2 28N 77 59W
Isdell →, Australia 124 C3 16 27 S 124 51 E
Ise, Japan 71 C8 34 25N 136 45 E
Ise-Heiya, Japan 71 C8 34 40N 136 30 E
Ise-Wan, Japan 71 C8 34 43N 136 43 E
Isefjord, Denmark 17 J5 55 53N 11 50 E
Isel →, Austria 34 E5 46 50N 12 47 E
Iseltwald, Switz. 32 C5 46 43N 7 58 E
Isenthal, Switz. 33 C7 46 55N 8 34 E
Iseo, Italy 44 C7 45 39N 10 3 E
Iseo, L. d', Italy 44 C7 45 43N 10 4 E
Iseramagazi, Tanzania 118 C3 4 37 S 32 10 E
Isère □, France 29 C9 45 15N 5 40 E
Isère →, France 29 D8 44 59N 4 51 E
Iserlohn, Germany 30 D3 51 22N 7 41 E
Isérnia, Italy 47 A7 41 36N 14 14 E
Isesaki, Japan 71 A11 36 19N 139 12 E
Iseyin, Nigeria 113 D5 8 0N 3 36 E
Isfara, Tajikistan 63 C5 40 7N 70 38 E
Isfjorden, Norway 18 B4 62 35N 7 49 E
Isherton, Guyana 169 C6 2 20N 59 25W
Ishigaki-Shima, Japan 69 M2 24 20N 124 10 E
Ishikari-Gawa →, Japan 68 C10 43 15N 141 23 E
Ishikari-Sammyaku, Japan 68 C11 43 30N 143 0 E
Ishikari-Wan, Japan 68 C10 43 25N 141 1 E
Ishikawa □, Japan 71 A8 36 30N 136 30 E
Ishim, Russia 64 D7 56 10N 69 30 E
Ishim →, Russia 64 D8 57 45N 71 10 E
Ishimbay, Russia 62 E6 53 28N 56 2 E
Ishinomaki, Japan 68 E10 38 32N 141 20 E
Ishioka, Japan 71 A12 36 11N 140 16 E
Ishizuchi-Yama, Japan 70 D5 33 45N 133 6 E
Ishkashim = Eshkāshem, Tajikistan 63 E5 36 44N 71 37 E
Ishkuman, Pakistan 93 A5 36 30N 73 50 E
Ishmi, Albania 50 E3 41 33N 19 34 E
Ishpeming, U.S.A. 148 B2 46 29N 87 40W
Ishurdi, Bangla. 90 C2 24 9N 89 3 E
Isigny-sur-Mer, France 26 C5 49 19N 1 6W
Isıklar Dağı, Turkey 51 F11 40 45N 27 15 E
Işıklı, Turkey 49 C11 38 19N 29 51 E
Isil Kul, Russia 64 D8 54 55N 71 16 E
Ísili, Italy 46 C2 39 44N 9 6 E
Isiolo, Kenya 118 B4 0 24N 37 33 E
Isiolo □, Kenya 118 B4 2 30N 37 30 E
Isiro, Dem. Rep. of the Congo 118 B2 2 53N 27 40 E
Isisford, Australia 126 C3 24 15 S 144 21 E
Iskandar, Uzbekistan 63 C4 41 36N 69 41 E
Iskenderun, Turkey 100 D7 36 32N 36 10 E
Iskenderun Körfezi, Turkey 100 D6 36 40N 35 50 E
Iski-Naukat, Kyrgyzstan 63 C6 40 16N 72 36 E
Iskilip, Turkey 100 B6 40 45N 34 29 E
Iskŭr →, Bulgaria 51 C8 43 45N 24 25 E
Iskŭr, Yazovir, Bulgaria 50 D7 42 23N 23 30 E
Iskut →, Canada 142 B2 56 45N 131 49W
Isla →, U.K. 22 E5 56 32N 3 20W
Isla Cristina, Spain 43 H3 37 13N 7 17W
Isla Vista, U.S.A. 161 L7 34 25N 119 53W
Islâhiye, Turkey 100 D7 37 0N 36 35 E
Islamabad, Pakistan 91 B4 33 40N 73 10 E
Islamkot, Pakistan 92 G4 24 42N 70 13 E
Islamorada, U.S.A. 153 L9 24 56N 80 37W
Islampur, India 94 F2 17 2N 74 20 E
Island →, Canada 142 A4 60 25N 121 12W
Island Bay, Phil. 81 G2 9 6N 118 10 E
Island Falls, Canada 140 C3 49 35N 81 20W
Island Falls, U.S.A. 141 C6 46 1N 68 16W
Island L., Canada 143 C10 53 47N 94 25W
Island Lagoon, Australia 128 A2 31 30 S 136 40 E
Island Pond, U.S.A. 151 B13 44 49N 71 53W
Islands, B. of, Canada 141 C8 49 11N 58 15W
Islands, B. of, N.Z. 130 B3 35 15 S 174 6 E
Islay, U.K. 22 F2 55 46N 6 10W
Isle →, France 28 D3 44 55N 0 15W
Isle aux Morts, Canada 141 C8 47 35N 59 0W
Isle of Hope, U.S.A. 152 D8 31 58N 81 5W
Isle of Wight □, U.K. 21 G6 50 41N 1 17W
Isle Royale, U.S.A. 154 B10 48 0N 88 54W
Isleta, U.S.A. 159 J10 34 55N 106 42W
Isleton, U.S.A. 160 G5 38 10N 121 37W
Ismail = Izmayil, Ukraine 59 K5 45 22N 28 46 E
Ismâ'ilîya, Egypt 106 H8 30 37N 32 18 E
Ismaning, Germany 31 G7 48 13N 11 40 E
Ismay, U.S.A. 154 B2 46 30N 104 48W
Isna, Egypt 106 B3 25 17N 32 30 E
Isogstalo, India 93 B8 34 15N 78 46 E
Ísola del Liri, Italy 45 G10 41 41N 13 34 E
Ísola della Scala, Italy 44 C7 45 16N 11 0 E
Ísola di Capo Rizzuto, Italy 47 D10 38 58N 17 6 E
Isparta, Turkey 57 G5 37 47N 30 30 E
Isperikh, Bulgaria 51 C10 43 43N 26 50 E
Íspica, Italy 47 F7 36 47N 14 55 E
Israel ■, Asia 103 D3 32 0N 34 50 E
Issano, Guyana 169 B6 5 49N 59 26W
Issia, Ivory C. 112 D3 6 33N 6 33W
Issoire, France 28 C7 45 32N 3 15 E
Issoudun, France 27 F8 46 57N 1 59 E
Issyk-Kul = Ysyk-Köl, Kyrgyzstan 63 B8 42 26N 76 12 E
Issyk-Kul, Ozero = Ysyk-Köl, Ozero, Kyrgyzstan 63 B8 42 25N 77 15 E
Ist, Croatia 45 D11 44 17N 14 47 E
Istaihah, U.A.E. 99 F7 23 19N 54 4 E
Istállós-kő, Hungary 52 B5 48 4N 20 26 E
İstanbul, Turkey 51 E12 41 0N 29 0 E
İstanbul □, Turkey 51 E12 41 0N 29 0 E
İstanbul Boğazı, Turkey 51 E13 41 10N 29 10 E
Isteren, Norway 18 B8 61 58N 11 47 E
Istiaía, Greece 48 C5 38 57N 23 9 E
Istmina, Colombia 168 B2 5 10N 76 39W
Isto, Mt., U.S.A. 144 B12 69 12N 143 48W
Istok, Serbia, Yug. 50 D4 42 45N 20 24 E
Istokpoga, L., U.S.A. 149 M5 27 23N 81 17W
Istra, Croatia 45 C10 45 10N 14 0 E
Istres, France 29 E8 43 31N 4 59 E
Istria = Istra, Croatia 45 C10 45 10N 14 0 E
Isulan, Phil. 81 H5 6 30N 124 29 E
Itá, Paraguay 174 B4 25 29 S 57 21W
'Itāb, Yemen 99 D5 15 20N 51 29 E
Itabaiana, Paraíba, Brazil 170 C4 7 18 S 35 19W
Itabaiana, Sergipe, Brazil 170 D4 10 41 S 37 37W
Itabaianinha, Brazil 170 D4 11 16 S 37 47W
Itaberaba, Brazil 171 D3 12 32 S 40 18W
Itaberaí, Brazil 171 E2 16 2 S 49 48W
Itabira, Brazil 171 E3 19 37 S 43 13W
Itabirito, Brazil 171 F3 20 15 S 43 48W
Itaboca, Brazil 169 D5 4 50 S 62 40W
Itabuna, Brazil 171 D4 14 48 S 39 16W
Itacajá, Brazil 170 C2 8 19 S 47 46W
Itacaunas →, Brazil 170 C2 5 21 S 49 8W
Itacoatiara, Brazil 169 D6 3 8 S 58 25W
Itacuaí →, Brazil 172 A3 4 20 S 70 12W
Itaguaçu, Brazil 171 E3 19 48 S 40 51W
Itaguari →, Brazil 171 D3 14 11 S 44 40W
Itaguatins, Brazil 170 C2 5 47 S 47 29W
Itaim →, Brazil 170 C3 7 2 S 42 2W
Itainópolis, Brazil 170 C3 7 24 S 41 31W
Itaipú, Représa de, Brazil 175 B5 25 30 S 54 30W
Itaituba, Brazil 169 D6 4 10 S 55 50W
Itajaí, Brazil 175 B6 27 50 S 48 39W
Itajubá, Brazil 171 F2 22 24 S 45 30W
Itajuípe, Brazil 171 D4 14 41 S 39 22W
Itaka, Tanzania 119 D3 8 50 S 32 49 E
Itako, Japan 71 B12 35 56N 140 33 E
Italy ■, Europe 13 G8 42 0N 13 0 E
Itamaraté, Brazil 170 B2 2 16 S 46 24W
Itambacuri, Brazil 171 E3 18 1 S 41 42W
Itambé, Brazil 171 E3 15 15 S 40 37W
Itampolo, Madag. 117 C7 24 41 S 43 57 E
Itanhauã →, Brazil 169 D5 4 45 S 63 48W
Itanhém, Brazil 171 E3 17 9 S 40 20W
Itano, Japan 70 C6 34 7N 134 28 E
Itapaci, Brazil 171 D2 14 57 S 49 34W
Itapagé, Brazil 170 B4 3 41 S 39 34W
Itaparica, I. de, Brazil 171 D4 12 54 S 38 42W
Itapebi, Brazil 171 E4 15 56 S 39 32W
Itapecuru-Mirim, Brazil 170 B3 3 24 S 44 20W
Itaperuna, Brazil 171 F3 21 10 S 41 54W
Itapetinga, Brazil 171 E3 15 15 S 40 15W
Itapetininga, Brazil 175 A6 23 36 S 48 7W
Itapeva, Brazil 175 A6 23 59 S 48 59W
Itapicuru →, Bahia, Brazil 170 D4 11 47 S 37 32W
Itapicuru →, Maranhão, Brazil 170 B3 2 52 S 44 12W
Itapinima, Brazil 173 B5 5 25 S 60 44W
Itapipoca, Brazil 170 B4 3 30 S 39 35W
Itapiranga, Brazil 169 D6 2 45 S 58 1W
Itapiúna, Brazil 170 B4 4 33 S 38 57W
Itaporanga, Brazil 170 C4 7 18 S 38 0W
Itapuá □, Paraguay 175 B4 26 40 S 55 40W
Itapuranga, Brazil 171 E2 15 40 S 49 59W
Itaquari, Brazil 171 F3 20 20 S 40 25W
Itaquatiara, Brazil 169 D6 2 58 S 58 30W
Itaquí, Brazil 174 B4 29 8 S 56 30W
Itararé, Brazil 175 A6 24 6 S 49 23W
Itarsi, India 92 H7 22 36N 77 51 E
Itarumã, Brazil 171 E1 18 42 S 51 25W
Itatí, Argentina 174 B4 27 16 S 58 15W
Itatira, Brazil 170 B4 4 30 S 39 37W
Itatuba, Brazil 173 B5 5 46 S 63 20W
Itatupa, Brazil 169 D7 0 37 S 51 12W
Itaueira, Brazil 170 C3 7 36 S 43 2W
Itaueira →, Brazil 170 C3 6 41 S 42 55W
Itaúna, Brazil 171 F3 20 4 S 44 34W
Itbayat, Phil. 80 A3 20 47N 121 51 E
Itbayat I., Phil. 80 A3 20 46N 121 50 E
Itchen →, U.K. 21 G6 50 55N 1 22W
Ite, Peru 172 D3 17 55 S 70 57W
Itéa, Greece 48 C4 38 25N 22 25 E
Itezhi Tezhi, L., Zambia 119 F2 15 30 S 25 30 E
Ithaca = Itháki, Greece 48 C2 38 25N 20 40 E
Ithaca, U.S.A. 151 D8 42 27N 76 30W
Itháki, Greece 48 C2 38 25N 20 40 E
Itinga, Brazil 171 E3 16 36 S 41 47W
Itiquira, Brazil 173 D7 17 12 S 54 7W
Itiquira →, Brazil 173 D6 17 18 S 56 44W
Itiruçu, Brazil 171 D3 13 31 S 40 9W
Itiúba, Brazil 170 D4 10 43 S 39 51W
Itkilik →, U.S.A. 144 A10 70 9N 150 56W
Ito, Japan 71 C11 34 58N 139 5 E
Itoigawa, Japan 69 F8 37 2N 137 51 E
Iton →, France 26 C8 49 9N 1 12 E
Itonamas →, Bolivia 173 C5 12 28 S 64 24W
Itri, Italy 46 A6 41 17N 13 32 E
Itsa, Egypt 106 J7 29 15N 30 47 E
Itsukaichi, Japan 70 C4 34 22N 132 22 E
Itsuki, Japan 70 E2 32 24N 130 50 E
Ittiri, Italy 46 B1 40 36N 8 34 E
Ittoqqortoormiit = Scoresbysund, Greenland 10 C8 70 20N 23 0W
Itu, Brazil 175 A6 23 17 S 47 15W
Itu, Nigeria 113 D6 5 10N 7 58 E
Ituaçu, Brazil 171 D3 13 50 S 41 18W
Ituango, Colombia 168 B2 7 4N 75 45W
Ituiutaba, Brazil 171 E2 19 0 S 49 25W

Karoi 231

Kamensk-Shakhtinskiy, *Russia* **61 F5** 48 23N 40 20 E
Kamensk Uralskiy, *Russia* **62 C9** 56 25N 62 2 E
Kamenskiy, *Russia* **60 E7** 50 48N 45 25 E
Kamenskoye, *Russia* **65 C17** 62 45N 165 30 E
Kamenyak, *Bulgaria* **51 C10** 43 24N 26 57 E
Kamenz, *Germany* **30 D10** 51 15N 14 5 E
Kameoka, *Japan* **71 C7** 35 0N 135 35 E
Kameyama, *Japan* **71 C8** 34 51N 136 27 E
Kami, *Albania* **50 D4** 42 17N 20 18 E
Kami-Jima, *Japan* **70 E2** 32 27N 130 20 E
Kami-koshiki-Jima, *Japan* **70 F1** 31 50N 129 52 E
Kamiah, *U.S.A.* **158 C5** 46 14N 116 2W
Kamień Krajeński, *Poland* **54 E4** 53 32N 17 32 E
Kamień Pomorski, *Poland* **54 E1** 53 57N 14 43 E
Kamienna →, *Poland* **55 G8** 51 6N 21 47 E
Kamienna Góra, *Poland* **55 H3** 50 47N 16 2 E
Kamieńsk, *Poland* **55 G6** 51 12N 19 29 E
Kamieskroon, *S. Africa* **116 E2** 30 9 S 17 56 E
Kamiita, *Japan* **70 C6** 34 6N 134 22 E
Kamilukuak, L., *Canada* **143 A8** 62 22N 101 40W
Kamin-Kashyrskyy, *Ukraine* **59 G3** 51 39N 24 56 E
Kamina, *Dem. Rep. of the Congo* **115 D5** 8 45 S 25 0 E
Kaminak L., *Canada* **143 A10** 62 10N 95 0W
Kaminka, *Ukraine* **59 H7** 49 3N 32 6 E
Kaminoyama, *Japan* **68 E10** 38 9N 140 17 E
Kamioka, *Japan* **71 A9** 36 25N 137 15 E
Kamiros, *Greece* **38 C9** 36 20N 27 56 E
Kamishak Bay, *U.S.A.* **144 G9** 59 15N 153 45W
Kamituga, *Dem. Rep. of the Congo* **118 C2** 3 2 S 28 10 E
Kamloops, *Canada* **142 C4** 50 40N 120 20W
Kamnik, *Slovenia* **45 B11** 46 14N 14 37 E
Kamo, *Armenia* **61 K7** 40 21N 45 7 E
Kamo, *Japan* **68 F9** 37 39N 139 3 E
Kamo, *N.Z.* **130 B3** 35 42 S 174 20 E
Kamoa Mts., *Guyana* **169 C6** 1 30N 59 0W
Kamogawa, *Japan* **71 B12** 35 5N 140 5 E
Kamoke, *Pakistan* **92 C6** 32 4N 74 4 E
Kamooloa, *U.S.A.* **145 J13** 21 34N 158 7W
Kamp →, *Austria* **34 C8** 48 23N 15 42 E
Kampala, *Uganda* **118 B3** 0 20N 32 30 E
Kampang Chhnang, *Cambodia* **87 F5** 12 20N 104 35 E
Kampar, *Malaysia* **87 K3** 4 18N 101 9 E
Kampar →, *Indonesia* **84 B2** 0 30N 103 8 E
Kampen, *Neths.* **24 B5** 52 33N 5 53 E
Kamphaeng Phet, *Thailand* **86 D2** 16 28N 99 30 E
Kampolombo, L., *Zambia* **119 E2** 11 37 S 29 42 E
Kampong Saom, *Cambodia* **87 G4** 10 38N 103 30 E
Kampong Saom, Chaak, *Cambodia* **87 G4** 10 50N 103 32 E
Kampong To, *Thailand* **87 J3** 6 3N 101 13 E
Kampot, *Cambodia* **87 G5** 10 36N 104 10 E
Kampsville, *U.S.A.* **156 E6** 39 18N 90 37W
Kamptee, *India* **94 D4** 21 9N 79 19 E
Kampti, *Burkina Faso* **112 C4** 10 7N 3 25W
Kampuchea = Cambodia ■, *Asia* **86 F5** 12 15N 105 0 E
Kampung →, *Indonesia* **83 C5** 5 44 S 138 24 E
Kampung Air Putih, *Malaysia* **87 K4** 4 15N 103 10 E
Kampung Jerangau, *Malaysia* **87 K4** 4 50N 103 10 E
Kampung Raja, *Malaysia* **87 K4** 5 45N 102 35 E
Kampungbaru = Tolitoli, *Indonesia* **82 A2** 1 5N 120 50 E
Kamrau, Teluk, *Indonesia* **83 B4** 3 30 S 133 36 E
Kamsack, *Canada* **143 C8** 51 34N 101 54W
Kamskoye Ustye, *Russia* **60 C9** 55 10N 49 20 E
Kamskoye Vdkhr., *Russia* **62 B6** 58 41N 56 7 E
Kamuchawie L., *Canada* **143 B8** 56 18N 101 59W
Kamuela, *U.S.A.* **145 C6** 20 1N 155 41W
Kamui-Misaki, *Japan* **68 C10** 43 20N 140 21 E
Kamyanets-Podilskyy, *Ukraine* **59 H4** 48 45N 26 40 E
Kamyanka-Buzka, *Ukraine* **59 G3** 50 8N 24 16 E
Kamyanka-Dniprovska, *Ukraine* **59 J8** 47 29N 34 28 E
Kāmyārān, *Iran* **101 E12** 34 47N 46 56 E
Kamyshin, *Russia* **60 E7** 50 10N 45 24 E
Kamyshlov, *Russia* **62 C9** 56 50N 62 43 E
Kamyzyak, *Russia* **61 G9** 46 4N 48 10 E
Kan, *Burma* **90 D5** 22 25N 94 5 E
Kanaaupscow, *Canada* **140 B4** 54 2N 76 30W
Kanaaupscow →, *Canada* **139 C12** 53 39N 77 9W
Kanab, *U.S.A.* **159 H7** 37 3N 112 32W
Kanab →, *U.S.A.* **159 H7** 36 24N 112 38W
Kanagawa □, *Japan* **71 B11** 35 20N 139 20 E
Kanagi, *Japan* **68 D10** 40 54N 140 27 E
Kanairiktok →, *Canada* **141 A7** 55 2N 60 18W
K'anak, *Greenland* **10 B4** 77 30N 69 0W
Kanakapura, *India* **95 H3** 12 33N 77 28 E
Kanália, *Greece* **48 B4** 39 30N 22 53 E
Kananga, *Dem. Rep. of the Congo* **115 D4** 5 55 S 22 18 E
Kanarraville, *U.S.A.* **159 H7** 37 32N 113 11W
Kanash, *Russia* **60 C8** 55 30N 47 32 E
Kanaskat, *U.S.A.* **160 C5** 47 19N 121 54W
Kanastraíon, Ákra = Palioúrion, Ákra, *Greece* **50 G7** 39 57N 23 45 E
Kanawha →, *U.S.A.* **148 F4** 38 50N 82 9W
Kanazawa, *Japan* **71 A8** 36 30N 136 38 E
Kanbalu, *Burma* **90 D5** 23 12N 95 31 E
Kanchanaburi, *Thailand* **86 E2** 14 2N 99 31 E
Kanchenjunga, *Nepal* **93 F13** 27 50N 88 10 E
Kanchipuram, *India* **95 H4** 12 52N 79 45 E
Kańczuga, *Poland* **55 J9** 49 59N 22 25 E
Kanda Kanda, *Dem. Rep. of the Congo* **115 D4** 6 52 S 23 48 E
Kandahar = Qandahār, *Afghan.* **91 C2** 31 32N 65 30 E
Kandalaksha, *Russia* **56 A5** 67 9N 32 30 E
Kandalakshkiy Zaliv, *Russia* **56 A6** 66 0N 35 0 E
Kandangan, *Indonesia* **85 C5** 2 50 S 115 20 E
Kandanos, *Greece* **38 D5** 35 19N 23 44 E
Kandava, *Latvia* **54 A9** 57 2N 22 46 E
Kandavu, *Fiji* **133 B2** 19 0 S 178 15 E
Kandavu Passage, *Fiji* **133 B2** 18 45 S 178 0 E
Kandep, *Papua N. G.* **132 C2** 5 54 S 143 32 E
Kander →, *Switz.* **32 C5** 46 33N 7 38 E
Kandersteg, *Switz.* **32 D5** 46 28N 7 40 E
Kandhíla, *Greece* **48 D4** 37 46N 22 22 E
Kandhkot, *Pakistan* **92 E3** 28 16N 69 8 E
Kandhla, *India* **92 E7** 29 18N 77 19 E
Kandi, *Benin* **113 C5** 11 7N 2 55 E
Kandi, *India* **93 H13** 23 58N 88 5 E
Kandıra, *Turkey* **100 B4** 41 4N 30 9 E
Kandla, *India* **92 H4** 23 0N 70 10 E
Kandos, *Australia* **129 B8** 32 45 S 149 58 E
Kandrian, *Papua N. G.* **132 D5** 6 14 S 149 37 E
Kandy, *Sri Lanka* **95 L5** 7 18N 80 43 E
Kane, *U.S.A.* **150 E6** 41 40N 78 49W
Kane Basin, *Greenland* **10 B4** 79 1N 70 0W
Kaneilio Pt., *U.S.A.* **145 K13** 21 27N 158 12W
Kaneohe B., *U.S.A.* **145 K14** 21 30N 157 50W
Kanevskaya, *Russia* **61 G4** 46 3N 38 57 E
Kanfanar, *Croatia* **45 C10** 45 7N 13 50 E
Kangaba, *Mali* **112 C3** 11 56N 8 25W
Kangal, *Turkey* **100 C7** 39 14N 37 23 E
Kangâmiut, *Greenland* **10 D5** 65 50N 53 20W
Kangān, *Fārs, Iran* **97 E7** 27 50N 52 3 E
Kangān, *Hormozgān, Iran* **97 E8** 25 48N 57 28 E
Kangar, *Malaysia* **87 J3** 6 27N 100 12 E
Kangaroo I., *Australia* **128 C2** 35 45 S 137 0 E
Kangasala, *Finland* **15 F21** 61 28N 24 4 E
Kangāvar, *Iran* **97 C6** 34 40N 48 0 E
Kangding, *China* **76 B3** 30 2N 101 57 E
Kāngdong, *N. Korea* **75 E14** 39 9N 126 5 E
Kangean, Kepulauan, *Indonesia* **85 D5** 6 55 S 115 23 E
Kangean Is. = Kangean, Kepulauan, *Indonesia* **85 D5** 6 55 S 115 23 E
Kangerdlugssuak, *Greenland* **10 D7** 68 10N 32 20W
Kangerluarsoruseet = Færingehavn, *Greenland* **10 E5** 63 45N 51 27W
Kanggye, *N. Korea* **75 D14** 41 0N 126 35 E
Kanggyŏng, *S. Korea* **75 F14** 36 10N 127 0 E
Kanghwa, *S. Korea* **75 F14** 37 45N 126 30 E
Kangilinnguit = Grønnedal, *Greenland* **10 E6** 61 20N 47 57W
Kangiqsualujjuaq, *Canada* **139 C13** 58 30N 65 59W
Kangiqsujuaq, *Canada* **139 B12** 61 30N 72 0W
Kangirsuk, *Canada* **139 C13** 60 0N 70 0W
Kangnūng, *S. Korea* **75 F15** 37 45N 128 54 E
Kango, *Gabon* **114 B2** 0 11N 10 5 E
Kangoya, *Dem. Rep. of the Congo* **115 D4** 9 55 S 22 48 E
Kangping, *China* **75 C12** 42 43N 123 18 E
Kangpokpi, *India* **90 C4** 25 8N 93 58 E
Kangyidaung, *Burma* **90 G5** 16 56N 94 54 E
Kanhangad, *India* **95 H2** 12 21N 74 58 E
Kanheri, *India* **94 E1** 19 13N 72 50 E
Kani, *Ivory C.* **112 D3** 8 29N 6 36W
Kaniama, *Dem. Rep. of the Congo* **115 D4** 7 30 S 24 12 E
Kaniapiskau →, *Canada* **141 A6** 56 40N 69 30W
Kaniapiskau L., *Canada* **141 B6** 54 10N 69 55W
Kanibadam, *Tajikistan* **63 C5** 40 17N 70 25 E
Kaniere, L., *N.Z.* **131 C6** 42 50 S 171 10 E
Kanin, Poluostrov, *Russia* **56 A8** 68 0N 45 0 E
Kanin Nos, Mys, *Russia* **56 A7** 68 39N 43 32 E
Kanin Pen. = Kanin, Poluostrov, *Russia* **56 A8** 68 0N 45 0 E
Kanina, *Albania* **50 F3** 40 23N 19 30 E
Kaniva, *Australia* **128 D4** 36 22 S 141 18 E
Kanjiža, *Serbia, Yug.* **52 D5** 46 3N 20 4 E
Kanjut Sar, *Pakistan* **93 A6** 36 7N 75 25 E
Kankaanpää, *Finland* **15 F20** 61 44N 22 50 E
Kankakee, *U.S.A.* **157 C9** 41 7N 87 52W
Kankakee →, *U.S.A.* **157 C8** 41 23N 88 15W
Kankan, *Guinea* **112 C3** 10 23N 9 15W
Kankendy = Xankändi, *Azerbaijan* **101 C12** 39 52N 46 49 E
Kanker, *India* **94 D5** 20 10N 81 40 E
Kanmuri-Yama, *Japan* **70 C4** 34 30N 132 4 E
Kannabe, *Japan* **70 C5** 34 32N 133 23 E
Kannapolis, *U.S.A.* **149 H5** 35 30N 80 37W
Kannauj, *India* **93 F8** 27 3N 79 56 E
Kano, *Nigeria* **113 C6** 12 2N 8 30 E
Kano □, *Nigeria* **113 C6** 11 30N 8 30 E
Kan'onji, *Japan* **70 C5** 34 7N 133 39 E
Kanoroba, *Ivory C.* **112 D3** 9 7N 6 8W
Kanowha, *U.S.A.* **156 B3** 42 57N 93 47W
Kanowit, *Malaysia* **85 B4** 2 14N 112 20 E
Kanowna, *Australia* **125 F3** 30 32 S 121 31 E
Kanoya, *Japan* **70 F2** 31 25N 130 50 E
Kanpetlet, *Burma* **90 E4** 21 10N 93 59 E
Kanpur, *India* **93 F9** 26 28N 80 20 E
Kansas, *U.S.A.* **157 E9** 39 33N 87 56W
Kansas □, *U.S.A.* **154 F6** 38 30N 99 0W
Kansas →, *U.S.A.* **154 F7** 39 7N 94 37W
Kansas City, *Kans., U.S.A.* **156 E2** 39 7N 94 38W
Kansas City, *Mo., U.S.A.* **156 E2** 39 6N 94 35W
Kansenia, *Dem. Rep. of the Congo* **119 E2** 10 20 S 26 0 E
Kansk, *Russia* **65 D10** 56 20N 95 37 E
Kansŏng, *S. Korea* **75 E15** 38 24N 128 30 E
Kansu = Gansu □, *China* **74 G3** 36 0N 104 0 E
Kant, *Kyrgyzstan* **63 B7** 42 53N 74 51 E
Kantché, *Niger* **109 F1** 13 31N 8 30 E
Kanté, *Togo* **113 D5** 9 57N 1 3 E
Kantemirovka, *Russia* **59 H10** 49 43N 39 55 E
Kantharalak, *Thailand* **86 E5** 14 39N 104 39 E
Kantishna →, *U.S.A.* **144 D10** 64 45N 149 58W
Kantō □, *Japan* **71 A11** 36 15N 139 30 E
Kantō-Heiya, *Japan* **71 B11** 36 0N 139 30 E
Kantō-Sanchi, *Japan* **71 B10** 35 59N 138 50 E
Kantu-long, *Burma* **90 F6** 19 57N 97 36 E
Kanturk, *Ireland* **23 D3** 52 11N 8 54W
Kanuma, *Japan* **71 A11** 36 34N 139 42 E
Kanus, *Namibia* **116 D2** 27 50 S 18 39 E
Kanye, *Botswana* **116 C4** 24 55 S 25 28 E
Kanzenze, *Dem. Rep. of the Congo* **115 E5** 10 30 S 25 12 E
Kanzi, Ras, *Tanzania* **118 D4** 7 1 S 39 33 E
Kao, *Fiji* **133 P13** 19 40 S 175 1W
Kaohsiung, *Taiwan* **77 F13** 22 35N 120 16 E
Kaokoveld, *Namibia* **116 B1** 19 15 S 14 30 E
Kaolack, *Senegal* **112 C1** 14 5N 16 8W
Kaoshan, *China* **75 B13** 44 38N 124 50 E
Kaouar, *Niger* **109 E2** 19 5N 12 52 E
Kapadvanj, *India* **92 H5** 23 5N 73 0 E
Kapagere, *Papua N. G.* **132 E4** 9 46 S 147 42 E
Kapahulu, *U.S.A.* **145 K14** 21 16N 157 49W
Kapaklı, *Turkey* **51 E11** 41 19N 27 59 E
Kapan, *Armenia* **101 C12** 39 18N 46 27 E
Kapanga, *Dem. Rep. of the Congo* **115 D4** 8 30 S 22 40 E
Kapapa I., *U.S.A.* **145 K14** 21 29N 157 48W
Kapatagan, *Phil.* **81 H4** 7 52N 123 44 E
Kapchagai = Qapshaghay, *Kazakstan* **63 B8** 43 51N 77 14 E
Kapchagaiskoye Vdkhr. = Qapshaghay Bögeni, *Kazakstan* **63 B8** 43 45N 77 50 E
Kapela = Velika Kapela, *Croatia* **45 C12** 45 10N 15 5 E
Kapéllo, Ákra, *Greece* **48 E5** 36 9N 23 3 E
Kapema, *Dem. Rep. of the Congo* **119 E2** 10 45 S 28 22 E
Kapfenberg, *Austria* **34 D8** 47 26N 15 18 E
Kapı Dağı, *Turkey* **51 F11** 40 28N 27 50 E
Kapia, *Dem. Rep. of the Congo* **115 C3** 4 17 S 19 46 E
Kapiri Mposhi, *Zambia* **119 E2** 13 59 S 28 43 E
Kāpīsā □, *Afghan.* **91 B3** 35 0N 69 20 E
Kapiskau →, *Canada* **140 B3** 52 47N 81 55W
Kapit, *Malaysia* **85 B4** 2 0N 112 55 E
Kapiti I., *N.Z.* **130 G3** 40 50 S 174 56 E
Kapka, Massif du, *Chad* **109 E4** 15 7N 21 45 E
Kaplice, *Czech Rep.* **34 C7** 48 42N 14 30 E
Kapoe, *Thailand* **87 H2** 9 34N 98 32 E
Kapoeta, *Sudan* **107 G3** 4 50N 33 35 E
Kápolnásnyék, *Hungary* **52 C3** 47 16N 18 41 E
Kaponga, *N.Z.* **130 F3** 39 29 S 174 9 E
Kapos →, *Hungary* **52 D3** 46 44N 18 30 E
Kaposvár, *Hungary* **52 D2** 46 25N 17 47 E
Kapowsin, *U.S.A.* **160 D4** 46 59N 122 13W
Kapp, *Norway* **18 D7** 60 43N 10 52 E
Kappeln, *Germany* **30 A5** 54 40N 9 55 E
Kappelshamn, *Sweden* **17 G12** 57 52N 18 47 E
Kapps, *Namibia* **116 C2** 22 32 S 17 18 E
Kaprije, *Croatia* **45 E12** 43 42N 15 43 E
Kapsan, *N. Korea* **75 D15** 41 4N 128 19 E
Kapsukas = Marijampolė, *Lithuania* **15 J20** 54 33N 23 19 E
Kapuas, *Indonesia* **85 C4** 3 10 S 114 5 E
Kapuas →, *Indonesia* **85 C3** 0 25 S 109 20 E
Kapuas Hulu, Pegunungan, *Malaysia* **85 B4** 1 30N 113 30 E
Kapuas Hulu Ra. = Kapuas Hulu, Pegunungan, *Malaysia* **85 B4** 1 30N 113 30 E
Kapulo, *Dem. Rep. of the Congo* **119 D2** 8 18 S 29 15 E
Kapunda, *Australia* **128 C3** 34 20 S 138 56 E
Kapuni, *N.Z.* **130 F3** 39 29 S 174 8 E
Kapurthala, *India* **92 D6** 31 23N 75 25 E
Kapuskasing, *Canada* **140 C3** 49 25N 82 30W
Kapuskasing →, *Canada* **140 C3** 49 49N 82 0W
Kapustin Yar, *Russia* **61 F7** 48 37N 45 40 E
Kaputar, *Australia* **127 E5** 30 15 S 150 10 E
Kaputir, *Kenya* **118 B4** 2 5N 35 28 E
Kapuvár, *Hungary* **52 C2** 47 36N 17 1 E
Kara, *Russia* **64 C7** 69 10N 65 0 E
Kara Ada, *Turkey* **49 E9** 36 58N 27 28 E
Kara-Balta, *Kyrgyzstan* **63 B6** 42 50N 73 49 E
Kara Bogaz Gol, Zaliv = Garabogazköl Aylagy, *Turkmenistan* **57 F9** 41 0N 53 30 E
Kara Burun, *Turkey* **49 E9** 36 32N 27 58 E
Kara Kalpak Republic □ = Karakalpakstan □, *Uzbekistan* **64 E6** 43 0N 58 0 E
Kara Kum, *Turkmenistan* **64 F7** 39 30N 60 0 E
Kara-Saki, *Japan* **70 C1** 34 41N 129 30 E
Kara Sea, *Russia* **64 B8** 75 0N 70 0 E
Kara Su, *Kyrgyzstan* **63 C6** 40 44N 72 53 E
Karaadilli, *Turkey* **49 C12** 38 18N 30 37 E
Karabash, *Russia* **62 D8** 55 29N 60 14 E
Karabekaul = Garabekewül, *Turkmenistan* **63 D2** 38 30N 64 8 E
Karabiğa, *Turkey* **51 F11** 40 23N 27 17 E
Karabük, *Turkey* **100 B5** 41 12N 32 37 E
Karabulak, *Kazakstan* **63 A9** 44 54N 78 30 E
Karaburun, *Turkey* **49 C8** 38 41N 26 28 E
Karaburuni, *Albania* **50 F3** 40 25N 19 20 E
Karabutak = Qarabutaq, *Kazakstan* **62 G8** 49 59N 60 14 E
Karacabey, *Turkey* **51 F12** 40 12N 28 21 E
Karacakılavuz, *Turkey* **51 E11** 41 8N 27 21 E
Karacaköy, *Turkey* **51 E12** 41 24N 28 22 E
Karacasu, *Turkey* **49 D10** 37 43N 28 35 E
Karachala = Qaraçala, *Azerbaijan* **61 L9** 39 45N 48 53 E
Karachayevsk, *Russia* **61 J5** 43 50N 41 55 E
Karachev, *Russia* **59 F8** 53 10N 35 5 E
Karachey-Cherkessia □, *Russia* **61 J5** 43 40N 41 30 E
Karachi, *Pakistan* **91 D2** 24 53N 67 0 E
Karad, *India* **94 F2** 17 15N 74 10 E
Karadirek, *Turkey* **49 C12** 38 38N 30 11 E
Karaga, *Ghana* **113 D4** 9 58N 0 28W
Karaganda = Qaraghandy, *Kazakstan* **64 E8** 49 50N 73 10 E
Karagayly, *Kazakstan* **64 E8** 49 26N 76 0 E
Karaginskiy, Ostrov, *Russia* **65 D17** 58 45N 164 0 E
Karagiye, Vpadina, *Kazakstan* **57 F9** 43 27N 51 45 E
Karagiye Depression = Karagiye, Vpadina, *Kazakstan* **57 F9** 43 27N 51 45 E
Karagüney Dağları, *Turkey* **100 B6** 40 30N 34 40 E
Karagwe □, *Tanzania* **118 C3** 2 0 S 31 0 E
Karahallı, *Turkey* **49 C11** 38 21N 29 33 E
Karaikal, *India* **95 J4** 10 59N 79 50 E
Karaikkudi, *India* **95 J4** 10 5N 78 45 E
Karaisali, *Turkey* **100 D6** 37 16N 35 2 E
Karaitivu I., *Sri Lanka* **95 K4** 9 45N 79 52 E
Karaj, *Iran* **97 C6** 35 48N 51 0 E
Karak, *Malaysia* **87 L4** 3 25N 102 2 E
Karakalpakstan □, *Uzbekistan* **64 E6** 43 0N 58 0 E
Karakitang, *Indonesia* **82 A3** 3 14N 125 28 E
Karaklis = Vanadzor, *Armenia* **61 K7** 40 48N 44 30 E
Karakoçan, *Turkey* **101 C9** 38 57N 40 2 E
Karakoram Pass, *Pakistan* **93 B7** 35 33N 77 50 E
Karakoram Ra., *Pakistan* **93 B7** 35 30N 77 0 E
Karakul, *Tajikistan* **63 D6** 39 2N 73 33 E
Karakul, *Uzbekistan* **63 D1** 39 22N 63 50 E
Karakuldzha, *Kyrgyzstan* **63 C6** 40 39N 73 26 E
Karakurt, *Turkey* **101 B10** 40 10N 42 37 E
Karal, *Chad* **109 F2** 12 50N 14 46 E
Karalon, *Russia* **65 D12** 57 5N 115 50 E
Karaman, *Balıkesir, Turkey* **49 B9** 39 39N 28 0 E
Karaman, *Konya, Turkey* **100 D5** 37 14N 33 13 E
Karamanlı, *Turkey* **49 D11** 37 23N 29 47 E
Karamay, *China* **72 B3** 45 30N 84 58 E
Karambu, *Indonesia* **85 C5** 3 53 S 116 6 E
Karamea, *N.Z.* **131 B7** 41 14 S 172 6 E
Karamea →, *N.Z.* **131 B7** 41 13 S 172 26 E
Karamea Bight, *N.Z.* **131 B6** 41 22 S 171 40 E
Karamet Niyaz = Garamätnyyaz, *Turkmenistan* **63 E2** 37 45N 64 34 E
Karamsad, *India* **92 H5** 22 35N 72 50 E
Karamürsel, *Turkey* **51 F13** 40 41N 29 36 E
Karand, *Iran* **101 E12** 34 16N 46 15 E
Karanganyar, *Indonesia* **85 D3** 7 38 S 109 37 E
Karanja, *India* **94 D3** 20 29N 77 31 E
Karaova, *Turkey* **49 D9** 37 5N 27 40 E
Karapınar, *Turkey* **100 D5** 37 41N 33 30 E
Karapiro, *N.Z.* **130 D4** 37 53 S 175 32 E
Karasburg, *Namibia* **116 D2** 28 0 S 18 44 E
Karasino, *Russia* **64 C9** 66 50N 86 50 E
Karasjok, *Norway* **14 B21** 69 27N 25 30 E
Karasu, *Turkey* **100 B4** 41 4N 30 46 E
Karasu →, *Turkey* **49 E12** 36 18N 30 10 E
Karasuk, *Russia* **64 D8** 53 44N 78 2 E
Karasuyama, *Japan* **71 A12** 36 39N 140 9 E
Karataş, *Adana, Turkey* **100 D6** 36 36N 35 21 E
Karataş, *Manisa, Turkey* **49 C10** 38 35N 28 16 E
Karataş Burnu, *Turkey* **100 D6** 36 31N 35 24 E
Karatau = Qarataū, *Kazakstan* **63 B5** 43 10N 70 28 E
Karatau, Khrebet, *Kazakstan* **63 B4** 43 30N 69 30 E
Karativu, *Sri Lanka* **95 K4** 8 22N 79 47 E
Karatobe, *Kazakstan* **62 G4** 49 44N 53 30 E
Karatoprak, *Turkey* **49 D9** 37 2N 27 15 E
Karatoya →, *India* **90 C2** 24 7N 89 36 E
Karaturuk, *Kazakstan* **63 B8** 43 35N 77 50 E
Karaul-Bazar, *Uzbekistan* **63 D2** 39 30N 64 48 E
Karauli, *India* **92 F7** 26 30N 77 4 E
Karavastasë, L. e, *Albania* **50 F3** 40 55N 19 30 E
Karávi, *Greece* **48 E5** 36 49N 23 37 E
Karavostasi, *Cyprus* **38 D11** 35 8N 32 50 E
Karawa, *Dem. Rep. of the Congo* **114 B4** 3 18N 20 17 E
Karawang, *Indonesia* **85 D3** 6 30 S 107 15 E
Karawanken, *Europe* **34 E7** 46 30N 14 40 E
Karayazı, *Turkey* **101 C10** 39 41N 42 9 E
Karazhal, *Kazakstan* **64 E8** 48 2N 70 49 E
Karbalā, *Iraq* **101 F11** 32 36N 44 3 E
Kårböle, *Sweden* **16 C9** 61 59N 15 22 E
Karcag, *Hungary* **52 C5** 47 19N 20 57 E
Karcha →, *Pakistan* **93 B7** 34 45N 76 10 E
Karczew, *Poland* **55 F8** 52 5N 21 15 E
Kardam, *Bulgaria* **51 C12** 43 45N 28 6 E
Kardeljovo = Ploče, *Croatia* **45 E14** 43 4N 17 26 E
Kardhámila, *Greece* **49 C8** 38 35N 26 5 E
Kardhamíli, *Greece* **48 E4** 36 53N 22 13 E
Kardhítsa, *Greece* **48 B3** 39 23N 21 54 E
Kardhítsa □, *Greece* **48 B3** 39 15N 21 50 E
Kärdla, *Estonia* **15 G20** 58 50N 22 40 E
Kareeberge, *S. Africa* **116 E3** 30 59 S 21 50 E
Kareima, *Sudan* **106 D3** 18 30N 31 49 E
Karelia □, *Russia* **56 A5** 65 30N 32 30 E
Karelian Republic □ = Karelia □, *Russia* **56 A5** 65 30N 32 30 E
Karema, *Papua N. G.* **132 E4** 9 12 S 147 18 E
Kārevāndar, *Iran* **97 E9** 27 53N 60 44 E
Kargasok, *Russia* **64 D9** 59 3N 80 53 E
Kargat, *Russia* **64 D9** 55 10N 80 15 E
Kargı, *Turkey* **100 B6** 41 11N 34 30 E
Kargil, *India* **93 B7** 34 32N 76 12 E
Kargopol, *Russia* **58 B10** 61 30N 38 58 E
Kargowa, *Poland* **55 F2** 52 5N 15 51 E
Karguéri, *Niger* **109 F2** 13 27N 10 30 E
Kariá, *Greece* **48 C2** 38 45N 20 39 E
Karia ba Mohammed, *Morocco* **110 B3** 34 22N 5 12W
Kariaí, *Greece* **51 F8** 40 14N 24 19 E
Karīān, *Iran* **97 E8** 26 57N 57 14 E
Kariba, *Zimbabwe* **119 F2** 16 28 S 28 50 E
Kariba, L., *Zimbabwe* **119 F2** 16 40 S 28 25 E
Kariba Dam, *Zimbabwe* **119 F2** 16 30 S 28 35 E
Kariba Gorge, *Zambia* **119 F2** 16 30 S 28 50 E
Karibib, *Namibia* **116 C2** 22 0 S 15 56 E
Karikari, C., *N.Z.* **130 A2** 34 46 S 173 24 E
Karimata, Kepulauan, *Indonesia* **85 C3** 1 25 S 109 0 E
Karimata, Selat, *Indonesia* **85 C3** 2 0 S 108 40 E
Karimata Is. = Karimata, Kepulauan, *Indonesia* **85 C3** 1 25 S 109 0 E
Karimnagar, *India* **94 E4** 18 26N 79 10 E
Karimunjawa, Kepulauan, *Indonesia* **85 D4** 5 50 S 110 30 E
Karin, *Somali Rep.* **120 B3** 10 50N 45 52 E
Káristos, *Greece* **48 C6** 38 1N 24 29 E
Karīt, *Iran* **97 C8** 33 29N 56 55 E
Kariya, *Japan* **71 C9** 34 58N 137 1 E
Karjala, *Finland* **58 A5** 62 0N 30 25 E
Karkal, *India* **95 H2** 13 15N 74 56 E
Karkar I., *Papua N. G.* **132 C4** 4 40 S 146 0 E
Karkaralinsk = Qarqaraly, *Kazakstan* **64 E8** 49 26N 75 30 E
Karkinitska Zatoka, *Ukraine* **59 K7** 45 56N 33 0 E
Karkinitskiy Zaliv = Karkinitska Zatoka, *Ukraine* **59 K7** 45 56N 33 0 E
Karkur Tohl, *Egypt* **106 C2** 22 5N 25 5 E
Karl Liebknecht, *Russia* **59 G8** 51 40N 35 35 E
Karl-Marx-Stadt = Chemnitz, *Germany* **30 E8** 50 51N 12 54 E
Karlholmsbruk, *Sweden* **16 D11** 60 31N 17 37 E
Karlino, *Poland* **54 D2** 54 3N 15 53 E
Karlivka, *Ukraine* **59 H8** 49 29N 35 8 E
Karlobag, *Croatia* **45 D12** 44 32N 15 5 E
Karlovac, *Croatia* **45 C12** 45 31N 15 36 E
Karlovka = Karlivka, *Ukraine* **59 H8** 49 29N 35 8 E
Karlovo, *Bulgaria* **51 D8** 42 38N 24 47 E
Karlovy Vary, *Czech Rep.* **34 A5** 50 13N 12 51 E
Karlsbad = Karlovy Vary, *Czech Rep.* **34 A5** 50 13N 12 51 E
Karlsborg, *Sweden* **17 F8** 58 33N 14 33 E
Karlshamn, *Sweden* **17 H8** 56 10N 14 51 E
Karlshus, *Norway* **18 E7** 59 21N 10 52 E
Karlskoga, *Sweden* **16 E8** 59 28N 14 33 E
Karlskrona, *Sweden* **17 H9** 56 10N 15 35 E
Karlsruhe, *Germany* **31 F4** 49 0N 8 23 E
Karlstad, *Sweden* **16 E7** 59 23N 13 30 E
Karlstad, *U.S.A.* **154 A6** 48 35N 96 31W
Karlstadt, *Germany* **31 F5** 49 57N 9 47 E
Karluk, *U.S.A.* **144 H9** 57 34N 154 28W
Karluk Indian Reservation, *U.S.A.* **144 H9** 57 35N 154 20W
Karmėlava, *Lithuania* **54 D11** 54 58N 24 4 E
Karmøy, *Norway* **18 E2** 59 15N 5 15 E
Karnal, *India* **92 E7** 29 42N 77 2 E
Karnali →, *Nepal* **93 E9** 28 45N 81 16 E
Karnaphuli Res., *Bangla.* **90 D4** 22 40N 92 20 E
Karnataka □, *India* **95 H3** 13 15N 77 0 E
Karnes City, *U.S.A.* **155 L6** 28 53N 97 54W
Karnische Alpen, *Europe* **34 E6** 46 36N 13 0 E
Karnobat, *Bulgaria* **51 D10** 42 39N 26 59 E
Kärnten □, *Austria* **34 E6** 46 52N 13 30 E
Karo, *Mali* **112 C4** 12 16N 3 18W
Karoi, *Zimbabwe* **119 F2** 16 48 S 29 45 E

Kilifi 233

Kendrew, S. Africa 116 E3 32 32 S 24 30 E
Kendrick, Fla., U.S.A. 153 F7 29 15N 82 10W
Kendrick, Idaho, U.S.A. 158 C5 46 37N 116 39W
Kene Thao, Laos 86 D3 17 44N 101 10 E
Kenedy, U.S.A. 155 L6 28 49N 97 51W
Kenema, S. Leone 112 D2 7 50N 11 14W
Keng Kok, Laos 86 D5 16 26N 105 12 E
Keng Tawng, Burma 90 E7 20 45N 98 18 E
Kengani, Dem. Rep. of the Congo 114 C3 2 59 S 17 36 E
Kenge, Dem. Rep. of the Congo 115 C3 4 50 S 17 4 E
Kengeja, Tanzania 118 D4 5 26 S 39 45 E
Kenhardt, S. Africa 116 D3 29 19 S 21 12 E
Kenimekh, Uzbekistan 63 C2 40 16N 65 7 E
Kenitra, Morocco 110 B3 34 15N 6 40W
Kenli, China 75 F10 37 30N 118 20 E
Kenmare, Ireland 23 E2 51 53N 9 36W
Kenmare, U.S.A. 154 A3 48 41N 102 5W
Kenmare River, Ireland 23 E2 51 48N 9 51W
Kennebec, U.S.A. 154 D5 43 54N 99 52W
Kennedy, Zimbabwe 119 F2 18 52 S 27 10 E
Kennedy Kanal, Arctic 10 A4 80 50N 66 0W
Kennedy Ra., Australia 125 D2 24 45 S 115 10 E
Kenner, U.S.A. 155 L9 29 59N 90 15W
Kennesaw, U.S.A. 152 A5 34 1N 84 37W
Kennet →, U.K. 21 F7 51 27N 0 57W
Kenneth Ra., Australia 124 D2 23 50 S 117 8 E
Kennett, U.S.A. 155 G9 36 14N 90 3W
Kennewick, U.S.A. 158 C4 46 12N 119 7W
Kénogami, Canada 141 C5 48 25N 71 15W
Kenogami →, Canada 140 B3 51 6N 84 28W
Kenora, Canada 143 D10 49 47N 94 29W
Kenosha, U.S.A. 157 B9 42 35N 87 49W
Kensington, Canada 141 C7 46 28N 63 34W
Kensington, U.S.A. 154 F5 39 46N 99 2W
Kensington Downs, Australia 126 C3 22 31 S 144 19 E
Kent, Ohio, U.S.A. 150 E3 41 9N 81 22W
Kent, Oreg., U.S.A. 158 D3 45 12N 120 42W
Kent, Tex., U.S.A. 155 K2 31 4N 104 13W
Kent, Wash., U.S.A. 160 C4 47 23N 122 14W
Kent □, U.K. 21 F8 51 12N 0 40 E
Kent Group, Australia 126 F4 39 30 S 147 20 E
Kent Pen., Canada 138 B9 68 30N 107 0W
Kentau, Kazakstan 63 B4 43 32N 68 36 E
Kentland, U.S.A. 157 D9 40 46N 87 27W
Kenton, U.S.A. 157 D13 40 39N 83 37W
Kentucky, Australia 129 A9 30 45 S 151 28 E
Kentucky □, U.S.A. 148 G3 37 0N 84 0W
Kentucky →, U.S.A. 157 F11 38 41N 85 11W
Kentucky L., U.S.A. 149 G2 37 1N 88 16W
Kentville, Canada 141 C7 45 6N 64 29W
Kentwood, U.S.A. 155 K9 30 56N 90 31W
Kenya ■, Africa 118 B4 1 0N 38 0 E
Kenya, Mt., Kenya 118 C4 0 10 S 37 18 E
Kenzou, Cameroon 114 B3 4 10N 15 2 E
Keo Neua, Deo, Vietnam 86 C5 18 23N 105 10 E
Keokea, U.S.A. 145 C5 20 43N 156 22W
Keokuk, U.S.A. 156 D5 40 24N 91 24W
Keosauqua, U.S.A. 156 D5 40 44N 91 58W
Keota, U.S.A. 156 C5 41 22N 91 57W
Kep, Cambodia 87 G5 10 29N 104 19 E
Kep, Vietnam 86 B6 21 24N 106 16 E
Kepez, Turkey 51 F10 40 5N 26 24 E
Kepi, Indonesia 83 C5 6 32 S 139 19 E
Kępice, Poland 54 D3 54 16N 16 51 E
Kepler Mts., N.Z. 131 F2 45 25 S 167 20 E
Kępno, Poland 55 G4 51 18N 17 58 E
Kepsut, Turkey 49 B10 39 40N 28 9 E
Kepuhi Pt., U.S.A. 145 K13 21 29N 158 14W
Kerala □, India 95 J3 11 0N 76 15 E
Kerama-Rettō, Japan 69 L3 26 5N 127 15 E
Keran, Pakistan 93 B5 34 35N 73 59 E
Kerang, Australia 128 C5 35 40 S 143 55 E
Keratéa, Greece 48 D5 37 48N 23 58 E
Keraudren, C., Australia 124 C2 19 58 S 119 45 E
Kerava, Finland 15 F21 60 25N 25 5 E
Keravat, Papua N. G. 132 C7 4 17 S 152 2 E
Kerch, Ukraine 59 K9 45 20N 36 20 E
Kerchenskiy Proliv, Black Sea 59 K9 45 10N 36 30 E
Kerchoual, Mali 113 B5 17 12N 0 20 E
Kerema, Papua N. G. 132 D3 7 58 S 145 50 E
Kerempe Burnu, Turkey 100 A5 42 2N 33 20 E
Keren, Eritrea 107 D4 15 45N 38 28 E
Kerewan, Gambia 112 C1 13 29N 16 10W
Kerguelen, Ind. Oc. 121 J5 49 15 S 69 10 E
Keri, Greece 48 D2 37 40N 20 49 E
Keri Kera, Sudan 107 E3 12 21N 32 42 E
Kericho, Kenya 118 C4 0 22 S 35 15 E
Kericho □, Kenya 118 C4 0 30 S 35 15 E
Kerikeri, N.Z. 130 B2 35 12 S 173 59 E
Kerinci, Indonesia 84 C2 1 40 S 101 15 E
Kerkenna, Is., Tunisia 108 B2 34 48N 11 11 E
Kerki, Turkmenistan 63 E2 37 50N 65 12 E
Kerkinítis, Límni, Greece 50 E7 41 12N 23 10 E
Kérkira, Greece 48 B1 39 37N 19 57 E
Kérkira □, Greece 48 B1 39 37N 19 50 E
Kerkrade, Neths. 24 D6 50 53N 6 4 E
Kerma, Sudan 106 D3 19 33N 30 32 E
Kermadec Is., Pac. Oc. 134 L10 30 0 S 178 15W
Kermadec Trench, Pac. Oc. 134 L10 30 30 S 176 0W
Kermān, Iran 97 D8 30 15N 57 1 E
Kerman, U.S.A. 160 J6 36 43N 120 4W
Kermān □, Iran 97 D8 30 0N 57 0 E
Kermānshāh = Bākhtarān, Iran 101 E12 34 23N 47 0 E
Kermen, Bulgaria 51 D10 42 30N 26 16 E
Kermit, U.S.A. 155 K3 31 52N 103 6W
Kern →, U.S.A. 161 K7 35 16N 119 18W
Kernhof, Austria 34 D8 47 49N 15 32 E
Kerns, Switz. 33 C6 46 54N 8 17 E
Kernville, U.S.A. 161 K8 35 45N 118 26W
Keroh, Malaysia 87 K3 5 43N 101 1 E
Kerpen, Germany 30 E2 50 51N 6 41 E
Kerrera, U.K. 22 E3 56 24N 5 33W
Kerrobert, Canada 143 C7 51 56N 109 8W
Kerrville, U.S.A. 155 K5 30 3N 99 8W
Kerry □, Ireland 23 D2 52 7N 9 35W
Kerry Hd., Ireland 23 D2 52 25N 9 56W
Kersa, Ethiopia 107 F5 9 28N 41 48 E
Kertosono, Indonesia 85 D4 7 38 S 112 9 E
Kerulen →, Asia 73 B6 48 48N 117 0 E
Kerzaz, Algeria 111 C4 29 29N 1 37W
Kerzers, Switz. 32 C4 46 59N 7 12 E
Kesagami →, Canada 140 B4 51 40N 79 45W
Kesagami L., Canada 140 B3 50 23N 80 15W
Keşan, Turkey 51 F10 40 49N 26 38 E
Kesch, Piz, Switz. 33 C9 46 38N 9 53 E
Kesennuma, Japan 68 E10 38 54N 141 35 E
Keshit, Iran 97 D8 29 43N 58 17 E
Keşiş Dağ, Turkey 101 C8 39 47N 39 46 E
Keskin, Turkey 100 C5 39 40N 33 36 E
Kestell, S. Africa 117 D4 28 17 S 28 42 E
Kestenga, Russia 56 A5 65 50N 31 45 E
Keswick, U.K. 20 C4 54 36N 3 8W
Keszthely, Hungary 52 D2 46 50N 17 15 E
Ket →, Russia 64 D9 58 55N 81 32 E
Keta, Ghana 113 D5 5 49N 1 0 E
Ketapang, Indonesia 85 C4 1 55 S 110 0 E
Ketchikan, U.S.A. 138 C6 55 21N 131 39W
Ketchum, U.S.A. 158 E6 43 41N 114 22W
Kete Krachi, Ghana 113 D4 7 46N 0 1W
Ketef, Khalîg Umm el, Egypt 106 C4 23 40N 35 35 E
Keti Bandar, Pakistan 92 G2 24 8N 67 27 E
Ketri, India 92 E6 28 1N 75 50 E
Kętrzyn, Poland 54 D8 54 7N 21 22 E
Kettering, U.K. 21 E7 52 24N 0 43W
Kettering, U.S.A. 157 E12 39 41N 84 10W
Kettle →, Canada 143 B11 56 40N 89 34W
Kettle Falls, U.S.A. 158 B4 48 37N 118 3W
Kettleman City, U.S.A. 160 J7 36 1N 119 58W
Kęty, Poland 55 J6 49 51N 19 16 E
Keuruu, Finland 15 E21 62 16N 24 41 E
Kevelaer, Germany 30 D2 51 36N 6 15 E
Kevin, U.S.A. 158 B8 48 45N 111 58W
Kewanee, U.S.A. 156 C7 41 14N 89 56W
Kewanna, U.S.A. 157 C10 41 1N 86 25W
Kewaunee, U.S.A. 148 C2 44 27N 87 31W
Keweenaw B., U.S.A. 148 B1 47 0N 88 15W
Keweenaw Pen., U.S.A. 148 B2 47 30N 88 0W
Keweenaw Pt., U.S.A. 148 B2 47 25N 87 43W
Key Biscayne, U.S.A. 153 K9 25 42N 80 10W
Key Colony Beach, U.S.A. 153 L9 24 45N 80 57W
Key Harbour, Canada 140 C3 45 50N 80 45W
Key Largo, U.S.A. 153 K9 25 5N 80 27W
Key West, U.S.A. 164 B3 24 33N 81 48W
Keyesport, U.S.A. 156 F7 38 45N 89 17W
Keynsham, U.K. 21 F5 51 24N 2 29W
Keyser, U.S.A. 148 F6 39 26N 78 59W
Keystone, U.S.A. 154 D3 43 54N 103 25W
Keysville, U.S.A. 152 B7 33 14N 82 14W
Keytesville, U.S.A. 156 E4 39 26N 92 56W
Kez, Russia 62 C4 57 55N 53 46 E
Kezhma, Russia 65 D11 58 59N 101 9 E
Kežmarok, Slovak Rep. 35 B13 49 10N 20 28 E
Khabarovsk, Russia 65 E14 48 30N 135 5 E
Khabr, Iran 97 D8 28 51N 56 22 E
Khābūr →, Syria 101 E9 35 17N 40 35 E
Khachmas = Xaçmaz, Azerbaijan 61 K9 41 31N 48 42 E
Khachrod, India 92 H6 23 25N 75 20 E
Khadari, W. el →, Sudan 107 E2 10 29N 27 15 E
Khadro, Pakistan 92 F3 26 11N 68 50 E
Khadyzhensk, Russia 61 H4 44 26N 39 32 E
Khadzhilyangar, India 93 B8 35 45N 79 20 E
Khagaria, India 93 G12 25 30N 86 32 E
Khaipur, Bahawalpur, Pakistan 92 E5 29 34N 72 17 E
Khaipur, Hyderabad, Pakistan 92 F3 27 32N 68 49 E
Khair, India 92 F7 27 57N 77 46 E
Khairabad, India 93 F9 27 33N 80 47 E
Khairagarh, India 93 J9 21 27N 81 2 E
Khairpur, Pakistan 91 D3 27 32N 68 49 E
Khāk Dow, Afghan. 91 B2 34 57N 67 16 E
Khakassia □, Russia 64 D9 53 0N 90 0 E
Khakhea, Botswana 116 C3 24 48 S 23 22 E
Khalafābād, Iran 97 D6 30 54N 49 24 E
Khalfallah, Algeria 111 B5 34 20N 0 16 E
Khalfūt, Yemen 99 D6 15 52N 52 10 E
Khalilabad, India 93 F10 26 48N 83 5 E
Khalīlī, Iran 97 E7 27 38N 53 17 E
Khalkhāl, Iran 97 B6 37 37N 48 32 E
Khálki, Dhodhekánisos, Greece 49 E9 36 17N 27 35 E
Khálki, Thessalía, Greece 48 B4 39 36N 22 30 E
Khalkidhikí □, Greece 50 F7 40 25N 23 20 E
Khalkís, Greece 48 C5 38 27N 23 42 E
Khalmer-Sede = Tazovskiy, Russia 64 C8 67 30N 78 44 E
Khalmer Yu, Russia 56 A12 67 58N 65 1 E
Khalturin, Russia 62 B2 58 40N 48 50 E
Khalūf, Oman 102 C6 20 30N 58 13 E
Kham Keut, Laos 86 C5 18 15N 104 43 E
Khamaria, India 94 C5 23 10N 80 52 E
Khamas Country, Botswana 116 C4 21 45 S 26 30 E
Khambhaliya, India 92 H3 22 14N 69 41 E
Khambhat, India 92 H5 22 23N 72 33 E
Khambhat, G. of, India 92 J5 20 45N 72 30 E
Khamgaon, India 94 D3 20 42N 76 37 E
Khamilonísion, Greece 49 F8 35 50N 26 15 E
Khamīr, Iran 97 E7 26 57N 55 36 E
Khamir, Yemen 98 C4 16 2N 44 0 E
Khamīs Mushayṭ, Si. Arabia 98 C3 18 18N 42 44 E
Khammam, India 94 F5 17 11N 80 6 E
Khamsa, Egypt 103 E1 30 27N 32 23 E
Khān Abū Shāmat, Syria 103 B5 33 39N 36 53 E
Khān Azād, Iraq 96 C5 33 7N 44 22 E
Khān Mujiddah, Iraq 96 C4 32 21N 43 48 E
Khān Shaykhūn, Syria 100 E7 35 26N 36 38 E
Khān Yūnis, Gaza Strip 103 D3 31 21N 34 18 E
Khānābād, Afghan. 91 A3 36 45N 69 5 E
Khanabad, Uzbekistan 63 C5 40 59N 70 38 E
Khānaqīn, Iraq 101 E11 34 23N 45 25 E
Khānbāghī, Iran 97 B7 36 10N 55 25 E
Khandrá, Greece 49 F8 35 3N 26 8 E
Khandwa, India 94 D3 21 49N 76 22 E
Khandyga, Russia 65 C14 62 42N 135 35 E
Khāneh, Iran 96 B5 36 41N 45 8 E
Khanewal, Pakistan 91 C3 30 20N 71 55 E
Khanh Duong, Vietnam 86 F7 12 44N 108 44 E
Khaniá, Greece 38 D6 35 30N 24 4 E
Khaniá □, Greece 38 D6 35 30N 24 0 E
Khaníon, Kólpos, Greece 38 D5 35 33N 23 55 E
Khanka, L., Asia 68 B6 45 0N 132 24 E
Khankendy = Xankändi, Azerbaijan 101 C12 39 52N 46 49 E
Khanna, India 92 D7 30 42N 76 16 E
Khanpur, Pakistan 91 C3 28 42N 70 35 E
Khantau, Kazakstan 63 A6 44 13N 73 48 E
Khanty-Mansiysk, Russia 64 C7 61 0N 69 0 E
Khapalu, Pakistan 93 B7 35 10N 76 20 E
Khapcheranga, Russia 65 E12 49 42N 112 24 E
Kharabali, Russia 61 G8 47 25N 47 15 E
Kharagpur, India 93 H12 22 20N 87 25 E
Khárakas, Greece 38 D7 35 1N 25 7 E
Kharan Kalat, Pakistan 91 C2 28 34N 65 21 E
Kharānaq, Iran 97 C7 32 20N 54 45 E
Kharda, India 94 E2 18 40N 75 34 E
Khardung La, India 93 B7 34 20N 77 43 E
Khârga, El Wâhât el, Egypt 106 B3 25 10N 30 35 E
Khargon, India 94 D2 21 45N 75 40 E
Kharit, Wadi el →, Egypt 106 C3 24 26N 33 3 E
Khārk, Jazireh, Iran 97 D6 29 15N 50 28 E
Kharkiv, Ukraine 59 H9 49 58N 36 20 E
Kharkov = Kharkiv, Ukraine 59 H9 49 58N 36 20 E
Kharmanli, Bulgaria 51 E9 41 55N 25 55 E
Kharovsk, Russia 58 C11 59 56N 40 13 E
Kharta, Turkey 100 B3 40 55N 29 7 E
Khartoum = El Khartûm, Sudan 107 D3 15 31N 32 35 E
Khasan, Russia 68 C5 42 25N 130 40 E
Khasavyurt, Russia 61 J8 43 16N 46 40 E
Khāsh, Iran 97 D9 28 15N 61 15 E
Khashm el Girba, Sudan 107 E4 14 59N 35 58 E
Khashuri, Georgia 61 J6 42 3N 43 35 E
Khasi Hills, India 90 C3 25 30N 91 30 E
Khaskovo, Bulgaria 51 E9 41 56N 25 30 E
Khaskovo □, Bulgaria 51 E9 42 0N 25 40 E
Khatanga, Russia 65 B11 72 0N 102 20 E
Khatanga →, Russia 65 B11 72 55N 106 0 E
Khatauli, India 92 E7 29 17N 77 43 E
Khātūnābād, Iran 97 C6 35 30N 51 40 E
Khatyrchi, Uzbekistan 63 C2 40 20N 65 58 E
Khatyrka, Russia 65 C18 62 3N 175 15 E
Khavast, Uzbekistan 63 C4 40 10N 68 49 E
Khawlaf, Ra's, Yemen 99 D6 12 40N 54 7 E
Khay', Si. Arabia 98 C3 18 45N 41 24 E
Khaybar, Harrat, Si. Arabia 96 E4 25 45N 40 0 E
Khaydarken, Kyrgyzstan 63 D5 39 57N 71 20 E
Khāzimiyah, Iraq 96 C4 34 46N 43 37 E
Khazzân Jabal el Awliyâ, Sudan 107 D3 15 24N 32 20 E
Khe Bo, Vietnam 86 C5 19 8N 104 41 E
Khe Long, Vietnam 86 B5 21 29N 104 46 E
Khed, Maharashtra, India 94 F1 17 43N 73 27 E
Khed, Maharashtra, India 94 E1 18 51N 73 56 E
Khekra, India 92 E7 28 52N 77 20 E
Khemarak Phouminville, Cambodia 87 G4 11 37N 102 59 E
Khemis Miliana, Algeria 111 A5 36 11N 2 14 E
Khemissèt, Morocco 110 B3 33 50N 6 1W
Khemmarat, Thailand 86 D5 16 10N 105 15 E
Khenāmān, Iran 97 D8 30 27N 56 29 E
Khenchela, Algeria 111 A6 35 28N 7 11 E
Khenifra, Morocco 110 B3 32 58N 5 46W
Kherrata, Algeria 111 A6 36 27N 5 13 E
Khérson, Greece 50 E6 41 5N 22 47 E
Kherson, Ukraine 59 J7 46 35N 32 35 E
Khersónisos Akrotíri, Greece 38 D6 35 30N 24 10 E
Kheta →, Russia 65 B11 71 54N 102 6 E
Khiliomódhion, Greece 48 D4 37 48N 22 51 E
Khilok, Russia 65 D12 51 30N 110 45 E
Khimki, Russia 58 E9 55 50N 37 20 E
Khíos, Greece 49 C8 38 27N 26 9 E
Khíos □, Greece 49 C8 38 27N 26 9 E
Khiuma = Hiiumaa, Estonia 15 G20 58 50N 22 45 E
Khiva, Uzbekistan 64 E7 41 30N 60 18 E
Khīyāv, Iran 96 B5 38 30N 47 45 E
Khlebarovo, Bulgaria 51 C10 43 37N 26 15 E
Khlong Khlung, Thailand 86 D2 16 12N 99 43 E
Khmelnik, Ukraine 59 H4 49 33N 27 58 E
Khmelnitskiy = Khmelnytskyy, Ukraine 59 H4 49 23N 27 0 E
Khmelnytskyy, Ukraine 59 H4 49 23N 27 0 E
Khmer Rep. = Cambodia ■, Asia 86 F5 12 15N 105 0 E
Khoai, Hon, Vietnam 87 H5 8 26N 104 50 E
Khodoriv, Ukraine 59 H3 49 24N 24 19 E
Khodzent = Khudzhand, Tajikistan 63 C4 40 17N 69 37 E
Khojak Pass, Afghan. 91 C2 30 55N 66 30 E
Khok Kloi, Thailand 87 H2 8 17N 98 19 E
Khok Pho, Thailand 87 J3 6 43N 101 6 E
Kholm, Afghan. 91 A2 36 45N 67 40 E
Kholm, Russia 58 D6 57 10N 31 15 E
Kholmsk, Russia 65 E15 47 40N 142 5 E
Khomas Hochland, Namibia 116 C2 22 40 S 16 0 E
Khomeyn, Iran 97 C6 33 40N 50 7 E
Khon Kaen, Thailand 86 D4 16 30N 102 47 E
Khong →, Cambodia 86 F5 13 32N 105 58 E
Khong Sedone, Laos 86 E5 15 34N 105 49 E
Khonuu, Russia 65 C15 66 30N 143 12 E
Khoper →, Russia 60 F6 49 30N 42 20 E
Khor el 'Atash, Sudan 107 E3 13 20N 34 15 E
Khóra, Greece 48 D3 37 3N 21 42 E
Khóra Sfakíon, Greece 38 D6 35 15N 24 9 E
Khorāsān □, Iran 97 C8 34 0N 58 0 E
Khorat = Nakhon Ratchasima, Thailand 86 E4 14 59N 102 12 E
Khorat, Cao Nguyen, Thailand 86 E4 15 30N 102 50 E
Khorb el Ethel, Algeria 110 C3 28 30N 6 17W
Khorixas, Namibia 116 C1 20 16 S 14 59 E
Khorol, Ukraine 59 H7 49 48N 33 15 E
Khorramābād, Khorāsān, Iran 97 C8 35 6N 57 57 E
Khorramābād, Lorestān, Iran 97 C6 33 30N 48 25 E
Khorrāmshahr, Iran 97 D6 30 29N 48 15 E
Khorugh, Tajikistan 63 E5 37 30N 71 36 E
Khosravī, Iran 97 D6 30 48N 51 28 E
Khosrowābād, Khuzestān, Iran 97 D6 30 10N 48 25 E
Khosrowābād, Kordestān, Iran 101 E12 35 31N 47 38 E
Khosūyeh, Iran 97 D7 28 32N 54 26 E
Khotyn, Ukraine 59 H4 48 31N 26 27 E
Khouribga, Morocco 110 B3 32 58N 6 57W
Khowai, Bangla. 90 C3 24 5N 91 40 E
Khoyniki, Belarus 59 G5 51 54N 29 55 E
Khrami →, Georgia 61 K7 41 25N 45 0 E
Khrenovoye, Russia 60 E5 51 4N 40 16 E
Khrisoúpolis, Greece 51 F8 40 58N 24 42 E
Khristianá, Greece 49 E7 36 14N 25 13 E
Khromtau, Kazakstan 62 F7 50 17N 58 27 E
Khrysokhou B., Cyprus 38 D11 35 6N 32 25 E
Khtapodhiá, Greece 49 D7 37 24N 25 34 E
Khu Khan, Thailand 86 E5 14 42N 104 12 E
Khudrah, W. →, Yemen 99 C5 18 10N 50 20 E
Khudzhand, Tajikistan 63 C4 40 17N 69 37 E
Khuff, Si. Arabia 96 E5 24 55N 44 53 E
Khūgīānī, Qandahar, Afghan. 91 C2 31 34N 66 32 E
Khūgīānī, Qandahar, Afghan. 91 C2 31 28N 65 14 E
Khulayṣ, Si. Arabia 98 B2 22 9N 39 19 E
Khulna, Bangla. 90 D2 22 45N 89 34 E
Khulna □, Bangla. 90 D2 22 25N 89 35 E
Khulo, Georgia 61 K6 41 33N 42 19 E
Khumago, Botswana 116 C3 20 26 S 24 32 E
Khumrah, Si. Arabia 98 B2 21 22N 39 13 E
Khūnsorkh, Iran 97 E8 27 9N 56 7 E
Khūr, Iran 97 C8 32 55N 58 18 E
Khurai, India 92 G8 24 3N 78 23 E
Khuraydah, Yemen 99 D5 15 33N 48 18 E
Khurayṣ, Si. Arabia 97 E6 25 6N 48 2 E
Khurīyā Murīyā, Jazā 'ir, Oman 99 C6 17 30N 55 58 E
Khurja, India 92 E7 28 15N 77 58 E
Khūsf, Iran 97 C8 32 46N 58 53 E
Khushab, Pakistan 91 B4 32 20N 72 20 E
Khust, Ukraine 59 H2 48 10N 23 18 E
Khuzdar, Pakistan 91 D2 27 52N 66 30 E
Khūzestān □, Iran 97 D6 31 0N 49 0 E
Khvājeh, Iran 96 B5 38 9N 46 35 E
Khvājeh Moḥammad, Kūh-e, Afghan. 91 A3 36 22N 70 17 E
Khvalynsk, Russia 60 D9 52 30N 48 2 E
Khvānsār, Iran 97 D7 29 56N 54 8 E
Khvatovka, Russia 60 D8 52 24N 46 32 E
Khvor, Iran 97 C7 33 45N 55 0 E
Khvorgū, Iran 97 E8 27 34N 56 27 E
Khvormūj, Iran 97 D6 28 40N 51 30 E
Khvoy, Iran 101 C11 38 35N 45 0 E
Khvoynaya, Russia 58 C8 58 58N 34 28 E
Khyber Pass, Afghan. 91 B3 34 10N 71 8 E
Kia, Solomon Is. 133 L10 7 32 S 158 26 E
Kiabukwa, Dem. Rep. of the Congo 115 D4 8 40 S 24 48 E
Kiadho →, India 94 E3 19 37N 77 40 E
Kiama, Australia 129 C9 34 40 S 150 50 E
Kiamba, Phil. 81 H5 6 2N 124 46 E
Kiambi, Dem. Rep. of the Congo 118 D2 7 15 S 28 0 E
Kiambu, Kenya 118 C4 1 8 S 36 50 E
Kiana, U.S.A. 144 C7 66 58N 160 26W
Kiangsi = Jiangxi □, China 77 D11 27 30N 116 0 E
Kiangsu = Jiangsu □, China 75 H11 33 0N 120 0 E
Kiáton, Greece 48 C4 38 1N 22 45 E
Kibæk, Denmark 17 H2 56 2N 8 51 E
Kibanga Port, Uganda 118 B3 0 10N 32 58 E
Kibangou, Congo 114 C2 3 26 S 12 22 E
Kibara, Tanzania 118 C3 2 8 S 33 30 E
Kibare, Mts., Dem. Rep. of the Congo 118 D2 8 25 S 27 10 E
Kibawe, Phil. 81 H5 7 34N 125 0 E
Kibombo, Dem. Rep. of the Congo 115 C5 3 57 S 25 53 E
Kibondo, Tanzania 118 C3 3 35 S 30 45 E
Kibondo □, Tanzania 118 C3 4 0 S 30 55 E
Kibumbu, Burundi 118 C2 3 32 S 29 45 E
Kibungo, Rwanda 118 C3 2 10 S 30 32 E
Kibuye, Burundi 118 C2 3 39 S 29 59 E
Kibuye, Rwanda 118 C2 2 3 S 29 21 E
Kibwesa, Tanzania 118 D2 6 30 S 29 58 E
Kibwezi, Kenya 118 C4 2 27 S 37 57 E
Kicasalih, Turkey 51 E10 41 23N 26 48 E
Kičevo, Macedonia 50 E4 41 34N 20 59 E
Kicking Horse Pass, Canada 142 C5 51 28N 116 16W
Kidal, Mali 113 B5 18 26N 1 22 E
Kidapawan, Phil. 81 H5 7 1N 125 3 E
Kidderminster, U.K. 21 E5 52 24N 2 15W
Kidete, Tanzania 118 D4 6 25 S 37 17 E
Kidira, Senegal 112 C2 14 28N 12 13W
Kidnappers, C., N.Z. 130 F6 39 38 S 177 5 E
Kidsgrove, U.K. 20 D5 53 5N 2 14W
Kidston, Australia 126 B3 18 52 S 144 8 E
Kidugallo, Tanzania 118 D4 6 49 S 38 15 E
Kidurong, Tanjong, Malaysia 85 B4 3 16N 113 3 E
Kiel, Germany 30 A6 54 19N 10 8 E
Kiel Canal = Nord-Ostsee-Kanal →, Germany 30 A5 54 12N 9 32 E
Kielce, Poland 55 H7 50 52N 20 42 E
Kielce □, Poland 55 H7 50 40N 20 40 E
Kielder Water, U.K. 20 B5 55 11N 2 31W
Kieler Bucht, Germany 30 A6 54 35N 10 25 E
Kien Binh, Vietnam 87 H5 9 55N 105 19 E
Kien Tan, Vietnam 87 G5 10 7N 105 17 E
Kienge, Dem. Rep. of the Congo 119 E2 10 30 S 27 30 E
Kiessé, Niger 113 C5 13 29N 4 1 E
Kieta, Papua N. G. 132 D8 6 12 S 155 36 E
Kiev = Kyyiv, Ukraine 59 G6 50 30N 30 28 E
Kiffa, Mauritania 112 B2 16 37N 11 24W
Kifisiá, Greece 48 C5 38 4N 23 49 E
Kifissós →, Greece 48 C5 38 35N 23 20 E
Kifrī, Iraq 101 E11 34 45N 45 0 E
Kigali, Rwanda 118 C3 1 59 S 30 4 E
Kigarama, Tanzania 118 C3 1 1 S 31 50 E
Kigoma □, Tanzania 118 D3 5 0 S 30 0 E
Kigoma-Ujiji, Tanzania 118 C2 4 55 S 29 36 E
Kigomasha, Ras, Tanzania 118 C4 4 58 S 38 58 E
Kihee, Australia 127 D3 27 23 S 142 37 E
Kihei, U.S.A. 145 C5 20 47N 156 28W
Kihikihi, N.Z. 130 E4 38 2 S 175 22 E
Kihnu, Estonia 15 G21 58 9N 24 1 E
Kiholo B., U.S.A. 145 D6 19 50N 155 55W
Kii-Hantō, Japan 71 D7 34 0N 135 45 E
Kii-Sanchi, Japan 71 C8 34 20N 136 0 E
Kii-Suidō, Japan 70 D6 33 40N 134 45 E
Kikaiga-Shima, Japan 69 K4 28 19N 129 59 E
Kikinda, Serbia, Yug. 52 E5 45 50N 20 30 E
Kikládhes, Greece 48 E6 37 0N 24 30 E
Kikládhes □, Greece 48 D6 37 0N 25 0 E
Kikoira, Australia 129 B7 33 39 S 146 40 E
Kikori, Papua N. G. 132 D3 7 25 S 144 15 E
Kikori →, Papua N. G. 132 D3 7 38 S 144 20 E
Kikuchi, Japan 70 E2 32 59N 130 47 E
Kikwit, Dem. Rep. of the Congo 115 D3 5 0 S 18 45 E
Kil, Sweden 16 E7 59 30N 13 20 E
Kila' Drosh, Pakistan 91 B3 35 33N 71 52 E
Kilafors, Sweden 16 C10 61 14N 16 36 E
Kilakkarai, India 95 K4 9 12N 78 47 E
Kilauea Crater, U.S.A. 146 J17 19 25N 155 17W
Kilbrannan Sd., U.K. 22 F3 55 37N 5 26W
Kilchberg, Switz. 33 B7 47 18N 8 33 E
Kilchu, N. Korea 75 D15 40 57N 129 25 E
Kilcoy, Australia 127 D5 26 59 S 152 30 E
Kildare, Ireland 23 C5 53 9N 6 55W
Kildare, U.S.A. 152 C8 32 32N 81 27W
Kildare □, Ireland 23 C5 53 10N 6 50W
Kilembe, Dem. Rep. of the Congo 115 D3 5 42 S 19 55 E
Kilen, Norway 18 E5 59 20N 8 49 E
Kilfinnane, Ireland 23 D3 52 21N 8 28W
Kilgore, U.S.A. 155 J7 32 23N 94 53W
Kilifi, Kenya 118 C4 3 40 S 39 48 E
Kilifi □, Kenya 118 C4 3 30 S 39 40 E

Koronadal 235

Klipplaat, *S. Africa* **116 E3** 33 1S 24 22 E
Klisura, *Bulgaria* **51 D8** 42 40N 24 28 E
Kljajićevo, *Serbia, Yug.* **52 E4** 45 45N 19 17 E
Ključ, *Bos.-H.* **45 D13** 44 32N 16 48 E
Kłobuck, *Poland* **55 H5** 50 55N 18 55 E
Klockestrand, *Sweden* **16 B11** 62 53N 17 55 E
Kłodawa, *Poland* **55 F5** 52 15N 18 55 E
Kłodzko, *Poland* **55 H3** 50 28N 16 38 E
Kløfta, *Norway* **18 D8** 60 4N 11 10 E
Klosi, *Albania* **50 E4** 41 28N 20 10 E
Klosterneuburg, *Austria* **35 C9** 48 18N 16 19 E
Klosters, *Switz.* **33 C9** 46 52N 9 52 E
Kloten, *Switz.* **33 B7** 47 27N 8 35 E
Klötze, *Germany* **30 C7** 52 37N 11 10 E
Klouto, *Togo* **113 D5** 6 57N 0 44 E
Kluane L., *Canada* **138 B6** 61 15N 138 40W
Kluczbork, *Poland* **55 H5** 50 58N 18 12 E
Klukwan, *U.S.A.* **144 G14** 59 24N 135 54W
Klyetsk, *Belarus* **59 F4** 53 5N 26 45 E
Klyuchevskaya, Gora, *Russia* **65 D17** 55 50N 160 30 E
Knaben, *Norway* **18 F4** 58 40N 7 4 E
Knappavellir, *Iceland* **11 D10** 63 54N 16 36W
Knäred, *Sweden* **17 H7** 56 31N 13 19 E
Knaresborough, *U.K.* **20 C6** 54 1N 1 28W
Knarvik, *Norway* **18 D2** 60 32N 5 19 E
Knee L., *Man., Canada* **143 B10** 55 3N 94 45W
Knee L., *Sask., Canada* **143 B7** 55 51N 107 0W
Kneïss, Is., *Tunisia* **108 B2** 34 22N 10 18 E
Knezha, *Bulgaria* **51 C8** 43 30N 24 5 E
Knić, *Serbia, Yug.* **50 C4** 43 53N 20 42 E
Knight I., *U.S.A.* **144 F11** 60 21N 147 45W
Knight Inlet, *Canada* **142 C3** 50 45N 125 40W
Knighton, *U.K.* **21 E4** 52 21N 3 3W
Knights Ferry, *U.S.A.* **160 H6** 37 50N 120 40W
Knights Landing, *U.S.A.* **160 G5** 38 48N 121 43W
Knightstown, *U.S.A.* **157 E11** 39 48N 85 32W
Knin, *Croatia* **45 D13** 44 3N 16 17 E
Knislinge, *Sweden* **17 H8** 56 12N 14 5 E
Knittelfeld, *Austria* **34 D7** 47 13N 14 51 E
Knivsta, *Sweden* **16 E11** 59 43N 17 48 E
Knjaževac, *Serbia, Yug.* **50 C6** 43 35N 22 18 E
Knob, C., *Australia* **125 F2** 34 32 S 119 16 E
Knock, *Ireland* **23 C3** 53 48N 8 55W
Knockmealdown Mts., *Ireland* **23 D4** 52 14N 7 56W
Knokke-Heist, *Belgium* **24 C3** 51 21N 3 17 E
Knossós, *Greece* **38 D7** 35 16N 25 10 E
Knox, *U.S.A.* **157 C10** 41 18N 86 37W
Knox, C., *Canada* **142 C2** 54 11N 133 5W
Knox City, *U.S.A.* **155 J5** 33 25N 99 49W
Knox Coast, *Antarctica* **7 C8** 66 30 S 108 0 E
Knoxville, *Ga., U.S.A.* **152 C6** 32 47N 83 59W
Knoxville, *Iowa, U.S.A.* **156 C4** 41 19N 93 6W
Knoxville, *Tenn., U.S.A.* **149 H4** 35 58N 83 55W
Knud Rasmussen Land, *Greenland* **10 B4** 79 0N 60 0W
Knysna, *S. Africa* **116 E3** 34 2 S 23 2 E
Knyszyn, *Poland* **54 E9** 53 20N 22 56 E
Ko Kha, *Thailand* **86 C2** 18 11N 99 24 E
Kō-Saki, *Japan* **70 C1** 34 5N 129 13 E
Koartac = Quaqtaq, *Canada* **139 B13** 60 55N 69 40W
Koba, *Aru, Indonesia* **83 C4** 6 37 S 134 37 E
Koba, *Bangka, Indonesia* **84 C3** 2 26 S 106 14 E
Kobarid, *Slovenia* **45 B10** 46 15N 13 30 E
Kobayashi, *Japan* **70 F2** 31 56N 130 59 E
Kobdo = Hovd, *Mongolia* **72 B4** 48 2N 91 37 E
Kōbe, *Japan* **71 C7** 34 45N 135 10 E
Kobelyaky, *Ukraine* **59 H8** 49 11N 34 9 E
København, *Denmark* **17 J6** 55 41N 12 34 E
Københavns Amtskommune □, *Denmark* **17 J6** 55 42N 12 21 E
Kōbi-Sho, *Japan* **69 M1** 25 56N 123 41 E
Koblenz, *Germany* **31 E3** 50 21N 7 36 E
Koblenz, *Switz.* **32 A6** 47 37N 8 14 E
Kobo, *Dem. Rep. of the Congo* **115 C3** 4 54 S 17 9 E
Kobo, *Ethiopia* **107 E4** 12 2N 39 56 E
Kobroor, Kepulauan, *Indonesia* **83 C4** 6 10 S 134 30 E
Kobryn, *Belarus* **59 F3** 52 15N 24 22 E
Kobuchizawa, *Japan* **71 B10** 35 52N 138 19 E
Kobuk →, *U.S.A.* **144 C7** 66 54N 160 38W
Kobuleti, *Georgia* **61 K5** 41 55N 41 45 E
Kobylin, *Poland* **55 G4** 51 43N 17 12 E
Kobyłka, *Poland* **55 F8** 52 21N 21 10 E
Kobylkino, *Russia* **60 C6** 54 8N 43 56 E
Koca →, *Turkey* **51 F11** 40 8N 27 57 E
Kocabaş, *Turkey* **49 D11** 37 49N 29 20 E
Kocaeli, *Turkey* **51 F13** 40 45N 29 50 E
Kocaeli □, *Turkey* **51 F13** 40 45N 29 55 E
Kočane, *Serbia, Yug.* **50 C5** 43 12N 21 52 E
Kočani, *Macedonia* **50 E6** 41 55N 22 25 E
Koçarlı, *Turkey* **49 D9** 37 45N 27 43 E
Koceljevo, *Serbia, Yug.* **50 B3** 44 28N 19 50 E
Kočevje, *Slovenia* **45 C11** 45 39N 14 50 E
Koch Bihar, *India* **90 B2** 26 22N 89 29 E
Kochang, *S. Korea* **75 G14** 35 41N 127 55 E
Kochas, *India* **93 G10** 25 15N 83 56 E
Kocher →, *Germany* **31 F5** 49 13N 9 12 E
Kōchi, *Japan* **70 D5** 33 30N 133 35 E
Kōchi □, *Japan* **70 D5** 33 40N 133 30 E
Kōchi-Heiya, *Japan* **70 D5** 33 28N 133 30 E
Kochiu = Gejiu, *China* **76 F4** 23 20N 103 10 E
Kochkor-Ata, *Kyrgyzstan* **63 C6** 41 1N 72 29 E
Kochkorka, *Kyrgyzstan* **63 B7** 42 13N 75 46 E
Kock, *Poland* **55 G9** 51 38N 22 27 E
Kodaira, *Japan* **71 B11** 35 44N 139 29 E
Koddiyar B., *Sri Lanka* **95 K5** 8 33N 81 15 E
Kode, *Sweden* **17 G5** 57 57N 11 51 E
Kodiak, *U.S.A.* **138 C4** 57 47N 152 24W
Kodiak I., *U.S.A.* **138 C4** 57 30N 152 45W
Kodinar, *India* **92 J4** 20 46N 70 46 E
Kodori →, *Georgia* **61 J5** 42 47N 41 10 E
Koes, *Namibia* **116 D2** 26 0 S 19 15 E
Kofçaz, *Turkey* **51 E11** 41 58N 27 12 E
Koffiefontein, *S. Africa* **116 D4** 29 30 S 25 0 E
Kofiau, *Indonesia* **83 B3** 1 11 S 129 50 E
Köflach, *Austria* **34 D8** 47 4N 15 5 E
Koforidua, *Ghana* **113 D4** 6 3N 0 17W
Kōfu, *Japan* **71 B10** 35 40N 138 30 E
Koga, *Japan* **71 A11** 36 11N 139 43 E
Kogaluk →, *Canada* **141 A7** 56 12N 61 44W
Kogan, *Australia* **127 D5** 27 2 S 150 40 E
Køge, *Denmark* **17 J6** 55 27N 12 11 E
Køge Bugt, *Denmark* **17 J6** 55 30N 12 20 E
Kogi □, *Nigeria* **113 D6** 7 45N 6 45 E
Kogin Baba, *Nigeria* **113 D7** 7 55N 11 35 E
Koh-i-Bābā, *Afghan.* **91 B2** 34 30N 67 0 E
Koh-i-Khurd, *Afghan.* **92 C1** 33 30N 65 59 E
Kohala Mts., *U.S.A.* **145 C6** 20 5N 155 45W
Kohat, *Pakistan* **91 B3** 33 40N 71 29 E
Kohima, *India* **90 C5** 25 35N 94 10 E
Kohkīlūyeh va Būyer Aḥmadi □, *Iran* **97 D6** 31 30N 50 30 E
Kohler Ra., *Antarctica* **7 D15** 77 0 S 110 0W
Kohtla-Järve, *Estonia* **15 G22** 59 20N 27 20 E
Kohukohu, *N.Z.* **130 B2** 35 22 S 173 38 E
Koillismaa, *Finland* **14 D23** 65 44N 28 36 E
Koin-dong, *N. Korea* **75 D14** 40 28N 126 18 E
Koinare, *Bulgaria* **51 C8** 43 21N 24 8 E
Kojetín, *Czech Rep.* **35 B10** 49 21N 17 20 E
Kojima, *Japan* **70 C5** 34 30N 133 50 E
Kōjo, *Japan* **70 C5** 34 33N 133 55 E
Kojŏ, *N. Korea* **75 E14** 38 58N 127 58 E
Kojonup, *Australia* **125 F2** 33 48 S 117 10 E
Kojūr, *Iran* **97 B6** 36 23N 51 43 E
Kok Yangak, *Kyrgyzstan* **63 C6** 41 2N 73 12 E
Koka, *Sudan* **106 C3** 20 5N 30 35 E
Kokand = Qŭqon, *Uzbekistan* **63 C5** 40 30N 70 57 E
Kokanee Glacier Prov. Park, *Canada* **142 D5** 49 47N 117 10W
Kokas, *Indonesia* **83 B4** 2 42 S 132 26 E
Kokava, *Slovak Rep.* **35 C12** 48 35N 19 50 E
Kokchetav = Kökshetaū, *Kazakstan* **64 D7** 53 20N 69 25 E
Kokemäenjoki →, *Finland* **15 F19** 61 32N 21 44 E
Kokerite, *Guyana* **169 B6** 7 12N 59 35W
Kokhma, *Russia* **60 B5** 56 57N 41 8 E
Kokiri, *N.Z.* **131 C6** 42 29 S 171 25 E
Kokkola, *Finland* **14 E20** 63 50N 23 8 E
Koko, *Nigeria* **113 C5** 11 28N 4 29 E
Koko Head, *U.S.A.* **145 K14** 21 16N 157 43W
Kokoda, *Papua N. G.* **132 E4** 8 54 S 147 47 E
Kokolopozo, *Ivory C.* **112 D3** 5 8N 6 5W
Kokomo, *U.S.A.* **157 D10** 40 29N 86 8W
Kokonau, *Indonesia* **83 B5** 4 43 S 136 26 E
Kokopo, *Papua N. G.* **132 C7** 4 22 S 152 19 E
Kokoro, *Niger* **113 C5** 14 12N 0 55 E
Koksan, *N. Korea* **75 E14** 38 46N 126 40 E
Köksengir, Gora, *Kazakstan* **63 A2** 44 21N 65 6 E
Kökshetaū, *Kazakstan* **64 D7** 53 20N 69 25 E
Koksoak →, *Canada* **139 C13** 58 30N 68 10W
Kokstad, *S. Africa* **117 E4** 30 32 S 29 29 E
Kokubu, *Japan* **70 F2** 31 44N 130 46 E
Kola, *Indonesia* **83 C4** 5 35 S 134 30 E
Kola, *Russia* **56 A5** 68 45N 33 8 E
Kola Pen. = Kolskiy Poluostrov, *Russia* **56 A6** 67 30N 38 0 E
Kolachel, *India* **95 K3** 8 10N 77 15 E
Kolahoi, *India* **93 B6** 34 12N 75 22 E
Kolahun, *Liberia* **112 D2** 8 15N 10 4W
Kolaka, *Indonesia* **82 B2** 4 3 S 121 46 E
Kolar, *India* **95 H4** 13 12N 78 15 E
Kolar Gold Fields, *India* **95 H4** 12 58N 78 16 E
Kolari, *Finland* **14 C20** 67 20N 23 48 E
Kolárovo, *Slovak Rep.* **35 D10** 47 54N 18 0 E
Kolašin, *Montenegro, Yug.* **50 D3** 42 50N 19 31 E
Kolbäck, *Sweden* **16 E10** 59 34N 16 15 E
Kolbäcksån →, *Sweden* **16 E10** 59 36N 16 16 E
Kolbeinsstaðir, *Iceland* **11 C4** 64 59N 22 16W
Kolbermoor, *Germany* **31 H8** 47 51N 12 4 E
Kolbu, *Norway* **18 D7** 60 39N 10 45 E
Kolbuszowa, *Poland* **55 H8** 50 15N 21 46 E
Kolchugino = Leninsk-Kuznetskiy, *Russia* **64 D9** 54 44N 86 10 E
Kolchugino, *Russia* **58 D10** 56 17N 39 22 E
Kolda, *Senegal* **112 C2** 12 55N 14 57W
Kolding, *Denmark* **17 J3** 55 30N 9 29 E
Kole, *Dem. Rep. of the Congo* **114 C4** 3 16 S 22 42 E
Koléa, *Algeria* **111 A5** 36 38N 2 46 E
Kolepom = Dolak, Pulau, *Indonesia* **83 C5** 8 0 S 138 30 E
Kolguyev, Ostrov, *Russia* **56 A8** 69 20N 48 30 E
Kolhapur, *India* **94 F2** 16 43N 74 15 E
Kolia, *Ivory C.* **112 D3** 9 46N 6 28W
Koliganek, *U.S.A.* **144 G8** 59 48N 157 25W
Kolín, *Czech Rep.* **34 A8** 50 2N 15 9 E
Kolind, *Denmark* **17 H4** 56 21N 10 34 E
Kolkas rags, *Latvia* **15 H20** 57 46N 22 37 E
Kollabúðir, *Iceland* **11 B4** 65 37N 22 4W
Kölleda, *Germany* **30 D7** 51 11N 11 15 E
Kollegal, *India* **95 H3** 12 9N 77 9 E
Kolleru L., *India* **94 F5** 16 40N 81 10 E
Kollsvík, *Iceland* **11 B2** 65 37N 24 19W
Kollum, *Neths.* **24 A6** 53 17N 6 10 E
Kolmanskop, *Namibia* **116 D2** 26 45 S 15 14 E
Köln, *Germany* **30 E2** 50 56N 6 57 E
Kolno, *Poland* **54 E8** 53 25N 21 56 E
Koło, *Poland* **55 F5** 52 14N 18 40 E
Koloa, *U.S.A.* **145 B2** 21 55N 159 28W
Kołobrzeg, *Poland* **54 D2** 54 10N 15 35 E
Kolokani, *Mali* **112 C3** 13 35N 7 45W
Kolombangara, *Solomon Is.* **133 M9** 8 0 S 157 5 E
Kolomna, *Russia* **58 E10** 55 8N 38 45 E
Kolomyya, *Ukraine* **59 H3** 48 31N 25 2 E
Kolondiéba, *Mali* **112 C3** 11 5N 6 54W
Kolonodale, *Indonesia* **82 B2** 2 3 S 121 25 E
Kolonowskie, *Poland* **55 H5** 50 39N 18 22 E
Kolosib, *India* **90 C4** 24 15N 92 45 E
Kolpashevo, *Russia* **64 D9** 58 20N 83 5 E
Kolpino, *Russia* **58 C6** 59 44N 30 39 E
Kolpny, *Russia* **59 F9** 52 17N 37 1 E
Kolskiy Poluostrov, *Russia* **56 A6** 67 30N 38 0 E
Kolskiy Zaliv, *Russia* **56 A5** 69 23N 34 0 E
Kolsva, *Sweden* **16 E9** 59 36N 15 51 E
Kolubara →, *Serbia, Yug.* **50 B4** 44 35N 20 15 E
Koluszki, *Poland* **55 G6** 51 45N 19 46 E
Kolwezi, *Dem. Rep. of the Congo* **119 E2** 10 40 S 25 25 E
Kolyma →, *Russia* **65 C17** 69 30N 161 0 E
Kolymskoye Nagorye, *Russia* **65 C16** 63 0N 157 0 E
Kôm Ombo, *Egypt* **106 C3** 24 25N 32 52 E
Komagene, *Japan* **71 B9** 35 44N 137 58 E
Komaki, *Japan* **71 B8** 35 17N 136 55 E
Komandorskiye Is. = Komandorskiye Ostrova, *Russia* **65 D17** 55 0N 167 0 E
Komandorskiye Ostrova, *Russia* **65 D17** 55 0N 167 0 E
Komárno, *Slovak Rep.* **35 D11** 47 49N 18 5 E
Komárom, *Hungary* **52 C3** 47 43N 18 7 E
Komárom-Esztergom □, *Hungary* **52 C3** 47 35N 18 20 E
Komatipoort, *S. Africa* **117 D5** 25 25 S 31 55 E
Komatou Yialou, *Cyprus* **38 D13** 35 25N 34 8 E
Komatsu, *Japan* **71 A8** 36 25N 136 30 E
Komatsujima, *Japan* **70 D6** 34 0N 134 35 E
Kombissiri, *Burkina Faso* **113 C4** 12 4N 1 20W
Kombo, *Gabon* **114 C2** 0 20 S 12 22 E
Kombori, *Burkina Faso* **112 C4** 13 26N 3 56W
Kombóti, *Greece* **48 B3** 39 6N 21 5 E
Komen, *Slovenia* **45 C10** 45 49N 13 45 E
Komenda, *Ghana* **113 D4** 5 4N 1 28W
Komi □, *Russia* **56 B10** 64 0N 55 0 E
Komiža, *Croatia* **45 E13** 43 3N 16 11 E
Komló, *Hungary* **52 D3** 46 15N 18 16 E
Kommamur Canal, *India* **95 G5** 16 0N 80 25 E
Kommunarsk = Alchevsk, *Ukraine* **59 H10** 48 30N 38 45 E
Kommunizma, Pik, *Tajikistan* **63 D6** 39 0N 72 2 E
Komodo, *Indonesia* **82 C1** 8 37 S 119 20 E
Komoé, *Ivory C.* **112 D4** 5 12N 3 44W
Komono, *Congo* **114 C2** 3 10 S 13 20 E
Komoran, Pulau, *Indonesia* **83 C5** 8 18 S 138 45 E
Komoro, *Japan* **71 A10** 36 19N 138 26 E
Komotini, *Greece* **51 E9** 41 9N 25 26 E
Komovi, *Montenegro, Yug.* **50 D3** 42 41N 19 39 E
Kompasberg, *S. Africa* **116 E3** 31 45 S 24 32 E
Kompong Bang, *Cambodia* **87 F5** 12 24N 104 40 E
Kompong Cham, *Cambodia* **87 G5** 12 0N 105 30 E
Kompong Chhnang = Kampang Chhnang, *Cambodia* **87 F5** 12 20N 104 35 E
Kompong Chikreng, *Cambodia* **86 F5** 13 5N 104 18 E
Kompong Kleang, *Cambodia* **86 F5** 13 6N 104 8 E
Kompong Luong, *Cambodia* **87 G5** 11 49N 104 48 E
Kompong Pranak, *Cambodia* **86 F5** 13 35N 104 55 E
Kompong Som = Kampong Saom, *Cambodia* **87 G4** 10 38N 103 30 E
Kompong Som, Chhung = Kampong Saom, Chaak, *Cambodia* **87 G4** 10 50N 103 32 E
Kompong Speu, *Cambodia* **87 G5** 11 26N 104 32 E
Kompong Sralao, *Cambodia* **86 E5** 14 5N 105 46 E
Kompong Thom, *Cambodia* **86 F5** 12 35N 104 51 E
Kompong Trabeck, *Cambodia* **86 F5** 13 6N 105 14 E
Kompong Trabeck, *Cambodia* **87 G5** 11 9N 105 28 E
Kompong Trach, *Cambodia* **87 G5** 11 25N 105 48 E
Kompong Tralach, *Cambodia* **87 G5** 11 54N 104 47 E
Komrat = Comrat, *Moldova* **53 D13** 46 18N 28 40 E
Komsberg, *S. Africa* **116 E3** 32 40 S 20 45 E
Komsomolabad, *Tajikistan* **63 D4** 38 50N 69 55 E
Komsomolets, *Kazakstan* **62 E9** 53 45N 62 2 E
Komsomolets, Ostrov, *Russia* **65 A10** 80 30N 95 0 E
Komsomolsk, *Amur, Russia* **65 D14** 50 30N 137 0 E
Komsomolsk, *Ivanovo, Russia* **58 D11** 57 2N 40 20 E
Komsomolsk, *Turkmenistan* **63 D1** 39 2N 63 36 E
Komsomolskiy, *Russia* **60 C7** 54 27N 45 33 E
Kömür Burnu, *Turkey* **49 C8** 38 39N 26 12 E
Kon Tum, *Vietnam* **86 E7** 14 24N 108 0 E
Kon Tum, Plateau du, *Vietnam* **86 E7** 14 30N 108 30 E
Konakovo, *Russia* **58 D9** 56 40N 36 51 E
Konarhá □, *Afghan.* **91 B3** 35 30N 71 3 E
Konārī, *Iran* **97 D6** 28 13N 51 36 E
Konawa, *U.S.A.* **155 H6** 34 58N 96 45W
Konch, *India* **93 G8** 26 0N 79 10 E
Kondagaon, *India* **94 E5** 19 35N 81 35 E
Konde, *Tanzania* **118 C4** 4 57 S 39 45 E
Kondiá, *Greece* **49 B7** 39 49N 25 10 E
Kondinin, *Australia* **125 F2** 32 34 S 118 8 E
Kondo, *Dem. Rep. of the Congo* **115 D2** 5 35 S 13 0 E
Kondoa, *Tanzania* **118 C4** 4 55 S 35 50 E
Kondoa □, *Tanzania* **118 D4** 5 0 S 36 0 E
Kondókali, *Greece* **38 A3** 39 38N 19 51 E
Kondopaga, *Russia* **58 A8** 62 12N 34 17 E
Kondratyevo, *Russia* **65 D10** 57 22N 98 15 E
Kondrovo, *Russia* **58 E8** 54 48N 35 56 E
Konduga, *Nigeria* **113 C7** 11 35N 13 26 E
Kondukur, *India* **95 G4** 15 12N 79 57 E
Koné, *N. Cal.* **133 U18** 21 4 S 164 52 E
Köneürgench, *Turkmenistan* **64 E6** 42 19N 59 10 E
Konevo, *Russia* **58 A10** 62 8N 39 20 E
Kong, *Ivory C.* **112 D4** 8 54N 4 36W
Kong → = Khong →, *Cambodia* **86 F5** 13 32N 105 58 E
Kong, Koh, *Cambodia* **87 G4** 11 20N 103 0 E
Kong Christian IX.s Land, *Greenland* **10 D7** 68 0N 36 0W
Kong Christian X.s Land, *Greenland* **10 C8** 74 0N 29 0W
Kong Franz Joseph Fd., *Greenland* **10 C8** 73 30N 24 30W
Kong Frederik IX.s Land, *Greenland* **10 D5** 67 0N 52 0W
Kong Frederik VI.s Kyst, *Greenland* **10 E6** 63 0N 43 0W
Kong Frederik VIII.s Land, *Greenland* **10 B8** 78 30N 26 0W
Kong Oscar Fjord, *Greenland* **10 C8** 72 20N 24 0W
Kongbo, *C.A.R.* **114 B4** 4 44N 21 23 E
Kongeå →, *Denmark* **17 J2** 55 23N 8 39 E
Kongerslev, *Denmark* **17 H4** 56 54N 10 8 E
Kongju, *S. Korea* **75 F14** 36 30N 127 0 E
Kongkemul, *Indonesia* **85 B4** 1 52N 112 11 E
Konglu, *Burma* **90 B6** 27 13N 97 57 E
Kongolo, *Kasai Or., Dem. Rep. of the Congo* **115 D4** 5 26 S 24 49 E
Kongolo, *Shaba, Dem. Rep. of the Congo* **118 D2** 5 22 S 27 0 E
Kongor, *Sudan* **107 F3** 7 1N 31 27 E
Kongoussi, *Burkina Faso* **113 C4** 13 19N 1 32W
Kongsberg, *Norway* **15 G13** 59 39N 9 39 E
Kongsvinger, *Norway* **15 F15** 60 12N 12 2 E
Kongwa, *Tanzania* **118 D4** 6 11 S 36 26 E
Koni, *Dem. Rep. of the Congo* **119 E2** 10 40 S 27 11 E
Koni, Mts., *Dem. Rep. of the Congo* **119 E2** 10 36 S 27 10 E
Koniecpol, *Poland* **55 H6** 50 46N 19 40 E
Königs Wusterhausen, *Germany* **30 C9** 52 19N 13 38 E
Königsberg = Kaliningrad, *Russia* **56 D3** 54 42N 20 32 E
Königsbrunn, *Germany* **31 G6** 48 16N 10 54 E
Königslutter, *Germany* **30 C6** 52 15N 10 49 E
Konin, *Poland* **55 F5** 52 12N 18 15 E
Konin □, *Poland* **55 F5** 52 15N 18 30 E
Konispoli, *Albania* **50 G4** 39 42N 20 10 E
Kónitsa, *Greece* **48 A2** 40 5N 20 48 E
Köniz, *Switz.* **32 C4** 46 56N 7 25 E
Konjic, *Bos.-H.* **52 G2** 43 42N 17 58 E
Konkiep, *Namibia* **116 D2** 26 49 S 17 15 E
Konkouré →, *Guinea* **112 D2** 9 50N 13 42W
Könnern, *Germany* **30 D7** 51 41N 11 47 E
Konnur, *India* **95 F2** 16 14N 74 49 E
Kono, *S. Leone* **112 D2** 8 30N 11 5W
Konolfingen, *Switz.* **32 C5** 46 54N 7 38 E
Konongo, *Ghana* **113 D4** 6 40N 1 15W
Konos, *Papua N. G.* **132 B6** 3 10 S 151 44 E
Konosha, *Russia* **58 B11** 61 0N 40 5 E
Kōnosu, *Japan* **71 A11** 36 3N 139 31 E
Konotop, *Ukraine* **59 G7** 51 12N 33 7 E
Końskie, *Poland* **55 G7** 51 15N 20 23 E
Konsmo, *Norway* **18 F4** 58 16N 7 23 E
Konstancin-Jeziorna, *Poland* **55 F8** 52 5N 21 7 E
Konstantinovka = Kostyantynivka, *Ukraine* **59 H9** 48 32N 37 39 E
Konstantinovsk, *Russia* **61 G5** 47 33N 41 10 E
Konstantynów Łódźki, *Poland* **55 G6** 51 45N 19 20 E
Konstanz, *Germany* **31 H5** 47 40N 9 10 E
Kont, *Iran* **97 E9** 26 55N 61 50 E
Kontagora, *Nigeria* **113 C6** 10 23N 5 27 E
Konya, *Turkey* **100 D5** 37 52N 32 35 E
Konya Ovası, *Turkey* **100 C5** 38 9N 33 5 E
Konyin, *Burma* **90 D5** 22 58N 94 42 E
Konz, *Germany* **31 F2** 49 42N 6 34 E
Konza, *Kenya* **118 C4** 1 45 S 37 7 E
Konzhakovskiy Kamen, Gora, *Russia* **62 B7** 59 38N 59 8 E
Kookynie, *Australia* **125 E3** 29 17 S 121 22 E
Koolau Range, *U.S.A.* **145 J14** 21 35N 157 50W
Kooline, *Australia* **124 D2** 22 57 S 116 20 E
Kooloonong, *Australia* **128 C5** 34 48 S 143 10 E
Koolyanobbing, *Australia* **125 F2** 30 48 S 119 36 E
Koondrook, *Australia* **128 C6** 35 33 S 144 8 E
Koonibba, *Australia* **127 E1** 31 54 S 133 25 E
Koorawatha, *Australia* **129 C8** 34 2 S 148 33 E
Koorda, *Australia* **125 F2** 30 48 S 117 35 E
Kooskia, *U.S.A.* **158 C6** 46 9N 115 59W
Kootenai →, *Canada* **158 B5** 49 15N 117 39W
Kootenay L., *Canada* **142 D5** 49 45N 116 50W
Kootenay Nat. Park, *Canada* **142 C5** 51 0N 116 0W
Kootjieskolk, *S. Africa* **116 E3** 31 15 S 20 21 E
Kopa, *Kazakstan* **63 B7** 43 31N 75 50 E
Kopanovka, *Russia* **61 G8** 47 28N 46 50 E
Kopaonik, *Serbia, Yug.* **50 C4** 43 10N 20 50 E
Kopargaon, *India* **94 E2** 19 51N 74 28 E
Kópasker, *Iceland* **11 A10** 66 18N 16 27W
Kópavogur, *Iceland* **11 C5** 64 6N 21 55W
Koper, *Slovenia* **45 C10** 45 31N 13 44 E
Kopervik, *Norway* **15 G11** 59 17N 5 17 E
Kopeysk, *Russia* **62 D8** 55 7N 61 37 E
Kopi, *Australia* **127 E2** 33 24 S 135 40 E
Köping, *Sweden* **16 E10** 59 31N 16 3 E
Köpingsvik, *Sweden* **17 H10** 56 53N 16 43 E
Kopište, *Croatia* **45 F13** 42 48N 16 42 E
Kopliku, *Albania* **50 D3** 42 15N 19 25 E
Köpmanholmen, *Sweden* **16 A12** 63 10N 18 35 E
Koppal, *India* **95 G3** 15 23N 76 5 E
Koppang, *Norway* **18 C8** 61 34N 11 3 E
Kopparberg, *Sweden* **16 E9** 59 52N 15 0 E
Kopparbergs län □, *Sweden* **16 C8** 61 0N 14 15 E
Koppeh Dāgh, *Asia* **97 B8** 38 0N 58 0 E
Kopperå, *Norway* **18 A8** 63 24N 11 50 E
Koppies, *S. Africa* **117 D4** 27 20 S 27 30 E
Koppio, *Australia* **128 C1** 34 26 S 135 51 E
Koppom, *Sweden* **16 E6** 59 43N 12 10 E
Koprivlen, *Bulgaria* **50 E7** 41 31N 23 53 E
Koprivnica, *Croatia* **45 B13** 46 12N 16 45 E
Kopřivnice, *Czech Rep.* **35 B11** 49 36N 18 9 E
Koprivshtitsa, *Bulgaria* **51 D8** 42 40N 24 19 E
Köprübaşı, *Turkey* **49 C10** 38 43N 28 23 E
Kopychyntsi, *Ukraine* **59 H3** 49 7N 25 58 E
Korab, *Macedonia* **50 E4** 41 44N 20 40 E
Korakiána, *Greece* **38 A3** 39 42N 19 45 E
Koraput, *India* **94 E6** 18 50N 82 40 E
Korba, *India* **93 H10** 22 20N 82 45 E
Korbach, *Germany* **30 D4** 51 16N 8 52 E
Korbu, G., *Malaysia* **87 K3** 4 41N 101 18 E
Korça, *Albania* **50 F4** 40 37N 20 50 E
Korce = Korça, *Albania* **50 F4** 40 37N 20 50 E
Korčula, *Croatia* **45 F13** 42 56N 16 57 E
Korčulanski Kanal, *Croatia* **45 E13** 43 3N 16 40 E
Kord Kūy, *Iran* **97 B7** 36 48N 54 7 E
Kord Sheykh, *Iran* **97 D7** 28 31N 52 53 E
Kordestān □, *Iran* **96 C5** 36 0N 47 0 E
Korea, North ■, *Asia* **75 E14** 40 0N 127 0 E
Korea, South ■, *Asia* **75 G15** 36 0N 128 0 E
Korea Bay, *Korea* **75 E13** 39 0N 124 0 E
Korea Strait, *Asia* **75 H15** 34 0N 129 30 E
Koregaon, *India* **94 F2** 17 40N 74 10 E
Korenevo, *Russia* **59 G8** 51 27N 34 55 E
Korenovsk, *Russia* **61 H4** 45 30N 39 22 E
Korets, *Ukraine* **59 G4** 50 40N 27 5 E
Korfantów, *Poland* **55 H4** 50 29N 17 36 E
Korgan, *Turkey* **100 B7** 40 44N 37 13 E
Korgus, *Sudan* **106 D3** 19 16N 33 29 E
Korhogo, *Ivory C.* **112 D3** 9 29N 5 28W
Koribundu, *S. Leone* **112 D2** 7 41N 11 46W
Korim, *Indonesia* **83 B5** 0 58 S 136 10 E
Korinthía □, *Greece* **48 D4** 37 50N 22 35 E
Korinthiakós Kólpos, *Greece* **48 C4** 38 16N 22 30 E
Kórinthos, *Greece* **48 D4** 37 56N 22 55 E
Korioumé, *Mali* **112 B4** 16 35N 3 0W
Koríssa, Límni, *Greece* **38 B3** 39 27N 19 53 E
Kōriyama, *Japan* **68 F10** 37 24N 140 23 E
Korkino, *Russia* **62 D8** 54 54N 61 23 E
Korkuteli, *Turkey* **49 D12** 37 4N 30 13 E
Korla, *China* **72 B3** 41 45N 86 4 E
Kormakiti, C., *Cyprus* **38 D11** 35 23N 32 56 E
Körmend, *Hungary* **52 C1** 47 5N 16 35 E
Kornat, *Croatia* **45 E12** 43 50N 15 20 E
Korneshty = Cornești, *Moldova* **53 C13** 47 21N 28 1 E
Korneuburg, *Austria* **35 C9** 48 20N 16 20 E
Kórnik, *Poland* **55 F4** 52 15N 17 6 E
Kornsjø, *Norway* **18 F8** 58 57N 11 39 E
Koro, *Fiji* **133 A2** 17 19 S 179 23 E
Koro, *Ivory C.* **112 D3** 8 32N 7 30W
Koro, *Mali* **112 C4** 14 1N 2 58W
Koro Sea, *Fiji* **133 A3** 17 30 S 179 45W
Koro Toro, *Chad* **109 E3** 16 5N 18 30 E
Koroba, *Papua N. G.* **132 C2** 5 44 S 142 47 E
Korocha, *Russia* **59 G9** 50 54N 37 19 E
Köroğlu Dağları, *Turkey* **100 B5** 40 38N 33 0 E
Korogwe, *Tanzania* **118 D4** 5 5 S 38 25 E
Korogwe □, *Tanzania* **118 D4** 5 0 S 38 20 E
Koroit, *Australia* **128 E5** 38 18 S 142 24 E
Korona, *U.S.A.* **153 F8** 29 25N 81 12W
Koronadal, *Phil.* **81 H5** 6 12N 125 1 E

L

Lawrenceburg 239

Lakewood, N.J., U.S.A. **151 F10** 40 6N 74 13W
Lakewood, Ohio, U.S.A. **150 E3** 41 29N 81 48W
Lakewood Center, U.S.A. **160 C4** 47 11N 122 32W
Lakhaniá, Greece **38 D9** 35 58N 27 54 E
Lakhipur, Assam, India **90 C4** 24 48N 93 0 E
Lakhipur, Assam, India **90 B3** 26 2N 90 18 E
Lakhonpheng, Laos **86 E5** 15 54N 105 34 E
Lakhpat, India **92 H3** 23 48N 68 47 E
Läki, Azerbaijan **61 K8** 40 34N 47 22 E
Laki, Iceland **11 C8** 64 4N 18 14W
Lakin, U.S.A. **155 G4** 37 57N 101 15W
Lakitusaki →, Canada **140 B3** 54 21N 82 25W
Lákkoi, Greece **38 D5** 35 24N 23 57 E
Lakonía □, Greece **48 E4** 36 55N 22 30 E
Lakonikós Kólpos, Greece **48 E4** 36 40N 22 40 E
Lakor, Indonesia **82 C3** 8 15 S 128 17 E
Lakota, Ivory C. **112 D3** 5 50N 5 30W
Lakota, U.S.A. **154 A5** 48 2N 98 21W
Laksefjorden, Norway **14 A22** 70 45N 26 50 E
Lakselv, Norway **14 A21** 70 2N 25 0 E
Lakshadweep Is., Ind. Oc. **121 C6** 10 0N 72 30 E
Laksham, Bangla. **90 D3** 23 14N 91 8 E
Lakshmeshwar, India **95 G2** 15 9N 75 28 E
Lakshmikantapur, India **93 H13** 22 5N 88 20 E
Lakshmipur, Bangla. **90 D3** 22 58N 90 50 E
Lakuramau, Papua N. G. **132 B6** 2 54 S 151 15 E
Lal-lo, Phil. **80 B3** 18 12N 121 40 E
Lala, Phil. **81 H4** 7 59N 123 46 E
Lala Musa, Pakistan **92 C5** 32 40N 73 57 E
Lalago, Tanzania **118 C3** 3 28 S 33 58 E
Lalapanzi, Zimbabwe **119 F3** 19 20 S 30 15 E
Lalapaşa, Turkey **51 E10** 41 49N 26 44 E
Lalbenque, France **28 D5** 44 19N 1 34 E
L'Albufera, Spain **41 F4** 39 20N 0 27W
Lalganj, India **93 G11** 25 52N 85 13 E
Lalibela, Ethiopia **107 E4** 12 2N 39 2 E
Lalin, China **75 B14** 45 12N 127 0 E
Lalín, Spain **42 C2** 42 40N 8 5W
Lalin He →, China **75 B13** 45 32N 125 40 E
Lalinde, France **28 D4** 44 50N 0 44 E
Lalitpur, India **93 G8** 24 42N 78 28 E
Lalm, Norway **18 C6** 61 50N 9 17 E
Lam, Vietnam **86 B6** 21 21N 106 31 E
Lam Pao Res., Thailand **86 D4** 16 50N 103 15 E
Lama Kara, Togo **113 D5** 9 30N 1 15 E
Lamag, Malaysia **85 A5** 5 29N 117 49 E
Lamaipum, Burma **90 C6** 25 40N 97 57 E
Lamap, Vanuatu **133 F5** 16 26 S 167 43 E
Lamar, Colo., U.S.A. **154 F3** 38 5N 102 37W
Lamar, Mo., U.S.A. **155 G7** 37 30N 94 16W
Lamarque, Argentina **176 A3** 39 24 S 65 40W
Lamas, Peru **172 B2** 6 28 S 76 31W
Lamastre, France **29 D8** 44 59N 4 35 E
Lambach, Austria **34 C6** 48 6N 13 51 E
Lamballe, France **26 D4** 48 29N 2 31W
Lambaréné, Gabon **114 C2** 0 41 S 10 12 E
Lambasa, Fiji **133 A2** 16 30 S 179 10 E
Lambay I., Ireland **23 C5** 53 29N 6 1W
Lambayeque □, Peru **172 B2** 6 45 S 80 0W
Lambert, U.S.A. **154 B2** 47 41N 104 37W
Lambert, C., Papua N. G. **132 C6** 4 11 S 151 31 E
Lambert Glacier, Antarctica **7 D6** 71 0 S 70 0 E
Lamberts Bay, S. Africa **116 E2** 32 5 S 18 17 E
Lambesc, France **29 E9** 43 39N 5 16 E
Lambi Kyun, Burma **87 G2** 10 50N 98 20 E
Lámbia, Greece **48 D3** 37 52N 21 53 E
Lambon, Papua N. G. **132 C7** 4 45 S 152 48 E
Lambro →, Italy **44 C6** 45 8N 9 32 E
Lambunao, Phil. **81 F4** 11 3N 122 29 E
Lame, Nigeria **113 C6** 10 30N 9 20 E
Lame Deer, U.S.A. **158 D10** 45 37N 106 40W
Lamego, Portugal **42 D3** 41 5N 7 52W
Lamèque, Canada **141 C7** 47 45N 64 38W
Lameroo, Australia **128 C4** 35 19 S 140 33 E
Lamesa, U.S.A. **155 J4** 32 44N 101 58W
Lamía, Greece **48 C4** 38 55N 22 26 E
Lamitan, Phil. **81 H4** 6 39N 122 8 E
Lammermuir Hills, U.K. **22 F6** 55 50N 2 40W
Lammhult, Sweden **17 G8** 57 10N 14 35 E
Lamon B., Phil. **80 D4** 14 30N 122 20 E
Lamongan, Indonesia **85 D4** 7 7 S 112 25 E
Lamoni, U.S.A. **156 D3** 40 37N 93 56W
Lamont, Canada **142 C6** 53 46N 112 50W
Lamont, Calif., U.S.A. **161 K8** 35 15N 118 55W
Lamont, Fla., U.S.A. **152 E6** 30 23N 83 49W
Lamont, Iowa, U.S.A. **156 B5** 42 35N 91 40W
Lamotte-Beuvron, France **27 E9** 47 36N 2 2 E
Lampa, Peru **172 D3** 15 22 S 70 22W
Lampang, Thailand **86 C2** 18 16N 99 32 E
Lampasas, U.S.A. **155 K5** 31 4N 98 11W
Lampazos de Naranjo, Mexico **162 B4** 27 2N 100 32W
Lampertheim, Germany **31 F4** 49 35N 8 27 E
Lampeter, U.K. **21 E3** 52 7N 4 4W
Lampione, Medit. S. **108 A2** 35 33N 12 20 E
Lampman, Canada **143 D8** 49 25N 102 50W
Lamprechtshausen, Austria **34 D5** 48 0N 12 58 E
Lamprey, Canada **143 B10** 58 33N 94 8W
Lampung □, Indonesia **84 D2** 5 30 S 104 30 E
Lamu, Burma **90 F5** 19 14N 94 10 E
Lamu, Kenya **118 C5** 2 16 S 40 55 E
Lamu □, Kenya **118 C5** 2 0 S 40 45 E
Lamud, Peru **172 B2** 6 10 S 77 57W
Lamut, Phil. **80 C3** 16 39N 121 14 E
Lamy, U.S.A. **159 J11** 35 29N 105 53W
Lan Xian, China **74 E6** 38 15N 111 35 E
Lanai, Hawaii, U.S.A. **145 C5** 20 50N 156 55W
Lanai, Hawaii, U.S.A. **146 H16** 20 50N 156 55W
Lanaihale, U.S.A. **145 C5** 20 49N 156 53W
Lanak La, India **93 B8** 34 27N 79 32 E
Lanak'o Shank'ou = Lanak La, India **93 B8** 34 27N 79 32 E
Lanao, L., Phil. **81 H5** 7 52N 124 15 E
Lanao del Norte □, Phil. **81 H5** 8 0N 124 10 E
Lanao del Sur □, Phil. **81 H5** 7 40N 124 15 E
Lanark, Canada **151 A8** 45 1N 76 22W
Lanark, U.K. **22 F5** 55 40N 3 47W
Lanark Village, U.S.A. **152 F5** 29 53N 84 36W
Lancang, China **76 F2** 22 36N 99 58 E
Lancang Jiang →, China **76 G3** 21 40N 101 10 E
Lancashire □, U.K. **20 D5** 53 50N 2 48W
Lancaster, Canada **151 A10** 45 10N 74 30W
Lancaster, U.K. **20 C5** 54 3N 2 48W
Lancaster, Calif., U.S.A. **161 L8** 34 42N 118 8W
Lancaster, Ky., U.S.A. **148 G3** 37 37N 84 35W
Lancaster, Mo., U.S.A. **156 D4** 40 31N 92 32W
Lancaster, N.H., U.S.A. **151 B13** 44 29N 71 34W
Lancaster, N.Y., U.S.A. **150 D6** 42 54N 78 40W
Lancaster, Pa., U.S.A. **151 F8** 40 2N 76 19W
Lancaster, S.C., U.S.A. **149 H5** 34 43N 80 46W
Lancaster, Wis., U.S.A. **156 B6** 42 51N 90 43W
Lancaster Sd., Canada **139 A11** 74 13N 84 0W
Lancer, Canada **143 C7** 50 48N 108 53W
Lanchow = Lanzhou, China **74 F2** 36 1N 103 52 E
Lanciano, Italy **45 F11** 42 14N 14 23 E
Lanco, Chile **176 A2** 39 24 S 72 46W
Lancones, Peru **172 A1** 4 30 S 80 30W
Lancun, China **75 F11** 36 25N 120 10 E
Łańcut, Poland **55 H9** 50 10N 22 13 E
Lancy, Switz. **32 D2** 46 12N 6 8 E
Landau, Bayern, Germany **31 G8** 48 40N 12 41 E
Landau, Rhld-Pfz., Germany **31 F4** 49 12N 8 6 E
Landay, Afghan. **91 C1** 30 31N 63 47 E
Landeck, Austria **34 D3** 47 9N 10 34 E
Lander, U.S.A. **158 E9** 42 50N 108 44W
Lander →, Australia **124 D5** 22 0 S 132 0 E
Landerneau, France **26 D2** 48 28N 4 17W
Landeryd, Sweden **17 G7** 57 7N 13 15 E
Landes, France **28 D2** 44 0N 1 0W
Landes □, France **28 E3** 43 57N 0 48W
Landete, Spain **40 F3** 39 56N 1 25W
Landi Kotal, Pakistan **91 B3** 34 7N 71 6 E
Landivisiau, France **26 D2** 48 31N 4 6W
Landor, Australia **125 E2** 25 10 S 116 54 E
Landquart, Switz. **33 C9** 46 58N 9 32 E
Landquart →, Switz. **33 C9** 46 50N 9 47 E
Landrecies, France **27 B10** 50 7N 3 40 E
Land's End, U.K. **21 G2** 50 4N 5 44W
Landsberg, Germany **31 G6** 48 2N 10 53 E
Landsborough Cr. →, Australia **126 C3** 22 28 S 144 35 E
Landsbro, Sweden **17 G8** 57 24N 14 56 E
Landshut, Germany **31 G8** 48 34N 12 8 E
Landskrona, Sweden **17 J6** 55 53N 12 50 E
Landstuhl, Germany **31 F3** 49 24N 7 33 E
Landvetter, Sweden **17 G6** 57 41N 12 17 E
Lane, U.S.A. **152 B10** 33 32N 79 53W
Lanesboro, U.S.A. **151 E9** 41 57N 75 34W
Lanester, France **26 E3** 47 46N 3 22W
Lanett, U.S.A. **152 C4** 32 52N 85 12W
Lang Bay, Canada **142 D4** 49 45N 124 21W
Lang Qua, Vietnam **86 A5** 22 16N 104 27 E
Lang Shan, China **74 D4** 41 0N 106 30 E
Lang Son, Vietnam **86 B6** 21 52N 106 42 E
Lang Suan, Thailand **87 H2** 9 57N 99 4 E
Langå, Denmark **17 H3** 56 23N 9 54 E
Lángadhás, Greece **50 F7** 40 46N 23 6 E
Langádhia, Greece **48 D4** 37 43N 22 1 E
Långan →, Sweden **16 A8** 63 19N 14 44 E
Langanes, Iceland **11 A12** 66 20N 14 53W
Langar, Iran **97 C9** 35 23N 60 25 E
Langara I., Canada **142 C2** 54 14N 133 1W
Långås, Sweden **17 H6** 56 58N 12 26 E
Langatabbetje, Surinam **169 C7** 4 59N 54 28W
Langdai, China **76 D5** 26 6N 105 21 E
Langdon, U.S.A. **154 A5** 48 45N 98 22W
Långe Jan = Ölands södra udde, Sweden **17 H10** 56 12N 16 23 E
Langeac, France **28 C7** 45 7N 3 29 E
Langeais, France **26 E7** 47 20N 0 24 E
Langeb Baraka →, Sudan **106 D4** 17 28N 36 50 E
Langeberg, S. Africa **116 E3** 33 55 S 21 0 E
Langeberge, S. Africa **116 D3** 28 15 S 22 33 E
Langeland, Denmark **17 K4** 54 56N 10 48 E
Langelands Bælt, Denmark **17 K4** 54 50N 10 55 E
Langen, Hessen, Germany **31 F4** 49 59N 8 40 E
Langen, Niedersachsen, Germany **30 B4** 53 36N 8 36 E
Langenburg, Canada **143 C8** 50 51N 101 43W
Langeneß, Germany **30 A4** 54 38N 8 36 E
Langenlois, Austria **34 C8** 48 29N 15 40 E
Langenthal, Switz. **32 B5** 47 13N 7 47 E
Langeoog, Germany **30 B3** 53 45N 7 32 E
Langeskov, Denmark **17 J4** 55 22N 10 35 E
Langesund, Norway **18 F6** 59 0N 9 45 E
Langevåg, Norway **18 B3** 62 26N 6 13 E
Långhem, Sweden **17 G7** 57 36N 13 14 E
Langhirano, Italy **44 D7** 44 37N 10 16 E
Langholm, U.K. **22 F5** 55 9N 3 0W
Langidoon, Australia **128 A5** 31 36 S 142 2 E
Langjökull, Iceland **11 C6** 64 39N 20 12W
Langkawi, Pulau, Malaysia **87 J2** 6 25N 99 45 E
Langklip, S. Africa **116 D3** 28 12 S 20 20 E
Langkon, Malaysia **85 A5** 6 30N 116 40 E
Langlade, St- P. & M. **141 C8** 46 50N 56 20W
Langlois, U.S.A. **158 E1** 42 56N 124 27W
Langnau, Switz. **32 C5** 46 56N 7 47 E
Langogne, France **28 D7** 44 43N 3 50 E
Langon, France **28 D3** 44 33N 0 16W
Langøya, Norway **14 B16** 68 45N 14 50 E
Langreo, Spain **42 B5** 43 18N 5 40W
Langres, France **27 E12** 47 52N 5 20 E
Langres, Plateau de, France **27 E12** 47 45N 5 3 E
Langsa, Indonesia **84 B1** 4 30N 97 57 E
Långsele, Sweden **16 A11** 63 12N 17 4 E
Långshyttan, Sweden **16 D10** 60 27N 16 2 E
Langtao, Burma **90 B6** 27 15N 97 34 E
Langting, India **90 C4** 25 31N 93 7 E
Langtry, U.S.A. **155 L4** 29 49N 101 34W
Langu, Thailand **87 J2** 6 53N 99 47 E
Languedoc, France **28 E7** 43 58N 3 55 E
Languedoc-Roussillon □, France **28 E6** 43 25N 3 0 E
Langwies, Switz. **33 C9** 46 50N 9 44 E
Langxi, China **77 B12** 31 10N 119 12 E
Langxiangzhen, China **74 E9** 39 43N 116 8 E
Langzhong, China **76 B5** 31 38N 105 58 E
Lanigan, Canada **143 C7** 51 51N 105 2W
Lankao, China **74 G8** 34 48N 114 50 E
Länkäran, Azerbaijan **101 C13** 38 48N 48 52 E
Lanmeur, France **26 D3** 48 39N 3 43W
Lannemezan, France **28 E4** 43 8N 0 23 E
Lannilis, France **26 D2** 48 35N 4 32W
Lannion, France **26 D3** 48 46N 3 29W
L'Annonciation, Canada **140 C5** 46 25N 74 55W
Lanouaille, France **28 C5** 45 24N 1 9 E
Lanping, China **76 D2** 26 28N 99 15 E
Lansdale, U.S.A. **151 F9** 40 14N 75 17W
Lansdowne, Australia **129 A10** 31 48 S 152 30 E
Lansdowne, Canada **151 B8** 44 24N 76 1W
Lansdowne House, Canada **140 B2** 52 14N 87 53W
L'Anse, U.S.A. **140 C2** 46 45N 88 27W
L'Anse au Loup, Canada **141 B8** 51 32N 56 50W
Lansford, U.S.A. **151 F9** 40 50N 75 53W
Lanshan, China **77 E9** 25 24N 112 10 E
Lansing, U.S.A. **157 B12** 42 44N 84 33W
Lanslebourg-Mont-Cenis, France **29 C10** 45 17N 6 52 E
Lanta Yai, Ko, Thailand **87 J2** 7 35N 99 3 E
Lantana, U.S.A. **153 J9** 26 35N 80 3W
Lantian, China **74 G5** 34 11N 109 20 E
Lanus, Argentina **174 C4** 34 44 S 58 27W
Lanusei, Italy **46 C2** 39 52N 9 34 E
Lanuza, Phil. **81 G6** 9 14N 126 4 E
Lanxi, China **77 C12** 29 13N 119 28 E
Lanzarote, Canary Is. **39 F6** 29 0N 13 40W
Lanzhou, China **74 F2** 36 1N 103 52 E
Lanzo Torinese, Italy **44 C4** 45 16N 7 28 E
Lao →, Italy **47 C8** 39 47N 15 48 E
Lao Bao, Laos **86 D6** 16 35N 106 30 E
Lao Cai, Vietnam **86 A4** 22 30N 103 57 E
Laoag, Phil. **80 B3** 18 7N 120 34 E
Laoang, Phil. **80 E5** 12 32N 125 8 E
Laoha He →, China **75 C11** 43 25N 120 35 E
Laois □, Ireland **23 D4** 52 57N 7 36W
Laon, France **27 C10** 49 33N 3 35 E
Laona, U.S.A. **148 C1** 45 34N 88 40W
Laos ■, Asia **86 D5** 17 45N 105 0 E
Lapa, Brazil **175 B6** 25 46 S 49 44W
Lapalisse, France **27 F10** 46 15N 3 38 E
Lapeer, U.S.A. **157 A13** 43 3N 83 19W
Lapeyrade, France **28 D3** 44 4N 0 3W
Lapithos, Cyprus **38 D12** 35 21N 33 11 E
Lapland = Lappland, Europe **14 B21** 68 7N 24 0 E
Lapog, Phil. **80 C3** 17 45N 120 27 E
Laporte, U.S.A. **151 E8** 41 25N 76 30W
Lapovo, Serbia, Yug. **50 B5** 44 10N 21 7 E
Lappeenranta, Finland **15 F23** 61 3N 28 12 E
Lappland, Europe **14 B21** 68 7N 24 0 E
Laprida, Argentina **174 D3** 37 34 S 60 45W
Lapseki, Turkey **100 B2** 40 20N 26 41 E
Laptev Sea, Russia **65 B13** 76 0N 125 0 E
Lapu-Lapu, Phil. **81 F4** 10 20N 123 55 E
Lapua, Finland **14 E20** 62 58N 23 0 E
Lăpuş →, Romania **53 C8** 47 25N 23 40 E
Lapuş, Munţii, Romania **53 C8** 47 20N 23 50 E
Lăpuşna, Moldova **53 D13** 46 53N 28 25 E
Łapy, Poland **55 F9** 52 59N 22 52 E
L'Aquila, Italy **45 F10** 42 22N 13 22 E
Lār, Āzarbājān-e Sharqī, Iran **96 B5** 38 30N 47 52 E
Lār, Fārs, Iran **97 E7** 27 40N 54 14 E
Lara, Australia **128 E6** 38 2 S 144 26 E
Lara, Phil. **81 G1** 8 48N 117 52 E
Lara □, Venezuela **168 A4** 10 10N 69 50W
Larabanga, Ghana **112 D4** 9 16N 1 56W
Larache, Morocco **110 A3** 35 10N 6 5W
Laragne-Montéglin, France **29 D9** 44 18N 5 49 E
Laramie, U.S.A. **154 E2** 41 19N 105 35W
Laramie Mts., U.S.A. **154 E2** 42 0N 105 30W
Laranjeiras, Brazil **170 D4** 10 48 S 37 10W
Laranjeiras do Sul, Brazil **175 B5** 25 23 S 52 23W
Larantuka, Indonesia **82 C2** 8 21 S 122 55 E
Larap, Phil. **80 D4** 14 18N 122 39 E
Larat, Indonesia **83 C4** 7 0 S 132 0 E
L'Arbresle, France **29 C8** 45 50N 4 36 E
Lärbro, Sweden **17 G12** 57 47N 18 50 E
Lårdal, Norway **18 E5** 59 25N 8 10 E
Larde, Mozam. **119 F4** 16 28 S 39 43 E
Larder Lake, Canada **140 C4** 48 5N 79 40W
Lardhos, Ákra = Líndhos, Ákra, Greece **38 C10** 36 4N 28 10 E
Lardhos, Órmos, Greece **38 C10** 36 4N 28 2 E
Laredo, Spain **42 B7** 43 26N 3 28W
Laredo, U.S.A. **155 M5** 27 30N 99 30W
Laredo Sd., Canada **142 C3** 52 30N 128 53W
Larena, Phil. **81 G4** 9 15N 123 35 E
Largentière, France **29 D8** 44 34N 4 18 E
L'Argentière-la-Bessée, France **29 D10** 44 47N 6 33 E
Largo, U.S.A. **149 M4** 27 55N 82 47W
Largo Key, U.S.A. **153 K9** 25 15N 80 15W
Largs, U.K. **22 F4** 55 47N 4 52W
Lari, Italy **44 E7** 43 34N 10 35 E
Lariang, Indonesia **82 B1** 1 26 S 119 17 E
Larimore, U.S.A. **154 B6** 47 54N 97 38W
Lārīn, Iran **97 C7** 35 55N 52 19 E
Larino, Italy **45 G11** 41 48N 14 54 E
Lárisa, Greece **48 B4** 39 36N 22 27 E
Lárisa □, Greece **48 B4** 39 39N 22 24 E
Larkana, Pakistan **91 D3** 27 32N 68 18 E
Larnaca, Cyprus **38 E12** 34 55N 33 38 E
Larnaca Bay, Cyprus **38 E12** 34 53N 33 45 E
Larne, U.K. **23 B6** 54 51N 5 51W
Larned, U.S.A. **154 F5** 38 11N 99 6W
Laroquebrou, France **28 D6** 44 58N 2 12 E
Larrimah, Australia **124 C5** 15 35 S 133 12 E
Larsen Bay, U.S.A. **144 H9** 57 32N 153 59W
Larsen Ice Shelf, Antarctica **7 C17** 67 0 S 62 0W
Laruns, France **28 F3** 43 0N 0 26W
Larvik, Norway **15 G14** 59 4N 10 2 E
Larzac, Causse du, France **28 E7** 43 50N 3 17 E
Las Alpujarras, Spain **41 J1** 36 55N 3 20W
Las Animas, U.S.A. **154 F3** 38 4N 103 13W
Las Anod, Somali Rep. **120 C3** 8 26N 47 19 E
Las Arenas, Spain **42 B6** 43 17N 4 50W
Las Brenãs, Argentina **174 B3** 27 5 S 61 7W
Las Cabezas de San Juan, Spain **43 J5** 36 57N 5 58W
Las Chimeneas, Mexico **161 N10** 32 8N 116 5W
Las Coloradas, Argentina **176 A2** 39 34 S 70 36W
Las Cruces, U.S.A. **159 K10** 32 19N 106 47W
Las Flores, Argentina **174 D4** 36 10 S 59 7W
Las Heras, Argentina **174 C2** 32 51 S 68 49W
Las Horquetas, Argentina **176 C2** 48 14 S 71 11W
Las Khoreh, Somali Rep. **120 B3** 11 10N 48 20 E
Las Lajas, Argentina **176 A2** 38 30 S 70 25W
Las Lomas, Peru **172 A1** 4 40 S 80 10W
Las Lomitas, Argentina **174 A3** 24 43 S 60 35W
Las Marismas, Spain **43 H4** 37 5N 6 20W
Las Mercedes, Venezuela **168 B4** 9 7N 66 24W
Las Minas, Spain **41 G3** 38 20N 1 41W
Las Navas de la Concepción, Spain **43 H5** 37 56N 5 30W
Las Navas del Marqués, Spain **42 E6** 40 36N 4 20W
Las Palmas, Argentina **174 B4** 27 8 S 58 45W
Las Palmas, Canary Is. **39 F4** 28 7N 15 26W
Las Palmas →, Mexico **161 N10** 32 26N 116 54W
Las Pedroñas, Spain **41 F2** 39 26N 2 40W
Las Piedras, Uruguay **175 C4** 34 44 S 56 14W
Las Pipinas, Argentina **174 D4** 35 30 S 57 19W
Las Plumas, Argentina **176 B3** 43 40 S 67 15W
Las Rosas, Argentina **174 C3** 32 30 S 61 35W
Las Rozas, Spain **42 E7** 40 29N 3 52W
Las Tablas, Panama **164 E3** 7 49N 80 14W
Las Termas, Argentina **174 B3** 27 29 S 64 52W
Las Truchas, Mexico **162 D4** 17 57N 102 13W
Las Varillas, Argentina **174 C3** 31 50 S 62 50W
Las Vegas, N. Mex., U.S.A. **159 J11** 35 36N 105 13W
Las Vegas, Nev., U.S.A. **161 J11** 36 10N 115 9W
Lasarte, Spain **40 B2** 43 16N 2 1W
Lascano, Uruguay **175 C5** 33 35 S 54 12W
Lashburn, Canada **143 C7** 53 10N 109 40W
Lashio, Burma **90 D6** 22 56N 97 45 E
Lashkar, India **92 F8** 26 10N 78 10 E
Lashkar Gāh, Afghan. **91 C2** 31 35N 64 21 E
Łasin, Poland **54 E6** 53 30N 19 2 E
Lasíthi, Greece **38 D7** 35 11N 25 31 E
Lasíthi □, Greece **38 D7** 35 5N 25 50 E
Lask, Poland **55 G6** 51 34N 19 8 E
Łaskarzew, Poland **55 G8** 51 48N 21 36 E
Laško, Slovenia **45 B12** 46 10N 15 16 E
Lassance, Brazil **171 E3** 17 54 S 44 34W
Lassay-les-Châteaux, France **26 D6** 48 27N 0 30W
Lassen Pk., U.S.A. **158 F3** 40 29N 121 31W
Last Mountain L., Canada **143 C7** 51 5N 105 14W
Lastchance Cr. →, U.S.A. **160 E5** 40 2N 121 15W
Lastoursville, Gabon **114 C2** 0 55 S 12 38 E
Lastovo, Croatia **45 F13** 42 46N 16 55 E
Lastovski Kanal, Croatia **45 F14** 42 50N 17 0 E
Lat Yao, Thailand **86 E2** 15 45N 99 48 E
Latacunga, Ecuador **168 D2** 0 50 S 78 35W
Latakia = Al Lādhiqīyah, Syria **100 E6** 35 30N 35 45 E
Latchford, Canada **140 C4** 47 20N 79 50W
Late, Tonga **133 P13** 18 48 S 174 39W
Laterza, Italy **47 B9** 40 37N 16 48 E
Latham, Australia **125 E2** 29 44 S 116 20 E
Lathen, Germany **30 C3** 52 52N 7 19 E
Lathrop, U.S.A. **156 E2** 39 33N 94 20W
Lathrop Wells, U.S.A. **161 J10** 36 39N 116 24W
Latiano, Italy **47 B10** 40 33N 17 43 E
Latina, Italy **46 A5** 41 28N 12 52 E
Latisana, Italy **45 C10** 45 47N 13 0 E
Latium = Lazio □, Italy **45 F9** 42 10N 12 30 E
Laton, U.S.A. **160 J7** 36 26N 119 41W
Latorytsya →, Slovak Rep. **35 C14** 48 28N 21 50 E
Latouche Treville, C., Australia **124 C3** 18 27 S 121 49 E
Látrar, Iceland **11 A3** 66 24N 23 2W
Latrobe, Australia **126 G4** 41 14 S 146 30 E
Latrobe, U.S.A. **150 F5** 40 19N 79 23W
Latrónico, Italy **47 B9** 40 5N 16 1 E
Latur, India **94 E3** 18 25N 76 40 E
Latvia ■, Europe **15 H20** 56 50N 24 0 E
Lau Group, Fiji **133 A3** 17 0 S 178 30W
Lauca →, Bolivia **172 D4** 19 9 S 68 10W
Lauchhammer, Germany **30 D9** 51 29N 13 47 E
Lauda-Königshofen, Germany **31 F5** 49 33N 9 42 E
Laudal, Norway **18 F4** 58 15N 7 30 E
Lauenburg, Germany **30 B6** 53 22N 10 32 E
Lauf, Germany **31 F7** 49 30N 11 16 E
Laufás, Iceland **11 B8** 65 53N 18 4W
Läufelfingen, Switz. **32 B5** 47 24N 7 52 E
Laufen, Switz. **32 B5** 47 25N 7 30 E
Laugarbakki, Iceland **11 B6** 65 20N 20 55W
Laugarvatn, Iceland **11 C6** 64 13N 20 44W
Laujar de Andarax, Spain **41 H2** 37 0N 2 54W
Laukaa, Finland **15 E21** 62 24N 25 56 E
Launceston, Australia **126 G4** 41 24 S 147 8 E
Launceston, U.K. **21 G3** 50 38N 4 22W
Laune →, Ireland **23 D2** 52 7N 9 47W
Launglon Bok, Burma **86 F1** 13 50N 97 54 E
Laupheim, Germany **31 G5** 48 14N 9 52 E
Laur, Phil. **80 D3** 15 35N 121 11 E
Laura, Queens., Australia **126 B3** 15 32 S 144 32 E
Laura, S. Austral., Australia **128 B3** 33 10 S 138 18 E
Laureana di Borrello, Italy **47 D9** 38 30N 16 5 E
Laurel, Fla., U.S.A. **153 H7** 27 8N 82 27W
Laurel, Ind., U.S.A. **157 E11** 39 31N 85 11W
Laurel, Miss., U.S.A. **155 K10** 31 41N 89 8W
Laurel, Mont., U.S.A. **158 D9** 45 40N 108 46W
Laurel Bay, U.S.A. **152 C9** 32 27N 80 47W
Laurencekirk, U.K. **22 E6** 56 50N 2 28W
Laurens, U.S.A. **149 H4** 34 30N 82 1W
Laurentian Plateau, Canada **141 B6** 52 0N 70 0W
Laurentides, Parc Prov. des, Canada **141 C5** 47 45N 71 15W
Lauria, Italy **47 B8** 40 2N 15 50 E
Laurie L., Canada **143 B8** 56 35N 101 57W
Laurinburg, U.S.A. **149 H6** 34 47N 79 28W
Laurium, U.S.A. **148 B1** 47 14N 88 27W
Lausanne, Switz. **32 C3** 46 32N 6 38 E
Laut, Indonesia **85 B3** 4 45N 108 0 E
Laut, Pulau, Indonesia **85 C5** 3 40 S 116 10 E
Laut Kecil, Kepulauan, Indonesia **85 C5** 4 45 S 115 40 E
Lautaro, Chile **176 A2** 38 31 S 72 27W
Lauterbach, Germany **30 E5** 50 37N 9 24 E
Lauterbrunnen, Switz. **32 C5** 46 36N 7 55 E
Lauterecken, Germany **31 F3** 49 38N 7 35 E
Lautoka, Fiji **133 A1** 17 37 S 177 27 E
Lauzès, France **28 D5** 44 34N 1 35 E
Lauzon, Canada **141 C5** 46 48N 71 10W
Lava Hot Springs, U.S.A. **158 E7** 42 37N 112 1W
Lavagh More, Ireland **23 B3** 54 46N 8 6W
Lavagna, Italy **44 D6** 44 18N 9 20 E
Laval, France **26 D6** 48 4N 0 48W
Lavalle, Argentina **174 B2** 28 15 S 65 15W
Lávara, Greece **51 E10** 41 19N 26 22 E
Lavardac, France **28 D4** 44 12N 0 20 E
Lavaur, France **28 E5** 43 40N 1 49 E
Lavaux, Switz. **32 D3** 46 30N 6 45 E
Lavelanet, France **28 F5** 42 57N 1 51 E
Lavello, Italy **47 A8** 41 3N 15 48 E
Laverne, U.S.A. **155 G5** 36 43N 99 54W
Lavers Hill, Australia **128 E5** 38 40 S 143 25 E
Laverton, Australia **125 E3** 28 44 S 122 29 E
Lavik, Norway **18 C2** 61 6N 5 25 E
Lavìs, Italy **44 B8** 46 8N 11 7 E
Lávkos, Greece **48 B5** 39 9N 23 14 E
Lavos, Portugal **42 E2** 40 6N 8 49W
Lavradio, Portugal **43 G1** 38 40N 9 3W
Lavras, Brazil **171 F3** 21 20 S 45 0W
Lavre, Portugal **43 G2** 38 46N 8 22W
Lávrion, Greece **48 D6** 37 40N 24 4 E
Lávris, Greece **38 D6** 35 25N 24 40 E
Lavumisa, Swaziland **117 D5** 27 20 S 31 55 E
Lawa, Phil. **81 H5** 6 12N 125 41 E
Lawa-an, Phil. **81 F5** 11 51N 125 5 E
Lawas, Malaysia **85 B5** 4 55N 115 25 E
Lawdar, Yemen **98 D4** 13 53N 45 52 E
Lawele, Indonesia **82 C2** 5 16 S 123 3 E
Lawksawk, Burma **90 E6** 21 15N 96 52 E
Lawn Hill, Australia **126 B2** 18 36 S 138 33 E
Lawqah, Si. Arabia **96 D4** 29 49N 42 45 E
Lawra, Ghana **112 C4** 10 39N 2 51W
Lawrence, N.Z. **131 F4** 45 55 S 169 41 E
Lawrence, Ind., U.S.A. **157 E10** 39 50N 86 2W
Lawrence, Kans., U.S.A. **154 F7** 38 58N 95 14W
Lawrence, Mass., U.S.A. **151 D13** 42 43N 71 10W
Lawrenceburg, Ind., U.S.A. **157 E12** 39 6N 84 52W
Lawrenceburg, Ky., U.S.A. **157 F12** 38 2N 84 54W

Litang 241

Levie, France 29 G13 41 40N 9 7 E
Levier, France 27 F13 46 58N 6 8 E
Levin, N.Z. 130 G4 40 37 S 175 18 E
Lévis, Canada 141 C5 46 48N 71 9W
Levis, L., Canada 142 A5 62 37N 117 58W
Levítha, Greece 49 D8 37 0N 26 28 E
Levittown, N.Y., U.S.A. 151 F11 40 44N 73 31W
Levittown, Pa., U.S.A. 151 F10 40 9N 74 51W
Levka, Bulgaria 51 E10 41 52N 26 15 E
Levkás, Greece 48 C2 38 40N 20 43 E
Levkás □, Greece 48 C2 38 40N 20 30 E
Levkímmi, Greece 38 B4 39 25N 20 3 E
Levkímmi, Ákra, Greece 38 B4 39 29N 20 4 E
Levkôsia = Nicosia, Cyprus 38 D12 35 10N 33 25 E
Levoča, Slovak Rep. 35 B13 49 2N 20 35 E
Levroux, France 27 F8 46 59N 1 38 E
Levski, Bulgaria 51 C9 43 21N 25 10 E
Levskigrad = Karlovo, Bulgaria 51 D8 42 38N 24 47 E
Levuka, Fiji 133 A2 17 34 S 179 0 E
Lewe, Burma 90 F6 19 38N 96 7 E
Lewellen, U.S.A. 154 E3 41 20N 102 9W
Lewes, U.K. 21 G8 50 52N 0 1 E
Lewes, U.S.A. 148 F8 38 46N 75 9W
Lewin Brzeski, Poland 55 H4 50 45N 17 37 E
Lewis, U.K. 22 C2 58 9N 6 40W
Lewis →, U.S.A. 160 E4 45 51N 122 48W
Lewis, Butt of, U.K. 22 C2 58 31N 6 16W
Lewis Ra., Australia 124 D4 20 3 S 128 50 E
Lewis Range, U.S.A. 158 C7 48 5N 113 5W
Lewisburg, Ohio, U.S.A. 157 E12 39 51N 84 33W
Lewisburg, Pa., U.S.A. 150 F8 40 58N 76 54W
Lewisburg, Tenn., U.S.A. 149 H2 35 27N 86 48W
Lewisport, U.S.A. 157 G10 37 56N 86 54W
Lewisporte, Canada 141 C8 49 15N 55 3W
Lewiston, Idaho, U.S.A. 158 C5 46 25N 117 1W
Lewiston, Maine, U.S.A. 149 C11 44 6N 70 13W
Lewistown, Ill., U.S.A. 156 D6 40 24N 90 9W
Lewistown, Mont., U.S.A. 158 C9 47 4N 109 26W
Lewistown, Pa., U.S.A. 150 F7 40 36N 77 34W
Lexington, Ga., U.S.A. 152 B6 33 52N 83 7W
Lexington, Ill., U.S.A. 154 E10 40 39N 88 47W
Lexington, Ky., U.S.A. 157 F12 38 3N 84 30W
Lexington, Miss., U.S.A. 155 J9 33 7N 90 3W
Lexington, Mo., U.S.A. 156 E3 39 11N 93 52W
Lexington, N.C., U.S.A. 149 H5 35 49N 80 15W
Lexington, Nebr., U.S.A. 154 E5 40 47N 99 45W
Lexington, Ohio, U.S.A. 150 F2 40 41N 82 35W
Lexington, Oreg., U.S.A. 158 D4 45 27N 119 42W
Lexington, S.C., U.S.A. 152 B9 33 59N 81 11W
Lexington, Tenn., U.S.A. 149 H1 35 39N 88 24W
Lexington Park, U.S.A. 148 F7 38 16N 76 27W
Leyburn, U.K. 20 C6 54 19N 1 48W
Leye, China 76 E6 24 48N 106 29 E
Leyland, U.K. 20 D5 53 42N 2 43W
Leyre →, France 28 D2 44 39N 1 1W
Leysin, Switz. 32 D4 46 21N 7 0 E
Leyte, Phil. 81 F5 11 0N 125 0 E
Leyte Gulf, Phil. 81 F5 10 50N 125 25 E
Leżajsk, Poland 55 H9 50 16N 22 25 E
Lezay, France 28 B3 46 15N 0 1W
Lezha, Albania 50 E3 41 47N 19 39 E
Lezhi, China 76 B5 30 19N 104 58 E
Lézignan-Corbières, France 28 E6 43 13N 2 43 E
Lezoux, France 28 C7 45 49N 3 21 E
Lgov, Russia 59 G8 51 42N 35 16 E
Lhasa, China 72 D4 29 25N 90 58 E
Lhazê, China 72 D3 29 5N 87 38 E
Lhokkruet, Indonesia 84 B1 4 55N 95 24 E
Lhokseumawe, Indonesia 84 A1 5 10N 97 10 E
L'Hospitalet de Llobregat, Spain 40 D7 41 21N 2 6 E
Lhuntsi Dzong, India 90 B3 27 39N 91 10 E
Li, Thailand 86 D2 17 48N 98 57 E
Li Shui →, China 77 C9 29 24N 112 1 E
Li Xian, Gansu, China 74 G3 34 10N 105 5 E
Li Xian, Hebei, China 74 E8 38 30N 115 35 E
Li Xian, Hunan, China 77 C8 29 36N 111 42 E
Li Xian, Sichuan, China 76 B4 31 23N 103 13 E
Lia-Moya, C.A.R. 114 A3 6 54N 16 17 E
Liádhoi, Greece 49 E8 36 50N 26 11 E
Lian, Phil. 80 D3 14 3N 120 39 E
Lian Xian, China 77 E9 24 51N 112 22 E
Liancheng, China 77 E11 25 42N 116 40 E
Lianga, Phil. 81 G6 8 38N 126 6 E
Lianga Bay, Phil. 81 G6 8 37N 126 12 E
Liangcheng, Nei Mongol Zizhiqu, China 74 D7 40 28N 112 25 E
Liangcheng, Shandong, China 75 G10 35 32N 119 37 E
Liangdang, China 74 H4 33 56N 106 18 E
Lianghekou, China 76 C7 29 11N 108 44 E
Liangping, China 76 B6 30 38N 107 47 E
Lianhua, China 77 D9 27 3N 113 54 E
Lianjiang, Fujian, China 77 D12 26 12N 119 27 E
Lianjiang, Guangdong, China 77 G8 21 40N 110 20 E
Lianping, China 77 E10 24 26N 114 30 E
Lianshan, China 77 E9 24 38N 112 8 E
Lianshanguan, China 75 D12 40 53N 123 43 E
Lianshui, China 75 H10 33 42N 119 20 E
Lianyuan, China 77 D8 27 40N 111 38 E
Lianyungang, China 75 G10 34 40N 119 11 E
Liao He →, China 75 D11 41 0N 121 50 E
Liaocheng, China 74 F8 36 28N 115 58 E
Liaodong Bandao, China 75 E12 40 0N 122 30 E
Liaodong Wan, China 75 D11 40 20N 121 10 E
Liaoning □, China 75 D12 41 40N 122 30 E
Liaoyang, China 75 D12 41 15N 122 58 E
Liaoyuan, China 75 C13 42 58N 125 2 E
Liaozhong, China 75 D12 41 23N 122 50 E
Liapádhes, Greece 48 B1 39 42N 19 40 E
Liard →, Canada 142 A4 61 51N 121 18W
Liari, Pakistan 92 G2 25 37N 66 30 E
Líbano, Colombia 168 C2 4 55N 75 4W
Libau = Liepāja, Latvia 15 H19 56 30N 21 0 E
Libby, U.S.A. 158 B6 48 23N 115 33W
Libenge, Dem. Rep. of the Congo 114 B3 3 40N 18 55 E
Liberal, Kans., U.S.A. 155 G4 37 3N 100 55W
Liberal, Mo., U.S.A. 155 G7 37 34N 94 31W
Liberdade, Brazil 172 C3 10 5 S 70 20W
Liberdade →, Brazil 173 B7 9 40 S 52 17W
Liberec, Czech Rep. 34 A8 50 47N 15 7 E
Liberia, Costa Rica 164 D2 10 40N 85 30W
Liberia ■, W. Afr. 112 D3 6 30N 9 30W
Libertad, Panay, Phil. 81 F3 11 46N 121 55 E
Libertad, Tablas, Phil. 80 E4 12 27N 122 0 E
Libertad, Venezuela 168 B4 8 20N 69 37W
Liberty, Ind., U.S.A. 157 E12 39 38N 84 56W
Liberty, Mo., U.S.A. 156 E2 39 15N 94 25W
Liberty, Tex., U.S.A. 155 K7 30 3N 94 48W
Liberty Center, U.S.A. 157 C12 41 27N 84 1W
Libertyville, U.S.A. 157 B9 42 18N 87 57W
Libiąż, Poland 55 H6 50 7N 19 21 E
Libibi, Angola 115 E3 14 42 S 17 44 E
Lîbîya, Sahrâ', Africa 108 C4 25 0N 25 0 E
Libmanan, Phil. 80 E4 13 42N 123 4 E
Libo, China 76 E6 25 22N 107 53 E
Libobo, Tanjung, Indonesia 82 B3 0 54 S 128 28 E
Libode, S. Africa 117 E4 31 33 S 29 2 E
Libohava, Albania 50 F4 40 3N 20 10 E
Libona, Phil. 81 G5 8 20N 124 44 E
Libonda, Zambia 115 E4 14 28 S 23 12 E
Libourne, France 28 D3 44 55N 0 14W
Libramont, Belgium 24 E5 49 55N 5 23 E
Librazhdi, Albania 50 E4 41 12N 20 22 E
Libreville, Gabon 114 B1 0 25N 9 26 E
Libya ■, N. Afr. 108 C3 27 0N 17 0 E
Libyan Desert = Lîbîya, Sahrâ', Africa 108 C4 25 0N 25 0 E
Libyan Plateau = Ed-Déffa, Egypt 106 A2 30 40N 26 30 E
Licantén, Chile 174 D1 35 55 S 72 0W
Licata, Italy 46 E6 37 6N 13 56 E
Lice, Turkey 101 C9 38 27N 40 39 E
Licheng, China 74 F7 36 28N 113 20 E
Lichfield, U.K. 21 E6 52 41N 1 49W
Lichinga, Mozam. 119 E4 13 13 S 35 11 E
Lichtenburg, S. Africa 116 D4 26 8 S 26 8 E
Lichtenfels, Germany 31 E7 50 8N 11 4 E
Lichuan, Hubei, China 76 B7 30 18N 108 57 E
Lichuan, Jiangxi, China 77 D11 27 18N 116 55 E
Licking →, U.S.A. 157 F12 39 6N 84 30W
Licosa, Punta, Italy 47 B7 40 15N 14 54 E
Lida, Belarus 15 K21 53 53N 25 15 E
Lida, U.S.A. 159 H5 37 28N 117 30W
Liden, Sweden 16 B10 62 42N 16 48 E
Lidhoríkion, Greece 48 C4 38 32N 22 12 E
Lidhult, Sweden 17 H7 56 50N 13 27 E
Lidköping, Sweden 17 F7 58 31N 13 7 E
Lidlidda, Phil. 80 C3 17 15N 120 31 E
Lido, Italy 45 C9 45 25N 12 22 E
Lido, Niger 113 C5 12 54N 3 44 E
Lido di Roma = Óstia, Lido di, Italy 45 G9 41 43N 12 17 E
Lidzbark, Poland 55 E6 53 15N 19 49 E
Lidzbark Warmiński, Poland 54 D7 54 7N 20 34 E
Liebenwalde, Germany 30 C9 52 52N 13 24 E
Lieberose, Germany 30 D10 51 59N 14 17 E
Liebig, Mt., Australia 124 D5 23 18 S 131 22 E
Liebling, Romania 52 E6 45 36N 21 20 E
Liechtenstein ■, Europe 33 B9 47 8N 9 35 E
Liège, Belgium 24 D5 50 38N 5 35 E
Liège □, Belgium 24 D5 50 32N 5 35 E
Liegnitz = Legnica, Poland 55 G3 51 12N 16 10 E
Lienart, Dem. Rep. of the Congo 118 B2 3 3N 25 31 E
Lienyünchiangshih = Lianyungang, China 75 G10 34 40N 119 11 E
Lienz, Austria 34 E5 46 50N 12 46 E
Liepāja, Latvia 15 H19 56 30N 21 0 E
Liepāja □, Latvia 54 B8 56 30N 21 30 E
Liepājas ezers, Latvia 54 B8 56 27N 21 3 E
Lier, Belgium 24 C4 51 7N 4 34 E
Liernais, France 27 E11 47 13N 4 16 E
Liestal, Switz. 32 B5 47 29N 7 44 E
Liești, Romania 53 E12 45 38N 27 34 E
Liévin, France 27 B9 50 24N 2 47 E
Lièvre →, Canada 140 C4 45 31N 75 26W
Liezen, Austria 34 D7 47 34N 14 15 E
Liffey →, Ireland 23 C5 53 21N 6 13W
Lifford, Ireland 23 B4 54 51N 7 29W
Liffré, France 26 D5 48 12N 1 30W
Lifjell, Norway 18 E5 59 27N 8 45 E
Lifudzin, Russia 68 B7 44 21N 134 58 E
Lifuka, Tonga 133 P13 19 48 S 174 21W
Ligao, Phil. 80 E4 13 14N 123 32 E
Lighthouse Point, U.S.A. 153 J9 26 15N 80 7W
Lighthouse Pt., U.S.A. 152 F5 29 54N 84 21W
Lightning Ridge, Australia 127 D4 29 22 S 148 0 E
Lignano Sabbiadoro, Italy 45 C10 45 42N 13 9 E
Ligny-en-Barrois, France 27 D12 48 36N 5 20 E
Ligoúrion, Greece 48 D5 37 37N 23 4 E
Ligueil, France 26 E7 47 2N 0 49 E
Liguria □, Italy 44 D5 44 30N 8 50 E
Ligurian Sea, Medit. S. 12 G7 43 20N 9 0 E
Lihir Group, Papua N. G. 132 B7 3 0 S 152 35 E
Lihou Reefs and Cays, Australia 126 B5 17 25 S 151 40 E
Lihue, U.S.A. 146 H15 21 59N 159 23W
Lijiang, China 76 D3 26 55N 100 20 E
Likasi, Dem. Rep. of the Congo 119 E2 10 55 S 26 48 E
Likati, Dem. Rep. of the Congo 114 B4 3 20N 24 0 E
Likenäs, Sweden 16 D8 60 37N 13 3 E
Likhoslavl, Russia 58 D8 57 12N 35 30 E
Likhovskoy, Russia 59 H11 48 10N 40 10 E
Likisia, Indonesia 82 C3 8 36 S 125 19 E
Liknes, Norway 18 F3 58 19N 6 59 E
Likokou, Gabon 114 C2 0 12 S 12 48 E
Likoma I., Malawi 119 E3 12 3 S 34 45 E
Likumburu, Tanzania 119 D4 9 43 S 35 8 E
L'Île-Bouchard, France 26 E7 47 7N 0 26 E
L'Île-Rousse, France 29 F12 42 38N 8 57 E
Liling, China 77 D9 27 42N 113 29 E
Lilla Edet, Sweden 17 F6 58 9N 12 8 E
Lille, France 27 B10 50 38N 3 3 E
Lille Bælt, Denmark 17 J3 55 20N 9 45 E
Lillebonne, France 26 C7 49 30N 0 32 E
Lillehammer, Norway 15 F14 61 8N 10 30 E
Lillesand, Norway 15 G13 58 15N 8 23 E
Lillestrøm, Norway 18 E8 59 58N 11 5 E
Lillhärdal, Sweden 16 C8 61 51N 14 5 E
Lillian Point, Mt., Australia 125 E4 27 40 S 126 6 E
Lillo, Spain 42 F7 39 45N 3 20W
Lillooet →, Canada 142 D4 49 15N 121 57W
Lilongwe, Malawi 119 E3 14 0 S 33 48 E
Liloy, Phil. 81 G4 8 4N 122 39 E
Lim →, Bos.-H. 50 C3 43 45N 19 15 E
Lima, Indonesia 82 B3 3 37 S 128 4 E
Lima, Peru 172 C2 12 0 S 77 0W
Lima, Mont., U.S.A. 158 D7 44 38N 112 36W
Lima, Ohio, U.S.A. 157 D12 40 44N 84 6W
Lima □, Peru 172 C2 12 3 S 77 3W
Lima →, Portugal 42 D2 41 41N 8 50W
Limages, Canada 151 A9 45 20N 75 16W
Liman, Russia 61 H8 45 45N 47 12 E
Limanowa, Poland 55 J7 49 42N 20 22 E
Limassol, Cyprus 38 E12 34 42N 33 1 E
Limavady, U.K. 23 A5 55 3N 6 56W
Limay →, Argentina 176 A3 39 0 S 68 0W
Limay Mahuida, Argentina 174 D2 37 10 S 66 45W
Limbach-Oberfrohna, Germany 30 E8 50 52N 12 43 E
Limbang, Brunei 85 B5 4 42N 115 6 E
Limbara, Mte., Italy 46 B2 40 51N 9 10 E
Limbaži, Latvia 15 H21 57 31N 24 42 E
Limbdi, India 92 H4 22 34N 71 51 E
Limbe, Cameroon 113 E6 4 1N 9 10 E
Limbri, Australia 129 A9 31 3 S 151 5 E
Limbueta, Angola 115 E3 12 30 S 18 42 E
Limbunya, Australia 124 C4 17 14 S 129 50 E
Limburg, Germany 31 E4 50 22N 8 4 E
Limburg □, Belgium 24 C5 51 2N 5 25 E
Limburg □, Neths. 24 C5 51 20N 5 55 E
Lime Village, U.S.A. 144 F9 61 21N 155 28W
Limedsforsen, Sweden 16 D7 60 52N 13 25 E
Limeira, Brazil 175 A6 22 35 S 47 28W
Limenária, Greece 51 F8 40 38N 24 32 E
Limerick, Ireland 23 D3 52 40N 8 37W
Limerick □, Ireland 23 D3 52 30N 8 50W
Limestone, U.S.A. 150 D6 42 2N 78 38W
Limestone →, Canada 143 B10 56 31N 94 7W
Limfjorden, Denmark 17 H3 56 55N 9 0 E
Limia = Lima →, Portugal 42 D2 41 41N 8 50W
Limín Khersonísou, Greece 49 F7 35 18N 25 21 E
Limingen, Norway 14 D15 64 48N 13 35 E
Limmared, Sweden 17 G7 57 34N 13 20 E
Limmat →, Switz. 33 B6 47 26N 8 20 E
Limmen Bight, Australia 126 A2 14 40 S 135 35 E
Limmen Bight →, Australia 126 B2 15 7 S 135 44 E
Límni, Greece 48 C5 38 43N 23 18 E
Límnos, Greece 49 B7 39 50N 25 5 E
Limoeiro, Brazil 170 C4 7 52 S 35 27W
Limoeiro do Norte, Brazil 170 C4 5 5 S 38 0W
Limoges, France 28 C5 45 50N 1 15 E
Limón, Costa Rica 164 E3 10 0N 83 2W
Limon, U.S.A. 154 F3 39 16N 103 41W
Limone Piemonte, Italy 44 D4 44 12N 7 34 E
Limousin, France 28 C5 45 30N 1 30 E
Limousin, Plateaux du, France 28 C5 45 45N 1 15 E
Limoux, France 28 E6 43 4N 2 12 E
Limpopo →, Africa 117 D5 25 5 S 33 30 E
Limuru, Kenya 118 C4 1 2 S 36 35 E
Lin Xian, China 74 F6 37 57N 110 58 E
Lin'an, China 77 B12 30 15N 119 42 E
Linapacan, Phil. 81 F2 11 30N 119 52 E
Linapacan I., Phil. 81 F2 11 27N 119 49 E
Linapacan Str., Phil. 81 F2 11 37N 119 56 E
Linares, Chile 174 D1 35 50 S 71 40W
Linares, Colombia 168 C2 1 23N 77 31W
Linares, Mexico 163 C5 24 50N 99 40W
Linares, Spain 43 G7 38 10N 3 40W
Linares □, Chile 174 D1 36 0 S 71 0W
Linaro, Capo, Italy 45 F8 42 2N 11 50 E
Línas Mte., Italy 46 C1 39 25N 8 38 E
Lincang, China 76 F3 23 58N 100 1 E
Lincheng, China 74 F8 37 25N 114 30 E
Linchuan, China 77 D11 27 57N 116 15 E
Lincoln, Argentina 174 C3 34 55 S 61 30W
Lincoln, N.Z. 131 D7 43 38 S 172 30 E
Lincoln, U.K. 20 D7 53 14N 0 32W
Lincoln, Calif., U.S.A. 160 G5 38 54N 121 17W
Lincoln, Ill., U.S.A. 156 D7 40 9N 89 22W
Lincoln, Kans., U.S.A. 154 F5 39 3N 98 9W
Lincoln, Maine, U.S.A. 141 C6 45 22N 68 30W
Lincoln, N.H., U.S.A. 151 B13 44 3N 71 40W
Lincoln, N. Mex., U.S.A. 159 K11 33 30N 105 23W
Lincoln, Nebr., U.S.A. 154 E6 40 49N 96 41W
Lincoln Hav = Lincoln Sea, Arctic 10 A5 84 0N 55 0W
Lincoln Park, Ga., U.S.A. 152 A5 32 52N 84 20W
Lincoln Park, Mich., U.S.A. 157 B13 42 15N 83 11W
Lincoln Sea, Arctic 10 A5 84 0N 55 0W
Lincolnshire □, U.K. 20 D7 53 14N 0 32W
Lincolnshire Wolds, U.K. 20 D7 53 26N 0 13W
Lincolnton, Ga., U.S.A. 152 B7 33 48N 82 29W
Lincolnton, N.C., U.S.A. 149 H5 35 29N 81 16W
L'Incudine, France 29 G13 41 50N 9 12 E
Lind, U.S.A. 158 C4 46 58N 118 37W
Linda, U.S.A. 160 F5 39 8N 121 34W
Lindale, U.S.A. 152 A4 34 11N 85 11W
Lindås, Norway 18 D2 60 44N 5 9 E
Lindau, Germany 31 H5 47 33N 9 42 E
Linden, Guyana 169 B6 6 0N 58 10W
Linden, Calif., U.S.A. 160 G5 38 1N 121 5W
Linden, Ind., U.S.A. 157 D10 40 11N 86 54W
Linden, Mich., U.S.A. 157 B13 42 49N 83 47W
Linden, Tex., U.S.A. 155 J7 33 1N 94 22W
Lindenhurst, U.S.A. 151 F11 40 41N 73 23W
Lindenow Fjord, Greenland 10 E6 60 30N 43 25W
Lindesberg, Sweden 16 E9 59 36N 15 15 E
Lindesnes, Norway 15 H12 57 58N 7 3 E
Líndhos, Greece 38 C10 36 6N 28 4 E
Líndhos, Ákra, Greece 38 C10 36 4N 28 10 E
Lindi, Tanzania 119 D4 9 58 S 39 38 E
Lindi □, Tanzania 119 D4 9 40 S 38 30 E
Lindi →, Dem. Rep. of the Congo 118 B2 0 33N 25 5 E
Lindö, Sweden 17 F10 58 37N 16 15 E
Lindome, Sweden 17 G6 57 35N 12 5 E
Lindoso, Portugal 42 D2 41 52N 8 11W
Lindow, Germany 30 C8 52 58N 12 59 E
Lindsay, Canada 140 D4 44 22N 78 43W
Lindsay, Calif., U.S.A. 160 J7 36 12N 119 5W
Lindsay, Okla., U.S.A. 155 H6 34 50N 97 38W
Lindsborg, U.S.A. 154 F6 38 35N 97 40W
Lindsdal, Sweden 17 H10 56 44N 16 18 E
Lineville, Ala., U.S.A. 152 B4 33 19N 85 45W
Lineville, Iowa, U.S.A. 156 D3 40 35N 93 32W
Linfen, China 74 F6 36 3N 111 30 E
Ling Xian, Hunan, China 77 D9 26 29N 113 48 E
Ling Xian, Shandong, China 74 F9 37 22N 116 30 E
Lingao, China 86 C7 19 56N 109 42 E
Lingayen, Phil. 80 C3 16 1N 120 14 E
Lingayen G., Phil. 80 C3 16 10N 120 15 E
Lingbi, China 75 H9 33 33N 117 33 E
Lingbo, Sweden 16 C10 61 3N 16 41 E
Lingchuan, Guangxi Zhuangzu, China 77 E8 25 26N 110 21 E
Lingchuan, Shanxi, China 74 G7 35 45N 113 12 E
Lingen, Germany 30 C3 52 31N 7 19 E
Lingga, Indonesia 84 C2 0 12 S 104 37 E
Lingga, Kepulauan, Indonesia 84 C2 0 10 S 104 30 E
Lingga Arch. = Lingga, Kepulauan, Indonesia 84 C2 0 10 S 104 30 E
Linghem, Sweden 17 F9 58 26N 15 47 E
Lingle, U.S.A. 154 D2 42 8N 104 21W
Lingling, China 77 D8 26 17N 111 37 E
Lingqiu, China 74 E8 39 28N 114 22 E
Lingshan, China 76 F7 22 25N 109 18 E
Lingshi, China 74 F6 36 48N 111 48 E
Lingshou, China 74 E8 38 20N 114 20 E
Lingshui, China 86 C8 18 27N 110 0 E
Lingtai, China 74 G4 35 0N 107 40 E
Linguère, Senegal 112 B1 15 25N 15 5W
Linguisan, Phil. 81 H4 7 30N 122 27 E
Lingwu, China 74 E4 38 6N 106 20 E
Lingyuan, China 75 D10 41 10N 119 15 E
Lingyun, China 76 E6 25 2N 106 35 E
Linhai, China 77 C13 28 50N 121 8 E
Linhares, Brazil 171 E3 19 25 S 40 4W
Linhe, China 74 D4 40 48N 107 20 E
Linjiang, China 75 D14 41 50N 127 0 E
Linköping, Sweden 17 F9 58 28N 15 36 E
Linkou, China 75 B16 45 15N 130 18 E
Linli, China 77 C8 29 27N 111 30 E
Linn, U.S.A. 156 F5 38 29N 91 51W
Linneus, U.S.A. 156 E3 39 53N 93 11W
Linnhe, L., U.K. 22 E3 56 36N 5 25W
Linosa, I., Medit. S. 108 A2 35 51N 12 50 E
Linqi, China 74 G7 35 45N 113 52 E
Linqing, China 74 F8 36 50N 115 42 E
Linqu, China 75 F10 36 25N 118 30 E
Linru, China 74 G7 34 11N 112 52 E
Lins, Brazil 175 A6 21 40 S 49 44W
Linshui, China 76 B6 30 21N 106 57 E
Lintao, China 74 G2 35 18N 103 52 E
Linth →, Switz. 31 H5 47 7N 9 7 E
Linthal, Switz. 33 C8 46 54N 9 0 E
Lintlaw, Canada 143 C8 52 4N 103 14W
Linton, Canada 141 C5 47 15N 72 16W
Linton, Ind., U.S.A. 157 F9 39 2N 87 10W
Linton, N. Dak., U.S.A. 154 B4 46 16N 100 14W
Lintong, China 74 G5 34 20N 109 10 E
Linville, Australia 127 D5 26 50 S 152 11 E
Linwood, Canada 150 C4 43 35N 80 43W
Linwood, U.S.A. 152 D4 31 56N 85 52W
Linwu, China 77 E9 25 19N 112 31 E
Linxi, China 75 C10 43 36N 118 2 E
Linxia, China 72 C5 35 36N 103 10 E
Linxiang, China 77 C9 29 28N 113 23 E
Linyanti →, Africa 116 B4 17 50 S 25 5 E
Linyi, China 75 G10 35 5N 118 21 E
Linz, Austria 34 C7 48 18N 14 18 E
Linz, Germany 30 E3 50 34N 7 17 E
Linzhenzhen, China 74 F5 36 30N 109 59 E
Linzi, China 75 F10 36 50N 118 20 E
Liomseter, Norway 18 C6 61 15N 9 35 E
Lion, G. du, France 28 E7 43 10N 4 0 E
Lionárisso, Cyprus 38 D13 35 28N 34 8 E
Lioni, Italy 47 B8 40 52N 15 11 E
Lions, G. of = Lion, G. du, France 28 E7 43 10N 4 0 E
Lion's Den, Zimbabwe 119 F3 17 15 S 30 5 E
Lion's Head, Canada 140 D3 44 58N 81 15W
Liouesso, Congo 114 B3 1 2N 15 43 E
Liozno = Lyozna, Belarus 58 E6 55 0N 30 50 E
Lipa, Phil. 80 E3 13 57N 121 10 E
Lipali, Mozam. 119 F4 15 50 S 35 50 E
Lipany, Slovak Rep. 35 B13 49 9N 20 58 E
Lípari, Italy 47 D7 38 26N 14 58 E
Lípari, Is. = Eólie, Ís., Italy 47 D7 38 30N 14 57 E
Lipcani, Moldova 53 B11 48 14N 26 48 E
Lipetsk, Russia 59 F10 52 37N 39 35 E
Lipiany, Poland 55 E1 53 2N 14 58 E
Liping, China 76 D7 26 15N 109 7 E
Lipkany = Lipcani, Moldova 53 B11 48 14N 26 48 E
Lipljan, Serbia, Yug. 50 D5 42 31N 21 7 E
Lipník nad Bečvou, Czech Rep. 35 B10 49 32N 17 36 E
Lipno, Poland 55 F6 52 49N 19 15 E
Lipova, Romania 52 D6 46 8N 21 42 E
Lipovcy Manzovka, Russia 68 B6 44 12N 132 26 E
Lipovets, Ukraine 59 H5 49 12N 29 1 E
Lippe →, Germany 30 D2 51 39N 6 36 E
Lippstadt, Germany 30 D4 51 41N 8 22 E
Lipscomb, U.S.A. 155 G4 36 14N 100 16W
Lipsk, Poland 54 E10 53 44N 23 24 E
Lipsko, Poland 55 G8 51 9N 21 40 E
Lipsói, Greece 49 D8 37 19N 26 50 E
Liptovský Hrádok, Slovak Rep. 35 B12 49 2N 19 44 E
Liptovský Milkuláš, Slovak Rep. 35 B12 49 6N 19 35 E
Liptrap C., Australia 129 E6 38 50 S 145 55 E
Lipu, China 77 E8 24 30N 110 22 E
Lira, Uganda 118 B3 2 17N 32 57 E
Liri →, Italy 46 A6 41 25N 13 52 E
Liria = Lliria, Spain 41 F4 39 37N 0 35W
Lisakovsk, Kazakstan 62 E9 52 33N 62 37 E
Lisala, Dem. Rep. of the Congo 114 B4 2 12N 21 38 E
Lisboa, Portugal 43 G1 38 42N 9 10W
Lisboa □, Portugal 43 F1 39 0N 9 12W
Lisbon = Lisboa, Portugal 43 G1 38 42N 9 10W
Lisbon, N. Dak., U.S.A. 154 B6 46 27N 97 41W
Lisbon, N.H., U.S.A. 151 B13 44 13N 71 55W
Lisbon, Ohio, U.S.A. 150 F4 40 46N 80 46W
Lisburn, U.K. 23 B5 54 31N 6 3W
Liscannor, B., Ireland 23 C2 52 55N 9 24W
Liscia →, Italy 46 A2 41 11N 9 9 E
Lishe Jiang →, China 76 E3 24 15N 101 35 E
Lishi, China 74 F6 37 31N 111 8 E
Lishu, China 75 C13 43 20N 124 18 E
Lishui, Jiangsu, China 77 B12 31 38N 119 2 E
Lishui, Zhejiang, China 77 C12 28 28N 119 54 E
Lisianski I., Pac. Oc. 134 E10 26 2N 174 0W
Lisianski I., U.S.A. 145 F9 26 2N 174 0W
Lisichansk = Lysychansk, Ukraine 59 H10 48 55N 38 30 E
Lisieux, France 26 C7 49 10N 0 12 E
Liski, Russia 59 G10 51 3N 39 30 E
L'Isle-Jourdain, Gers, France 28 E5 43 36N 1 5 E
L'Isle-Jourdain, Vienne, France 28 B4 46 13N 0 31 E
L'Isle-sur-la-Sorgue, France 29 E9 43 54N 5 2 E
Lisle-sur-Tarn, France 28 E5 43 52N 1 49 E
Lismore, Australia 127 D5 28 44 S 153 21 E
Lismore, Ireland 23 D4 52 8N 7 55W
Lista, Norway 15 G12 58 7N 6 39 E
Lister, Mt., Antarctica 7 D11 78 0 S 162 0 E
Liston, Australia 127 D5 28 39 S 152 6 E
Listowel, Canada 140 D3 43 44N 80 58W
Listowel, Ireland 23 D2 52 27N 9 29W
Lit, Sweden 16 A8 63 19N 14 51 E
Lit-et-Mixe, France 28 D2 44 2N 1 15W
Litang, Guangxi Zhuangzu, China 76 F7 23 12N 109 8 E
Litang, Sichuan, China 76 B3 30 1N 100 17 E

244 Lusambo

Lusambo, Dem. Rep. of the Congo . 115 C4 4 58 S 23 28 E
Lusangaye, Dem. Rep. of the Congo . 115 C5 4 54 S 26 0 E
Luseland, Canada . 143 C7 52 5N 109 24W
Lushan, Henan, China . 74 H7 33 45N 112 55 E
Lushan, Sichuan, China . 76 B4 30 12N 102 52 E
Lushi, China . 74 G6 34 3N 111 3 E
Lushnja, Albania . 50 F3 40 55N 19 41 E
Lushoto, Tanzania . 118 C4 4 47 S 38 20 E
Lushoto □, Tanzania . 118 C4 4 45 S 38 20 E
Lushui, China . 76 E2 25 58N 98 44 E
Lüshun, China . 75 E11 38 45N 121 15 E
Lusignan, France . 28 B4 46 26N 0 8 E
Lusigny-sur-Barse, France . 27 D11 48 16N 4 15 E
Lusk, U.S.A. . 154 D2 42 46N 104 27W
Lussac-les-Châteaux, France . 28 B4 46 24N 0 43 E
Lussanvira, Brazil . 171 F1 20 42 S 51 7W
Lustenau, Austria . 34 D2 47 26N 9 39 E
Lustrafjorden, Norway . 18 C4 61 23N 7 25 E
Luta = Dalian, China . 75 E11 38 50N 121 40 E
Luterabo, Angola . 115 E4 13 26 S 21 16 E
Lutherstadt Wittenberg, Germany . 30 D8 51 53N 12 39 E
Luthersville, U.S.A. . 152 B5 33 13N 84 45W
Luti, Solomon Is. . 133 L9 7 14 S 157 0 E
Luton, U.K. . 21 F7 51 53N 0 24W
Luton □, U.K. . 21 F7 51 53N 0 24W
Lutong, Malaysia . 85 B4 4 28N 114 0 E
Lutry, Switz. . 32 C3 46 31N 6 42 E
Lutselke, Canada . 143 A6 62 24N 110 44W
Lutsk, Ukraine . 59 G3 50 50N 25 15 E
Lutuai, Angola . 115 E4 12 41 S 20 7 E
Lutz, U.S.A. . 153 G7 28 9N 82 28W
Lützow Holmbukta, Antarctica . 7 C4 69 10 S 37 30 E
Lutzputs, S. Africa . 116 D3 28 3 S 20 40 E
Luverne, Ala., U.S.A. . 152 D3 31 43N 86 16W
Luverne, Minn., U.S.A. . 154 D6 43 39N 96 13W
Luvo, Angola . 115 D2 5 51 S 14 5 E
Luvua, Dem. Rep. of the Congo . 115 D5 8 48 S 25 17 E
Luvua →, Dem. Rep. of the Congo . 118 D2 6 50 S 27 30 E
Luwegu →, Tanzania . 119 D4 8 31 S 37 23 E
Luwuk, Indonesia . 82 B2 0 56 S 122 47 E
Luxembourg, Lux. . 24 E6 49 37N 6 9 E
Luxembourg □, Belgium . 24 E5 49 58N 5 30 E
Luxembourg ■, Europe . 13 F7 49 45N 6 0 E
Luxeuil-les-Bains, France . 27 E13 47 49N 6 24 E
Luxi, Hunan, China . 77 C8 28 20N 110 7 E
Luxi, Yunnan, China . 76 E4 24 40N 103 55 E
Luxi, Yunnan, China . 76 E2 24 27N 98 36 E
Luxor = El Uqsur, Egypt . 106 B3 25 41N 32 38 E
Luy-de-Béarn →, France . 28 E3 43 39N 0 48W
Luy-de-France →, France . 28 E3 43 39N 0 48W
Luyi, China . 74 H8 33 50N 115 35 E
Luz-St-Sauveur, France . 28 F4 42 53N 0 0 E
Luza, Russia . 56 B8 60 39N 47 10 E
Luzern, Switz. . 33 B6 47 3N 8 18 E
Luzern □, Switz. . 32 B5 47 2N 7 55 E
Luzhai, China . 76 E7 24 29N 109 42 E
Luzhou, China . 76 C5 28 52N 105 20 E
Luziânia, Brazil . 171 E2 16 20 S 48 0W
Luzilândia, Brazil . 170 B3 3 28 S 42 22W
Lužnice →, Czech Rep. . 34 B7 49 14N 14 23 E
Luzon, Phil. . 80 C3 16 0N 121 0 E
Luzy, France . 27 F10 46 47N 3 58 E
Luzzi, Italy . 47 C9 39 27N 16 17 E
Lviv, Ukraine . 59 H3 49 50N 24 0 E
Lvov = Lviv, Ukraine . 59 H3 49 50N 24 0 E
Lwówek, Poland . 55 F3 52 28N 16 10 E
Lwówek Śląski, Poland . 55 G2 51 7N 15 38 E
Lyakhavichy, Belarus . 59 F4 53 2N 26 32 E
Lyakhovskiye, Ostrova, Russia . 65 B15 73 40N 141 0 E
Lyaki = Läki, Azerbaijan . 61 K8 40 34N 47 22 E
Lyall Mt., N.Z. . 131 F2 45 16 S 167 32 E
Lyallpur = Faisalabad, Pakistan . 91 C4 31 30N 73 5 E
Lyalya →, Russia . 62 B8 59 9N 61 29 E
Lyaskovets, Bulgaria . 51 C9 43 6N 25 44 E
Lybster, U.K. . 22 C5 58 18N 3 15W
Lycaonia, Turkey . 100 D5 38 0N 33 0 E
Lychen, Germany . 30 B9 53 12N 13 18 E
Lychkova, Russia . 58 D7 57 55N 32 24 E
Lycia, Turkey . 49 E11 36 30N 29 30 E
Lycksbyån →, Sweden . 17 H9 56 12N 15 39 E
Lycksele, Sweden . 14 D18 64 38N 18 40 E
Lycosura, Greece . 48 D4 37 20N 22 3 E
Lydda = Lod, Israel . 103 D3 31 57N 34 54 E
Lydenburg, S. Africa . 117 D5 25 10 S 30 29 E
Lydia, Turkey . 49 C10 38 48N 28 19 E
Łydynia →, Poland . 55 F7 52 43N 20 26 E
Lyell, N.Z. . 131 B7 41 48 S 172 4 E
Lyell I., Canada . 142 C2 52 40N 131 35W
Lyepyel, Belarus . 58 E5 54 50N 28 40 E
Lygnern, Sweden . 17 G6 57 30N 12 15 E
Lyman, U.S.A. . 158 F8 41 20N 110 18W
Lyme B., U.K. . 21 G4 50 42N 2 53W
Lyme Regis, U.K. . 21 G5 50 43N 2 57W
Lymington, U.K. . 21 G6 50 45N 1 32W
Łyna →, Poland . 15 J19 54 37N 21 14 E
Lynchburg, Ohio, U.S.A. . 157 E13 39 15N 83 48W
Lynchburg, S.C., U.S.A. . 152 A9 34 3N 80 4W
Lynchburg, Va., U.S.A. . 148 G6 37 25N 79 9W
Lynd →, Australia . 126 B3 16 28 S 143 18 E
Lynd Ra., Australia . 127 D4 25 30 S 149 20 E
Lynden, Canada . 150 C4 43 14N 80 9W
Lynden, U.S.A. . 160 B4 48 57N 122 27W
Lyndhurst, Queens., Australia . 126 B3 19 12 S 144 20 E
Lyndhurst, S. Austral., Australia . 127 E2 30 15 S 138 18 E
Lyndon →, Australia . 125 D1 23 29 S 114 6 E
Lyndonville, N.Y., U.S.A. . 150 C6 43 20N 78 23W
Lyndonville, Vt., U.S.A. . 151 B12 44 31N 72 1W
Lyngdal, Buskerud, Norway . 18 E6 59 54N 9 32 E
Lyngdal, Vest-Agder, Norway . 18 F4 58 8N 7 7 E
Lyngen, Norway . 14 B19 69 45N 20 30 E
Lyngør, Norway . 18 F6 58 38N 9 8 E
Lynher Reef, Australia . 124 C3 15 27 S 121 55 E
Lynn, Ind., U.S.A. . 157 D12 40 3N 84 56W
Lynn, Mass., U.S.A. . 151 D14 42 28N 70 57W
Lynn Canal, U.S.A. . 142 B1 58 50N 135 15W
Lynn Haven, U.S.A. . 152 E4 30 15N 85 39W
Lynn Lake, Canada . 143 B8 56 51N 101 3W
Lynne, U.S.A. . 153 F8 29 12N 81 55W
Lynnwood, U.S.A. . 160 C4 47 49N 122 19W
Lynton, U.K. . 21 F4 51 13N 3 50W
Lyntupy, Belarus . 15 J22 55 4N 26 23 E
Lynx L., Canada . 143 A7 62 25N 106 15W
Lyon, France . 29 C8 45 46N 4 50 E
Lyonnais, France . 29 C8 45 45N 4 15 E
Lyons = Lyon, France . 29 C8 45 46N 4 50 E
Lyons, Colo., U.S.A. . 154 E2 40 14N 105 16W
Lyons, Ga., U.S.A. . 152 C7 32 12N 82 19W
Lyons, Kans., U.S.A. . 154 F5 38 21N 98 12W
Lyons, N.Y., U.S.A. . 150 C8 43 5N 77 0W
Lyozna, Belarus . 58 E6 55 0N 30 50 E
Lys = Leie →, Belgium . 24 C3 51 2N 3 45 E
Lysá nad Labem, Czech Rep. . 34 A7 50 11N 14 51 E
Lysebotn, Norway . 18 E3 59 3N 6 37 E
Lysefjorden, Norway . 18 E3 59 0N 6 23 E
Lysekil, Sweden . 17 F5 58 17N 11 26 E
Lyskovo, Russia . 60 B7 56 0N 45 3 E
Lyss, Switz. . 32 B4 47 4N 7 19 E
Lystrup, Denmark . 17 H4 56 14N 10 14 E
Lysva, Russia . 62 B6 58 7N 57 49 E
Lysvik, Sweden . 16 D7 60 1N 13 9 E
Lysychansk, Ukraine . 59 H10 48 55N 38 30 E
Lytham St. Anne's, U.K. . 20 D4 53 45N 3 0W
Lytle, U.S.A. . 155 L5 29 14N 98 48W
Lyttelton, N.Z. . 131 D7 43 35 S 172 44 E
Lytton, Canada . 142 C4 50 13N 121 31W
Lyuban, Russia . 58 C6 59 16N 31 18 E
Lyubertsy, Russia . 58 E9 55 39N 37 50 E
Lyubim, Russia . 58 C11 58 20N 40 39 E
Lyubimets, Bulgaria . 51 E10 41 50N 26 5 E
Lyuboml, Ukraine . 59 G3 51 11N 24 4 E
Lyubotyn, Ukraine . 59 H8 50 0N 36 0 E
Lyubytino, Russia . 58 C7 58 50N 33 16 E
Lyudinovo, Russia . 58 F8 53 52N 34 28 E

M

Ma →, Vietnam . 86 C5 19 47N 105 56 E
Ma'adaba, Jordan . 103 E4 30 43N 35 47 E
Maamba, Zambia . 116 B4 17 17 S 26 28 E
Ma'ān, Jordan . 103 E4 30 12N 35 44 E
Ma'ān □, Jordan . 103 F5 30 0N 36 0 E
Maanselkä, Finland . 14 C23 63 52N 28 32 E
Ma'anshan, China . 77 B12 31 44N 118 29 E
Maarianhamina, Finland . 15 F18 60 5N 19 55 E
Ma'arrat an Nu'mān, Syria . 100 E7 35 43N 36 43 E
Maas →, Neths. . 24 C4 51 45N 4 32 E
Maaseik, Belgium . 24 C5 51 6N 5 45 E
Maastricht, Neths. . 24 D5 50 50N 5 40 E
Maave, Mozam. . 117 C5 21 4 S 34 47 E
Ma'bar, Yemen . 98 D4 14 48N 44 17 E
Mabaruma, Guyana . 169 B6 8 10N 59 50W
Mabein, Burma . 90 D6 23 29N 96 37 E
Mabel L., Canada . 142 C5 50 35N 118 43W
Mabenge, Dem. Rep. of the Congo . 118 B1 4 15N 24 12 E
Mabian, China . 76 C4 28 47N 103 37 E
Mablethorpe, U.K. . 20 D8 53 20N 0 15 E
Mableton, U.S.A. . 152 B5 33 49N 84 35W
Mably, France . 27 F11 46 5N 4 4 E
Maboma, Dem. Rep. of the Congo . 118 B2 2 30N 28 10 E
Maboukou, Congo . 114 C2 3 39 S 12 31 E
Mabrouk, Mali . 113 B4 19 29N 1 15W
Mabton, U.S.A. . 158 C3 46 13N 120 0W
Mabungo, Somali Rep. . 120 D2 0 49N 42 35 E
Mac Bac, Vietnam . 87 H6 9 46N 106 7 E
Macachín, Argentina . 174 D3 37 10 S 63 43W
Macaé, Brazil . 171 F3 22 20 S 41 43W
Macael, Spain . 41 H2 37 20N 2 18W
Macaíba, Brazil . 170 C4 5 51 S 35 21W
Macajuba, Brazil . 171 D3 12 9 S 40 22W
Macalelon, Phil. . 80 E4 13 45N 122 8 E
McAlester, U.S.A. . 155 H7 34 56N 95 46W
McAllen, U.S.A. . 155 M5 26 12N 98 14W
McAlpin, U.S.A. . 152 E7 30 8N 82 57W
Macamic, Canada . 140 C4 48 45N 79 0W
Macao = Macau ■, Asia . 77 F9 22 16N 113 35 E
Macão, Portugal . 43 F3 39 35N 7 59W
Macapá, Brazil . 169 C7 0 5N 51 4W
Macará, Ecuador . 168 D2 4 23 S 79 57W
Macarani, Brazil . 171 E3 15 33 S 40 24W
Macarena, Serranía de la, Colombia . 168 C3 2 45N 73 55W
Macarthur, Australia . 128 E5 38 5 S 142 0 E
McArthur →, Australia . 126 B2 15 54 S 136 40 E
McArthur, Port, Australia . 126 B2 16 4 S 136 23 E
McArthur River, Australia . 126 B2 16 27 S 136 7 E
Macas, Ecuador . 168 D2 2 19 S 78 7W
Macate, Peru . 172 B2 8 48 S 78 7W
Macau, Brazil . 170 C4 5 15 S 36 40W
Macau ■, Asia . 77 F9 22 16N 113 35 E
Macaúbas, Brazil . 171 D3 13 2 S 42 42W
Macaya →, Colombia . 168 C3 0 59N 72 20W
McBride, Canada . 142 C4 53 20N 120 19W
McCall, U.S.A. . 158 D5 44 55N 116 6W
McCamey, U.S.A. . 155 K3 31 8N 102 14W
McCammon, U.S.A. . 158 E7 42 39N 112 12W
McCauley I., Canada . 142 C2 53 40N 130 15W
McCleary, U.S.A. . 160 C3 47 3N 123 16W
Macclenny, U.S.A. . 152 E7 30 17N 82 7W
Macclesfield, U.K. . 20 D5 53 15N 2 8W
McClintock, Canada . 143 B10 57 50N 94 10W
M'Clintock Chan., Canada . 138 A9 72 0N 102 0W
McClintock Ra., Australia . 124 C4 18 44 S 127 38 E
McCloud, U.S.A. . 158 F2 41 15N 122 8W
McCluer I., Australia . 124 B5 11 5 S 133 0 E
McClure, U.S.A. . 150 F7 40 42N 77 19W
McClure, L., U.S.A. . 160 H6 37 35N 120 16W
M'Clure Str., Canada . 6 B2 75 0N 119 0W
McClusky, U.S.A. . 154 B4 47 29N 100 27W
McComb, U.S.A. . 155 K9 31 15N 90 27W
McConaughy, L., U.S.A. . 154 E4 41 14N 101 40W
McCook, U.S.A. . 154 E4 40 12N 100 38W
McCormick, U.S.A. . 152 B7 33 55N 82 17W
McCullough Mt., U.S.A. . 161 K11 35 35N 115 13W
McCusker →, Canada . 143 B7 55 32N 108 39W
McDame, Canada . 142 B3 59 44N 128 59W
McDavid, U.S.A. . 153 E2 30 52N 87 19W
McDermitt, U.S.A. . 158 F5 41 59N 117 43W
Macdonald, L., Australia . 124 D4 23 30 S 129 0 E
Macdonald, Mt., Vanuatu . 133 G6 17 36 S 168 23 E
McDonald Is., Ind. Oc. . 121 K6 53 0 S 73 0 E
Macdonnell Ranges, Australia . 124 D5 23 40 S 133 0 E
McDonough, U.S.A. . 152 B5 33 27N 84 9W
McDouall Peak, Australia . 127 D1 29 51 S 134 55 E
McDougalls Well, Australia . 128 A4 31 8 S 141 15 E
MacDowell L., Canada . 140 B1 52 15N 92 45W
Macduff, U.K. . 22 D6 57 40N 2 31W
Maceda, Spain . 42 C3 42 16N 7 39W
Macedonia ■, Europe . 50 E5 41 53N 21 40 E
Maceió, Brazil . 170 C4 9 40 S 35 41W
Maceira, Portugal . 42 F2 39 41N 8 55W
Macenta, Guinea . 112 D3 8 35N 9 32W
Macerata, Italy . 45 E10 43 18N 13 27 E
McFarland, U.S.A. . 161 K7 35 41N 119 14W
McFarlane →, Canada . 143 B7 59 12N 107 58W
Macfarlane, L., Australia . 128 B2 32 0 S 136 40 E
McGehee, U.S.A. . 155 J9 33 38N 91 24W
McGill, U.S.A. . 158 G6 39 23N 114 47W
Macgillycuddy's Reeks, Ireland . 23 E2 51 58N 9 45W
McGrath, U.S.A. . 144 E9 62 58N 155 36W
MacGregor, Canada . 143 D9 49 57N 98 48W
McGregor, U.S.A. . 156 A5 43 1N 91 11W
McGregor →, Canada . 142 B4 55 10N 122 0W
McGregor Ra., Australia . 127 D3 27 0 S 142 45 E
Māch Kowr, Iran . 97 E9 25 48N 61 28 E
Machacalis, Brazil . 171 E3 17 5 S 40 45W
Machado = Jiparaná →, Brazil . 173 B5 8 3 S 62 52W
Machagai, Argentina . 174 B3 26 56 S 60 2W
Machakos, Kenya . 118 C4 1 30 S 37 15 E
Machakos □, Kenya . 118 C4 1 30 S 37 15 E
Machala, Ecuador . 168 D2 3 20 S 79 57W
Machanga, Mozam. . 117 C6 20 59 S 35 0 E
Machattie, L., Australia . 126 C2 24 50 S 139 48 E
Machault, France . 27 C11 49 21N 4 29 E
Machava, Mozam. . 117 D5 25 54 S 32 28 E
Machece, Mozam. . 119 F4 19 15 S 35 32 E
Machecoul, France . 26 F5 47 0N 1 49W
Macheng, China . 77 B10 31 12N 115 2 E
McHenry, U.S.A. . 157 B8 42 21N 88 16W
Machero, Spain . 43 F6 39 21N 4 20W
Machias, U.S.A. . 141 D6 44 43N 67 28W
Machichi →, Canada . 143 B10 57 3N 92 6W
Machico, Madeira . 39 D3 32 43N 16 44W
Machida, Japan . 71 B11 35 28N 139 23 E
Machilipatnam, India . 95 F5 16 12N 81 8 E
Machiques, Venezuela . 168 A3 10 4N 72 34W
Machupicchu, Peru . 172 C3 13 8 S 72 30W
Machynlleth, U.K. . 21 E4 52 35N 3 50W
Maciejowice, Poland . 55 G8 51 36N 21 26 E
McIlwraith Ra., Australia . 126 A3 13 50 S 143 20 E
Măcin, Romania . 53 E13 45 16N 28 8 E
Macina, Mali . 112 C4 14 50N 5 0W
McIntosh, U.S.A. . 154 C4 45 55N 101 21W
McIntosh L., Canada . 143 B8 55 45N 105 0W
Macintosh Ra., Australia . 125 E4 27 39 S 125 32 E
Macintyre →, Australia . 127 D5 28 37 S 150 47 E
Macizo Galaico, Spain . 42 C3 42 30N 7 30W
Mackay, Australia . 126 C4 21 8 S 149 11 E
Mackay, U.S.A. . 158 E7 43 55N 113 37W
MacKay →, Canada . 142 B6 57 10N 111 38W
Mackay, L., Australia . 124 D4 22 30 S 129 0 E
McKay Ra., Australia . 124 D3 23 0 S 122 30 E
McKeesport, U.S.A. . 150 F5 40 21N 79 52W
McKenna, U.S.A. . 160 D4 46 56N 122 33W
Mackenzie, Canada . 142 B4 55 20N 123 5W
Mackenzie, Guyana . 169 B6 6 0N 58 17W
McKenzie, U.S.A. . 149 G1 36 8N 88 31W
Mackenzie →, Australia . 126 C4 23 38 S 149 46 E
Mackenzie →, Canada . 138 B6 69 10N 134 20W
McKenzie →, U.S.A. . 158 D2 44 7N 123 6W
Mackenzie Bay, Canada . 6 B1 69 0N 137 30W
Mackenzie City = Linden, Guyana . 169 B6 6 0N 58 10W
Mackenzie Highway, Canada . 142 B5 58 0N 117 15W
Mackenzie Mts., Canada . 138 B7 64 0N 130 0W
Mackenzie Plains, N.Z. . 131 E5 44 10 S 170 25 E
McKerrow L., N.Z. . 131 E3 44 25 S 168 5 E
Mackinaw, U.S.A. . 156 D7 40 32N 89 21W
Mackinaw →, U.S.A. . 156 D7 40 33N 89 44W
Mackinaw City, U.S.A. . 148 C3 45 47N 84 44W
McKinlay, Australia . 126 C3 21 16 S 141 18 E
McKinlay →, Australia . 126 C3 20 50 S 141 28 E
McKinley, Mt., U.S.A. . 138 B4 63 4N 151 0W
McKinley Park, U.S.A. . 144 E10 63 44N 148 55W
McKinley Sea, Arctic . 10 A11 82 0N 0 0 E
McKinney, U.S.A. . 155 J6 33 12N 96 37W
McKinnon, U.S.A. . 152 D8 31 25N 81 56W
McKinnon Pass, N.Z. . 131 E3 44 52 S 168 12 E
Mackinnon Road, Kenya . 118 C4 3 40 S 39 1 E
Macksville, Australia . 129 A10 30 40 S 152 56 E
McLaren Vale, Australia . 128 C3 35 13 S 138 31 E
McLaughlin, U.S.A. . 154 C4 45 49N 100 49W
Maclean, Australia . 127 D5 29 26 S 153 16 E
McLean, Ill., U.S.A. . 156 D7 40 19N 89 10W
McLean, Tex., U.S.A. . 155 H4 35 14N 100 36W
McLeansboro, U.S.A. . 154 F10 38 6N 88 32W
Maclear, S. Africa . 117 E4 31 2 S 28 23 E
Macleay →, Australia . 129 A10 30 56 S 153 0 E
McLennan, Canada . 142 B5 55 42N 116 50W
MacLeod, B., Canada . 143 A7 62 53N 110 0W
McLeod, L., Australia . 125 D1 24 9 S 113 47 E
MacLeod Lake, Canada . 142 C4 54 58N 123 0W
McLoughlin, Mt., U.S.A. . 158 E2 42 27N 122 19W
McLure, Canada . 142 C4 51 2N 120 13W
McMechen, U.S.A. . 150 G4 39 57N 80 44W
McMillan, L., U.S.A. . 155 J2 32 36N 104 21W
McMinnville, Oreg., U.S.A. . 158 D2 45 13N 123 12W
McMinnville, Tenn., U.S.A. . 149 H3 35 41N 85 46W
McMorran, Canada . 143 C7 51 19N 108 42W
McMurdo Sd., Antarctica . 7 D11 77 0 S 170 0 E
McMurray = Fort McMurray, Canada . 142 B6 56 44N 111 7W
McMurray, U.S.A. . 160 B4 48 19N 122 14W
McNary, U.S.A. . 159 J9 34 4N 109 51W
MacNutt, Canada . 143 C8 51 5N 101 36W
Maco, Phil. . 81 H5 7 20N 125 50 E
Macocolo, Angola . 115 D3 6 47 S 16 8 E
Macodoene, Mozam. . 117 C6 23 32 S 35 5 E
Macomb, U.S.A. . 156 D6 40 27N 90 40W
Macomer, Italy . 46 B1 40 16N 8 47 E
Mâcon, France . 27 F11 46 19N 4 50 E
Macon, Ga., U.S.A. . 152 C6 32 51N 83 38W
Macon, Ill., U.S.A. . 156 E8 39 43N 89 0W
Macon, Miss., U.S.A. . 149 J1 33 7N 88 34W
Macon, Mo., U.S.A. . 156 E4 39 44N 92 28W
Macondo, Angola . 115 E4 12 37 S 23 46 E
Macossa, Mozam. . 119 F3 17 55 S 33 56 E
Macoun L., Canada . 143 B8 56 32N 103 40W
Macoupin Cr. →, U.S.A. . 156 E6 39 11N 90 38W
Macovane, Mozam. . 117 C6 21 30 S 35 2 E
McPherson, U.S.A. . 154 F6 38 22N 97 40W
McPherson Pk., U.S.A. . 161 L7 34 53N 119 53W
McPherson Ra., Australia . 127 D5 28 15 S 153 15 E
Macquarie Harbour, Australia . 126 G4 42 15 S 145 23 E
Macquarie Is., Pac. Oc. . 134 N7 54 36 S 158 55 E
McRae, U.S.A. . 152 C7 32 4N 82 54W
MacRobertson Land, Antarctica . 7 D6 71 0 S 64 0 E
Macroom, Ireland . 23 E3 51 54N 8 57W
Macroy, Australia . 124 D2 20 53 S 118 2 E
MacTier, Canada . 150 A5 45 9N 79 46W
Macubela, Mozam. . 119 F4 16 53 S 37 49 E
Macugnaga, Italy . 44 C4 45 58N 7 58 E
Macuiza, Mozam. . 119 F3 18 7 S 34 29 E
Macujer, Colombia . 168 C3 0 24N 73 10W
Macusani, Peru . 172 C3 14 4 S 70 29W
Macuse, Mozam. . 119 F4 17 45 S 37 10 E
Macuspana, Mexico . 163 D6 17 46N 92 36W
Macusse, Angola . 115 F4 17 48 S 20 23 E
McVille, U.S.A. . 154 B5 47 46N 98 11W
Madadeni, S. Africa . 117 D5 27 43 S 30 3 E
Madadi, Chad . 109 E4 18 28N 20 45 E
Madagali, Nigeria . 113 C7 10 56N 13 33 E
Madagascar ■, Africa . 117 C8 20 0 S 47 0 E
Madā'in Sālih, Si. Arabia . 96 E3 26 46N 37 57 E
Madalag, Phil. . 81 F4 11 32N 122 18 E
Madama, Niger . 109 D2 22 0N 13 40 E
Madame I., Canada . 141 C7 45 30N 60 58W
Madan, Bulgaria . 51 E8 41 30N 24 57 E
Madanapalle, India . 95 H4 13 33N 78 28 E
Madang, Papua N. G. . 132 C3 5 12 S 145 49 E
Madaoua, Niger . 113 C6 14 5N 6 27 E
Madara, Nigeria . 113 C7 11 45N 10 35 E
Madaripur, Bangla. . 90 D3 23 19N 90 15 E
Madauk, Burma . 90 G6 17 56N 96 52 E
Madawaska, Canada . 150 A7 45 30N 78 0W
Madawaska →, Canada . 140 C4 45 27N 76 21W
Madaya, Burma . 90 D6 22 12N 96 10 E
Madbar, Sudan . 107 F3 6 17N 30 45 E
Maddalena, Italy . 46 A2 41 16N 9 23 E
Maddaloni, Italy . 47 A7 41 2N 14 23 E
Madeira, Atl. Oc. . 39 D3 32 50N 17 0W
Madeira, U.S.A. . 157 E12 39 11N 84 22W
Madeira →, Brazil . 169 D6 3 22 S 58 45W
Madeira Beach, U.S.A. . 153 H7 27 48N 82 48W
Madeleine, Is. de la, Canada . 141 C7 47 30N 61 40W
Maden, Turkey . 101 C8 38 23N 39 40 E
Madera, U.S.A. . 160 J6 36 57N 120 3W
Madgaon, India . 95 G1 15 12N 73 58 E
Madha, India . 94 F2 18 0N 75 30 E
Madhubani, India . 93 F12 26 21N 86 7 E
Madhumati →, Bangla. . 90 D2 22 53N 89 52 E
Madhya Pradesh □, India . 92 J8 22 50N 78 0 E
Madian, China . 77 A11 33 0N 116 6 E
Madidi →, Bolivia . 172 C4 12 32 S 66 52W
Madikeri, India . 95 H2 12 30N 75 45 E
Madill, U.S.A. . 155 H6 34 6N 96 46W
Madimba, Angola . 115 D2 6 36 S 14 23 E
Madimba, Dem. Rep. of the Congo . 115 C3 4 58 S 15 5 E
Ma'din, Syria . 101 E8 35 45N 39 36 E
Madīnat ash Sha'b, Yemen . 98 D4 12 50N 45 0 E
Madingou, Congo . 114 C2 4 10 S 13 33 E
Madirovalo, Madag. . 117 B8 16 26 S 46 32 E
Madison, Calif., U.S.A. . 160 G5 38 41N 121 59W
Madison, Fla., U.S.A. . 152 E6 30 28N 83 25W
Madison, Ga., U.S.A. . 152 B6 33 36N 83 28W
Madison, Ind., U.S.A. . 157 F11 38 44N 85 23W
Madison, Mo., U.S.A. . 156 E4 39 28N 92 13W
Madison, Nebr., U.S.A. . 154 E6 41 50N 97 27W
Madison, Ohio, U.S.A. . 150 E3 41 46N 81 3W
Madison, S. Dak., U.S.A. . 154 D6 44 0N 97 7W
Madison, Wis., U.S.A. . 156 A7 43 4N 89 24W
Madison →, U.S.A. . 158 D8 45 56N 111 31W
Madisonville, Ky., U.S.A. . 148 G2 37 20N 87 30W
Madisonville, Tex., U.S.A. . 155 K7 30 57N 95 55W
Madista, Botswana . 116 C4 21 15 S 25 6 E
Madiun, Indonesia . 85 D4 7 38 S 111 32 E
Madol, Sudan . 107 F2 9 3N 27 45 E
Madon →, France . 27 D13 48 36N 6 6 E
Madona, Latvia . 15 H22 56 53N 26 5 E
Madonie, Italy . 46 E6 37 50N 13 50 E
Madonna di Campíglio, Italy . 44 B7 46 14N 10 49 E
Madra Dağı, Turkey . 49 B9 39 23N 27 12 E
Madrakah, Ra's al, Oman . 99 C7 19 0N 57 50 E
Madras = Chennai, India . 95 H5 13 8N 80 19 E
Madras = Tamil Nadu □, India . 95 J3 11 0N 77 0 E
Madras, U.S.A. . 158 D3 44 38N 121 8W
Madre, L., Mexico . 163 C5 25 0N 97 30W
Madre, Laguna, U.S.A. . 155 M6 27 0N 97 30W
Madre, Sierra, Phil. . 80 C4 17 0N 122 0 E
Madre de Dios □, Peru . 172 C3 12 0 S 70 15W
Madre de Dios →, Bolivia . 172 C4 10 59 S 66 8W
Madre de Dios, I., Chile . 176 D1 50 20 S 75 10W
Madre del Sur, Sierra, Mexico . 163 D5 17 30N 100 0W
Madre Occidental, Sierra, Mexico . 162 B3 27 0N 107 0W
Madre Oriental, Sierra, Mexico . 162 C5 25 0N 100 0W
Madri, India . 92 G5 24 16N 73 32 E
Madrid, Spain . 42 E7 40 25N 3 45W
Madrid, Ala., U.S.A. . 152 D4 31 2N 85 24W
Madrid, Iowa, U.S.A. . 156 C3 41 53N 93 49W
Madrid □, Spain . 42 E7 40 30N 3 45W
Madridejos, Spain . 43 F7 39 28N 3 33W
Madrigal de las Altas Torres, Spain . 42 D6 41 5N 5 0W
Madrona, Sierra, Spain . 43 G6 38 27N 4 16W
Madroñera, Spain . 43 F5 39 26N 5 42W
Madu, Sudan . 107 E2 14 37N 26 4 E
Madura, Selat, Indonesia . 85 D4 7 30 S 113 20 E
Madura Motel, Australia . 125 F4 31 55 S 127 0 E
Madurai, India . 95 K4 9 55N 78 10 E
Madurantakam, India . 95 H4 12 30N 79 50 E
Madzhalis, Russia . 61 J8 42 9N 47 47 E
Mae Chan, Thailand . 86 B2 20 9N 99 52 E
Mae Hong Son, Thailand . 86 C2 19 16N 97 56 E
Mae Khlong →, Thailand . 86 F3 13 24N 100 0 E
Mae Phrik, Thailand . 86 D2 17 27N 99 7 E
Mae Ramat, Thailand . 86 D2 16 58N 98 31 E
Mae Rim, Thailand . 86 C2 18 54N 98 57 E
Mae Sot, Thailand . 86 D2 16 43N 98 34 E
Mae Suai, Thailand . 86 C2 19 39N 99 33 E
Mae Tha, Thailand . 86 C2 18 28N 99 8 E
Maebaru, Japan . 70 D2 33 33N 130 12 E
Maebashi, Japan . 71 A11 36 24N 139 4 E
Maella, Spain . 40 D5 41 8N 0 7 E
Maesteg, U.K. . 21 F4 51 36N 3 40W
Maestra, Sierra, Cuba . 164 B4 20 15N 77 0W
Maestrazgo, El, Spain . 40 E4 40 30N 0 25W
Maestre de Campo I., Phil. . 80 E3 12 56N 121 42 E
Maevatanana, Madag. . 117 B8 16 56 S 46 49 E
Maéwo, Vanuatu . 133 E6 15 10 S 168 10 E
Ma'fan, Libya . 108 C2 25 56N 14 29 E

Maştağa 247

Marawi City, Phil. 81 G5 8 0N 124 21 E
Marāwih, U.A.E. 97 E7 24 18N 53 18 E
Marbella, Spain 43 J6 36 30N 4 57W
Marble Bar, Australia 124 D2 21 9 S 119 44 E
Marble Falls, U.S.A. 155 K5 30 35N 98 16W
Marblehead, U.S.A. 151 D14 42 30N 70 51W
Mårbu, Norway 18 D5 60 11N 8 9 E
Marburg, Germany 30 E4 50 47N 8 46 E
Marcal →, Hungary 52 C2 47 41N 17 40 E
Marcali, Hungary 52 D2 46 35N 17 25 E
Marcapata, Peru 172 C3 13 31 S 70 52W
Marcaria, Italy 44 C7 45 7N 10 32 E
Mărcăuţi, Moldova 53 B12 48 20N 27 14 E
Marceline, U.S.A. 156 E4 39 43N 92 57W
March, U.K. 21 E8 52 33N 0 5 E
Marchal, Dem. Rep. of the Congo 115 D2 5 16 S 14 58 E
Marchand = Rommani, Morocco 110 B3 33 31N 6 40W
Marche, France 28 B5 46 5N 1 20 E
Marche □, Italy 45 E10 43 30N 13 15 E
Marche-en-Famenne, Belgium 24 D5 50 14N 5 19 E
Marchena, Spain 43 H5 37 18N 5 23W
Marches = Marche □, Italy 45 E10 43 30N 13 15 E
Marciana Marina, Italy 44 F7 42 48N 10 12 E
Marcianise, Italy 47 A7 41 2N 14 17 E
Marcigny, France 27 F11 46 17N 4 2 E
Marcillat-en-Combraille, France 27 F9 46 12N 2 38 E
Marck, France 27 B8 50 57N 1 57 E
Marckolsheim, France 27 D14 48 10N 7 30 E
Marco, U.S.A. 153 K8 25 58N 81 44W
Marcona, Peru 172 D3 15 10 S 75 0W
Marcos Juárez, Argentina 174 C3 32 42 S 62 5W
Mărculeşti, Moldova 53 C13 47 52N 28 14 E
Marcus Baker, Mt., U.S.A. 144 F11 61 26N 147 45W
Marcus I. = Minami-Tori-Shima, Pac. Oc. 134 E7 24 0N 153 45 E
Marcus Necker Ridge, Pac. Oc. 134 F9 20 0N 175 0 E
Marcy, Mt., U.S.A. 151 B11 44 7N 73 56W
Mardan, Pakistan 91 B4 34 20N 72 0 E
Mardie, Australia 124 D2 21 12 S 115 59 E
Mardin, Turkey 101 D9 37 20N 40 43 E
Mårdsjön, Sweden 16 A9 63 18N 15 35 E
Maré, I., N. Cal. 133 U22 21 30 S 168 0 E
Marécchia →, Italy 45 D9 44 4N 12 34 E
Marechal Deodoro, Brazil 170 C4 9 43 S 35 54W
Maree, L., U.K. 22 D3 57 40N 5 26W
Mareeba, Australia 126 B4 16 59 S 145 28 E
Marek, Indonesia 82 B2 4 41 S 120 24 E
Maremma, Italy 45 F8 42 30N 11 30 E
Maréna, Mali 112 C3 14 0N 7 20W
Marengo, U.S.A. 156 C4 41 48N 92 4W
Marennes, France 28 C2 45 49N 1 7W
Marenyi, Kenya 118 C4 4 22 S 39 8 E
Marerano, Madag. 117 C7 21 23 S 44 52 E
Maréttimo, Italy 46 E5 37 58N 12 4 E
Mareuil, France 28 C4 45 26N 0 29 E
Marfa, U.S.A. 155 K2 30 19N 104 1W
Marfa Pt., Malta 38 D1 35 59N 14 19 E
Marganets = Marhanets, Ukraine 59 J8 47 40N 34 40 E
Margaret →, Australia 124 C4 18 9 S 125 41 E
Margaret Bay, Canada 142 C3 51 20N 127 35W
Margaret L., Canada 142 B5 58 56N 115 25W
Margaret River, Australia 124 C4 18 38 S 126 52 E
Margarita, I. de, Venezuela 169 A5 11 0N 64 0W
Margarítion, Greece 48 B2 39 22N 20 26 E
Margaritovo, Russia 68 C7 43 25N 134 45 E
Margate, S. Africa 117 E5 30 50 S 30 20 E
Margate, U.K. 21 F9 51 23N 1 23 E
Margate, U.S.A. 153 J9 26 15N 80 12W
Margelan = Marghilon, Uzbekistan 63 C5 40 27N 71 42 E
Margeride, Mts. de la, France 28 D7 44 43N 3 38 E
Margherita, India 90 B5 27 16N 95 40 E
Margherita di Savóia, Italy 47 A9 41 22N 16 9 E
Marghilon, Uzbekistan 63 C5 40 27N 71 42 E
Marghita, Romania 52 C7 47 22N 22 22 E
Margonin, Poland 55 F4 52 58N 17 5 E
Margosatubig, Phil. 81 H4 7 34N 123 10 E
Marguerite, Canada 142 C4 52 30N 122 25W
Marhanets, Ukraine 59 J8 47 40N 34 40 E
Marhoum, Algeria 111 B4 34 27N 0 11W
Mari El □, Russia 60 B8 56 30N 48 0 E
Mari Republic □ = Mari El □, Russia 60 B8 56 30N 48 0 E
María, Sa. de, Spain 41 H2 37 39N 2 14W
María Elena, Chile 174 A2 22 18 S 69 40W
María Grande, Argentina 174 C4 31 45 S 59 55W
Maria I., N. Terr., Australia 126 A2 14 52 S 135 45 E
Maria I., Tas., Australia 126 G4 42 35 S 148 0 E
Maria van Diemen, C., N.Z. 130 A1 34 29 S 172 40 E
Mariager, Denmark 17 H3 56 40N 9 59 E
Mariager Fjord, Denmark 17 H4 56 42N 10 19 E
Mariakani, Kenya 118 C4 3 50 S 39 27 E
Marian, L., U.S.A. 153 H8 27 53N 81 6W
Marian L., Canada 142 A5 63 0N 116 15W
Mariana Trench, Pac. Oc. 134 F6 13 0N 145 0 E
Marianao, Cuba 164 B3 23 8N 82 24W
Mariani, India 90 B5 26 39N 94 19 E
Marianna, Ark., U.S.A. 155 H9 34 46N 90 46W
Marianna, Fla., U.S.A. 152 E4 30 46N 85 14W
Mariannelund, Sweden 17 G9 57 37N 15 35 E
Mariánské Lázně, Czech Rep. 34 B5 49 58N 12 41 E
Marias →, U.S.A. 158 C8 47 56N 110 30W
Mariato, Punta, Panama 164 E3 7 12N 80 52W
Mariazell, Austria 34 D8 47 47N 15 19 E
Ma'rib, Yemen 98 D4 15 25N 45 21 E
Maribo, Denmark 17 K5 54 48N 11 30 E
Maribor, Slovenia 45 B12 46 36N 15 40 E
Maricaban I., Phil. 80 E3 13 39N 120 53 E
Maricalom, Phil. 81 G4 9 42N 122 25 E
Marico →, Africa 116 C4 23 35 S 26 57 E
Maricopa, Ariz., U.S.A. 159 K7 33 4N 112 3W
Maricopa, Calif., U.S.A. 161 K7 35 4N 119 24W
Marīdī, Sudan 107 G2 4 55N 29 25 E
Maridi, Wadi →, Sudan 107 F2 6 15N 29 21 E
Marié →, Brazil 168 D4 0 27 S 66 26W
Marie Byrd Land, Antarctica 7 D14 79 30 S 125 0W
Marie-Galante, Guadeloupe 165 C7 15 56N 61 16W
Mariecourt = Kangiqsujuaq, Canada 139 B12 61 30N 72 0W
Mariefred, Sweden 16 E11 59 15N 17 12 E
Marieholm, Sweden 17 J7 55 53N 13 10 E
Mariembourg, Belgium 24 D4 50 6N 4 31 E
Marienbad = Mariánské Lázně, Czech Rep. 34 B5 49 58N 12 41 E
Marienberg, Germany 30 E9 50 39N 13 9 E
Mariental, Namibia 116 C2 24 36 S 18 0 E
Marienville, U.S.A. 150 E5 41 28N 79 8W
Mariestad, Sweden 17 F7 58 43N 13 50 E
Marietta, Ga., U.S.A. 152 B5 33 57N 84 33W
Marietta, Ohio, U.S.A. 148 F5 39 25N 81 27W
Marieville, Canada 151 A11 45 26N 73 10W
Marignane, France 29 E9 43 25N 5 13 E
Marihatag, Phil. 81 G6 8 48N 126 18 E
Mariinsk, Russia 64 D9 56 10N 87 20 E
Mariinskiy Posad, Russia 60 B8 56 10N 47 45 E
Marijampolė, Lithuania 15 J20 54 33N 23 19 E
Marijampolės □, Lithuania 54 D10 54 34N 23 21 E
Marília, Brazil 175 A6 22 13 S 50 0W
Marillana, Australia 124 D2 22 37 S 119 16 E
Marimba, Angola 115 D3 8 28 S 17 8 E
Marín, Spain 42 C2 42 23N 8 42W
Marina, U.S.A. 160 J5 36 41N 121 48W
Marina Plains, Australia 126 A3 14 37 S 143 57 E
Marinduque, Phil. 80 E3 13 25N 122 0 E
Marine City, U.S.A. 148 D4 42 43N 82 30W
Marineland, U.S.A. 152 F8 29 40N 81 13W
Marineo, Italy 46 E6 37 57N 13 25 E
Marinette, U.S.A. 148 C2 45 6N 87 38W
Maringá, Brazil 175 A5 23 26 S 52 2W
Marinha Grande, Portugal 42 F2 39 45N 8 56W
Marino, Italy 45 G9 41 46N 12 39 E
Marion, Ala., U.S.A. 149 J2 32 38N 87 19W
Marion, Ill., U.S.A. 155 G10 37 44N 88 56W
Marion, Ind., U.S.A. 157 D11 40 32N 85 40W
Marion, Iowa, U.S.A. 156 B5 42 2N 91 36W
Marion, Kans., U.S.A. 154 F6 38 21N 97 1W
Marion, Mich., U.S.A. 148 C3 44 6N 85 9W
Marion, N.C., U.S.A. 149 H5 35 41N 82 1W
Marion, Ohio, U.S.A. 157 D13 40 35N 83 8W
Marion, S.C., U.S.A. 149 H6 34 11N 79 24W
Marion, Va., U.S.A. 149 G5 36 50N 81 31W
Marion, L., U.S.A. 152 B9 33 28N 80 10W
Marion Bay, Australia 128 C2 35 12 S 136 59 E
Marion I., Ind. Oc. 121 J2 47 0 S 38 0 E
Maripa, Venezuela 169 B4 7 26N 65 9W
Maripasoula, Fr. Guiana 169 C7 3 40N 54 4W
Maripipi I., Phil. 81 F5 11 47N 124 19 E
Mariposa, U.S.A. 160 H7 37 29N 119 58W
Mariscal Estigarribia, Paraguay 174 A3 22 3 S 60 40W
Maritime Alps = Maritimes, Alpes, Europe 29 D11 44 10N 7 10 E
Maritimes, Alpes, Europe 29 D11 44 10N 7 10 E
Maritsa = Évros →, Bulgaria 100 B2 41 40N 26 34 E
Maritsá, Greece 38 C10 36 22N 28 8 E
Mariupol, Ukraine 59 J9 47 5N 37 31 E
Marīvān, Iran 101 E12 35 30N 46 25 E
Markah, W. →, Yemen 98 D4 14 59N 46 36 E
Markam, China 76 C2 29 42N 98 38 E
Markapur, India 95 G4 15 44N 79 19 E
Markaryd, Sweden 17 H7 56 28N 13 35 E
Markazī □, Iran 97 C6 35 0N 49 30 E
Markdale, Canada 150 B4 44 19N 80 39W
Marked Tree, U.S.A. 155 H9 35 32N 90 25W
Markelsdorfer Huk, Germany 30 A7 54 33N 11 4 E
Market Drayton, U.K. 20 E5 52 54N 2 29W
Market Harborough, U.K. 21 E7 52 29N 0 55W
Market Rasen, U.K. 20 D7 53 24N 0 20W
Markham, Canada 150 C5 43 52N 79 16W
Markham →, Papua N. G. 132 D4 6 41 S 147 2 E
Markham, Mt., Antarctica 7 E11 83 0 S 164 0 E
Markham L., Canada 143 A8 62 30N 102 35W
Marki, Poland 55 F8 52 20N 21 2 E
Markkleeberg, Germany 30 D8 51 16N 12 23 E
Markleeville, U.S.A. 160 G7 38 42N 119 47W
Markopoulon, Greece 48 D5 37 53N 23 57 E
Markovac, Serbia, Yug. 50 B5 44 14N 21 7 E
Markovo, Russia 65 C17 64 40N 170 24 E
Markoye, Burkina Faso 113 C5 14 39N 0 2 E
Marks, Russia 60 E8 51 45N 46 50 E
Marksville, U.S.A. 155 K8 31 8N 92 4W
Markt Schwaben, Germany 31 G7 48 11N 11 52 E
Marktoberdorf, Germany 31 H6 47 45N 10 37 E
Marktredwitz, Germany 31 E8 50 1N 12 6 E
Marl, Germany 30 D3 51 39N 7 4 E
Marla, Australia 127 D1 27 19 S 133 33 E
Marlboro, U.S.A. 151 D13 42 19N 71 33W
Marlborough, Australia 126 C4 22 46 S 149 52 E
Marlborough, U.K. 21 F6 51 25N 1 43W
Marlborough Downs, U.K. 21 F6 51 27N 1 53W
Marle, France 27 C10 49 43N 3 47 E
Marlin, U.S.A. 155 K6 31 18N 96 54W
Marlow, Germany 30 A8 54 9N 12 33 E
Marlow, Ga., U.S.A. 152 C8 32 16N 81 23W
Marlow, Okla., U.S.A. 155 H6 34 39N 97 58W
Marly-le-Grand, Switz. 32 C4 46 47N 7 10 E
Marmagao, India 95 G1 15 25N 73 56 E
Marmande, France 28 D4 44 30N 0 10 E
Marmara, Turkey 51 F11 40 35N 27 38 E
Marmara, Sea of = Marmara Denizi, Turkey 51 F12 40 45N 28 15 E
Marmara Denizi, Turkey 51 F12 40 45N 28 15 E
Marmara Gölü, Turkey 49 C10 38 37N 28 2 E
Marmaris, Turkey 49 E10 36 50N 28 14 E
Marmaris Limanı, Turkey 49 E10 36 50N 28 15 E
Marmarth, U.S.A. 154 B3 46 18N 103 54W
Marmelos →, Brazil 173 B5 6 6 S 61 46W
Marmion, Mt., Australia 125 E2 29 16 S 119 50 E
Marmion L., Canada 140 C1 48 55N 91 20W
Marmolada, Mte., Italy 45 B8 46 26N 11 51 E
Marmolejo, Spain 43 G6 38 3N 4 13W
Marmora, Canada 140 D4 44 28N 77 41W
Mármora, La, Italy 46 C2 39 59N 9 20 E
Mârmorilik, Greenland 10 C5 71 3N 51 0W
Marnay, France 27 E12 47 16N 5 48 E
Marne, Germany 30 B5 53 56N 9 2 E
Marne □, France 27 D11 48 50N 4 10 E
Marne →, France 27 D9 48 48N 2 24 E
Marneuli, Georgia 61 K7 41 30N 44 48 E
Maro, Chad 109 G3 8 30N 19 0 E
Maro Reef, U.S.A. 145 F9 25 25N 170 35W
Maroa, Venezuela 168 C4 2 43N 67 33W
Maroala, Madag. 117 B8 15 23 S 47 59 E
Maroantsetra, Madag. 117 B8 15 26 S 49 44 E
Maromandia, Madag. 117 A8 14 13 S 48 5 E
Marondera, Zimbabwe 119 F3 18 5 S 31 42 E
Maroni →, Fr. Guiana 169 B7 5 30N 54 0W
Marónia, Greece 51 F9 40 53N 25 30 E
Maronne →, France 28 C5 45 5N 1 56 E
Maroochydore, Australia 127 D5 26 29 S 153 5 E
Maroona, Australia 128 D5 37 27 S 142 54 E
Maros, Indonesia 82 C1 5 0 S 119 34 E
Maros →, Hungary 52 D5 46 15N 20 13 E
Marosakoa, Madag. 117 B8 15 26 S 46 38 E
Maróstica, Italy 45 C8 45 44N 11 40 E
Maroua, Cameroon 113 C7 10 40N 14 20 E
Marovoay, Madag. 117 B8 16 6 S 46 39 E
Marowijne □, Surinam 169 C7 4 0N 55 0W
Marowijne →, Surinam 169 B7 5 45N 53 58W
Marquard, S. Africa 116 D4 28 40 S 27 28 E
Marquesas Is. = Marquises, Is., Pac. Oc. 135 H14 9 30 S 140 0W
Marquesas Keys, U.S.A. 153 L7 24 35N 82 10W
Marquette, U.S.A. 148 B2 46 33N 87 24W
Marquise, France 27 B8 50 50N 1 40 E
Marquises, Is., Pac. Oc. 135 H14 9 30 S 140 0W
Marra, Gebel, Sudan 107 F2 7 20N 27 35 E
Marracuene, Mozam. 117 D5 25 45 S 32 35 E
Marradi, Italy 45 D8 44 4N 11 37 E
Marrakech, Morocco 110 B3 31 9N 8 0W
Marratxi, Spain 40 F7 39 39N 2 48 E
Marrawah, Australia 126 G3 40 55 S 144 42 E
Marrecas, Serra das, Brazil 170 C3 9 0 S 41 0W
Marree, Australia 127 D2 29 39 S 138 1 E
Marrilla, Australia 124 D1 22 31 S 114 25 E
Marrimane, Mozam. 117 C5 22 58 S 33 34 E
Marromeu, Mozam. 117 B6 18 15 S 36 25 E
Marroquí, Punta, Spain 43 K5 36 0N 5 37W
Marrowie Cr. →, Australia 129 B6 33 23 S 145 40 E
Marrubane, Mozam. 119 F4 18 0 S 37 0 E
Marrúbiu, Italy 46 C1 39 40N 8 35 E
Marrupa, Mozam. 119 E4 13 8 S 37 30 E
Marsa el Brega, Libya 108 B3 30 24N 19 37 E
Marsá Matrûh, Egypt 106 A2 31 19N 27 9 E
Marsá Susah, Libya 108 B4 32 52N 21 59 E
Marsabit, Kenya 118 B4 2 18N 38 0 E
Marsabit □, Kenya 118 B4 2 45N 37 45 E
Marsala, Italy 46 E5 37 48N 12 26 E
Marsalforn, Malta 38 C1 36 4N 14 15 E
Mârşani, Romania 53 F9 44 1N 24 1 E
Marsberg, Germany 30 D4 51 28N 8 52 E
Marsciano, Italy 45 F9 42 54N 12 20 E
Marsden, Australia 129 B7 33 47 S 147 32 E
Marseillan, France 28 E7 43 23N 3 31 E
Marseille, France 29 E9 43 18N 5 23 E
Marseilles = Marseille, France 29 E9 43 18N 5 23 E
Marseilles, U.S.A. 157 C8 41 20N 88 43W
Marsh I., U.S.A. 155 L9 29 34N 91 53W
Marsh L., U.S.A. 154 C7 45 5N 96 0W
Marshall, Liberia 112 D2 6 8N 10 22W
Marshall, Ark., U.S.A. 155 H8 35 55N 92 38W
Marshall, Ill., U.S.A. 157 E9 39 23N 87 42W
Marshall, Mich., U.S.A. 157 B12 42 16N 84 58W
Marshall, Minn., U.S.A. 154 C7 44 25N 95 45W
Marshall, Mo., U.S.A. 156 E3 39 7N 93 12W
Marshall, Tex., U.S.A. 155 J7 32 33N 94 23W
Marshall →, Australia 126 C2 22 59 S 136 59 E
Marshall Is. ■, Pac. Oc. 134 G9 9 0N 171 0 E
Marshalltown, U.S.A. 156 B4 42 3N 92 55W
Marshallville, U.S.A. 152 C6 32 27N 83 56W
Marshfield, Mo., U.S.A. 155 G8 37 15N 92 54W
Marshfield, Wis., U.S.A. 154 C9 44 40N 90 10W
Marshūn, Iran 97 B6 36 19N 49 23 E
Mársico Nuovo, Italy 47 B8 40 25N 15 44 E
Märsta, Sweden 16 E11 59 37N 17 52 E
Marstal, Denmark 17 K4 54 51N 10 30 E
Marstrand, Sweden 17 G5 57 53N 11 35 E
Mart, U.S.A. 155 K6 31 33N 96 50W
Marta →, Italy 45 F8 42 14N 11 42 E
Martaban, Burma 90 G6 16 30N 97 35 E
Martaban, G. of, Burma 90 G6 16 5N 96 30 E
Martano, Italy 47 B11 40 12N 18 18 E
Martapura, Kalimantan, Indonesia 85 C4 3 22 S 114 47 E
Martapura, Sumatera, Indonesia 84 C2 4 19 S 104 22 E
Marte, Nigeria 113 C7 12 23N 13 46 E
Martel, France 28 D5 44 57N 1 37 E
Martelange, Belgium 24 E5 49 49N 5 43 E
Martellago, Italy 45 C9 45 33N 12 9 E
Martensdale, U.S.A. 156 C3 41 23N 93 45W
Martés, Sierra, Spain 41 F4 39 20N 1 0W
Martfű, Hungary 52 C5 47 1N 20 17 E
Martha's Vineyard, U.S.A. 151 E14 41 25N 70 38W
Martigné-Ferchaud, France 26 E5 47 50N 1 20W
Martigny, Switz. 32 D4 46 6N 7 3 E
Martigues, France 29 E9 43 24N 5 4 E
Martil, Morocco 110 A3 35 36N 5 15W
Martin, Slovak Rep. 35 B11 49 6N 18 58 E
Martin, S. Dak., U.S.A. 154 D4 43 11N 101 44W
Martin, Tenn., U.S.A. 155 G10 36 21N 88 51W
Martín →, Spain 40 D4 41 18N 0 19W
Martin L., U.S.A. 152 C4 32 41N 85 55W
Martin Pt., U.S.A. 144 A12 70 8N 143 16W
Martina, Switz. 33 C10 46 53N 10 28 E
Martina Franca, Italy 47 B10 40 42N 17 20 E
Martinborough, N.Z. 130 H4 41 14 S 175 29 E
Martinez, U.S.A. 160 G4 38 1N 122 8W
Martinho Campos, Brazil 171 E2 19 20 S 45 13W
Martinique ■, W. Indies 165 D7 14 40N 61 0W
Martinique Passage, W. Indies 165 C7 15 15N 61 0W
Martínon, Greece 48 C5 38 35N 23 12 E
Martinópolis, Brazil 175 A5 22 11 S 51 12W
Martins Ferry, U.S.A. 150 F4 40 6N 80 44W
Martinsberg, Austria 34 C8 48 22N 15 9 E
Martinsburg, Pa., U.S.A. 150 F6 40 19N 78 20W
Martinsburg, W. Va., U.S.A. 148 F7 39 27N 77 58W
Martinsicuro, Italy 45 F10 42 54N 13 54 E
Martinsville, Ill., U.S.A. 157 E9 39 20N 87 53W
Martinsville, Ind., U.S.A. 157 E10 39 26N 86 25W
Martinsville, Va., U.S.A. 149 G6 36 41N 79 52W
Marton, N.Z. 130 G4 40 4 S 175 23 E
Martorell, Spain 40 D6 41 28N 1 56 E
Martos, Spain 43 H7 37 44N 3 58W
Martūbah, Libya 108 B4 32 35N 22 46 E
Martuk, Kazakstan 62 F6 50 46N 56 31 E
Martuni, Armenia 61 K7 40 8N 45 20 E
Maru, Nigeria 113 C6 12 22N 6 22 E
Marudi, Malaysia 85 B4 4 11N 114 19 E
Ma'ruf, Afghan. 91 C2 31 30N 67 6 E
Marugame, Japan 70 C5 34 15N 133 40 E
Marui, Papua N. G. 132 C2 4 4 S 143 2 E
Maruia →, N.Z. 131 B7 41 47 S 172 13 E
Maruim, Brazil 170 D4 10 45 S 37 5W
Marulan, Australia 129 C9 34 43 S 150 3 E
Marum, Mt., Vanuatu 133 F6 16 15 S 168 7 E
Marunga, Angola 115 F4 17 28 S 20 2 E
Marungu, Mts., Dem. Rep. of the Congo 118 D3 7 30 S 30 0 E
Maruoka, Japan 71 A8 36 9N 136 16 E
Marvast, Iran 97 D7 30 30N 54 15 E
Marvejols, France 28 D7 44 33N 3 19 E
Marwar, India 92 G5 25 43N 73 45 E
Mary, Turkmenistan 64 F7 37 40N 61 50 E
Mary Frances L., Canada 143 A7 63 19N 106 13W
Mary Kathleen, Australia 126 C2 20 44 S 139 48 E
Maryborough = Port Laoise, Ireland 23 C4 53 2N 7 18W
Maryborough, Queens., Australia 127 D5 25 31 S 152 37 E
Maryborough, Vic., Australia 128 D5 37 0 S 143 44 E
Maryfield, Canada 143 D8 49 50N 101 35W
Maryland □, U.S.A. 148 F7 39 0N 76 30W
Maryland Junction, Zimbabwe 119 F3 17 45 S 30 31 E
Maryport, U.K. 20 C4 54 44N 3 28W
Mary's Harbour, Canada 141 B8 52 18N 55 51W
Marystown, Canada 141 C8 47 10N 55 10W
Marysvale, U.S.A. 159 G7 38 27N 112 14W
Marysville, Canada 142 D5 49 35N 116 0W
Marysville, Calif., U.S.A. 160 F5 39 9N 121 35W
Marysville, Kans., U.S.A. 154 F6 39 51N 96 39W
Marysville, Mich., U.S.A. 150 D2 42 54N 82 29W
Marysville, Ohio, U.S.A. 157 D13 40 14N 83 22W
Marysville, Wash., U.S.A. 160 B4 48 3N 122 11W
Maryvale, Australia 127 D5 28 4 S 152 12 E
Maryville, Mo., U.S.A. 156 D2 40 21N 94 52W
Maryville, Tenn., U.S.A. 149 H4 35 46N 83 58W
Marzo, Punta, Colombia 168 B2 6 50N 77 42W
Marzūq, Libya 108 C2 25 53N 13 57 E
Masahunga, Tanzania 118 C3 2 6 S 33 18 E
Masai Steppe, Tanzania 118 C4 4 30 S 36 30 E
Masaka, Uganda 118 C3 0 21 S 31 45 E
Masalembo, Kepulauan, Indonesia 85 D4 5 35 S 114 30 E
Masalima, Kepulauan, Indonesia 85 D5 5 4 S 117 5 E
Masallı, Azerbaijan 101 C13 39 3N 48 40 E
Masamba, Indonesia 82 B2 2 30 S 120 15 E
Masan, S. Korea 75 G15 35 11N 128 32 E
Masaryktown, U.S.A. 153 G7 28 27N 82 27W
Masasi, Tanzania 119 E4 10 45 S 38 52 E
Masasi □, Tanzania 119 E4 10 45 S 38 50 E
Masaya, Nic. 164 D2 12 0N 86 7W
Masba, Nigeria 113 C7 10 35N 13 1 E
Masbate, Phil. 80 E4 12 21N 123 36 E
Masbate Pass, Phil. 80 E4 12 30N 123 35 E
Máscali, Italy 47 E8 37 45N 15 12 E
Mascara, Algeria 111 A5 35 26N 0 6 E
Mascarene Is., Ind. Oc. 121 G4 22 0 S 55 0 E
Mascota, Mexico 162 C4 20 30N 104 50W
Mascoutah, U.S.A. 156 F7 38 29N 89 48W
Masela, Indonesia 83 C3 8 9 S 129 51 E
Maseru, Lesotho 116 D4 29 18 S 27 30 E
Masfjorden, Norway 18 D2 60 48N 5 12 E
Mashaba, Zimbabwe 119 G3 20 2 S 30 29 E
Mashābih, Si. Arabia 96 E3 25 35N 36 30 E
Mashan, China 76 F7 23 40N 108 11 E
Masherbrum, Pakistan 93 B7 35 38N 76 18 E
Mashhad, Iran 97 B8 36 20N 59 35 E
Mashi, Nigeria 113 C6 13 0N 7 54 E
Mashiki, Japan 70 E2 32 51N 130 53 E
Mashīz, Iran 97 D8 29 56N 56 37 E
Mashkel, Hamun-i-, Pakistan 91 C1 28 30N 63 0 E
Mashki Chāh, Pakistan 91 C1 29 5N 62 30 E
Mashonaland Central □, Zimbabwe 117 B5 17 30 S 31 0 E
Mashonaland East □, Zimbabwe 117 B5 18 0 S 32 0 E
Mashonaland West □, Zimbabwe 117 B4 17 30 S 29 30 E
Mashtaga = Maştağa, Azerbaijan 61 K10 40 35N 49 57 E
Masi Manimba, Dem. Rep. of the Congo 115 C3 4 40 S 17 54 E
Masindi, Uganda 118 B3 1 40N 31 43 E
Masindi Port, Uganda 118 B3 1 43N 32 2 E
Masinloc, Phil. 80 D2 15 32N 119 57 E
Maşīrah, Khalīj, Oman 99 B7 20 10N 58 10 E
Maşīrah, Tur'at, Oman 99 B7 20 30N 58 40 E
Masisea, Peru 172 B3 8 35 S 74 22W
Masisi, Dem. Rep. of the Congo 118 C2 1 23 S 28 49 E
Masjed Soleyman, Iran 97 D6 31 55N 49 18 E
Mask, L., Ireland 23 C2 53 36N 9 22W
Maskelyne Is., Vanuatu 133 F5 16 32 S 167 49 E
Maski, India 95 G3 15 56N 76 46 E
Maslen Nos, Bulgaria 51 D11 42 18N 27 48 E
Maslinica, Croatia 45 E13 43 24N 16 13 E
Maşna'ah, Yemen 99 D5 14 27N 48 17 E
Masnou = El Masnou, Spain 40 D7 41 28N 2 20 E
Masoala, Tanjon' i, Madag. 117 B9 15 59 S 50 13 E
Masoarivo, Madag. 117 B7 19 3 S 44 19 E
Masomeloka, Madag. 117 C8 20 17 S 48 37 E
Mason, Mich., U.S.A. 157 B12 42 35N 84 27W
Mason, Nev., U.S.A. 160 G7 38 56N 119 8W
Mason, Ohio, U.S.A. 157 E12 39 22N 84 19W
Mason, Tex., U.S.A. 155 K5 30 45N 99 14W
Mason B., N.Z. 131 M1 46 55 S 167 45 E
Mason City, Ill., U.S.A. 156 D7 40 12N 89 42W
Mason City, Iowa, U.S.A. 156 A3 43 9N 93 12W
Maspalomas, Canary Is. 39 G4 27 46N 15 35W
Maspalomas, Pta., Canary Is. 39 G4 27 43N 15 36W
Masqat, Oman 99 B7 23 37N 58 36 E
Massa, Congo 114 C3 3 45 S 15 29 E
Massa, Italy 44 D7 44 1N 10 9 E
Massa, O. →, Morocco 110 B3 30 2N 9 40W
Massa Maríttima, Italy 44 E7 43 3N 10 52 E
Massachusetts □, U.S.A. 151 D13 42 30N 72 0W
Massachusetts B., U.S.A. 151 D14 42 20N 70 50W
Massafra, Italy 47 B10 40 35N 17 7 E
Massaguet, Chad 109 F3 12 28N 15 26 E
Massakory, Chad 109 F3 13 0N 15 49 E
Massanella, Spain 39 B9 39 48N 2 51 E
Massangena, Mozam. 117 C5 21 34 S 33 0 E
Massapê, Brazil 170 B3 3 31 S 40 19W
Massat, France 28 F5 42 53N 1 21 E
Massawa = Mitsiwa, Eritrea 107 D4 15 35N 39 25 E
Massena, U.S.A. 151 B10 44 56N 74 54W
Massénya, Chad 109 F3 11 21N 16 9 E
Masset, Canada 142 C2 54 2N 132 10W
Masseube, France 28 E4 43 25N 0 34 E
Massiac, France 28 C7 45 15N 3 11 E
Massif Central, France 28 D7 44 55N 3 0 E
Massillon, U.S.A. 150 F3 40 48N 81 32W
Massinga, Mozam. 117 C6 23 15 S 35 22 E
Mässlingen, Sweden 16 B6 62 40N 12 50 E
Masson, Canada 151 A9 45 32N 75 25W
Masson I., Antarctica 7 C7 66 10 S 93 20 E
Mastābah, Si. Arabia 98 B2 20 49N 39 26 E
Maştağa, Azerbaijan 61 K10 40 35N 49 57 E

248 Mastanli

Mastanli = Momchilgrad, *Bulgaria* 51 E9 41 33N 25 23 E
Masterton, *N.Z.* 130 G4 40 56 S 175 39 E
Mástikho, Ákra, *Greece* 49 C8 38 10N 26 2 E
Mastuj, *Pakistan* 93 A5 36 20N 72 36 E
Mastung, *Pakistan* 91 C2 29 50N 66 56 E
Mastūrah, *Si. Arabia* 98 B2 23 7N 38 52 E
Masty, *Belarus* 58 F3 53 27N 24 38 E
Masuda, *Japan* 70 C3 34 40N 131 51 E
Masuika, *Dem. Rep. of the Congo* 115 D4 7 37 S 22 32 E
Masvingo, *Zimbabwe* 119 G3 20 8 S 30 49 E
Masvingo □, *Zimbabwe* 119 G3 21 0 S 31 30 E
Maswa □, *Tanzania* 118 C3 3 30 S 34 0 E
Maşyāf, *Syria* 100 E7 35 4N 36 20 E
Maszewo, *Poland* 54 E2 53 29N 15 3 E
Mata de São João, *Brazil* 171 D4 12 31 S 38 17W
Mata Utu, *Wall. & F. Is.* 123 C15 13 17 S 176 8W
Matabeleland North □, *Zimbabwe* 119 F2 19 0 S 28 0 E
Matabeleland South □, *Zimbabwe* 119 G2 21 0 S 29 0 E
Mataboor, *Indonesia* 83 B5 1 41 S 138 3 E
Matachel →, *Spain* 43 G4 38 50N 6 17W
Matachewan, *Canada* 140 C3 47 56N 80 39W
Matacuni →, *Venezuela* 169 C4 3 2N 65 16W
Matadi, *Dem. Rep. of the Congo* 115 D2 5 52 S 13 31 E
Matagalpa, *Nic.* 164 D2 13 0N 85 58W
Matagami, *Canada* 140 C4 49 45N 77 34W
Matagami, L., *Canada* 140 C4 49 50N 77 40W
Matagorda, *U.S.A.* 155 L7 28 42N 95 58W
Matagorda B., *U.S.A.* 155 L6 28 40N 96 0W
Matagorda I., *U.S.A.* 155 L6 28 15N 96 30W
Mataguinao, *Phil.* 80 E5 12 5N 124 55 E
Matak, *Indonesia* 87 L6 3 18N 106 16 E
Matakana, *Australia* 129 B6 32 59 S 145 54 E
Matakana, *N.Z.* 130 C3 36 21 S 174 43 E
Matakana I., *N.Z.* 130 C3 36 21 S 174 43 E
Matala, *Angola* 115 E3 14 46 S 15 4 E
Mátala, *Greece* 38 E6 34 59N 24 45 E
Matalaque, *Peru* 172 D3 16 26 S 70 49W
Matale, *Sri Lanka* 95 L5 7 30N 80 37 E
Matam, *Phil.* 81 G4 8 25N 123 19 E
Matam, *Senegal* 112 B2 15 34N 13 17W
Matamata, *N.Z.* 130 D4 37 48 S 175 47 E
Matameye, *Niger* 109 F1 13 26N 8 28 E
Matamoros, *Campeche, Mexico* 163 D6 18 50N 90 50W
Matamoros, *Coahuila, Mexico* 162 B4 25 33N 103 15W
Matamoros, *Puebla, Mexico* 163 D5 18 2N 98 17W
Matamoros, *Tamaulipas, Mexico* 163 B5 25 50N 97 30W
Ma'ṭan as Sarra, *Libya* 109 D4 21 45N 22 0 E
Matana, Danau, *Indonesia* 82 B2 2 28 S 121 20 E
Matandu →, *Tanzania* 119 D3 8 45 S 34 19 E
Matane, *Canada* 141 C6 48 50N 67 33W
Matang, *China* 76 F5 23 30N 104 7 E
Matankari, *Niger* 113 C5 13 46N 4 1 E
Matanzas, *Cuba* 164 B3 23 0N 81 40W
Matapan, C. = Taínaron, Ákra, *Greece* 48 E4 36 22N 22 27 E
Matapédia, *Canada* 141 C6 48 0N 66 59W
Matara, *Sri Lanka* 95 M5 5 58N 80 30 E
Mataram, *Indonesia* 85 D5 8 41 S 116 10 E
Matarani, *Peru* 172 D3 17 0 S 72 10W
Mataranka, *Australia* 124 B5 14 55 S 133 4 E
Matarma, Râs, *Egypt* 103 E1 30 27N 32 44 E
Mataró, *Spain* 40 D7 41 32N 2 29 E
Matarraña →, *Spain* 40 D5 41 14N 0 22 E
Mataruška Banja, *Serbia, Yug.* 50 C4 43 40N 20 40 E
Mataso, *Vanuatu* 133 G6 17 14 S 168 26 E
Matata, *N.Z.* 130 D5 37 54 S 176 48 E
Matatiele, *S. Africa* 117 E4 30 20 S 28 49 E
Mataura, *N.Z.* 131 G3 46 11 S 168 51 E
Mataura →, *N.Z.* 131 G3 46 34 S 168 44 E
Mategua, *Bolivia* 173 C5 13 1 S 62 48W
Matehuala, *Mexico* 162 C4 23 40N 100 40W
Mateira, *Brazil* 171 E1 18 54 S 50 30W
Mateke Hills, *Zimbabwe* 119 G3 21 48 S 31 0 E
Matera, *Italy* 47 B9 40 40N 16 36 E
Matese, Monti del, *Italy* 47 A7 41 27N 14 22 E
Mátészalka, *Hungary* 52 C7 47 58N 22 20 E
Matetsi, *Zimbabwe* 119 F2 18 12 S 26 0 E
Mateur, *Tunisia* 108 A1 37 0N 9 40 E
Matfors, *Sweden* 16 B11 62 21N 17 2 E
Matha, *France* 28 C3 45 52N 0 20W
Matheson Island, *Canada* 143 C9 51 45N 96 56W
Mathis, *U.S.A.* 155 L6 28 6N 97 50W
Mathoura, *Australia* 129 C6 35 50 S 144 55 E
Mathráki, *Greece* 38 A3 39 48N 19 31 E
Mathura, *India* 92 F7 27 30N 77 40 E
Mati, *Phil.* 81 H6 6 55N 126 15 E
Mati →, *Albania* 50 E3 41 40N 19 35 E
Matías Romero, *Mexico* 163 D5 16 53N 95 2W
Matibane, *Mozam.* 119 E5 14 49 S 40 45 E
Matican, *Phil.* 81 H3 6 39N 121 53 E
Matima, *Botswana* 116 C3 20 15 S 24 26 E
Matiri Ra., *N.Z.* 131 B7 41 38 S 172 20 E
Matlock, *U.K.* 20 D6 53 9N 1 33W
Matmata, *Tunisia* 108 B1 33 37N 9 59 E
Matna, *Sudan* 107 E4 13 49N 35 10 E
Matnog, *Phil.* 80 E5 12 35N 124 5 E
Mato →, *Venezuela* 169 B4 7 9N 65 7W
Mato, Serrania de, *Venezuela* 168 B4 6 25N 65 25W
Mato Grosso □, *Brazil* 173 C7 14 0 S 55 0W
Mato Grosso, Planalto do, *Brazil* 173 D7 15 0 S 55 0W
Mato Grosso, Plateau of, *Brazil* 166 E5 15 0 S 54 0W
Mato Grosso do Sul □, *Brazil* 173 D7 18 0 S 55 0W
Matochkin Shar, *Russia* 64 B6 73 10N 56 40 E
Matong, *Papua N. G.* 132 C6 5 36 S 151 50 E
Matopo Hills, *Zimbabwe* 119 G2 20 36 S 28 20 E
Matopos, *Zimbabwe* 119 G2 20 20 S 28 29 E
Matosinhos, *Portugal* 42 D2 41 11N 8 42W
Matour, *France* 27 F11 46 19N 4 29 E
Matrah, *Oman* 99 B7 23 37N 58 30 E
Matsena, *Nigeria* 113 C7 13 5N 10 5 E
Matsesta, *Russia* 61 J4 43 34N 39 51 E
Matsu Tao, *Taiwan* 77 E13 26 9N 119 56 E
Matsubara, *Japan* 71 C7 34 33N 135 34 E
Matsudo, *Japan* 71 B11 35 47N 139 54 E
Matsue, *Japan* 70 B5 35 25N 133 10 E
Matsumae, *Japan* 68 D10 41 26N 140 7 E
Matsumoto, *Japan* 71 A10 36 15N 138 0 E
Matsusaka, *Japan* 71 C8 34 34N 136 32 E
Matsutō, *Japan* 71 A8 36 31N 136 34 E
Matsuura, *Japan* 70 D1 33 20N 129 49 E
Matsuyama, *Japan* 70 D4 33 45N 132 45 E
Matsuzaki, *Japan* 71 C10 34 43N 138 50 E
Mattagami →, *Canada* 140 B3 50 43N 81 29W
Mattancheri, *India* 95 K3 9 50N 76 15 E
Mattawa, *Canada* 140 C4 46 20N 78 45W
Mattawamkeag, *U.S.A.* 141 C6 45 32N 68 21W
Matterhorn, *Switz.* 32 E5 45 58N 7 39 E
Mattersburg, *Austria* 35 D9 47 44N 16 24 E
Matteson, *U.S.A.* 157 C9 41 30N 87 42W
Matthew Town, *Bahamas* 165 B5 20 57N 73 40W
Matthews, *U.S.A.* 157 D11 40 23N 85 30W
Matthew's Ridge, *Guyana* 169 B5 7 37N 60 10W
Mattice, *Canada* 140 C3 49 40N 83 20W
Mattituck, *U.S.A.* 151 F12 40 59N 72 32W
Matuba, *Mozam.* 117 C5 24 28 S 32 49 E
Matucana, *Peru* 172 C2 11 55 S 76 25W
Matuku, *Fiji* 133 B2 19 10 S 179 44 E
Matun, *Afghan.* 92 C3 33 22N 69 58 E
Maturín, *Venezuela* 169 B5 9 45N 63 11W
Matutum, Mt., *Phil.* 81 H5 6 22N 125 5 E
Matveyev Kurgan, *Russia* 59 J10 47 35N 38 57 E
Matxitxako, C., *Spain* 40 B2 43 28N 2 47W
Mau, *India* 93 G10 25 56N 83 33 E
Mau Escarpment, *Kenya* 118 C4 0 40 S 36 0 E
Mau Ranipur, *India* 93 G8 25 16N 79 8 E
Mauban, *Phil.* 80 D3 14 12N 121 44 E
Maubeuge, *France* 27 B10 50 17N 3 57 E
Maubourguet, *France* 28 E4 43 29N 0 1 E
Maud, Pt., *Australia* 124 D1 23 6 S 113 45 E
Maude, *Australia* 128 C6 34 29 S 144 18 E
Maués, *Brazil* 169 D6 3 20 S 57 45W
Maughold Hd., *U.K.* 20 C3 54 18N 4 18W
Mauguio, *France* 28 E7 43 37N 4 1 E
Maui, *U.S.A.* 146 H16 20 48N 156 20W
Maulamyaing = Moulmein, *Burma* 90 G6 16 30N 97 40 E
Maule □, *Chile* 174 D1 36 5 S 72 30W
Mauléon-Licharre, *France* 28 E3 43 14N 0 54W
Maullín, *Chile* 176 B2 41 38 S 73 37W
Maulvibazar, *Bangla.* 90 C3 24 29N 91 42 E
Maumee, *U.S.A.* 157 C13 41 34N 83 39W
Maumee →, *U.S.A.* 157 C13 41 42N 83 28W
Maumere, *Indonesia* 82 C2 8 38 S 122 13 E
Maumusson, Pertuis de, *France* 28 C2 45 48N 1 14W
Maun, *Botswana* 116 C3 20 0 S 23 26 E
Mauna Kea, *U.S.A.* 146 J17 19 50N 155 28W
Mauna Loa, *U.S.A.* 146 J17 19 30N 155 35W
Maunaloa, *U.S.A.* 145 B4 21 8N 157 13W
Maunalua B., *U.S.A.* 145 K14 21 15N 157 45W
Maunawili, *U.S.A.* 145 K14 21 23N 157 46W
Maungaturoto, *N.Z.* 130 C3 36 6 S 174 23 E
Maungdaw, *Burma* 90 E4 20 50N 92 21 E
Maungmagan Is., *Burma* 86 F1 14 0N 97 30 E
Maupin, *U.S.A.* 158 D3 45 11N 121 5W
Maure-de-Bretagne, *France* 26 E5 47 59N 1 58W
Maurepas, L., *U.S.A.* 155 K9 30 15N 90 30W
Maures, *France* 29 E10 43 15N 6 15 E
Mauriac, *France* 28 C6 45 13N 2 19 E
Maurice, L., *Australia* 125 E5 29 30 S 131 0 E
Mauriceville, *N.Z.* 130 G4 40 45 S 175 42 E
Maurienne, *France* 29 C10 45 13N 6 30 E
Mauritania ■, *Africa* 110 D3 20 50N 10 0W
Mauritius ■, *Ind. Oc.* 121 G4 20 0 S 57 0 E
Mauron, *France* 26 D4 48 9N 2 18W
Maurs, *France* 28 D6 44 43N 2 12 E
Mauston, *U.S.A.* 154 D9 43 48N 90 5W
Mauterndorf, *Austria* 34 D6 47 9N 13 40 E
Mauthen, *Austria* 34 E6 46 40N 13 0 E
Mauvezin, *France* 28 E4 43 44N 0 53 E
Mauzé-sur-le-Mignon, *France* 28 B3 46 12N 0 41W
Mavaca →, *Venezuela* 169 C4 2 31N 65 11W
Mavelikara, *India* 95 K3 9 14N 76 32 E
Mavinga, *Angola* 115 F4 15 50 S 20 21 E
Mavli, *India* 92 G5 24 45N 73 55 E
Mavrova, *Albania* 50 F3 40 26N 19 32 E
Mavuradonha Mts., *Zimbabwe* 119 F3 16 30 S 31 30 E
Mawa, *Dem. Rep. of the Congo* 118 B2 2 45N 26 40 E
Mawana, *India* 92 E7 29 6N 77 58 E
Mawand, *Pakistan* 92 E3 29 33N 68 38 E
Mawk Mai, *Burma* 90 E6 20 14N 97 37 E
Mawlaik, *Burma* 90 D5 23 40N 94 26 E
Mawlawkho, *Burma* 90 G6 17 50N 97 38 E
Mawquq, *Si. Arabia* 96 E4 27 25N 41 8 E
Mawshij, *Yemen* 98 D3 13 43N 43 17 E
Mawson Coast, *Antarctica* 7 C6 68 30 S 63 0 E
Max, *U.S.A.* 154 B4 47 49N 101 18W
Maxcanú, *Mexico* 163 C6 20 40N 92 0W
Maxesibeni, *S. Africa* 117 E4 30 49 S 29 23 E
Maxeys, *U.S.A.* 152 B6 33 45N 83 11W
Maxhamish L., *Canada* 142 B4 59 50N 123 17W
Maxixe, *Mozam.* 117 C6 23 54 S 35 17 E
Maxville, *Canada* 151 A10 45 17N 74 51W
Maxwell, *N.Z.* 130 F3 39 51 S 174 49 E
Maxwell, *U.S.A.* 160 F4 39 17N 122 11W
Maxwelton, *Australia* 126 C3 20 43 S 142 41 E
May Downs, *Australia* 126 C4 22 38 S 148 55 E
May Pen, *Jamaica* 164 C4 17 58N 77 15W
May River, *Papua N. G.* 132 C1 4 19 S 141 58 E
Maya, *Indonesia* 85 C3 1 10 S 109 35 E
Maya →, *Russia* 65 D14 60 28N 134 28 E
Maya Mts., *Belize* 163 D7 16 30N 89 0W
Mayaguana, *Bahamas* 165 B5 22 30N 72 44W
Mayagüez, *Puerto Rico* 165 C6 18 12N 67 9W
Mayahi, *Niger* 113 C6 13 58N 7 40 E
Mayals = Maials, *Spain* 40 D5 41 22N 0 30 E
Mayama, *Congo* 114 C2 3 51 S 14 54 E
Mayāmey, *Iran* 97 B7 36 24N 55 42 E
Mayang, *China* 76 D7 27 53N 109 49 E
Mayarí, *Cuba* 165 B4 20 40N 75 41W
Mayavaram = Mayuram, *India* 95 J4 11 3N 79 42 E
Maybell, *U.S.A.* 158 F9 40 31N 108 5W
Maybole, *U.K.* 22 F4 55 21N 4 42W
Maychew, *Ethiopia* 107 E4 12 50N 39 31 E
Maydān, *Iraq* 101 E11 34 55N 45 37 E
Maydena, *Australia* 126 G4 42 45 S 146 30 E
Maydī, *Yemen* 98 C3 16 19N 42 48 E
Mayen, *Germany* 31 E3 50 19N 7 13 E
Mayenne, *France* 26 D6 48 20N 0 38W
Mayenne □, *France* 26 D6 48 10N 0 40W
Mayenne →, *France* 26 E6 47 30N 0 32W
Mayer, *U.S.A.* 159 J7 34 24N 112 14W
Mayerthorpe, *Canada* 142 C5 53 57N 115 8W
Mayesville, *U.S.A.* 152 A9 34 0N 80 12W
Mayfield, *Ga., U.S.A.* 152 B7 33 21N 82 48W
Mayfield, *Ky., U.S.A.* 149 G1 36 44N 88 38W
Mayhill, *U.S.A.* 159 K11 32 53N 105 29W
Maykop, *Russia* 61 H5 44 35N 40 10 E
Mayli-Say, *Kyrgyzstan* 63 C6 41 17N 72 24 E
Maymyo, *Burma* 86 A1 22 2N 96 28 E
Maynard, *U.S.A.* 160 C4 47 59N 122 55W
Maynard Hills, *Australia* 125 E2 28 28 S 119 49 E
Mayne →, *Australia* 126 C3 23 40 S 141 55 E
Maynooth, *Ireland* 23 C5 53 23N 6 34W
Mayo, *Canada* 138 B6 63 38N 135 57W
Mayo, *U.S.A.* 152 E6 30 3N 83 10W
Mayo □, *Ireland* 23 C2 53 53N 9 3W
Mayo →, *Argentina* 176 C3 45 45 S 69 45W
Mayo →, *Peru* 172 B2 6 38 S 76 15W
Mayo Bay, *Phil.* 81 H6 6 56N 126 22 E
Mayoko, *Dem. Rep. of the Congo* 114 C2 2 18 S 12 49 E
Mayon Volcano, *Phil.* 80 E4 13 15N 123 41 E
Mayor I., *N.Z.* 130 D5 37 16 S 176 17 E
Mayorga, *Spain* 42 C5 42 10N 5 16W
Mayotte, I., *Mayotte* 121 F3 12 50 S 45 10 E
Mayoyao, *Phil.* 80 C3 16 59N 121 14 E
Mayraira Pt., *Phil.* 80 B3 18 39N 120 51 E
Mayskiy, *Russia* 61 J7 43 47N 44 2 E
Mayson L., *Canada* 143 B7 57 55N 107 10W
Maysville, *Ky., U.S.A.* 157 F13 38 39N 83 46W
Maysville, *Mo., U.S.A.* 156 E2 39 53N 94 22W
Mayu, *Indonesia* 82 A3 1 30N 126 30 E
Mayumba, *Gabon* 114 C2 3 25 S 10 39 E
Mayuram, *India* 95 J4 11 3N 79 42 E
Mayville, *N. Dak., U.S.A.* 154 B6 47 30N 97 20W
Mayville, *N.Y., U.S.A.* 150 D5 42 15N 79 30W
Mayya, *Russia* 65 C14 61 44N 130 18 E
Mazabuka, *Zambia* 119 F2 15 52 S 27 44 E
Mazagán = El Jadida, *Morocco* 110 B3 33 11N 8 17W
Mazagão, *Brazil* 169 D7 0 7 S 51 16W
Mazamet, *France* 28 E6 43 30N 2 20 E
Mazán, *Peru* 168 D3 3 30 S 73 0W
Māzandarān □, *Iran* 97 B7 36 30N 52 0 E
Mazapil, *Mexico* 162 C4 24 38N 101 34W
Mazar, O. →, *Algeria* 111 B5 31 50N 1 36 E
Mazar-e Sharīf, *Afghan.* 91 A2 36 41N 67 0 E
Mazara del Vallo, *Italy* 46 E5 37 39N 12 35 E
Mazarredo, *Argentina* 176 C3 47 10 S 66 50W
Mazarrón, *Spain* 41 H3 37 38N 1 19W
Mazarrón, G. de, *Spain* 41 H3 37 27N 1 19W
Mazaruni →, *Guyana* 169 B6 6 25N 58 35W
Mazatán, *Mexico* 162 B2 29 0N 110 8W
Mazatenango, *Guatemala* 164 D1 14 35N 91 30W
Mazatlán, *Mexico* 162 C3 23 13N 106 25W
Mažeikiai, *Lithuania* 15 H20 56 20N 22 20 E
Māzhān, *Iran* 97 C8 32 30N 59 0 E
Mazīnān, *Iran* 97 B8 36 19N 56 56 E
Mazoe, *Mozam.* 119 F3 16 42 S 33 7 E
Mazoe →, *Mozam.* 119 F3 16 20 S 33 30 E
Mazomanie, *U.S.A.* 156 A7 43 11N 89 48W
Mazon, *U.S.A.* 157 C8 41 14N 88 25W
Mazowe, *Zimbabwe* 119 F3 17 28 S 30 58 E
Mazrûb, *Sudan* 107 E2 14 0N 29 20 E
Mazu Dao, *China* 77 D12 26 10N 119 55 E
Mazurian Lakes = Mazurski, Pojezierze, *Poland* 54 E7 53 50N 21 0 E
Mazurski, Pojezierze, *Poland* 54 E7 53 50N 21 0 E
Mazyr, *Belarus* 59 F5 51 59N 29 15 E
Mba, *Fiji* 133 A1 17 33 S 177 41 E
Mbaba, *Senegal* 112 C1 14 59N 16 44W
Mbabane, *Swaziland* 117 D5 26 18 S 31 6 E
Mbagne, *Mauritania* 112 B2 16 6N 14 47W
M'bahiakro, *Ivory C.* 112 D4 7 33N 4 19W
Mbaïki, *C.A.R.* 114 B3 3 53N 18 1 E
Mbakana, Mt. de, *Cameroon* 114 A3 7 57N 15 6 E
Mbala, *Zambia* 119 D3 8 46 S 31 24 E
Mbale, *Uganda* 118 B3 1 8N 34 12 E
Mbalmayo, *Cameroon* 113 E7 3 33N 11 33 E
Mbamba Bay, *Tanzania* 119 E3 11 13 S 34 49 E
Mbandaka, *Dem. Rep. of the Congo* 114 B3 0 1N 18 18 E
Mbanga, *Cameroon* 113 E6 4 30N 9 33 E
Mbanza Congo, *Angola* 115 D2 6 18 S 14 16 E
Mbanza Ngungu, *Dem. Rep. of the Congo* 115 D2 5 12 S 14 53 E
Mbarara, *Uganda* 118 C3 0 35 S 30 40 E
Mbashe →, *S. Africa* 117 E4 32 15 S 28 54 E
Mbatto, *Ivory C.* 112 D4 6 28N 4 22W
Mbengga, *Fiji* 133 B2 18 23 S 178 8 E
Mbenkuru →, *Tanzania* 119 D4 9 25 S 39 50 E
Mberengwa, *Zimbabwe* 119 G2 20 29 S 29 57 E
Mberengwa, Mt., *Zimbabwe* 119 G2 20 37 S 29 55 E
Mberubu, *Nigeria* 113 D6 6 10N 7 38 E
Mbesuma, *Zambia* 119 E3 10 0 S 32 2 E
Mbeya, *Tanzania* 119 D3 8 54 S 33 29 E
Mbeya □, *Tanzania* 118 D3 8 15 S 33 30 E
Mbigou, *Gabon* 114 C2 1 53 S 11 56 E
Mbinga, *Tanzania* 119 E4 10 50 S 35 0 E
Mbinga □, *Tanzania* 119 E4 10 50 S 35 0 E
Mbini □, *Eq. Guin.* 114 B2 1 30N 10 0 E
Mboki, *C.A.R.* 107 F2 5 19N 25 58 E
Mboli, *Dem. Rep. of the Congo* 114 B4 4 8N 23 9 E
Mboro, *Senegal* 112 B1 15 9N 16 54W
Mboune, *Senegal* 112 C2 14 42N 13 34W
Mbouoma, *Congo* 114 C3 0 52 S 15 4 E
Mbour, *Senegal* 112 C1 14 22N 16 54W
Mbout, *Mauritania* 112 B2 16 1N 12 38W
Mbozi □, *Tanzania* 119 D3 9 0 S 32 50 E
Mbrés, *C.A.R.* 114 A3 6 40N 19 48 E
Mbuji-Mayi, *Dem. Rep. of the Congo* 115 D4 6 9 S 23 40 E
Mbulu, *Tanzania* 118 C4 3 45 S 35 30 E
Mbulu □, *Tanzania* 118 C4 3 52 S 35 33 E
Mburucuyá, *Argentina* 174 B4 28 1 S 58 14W
Mcherrah, *Algeria* 110 C4 27 0N 4 30W
Mchinja, *Tanzania* 119 D4 9 44 S 39 45 E
Mchinji, *Malawi* 119 E3 13 47 S 32 58 E
Mdennah, *Mauritania* 110 D3 24 37N 6 0W
Mead, L., *U.S.A.* 161 J12 36 1N 114 44W
Meade, *U.S.A.* 155 G4 37 17N 100 20W
Meade →, *U.S.A.* 144 A9 70 52N 155 55W
Meade River, *U.S.A.* 144 A8 70 28N 157 24W
Meadow, *Australia* 125 E1 26 35 S 114 40 E
Meadow Lake, *Canada* 143 C7 54 10N 108 26W
Meadow Lake Prov. Park, *Canada* 143 C7 54 27N 109 0W
Meadow Valley Wash →, *U.S.A.* 161 J12 36 40N 114 34W
Meadville, *Mo., U.S.A.* 156 E3 39 47N 93 18W
Meadville, *Pa., U.S.A.* 150 E4 41 39N 80 9W
Meaford, *Canada* 140 D3 44 36N 80 35W
Mealhada, *Portugal* 42 E2 40 22N 8 27W
Mealy Mts., *Canada* 141 B8 53 10N 58 0W
Meander River, *Canada* 142 B5 59 2N 117 42W
Meansville, *U.S.A.* 152 B5 33 3N 84 18W
Meares, C., *U.S.A.* 158 D2 45 37N 124 0W
Mearim →, *Brazil* 170 B3 3 4 S 44 35W
Meath □, *Ireland* 23 C5 53 40N 6 57W
Meath Park, *Canada* 143 C7 53 27N 105 22W
Meatian, *Australia* 128 C5 35 34 S 143 21 E
Meaulne, *France* 27 F9 46 36N 2 36 E
Meaux, *France* 27 D9 48 58N 2 50 E
Mebechi-Gawa →, *Japan* 68 D10 40 31N 141 31 E
Mebonden, *Norway* 18 A8 63 13N 11 2 E
Mecanhelas, *Mozam.* 119 F4 15 12 S 35 54 E
Mecaya →, *Colombia* 168 C2 0 29N 75 11W
Mecca = Makkah, *Si. Arabia* 98 B2 21 30N 39 54 E
Mecca, *U.S.A.* 161 M10 33 34N 116 5W
Mechanicsburg, *U.S.A.* 150 F8 40 13N 77 1W
Mechanicsville, *U.S.A.* 156 C5 41 54N 91 16W
Mechanicville, *U.S.A.* 151 D11 42 54N 73 41W
Mechara, *Ethiopia* 107 F5 8 36N 40 20 E
Mechelen, *Belgium* 24 C4 51 2N 4 29 E
Mecheria, *Algeria* 111 B4 33 35N 0 18W
Mechernich, *Germany* 30 E2 50 35N 6 39 E
Mechetinskaya, *Russia* 61 G5 46 45N 40 32 E
Mechra Benâbbou, *Morocco* 110 B3 32 39N 7 48W
Mecidiye, *Turkey* 51 F10 40 38N 26 32 E
Mecitözü, *Turkey* 100 B6 40 32N 35 17 E
Mecklenburg-Vorpommern □, *Germany* 30 B8 53 45N 12 15 E
Mecklenburger Bucht, *Germany* 30 A7 54 20N 11 40 E
Meconta, *Mozam.* 119 E4 14 59 S 39 50 E
Mecsek, *Hungary* 52 D3 46 10N 18 18 E
Meda, *Australia* 124 C3 17 22 S 123 59 E
Meda, *Portugal* 42 E3 40 57N 7 18W
Medak, *India* 94 E4 18 1N 78 15 E
Medan, *Indonesia* 84 B1 3 40N 98 38 E
Médanos, *Argentina* 176 A4 38 50 S 62 42W
Medanosa, Pta., *Argentina* 176 C3 48 8 S 66 0W
Medart, *U.S.A.* 152 E5 30 5N 84 23W
Medaryville, *U.S.A.* 157 C10 41 5N 86 55W
Medawachchiya, *Sri Lanka* 95 K5 8 30N 80 30 E
Mede, *Italy* 44 C5 45 6N 8 44 E
Médéa, *Algeria* 111 A5 36 12N 2 50 E
Mededa, *Bos.-H.* 52 G4 43 44N 19 10 E
Médégué, *Gabon* 114 B2 0 37N 10 8 E
Medeiros Neto, *Brazil* 171 E3 17 20 S 40 14W
Medel, Pic, *Switz.* 33 C7 46 34N 8 55 E
Medellín, *Colombia* 168 B2 6 15N 75 35W
Medelpad, *Sweden* 16 B10 62 33N 16 30 E
Medemblik, *Neths.* 24 B5 52 46N 5 8 E
Médenine, *Tunisia* 108 B2 33 21N 10 30 E
Mederdra, *Mauritania* 112 B1 17 0N 15 38W
Medford, *Mass., U.S.A.* 151 D13 42 25N 71 7W
Medford, *Oreg., U.S.A.* 158 E2 42 19N 122 52W
Medford, *Wis., U.S.A.* 154 C9 45 9N 90 20W
Medgidia, *Romania* 53 F13 44 15N 28 19 E
Medi, *Sudan* 107 F3 5 4N 30 42 E
Media Agua, *Argentina* 174 C2 31 58 S 68 25W
Media Luna, *Argentina* 174 C2 34 45 S 66 44W
Mediapolis, *U.S.A.* 156 D5 41 0N 91 10W
Mediaş, *Romania* 53 D9 46 9N 24 22 E
Medical Lake, *U.S.A.* 158 C5 47 34N 117 41W
Medicina, *Italy* 45 D8 44 28N 11 38 E
Medicine Bow, *U.S.A.* 158 F10 41 54N 106 12W
Medicine Bow Pk., *U.S.A.* 158 F10 41 21N 106 19W
Medicine Bow Ra., *U.S.A.* 158 F10 41 10N 106 25W
Medicine Hat, *Canada* 143 D6 50 0N 110 45W
Medicine Lake, *U.S.A.* 154 A2 48 30N 104 30W
Medicine Lodge, *U.S.A.* 155 G5 37 17N 98 35W
Medina = Al Madīnah, *Si. Arabia* 96 E3 24 35N 39 52 E
Medina, *Brazil* 171 E3 16 15 S 41 29W
Medina, *Colombia* 168 C3 4 30N 73 21W
Medina, *N. Dak., U.S.A.* 154 B5 46 54N 99 18W
Medina, *N.Y., U.S.A.* 150 C6 43 13N 78 23W
Medina, *Ohio, U.S.A.* 150 E3 41 8N 81 52W
Medina →, *U.S.A.* 155 L5 29 16N 98 29W
Medina de Pomar, *Spain* 42 C7 42 56N 3 29W
Medina de Ríoseco, *Spain* 42 D5 41 53N 5 3W
Medina del Campo, *Spain* 42 D6 41 18N 4 55W
Medina L., *U.S.A.* 155 L5 29 32N 98 56W
Medina Sidonia, *Spain* 43 J5 36 28N 5 57W
Medinaceli, *Spain* 40 D2 41 12N 2 30W
Medinipur, *India* 93 H12 22 25N 87 21 E
Mediterranean Sea, *Europe* 12 H7 35 0N 15 0 E
Medjerda, O. →, *Tunisia* 108 A2 37 7N 10 13 E
Medley, *Canada* 143 C6 54 25N 110 16W
Mednogorsk, *Russia* 62 F6 51 24N 57 37 E
Médoc, *France* 28 C3 45 10N 0 50W
Medora, *U.S.A.* 157 F10 38 49N 86 10W
Médouneu, *Gabon* 114 B2 0 57N 10 47 E
Medstead, *Canada* 143 C7 53 19N 108 5W
Medulin, *Croatia* 45 D10 44 49N 13 55 E
Medveđa, *Serbia, Yug.* 50 D5 42 50N 21 32 E
Medvedevo, *Russia* 60 B8 56 37N 47 47 E
Medveditsa →, *Tver, Russia* 58 D9 57 5N 37 30 E
Medveditsa →, *Volgograd, Russia* 60 F6 49 35N 42 41 E
Medvedok, *Russia* 60 B10 57 20N 50 1 E
Medvezhi, Ostrava, *Russia* 65 B17 71 0N 161 0 E
Medvezhyegorsk, *Russia* 56 B5 63 0N 34 25 E
Medway →, *U.K.* 21 F8 51 27N 0 46 E
Medway Towns □, *U.K.* 21 F8 51 25N 0 32 E
Medzev, *Slovak Rep.* 35 C13 48 43N 20 55 E
Medzilaborce, *Slovak Rep.* 35 B14 49 17N 21 52 E
Medžitlija, *Macedonia* 50 F5 40 56N 21 26 E
Meeberrie, *Australia* 125 E2 26 57 S 115 51 E
Meekatharra, *Australia* 125 E2 26 32 S 118 29 E
Meeker, *U.S.A.* 158 F10 40 2N 107 55W
Meeniyan, *Australia* 129 E7 38 35 S 146 0 E
Meersburg, *Germany* 31 H5 47 41N 9 16 E
Meerut, *India* 92 E7 29 1N 77 42 E
Meeteetse, *U.S.A.* 158 D9 44 9N 108 52W
Mega, *Ethiopia* 107 G4 3 57N 38 19 E
Megálo Khorío, *Greece* 49 E9 36 27N 27 24 E
Megálo Petalí, *Greece* 48 D6 38 0N 24 15 E
Megalópolis, *Greece* 48 D4 37 25N 22 7 E
Meganísi, *Greece* 48 C2 38 39N 20 48 E
Mégara, *Greece* 48 D5 37 58N 23 22 E
Megdhova →, *Greece* 48 B3 39 10N 21 45 E
Megève, *France* 29 C10 45 51N 6 37 E
Meghalaya □, *India* 90 C3 25 50N 91 0 E
Meghezez, *Ethiopia* 107 F4 9 18N 39 26 E
Meghna →, *Bangla.* 90 D3 22 50N 90 50 E
Mégiscane, L., *Canada* 140 C4 48 35N 75 55W
Megiste, *Greece* 49 E11 36 8N 29 34 E
Megra, *Russia* 58 B9 60 11N 37 14 E
Mehadia, *Romania* 52 F7 44 56N 22 23 E
Mehaïguene, O. →, *Algeria* 111 B5 32 15N 2 59 E
Mehedeby, *Sweden* 16 D11 60 27N 17 25 E
Mehedinţi □, *Romania* 52 F7 44 40N 22 45 E
Meheisa, *Sudan* 106 D3 19 38N 32 57 E
Mehndawal, *India* 93 F10 26 58N 83 5 E

250 Middelburg

Middelburg, *Mpumalanga, S. Africa* **117 D4** 25 49 S 29 28 E
Middelfart, *Denmark* **17 J3** 55 30N 9 43 E
Middelwit, *S. Africa* **116 C4** 24 51 S 27 3 E
Middle →, *U.S.A.* **156 C3** 41 26N 93 30W
Middle Alkali L., *U.S.A.* **158 F3** 41 27N 120 5W
Middle Fork Feather →, *U.S.A.* **160 F5** 38 33N 121 30W
Middle I., *Australia* **125 F3** 34 6 S 123 11 E
Middle Loup →, *U.S.A.* **154 E5** 41 17N 98 24W
Middle Raccoon →, *U.S.A.* **156 C3** 41 35N 93 35W
Middleboro, *U.S.A.* **151 E14** 41 54N 70 55W
Middleburg, *Fla., U.S.A.* **152 E8** 30 4N 81 52W
Middleburg, *N.Y., U.S.A.* **151 D10** 42 36N 74 20W
Middleburg, *Pa., U.S.A.* **150 F7** 40 47N 77 3W
Middlebury, *Ind., U.S.A.* **157 C11** 41 41N 85 42W
Middlebury, *Vt., U.S.A.* **151 B11** 44 1N 73 10W
Middlemarch, *N.Z.* **131 F5** 45 30 S 170 9 E
Middleport, *U.S.A.* **148 F4** 39 0N 82 3W
Middlesboro, *U.S.A.* **149 G4** 36 36N 83 43W
Middlesbrough, *U.K.* **20 C6** 54 35N 1 13W
Middlesbrough □, *U.K.* **20 C6** 54 28N 1 13W
Middlesex, *Belize* **164 C2** 17 2N 88 31W
Middlesex, *U.S.A.* **151 F10** 40 36N 74 30W
Middleton, *Australia* **126 C3** 22 22 S 141 32 E
Middleton, *Canada* **141 D6** 44 57N 65 4W
Middleton, *U.S.A.* **156 A7** 43 6N 89 30W
Middletown, *U.K.* **23 B5** 54 17N 6 51W
Middletown, *Calif., U.S.A.* **160 G4** 38 45N 122 37W
Middletown, *Conn., U.S.A.* **151 E12** 41 34N 72 39W
Middletown, *N.Y., U.S.A.* **151 E10** 41 27N 74 25W
Middletown, *Ohio, U.S.A.* **157 E12** 39 31N 84 24W
Middletown, *Pa., U.S.A.* **151 F8** 40 12N 76 44W
Middleville, *U.S.A.* **157 B11** 42 43N 85 28W
Midelt, *Morocco* **110 B4** 32 46N 4 44W
Miðgarður, *Iceland* **11 A9** 66 32N 18 0W
Midhirst, *N.Z.* **130 F3** 39 17 S 174 18 E
Miðsandur, *Iceland* **11 C5** 64 24N 21 28W
Midhurst, *U.K.* **21 G7** 50 59N 0 44W
Midi, Canal du →, *France* **28 E5** 43 45N 1 21 E
Midi d'Ossau, Pic du, *France* **28 F3** 42 50N 0 26W
Midi-Pyrénées □, *France* **28 E5** 43 55N 1 45 E
Midland, *Canada* **140 D4** 44 45N 79 50W
Midland, *Calif., U.S.A.* **161 M12** 33 52N 114 48W
Midland, *Mich., U.S.A.* **148 D3** 43 37N 84 14W
Midland, *Pa., U.S.A.* **150 F4** 40 39N 80 27W
Midland, *Tex., U.S.A.* **155 K3** 32 0N 102 3W
Midlands □, *Zimbabwe* **119 F2** 19 40 S 29 0 E
Midleton, *Ireland* **23 E3** 51 55N 8 10W
Midlothian, *U.S.A.* **155 J6** 32 30N 97 0W
Midlothian □, *U.K.* **22 F5** 55 51N 3 5W
Midongy, Tangorombohitr' i, *Madag.* **117 C8** 23 30 S 47 0 E
Midongy Atsimo, *Madag.* **117 C8** 23 35 S 47 1 E
Midou →, *France* **28 E3** 43 54N 0 30W
Midouze →, *France* **28 E3** 43 48N 0 51W
Midsayap, *Phil.* **81 H5** 7 12N 124 32 E
Midsund, *Norway* **18 B3** 62 41N 6 40 E
Midtgulen, *Norway* **18 C2** 61 44N 5 11 E
Midu, *China* **76 E3** 25 18N 100 30 E
Midville, *U.S.A.* **152 C7** 32 49N 82 14W
Midway, *Ala., U.S.A.* **152 C4** 32 5N 85 31W
Midway, *Fla., U.S.A.* **152 E5** 30 30N 84 27W
Midway Is., *Pac. Oc.* **134 E10** 28 13N 177 22W
Midway Wells, *U.S.A.* **161 N11** 32 41N 115 7W
Midwest, *U.S.A.* **147 B9** 42 0N 90 0W
Midwest, *Wyo., U.S.A.* **158 E10** 43 25N 106 16W
Midwest City, *U.S.A.* **155 H6** 35 27N 97 24W
Midyat, *Turkey* **101 D9** 37 25N 41 23 E
Midzŏr, *Bulgaria* **50 C6** 43 24N 22 40 E
Mie □, *Japan* **71 C8** 34 30N 136 10 E
Miechów, *Poland* **55 H7** 50 21N 20 5 E
Miedwie, Jezioro, *Poland* **55 E1** 53 17N 14 54 E
Międzybórz, *Poland* **55 G4** 51 25N 17 34 E
Międzychód, *Poland* **55 F2** 52 35N 15 53 E
Międzylesie, *Poland* **55 H3** 50 8N 16 40 E
Międzyrzec Podlaski, *Poland* **55 G9** 51 58N 22 45 E
Międzyrzecz, *Poland* **55 F2** 52 26N 15 35 E
Międzyzdroje, *Poland* **54 E1** 53 56N 14 26 E
Miejska Górka, *Poland* **55 G3** 51 39N 16 58 E
Miélan, *France* **28 E4** 43 27N 0 19 E
Mielec, *Poland* **55 H8** 50 15N 21 25 E
Mienga, *Angola* **115 F3** 17 12 S 19 48 E
Miercurea-Ciuc, *Romania* **53 D10** 46 21N 25 48 E
Miercurea Sibiului, *Romania* **53 E8** 45 53N 23 48 E
Mieres, *Spain* **42 B5** 43 18N 5 48W
Mieroszów, *Poland* **55 H3** 50 40N 16 11 E
Mieso, *Ethiopia* **107 F5** 9 15N 40 43 E
Mieszkowice, *Poland* **55 F1** 52 47N 14 30 E
Mifflintown, *U.S.A.* **150 F7** 40 34N 77 24W
Mifraz Ḥefa, *Israel* **103 C4** 32 52N 35 0 E
Migennes, *France* **27 E10** 47 58N 3 31 E
Migliarino, *Italy* **45 D8** 44 46N 11 56 E
Miguel Alemán, Presa, *Mexico* **163 D5** 18 15N 96 40W
Miguel Alves, *Brazil* **170 B3** 4 11 S 42 55W
Miguel Calmon, *Brazil* **170 D3** 11 26 S 40 36W
Miguelturra, *Spain* **43 G7** 38 58N 3 53W
Mihăileni, *Romania* **53 C11** 47 58N 26 9 E
Mihăileşti, *Romania* **53 F10** 44 20N 25 54 E
Mihailovca, *Moldova* **53 D13** 46 33N 28 56 E
Mihalgazi, *Turkey* **49 A12** 40 2N 30 34 E
Mihaliççık, *Turkey* **100 C4** 39 53N 31 30 E
Mihara, *Japan* **70 C5** 34 24N 133 5 E
Mihara-Yama, *Japan* **71 C11** 34 43N 139 23 E
Miheşu de Cîmpie, *Romania* **53 D9** 46 41N 24 9 E
Mijas, *Spain* **43 J6** 36 36N 4 40W
Mikese, *Tanzania* **118 D4** 6 48 S 37 55 E
Mikha-Tskhakaya = Senaki, *Georgia* **61 J6** 42 15N 42 7 E
Mikhailovka = Mykhaylivka, *Ukraine* **59 J8** 47 12N 35 15 E
Mikhaylov, *Russia* **58 E10** 54 14N 39 0 E
Mikhaylovgrad = Montana, *Bulgaria* **50 C7** 43 27N 23 16 E
Mikhaylovka, *Russia* **60 E6** 50 3N 43 5 E
Mikhaylovski, *Russia* **62 C7** 56 27N 59 7 E
Mikhnevo, *Russia* **58 E9** 55 4N 37 59 E
Miki, *Hyōgo, Japan* **70 C6** 34 48N 134 59 E
Miki, *Kagawa, Japan* **70 C6** 34 12N 134 7 E
Mikínai, *Greece* **48 D4** 37 43N 22 46 E
Mikkeli, *Finland* **15 F22** 61 43N 27 15 E
Mikkwa →, *Canada* **142 B6** 58 25N 114 46W
Mikniya, *Sudan* **107 D3** 17 0N 33 45 E
Mikołajki, *Poland* **54 E8** 53 49N 21 37 E
Míkonos, *Greece* **49 D7** 37 30N 25 25 E
Mikrí Préspa, Límni, *Greece* **50 F5** 40 47N 21 3 E
Mikrón Dhérion, *Greece* **51 E10** 41 19N 26 6 E
Mikstat, *Poland* **55 G4** 51 32N 17 59 E
Mikulov, *Czech Rep.* **35 C9** 48 48N 16 39 E
Mikumi, *Tanzania* **118 D4** 7 26 S 37 0 E
Mikun, *Russia* **56 B9** 62 20N 50 0 E
Mikuni, *Japan* **71 A8** 36 13N 136 9 E
Mikuni-Tōge, *Japan* **71 A10** 36 50N 138 50 E
Mikura-Jima, *Japan* **71 D11** 33 52N 139 36 E
Milaca, *U.S.A.* **154 C8** 45 45N 93 39W
Milagro, *Ecuador* **168 D2** 2 11 S 79 36W
Milagros, *Phil.* **80 E4** 12 13N 123 30 E
Milan = Milano, *Italy* **44 C6** 45 28N 9 12 E
Milan, *Ga., U.S.A.* **152 C6** 32 1N 83 4W
Milan, *Ill., U.S.A.* **156 C6** 41 27N 90 34W
Milan, *Mich., U.S.A.* **157 B13** 42 5N 83 41W
Milan, *Mo., U.S.A.* **156 D3** 40 12N 93 7W
Milan, *Tenn., U.S.A.* **149 H1** 35 55N 88 46W
Miland, *Norway* **18 E5** 59 54N 8 45 E
Milang, *S. Austral., Australia* **127 E2** 32 2 S 139 10 E
Milang, *S. Austral., Australia* **128 C3** 35 24 S 138 58 E
Milange, *Mozam.* **119 F4** 16 3 S 35 45 E
Milano, *Italy* **44 C6** 45 28N 9 12 E
Milâs, *Turkey* **57 G4** 37 20N 27 50 E
Milatos, *Greece* **38 D7** 35 18N 25 34 E
Milazzo, *Italy* **47 D8** 38 13N 15 15 E
Milbank, *U.S.A.* **154 C6** 45 13N 96 38W
Milden, *Canada* **143 C7** 51 29N 107 32W
Mildenhall, *U.K.* **21 E8** 52 21N 0 32 E
Mildmay, *Canada* **150 B3** 44 3N 81 7W
Mildura, *Australia* **128 C5** 34 13 S 142 9 E
Mile, *China* **76 E4** 24 28N 103 20 E
Miléai, *Greece* **48 B5** 39 20N 23 9 E
Miles, *Australia* **127 D5** 26 40 S 150 9 E
Miles, *U.S.A.* **155 K4** 31 36N 100 11W
Miles City, *U.S.A.* **154 B2** 46 25N 105 51W
Mileşti, *Moldova* **53 C13** 47 13N 28 3 E
Milestone, *Canada* **143 D8** 49 59N 104 31W
Mileto, *Italy* **47 D9** 38 36N 16 4 E
Miletto, Mte., *Italy* **47 A7** 41 27N 14 22 E
Miletus, *Turkey* **49 D9** 37 30N 27 18 E
Mileura, *Australia* **125 E2** 26 22 S 117 20 E
Milevsko, *Czech Rep.* **34 B7** 49 27N 14 21 E
Milford, *Calif., U.S.A.* **160 E6** 40 10N 120 22W
Milford, *Conn., U.S.A.* **151 E11** 41 14N 73 3W
Milford, *Del., U.S.A.* **148 F8** 38 55N 75 26W
Milford, *Ga., U.S.A.* **152 D5** 31 23N 84 33W
Milford, *Ill., U.S.A.* **157 D9** 40 38N 87 42W
Milford, *Mass., U.S.A.* **151 D13** 42 8N 71 31W
Milford, *Mich., U.S.A.* **157 B13** 42 35N 83 36W
Milford, *Pa., U.S.A.* **151 E10** 41 19N 74 48W
Milford, *Utah, U.S.A.* **159 G7** 38 24N 113 1W
Milford Haven, *U.K.* **21 F2** 51 42N 5 7W
Milford Sd., *N.Z.* **131 E2** 44 41 S 167 47 E
Milgun, *Australia* **125 D2** 24 56 S 118 18 E
Milḥ, Baḥr al, *Iraq* **101 F10** 32 40N 43 35 E
Miliana, *Aïn Salah, Algeria* **111 C5** 27 20N 2 32 E
Miliana, *Médéa, Algeria* **111 A5** 36 20N 2 15 E
Milicz, *Poland* **55 G4** 51 31N 17 19 E
Mililani Town, *U.S.A.* **145 K13** 21 28N 158 1W
Miling, *Australia* **125 F2** 30 30 S 116 17 E
Militello in Val di Catánia, *Italy* **47 E7** 37 16N 14 48 E
Milk →, *U.S.A.* **158 B10** 48 4N 106 19W
Milk, Wadi el →, *Sudan* **106 D3** 17 55N 30 20 E
Milk River, *Canada* **142 D6** 49 10N 112 5W
Mill City, *U.S.A.* **158 D2** 44 45N 122 29W
Mill I., *Antarctica* **7 C8** 66 0 S 101 30 E
Mill Shoals, *U.S.A.* **157 F8** 38 15N 88 21W
Mill Valley, *U.S.A.* **160 H4** 37 54N 122 32W
Millárs →, *Spain* **41 F4** 39 55N 0 1W
Millau, *France* **28 D7** 44 8N 3 4 E
Millbridge, *Canada* **150 B7** 44 41N 77 36W
Millbrook, *Canada* **150 B6** 44 10N 78 29W
Mille Lacs, L. des, *Canada* **140 C1** 48 45N 90 35W
Mille Lacs L., *U.S.A.* **154 B8** 46 15N 93 39W
Milledgeville, *Ga., U.S.A.* **152 B6** 33 5N 83 14W
Milledgeville, *Ill., U.S.A.* **156 C7** 41 58N 89 46W
Millen, *U.S.A.* **152 C8** 32 48N 81 57W
Miller, *U.S.A.* **154 C5** 44 31N 98 59W
Millerovo, *Russia* **61 F5** 48 57N 40 28 E
Miller's Flat, *N.Z.* **131 F4** 45 39 S 169 23 E
Millersburg, *Ind., U.S.A.* **157 C11** 41 32N 85 42W
Millersburg, *Ohio, U.S.A.* **150 F3** 40 33N 81 55W
Millersburg, *Pa., U.S.A.* **150 F8** 40 32N 76 58W
Millerton, *N.Z.* **131 B6** 41 39 S 171 54 E
Millerton, *U.S.A.* **151 E11** 41 57N 73 31W
Millerton L., *U.S.A.* **160 J7** 37 1N 119 41W
Millevaches, Plateau de, *France* **28 C6** 45 45N 2 0 E
Millicent, *Australia* **128 D4** 37 34 S 140 21 E
Milligan, *U.S.A.* **153 E3** 30 45N 86 38W
Millinocket, *U.S.A.* **141 C6** 45 39N 68 43W
Millmerran, *Australia* **127 D5** 27 53 S 151 16 E
Millom, *U.K.* **20 C4** 54 13N 3 16W
Mills L., *Canada* **142 A5** 61 30N 118 20W
Millsboro, *U.S.A.* **150 G5** 40 0N 80 0W
Milltown Malbay, *Ireland* **23 D2** 52 52N 9 24W
Millville, *U.S.A.* **148 F8** 39 24N 75 2W
Millwood, *U.S.A.* **152 D7** 31 16N 82 40W
Millwood L., *U.S.A.* **155 J8** 33 42N 93 58W
Milna, *Croatia* **45 E13** 43 20N 16 28 E
Milne →, *Australia* **126 C2** 21 10 S 137 33 E
Milne Land, *Greenland* **10 C8** 70 40N 26 30W
Milnor, *U.S.A.* **154 B6** 46 16N 97 27W
Milo, *Canada* **142 C6** 50 34N 112 53W
Mílos, *Greece* **48 E6** 36 44N 24 25 E
Miłosław, *Poland* **55 F4** 52 12N 17 32 E
Milot, *Albania* **50 E3** 41 41N 19 43 E
Milparinka P.O., *Australia* **127 D3** 29 46 S 141 57 E
Milroy, *U.S.A.* **157 E11** 39 30N 85 28W
Miltenberg, *Germany* **31 F5** 49 41N 9 16 E
Milton, *Canada* **150 C5** 43 31N 79 53W
Milton, *N.Z.* **131 G4** 46 7 S 169 59 E
Milton, *Calif., U.S.A.* **160 G6** 38 3N 120 51W
Milton, *Fla., U.S.A.* **149 K2** 30 38N 87 3W
Milton, *Iowa, U.S.A.* **156 D4** 40 41N 92 10W
Milton, *Pa., U.S.A.* **150 F8** 41 1N 76 51W
Milton, *Wis., U.S.A.* **157 B8** 42 47N 88 56W
Milton-Freewater, *U.S.A.* **158 D4** 45 56N 118 23W
Milton Keynes, *U.K.* **21 E7** 52 1N 0 44W
Milton Keynes □, *U.K.* **21 E7** 52 1N 0 44W
Miltou, *Chad* **109 F3** 10 14N 17 26 E
Milverton, *Canada* **150 C4** 43 34N 80 55W
Milwaukee, *U.S.A.* **157 A9** 43 2N 87 55W
Milwaukee Deep, *Atl. Oc.* **8 G2** 19 50N 68 0W
Milwaukie, *U.S.A.* **160 E4** 45 27N 122 38W
Mim, *Ghana* **112 D4** 6 57N 2 33W
Mimizan, *France* **28 D2** 44 12N 1 13W
Mimoň, *Czech Rep.* **34 A7** 50 38N 14 43 E
Mimongo, *Gabon* **114 C2** 1 11 S 11 36 E
Mimoso, *Brazil* **171 E2** 15 10 S 48 5W
Mims, *U.S.A.* **153 G9** 28 40N 80 51W
Min Jiang →, *Fujian, China* **77 E12** 26 0N 119 35 E
Min Jiang →, *Sichuan, China* **76 C5** 28 45N 104 40 E
Min-Kush, *Kyrgyzstan* **63 C7** 41 40N 74 28 E
Min Xian, *China* **74 G3** 34 25N 104 5 E
Mina, *U.S.A.* **159 G4** 38 24N 118 7W
Mina Pirquitas, *Argentina* **174 A2** 22 40 S 66 30W
Mīnā Su'ud, *Si. Arabia* **97 D6** 28 45N 48 28 E
Mīnā'al Aḥmadī, *Kuwait* **97 D6** 29 5N 48 10 E
Mīnāb, *Iran* **97 E8** 27 10N 57 1 E
Minago →, *Canada* **143 C9** 54 33N 98 59W
Minakami, *Japan* **71 A10** 36 49N 138 59 E
Minaki, *Canada* **143 D10** 49 59N 94 40W
Minakuchi, *Japan* **71 C8** 34 58N 136 10 E
Minamata, *Japan* **70 E2** 32 10N 130 30 E
Minami-Tori-Shima, *Pac. Oc.* **134 E7** 24 0N 153 45 E
Minas, *Uruguay* **175 C4** 34 20 S 55 10W
Minas, Sierra de las, *Guatemala* **164 C2** 15 9N 89 31W
Minas Basin, *Canada* **141 C7** 45 20N 64 12W
Minas de Rio Tinto = Minas de Riotinto, *Spain* **43 H4** 37 42N 6 35W
Minas de Riotinto, *Spain* **43 H4** 37 42N 6 35W
Minas Gerais □, *Brazil* **171 E2** 18 50 S 46 0W
Minas Novas, *Brazil* **171 E3** 17 15 S 42 36W
Minatitlán, *Mexico* **163 D6** 17 59N 94 31W
Minbu, *Burma* **90 E5** 20 10N 94 52 E
Minbya, *Burma* **90 E4** 20 22N 93 16 E
Mincio →, *Italy* **44 C7** 45 4N 10 59 E
Minčol, *Slovak Rep.* **35 B13** 49 15N 20 58 E
Mindanao, *Phil.* **81 H5** 8 0N 125 0 E
Mindanao Sea = Bohol Sea, *Phil.* **81 G5** 9 0N 124 0 E
Mindanao Trench, *Pac. Oc.* **80 E5** 12 0N 126 6 E
Mindel →, *Germany* **31 G6** 48 31N 10 23 E
Mindelheim, *Germany* **31 G6** 48 2N 10 29 E
Minden, *Canada* **150 B6** 44 55N 78 43W
Minden, *Germany* **30 C4** 52 17N 8 55 E
Minden, *La., U.S.A.* **155 J8** 32 37N 93 17W
Minden, *Nev., U.S.A.* **160 G7** 38 57N 119 46W
Mindiptana, *Indonesia* **83 C6** 5 55 S 140 22 E
Mindon, *Burma* **90 F5** 19 21N 94 44 E
Mindoro, *Phil.* **80 E3** 13 0N 121 0 E
Mindoro Occidental □, *Phil.* **80 E3** 13 0N 120 55 E
Mindoro Oriental □, *Phil.* **80 E3** 13 0N 121 5 E
Mindoro Str., *Phil.* **80 E3** 12 30N 120 30 E
Mindouli, *Congo* **115 C2** 4 12 S 14 28 E
Mine, *Japan* **70 C3** 34 12N 131 7 E
Minehead, *U.K.* **21 F4** 51 12N 3 29W
Mineiros, *Brazil* **173 D7** 17 34 S 52 34W
Mineola, *U.S.A.* **155 J7** 32 40N 95 29W
Mineral King, *U.S.A.* **160 J8** 36 27N 118 36W
Mineral Point, *U.S.A.* **156 B6** 42 52N 90 11W
Mineral Wells, *U.S.A.* **155 J5** 32 48N 98 7W
Mineralnyye Vody, *Russia* **61 H6** 44 15N 43 8 E
Minersville, *Pa., U.S.A.* **151 F8** 40 41N 76 16W
Minersville, *Utah, U.S.A.* **159 G7** 38 13N 112 56W
Minerva, *U.S.A.* **150 F3** 40 44N 81 6W
Minervino Murge, *Italy* **47 A9** 41 5N 16 5 E
Minetto, *U.S.A.* **151 C8** 43 24N 76 28W
Mingäçevir, *Azerbaijan* **61 K8** 40 45N 47 0 E
Mingäçevir Su Anbarı, *Azerbaijan* **61 K8** 40 57N 46 50 E
Mingan, *Canada* **141 B7** 50 20N 64 0W
Mingary, *Australia* **128 B4** 32 8 S 140 45 E
Mingechaur = Mingäçevir, *Azerbaijan* **61 K8** 40 45N 47 0 E
Mingechaurskoye Vdkhr. = Mingäçevir Su Anbarı, *Azerbaijan* **61 K8** 40 57N 46 50 E
Mingela, *Australia* **126 B4** 19 52 S 146 38 E
Mingenew, *Australia* **125 E2** 29 12 S 115 21 E
Mingera Cr. →, *Australia* **126 C2** 20 38 S 137 45 E
Minggang, *China* **77 A10** 32 24N 114 3 E
Mingin, *Burma* **90 D5** 22 50N 94 30 E
Mingir, *Moldova* **53 D13** 46 40N 28 20 E
Minglanilla, *Spain* **41 F3** 39 34N 1 38W
Minglun, *China* **76 E7** 25 10N 108 21 E
Mingorria, *Spain* **42 E6** 40 45N 4 40W
Mingt'iehkaitafan = Mintaka Pass, *Pakistan* **93 A6** 37 0N 74 58 E
Mingxi, *China* **77 D11** 26 18N 117 12 E
Mingyuegue, *China* **75 C15** 43 2N 128 50 E
Minho = Miño →, *Spain* **42 D2** 41 52N 8 40W
Minhou, *China* **77 E12** 26 0N 119 15 E
Minićevo, *Serbia, Yug.* **52 G7** 43 42N 22 18 E
Minidoka, *U.S.A.* **158 E7** 42 45N 113 29W
Minier, *U.S.A.* **156 D7** 40 26N 89 19W
Minigwal, L., *Australia* **125 E3** 29 31 S 123 14 E
Minilya, *Australia* **125 D1** 23 55 S 114 0 E
Minilya →, *Australia* **125 D1** 23 45 S 114 0 E
Mininera, *Australia* **128 D5** 37 37 S 142 58 E
Minipi, L., *Canada* **141 B7** 52 25N 60 45W
Minj, *Papua N. G.* **132 C3** 5 54 S 144 37 E
Mink L., *Canada* **142 A5** 61 54N 117 40W
Minlaton, *Australia* **128 C2** 34 45 S 137 35 E
Minna, *Nigeria* **113 D6** 9 37N 6 30 E
Minneapolis, *Kans., U.S.A.* **154 F6** 39 8N 97 42W
Minneapolis, *Minn., U.S.A.* **154 C8** 44 59N 93 16W
Minnedosa, *Canada* **143 C9** 50 14N 99 50W
Minnesota □, *U.S.A.* **154 B8** 46 0N 94 15W
Minnesund, *Norway* **18 D8** 60 23N 11 14 E
Minnie Creek, *Australia* **125 D2** 24 3 S 115 42 E
Minnipa, *Australia* **127 E2** 32 51 S 135 9 E
Minnitaki L., *Canada* **140 C1** 49 57N 92 10W
Mino, *Japan* **71 B8** 35 32N 136 55 E
Miño, *Spain* **42 B2** 43 21N 8 12W
Miño →, *Spain* **42 D2** 41 52N 8 40W
Mino-Kamo, *Japan* **71 B9** 35 23N 137 2 E
Mino-Mikawa-Kōgen, *Japan* **71 B9** 35 10N 137 23 E
Minoa, *Greece* **49 F7** 35 6N 25 45 E
Minobu, *Japan* **71 B10** 35 22N 138 26 E
Minobu-Sanchi, *Japan* **71 B10** 35 14N 138 20 E
Minonk, *U.S.A.* **156 D7** 40 54N 89 2W
Minooka, *U.S.A.* **157 C8** 41 27N 88 16W
Minorca = Menorca, *Spain* **39 B11** 40 0N 4 0 E
Minore, *Australia* **129 B8** 32 14 S 148 27 E
Minot, *U.S.A.* **154 A4** 48 14N 101 18W
Minqin, *China* **74 E2** 38 38N 103 20 E
Minqing, *China* **77 D12** 26 15N 118 50 E
Minsen, *Germany* **30 B3** 53 41N 7 58 E
Minsk, *Belarus* **58 F4** 53 52N 27 30 E
Mińsk Mazowiecki, *Poland* **55 F8** 52 10N 21 33 E
Minster, *U.S.A.* **157 D12** 40 24N 84 23W
Mintaka Pass, *Pakistan* **93 A6** 37 0N 74 58 E
Minthami, *Burma* **90 D5** 23 55N 94 16 E
Minton, *Canada* **143 D8** 49 10N 104 35W
Mintoum, *Gabon* **114 B2** 0 27N 12 16 E
Minturn, *U.S.A.* **158 G10** 39 35N 106 26W
Minturno, *Italy* **46 A6** 41 15N 13 45 E
Minûf, *Egypt* **106 H7** 30 26N 30 52 E
Minusinsk, *Russia* **65 D10** 53 43N 91 20 E
Minutang, *India* **90 A6** 28 15N 96 30 E
Minvoul, *Gabon* **114 B2** 2 9N 12 8 E
Minwakh, *Yemen* **99 C5** 16 48N 48 6 E
Minya el Qamh, *Egypt* **106 H7** 30 31N 31 21 E
Minyar, *Russia* **62 D6** 55 4N 57 33 E
Minyip, *Australia* **128 D5** 36 29 S 142 36 E
Mionica, *Bos.-H.* **52 F3** 44 51N 18 29 E
Mionica, *Serbia, Yug.* **50 B4** 44 14N 20 6 E
Mir, *Niger* **109 F2** 14 5N 11 59 E
Mīr Kūh, *Iran* **97 E8** 26 22N 58 55 E
Mīr Shahdād, *Iran* **97 E8** 26 15N 58 29 E
Mira, *Italy* **45 C9** 45 26N 12 8 E
Mira, *Portugal* **42 E2** 40 26N 8 44W
Mira →, *Colombia* **168 C2** 1 36N 79 1W
Mira →, *Portugal* **43 H2** 37 43N 8 47W
Mira por vos Cay, *Bahamas* **165 B5** 22 9N 74 30W
Mīrābād, *Afghan.* **91 C1** 30 25N 61 50 E
Mirabella Eclano, *Italy* **47 A7** 41 2N 14 59 E
Miracema do Norte, *Brazil* **170 C2** 9 33 S 48 24W
Mirador, *Brazil* **170 C3** 6 22 S 44 22W
Miraflores, *Colombia* **168 C3** 1 25N 72 13W
Miraj, *India* **94 F2** 16 50N 74 45 E
Miram Shah, *Pakistan* **91 B3** 33 0N 70 2 E
Miramar, *Argentina* **174 D4** 38 15 S 57 50W
Miramar, *Mozam.* **117 C6** 23 50 S 35 35 E
Miramar, *U.S.A.* **153 K9** 25 59N 80 15W
Miramas, *France* **29 E8** 43 33N 4 59 E
Mirambeau, *France* **28 C3** 45 23N 0 35W
Miramichi B., *Canada* **141 C7** 47 15N 65 0W
Miramont-de-Guyenne, *France* **28 D4** 44 37N 0 21 E
Miranda, *Brazil* **173 E6** 20 10 S 56 15W
Miranda □, *Venezuela* **168 A4** 10 15N 66 25W
Miranda →, *Brazil* **173 D6** 19 25 S 57 20W
Miranda de Ebro, *Spain* **40 C2** 42 41N 2 57W
Miranda do Corvo, *Spain* **42 E2** 40 6N 8 20W
Miranda do Douro, *Portugal* **42 D4** 41 30N 6 16W
Mirande, *France* **28 E4** 43 31N 0 25 E
Mirandela, *Portugal* **42 D3** 41 32N 7 10W
Mirando City, *U.S.A.* **155 M5** 27 26N 99 0W
Mirándola, *Italy* **44 D8** 44 53N 11 4 E
Mirandópolis, *Brazil* **175 A5** 21 9 S 51 6W
Mirango, *Malawi* **119 E3** 13 32 S 34 58 E
Mirani, *Australia* **126 C4** 21 9 S 148 53 E
Mirano, *Italy* **45 C9** 45 30N 12 7 E
Miras, *Albania* **50 F4** 40 30N 20 56 E
Mirassol, *Brazil* **175 A6** 20 46 S 49 28W
Mirbāţ, *Oman* **99 C6** 17 0N 54 45 E
Mirboo North, *Australia* **129 E7** 38 24 S 146 10 E
Mirear, *Egypt* **106 C4** 23 15N 35 41 E
Mirebeau, *Côte-d'Or, France* **27 E12** 47 25N 5 20 E
Mirebeau, *Vienne, France* **26 F7** 46 49N 0 10 E
Mirecourt, *France* **27 D13** 48 20N 6 10 E
Mirgorod = Myrhorod, *Ukraine* **59 H7** 49 58N 33 37 E
Miri, *Malaysia* **85 B4** 4 23N 113 59 E
Miriam Vale, *Australia* **126 C5** 24 20 S 151 33 E
Miribel, *France* **27 G11** 45 50N 4 57 E
Mirim, L., *S. Amer.* **175 C5** 32 45 S 52 50W
Mirimire, *Venezuela* **168 A4** 11 10N 68 43W
Miriti, *Brazil* **173 B6** 6 15 S 59 0W
Mirnyy, *Russia* **65 C12** 62 33N 113 53 E
Miroč, *Serbia, Yug.* **50 B6** 44 32N 22 16 E
Mirond L., *Canada* **143 B8** 55 6N 102 47W
Mirosławiec, *Poland* **54 E3** 53 20N 16 5 E
Mirpur, *Pakistan* **91 B4** 33 32N 73 56 E
Mirpur Bibiwari, *Pakistan* **92 E2** 28 33N 67 44 E
Mirpur Khas, *Pakistan* **91 D3** 25 30N 69 0 E
Mirpur Sakro, *Pakistan* **92 G2** 24 33N 67 41 E
Mirria, *Niger* **109 F1** 13 43N 9 7 E
Mirror, *Canada* **142 C6** 52 30N 113 7W
Mirsk, *Poland* **55 H2** 50 58N 15 23 E
Miryang, *S. Korea* **75 G15** 35 31N 128 44 E
Mirzaani, *Georgia* **61 K8** 41 24N 46 5 E
Mirzapur, *India* **93 G10** 25 10N 82 34 E
Mirzapur-cum-Vindhyachal = Mirzapur, *India* **93 G10** 25 10N 82 34 E
Misamis Occidental □, *Phil.* **81 G4** 8 20N 123 42 E
Misamis Oriental □, *Phil.* **81 G5** 8 45N 125 0 E
Misantla, *Mexico* **163 D5** 19 56N 96 50W
Misawa, *Japan* **68 D10** 40 41N 141 24 E
Miscou I., *Canada* **141 C7** 47 57N 64 31W
Mish'āb, Ra'as al, *Si. Arabia* **97 D6** 28 15N 48 43 E
Mishagua →, *Peru* **172 C3** 11 12 S 72 58W
Mishan, *China* **73 B8** 45 37N 131 48 E
Mishawaka, *U.S.A.* **157 C10** 41 40N 86 11W
Mishbih, Gebel, *Egypt* **106 C3** 22 38N 34 44 E
Mishima, *Japan* **71 B10** 35 10N 138 52 E
Mishmi Hills, *India* **90 A6** 29 0N 96 0 E
Misima I., *Papua N. G.* **132 F7** 10 40 S 152 45 E
Misión, *Mexico* **161 N10** 32 6N 116 53W
Misión Fagnano, *Argentina* **176 D3** 54 32 S 67 17W
Misiones □, *Argentina* **175 B5** 27 0 S 55 0W
Misiones □, *Paraguay* **174 B4** 27 0 S 56 0W
Miskah, *Si. Arabia* **96 E4** 24 49N 42 56 E
Miskitos, Cayos, *Nic.* **164 D3** 14 26N 82 50W
Miskolc, *Hungary* **52 B5** 48 7N 20 50 E
Misoke, *Dem. Rep. of the Congo* **118 C2** 0 42 S 28 2 E
Misool, *Indonesia* **83 B4** 1 52 S 130 10 E
Misrātah, *Libya* **108 B3** 32 24N 15 3 E
Misrātah □, *Libya* **108 C3** 33 30N 15 0 E
Missanabie, *Canada* **140 C3** 48 20N 84 6W
Missão Velha, *Brazil* **170 C4** 7 15 S 39 10W
Missinaibi →, *Canada* **140 B3** 50 43N 81 29W
Missinaibi L., *Canada* **140 C3** 48 23N 83 40W
Mission, *S. Dak., U.S.A.* **154 D4** 43 18N 100 39W
Mission, *Tex., U.S.A.* **155 M5** 26 13N 98 20W
Mission City, *Canada* **142 D4** 49 10N 122 15W
Mission Viejo, *U.S.A.* **161 M9** 33 36N 117 40W
Missisa L., *Canada* **140 B2** 52 20N 85 7W
Missisagi →, *Canada* **140 C3** 46 15N 83 9W
Mississinewa Res., *U.S.A.* **157 D10** 40 46N 86 3W
Mississippi □, *U.S.A.* **155 J10** 33 0N 90 0W
Mississippi →, *U.S.A.* **155 L10** 29 9N 89 15W
Mississippi L., *Canada* **151 A8** 45 5N 76 10W
Mississippi River Delta, *U.S.A.* **155 L9** 29 10N 89 15W
Mississippi Sd., *U.S.A.* **155 K10** 30 20N 89 0W
Missoula, *U.S.A.* **158 C7** 46 52N 114 1W
Missour, *Morocco* **110 B4** 33 3N 4 0W
Missouri □, *U.S.A.* **154 F8** 38 25N 92 30W
Missouri →, *U.S.A.* **154 F9** 38 49N 90 7W
Missouri Valley, *U.S.A.* **154 E7** 41 34N 95 53W
Mist, *U.S.A.* **160 E3** 45 59N 123 15W
Mistake B., *Canada* **143 A10** 62 8N 93 0W
Mistassini →, *Canada* **141 C5** 48 42N 72 20W
Mistassini L., *Canada* **140 B5** 51 0N 73 30W
Mistastin L., *Canada* **141 A7** 55 57N 63 20W
Mistatim, *Canada* **143 C8** 52 52N 103 22W
Mistelbach, *Austria* **35 C9** 48 34N 16 34 E
Misterbianco, *Italy* **47 E8** 37 31N 15 1 E
Mistretta, *Italy* **47 E7** 37 56N 14 22 E

Munchŏn 253

Mosby, *Norway* **18 F4** 58 12N 7 55 E
Mošćenice, *Croatia* **45 C11** 45 17N 14 16 E
Mosciano Sant' Ángelo, *Italy* **45 F10** 42 42N 13 52 E
Moscos Is. = Maungmagan Is., *Burma* **86 F1** 14 0N 97 30 E
Moscow = Moskva, *Russia* **58 E9** 55 45N 37 35 E
Moscow, *U.S.A.* **158 C5** 46 44N 117 0W
Mosel →, *Europe* **27 B14** 50 22N 7 36 E
Moselle = Mosel →, *Europe* **27 B14** 50 22N 7 36 E
Moselle □, *France* **27 D13** 48 59N 6 33 E
Moses Lake, *U.S.A.* **158 C4** 47 8N 119 17W
Mosgiel, *N.Z.* **131 F5** 45 53 S 170 21 E
Moshi, *Tanzania* **118 C4** 3 22 S 37 18 E
Moshi □, *Tanzania* **118 C4** 3 22 S 37 18 E
Moshupa, *Botswana* **116 C4** 24 46 S 25 29 E
Mosina, *Poland* **55 F3** 52 15N 16 50 E
Mosjøen, *Norway* **14 D15** 65 51N 13 12 E
Moskenesøya, *Norway* **14 C15** 67 58N 13 0 E
Moskenstraumen, *Norway* **14 C15** 67 47N 12 45 E
Moskog, *Norway* **18 C2** 61 26N 6 0 E
Moskva, *Russia* **58 E9** 55 45N 37 35 E
Moskva →, *Russia* **58 E9** 55 5N 38 51 E
Moslavačka Gora, *Croatia* **45 C13** 45 40N 16 37 E
Moso, *Vanuatu* **133 G6** 17 30 S 168 15 E
Mosomane, *Botswana* **116 C4** 24 2 S 26 19 E
Moson-magyaróvár, *Hungary* **52 C2** 47 52N 17 18 E
Mošorin, *Serbia, Yug.* **52 E5** 45 19N 20 4 E
Mospino, *Ukraine* **59 J9** 47 52N 38 0 E
Mosquera, *Colombia* **168 C2** 2 35N 78 24W
Mosquero, *U.S.A.* **155 H3** 35 47N 103 58W
Mosqueruela, *Spain* **40 E4** 40 21N 0 27W
Mosquitia, *Honduras* **164 C3** 15 20N 84 10W
Mosquitos, G. de los, *Panama* **164 E3** 9 15N 81 10W
Moss, *Norway* **15 G14** 59 27N 10 40 E
Moss Vale, *Australia* **129 C9** 34 32 S 150 25 E
Mossaka, *Congo* **114 C3** 1 15 S 16 45 E
Mossâmedes, *Brazil* **171 E1** 16 7 S 50 11W
Mossbank, *Canada* **143 D7** 49 56N 105 56W
Mossburn, *N.Z.* **131 F3** 45 41 S 168 15 E
Mosselbaai, *S. Africa* **116 E3** 34 11 S 22 8 E
Mossendjo, *Congo* **114 C2** 2 55 S 12 42 E
Mosses, Col des, *Switz.* **32 D4** 46 25N 7 7 E
Mossgiel, *Australia* **128 B6** 33 15 S 144 5 E
Mossingen, *Germany* **31 G5** 48 24N 9 4 E
Mossman, *Australia* **126 B4** 16 21 S 145 15 E
Mossoró, *Brazil* **170 C4** 5 10 S 37 15W
Mossuril, *Mozam.* **119 E5** 14 58 S 40 42 E
Mossy →, *Canada* **143 C8** 54 5N 102 58W
Mossy Head, *U.S.A.* **153 E3** 30 45N 86 19W
Most, *Czech Rep.* **34 A6** 50 31N 13 38 E
Mosta, *Malta* **38 D1** 35 54N 14 24 E
Moṣṭafáābād, *Iran* **97 C7** 33 39N 54 53 E
Mostaganem, *Algeria* **111 A5** 35 54N 0 5 E
Mostar, *Bos.-H.* **52 G2** 43 22N 17 50 E
Mostardas, *Brazil* **175 C5** 31 2 S 50 51W
Mostefa, Rass, *Tunisia* **108 A2** 36 55N 11 3 E
Mosterhamn, *Norway* **18 E2** 59 42N 5 21 E
Mostiska = Mostyska, *Ukraine* **59 H2** 49 48N 23 4 E
Móstoles, *Spain* **42 E7** 40 19N 3 53W
Mosty = Masty, *Belarus* **58 F3** 53 27N 24 38 E
Mostyska, *Ukraine* **59 H2** 49 48N 23 4 E
Mosul = Al Mawṣil, *Iraq* **101 D10** 36 15N 43 5 E
Mosulpo, *S. Korea* **75 H14** 33 20N 126 17 E
Møsvatnet, *Norway* **18 E5** 59 52N 8 5 E
Mota, *Vanuatu* **133 C5** 13 49 S 167 42 E
Mota del Cuervo, *Spain* **41 F2** 39 30N 2 52W
Mota del Marqués, *Spain* **42 D5** 41 38N 5 11W
Mota Lava, *Vanuatu* **133 C5** 13 40 S 167 40 E
Motagua →, *Guatemala* **164 C2** 15 44N 88 14W
Motala, *Sweden* **17 F9** 58 32N 15 1 E
Moțca, *Romania* **53 C11** 47 15N 26 37 E
Motegi, *Japan* **71 A12** 36 32N 140 11 E
Motherwell, *U.K.* **22 F5** 55 47N 3 58W
Motihari, *India* **93 F11** 26 30N 84 55 E
Motilla del Palancar, *Spain* **41 F3** 39 34N 1 55W
Motiti I., *N.Z.* **130 D5** 37 38 S 176 25 E
Motnik, *Slovenia* **45 B11** 46 14N 14 54 E
Motocurunya, *Venezuela* **169 C5** 4 24N 64 5W
Motovun, *Croatia* **45 C10** 45 20N 13 50 E
Motozintla de Mendoza, *Mexico* **163 D6** 15 21N 92 14W
Motril, *Spain* **43 J7** 36 31N 3 37W
Motru, *Romania* **52 F7** 44 48N 22 59 E
Motru →, *Romania* **53 F8** 44 32N 23 31 E
Mott, *U.S.A.* **154 B3** 46 23N 102 20W
Móttola, *Italy* **47 B10** 40 38N 17 2 E
Motu, *N.Z.* **130 E6** 38 18 S 177 40 E
Motu →, *N.Z.* **130 D6** 37 51 S 177 35 E
Motueka, *N.Z.* **131 B8** 41 7 S 173 1 E
Motueka →, *N.Z.* **131 B8** 41 5 S 173 1 E
Motul, *Mexico* **163 C7** 21 0N 89 20W
Motupena Pt., *Papua N. G.* **132 D8** 6 30 S 155 10 E
Mouanda, *Gabon* **114 C2** 1 28 S 13 7 E
Mouchalagane →, *Canada* **141 B6** 50 56N 68 41W
Moúdhros, *Greece* **49 B7** 39 50N 25 18 E
Mouding, *China* **76 E3** 25 20N 101 28 E
Moudjeria, *Mauritania* **112 B2** 17 50N 12 28W
Moudon, *Switz.* **32 C3** 46 40N 6 49 E
Mougoundou, *Congo* **114 C2** 2 40 S 12 41 E
Mouila, *Gabon* **114 C2** 1 50 S 11 0 E
Mouka, *C.A.R.* **114 A4** 7 16N 21 52 E
Moulamein, *Australia* **128 C6** 35 3 S 144 1 E
Mouliana, *Greece* **38 D7** 35 10N 25 59 E
Moulins, *France* **27 F10** 46 35N 3 19 E
Moulmein, *Burma* **90 G6** 16 30N 97 40 E
Moulmeingyun, *Burma* **90 G5** 16 23N 95 16 E
Moulouya, O. →, *Morocco* **111 A4** 35 5N 2 25W
Moulton, *Iowa, U.S.A.* **156 D4** 40 41N 92 41W
Moulton, *Tex., U.S.A.* **155 L6** 29 35N 97 9W
Moultrie, *U.S.A.* **152 D6** 31 11N 83 47W
Moultrie, L., *U.S.A.* **152 B9** 33 20N 80 5W
Mound City, *Mo., U.S.A.* **154 E7** 40 7N 95 14W
Mound City, *S. Dak., U.S.A.* **154 C4** 45 44N 100 4W
Moúnda, Ákra, *Greece* **48 C2** 38 5N 20 45 E
Moundou, *Chad* **109 G3** 8 40N 16 10 E
Moundsville, *U.S.A.* **150 G4** 39 55N 80 44W
Mounembé, *Congo* **114 C2** 3 20 S 12 32 E
Moung, *Cambodia* **86 F4** 12 46N 103 27 E
Moungoudi, *Congo* **114 C2** 2 45 S 11 46 E
Mount Airy, *U.S.A.* **149 G5** 36 31N 80 37W
Mount Albert, *Canada* **150 B5** 44 8N 79 19W
Mount Amherst, *Australia* **124 C4** 18 24 S 126 58 E
Mount Angel, *U.S.A.* **158 D2** 45 4N 122 48W
Mount Augustus, *Australia* **124 D2** 24 20 S 116 56 E
Mount Ayr, *U.S.A.* **156 D2** 40 43N 94 14W
Mount Barker, *S. Austral., Australia* **128 C3** 35 5 S 138 52 E
Mount Barker, *W. Austral., Australia* **125 F2** 34 38 S 117 40 E
Mount Beauty, *Australia* **129 D7** 36 47 S 147 10 E
Mount Carmel, *U.S.A.* **157 F9** 38 25N 87 46W
Mount Carroll, *U.S.A.* **156 B7** 42 6N 89 59W
Mount Clemens, *U.S.A.* **140 D3** 42 35N 82 53W
Mount Coolon, *Australia* **126 C4** 21 25 S 147 25 E
Mount Darwin, *Zimbabwe* **119 F3** 16 47 S 31 38 E
Mount Desert I., *U.S.A.* **141 D6** 44 21N 68 20W
Mount Dora, *U.S.A.* **149 L5** 28 48N 81 38W
Mount Douglas, *Australia* **126 C4** 21 35 S 146 50 E
Mount Eba, *Australia* **127 E2** 30 11 S 135 40 E
Mount Eden, *U.S.A.* **157 F11** 38 3N 85 9W
Mount Edgecumbe, *U.S.A.* **142 B1** 57 3N 135 21W
Mount Elizabeth, *Australia* **124 C4** 16 0 S 125 50 E
Mount Fletcher, *S. Africa* **117 E4** 30 40 S 28 30 E
Mount Forest, *Canada* **140 D3** 43 59N 80 43W
Mount Gambier, *Australia* **128 D4** 37 50 S 140 46 E
Mount Garnet, *Australia* **126 B4** 17 37 S 145 6 E
Mount Hagen, *Papua N. G.* **132 C3** 5 52 S 144 16 E
Mount Hope, *N.S.W., Australia* **129 B6** 32 51 S 145 51 E
Mount Hope, *S. Austral., Australia* **127 E2** 34 7 S 135 23 E
Mount Hope, *U.S.A.* **148 G5** 37 54N 81 10W
Mount Horeb, *U.S.A.* **156 B7** 43 1N 89 44W
Mount Howitt, *Australia* **127 D3** 26 31 S 142 16 E
Mount Isa, *Australia* **126 C2** 20 42 S 139 26 E
Mount Keith, *Australia* **125 E3** 27 15 S 120 30 E
Mount Laguna, *U.S.A.* **161 N10** 32 52N 116 25W
Mount Larcom, *Australia* **126 C5** 23 48 S 150 59 E
Mount Lofty Ra., *Australia* **128 C3** 34 35 S 139 5 E
Mount Magnet, *Australia* **125 E2** 28 2 S 117 47 E
Mount Manara, *Australia* **128 B5** 32 29 S 143 58 E
Mount Margaret, *Australia* **127 D3** 26 54 S 143 21 E
Mount Maunganui, *N.Z.* **130 D5** 37 40 S 176 14 E
Mount Molloy, *Australia* **126 B4** 16 42 S 145 20 E
Mount Monger, *Australia* **125 F3** 31 0 S 122 0 E
Mount Morgan, *Australia* **126 C5** 23 40 S 150 25 E
Mount Morris, *U.S.A.* **150 D7** 42 44N 77 52W
Mount Mulligan, *Australia* **126 B3** 16 45 S 144 47 E
Mount Narryer, *Australia* **125 E2** 26 30 S 115 55 E
Mount Olive, *U.S.A.* **156 E7** 39 4N 89 44W
Mount Olivet, *U.S.A.* **157 F12** 38 32N 84 2W
Mount Orab, *U.S.A.* **157 E13** 39 2N 83 55W
Mount Oxide Mine, *Australia* **126 B2** 19 30 S 139 29 E
Mount Pearl, *Canada* **141 C9** 47 31N 52 47W
Mount Perry, *Australia* **127 D5** 25 13 S 151 42 E
Mount Phillips, *Australia* **124 D2** 24 25 S 116 15 E
Mount Pleasant, *Iowa, U.S.A.* **156 D5** 40 58N 91 33W
Mount Pleasant, *Mich., U.S.A.* **148 D3** 43 36N 84 46W
Mount Pleasant, *Pa., U.S.A.* **150 F5** 40 9N 79 33W
Mount Pleasant, *S.C., U.S.A.* **152 C10** 32 47N 79 52W
Mount Pleasant, *Tenn., U.S.A.* **149 H2** 35 32N 87 12W
Mount Pleasant, *Tex., U.S.A.* **155 J7** 33 9N 94 58W
Mount Pleasant, *Utah, U.S.A.* **158 G8** 39 33N 111 27W
Mount Pocono, *U.S.A.* **151 E9** 41 7N 75 22W
Mount Pulaski, *U.S.A.* **156 D7** 40 1N 89 17W
Mount Rainier National Park, *U.S.A.* **160 D5** 46 55N 121 50W
Mount Revelstoke Nat. Park, *Canada* **142 C5** 51 5N 118 30W
Mount Robson Prov. Park, *Canada* **142 C5** 53 0N 119 0W
Mount Roskill, *N.Z.* **130 C3** 36 55 S 174 45 E
Mount Sandiman, *Australia* **125 D2** 24 25 S 115 30 E
Mount Shasta, *U.S.A.* **158 F2** 41 19N 122 19W
Mount Signal, *U.S.A.* **161 N11** 32 39N 115 37W
Mount Somers, *N.Z.* **131 D6** 43 45 S 171 27 E
Mount Sterling, *Ill., U.S.A.* **156 E6** 39 59N 90 45W
Mount Sterling, *Ky., U.S.A.* **157 F13** 38 4N 83 56W
Mount Sterling, *Ohio, U.S.A.* **157 E13** 39 43N 83 16W
Mount Surprise, *Australia* **126 B3** 18 10 S 144 17 E
Mount Union, *U.S.A.* **150 F7** 40 23N 77 53W
Mount Vernon, *Australia* **124 D2** 24 9 S 118 2 E
Mount Vernon, *Ga., U.S.A.* **152 C7** 32 11N 82 36W
Mount Vernon, *Ind., U.S.A.* **154 F10** 38 17N 88 57W
Mount Vernon, *Ind., U.S.A.* **157 F8** 37 56N 87 54W
Mount Vernon, *Iowa, U.S.A.* **156 C5** 41 55N 91 23W
Mount Vernon, *N.Y., U.S.A.* **151 F11** 40 55N 73 50W
Mount Vernon, *Ohio, U.S.A.* **150 F2** 40 23N 82 29W
Mount Vernon, *Wash., U.S.A.* **160 B4** 48 25N 122 20W
Mount Victor, *Australia* **128 B3** 32 11 S 139 44 E
Mount Washington, *U.S.A.* **157 F11** 38 3N 85 33W
Mount Wellington, *N.Z.* **130 C3** 36 55 S 174 52 E
Mount Zion, *U.S.A.* **157 E8** 39 46N 88 53W
Mountain □, *Phil.* **80 C3** 17 20N 121 10 E
Mountain Ash, *U.K.* **21 F4** 51 40N 3 23W
Mountain Center, *U.S.A.* **161 M10** 33 42N 116 44W
Mountain City, *Nev., U.S.A.* **158 F6** 41 50N 115 58W
Mountain City, *Tenn., U.S.A.* **149 G5** 36 29N 81 48W
Mountain Grove, *U.S.A.* **155 G8** 37 8N 92 16W
Mountain Home, *Ark., U.S.A.* **155 G8** 36 20N 92 23W
Mountain Home, *Idaho, U.S.A.* **158 E6** 43 8N 115 41W
Mountain Iron, *U.S.A.* **154 B8** 47 32N 92 37W
Mountain Park, *Canada* **142 C5** 52 50N 117 15W
Mountain Pass, *U.S.A.* **161 K11** 35 29N 115 35W
Mountain View, *Ark., U.S.A.* **155 H8** 35 52N 92 7W
Mountain View, *Calif., U.S.A.* **160 H4** 37 23N 122 5W
Mountain View, *Hawaii, U.S.A.* **145 D6** 19 33N 155 7W
Mountainair, *U.S.A.* **159 J10** 34 31N 106 15W
Mountmellick, *Ireland* **23 C4** 53 7N 7 20W
Mountrath, *Ireland* **23 D4** 53 0N 7 28W
Moura, *Australia* **126 C4** 24 35 S 149 58 E
Moura, *Brazil* **169 D5** 1 32 S 61 38W
Moura, *Portugal* **43 G3** 38 7N 7 30W
Mourão, *Portugal* **43 G3** 38 22N 7 22W
Mourdi, Dépression du, *Chad* **109 E4** 18 10N 23 0 E
Mourdiah, *Mali* **112 C3** 14 35N 7 25W
Mourenx-Ville-Nouvelle, *France* **28 E3** 43 22N 0 38W
Mouri, *Ghana* **113 D4** 5 6N 1 14W
Mourilyan, *Australia* **126 B4** 17 35 S 146 3 E
Mourmelon-le-Grand, *France* **27 C11** 49 8N 4 22 E
Mourne →, *U.K.* **23 B4** 54 52N 7 26W
Mourne Mts., *U.K.* **23 B5** 54 10N 6 0W
Mourniaí, *Greece* **38 D6** 35 29N 24 1 E
Mournies = Mourniaí, *Greece* **38 D6** 35 29N 24 1 E
Mouscron, *Belgium* **24 D3** 50 45N 3 12 E
Moussoro, *Chad* **109 F3** 13 41N 16 35 E
Mouthe, *France* **27 F13** 46 44N 6 12 E
Moutier, *Switz.* **32 B4** 47 16N 7 21 E
Moûtiers, *France* **29 C10** 45 29N 6 32 E
Moutohara, *N.Z.* **130 E6** 38 27 S 177 32 E
Moutong, *Indonesia* **82 A2** 0 28N 121 13 E
Mouy, *France* **27 C9** 49 18N 2 20 E
Mouzáki, *Greece* **48 B3** 39 25N 21 37 E
Mouzon, *France* **27 C12** 49 36N 5 3 E
Movas, *Mexico* **162 B3** 28 10N 109 25W
Moville, *Ireland* **23 A4** 55 11N 7 3W
Moweaqua, *U.S.A.* **156 E7** 39 38N 89 1W
Moxico □, *Angola* **115 E4** 12 0 S 20 30 E
Moxotó →, *Brazil* **170 C4** 9 19 S 38 14W
Moy →, *Ireland* **23 B2** 54 8N 9 8W
Moyale, *Kenya* **107 G4** 3 30N 39 0 E
Moyamba, *S. Leone* **112 D2** 8 4N 12 30W
Moyen Atlas, *Morocco* **110 B4** 33 0N 5 0W
Moyo, *Indonesia* **82 C1** 8 10 S 117 40 E
Moyobamba, *Peru* **172 B2** 6 0 S 77 0W
Moyyero →, *Russia* **65 C11** 68 44N 103 42 E
Moyynty, *Kazakstan* **64 E8** 47 10N 73 18 E
Mozambique = Moçambique, *Mozam.* **119 F5** 15 3 S 40 42 E
Mozambique ■, *Africa* **119 F4** 19 0 S 35 0 E
Mozambique Chan., *Africa* **117 B7** 17 30 S 42 30 E
Mozdok, *Russia* **61 J7** 43 45N 44 48 E
Mozdūrān, *Iran* **97 B9** 36 9N 60 35 E
Mozhaysk, *Russia* **58 E9** 55 30N 36 2 E
Mozhga, *Russia* **60 B11** 56 26N 52 15 E
Mozhnābād, *Iran* **97 C9** 34 7N 60 6 E
Mozirje, *Slovenia* **45 B11** 46 22N 14 58 E
Mozyr = Mazyr, *Belarus* **59 F5** 51 59N 29 15 E
Mpanda, *Tanzania* **118 D3** 6 23 S 31 1 E
Mpanda □, *Tanzania* **118 D3** 6 23 S 31 40 E
Mpésoba, *Mali* **112 C3** 12 31N 5 39W
Mpika, *Zambia* **119 E3** 11 51 S 31 25 E
Mpulungu, *Zambia* **119 D3** 8 51 S 31 5 E
Mpumalanga, *S. Africa* **117 D5** 29 50 S 30 33 E
Mpumalanga □, *S. Africa* **117 B5** 26 0 S 30 0 E
Mpwapwa, *Tanzania* **118 D4** 6 23 S 36 30 E
Mpwapwa □, *Tanzania* **118 D4** 6 30 S 36 20 E
Mqinvartsveri = Kazbek, *Russia* **61 J7** 42 42N 44 30 E
Mrągowo, *Poland* **54 E8** 53 52N 21 18 E
Mramor, *Serbia, Yug.* **50 C5** 43 20N 21 45 E
Mrimina, *Morocco* **110 C3** 29 50N 7 9W
Mrkonjić Grad, *Bos.-H.* **52 F2** 44 26N 17 4 E
Mrkopalj, *Croatia* **45 C11** 45 21N 14 52 E
Mrocza, *Poland* **55 E4** 53 16N 17 35 E
Msab, Oued en →, *Algeria* **111 B6** 32 15N 5 0 E
Msaken, *Tunisia* **108 A2** 35 49N 10 33 E
Msambansovu, *Zimbabwe* **119 F3** 15 50 S 30 3 E
M'sila, *Algeria* **111 A5** 35 46N 4 30 E
Msoro, *Zambia* **119 E3** 13 35 S 31 50 E
Msta →, *Russia* **58 C6** 58 25N 31 20 E
Mstislavl = Mstsislaw, *Belarus* **58 E6** 54 0N 31 50 E
Mstsislaw, *Belarus* **58 E6** 54 0N 31 50 E
Mszana Dolna, *Poland* **55 J7** 49 41N 20 5 E
Mszczonów, *Poland* **55 G7** 51 58N 20 33 E
Mtama, *Tanzania* **119 E4** 10 17 S 39 21 E
Mtilikwe →, *Zimbabwe* **119 G3** 21 9 S 31 30 E
Mtsensk, *Russia* **58 F9** 53 17N 36 36 E
Mtskheta, *Georgia* **61 K7** 41 52N 44 45 E
Mtubatuba, *S. Africa* **117 D5** 28 30 S 32 8 E
Mtwara-Mikindani, *Tanzania* **119 E5** 10 20 S 40 20 E
Mu →, *Burma* **90 E5** 21 56N 95 38 E
Mu Gia, Deo, *Vietnam* **86 D5** 17 40N 105 47 E
Mu Us Shamo, *China* **74 E5** 39 0N 109 0 E
Muacandalo, *Angola* **115 E3** 10 2 S 19 40 E
Muaná, *Brazil* **170 B2** 1 25 S 49 15W
Muanda, *Dem. Rep. of the Congo* **115 D2** 6 0 S 12 20 E
Muang Chiang Rai, *Thailand* **86 C2** 19 52N 99 50 E
Muang Khong, *Laos* **86 E5** 14 7N 105 51 E
Muang Lamphun, *Thailand* **86 C2** 18 40N 99 2 E
Muang Pak Beng, *Laos* **86 C3** 19 54N 101 8 E
Muar, *Malaysia* **87 L4** 2 3N 102 34 E
Muarabungo, *Indonesia* **84 C2** 1 28 S 102 52 E
Muaraenim, *Indonesia* **84 C2** 3 40 S 103 50 E
Muarajuloi, *Indonesia* **85 C4** 0 12 S 114 3 E
Muarakaman, *Indonesia* **85 C5** 0 2 S 116 45 E
Muaratebo, *Indonesia* **84 C2** 1 30 S 102 26 E
Muaratembesi, *Indonesia* **84 C2** 1 42 S 103 8 E
Muaratewe, *Indonesia* **85 C4** 0 58 S 114 52 E
Mubarakpur, *India* **93 F10** 26 6N 83 18 E
Mubarraz = Al Mubarraz, *Si. Arabia* **97 E6** 25 30N 49 40 E
Mubende, *Uganda* **118 B3** 0 33N 31 22 E
Mubi, *Nigeria* **113 C7** 10 18N 13 16 E
Mubur, P., *Indonesia* **87 L6** 3 20N 106 12 E
Mucajaí →, *Brazil* **169 C5** 2 25N 60 52W
Mucajaí, Serra do, *Brazil* **169 C5** 2 23N 61 10W
Mucari, *Angola* **115 D3** 9 30 S 16 54 E
Muchachos, Roque de los, *Canary Is.* **39 F2** 28 44N 17 52W
Mücheln, *Germany* **30 D7** 51 17N 11 47 E
Muchinga Mts., *Zambia* **119 E3** 11 30 S 31 30 E
Muchkapskiy, *Russia* **60 E6** 51 52N 42 28 E
Muck, *U.K.* **22 E2** 56 50N 6 15W
Muckadilla, *Australia* **127 D4** 26 35 S 148 23 E
Muckalee Cr. →, *U.S.A.* **152 D5** 31 38N 84 9W
Muco →, *Colombia* **168 C3** 4 15N 70 21W
Mucoma, *Angola* **115 F2** 15 18 S 13 39 E
Muconda, *Angola* **115 E4** 10 31 S 21 15 E
Mucuim →, *Brazil* **173 B5** 6 33 S 64 18W
Mucur, *Turkey* **100 C6** 39 3N 34 22 E
Mucura, *Brazil* **169 D5** 2 31 S 62 43W
Mucuri, *Brazil* **171 E4** 18 0 S 39 36W
Mucurici, *Brazil* **171 E3** 18 6 S 40 31W
Mucusso, *Angola* **115 F4** 18 1 S 21 25 E
Muda, *Canary Is.* **39 F6** 28 34N 13 57W
Mudan Jiang →, *China* **75 A15** 46 20N 129 30 E
Mudanjiang, *China* **75 B15** 44 38N 129 30 E
Mudanya, *Turkey* **51 F12** 40 25N 28 50 E
Muddy Cr. →, *U.S.A.* **159 H8** 38 24N 110 42W
Mudgee, *Australia* **129 B8** 32 32 S 149 31 E
Mudjatik →, *Canada* **143 B7** 56 1N 107 36W
Mudon, *Burma* **90 G6** 16 15N 97 44 E
Mudugh, *Somali Rep.* **120 C3** 7 0N 47 30 E
Mudurnu, *Turkey* **100 B4** 40 27N 31 12 E
Muecate, *Mozam.* **119 E4** 14 55 S 39 40 E
Mueda, *Mozam.* **119 E4** 11 36 S 39 28 E
Mueller Ra., *Australia* **124 C4** 18 18 S 126 46 E
Muende, *Mozam.* **119 E3** 14 28 S 33 0 E
Muerto, Mar, *Mexico* **163 D6** 16 10N 94 10W
Mufindi □, *Tanzania* **119 D4** 8 30 S 35 20 E
Mufu Shan, *China* **77 C10** 29 20N 114 30 E
Mufulira, *Zambia* **119 E2** 12 32 S 28 15 E
Mufumbiro Range, *Africa* **118 C2** 1 25 S 29 30 E
Mugardos, *Spain* **42 B2** 43 27N 8 15W
Muge →, *Portugal* **43 F2** 39 8N 8 44W
Múggia, *Italy* **45 C10** 45 36N 13 46 E
Mughayrā', *Si. Arabia* **96 D3** 29 17N 37 41 E
Mugi, *Japan* **70 D6** 33 40N 134 25 E
Mugia = Muxía, *Spain* **42 B1** 43 3N 9 10W
Mugila, Mts., *Dem. Rep. of the Congo* **118 D2** 7 0 S 28 50 E
Muğla, *Turkey* **57 G4** 37 15N 28 22 E
Muğla □, *Turkey* **49 D10** 37 15N 28 0 E
Mŭglizh, *Bulgaria* **51 D9** 42 37N 25 32 E
Mugu, *Nepal* **93 E10** 29 45N 82 30 E
Muhammad, Râs, *Egypt* **106 B3** 27 44N 34 16 E
Muhammad Qol, *Sudan* **106 C4** 20 53N 37 9 E
Muhammadabad, *India* **93 F10** 26 4N 83 25 E
Muḩayriqah, *Si. Arabia* **98 B4** 23 59N 45 4 E
Muhesi →, *Tanzania* **118 D4** 7 0 S 35 20 E
Muheza □, *Tanzania* **118 D4** 5 0 S 39 0 E
Mühlacker, *Germany* **31 G4** 48 57N 8 51 E
Mühldorf, *Germany* **31 G8** 48 14N 12 32 E
Mühlhausen, *Germany* **30 D6** 51 12N 10 27 E
Mühlig Hofmann fjell, *Antarctica* **7 D3** 72 30 S 5 0 E
Mühlviertel, *Austria* **34 C7** 48 30N 14 10 E
Muhos, *Finland* **14 D22** 64 47N 25 59 E
Muhu, *Estonia* **15 G20** 58 36N 23 11 E
Muhutwe, *Tanzania* **118 C3** 1 35 S 31 45 E
Muikamachi, *Japan* **69 F9** 37 15N 138 50 E
Muine Bheag, *Ireland* **23 D5** 52 42N 6 58W
Muir, L., *Australia* **125 F2** 34 30 S 116 40 E
Mukacheve, *Ukraine* **59 H2** 48 27N 22 45 E
Mukachevo = Mukacheve, *Ukraine* **59 H2** 48 27N 22 45 E
Mukah, *Malaysia* **85 B4** 2 55N 112 5 E
Mukawwa, Geziret, *Egypt* **106 C4** 23 55N 35 53 E
Mukdahan, *Thailand* **86 D5** 16 32N 104 43 E
Mukden = Shenyang, *China* **75 D12** 41 48N 123 27 E
Mukhtolovo, *Russia* **60 C6** 55 29N 43 15 E
Mukhtuya = Lensk, *Russia* **65 C12** 60 48N 114 55 E
Mukinbudin, *Australia* **125 F2** 30 55 S 118 5 E
Mukishi, *Dem. Rep. of the Congo* **115 D4** 8 30 S 24 44 E
Mukomuko, *Indonesia* **84 C2** 2 30 S 101 10 E
Mukomwenze, *Dem. Rep. of the Congo* **118 D2** 6 49 S 27 15 E
Mukry, *Turkmenistan* **63 E2** 37 54N 65 12 E
Muktsar, *India* **92 D6** 30 30N 74 30 E
Mukur, *Afghan.* **92 C2** 32 50N 67 42 E
Mukutawa →, *Canada* **143 C9** 53 10N 97 24W
Mukwela, *Zambia* **119 F2** 17 0 S 26 40 E
Mukwonago, *U.S.A.* **157 B8** 42 52N 88 20W
Mula, *Spain* **41 G3** 38 3N 1 33W
Mula →, *India* **94 E2** 18 34N 74 21 E
Mulanay, *Phil.* **80 E4** 13 31N 122 24 E
Mulange, *Dem. Rep. of the Congo* **118 C2** 3 40 S 27 10 E
Mulanje, *Malawi* **119 F4** 16 2 S 35 33 E
Mulberry, *U.S.A.* **153 H8** 27 54N 81 59W
Mulberry Grove, *U.S.A.* **156 F7** 38 56N 89 16W
Mulchatna →, *U.S.A.* **144 G8** 59 40N 157 7W
Mulchén, *Chile* **174 D1** 37 45 S 72 20W
Mulde →, *Germany* **30 D8** 51 53N 12 15 E
Muldraugh, *U.S.A.* **157 G11** 37 56N 85 59W
Mule Creek, *U.S.A.* **154 D2** 43 19N 104 8W
Muleba, *Tanzania* **118 C3** 1 50 S 31 37 E
Muleba □, *Tanzania* **118 C3** 2 0 S 31 30 E
Mulegns, *Switz.* **33 C9** 46 32N 9 38 E
Muleshoe, *U.S.A.* **155 H3** 34 13N 102 43W
Mulga Valley, *Australia* **128 A4** 31 8 S 141 3 E
Mulgathing, *Australia* **127 E1** 30 15 S 134 8 E
Mulgrave, *Canada* **141 C7** 45 38N 61 31W
Mulgrave I., *Papua N. G.* **132 F2** 10 5 S 142 10 E
Mulhacén, *Spain* **43 H7** 37 4N 3 20W
Mülheim, *Germany* **30 D2** 51 25N 6 54 E
Mulhouse, *France* **27 E14** 47 40N 7 20 E
Muli, *China* **76 D3** 27 52N 101 8 E
Mulifanua, *W. Samoa* **133 W24** 13 50 S 171 59W
Muling, *China* **75 B16** 44 35N 130 10 E
Mull, *U.K.* **22 E3** 56 25N 5 56W
Mull, Sound of, *U.K.* **22 E3** 56 30N 5 50W
Mullaittivu, *Sri Lanka* **95 K5** 9 15N 80 49 E
Mullen, *U.S.A.* **154 D4** 42 3N 101 1W
Mullengudgery, *Australia* **129 A7** 31 43 S 147 23 E
Mullens, *U.S.A.* **148 G5** 37 35N 81 23W
Muller, Pegunungan, *Indonesia* **85 B4** 0 30N 113 30 E
Mullet Pen., *Ireland* **23 B1** 54 13N 10 2W
Mullewa, *Australia* **125 E2** 28 29 S 115 30 E
Müllheim, *Germany* **31 H3** 47 47N 7 36 E
Mulligan →, *Australia* **126 D2** 25 0 S 139 0 E
Mullin, *U.S.A.* **155 K5** 31 33N 98 40W
Mullingar, *Ireland* **23 C4** 53 31N 7 21W
Mullins, *U.S.A.* **149 H6** 34 12N 79 15W
Mullsjö, *Sweden* **17 G7** 57 56N 13 55 E
Mullumbimby, *Australia* **127 D5** 28 30 S 153 30 E
Mulobezi, *Zambia* **119 F2** 16 45 S 25 7 E
Mulroy B., *Ireland* **23 A4** 55 15N 7 46W
Mulshi L., *India* **94 E1** 18 30N 73 48 E
Multai, *India* **94 D4** 21 50N 78 21 E
Multan, *Pakistan* **91 C3** 30 15N 71 36 E
Mulu, Gunong, *Malaysia* **85 B4** 4 3N 114 56 E
Mulumbe, Mts., *Dem. Rep. of the Congo* **119 D2** 8 40 S 27 30 E
Mulungushi Dam, *Zambia* **119 E2** 14 48 S 28 48 E
Mulvane, *U.S.A.* **155 G6** 37 29N 97 15W
Mulwad, *Sudan* **106 D3** 18 45N 30 39 E
Mulwala, *Australia* **129 C7** 35 59 S 146 0 E
Mumbai, *India* **94 E1** 18 55N 72 50 E
Mumbondo, *Angola* **115 E2** 10 9 S 14 15 E
Mumbwa, *Zambia* **119 F2** 15 0 S 27 0 E
Mumeng, *Papua N. G.* **132 D4** 7 1 S 146 37 E
Mumra, *Russia* **61 H8** 45 45N 47 41 E
Mun →, *Thailand* **86 E5** 15 19N 105 30 E
Muna, *Indonesia* **82 C2** 5 0 S 122 30 E
Munamagi, *Estonia* **15 H22** 57 43N 27 4 E
Münchberg, *Germany* **31 E7** 50 11N 11 47 E
Müncheberg, *Germany* **30 C10** 52 30N 14 9 E
München, *Germany* **31 G7** 48 8N 11 34 E
Munchen-Gladbach = Mönchengladbach, *Germany* **30 D2** 51 11N 6 27 E
Muncho Lake, *Canada* **142 B3** 59 0N 125 50W
Munchŏn, *N. Korea* **75 E14** 39 14N 127 19 E

Ndali 255

Nahîya, W. →, Egypt 106 J7 28 55N 31 0 E
Nahlin, Canada 142 B2 58 55N 131 38W
Nahuel Huapi, L., Argentina 176 B2 41 0 S 71 32W
Nahunta, U.S.A. 152 D8 31 12N 81 59W
Naicá, Mexico 162 B3 27 53N 105 31W
Naicam, Canada 143 C8 52 30N 104 30W
Naila, Germany 31 E7 50 19N 11 42 E
Nain, Canada 141 A7 56 34N 61 40W
Nā'īn, Iran 97 C7 32 54N 53 0 E
Naini Tal, India 93 E8 29 30N 79 30 E
Naintré, France 26 F7 46 46N 0 29 E
Naipu, Romania 53 F10 44 12N 25 47 E
Nairn, U.K. 22 D5 57 35N 3 53W
Nairobi, Kenya 118 C4 1 17 S 36 48 E
Naissaar, Estonia 15 G21 59 34N 24 29 E
Naivasha, Kenya 118 C4 0 40 S 36 30 E
Naivasha, L., Kenya 118 C4 0 48 S 36 20 E
Najac, France 28 D5 44 14N 1 58 E
Najafābād, Iran 97 C6 32 40N 51 15 E
Nájera, Spain 40 C2 42 26N 2 48W
Najerilla →, Spain 40 C2 42 32N 2 48W
Najibabad, India 92 E8 29 40N 78 20 E
Najin, N. Korea 75 C16 42 12N 130 15 E
Najmah, Si. Arabia 97 E6 26 42N 50 6 E
Naju, S. Korea 75 G14 35 3N 126 43 E
Naka →, Japan 71 A12 36 20N 140 36 E
Nakadōri-Shima, Japan 69 H4 32 57N 129 4 E
Nakalagba,
Dem. Rep. of the Congo 118 B2 2 50N 27 58 E
Nakama, Japan 70 D2 33 56N 130 43 E
Nakaminato, Japan 71 A12 36 21N 140 36 E
Nakamura, Japan 70 E4 32 59N 132 56 E
Nakanai Mts., Papua N. G. 132 C6 5 40 S 151 0 E
Nakano, Japan 71 A10 36 45N 138 22 E
Nakano-Shima, Japan 69 K4 29 51N 129 52 E
Nakanojō, Japan 71 A10 36 35N 138 51 E
Nakashibetsu, Japan 68 C12 43 33N 144 59 E
Nakatsu, Japan 70 D3 33 34N 131 15 E
Nakatsugawa, Japan 71 B9 35 29N 137 30 E
Nakfa, Eritrea 107 D4 16 40N 38 32 E
Nakhichevan = Naxçıvan,
Azerbaijan 101 C11 39 12N 45 15 E
Nakhichevan Republic □ =
Naxçıvan □, Azerbaijan 101 C11 39 25N 45 26 E
Nakhl, Egypt 103 F2 29 55N 33 43 E
Nakhl-e Taqī, Iran 97 E7 27 28N 52 36 E
Nakhodka, Russia 68 C6 42 53N 132 54 E
Nakhon Nayok, Thailand 86 E3 14 12N 101 13 E
Nakhon Pathom, Thailand 86 F3 13 49N 100 3 E
Nakhon Phanom, Thailand 86 D5 17 23N 104 43 E
Nakhon Ratchasima,
Thailand 86 E4 14 59N 102 12 E
Nakhon Sawan, Thailand 86 E3 15 35N 100 10 E
Nakhon Si Thammarat,
Thailand 87 H3 8 29N 100 0 E
Nakhon Thai, Thailand 86 D3 17 5N 100 44 E
Nakina, B.C., Canada 142 B2 59 12N 132 52W
Nakina, Ont., Canada 140 B2 50 10N 86 40W
Nakło nad Notecią, Poland 55 E4 53 9N 17 38 E
Nakodar, India 92 D6 31 8N 75 31 E
Nakskov, Denmark 17 K5 54 50N 11 8 E
Naktong →, S. Korea 75 G15 35 7N 128 57 E
Nakuru, Kenya 118 C4 0 15 S 36 4 E
Nakuru □, Kenya 118 C4 0 15 S 35 5 E
Nakuru, L., Kenya 118 C4 0 23 S 36 5 E
Nakusp, Canada 142 C5 50 20N 117 45W
Nal →, Pakistan 91 D2 25 20N 65 30 E
Nalchik, Russia 61 J6 43 30N 43 33 E
Nałęczów, Poland 55 G9 51 17N 22 9 E
Nalerigu, Ghana 113 C4 10 35N 0 25W
Nalgonda, India 94 F4 17 6N 79 15 E
Nalhati, India 93 G12 24 17N 87 52 E
Nallamalai Hills, India 95 G4 15 30N 78 50 E
Nallıhan, Turkey 100 B4 40 11N 31 20 E
Nalón →, Spain 42 B4 43 32N 6 4W
Nālūt, Libya 108 B2 31 54N 11 0 E
Nam Can, Vietnam 87 H5 8 46N 104 59 E
Nam Co, China 72 C4 30 30N 90 45 E
Nam Dinh, Vietnam 86 B6 20 25N 106 5 E
Nam Du, Hon, Vietnam 87 H5 9 41N 104 21 E
Nam Ngum Dam, Laos 86 C4 18 35N 102 34 E
Nam-Phan = Cochin China,
Vietnam 87 G6 10 30N 106 0 E
Nam Phong, Thailand 86 D4 16 42N 102 52 E
Nam Tha, Laos 86 B3 20 58N 101 30 E
Nam Tok, Thailand 86 E2 14 21N 99 4 E
Namachire, Angola 115 E4 11 26 S 22 43 E
Namacunde, Angola 115 F3 17 18 S 15 50 E
Namacurra, Mozam. 117 B6 17 30 S 36 50 E
Namak, Daryācheh-ye, Iran 97 C7 34 30N 52 0 E
Namak, Kavir-e, Iran 97 C8 34 30N 57 30 E
Namakkal, India 95 J4 11 13N 78 13 E
Namaland, Namibia 116 C2 26 0 S 17 0 E
Namangan, Uzbekistan 63 C5 41 0N 71 40 E
Namapa, Mozam. 119 E4 13 43 S 39 50 E
Namaqualand, S. Africa 116 E2 30 0 S 17 25 E
Namasagali, Uganda 118 B3 1 2N 33 0 E
Namatanai, Papua N. G. 132 B7 3 40 S 152 29 E
Namber, Indonesia 83 B4 1 2 S 134 49 E
Nambour, Australia 127 D5 26 32 S 152 58 E
Nambouwalu, Fiji 133 A2 17 0 S 178 45 E
Nambucca Heads, Australia 129 A10 30 37 S 153 0 E
Namcha Barwa, China 72 D4 29 40N 95 10 E
Namche Bazar, Nepal 93 F12 27 51N 86 47 E
Namchonjŏm, N. Korea 75 E14 38 15N 126 26 E
Namecunda, Mozam. 119 E4 14 54 S 37 37 E
Nameh, Indonesia 85 B5 2 34N 116 21 E
Nameponda, Mozam. 119 F4 15 50 S 39 50 E
Namerikawa, Japan 71 A9 36 46N 137 20 E
Náměšť nad Oslavou,
Czech Rep. 35 B9 49 12N 16 10 E
Námestovo, Slovak Rep. 35 B12 49 24N 19 25 E
Nametil, Mozam. 119 F4 15 40 S 39 21 E
Namew L., Canada 143 C8 54 14N 101 56W
Namhsan, Burma 90 D6 22 48N 97 2 E
Namib Desert =
Namibwoestyn, Namibia 116 C2 22 30 S 15 0 E
Namibe, Angola 115 F2 15 7 S 12 11 E
Namibe □, Angola 115 F2 16 35 S 12 30 E
Namibia ■, Africa 116 C2 22 0 S 18 9 E
Namibwoestyn, Namibia 116 C2 22 30 S 15 0 E
Namīn, Iran 101 C13 38 25N 48 30 E
Namkhan, Burma 90 D6 23 50N 97 41 E
Namlea, Indonesia 82 B3 3 18 S 127 5 E
Namoi →, Australia 129 A8 30 12 S 149 30 E
Namous, O. en →, Algeria 111 B4 31 0N 0 15W
Nampa, U.S.A. 158 E5 43 34N 116 34W
Nampo, N. Korea 75 E13 38 52N 125 10 E
Nampō-Shotō, Japan 69 J10 32 0N 140 0 E
Nampula, Mozam. 119 F4 15 6 S 39 15 E
Namrole, Indonesia 82 B3 3 46 S 126 46 E
Namsen →, Norway 14 D14 64 28N 11 37 E
Namsos, Norway 14 D14 64 29N 11 30 E
Namtsy, Russia 65 C13 62 43N 129 37 E
Namtu, Burma 90 D6 23 5N 97 28 E
Namtumbo, Tanzania 119 E4 10 30 S 36 4 E
Namu, Canada 142 C3 51 52N 127 50W
Namuac, Phil. 80 B3 18 37N 121 10 E
Namur, Belgium 24 D4 50 27N 4 52 E
Namur □, Belgium 24 D4 50 17N 5 0 E
Namutoni, Namibia 116 B2 18 49 S 16 55 E
Namwala, Zambia 119 F2 15 44 S 26 30 E
Namwŏn, S. Korea 75 G14 35 23N 127 23 E
Namysłów, Poland 55 G4 51 6N 17 42 E
Nan, Thailand 86 C3 18 48N 100 46 E
Nan →, Thailand 86 E3 15 42N 100 9 E
Nan Xian, China 77 C9 29 20N 112 22 E
Nana, Romania 53 F11 44 17N 26 34 E
Nanaimo, Canada 142 D4 49 10N 124 0W
Nanakuli, U.S.A. 145 K13 21 24N 158 9W
Nanam, N. Korea 75 D15 41 44N 129 40 E
Nanan, China 77 E12 24 59N 118 21 E
Nanango, Australia 127 D5 26 40 S 152 0 E
Nan'ao, China 77 F11 23 28N 117 5 E
Nanao, Japan 69 F8 37 0N 137 0 E
Nanbu, China 76 B6 31 18N 106 3 E
Nanchang, China 77 C10 28 42N 115 55 E
Nancheng, China 77 D11 27 33N 116 35 E
Nanching = Nanjing, China 77 A12 32 2N 118 47 E
Nanchong, China 76 B6 30 43N 106 2 E
Nanchuan, China 76 C6 29 9N 107 6 E
Nancy, France 27 D13 48 42N 6 12 E
Nanda Devi, India 93 D8 30 23N 79 59 E
Nandan, China 76 E6 24 58N 107 29 E
Nandan, Japan 70 C6 34 10N 134 42 E
Nanded, India 94 E3 19 10N 77 20 E
Nandewar Ra., Australia 127 E5 30 15 S 150 35 E
Nandi □, Kenya 118 B4 0 15N 35 0 E
Nandikotkur, India 95 G4 15 52N 78 18 E
Nandura, India 94 D3 20 52N 76 25 E
Nandurbar, India 94 D2 21 20N 74 15 E
Nandyal, India 95 G4 15 30N 78 30 E
Nanfeng, Guangdong, China 77 F8 23 45N 111 47 E
Nanfeng, Jiangxi, China 77 D11 27 12N 116 28 E
Nanga, Australia 125 E1 26 7 S 113 45 E
Nanga-Eboko, Cameroon 113 E7 4 41N 12 22 E
Nanga Parbat, Pakistan 93 B6 35 10N 74 35 E
Nangade, Mozam. 119 E4 11 5 S 39 36 E
Nangapinoh, Indonesia 85 C4 0 20 S 111 44 E
Nangarhár □, Afghan. 91 B3 34 20N 70 0 E
Nangatayap, Indonesia 85 C4 1 32 S 110 34 E
Nangeya Mts., Uganda 118 B3 3 30N 33 30 E
Nangis, France 27 D10 48 33N 3 1 E
Nangong, China 74 F8 37 23N 115 22 E
Nangwarry, Australia 128 D4 37 33 S 140 48 E
Nanhua, China 76 E3 25 13N 101 21 E
Nanhuang, China 75 F11 36 58N 121 48 E
Nanhui, China 77 B13 31 5N 121 44 E
Nanjangud, India 95 H3 12 6N 76 43 E
Nanjeko, Zambia 119 F1 15 31 S 23 30 E
Nanji Shan, China 77 D13 27 27N 121 4 E
Nanjian, China 76 E3 25 2N 100 25 E
Nanjiang, China 76 A6 32 28N 106 51 E
Nanjing, Fujian, China 77 E11 24 25N 117 20 E
Nanjing, Jiangsu, China 77 A12 32 2N 118 47 E
Nanjirinji, Tanzania 119 D4 9 41 S 39 5 E
Nankana Sahib, Pakistan 92 D5 31 27N 73 38 E
Nankang, China 77 E10 25 40N 114 45 E
Nanking = Nanjing, China 77 A12 32 2N 118 47 E
Nankoku, Japan 70 D5 33 39N 133 44 E
Nanling, China 77 B12 30 55N 118 20 E
Nanning, China 76 F7 22 48N 108 20 E
Nannup, Australia 125 F2 33 59 S 115 48 E
Nanortalik, Greenland 10 E6 60 10N 45 17W
Nanpan Jiang →, China 76 E6 25 10N 106 5 E
Nanpara, India 93 F9 27 52N 81 33 E
Nanpi, China 74 E9 38 2N 116 45 E
Nanping, Fujian, China 77 D12 26 38N 118 10 E
Nanping, Henan, China 77 C9 29 55N 112 3 E
Nanri Dao, China 77 E12 25 15N 119 25 E
Nanripe, Mozam. 119 E4 13 52 S 38 52 E
Nansei-Shotō = Ryūkyū-
rettō, Japan 69 M3 26 0N 126 0 E
Nansen Land, Greenland 10 A6 83 0N 43 0W
Nansen Sd., Canada 6 A3 81 0N 91 0W
Nansio, Tanzania 118 C3 2 3 S 33 4 E
Nant, France 28 D7 44 1N 3 18 E
Nanterre, France 27 D9 48 53N 2 13 E
Nantes, France 26 E5 47 12N 1 33W
Nantiat, France 28 B5 46 1N 1 11 E
Nanticoke, U.S.A. 151 E8 41 12N 76 0W
Nanton, Canada 142 C6 50 21N 113 46W
Nantong, China 77 A13 32 1N 120 52 E
Nantua, France 27 F12 46 10N 5 35 E
Nantucket I., U.S.A. 136 E12 41 16N 70 5W
Nantwich, U.K. 20 D5 53 4N 2 31W
Nanuku Passage, Fiji 133 A3 16 45 S 179 15W
Nanuque, Brazil 171 E3 17 50 S 40 21W
Nanutarra, Australia 124 D2 22 32 S 115 30 E
Nanxiong, China 77 E10 25 6N 114 15 E
Nanyang, China 74 H7 33 11N 112 30 E
Nanyi Hu, China 77 B12 31 5N 119 0 E
Nan'yō, Japan 70 C3 34 3N 131 49 E
Nanyuan, China 74 E9 39 44N 116 22 E
Nanyuki, Kenya 118 B4 0 2N 37 4 E
Nanzhang, China 77 B8 31 45N 111 50 E
Nao, C. de la, Spain 41 G5 38 44N 0 14 E
Naococane L., Canada 141 B5 52 50N 70 45W
Naoetsu, Japan 69 F9 37 12N 138 10 E
Naogaon, Bangla. 90 C2 24 52N 88 52 E
Náousa, Imathía, Greece 50 F6 40 42N 22 9 E
Náousa, Kikládhes, Greece 49 D7 37 7N 25 14 E
Naozhou Dao, China 77 G8 20 55N 110 20 E
Napa, U.S.A. 160 G4 38 18N 122 17W
Napa →, U.S.A. 160 G4 38 10N 122 19W
Napakiak, U.S.A. 144 F7 60 42N 161 57W
Napamute, U.S.A. 144 F8 61 33N 158 42W
Napanee, Canada 140 D4 44 15N 77 0W
Napanoch, U.S.A. 151 E10 41 44N 74 22W
Napaskiak, U.S.A. 144 F7 60 43N 161 55W
Nape, Laos 86 C5 18 18N 105 6 E
Nape Pass = Keo Neua,
Deo, Vietnam 86 C5 18 23N 105 10 E
Naperville, U.S.A. 157 C8 41 46N 88 9W
Napf, Switz. 32 B5 47 1N 7 56 E
Napier, N.Z. 130 F5 39 30 S 176 56 E
Napier Broome B., Australia 124 B4 14 2 S 126 37 E
Napier Downs, Australia 124 C3 17 11 S 124 36 E
Napier Pen., Australia 126 A2 12 4 S 135 43 E
Naples = Nápoli, Italy 47 B7 40 50N 14 15 E
Naples, U.S.A. 149 M5 26 8N 81 48W
Naples Park, U.S.A. 153 J8 26 17N 81 46W
Napo, China 76 F5 23 22N 105 50 E
Napo □, Ecuador 168 D2 0 30 S 77 0W
Napo →, Peru 168 D3 3 20 S 72 40W
Napoleon, N. Dak., U.S.A. 154 B5 46 30N 99 46W
Napoleon, Ohio, U.S.A. 157 C12 41 23N 84 8W
Nápoli, Italy 47 B7 40 50N 14 15 E
Nápoli, G. di, Italy 47 B7 40 43N 14 10 E
Napopo,
Dem. Rep. of the Congo 118 B2 4 15N 28 0 E
Nappa Merrie, Australia 127 D3 27 36 S 141 7 E
Nappanee, U.S.A. 157 C11 41 27N 86 0W
Naqâda, Egypt 106 B3 25 53N 32 42 E
Naqadeh, Iran 101 D11 36 57N 45 23 E
Naqqāsh, Iran 97 C6 35 40N 49 6 E
Nara, Japan 71 C7 34 40N 135 49 E
Nara, Mali 112 B3 15 10N 7 20W
Nara □, Japan 71 C8 34 30N 136 0 E
Nara Canal, Pakistan 92 G3 24 30N 69 20 E
Nara Visa, U.S.A. 155 H3 35 37N 103 6W
Naracoorte, Australia 128 D4 36 58 S 140 45 E
Naradhan, Australia 129 B7 33 34 S 146 17 E
Narasapur, India 95 F5 16 26N 81 40 E
Narasaropet, India 95 F5 16 14N 80 4 E
Narathiwat, Thailand 87 J3 6 30N 101 48 E
Narayanganj, Bangla. 90 D3 23 40N 90 33 E
Narayanpet, India 94 F3 16 45N 77 30 E
Narbonne, France 28 E7 43 11N 3 0 E
Narbuvollen, Norway 18 B8 62 21N 11 27 E
Narcea →, Spain 42 B4 43 33N 6 44W
Nardīn, Iran 97 B7 37 3N 55 59 E
Nardò, Italy 47 B11 40 11N 18 2 E
Narembeen, Australia 125 F2 32 7 S 118 24 E
Nares Str., Arctic 10 B3 80 0N 70 0W
Naretha, Australia 125 F3 31 0 S 124 45 E
Narew →, Poland 55 F7 52 26N 20 41 E
Nari →, Pakistan 92 F2 28 0N 67 40 E
Narindra, Helodranon' i,
Madag. 117 A8 14 55 S 47 30 E
Narino □, Colombia 168 C2 1 30N 78 0W
Narita, Japan 71 B12 35 47N 140 19 E
Närke, Sweden 16 E8 59 10N 15 0 E
Narmada →, India 92 J5 21 38N 72 36 E
Narman, Turkey 101 B9 40 26N 41 57 E
Narmland, Sweden 15 F15 60 0N 13 30 E
Narnaul, India 92 E7 28 5N 76 11 E
Narni, Italy 45 F9 42 31N 12 30 E
Naro, Ghana 112 C4 10 22N 2 27W
Naro Fominsk, Russia 58 E9 55 23N 36 43 E
Narodnaya, Russia 56 A10 65 5N 59 58 E
Narok, Kenya 118 C4 1 55 S 35 52 E
Narok □, Kenya 118 C4 1 20 S 36 30 E
Narón, Spain 42 B2 43 32N 8 9W
Narooma, Australia 129 D9 36 14 S 150 4 E
Narowal, Pakistan 91 B4 32 6N 74 52 E
Narrabri, Australia 127 E4 30 19 S 149 46 E
Narran →, Australia 127 D4 28 37 S 148 12 E
Narrandera, Australia 129 C7 34 42 S 146 31 E
Narraway →, Canada 142 B5 55 44N 119 55W
Narrogin, Australia 125 F2 32 58 S 117 14 E
Narromine, Australia 129 B8 32 12 S 148 12 E
Narsampet, India 94 F4 17 57N 79 58 E
Narsaq, Greenland 10 E6 60 57N 46 4W
Narsimhapur, India 93 H8 22 54N 79 14 E
Nartes, L. e, Albania 50 F3 40 32N 19 25 E
Nartkala, Russia 61 J6 43 33N 43 51 E
Naruto, Kantō, Japan 70 C6 34 11N 134 37 E
Narutō, Shikoku, Japan 71 B12 35 36N 140 25 E
Naruto-Kaikyō, Japan 70 C6 34 14N 134 39 E
Narva, Estonia 58 C5 59 23N 28 12 E
Narva →, Russia 15 G22 59 27N 28 2 E
Narvacan, Phil. 80 C3 17 25N 120 28 E
Narvik, Norway 14 B17 68 28N 17 26 E
Narvskoye Vdkhr., Russia 58 C5 59 18N 28 14 E
Narwana, India 92 E7 29 39N 76 6 E
Naryan-Mar, Russia 56 A9 67 42N 53 12 E
Naryilco, Australia 127 D3 28 37 S 141 53 E
Narym, Russia 64 D9 59 0N 81 30 E
Naryn, Kyrgyzstan 63 C7 41 26N 75 58 E
Naryn →, Uzbekistan 63 C5 40 52N 71 36 E
Nasa, Norway 14 C16 66 29N 15 23 E
Nasarawa, Nigeria 113 D6 8 32N 7 41 E
Năsăud, Romania 53 C9 47 19N 24 29 E
Nasawa, Vanuatu 133 E6 15 0 S 168 0 E
Naseby, N.Z. 131 F5 45 1 S 170 10 E
Naselle, U.S.A. 160 D3 46 22N 123 49W
Naser, Buheirat en, Egypt 106 C3 23 0N 32 30 E
Nashua, Iowa, U.S.A. 156 B4 42 57N 92 32W
Nashua, Mont., U.S.A. 158 B10 48 8N 106 22W
Nashua, N.H., U.S.A. 151 D13 42 45N 71 28W
Nashville, Ark., U.S.A. 155 J8 33 57N 93 51W
Nashville, Ga., U.S.A. 152 D6 31 12N 83 15W
Nashville, Ill., U.S.A. 156 F7 38 21N 89 23W
Nashville, Ind., U.S.A. 157 E10 39 12N 86 15W
Nashville, Mich., U.S.A. 157 B11 42 36N 85 5W
Nashville, Tenn., U.S.A. 149 G2 36 10N 86 47W
Našice, Croatia 52 E3 45 32N 18 4 E
Nasielsk, Poland 55 F7 52 35N 20 50 E
Nasik, India 94 E1 19 58N 73 50 E
Nasipit, Phil. 81 G5 8 57N 125 19 E
Nasirabad, India 92 F6 26 15N 74 45 E
Naskaupi →, Canada 141 B7 53 47N 60 51W
Naso, Italy 47 D7 38 7N 14 47 E
Naso Pt., Phil. 81 F3 10 25N 121 57 E
Naṣrīān-e Pā'īn, Iran 96 C5 32 52N 46 52 E
Nass →, Canada 142 C3 55 0N 129 40W
Nassau, Bahamas 164 A4 25 5N 77 20W
Nassau, U.S.A. 151 D11 42 31N 73 37W
Nassau, B., Chile 176 E3 55 20 S 68 0W
Nasser, L. = Naser, Buheirat
en, Egypt 106 C3 23 0N 32 30 E
Nasser City = Kôm Ombo,
Egypt 106 C3 24 25N 32 52 E
Nassian, Ivory C. 112 D4 8 28N 3 28W
Nässjö, Sweden 17 G8 57 39N 14 42 E
Nasugbu, Phil. 80 D3 14 5N 120 38 E
Näsum, Sweden 17 H8 56 10N 14 29 E
Näsviken, Sweden 16 C10 61 46N 16 52 E
Nat Kyizin, Burma 86 E1 14 57N 97 59 E
Nata, Botswana 116 C4 20 12 S 26 12 E
Natagaima, Colombia 168 C2 3 37N 75 6W
Natal, Brazil 170 C4 5 47 S 35 13W
Natal, Canada 142 D6 49 43N 114 51W
Natal, Indonesia 84 B1 0 35N 99 7 E
Natalinci, Serbia, Yug. 52 F5 44 15N 20 49 E
Naṭanz, Iran 97 C6 33 30N 51 55 E
Natashquan, Canada 141 B7 50 14N 61 46W
Natashquan →, Canada 141 B7 50 7N 61 50W
Natchez, U.S.A. 155 K9 31 34N 91 24W
Natchitoches, U.S.A. 155 K8 31 46N 93 5W
Naters, Switz. 32 D5 46 19N 7 58 E
Natewa B., Fiji 133 A2 16 35 S 179 40 E
Nathalia, Australia 129 D6 36 1 S 145 13 E
Nathdwara, India 92 G5 24 55N 73 50 E
Nati, Pta., Spain 39 A10 40 3N 3 50 E
Natimuk, Australia 128 D5 36 42 S 142 0 E
Nation →, Canada 142 B4 55 30N 123 32W
National City, U.S.A. 161 N9 32 41N 117 6W
Natitingou, Benin 113 C5 10 20N 1 26 E
Natividad, I., Mexico 162 B1 27 50N 115 10W
Natogyi, Burma 90 E5 21 25N 95 39 E
Natoma, U.S.A. 154 F5 39 11N 99 2W
Natonin, Phil. 80 C3 17 6N 121 18 E
Natron, L., Tanzania 118 C4 2 20 S 36 0 E
Natrona Heights, U.S.A. 150 F5 40 37N 79 44W
Natrûn, W. el →, Egypt 106 H7 30 25N 30 13 E
Nättraby, Sweden 17 H9 56 13N 15 31 E
Natuna Besar, Kepulauan,
Indonesia 87 L7 4 0N 108 15 E
Natuna Is. = Natuna Besar,
Kepulauan, Indonesia 87 L7 4 0N 108 15 E
Natuna Selatan, Kepulauan,
Indonesia 85 B3 2 45N 109 0 E
Natural Bridge, U.S.A. 151 B9 44 5N 75 30W
Naturaliste, C., Australia 126 G4 40 50 S 148 15 E
Natya, Australia 128 C5 34 57 S 143 13 E
Nau, Tajikistan 63 C4 40 9N 69 22 E
Nau Qala, Afghan. 92 B3 34 5N 68 5 E
Naubinway, U.S.A. 140 C2 46 6N 85 27W
Naucelle, France 28 D6 44 13N 2 20 E
Nauders, Austria 34 E3 46 54N 10 30 E
Nauen, Germany 30 C8 52 36N 12 52 E
Naugatuck, U.S.A. 151 E11 41 30N 73 3W
Naujan, Phil. 80 E3 13 20N 121 18 E
Naujoji Akmenė, Lithuania 54 B9 56 19N 22 54 E
Naumburg, Germany 30 D7 51 9N 11 47 E
Nā'ūr at Tunayb, Jordan 103 D4 31 48N 35 57 E
Nauru ■, Pac. Oc. 134 H8 1 0 S 166 0 E
Naushahra = Nowshera,
Pakistan 91 B4 34 0N 72 0 E
Nausori, Fiji 133 B2 18 2 S 178 32 E
Naustdal, Norway 18 C2 61 31N 5 43 E
Nauta, Peru 168 D3 4 31 S 73 35W
Nauteyri, Iceland 11 B4 65 55N 22 21W
Nautla, Mexico 163 C5 20 20N 96 50W
Nauvoo, U.S.A. 156 D5 40 33N 91 23W
Nava, Mexico 162 B4 28 25N 100 46W
Nava, Spain 42 B5 43 21N 5 31W
Nava del Rey, Spain 42 D5 41 22N 5 6W
Navadwip, India 93 H13 23 34N 88 20 E
Navahermosa, Spain 43 F6 39 41N 4 28W
Navahrudak, Belarus 58 F3 53 40N 25 50 E
Navajo Reservoir, U.S.A. 159 H10 36 48N 107 36W
Naval, Phil. 81 F5 11 34N 124 23 E
Navalcarnero, Spain 42 E6 40 17N 4 5W
Navalmoral de la Mata,
Spain 42 F5 39 52N 5 33W
Navalvillar de Pela, Spain 43 F5 39 9N 5 24W
Navan = An Uaimh, Ireland 23 C5 53 39N 6 41W
Navapolatsk, Belarus 58 E5 55 32N 28 37 E
Navarino, I., Chile 176 E3 55 0 S 67 40W
Navarra □, Spain 40 C3 42 40N 1 40W
Navarre, Fla., U.S.A. 153 E3 30 24N 86 52W
Navarre, Ohio, U.S.A. 150 F3 40 43N 81 31W
Navarro →, U.S.A. 160 F3 39 11N 123 45W
Navas de San Juan, Spain 43 G7 38 30N 3 19W
Navasota, U.S.A. 155 K6 30 23N 96 5W
Navassa, W. Indies 165 C5 18 30N 75 0W
Nävekvarn, Sweden 17 F10 58 38N 16 49 E
Naver →, U.K. 22 C4 58 32N 4 14W
Navia, Spain 42 B4 43 35N 6 42W
Navia →, Spain 42 B4 43 15N 6 50W
Navia de Suarna, Spain 42 C3 42 58N 7 3W
Navidad, Chile 174 C1 33 57 S 71 50W
Navlya, Russia 59 F8 52 53N 34 30 E
Năvodari, Romania 53 F13 44 19N 28 36 E
Navoi = Nawoiy, Uzbekistan 63 C2 40 9N 65 22 E
Navojoa, Mexico 162 B3 27 0N 109 30W
Navolato, Mexico 162 C3 24 47N 107 42W
Návpaktos, Greece 48 C3 38 24N 21 50 E
Návplion, Greece 48 D4 37 33N 22 50 E
Navrongo, Ghana 113 C4 10 51N 1 3W
Navsari, India 94 D1 20 57N 72 59 E
Nawa Kot, Pakistan 92 E4 28 21N 71 24 E
Nawabganj, Bangla. 90 C2 24 35N 88 14 E
Nawabganj, Ut. P., India 93 F9 26 56N 81 14 E
Nawabganj, Ut. P., India 93 E8 28 32N 79 40 E
Nawabshah, Pakistan 91 D3 26 15N 68 25 E
Nawada, India 93 G11 24 50N 85 33 E
Nāwah, Afghan. 91 B2 32 19N 67 53 E
Nawakot, Nepal 93 F11 27 55N 85 10 E
Nawalgarh, India 92 F6 27 50N 75 15 E
Nawanshahr, India 93 C6 32 33N 74 48 E
Nawapara, India 94 D6 20 46N 82 33 E
Nawāsīf, Harrat, Si. Arabia 98 B3 21 20N 42 10 E
Nawi, Sudan 106 D3 18 32N 30 50 E
Nawng Hpa, Burma 90 D7 22 30N 98 30 E
Nawoiy, Uzbekistan 63 C2 40 9N 65 22 E
Naws, Ra's, Oman 99 C6 17 15N 55 16 E
Naxçıvan, Azerbaijan 101 C11 39 12N 45 15 E
Naxçıvan □, Azerbaijan 101 C11 39 25N 45 26 E
Náxos, Greece 49 D7 37 8N 25 25 E
Nay, France 28 E3 43 10N 0 18W
Nāy Band, Iran 97 E7 27 20N 52 40 E
Naya →, Colombia 168 C2 3 13N 77 22W
Nayakhan, Russia 65 C16 61 56N 159 0 E
Nayarit □, Mexico 162 C4 22 0N 105 0W
Nayé, Senegal 112 C2 14 28N 12 12W
Nayong, China 76 D5 26 50N 105 20 E
Nayoro, Japan 68 B11 44 21N 142 28 E
Nayyāl, W. →, Si. Arabia 96 D3 28 35N 39 4 E
Nazaré, Bahia, Brazil 171 D4 13 2 S 39 0W
Nazaré, Pará, Brazil 173 B7 6 25 S 52 29W
Nazaré, Tocantins, Brazil 170 C2 6 23 S 47 40W
Nazaré, Portugal 43 F1 39 36N 9 4W
Nazareth = Nazerat, Israel 103 C4 32 42N 35 17 E
Nazas, Mexico 162 B4 25 10N 104 6W
Nazas →, Mexico 162 B4 25 35N 103 25W
Nazca, Peru 172 C2 14 53 S 74 54W
Naze, The, U.K. 21 F9 51 53N 1 18 E
Nazerat, Israel 103 C4 32 42N 35 17 E
Nāzīk, Iran 101 C11 39 1N 45 4 E
Nazilli, Turkey 49 D10 37 55N 28 15 E
Nazir Hat, Bangla. 90 D3 22 35N 91 49 E
Nazko, Canada 142 C4 53 1N 123 37W
Nazko →, Canada 142 C4 53 7N 123 34W
Nazret, Ethiopia 107 F4 8 32N 39 22 E
Nazwá, Oman 99 B7 22 56N 57 32 E
Nchanga, Zambia 119 E2 12 30 S 27 49 E
Ncheu, Malawi 119 E3 14 50 S 34 47 E
Ndala, Tanzania 118 C3 4 45 S 33 15 E
Ndalatando, Angola 115 D2 9 12 S 14 48 E
Ndali, Benin 113 D5 9 50N 2 46 E

Ohau, L. 259

Noyes I., *U.S.A.* **142 B2** 55 30N 133 40W
Noyon, *France* .... **27 C9** 49 34N 2 59 E
Noyon, *Mongolia* .... **74 C2** 43 2N 102 4 E
Nozay, *France* **26 E5** 47 34N 1 38W
Nsa, O. en →, *Algeria* .... **111 B6** 32 28N 5 24 E
Nsa, Plateau de, *Congo* .... **114 C3** 2 26 S 15 20 E
Nsah, *Congo* .... **114 C3** 2 22 S 15 19 E
Nsanje, *Malawi* .... **119 F4** 16 55 S 35 12 E
Nsawam, *Ghana* **113 D4** 5 50N 0 24W
Nsomba, *Zambia* .... **119 E2** 10 45 S 29 51 E
Nsopzup, *Burma* .... **90 C6** 25 51N 97 30 E
Nsukka, *Nigeria* .... **113 D6** 6 51N 7 29 E
Ntoum, *Gabon* .... **114 B1** 0 22N 9 47 E
Nu Jiang →, *China* ...... **76 C1** 29 58N 97 25 E
Nu Shan, *China* .... **76 E2** 26 0N 99 20 E
Nuba Mts. = Nubah, Jibalan, *Sudan* .... **107 E3** 12 0N 31 0 E
Nubah, Jibalan, *Sudan* ..... **107 E3** 12 0N 31 0 E
Nubia, *Africa* .... **104 D7** 21 0N 32 0 E
Nubian Desert = Nûbîya, Es Sahrâ en, *Sudan* .... **106 C3** 21 30N 33 30 E
Nûbîya, Es Sahrâ en, *Sudan* **106 C3** 21 30N 33 30 E
Ñuble □, *Chile* .... **174 D1** 37 0 S 72 0W
Nubledo, *Spain* **42 B5** 43 31N 5 52W
Nuboai, *Indonesia* .... **83 B5** 2 10 S 136 30 E
Nubra →, *India* .... **93 B7** 34 35N 77 35 E
Nucet, *Romania* .... **52 D7** 46 28N 22 35 E
Nueces →, *U.S.A.* **155 M6** 27 51N 97 30W
Nueltin L., *Canada* **143 A9** 60 30N 99 30W
Nueva, I., *Chile* .... **176 E3** 55 13 S 66 30W
Nueva Antioquia, *Colombia* **168 B4** 6 5N 69 26W
Nueva Asunción □, *Paraguay* .... **174 A3** 21 0 S 61 0W
Nueva Carteya, *Spain* **43 H6** 37 35N 4 28W
Nueva Ecija □, *Phil.* ...... **80 D3** 15 35N 121 0 E
Nueva Esparta □, *Venezuela* **169 A5** 11 0N 64 0W
Nueva Gerona, *Cuba* **164 B3** 21 53N 82 49W
Nueva Imperial, *Chile* ..... **176 A2** 38 45 S 72 58W
Nueva Palmira, *Uruguay* .... **174 C4** 33 52 S 58 20W
Nueva Rosita, *Mexico* **162 B4** 28 0N 101 11W
Nueva San Salvador, *El Salv.* **164 D2** 13 40N 89 18W
Nueva Tabarca, *Spain* **41 G4** 38 17N 0 30W
Nueva Vizcaya □, *Phil.* .... **80 C3** 16 20N 121 20 E
Nuéve de Julio, *Argentina* .. **174 D3** 35 30 S 61 0W
Nuevitas, *Cuba* **164 B4** 21 30N 77 20W
Nuevo, G., *Argentina* ...... **176 B4** 43 0 S 64 30W
Nuevo Guerrero, *Mexico* **163 B5** 26 34N 99 15W
Nuevo Laredo, *Mexico* **163 B5** 27 30N 99 30W
Nuevo León □, *Mexico* **162 C5** 25 0N 100 0W
Nuevo Mundo, Cerro, *Bolivia* .... **172 E4** 21 55 S 66 53W
Nuevo Rocafuerte, *Ecuador* **168 D2** 0 55 S 75 27W
Nugget Pt., *N.Z.* .... **131 G4** 46 27 S 169 50 E
Nugrus, Gebel, *Egypt* ...... **106 C3** 24 47N 34 35 E
Nuhaka, *N.Z.* .... **130 F6** 39 3 S 177 45 E
Nuits-St-Georges, *France* ... **27 E11** 47 10N 4 56 E
Nûk, *Greenland* **10 E5** 64 10N 51 46W
Nukey Bluff, *Australia* ..... **127 E2** 32 26 S 135 29 E
Nukheila, *Sudan* .... **106 D2** 19 1N 26 21 E
Nukhuyb, *Iraq* .... **101 F10** 32 4N 42 3 E
Nuku'alofa, *Tonga* .... **133 Q14** 21 10 S 174 0W
Nukus, *Uzbekistan* .... **64 E6** 42 27N 59 41 E
Nules, *Spain* **40 F4** 39 51N 0 9W
Nullagine →, *Australia* .... **124 D3** 21 20 S 120 20 E
Nullarbor, *Australia* .... **125 F5** 31 28 S 130 55 E
Nullarbor Plain, *Australia* .. **125 F4** 31 10 S 129 0 E
Numalla, L., *Australia* ..... **127 D3** 28 43 S 144 20 E
Numan, *Nigeria* .... **113 D7** 9 29N 12 3 E
Numata, *Japan* .... **71 A11** 36 45N 139 4 E
Numatinna →, *Sudan* ...... **107 F2** 7 38N 27 20 E
Numazu, *Japan* .... **71 B10** 35 7N 138 51 E
Numbulwar, *Australia* ..... **126 A2** 14 15 S 135 45 E
Numedal, *Norway* .... **18 D6** 60 6N 9 6 E
Numfoor, *Indonesia* .... **83 B4** 1 0 S 134 50 E
Numurkah, *Australia* ...... **129 D6** 36 5 S 145 26 E
Nunaksaluk I., *Canada* **141 A7** 55 49N 60 20W
Nunavut □, *Canada* **139 B11** 66 0N 85 0W
Nungo, *Mozam.* .... **119 E4** 13 23 S 37 43 E
Nungwe, *Tanzania* .... **118 C3** 2 48 S 32 2 E
Nunivak I., *U.S.A.* **138 C3** 60 10N 166 30W
Nunkun, *India* .... **93 C7** 33 57N 76 2 E
Nùoro, *Italy* .... **46 B2** 40 20N 9 20 E
Núpur, *Iceland* **11 B3** 65 56N 23 36W
Nuqayy, Jabal, *Libya* ...... **108 D3** 23 11N 19 30 E
Nuqūb, *Yemen* .... **98 D4** 14 59N 45 48 E
Nuquí, *Colombia* **168 B2** 5 42N 77 17W
Nūrābād, *Iran* .... **97 E8** 27 47N 57 12 E
Nurata, *Uzbekistan* .... **63 C2** 40 33N 65 41 E
Nuratau, Khrebet, *Uzbekistan* .... **63 C3** 40 40N 66 30 E
Nure →, *Italy* .... **44 C6** 45 3N 9 49 E
Nuremberg = Nürnberg, *Germany* .... **31 F7** 49 27N 11 3 E
Nūrestān, *Afghan.* .... **91 B3** 35 30N 70 45 E
Nuri, *Mexico* **162 B3** 28 2N 109 22W
Nurina, *Australia* .... **125 F4** 30 56 S 126 33 E
Nuriootpa, *Australia* ...... **128 C3** 34 27 S 139 0 E
Nurlat, *Russia* .... **60 C10** 54 29N 50 45 E
Nurmes, *Finland* .... **14 E23** 63 33N 29 10 E
Nürnberg, *Germany* .... **31 F7** 49 27N 11 3 E
Nurra, La, *Italy* .... **46 B1** 40 45N 8 15 E
Nurran, L. = Terewah, L., *Australia* .... **127 D4** 29 52 S 147 35 E
Nurrari Lakes, *Australia* .... **125 E5** 29 1 S 130 5 E
Nurri, *Italy* .... **46 C2** 39 43N 9 14 E
Nürtingen, *Germany* ...... **31 G5** 48 37N 9 19 E
Nurzec →, *Poland* .... **55 F9** 52 37N 22 25 E
Nus, *Italy* .... **44 C4** 45 45N 7 28 E
Nusa Barung, *Indonesia* .... **85 D4** 8 30 S 113 30 E
Nusa Kambangan, *Indonesia* **85 D3** 7 40 S 108 10 E
Nusa Tenggara Barat □, *Indonesia* .... **85 D5** 8 50 S 117 30 E
Nusa Tenggara Timur □, *Indonesia* .... **82 C2** 9 30 S 122 0 E
Nusaybin, *Turkey* .... **101 D9** 37 3N 41 10 E
Nushki, *Pakistan* .... **91 C2** 29 35N 66 0 E
Nutwood Downs, *Australia* . **126 B1** 15 49 S 134 10 E
Nuuk, *Greenland* **10 E5** 64 10N 51 35W
Nuussauq = Kraulshavn, *Greenland* **10 C5** 74 8N 57 3W
Nuwakot, *Nepal* .... **93 E10** 28 10N 83 55 E
Nuwara Eliya, *Sri Lanka* .... **95 L5** 6 58N 80 48 E
Nuweiba', *Egypt* .... **106 B3** 28 59N 34 39 E
Nuweveldberge, *S. Africa* ... **116 E3** 32 10 S 21 45 E
Nuyts, C., *Australia* .... **125 F5** 32 2 S 132 21 E
Nuyts Arch., *Australia* ..... **127 E1** 32 35 S 133 20 E
Nuzvid, *India* .... **94 F5** 16 47N 80 53 E
Nxau-Nxau, *Botswana* ..... **116 B3** 18 57 S 21 4 E
Nyaake, *Liberia* **112 E3** 4 52N 7 37W
Nyack, *U.S.A.* **151 E11** 41 5N 73 55W
Nyah West, *Australia* ...... **128 C5** 35 16 S 143 21 E
Nyahanga, *Tanzania* ...... **118 C3** 2 20 S 33 37 E
Nyahua, *Tanzania* .... **118 D3** 5 25 S 33 23 E
Nyahururu, *Kenya* .... **118 B4** 0 2N 36 27 E
Nyainqentanglha Shan, *China* **72 D4** 30 0N 90 0 E
Nyakanazi, *Tanzania* ...... **118 C3** 3 2 S 31 10 E
Nyakrom, *Ghana* **113 D4** 5 40N 0 50W
Nyâlâ, *Sudan* .... **107 E1** 12 2N 24 58 E
Nyamandhlovu, *Zimbabwe* . **119 F2** 19 55 S 28 16 E
Nyambiti, *Tanzania* .... **118 C3** 2 48 S 33 27 E
Nyamwaga, *Tanzania* ...... **118 C3** 1 27 S 34 33 E
Nyandekwa, *Tanzania* ..... **118 C3** 3 57 S 32 32 E
Nyanding →, *Sudan* ...... **107 F3** 8 40N 32 41 E
Nyandoma, *Russia* .... **58 B11** 61 40N 40 12 E
Nyanga →, *Gabon* .... **114 C2** 2 58 S 10 15 E
Nyangana, *Namibia* .... **116 B3** 18 0 S 20 40 E
Nyanguge, *Tanzania* ...... **118 C3** 2 30 S 33 12 E
Nyankpala, *Ghana* **113 D4** 9 21N 0 58W
Nyanza, *Rwanda* .... **118 C2** 2 20 S 29 42 E
Nyanza □, *Kenya* .... **118 C3** 0 10 S 34 15 E
Nyanza-Lac, *Burundi* ...... **118 C2** 4 21 S 29 36 E
Nyarling →, *Canada* **142 A6** 60 41N 113 23W
Nyasa, L., *Africa* .... **119 E3** 12 30 S 34 30 E
Nyasvizh, *Belarus* .... **59 F4** 53 14N 26 38 E
Nyaunglebin, *Burma* .... **90 G6** 17 52N 96 42 E
Nyazepetrovsk, *Russia* ..... **62 C7** 56 3N 59 36 E
Nyazura, *Zimbabwe* .... **119 F3** 18 40 S 32 16 E
Nyazwidzi →, *Zimbabwe* .. **119 G3** 20 0 S 31 17 E
Nybergsund, *Norway* ...... **18 C9** 61 15N 12 19 E
Nyborg, *Denmark* .... **17 J4** 55 18N 10 47 E
Nybro, *Sweden* .... **17 H9** 56 44N 15 55 E
Nyda, *Russia* .... **64 C8** 66 40N 72 58 E
Nyeboe Land, *Greenland* **10 A5** 82 0N 57 0W
Nyeri, *Kenya* .... **118 C4** 0 23 S 36 56 E
Nyerol, *Sudan* .... **107 F3** 8 41N 32 1 E
Nyhammar, *Sweden* .... **16 D8** 60 17N 14 58 E
Nyiel, *Sudan* .... **107 F3** 6 9N 31 13 E
Nyinahin, *Ghana* **112 D4** 6 43N 2 3W
Nyíradony, *Hungary* ...... **52 C6** 47 41N 21 55 E
Nyírbátor, *Hungary* .... **52 C7** 47 49N 22 9 E
Nyíregyháza, *Hungary* ..... **52 C6** 47 58N 21 47 E
Nykirke, *Norway* .... **18 D7** 60 54N 10 19 E
Nykøbing, *Storstrøm, Denmark* .... **17 K5** 54 56N 11 52 E
Nykøbing, *Vestsjælland, Denmark* .... **17 J5** 55 55N 11 40 E
Nykøbing, *Viborg, Denmark* **17 H2** 56 48N 8 51 E
Nyköping, *Sweden* .... **17 F11** 58 45N 17 1 E
Nykroppa, *Sweden* .... **16 E8** 59 37N 14 18 E
Nykvarn, *Sweden* .... **16 E11** 59 11N 17 25 E
Nyland, *Sweden* .... **16 A11** 63 1N 17 45 E
Nylstroom, *S. Africa* ...... **117 C4** 24 42 S 28 22 E
Nymagee, *Australia* .... **129 B7** 32 7 S 146 20 E
Nymburk, *Czech Rep.* ...... **34 A8** 50 10N 15 1 E
Nynäshamn, *Sweden* ...... **17 F11** 58 54N 17 57 E
Nyngan, *Australia* .... **127 E4** 31 30 S 147 8 E
Nyoman = Neman →, *Lithuania* .... **15 J20** 55 25N 21 10 E
Nyon, *Switz.* .... **32 D2** 46 23N 6 14 E
Nyong →, *Cameroon* ...... **113 E6** 3 17N 9 54 E
Nyons, *France* .... **29 D9** 44 22N 5 10 E
Nyora, *Australia* .... **129 E6** 38 20 S 145 41 E
Nyou, *Burkina Faso* **113 C4** 12 42N 2 1W
Nýrsko, *Czech Rep.* .... **34 B6** 49 18N 13 9 E
Nysa, *Poland* .... **55 H4** 50 30N 17 22 E
Nysa →, *Europe* .... **30 C10** 52 4N 14 46 E
Nysa Kłodzka →, *Poland* ... **55 H4** 50 49N 17 40 E
Nysäter, *Sweden* .... **16 E6** 59 17N 12 47 E
Nyseter, *Norway* .... **18 B5** 62 2N 8 20 E
Nyssa, *U.S.A.* **158 E5** 43 53N 117 0W
Nysted, *Denmark* .... **17 K5** 54 40N 11 44 E
Nytva, *Russia* .... **62 C5** 57 56N 55 20 E
Nyūgawa, *Japan* .... **70 D5** 33 56N 133 5 E
Nyunzu, *Dem. Rep. of the Congo* . **118 D2** 5 57 S 27 58 E
Nyurba, *Russia* .... **65 C12** 63 17N 118 28 E
Nyzhnohirskyy, *Ukraine* .... **59 K8** 45 27N 34 38 E
Nzega, *Tanzania* .... **118 C3** 4 10 S 33 12 E
Nzega □, *Tanzania* .... **118 C3** 4 10 S 33 10 E
N'zérékoré, *Guinea* **112 D3** 7 49N 8 48W
Nzeto, *Angola* .... **115 D2** 7 10 S 12 52 E
Nzilo, Chutes de, *Dem. Rep. of the Congo* . **115 E5** 10 18 S 25 27 E
Nzubuka, *Tanzania* .... **118 C3** 4 45 S 32 50 E

O

O Barco, *Spain* **42 C4** 42 23N 6 58W
O Carballiño, *Spain* **42 C2** 42 26N 8 5W
O Corgo, *Spain* **42 C3** 42 56N 7 25W
O Pino, *Spain* **42 C2** 42 56N 8 20W
O Porriño, *Spain* **42 C2** 42 10N 8 37W
Ō-Shima, *Fukuoka, Japan* .. **70 D2** 33 54N 130 25 E
Ō-Shima, *Nagasaki, Japan* .. **70 C1** 34 29N 129 33 E
Ō-Shima, *Shizuoka, Japan* .. **71 C11** 34 44N 139 24 E
Oa, Mull of, *U.K.* **22 F2** 55 35N 6 20W
Oacoma, *U.S.A.* **154 D5** 43 48N 99 24W
Oahe, L., *U.S.A.* **154 C4** 44 27N 100 24W
Oahe Dam, *U.S.A.* **154 C4** 44 27N 100 24W
Oahu, *U.S.A.* **146 H16** 21 28N 157 58W
Oak Creek, *Colo., U.S.A.* ... **158 F10** 40 16N 106 57W
Oak Creek, *Wis., U.S.A.* **157 B9** 42 52N 87 55W
Oak Harbor, *U.S.A.* **160 B4** 48 18N 122 39W
Oak Hill, *Fla., U.S.A.* **153 G9** 28 52N 80 51W
Oak Hill, *W. Va., U.S.A.* ... **148 G5** 37 59N 81 9W
Oak Lawn, *U.S.A.* **157 C9** 41 43N 87 44W
Oak Park, *Ga., U.S.A.* **152 C7** 32 22N 82 19W
Oak Park, *Ill., U.S.A.* **157 C9** 41 53N 87 47W
Oak Ridge, *U.S.A.* **149 G3** 36 1N 84 16W
Oak View, *U.S.A.* **161 L7** 34 24N 119 18W
Oakan-Dake, *Japan* .... **68 C12** 43 27N 144 10 E
Oakbank, *Australia* .... **128 B4** 33 4 S 140 33 E
Oakdale, *Calif., U.S.A.* **160 H6** 37 46N 120 51W
Oakdale, *La., U.S.A.* **155 K8** 30 49N 92 40W
Oakes, *U.S.A.* **154 B5** 46 8N 98 6W
Oakesdale, *U.S.A.* **158 C5** 47 8N 117 15W
Oakey, *Australia* .... **127 D5** 27 25 S 151 43 E
Oakfield, *U.S.A.* **152 D6** 31 47N 83 58W
Oakford, *U.S.A.* **156 D7** 40 6N 89 58W
Oakham, *U.K.* **21 E7** 52 40N 0 43W
Oakhurst, *U.S.A.* **160 H7** 37 19N 119 40W
Oakland, *Calif., U.S.A.* **160 H4** 37 49N 122 16W
Oakland, *Ill., U.S.A.* **157 E8** 39 39N 88 2W
Oakland, *Oreg., U.S.A.* **158 E2** 43 25N 123 18W
Oakland City, *U.S.A.* **157 F9** 38 20N 87 21W
Oakland Park, *U.S.A.* **153 J9** 26 10N 80 8W
Oaklands, *Australia* .... **129 C7** 35 34 S 146 10 E
Oakley, *Idaho, U.S.A.* **158 E7** 42 15N 113 53W
Oakley, *Kans., U.S.A.* **154 F4** 39 8N 100 51W
Oakley Creek, *Australia* ... **129 A8** 31 37 S 149 46 E
Oakover →, *Australia* .... **124 D3** 21 0 S 120 40 E
Oakridge, *U.S.A.* **158 E2** 43 45N 122 28W
Oaktown, *U.S.A.* **157 F9** 38 52N 87 27W
Oakville, *U.S.A.* **160 D3** 46 51N 123 14W
Oakwood, *U.S.A.* **157 C12** 41 6N 84 23W
Oamaru, *N.Z.* .... **131 F5** 45 5 S 170 59 E
Ōamishirasato, *Japan* ..... **71 B12** 35 31N 140 18 E
Oancea, *Romania* .... **53 E12** 45 21N 27 42 E
Oarai, *Japan* .... **71 A12** 36 21N 140 34 E
Oasis, *Calif., U.S.A.* **161 M10** 33 28N 116 6W
Oasis, *Nev., U.S.A.* **160 H9** 37 29N 117 55W
Oates Land, *Antarctica* .... **7 C11** 69 0 S 160 0 E
Oatman, *U.S.A.* **161 K12** 35 1N 114 19W
Oaxaca, *Mexico* **163 D5** 17 2N 96 40W
Oaxaca □, *Mexico* **163 D5** 17 0N 97 0W
Ob →, *Russia* .... **64 C7** 66 45N 69 30 E
Oba, *Canada* **140 C3** 49 4N 84 7W
Obala, *Cameroon* .... **113 E7** 4 9N 11 32 E
Obama, *Fukui, Japan* ..... **71 B7** 35 30N 135 45 E
Obama, *Nagasaki, Japan* ... **70 E2** 32 43N 130 13 E
Oban, *U.K.* **22 E3** 56 25N 5 29W
Obbia, *Somali Rep.* .... **120 C3** 5 25N 48 30 E
Obed, *Canada* **142 C5** 53 30N 117 10W
Ober-Aagau, *Switz.* .... **32 B5** 47 10N 7 45 E
Obera, *Argentina* .... **175 B4** 27 21 S 55 2W
Oberalppass, *Switz.* ...... **33 C7** 46 39N 8 35 E
Oberalpstock, *Switz.* ...... **33 C7** 46 45N 8 47 E
Oberammergau, *Germany* ... **31 H7** 47 36N 11 4 E
Oberasbach, *Germany* ..... **31 F6** 49 25N 10 57 E
Oberbayern □, *Germany* ... **31 G7** 48 5N 11 50 E
Oberdrauburg, *Austria* ..... **34 E5** 46 44N 12 58 E
Oberengadin, *Switz.* ...... **33 C9** 46 35N 9 55 E
Oberentfelden, *Switz.* ..... **32 B6** 47 21N 8 2 E
Oberfranken □, *Germany* .. **31 E7** 50 10N 11 20 E
Oberhausen, *Germany* ..... **30 D2** 51 28N 6 51 E
Oberkirch, *Germany* ...... **31 G4** 48 31N 8 4 E
Oberland, *Switz.* .... **32 C5** 46 35N 7 38 E
Oberlausitz, *Germany* ..... **30 D10** 51 16N 14 18 E
Oberlin, *Kans., U.S.A.* **154 F4** 39 49N 100 32W
Oberlin, *La., U.S.A.* **155 K8** 30 37N 92 46W
Oberlin, *Ohio, U.S.A.* **150 E2** 41 18N 82 13W
Obernai, *France* .... **27 D14** 48 28N 7 30 E
Oberndorf, *Germany* ...... **31 G4** 48 17N 8 34 E
Oberon, *Australia* .... **129 B8** 33 45 S 149 52 E
Oberösterreich □, *Austria* .. **34 C7** 48 10N 14 0 E
Oberpfalz □, *Germany* .... **31 F8** 49 20N 12 10 E
Oberpfälzer Wald, *Germany* **31 F8** 49 30N 12 30 E
Obersiggenthal, *Switz.* .... **33 B6** 47 29N 8 18 E
Oberstdorf, *Germany* ...... **31 H6** 47 24N 10 15 E
Oberting, *Gabon* .... **114 C1** 0 22 S 9 46 E
Oberursel, *Germany* ...... **31 E4** 50 11N 8 35 E
Oberwart, *Austria* .... **35 D9** 47 17N 16 12 E
Oberwil, *Switz.* .... **32 A5** 47 32N 7 33 E
Obi, Kepulauan, *Indonesia* . **82 B3** 1 23 S 127 45 E
Obi Is. = Obi, Kepulauan, *Indonesia* .... **82 B3** 1 23 S 127 45 E
Obiaruku, *Nigeria* .... **113 D6** 5 51N 6 9 E
Óbidos, *Brazil* .... **169 D6** 1 50 S 55 30W
Óbidos, *Portugal* **43 F1** 39 19N 9 10W
Obihiro, *Japan* .... **68 C11** 42 56N 143 12 E
Obilatu, *Indonesia* .... **82 B3** 1 25 S 127 20 E
Obilnoye, *Russia* .... **61 G7** 47 32N 44 30 E
Obing, *Germany* .... **31 G8** 48 0N 12 24 E
Objat, *France* .... **28 C5** 45 16N 1 24 E
Oblong, *U.S.A.* **157 F9** 39 0N 87 55W
Obluchye, *Russia* .... **65 E14** 49 1N 131 4 E
Obninsk, *Russia* .... **58 E9** 55 8N 36 37 E
Obo, *C.A.R.* .... **114 A5** 5 20N 26 32 E
Obo, *Ethiopia* .... **107 G4** 3 46N 38 52 E
Oboa, Mt., *Uganda* ...... **118 B3** 1 45N 34 45 E
Obock, *Djibouti* .... **107 E5** 12 0N 43 20 E
Oborniki, *Poland* .... **55 F3** 52 39N 16 50 E
Oborniki Śląskie, *Poland* .. **55 G3** 51 17N 16 53 E
Obouya, *Congo* .... **114 C3** 0 56 S 15 43 E
Oboyan, *Russia* .... **59 G9** 51 15N 36 21 E
Obozerskaya = Obozerskiy, *Russia* .... **64 C5** 63 34N 40 21 E
Obozerskiy, *Russia* .... **64 C5** 63 34N 40 21 E
Obrenovac, *Serbia, Yug.* ... **50 B4** 44 40N 20 11 E
O'Brien, *U.S.A.* **152 E7** 30 2N 82 57W
Obrovac, *Croatia* .... **45 D12** 44 11N 15 41 E
Obruk, *Turkey* .... **100 C5** 38 7N 33 12 E
Obrzycko, *Poland* .... **55 F3** 52 42N 16 32 E
Observatory Inlet, *Canada* . **142 B3** 55 10N 129 54W
Obshchi Syrt, *Russia* ...... **62 E4** 52 0N 53 0 E
Obskaya Guba, *Russia* ..... **64 C8** 69 0N 73 0 E
Obuasi, *Ghana* **113 D4** 6 17N 1 40W
Obubra, *Nigeria* .... **113 D6** 6 8N 8 20 E
Obwalden □, *Switz.* ...... **32 C6** 46 55N 8 15 E
Obzor, *Bulgaria* .... **51 D11** 42 50N 27 52 E
Ocala, *U.S.A.* **149 L4** 29 11N 82 8W
Ocamo →, *Venezuela* **169 C4** 2 48N 65 14W
Ocampo, *Mexico* **162 B3** 28 9N 108 24W
Ocaña, *Colombia* **168 B3** 8 15N 73 20W
Ocaña, *Spain* **42 F7** 39 55N 3 30W
Ocanomowoc, *U.S.A.* **154 D10** 43 7N 88 30W
Ocate, *U.S.A.* **155 G2** 36 11N 105 3W
Occidental, Cordillera, *Colombia* **168 C2** 5 0N 76 0W
Occidental, Cordillera, *Peru* **172 C3** 14 0 S 74 0W
Ocean City, *N.J., U.S.A.* ... **148 F8** 39 17N 74 35W
Ocean City, *Wash., U.S.A.* . **160 C2** 47 4N 124 10W
Ocean I. = Banaba, *Kiribati* **134 H8** 0 45 S 169 50 E
Ocean Park, *U.S.A.* **160 D2** 46 30N 124 3W
Oceano, *U.S.A.* **161 K6** 35 6N 120 37W
Oceanport, *U.S.A.* **151 F10** 40 19N 74 3W
Oceanside, *U.S.A.* **161 M9** 33 12N 117 23W
Ochagavía, *Spain* **40 C3** 42 55N 1 5W
Ochakiv, *Ukraine* .... **59 J6** 46 37N 31 33 E
Ochamchira, *Georgia* ..... **61 J5** 42 46N 41 32 E
Ocher, *Russia* .... **62 C5** 57 53N 54 42 E
Ochiai, *Japan* .... **70 B5** 35 1N 133 45 E
Ochil Hills, *U.K.* **22 E5** 56 14N 3 40W
Ochlocknee, *U.S.A.* **152 E5** 30 58N 84 3W
Ochlockonee →, *U.S.A.* ... **152 F5** 29 59N 84 26W
Ochopee, *U.S.A.* **153 K8** 25 54N 81 18W
Ochre River, *Canada* **143 C9** 51 4N 99 47W
Ochsenfurt, *Germany* ..... **31 F6** 49 40N 10 4 E
Ochsenhausen, *Germany* ... **31 G5** 48 4N 9 57 E
Ocilla, *U.S.A.* **152 D6** 31 36N 83 15W
Ockelbo, *Sweden* .... **16 D10** 60 54N 16 45 E
Ocmulgee →, *U.S.A.* **152 D7** 31 58N 82 33W
Ocna Mureş, *Romania* ..... **53 D8** 46 23N 23 55 E
Ocna Sibiului, *Romania* .... **53 E9** 45 52N 24 2 E
Ocnele Mari, *Romania* ..... **53 E9** 45 8N 24 18 E
Ocniţa, *Moldova* .... **53 B12** 48 25N 27 30 E
Ocoee, *U.S.A.* **153 G8** 28 34N 81 33W
Ocoña, *Peru* .... **172 D3** 16 26 S 73 8W
Ocoña →, *Peru* .... **172 D3** 16 28 S 73 8W
Oconee →, *U.S.A.* **152 D7** 31 58N 82 33W
Oconee, L., *U.S.A.* **152 B6** 33 28N 83 15W
Oconee National Forest, *U.S.A.* **152 B6** 33 15N 83 45W
Oconomowoc, *U.S.A.* **157 A8** 43 7N 88 30W
Oconto, *U.S.A.* **148 C2** 44 53N 87 52W
Oconto Falls, *U.S.A.* **148 C1** 44 52N 88 9W
Ocosingo, *Mexico* **163 D6** 17 10N 92 15W
Ocotal, *Nic.* **164 D2** 13 41N 86 31W
Ocotlán, *Mexico* **162 C4** 20 21N 102 42W
Ocreza →, *Portugal* **43 F3** 39 32N 7 50W
Öcsa, *Hungary* .... **52 C4** 47 17N 19 15 E
Octave, *U.S.A.* **159 J7** 34 10N 112 43W
Octeville, *France* **26 C5** 49 38N 1 40W
Ocumare del Tuy, *Venezuela* **168 A4** 10 7N 66 46W
Ocuri, *Bolivia* .... **173 D4** 18 45 S 65 50W
Oda, *Ghana* **113 D4** 5 50N 0 51W
Oda, *Ehime, Japan* .... **70 D4** 33 36N 132 53 E
Ōda, *Shimane, Japan* ..... **70 B4** 35 11N 132 30 E
Oda, J., *Sudan* .... **106 C4** 20 21N 36 39 E
Ódáðahraun, *Iceland* **11 B9** 65 5N 17 0W
Ödåkra, *Sweden* .... **17 H6** 56 7N 12 45 E
Odate, *Japan* .... **68 D10** 40 16N 140 34 E
Odawara, *Japan* .... **71 B11** 35 20N 139 6 E
Odda, *Norway* .... **15 F12** 60 3N 6 35 E
Odder, *Denmark* .... **17 J4** 55 58N 10 10 E
Oddi, *Iceland* **11 D6** 63 46N 20 24W
Oddur, *Somali Rep.* .... **120 D2** 4 11N 43 52 E
Odei →, *Canada* **143 B9** 56 6N 96 54W
Odell, *U.S.A.* **157 D8** 41 0N 88 31W
Odemira, *Portugal* **43 H2** 37 35N 8 40W
Ödemiş, *Turkey* .... **49 C9** 38 15N 28 0 E
Odendaalsrus, *S. Africa* .... **116 D4** 27 48 S 26 45 E
Odensbacken, *Sweden* ..... **16 E9** 59 10N 15 32 E
Odense, *Denmark* .... **17 J4** 55 22N 10 23 E
Odenwald, *Germany* ...... **31 F5** 49 35N 9 0 E
Oder →, *Europe* .... **30 B10** 53 33N 14 38 E
Oder-Havel Kanal, *Germany* **30 C10** 52 52N 14 2 E
Oderzo, *Italy* .... **45 C9** 45 47N 12 29 E
Odesa, *Ukraine* .... **59 J6** 46 30N 30 45 E
Ödeshög, *Sweden* .... **17 F8** 58 14N 14 39 E
Odessa = Odesa, *Ukraine* .. **59 J6** 46 30N 30 45 E
Odessa, *Canada* **151 B8** 44 17N 76 43W
Odessa, *Mo., U.S.A.* **156 F3** 39 0N 93 57W
Odessa, *Tex., U.S.A.* **155 K3** 31 52N 102 23W
Odessa, *Wash., U.S.A.* **158 C4** 47 20N 118 41W
Odiakwe, *Botswana* .... **116 C4** 20 12 S 25 17 E
Odiel →, *Spain* **43 H4** 37 10N 6 55W
Odienné, *Ivory C.* **112 D3** 9 30N 7 34W
Odintsovo, *Russia* .... **58 E9** 55 39N 37 15 E
Odiongan, *Phil.* .... **80 E3** 12 24N 121 59 E
Odobeşti, *Romania* .... **53 E12** 45 43N 27 4 E
Odolanów, *Poland* .... **55 G4** 51 34N 17 40 E
O'Donnell, *Phil.* .... **80 D3** 15 21N 120 27 E
O'Donnell, *U.S.A.* **155 J4** 32 58N 101 50W
Odorheiu Secuiesc, *Romania* **53 D10** 46 21N 25 21 E
Odoyevo, *Russia* .... **58 F9** 53 56N 36 42 E
Odra = Oder →, *Europe* . **30 B10** 53 33N 14 38 E
Odra →, *Europe* .... **54 E1** 53 33N 14 38 E
Odra →, *Spain* **42 C6** 42 14N 4 17W
Odum, *U.S.A.* **152 D7** 31 40N 82 2W
Odweina, *Somali Rep.* ..... **120 C3** 9 25N 45 4 E
Odžaci, *Serbia, Yug.* ...... **52 E4** 45 30N 19 17 E
Odžak, *Bos.-H.* .... **52 E3** 45 3N 18 18 E
Odzi, *Zimbabwe* .... **117 B5** 19 0 S 32 20 E
Oebisfelde, *Germany* ...... **30 C6** 52 27N 10 57 E
Oeiras, *Brazil* .... **170 C3** 7 0 S 42 8W
Oeiras, *Portugal* **43 G1** 38 41N 9 18W
Oelrichs, *U.S.A.* **154 D3** 43 11N 103 14W
Oelsnitz, *Germany* .... **31 E8** 50 24N 12 10 E
Oelwein, *U.S.A.* **154 D9** 42 41N 91 55W
Oenpelli, *Australia* .... **124 B5** 12 20 S 133 4 E
Oetz, *Austria* .... **34 D3** 47 13N 10 53 E
Of, *Turkey* .... **101 B9** 40 59N 40 23 E
O'Fallon, *U.S.A.* **156 F6** 38 49N 90 42W
Ofanto →, *Italy* .... **47 A9** 41 22N 16 13 E
Offa, *Nigeria* .... **113 D5** 8 13N 4 42 E
Offaly □, *Ireland* **23 C4** 53 15N 7 30W
Offenbach, *Germany* ...... **31 E4** 50 6N 8 44 E
Offenburg, *Germany* ...... **31 G3** 48 28N 7 56 E
Offida, *Italy* .... **45 F10** 42 56N 13 41 E
Ofidhousa, *Greece* .... **49 E8** 36 33N 26 8 E
Ofotfjorden, *Norway* ...... **14 B17** 68 27N 17 0 E
Ofte, *Norway* .... **18 E5** 59 30N 8 12 E
Ofu, *Amer. Samoa* .... **133 X25** 14 11 S 169 41W
Ōfunato, *Japan* .... **68 E10** 39 4N 141 43 E
Oga, *Japan* .... **68 E9** 39 55N 139 50 E
Oga-Hantō, *Japan* .... **68 E9** 39 58N 139 47 E
Ogaden, *Ethiopia* .... **120 C3** 7 30N 45 30 E
Ogahalla, *Canada* **140 B2** 50 6N 85 51W
Ōgaki, *Japan* .... **71 B8** 35 21N 136 37 E
Ogallala, *U.S.A.* **154 E4** 41 8N 101 43W
Ogan →, *Indonesia* ...... **84 C2** 3 1 S 104 44 E
Ogasawara Gunto, *Pac. Oc.* **134 E6** 27 0N 142 0 E
Ogbomosho, *Nigeria* ...... **113 D5** 8 1N 4 11 E
Ogden, *Iowa, U.S.A.* **156 B3** 42 2N 94 2W
Ogden, *Utah, U.S.A.* **158 F7** 41 13N 111 58W
Ogdensburg, *U.S.A.* **151 B9** 44 42N 75 30W
Ogeechee →, *U.S.A.* **152 B8** 31 50N 81 3W
Ogilby, *U.S.A.* **161 N12** 32 49N 114 50W
Oglesby, *U.S.A.* **156 C7** 41 18N 89 4W
Oglethorpe, *U.S.A.* **152 C5** 32 18N 84 4W
Oglio →, *Italy* .... **44 C7** 45 2N 10 39 E
Ogmore, *Australia* .... **126 C4** 22 37 S 149 35 E
Ognon →, *France* .... **27 E12** 47 16N 5 28 E
Ogoamas, *Indonesia* ...... **82 A2** 0 50N 120 5 E
Ogoja, *Nigeria* .... **113 D6** 6 38N 8 39 E
Ogoki →, *Canada* **140 B2** 51 38N 85 57W
Ogoki L., *Canada* **140 B2** 50 50N 87 10W
Ogoki Res., *Canada* **140 B2** 50 45N 88 15W
Ogooué →, *Gabon* .... **114 C1** 1 0 S 9 0 E
Ōgori, *Japan* .... **70 C3** 34 6N 131 24 E
Ogosta →, *Bulgaria* ...... **50 C7** 43 48N 23 55 E
Ogowe = Ogooué →, *Gabon* .... **114 C1** 1 0 S 9 0 E
Ogr = Sharafa, *Sudan* ..... **107 E2** 11 59N 27 7 E
Ograźden, *Macedonia* ..... **50 E6** 41 30N 22 50 E
Ogre, *Latvia* .... **15 H21** 56 49N 24 36 E
Ogrein, *Sudan* .... **106 D3** 17 55N 34 50 E
Ogulin, *Croatia* .... **45 C12** 45 16N 15 16 E
Ogun □, *Nigeria* .... **113 D5** 7 0N 3 0 E
Oguni, *Japan* .... **70 D3** 33 11N 131 8 E
Ögur, *Iceland* **11 A4** 66 2N 22 44W
Oguta, *Nigeria* .... **113 D6** 5 44N 6 44 E
Ogwashi-Uku, *Nigeria* ..... **113 D6** 6 15N 6 30 E
Ogwe, *Nigeria* .... **113 E6** 5 0N 7 14 E
Ohai, *N.Z.* .... **131 F3** 45 55 S 168 0 E
Ohakune, *N.Z.* .... **130 F4** 39 24 S 175 24 E
Ohanet, *Algeria* .... **111 C6** 28 44N 8 46 E
Ōhara, *Japan* .... **71 B12** 35 15N 140 23 E
Ohata, *Japan* .... **68 D10** 41 24N 141 10 E
Ohatchee, *U.S.A.* **152 B4** 33 47N 86 0W
Ohau, L., *N.Z.* .... **131 E4** 44 15 S 169 53 E

260 Ohaupo

Ohaupo, N.Z. 130 D4 37 56 S 175 20 E
Ohio □, U.S.A. 148 E3 40 15N 82 45W
Ohio →, U.S.A. 148 G1 36 59N 89 8W
Ohio City, U.S.A. 157 D12 40 46N 84 37W
Ohiwa Harbour, N.Z. 130 D6 37 59 S 177 10 E
Ohře →, Czech Rep. 34 A7 50 30N 14 10 E
Ohre →, Germany 30 C7 52 18N 11 46 E
Ohrid, Macedonia 50 E4 41 8N 20 52 E
Ohridsko Jezero, Macedonia 50 E4 41 8N 20 52 E
Ohrigstad, S. Africa 117 C5 24 39 S 30 36 E
Öhringen, Germany 31 F5 49 12N 9 31 E
Ohura, N.Z. 130 E3 38 51 S 174 59 E
Oiapoque →, Brazil 169 C7 4 8N 51 40W
Oikou, China 75 E9 38 35N 117 42 E
Oil City, U.S.A. 150 E5 41 26N 79 42W
Oildale, U.S.A. 161 K7 35 25N 119 1W
Oinousa, Greece 49 C8 38 33N 26 14 E
Oise □, France 27 C9 49 28N 2 30 E
Oise →, France 27 C9 49 0N 2 4 E
Ōita, Japan 70 D3 33 14N 131 36 E
Ōita □, Japan 70 D3 33 15N 131 30 E
Oiticica, Brazil 170 C3 5 3 S 41 5W
Ojai, U.S.A. 161 L7 34 27N 119 15W
Ojinaga, Mexico 162 B4 29 34N 104 25W
Ojiya, Japan 69 F9 37 18N 138 48 E
Ojos del Salado, Cerro, Argentina 174 B2 27 0 S 68 40W
Oka →, Russia 60 B7 56 20N 43 59 E
Okaba, Indonesia 83 C5 8 6 S 139 42 E
Okahandja, Namibia 116 C2 22 0 S 16 59 E
Okahukura, N.Z. 130 E4 38 48 S 175 14 E
Okaihau, N.Z. 130 B2 35 19 S 173 47 E
Okanagan L., Canada 142 D5 50 0N 119 30W
Okandja, Gabon 114 C2 0 35 S 13 45 E
Okanogan, U.S.A. 158 B4 48 22N 119 35W
Okanogan →, U.S.A. 158 B4 48 6N 119 44W
Okány, Hungary 52 D6 46 52N 21 21 E
Okapa, Papua N. G. 132 D3 6 38 S 145 39 E
Okaputa, Namibia 116 C2 20 5 S 17 0 E
Okara, Pakistan 91 C4 30 50N 73 31 E
Okarito, N.Z. 131 D5 43 15 S 170 9 E
Okato, N.Z. 130 F2 39 12 S 173 53 E
Okaukuejo, Namibia 116 B2 19 10 S 16 0 E
Okavango Swamps, Botswana 116 B3 18 45 S 22 45 E
Okawa, Japan 70 D2 33 9N 130 21 E
Okawville, U.S.A. 156 F7 38 26N 89 33W
Okaya, Japan 71 A10 36 5N 138 10 E
Okayama, Japan 70 C5 34 40N 133 54 E
Okayama □, Japan 70 C5 35 0N 133 50 E
Okazaki, Japan 71 C9 34 57N 137 10 E
Oke-Iho, Nigeria 113 D5 8 1N 3 18 E
Okeechobee, U.S.A. 149 M5 27 15N 80 50W
Okeechobee, L., U.S.A. 149 M5 27 0N 80 50W
Okefenokee Swamp, U.S.A. 152 E7 30 40N 82 20W
Okehampton, U.K. 21 G4 50 44N 4 0W
Okene, Nigeria 113 D6 7 32N 6 11 E
Oker →, Germany 30 C6 52 32N 10 22 E
Okha, Russia 65 D15 53 40N 143 0 E
Ókhi Óros, Greece 48 C6 38 5N 24 25 E
Okhotsk, Russia 65 D15 59 20N 143 10 E
Okhotsk, Sea of, Asia 65 D15 55 0N 145 0 E
Okhotskiy Perevoz, Russia 65 C14 61 52N 135 35 E
Okhtyrka, Ukraine 59 G8 50 25N 35 0 E
Oki-no-Shima, Japan 70 E4 32 44N 132 33 E
Oki-Shotō, Japan 70 A5 36 5N 133 15 E
Okiep, S. Africa 116 D2 29 39 S 17 53 E
Okigwi, Nigeria 113 D6 5 52N 7 20 E
Okija, Nigeria 113 D6 5 54N 6 55 E
Okinawa □, Japan 69 L4 26 40N 128 0 E
Okinawa-Guntō, Japan 69 L4 26 40N 128 0 E
Okinawa-Jima, Japan 69 L4 26 32N 128 0 E
Okino-erabu-Shima, Japan 69 L4 27 21N 128 33 E
Okitipupa, Nigeria 113 D5 6 31N 4 50 E
Oklahoma □, U.S.A. 155 H6 35 20N 97 30W
Oklahoma City, U.S.A. 155 H6 35 30N 97 30W
Oklawaha →, U.S.A. 153 F8 29 28N 81 41W
Oklawaha, L., U.S.A. 153 F8 29 30N 81 45W
Okmulgee, U.S.A. 155 H7 35 37N 95 58W
Oknitsa = Ocniţa, Moldova 53 B12 48 25N 27 30 E
Okolo, Uganda 118 B3 2 37N 31 8 E
Okolona, Ky., U.S.A. 157 F11 38 8N 85 41W
Okolona, Miss., U.S.A. 155 J10 34 0N 88 45W
Okonek, Poland 54 E3 53 32N 16 51 E
Okrika, Nigeria 113 E6 4 40N 7 10 E
Øksendal, Norway 18 B5 62 42N 8 27 E
Oksibil, Indonesia 83 B6 4 59 S 140 35 E
Øksna, Norway 18 D8 60 58N 11 27 E
Oksovskiy, Russia 56 B6 62 33N 39 57 E
Oktabrsk = Oktyabrsk, Kazakstan 57 E10 49 28N 57 25 E
Oktyabr, Kazakstan 63 B8 43 41N 77 12 E
Oktyabrsk, Kazakstan 57 E10 49 28N 57 25 E
Oktyabrsk, Russia 60 D9 53 11N 48 40 E
Oktyabrskiy = Aktsyabrski, Belarus 59 F5 52 38N 28 53 E
Oktyabrskiy, Bashkortostan, Russia 62 D4 54 28N 53 28 E
Oktyabrskiy, Perm, Russia 62 C6 56 31N 57 12 E
Oktyabrskiy, Rostov, Russia 61 G5 47 30N 40 4 E
Oktyabrskoy Revolyutsii, Ostrov, Russia 65 B10 79 30N 97 0 E
Oktyabrskoye = Zhovtneve, Ukraine 59 J7 46 54N 32 3 E
Oktyabrskoye, Russia 62 D9 54 26N 62 44 E
Ōkuchi, Japan 70 E2 32 4N 130 37 E
Okulovka, Russia 58 C7 58 25N 33 19 E
Okuru, N.Z. 131 D3 43 55 S 168 55 E
Okushiri-Tō, Japan 68 C9 42 15N 139 30 E
Okuta, Nigeria 113 D5 9 14N 3 12 E
Okwa →, Botswana 116 C3 22 30 S 23 0 E
Ola, U.S.A. 155 H8 35 2N 93 13W
Ólafsfjörður, Iceland 11 A8 66 4N 18 39W
Ólafsvík, Iceland 11 C3 64 53N 23 43W
Olaine, Latvia 54 B10 56 48N 23 59 E
Olancha, U.S.A. 161 J8 36 17N 118 1W
Olancha Pk., U.S.A. 161 J8 36 15N 118 7W
Olanchito, Honduras 164 C2 15 30N 86 30W
Öland, Sweden 17 H10 56 45N 16 38 E
Ölands norra udde, Sweden 17 G11 57 22N 17 5 E
Ölands södra udde, Sweden 17 H10 56 12N 16 23 E
Olanta, U.S.A. 152 B10 33 56N 79 56W
Olar, U.S.A. 152 B9 33 11N 81 11W
Olargues, France 28 E6 43 34N 2 53 E
Olary, Australia 128 B4 32 18 S 140 19 E
Olascoaga, Argentina 174 D3 35 15 S 60 39W
Olathe, U.S.A. 154 F7 38 53N 94 49W
Olavarría, Argentina 174 D3 36 55 S 60 20W
Oława, Poland 55 H4 50 57N 17 20 E
Olbernhau, Germany 30 E9 50 40N 13 19 E
Ólbia, Italy 46 B2 40 55N 9 31 E
Ólbia, G. di, Italy 46 B2 40 55N 9 39 E
Olching, Germany 31 G7 48 12N 11 21 E
Old Bahama Chan. = Bahama, Canal Viejo de, W. Indies 164 B4 22 10N 77 30W
Old Baldy Pk. = San Antonio, Mt., U.S.A. 161 L9 34 17N 117 38W
Old Cork, Australia 126 C3 22 57 S 141 52 E
Old Crow, Canada 138 B6 67 30N 139 55W
Old Dale, U.S.A. 161 L11 34 8N 115 47W
Old Dongola, Sudan 106 D3 18 11N 30 44 E
Old Forge, N.Y., U.S.A. 151 C10 43 43N 74 58W
Old Forge, Pa., U.S.A. 151 E9 41 22N 75 45W
Old Fort →, Canada 143 B6 58 36N 110 24W
Old Shinyanga, Tanzania 118 C3 3 33 S 33 27 E
Old Speck Mt., U.S.A. 151 B14 44 34N 70 57W
Old Town, Fla., U.S.A. 153 F7 29 36N 82 59W
Old Town, Maine, U.S.A. 141 D6 44 56N 68 39W
Old Wives L., Canada 143 C7 50 5N 106 0W
Oldbury, U.K. 21 F5 51 38N 2 33W
Oldcastle, Ireland 23 C4 53 46N 7 10W
Oldeani, Tanzania 118 C4 3 22 S 35 35 E
Olden, Norway 18 C3 61 49N 6 49 E
Oldenburg, Niedersachsen, Germany 30 B4 53 9N 8 13 E
Oldenburg, Schleswig-Holstein, Germany 30 A6 54 17N 10 52 E
Oldenzaal, Neths. 24 B6 52 19N 6 53 E
Oldham, U.K. 20 D5 53 33N 2 7W
Oldman →, Canada 142 D6 49 57N 111 42W
Oldmeldrum, U.K. 22 D6 57 20N 2 19W
Olds, Canada 142 C6 51 50N 114 10W
Oldsmar, U.S.A. 153 G7 28 2N 82 40W
Ole Rømer Land, Greenland 10 C8 74 10N 24 30W
Olean, U.S.A. 150 D6 42 5N 78 26W
Olecko, Poland 54 D9 54 2N 22 31 E
Oléggio, Italy 44 C5 45 36N 8 38 E
Oleiros, Portugal 42 F3 39 56N 7 56W
Oleiros, Spain 42 B2 43 20N 8 19W
Olekma →, Russia 65 C13 60 22N 120 42 E
Olekminsk, Russia 65 C13 60 25N 120 30 E
Oleksandriya, Kirovohrad, Ukraine 59 H7 48 42N 33 3 E
Oleksandriya, Rivne, Ukraine 59 G4 50 37N 26 19 E
Oleksandrovka, Ukraine 59 H7 48 55N 32 20 E
Olema, U.S.A. 160 G4 38 3N 122 47W
Ølen, Norway 18 E2 59 36N 5 48 E
Olenegorsk, Russia 56 A5 68 9N 33 18 E
Olenek, Russia 65 C12 68 28N 112 18 E
Olenek →, Russia 65 B13 73 0N 120 10 E
Olenino, Russia 58 D7 56 15N 33 30 E
Oléron, Î. d', France 28 C2 45 55N 1 15W
Oleśnica, Poland 55 G4 51 13N 17 22 E
Olesno, Poland 55 H5 50 51N 18 26 E
Olevsk, Ukraine 59 G4 51 12N 27 39 E
Olga, Russia 65 E14 43 50N 135 14 E
Olga, L., Canada 140 C4 49 47N 77 15W
Olga, Mt., Australia 125 E5 25 20 S 130 50 E
Ølgod, Denmark 17 J2 55 49N 8 36 E
Olhão, Portugal 43 H3 37 3N 7 48W
Olib, Croatia 45 D11 44 23N 14 44 E
Oliena, Italy 46 B2 40 16N 9 24 E
Oliete, Spain 40 D4 41 1N 0 41W
Olifants →, Africa 117 C5 23 57 S 31 58 E
Olifantshoek, S. Africa 116 D3 27 57 S 22 42 E
Ólimbos, Greece 49 F9 35 44N 27 11 E
Ólimbos, Óros, Greece 50 F6 40 6N 22 23 E
Olímpia, Brazil 175 A6 20 44 S 48 54W
Olin, U.S.A. 156 C5 42 0N 91 9W
Olinda, Brazil 170 C5 8 1 S 34 51W
Olindiná, Brazil 170 D4 11 22 S 38 21W
Olite, Spain 40 C3 42 29N 1 40W
Oliva, Argentina 174 C3 32 0 S 63 38W
Oliva, Spain 41 G4 38 58N 0 9W
Oliva, Punta del, Spain 42 B5 43 37N 5 28W
Oliva de la Frontera, Spain 43 G4 38 17N 6 54W
Olivares, Spain 40 F2 39 46N 2 20W
Olive Hill, U.S.A. 157 F13 38 18N 83 13W
Olivehurst, U.S.A. 160 F5 39 6N 121 34W
Oliveira, Brazil 171 F3 20 39 S 44 50W
Oliveira de Azeméis, Portugal 42 E2 40 49N 8 29W
Oliveira do Douro, Portugal 42 D2 41 5N 8 2W
Oliveira dos Brejinhos, Brazil 171 D3 12 19 S 42 54W
Olivenza, Spain 43 G3 38 41N 7 9W
Oliver, Canada 142 D5 49 13N 119 37W
Oliver, U.S.A. 152 C8 32 31N 81 32W
Oliver L., Canada 143 B8 56 56N 103 22W
Olivet, France 27 E8 47 51N 1 55 E
Olivine Ra., N.Z. 131 E3 44 15 S 168 30 E
Olivone, Switz. 33 C7 46 32N 8 57 E
Olkhovka, Russia 60 F7 49 48N 44 32 E
Olkusz, Poland 55 H6 50 18N 19 33 E
Ollagüe, Chile 174 A2 21 15 S 68 10W
Olmaliq, Uzbekistan 63 C4 40 50N 69 35 E
Olmedo, Spain 42 D6 41 20N 4 43W
Olmeto, France 29 G12 41 43N 8 55 E
Olmos, Peru 172 B2 5 59 S 79 46W
Olney, Ill., U.S.A. 157 F8 38 44N 88 5W
Olney, Tex., U.S.A. 155 J5 33 22N 98 45W
Olofström, Sweden 17 H8 56 17N 14 32 E
Oloma, Cameroon 113 E7 3 29N 11 19 E
Olomane →, Canada 141 B7 50 14N 60 37W
Olombo, Congo 114 C3 1 18 S 15 53 E
Olomouc, Czech Rep. 35 B10 49 38N 17 12 E
Olonets, Russia 58 B7 61 0N 32 54 E
Olongapo, Phil. 80 D3 14 50N 120 18 E
Olonne-sur-Mer, France 28 B2 46 32N 1 47W
Oloron, Gave d' →, France 28 E2 43 33N 1 5W
Oloron-Ste-Marie, France 28 E3 43 11N 0 38W
Olot, Spain 40 C7 42 11N 2 30 E
Olovo, Bos.-H. 52 F3 44 8N 18 35 E
Olovyannaya, Russia 65 D12 50 58N 115 35 E
Olowalu, U.S.A. 145 C5 20 49N 156 38W
Oloy →, Russia 65 C16 66 29N 159 29 E
Olsberg, Germany 30 D4 51 21N 8 31 E
Olshammar, Sweden 17 F8 58 45N 14 48 E
Olshanka, Ukraine 59 H6 48 16N 30 58 E
Olshany, Ukraine 59 G8 50 3N 35 53 E
Olsztyn, Poland 54 E7 53 48N 20 29 E
Olsztyn □, Poland 54 E7 53 30N 20 30 E
Olsztynek, Poland 54 E7 53 34N 20 19 E
Olt □, Romania 53 F9 44 20N 24 30 E
Olt →, Romania 53 G9 43 43N 24 51 E
Oltedal, Norway 18 F3 58 49N 6 2 E
Olten, Switz. 32 B5 47 21N 7 53 E
Olteniţa, Romania 53 F11 44 7N 26 42 E
Olton, U.S.A. 155 H3 34 11N 102 8W
Oltu, Turkey 101 B9 40 35N 41 58 E
Olula del Río, Spain 41 H2 37 21N 2 18W
Olur, Turkey 101 B10 40 49N 42 8 E
Olustee, U.S.A. 152 E7 30 12N 82 26W
Olutanga, Phil. 81 H4 7 26N 122 54 E
Olutanga I., Phil. 81 H4 7 22N 122 52 E
Olvega, Spain 40 D2 41 47N 2 0W
Olvera, Spain 43 J5 36 55N 5 18W
Olymbos, Cyprus 38 D12 35 21N 33 45 E
Olympia, Greece 48 D3 37 39N 21 39 E
Olympia, U.S.A. 160 D4 47 3N 122 53W
Olympic Mts., U.S.A. 160 C3 47 55N 123 45W
Olympic Nat. Park, U.S.A. 160 C3 47 48N 123 30W
Olympus, Cyprus 38 E11 34 56N 32 52 E
Olympus, Mt. = Ólimbos, Óros, Greece 50 F6 40 6N 22 23 E
Olympus, Mt. = Uludağ, Turkey 51 F13 40 4N 29 13 E
Olympus, Mt., U.S.A. 160 C3 47 48N 123 43W
Olyphant, U.S.A. 151 E9 41 27N 75 36W
Om →, Russia 64 D8 54 59N 73 22 E
Om Hajer, Eritrea 107 E4 14 20N 36 41 E
Om Koi, Thailand 86 D2 17 48N 98 22 E
Ōma, Japan 68 D10 41 45N 141 5 E
Ōmachi, Japan 71 A9 36 30N 137 50 E
Omae-Zaki, Japan 71 C10 34 36N 138 14 E
Ōmagari, Japan 68 E10 39 27N 140 29 E
Omagh, U.K. 23 B4 54 36N 7 19W
Omagh □, U.K. 23 B4 54 35N 7 15W
Omaha, U.S.A. 154 E7 41 17N 95 58W
Omak, U.S.A. 158 B4 48 25N 119 31W
Omalos, Greece 38 D5 35 19N 23 55 E
Oman ■, Asia 99 B7 23 0N 58 0 E
Oman, G. of, Asia 97 E8 24 30N 58 30 E
Omapere, N.Z. 130 B2 35 37 S 173 25 E
Omar Combon, Somali Rep. 120 D3 3 10N 45 47 E
Omaruru, Namibia 116 C2 21 26 S 16 0 E
Omaruru →, Namibia 116 C1 22 7 S 14 15 E
Omate, Peru 172 D3 16 45 S 71 0W
Ombai, Selat, Indonesia 82 C2 8 30 S 124 50 E
Omboué, Gabon 114 C1 1 35 S 9 15 E
Ombrone →, Italy 44 F8 42 42N 11 5 E
Omchi, Chad 109 D3 21 22N 17 53 E
Omdurmân, Sudan 107 D3 15 40N 32 28 E
Ōme, Japan 71 B11 35 47N 139 15 E
Omega, U.S.A. 152 D6 31 21N 83 36W
Omegna, Italy 44 C5 45 53N 8 24 E
Omeonga, Dem. Rep. of the Congo 114 C4 3 40 S 24 22 E
Ometepe, I. de, Nic. 164 D2 11 32N 85 35W
Ometepec, Mexico 163 D5 16 39N 98 23W
Ōmi-Shima, Ehime, Japan 70 C5 34 15N 133 0 E
Ōmi-Shima, Yamaguchi, Japan 70 C3 34 25N 131 9 E
Omihachiman, Japan 71 B8 35 7N 136 3 E
Ominato, Japan 68 D10 41 17N 141 10 E
Omineca →, Canada 142 B4 56 3N 124 16W
Omiš, Croatia 45 E13 43 28N 16 40 E
Omišalj, Croatia 45 C11 45 13N 14 32 E
Omitara, Namibia 116 C2 22 16 S 18 2 E
Ōmiya, Japan 71 B11 35 54N 139 38 E
Ommaney, C., U.S.A. 144 H14 56 10N 134 40W
Omme Å →, Denmark 17 J2 55 56N 8 32 E
Ommen, Neths. 24 B6 52 31N 6 26 E
Ömnögovĭ □, Mongolia 74 C3 43 15N 104 0 E
Omo →, Ethiopia 107 F4 6 25N 36 10 E
Omodeo, L., Italy 46 B1 40 8N 8 56 E
Omodhos, Cyprus 38 E11 34 51N 32 48 E
Omolon →, Russia 65 C16 68 42N 158 36 E
Omono-Gawa →, Japan 68 E10 39 46N 140 3 E
Omsk, Russia 64 D8 55 0N 73 12 E
Omsukchan, Russia 65 C16 62 32N 155 48 E
Ōmu, Japan 68 B11 44 34N 142 58 E
Omul, Vf., Romania 53 E10 45 27N 25 29 E
Omulew →, Poland 55 E8 53 5N 21 33 E
Ōmura, Japan 70 E1 32 56N 129 57 E
Omura-Wan, Japan 70 E1 32 57N 129 52 E
Omurtag, Bulgaria 51 C10 43 8N 26 26 E
Ōmuta, Japan 70 D2 33 5N 130 26 E
Omutninsk, Russia 62 B4 58 45N 52 4 E
On-Take, Japan 70 F2 31 35N 130 39 E
Oña, Spain 42 C7 42 43N 3 25W
Ona, U.S.A. 153 H8 27 29N 81 55W
Onaga, U.S.A. 154 F6 39 29N 96 10W
Onalaska, U.S.A. 154 D9 43 53N 91 14W
Onamia, U.S.A. 154 B8 46 4N 93 40W
Onancock, U.S.A. 148 G8 37 43N 75 45W
Onang, Indonesia 82 B1 3 2 S 118 49 E
Onaping L., Canada 140 C3 47 3N 81 30W
Onarga, U.S.A. 157 D8 40 43N 88 1W
Onarhā, Afghan. 91 B3 35 30N 71 0 E
Oñati, Spain 40 B2 43 3N 2 25W
Onavas, Mexico 162 B3 28 28N 109 30W
Onawa, U.S.A. 154 D6 42 2N 96 6W
Onaway, U.S.A. 148 C3 45 21N 84 14W
Oncócua, Angola 115 F2 16 30 S 13 25 E
Onda, Spain 40 F4 39 55N 0 17W
Ondaejin, N. Korea 75 D15 41 34N 129 40 E
Ondangua, Namibia 116 B2 17 57 S 16 4 E
Ondarroa, Spain 40 B2 43 19N 2 25W
Ondas →, Brazil 171 D3 12 8 S 44 55W
Ondava →, Slovak Rep. 35 C14 48 27N 21 48 E
Ondjiva, Angola 115 F3 16 48 S 15 50 E
Ondo, Japan 70 C4 34 11N 132 32 E
Ondo, Nigeria 113 D5 7 4N 4 47 E
Ondo □, Nigeria 113 D6 7 0N 5 0 E
Öndörshil, Mongolia 74 B5 45 13N 108 5 E
Öndverðarnes, Iceland 11 C2 64 52N 24 0W
Oneco, U.S.A. 153 H7 27 25N 82 31W
Onega, Russia 56 B6 64 0N 38 10 E
Onega →, Russia 56 B6 63 58N 38 2 E
Onega, G. of = Onezhskaya Guba, Russia 56 B6 64 24N 36 38 E
Onega, L. = Onezhskoye Ozero, Russia 58 B8 61 44N 35 22 E
Onehunga, N.Z. 130 C3 36 55 S 174 48 E
Oneida, Ill., U.S.A. 156 C6 41 4N 90 13W
Oneida, N.Y., U.S.A. 151 C9 43 6N 75 39W
Oneida L., U.S.A. 151 C9 43 12N 75 54W
O'Neill, U.S.A. 154 D5 42 27N 98 39W
Onekotan, Ostrov, Russia 65 E16 49 25N 154 45 E
Onema, Dem. Rep. of the Congo 115 C4 4 35 S 24 30 E
Oneonta, Ala., U.S.A. 149 J2 33 57N 86 28W
Oneonta, N.Y., U.S.A. 151 D9 42 27N 75 4W
Onerahi, N.Z. 130 B3 35 45 S 174 22 E
Oneşti, Romania 53 D11 46 17N 26 47 E
Onezhskaya Guba, Russia 56 B6 64 24N 36 38 E
Onezhskoye Ozero, Russia 58 B8 61 44N 35 22 E
Ongarue, N.Z. 130 E4 38 42 S 175 19 E
Ongea Levu, Fiji 133 B3 19 8 S 178 24W
Ongerup, Australia 125 F2 33 58 S 118 28 E
Ongjin, N. Korea 75 F13 37 56N 125 21 E
Ongkharak, Thailand 86 E3 14 8N 101 1 E
Ongniud Qi, China 75 C10 43 0N 118 38 E
Ongoka, Dem. Rep. of the Congo 118 C2 1 20 S 26 0 E
Ongole, India 95 G5 15 33N 80 2 E
Ongon, Mongolia 74 B7 45 41N 113 5 E
Oni, Georgia 61 J6 42 33N 43 26 E
Onida, U.S.A. 154 C4 44 42N 100 4W
Onilahy →, Madag. 117 C7 23 34 S 43 45 E
Onitsha, Nigeria 113 D6 6 6N 6 42 E
Onmaka, Burma 90 D6 22 17N 96 41 E
Ono, Fiji 133 B2 18 55 S 178 29 E
Ono, Fukui, Japan 71 B8 35 59N 136 29 E
Ono, Hyōgo, Japan 70 C6 34 51N 134 56 E
Onoda, Japan 70 C3 34 2N 131 25 E
Onoke, L., N.Z. 130 H4 41 22 S 175 8 E
Onomichi, Japan 70 C5 34 25N 133 12 E
Onpyŏng-ni, S. Korea 75 H14 33 25N 126 55 E
Ons, I. de, Spain 42 C2 42 23N 8 55W
Onslow, Australia 124 D2 21 40 S 115 12 E
Onslow B., U.S.A. 149 H7 34 20N 77 15W
Ontake-San, Japan 71 B9 35 53N 137 29 E
Ontario, Calif., U.S.A. 161 L9 34 4N 117 39W
Ontario, Oreg., U.S.A. 158 D5 44 2N 116 58W
Ontario □, Canada 140 B2 48 0N 83 0W
Ontario, L., U.S.A. 140 D4 43 20N 78 0W
Ontinyent, Spain 41 G4 38 50N 0 35W
Ontonagon, U.S.A. 154 B10 46 52N 89 19W
Ontur, Spain 41 G3 38 38N 1 29W
Onyx, U.S.A. 161 K8 35 41N 118 14W
Oodnadatta, Australia 127 D2 27 33 S 135 30 E
Ooldea, Australia 125 F5 30 27 S 131 50 E
Oombulgurri, Australia 124 C4 15 15 S 127 45 E
Oona River, Canada 142 C2 53 57N 130 16W
Oorindi, Australia 126 C3 20 40 S 141 1 E
Oost-Vlaanderen □, Belgium 24 C3 51 5N 3 50 E
Oostende, Belgium 24 C2 51 15N 2 54 E
Oosterhout, Neths. 24 C4 51 39N 4 47 E
Oosterschelde, Neths. 24 C4 51 33N 4 0 E
Oosterwolde, Neths. 24 B6 53 0N 6 17 E
Ootacamund = Udagamandalam, India 95 J3 11 30N 76 44 E
Ootha, Australia 129 B7 33 6 S 147 29 E
Ootsa L., Canada 142 C3 53 50N 126 2W
Opaka, Bulgaria 51 C10 43 28N 26 10 E
Opala, Dem. Rep. of the Congo 114 C4 0 40 S 24 20 E
Opalenica, Poland 55 F3 52 18N 16 24 E
Opan, Bulgaria 51 D9 42 13N 25 41 E
Opanake, Sri Lanka 95 L5 6 35N 80 40 E
Opapa, N.Z. 130 F5 39 47 S 176 42 E
Opasatika, Canada 140 C3 49 30N 82 50W
Opasquia, Canada 143 C10 53 16N 93 34W
Opatija, Croatia 45 C11 45 21N 14 17 E
Opatów, Poland 55 H8 50 50N 21 27 E
Opava, Czech Rep. 35 B10 49 57N 17 58 E
Opelika, U.S.A. 152 C4 32 39N 85 23W
Opelousas, U.S.A. 155 K8 30 32N 92 5W
Opémisca, L., Canada 140 C5 49 56N 74 52W
Open Bay Is., N.Z. 131 D3 43 51 S 168 51 E
Opheim, U.S.A. 158 B10 48 51N 106 24W
Ophthalmia Ra., Australia 124 D2 23 15 S 119 30 E
Opi, Nigeria 113 D6 6 36N 7 28 E
Opihikao, U.S.A. 145 D7 19 26N 154 53W
Opinaca →, Canada 140 B4 52 15N 78 2W
Opinaca L., Canada 140 B4 52 39N 76 20W
Opiskotish, L., Canada 141 B6 53 10N 67 50W
Opobo, Nigeria 113 E6 4 35N 7 34 E
Opochka, Russia 58 D5 56 42N 28 45 E
Opoczno, Poland 55 G7 51 22N 20 18 E
Opol, Phil. 81 G5 8 31N 124 34 E
Opole, Poland 55 H4 50 42N 17 58 E
Opole □, Poland 55 H4 50 40N 17 56 E
Opole Lubelskie, Poland 55 G8 51 9N 21 58 E
Opon = Lapu-Lapu, Phil. 81 F4 10 20N 123 55 E
Oporto = Porto, Portugal 42 D2 41 8N 8 40W
Opotiki, N.Z. 130 E6 38 1 S 177 19 E
Opp, U.S.A. 152 D3 31 17N 86 16W
Oppdal, Norway 15 E13 62 35N 9 41 E
Óppido Mamertina, Italy 47 D8 38 16N 15 59 E
Oppland □, Norway 18 C6 61 15N 9 40 E
Oprişor, Romania 52 F8 44 17N 23 5 E
Oprtalj, Croatia 45 C10 45 23N 13 50 E
Opua, N.Z. 130 B3 35 19 S 174 9 E
Opunake, N.Z. 130 F2 39 26 S 173 52 E
Opuzen, Croatia 45 E14 43 1N 17 34 E
Oquawka, U.S.A. 156 D6 40 56N 90 57W
Ora, Cyprus 38 E12 34 51N 33 12 E
Ora Banda, Australia 125 F3 30 20 S 121 0 E
Oracle, U.S.A. 159 K8 32 37N 110 46W
Oradea, Romania 52 C6 47 2N 21 58 E
Öræfajökull, Iceland 11 C10 64 2N 16 39W
Orahovac, Serbia, Yug. 50 D4 42 24N 20 40 E
Orahovica, Croatia 52 E2 45 35N 17 52 E
Orai, India 93 G8 25 58N 79 30 E
Oraison, France 29 E9 43 55N 5 55 E
Oral = Zhayyq →, Kazakstan 57 E9 47 0N 51 48 E
Oral, Kazakstan 60 E10 51 20N 51 20 E
Oran, Algeria 111 A4 35 45N 0 39W
Oran, Argentina 174 A3 23 10 S 64 20W
Orange, Australia 129 B8 33 15 S 149 7 E
Orange, France 29 D8 44 8N 4 47 E
Orange, Calif., U.S.A. 161 M9 33 47N 117 51W
Orange, Mass., U.S.A. 151 D12 42 35N 72 19W
Orange, Tex., U.S.A. 155 K8 30 6N 93 44W
Orange, Va., U.S.A. 148 F6 38 15N 78 7W
Orange →, S. Africa 116 D2 28 41 S 16 28 E
Orange, C., Brazil 169 C7 4 20N 51 30W
Orange City, U.S.A. 153 G8 28 57N 81 18W
Orange Cove, U.S.A. 160 J7 36 38N 119 19W
Orange Free State □ = Free State □, S. Africa 116 D4 28 30 S 27 0 E
Orange Grove, U.S.A. 155 M6 27 58N 97 56W
Orange L., U.S.A. 153 F7 29 25N 82 13W
Orange Park, U.S.A. 152 E8 30 10N 81 42W
Orange Walk, Belize 163 D7 18 6N 88 33W
Orangeburg, U.S.A. 152 B9 33 30N 80 52W
Orangeville, Canada 140 D3 43 55N 80 5W
Orangeville, U.S.A. 156 B7 42 28N 89 39W
Orani, Phil. 80 D3 14 49N 120 32 E
Oranienburg, Germany 30 C9 52 45N 13 14 E
Oranje = Orange →, S. Africa 116 D2 28 41 S 16 28 E
Oranje Vrystaat □ = Free State □, S. Africa 116 D4 28 30 S 27 0 E
Oranjemund, Namibia 116 D2 28 38 S 16 29 E
Oranjerivier, S. Africa 116 D3 29 40 S 24 12 E
Oras, Phil. 80 E5 12 9N 125 28 E
Orašje, Bos.-H. 52 E3 45 1N 18 42 E

Ouezzane 261

Orăştie, *Romania* 53 E8 45 50N 23 10 E
Oraşul Stalin = Braşov,
Romania 53 E10 45 38N 25 35 E
Orava →, *Slovak Rep.* 35 B12 49 9N 19 8 E
Orava, Vodna nádrž,
Slovak Rep. 35 B12 49 25N 19 35 E
Oraviţa, *Romania* 52 E6 45 2N 21 43 E
Orawia, *N.Z.* 131 G2 46 1 S 167 50 E
Orb →, *France* 28 E7 43 15N 3 18 E
Orba →, *Italy* 44 D5 44 53N 8 37 E
Ørbæk, *Denmark* 17 J4 55 17N 10 39 E
Orbe, *Switz.* 32 C3 46 43N 6 32 E
Orbec, *France* 26 C7 49 1N 0 23 E
Orbetello, *Italy* 45 F8 42 27N 11 13 E
Órbigo →, *Spain* 42 C5 42 5N 5 42W
Orbost, *Australia* 129 D8 37 40 S 148 29 E
Örbyhus, *Sweden* 16 D11 60 15N 17 43 E
Orce, *Spain* 41 H2 37 44N 2 28W
Orce →, *Spain* 41 H2 37 44N 2 28W
Orchies, *France* 27 B10 50 28N 3 14 E
Orchila, I., *Venezuela* 168 A4 11 48N 66 10W
Orcia →, *Italy* 45 F8 42 58N 11 21 E
Orco →, *Italy* 44 C4 45 10N 7 52 E
Orcopampa, *Peru* 172 D3 15 20 S 72 23W
Orcutt, *U.S.A.* 161 L6 34 52N 120 27W
Ord →, *Australia* 124 C4 15 33 S 128 15 E
Ord, Mt., *Australia* 124 C4 17 20 S 125 34 E
Ordenes = Ordes, *Spain* 42 B2 43 5N 8 29W
Orderville, *U.S.A.* 159 H7 37 17N 112 38W
Ordes, *Spain* 42 B2 43 5N 8 29W
Ording = St-Peter-Ording,
Germany 30 A4 54 20N 8 36 E
Ordos = Mu Us Shamo,
China 74 E5 39 0N 109 0 E
Ordu, *Turkey* 100 B7 40 55N 37 53 E
Ordubad, *Azerbaijan* 101 C12 38 54N 46 1 E
Orduña, *Álava, Spain* 40 C2 42 58N 2 58W
Orduña, *Granada, Spain* 43 H7 37 20N 3 30W
Ordway, *U.S.A.* 154 F3 38 13N 103 46W
Ordzhonikidze =
Vladikavkaz, *Russia* 61 J7 43 0N 44 35 E
Ordzhonikidze, *Kazakstan* 62 E8 52 27N 61 39 E
Ordzhonikidze, *Ukraine* 59 J8 47 39N 34 3 E
Ordzhonikidze, *Uzbekistan* 63 C4 41 21N 69 22 E
Ordzhonikidzeabad,
Tajikistan 63 D4 38 34N 69 1 E
Ore,
Dem. Rep. of the Congo 118 B2 3 17N 29 30 E
Ore Mts. = Erzgebirge,
Germany 30 E8 50 27N 12 55 E
Orealla, *Guyana* 169 B6 5 15N 57 23W
Orebić, *Croatia* 45 F14 43 0N 17 11 E
Örebro, *Sweden* 16 E9 59 20N 15 18 E
Örebro län □, *Sweden* 16 E8 59 27N 15 0 E
Oregon, *Ill., U.S.A.* 156 B7 42 1N 89 20W
Oregon, *Ohio, U.S.A.* 157 C13 41 38N 83 25W
Oregon, *Wis., U.S.A.* 156 B7 42 56N 89 23W
Oregon □, *U.S.A.* 158 E3 44 0N 121 0W
Oregon City, *U.S.A.* 160 E4 45 21N 122 36W
Öregrund, *Sweden* 16 D12 60 21N 18 30 E
Öregrundsgrepen, *Sweden* 16 D12 60 25N 18 15 E
Orekhov = Orikhiv, *Ukraine* 59 J8 47 30N 35 48 E
Orekhovo-Zuyevo, *Russia* 58 E10 55 50N 38 55 E
Orel, *Russia* 59 F9 52 57N 36 3 E
Orel →, *Ukraine* 59 H8 48 40N 34 39 E
Orellana, *Spain* 43 F5 39 1N 5 32W
Orellana, Canal de, *Spain* 43 F5 39 2N 6 0W
Orellana, Embalse de, *Spain* 43 F5 39 5N 5 10W
Orem, *U.S.A.* 158 F8 40 19N 111 42W
Ören, *Turkey* 49 D9 37 3N 27 57 E
Orenburg, *Russia* 62 F5 51 45N 55 6 E
Örencik, *Turkey* 49 B11 39 16N 29 33 E
Orense = Ourense, *Spain* 42 C3 42 19N 7 55W
Orense □, *Spain* 42 C3 42 15N 7 51W
Orepuki, *N.Z.* 131 G2 46 19 S 167 46 E
Orestiás, *Greece* 51 E10 41 30N 26 33 E
Øresund, *Europe* 17 J6 55 45N 12 45 E
Oreti →, *N.Z.* 131 G3 46 28 S 168 14 E
Orford Ness, *U.K.* 21 E9 52 5N 1 35 E
Organà = Organyà, *Spain* 40 C6 42 13N 1 20 E
Organos, Pta. de los,
Canary Is. 39 F2 28 12N 17 17W
Organyà, *Spain* 40 C6 42 13N 1 20 E
Orgaz, *Spain* 43 F7 39 39N 3 53W
Ørgenvika, *Norway* 18 D6 60 17N 9 42 E
Orgeyev = Orhei, *Moldova* 53 C13 47 24N 28 50 E
Orgūn, *Afghan.* 91 B3 32 55N 69 12 E
Orhaneli, *Turkey* 51 G12 39 54N 28 59 E
Orhaneli →, *Turkey* 51 G12 39 50N 28 55 E
Orhangazi, *Turkey* 51 F13 40 29N 29 18 E
Orhei, *Moldova* 53 C13 47 24N 28 50 E
Orhon Gol →, *Mongolia* 72 A5 50 21N 106 0 E
Ória, *Italy* 47 B10 40 30N 17 38 E
Orient, *Australia* 127 D3 28 7 S 142 50 E
Orient, *U.S.A.* 156 C2 41 12N 94 25W
Oriental, Cordillera, *Bolivia* 173 D4 17 0 S 66 0W
Oriental, Cordillera,
Colombia 168 B3 6 0N 73 0W
Oriente, *Argentina* 174 D3 38 44 S 60 37W
Orihuela, *Spain* 41 G4 38 7N 0 55W
Orihuela del Tremedal, *Spain* 40 E3 40 33N 1 39W
Orikhiv, *Ukraine* 59 J8 47 30N 35 48 E
Oriku, *Albania* 50 F3 40 20N 19 26 E
Orinduik, *Guyana* 169 C5 4 40N 60 3W
Orinoco →, *Venezuela* 169 B5 9 15N 61 30W
Orion, *Ala., U.S.A.* 152 D4 31 58N 86 0W
Orion, *Ill., U.S.A.* 156 C6 41 21N 90 23W
Orissa □, *India* 94 E7 20 0N 84 0 E
Orissaare, *Estonia* 15 G20 58 34N 23 5 E
Oristano, *Italy* 46 C1 39 54N 8 36 E
Oristano, G. di, *Italy* 46 C1 39 50N 8 29 E
Orituco →, *Venezuela* 168 B4 8 45N 67 27W
Orizaba, *Mexico* 163 D5 18 51N 97 6W
Orizare, *Bulgaria* 51 D11 42 44N 27 39 E
Orizona, *Brazil* 171 E2 17 3 S 48 18W
Ørje, *Norway* 18 E8 59 29N 11 39 E
Orjen, *Bos.-H.* 50 D2 42 35N 18 34 E
Orjiva, *Spain* 43 J7 36 53N 3 24W
Orkanger, *Norway* 14 E13 63 18N 9 52 E
Örkelljunga, *Sweden* 17 H7 56 17N 13 17 E
Örken, *Sweden* 17 G9 57 6N 15 1 E
Örkény, *Hungary* 52 C4 47 9N 19 26 E
Orkla →, *Norway* 14 E13 63 18N 9 51 E
Orkney, *S. Africa* 116 D4 26 58 S 26 40 E
Orkney □, *U.K.* 22 B5 59 2N 3 13W
Orkney Is., *U.K.* 22 B6 59 0N 3 0W
Orland, *Calif., U.S.A.* 160 F4 39 45N 122 12W
Orland, *Ind., U.S.A.* 157 C11 41 47N 85 12W
Orlando, *U.S.A.* 149 L5 28 33N 81 23W
Orlando, C. d', *Italy* 47 D7 38 10N 14 43 E
Orléanais, *France* 27 E9 48 0N 2 0 E
Orléans, *France* 27 E8 47 54N 1 52 E
Orleans, *U.S.A.* 151 B12 44 49N 72 12W
Orléans, I. d', *Canada* 141 C5 46 54N 70 58W
Orlice →, *Czech Rep.* 34 A8 50 13N 15 50 E
Orlov, *Slovak Rep.* 35 B13 49 17N 20 51 E
Orlov Gay, *Russia* 60 E9 50 56N 48 19 E
Orlová, *Czech Rep.* 35 B11 49 51N 18 26 E
Orlovat, *Serbia, Yug.* 52 E5 45 14N 20 33 E
Ormara, *Pakistan* 91 D2 25 16N 64 33 E
Ormea, *Italy* 44 D4 44 9N 7 54 E
Ormília, *Greece* 50 F7 40 16N 23 39 E
Ormoc, *Phil.* 81 F5 11 0N 124 37 E
Ormond, *N.Z.* 130 E6 38 33 S 177 56 E
Ormond Beach, *U.S.A.* 149 L5 29 17N 81 3W
Ormond by the Sea, *U.S.A.* 153 F8 29 21N 81 4W
Ormondville, *N.Z.* 130 G5 40 5 S 176 19 E
Ormož, *Slovenia* 45 B13 46 25N 16 10 E
Ormskirk, *U.K.* 20 D5 53 35N 2 54W
Ormstown, *Canada* 151 A11 45 8N 74 0W
Ornans, *France* 27 E13 47 7N 6 10 E
Orne □, *France* 26 D7 48 40N 0 5 E
Orne →, *France* 26 C6 49 18N 0 15W
Orneta, *Poland* 54 D7 54 8N 20 9 E
Ornö, *Sweden* 16 E12 59 4N 18 24 E
Örnsköldsvik, *Sweden* 16 A12 63 17N 18 40 E
Oro, *N. Korea* 75 D14 40 1N 127 27 E
Oro →, *Mexico* 162 B3 25 35N 105 2W
Oro Grande, *U.S.A.* 161 L9 34 36N 117 20W
Orobie, Alpi, *Italy* 44 B6 46 7N 10 0 E
Orocué, *Colombia* 168 C3 4 48N 71 20W
Orodo, *Nigeria* 113 D6 5 34N 7 4 E
Orogrande, *U.S.A.* 159 K10 32 24N 106 5W
Orol Dengizi = Aral Sea,
Asia 64 E7 44 30N 60 0 E
Oromocto, *Canada* 141 C6 45 54N 66 29W
Oron, *Nigeria* 113 E6 4 48N 8 14 E
Oron, *Switz.* 32 C3 46 34N 6 50 E
Orono, *Canada* 150 C6 43 59N 78 37W
Oronsay, *U.K.* 22 E2 56 1N 6 15W
Oropesa, *Spain* 42 F5 39 57N 5 10W
Oroqen Zizhiqi, *China* 73 A7 50 34N 123 43 E
Oroquieta, *Phil.* 81 G4 8 32N 123 44 E
Orós, *Brazil* 170 C4 6 15 S 38 55W
Orosei, *Italy* 46 B2 40 23N 9 42 E
Orosei, G. di, *Italy* 46 B2 40 15N 9 44 E
Orosháza, *Hungary* 52 D5 46 32N 20 42 E
Oroszlány, *Hungary* 52 C3 47 29N 18 19 E
Orote Pen., *Guam* 133 R15 13 26N 144 38 E
Orotukan, *Russia* 65 C16 62 16N 151 42 E
Oroville, *Calif., U.S.A.* 160 F5 39 31N 121 33W
Oroville, *Wash., U.S.A.* 158 B4 48 56N 119 26W
Oroville, L., *U.S.A.* 160 F5 39 33N 121 29W
Orrefors, *Sweden* 17 H9 56 50N 15 45 E
Orrick, *U.S.A.* 156 E2 39 13N 94 7W
Orroroo, *Australia* 128 B3 32 43 S 138 38 E
Orrviken, *Sweden* 16 A8 63 6N 14 26 E
Orrville, *U.S.A.* 150 F3 40 50N 81 46W
Orsa, *Sweden* 16 C8 61 7N 14 37 E
Orsara di Púglia, *Italy* 47 A8 41 17N 15 16 E
Orsasjön, *Sweden* 16 C8 61 7N 14 37 E
Orsha, *Belarus* 58 E6 54 30N 30 25 E
Orsières, *Switz.* 32 D4 46 2N 7 9 E
Örsjö, *Sweden* 17 H9 56 42N 15 45 E
Orsk, *Russia* 62 F7 51 12N 58 34 E
Orşova, *Romania* 52 F7 44 41N 22 25 E
Ørsta, *Norway* 18 B3 62 13N 6 8 E
Ørsted, *Denmark* 17 H4 56 30N 10 20 E
Örsundsbro, *Sweden* 16 E11 59 44N 17 18 E
Orta, L. d', *Italy* 44 C5 45 49N 8 24 E
Orta Nova, *Italy* 47 A8 41 19N 15 42 E
Ortaca, *Turkey* 49 E10 36 49N 28 45 E
Ortakent, *Turkey* 49 D9 37 5N 27 21 E
Ortaklar, *Turkey* 49 D9 37 53N 27 30 E
Ortaköy, *Çorum, Turkey* 100 B6 40 16N 35 15 E
Ortaköy, *Niğde, Turkey* 100 C6 38 44N 34 3 E
Orte, *Italy* 45 F9 42 27N 12 23 E
Ortegal, C., *Spain* 42 B3 43 43N 7 52W
Orteguaza →, *Colombia* 168 C2 0 43N 75 16W
Orthez, *France* 28 E3 43 29N 0 48W
Ortigueira, *Spain* 42 B3 43 40N 7 50W
Orting, *U.S.A.* 160 C4 47 6N 122 12W
Ortisei, *Italy* 45 B8 46 34N 11 40 E
Ortles, *Italy* 44 B7 46 31N 10 33 E
Ortnevik, *Norway* 18 C3 61 6N 6 7 E
Orto, Tokay, *Kyrgyzstan* 63 B8 42 20N 76 1 E
Ortón →, *Bolivia* 172 C4 10 50 S 67 0W
Ortona, *Italy* 45 F11 42 21N 14 24 E
Orūmīyeh, *Iran* 101 D11 37 40N 45 0 E
Orūmīyeh, Daryācheh-ye,
Iran 101 D11 37 50N 45 30 E
Orune, *Italy* 46 B2 40 24N 9 22 E
Oruro, *Bolivia* 172 D4 18 0 S 67 9W
Oruro □, *Bolivia* 172 D4 18 40 S 67 30W
Orust, *Sweden* 17 F5 58 10N 11 40 E
Oruzgān □, *Afghan.* 91 B2 33 30N 66 0 E
Orvault, *France* 26 E5 47 17N 1 38W
Orvieto, *Italy* 45 F9 42 43N 12 7 E
Orwell, *U.S.A.* 150 E4 41 32N 80 52W
Orwell →, *U.K.* 21 F9 51 59N 1 18 E
Oryakhovo, *Bulgaria* 50 C7 43 40N 23 57 E
Orzinuovi, *Italy* 44 C6 45 24N 9 55 E
Orzyc →, *Poland* 55 F8 52 46N 21 14 E
Orzysz, *Poland* 54 E8 53 50N 21 58 E
Os, *Norway* 18 B8 62 30N 11 14 E
Osa, *Russia* 62 C5 57 17N 55 26 E
Osa →, *Norway* 18 C8 61 18N 11 46 E
Osa →, *Poland* 54 E5 53 33N 18 46 E
Osa, Pen. de, *Costa Rica* 164 E3 8 0N 84 0W
Osage, *Iowa, U.S.A.* 154 D8 43 17N 92 49W
Osage, *Wyo., U.S.A.* 154 D2 43 59N 104 25W
Osage →, *U.S.A.* 156 F5 38 35N 91 57W
Osage City, *U.S.A.* 154 F7 38 38N 95 50W
Ōsaka, *Japan* 71 C7 34 40N 135 30 E
Ōsaka □, *Japan* 71 C7 34 30N 135 30 E
Ōsaka-Wan, *Japan* 71 C7 34 30N 135 18 E
Osan, *S. Korea* 75 F14 37 11N 127 4 E
Osawatomie, *U.S.A.* 154 F7 38 31N 94 57W
Osborne, *U.S.A.* 154 F5 39 26N 98 42W
Osby, *Sweden* 17 H7 56 23N 13 59 E
Osceola, *Ark., U.S.A.* 155 H10 35 42N 89 58W
Osceola, *Iowa, U.S.A.* 156 C3 41 2N 93 46W
Osceola, *Mo., U.S.A.* 156 F3 38 3N 93 42W
Osceola National Forest,
U.S.A. 152 E7 30 20N 82 30W
Oschatz, *Germany* 30 D9 51 17N 13 6 E
Oschersleben, *Germany* 30 C7 52 2N 11 14 E
Öschiri, *Italy* 46 B2 40 43N 9 6 E
Oscoda, *U.S.A.* 150 B1 44 26N 83 20W
Osečina, *Serbia, Yug.* 50 B3 44 23N 19 34 E
Ösel = Saaremaa, *Estonia* 15 G20 58 30N 22 30 E
Osensjøen, *Norway* 18 C8 61 13N 11 50 E
Osery, *Russia* 58 E10 54 52N 38 28 E
Osgood, *U.S.A.* 157 E11 39 8N 85 18W
Osh, *Kyrgyzstan* 63 C6 40 37N 72 49 E
Oshawa, *Canada* 140 D4 43 50N 78 50W
Oshima, *Japan* 70 D4 33 55N 132 14 E
Oshkosh, *Nebr., U.S.A.* 154 E3 41 24N 102 21W
Oshkosh, *Wis., U.S.A.* 154 C10 44 1N 88 33W
Oshmyany = Ashmyany,
Belarus 15 J21 54 26N 25 52 E
Oshnovīyeh, *Iran* 96 B5 37 2N 45 6 E
Oshogbo, *Nigeria* 113 D5 7 48N 4 37 E
Oshtorīnān, *Iran* 97 C6 34 1N 48 38 E
Oshwe,
Dem. Rep. of the Congo 114 C3 3 25 S 19 28 E
Osieczna, *Poland* 55 G3 51 55N 16 40 E
Osierfield, *U.S.A.* 152 D6 31 40N 83 7W
Osijek, *Croatia* 52 E3 45 34N 18 41 E
Òsilo, *Italy* 46 B1 40 45N 8 40 E
Ósimo, *Italy* 45 E10 43 28N 13 30 E
Osintorf, *Belarus* 58 E6 54 40N 30 39 E
Osipenko = Berdyansk,
Ukraine 59 J9 46 45N 36 50 E
Osipovichi = Asipovichy,
Belarus 58 F5 53 19N 28 33 E
Osizweni, *S. Africa* 117 D5 27 49 S 30 7 E
Oskaloosa, *U.S.A.* 156 C4 41 18N 92 39W
Oskarshamn, *Sweden* 17 G10 57 15N 16 27 E
Oskarström, *Sweden* 17 H6 56 48N 12 58 E
Oskélanéo, *Canada* 140 C4 48 5N 75 15W
Öskemen, *Kazakstan* 64 E9 50 0N 82 36 E
Oskol →, *Ukraine* 59 H9 49 6N 37 25 E
Oslo, *Norway* 15 G14 59 55N 10 45 E
Oslo □, *Norway* 18 D7 59 54N 10 43 E
Oslob, *Phil.* 81 G4 9 31N 123 26 E
Oslofjorden, *Norway* 15 G14 59 20N 10 35 E
Osmanabad, *India* 94 E3 18 5N 76 10 E
Osmancık, *Turkey* 100 B6 40 58N 34 47 E
Osmaniye, *Turkey* 100 D7 37 5N 36 10 E
Osmanlı, *Turkey* 51 E10 41 35N 26 51 E
Ösmo, *Sweden* 16 F11 58 58N 17 55 E
Osnabrück, *Germany* 30 C4 52 17N 8 3 E
Ośno Lubuskie, *Poland* 55 F1 52 28N 14 51 E
Osoblaha, *Czech Rep.* 35 A10 50 17N 17 44 E
Osogovska Planina,
Macedonia 50 D6 42 10N 22 30 E
Osor, *Italy* 45 D11 44 42N 14 24 E
Osorio, *Brazil* 175 B5 29 53 S 50 17W
Osorno, *Chile* 176 B2 40 25 S 73 0W
Osorno, *Spain* 42 C6 42 24N 4 22W
Osorno □, *Chile* 176 B2 40 34 S 73 9W
Osorno, Vol., *Chile* 176 B2 41 0 S 72 30W
Osoyoos, *Canada* 142 D5 49 0N 119 30W
Osøyro, *Norway* 15 F11 60 9N 5 30 E
Óspakseyri, *Iceland* 11 B5 65 27N 21 26W
Ospika →, *Canada* 142 B4 56 20N 124 0W
Osprey, *U.S.A.* 153 H7 27 12N 82 29W
Osprey Reef, *Australia* 126 A4 13 52 S 146 36 E
Oss, *Neths.* 24 C5 51 46N 5 32 E
Ossa, Mt., *Australia* 126 G4 41 52 S 146 3 E
Óssa, Óros, *Greece* 48 B4 39 47N 22 42 E
Ossa de Montiel, *Spain* 41 G2 38 58N 2 45W
Ossabaw I., *U.S.A.* 152 D8 31 50N 81 5W
Ossabaw Sd., *U.S.A.* 152 D8 31 50N 81 6W
Osse →, *France* 28 D4 44 7N 0 17 E
Ossi, *Italy* 46 B1 40 40N 8 35 E
Ossining, *U.S.A.* 151 E11 41 10N 73 55W
Ossipee, *U.S.A.* 151 C13 43 41N 71 7W
Ossokmanuan L., *Canada* 141 B7 53 25N 65 0W
Ossora, *Russia* 65 D17 59 20N 163 13 E
Ostashkov, *Russia* 58 D7 57 4N 33 2 E
Östavall, *Sweden* 16 B9 62 26N 15 29 E
Østby, *Norway* 18 C9 61 15N 12 33 E
Oste →, *Germany* 30 B5 53 33N 9 2 E
Ostend = Oostende, *Belgium* 24 C2 51 15N 2 54 E
Oster, *Ukraine* 59 G6 50 57N 30 53 E
Osterburg, *Germany* 30 C7 52 47N 11 45 E
Osterburken, *Germany* 31 F5 49 25N 9 26 E
Österbybruk, *Sweden* 16 D11 60 13N 17 55 E
Österbymo, *Sweden* 17 G9 57 49N 15 15 E
Österdalälven, *Sweden* 16 C7 61 30N 13 45 E
Østerdalen, *Norway* 15 F14 61 40N 10 50 E
Österfärnebo, *Sweden* 16 D10 60 19N 16 48 E
Österforse, *Sweden* 16 A11 63 9N 17 3 E
Östergötlands län □, *Sweden* 17 F9 58 35N 15 45 E
Osterholz-Scharmbeck,
Germany 30 B4 53 13N 8 47 E
Østerild, *Denmark* 17 G2 57 2N 8 51 E
Ostermundigen, *Switz.* 32 C4 46 58N 7 27 E
Osterode, *Germany* 30 D6 51 43N 10 15 E
Östersund, *Sweden* 16 A8 63 10N 14 38 E
Östervåla, *Sweden* 16 D11 60 11N 17 11 E
Østfold □, *Norway* 18 E8 59 25N 11 25 E
Ostfriesische Inseln,
Germany 30 B3 53 42N 7 0 E
Ostfriesland, *Germany* 30 B3 53 20N 7 30 E
Östhammar, *Sweden* 16 D12 60 16N 18 22 E
Óstia, Lido di, *Italy* 45 G9 41 43N 12 17 E
Ostíglia, *Italy* 45 C8 45 4N 11 8 E
Östmark, *Sweden* 16 D6 60 17N 12 45 E
Östra Husby, *Sweden* 17 F10 58 35N 16 33 E
Ostrava, *Czech Rep.* 35 B11 49 51N 18 18 E
Ostróda, *Poland* 54 E6 53 42N 19 58 E
Ostrogozhsk, *Russia* 59 G10 50 55N 39 7 E
Ostroh, *Ukraine* 59 G4 50 20N 26 30 E
Ostrołęka, *Poland* 55 E8 53 4N 21 32 E
Ostrołęka □, *Poland* 55 F8 53 0N 21 30 E
Ostrov, *Bulgaria* 51 C8 43 40N 24 9 E
Ostrov, *Czech Rep.* 34 A5 50 18N 12 57 E
Ostrov, *Romania* 53 F12 44 6N 27 24 E
Ostrov, *Russia* 58 D5 57 25N 28 20 E
Ostrów Lubelski, *Poland* 55 G9 51 29N 22 51 E
Ostrów Mazowiecka, *Poland* 55 F8 52 50N 21 51 E
Ostrów Wielkopolski, *Poland* 55 G4 51 36N 17 44 E
Ostrowiec-Świętokrzyski,
Poland 55 H8 50 55N 21 22 E
Ostrožac, *Bos.-H.* 52 G2 43 43N 17 49 E
Ostrzeszów, *Poland* 55 G4 51 25N 17 52 E
Ostseebad Kühlungsborn,
Germany 30 A7 54 8N 11 44 E
Osttirol □, *Austria* 34 E5 46 50N 12 30 E
Ostuni, *Italy* 47 B10 40 44N 17 35 E
Osŭm →, *Bulgaria* 51 C8 43 40N 24 50 E
Osumi →, *Albania* 50 F4 40 40N 20 10 E
Ōsumi-Hantō, *Japan* 70 F2 31 20N 130 55 E
Ōsumi-Kaikyō, *Japan* 69 J5 30 55N 131 0 E
Ōsumi-Shotō, *Japan* 69 J5 30 30N 130 0 E
Osun □, *Nigeria* 113 D5 7 30N 4 30 E
Osuna, *Spain* 43 H5 37 14N 5 8W
Oswego, *U.S.A.* 151 C8 43 27N 76 31W
Oswestry, *U.K.* 20 E4 52 52N 3 3W
Oświęcim, *Poland* 55 H6 50 2N 19 11 E
Ōta, *Japan* 71 A11 36 18N 139 22 E
Ota-Gawa →, *Japan* 70 C4 34 21N 132 18 E
Otaci, *Moldova* 53 B12 48 27N 27 47 E
Otago □, *N.Z.* 131 E4 45 15 S 170 0 E
Otago Harbour, *N.Z.* 131 F5 45 47 S 170 42 E
Otago Pen., *N.Z.* 131 F5 45 48 S 170 39 E
Otahuhu, *N.Z.* 130 C3 36 56 S 174 51 E
Ōtake, *Japan* 70 C4 34 12N 132 13 E
Ōtaki, *Japan* 71 B12 35 17N 140 15 E
Otaki, *N.Z.* 130 G4 40 45 S 175 10 E
Otane, *N.Z.* 130 F5 39 54 S 176 39 E
Otar, *Kazakstan* 63 B7 43 32N 75 12 E
Otaru, *Japan* 68 C10 43 10N 141 0 E
Otaru-Wan = Ishikari-Wan,
Japan 68 C10 43 25N 141 1 E
Otautau, *N.Z.* 131 G3 46 9 S 168 1 E
Otava →, *Czech Rep.* 34 B7 49 26N 14 12 E
Otavalo, *Ecuador* 168 C2 0 13N 78 20W
Otavi, *Namibia* 116 B2 19 40 S 17 24 E
Otchinjau, *Angola* 115 F2 16 30 S 13 56 E
Otelec, *Romania* 52 E5 45 36N 20 50 E
Oţelu Roşu, *Romania* 52 E7 45 32N 22 22 E
Otero de Rey = Outeiro de
Rei, *Spain* 42 B3 43 6N 7 36W
Othello, *U.S.A.* 158 C4 46 50N 119 10W
Othonoí, *Greece* 48 B1 39 52N 19 22 E
Óthris, Óros, *Greece* 48 B4 39 2N 22 37 E
Otira, *N.Z.* 131 C6 42 49 S 171 35 E
Otira Gorge, *N.Z.* 131 C6 42 53 S 171 33 E
Otis, *U.S.A.* 154 E3 40 9N 102 58W
Otjiwarongo, *Namibia* 116 C2 20 30 S 16 33 E
Otmuchów, *Poland* 55 H4 50 28N 17 10 E
Oto Tolu Group, *Tonga* 133 Q13 20 21 S 174 32W
Otočac, *Croatia* 45 D12 44 53N 15 12 E
Otoineppu, *Japan* 68 B11 44 44N 142 16 E
Otok, *Croatia* 45 E13 43 42N 16 44 E
Oton, *Phil.* 81 F4 10 42N 122 29 E
Otorohanga, *N.Z.* 130 E4 38 12 S 175 14 E
Otoskwin →, *Canada* 140 B2 52 13N 88 6W
Otosquen, *Canada* 143 C8 53 17N 102 1W
Ōtoyo, *Japan* 70 D5 33 43N 133 45 E
Otra →, *Norway* 15 G13 58 9N 8 1 E
Otradnyy, *Russia* 60 D10 53 22N 51 21 E
Otranto, *Italy* 47 B11 40 9N 18 28 E
Otranto, C. d', *Italy* 47 B11 40 7N 18 30 E
Otranto, Str. of, *Italy* 47 B11 40 15N 18 40 E
Otrokovice, *Czech Rep.* 35 B10 49 12N 17 32 E
Otse, *S. Africa* 116 D4 25 2 S 25 45 E
Otsego, *U.S.A.* 157 B11 42 27N 85 42W
Ōtsu, *Japan* 71 C7 35 0N 135 50 E
Ōtsuki, *Japan* 71 B10 35 36N 138 57 E
Otta, *Norway* 18 C6 61 46N 9 32 E
Otta →, *Norway* 18 C6 61 46N 9 31 E
Ottapalam, *India* 95 J3 10 46N 76 23 E
Ottawa = Outaouais →,
Canada 140 C5 45 27N 74 8W
Ottawa, *Canada* 140 C4 45 27N 75 42W
Ottawa, *Ill., U.S.A.* 154 E10 41 21N 88 51W
Ottawa, *Kans., U.S.A.* 154 F7 38 37N 95 16W
Ottawa, *Ohio, U.S.A.* 157 C12 41 1N 84 3W
Ottawa Is., *Canada* 139 C11 59 35N 80 10W
Ottélé, *Cameroon* 113 E7 3 38N 11 19 E
Ottensheim, *Austria* 34 C7 48 21N 14 12 E
Otter Creek, *U.S.A.* 153 F7 29 19N 82 46W
Otter L., *Canada* 143 B8 55 35N 104 39W
Otter Rapids, *Ont., Canada* 140 B3 50 11N 81 39W
Otter Rapids, *Sask., Canada* 143 B8 55 38N 104 44W
Otterbein, *U.S.A.* 157 D9 40 29N 87 6W
Otterndorf, *Germany* 30 B4 53 48N 8 53 E
Otterøya, *Norway* 18 B3 62 45N 6 50 E
Otterup, *Denmark* 17 J4 55 30N 10 22 E
Otterville, *Canada* 150 D4 42 55N 80 36W
Otterville, *U.S.A.* 156 F4 38 42N 93 0W
Ottery St. Mary, *U.K.* 21 G4 50 44N 3 17W
Otto Beit Bridge, *Zimbabwe* 119 F2 15 59 S 28 56 E
Ottosdal, *S. Africa* 116 D4 26 46 S 25 59 E
Ottoville, *U.S.A.* 157 D12 40 57N 84 22W
Ottumwa, *U.S.A.* 156 D4 41 1N 92 25W
Otu, *Nigeria* 113 D5 8 14N 3 22 E
Otukpa, *Nigeria* 113 D6 7 9N 7 41 E
Oturkpo, *Nigeria* 113 D6 7 16N 8 8 E
Otway, B., *Chile* 176 D2 53 30 S 74 0W
Otway, C., *Australia* 128 E5 38 52 S 143 30 E
Otwock, *Poland* 55 F8 52 5N 21 20 E
Ötztaler Ache →, *Austria* 34 D3 47 14N 10 50 E
Ötztaler Alpen, *Austria* 34 E3 46 56N 11 0 E
Ou →, *Laos* 86 B4 20 4N 102 13 E
Ou Neua, *Laos* 86 A3 22 18N 101 48 E
Ou-Sammyaku, *Japan* 68 E10 39 20N 140 35 E
Ouachita →, *U.S.A.* 155 K9 31 38N 91 49W
Ouachita, L., *U.S.A.* 155 H8 34 34N 93 12W
Ouachita Mts., *U.S.A.* 155 H7 34 40N 94 25W
Ouaco, *N. Cal.* 133 T18 20 50 S 164 29 E
Ouadâne, *Mauritania* 110 D2 20 50N 11 40W
Ouadda, *C.A.R.* 114 A4 8 15N 22 20 E
Ouagadougou, *Burkina Faso* 113 C4 12 25N 1 30W
Ouagam, *Chad* 109 F2 14 22N 14 42 E
Ouahigouya, *Burkina Faso* 112 C4 13 31N 2 25W
Ouahila, *Algeria* 110 C4 27 50N 5 0W
Ouahran = Oran, *Algeria* 111 A4 35 45N 0 39W
Oualâta, *Mauritania* 112 B3 17 20N 6 55W
Ouallene, *Algeria* 111 D5 24 41N 1 11 E
Ouanda Djallé, *C.A.R.* 114 A4 8 55N 22 53 E
Ouandago, *C.A.R.* 114 A3 7 13N 18 50 E
Ouango, *C.A.R.* 114 B4 4 19N 22 30 E
Ouarâne, *Mauritania* 110 D2 21 0N 10 30W
Ouargla, *Algeria* 111 B6 31 59N 5 16 E
Ouarkziz, Djebel, *Algeria* 110 C3 28 50N 8 0W
Ouarzazate, *Morocco* 110 B3 30 55N 6 50W
Ouatagouna, *Mali* 113 B5 15 11N 0 43 E
Ouatere, *C.A.R.* 114 A3 5 30N 19 8 E
Oubangi →,
Dem. Rep. of the Congo 114 C3 0 30 S 17 50 E
Oubarakai, O. →, *Algeria* 111 C6 27 20N 9 0 E
Oubatche, *N. Cal.* 133 T18 20 26 S 164 39 E
Ouche →, *France* 27 E12 47 6N 5 16 E
Ouddorp, *Neths.* 24 C3 51 50N 3 57 E
Oude Rijn →, *Neths.* 24 B4 52 12N 4 24 E
Oudenaarde, *Belgium* 24 D3 50 50N 3 37 E
Oudon →, *France* 26 E6 47 41N 0 53W
Oudtshoorn, *S. Africa* 116 E3 33 35 S 22 14 E
Oued Zem, *Morocco* 110 B3 32 52N 6 34W
Ouégoa, *N. Cal.* 133 T18 20 20 S 164 26 E
Ouellé, *Ivory C.* 112 D4 7 26N 4 1W
Ouen, I., *N. Cal.* 133 V20 22 26 S 166 49 E
Ouenza, *Algeria* 111 A6 35 57N 8 4 E
Ouessa, *Burkina Faso* 112 C4 11 4N 2 47W
Ouessant, Î. d', *France* 26 D1 48 28N 5 6W
Ouesso, *Congo* 114 B3 1 37N 16 5 E
Ouest, Pte., *Canada* 141 C7 49 52N 64 40W
Ouezzane, *Morocco* 110 B3 34 51N 5 35W

262 Oughterard

Oughterard, *Ireland* **23 C2** 53 26N 9 18W
Ouidah, *Benin* **113 D5** 6 25N 2 0 E
Ouistreham, *France* **26 C6** 49 17N 0 18W
Oujda, *Morocco* **111 B4** 34 41N 1 55W
Oujeft, *Mauritania* **110 D2** 20 2N 13 0W
Oulainen, *Finland* **14 D21** 64 17N 24 47 E
Ould Yenjé, *Mauritania* **112 B2** 15 38N 12 16W
Ouled Djellal, *Algeria* **111 B6** 34 28N 5 2 E
Ouled Naïl, Mts. des, *Algeria* **111 B5** 34 30N 3 30 E
Oullins, *France* **29 C8** 45 43N 4 49 E
Oulmès, *Morocco* **110 B3** 33 17N 6 0W
Oulu, *Finland* **14 D21** 65 1N 25 29 E
Oulujärvi, *Finland* **14 D22** 64 25N 27 15 E
Oulujoki →, *Finland* **14 D21** 65 1N 25 30 E
Oulx, *Italy* **44 C3** 45 2N 6 50 E
Oum Chalouba, *Chad* **109 E4** 15 48N 20 46 E
Oum-el-Bouaghi, *Algeria* **111 A6** 35 55N 7 6 E
Oum el Ksi, *Algeria* **110 C3** 29 4N 6 59W
Oum-er-Rbia, O. →, *Morocco* **110 B3** 33 19N 8 21W
Oum Hadjer, *Chad* **109 F3** 13 18N 19 41 E
Oumé, *Ivory C.* **112 D3** 6 21N 5 27W
Ounane, Dj., *Algeria* **111 C6** 25 4N 7 19 E
Ounasjoki →, *Finland* **14 C21** 66 31N 25 40 E
Ounguati, *Namibia* **116 C2** 22 0 S 15 46 E
Ounianga-Kébir, *Chad* **109 E4** 19 4N 20 29 E
Ounianga Sérir, *Chad* **109 E4** 18 54N 20 51 E
Our →, *Lux.* **24 E6** 49 55N 6 5 E
Ouranópolis, *Greece* **50 F7** 40 20N 23 59 E
Ouray, *U.S.A.* **159 G10** 38 1N 107 40W
Ourcq →, *France* **27 C10** 49 1N 3 1 E
Ourém, *Brazil* **170 B2** 1 33 S 47 6W
Ourense, *Spain* **42 C3** 42 19N 7 55W
Ouricuri, *Brazil* **170 C3** 7 53 S 40 5W
Ourinhos, *Brazil* **175 A6** 23 0 S 49 54W
Ourique, *Portugal* **43 H2** 37 38N 8 16W
Ouro Fino, *Brazil* **175 A6** 22 16 S 46 25W
Ouro Prêto, *Brazil* **171 F3** 20 20 S 43 30W
Ouro Sogui, *Senegal* **112 B2** 15 36N 13 19W
Oursi, *Burkina Faso* **113 C4** 14 41N 0 27W
Ourthe →, *Belgium* **24 D5** 50 29N 5 35 E
Ouse, *Australia* **126 G4** 42 38 S 146 42 E
Ouse →, *E. Susx., U.K.* **21 G8** 50 47N 0 4 E
Ouse →, *N. Yorks., U.K.* **20 D7** 53 44N 0 55W
Oust, *France* **28 F5** 42 52N 1 13 E
Oust →, *France* **26 E4** 47 35N 2 6W
Outaouais →, *Canada* **140 C5** 45 27N 74 8W
Outardes →, *Canada* **141 C6** 49 24N 69 30W
Outat Oulad el Haj, *Morocco* **111 B4** 33 22N 3 42W
Outeiro de Rei, *Spain* **42 B3** 43 6N 7 36W
Outer Hebrides, *U.K.* **22 D1** 57 30N 7 40W
Outer I., *Canada* **141 B8** 51 10N 58 35W
Outes = Serra de Outes, *Spain* **42 C2** 42 52N 8 55W
Outjo, *Namibia* **116 C2** 20 5 S 16 7 E
Outlook, *Canada* **143 C7** 51 30N 107 0W
Outlook, *U.S.A.* **154 A2** 48 53N 104 47W
Outokumpu, *Finland* **14 E23** 62 43N 29 1 E
Outreau, *France* **27 B8** 50 40N 1 36 E
Ouvèze →, *France* **29 E8** 43 59N 4 51 E
Ouyen, *Australia* **128 C5** 35 1 S 142 22 E
Ouzinkie, *U.S.A.* **144 H9** 57 56N 152 30W
Ouzouer-le-Marché, *France* **27 E8** 47 54N 1 32 E
Ovada, *Italy* **44 D5** 44 38N 8 38 E
Ovalau, *Fiji* **133 A2** 17 40 S 178 48 E
Ovalle, *Chile* **174 C1** 30 33 S 71 18W
Ovamboland, *Namibia* **116 B2** 18 30 S 16 0 E
Ovar, *Portugal* **42 E2** 40 51N 8 40W
Ovejas, *Colombia* **168 B2** 9 32N 75 14W
Ovens, *Australia* **129 D7** 36 35 S 146 46 E
Overath, *Germany* **30 E3** 50 56N 7 17 E
Overflakkee, *Neths.* **24 C4** 51 44N 4 10 E
Overijssel □, *Neths.* **24 B6** 52 25N 6 35 E
Overland, *U.S.A.* **156 F6** 38 41N 90 22W
Overland Park, *U.S.A.* **154 F7** 38 55N 94 50W
Overton, *U.S.A.* **161 J12** 36 33N 114 27W
Övertorneå, *Sweden* **14 C20** 66 23N 23 38 E
Överum, *Sweden* **17 F10** 58 0N 16 20 E
Ovid, *Colo., U.S.A.* **154 E3** 40 58N 102 23W
Ovid, *Mich., U.S.A.* **157 A12** 43 1N 84 22W
Ovidiopol, *Ukraine* **59 J6** 46 15N 30 30 E
Ovidiu, *Romania* **53 F13** 44 16N 28 34 E
Oviedo, *Spain* **42 B5** 43 25N 5 50W
Oviedo, *U.S.A.* **153 G8** 28 40N 81 13W
Oviksfjällen, *Sweden* **16 A7** 63 0N 13 49 E
Oviši, *Latvia* **15 H19** 57 33N 21 44 E
Övör Hangay □, *Mongolia* **74 B2** 45 0N 102 30 E
Ovoro, *Nigeria* **113 D6** 5 26N 7 16 E
Øvre Årdal, *Norway* **15 F12** 61 19N 7 48 E
Övre Fryken, *Sweden* **16 E7** 60 0N 13 7 E
Øvre Rendal, *Norway* **18 C8** 61 54N 11 4 E
Øvre Rindal, *Norway* **18 A6** 63 6N 9 10 E
Øvre Sirdal, *Norway* **18 F3** 58 48N 6 43 E
Ovruch, *Ukraine* **59 G5** 51 25N 28 45 E
Owaka, *N.Z.* **131 G4** 46 27 S 169 40 E
Owambo = Ovamboland, *Namibia* **116 B2** 18 30 S 16 0 E
Owando, *Congo* **114 C3** 0 29 S 15 55 E
Owase, *Japan* **71 C8** 34 7N 136 12 E
Owatonna, *U.S.A.* **154 C8** 44 5N 93 14W
Owbeh, *Afghan.* **91 B1** 34 28N 63 10 E
Owego, *U.S.A.* **151 D8** 42 6N 76 16W
Owen, *Australia* **128 C3** 34 15 S 138 32 E
Owen Falls Dam, *Uganda* **118 B3** 0 30N 33 5 E
Owen Mt., *N.Z.* **131 B7** 41 35 S 172 33 E
Owen Sound, *Canada* **140 D3** 44 35N 80 55W
Owen Stanley Ra., *Papua N. G.* **132 E4** 8 30 S 147 0 E
Owendo, *Gabon* **114 B1** 0 17N 9 30 E
Owens →, *U.S.A.* **160 J9** 36 32N 117 59W
Owens L., *U.S.A.* **161 J9** 36 26N 117 57W
Owensboro, *U.S.A.* **157 G9** 37 46N 87 7W
Owensville, *Ind., U.S.A.* **157 F9** 38 16N 87 41W
Owensville, *Mo., U.S.A.* **156 F5** 38 21N 91 30W
Owenton, *U.S.A.* **157 F12** 38 32N 84 50W
Owerri, *Nigeria* **113 D6** 5 29N 7 0 E
Owhango, *N.Z.* **130 F4** 39 0 S 175 23 E
Owingsville, *U.S.A.* **157 F13** 38 9N 83 46W
Owl →, *Canada* **143 B10** 57 51N 92 44W
Owo, *Nigeria* **113 D6** 7 10N 5 39 E
Owosso, *U.S.A.* **157 B12** 43 0N 84 10W
Owyhee, *U.S.A.* **158 F5** 41 57N 116 6W
Owyhee →, *U.S.A.* **158 E5** 43 49N 117 2W
Owyhee, L., *U.S.A.* **158 E5** 43 38N 117 14W
Ox Mts. = Slieve Gamph, *Ireland* **23 B3** 54 6N 9 0W
Oxapampa, *Peru* **172 C2** 10 33 S 75 26W
Öxarfjörður, *Iceland* **11 A10** 66 15N 16 45W
Oxelösund, *Sweden* **17 F11** 58 43N 17 5 E
Oxford, *N.Z.* **131 D7** 43 18 S 172 11 E
Oxford, *U.K.* **21 F6** 51 46N 1 15W
Oxford, *Ala., U.S.A.* **152 B4** 33 36N 85 51W
Oxford, *Iowa, U.S.A.* **156 C5** 41 43N 91 47W
Oxford, *Mich., U.S.A.* **157 B13** 42 49N 83 16W
Oxford, *Miss., U.S.A.* **155 H10** 34 22N 89 31W
Oxford, *N.C., U.S.A.* **149 G6** 36 19N 78 35W
Oxford, *Ohio, U.S.A.* **157 E12** 39 31N 84 45W
Oxford L., *Canada* **143 C9** 54 51N 95 37W
Oxfordshire □, *U.K.* **21 F6** 51 48N 1 16W
Oxía, *Greece* **48 C3** 38 16N 21 5 E
Oxie, *Sweden* **17 J7** 55 33N 13 6 E
Oxílithos, *Greece* **48 C6** 38 35N 24 7 E
Oxley, *Australia* **128 C6** 34 11 S 144 6 E
Oxnard, *U.S.A.* **161 L7** 34 12N 119 11W
Oxsjövålen, *Sweden* **16 B7** 62 34N 13 57 E
Oxus = Amudarya →, *Uzbekistan* **64 E6** 43 58N 59 34 E
Oya, *Malaysia* **85 B4** 2 55N 111 55 E
Oyabe, *Japan* **71 A8** 36 47N 136 56 E
Oyama, *Japan* **71 A11** 36 18N 139 48 E
Oyana, *Japan* **70 E2** 32 32N 130 30 E
Oyapock →, *Fr. Guiana* **169 C7** 4 8N 51 40W
Øye, *Norway* **18 F3** 58 16N 6 49 E
Oyem, *Gabon* **114 B2** 1 34N 11 31 E
Oyen, *Canada* **143 C6** 51 22N 110 28W
Øyer, *Norway* **18 C7** 61 16N 10 25 E
Øyeren, *Norway* **18 E8** 59 50N 11 15 E
Oykel →, *U.K.* **22 D4** 57 56N 4 26W
Oymyakon, *Russia* **65 C15** 63 25N 142 44 E
Oyo, *Nigeria* **113 D5** 7 46N 3 56 E
Oyo □, *Nigeria* **113 D5** 8 15N 3 30 E
Oyón, *Peru* **172 C2** 10 37 S 76 47W
Oyonnax, *France* **27 F12** 46 16N 5 40 E
Øyslebø, *Norway* **18 F4** 58 9N 7 34 E
Oyster Bay, *U.S.A.* **151 F11** 40 52N 73 32W
Øystese, *Norway* **18 D3** 60 22N 6 9 E
Oytal, *Kazakstan* **63 B6** 42 54N 73 17 E
Ōyūbari, *Japan* **68 C11** 43 1N 142 5 E
Özalp, *Turkey* **101 C10** 38 39N 43 59 E
Ozamiz, *Phil.* **81 G4** 8 15N 123 50 E
Ozark, *Ala., U.S.A.* **152 D4** 31 28N 85 39W
Ozark, *Ark., U.S.A.* **155 H8** 35 29N 93 50W
Ozark, *Mo., U.S.A.* **155 G8** 37 1N 93 12W
Ozark Plateau, *U.S.A.* **155 G9** 37 20N 91 40W
Ozarks, L. of the, *U.S.A.* **156 F4** 38 12N 92 38W
Ożarów, *Poland* **55 H8** 50 53N 21 40 E
Ózd, *Hungary* **52 B5** 48 14N 20 15 E
Ozernoye, *Russia* **60 E10** 51 46N 51 28 E
Ozërnyy, *Russia* **62 F8** 51 8N 60 50 E
Ozette L., *U.S.A.* **160 B2** 48 6N 124 38W
Özgön, *Kyrgyzstan* **63 C6** 40 46N 73 18 E
Ozieri, *Italy* **46 B2** 40 35N 9 0 E
Ozimek, *Poland* **55 H5** 50 41N 18 11 E
Ozinki, *Russia* **60 E9** 51 12N 49 44 E
Ozona, *U.S.A.* **155 K4** 30 43N 101 12W
Ozorków, *Poland* **55 G6** 51 57N 19 16 E
Ozren, *Bos.-H.* **52 G3** 43 55N 18 29 E
Ozu, *Ehime, Japan* **70 D4** 33 30N 132 33 E
Ozu, *Kumamoto, Japan* **70 E2** 32 52N 130 52 E
Ozuluama, *Mexico* **163 C5** 21 40N 97 50W
Ozun, *Romania* **53 E10** 45 47N 25 50 E
Ozurgeti, *Georgia* **61 K5** 41 55N 42 2 E

P

Pa, *Burkina Faso* **112 C4** 11 33N 3 19W
Pa-an, *Burma* **90 G6** 16 51N 97 40 E
Pa Mong Dam, *Thailand* **86 D4** 18 0N 102 22 E
Paagoumène, *N. Cal.* **133 T18** 20 29 S 164 11 E
Paama, *Vanuatu* **133 F6** 16 28 S 168 14 E
Paamiut = Frederikshåb, *Greenland* **10 E6** 62 0N 49 43W
Paar →, *Germany* **31 G7** 48 46N 11 36 E
Paarl, *S. Africa* **116 E2** 33 45 S 18 56 E
Paauilo, *U.S.A.* **146 H17** 20 2N 155 22W
Pab Hills, *Pakistan* **91 D2** 26 30N 66 45 E
Pabbay, *U.K.* **22 D1** 57 46N 7 14W
Pabianice, *Poland* **55 G6** 51 40N 19 20 E
Pabna, *Bangla.* **90 C2** 24 1N 89 18 E
Pabo, *Uganda* **118 B3** 3 1N 32 10 E
Pacaás Novos, Serra dos, *Brazil* **173 C5** 10 45 S 64 15W
Pacaipampa, *Peru* **172 B2** 5 35 S 79 39W
Pacaja →, *Brazil* **170 B1** 1 56 S 50 50W
Pacajus, *Brazil* **170 B4** 4 10 S 38 31W
Pacaraima, Sierra, *Venezuela* **169 C5** 4 0N 62 30W
Pacarán, *Peru* **172 C2** 12 50 S 76 3W
Pacaraos, *Peru* **172 C2** 11 12 S 76 42W
Pacasmayo, *Peru* **172 B2** 7 20 S 79 35W
Pace, *U.S.A.* **153 E2** 30 36N 87 10W
Paceco, *Italy* **46 E5** 37 59N 12 33 E
Pachacamac, *Peru* **172 C2** 12 14 S 77 53W
Pachhar, *India* **92 G7** 24 40N 77 42 E
Pachino, *Italy* **47 F8** 36 43N 15 5 E
Pachitea →, *Peru* **172 B3** 8 46 S 74 33W
Pachiza, *Peru* **172 B2** 7 16 S 76 46W
Pacho, *Colombia* **168 B3** 5 8N 74 10W
Pachora, *India* **94 D2** 20 38N 75 29 E
Pachuca, *Mexico* **163 C5** 20 10N 98 40W
Pacific, *Canada* **142 C3** 54 48N 128 28W
Pacific, *U.S.A.* **156 F6** 38 29N 90 45W
Pacific-Antarctic Ridge, *Pac. Oc.* **135 M16** 43 0 S 115 0W
Pacific Grove, *U.S.A.* **160 J5** 36 38N 121 56W
Pacific Ocean, *Pac. Oc.* **135 G14** 10 0N 140 0W
Pacific Palisades, *U.S.A.* **145 K14** 21 25N 157 58W
Pacifica, *U.S.A.* **160 H4** 37 36N 122 30W
Pacitan, *Indonesia* **85 D4** 8 12 S 111 7 E
Packsaddle, *Australia* **128 A4** 30 36 S 141 58 E
Packwood, *U.S.A.* **160 D5** 46 36N 121 40W
Pacov, *Czech Rep.* **34 B8** 49 27N 15 0 E
Pacuí →, *Brazil* **171 E2** 16 46 S 45 1W
Pacy-sur-Eure, *France* **26 C8** 49 1N 1 23 E
Padaido, Kepulauan, *Indonesia* **83 B5** 1 5 S 138 0 E
Padang, *Indonesia* **84 C2** 1 0 S 100 20 E
Padang Endau, *Malaysia* **87 L4** 2 40N 103 38 E
Padangpanjang, *Indonesia* **84 C2** 0 40 S 100 20 E
Padangsidempuan, *Indonesia* **84 B1** 1 30N 99 15 E
Padangtikar, *Indonesia* **85 C3** 0 44 S 109 15 E
Padatchuang, *Burma* **90 F5** 19 46N 94 48 E
Padauari →, *Brazil* **169 D5** 0 15 S 64 5W
Padborg, *Denmark* **17 K3** 54 49N 9 21 E
Padcaya, *Bolivia* **173 E5** 21 52 S 64 48W
Paddockwood, *Canada* **143 C7** 53 30N 105 30W
Paderborn, *Germany* **30 D4** 51 42N 8 45 E
Padeș, Vf., *Romania* **52 E7** 45 40N 22 22 E
Padilla, *Bolivia* **173 D5** 19 19 S 64 20W
Padina, *Romania* **53 F12** 44 50N 27 8 E
Padma →, *Bangla.* **90 D3** 23 22N 90 32 E
Padmanabhapuram, *India* **95 K3** 8 16N 77 17 E
Pádova, *Italy* **45 C8** 45 25N 11 53 E
Padra, *India* **92 H5** 22 15N 73 7 E
Padrauna, *India* **93 F10** 26 54N 83 59 E
Padre Burgos, *Phil.* **81 F5** 10 1N 125 0 E
Padre I., *U.S.A.* **155 M6** 27 10N 97 25W
Padrón, *Spain* **42 C2** 42 41N 8 39W
Padstow, *U.K.* **21 G3** 50 33N 4 58W
Padua = Pádova, *Italy* **45 C8** 45 25N 11 53 E
Paducah, *Ky., U.S.A.* **148 G1** 37 5N 88 37W
Paducah, *Tex., U.S.A.* **155 H4** 34 1N 100 18W
Padul, *Spain* **43 H7** 37 1N 3 38W
Padwa, *India* **94 E6** 18 27N 82 47 E
Paekakariki, *N.Z.* **130 G3** 40 59 S 174 58 E
Paengaroa, *N.Z.* **130 D5** 37 49 S 176 29 E
Paengnyong-do, *S. Korea* **75 F13** 37 57N 124 40 E
Paeroa, *N.Z.* **130 D4** 37 23 S 175 41 E
Paesana, *Italy* **44 D4** 44 41N 7 16 E
Paete, *Phil.* **80 D3** 14 23N 121 29 E
Pafúri, *Mozam.* **117 C5** 22 28 S 31 17 E
Pag, *Croatia* **45 D12** 44 25N 15 3 E
Paga, *Ghana* **113 C4** 11 1N 1 8W
Pagadian, *Phil.* **81 H4** 7 55N 123 30 E
Pagai Selatan, *Indonesia* **84 C2** 3 0 S 100 15 E
Pagai Utara, Pulau, *Indonesia* **84 C2** 2 35 S 100 0 E
Pagalu = Annobón, *Atl. Oc.* **105 G4** 1 25 S 5 36 E
Pagastikós Kólpos, *Greece* **48 B5** 39 15N 23 0 E
Pagatan, *Indonesia* **85 C5** 3 33 S 115 59 E
Page, *Ariz., U.S.A.* **159 H8** 36 57N 111 27W
Page, *N. Dak., U.S.A.* **154 B6** 47 10N 97 34W
Pagėgiai, *Lithuania* **54 C8** 55 9N 21 54 E
Pago Pago, *Amer. Samoa* **133 X24** 14 16 S 170 43W
Pagosa Springs, *U.S.A.* **159 H10** 37 16N 107 1W
Pagwa River, *Canada* **140 B2** 50 2N 85 14W
Pahala, *U.S.A.* **146 J17** 19 12N 155 29W
Pahang □, *Malaysia* **84 B2** 3 30N 102 45 E
Pahang →, *Malaysia* **87 L4** 3 30N 103 9 E
Pahia Pt., *N.Z.* **131 G2** 46 20 S 167 41 E
Pahiatua, *N.Z.* **130 G4** 40 27 S 175 50 E
Pahokee, *U.S.A.* **149 M5** 26 50N 80 40W
Pahrump, *U.S.A.* **161 J11** 36 12N 115 59W
Pahute Mesa, *U.S.A.* **160 H10** 37 20N 116 45W
Pai, *Thailand* **86 C2** 19 19N 98 27 E
Paia, *U.S.A.* **146 H16** 20 54N 156 22W
Paicines, *U.S.A.* **160 J5** 36 44N 121 17W
Paide, *Estonia* **15 G21** 58 57N 25 31 E
Paignton, *U.K.* **21 G4** 50 26N 3 35W
Paiho, *Taiwan* **77 F13** 23 21N 120 25 E
Paiján, *Peru* **172 B2** 7 42 S 79 20W
Päijänne, *Finland* **15 F21** 61 30N 25 30 E
Pailin, *Cambodia* **86 F4** 12 46N 102 36 E
Paimpol, *France* **26 D3** 48 48N 3 4W
Painan, *Indonesia* **84 C2** 1 21 S 100 34 E
Painesville, *U.S.A.* **150 E3** 41 43N 81 15W
Paint Hills = Wemindji, *Canada* **140 B4** 53 0N 78 49W
Paint L., *Canada* **143 B9** 55 28N 97 57W
Paint Rock, *U.S.A.* **155 K5** 31 31N 99 55W
Painted Desert, *U.S.A.* **159 J8** 36 0N 111 0W
Paintsville, *U.S.A.* **148 G4** 37 49N 82 48W
País Vasco □, *Spain* **40 C2** 42 50N 2 45W
Paisley, *Canada* **150 B3** 44 18N 81 16W
Paisley, *U.K.* **22 F4** 55 50N 4 25W
Paisley, *U.S.A.* **158 E3** 42 42N 120 32W
Païta, *N. Cal.* **133 V20** 22 8 S 166 22 E
Paita, *Peru* **172 B1** 5 11 S 81 9W
Paiva →, *Portugal* **42 D2** 41 4N 8 16W
Paizhou, *China* **77 B9** 30 12N 113 55 E
Pajares, *Spain* **42 B5** 43 1N 5 46W
Pajares, Puerto de, *Spain* **42 C5** 42 58N 5 46W
Pajęczno, *Poland* **55 G5** 51 10N 19 0 E
Pak Lay, *Laos* **86 C3** 18 15N 101 27 E
Pak Phanang, *Thailand* **87 H3** 8 21N 100 12 E
Pak Sane, *Laos* **86 C4** 18 22N 103 39 E
Pak Song, *Laos* **86 E6** 15 11N 106 14 E
Pak Suong, *Laos* **86 C4** 19 58N 102 15 E
Pakala, *India* **95 H4** 13 29N 79 8 E
Pakaraima Mts., *Guyana* **169 B6** 6 0N 60 0W
Pakenham, *Australia* **129 E6** 38 6 S 145 30 E
Pákhnes, *Greece* **38 D6** 35 16N 24 4 E
Pakhtakor, *Uzbekistan* **63 C2** 40 2N 65 46 E
Pakistan ■, *Asia* **91 C3** 30 0N 70 0 E
Pakkading, *Laos* **86 C4** 18 19N 103 59 E
Pakokku, *Burma* **90 E5** 21 20N 95 0 E
Pakość, *Poland* **55 F5** 52 48N 18 6 E
Pakpattan, *Pakistan* **91 C4** 30 25N 73 27 E
Pakrac, *Croatia* **52 E2** 45 27N 17 12 E
Pakruojis, *Lithuania* **54 C10** 55 58N 23 52 E
Paks, *Hungary* **52 D3** 46 38N 18 55 E
Paktīā □, *Afghan.* **91 B3** 33 0N 69 15 E
Paktīkā □, *Afghan.* **91 B3** 32 30N 69 0 E
Pakwach, *Uganda* **118 B3** 2 28N 31 27 E
Pakxe, *Laos* **86 E5** 15 5N 105 52 E
Pala, *Chad* **109 G3** 9 25N 15 5 E
Pala, *Dem. Rep. of the Congo* **118 D2** 6 45 S 29 30 E
Pala, *U.S.A.* **161 M9** 33 22N 117 5W
Palabek, *Uganda* **118 B3** 3 22N 32 33 E
Palacios, *U.S.A.* **155 L6** 28 42N 96 13W
Palafrugell, *Spain* **40 D8** 41 55N 3 10 E
Palagiano, *Italy* **47 B10** 40 35N 17 2 E
Palagonía, *Italy* **47 E7** 37 19N 14 45 E
Palagruža, *Croatia* **45 F13** 42 24N 16 15 E
Palaiókastron, *Greece* **38 D8** 35 12N 26 15 E
Palaiokhóra, *Greece* **38 D5** 35 16N 23 39 E
Pálairos, *Greece* **48 C2** 38 45N 20 51 E
Palaiseau, *France* **27 D9** 48 43N 2 15 E
Palakol, *India* **95 F5** 16 31N 81 46 E
Palam, *India* **94 E3** 19 0N 77 0 E
Palamás, *Greece* **48 B4** 39 26N 22 4 E
Palamòs, *Spain* **40 D8** 41 50N 3 10 E
Palampur, *India* **92 C7** 32 10N 76 30 E
Palamut, *Turkey* **49 C9** 38 59N 27 41 E
Palana, *Australia* **126 F4** 39 45 S 147 55 E
Palana, *Russia* **65 D16** 59 10N 159 59 E
Palanan, *Phil.* **80 C4** 17 8N 122 29 E
Palanan Bay, *Phil.* **80 C4** 17 9N 122 27 E
Palanan Pt., *Phil.* **80 C4** 17 17N 122 30 E
Palandri, *Pakistan* **93 C5** 33 42N 73 40 E
Palanga, *Lithuania* **15 J19** 55 58N 21 3 E
Palangkaraya, *Indonesia* **85 C4** 2 16 S 113 56 E
Palani, *India* **95 J3** 10 30N 77 30 E
Palani Hills, *India* **95 J3** 10 14N 77 33 E
Palanpur, *India* **92 G5** 24 10N 72 25 E
Palanro, *Indonesia* **82 B1** 3 21 S 119 23 E
Palaoa Pt., *U.S.A.* **145 C5** 20 44N 156 58W
Palapye, *Botswana* **116 C4** 22 30 S 27 7 E
Palar →, *India* **95 H5** 12 27N 80 13 E
Palas, *Pakistan* **93 B5** 35 4N 73 14 E
Palas de Rei, *Spain* **42 C3** 42 52N 7 52W
Palatine, *U.S.A.* **157 B8** 42 7N 88 3W
Palatka, *Russia* **65 C16** 60 6N 150 54 E
Palatka, *U.S.A.* **152 F8** 29 39N 81 38W
Palau, *Italy* **46 A2** 41 11N 9 23 E
Palau ■, *Pac. Oc.* **134 G5** 7 30N 134 30 E
Palauk, *Burma* **86 F2** 13 10N 98 40 E
Palawan, *Phil.* **81 G2** 9 30N 118 30 E
Palawan □, *Phil.* **81 G2** 10 0N 119 0 E
Palawan Passage, *Phil.* **81 G2** 10 0N 118 0 E
Palayankottai, *India* **95 K3** 8 45N 77 45 E
Palazzo, Pte., *France* **29 F12** 42 28N 8 30 E
Palazzo San Gervásio, *Italy* **47 B8** 40 56N 15 59 E
Palazzolo Acréide, *Italy* **47 E7** 37 4N 14 54 E
Palca, *Chile* **172 D4** 19 7 S 69 9W
Paldiski, *Estonia* **15 G21** 59 23N 24 9 E
Pale, *Bos.-H.* **52 G3** 43 50N 18 38 E
Palel, *India* **90 C5** 24 27N 94 2 E
Paleleh, *Indonesia* **82 A2** 1 10N 121 50 E
Palembang, *Indonesia* **84 C2** 3 0 S 104 50 E
Palena →, *Chile* **176 B2** 43 50 S 73 50W
Palena, L., *Chile* **176 B2** 43 55 S 71 40W
Palencia, *Spain* **42 C6** 42 1N 4 34W
Palencia □, *Spain* **42 C6** 42 31N 4 33W
Paleokastrítsa, *Greece* **38 A3** 39 40N 19 41 E
Paleometokho, *Cyprus* **38 D12** 35 7N 33 11 E
Palermo, *Colombia* **168 C2** 2 54N 75 26W
Palermo, *Italy* **46 D6** 38 7N 13 22 E
Palermo, *U.S.A.* **158 G3** 39 26N 121 33W
Palestine, *Asia* **103 D4** 32 0N 35 0 E
Palestine, *U.S.A.* **155 K7** 31 46N 95 38W
Palestrina, *Italy* **45 G9** 41 50N 12 53 E
Paletwa, *Burma* **90 E4** 21 10N 92 50 E
Palghat, *India* **95 J3** 10 46N 76 42 E
Palgrave, Mt., *Australia* **124 D2** 23 22 S 115 58 E
Pali, *India* **92 G5** 25 50N 73 20 E
Palikea Pk., *U.S.A.* **145 K13** 21 26N 158 6W
Palin, Mt., *Malaysia* **85 A5** 6 10N 117 10 E
Palinit, *Phil.* **80 E5** 12 15N 124 20 E
Palinuro, *Italy* **47 B8** 40 2N 15 17 E
Palinuro, C., *Italy* **47 B8** 40 2N 15 16 E
Palioúrion, Ákra, *Greece* **50 G7** 39 57N 23 45 E
Palisade, *U.S.A.* **154 E4** 40 21N 101 7W
Paliseul, *Belgium* **24 E5** 49 54N 5 8 E
Palitana, *India* **92 J4** 21 32N 71 49 E
Palizada, *Mexico* **163 D6** 18 18N 92 8W
Palk Bay, *Asia* **95 K4** 9 30N 79 15 E
Palk Strait, *Asia* **95 K4** 10 0N 79 45 E
Palkānah, *Iraq* **96 C5** 35 49N 44 26 E
Palkonda, *India* **94 E6** 18 36N 83 48 E
Palkonda Ra., *India* **95 H4** 13 50N 79 20 E
Palla Road = Dinokwe, *Botswana* **116 C4** 23 29 S 26 37 E
Pallanza = Verbánia, *Italy* **44 C5** 45 56N 8 33 E
Pallasovka, *Russia* **60 E8** 50 4N 47 0 E
Palleru →, *India* **94 F5** 16 45N 80 2 E
Pallës, Bishti i, *Albania* **50 E3** 41 24N 19 24 E
Pallisa, *Uganda* **118 B3** 1 12N 33 43 E
Palliser, C., *N.Z.* **130 H4** 41 37 S 175 14 E
Palliser B., *N.Z.* **130 H4** 41 26 S 175 5 E
Pallu, *India* **92 E6** 28 59N 74 14 E
Palm Bay, *U.S.A.* **149 L5** 28 2N 80 35W
Palm Beach, *U.S.A.* **149 M6** 26 43N 80 2W
Palm Desert, *U.S.A.* **161 M10** 33 43N 116 22W
Palm Harbor, *U.S.A.* **153 G7** 28 5N 82 47W
Palm Is., *Australia* **126 B4** 18 40 S 146 35 E
Palm Springs, *U.S.A.* **161 M10** 33 50N 116 33W
Palma, *Mozam.* **119 E5** 10 46 S 40 29 E
Palma →, *Brazil* **171 D2** 12 33 S 47 52W
Palma, B. de, *Spain* **39 B9** 39 30N 2 39 E
Palma de Mallorca, *Spain* **39 B9** 39 35N 2 39 E
Palma del Río, *Spain* **43 H5** 37 43N 5 17W
Palma di Montechiaro, *Italy* **46 E6** 37 11N 13 46 E
Palma Soriano, *Cuba* **164 B4** 20 15N 76 0W
Palmares, *Brazil* **170 C4** 8 41 S 35 28W
Palmarito, *Venezuela* **168 B3** 7 37N 70 10W
Palmarola, *Italy* **46 B5** 40 56N 12 51 E
Palmas, *Brazil* **175 B5** 26 29 S 52 0W
Palmas, C., *Liberia* **112 E3** 4 27N 7 46W
Pálmas, G. di, *Italy* **46 D1** 39 0N 8 30 E
Palmas de Monte Alto, *Brazil* **171 D3** 14 16 S 43 10W
Palmdale, *Calif., U.S.A.* **161 L8** 34 35N 118 7W
Palmdale, *Fla., U.S.A.* **153 J8** 26 57N 81 19W
Palmeira, *Brazil* **171 G2** 25 25 S 50 0W
Palmeira dos Índios, *Brazil* **170 C4** 9 25 S 36 37W
Palmeirais, *Brazil* **170 C3** 6 0 S 43 0W
Palmeiras →, *Brazil* **171 D2** 12 22 S 47 8W
Palmeirinhas, Pta. das, *Angola* **115 D2** 9 2 S 12 57 E
Palmela, *Portugal* **43 G2** 38 32N 8 57W
Palmelo, *Brazil* **171 E2** 17 20 S 48 27W
Palmer, *U.S.A.* **138 B5** 61 36N 149 7W
Palmer →, *Australia* **126 B3** 16 0 S 142 26 E
Palmer Arch., *Antarctica* **7 C17** 64 15 S 65 0W
Palmer Lake, *U.S.A.* **154 F2** 39 7N 104 55W
Palmer Land, *Antarctica* **7 D18** 73 0 S 63 0W
Palmerston, *Canada* **150 C4** 43 50N 80 51W
Palmerston, *N.Z.* **131 F5** 45 29 S 170 43 E
Palmerston North, *N.Z.* **130 G4** 40 21 S 175 39 E
Palmerton, *U.S.A.* **151 F9** 40 48N 75 37W
Palmetto, *Fla., U.S.A.* **149 M4** 27 31N 82 34W
Palmetto, *Ga., U.S.A.* **152 B5** 33 31N 84 40W
Palmi, *Italy* **47 D8** 38 21N 15 51 E
Palmira, *Argentina* **174 C2** 32 59 S 68 34W
Palmira, *Colombia* **168 C2** 3 32N 76 16W
Palmyra = Tudmur, *Syria* **101 E8** 34 36N 38 15 E
Palmyra, *Ill., U.S.A.* **156 E7** 39 26N 90 0W
Palmyra, *Mo., U.S.A.* **156 E5** 39 48N 91 32W
Palmyra, *N.Y., U.S.A.* **150 C7** 43 5N 77 18W
Palmyra, *Wis., U.S.A.* **157 B8** 42 52N 88 36W
Palmyra Is., *Pac. Oc.* **135 G11** 5 52N 162 5W
Palo, *Phil.* **81 F5** 11 10N 124 59 E
Palo Alto, *U.S.A.* **160 H4** 37 27N 122 10W
Palo Verde, *U.S.A.* **161 M12** 33 26N 114 44W
Palompon, *Phil.* **81 F5** 11 3N 124 23 E
Palopo, *Indonesia* **82 B2** 3 0 S 120 16 E
Palos, C. de, *Spain* **41 H4** 37 38N 0 40W
Palos de la Frontera, *Spain* **43 H4** 37 14N 6 53W
Palos Verdes, *U.S.A.* **161 M8** 33 48N 118 23W
Palos Verdes, Pt., *U.S.A.* **161 M8** 33 43N 118 26W
Palouse, *U.S.A.* **158 C5** 46 55N 117 4W
Palpa, *Peru* **172 C2** 14 30 S 75 15W
Palparara, *Australia* **126 C3** 24 47 S 141 28 E
Pålsboda, *Sweden* **16 E9** 59 3N 15 22 E
Palu, *Indonesia* **82 B1** 1 0 S 119 52 E
Palu, *Turkey* **101 C9** 38 45N 40 0 E
Paluan, *Phil.* **80 E3** 13 26N 120 29 E
Paluzza, *Italy* **45 B10** 46 32N 13 1 E
Palwal, *India* **92 E7** 28 8N 77 19 E
Pama, *Burkina Faso* **113 C5** 11 19N 0 44 E

Patrocínio 263

Pamanukan, Indonesia 85 D3 6 16 S 107 49 E
Pamban I., India 95 K4 9 15N 79 20 E
Pambuhan, Phil. 80 E4 13 59N 123 5 E
Pamekasan, Indonesia 85 D4 7 10 S 113 28 E
Pamiers, France 28 E5 43 7N 1 39 E
Pamir, Tajikistan 63 E6 37 40N 73 0 E
Pamir →, Tajikistan 63 E6 37 1N 72 41 E
Pâmiut, Greenland 10 E6 62 0N 49 50W
Pamlico →, U.S.A. 149 H7 35 20N 76 28W
Pamlico Sd., U.S.A. 149 H8 35 20N 76 0W
Pampa, U.S.A. 155 H4 35 32N 100 58W
Pampa de Agma, Argentina 176 B3 43 45 S 69 40W
Pampa de las Salinas, Argentina 174 C2 32 1 S 66 58W
Pampa Grande, Bolivia 173 D5 18 5 S 64 6W
Pampa Hermosa, Peru 172 B2 7 7 S 75 4W
Pampanga □, Phil. 80 D3 15 4N 120 40 E
Pampanua, Indonesia 82 B2 4 16 S 120 8 E
Pampas, Argentina 174 D3 35 0 S 63 0W
Pampas, Peru 172 C3 12 20 S 74 50W
Pampas →, Peru 172 C3 13 24 S 73 12W
Pamphylia, Turkey 100 D4 37 0N 31 20 E
Pamplona, Colombia 168 B3 7 23N 72 39W
Pamplona, Phil. 80 B3 18 31N 121 20 E
Pamplona, Spain 40 C3 42 48N 1 38W
Pampoenpoort, S. Africa 116 E3 31 3 S 22 40 E
Pamukçu, Turkey 49 B9 39 30N 27 54 E
Pamukkale, Turkey 49 D11 37 55N 29 8 E
Pan Xian, China 76 E5 25 46N 104 38 E
Pana, U.S.A. 156 E7 39 23N 89 5W
Panabo, Phil. 81 H5 7 19N 125 42 E
Panaca, U.S.A. 159 H6 37 47N 114 23W
Panacea, U.S.A. 152 E5 30 2N 84 23W
Panagyurishte, Bulgaria 51 D8 42 30N 24 15 E
Panaitan, Indonesia 84 D3 6 36 S 105 12 E
Panaji, India 95 G1 15 25N 73 50 E
Panamá, Panama 164 E4 9 0N 79 25W
Panama ■, Cent. Amer. 164 E4 8 48N 79 55W
Panamá, G. de, Panama 164 E4 8 4N 79 20W
Panama Canal, Panama 164 E4 9 10N 79 37W
Panama City, U.S.A. 152 E4 30 10N 85 40W
Panama City Beach, U.S.A. 152 E4 30 11N 85 48W
Panamint Range, U.S.A. 161 J9 36 20N 117 20W
Panamint Springs, U.S.A. 161 J9 36 20N 117 28W
Panão, Peru 172 B2 9 55 S 75 55W
Panaon I., Phil. 81 F5 10 3N 125 13 E
Panare, Thailand 87 J3 6 51N 101 30 E
Panarea, Italy 47 D8 38 38N 15 4 E
Panaro →, Italy 45 D8 44 55N 11 25 E
Panarukan, Indonesia 85 D4 7 42 S 113 56 E
Panay, Phil. 81 F4 11 10N 122 30 E
Panay, G., Phil. 81 F4 11 0N 122 30 E
Pancake Range, U.S.A. 159 G6 38 30N 115 50W
Pančevo, Serbia, Yug. 52 F5 44 52N 20 41 E
Panciu, Romania 53 E12 45 54N 27 8 E
Pancol, Phil. 81 F2 10 52N 119 25 E
Pancorbo, Desfiladero, Spain 42 C7 42 32N 3 5W
Pâncota, Romania 52 D6 46 20N 21 45 E
Pandan, Antique, Phil. 81 F4 11 45N 122 10 E
Pandan, Catanduanes, Phil. 80 D5 14 3N 124 10 E
Pandan Bay, Phil. 81 F4 11 43N 122 0 E
Pandegelang, Indonesia 84 D3 6 25 S 106 5 E
Pandharpur, India 94 F2 17 41N 75 20 E
Pandhurna, India 94 D4 21 36N 78 35 E
Pando, Uruguay 175 C4 34 44 S 56 0W
Pando □, Bolivia 172 C4 11 20 S 67 40W
Pando, L. = Hope, L., Australia 127 D2 28 24 S 139 18 E
Pandokrátor, Greece 38 A3 39 45N 19 50 E
Pandora, Costa Rica 164 E3 9 43N 83 3W
Pandrup, Denmark 17 G3 57 14N 9 40 E
Pandu, Dem. Rep. of the Congo 114 B3 4 59N 19 16 E
Panevėžys, Lithuania 15 J21 55 42N 24 25 E
Panfilov, Kazakstan 64 E9 44 10N 80 0 E
Panfilovo, Russia 60 E6 50 25N 42 46 E
Panga, Dem. Rep. of the Congo 118 B2 1 52N 26 18 E
Pangaíon Óros, Greece 51 F8 40 50N 24 0 E
Pangala, Congo 114 C2 4 1 S 13 52 E
Pangalanes, Canal des, Madag. 117 C8 22 48 S 47 50 E
Pangani, Tanzania 118 D4 5 25 S 38 58 E
Pangani □, Tanzania 118 D4 5 25 S 39 0 E
Pangani →, Tanzania 118 D4 5 26 S 38 58 E
Panganiban, Phil. 80 E5 13 55N 124 18 E
Panganuran, Phil. 81 G4 8 2N 122 22 E
Pangasinan □, Phil. 80 D3 15 55N 120 20 E
Pangfou = Bengbu, China 75 H9 32 58N 117 20 E
Pangil, Dem. Rep. of the Congo 118 C2 3 10 S 26 35 E
Pangkah, Tanjung, Indonesia 85 D4 6 51 S 112 33 E
Pangkai, Burma 90 D7 22 40N 98 40 E
Pangkajene, Indonesia 82 B1 4 46 S 119 34 E
Pangkalanbrandan, Indonesia 84 B1 4 1N 98 20 E
Pangkalanbuun, Indonesia 85 C4 2 41 S 111 37 E
Pangkalansusu, Indonesia 84 B1 4 2N 98 13 E
Pangkalpinang, Indonesia 84 C3 2 0 S 106 0 E
Pangkoh, Indonesia 85 C4 3 5 S 114 8 E
Panglao, Phil. 81 G4 9 35N 123 45 E
Panglao I., Phil. 81 G4 9 35N 123 48 E
Pangnirtung, Canada 139 B13 66 8N 65 54W
Pangrango, Indonesia 84 D3 6 46 S 107 1 E
Pangsau Pass, Burma 90 B6 27 15N 96 10 E
Pangtara, Burma 90 E6 20 57N 96 40 E
Panguipulli, Chile 176 A2 39 38 S 72 20W
Panguitch, U.S.A. 159 H7 37 50N 112 26W
Pangutaran, Phil. 81 H3 6 18N 120 35 E
Pangutaran Group, Phil. 81 H3 6 18N 120 34 E
Panhandle, U.S.A. 155 H4 35 21N 101 23W
Pani Mines, India 92 H5 22 29N 73 50 E
Pania-Mutombo, Dem. Rep. of the Congo 115 D4 5 11 S 23 51 E
Paniau, U.S.A. 145 B1 21 56N 160 5W
Panié, Mt., N. Cal. 133 T18 20 36 S 164 46 E
Panipat, India 92 E7 29 25N 77 2 E
Panitan, Phil. 81 F4 11 28N 122 46 E
Panjal Range, India 92 C7 32 30N 76 50 E
Panjgur, Pakistan 91 D2 27 0N 64 5 E
Panji Poyon, Tajikistan 63 E4 37 12N 68 35 E
Panjim = Panaji, India 95 G1 15 25N 73 50 E
Panjwai, Afghan. 92 D1 31 26N 65 27 E
Pankshin, Nigeria 113 D6 9 16N 9 25 E
Panmunjŏm, N. Korea 75 F14 37 59N 126 38 E
Panna, India 93 G9 24 40N 80 15 E
Panna Hills, India 93 G9 24 40N 81 15 E
Pano Lefkara, Cyprus 38 E12 34 53N 33 20 E
Pano Panayia, Cyprus 38 E11 34 55N 32 38 E
Panora, U.S.A. 156 C2 41 42N 94 22W
Panorama, Brazil 175 A5 21 21 S 51 51W
Pánormon, Greece 38 D6 35 25N 24 41 E
Panruti, India 95 J4 11 46N 79 35 E
Panshan, China 75 D12 41 3N 122 2 E
Panshi, China 75 C14 42 58N 126 5 E
Pantao, Phil. 80 E4 13 12N 123 20 E
Pantar, Indonesia 82 C2 8 28 S 124 10 E
Pante Macassar, Indonesia 82 C2 9 30 S 123 58 E
Pantelleria, Italy 46 F4 36 50N 11 57 E
Pantha, Burma 90 D5 23 55N 94 35 E
Pantin Sakan, Burma 90 F6 18 38N 97 33 E
Pantón, Spain 42 C3 42 31N 7 37W
Pánuco, Mexico 163 C5 22 0N 98 15W
Panukulan, Phil. 80 D3 14 56N 121 49 E
Panyam, Nigeria 113 D6 9 27N 9 8 E
Panyu, China 77 F9 22 51N 113 20 E
Pao →, Anzoátegui, Venezuela 169 B5 8 6N 64 17W
Pao →, Apure, Venezuela 168 B4 8 33N 68 1W
Páola, Italy 47 C9 39 21N 16 2 E
Paola, Malta 38 D2 35 52N 14 30 E
Paola, U.S.A. 154 F7 38 35N 94 53W
Paoli, U.S.A. 157 F10 38 33N 86 28W
Paonia, U.S.A. 159 G10 38 52N 107 36W
Paoting = Baoding, China 74 E8 38 50N 115 28 E
Paot'ou = Baotou, China 74 D6 40 32N 110 2 E
Paoua, C.A.R. 114 A3 7 9N 16 20 E
Pápa, Hungary 52 C2 47 22N 17 30 E
Papa, U.S.A. 145 D6 19 13N 155 52W
Papa Stour, U.K. 22 A7 60 20N 1 42W
Papa Westray, U.K. 22 B6 59 20N 2 55W
Papaaloa, U.S.A. 145 D6 19 59N 155 13W
Papagayo →, Mexico 163 D5 16 36N 99 43W
Papagayo, G. de, Costa Rica 164 D2 10 30N 85 50W
Papagni →, India 95 G3 15 35N 77 45 E
Papakura, N.Z. 130 D3 37 4 S 174 59 E
Papantla, Mexico 163 C5 20 30N 97 30W
Paparoa, N.Z. 130 C3 36 6 S 174 16 E
Paparoa Nat. Park, N.Z. 131 C6 42 7 S 171 26 E
Paparoa Ra., N.Z. 131 C6 42 5 S 171 35 E
Pápas, Ákra, Greece 48 C3 38 13N 21 20 E
Papatoetoe, N.Z. 130 C3 36 59 S 174 51 E
Papawai Pt., U.S.A. 145 C5 20 47N 156 32W
Papeete, Tahiti 133 S16 17 32 S 149 34W
Papenburg, Germany 30 B3 53 5N 7 23 E
Paphlagonia, Turkey 100 B5 41 30N 33 0 E
Paphos, Cyprus 38 E11 34 46N 32 25 E
Papien Chiang = Da →, Vietnam 86 B5 21 15N 105 20 E
Papigochic →, Mexico 162 B3 29 9N 109 40W
Paposo, Chile 174 B1 25 0 S 70 30W
Papoutsa, Cyprus 38 E12 34 54N 33 4 E
Papua, G. of, Papua N. G. 132 E3 9 0 S 144 50 E
Papua New Guinea ■, Oceania 132 E3 8 0 S 145 0 E
Papudo, Chile 174 C1 32 29 S 71 27W
Papuk, Croatia 52 E2 45 30N 17 30 E
Papun, Burma 90 F6 18 2N 97 30 E
Papunya, Australia 124 D5 23 15 S 131 54 E
Pará = Belém, Brazil 170 B2 1 20 S 48 30W
Pará □, Brazil 173 A7 3 20 S 52 0W
Pará □, Surinam 169 B6 5 20N 55 5W
Paraburdoo, Australia 124 D2 23 14 S 117 32 E
Paracale, Phil. 80 D4 14 17N 122 48 E
Paracas, Pen., Peru 172 C2 13 53 S 76 20W
Paracatu, Brazil 171 E2 17 10 S 46 50W
Paracatu →, Brazil 171 E2 16 30 S 45 4W
Parachilna, Australia 128 A3 31 10 S 138 21 E
Parachinar, Pakistan 91 B3 33 55N 70 5 E
Paraćin, Serbia, Yug. 50 C5 43 54N 21 27 E
Paracuru, Brazil 170 B4 3 24 S 39 4W
Paradas, Punta, Peru 172 D2 15 22 S 75 11W
Paradas, Spain 43 H5 37 18N 5 29W
Paradela, Spain 42 C3 42 44N 7 37W
Paradhísi, Greece 38 C10 36 18N 28 7 E
Paradip, India 94 D8 20 15N 86 35 E
Paradise, Calif., U.S.A. 160 F5 39 46N 121 37W
Paradise, Mont., U.S.A. 158 C6 47 23N 114 48W
Paradise, Nev., U.S.A. 161 J11 36 9N 115 10W
Paradise →, Canada 141 B8 53 27N 57 19W
Paradise Valley, U.S.A. 158 F5 41 30N 117 32W
Parado, Indonesia 85 D5 8 42 S 118 30 E
Paragould, U.S.A. 155 G9 36 3N 90 29W
Paraguá →, Bolivia 173 C5 13 34 S 61 53W
Paragua →, Venezuela 169 B5 6 55N 62 55W
Paraguaçu →, Brazil 171 D4 12 45 S 38 54W
Paraguaçu Paulista, Brazil 175 A5 22 22 S 50 35W
Paraguaipoa, Venezuela 168 A3 11 21N 71 57W
Paraguaná, Pen. de, Venezuela 168 A4 12 0N 70 0W
Paraguarí, Paraguay 174 B4 25 36 S 57 0W
Paraguarí □, Paraguay 174 B4 26 0 S 57 10W
Paraguay ■, S. Amer. 174 A4 23 0 S 57 0W
Paraguay →, Paraguay 174 B4 27 18 S 58 38W
Paraíba = João Pessoa, Brazil 170 C5 7 10 S 34 52W
Paraíba □, Brazil 170 C4 7 0 S 36 0W
Paraíba do Sul →, Brazil 171 F3 21 37 S 41 3W
Parainen, Finland 15 F20 60 18N 22 18 E
Paraiso, Mexico 163 D6 18 24N 93 14W
Parak, Iran 97 E7 27 38N 52 25 E
Parakhino Paddubye, Russia 58 C7 58 26N 33 10 E
Parakou, Benin 113 D5 9 25N 2 40 E
Parakylia, Australia 128 A2 30 24 S 136 25 E
Paralimni, Cyprus 38 D12 35 2N 33 58 E
Parálion-Astrous, Greece 48 D4 37 25N 22 45 E
Paramakkudi, India 95 K4 9 31N 78 39 E
Paramaribo, Surinam 169 B6 5 50N 55 10W
Parambu, Brazil 170 C3 6 13 S 40 43W
Paramillo, Nudo del, Colombia 168 B2 7 4N 75 55W
Paramirim, Brazil 171 D3 13 26 S 42 15W
Paramirim →, Brazil 171 D3 11 34 S 43 18W
Paramithiá, Greece 48 B2 39 30N 20 35 E
Paramushir, Ostrov, Russia 65 D16 50 24N 156 0 E
Paran →, Israel 103 E4 30 20N 35 10 E
Paraná, Argentina 174 C3 31 45 S 60 30W
Paranã, Brazil 171 D2 12 30 S 47 48W
Paraná □, Brazil 175 A5 24 30 S 51 0W
Paraná →, Argentina 174 C4 33 43 S 59 15W
Paranaguá, Brazil 175 B6 25 30 S 48 30W
Paranaíba →, Brazil 171 F1 20 6 S 51 4W
Paranapanema →, Brazil 175 A5 22 40 S 53 9W
Paranapiacaba, Serra do, Brazil 175 A6 24 31 S 48 35W
Paranavaí, Brazil 175 A5 23 4 S 52 56W
Parang, Jolo, Phil. 81 J3 5 55N 120 54 E
Parang, Mindanao, Phil. 81 H5 7 23N 124 16 E
Parangaba, Brazil 170 B4 3 45 S 38 33W
Parangippettai, India 95 J4 11 30N 79 38 E
Parângul Mare, Vf., Romania 53 E8 45 20N 23 37 E
Paraparauma, N.Z. 130 G4 40 57 S 175 3 E
Parapóla, Greece 48 E5 36 55N 23 27 E
Paraspóri, Ákra, Greece 49 F9 35 55N 27 15 E
Paratinga, Brazil 171 D3 12 40 S 43 10W
Paratoo, Australia 128 B3 32 42 S 139 20 E
Parattah, Australia 126 G4 42 22 S 147 23 E
Paraúna, Brazil 171 E1 16 55 S 50 26W
Paray-le-Monial, France 27 F11 46 27N 4 7 E
Parbati →, India 92 G7 25 50N 76 30 E
Parbatipur, Bangla. 90 C2 25 39N 88 55 E
Parbhani, India 94 E3 19 8N 76 52 E
Parchim, Germany 30 B7 53 26N 11 52 E
Parczew, Poland 55 G9 51 40N 22 52 E
Pardes Hanna-Karkur, Israel 103 C3 32 28N 34 57 E
Pardilla, Spain 42 D7 41 33N 3 43W
Pardo →, Bahia, Brazil 171 E4 15 40 S 39 0W
Pardo →, Mato Grosso, Brazil 175 A5 21 46 S 52 9W
Pardo →, Minas Gerais, Brazil 171 E3 15 48 S 44 48W
Pardo →, São Paulo, Brazil 171 F2 20 10 S 48 38W
Pardubice, Czech Rep. 34 A8 50 3N 15 45 E
Pare, Indonesia 85 D4 7 43 S 112 12 E
Pare □, Tanzania 118 C4 4 10 S 38 0 E
Pare Mts., Tanzania 118 C4 4 0 S 37 45 E
Parecis, Serra dos, Brazil 173 C6 13 0 S 60 0W
Paredes de Nava, Spain 42 C6 42 9N 4 42W
Pareh, Iran 96 B5 38 52N 45 42 E
Parelhas, Brazil 170 C4 6 41 S 36 39W
Paren, Russia 65 C17 62 30N 163 15 E
Parengarenga Harbour, N.Z. 130 A2 34 31 S 173 0 E
Parent, Canada 140 C5 47 55N 74 35W
Parent, L., Canada 140 C4 48 31N 77 1W
Parentis-en-Born, France 28 D2 44 21N 1 4W
Parepare, Indonesia 82 B1 4 0 S 119 40 E
Parfino, Russia 58 D6 57 59N 31 34 E
Párga, Greece 48 B2 39 15N 20 29 E
Pargo, Pta. do, Madeira 39 D2 32 49N 17 17W
Parguba, Russia 56 B5 62 20N 34 27 E
Paria, G. de, Venezuela 169 A5 10 20N 62 0W
Paria, Pen. de, Venezuela 169 A5 10 50N 62 30W
Pariaguán, Venezuela 169 B5 8 51N 64 34W
Pariaman, Indonesia 84 C2 0 47 S 100 11 E
Paricatuba, Brazil 169 D5 4 26 S 61 53W
Paricutín, Cerro, Mexico 162 D4 19 28N 102 15W
Parigi, Java, Indonesia 85 D3 7 42 S 108 29 E
Parigi, Sulawesi, Indonesia 82 B2 0 50 S 120 5 E
Parika, Guyana 169 B6 6 50N 58 20W
Parikkala, Finland 58 B5 61 33N 29 31 E
Parima, Serra, Brazil 169 C5 2 30N 64 0W
Parinari, Peru 172 A3 4 35 S 74 25W
Pariñas, Pta., S. Amer. 166 D2 4 30 S 82 0W
Parincea, Romania 53 D12 46 27N 27 9 E
Parintins, Brazil 169 D6 2 40 S 56 50W
Paris, Canada 140 D3 43 12N 80 25W
Paris, France 27 D9 48 50N 2 20 E
Paris, Idaho, U.S.A. 158 E8 42 14N 111 24W
Paris, Ill., U.S.A. 157 E9 39 36N 87 42W
Paris, Ky., U.S.A. 157 F12 38 13N 84 15W
Paris, Mo., U.S.A. 156 E5 39 29N 92 0W
Paris, Tenn., U.S.A. 149 G1 36 18N 88 19W
Paris, Tex., U.S.A. 155 J7 33 40N 95 33W
Paris, Ville de □, France 27 D9 48 50N 2 20 E
Parish, U.S.A. 151 C8 43 25N 76 8W
Pariti, Indonesia 82 D2 10 15 S 123 45 E
Park, U.S.A. 160 B4 48 45N 122 18W
Park City, U.S.A. 158 F8 40 39N 111 30W
Park Falls, U.S.A. 154 C9 45 56N 90 27W
Park Forest, U.S.A. 157 C9 41 29N 87 40W
Park Range, U.S.A. 158 G10 40 0N 106 30W
Park Rapids, U.S.A. 154 B7 46 55N 95 4W
Park Ridge, U.S.A. 157 B9 42 2N 87 51W
Park River, U.S.A. 154 A6 48 24N 97 45W
Park Rynie, S. Africa 117 E5 30 25 S 30 45 E
Parkā Bandar, Iran 97 E8 25 55N 59 35 E
Parkano, Finland 15 E20 62 1N 23 0 E
Parkent, Uzbekistan 63 C4 41 18N 69 40 E
Parker, Ariz., U.S.A. 161 L12 34 9N 114 17W
Parker, S. Dak., U.S.A. 154 D6 43 24N 97 8W
Parker Dam, U.S.A. 161 L12 34 18N 114 8W
Parkersburg, Iowa, U.S.A. 156 B4 42 35N 92 47W
Parkersburg, W. Va., U.S.A. 148 F5 39 16N 81 34W
Parkerview, Canada 143 C8 51 21N 103 18W
Parkes, Australia 129 B8 33 9 S 148 11 E
Parkfield, U.S.A. 160 K6 35 54N 120 26W
Parkhar, Tajikistan 63 E4 37 30N 69 34 E
Parkland, U.S.A. 160 C4 47 9N 122 26W
Parkside, Canada 143 C7 53 10N 106 33W
Parkston, U.S.A. 154 D6 43 24N 97 59W
Parksville, Canada 142 D4 49 20N 124 21W
Parksville, U.S.A. 152 B7 33 47N 82 13W
Parla, Spain 42 E7 40 14N 3 46W
Parlakimidi, India 94 E7 18 45N 84 5 E
Parli, India 94 E3 18 50N 76 35 E
Pârliţa, Moldova 53 C12 47 19N 27 52 E
Parma, Italy 44 D7 44 48N 10 20 E
Parma, Idaho, U.S.A. 158 E5 43 47N 116 57W
Parma, Ohio, U.S.A. 150 E3 41 23N 81 43W
Parma →, Italy 44 D7 44 56N 10 26 E
Parnaguá, Brazil 170 D3 10 10 S 44 38W
Parnaíba, Piauí, Brazil 170 B3 2 54 S 41 47W
Parnaíba, São Paulo, Brazil 173 D7 19 34 S 51 14W
Parnaíba →, Brazil 170 B3 3 0 S 41 50W
Parnamirim, Brazil 170 C4 8 5 S 39 34W
Parnarama, Brazil 170 C3 5 31 S 43 6W
Parnassós, Greece 48 C4 38 35N 22 30 E
Parnassus, N.Z. 131 C8 42 42 S 173 23 E
Párnis, Greece 48 C5 38 14N 23 45 E
Párnon Óros, Greece 48 D4 37 15N 22 45 E
Pärnu, Estonia 15 G21 58 28N 24 33 E
Parola, India 94 D2 20 47N 75 7 E
Paroo →, Australia 127 E3 31 28 S 143 32 E
Páros, Greece 49 D7 37 6N 25 11 E
Parowan, U.S.A. 159 H7 37 51N 112 50W
Parpaillon, France 29 D10 44 30N 6 40 E
Parral, Chile 174 D1 36 10 S 71 52W
Parramatta, Australia 129 B9 33 48 S 151 1 E
Parras, Mexico 162 B4 25 30N 102 20W
Parrett →, U.K. 21 F4 51 12N 3 1W
Parris I., U.S.A. 152 C9 32 20N 80 41W
Parrish, U.S.A. 153 H7 27 35N 82 26W
Parrott, U.S.A. 152 D5 31 54N 84 31W
Parrsboro, Canada 141 C7 45 30N 64 25W
Parry Is., Canada 6 B2 77 0N 110 0W
Parry Sound, Canada 140 C4 45 20N 80 0W
Parsberg, Germany 31 F7 49 10N 11 43 E
Parsęta →, Poland 54 D2 54 11N 15 34 E
Parshall, U.S.A. 154 B3 47 57N 102 8W
Parsnip →, Canada 142 B4 55 10N 123 2W
Parsons, U.S.A. 155 G7 37 20N 95 16W
Parsons Ra., Australia 126 A2 13 30 S 135 15 E
Partabpur, India 94 E5 20 0N 80 42 E
Partanna, Italy 46 E5 37 43N 12 53 E
Parthenay, France 26 F6 46 38N 0 16W
Partinico, Italy 46 D6 38 3N 13 7 E
Partizánske, Slovak Rep. 35 C11 48 38N 18 23 E
Partur, India 94 E3 19 40N 76 14 E
Paru →, Brazil 169 D7 1 33 S 52 38W
Parú →, Venezuela 168 C4 4 20N 66 27W
Paru de Oeste →, Brazil 169 C6 1 30N 56 0W
Parubcan, Phil. 80 E4 13 43N 123 45 E
Parucito →, Venezuela 168 B4 5 18N 65 59W
Parur, India 95 J3 10 13N 76 14 E
Paruro, Peru 172 C3 13 45 S 71 50W
Parvān □, Afghan. 91 B3 35 0N 69 0 E
Parvatipuram, India 94 E6 18 50N 83 25 E
Påryd, Sweden 17 H9 56 34N 15 55 E
Parys, S. Africa 116 D4 26 52 S 27 29 E
Pas-de-Calais □, France 27 B9 50 30N 2 10 E
Pasada, Spain 42 B5 43 23N 5 40W
Pasadena, Calif., U.S.A. 161 L8 34 9N 118 9W
Pasadena, Tex., U.S.A. 155 L7 29 43N 95 13W
Pasaje, Ecuador 168 D2 3 23 S 79 50W
Pasaje →, Argentina 174 B3 25 39 S 63 56W
Paşalimanı, Turkey 51 F11 40 29N 27 36 E
Pasay, Phil. 80 D3 14 33N 121 0 E
Pascagoula, U.S.A. 155 K10 30 21N 88 33W
Pascagoula →, U.S.A. 155 K10 30 23N 88 37W
Paşcani, Romania 53 C11 47 14N 26 45 E
Pasco, U.S.A. 158 C4 46 14N 119 6W
Pasco □, Peru 172 C3 10 40 S 75 0W
Pasco, Cerro de, Peru 172 C2 10 45 S 76 10W
Pascua, I. de, Pac. Oc. 135 K17 27 0 S 109 0W
Pasewalk, Germany 30 B9 53 30N 13 58 E
Pasfield L., Canada 143 B7 58 24N 105 20W
Pasha →, Russia 58 B7 60 29N 32 55 E
Pashiwari, Pakistan 93 B6 34 40N 75 10 E
Pashiya, Russia 62 B7 58 33N 58 26 E
Pashmakli = Smolyan, Bulgaria 51 E8 41 36N 24 38 E
Pasighat, India 90 A5 28 4N 95 21 E
Pasinler, Turkey 101 C9 39 59N 41 41 E
Pasir Mas, Malaysia 87 J4 6 2N 102 8 E
Pasirian, Indonesia 85 D4 8 13 S 113 8 E
Pasirkuning, Indonesia 84 C2 0 30 S 104 33 E
Påskallavik, Sweden 17 G10 57 10N 16 26 E
Paskūh, Iran 97 E9 27 34N 61 39 E
Pasłęk, Poland 54 D6 54 3N 19 41 E
Pasłęka →, Poland 54 D6 54 26N 19 46 E
Pasley, C., Australia 125 F3 33 52 S 123 35 E
Pašman, Croatia 45 E12 43 58N 15 20 E
Pasmore →, Australia 128 A3 31 5 S 139 49 E
Pasni, Pakistan 91 D1 25 15N 63 27 E
Paso Cantinela, Mexico 161 N11 32 33N 115 47W
Paso de Indios, Argentina 176 B3 43 55 S 69 0W
Paso de los Libres, Argentina 174 B4 29 44 S 57 10W
Paso de los Toros, Uruguay 174 C4 32 45 S 56 30W
Paso Flores, Argentina 176 B2 40 35 S 70 38W
Paso Robles, U.S.A. 159 J3 35 38N 120 41W
Pasorapa, Bolivia 173 D5 18 16 S 64 37W
Paspébiac, Canada 141 C6 48 3N 65 17W
Pasrur, Pakistan 92 C6 32 16N 74 43 E
Passage West, Ireland 23 E3 51 52N 8 21W
Passaic, U.S.A. 151 F10 40 51N 74 7W
Passau, Germany 31 G9 48 34N 13 28 E
Passero, C., Italy 47 F8 36 41N 15 10 E
Passi, Phil. 81 F4 11 6N 122 38 E
Passo Fundo, Brazil 175 B5 28 10 S 52 20W
Passos, Brazil 171 F2 20 45 S 46 37W
Passow, Germany 30 B10 53 8N 14 6 E
Passwang, Switz. 32 B5 47 22N 7 41 E
Passy, France 29 C10 45 55N 6 41 E
Pastavy, Belarus 15 J22 55 4N 26 50 E
Pastaza □, Ecuador 168 D2 2 0 S 77 0W
Pastaza →, Peru 168 D2 4 50 S 76 52W
Pasto, Colombia 168 C2 1 13N 77 17W
Pastol B., U.S.A. 144 E7 63 7N 163 15W
Pastos Bons, Brazil 170 C3 6 36 S 44 5W
Pastrana, Spain 40 E2 40 27N 2 53W
Pasuquin, Phil. 80 B3 18 20N 120 37 E
Pasuruan, Indonesia 85 D4 7 40 S 112 44 E
Pasym, Poland 54 E7 53 48N 20 49 E
Pásztó, Hungary 52 C4 47 52N 19 43 E
Patagonia, Argentina 176 C3 45 0 S 69 0W
Patagonia, U.S.A. 159 L8 31 33N 110 45W
Patambar, Iran 97 D9 29 45N 60 17 E
Patan, Gujarat, India 94 F1 17 22N 73 57 E
Patan, Maharashtra, India 92 H5 23 54N 72 14 E
Patani, Indonesia 82 A3 0 20N 128 50 E
Pătârlagele, Romania 53 E11 45 19N 26 21 E
Pataudi, India 92 E7 28 18N 76 48 E
Patchewollock, Australia 128 C5 35 22 S 142 12 E
Patchogue, U.S.A. 151 F11 40 46N 73 1W
Patea, N.Z. 130 F3 39 45 S 174 30 E
Pategi, Nigeria 113 D6 8 50N 5 45 E
Patensie, S. Africa 116 E3 33 46 S 24 49 E
Paterna, Spain 41 F4 39 30N 0 26W
Paternion, Austria 34 E6 46 43N 13 38 E
Paternò, Italy 47 E7 37 34N 14 54 E
Pateros, U.S.A. 158 B4 48 3N 119 54W
Paterson, Australia 129 B9 32 35 S 151 36 E
Paterson, U.S.A. 151 F10 40 55N 74 11W
Paterson Inlet, N.Z. 131 G3 46 56 S 168 12 E
Paterson Ra., Australia 124 D3 21 45 S 122 10 E
Pathankot, India 92 C6 32 18N 75 45 E
Patharghata, Bangla. 90 D2 22 2N 89 58 E
Pathfinder Reservoir, U.S.A. 158 E10 42 28N 106 51W
Pathiu, Thailand 87 G2 10 42N 99 19 E
Pathum Thani, Thailand 86 E3 14 1N 100 32 E
Pati, Indonesia 85 D4 6 45 S 111 1 E
Pati Pt., Guam 133 R15 13 40N 144 50 E
Patía, Colombia 168 C2 2 4N 77 4W
Patía →, Colombia 168 C2 2 13N 78 40W
Patiala, India 92 D7 30 23N 76 26 E
Patine Kouka, Senegal 112 C2 12 45N 13 45W
Patitíron, Greece 48 B5 39 8N 23 50 E
Pativilca, Peru 172 C2 10 42 S 77 48W
Patkai Bum, India 90 B5 27 0N 95 30 E
Pátmos, Greece 49 D8 37 21N 26 36 E
Patna, India 93 G11 25 35N 85 12 E
Patnongon, Phil. 81 F4 10 55N 122 0 E
Patnos, Turkey 101 C10 39 13N 42 51 E
Patonga, Uganda 118 B3 2 45N 33 15 E
Patos, Brazil 170 C4 6 55 S 37 16W
Patos, L. dos, Brazil 175 C5 31 20 S 51 0W
Patos de Minas, Brazil 171 E2 18 35 S 46 32W
Patosi, Albania 50 F3 40 42N 19 38 E
Patquía, Argentina 174 C2 30 2 S 66 55W
Pátrai, Greece 48 C3 38 14N 21 47 E
Pátraikós Kólpos, Greece 48 C3 38 17N 21 30 E
Patras = Pátrai, Greece 48 C3 38 14N 21 47 E
Patricio Lynch, I., Chile 176 C1 48 35 S 75 30W
Patrocínio, Brazil 171 E2 18 57 S 47 0W

Piombino, Canale di 265

Pervomayskiy, *Russia* **62 F5** 51 32N 55 2 E
Pervouralsk, *Russia* **62 C7** 56 59N 59 59 E
Pes, Pta. del, *Spain* **39 C7** 38 46N 1 26 E
Pésaro, *Italy* **45 E9** 43 54N 12 55 E
Pescara, *Italy* **45 F11** 42 28N 14 13 E
Pescara →, *Italy* **45 F11** 42 28N 14 13 E
Peschanokopskoye, *Russia* **61 G5** 46 14N 41 4 E
Péscia, *Italy* **44 E7** 43 54N 10 41 E
Pescina, *Italy* **45 F10** 42 2N 13 39 E
Peseux, *Switz.* **32 C3** 46 59N 6 53 E
Peshawar, *Pakistan* **91 B3** 34 2N 71 37 E
Peshkopi, *Albania* **50 E4** 41 41N 20 25 E
Peshtera, *Bulgaria* **51 D8** 42 2N 24 18 E
Peshtigo, *U.S.A.* **148 C2** 45 4N 87 46W
Peski, *Russia* **60 E6** 51 14N 42 29 E
Peskovka, *Russia* **62 B4** 59 4N 52 22 E
Pêso da Régua, *Portugal* **42 D3** 41 10N 7 47W
Pesqueira, *Brazil* **170 C4** 8 20 S 36 42W
Pessac, *France* **28 D3** 44 48N 0 37W
Pest □, *Hungary* **52 C4** 47 29N 19 5 E
Pestovo, *Russia* **58 C8** 58 33N 35 42 E
Pestravka, *Russia* **60 D9** 52 28N 49 57 E
Péta, *Greece* **48 B3** 39 10N 21 2 E
Petah Tiqwa, *Israel* **103 C3** 32 6N 34 53 E
Petalídhion, *Greece* **48 E3** 36 57N 21 55 E
Petaling Jaya, *Malaysia* **87 L3** 3 4N 101 42 E
Petaloudhes, *Greece* **38 C10** 36 18N 28 5 E
Petaluma, *U.S.A.* **160 G4** 38 14N 122 39W
Pétange, *Lux.* **24 E5** 49 33N 5 55 E
Petatlán, *Mexico* **162 D4** 17 31N 101 16W
Petauke, *Zambia* **119 E3** 14 14 S 31 20 E
Petawawa, *Canada* **140 C4** 45 54N 77 17W
Petén Itzá, L., *Guatemala* **164 C2** 16 58N 89 50W
Peter I.s Øy, *Antarctica* **7 C16** 69 0 S 91 0W
Peter Pond L., *Canada* **143 B7** 55 55N 108 44W
Peterbell, *Canada* **140 C3** 48 36N 83 21W
Peterborough, *Australia* **128 B3** 32 58 S 138 51 E
Peterborough, *Canada* **150 B6** 44 20N 78 20W
Peterborough, *U.K.* **21 E7** 52 35N 0 15W
Peterborough, *U.S.A.* **151 D13** 42 53N 71 57W
Peterborough □, *U.K.* **21 E7** 52 35N 0 15W
Peterculter, *U.K.* **22 D6** 57 6N 2 16W
Peterhead, *U.K.* **22 D7** 57 31N 1 48W
Peterlee, *U.K.* **20 C6** 54 47N 1 20W
Petermann Bjerg, *Greenland* **10 C8** 73 7N 28 25W
Petermann Gletscher, *Greenland* **10 A4** 80 30N 60 0W
Peter's Mine, *Guyana* **169 B6** 6 14N 59 20W
Petersburg, *Alaska, U.S.A.* **142 B2** 56 48N 132 58W
Petersburg, *Ill., U.S.A.* **156 D7** 40 1N 89 51W
Petersburg, *Ind., U.S.A.* **157 F9** 38 30N 87 17W
Petersburg, *Va., U.S.A.* **148 G7** 37 14N 77 24W
Petersburg, *W. Va., U.S.A.* **148 F6** 39 1N 79 5W
Petersfield, *U.K.* **21 F7** 51 1N 0 56W
Petershagen, *Germany* **30 C4** 52 23N 8 58 E
Petford, *Australia* **126 B3** 17 20 S 144 58 E
Petília Policastro, *Italy* **47 C9** 39 7N 16 48 E
Petit Bois I., *U.S.A.* **149 K1** 30 12N 88 26W
Petit-Cap, *Canada* **141 C7** 49 3N 64 30W
Petit Goâve, *Haiti* **165 C5** 18 27N 72 51W
Petit Lac Manicouagan, *Canada* **141 B6** 51 25N 67 40W
Petit Saint Bernard, Col du, *Italy* **29 C10** 45 40N 6 52 E
Petitcodiac, *Canada* **141 C6** 45 57N 65 11W
Petite Baleine →, *Canada* **140 A4** 56 0N 76 45W
Petite Saguenay, *Canada* **141 C5** 48 15N 70 4W
Petitsikapau, L., *Canada* **141 B6** 54 37N 66 25W
Petlad, *India* **92 H5** 22 30N 72 45 E
Peto, *Mexico* **163 C7** 20 10N 88 53W
Petone, *N.Z.* **130 H3** 41 13 S 174 53 E
Petoskey, *U.S.A.* **148 C3** 45 22N 84 57W
Petra, *Jordan* **103 E4** 30 20N 35 22 E
Petra, *Spain* **39 B10** 39 37N 3 6 E
Petra, Ostrova, *Russia* **6 B13** 76 15N 118 30 E
Petra Velikogo, Zaliv, *Russia* **68 C6** 42 40N 132 0 E
Petrel = Petrer, *Spain* **41 G4** 38 30N 0 46W
Petrella, Monte, *Italy* **46 A6** 41 18N 13 40 E
Petrer, *Spain* **41 G4** 38 30N 0 46W
Petreto-Bicchisano, *France* **29 G12** 41 47N 8 58 E
Petrey, *U.S.A.* **152 D3** 31 51N 86 13W
Petrich, *Bulgaria* **50 E7** 41 24N 23 13 E
Petrijanec, *Croatia* **45 B13** 46 23N 16 17 E
Petrikov = Pyetrikaw, *Belarus* **59 F5** 52 11N 28 29 E
Petrila, *Romania* **53 E8** 45 29N 23 29 E
Petrinja, *Croatia* **45 C13** 45 28N 16 18 E
Petrodvorets, *Russia* **58 C5** 59 52N 29 54 E
Petrograd = Sankt-Peterburg, *Russia* **58 C6** 59 55N 30 20 E
Petrolândia, *Brazil* **170 C4** 9 5 S 38 20W
Petrolia, *Canada* **140 D3** 42 54N 82 9W
Petrolina, *Brazil* **170 C3** 9 24 S 40 30W
Petropavl, *Kazakstan* **64 D7** 54 53N 69 13 E
Petropavlovsk = Petropavl, *Kazakstan* **64 D7** 54 53N 69 13 E
Petropavlovsk-Kamchatskiy, *Russia* **65 D16** 53 3N 158 43 E
Petropavlovskiy = Akhtubinsk, *Russia* **61 F8** 48 13N 46 7 E
Petrópolis, *Brazil* **171 F3** 22 33 S 43 9W
Petroşani, *Romania* **53 E8** 45 28N 23 20 E
Petrova Gora, *Croatia* **45 C12** 45 15N 15 45 E
Petrovac, *Montenegro, Yug.* **50 D2** 42 13N 18 57 E
Petrovac, *Serbia, Yug.* **50 B5** 44 22N 21 26 E
Petrovaradin, *Serbia, Yug.* **52 E4** 45 16N 19 55 E
Petrovsk, *Russia* **60 D7** 52 22N 45 19 E
Petrovsk-Zabaykalskiy, *Russia* **65 D11** 51 20N 108 55 E
Petrovskaya, *Russia* **59 K9** 45 25N 37 58 E
Petrovskoye = Svetlograd, *Russia* **61 H6** 45 25N 42 58 E
Petrovskoye, *Russia* **62 E6** 53 37N 56 23 E
Petrozavodsk, *Russia* **58 B8** 61 41N 34 20 E
Petrus Steyn, *S. Africa* **117 D4** 27 38 S 28 8 E
Petrusburg, *S. Africa* **116 D4** 29 4 S 25 26 E
Pettitts, *Australia* **129 C8** 34 56 S 148 10 E
Petzeck, *Austria* **34 E5** 46 57N 12 48 E
Peumo, *Chile* **174 C1** 34 21 S 71 12W
Peureulak, *Indonesia* **84 B1** 4 48N 97 45 E
Peusangan →, *Indonesia* **84 A1** 5 16N 96 51 E
Pevek, *Russia* **65 C18** 69 41N 171 19 E
Peveragno, *Italy* **44 D4** 44 20N 7 37 E
Peyrehorade, *France* **28 E2** 43 34N 1 7W
Peyruis, *France* **29 D9** 44 1N 5 56 E
Pézenas, *France* **28 E7** 43 28N 3 24 E
Pezinok, *Slovak Rep.* **35 C10** 48 17N 17 17 E
Pfaffenhofen, *Germany* **31 G7** 48 31N 11 31 E
Pfäffikon, *Switz.* **33 B7** 47 13N 8 46 E
Pfarrkirchen, *Germany* **31 G8** 48 25N 12 56 E
Pfeffenhausen, *Germany* **31 G7** 48 39N 11 58 E
Pforzheim, *Germany* **31 G4** 48 52N 8 41 E
Pfullendorf, *Germany* **31 H5** 47 55N 9 15 E
Pfungstadt, *Germany* **31 F4** 49 48N 8 35 E
Phaistós, *Greece* **38 D6** 35 2N 24 50 E
Phala, *Botswana* **116 C4** 23 45 S 26 50 E
Phalera = Phulera, *India* **92 F6** 26 52N 75 16 E
Phalodi, *India* **92 F5** 27 12N 72 24 E
Phalsbourg, *France* **27 D14** 48 46N 7 15 E
Phan, *Thailand* **86 C2** 19 28N 99 43 E
Phan Rang, *Vietnam* **87 G7** 11 34N 109 0 E
Phan Ri = Hoa Da, *Vietnam* **87 G7** 11 16N 108 40 E
Phan Thiêt, *Vietnam* **87 G7** 11 1N 108 9 E
Phanae, *Greece* **49 C7** 38 8N 25 57 E
Phanat Nikhom, *Thailand* **86 F3** 13 27N 101 11 E
Phangan, Ko, *Thailand* **87 H3** 9 45N 100 0 E
Phangnga, *Thailand* **87 H2** 8 28N 98 30 E
Phanh Bho Ho Chi Minh, *Vietnam* **87 G6** 10 58N 106 40 E
Phanom Sarakham, *Thailand* **86 F3** 13 45N 101 21 E
Pharenda, *India* **93 F10** 27 5N 83 17 E
Phatthalung, *Thailand* **87 J3** 7 39N 100 6 E
Phayao, *Thailand* **86 C2** 19 11N 99 55 E
Phelps, *N.Y., U.S.A.* **150 D7** 42 58N 77 3W
Phelps, *Wis., U.S.A.* **154 B10** 46 4N 89 5W
Phelps L., *Canada* **143 B8** 59 15N 103 15W
Phenix City, *U.S.A.* **149 J3** 32 28N 85 0W
Phet Buri, *Thailand* **86 F2** 13 1N 99 55 E
Phetchabun, *Thailand* **86 D3** 16 25N 101 8 E
Phetchabun, Thiu Khao, *Thailand* **86 E3** 16 0N 101 20 E
Phetchaburi = Phet Buri, *Thailand* **86 F2** 13 1N 99 55 E
Phi Phi, Ko, *Thailand* **87 J2** 7 45N 98 46 E
Phiafay, *Laos* **86 E6** 14 48N 106 0 E
Phibun Mangsahan, *Thailand* **86 E5** 15 14N 105 14 E
Phichai, *Thailand* **86 D3** 17 22N 100 10 E
Phichit, *Thailand* **86 D3** 16 26N 100 22 E
Philadelphia, *Miss., U.S.A.* **155 J10** 32 46N 89 7W
Philadelphia, *N.Y., U.S.A.* **151 B9** 44 9N 75 43W
Philadelphia, *Pa., U.S.A.* **151 G9** 39 57N 75 10W
Philip, *U.S.A.* **154 C4** 44 2N 101 40W
Philip Smith Mts., *U.S.A.* **144 C11** 68 0N 148 0W
Philippeville, *Belgium* **24 D4** 50 12N 4 33 E
Philippi, *Greece* **51 E8** 41 1N 24 16 E
Philippi L., *Australia* **126 C2** 24 20 S 138 55 E
Philippines ■, *Asia* **80 E4** 12 0N 123 0 E
Philippolis, *S. Africa* **116 E4** 30 15 S 25 16 E
Philippopolis = Plovdiv, *Bulgaria* **51 D8** 42 8N 24 44 E
Philipsburg, *Mont., U.S.A.* **158 C7** 46 20N 113 18W
Philipsburg, *Pa., U.S.A.* **150 F6** 40 54N 78 13W
Philipstown = Daingean, *Ireland* **23 C4** 53 18N 7 17W
Philipstown, *S. Africa* **116 E3** 30 28 S 24 30 E
Phillip I., *Australia* **129 E6** 38 30 S 145 12 E
Phillips, *Tex., U.S.A.* **155 H4** 35 42N 101 22W
Phillips, *Wis., U.S.A.* **154 C9** 45 42N 90 24W
Phillipsburg, *Ga., U.S.A.* **152 D6** 31 25N 83 30W
Phillipsburg, *Kans., U.S.A.* **154 F5** 39 45N 99 19W
Phillipsburg, *N.J., U.S.A.* **151 F9** 40 42N 75 12W
Phillott, *Australia* **127 D4** 27 53 S 145 50 E
Philmont, *U.S.A.* **151 D11** 42 15N 73 39W
Philomath, *Ga., U.S.A.* **152 B7** 33 44N 82 59W
Philomath, *Oreg., U.S.A.* **158 D2** 44 32N 123 22W
Phimai, *Thailand* **86 E4** 15 13N 102 30 E
Phitsanulok, *Thailand* **86 D3** 16 50N 100 12 E
Phnom Dangrek, *Thailand* **86 E5** 14 20N 104 0 E
Phnom Penh, *Cambodia* **87 G5** 11 33N 104 55 E
Phnum Penh = Phnom Penh, *Cambodia* **87 G5** 11 33N 104 55 E
Phoenix, *Ariz., U.S.A.* **159 K7** 33 27N 112 4W
Phoenix, *N.Y., U.S.A.* **151 C8** 43 14N 76 18W
Phoenix Is., *Kiribati* **134 H10** 3 30 S 172 0W
Phoenixville, *U.S.A.* **151 F9** 40 8N 75 31W
Phon, *Thailand* **86 E4** 15 49N 102 36 E
Phon Tiou, *Laos* **86 D5** 17 53N 104 37 E
Phong →, *Thailand* **86 D4** 16 23N 102 56 E
Phong Saly, *Laos* **86 B4** 21 42N 102 9 E
Phong Tho, *Vietnam* **86 A4** 22 32N 103 21 E
Phonhong, *Laos* **86 C4** 18 30N 102 25 E
Phonum, *Thailand* **87 H2** 8 49N 98 48 E
Phosphate Hill, *Australia* **126 C2** 21 53 S 139 58 E
Photharam, *Thailand* **86 F2** 13 41N 99 51 E
Phra Nakhon Si Ayutthaya, *Thailand* **86 E3** 14 25N 100 30 E
Phra Thong, Ko, *Thailand* **87 H2** 9 5N 98 17 E
Phrae, *Thailand* **86 C3** 18 7N 100 9 E
Phrom Phiram, *Thailand* **86 D3** 17 2N 100 12 E
Phrygia, *Turkey* **100 C4** 38 40N 30 0 E
Phu Dien, *Vietnam* **86 C5** 18 58N 105 31 E
Phu Loi, *Laos* **86 B4** 20 14N 103 14 E
Phu Ly, *Vietnam* **86 B5** 20 35N 105 50 E
Phu Quoc, Dao, *Vietnam* **87 G4** 10 20N 104 0 E
Phu Tho, *Vietnam* **86 B5** 21 24N 105 13 E
Phuc Yen, *Vietnam* **86 B5** 21 16N 105 45 E
Phuket, *Thailand* **87 J2** 7 52N 98 22 E
Phuket, Ko, *Thailand* **87 J2** 8 0N 98 22 E
Phulbari, *India* **90 C3** 25 55N 90 2 E
Phulera, *India* **92 F6** 26 52N 75 16 E
Phun Phin, *Thailand* **87 H2** 9 7N 99 12 E
Piacá, *Brazil* **170 C2** 7 42 S 47 18W
Piacenza, *Italy* **44 C6** 45 1N 9 40 E
Piaçubaçu, *Brazil* **170 D4** 10 24 S 36 25W
Piako →, *N.Z.* **130 D4** 37 12 S 175 30 E
Pialba, *Australia* **127 D5** 25 20 S 152 45 E
Pian Cr. →, *Australia* **127 E4** 30 2 S 148 12 E
Piana, *France* **29 F12** 42 15N 8 34 E
Pianella, *Italy* **45 F11** 42 24N 14 2 E
Piangil, *Australia* **128 C5** 35 5 S 143 20 E
Pianosa, *Puglia, Italy* **45 F12** 42 12N 15 44 E
Pianosa, *Toscana, Italy* **44 F7** 42 35N 10 5 E
Piapot, *Canada* **143 D7** 49 59N 109 8W
Pias, *Portugal* **43 G3** 38 1N 7 29W
Piaseczno, *Poland* **55 F8** 52 5N 21 2 E
Piaski, *Poland* **55 G9** 51 8N 22 52 E
Piastów, *Poland* **55 F7** 52 12N 20 48 E
Piatã, *Brazil* **171 D3** 13 9 S 41 48W
Piatra, *Romania* **53 G10** 43 51N 25 9 E
Piatra Neamţ, *Romania* **53 D11** 46 56N 26 21 E
Piatra Olt, *Romania* **53 F9** 44 22N 24 16 E
Piauí □, *Brazil* **170 C3** 7 0 S 43 0W
Piaui →, *Brazil* **170 C3** 6 38 S 42 42W
Piave →, *Italy* **45 C9** 45 32N 12 44 E
Piazza Ármerina, *Italy* **47 E7** 37 21N 14 20 E
Pibor →, *Sudan* **107 F3** 7 35N 33 0 E
Pibor Post, *Sudan* **107 F3** 6 47N 33 3 E
Pica, *Chile* **172 E4** 20 35 S 69 25W
Picardie, *France* **27 C10** 49 50N 3 0 E
Picardie, Plaine de, *France* **27 C9** 50 0N 2 0 E
Picardy = Picardie, *France* **27 C10** 49 50N 3 0 E
Picayune, *U.S.A.* **155 K10** 30 32N 89 41W
Picerno, *Italy* **47 B8** 40 38N 15 38 E
Pichilemu, *Chile* **174 C1** 34 22 S 72 0W
Pichincha, □, *Ecuador* **168 D2** 0 10 S 78 40W
Pickerel L., *Canada* **140 C1** 48 40N 91 25W
Pickering, *U.K.* **20 C7** 54 15N 0 46W
Pickering, Vale of, *U.K.* **20 C7** 54 14N 0 45W
Pickle Lake, *Canada* **140 B1** 51 30N 90 12W
Pico Truncado, *Argentina* **176 C3** 46 40 S 68 0W
Picos, *Brazil* **170 C3** 7 5 S 41 28W
Picota, *Peru* **172 B2** 6 54 S 76 24W
Picton, *Australia* **129 C9** 34 12 S 150 34 E
Picton, *Canada* **140 D4** 44 1N 77 9W
Picton, *N.Z.* **131 B9** 41 18 S 174 3 E
Picton, I., *Chile* **176 E3** 55 2 S 66 57W
Pictou, *Canada* **141 C7** 45 41N 62 42W
Picture Butte, *Canada* **142 D6** 49 55N 112 45W
Picuí, *Brazil* **170 C4** 6 31 S 36 21W
Picún Leufú, *Argentina* **176 A3** 39 30 S 69 5W
Pidurutalagala, *Sri Lanka* **95 L5** 7 10N 80 50 E
Piechowice, *Poland* **55 H2** 50 51N 15 36 E
Piedecuesta, *Colombia* **168 B3** 6 59N 73 3W
Piedmont = Piemonte □, *Italy* **44 D5** 45 0N 8 0 E
Piedmont, *U.S.A.* **152 B4** 33 55N 85 37W
Piedmont Plateau, *U.S.A.* **149 J5** 34 0N 81 30W
Piedmonte Matese, *Italy* **47 A7** 41 22N 14 22 E
Piedra →, *Spain* **40 D3** 41 18N 1 47W
Piedra del Anguila, *Argentina* **176 B2** 40 2 S 70 4W
Piedra Lais, *Venezuela* **168 C4** 3 10N 65 50W
Piedrabuena, *Spain* **43 G6** 39 0N 4 10W
Piedrahita, *Spain* **42 E5** 40 28N 5 23W
Piedralaves, *Spain* **42 E6** 40 19N 4 42W
Piedras, R. de las →, *Peru* **172 C4** 12 30 S 69 15W
Piedras Blancas, *Spain* **42 B5** 43 33N 5 58W
Piedras Negras, *Mexico* **162 B4** 28 42N 100 31W
Piedras Pt., *Phil.* **81 F2** 10 11N 118 48 E
Piekary Śląskie, *Poland* **55 H5** 50 24N 18 57 E
Pieksämäki, *Finland* **15 E22** 62 18N 27 10 E
Piemonte □, *Italy* **44 D5** 45 0N 8 0 E
Pieniężno, *Poland* **54 D7** 54 14N 20 8 E
Pieńsk, *Poland* **55 G2** 51 16N 15 2 E
Pier Millan, *Australia* **128 C5** 35 14 S 142 40 E
Pierce, *U.S.A.* **158 C6** 46 30N 115 48W
Piercefield, *U.S.A.* **151 B10** 44 13N 74 35W
Piería □, *Greece* **50 F6** 40 13N 22 25 E
Pierre, *U.S.A.* **154 C4** 44 22N 100 21W
Pierre-Buffière, *France* **28 C5** 45 41N 1 22 E
Pierre-de-Bresse, *France* **27 F12** 46 54N 5 13 E
Pierrefontaine-les-Varans, *France* **27 E13** 47 14N 6 32 E
Pierrefort, *France* **28 D6** 44 55N 2 50 E
Pierrelatte, *France* **29 D8** 44 23N 4 43 E
Pierson, *U.S.A.* **153 F8** 29 14N 81 28W
Piešťany, *Slovak Rep.* **35 C10** 48 38N 17 55 E
Piesting →, *Austria* **35 C9** 48 6N 16 40 E
Pieszyce, *Poland* **55 H3** 50 43N 16 33 E
Piet Retief, *S. Africa* **117 D5** 27 1 S 30 50 E
Pietarsaari, *Finland* **14 E20** 63 40N 22 43 E
Pietermaritzburg, *S. Africa* **117 D5** 29 35 S 30 25 E
Pietersburg, *S. Africa* **117 C4** 23 54 S 29 25 E
Pietragalla, *Italy* **47 B8** 40 45N 15 53 E
Pietrasanta, *Italy* **44 E7** 43 57N 10 14 E
Pietroşiţa, *Romania* **53 E10** 45 11N 25 26 E
Pietrosul, Vf., *Maramureş, Romania* **53 C9** 47 35N 24 43 E
Pietrosul, Vf., *Suceava, Romania* **53 C10** 47 12N 25 18 E
Pieve di Cadore, *Italy* **45 B9** 46 26N 12 22 E
Pieve di Teco, *Italy* **44 D4** 44 3N 7 56 E
Pievepélago, *Italy* **44 D7** 44 12N 10 37 E
Pigadhítsa, *Greece* **50 G5** 39 59N 21 23 E
Pigeon, *U.S.A.* **148 D4** 43 50N 83 16W
Pigeon I., *India* **95 G2** 14 2N 74 20 E
Piggott, *U.S.A.* **155 G9** 36 23N 90 11W
Pigna, *Italy* **44 E4** 43 56N 7 40 E
Pigüe, *Argentina* **174 D3** 37 36 S 62 25W
Pihani, *India* **93 F9** 27 36N 80 15 E
Pihlajavesi, *Finland* **15 F23** 61 45N 28 45 E
Pikalevo, *Russia* **58 C8** 59 37N 34 9 E
Pike Road, *U.S.A.* **152 C3** 32 17N 86 6W
Pikes Peak, *U.S.A.* **154 F2** 38 50N 105 3W
Piketberg, *S. Africa* **116 E2** 32 55 S 18 40 E
Pikeville, *U.S.A.* **148 G4** 37 29N 82 31W
Pikou, *China* **75 E12** 39 18N 122 22 E
Pikwitonei, *Canada* **143 B9** 55 35N 97 9W
Piła, *Poland* **55 E3** 53 10N 16 48 E
Pila, *Spain* **41 G3** 38 16N 1 11W
Piła □, *Poland* **55 E3** 53 0N 17 0 E
Pilaía, *Greece* **50 F6** 40 32N 22 59 E
Pilani, *India* **92 E6** 28 22N 75 33 E
Pilar, *Brazil* **170 C4** 9 36 S 35 56W
Pilar, *Paraguay* **174 B4** 26 50 S 58 20W
Pilar de la Horadada, *Spain* **41 H4** 37 52N 0 47W
Pilas Group, *Phil.* **81 H3** 6 45N 121 35 E
Pilawa, *Poland* **55 G8** 51 57N 21 32 E
Pilaya →, *Bolivia* **173 E5** 20 55 S 64 4W
Pilcomayo →, *Paraguay* **174 B4** 25 21 S 57 42W
Pilgrimstad, *Sweden* **16 B9** 62 57N 15 2 E
Píli, *Greece* **49 E9** 36 50N 27 15 E
Pili, *Phil.* **80 E4** 13 33N 123 19 E
Pilibhit, *India* **93 E8** 28 40N 79 50 E
Pilica →, *Poland* **55 G8** 51 52N 21 17 E
Pilion, *Greece* **48 B5** 39 27N 23 3 E
Pilis, *Hungary* **52 C4** 47 17N 19 35 E
Pilisvörösvár, *Hungary* **52 C3** 47 38N 18 55 E
Pilkhawa, *India* **92 E7** 28 43N 77 42 E
Pillaro, *Ecuador* **168 D2** 1 10 S 78 32W
Pílos, *Greece* **48 E3** 36 55N 21 42 E
Pilot Grove, *U.S.A.* **156 F4** 38 53N 92 55W
Pilot Mound, *Canada* **143 D9** 49 15N 98 54W
Pilot Point, *Alaska, U.S.A.* **144 H8** 57 34N 157 35W
Pilot Point, *Tex., U.S.A.* **155 J6** 33 24N 96 58W
Pilot Rock, *U.S.A.* **158 D4** 45 29N 118 50W
Pilot Station, *U.S.A.* **144 F7** 61 56N 162 53W
Pilsen = Plzeň, *Czech Rep.* **34 B6** 49 45N 13 22 E
Pilštanj, *Slovenia* **45 B12** 46 8N 15 39 E
Piltene, *Latvia* **54 A8** 57 13N 21 40 E
Pilzno, *Poland* **55 J8** 49 58N 21 16 E
Pima, *U.S.A.* **159 K9** 32 54N 109 50W
Pimba, *Australia* **128 A2** 31 18 S 136 46 E
Pimenta Bueno, *Brazil* **173 C5** 11 35 S 61 10W
Pimentel, *Peru* **172 B2** 6 45 S 79 55W
Pina de Ebro, *Spain* **40 D4** 41 29N 0 33W
Pinamalayan, *Phil.* **80 E3** 13 2N 121 29 E
Pinang, *Malaysia* **87 K3** 5 25N 100 15 E
Pinang □, *Malaysia* **84 A2** 5 20N 100 20 E
Pinar, C. del, *Spain* **39 B10** 39 53N 3 12 E
Pinar del Río, *Cuba* **164 B3** 22 26N 83 40W
Pinarbaşı, *Çanakkale, Turkey* **49 B8** 39 53N 26 15 E
Pinarbaşı, *Kayseri, Turkey* **100 C7** 38 43N 36 23 E
Pinarhisar, *Turkey* **51 E11** 41 37N 27 30 E
Pinatubo, *Phil.* **80 D3** 15 8N 120 21 E
Pincehely, *Hungary* **52 D3** 46 41N 18 27 E
Pinchang, *China* **76 B6** 31 36N 107 3 E
Pincher Creek, *Canada* **142 D6** 49 30N 113 57W
Pinchi L., *Canada* **142 C4** 54 38N 124 30W
Pinckard, *U.S.A.* **152 D4** 31 19N 85 33W
Pinckneyville, *U.S.A.* **156 F7** 38 5N 89 23W
Pińczów, *Poland* **55 H7** 50 32N 20 32 E
Pind Dadan Khan, *Pakistan* **92 C5** 32 36N 73 7 E
Pindar, *Australia* **125 E2** 28 30 S 115 47 E
Pindaré →, *Brazil* **170 B3** 3 17 S 44 47W
Pindaré Mirim, *Brazil* **170 B2** 3 37 S 45 21W
Pindi Gheb, *Pakistan* **92 C5** 33 14N 72 21 E
Pindiga, *Nigeria* **113 D7** 9 58N 10 53 E
Pindobal, *Brazil* **170 B2** 3 16 S 48 25W
Pindos Óros, *Greece* **48 B3** 40 0N 21 0 E
Pindus Mts. = Pindos Óros, *Greece* **48 B3** 40 0N 21 0 E
Pine, *U.S.A.* **159 J8** 34 23N 111 27W
Pine →, *Canada* **143 B7** 58 50N 105 38W
Pine, C., *Canada* **141 C9** 46 37N 53 32W
Pine Bluff, *U.S.A.* **155 H9** 34 13N 92 1W
Pine City, *U.S.A.* **154 C8** 45 50N 92 59W
Pine Falls, *Canada* **143 C9** 50 34N 96 11W
Pine Flat L., *U.S.A.* **160 J7** 36 50N 119 20W
Pine Hill, *U.S.A.* **153 G8** 28 32N 81 28W
Pine Is., *U.S.A.* **153 J7** 26 36N 82 7W
Pine Level, *U.S.A.* **152 C3** 32 4N 86 4W
Pine Mountain, *U.S.A.* **152 C5** 32 52N 84 51W
Pine Pass, *Canada* **142 B4** 55 25N 122 42W
Pine Point, *Canada* **142 A6** 60 50N 114 28W
Pine Ridge, *Australia* **129 A9** 31 30 S 150 28 E
Pine Ridge, *U.S.A.* **154 D3** 43 2N 102 33W
Pine River, *Canada* **143 C8** 51 45N 100 30W
Pine River, *U.S.A.* **154 B7** 46 43N 94 24W
Pine Valley, *U.S.A.* **161 N10** 32 50N 116 32W
Pinecrest, *U.S.A.* **160 G6** 38 12N 120 1W
Pineda de Mar, *Spain* **40 D7** 41 37N 2 42 E
Pinedale, *U.S.A.* **160 J7** 36 50N 119 48W
Pinega →, *Russia* **56 B8** 64 30N 44 19 E
Pinehill, *Australia* **126 C4** 23 38 S 146 57 E
Pinehurst, *U.S.A.* **152 C6** 32 12N 83 46W
Pinellas Park, *U.S.A.* **153 H7** 27 50N 82 43W
Pinerolo, *Italy* **44 D4** 44 53N 7 21 E
Pineto, *Italy* **45 F11** 42 36N 14 4 E
Pinetop, *U.S.A.* **159 J9** 34 8N 109 56W
Pinetown, *S. Africa* **117 D5** 29 48 S 30 54 E
Pinetree, *U.S.A.* **158 E11** 43 42N 105 52W
Pinetta, *U.S.A.* **152 E6** 30 36N 83 21W
Pineview, *U.S.A.* **152 C6** 32 7N 83 30W
Pineville, *Ky., U.S.A.* **149 G4** 36 46N 83 42W
Pineville, *La., U.S.A.* **155 K8** 31 19N 92 26W
Pineville, *S.C., U.S.A.* **152 B9** 33 26N 80 1W
Pinewood, *U.S.A.* **152 B9** 33 44N 80 27W
Piney, *France* **27 D11** 48 22N 4 21 E
Ping →, *Thailand* **86 E3** 15 42N 100 9 E
Pingaring, *Australia* **125 F2** 32 40 S 118 32 E
Pingba, *China* **76 D6** 26 23N 106 12 E
Pingchuan, *China* **76 D3** 27 35N 101 55 E
Pingding, *China* **74 F7** 37 47N 113 38 E
Pingdingshan, *China* **74 H7** 33 43N 113 27 E
Pingdong, *Taiwan* **77 F13** 22 39N 120 30 E
Pingdu, *China* **75 F10** 36 42N 119 59 E
Pingelly, *Australia* **125 F2** 32 32 S 117 5 E
Pingguo, *China* **76 F6** 23 19N 107 36 E
Pinghe, *China* **77 E11** 24 17N 117 21 E
Pinghu, *China* **77 B13** 30 40N 121 2 E
Pingjiang, *China* **77 C9** 28 45N 113 36 E
Pingle, *China* **77 E8** 24 40N 110 40 E
Pingli, *China* **76 A7** 32 27N 109 22 E
Pingliang, *China* **74 G4** 35 35N 106 31 E
Pinglu, *China* **74 E7** 39 31N 112 30 E
Pingluo, *China* **74 E4** 38 52N 106 30 E
Pingnan, *Fujian, China* **77 D12** 26 55N 119 0 E
Pingnan, *Guangxi Zhuangzu, China* **77 F8** 23 33N 110 22 E
Pingquan, *China* **75 D10** 41 1N 118 37 E
Pingrup, *Australia* **125 F2** 33 32 S 118 29 E
Pingtan, *China* **77 E12** 25 31N 119 47 E
Pingtang, *China* **76 E6** 25 49N 107 17 E
P'ingtung, *Taiwan* **77 F13** 22 38N 120 30 E
Pingwu, *China* **74 H3** 32 25N 104 30 E
Pingxiang, *Guangxi Zhuangzu, China* **76 F6** 22 6N 106 46 E
Pingxiang, *Jiangxi, China* **77 D9** 27 43N 113 48 E
Pingyao, *China* **74 F7** 37 12N 112 10 E
Pingyi, *China* **75 G9** 35 30N 117 35 E
Pingyin, *China* **74 F9** 36 20N 116 25 E
Pingyuan, *Guangdong, China* **77 E10** 24 37N 115 57 E
Pingyuan, *Shandong, China* **74 F9** 37 10N 116 22 E
Pingyuanjie, *China* **76 F4** 23 45N 103 48 E
Pinhal, *Brazil* **175 A6** 22 10 S 46 46W
Pinhal Novo, *Portugal* **43 G2** 38 38N 8 55W
Pinheiro, *Brazil* **170 B2** 2 31 S 45 5W
Pinhel, *Portugal* **42 E3** 40 50N 7 1W
Pinhuá →, *Brazil* **173 B5** 6 21 S 65 0W
Pini, *Indonesia* **84 B1** 0 10N 98 40 E
Piniós →, *Ilía, Greece* **48 D3** 37 48N 21 20 E
Piniós →, *Tríkkala, Greece* **48 B4** 39 55N 22 41 E
Pinjarra, *Australia* **125 F2** 32 37 S 115 52 E
Pink →, *Canada* **143 B8** 56 50N 103 50W
Pinkafeld, *Austria* **35 D9** 47 22N 16 9 E
Pinlebu, *Burma* **90 C5** 24 5N 95 22 E
Pinnacles, *Australia* **125 E3** 28 12 S 120 26 E
Pinnacles, *U.S.A.* **160 J5** 36 33N 121 19W
Pinnaroo, *Australia* **128 C4** 35 17 S 140 53 E
Pinneberg, *Germany* **30 B5** 53 40N 9 48 E
Pínnes, Ákra, *Greece* **51 F8** 40 5N 24 20 E
Pino Hachado, Paso, *S. Amer.* **176 A2** 38 39 S 70 54W
Pinon Hills, *U.S.A.* **161 L9** 34 26N 117 39W
Pinos, *Mexico* **162 C4** 22 20N 101 40W
Pinos, Mt., *U.S.A.* **161 L7** 34 49N 119 8W
Pinos Pt., *U.S.A.* **159 H3** 36 38N 121 57W
Pinos Puente, *Spain* **43 H7** 37 15N 3 45W
Pinotepa Nacional, *Mexico* **163 D5** 16 19N 98 3W
Pinrang, *Indonesia* **82 B1** 3 46 S 119 41 E
Pins, I. des, *N. Cal.* **133 V21** 22 37 S 167 30 E
Pinsk, *Belarus* **59 F4** 52 10N 26 1 E
Pintados, *Chile* **172 E4** 20 35 S 69 40W
Pintumba, *Australia* **125 F5** 31 30 S 132 12 E
Pintuyan, *Phil.* **81 G5** 9 57N 125 15 E
Pinukpuk, *Phil.* **80 C3** 17 35N 121 22 E
Pinyang, *China* **77 D13** 27 42N 120 31 E
Pinyug, *Russia* **62 A1** 60 5N 48 0 E
Pio V. Corpuz, *Phil.* **81 F5** 11 55N 124 2 E
Pio XII, *Brazil* **170 B2** 3 53 S 45 17W
Pioche, *U.S.A.* **159 H6** 37 56N 114 27W
Pioduran, *Phil.* **80 E4** 13 2N 123 25 E
Piombino, *Italy* **44 F7** 42 55N 10 32 E
Piombino, Canale di, *Italy* **44 F7** 42 53N 10 30 E

268 Powell, L.

Powell, L., U.S.A. **159 H8** 36 57N 111 29W
Powell River, Canada **142 D4** 49 50N 124 35W
Powelton, U.S.A. **152 B7** 33 26N 82 52W
Powers, Mich., U.S.A. **148 C2** 45 41N 87 32W
Powers, Oreg., U.S.A. **158 E1** 42 53N 124 4W
Powers Lake, U.S.A. **154 A3** 48 34N 102 39W
Powys □, U.K. **21 E4** 52 20N 3 20W
Poxoreu, Brazil **173 D7** 15 50S 54 23W
Poya, N. Cal. **133 U19** 21 19S 165 7E
Poyang Hu, China **77 C11** 29 5N 116 20E
Poyarkovo, Russia **65 E13** 49 36N 128 41E
Poysdorf, Austria **35 C9** 48 40N 16 37E
Poza de la Sal, Spain **42 C7** 42 35N 3 31W
Poza Rica, Mexico **163 C5** 20 33N 97 27W
Pozanti, Turkey **100 D6** 37 25N 34 50E
Požarevac, Serbia, Yug. **50 B5** 44 35N 21 18E
Pozazal, Puerto, Spain **42 C6** 42 56N 4 10W
Požega, Croatia **52 E2** 45 20N 17 40E
Požega, Serbia, Yug. **50 C4** 43 53N 20 2E
Pozhva, Russia **62 B6** 59 5N 56 5E
Poznań, Poland **55 F3** 52 25N 16 55E
Poznań □, Poland **55 F3** 52 30N 17 0E
Pozo, U.S.A. **161 K6** 35 20N 120 24W
Pozo Alcón, Spain **43 H8** 37 42N 2 56W
Pozo Almonte, Chile **172 E4** 20 10S 69 50W
Pozo Colorado, Paraguay **174 A4** 23 30S 58 45W
Pozo del Dátil, Mexico **162 B2** 30 0N 112 15W
Pozoblanco, Spain **43 G6** 38 23N 4 51W
Pozorrubio, Phil. **80 C3** 16 7N 120 33E
Pozuzo, Peru **172 C2** 10 5S 75 35W
Pozzallo, Italy **47 F7** 36 43N 14 51E
Pozzomaggiore, Italy **46 B1** 40 24N 8 39E
Pozzuoli, Italy **47 B7** 40 49N 14 7E
Pra →, Ghana **113 D4** 5 1N 1 37W
Prabuty, Poland **54 E6** 53 47N 19 15E
Prača, Bos.-H. **52 G3** 43 47N 18 43E
Prachatice, Czech Rep. **34 B6** 49 1N 14 0E
Prachin Buri, Thailand **86 F3** 14 0N 101 25E
Prachuap Khiri Khan, Thailand **87 G2** 11 49N 99 48E
Pradelles, France **28 D7** 44 46N 3 52E
Pradera, Colombia **168 C2** 3 25N 76 15W
Prades, France **28 F6** 42 38N 2 23E
Prado, Brazil **171 E4** 17 20S 39 13W
Prado del Rey, Spain **43 J5** 36 48N 5 33W
Præstø, Denmark **17 J6** 55 8N 12 2E
Pragersko, Slovenia **45 B12** 46 27N 15 42E
Prague = Praha, Czech Rep. **34 A7** 50 5N 14 22E
Praha, Czech Rep. **34 A7** 50 5N 14 22E
Prahecq, France **28 B3** 46 19N 0 26W
Prahita →, India **94 E4** 19 0N 79 55E
Prahova □, Romania **53 E10** 45 10N 26 0E
Prahova →, Romania **53 F10** 44 50N 25 50E
Prahovo, Serbia, Yug. **50 B6** 44 18N 22 39E
Praia, C. Verde Is. **8 G6** 14 55N 23 30W
Práia a Mare, Italy **47 C8** 39 50N 15 45E
Praid, Romania **53 D10** 46 32N 25 10E
Prainha, Amazonas, Brazil **173 B5** 7 10S 60 30W
Prainha, Pará, Brazil **169 D7** 1 45S 53 30W
Prairie, Australia **126 C3** 20 50S 144 35E
Prairie →, U.S.A. **155 H5** 34 30N 99 23W
Prairie City, U.S.A. **158 D4** 44 28N 118 43W
Prairie du Chien, U.S.A. **156 A5** 43 3N 91 9W
Prairie du Rocher, U.S.A. **156 F6** 38 5N 90 6W
Pramánda, Greece **48 B3** 39 32N 21 8E
Pran Buri, Thailand **86 F2** 12 23N 99 55E
Prándarjökull, Iceland **11 C12** 64 40N 14 55W
Prang, Ghana **113 D4** 8 1N 0 56W
Prasonísi, Ákra, Greece **38 D9** 35 42N 27 46E
Prästmon, Sweden **16 A11** 63 5N 17 45E
Praszka, Poland **55 G5** 51 5N 18 31E
Prata, Brazil **171 E2** 19 25S 48 54W
Pratapgarh, India **92 G6** 24 2N 74 40E
Prätigau, Switz. **33 C9** 46 56N 9 44E
Prato, Italy **44 E8** 43 53N 11 6E
Prátola Peligna, Italy **45 F10** 42 6N 13 52E
Prats-de-Mollo-la-Preste, France **28 F6** 42 25N 2 27E
Pratt, U.S.A. **155 G5** 37 39N 98 44W
Pratteln, Switz. **32 A5** 47 31N 7 41E
Prattville, U.S.A. **149 J2** 32 28N 86 29W
Pravara →, India **94 E2** 19 35N 74 45E
Pravdinsk, Russia **60 B6** 56 29N 43 28E
Pravets, Bulgaria **50 D7** 42 53N 23 55E
Pravia, Spain **42 B4** 43 30N 6 12W
Praya, Indonesia **85 D5** 8 39S 116 17E
Pré-en-Pail, France **26 D6** 48 28N 0 12W
Precordillera, Argentina **174 C2** 30 0S 69 1W
Predáppio, Italy **45 D8** 44 6N 11 59E
Predazzo, Italy **45 B8** 46 19N 11 36E
Predeal, Romania **53 E10** 45 30N 25 34E
Predejane, Serbia, Yug. **50 D6** 42 51N 22 9E
Preeceville, Canada **143 C8** 51 57N 102 40W
Preetz, Germany **30 A6** 54 14N 10 18E
Pregonero, Venezuela **168 B3** 8 1N 71 46W
Pregrada, Croatia **45 B12** 46 11N 15 45E
Preiļi, Latvia **15 H22** 56 18N 26 43E
Preko, Croatia **45 D12** 44 7N 15 10E
Prelate, Canada **143 C7** 50 51N 109 24W
Prelog, Croatia **45 B13** 46 18N 16 32E
Prémery, France **27 E10** 47 10N 3 18E
Premià de Mar, Spain **40 D7** 41 29N 2 22E
Premier, Canada **142 B3** 56 4N 129 56W
Premont, U.S.A. **155 M5** 27 22N 98 7W
Premuda, Croatia **45 D11** 44 20N 14 36E
Prenjasi, Albania **50 E4** 41 4N 20 32E
Prentice, U.S.A. **154 C9** 45 33N 90 17W
Prenzlau, Germany **30 B9** 53 19N 13 51E
Preobrazheniye, Russia **68 C6** 42 54N 133 54E
Přerov, Czech Rep. **35 B10** 49 28N 17 27E
Prescott, Canada **140 D4** 44 45N 75 30W
Prescott, Ariz., U.S.A. **159 J7** 34 33N 112 28W
Prescott, Ark., U.S.A. **155 J8** 33 48N 93 23W
Preservation Inlet, N.Z. **131 G1** 46 8S 166 35E
Preševo, Serbia, Yug. **50 D5** 42 19N 21 39E
Presho, U.S.A. **154 D4** 43 54N 100 3W
Presicce, Italy **47 C11** 39 54N 18 16E
Presidencia de la Plaza, Argentina **174 B4** 27 0S 59 50W
Presidencia Roque Saenz Peña, Argentina **174 B3** 26 45S 60 30W
Presidente Epitácio, Brazil **171 F1** 21 56S 52 6W
Presidente Hayes □, Paraguay **174 A4** 24 0S 59 0W
Presidente Hermes, Brazil **173 C5** 11 17S 61 55W
Presidente Prudente, Brazil **175 A5** 22 5S 51 25W
Presidente Roxas, Phil. **81 F4** 11 26N 122 56E
Presidio, Mexico **162 B4** 29 29N 104 23W
Presidio, U.S.A. **155 L2** 29 34N 104 22W
Preslav, Bulgaria **51 C10** 43 10N 26 52E
Preslavska Planina, Bulgaria **51 C10** 43 10N 26 45E
Prešov, Slovak Rep. **35 B14** 49 0N 21 15E
Prešovský □, Slovak Rep. **35 B13** 49 10N 21 0E
Prespa, Bulgaria **51 E8** 41 44N 24 55E
Prespa, L. = Prespansko Jezero, Macedonia **50 F5** 40 55N 21 0E
Prespansko Jezero, Macedonia **50 F5** 40 55N 21 0E
Presque Isle, U.S.A. **141 C6** 46 41N 68 1W
Prestatyn, U.K. **20 D4** 53 20N 3 24W
Prestea, Ghana **112 D4** 5 22N 2 7W
Presteigne, U.K. **21 E5** 52 17N 3 0W
Přeštice, Czech Rep. **34 B6** 49 34N 13 20E
Presto, Bolivia **173 D5** 18 55S 64 56W
Preston, Canada **150 C4** 43 23N 80 21W
Preston, U.K. **20 D5** 53 46N 2 42W
Preston, Ga., U.S.A. **152 C5** 32 4N 84 32W
Preston, Idaho, U.S.A. **158 E8** 42 6N 111 53W
Preston, Iowa, U.S.A. **156 B6** 42 3N 90 24W
Preston, Minn., U.S.A. **154 D8** 43 40N 92 5W
Preston, Nev., U.S.A. **158 G6** 38 55N 115 4W
Preston, C., Australia **124 D2** 20 51S 116 12E
Prestranda, Norway **18 E6** 59 6N 9 4E
Prestwick, U.K. **22 F4** 55 29N 4 37W
Prêto →, Amazonas, Brazil **169 D5** 0 8S 64 6W
Prêto →, Bahia, Brazil **170 D3** 11 21S 43 52W
Prêto do Igapó-Açu →, Brazil **169 D6** 4 26S 59 48W
Pretoria, S. Africa **117 D4** 25 44S 28 12E
Preuilly-sur-Claise, France **26 F7** 46 51N 0 56E
Préveza, Greece **48 C2** 38 57N 20 47E
Préveza □, Greece **48 B2** 39 20N 20 40E
Prey Veng, Cambodia **87 G5** 11 35N 105 29E
Priazovskoye, Ukraine **59 J8** 46 44N 35 40E
Pribilof Is., U.S.A. **144 H5** 57 0N 170 0W
Priboj, Serbia, Yug. **50 C3** 43 35N 19 32E
Příbram, Czech Rep. **34 B7** 49 41N 14 2E
Price, U.S.A. **158 G8** 39 36N 110 49W
Price I., Canada **142 C3** 52 23N 128 41W
Prichard, U.S.A. **149 K1** 30 44N 88 5W
Priego, Spain **40 E2** 40 26N 2 21W
Priego de Córdoba, Spain **43 H6** 37 27N 4 12W
Priekule, Latvia **15 H19** 56 26N 21 35E
Prien, Germany **31 H8** 47 51N 12 20E
Prienai, Lithuania **54 D10** 54 38N 23 57E
Prieska, S. Africa **116 D3** 29 40S 22 42E
Priest →, U.S.A. **158 B5** 48 12N 116 54W
Priest L., U.S.A. **158 B5** 48 35N 116 52W
Priest Valley, U.S.A. **160 J6** 36 10N 120 39W
Priestly, Canada **142 C3** 54 8N 125 20W
Prieto Diaz, Phil. **80 E5** 13 2N 124 12E
Prievidza, Slovak Rep. **35 C11** 48 46N 18 36E
Prignitz, Germany **30 B7** 53 6N 11 45E
Prijedor, Bos.-H. **45 D13** 44 58N 16 41E
Prijepolje, Serbia, Yug. **50 C3** 43 27N 19 40E
Prikaspiyskaya Nizmennost = Caspian Depression, Eurasia **61 G9** 47 0N 48 0E
Prikubanskaya Nizmennost, Russia **59 K10** 45 39N 38 33E
Prilep, Macedonia **50 E5** 41 21N 21 32E
Priluki = Pryluky, Ukraine **59 G7** 50 30N 32 24E
Prime Seal I., Australia **126 G4** 40 3S 147 43E
Primeira Cruz, Brazil **170 B3** 2 30S 43 26W
Primorsk, Russia **58 B5** 60 22N 28 37E
Primorsko, Bulgaria **51 D11** 42 15N 27 44E
Primorsko-Akhtarsk, Russia **59 J10** 46 2N 38 10E
Primorskoye, Ukraine **59 J9** 46 48N 36 20E
Primrose L., Canada **143 C7** 54 55N 109 45W
Prince Albert, Canada **143 C7** 53 15N 105 50W
Prince Albert, S. Africa **116 E3** 33 12S 22 2E
Prince Albert Mts., Antarctica **7 D11** 76 0S 161 30E
Prince Albert Nat. Park, Canada **143 C7** 54 0N 106 25W
Prince Albert Pen., Canada **138 A8** 72 30N 116 0W
Prince Albert Sd., Canada **138 A8** 70 25N 115 0W
Prince Alfred, C., Canada **6 B1** 74 20N 124 40W
Prince Charles I., Canada **139 B12** 67 47N 76 12W
Prince Charles Mts., Antarctica **7 D6** 72 0S 67 0E
Prince Edward I. □, Canada **141 C7** 46 20N 63 20W
Prince Edward Is., Ind. Oc. **121 J2** 46 35S 38 0E
Prince George, Canada **142 C4** 53 55N 122 50W
Prince of Wales, C., U.S.A. **136 C3** 65 36N 168 5W
Prince of Wales I., Australia **126 A3** 10 40S 142 10E
Prince of Wales I., Canada **138 A10** 73 0N 99 0W
Prince of Wales I., U.S.A. **142 B2** 55 47N 132 50W
Prince Patrick I., Canada **6 B2** 77 0N 120 0W
Prince Regent Inlet, Canada **6 B3** 73 0N 90 0W
Prince Rupert, Canada **142 C2** 54 20N 130 20W
Princesa Isabel, Brazil **170 C4** 7 44S 38 0W
Princess Charlotte B., Australia **126 A3** 14 25S 144 0E
Princess May Ranges, Australia **124 C4** 15 30S 125 30E
Princess Royal I., Canada **142 C3** 53 0N 128 40W
Princeton, Canada **142 D4** 49 27N 120 30W
Princeton, Calif., U.S.A. **160 F4** 39 24N 122 1W
Princeton, Ill., U.S.A. **156 C7** 41 23N 89 28W
Princeton, Ind., U.S.A. **157 F9** 38 21N 87 34W
Princeton, Ky., U.S.A. **148 G2** 37 7N 87 53W
Princeton, Mo., U.S.A. **156 D3** 40 24N 93 35W
Princeton, N.J., U.S.A. **151 F10** 40 21N 74 39W
Princeton, W. Va., U.S.A. **148 G5** 37 22N 81 6W
Princeville, U.S.A. **156 D7** 40 56N 89 46W
Principe, I. de, Atl. Oc. **114 B1** 1 37N 7 27E
Principe Chan., Canada **142 C3** 53 28N 130 0W
Principe da Beira, Brazil **173 C5** 12 20S 64 30W
Prineville, U.S.A. **158 D3** 44 18N 120 51W
Prins Christian Sund, Greenland **10 E6** 60 4N 43 10W
Prins Harald Kyst, Antarctica **7 D4** 70 0S 35 1E
Prinsesse Astrid Kyst, Antarctica **7 D3** 70 45S 12 30E
Prinsesse Ragnhild Kyst, Antarctica **7 D4** 70 15S 27 30E
Prinzapolca, Nic. **164 D3** 13 20N 83 35W
Prior, C., Spain **42 B2** 43 34N 8 17W
Priozersk, Russia **58 B6** 61 2N 30 7E
Pripet → = Prypyat →, Europe **59 G6** 51 20N 30 15E
Pripet Marshes, Europe **59 F5** 52 10N 28 10E
Pripyat Marshes = Pripet Marshes, Europe **59 F5** 52 10N 28 10E
Pripyats = Prypyat →, Europe **59 G6** 51 20N 30 15E
Prislop, Pasul, Romania **53 C9** 47 37N 24 48E
Pristen, Russia **59 G9** 51 15N 36 44E
Priština, Serbia, Yug. **50 D5** 42 40N 21 13E
Pritzwalk, Germany **30 B8** 53 9N 12 10E
Privas, France **29 D8** 44 45N 4 37E
Priverno, Italy **46 A6** 41 28N 13 11E
Privolzhsk, Russia **60 B5** 57 23N 41 16E
Privolzhskaya Vozvyshennost, Russia **60 E7** 51 0N 46 0E
Privolzhskiy, Russia **60 E8** 51 25N 46 3E
Privolzhye, Russia **60 D9** 52 52N 48 33E
Priyutnoye, Russia **61 G6** 46 12N 43 40E
Priyutovo, Russia **62 E4** 53 55N 53 59E
Prizren, Serbia, Yug. **50 D4** 42 13N 20 45E
Prizzi, Italy **46 E6** 37 43N 13 26E
Prnjavor, Bos.-H. **52 F2** 44 52N 17 43E
Probolinggo, Indonesia **85 D4** 7 46S 113 13E
Prochowice, Poland **55 G3** 51 17N 16 20E
Proddatur, India **95 G4** 14 45N 78 30E
Prodhromos, Cyprus **38 E11** 34 57N 32 50E
Proença-a-Nova, Portugal **42 F3** 39 45N 7 54W
Profítis Ilías, Greece **38 C9** 36 17N 27 56E
Profondeville, Belgium **24 D4** 50 23N 4 52E
Progreso, Mexico **163 C7** 21 20N 89 40W
Prokhladnyy, Russia **61 J7** 43 50N 44 2E
Prokletije, Albania **50 D3** 42 30N 19 45E
Prokopyevsk, Russia **64 D9** 54 0N 86 45E
Prokuplje, Serbia, Yug. **50 C5** 43 16N 21 36E
Proletarsk, Russia **61 G5** 46 42N 41 50E
Prome = Pyè, Burma **90 F5** 18 49N 95 13E
Prophet →, Canada **142 B4** 58 48N 122 40W
Prophetstown, U.S.A. **156 C7** 41 40N 89 56W
Propriá, Brazil **170 D4** 10 13S 36 51W
Propriano, France **29 G12** 41 41N 8 52E
Proserpine, Australia **126 C4** 20 21S 148 36E
Prosna →, Poland **55 F4** 52 6N 17 44E
Prosperidad, Phil. **81 G5** 8 34N 125 52E
Prosser, U.S.A. **158 C4** 46 12N 119 46W
Prostějov, Czech Rep. **35 B10** 49 30N 17 9E
Prostki, Poland **54 E9** 53 42N 22 25E
Proston, Australia **127 D5** 26 8S 151 32E
Proszowice, Poland **55 H7** 50 13N 20 16E
Protection, U.S.A. **155 G5** 37 12N 99 29W
Próti, Greece **48 D3** 37 5N 21 32E
Provadiya, Bulgaria **51 C11** 43 12N 27 30E
Provence, France **29 E9** 43 40N 5 46E
Provence-Alpes-Côte d'Azur □, France **29 D10** 44 0N 6 15E
Providence, Ky., U.S.A. **148 G2** 37 24N 87 46W
Providence, R.I., U.S.A. **151 E13** 41 49N 71 24W
Providence Bay, Canada **140 C3** 45 41N 82 15W
Providence C., N.Z. **131 F1** 45 59S 166 29E
Providence Mts., U.S.A. **159 J6** 35 10N 115 15W
Providencia, Ecuador **168 D2** 0 28S 76 28W
Providencia, I. de, Colombia **164 D3** 13 25N 81 26W
Provideniya, Russia **65 C19** 64 23N 173 18W
Provins, France **27 D10** 48 33N 3 15E
Provo, U.S.A. **158 F8** 40 14N 111 39W
Provost, Canada **143 C6** 52 25N 110 20W
Prozor, Bos.-H. **52 G2** 43 50N 17 34E
Prudentópolis, Brazil **171 G1** 25 12S 50 57W
Prud'homme, Canada **143 C7** 52 20N 105 54W
Prudnik, Poland **55 H4** 50 20N 17 38E
Prüm, Germany **31 E2** 50 12N 6 25E
Prundu, Romania **53 F11** 44 6N 26 14E
Pruszcz Gdański, Poland **54 D5** 54 17N 18 40E
Pruszków, Poland **55 F7** 52 9N 20 49E
Prut →, Romania **53 E13** 45 28N 28 10E
Pruzhany, Belarus **59 F3** 52 33N 24 28E
Prvič, Croatia **45 D11** 44 55N 14 47E
Prydz B., Antarctica **7 C6** 69 0S 74 0E
Pryluky, Ukraine **59 G7** 50 30N 32 24E
Pryor, U.S.A. **155 G7** 36 19N 95 19W
Prypyat →, Europe **59 G6** 51 20N 30 15E
Przasnysz, Poland **55 E7** 53 2N 20 54E
Przedbórz, Poland **55 G6** 51 6N 19 53E
Przedecz, Poland **55 F5** 52 20N 18 53E
Przemków, Poland **55 G2** 51 31N 15 48E
Przemyśl, Poland **55 J9** 49 50N 22 45E
Przemyśl □, Poland **55 J9** 50 0N 22 45E
Przeworsk, Poland **55 H9** 50 6N 22 32E
Przewóz, Poland **55 G1** 51 28N 14 57E
Przhevalsk, Kyrgyzstan **63 B9** 42 30N 78 20E
Przysucha, Poland **55 G7** 51 22N 20 38E
Psakhná, Greece **48 C5** 38 34N 23 35E
Psará, Greece **49 C7** 38 37N 25 38E
Psathoúra, Greece **48 B6** 39 30N 24 12E
Psel →, Ukraine **59 H7** 49 10N 33 37E
Pserimos, Greece **49 E9** 36 56N 27 8E
Psíra, Greece **38 D7** 35 12N 25 52E
Pskem →, Uzbekistan **63 C5** 41 38N 70 1E
Pskemskiy Khrebet, Uzbekistan **63 C5** 42 0N 70 45E
Pskent, Uzbekistan **63 C4** 40 54N 69 20E
Pskov, Russia **58 D5** 57 50N 28 25E
Pskovskoye, Ozero, Russia **15 H22** 58 0N 27 58E
Psunj, Croatia **52 E2** 45 25N 17 19E
Pteleón, Greece **48 B4** 39 3N 22 57E
Ptich = Ptsich →, Belarus **59 F5** 52 9N 28 52E
Ptolemaís, Greece **50 F5** 40 30N 21 43E
Ptsich →, Belarus **59 F5** 52 9N 28 52E
Ptuj, Slovenia **45 B12** 46 28N 15 50E
Ptujska Gora, Slovenia **45 B12** 46 23N 15 47E
Pu Xian, China **74 F6** 36 24N 111 6E
Pua, Thailand **86 C3** 19 11N 100 55E
Puaena Pt., U.S.A. **145 J13** 21 36N 158 6W
Puán, Argentina **174 D3** 37 30S 62 45W
Pu'an, China **76 E5** 25 46N 104 57E
Puan, S. Korea **75 G14** 35 44N 126 44E
Pu'apu'a, W. Samoa **133 W23** 13 34S 172 9W
Pubei, China **76 F7** 22 16N 109 31E
Pucacuro →, Peru **168 D3** 3 20S 74 58W
Pucallpa, Peru **172 B3** 8 25S 74 30W
Pucará, Bolivia **173 D5** 18 43S 64 11W
Pucará, Peru **172 D3** 15 5S 70 24W
Pucarani, Bolivia **172 D4** 16 23S 68 30W
Pucheng, China **77 D12** 27 59N 118 31E
Pucheni, Romania **53 E10** 45 12N 25 17E
Puchheim, Germany **31 G7** 48 9N 11 21E
Púchov, Slovak Rep. **35 B11** 49 8N 18 20E
Pucio Pt., Phil. **81 F3** 11 46N 121 51E
Pucioasa, Romania **53 E10** 45 5N 25 25E
Pučišća, Croatia **45 E13** 43 22N 16 43E
Puck, Poland **54 D5** 54 45N 18 23E
Pucka, Zatoka, Poland **54 D5** 54 30N 18 40E
Puçol, Spain **41 F4** 39 37N 0 18W
Pudasjärvi, Finland **14 D22** 65 23N 26 53E
Puding, China **76 D5** 26 18N 105 44E
Pudozh, Russia **58 B9** 61 48N 36 32E
Pudtol, Phil. **80 B3** 18 13N 121 22E
Pudukkottai, India **95 J4** 10 28N 78 47E
Puebla, Mexico **163 D5** 19 3N 98 12W
Puebla □, Mexico **163 D5** 18 30N 98 0W
Puebla de Alcocer, Spain **43 G5** 38 59N 5 14W
Puebla de Don Fadrique, Spain **41 H2** 37 58N 2 25W
Puebla de Don Rodrigo, Spain **43 F6** 39 5N 4 37W
Puebla de Guzmán, Spain **43 H3** 37 37N 7 15W
Puebla de la Calzada, Spain **43 G4** 38 54N 6 37W
Puebla de Sanabria, Spain **42 C4** 42 4N 6 38W
Puebla de Trives = Pobra de Trives, Spain **42 C3** 42 20N 7 10W
Pueblo, U.S.A. **154 F2** 38 16N 104 37W
Pueblo Hundido, Chile **174 B1** 26 20S 70 5W
Pueblo Nuevo, Venezuela **168 B3** 8 26N 71 26W
Puelches, Argentina **174 D2** 38 5S 65 51W
Puelén, Argentina **174 D2** 37 32S 67 38W
Puente Alto, Chile **174 C1** 33 32S 70 35W
Puente-Genil, Spain **43 H6** 37 22N 4 47W
Puente la Reina, Spain **40 C3** 42 40N 1 49W
Puenteareas = Ponteareas, Spain **42 C2** 42 10N 8 28W
Puentedeume = Pontedeume, Spain **42 B2** 43 24N 8 10W
Puentes de Garcia Rodriguez = As Pontes de García Rodríquez, Spain **42 B3** 43 27N 7 50W
Pueo Pt., U.S.A. **145 B1** 21 54N 160 4W
Pu'er, China **76 F3** 23 0N 101 15E
Puerco →, U.S.A. **159 J10** 34 22N 107 50W
Puerta Galera, Phil. **80 E3** 13 30N 120 57E
Puerto, Canary Is. **39 F2** 28 5N 17 20W
Puerto Acosta, Bolivia **172 D4** 15 32S 69 15W
Puerto Aisén, Chile **176 C2** 45 27S 73 0W
Puerto Ángel, Mexico **163 D5** 15 40N 96 29W
Puerto Arista, Mexico **163 D6** 15 56N 93 48W
Puerto Armuelles, Panama **164 E3** 8 20N 82 51W
Puerto Ayacucho, Venezuela **168 B4** 5 40N 67 35W
Puerto Barrios, Guatemala **164 C2** 15 40N 88 32W
Puerto Bermejo, Argentina **174 B4** 26 55S 58 34W
Puerto Bermúdez, Peru **172 C3** 10 20S 74 58W
Puerto Bolívar, Ecuador **168 D2** 3 19S 79 55W
Puerto Cabello, Venezuela **168 A4** 10 28N 68 1W
Puerto Cabezas, Nic. **164 D3** 14 0N 83 30W
Puerto Cabo Gracias á Dios, Nic. **164 D3** 15 0N 83 10W
Puerto Capaz = Jebba, Morocco **110 A4** 35 11N 4 43W
Puerto Carreño, Colombia **168 B4** 6 12N 67 22W
Puerto Castilla, Honduras **164 C2** 16 0N 86 0W
Puerto Chicama, Peru **172 B2** 7 45S 79 20W
Puerto Coig, Argentina **176 D3** 50 54S 69 15W
Puerto Cortés, Costa Rica **164 E3** 8 55N 84 0W
Puerto Cortés, Honduras **164 C2** 15 51N 88 0W
Puerto Cumarebo, Venezuela **168 A4** 11 29N 69 30W
Puerto de Alcudia, Spain **39 B10** 39 50N 3 7E
Puerto de Andraitx, Spain **39 B9** 39 32N 2 23E
Puerto de Cabrera, Spain **39 B9** 39 8N 2 56E
Puerto de Gran Tarajal, Canary Is. **39 F5** 28 13N 14 1W
Puerto de la Cruz, Canary Is. **39 F3** 28 24N 16 32W
Puerto de Mazarrón, Spain **41 H3** 37 34N 1 15W
Puerto de Pozo Negro, Canary Is. **39 F6** 28 19N 13 55W
Puerto de Sóller, Spain **39 B9** 39 48N 2 42E
Puerto de Somosierra, Spain **42 D7** 41 9N 3 35W
Puerto del Carmen, Canary Is. **39 F6** 28 55N 13 38W
Puerto del Rosario, Canary Is. **39 F6** 28 30N 13 52W
Puerto Deseado, Argentina **176 C3** 47 55S 66 0W
Puerto Guaraní, Paraguay **173 E6** 21 18S 57 55W
Puerto Heath, Bolivia **172 C4** 12 34S 68 39W
Puerto Huitoto, Colombia **168 C3** 0 18N 74 3W
Puerto Inca, Peru **172 B3** 9 22S 74 54W
Puerto Juárez, Mexico **163 C7** 21 11N 86 49W
Puerto La Cruz, Venezuela **169 A5** 10 13N 64 38W
Puerto Leguízamo, Colombia **168 D3** 0 12S 74 46W
Puerto Limón, Colombia **168 C3** 3 23N 73 30W
Puerto Lobos, Argentina **176 B3** 42 0S 65 3W
Puerto López, Colombia **168 C3** 4 5N 72 58W
Puerto Lumbreras, Spain **41 H3** 37 34N 1 48W
Puerto Madryn, Argentina **176 B3** 42 48S 65 4W
Puerto Maldonado, Peru **172 C4** 12 30S 69 10W
Puerto Manotí, Cuba **164 B4** 21 22N 76 50W
Puerto Mazarrón = Puerto de Mazarrón, Spain **41 H3** 37 34N 1 15W
Puerto Mercedes, Colombia **168 C3** 1 11N 72 53W
Puerto Miraña, Colombia **168 D3** 1 20S 70 19W
Puerto Montt, Chile **176 B2** 41 28S 73 0W
Puerto Morelos, Mexico **163 C7** 20 49N 86 52W
Puerto Nariño, Colombia **168 C4** 4 56N 67 48W
Puerto Natales, Chile **176 D2** 51 45S 72 15W
Puerto Nuevo, Colombia **168 B4** 5 53N 69 56W
Puerto Nutrias, Venezuela **168 B4** 8 5N 69 18W
Puerto Ordaz, Venezuela **169 B5** 8 16N 62 44W
Puerto Padre, Cuba **164 B4** 21 13N 76 35W
Puerto Páez, Venezuela **168 B4** 6 13N 67 28W
Puerto Peñasco, Mexico **162 A2** 31 20N 113 33W
Puerto Pinasco, Paraguay **174 A4** 22 36S 57 50W
Puerto Pirámides, Argentina **176 B4** 42 35S 64 20W
Puerto Plata, Dom. Rep. **165 C5** 19 48N 70 45W
Puerto Pollensa, Spain **39 B10** 39 54N 3 4E
Puerto Portillo, Peru **172 B3** 9 45S 72 42W
Puerto Princesa, Phil. **81 G2** 9 46N 118 45E
Puerto Quellón, Chile **176 B2** 43 7S 73 37W
Puerto Quepos, Costa Rica **164 E3** 9 29N 84 6W
Puerto Real, Spain **43 J4** 36 33N 6 12W
Puerto Rico, Bolivia **172 C4** 11 5S 67 38W
Puerto Rico, Canary Is. **39 G4** 27 47N 15 42W
Puerto Rico ■, W. Indies **165 C6** 18 15N 66 45W
Puerto Rico Trench, Atl. Oc. **165 C6** 19 50N 66 0W
Puerto Saavedra, Chile **176 A2** 38 47S 73 24W
Puerto Sastre, Paraguay **174 A4** 22 2S 57 55W
Puerto Serrano, Spain **43 J5** 36 56N 5 33W
Puerto Siles, Bolivia **173 C4** 12 48S 65 5W
Puerto Suárez, Bolivia **173 D6** 18 58S 57 52W
Puerto Tejada, Colombia **168 C2** 3 14N 76 24W
Puerto Umbría, Colombia **168 C2** 0 52N 76 33W
Puerto Vallarta, Mexico **162 C3** 20 36N 105 15W
Puerto Varas, Chile **176 B2** 41 19S 72 59W
Puerto Villazón, Bolivia **173 C5** 13 32S 61 57W
Puerto Wilches, Colombia **168 B3** 7 21N 73 54W
Puertollano, Spain **43 G6** 38 43N 4 7W
Puesto Cunambo, Peru **168 D2** 2 10S 76 0W
Pueyrredón, L., Argentina **176 C2** 47 20S 72 0W
Puffin I., Ireland **23 E1** 51 50N 10 24W
Pugachev, Russia **60 D9** 52 0N 48 49E
Puge, China **76 D4** 27 20N 102 31E
Puge, Tanzania **118 C3** 4 45S 33 11E
Puget Sound, U.S.A. **158 C2** 47 50N 122 30W
Puget-Théniers, France **29 E10** 43 58N 6 53E
Púglia □, Italy **47 A9** 41 15N 16 15E
Pugo, Phil. **80 C3** 16 18N 121 30E
Pugŏdong, N. Korea **75 C16** 42 5N 130 0E
Pugu, Tanzania **118 D4** 6 55S 39 4E

Q

Rzhev 273

Rønne, *Denmark* 17 J8 55 6N 14 43 E
Ronne Ice Shelf, *Antarctica* 7 D18 78 0 S 60 0W
Ronneby, *Sweden* 17 H9 56 12N 15 17 E
Ronnebyån →, *Sweden* 17 H9 56 11N 15 18 E
Rönneshytta, *Sweden* 17 F9 58 56N 15 2 E
Ronsard, C., *Australia* 125 D1 24 46 S 113 10 E
Ronse, *Belgium* 24 D3 50 45N 3 35 E
Ronuro →, *Brazil* 173 C7 11 56 S 53 33W
Roodepoort, *S. Africa* 117 D4 26 11 S 27 54 E
Roodhouse, *U.S.A.* 156 E6 39 29N 90 24W
Roof Butte, *U.S.A.* 159 H9 36 28N 109 5W
Roopville, *U.S.A.* 152 B4 33 27N 85 8W
Roorkee, *India* 92 E7 29 52N 77 59 E
Roosendaal, *Neths.* 24 C4 51 32N 4 29 E
Roosevelt, *Minn., U.S.A.* 154 A7 48 48N 95 6W
Roosevelt, *Utah, U.S.A.* 158 F8 40 18N 109 59W
Roosevelt →, *Brazil* 173 B5 7 35 S 60 20W
Roosevelt, Mt., *Canada* 142 B3 58 26N 125 20W
Roosevelt I., *Antarctica* 7 D12 79 30 S 162 0W
Roosevelt Res., *U.S.A.* 159 K8 33 46N 111 0W
Ropczyce, *Poland* 55 H8 50 4N 21 38 E
Roper →, *Australia* 126 A2 14 43 S 135 27 E
Ropesville, *U.S.A.* 155 J3 33 26N 102 9W
Roque Pérez, *Argentina* 174 D4 35 25 S 59 24W
Roquefort, *France* 28 D3 44 2N 0 20W
Roquemaure, *France* 29 D8 44 3N 4 48 E
Roquetas de Mar, *Spain* 41 J2 36 46N 2 36W
Roquetes, *Spain* 40 E5 40 50N 0 30 E
Roquevaire, *France* 29 E9 43 20N 5 36 E
Roraima □, *Brazil* 169 C5 2 0N 61 30W
Roraima, Mt., *Venezuela* 169 B5 5 10N 60 40W
Rorketon, *Canada* 143 C9 51 24N 99 35W
Røros, *Norway* 15 E14 62 35N 11 23 E
Rorschach, *Switz.* 33 B8 47 28N 9 28 E
Rosa, *Zambia* 119 D3 9 33 S 31 15 E
Rosa, C., *Algeria* 111 A6 37 0N 8 16 E
Rosa, Monte, *Europe* 32 E5 45 57N 7 53 E
Rosa, Monte, *Italy* 44 C4 45 55N 7 53 E
Rosal de la Frontera, *Spain* 43 H3 37 59N 7 13W
Rosales, *Phil.* 80 D3 15 54N 120 38 E
Rosalia, *U.S.A.* 158 C5 47 14N 117 22W
Rosamond, *U.S.A.* 161 L8 34 52N 118 10W
Rosans, *France* 29 D9 44 24N 5 29 E
Rosario, *Argentina* 174 C3 33 0 S 60 40W
Rosário, *Brazil* 170 B3 3 0 S 44 15W
Rosario, *Baja Calif., Mexico* 162 B1 30 0N 115 50W
Rosario, *Sinaloa, Mexico* 162 C3 23 0N 105 52W
Rosario, *Paraguay* 174 A4 24 30 S 57 35W
Rosario, *Phil.* 81 G5 8 24N 125 59 E
Rosario, Villa del, *Venezuela* 168 A3 10 19N 72 19W
Rosario de la Frontera, *Argentina* 174 B3 25 50 S 65 0W
Rosario de Lerma, *Argentina* 174 A2 24 59 S 65 35W
Rosario del Tala, *Argentina* 174 C4 32 20 S 59 10W
Rosário do Sul, *Brazil* 175 C5 30 15 S 54 55W
Rosário Oeste, *Brazil* 173 C6 14 50 S 56 25W
Rosarito, *Mexico* 161 N9 32 18N 117 4W
Rosarno, *Italy* 47 D8 38 29N 15 58 E
Rosas = Roses, *Spain* 40 C8 42 19N 3 10 E
Roscoe, *Miss., U.S.A.* 156 G3 37 58N 93 48W
Roscoe, *S. Dak., U.S.A.* 154 C5 45 27N 99 20W
Roscoff, *France* 26 D3 48 44N 3 58W
Roscommon, *Ireland* 23 C3 53 38N 8 11W
Roscommon, *U.S.A.* 148 C3 44 30N 84 35W
Roscommon □, *Ireland* 23 C3 53 49N 8 23W
Roscrea, *Ireland* 23 D4 52 57N 7 49W
Rose →, *Australia* 126 A2 14 16 S 135 45 E
Rose Blanche, *Canada* 141 C8 47 38N 58 45W
Rose Harbour, *Canada* 142 C2 52 15N 131 10W
Rose Pt., *Canada* 142 C2 54 11N 131 39W
Rose Valley, *Canada* 143 C8 52 19N 103 49W
Roseau, *Domin.* 165 C7 15 20N 61 24W
Roseau, *U.S.A.* 154 A7 48 51N 95 46W
Rosebery, *Australia* 126 G4 41 46 S 145 33 E
Rosebud, *U.S.A.* 155 K6 31 4N 96 59W
Roseburg, *U.S.A.* 158 E2 43 13N 123 20W
Rosedale, *Australia* 126 C5 24 38 S 151 53 E
Rosedale, *U.S.A.* 155 J9 33 51N 91 2W
Roseland, *U.S.A.* 160 G4 38 25N 122 43W
Rosemary, *Canada* 142 C6 50 46N 112 5W
Rosenberg, *U.S.A.* 155 L7 29 34N 95 49W
Rosendaël, *France* 27 A9 51 3N 2 24 E
Rosendal, *Norway* 18 E3 59 59N 6 0 E
Rosendale, *U.S.A.* 156 D2 40 4N 94 51W
Rosenheim, *Germany* 31 H8 47 51N 12 7 E
Roses, *Spain* 40 C8 42 19N 3 10 E
Roses, G. de, *Spain* 40 C8 42 10N 3 15 E
Roseto degli Abruzzi, *Italy* 45 F11 42 41N 14 1 E
Rosetown, *Canada* 143 C7 51 35N 107 59W
Rosetta = Rashîd, *Egypt* 106 H7 31 21N 30 22 E
Roseville, *Calif., U.S.A.* 160 G5 38 45N 121 17W
Roseville, *Ill., U.S.A.* 156 D6 40 44N 90 40W
Roseville, *Mich., U.S.A.* 157 B14 42 30N 82 56W
Rosewood, *N.S.W., Australia* 129 C7 35 38 S 147 52 E
Rosewood, *N. Terr., Australia* 124 C4 16 28 S 128 58 E
Rosewood, *Queens., Australia* 127 D5 27 38 S 152 36 E
Roshkhvār, *Iran* 97 C8 34 58N 59 37 E
Rosier, *U.S.A.* 152 C7 32 59N 82 15W
Rosières-en-Santerre, *France* 27 C9 49 49N 2 42 E
Rosignano Marittimo, *Italy* 44 E7 43 24N 10 28 E
Rosignol, *Guyana* 169 B6 6 15N 57 30W
Roșiori de Vede, *Romania* 53 F10 44 9N 25 0 E
Rositsa, *Bulgaria* 51 C11 43 57N 27 57 E
Rositsa →, *Bulgaria* 51 C9 43 10N 25 30 E
Roskilde, *Denmark* 17 J6 55 38N 12 3 E
Roskilde Amtskommune □, *Denmark* 17 J6 55 35N 12 5 E
Roskovec, *Albania* 50 F3 40 44N 19 43 E
Roslavl, *Russia* 58 F7 53 57N 32 55 E
Roslyn, *Australia* 129 C8 34 29 S 149 37 E
Rosmaninhal, *Portugal* 42 F3 39 44N 7 5W
Rosmead, *S. Africa* 116 E4 31 29 S 25 8 E
Røsnæs, *Denmark* 17 J4 55 44N 10 55 E
Rosolini, *Italy* 47 F7 36 49N 14 57 E
Rosporden, *France* 26 E3 47 57N 3 50W
Ross, *Australia* 126 G4 42 2 S 147 30 E
Ross, *N.Z.* 131 C5 42 53 S 170 49 E
Ross I., *Antarctica* 7 D11 77 30 S 168 0 E
Ross Ice Shelf, *Antarctica* 7 E12 80 0 S 180 0 E
Ross L., *U.S.A.* 158 B3 48 44N 121 4W
Ross-on-Wye, *U.K.* 21 F5 51 54N 2 34W
Ross Sea, *Antarctica* 7 D11 74 0 S 178 0 E
Rossa, *Switz.* 33 D8 46 23N 9 8 E
Rossall Pt., *U.K.* 20 D4 53 55N 3 3W
Rossan Pt., *Ireland* 23 B3 54 42N 8 47W
Rossano, *Italy* 47 C9 39 36N 16 39 E
Rossburn, *Canada* 143 C8 50 40N 100 49W
Rosseau, *Canada* 150 A5 45 16N 79 39W
Rossel, C., *Vanuatu* 133 K4 20 23 S 166 36 E
Rosses, The, *Ireland* 23 A3 55 2N 8 20W
Rossford, *U.S.A.* 157 C13 41 36N 83 34W
Rossignol, L., *Canada* 140 B5 52 43N 73 40W
Rossignol Res., *Canada* 141 D6 44 12N 65 10W
Rosskreppfjorden, *Norway* 18 E4 59 4N 7 10 E
Rossland, *Canada* 142 D5 49 6N 117 50W
Rosslare, *Ireland* 23 D5 52 17N 6 24W
Rosslau, *Germany* 30 D8 51 52N 12 15 E
Rosso, *Mauritania* 112 B1 16 40N 15 45W
Rosso, C., *France* 29 F12 42 13N 8 32 E
Rossosh, *Russia* 59 G10 50 15N 39 28 E
Rossport, *Canada* 140 C2 48 50N 87 30W
Røssvatnet, *Norway* 14 D16 65 45N 14 5 E
Rossville, *Australia* 126 B4 15 48 S 145 15 E
Rossville, *U.S.A.* 157 D10 40 25N 86 36W
Røst, *Norway* 14 C15 67 32N 12 0 E
Rostāq, *Afghan.* 91 A3 37 7N 69 49 E
Rosthern, *Canada* 143 C7 52 40N 106 20W
Rostock, *Germany* 30 A8 54 5N 12 8 E
Rostov, *Don, Russia* 59 J10 47 15N 39 45 E
Rostov, *Yaroslavl, Russia* 58 D10 57 14N 39 25 E
Rostrenen, *France* 26 D3 48 14N 3 21W
Roswell, *Ga., U.S.A.* 152 A5 34 2N 84 22W
Roswell, *N. Mex., U.S.A.* 155 J2 33 24N 104 32W
Rota, *Spain* 43 J4 36 37N 6 20W
Rotan, *U.S.A.* 155 J4 32 51N 100 28W
Rotenburg, *Hessen, Germany* 30 E5 50 59N 9 44 E
Rotenburg, *Niedersachsen, Germany* 30 B5 53 6N 9 25 E
Roth, *Germany* 31 F7 49 15N 11 5 E
Rothaargebirge, *Germany* 30 D4 51 2N 8 13 E
Rothenburg, *Switz.* 33 B6 47 6N 8 16 E
Rothenburg ob der Tauber, *Germany* 31 F6 49 23N 10 11 E
Rother →, *U.K.* 21 G8 50 59N 0 45 E
Rotherham, *U.K.* 20 D6 53 26N 1 20W
Rothes, *U.K.* 22 D5 57 32N 3 13W
Rothesay, *Canada* 141 C6 45 23N 66 0W
Rothesay, *U.K.* 22 F3 55 50N 5 3W
Rothrist, *Switz.* 32 B5 47 18N 7 54 E
Roti, *Indonesia* 82 D2 10 50 S 123 0 E
Rotja, Pta., *Spain* 41 G6 38 38N 1 35 E
Rotnes, *Norway* 18 D7 60 3N 10 51 E
Roto, *Australia* 129 B6 33 0 S 145 30 E
Roto Aira L., *N.Z.* 130 F4 39 3 S 175 45 E
Rotoehu L., *N.Z.* 130 E5 38 1 S 176 32 E
Rotoiti, L., *N.Z.* 130 E5 38 2 S 176 26 E
Rotoiti L., *N.Z.* 131 B7 41 51 S 172 49 E
Rotoma L., *N.Z.* 130 E5 38 2 S 176 35 E
Rotoroa, L., *N.Z.* 131 B7 41 55 S 172 39 E
Rotorua, *N.Z.* 130 E5 38 9 S 176 16 E
Rotorua, L., *N.Z.* 130 E5 38 5 S 176 18 E
Rott →, *Germany* 31 G9 48 27N 13 25 E
Rotten →, *Switz.* 32 D5 46 18N 7 36 E
Rottenburg, *Germany* 31 G4 48 28N 8 55 E
Rottenmann, *Austria* 34 D7 47 31N 14 22 E
Rotterdam, *Neths.* 24 C4 51 55N 4 30 E
Rottne, *Sweden* 17 G8 57 1N 14 54 E
Rottnest I., *Australia* 125 F2 32 0 S 115 27 E
Rottumeroog, *Neths.* 24 A6 53 33N 6 34 E
Rottweil, *Germany* 31 G4 48 9N 8 37 E
Rotuma, *Fiji* 134 J9 12 25 S 177 5 E
Roubaix, *France* 27 B10 50 40N 3 10 E
Roudnice nad Labem, *Czech Rep.* 34 A7 50 25N 14 15 E
Rouen, *France* 26 C8 49 27N 1 4 E
Rouergue, *France* 28 D5 44 15N 2 0 E
Rough Ridge, *N.Z.* 131 F4 45 10 S 169 55 E
Rouillac, *France* 28 C3 45 47N 0 4W
Rouleau, *Canada* 143 C8 50 10N 104 56W
Round Mountain, *U.S.A.* 158 G5 38 43N 117 4W
Round Mt., *Australia* 127 E5 30 26 S 152 16 E
Round Oak, *U.S.A.* 152 B6 33 7N 83 37W
Roundup, *U.S.A.* 158 C9 46 27N 108 33W
Roura, *Fr. Guiana* 169 C7 4 44N 52 20W
Rousay, *U.K.* 22 B5 59 10N 3 2W
Rouses Point, *U.S.A.* 151 B11 44 59N 73 22W
Roussillon, *Isère, France* 29 C8 45 24N 4 49 E
Roussillon, *Pyrénées-Or., France* 28 F6 42 30N 2 35 E
Roussin, C., *N. Cal.* 133 U21 21 20 S 167 59 E
Rouxville, *S. Africa* 116 E4 30 25 S 26 50 E
Rouyn-Noranda, *Canada* 140 C4 48 20N 79 0W
Rovaniemi, *Finland* 14 C21 66 29N 25 41 E
Rovato, *Italy* 44 C7 45 34N 10 0 E
Rovenki, *Ukraine* 59 H10 48 5N 39 21 E
Rovereto, *Italy* 44 C8 45 53N 11 3 E
Roverud, *Norway* 18 D9 60 15N 12 3 E
Rovigo, *Italy* 45 C8 45 4N 11 47 E
Rovinj, *Croatia* 45 C10 45 5N 13 40 E
Rovira, *Colombia* 168 C2 4 15N 75 20W
Rovno = Rivne, *Ukraine* 59 G4 50 40N 26 10 E
Rovnoye, *Russia* 60 E8 50 52N 46 3 E
Rovuma = Ruvuma →, *Tanzania* 119 E5 10 29 S 40 28 E
Row'ān, *Iran* 97 C6 35 8N 48 51 E
Rowena, *Australia* 127 D4 29 48 S 148 55 E
Rowes, *Australia* 129 D8 37 0 S 149 6 E
Rowesville, *U.S.A.* 152 B9 33 22N 80 50W
Rowley Shoals, *Australia* 124 C2 17 30 S 119 0 E
Roxa, *Guinea-Biss.* 112 C1 11 15N 15 45W
Roxas = Barbacan, *Phil.* 81 F2 10 20N 119 21 E
Roxas, *Capiz, Phil.* 81 F4 11 36N 122 49 E
Roxas, *Isabela, Phil.* 80 C3 17 8N 121 36 E
Roxas, *Mindoro, Phil.* 80 E3 12 35N 121 31 E
Roxboro, *U.S.A.* 149 G6 36 24N 78 59W
Roxborough Downs, *Australia* 126 C2 22 30 S 138 45 E
Roxburgh, *N.Z.* 131 F4 45 33 S 169 19 E
Roxen, *Sweden* 17 F9 58 30N 15 40 E
Roy, *Fla., U.S.A.* 153 F8 29 37N 81 29W
Roy, *Mont., U.S.A.* 158 C9 47 20N 108 58W
Roy, *N. Mex., U.S.A.* 155 H2 35 57N 104 12W
Roy Hill, *Australia* 124 D2 22 37 S 119 58 E
Royal Canal, *Ireland* 23 C4 53 30N 7 13W
Royal Center, *U.S.A.* 157 D10 40 52N 86 30W
Royal Leamington Spa, *U.K.* 21 E6 52 18N 1 31W
Royal Tunbridge Wells, *U.K.* 21 F8 51 7N 0 16 E
Royalla, *Australia* 129 C8 35 30 S 149 9 E
Royan, *France* 28 C2 45 37N 1 2W
Roye, *France* 27 C9 49 42N 2 48 E
Royston, *U.K.* 21 E7 52 3N 0 0 E
Rožaj, *Montenegro, Yug.* 50 D4 42 50N 20 11 E
Różan, *Poland* 55 F8 52 52N 21 25 E
Rozay-en-Brie, *France* 27 D9 48 41N 2 58 E
Rozdilna, *Ukraine* 59 J6 46 50N 30 2 E
Rozhyshche, *Ukraine* 59 G3 50 54N 25 15 E
Rožmitál pod Třemšínem, *Czech Rep.* 34 B6 49 36N 13 53 E
Rožňava, *Slovak Rep.* 35 C13 48 37N 20 35 E
Rozogi, *Poland* 54 E8 53 28N 21 19 E
Rozoy-sur-Serre, *France* 27 C11 49 40N 4 8 E
Rozzano, *Italy* 44 C6 45 22N 9 10 E
Rrësheni, *Albania* 50 E3 41 47N 19 49 E
Rrogozhino, *Albania* 50 E3 41 4N 19 50 E
Rtanj, *Serbia, Yug.* 50 C5 43 45N 21 50 E
Rtishchevo, *Russia* 60 D6 52 18N 43 46 E
Rúa = A Rúa, *Spain* 42 C3 42 24N 7 6W
Ruacaná, *Angola* 115 F2 17 20 S 14 12 E
Ruahine Ra., *N.Z.* 130 F5 39 55 S 176 2 E
Ruamahanga →, *N.Z.* 130 H4 41 24 S 175 8 E
Ruapehu, *N.Z.* 130 F4 39 17 S 175 35 E
Ruapuke I., *N.Z.* 131 G3 46 46 S 168 31 E
Ruâq, W. →, *Egypt* 103 F2 30 0N 33 49 E
Ruatoria, *N.Z.* 130 D7 37 55 S 178 20 E
Ruawai, *N.Z.* 130 C2 36 8 S 173 59 E
Rub' al Khālī, *Si. Arabia* 99 C5 18 0N 48 0 E
Rubeho Mts., *Tanzania* 118 D4 6 50 S 36 25 E
Rubezhnoye = Rubizhne, *Ukraine* 59 H10 49 6N 38 25 E
Rubh a' Mhail, *U.K.* 22 F2 55 56N 6 8W
Rubha Hunish, *U.K.* 22 D2 57 42N 6 20W
Rubha Robhanais = Lewis, Butt of, *U.K.* 22 C2 58 31N 6 16W
Rubi, *Spain* 40 D7 41 29N 2 2 E
Rubiataba, *Brazil* 171 E2 15 8 S 49 48W
Rubicon →, *U.S.A.* 160 G5 38 53N 121 4W
Rubicone →, *Italy* 45 D9 44 8N 12 28 E
Rubik, *Albania* 50 E3 41 46N 19 47 E
Rubinéia, *Brazil* 171 F1 20 13 S 51 2W
Rubino, *Ivory C.* 112 D4 6 4N 4 18W
Rubio, *Venezuela* 168 B3 7 43N 72 22W
Rubizhne, *Ukraine* 59 H10 49 6N 38 25 E
Rubtsovsk, *Russia* 64 D9 51 30N 81 10 E
Ruby L., *U.S.A.* 158 F6 40 10N 115 28W
Ruby Mts., *U.S.A.* 158 F6 40 30N 115 20W
Rucheng, *China* 77 E9 25 33N 113 38 E
Ruciane-Nida, *Poland* 54 E8 53 40N 21 32 E
Rūd Sar, *Iran* 97 B6 37 8N 50 18 E
Ruda, *Sweden* 17 G10 57 6N 16 7 E
Ruda Śląska, *Poland* 55 H5 50 16N 18 50 E
Rudall, *Australia* 128 B2 33 43 S 136 17 E
Rudall →, *Australia* 124 D3 22 34 S 122 13 E
Rūdbār, *Afghan.* 91 C1 30 9N 62 36 E
Rüdersdorf, *Germany* 30 C9 52 27N 13 47 E
Rudewa, *Tanzania* 119 E3 10 7 S 34 40 E
Rudkøbing, *Denmark* 17 K4 54 56N 10 41 E
Rudna, *Poland* 55 G3 51 30N 16 17 E
Rudnichnyy, *Russia* 56 C9 59 38N 52 26 E
Rudnik, *Bulgaria* 51 D11 42 36N 27 30 E
Rudnik, *Poland* 55 H9 50 26N 22 15 E
Rudnik, *Serbia, Yug.* 50 B4 44 7N 20 35 E
Rudnya, *Russia* 58 E6 54 55N 31 7 E
Rudnyy, *Kazakstan* 62 E9 52 57N 63 7 E
Rudo, *Bos.-H.* 50 C3 43 41N 19 23 E
Rudolfa, Ostrov, *Russia* 64 A6 81 45N 58 30 E
Rudolstadt, *Germany* 30 E7 50 44N 11 19 E
Rudong, *China* 77 A13 32 20N 121 12 E
Rudozem, *Bulgaria* 51 E8 41 29N 24 51 E
Rudyard, *U.S.A.* 148 B3 46 14N 84 36W
Rue, *France* 27 B8 50 15N 1 40 E
Rufa'a, *Sudan* 107 E3 14 44N 33 22 E
Rufflin, *U.S.A.* 152 B9 33 0N 80 49W
Rufiji □, *Tanzania* 118 D4 8 0 S 38 30 E
Rufiji →, *Tanzania* 118 D4 7 50 S 39 15 E
Rufino, *Argentina* 174 C3 34 20 S 62 50W
Rufisque, *Senegal* 112 C1 14 40N 17 15W
Rufunsa, *Zambia* 119 F2 15 4 S 29 34 E
Rugao, *China* 77 A13 32 23N 120 31 E
Rugby, *U.K.* 21 E6 52 23N 1 16W
Rugby, *U.S.A.* 154 A5 48 22N 100 0W
Rügen, *Germany* 30 A9 54 22N 13 24 E
Rugles, *France* 26 D7 48 50N 0 40 E
Ruhea, *Bangla.* 90 B2 26 10N 88 25 E
Ruhengeri, *Rwanda* 118 C2 1 30 S 29 36 E
Ruhla, *Germany* 30 E6 50 54N 10 23 E
Ruhland, *Germany* 30 D9 51 27N 13 51 E
Ruhnu, *Estonia* 15 H20 57 48N 23 15 E
Ruhr →, *Germany* 30 D2 51 27N 6 43 E
Ruhuhu →, *Tanzania* 119 E3 10 31 S 34 34 E
Rui Barbosa, *Brazil* 171 D3 12 18 S 40 27W
Rui'an, *China* 77 D13 27 47N 120 40 E
Ruichang, *China* 77 C10 29 40N 115 39 E
Ruidosa, *U.S.A.* 155 L2 29 59N 104 41W
Ruidoso, *U.S.A.* 159 K11 33 20N 105 41W
Ruili, *China* 76 E1 24 1N 97 43 E
Ruivo, Pico, *Madeira* 39 D3 32 45N 16 56W
Ruj, *Bulgaria* 50 D6 42 52N 22 34 E
Rujen, *Macedonia* 50 D6 42 9N 22 30 E
Rujm Tal'at al Jamā'ah, *Jordan* 103 E4 30 24N 35 30 E
Ruk, *Pakistan* 92 F3 27 50N 68 42 E
Rukwa □, *Tanzania* 118 D3 7 0 S 31 30 E
Rukwa, L., *Tanzania* 118 D3 8 0 S 32 20 E
Rulhieres, C., *Australia* 124 B4 13 56 S 127 22 E
Rum = Rhum, *U.K.* 22 E2 57 0N 6 20W
Rum Cay, *Bahamas* 165 B5 23 40N 74 58W
Rum Jungle, *Australia* 124 B5 13 0 S 130 59 E
Ruma, *Serbia, Yug.* 52 E4 45 0N 19 50 E
Rumāḥ, *Si. Arabia* 96 E5 25 29N 47 10 E
Rumādah, *Yemen* 98 D3 13 34N 43 52 E
Rumania = Romania ■, *Europe* 53 D10 46 0N 25 0 E
Rumaylah, *Iraq* 96 D5 30 47N 47 37 E
Rumaylah, 'Urūq ar, *Si. Arabia* 98 B4 21 0N 47 30 E
Rumbalara, *Australia* 126 D1 25 20 S 134 29 E
Rumbêk, *Sudan* 107 F2 6 54N 29 37 E
Rumburk, *Czech Rep.* 34 A7 50 57N 14 32 E
Rumford, *U.S.A.* 151 B14 44 33N 70 33W
Rumia, *Poland* 54 D5 54 37N 18 25 E
Rumilly, *France* 29 C9 45 53N 5 56 E
Rumoi, *Japan* 68 C10 43 56N 141 39 E
Rumonge, *Burundi* 118 C2 3 59 S 29 26 E
Rumsey, *Canada* 142 C6 51 51N 112 48W
Rumula, *Australia* 126 B4 16 35 S 145 20 E
Rumuruti, *Kenya* 118 B4 0 17N 36 32 E
Runan, *China* 74 H8 33 0N 114 30 E
Runanga, *N.Z.* 131 C6 42 25 S 171 15 E
Runaway, C., *N.Z.* 130 D6 37 32 S 177 59 E
Runcorn, *U.K.* 20 D5 53 21N 2 44W
Rungwa, *Tanzania* 118 D3 6 55 S 33 32 E
Rungwa →, *Tanzania* 118 D3 7 36 S 31 50 E
Rungwe, *Tanzania* 119 D3 9 11 S 33 32 E
Rungwe □, *Tanzania* 119 D3 9 25 S 33 32 E
Runka, *Nigeria* 113 C6 12 28N 7 20 E
Runn, *Sweden* 16 D9 60 30N 15 40 E
Runton Ra., *Australia* 124 D3 23 31 S 123 6 E
Ruokolahti, *Finland* 58 B5 61 17N 28 50 E
Ruoqiang, *China* 72 C3 38 55N 88 10 E
Rupa, *India* 90 B4 27 15N 92 21 E
Rupar, *India* 92 D7 31 2N 76 38 E
Rupat, *Indonesia* 84 B2 1 45N 101 40 E
Rupea, *Romania* 53 D10 46 2N 25 13 E
Rupert →, *Canada* 140 B4 51 29N 78 45W
Rupert House = Waskaganish, *Canada* 140 B4 51 30N 78 40W
Rupsa, *Bangla.* 90 E2 21 44N 89 30 E
Rupununi →, *Guyana* 169 C6 4 3N 58 35W
Rur →, *Germany* 30 D1 51 11N 5 59 E
Rurrenabaque, *Bolivia* 172 C4 14 30 S 67 32W
Rus →, *Spain* 41 F2 39 30N 2 30W
Rusambo, *Zimbabwe* 119 F3 16 30 S 32 4 E
Rusape, *Zimbabwe* 119 F3 18 35 S 32 8 E
Ruschuk = Ruse, *Bulgaria* 51 C9 43 48N 25 59 E
Ruse, *Bulgaria* 51 C9 43 48N 25 59 E
Ruse □, *Bulgaria* 51 C10 43 35N 26 20 E
Rușețu, *Romania* 53 F12 44 57N 27 14 E
Rush, *Ireland* 23 C5 53 31N 6 6W
Rushan, *China* 75 F11 36 56N 121 30 E
Rushden, *U.K.* 21 E7 52 18N 0 35W
Rushford, *U.S.A.* 154 D9 43 49N 91 46W
Rushville, *Ill., U.S.A.* 156 D6 40 7N 90 34W
Rushville, *Ind., U.S.A.* 157 E11 39 37N 85 27W
Rushville, *Nebr., U.S.A.* 154 D3 42 43N 102 28W
Rushworth, *Australia* 129 D6 36 32 S 145 1 E
Ruskin, *U.S.A.* 153 H7 27 43N 82 26W
Russas, *Brazil* 170 B4 4 55 S 37 50W
Russell, *Canada* 143 C8 50 50N 101 20W
Russell, *N.Z.* 130 B3 35 16 S 174 10 E
Russell, *Fla., U.S.A.* 152 E8 30 3N 81 45W
Russell, *Kans., U.S.A.* 154 F5 38 54N 98 52W
Russell Is., *Solomon Is.* 133 M10 9 4 S 159 12 E
Russell L., *Man., Canada* 143 B8 56 15N 101 30W
Russell L., *N.W.T., Canada* 142 A5 63 5N 115 44W
Russellkonda, *India* 94 E7 19 57N 84 42 E
Russellville, *Ala., U.S.A.* 149 H2 34 30N 87 44W
Russellville, *Ark., U.S.A.* 155 H8 35 17N 93 8W
Russellville, *Ky., U.S.A.* 149 G2 36 51N 86 53W
Rüsselsheim, *Germany* 31 F4 49 59N 8 23 E
Russi, *Italy* 45 D9 44 22N 12 2 E
Russia ■, *Eurasia* 65 C11 62 0N 105 0 E
Russian →, *U.S.A.* 160 G3 38 27N 123 8W
Russiaville, *U.S.A.* 157 D10 40 25N 86 16W
Russkoye Ustie, *Russia* 6 B15 71 0N 149 0 E
Rust, *Austria* 35 D9 47 49N 16 42 E
Rustam, *Pakistan* 92 B5 34 25N 72 13 E
Rustam Shahr, *Pakistan* 92 F2 26 58N 66 6 E
Rustavi, *Georgia* 61 K7 41 30N 45 0 E
Rustenburg, *S. Africa* 116 D4 25 41 S 27 14 E
Ruston, *U.S.A.* 155 J8 32 32N 92 38W
Ruswil, *Switz.* 32 B6 47 5N 8 8 E
Rutana, *Burundi* 118 C3 3 55 S 30 0 E
Rute, *Spain* 43 H6 37 19N 4 23W
Ruteng, *Indonesia* 82 C2 8 35 S 120 30 E
Ruth, *Mich., U.S.A.* 150 C2 43 42N 82 45W
Ruth, *Nev., U.S.A.* 158 G6 39 17N 114 59W
Rutherford, *U.S.A.* 160 G4 38 26N 122 24W
Rutherglen, *Australia* 129 D7 36 5 S 146 29 E
Rüti, *Switz.* 33 B7 47 16N 8 51 E
Rutland □, *U.K.* 21 E7 52 38N 0 40W
Rutland Plains, *Australia* 126 B3 15 38 S 141 43 E
Rutland Water, *U.K.* 21 E7 52 39N 0 38W
Rutledal, *Norway* 18 C2 61 4N 5 10 E
Rutledge, *U.S.A.* 152 B6 33 38N 83 37W
Rutledge →, *Canada* 143 A6 61 4N 112 0W
Rutledge L., *Canada* 143 A6 61 33N 110 47W
Rutqa, W. →, *Syria* 101 E9 34 30N 41 3 E
Rutshuru, *Dem. Rep. of the Congo* 118 C2 1 13 S 29 25 E
Ruvo di Púglia, *Italy* 47 A9 41 7N 16 29 E
Ruvu, *Tanzania* 118 D4 6 49 S 38 43 E
Ruvu →, *Tanzania* 118 D4 6 23 S 38 52 E
Ruvuma □, *Tanzania* 119 E4 10 20 S 36 0 E
Ruvuma →, *Tanzania* 119 E5 10 29 S 40 28 E
Ruwais, *U.A.E.* 97 E7 24 5N 52 50 E
Ruwenzori, *Africa* 118 B2 0 30N 29 55 E
Ruyigi, *Burundi* 118 C3 3 29 S 30 15 E
Ruyuan, *China* 77 E9 24 46N 113 16 E
Ruzayevka, *Russia* 60 C7 54 4N 45 0 E
Růzhevo Konare, *Bulgaria* 51 D8 42 23N 24 46 E
Ružomberok, *Slovak Rep.* 35 B12 49 3N 19 17 E
Rwanda ■, *Africa* 118 C3 2 0 S 30 0 E
Ryakhovo, *Bulgaria* 51 C10 43 58N 26 18 E
Ryan, L., *U.K.* 22 G3 55 0N 5 2W
Ryazan, *Russia* 58 E10 54 40N 39 40 E
Ryazhsk, *Russia* 58 F11 53 45N 40 3 E
Rybache = Rybachye, *Kazakstan* 64 E9 46 40N 81 20 E
Rybachiy Poluostrov, *Russia* 56 A5 69 43N 32 0 E
Rybachye = Ysyk-Köl, *Kyrgyzstan* 63 B8 42 26N 76 12 E
Rybachye, *Kazakstan* 64 E9 46 40N 81 20 E
Rybinsk, *Russia* 58 C10 58 5N 38 50 E
Rybinskoye Vdkhr., *Russia* 58 C10 58 30N 38 25 E
Rybnik, *Poland* 55 H5 50 6N 18 32 E
Rybnitsa = Râbnița, *Moldova* 53 C14 47 45N 29 0 E
Rybnoye, *Russia* 58 E10 54 45N 39 30 E
Rychnov nad Kněžnou, *Czech Rep.* 35 A9 50 10N 16 17 E
Rychwał, *Poland* 55 F5 52 4N 18 10 E
Ryd, *Sweden* 17 H8 56 27N 14 42 E
Rydaholm, *Sweden* 17 H8 56 59N 14 18 E
Ryde, *U.K.* 21 G6 50 43N 1 9W
Ryderwood, *U.S.A.* 160 D3 46 23N 123 3W
Rydzyna, *Poland* 55 G3 51 47N 16 39 E
Rye, *U.K.* 21 G8 50 57N 0 45 E
Rye →, *U.K.* 20 C7 54 11N 0 44W
Rye Bay, *U.K.* 21 G8 50 52N 0 49 E
Rye Patch Reservoir, *U.S.A.* 158 F4 40 28N 118 19W
Ryegate, *U.S.A.* 158 C9 46 18N 109 15W
Ryfylke, *Norway* 18 E3 59 25N 6 25 E
Rykene, *Norway* 18 F5 58 24N 8 37 E
Ryki, *Poland* 55 G8 51 38N 21 56 E
Rylsk, *Russia* 59 G8 51 36N 34 43 E
Rylstone, *Australia* 129 B8 32 46 S 149 58 E
Rymanów, *Poland* 55 J8 49 35N 21 51 E
Ryn, *Poland* 54 E8 53 57N 21 34 E
Ryn Peski, *Kazakstan* 61 G9 47 30N 49 0 E
Ryōhaku-Sanchi, *Japan* 71 A8 36 9N 136 49 E
Ryōthu, *Japan* 68 E9 38 5N 138 26 E
Rypin, *Poland* 55 E6 53 3N 19 25 E
Ryssby, *Sweden* 17 H8 56 52N 14 10 E
Ryūgasaki, *Japan* 71 B12 35 54N 140 11 E
Ryūkyū Is. = Ryūkyū-rettō, *Japan* 69 M3 26 0N 126 0 E
Ryūkyū-rettō, *Japan* 69 M3 26 0N 126 0 E
Rzepin, *Poland* 55 F1 52 20N 14 49 E
Rzeszów, *Poland* 55 H8 50 5N 21 58 E
Rzeszów □, *Poland* 55 J8 50 0N 22 0 E
Rzhev, *Russia* 58 D8 56 20N 34 20 E

S

Sa, *Thailand* **86 C3** 18 34N 100 45 E
Sa Conillera, *Spain* **39 C7** 38 59N 1 13 E
Sa Dec, *Vietnam* **87 G5** 10 20N 105 46 E
Sa Dragonera, , *Spain* **39 B9** 39 35N 2 19 E
Sa-koi, *Burma* **90 F6** 19 54N 97 3 E
Sa Pobla, *Spain* **40 F8** 39 46N 3 1 E
Sa'ādatābād, *Fārs, Iran* **97 D7** 30 10N 53 5 E
Sa'ādatābād, *Kermān, Iran* **97 D7** 28 3N 55 53 E
Saale →, *Germany* **30 D7** 51 56N 11 54 E
Saaler Bodden, *Germany* **30 A8** 54 20N 12 27 E
Saalfeld, *Germany* **30 E7** 50 38N 11 21 E
Saalfelden, *Austria* **34 D5** 47 25N 12 51 E
Saane →, *Switz.* **32 B4** 47 8N 7 10 E
Saar →, *Europe* **24 E6** 49 41N 6 32 E
Saarbrücken, *Germany* **31 F2** 49 14N 6 59 E
Saarburg, *Germany* **31 F2** 49 36N 6 32 E
Saaremaa, *Estonia* **15 G20** 58 30N 22 30 E
Saarijärvi, *Finland* **15 E21** 62 43N 25 16 E
Saariselkä, *Finland* **14 B23** 68 16N 28 15 E
Saarland □, *Germany* **31 F2** 49 20N 7 0 E
Saarlouis, *Germany* **31 F2** 49 18N 6 45 E
Saas Fee, *Switz.* **32 D5** 46 7N 7 56 E
Sab 'Ābar, *Syria* **100 F7** 33 46N 37 41 E
Saba, *W. Indies* **165 C7** 17 42N 63 26W
Šabac, *Serbia, Yug.* **50 B3** 44 48N 19 42 E
Sabadell, *Spain* **40 D7** 41 28N 2 7 E
Sabae, *Japan* **71 B8** 35 57N 136 11 E
Sabah □, *Malaysia* **85 A5** 6 0N 117 0 E
Sabak Bernam, *Malaysia* **87 L3** 3 46N 100 58 E
Sabalān, Kūhhā-ye, *Iran* **101 C12** 38 15N 47 45 E
Sabalana, Kepulauan,
Indonesia **82 C1** 6 45 S 118 50 E
Sábana de la Mar,
Dom. Rep. **165 C6** 19 7N 69 24W
Sábanalarga, *Colombia* **168 A3** 10 38N 74 55W
Sabang, *Indonesia* **84 A1** 5 50N 95 15 E
Sabangan, *Phil.* **80 C3** 17 0N 120 55 E
Săbăoani, *Romania* **53 C11** 47 1N 26 51 E
Sabará, *Brazil* **171 E3** 19 55 S 43 46W
Sabari →, *India* **94 F5** 17 35N 81 16 E
Sab'atayn, Ramlat as, *Yemen* **98 D4** 15 30N 46 10 E
Sabattis, *U.S.A.* **151 B10** 44 6N 74 40W
Sabáudia, *Italy* **46 A6** 41 18N 13 1 E
Sabaya, *Bolivia* **172 D4** 19 1 S 68 23W
Sabāyā, Jaz., *Si. Arabia* **98 C3** 18 35N 41 3 E
Saberania, *Indonesia* **83 B5** 2 5 S 138 18 E
Sabhah, *Libya* **108 C2** 27 9N 14 29 E
Sabhah □, *Libya* **108 C2** 26 0N 14 0 E
Sabie, *S. Africa* **117 D5** 25 10 S 30 48 E
Sabina, *U.S.A.* **157 E13** 39 29N 83 38W
Sabinal, *Mexico* **162 A3** 30 58N 107 25W
Sabinal, *U.S.A.* **155 L5** 29 19N 99 28W
Sabiñánigo, *Spain* **40 C4** 42 31N 0 22W
Sabinar, Punta del, *Spain* **41 J2** 36 43N 2 44W
Sabinas, *Mexico* **162 B4** 27 50N 101 10W
Sabinas →, *Mexico* **162 B4** 27 37N 100 42W
Sabinas Hidalgo, *Mexico* **162 B4** 26 33N 100 10W
Sabine →, *U.S.A.* **155 L8** 29 59N 93 47W
Sabine L., *U.S.A.* **155 L8** 29 53N 93 51W
Sabine Pass, *U.S.A.* **155 L8** 29 44N 93 54W
Sabinópolis, *Brazil* **171 E3** 18 40 S 43 6W
Sabinov, *Slovak Rep.* **35 B14** 49 6N 21 5 E
Sabirabad, *Azerbaijan* **61 K9** 40 5N 48 30 E
Sabkhat Tāwurghā', *Libya* **108 B3** 31 51N 15 15 E
Sabkhet el Bardawîl, *Egypt* **103 D2** 31 10N 33 15 E
Sablayan, *Phil.* **80 E3** 12 50N 120 50 E
Sable, C., *Canada* **141 D6** 43 29N 65 38W
Sable, C., *U.S.A.* **164 A3** 25 9N 81 8W
Sable I., *Canada* **141 D8** 44 0N 60 0W
Sablé-sur-Sarthe, *France* **26 E6** 47 50N 0 20W
Saboeiro, *Brazil* **170 C4** 6 32 S 39 54W
Sabor →, *Portugal* **42 D3** 41 10N 7 7W
Sabou, *Burkina Faso* **112 C4** 12 1N 2 15W
Sabrātah, *Libya* **108 B2** 32 47N 12 29 E
Sabres, *France* **28 D3** 44 9N 0 43W
Sabria, *Tunisia* **108 B1** 33 22N 8 45 E
Sabrina Coast, *Antarctica* **7 C9** 68 0 S 120 0 E
Sabtang I., *Phil.* **80 A3** 20 19N 121 52 E
Sabugal, *Portugal* **42 E3** 40 20N 7 5W
Sabula, *U.S.A.* **156 B6** 42 4N 90 10W
Sabulubbek, *Indonesia* **84 C1** 1 36 S 98 40 E
Sabuncu, *Turkey* **49 B12** 39 33N 30 12 E
Şabyā, *Si. Arabia* **98 C3** 17 9N 42 37 E
Sabzevār, *Iran* **97 B8** 36 15N 57 40 E
Sabzvārān, *Iran* **97 D8** 28 45N 57 50 E
Sac City, *U.S.A.* **156 B2** 42 25N 95 0W
Sacedón, *Spain* **40 E2** 40 29N 2 41W
Săcele, *Romania* **53 E10** 45 37N 25 41 E
Sachigo →, *Canada* **140 A2** 55 6N 88 58W
Sachigo, L., *Canada* **140 B1** 53 50N 92 12W
Sachkhere, *Georgia* **61 J6** 42 25N 43 28 E
Sachseln, *Switz.* **33 C6** 46 52N 8 15 E
Sachsen □, *Germany* **30 E9** 50 55N 13 10 E
Sachsen-Anhalt □, *Germany* **30 D7** 52 0N 12 0 E
Sacile, *Italy* **45 C9** 45 57N 12 30 E
Sackets Harbor, *U.S.A.* **151 C8** 43 57N 76 7W
Saco, *Maine, U.S.A.* **149 D10** 43 30N 70 27W
Saco, *Mont., U.S.A.* **158 B10** 48 28N 107 21W
Sacramento, *Brazil* **171 E2** 19 53 S 47 27W
Sacramento, *U.S.A.* **160 G5** 38 35N 121 29W
Sacramento →, *U.S.A.* **160 G5** 38 3N 121 56W
Sacramento Mts., *U.S.A.* **159 K11** 32 30N 105 30W
Sacramento Valley, *U.S.A.* **160 G5** 39 30N 122 0W
Sacratif, C., *Spain* **43 J7** 36 42N 3 28W
Săcueni, *Romania* **52 C7** 47 20N 22 5 E
Sada, *Spain* **42 B2** 43 22N 8 15W
Sada-Misaki-Hantō, *Japan* **70 D4** 33 22N 132 1 E
Sádaba, *Spain* **40 C3** 42 19N 1 12W
Sadani, *Tanzania* **118 D4** 5 58 S 38 35 E
Sadao, *Thailand* **87 J3** 6 38N 100 26 E
Sadaseopet, *India* **94 F3** 17 38N 77 59 E
Sadd el Aali, *Egypt* **106 C3** 23 54N 32 54 E
Saddle Mt., *U.S.A.* **160 E3** 45 58N 123 41W
Sade, *Nigeria* **113 C7** 11 22N 10 45 E
Şadh, *Oman* **99 C6** 17 3N 55 4 E
Sadieville, *U.S.A.* **157 F12** 38 23N 84 32W
Sadimi,
Dem. Rep. of the Congo **115 D4** 9 25 S 23 32 E
Sadiya, *India* **90 B5** 27 50N 95 40 E
Sa'dīyah, Hawr as, *Iraq* **101 F12** 32 15N 46 30 E
Sado, *Japan* **68 F9** 38 0N 138 25 E
Sado →, *Portugal* **43 G2** 38 29N 8 55W
Sadon, *Russia* **61 J6** 42 52N 43 58 E
Sæbøvik, *Norway* **18 E2** 59 47N 5 40 E
Sæby, *Denmark* **17 G4** 57 21N 10 30 E
Saegerstown, *U.S.A.* **150 E4** 41 43N 80 9W
Saelices, *Spain* **40 F2** 39 55N 2 49W
Sætre, *Norway* **18 E7** 59 41N 10 33 E
Sævareid, *Norway* **18 D2** 60 11N 5 46 E
Safaalan, *Turkey* **51 E12** 41 26N 28 6 E
Safaga, *Egypt* **106 B3** 26 42N 34 0 E
Şafājah, *Si. Arabia* **96 E3** 26 25N 39 0 E
Šafárikovo = Tornal'a,
Slovak Rep. **35 C13** 48 25N 20 20 E
Safata B., *W. Samoa* **133 X24** 14 0 S 171 50W
Safed Koh, *Afghan.* **91 B3** 34 0N 70 0 E
Säffle, *Sweden* **16 E6** 59 8N 12 55 E
Safford, *U.S.A.* **159 K9** 32 50N 109 43W
Saffron Walden, *U.K.* **21 E8** 52 1N 0 16 E
Safi, *Morocco* **110 B3** 32 18N 9 20W
Şafīābād, *Iran* **97 B8** 36 45N 57 58 E
Safīd Dasht, *Iran* **97 C6** 33 27N 48 11 E
Safīd Kūh, *Afghan.* **91 B1** 34 45N 63 0 E
Safonovo, *Russia* **58 E7** 55 4N 33 16 E
Safranbolu, *Turkey* **100 B5** 41 15N 32 41 E
Safwān, *Iraq* **96 D5** 30 7N 47 43 E
Sag Harbor, *U.S.A.* **151 F12** 41 0N 72 18W
Sag Sag, *Papua N. G.* **132 C5** 5 32 S 148 23 E
Saga, *Indonesia* **83 B4** 2 40 S 132 55 E
Saga, *Kōchi, Japan* **70 D5** 33 5N 133 6 E
Saga, *Saga, Japan* **70 D2** 33 15N 130 16 E
Saga □, *Japan* **70 D2** 33 15N 130 20 E
Sagae, *Japan* **68 E10** 38 22N 140 17 E
Sagaing □, *Burma* **90 D5** 23 55N 95 56 E
Sagala, *Mali* **112 C3** 14 9N 6 38W
Sagami-Nada, *Japan* **71 C11** 34 58N 139 30 E
Sagami-Wan, *Japan* **71 B11** 35 15N 139 25 E
Sagamihara, *Japan* **71 B11** 35 33N 139 25 E
Saganoseki, *Japan* **70 D3** 33 15N 131 53 E
Sagar, *India* **95 G2** 14 14N 75 6 E
Sagara, *Japan* **71 C10** 34 41N 138 12 E
Sagara, L., *Tanzania* **118 D3** 5 20 S 31 0 E
Sagavanirktok →, *U.S.A.* **144 A11** 70 19N 147 53W
Sagawa, *Japan* **70 D5** 33 28N 133 11 E
Sagay, *Phil.* **81 F4** 10 57N 123 25 E
Saginaw, *U.S.A.* **148 D4** 43 26N 83 56W
Saginaw B., *U.S.A.* **148 D4** 43 50N 83 40W
Sagleipie, *Liberia* **112 D3** 7 0N 8 52W
Saglouc = Salluit, *Canada* **139 B12** 62 14N 75 38W
Sagŏ-ri, *S. Korea* **75 G14** 35 25N 126 49 E
Sagone, *France* **29 F12** 42 7N 8 42 E
Sagone, G. de, *France* **29 F12** 42 4N 8 40 E
Sagres, *Portugal* **43 J2** 37 0N 8 58W
Sagu, *Burma* **90 E5** 20 13N 94 46 E
Sagua la Grande, *Cuba* **164 B3** 22 50N 80 10W
Saguache, *U.S.A.* **159 G10** 38 5N 106 8W
Saguenay →, *Canada* **141 C5** 48 22N 71 0W
Sagunt, *Spain* **40 F4** 39 42N 0 18W
Sagunto = Sagunt, *Spain* **40 F4** 39 42N 0 18W
Sagvåg, *Norway* **18 E2** 59 46N 5 25 E
Sahaba, *Sudan* **106 D3** 18 57N 30 25 E
Sahagún, *Colombia* **168 B2** 8 57N 75 27W
Sahagún, *Spain* **42 C5** 42 18N 5 2W
Saḩam al Jawlān, *Syria* **103 C4** 32 45N 35 55 E
Sahand, Kūh-e, *Iran* **101 D12** 37 44N 46 27 E
Sahara, *Africa* **104 D4** 23 0N 5 0 E
Saharan Atlas = Saharien,
Atlas, *Algeria* **111 B5** 33 30N 1 0 E
Saharanpur, *India* **92 E7** 29 58N 77 33 E
Saharien, Atlas, *Algeria* **111 B5** 33 30N 1 0 E
Sahasinaka, *Madag.* **117 C8** 21 49 S 47 49 E
Sahaswan, *India* **93 E8** 28 5N 78 45 E
Sahel, Canal du, *Mali* **112 C3** 14 20N 6 0W
Sahibganj, *India* **93 G12** 25 12N 87 40 E
Sāḩilīyah, *Iraq* **101 F10** 33 43N 42 42 E
Sahiwal, *Pakistan* **91 C4** 30 45N 73 8 E
Şahneh, *Iran* **101 E12** 34 29N 47 41 E
Sahtaneh →, *Canada* **142 B4** 59 2N 122 28W
Sahuaripa, *Mexico* **162 B3** 29 0N 109 13W
Sahuarita, *U.S.A.* **159 L8** 31 57N 110 58W
Sahuayo, *Mexico* **162 C4** 20 4N 102 43W
Šahy, *Slovak Rep.* **35 C11** 48 4N 18 55 E
Sai Buri, *Thailand* **87 J3** 6 43N 101 45 E
Sai-Cinza, *Brazil* **173 B6** 6 17 S 57 42W
Saibai I., *Australia* **132 E2** 9 25 S 142 40 E
Sa'id Bundas, *Sudan* **109 G4** 8 24N 24 48 E
Saïda, *Algeria* **111 B5** 34 50N 0 11 E
Sa'īdābād, *Kermān, Iran* **97 D7** 29 30N 55 45 E
Sa'īdābād, *Semnān, Iran* **97 B7** 36 8N 54 11 E
Saïdia, *Morocco* **111 A4** 35 5N 2 14W
Sa'īdīyeh, *Iran* **97 B6** 36 20N 48 55 E
Saidor, *Papua N. G.* **132 C4** 5 40 S 146 29 E
Saidpur, *Bangla.* **90 C2** 25 48N 89 0 E
Saidu, *Pakistan* **91 B4** 34 43N 72 24 E
Saignelégier, *Switz.* **32 B4** 47 15N 7 0 E
Saignes, *France* **28 C6** 45 20N 2 31 E
Saigō, *Japan* **70 A5** 36 12N 133 20 E
Saigon = Phanh Bho Ho Chi
Minh, *Vietnam* **87 G6** 10 58N 106 40 E
Saijō, *Ehime, Japan* **70 D5** 33 55N 133 11 E
Saijō, *Hiroshima, Japan* **70 C4** 34 25N 132 45 E
Saiki, *Japan* **70 E3** 32 58N 131 51 E
Saillans, *France* **29 D9** 44 42N 5 12 E
Sailolof, *Indonesia* **83 B4** 1 7 S 130 46 E
Saimaa, *Finland* **15 F23** 61 15N 28 15 E
Saimbeyli, *Turkey* **100 D7** 37 59N 36 6 E
Şa'in Dezh, *Iran* **101 D12** 36 40N 46 25 E
St. Abb's Head, *U.K.* **22 F6** 55 55N 2 8W
St-Affrique, *France* **28 E6** 43 57N 2 53 E
St-Agrève, *France* **29 C8** 45 0N 4 23 E
St-Aignan, *France* **26 E8** 47 16N 1 22 E
St. Alban's, *Canada* **141 C8** 47 51N 55 50W
St. Albans, *U.K.* **21 F7** 51 45N 0 19W
St. Albans, *Vt., U.S.A.* **151 B11** 44 49N 73 5W
St. Albans, *W. Va., U.S.A.* **148 F5** 38 23N 81 50W
St. Alban's Head, *U.K.* **21 G5** 50 34N 2 4W
St. Albert, *Canada* **142 C6** 53 37N 113 32W
St-Amand-en-Puisaye, *France* **27 E10** 47 32N 3 5 E
St-Amand-les-Eaux, *France* **27 B10** 50 27N 3 25 E
St-Amand-Montrond, *France* **27 F9** 46 43N 2 30 E
St-Amarin, *France* **27 E14** 47 54N 7 2 E
St-Amour, *France* **27 F12** 46 26N 5 21 E
St-André-de-Cubzac, *France* **28 D3** 44 59N 0 26W
St-André-les-Alpes, *France* **29 E10** 43 58N 6 30 E
St. Andrew Sd., *U.S.A.* **152 E8** 31 0N 81 25W
St. Andrew's, *Canada* **141 C8** 47 45N 59 15W
St. Andrews, *N.Z.* **131 E6** 44 33 S 171 10 E
St. Andrews, *U.K.* **22 E6** 56 20N 2 47W
St. Andrews, *U.S.A.* **152 C9** 32 47N 80 0W
St-Anicet, *Canada* **151 A10** 45 8N 74 22W
St. Ann B., *Canada* **141 C7** 46 22N 60 25W
St. Anne, *U.S.A.* **157 C9** 41 1N 87 43W
St. Ann's Bay, *Jamaica* **164 C4** 18 26N 77 15W
St. Anthony, *Canada* **141 B8** 51 22N 55 35W
St. Anthony, *U.S.A.* **158 E8** 43 58N 111 41W
St-Antonin-Noble-Val,
France **28 D5** 44 10N 1 45 E
St. Arnaud, *Australia* **128 D5** 36 40 S 143 16 E
St. Arnaud Ra., *N.Z.* **131 C7** 42 1 S 172 53 E
St. Arthur, *Canada* **141 C6** 47 33N 67 46W
St-Astier, *France* **28 C4** 45 8N 0 31 E
St.-Aubin, *Switz.* **32 C3** 46 54N 6 47 E
St-Aubin-du-Cormier, *France* **26 D5** 48 15N 1 26W
St-Augustin-Saguenay,
Canada **141 B8** 51 13N 58 38W
St. Augustine, *U.S.A.* **152 F8** 29 54N 81 19W
St. Augustine Beach, *U.S.A.* **152 F8** 29 51N 81 16W
St-Aulaye, *France* **28 C4** 45 12N 0 9 E
St. Austell, *U.K.* **21 G3** 50 20N 4 47W
St-Avold, *France* **27 C13** 49 6N 6 43 E
St-Barthélemy, *W. Indies* **165 C7** 17 50N 62 50W
St. Bathans, *N.Z.* **131 E4** 44 53 S 169 50 E
St. Bathan's Mt., *N.Z.* **131 E4** 44 45 S 169 45 E
St-Béat, *France* **28 F4** 42 55N 0 41 E
St. Bees Hd., *U.K.* **20 C4** 54 31N 3 38W
St-Benoît-du-Sault, *France* **28 B5** 46 26N 1 24 E
St-Bernard, Col du Grand,
Europe **32 E4** 45 53N 7 11 E
St-Blaise, *Switz.* **32 B3** 47 1N 6 59 E
St. Boniface, *Canada* **143 D9** 49 53N 97 5W
St-Bonnet, *France* **29 D10** 44 40N 6 5 E
St-Brévin-les-Pins, *France* **26 E4** 47 14N 2 10W
St-Brice-en-Coglès, *France* **26 D5** 48 25N 1 22W
St. Bride's, *Canada* **141 C9** 46 56N 54 10W
St. Brides B., *U.K.* **21 F2** 51 49N 5 9W
St-Brieuc, *France* **26 D4** 48 30N 2 46W
St-Calais, *France* **26 E7** 47 55N 0 45 E
St-Cast-le-Guildo, *France* **26 D4** 48 37N 2 18W
St. Catharines, *Canada* **140 D4** 43 10N 79 15W
St. Catherines I., *U.S.A.* **152 D8** 31 40N 81 10W
St. Catherine's Pt., *U.K.* **21 G6** 50 34N 1 18W
St-Céré, *France* **28 D5** 44 51N 1 54 E
St-Cergue, *Switz.* **32 D2** 46 27N 6 10 E
St-Cernin, *France* **28 C6** 45 5N 2 25 E
St-Chamond, *France* **29 C8** 45 28N 4 31 E
St. Charles, *Ill., U.S.A.* **157 C8** 41 54N 88 19W
St. Charles, *Mo., U.S.A.* **156 F6** 38 47N 90 29W
St-Chély-d'Apcher, *France* **28 D7** 44 48N 3 17 E
St-Chinian, *France* **28 E6** 43 25N 2 56 E
St. Christopher = St. Kitts,
W. Indies **165 C7** 17 20N 62 40W
St. Christopher-Nevis ■ =
St. Kitts & Nevis ■,
W. Indies **165 C7** 17 20N 62 40W
St-Ciers-sur-Gironde, *France* **28 C3** 45 17N 0 37W
St. Clair, *Ga., U.S.A.* **152 B7** 33 9N 82 13W
St. Clair, *Mich., U.S.A.* **150 D2** 42 50N 82 30W
St. Clair, *Mo., U.S.A.* **156 F6** 38 21N 90 59W
St. Clair, *Pa., U.S.A.* **151 F8** 40 43N 76 12W
St. Clair, L., *Canada* **140 D3** 42 30N 82 45W
St. Clair Shores, *U.S.A.* **157 B14** 42 30N 82 53W
St. Clairsville, *U.S.A.* **150 F4** 40 5N 80 54W
St-Claud, *France* **28 C4** 45 54N 0 28 E
St. Claude, *Canada* **143 D9** 49 40N 98 20W
St-Claude, *France* **27 F12** 46 22N 5 52 E
St. Cloud, *Fla., U.S.A.* **149 L5** 28 15N 81 17W
St. Cloud, *Minn., U.S.A.* **154 C7** 45 34N 94 10W
St-Coeur de Marie, *Canada* **141 C5** 48 39N 71 43W
St. Cricq, C., *Australia* **125 E1** 25 17 S 113 6 E
St. Croix, *Virgin Is.* **165 C7** 17 45N 64 45W
St. Croix →, *U.S.A.* **154 C8** 44 45N 92 48W
St. Croix Falls, *U.S.A.* **154 C8** 45 24N 92 38W
St-Cyprien, *France* **28 F7** 42 37N 3 2 E
St-Cyr-sur-Mer, *France* **29 E9** 43 11N 5 43 E
St. David, *U.S.A.* **156 D6** 40 30N 90 3W
St. David's, *Canada* **141 C8** 48 12N 58 52W
St. David's, *U.K.* **21 F2** 51 53N 5 16W
St. David's Head, *U.K.* **21 F2** 51 54N 5 19W
St-Denis, *France* **27 D9** 48 56N 2 22 E
St-Denis, *Réunion* **121 G4** 20 52 S 55 27 E
St-Dié, *France* **27 D13** 48 17N 6 56 E
St-Dizier, *France* **27 D11** 48 38N 4 56 E
St-Égrève, *France* **29 C9** 45 14N 5 41 E
St. Elias, Mt., *U.S.A.* **138 B5** 60 18N 140 56W
St. Elias Mts., *Canada* **142 A1** 60 33N 139 28W
St. Elias Mts., *U.S.A.* **144 G13** 60 0N 138 0W
St.-Élie, *Fr. Guiana* **169 C7** 4 49N 53 17W
St. Elmo, *U.S.A.* **157 E8** 39 2N 88 51W
St-Eloy-les-Mines, *France* **27 F9** 46 10N 2 51 E
St-Émilion, *France* **28 D3** 44 53N 0 9W
St-Étienne, *France* **29 C8** 45 27N 4 22 E
St-Étienne-de-Tinée, *France* **29 D10** 44 16N 6 56 E
St-Étienne-du-Rouvray,
France **26 C8** 49 23N 1 6 E
St. Eugène, *Canada* **151 A10** 45 30N 74 28W
St. Eustatius, *W. Indies* **165 C7** 17 20N 63 0W
St-Fargeau, *France* **27 E10** 47 39N 3 4 E
St-Félicien, *Canada* **140 C5** 48 40N 72 25W
St-Florent, *France* **29 F13** 42 41N 9 18 E
St-Florent, G. de, *France* **29 F13** 42 47N 9 12 E
St-Florent-sur-Cher, *France* **27 F9** 46 59N 2 15 E
St-Florentin, *France* **27 E10** 48 0N 3 45 E
St-Flour, *France* **28 C7** 45 2N 3 6 E
St. Francis, *U.S.A.* **154 F4** 39 47N 101 48W
St. Francis →, *U.S.A.* **155 H9** 34 38N 90 36W
St. Francis, C., *S. Africa* **116 E3** 34 14 S 24 49 E
St. Francisville, *Ill., U.S.A.* **157 F9** 38 36N 87 39W
St. Francisville, *La., U.S.A.* **155 K9** 30 47N 91 23W
St-François, L., *Canada* **151 A10** 45 10N 74 22W
St-Fulgent, *France* **26 F5** 46 50N 1 10W
St-Gabriel-de-Brandon,
Canada **140 C5** 46 17N 73 24W
St. Gallen = Sankt Gallen,
Switz. **33 B8** 47 26N 9 22 E
St-Galmier, *France* **27 G11** 45 35N 4 19 E
St-Gaudens, *France* **28 E4** 43 6N 0 44 E
St-Gaultier, *France* **26 F8** 46 39N 1 26 E
St-Gengoux-le-National,
France **27 F11** 46 37N 4 40 E
St-Geniez-d'Olt, *France* **28 D6** 44 27N 2 58 E
St. George, *Australia* **127 D4** 28 1 S 148 30 E
St. George, *Canada* **141 C6** 45 11N 66 50W
St. George, *Ga., U.S.A.* **152 E7** 30 31N 82 2W
St. George, *S.C., U.S.A.* **152 B9** 33 11N 80 35W
St. George, *Utah, U.S.A.* **159 H7** 37 6N 113 35W
St. George, C., *Canada* **141 C8** 48 30N 59 16W
St. George, C., *Papua N. G.* **132 C7** 4 49 S 152 53 E
St. George, C., *U.S.A.* **153 F4** 29 40N 85 5W
St. George I., *Alaska,*
U.S.A. **144 H5** 56 35N 169 35W
St. George I., *Fla., U.S.A.* **153 F5** 29 35N 84 55W
St. George Ra., *Australia* **124 C4** 18 40 S 125 0 E
St. George's, *Canada* **141 C8** 48 26N 58 31W
St-Georges, *Canada* **141 C5** 46 8N 70 40W
St-Georges, *Fr. Guiana* **169 C7** 4 0N 52 0W
St. George's, *Grenada* **165 D7** 12 5N 61 43W
St. George's B., *Canada* **141 C8** 48 24N 58 53W
St. Georges Basin, *Australia* **124 C4** 15 23 S 125 2 E
St. George's Channel,
Europe **23 E6** 52 0N 6 0W
St. George's Channel,
Papua N. G. **132 C7** 4 10 S 152 20 E
St. Georges Hd., *Australia* **129 C9** 35 12 S 150 42 E
St-Georges-lès-Baillargeaux,
France **28 B4** 46 41N 0 22 E
St-Germain-de-Calberte,
France **28 D7** 44 13N 3 48 E
St-Germain-en-Laye, *France* **27 D9** 48 54N 2 6 E
St-Germain-Lembron, *France* **28 C7** 45 27N 3 14 E
St-Gervais-d'Auvergne,
France **27 F9** 46 4N 2 50 E
St-Gervais-les-Bains, *France* **29 C10** 45 53N 6 42 E
St-Gildas, Pte. de, *France* **26 E4** 47 8N 2 14W
St-Gilles, *France* **29 E8** 43 40N 4 26 E
St-Gingolph, *Switz.* **32 D3** 46 24N 6 48 E
St-Girons, *Ariège, France* **28 F5** 42 59N 1 8 E
St-Girons, *Landes, France* **28 E2** 43 56N 1 18W
St. Gotthard P. = San
Gottardo, P. del, *Switz.* **33 C7** 46 33N 8 33 E
St. Helena, *U.S.A.* **158 G2** 38 30N 122 28W
St. Helena ■, *Atl. Oc.* **9 K8** 15 55 S 5 44W
St. Helena, Mt., *U.S.A.* **160 G4** 38 40N 122 36W
St. Helena B., *S. Africa* **116 E2** 32 40 S 18 10 E
St. Helena Sd., *U.S.A.* **152 C9** 32 15N 80 25W
St. Helens, *Australia* **126 G4** 41 20 S 148 15 E
St. Helens, *U.K.* **20 D5** 53 27N 2 44W
St. Helens, *U.S.A.* **160 E4** 45 52N 122 48W
St. Helens, Mt., *U.S.A.* **160 D4** 46 12N 122 12W
St. Helier, *U.K.* **21 H5** 49 10N 2 7W
St-Herblain, *France* **26 E5** 47 13N 1 40W
St-Hilaire-du-Harcouët,
France **26 D5** 48 35N 1 5W
St-Hippolyte, *France* **27 E13** 47 19N 6 50 E
St-Hippolyte-du-Fort, *France* **28 E7** 43 58N 3 52 E
St-Honoré-les-Bains, *France* **27 F10** 46 54N 3 50 E
St-Hubert, *Belgium* **25 D5** 50 2N 5 23 E
St.-Hyacinthe, *Canada* **140 C5** 45 40N 72 58W
St. Ignace, *U.S.A.* **148 C3** 45 52N 84 44W
St. Ignace I., *Canada* **140 C2** 48 45N 88 0W
St. Ignatius, *U.S.A.* **158 C6** 47 19N 114 6W
St-Imier, *Switz.* **32 B3** 47 9N 6 58 E
St. Ives, *U.K.* **21 G2** 50 12N 5 30W
St-James, *France* **26 D5** 48 31N 1 20W
St. James, *Minn., U.S.A.* **154 D7** 43 59N 94 38W
St. James, *Mo., U.S.A.* **156 G5** 38 0N 91 37W
St. James City, *U.S.A.* **153 J7** 26 29N 82 5W
St-Jean, *Canada* **140 C5** 45 20N 73 20W
St-Jean →, *Canada* **141 B7** 50 17N 64 20W
St-Jean, L., *Canada* **141 C5** 48 40N 72 0W
St. Jean Baptiste, *Canada* **143 D9** 49 15N 97 20W
St-Jean-d'Angély, *France* **28 C3** 45 57N 0 31W
St-Jean-de-Braye, *France* **27 E8** 47 53N 1 58 E
St-Jean-de-Luz, *France* **28 E2** 43 23N 1 39W
St-Jean-de-Maurienne,
France **29 C10** 45 16N 6 21 E
St-Jean-de-Monts, *France* **26 F4** 46 47N 2 4W
St-Jean-du-Gard, *France* **28 D7** 44 7N 3 52 E
St-Jean-en-Royans, *France* **29 C9** 45 1N 5 18 E
St-Jean-Pied-de-Port, *France* **28 E2** 43 10N 1 14W
St-Jean-Port-Joli, *Canada* **141 C5** 47 15N 70 13W
St-Jérôme, *Qué., Canada* **140 C5** 45 47N 74 0W
St-Jérôme, *Qué., Canada* **141 C5** 48 26N 71 53W
St. Joe, *U.S.A.* **157 C12** 41 19N 84 54W
St. John, *Canada* **141 C6** 45 20N 66 8W
St. John, *Kans., U.S.A.* **155 G5** 38 0N 98 46W
St. John, *N. Dak., U.S.A.* **154 A5** 48 57N 99 43W
St. John →, *U.S.A.* **141 C6** 45 12N 66 5W
St. John, C., *Canada* **141 C8** 50 0N 55 32W
St. John's, *Antigua* **165 C7** 17 6N 61 51W
St. John's, *Canada* **141 C9** 47 35N 52 40W
St. Johns, *Ariz., U.S.A.* **159 J9** 34 30N 109 22W
St. Johns, *Mich., U.S.A.* **157 B12** 43 0N 84 33W
St. Johns →, *U.S.A.* **152 E8** 30 24N 81 24W
St. John's Pt., *Ireland* **23 B3** 54 34N 8 27W
St. Johnsbury, *U.S.A.* **151 B12** 44 25N 72 1W
St. Johnsville, *U.S.A.* **151 D10** 43 0N 74 43W
St-Joseph, *N. Cal.* **133 K4** 20 27 S 166 36 E
St. Joseph, *Ill., U.S.A.* **157 D8** 40 7N 88 2W
St. Joseph, *La., U.S.A.* **155 K9** 31 55N 91 14W
St. Joseph, *Mich., U.S.A.* **157 B10** 42 6N 86 29W
St. Joseph, *Mo., U.S.A.* **156 E2** 39 46N 94 50W
St. Joseph →, *U.S.A.* **157 B10** 42 7N 86 29W
St. Joseph, I., *Canada* **140 C3** 46 12N 83 58W
St. Joseph, L., *Canada* **140 B1** 51 10N 90 35W
St. Joseph Pt., *U.S.A.* **152 F4** 29 52N 85 24W
St-Jovite, *Canada* **140 C5** 46 8N 74 38W
St-Juéry, *France* **28 E6** 43 57N 2 12 E
St-Julien-Chapteuil, *France* **29 C8** 45 2N 4 4 E
St-Julien-de-Vouvantes,
France **26 E5** 47 38N 1 13W
St-Julien-en-Genevois,
France **27 F13** 46 9N 6 5 E
St-Junien, *France* **28 C4** 45 53N 0 55 E
St-Just-en-Chaussée, *France* **27 C9** 49 30N 2 25 E
St-Just-en-Chevalet, *France* **28 C7** 45 55N 3 50 E
St. Kilda, *N.Z.* **131 F5** 45 53 S 170 31 E
St. Kitts, *W. Indies* **165 C7** 17 20N 62 40W
St. Kitts & Nevis ■,
W. Indies **165 C7** 17 20N 62 40W
St. Laurent, *Canada* **143 C9** 50 25N 97 58W
St-Laurent, *Fr. Guiana* **169 B7** 5 29N 54 3W
St-Laurent-de-la-Salanque,
France **28 F6** 42 46N 2 59 E
St-Laurent-du-Pont, *France* **29 C9** 45 23N 5 45 E
St-Laurent-en-Grandvaux,
France **27 F12** 46 35N 5 58 E
St-Laurent-et-Benon, *France* **28 C3** 45 8N 0 49W
St. Lawrence, *Australia* **126 C4** 22 16 S 149 31 E
St. Lawrence, *Canada* **141 C8** 46 54N 55 23W
St. Lawrence →, *Canada* **141 C6** 49 30N 66 0W
St. Lawrence, Gulf of,
Canada **141 C7** 48 25N 62 0W
St. Lawrence I., *U.S.A.* **138 B3** 63 30N 170 30W
St. Leonard, *Canada* **141 C6** 47 12N 67 58W
St-Léonard-de-Noblat,
France **28 C5** 45 49N 1 29 E
St. Lewis →, *Canada* **141 B8** 52 26N 56 11W
St-Lô, *France* **26 C5** 49 7N 1 5W
St-Louis, *France* **27 E14** 47 30N 7 34 E
St-Louis, *Senegal* **112 B1** 16 8N 16 27W
St. Louis, *Mich., U.S.A.* **148 D3** 43 25N 84 36W
St. Louis, *Mo., U.S.A.* **156 F6** 38 37N 90 12W
St. Louis →, *U.S.A.* **154 B8** 47 15N 92 45W
St-Loup-sur-Semouse, *France* **27 E13** 47 53N 6 16 E
St. Lucia ■, *W. Indies* **165 D7** 14 0N 60 50W
St. Lucia, L., *S. Africa* **117 D5** 28 5 S 32 30 E
St. Lucia Channel, *W. Indies* **165 D7** 14 15N 61 0W
St. Lucie, *U.S.A.* **153 H9** 27 29N 80 20W
St. Lucie Canal, *U.S.A.* **153 H9** 27 10N 80 18W
St. Lunaire-Griquet, *Canada* **141 B8** 51 31N 55 28W
St. Maarten, *W. Indies* **165 C7** 18 0N 63 5W

Santiago 277

San Sebastián, *Venezuela* 168 B4 9 57N 67 11W
San Sebastian de la Gomera, *Canary Is.* 39 F2 28 5N 17 7W
San Serra, *Spain* 39 B10 39 43N 3 13 E
San Serverino Marche, *Italy* 45 E10 43 13N 13 10 E
San Severo, *Italy* 45 G12 41 41N 15 23 E
San Simeon, *U.S.A.* 160 K5 35 39N 121 11W
San Simon, *U.S.A.* 159 K9 32 16N 109 14W
San Stéfano di Cadore, *Italy* 45 B9 46 34N 12 33 E
San Stino di Livenza, *Italy* 45 C9 45 44N 12 41 E
San Telmo, *Mexico* 162 A1 30 58N 116 6W
San Telmo, *Spain* 39 B9 39 35N 2 21 E
San Teodoro, *Phil.* 80 E3 13 26N 121 1 E
San Tiburcio, *Mexico* 162 C4 24 8N 101 32W
San Valentin, Mte., *Chile* 176 C2 46 30 S 73 30W
San Vicente, *Phil.* 80 B4 18 30N 122 8 E
San Vicente de Alcántara, *Spain* 43 F3 39 22N 7 8W
San Vicente de la Barquera, *Spain* 42 B6 43 23N 4 29W
San Vicente del Caguán, *Colombia* 168 C3 2 7N 74 46W
San Vincente del Raspeig, *Spain* 41 G4 38 24N 0 31W
San Vincenzo, *Italy* 44 E7 43 6N 10 32 E
San Vito, *Italy* 46 C2 39 26N 9 32 E
San Vito, C., *Italy* 46 D5 38 11N 12 41 E
San Vito al Tagliamento, *Italy* 45 C9 45 54N 12 52 E
San Vito Chietino, *Italy* 45 F11 42 18N 14 27 E
San Vito dei Normanni, *Italy* 47 B10 40 39N 17 42 E
San Yanaro, *Colombia* 168 C4 2 47N 69 42W
San Ygnacio, *U.S.A.* 155 M5 27 3N 99 26W
Saña, *Peru* 172 B2 6 54 S 79 36W
Sana', *Yemen* 98 D4 15 27N 44 12 E
Sana →, *Bos.-H.* 45 C13 45 3N 16 23 E
Sanaba, *Burkina Faso* 112 C4 12 25N 3 47W
Şanāfīr, *Si. Arabia* 106 B3 27 56N 34 42 E
Sanaga →, *Cameroon* 113 E6 3 35N 9 38 E
Sanaloa, Presa, *Mexico* 162 C3 24 50N 107 20W
Sanām, *Si. Arabia* 98 B4 23 40N 44 45 E
Sanana, *Indonesia* 82 B3 2 4 S 125 58 E
Sanand, *India* 92 H5 22 59N 72 25 E
Sanandaj, *Iran* 101 E12 35 18N 47 1 E
Sanandita, *Bolivia* 174 A3 21 40 S 63 45W
Sanary-sur-Mer, *France* 29 E9 43 7N 5 49 E
Sanāw, *Yemen* 99 C5 17 50N 51 5 E
Sanawad, *India* 92 H7 22 11N 76 5 E
Sanbe-San, *Japan* 70 B4 35 6N 132 38 E
Sancellas, *Spain* 39 B9 39 39N 2 54 E
Sancergues, *France* 27 E9 47 10N 2 54 E
Sancerre, *France* 27 E9 47 20N 2 50 E
Sancerrois, Collines du, *France* 27 E9 47 20N 2 40 E
Sancha He →, *China* 76 D6 26 48N 106 7 E
Sanchahe, *China* 75 B14 44 50N 126 2 E
Sánchez, *Dom. Rep.* 165 C6 19 15N 69 36W
Sanchor, *India* 92 G4 24 45N 71 55 E
Sanco Pt., *Phil.* 81 G6 8 15N 126 27 E
Sancoins, *France* 27 F9 46 47N 2 55 E
Sancti Spíritus, *Cuba* 164 B4 21 52N 79 33W
Sancy, Puy de, *France* 28 C6 45 32N 2 50 E
Sand, *Norway* 18 E3 59 29N 6 16 E
Sand →, *S. Africa* 117 C5 22 25 S 30 5 E
Sand Cr. →, *U.S.A.* 157 E11 39 3N 85 51W
Sand I., *U.S.A.* 145 K14 21 19N 157 53W
Sand Springs, *U.S.A.* 155 G6 36 9N 96 7W
Sanda, *Japan* 71 C7 34 53N 135 14 E
Sandakan, *Malaysia* 85 A5 5 53N 118 4 E
Sandalwood, *Australia* 128 C4 34 55 S 140 9 E
Sandan = Sambor, *Cambodia* 86 F6 12 46N 106 0 E
Sandane, *Norway* 18 C3 61 46N 6 13 E
Sandanski, *Bulgaria* 50 E7 41 35N 23 16 E
Sandaré, *Mali* 112 C2 14 40N 10 15W
Sandared, *Sweden* 17 G6 57 43N 12 47 E
Sandarne, *Sweden* 16 C11 61 16N 17 9 E
Sanday, *U.K.* 22 B6 59 16N 2 31W
Sande, *Møre og Romsdal, Norway* 18 B2 62 15N 5 27 E
Sande, *Sogn og Fjordane, Norway* 18 C2 61 20N 5 47 E
Sande, *Vestfold, Norway* 18 E7 59 36N 10 12 E
Sandefjord, *Norway* 15 G14 59 10N 10 15 E
Sandeid, *Norway* 18 E2 59 33N 5 52 E
Sanders, *Ariz., U.S.A.* 159 J9 35 13N 109 20W
Sanders, *Ky., U.S.A.* 157 F12 38 40N 84 56W
Sanderson, *Fla., U.S.A.* 152 E7 30 15N 82 16W
Sanderson, *Tex., U.S.A.* 155 K3 30 9N 102 24W
Sanderston, *Australia* 128 C3 34 46 S 139 15 E
Sandersville, *U.S.A.* 152 C7 32 59N 82 48W
Sandfloegga, *Norway* 18 E4 59 58N 7 10 E
Sandfly L., *Canada* 143 B7 55 43N 106 6W
Sandgate, *Australia* 127 D5 27 18 S 153 3 E
Sandgerði, *Iceland* 11 C4 64 3N 22 42W
Sandhammaren, C., *Sweden* 17 J8 55 23N 14 14 E
Sandía, *Peru* 172 C4 14 10 S 69 30W
Sandıklı, *Turkey* 49 C12 38 28N 30 17 E
Sandnes, *Aust-Agder, Norway* 18 F4 58 53N 7 45 E
Sandnes, *Rogaland, Norway* 15 G11 58 50N 5 45 E
Sandnessjøen, *Norway* 14 C15 66 2N 12 38 E
Sandoa, *Dem. Rep. of the Congo* 115 D4 9 41 S 23 0 E
Sandomierz, *Poland* 55 H8 50 40N 21 43 E
Sândominic, *Romania* 53 D10 46 35N 25 47 E
Sandona, *Colombia* 168 C2 1 17N 77 28W
Sandongo, *Angola* 115 F4 15 30 S 21 28 E
Sandoval, *U.S.A.* 156 F7 38 37N 89 7W
Sandover →, *Australia* 126 C2 21 43 S 136 32 E
Sandoy, *Færoe Is.* 14 F9 61 52N 6 46W
Sandpoint, *U.S.A.* 158 B5 48 17N 116 33W
Sandray, *U.K.* 22 E1 56 53N 7 31W
Sandringham, *U.K.* 20 E8 52 51N 0 31 E
Sandspit, *Canada* 142 C2 53 14N 131 49W
Sandstone, *Australia* 125 E2 27 59 S 119 16 E
Sandu, *China* 76 E6 26 0N 107 52 E
Sandusky, *Mich., U.S.A.* 140 D3 43 25N 82 50W
Sandusky, *Ohio, U.S.A.* 150 E2 41 27N 82 42W
Sandusky →, *U.S.A.* 157 C14 41 27N 83 0W
Sandvig, *Sweden* 17 J8 55 18N 14 47 E
Sandvika, *Norway* 18 E7 59 54N 10 31 E
Sandviken, *Sweden* 16 D10 60 38N 16 46 E
Sandwich, *U.S.A.* 157 C8 41 39N 88 37W
Sandwich, C., *Australia* 126 B4 18 14 S 146 18 E
Sandwich B., *Canada* 141 B8 53 40N 57 15W
Sandwich B., *Namibia* 116 C1 23 25 S 14 20 E
Sandy, *Nev., U.S.A.* 161 K11 35 49N 115 36W
Sandy, *Oreg., U.S.A.* 160 E4 45 24N 122 16W
Sandy, *Utah, U.S.A.* 158 F8 40 35N 111 50W
Sandy Bight, *Australia* 125 F3 33 50 S 123 20 E
Sandy C., *Queens., Australia* 126 C5 24 42 S 153 15 E
Sandy C., *Tas., Australia* 126 G3 41 25 S 144 45 E
Sandy Cay, *Bahamas* 165 B4 23 13N 75 18W
Sandy Cr. →, *U.S.A.* 158 F9 41 51N 109 47W
Sandy L., *Canada* 140 B1 53 2N 93 0W
Sandy Lake, *Canada* 140 B1 53 0N 93 15W
Sandy Narrows, *Canada* 143 B8 55 5N 103 4W
Sandy Springs, *U.S.A.* 152 B5 33 56N 84 23W
Sanford, *Fla., U.S.A.* 149 L5 28 48N 81 16W
Sanford, *Maine, U.S.A.* 151 C14 43 27N 70 47W
Sanford, *N.C., U.S.A.* 149 H6 35 29N 79 10W
Sanford →, *Australia* 125 E2 27 22 S 115 53 E
Sanford, Mt., *U.S.A.* 138 B5 62 13N 144 8W
Sang-i-Masha, *Afghan.* 92 C2 33 8N 67 27 E
Sanga, *Mozam.* 119 E4 12 22 S 35 21 E
Sanga →, *Congo* 114 C3 1 5 S 17 0 E
Sangamner, *India* 94 E2 19 37N 74 15 E
Sangamon →, *U.S.A.* 156 D6 40 7N 90 20W
Sangar, *Afghan.* 92 C1 32 56N 65 30 E
Sangar, *Russia* 65 C13 64 2N 127 31 E
Sangar Sarai, *Afghan.* 92 B4 34 27N 70 35 E
Sangasangadalam, *Indonesia* 85 C5 0 36 S 117 13 E
Sangatte, *France* 27 B8 50 56N 1 44 E
Sangay, *Ecuador* 168 D2 2 0 S 78 20W
Sange, *Dem. Rep. of the Congo* 118 D2 6 58 S 28 21 E
Sangeang, *Indonesia* 82 C1 8 12 S 119 6 E
Sângeorz-Băi, *Romania* 53 C9 47 22N 24 41 E
Sanger, *U.S.A.* 160 J7 36 42N 119 33W
Sângera, *Moldova* 53 D13 46 55N 28 58 E
Sangerhausen, *Germany* 30 D7 51 28N 11 18 E
Sanggan He →, *China* 74 E9 38 12N 117 15 E
Sanggau, *Indonesia* 85 B4 0 5N 110 30 E
Sangihe, Kepulauan, *Indonesia* 82 A3 3 0N 126 0 E
Sangihe, Pulau, *Indonesia* 82 A3 3 45N 125 30 E
Sangju, *S. Korea* 75 F15 36 25N 128 10 E
Sangkapura, *Indonesia* 85 D4 5 52 S 112 40 E
Sangkhla, *Thailand* 86 E2 14 57N 98 28 E
Sangli, *India* 94 F2 16 55N 74 33 E
Sangmélima, *Cameroon* 113 E7 2 57N 12 1 E
Sangpang Bum, *Burma* 90 B5 26 30N 95 50 E
Sangre de Cristo Mts., *U.S.A.* 155 G2 37 0N 105 0W
Sangro →, *Italy* 45 F11 42 14N 14 32 E
Sangudo, *Canada* 142 C6 53 50N 114 54W
Sangue →, *Brazil* 173 C6 11 1 S 58 39W
Sangüesa, *Spain* 40 C3 42 37N 1 17W
Sanguinaires, Îs., *France* 29 G12 41 51N 8 36 E
Sangzhi, *China* 77 C8 29 25N 110 12 E
Sanhala, *Ivory C.* 112 C3 10 3N 6 51W
Sanibel I., *U.S.A.* 153 J7 26 26N 82 6W
Sanje, *Uganda* 118 C3 0 49 S 31 30 E
Sanjiang, *China* 76 E7 25 48N 109 37 E
Sanjo, *Japan* 68 F9 37 37N 138 57 E
Sankarankovil, *India* 95 K3 9 10N 77 35 E
Sankeshwar, *India* 95 F2 16 23N 74 32 E
Sankosh →, *India* 90 B2 26 24N 89 47 E
Sankt Andrä, *Austria* 34 E7 46 46N 14 50 E
Sankt Antönien, *Switz.* 33 C9 46 58N 9 48 E
Sankt Augustin, *Germany* 30 E3 50 45N 7 10 E
Sankt Blasien, *Germany* 31 H4 47 47N 8 7 E
Sankt Gallen, *Switz.* 33 B8 47 26N 9 22 E
Sankt Gallen □, *Switz.* 33 B8 47 25N 9 22 E
Sankt Goar, *Germany* 31 E3 50 12N 7 43 E
Sankt Ingbert, *Germany* 31 F3 49 16N 7 6 E
Sankt Johann im Pongau, *Austria* 34 D6 47 22N 13 12 E
Sankt Johann in Tirol, *Austria* 34 D5 47 30N 12 25 E
Sankt Margrethen, *Switz.* 33 B9 47 28N 9 37 E
Sankt Moritz, *Switz.* 33 D9 46 30N 9 50 E
Sankt-Peterburg, *Russia* 58 C6 59 55N 30 20 E
Sankt Pölten, *Austria* 34 C8 48 12N 15 38 E
Sankt Ulrich = Ortisei, *Italy* 45 B8 46 34N 11 40 E
Sankt Valentin, *Austria* 34 C7 48 11N 14 33 E
Sankt Veit an der Glan, *Austria* 34 E7 46 47N 14 22 E
Sankt Wendel, *Germany* 31 F3 49 27N 7 9 E
Sankt Wolfgang, *Austria* 34 D6 47 43N 13 27 E
Sankuru →, *Dem. Rep. of the Congo* 115 C4 4 17 S 20 25 E
Sanliurfa, *Turkey* 101 D8 37 12N 38 50 E
Sanlúcar de Barrameda, *Spain* 43 J4 36 46N 6 21W
Sanluri, *Italy* 46 C1 39 34N 8 54 E
Sânmartin, *Romania* 53 D10 46 19N 25 58 E
Sanmenxia, *China* 74 G6 34 47N 111 12 E
Sanming, *China* 77 D11 26 15N 117 40 E
Sannan, *Japan* 71 B7 35 2N 135 1 E
Sannaspos, *S. Africa* 116 D4 29 6 S 26 34 E
Sannicandro Gargánico, *Italy* 45 G12 41 50N 15 34 E
Sânnicolau Mare, *Romania* 52 D5 46 5N 20 39 E
Sannieshof, *S. Africa* 116 D4 26 30 S 25 47 E
Sannīn, J., *Lebanon* 103 B4 33 57N 35 52 E
Sano, *Japan* 71 A11 36 19N 139 35 E
Sanok, *Poland* 55 J9 49 35N 22 10 E
Sanquhar, *U.K.* 22 F5 55 22N 3 54W
Sansanding Dam, *Mali* 112 C3 13 48N 6 0W
Sansepolcro, *Italy* 45 E9 43 34N 12 8 E
Sansha, *China* 77 D13 26 58N 120 12 E
Sanshui, *China* 77 F9 23 10N 112 56 E
Sanski Most, *Bos.-H.* 45 D13 44 46N 16 40 E
Sansui, *China* 76 D7 26 58N 108 39 E
Sant Antoni Abat, *Spain* 39 C7 38 59N 1 19 E
Sant Boi de Llobregat, *Spain* 40 D7 41 21N 2 2 E
Sant Carles de la Ràpita, *Spain* 40 E5 40 37N 0 35 E
Sant Celoni, *Spain* 40 D7 41 42N 2 30 E
Sant' Egídio alla Vibrata, *Italy* 45 F10 42 49N 13 42 E
Sant Feliu de Guíxols, *Spain* 40 D8 41 45N 3 1 E
Sant Feliu de Llobregat, *Spain* 40 D7 41 23N 2 2 E
Sant Francesc de Formentera, *Spain* 39 C7 38 42N 1 26 E
Sant Joan Baptista, *Spain* 39 B8 39 5N 1 31 E
Sant Jordi, G. de, *Spain* 40 E6 40 53N 1 2 E
Sant Llorenç de Morunys, *Spain* 40 C6 42 8N 1 35 E
Sant Mateu, *Spain* 40 E5 40 28N 0 10 E
Sant Miquel, *Spain* 39 B7 39 3N 1 26 E
Santa, *Peru* 172 B2 8 59 S 78 40W
Sant' Ágata Militello, *Italy* 47 D7 38 2N 14 8 E
Santa Ana, *Beni, Bolivia* 173 C4 13 50 S 65 40W
Santa Ana, *Santa Cruz, Bolivia* 173 D6 18 43 S 58 44W
Santa Ana, *Santa Cruz, Bolivia* 173 D5 16 37 S 60 43W
Santa Ana, *Ecuador* 168 D1 1 16 S 80 20W
Santa Ana, *El Salv.* 164 D2 14 0N 89 31W
Santa Ana, *Mexico* 162 A2 30 31N 111 8W
Santa Ana, *Phil.* 80 B4 18 28N 122 20 E
Santa Ana, *U.S.A.* 161 M9 33 46N 117 52W
Santa Ana →, *Venezuela* 168 B3 9 30N 71 57W
Sant' Ángelo Lodigiano, *Italy* 44 C6 45 14N 9 25 E
Sant'Antíoco, *Italy* 46 C1 39 4N 8 27 E
Santa Bárbara, *Colombia* 168 B2 5 53N 75 35W
Santa Bárbara, *Honduras* 164 D2 14 53N 88 14W
Santa Bárbara, *Mexico* 162 B3 26 48N 105 50W
Santa Barbara, *Phil.* 81 F4 10 50N 122 32 E
Santa Bárbara, *Spain* 40 E5 40 42N 0 29 E
Santa Barbara, *U.S.A.* 161 L7 34 25N 119 42W
Santa Bárbara, *Venezuela* 168 B3 7 47N 71 10W
Santa Bárbara, Mt., *Spain* 41 H2 37 23N 2 50W
Santa Barbara Channel, *U.S.A.* 161 L7 34 15N 120 0W
Santa Barbara I., *U.S.A.* 161 M7 33 29N 119 2W
Santa Catalina, *Colombia* 168 A2 10 36N 75 17W
Santa Catalina, *Mexico* 162 B2 25 40N 110 50W
Santa Catalina, Gulf of, *U.S.A.* 161 N9 33 10N 117 50W
Santa Catalina I., *U.S.A.* 161 M8 33 23N 118 25W
Santa Catarina □, *Brazil* 175 B6 27 25 S 48 30W
Santa Catarina, I. de, *Brazil* 175 B6 27 30 S 48 40W
Santa Caterina di Pittinuri, *Italy* 46 B1 40 6N 8 27 E
Santa Caterina Villarmosa, *Italy* 47 E7 37 35N 14 2 E
Santa Cecília, *Brazil* 175 B5 26 56 S 50 18W
Santa Clara, *Cuba* 164 B4 22 20N 80 0W
Santa Clara, *Calif., U.S.A.* 160 H5 37 21N 121 57W
Santa Clara, *Utah, U.S.A.* 159 H7 37 8N 113 39W
Santa Clara de Olimar, *Uruguay* 175 C5 32 50 S 54 54W
Santa Clotilde, *Peru* 168 D3 2 33 S 73 45W
Santa Coloma de Farners, *Spain* 40 D7 41 50N 2 39 E
Santa Coloma de Gramenet, *Spain* 40 D7 41 27N 2 13 E
Santa Comba, *Spain* 42 B2 43 2N 8 49W
Santa Croce Camerina, *Italy* 47 F7 36 50N 14 31 E
Santa Croce di Magliano, *Italy* 45 G11 41 42N 14 59 E
Santa Cruz, *Argentina* 176 D3 50 0 S 68 32W
Santa Cruz, *Bolivia* 173 D5 17 43 S 63 10W
Santa Cruz, *Brazil* 170 C4 6 13 S 36 1W
Santa Cruz, *Chile* 174 C1 34 38 S 71 27W
Santa Cruz, *Costa Rica* 164 D2 10 15N 85 35W
Santa Cruz, *Madeira* 39 D3 32 42N 16 46W
Santa Cruz, *Peru* 172 B2 5 40 S 75 56W
Santa Cruz, *Davao del S., Phil.* 81 H5 6 50N 125 25 E
Santa Cruz, *Laguna, Phil.* 80 D3 14 20N 121 24 E
Santa Cruz, *Marinduque, Phil.* 80 E4 13 28N 122 2 E
Santa Cruz, *U.S.A.* 160 J4 36 58N 122 1W
Santa Cruz, *Venezuela* 169 B5 8 3N 64 27W
Santa Cruz □, *Argentina* 176 C3 49 0 S 70 0W
Santa Cruz □, *Bolivia* 173 D5 17 43 S 63 10W
Santa Cruz →, *Argentina* 176 D3 50 10 S 68 20W
Santa Cruz Cabrália, *Brazil* 171 E4 16 17 S 39 2W
Santa Cruz de la Palma, *Canary Is.* 39 F2 28 41N 17 46W
Santa Cruz de Mudela, *Spain* 43 G7 38 39N 3 28W
Santa Cruz de Tenerife, *Canary Is.* 39 F3 28 28N 16 15W
Santa Cruz del Norte, *Cuba* 164 B3 23 9N 81 55W
Santa Cruz del Retamar, *Spain* 42 E6 40 8N 4 14W
Santa Cruz del Sur, *Cuba* 164 B4 20 44N 78 0W
Santa Cruz do Rio Pardo, *Brazil* 175 A6 22 54 S 49 37W
Santa Cruz do Sul, *Brazil* 175 B5 29 42 S 52 25W
Santa Cruz I., *U.S.A.* 161 M7 34 1N 119 43W
Santa Cruz Is., *Solomon Is.* 134 J8 10 30 S 166 0 E
Santa Domingo, Cay, *Bahamas* 164 B4 21 25N 75 15W
Santa Elena, *Argentina* 174 C4 30 58 S 59 47W
Santa Elena, *Ecuador* 168 D1 2 16 S 80 52W
Santa Elena, C., *Costa Rica* 164 D2 10 54N 85 56W
Sant' Eufémia, G. di, *Italy* 47 D9 38 51N 16 4 E
Santa Eugenia, Pta., *Mexico* 162 B1 27 50N 115 5W
Santa Eulàlia des Riu, *Spain* 39 C8 38 59N 1 32 E
Santa Fe, *Argentina* 174 C3 31 35 S 60 41W
Santa Fe, *Nueva Viscaya, Phil.* 80 C3 16 10N 120 57 E
Santa Fe, *Tablas, Phil.* 80 E4 12 10N 122 0 E
Santa Fe, *Spain* 43 H7 37 11N 3 43W
Santa Fe, *U.S.A.* 159 J11 35 41N 105 57W
Santa Fé □, *Argentina* 174 C3 31 50 S 60 55W
Santa Fe, L., *U.S.A.* 152 F7 29 45N 82 5W
Santa Filomena, *Brazil* 170 C2 9 6 S 45 50W
Santa Fiora, *Italy* 45 F8 42 50N 11 35 E
Santa Galdana, *Spain* 39 B10 39 56N 3 58 E
Santa Gertrudis, *Spain* 39 C7 39 0N 1 26 E
Santa Giustina, *Italy* 45 B9 46 10N 12 5 E
Santa Helena, *Brazil* 170 B2 2 14 S 45 18W
Santa Helena de Goiás, *Brazil* 171 E1 17 53 S 50 35W
Santa Inês, *Brazil* 171 D4 13 17 S 39 48W
Santa Inés, *Baleares, Spain* 39 B7 39 3N 1 21 E
Santa Inés, *Extremadura, Spain* 43 G5 38 32N 5 37W
Santa Inés, I., *Chile* 176 D2 54 0 S 73 0W
Santa Isabel = Rey Malabo, *Eq. Guin.* 113 E6 3 45N 8 50 E
Santa Isabel, *Argentina* 174 D2 36 10 S 66 54W
Santa Isabel, *Brazil* 171 D1 11 45 S 51 30W
Santa Isabel, *Solomon Is.* 133 M10 8 0 S 159 0 E
Santa Isabel, Pico, *Eq. Guin.* 113 E6 3 36N 8 49 E
Santa Isabel do Araguaia, *Brazil* 170 C2 6 7 S 48 19W
Santa Isabel do Morro, *Brazil* 171 D1 11 34 S 50 40W
Santa Lucía, *Corrientes, Argentina* 174 B4 28 58 S 59 5W
Santa Lucía, *San Juan, Argentina* 174 C2 31 30 S 68 30W
Santa Lucia, *Phil.* 80 C3 17 7N 120 27 E
Santa Lucía, *Spain* 41 H4 37 35N 0 58W
Santa Lucía, *Uruguay* 174 C4 34 27 S 56 24W
Santa Lucia Range, *U.S.A.* 160 K5 36 0N 121 20W
Santa Magdalena, I., *Mexico* 162 C2 24 40N 112 15W
Santa Margarita, *Argentina* 174 D3 38 28 S 61 35W
Santa Margarita, *Mexico* 162 C2 24 30N 111 50W
Santa Margarita, *Spain* 39 B10 39 42N 3 6 E
Santa Margarita, *U.S.A.* 160 K6 35 23N 120 37W
Santa Margarita →, *U.S.A.* 161 M9 33 13N 117 23W
Santa Margherita, *Italy* 46 D1 38 58N 8 58 E
Santa Margherita Ligure, *Italy* 44 D6 44 20N 9 11 E
Santa María, *Argentina* 174 B2 26 40 S 66 0W
Santa Maria, *Brazil* 175 B5 29 40 S 53 48W
Santa Maria, *Ilocos S., Phil.* 80 C3 17 22N 120 29 E
Santa Maria, *Isabela, Phil.* 80 C3 17 28N 121 45 E
Santa Maria, *Spain* 39 B9 39 38N 2 47 E
Santa Maria, *Switz.* 33 C10 46 36N 10 25 E
Santa Maria, *U.S.A.* 161 L6 34 57N 120 26W
Santa María →, *Mexico* 162 A3 31 0N 107 14W
Santa María, B. de, *Mexico* 162 B3 25 10N 108 40W
Santa Maria, C. de, *Portugal* 43 J3 36 58N 7 53W
Santa Maria Cápua Vétere, *Italy* 47 A7 41 5N 14 15 E
Santa Maria da Feira, *Portugal* 42 E2 40 55N 8 35W
Santa Maria da Vitória, *Brazil* 171 D3 13 24 S 44 12W
Santa María de Ipire, *Venezuela* 169 B4 8 49N 65 19W
Santa Maria di Léuca, C., *Italy* 47 C11 39 47N 18 22 E
Santa Maria do Suaçuí, *Brazil* 171 E3 18 12 S 42 25W
Santa Maria dos Marmelos, *Brazil* 173 B5 6 7 S 61 51W
Santa María la Real de Nieva, *Spain* 42 D6 41 4N 4 24W
Santa Marinella, *Italy* 45 F8 42 2N 11 52 E
Santa Marta, *Colombia* 168 A3 11 15N 74 13W
Santa Marta, Sierra Nevada de, *Colombia* 168 A3 10 55N 73 50W
Santa Marta de Tormes, *Spain* 42 E5 40 57N 5 38W
Santa Marta Grande, C., *Brazil* 175 B6 28 43 S 48 50W
Santa Marta Ortigueira, Ría de, *Spain* 42 B3 43 44N 7 45W
Santa Monica, *U.S.A.* 161 M8 34 1N 118 29W
Santa Olalla, *Huelva, Spain* 43 H4 37 54N 6 14W
Santa Olalla, *Toledo, Spain* 42 E6 40 2N 4 25W
Santa Pola, *Spain* 41 G4 38 13N 0 35W
Santa Ponsa, *Spain* 39 B9 39 30N 2 28 E
Santa Quitéria, *Brazil* 170 B3 4 20 S 40 10W
Santa Rita, *U.S.A.* 159 K10 32 48N 108 4W
Santa Rita, *Guarico, Venezuela* 168 B4 8 8N 66 16W
Santa Rita, *Zulia, Venezuela* 168 A3 10 32N 71 32W
Santa Rita do Araquaia, *Brazil* 173 D7 17 20 S 53 12W
Santa Rosa, *La Pampa, Argentina* 174 D3 36 40 S 64 17W
Santa Rosa, *San Luis, Argentina* 174 C2 32 21 S 65 10W
Santa Rosa, *Bolivia* 172 C4 10 36 S 67 20W
Santa Rosa, *Brazil* 175 B5 27 52 S 54 29W
Santa Rosa, *Colombia* 168 C4 3 32N 69 48W
Santa Rosa, *Ecuador* 168 D2 3 27 S 79 58W
Santa Rosa, *Peru* 172 C3 14 30 S 70 50W
Santa Rosa, *Phil.* 80 D3 15 25N 120 57 E
Santa Rosa, *Calif., U.S.A.* 160 G4 38 26N 122 43W
Santa Rosa, *N. Mex., U.S.A.* 155 H2 34 57N 104 41W
Santa Rosa, *Venezuela* 168 C4 1 29N 66 55W
Santa Rosa Beach, *U.S.A.* 152 E3 30 22N 86 14W
Santa Rosa de Cabal, *Colombia* 168 C2 4 52N 75 38W
Santa Rosa de Copán, *Honduras* 164 D2 14 47N 88 46W
Santa Rosa de Osos, *Colombia* 168 B2 6 39N 75 28W
Santa Rosa de Río Primero, *Argentina* 174 C3 31 8 S 63 20W
Santa Rosa de Viterbo, *Colombia* 168 B3 5 53N 72 59W
Santa Rosa del Palmar, *Bolivia* 173 D5 16 54 S 62 24W
Santa Rosa I., *Calif., U.S.A.* 161 M6 33 58N 120 6W
Santa Rosa I., *Fla., U.S.A.* 149 K2 30 20N 86 50W
Santa Rosa Range, *U.S.A.* 158 F5 41 45N 117 40W
Santa Rosalía, *Mexico* 162 B2 27 20N 112 20W
Santa Sylvina, *Argentina* 174 B3 27 50 S 61 10W
Santa Tecla = Nueva San Salvador, *El Salv.* 164 D2 13 40N 89 18W
Santa Teresa, *Argentina* 174 C3 33 25 S 60 47W
Santa Teresa, *Brazil* 171 E3 19 55 S 40 36W
Santa Teresa, *Mexico* 163 B5 25 17N 97 51W
Santa Teresa, *Venezuela* 169 C5 4 43N 61 4W
Santa Teresa di Riva, *Italy* 47 E8 37 57N 15 22 E
Santa Teresa Gallura, *Italy* 46 A2 41 14N 9 11 E
Santa Uxía, *Spain* 42 C2 42 36N 8 58W
Santa Vitória, *Brazil* 171 E1 18 50 S 50 8W
Santa Vitória do Palmar, *Brazil* 175 C5 33 32 S 53 25W
Santa Ynez →, *U.S.A.* 161 L6 35 41N 120 36W
Santa Ynez Mts., *U.S.A.* 161 L6 34 30N 120 0W
Santa Ysabel, *U.S.A.* 161 M10 33 7N 116 40W
Santadi, *Italy* 46 C1 39 5N 8 43 E
Santaella, *Spain* 43 H6 37 34N 4 51W
Santahar, *Bangla.* 90 C2 24 48N 88 59 E
Santai, *China* 76 B5 31 5N 104 58 E
Santaluz, *Brazil* 170 D4 11 15 S 39 22W
Santana, *Brazil* 171 D3 13 2 S 44 5W
Santana, *Madeira* 39 D3 32 48N 16 52W
Sântana, *Romania* 52 D6 46 20N 21 30 E
Santana, Coxilha de, *Brazil* 175 C4 30 50 S 55 35W
Santana do Ipanema, *Brazil* 170 C4 9 22 S 37 14W
Santana do Livramento, *Brazil* 175 C4 30 55 S 55 30W
Santander, *Colombia* 168 C2 3 1N 76 28W
Santander, *Phil.* 81 G4 9 25N 123 20 E
Santander, *Spain* 42 B7 43 27N 3 51W
Santander Jiménez, *Mexico* 163 C5 24 11N 98 29W
Santanyí, *Spain* 39 B10 39 20N 3 5 E
Santaquin, *U.S.A.* 158 G8 39 59N 111 47W
Santarcángelo di Romagna, *Italy* 45 D9 44 4N 12 26 E
Santarém, *Brazil* 169 D7 2 25 S 54 42W
Santarém, *Portugal* 43 F2 39 12N 8 42W
Santarém □, *Portugal* 43 F2 39 10N 8 40W
Santaren Channel, *W. Indies* 164 B4 24 0N 79 30W
Santee, *U.S.A.* 161 N10 32 50N 116 58W
Santéramo in Colle, *Italy* 47 B9 40 49N 16 45 E
Santerno →, *Italy* 45 D8 44 34N 11 58 E
Santhià, *Italy* 44 C5 45 22N 8 10 E
Santiago, *Bolivia* 173 D6 18 19 S 59 34W
Santiago, *Brazil* 175 B5 29 11 S 54 52W
Santiago, *C. Verde Is.* 8 G6 15 10N 23 30W
Santiago, *Chile* 174 C1 33 24 S 70 40W
Santiago, *Panama* 164 E3 8 0N 81 0W
Santiago, *Peru* 172 C2 14 11 S 75 43W
Santiago, *Ilocos S., Phil.* 80 C3 17 18N 120 27 E
Santiago, *Isabela, Phil.* 80 C3 16 41N 121 33 E
Santiago □, *Chile* 174 C1 33 30 S 70 50W

Sennâr 279

Saynshand, *Mongolia* **74 B6** 44 55N 110 11 E
Sayō, *Japan* **70 C6** 34 59N 134 22 E
Sayre, *Okla., U.S.A.* **155 H5** 35 18N 99 38W
Sayre, *Pa., U.S.A.* **151 E8** 41 59N 76 32W
Sayula, *Mexico* **162 D4** 19 50N 103 40W
Saywūn, *Yemen* **99 D5** 15 56N 48 47 E
Sazanit, *Albania* **50 F3** 40 30N 19 20 E
Sázava →, *Czech Rep.* **34 B7** 49 53N 14 24 E
Sazin, *Pakistan* **93 B5** 35 35N 73 30 E
Sazlika →, *Bulgaria* **51 E9** 41 59N 25 50 E
Sbeïtla, *Tunisia* **108 A1** 35 12N 9 7 E
Scaër, *France* **26 D3** 48 2N 3 42W
Scafell Pike, *U.K.* **20 C4** 54 27N 3 14W
Scalea, *Italy* **47 C8** 39 49N 15 47 E
Scalloway, *U.K.* **22 A7** 60 9N 1 17W
Scalpay, *U.K.* **22 D3** 57 18N 6 0W
Scandia, *Canada* **142 C6** 50 20N 112 0W
Scandiano, *Italy* **44 D7** 44 36N 10 43 E
Scandicci, *Italy* **45 E8** 43 45N 11 11 E
Scandinavia, *Europe* **12 C8** 64 0N 12 0 E
Scansano, *Italy* **45 F8** 42 41N 11 20 E
Scapa Flow, *U.K.* **22 C5** 58 53N 3 3W
Scappoose, *U.S.A.* **160 E4** 45 45N 122 53W
Scarámia, Capo, *Italy* **47 F7** 36 47N 14 29 E
Scarba, *U.K.* **22 E3** 56 11N 5 43W
Scarborough, *Trin. & Tob.* **165 D7** 11 11N 60 42W
Scarborough, *U.K.* **20 C7** 54 17N 0 24W
Scargill, *N.Z.* **131 C7** 42 56 S 172 58 E
Scariff I., *Ireland* **23 E1** 51 44N 10 15W
Scarp, *U.K.* **22 C1** 58 1N 7 8W
Scarsdale, *Australia* **128 D5** 37 41 S 143 39 E
Scebeli, Wabi →, *Somali Rep.* **107 G5** 2 0N 44 0 E
Šćedro, *Croatia* **45 E13** 43 6N 16 43 E
Scenic, *U.S.A.* **154 D3** 43 47N 102 33W
Schaal See, *Germany* **30 B6** 53 36N 10 55 E
Schaan, *Liech.* **33 B9** 47 10N 9 31 E
Schaffhausen, *Switz.* **33 A7** 47 42N 8 39 E
Schaffhausen □, *Switz.* **33 A7** 47 42N 8 36 E
Schagen, *Neths.* **24 B4** 52 49N 4 48 E
Schangnau, *Switz.* **32 C5** 46 50N 7 47 E
Schänis, *Switz.* **33 B8** 47 10N 9 3 E
Schärding, *Austria* **34 C6** 48 27N 13 27 E
Scharhörn, *Germany* **30 B4** 53 57N 8 24 E
Schaumburg, *U.S.A.* **157 B8** 42 2N 88 5W
Scheessel, *Germany* **30 B5** 53 10N 9 29 E
Schefferville, *Canada* **141 B6** 54 48N 66 50W
Scheibbs, *Austria* **34 C8** 48 1N 15 9 E
Schelde →, *Belgium* **24 C4** 51 15N 4 16 E
Schell City, *U.S.A.* **156 F2** 38 1N 94 7W
Schell Creek Ra., *U.S.A.* **158 G6** 39 15N 114 30W
Schenectady, *U.S.A.* **151 D11** 42 49N 73 57W
Scherfede, *Germany* **30 D5** 51 32N 9 2 E
Schesaplana, *Switz.* **33 B9** 47 5N 9 43 E
Schesslitz, *Germany* **31 F7** 49 58N 11 1 E
Schiedam, *Neths.* **24 C4** 51 55N 4 25 E
Schiermonnikoog, *Neths.* **24 A6** 53 30N 6 15 E
Schiers, *Switz.* **33 C9** 46 58N 9 41 E
Schiltigheim, *France* **27 D14** 48 35N 7 45 E
Schio, *Italy* **45 C8** 45 43N 11 21 E
Schladming, *Austria* **34 D6** 47 23N 13 41 E
Schlanders = Silandro, *Italy* **44 B7** 46 38N 10 46 E
Schlei →, *Germany* **30 A5** 54 40N 10 0 E
Schleiden, *Germany* **30 E2** 50 31N 6 28 E
Schleiz, *Germany* **30 E7** 50 35N 11 49 E
Schleswig, *Germany* **30 A5** 54 31N 9 34 E
Schleswig-Holstein □, *Germany* **30 A5** 54 30N 9 30 E
Schlieren, *Switz.* **33 B6** 47 26N 8 27 E
Schlüchtern, *Germany* **31 E5** 50 20N 9 32 E
Schmalkalden, *Germany* **30 E6** 50 44N 10 26 E
Schmölln, *Germany* **30 E8** 50 54N 12 19 E
Schneeberg, *Austria* **34 D8** 47 47N 15 48 E
Schneeberg, *Germany* **30 E8** 50 35N 12 38 E
Schneider, *U.S.A.* **157 C9** 41 13N 87 28W
Schneverdingen, *Germany* **30 B5** 53 7N 9 48 E
Schofield, *U.S.A.* **154 C10** 44 54N 89 36W
Scholls, *U.S.A.* **160 E4** 45 24N 122 56W
Schönberg, *Mecklenburg-Vorpommern, Germany* **30 B6** 53 52N 10 56 E
Schönberg, *Schleswig-Holstein, Germany* **30 A6** 54 23N 10 21 E
Schönebeck, *Germany* **30 C7** 52 2N 11 44 E
Schönenwerd, *Switz.* **32 B6** 47 23N 8 0 E
Schongau, *Germany* **31 H6** 47 47N 10 53 E
Schöningen, *Germany* **30 C6** 52 8N 10 56 E
Schoolcraft, *U.S.A.* **157 B11** 42 7N 85 38W
Schopfheim, *Germany* **31 H3** 47 38N 7 50 E
Schorndorf, *Germany* **31 G5** 48 47N 9 32 E
Schortens, *Germany* **30 B3** 53 31N 7 56 E
Schouten I., *Australia* **126 G4** 42 20 S 148 20 E
Schouten Is. = Supiori, *Indonesia* **83 B5** 1 0 S 136 0 E
Schouwen, *Neths.* **24 C3** 51 43N 3 45 E
Schramberg, *Germany* **31 G4** 48 13N 8 22 E
Schrankogel, *Austria* **34 D4** 47 3N 11 7 E
Schreckhorn, *Switz.* **32 C6** 46 36N 8 7 E
Schreiber, *Canada* **140 C2** 48 45N 87 20W
Schrems, *Austria* **34 C8** 48 47N 15 4 E
Schrobenhausen, *Germany* **31 G7** 48 34N 11 16 E
Schruns, *Austria* **34 D2** 47 5N 9 56 E
Schuler, *Canada* **143 C6** 50 20N 110 6W
Schuls, *Switz.* **33 C10** 46 48N 10 18 E
Schumacher, *Canada* **140 C3** 48 30N 81 16W
Schüpfen, *Switz.* **32 B4** 47 2N 7 24 E
Schüpfheim, *Switz.* **32 C6** 46 57N 8 2 E
Schurz, *U.S.A.* **158 G4** 38 57N 118 49W
Schuyler, *U.S.A.* **154 E6** 41 27N 97 4W
Schuylkill Haven, *U.S.A.* **151 F8** 40 37N 76 11W
Schwabach, *Germany* **31 F7** 49 19N 11 2 E
Schwaben □, *Germany* **31 G6** 48 15N 10 30 E
Schwäbisch Gmünd, *Germany* **31 G5** 48 48N 9 47 E
Schwäbisch Hall, *Germany* **31 F5** 49 6N 9 44 E
Schwäbische Alb, *Germany* **31 G5** 48 20N 9 30 E
Schwabmünchen, *Germany* **31 G6** 48 10N 10 46 E
Schwalmstadt, *Germany* **30 E5** 50 55N 9 10 E
Schwanden, *Switz.* **33 C8** 46 58N 9 5 E
Schwandorf, *Germany* **31 F8** 49 20N 12 7 E
Schwaner, Pegunungan, *Indonesia* **85 C4** 1 0 S 112 30 E
Schwanewede, *Germany* **30 B4** 53 14N 8 35 E
Schwarmstedt, *Germany* **30 C5** 52 39N 9 38 E
Schwarze Elster →, *Germany* **30 D8** 51 48N 12 50 E
Schwarzenberg, *Germany* **30 E8** 50 32N 12 47 E
Schwarzenburg, *Switz.* **32 C4** 46 49N 7 20 E
Schwarzwald, *Germany* **31 G4** 48 30N 8 20 E
Schwatka Mts., *U.S.A.* **144 C8** 67 20N 156 30W
Schwaz, *Austria* **34 D4** 47 20N 11 44 E
Schwechat, *Austria* **35 C9** 48 8N 16 28 E
Schwedt, *Germany* **30 B10** 53 3N 14 16 E
Schweinfurt, *Germany* **31 E6** 50 3N 10 14 E
Schweizer Mittelland, *Switz.* **32 C4** 47 0N 7 15 E
Schweizer-Reneke, *S. Africa* **116 D4** 27 11 S 25 18 E
Schwenningen = Villingen-Schwenningen, *Germany* **31 G4** 48 3N 8 26 E
Schwerin, *Germany* **30 B7** 53 36N 11 22 E
Schweriner See, *Germany* **30 B7** 53 43N 11 28 E
Schwetzingen, *Germany* **31 F4** 49 23N 8 35 E
Schwyz, *Switz.* **33 B7** 47 2N 8 39 E
Schwyz □, *Switz.* **33 B7** 47 2N 8 39 E
Sciacca, *Italy* **46 E6** 37 31N 13 3 E
Sciao, *Somali Rep.* **120 D3** 3 26N 45 21 E
Scicli, *Italy* **47 F7** 36 47N 14 42 E
Scilla, *Italy* **47 D8** 38 15N 15 43 E
Scilly, Isles of, *U.K.* **21 H1** 49 56N 6 22W
Ścinawa, *Poland* **55 G3** 51 25N 16 26 E
Scione, *Greece* **50 G7** 39 57N 23 36 E
Scioto →, *U.S.A.* **148 F4** 38 44N 83 1W
Scobey, *U.S.A.* **154 A2** 48 47N 105 25W
Scone, *Australia* **129 B9** 32 5 S 150 52 E
Scordia, *Italy* **47 E7** 37 18N 14 51 E
Scoresby Land, *Greenland* **10 C8** 71 50N 24 30W
Scoresby Sund, *Greenland* **10 C8** 70 28N 21 46W
Scoresbysund, *Greenland* **10 C8** 70 20N 23 0W
Scorniceşti, *Romania* **53 F9** 44 34N 24 33 E
Scotia, *Calif., U.S.A.* **158 F1** 40 29N 124 6W
Scotia, *N.Y., U.S.A.* **151 D11** 42 50N 73 58W
Scotia, *S.C., U.S.A.* **152 C8** 32 41N 81 15W
Scotia Sea, *Antarctica* **7 B18** 56 5 S 56 0W
Scotland, *U.S.A.* **154 D6** 43 9N 97 43W
Scotland □, *U.K.* **22 E5** 57 0N 4 0W
Scotland Neck, *U.S.A.* **149 G7** 36 8N 77 25W
Scott, C., *Australia* **124 B4** 13 30 S 129 49 E
Scott City, *U.S.A.* **154 F4** 38 29N 100 54W
Scott Glacier, *Antarctica* **7 C8** 66 15 S 100 5 E
Scott I., *Antarctica* **7 C11** 67 0 S 179 0 E
Scott Is., *Canada* **142 C3** 50 48N 128 40W
Scott L., *Canada* **143 B7** 59 55N 106 18W
Scott Reef, *Australia* **124 B3** 14 0 S 121 50 E
Scottburgh, *S. Africa* **117 E5** 30 15 S 30 47 E
Scottdale, *U.S.A.* **150 F5** 40 6N 79 35W
Scottish Borders □, *U.K.* **22 F6** 55 35N 2 50W
Scottsbluff, *U.S.A.* **154 E3** 41 52N 103 40W
Scottsboro, *U.S.A.* **149 H3** 34 40N 86 2W
Scottsburg, *U.S.A.* **157 F11** 38 41N 85 47W
Scottsdale, *Australia* **126 G4** 41 9 S 147 31 E
Scottsdale, *U.S.A.* **159 K7** 33 29N 111 56W
Scottsville, *Ky., U.S.A.* **149 G2** 36 45N 86 11W
Scottsville, *N.Y., U.S.A.* **150 C7** 43 2N 77 47W
Scottville, *U.S.A.* **148 D2** 43 58N 86 17W
Scranton, *Iowa, U.S.A.* **156 B2** 42 1N 94 33W
Scranton, *Pa., U.S.A.* **151 E9** 41 25N 75 40W
Screven, *U.S.A.* **152 D7** 31 29N 82 1W
Scugog, L., *Canada* **150 B6** 44 10N 78 55W
Sculeni, *Moldova* **53 C12** 47 20N 27 37 E
Scunthorpe, *U.K.* **20 D7** 53 36N 0 39W
Scuol, *Switz.* **33 C10** 46 48N 10 17 E
Scusciuban, *Somali Rep.* **120 B4** 10 18N 50 12 E
Scutari = Üsküdar, *Turkey* **57 F4** 41 0N 29 5 E
Seabra, *Brazil* **171 D3** 12 25 S 41 46W
Seabrook, L., *Australia* **125 F2** 30 55 S 119 40 E
Seaford, *U.K.* **21 G8** 50 47N 0 7 E
Seaford, *U.S.A.* **148 F8** 38 39N 75 37W
Seaforth, *Canada* **140 D3** 43 35N 81 25W
Seaforth, L., *U.K.* **22 D2** 57 52N 6 36W
Seagraves, *U.S.A.* **155 J3** 32 57N 102 34W
Seaham, *U.K.* **20 C6** 54 50N 1 20W
Seal →, *Canada* **143 B10** 59 4N 94 48W
Seal Cove, *Canada* **141 C8** 49 57N 56 22W
Seal L., *Canada* **141 B7** 54 20N 61 30W
Seale, *U.S.A.* **152 C4** 32 18N 85 10W
Sealy, *U.S.A.* **155 L6** 29 47N 96 9W
Seaman, *U.S.A.* **157 F13** 38 57N 83 34W
Searchlight, *U.S.A.* **161 K12** 35 28N 114 55W
Searcy, *U.S.A.* **155 H9** 35 15N 91 44W
Searles L., *U.S.A.* **161 K9** 35 44N 117 21W
Seascale, *U.K.* **20 C4** 54 24N 3 29W
Seaside, *Calif., U.S.A.* **160 J5** 36 37N 121 50W
Seaside, *Oreg., U.S.A.* **160 E3** 46 0N 123 56W
Seaspray, *Australia* **129 E7** 38 25 S 147 15 E
Seattle, *U.S.A.* **160 C4** 47 36N 122 20W
Seaview Ra., *Australia* **126 B4** 18 40 S 145 45 E
Seaward Kaikouras, *N.Z.* **131 C8** 42 10 S 173 44 E
Sebangka, *Indonesia* **84 B2** 0 7N 104 36 E
Sebastian, *U.S.A.* **153 H9** 27 49N 80 28W
Sebastián Vizcaíno, B., *Mexico* **162 B2** 28 0N 114 30W
Sebastopol = Sevastopol, *Ukraine* **59 K7** 44 35N 33 30 E
Sebastopol, *U.S.A.* **160 G4** 38 24N 122 49W
Sebderat, *Eritrea* **107 D4** 15 26N 36 42 E
Sebdou, *Algeria* **111 B4** 34 38N 1 19W
Seben, *Turkey* **100 B4** 40 24N 31 34 E
Sebeş, *Romania* **53 E8** 45 58N 23 34 E
Sebeşului, Munţii, *Romania* **53 E8** 45 36N 23 40 E
Sebewaing, *U.S.A.* **148 D4** 43 44N 83 27W
Sebezh, *Russia* **58 D5** 56 14N 28 22 E
Sebha = Sabhah, *Libya* **108 C2** 27 9N 14 29 E
Sébi, *Mali* **112 B4** 15 50N 4 12W
Şebinkarahisar, *Turkey* **101 B8** 40 22N 38 28 E
Sebiş, *Romania* **52 D7** 46 23N 22 13 E
Sebkhet Te-n-Dghâmcha, *Mauritania* **112 B1** 18 30N 15 55W
Sebkra Azzel Mati, *Algeria* **111 C5** 26 10N 0 43 E
Sebkra Mekerghene, *Algeria* **111 C5** 26 21N 1 30 E
Seblat, *Indonesia* **84 C2** 3 14 S 101 38 E
Sebnitz, *Germany* **30 E10** 50 58N 14 15 E
Sebou, Oued →, *Morocco* **110 B3** 34 16N 6 40W
Sebring, *Fla., U.S.A.* **149 M5** 27 30N 81 27W
Sebring, *Ohio, U.S.A.* **150 F3** 40 55N 81 2W
Sebringville, *Canada* **150 C3** 43 24N 81 4W
Sebta = Ceuta, *N. Afr.* **110 A3** 35 52N 5 18W
Sebuku, *Indonesia* **85 C5** 3 30 S 116 25 E
Sebuku, Teluk, *Malaysia* **85 B5** 4 0N 118 10 E
Sečanj, *Serbia, Yug.* **52 E5** 45 25N 20 47 E
Secchia →, *Italy* **44 C8** 45 4N 11 0 E
Sechelt, *Canada* **142 D4** 49 25N 123 42W
Sechura, *Peru* **172 B1** 5 39 S 80 50W
Sechura, Desierto de, *Peru* **172 B1** 6 0 S 80 30W
Seclin, *France* **27 B10** 50 33N 3 2 E
Secondigny, *France* **26 F6** 46 37N 0 26W
Sečovce, *Slovak Rep.* **35 C14** 48 42N 21 40 E
Secretary I., *N.Z.* **131 F1** 45 15 S 166 56 E
Secunderabad, *India* **94 F4** 17 28N 78 30 E
Sécure →, *Bolivia* **173 D5** 15 10 S 64 52W
Sedalia, *U.S.A.* **156 F3** 38 42N 93 14W
Sedan, *Australia* **128 C3** 34 34 S 139 19 E
Sedan, *France* **27 C11** 49 43N 4 57 E
Sedan, *U.S.A.* **155 G6** 37 8N 96 11W
Sedano, *Spain* **42 C7** 42 43N 3 49W
Seddon, *N.Z.* **131 B9** 41 40 S 174 7 E
Seddonville, *N.Z.* **131 B7** 41 33 S 172 1 E
Sedeh, *Fārs, Iran* **97 D7** 30 45N 52 11 E
Sedeh, *Khorāsān, Iran* **97 C8** 33 20N 59 14 E
Séderon, *France* **29 D9** 44 12N 5 32 E
Sederot, *Israel* **103 D3** 31 32N 34 37 E
Sedgewick, *Canada* **142 C6** 52 48N 111 41W
Sédhiou, *Senegal* **112 C1** 12 44N 15 30W
Sedico, *Italy* **45 B9** 46 8N 12 6 E
Sedlčany, *Czech Rep.* **34 B7** 49 40N 14 25 E
Sedley, *Canada* **143 C8** 50 10N 104 0W
Sedova, Pik, *Russia* **64 B6** 73 29N 54 58 E
Sedrata, *Algeria* **111 A6** 36 7N 7 31 E
Sedro Woolley, *U.S.A.* **160 B4** 48 30N 122 14W
Sedrun, *Switz.* **33 C7** 46 36N 8 47 E
Šeduva, *Lithuania* **54 C10** 55 45N 23 45 E
Sędziszów, *Poland* **55 H7** 50 35N 20 4 E
Sędziszów Małapolski, *Poland* **55 H8** 50 5N 21 45 E
Seebad Ahlbeck, *Germany* **30 B10** 53 56N 14 10 E
Seefeld in Tirol, *Austria* **34 D4** 47 19N 11 13 E
Seehausen, *Germany* **30 C7** 52 54N 11 45 E
Seeheim, *Namibia* **116 D2** 26 50 S 17 45 E
Seeheim-Jugenheim, *Germany* **31 F4** 49 49N 8 40 E
Seekoei →, *S. Africa* **116 E4** 30 18 S 25 1 E
Seelow, *Germany* **30 C10** 52 32N 14 23 E
Sées, *France* **26 D7** 48 38N 0 10 E
Seesen, *Germany* **30 D6** 51 54N 10 10 E
Seevetal, *Germany* **30 B6** 53 26N 10 1 E
Sefadu, *S. Leone* **112 D2** 8 35N 10 58W
Seferihisar, *Turkey* **49 C8** 38 10N 26 50 E
Séféto, *Mali* **112 C3** 14 8N 9 49W
Sefrou, *Morocco* **110 B4** 33 52N 4 52W
Sefton, *N.Z.* **131 D7** 43 15 S 172 41 E
Sefuri-San, *Japan* **70 D2** 33 28N 130 18 E
Sefwi Bekwai, *Ghana* **112 D4** 6 10N 2 25W
Seg-ozero, *Russia* **56 B5** 63 20N 33 46 E
Segag, *Ethiopia* **120 C2** 7 39N 42 50 E
Segamat, *Malaysia* **87 L4** 2 30N 102 50 E
Şegarcea, *Romania* **53 F8** 44 6N 23 43 E
Segbwema, *S. Leone* **112 D2** 8 0N 11 0W
Seget, *Indonesia* **83 B4** 1 24 S 130 58 E
Segezha, *Russia* **56 B5** 63 44N 34 19 E
Seggueur, O. →, *Algeria* **111 B5** 32 14N 1 48 E
Segonzac, *France* **28 C3** 45 36N 0 14W
Segorbe, *Spain* **40 F4** 39 50N 0 30W
Ségou, *Mali* **112 C3** 13 30N 6 16W
Segovia = Coco →, *Cent. Amer.* **164 D3** 15 0N 83 8W
Segovia, *Colombia* **168 B3** 7 7N 74 42W
Segovia, *Spain* **42 E6** 40 57N 4 10W
Segovia □, *Spain* **42 E6** 40 55N 4 10W
Segré, *France* **26 E6** 47 40N 0 52W
Segre →, *Spain* **40 D5** 41 40N 0 43 E
Séguéla, *Ivory C.* **112 D3** 7 55N 6 40W
Seguin, *U.S.A.* **155 L6** 29 34N 97 58W
Segundo →, *Argentina* **174 C3** 30 53 S 62 44W
Segura →, *Spain* **41 G4** 38 3N 0 44W
Segura, Sierra de, *Spain* **41 G2** 38 5N 2 45W
Seh Qal'eh, *Iran* **97 C8** 33 40N 58 24 E
Sehitwa, *Botswana* **116 C3** 20 30 S 22 30 E
Sehore, *India* **92 H7** 23 10N 77 5 E
Sehwan, *Pakistan* **91 D2** 26 28N 67 53 E
Şeica Mare, *Romania* **53 D9** 46 1N 24 7 E
Seikpyu, *Burma* **90 E5** 20 54N 94 48 E
Seil, *U.K.* **22 E3** 56 18N 5 38W
Seiland, *Norway* **14 A20** 70 25N 23 15 E
Seilhac, *France* **28 C5** 45 22N 1 43 E
Seiling, *U.S.A.* **155 G5** 36 9N 98 56W
Seille →, *Moselle, France* **27 C13** 49 7N 6 11 E
Seille →, *Saône-et-Loire, France* **27 F11** 46 31N 4 57 E
Sein, Î. de, *France* **26 D2** 48 2N 4 52W
Seinäjoki, *Finland* **15 E20** 62 40N 22 51 E
Seine →, *France* **26 C7** 49 26N 0 26 E
Seine, B. de la, *France* **26 C6** 49 40N 0 40W
Seine-et-Marne □, *France* **27 D10** 48 45N 3 0 E
Seine-Maritime □, *France* **26 C7** 49 40N 1 0 E
Seine-St-Denis □, *France* **27 D9** 48 58N 2 24 E
Seini, *Romania* **53 C8** 47 44N 23 21 E
Seirijai, *Lithuania* **54 D10** 54 14N 23 49 E
Seistan, *Iran* **97 D9** 30 50N 61 0 E
Seistan, Daryācheh-ye, *Iran* **97 D9** 31 0N 61 0 E
Sejerø, *Denmark* **17 J5** 55 54N 11 9 E
Sejerø Bugt, *Denmark* **17 J5** 55 53N 11 15 E
Sejny, *Poland* **54 D10** 54 6N 23 21 E
Seka, *Ethiopia* **107 F4** 8 10N 36 52 E
Sekayu, *Indonesia* **84 C2** 2 51 S 103 51 E
Seke, *Tanzania* **118 C3** 3 20 S 33 31 E
Seke-Banza, *Dem. Rep. of the Congo* **115 D2** 5 20 S 13 16 E
Sekenke, *Tanzania* **118 C3** 4 18 S 34 11 E
Seki, *Japan* **71 B8** 35 29N 136 55 E
Seki, *Turkey* **49 E11** 36 48N 29 33 E
Sekigahara, *Japan* **71 B8** 35 22N 136 28 E
Sekondi-Takoradi, *Ghana* **112 E4** 4 58N 1 45W
Seksna, *Russia* **58 C10** 59 13N 38 30 E
Sekuma, *Botswana* **116 C3** 24 36 S 23 50 E
Selah, *U.S.A.* **158 C3** 46 39N 120 32W
Selama, *Malaysia* **87 K3** 5 12N 100 42 E
Selangor □, *Malaysia* **84 B2** 3 10N 101 30 E
Selárgius, *Italy* **46 C2** 39 16N 9 10 E
Selaru, *Indonesia* **83 C4** 8 9 S 131 0 E
Selawik L., *U.S.A.* **144 C7** 66 30N 160 45W
Selb, *Germany* **31 E8** 50 10N 12 7 E
Selbusjøen, *Norway* **18 A7** 63 15N 10 50 E
Selby, *U.K.* **20 D6** 53 47N 1 5W
Selby, *U.S.A.* **154 C4** 45 31N 100 2W
Selca, *Croatia* **45 E13** 43 20N 16 50 E
Selçuk, *Turkey* **49 D9** 37 56N 27 22 E
Selden, *U.S.A.* **154 F4** 39 33N 100 34W
Sele →, *Italy* **47 B7** 40 29N 14 56 E
Selebi-Pikwe, *Botswana* **117 C4** 21 58 S 27 48 E
Selemdzha →, *Russia* **65 D13** 51 42N 128 53 E
Selendi, *Manisa, Turkey* **49 C10** 38 43N 28 50 E
Selendi, *Manisa, Turkey* **49 C9** 38 46N 27 53 E
Selenga = Selenge Mörön →, *Asia* **72 A5** 52 16N 106 16 E
Selenge, *Dem. Rep. of the Congo* **114 C3** 1 58 S 18 11 E
Selenge Mörön →, *Asia* **72 A5** 52 16N 106 16 E
Selenica, *Albania* **50 F3** 40 33N 19 39 E
Selenter See, *Germany* **30 A6** 54 18N 10 26 E
Sélestat, *France* **27 D14** 48 16N 7 26 E
Seletan, Tanjung, *Indonesia* **85 C4** 4 10 S 114 40 E
Selevac, *Serbia, Yug.* **50 B4** 44 28N 20 52 E
Selfoss, *Iceland* **11 D6** 63 56N 21 0W
Selfridge, *U.S.A.* **154 B4** 46 2N 100 56W
Sélibabi, *Mauritania* **112 B2** 15 10N 12 15W
Seliger, Ozero, *Russia* **58 D7** 57 15N 33 0 E
Seligman, *U.S.A.* **159 J7** 35 20N 112 53W
Şelim, *Turkey* **101 B10** 40 30N 42 46 E
Selîma, El Wâhât el, *Sudan* **106 C2** 21 22N 29 19 E
Selimiye, *Turkey* **49 D9** 37 24N 27 40 E
Selinda Spillway, *Botswana* **116 B3** 18 35 S 23 10 E
Selinoús, *Greece* **48 D3** 37 35N 21 37 E
Selizharovo, *Russia* **58 D7** 56 51N 33 27 E
Selje, *Norway* **18 B2** 62 3N 5 22 E
Seljord, *Norway* **18 E5** 59 30N 8 40 E
Selkirk, *Canada* **143 C9** 50 10N 96 55W
Selkirk, *U.K.* **22 F6** 55 33N 2 50W
Selkirk I., *Canada* **143 C9** 53 20N 99 6W
Selkirk Mts., *Canada* **142 C5** 51 15N 117 40W
Selliá, *Greece* **38 D6** 35 12N 24 23 E
Sellières, *France* **27 F12** 46 50N 5 32 E
Sells, *U.S.A.* **159 L8** 31 55N 111 53W
Sellye, *Hungary* **52 E2** 45 52N 17 51 E
Selma, *Ala., U.S.A.* **149 J2** 32 25N 87 1W
Selma, *Calif., U.S.A.* **160 J7** 36 34N 119 37W
Selma, *N.C., U.S.A.* **149 H6** 35 32N 78 17W
Selmer, *U.S.A.* **149 H1** 35 10N 88 36W
Selong, *Indonesia* **85 D5** 8 39 S 116 32 E
Selongey, *France* **27 E12** 47 36N 5 11 E
Selowandoma Falls, *Zimbabwe* **119 G3** 21 15 S 31 50 E
Selpele, *Indonesia* **83 B4** 0 1 S 130 5 E
Selsey Bill, *U.K.* **21 G7** 50 43N 0 47W
Seltso, *Russia* **58 F8** 53 22N 34 4 E
Seltz, *France* **27 D15** 48 54N 8 4 E
Selu, *Indonesia* **83 C4** 7 32 S 130 55 E
Sélune →, *France* **26 D5** 48 38N 1 22W
Selva = La Selva del Camp, *Spain* **40 D6** 41 13N 1 8 E
Selva, *Argentina* **174 B3** 29 50 S 62 0W
Selvas, *Brazil* **172 B4** 6 30 S 67 0W
Selwyn, *Australia* **126 C3** 21 32 S 140 30 E
Selwyn L., *Canada* **143 B8** 60 0N 104 30W
Selwyn Passage, *Vanuatu* **133 F6** 16 3 S 168 12 E
Selwyn Ra., *Australia* **126 C3** 21 10 S 140 0 E
Sem, *Norway* **18 E7** 59 14N 10 17 E
Semani →, *Albania* **50 F3** 40 47N 19 30 E
Semara, *W. Sahara* **110 C2** 26 48N 11 41W
Semarang, *Indonesia* **85 D4** 7 0 S 110 26 E
Sematan, *Malaysia* **85 B3** 1 48N 109 46 E
Semau, *Indonesia* **82 D2** 10 13 S 123 22 E
Sembabule, *Uganda* **118 C3** 0 4 S 31 25 E
Sembé, *Congo* **114 B2** 1 39N 14 36 E
Şemdinli, *Turkey* **101 D11** 37 18N 44 35 E
Sémé, *Senegal* **112 B2** 15 4N 13 41W
Semeih, *Sudan* **107 E3** 12 43N 30 53 E
Semenov, *Russia* **60 B7** 56 43N 44 30 E
Semenovka, *Chernihiv, Ukraine* **59 F7** 52 8N 32 36 E
Semenovka, *Kremenchuk, Ukraine* **59 H7** 49 37N 33 10 E
Semeru, *Indonesia* **85 D4** 8 4 S 112 55 E
Semey, *Kazakstan* **64 D9** 50 30N 80 10 E
Semichi Is., *U.S.A.* **144 K1** 52 42N 174 0 E
Semikarakorskiy, *Russia* **61 G5** 47 31N 40 48 E
Semiluki, *Russia* **59 G10** 51 41N 39 2 E
Seminoe Reservoir, *U.S.A.* **158 F10** 42 9N 106 55W
Seminole, *Fla., U.S.A.* **153 H7** 27 50N 82 47W
Seminole, *Okla., U.S.A.* **155 H6** 35 14N 96 41W
Seminole, *Tex., U.S.A.* **155 J3** 32 43N 102 39W
Seminole, L., *U.S.A.* **152 E5** 30 43N 84 52W
Semipalatinsk = Semey, *Kazakstan* **64 D9** 50 30N 80 10 E
Semirara I., *Phil.* **80 E3** 12 4N 121 23 E
Semirara Is., *Phil.* **81 F3** 12 0N 121 20 E
Semitau, *Indonesia* **85 B4** 0 29N 111 57 E
Semiyarka, *Kazakstan* **64 D8** 50 55N 78 23 E
Semiyarskoye = Semiyarka, *Kazakstan* **64 D8** 50 55N 78 23 E
Semmering P., *Austria* **34 D8** 47 41N 15 45 E
Semnān, *Iran* **97 C7** 35 40N 53 23 E
Semnān □, *Iran* **97 C7** 36 0N 54 0 E
Sempang Mengayou, Tanjong, *Malaysia* **85 A5** 7 0N 116 40 E
Semporna, *Malaysia* **85 B5** 4 30N 118 33 E
Semuda, *Indonesia* **85 C4** 2 51 S 112 58 E
Semur-en-Auxois, *France* **27 E11** 47 30N 4 20 E
Sena, *Bolivia* **172 C4** 11 32 S 67 11W
Senā, *Iran* **97 D6** 28 27N 51 36 E
Sena, *Mozam.* **119 F4** 17 25 S 35 0 E
Sena →, *Bolivia* **172 C4** 11 31 S 67 11W
Sena Madureira, *Brazil* **172 B4** 9 5 S 68 45W
Senador Pompeu, *Brazil* **170 C4** 5 40 S 39 20W
Senaja, *Malaysia* **85 A5** 6 45N 117 3 E
Senaki, *Georgia* **61 J6** 42 15N 42 7 E
Senanga, *Zambia* **116 B3** 16 2 S 23 14 E
Senatobia, *U.S.A.* **155 H10** 34 37N 89 58W
Sendafa, *Ethiopia* **107 F4** 9 11N 39 3 E
Sendai, *Kagoshima, Japan* **70 F2** 31 50N 130 20 E
Sendai, *Miyagi, Japan* **68 E10** 38 15N 140 53 E
Sendai-Wan, *Japan* **68 E10** 38 15N 141 0 E
Sendamangalam, *India* **95 J4** 11 17N 78 17 E
Senden, *Bayern, Germany* **31 G6** 48 19N 10 4 E
Senden, *Nordrhein-Westfalen, Germany* **30 D3** 51 52N 7 22 E
Sendurjana, *India* **94 D4** 21 32N 78 17 E
Senec, *Slovak Rep.* **35 C10** 48 12N 17 23 E
Seneca, *Oreg., U.S.A.* **158 D4** 44 8N 118 58W
Seneca, *S.C., U.S.A.* **149 H4** 34 41N 82 57W
Seneca Falls, *U.S.A.* **151 D8** 42 55N 76 48W
Seneca L., *U.S.A.* **150 D8** 42 40N 76 54W
Senegal ■, *W. Afr.* **112 C2** 14 30N 14 30W
Senegal →, *W. Afr.* **112 B1** 15 48N 16 32W
Senegambia, *Africa* **104 E2** 12 45N 12 0W
Senekal, *S. Africa* **117 D4** 28 20 S 27 36 E
Senftenberg, *Germany* **30 D10** 51 32N 14 0 E
Senga Hill, *Zambia* **119 D3** 9 19 S 31 11 E
Senge Khambab = Indus →, *Pakistan* **91 D2** 24 20N 67 47 E
Sengerema □, *Tanzania* **118 C3** 2 10 S 32 20 E
Sengiley, *Russia* **60 D9** 53 58N 48 46 E
Sengua →, *Zimbabwe* **119 F2** 17 7 S 28 5 E
Senguerr →, *Argentina* **176 C3** 45 35 S 68 50W
Senhor-do-Bonfim, *Brazil* **170 D3** 10 30 S 40 10W
Senica, *Slovak Rep.* **35 C10** 48 41N 17 25 E
Senigállia, *Italy* **45 E10** 43 43N 13 13 E
Seniku, *Burma* **90 C6** 25 32N 97 48 E
Senio →, *Italy* **45 D9** 44 35N 12 15 E
Senirkent, *Turkey* **49 C12** 38 6N 30 33 E
Senise, *Italy* **47 B9** 40 9N 16 17 E
Senj, *Croatia* **45 D11** 45 0N 14 58 E
Senja, *Norway* **14 B17** 69 25N 17 30 E
Senlis, *France* **27 C9** 49 13N 2 35 E
Senmonorom, *Cambodia* **86 F6** 12 27N 107 12 E
Sennâr, *Sudan* **107 E3** 13 30N 33 35 E

Silver City 281

Shencottah, India 95 K3 8 59N 77 18 E
Shendam, Nigeria 113 D6 8 49N 9 30 E
Shendî, Sudan 107 D3 16 46N 33 22 E
Shendurni, India 94 D2 20 39N 75 36 E
Sheng Xian, China 77 C13 29 35N 120 50 E
Shengfang, China 74 E9 39 3N 116 42 E
Shëngjergji, Albania 50 E4 41 17N 20 10 E
Shëngjin, Albania 50 E3 41 50N 19 35 E
Shenjingzi, China 75 B13 44 40N 124 30 E
Shenmëria, Albania 50 D4 42 7N 20 13 E
Shenmu, China 74 E6 38 50N 110 29 E
Shennongjia, China 77 B8 31 43N 110 44 E
Shenqiu, China 74 H8 33 25N 115 5 E
Shenqiucheng, China 74 H8 33 24N 115 2 E
Shensi = Shaanxi □, China 74 G5 35 0N 109 0 E
Shenyang, China 75 D12 41 48N 123 27 E
Shenzhen, China 77 F10 22 27N 114 10 E
Shepetivka, Ukraine 59 G4 50 10N 27 10 E
Shepherd Is., Vanuatu 133 F6 16 55 S 168 36 E
Shepherdsville, U.S.A. 157 G11 37 59N 85 43W
Shepparton, Australia 129 D6 36 23 S 145 26 E
Sheppey, I. of, U.K. 21 F8 51 25N 0 48 E
Shepton Mallet, U.K. 21 F5 51 11N 2 33W
Sheqi, China 74 H7 33 12N 112 57 E
Sher Qila, Pakistan 93 A6 36 7N 74 2 E
Sherabad, Uzbekistan 63 E3 37 40N 67 1 E
Sherborne, U.K. 21 G5 50 57N 2 31W
Sherbro I., S. Leone 112 D2 7 30N 12 40W
Sherbrooke, Canada 141 C5 45 28N 71 57W
Sherda, Chad 109 D3 20 7N 16 46 E
Shereik, Sudan 106 D3 18 44N 33 47 E
Sheridan, Ark., U.S.A. 155 H8 34 19N 92 24W
Sheridan, Ill., U.S.A. 157 C8 41 32N 88 41W
Sheridan, Ind., U.S.A. 157 D10 40 8N 86 13W
Sheridan, Mo., U.S.A. 156 D2 40 31N 94 37W
Sheridan, Wyo., U.S.A. 158 D10 44 48N 106 58W
Sheringham, U.K. 20 E9 52 56N 1 13 E
Sherkin I., Ireland 23 E2 51 28N 9 26W
Sherkot, India 93 E8 29 22N 78 35 E
Sherman, U.S.A. 155 J6 33 40N 96 35W
Sherpur, Afghan. 91 B3 34 32N 69 10 E
Sherpur, Bangla. 90 C3 25 0N 90 0 E
Sherridon, Canada 143 B8 55 8N 101 5W
Sherwood, N. Dak., U.S.A. 154 A4 48 57N 101 38W
Sherwood, Ohio, U.S.A. 157 C12 41 17N 84 33W
Sherwood, Tex., U.S.A. 155 K4 31 18N 100 45W
Sherwood Forest, U.K. 20 D6 53 6N 1 7W
Sheslay, Canada 142 B2 58 17N 131 52W
Sheslay →, Canada 142 B2 58 48N 132 5W
Shethanei L., Canada 143 B9 58 48N 97 50W
Shetland □, U.K. 22 A7 60 30N 1 30W
Shetland Is., U.K. 22 A7 60 30N 1 30W
Shevaroy Hills, India 95 J4 11 58N 78 12 E
Shewa □, Ethiopia 107 F4 9 33N 38 10 E
Shewa Gimira, Ethiopia 107 F4 7 4N 35 51 E
Sheyenne, U.S.A. 154 B5 47 50N 99 7W
Sheyenne →, U.S.A. 154 B6 47 2N 96 50W
Shibām, Yemen 99 D5 16 0N 48 36 E
Shibata, Japan 68 F9 37 57N 139 20 E
Shibecha, Japan 68 C12 43 17N 144 36 E
Shibetsu, Japan 68 B11 44 10N 142 23 E
Shibîn el Kôm, Egypt 106 H7 30 31N 30 55 E
Shibîn el Qanâtir, Egypt 106 H7 30 19N 31 19 E
Shibing, China 76 D7 27 2N 108 7 E
Shibogama L., Canada 140 B2 53 35N 88 15W
Shibukawa, Japan 71 A11 36 29N 139 0 E
Shibushi, Japan 70 F3 31 25N 131 8 E
Shibushi-Wan, Japan 70 F3 31 24N 131 8 E
Shicheng, China 77 D11 26 22N 116 20 E
Shickshock Mts. = Chic-Chocs, Mts., Canada 141 C6 48 55N 66 0W
Shidād, Si. Arabia 98 B3 21 19N 40 3 E
Shidao, China 75 F12 36 50N 122 25 E
Shidian, China 76 E2 24 40N 99 5 E
Shido, Japan 70 C6 34 19N 134 10 E
Shiel, L., U.K. 22 E3 56 48N 5 34W
Shield, C., Australia 126 A2 13 20 S 136 20 E
Shiga □, Japan 71 B8 35 20N 136 0 E
Shigaib, Sudan 109 E4 15 5N 23 35 E
Shigaraki, Japan 71 C8 34 57N 136 2 E
Shigu, China 76 D2 26 51N 99 56 E
Shiguaigou, China 74 D6 40 52N 110 15 E
Shihan, W. →, Yemen 99 C5 17 24N 51 26 E
Shihchiachuangi = Shijiazhuang, China 74 E8 38 2N 114 28 E
Shiiba, Japan 70 E3 32 29N 131 4 E
Shijaku, Albania 50 E3 41 21N 19 33 E
Shijiazhuang, China 74 E8 38 2N 114 28 E
Shijiu Hu, China 77 B12 31 25N 118 50 E
Shikarpur, India 92 E8 28 17N 78 7 E
Shikarpur, Pakistan 91 D3 27 57N 68 39 E
Shikine-Jima, Japan 71 C11 34 19N 139 13 E
Shikoku, Japan 70 D5 33 30N 133 30 E
Shikoku □, Japan 70 D5 33 30N 133 30 E
Shikoku-Sanchi, Japan 70 D5 33 30N 133 30 E
Shiliguri, India 90 B2 26 45N 88 25 E
Shilka, Russia 65 D12 52 0N 115 55 E
Shilka →, Russia 65 D13 53 20N 121 26 E
Shillelagh, Ireland 23 D5 52 45N 6 32W
Shillong, India 90 C3 25 35N 91 53 E
Shilo, West Bank 103 C4 32 4N 35 18 E
Shiloh, U.S.A. 152 C5 32 49N 84 42W
Shilong, China 77 F9 23 5N 113 52 E
Shilou, China 74 F6 37 0N 110 48 E
Shilovo, Russia 60 C5 54 25N 40 57 E
Shima-Hantō, Japan 71 C8 34 22N 136 45 E
Shimabara, Japan 70 E2 32 48N 130 20 E
Shimada, Japan 71 C10 34 49N 138 10 E
Shimane □, Japan 70 C4 35 0N 132 30 E
Shimane-Hantō, Japan 70 B5 35 30N 133 0 E
Shimanovsk, Russia 65 D13 52 15N 127 30 E
Shimen, China 77 C8 29 35N 111 20 E
Shimenjie, China 77 C11 29 29N 116 48 E
Shimian, China 76 C4 29 17N 102 23 E
Shimizu, Japan 71 C10 35 0N 138 30 E
Shimo-Jima, Japan 70 E2 32 15N 130 7 E
Shimo-Koshiki-Jima, Japan 70 F1 31 40N 129 43 E
Shimoda, Japan 71 C10 34 40N 138 57 E
Shimodate, Japan 71 A11 36 20N 139 55 E
Shimoga, India 95 H2 13 57N 75 32 E
Shimoni, Kenya 118 C4 4 38 S 39 20 E
Shimonita, Japan 71 A10 36 13N 138 47 E
Shimonoseki, Japan 70 D2 33 58N 130 55 E
Shimotsuma, Japan 71 A11 36 11N 139 58 E
Shimpuru Rapids, Angola 115 F3 17 45 S 19 55 E
Shimsha →, India 95 H3 13 15N 77 10 E
Shimsk, Russia 58 C6 58 15N 30 50 E
Shin, L., U.K. 22 C4 58 7N 4 30W
Shin-Tone →, Japan 71 B12 35 44N 140 51 E
Shinan, China 76 F7 22 44N 109 53 E
Shinano →, Japan 69 F9 36 50N 138 30 E
Shīndand, Afghan. 91 B1 33 12N 62 8 E
Shingbwiyang, Burma 90 B6 26 41N 96 13 E
Shingler, U.S.A. 152 D6 31 35N 83 47W
Shingleton, U.S.A. 140 C2 46 21N 86 28W
Shingū, Japan 71 D7 33 40N 135 55 E
Shinji, Japan 70 B4 35 24N 132 54 E
Shinji Ko, Japan 70 B4 35 26N 132 57 E
Shinjō, Japan 68 E10 38 46N 140 18 E
Shinkafe, Nigeria 113 C6 13 8N 6 29 E
Shīnkay, Afghan. 91 C2 31 57N 67 26 E
Shinminato, Japan 71 A9 36 47N 137 4 E
Shinonoi, Japan 71 A10 36 35N 138 9 E
Shinshār, Syria 103 A5 34 36N 36 43 E
Shinshiro, Japan 71 C9 34 54N 137 30 E
Shinyanga, Tanzania 118 C3 3 45 S 33 27 E
Shinyanga □, Tanzania 118 C3 3 50 S 34 0 E
Shio-no-Misaki, Japan 71 D7 33 25N 135 45 E
Shiogama, Japan 68 E10 38 19N 141 1 E
Shiojiri, Japan 71 A9 36 6N 137 58 E
Ship I., U.S.A. 155 K10 30 13N 88 55W
Shipchenski Prokhod, Bulgaria 51 D9 42 45N 25 15 E
Shiping, China 76 F4 23 45N 102 23 E
Shippegan, Canada 141 C7 47 45N 64 45W
Shippensburg, U.S.A. 150 F7 40 3N 77 31W
Shiprock, U.S.A. 159 H9 36 47N 108 41W
Shiqian, China 76 D7 27 32N 108 13 E
Shiqma, N. →, Israel 103 D3 31 37N 34 30 E
Shiquan, China 74 H5 33 5N 108 15 E
Shīr Kūh, Iran 97 D7 31 39N 54 3 E
Shirabad = Sherabad, Uzbekistan 63 E3 37 40N 67 1 E
Shiragami-Misaki, Japan 68 D10 41 24N 140 12 E
Shirahama, Japan 71 D7 33 41N 135 20 E
Shirakawa, Fukushima, Japan 69 F10 37 7N 140 13 E
Shirakawa, Gifu, Japan 71 A8 36 17N 136 56 E
Shirane-San, Gumma, Japan 71 A11 36 48N 139 22 E
Shirane-San, Yamanashi, Japan 71 B10 35 42N 138 9 E
Shiraoi, Japan 68 C10 42 33N 141 21 E
Shīrāz, Iran 97 D7 29 42N 52 30 E
Shirbin, Egypt 106 H7 31 11N 31 32 E
Shire →, Africa 119 F4 17 42 S 35 19 E
Shiretoko-Misaki, Japan 68 B12 44 21N 145 20 E
Shirinab →, Pakistan 92 D2 30 15N 66 28 E
Shiriya-Zaki, Japan 68 D10 41 25N 141 30 E
Shirley, U.S.A. 157 E11 39 53N 85 35W
Shiroishi, Japan 68 F10 38 0N 140 37 E
Shirol, India 94 F2 16 47N 74 41 E
Shirpur, India 94 D2 21 21N 74 57 E
Shirvān, Iran 97 B8 37 30N 57 50 E
Shirwa, L. = Chilwa, L., Malawi 119 F4 15 15 S 35 40 E
Shishaldin Volcano, U.S.A. 144 J7 54 45N 163 58W
Shishou, China 77 C9 29 38N 112 22 E
Shitai, China 77 B11 30 12N 117 25 E
Shively, U.S.A. 157 F11 38 12N 85 49W
Shivpuri, India 92 G7 25 26N 77 42 E
Shixian, China 75 C15 43 5N 129 50 E
Shixing, China 77 E10 24 46N 114 5 E
Shiyan, China 77 A8 32 35N 110 45 E
Shiyata, Egypt 106 B2 29 25N 25 7 E
Shizhu, China 76 C7 29 58N 108 7 E
Shizong, China 76 E5 24 50N 104 0 E
Shizuishan, China 74 E4 39 15N 106 50 E
Shizuoka, Japan 71 C10 34 57N 138 24 E
Shizuoka □, Japan 71 B10 35 15N 138 40 E
Shklov = Shklow, Belarus 58 E6 54 16N 30 15 E
Shklow, Belarus 58 E6 54 16N 30 15 E
Shkoder = Shkodra, Albania 50 D3 42 4N 19 32 E
Shkodra, Albania 50 D3 42 4N 19 32 E
Shkumbini →, Albania 50 E3 41 2N 19 31 E
Shmidta, Ostrov, Russia 65 A10 81 0N 91 0 E
Shō-Gawa →, Japan 71 A9 36 47N 137 4 E
Shoal Cr. →, U.S.A. 156 E3 39 44N 93 32W
Shoal Lake, Canada 143 C8 50 30N 100 35W
Shoals, U.S.A. 157 F10 38 40N 86 47W
Shōbara, Japan 70 C5 34 51N 133 1 E
Shōdo-Shima, Japan 70 C6 34 30N 134 15 E
Shokpar, Kazakstan 63 B7 43 49N 74 21 E
Sholapur = Solapur, India 94 F2 17 43N 75 56 E
Shologontsy, Russia 65 C12 66 13N 114 0 E
Shōmrōn, West Bank 103 C4 32 15N 35 13 E
Shoranur, India 95 J3 10 46N 76 19 E
Shorapur, India 95 F3 16 31N 76 48 E
Shoreham by Sea, U.K. 21 G7 50 50N 0 16W
Shorter, U.S.A. 152 C4 32 24N 85 57W
Shorterville, U.S.A. 152 D4 31 34N 85 6W
Shortland I., Solomon Is. 133 L8 7 0 S 155 45 E
Shoshone, Calif., U.S.A. 161 K10 35 58N 116 16W
Shoshone, Idaho, U.S.A. 158 E6 42 56N 114 25W
Shoshone L., U.S.A. 158 D8 44 22N 110 43W
Shoshone Mts., U.S.A. 158 G5 39 20N 117 25W
Shoshong, Botswana 116 C4 22 56 S 26 31 E
Shoshoni, U.S.A. 158 E9 43 14N 108 7W
Shostka, Ukraine 59 G7 51 57N 33 32 E
Shou Xian, China 77 A11 32 37N 116 42 E
Shouchang, China 77 C12 29 18N 119 12 E
Shouguang, China 75 F10 37 52N 118 45 E
Shouning, China 77 D12 27 27N 119 31 E
Shouyang, China 74 F7 37 54N 113 8 E
Show Low, U.S.A. 159 J9 34 15N 110 2W
Shpola, Ukraine 59 H6 49 1N 31 30 E
Shreveport, U.S.A. 155 J8 32 31N 93 45W
Shrewsbury, U.K. 21 E5 52 43N 2 45W
Shrirampur, India 93 H13 22 44N 88 21 E
Shrirangapattana, India 95 H3 12 26N 76 43 E
Shropshire □, U.K. 21 E5 52 36N 2 45W
Shu, Kazakstan 63 B6 43 36N 73 42 E
Shu →, Kazakstan 63 A3 45 0N 67 44 E
Shuangbai, China 76 E3 24 42N 101 38 E
Shuangcheng, China 75 B14 45 20N 126 15 E
Shuangfeng, China 77 D9 27 29N 112 11 E
Shuanggou, China 75 G9 34 2N 117 30 E
Shuangjiang, China 76 F2 23 26N 99 58 E
Shuangliao, China 75 C12 43 29N 123 30 E
Shuangshanzi, China 75 D10 40 20N 119 8 E
Shuangyang, China 75 C13 43 28N 125 40 E
Shuangyashan, China 73 B8 46 28N 131 5 E
Shu'b, Ra's, Yemen 99 D6 12 30N 53 25 E
Shucheng, China 77 B11 31 28N 116 57 E
Shugozero, Russia 58 C8 59 54N 34 10 E
Shuguri Falls, Tanzania 119 D4 8 33 S 37 22 E
Shuhayr, Yemen 99 D5 14 41N 49 23 E
Shuiji, China 77 D12 27 13N 118 20 E
Shuiye, China 74 F8 36 7N 114 8 E
Shujalpur, India 92 H7 23 18N 76 46 E
Shukpa Kunzang, India 93 B8 34 22N 78 22 E
Shulan, China 75 B14 44 28N 127 0 E
Shulaveri, Georgia 61 K7 41 22N 44 45 E
Shule, China 72 C2 39 25N 76 3 E
Shullsburg, U.S.A. 156 B6 42 35N 90 13W
Shumagin Is., U.S.A. 138 C4 55 7N 160 30W
Shumen, Bulgaria 51 C10 43 18N 26 55 E
Shumerlya, Russia 60 C8 55 30N 46 25 E
Shumikha, Russia 62 D9 55 10N 63 15 E
Shunchang, China 77 D11 26 54N 117 48 E
Shunde, China 77 F9 22 42N 113 14 E
Shungay, Kazakstan 61 F8 48 30N 46 45 E
Shuo Xian, China 74 E7 39 20N 112 33 E
Shūr →, Iran 97 D7 28 30N 55 0 E
Shūr Āb, Iran 97 C6 34 23N 51 11 E
Shūr Gaz, Iran 97 D8 29 10N 59 20 E
Shūrāb, Iran 97 C8 33 43N 56 29 E
Shurab, Tajikistan 63 C5 40 3N 70 33 E
Shurchi, Uzbekistan 63 E3 37 59N 67 47 E
Shūrjestān, Iran 97 D7 31 24N 52 25 E
Shurkhua, Burma 90 D4 22 15N 93 38 E
Shurugwi, Zimbabwe 119 F3 19 40 S 30 0 E
Shūsf, Iran 97 D9 31 50N 60 5 E
Shūsh, Iran 101 F13 32 11N 48 15 E
Shūshtar, Iran 97 D6 32 0N 48 50 E
Shuswap L., Canada 142 C5 50 55N 119 3W
Shuya, Russia 60 B5 56 50N 41 28 E
Shuyang, China 75 G10 34 10N 118 42 E
Shuzenji, Japan 71 C10 34 58N 138 56 E
Shūzū, Iran 97 D7 29 52N 54 30 E
Shwebo, Burma 90 D5 22 30N 95 45 E
Shwegu, Burma 90 C6 24 15N 96 26 E
Shwegun, Burma 90 G6 17 9N 97 39 E
Shwenyaung, Burma 90 E6 20 46N 96 57 E
Shymkent, Kazakstan 63 B4 42 18N 69 36 E
Shyok, India 93 B8 34 15N 78 12 E
Shyok →, Pakistan 93 B6 35 13N 75 53 E
Si Chon, Thailand 87 H2 9 0N 99 54 E
Si Kiang = Xi Jiang →, China 77 F9 22 5N 113 20 E
Si-ngan = Xi'an, China 74 G5 34 15N 109 0 E
Si Prachan, Thailand 86 E3 14 37N 100 9 E
Si Racha, Thailand 86 F3 13 10N 100 48 E
Si Xian, China 75 H9 33 30N 117 50 E
Siahan Range, Pakistan 91 D2 27 30N 64 40 E
Siak →, Indonesia 84 B2 1 13N 102 9 E
Siaksriindrapura, Indonesia 84 B2 0 51N 102 0 E
Sialkot, Pakistan 91 B4 32 32N 74 30 E
Sialsuk, India 90 D4 23 24N 92 45 E
Siam = Thailand ■, Asia 86 E4 16 0N 102 0 E
Siam, Australia 128 B2 32 35 S 136 41 E
Sianów, Poland 54 D3 54 13N 16 18 E
Siantan, Indonesia 84 B3 3 10N 106 15 E
Siàpo →, Venezuela 168 C4 2 7N 66 28W
Sīāreh, Iran 97 D9 28 5N 60 14 E
Siargao, Phil. 81 G6 9 52N 126 3 E
Siari, Pakistan 93 B7 34 55N 76 40 E
Siari, Phil. 81 G4 8 19N 122 58 E
Siasi I., Phil. 81 J3 5 33N 120 51 E
Siassi, Papua N. G. 132 C4 5 40 S 147 51 E
Siátista, Greece 50 F5 40 15N 21 33 E
Siaton, Phil. 81 G4 9 4N 123 2 E
Siau, Indonesia 82 A3 2 50N 125 25 E
Šiauliai, Lithuania 15 J20 55 56N 23 15 E
Šiauliai □, Lithuania 54 C10 55 56N 23 19 E
Siaya □, Kenya 118 C3 0 0 34 20 E
Siazan = Siyäzän, Azerbaijan 61 K9 41 3N 49 10 E
Sibâi, Gebel el, Egypt 106 B3 25 45N 34 10 E
Sibang, Gabon 114 B1 0 25N 9 31 E
Sibay, Russia 62 E7 52 42N 58 39 E
Sibay I., Phil. 81 F3 11 51N 121 29 E
Sibayi, L., S. Africa 117 D5 27 20 S 32 45 E
Šibenik, Croatia 45 E12 43 48N 15 54 E
Siberia, Russia 6 D13 60 0N 100 0 E
Siberut, Indonesia 84 C1 1 30 S 99 0 E
Sibi, Pakistan 91 C2 29 30N 67 54 E
Sibil = Oksibil, Indonesia 83 B6 4 59 S 140 35 E
Sibiti, Congo 114 C2 3 38 S 13 19 E
Sibiu, Romania 53 E9 45 45N 24 9 E
Sibiu □, Romania 53 E9 45 50N 24 15 E
Sibley, Ill., U.S.A. 157 D8 40 35N 88 23W
Sibley, Iowa, U.S.A. 154 D7 43 24N 95 45W
Sibley, La., U.S.A. 155 J8 32 33N 93 18W
Sibolga, Indonesia 84 B1 1 42N 98 45 E
Sibsagar, India 90 B5 27 0N 94 36 E
Sibu, Malaysia 85 B4 2 18N 111 49 E
Sibuco, Phil. 81 H4 7 20N 122 10 E
Sibuguey B., Phil. 81 H4 7 50N 122 45 E
Sibut, C.A.R. 114 A3 5 46N 19 10 E
Sibutu, Phil. 81 J2 4 45N 119 30 E
Sibutu Group, Phil. 81 J2 4 45N 119 20 E
Sibutu Passage, E. Indies 81 J3 4 50N 120 0 E
Sibuyan, Phil. 80 E4 12 25N 122 40 E
Sibuyan Sea, Phil. 80 E4 12 30N 122 20 E
Sic, Romania 53 D8 46 56N 23 53 E
Sicamous, Canada 142 C5 50 49N 119 0W
Sicapoo, Mt., Phil. 80 B3 18 1N 120 56 E
Sichuan □, China 76 B5 30 30N 103 0 E
Sicilia, Italy 47 E7 37 30N 14 30 E
Sicily = Sicilia, Italy 47 E7 37 30N 14 30 E
Sicuani, Peru 172 C3 14 21 S 71 10W
Šid, Serbia, Yug. 52 E4 45 8N 19 14 E
Sidamo □, Ethiopia 107 G4 5 0N 37 50 E
Sidaouet, Niger 109 E1 18 34N 8 3 E
Sidári, Greece 38 A3 39 47N 19 41 E
Siddhapur, India 92 H5 23 56N 72 25 E
Siddipet, India 94 E4 18 5N 78 51 E
Sidell, U.S.A. 157 E9 39 55N 87 49W
Sidensjö, Sweden 16 A12 63 18N 18 17 E
Sidéradougou, Burkina Faso 112 C4 10 42N 4 12W
Siderno, Italy 47 D9 38 16N 16 18 E
Sídheros, Ákra, Greece 38 D8 35 19N 26 19 E
Sidhirókastron, Greece 50 E7 41 13N 23 24 E
Sîdi Abd el Rahmân, Egypt 106 H6 30 55N 29 44 E
Sîdi Barrâni, Egypt 106 A2 31 38N 25 58 E
Sidi-bel-Abbès, Algeria 111 A4 35 13N 0 39W
Sidi Bennour, Morocco 110 B3 32 40N 8 25W
Sidi Haneish, Egypt 106 A2 31 10N 27 35 E
Sidi Kacem, Morocco 110 B3 34 11N 5 49W
Sidi Omar, Egypt 106 A1 31 24N 24 57 E
Sidi Slimane, Morocco 110 B3 34 16N 5 56W
Sidi Smaïl, Morocco 110 B3 32 50N 8 31W
Sidi 'Uzayz, Libya 108 B4 31 41N 24 55 E
Sidlaw Hills, U.K. 22 E5 56 32N 3 2W
Sidley, Mt., Antarctica 7 D14 77 2 S 126 2W
Sidmouth, U.K. 21 G4 50 40N 3 15W
Sidmouth, C., Australia 126 A3 13 25 S 143 36 E
Sidney, Canada 142 D4 48 39N 123 24W
Sidney, Mont., U.S.A. 154 B2 47 43N 104 9W
Sidney, N.Y., U.S.A. 151 D9 42 19N 75 24W
Sidney, Nebr., U.S.A. 154 E3 41 8N 102 59W
Sidney, Ohio, U.S.A. 157 D12 40 17N 84 9W
Sidney Lanier L., U.S.A. 152 A5 34 10N 84 4W
Sidoarjo, Indonesia 85 D4 7 27 S 112 43 E
Sidoktaya, Burma 90 E5 20 27N 94 15 E
Sidon = Saydā, Lebanon 103 B4 33 35N 35 25 E
Sidra, G. of = Surt, Khalīj, Libya 108 B3 31 40N 18 30 E
Siedlce, Poland 55 F9 52 10N 22 20 E
Siedlce □, Poland 55 F9 52 20N 22 0 E
Sieg →, Germany 30 E3 50 46N 7 6 E
Siegburg, Germany 30 E3 50 47N 7 12 E
Siegen, Germany 30 E4 50 51N 8 0 E
Siem Pang, Cambodia 86 E6 14 7N 106 23 E
Siem Reap = Siemreab, Cambodia 86 F4 13 20N 103 52 E
Siemiatycze, Poland 55 F9 52 27N 22 53 E
Siemreab, Cambodia 86 F4 13 20N 103 52 E
Siena, Italy 45 E8 43 19N 11 21 E
Sieniawa, Poland 55 H9 50 11N 22 38 E
Sieradz, Poland 55 G5 51 37N 18 41 E
Sieradz □, Poland 55 G5 51 30N 18 45 E
Sieraków, Poland 55 F3 52 39N 16 2 E
Sierck-les-Bains, France 27 C13 49 26N 6 20 E
Sierning, Austria 34 C7 48 2N 14 18 E
Sierpc, Poland 55 F6 52 55N 19 43 E
Sierpe, Bocas de la, Venezuela 169 B5 10 0N 61 30W
Sierra Blanca, U.S.A. 159 L11 31 11N 105 22W
Sierra Blanca Peak, U.S.A. 159 K11 33 23N 105 49W
Sierra City, U.S.A. 160 F6 39 34N 120 38W
Sierra Colorada, Argentina 176 B3 40 35 S 67 50W
Sierra de Yeguas, Spain 43 H6 37 7N 4 52W
Sierra Gorda, Chile 174 A2 22 50 S 69 15W
Sierra Grande, Argentina 176 B3 41 36 S 65 22W
Sierra Leone ■, W. Afr. 112 D2 9 0N 12 0W
Sierra Madre, Mexico 163 D6 16 0N 93 0W
Sierra Mojada, Mexico 162 B4 27 19N 103 42W
Sierraville, U.S.A. 160 F6 39 36N 120 22W
Sierre, Switz. 32 D5 46 17N 7 31 E
Sífnos, Greece 48 E6 37 0N 24 45 E
Sifton, Canada 143 C8 51 21N 100 8W
Sifton Pass, Canada 142 B3 57 52N 126 15W
Sig, Algeria 111 A4 35 32N 0 12W
Sigaboy, Phil. 81 H6 6 39N 126 5 E
Sigdal, Norway 18 D6 60 3N 9 38 E
Sigean, France 28 E6 43 2N 2 58 E
Sighetu-Marmaţiei, Romania 53 C8 47 57N 23 52 E
Sighişoara, Romania 53 D9 46 12N 24 50 E
Sigira, Yemen 99 D6 12 37N 54 20 E
Sigli, Indonesia 84 A1 5 25N 96 0 E
Siglufjörður, Iceland 11 A8 66 12N 18 55W
Siglunes, Iceland 11 A8 66 12N 18 50W
Sigmaringen, Germany 31 G5 48 5N 9 12 E
Signa, Italy 44 E8 43 45N 11 10 E
Signakhi = Tsnori, Georgia 61 K7 41 40N 45 57 E
Signal, U.S.A. 161 L13 34 30N 113 38W
Signal Pk., U.S.A. 161 M12 33 20N 114 2W
Signau, Switz. 32 C5 46 56N 7 45 E
Signy-l'Abbaye, France 27 C11 49 40N 4 25 E
Sigourney, U.S.A. 156 C4 41 20N 92 12W
Sigsbee, U.S.A. 152 D6 31 16N 83 52W
Sigsig, Ecuador 168 D2 3 0 S 78 50W
Sigüenza, Spain 40 D2 41 3N 2 40W
Siguiri, Guinea 112 C3 11 31N 9 10W
Sigulda, Latvia 15 H21 57 10N 24 55 E
Sigurd, U.S.A. 159 G8 38 50N 111 58W
Sihanoukville = Kampong Saom, Cambodia 87 G4 10 38N 103 30 E
Sihaus, Peru 172 B2 8 40 S 77 40W
Sihui, China 77 F9 23 20N 112 40 E
Siikajoki →, Finland 14 D21 64 50N 24 43 E
Siilinjärvi, Finland 14 E22 63 4N 27 39 E
Siirt, Turkey 101 D9 37 57N 41 55 E
Siit, Phil. 81 J5 5 59N 124 13 E
Sijarira Ra., Zimbabwe 119 F2 17 36 S 27 45 E
Sijunjung, Indonesia 84 C2 0 42 S 100 58 E
Sikao, Thailand 87 J2 7 34N 99 21 E
Sikar, India 92 F6 27 33N 75 10 E
Sikasso, Mali 112 C3 11 18N 5 35W
Sikeston, U.S.A. 155 G10 36 53N 89 35W
Sikhote Alin, Khrebet, Russia 68 B8 45 0N 136 0 E
Sikhote Alin Ra. = Sikhote Alin, Khrebet, Russia 68 B8 45 0N 136 0 E
Sikiá, Greece 50 F7 40 2N 23 56 E
Síkinos, Greece 49 E7 36 40N 25 8 E
Sikkani Chief →, Canada 142 B4 57 47N 122 15W
Sikkim □, India 90 B2 27 50N 88 30 E
Siklós, Hungary 52 E3 45 50N 18 19 E
Sikotu-Ko, Japan 68 C10 42 45N 141 25 E
Sil →, Spain 42 C3 42 27N 7 43W
Silacayoapan, Mexico 163 D5 17 30N 98 9W
Šilalė, Lithuania 54 C9 55 28N 22 12 E
Silandro, Italy 44 B7 46 38N 10 46 E
Silanga, Phil. 81 F2 11 1N 119 34 E
Silay, Phil. 81 F4 10 47N 123 14 E
Silba, Croatia 45 D11 44 24N 14 41 E
Silchar, India 90 C4 24 49N 92 48 E
Silcox, Canada 143 B10 57 12N 94 10W
Sildegapet, Norway 18 B2 62 5N 5 0 E
Şile, Turkey 51 E13 41 10N 29 37 E
Siler City, U.S.A. 149 H6 35 44N 79 28W
Sileru →, India 94 F5 17 49N 81 24 E
Silet, Algeria 111 D5 22 44N 4 37 E
Silgarhi Doti, Nepal 93 E9 29 15N 81 0 E
Silghat, India 90 B4 26 35N 93 0 E
Silifke, Turkey 100 D5 36 22N 33 58 E
Siliguri = Shiliguri, India 90 B2 26 45N 88 25 E
Siling Co, China 72 C3 31 50N 89 20 E
Silistea Nouă, Romania 53 F10 44 23N 25 1 E
Silistra, Bulgaria 51 B11 44 6N 27 19 E
Silivri, Turkey 51 E12 41 4N 28 14 E
Siljan, Norway 18 E6 59 18N 9 42 E
Siljan, Sweden 16 D8 60 55N 14 45 E
Siljansnäs, Sweden 16 D8 60 47N 14 52 E
Silkeborg, Denmark 17 H3 56 10N 9 32 E
Silla, Spain 41 F4 39 22N 0 25W
Sillajhuay, Cordillera, Chile 172 D4 19 46 S 68 40W
Sillamäe, Estonia 15 G22 59 24N 27 45 E
Sillé-le-Guillaume, France 26 D6 48 10N 0 8W
Silleda, Spain 42 C2 42 42N 8 14W
Silloth, U.K. 20 C4 54 52N 3 23W
Sillustani, Peru 172 D3 15 50 S 70 7W
Sílo, Greece 51 E9 41 10N 25 53 E
Siloam, U.S.A. 152 B6 33 32N 83 5W
Siloam Springs, U.S.A. 155 G7 36 11N 94 32W
Silopi, Turkey 101 D10 37 15N 42 27 E
Silsbee, U.S.A. 155 K7 30 21N 94 11W
Šilutė, Lithuania 15 J19 55 21N 21 33 E
Silva Porto = Kuito, Angola 115 E3 12 22 S 16 55 E
Silvan, Turkey 101 C9 38 7N 41 2 E
Silvaplana, Switz. 33 D9 46 28N 9 48 E
Silver City, N. Mex., U.S.A. 159 K9 32 46N 108 17W

Sorrento 283

Slonim, Belarus 59 F3 53 4N 25 19 E
Slough, U.K. 21 F7 51 30N 0 36W
Slough □, U.K. 21 F7 51 30N 0 36W
Sloughhouse, U.S.A. 160 G5 38 26N 121 12W
Slovak Rep. ■, Europe 35 C13 48 30N 20 0 E
Slovakia = Slovak Rep. ■, Europe 35 C13 48 30N 20 0 E
Slovakian Ore Mts. = Slovenské Rudohorie, Slovak Rep. 35 C12 48 45N 20 0 E
Slovenia ■, Europe 45 C11 45 58N 14 30 E
Slovenija = Slovenia ■, Europe 45 C11 45 58N 14 30 E
Slovenj Gradec, Slovenia 45 B12 46 31N 15 5 E
Slovenska Bistrica, Slovenia 45 B12 46 24N 15 35 E
Slovenská Republika = Slovak Rep. ■, Europe 35 C13 48 30N 20 0 E
Slovenske Konjice, Slovenia 45 B12 46 20N 15 28 E
Slovenské Rudohorie, Slovak Rep. 35 C12 48 45N 20 0 E
Slovyansk, Ukraine 59 H9 48 55N 37 36 E
Słubice, Poland 55 F1 52 22N 14 35 E
Sluch →, Ukraine 59 G4 51 37N 26 38 E
Sluis, Neths. 24 C3 51 18N 3 23 E
Slŭnchev Bryag, Bulgaria 51 D11 42 40N 27 41 E
Slunj, Croatia 45 C12 45 6N 15 33 E
Słupca, Poland 55 F4 52 15N 17 52 E
Słupia →, Poland 54 D3 54 35N 16 51 E
Słupsk, Poland 54 D4 54 30N 17 3 E
Słupsk □, Poland 54 D4 54 15N 17 30 E
Slurry, S. Africa 116 D4 25 49 S 25 42 E
Slutsk, Belarus 59 F4 53 2N 27 31 E
Slyne Hd., Ireland 23 C1 53 25N 10 10W
Slyudyanka, Russia 65 D11 51 40N 103 40 E
Småland, Sweden 17 G9 57 15N 15 25 E
Smålandsfarvandet, Denmark 17 J5 55 10N 11 20 E
Smålandsstenar, Sweden 17 G7 57 10N 13 25 E
Small Nggela, Solomon Is. 133 M11 9 0 S 160 0 E
Smalltree L., Canada 143 A8 61 0N 105 0W
Smallwood Res., Canada 141 B7 54 0N 64 0W
Smarhon, Belarus 58 E4 54 20N 26 24 E
Smarje, Slovenia 45 B12 46 15N 15 34 E
Smarr, U.S.A. 152 C6 32 59N 83 53W
Smartt Syndicate Dam, S. Africa 116 E3 30 45 S 23 10 E
Smartville, U.S.A. 160 F5 39 13N 121 18W
Smeaton, Canada 143 C8 53 30N 104 49W
Smedby, Sweden 17 H10 56 41N 16 13 E
Smederevo, Serbia, Yug. 50 B4 44 40N 20 57 E
Smederevska Palanka, Serbia, Yug. 50 B4 44 22N 20 58 E
Smedjebacken, Sweden 16 D9 60 8N 15 25 E
Smela = Smila, Ukraine 59 H6 49 15N 31 58 E
Smerwick Harbour, Ireland 23 D1 52 12N 10 23W
Smethport, U.S.A. 150 E6 41 49N 78 27W
Smidovich, Russia 65 E14 48 36N 133 49 E
Śmigiel, Poland 55 F3 52 1N 16 32 E
Smila, Ukraine 59 H6 49 15N 31 58 E
Smiley, Canada 143 C7 51 38N 109 29W
Smilyan, Bulgaria 51 E8 41 29N 24 46 E
Smith, Canada 142 B6 55 10N 114 0W
Smith →, Canada 142 B3 59 34N 126 30W
Smith B., U.S.A. 144 A9 70 30N 154 20W
Smith Center, U.S.A. 154 F5 39 47N 98 47W
Smith Sund, Greenland 10 B3 78 30N 74 0W
Smithburne →, Australia 126 B3 17 3 S 140 57 E
Smithers, Canada 142 C3 54 45N 127 10W
Smithfield, S. Africa 117 E4 30 9 S 26 30 E
Smithfield, N.C., U.S.A. 149 H6 35 31N 78 21W
Smithfield, Utah, U.S.A. 158 F8 41 50N 111 50W
Smiths, U.S.A. 152 C4 32 32N 85 6W
Smiths Falls, Canada 140 D4 44 55N 76 0W
Smithton, Australia 126 G4 40 53 S 145 6 E
Smithtown, Australia 129 A10 30 58 S 152 48 E
Smithville, Canada 150 C5 43 6N 79 33W
Smithville, Ga., U.S.A. 152 D5 31 54N 84 15W
Smithville, Mo., U.S.A. 156 E2 39 23N 94 35W
Smithville, Tex., U.S.A. 155 K6 30 1N 97 10W
Smoaks, U.S.A. 152 B9 33 5N 80 49W
Smoky →, Canada 142 B5 56 10N 117 21W
Smoky Bay, Australia 127 E1 32 22 S 134 13 E
Smoky Falls, Canada 140 B3 50 4N 82 10W
Smoky Hill →, U.S.A. 154 F6 39 4N 96 48W
Smoky Lake, Canada 142 C6 54 10N 112 30W
Smøla, Norway 14 E13 63 23N 8 3 E
Smolensk, Russia 58 E7 54 45N 32 5 E
Smolikas, Óros, Greece 50 F4 40 9N 20 58 E
Smolník, Slovak Rep. 35 C13 48 43N 20 44 E
Smolyan, Bulgaria 51 E8 41 36N 24 38 E
Smooth Rock Falls, Canada 140 C3 49 17N 81 37W
Smoothstone L., Canada 143 C7 54 40N 106 50W
Smorgon = Smarhon, Belarus 58 E4 54 20N 26 24 E
Smulţi, Romania 53 E12 45 57N 27 44 E
Smyadovo, Bulgaria 51 C11 43 2N 27 1 E
Smygehamn, Sweden 17 J7 55 21N 13 22 E
Smyrna = Izmir, Turkey 57 G4 38 25N 27 8 E
Smyrna, U.S.A. 152 B5 33 53N 84 31W
Snæfell, Iceland 11 C11 64 48N 15 34W
Snaefell, U.K. 20 C3 54 16N 4 27W
Snæfellsjökull, Iceland 11 C3 64 49N 23 46W
Snæfellsnessýsla □, Iceland 11 C3 65 0N 23 0W
Snake →, U.S.A. 158 C4 46 12N 119 2W
Snake I., Australia 129 E7 38 47 S 146 33 E
Snake L., Canada 143 B7 55 32N 106 35W
Snake Range, U.S.A. 158 G6 39 0N 114 20W
Snake River Plain, U.S.A. 158 E7 42 50N 114 0W
Snasahögarna, Sweden 16 A6 63 13N 12 21 E
Snåsavatnet, Norway 14 D14 64 12N 12 0 E
Snedsted, Denmark 17 H2 56 55N 8 32 E
Sneek, Neths. 24 A5 53 2N 5 40 E
Sneeuberge, S. Africa 116 E3 31 46 S 24 20 E
Snejbjerg, Denmark 17 H2 56 8N 8 54 E
Snelling, Calif., U.S.A. 160 H6 37 31N 120 26W
Snelling, S.C., U.S.A. 152 B9 33 15N 81 27W
Snezhnoye, Ukraine 59 J10 48 0N 38 58 E
Snežnik, Slovenia 45 C11 45 36N 14 35 E
Śniadowo, Poland 55 E8 53 2N 22 0 E
Śniardwy, Jezioro, Poland 54 E8 53 48N 21 50 E
Śnieżka, Europe 34 A8 50 44N 15 44 E
Snigirevka = Snihurivka, Ukraine 59 J7 47 2N 32 49 E
Snihurivka, Ukraine 59 J7 47 2N 32 49 E
Snillfjord, Norway 18 A6 63 24N 9 30 E
Snina, Slovak Rep. 35 C15 48 58N 22 9 E
Snizort, L., U.K. 22 D2 57 33N 6 28W
Snøhetta, Norway 15 E13 62 19N 9 16 E
Snohomish, U.S.A. 160 C4 47 55N 122 6W
Snønuten, Norway 18 E3 59 31N 6 52 E
Snoul, Cambodia 87 F6 12 4N 106 26 E
Snow Hill, U.S.A. 148 F8 38 11N 75 24W
Snow Lake, Canada 143 C8 54 52N 100 3W
Snow Mt., U.S.A. 160 F4 39 23N 122 45W
Snowbird L., Canada 143 A8 60 45N 103 0W
Snowdon, U.K. 20 D3 53 4N 4 5W
Snowdoun, U.S.A. 152 C3 32 15N 86 18W
Snowdrift →, Canada 143 A6 62 24N 110 44W
Snowflake, U.S.A. 159 J8 34 30N 110 5W
Snowshoe Pk., U.S.A. 158 B6 48 13N 115 41W
Snowtown, Australia 128 B3 33 46 S 138 14 E
Snowville, U.S.A. 158 F7 41 58N 112 43W
Snowy →, Australia 129 D8 37 46 S 148 30 E
Snowy Mts., Australia 129 D8 36 30 S 148 20 E
Snug Corner, Bahamas 165 B5 22 33N 73 52W
Snyatyn, Ukraine 59 H3 48 27N 25 38 E
Snyder, Okla., U.S.A. 155 H5 34 40N 98 57W
Snyder, Tex., U.S.A. 155 J4 32 44N 100 55W
Soacha, Colombia 168 C3 4 35N 74 13W
Soahanina, Madag. 117 B7 18 42 S 44 13 E
Soalala, Madag. 117 B8 16 6 S 45 20 E
Soan →, Pakistan 92 C4 33 1N 71 44 E
Soanierana-Ivongo, Madag. 117 B8 16 55 S 49 35 E
Soap Lake, U.S.A. 158 C4 47 23N 119 29W
Şoarş, Romania 53 E9 45 56N 24 55 E
Sobat, Nahr →, Sudan 107 F3 9 22N 31 33 E
Soběslav, Czech Rep. 34 B7 49 16N 14 45 E
Sobhapur, India 92 H8 22 47N 78 17 E
Sobinka, Russia 58 E11 56 0N 40 0 E
Sobo-Yama, Japan 70 E3 32 51N 131 22 E
Sobótka, Poland 55 H3 50 54N 16 44 E
Sobra, Croatia 45 F14 42 44N 17 34 E
Sobradinho, Reprêsa de, Brazil 170 C3 9 30 S 42 0 E
Sobral, Brazil 170 B3 3 50 S 40 20W
Sobrance, Slovak Rep. 35 C15 48 45N 22 11 E
Sobreira Formosa, Portugal 42 F3 39 46N 7 51W
Soc Giang, Vietnam 86 A6 22 54N 106 1 E
Soc Trang, Vietnam 87 H5 9 37N 105 50 E
Soča →, Europe 34 E6 46 20N 13 40 E
Sochaczew, Poland 55 F7 52 15N 20 13 E
Soch'e = Shache, China 72 C2 38 20N 77 10 E
Sochi, Russia 61 J4 43 35N 39 40 E
Social Circle, U.S.A. 152 B6 33 39N 83 43W
Société, Is. de la, Pac. Oc. 135 J12 17 0 S 151 0W
Society Hill, U.S.A. 152 C4 32 26N 85 27W
Society Is. = Société, Is. de la, Pac. Oc. 135 J12 17 0 S 151 0W
Socompa, Portezuelo de, Chile 174 A2 24 27 S 68 18W
Socorro, Colombia 168 B3 6 29N 73 16W
Socorro, Phil. 81 G5 9 37N 125 58 E
Socorro, U.S.A. 159 J10 34 4N 106 54W
Socorro, I., Mexico 162 D2 18 45N 110 58W
Socotra, Ind. Oc. 99 D6 12 30N 54 0 E
Socovos, Spain 41 G3 38 20N 1 58W
Socuéllamos, Spain 41 F2 39 16N 2 47W
Soda L., U.S.A. 159 J5 35 10N 116 4W
Soda Plains, India 93 B8 35 30N 79 0 E
Soda Springs, U.S.A. 158 E8 42 39N 111 36W
Sodankylä, Finland 14 C22 67 29N 26 40 E
Söderala, Sweden 16 C10 61 17N 16 55 E
Söderbärke, Sweden 16 D9 60 5N 15 33 E
Söderfors, Sweden 16 D11 60 23N 17 25 E
Söderhamn, Sweden 16 C11 61 18N 17 10 E
Söderköping, Sweden 17 F10 58 31N 16 20 E
Södermanland, Sweden 15 G17 58 56N 16 55 E
Södermanlands län □, Sweden 16 E10 59 10N 16 30 E
Södertälje, Sweden 16 E11 59 12N 17 39 E
Sodiri, Sudan 107 E2 14 27N 29 0 E
Sodo, Ethiopia 107 F4 7 0N 37 41 E
Södra Dellen, Sweden 16 C10 61 48N 16 43 E
Södra Finnskoga, Sweden 16 D6 60 42N 12 34 E
Södra Sandby, Sweden 17 J7 55 43N 13 21 E
Södra Ulvön, Sweden 16 B12 62 59N 18 38 E
Södra Vi, Sweden 17 G9 57 45N 15 45 E
Sodražica, Slovenia 45 C11 45 45N 14 39 E
Sodus, U.S.A. 150 C7 43 14N 77 4W
Soe, Indonesia 82 C2 9 52 S 124 17 E
Soekmekaar, S. Africa 117 C4 23 30 S 29 55 E
Soest, Germany 30 D4 51 34N 8 7 E
Soest, Neths. 24 B5 52 9N 5 19 E
Sofádhes, Greece 48 B4 39 20N 22 4 E
Sofara, Mali 112 C4 13 59N 4 9W
Sofia = Sofiya, Bulgaria 50 D7 42 45N 23 20 E
Sofia →, Madag. 117 B8 15 27 S 47 23 E
Sofievka, Ukraine 59 H7 48 6N 33 55 E
Sofikón, Greece 48 D5 37 47N 23 3 E
Sofiya, Bulgaria 50 D7 42 45N 23 20 E
Sofiya □, Bulgaria 50 D7 42 15N 23 20 E
Sōfu-Gan, Japan 69 K10 29 49N 140 21 E
Sogakofe, Ghana 113 D5 6 2N 0 39 E
Sogamoso, Colombia 168 B3 5 43N 72 56W
Sogār, Iran 97 E8 25 53N 58 6 E
Sögel, Germany 30 C3 52 50N 7 31 E
Sogeri, Papua N. G. 132 E4 9 26 S 147 35 E
Sogn og Fjordane □, Norway 18 C3 61 40N 6 45 E
Sogndalsfjøra, Norway 15 F12 61 14N 7 5 E
Søgne, Norway 15 G12 58 5N 7 48 E
Sognefjorden, Norway 15 F11 61 10N 5 50 E
Söğüt, Bilecik, Turkey 49 A12 40 2N 30 11 E
Söğüt, Burdur, Turkey 49 D11 37 2N 29 50 E
Söğüt Dağı, Turkey 49 D11 37 50N 29 55 E
Söğütköy, Turkey 49 E10 36 40N 28 8 E
Sŏgwi-po, S. Korea 75 H14 33 13N 126 34 E
Soh, Iran 97 C6 33 26N 51 27 E
Sohâg, Egypt 106 B3 26 33N 31 43 E
Sohano, Papua N. G. 132 C8 5 22 S 154 37 E
Sŏhori, N. Korea 75 D15 40 7N 128 23 E
Soignies, Belgium 24 D4 50 35N 4 5 E
Soira, Eritrea 107 E4 14 45N 39 30 E
Soissons, France 27 C10 49 25N 3 19 E
Sōja, Japan 70 C5 34 40N 133 45 E
Sojat, India 92 G5 25 55N 73 45 E
Sok →, Russia 60 D10 53 24N 50 8 E
Sokal, Ukraine 59 G3 50 31N 24 15 E
Söke, Turkey 49 D9 37 48N 27 28 E
Sokelo, Dem. Rep. of the Congo 115 D4 9 55 S 24 36 E
Sokhós, Greece 50 F7 40 48N 23 22 E
Sokhumi, Georgia 61 J5 43 0N 41 0 E
Sokki, Oued In →, Algeria 111 C5 29 30N 3 42 E
Sokna, Norway 18 D6 60 16N 9 58 E
Soknedal, Norway 18 B7 62 57N 10 13 E
Soko Banja, Serbia, Yug. 50 C5 43 40N 21 51 E
Sokodé, Togo 113 D5 9 0N 1 11 E
Sokol, Russia 58 C11 59 30N 40 5 E
Sokolac, Bos.-H. 52 G3 43 56N 18 48 E
Sokółka, Poland 54 E10 53 25N 23 30 E
Sokolo, Mali 112 C3 14 53N 6 8W
Sokolov, Czech Rep. 34 A5 50 12N 12 40 E
Sokołów Małpolski, Poland 55 H9 50 12N 22 7 E
Sokołów Podlaski, Poland 55 F9 52 25N 22 15 E
Sokoły, Poland 55 F9 52 59N 22 42 E
Sokoto, Nigeria 113 C6 13 2N 5 16 E
Sokoto □, Nigeria 113 C6 12 30N 6 0 E
Sokoto →, Nigeria 113 C5 11 20N 4 10 E
Sokuluk, Kyrgyzstan 63 B7 42 52N 74 18 E
Sol Iletsk, Russia 62 F5 51 10N 55 0 E
Sola, Norway 18 F2 58 53N 5 36 E
Sola →, Poland 55 H6 50 4N 19 15 E
Solai, Kenya 118 B4 0 2N 36 12 E
Solana, Phil. 80 C3 17 39N 121 41 E
Solander I., N.Z. 131 G1 46 34 S 166 54 E
Solano, Phil. 80 C3 16 31N 121 15 E
Solapur, India 94 F2 17 43N 75 56 E
Solca, Romania 53 C10 47 40N 25 50 E
Solda Gölü, Turkey 49 D11 37 33N 29 42 E
Soldăneşti, Moldova 53 C13 47 49N 28 48 E
Soldotna, U.S.A. 144 F10 60 29N 151 3W
Soléa □, Cyprus 38 D12 35 5N 33 4 E
Solec Kujawski, Poland 55 E5 53 5N 18 14 E
Soledad, Colombia 168 A3 10 55N 74 46W
Soledad, U.S.A. 160 J5 36 26N 121 20W
Soledad, Venezuela 169 B5 8 10N 63 34W
Sølen, Norway 18 C8 61 53N 11 31 E
Solent, The, U.K. 21 G6 50 45N 1 25W
Solenzara, France 29 G13 41 53N 9 23 E
Solesmes, France 27 B10 50 10N 3 30 E
Solfonn, Norway 15 F12 60 2N 6 57 E
Solhan, Turkey 101 C9 38 57N 41 3 E
Sølheim, Norway 18 D2 60 53N 5 27 E
Soligalich, Russia 56 C7 59 5N 42 10 E
Soligorsk = Salihorsk, Belarus 59 F4 52 51N 27 27 E
Solihull, U.K. 21 E6 52 26N 1 47W
Solikamsk, Russia 62 B6 59 38N 56 50 E
Solila, Madag. 117 C8 21 25 S 46 37 E
Solimões = Amazonas →, S. Amer. 169 D8 0 5 S 50 0W
Solin, Croatia 45 E13 43 33N 16 30 E
Solingen, Germany 30 D3 51 10N 7 5 E
Sollebrunn, Sweden 17 F6 58 8N 12 32 E
Sollefteå, Sweden 16 A11 63 12N 17 20 E
Sollentuna, Sweden 16 E11 59 26N 17 56 E
Sóller, Spain 39 B9 39 46N 2 43 E
Sollerön, Sweden 16 D8 60 55N 14 37 E
Solling, Germany 30 D5 51 42N 9 38 E
Solnechnogorsk, Russia 58 D9 56 10N 36 57 E
Solofra, Italy 47 B7 40 50N 14 51 E
Sologne, France 27 E8 47 40N 1 45 E
Solok, Indonesia 84 C2 0 45 S 100 40 E
Sololá, Guatemala 164 D1 14 49N 91 10W
Solomon, N. Fork →, U.S.A. 154 F5 39 29N 98 26W
Solomon, S. Fork →, U.S.A. 154 F5 39 25N 99 12W
Solomon Is. ■, Pac. Oc. 133 L8 6 0 S 155 0 E
Solomon Sea, Papua N. G. 132 D6 7 0 S 150 0 E
Solon, China 73 B7 46 32N 121 10 E
Solon Springs, U.S.A. 154 B9 46 22N 91 49W
Solonópole, Brazil 170 C4 5 44 S 39 1W
Solor, Indonesia 82 C2 8 27 S 123 0 E
Solotcha, Russia 58 E10 54 48N 39 53 E
Solothurn, Switz. 32 B5 47 13N 7 32 E
Solothurn □, Switz. 32 B5 47 18N 7 40 E
Solotobe, Kazakstan 63 A3 44 37N 66 3 E
Solsona, Spain 40 C6 42 0N 1 31 E
Solsvik, Norway 18 D1 60 26N 4 58 E
Solt, Hungary 52 D4 46 45N 19 1 E
Šolta, Croatia 45 E13 43 24N 16 15 E
Solţānābād, Khorāsān, Iran 97 C8 34 13N 59 58 E
Solţānābād, Khorāsān, Iran 97 B8 36 29N 58 5 E
Solţānābād, Markazī, Iran 97 C6 35 31N 51 10 E
Soltau, Germany 30 C5 52 59N 9 50 E
Soltsy, Russia 58 C6 58 10N 30 30 E
Solund, Norway 18 C1 61 5N 4 50 E
Solunska Glava, Macedonia 50 E5 41 44N 21 31 E
Solvang, U.S.A. 161 L6 34 36N 120 8W
Solvay, U.S.A. 151 C8 43 3N 76 13W
Sölvesborg, Sweden 17 H8 56 5N 14 35 E
Solvychegodsk, Russia 56 B8 61 21N 46 56 E
Solway Firth, U.K. 20 C4 54 49N 3 35W
Solwezi, Zambia 119 E2 12 11 S 26 21 E
Sōma, Japan 68 F10 37 40N 140 50 E
Soma, Turkey 49 B9 39 10N 27 35 E
Somali Pen., Africa 104 F8 7 0N 46 0 E
Somali Rep. ■, Africa 120 C3 7 0N 47 0 E
Somalia = Somali Rep. ■, Africa 120 C3 7 0N 47 0 E
Sombe Dzong, Bhutan 90 B2 27 13N 89 8 E
Sombernon, France 27 E11 47 20N 4 40 E
Sombor, Serbia, Yug. 52 E4 45 46N 19 9 E
Sombra, Canada 150 D2 42 43N 82 29W
Sombrerete, Mexico 162 C4 23 40N 103 40W
Sombrero, Anguilla 165 C7 18 37N 63 30W
Şomcuta Mare, Romania 53 C8 47 31N 23 28 E
Somers, U.S.A. 158 B6 48 5N 114 13W
Somerset, Canada 143 D9 49 25N 98 39W
Somerset, Colo., U.S.A. 159 G10 38 56N 107 28W
Somerset, Ky., U.S.A. 148 G3 37 5N 84 36W
Somerset, Mass., U.S.A. 151 E13 41 47N 71 8W
Somerset, Pa., U.S.A. 150 F5 40 1N 79 5W
Somerset □, U.K. 21 F5 51 9N 3 0W
Somerset East, S. Africa 116 E4 32 42 S 25 35 E
Somerset I., Canada 138 A10 73 30N 93 0W
Somerset West, S. Africa 116 E2 34 8 S 18 50 E
Somerton, U.S.A. 159 K6 32 36N 114 43W
Somerville, U.S.A. 151 F10 40 35N 74 38W
Someş →, Romania 52 C7 47 49N 22 43 E
Someşul Mare →, Romania 53 C8 47 9N 23 55 E
Sommariva, Australia 127 D4 26 24 S 146 36 E
Somme □, France 27 C9 49 57N 2 20 E
Somme →, France 27 B8 50 11N 1 38 E
Somme, B. de la, France 26 B8 50 14N 1 33 E
Sommen, Jönköping, Sweden 17 F8 58 12N 14 58 E
Sommen, Östergötland, Sweden 17 F9 58 0N 15 15 E
Sommepy-Tahure, France 27 C11 49 15N 4 31 E
Sömmerda, Germany 30 D7 51 9N 11 7 E
Sommesous, France 27 D11 48 44N 4 12 E
Sommières, France 29 E8 43 47N 4 6 E
Somogy □, Hungary 52 D2 46 19N 17 30 E
Somogyszob, Hungary 52 D2 46 18N 17 20 E
Somosomo Str., Fiji 133 A3 16 0 S 180 0 E
Somoto, Nic. 164 D2 13 28N 86 37W
Sompolno, Poland 55 F5 52 26N 18 30 E
Somport, Puerto de, Spain 40 C4 42 48N 0 31W
Somuncurá, Meseta de, Argentina 176 B3 41 30 S 67 0W
Son, Norway 18 E7 59 32N 10 42 E
Son Ha, Vietnam 86 E7 15 3N 108 34 E
Son Hoa, Vietnam 86 F7 13 2N 108 58 E
Son La, Vietnam 86 B4 21 20N 103 50 E
Son Servera, Spain 40 F8 39 37N 3 21 E
Son Tay, Vietnam 86 B5 21 8N 105 30 E
Soná, Panama 164 E3 8 0N 81 20W
Sonamarg, India 93 B6 34 18N 75 21 E
Sonamukhi, India 93 H12 23 18N 87 27 E
Sonamura, India 90 D3 23 29N 91 15 E
Sŏnchŏn, N. Korea 75 E13 39 48N 124 55 E
Sondags →, S. Africa 116 E4 33 44 S 25 51 E
Sóndalo, Italy 44 B7 46 20N 10 19 E
Sondar, India 93 C6 33 28N 75 56 E
Søndeled, Norway 18 F6 58 46N 9 3 E
Sønder Felding, Denmark 17 J2 55 57N 8 47 E
Sønder Omme, Denmark 17 J2 55 50N 8 54 E
Sønderborg, Denmark 17 K3 54 55N 9 49 E
Sønderjyllands Amtskommune □, Denmark 17 J3 55 10N 9 10 E
Sondershausen, Germany 30 D6 51 22N 10 51 E
Søndre Strømfjord, Greenland 10 D5 66 59N 50 40W
Sóndrio, Italy 44 B6 46 10N 9 52 E
Sone, Mozam. 119 F3 17 23 S 34 55 E
Sonepur, India 94 D6 20 55N 83 50 E
Song, Thailand 86 C3 18 28N 100 11 E
Song Cau, Vietnam 86 F7 13 27N 109 18 E
Song Xian, China 74 G7 34 12N 112 8 E
Songavatnet, Norway 18 E4 59 52N 7 32 E
Songchŏn, N. Korea 75 E14 39 12N 126 15 E
Songea, Tanzania 119 E4 10 40 S 35 40 E
Songea □, Tanzania 119 E4 10 30 S 36 0 E
Songeons, France 27 C8 49 32N 1 50 E
Songhua Hu, China 75 C14 43 35N 126 50 E
Songhua Jiang →, China 73 B8 47 45N 132 30 E
Songjiang, China 77 B13 31 1N 121 12 E
Songjin, N. Korea 75 D15 40 40N 129 10 E
Songjŏng-ni, S. Korea 75 G14 35 8N 126 47 E
Songkan, China 76 C6 28 35N 106 52 E
Songkhla, Thailand 87 J3 7 13N 100 37 E
Songming, China 76 E4 25 12N 103 2 E
Songnim, N. Korea 75 E13 38 45N 125 39 E
Songo, Angola 115 D2 7 22 S 14 51 E
Songololo, Dem. Rep. of the Congo 115 D2 5 42 S 14 2 E
Songpan, China 76 A4 32 40N 103 30 E
Songtao, China 76 C7 28 11N 109 10 E
Songwe, Dem. Rep. of the Congo 118 C2 3 20 S 26 16 E
Songwe →, Africa 119 D3 9 44 S 33 58 E
Songxi, China 77 D12 27 31N 118 44 E
Songzi, China 77 B8 30 12N 111 45 E
Sonid Youqi, China 74 C7 42 45N 112 48 E
Sonipat, India 92 E7 29 0N 77 5 E
Sonkel, Ozero, Kyrgyzstan 63 C7 41 50N 75 12 E
Sonkovo, Russia 58 D9 57 50N 37 5 E
Sonmiani, Pakistan 91 D2 25 25N 66 40 E
Sonnino, Italy 46 A6 41 25N 13 14 E
Sono →, Minas Gerais, Brazil 171 E2 17 2 S 45 32W
Sono →, Tocantins, Brazil 170 C2 9 58 S 48 11W
Sonobe, Japan 71 B7 35 6N 135 28 E
Sonogno, Switz. 33 D7 46 22N 8 47 E
Sonora, Calif., U.S.A. 160 H6 37 59N 120 23W
Sonora, Tex., U.S.A. 155 K4 30 34N 100 39W
Sonora □, Mexico 162 B2 29 0N 111 0W
Sonora →, Mexico 162 B2 28 50N 111 33W
Sonora Desert, U.S.A. 161 L12 33 40N 114 15W
Sonoyta, Mexico 162 A2 31 51N 112 50W
Sonqor, Iran 101 E12 34 47N 47 36 E
Sŏnsan, S. Korea 75 F15 36 14N 128 17 E
Sonseca, Spain 43 F7 39 42N 3 57W
Sonsonate, El Salv. 164 D2 13 43N 89 44W
Sonstorp, Sweden 17 F9 58 44N 15 38 E
Sonthofen, Germany 31 H6 47 30N 10 16 E
Soochow = Suzhou, China 77 B13 31 19N 120 38 E
Sop Hao, Laos 86 B5 20 33N 104 27 E
Sop Prap, Thailand 86 D2 17 53N 99 20 E
Sopachuy, Bolivia 173 D5 19 29 S 64 31W
Sopchoppy, U.S.A. 152 E5 30 4N 84 29W
Sopelana, Spain 40 B2 43 23N 2 58W
Soperton, U.S.A. 152 C7 32 23N 82 35W
Sopi, Indonesia 82 A3 2 34N 128 28 E
Sopo, Nahr →, Sudan 107 F2 8 40N 26 30 E
Sopot, Bulgaria 51 D8 42 39N 24 45 E
Sopot, Poland 54 D5 54 27N 18 31 E
Sopot, Serbia, Yug. 50 B4 44 29N 20 36 E
Sopotnica, Macedonia 50 E5 41 18N 21 13 E
Sopron, Hungary 52 C1 47 45N 16 32 E
Sop's Arm, Canada 141 C8 49 46N 56 56W
Sopur, India 93 B6 34 18N 74 27 E
Sør-Rondane, Antarctica 7 D4 72 0 S 25 0 E
Sør-Trøndelag □, Norway 18 A7 63 0N 11 0 E
Sora, Italy 45 G10 41 43N 13 37 E
Sorada, India 94 E7 19 45N 84 26 E
Sorah, Pakistan 92 F3 27 13N 68 56 E
Söråker, Sweden 16 B11 62 30N 17 32 E
Sorano, Italy 45 F8 42 41N 11 43 E
Sorata, Bolivia 172 D4 15 50 S 68 40W
Sorbas, Spain 41 H2 37 6N 2 7W
Sörbygden, Sweden 16 B10 62 48N 16 12 E
Sore, France 28 D3 44 18N 0 35W
Sorel, Canada 140 C5 46 0N 73 10W
Sörenberg, Switz. 32 C6 46 49N 8 2 E
Sorento, U.S.A. 156 F7 39 1N 89 35W
Soresina, Italy 44 C6 45 17N 9 51 E
Sørfjorden, Norway 18 D3 60 20N 6 37 E
Sörforsa, Sweden 16 C10 61 43N 16 58 E
Sórgono, Italy 46 B2 40 1N 9 6 E
Sorgues, France 29 D8 44 1N 4 53 E
Sorgun, Turkey 100 C6 39 46N 35 11 E
Soria, Spain 40 D2 41 43N 2 32W
Soria □, Spain 40 D2 41 46N 2 28W
Soriano, Uruguay 174 C4 33 24 S 58 19W
Soriano nel Cimino, Italy 45 F9 42 25N 12 14 E
Sorkh, Kuh-e, Iran 97 C8 35 40N 58 30 E
Sorø, Denmark 17 J5 55 26N 11 32 E
Soro, Guinea 112 C3 10 9N 9 48W
Soroca, Moldova 53 B13 48 8N 28 12 E
Sorocaba, Brazil 175 A6 23 31 S 47 27W
Sorochinsk, Russia 62 E4 52 26N 53 10 E
Soroki = Soroca, Moldova 53 B13 48 8N 28 12 E
Soron, India 93 F8 27 55N 78 45 E
Sorong, Indonesia 83 B4 0 55 S 131 15 E
Soroní, Greece 38 C10 36 21N 28 1 E
Soroti, Uganda 118 B3 1 43N 33 35 E
Sørøya, Norway 14 A20 70 40N 22 30 E
Sørøyane, Norway 18 B2 62 25N 5 32 E
Sørøysundet, Norway 14 A20 70 25N 23 0 E
Sorraia →, Portugal 43 G2 38 55N 8 53W
Sorrento, Australia 127 F3 38 22 S 144 47 E
Sorrento, Italy 47 B7 40 37N 14 22 E

Süderbrarup 285

Starachowice, Poland 55 G8 51 3N 21 2 E
Staraya Russa, Russia 58 D6 57 58N 31 23 E
Starbuck I., Kiribati 135 H12 5 37 S 155 55W
Starchiojd, Romania 53 E11 45 19N 26 11 E
Stargard Szczeciński, Poland 54 E2 53 20N 15 0 E
Stårheim, Norway 18 C2 61 56N 5 40 E
Stari Bar, Montenegro, Yug. 50 D3 42 7N 19 10 E
Stari Trg, Slovenia 45 C12 45 29N 15 7 E
Staritsa, Russia 58 D8 56 33N 34 55 E
Starke, U.S.A. 152 F7 29 57N 82 7W
Starkville, Colo., U.S.A. 155 G2 37 8N 104 30W
Starkville, Miss., U.S.A. 149 J1 33 28N 88 49W
Starnberg, Germany 31 H7 48 0N 11 21 E
Starnberger See, Germany 31 H7 47 54N 11 19 E
Starobilsk, Ukraine 59 H10 49 16N 39 0 E
Starodub, Russia 59 F7 52 30N 32 50 E
Starogard Gdański, Poland 54 E5 53 59N 18 30 E
Starokonstantinov = Starokonstyantyniv, Ukraine 59 H4 49 48N 27 10 E
Starokonstyantyniv, Ukraine 59 H4 49 48N 27 10 E
Starominskaya, Russia 59 J10 46 33N 39 0 E
Staroshcherbinovskaya, Russia 59 J10 46 40N 38 53 E
Stars Mill, U.S.A. 152 B5 33 19N 84 31W
Start Pt., U.K. 21 G4 50 13N 3 39W
Stary Sącz, Poland 55 J7 49 33N 20 35 E
Staryy Biryuzyak, Russia 61 H8 44 46N 46 50 E
Staryy Chartoriysk, Ukraine 59 G3 51 15N 25 54 E
Staryy Krym, Ukraine 59 K8 45 3N 35 8 E
Staryy Oskol, Russia 59 G9 51 19N 37 55 E
Stassfurt, Germany 30 D7 51 51N 11 35 E
Staszów, Poland 55 H8 50 33N 21 10 E
State Center, U.S.A. 156 B3 42 1N 93 10W
State College, U.S.A. 150 F7 40 48N 77 52W
Stateline, U.S.A. 160 G7 38 57N 119 56W
Staten, I. = Estados, I. de Los, Argentina 176 D4 54 40 S 64 30W
Staten I., U.S.A. 151 F10 40 35N 74 9W
Statenville, U.S.A. 152 E6 30 42N 83 2W
Statesboro, U.S.A. 152 C8 32 27N 81 47W
Statesville, U.S.A. 149 H5 35 47N 80 53W
Statham, U.S.A. 152 B6 33 58N 83 35W
Stathelle, Norway 18 E6 59 3N 9 41 E
Stauffer, U.S.A. 161 L7 34 45N 119 3W
Staunton, Ill., U.S.A. 156 F7 39 1N 89 47W
Staunton, Va., U.S.A. 148 F6 38 9N 79 4W
Stavanger, Norway 15 G11 58 57N 5 40 E
Staveley, N.Z. 131 D6 43 40 S 171 32 E
Stavelot, Belgium 24 D5 50 23N 5 55 E
Stavern, Norway 15 G14 59 0N 10 1 E
Stavoren, Neths. 24 B5 52 53N 5 22 E
Stavropol, Russia 61 H6 45 5N 42 0 E
Stavros, Cyprus 38 D11 35 1N 32 38 E
Stavrós, Greece 38 D6 35 12N 24 45 E
Stavros, Ákra, Greece 38 D6 35 26N 24 58 E
Stavroúpolis, Greece 51 E8 41 12N 24 45 E
Stawell, Australia 128 D5 37 5 S 142 47 E
Stawell →, Australia 126 C3 20 20 S 142 55 E
Stawiski, Poland 54 E9 53 22N 22 9 E
Stawiszyn, Poland 55 G5 51 56N 18 4 E
Stayner, Canada 150 B4 44 25N 80 5W
Steamboat Springs, U.S.A. 158 F10 40 29N 106 50W
Steane, Norway 18 E5 59 16N 8 33 E
Stebbins, U.S.A. 144 E7 63 31N 162 17W
Stebleva, Albania 50 E4 41 23N 20 33 E
Steckborn, Switz. 33 A7 47 44N 8 59 E
Steele, Ala., U.S.A. 152 B3 33 56N 86 12W
Steele, N. Dak., U.S.A. 154 B5 46 51N 99 55W
Steelton, U.S.A. 150 F8 40 14N 76 50W
Steelville, U.S.A. 155 G9 37 58N 91 22W
Steen River, Canada 142 B5 59 40N 117 12W
Steenkool = Bintuni, Indonesia 83 B4 2 7 S 133 32 E
Steenstrup Gletscher, Greenland 10 B5 75 15N 57 0W
Steenwijk, Neths. 24 B6 52 47N 6 7 E
Steep Pt., Australia 125 E1 26 8 S 113 8 E
Steep Rock, Canada 143 C9 51 30N 98 48W
Ştefan Vodă, Moldova 53 D14 46 27N 29 42 E
Ştefăneşti, Romania 53 C12 47 44N 27 15 E
Stefanie L. = Chew Bahir, Ethiopia 107 G4 4 40N 36 50 E
Stefansson Bay, Antarctica 7 C5 67 20 S 59 8 E
Steffisburg, Switz. 32 C5 46 47N 7 38 E
Stege, Denmark 17 K6 54 59N 12 18 E
Ştei, Romania 52 D7 46 32N 22 27 E
Steiermark □, Austria 34 D8 47 26N 15 0 E
Steigerwald, Germany 31 F6 49 44N 10 26 E
Steilacoom, U.S.A. 160 C4 47 10N 122 36W
Steinbach, Canada 143 D9 49 32N 96 40W
Steinfurt, Germany 30 C3 52 9N 7 20 E
Steinhatchee, U.S.A. 152 F6 29 40N 83 23W
Steinheim, Germany 30 D5 51 51N 9 5 E
Steinhuder Meer, Germany 30 C5 52 29N 9 21 E
Steinkjer, Norway 14 D14 64 1N 11 31 E
Steinkopf, S. Africa 116 D2 29 18 S 17 43 E
Steinshamn, Norway 18 B3 62 47N 6 28 E
Stellarton, Canada 141 C7 45 32N 62 30W
Stellenbosch, S. Africa 116 E2 33 58 S 18 50 E
Stelvio, Paso dello, Italy 33 C10 46 32N 10 27 E
Stenay, France 27 C12 49 29N 5 12 E
Stendal, Germany 30 C7 52 36N 11 53 E
Stende, Latvia 54 A9 57 11N 22 33 E
Stenhamra, Sweden 16 E11 59 20N 17 41 E
Stenstorp, Sweden 17 F7 58 17N 13 45 E
Stenungsund, Sweden 17 F5 58 6N 11 50 E
Steornabhaigh = Stornoway, U.K. 22 C2 58 13N 6 23W
Stepanakert = Xankändi, Azerbaijan 101 C12 39 52N 46 49 E
Stepanavan, Armenia 61 K7 41 1N 44 23 E
Stephen, U.S.A. 154 A6 48 27N 96 53W
Stephens, C., N.Z. 131 A8 40 42 S 173 58 E
Stephens Creek, Australia 128 A4 31 50 S 141 30 E
Stephens I., Canada 142 C2 54 10N 130 45W
Stephens I., N.Z. 131 A9 40 40 S 174 1 E
Stephenville, Canada 141 C8 48 31N 58 35W
Stephenville, U.S.A. 155 J5 32 13N 98 12W
Stepnica, Poland 54 E1 53 38N 14 36 E
Stepnoi = Elista, Russia 61 G7 46 16N 44 14 E
Stepnoye, Russia 62 D8 54 4N 60 26 E
Steppe, Asia 66 D9 50 0N 50 0 E
Stereá Ellas □, Greece 48 C4 38 50N 23 0 E
Sterkstroom, S. Africa 116 E4 31 32 S 26 32 E
Sterling, Alaska, U.S.A. 144 F10 60 32N 150 46W
Sterling, Colo., U.S.A. 154 E3 40 37N 103 13W
Sterling, Ga., U.S.A. 152 D8 31 16N 81 34W
Sterling, Ill., U.S.A. 156 C7 41 48N 89 42W
Sterling, Kans., U.S.A. 154 F5 38 13N 98 12W
Sterling City, U.S.A. 155 K4 31 51N 101 0W
Sterling Heights, U.S.A. 157 B13 42 35N 83 0W
Sterling Run, U.S.A. 150 E6 41 25N 78 12W
Sterlitamak, Russia 62 E6 53 40N 56 0 E
Sternberg, Germany 30 B7 53 42N 11 50 E
Šternberk, Czech Rep. 35 B10 49 45N 17 15 E
Stérnes, Greece 38 D6 35 30N 24 9 E
Sterzing = Vipiteno, Italy 45 B8 46 54N 11 26 E
Stettin = Szczecin, Poland 54 E1 53 27N 14 27 E
Stettiner Haff, Germany 30 B10 53 47N 14 15 E
Stettler, Canada 142 C6 52 19N 112 40W
Steubenville, U.S.A. 150 F4 40 22N 80 37W
Stevenage, U.K. 21 F7 51 55N 0 13W
Stevens Point, U.S.A. 154 C10 44 31N 89 34W
Stevens Pottery, U.S.A. 152 C6 32 57N 83 17W
Stevenson, U.S.A. 160 E5 45 42N 121 53W
Stevenson L., Canada 143 C9 53 55N 96 0W
Stevns Klint, Denmark 17 J6 55 17N 12 28 E
Steward, U.S.A. 156 C7 41 51N 89 1W
Stewardson, U.S.A. 157 E8 39 16N 88 38W
Stewart, Canada 142 B3 55 56N 129 57W
Stewart, Ga., U.S.A. 152 B6 33 25N 83 52W
Stewart, Nev., U.S.A. 160 F7 39 5N 119 46W
Stewart, C., Australia 126 A1 11 57 S 134 56 E
Stewart, I., Chile 176 D2 54 50 S 71 15W
Stewart I., N.Z. 131 G2 46 58 S 167 54 E
Stewarts Point, U.S.A. 160 G3 38 39N 123 24W
Stewartsville, U.S.A. 156 E2 39 45N 94 30W
Stewiacke, Canada 141 C7 45 9N 63 22W
Steynsburg, S. Africa 116 E4 31 15 S 25 49 E
Steyr, Austria 34 C7 48 3N 14 25 E
Steyr →, Austria 34 C7 48 3N 14 25 E
Steytlerville, S. Africa 116 E3 33 17 S 24 19 E
Stia, Italy 45 E8 43 48N 11 42 E
Stigler, U.S.A. 155 H7 35 15N 95 8W
Stigliano, Italy 47 B9 40 24N 16 14 E
Stigtomta, Sweden 17 F10 58 47N 16 48 E
Stikine →, Canada 142 B2 56 40N 132 30W
Stilfontein, S. Africa 116 D4 26 51 S 26 50 E
Stilís, Greece 48 C4 38 55N 22 47 E
Stillmore, U.S.A. 152 C7 32 27N 82 13W
Stillwater, N.Z. 131 C6 42 27 S 171 20 E
Stillwater, Minn., U.S.A. 154 C8 45 3N 92 49W
Stillwater, N.Y., U.S.A. 151 D11 42 55N 73 41W
Stillwater, Okla., U.S.A. 155 G6 36 7N 97 4W
Stillwater Range, U.S.A. 158 G4 39 50N 118 5W
Stillwell, U.S.A. 152 C8 32 23N 81 15W
Stilo, Pta., Italy 47 D9 38 25N 16 35 E
Stilwell, U.S.A. 155 H7 35 49N 94 38W
Štip, Macedonia 50 E6 41 42N 22 10 E
Stíra, Greece 48 C6 38 9N 24 14 E
Stirling, Australia 126 B3 17 12 S 141 35 E
Stirling, Canada 142 D6 49 30N 112 30W
Stirling, N.Z. 131 G4 46 14 S 169 49 E
Stirling, U.K. 22 E5 56 8N 3 57W
Stirling □, U.K. 22 E4 56 12N 4 18W
Stirling Ra., Australia 125 F2 34 23 S 118 0 E
Stittsville, Canada 151 A9 45 15N 75 55W
Stjernøya, Norway 14 A20 70 20N 22 40 E
Stjørdalshalsen, Norway 14 E14 63 29N 10 51 E
Stock Island, U.S.A. 153 L8 24 32N 81 34W
Stockach, Germany 31 H5 47 50N 9 1 E
Stockaryd, Sweden 17 G8 57 19N 14 36 E
Stockbridge, Ga., U.S.A. 152 B5 33 33N 84 14W
Stockbridge, Mich., U.S.A. 157 B12 42 27N 84 11W
Stockerau, Austria 35 C9 48 24N 16 12 E
Stockett, U.S.A. 158 C8 47 21N 111 10W
Stockholm, Sweden 16 E12 59 20N 18 3 E
Stockholms län □, Sweden 16 E12 59 30N 18 20 E
Stockhorn, Switz. 32 C5 46 42N 7 33 E
Stockport, U.K. 20 D5 53 25N 2 9W
Stocksbridge, U.K. 20 D6 53 29N 1 35W
Stockton, Australia 129 B9 32 50 S 151 47 E
Stockton, Calif., U.S.A. 160 H5 37 58N 121 17W
Stockton, Ill., U.S.A. 156 B6 42 21N 90 1W
Stockton, Kans., U.S.A. 154 F5 39 26N 99 16W
Stockton, Mo., U.S.A. 155 G8 37 42N 93 48W
Stockton-on-Tees, U.K. 20 C6 54 35N 1 19W
Stockton-on-Tees □, U.K. 20 C6 54 35N 1 19W
Stoczek Łukowski, Poland 55 G8 51 58N 21 58 E
Stöde, Sweden 16 B10 62 28N 16 35 E
Stoeng Treng, Cambodia 86 F5 13 31N 105 58 E
Stoer, Pt. of, U.K. 22 C3 58 16N 5 23W
Stogovo, Macedonia 50 E4 41 31N 20 38 E
Stoholm, Denmark 17 H3 56 30N 9 8 E
Stoke, N.Z. 131 B8 41 19 S 173 14 E
Stoke-on-Trent, U.K. 20 D5 53 1N 2 11W
Stoke-on-Trent □, U.K. 20 D5 53 1N 2 11W
Stokes Bay, Canada 140 D3 45 0N 81 28W
Stokes Pt., Australia 126 G3 40 10 S 143 56 E
Stokes Ra., Australia 124 C5 15 50 S 130 50 E
Stokkseyri, Iceland 11 D5 63 50N 21 2W
Stokksnes, Iceland 11 C12 64 14N 14 58W
Stokmarknes, Norway 14 B16 68 34N 14 54 E
Stolac, Bos.-H. 50 C1 43 5N 17 59 E
Stolberg, Germany 30 E2 50 47N 6 13 E
Stolbovoy, Ostrov, Russia 65 D17 74 44N 135 14 E
Stolbtsy = Stowbtsy, Belarus 58 F4 53 30N 26 43 E
Stolin, Belarus 59 G4 51 53N 26 50 E
Stöllet, Sweden 16 D7 60 26N 13 15 E
Stolnici, Romania 53 F9 44 31N 24 48 E
Stomíon, Greece 38 D5 35 21N 23 32 E
Ston, Croatia 45 F14 42 51N 17 43 E
Stone, U.K. 20 E5 52 55N 2 9W
Stone Mountain, U.S.A. 152 B5 33 49N 84 10W
Stonehaven, U.K. 22 E6 56 59N 2 12W
Stonehenge, Australia 126 C3 24 22 S 143 17 E
Stonehenge, U.K. 21 F6 51 9N 1 45W
Stonewall, Canada 143 C9 50 10N 97 19W
Stongfjorden, Norway 18 C2 61 26N 5 12 E
Stonington, U.S.A. 156 E7 39 44N 89 12W
Stony L., Man., Canada 143 B9 58 51N 98 40W
Stony L., Ont., Canada 150 B6 44 30N 78 5W
Stony Rapids, Canada 143 B7 59 16N 105 50W
Stony Tunguska = Tunguska, Podkamennaya →, Russia 65 C10 61 50N 90 13 E
Stonyford, U.S.A. 160 F4 39 23N 122 33W
Stopnica, Poland 55 H7 50 27N 20 57 E
Storå, Sweden 16 E9 59 42N 15 6 E
Storå →, Denmark 17 H2 56 20N 8 19 E
Stora Gla, Sweden 16 E6 59 30N 12 30 E
Stora Le, Sweden 16 E5 59 5N 11 55 E
Stora Lulevatten, Sweden 14 C18 67 10N 19 30 E
Stóra-Vatnshorn, Iceland 11 B5 65 4N 21 33W
Storavan, Sweden 14 D18 65 45N 18 10 E
Stord, Norway 15 G11 59 52N 5 23 E
Stordal, Norway 18 B4 62 23N 7 0 E
Store Bælt, Denmark 17 J4 55 20N 11 0 E
Store Creek, Australia 129 B8 32 54 S 149 6 E
Store Heddinge, Denmark 17 J6 55 18N 12 23 E
Store-Jukleeggi, Norway 18 C5 61 3N 8 12 E
Store Koldewey, Greenland 10 B9 76 30N 19 0W
Store Sølnkletten, Norway 18 C7 61 59N 10 16 E
Store Sotra, Norway 18 D1 60 18N 5 4 E
Storebro, Sweden 17 G9 57 35N 15 52 E
Støren, Norway 18 A7 63 3N 10 18 E
Storerikvollen, Norway 18 A8 63 7N 11 58 E
Storfjellseter, Norway 18 C7 61 40N 10 30 E
Storfjorden, Møre og Romsdal, Norway 18 B3 62 8N 6 33 E
Storfjorden, Møre og Romsdal, Norway 18 B3 62 28N 6 35 E
Storfors, Sweden 16 E8 59 32N 14 17 E
Stóridalur, Iceland 11 D7 63 38N 19 57W
Stórinúpur, Iceland 11 C6 64 3N 20 10W
Storli, Norway 18 B6 62 42N 9 5 E
Storlien, Sweden 16 A6 63 20N 12 5 E
Storm B., Australia 126 G4 43 10 S 147 30 E
Storm Lake, U.S.A. 154 D7 42 39N 95 13W
Stormberge, S. Africa 116 E4 31 16 S 26 17 E
Stormsrivier, S. Africa 116 E3 33 59 S 23 52 E
Stornoway, U.K. 22 C2 58 13N 6 23W
Storo, Italy 44 C7 45 51N 10 35 E
Storozhinets = Storozhynets, Ukraine 59 H3 48 14N 25 45 E
Storozhynets, Ukraine 59 H3 48 14N 25 45 E
Storsjøen, Hedmark, Norway 18 D8 60 20N 11 40 E
Storsjøen, Hedmark, Norway 18 C8 61 30N 11 14 E
Storsjön, Gävleborg, Sweden 16 D10 60 35N 16 45 E
Storsjön, Jämtland, Sweden 16 C7 62 48N 13 7 E
Storsjön, Jämtland, Sweden 16 A8 63 9N 14 30 E
Storstrøms Amtskommune □, Denmark 17 J5 54 50N 11 45 E
Storuman, Sweden 14 D17 65 5N 17 10 E
Storuman, sjö, Sweden 14 D17 65 13N 16 50 E
Storvätteshågna, Sweden 16 B6 62 6N 12 30 E
Storvigelen, Norway 18 B9 62 32N 12 2 E
Storvik, Sweden 16 D10 60 35N 16 33 E
Storvreta, Sweden 16 E11 59 58N 17 44 E
Story City, U.S.A. 156 B3 42 11N 93 36W
Stoughton, Canada 143 D8 49 40N 103 0W
Stoughton, U.S.A. 156 B8 42 55N 89 13W
Stour →, Dorset, U.K. 21 G6 50 43N 1 47W
Stour →, Kent, U.K. 21 F9 51 18N 1 22 E
Stour →, Suffolk, U.K. 21 F9 51 57N 1 4 E
Stourbridge, U.K. 21 E5 52 28N 2 8W
Stout, L., Canada 143 C10 52 0N 94 40W
Stovall, U.S.A. 152 C5 32 58N 84 51W
Stove Pipe Wells Village, U.S.A. 161 J9 36 35N 117 11W
Støvring, Denmark 17 H3 56 54N 9 50 E
Stowbtsy, Belarus 58 F4 53 30N 26 43 E
Stowmarket, U.K. 21 E9 52 12N 1 0 E
Strabane, U.K. 23 B4 54 50N 7 27W
Stracin, Macedonia 50 D6 42 13N 22 2 E
Stradella, Italy 44 C6 45 5N 9 18 E
Strahan, Australia 126 G4 42 9 S 145 20 E
Strajitsa, Bulgaria 51 C9 43 14N 25 58 E
Strakonice, Czech Rep. 34 B6 49 15N 13 53 E
Straldzha, Bulgaria 51 D10 42 35N 26 40 E
Stralsund, Germany 30 A9 54 18N 13 4 E
Strand, Norway 18 C8 61 17N 11 17 E
Strand, S. Africa 116 E2 34 9 S 18 48 E
Stranda, Møre og Romsdal, Norway 15 E12 62 19N 6 58 E
Stranda, Nord-Trøndelag, Norway 14 E14 63 33N 10 14 E
Strandarkirkja, Iceland 11 D5 63 50N 21 42W
Strandasýsla □, Iceland 11 B5 65 45N 21 45W
Strandby, Denmark 17 G4 57 30N 10 29 E
Strangford L., U.K. 23 B6 54 30N 5 37W
Strängnäs, Sweden 16 E11 59 23N 17 2 E
Strangsville, U.S.A. 150 E3 41 19N 81 50W
Stranraer, U.K. 22 G3 54 54N 5 1W
Strasbourg, Canada 143 C8 51 4N 104 55W
Strasbourg, France 27 D14 48 35N 7 42 E
Strasburg, Germany 30 B9 53 30N 13 43 E
Strasburg, U.S.A. 154 B4 46 8N 100 10W
Străşeni, Moldova 53 C13 47 8N 28 36 E
Stråssa, Sweden 16 E9 59 44N 15 12 E
Stratford, N.S.W., Australia 129 B9 32 7 S 151 55 E
Stratford, Vic., Australia 129 D7 37 59 S 147 7 E
Stratford, Canada 140 D3 43 23N 81 0W
Stratford, N.Z. 130 F3 39 20 S 174 19 E
Stratford, Calif., U.S.A. 160 J7 36 11N 119 49W
Stratford, Conn., U.S.A. 151 E11 41 12N 73 8W
Stratford, Tex., U.S.A. 155 G3 36 20N 102 4W
Stratford-upon-Avon, U.K. 21 E6 52 12N 1 42W
Strath Spey, U.K. 22 D5 57 9N 3 49W
Strathalbyn, Australia 128 C3 35 13 S 138 53 E
Strathaven, U.K. 22 F4 55 40N 4 5W
Strathcona Prov. Park, Canada 142 D3 49 38N 125 40W
Strathmore, Australia 126 B3 17 50 S 142 35 E
Strathmore, Canada 142 C6 51 5N 113 18W
Strathmore, U.K. 22 E5 56 37N 3 7W
Strathmore, U.S.A. 160 J7 36 9N 119 4W
Strathnaver, Canada 142 C4 53 20N 122 33W
Strathpeffer, U.K. 22 D4 57 35N 4 32W
Strathroy, Canada 140 D3 42 58N 81 38W
Strathy Pt., U.K. 22 C4 58 36N 4 1W
Stratton, U.S.A. 154 F3 39 19N 102 36W
Straubing, Germany 31 G8 48 52N 12 34 E
Straumnes, Iceland 11 A3 66 26N 23 8W
Strausberg, Germany 30 C9 52 35N 13 54 E
Strawberry Point, U.S.A. 156 B5 42 41N 91 32W
Strawberry Reservoir, U.S.A. 158 F8 40 8N 111 9W
Strawn, U.S.A. 155 J5 32 33N 98 30W
Strážnice, Czech Rep. 35 C10 48 54N 17 19 E
Streaky B., Australia 127 E1 32 48 S 134 13 E
Streaky Bay, Australia 127 E1 32 51 S 134 18 E
Streator, U.S.A. 154 E10 41 8N 88 50W
Středočeský □, Czech Rep. 34 B7 49 55N 14 30 E
Streeter, U.S.A. 154 B5 46 39N 99 21W
Streetsville, Canada 150 C5 43 35N 79 42W
Strehaia, Romania 53 F8 44 37N 23 10 E
Strelcha, Bulgaria 51 D8 42 25N 24 19 E
Strelka, Russia 65 D10 58 5N 93 3 E
Streng →, Cambodia 86 F4 13 12N 103 37 E
Stresa, Italy 44 C5 45 52N 8 28 E
Streymoy, Færoe Is. 14 E9 62 8N 7 5W
Strezhevoy, Russia 64 C8 60 42N 77 34 E
Střibro, Czech Rep. 34 A6 49 44N 13 0 E
Strickland →, Papua N. G. 132 D1 7 35 S 141 36 E
Strimón →, Greece 50 F7 40 46N 23 51 E
Strimonikós Kólpos, Greece 50 F7 40 33N 24 0 E
Stroeder, Argentina 176 B4 40 12 S 62 37W
Strofádhes, Greece 48 D3 37 15N 21 0 E
Stroma, U.K. 22 C5 58 41N 3 7W
Strómboli, Italy 47 D8 38 47N 15 13 E
Stromeferry, U.K. 22 D3 57 21N 5 33W
Strømmen, Norway 18 E7 59 58N 10 59 E
Stromness, U.K. 22 C5 58 58N 3 17W
Strömsbruk, Sweden 16 C11 61 52N 17 18 E
Stromsburg, U.S.A. 154 E6 41 7N 97 36W
Strömsnäsbruk, Sweden 17 H7 56 35N 13 45 E
Strömstad, Sweden 17 F5 58 56N 11 10 E
Strömsund, Sweden 14 E16 63 51N 15 33 E
Stronghurst, U.S.A. 156 D6 40 45N 90 55W
Strongilí, Greece 49 E11 36 6N 29 42 E
Stróngoli, Italy 47 C10 39 16N 17 3 E
Stronie Śląskie, Poland 55 H3 50 18N 16 53 E
Stronsay, U.K. 22 B6 59 7N 2 35W
Stropkov, Slovak Rep. 35 B14 49 13N 21 39 E
Stroud, U.K. 21 F5 51 45N 2 13W
Stroud Road, Australia 129 B9 32 18 S 151 57 E
Stroudsburg, U.S.A. 151 F9 40 59N 75 12W
Stroumbi, Cyprus 38 E11 34 53N 32 29 E
Struer, Denmark 17 H2 56 30N 8 35 E
Struga, Macedonia 50 E4 41 11N 20 44 E
Strugi Krasnyye, Russia 58 C5 58 21N 29 1 E
Strumica, Macedonia 50 E6 41 28N 22 41 E
Strumica →, Europe 50 E7 41 20N 23 22 E
Struthers, Canada 140 C2 48 41N 85 51W
Struthers, U.S.A. 150 E4 41 4N 80 39W
Stryama, Bulgaria 51 D8 42 16N 24 54 E
Stryker, U.S.A. 158 B6 48 41N 114 46W
Stryków, Poland 55 G6 51 55N 19 33 E
Stryn, Norway 18 C3 61 54N 6 43 E
Stryy, Ukraine 59 H2 49 16N 23 48 E
Strzegom, Poland 55 H3 50 58N 16 20 E
Strzelce Krajeńskie, Poland 55 F2 52 52N 15 33 E
Strzelce Opolskie, Poland 55 H5 50 31N 18 18 E
Strzelecki Cr. →, Australia 127 D2 29 37 S 139 59 E
Strzelin, Poland 55 H4 50 46N 17 2 E
Strzelno, Poland 55 F5 52 35N 18 9 E
Strzybnica, Poland 55 H5 50 28N 18 48 E
Strzyżów, Poland 55 J8 49 52N 21 47 E
Stuart, Fla., U.S.A. 149 M5 27 12N 80 15W
Stuart, Iowa, U.S.A. 156 C2 41 30N 94 19W
Stuart, Nebr., U.S.A. 154 D5 42 36N 99 8W
Stuart →, Canada 142 C4 54 0N 123 35W
Stuart Bluff Ra., Australia 124 D5 22 50 S 131 52 E
Stuart I., U.S.A. 144 E7 63 35N 162 30W
Stuart L., Canada 142 C4 54 30N 124 30W
Stuart Mts., N.Z. 131 F2 45 2 S 167 39 E
Stuart Ra., Australia 127 D1 29 10 S 134 56 E
Stubbekøbing, Denmark 17 K6 54 53N 12 9 E
Stuben, Austria 34 D3 47 10N 10 8 E
Studen Kladenets, Yazovir, Bulgaria 51 E9 41 37N 25 30 E
Studenka, Czech Rep. 35 B11 49 44N 18 5 E
Studholme, N.Z. 131 E6 44 42 S 171 9 E
Stugudal, Norway 18 B8 62 53N 11 53 E
Stugun, Sweden 16 A9 63 10N 15 40 E
Stuhr, Germany 30 B4 53 5N 8 44 E
Stull, L., Canada 140 B1 54 24N 92 34W
Stung Treng = Stoeng Treng, Cambodia 86 F5 13 31N 105 58 E
Stupart →, Canada 143 B10 56 0N 93 25W
Stupava, Slovak Rep. 35 C10 48 17N 17 2 E
Stupino, Russia 58 E10 54 57N 38 2 E
Sturgeon B., Canada 143 C9 52 0N 97 50W
Sturgeon Bay, U.S.A. 148 C2 44 50N 87 23W
Sturgeon Falls, Canada 140 C4 46 25N 79 57W
Sturgeon L., Alta., Canada 142 B5 55 6N 117 32W
Sturgeon L., Ont., Canada 140 C1 50 0N 90 45W
Sturgeon L., Ont., Canada 150 B6 44 28N 78 43W
Sturgis, Mich., U.S.A. 157 C11 41 48N 85 25W
Sturgis, S. Dak., U.S.A. 154 C3 44 25N 103 31W
Sturkö, Sweden 17 H9 56 5N 15 42 E
Štúrovo, Slovak Rep. 35 D11 47 48N 18 41 E
Sturt Cr. →, Australia 124 C4 19 8 S 127 50 E
Sturt Creek, Australia 124 C4 19 12 S 128 8 E
Sturts Meadows, Australia 128 A4 31 18 S 141 42 E
Stutterheim, S. Africa 116 E4 32 33 S 27 28 E
Stuttgart, Germany 31 G5 48 48N 9 11 E
Stuttgart, U.S.A. 155 H9 34 30N 91 33W
Stuyvesant, U.S.A. 151 D11 42 23N 73 45W
Stykkishólmur, Iceland 11 B4 65 2N 22 40W
Styria = Steiermark □, Austria 34 D8 47 26N 15 0 E
Styrsö, Sweden 17 G5 57 37N 11 46 E
Su-no-Saki, Japan 71 C11 34 58N 139 45 E
Su Xian, China 74 H9 33 41N 116 59 E
Suai, Indonesia 82 C3 9 21 S 125 17 E
Suakin, Sudan 106 D4 19 8N 37 20 E
Sual, Phil. 80 C3 16 4N 120 5 E
Suan, N. Korea 75 E14 38 42N 126 22 E
Suapure →, Venezuela 168 B4 6 48N 67 1W
Suaqui, Mexico 162 B3 29 12N 109 41W
Suatá →, Venezuela 169 B4 7 52N 65 22W
Subang, Indonesia 85 D3 6 34 S 107 45 E
Subansiri →, India 90 B4 26 48N 93 50 E
Subayhah, Si. Arabia 96 D3 30 2N 38 50 E
Subcetate, Romania 52 E8 45 36N 23 0 E
Subi, Indonesia 85 B3 2 58N 108 50 E
Subiaco, Italy 45 G10 41 56N 13 5 E
Subotica, Serbia, Yug. 52 D4 46 6N 19 39 E
Success, Canada 143 C7 50 28N 108 6W
Suceava, Romania 53 C11 47 38N 26 16 E
Suceava □, Romania 53 C10 47 37N 25 40 E
Suceava →, Romania 53 C11 47 32N 26 32 E
Sucha-Beskidzka, Poland 55 J6 49 44N 19 35 E
Suchań, Poland 55 E2 53 18N 15 18 E
Suchan, Russia 68 C6 43 8N 133 9 E
Suchedniów, Poland 55 G7 51 3N 20 49 E
Suchitoto, El Salv. 164 D2 13 56N 89 0W
Suchou = Suzhou, China 77 B13 31 19N 120 38 E
Süchow = Xuzhou, China 75 G9 34 18N 117 10 E
Suchowola, Poland 54 E10 53 33N 23 3 E
Sucio →, Colombia 168 B2 7 27N 77 7W
Suck →, Ireland 23 C3 53 17N 8 3W
Suckling, Mt., Papua N. G. 132 E5 9 49 S 148 53 E
Sucre, Bolivia 173 D4 19 0 S 65 15W
Sucre, Colombia 168 B3 8 49N 74 44W
Sucre □, Colombia 168 B2 8 50N 75 40W
Sucre □, Venezuela 169 A5 10 25N 63 30W
Sucuaro, Colombia 168 C4 4 34N 68 50W
Sućuraj, Croatia 45 E14 43 10N 17 8 E
Sucuriju, Brazil 170 A2 1 39N 49 57W
Sucuriú →, Brazil 173 E7 20 47 S 51 38W
Sud, Pte., Canada 141 C7 49 3N 62 14W
Sud-Ouest, Pte. du, Canada 141 C7 49 23N 63 36W
Suda →, Russia 58 C9 59 0N 37 40 E
Sudak, Ukraine 59 K8 44 51N 34 57 E
Sudan, U.S.A. 155 H3 34 4N 102 32W
Sudan ■, Africa 107 E3 15 0N 30 0 E
Sudbury, Canada 140 C3 46 30N 81 0W
Sudbury, U.K. 21 E8 52 2N 0 45 E
Sûdd, Sudan 107 F3 8 20N 30 0 E
Suddie, Guyana 169 B6 7 8N 58 29W
Süderbrarup, Germany 30 A5 54 38N 9 45 E

Tamarinda 287

Swan L., Canada 143 C8 52 30N 100 40W
Swan Reach, Australia 128 C3 34 35 S 139 37 E
Swan River, Canada 143 C8 52 10N 101 16W
Swanage, U.K. 21 G6 50 36N 1 58W
Swansea, Australia 129 B9 33 3 S 151 35 E
Swansea, U.K. 21 F4 51 37N 3 57W
Swansea, U.S.A. 152 B9 33 44N 81 6W
Swansea □, U.K. 21 F3 51 38N 4 3W
Swar →, Pakistan 93 B5 34 40N 72 5 E
Swartberge, S. Africa 116 E3 33 20 S 22 0 E
Swartmodder, S. Africa 116 D3 28 1 S 20 32 E
Swartruggens, S. Africa 116 D4 25 39 S 26 42 E
Swarzędz, Poland 55 F4 52 25N 17 4 E
Swastika, Canada 140 C3 48 7N 80 6W
Swatow = Shantou, China 77 F11 23 18N 116 40 E
Swaziland ■, Africa 117 D5 26 30 S 31 30 E
Sweden ■, Europe 15 G16 57 0N 15 0 E
Swedru, Ghana 113 D4 5 32N 0 41W
Sweet Home, U.S.A. 158 D2 44 24N 122 44W
Sweet Springs, U.S.A. 156 F3 38 58N 93 25W
Sweetwater, Nev., U.S.A. 160 G7 38 27N 119 9W
Sweetwater, Tex., U.S.A. 155 J4 32 28N 100 25W
Sweetwater →, U.S.A. 158 E10 42 31N 107 2W
Swellendam, S. Africa 116 E3 34 1 S 20 26 E
Swider →, Poland 55 F8 52 6N 21 14 E
Świdnica, Poland 55 H3 50 50N 16 30 E
Świdnik, Poland 55 G9 51 13N 22 39 E
Świdwin, Poland 54 E2 53 47N 15 49 E
Świebodzice, Poland 55 H3 50 51N 16 20 E
Świebodzin, Poland 55 F2 52 15N 15 31 E
Świecie, Poland 54 E5 53 25N 18 30 E
Swierzawa, Poland 55 G2 51 1N 15 54 E
Świętokrzyskie, Góry, Poland 55 H7 51 0N 20 30 E
Swift Current, Canada 143 C7 50 20N 107 45W
Swiftcurrent →, Canada 143 C7 50 38N 107 44W
Swilly, L., Ireland 23 A4 55 12N 7 33W
Swindle, I., Canada 142 C3 52 30N 128 35W
Swindon, U.K. 21 F6 51 34N 1 46W
Swindon □, U.K. 21 F6 51 34N 1 46W
Swinemünde = Świnoujście, Poland 54 E1 53 54N 14 16 E
Swinford, Ireland 23 C3 53 57N 8 58W
Świnoujście, Poland 54 E1 53 54N 14 16 E
Switzerland ■, Europe 32 D6 46 30N 8 0 E
Swords, Ireland 23 C5 53 28N 6 13W
Swords, U.S.A. 152 B6 33 33N 83 18W
Syasstroy, Russia 58 B7 60 9N 32 33 E
Sycamore, Ga., U.S.A. 152 D6 31 40N 83 38W
Sycamore, S.C., U.S.A. 152 B9 33 2N 81 13W
Sychevka, Russia 58 E8 55 59N 34 16 E
Syców, Poland 55 G4 51 19N 17 40 E
Sydney, Australia 129 B9 33 53 S 151 10 E
Sydney, Canada 141 C7 46 7N 60 7W
Sydney Mines, Canada 141 C7 46 18N 60 15W
Sydprøven, Greenland 10 E6 60 30N 45 35W
Sydra, G. of = Surt, Khalīj, Libya 108 B3 31 40N 18 30 E
Syeverodonetsk, Ukraine 59 H10 48 58N 38 35 E
Syfteland, Norway 18 D2 60 14N 5 27 E
Syke, Germany 30 C4 52 55N 8 50 E
Sykkylven, Norway 18 B3 62 23N 6 35 E
Syktyvkar, Russia 56 B9 61 45N 50 40 E
Sylacauga, U.S.A. 153 B3 33 10N 86 15W
Sylarna, Sweden 14 E15 63 2N 12 13 E
Sylhet, Bangla. 90 C3 24 54N 91 52 E
Sylt, Germany 30 A4 54 54N 8 22 E
Sylte, Norway 18 B4 62 18N 7 17 E
Sylva →, Russia 62 B6 58 0N 56 54 E
Sylvan Lake, Canada 142 C6 52 20N 114 3W
Sylvania, Ga., U.S.A. 152 C8 32 45N 81 38W
Sylvania, Ohio, U.S.A. 157 C13 41 43N 83 42W
Sylvester, U.S.A. 152 D6 31 32N 83 50W
Sym, Russia 64 C9 60 20N 88 18 E
Symón, Mexico 162 C4 24 42N 102 35W
Synelnykove, Ukraine 59 H8 48 25N 35 30 E
Synnfjell, Norway 18 C6 61 5N 9 46 E
Synnott Ra., Australia 124 C4 16 30 S 125 20 E
Syracuse, Ind., U.S.A. 157 C11 41 26N 85 45W
Syracuse, Kans., U.S.A. 155 G4 37 59N 101 45W
Syracuse, N.Y., U.S.A. 151 C8 43 3N 76 9W
Syrdarya = Sirdaryo, Uzbekistan 63 C4 40 50N 68 40 E
Syrdarya →, Kazakstan 64 E7 46 3N 61 0 E
Syria ■, Asia 101 E8 35 0N 38 0 E
Syriam, Burma 90 G6 16 44N 96 19 E
Syrian Desert = Ash Shām, Bādiyat, Asia 66 F7 32 0N 40 0 E
Sysert, Russia 62 C8 56 29N 60 49 E
Sysslebäck, Sweden 16 D6 60 44N 12 52 E
Syvde, Norway 18 B2 62 5N 5 44 E
Syzran, Russia 60 D9 53 12N 48 30 E
Szabolcs-Szatmár-Bereg □, Hungary 52 B6 48 2N 21 45 E
Szadek, Poland 55 G5 51 41N 18 59 E
Szamocin, Poland 55 E4 53 2N 17 7 E
Szamos →, Hungary 52 B7 48 7N 22 20 E
Szamotuły, Poland 55 F3 52 37N 16 33 E
Száraz →, Hungary 52 D6 46 10N 21 15 E
Szarvas, Hungary 52 D5 46 50N 20 38 E
Százhalombatta, Hungary 52 C3 47 20N 18 58 E
Szczawnica, Poland 55 J7 49 26N 20 30 E
Szczebrzeszyn, Poland 55 H9 50 42N 22 59 E
Szczecin, Poland 54 E1 53 27N 14 27 E
Szczecin □, Poland 54 E1 53 25N 14 32 E
Szczecinek, Poland 54 E3 53 43N 16 41 E
Szczeciński, Zalew = Stettiner Haff, Germany 30 B10 53 47N 14 15 E
Szczekociny, Poland 55 H6 50 38N 19 48 E
Szczucin, Poland 55 H8 50 18N 21 4 E
Szczuczyn, Poland 54 E9 53 36N 22 19 E
Szczyrk, Poland 55 J6 49 43N 19 2 E
Szczytna, Poland 55 H3 50 25N 16 28 E
Szczytno, Poland 54 E7 53 33N 21 0 E
Szechwan = Sichuan □, China 76 B5 30 30N 103 0 E
Szécsény, Hungary 52 B4 48 7N 19 30 E
Szeged, Hungary 52 D5 46 16N 20 10 E
Szeghalom, Hungary 52 C6 47 1N 21 10 E
Székesfehérvár, Hungary 52 C3 47 15N 18 25 E
Szekszárd, Hungary 52 D3 46 22N 18 42 E
Szendrő, Hungary 52 B5 48 24N 20 41 E
Szentendre, Hungary 52 C4 47 39N 19 4 E
Szentes, Hungary 52 D5 46 39N 20 21 E
Szentgotthárd, Hungary 52 D1 46 58N 16 19 E
Szentlőrinc, Hungary 52 D3 46 3N 18 1 E
Szerencs, Hungary 52 B6 48 10N 21 12 E
Szigetszentmiklós, Hungary 52 C4 47 21N 19 3 E
Szigetvár, Hungary 52 D2 46 3N 17 46 E
Szikszó, Hungary 52 B5 48 12N 20 56 E
Szklarska Poreba, Poland 55 H2 50 50N 15 33 E
Szkwa →, Poland 55 E8 53 11N 21 43 E
Szlichtyngowa, Poland 55 G3 51 42N 16 15 E
Szob, Hungary 52 C3 47 48N 18 53 E
Szolnok, Hungary 52 C5 47 10N 20 15 E
Szombathely, Hungary 52 C1 47 14N 16 38 E
Szprotawa, Poland 55 G2 51 33N 15 35 E
Sztum, Poland 54 E6 53 55N 19 1 E
Sztutowo, Poland 54 D6 54 20N 19 15 E
Szubin, Poland 55 E4 53 1N 17 45 E
Szydłowiec, Poland 55 G7 51 15N 20 51 E
Szypliszki, Poland 54 D10 54 17N 23 2 E

T

Ta Khli Khok, Thailand 86 E3 15 18N 100 20 E
Ta Lai, Vietnam 87 G6 11 24N 107 23 E
Tab, Hungary 52 D3 46 44N 18 2 E
Tabacal, Argentina 174 A3 23 15 S 64 15W
Tabaco, Phil. 80 E4 13 22N 123 44 E
Tabagné, Ivory C. 112 D4 7 59N 3 4W
Ţābah, Si. Arabia 96 E4 26 55N 42 38 E
Tabajara, Brazil 173 B5 8 56 S 62 8W
Tabalos, Peru 172 B2 6 26 S 76 37W
Tabango, Phil. 81 F5 11 19N 124 22 E
Tabar Is., Papua N. G. 132 B7 2 50 S 152 0 E
Tabarka, Tunisia 108 A1 36 56N 8 46 E
Ţabas, Khorāsān, Iran 97 C9 32 48N 60 12 E
Ţabas, Khorāsān, Iran 97 C8 33 35N 56 55 E
Tabasará, Serranía de, Panama 164 E3 8 35N 81 40W
Tabasco □, Mexico 163 D6 17 45N 93 30W
Tabatinga, Serra da, Brazil 170 D3 10 30 S 44 0W
Tabayin, Burma 90 D5 22 42N 95 20 E
Tabāzīn, Iran 97 D8 31 12N 57 54 E
Tabelbala, Kahal de, Algeria 111 C4 28 47N 2 0W
Taber, Canada 142 D6 49 47N 112 8W
Taberg, Sweden 17 G8 57 40N 14 6 E
Tabi, Angola 115 D2 8 10 S 13 18 E
Tabira, Brazil 170 C4 7 35 S 37 33W
Tablas, Phil. 80 E4 12 25N 122 2 E
Tablas Strait, Phil. 80 E3 12 40N 121 48 E
Table B. = Tafelbaai, S. Africa 116 E2 33 35 S 18 25 E
Table B., Canada 141 B8 53 40N 56 25W
Table Grove, U.S.A. 156 D6 40 20N 90 27W
Table Mt., S. Africa 116 E2 34 0 S 18 22 E
Tableland, Australia 124 C4 17 16 S 126 51 E
Tabletop, Mt., Australia 126 C4 23 24 S 147 11 E
Tabogon, Phil. 81 F5 10 57N 124 2 E
Tábor, Czech Rep. 34 B7 49 25N 14 39 E
Tabora, Tanzania 118 D3 5 2 S 32 50 E
Tabora □, Tanzania 118 D3 5 0 S 33 0 E
Tabou, Ivory C. 112 E3 4 30N 7 20W
Tabrīz, Iran 101 C12 38 7N 46 20 E
Tabuaeran, Pac. Oc. 135 G12 3 51N 159 22W
Tabuelan, Phil. 81 F4 10 49N 123 52 E
Tabuenca, Spain 40 D3 41 42N 1 33W
Tabuk, Phil. 80 C3 17 24N 121 25 E
Tabūk, Si. Arabia 96 D3 28 23N 36 36 E
Tabwemasana, Mt., Vanuatu 133 E4 15 20 S 166 44 E
Täby, Sweden 16 E12 59 28N 18 4 E
Tacámbaro de Codallos, Mexico 162 D4 19 14N 101 28W
Tacheng, China 72 B3 46 40N 82 58 E
Tachia, Taiwan 77 E13 24 25N 120 28 E
Tachibana-Wan, Japan 70 E2 32 45N 130 7 E
Tachikawa, Japan 71 B11 35 42N 139 25 E
Tach'ing Shan = Daqing Shan, China 74 D6 40 40N 111 0 E
Táchira □, Venezuela 168 B3 8 7N 72 15W
Tachov, Czech Rep. 34 B5 49 47N 12 39 E
Tácina →, Italy 47 D9 38 57N 16 55 E
Tacloban, Phil. 81 F5 11 15N 124 58 E
Tacna, Peru 172 D3 18 0 S 70 20W
Tacna □, Peru 172 D3 17 40 S 70 20W
Tacoma, U.S.A. 160 C4 47 14N 122 26W
Tacuarembó, Uruguay 175 C4 31 45 S 56 0W
Tacutu →, Brazil 169 C5 3 1N 60 29W
Tademaït, Plateau du, Algeria 111 C5 28 30N 2 30 E
Tadent, O. →, Algeria 111 D6 22 25N 6 40 E
Tadjerdjeri, O. →, Algeria 111 C6 26 0N 8 0 E
Tadjerouna, Algeria 111 B5 33 31N 2 3 E
Tadjettaret, O. →, Algeria 111 D6 21 20N 7 22 E
Tadjmout, Oasis, Algeria 111 B5 33 52N 2 30 E
Tadjmout, Saoura, Algeria 111 C5 25 37N 3 48 E
Tadjoura, Djibouti 107 E5 11 50N 42 55 E
Tadjoura, Golfe de, Djibouti 107 E5 11 50N 43 0 E
Tadmor, N.Z. 131 B7 41 27 S 172 45 E
Tadotsu, Japan 70 C5 34 16N 133 45 E
Tadoule, L., Canada 143 B9 58 36N 98 20W
Tadoussac, Canada 141 C6 48 11N 69 42W
Tadzhikistan = Tajikistan ■, Asia 63 D5 38 30N 70 0 E
Taechŏn-ni, S. Korea 75 F14 36 21N 126 36 E
Taegu, S. Korea 75 G15 35 50N 128 37 E
Taegwan, N. Korea 75 D13 40 13N 125 12 E
Taejŏn, S. Korea 75 F14 36 20N 127 28 E
Tafalla, Spain 40 C3 42 30N 1 41W
Tafar, Sudan 107 F2 6 52N 28 15 E
Tafassasset, O. →, Algeria 111 D6 22 0N 9 57 E
Tafelbaai, S. Africa 116 E2 33 35 S 18 25 E
Tafelney, C., Morocco 110 B3 31 3N 9 51W
Tafermaar, Indonesia 83 C4 6 47 S 134 10 E
Taffermit, Morocco 110 C3 29 37N 9 15W
Tafí Viejo, Argentina 174 B2 26 43 S 65 17W
Tafīhān, Iran 97 D7 29 25N 52 39 E
Tafiré, Ivory C. 112 D3 9 4N 5 4W
Tafjord, Norway 18 B4 62 14N 7 24 E
Tafnidilt, Morocco 110 C2 28 47N 10 58W
Tafraoute, Morocco 110 C3 29 50N 8 58W
Taft, Iran 97 D7 31 45N 54 14 E
Taft, Phil. 81 F5 11 57N 125 30 E
Taft, Calif., U.S.A. 161 K7 35 8N 119 28W
Taft, Fla., U.S.A. 153 G8 28 26N 81 22W
Taft, Tex., U.S.A. 155 M6 27 59N 97 24W
Taga, W. Samoa 133 W23 13 46 S 172 28W
Taga Dzong, Bhutan 90 B2 27 5N 89 55 E
Tagana-an, Phil. 81 G5 9 42N 125 35 E
Taganrog, Russia 59 J10 47 12N 38 50 E
Taganrogskiy Zaliv, Russia 59 J10 47 0N 38 30 E
Tagânt, Mauritania 112 B2 18 20N 11 0W
Tagap Ga, Burma 90 B6 26 56N 96 13 E
Tagapula I., Phil. 80 E5 12 4N 124 12 E
Tagatay, Phil. 80 D3 14 6N 120 56 E
Tagauayan I., Phil. 81 F3 10 58N 121 13 E
Tagbilaran, Phil. 81 G4 9 39N 123 51 E
Tage, Papua N. G. 132 D2 6 19 S 143 20 E
Tággia, Italy 44 E4 43 52N 7 51 E
Taghzout, Morocco 110 B4 33 30N 4 49W
Tagish, Canada 142 A2 60 19N 134 16W
Tagish L., Canada 142 A2 60 10N 134 20W
Tagkawayan, Phil. 80 E4 13 58N 122 32 E
Tagliacozzo, Italy 45 F10 42 4N 13 14 E
Tagliamento →, Italy 45 C10 45 38N 13 6 E
Táglio di Po, Italy 45 D9 45 0N 12 12 E
Tagna, Colombia 168 D3 2 24 S 70 37W
Tago, Phil. 81 G6 9 2N 126 13 E
Tago, Mt., Phil. 81 G5 8 23N 125 5 E
Tagomago, Spain 39 B8 39 2N 1 39 E
Taguatinga, Brazil 171 D3 12 16 S 42 26W
Tagudin, Phil. 80 C3 16 56N 120 27 E
Tagula, Papua N. G. 132 F7 11 22 S 153 15 E
Tagula I., Papua N. G. 132 F7 11 30 S 153 30 E
Tagum, Phil. 81 H5 7 33N 125 53 E
Tagus = Tejo →, Europe 43 F2 38 40N 9 24W
Tahakopa, N.Z. 131 G4 46 30 S 169 23 E
Tahala, Morocco 110 B4 34 0N 4 28W
Tahan, Gunong, Malaysia 87 K4 4 34N 102 17 E
Tahānah-ye sūr Gol, Afghan. 91 C2 31 43N 67 53 E
Tahara, Japan 71 C9 34 40N 137 16 E
Tahat, Algeria 111 D6 23 18N 5 33 E
Tāherī, Iran 97 E7 27 43N 52 20 E
Tahiti, Pac. Oc. 135 J13 17 37 S 149 27W
Tahoe, L., U.S.A. 160 G6 39 6N 120 2W
Tahoe City, U.S.A. 160 F6 39 10N 120 9W
Taholah, U.S.A. 160 C2 47 21N 124 17W
Tahora, N.Z. 130 F3 39 2 S 174 49 E
Tahoua, Niger 113 C6 14 57N 5 16 E
Tahta, Egypt 106 B3 26 44N 31 32 E
Tahtaköprü, Turkey 51 G13 39 57N 29 39 E
Tahtalı Dağları, Turkey 100 C7 38 20N 36 0 E
Tahuamanu →, Bolivia 172 C4 11 6 S 67 36W
Tahulandang, Indonesia 82 A3 2 27N 125 23 E
Tahuna, Indonesia 82 A3 3 38N 125 30 E
Taï, Ivory C. 112 D3 5 55N 7 30W
Tai Shan, China 75 F9 36 25N 117 20 E
Tai Xian, China 77 A13 32 30N 120 7 E
Tai'an, China 75 F9 36 12N 117 8 E
Taibei = T'aipei, Taiwan 77 E13 25 2N 121 30 E
Taibique, Canary Is. 39 G2 27 42N 17 58W
Taibus Qi, China 74 D8 41 54N 115 22 E
T'aichung, Taiwan 77 E13 24 9N 120 37 E
Taieri →, N.Z. 131 G5 46 3 S 170 12 E
Taiga Madema, Libya 108 D3 23 46N 15 25 E
Taigu, China 74 F7 37 28N 112 30 E
Taihang Shan, China 74 G7 36 0N 113 30 E
Taihape, N.Z. 130 F4 39 41 S 175 48 E
Taihe, Anhui, China 74 H8 33 20N 115 42 E
Taihe, Jiangxi, China 77 D10 26 47N 114 52 E
Taihu, China 77 B11 30 22N 116 20 E
Taijiang, China 76 D7 26 39N 108 21 E
Taikang, China 74 G8 34 5N 114 50 E
Taikkyi, Burma 90 G6 17 20N 96 0 E
Tailem Bend, Australia 128 C3 35 12 S 139 29 E
Tailfingen, Germany 31 G5 48 15N 9 1 E
Taimyr Peninsula = Taymyr, Poluostrov, Russia 65 B11 75 0N 100 0 E
Tain, U.K. 22 D4 57 49N 4 4W
T'ainan, Taiwan 77 F13 23 0N 120 10 E
Taínaron, Ákra, Greece 48 E4 36 22N 22 27 E
Tainggyo, Burma 90 G5 17 49N 94 29 E
Taining, China 77 D11 26 54N 117 9 E
Taiobeiras, Brazil 171 E3 15 49 S 42 14W
T'aipei, Taiwan 77 E13 25 2N 121 30 E
Taiping, China 77 B12 30 15N 118 6 E
Taiping, Malaysia 87 K3 4 51N 100 44 E
Taipingzhen, China 74 H6 33 35N 111 42 E
Taipu, Brazil 170 C4 5 37 S 35 36W
Tairbeart = Tarbert, U.K. 22 D2 57 54N 6 49W
Taisha, Japan 70 B4 35 24N 132 40 E
Taishan, China 77 F9 22 14N 112 41 E
Taishun, China 77 D12 27 30N 119 42 E
Taita □, Kenya 118 C4 4 0 S 38 30 E
Taita Hills, Kenya 118 C4 3 25 S 38 15 E
Taitao, C., Chile 176 C1 45 53 S 75 5W
Taitao, Pen. de, Chile 176 C2 46 30 S 75 0W
T'aitung, Taiwan 77 F13 22 43N 121 4 E
Taivalkoski, Finland 14 D23 65 33N 28 12 E
Taiwan ■, Asia 77 F13 23 30N 121 0 E
Taixing, China 77 A13 32 11N 120 0 E
Taïyetos Óros, Greece 48 D4 37 0N 22 23 E
Taiyiba, Israel 103 C4 32 36N 35 27 E
Taiyuan, China 74 F7 37 52N 112 33 E
Taizhong = T'aichung, Taiwan 77 E13 24 9N 120 37 E
Taizhou, China 77 A12 32 28N 119 55 E
Taizhou Liedao, China 77 C13 28 30N 121 55 E
Ta'izz, Yemen 98 D4 13 35N 44 2 E
Tājābād, Iran 97 D7 30 2N 54 24 E
Tajapuru, Furo do, Brazil 170 B1 1 50 S 50 25W
Tajarḥī, Libya 108 D2 24 21N 14 28 E
Tajikistan ■, Asia 63 D5 38 30N 70 0 E
Tajima, Japan 69 F9 37 12N 139 46 E
Tajimi, Japan 71 B9 35 19N 137 8 E
Tajo = Tejo →, Europe 43 F2 38 40N 9 24W
Tajrīsh, Iran 97 C6 35 48N 51 25 E
Tājūrā, Libya 108 B2 32 51N 13 21 E
Tak, Thailand 86 D2 16 52N 99 8 E
Takāb, Iran 101 D12 36 24N 47 7 E
Takachiho, Japan 70 E3 32 42N 131 18 E
Takada, Japan 69 F9 37 7N 138 15 E
Takahagi, Japan 69 F10 36 43N 140 45 E
Takahashi, Japan 70 C5 34 51N 133 39 E
Takaka, N.Z. 131 A7 40 51 S 172 50 E
Takamatsu, Japan 70 C6 34 20N 134 5 E
Takanabe, Japan 70 E3 32 8N 131 30 E
Takaoka, Japan 71 A9 36 47N 137 0 E
Takapau, N.Z. 130 G5 40 2 S 176 21 E
Takapuna, N.Z. 130 C3 36 47 S 174 47 E
Takasago, Japan 70 C6 34 45N 134 48 E
Takasaki, Japan 71 A11 36 20N 139 0 E
Takase, Japan 70 C5 34 7N 133 48 E
Takatsuki, Japan 71 C7 34 51N 135 37 E
Takaungu, Kenya 118 C4 3 38 S 39 52 E
Takawa, Japan 70 D2 33 38N 130 51 E
Takayama, Japan 71 A9 36 18N 137 11 E
Takayama-Bonchi, Japan 71 B9 36 0N 137 18 E
Take-Shima, Japan 69 J5 30 49N 130 26 E
Takefu, Japan 71 B8 35 50N 136 10 E
Takehara, Japan 70 C4 34 21N 132 55 E
Takengon, Indonesia 84 B1 4 45N 96 50 E
Takeo, Japan 70 D2 33 12N 130 1 E
Tåkern, Sweden 17 F8 58 22N 14 45 E
Tākestān, Iran 97 C6 36 0N 49 40 E
Taketa, Japan 70 E3 32 58N 131 24 E
Takev, Cambodia 87 G5 10 59N 104 47 E
Takh, India 93 C7 33 6N 77 32 E
Takhār □, Afghan. 91 A3 36 40N 70 0 E
Taki, Papua N. G. 132 D8 6 29 S 155 52 E
Takikawa, Japan 68 C10 43 33N 141 54 E
Takla L., Canada 142 B3 55 15N 125 45W
Takla Landing, Canada 142 B3 55 30N 125 50W
Takla Makan = Taklamakan Shamo, China 72 C3 38 0N 83 0 E
Taklamakan Shamo, China 72 C3 38 0N 83 0 E
Takotna, U.S.A. 144 E8 62 59N 156 4W
Taku, Japan 70 D2 33 18N 130 3 E
Taku →, Canada 142 B2 58 30N 133 50W
Takum, Nigeria 113 D6 7 18N 9 36 E
Takuma, Japan 70 C5 34 13N 133 40 E
Takundi, Dem. Rep. of the Congo 115 C3 4 45 S 16 34 E
Takuran, Phil. 81 H4 7 51N 123 34 E
Takutu →, Guyana 169 C5 3 1N 60 29W
Tal Halāl, Iran 97 D7 28 54N 55 1 E
Tala, Uruguay 175 C4 34 21 S 55 46W
Talachyn, Belarus 58 E5 54 25N 29 42 E
Talacogan, Phil. 81 G5 8 32N 125 39 E
Talagante, Chile 174 C1 33 40 S 70 50W
Talaïnt, Morocco 110 C3 29 41N 9 40W
Talak, Niger 113 B6 18 0N 5 0 E
Talakag, Phil. 81 G5 8 16N 124 37 E
Talamanca, Cordillera de, Cent. Amer. 164 E3 9 20N 83 20W
Talant, France 27 E11 47 19N 4 58 E
Talara, Peru 172 A1 4 38 S 81 18W
Talas, Kyrgyzstan 63 B6 42 30N 72 13 E
Talas, Turkey 100 C6 38 41N 35 33 E
Talas →, Kazakstan 63 B5 44 0N 70 20 E
Talasea, Papua N. G. 132 C6 5 20 S 150 2 E
Talasskiy Alatau, Khrebet, Kyrgyzstan 63 B6 42 15N 72 0 E
Talâta, Egypt 103 E1 30 36N 32 20 E
Talata Mafara, Nigeria 113 C6 12 38N 6 4 E
Talaud, Kepulauan, Indonesia 82 A3 4 30N 127 10 E
Talaud Is. = Talaud, Kepulauan, Indonesia 82 A3 4 30N 127 10 E
Talavera de la Reina, Spain 42 F6 39 55N 4 46W
Talavera la Real, Spain 43 G4 38 53N 6 46W
Talawana, Australia 124 D3 22 51 S 121 9 E
Talawgyi, Burma 90 C6 25 4N 97 19 E
Talayan, Phil. 81 H5 6 52N 124 24 E
Talayuela, Spain 42 F5 39 59N 5 36W
Talbert, Sillon de, France 26 D3 48 53N 3 5W
Talbot, C., Australia 124 B4 13 48 S 126 43 E
Talbotton, U.S.A. 152 C5 32 41N 84 32W
Talbragar →, Australia 129 B8 32 12 S 148 37 E
Talca, Chile 174 D1 35 28 S 71 40W
Talca □, Chile 174 D1 35 20 S 71 46W
Talcahuano, Chile 174 D1 36 40 S 73 10W
Talcher, India 94 D7 21 0N 85 18 E
Talcho, Niger 113 C5 14 44N 3 28 E
Taldy Kurgan = Taldyqorghan, Kazakstan 64 E8 45 10N 78 45 E
Taldyqorghan, Kazakstan 64 E8 45 10N 78 45 E
Tālesh, Iran 97 B6 37 58N 48 58 E
Ţālesh, Kūhhā-ye, Iran 97 B6 37 42N 48 55 E
Talgar, Kazakstan 63 B8 43 19N 77 15 E
Talgar, Pik, Kazakstan 63 B8 43 5N 77 20 E
Talguharai, Sudan 106 D4 18 19N 35 56 E
Tali Post, Sudan 107 F3 5 55N 30 44 E
Talibon, Phil. 81 F5 10 9N 124 20 E
Talibong, Ko, Thailand 87 J2 7 15N 99 23 E
Talihina, U.S.A. 155 H7 34 45N 95 3W
Talikota, India 95 F3 16 29N 76 17 E
Talimardzhan = Tallymerjen, Turkmenistan 63 D2 38 23N 65 37 E
Talisay, Phil. 81 F4 10 44N 122 58 E
Talisayan, Phil. 81 G5 9 0N 124 55 E
Talitsa, Russia 62 C9 57 0N 63 43 E
Taliwang, Indonesia 82 C1 8 50 S 116 55 E
Tall 'Afar, Iraq 101 D10 36 22N 42 27 E
Tall Kalakh, Syria 103 A5 34 41N 36 15 E
Talla, Egypt 106 J7 28 5N 30 43 E
Talladega, U.S.A. 152 B3 33 26N 86 6W
Tallahassee, U.S.A. 152 E5 30 27N 84 17W
Tallangatta, Australia 129 D7 36 15 S 147 19 E
Tallapoosa, U.S.A. 152 B4 33 45N 85 17W
Tallapoosa →, U.S.A. 152 C3 32 30N 86 16W
Tallard, France 29 D10 44 28N 6 3 E
Tallarook, Australia 129 D6 37 5 S 145 6 E
Tallassee, U.S.A. 152 C4 32 32N 85 54W
Tallawang, Australia 129 B8 32 12 S 149 28 E
Tällberg, Sweden 16 D9 60 51N 15 2 E
Tallering Pk., Australia 125 E2 28 6 S 115 37 E
Tallinn, Estonia 15 G21 59 22N 24 48 E
Tallulah, U.S.A. 155 J9 32 25N 91 11W
Tallymerjen, Turkmenistan 63 D2 38 23N 65 37 E
Tălmaciu, Romania 53 E9 45 38N 24 19 E
Talmest, Morocco 110 B3 31 48N 9 21W
Talmont-St-Hilaire, France 28 B2 46 27N 1 37W
Talne, Ukraine 59 H6 48 50N 30 44 E
Talnoye = Talne, Ukraine 59 H6 48 50N 30 44 E
Taloda, India 94 D2 21 34N 74 11 E
Talodi, Sudan 107 E3 10 35N 30 22 E
Talomo, Phil. 81 H5 7 3N 125 32 E
Tāloqān, Afghan. 91 A3 36 44N 69 33 E
Talovaya, Russia 60 E5 51 6N 40 45 E
Taloyoak, Canada 138 B10 69 32N 93 32W
Talpa de Allende, Mexico 162 C4 20 23N 104 51W
Talquin, L., U.S.A. 152 E5 30 23N 84 39W
Talsi, Latvia 15 H20 57 10N 22 30 E
Talsi □, Latvia 54 A9 57 20N 22 40 E
Talsinnt, Morocco 111 B4 32 33N 3 27W
Taltal, Chile 174 B1 25 23 S 70 33W
Taltson →, Canada 142 A6 61 24N 112 46W
Talwood, Australia 129 A8 28 29 S 149 29 E
Talyawalka Cr. →, Australia 128 B5 32 28 S 142 22 E
Tam Chau, Vietnam 87 G5 10 48N 105 12 E
Tam Ky, Vietnam 86 E7 15 34N 108 29 E
Tam Quan, Vietnam 86 E7 14 35N 109 3 E
Tama, U.S.A. 156 C4 41 58N 92 35W
Tamala, Australia 125 E1 26 42 S 113 47 E
Tamalameque, Colombia 168 B3 8 52N 73 49W
Tamale, Ghana 113 D4 9 22N 0 50W
Taman, Russia 59 K9 45 14N 36 41 E
Tamana, Japan 70 E2 32 58N 130 32 E
Tamanar, Morocco 110 B3 31 1N 9 46W
Tamano, Japan 70 C5 34 29N 133 59 E
Tamanrasset, Algeria 111 D6 22 50N 5 30 E
Tamanrasset, O. →, Algeria 111 D5 22 0N 2 0 E
Tamanthi, Burma 90 C5 25 19N 95 17 E
Tamaqua, U.S.A. 151 F9 40 48N 75 58W
Tamar →, U.K. 21 G3 50 27N 4 15W
Támara, Colombia 168 B3 5 50N 72 10W
Tamarac, U.S.A. 153 J9 26 12N 80 10W
Tamarang, Australia 129 A9 31 27 S 150 5 E
Tamarinda, Spain 39 B10 39 55N 3 49 E

Torres Vedras 291

Tîrgu Mureş = Târgu Mureş, *Romania* **53 D9** 46 31N 24 38 E
Tirich Mir, *Pakistan* **91 A3** 36 15N 71 55 E
Tiriolo, *Italy* **47 D9** 38 57N 16 30 E
Tiririca, Serra da, *Brazil* **171 E2** 17 6S 47 6W
Tiris, *W. Sahara* **110 D2** 23 10N 13 20W
Tirlyanskiy, *Russia* **62 D7** 54 14N 58 35 E
Tirna →, *India* **94 E3** 18 4N 76 57 E
Tîrnavos, *Greece* **48 B4** 39 45N 22 18 E
Tirodi, *India* **94 D4** 21 40N 79 44 E
Tirol □, *Austria* **34 D3** 47 3N 10 43 E
Tiros, *Brazil* **171 E2** 19 0S 45 58W
Tirschenreuth, *Germany* **31 F8** 49 53N 12 19 E
Tirso →, *Italy* **46 C1** 39 53N 8 32 E
Tirstrup, *Denmark* **17 H4** 56 18N 10 42 E
Tirua, Pt., *N.Z.* **130 E3** 38 25 S 174 40 E
Tiruchchendur, *India* **95 K4** 8 30N 78 11 E
Tiruchchirappalli, *India* **95 J4** 10 45N 78 45 E
Tiruchengodu, *India* **95 J3** 11 23N 77 56 E
Tirumangalam, *India* **95 K3** 9 49N 77 58 E
Tirunelveli, *India* **95 K3** 8 45N 77 45 E
Tirupati, *India* **95 H4** 13 39N 79 25 E
Tiruppattur, *India* **95 H4** 12 30N 78 30 E
Tiruppur, *India* **95 J3** 11 5N 77 22 E
Tirutturaippundi, *India* **95 J4** 10 32N 79 41 E
Tiruvadaimarudur, *India* **95 J4** 11 2N 79 27 E
Tiruvallar, *India* **95 H4** 13 9N 79 57 E
Tiruvannamalai, *India* **95 H4** 12 15N 79 5 E
Tiruvettipuram, *India* **95 H4** 12 39N 79 33 E
Tiruvottiyur, *India* **95 H5** 13 10N 80 22 E
Tisa →, *Serbia, Yug.* **52 E5** 45 15N 20 17 E
Tisdale, *Canada* **143 C8** 52 50N 104 0W
Tishomingo, *U.S.A.* **155 H6** 34 14N 96 41W
Tisjön, *Sweden* **16 D7** 60 56N 13 0 E
Tisnaren, *Sweden* **17 F9** 58 58N 15 56 E
Tišnov, *Czech Rep.* **35 B9** 49 21N 16 25 E
Tisovec, *Slovak Rep.* **35 C12** 48 41N 19 56 E
Tissemsilt, *Algeria* **111 A5** 35 35N 1 50 E
Tissint, *Morocco* **110 C3** 29 57N 7 16W
Tista →, *India* **90 C2** 25 23N 89 43 E
Tistedal, *Norway* **18 E8** 59 8N 11 27 E
Tisza = Tisa →, *Serbia, Yug.* **52 E5** 45 15N 20 17 E
Tiszaföldvár, *Hungary* **52 D5** 46 58N 20 14 E
Tiszafüred, *Hungary* **52 C5** 47 38N 20 50 E
Tiszalök, *Hungary* **52 B6** 48 1N 21 20 E
Tiszavasvári, *Hungary* **52 C6** 47 58N 21 18 E
Tit, *Ahaggar, Algeria* **111 D6** 23 0N 5 10 E
Tit, *Tademait, Algeria* **111 C5** 27 0N 1 29 E
Tit-Ary, *Russia* **65 B13** 71 55N 127 2 E
Titaguas, *Spain* **40 F3** 39 53N 1 6W
Titahi Bay, *N.Z.* **130 H3** 41 6S 174 50 E
Titel, *Serbia, Yug.* **52 E5** 45 10N 20 18 E
Tithwal, *Pakistan* **93 B5** 34 21N 73 50 E
Titicaca, L., *S. Amer.* **172 D4** 15 30 S 69 30W
Titisee, *Germany* **31 H4** 47 54N 8 10 E
Tititira Hd., *N.Z.* **131 D4** 43 36 S 169 25 E
Titiwa, *Nigeria* **113 C7** 12 14N 12 53 E
Titlagarh, *India* **94 D6** 20 15N 83 11 E
Titlis, *Switz.* **33 C6** 46 46N 8 27 E
Tito, *Italy* **47 B8** 40 35N 15 40 E
Titograd = Podgorica, *Montenegro, Yug.* **50 D3** 42 30N 19 19 E
Titova Korenica, *Croatia* **45 D12** 44 45N 15 41 E
Titu, *Romania* **53 F10** 44 39N 25 32 E
Titule, *Dem. Rep. of the Congo* **118 B2** 3 15N 25 31 E
Titumate, *Colombia* **168 B2** 8 19N 77 5W
Titusville, *Fla., U.S.A.* **149 L5** 28 37N 80 49W
Titusville, *Pa., U.S.A.* **150 E5** 41 38N 79 41W
Tivaouane, *Senegal* **112 C1** 14 56N 16 45W
Tivat, *Montenegro, Yug.* **50 D2** 42 28N 18 43 E
Tiverton, *U.K.* **21 G4** 50 54N 3 29W
Tívoli, *Italy* **45 G9** 41 58N 12 45 E
Tiwī, *Oman* **99 B7** 22 45N 59 12 E
Tiyo, *Eritrea* **107 E5** 14 41N 40 15 E
Tizga, *Morocco* **110 B3** 32 1N 5 9W
Ti'zi N'Isli, *Morocco* **110 B3** 32 28N 5 47W
Tizi-Ouzou, *Algeria* **111 A5** 36 42N 4 3 E
Tizimín, *Mexico* **163 C7** 21 0N 88 1W
Tiznados →, *Venezuela* **168 B4** 8 16N 67 47W
Tiznit, *Morocco* **110 C3** 29 48N 9 45W
Tjæreborg, *Denmark* **17 J2** 55 28N 8 36 E
Tjällmo, *Sweden* **17 F9** 58 43N 15 21 E
Tjeggelvas, *Sweden* **14 C17** 66 37N 17 45 E
Tjirebon = Cirebon, *Indonesia* **85 D3** 6 45 S 108 32 E
Tjøme, *Norway* **18 E7** 59 8N 10 26 E
Tjörn, *Sweden* **17 F5** 58 0N 11 35 E
Tjörnes, *Iceland* **11 A9** 66 12N 17 9W
Tkibuli = Tqibuli, *Georgia* **61 J6** 42 26N 43 0 E
Tkvarcheli = Tqvarcheli, *Georgia* **61 J5** 42 47N 41 42 E
Tlacotalpan, *Mexico* **163 D5** 18 37N 95 40W
Tlahualilo, *Mexico* **162 B4** 26 20N 103 30W
Tlaquepaque, *Mexico* **162 C4** 20 39N 103 19W
Tlaxcala, *Mexico* **163 D5** 19 20N 98 14W
Tlaxcala □, *Mexico* **163 D5** 19 30N 98 20W
Tlaxiaco, *Mexico* **163 D5** 17 18N 97 40W
Tlell, *Canada* **142 C2** 53 34N 131 56W
Tlemcen, *Algeria* **111 B4** 34 52N 1 21W
Tleta Sidi Bouguedra, *Morocco* **110 B3** 32 16N 9 59W
Tłuszcz, *Poland* **55 F8** 52 25N 21 25 E
Tlyarata, *Russia* **61 J8** 42 9N 46 26 E
Tmassah, *Libya* **108 C3** 26 19N 15 51 E
Tnine d'Anglou, *Morocco* **110 C3** 29 50N 9 50W
To Bong, *Vietnam* **86 F7** 12 45N 109 16 E
To-Shima, *Japan* **71 C11** 34 31N 139 17 E
Toad →, *Canada* **142 B4** 59 25N 124 57W
Toamasina, *Madag.* **117 B8** 18 10 S 49 25 E
Toamasina □, *Madag.* **117 B8** 18 0S 49 0 E
Toay, *Argentina* **174 D3** 36 43 S 64 38W
Toba, *Japan* **71 C8** 34 30N 136 51 E
Toba, Danau, *Indonesia* **84 B1** 2 30N 97 30 E
Toba Kakar, *Pakistan* **91 C3** 31 30N 69 0 E
Toba Tek Singh, *Pakistan* **92 D5** 30 55N 72 25 E
Tobago, *W. Indies* **165 D7** 11 10N 60 30W
Tobarra, *Spain* **41 G3** 38 37N 1 44W
Tobelo, *Indonesia* **82 A3** 1 45N 127 56 E
Tobermorey, *Australia* **126 C2** 22 12 S 138 0 E
Tobermory, *Canada* **140 C3** 45 12N 81 40W
Tobermory, *U.K.* **22 E2** 56 38N 6 5W
Tobin, *U.S.A.* **160 F5** 39 55N 121 19W
Tobin, L., *Australia* **124 D4** 21 45 S 125 49 E
Tobin L., *Canada* **143 C8** 53 35N 103 30W
Toblach = Dobbiaco, *Italy* **45 B9** 46 44N 12 14 E
Toboali, *Indonesia* **84 C3** 3 0S 106 25 E
Tobol, *Kazakstan* **62 E9** 52 40N 62 39 E
Tobol →, *Russia* **64 D7** 58 10N 68 12 E
Toboli, *Indonesia* **82 B2** 0 38 S 120 5 E
Tobolsk, *Russia* **64 D7** 58 15N 68 10 E
Toboso, *Phil.* **81 F4** 10 43N 123 31 E
Tobruk = Tubruq, *Libya* **108 B4** 32 7N 23 55 E
Tobyhanna, *U.S.A.* **151 E9** 41 11N 75 25W
Tobyl = Tobol →, *Russia* **64 D7** 58 10N 68 12 E
Tocache Nuevo, *Peru* **172 B2** 8 9S 76 26W
Tocantínia, *Brazil* **170 C2** 9 33 S 48 22W
Tocantinópolis, *Brazil* **170 C2** 6 20 S 47 25W
Tocantins □, *Brazil* **170 D2** 10 0S 48 0W
Tocantins →, *Brazil* **170 B2** 1 45 S 49 10W
Toccoa, *U.S.A.* **149 H4** 34 35N 83 19W
Toce →, *Italy* **44 C5** 45 56N 8 29 E
Tochigi, *Japan* **71 A11** 36 25N 139 45 E
Tochigi □, *Japan* **71 A11** 36 45N 139 45 E
Tocina, *Spain* **43 H5** 37 37N 5 44W
Töcksfors, *Sweden* **16 E5** 59 31N 11 52 E
Tocopilla, *Chile* **174 A1** 22 5S 70 10W
Tocumwal, *Australia* **129 C6** 35 51 S 145 31 E
Tocuyo →, *Venezuela* **168 A4** 11 3N 68 23W
Tocuyo de la Costa, *Venezuela* **168 A4** 11 2N 68 23W
Todal, *Norway* **18 B5** 62 49N 8 44 E
Todd →, *Australia* **126 C2** 24 52 S 135 48 E
Todeli, *Indonesia* **82 B2** 1 38 S 124 34 E
Todenyang, *Kenya* **118 B4** 4 35N 35 56 E
Todi, *Italy* **45 F9** 42 47N 12 24 E
Tödi, *Switz.* **33 C7** 46 48N 8 55 E
Todos os Santos, B. de, *Brazil* **171 D4** 12 48 S 38 38W
Todos Santos, *Mexico* **162 C2** 23 27N 110 13W
Todtnau, *Germany* **31 H3** 47 49N 7 56 E
Toe Hd., *U.K.* **22 D1** 57 50N 7 8W
Toecé, *Burkina Faso* **113 C4** 11 50N 1 16W
Toetoes B., *N.Z.* **131 G3** 46 42 S 168 41 E
Tofield, *Canada* **142 C6** 53 25N 112 40W
Tofino, *Canada* **142 D3** 49 11N 125 55W
Tofte, *Norway* **18 E7** 59 33N 10 34 E
Tofua, *Tonga* **133 P11** 19 45 S 175 5W
Toga, *Vanuatu* **133 C4** 13 26 S 166 42 E
Tōgane, *Japan* **71 B12** 35 33N 140 22 E
Togba, *Mauritania* **112 B2** 17 26N 10 12W
Togbo, *C.A.R.* **114 A3** 6 0N 17 27 E
Toggenburg, *Switz.* **33 B8** 47 16N 9 9 E
Togiak, *U.S.A.* **144 G7** 59 4N 160 24W
Togian, Kepulauan, *Indonesia* **82 B2** 0 20 S 121 50 E
Togliatti, *Russia* **60 D9** 53 32N 49 24 E
Togo ■, *W. Afr.* **113 D5** 8 30N 1 35 E
Togtoh, *China* **74 D6** 40 15N 111 10 E
Toguzak →, *Kazakstan* **62 D9** 54 3N 62 44 E
Tohma →, *Turkey* **100 C7** 38 29N 38 23 E
Tōhoku □, *Japan* **68 E10** 39 50N 141 45 E
Tohopekaliga L., *U.S.A.* **153 G8** 28 12N 81 24W
Toi, *Japan* **71 C10** 34 54N 138 47 E
Toinya, *Sudan* **107 F2** 6 17N 29 46 E
Tojikiston = Tajikistan ■, *Asia* **63 D5** 38 30N 70 0 E
Tojo, *Indonesia* **82 B2** 1 20 S 121 15 E
Tōjō, *Japan* **70 C5** 34 53N 133 16 E
Tok, *U.S.A.* **144 E12** 63 20N 142 59W
Tok →, *Russia* **62 E4** 52 46N 52 22 E
Toka, *Guyana* **169 C6** 3 58N 59 17W
Tokaanu, *N.Z.* **130 E4** 38 58 S 175 46 E
Tokachi-Dake, *Japan* **68 C11** 43 17N 142 5 E
Tokachi-Gawa →, *Japan* **68 C11** 42 44N 143 42 E
Tokai, *Japan* **71 B8** 35 2N 136 55 E
Tokaj, *Hungary* **52 B6** 48 8N 21 27 E
Tokala, *Indonesia* **82 B2** 1 30 S 121 40 E
Tōkamachi, *Japan* **69 F9** 37 8N 138 43 E
Tokanui, *N.Z.* **131 G3** 46 34 S 168 56 E
Tokar, *Sudan* **106 D4** 18 27N 37 56 E
Tokara-Rettō, *Japan* **69 K4** 29 37N 129 43 E
Tokarahi, *N.Z.* **131 E5** 44 56 S 170 39 E
Tokashiki-Shima, *Japan* **69 L3** 26 11N 127 21 E
Tokat, *Turkey* **100 B7** 40 22N 36 35 E
Tŏkchŏn, *N. Korea* **75 E14** 39 45N 126 18 E
Tokeland, *U.S.A.* **160 D3** 46 42N 123 59W
Tokelau Is., *Pac. Oc.* **134 H10** 9 0S 171 45W
Toki, *Japan* **71 B9** 35 18N 137 8 E
Tokmak, *Kyrgyzstan* **63 B7** 42 49N 75 15 E
Tokmak, *Ukraine* **59 J8** 47 16N 35 42 E
Toko Ra., *Australia* **126 C2** 23 5S 138 20 E
Tokomaru Bay, *N.Z.* **130 E7** 38 8S 178 22 E
Tokoname, *Japan* **71 C8** 34 53N 136 51 E
Tokoro-Gawa →, *Japan* **68 B12** 44 7N 144 5 E
Tokoroa, *N.Z.* **130 E4** 38 13 S 175 50 E
Tokorozawa, *Japan* **71 B11** 35 47N 139 28 E
Toksook Bay, *U.S.A.* **144 F6** 60 32N 165 0W
Toktogul, *Kyrgyzstan* **63 C6** 41 50N 72 50 E
Toku, *Tonga* **133 P13** 18 10 S 174 11W
Tokuji, *Japan* **70 C3** 34 11N 131 42 E
Tokuno-Shima, *Japan* **69 L4** 27 56N 128 55 E
Tokushima, *Japan* **70 C6** 34 4N 134 34 E
Tokushima □, *Japan* **70 D6** 33 55N 134 0 E
Tokuyama, *Japan* **70 C3** 34 3N 131 50 E
Tōkyō, *Japan* **71 B11** 35 45N 139 45 E
Tōkyō □, *Japan* **71 B11** 35 40N 139 30 E
Tōkyō-Wan, *Japan* **71 B11** 35 25N 139 47 E
Tokzār, *Afghan.* **91 B2** 35 52N 66 26 E
Tolaga Bay, *N.Z.* **130 E7** 38 21 S 178 20 E
Tolbukhin = Dobrich, *Bulgaria* **51 C11** 43 37N 27 49 E
Toledo, *Phil.* **81 F4** 10 23N 123 38 E
Toledo, *Spain* **42 F6** 39 50N 4 2W
Toledo, *Ill., U.S.A.* **157 E8** 39 16N 88 15W
Toledo, *Iowa, U.S.A.* **156 C4** 42 0N 92 35W
Toledo, *Ohio, U.S.A.* **157 C13** 41 39N 83 33W
Toledo, *Oreg., U.S.A.* **158 D2** 44 37N 123 56W
Toledo, *Wash., U.S.A.* **158 C2** 46 26N 122 51W
Toledo, Montes de, *Spain* **43 F6** 39 33N 4 20W
Tolentino, *Italy* **45 E10** 43 12N 13 17 E
Tolfa, *Italy* **45 F8** 42 9N 11 56 E
Tolga, *Algeria* **111 B6** 34 40N 5 22 E
Tolga, *Norway* **18 B8** 62 26N 11 1 E
Toliara, *Madag.* **117 C7** 23 21 S 43 40 E
Toliara □, *Madag.* **117 C8** 21 0S 45 0 E
Tolima, *Colombia* **168 C2** 4 40N 75 19W
Tolima □, *Colombia* **168 C2** 3 45N 75 15W
Tolitoli, *Indonesia* **82 A2** 1 5N 120 50 E
Tolkmicko, *Poland* **54 D6** 54 19N 19 31 E
Tollarp, *Sweden* **17 J7** 55 55N 13 58 E
Tollensesee, *Germany* **30 B9** 53 30N 13 13 E
Tollhouse, *U.S.A.* **160 H7** 37 1N 119 24W
Tolmachevo, *Russia* **58 C5** 58 56N 29 51 E
Tolmezzo, *Italy* **45 B10** 46 24N 13 1 E
Tolmin, *Slovenia* **45 B10** 46 11N 13 45 E
Tolna, *Hungary* **52 D3** 46 25N 18 48 E
Tolna □, *Hungary* **52 D3** 46 30N 18 30 E
Tolo, *Dem. Rep. of the Congo* **114 C3** 2 55 S 18 34 E
Tolo, Teluk, *Indonesia* **82 B2** 2 20 S 122 10 E
Tolochin = Talachyn, *Belarus* **58 E5** 54 25N 29 42 E
Tolong Bay, *Phil.* **81 G4** 9 20N 122 49 E
Tolono, *U.S.A.* **157 E8** 39 59N 88 16W
Tolosa, *Spain* **40 B2** 43 8N 2 5W
Tolox, *Spain* **43 J6** 36 41N 4 54W
Toltén, *Chile* **176 A2** 39 13 S 74 14W
Toluca, *Mexico* **163 D5** 19 20N 99 40W
Tolybay, *Kazakstan* **62 F9** 50 31N 62 19 E
Tom Burke, *S. Africa* **117 C4** 23 5S 28 0 E
Tom Price, *Australia* **124 D2** 22 40 S 117 48 E
Tomah, *U.S.A.* **154 D9** 43 59N 90 30W
Tomahawk, *U.S.A.* **154 C10** 45 28N 89 44W
Tomai, *Moldova* **53 D13** 46 34N 28 19 E
Tomakomai, *Japan* **68 C10** 42 38N 141 36 E
Tomales, *U.S.A.* **160 G4** 38 15N 122 53W
Tomales B., *U.S.A.* **160 G3** 38 15N 123 58W
Tomanlivi, *Fiji* **133 A2** 17 37 S 178 1 E
Tomar, *Portugal* **43 F2** 39 36N 8 25W
Tómaros, Óros, *Greece* **48 B2** 39 29N 20 48 E
Tomarza, *Turkey* **100 C6** 38 27N 35 48 E
Tomás Barrón, *Bolivia* **172 D4** 17 35 S 67 31W
Tomaszów Lubelski, *Poland* **55 H10** 50 27N 23 25 E
Tomaszów Mazowiecki, *Poland* **55 G7** 51 30N 20 2 E
Tomatlán, *Mexico* **162 D3** 19 56N 105 15W
Tombador, Serra do, *Brazil* **173 C6** 12 0S 58 0W
Tombé, *Sudan* **107 F3** 5 53N 31 40 E
Tombigbee →, *U.S.A.* **149 K2** 31 8N 87 57W
Tombôco, *Angola* **115 D2** 6 48 S 13 18 E
Tombouctou, *Mali* **112 B4** 16 50N 3 0W
Tombstone, *U.S.A.* **159 L8** 31 43N 110 4W
Tombua, *Angola* **115 F2** 15 55 S 11 55 E
Tomé, *Chile* **174 D1** 36 36 S 72 57W
Tomé-Açu, *Brazil* **170 B2** 2 25 S 48 9W
Tomelilla, *Sweden* **17 J7** 55 33N 13 58 E
Tomelloso, *Spain* **43 F7** 39 10N 3 2W
Tomingley, *Australia* **129 B8** 32 26 S 148 16 E
Tomini, *Indonesia* **82 A2** 0 30N 120 30 E
Tomini, Teluk, *Indonesia* **82 B2** 0 10 S 122 0 E
Tominian, *Mali* **112 C4** 13 17N 4 35W
Tomiño, *Spain* **42 D2** 41 59N 8 46W
Tomintoul, *U.K.* **22 D5** 57 15N 3 23W
Tomislavgrad, *Bos.-H.* **52 G2** 43 42N 17 13 E
Tomkinson Ranges, *Australia* **125 E4** 26 11 S 129 5 E
Tommot, *Russia* **65 D13** 59 4N 126 20 E
Tomnop Ta Suos, *Cambodia* **87 G5** 11 20N 104 15 E
Tomo, *Colombia* **168 C4** 2 38N 67 32W
Tomo, *Japan* **70 C5** 34 23N 133 23 E
Tomo →, *Colombia* **168 B4** 5 20N 67 48W
Tomobe, *Japan* **71 A12** 36 20N 140 20 E
Tomra, *Norway* **18 B3** 62 34N 6 56 E
Toms Place, *U.S.A.* **160 H8** 37 34N 118 41W
Toms River, *U.S.A.* **151 G10** 39 58N 74 12W
Tomsk, *Russia* **64 D9** 56 30N 85 5 E
Tomtabacken, *Sweden* **17 G8** 57 30N 14 30 E
Tona, *Spain* **40 D7** 41 51N 2 14 E
Tonalá, *Mexico* **163 D6** 16 8N 93 41W
Tonale, Passo del, *Italy* **44 B7** 46 16N 10 35 E
Tonalea, *U.S.A.* **159 H8** 36 19N 110 56W
Tonami, *Japan* **71 A8** 36 40N 136 58 E
Tonantins, *Brazil* **168 D4** 2 45 S 67 45W
Tonasket, *U.S.A.* **158 B4** 48 42N 119 26W
Tonate, *Fr. Guiana* **169 C7** 5 0N 52 28W
Tonawanda, *U.S.A.* **150 D6** 43 1N 78 53W
Tonbridge, *U.K.* **21 F8** 51 11N 0 17 E
Tondano, *Indonesia* **82 A2** 1 35N 124 54 E
Tondela, *Portugal* **42 E2** 40 31N 8 5W
Tønder, *Denmark* **17 K2** 54 58N 8 50 E
Tondi, *India* **95 K4** 9 45N 79 4 E
Tondi Kiwindi, *Niger* **113 C5** 14 28N 2 2 E
Tondibi, *Mali* **113 B4** 16 39N 0 14W
Tonekābon, *Iran* **97 B6** 36 45N 51 12 E
Tong Xian, *China* **74 E9** 39 55N 116 35 E
Tonga ■, *Pac. Oc.* **133 P13** 19 50 S 174 30W
Tonga Trench, *Pac. Oc.* **134 J10** 18 0S 173 0W
Tongaat, *S. Africa* **117 D5** 29 33 S 31 9 E
Tongala, *Australia* **129 D6** 36 14 S 144 56 E
Tong'an, *China* **77 E12** 24 37N 118 8 E
Tongareva, *Cook Is.* **135 H12** 9 0S 158 0W
Tongass National Forest, *U.S.A.* **144 H14** 56 30N 134 0W
Tongatapu, *Tonga* **133 Q14** 21 10 S 174 0W
Tongatapu Group, *Tonga* **133 Q13** 21 0S 175 0W
Tongbai, *China* **77 A9** 32 20N 113 23 E
Tongcheng, *Anhui, China* **77 B11** 31 4N 116 56 E
Tongcheng, *Hubei, China* **77 C9** 29 15N 113 50 E
Tongchŏn-ni, *N. Korea* **75 E14** 39 50N 127 25 E
Tongchuan, *China* **74 G5** 35 6N 109 3 E
Tongdao, *China* **76 D7** 26 10N 109 42 E
Tongeren, *Belgium* **24 D5** 50 47N 5 28 E
Tongguan, *China* **77 C10** 28 31N 114 20 E
Tongguan, *China* **74 G6** 34 40N 110 25 E
Tonghai, *China* **76 E4** 24 10N 102 53 E
Tonghua, *China* **75 D13** 41 42N 125 58 E
Tongjiang, *China* **76 B6** 31 58N 107 11 E
Tongjosŏn Man, *N. Korea* **75 E15** 39 30N 128 0 E
Tongking, G. of = Tonkin, G. of, *Asia* **72 E5** 20 0N 108 0 E
Tongliang, *China* **76 C6** 29 50N 106 3 E
Tongliao, *China* **75 C12** 43 38N 122 18 E
Tongling, *China* **77 B11** 30 55N 117 48 E
Tonglu, *China* **77 C12** 29 45N 119 37 E
Tongnae, *S. Korea* **75 G15** 35 12N 129 5 E
Tongnan, *China* **76 B5** 30 9N 105 50 E
Tongoa, *Vanuatu* **133 F6** 16 54 S 168 34 E
Tongobory, *Madag.* **117 C7** 23 32 S 44 20 E
Tongoy, *Chile* **174 C1** 30 16 S 71 31W
Tongren, *China* **76 D7** 27 43N 109 11 E
Tongres = Tongeren, *Belgium* **24 D5** 50 47N 5 28 E
Tongsa Dzong, *Bhutan* **90 B3** 27 31N 90 31 E
Tongue, *U.K.* **22 C4** 58 29N 4 25W
Tongue →, *U.S.A.* **154 B2** 46 25N 105 52W
Tongwei, *China* **74 G3** 35 0N 105 5 E
Tongxin, *China* **74 F3** 36 59N 105 58 E
Tongyang, *N. Korea* **75 E14** 39 9N 126 53 E
Tongyu, *China* **75 B12** 44 45N 123 4 E
Tongzi, *China* **76 C6** 28 9N 106 49 E
Tonica, *U.S.A.* **156 C7** 41 13N 89 4W
Tonj, *Sudan* **107 F2** 7 20N 28 44 E
Tonk, *India* **92 F6** 26 6N 75 54 E
Tonkawa, *U.S.A.* **155 G6** 36 41N 97 18W
Tonkin = Bac Phan, *Vietnam* **86 B5** 22 0N 105 0 E
Tonkin, G. of, *Asia* **72 E5** 20 0N 108 0 E
Tonle Sap, *Cambodia* **86 F5** 13 0N 104 0 E
Tonnay-Charente, *France* **28 C3** 45 56N 0 55W
Tonneins, *France* **28 D4** 44 23N 0 19 E
Tonnerre, *France* **27 E10** 47 51N 3 59 E
Tönning, *Germany* **30 A4** 54 19N 8 56 E
Tono, *Japan* **68 E10** 39 19N 141 32 E
Tonopah, *U.S.A.* **159 G5** 38 4N 117 14W
Tonoshō, *Japan* **70 C6** 34 29N 134 11 E
Tonosí, *Panama* **164 E3** 7 20N 80 20W
Tønsberg, *Norway* **15 G14** 59 19N 10 25 E
Tonsina, *U.S.A.* **144 F11** 61 39N 145 11W
Tonstad, *Norway* **18 F3** 58 40N 6 45 E
Tonumea, *Tonga* **133 Q13** 20 30 S 174 30W
Tonya, *Turkey* **101 B8** 40 53N 39 16 E
Tonzang, *Burma* **90 D4** 23 36N 93 42 E
Tonzi, *Burma* **90 C5** 24 39N 94 57 E
Tooele, *U.S.A.* **158 F7** 40 32N 112 18W
Toolondo, *Australia* **128 D4** 36 58 S 141 58 E
Toompine, *Australia* **127 D3** 27 15 S 144 19 E
Toomsboro, *U.S.A.* **152 C6** 32 50N 83 5W
Toongi, *Australia* **129 B8** 32 28 S 148 30 E
Toonpan, *Australia* **126 B4** 19 28 S 146 48 E
Toora, *Australia* **129 E7** 38 39 S 146 23 E
Toora-Khem, *Russia* **65 D10** 52 28N 96 17 E
Toowoomba, *Australia* **127 D5** 27 32 S 151 56 E
Top-ozero, *Russia* **56 A5** 65 35N 32 0 E
Topalu, *Romania* **53 F13** 44 31N 28 3 E
Topaz, *U.S.A.* **160 G7** 38 41N 119 30W
Topeka, *U.S.A.* **154 F7** 39 3N 95 40W
Topl'a →, *Slovak Rep.* **35 C14** 48 45N 21 45 E
Topley, *Canada* **142 C3** 54 49N 126 18W
Toplica →, *Serbia, Yug.* **50 C5** 43 15N 21 49 E
Toplița, *Romania* **53 D10** 46 55N 25 20 E
Topocalma, Pta., *Chile* **174 C1** 34 10 S 72 2W
Topock, *U.S.A.* **161 L12** 34 46N 114 29W
Topola, *Serbia, Yug.* **50 B4** 44 17N 20 41 E
Topolčani, *Macedonia* **50 E5** 41 14N 21 25 E
Topoľčany, *Slovak Rep.* **35 C11** 48 35N 18 12 E
Topolnitsa →, *Bulgaria* **51 D8** 42 11N 24 18 E
Topolobampo, *Mexico* **162 B3** 25 40N 109 4W
Topoloveni, *Romania* **53 F10** 44 49N 25 5 E
Topolovgrad, *Bulgaria* **51 D10** 42 5N 26 20 E
Topolvățu Mare, *Romania* **52 E6** 45 46N 21 41 E
Toppenish, *U.S.A.* **158 C3** 46 23N 120 19W
Topraisar, *Romania* **53 F13** 44 1N 28 27 E
Topusko, *Croatia* **45 C12** 45 18N 15 59 E
Toquepala, *Peru* **172 D3** 17 24 S 70 25W
Torà, *Spain* **40 D6** 41 49N 1 25 E
Tora Kit, *Sudan* **107 E3** 11 2N 32 36 E
Toraka Vestale, *Madag.* **117 B7** 16 20 S 43 58 E
Torata, *Peru* **172 D3** 17 23 S 70 1W
Torbalı, *Turkey* **49 C9** 38 10N 27 21 E
Torbay, *Canada* **141 C9** 47 40N 52 42W
Torbay □, *U.K.* **21 G4** 50 26N 3 31W
Tørberget, *Norway* **18 C9** 61 8N 12 7 E
Torbjörntorp, *Sweden* **17 F7** 58 12N 13 36 E
Tordesillas, *Spain* **42 D6** 41 30N 5 0W
Töreboda, *Sweden* **17 F8** 58 41N 14 7 E
Torekov, *Sweden* **17 H6** 56 26N 12 37 E
Torellò, *Spain* **40 C7** 42 3N 2 16 E
Toreno, *Spain* **42 C4** 42 42N 6 30W
Torfaen □, *U.K.* **21 F4** 51 43N 3 3W
Torfajökull, *Iceland* **11 D7** 63 54N 19 0W
Torfastaðir, *Iceland* **11 C6** 64 10N 20 30W
Torgau, *Germany* **30 D8** 51 34N 13 0 E
Torgelow, *Germany* **30 B10** 53 37N 14 1 E
Torhamn, *Sweden* **17 H9** 56 6N 15 50 E
Torhout, *Belgium* **24 C3** 51 5N 3 7 E
Tori, *Ethiopia* **107 F3** 7 53N 33 35 E
Tori-Shima, *Japan* **69 J10** 30 29N 140 19 E
Torigni-sur-Vire, *France* **26 C6** 49 3N 0 58W
Torija, *Spain* **40 E1** 40 44N 3 2W
Torin, *Mexico* **162 B2** 27 33N 110 15W
Torino, *Italy* **44 C4** 45 3N 7 40 E
Torit, *Sudan* **107 G3** 4 27N 32 31 E
Torkamān, *Iran* **101 D12** 37 35N 47 23 E
Torkovichi, *Russia* **58 C6** 58 51N 30 21 E
Tormac, *Romania* **52 E6** 45 30N 21 30 E
Tormes →, *Spain* **42 D4** 41 18N 6 29W
Tornado Mt., *Canada* **142 D6** 49 55N 114 40W
Tornal'a, *Slovak Rep.* **35 C13** 48 25N 20 20 E
Torne älv →, *Sweden* **14 D21** 65 50N 24 12 E
Torneå = Tornio, *Finland* **14 D21** 65 50N 24 12 E
Torneträsk, *Sweden* **14 B18** 68 24N 19 15 E
Tornio, *Finland* **14 D21** 65 50N 24 12 E
Tornionjoki →, *Finland* **14 D21** 65 50N 24 12 E
Tornquist, *Argentina* **174 D3** 38 8S 62 15W
Toro, *Baleares, Spain* **39 B11** 39 59N 4 8 E
Toro, *Zamora, Spain* **42 D5** 41 35N 5 24W
Torö, *Sweden* **17 F11** 58 48N 17 50 E
Toro, Cerro del, *Chile* **174 B2** 29 10 S 69 50W
Toro Pk., *U.S.A.* **161 M10** 33 34N 116 24W
Törökszentmiklós, *Hungary* **52 C5** 47 11N 20 27 E
Toronîos Kólpos, *Greece* **50 F7** 40 5N 23 30 E
Toronto, *Australia* **129 B9** 33 0S 151 30 E
Toronto, *Canada* **140 D4** 43 39N 79 20W
Toronto, *U.S.A.* **150 F4** 40 28N 80 36W
Toropets, *Russia* **58 D6** 56 30N 31 40 E
Tororo, *Uganda* **118 B3** 0 45N 34 12 E
Toros Dağları, *Turkey* **100 D5** 37 0N 32 30 E
Torotoro, *Bolivia* **173 D4** 18 7S 65 46W
Torpo, *Norway* **18 D5** 60 40N 8 43 E
Torquay, *Australia* **128 E6** 38 20 S 144 19 E
Torquay, *Canada* **143 D8** 49 9N 103 30W
Torquay, *U.K.* **21 G4** 50 27N 3 32W
Torquemada, *Spain* **42 C6** 42 2N 4 19W
Torrance, *U.S.A.* **161 M8** 33 50N 118 19W
Torrão, *Portugal* **43 G2** 38 16N 8 11W
Torre Annunziata, *Italy* **47 B7** 40 45N 14 27 E
Torre de Moncorvo, *Portugal* **42 D3** 41 12N 7 8W
Torre del Campo, *Spain* **43 H7** 37 46N 3 53W
Torre del Greco, *Italy* **47 B7** 40 47N 14 22 E
Torre del Mar, *Spain* **43 J6** 36 44N 4 6W
Torre-Pacheco, *Spain* **41 H4** 37 44N 0 57W
Torre Péllice, *Italy* **44 D4** 44 49N 7 13 E
Torreblanca, *Spain* **40 E5** 40 14N 0 12 E
Torrecampo, *Spain* **43 G6** 38 29N 4 41W
Torrecilla en Cameros, *Spain* **40 C2** 42 15N 2 38W
Torredembarra, *Spain* **40 D6** 41 9N 1 24 E
Torredonjimeno, *Spain* **43 H7** 37 46N 3 57W
Torrejón de Ardoz, *Spain* **42 E7** 40 27N 3 29W
Torrejoncillo, *Spain* **42 F4** 39 54N 6 28W
Torrelaguna, *Spain* **42 E7** 40 50N 3 38W
Torrelavega, *Spain* **42 B6** 43 20N 4 5W
Torremaggiore, *Italy* **45 G12** 41 41N 15 17 E
Torremolinos, *Spain* **43 J6** 36 38N 4 30W
Torrens, L., *Australia* **128 A2** 31 0S 137 50 E
Torrens Cr. →, *Australia* **126 C4** 22 23 S 145 9 E
Torrens Creek, *Australia* **126 C4** 20 48 S 145 3 E
Torrent, *Spain* **41 F4** 39 27N 0 28W
Torrenueva, *Spain* **43 G7** 38 38N 3 22W
Torreón, *Mexico* **162 B4** 25 33N 103 26W
Torreperogil, *Spain* **43 G7** 38 2N 3 17W
Torres, *Mexico* **162 B2** 28 46N 110 47W
Torres, Is., *Vanuatu* **133 C4** 13 15 S 166 37 E
Torres Novas, *Portugal* **43 F2** 39 27N 8 33W
Torres Strait, *Australia* **132 E2** 9 50 S 142 20 E
Torres Vedras, *Portugal* **43 F1** 39 5N 9 15W

292 Torrevieja

Torrevieja, Spain 41 H4 37 59N 0 42W
Torrey, U.S.A. 159 G8 38 18N 111 25W
Torridge →, U.K. 21 G3 51 0N 4 13W
Torridon, L., U.K. 22 D3 57 35N 5 50W
Torrijos, Phil. 80 E4 13 19N 122 5 E
Torrijos, Spain 42 F6 39 59N 4 18W
Tørring, Denmark 17 J3 55 52N 9 29 E
Torrington, Conn., U.S.A. 151 E11 41 48N 73 7W
Torrington, Wyo., U.S.A. 154 D2 42 4N 104 11W
Torroella de Montgrì, Spain 40 C8 42 2N 3 8 E
Torrox, Spain 43 J7 36 46N 3 57W
Torsås, Sweden 17 H9 56 24N 16 0 E
Torsby, Sweden 16 D6 60 7N 13 0 E
Torshälla, Sweden 16 E10 59 25N 16 28 E
Tórshavn, Færoe Is. 14 E9 62 5N 6 56W
Torslanda, Sweden 17 G5 57 44N 11 45 E
Torsö, Sweden 17 F7 58 48N 13 45 E
Tortola, Virgin Is. 165 C7 18 19N 64 45W
Tórtoles de Esgueva, Spain 42 D6 41 49N 4 2W
Tortolì, Italy 46 C2 39 55N 9 39 E
Tortona, Italy 44 D5 44 54N 8 52 E
Tortorici, Italy 47 D7 38 2N 14 49 E
Tortosa, Spain 40 E5 40 49N 0 31 E
Tortosa, C., Spain 40 E5 40 41N 0 52 E
Tortosendo, Portugal 42 E3 40 15N 7 31W
Tortue, I. de la, Haiti 165 B5 20 5N 72 57W
Tortum, Turkey 101 B9 40 19N 41 35 E
Ţorūd, Iran 97 C7 35 25N 55 5 E
Torul, Turkey 101 B8 40 34N 39 18 E
Toruń, Poland 55 E5 53 2N 18 39 E
Toruń □, Poland 55 E5 53 20N 19 0 E
Tory I., Ireland 23 A3 55 16N 8 14W
Torysa →, Slovak Rep. 35 C14 48 39N 21 21 E
Torzhok, Russia 58 D8 57 5N 34 55 E
Torzym, Poland 55 F2 52 19N 15 5 E
Tosa, Japan 70 D5 33 24N 133 23 E
Tosa-Shimizu, Japan 70 E4 32 52N 132 58 E
Tosa-Wan, Japan 70 D5 33 15N 133 30 E
Tosa-yamada, Japan 70 D5 33 36N 133 38 E
Toscana □, Italy 44 E8 43 25N 11 0 E
Toscano, Arcipelago, Italy 44 F7 42 30N 10 30 E
Toshkent, Uzbekistan 63 C4 41 20N 69 10 E
Tosno, Russia 58 C6 59 38N 30 46 E
Tossa de Mar, Spain 40 D7 41 43N 2 56 E
Tösse, Sweden 17 F6 58 58N 12 39 E
Tostado, Argentina 174 B3 29 15 S 61 50W
Tostedt, Germany 30 B5 53 17N 9 42 E
Tostón, Pta. de, Canary Is. 39 F5 28 42N 14 2W
Tosu, Japan 70 D2 33 22N 130 31 E
Tosya, Turkey 100 B6 41 1N 34 2 E
Toszek, Poland 55 H5 50 27N 18 32 E
Totak, Norway 18 E5 59 40N 8 0 E
Totana, Spain 41 H3 37 45N 1 30W
Totebo, Sweden 17 G10 57 38N 16 12 E
Toteng, Botswana 116 C3 20 22 S 22 58 E
Tôtes, France 26 C8 49 41N 1 2 E
Tótkomlós, Hungary 52 D5 46 24N 20 45 E
Totland, Norway 18 C2 61 56N 5 23 E
Totma, Russia 56 C7 60 0N 42 40 E
Totnes, U.K. 21 G4 50 26N 3 42W
Totness, Surinam 169 B6 5 53N 56 19W
Totonicapán, Guatemala 164 D1 14 58N 91 12W
Totora, Bolivia 173 D4 17 42 S 65 9W
Totoya, I., Fiji 133 B3 18 57 S 179 50W
Totskoye, Russia 62 E4 52 32N 52 45 E
Totten Glacier, Antarctica 7 C8 66 45 S 116 10 E
Tottenham, Australia 129 B7 32 14 S 147 21 E
Tottenham, Canada 150 B5 44 1N 79 49W
Tottori, Japan 70 B6 35 30N 134 15 E
Tottori □, Japan 70 B6 35 30N 134 12 E
Touat, Algeria 111 C5 27 27N 0 30 E
Touba, Ivory C. 112 D3 8 22N 7 40W
Toubkal, Djebel, Morocco 110 B3 31 0N 8 0W
Toucy, France 27 E10 47 44N 3 15 E
Tougan, Burkina Faso 112 C4 13 11N 2 58W
Touggourt, Algeria 111 B6 33 6N 6 4 E
Tougué, Guinea 112 C2 11 25N 11 50W
Touho, N. Cal. 133 T19 20 47 S 165 14 E
Toukmatine, Algeria 111 D6 24 49N 7 11 E
Toul, France 27 D12 48 40N 5 53 E
Toulepleu, Ivory C. 112 D3 6 32N 8 24W
Toulon, France 29 E9 43 10N 5 55 E
Toulon, U.S.A. 156 C7 41 6N 89 52W
Toulouse, France 28 E5 43 37N 1 27 E
Toummo, Niger 108 D2 22 45N 14 8 E
Toummo Dhoba, Niger 108 D2 22 30N 14 31 E
Toumodi, Ivory C. 112 D3 6 32N 5 4W
Tounan, Taiwan 77 F13 23 41N 120 28 E
Tounassine, Hamada, Algeria 110 C4 28 48N 5 0W
Toungoo, Burma 90 F6 19 0N 96 30 E
Touques →, France 26 C7 49 22N 0 8 E
Touraine, France 26 E7 47 20N 0 30 E
Tourane = Da Nang, Vietnam 86 D7 16 4N 108 13 E
Tourcoing, France 27 B10 50 42N 3 10 E
Touriñán, C., Spain 42 B1 43 3N 9 17W
Tourine, Mauritania 110 D2 22 23N 11 50W
Tournai, Belgium 24 D3 50 35N 3 25 E
Tournan-en-Brie, France 27 D9 48 44N 2 46 E
Tournay, France 28 E4 43 13N 0 13 E
Tournon-St-Martin, France 26 F7 46 45N 0 58 E
Tournon-sur-Rhône, France 29 C8 45 4N 4 50 E
Tournus, France 27 F11 46 35N 4 54 E
Touros, Brazil 170 C4 5 12 S 35 28W
Tours, France 26 E7 47 22N 0 40 E
Touside, Pic, Chad 109 D3 21 1N 16 29 E
Touwsrivier, S. Africa 116 E3 33 20 S 20 2 E
Tovar, Venezuela 168 B3 8 20N 71 46W
Tovarkovskiy, Russia 58 F10 53 40N 38 14 E
Tovdal, Norway 18 F5 58 47N 8 10 E
Tovdalselva →, Norway 18 F5 58 11N 8 7 E
Tovuz, Azerbaijan 61 K7 41 0N 45 40 E
Towada, Japan 68 D10 40 37N 141 13 E
Towada-Ko, Japan 68 D10 40 28N 140 55 E
Towamba, Australia 129 D8 37 6 S 149 43 E
Towanda, Ill., U.S.A. 157 D8 40 36N 88 53W
Towanda, Pa., U.S.A. 151 E8 41 46N 76 27W
Tower, U.S.A. 154 B8 47 48N 92 17W
Towerhill Cr. →, Australia 126 C3 22 28 S 144 35 E
Towner, U.S.A. 154 A4 48 21N 100 25W
Towns, U.S.A. 152 D7 32 0N 82 45W
Townsend, Ga., U.S.A. 152 D8 31 33N 81 31W
Townsend, Mont., U.S.A. 158 C8 46 19N 111 31W
Townshend I., Australia 126 C5 22 10 S 150 31 E
Townsville, Australia 126 B4 19 15 S 146 45 E
Towson, U.S.A. 148 F7 39 24N 76 36W
Towuti, Danau, Indonesia 82 B2 2 45 S 121 32 E
Toya-Ko, Japan 68 C10 42 35N 140 51 E
Toyah, U.S.A. 155 K3 31 19N 103 48W
Toyahvale, U.S.A. 155 K3 30 57N 103 47W
Toyama, Japan 71 A9 36 40N 137 15 E
Toyama □, Japan 71 A9 36 45N 137 30 E
Toyama-Wan, Japan 69 F8 37 0N 137 30 E
Tōyō, Japan 70 D6 33 26N 134 16 E
Toyohashi, Japan 71 C9 34 45N 137 25 E
Toyokawa, Japan 71 C9 34 48N 137 27 E
Toyonaka, Japan 71 C7 34 50N 135 28 E
Toyooka, Japan 70 B6 35 35N 134 48 E
Toyota, Japan 71 B9 35 3N 137 7 E
Toyoura, Japan 70 C2 34 6N 130 57 E
Toytepa, Uzbekistan 63 C4 41 3N 69 20 E
Tozeur, Tunisia 108 B1 33 56N 8 8 E
Tqibuli, Georgia 61 J6 42 26N 43 0 E
Tqvarcheli, Georgia 61 J5 42 47N 41 42 E
Trá Li = Tralee, Ireland 23 D2 52 16N 9 42W
Tra On, Vietnam 87 H5 9 58N 105 55 E
Trabancos →, Spain 42 D5 41 36N 5 15W
Traben-Trarbach, Germany 31 F3 49 57N 7 7 E
Trabzon, Turkey 101 B8 41 0N 39 45 E
Tracadie, Canada 141 C7 47 30N 64 55W
Tracy, Calif., U.S.A. 160 H5 37 44N 121 26W
Tracy, Minn., U.S.A. 154 C7 44 14N 95 37W
Tradate, Italy 44 C5 45 43N 8 54 E
Traer, U.S.A. 156 B4 42 12N 92 28W
Trafalgar, Australia 129 E7 38 14 S 146 12 E
Trafalgar, C., Spain 43 J4 36 10N 6 2W
Trāghān, Libya 108 C2 26 0N 14 30 E
Tragowel, Australia 128 C6 35 50 S 144 0 E
Traian, Brăila, Romania 53 E12 45 11N 27 44 E
Traian, Tulcea, Romania 53 E13 45 2N 28 15 E
Traiguén, Chile 176 A2 38 15 S 72 41W
Trail, Canada 142 D5 49 5N 117 40W
Traill Ø, Greenland 10 C8 72 30N 23 0W
Trainor L., Canada 142 A4 60 24N 120 17W
Traíra →, Brazil 168 D4 1 4 S 69 26W
Trákhonas, Cyprus 38 D12 35 12N 33 21 E
Tralee, Ireland 23 D2 52 16N 9 42W
Tralee B., Ireland 23 D2 52 17N 9 55W
Tramelan, Switz. 32 B4 47 13N 7 7 E
Tramore, Ireland 23 D4 52 10N 7 10W
Tramore B., Ireland 23 D4 52 9N 7 10W
Tran Ninh, Cao Nguyen, Laos 86 C4 19 30N 103 10 E
Tranås, Sweden 17 F8 58 3N 14 59 E
Tranbjerg, Denmark 17 H4 56 6N 10 9 E
Tranby, Norway 18 E7 59 49N 10 15 E
Trancas, Argentina 174 B2 26 11 S 65 20W
Trancoso, Portugal 42 E3 40 49N 7 21W
Tranebjerg, Denmark 17 J4 55 51N 10 36 E
Tranemo, Sweden 17 G7 57 30N 13 20 E
Trang, Thailand 87 J2 7 33N 99 38 E
Trangahy, Madag. 117 B7 19 7 S 44 31 E
Trangan, Indonesia 83 C4 6 40 S 134 20 E
Trangie, Australia 129 B8 32 4 S 148 0 E
Trångsviken, Sweden 16 A7 63 19N 13 59 E
Trani, Italy 47 A9 41 17N 16 25 E
Tranoroa, Madag. 117 C8 24 42 S 45 4 E
Tranquebar, India 95 J4 11 1N 79 54 E
Tranqueras, Uruguay 175 C4 31 13 S 55 45W
Trans Nzoia □, Kenya 118 B4 1 0N 35 0 E
Transantarctic Mts., Antarctica 7 E12 85 0 S 170 0W
Transcaucasia = Zakavkazye, Asia 57 F7 42 0N 44 0 E
Transcona, Canada 143 D9 49 55N 97 0W
Transilvania, Romania 53 D9 46 30N 24 0 E
Transilvanian Alps = Carpații Meridionali, Romania 53 E9 45 30N 25 0 E
Transtrand, Sweden 16 C7 61 6N 13 20 E
Transtrandsfjällen, Sweden 16 C6 61 8N 13 0 E
Transylvania = Transilvania, Romania 53 D9 46 30N 24 0 E
Trápani, Italy 46 D5 38 1N 12 29 E
Trapper Pk., U.S.A. 158 D6 45 54N 114 18W
Traralgon, Australia 129 E7 38 12 S 146 34 E
Trarza, Mauritania 112 B2 17 30N 15 0W
Trás-os-Montes, Angola 115 E3 10 17 S 19 5 E
Trasacco, Italy 45 G10 41 57N 13 32 E
Trăscău, Munții, Romania 53 D8 46 14N 23 14 E
Trasimeno, L., Italy 45 E9 43 8N 12 6 E
Träslövsläge, Sweden 17 G6 57 4N 12 16 E
Trasvase Tajo-Segura, Canal de, Spain 40 E2 40 15N 2 55W
Trat, Thailand 87 F4 12 14N 102 33 E
Traun, Austria 34 C7 48 14N 14 15 E
Traunreut, Germany 31 H8 47 57N 12 36 E
Traunsee, Austria 34 D6 47 55N 13 50 E
Traunstein, Germany 31 H8 47 52N 12 37 E
Traveller's L., Australia 128 B5 33 20 S 142 0 E
Travemünde, Germany 30 B6 53 57N 10 52 E
Travers, Mt., N.Z. 131 C7 42 1 S 172 45 E
Traverse City, U.S.A. 148 C3 44 46N 85 38W
Travnik, Bos.-H. 52 F2 44 17N 17 39 E
Trayning, Australia 125 F2 31 7 S 117 40 E
Trbovlje, Slovenia 45 B12 46 12N 15 5 E
Treasure Island, U.S.A. 153 H7 27 46N 82 46W
Treasury Is., Solomon Is. 133 L8 7 22 S 155 37 E
Trébbia →, Italy 44 C6 45 4N 9 41 E
Trebel →, Germany 30 B9 53 54N 13 2 E
Trébeurden, France 26 D3 48 46N 3 35W
Třebíč, Czech Rep. 34 B8 49 14N 15 55 E
Trebinje, Bos.-H. 50 D2 42 44N 18 22 E
Trebisacce, Italy 47 C9 39 52N 16 32 E
Trebišnjica →, Bos.-H. 50 D2 42 47N 18 8 E
Trebišov, Slovak Rep. 35 C14 48 38N 21 41 E
Trebižat →, Bos.-H. 45 E14 43 15N 17 30 E
Trebnje, Slovenia 45 C12 45 54N 15 1 E
Třeboň, Czech Rep. 34 B7 49 1N 14 48 E
Trebujena, Spain 43 J4 36 52N 6 11W
Trecate, Italy 44 C5 45 26N 8 44 E
Trece Martires, Phil. 80 D3 14 20N 120 50 E
Tregaron, U.K. 21 E4 52 14N 3 56W
Tregnago, Italy 45 C8 45 31N 11 10 E
Tregrosse Is., Australia 126 B5 17 41 S 150 43 E
Tréguier, France 26 D3 48 47N 3 16W
Trégunc, France 26 E3 47 51N 3 51W
Treherne, Canada 143 D9 49 38N 98 42W
Tréia, Italy 45 E10 43 19N 13 19 E
Treignac, France 28 C5 45 32N 1 48 E
Treinta y Tres, Uruguay 175 C5 33 16 S 54 17W
Treis-karden, Germany 31 E3 50 10N 7 18 E
Treklyano, Bulgaria 50 D6 42 33N 22 36 E
Trélazé, France 26 E6 47 26N 0 30W
Trelew, Argentina 176 B3 43 10 S 65 20W
Trélissac, France 28 C4 45 11N 0 47 E
Trelleborg, Sweden 17 J7 55 20N 13 10 E
Tremadog Bay, U.K. 20 E3 52 51N 4 18W
Trémiti, Italy 45 F12 42 8N 15 30 E
Tremonton, U.S.A. 158 F7 41 43N 112 10W
Tremp, Spain 40 C5 42 10N 0 52 E
Trenche →, Canada 140 C5 47 46N 72 53W
Trenčiansky □, Slovak Rep. 35 C11 48 45N 18 20 E
Trenčín, Slovak Rep. 35 C11 48 52N 18 4 E
Trengereid, Norway 18 D2 60 26N 5 37 E
Trenggalek, Indonesia 85 D4 8 3 S 111 43 E
Trenque Lauquen, Argentina 174 D3 36 5 S 62 45W
Trent →, U.K. 20 D7 53 41N 0 42W
Trentino-Alto Adige □, Italy 45 B8 46 30N 11 20 E
Trento, Italy 44 B8 46 4N 11 8 E
Trenton, Canada 140 D4 44 10N 77 34W
Trenton, Fla., U.S.A. 153 F7 29 37N 82 49W
Trenton, Mich., U.S.A. 157 B13 42 8N 83 11W
Trenton, Mo., U.S.A. 156 D3 40 5N 93 37W
Trenton, N.J., U.S.A. 151 F10 40 14N 74 46W
Trenton, Nebr., U.S.A. 154 E4 40 11N 101 1W
Trenton, S.C., U.S.A. 152 B9 33 45N 81 51W
Trenton, Tenn., U.S.A. 155 H10 35 59N 88 56W
Trepassey, Canada 141 C9 46 43N 53 25W
Trepuzzi, Italy 47 B11 40 24N 18 4 E
Tres Arroyos, Argentina 174 D3 38 26 S 60 20W
Três Corações, Brazil 171 F2 21 44 S 45 15W
Três Lagoas, Brazil 171 F1 20 50 S 51 43W
Tres Lagos →, Argentina 176 C2 49 35 S 71 25W
Tres Marías, Mexico 162 C3 21 25N 106 28W
Três Marias, Reprêsa, Brazil 171 E2 18 12 S 45 15W
Tres Montes, C., Chile 176 C1 46 50 S 75 30W
Tres Pinos, U.S.A. 160 J5 36 48N 121 19W
Três Pontas, Brazil 171 F2 21 23 S 45 29W
Tres Puentes, Chile 174 B1 27 50 S 70 15W
Tres Puntas, C., Argentina 176 C3 47 0 S 66 0W
Três Rios, Brazil 171 F3 22 6 S 43 15W
Tres Valles, Mexico 163 D5 18 15N 96 8W
Tresco, U.K. 21 H1 49 57N 6 20W
Tresfjord, Norway 18 B4 62 31N 7 7 E
Treska →, Macedonia 50 E5 42 0N 21 20 E
Treskavica, Bos.-H. 52 G3 43 40N 18 20 E
Trespaderne, Spain 42 C7 42 47N 3 24W
Trets, France 29 E9 43 27N 5 41 E
Treuchtlingen, Germany 31 G6 48 58N 10 54 E
Treuenbrietzen, Germany 30 C8 52 5N 12 52 E
Treungen, Norway 18 E5 59 1N 8 31 E
Trevi, Italy 45 F9 42 52N 12 45 E
Trevíglio, Italy 44 C6 45 31N 9 35 E
Trevínca, Peña, Spain 42 C4 42 15N 6 46W
Treviso, Italy 45 C9 45 40N 12 15 E
Trévoux, France 29 C8 45 57N 4 47 E
Trgovište, Serbia, Yug. 50 D6 42 20N 22 10 E
Triabunna, Australia 126 G4 42 30 S 147 55 E
Triánda, Greece 38 C10 36 25N 28 10 E
Triaucourt-en-Argonne, France 27 D12 48 59N 5 2 E
Tribly, U.S.A. 153 G7 28 28N 82 12W
Tribsees, Germany 30 A8 54 5N 12 44 E
Tribulation, C., Australia 126 B4 16 5 S 145 29 E
Tribune, U.S.A. 154 F4 38 28N 101 45W
Tricárico, Italy 47 B9 40 37N 16 9 E
Tricase, Italy 47 C11 39 56N 18 22 E
Trichinopoly = Tiruchchirappalli, India 95 J4 10 45N 78 45 E
Trichur, India 95 J3 10 30N 76 18 E
Trida, Australia 129 B6 33 1 S 145 1 E
Trier, Germany 31 F2 49 45N 6 38 E
Trieste, Italy 45 C10 45 40N 13 46 E
Trieste, G. di, Italy 45 C10 45 40N 13 35 E
Trieux →, France 26 D3 48 43N 3 9W
Triggiano, Italy 47 A9 41 4N 16 55 E
Triglav, Slovenia 45 B10 46 21N 13 50 E
Trigno →, Italy 45 F11 42 4N 14 48 E
Trigueros, Spain 43 H4 37 24N 6 50W
Tríkeri, Greece 48 B5 39 6N 23 5 E
Trikhonis, Límni, Greece 48 C3 38 34N 21 30 E
Tríkkala, Greece 48 B3 39 34N 21 47 E
Tríkkala □, Greece 48 B3 39 41N 21 30 E
Trikomo, Cyprus 38 D12 35 17N 33 52 E
Trikora, Puncak, Indonesia 83 B5 4 15 S 138 45 E
Trilj, Croatia 45 E13 43 38N 16 42 E
Trillo, Spain 40 E2 40 42N 2 35W
Trim, Ireland 23 C5 53 33N 6 48W
Trincomalee, Sri Lanka 95 K5 8 38N 81 15 E
Trindade, Brazil 171 E2 16 40 S 49 30W
Trindade, I., Atl. Oc. 9 L6 20 20 S 29 50W
Třinec, Czech Rep. 35 B11 49 41N 18 39 E
Trinidad, Bolivia 173 C5 14 46 S 64 50W
Trinidad, Colombia 168 B3 5 25N 71 40W
Trinidad, Cuba 164 B4 21 48N 80 0W
Trinidad, Uruguay 174 C4 33 30 S 56 50W
Trinidad, U.S.A. 155 G2 37 10N 104 31W
Trinidad, W. Indies 165 D7 10 30N 61 15W
Trinidad →, Mexico 163 D5 17 49N 95 9W
Trinidad, G., Chile 176 C1 49 55 S 75 25W
Trinidad, I., Argentina 176 A4 39 10 S 62 0W
Trinidad & Tobago ■, W. Indies 165 D7 10 30N 61 20W
Trinitápoli, Italy 47 A9 41 21N 16 5 E
Trinity, Canada 141 C9 48 59N 53 55W
Trinity, U.S.A. 155 K7 30 57N 95 22W
Trinity →, Calif., U.S.A. 158 F2 41 11N 123 42W
Trinity →, Tex., U.S.A. 155 L7 29 45N 94 43W
Trinity B., Canada 141 C9 48 20N 53 10W
Trinity Is., U.S.A. 144 H9 56 33N 154 25W
Trinity Range, U.S.A. 158 F4 40 15N 118 45W
Trinkitat, Sudan 106 D4 18 45N 37 51 E
Trino, Italy 44 C5 45 12N 8 18 E
Trion, U.S.A. 149 H3 34 33N 85 19W
Trionto, C., Italy 47 C9 39 37N 16 43 E
Triora, Italy 44 D4 44 1N 7 46 E
Tripoli = Tarābulus, Lebanon 103 A4 34 31N 35 50 E
Tripoli = Tarābulus, Libya 108 B2 32 49N 13 7 E
Tripoli, U.S.A. 156 B4 42 49N 92 16W
Trípolis, Greece 48 D4 37 31N 22 25 E
Tripolitania, Libya 108 B2 31 0N 12 0 E
Tripp, U.S.A. 154 D6 43 13N 97 58W
Tripura □, India 90 D4 24 0N 92 0 E
Tripylos, Cyprus 38 E11 34 59N 32 41 E
Trischen, Germany 30 A4 54 4N 8 40 E
Tristan da Cunha, Atl. Oc. 9 M7 37 6 S 12 20W
Trivandrum, India 95 K3 8 41N 77 0 E
Trivento, Italy 45 G11 41 47N 14 33 E
Trnava, Slovak Rep. 35 C10 48 23N 17 35 E
Trnavský □, Slovak Rep. 35 C10 48 30N 17 45 E
Troarn, France 26 C6 49 11N 0 11W
Trobriand Is., Papua N. G. 132 E6 8 30 S 151 0 E
Trochu, Canada 142 C6 51 50N 113 13W
Trodely I., Canada 140 B4 52 15N 79 26W
Troezen, Greece 48 D5 37 25N 23 15 E
Trogir, Croatia 45 E13 43 32N 16 15 E
Troglav, Croatia 45 E13 43 56N 16 36 E
Tróia, Italy 47 A8 41 22N 15 18 E
Troilus, L., Canada 140 B5 50 50N 74 35W
Troina, Italy 47 E7 37 47N 14 36 E
Trois Fourches, Cap des, Morocco 111 A4 35 26N 2 58W
Trois-Pistoles, Canada 141 C6 48 5N 69 10W
Trois-Rivières, Canada 140 C5 46 25N 72 34W
Troisdorf, Germany 30 E3 50 48N 7 11 E
Troitsk, Russia 62 D8 54 10N 61 35 E
Troitskiy, Russia 62 C9 57 5N 63 43 E
Troitsko Pechorsk, Russia 56 B10 62 40N 56 10 E
Trölladyngja, Iceland 11 C9 64 54N 17 16W
Trollhättan, Sweden 17 F6 58 17N 12 20 E
Trollheimen, Norway 14 E13 62 46N 9 1 E
Trombetas →, Brazil 169 D6 1 55 S 55 35W
Tromelin I., Ind. Oc. 121 F4 15 52 S 54 25 E
Tromøy, Norway 18 F5 58 27N 8 51 E
Tromsø, Norway 14 B18 69 40N 18 56 E
Trona, U.S.A. 161 K9 35 46N 117 23W
Tronador, Argentina 176 B2 41 10 S 71 50W
Trøndelag, Norway 14 D14 64 17N 11 50 E
Trondheim, Norway 14 E14 63 36N 10 25 E
Trondheimsfjorden, Norway 14 E14 63 35N 10 30 E
Trondheimsleia, Norway 18 A5 63 25N 8 30 E
Trönninge, Sweden 17 H6 56 37N 12 51 E
Tronto →, Italy 45 F10 42 54N 13 55 E
Troodos, Cyprus 38 E11 34 55N 32 52 E
Troon, U.K. 22 F4 55 33N 4 39W
Tropea, Italy 47 D8 38 41N 15 54 E
Tropic, U.S.A. 159 H7 37 37N 112 5W
Tropoja, Albania 50 D4 42 23N 20 10 E
Trosa, Sweden 17 F11 58 54N 17 33 E
Trostan, U.K. 23 A5 55 3N 6 10W
Trostberg, Germany 31 G8 48 1N 12 33 E
Trostyanets, Ukraine 59 G8 50 33N 34 59 E
Troup, U.S.A. 155 J7 32 9N 95 7W
Trout →, Canada 142 A5 61 19N 119 51W
Trout L., N.W.T., Canada 142 A4 60 40N 121 14W
Trout L., Ont., Canada 143 C10 51 20N 93 15W
Trout Lake, Mich., U.S.A. 140 C2 46 12N 85 1W
Trout Lake, Wash., U.S.A. 160 E5 46 0N 121 32W
Trout River, Canada 141 C8 49 29N 58 8W
Trouville-sur-Mer, France 26 C7 49 21N 0 5 E
Trowbridge, U.K. 21 F5 51 18N 2 12W
Troy, Turkey 49 B8 39 57N 26 12 E
Troy, Ala., U.S.A. 152 D4 31 48N 85 58W
Troy, Idaho, U.S.A. 158 C5 46 44N 116 46W
Troy, Ill., U.S.A. 156 F7 38 44N 89 54W
Troy, Ind., U.S.A. 157 G10 37 59N 86 55W
Troy, Kans., U.S.A. 154 F7 39 47N 95 5W
Troy, Mich., U.S.A. 157 B13 42 37N 83 9W
Troy, Mo., U.S.A. 156 F6 38 59N 90 59W
Troy, Mont., U.S.A. 158 B6 48 28N 115 53W
Troy, N.Y., U.S.A. 151 D11 42 44N 73 41W
Troy, Ohio, U.S.A. 157 D12 40 2N 84 12W
Troy, S.C., U.S.A. 152 B7 33 59N 82 17W
Troyan, Bulgaria 51 D8 42 57N 24 43 E
Troyes, France 27 D11 48 19N 4 3 E
Trpanj, Croatia 45 E14 43 1N 17 15 E
Trstenik, Serbia, Yug. 50 C5 43 36N 21 0 E
Trubchevsk, Russia 59 F7 52 33N 33 47 E
Trucial States = United Arab Emirates ■, Asia 97 F7 23 50N 54 0 E
Truckee, U.S.A. 160 F6 39 20N 120 11W
Trudfront, Russia 61 H8 45 56N 47 40 E
Trudovoye, Russia 68 C6 43 17N 132 5 E
Trujillo, Colombia 168 C2 4 10N 76 19W
Trujillo, Honduras 164 C2 16 0N 86 0W
Trujillo, Peru 172 B2 8 6 S 79 0W
Trujillo, Spain 43 F5 39 28N 5 55W
Trujillo, U.S.A. 155 H2 35 32N 104 42W
Trujillo, Venezuela 168 B3 9 22N 70 38W
Trujillo □, Venezuela 168 B3 9 25N 70 30W
Truk, Pac. Oc. 134 G7 7 25N 151 46 E
Trumann, U.S.A. 155 H9 35 41N 90 31W
Trumbull, Mt., U.S.A. 159 H7 36 25N 113 8W
Trŭn, Bulgaria 50 D6 42 51N 22 38 E
Trun, France 26 D7 48 50N 0 2 E
Trun, Switz. 33 C7 46 45N 8 59 E
Trundle, Australia 129 B7 32 53 S 147 35 E
Trung-Phan = Annam, Vietnam 86 E7 16 0N 108 0 E
Truro, Australia 128 C3 34 24 S 139 9 E
Truro, Canada 141 C7 45 21N 63 14W
Truro, U.K. 21 G2 50 16N 5 4W
Truskavets, Ukraine 59 H2 49 17N 23 30 E
Truslove, Australia 125 F3 33 20 S 121 45 E
Trŭstenik, Bulgaria 51 C8 43 31N 24 28 E
Trustrup, Denmark 17 H4 56 20N 10 46 E
Truth or Consequences, U.S.A. 159 K10 33 8N 107 15W
Trutnov, Czech Rep. 34 A8 50 37N 15 54 E
Truyère →, France 28 D6 44 38N 2 34 E
Tryavna, Bulgaria 51 D9 42 54N 25 25 E
Tryon, U.S.A. 149 H4 35 13N 82 14W
Tryonville, U.S.A. 150 E5 41 42N 79 48W
Trysilelva →, Norway 18 C9 61 2N 12 35 E
Trzcianka, Poland 55 E3 53 3N 16 25 E
Trzciel, Poland 55 F2 52 23N 15 50 E
Trzcińsko Zdrój, Poland 55 F1 52 58N 14 35 E
Trzebiatów, Poland 54 D2 54 3N 15 18 E
Trzebiez, Poland 54 E1 53 38N 14 31 E
Trzebnica, Poland 55 G4 51 20N 17 1 E
Trzemeszno, Poland 55 F4 52 33N 17 48 E
Tržič, Slovenia 45 B11 46 22N 14 18 E
Tsagan Aman, Russia 61 G8 47 34N 46 43 E
Tsala Apopka L., U.S.A. 153 G7 28 53N 82 19W
Tsamandás, Greece 48 B2 39 46N 20 21 E
Tsaratanana, Madag. 117 B8 16 47 S 47 39 E
Tsaratanana, Mt. de, Madag. 117 A8 14 0 S 49 0 E
Tsarevo = Michurin, Bulgaria 51 D11 42 9N 27 51 E
Tsarevo, Bulgaria 51 D9 42 28N 25 52 E
Tsaritsáni, Greece 48 B4 39 53N 22 14 E
Tsau, Botswana 116 C3 20 8 S 22 22 E
Tsebrykove, Ukraine 59 J6 47 9N 30 10 E
Tselinograd = Aqmola, Kazakstan 64 D8 51 10N 71 30 E
Tsetserleg, Mongolia 72 B5 47 36N 101 32 E
Tshabong, Botswana 116 D3 26 2 S 22 29 E
Tshane, Botswana 116 C3 24 5 S 21 54 E
Tshela, Dem. Rep. of the Congo 115 C2 4 57 S 13 4 E
Tshesebe, Botswana 117 C4 21 51 S 27 32 E
Tshibeke, Dem. Rep. of the Congo 118 C2 2 40 S 28 35 E
Tshibinda, Dem. Rep. of the Congo 118 C2 2 23 S 28 43 E
Tshikapa, Dem. Rep. of the Congo 115 D4 6 28 S 20 48 E
Tshilenge, Dem. Rep. of the Congo 115 D4 6 17 S 23 48 E
Tshinsenda, Dem. Rep. of the Congo 119 E2 12 20 S 28 0 E
Tshofa, Dem. Rep. of the Congo 115 D5 5 13 S 25 16 E
Tshwane, Botswana 116 C3 22 24 S 22 1 E
Tsigara, Botswana 116 C4 20 22 S 25 54 E
Tsihombe, Madag. 117 D8 25 10 S 45 41 E

Uberaba 293

Tsimlyansk, *Russia* **61 G6** 47 40N 42 6 E
Tsimlyansk Res. = Tsimlyanskoye Vdkhr., *Russia* **61 F6** 48 0N 43 0 E
Tsimlyanskoye Vdkhr., *Russia* **61 F6** 48 0N 43 0 E
Tsinan = Jinan, *China* **74 F9** 36 38N 117 1 E
Tsineng, *S. Africa* **116 D3** 27 5 S 23 5 E
Tsínga, *Greece* **51 E8** 41 23N 24 44 E
Tsinghai = Qinghai □, *China* **72 C4** 36 0N 98 0 E
Tsingtao = Qingdao, *China* **75 F11** 36 5N 120 20 E
Tsinjomitondraka, *Madag.* **117 B8** 15 40 S 47 8 E
Tsiroanomandidy, *Madag.* **117 B8** 18 46 S 46 2 E
Tsiteli-Tsqaro, *Georgia* **61 K8** 41 33N 46 0 E
Tsivilsk, *Russia* **60 C8** 55 50N 47 25 E
Tsivory, *Madag.* **117 C8** 24 4 S 46 5 E
Tskhinvali, *Georgia* **61 J7** 42 14N 44 1 E
Tsna →, *Russia* **60 C6** 54 55N 41 58 E
Tsnori, *Georgia* **61 K7** 41 40N 45 57 E
Tso Moriri, L., *India* **93 C8** 32 50N 78 20 E
Tsodilo Hill, *Botswana* **116 B3** 18 49 S 21 43 E
Tsogttsetsiy, *Mongolia* **74 C3** 43 43N 105 35 E
Tsolo, *S. Africa* **117 E4** 31 18 S 28 37 E
Tsomo, *S. Africa* **117 E4** 32 0 S 27 42 E
Tsu, *Japan* **71 C8** 34 45N 136 25 E
Tsu L., *Canada* **142 A6** 60 40N 111 52W
Tsuchiura, *Japan* **71 A12** 36 5N 140 15 E
Tsugaru-Kaikyō, *Japan* **68 D10** 41 35N 141 0 E
Tsukumi, *Japan* **70 D3** 33 4N 131 52 E
Tsukushi-Sanchi, *Japan* **70 D2** 33 25N 130 30 E
Tsumeb, *Namibia* **116 B2** 19 9 S 17 44 E
Tsumis, *Namibia* **116 C2** 23 39 S 17 29 E
Tsuna, *Japan* **70 C6** 34 28N 134 56 E
Tsuno-Shima, *Japan* **70 C2** 34 21N 130 52 E
Tsuru, *Japan* **71 B10** 35 31N 138 57 E
Tsuruga, *Japan* **71 B8** 35 45N 136 2 E
Tsuruga-Wan, *Japan* **71 B8** 35 50N 136 3 E
Tsurugi, *Japan* **71 A8** 36 29N 136 37 E
Tsurugi-San, *Japan* **70 D6** 33 51N 134 6 E
Tsurumi-Saki, *Japan* **70 E4** 32 56N 132 5 E
Tsuruoka, *Japan* **68 E9** 38 44N 139 50 E
Tsurusaki, *Japan* **70 D3** 33 14N 131 41 E
Tsushima, *Gifu, Japan* **71 B8** 35 10N 136 43 E
Tsushima, *Nagasaki, Japan* **70 C1** 34 20N 129 20 E
Tsvetkovo, *Ukraine* **59 H6** 49 8N 31 33 E
Tsyelyakhany, *Belarus* **59 F3** 52 30N 25 46 E
Tu →, *Burma* **90 E6** 21 50N 96 15 E
Tua →, *Portugal* **42 D3** 41 13N 7 26W
Tuai, *N.Z.* **130 E6** 38 47 S 177 10 E
Tuakau, *N.Z.* **130 D3** 37 16 S 174 59 E
Tual, *Indonesia* **83 C4** 5 38 S 132 44 E
Tuam, *Ireland* **23 C3** 53 31N 8 51W
Tuamarina, *N.Z.* **131 B8** 41 25 S 173 59 E
Tuamotu Arch. = Tuamotu Is., *Pac. Oc.* **135 J13** 17 0 S 144 0W
Tuamotu Is., *Pac. Oc.* **135 J13** 17 0 S 144 0W
Tuamotu Ridge, *Pac. Oc.* **135 K14** 20 0 S 138 0W
Tuanfeng, *China* **77 B10** 30 38N 114 52 E
Tuanxi, *China* **76 D6** 27 28N 107 8 E
Tuao, *Phil.* **80 C3** 17 55N 121 22 E
Tuapse, *Russia* **61 H4** 44 5N 39 10 E
Tuas, *Singapore* **84 B2** 1 19N 103 39 E
Tuatapere, *N.Z.* **131 G2** 46 8 S 167 41 E
Tuba City, *U.S.A.* **159 H8** 36 8N 111 14W
Tuban, *Indonesia* **85 D4** 6 54 S 112 3 E
Tubarão, *Brazil* **175 B6** 28 30 S 49 0W
Tūbās, *West Bank* **103 C4** 32 20N 35 22 E
Tubau, *Malaysia* **85 B4** 3 10N 113 40 E
Tübingen, *Germany* **31 G5** 48 31N 9 4 E
Tubruq, *Libya* **108 B4** 32 7N 23 55 E
Tubuai Is., *Pac. Oc.* **135 K13** 25 0 S 150 0W
Tuburan, *Phil.* **81 H4** 6 39N 122 16 E
Tuc Trung, *Vietnam* **87 G6** 11 1N 107 12 E
Tucacas, *Venezuela* **168 A4** 10 48N 68 19W
Tucano, *Brazil* **170 D4** 10 58 S 38 48W
T'uch'ang, *Taiwan* **77 E13** 24 42N 121 25 E
Tuchodi →, *Canada* **142 B4** 58 17N 123 42W
Tuchola, *Poland* **54 E4** 53 33N 17 52 E
Tuchów, *Poland* **55 J8** 49 54N 21 1 E
Tucker, *U.S.A.* **152 B5** 33 51N 84 13W
Tucson, *U.S.A.* **159 K8** 32 13N 110 58W
Tucumán □, *Argentina* **174 B2** 26 48 S 66 2W
Tucumcari, *U.S.A.* **155 H3** 35 10N 103 44W
Tucunaré, *Brazil* **173 B6** 5 18 S 55 51W
Tucupido, *Venezuela* **168 B4** 9 17N 65 47W
Tucupita, *Venezuela* **169 B5** 9 2N 62 3W
Tucuruí, *Brazil* **170 B2** 3 42 S 49 44W
Tucuruí, Reprêsa de, *Brazil* **170 B2** 4 0 S 49 30W
Tuczno, *Poland* **55 E3** 53 13N 16 10 E
Tuddal, *Norway* **18 E5** 59 46N 8 49 E
Tudela, *Spain* **40 C3** 42 4N 1 39W
Tudmur, *Syria* **101 E8** 34 36N 38 15 E
Tudor, L., *Canada* **141 A6** 55 50N 65 25W
Tudora, *Romania* **53 C11** 47 31N 26 45 E
Tuella →, *Portugal* **42 D3** 41 30N 7 12W
Tuen, *Australia* **127 D4** 28 33 S 145 37 E
Tueré →, *Brazil* **170 B1** 2 48 S 50 59W
Tufi, *Papua N. G.* **132 E5** 9 8 S 149 19 E
Tufsingdalen, *Norway* **18 B8** 62 18N 11 44 E
Tugela →, *S. Africa* **117 D5** 29 14 S 31 30 E
Tuguegarao, *Phil.* **80 C3** 17 35N 121 42 E
Tugur, *Russia* **65 D14** 53 44N 136 45 E
Tui, *Spain* **42 C2** 42 3N 8 39W
Tuineje, *Canary Is.* **39 F5** 28 19N 14 3W
Tukangbesi, Kepulauan, *Indonesia* **82 C2** 6 0 S 124 0 E
Tukarak I., *Canada* **140 A4** 56 15N 78 45W
Tukayyid, *Iraq* **96 D5** 29 47N 45 36 E
Tûkh, *Egypt* **106 H7** 30 21N 31 12 E
Tukituki →, *N.Z.* **130 F5** 39 36 S 176 56 E
Tukobo, *Ghana* **112 D4** 5 1N 2 47W
Tūkrah, *Libya* **108 B4** 32 30N 20 37 E
Tuktoyaktuk, *Canada* **138 B6** 69 27N 133 2W
Tukums, *Latvia* **15 H20** 56 58N 23 10 E
Tukums □, *Latvia* **54 B10** 56 55N 23 0 E
Tukuyu, *Tanzania* **119 D3** 9 17 S 33 35 E
Tula, *Hidalgo, Mexico* **163 C5** 20 5N 99 20W
Tula, *Tamaulipas, Mexico* **163 C5** 23 0N 99 40W
Tula, *Nigeria* **113 D7** 9 51N 11 27 E
Tula, *Russia* **58 E9** 54 13N 37 38 E
Tulak, *Afghan.* **91 B1** 33 55N 63 40 E
Tulancingo, *Mexico* **163 C5** 20 5N 99 22W
Tulangbawang →, *Indonesia* **84 C3** 4 24 S 105 52 E
Tulare, *Serbia, Yug.* **50 D5** 42 48N 21 28 E
Tulare, *U.S.A.* **160 J7** 36 13N 119 21W
Tulare Lake Bed, *U.S.A.* **160 K7** 36 0N 119 48W
Tularosa, *U.S.A.* **159 K10** 33 5N 106 1W
Tulbagh, *S. Africa* **116 E2** 33 16 S 19 6 E
Tulcán, *Ecuador* **168 C2** 0 48N 77 43W
Tulcea, *Romania* **53 E13** 45 13N 28 46 E
Tulcea □, *Romania* **53 E13** 45 0N 28 30 E
Tulchyn, *Ukraine* **59 H5** 48 41N 28 49 E
Tūleh, *Iran* **97 C7** 34 35N 52 33 E
Tulemalu L., *Canada* **143 A9** 62 58N 99 25W
Tulgheş, *Romania* **53 D10** 46 58N 25 45 E
Tuli, *Indonesia* **82 B2** 1 24 S 122 26 E
Tuli, *Zimbabwe* **119 G2** 21 58 S 29 13 E
Tulia, *U.S.A.* **155 H4** 34 32N 101 46W
Tuliszków, *Poland* **55 F5** 52 5N 18 18 E
Tulita, *Canada* **138 B7** 64 57N 125 30W
Ţulkarm, *West Bank* **103 C4** 32 19N 35 2 E
Tulla, *Ireland* **23 D3** 52 53N 8 46W
Tullahoma, *U.S.A.* **149 H2** 35 22N 86 13W
Tullamore, *Australia* **129 B7** 32 39 S 147 36 E
Tullamore, *Ireland* **23 C4** 53 16N 7 31W
Tulle, *France* **28 C5** 45 16N 1 46 E
Tullibigeal, *Australia* **129 B7** 33 25 S 146 44 E
Tulln, *Austria* **34 C9** 48 20N 16 4 E
Tullow, *Ireland* **23 D5** 52 49N 6 45W
Tullus, *Sudan* **107 E1** 11 7N 24 31 E
Tully, *Australia* **126 B4** 17 56 S 145 55 E
Ţulmaythah, *Libya* **108 B4** 32 40N 20 55 E
Tulmur, *Australia* **126 C3** 22 40 S 142 20 E
Tulnici, *Romania* **53 E11** 45 51N 26 38 E
Tulovo, *Bulgaria* **51 D9** 42 33N 25 32 E
Tulsa, *U.S.A.* **155 G7** 36 10N 95 55W
Tulsequah, *Canada* **142 B2** 58 39N 133 35W
Tulu Milki, *Ethiopia* **107 F4** 9 55N 38 20 E
Tulu Welel, *Ethiopia* **107 F3** 8 56N 34 47 E
Tulua, *Colombia* **168 C2** 4 6N 76 11W
Tulucești, *Romania* **53 E13** 45 34N 28 2 E
Tuluksak, *U.S.A.* **144 F7** 61 6N 160 58W
Tulun, *Russia* **65 D11** 54 32N 100 35 E
Tulungagung, *Indonesia* **85 D4** 8 5 S 111 54 E
Tuma, *Russia* **58 E11** 55 10N 40 30 E
Tuma →, *Nic.* **164 D3** 13 6N 84 35W
Tumaco, *Colombia* **168 C2** 1 50N 78 45W
Tumaco, Ensenada, *Colombia* **168 C2** 1 55N 78 45W
Tumatumari, *Guyana* **169 B6** 5 20N 58 55W
Tumauini, *Phil.* **80 C3** 17 17N 121 49 E
Tumba, *Sweden* **16 E11** 59 12N 17 48 E
Tumba, L., *Dem. Rep. of the Congo* **114 C3** 0 50 S 18 0 E
Tumbarumba, *Australia* **129 C8** 35 44 S 148 0 E
Tumbaya, *Argentina* **174 A2** 23 50 S 65 26W
Tumbes, *Peru* **172 A1** 3 37 S 80 27W
Tumbes □, *Peru* **172 A1** 3 50 S 80 30W
Tumbwe, *Dem. Rep. of the Congo* **119 E2** 11 25 S 27 15 E
Tumby Bay, *Australia* **128 C2** 34 21 S 136 8 E
Tumd Youqi, *China* **74 D6** 40 30N 110 30 E
Tumen, *China* **75 C15** 43 0N 129 50 E
Tumen Jiang →, *China* **75 C16** 42 20N 130 35 E
Tumeremo, *Venezuela* **169 B5** 7 18N 61 30W
Tumiritinga, *Brazil* **171 E3** 18 58 S 41 38W
Tumkur, *India* **95 H3** 13 18N 77 6 E
Tump, *Pakistan* **91 D1** 26 7N 62 16 E
Tumpat, *Malaysia* **87 J4** 6 11N 102 10 E
Tumsar, *India* **94 D4** 21 26N 79 45 E
Tumu, *Ghana* **112 C4** 10 56N 1 56W
Tumucumaque, Serra, *Brazil* **169 C7** 2 0N 55 0W
Tumupasa, *Bolivia* **172 C4** 14 9 S 67 55W
Tumut, *Australia* **129 C8** 35 16 S 148 13 E
Tumwater, *U.S.A.* **158 C2** 47 1N 122 54W
Tunadal, *Sweden* **16 B11** 62 26N 17 22 E
Tunas de Zaza, *Cuba* **164 B4** 21 39N 79 34W
Tunbridge Wells = Royal Tunbridge Wells, *U.K.* **21 F8** 51 7N 0 16 E
Tunçbilek, *Turkey* **49 B11** 39 37N 29 29 E
Tunceli, *Turkey* **101 C8** 39 6N 39 31 E
Tuncurry, *Australia* **129 B10** 32 17 S 152 29 E
Tunduru, *Tanzania* **119 E4** 11 8 S 37 25 E
Tunduru □, *Tanzania* **119 E4** 11 5 S 37 22 E
Tundzha →, *Bulgaria* **51 E10** 41 40N 26 35 E
Tunga →, *India* **95 G2** 15 0N 75 50 E
Tunga Pass, *India* **90 A5** 29 0N 94 14 E
Tungabhadra →, *India* **95 G4** 15 57N 78 15 E
Tungabhadra Dam, *India* **95 G2** 15 0N 75 50 E
Tungaru, *Sudan* **107 E3** 10 9N 30 52 E
Tungi, *Bangla.* **90 D3** 23 53N 90 24 E
Tungla, *Nic.* **164 D3** 13 24N 84 21W
Tungnafellsjökull, *Iceland* **11 C9** 64 45N 17 55W
Tungshih, *Taiwan* **77 E13** 24 12N 120 43 E
Tungsten, *Canada* **142 A3** 61 57N 128 16W
Tungufell, *Iceland* **11 C6** 64 17N 20 10W
Tungurahua □, *Ecuador* **168 D2** 1 15 S 78 35W
Tunguska, Nizhnyaya →, *Russia* **65 C9** 65 48N 88 4 E
Tunguska, Podkamennaya →, *Russia* **65 C10** 61 50N 90 13 E
Tuni, *India* **94 F6** 17 22N 82 36 E
Tunia, *Colombia* **168 C2** 2 41N 76 31W
Tunica, *U.S.A.* **155 H9** 34 41N 90 23W
Tunis, *Tunisia* **108 A2** 36 50N 10 11 E
Tunis, Golfe de, *Tunisia* **108 A2** 37 0N 10 30 E
Tunisia ■, *Africa* **108 B1** 33 30N 9 10 E
Tunja, *Colombia* **168 B3** 5 33N 73 25W
Tunkhannock, *U.S.A.* **151 E9** 41 32N 75 57W
Tunliu, *China* **74 F7** 36 13N 112 52 E
Tunnsjøen, *Norway* **14 D15** 64 45N 13 25 E
Tunø, *Denmark* **17 J4** 55 57N 10 27 E
Tunungayualok I., *Canada* **141 A7** 56 0N 61 0W
Tunuyán, *Argentina* **174 C2** 33 35 S 69 0W
Tunuyán →, *Argentina* **174 C2** 33 33 S 67 30W
Tunxi, *China* **77 C12** 29 42N 118 25 E
Tuo Jiang →, *China* **76 C5** 28 50N 105 35 E
Tuolumne, *U.S.A.* **160 H6** 37 58N 120 15W
Tuolumne →, *U.S.A.* **160 H5** 37 36N 121 13W
Tūp Āghāj, *Iran* **101 D12** 36 3N 47 50 E
Tupã, *Brazil* **175 A5** 21 57 S 50 28W
Tupaciguara, *Brazil* **171 E2** 18 35 S 48 42W
Tupelo, *U.S.A.* **149 H1** 34 16N 88 43W
Tupik, *Russia* **58 E7** 55 42N 33 22 E
Tupinambaranas, *Brazil* **169 D6** 3 0 S 58 0W
Tupirama, *Brazil* **170 C2** 8 58 S 48 12W
Tupiratins, *Brazil* **170 C2** 8 23 S 48 8W
Tupiza, *Bolivia* **174 A2** 21 30 S 65 40W
Tupižnica, *Serbia, Yug.* **50 C6** 43 43N 22 10 E
Tupman, *U.S.A.* **161 K7** 35 18N 119 21W
Tupper, *Canada* **142 B4** 55 32N 120 1W
Tupper Lake, *U.S.A.* **151 B10** 44 14N 74 28W
Tupungato, Cerro, *S. Amer.* **174 C2** 33 15 S 69 50W
Tuquan, *China* **75 B11** 45 18N 121 38 E
Túquerres, *Colombia* **168 C2** 1 5N 77 37W
Tura, *India* **90 C3** 25 30N 90 16 E
Tura, *Russia* **65 C11** 64 20N 100 17 E
Turabah, *Si. Arabia* **96 D4** 28 20N 43 15 E
Turagua, Serranía, *Venezuela* **169 B5** 7 20N 64 35W
Turaiyur, *India* **95 J4** 11 9N 78 38 E
Turakina, *N.Z.* **130 G4** 40 3 S 175 16 E
Turakina →, *N.Z.* **130 G4** 40 5 S 175 8 E
Turakirae Hd., *N.Z.* **130 H3** 41 26 S 174 56 E
Tūrān, *Iran* **97 C8** 35 39N 56 42 E
Turan, *Russia* **65 D10** 51 55N 95 0 E
Turayf, *Si. Arabia* **96 D3** 31 41N 38 39 E
Turbacz, *Poland* **55 J7** 49 30N 20 8 E
Turbe, *Bos.-H.* **52 F2** 44 15N 17 35 E
Turbenthal, *Switz.* **33 B7** 47 27N 8 51 E
Turbeville, *U.S.A.* **152 B9** 33 54N 80 1W
Turčianske Teplice, *Slovak Rep.* **35 C11** 48 52N 18 52 E
Turcoaia, *Romania* **53 E13** 45 7N 28 11 E
Turda, *Romania* **53 D8** 46 34N 23 47 E
Turek, *Poland* **55 F5** 52 3N 18 30 E
Turen, *Venezuela* **168 B4** 9 17N 69 6W
Turfan = Turpan, *China* **72 B3** 43 58N 89 10 E
Turfan Depression = Turpan Hami, *China* **66 E12** 42 40N 89 25 E
Tŭrgovishte, *Bulgaria* **51 C10** 43 17N 26 38 E
Turgut, *Turkey* **49 D10** 37 22N 28 4 E
Turgutlu, *Turkey* **57 G4** 38 30N 27 43 E
Turhal, *Turkey* **100 B7** 40 24N 36 5 E
Turia →, *Spain* **41 F4** 39 27N 0 19W
Turiaçu, *Brazil* **170 B2** 1 40 S 45 19W
Turiaçu →, *Brazil* **170 B2** 1 36 S 45 19W
Turiec →, *Slovak Rep.* **35 B11** 49 7N 18 55 E
Turin = Torino, *Italy* **44 C4** 45 3N 7 40 E
Turin, *Canada* **142 D6** 49 58N 112 31W
Turinsk, *Russia* **62 B9** 58 3N 63 42 E
Turkana □, *Kenya* **118 B4** 3 0N 35 30 E
Turkana, L., *Africa* **118 B4** 3 30N 36 5 E
Türkeli, *Turkey* **51 F11** 40 30N 27 30 E
Turkestan = Türkistan, *Kazakstan* **63 B4** 43 17N 68 16 E
Turkestanskiy, Khrebet, *Tajikistan* **63 D4** 39 35N 69 0 E
Túrkeve, *Hungary* **52 C5** 47 6N 20 44 E
Turkey ■, *Eurasia* **100 C7** 39 0N 36 0 E
Turkey →, *U.S.A.* **156 B5** 42 43N 91 2W
Turkey Creek, *Australia* **124 C4** 17 2 S 128 12 E
Turki, *Russia* **60 D6** 52 0N 43 15 E
Türkistan, *Kazakstan* **63 B4** 43 17N 68 16 E
Türkmenbashi, *Turkmenistan* **57 G9** 40 5N 53 5 E
Turkmenistan ■, *Asia* **64 F6** 39 0N 59 0 E
Türkmenli, *Turkey* **49 B8** 39 45N 26 30 E
Türkoğlu, *Turkey* **100 D7** 37 23N 36 50 E
Turks & Caicos Is. ■, *W. Indies* **165 B5** 21 20N 71 20W
Turks Island Passage, *W. Indies* **165 B5** 21 30N 71 30W
Turku, *Finland* **15 F20** 60 30N 22 19 E
Turkwel →, *Kenya* **118 B4** 3 6N 36 6 E
Turlock, *U.S.A.* **160 H6** 37 30N 120 51W
Turnagain →, *Canada* **142 B3** 59 12N 127 35W
Turnagain, C., *N.Z.* **130 G5** 40 28 S 176 38 E
Turneffe Is., *Belize* **163 D7** 17 20N 87 50W
Turner, *Australia* **124 C4** 17 52 S 128 16 E
Turner, *U.S.A.* **158 B9** 48 51N 108 24W
Turner Pt., *Australia* **126 A1** 11 47 S 133 32 E
Turner Valley, *Canada* **142 C6** 50 40N 114 17W
Turners Falls, *U.S.A.* **151 D12** 42 36N 72 33W
Turnhout, *Belgium* **24 C4** 51 19N 4 57 E
Türnitz, *Austria* **34 D8** 47 55N 15 29 E
Turnor L., *Canada* **143 B7** 56 35N 108 35W
Turnov, *Czech Rep.* **34 A8** 50 34N 15 10 E
Tŭrnovo = Veliko Tŭrnovo, *Bulgaria* **51 C9** 43 5N 25 41 E
Turnu Măgurele, *Romania* **53 G9** 43 46N 24 56 E
Turnu Roşu, P., *Romania* **53 E9** 45 33N 24 17 E
Turobin, *Poland* **55 H9** 50 50N 22 44 E
Turon, *U.S.A.* **155 G5** 37 48N 98 26W
Tuross Head, *Australia* **129 D9** 36 3 S 150 8 E
Turpan, *China* **72 B3** 43 58N 89 10 E
Turpan Hami, *China* **66 E12** 42 40N 89 25 E
Turrës, Kalaja e, *Albania* **50 E3** 41 10N 19 28 E
Turriff, *U.K.* **22 D6** 57 32N 2 27W
Tursāq, *Iraq* **101 F11** 33 27N 45 47 E
Tursi, *Italy* **47 B9** 40 15N 16 28 E
Turtle Head I., *Australia* **126 A3** 10 56 S 142 37 E
Turtle Is., *Phil.* **81 H2** 6 7N 118 14 E
Turtle L., *Canada* **143 C7** 53 36N 108 38W
Turtle Lake, *N. Dak., U.S.A.* **154 B4** 47 31N 100 53W
Turtle Lake, *Wis., U.S.A.* **154 C8** 45 24N 92 8W
Turtleford, *Canada* **143 C7** 53 23N 108 57W
Turua, *N.Z.* **130 D4** 37 14 S 175 35 E
Turugart, Pereval, *Kyrgyzstan* **63 C7** 40 32N 75 24 E
Turukhansk, *Russia* **65 C9** 65 21N 88 5 E
Turzovka, *Slovak Rep.* **35 B11** 49 25N 18 35 E
Tuscaloosa, *U.S.A.* **149 J2** 33 12N 87 34W
Tuscánia, *Italy* **45 F8** 42 25N 11 52 E
Tuscany = Toscana □, *Italy* **44 E8** 43 25N 11 0 E
Tuscola, *Ill., U.S.A.* **157 E8** 39 48N 88 17W
Tuscola, *Tex., U.S.A.* **155 J5** 32 12N 99 48W
Tuscumbia, *Ala., U.S.A.* **149 H2** 34 44N 87 42W
Tuscumbia, *Mo., U.S.A.* **156 F4** 38 14N 92 28W
Tuskegee, *U.S.A.* **152 C4** 32 25N 85 42W
Tustin, *U.S.A.* **161 M9** 33 44N 117 49W
Tustna, *Norway* **18 A5** 63 10N 8 5 E
Tuszyn, *Poland* **55 G6** 51 36N 19 33 E
Tutak, *Turkey* **101 C10** 39 31N 42 46 E
Tutayev, *Russia* **58 D10** 57 53N 39 32 E
Tuticorin, *India* **95 K4** 8 50N 78 12 E
Tutin, *Serbia, Yug.* **50 D4** 42 58N 20 20 E
Tutóia, *Brazil* **170 B3** 2 45 S 42 20W
Tutong, *Brunei* **85 B4** 4 47N 114 40 E
Tutova →, *Romania* **53 D12** 46 7N 27 30 E
Tutrakan, *Bulgaria* **51 B10** 44 2N 26 40 E
Tutshi L., *Canada* **142 B2** 59 56N 134 30W
Tuttle, *U.S.A.* **154 B5** 47 9N 100 0W
Tuttlingen, *Germany* **31 H4** 47 58N 8 48 E
Tutuala, *Indonesia* **82 C3** 8 25 S 127 15 E
Tutuila, *Amer. Samoa* **133 X24** 14 19 S 170 50W
Tutuko Mt., *N.Z.* **131 E3** 44 35 S 168 1 E
Tututepec, *Mexico* **163 D5** 16 9N 97 38W
Tutye, *Australia* **128 C4** 35 12 S 141 29 E
Tuva □, *Russia* **65 D10** 51 30N 95 0 E
Tuvalu ■, *Pac. Oc.* **134 H9** 8 0 S 178 0 E
Tuwal, *Si. Arabia* **98 B2** 22 17N 39 6 E
Tuxer Alpen, *Austria* **34 D4** 47 10N 11 45 E
Tuxpan, *Mexico* **163 C5** 20 58N 97 23W
Tuxtla Gutiérrez, *Mexico* **163 D6** 16 50N 93 10W
Tuy = Tui, *Spain* **42 C2** 42 3N 8 39W
Tuy An, *Vietnam* **86 F7** 13 17N 109 16 E
Tuy Duc, *Vietnam* **87 F6** 12 15N 107 27 E
Tuy Hoa, *Vietnam* **86 F7** 13 5N 109 10 E
Tuy Phong, *Vietnam* **87 G7** 11 14N 108 43 E
Tuya L., *Canada* **142 B2** 59 7N 130 35W
Tuyen Hoa, *Vietnam* **86 D6** 17 50N 106 10 E
Tuyen Quang, *Vietnam* **86 B5** 21 50N 105 10 E
Tuymazy, *Russia* **62 D4** 54 36N 53 42 E
Tūysarkān, *Iran* **97 C6** 34 33N 48 27 E
Tuz Gölü, *Turkey* **100 C5** 38 42N 33 18 E
Ţūz Khurmātū, *Iraq* **101 E11** 34 56N 44 38 E
Tuzi, *Montenegro, Yug.* **50 D3** 42 22N 19 20 E
Tuzkan, Ozero, *Uzbekistan* **63 C3** 40 35N 67 28 E
Tuzla, *Bos.-H.* **52 F3** 44 34N 18 41 E
Tuzlov →, *Russia* **59 J10** 47 17N 39 57 E
Tuzluca, *Turkey* **101 B10** 40 3N 43 39 E
Tvååker, *Sweden* **17 G6** 57 4N 12 25 E
Tvardiţa, *Moldova* **53 D13** 46 9N 28 58 E
Tvedestrand, *Norway* **18 F5** 58 38N 8 58 E
Tver, *Russia* **58 D8** 56 55N 35 55 E
Tvrdošin, *Slovak Rep.* **35 B12** 49 21N 19 35 E
Tvrdošovce, *Slovak Rep.* **35 C11** 48 6N 18 4 E
Tvŭrditsa, *Bulgaria* **51 D9** 42 42N 25 53 E
Twain, *U.S.A.* **160 E5** 40 1N 121 3W
Twain Harte, *U.S.A.* **160 G6** 38 2N 120 14W
Twardogóra, *Poland* **55 G4** 51 23N 17 28 E
Tweed, *Canada* **150 B7** 44 29N 77 19W
Tweed →, *U.K.* **22 F6** 55 45N 2 0W
Tweed Heads, *Australia* **127 D5** 28 10 S 153 31 E
Tweedsmuir Prov. Park, *Canada* **142 C3** 53 0N 126 20W
Twentynine Palms, *U.S.A.* **161 L10** 34 8N 116 3W
Twillingate, *Canada* **141 C9** 49 42N 54 45W
Twin Bridges, *U.S.A.* **158 D7** 45 33N 112 20W
Twin City, *U.S.A.* **152 C7** 32 35N 82 10W
Twin Falls, *U.S.A.* **158 E6** 42 34N 114 28W
Twin Hills, *U.S.A.* **144 G8** 59 23N 159 58W
Twin Lakes, *U.S.A.* **152 E6** 30 43N 83 13W
Twin Valley, *U.S.A.* **154 B6** 47 16N 96 16W
Twinnge, *Burma* **90 D6** 23 10N 96 2 E
Twisp, *U.S.A.* **158 B3** 48 22N 120 7W
Twistringen, *Germany* **30 C4** 52 48N 8 37 E
Two Harbors, *U.S.A.* **154 B9** 47 2N 91 40W
Two Hills, *Canada* **142 C6** 53 43N 111 52W
Two Rivers, *U.S.A.* **148 C2** 44 9N 87 34W
Two Thumbs Ra., *N.Z.* **131 D5** 43 45 S 170 44 E
Twofold B., *Australia* **129 D8** 37 8 S 149 59 E
Ty Ty, *U.S.A.* **152 D6** 31 28N 83 39W
Tyachiv, *Ukraine* **59 H2** 48 1N 23 35 E
Tychy, *Poland* **55 H5** 50 9N 18 59 E
Tyczyn, *Poland* **55 J9** 49 58N 22 2 E
Tydal, *Norway* **18 A8** 63 4N 11 34 E
Tyin, *Norway* **18 C5** 61 18N 8 15 E
Tykocin, *Poland* **55 E9** 53 13N 22 46 E
Tyler, *U.S.A.* **147 D7** 32 18N 95 17W
Tyler, *Minn., U.S.A.* **154 C6** 44 18N 96 8W
Tyler, *Tex., U.S.A.* **155 J7** 32 21N 95 18W
Tyligul →, *Ukraine* **59 J6** 47 4N 30 57 E
Tylldal, *Norway* **18 B7** 62 8N 10 48 E
Týn nad Vltavou, *Czech Rep.* **34 B7** 49 13N 14 26 E
Tynda, *Russia* **65 D13** 55 10N 124 43 E
Tyne →, *U.K.* **20 C6** 54 59N 1 32W
Tyne & Wear □, *U.K.* **20 B6** 55 6N 1 17W
Týnec nad Sázavou, *Czech Rep.* **34 B7** 49 50N 14 36 E
Tynemouth, *U.K.* **20 B6** 55 1N 1 26W
Tynset, *Norway* **18 B7** 62 17N 10 47 E
Tyonek, *U.S.A.* **144 F10** 61 4N 151 8W
Tyonek Indian Reservation, *U.S.A.* **144 F10** 61 5N 151 10W
Tyre = Sūr, *Lebanon* **103 B4** 33 19N 35 16 E
Tyrifjorden, *Norway* **15 F14** 60 2N 10 8 E
Tyringe, *Sweden* **17 H7** 56 9N 13 35 E
Tyristrand, *Norway* **18 D7** 60 4N 10 6 E
Tyrnyauz, *Russia* **61 J6** 43 21N 42 45 E
Tyrol = Tirol □, *Austria* **34 D3** 47 3N 10 43 E
Tyrone, *U.S.A.* **150 F6** 40 40N 78 14W
Tyrone □, *U.K.* **23 B4** 54 38N 7 11W
Tyrrell →, *Australia* **128 C5** 35 26 S 142 51 E
Tyrrell, L., *Australia* **128 C5** 35 20 S 142 50 E
Tyrrell Arm, *Canada* **143 A9** 62 27N 97 30W
Tyrrell L., *Canada* **143 A7** 63 7N 105 27W
Tyrrhenian Sea, *Medit. S.* **12 G8** 40 0N 12 30 E
Tysfjorden, *Norway* **14 B17** 68 7N 16 25 E
Tysnes, *Norway* **18 D2** 60 1N 5 30 E
Tysnesøya, *Norway* **18 D2** 60 0N 5 35 E
Tysse, *Norway* **18 D2** 60 23N 5 47 E
Tyssedal, *Norway* **18 D3** 60 7N 6 35 E
Tystberga, *Sweden* **17 F11** 58 51N 17 15 E
Tytuvėnai, *Lithuania* **54 C10** 55 36N 23 12 E
Tyub Karagan, Mys, *Kazakstan* **61 H10** 44 40N 50 19 E
Tyuleni, Ostrova, *Kazakstan* **61 H10** 45 2N 50 16 E
Tyuleniy, *Russia* **61 H8** 44 28N 47 30 E
Tyuleniy, Mys, *Azerbaijan* **61 K10** 40 12N 50 22 E
Tyulgan, *Russia* **62 E6** 52 22N 56 12 E
Tyumen, *Russia* **64 D7** 57 11N 65 29 E
Tyumen-Aryk, *Kazakstan* **63 A3** 44 2N 67 1 E
Tyup, *Kyrgyzstan* **63 B9** 42 45N 78 20 E
Tywi →, *U.K.* **21 F3** 51 48N 4 21W
Tywyn, *U.K.* **21 E3** 52 35N 4 5W
Tzaneen, *S. Africa* **117 C5** 23 47 S 30 9 E
Tzermiádhes, *Greece* **38 D7** 35 12N 25 29 E
Tzoumérka, Óros, *Greece* **48 B3** 39 30N 21 26 E
Tzukong = Zigong, *China* **76 C5** 29 15N 104 48 E

U

U Taphao, *Thailand* **86 F3** 12 35N 101 0 E
U.S.A. = United States of America ■, *N. Amer.* **146 C7** 37 0N 96 0W
Uacalla Iero, *Somali Rep.* **120 D2** 1 48N 42 38 E
Uachadi, Sierra, *Venezuela* **169 C4** 4 54N 65 18W
Uainambi, *Colombia* **168 C4** 1 43N 69 51W
Uanda, *Australia* **126 C3** 21 37 S 144 55 E
Uanle Uen, *Somali Rep.* **120 D2** 2 37N 44 54 E
Uarsciek, *Somali Rep.* **120 D3** 2 28N 45 55 E
Uascen, *Somali Rep.* **120 D2** 4 11N 43 13 E
Uasin □, *Kenya* **118 B4** 0 30N 35 20 E
Uato-Udo, *Indonesia* **82 C3** 9 7 S 125 36 E
Uatumã →, *Brazil* **169 D6** 2 26 S 57 37W
Uauá, *Brazil* **170 C4** 9 50 S 39 28W
Uaupés, *Brazil* **168 D4** 0 8 S 67 5W
Uaupés →, *Brazil* **168 C4** 0 2N 67 16W
Uaxactún, *Guatemala* **164 C2** 17 25N 89 29W
Ub, *Serbia, Yug.* **50 B4** 44 28N 20 6 E
Ubá, *Brazil* **171 F3** 21 8 S 43 0W
Ubaitaba, *Brazil* **171 D4** 14 18 S 39 20W
Ubangi = Oubangi →, *Dem. Rep. of the Congo* **114 C3** 0 30 S 17 50 E
Ubaté, *Colombia* **168 B3** 5 19N 73 49W
Ubauro, *Pakistan* **92 E3** 28 15N 69 45 E
Ubay, *Phil.* **81 F5** 10 3N 124 28 E
'Ubaydīyah, *Yemen* **98 D3** 13 7N 43 20 E
Ubaye →, *France* **29 D10** 44 28N 6 18 E
Ubayyiḍ, W. al →, *Iraq* **101 F10** 32 34N 43 48 E
Ube, *Japan* **70 D3** 33 56N 131 15 E
Úbeda, *Spain* **43 G7** 38 3N 3 23W
Uberaba, *Brazil* **171 E2** 19 50 S 47 55W

Vaygach, Ostrov 295

Ústica, *Italy* 46 D6 38 42N 13 11 E
Ustinov = Izhevsk, *Russia* 62 C4 56 51N 53 14 E
Ustka, *Poland* 54 D3 54 35N 16 55 E
Ustroń, *Poland* 55 J5 49 43N 18 48 E
Ustrzyki Dolne, *Poland* 55 J9 49 27N 22 40 E
Ustyurt Plateau, *Asia* 64 E6 44 0N 55 0 E
Ustyuzhna, *Russia* 58 C9 58 50N 36 32 E
Usu, *China* 72 B3 44 27N 84 40 E
Usuki, *Japan* 70 D3 33 8N 131 49 E
Usulután, *El Salv.* 164 D2 13 25N 88 28W
Usumacinta →, *Mexico* 163 D6 17 0N 91 0W
Usumbura = Bujumbura, *Burundi* 118 C2 3 16 S 29 18 E
Usure, *Tanzania* 118 C3 4 40 S 34 22 E
Usva, *Russia* 62 B6 58 41N 57 37 E
Uta, *Indonesia* 83 B5 4 33 S 136 0 E
'Uta Vava'u, *Tonga* 133 P14 18 36 S 174 0W
Utah □, *U.S.A.* 158 G8 39 20N 111 30W
Utah L., *U.S.A.* 158 F8 40 10N 111 58W
Utansjö, *Sweden* 16 B11 62 46N 17 55 E
Ute Creek →, *U.S.A.* 155 H3 35 21N 103 50W
Utebo, *Spain* 40 D3 41 43N 1 0W
Utena, *Lithuania* 15 J21 55 27N 25 40 E
Utete, *Tanzania* 118 D4 8 0 S 38 45 E
Uthai Thani, *Thailand* 86 E3 15 22N 100 3 E
Uthal, *Pakistan* 92 G2 25 44N 66 40 E
Utiariti, *Brazil* 173 C6 13 0 S 58 10W
Utica, *N.Y., U.S.A.* 151 C9 43 6N 75 14W
Utica, *Ohio, U.S.A.* 150 F2 40 14N 82 27W
Utiel, *Spain* 41 F3 39 37N 1 11W
Utik L., *Canada* 143 B9 55 15N 96 0W
Utikuma L., *Canada* 142 B5 55 50N 115 30W
Utinga, *Brazil* 171 D3 12 6 S 41 5W
Utne, *Norway* 18 D3 60 25N 6 37 E
Uto, *Japan* 70 E2 32 41N 130 40 E
Utö, *Sweden* 16 F12 58 56N 18 16 E
Utrecht, *Neths.* 24 B5 52 5N 5 8 E
Utrecht, *S. Africa* 117 D5 27 38 S 30 20 E
Utrecht □, *Neths.* 24 B5 52 6N 5 7 E
Utrera, *Spain* 43 H5 37 12N 5 48W
Utsira, *Norway* 18 E1 59 19N 4 53 E
Utsjoki, *Finland* 14 B22 69 51N 26 59 E
Utsunomiya, *Japan* 71 A11 36 30N 139 50 E
Uttar Pradesh □, *India* 93 F9 27 0N 80 0 E
Uttaradit, *Thailand* 86 D3 17 36N 100 5 E
Uttoxeter, *U.K.* 20 E6 52 54N 1 52W
Utva →, *Kazakstan* 62 F4 51 28N 52 40 E
Uummannarsuaq = Farvel, Kap, *Greenland* 10 F6 59 48N 43 55W
Uusikaarlepyy, *Finland* 14 E20 63 32N 22 31 E
Uusikaupunki, *Finland* 15 F19 60 47N 21 25 E
Uva, *Russia* 60 B11 56 59N 52 13 E
Uvá →, *Colombia* 168 C3 3 41N 70 3W
Uvac →, *Serbia, Yug.* 50 C3 43 35N 19 30 E
Uvalda, *U.S.A.* 152 C7 32 2N 82 31W
Uvalde, *U.S.A.* 155 L5 29 13N 99 47W
Uvarovo, *Russia* 60 E6 51 59N 42 14 E
Uvat, *Russia* 64 D7 59 5N 68 50 E
Uvdal, *Norway* 18 D5 60 17N 8 48 E
Uvéa, I., *Vanuatu* 123 E12 20 30 S 166 35 E
Uvelskiy, *Russia* 62 D8 54 26N 61 22 E
Uvinza, *Tanzania* 118 D3 5 5 S 30 24 E
Uvira, *Dem. Rep. of the Congo* 118 C2 3 22 S 29 3 E
Uvs Nuur, *Mongolia* 72 A4 50 20N 92 30 E
Uwa, *Japan* 70 D4 33 22N 132 31 E
Uwajima, *Japan* 70 D4 33 10N 132 35 E
'Uwayfī, *Oman* 99 B7 22 15N 56 59 E
Uweinat, Jebel, *Sudan* 106 C1 21 54N 24 58 E
Uxbridge, *Canada* 150 B5 44 6N 79 7W
Uxin Qi, *China* 74 E5 38 50N 109 5 E
Uxmal, *Mexico* 163 C7 20 22N 89 46W
Uyak, *U.S.A.* 144 H9 57 38N 154 0W
Uyo, *Nigeria* 113 D6 5 1N 7 53 E
Uyu →, *Burma* 90 C5 24 51N 94 57 E
Uyuk, *Kazakstan* 63 B5 43 36N 71 16 E
Üyüklü Tepe, *Turkey* 49 D9 37 5N 27 21 E
Uyûn Mûsa, *Egypt* 103 F1 29 53N 32 40 E
Uyuni, *Bolivia* 172 E4 20 28 S 66 47W
Uzbekistan ■, *Asia* 63 C2 41 30N 65 0 E
Uzen, *Kazakstan* 57 F9 43 29N 52 54 E
Uzen, Bolshoi →, *Kazakstan* 61 F9 49 6N 49 56 E
Uzen, Mal →, *Kazakstan* 61 F9 49 4N 49 44 E
Uzerche, *France* 28 C5 45 25N 1 34 E
Uzès, *France* 29 D8 44 1N 4 26 E
Uzgen = Özgön, *Kyrgyzstan* 63 B6 40 46N 73 18 E
Uzh →, *Ukraine* 59 G6 51 15N 30 12 E
Uzhgorod = Uzhhorod, *Ukraine* 59 H2 48 36N 22 18 E
Uzhhorod, *Ukraine* 59 H2 48 36N 22 18 E
Užice, *Serbia, Yug.* 50 C3 43 55N 19 50 E
Uzlovaya, *Russia* 58 F10 54 0N 38 5 E
Üzümlü, *Turkey* 49 E11 36 44N 29 14 E
Uzun-Agach, *Kazakstan* 63 B8 43 35N 76 20 E
Uzunköprü, *Turkey* 51 E10 41 16N 26 43 E
Uzunkuyu, *Turkey* 49 C8 38 17N 26 33 E
Uzwil, *Switz.* 33 B8 47 26N 9 9 E

V

Vaal →, *S. Africa* 116 D3 29 4 S 23 38 E
Vaal Dam, *S. Africa* 117 D4 27 0 S 28 14 E
Vaalwater, *S. Africa* 117 C4 24 15 S 28 8 E
Vaasa, *Finland* 14 E19 63 6N 21 38 E
Vabre, *France* 28 E6 43 42N 2 24 E
Vác, *Hungary* 52 C4 47 49N 19 10 E
Vacaria, *Brazil* 175 B5 28 31 S 50 52W
Vacaville, *U.S.A.* 160 G5 38 21N 121 59W
Vaccarès, Étang de, *France* 29 E8 43 32N 4 34 E
Vach → = Vakh →, *Russia* 64 C8 60 45N 76 45 E
Vache, Î. à, *Haiti* 165 C5 18 2N 73 35W
Väckelsång, *Sweden* 17 H8 56 37N 14 58 E
Väddö, *Sweden* 16 D12 60 0N 18 50 E
Väderstad, *Sweden* 17 F8 58 19N 14 55 E
Vadheim, *Norway* 18 C2 61 13N 5 49 E
Vadnagar, *India* 92 H5 23 47N 72 40 E
Vado Ligure, *Italy* 44 D5 44 17N 8 26 E
Vadodara, *India* 92 H5 22 20N 73 10 E
Vadsø, *Norway* 14 A23 70 3N 29 50 E
Vadstena, *Sweden* 17 F8 58 28N 14 54 E
Vaduz, *Liech.* 33 B9 47 8N 9 31 E
Værlandet, *Norway* 18 C1 61 18N 4 44 E
Værøy, *Norway* 14 C15 67 40N 12 40 E
Vågåmo, *Norway* 18 C6 61 52N 9 6 E
Vágar, *Færoe Is.* 14 E9 62 5N 7 15W
Vaggeryd, *Sweden* 17 G8 57 30N 14 10 E
Vagney, *France* 27 D13 48 1N 6 43 E
Vagnhärad, *Sweden* 17 F11 58 57N 17 33 E
Vagos, *Portugal* 42 E2 40 33N 8 42W
Vågsfjorden, *Norway* 14 B17 68 50N 16 50 E
Váh →, *Slovak Rep.* 35 D11 47 43N 18 7 E
Vahsel B., *Antarctica* 7 D1 75 0 S 35 0W
Vaï, *Greece* 38 D8 35 15N 26 18 E
Vaigach, *Russia* 64 B6 70 10N 59 0 E
Vaigai →, *India* 95 K4 9 15N 79 10 E
Vaiges, *France* 26 D6 48 2N 0 30W
Vaihingen, *Germany* 31 G4 48 54N 8 57 E
Vaijapur, *India* 94 E2 19 58N 74 45 E
Vaikam, *India* 95 K3 9 45N 76 25 E
Vailly-sur-Aisne, *France* 27 C10 49 24N 3 31 E
Vaippar →, *India* 95 K4 9 0N 78 25 E
Vaison-la-Romaine, *France* 29 D9 44 14N 5 4 E
Vajpur, *India* 94 D1 21 24N 73 17 E
Vakarel, *Bulgaria* 50 D7 42 35N 23 40 E
Vakfikebir, *Turkey* 101 B8 41 2N 39 17 E
Vakh →, *Russia* 64 C8 60 45N 76 45 E
Vakhsh →, *Tajikistan* 63 E4 37 6N 68 18 E
Vakhtan, *Russia* 60 B8 57 53N 46 47 E
Vaksdal, *Norway* 18 D2 60 29N 5 45 E
Vál, *Hungary* 52 C3 47 22N 18 40 E
Val-de-Marne □, *France* 27 D9 48 45N 2 28 E
Val-d'Isère, *France* 29 C10 45 27N 6 59 E
Val-d'Oise □, *France* 27 C9 49 5N 2 10 E
Val-d'Or, *Canada* 140 C4 48 7N 77 47W
Val Marie, *Canada* 143 D7 49 15N 107 45W
Valaam, *Russia* 58 B6 61 22N 30 57 E
Valadares, *Portugal* 42 D2 41 5N 8 38W
Valahia, *Romania* 53 F9 44 35N 25 0 E
Valais □, *Switz.* 32 D5 46 12N 7 45 E
Valais, Alpes du, *Switz.* 32 D5 46 5N 7 35 E
Valandovo, *Macedonia* 50 E6 41 19N 22 34 E
Valašské Meziříčí, *Czech Rep.* 35 B10 49 29N 17 59 E
Valáxa, *Greece* 48 C6 38 50N 24 29 E
Vålberg, *Sweden* 16 E7 59 23N 13 11 E
Valbo, *Sweden* 16 D10 60 40N 17 0 E
Valbondione, *Italy* 44 B7 46 2N 10 1 E
Vâlcani, *Romania* 52 D5 46 0N 20 26 E
Vâlcea □, *Romania* 53 F9 45 0N 24 10 E
Valcheta, *Argentina* 176 B3 40 40 S 66 8W
Valdagno, *Italy* 45 C8 45 39N 11 18 E
Valdahon, *France* 27 E13 47 8N 6 21 E
Valday, *Russia* 58 D7 57 58N 33 9 E
Valdayskaya Vozvyshennost, *Russia* 58 D7 57 0N 33 30 E
Valdeazogues →, *Spain* 43 G6 38 45N 4 55W
Valdecañas, Embalse de, *Spain* 42 F5 39 45N 5 25W
Valdemarsvik, *Sweden* 17 F10 58 14N 16 40 E
Valdemoro, *Spain* 42 E7 40 12N 3 40W
Valdepeñas, *Spain* 43 G7 38 43N 3 25W
Valderaduey →, *Spain* 42 D5 41 31N 5 42W
Valdérice, *Italy* 46 D5 38 4N 12 37 E
Valderrobres, *Spain* 40 E5 40 53N 0 9 E
Valdés, Pen., *Argentina* 176 B4 42 30 S 63 45W
Valdez, *Ecuador* 168 C2 1 15N 79 0W
Valdez, *U.S.A.* 138 B5 61 7N 146 16W
Valdivia, *Chile* 176 A2 39 50 S 73 14W
Valdivia, *Colombia* 168 B2 7 11N 75 27W
Valdivia □, *Chile* 176 B2 40 0 S 73 0W
Valdobbiádene, *Italy* 45 C8 45 54N 12 0 E
Valdosta, *U.S.A.* 152 E6 30 50N 83 17W
Valdoviño, *Spain* 42 B2 43 36N 8 8W
Valdres, *Norway* 15 F13 61 5N 9 5 E
Vale, *Georgia* 61 K6 41 30N 42 58 E
Vale, *U.S.A.* 158 E5 43 59N 117 15W
Vale of Glamorgan □, *U.K.* 21 F4 51 28N 3 25W
Valea lui Mihai, *Romania* 52 C7 47 32N 22 11 E
Valea Mărului, *Romania* 53 E12 45 49N 27 42 E
Valença, *Brazil* 171 D4 13 20 S 39 5W
Valença, *Portugal* 42 C2 42 1N 8 34W
Valença do Piauí, *Brazil* 170 C3 6 20 S 41 45W
Valençay, *France* 27 E8 47 9N 1 34 E
Valence = Valence d'Agen, *France* 28 D4 44 6N 0 53 E
Valence, *France* 29 D8 44 57N 4 54 E
Valence d'Agen, *France* 28 D4 44 6N 0 53 E
Valencia, *Phil.* 81 H5 7 57N 125 3 E
Valencia, *Spain* 41 F4 39 27N 0 23W
Valencia, *Venezuela* 168 A4 10 11N 68 0W
Valencia □, *Spain* 41 F4 39 20N 0 40W
Valencia, G. de, *Spain* 41 F5 39 30N 0 20 E
Valencia de Alcántara, *Spain* 43 F3 39 25N 7 14W
Valencia de Don Juan, *Spain* 42 C5 42 17N 5 31W
Valencia I., *Ireland* 23 E1 51 54N 10 22W
Valenciennes, *France* 27 B10 50 20N 3 34 E
Văleni, *Romania* 53 F9 44 15N 24 45 E
Vălenii de Munte, *Romania* 53 E11 45 11N 26 2 E
Valensole, *France* 29 E9 43 50N 5 59 E
Valentigney, *France* 27 E13 47 27N 6 51 E
Valentim, Sa. do, *Brazil* 170 C3 6 0 S 43 30W
Valentin, *Russia* 68 C7 43 8N 134 17 E
Valentine, *Nebr., U.S.A.* 154 D4 42 52N 100 33W
Valentine, *Tex., U.S.A.* 155 K2 30 35N 104 30W
Valenza, *Italy* 44 C5 45 1N 8 38 E
Våler, *Hedmark, Norway* 18 D8 60 41N 11 50 E
Våler, *Østfold, Norway* 18 E7 59 29N 10 51 E
Valera, *Venezuela* 168 B3 9 19N 70 37W
Valestrand, *Norway* 18 E2 59 40N 5 24 E
Valga, *Estonia* 15 H22 57 47N 26 2 E
Valguarnera Caropepe, *Italy* 47 E7 37 30N 14 23 E
Valier, *U.S.A.* 158 B7 48 18N 112 16W
Valinco, G. de, *France* 29 G12 41 40N 8 52 E
Valjevo, *Serbia, Yug.* 50 B3 44 18N 19 53 E
Valka, *Latvia* 15 H21 57 42N 25 57 E
Valkeakoski, *Finland* 15 F20 61 16N 24 2 E
Valkenswaard, *Neths.* 24 C5 51 21N 5 29 E
Vall de Uxó = La Vall d'Uixó, *Spain* 40 F4 39 49N 0 15W
Valla, *Sweden* 16 E10 59 2N 16 20 E
Valladolid, *Mexico* 163 C7 20 40N 88 11W
Valladolid, *Spain* 42 D6 41 38N 4 43W
Valladolid □, *Spain* 42 D6 41 38N 4 43W
Vallata, *Italy* 47 A8 41 2N 15 15 E
Valldemossa, *Spain* 39 B9 39 43N 2 37 E
Valle, *Norway* 18 E4 59 13N 7 33 E
Valle d'Aosta □, *Italy* 44 C4 45 45N 7 15 E
Valle de Arán, *Spain* 40 C5 42 50N 0 55 E
Valle de la Pascua, *Venezuela* 168 B4 9 13N 66 0W
Valle de las Palmas, *Mexico* 161 N10 32 20N 116 43W
Valle de Santiago, *Mexico* 162 C4 20 25N 101 15W
Valle de Suchil, *Mexico* 162 C4 23 38N 103 55W
Valle de Zaragoza, *Mexico* 162 B3 27 28N 105 49W
Valle del Cauca □, *Colombia* 168 C2 3 45N 76 30W
Valle Fértil, Sierra del, *Argentina* 174 C2 30 20 S 68 0W
Valle Hermoso, *Mexico* 163 B5 25 35N 97 40W
Valledupar, *Colombia* 168 A3 10 29N 73 15W
Vallehermoso, *Canary Is.* 39 F2 28 10N 17 15W
Vallejo, *U.S.A.* 160 G4 38 7N 122 14W
Vallenar, *Chile* 174 B1 28 30 S 70 50W
Vallentuna, *Sweden* 16 E12 59 32N 18 5 E
Valleraugue, *France* 28 D7 44 6N 3 39 E
Vallet, *France* 26 E5 47 10N 1 15W
Valletta, *Malta* 38 D2 35 54N 14 31 E
Valley Center, *U.S.A.* 161 M9 33 13N 117 2W
Valley City, *U.S.A.* 154 B6 46 55N 98 0W
Valley Falls, *U.S.A.* 158 E3 42 29N 120 17W
Valley Park, *U.S.A.* 156 F6 38 33N 90 29W
Valley Springs, *U.S.A.* 160 G6 38 12N 120 50W
Valley Station, *U.S.A.* 157 F11 38 6N 85 52W
Valley Wells, *U.S.A.* 161 K11 35 27N 115 46W
Valleyview, *Canada* 142 B5 55 5N 117 17W
Valli di Comácchio, *Italy* 45 D9 44 40N 12 15 E
Vallimanca, Arroyo, *Argentina* 174 D4 35 40 S 59 10W
Vallo della Lucánia, *Italy* 47 B8 40 14N 15 16 E
Vallon-Pont-d'Arc, *France* 29 D8 44 24N 4 24 E
Vallorbe, *Switz.* 32 C2 46 42N 6 20 E
Valls, *Spain* 40 D6 41 18N 1 15 E
Valmaseda = Balmaseda, *Spain* 40 B1 43 11N 3 12W
Valmeyer, *U.S.A.* 156 F6 38 18N 90 19W
Valmiera, *Latvia* 15 H21 57 37N 25 29 E
Valnera, *Spain* 42 B7 43 9N 3 40W
Valognes, *France* 26 C5 49 30N 1 28W
Valona = Vlóra, *Albania* 50 F3 40 32N 19 28 E
Valongo, *Portugal* 42 D2 41 8N 8 30W
Valozhyn, *Belarus* 58 E4 54 3N 26 30 E
Valpaços, *Portugal* 42 D3 41 36N 7 17W
Valparaíso, *Chile* 174 C1 33 2 S 71 40W
Valparaíso, *Mexico* 162 C4 22 50N 103 32W
Valparaiso, *Fla., U.S.A.* 153 E3 30 29N 86 30W
Valparaiso, *Ind., U.S.A.* 157 C9 41 28N 87 4W
Valparaíso □, *Chile* 174 C1 33 2 S 71 40W
Valpovo, *Croatia* 52 E3 45 39N 18 25 E
Valréas, *France* 29 D9 44 24N 5 0 E
Vals, *Switz.* 33 C8 46 39N 9 11 E
Vals →, *S. Africa* 116 D4 27 23 S 26 30 E
Vals, Tanjung, *Indonesia* 83 C5 8 26 S 137 25 E
Vals-les-Bains, *France* 29 D8 44 42N 4 24 E
Valsad, *India* 94 D1 20 40N 72 58 E
Valtellina, *Italy* 44 B6 46 11N 9 55 E
Valþjofsstaður, *Iceland* 11 B12 65 1N 14 59W
Valuyki, *Russia* 59 G10 50 10N 38 5 E
Valverde, *Canary Is.* 39 G2 27 48N 17 55W
Valverde del Camino, *Spain* 43 H4 37 35N 6 47W
Valverde del Fresno, *Spain* 42 E4 40 15N 6 51W
Vama, *Romania* 53 C10 47 34N 25 42 E
Vamdrup, *Denmark* 17 J3 55 25N 9 17 E
Våmhus, *Sweden* 16 C8 61 7N 14 29 E
Vammala, *Finland* 15 F20 61 20N 22 54 E
Vámos, *Greece* 38 D6 35 24N 24 13 E
Vamsadhara →, *India* 94 E7 18 21N 84 8 E
Van, *Turkey* 101 C10 38 30N 43 20 E
Van, L. = Van Gölü, *Turkey* 101 C10 38 30N 43 0 E
Van Alstyne, *U.S.A.* 155 J6 33 25N 96 35W
Van Blommestein Meer, *Surinam* 169 C6 4 45N 55 5W
Van Bruyssel, *Canada* 141 C5 47 56N 72 9W
Van Buren, *Canada* 141 C6 47 10N 67 55W
Van Buren, *Ark., U.S.A.* 155 H7 35 26N 94 21W
Van Buren, *Maine, U.S.A.* 149 B11 47 10N 67 58W
Van Buren, *Mo., U.S.A.* 155 G9 37 0N 91 1W
Van Canh, *Vietnam* 86 F7 13 37N 109 0 E
Van Diemen, C., *N. Terr., Australia* 124 B5 11 9 S 130 24 E
Van Diemen, C., *Queens., Australia* 126 B2 16 30 S 139 46 E
Van Diemen G., *Australia* 124 B5 11 45 S 132 0 E
Van Gölü, *Turkey* 101 C10 38 30N 43 0 E
Van Horn, *U.S.A.* 155 K2 31 3N 104 50W
Van Horne, *U.S.A.* 156 B4 42 1N 92 4W
Van Ninh, *Vietnam* 86 F7 12 42N 109 14 E
Van Rees, Pegunungan, *Indonesia* 83 B5 2 35 S 138 15 E
Van Tassell, *U.S.A.* 154 D2 42 40N 104 5W
Van Tivu, *India* 95 K4 8 51N 78 15 E
Van Wert, *U.S.A.* 157 D12 40 52N 84 35W
Van Yen, *Vietnam* 86 B5 21 4N 104 42 E
Vanadzor, *Armenia* 61 K7 40 48N 44 30 E
Vanavara, *Russia* 65 C11 60 22N 102 16 E
Vance, *U.S.A.* 152 B9 33 26N 80 25W
Vanceburg, *U.S.A.* 157 F13 38 36N 83 19W
Vancouver, *Canada* 142 D4 49 15N 123 10W
Vancouver, *U.S.A.* 160 E4 45 38N 122 40W
Vancouver, C., *Australia* 125 G2 35 2 S 118 11 E
Vancouver, Mt., *U.S.A.* 144 F13 60 20N 139 41W
Vancouver I., *Canada* 142 D3 49 50N 126 0W
Vandalia, *Ill., U.S.A.* 156 F7 38 58N 89 6W
Vandalia, *Mo., U.S.A.* 156 E5 39 19N 91 29W
Vandalia, *Ohio, U.S.A.* 157 E12 39 54N 84 12W
Vandavasi, *India* 95 H4 12 30N 79 30 E
Vandeloos B., *Sri Lanka* 95 L5 8 0N 81 45 E
Vandenburg, *U.S.A.* 161 L6 34 35N 120 33W
Vanderbijlpark, *S. Africa* 117 D4 26 42 S 27 54 E
Vandergrift, *U.S.A.* 150 F5 40 36N 79 34W
Vanderhoof, *Canada* 142 C4 54 0N 124 0W
Vanderkloof Dam, *S. Africa* 116 E3 30 4 S 24 40 E
Vanderlin I., *Australia* 126 B2 15 44 S 137 2 E
Vandyke, *Australia* 126 C4 24 10 S 147 51 E
Vänern, *Sweden* 17 F7 58 47N 13 30 E
Vänersborg, *Sweden* 17 F6 58 26N 12 19 E
Vang, *Norway* 18 C5 61 7N 8 34 E
Vang Vieng, *Laos* 86 C4 18 58N 102 32 E
Vanga, *Kenya* 118 C4 4 35 S 39 12 E
Vangaindrano, *Madag.* 117 C8 23 21 S 47 36 E
Vangsnes, *Norway* 18 C3 61 9N 6 39 E
Vanguard, *Canada* 143 D7 49 55N 107 20W
Vangunu, *Solomon Is.* 133 M10 8 40 S 158 5 E
Vanier, *Canada* 140 C4 45 27N 75 40W
Vanimo, *Papua N. G.* 132 B1 2 42 S 141 21 E
Vanino, *Russia* 65 E15 48 50N 140 5 E
Vanivilasa Sagara, *India* 95 H3 13 45N 76 30 E
Vaniyambadi, *India* 95 H4 12 46N 78 44 E
Vânju Mare, *Romania* 52 F7 44 25N 22 52 E
Vankleek Hill, *Canada* 140 C5 45 32N 74 40W
Vanna, *Norway* 14 A18 70 6N 19 50 E
Vännäs, *Sweden* 14 E18 63 58N 19 48 E
Vannes, *France* 26 E4 47 40N 2 47W
Vanoise, *France* 29 C10 45 25N 6 40 E
Vanrhynsdorp, *S. Africa* 116 E2 31 36 S 18 44 E
Vanrook, *Australia* 126 B3 16 57 S 141 57 E
Vansbro, *Sweden* 16 D8 60 32N 14 15 E
Vanse, *Norway* 18 F3 58 6N 6 41 E
Vansittart B., *Australia* 124 B4 14 3 S 126 17 E
Vantaa, *Finland* 15 F21 60 18N 24 58 E
Vanthli, *India* 92 J4 21 28N 70 25 E
Vanua Levu, *Fiji* 133 A2 16 33 S 179 15 E
Vanuatu ■, *Pac. Oc.* 133 E6 15 0 S 168 0 E
Vanwyksvlei, *S. Africa* 116 E3 30 18 S 21 49 E
Vanzylsrus, *S. Africa* 116 D3 26 52 S 22 4 E
Vapnyarka, *Ukraine* 59 H5 48 32N 28 45 E
Var □, *France* 29 E10 43 27N 6 18 E
Var →, *France* 29 E11 43 39N 7 12 E
Vara, *Sweden* 17 F6 58 16N 12 55 E
Varada →, *India* 95 G2 15 0N 75 40 E
Varades, *France* 26 E5 47 25N 1 1W
Varáita →, *Italy* 44 D4 44 9N 7 53 E
Varaldsøy, *Norway* 18 D2 60 6N 5 59 E
Varallo, *Italy* 44 C5 45 49N 8 15 E
Varanasi, *India* 93 G10 25 22N 83 0 E
Varanger-halvøya, *Norway* 14 A23 70 25N 29 30 E
Varangerfjorden, *Norway* 14 A23 70 3N 29 25 E
Varano, Lago di, *Italy* 45 G12 41 53N 15 45 E
Varaždin, *Croatia* 45 B13 46 20N 16 20 E
Varazze, *Italy* 44 D5 44 22N 8 34 E
Varberg, *Sweden* 17 G6 57 6N 12 20 E
Vardar = Axiós →, *Greece* 50 F6 40 57N 22 35 E
Varde, *Denmark* 17 J2 55 38N 8 29 E
Varde Å →, *Denmark* 17 J2 55 35N 8 19 E
Vardø, *Norway* 14 A24 70 23N 31 5 E
Varel, *Germany* 30 B4 53 23N 8 8 E
Varella, Mui, *Vietnam* 86 F7 12 54N 109 26 E
Varėna, *Lithuania* 15 J21 54 12N 24 30 E
Varennes-sur-Allier, *France* 27 F10 46 19N 3 24 E
Varennes-Vauzelles, *France* 27 E10 47 3N 3 9 E
Vareš, *Bos.-H.* 52 F3 44 12N 18 23 E
Varese, *Italy* 44 C5 45 48N 8 50 E
Vârfurile, *Romania* 52 D7 46 19N 22 31 E
Vårgårda, *Sweden* 17 F6 58 2N 12 49 E
Vargem Bonita, *Brazil* 171 F2 20 20 S 46 22W
Vargem Grande, *Brazil* 170 B3 3 33 S 43 56W
Varginha, *Brazil* 175 A6 21 33 S 45 25W
Vargön, *Sweden* 17 F6 58 22N 12 20 E
Varhaug, *Norway* 18 F2 58 37N 5 41 E
Variadero, *U.S.A.* 155 H2 35 43N 104 17W
Varillas, *Chile* 174 A1 24 0 S 70 10W
Varkaus, *Finland* 15 E22 62 19N 27 50 E
Varmahlíð, *Iceland* 11 B7 65 33N 19 28W
Värmdölandet, *Sweden* 16 E12 59 20N 18 33 E
Värmeln, *Sweden* 16 E6 59 35N 12 54 E
Värmlands Bro, *Sweden* 16 E7 59 11N 13 0 E
Värmlands län □, *Sweden* 16 E6 60 0N 13 20 E
Varna, *Bulgaria* 51 C11 43 13N 27 56 E
Varna, *Russia* 62 E8 53 24N 60 58 E
Varna, *U.S.A.* 156 C7 41 2N 89 14W
Varna □, *Bulgaria* 51 C11 43 20N 27 30 E
Varna →, *India* 94 F2 16 48N 74 32 E
Värnamo, *Sweden* 17 G8 57 10N 14 3 E
Varnsdorf, *Czech Rep.* 34 A7 50 55N 14 35 E
Varnville, *U.S.A.* 152 C8 32 51N 81 5W
Várpalota, *Hungary* 52 C3 47 12N 18 8 E
Vars, *Canada* 151 A9 45 21N 75 21W
Vars, *France* 29 D10 44 37N 6 42 E
Vartdal, *Norway* 18 B3 62 20N 6 8 E
Varto, *Turkey* 101 C9 39 10N 41 27 E
Varvarin, *Serbia, Yug.* 50 C5 43 43N 21 20 E
Varzaneh, *Iran* 97 C7 32 25N 52 40 E
Várzea Alegre, *Brazil* 170 C4 6 47 S 39 17W
Várzea da Palma, *Brazil* 171 E3 17 36 S 44 44W
Várzea Grande, *Brazil* 173 D6 15 39 S 56 8W
Varzi, *Italy* 44 D6 44 49N 9 12 E
Varzo, *Italy* 44 B5 46 12N 8 15 E
Varzy, *France* 27 E10 47 22N 3 20 E
Vas □, *Hungary* 52 C1 47 10N 16 55 E
Vasa Barris →, *Brazil* 170 D4 11 10 S 37 10W
Vásárosnamény, *Hungary* 52 B7 48 9N 22 19 E
Vascão →, *Portugal* 43 H3 37 31N 7 31W
Vaşcău, *Romania* 52 D7 46 28N 22 30 E
Vascongadas = País Vasco □, *Spain* 40 C2 42 50N 2 45W
Vāshīr, *Afghan.* 91 B1 32 16N 63 51 E
Vasht = Khāsh, *Iran* 97 D9 28 15N 61 15 E
Vasilevichi, *Belarus* 59 F5 52 15N 29 50 E
Vasilikón, *Greece* 48 C5 38 25N 23 40 E
Vasilkov = Vasylkiv, *Ukraine* 59 G6 50 7N 30 15 E
Vaslui, *Romania* 53 D12 46 38N 27 42 E
Vaslui □, *Romania* 53 D12 46 30N 27 45 E
Väsman, *Sweden* 16 D9 60 9N 15 5 E
Vassar, *Canada* 143 D9 49 10N 95 55W
Vassar, *U.S.A.* 148 D4 43 22N 83 35W
Vassfaret, *Norway* 18 D6 60 38N 9 28 E
Västerås, *Sweden* 16 E10 59 37N 16 38 E
Västerbotten, *Sweden* 14 D18 64 36N 20 4 E
Västerdalälven →, *Sweden* 16 D8 60 30N 14 7 E
Västergötland, *Sweden* 17 F7 58 0N 13 10 E
Västerhaninge, *Sweden* 16 E12 59 7N 18 6 E
Västervik, *Sweden* 17 G10 57 43N 16 33 E
Västmanland, *Sweden* 15 G16 59 45N 16 20 E
Västmanlands län □, *Sweden* 16 E10 59 45N 16 20 E
Vasto, *Italy* 45 F11 42 8N 14 40 E
Vasvár, *Hungary* 52 C1 47 3N 16 47 E
Vasylkiv, *Ukraine* 59 G6 50 7N 30 15 E
Vatan, *France* 27 E8 47 4N 1 50 E
Vaté = Efate, I., *Vanuatu* 133 G6 17 40 S 168 25 E
Vatersay, *U.K.* 22 E1 56 55N 7 32W
Váthia, *Greece* 48 E4 36 29N 22 29 E
Vatican City ■, *Europe* 45 G9 41 54N 12 27 E
Vaticano, C., *Italy* 47 D8 38 37N 15 50 E
Vatili, *Cyprus* 38 D12 35 6N 33 40 E
Vatin, *Serbia, Yug.* 52 E6 45 12N 21 20 E
Vatnajökull, *Iceland* 11 C10 64 30N 16 48W
Vatnås, *Norway* 18 E6 59 58N 9 37 E
Vatneyri, *Iceland* 11 B2 65 35N 24 0W
Vatólakkos, *Greece* 50 F5 40 30N 21 50 E
Vatoloha, *Madag.* 117 B8 17 52 S 47 48 E
Vatomandry, *Madag.* 117 B8 19 20 S 48 59 E
Vatra-Dornei, *Romania* 53 C10 47 22N 25 22 E
Vättern, *Sweden* 17 F8 58 25N 14 30 E
Vättis, *Switz.* 33 C8 46 55N 9 27 E
Vatulele, *Fiji* 133 B1 18 33 S 177 37 E
Vaucluse, *U.S.A.* 152 B9 33 37N 81 49W
Vaucluse □, *France* 29 E9 43 50N 5 20 E
Vaucouleurs, *France* 27 D12 48 37N 5 40 E
Vaud □, *Switz.* 32 C3 46 35N 6 30 E
Vaughn, *Mont., U.S.A.* 158 C8 47 33N 111 33W
Vaughn, *N. Mex., U.S.A.* 159 J11 34 36N 105 13W
Vaulruz, *Switz.* 32 C3 46 38N 6 59 E
Vaupés = Uaupés →, *Brazil* 168 C4 0 2N 67 16W
Vaupes □, *Colombia* 168 C3 1 0N 71 0W
Vauvert, *France* 29 E8 43 42N 4 17 E
Vauxhall, *Canada* 142 C6 50 5N 112 9W
Vava'u, *Tonga* 133 P14 18 36 S 174 0W
Vavoua, *Ivory C.* 112 D3 7 23N 6 29W
Vawkavysk, *Belarus* 59 F3 53 9N 24 30 E
Vaxholm, *Sweden* 16 E12 59 25N 18 20 E
Växjö, *Sweden* 17 H8 56 52N 14 50 E
Våxtorp, *Sweden* 17 H7 56 25N 13 8 E
Vaygach, Ostrov, *Russia* 64 C7 70 0N 60 0 E

296 Váyia

Váyia, *Greece* **48 C5** 38 19N 23 11 E
Váyia, Ákra, *Greece* **38 C10** 36 15N 28 11 E
Veadeiros, *Brazil* **171 D2** 14 7 S 47 31W
Vechelde, *Germany* **30 C6** 52 16N 10 22 E
Vechta, *Germany* **30 C4** 52 44N 8 17 E
Vechte →, *Neths.* **24 B6** 52 34N 6 6 E
Vecsés, *Hungary* **52 C4** 47 26N 19 19 E
Vedaranniyam, *India* **95 J4** 10 25N 79 50 E
Vedavågen, *Norway* **18 E2** 59 17N 5 12 E
Veddige, *Sweden* **17 G6** 57 17N 12 20 E
Vedea →, *Romania* **53 G10** 43 42N 25 41 E
Vedia, *Argentina* **174 C3** 34 30 S 61 31W
Vedum, *Sweden* **17 F7** 58 11N 13 0 E
Veendam, *Neths.* **24 A6** 53 5N 6 52 E
Veenendaal, *Neths.* **24 B5** 52 2N 5 34 E
Vefsna →, *Norway* **14 D15** 65 48N 13 10 E
Vega, *Norway* **14 D14** 65 40N 11 55 E
Vega, *U.S.A.* **155 H3** 35 15N 102 26W
Vegadeo, *Spain* **42 B3** 43 27N 7 4W
Vegårshei, *Norway* **18 F5** 58 44N 8 51 E
Veggli, *Norway* **18 D6** 60 3N 9 9 E
Vegorrítis, Límni, *Greece* **50 F5** 40 45N 21 45 E
Vegreville, *Canada* **142 C6** 53 30N 112 5W
Veidholmen, *Norway* **18 A4** 63 31N 7 58 E
Veinge, *Sweden* **17 H7** 56 33N 13 4 E
Veisiejai, *Lithuania* **54 D10** 54 6N 23 42 E
Veitch, *Australia* **128 C4** 34 39 S 140 31 E
Vejbystrand, *Sweden* **17 H6** 56 19N 12 45 E
Vejen, *Denmark* **17 J3** 55 30N 9 9 E
Vejer de la Frontera, *Spain* **43 J5** 36 15N 5 59W
Vejle, *Denmark* **17 J3** 55 43N 9 30 E
Vejle Amtskommune □, *Denmark* **17 J3** 55 45N 9 20 E
Vejle Fjord, *Denmark* **17 J3** 55 40N 9 50 E
Vela Luka, *Croatia* **45 F13** 42 59N 16 44 E
Velanai I., *Sri Lanka* **95 K4** 9 45N 79 45 E
Velas, C., *Costa Rica* **164 D2** 10 21N 85 52W
Velasco, Sierra de, *Argentina* **174 B2** 29 20 S 67 10W
Velay, Mts. du, *France* **28 D7** 45 0N 3 40 E
Velbert, *Germany* **30 D3** 51 20N 7 3 E
Velddrif, *S. Africa* **116 E2** 32 42 S 18 11 E
Velebit Planina, *Croatia* **45 D12** 44 50N 15 20 E
Velebitski Kanal, *Croatia* **45 D11** 44 45N 14 55 E
Veleka →, *Bulgaria* **51 D11** 42 4N 27 58 E
Velencei-tó, *Hungary* **52 C3** 47 13N 18 36 E
Velenje, *Slovenia* **45 B12** 46 23N 15 8 E
Veles, *Macedonia* **50 E5** 41 46N 21 47 E
Velestínon, *Greece* **48 B4** 39 23N 22 43 E
Vélez, *Colombia* **168 B3** 6 1N 73 41W
Vélez-Málaga, *Spain* **43 J6** 36 48N 4 5W
Vélez Rubio, *Spain* **41 H2** 37 41N 2 5W
Velhas →, *Brazil* **171 E3** 17 13 S 44 49W
Velika, *Croatia* **52 E2** 45 27N 17 40 E
Velika Gorica, *Croatia* **45 C13** 45 44N 16 5 E
Velika Kapela, *Croatia* **45 C12** 45 10N 15 5 E
Velika Kladuša, *Bos.-H.* **45 C12** 45 11N 15 48 E
Velika Morava →, *Serbia, Yug.* **50 B5** 44 43N 21 3 E
Velika Plana, *Serbia, Yug.* **50 B5** 44 20N 21 4 E
Velikaya →, *Russia* **58 D5** 57 48N 28 10 E
Velikaya Kema, *Russia* **68 B8** 45 30N 137 12 E
Velikaya Lepetikha, *Ukraine* **59 J7** 47 2N 33 58 E
Veliké Kapušany, *Slovak Rep.* **35 C15** 48 34N 22 5 E
Velike Lašče, *Slovenia* **45 C11** 45 49N 14 45 E
Veliki Jastrebac, *Serbia, Yug.* **50 C5** 43 25N 21 30 E
Veliki Kanal, *Serbia, Yug.* **52 E4** 45 45N 19 15 E
Veliki Popović, *Serbia, Yug.* **50 B5** 44 8N 21 18 E
Veliki Ustyug, *Russia* **56 B8** 60 47N 46 20 E
Velikiye Luki, *Russia* **58 D6** 56 25N 30 32 E
Veliko Gradište, *Serbia, Yug.* **50 B5** 44 46N 21 29 E
Veliko Tŭrnovo, *Bulgaria* **51 C9** 43 5N 25 41 E
Velikonda Range, *India* **95 G4** 14 45N 79 10 E
Velingrad, *Bulgaria* **50 D7** 42 4N 23 58 E
Velino, Mte., *Italy* **45 F10** 42 9N 13 23 E
Velizh, *Russia* **58 E6** 55 36N 31 11 E
Velké Karlovice, *Czech Rep.* **35 B11** 49 20N 18 17 E
Velke Meziříčí, *Czech Rep.* **34 B9** 49 21N 16 1 E
Vel'ký Javorník, *Slovak Rep.* **35 B11** 49 19N 18 22 E
Vel'ký Krtíš, *Slovak Rep.* **35 C12** 48 12N 19 21 E
Vel'ký Meder, *Slovak Rep.* **35 D10** 47 52N 17 46 E
Vel'ký Tribeč, *Slovak Rep.* **35 C11** 48 28N 18 15 E
Vella G., *Solomon Is.* **133 M9** 8 0 S 156 50 E
Vella Lavella, *Solomon Is.* **133 L9** 7 45 S 156 40 E
Vellar →, *India* **95 J4** 11 30N 79 36 E
Velletri, *Italy* **46 A5** 41 41N 12 47 E
Vellinge, *Sweden* **17 J6** 55 29N 13 0 E
Vellmar, *Germany* **30 D5** 51 22N 9 28 E
Vellore, *India* **95 H4** 12 57N 79 10 E
Velsk, *Russia* **58 B11** 61 10N 42 5 E
Velten, *Germany* **30 C9** 52 42N 13 10 E
Velva, *U.S.A.* **154 A4** 48 4N 100 56W
Velvendós, *Greece* **50 F6** 40 15N 22 6 E
Vemb, *Denmark* **17 H2** 56 21N 8 21 E
Vembanad L., *India* **95 K3** 9 36N 76 15 E
Vemdalen, *Sweden* **16 B7** 62 27N 13 51 E
Ven, *Sweden* **17 J6** 55 55N 12 45 E
Venaco, *France* **29 F13** 42 14N 9 11 E
Venado Tuerto, *Argentina* **174 C3** 33 50 S 62 0W
Venafro, *Italy* **47 A7** 41 29N 14 2 E
Venarey-les-Laumes, *France* **27 E11** 47 32N 4 26 E
Venaría, *Italy* **44 C4** 45 8N 7 38 E
Venčane, *Serbia, Yug.* **50 B4** 44 24N 20 28 E
Vence, *France* **29 E11** 43 43N 7 6 E
Vendas Novas, *Portugal* **43 G2** 38 39N 8 27W
Vendée □, *France* **26 F5** 46 50N 1 35W
Vendée →, *France* **26 F5** 46 20N 1 10W
Vendéen, Bocage, *France* **28 B2** 46 40N 1 20W
Vendeuvre-sur-Barse, *France* **27 D11** 48 14N 4 28 E
Vendôme, *France* **26 E8** 47 47N 1 3 E
Vendrell = El Vendrell, *Spain* **40 D6** 41 10N 1 30 E
Vendsyssel, *Denmark* **17 G4** 57 22N 10 0 E
Venelles, *France* **29 E9** 43 35N 5 28 E
Véneta, L., *Italy* **45 C9** 45 23N 12 25 E
Venetie Indian Reservation, *U.S.A.* **144 C11** 67 20N 146 0W
Véneto □, *Italy* **45 C9** 45 30N 12 0 E
Venev, *Russia* **58 E10** 54 22N 38 17 E
Venézia, *Italy* **45 C9** 45 27N 12 21 E
Venézia, G. di, *Italy* **45 C10** 45 15N 13 0 E
Venezuela ■, *S. Amer.* **168 B4** 8 0N 66 0W
Venezuela, G. de, *Venezuela* **168 A3** 11 30N 71 0W
Vengurla, *India* **95 G1** 15 53N 73 45 E
Vengurla Rocks, *India* **95 G1** 15 55N 73 22 E
Venice = Venézia, *Italy* **45 C9** 45 27N 12 21 E
Venice, *U.S.A.* **153 H7** 27 6N 82 27W
Vénissieux, *France* **29 C8** 45 42N 4 53 E
Venjansjön, *Sweden* **16 D8** 60 54N 14 0 E
Venkatagiri, *India* **95 H4** 14 0N 79 35 E
Venkatapuram, *India* **94 E5** 18 20N 80 30 E
Venlo, *Neths.* **24 C6** 51 22N 6 11 E
Vennesla, *Norway* **15 G12** 58 15N 7 59 E
Venosa, *Italy* **47 B8** 40 58N 15 49 E
Venray, *Neths.* **24 C6** 51 31N 6 0 E
Venta, *Lithuania* **54 B9** 56 12N 22 42 E
Venta →, *Latvia* **54 A8** 57 24N 21 33 E
Venta de Baños, *Spain* **42 D6** 41 55N 4 30W
Venta de Cardeña = Cardeña, *Spain* **43 G6** 38 16N 4 20W
Ventana, Punta de la, *Mexico* **162 C3** 24 4N 109 48W
Ventana, Sa. de la, *Argentina* **174 D3** 38 0 S 62 30W
Ventersburg, *S. Africa* **116 D4** 28 7 S 27 9 E
Venterstad, *S. Africa* **116 E4** 30 47 S 25 48 E
Ventimíglia, *Italy* **44 E4** 43 47N 7 36 E
Ventnor, *U.K.* **21 G6** 50 36N 1 12W
Ventoténe, *Italy* **46 B6** 40 47N 13 25 E
Ventoux, Mt., *France* **29 D9** 44 10N 5 17 E
Ventspils, *Latvia* **15 H19** 57 25N 21 32 E
Ventspils □, *Latvia* **54 A8** 57 20N 21 50 E
Ventuarí →, *Venezuela* **168 C4** 3 58N 67 2W
Ventucopa, *U.S.A.* **161 L7** 34 50N 119 29W
Ventura, *U.S.A.* **161 L7** 34 17N 119 18W
Venus, *U.S.A.* **153 H8** 27 4N 81 22W
Venus B., *Australia* **129 E6** 38 40 S 145 42 E
Vera, *Argentina* **174 B3** 29 30 S 60 20W
Vera, *Spain* **41 H3** 37 15N 1 51W
Veracruz, *Mexico* **163 D5** 19 10N 96 10W
Veracruz □, *Mexico* **163 D5** 19 0N 96 15W
Veraval, *India* **92 J4** 20 53N 70 27 E
Verbánia, *Italy* **44 C5** 45 56N 8 33 E
Verbicaro, *Italy* **47 C8** 39 45N 15 55 E
Verbier, *Switz.* **32 D4** 46 6N 7 13 E
Vercelli, *Italy* **44 C5** 45 19N 8 25 E
Verchovchevo, *Ukraine* **59 H8** 48 32N 34 10 E
Verdalsøra, *Norway* **14 E14** 63 48N 11 30 E
Verde →, *Argentina* **176 B3** 41 56 S 65 5W
Verde →, *Goiás, Brazil* **171 E1** 19 11 S 50 44W
Verde →, *Goiás, Brazil* **171 E1** 18 1 S 50 14W
Verde →, *Mato Grosso, Brazil* **173 C6** 11 54 S 55 48W
Verde →, *Mato Grosso do Sul, Brazil* **173 E7** 21 25 S 52 20W
Verde →, *Chihuahua, Mexico* **162 B3** 26 29N 107 58W
Verde →, *Oaxaca, Mexico* **163 D5** 15 59N 97 50W
Verde →, *Veracruz, Mexico* **162 C4** 21 10N 102 50W
Verde →, *Paraguay* **174 A4** 23 9 S 57 37W
Verde, Cay, *Bahamas* **164 B4** 23 0N 75 5W
Verde Grande →, *Brazil* **171 E3** 16 13 S 43 49W
Verde I., *Phil.* **80 E3** 13 33N 121 5 E
Verde Island Pass, *Phil.* **80 E3** 13 34N 120 51 E
Verde Pequeno →, *Brazil* **171 D3** 14 48 S 43 31W
Verden, *Germany* **30 C5** 52 55N 9 14 E
Verdery, *U.S.A.* **152 A7** 34 7N 82 15W
Verdhikoúsa, *Greece* **48 B3** 39 47N 21 59 E
Verdi, *U.S.A.* **160 F7** 39 31N 119 59W
Verdigre, *U.S.A.* **154 D6** 42 36N 98 2W
Verdon →, *France* **29 E9** 43 43N 5 46 E
Verdun, *France* **27 C12** 49 9N 5 24 E
Verdun-sur-le-Doubs, *France* **27 F12** 46 54N 5 2 E
Vereeniging, *S. Africa* **117 D4** 26 38 S 27 57 E
Vérendrye, Parc Prov. de la, *Canada* **140 C4** 47 20N 76 40W
Vereshchagino, *Russia* **62 B5** 58 5N 54 40 E
Verga, C., *Guinea* **112 C2** 10 30N 14 10W
Vergato, *Italy* **44 D8** 44 17N 11 7 E
Vergemont, *Australia* **126 C3** 23 33 S 143 1 E
Vergemont Cr. →, *Australia* **126 C3** 24 16 S 143 16 E
Vergennes, *U.S.A.* **151 B11** 44 10N 73 15W
Vergt, *France* **28 C4** 45 2N 0 43 E
Verín, *Spain* **42 D3** 41 57N 7 27W
Verkhnedvinsk = Vyerkhnyadzvinsk, *Belarus* **58 E4** 55 45N 27 58 E
Verkhneuralsk, *Russia* **62 E7** 53 53N 59 13 E
Verkhnevilyuysk, *Russia* **65 C13** 63 27N 120 18 E
Verkhniy Avzyan, *Russia* **62 E6** 53 32N 57 33 E
Verkhniy Baskunchak, *Russia* **61 F8** 48 14N 46 44 E
Verkhniy Tagil, *Russia* **62 C7** 57 22N 59 56 E
Verkhniy Ufaley, *Russia* **62 C8** 56 4N 60 14 E
Verkhniye Kigi, *Russia* **62 D7** 55 25N 58 37 E
Verkhnyaya Salda, *Russia* **62 C8** 58 2N 60 33 E
Verkhnyaya Tura, *Russia* **62 B7** 58 22N 59 50 E
Verkhoturye, *Russia* **62 B8** 58 52N 60 48 E
Verkhovye, *Russia* **59 F9** 52 55N 37 15 E
Verkhoyansk, *Russia* **65 C14** 67 35N 133 25 E
Verkhoyansk Ra. = Verkhoyanskiy Khrebet, *Russia* **65 C13** 66 0N 129 0 E
Verkhoyanskiy Khrebet, *Russia* **65 C13** 66 0N 129 0 E
Verlo, *Canada* **143 C7** 50 19N 108 35W
Verma, *Norway* **18 B5** 62 21N 8 3 E
Vermenton, *France* **27 E10** 47 40N 3 42 E
Vermilion, *Canada* **143 C6** 53 20N 110 50W
Vermilion →, *Alta., Canada* **143 C6** 53 22N 110 51W
Vermilion →, *Qué., Canada* **140 C5** 47 38N 72 56W
Vermilion →, *Ill., U.S.A.* **156 C7** 41 19N 89 4W
Vermilion →, *Ind., U.S.A.* **157 E9** 39 57N 87 27W
Vermilion, B., *U.S.A.* **155 L9** 29 45N 91 55W
Vermilion Bay, *Canada* **143 D10** 49 51N 93 34W
Vermilion Chutes, *Canada* **142 B6** 58 22N 114 51W
Vermilion L., *U.S.A.* **154 B8** 47 53N 92 26W
Vermillion, *U.S.A.* **154 D6** 42 47N 96 56W
Vermont, *U.S.A.* **156 D6** 40 18N 90 26W
Vermont □, *U.S.A.* **151 C12** 44 0N 73 0W
Vermosh, *Albania* **50 D3** 42 35N 19 42 E
Verna, *U.S.A.* **153 H7** 27 23N 82 16W
Vernal, *U.S.A.* **158 F9** 40 27N 109 32W
Vernalis, *U.S.A.* **160 H5** 37 36N 121 17W
Vernayaz, *Switz.* **32 D4** 46 8N 7 3 E
Vernazza, *Italy* **44 D6** 44 10N 9 45 E
Verner, *Canada* **140 C3** 46 25N 80 8W
Verneuil-sur-Avre, *France* **26 D7** 48 45N 0 55 E
Verneukpan, *S. Africa* **116 E3** 30 0 S 21 0 E
Vernier, *Switz.* **32 D2** 46 13N 6 5 E
Vérnio, *Italy* **44 D8** 44 3N 11 9 E
Vernon, *Canada* **142 C5** 50 20N 119 15W
Vernon, *France* **26 C8** 49 5N 1 30 E
Vernon, *Ill., U.S.A.* **156 F7** 38 48N 89 5W
Vernon, *Ind., U.S.A.* **157 F11** 38 59N 85 36W
Vernon, *Tex., U.S.A.* **155 H5** 34 9N 99 17W
Vernonia, *U.S.A.* **160 E3** 45 52N 123 11W
Vernouillet, *France* **26 D8** 48 58N 1 58 E
Vero Beach, *U.S.A.* **149 M5** 27 38N 80 24W
Véroia, *Greece* **50 F6** 40 34N 22 12 E
Véroli, *Italy* **45 G10** 41 41N 13 25 E
Verona, *Italy* **44 C7** 45 27N 10 59 E
Verona, *U.S.A.* **156 B7** 42 59N 89 32W
Verrès, *Italy* **44 C4** 45 40N 7 42 E
Versailles, *France* **27 D9** 48 48N 2 8 E
Versailles, *Ill., U.S.A.* **156 E6** 39 53N 90 39W
Versailles, *Ind., U.S.A.* **157 E11** 39 4N 85 15W
Versailles, *Ky., U.S.A.* **157 F12** 38 3N 84 44W
Versailles, *Mo., U.S.A.* **156 F4** 38 26N 92 51W
Versailles, *Ohio, U.S.A.* **157 D12** 40 13N 84 29W
Versalles, *Bolivia* **173 C5** 12 44 S 63 18W
Versmold, *Germany* **30 C4** 52 2N 8 9 E
Versoix, *Switz.* **32 D2** 46 17N 6 10 E
Vert, C., *Senegal* **112 C1** 14 45N 17 30W
Vertou, *France* **26 E5** 47 10N 1 28W
Vertus, *France* **27 D11** 48 54N 4 2 E
Verulam, *S. Africa* **117 D5** 29 38 S 31 2 E
Verviers, *Belgium* **24 D5** 50 37N 5 52 E
Vervins, *France* **27 C10** 49 50N 3 53 E
Veržej, *Slovenia* **45 B13** 46 34N 16 13 E
Verzy, *France* **27 C11** 49 9N 4 10 E
Vescovato, *France* **29 F13** 42 30N 9 27 E
Veselí nad Lužnicí, *Czech Rep.* **34 B7** 49 12N 14 43 E
Veselie, *Bulgaria* **51 D11** 42 18N 27 38 E
Veselovskoye Vdkhr., *Russia* **61 G5** 46 58N 41 25 E
Veshenskaya, *Russia* **60 F5** 49 35N 41 44 E
Vesle →, *France* **27 C10** 49 23N 3 28 E
Veslyana →, *Russia* **62 A4** 60 20N 54 0 E
Vesoul, *France* **27 E13** 47 40N 6 11 E
Vessigebro, *Sweden* **17 H6** 56 58N 12 40 E
Vest-Agder □, *Norway* **18 F4** 58 30N 7 15 E
Vesta, *U.S.A.* **152 B7** 33 58N 82 56W
Vestbygd, *Norway* **18 F3** 58 6N 6 34 E
Vestdalseyri, *Iceland* **11 B13** 65 17N 13 59W
Vesterålen, *Norway* **14 B16** 68 45N 15 0 E
Vestfjorden, *Norway* **14 C15** 67 55N 14 0 E
Vestfold □, *Norway* **18 E7** 59 15N 10 0 E
Vestfossen, *Norway* **18 E6** 59 44N 9 52 E
Vestgrønland □, *Greenland* **10 C6** 70 0N 47 0W
Vestmannaeyjar, *Iceland* **11 D6** 63 27N 20 15W
Vestnes, *Norway* **18 B4** 62 39N 7 5 E
Vestre Gausdal, *Norway* **18 C7** 61 12N 10 8 E
Vestre Slidre, *Norway* **18 C5** 61 5N 8 58 E
Vestsjællands Amtskommune □, *Denmark* **17 J5** 55 30N 11 20 E
Vestspitsbergen, *Svalbard* **6 B8** 78 40N 17 0 E
Vestur-skaftafellssýsla □, *Iceland* **11 D8** 63 50N 18 30W
Vestvågøy, *Norway* **14 B15** 68 18N 13 50 E
Vesuvio, *Italy* **47 B7** 40 49N 14 26 E
Vesuvius, Mt. = Vesuvio, *Italy* **47 B7** 40 49N 14 26 E
Vesyegonsk, *Russia* **58 C9** 58 40N 37 16 E
Veszprém, *Hungary* **52 C2** 47 8N 17 57 E
Veszprém □, *Hungary* **52 C2** 47 5N 17 55 E
Vésztő, *Hungary* **52 D6** 46 55N 21 16 E
Vetapalem, *India* **95 G5** 15 47N 80 18 E
Vetlanda, *Sweden* **17 G9** 57 24N 15 3 E
Vetluga, *Russia* **60 B7** 57 53N 45 45 E
Vetlugu →, *Russia* **60 B8** 56 36N 46 4 E
Vetluzhskiy, *Kostroma, Russia* **60 A7** 58 23N 45 26 E
Vetluzhskiy, *Nizhniy Novgorod, Russia* **60 B7** 57 17N 45 12 E
Vetovo, *Bulgaria* **51 C10** 43 42N 26 16 E
Vetralla, *Italy* **45 F9** 42 20N 12 2 E
Vetren, *Bulgaria* **51 D8** 42 15N 24 3 E
Vettore, Mte., *Italy* **45 F10** 42 49N 13 16 E
Veurne, *Belgium* **24 C2** 51 5N 2 40 E
Vevay, *U.S.A.* **157 F11** 38 45N 85 4W
Vevey, *Switz.* **32 D3** 46 28N 6 51 E
Vévi, *Greece* **50 F5** 40 47N 21 38 E
Veynes, *France* **29 D9** 44 32N 5 49 E
Veys, *Iran* **97 D6** 31 30N 49 0 E
Vézelay, *France* **27 E10** 47 27N 3 45 E
Vézelise, *France* **27 D13** 48 30N 6 5 E
Vézère →, *France* **28 D4** 44 53N 0 53 E
Vezhen, *Bulgaria* **51 D8** 42 50N 24 20 E
Vezirköprü, *Turkey* **100 B6** 41 8N 35 27 E
Vezzani, *France* **29 F13** 42 10N 9 15 E
Vi Thanh, *Vietnam* **87 H5** 9 42N 105 26 E
Viacha, *Bolivia* **172 D4** 16 39 S 68 18W
Viadana, *Italy* **44 D7** 44 56N 10 31 E
Viamão, *Brazil* **175 C5** 30 5 S 51 0W
Viana, *Brazil* **170 B3** 3 13 S 44 55W
Viana, *Spain* **40 C2** 42 31N 2 22W
Viana do Alentejo, *Portugal* **43 G3** 38 17N 7 59W
Viana do Bolo, *Spain* **42 C3** 42 11N 7 6W
Viana do Castelo, *Portugal* **42 D2** 41 42N 8 50W
Viana do Castelo □, *Portugal* **42 D2** 41 50N 8 30W
Vianden, *Lux.* **24 E6** 49 56N 6 12 E
Vianópolis, *Brazil* **171 E2** 16 40 S 48 35W
Viar →, *Spain* **43 H5** 37 36N 5 50W
Viaréggio, *Italy* **44 E7** 43 52N 10 14 E
Viaur →, *France* **28 D5** 44 8N 1 58 E
Vibank, *Canada* **143 C8** 50 20N 103 56W
Vibble, *Sweden* **17 G12** 57 37N 18 16 E
Vibo Valéntia, *Italy* **47 D9** 38 40N 16 6 E
Viborg, *Denmark* **17 H3** 56 27N 9 23 E
Viborg Amtskommune □, *Denmark* **17 H3** 56 30N 9 30 E
Vibraye, *France* **26 D7** 48 3N 0 44 E
Vic, *Spain* **40 D7** 41 58N 2 19 E
Vic, Étang de, *France* **28 E7** 43 29N 3 50 E
Vic-en-Bigorre, *France* **28 E4** 43 24N 0 3 E
Vic-Fézensac, *France* **28 E4** 43 47N 0 19 E
Vic-le-Comte, *France* **27 G10** 45 39N 3 14 E
Vic-sur-Cère, *France* **28 D6** 44 59N 2 38 E
Vícar, *Spain* **41 J2** 36 50N 2 38W
Vicenza, *Italy* **45 C8** 45 33N 11 33 E
Vich = Vic, *Spain* **40 D7** 41 58N 2 19 E
Vichada □, *Colombia* **168 C4** 5 0N 69 30W
Vichada →, *Colombia* **168 C4** 4 55N 67 50W
Vichuga, *Russia* **60 B5** 57 12N 41 55 E
Vichy, *France* **27 F10** 46 9N 3 26 E
Vicksburg, *Ariz., U.S.A.* **161 M13** 33 45N 113 45W
Vicksburg, *Mich., U.S.A.* **157 B11** 42 7N 85 32W
Vicksburg, *Miss., U.S.A.* **155 J9** 32 21N 90 53W
Vico, *France* **29 F12** 42 10N 8 49 E
Vico, L. di, *Italy* **45 F9** 42 19N 12 10 E
Vico del Gargano, *Italy* **45 G12** 41 54N 15 57 E
Viçosa, *Brazil* **170 C4** 9 28 S 36 14W
Viçosa do Ceará, *Brazil* **170 B3** 3 34 S 41 5W
Vicosoprano, *Switz.* **33 D9** 46 22N 9 38 E
Vicovu de Sus, *Romania* **53 C10** 47 56N 25 41 E
Victor, *India* **92 J4** 21 0N 71 30 E
Victor, *Colo., U.S.A.* **154 F2** 38 43N 105 9W
Victor, *N.Y., U.S.A.* **150 D7** 42 58N 77 24W
Victor Emanuel Ra., *Papua N. G.* **132 C2** 5 20 S 142 15 E
Victor Harbor, *Australia* **127 F2** 35 30 S 138 37 E
Victoria = Labuan, *Malaysia* **85 A5** 5 20N 115 14 E
Victoria, *Argentina* **174 C3** 32 40 S 60 10W
Victoria, *Canada* **142 D4** 48 30N 123 25W
Victoria, *Chile* **176 A2** 38 13 S 72 20W
Victoria, *Guinea* **112 C2** 10 50N 14 32W
Victoria, *Malta* **38 C1** 36 2N 14 14 E
Victoria, *Mindoro, Phil.* **80 E3** 13 12N 121 12 E
Victoria, *Tarlac, Phil.* **80 D3** 15 35N 120 41 E
Victoria, *Romania* **53 E9** 45 44N 24 41 E
Victoria, *Seychelles* **121 E4** 5 0 S 55 40 E
Victoria, *Ill., U.S.A.* **156 C6** 41 2N 90 6W
Victoria, *Kans., U.S.A.* **154 F5** 38 52N 99 9W
Victoria, *Tex., U.S.A.* **155 L6** 28 48N 97 0W
Victoria □, *Australia* **128 D6** 37 0 S 144 0 E
Victoria →, *Australia* **124 C4** 15 10 S 129 40 E
Victoria, Grand L., *Canada* **140 C4** 47 31N 77 30W
Victoria, L., *Africa* **118 C3** 1 0 S 33 0 E
Victoria, L., *Australia* **128 B4** 33 57 S 141 15 E
Victoria, Mt., *Burma* **90 E4** 21 15N 93 55 E
Victoria, Mt., *Papua N. G.* **132 E4** 8 55 S 147 32 E
Victoria Beach, *Canada* **143 C9** 50 40N 96 35W
Victoria de Durango = Durango, *Mexico* **162 C4** 24 3N 104 39W
Victoria de las Tunas, *Cuba* **164 B4** 20 58N 76 59W
Victoria Falls, *Zimbabwe* **119 F2** 17 58 S 25 52 E
Victoria Harbour, *Canada* **140 D4** 44 45N 79 45W
Victoria I., *Canada* **138 A8** 71 0N 111 0W
Victoria Ld., *Antarctica* **7 D11** 75 0 S 160 0 E
Victoria Nile →, *Uganda* **118 B3** 2 14N 31 26 E
Victoria Peaks, *Phil.* **81 G2** 9 22N 118 20 E
Victoria Ra., *N.Z.* **131 C7** 42 12 S 172 7 E
Victoria Res., *Canada* **141 C8** 48 20N 57 27W
Victoria River Downs, *Australia* **124 C5** 16 25 S 131 0 E
Victoria West, *S. Africa* **116 E3** 31 25 S 23 4 E
Victorias, *Phil.* **81 F4** 10 54N 123 5 E
Victoriaville, *Canada* **141 C5** 46 4N 71 56W
Victorica, *Argentina* **174 D2** 36 20 S 65 30W
Victorville, *U.S.A.* **161 L9** 34 32N 117 18W
Vicuña, *Chile* **174 C1** 30 0 S 70 50W
Vicuña Mackenna, *Argentina* **174 C3** 33 53 S 64 25W
Vidal, *U.S.A.* **161 L12** 34 7N 114 31W
Vidal Junction, *U.S.A.* **161 L12** 34 11N 114 34W
Vidalia, *U.S.A.* **152 C7** 32 13N 82 25W
Vidauban, *France* **29 E10** 43 25N 6 27 E
Videbæk, *Denmark* **17 H2** 56 6N 8 38 E
Videle, *Romania* **53 F10** 44 17N 25 31 E
Videseter, *Norway* **18 C4** 61 57N 7 14 E
Vidette, *U.S.A.* **152 B7** 33 2N 82 15W
Víðirhóll, *Iceland* **11 B10** 65 44N 16 2W
Vídho, *Greece* **38 A3** 39 38N 19 55 E
Vidigueira, *Portugal* **43 G3** 38 12N 7 48W
Vidin, *Bulgaria* **50 C6** 43 59N 22 50 E
Vidio, C., *Spain* **42 B4** 43 35N 6 14W
Vidisha, *India* **92 H7** 23 28N 77 53 E
Vidra, *Romania* **53 E11** 45 56N 26 55 E
Viduša, *Bos.-H.* **50 D2** 42 55N 18 21 E
Vidzy, *Belarus* **15 J22** 55 23N 26 37 E
Viechtach, *Germany* **31 F8** 49 4N 12 53 E
Viedma, *Argentina* **176 B4** 40 50 S 63 0W
Viedma, L., *Argentina* **176 C2** 49 30 S 72 30W
Vieira do Minho, *Portugal* **42 D2** 41 38N 8 8W
Vielha, *Spain* **40 C5** 42 43N 0 44 E
Viella = Vielha, *Spain* **40 C5** 42 43N 0 44 E
Vielsalm, *Belgium* **24 D5** 50 17N 5 54 E
Vienenburg, *Germany* **30 D6** 51 57N 10 34 E
Vieng Pou Kha, *Laos* **86 B3** 20 41N 101 4 E
Vienna = Wien, *Austria* **35 C9** 48 12N 16 22 E
Vienna, *Ga., U.S.A.* **152 C6** 32 6N 83 47W
Vienna, *Ill., U.S.A.* **155 G10** 37 25N 88 54W
Vienna, *Mo., U.S.A.* **156 F5** 38 11N 91 57W
Vienne, *France* **29 C8** 45 31N 4 53 E
Vienne □, *France* **28 B4** 46 30N 0 42 E
Vienne →, *France* **26 E7** 47 13N 0 5 E
Vientiane, *Laos* **86 D4** 17 58N 102 36 E
Vientos, Paso de los, *Caribbean* **165 C5** 20 0N 74 0W
Viernheim, *Germany* **31 F4** 49 31N 8 35 E
Viersen, *Germany* **30 D2** 51 15N 6 23 E
Vierwaldstättersee, *Switz.* **33 C7** 47 0N 8 30 E
Vierzon, *France* **27 E9** 47 13N 2 5 E
Vieste, *Italy* **45 G13** 41 53N 16 10 E
Vietnam ■, *Asia* **86 C6** 19 0N 106 0 E
Vieux-Boucau-les-Bains, *France* **28 E2** 43 48N 1 23W
Vif, *France* **29 C9** 45 5N 5 41 E
Vigan, *Phil.* **80 C3** 17 35N 120 28 E
Vigévano, *Italy* **44 C5** 45 19N 8 51 E
Vigia, *Brazil* **170 B2** 0 50 S 48 5W
Vigía Chico, *Mexico* **163 D7** 19 46N 87 35W
Víglas, Ákra, *Greece* **38 D9** 35 54N 27 51 E
Vignemalle, *France* **28 F3** 42 47N 0 10W
Vigneulles-lès-Hattonchâtel, *France* **27 D12** 48 59N 5 43 E
Vignola, *Italy* **44 D8** 44 29N 11 1 E
Vigo, *Spain* **42 C2** 42 12N 8 41W
Vigo, Ría de, *Spain* **42 C2** 42 15N 8 45W
Vigrestad, *Norway* **18 F2** 58 34N 5 42 E
Vigsø Bugt, *Denmark* **17 G2** 57 8N 8 47 E
Vihiers, *France* **26 E6** 47 10N 0 30W
Vijayadurg, *India* **94 F1** 16 30N 73 25 E
Vijayawada, *India* **95 F5** 16 31N 80 39 E
Vík, *Iceland* **11 D7** 63 25N 19 1W
Vik, *Norway* **18 C3** 61 21N 6 6 E
Vika, *Sweden* **16 D8** 60 57N 14 28 E
Vikarbyn, *Sweden* **16 D9** 60 55N 15 1 E
Vike, *Norway* **18 D2** 60 42N 5 35 E
Vikedal, *Norway* **18 E2** 59 30N 5 55 E
Vikeke, *Indonesia* **82 C3** 8 52 S 126 23 E
Vikeland, *Norway* **18 F4** 58 5N 7 18 E
Viken, *Malmöhus, Sweden* **17 H6** 56 9N 12 34 E
Viken, *Skaraborg, Sweden* **17 F8** 58 39N 14 20 E
Vikersund, *Norway* **18 E6** 59 58N 9 59 E
Vikeså, *Norway* **18 F3** 58 38N 6 3 E
Vikevåg, *Norway* **18 E2** 59 5N 5 41 E
Viking, *Canada* **142 C6** 53 7N 111 50W
Vikmanshyttan, *Sweden* **16 D9** 60 18N 15 50 E
Vikna, *Norway* **14 D14** 64 55N 10 58 E
Vikramasingapuram, *India* **95 K3** 8 40N 76 47 E
Viksøyri, *Norway* **18 C3** 61 4N 6 34 E
Vila da Maganja, *Mozam.* **119 F4** 17 18 S 37 30 E
Vila de João Belo = Xai-Xai, *Mozam.* **117 D5** 25 6 S 33 31 E
Vila de Rei, *Portugal* **42 F2** 39 41N 8 9W
Vila do Bispo, *Portugal* **43 H2** 37 5N 8 53W
Vila do Chibuto, *Mozam.* **117 C5** 24 40 S 33 33 E
Vila do Conde, *Portugal* **42 D2** 41 21N 8 45W
Vila Franca de Xira, *Portugal* **43 G2** 38 57N 8 59W
Vila Gamito, *Mozam.* **119 E3** 14 12 S 33 0 E
Vila Gomes da Costa, *Mozam.* **117 C5** 24 20 S 33 37 E
Vila Machado, *Mozam.* **119 F3** 19 15 S 34 14 E
Vila Mouzinho, *Mozam.* **119 E3** 14 48 S 34 25 E
Vila Nova de Famalicão, *Portugal* **42 D2** 41 25N 8 32W

Voltaire, C. 297

Vila Nova de Fos Côa, *Portugal* 42 D3 41 5N 7 9W
Vila Nova de Foscôa = Vila Nova de Fos Côa, *Portugal* 42 D3 41 5N 7 9W
Vila Nova de Gaia, *Portugal* 42 D2 41 4N 8 40W
Vila Nova de Ourém, *Portugal* 42 F2 39 40N 8 35W
Vila Pouca de Aguiar, *Portugal* 42 D3 41 30N 7 38W
Vila Real, *Portugal* 42 D3 41 17N 7 48W
Vila Real □, *Portugal* 42 D3 41 36N 7 35W
Vila-real de los Infantes, *Spain* 40 F4 39 55N 0 3W
Vila Real de Santo António, *Portugal* 43 H3 37 10N 7 28W
Vila Vasco da Gama, *Mozam.* 119 E3 14 54 S 32 14 E
Vila Velha, *Amapá, Brazil* 169 C7 3 13N 51 13W
Vila Velha, *Espírito Santo, Brazil* 171 F3 20 20 S 40 17W
Vila Viçosa, *Portugal* 43 G3 38 45N 7 27W
Vilafranca del Maestrat, *Spain* 40 E4 40 26N 0 16W
Vilafranca del Penedès, *Spain* 40 D6 41 21N 1 40 E
Vilagarcía de Arousa, *Spain* 42 C2 42 34N 8 46W
Vilaine →, *France* 26 E4 47 30N 2 27W
Vilanandro, Tanjona, *Madag.* 117 B7 16 11 S 44 27 E
Vilanculos, *Mozam.* 117 C6 22 1 S 35 17 E
Vilanova de Castelló, *Spain* 41 F4 39 5N 0 31W
Vilanova i la Geltrú, *Spain* 40 D6 41 13N 1 40 E
Vilar Formosa, *Portugal* 42 E4 40 38N 6 45W
Vilaseca, *Spain* 40 D6 41 7N 1 9 E
Vilaseca-Salou = Vilaseca, *Spain* 40 D6 41 7N 1 9 E
Vilbjerg, *Denmark* 17 H2 56 12N 8 46 E
Vilcabamba, Cordillera, *Peru* 172 C3 13 0 S 73 0W
Vilcanchos, *Peru* 172 C3 13 40 S 74 25W
Vilches, *Spain* 43 G7 38 12N 3 30W
Vileyka, *Belarus* 58 E4 54 30N 26 53 E
Vilhelmina, *Sweden* 14 D17 64 35N 16 39 E
Vilhena, *Brazil* 173 C5 12 40 S 60 5W
Viliga, *Russia* 65 C16 61 36N 156 56 E
Viliya →, *Lithuania* 15 J21 55 8N 24 16 E
Viljandi, *Estonia* 15 G21 58 28N 25 30 E
Vilkaviškis, *Lithuania* 54 D10 54 39N 23 2 E
Vilkija, *Lithuania* 54 C10 55 3N 23 35 E
Vilkitskogo, Proliv, *Russia* 65 B11 78 0N 103 0 E
Vilkovo = Vylkove, *Ukraine* 59 K5 45 28N 29 32 E
Villa Abecia, *Bolivia* 174 A2 21 0 S 68 18W
Villa Ahumada, *Mexico* 162 A3 30 38N 106 30W
Villa Ana, *Argentina* 174 B4 28 28 S 59 40W
Villa Ángela, *Argentina* 174 B3 27 34 S 60 45W
Villa Bella, *Bolivia* 173 C4 10 25 S 65 22W
Villa Bens = Tarfaya, *Morocco* 110 C2 27 55N 12 55W
Villa Cañás, *Argentina* 174 C3 34 0 S 61 35W
Villa Carlos, *Spain* 39 B11 39 53N 4 17 E
Villa Cisneros = Dakhla, *W. Sahara* 110 D1 23 50N 15 53W
Villa Colón, *Argentina* 174 C2 31 38 S 68 20W
Villa Constitución, *Argentina* 174 C3 33 15 S 60 20W
Villa de Cura, *Venezuela* 168 A4 10 2N 67 29W
Villa de María, *Argentina* 174 B3 29 55 S 63 43W
Villa del Rio, *Spain* 43 H6 37 59N 4 17W
Villa del Rosario, *Venezuela* 168 A3 10 19N 72 19W
Villa Dolores, *Argentina* 174 C2 31 58 S 65 15W
Villa Frontera, *Mexico* 162 B4 26 56N 101 27W
Villa Grove, *U.S.A.* 157 E8 39 52N 88 10W
Villa Guillermina, *Argentina* 174 B4 28 15 S 59 29W
Villa Hayes, *Paraguay* 174 B4 25 5 S 57 20W
Villa Iris, *Argentina* 174 D3 38 12 S 63 12W
Villa Juárez, *Mexico* 162 B4 27 37N 100 44W
Villa María, *Argentina* 174 C3 32 20 S 63 10W
Villa Mazán, *Argentina* 174 B2 28 40 S 66 30W
Villa Minozzo, *Italy* 44 D7 44 22N 10 28 E
Villa Montes, *Bolivia* 174 A3 21 10 S 63 30W
Villa Ocampo, *Argentina* 174 B4 28 30 S 59 20W
Villa Ocampo, *Mexico* 162 B3 26 29N 105 30W
Villa Ojo de Agua, *Argentina* 174 B3 29 30 S 63 44W
Villa Rica, *U.S.A.* 152 B5 33 44N 84 55W
Villa San Giovanni, *Italy* 47 D8 38 13N 15 38 E
Villa San José, *Argentina* 174 C4 32 12 S 58 15W
Villa San Martín, *Argentina* 174 B3 28 15 S 64 9W
Villa Santina, *Italy* 45 B9 46 24N 12 55 E
Villa Unión, *Mexico* 162 C3 23 12N 106 14W
Villaba, *Phil.* 81 F5 11 13N 124 24 E
Villablino, *Spain* 42 C4 42 57N 6 19W
Villacarriedo, *Spain* 42 B7 43 14N 3 48W
Villacarrillo, *Spain* 43 G7 38 7N 3 3W
Villacastín, *Spain* 42 E6 40 46N 4 25W
Villach, *Austria* 34 E6 46 37N 13 51 E
Villacidro, *Italy* 46 C1 39 27N 8 44 E
Villada, *Spain* 42 C6 42 15N 4 59W
Villadiego, *Spain* 42 C6 42 31N 4 1W
Villadóssola, *Italy* 44 B5 46 4N 8 16 E
Villafeliche, *Spain* 40 D3 41 10N 1 30W
Villafranca, *Spain* 40 C3 42 17N 1 46W
Villafranca de los Barros, *Spain* 43 G4 38 35N 6 18W
Villafranca de los Caballeros, *Baleares, Spain* 39 B10 39 34N 3 25 E
Villafranca de los Caballeros, *Toledo, Spain* 43 F7 39 26N 3 21W
Villafranca del Cid = Vilafranca del Maestrat, *Spain* 40 E4 40 26N 0 16W
Villafranca del Panadés = Vilafranca del Penedès, *Spain* 40 D6 41 21N 1 40 E
Villafranca di Verona, *Italy* 44 C7 45 21N 10 50 E
Villafranca Tirrena, *Italy* 47 D8 38 20N 15 25 E
Villagrán, *Mexico* 163 C5 24 29N 99 29W
Villaguay, *Argentina* 174 C4 32 0 S 59 0W
Villaharta, *Spain* 43 G6 38 9N 4 54W
Villahermosa, *Mexico* 163 D6 17 59N 92 55W
Villahermosa, *Spain* 41 G2 38 46N 2 52W
Villaines-la-Juhel, *France* 26 D6 48 21N 0 20W
Villajoyosa, *Spain* 41 G4 38 30N 0 12W
Villalba, *Spain* 42 B3 43 26N 7 40W
Villalba de Guardo, *Spain* 42 C6 42 42N 4 49W
Villalón de Campos, *Spain* 42 C5 42 5N 5 4W
Villalpando, *Spain* 42 D5 41 51N 5 25W
Villaluenga, *Spain* 42 E7 40 2N 3 54W
Villamanán, *Spain* 42 C5 42 19N 5 35W
Villamartín, *Spain* 43 J5 36 52N 5 38W
Villamayor de Santiago, *Spain* 40 F2 39 50N 2 59W
Villamblard, *France* 28 C4 45 2N 0 32 E
Villanova Monteleone, *Italy* 46 B1 40 30N 8 28 E
Villanueva, *Colombia* 168 A3 10 37N 72 59W
Villanueva, *U.S.A.* 159 J11 35 16N 105 22W
Villanueva de Castellón = Vilanova de Castelló, *Spain* 41 F4 39 5N 0 31W
Villanueva de Córdoba, *Spain* 43 G6 38 20N 4 38W
Villanueva de la Fuente, *Spain* 41 G2 38 42N 2 42W
Villanueva de la Serena, *Spain* 43 G5 38 59N 5 50W
Villanueva de la Sierra, *Spain* 42 E4 40 12N 6 24W
Villanueva de los Castillejos, *Spain* 43 H3 37 30N 7 15W
Villanueva de los Infantes, *Spain* 43 G7 38 43N 3 1W
Villanueva del Arzobispo, *Spain* 41 G2 38 10N 3 0W
Villanueva del Fresno, *Spain* 43 G3 38 23N 7 10W
Villanueva y Geltrú = Vilanova i la Geltrú, *Spain* 40 D6 41 13N 1 40 E
Villaputzu, *Italy* 46 C2 39 26N 9 34 E
Villaquilambre, *Spain* 42 C5 42 39N 5 33W
Villar del Arzobispo, *Spain* 40 F4 39 44N 0 50W
Villar del Rey, *Spain* 43 F4 39 7N 6 50W
Villard-de-Lans, *France* 29 C9 45 3N 5 33 E
Villarramiel, *Spain* 42 C6 42 2N 4 55W
Villarreal = Vila-real de los Infantes, *Spain* 40 F4 39 55N 0 3W
Villarrica, *Chile* 176 A2 39 15 S 72 15W
Villarrica, *Paraguay* 174 B4 25 40 S 56 30W
Villarrobledo, *Spain* 41 F2 39 18N 2 36W
Villarroya de la Sierra, *Spain* 40 D3 41 27N 1 46W
Villarrubia de los Ojos, *Spain* 43 F7 39 14N 3 36W
Villars-les-Dombes, *France* 27 F12 46 0N 5 3 E
Villasayas, *Spain* 40 D2 41 24N 2 39W
Villaseca de los Gamitos = Villaseco de los Gamitos, *Spain* 42 D4 41 2N 6 7W
Villaseco de los Gamitos, *Spain* 42 D4 41 2N 6 7W
Villasimíus, *Italy* 46 C2 39 8N 9 31 E
Villastar, *Spain* 40 E3 40 17N 1 9W
Villatobas, *Spain* 42 F7 39 54N 3 20W
Villavicencio, *Argentina* 174 C2 32 28 S 69 0W
Villavicencio, *Colombia* 168 C3 4 9N 73 37W
Villaviciosa, *Spain* 42 B5 43 32N 5 27W
Villazón, *Bolivia* 174 A2 22 0 S 65 35W
Ville-Marie, *Canada* 140 C4 47 20N 79 30W
Ville Platte, *U.S.A.* 155 K8 30 41N 92 17W
Villedieu-les-Poêles, *France* 26 D5 48 50N 1 13W
Villefort, *France* 28 D7 44 28N 3 56 E
Villefranche-de-Lauragais, *France* 28 E5 43 25N 1 44 E
Villefranche-de-Rouergue, *France* 28 D6 44 21N 2 2 E
Villefranche-du-Périgord, *France* 28 D5 44 38N 1 5 E
Villefranche-sur-Saône, *France* 29 C8 45 59N 4 43 E
Villegrande, *Bolivia* 173 D5 18 30 S 64 10W
Villel, *Spain* 40 E3 40 14N 1 12W
Villemur-sur-Tarn, *France* 28 E5 43 51N 1 31 E
Villena, *Spain* 41 G4 38 39N 0 52W
Villenauxe-la-Grande, *France* 27 D10 48 35N 3 33 E
Villenave-d'Ornon, *France* 28 D3 44 46N 0 33W
Villeneuve, *Switz.* 32 D3 46 24N 6 56 E
Villeneuve-d'Ascq, *France* 27 B10 50 38N 3 9 E
Villeneuve-l'Archevêque, *France* 27 D10 48 14N 3 32 E
Villeneuve-lès-Avignon, *France* 29 E8 43 58N 4 49 E
Villeneuve-sur-Allier, *France* 27 F10 46 40N 3 13 E
Villeneuve-sur-Lot, *France* 28 D4 44 24N 0 42 E
Villeneuve-sur-Yonne, *France* 27 D10 48 5N 3 18 E
Villeréal, *France* 28 D4 44 38N 0 45 E
Villers-Bocage, *France* 26 C6 49 3N 0 40W
Villers-Cotterêts, *France* 27 C10 49 15N 3 4 E
Villers-sur-Mer, *France* 26 C6 49 21N 0 2W
Villersexel, *France* 27 E13 47 33N 6 26 E
Villerupt, *France* 27 C12 49 28N 5 55 E
Villeurbanne, *France* 29 C8 45 46N 4 55 E
Villiers, *S. Africa* 117 D4 27 2S 28 36 E
Villingen-Schwenningen, *Germany* 31 G4 48 3N 8 26 E
Villisca, *U.S.A.* 156 D2 40 56N 94 59W
Villupuram, *India* 95 J4 11 59N 79 31 E
Vilna, *Canada* 142 C6 54 7N 111 55W
Vilnius, *Lithuania* 15 J21 54 38N 25 19 E
Vils, *Austria* 34 D3 47 33N 10 38 E
Vils →, *Bayern, Germany* 31 G9 48 37N 13 11 E
Vils →, *Bayern, Germany* 31 F7 49 10N 11 57 E
Vilsbiburg, *Germany* 31 G8 48 26N 12 22 E
Vilshofen, *Germany* 31 G9 48 37N 13 11 E
Vilusi, *Montenegro, Yug.* 50 D2 42 44N 18 34 E
Vilvoorde, *Belgium* 24 D4 50 56N 4 26 E
Vilyuy →, *Russia* 65 C13 64 24N 126 26 E
Vilyuysk, *Russia* 65 C13 63 40N 121 35 E
Vimianzo, *Spain* 42 B1 43 7N 9 2W
Vimioso, *Portugal* 42 D4 41 35N 6 31W
Vimmerby, *Sweden* 17 G9 57 40N 15 55 E
Vimoutiers, *France* 26 D7 48 57N 0 10 E
Vimperk, *Czech Rep.* 34 B6 49 3N 13 46 E
Viña del Mar, *Chile* 174 C1 33 0 S 71 30W
Vinarós, *Spain* 40 E5 40 30N 0 27 E
Vincennes, *U.S.A.* 157 F9 38 41N 87 32W
Vincent, *U.S.A.* 161 L8 34 33N 118 11W
Vinces, *Ecuador* 168 D2 1 32 S 79 45W
Vinchina, *Argentina* 174 B2 28 45 S 68 15W
Vindelälven →, *Sweden* 14 E18 63 55N 19 50 E
Vindeln, *Sweden* 14 D18 64 12N 19 43 E
Vinderup, *Denmark* 17 H2 56 29N 8 45 E
Vindhya Ra., *India* 92 H7 22 50N 77 0 E
Vine Grove, *U.S.A.* 157 G11 37 49N 85 59W
Vineland, *U.S.A.* 148 F8 39 29N 75 2W
Vinga, *Romania* 52 D6 46 1N 21 14 E
Vingåker, *Sweden* 16 E9 59 2N 15 52 E
Vingelen, *Norway* 18 B7 62 25N 10 52 E
Vingnes, *Norway* 18 C7 61 7N 10 26 E
Vinh, *Vietnam* 86 C5 18 45N 105 38 E
Vinh Linh, *Vietnam* 86 D6 17 4N 107 2 E
Vinh Long, *Vietnam* 87 G5 10 16N 105 57 E
Vinh Yen, *Vietnam* 86 B5 21 21N 105 35 E
Vinhais, *Portugal* 42 D3 41 50N 7 5W
Vinica, *Croatia* 45 B13 46 20N 16 9 E
Vinica, *Macedonia* 50 E6 41 53N 22 30 E
Vinica, *Slovenia* 45 C12 45 28N 15 16 E
Vinita, *U.S.A.* 155 G7 36 39N 95 9W
Vinje, *Hordaland, Norway* 18 D3 60 48N 6 30 E
Vinje, *Sør-Trøndelag, Norway* 18 A5 63 12N 9 0 E
Vinje, *Telemark, Norway* 18 E4 59 37N 7 51 E
Vinkovci, *Croatia* 52 E3 45 19N 18 48 E
Vinnitsa = Vinnytsya, *Ukraine* 59 H5 49 15N 28 30 E
Vinnytsya, *Ukraine* 59 H5 49 15N 28 30 E
Vinslöv, *Sweden* 17 H7 56 7N 13 55 E
Vinstra, *Norway* 18 C6 61 37N 9 44 E
Vinstra →, *Norway* 18 C6 61 37N 9 44 E
Vintar, *Phil.* 80 B3 18 14N 120 39 E
Vintjärn, *Sweden* 16 D10 60 50N 16 4 E
Vinton, *Calif., U.S.A.* 160 F6 39 48N 120 10W
Vinton, *Iowa, U.S.A.* 156 B4 42 10N 92 1W
Vinton, *La., U.S.A.* 155 K8 30 11N 93 35W
Vinţu de Jos, *Romania* 53 D8 46 0N 23 30 E
Viöl, *Germany* 30 A5 54 34N 9 11 E
Viola, *U.S.A.* 156 C6 41 12N 90 35W
Violet Town, *Australia* 129 D6 36 38 S 145 42 E
Vipava, *Slovenia* 45 C10 45 51N 13 58 E
Vipiteno, *Italy* 45 B8 46 54N 11 26 E
Vir, *Croatia* 45 D12 44 17N 15 3 E
Vir, *Tajikistan* 63 E6 37 45N 72 5 E
Virac, *Phil.* 80 E5 13 30N 124 20 E
Virachei, *Cambodia* 86 F6 13 59N 106 49 E
Virago Sd., *Canada* 142 C2 54 0N 132 30W
Virajpet = Virarajendrapet, *India* 95 H2 12 10N 75 50 E
Viramgam, *India* 92 H5 23 5N 72 0 E
Viranşehir, *Turkey* 101 D8 37 13N 39 45 E
Virarajendrapet, *India* 95 H2 12 10N 75 50 E
Viravanallur, *India* 95 K3 8 40N 77 30 E
Virbalis, *Lithuania* 54 D9 54 39N 22 49 E
Virden, *Canada* 143 D8 49 50N 100 56W
Virden, *U.S.A.* 156 E7 39 30N 89 46W
Vire, *France* 26 D6 48 50N 0 53W
Vire →, *France* 26 C5 49 20N 1 7W
Virgem da Lapa, *Brazil* 171 E3 16 49 S 42 21W
Vírgenes, C., *Argentina* 176 D3 52 19 S 68 21W
Virgin →, *Canada* 143 B7 57 2N 108 17W
Virgin →, *U.S.A.* 159 H6 36 28N 114 21W
Virgin Gorda, *Virgin Is.* 165 C7 18 30N 64 26W
Virgin Is. (British) ■, *W. Indies* 165 C7 18 30N 64 30W
Virgin Is. (U.S.) ■, *W. Indies* 165 C7 18 20N 65 0W
Virginia, *S. Africa* 116 D4 28 8 S 26 55 E
Virginia, *Ill., U.S.A.* 156 E6 39 57N 90 13W
Virginia, *Minn., U.S.A.* 154 B8 47 31N 92 32W
Virginia □, *U.S.A.* 148 G7 37 30N 78 45W
Virginia Beach, *U.S.A.* 148 G8 36 51N 75 59W
Virginia City, *Mont., U.S.A.* 158 D8 45 18N 111 56W
Virginia City, *Nev., U.S.A.* 160 F7 39 19N 119 39W
Virginia Falls, *Canada* 142 A3 61 38N 125 42W
Virginiatown, *Canada* 140 C4 48 9N 79 36W
Virje, *Croatia* 45 B13 46 4N 16 59 E
Viroqua, *U.S.A.* 154 D9 43 34N 90 53W
Virovitica, *Croatia* 52 E2 45 51N 17 21 E
Virpazar, *Montenegro, Yug.* 50 D3 42 14N 19 6 E
Virserum, *Sweden* 17 G9 57 20N 15 35 E
Virton, *Belgium* 24 E5 49 35N 5 32 E
Virú, *Peru* 172 B2 8 25 S 78 45W
Virudunagar, *India* 95 K3 9 30N 77 58 E
Vis, *Croatia* 45 E13 43 4N 16 10 E
Visalia, *U.S.A.* 160 J7 36 20N 119 18W
Visayan Sea, *Phil.* 81 F4 11 30N 123 30 E
Visby, *Sweden* 17 G12 57 37N 18 18 E
Viscount Melville Sd., *Canada* 6 B2 74 10N 108 0W
Visé, *Belgium* 24 D5 50 44N 5 41 E
Višegrad, *Bos.-H.* 52 G4 43 47N 19 17 E
Viseu, *Brazil* 170 B2 1 10 S 46 5W
Viseu, *Portugal* 42 E3 40 40N 7 55W
Viseu □, *Portugal* 42 E3 40 40N 7 55W
Vişeu de Sus, *Romania* 53 C9 47 45N 24 25 E
Vishakhapatnam, *India* 94 F6 17 45N 83 20 E
Vishera →, *Russia* 62 A6 59 55N 56 25 E
Vişina, *Romania* 53 G9 43 52N 24 27 E
Vişineşti, *Moldova* 53 D13 46 20N 28 27 E
Visingsö, *Sweden* 17 F8 58 2N 14 20 E
Viskafors, *Sweden* 17 G6 57 37N 12 50 E
Viskan →, *Sweden* 17 G6 57 14N 12 12 E
Viški Kanal, *Croatia* 45 E13 43 4N 16 5 E
Vislanda, *Sweden* 17 H8 56 46N 14 30 E
Visnagar, *India* 92 H5 23 45N 72 32 E
Višnja Gora, *Slovenia* 45 C11 45 58N 14 45 E
Viso, Mte., *Italy* 44 D4 44 38N 7 5 E
Viso del Marqués, *Spain* 43 G7 38 32N 3 34W
Visoko, *Bos.-H.* 52 G3 43 58N 18 10 E
Visokoi I., *Antarctica* 7 B1 56 43 S 27 15W
Visp, *Switz.* 32 D5 46 17N 7 52 E
Vispa →, *Switz.* 32 D5 46 9N 7 48 E
Vissefjärda, *Sweden* 17 H9 56 32N 15 35 E
Visselhövede, *Germany* 30 C5 52 59N 9 34 E
Vissenbjerg, *Denmark* 17 J4 55 23N 10 7 E
Vissoie, *Switz.* 32 D5 46 13N 7 36 E
Vista, *U.S.A.* 161 M9 33 12N 117 14W
Vistonikos, Ormos = Vistonís, Límni, *Greece* 51 E9 41 0N 25 7 E
Vistonís, Límni, *Greece* 51 E9 41 0N 25 7 E
Vistula = Wisła →, *Poland* 54 D5 54 22N 18 55 E
Vit →, *Bulgaria* 51 C8 43 30N 24 30 E
Vitanje, *Slovenia* 45 B12 46 25N 15 18 E
Vitebsk = Vitsyebsk, *Belarus* 58 E6 55 10N 30 15 E
Viterbo, *Italy* 45 F9 42 25N 12 6 E
Vitez, *Bos.-H.* 52 F2 44 10N 17 48 E
Viti Levu, *Fiji* 133 A1 17 30 S 177 30 E
Vitiaz Str., *Papua N. G.* 132 C4 5 40 S 147 10 E
Vitigudino, *Spain* 42 D4 41 1N 6 26W
Vitim, *Russia* 65 D12 59 28N 112 35 E
Vitim →, *Russia* 65 D12 59 26N 112 34 E
Vitina, *Bos.-H.* 45 E14 43 17N 17 29 E
Vitína, *Greece* 48 D4 37 40N 22 10 E
Vítkov, *Czech Rep.* 35 B10 49 46N 17 45 E
Vitória, *Brazil* 171 F3 20 20 S 40 22W
Vitória da Conquista, *Brazil* 171 D3 14 51 S 40 51W
Vitória de São Antão, *Brazil* 170 C4 8 10 S 35 20W
Vitoria-Gasteiz, *Spain* 40 C2 42 50N 2 41W
Vitorino Friere, *Brazil* 170 B2 4 4 S 45 10W
Vitré, *France* 26 D5 48 8N 1 12W
Vitry-le-François, *France* 27 D11 48 43N 4 33 E
Vitry-sur-Seine, *France* 27 D9 48 47N 2 24 E
Vitsand, *Sweden* 16 D7 60 20N 13 0 E
Vitsi, Óros, *Greece* 50 F5 40 40N 21 25 E
Vitsyebsk, *Belarus* 58 E6 55 10N 30 15 E
Vittaryd, *Sweden* 17 H7 56 58N 13 57 E
Vitteaux, *France* 27 E11 47 24N 4 30 E
Vittel, *France* 27 D12 48 12N 5 57 E
Vittória, *Italy* 47 F7 36 57N 14 32 E
Vittório Véneto, *Italy* 45 C9 45 59N 12 18 E
Vittsjö, *Sweden* 17 H7 56 20N 13 40 E
Vitu Is., *Papua N. G.* 132 C5 4 50 S 149 25 E
Viveiro, *Spain* 42 B3 43 39N 7 38W
Viviers, *France* 29 D8 44 30N 4 40 E
Vivonne, *Australia* 128 C2 35 59 S 137 9 E
Vivonne, *France* 28 B4 46 25N 0 15 E
Vivonne B., *Australia* 128 C2 35 59 S 137 9 E
Vizcaíno, Desierto de, *Mexico* 162 B2 27 40N 113 50W
Vizcaíno, Sierra, *Mexico* 162 B2 27 30N 114 0W
Vizcaya □, *Spain* 40 B2 43 15N 2 45W
Vize, *Turkey* 51 E11 41 34N 27 45 E
Vizianagaram, *India* 94 E6 18 6N 83 30 E
Vizille, *France* 29 C9 45 5N 5 46 E
Viziñada, *Croatia* 45 C10 45 20N 13 46 E
Viziru, *Romania* 53 E12 45 0N 27 43 E
Vizzini, *Italy* 47 E7 37 10N 14 45 E
Vjosa →, *Albania* 50 F3 40 37N 19 24 E
Vlaardingen, *Neths.* 24 C4 51 55N 4 21 E
Vlădeasa, Vf., *Romania* 52 D7 46 47N 22 50 E
Vladičin Han, *Serbia, Yug.* 50 D6 42 42N 22 1 E
Vladikavkaz, *Russia* 61 J7 43 0N 44 35 E
Vladimir, *Russia* 58 D11 56 15N 40 30 E
Vladimir Volynskiy = Volodymyr-Volynskyy, *Ukraine* 59 G3 50 50N 24 18 E
Vladimirci, *Serbia, Yug.* 50 B3 44 36N 19 50 E
Vladimirovac, *Serbia, Yug.* 52 E5 45 1N 20 53 E
Vladimirovka, *Russia* 61 F8 48 27N 46 10 E
Vladimirovo, *Bulgaria* 50 C7 43 32N 23 22 E
Vladimorvka, *Kazakstan* 60 E10 50 51N 51 8 E
Vladislavovka, *Ukraine* 59 K8 45 12N 35 29 E
Vladivostok, *Russia* 68 C5 43 10N 131 53 E
Vlăhiţa, *Romania* 53 D10 46 21N 25 31 E
Vlakhiótis, *Greece* 48 E4 36 52N 22 42 E
Vlasenica, *Bos.-H.* 52 F3 44 11N 18 59 E
Vlašić, *Bos.-H.* 52 F2 44 19N 17 37 E
Vlašim, *Czech Rep.* 34 B7 49 40N 14 53 E
Vlasinsko Jezero, *Serbia, Yug.* 50 D6 42 44N 22 22 E
Vlasotince, *Serbia, Yug.* 50 D6 42 59N 22 7 E
Vlieland, *Neths.* 24 A4 53 16N 4 55 E
Vlissingen, *Neths.* 24 C3 51 26N 3 34 E
Vlóra, *Albania* 50 F3 40 32N 19 28 E
Vlorës, Gjiri i, *Albania* 50 F3 40 29N 19 27 E
Vltava →, *Czech Rep.* 34 A7 50 21N 14 30 E
Vo Dat, *Vietnam* 87 G6 11 9N 107 31 E
Vobarno, *Italy* 44 C7 45 39N 10 30 E
Voćin, *Croatia* 52 E2 45 37N 17 33 E
Vöcklabruck, *Austria* 34 C6 48 1N 13 39 E
Vodice, *Croatia* 45 E12 43 47N 15 47 E
Vodňany, *Czech Rep.* 34 B7 49 9N 14 11 E
Vodnjan, *Croatia* 45 D10 44 59N 13 52 E
Voe, *U.K.* 22 A7 60 21N 1 16W
Vogar, *Iceland* 11 D4 63 58N 22 22W
Vogelkop = Doberai, Jazirah, *Indonesia* 83 B4 1 25 S 133 0 E
Vogelsberg, *Germany* 30 E5 50 31N 9 12 E
Voghera, *Italy* 44 D6 44 59N 9 1 E
Voh, *N. Cal.* 133 T18 20 58 S 164 42 E
Vohibinany, *Madag.* 117 B8 18 49 S 49 4 E
Vohimarina = Iharana, *Madag.* 117 A9 13 25 S 50 0 E
Vohimena, Tanjon' i, *Madag.* 117 D8 25 36 S 45 8 E
Vohipeno, *Madag.* 117 C8 22 22 S 47 51 E
Voi, *Kenya* 118 C4 3 25 S 38 32 E
Void-Vacon, *France* 27 D12 48 40N 5 36 E
Voineşti, *Iaşi, Romania* 53 C12 47 5N 27 27 E
Voineşti, *Prahova, Romania* 53 E10 45 5N 25 14 E
Voiotía □, *Greece* 48 C5 38 20N 23 0 E
Voiron, *France* 29 C9 45 22N 5 35 E
Voisey B., *Canada* 141 A7 56 15N 61 50W
Voitsberg, *Austria* 34 D8 47 3N 15 9 E
Vojens, *Denmark* 17 J3 55 16N 9 18 E
Vojmsjön, *Sweden* 14 D17 64 55N 16 40 E
Vojnić, *Croatia* 45 C12 45 19N 15 43 E
Vojnik, *Italy* 45 B12 46 18N 15 19 E
Vojvodina □, *Serbia, Yug.* 52 E5 45 20N 20 0 E
Vokhtoga, *Russia* 58 C11 58 46N 41 8 E
Volary, *Czech Rep.* 34 C6 48 54N 13 52 E
Volborg, *U.S.A.* 154 C2 45 51N 105 41W
Volcano, *U.S.A.* 145 D6 19 26N 155 14W
Volcano Is. = Kazan-Rettō, *Pac. Oc.* 134 E6 25 0N 141 0 E
Volchansk = Vovchansk, *Ukraine* 59 G9 50 17N 36 58 E
Volchansk, *Russia* 62 B8 59 56N 60 4 E
Volchya →, *Ukraine* 59 H8 48 32N 36 0 E
Volda, *Norway* 15 E12 62 9N 6 5 E
Volga, *Russia* 58 C10 57 58N 38 16 E
Volga →, *Russia* 61 G9 46 0N 48 30 E
Volga Hts. = Privolzhskaya Vozvyshennost, *Russia* 60 E7 51 0N 46 0 E
Volgo-Baltiyskiy Kanal, *Russia* 58 B9 60 0N 38 0 E
Volgo-Donskoy Kanal, *Russia* 61 F7 48 40N 43 37 E
Volgodonsk, *Russia* 61 G6 47 33N 42 5 E
Volgograd, *Russia* 61 F7 48 40N 44 25 E
Volgogradskoye Vdkhr., *Russia* 60 E8 50 0N 45 20 E
Volgorechensk, *Russia* 60 B5 57 28N 41 14 E
Volímai, *Greece* 48 D2 37 53N 20 35 E
Volintiri, *Moldova* 53 D14 46 26N 29 37 E
Volissós, *Greece* 49 C7 38 29N 25 54 E
Volkach, *Germany* 31 F6 49 52N 10 14 E
Völkermarkt, *Austria* 34 E7 46 39N 14 39 E
Volkhov, *Russia* 58 C7 59 55N 32 15 E
Volkhov →, *Russia* 58 B7 60 8N 32 20 E
Völklingen, *Germany* 31 F2 49 15N 6 50 E
Volkovysk = Vawkavysk, *Belarus* 59 F3 53 9N 24 30 E
Volksrust, *S. Africa* 117 D4 27 24 S 29 53 E
Voll, *Norway* 18 B4 62 31N 7 27 E
Volnansk, *Ukraine* 59 H8 48 2N 35 29 E
Volnovakha, *Ukraine* 59 J9 47 35N 37 30 E
Volochanka, *Russia* 65 B10 71 0N 94 28 E
Volodarsk, *Russia* 60 B6 56 12N 43 15 E
Volodymyr-Volynskyy, *Ukraine* 59 G3 50 50N 24 18 E
Vologda, *Russia* 58 C10 59 10N 39 45 E
Volokolamsk, *Russia* 58 D8 56 5N 35 57 E
Volokonovka, *Russia* 59 G9 50 33N 37 52 E
Vólos, *Greece* 48 B4 39 24N 22 59 E
Volosovo, *Russia* 58 C5 59 27N 29 32 E
Volovets, *Ukraine* 59 H2 48 43N 23 11 E
Volovo, *Russia* 58 F10 53 35N 38 1 E
Volozhin = Valozhyn, *Belarus* 58 E4 54 3N 26 30 E
Volsk, *Russia* 60 D8 52 5N 47 22 E
Volta →, *Ghana* 113 D5 5 46N 0 41 E
Volta, L., *Ghana* 113 D5 7 30N 0 0 E
Volta Blanche = White Volta →, *Ghana* 113 D4 9 10N 1 15W
Volta Redonda, *Brazil* 171 F3 22 31 S 44 5W
Voltaire, C., *Australia* 124 B4 14 16 S 125 35 E

Xifei He 301

Windflower L., Canada 142 A5 62 52N 118 30W
Windhoek, Namibia 116 C2 22 35 S 17 4 E
Windischgarsten, Austria 34 D7 47 42N 14 21 E
Windom, U.S.A. 154 D7 43 52N 95 7W
Windorah, Australia 126 D3 25 24 S 142 36 E
Window Rock, U.S.A. 159 J9 35 41N 109 3W
Windrush →, U.K. 21 F6 51 43N 1 24W
Windsor, Australia 129 B9 33 37 S 150 50 E
Windsor, N.S., Canada 141 D7 44 59N 64 5W
Windsor, Nfld., Canada 141 C8 48 57N 55 40W
Windsor, Ont., Canada 140 D3 42 18N 83 0W
Windsor, N.Z. 131 E5 44 59 S 170 49 E
Windsor, U.K. 21 F7 51 29N 0 36W
Windsor, Colo., U.S.A. 154 E2 40 29N 104 54W
Windsor, Conn., U.S.A. 151 E12 41 50N 72 39W
Windsor, Ill., U.S.A. 157 E8 39 26N 88 36W
Windsor, Mo., U.S.A. 156 F3 38 32N 93 31W
Windsor, N.Y., U.S.A. 151 D9 42 5N 75 37W
Windsor, S.C., U.S.A. 152 B9 33 29N 81 31W
Windsor, Vt., U.S.A. 151 C12 43 29N 72 24W
Windsor & Maidenhead □, U.K. 21 F7 51 29N 0 40W
Windsor Forest, U.S.A. 152 D8 31 59N 81 5W
Windsorton, S. Africa 116 D3 28 16 S 24 44 E
Windward Is., W. Indies 165 D7 13 0N 61 0W
Windward Passage = Vientos, Paso de los, Caribbean 165 C5 20 0N 74 0W
Windy L., Canada 143 A8 60 20N 100 2W
Winefred L., Canada 143 B6 55 30N 110 30W
Winejok, Sudan 107 F2 9 1N 27 30 E
Winfield, Iowa, U.S.A. 156 C5 41 7N 91 26W
Winfield, Kans., U.S.A. 155 G6 37 15N 96 59W
Winfield, Mo., U.S.A. 156 F6 39 0N 90 44W
Wingate Mts., Australia 124 B5 14 25 S 130 40 E
Wingen, Australia 129 A9 31 54 S 150 54 E
Wingham, Australia 129 A10 31 48 S 152 22 E
Wingham, Canada 140 D3 43 55N 81 20W
Winifred, U.S.A. 158 C9 47 34N 109 23W
Winisk, Canada 140 A2 55 20N 85 15W
Winisk →, Canada 140 A2 55 17N 85 5W
Winisk L., Canada 140 B2 52 55N 87 22W
Wink, U.S.A. 155 K3 31 45N 103 9W
Winkler, Canada 143 D9 49 10N 97 56W
Winklern, Austria 34 E5 46 52N 12 52 E
Winlock, U.S.A. 160 D4 46 30N 122 56W
Winneba, Ghana 113 D4 5 25N 0 36W
Winnebago, Ill., U.S.A. 156 B7 42 16N 89 15W
Winnebago, Minn., U.S.A. 154 D7 43 46N 94 10W
Winnebago, L., U.S.A. 148 D1 44 0N 88 26W
Winnecke Cr. →, Australia 124 C5 18 35 S 131 34 E
Winnemucca, U.S.A. 158 F5 40 58N 117 44W
Winnemucca L., U.S.A. 158 F4 40 7N 119 21W
Winner, U.S.A. 154 D5 43 22N 99 52W
Winnett, U.S.A. 158 C9 47 0N 108 21W
Winnfield, U.S.A. 155 K8 31 56N 92 38W
Winnibigoshish, L., U.S.A. 154 B7 47 27N 94 13W
Winning, Australia 124 D1 23 9 S 114 30 E
Winnipeg, Canada 143 D9 49 54N 97 9W
Winnipeg →, Canada 143 C9 50 38N 96 19W
Winnipeg, L., Canada 143 C9 52 0N 97 0W
Winnipeg Beach, Canada 143 C9 50 30N 96 58W
Winnipegosis, Canada 143 C9 51 39N 99 55W
Winnipegosis L., Canada 143 C9 52 30N 100 0W
Winnipesaukee, L., U.S.A. 151 C13 43 38N 71 21W
Winnsboro, La., U.S.A. 155 J9 32 10N 91 43W
Winnsboro, S.C., U.S.A. 149 H5 34 23N 81 5W
Winnsboro, Tex., U.S.A. 155 J7 32 58N 95 17W
Winokapau, L., Canada 141 B7 53 15N 62 50W
Winona, Minn., U.S.A. 154 C9 44 3N 91 39W
Winona, Miss., U.S.A. 155 J10 33 29N 89 44W
Winooski, U.S.A. 151 B11 44 29N 73 11W
Winschoten, Neths. 24 A7 53 9N 7 3 E
Winsen, Germany 30 B6 53 22N 10 13 E
Winsford, U.K. 20 D5 53 12N 2 31W
Winslow, Ariz., U.S.A. 159 J8 35 2N 110 42W
Winslow, Ind., U.S.A. 157 F9 38 23N 87 13W
Winslow, Wash., U.S.A. 160 C4 47 38N 122 31W
Winsted, U.S.A. 151 E11 41 55N 73 4W
Winston-Salem, U.S.A. 149 G5 36 6N 80 15W
Winter Beach, U.S.A. 153 H9 27 43N 80 25W
Winter Garden, U.S.A. 149 L5 28 34N 81 35W
Winter Haven, U.S.A. 149 M5 28 1N 81 44W
Winter Park, U.S.A. 149 L5 28 36N 81 20W
Winterberg, Germany 30 D4 51 11N 8 33 E
Winterhaven, U.S.A. 161 N12 32 47N 114 39W
Winters, Calif., U.S.A. 160 G5 38 32N 121 58W
Winters, Tex., U.S.A. 155 K5 31 58N 99 58W
Winterset, U.S.A. 156 C3 41 20N 94 1W
Wintersville, U.S.A. 150 F4 40 23N 80 42W
Winterswijk, Neths. 24 C6 51 58N 6 43 E
Winterthur, Switz. 33 B7 47 30N 8 44 E
Winthrop, Minn., U.S.A. 154 C7 44 32N 94 22W
Winthrop, Wash., U.S.A. 158 B3 48 28N 120 10W
Winton, Australia 126 C3 22 24 S 143 3 E
Winton, N.Z. 131 G3 46 8 S 168 20 E
Winton, U.S.A. 149 G7 36 24N 76 56W
Wipper →, Germany 30 D7 51 16N 11 12 E
Wirraminna, Australia 128 A2 31 12 S 136 13 E
Wirrulla, Australia 127 E1 32 24 S 134 31 E
Wisacky, U.S.A. 152 A9 34 9N 80 12W
Wisbech, U.K. 21 E8 52 41N 0 9 E
Wisconsin □, U.S.A. 154 C10 44 45N 89 30W
Wisconsin →, U.S.A. 154 D9 43 0N 91 15W
Wisconsin Dells, U.S.A. 154 D10 43 38N 89 46W
Wisconsin Rapids, U.S.A. 154 C10 44 23N 89 49W
Wisdom, U.S.A. 158 D7 45 37N 113 27W
Wishaw, U.K. 22 F5 55 46N 3 54W
Wishek, U.S.A. 154 B5 46 16N 99 33W
Wisła, Poland 55 J5 49 38N 18 53 E
Wisła →, Poland 54 D5 54 22N 18 55 E
Wisłok →, Poland 55 H9 50 13N 22 32 E
Wisłoka →, Poland 55 H8 50 27N 21 23 E
Wismar, Germany 30 B7 53 54N 11 29 E
Wismar, Guyana 169 B6 5 59N 58 18W
Wisner, U.S.A. 154 E6 41 59N 96 55W
Wissant, France 27 B8 50 52N 1 40 E
Wissembourg, France 27 C14 49 2N 7 57 E
Wisznice, Poland 55 G10 51 48N 23 13 E
Witbank, S. Africa 117 D4 25 51 S 29 14 E
Witdraai, S. Africa 116 D3 26 58 S 20 48 E
Witham, U.K. 21 F8 51 48N 0 40 E
Witham →, U.K. 20 E7 52 59N 0 2W
Withernsea, U.K. 20 D8 53 44N 0 1 E
Withlacoochee →, Fla., U.S.A. 152 E6 30 24N 83 10W
Withlacoochee →, Fla., U.S.A. 153 G7 29 0N 82 45W
Witkowo, Poland 55 F4 52 26N 17 45 E
Witney, U.K. 21 F6 51 48N 1 28W
Witnica, Poland 55 F1 52 40N 14 54 E
Witnossob →, Namibia 116 D3 26 55 S 20 37 E
Wittdün, Germany 30 A4 54 38N 8 23 E
Witten, Germany 30 D3 51 26N 7 20 E
Wittenberge, Germany 30 B7 53 0N 11 45 E
Wittenburg, Germany 30 B7 53 31N 11 4 E
Wittenheim, France 27 E14 47 44N 7 20 E
Wittenoom, Australia 124 D2 22 15 S 118 20 E
Witti, Banjaran, Malaysia 85 A5 5 11N 116 29 E
Wittingen, Germany 30 C6 52 44N 10 44 E
Wittlich, Germany 31 F2 49 59N 6 53 E
Wittmund, Germany 30 B3 53 34N 7 46 E
Wittow, Germany 30 A9 54 38N 13 20 E
Wittstock, Germany 30 B8 53 10N 12 28 E
Witzenhausen, Germany 30 D5 51 20N 9 51 E
Wkra →, Poland 55 F7 52 27N 20 44 E
Władysławowo, Poland 54 D5 54 48N 18 25 E
Wleń, Poland 55 G2 51 2N 15 39 E
Wlingi, Indonesia 85 D4 8 5 S 112 25 E
Włocławek, Poland 55 F6 52 40N 19 3 E
Włocławek □, Poland 55 F6 52 50N 19 10 E
Włodawa, Poland 55 G10 51 33N 23 31 E
Włoszczowa, Poland 55 H6 50 50N 19 55 E
Woburn, U.S.A. 151 D13 42 29N 71 9W
Wodian, China 74 H7 32 50N 112 35 E
Wodonga, Australia 129 D7 36 5 S 146 50 E
Wodzisław Śląski, Poland 55 H5 50 1N 18 26 E
Wœrth, France 27 D14 48 57N 7 45 E
Wohlen, Switz. 33 B6 47 21N 8 17 E
Woinbogoin, China 76 A2 32 51N 98 39 E
Woippy, France 27 C13 49 10N 6 8 E
Wojcieszow, Poland 55 H2 50 58N 15 55 E
Wokam, Indonesia 83 C4 5 45 S 134 28 E
Wokha, India 90 B5 26 6N 94 16 E
Woking, U.K. 21 F7 51 19N 0 34W
Wokingham □, U.K. 21 F7 51 25N 0 51W
Wolbrom, Poland 55 H6 50 24N 19 45 E
Wolcottville, U.S.A. 157 C11 41 32N 85 22W
Wołczyn, Poland 55 G5 51 1N 18 3 E
Woldegk, Germany 30 B9 53 27N 13 34 E
Wolf →, Canada 142 A2 60 17N 132 33W
Wolf Creek, U.S.A. 158 C7 47 0N 112 4W
Wolf L., Canada 142 A2 60 24N 131 40W
Wolf Point, U.S.A. 154 A2 48 5N 105 39W
Wolfe I., Canada 140 D4 44 7N 76 20W
Wolfen, Germany 30 D8 51 39N 12 15 E
Wolfenbüttel, Germany 30 C6 52 10N 10 33 E
Wolfratshausen, Germany 31 H7 47 54N 11 24 E
Wolfsberg, Austria 34 E7 46 50N 14 52 E
Wolfsburg, Germany 30 C6 52 27N 10 48 E
Wolgast, Germany 30 A9 54 3N 13 44 E
Wolhusen, Switz. 32 B6 47 4N 8 4 E
Wolin, Poland 54 E1 53 50N 14 37 E
Wollaston, Is., Chile 176 E3 55 40 S 67 30W
Wollaston Forland, Greenland 10 C9 74 25N 19 40W
Wollaston L., Canada 143 B8 58 7N 103 10W
Wollaston Pen., Canada 138 B8 69 30N 115 0W
Wollogorang, Australia 126 B2 17 13 S 137 57 E
Wollongong, Australia 129 C9 34 25 S 150 54 E
Wolmaransstad, S. Africa 116 D4 27 12 S 25 59 E
Wolmirstedt, Germany 30 C7 52 14N 11 37 E
Wołomin, Poland 55 F8 52 19N 21 15 E
Wołów, Poland 55 G3 51 20N 16 38 E
Wolseley, Australia 128 D4 36 23 S 140 54 E
Wolseley, Canada 143 C8 50 25N 103 15W
Wolseley, S. Africa 116 E2 33 26 S 19 7 E
Wolstenholme, C., Canada 136 C12 62 35N 77 30W
Wolsztyn, Poland 55 F3 52 8N 16 5 E
Wolvega, Neths. 24 B6 52 52N 6 0 E
Wolverhampton, U.K. 21 E5 52 35N 2 7W
Wonarah, Australia 126 B2 19 55 S 136 20 E
Wonboyn, Australia 129 D8 37 15 S 149 55 E
Wondai, Australia 127 D5 26 20 S 151 49 E
Wongalarroo L., Australia 128 A6 31 32 S 144 0 E
Wongan Hills, Australia 125 F2 30 51 S 116 37 E
Wongawol, Australia 125 E3 26 5 S 121 55 E
Wŏnju, S. Korea 75 F14 37 22N 127 58 E
Wonosari, Indonesia 85 D4 7 58 S 110 36 E
Wonosobo, Indonesia 85 D3 7 22 S 109 54 E
Wŏnsan, N. Korea 75 E14 39 11N 127 27 E
Wonthaggi, Australia 129 E6 38 37 S 145 37 E
Woocalla, Australia 128 A2 31 42 S 137 12 E
Wood Buffalo Nat. Park, Canada 142 B6 59 0N 113 41W
Wood Is., Australia 124 C3 16 24 S 123 19 E
Wood L., Canada 143 B8 55 17N 103 17W
Wood Lake, U.S.A. 154 D4 42 38N 100 14W
Wood River, U.S.A. 156 F6 38 52N 90 5W
Woodah I., Australia 126 A2 13 27 S 136 10 E
Woodanilling, Australia 125 F2 33 31 S 117 24 E
Woodbine, U.S.A. 152 E8 30 58N 81 44W
Woodbridge, Canada 150 C5 43 47N 79 36W
Woodbridge, U.K. 21 E9 52 6N 1 20 E
Woodburn, Australia 127 D5 29 6 S 153 23 E
Woodbury, U.S.A. 152 C5 32 59N 84 35W
Woodenbong, Australia 127 D5 28 24 S 152 39 E
Woodend, Australia 128 D6 37 20 S 144 33 E
Woodford, U.S.A. 152 B9 33 40N 81 7W
Woodfords, U.S.A. 160 G7 38 47N 119 50W
Woodgreen, Australia 126 C1 22 26 S 134 12 E
Woodlake, U.S.A. 160 J7 36 25N 119 6W
Woodland, U.S.A. 160 G5 38 41N 121 46W
Woodlands, Australia 124 D2 24 46 S 118 8 E
Woodlark I., Papua N. G. 132 E7 9 10 S 152 50 E
Woodpecker, Canada 142 C4 53 30N 122 40W
Woodridge, Canada 143 D9 49 20N 96 9W
Woodroffe, Mt., Australia 125 E5 26 20 S 131 45 E
Woodruff, Ariz., U.S.A. 159 J8 34 51N 110 1W
Woodruff, Utah, U.S.A. 158 F8 41 31N 111 10W
Woodruff, L., U.S.A. 153 F8 29 6N 81 24W
Woods, L., Australia 126 B1 17 50 S 133 30 E
Woods, L., Canada 141 B6 54 30N 65 13W
Woods, L. of the, Canada 143 D10 49 15N 94 45W
Woodside, S. Austral., Australia 128 C3 34 58 S 138 52 E
Woodside, Vic., Australia 129 E7 38 31 S 146 52 E
Woodstock, N.S.W., Australia 129 B8 33 45 S 148 53 E
Woodstock, Queens., Australia 126 B4 19 35 S 146 50 E
Woodstock, W. Austral., Australia 124 D2 21 41 S 118 57 E
Woodstock, N.B., Canada 141 C6 46 11N 67 37W
Woodstock, Ont., Canada 140 D3 43 10N 80 45W
Woodstock, U.K. 21 F6 51 51N 1 20W
Woodstock, Ga., U.S.A. 152 A5 34 6N 84 31W
Woodstock, Ill., U.S.A. 154 D10 42 19N 88 27W
Woodstock, Vt., U.S.A. 151 C12 43 37N 72 31W
Woodsville, U.S.A. 151 B13 44 9N 72 2W
Woodville, N.Z. 130 G4 40 20 S 175 53 E
Woodville, Fla., U.S.A. 152 E5 30 19N 84 15W
Woodville, Ga., U.S.A. 152 B6 33 40N 83 7W
Woodville, Ohio, U.S.A. 157 C13 41 27N 83 22W
Woodville, Tex., U.S.A. 155 K7 30 47N 94 25W
Woodward, U.S.A. 155 G5 36 26N 99 24W
Woody, U.S.A. 161 K8 35 42N 118 50W
Woolamai, C., Australia 129 E6 38 30 S 145 23 E
Wooler, U.K. 20 B5 55 33N 2 1W
Woolgoolga, Australia 127 E5 30 6 S 153 11 E
Woombye, Australia 127 D5 26 40 S 152 55 E
Woomera, Australia 128 A2 31 5 S 136 50 E
Woonona, Australia 129 C9 34 21 S 150 54 E
Woonsocket, R.I., U.S.A. 151 E13 42 0N 71 31W
Woonsocket, S. Dak., U.S.A. 154 C5 44 3N 98 17W
Wooramel, Australia 125 E1 25 45 S 114 17 E
Wooramel →, Australia 125 E1 25 47 S 114 10 E
Wooroloo, Australia 125 F2 31 48 S 116 18 E
Wooster, U.S.A. 150 F3 40 48N 81 56W
Worb, Switz. 32 C5 46 56N 7 33 E
Worcester, S. Africa 116 E2 33 39 S 19 27 E
Worcester, U.K. 21 E5 52 11N 2 12W
Worcester, Mass., U.S.A. 151 D13 42 16N 71 48W
Worcester, N.Y., U.S.A. 151 D10 42 36N 74 45W
Worcestershire □, U.K. 21 E5 52 13N 2 10W
Worden, U.S.A. 156 F7 38 56N 89 50W
Wörgl, Austria 34 D5 47 29N 12 3 E
Workington, U.K. 20 C4 54 39N 3 33W
Worksop, U.K. 20 D6 53 18N 1 7W
Workum, Neths. 24 B5 52 59N 5 26 E
Worland, U.S.A. 158 D10 44 1N 107 57W
Wormhout, France 27 B9 50 52N 2 28 E
Worms, Germany 31 F4 49 37N 8 21 E
Wörth, Germany 31 F8 49 1N 12 24 E
Wortham, U.S.A. 155 K6 31 47N 96 28W
Wörther See, Austria 34 E7 46 37N 14 10 E
Worthing, U.K. 21 G7 50 49N 0 21W
Worthington, Ind., U.S.A. 157 E10 39 7N 86 59W
Worthington, Minn., U.S.A. 154 D7 43 37N 95 36W
Worthington, Ohio, U.S.A. 157 D13 40 5N 83 1W
Wosi, Indonesia 82 B3 0 15 S 128 0 E
Wou-han = Wuhan, China 77 B10 30 31N 114 18 E
Wour, Chad 109 D3 21 14N 16 0 E
Wousi = Wuxi, China 77 B13 31 33N 120 18 E
Wowoni, Indonesia 82 B2 4 5 S 123 5 E
Woy Woy, Australia 129 B9 33 30 S 151 19 E
Wrangel I. = Vrangelya, Ostrov, Russia 65 B19 71 0N 180 0 E
Wrangell, U.S.A. 138 C6 56 28N 132 23W
Wrangell I., U.S.A. 142 B2 56 16N 132 12W
Wrangell Mts., U.S.A. 138 B5 61 30N 142 0W
Wrath, C., U.K. 22 C3 58 38N 5 1W
Wray, U.S.A. 154 E3 40 5N 102 13W
Wrekin, The, U.K. 21 E5 52 41N 2 32W
Wrens, U.S.A. 152 B7 33 12N 82 23W
Wrexham, U.K. 20 D4 53 3N 3 0W
Wrexham □, U.K. 20 D5 53 1N 2 58W
Wriezen, Germany 30 C10 52 42N 14 7 E
Wright, Canada 142 C4 51 52N 121 40W
Wright, Phil. 81 F5 11 42N 125 2 E
Wrightson Mt., U.S.A. 159 L8 31 42N 110 51W
Wrightsville, U.S.A. 152 C7 32 44N 82 43W
Wrightwood, U.S.A. 161 L9 34 21N 117 38W
Wrigley, Canada 138 B7 63 16N 123 37W
Wrocław, Poland 55 G4 51 5N 17 5 E
Wrocław □, Poland 55 G4 51 0N 17 0 E
Wronki, Poland 55 F3 52 41N 16 21 E
Września, Poland 55 F4 52 21N 17 36 E
Wschowa, Poland 55 G3 51 48N 16 20 E
Wu Jiang →, China 76 C6 29 40N 107 20 E
Wu'an, China 74 F8 36 40N 114 15 E
Wubin, Australia 125 F2 30 6 S 116 37 E
Wubu, China 74 F6 37 28N 110 42 E
Wuchang, China 75 B14 44 55N 127 5 E
Wucheng, China 74 F9 37 12N 116 20 E
Wuchuan, Guangdong, China 77 G8 21 33N 110 43 E
Wuchuan, Guizhou, China 76 C7 28 25N 108 3 E
Wuchuan, Nei Mongol Zizhiqu, China 74 D6 41 5N 111 28 E
Wuday'ah, Si. Arabia 98 C4 17 2N 47 7 E
Wudi, China 75 F9 37 40N 117 35 E
Wuding, China 76 E4 25 24N 102 21 E
Wuding He →, China 74 F6 37 2N 110 23 E
Wudu, China 74 H3 33 22N 104 54 E
Wufeng, China 77 B8 30 12N 110 42 E
Wugang, China 77 D8 26 44N 110 35 E
Wugong Shan, China 77 D10 27 30N 114 0 E
Wuhan, China 77 B10 30 31N 114 18 E
Wuhe, China 75 H9 33 10N 117 50 E
Wuhsi = Wuxi, China 77 B13 31 33N 120 18 E
Wuhu, China 77 B12 31 22N 118 21 E
Wujiang, China 77 B13 31 10N 120 38 E
Wukari, Nigeria 113 D6 7 51N 9 42 E
Wulajie, China 75 B14 44 6N 126 33 E
Wulanbulang, China 74 D6 41 5N 110 55 E
Wulehe, Ghana 113 D5 8 39N 0 0 E
Wulff Land, Greenland 10 A6 82 0N 49 0W
Wulian, China 75 G10 35 40N 119 12 E
Wuliang Shan, China 76 E3 24 30N 100 40 E
Wuliaru, Indonesia 83 C4 7 27 S 131 0 E
Wuluk'omushih Ling, China 72 C3 36 25N 87 25 E
Wulumuchi = Ürümqi, China 64 E9 43 45N 87 45 E
Wum, Cameroon 113 D7 6 24N 10 2 E
Wuming, China 76 F7 23 12N 108 18 E
Wuning, China 77 C10 29 17N 115 5 E
Wunnummin L., Canada 140 B2 52 55N 89 10W
Wunsiedel, Germany 31 E8 50 2N 12 0 E
Wunstorf, Germany 30 C5 52 25N 9 26 E
Wuntho, Burma 90 D5 23 55N 95 45 E
Wuping, China 77 E11 25 5N 116 5 E
Wuppertal, Germany 30 D3 51 16N 7 12 E
Wuppertal, S. Africa 116 E2 32 13 S 19 12 E
Wuqing, China 75 E9 39 23N 117 4 E
Würenlingen, Switz. 33 A6 47 32N 8 16 E
Wurung, Australia 126 B3 19 13 S 140 38 E
Würzburg, Germany 31 F5 49 46N 9 55 E
Wurzen, Germany 30 D8 51 22N 12 44 E
Wushan, Gansu, China 74 G3 34 43N 104 53 E
Wushan, Sichuan, China 76 B7 31 7N 109 54 E
Wusuli Jiang = Ussuri →, Asia 68 A7 48 27N 135 0 E
Wutach →, Germany 31 H4 47 37N 8 15 E
Wutai, China 74 E7 38 40N 113 12 E
Wuting = Huimin, China 75 F9 37 27N 117 28 E
Wutong, China 77 E8 25 24N 110 4 E
Wutonghaolai, China 75 C11 42 50N 120 5 E
Wutongqiao, China 76 C4 29 22N 103 50 E
Wuwei, Anhui, China 77 B11 31 18N 117 54 E
Wuwei, Gansu, China 72 C5 37 57N 102 34 E
Wuxi, Jiangsu, China 77 B13 31 33N 120 18 E
Wuxi, Sichuan, China 76 B7 31 23N 109 35 E
Wuxiang, China 74 F7 36 49N 112 50 E
Wuxing, China 77 B13 30 51N 120 8 E
Wuxuan, China 76 F7 23 34N 109 38 E
Wuyang, China 74 H7 33 25N 113 35 E
Wuyi, Hebei, China 74 F8 37 46N 115 56 E
Wuyi, Zhejiang, China 77 C12 28 52N 119 50 E
Wuyi Shan, China 77 D11 27 0N 117 0 E
Wuyo, Nigeria 113 C7 10 23N 11 50 E
Wuyuan, Jiangxi, China 77 C11 29 15N 117 50 E
Wuyuan, Nei Mongol Zizhiqu, China 74 D5 41 2N 108 20 E
Wuzhai, China 74 E6 38 54N 111 48 E
Wuzhi Shan, China 86 C7 18 45N 109 45 E
Wuzhong, China 74 E4 38 2N 106 12 E
Wuzhou, China 77 F8 23 30N 111 18 E
Wyaaba Cr. →, Australia 126 B3 16 27 S 141 35 E
Wyalkatchem, Australia 125 F2 31 8 S 117 22 E
Wyalusing, U.S.A. 151 E8 41 40N 76 16W
Wyandotte, U.S.A. 157 B13 42 12N 83 9W
Wyandra, Australia 127 D4 27 12 S 145 56 E
Wyangala Res., Australia 129 B8 33 54 S 149 0 E
Wyara, L., Australia 127 D3 28 42 S 144 14 E
Wycheproof, Australia 128 D5 36 5 S 143 17 E
Wye →, U.K. 21 F5 51 38N 2 40W
Wyemandoo, Australia 125 E2 28 28 S 118 29 E
Wyk, Germany 30 A4 54 41N 8 33 E
Wymondham, U.K. 21 E9 52 35N 1 7 E
Wymore, U.S.A. 154 E6 40 7N 96 40W
Wynbring, Australia 127 E1 30 33 S 133 32 E
Wyndham, Australia 124 C4 15 33 S 128 3 E
Wyndham, N.Z. 131 G3 46 20 S 168 51 E
Wyndmere, U.S.A. 154 B6 46 16N 97 8W
Wynne, U.S.A. 155 H9 35 14N 90 47W
Wynnum, Australia 127 D5 27 27 S 153 9 E
Wynyard, Australia 129 G4 41 5 S 145 44 E
Wynyard, Canada 143 C8 51 45N 104 10W
Wyola, L., Australia 125 E5 29 8 S 130 17 E
Wyoming, Ill., U.S.A. 156 C7 41 4N 89 47W
Wyoming, Iowa, U.S.A. 156 B6 42 4N 91 0W
Wyoming, Mich., U.S.A. 157 B11 42 54N 85 42W
Wyoming □, U.S.A. 158 E10 43 0N 107 30W
Wyong, Australia 129 B9 33 14 S 151 24 E
Wyrzysk, Poland 55 E4 53 10N 17 17 E
Wyśmierzyce, Poland 55 G7 51 37N 20 50 E
Wysoka, Poland 55 E4 53 13N 17 2 E
Wysokie, Poland 55 H9 50 55N 22 40 E
Wysokie Mazowieckie, Poland 55 F9 52 55N 22 30 E
Wyszków, Poland 55 F8 52 36N 21 25 E
Wyszogród, Poland 55 F7 52 23N 20 9 E
Wytheville, U.S.A. 148 G5 36 57N 81 5W
Wyżyna Małopolska, Poland 55 H7 50 45N 20 0 E

X

Xa-Muteba, Angola 115 D3 9 34 S 17 50 E
Xaçmaz, Azerbaijan 61 K9 41 31N 48 42 E
Xai-Xai, Mozam. 117 D5 25 6 S 33 31 E
Xainza, China 72 C3 30 58N 88 35 E
Xambioá, Brazil 170 C2 6 25 S 48 40W
Xangongo, Angola 115 F3 16 45 S 15 5 E
Xankändi, Azerbaijan 101 C12 39 52N 46 49 E
Xanlar, Azerbaijan 61 K8 40 37N 46 12 E
Xanten, Germany 30 D2 51 39N 6 26 E
Xánthi, Greece 51 E8 41 10N 24 58 E
Xánthi □, Greece 51 E8 41 10N 24 58 E
Xanthos, Turkey 49 E11 36 19N 29 18 E
Xapuri, Brazil 172 C4 10 35 S 68 35W
Xar Moron He →, China 75 C11 43 25N 120 35 E
Xarrë, Albania 50 G4 39 44N 20 3 E
Xátiva, Spain 41 G4 38 59N 0 32W
Xau, L., Botswana 116 C3 21 15 S 24 44 E
Xavantina, Brazil 175 A5 21 15 S 52 48W
Xenia, Ill., U.S.A. 157 F8 38 38N 88 38W
Xenia, Ohio, U.S.A. 157 E13 39 41N 83 56W
Xeropotamos →, Cyprus 38 E11 34 42N 32 33 E
Xertigny, France 27 D13 48 3N 6 24 E
Xhora, S. Africa 117 E4 31 55 S 28 38 E
Xhumo, Botswana 116 C3 21 7 S 24 35 E
Xi Jiang →, China 77 F9 22 5N 113 20 E
Xi Xian, Henan, China 77 A10 32 20N 114 43 E
Xi Xian, Shanxi, China 74 F6 36 41N 110 58 E
Xia Xian, China 74 G6 35 8N 111 12 E
Xiachengzi, China 75 B16 44 40N 130 18 E
Xiachuan Dao, China 77 G9 21 40N 112 40 E
Xiaguan, China 76 E3 25 32N 100 16 E
Xiajiang, China 77 D10 27 30N 115 10 E
Xiajin, China 74 F9 36 56N 116 0 E
Xiamen, China 77 E12 24 25N 118 4 E
Xi'an, China 74 G5 34 15N 109 0 E
Xian Xian, China 74 E9 38 12N 116 6 E
Xianfeng, China 76 C7 29 40N 109 8 E
Xiang Jiang →, China 77 C9 28 55N 112 50 E
Xiangcheng, Henan, China 74 H8 33 29N 114 52 E
Xiangcheng, Henan, China 74 H7 33 50N 113 27 E
Xiangcheng, Sichuan, China 76 C2 28 53N 99 47 E
Xiangdu, China 76 F6 23 13N 106 58 E
Xiangfan, China 77 A9 32 2N 112 8 E
Xianghuang Qi, China 74 C7 42 2N 113 50 E
Xiangning, China 74 G6 35 58N 110 50 E
Xiangquan, China 74 F7 36 30N 113 1 E
Xiangshan, China 77 C13 29 29N 121 51 E
Xiangshui, China 75 G10 34 12N 119 33 E
Xiangtan, China 77 D9 27 51N 112 54 E
Xiangxiang, China 77 D9 27 43N 112 28 E
Xiangyin, China 77 C9 28 38N 112 54 E
Xiangyun, China 76 E3 25 34N 100 35 E
Xiangzhou, China 76 F7 23 58N 109 40 E
Xianju, China 77 C13 28 51N 120 44 E
Xianning, China 77 C10 29 51N 114 16 E
Xianshui He →, China 76 B3 30 10N 100 59 E
Xianyang, China 74 G5 34 20N 108 40 E
Xianyou, China 77 E12 25 22N 118 38 E
Xiao Hinggan Ling, China 73 B7 49 0N 127 0 E
Xiao Xian, China 74 G9 34 15N 116 55 E
Xiaofeng, China 77 B12 30 35N 119 32 E
Xiaogan, China 77 B9 30 52N 113 55 E
Xiaojin, China 76 B4 30 59N 102 21 E
Xiaolan, China 77 F9 22 38N 113 13 E
Xiaoshan, China 77 B13 30 12N 120 18 E
Xiaoyi, China 74 F6 37 8N 111 48 E
Xiapu, China 77 D12 26 54N 119 59 E
Xiawa, China 75 C11 42 35N 120 38 E
Xiayi, China 74 G9 34 15N 116 10 E
Xichang, China 76 D4 27 51N 102 19 E
Xichong, China 76 B5 30 57N 105 54 E
Xichuan, China 74 H6 33 0N 111 30 E
Xiemahe, China 77 B8 31 38N 111 12 E
Xieng Khouang, Laos 86 C4 19 17N 103 25 E
Xifei He →, China 74 H9 32 45N 116 40 E

302 Xifeng

Xifeng, *Guizhou, China* **76 D6** 27 7N 106 42 E
Xifeng, *Liaoning, China* **75 C13** 42 42N 124 45 E
Xifengzhen, *China* **74 G4** 35 40N 107 40 E
Xigazê, *China* **72 D3** 29 5N 88 45 E
Xihe, *China* **74 G3** 34 2N 105 20 E
Xihua, *China* **74 H8** 33 45N 114 30 E
Xilaganí, *Greece* **51 F9** 40 58N 25 28 E
Xiliao He →, *China* **75 C12** 43 32N 123 35 E
Xilin, *China* **76 E5** 24 30N 105 6 E
Xilókastron, *Greece* **48 C4** 38 5N 22 38 E
Xin Jiang →, *China* **77 C11** 28 45N 116 35 E
Xin Xian, *China* **74 E7** 38 22N 112 46 E
Xinavane, *Mozam.* **117 D5** 25 2S 32 47 E
Xinbin, *China* **75 D13** 41 40N 125 2 E
Xincai, *China* **77 A10** 32 43N 114 58 E
Xinchang, *China* **77 C13** 29 28N 120 52 E
Xincheng,
Guangxi Zhuangzu, China **76 E7** 24 5N 108 39 E
Xincheng, *Jiangxi, China* **77 D10** 26 48N 114 6 E
Xinfeng, *Guangdong, China* **77 E10** 24 5N 114 16 E
Xinfeng, *Jiangxi, China* **77 D11** 27 7N 116 11 E
Xinfeng, *Jiangxi, China* **77 E10** 25 27N 114 58 E
Xing Xian, *China* **74 E6** 38 27N 111 7 E
Xing'an, *Guangxi Zhuangzu, China* **77 E8** 25 38N 110 40 E
Xingan, *Jiangxi, China* **77 D10** 27 46N 115 20 E
Xingcheng, *China* **75 D11** 40 40N 120 45 E
Xingguo, *China* **77 D10** 26 21N 115 21 E
Xinghe, *China* **74 D7** 40 55N 113 55 E
Xinghua, *China* **75 H10** 32 58N 119 48 E
Xinghua Wan, *China* **77 E12** 25 15N 119 20 E
Xinglong, *China* **75 D9** 40 25N 117 30 E
Xingning, *China* **77 E10** 24 3N 115 42 E
Xingping, *China* **74 G5** 34 20N 108 28 E
Xingren, *China* **76 E5** 25 24N 105 11 E
Xingshan, *China* **77 B8** 31 15N 110 45 E
Xingtai, *China* **74 F8** 37 3N 114 32 E
Xingu →, *Brazil* **169 D7** 1 30 S 51 53W
Xingyang, *China* **74 G7** 34 45N 112 52 E
Xinhe, *China* **74 F8** 37 30N 115 15 E
Xinhua, *China* **77 D8** 27 42N 111 13 E
Xinhuang, *China* **76 D7** 27 21N 109 12 E
Xinhui, *China* **77 F9** 22 25N 113 0 E
Xining, *China* **72 C5** 36 34N 101 40 E
Xinjiang, *China* **74 G6** 35 34N 111 11 E
Xinjiang Uygur Zizhiqu □, *China* **72 C3** 42 0N 86 0 E
Xinjie, *China* **76 D3** 26 48N 101 15 E
Xinjin, *Liaoning, China* **75 E11** 39 25N 121 58 E
Xinjin, *Sichuan, China* **76 B4** 30 24N 103 47 E
Xinkai He →, *China* **75 C12** 43 32N 123 35 E
Xinle, *China* **74 E8** 38 25N 114 40 E
Xinlitun, *China* **75 D12** 42 0N 122 8 E
Xinlong, *China* **76 B3** 30 57N 100 12 E
Xinmin, *China* **75 D12** 41 59N 122 50 E
Xinning, *China* **77 D8** 26 28N 110 50 E
Xinping, *China* **76 E3** 24 5N 101 59 E
Xinshao, *China* **77 D8** 27 21N 111 26 E
Xintai, *China* **75 G9** 35 55N 117 45 E
Xintian, *China* **77 E9** 25 55N 112 13 E
Xinxiang, *China* **74 G7** 35 18N 113 50 E
Xinxing, *China* **77 F9** 22 35N 112 15 E
Xinyang, *China* **77 A10** 32 6N 114 3 E
Xinye, *China* **77 A9** 32 30N 112 21 E
Xinyi, *China* **77 F8** 22 25N 111 0 E
Xinyu, *China* **77 D10** 27 49N 114 58 E
Xinzhan, *China* **75 C14** 43 50N 127 18 E
Xinzheng, *China* **74 G7** 34 20N 113 45 E
Xinzhou, *China* **77 B10** 30 50N 114 48 E
Xinzo de Limia, *Spain* **42 C3** 42 3N 7 47W
Xiong Xian, *China* **74 E9** 38 59N 116 8 E
Xiongyuecheng, *China* **75 D12** 40 12N 122 5 E
Xiping, *Henan, China* **74 H8** 33 22N 114 5 E
Xiping, *Henan, China* **74 H6** 33 25N 111 8 E
Xiping, *Zhejiang, China* **77 C12** 28 16N 119 29 E
Xique-Xique, *Brazil* **170 D3** 10 50 S 42 40W
Xiruá →, *Brazil* **172 B4** 6 3 S 67 50W
Xishui, *China* **77 B10** 30 30N 115 15 E
Xituozhen, *China* **76 B7** 30 22N 108 11 E
Xiuning, *China* **77 C12** 29 45N 118 10 E
Xiuren, *China* **77 E8** 24 27N 110 12 E
Xiushan, *China* **76 C7** 28 25N 108 57 E
Xiushui, *China* **77 C10** 29 2N 114 33 E
Xiuwen, *China* **76 D6** 26 49N 106 32 E
Xiuyan, *China* **75 D12** 40 18N 123 11 E
Xixia, *China* **74 H6** 33 25N 111 29 E
Xixiang, *China* **74 H4** 33 0N 107 44 E
Xiyang, *China* **74 F7** 37 38N 113 38 E
Xizang Zizhiqu □, *China* **72 C3** 32 0N 88 0 E
Xlendi, *Malta* **38 C1** 36 1N 14 12 E
Xu Jiang →, *China* **77 D11** 28 0N 116 25 E
Xuan Loc, *Vietnam* **87 G6** 10 56N 107 14 E
Xuancheng, *China* **77 B12** 30 56N 118 43 E
Xuan'en, *China* **76 C7** 30 0N 109 30 E
Xuanhan, *China* **76 B6** 31 18N 107 38 E
Xuanhua, *China* **74 D8** 40 40N 115 2 E
Xuchang, *China* **74 G7** 34 2N 113 48 E
Xudat, *Azerbaijan* **61 K9** 41 38N 48 41 E
Xuefeng Shan, *China* **77 D8** 27 5N 110 35 E
Xuejiaping, *China* **77 B8** 31 39N 110 16 E
Xun Jiang →, *China* **77 F8** 23 35N 111 30 E
Xun Xian, *China* **74 G8** 35 42N 114 33 E
Xundian, *China* **76 E4** 25 36N 103 15 E
Xunwu, *China* **77 E10** 24 54N 115 37 E
Xunyang, *China* **74 H5** 32 48N 109 22 E
Xunyi, *China* **74 G5** 35 8N 108 20 E
Xupu, *China* **77 D8** 27 53N 110 32 E
Xúquer →, *Spain* **41 F4** 39 5N 0 10W
Xushui, *China* **74 E8** 39 2N 115 40 E
Xuwen, *China* **77 G8** 20 20N 110 10 E
Xuyen Moc, *Vietnam* **87 G6** 10 34N 107 25 E
Xuyong, *China* **76 C5** 28 10N 105 22 E
Xuzhou, *China* **75 G9** 34 18N 117 10 E
Xylophagou, *Cyprus* **38 E12** 34 54N 33 51 E

Y

Ya Xian, *China* **86 C7** 18 14N 109 29 E
Yaamba, *Australia* **126 C5** 23 8 S 150 22 E
Ya'an, *China* **76 C4** 29 58N 103 5 E
Yaapeet, *Australia* **128 C5** 35 45 S 142 3 E
Yabassi, *Cameroon* **113 E6** 4 30N 9 57 E
Yabba North, *Australia* **129 D6** 36 13 S 145 42 E
Yabelo, *Ethiopia* **107 G4** 4 50N 38 8 E
Yablanitsa, *Bulgaria* **51 C8** 43 2N 24 5 E
Yablonovy Ra. = Yablonovyy Khrebet, *Russia* **65 D12** 53 0N 114 0 E
Yablonovyy Khrebet, *Russia* **65 D12** 53 0N 114 0 E
Yabrai Shan, *China* **74 E2** 39 40N 103 0 E
Yabrūd, *Syria* **103 B5** 33 58N 36 39 E
Yacheng, *China* **73 E5** 18 22N 109 6 E
Yacuiba, *Bolivia* **174 A3** 22 0 S 63 43W
Yacuma →, *Bolivia* **173 C4** 13 38 S 65 23W
Yadgir, *India* **94 F3** 16 45N 77 5 E
Yadkin →, *U.S.A.* **149 H5** 35 29N 80 9W
Yadrin, *Russia* **60 C8** 55 57N 46 12 E
Yagaba, *Ghana* **113 C4** 10 14N 1 20W
Yağcılar, *Turkey* **49 B10** 39 25N 28 23 E
Yagodnoye, *Russia* **65 C15** 62 33N 149 40 E
Yagoua, *Cameroon* **114 A3** 10 20N 15 13 E
Yaguas →, *Peru* **168 D3** 2 45 S 70 10W
Yahila, *Dem. Rep. of the Congo* **114 B4** 0 13N 24 28 E
Yahk, *Canada* **142 D5** 49 6N 116 10W
Yahotyn, *Ukraine* **59 G6** 50 17N 31 46 E
Yahuma, *Dem. Rep. of the Congo* **114 B4** 1 0N 23 10 E
Yahyalı, *Turkey* **100 C6** 38 5N 35 2 E
Yaita, *Japan* **69 F9** 36 48N 139 56 E
Yaiza, *Canary Is.* **39 F6** 28 57N 13 46W
Yaizu, *Japan* **71 C10** 34 52N 138 20 E
Yajiang, *China* **76 B3** 30 2N 100 57 E
Yajua, *Nigeria* **113 C7** 11 27N 12 49 E
Yakage, *Japan* **70 C5** 34 37N 133 35 E
Yakamba, *Dem. Rep. of the Congo* **114 B3** 2 42N 19 38 E
Yakima, *U.S.A.* **158 C3** 46 36N 120 31W
Yakima →, *U.S.A.* **158 C3** 47 0N 120 30W
Yako, *Burkina Faso* **112 C4** 12 59N 2 15W
Yakoma, *Dem. Rep. of the Congo* **114 B4** 4 5N 22 27 E
Yakoruda, *Bulgaria* **50 D7** 42 1N 23 39 E
Yakovlevka, *Russia* **68 B6** 44 26N 133 28 E
Yakshur Bodya, *Russia* **62 C4** 57 11N 53 7 E
Yaku-Shima, *Japan* **69 J5** 30 20N 130 30 E
Yakutat, *U.S.A.* **138 C6** 59 33N 139 44W
Yakutat B., *U.S.A.* **144 G12** 59 45N 140 45W
Yakutia = Sakha □, *Russia* **65 C14** 66 0N 130 0 E
Yakutsk, *Russia* **65 C13** 62 5N 129 50 E
Yala, *Thailand* **87 J3** 6 33N 101 18 E
Yalbalgo, *Australia* **125 E1** 25 10 S 114 45 E
Yalboroo, *Australia* **126 C4** 20 50 S 148 40 E
Yale, *U.S.A.* **150 C2** 43 8N 82 48W
Yalgoo, *Australia* **125 E2** 28 16 S 116 39 E
Yali, *Dem. Rep. of the Congo* **114 B4** 0 4N 21 3 E
Yaligimba, *Dem. Rep. of the Congo* **114 B4** 2 13N 22 56 E
Yalinga, *C.A.R.* **114 A4** 6 33N 23 10 E
Yalkubul, Punta, *Mexico* **163 C7** 21 32N 88 37W
Yalleroi, *Australia* **126 C4** 24 3 S 145 42 E
Yalobusha →, *U.S.A.* **155 J9** 33 33N 90 10W
Yaloke, *C.A.R.* **114 A3** 5 19N 17 5 E
Yalong Jiang →, *China* **76 D3** 26 40N 101 55 E
Yalova, *Turkey* **51 F13** 40 41N 29 15 E
Yalta, *Ukraine* **59 K8** 44 30N 34 10 E
Yalu Jiang →, *China* **75 E13** 40 0N 124 22 E
Yalvaç, *Turkey* **100 C4** 38 17N 31 10 E
Yam Ha Melah = Dead Sea, *Asia* **103 D4** 31 30N 35 30 E
Yam Kinneret, *Israel* **103 C4** 32 45N 35 35 E
Yamada, *Japan* **70 D2** 33 33N 130 49 E
Yamaga, *Japan* **70 D2** 33 1N 130 41 E
Yamagata, *Japan* **68 E10** 38 15N 140 15 E
Yamagata □, *Japan* **68 E10** 38 30N 140 0 E
Yamagawa, *Japan* **70 F2** 31 12N 130 39 E
Yamaguchi, *Japan* **70 C3** 34 10N 131 32 E
Yamaguchi □, *Japan* **70 C3** 34 20N 131 40 E
Yamal, Poluostrov, *Russia* **64 B8** 71 0N 70 0 E
Yamal Pen. = Yamal, Poluostrov, *Russia* **64 B8** 71 0N 70 0 E
Yamanaka, *Japan* **71 A8** 36 15N 136 22 E
Yamanashi □, *Japan* **71 B10** 35 40N 138 40 E
Yamantau, Gora, *Russia* **62 D7** 54 15N 58 6 E
Yamato, *Japan* **71 B11** 35 27N 139 25 E
Yamatotakada, *Japan* **71 C7** 34 31N 135 45 E
Yamazaki, *Japan* **70 C6** 35 0N 134 32 E
Yamba, *N.S.W., Australia* **127 D5** 29 26 S 153 23 E
Yamba, *S. Austral., Australia* **128 C4** 34 10 S 140 52 E
Yambah, *Australia* **126 C1** 23 10 S 133 50 E
Yambarran Ra., *Australia* **124 C5** 15 10 S 130 25 E
Yambata, *Dem. Rep. of the Congo* **114 B4** 2 26N 21 58 E
Yâmbiô, *Sudan* **107 G2** 4 35N 28 16 E
Yambol, *Bulgaria* **51 D10** 42 30N 26 30 E
Yamdena, *Indonesia* **83 C4** 7 45 S 131 20 E
Yame, *Japan* **70 D2** 33 13N 130 35 E
Yamethin, *Burma* **90 E6** 20 29N 96 18 E
Yamil, *Nigeria* **113 C6** 12 53N 8 4 E
Yamma-Yamma, L., *Australia* **127 D3** 26 16 S 141 20 E
Yamoussoukro, *Ivory C.* **112 D3** 6 49N 5 17W
Yampa →, *U.S.A.* **158 F9** 40 32N 108 59W
Yampi Sd., *Australia* **124 C3** 16 8 S 123 38 E
Yampil, *Moldova* **59 H5** 48 15N 28 15 E
Yampol = Yampil, *Moldova* **59 H5** 48 15N 28 15 E
Yamrat, *Nigeria* **113 C6** 10 11N 9 55 E
Yamrukchal = Botev, *Bulgaria* **51 D8** 42 44N 24 52 E
Yamuna →, *India* **93 G9** 25 30N 81 53 E
Yamzho Yumco, *China* **72 D4** 28 48N 90 35 E
Yan, *Nigeria* **113 C7** 10 5N 12 11 E
Yan →, *Sri Lanka* **95 K5** 9 0N 81 10 E
Yana →, *Russia* **65 B14** 71 30N 136 0 E
Yanac, *Australia* **128 D4** 36 8 S 141 25 E
Yanagawa, *Japan* **70 D2** 33 10N 130 24 E
Yanahara, *Japan* **70 C6** 34 58N 134 2 E
Yanai, *Japan* **70 D4** 33 58N 132 7 E
Yanam, *India* **94 F6** 16 47N 82 15 E
Yan'an, *China* **74 F5** 36 35N 109 26 E
Yanaul, *Russia* **62 C5** 56 25N 55 0 E
Yanbian, *China* **76 D3** 26 47N 101 31 E
Yanbu 'al Baḩr, *Si. Arabia* **96 F3** 24 0N 38 5 E
Yancannia, *Australia* **127 E3** 30 12 S 142 35 E
Yanchang, *China* **74 F6** 36 43N 110 1 E
Yancheng, *Henan, China* **74 H8** 33 35N 114 0 E
Yancheng, *Jiangsu, China* **75 H11** 33 23N 120 8 E
Yanchi, *China* **74 F4** 37 48N 107 20 E
Yanchuan, *China* **74 F6** 36 51N 110 10 E
Yanco, *Australia* **129 C7** 34 38 S 146 27 E
Yanco Cr. →, *Australia* **129 C6** 35 14 S 145 35 E
Yandal, *Australia* **125 E3** 27 35 S 121 10 E
Yandanooka, *Australia* **125 E2** 29 18 S 115 29 E
Yandaran, *Australia* **126 C5** 24 43 S 152 6 E
Yandé, I., *N. Cal.* **133 T17** 20 3 S 163 49 E
Yandina, *Solomon Is.* **133 M10** 9 7 S 159 13 E
Yandja, *Dem. Rep. of the Congo* **114 C3** 1 41 S 17 43 E
Yandongi, *Dem. Rep. of the Congo* **114 B4** 2 51N 22 16 E
Yandoon, *Burma* **90 G5** 17 0N 95 40 E
Yanfeng, *China* **76 E3** 25 52N 101 8 E
Yanfolila, *Mali* **112 C3** 11 11N 8 9W
Yang Xian, *China* **74 H4** 33 15N 107 30 E
Yangambi, *Dem. Rep. of the Congo* **118 B1** 0 47N 24 20 E
Yangbi, *China* **76 E2** 25 41N 99 58 E
Yangcheng, *China* **74 G7** 35 28N 112 22 E
Yangch'ü = Taiyuan, *China* **74 F7** 37 52N 112 33 E
Yangchun, *China* **77 F8** 22 11N 111 48 E
Yanggao, *China* **74 D7** 40 21N 113 55 E
Yanggu, *China* **74 F8** 36 8N 115 43 E
Yangibazar, *Kyrgyzstan* **63 C5** 41 40N 70 53 E
Yangikishlak, *Uzbekistan* **63 C3** 40 25N 67 10 E
Yangiyul, *Uzbekistan* **63 C4** 41 0N 69 3 E
Yangjiang, *China* **77 G8** 21 50N 111 59 E
Yangliuqing, *China* **75 E9** 39 2N 117 5 E
Yangon = Rangoon, *Burma* **90 G6** 16 45N 96 20 E
Yangping, *China* **77 B8** 31 12N 111 25 E
Yangpingguan, *China* **74 H4** 32 58N 106 5 E
Yangquan, *China* **74 F7** 37 58N 113 31 E
Yangshan, *China* **77 E9** 24 30N 112 40 E
Yangshuo, *China* **77 E8** 24 48N 110 29 E
Yangtse = Chang Jiang →, *China* **77 B13** 31 48N 121 10 E
Yangtze Kiang = Chang Jiang →, *China* **77 B13** 31 48N 121 10 E
Yangxin, *China* **77 C10** 29 50N 115 12 E
Yangyang, *S. Korea* **75 E15** 38 4N 128 38 E
Yangyuan, *China* **74 D8** 40 1N 114 10 E
Yangzhou, *China* **77 A12** 32 21N 119 26 E
Yanhe, *China* **76 C7** 28 31N 108 29 E
Yanji, *China* **75 C15** 42 59N 129 30 E
Yanjin, *China* **76 C5** 28 5N 104 18 E
Yanjing, *China* **76 C2** 29 7N 98 33 E
Yankton, *U.S.A.* **154 D6** 42 53N 97 23W
Yanna, *Australia* **127 D4** 26 58 S 146 0 E
Yanonge, *Dem. Rep. of the Congo* **114 B4** 0 35N 24 38 E
Yanqi, *China* **72 B3** 42 5N 86 35 E
Yanqing, *China* **74 D8** 40 30N 115 58 E
Yanshan, *Hebei, China* **75 E9** 38 4N 117 22 E
Yanshan, *Jiangxi, China* **77 C11** 28 15N 117 41 E
Yanshan, *Yunnan, China* **76 F5** 23 35N 104 20 E
Yanshou, *China* **75 B15** 45 28N 128 22 E
Yantabulla, *Australia* **127 D4** 29 21 S 145 0 E
Yantai, *China* **75 F11** 37 34N 121 22 E
Yanting, *China* **76 B5** 31 11N 105 24 E
Yantra →, *Bulgaria* **51 C9** 43 40N 25 37 E
Yanwa, *China* **76 D2** 27 35N 98 55 E
Yanykurgan, *Kazakstan* **63 B3** 43 50N 68 48 E
Yanyuan, *China* **76 D3** 27 25N 101 30 E
Yanzhou, *China* **74 G9** 35 35N 116 49 E
Yao, *Chad* **109 F3** 12 56N 17 33 E
Yao, *Japan* **71 C7** 34 32N 135 36 E
Yao Xian, *China* **74 G5** 34 55N 108 59 E
Yao Yai, Ko, *Thailand* **87 J2** 8 0N 98 35 E
Yao'an, *China* **76 E3** 25 31N 101 18 E
Yaodu, *China* **76 A5** 32 45N 105 22 E
Yaoundé, *Cameroon* **113 E7** 3 50N 11 35 E
Yaowan, *China* **75 G10** 34 15N 118 3 E
Yap I., *Pac. Oc.* **134 G5** 9 30N 138 10 E
Yapen, *Indonesia* **83 B5** 1 50 S 136 0 E
Yapen, Selat, *Indonesia* **83 B5** 1 20 S 136 10 E
Yappar →, *Australia* **126 B3** 18 22 S 141 16 E
Yaqui →, *Mexico* **162 B2** 27 37N 110 39W
Yar, *Russia* **62 B4** 58 14N 52 5 E
Yar-Sale, *Russia* **64 C8** 66 50N 70 50 E
Yaracuy □, *Venezuela* **168 A4** 10 20N 68 45W
Yaracuy →, *Venezuela* **168 A4** 10 33N 68 15W
Yaraka, *Australia* **126 C3** 24 53 S 144 3 E
Yaransk, *Russia* **60 B8** 57 22N 47 49 E
Yarbasan, *Turkey* **49 C10** 38 59N 28 49 E
Yardea P.O., *Australia* **127 E2** 32 23 S 135 32 E
Yardımcı Burnu, *Turkey* **49 E12** 36 13N 30 25 E
Yare →, *U.K.* **21 E9** 52 35N 1 38 E
Yaremcha, *Ukraine* **59 H3** 48 27N 24 33 E
Yarensk, *Russia* **56 B8** 62 11N 49 15 E
Yarí →, *Colombia* **168 D3** 0 20 S 72 20W
Yaritagua, *Venezuela* **168 A4** 10 5N 69 8W
Yarkand = Shache, *China* **72 C2** 38 20N 77 10 E
Yarker, *Canada* **151 B8** 44 23N 76 46W
Yarkhun →, *Pakistan* **93 A5** 36 17N 72 30 E
Yarmouth, *Canada* **141 D6** 43 50N 66 7W
Yarmūk →, *Syria* **103 C4** 32 42N 35 40 E
Yaroslavl, *Russia* **58 D10** 57 35N 39 55 E
Yarqa, W. →, *Egypt* **103 F2** 30 0N 33 49 E
Yarra Yarra Lakes, *Australia* **125 E2** 29 40 S 115 45 E
Yarraden, *Australia* **126 A3** 14 17 S 143 15 E
Yarraloola, *Australia* **124 D2** 21 33 S 115 52 E
Yarram, *Australia* **129 E7** 38 29 S 146 39 E
Yarraman, *Australia* **127 D5** 26 50 S 152 0 E
Yarranvale, *Australia* **127 D4** 26 50 S 145 20 E
Yarras, *Australia* **129 A10** 31 25 S 152 20 E
Yarrawonga, *Australia* **129 D7** 36 0 S 146 0 E
Yarrowmere, *Australia* **126 C4** 21 27 S 145 53 E
Yarto, *Australia* **128 C5** 35 28 S 142 16 E
Yartsevo, *Russia* **58 E7** 55 6N 32 43 E
Yartsevo, *Russia* **65 C10** 60 20N 90 0 E
Yarumal, *Colombia* **168 B2** 6 58N 75 24W
Yasawa, *Fiji* **133 A1** 16 47 S 177 31 E
Yasawa Group, *Fiji* **133 A1** 17 0 S 177 23 E
Yaselda, *Belarus* **59 F4** 52 7N 26 28 E
Yashbum, *Yemen* **98 D4** 14 19N 46 56 E
Yashi, *Nigeria* **113 C6** 12 23N 7 54 E
Yashiro-Jima, *Japan* **70 D4** 33 55N 132 15 E
Yashkul, *Russia* **61 G7** 46 11N 45 21 E
Yasin, *Pakistan* **93 A5** 36 24N 73 23 E
Yasinovataya, *Ukraine* **59 H9** 48 7N 37 57 E
Yasinski, L., *Canada* **140 B4** 53 16N 77 35W
Yasinya, *Ukraine* **59 H3** 48 16N 24 21 E
Yasnyy, *Russia* **62 F7** 51 1N 59 58 E
Yasothon, *Thailand* **86 E5** 15 50N 104 10 E
Yass, *Australia* **129 C8** 34 49 S 148 54 E
Yasugi, *Japan* **70 B5** 35 26N 133 15 E
Yata →, *Bolivia* **173 C4** 10 29 S 65 26W
Yatağan, *Turkey* **49 D10** 37 20N 28 10 E
Yates Center, *U.S.A.* **155 G7** 37 53N 95 44W
Yates Pt., *N.Z.* **131 E2** 44 29 S 167 49 E
Yatesville, *U.S.A.* **152 C5** 32 55N 84 9W
Yathkyed L., *Canada* **143 A9** 62 40N 98 0W
Yathong, *Australia* **129 B6** 32 37 S 145 33 E
Yatsuo, *Japan* **71 A9** 36 34N 137 8 E
Yatsushiro, *Japan* **70 E2** 32 30N 130 40 E
Yatsushiro-Kai, *Japan* **70 E2** 32 30N 130 25 E
Yatta Plateau, *Kenya* **118 C4** 2 0 S 38 0 E
Yauca, *Peru* **172 D3** 15 39 S 74 35W
Yauya, *Peru* **172 B2** 8 59 S 77 17W
Yauyos, *Peru* **172 C2** 12 19 S 75 50W
Yaval, *India* **94 D2** 21 10N 75 42 E
Yavan, *Tajikistan* **63 D4** 38 19N 69 2 E
Yavari →, *Peru* **172 A3** 4 21 S 70 2W
Yavatmal, *India* **94 D4** 20 20N 78 15 E
Yavne, *Israel* **103 D3** 31 52N 34 45 E
Yavoriv, *Ukraine* **59 H2** 49 55N 23 20 E
Yavorov = Yavoriv, *Ukraine* **59 H2** 49 55N 23 20 E
Yavuzeli, *Turkey* **100 D7** 37 18N 37 24 E
Yawatahama, *Japan* **70 D4** 33 27N 132 24 E
Yawri B., *S. Leone* **112 D2** 8 22N 13 0W
Yaxi, *China* **76 D6** 27 33N 106 41 E
Yayama-Rettō, *Japan* **69 M1** 24 30N 123 40 E
Yazagyo, *Burma* **90 D5** 23 30N 94 6 E
Yazd, *Iran* **97 D7** 31 55N 54 27 E
Yazd □, *Iran* **97 D7** 32 0N 55 0 E
Yazdān, *Iran* **91 B1** 33 30N 60 50 E
Yazıköy, *Turkey* **49 E9** 36 40N 27 20 E
Yazoo →, *U.S.A.* **155 J9** 32 22N 90 54W
Yazoo City, *U.S.A.* **155 J9** 32 51N 90 25W
Ybbs, *Austria* **34 C8** 48 12N 15 4 E
Yding Skovhøj, *Denmark* **17 J3** 55 59N 9 46 E
Ydrim, *Yemen* **98 D4** 14 20N 44 22 E
Ye Xian, *Henan, China* **74 H7** 33 35N 113 25 E
Ye Xian, *Shandong, China* **75 F10** 37 8N 119 57 E
Yea, *Australia* **129 D6** 37 14 S 145 26 E
Yealering, *Australia* **125 F2** 32 36 S 117 36 E
Yearinan, *Australia* **129 A8** 31 10 S 149 11 E
Yebbi-Souma, *Chad* **109 D3** 21 7N 17 54 E
Yebyu, *Burma* **86 E2** 14 15N 98 13 E
Yechŏn, *S. Korea* **75 F15** 36 39N 128 27 E
Yecla, *Spain* **41 G3** 38 35N 1 5W
Yécora, *Mexico* **162 B3** 28 20N 108 58W
Yedashe, *Burma* **90 F6** 19 10N 96 20 E
Yedintsy = Edineţ, *Moldova* **53 B12** 48 9N 27 18 E
Yeeda, *Australia* **124 C3** 17 31 S 123 38 E
Yeelanna, *Australia* **127 E2** 34 9 S 135 45 E
Yefremov, *Russia* **58 F10** 53 8N 38 3 E
Yeghegnadzor, *Armenia* **101 C11** 39 44N 45 19 E
Yegorlyk →, *Russia* **61 G5** 46 35N 41 57 E
Yegorlykskaya, *Russia* **61 G5** 46 35N 40 35 E
Yegoryevsk, *Russia* **58 E10** 55 27N 38 55 E
Yegros, *Paraguay* **174 B4** 26 20 S 56 25W
Yehuda, Midbar, *Israel* **103 D4** 31 35N 35 15 E
Yei, *Sudan* **107 G3** 4 9N 30 40 E
Yei, Nahr →, *Sudan* **107 F3** 6 15N 30 13 E
Yejmiadzin, *Armenia* **61 K7** 40 12N 44 19 E
Yekaterinburg, *Russia* **62 C8** 56 50N 60 30 E
Yekaterinodar = Krasnodar, *Russia* **61 H4** 45 5N 39 0 E
Yekumbe, *Dem. Rep. of the Congo* **114 C4** 1 2S 23 27 E
Yelabuga, *Russia* **60 C11** 55 45N 52 4 E
Yelan, *Russia* **60 E6** 50 55N 43 43 E
Yelandur, *India* **95 H3** 12 6N 77 0 E
Yelarbon, *Australia* **127 D5** 28 33 S 150 38 E
Yelatma, *Russia* **60 C5** 55 0N 41 45 E
Yelcho, L., *Chile* **176 B2** 43 18 S 72 18W
Yelets, *Russia* **59 F10** 52 40N 38 30 E
Yélimané, *Mali* **112 B2** 15 9N 10 34W
Yelizavetgrad = Kirovohrad, *Ukraine* **59 H7** 48 35N 32 20 E
Yelizavetinka, *Russia* **62 F7** 51 46N 59 45 E
Yell, *U.K.* **22 A7** 60 35N 1 5W
Yell Sd., *U.K.* **22 A7** 60 33N 1 15W
Yellamanchilli = Elamanchili, *India* **94 F6** 17 33N 82 50 E
Yellow →, *U.S.A.* **153 E3** 30 30N 87 0W
Yellow Sea, *China* **75 G12** 35 0N 123 0 E
Yellowhead Pass, *Canada* **142 C5** 52 53N 118 25W
Yellowknife, *Canada* **142 A6** 62 27N 114 29W
Yellowknife →, *Canada* **142 A6** 62 31N 114 19W
Yellowstone →, *U.S.A.* **154 B3** 47 59N 103 59W
Yellowstone L., *U.S.A.* **158 D8** 44 27N 110 22W
Yellowstone National Park, *U.S.A.* **158 D9** 44 40N 110 30W
Yellowtail Res., *U.S.A.* **158 D9** 45 6N 108 8W
Yelnya, *Russia* **58 E7** 54 35N 33 15 E
Yelsk, *Belarus* **59 G5** 51 50N 29 10 E
Yelvertoft, *Australia* **126 C2** 20 13 S 138 45 E
Yelwa, *Nigeria* **113 C5** 10 49N 4 41 E
Yemanzhelinsk, *Russia* **62 D8** 54 58N 61 18 E
Yemassee, *U.S.A.* **152 C9** 32 41N 80 51W
Yembongo, *Dem. Rep. of the Congo* **114 B3** 3 12N 19 2 E
Yemen ■, *Asia* **98 D4** 15 0N 44 0 E
Yen Bai, *Vietnam* **86 B5** 21 42N 104 52 E
Yenakiyeve, *Ukraine* **59 H10** 48 15N 38 15 E
Yenakiyevo = Yenakiyeve, *Ukraine* **59 H10** 48 15N 38 15 E
Yenangyaung, *Burma* **90 E5** 20 30N 95 0 E
Yenanma, *Burma* **90 F5** 19 46N 94 49 E
Yenbo = Yanbu 'al Baḩr, *Si. Arabia* **96 F3** 24 0N 38 5 E
Yenda, *Australia* **129 C7** 34 13 S 146 14 E
Yendéré, *Ivory C.* **112 C4** 10 12N 4 59W
Yendi, *Ghana* **113 D4** 9 29N 0 1W
Yengo, *Congo* **114 B3** 0 22N 15 29 E
Yenice, *Ankara, Turkey* **100 C5** 39 14N 32 42 E
Yenice, *Aydın, Turkey* **49 D10** 37 49N 28 35 E
Yenice, *Çanakkale, Turkey* **49 B9** 39 55N 27 17 E
Yenice, *Edirne, Turkey* **51 F10** 40 42N 26 9 E
Yenice →, *Turkey* **100 D6** 37 37N 35 33 E
Yenifoça, *Turkey* **49 C8** 38 44N 26 51 E
Yenihisar, *Turkey* **49 D9** 37 22N 27 16 E
Yeniköy, *Bursa, Turkey* **51 F13** 40 31N 29 22 E
Yeniköy, *Çanakkale, Turkey* **49 B8** 39 55N 26 10 E
Yeniköy, *Kütahya, Turkey* **49 C11** 38 52N 29 17 E
Yenipazar, *Turkey* **49 D10** 37 49N 28 11 E
Yenisaía, *Greece* **51 E8** 41 1N 24 57 E
Yenişehir, *Turkey* **51 F13** 40 16N 29 38 E
Yenisey →, *Russia* **64 B9** 71 50N 82 40 E
Yeniseysk, *Russia* **65 D10** 58 27N 92 13 E
Yeniseyskiy Zaliv, *Russia* **64 B9** 72 20N 81 0 E
Yennádhi, *Greece* **38 C9** 36 2N 27 56 E
Yenne, *France* **29 C9** 45 43N 5 44 E
Yenotayevka, *Russia* **61 G8** 47 15N 47 0 E
Yenyuka, *Russia* **65 D13** 57 57N 121 15 E
Yeo →, *U.K.* **21 G5** 51 2N 2 49W
Yeo, L., *Australia* **125 E3** 28 0 S 124 30 E
Yeola, *India* **94 D2** 20 2N 74 30 E
Yeoryioúpolis, *Greece* **38 D6** 35 20N 24 15 E
Yeoval, *Australia* **129 B8** 32 47 S 148 40 E
Yeovil, *U.K.* **21 G5** 50 57N 2 38W
Yepes, *Spain* **42 F7** 39 55N 3 39W
Yeppoon, *Australia* **126 C5** 23 5 S 150 47 E
Yeráki, *Greece* **48 D4** 37 0N 22 42 E
Yerbent, *Turkmenistan* **64 F6** 39 30N 58 50 E
Yerbogachen, *Russia* **65 C11** 61 16N 108 0 E
Yerevan, *Armenia* **61 K7** 40 10N 44 31 E
Yerilla, *Australia* **125 E3** 29 24 S 121 47 E
Yerkesik, *Turkey* **49 D10** 37 7N 28 19 E
Yerköy, *Turkey* **100 C6** 39 38N 34 28 E
Yerla →, *India* **94 F2** 16 50N 74 30 E
Yermak, *Kazakstan* **64 D8** 52 2N 76 55 E
Yermo, *U.S.A.* **161 L10** 34 54N 116 50W

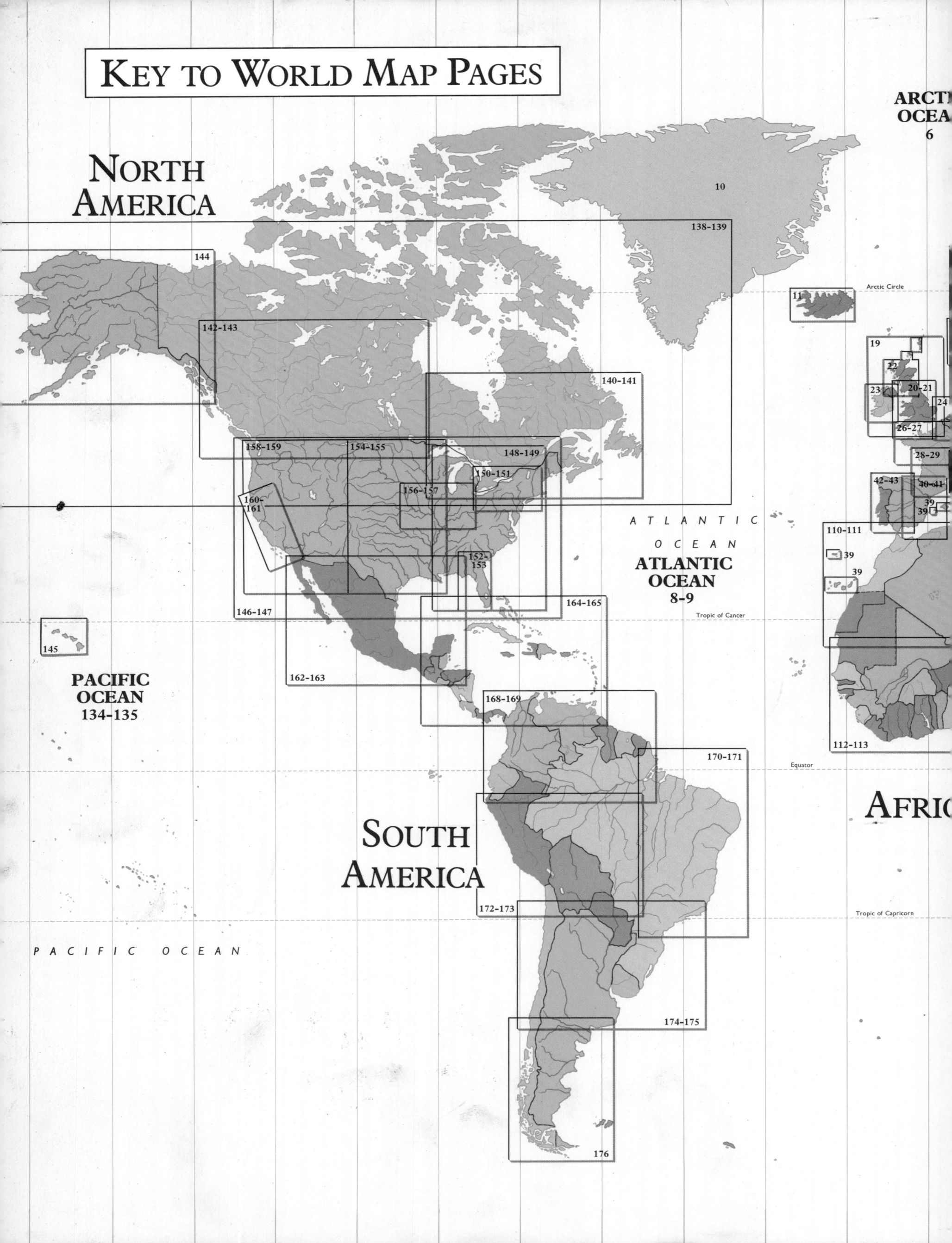

KEY TO WORLD MAP PAGES

NORTH AMERICA

ARCTIC
OCEAN
6

10

138-139

144

142-143

Arctic Circle

11

19

22

140-141

23

20-21

24

26-27

158-159

154-155

148-149

28-29

150-151

156-157

42-43

30-41

39
39

160-161

ATLANTIC

OCEAN

110-111

39

39

ATLANTIC
OCEAN
8-9

152-153

146-147

164-165

Tropic of Cancer

145

162-163

112-113

PACIFIC
OCEAN
134-135

168-169

Equator

AFRIC

170-171

SOUTH

AMERICA

172-173

Tropic of Capricorn

PACIFIC   OCEAN

174-175

176